THE
YOUTH BIBLE

is presented to

Nola Verna

by

Dad, mom, Nicole + Natasha

on

May 25, 1997
your
Confirmation Day

ACKNOWLEDGMENTS

The following people contributed to *The Youth Bible:*

Group Publishing editorial team: Eugene C. Roehlkepartain (general editor), Thom Schultz, Joani Schultz, Paul Woods, Michael D. Warden, Chris Yount, Lee Sparks, Cindy Sauer, and DeAnne Trujillo.

Word, Inc. team: Dan Rich, Kip Jordon, Carol Bartley, Carey Moore, Dave Moberg, Rob Birkhead, Ed Curtis, Jill Sciacca, Jim Burns, and Matt Barnhill.

Writers: Timothy R. Anderson, Nancy Brumbaugh Bayne, J. Brent Bill, Ann B. Cannon, Michael C. Carson, Dave Carver, Rick Chromey, L. Katherine Cook, Vaughn CroweTipton, Bob Darden, Karen Dockrey, Thomas J. Everson, Jim Farris, Dean Feldmeyer, Karen J. Fisher, Marty Fuller, Mike Gillespie, Mark Gilroy, Vicki Grove, Sam D. Halverson, Cindy S. Hansen, Mike Hertenstein, Margaret R. Hinchey, Tom Klaus, Rick Lawrence, Cynthia Cornwell McCachern, Elaine McCalla, Robert J. McCarty, Kevin A. Miller, Amy L.W. Nappa, Mike D.F. Nappa, Jolene L. Roehlkepartain, Ron Scates, Bob Searl, Yvonne L.D. Steindal, Gary B. Swanson, Jeffrey E. Tucker, Ramona Cramer Tucker, Annie Wamberg, Steve Wamberg, Mark Winter, Twyla Gill Wright, and Carol Davis Younger.

Designers and artists: Richard Slaton, Brian Peterson, Pat Reinheimer, David Martin, and Glyn Powell.

We would also like to thank all the young people, families and youth leaders who allowed their stories to be used in this Bible. Names and details have been changed to maintain their privacy.

PREFACE

The Bible is God's message to humanity. He has spoken to all peoples and all generations. Of course, God first accomplished this by directly addressing his people, the Israelites in the Old Testament and the young church in the New Testament, in a language they could understand.

The original text of the Bible was written in Hebrew, Aramaic, and Greek—languages of the people. Since God intends to address all people of all ages through his Word, each generation and language group must translate the Bible into its own language.

These facts, that the Bible is God's message and that it is ultimately addressed to all people in every age, require that a translation be both accurate and clear. These are the two overarching principles that stand behind the *New Century Version*.

An Accurate Translation

The first concern of the *New Century Version* is that the translation be faithful to the manuscripts in the original languages. A team composed of the World Bible Translation Center and fifty additional, highly qualified and experienced Bible scholars and translators was assembled. This team included people with experience on the *New International Version*, the *New American Standard Bible*, and the *New King James Version*. The scholars came from a variety of theological colleges, universities, and seminaries in the United States, Canada, Australia, and Great Britain.

These translators recognize that the most accurate translations are those which pay close attention to the meanings of words in their broader context, rather than those which simply treat words as isolated entities. They understand that a contemporary English translation must sometimes depart from the word order of the original languages to reflect accurately the meaning of God's Word to a modern English-speaking audience.

Further, it is true that translation involves interpretive decisions. With this in mind, it is important to note that the breadth of scholarship which stands behind the *New Century Version* ensures an unbiased translation.

Last, it should be mentioned that the best available Hebrew and Greek texts were used, principally the third edition of the United Bible Societies' Greek text and the latest edition of the Biblia Hebraica, along with the Septuagint.

A Clear Translation

The second concern was to make the language clear enough for all people to read the Bible and understand it for themselves. In maintaining clear language, several guidelines were followed. Vocabulary choice has been based upon *The Living Word Vocabulary* by Dr. Edgar Dale and Dr. Joseph O'Rourke (Worldbook-Childcraft International, 1981), which is the standard used by the editors of *The World Book Encyclopedia* to determine appropriate vocabulary. For difficult words that have no simpler synonyms, footnotes and dictionary references are provided. Footnotes appear at the bottom of the page and are indicated in the text by a raised letter (*n*) for "note." The dictionary/topical concordance is located at the back of the Bible with references indicated in the text by a raised letter (*d*).

The *New Century Version* aids understanding by using contemporary references for measurements and geographical locations when it is feasible. For instance, terms such as "shekels," "cubits," "omer," and "hin" have been converted to modern equivalents. Where geographical references are identical, the modern name has been used, such as the "Mediterranean Sea" instead of "Great Sea" or "Western Sea." Also, to minimize confusion, the most familiar name for a place is used consistently, instead of using variant names for the same place. "Lake Galilee" is used throughout rather than its variant forms, "Sea of Kinnereth," "Lake Gennesaret," and "Sea of Tiberias."

Ancient customs are often unfamiliar to modern readers. Customs such as shaving a man's beard to shame him or ritually walking between the halves of a dead animal to seal an agreement are meaningless to many modern-day readers. So these are clarified either in the text or in a footnote.

Since *meanings* of words change with time, care has been taken to avoid potential misunderstandings. To do so, the *New Century Version* uses contemporary language in place of the archaic language often found in translations. Frequently in the Old Testament God tells his people to "devote" something to him, as when he tells the Israelites to devote Jericho and everything in it to him. While we might understand this to mean he is telling them to keep it safe and holy, the exact opposite is true. He is telling them to destroy it totally as an offering to him. The *New Century Version* communicates the idea clearly by translating "devoted," in these situations, as "destroyed as an offering to the Lord."

Where there was potential for confusion, *rhetorical questions* have been stated according to their implied answer. The psalmist's question, "Who, O God, is like you?" has been stated more directly as, "God, there is no one like you."

Figures of speech have been translated according to their meanings. For instance, the expression, "the Virgin Daughter of Zion," which is frequently used in the Old Testament, is simply and accurately translated "the people of Jerusalem" so that the meaning is not obscured by the figure of speech.

Idiomatic expressions of the biblical languages are translated to communicate the same meaning to today's reader that would have been understood by the original audience. For example, the Hebrew idiom "he rested with his fathers" is translated by its meaning—"he died."

Obscure terms have been clarified. Terms are often obscure in the Bible because they are part of the ancient culture which God directly addressed in his revelation. In the Old Testament, for instance, God frequently condemns the people for their "high places" and "Asherah poles." The *New Century Version* translates these according to their meanings, which would have been understood by the Hebrews. "High places" is translated "places where gods were worshiped" and "Asherah poles" is translated "Asherah idols."

Gender language has also been translated with a concern for clarity. To avoid the misconception that "man," "mankind," and "he" are exclusively masculine when they are being used in a generic sense, this translation has chosen to use less ambiguous language, such as "people," "humans," and "human beings," and has carefully worked throughout to choose gender language that would accurately convey the intent of the original writers. Specifically and exclusively masculine and feminine references in the text have been retained.

Following in the tradition of other English versions, the *New Century Version* indicates the divine name YHWH, the Tetragrammaton, by putting LORD, and sometimes GOD, in capital letters. This is to distinguish it from Adonai, another Hebrew word that is translated "Lord."

Every attempt has been made to maintain proper English style, while clarifying concepts and communication. The beauty of Hebrew parallelism in poetry has been retained, and the images of the ancient languages have been captured in equivalent English images wherever possible, but in all cases, clarity of communication with the modern reader has taken precedence over preservation of the ancient form.

Study Aids

Other features to enhance understanding of the text include full-color maps of Bible lands, subject headings throughout to identify speakers and topics, book introductions to give a synopsis of each book's theme, a dictionary/topical concordance of biblical words and concepts, and footnotes identifying Old Testament quotations in the New Testament.

Our Prayer

It is with great humility and prayerfulness that this Bible is presented. We acknowledge the infallibility of God's Word and yet our own human frailty. We pray that God has worked through us as his vessels so that we all might better learn his truth for ourselves and that it might richly grow in our lives. It is to his glory that this Bible is given.

NO DUSTING NECESSARY

According to a Search Institute study, 86 percent of Christian teenagers do not read the Bible when they are by themselves. Why?

"I sometimes don't understand it, so I stop."
–Mary in Nebraska

"I'm really confused."
–Andrew in Michigan

"I don't know how to read the Bible."
–Chris in Florida

If you are like most teenagers, you have had similar feelings. Sometimes the Bible seems hard to understand, hard to use, irrelevant, and even boring. So even though you know it's important, it often collects dust on a shelf.

The Youth Bible is designed specifically to help you find God's guidance in the everyday issues you face. It includes:

- The Bible text translated into clear, modern English. It's easier to read than a newspaper!
- Devotions that relate the Bible to everyday life.
- Introductions that help you understand each book of the Bible.
- "Sidelights" that give interesting–often humorous–insights into life in Bible times.

These features help you discover for yourself that the Bible is about everyday life. It's easy to use, interesting, and life-changing.

It's Easy to Use

You don't have to be a Bible scholar to use *The Youth Bible.* In fact, we have designed it so that people who have never studied the Bible can find help in God's Word. Here is all you have to do to use it.

- *Find what's on your mind* – When you are dealing with a topic or problem, just look it up in the "Topical Devotion Guide." This guide lists more than four hundred devotions on topics that interest teenagers.
- *Read the devotion* – The devotions tell true stories or give interesting information to help you think about the topic. Then read the related Bible passage and think about the questions, which will help you understand and apply the passage.
- *Find related passages* – Each devotion suggests other Bible passages that can speak to your need. Just look them up. And you don't have to already know where to find Malachi or 2 Timothy or 1 Chronicles in the Bible. Just use the page numbers listed beside each reference.
- *Learn about the Bible* – This Bible doesn't assume you know who people are or what events take place. It explains in simple language the ideas and events that are important for understanding Bible passages. And if you don't know where to find a story, use the quick guide "Where Do I Find . . . ?" to help you.

It's Interesting

On the surface, many parts of the Bible may seem boring. But when you start digging, you discover that even these kinds of books are fascinating. These features help bring the Bible to life:

- *Introductions* – Each book of the Bible has a short, easy-to-read introduction to help you understand the book and its purpose. Most introductions also include time lines and maps or diagrams to help you see when and where things happened.
- *Sidelights* – Throughout the Bible you'll find over three hundred boxes with interesting and fun information about life in Bible times and about the Bible itself. This information will

not only add interest to your Bible reading, but it will help you understand many passages. Besides, you will amaze your friends with your knowledge!

It's Life-Changing

One warning: Don't use this Bible unless you want your life to be changed. The devotions are written to challenge you to grow in your faith. They encourage you to examine your own life and to relate the scriptural principles to what you say, do, and think.

Of course, the Bible can do all these things even without the devotions, introductions, and sidelights that are added. It's God's Word, and it doesn't need our help. But sometimes *we* need help; we need guidance and direction to get us started. *The Youth Bible* gives that help. Once you start using it, it won't have much time to collect dust on the bookshelf.

The Editors, Group Publishing

FIVE BIBLE STUDY TIPS

1. Pray. Ask God to guide you as you read. Your prayer doesn't have to be fancy. You might just pray, "Help me, God, to discover you and your will as I read my Bible."

2. Read. Read a devotion and the Bible passage related to it. If the passage is not clear the first time you read it, read it again. Also check out the introduction at the beginning of the book that helps you understand the book's purpose.

3. Think. Think about the questions listed in the devotion. It may help to ask yourself: What's going on in the passage? How is the world similar or different than it was then? How does the passage fit into my faith?

4. Do. What is God saying to you through this passage? What changes or new directions does the passage call for? Decide what you can do to respond to the truth in the passage, and do it. Use the ideas in the devotional section labeled "Consider . . ." to get you started. It could change your life!

5. Ask. If a passage confuses or bothers you, talk to someone about it. Ask a parent, youth leader, pastor, Sunday school teacher, or trusted friend to help you understand.

USING THE YOUTH BIBLE IN GROUPS

Though designed especially for individual use, *The Youth Bible* has many features that also make it excellent for group use. Use it with your youth group or in a Bible study group with friends. Try these suggestions:

Decide – Find out what topics interest or concern group members. Then see the Topical Devotion Guide to find the devotions on those themes.

Compare – Have different people (or small groups) look at different devotions on the same topic. Compare the stories and the passages. Where do they overlap? What new insights do you gain from the differences?

Be open – Let people express their thoughts and feelings. Listen for different perspectives. When someone says something controversial, you might ask, "Would anyone like to respond to that?"

Commit – Decide specific ways group members can apply what they have learned from the Bible. Encourage each other to keep the commitments you make to yourselves and to God.

TOPICAL DEVOTION GUIDE

This devotion guide helps you find devotions on topics that interest or concern you. Refer to it when you are dealing with a particular problem or issue, or use it as a topical reading plan. Simply decide what topic you want to study and then read one devotion each day on that topic until you have read all the devotions and passages.

Where Do I Find ... ?

Have you ever known what you were looking for but didn't know where to find it in the Bible? A great event? A famous passage? A favorite story? Use this guide to help you find stories you remember but don't know where to find. The descriptions listed here are the common descriptions and are not always exactly the same as the descriptions in this Bible translation.

CONTENTS

OLD TESTAMENT

NEW TESTAMENT

OLD
TESTAMENT

GENESIS

Why Read This Book:

■ Reflect on the beauty and wonder of God's creation (Genesis 1—2).
■ Learn how God responds to rebellion against Him (Genesis 3—11).
■ Discover how God keeps his promises (Genesis 12—24).
■ See how God works for good even during bad times (Genesis 37—50).

Behind the Scenes:

For a week, you work tediously in art class creating a clay sculpture. You carefully shape the soft clay. On Friday, you leave the almost-finished sculpture to harden. Monday you return. You find your clay twisted into a chaotic, unrecognizable blob. Rage and sadness swell up in you. You must begin the painstaking work all over again.

Genesis tells a similar story. It's the story of God's loving care in creating the world. But the story has a dark, twisted side. Genesis tells of human rebellion, murder, and other human evil as people rebel against God.

Genesis falls naturally into two parts. Chapters 1—11 talk about the beginnings of the world. Here you'll read the famous stories of Adam and Eve, Cain and Abel, Noah, and the tower of Babel. Each story shows how people often twist and destroy the gifts God has given them.

Then chapters 12—50 talk specifically about the beginnings of the Hebrew people, later known as Israelites. You'll read about Abraham, the father of the nation, and his sons. And the book concludes with the story of Joseph, whom God was able to use for great things even after his brothers had sold him into slavery.

Genesis is one of the most important books in the Bible. Not only does the rest of the Bible build on the foundation laid in this book, but the book shows how, from the beginning, God has used special people to play important roles in his world.

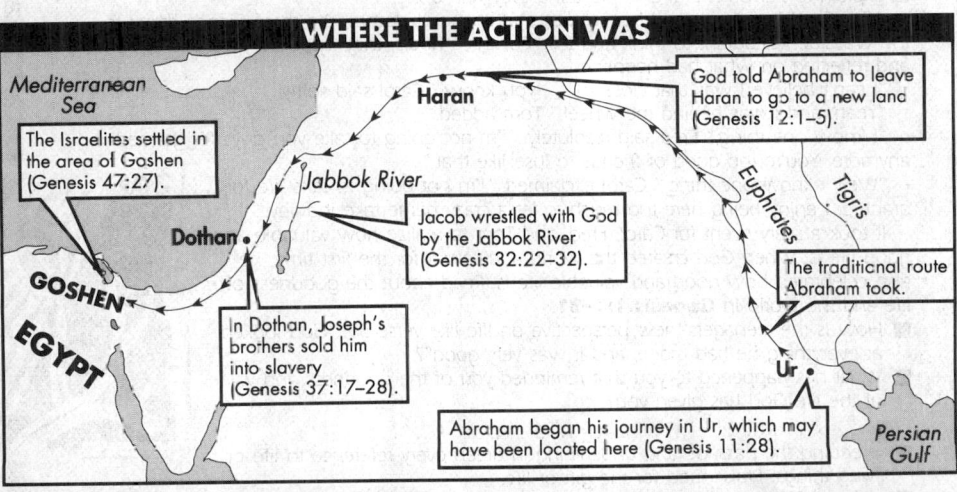

WHERE THE ACTION WAS

Mediterranean Sea

Haran

God told Abraham to leave Haran to go to a new land (Genesis 12:1—5).

The Israelites settled in the area of Goshen (Genesis 47:27).

Jabbok River

Dothan

Jacob wrestled with God by the Jabbok River (Genesis 32:22—32).

The traditional route Abraham took.

GOSHEN

EGYPT

In Dothan, Joseph's brothers sold him into slavery (Genesis 37:17—28).

Abraham began his journey in Ur, which may have been located here (Genesis 11:28).

Euphrates

Tigris

Ur

Persian Gulf

WHEN THE ACTION WAS

Abraham lived	Joseph was sold into slavery	The Israelites escaped from Egypt			Jesus was born
2000BC	1500BC	1000BC	500BC		BC/AD

◄ Creation, the Flood, the Tower

The Beginning of the World

1 In the beginning God created the sky and the earth. ²The earth was empty and had no form. Darkness covered the ocean, and God's Spirit*d* was moving over the water.

³Then God said, "Let there be light," and there was light. ⁴God saw that the light was good, so he divided the light from the darkness. ⁵God named the light "day" and the darkness "night." Evening passed, and morning came. This was the first day.

⁶Then God said, "Let there be something to divide the water in two." ⁷So God made the air and placed some of the water above the air and some below it. ⁸God named the air "sky." Evening passed, and morning came. This was the second day.

⁹Then God said, "Let the water under the sky be gathered together so the dry land will appear." And it happened. ¹⁰God named the dry land "earth" and the water that was gathered together "seas." God saw that this was good.

¹¹Then God said, "Let the earth produce plants — some to make grain for seeds and others to make fruits with seeds in them. Every seed will produce more of its own kind of plant." And it happened. ¹²The earth produced plants with grain for seeds and trees that made fruits with seeds in them. Each seed grew its own kind of plant. God

---

LIFE

The Good Things

Carol, Fred, and Tom had planned an evening packed with fun. The trunk of Tom's Honda was loaded with toilet paper and flashlights—the supplies they'd need to "t.p." Tanya's house in honor of her sixteenth birthday.

But first they went to the school parking lot for some fun with the car. Carol and Fred jumped on the hood, and Tom steered in wild, squealing circles. It was as fun as a roller coaster—until Carol lost her grip and flew off the hood. The tires screeched and swerved, barely missing Carol, who was lying on the ground. Her jeans were ripped, and one leg was bleeding.

"You okay?" Tom asked as he rushed out of the car.

"I think so," Carol responded, holding her leg. "Just shook up."

The three friends pulled themselves together, stunned by what had happened—and could have happened. Their original plans forgotten, they cautiously drove to Carol's house to explain to her parents the stupid thing they had done.

After Carol had bandaged her scrapes and changed clothes, the three friends drove to the Wayside Restaurant to think and talk. For three hours, they sipped on chocolate malts and reflected on what had happened.

"I can't believe I was that close to . . . you know," Carol said softly.

"Yeah, and I was behind the wheel," Tom added.

"I know one thing," Fred said resolutely. "I'm not going to take you guys for granted anymore. You're too good of friends to lose like that."

"Well, I know one thing," Carol exclaimed. "I'm not going to take life for granted. I enjoy being here too much to let a crazy game take it away."

It took a scary event for Carol, Fred, and Tom to realize how valuable and good life is. When God created the world and saw it for the first time, he also celebrated how good and valuable life is. Read about the goodness of life and the world in **Genesis 1:1–31**.

- How is the teenagers' new perspective on life like verse 31: "God looked at everything he had made, and it was very good"?
- What has happened to you that reminded you of the goodness and value of the life God has given you?

C O N S I D E R . . .

- rereading the passage and underlining in green every reference to life or living things. Praise God for the gift of life.
- giving a flower or small houseplant or doing a chore for someone who is valuable to you. Include a note that celebrates how he or she makes your life better.

F O R   M O R E ,   S E E . . .

- Genesis 2:4–17 (p. 3)
- Psalm 104:1–32 (p. 541)
- John 10:7–18 (p. 1074)

saw that all this was good. [13]Evening passed, and morning came. This was the third day.

[14]Then God said, "Let there be lights in the sky to separate day from night. These lights will be used for signs, seasons, days, and years. [15]They will be in the sky to give light to the earth." And it happened.

[16]So God made the two large lights. He made the brighter light to rule the day and made the smaller light to rule the night. He also made the stars. [17]God put all these in the sky to shine on the earth, [18]to rule over the day and over the night, and to separate the light from the darkness. God saw that all these things were good. [19]Evening passed, and morning came. This was the fourth day.

[20]Then God said, "Let the water be filled with living things, and let birds fly in the air above the earth."

[21]So God created the large sea animals and every living thing that moves in the sea. The sea is filled with these living things, with each one producing more of its own kind. He also made every bird that flies, and each bird produced more of its own kind. God saw that this was good. [22]God blessed them and said, "Have many young ones so that you may grow in number. Fill the water of the seas, and let the birds grow in number on the earth." [23]Evening passed, and morning came. This was the fifth day.

[24]Then God said, "Let the earth be filled with animals, each producing more of its own kind. Let there be tame animals and small crawling animals and wild animals, and let each produce more of its kind." And it happened.

[25]So God made the wild animals, the tame animals, and all the small crawling animals to produce more of their own kind. God saw that this was good.

[26]Then God said, "Let us make human beings in our image and likeness. And let them rule over the fish in the sea and the birds in the sky, over the tame animals, over all the earth, and over all the small crawling animals on the earth."

[27]So God created human beings in his image. In the image of God he created them. He created them male and female. [28]God blessed them and said, "Have many children and grow in number. Fill the earth and be its master. Rule over the fish in the sea and over the birds in the sky and over every living thing that moves on the earth."

[29]God said, "Look, I have given you all the plants that have grain for seeds and all the trees whose fruits have seeds in them. They will be food for you. [30]I have given all the green plants as food for every wild animal, every bird of the air, and every small crawling animal." And it happened. [31]God looked at everything he had made, and it was very good. Evening passed, and morning came. This was the sixth day.

The Seventh Day — Rest

2 So the sky, the earth, and all that filled them were finished. [2]By the seventh day God finished the work he had been doing, so he rested from all his work. [3]God blessed the seventh day and made it a holy day, because on that day he rested from all the work he had done in creating the world.

The First People

[4]This is the story of the creation of the sky and the earth. When the Lord God first made the earth and the sky, [5]there were still no plants on the earth. Nothing was growing in the fields because the Lord God had not yet made it rain on the land. And there was no person to care for the ground, [6]but a mist would rise up from the earth and water all the ground.

[7]Then the Lord God took dust from the ground and formed a man from it. He breathed the breath of life into the man's nose, and the man became a living person. [8]Then the Lord God planted a garden in the east, in a place called Eden, and put the man he had formed into it. [9]The Lord God caused every beautiful tree and every tree that was good for food to grow out of the ground. In the middle of the garden, God put the tree that gives life and also the tree that gives the knowledge of good and evil.

[10]A river flowed through Eden and watered the garden. From there the river branched out to become four rivers. [11]The first river, named Pishon, flows around the whole land of Havilah, where there is gold. [12]The gold of that land is excellent. Bdellium and onyx[n] are also found there. [13]The second river, named Gihon, flows around the whole land of Cush. [14]The third river, named Tigris, flows out of Assyria toward the east. The fourth river is the Euphrates.

[15]The Lord God put the man in the garden of Eden to care for it and work it. [16]The Lord God commanded him, "You may eat the fruit from any tree in the garden, [17]but you must not eat the fruit from the tree which gives the knowledge of good and evil. If you ever eat fruit from that tree, you will die!"

The First Woman

[18]Then the Lord God said, "It is not good for the man to be alone. I will make a helper who is right for him."

[19]From the ground God formed every wild ani-

---

bdellium and onyx Bdellium is an expensive, sweet-smelling resin like myrrh, and onyx is a gem.

mal and every bird in the sky, and he brought them to the man so the man could name them.

SIDELIGHT: Adam and Eve ate an apple in the garden, right? Probably not. The Bible never says what the fruit was. It's only described as "the fruit from the tree which gives the knowledge of good and evil" (Genesis 2:17). Doesn't sound much like the humble apple!

Whatever the man called each living thing, that became its name. [20]The man gave names to all the tame animals, to the birds in the sky, and to all the wild animals. But Adam[n] did not find a helper that was right for him. [21]So the LORD God caused the man to sleep very deeply, and while he was asleep, God removed one of the man's ribs. Then God closed up the man's skin at the place where he took the rib. [22]The LORD God used the rib from the man to make a woman, and then he brought the woman to the man.

[23]And the man said,
"Now, this is someone whose bones came
     from my bones,
  whose body came from my body.
I will call her 'woman,'
  because she was taken out of man."

[24]So a man will leave his father and mother and be united with his wife, and the two will become one body. [25]The man and his wife were naked, but they were not ashamed.

The Beginning of Sin

3 Now the snake was the most clever of all the wild animals the LORD God had made. One day the snake said to the woman, "Did God really

---

Adam   This is the name of the first man. It also means "humans," including men and women.

CREATION

Will We Ever Learn?

Five hundred years ago, Christopher Columbus wrote about the lush forests on the Haitian island of La Gonave. He described "thousands of kinds of trees so tall that they seem to be scratching heaven."

Today, the mountains of that island are almost barren. When the rain comes, the rich topsoil is eroded away, causing regular, devastating floods.

One year, thirty-three people in the small island town of Anse-a-Galets died in a flood. Three years later, the people were ready for the flooding. No one died, but two churches, four homes, and a drinking-water system were destroyed.

Some say the floods are natural disasters. But they happen, in part, because the people don't care for the land. They cut down trees to make charcoal to cook with or to sell. It's the only way they know to survive.

But it hurts them. Without trees, the highlands aren't protected. When rainfall comes, the good soil washes away, and the lowlands flood. So the cutting of trees to survive actually makes survival more difficult.

The people of La Gonave are experiencing the problems that come when people don't take care of the environment. Read **Genesis 2:4–17**— particularly verse 15—to see how God expects us to care for his world.

- How well do you think the people of La Gonave are fulfilling the responsibility of caring for God's "garden"?
- In what ways have you taken responsibility for caring for the world or "garden" God has given you?

CONSIDER . . .

- noting everything you throw away in a day or week. Decide which items you could avoid throwing away by recycling, reusing, or not purchasing.
- contributing to or getting involved with the National Forestry Association's Global ReLeaf campaign (Box 2000, Washington, DC 20013) or another organization that plants trees to repair damage people have caused by cutting down trees.

FOR MORE, SEE . . .

- Leviticus 25:1–7 (p. 121)
- Psalm 8:1–9 (p. 485)
- Colossians 1:15–20 (p. 1239)

say that you must not eat fruit from any tree in the garden?"

²The woman answered the snake, "We may eat fruit from the trees in the garden. ³But God told us, 'You must not eat fruit from the tree that is in the middle of the garden. You must not even touch it, or you will die.' "

⁴But the snake said to the woman, "You will not die. ⁵God knows that if you eat the fruit from that tree, you will learn about good and evil and you will be like God!"

⁶The woman saw that the tree was beautiful, that its fruit was good to eat, and that it would make her wise. So she took some of its fruit and ate it. She also gave some of the fruit to her husband, and he ate it.

⁷Then, it was as if their eyes were opened. They realized they were naked, so they sewed fig leaves together and made something to cover themselves.

⁸Then they heard the LORD God walking in the garden during the cool part of the day, and the man and his wife hid from the LORD God among the trees in the garden. ⁹But the LORD God called to the man and said, "Where are you?"

¹⁰The man answered, "I heard you walking in the garden, and I was afraid because I was naked, so I hid."

¹¹God asked, "Who told you that you were naked? Did you eat fruit from the tree from which I commanded you not to eat?"

¹²The man said, "You gave this woman to me and she gave me fruit from the tree, so I ate it."

¹³Then the LORD God said to the woman, "How could you have done such a thing?"

She answered, "The snake tricked me, so I ate the fruit."

¹⁴The LORD God said to the snake,
"Because you did this,
    a curse will be put on you.
You will be cursed as no other animal,
    tame or wild, will ever be.
You will crawl on your stomach,
    and you will eat dust all the days of your
        life.
¹⁵I will make you and the woman
    enemies to each other.
Your descendants*d* and her descendants
    will be enemies.
One of her descendants will crush your head,

One Body . . . Kind Of

"Connie, I'd like to talk about something."

"Sure, Jeff. Are you nervous about the wedding?"

"No, that's not it. I just wonder if you'd sign this with me. It's a pre-marriage agreement."

Connie scanned the document in disbelief. "This covers everything," she said. "Who'll get what if we divorce. How many children and how we'll raise them. How we'll pay the bills. Who's responsible for what around the house. . . . This reads like a business deal."

"Well, my lawyer . . ."

"Your lawyer! I thought we loved and trusted each other, Jeff."

"Of course I love you, Connie. I just want to be sure everything's clear. These agreements are good protection . . . you know, with the divorce rate and all."

"Will this piece of paper protect us more than sacred vows to love and cherish each other?"

Connie and Jeff discovered differences in their views of marriage—almost too late. Read **Genesis 2:18–24** to discover God's intention for marriage.

■ How could this passage help Connie and Jeff sort out their conflicting expectations for marriage?

■ How does this passage challenge or confirm your views of marriage?

C O N S I D E R . . .

■ listing in order of priority all the things that would be important to you if you married. Then decide whether those priorities are compatible with the theme of this scripture passage.

■ asking a parent or pastor to define a healthy Christian marriage.

F O R   M O R E ,   S E E . . .

■ Genesis 29:16–20 (p. 34)   ■ Ephesians 5:21–33 (p. 1225)
■ Matthew 19:3–6 (p. 941)

and you will bite his heel."

¹⁶Then God said to the woman,
"I will cause you to have much trouble
    when you are pregnant,
and when you give birth to children,
    you will have great pain.
You will greatly desire your husband,
    but he will rule over you."

¹⁷Then God said to the man, "You listened to what your wife said, and you ate fruit from the tree from which I commanded you not to eat. "So I will put a curse on the ground,
    and you will have to work very hard for
        your food.

In pain you will eat its food
    all the days of your life.
¹⁸The ground will produce thorns and weeds
        for you,
    and you will eat the plants of the field.
¹⁹You will sweat and work hard
    for your food.
Later you will return to the ground,
    because you were taken from it.
You are dust,
    and when you die, you will return to the
        dust."

²⁰The man named his wife Eve,[n] because she is the mother of everyone who has ever lived. ²¹The LORD God made clothes from animal

Eve   This name sounds like the Hebrew word meaning "alive."

SIN

An Expensive CD

Larry Rickers pulled the compact disc out from under his school jacket as he sauntered toward his car. His cool exterior disguised his excitement. A single from the CD had been at the top of the charts for five weeks straight, and he couldn't get it out of his head. He'd never wanted a recording this much, and now he had it. He couldn't wait to listen to it.

Suddenly, something came down hard on the back of his neck and made him crumple to his knees.

"Back inside, kid," an angry voice growled, as a security guard jerked Larry's arm behind his back. "I'll take that CD, thank you."

Larry felt humiliated as the guard escorted him through the mall, to the store manager's office. Then he sat awkwardly while the manager finished talking to the cops on the phone.

"An officer will be here in a few minutes," he said as he put down the receiver. "I won't press charges if you're a first-timer, but I need your home phone number. Your mom or dad will have to come get you."

Larry dictated the number as the manager dialed. "And, young man," the manager said as the phone rang, "I never want to see you in my store again."

Larry dreaded seeing his mom. She'd be so disappointed. Her eyes would be glassy-wet and red. She wouldn't look at him. That was the hardest part. He laid his head back and waited.

Larry experienced shame as Adam and Eve experienced shame when God caught them disobeying him. Read **Genesis 3:8–24** to learn what happened.

■ How does the store manager's punishment for shoplifting compare to God's punishment of Adam and Eve? What resulted from Adam and Eve's sin? Was Larry's punishment—and Adam and Eve's—appropriate?

■ In what ways do you, like Adam and Eve, try to hide from God when you disobey him?

CONSIDER . . .

■ interrupting the "blame chain" ("somebody else made me do it") by accepting responsibility for things you do.

■ *talking to someone you trust about a sin you've been hiding inside, then confessing the sin to God. Discover how the confession affects you.*

FOR   MORE,   SEE . . .

■ Psalm 119:9–16 (p. 550)
■ John 8:1–11 (p. 1070)

■ 1 John 1:5–10 (p. 1316)

skins for the man and his wife and dressed them. [22]Then the LORD God said, "The man has become like one of us; he knows good and evil. We must keep him from eating some of the fruit from the tree of life, or he will live forever." [23]So the LORD God forced the man out of the garden of Eden to work the ground from which he was taken. [24]After God forced the man out of the garden, he placed angels and a sword of fire that flashed around in every direction on its eastern border. This kept people from getting to the tree of life.

The First Family

4 Adam had sexual relations with his wife Eve, and she became pregnant and gave birth to Cain.[n] Eve said, "With the LORD's help, I have given birth to a man." [2]After that, Eve gave birth to Cain's brother Abel. Abel took care of flocks, and Cain became a farmer.

[3]Later, Cain brought some food from the ground as a gift to God. [4]Abel brought the best parts from some of the firstborn[d] of his flock. The LORD accepted Abel and his gift, [5]but he did not accept Cain and his gift. So Cain became very angry and felt rejected.

[6]The LORD asked Cain, "Why are you angry? Why do you look so unhappy? [7]If you do things well, I will accept you, but if you do not do them well, sin is ready to attack you. Sin wants you, but you must rule over it."

[8]Cain said to his brother Abel, "Let's go out into the field." While they were out in the field, Cain attacked his brother Abel and killed him.

[9]Later, the LORD said to Cain, "Where is your brother Abel?"

Cain answered, "I don't know. Is it my job to take care of my brother?"

[10]Then the LORD said, "What have you done? Your brother's blood is crying out to me from the ground. [11]And now you will be cursed in your work with the ground, the same ground where your brother's blood fell and where your hands killed him. [12]You will work the ground, but it will not grow good crops for you anymore, and you will wander around on the earth."

[13]Then Cain said to the LORD, "This punishment is more than I can stand! [14]Today you have forced me to stop working the ground, and now I must hide from you. I must wander around on the earth, and anyone who meets me can kill me."

[15]The LORD said to Cain, "No! If anyone kills you, I will punish that person seven times more." Then the LORD put a mark on Cain warning anyone who met him not to kill him.

Cain's Family

[16]So Cain went away from the LORD and lived in the land of Nod,[n] east of Eden. [17]He had sexual relations with his wife, and she became pregnant and gave birth to Enoch. At that time Cain was building a city, which he named after his son Enoch. [18]Enoch had a son named Irad, Irad had a son named Mehujael, Mehujael had a son named Methushael, and Methushael had a son named Lamech.

> ☀ **SIDELIGHT:** If one wife is a good idea, two wives must be twice as good. That's what Lamech thought (Genesis 4:19). The idea really caught on by the time it reached Solomon, who ended up with seven hundred wives (1 Kings 11:3, p. 315).

[19]Lamech married two women, Adah and Zillah. [20]Adah gave birth to Jabal, who became the first person to live in tents and raise cattle. [21]Jabal's brother was Jubal, the first person to play the harp and flute. [22]Zillah gave birth to Tubal-Cain, who made tools out of bronze and iron. The sister of Tubal-Cain was Naamah.

[23]Lamech said to his wives:
"Adah and Zillah, hear my voice!
    You wives of Lamech, listen to what I say.
I killed a man for wounding me,
    a young man for hitting me.
[24]If Cain's killer is punished seven times,
    then Lamech's killer will be punished
        seventy-seven times."

Adam and Eve Have a New Son

[25]Adam had sexual relations with his wife Eve again, and she gave birth to a son. She named him Seth[n] and said, "God has given me another child. He will take the place of Abel, who was killed by Cain." [26]Seth also had a son, and they named him Enosh. At that time people began to pray to the LORD.

Adam's Family History

5 This is the family history of Adam. When God created human beings, he made them in his own likeness. [2]He created them male and female, and on that day he blessed them and named them human beings.

[3]When Adam was 130 years old, he became the father of another son in his likeness and im-

---

Cain   This name sounds like the Hebrew word for "I have given birth."
Nod   This name sounds like the Hebrew word for "wander."
Seth   This name sounds like the Hebrew word for "to give."

age, and Adam named him Seth. 4After Seth was born, Adam lived 800 years and had other sons and daughters. 5So Adam lived a total of 930 years, and then he died.

6When Seth was 105 years old, he had a son named Enosh. 7After Enosh was born, Seth lived 807 years and had other sons and daughters. 8So Seth lived a total of 912 years, and then he died.

9When Enosh was 90 years old, he had a son named Kenan. 10After Kenan was born, Enosh lived 815 years and had other sons and daughters. 11So Enosh lived a total of 905 years, and then he died.

12When Kenan was 70 years old, he had a son named Mahalalel. 13After Mahalalel was born, Kenan lived 840 years and had other sons and daughters. 14So Kenan lived a total of 910 years, and then he died.

15When Mahalalel was 65 years old, he had a son named Jared. 16After Jared was born, Mahalalel lived 830 years and had other sons and daughters. 17So Mahalalel lived a total of 895 years, and then he died.

18When Jared was 162 years old, he had a son named Enoch. 19After Enoch was born, Jared lived 800 years and had other sons and daughters. 20So Jared lived a total of 962 years, and then he died.

21When Enoch was 65 years old, he had a son named Methuselah. 22After Methuselah was born, Enoch walked with God 300 years more and had other sons and daughters. 23So Enoch lived a total of 365 years. 24Enoch walked with God; one day Enoch could not be found, because God took him.

25When Methuselah was 187 years old, he had a son named Lamech. 26After Lamech was born, Methuselah lived 782 years and had other sons and daughters. 27So Methuselah lived a total of 969 years, and then he died.

SIDELIGHT: If you think older adults tell too many stories about "when I was your age," imagine how Methuselah's kids must have felt. Genesis 5:27 says he lived to be 969 years old. If he were born when Christopher Columbus discovered the Americas in 1492, he would only be middle-aged today!

28When Lamech was 182, he had a son. 29Lamech named his son Noah[n] and said, "He will comfort us in our work, which comes from the ground the LORD has cursed." 30After Noah was born, Lamech lived 595 years and had other sons

---

Noah This name sounds like the Hebrew word for "rest."

---

and daughters. 31So Lamech lived a total of 777 years, and then he died.

32After Noah was 500 years old, he became the father of Shem, Ham, and Japheth.

The Human Race Becomes Evil

6 The number of people on earth began to grow, and daughters were born to them. 2When the sons of God saw that these girls were beautiful, they married any of them they chose. 3The LORD said, "My Spirit[d] will not remain in human beings forever, because they are flesh. They will live only 120 years."

4The Nephilim[d] were on the earth in those days and also later. That was when the sons of God had sexual relations with the daughters of human beings. These women gave birth to children, who became famous and were the mighty warriors of long ago.

SIDELIGHT: Noah's boat described in Genesis 6:15 would have been huge for its time—about 450 feet long, the length of one and a half football fields. That's five times as long as the Mayflower in which the pilgrims sailed to North America in 1620. And it's more than half as long as a modern 860-foot ocean liner.

5The LORD saw that the human beings on the earth were very wicked and that everything they thought about was evil. 6He was sorry he had made human beings on the earth, and his heart was filled with pain. 7So the LORD said, "I will destroy all human beings that I made on the earth. And I will destroy every animal and everything that crawls on the earth and the birds of the air, because I am sorry I have made them." 8But Noah pleased the LORD.

Noah and the Great Flood

9This is the family history of Noah. Noah was a good man, the most innocent man of his time, and he walked with God. 10He had three sons: Shem, Ham, and Japheth.

11People on earth did what God said was evil, and violence was everywhere. 12When God saw that everyone on the earth did only evil, 13he said to Noah, "Because people have made the earth full of violence, I will destroy all of them from the earth. 14Build a boat of cypress wood for yourself. Make rooms in it and cover it inside and outside with tar. 15This is how big I want you to build the boat: four hundred fifty feet long, seventy-five feet wide, and forty-five feet high. 16Make an opening around the top of the boat that is eighteen inches high from the edge of the roof down. Put a door in the side of the boat. Make an upper, middle, and lower deck in it. [17]I will bring a flood of water on the earth to destroy all living things that live under the sky, including everything that has the breath of life. Everything on the earth will die. [18]But I will make an agreement with you — you, your sons, your wife, and your sons' wives will all go into the boat. [19]Also, you must bring into the boat two of every living thing, male and female. Keep them alive with you. [20]Two of every kind of bird, animal, and crawling thing will come to you to be kept alive. [21]Also gather some of every kind of food and store it on the boat as food for you and the animals."

[22]Noah did everything that God commanded him.

The Flood Begins

7 Then the LORD said to Noah, "I have seen that you are the best person among the people of this time, so you and your family can go into the boat. [2]Take with you seven pairs, each male with its female, of every kind of clean[d] animal, and take one pair, each male with its female, of every kind of unclean animal. [3]Take seven pairs of all the birds of the sky, each male with its female. This will allow all these animals to continue living on the earth after the flood. [4]Seven days from now I will send rain on the earth. It will rain forty days and forty nights, and I will wipe off from the earth every living thing that I have made."

[5]Noah did everything the LORD commanded him.

[6]Noah was six hundred years old when the flood came. [7]He and his wife and his sons and their wives went into the boat to escape the waters of the flood. [8]The clean animals, the unclean animals, the birds, and everything that crawls on the ground [9]came to Noah. They went into the boat in groups of two, male and female, just as God had commanded Noah. [10]Seven days later the flood started.

[11]When Noah was six hundred years old, the flood started. On the seventeenth day of the second month of that year the underground springs

---

EVIL

Quiet Cancer

The symptoms don't seem that bad. You feel kind of tired and short of breath. Your blood doesn't clot as well as it should, and you bruise easily.

But these seemingly minor problems can be symptoms of acute leukemia, a potentially deadly cancer.

Though the outward signs don't seem that bad, inside, the body is under siege. Cancerous cells have invaded the bone marrow and bloodstream. The body no longer produces enough healthy white blood cells, taking away the body's ability to fight off infections. Suddenly, the body feels sick and needs immediate medical attention. Untreated, a person can die within six weeks. Treatment can involve intravenous chemotherapy with drugs that kill the cancerous cells, but also kill normal cells.

The hope is that healthy cells will grow again after treatment . . . and that cancerous ones won't.

Like leukemia, evil can spread without people really noticing it. Yet it's deadly and difficult to get rid of. See how God feels about evil in the world by reading **Genesis 6:5–7:24**.

■ What parallels do you see between acute leukemia and the evil described in the passage? How is God's response to that evil like chemotherapy?

■ What kinds of evil described in the passage still exist today? How is God working in the world today to stop the spread of evil?

C O N S I D E R . . .

■ identifying a potential evil in your life and then talking to a parent or other trusted adult about how you can stop it before it grows into a bigger problem.

■ clipping newspaper articles that show evil in the world. Each day this week, pray for people who are trapped by that evil.

F O R   M O R E ,   S E E . . .

■ Psalm 43:1–5 (p. 507)   ■ 1 John 5:18–20 (p. 1321)
■ Romans 1:28–32 (p. 1141)

split open, and the clouds in the sky poured out rain. [12]The rain fell on the earth for forty days and forty nights.

[13]On that same day Noah and his wife, his sons Shem, Ham, and Japheth, and their wives went into the boat. [14]They had every kind of wild and tame animal, every kind of animal that crawls on the earth, and every kind of bird. [15]Every creature that had the breath of life came to Noah in the boat in groups of two. [16]One male and one female of every living thing came, just as God had commanded Noah. Then the LORD closed the door behind them.

[17]Water flooded the earth for forty days, and as it rose it lifted the boat off the ground. [18]The water continued to rise, and the boat floated on it above the earth. [19]The water rose so much that even the highest mountains under the sky were covered by it. [20]It continued to rise until it was more than twenty feet above the mountains.

[21]All living things that moved on the earth died. This included all the birds, tame animals, wild animals, and creatures that swarm on the earth, as well as all human beings. [22]So everything on dry land that had the breath of life in it died. [23]God destroyed from the earth every living thing that was on the land — every man, animal, crawling thing, and bird of the sky. All that was left was Noah and what was with him in the boat. [24]And the waters continued to cover the earth for one hundred fifty days.

The Flood Ends

8 But God remembered Noah and all the wild and tame animals with him in the boat. He made a wind blow over the earth, and the water went down. [2]The underground springs stopped flowing, and the clouds in the sky stopped pouring down rain. [3-4]The water that covered the earth began to go down. After one hundred fifty days it had gone down so much that the boat touched land again. It came to rest on one of the mountains of Ararat[n] on the seventeenth day of the seventh month. [5]The water continued to go down so that by the first day of the tenth month the tops of the mountains could be seen.

[6]Forty days later Noah opened the window he had made in the boat, and [7]he sent out a raven. It flew here and there until the water had dried up from the earth. [8]Then Noah sent out a dove to find out if the water had dried up from the ground. [9]The dove could not find a place to land *because water still covered the earth, so it* came back to the boat. Noah reached out his hand and took the bird and brought it back into the boat. [10]After seven days Noah again sent out the dove from the boat, [11]and that evening it came

back to him with a fresh olive leaf in its mouth. Then Noah knew that the ground was almost dry. [12]Seven days later he sent the dove out again, but this time it did not come back.

[13]When Noah was six hundred and one years old, in the first day of the first month of that year, the water was dried up from the land. Noah removed the covering of the boat and saw that the land was dry. [14]By the twenty-seventh day of the second month the land was completely dry.

[15]Then God said to Noah, [16]"You and your wife, your sons, and their wives should go out of the boat. [17]Bring every animal out of the boat with you — the birds, animals, and everything that crawls on the earth. Let them have many young ones so that they might grow in number."

[18]So Noah went out with his sons, his wife, and his sons' wives. [19]Every animal, everything that crawls on the earth, and every bird went out of the boat by families.

[20]Then Noah built an altar to the LORD. He took some of all the clean[d] birds and animals, and he burned them on the altar as offerings to God. [21]The LORD was pleased with these sacrifices and said to himself, "I will never again curse the ground because of human beings. Their thoughts are evil even when they are young, but I will never again destroy every living thing on the earth as I did this time.
[22]"As long as the earth continues,
planting and harvest,
cold and hot,
summer and winter,
day and night
will not stop."

The New Beginning

9 Then God blessed Noah and his sons and said to them, "Have many children; grow in number and fill the earth. [2]Every animal on earth, every bird in the sky, every animal that crawls on the ground, and every fish in the sea will respect and fear you. I have given them to you.

[3]"Everything that moves, everything that is alive, is yours for food. Earlier I gave you the green plants, but now I give you everything for food. [4]But you must not eat meat that still has blood in it, because blood gives life. [5]I will demand blood for life. I will demand the life of any animal that kills a person, and I will demand the life of anyone who takes another person's life.

[6]*"Whoever kills a human being*
will be killed by a human being,
because God made humans
in his own image.

[7]"As for you, Noah, I want you and your family

Ararat The ancient land of Urartu, an area in Eastern Turkey.

to have many children, to grow in number on the earth, and to become many."

⁸Then God said to Noah and his sons, ⁹"Now I am making my agreement with you and your people who will live after you, ¹⁰and with every living thing that is with you — the birds, the tame and the wild animals, and with everything that came out of the boat with you — with every living thing on earth. ¹¹I make this agreement with you: I will never again destroy all living things by a flood. A flood will never again destroy the earth."

¹²And God said, "This is the sign of the agreement between me and you and every living creature that is with you. ¹³I am putting my rainbow in the clouds as the sign of the agreement between me and the earth. ¹⁴When I bring clouds over the earth and a rainbow appears in them, ¹⁵I will remember my agreement between me and you and every living thing. Floods will never again destroy all life on the earth. ¹⁶When the rainbow appears in the clouds, I will see it and I will remember the agreement that continues forever between me and every living thing on the earth."

¹⁷So God said to Noah, "The rainbow is a sign of the agreement that I made with all living things on earth."

Noah and His Sons

¹⁸The sons of Noah who came out of the boat with him were Shem, Ham, and Japheth. (Ham was the father of Canaan.) ¹⁹These three men were Noah's sons, and all the people on earth came from these three sons.

²⁰Noah became a farmer and planted a vineyard. ²¹When he drank wine made from his grapes, he became drunk and lay naked in his tent. ²²Ham, the father of Canaan, looked at his naked father and told his brothers outside. ²³Then Shem and Japheth got a coat and, carrying it on both their shoulders, they walked backwards into the tent and covered their father. They turned their faces away so that they did not see their father's nakedness.

²⁴Noah was sleeping because of the wine. When he woke up and learned what his youngest son, Ham, had done to him, ²⁵he said, "May there be a curse on Canaan!

FUTURE

A Hope-Filled Dream

The future looked bleak for Miguel Rodriquez. Friends in his Brooklyn, New York neighborhood used drugs, spent time in jail, and dropped out of school. For them, life seemed hopeless and the future painful.

But Miguel had a friend who believed in him—Phill Carlos Archbold, his youth minister. Phill Carlos encouraged and supported Miguel, helped him with homework, and invited him over for meals. Sometimes he would even pay Miguel's bus fare so he could get to school.

"He was a father-figure to me," Miguel says. "He was—and still is—always there for me."

Phill Carlos's support and encouragement gave Miguel hope for the future. Though his friends dropped out of high school, he graduated and went on to earn a mechanical engineering degree.

Because of Phill Carlos's ministry, Miguel looked forward to a bright future. God's promise to Noah also pointed to a bright future. Read about it in **Genesis 9:8–17**.

■ How do you think God's promise to Noah gave him hope? How is that hope similar to the hope Phill Carlos gave to Miguel?
■ What signs—like the rainbow for Noah—do you see that give you hope and courage for the future?

C O N S I D E R . . .
■ drawing a rainbow on paper and posting it where you'll see it. Whenever something happens this week that encourages you about your future, write it on the paper.
■ watching the evening news to look for signs of hope. Thank God for those people who are working for a positive future.

F O R   M O R E ,   S E E . . .
■ Jeremiah 29:11 (p. 723)   ■ 2 Corinthians 4:16–18 (p. 1196)
■ Matthew 6:25–34 (p. 918)

May he be the lowest slave to his
brothers."
26Noah also said,
"May the Lord, the God of Shem, be
praised!
May Canaan be Shem's slave.
27May God give more land to Japheth.
May Japheth live in Shem's tents,
and may Canaan be their slave."
28After the flood Noah lived 350 years. 29He
lived a total of 950 years, and then he died.

Nations Grow and Spread

10 This is the family history of Shem, Ham,
and Japheth, the sons of Noah. After the
flood these three men had sons.

Japheth's Sons

2The sons of Japheth were Gomer, Magog,
Madai, Javan, Tubal, Meshech, and Tiras.
3The sons of Gomer were Ashkenaz, Riphath,
and Togarmah.
4The sons of Javan were Elishah, Tarshish, Kittim,n and Rodanim. 5Those who lived in the
lands around the Mediterranean Sea came from
these sons of Japheth. All the families grew and
became different nations, each nation with its
own land and its own language.

Ham's Sons

6The sons of Ham were Cush, Mizraim,n Put,
and Canaan.
7The sons of Cush were Seba, Havilah, Sabtah,
Raamah, and Sabteca.
The sons of Raamah were Sheba and Dedan.
8Cush also had a descendantd named Nimrod,
who became a very powerful man on earth. 9He
was a great hunter before the Lord, which is why
people say someone is "like Nimrod, a great
hunter before the Lord." 10At first Nimrod's kingdom covered Babylon, Erech, Akkad, and Calneh
in the land of Babylonia. 11From there he went to
Assyria, where he built the cities of Nineveh, Rehoboth Ir, and Calah. 12He also built Resen, the
great city between Nineveh and Calah.
13Mizraim was the father of the Ludites, Anamites, Lehabites, Naphtuhites, 14Pathrusites, Casluhites, and the people of Crete. (The Philistines
came from the Casluhites.)
15Canaan was the father of Sidon, his first son,
and of Heth. 16He was also the father of the Jebusites, Amorites, Girgashites, 17Hivites, Arkites, Sinites, 18Arvadites, Zemarites, and Hamathites.
The families of the Canaanites scattered. 19Their

land reached from Sidon to Gerar as far as Gaza,
and then to Sodom, Gomorrah, Admah, and Zeboiim, as far as Lasha.
20All these people were the sons of Ham, and
all these families had their own languages, their
own lands, and their own nations.

Shem's Sons

21Shem, Japheth's older brother, also had sons.
One of his descendantsd was the father of all the
sons of Eber.
22The sons of Shem were Elam, Asshur, Arphaxad, Lud, and Aram.
23The sons of Aram were Uz, Hul, Gether, and
Meshech.
24Arphaxad was the father of Shelah, who was
the father of Eber. 25Eber was the father of two
sons—one named Peleg,n because the earth was
divided during his life, and the other was named
Joktan.
26Joktan was the father of Almodad, Sheleph,
Hazarmaveth, Jerah, 27Hadoram, Uzal, Diklah,
28Obal, Abimael, Sheba, 29Ophir, Havilah, and Jobab. All these people were the sons of Joktan.
30They lived in the area between Mesha and Sephar in the hill country in the East.
31These are the people from the family of
Shem, arranged by families, languages, countries,
and nations.
32This is the list of the families from the sons of
Noah, arranged according to their nations. From
these families came all the nations who spread
across the earth after the flood.

The Languages Confused

11 At this time the whole world spoke one
language, and everyone used the same
words. 2As people moved from the east, they
found a plain in the land of Babylonia and settled
there.
3They said to each other, "Let's make bricks
and bake them to make them hard." So they used
bricks instead of stones, and tar instead of mortar.
4Then they said to each other, "Let's build a city
and a tower for ourselves, whose top will reach
high into the sky. We will become famous. Then
we will not be scattered over all the earth."
5The Lord came down to see the city and the
tower that the people had built. 6The Lord said,
"Now, these people are united, all speaking the
same language. This is only the beginning of what
they will do. They will be able to do anything they
want. 7Come, let us go down and confuse their
language so they will not be able to understand
each other."

Kittim His descendants were the people of Cyprus.
Mizraim This is another name for Egypt.
Peleg This name sounds like the Hebrew word for "divided."

⁸So the LORD scattered them from there over all the earth, and they stopped building the city. ⁹The place is called Babel* since that is where the LORD confused the language of the whole world. So the LORD caused them to spread out from there over the whole world.

SIDELIGHT: The tower described in Genesis 11:1–9 was probably a ziggurat—a multi-storied temple built to worship Babylonian gods. The "temple towers," which looked like staircase pyramids, were built in most major Babylonian cities.

The Story of Shem's Family

¹⁰This is the family history of Shem. Two years after the flood, when Shem was 100 years old, his son Arphaxad was born ¹¹After that, Shem lived 500 years and had other sons and daughters.

¹²When Arphaxad was 35 years old, his son Shelah was born. ¹³After that, Arphaxad lived 403 years and had other sons and daughters.

¹⁴When Shelah was 30 years old, his son Eber was born. ¹⁵After that, Shelah lived 403 years and had other sons and daughters.

¹⁶When Eber was 34 years old, his son Peleg was born. ¹⁷After that, Eber lived 430 years and had other sons and daughters.

¹⁸When Peleg was 30 years old, his son Reu was born. ¹⁹After that, Peleg lived 209 years and had other sons and daughters.

²⁰When Reu was 32 years old, his son Serug was born. ²¹After that, Reu lived 207 years and had other sons and daughters.

²²When Serug was 30 years old, his son Nahor was born. ²³After that, Serug lived 200 years and had other sons and daughters.

²⁴When Nahor was 29 years old, his son Terah was born. ²⁵After that, Nahor lived 119 years and had other sons and daughters.

²⁶After Terah was 70 years old, his sons Abram, Nahor, and Haran were born.

Babel This name sounds like the Hebrew word for "confused."

BRAGGING

Pride Hurts

Everyone was sure Susan Thompson would get the lead role of Maria in the spring musical, "West Side Story." Especially Susan. She regularly reminded everyone of her experience—being in every production since she was a freshman.

"I can make Maria come to life on the stage," she would proclaim. "Besides, this is my last high school show. Lots of people would be disappointed if I weren't cast as Maria."

Audition day came, and Susan was ready. She confidently sang and danced and acted. It felt great. "I was hot!" she told her best friend, Dee, on the phone that evening. "This is a great part. It'll really stretch me."

The next morning Susan rushed to the drama room to see the cast list and confirm what she already knew.

But she stared at the list in disbelief. Her name wasn't next to Maria. It was way down the page—a little part with just a few lines in Act 2. Humiliated, Susan left in tears.

Pride was at the root of Susan's problem. And it was at the heart of the events in **Genesis 11:1–9**, where the people built a tower in disobedience to God.

■ How did Susan's pride hurt her like pride hurt the tower builders?
■ What "towers" of pride are you building in your own life?

CONSIDER . . .

■ giving a compliment to another person when you're tempted to brag about yourself.
■ listing everything about yourself that makes you proud. Then put checkmarks beside items you think are appropriate forms of pride, and x's beside those that aren't. Decide how you'll begin overcoming one of the x's this week.

FOR MORE, SEE . . .

■ Proverbs 16:18–19 (p. 581)　　　　■ Philippians 2:1–11 (p. 1230)
■ Hosea 5:5–6 (p. 826)

The Story of Terah's Family

27This is the family history of Terah. Terah was the father of Abram, Nahor, and Haran. Haran was the father of Lot. 28While his father, Terah, was still alive, Haran died in Ur in Babylonia, where he was born. 29Abram and Nahor both married. Abram's wife was named Sarai, and Nahor's wife was named Milcah. She was the daughter of Haran, who was the father of both Milcah and Iscah. 30Sarai was not able to have children.

31Terah took his son Abram, his grandson Lot (Haran's son), and his daughter-in-law Sarai (Abram's wife) and moved out of Ur of Babylonia. They had planned to go to the land of Canaan, but when they reached the city of Haran, they settled there.

32Terah lived to be 205 years old, and then he died in Haran.

God Calls Abram

12 The LORD said to Abram, "Leave your country, your relatives, and your father's family, and go to the land I will show you.
2I will make you a great nation,
and I will bless you.
I will make you famous,
and you will be a blessing to others.
3I will bless those who bless you,
and I will place a curse on those who harm you.
And all the people on earth
will be blessed through you."

GOD'S WILL

Unknown Outcomes

Though it was the 1950s, the Auca Indians of Ecuador, South America were still a violent, Stone Age tribe.

But Jim Elliot felt God calling him to Ecuador to share the Gospel with the Aucas. Only one missionary had ever gone: Pedro Suarez, a Jesuit priest who, in 1667, was murdered at his remote jungle outpost.

Jim didn't let history deter him from what he knew God wanted. "My going to Ecuador is God's counsel," Jim wrote in his diary.

So Jim and four other missionaries left their families and boarded the ship for Ecuador. They built an encampment in Auca territory and began trying to befriend the Aucas. They would fly over their village in a small airplane, drop gifts and call out to them in the Auca language.

On January 6, 1956, they finally befriended one Auca, a young man they called "George." Now, they hoped, they could make more contact with the tribe.

That weekend, the Aucas attacked, killing all the missionaries, including Jim Elliot.

But that wasn't the end of the story. Jim's wife, Elisabeth, refused to let the murder of her husband keep her from following God's call to Ecuador. She and other missionaries returned to Auca territory.

Less than three years later, Elisabeth wrote: "Today I sit in a tiny leaf-thatched hut. . . . In another leaf house, just ten feet away, sit two of the seven men who killed my husband."

Jim Elliot followed God's will to seemingly tragic consequences. But God was at work even when his plan was difficult to see. And the missionary effort, started by Jim Elliot and continued by Elisabeth, prospered. Abram also left everything he knew to follow God to an unknown place. Read about his faith in **Genesis 12:1–9**.

■ In what ways was Jim Elliot's call similar to Abram's call in the passage?
■ Have you ever sensed that God wanted you to do something without your knowing what the result would be? How did you respond?

C O N S I D E R . . .

■ taking a step of faith by doing something you believe God wants you to do, such as sharing your faith with a friend or working on a bad habit.
■ *making a bookmark for your Bible with two big eyes on it to remind you to look for God's will as you read.*

F O R   M O R E ,   S E E . . .

■ Genesis 45:1–8 (p. 50)
■ Matthew 8:18–22 (p. 921)
■ James 4:13–17 (p. 1298)

[4]So Abram left Haran as the LORD had told him, and Lot went with him. At this time Abram was 75 years old. [5]He took his wife Sarai, his nephew Lot, and everything they owned, as well as all the servants they had gotten in Haran. They set out from Haran, planning to go to the land of Canaan, and in time they arrived there.

SIDELIGHT: When Abram left Egypt, he couldn't rent a moving truck to haul all his belongings when he moved from Haran to Canaan (Genesis 12:4–5). Instead, he probably lived in large animal-skin tents that were stretched over wooden poles. Some tents may have had several rooms.

---

[6]Abram traveled through that land as far as the great tree of Moreh at Shechem. The Canaanites were living in the land at that time. [7]The LORD appeared to Abram and said, "I will give this land to your descendants."[d] So Abram built an altar there to the LORD, who had appeared to him. [8]Then he traveled from Shechem to the mountain east of Bethel and set up his tent there. Bethel was to the west, and Ai was to the east. There Abram built another altar to the LORD and worshiped him. [9]After this, he traveled on toward southern Canaan.

Abram Goes to Egypt

[10]At this time there was not much food in the land, so Abram went down to Egypt to live because there was so little food. [11]Just before they arrived in Egypt, he said to his wife Sarai, "I know you are a very beautiful woman. [12]When the Egyptians see you, they will say, 'This woman is his wife.' Then they will kill me but let you live. [13]Tell them you are my sister so that things will go well with me and I may be allowed to live because of you."

[14]When Abram came to Egypt, the Egyptians saw that Sarai was very beautiful. [15]The Egyptian officers saw her and told the king of Egypt how beautiful she was. They took her to the king's palace, and [16]the king was kind to Abram because he thought Abram was her brother. He gave Abram sheep, cattle, male and female donkeys, male and female servants, and camels.

[17]But the LORD sent terrible diseases on the king and all the people in his house because of Abram's wife Sarai. [18]So the king sent for Abram and said, "What have you done to me? Why didn't you tell me Sarai was your wife? [19]Why did you say, 'She is my sister' so that I made her my wife? Now, here is your wife. Take her and leave!" [20]Then the king commanded his men to make Abram leave Egypt; so Abram and his wife left with everything they owned.

Abram and Lot Separate

13 So Abram, his wife, and Lot left Egypt, taking everything they owned, and traveled to southern Canaan. [2]Abram was very rich in cattle, silver, and gold.

[3]He left southern Canaan and went back to Bethel where he had camped before, between Bethel and Ai, [4]and where he had built an altar. So he worshiped the LORD there.

[5]During this time Lot was traveling with Abram, and Lot also had flocks, herds, and tents. [6]Abram and Lot had so many animals that the land could not support both of them together, [7]so Abram's herdsmen and Lot's herdsmen began to argue. The Canaanites and the Perizzites were living in the land at this time.

[8]Abram said to Lot, "There should be no arguing between you and me, or between your herdsmen and mine, because we are brothers. [9]We should separate. The whole land is there in front of you. If you go to the left, I will go to the right. If you go to the right, I will go to the left."

[10]Lot looked all around and saw the whole Jordan Valley, and that there was much water there. It was like the LORD's garden, like the land of Egypt in the direction of Zoar. (This was before the LORD destroyed Sodom and Gomorrah.) [11]So Lot chose to move east and live in the Jordan Valley. In this way Abram and Lot separated. [12]Abram lived in the land of Canaan, but Lot lived among the cities in the Jordan Valley, very near to Sodom. [13]Now the people of Sodom were very evil and were always sinning against the LORD.

[14]After Lot left, the LORD said to Abram, "Look all around you — to the north and south and east and west. [15]All this land that you see I will give to you and your descendants[d] forever. [16]I will make your descendants as many as the dust of the earth. If anyone could count the dust on the earth, he could count your people. [17]Get up! Walk through all this land because I am now giving it to you."

[18]So Abram moved his tents and went to live near the great trees of Mamre at the city of Hebron. There he built an altar to the LORD.

Lot Is Captured

14 Now Amraphel was king of Babylonia, Arioch was king of Ellasar, Kedorlaomer was king of Elam, and Tidal was king of Goiim. [2]All these kings went to war against several other kings: Bera king of Sodom, Birsha king of Gomorrah, Shinab king of Admah, Shemeber king of Zeboiim, and the king of Bela. (Bela is also called Zoar.)

³These kings who were attacked united their armies in the Valley of Siddim (now the Dead Sea*ᵈ*). ⁴They had served Kedorlaomer for twelve years, but in the thirteenth year, they all turned against him. ⁵Then in the fourteenth year, Kedorlaomer and the kings with him came and defeated the Rephaites*ᵈ* in Ashteroth Karnaim, the Zuzites in Ham, and the Emites in Shaveh Kiriathaim. ⁶They also defeated the Horites in the mountains of Edom to El Paran (near the desert). ⁷Then they turned back and went to En Mishpat (that is, Kadesh). They defeated all the Amalekites, as well as the Amorites who lived in Hazazon Tamar.

⁸At that time the kings of Sodom, Gomorrah, Admah, Zeboiim, and Bela went out to fight in the Valley of Siddim. (Bela is called Zoar.) ⁹They fought against Kedorlaomer king of Elam, Tidal king of Goiim, Amraphel king of Babylonia, and Arioch king of Ellasar — four kings fighting against five. ¹⁰There were many tar pits in the Valley of Siddim. When the kings of Sodom and Gomorrah and their armies ran away, some of the soldiers fell into the tar pits, but the others ran away to the mountains.

¹¹Now Kedorlaomer and his armies took everything the people of Sodom and Gomorrah owned, including their food. ¹²They took Lot, Abram's nephew who was living in Sodom, and everything he owned. Then they left. ¹³One of the men who was not captured went to Abram, the Hebrew, and told him what had happened. At that time Abram was camped near the great trees of Mamre the Amorite. Mamre was a brother of Eshcol and Aner, and they had all made an agreement to help Abram.

Abram Rescues Lot

¹⁴When Abram learned that Lot had been captured, he called out his 318 trained men who had been born in his camp. He led the men and chased the enemy all the way to the town of Dan. ¹⁵That night he divided his men into groups, and they made a surprise attack against the enemy. They chased them all the way to Hobah, north of Damascus. ¹⁶Then Abram brought back everything the enemy had stolen, the women and the other people, and Lot, and everything Lot owned.

¹⁷After defeating Kedorlaomer and the kings who were with him, Abram went home. As he was returning, the king of Sodom came out to *meet him in the Valley of Shaveh (now called* King's Valley).

¹⁸Melchizedek king of Salem brought out bread and wine. He was a priest for God Most High ¹⁹and blessed Abram, saying,

"Abram, may you be blessed by God Most High,

the God who made heaven and earth.
²⁰And we praise God Most High,
who has helped you to defeat your
enemies."

Then Abram gave Melchizedek a tenth of everything he had brought back from the battle.

²¹The king of Sodom said to Abram, "You may keep all these things for yourself. Just give me my people who were captured."

²²But Abram said to the king of Sodom, "I make a promise to the Lᴏʀᴅ, the God Most High, who made heaven and earth. ²³I promise that I will not keep anything that is yours. I will not keep even a thread or a sandal strap so that you cannot say, 'I made Abram rich.' ²⁴I will keep nothing but the food my young men have eaten. But give Aner, Eshcol, and Mamre their share of what we won, because they went with me into battle."

God's Agreement with Abram

15 After these things happened, the Lᴏʀᴅ spoke his word to Abram in a vision: "Abram, don't be afraid. I will defend you, and I will give you a great reward."

²But Abram said, "Lord Gᴏᴅ, what can you give me? I have no son, so my slave Eliezer from Damascus will get everything I own after I die." ³Abram said, "Look, you have given me no son, so a slave born in my house will inherit everything I have."

⁴Then the Lᴏʀᴅ spoke his word to Abram: "He will not be the one to inherit what you have. You will have a son of your own who will inherit what you have."

⁵Then God led Abram outside and said, "Look at the sky. There are so many stars you cannot count them. Your descendants*ᵈ* also will be too many to count."

⁶Abram believed the Lᴏʀᴅ. And the Lᴏʀᴅ accepted Abram's faith, and that faith made him right with God.

⁷God said to Abram, "I am the Lᴏʀᴅ who led you out of Ur of Babylonia so that I could give you this land to own."

⁸But Abram said, "Lord Gᴏᴅ, how can I be sure that I will own this land?"

⁹The Lᴏʀᴅ said to Abram, "Bring me a three-year-old cow, a three-year-old goat, a three-year-old male sheep, a dove, and a young pigeon."

¹⁰Abram brought them all to God. Then Abram killed the animals and cut each of them into two pieces, laying each half opposite the other half. *But he did not cut the birds in half.* ¹¹*Later, large* birds flew down to eat the animals, but Abram chased them away.

¹²As the sun was going down, Abram fell into a deep sleep. While he was asleep, a very terrible darkness came. ¹³Then the Lᴏʀᴅ said to Abram, "You can be sure that your descendants will be

strangers and travel in a land they don't own. The people there will make them slaves and be cruel to them for four hundred years. [14]But I will punish the nation where they are slaves. Then your descendants will leave that land, taking great wealth with them. [15]And you, Abram, will die in peace and will be buried at an old age. [16]After your great-great-grandchildren are born, your people will come to this land again. It will take that long, because I am not yet going to punish the Amorites for their evil behavior."

[17]After the sun went down, it was very dark. Suddenly a smoking firepot and a blazing torch passed between the halves of the dead animals.[n] [18]So on that day the LORD made an agreement with Abram and said, "I will give to your descendants the land between the river of Egypt and the great river Euphrates. [19]This is the land of the Kenites, Kenizzites, Kadmonites, [20]Hittites, Perizzites, Rephaites,[d] [21]Amorites, Canaanites, Girgashites, and Jebusites."

Ishmael Is Born

16 Sarai, Abram's wife, had no children, but she had a slave girl from Egypt named Hagar. [2]Sarai said to Abram, "Look, the LORD has not allowed me to have children, so have sexual relations with my slave girl. If she has a child, maybe I can have my own family through her."

Abram did what Sarai said. [3]It was after he had lived ten years in Canaan that Sarai gave Hagar to her husband Abram. (Hagar was her slave girl from Egypt.)

[4]Abram had sexual relations with Hagar, and she became pregnant. When Hagar learned she was pregnant, she began to treat her mistress Sarai badly. [5]Then Sarai said to Abram, "This is your fault. I gave my slave girl to you, and when she became pregnant, she began to treat me badly. Let the LORD decide who is right—you or me."

[6]But Abram said to Sarai, "You are Hagar's mistress. Do anything you want to her." Then Sarai was hard on Hagar, and Hagar ran away.

passed . . . animals This showed that God sealed the agreement between himself and Abram.

DISCOURAGEMENT

49,999 . . . and Counting

Thomas wanted to create something to store electricity. Time after time—in fact, fifty thousand times—he failed. But he kept trying and eventually succeeded. The first battery was invented.

Someone asked him, "Don't you get discouraged when you have to try fifty thousand experiments before you get any results?"

"Results?" Thomas replied. "Why, I've gotten a lot of results. I know fifty thousand things that won't work."

Thomas didn't get discouraged when he didn't get instant results. Perhaps that's why Thomas Edison is credited with almost thirteen hundred inventions, including record players, movies, microphones, light bulbs, and the transmitter that made telephones possible.

Just as Thomas Edison didn't expect instant results, Abram also waited for God's promises to come true. Read **Genesis 15:1–6** to see how he didn't give in to discouragement.
- What kept Thomas Edison from giving in to discouragement? What kept Abram from giving in? What's similar and different about the two situations?
- When have you been discouraged and tempted to give up on God as Abram was tempted? What happened?

CONSIDER . . .
- writing a letter of encouragement to yourself, then sealing the letter in an envelope to keep in your Bible. Open and read the letter sometime when you're discouraged.
- visiting a hospital's physical rehabilitation center. Ask a therapist what characteristics keep people from getting discouraged in recovery. Apply those characteristics in your own life.

FOR MORE, SEE . . .
- Psalm 77:1–15 (p. 526)
- Isaiah 40:27–31 (p. 656)
- Hebrews 6:13–19 (p. 1282)

7The angel of the LORD found Hagar beside a spring of water in the desert, by the road to Shur. 8The angel said, "Hagar, Sarai's slave girl, where have you come from? Where are you going?"

Hagar answered, "I am running away from my mistress Sarai."

9The angel of the LORD said to her, "Go home to your mistress and obey her." 10The angel also said, "I will give you so many descendants*d* they cannot be counted."

11The angel added,
"You are now pregnant,
 and you will have a son.
You will name him Ishmael,*n*
 because the LORD has heard your cries.
12Ishmael will be like a wild donkey.

He will be against everyone,
 and everyone will be against him.
He will attack all his brothers."

13The slave girl gave a name to the LORD who spoke to her: "You are 'God who sees me,' " because she said to herself, "Have I really seen God who sees me?" 14So the well there, between Kadesh and Bered, was called Beer Lahai Roi.*n*

15Hagar gave birth to a son for Abram, and Abram named him Ishmael. 16Abram was eighty-six years old when Hagar gave birth to Ishmael.

Proof of the Agreement

17 When Abram was ninety-nine years old, the LORD appeared to him and said, "I am God Almighty. Obey me and do what is right.

Ishmael The Hebrew words for "Ishmael" and "has heard" sound similar.
Beer Lahai Roi This means "the well of the Living One who sees me."

PROMISES

Trusting the Pilot

The clouds hid the airport at Nairobi, Kenya. The twin-engine Cessna was running low on fuel.

"We're going to have to set down at the Athi River strip," the pilot said. "We can't fly into that storm."

The missionary passengers—the Partain family—listened nervously to the pilot's decision. Ruth, the mother, was unconscious, lying on a stretcher in the back after a near-fatal car accident. They had to get to Nairobi for better medical care.

The plane touched down and bounced to a stop on the grassy landing strip. When the storm had passed, the pilot stepped out and paced the runway. "I think we can make it now," he concluded. "But it's a bit muddy. I don't think we should try it with this load. We'll have to leave the luggage here. And we'll need Gene and David to wait too."

The two teenagers looked apprehensive, knowing that the landing strip was near a wild game park. "Don't worry," the pilot assured, "I'll be back to get you as quickly as I can. And it's safe here. The fence will keep wild animals out."

So Gene and David sat on the luggage and waited, watching for herds of wildebeests and zebras. They didn't worry much, though, because they knew the pilot would be back—as he had promised.

An hour later, a small dot in the sky showed the pilot's promise coming true. And the pilot's plan helped everyone arrive safely in Nairobi.

As the two teenagers trusted the pilot to come back, Abraham knew he could trust God's promise in **Genesis 17:1–10**.

■ Why do you think Gene, David, and Abraham trusted the promises made to them?
■ What kind of assurance do you get from God's promise to Abraham?

CONSIDER...

■ changing something about yourself—such as a negative attitude or habit— as a sign that you believe and have responded to God's promise.
■ drawing up a blank agreement between you and God, and posting it in your bedroom. *When you find a promise from God in the Bible, write it on one side of the agreement. When you make a commitment to God, write it on the other side.*

FOR MORE, SEE...

■ Numbers 23:19 (p. 148)
■ Matthew 28:16–20 (p. 962)
■ Romans 4:18–25 (p. 1145)

[2]I will make an agreement between us, and I will make you the ancestor of many people."

[3]Then Abram bowed facedown on the ground. God said to him, [4]"I am making my agreement with you: I will make you the father of many nations. [5]I am changing your name from Abram[n] to Abraham[n] because I am making you a father of

---

---

many nations. [6]I will give you many descendants.[d] New nations will be born from you, and kings will come from you. [7]And I will make an agreement between me and you and all your descendants from now on: I will be your God and the God of all your descendants. [8]You live in the land of Canaan now as a stranger, but I will give you and your descendants all this land forever. And I will be the God of your descendants."

[9]Then God said to Abraham, "You and your descendants must keep this agreement from now on. [10]This is my agreement with you and all your descendants, which you must obey: Every male among you must be circumcised.[d] [11]Cut away your foreskin to show that you are prepared to follow the agreement between me and you. [12]From now on when a baby boy is eight days old, you will circumcise him. This includes any boy born among your people or any who is your slave, who is not one of your descendants. [13]Circumcise every baby boy whether he is born in your family or bought as a slave. Your bodies will be marked to show that you are part of my agreement that lasts forever. [14]Any male who is not circumcised will be cut off from his people, because he has broken my agreement."

Isaac — the Promised Son

[15]God said to Abraham, "I will change the name of Sarai,[n] your wife, to Sarah.[n] [16]I will bless her and give her a son, and you will be the father. She will be the mother of many nations. Kings of nations will come from her."

[17]Abraham bowed facedown on the ground and laughed. He said to himself, "Can a man have a child when he is a hundred years old? Can Sarah give birth to a child when she is ninety?" [18]Then Abraham said to God, "Please let Ishmael be the son you promised."

[19]God said, "No, Sarah your wife will have a son, and you will name him Isaac.[n] I will make my agreement with him to be an agreement that continues forever with all his descendants.[d]

[20]"As for Ishmael, I have heard you. I will bless him and give him many descendants. And I will cause their numbers to grow greatly. He will be the father of twelve great leaders, and I will make him into a great nation. [21]But I will make my agreement with Isaac, the son whom Sarah will have at this same time next year." [22]After God finished talking with Abraham, God rose and left him.

[23]Then Abraham gathered Ishmael, all the males born in his camp, and the slaves he had bought. So that day Abraham circumcised every man and boy in his camp as God told him to do. [24]Abraham was ninety-nine years old when he was circumcised. [25]And Ishmael, his son, was thirteen years old when he was circumcised. [26]Abraham and his son were circumcised on the same day. [27]Also on that day all the men in Abraham's camp were circumcised, including all those born in his camp and all the slaves he had bought from other nations.

The Three Visitors

18 Later, the LORD again appeared to Abraham near the great trees of Mamre. Abraham was sitting at the entrance of his tent during the hottest part of the day. [2]He looked up and saw three men standing near him. When Abraham saw them, he ran from his tent to meet them. He bowed facedown on the ground before them [3]and said, "Sir, if you think well of me, please stay awhile with me, your servant. [4]I will bring some water so all of you can wash your feet. You may rest under the tree, [5]and I will get some bread for you so you can regain your strength. Then you may continue your journey."

The three men said, "That is fine. Do as you said."

[6]Abraham hurried to the tent where Sarah was and said to her, "Hurry, prepare twenty quarts of fine flour, and make it into loaves of bread."

Abram This name means "honored father."
Abraham The end of the Hebrew word for "Abraham" sounds like the beginning of the Hebrew word for "many."
Sarai An Aramaic name meaning "princess."
Sarah A Hebrew name meaning "princess."
Isaac The Hebrew words for "he laughed" (vs. 17) and "Isaac" sound the same.

⁷Then Abraham ran to his herd and took one of his best calves. He gave it to a servant, who hurried to kill it and to prepare it for food. ⁸Abraham gave the three men the calf that had been cooked and milk curds and milk. While they ate, he stood under the tree near them.

⁹The men asked Abraham, "Where is your wife Sarah?"

"There, in the tent," said Abraham.

¹⁰Then the LORD said, "I will certainly return to you about this time a year from now. At that time your wife Sarah will have a son."

Sarah was listening at the entrance of the tent which was behind him. ¹¹Abraham and Sarah were very old. Since Sarah was past the age when women normally have children, ¹²she laughed to herself, "My husband and I are too old to have a baby."

¹³Then the LORD said to Abraham, "Why did Sarah laugh? Why did she say, 'I am too old to have a baby'? ¹⁴Is anything too hard for the LORD? No! I will return to you at the right time a year from now, and Sarah will have a son."

¹⁵Sarah was afraid, so she lied and said, "I didn't laugh."

But the LORD said, "No. You did laugh."

¹⁶Then the men got up to leave and started out toward Sodom. Abraham walked along with them a short time to send them on their way.

Abraham's Bargain with God

¹⁷The LORD said, "Should I tell Abraham what I am going to do now? ¹⁸Abraham's children will certainly become a great and powerful nation, and all nations on earth will be blessed through him. ¹⁹I have chosen him so he would command his children and his descendants*d* to live the way the LORD wants them to, to live right and be fair. Then I, the LORD, will give Abraham what I promised him."

DOUBT

Who, Me?

Tony Matthews avoided his church's youth group. It was small, and none of his friends went. Plus, Tony was the youngest teenager in his church.

One Sunday, Tony's youth leader, Sharon, stopped him in the hall after worship. "Going with us on the retreat?" she asked.

Tony shook his head. "Uhhhh . . . It sounds all right, but I don't think so. Nobody my age will be there."

"That's a problem, isn't it?" Sharon mused. "Why don't you invite some of your friends?"

"I'm not very good at asking," Tony replied. "Besides, they wouldn't go anyway."

"Why not give it a try?" Sharon prodded. "I'd really like you to go."

Tony decided to try, but it was tough. He was shy, and he'd never talked to anyone about his church.

Most of the kids he asked said no, but Tony was persistent. Finally, he found two buddies to go with him, and they had a great time at the retreat.

The next youth group event was a miniature golf outing. Sharon figured about a dozen young people would come. But Tony and his friends liked golf, and he was part of the reason twenty-seven people showed up.

Being shy, Tony had doubted he had the gifts needed to persuade other kids to come to church, but God knew otherwise. Abraham and Sarah also doubted God could use them. Read their story in **Genesis 17:15–19**.

■ How were Tony, Abraham, and Sarah similar and how were they different?

■ Have you ever felt like laughing when someone suggested how God could use you? How did you deal with your doubts?

C O N S I D E R . . .

■ asking a friend to tell you about gifts you have that you may not be aware of. Then commit yourself to using those gifts to serve God.

■ doing something you're not sure you could ever do (such as writing a song, leading a *Bible study, or sharing your faith*) to see if God has given you gifts you doubted you had.

F O R   M O R E ,   S E E . . .

■ Exodus 3:7–22 (p. 60)
■ Psalm 77:1–15 (p. 526)

■ John 20:24–29 (p. 1094)

²⁰Then the LORD said, "I have heard many complaints against the people of Sodom and Gomorrah. They are very evil. ²¹I will go down and see if they are as bad as I have heard. If not, I will know."

²²So the men turned and went toward Sodom, but Abraham stood there before the LORD. ²³Then Abraham approached him and asked, "Do you plan to destroy the good people along with the evil ones? ²⁴What if there are fifty good people in that city? Will you still destroy it? Surely you will save the city for the fifty good people living there. ²⁵Surely you will not destroy the good people along with the evil ones; then they would be treated the same. You are the judge of all the earth. Won't you do what is right?"

²⁶The LORD said, "If I find fifty good people in the city of Sodom, I will save the whole city because of them."

²⁷Then Abraham said, "Though I am only dust and ashes, I have been brave to speak to the Lord. ²⁸What if there are only forty-five good people in the city? Will you destroy the whole city for the lack of five good people?"

The LORD said, "If I find forty-five there, I will not destroy the city."

²⁹Again Abraham said to him, "If you find only forty good people there, will you destroy the city?"

The LORD said, "If I find forty, I will not destroy it."

³⁰Then Abraham said, "Lord, please don't be angry with me, but let me ask you this. If you find only thirty good people in the city, will you destroy it?"

He said, "If I find thirty good people there, I will not destroy the city."

³¹Then Abraham said, "I have been brave to speak to the Lord. But what if there are twenty good people in the city?"

He answered, "If I find twenty there, I will not destroy the city."

³²Then Abraham said, "Lord, please don't be angry with me, but let me bother you this one last time. What if you find ten there?"

He said, "If I find ten there, I will not destroy it."

³³When the LORD finished speaking to Abraham, he left, and Abraham returned home.

SERVICE

Gift for a Stranger

Unlike other leaders in India in the 1940s, V. P. Menon didn't have a fancy degree from a fancy university. He wasn't from a well-to-do or respected family. The oldest of thirteen children, he had to quit school at age thirteen to work in coal mines and factories.

As a young man, he went to Delhi to get a government job. On the way, everything he had—including his money and identification—was stolen at the railway station.

In desperation, he went to an elderly man standing nearby, explained his situation, and asked for a loan of fifteen rupees to buy food until he could get a job. The man gave him the money. Menon asked for his address so he could repay the loan, but the man said Menon didn't owe the debt to him, but owed any stranger in need. The help came from a stranger and should be repaid to a stranger.

Menon never forgot his debt, and his life was marked by constant generosity to those in need. The day before he died, a beggar came to the family home asking for money to buy new sandals. Menon asked his daughter to take fifteen rupees out of his wallet to give to the man.

It was his last conscious act.

V. P. Menon served strangers selflessly, just as Abraham provided food for strangers in **Genesis 18:1–16**. Read how that incident affected Abraham.

■ What attitudes cause people to share as Menon, Abraham and Sarah did?
■ How do you need to become more like Abraham and Sarah? When have *you served God by serving people you didn't know?*

C O N S I D E R . . .

■ inviting someone who's new at your school home for a Coke.
■ trying V. P. Menon's approach. Give five dollars to a stranger in need, and ask that he or she repay it to another stranger in need.

F O R   M O R E ,   S E E . . .

■ 1 Kings 17:10–16 (p. 322)
■ Hebrews 13:2 (p. 1290)

■ James 2:1–13 (p. 1294)

Lot Leaves Sodom

19 The two angels came to Sodom in the evening as Lot was sitting near the city gate. When he saw them, he got up and went to them and bowed facedown on the ground. ²Lot said, "Sirs, please come to my house and spend the night. There you can wash your feet, and then tomorrow you may continue your journey."

The angels answered, "No, we will spend the night in the city's public square."

³But Lot begged them to come, so they agreed and went to his house. Then Lot prepared a meal for them. He baked bread without yeast, and they ate it.

⁴Before bedtime, men both young and old and from every part of Sodom surrounded Lot's house. ⁵They called to Lot, "Where are the two men who came to you tonight? Bring them out to us so we can have sexual relations with them."

⁶Lot went outside to them, closing the door behind him. ⁷He said, "No, my brothers! Do not do this evil thing. ⁸Look! I have two daughters who have never slept with a man. I will give them to you, and you may do anything you want with them. But please don't do anything to these men. They have come to my house, and I must protect them."

⁹The men around the house answered, "Move out of the way!" Then they said to each other, "This man Lot came to our city as a stranger, and now he wants to tell us what to do!" They said to Lot, "We will do worse things to you than to them." They started pushing him back and were ready to break down the door.

GOD'S LOVE

A Second Chance

Most girls would love to have Amy Kennedy's looks. Her face. Her hair. Her figure. You would think she had it made.

But her good looks haven't kept her life from being a mess. At home, her alcoholic mom either neglected her or screamed at her. So she avoided home and hung out on street corners with other kids who didn't fit in.

At thirteen, Amy ran away from home for the fourth time and ended up in a juvenile detention center. While there, she decided to turn her life around and make something of herself—to give herself a second chance.

When she returned to school, things went great. She made new friends who didn't drink or party. Her life seemed to be coming together. But then a rumor started. "Amy sleeps around," people whispered at school. Nothing Amy said or did made any difference, and the rumor stuck. One by one, her new friends dumped her.

Except Mona. "I don't believe the rumor," she would tell Amy. "Besides, you deserve a second chance."

But Amy still felt rejected, so she went back to her old friends. She started dating Tim, who kept her comfortable with expensive gifts bought with drug money. "I love you," he would tell Amy. But she discovered that he only said it to get her to have sex with him. When she wouldn't, he dropped her, and so did all of her other old friends.

But Amy wasn't friendless. She still had Mona, and Mona's family took her in so she would have a place to live. Now, three years later, she feels like part of the family. She knows what it's like to have a second chance.

Like Amy, the people of Sodom and Gomorrah were given a second chance. Read how they responded to it in **Genesis 18:20—19:25**.

■ How are Amy's friend Mona and Abraham similar? different?
■ If you were Abraham, when would you have given up begging for the lives of the people?

C O N S I D E R . . .

■ giving a friend a second chance when he or she blows it and does *something that hurts you.*
■ keeping track of all the times people give you second chances. Thank them by baking cookies or running an errand—and learning from your mistake.

F O R   M O R E ,   S E E . . .

■ Joel 2:12–13 (p. 837)   ■ Acts 26:9–18 (p. 1135)
■ Zephaniah 3:14–20 (p. 884)

¹⁰But the two men staying with Lot opened the door, pulled him back inside the house, and then closed the door. ¹¹They struck those outside the door with blindness, so the men, both young and old, could not find the door.

¹²The two men said to Lot, "Do you have any other relatives in this city? Do you have any sons-in-law, sons, daughters, or any other relatives? If you do, tell them to leave now, ¹³because we are about to destroy this city. The LORD has heard of all the evil that is here, so he has sent us to destroy it."

¹⁴So Lot went out and said to his future sons-in-law who were pledged to marry his daughters, "Hurry and leave this city! The LORD is about to destroy it!" But they thought Lot was joking.

¹⁵At dawn the next morning, the angels begged Lot to hurry. They said, "Go! Take your wife and your two daughters with you so you will not be destroyed when the city is punished."

¹⁶But Lot delayed. So the two men took the hands of Lot, his wife, and his two daughters and led them safely out of the city. So the LORD was merciful to Lot and his family. ¹⁷After they brought them out of the city, one of the men said, "Run for your lives! Don't look back or stop anywhere in the valley. Run to the mountains, or you will be destroyed."

¹⁸But Lot said to one of them, "Sir, please don't force me to go so far! ¹⁹You have been merciful and kind to me and have saved my life. But I can't run to the mountains. The disaster will catch me, and I will die. ²⁰Look, that little town over there is not too far away. Let me run there. It's really just a little town, and I'll be safe there."

²¹The angel said to Lot, "Very well, I will allow you to do this also. I will not destroy that town. ²²But run there fast, because I cannot destroy Sodom until you are safely in that town." (That town is named Zoar,ⁿ because it is little.)

Sodom and Gomorrah Are Destroyed

²³The sun had already come up when Lot entered Zoar. ²⁴The LORD sent a rain of burning sulfur down from the sky on Socom and Gomorrah ²⁵and destroyed those cities. He also destroyed the whole Jordan Valley, everyone living in the cities, and even all the plants.

²⁶At that point Lot's wife looked back. When she did, she became a pillar of salt.

²⁷Early the next morning, Abraham got up and went to the place where he had stood before the LORD. ²⁸He looked down toward Sodom and Gomorrah and all the Jordan Valley and saw smoke rising from the land, like smoke from a furnace.

²⁹God destroyed the cities in the valley, but he remembered what Abraham had asked. So God saved Lot's life, but he destroyed the city where Lot had lived.

> ※ **SIDELIGHT:** When God destroyed the cities of Sodom and Gomorrah (Genesis 19:23–29), he made sure they weren't built again. Archaeologists believe the two cities are now under water in a shallow part of the Dead Sea. The waters may have risen because of an earthquake around 2000 B.C.

Lot and His Daughters

³⁰Lot was afraid to continue living in Zoar, so he and his two daughters went to live in the mountains in a cave. ³¹One day the older daughter said to the younger, "Our father is old. Everywhere on the earth women and men marry, but there are no men around here for us to marry. ³²Let's get our father drunk and have sexual relations with him. We can use him to have children and continue our family."

³³That night the two girls got their father drunk, and the older daughter went and had sexual relations with him. But Lot did not know when she lay down or when she got up.

³⁴The next day the older daughter said to the younger, "Last night I had sexual relations with my father. Let's get him drunk again tonight so you can go and have sexual relations with him, too. In this way we can use our father to have children to continue our family." ³⁵So that night they got their father drunk again, and the younger daughter went and had sexual relations with him. Again, Lot did not know when she lay down or when she got up.

³⁶So both of Lot's daughters became pregnant by their father. ³⁷The older daughter gave birth to a son and named him Moab. He is the ancestor of all the Moabite people who are still living today. ³⁸The younger daughter also gave birth to a son and named him Ben-Ammi. He is the father of all the Ammonite people who are still living today.

Abraham Tricks Abimelech

20 Abraham left Hebron and traveled to southern Canaan where he stayed awhile between Kadesh and Shur. When he moved to Gerar, ²he told people that his wife Sarah was his sister. Abimelech king of Gerar heard this, so he sent some servants to take her. ³But one night God spoke to Abimelech in a

---

Zoar This name sounds like the Hebrew word for "little."

dream and said, "You will die. The woman you took is married."

⁴But Abimelech had not gone near Sarah, so he said, "Lord, would you destroy an innocent nation? ⁵Abraham himself told me, 'This woman is my sister,' and she also said, 'He is my brother.' I am innocent. I did not know I was doing anything wrong."

⁶Then God said to Abimelech in the dream, "Yes, I know you did not realize what you were doing. So I did not allow you to sin against me and touch her. ⁷Give Abraham his wife back. He is a prophet.ᵈ He will pray for you, and you will not die. But if you do not give Sarah back, you and all your family will surely die."

⁸So early the next morning, Abimelech called all his officers and told them everything that had happened in the dream. They were very afraid. ⁹Then Abimelech called Abraham to him and said, "What have you done to us? What wrong did I do against you? Why did you bring this trouble to my kingdom? You should not have done these things to me. ¹⁰What were you thinking that caused you to do this?"

¹¹Then Abraham answered, "I thought no one in this place respected God and that someone would kill me to get Sarah. ¹²And it is true that she is my sister. She is the daughter of my father, but she is not the daughter of my mother. ¹³When God told me to leave my father's house and wander in many different places, I told Sarah, 'You must do a special favor for me. Everywhere we go tell people I am your brother.' "

¹⁴Then Abimelech gave Abraham some sheep, cattle, and male and female slaves. He also gave Sarah, Abraham's wife, back to him ¹⁵and said, "Look around you at my land. You may live anywhere you want."

¹⁶Abimelech said to Sarah, "I gave your brother Abraham twenty-five pounds of silver to make up for any wrong that people may think about you. I want everyone to know that you are innocent."

¹⁷Then Abraham prayed to God, and God healed Abimelech, his wife, and his servant girls so they could have children. ¹⁸The LORD had kept all the women in Abimelech's house from having children as a punishment on Abimelech for taking Abraham's wife Sarah.

A Baby for Sarah

21 The LORD cared for Sarah as he had said and did for her what he had promised. ²Sarah became pregnant and gave birth to a son for Abraham in his old age. Everything happened at the time God had said it would. ³Abraham named his son Isaac, the son Sarah gave birth to.

⁴He circumcisedᵈ Isaac when he was eight days old as God had commanded.

⁵Abraham was one hundred years old when his son Isaac was born. ⁶And Sarah said, "God has made me laugh.ⁿ Everyone who hears about this will laugh with me. ⁷No one thought that I would be able to have Abraham's child, but even though Abraham is old I have given him a son."

Hagar and Ishmael Leave

⁸Isaac grew, and when he became old enough to eat food, Abraham gave a great feast. ⁹But Sarah saw Ishmael making fun of Isaac. (Ishmael was the son of Abraham by Hagar, Sarah's Egyptian slave.) ¹⁰So Sarah said to Abraham, "Throw out this slave woman and her son. Her son should not inherit anything; my son Isaac should receive it all."

¹¹This troubled Abraham very much because Ishmael was also his son. ¹²But God said to Abraham, "Don't be troubled about the boy and the slave woman. Do whatever Sarah tells you. The descendantsᵈ I promised you will be from Isaac. ¹³I will also make the descendants of Ishmael into a great nation because he is your son, too."

¹⁴Early the next morning Abraham took some food and a leather bag full of water. He gave them to Hagar and sent her away. Carrying these things and her son, Hagar went and wandered in the desert of Beersheba.

¹⁵Later, when all the water was gone from the bag, Hagar put her son under a bush. ¹⁶Then she went away a short distance and sat down. She thought, "My son will die, and I cannot watch this happen." She sat there and he began to cry.

¹⁷God heard the boy crying, and God's angel called to Hagar from heaven. He said, "What is wrong, Hagar? Don't be afraid! God has heard the boy crying there. ¹⁸Help him up and take him by the hand. I will make his descendants into a great nation."

¹⁹Then God showed Hagar a well of water. So she went to the well and filled her bag with water and gave the boy a drink.

²⁰God was with the boy as he grew up. Ishmael lived in the desert and became an archer. ²¹He lived in the Desert of Paran, and his mother found a wife for him in Egypt.

Abraham's Bargain with Abimelech

²²Then Abimelech came with Phicol, the commander of his army, and said to Abraham, "God is with you in everything you do. ²³So make a promise to me here before God that you will be fair with me and my children and my descendants.ᵈ Be kind to me and to this land where you

laugh The Hebrew words for "he laughed" and "Isaac" sound the same.

have lived as a stranger—as kind as I have been to you."

²⁴And Abraham said, "I promise." ²⁵Then Abraham complained to Abimelech about Abimelech's servants who had seized a well of water.

²⁶But Abimelech said, "I don't know who did this. You never told me about this before today."

²⁷Then Abraham gave Abimelech some sheep and cattle, and they made an agreement. ²⁸Abraham also put seven female lambs in front of Abimelech.

²⁹Abimelech asked Abraham, "Why did you put these seven female lambs by themselves?"

³⁰Abraham answered, "Accept these lambs from me to prove that you believe I dug this well."

³¹So that place was called Beersheba[n] because they made a promise to each other there.

³²After Abraham and Abimelech made the agreement at Beersheba, Abimelech and Phicol, the commander of his army, went back to the land of the Philistines.

³³Abraham planted a tamarisk tree at Beersheba and prayed to the LORD, the God who lives forever. ³⁴And Abraham lived as a stranger in the land of the Philistines for a long time.

God Tests Abraham

22 After these things God tested Abraham's faith. God said to him, "Abraham!"

And he answered, "Here I am."

²Then God said, "Take your only son, Isaac, the son you love, and go to the land of Moriah. Kill

Beersheba This name means "well of the promise" or "well of seven."

PRIORITIES

Worth a Sacrifice

Jesse Poling couldn't sleep. He tossed restlessly in bed, wondering what to do. He had been planning to take a summer job at a local machine shop. The pay and hours looked great, and the work didn't sound bad.

But then, last week at school, he had seen a poster about a camp for disabled kids that needed someone to teach swimming and canoeing. He loved water sports, and his youth minister had encouraged him to consider volunteering to help at the camp.

Jesse wasn't prepared for the reaction when he mentioned the camp possibility to his dad. "That's the craziest idea you've come up with in a long time, Jesse," his dad fumed. "Why would you want to work for free when you could get paid? It's not like you're independently wealthy. And then you'll come running to me to pay your college tuition."

His dad had a point, Jesse reasoned as he stared up at the dark bedroom ceiling. But no matter how hard he tried, he couldn't forget about the camp—or those kids.

When Jesse's alarm woke him the next morning, he knew what he had to do. "Dad," he explained at breakfast, "some things are worth sacrificing for. Helping at that camp is important to me." His dad didn't understand, but he agreed to let Jesse stick with his priorities. So Jesse called the camp director.

Like Jesse, Abraham had tough decisions, but he also stuck with what he believed was right. Check out **Genesis 22:1–18** to see what happened.

■ What do Jesse's and Abraham's decisions say about their priorities?
■ When have you, like Abraham, had to make a tough decision because of what you believed God wanted? What happened?

CONSIDER . . .

■ writing out the issues involved in a tough decision. Keep the list by your bed or on your desk for a few days. Whenever you think of an option, benefit, or disadvantage, write it on the paper. Pray about your decision through the week and then make the decision, sticking to what you know to be right.
■ having a "What If" discussion over lunch with friends in the school cafeteria. Brainstorm together several situations that test your priorities. Then discuss what you would do if you were in a particular situation.

FOR MORE, SEE . . .

■ Proverbs 3 (p. 570)
■ Daniel 3:8–30 (p. 809)
■ Matthew 6:19–24 (p. 918)

him there and offer him as a whole burnt offering on one of the mountains I will tell you about."

3Abraham got up early in the morning and saddled his donkey. He took Isaac and two servants with him. After he cut the wood for the sacrifice, they went to the place God had told them to go. 4On the third day Abraham looked up and saw the place in the distance. 5He said to his servants, "Stay here with the donkey. My son and I will go over there and worship, and then we will come back to you."

6Abraham took the wood for the sacrifice and gave it to his son to carry, but he himself took the knife and the fire. So he and his son went on together.

7Isaac said to his father Abraham, "Father!"

Abraham answered, "Yes, my son."

Isaac said, "We have the fire and the wood, but where is the lamb we will burn as a sacrifice?"

8Abraham answered, "God will give us the lamb for the sacrifice, my son."

So Abraham and his son went on together 9and came to the place God had told him about. Abraham built an altar there. He laid the wood on it and then tied up his son Isaac and laid him on the wood on the altar. 10Then Abraham took his knife and was about to kill his son.

11But the angel of the LORD called to him from heaven and said, "Abraham! Abraham!"

Abraham answered, "Yes."

12The angel said, "Don't kill your son or hurt him in any way. Now I can see that you trust God and that you have not kept your son, your only son, from me."

13Then Abraham looked up and saw a male sheep caught in a bush by its horns. So Abraham went and took the sheep and killed it. He offered it as a whole burnt offering to God, and his son was saved. 14So Abraham named that place The LORD Provides. Even today people say, "On the mountain of the LORD it will be provided."

15The angel of the LORD called to Abraham from heaven a second time 16and said, "The LORD says, 'Because you did not keep back your son, your only son, from me, I make you this promise by my own name: 17I will surely bless you and give you many descendants.d They will be as many as the stars in the sky and the sand on the seashore, and they will capture the cities of their enemies. 18Through your descendants all the nations on the earth will be blessed, because you obeyed me.' "

19Then Abraham returned to his servants. They all traveled back to Beersheba, and Abraham stayed there.

20After these things happened, someone told Abraham: "Your brother Nahor and his wife Milcah have children now. 21The first son is Uz, and the second is Buz. The third son is Kemuel (the

father of Aram). 22Then there are Kesed, Hazo, Pildash, Jidlaph, and Bethuel." 23Bethuel became the father of Rebekah. Milcah was the mother of these eight sons, and Nahor, Abraham's brother, was the father. 24Also Nahor had four other sons by his slave womand Reumah. Their names were Tebah, Gaham, Tahash, and Maacah.

Sarah Dies

23 Sarah lived to be one hundred twenty-seven years old. 2She died in Kiriath Arba (that is, Hebron) in the land of Canaan. Abraham was very sad and cried because of her. 3After a while he got up from the side of his wife's body and went to talk to the Hittites. He said, 4"I am only a stranger and a foreigner here. Sell me some of your land so that I can bury my dead wife."

5The Hittites answered Abraham, 6"Sir, you are a great leader among us. You may have the best place we have to bury your dead. You may have any of our burying places that you want, and none of us will stop you from burying your dead wife."

7Abraham rose and bowed to the people of the land, the Hittites. 8He said to them, "If you truly want to help me bury my dead wife here, speak to Ephron, the son of Zohar for me. 9Ask him to sell me the cave of Machpelah at the edge of his field. I will pay him the full price. You can be the witnesses that I am buying it as a burial place."

10Ephron was sitting among the Hittites at the city gate. He answered Abraham, 11"No, sir. I will give you the land and the cave that is in it, with these people as witnesses. Bury your dead wife."

12Then Abraham bowed down before the Hittites. 13He said to Ephron before all the people, "Please let me pay you the full price for the field. Accept my money, and I will bury my dead there."

14Ephron answered Abraham, 15"Sir, the land is worth ten pounds of silver, but I won't argue with you over the price. Take the land, and bury your dead wife."

16Abraham agreed and paid Ephron in front of the Hittite witnesses. He weighed out the full price, ten pounds of silver, and they counted the weight as the traders normally did.

17-18So Ephron's field in Machpelah, east of Mamre, was sold. Abraham became the owner of the field, the cave in it, and all the trees that were in the field. The sale was made at the city gate, with the Hittites as witnesses. [19]After this, Abraham buried his wife Sarah in the cave in the field of Machpelah, near Mamre. (Mamre was later called Hebron in the land of Canaan.) [20]So Abraham bought the field and the cave in it from the Hittites to use as a burying place.

A Wife for Isaac

24 Abraham was now very old, and the LORD had blessed him in every way. [2]Abraham said to his oldest servant, who was in charge of everything he owned, "Put your hand

---

> ✴ **SIDELIGHT:** In Abraham's day, one way to show you'd keep your promise was to put your hand under the thigh of the person you were making the promise to (Genesis 24:2). Don't you like a simple promise better?

---

under my leg. [n] [3]Make a promise to me before the LORD, the God of heaven and earth. Don't get a wife for my son from the Canaanite girls who live around here. [4]Instead, go back to my country, to the land of my relatives, and get a wife for my son Isaac."

[5]The servant said to him, "What if this woman does not want to return with me to this land? Then, should I take your son with me back to your homeland?"

[6]Abraham said to him, "No! Don't take my son back there. [7]The LORD, the God of heaven, brought me from the home of my father and the land of my relatives. And he promised me, 'I will give this land to your descendants.' [d] The LORD will send his angel before you to help you get a wife for my son there. [8]If the girl won't come back with you, you will be free from this promise. But you must not take my son back there." [9]So the servant put his hand under his master's leg and made a promise to Abraham about this.

[10]The servant took ten of Abraham's camels and left, carrying with him many different kinds of beautiful gifts. He went to Northwest Mesopotamia to Nahor's city. [11]In the evening, when the women come out to get water, he made the camels kneel down at the well outside the city.

[12]The servant said, "LORD, God of my master Abraham, allow me to find a wife for his son today. Please show this kindness to my master Abraham. [13]Here I am, standing by the spring, and the girls from the city are coming out to get water. [14]I

will say to one of them, 'Please put your jar down so I can drink.' Then let her say, 'Drink, and I will also give water to your camels.' If that happens, I will know she is the right one for your servant Isaac and that you have shown kindness to my master."

[15]Before the servant had finished praying, Rebekah, the daughter of Bethuel, came out of the city. (Bethuel was the son of Milcah and Nahor, Abraham's brother.) Rebekah was carrying her water jar on her shoulder. [16]She was very pretty, a virgin; [i] she had never had sexual relations with a man. She went down to the spring and filled her jar, then came back up. [17]The servant ran to her and said, "Please give me a little water from your jar."

[18]Rebekah said, "Drink, sir." She quickly lowered the jar from her shoulder and gave him a drink. [19]After he finished drinking, Rebekah said, "I will also pour some water for your camels." [20]So she quickly poured all the water from her jar into the drinking trough for the camels. Then she kept running to the well until she had given all the camels enough to drink.

[21]The servant quietly watched her. He wanted to be sure the LORD had made his trip successful. [22]After the camels had finished drinking, he gave Rebekah a gold ring weighing one-fifth of an ounce and two gold arm bracelets weighing about four ounces each. [23]He asked, "Who is your father? Is there a place in his house for me and my men to spend the night?"

[24]Rebekah answered, "My father is Bethuel, the son of Milcah and Nahor." [25]Then she said, "And, yes, we have straw for your camels and a place for you to spend the night."

[26]The servant bowed and worshiped the LORD [27]and said, "Blessed is the LORD, the God of my master Abraham. The LORD has been kind and truthful to him and has led me to my master's relatives."

[28]Then Rebekah ran and told her mother's family about all these things. [29]She had a brother named Laban, who ran out to Abraham's servant, who was still at the spring. [30]Laban had heard what she had said and had seen the ring and the bracelets on his sister's arms. So he ran out to the well, and there was the man standing by the camels at the spring. [31]Laban said, "Sir, you are welcome to come in; you don't have to stand outside. I have prepared the house for you and also a place for your camels."

[32]So Abraham's servant went into the house. After Laban unloaded the camels and gave them straw and food, he gave water to Abraham's servant so he and the men with him could wash their feet. [33]Then Laban gave the servant food,

---

[ut . . . leg] This showed that a person would keep the promise.

but the servant said, "I will not eat until I have told you why I came."

So Laban said, "Then tell us."

³⁴He said, "I am Abraham's servant. ³⁵The LORD has greatly blessed my master in everything, and he has become a rich man. The LORD has given him many flocks of sheep, herds of cattle, silver and gold, male and female servants, camels, and horses. ³⁶Sarah, my master's wife, gave birth to a son when she was old, and my master has given everything he owns to that son. ³⁷My master had me make a promise to him and said, 'Don't get a wife for my son from the Canaanite girls who live around here. ³⁸Instead, you must go to my father's people and to my family. There you must get a wife for my son.' ³⁹I said to my master, 'What if the woman will not come back with me?' ⁴⁰But he said, 'I serve the LORD, who will send his angel with you and will help you. You will get a wife for my son from my family and my father's people. ⁴¹Then you will be free from the promise. But if they will not give you a wife for my son, you will be free from this promise.'

⁴²"Today I came to this spring. I said, 'LORD, God of my master Abraham, please make my trip successful. ⁴³I am standing by this spring. I will wait for a young woman to come out to get water, and I will say, "Please give me water from your jar to drink." ⁴⁴Then let her say, "Drink this water, and I will also get water for your camels." By this I will know the LORD has chosen her for my master's son.'

⁴⁵"Before I finished my silent prayer, Rebekah came out of the city with her water jar on her shoulder. She went down to the spring and got water. I said to her, 'Please give me a drink.' ⁴⁶She quickly lowered the jar from her shoulder and said, 'Drink this. I will also get water for your camels.' So I drank, and she gave water to my camels too. ⁴⁷When I asked her, 'Who is your father?' she answered, 'My father is Bethuel son of Milcah and Nahor.' Then I put the ring in her nose and the bracelets on her arms, ⁴⁸and I bowed my head and thanked the LORD. I praised the LORD, the God of my master Abraham, because he led me on the right road to get the granddaughter of my master's brother for his son. ⁴⁹Now, tell me, will you be kind and truthful to my master? And if not, tell me so. Then I will know what I should do."

⁵⁰Laban and Bethuel answered, "This is clearly from the LORD, and we cannot change what must happen. *⁵¹Rebekah is yours. Take her and go. Let her marry your master's son as the LORD has commanded.*"

⁵²When Abraham's servant heard these words, he bowed facedown on the ground before the LORD. ⁵³Then he gave Rebekah gold and silver jewelry and clothes. He also gave expensive gifts

to her brother and mother. ⁵⁴The servant and the men with him ate and drank and spent the night there. When they got up the next morning, the servant said, "Now let me go back to my master."

⁵⁵Rebekah's mother and her brother said, "Let Rebekah stay with us at least ten days. After that she may go."

⁵⁶But the servant said to them, "Do not make me wait, because the LORD has made my trip successful. Now let me go back to my master."

⁵⁷Rebekah's brother and mother said, "We will call Rebekah and ask her what she wants to do." ⁵⁸They called her and asked her, "Do you want to go with this man now?"

She said, "Yes, I do."

⁵⁹So they allowed Rebekah and her nurse to go with Abraham's servant and his men. ⁶⁰They blessed Rebekah and said,

"Our sister, may you be the mother of
  thousands of people,
and may your descendants*ᵈ* capture the
  cities of their enemies."

⁶¹Then Rebekah and her servant girls got on the camels and followed the servant and his men. So the servant took Rebekah and left.

⁶²At this time Isaac had left Beer Lahai Roi and was living in southern Canaan. ⁶³One evening when he went out to the field to think, he looked up and saw camels coming. ⁶⁴Rebekah also looked and saw Isaac. Then she jumped down from the camel ⁶⁵and asked the servant, "Who is that man walking in the field to meet us?"

The servant answered, "That is my master." So Rebekah covered her face with her veil.

⁶⁶The servant told Isaac everything that had happened. ⁶⁷Then Isaac brought Rebekah into the tent of Sarah, his mother, and she became his wife. Isaac loved her very much, and so he was comforted after his mother's death.

Abraham's Family

25 Abraham married again, and his new wife was Keturah. ²She gave birth to Zimran, Jokshan, Medan, Midian, Ishbak, and Shuah. ³Jokshan was the father of Sheba and Dedan. Dedan's descendants*ᵈ* were the people of Assyria, Letush, and Leum. ⁴The sons of Midian were Ephah, Epher, Hanoch, Abida, and Eldaah. All these were descendants of Keturah. ⁵Abraham left everything he owned to Isaac. ⁶But *before Abraham died, he did give gifts to the sons of his other wives, then sent them to the East to be* away from Isaac.

⁷Abraham lived to be one hundred seventy-five years old. ⁸He breathed his last breath and died at an old age, after a long and satisfying life. ⁹His sons Isaac and Ishmael buried him in the cave of Machpelah in the field of Ephron east of Mamre,

(Ephron was the son of Zohar the Hittite.) ¹⁰So Abraham was buried with his wife Sarah in the same field that he had bought from the Hittites. ¹¹After Abraham died, God blessed his son Isaac. Isaac was now living at Beer Lahai Roi.

¹²This is the family history of Ishmael, Abraham's son. (Hagar, Sarah's Egyptian servant, was Ishmael's mother.) ¹³These are the names of Ishmael's sons in the order they were born: Nebaioth, the first son, then Kedar, Adbeel, Mibsam, ¹⁴Mishma, Dumah, Massa, ¹⁵Hadad, Tema, Jetur, Naphish, and Kedemah. ¹⁶These were Ishmael's sons, and these are the names of the tribal leaders listed according to their settlements and camps. ¹⁷Ishmael lived one hundred thirty-seven years and then breathed his last breath and died. ¹⁸His descendants lived from Havilah to Shur, which is east of Egypt stretching toward Assyria. They often attacked the descendants of his brothers.

Isaac's Family

¹⁹This is the family history of Isaac. Abraham

Esau   This name may mean "hairy."

had a son named Isaac. ²⁰When Isaac was forty years old, he married Rebekah, who came from Northwest Mesopotamia. She was Bethuel's daughter and the sister of Laban the Aramean. ²¹Isaac's wife could not have children, so Isaac prayed to the LORD for her. The LORD heard Isaac's prayer, and Rebekah became pregnant.

²²While she was pregnant, the babies struggled inside her. She asked, "Why is this happening to me?" Then she went to get an answer from the LORD.

²³The LORD said to her,

"Two nations are in your body,
    and two groups of people will be taken
        from you.
One group will be stronger than the other,
    and the older will serve the younger."

²⁴When the time came, Rebekah gave birth to twins. ²⁵The first baby was born red. Since his skin was like a hairy robe, he was named Esau.ⁿ ²⁶When the second baby was born, he was holding on to Esau's heel, so that baby was named

---

FAMILY

Sibling Rivalry

According to the American Chicle Youth Poll, most teenagers in North America have one brother and one sister. Only 8 percent of teenagers have no brothers or sisters. But 12 percent have three or more brothers and sisters.

So how do they get along with their brothers and sisters?

Only 62 percent of young people in the poll say they're happy with their relationships with their brothers and sisters. It's the area of home life they're least satisfied with.

About 40 percent say getting along better with their brothers and sisters would improve their home life more than anything else.

Only 15 percent of teenagers say they can talk about their problems with their brothers. And only 19 percent say they can talk about their problems with their sisters.

Some tension between brothers and sisters is normal. Relationships with siblings have been tough for a long time. **Genesis 25:19–34** describes fierce sibling rivalry between Esau and Jacob. Read how their rivalry made life difficult for them.

■ If someone asked Jacob and Esau to respond to a survey about sibling relationships, what do you think the two of them would say?

■ How is your relationship with your brother and/or sister like or unlike the relationship between Jacob and Esau? Which of the two brothers do you most closely identify with?

CONSIDER . . .

■ sending your brother or sister a note—through the mail—giving a compliment for something he or she did recently.

■ asking a trusted adult for some help with your family conflicts.

FOR MORE, SEE . . .

■ Judges 9:1–6 (p. 225)   ■ 1 John 3:11–18 (p. 1318)
■ Luke 10:38–42 (p. 1024)

Jacob.[n] Isaac was sixty years old when they were born.

27When the boys grew up, Esau became a skilled hunter. He loved to be out in the fields. But Jacob was a quiet man and stayed among the tents. 28Isaac loved Esau because he hunted the wild animals that Isaac enjoyed eating. But Rebekah loved Jacob.

29One day Jacob was boiling a pot of vegetable soup. Esau came in from hunting in the fields, weak from hunger. 30So Esau said to Jacob, "Let me eat some of that red soup, because I am weak with hunger." (That is why people call him Edom.[n])

31But Jacob said, "You must sell me your rights as the firstborn son."[n]

32Esau said, "I am almost dead from hunger. If I die, all of my father's wealth will not help me."

33But Jacob said, "First, promise me that you will give it to me." So Esau made a promise to Jacob and sold his part of their father's wealth to Jacob. 34Then Jacob gave Esau bread and vegetable soup, and he ate and drank, and then left. So Esau showed how little he cared about his rights as the firstborn son.

Isaac Lies to Abimelech

26 Now there was a time of hunger in the land, besides the time of hunger that happened during Abraham's life. So Isaac went to the town of Gerar to see Abimelech king of the Philistines. 2The LORD appeared to Isaac and said, "Don't go down to Egypt, but live in the land where I tell you to live. 3Stay in this land, and I will be with you and bless you. I will give you and your descendants[d] all these lands, and I will keep the oath I made to Abraham your father. 4I will give you many descendants, as hard to count as the stars in the sky, and I will give them all these lands. Through your descendants all the nations on the earth will be blessed. 5I will do this because your father Abraham obeyed me. He did what I said and obeyed my commands, my teachings, and my rules."

6So Isaac stayed in Gerar. 7His wife Rebekah was very beautiful, and the men of that place asked Isaac about her. Isaac said, "She is my sister," because he was afraid to tell them she was his wife. He thought they might kill him so they could have her.

8Isaac lived there a long time. One day as Abimelech king of the Philistines looked out his window, he saw Isaac holding his wife Rebekah tenderly. 9Abimelech called for Isaac and said, "This woman is your wife. Why did you say she was your sister?"

Isaac said to him, "I was afraid you would kill me so you could have her."

10Abimelech said, "What have you done to us? One of our men might have had sexual relations with your wife. Then we would have been guilty of a great sin."

11So Abimelech warned everyone, "Anyone who touches this man or his wife will be put to death."

Isaac Becomes Rich

12Isaac planted seed in that land, and that year he gathered a great harvest. The LORD blessed him very much, 13and he became rich. He gathered more wealth until he became a very rich man. 14He had so many slaves and flocks and herds that the Philistines envied him. 15So they stopped up all the wells the servants of Isaac's father Abraham had dug. (They had dug them when Abraham was alive.) The Philistines filled those wells with dirt. 16And Abimelech said to Isaac, "Leave our country because you have become much more powerful than we are."

17So Isaac left that place and camped in the Valley of Gerar and lived there. 18Long before this time Abraham had dug many wells, but after he died, the Philistines filled them with dirt. So Isaac dug those wells again and gave them the same names his father had given them. 19Isaac's servants dug a well in the valley, from which a spring of water flowed. 20But the herdsmen of Gerar argued with them and said, "This water is ours." So Isaac named that well Argue because they argued with him. 21Then his servants dug another well. When the people also argued about it, Isaac named that well Fight. 22He moved from there and dug another well. No one argued about this one, so he named it Room Enough. Isaac said, "Now the LORD has made room for us, and we will be successful in this land."

23From there Isaac went to Beersheba. 24The LORD appeared to him that night and said, "I am the God of your father Abraham. Don't be afraid, because I am with you. I will bless you and give you many descendants[d] because of my servant Abraham." 25So Isaac built an altar and worshiped the LORD there. He also made a camp there, and his servants dug a well.

26Abimelech came from Gerar to see Isaac. He brought with him Ahuzzath, who advised him, and Phicol, the commander of his army. 27Isaac asked them, "Why have you come to see me? You

---

Jacob This name sounds like the Hebrew word for "heel." "Grabbing someone's heel" is a Hebrew saying for tricking someone.

Edom This name sounds like the Hebrew word for "red."

rights . . . son Usually the firstborn son had a high rank in the family. The firstborn son usually became the new head of the family.

were my enemy and forced me to leave your country."

28They answered, "Now we know that the LORD is with you. Let us swear an oath to each other. Let us make an agreement with you 29that since we did not hurt you, you will not hurt us. We were good to you and sent you away in peace. Now the LORD has blessed you."

30So Isaac prepared food for them, and they all ate and drank. 31Early the next morning the men swore an oath to each other. Then Isaac sent them away, and they left in peace.

32That day Isaac's servants came and told him about the well they had dug, saying, "We found water in that well." 33So Isaac named it Shibah*n* and that city is called Beersheba even now.

34When Esau was forty years old, he married two Hittite women — Judith daughter of Beeri and Basemath daughter of Elon. 35These women brought much sorrow to Isaac and Rebekah.

Shibah   This name sounds like the Hebrew words for "seven" and "promise."

HONESTY

Truth and Consequences

Marcus Baker couldn't wait to show up at Julius's "spring fling" party with Maria. Every guy in school drooled over Maria. For months, he had wanted to ask her out. Then when he invited her to the party, she had actually said, "I'd love to go with you."

When he had told his parents about the date, they asked about the party. "Will Julius's parents be there?"

"Of course," he said, without thinking.

Then he found out Julius's parents would be out of town. "That's the whole idea, guy!" Julius had boasted. "This is going to be a real party!"

The Thursday before the party, Marcus's parents spent the whole breakfast asking for details about the party. Usually he liked it when they showed interest, but it felt like they were prying this time.

He tried not to lie. Instead, he carefully worded his answers to avoid the exact truth about Julius's parents being gone. "I'm not sure exactly about the plans," he explained awkwardly. "But I'm sure Julius and his parents have everything worked out."

His parents seemed satisfied, and Marcus spent the day trying to put the conversation — and his white lies — out of his mind. But he couldn't. When he went to bed that night, he couldn't sleep. He didn't want to blow their trust in him over one party — even if he was taking Maria.

Finally, at 2 A.M., he climbed out of bed and went to his parents' room to wake them. He had to tell them and risk the consequences. And he could not sleep until he did.

And he was right about what his parents would say. They didn't let him go to the party. Friday morning, when he called Maria to explain, she was relieved. "To be honest," she said, "I was worried when I heard what the party would be like. Maybe we can do something else instead."

Marcus had struggled with telling the whole truth. Similarly, Isaac feared for his life if he told the king the truth. Read what happened to him in **Genesis 26:1–11**.

■ What were Marcus and Isaac afraid would happen if they told the truth? Was their concern legitimate?

■ When have you, like Isaac, told a lie to avoid potential trouble? What happened?

C O N S I D E R . . .

■ talking with your parent or a trusted adult friend about situations when you might be tempted not to tell the whole truth. Ask what he or she would do in that situation.

■ starting an honesty piggy bank. Every time you tell the truth when it's tough, put in a penny. Every time you tell a lie, take out a penny. Try to improve your "bank balance."

F O R   M O R E ,   S E E . . .

■ Genesis 20:1–13 (p. 23)   ■ Acts 5:1–11 (p. 1104)
■ Proverbs 3:3–4 (p. 570)

Jacob Tricks Isaac

27 When Isaac was old, his eyesight was poor, so he could not see clearly. One day he called his older son Esau to him and said, "Son."

Esau answered, "Here I am."

²Isaac said, "I am old and don't know when I might die. ³So take your bow and arrows and go hunting in the field for an animal for me to eat. ⁴When you prepare the tasty food that I love, bring it to me, and I will eat. Then I will bless you before I die." ⁵So Esau went out in the field to hunt.

Rebekah was listening as Isaac said this to his son Esau. ⁶She said to her son Jacob, "Listen, I heard your father saying to your brother Esau, ⁷'Kill an animal and prepare some tasty food for me to eat. Then I will bless you in the presence of the Lord before I die.' ⁸So obey me, my son, and do what I tell you. ⁹Go out to our goats and bring me two of the best young ones. I will prepare them just the way your father likes them. ¹⁰Then you will take the food to your father, and he will bless you before he dies."

¹¹But Jacob said to his mother Rebekah, "My brother Esau is a hairy man, and I am smooth! ¹²If my father touches me, he will know I am not Esau. Then he will not bless me but will place a curse on me because I tried to trick him."

¹³So Rebekah said to him, "If your father puts a curse on you, I will accept the blame. Just do what I said and go, get the goats for me."

¹⁴So Jacob went out and got two goats and brought them to his mother, and she cooked them in the special way Isaac enjoyed. ¹⁵She took the best clothes of her older son Esau that were in the house and put them on the younger son Jacob. ¹⁶She also took the skins of the goats and put them on Jacob's hands and neck. ¹⁷Then she gave Jacob the tasty food and the bread she had made.

¹⁸Jacob went in to his father and said, "Father."

And his father said, "Yes, my son. Who are you?"

¹⁹Jacob said to him, "I am Esau, your first son. I have done what you told me. Now sit up and eat some meat of the animal I hunted for you. Then bless me."

²⁰But Isaac asked his son, "How did you find and kill the animal so quickly?"

Jacob answered, "Because the Lord your God helped me to find it."

²¹Then Isaac said to Jacob, "Come near so I can touch you, my son. Then I will know if you are really my son Esau."

²²So Jacob came near to Isaac his father. Isaac touched him and said, "Your voice sounds like Jacob's voice, but your hands are hairy like the hands of Esau." ²³Isaac did not know it was Jacob, because his hands were hairy like Esau's hands, so Isaac blessed him. ²⁴Isaac asked, "Are you really my son Esau?"

Jacob answered, "Yes, I am."

²⁵Then Isaac said, "Bring me the food, and I will eat it and bless you." So Jacob gave him the food, and he ate. Jacob gave him wine, and he drank. ²⁶Then Isaac said to him, "My son, come near and kiss me." ²⁷So Jacob went to his father and kissed him. When Isaac smelled Esau's clothes, he blessed him and said,

"The smell of my son
  is like the smell of the field
  that the Lord has blessed.
²⁸May God give you plenty of rain
  and good soil
  so that you will have plenty of grain and
    new wine.
²⁹May nations serve you
  and peoples bow down to you.
May you be master over your brothers,
  and may your mother's sons bow down to
    you.
May everyone who curses you be cursed,
  and may everyone who blesses you be
    blessed."

> ✳ **SIDELIGHT:** Jacob was the world's first make-up artist. With some help from his mom, Rebekah, and some fancy cosmetic work, he tricked his father, Isaac, into thinking he was his older brother, Esau (Genesis 27:14–29). By mistakenly blessing Jacob instead of Esau, Isaac fulfilled God's promise to Rebekah in Genesis 25:23 (p. 29).

³⁰Isaac finished blessing Jacob. Then, just as Jacob left his father Isaac, Esau came in from hunting. ³¹He also prepared some tasty food and brought it to his father. He said, "Father, rise and eat the food that your son killed for you and then bless me."

³²Isaac asked, "Who are you?"

He answered, "I am your son—your firstborn son—Esau."

³³Then Isaac trembled greatly and said, "Then who was it that hunted the animals and brought me food before you came? I ate it, and I blessed him, and it is too late now to take back my blessing."

³⁴When Esau heard the words of his father, he let out a loud and bitter cry. He said to his father, "Bless me—me, too, my father!"

[35]But Isaac said, "Your brother came and tricked me. He has taken your blessing."

[36]Esau said, "Jacob is the right name for him. He has tricked me these two times. He took away my share of everything you own, and now he has taken away my blessing." Then Esau asked, "Haven't you saved a blessing for me?"

[37]Isaac answered, "I gave Jacob the power to be master over you, and all his brothers will be his servants. And I kept him strong with grain and new wine. There is nothing left to give you, my son."

[38]But Esau continued, "Do you have only one blessing, Father? Bless me, too, Father!" Then Esau began to cry out loud.

[39]Isaac said to him,
"You will live far away from the best land,
    far from the rain.
[40]You will live by using your sword,
    and you will be a slave to your brother.
But when you struggle,
    you will break free from him."

[41]After that Esau hated Jacob because of the blessing from Isaac. He thought to himself, "My father will soon die, and I will be sad for him. Then I will kill Jacob."

[42]Rebekah heard about Esau's plan to kill Jacob. So she sent for Jacob and said to him, "Listen, your brother Esau is comforting himself by planning to kill you. [43]So, my son, do what I say. My brother Laban is living in Haran. Go to him at once! [44]Stay with him for a while, until your brother is not so angry. [45]In time, your brother will not be angry, and he will forget what you did to him. Then I will send a servant to bring you back. I don't want to lose both of my sons on the same day."

[46]Then Rebekah said to Isaac, "I am tired of Hittite women. If Jacob marries one of these Hittite women here in this land, I want to die."

Jacob Searches for a Wife

28 Isaac called Jacob and blessed him and commanded him, "You must not marry a Canaanite woman. [2]Go to the house of Bethuel, your mother's father, in Northwest Mesopotamia. Laban, your mother's brother, lives there. Marry one of his daughters. [3]May God Almighty bless you and give you many children, and may you become a group of many peoples. [4]May he give you and your descendants[d] the blessing of Abraham so that you may own the land where you are now living as a stranger, the land God gave to Abraham." [5]So Isaac sent Jacob to Northwest Mesopotamia, to Laban the brother of Rebekah. Bethuel the Aramean was the father of Laban and Rebekah, and Rebekah was the mother of Jacob and Esau.

[6]Esau learned that Isaac had blessed Jacob and sent him to Northwest Mesopotamia to find a wife there. He also learned that Isaac had commanded Jacob not to marry a Canaanite woman [7]and that Jacob had obeyed his father and mother and had gone to Northwest Mesopotamia. [8]So Esau saw that his father Isaac did not want his sons to marry Canaanite women. [9]Now Esau already had wives, but he went to Ishmael son of Abraham, and he married Mahalath, Ishmael's daughter. Mahalath was the sister of Nebaioth.

Jacob's Dream at Bethel

[10]Jacob left Beersheba and set out for Haran. [11]When he came to a place, he spent the night there because the sun had set. He found a stone and laid his head on it to go to sleep. [12]Jacob dreamed that there was a ladder resting on the earth and reaching up into heaven, and he saw angels of God going up and coming down the ladder. [13]Then Jacob saw the LORD standing above the ladder, and he said, "I am the LORD, the God of Abraham your grandfather, and the God of Isaac. I will give you and your descendants[d] the land on which you are now sleeping. [14]Your descendants will be as many as the dust of the earth. They will spread west and east, north and south, and all the families of the earth will be blessed through you and your descendants. [15]I am with you and will protect you everywhere you go and will bring you back to this land. I will not leave you until I have done what I have promised you."

[16]Then Jacob woke from his sleep and said, "Surely the LORD is in this place, but I did not know it." [17]He was afraid and said, "This place frightens me! It is surely the house of God and the gate of heaven."

[18]Jacob rose early in the morning and took the stone he had slept on and set it up on its end. Then he poured olive oil on the top of it. [19]At first, the name of that city was Luz, but Jacob named it Bethel.[n]

[20]Then Jacob made a promise. He said, "I want God to be with me and to protect me on this journey. I want him to give me food to eat and clothes to wear [21]so I will be able to return in peace to my father's house. If the LORD does these things, he will be my God. [22]This stone which I have set up on its end will be the house of God. And I will give God one-tenth of all he gives me."

Jacob This name sounds like the Hebrew word for "heel." "Grabbing someone's heel" is a Hebrew saying for tricking someone.
Bethel This name means "house of God."

Jacob Arrives in Northwest Mesopotamia

29 Then Jacob continued his journey and came to the land of the people of the East. ²He looked and saw a well in the field and three flocks of sheep lying nearby, because they drank water from this well. A large stone covered the mouth of the well. ³When all the flocks would gather there, the shepherds would roll the stone away from the well and water the sheep. Then they would put the stone back in its place.

⁴Jacob said to the shepherds there, "My brothers, where are you from?"

They answered, "We are from Haran."

⁵Then Jacob asked, "Do you know Laban, grandson of Nahor?"

They answered, "We know him."

⁶Then Jacob asked, "How is he?"

They answered, "He is well. Look, his daughter Rachel is coming now with his sheep."

⁷Jacob said, "But look, it is still the middle of the day. It is not time for the sheep to be gathered for the night, so give them water and let them go back into the pasture."

⁸But they said, "We cannot do that until all the flocks are gathered. Then we will roll away the stone from the mouth of the well and water the sheep."

⁹While Jacob was talking with the shepherds, Rachel came with her father's sheep, because it was her job to care for the sheep. ¹⁰When Jacob saw Laban's daughter Rachel and Laban's sheep, he went to the well and rolled the stone from its mouth and watered Laban's sheep. Now Laban was the brother of Rebekah, Jacob's mother. ¹¹Then Jacob kissed Rachel and cried. ¹²He told her that he was from her father's family and that he was the son of Rebekah. So Rachel ran home and told her father.

¹³When Laban heard the news about his sister's son Jacob, he ran to meet him. Laban hugged him and kissed him and brought him to his house, where Jacob told Laban everything that had happened.

¹⁴Then Laban said, "You are my own flesh and blood."

Jacob Is Tricked

Jacob stayed there a month. ¹⁵Then Laban said to Jacob, "You are my relative, but it is not right for you to work for me without pay. What would you like me to pay you?"

¹⁶Now Laban had two daughters. The older was Leah, and the younger was Rachel. ¹⁷Leah had weak eyes, but Rachel was very beautiful. ¹⁸Jacob loved Rachel, so he said to Laban, "Let me marry your younger daughter Rachel. If you will, I will work seven years for you."

¹⁹Laban said, "It would be better for her to marry you than someone else, so stay here with me." ²⁰So Jacob worked for Laban seven years so he could marry Rachel. But they seemed like just a few days to him because he loved Rachel very much.

²¹After seven years Jacob said to Laban, "Give me Rachel so that I may marry her. The time I promised to work for you is over."

²²So Laban gave a feast for all the people there. ²³That evening he brought his daughter Leah to Jacob, and they had sexual relations. ²⁴(Laban gave his slave girl Zilpah to his daughter to be her servant.) ²⁵In the morning when Jacob saw that he had had sexual relations with Leah, he said to Laban, "What have you done to me? I worked hard for you so that I could marry Rachel! Why did you trick me?"

²⁶Laban said, "In our country we do not allow the younger daughter to marry before the older daughter. ²⁷But complete the full week of marriage ceremony with Leah, and I will give you Rachel to marry also. But you must serve me another seven years."

²⁸So Jacob did this, and when he had completed the week with Leah, Laban gave him his daughter Rachel as a wife. ²⁹(Laban gave his slave girl Bilhah to his daughter Rachel to be her servant.) ³⁰So Jacob had sexual relations with Rachel also, and Jacob loved Rachel more than Leah. Jacob worked for Laban for another seven years.

> ☀ **SIDELIGHT:** If you think it's hard to get a date with the right guy or girl, imagine how Jacob felt. He worked seven years to marry beautiful Rachel, only to be tricked into marrying her "weak-eyed" sister Leah. Then Jacob was given Rachel too, but he had to work for seven more years (Genesis 29:16–30). Jacob might have been tricked because the bride is brought to the wedding festivities wearing a veil.

Jacob's Family Grows

³¹When the LORD saw that Jacob loved Rachel more than Leah, he made it possible for Leah to have children, but not Rachel. ³²Leah became pregnant and gave birth to a son. She named him Reuben,ⁿ because she said, "The LORD has seen my troubles. Surely now my husband will love me."

Reuben   This name sounds like the Hebrew word for "he has seen my troubles."

[33]Leah became pregnant again and gave birth to another son. She named him Simeon[n] and said, "The LORD has heard that I am not loved, so he has given me this son."

[34]Leah became pregnant again and gave birth to another son. She named him Levi[n] and said, "Now, surely my husband will be close to me, because I have given him three sons."

[35]Then Leah gave birth to another son. She named him Judah,[n] because she said, "Now I will praise the LORD." Then Leah stopped having children.

30 When Rachel saw that she was not having children for Jacob, she envied her sister Leah. She said to Jacob, "Give me children, or I'll die!"

[2]Jacob became angry with her and said, "Can I do what only God can do? He is the one who has kept you from having children."

[3]Then Rachel said, "Here is my slave girl Bilhah. Have sexual relations with her so she can give birth to a child for me. Then I can have my own family through her."

[4]So Rachel gave Bilhah, her slave girl, to Jacob as a wife, and he had sexual relations with her. [5]She became pregnant and gave Jacob a son. [6]Rachel said, "God has judged me innocent. He has listened to my prayer and has given me a son," so she named him Dan.[n]

[7]Bilhah became pregnant again and gave Jacob a second son. [8]Rachel said, "I have struggled hard with my sister, and I have won." So she named that son Naphtali.[n]

[9]Leah saw that she had stopped having children, so she gave her slave girl Zilpah to Jacob as a wife. [10]When Zilpah had a son, [11]Leah said, "I am lucky," so she named him Gad.[n] [12]Zilpah gave birth to another son, [13]and Leah said, "I am very happy! Now women will call me happy," so she named him Asher.[n]

[14]During the wheat harvest Reuben went into the field and found some mandrake[n] plants and brought them to his mother Leah. But Rachel said to Leah, "Please give me some of your son's mandrakes."

[15]Leah answered, "You have already taken away my husband, and now you are trying to take away my son's mandrakes."

But Rachel answered, "If you will give me your son's mandrakes, you may sleep with Jacob tonight."

[16]When Jacob came in from the field that night, Leah went out to meet him. She said, "You will have sexual relations with me tonight because I have paid for you with my son's mandrakes." So Jacob slept with her that night.

[17]Then God answered Leah's prayer, and she became pregnant again. She gave birth to a fifth son [18]and said, "God has given me what I paid for, because I gave my slave girl to my husband." So Leah named her son Issachar.[n]

[19]Leah became pregnant again and gave birth to a sixth son. [20]She said, "God has given me a fine gift. Now surely Jacob will honor me, because I have given him six sons," so she named him Zebulun.[n]

[21]Later Leah gave birth to a daughter and named her Dinah.

[22]Then God remembered Rachel and answered her prayer, making it possible for her to have children. [23]When she became pregnant and gave birth to a son, she said, "God has taken away my shame," [24]and she named him Joseph.[n] Rachel said, "I wish the LORD would give me another son."

Jacob Tricks Laban

[25]After the birth of Joseph, Jacob said to Laban, "Now let me go to my own home and country. [26]Give me my wives and my children and let me go. I have earned them by working for you, and you know that I have served you well."

[27]Laban said to him, "If I have pleased you, please stay. I know the LORD has blessed me because of you. [28]Tell me what I should pay you, and I will give it to you."

[29]Jacob answered, "You know that I have worked hard for you, and your flocks have grown while I cared for them. [30]When I came, you had little, but now you have much. Every time I did something for you, the LORD blessed you. But when will I be able to do something for my own family?"

[31]Laban asked, "Then what should I give you?"

Jacob answered, "I don't want you to give me anything. Just do this one thing, and I will come back and take care of your flocks. [32]Today let me go through all your flocks. I will take every speck-

---

Simeon This name sounds like the Hebrew word for "has heard."
Levi This name sounds like the Hebrew word for "be close to."
Judah This name sounds like the Hebrew word for "praise."
Dan This name means "he has judged."
Naphtali This name sounds like the Hebrew word for "my struggle."
Gad This name may mean "lucky."
Asher This name may mean "happy."
mandrake A plant which was believed to cause a woman to become pregnant.
Issachar This name sounds like the Hebrew word for "paid for."
Zebulun This name sounds like the Hebrew word for "honor."
Joseph This name sounds like the Hebrew word for "he adds."

led or spotted sheep, every black lamb, and every spotted or speckled goat. That will be my pay. ³³In the future you can easily see if I am honest. When you come to look at my flocks, if I have any goat that isn't speckled or spotted or any lamb that isn't black, you will know I stole it."

³⁴Laban answered, "Agreed! We will do what you ask." ³⁵But that day Laban took away all the male goats that had streaks or spots, all the speckled and spotted female goats (all those that had white on them), and all the black sheep. He told his sons to watch over them. ³⁶Then he took these animals to a place that was three days' journey away from Jacob. Jacob took care of all the flocks that were left.

³⁷So Jacob cut green branches from poplar, almond, and plane trees and peeled off some of the bark so that the branches had white stripes on them. ³⁸He put the branches in front of the flocks at the watering places. When the animals came to drink, they also mated there, ³⁹so the flocks mated in front of the branches. Then the young that were born were streaked, speckled, or spotted. ⁴⁰Jacob separated the young animals from the others, and he made them face the streaked and dark animals in Laban's flock. Jacob kept his animals separate from Laban's. ⁴¹When the stronger animals in the flock were mating, Jacob put the branches before their eyes so they would mate near the branches. ⁴²But when the weaker animals mated, Jacob did not put the branches there. So the animals born from the weaker animals were Laban's, and those born from the stronger animals were Jacob's. ⁴³In this way Jacob became very rich. He had large flocks, many male and female servants, camels, and donkeys.

Jacob Runs Away

31 One day Jacob heard Laban's sons talking. They said, "Jacob has taken everything our father owned, and in this way he has become rich." ²Then Jacob noticed that Laban was not as friendly as he had been before. ³The LORD said to Jacob, "Go back to the land where your ancestors lived, and I will be with you."

⁴So Jacob told Rachel and Leah to meet him in the field where he kept his flocks. ⁵He said to them, "I have seen that your father is not as friendly with me as he used to be, but the God of my father has been with me. ⁶You both know that I have worked as hard as I could for your father, *but he cheated me and changed my pay ten* times. But God has not allowed your father to harm me. ⁸When Laban said, 'You can have all the speckled animals as your pay,' all the animals gave birth to speckled young ones. But when he said, 'You can have all the streaked animals as your pay,' all the flocks gave birth to streaked ba-

bies. ⁹So God has taken the animals away from your father and has given them to me.

¹⁰"I had a dream during the season when the flocks were mating. I saw that the only male goats who were mating were streaked, speckled, or spotted. ¹¹The angel of God spoke to me in that dream and said, 'Jacob!' I answered, 'Yes!' ¹²The angel said, 'Look! Only the streaked, speckled, or spotted male goats are mating. I have seen all the wrong things Laban has been doing to you. ¹³I am the God who appeared to you at Bethel, where you poured olive oil on the stone you set up on end and where you made a promise to me. Now I want you to leave here and go back to the land where you were born.'"

¹⁴Rachel and Leah answered Jacob, "Our father has nothing to give us when he dies. ¹⁵He has treated us like strangers. He sold us to you, and then he spent all of the money you paid for us. ¹⁶God took all this wealth from our father, and now it belongs to us and our children. So do whatever God has told you to do."

¹⁷So Jacob put his children and his wives on camels, ¹⁸and they began their journey back to Isaac, his father, in the land of Canaan. All the flocks of animals that Jacob owned walked ahead of them. He carried everything with him that he had gotten while he lived in Northwest Mesopotamia.

¹⁹While Laban was gone to cut the wool from his sheep, Rachel stole the idols that belonged to him. ²⁰And Jacob tricked Laban the Aramean by not telling him he was leaving. ²¹Jacob and his family left quickly, crossed the Euphrates River, and traveled toward the mountains of Gilead.

²²Three days later Laban learned that Jacob had run away, ²³so he gathered his relatives and began to chase him. After seven days Laban found him in the mountains of Gilead. ²⁴That night God came to Laban the Aramean in a dream and said, "Be careful! Do not say anything to Jacob, good or bad."

The Search for the Stolen Idols

²⁵So Laban caught up with Jacob. Now Jacob had made his camp in the mountains, so Laban and his relatives set up their camp in the mountains of Gilead. ²⁶Laban said to Jacob, "What have you done? You cheated me and took my daughters as if you had captured them in a war. ²⁷Why did you run away secretly and trick me? Why didn't you tell me? Then I could have sent you *away with joy and singing and with the music of* tambourines[d] and harps. ²⁸You did not even let me kiss my grandchildren and my daughters good-bye. You were very foolish to do this! ²⁹I have the power to harm you, but last night the God of your father spoke to me and warned me not to say anything to you, good or bad. ³⁰I know

you want to go back to your home, but why did you steal my idols?"

³¹Jacob answered Laban, "I left without telling you, because I was afraid you would take your daughters away from me. ³²If you find anyone here who has taken your idols, that person will be killed! Your relatives will be my witnesses. You may look for anything that belongs to you and take anything that is yours." (Now Jacob did not know that Rachel had stolen Laban's idols.)

³³So Laban looked in Jacob's tent, in Leah's tent, and in the tent where the two slave women stayed, but he did not find his idols. When he left Leah's tent, he went into Rachel's tent. ³⁴Rachel had hidden the idols inside her camel's saddle and was sitting on them. Although Laban looked through the whole tent, he did not find them.

³⁵Rachel said to her father, "Father, don't be angry with me. I am not able to stand up before you because I am having my monthly period." So Laban looked through the camp, but he did not find his idols.

³⁶Then Jacob became very angry and said, "What wrong have I done? What law have I broken to cause you to chase me? ³⁷You have looked through everything I own, but you have found nothing that belongs to you. If you have found anything, show it to everyone. Put it in front of your relatives and my relatives, and let them decide which one of us is right. ³⁸I have worked for you now for twenty years. During all that time none of the lambs and kids died during birth, and I have not eaten any of the male sheep from your flocks. ³⁹Any time an animal was killed by wild beasts, I did not bring it to you, but made up for the loss myself. You made me pay for any animal that was stolen during the day or night. ⁴⁰In the daytime the sun took away my strength, and at night I was cold and could not sleep. ⁴¹I worked like a slave for you for twenty years — the first fourteen to get your two daughters and the last six to earn your flocks. During that time you changed my pay ten times. ⁴²But the God of my father, the God of Abraham and the God of Isaac, was with me. Otherwise, you would have sent me away with nothing. But he saw the trouble I had and the hard work I did, and last night he corrected you."

Jacob and Laban's Agreement

⁴³Laban said to Jacob, "These girls are my daughters. Their children belong to me, and these flocks are mine. Everything you see here belongs to me, but I can do nothing to keep my daughters and their children. ⁴⁴Let us make an agreement, and let us set up a pile of stones to remind us of it."

⁴⁵So Jacob took a large rock and set it up on its end. ⁴⁶He told his relatives to gather rocks, so they took the rocks and piled them up; then they ate beside the pile. ⁴⁷Laban named that place in his language A Pile to Remind Us, and Jacob gave the place the same name in Hebrew.

⁴⁸Laban said to Jacob, "This pile of rocks will remind us of the agreement between us." That is why the place was called A Pile to Remind Us. ⁴⁹It was also called Mizpah,ⁿ because Laban said, "Let the LORD watch over us while we are separated from each other. ⁵⁰Remember that God is our witness even if no one else is around us. He will know if you harm my daughters or marry other women. ⁵¹Here is the pile of rocks that I have put between us and here is the rock I set up on end. ⁵²This pile of rocks and this rock set on end will remind us of our agreement. I will never go past this pile to hurt you, and you must never come to my side of them to hurt me. ⁵³Let the God of Abraham, who is the God of Nahor and the God of their fathers, punish either of us if we break this agreement."

So Jacob made a promise in the name of the God whom his father Isaac worshiped. ⁵⁴Then Jacob killed an animal and offered it as a sacrifice on the mountain, and he invited his relatives to share in the meal. After they finished eating, they spent the night on the mountain. ⁵⁵Early the next morning Laban kissed his grandchildren and his daughters and blessed them, and then he left to return home.

Jacob Meets Esau

32 When Jacob also went his way, the angels of God met him. ²When he saw them, he said, "This is the camp of God!" So he named that place Mahanaim.ⁿ

³Jacob's brother Esau was living in the area called Seir in the country of Edom. Jacob sent messengers to Esau, ⁴telling them, "Give this message to my master Esau: 'This is what Jacob, your servant, says: I have lived with Laban and have remained there until now. ⁵I have cattle, donkeys, flocks, and male and female servants. I send this message to you and ask you to accept us.'"

⁶The messengers returned to Jacob and said, "We went to your brother Esau. He is coming to meet you and has four hundred men with him." ⁷Then Jacob was very afraid and worried. He divided the people who were with him and all the flocks, herds, and camels into two camps. ⁸Jacob thought, "Esau might come and destroy one

Mizpah This name sounds like the Hebrew word for "watch."
Mahanaim This name means "two camps."

camp, but the other camp can run away and be saved."

⁹Then Jacob said, "God of my father Abraham! God of my father Isaac! LORD, you told me to return to my country and my family. You said that you would treat me well. ¹⁰I am not worthy of the kindness and continual goodness you have shown me. The first time I traveled across the Jordan River, I had only my walking stick, but now I own enough to have two camps. ¹¹Please save me from my brother Esau. I am afraid he will come and kill all of us, even the mothers with the children. ¹²You said to me, 'I will treat you well and will make your children as many as the sand of the seashore. There will be too many to count.' "

¹³Jacob stayed there for the night and prepared a gift for Esau from what he had with him: ¹⁴two hundred female goats and twenty male goats, two hundred female sheep and twenty male sheep, ¹⁵thirty female camels and their young, forty cows and ten bulls, twenty female donkeys, and ten male donkeys. ¹⁶Jacob gave each separate flock of animals to one of his servants and said to them, "Go ahead of me and keep some space between each herd." ¹⁷Jacob gave them their orders. To the servant with the first group of animals he said, "My brother Esau will come to you and ask, 'Whose servant are you? Where are you going and whose animals are these?' ¹⁸Then you will answer, 'They belong to your servant Jacob. He sent them as a gift to you, my master Esau, and he also is coming behind us.' "

¹⁹Jacob ordered the second servant, the third servant, and all the other servants to do the same thing. He said, "Say the same thing to Esau when you meet him. ²⁰Say, 'Your servant Jacob is coming behind us.' " Jacob thought, "If I send these gifts ahead of me, maybe Esau will forgive me. Then when I see him, perhaps he will accept me." ²¹So Jacob sent the gifts to Esau, but he himself stayed that night in the camp.

Jacob Wrestles with God

²²During the night Jacob rose and crossed the

Wrestling With God

Donald Cho, sixteen, sat silently through the youth council meeting at church. Usually bubbling with ideas, he sat back in his chair with his arms folded. The summer trip being planned just didn't interest him.

He and some friends had visited a home for the mentally retarded early that day, and he couldn't get it out of his mind.

Then, without warning or prompting, he interrupted the planning. "I get so disgusted sometimes when we sit here and haggle about what amusement parks to visit on our trip and all that junk," Donald said. "I mean, there are people living in old people's homes and hospitals and places for mentally retarded people. And nobody cares about. . . ."

His voice trailed off when he noticed everyone staring at him. "I just wish we did something that really mattered," he concluded. "What's the point of being a Christian otherwise?"

Donald's visit to the home for mentally retarded people had challenged him to struggle with what it means to follow God. Jacob also struggled with God—literally. Read **Genesis 32:22–32** and see what happened when Jacob wrestled with God.

■ How does Donald's struggle with what it means to follow God compare with Jacob's wrestling by the Jabbok River?

■ When have you "wrestled with God" like Jacob and grown in your faith because of the struggle?

CONSIDER . . .

■ writing a letter to God, honestly asking him the questions you have about him, your faith, and the world. Then decide one thing you'll start doing to discover some answers to those questions.

■ asking an athlete to tell you how the struggle of practice and physical exertion helps him or her improve physically. Compare the response to how "wrestling with God" can help you grow in your faith.

FOR MORE, SEE . . .

■ Job 23:1–14 (p. 466)   ■ John 20:24–29 (p. 1094)
■ Jonah 2:1–7 (p. 857)

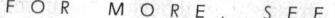

Jabbok River at the crossing, taking with him his two wives, his two slave girls, and his eleven sons. 23He sent his family and everything he had across the river. 24So Jacob was alone, and a man came and wrestled with him until the sun came up. 25When the man saw he could not defeat Jacob, he struck Jacob's hip and put it out of joint. 26Then he said to Jacob, "Let me go. The sun is coming up."

But Jacob said, "I will let you go if you will bless me."

27The man said to him, "What is your name?"

And he answered, "Jacob."

28Then the man said, "Your name will no longer be Jacob. Your name will now be Israel, *n* because you have wrestled with God and with people, and you have won."

29Then Jacob asked him, "Please tell me your name."

But the man said, "Why do you ask my name?" Then he blessed Jacob there.

30So Jacob named that place Peniel, *n* saying, "I have seen God face to face, but my life was saved." 31Then the sun rose as he was leaving that place, and Jacob was limping because of his leg. 32So even today the people of Israel do not eat the muscle that is on the hip joint of animals, because Jacob was touched there.

☼ SIDELIGHT: The first wrestling match in the Bible was no mere three-period event. It lasted a night. Jacob's opponent had out-of-this-world strength, but Jacob still ended the match undefeated— though he sustained a sports-related injury and was given a prize-fighter's name, Israel, which means "he struggles with God" (Genesis 32:22–32).

Jacob Shows His Bravery

33 Jacob looked up and saw Esau coming, and with him were four hundred men. So Jacob divided his children among Leah, Rachel, and the two slave girls. 2Jacob put the slave girls with their children first, then Leah and her children behind them, and Rachel and Joseph last. 3Jacob himself went out in front of them and bowed down flat on the ground seven times as he was walking toward his brother.

4But Esau ran to meet Jacob and put his arms around him and hugged him. Then Esau kissed him, and they both cried. 5When Esau looked up and saw the women and children, he asked, "Who are these people with you?"

Jacob answered, "These are the children God has given me. God has been good to me, your servant."

6Then the two slave girls and their children came up to Esau and bowed down flat on the earth before him. 7Leah and her children also came up to Esau and also bowed down flat on the earth. Last of all, Joseph and Rachel came up to Esau, and they, too, bowed down flat before him.

8Esau said, "I saw many herds as I was coming here. Why did you bring them?"

Jacob answered, "They were to please you, my master."

9But Esau said, "I already have enough, my brother. Keep what you have."

10Jacob said, "No! Please! If I have pleased you, then accept the gift I give you. I am very happy to see your face again. It is like seeing the face of God, because you have accepted me. 11So I beg you to accept the gift I give you. God has been very good to me, and I have more than I need." And because Jacob begged, Esau accepted the gift.

12Then Esau said, "Let us be going. I will travel with you."

13But Jacob said to him, "My master, you know that the children are weak. And I must be careful with my flocks and their young ones. If I force them to go too far in one day, all the animals will die. 14So, my master, you go on ahead of me, your servant. I will follow you slowly and let the animals and the children set the speed at which we travel. I will meet you, my master, in Edom."

15So Esau said, "Then let me leave some of my people with you."

"No, thank you," said Jacob. "I only want to please you, my master." 16So that day Esau started back to Edom. 17But Jacob went to Succoth, where he built a house for himself and shelters for his animals. That is why the place was named Succoth. *n*

18Jacob left Northwest Mesopotamia and arrived safely at the city of Shechem in the land of Canaan. There he camped east of the city. 19He bought a part of the field where he had camped from the sons of Hamor father of Shechem for one hundred pieces of silver. 20He built an altar there and named it after God, the God of Israel.

Dinah Is Attacked

34 At this time Dinah, the daughter of Leah and Jacob, went out to visit the women of the land. 2When Shechem son of Hamor the Hivite, the ruler of the land, saw her, he took her

---

Israel   This name means "he wrestles with God."
Peniel   This name means "the face of God."
Succoth   This name means "shelters."

and forced her to have sexual relations with him. ³Shechem fell in love with Dinah, and he spoke kindly to her. ⁴He told his father, Hamor, "Please get this girl for me so I can marry her."

⁵Jacob learned how Shechem had disgraced his daughter, but since his sons were out in the field with the cattle, Jacob said nothing until they came home. ⁶While he waited, Hamor father of Shechem went to talk with Jacob.

⁷When Jacob's sons heard what had happened, they came in from the field. They were very angry that Shechem had done such a wicked thing to Israel. It was wrong for him to have sexual relations with Jacob's daughter; a thing like this should not be done.

⁸But Hamor talked to Dinah's brothers and said, "My son Shechem is deeply in love with Dinah. Please let him marry her. ⁹Marry our people. Give your women to our men as wives and take our women for your men as wives. ¹⁰You can live in the same land with us. You will be free to own land and to trade here."

¹¹Shechem also talked to Jacob and to Dinah's brothers and said, "Please accept my offer. I will give anything you ask. ¹²Ask as much as you want for the payment for the bride, and I will give it to you. Just let me marry Dinah."

¹³Jacob's sons answered Shechem and his father with lies, because Shechem had disgraced their sister Dinah. ¹⁴The brothers said to them, "We cannot allow you to marry our sister, because you are not circumcised.ᵈ That would be a disgrace to us. ¹⁵But we will allow you to marry her if you do this one thing: Every man in your town must be circumcised like us. ¹⁶Then your men can marry our women, and our men can marry your women, and we will live in your land and become one people. ¹⁷If you refuse to be circumcised, we will take Dinah and leave."

¹⁸What they asked seemed fair to Hamor and Shechem. ¹⁹So Shechem quickly went to be circumcised because he loved Jacob's daughter.

Now Shechem was the most respected man in his family. ²⁰So Hamor and Shechem went to the gate of their city and spoke to the men of their city, saying, ²¹"These people want to be friends with us. So let them live in our land and trade here. There is enough land for all of us. Let us marry their women, and we can let them marry our women. ²²But we must agree to one thing: All our men must be circumcised as they are. Then they will agree to live in our land, and we will be one people. ²³If we do this, their cattle and their animals will belong to us. Let us do what they say, and they will stay in our land." ²⁴All the people who had come to the city gate heard this. They agreed with Hamor and Shechem, and every man was circumcised.

²⁵Three days later the men who were circum-cised were still in pain. Two of Jacob's sons, Simeon and Levi (Dinah's brothers), took their swords and made a surprise attack on the city, killing all the men there. ²⁶They killed Hamor and his son Shechem and then took Dinah out of Shechem's house and left. ²⁷Jacob's sons came upon the dead bodies and stole everything that was in the city, to pay them back for what Shechem had done to their sister. ²⁸So the brothers took the flocks, herds, and donkeys, and everything in the city and in the fields. ²⁹They took every valuable thing the people owned, even their wives and children and everything in the houses.

³⁰Then Jacob said to Simeon and Levi, "You have caused me a lot of trouble. Now the Canaanites and the Perizzites who live in the land will hate me. Since there are only a few of us, if they join together to attack us, my people and I will be destroyed."

³¹But the brothers said, "We will not allow our sister to be treated like a prostitute."ᵈ

Jacob in Bethel

35 God said to Jacob, "Go to the city of Bethel and live there. Make an altar to the God who appeared to you there when you were running away from your brother Esau."

²So Jacob said to his family and to all who were with him, "Put away the foreign gods you have, and make yourselves clean,ᵈ and change your clothes. ³We will leave here and go to Bethel. There I will build an altar to God, who has helped me during my time of trouble. He has been with me everywhere I have gone." ⁴So they gave Jacob all the foreign gods they had, and the earrings they were wearing, and he hid them under the great tree near the town of Shechem. ⁵Then Jacob and his sons left there. But God caused the people in the nearby cities to be afraid, so they did not follow them. ⁶And Jacob and all the people who were with him went to Luz, which is now called Bethel, in the land of Canaan. ⁷There Jacob built an altar and named the place Bethel, after God, because God had appeared to him there when he was running from his brother.

⁸Deborah, Rebekah's nurse, died and was buried under the oak tree at Bethel, so they named that place Oak of Crying.

Jacob's New Name

⁹When Jacob came back from Northwest Mesopotamia, God appeared to him again and blessed him. ¹⁰God said to him, "Your name is Jacob, but you will not be called Jacob any longer. Your new name will be Israel." So he called him Israel. ¹¹God said to him, "I am God Almighty. Have many children and grow in number as a nation. You will be the ancestor of many nations and kings. ¹²The same land I gave to Abraham and

Isaac I will give to you and your descendants."[d] [13]Then God left him. [14]Jacob set up a stone on edge in that place where God had talked to him, and he poured a drink offering and olive oil on it to make it special for God. [15]And Jacob named the place Bethel.

Rachel Dies Giving Birth

[16]Jacob and his group left Bethel. Before they came to Ephrath, Rachel began giving birth to her baby, [17]but she was having much trouble. When Rachel's nurse saw this, she said, "Don't be afraid, Rachel. You are giving birth to another son." [18]Rachel gave birth to the son, but she herself died. As she lay dying, she named the boy Son of My Suffering, but Jacob called him Benjamin.[n] [19]Rachel was buried on the road to Ephrath, a district of Bethlehem, [20]and Jacob set up a rock on her grave to honor her. That rock is still there. [21]Then Israel[n] continued his journey and camped just south of Migdal Eder.

[22]While Israel was there, Reuben had sexual relations with Israel's slave woman[d] Bilhah, and Israel heard about it.

The Family of Israel

Jacob had twelve sons. [23]He had six sons by his wife Leah: Reuben, his first son, then Simeon, Levi, Judah, Issachar, and Zebulun.

[24]He had two sons by his wife Rachel: Joseph and Benjamin.

[25]He had two sons by Rachel's slave girl Bilhah: Dan and Naphtali.

[26]And he had two sons by Leah's slave girl Zilpah: Gad and Asher.

These are Jacob's sons who were born in Northwest Mesopotamia.

[27]Jacob went to his father Isaac at Mamre near Hebron, where Abraham and Isaac had lived. [28]Isaac lived one hundred eighty years. [29]So Isaac breathed his last breath and died when he was very old, and his sons Esau and Jacob buried him.

Esau's Family

36 This is the family history of Esau (also called Edom).

[2]Esau married women from the land of Canaan: Adah daughter of Elon the Hittite; and Oholibamah daughter of Anah, the son of Zibeon the Hivite; [3]and Basemath, Ishmael's daughter, the sister of Nebaioth.

[4]Adah gave birth to Eliphaz for Esau. Basemath gave him Reuel, [5]and Oholibamah gave him Jeush, Jalam, and Korah. These were Esau's sons who were born in the land of Canaan.

[6]Esau took his wives, his sons, his daughters, and all the people who lived with him, his herds and other animals, and all the belongings he had gotten in Canaan, and he went to a land away from his brother Jacob. [7]Esau's and Jacob's belongings were becoming too many for them to live in the same land. The land where they had lived could not support both of them, because they had too many herds. [8]So Esau lived in the mountains of Edom. (Esau is also named Edom.)

[9]This is the family history of Esau. He is the ancestor of the Edomites, who live in the mountains of Edom.

[10]Esau's sons were Eliphaz, son of Adah and Esau, and Reuel, son of Basemath and Esau.

[11]Eliphaz had five sons: Teman, Omar, Zepho, Gatam, and Kenaz. [12]Eliphaz also had a slave woman[d] named Timna, and Timna and Eliphaz gave birth to Amalek. These were Esau's grandsons by his wife Adah.

[13]Reuel had four sons: Nahath, Zerah, Shammah, and Mizzah. These were Esau's grandsons by his wife Basemath.

[14]Esau's third wife was Oholibamah the daughter of Anah. (Anah was the son of Zibeon.) Esau and Oholibamah gave birth to Jeush, Jalam, and Korah.

[15]These were the leaders that came from Esau: Esau's first son was Eliphaz. From him came these leaders: Teman, Omar, Zepho, Kenaz, [16]Korah, Gatam, and Amalek. These were the leaders that came from Eliphaz in the land of Edom. They were the grandsons of Adah.

[17]Esau's son Reuel was the father of these leaders: Nahath, Zerah, Shammah, and Mizzah. These were the leaders that came from Reuel in the land of Edom. They were the grandsons of Esau's wife Basemath.

[18]Esau's wife Oholibamah gave birth to these leaders: Jeush, Jalam, and Korah. These are the leaders that came from Esau's wife Oholibamah the daughter of Anah. [19]These were the sons of Esau (also called Edom), and these were their leaders.

[20]These were the sons of Seir the Horite, who were living in the land: Lotan, Shobal, Zibeon, Anah, [21]Dishon, Ezer, and Dishan. These sons of Seir were the leaders of the Horites in Edom.

[22]The sons of Lotan were Hori and Homam. (Timna was Lotan's sister.)

[23]The sons of Shobal were Alvan, Manahath, Ebal, Shepho, and Onam.

[24]The sons of Zibeon were Aiah and Anah. Anah is the man who found the hot springs in the desert while he was caring for his father's donkeys.

Benjamin This name means "right-hand son" or "favorite son."
Israel Also called Jacob.

25The children of Anah were Dishon and Oholibamah daughter of Anah.

26The sons of Dishon were Hemdan, Eshban, Ithran, and Keran.

27The sons of Ezer were Bilhan, Zaavan, and Akan.

28The sons of Dishan were Uz and Aran.

29These were the names of the Horite leaders: Lotan, Shobal, Zibeon, Anah, 30Dishon, Ezer, and Dishan.

These men were the leaders of the Horite families who lived in the land of Edom.

31These are the kings who ruled in the land of Edom before the Israelites ever had a king:

32Bela son of Beor was the king of Edom. He came from the city of Dinhabah.

33When Bela died, Jobab son of Zerah became king. Jobab was from Bozrah.

34When Jobab died, Husham became king. He was from the land of the Temanites.

35When Husham died, Hadad son of Bedad, who had defeated Midian in the country of Moab, became king. Hadad was from the city of Avith.

36When Hadad died, Samlah became king. He was from Masrekah.

37When Samlah died, Shaul became king. He was from Rehoboth on the Euphrates River.

38When Shaul died, Baal-Hanan son of Acbor became king.

39When Baal-Hanan son of Acbor died, Hadad became king. He was from the city of Pau. His wife's name was Mehetabel daughter of Matred, who was the daughter of Me-Zahab.

40These Edomite leaders, listed by their families and regions, came from Esau. Their names were Timna, Alvah, Jetheth, 41Oholibamah, Elah, Pinon, 42Kenaz, Teman, Mibzar, 43Magdiel, and Iram. They were the leaders of Edom. (Esau was the father of the Edomites.) The area where each of these families lived was named after that family.

Joseph the Dreamer

37 Jacob lived in the land of Canaan, where his father had lived. 2This is the family history of Jacob:

Joseph was a young man, seventeen years old. He and his brothers, the sons of Bilhah and Zilpah, his father's wives, cared for the flocks. Joseph gave his father bad reports about his brothers. 3Since Joseph was born when his father Israel[n] was old, Israel loved him more than his *other sons. He made Joseph a special robe with long sleeves.* 4When Joseph's brothers saw that their father loved him more than he loved them, they hated their brother and could not speak to *him politely.*

Israel Also called Jacob.

5One time Joseph had a dream, and when he told his brothers about it, they hated him even more. 6Joseph said, "Listen to the dream I had. 7We were in the field tying bundles of wheat together. My bundle stood up, and your bundles of wheat gathered around it and bowed down to it."

✳ SIDELIGHT: Joseph's "coat of many colors" was likely a long robe with sleeves. Laborers wore shorter garments that freed their arms and legs. The coat upset Joseph's brothers because it signified that Joseph was special and didn't have to do any manual labor (Genesis 37:3–4).

8His brothers said, "Do you really think you will be king over us? Do you truly think you will rule over us?" His brothers hated him even more because of his dreams and what he had said.

9Then Joseph had another dream, and he told his brothers about it also. He said, "Listen, I had another dream. I saw the sun, moon, and eleven stars bowing down to me."

10Joseph also told his father about this dream, but his father scolded him, saying, "What kind of dream is this? Do you really believe that your mother, your brothers, and I will bow down to you?" 11Joseph's brothers were jealous of him, but his father thought about what all these things could mean.

12One day Joseph's brothers went to Shechem to graze their father's flocks. 13Israel said to Joseph, "Go to Shechem where your brothers are grazing the flocks."

Joseph answered, "I will go."

14His father said, "Go and see if your brothers and the flocks are all right. Then come back and tell me." So Joseph's father sent him from the Valley of Hebron.

When Joseph came to Shechem, 15a man found him wandering in the field and asked him, "What are you looking for?"

16Joseph answered, "I am looking for my brothers. Can you tell me where they are grazing the flocks?"

17The man said, "They have already gone. I heard them say they were going to Dothan." So Joseph went to look for his brothers and found them in Dothan.

Joseph Sold into Slavery

18Joseph's brothers saw him coming from far away. Before he reached them, they made a plan to kill him. 19They said to each other, "Here comes that dreamer. [20]Let's kill him and throw his body into one of the wells. We can tell our father that a wild animal killed him. Then we will see what will become of his dreams."

[21]But Reuben heard their plan and saved Joseph, saying, "Let's not kill him. [22]Don't spill any blood. Throw him into this well here in the desert, but don't hurt him!" Reuben planned to save Joseph later and send him back to his father. [23]So when Joseph came to his brothers, they pulled off his robe with long sleeves [24]and threw him into the well. It was empty, and there was no water in it.

[25]While Joseph was in the well, the brothers sat down to eat. When they looked up, they saw a group of Ishmaelites traveling from Gilead to Egypt. Their camels were carrying spices, balm,[d] and myrrh.[d]

[26]Then Judah said to his brothers, "What will we gain if we kill our brother and hide his death? [27]Let's sell him to these Ishmaelites. Then we will not be guilty of killing our own brother. After all, he is our brother, our own flesh and blood." And the other brothers agreed. [28]So when the Midianite traders came by, the brothers took Joseph out of the well and sold him to the Ishmaelites for eight ounces of silver. And the Ishmaelites took him to Egypt.

SIDELIGHT: Do you think your brother is mean? Joseph's brothers sold him as a slave into Egypt (Genesis 37:18–28). The payment of eight ounces of silver was the same amount the Israelites later gave when they dedicated a young man to God (see Leviticus 27:5, p. 124).

FAMILY

Family Feud

Another famous Wilson-sister fight was brewing. Usually Marianne was home from college for an hour or so before the anger boiled over. This time she didn't have her bag unpacked.

"How could you ruin my Creston High School jacket!" Marianne screamed the minute she opened her closet to hang up her clothes.

"I didn't fall off my bike on purpose," Sheila yelled from her room. "A car almost hit me. It's not my fault!"

"But you took my jacket," Marianne hissed, storming into her sister's room.

"Mom said I could wear anything in your closet," Sheila retorted hotly.

"But you should've known I'd never let you wear this. I can never replace it," Marianne shot back.

"It's just a stupid school jacket," Sheila sassed sarcastically. "I thought you were a big college girl now."

Marianne threw the torn jacket on Sheila's bed. "Mom lets you get away with everything," she said, seething with anger. "But not this time. You're going to pay, little sister." And she stormed out of the room.

Sheila sat down on the bed, and her anger turned to tears. Why do I have so much trouble with my sister?

Sheila and Marianne's constant clashes are a lot like the clashes between Joseph and his brothers. Read **Genesis 37:1–36** to see what their bad relationship led to.

■ What problems do you see in Marianne and Sheila's relationship that also show up in the relationship between Joseph and his brothers?
■ Are you more like Joseph (the one who gets picked on) or his brothers (the ones who become jealous)?

C O N S I D E R . . .

■ writing an "I'm sorry" or "I forgive you" note to a family member and taping it to a mirror he or she uses.
■ starting a "Something Nice" jar to collect notes about nice things other family members do for you. Look through the notes when you're angry at another family member.

F O R   M O R E ,   S E E . . .

■ Genesis 27:1–41 (p. 32)   ■ 1 John 2:9–11 (p. 1317)
■ Luke 10:38–41 (p. 1024)

²⁹When Reuben came back to the well and Joseph was not there, he tore his clothes to show he was upset. ³⁰Then he went back to his brothers and said, "The boy is not there! What shall I do?" ³¹The brothers killed a goat and dipped Joseph's robe in its blood. ³²Then they brought the long-sleeved robe to their father and said, "We found this robe. Look it over carefully and see if it is your son's robe."

³³Jacob looked it over and said, "It is my son's robe! Some savage animal has eaten him. My son Joseph has been torn to pieces!" ³⁴Then Jacob tore his clothes and put on rough cloth to show that he was upset, and he continued to be sad about his son for a long time. ³⁵All of his sons and daughters tried to comfort him, but he could not be comforted. He said, "I will be sad about my son until the day I die." So Jacob cried for his son Joseph.

³⁶Meanwhile the Midianites who had bought Joseph had taken him to Egypt. There they sold him to Potiphar, an officer to the king of Egypt and captain of the palace guard.

Judah and Tamar

38 About that time, Judah left his brothers and went to stay with a man named Hirah in the town of Adullam. ²There Judah met a Canaanite girl, the daughter of a man named Shua, and married her. Judah had sexual relations with her, ³and she became pregnant and gave birth to a son, whom Judah named Er. ⁴Later she gave birth to another son and named him Onan. ⁵Still later she had another son and named him Shelah. She was at Kezib when this third son was born.

⁶Judah chose a girl named Tamar to be the wife of his first son Er. ⁷But Er, Judah's oldest son, did what the LORD said was evil, so the LORD killed him. ⁸Then Judah said to Er's brother Onan, "Go and have sexual relations with your dead brother's wife.ⁿ It is your duty to provide children for your brother in this way."

⁹But Onan knew that the children would not belong to him, so when he was supposed to have sexual relations with Tamar he did not complete the sex act. This made it impossible for Tamar to become pregnant and for Er to have descendants.ᵈ ¹⁰The LORD was displeased by this wicked thing Onan had done, so the LORD killed Onan also. ¹¹Then Judah said to his daughter-in-law Tamar, "Go back to live in your father's house, and don't marry until my young son Shelah grows up." Judah was afraid that Shelah also would die like his brothers. So Tamar returned to her father's home.

¹²After a long time Judah's wife, the daughter of Shua, died. After Judah had gotten over his sorrow, he went to Timnah to his men who were cutting the wool from his sheep. His friend Hirah from Adullam went with him. ¹³Tamar learned that Judah, her father-in-law, was going to Timnah to cut the wool from his sheep. ¹⁴So she took off the clothes that showed she was a widow and covered her face with a veil to hide who she was. Then she sat down by the gate of Enaim on the road to Timnah. She did this because Judah's younger son Shelah had grown up, but Judah had not made plans for her to marry him.

¹⁵When Judah saw her, he thought she was a prostitute,ᵈ because she had covered her face with a veil. ¹⁶So Judah went to her and said, "Let me have sexual relations with you." He did not know that she was Tamar, his daughter-in-law.

She asked, "What will you give me if I let you have sexual relations with me?"

¹⁷Judah answered, "I will send you a young goat from my flock."

She answered, "First give me something to keep as a deposit until you send the goat."

¹⁸Judah asked, "What do you want me to give you as a deposit?"

Tamar answered, "Give me your seal and its cord,ⁿ and give me your walking stick." So Judah gave these things to her. Then Judah and Tamar had sexual relations, and Tamar became pregnant. ¹⁹When Tamar went home, she took off the veil that covered her face and put on the clothes that showed she was a widow.

²⁰Judah sent his friend Hirah with the young goat to find the woman and get back his seal and the walking stick he had given her, but Hirah could not find her. ²¹He asked some of the people at the town of Enaim, "Where is the prostitute who was here by the road?"

They answered, "There has never been a prostitute here."

²²So he went back to Judah and said, "I could not find the woman, and the people who lived there said, 'There has never been a prostitute here.' "

²³Judah said, "Let her keep the things. I don't want people to laugh at us. I sent her the goat as I promised, but you could not find her."

²⁴About three months later someone told Judah, "Tamar, your daughter-in-law, is guilty of acting like a prostitute, and now she is pregnant."

Go ... wife It was a custom in Israel that if a man died without children, one of his brothers would marry the widow. If a child was born, it would be considered the dead man's child.
seal ... cord A seal was used like a rubber stamp, and people ran a string through it to tie around the neck. They wrote a contract, folded it, put wax or clay on the contract, and pressed the seal onto it as a signature.

Then Judah said, "Bring her out and let her be burned to death."

25When the people went to bring Tamar out, she sent a message to her father-in-law that said, "The man who owns these things has made me pregnant. Look at this seal and its cord and this walking stick, and tell me whose they are."

26Judah recognized them and said, "She is more in the right than I. She did this because I did not give her to my son Shelah as I promised." And Judah did not have sexual relations with her again.

27When the time came for Tamar to give birth, there were twins in her body. 28While she was giving birth, one baby put his hand out. The nurse tied a red string on his hand and said, "This baby came out first." 29But he pulled his hand back in, so the other baby was born first. The nurse said, "So you are able to break out first," and they named him Perez. n 30After this, the baby with the red string on his hand was born, and they named him Zerah.

Joseph Is Sold to Potiphar

39 Now Joseph had been taken down to Egypt. An Egyptian named Potiphar was an officer to the king of Egypt and the captain of the palace guard. He bought Joseph from the Ishmaelites who had brought him down there. 2The LORD was with Joseph, and he became a successful man. He lived in the house of his master, Potiphar the Egyptian.

3Potiphar saw that the LORD was with Joseph and that the LORD made Joseph successful in everything he did. 4So Potiphar was very happy with Joseph and allowed him to be his personal servant. He put Joseph in charge of the house, trusting him with everything he owned. 5When Joseph was put in charge of the house and everything Potiphar owned, the LORD blessed the people in Potiphar's house because of Joseph. And the LORD blessed everything that belonged to Potiphar, both in the house and in the field. 6So Potiphar left Joseph in charge of everything he owned and was not concerned about anything except the food he ate.

Joseph Is Put into Prison

Now Joseph was well built and handsome. 7After some time the wife of Joseph's master began to desire Joseph, and one day she said to him, "Have sexual relations with me."

8But Joseph refused and said to her, "My master trusts me with everything in his house. He has put me in charge of everything he owns. 9There is no one in his house greater than I. He has not kept anything from me except you, because you

are his wife. How can I do such an evil thing? It is a sin against God."

10The woman talked to Joseph every day, but he refused to have sexual relations with her or even spend time with her.

11One day Joseph went into the house to do his work as usual and was the only man in the house at that time. 12His master's wife grabbed his coat and said to him, "Come and have sexual relations with me." But Joseph left his coat in her hand and ran out of the house.

13When she saw that Joseph had left his coat in her hands and had run outside, 14she called to the servants in her house and said, "Look! This Hebrew slave was brought here to shame us. He came in and tried to have sexual relations with me, but I screamed. 15My scream scared him and he ran away, but he left his coat with me." 16She kept his coat until her husband came home, 17and she told him the same story. She said, "This Hebrew slave you brought here came in to shame me! 18When he came near me, I screamed. He ran away, but he left his coat."

19When Joseph's master heard what his wife said Joseph had done, he became very angry. 20So Potiphar arrested Joseph and put him into the prison where the king's prisoners were put. And Joseph stayed there in the prison.

21But the LORD was with Joseph and showed him kindness and caused the prison warden to like Joseph. 22The prison warden chose Joseph to take care of all the prisoners, and he was responsible for whatever was done in the prison. 23The warden paid no attention to anything that was in Joseph's care because the LORD was with Joseph and made him successful in everything he did.

Joseph Interprets Two Dreams

40 After these things happened, two of the king's officers displeased the king — the man who served wine to the king and the king's baker. 2The king became angry with his officer who served him wine and his baker, 3so he put them in the prison of the captain of the guard, the same prison where Joseph was kept. 4The captain of the guard put the two prisoners in Joseph's care, and they stayed in prison for some time.

5One night both the king's officer who served him wine and the baker had a dream. Each had his own dream with its own meaning. 6When Joseph came to them the next morning, he saw they were worried. 7He asked the king's officers who were with him, "Why do you look so unhappy today?"

8The two men answered, "We both had dreams last night, but no one can explain their meaning to us."

Perez This name means "breaking out."

Joseph said to them, "God is the only One who can explain the meaning of dreams. Tell me your dreams."

9So the man who served wine to the king told Joseph his dream. He said, "I dreamed I saw a vine, and 10on the vine were three branches. I watched the branches bud and blossom, and then the grapes ripened. 11I was holding the king's cup, so I took the grapes and squeezed the juice into the cup. Then I gave it to the king."

12Then Joseph said, "I will explain the dream to you. The three branches stand for three days. 13Before the end of three days the king will free you, and he will allow you to return to your work. You will serve the king his wine just as you did before. 14But when you are free, remember me. Be kind to me, and tell the king about me so I can get out of this prison. 15I was taken by force from the land of the Hebrews, and I have done nothing here to deserve being put in prison."

16The baker saw that Joseph's explanation of the dream was good, so he said to him, "I also had a dream. I dreamed there were three bread baskets on my head. 17In the top basket were all kinds of baked food for the king, but the birds were eating this food out of the basket on my head."

18Joseph answered, "I will tell you what the dream means. The three baskets stand for three days. 19Before the end of three days, the king will cut off your head! He will hang your body on a pole, and the birds will eat your flesh."

20Three days later, on his birthday, the king gave a feast for all his officers. In front of his officers, he released from prison the chief officer who served his wine and the chief baker. 21The king gave his chief officer who served wine his old position, and once again he put the king's cup of wine into the king's hand. 22But the king hanged the baker on a pole. Everything happened just as Joseph had said it would, 23but the officer who served wine did not remember Joseph. He forgot all about him.

The King's Dreams

41 Two years later the king dreamed he was standing on the bank of the Nile River. 2He saw seven fat and beautiful cows come up out of the river, and they stood there, eating the grass. 3Then seven more cows came up out of the river, but they were thin and ugly. They stood beside the seven beautiful cows on the bank of the Nile. 4The seven thin and ugly cows ate the seven beautiful fat cows. Then the king woke up. 5The king slept again and dreamed a second time. In his dream he saw seven full and good heads of grain growing on one stalk. 6After that, seven more heads of grain sprang up, but they were thin and burned by the hot east wind. 7The thin heads of grain ate the seven full and good heads. Then the king woke up again, and he realized it was only a dream. 8The next morning the king was troubled about these dreams, so he sent for all the magicians and wise men of Egypt. The king told them his dreams, but no one could explain their meaning to him.

9Then the chief officer who served wine to the king said to him, "Now I remember something I promised to do, but I forgot about it. 10There was a time when you were angry with the baker and me, and you put us in prison in the house of the captain of the guard. 11In prison we each had a dream on the same night, and each dream had a different meaning. 12A young Hebrew man, a servant of the captain of the guard, was in the prison with us. When we told him our dreams, he explained their meanings to us. He told each man the meaning of his dream, and 13things happened exactly as he said they would: I was given back my old position, and the baker was hanged."

14So the king called for Joseph. The guards quickly brought him out of the prison, and he shaved, put on clean clothes, and went before the king.

15The king said to Joseph, "I have had a dream, but no one can explain its meaning to me. I have heard that you can explain a dream when someone tells it to you."

16Joseph answered the king, "I am not able to explain the meaning of dreams, but God will do this for the king."

17Then the king said to Joseph, "In my dream I was standing on the bank of the Nile River. 18I saw seven fat and beautiful cows that came up out of the river and ate the grass. 19Then I saw seven more cows come out of the river that were thin and lean and ugly—the worst looking cows I have seen in all the land of Egypt. 20And these thin and ugly cows ate the first seven fat cows, 21but after they had eaten the seven cows, no one could tell they had eaten them. They looked just as thin and ugly as they did in the beginning. Then I woke up.

22"I had another dream. I saw seven full and good heads of grain growing on one stalk. 23Then seven more heads of grain sprang up after them, but these heads were thin and ugly and were burned by the hot east wind. 24Then the thin heads ate the seven good heads. I told this dream to the magicians, but no one could explain its meaning to me."

Joseph Tells the Dreams' Meaning

25Then Joseph said to the king, "Both of these dreams mean the same thing. God is telling you what he is about to do. 26The seven good cows stand for seven years, and the seven good heads of grain stand for seven years. Both dreams mean the same thing. [27]The seven thin and ugly cows stand for seven years, and the seven thin heads of grain burned by the hot east wind stand for seven years of hunger. [28]This will happen as I told you. God is showing the king what he is about to do. [29]You will have seven years of good crops and plenty to eat in all the land of Egypt. [30]But after those seven years, there will come seven years of hunger, and all the food that grew in the land of Egypt will be forgotten. The time of hunger will eat up the land. [31]People will forget what it was like to have plenty of food, because the hunger that follows will be so great. [32]You had two dreams which mean the same thing. This shows that God has firmly decided that this will happen, and he will make it happen soon.

[33]"So let the king choose a man who is very wise and understanding and set him over the land of Egypt. [34]And let the king also appoint officers over the land, who should take one-fifth of all the food that is grown during the seven good years. [35]They should gather all the food that is produced during the good years that are coming, and under the king's authority they should store the grain in the cities and guard it. [36]That food should be saved to use during the seven years of hunger that will come on the land of Egypt. Then the people in Egypt will not die during the seven years of hunger."

Joseph Is Made Ruler over Egypt

[37]This seemed like a very good idea to the king, and all his officers agreed. [38]And the king asked them, "Can we find a better man than Joseph to take this job? God's spirit is truly in him!"

[39]So the king said to Joseph, "God has shown you all this. There is no one as wise and understanding as you are, so [40]I will put you in charge of my palace. All the people will obey your orders, and only I will be greater than you."

[41]Then the king said to Joseph, "Look! I have put you in charge of all the land of Egypt." [42]Then the king took off from his own finger his ring with the royal seal on it, and he put it on Joseph's finger. He gave Joseph fine linen clothes to wear, and he put a gold chain around Joseph's neck. [43]The king had Joseph ride in the second royal chariot, and people walked ahead of his chariot calling, "Bow down!" By doing these things, the king put Joseph in charge of all of Egypt.

[44]The king said to him, "I am the king, and I say that no one in all the land of Egypt may lift a hand or a foot without your permission." [45]The king gave Joseph the name Zaphenath-Paneah. He also gave Joseph a wife named Asenath, who was the daughter of Potiphera, priest of On. So Joseph traveled through all the land of Egypt.

[46]Joseph was thirty years old when he began serving the king of Egypt. And he left the king's court and traveled through all the land of Egypt.

[47]During the seven good years, the crops in the land grew well. [48]And Joseph gathered all the food which was produced in Egypt during those seven years of good crops and stored the food in the cities. In every city he stored grain that had been grown in the fields around that city. [49]Joseph stored much grain, as much as the sand of the seashore — so much that he could not measure it.

[50]Joseph's wife was Asenath daughter of Potiphera, the priest of On. Before the years of hunger came Joseph and Asenath had two sons. [51]Joseph named the first son Manasseh [a] and said, "God has made me forget all the troubles I have had and all my father's family." [52]Joseph named the second son Ephraim [n] and said, "God has given me children in the land of my troubles."

[53]The seven years of good crops came to an end in the land of Egypt. [54]Then the seven years of hunger began, just as Joseph had said. In all the lands people had nothing to eat, but in Egypt there was food. [55]The time of hunger became terrible in all of Egypt, and the people cried to the king for food. He said to all the Egyptians, "Go to Joseph and do whatever he tells you."

[56]The hunger was everywhere in that part of the world. And Joseph opened the storehouses and sold grain to the people of Egypt, because the time of hunger became terrible in Egypt. [57]And all the people in that part of the world came to Joseph in Egypt to buy grain because the hunger was terrible everywhere in that part of the world.

The Dreams Come True

42 Jacob learned that there was grain in Egypt, so he said to his sons, "Why are you just sitting here looking at one another? [2]I

Manasseh   This name sounds like the Hebrew word for "made me forget."
Ephraim   This name sounds like the Hebrew word for "given me children."

have heard that there is grain in Egypt. Go down there and buy grain for us to eat, so that we will live and not die."

3So ten of Joseph's brothers went down to buy grain from Egypt. 4But Jacob did not send Benjamin, Joseph's brother, with them, because he was afraid that something terrible might happen to him. 5Along with many other people, the sons of Israel[n] went to Egypt to buy grain, because the people in the land of Canaan were also hungry.

6Now Joseph was governor over Egypt. He was the one who sold the grain to people who came to buy it. So Joseph's brothers came to him and bowed facedown on the ground before him. 7When Joseph saw his brothers, he knew who they were, but he acted as if he didn't know them. He asked unkindly, "Where do you come from?"

They answered, "We have come from the land of Canaan to buy food."

8Joseph knew they were his brothers, but they did not know who he was. 9And Joseph remembered his dreams about his brothers bowing to him. He said to them, "You are spies! You came to learn where the nation is weak!"

10But his brothers said to him, "No, my master. We come as your servants just to buy food. 11We are all sons of the same father. We are honest men, not spies."

12Then Joseph said to them, "No! You have come to learn where this nation is weak!"

13And they said, "We are ten of twelve brothers, sons of the same father, and we live in the land of Canaan. Our youngest brother is there with our father right now, and our other brother is gone."

14But Joseph said to them, "I can see I was right! You are spies! 15But I will give you a way to prove you are telling the truth. As surely as the king lives, you will not leave this place until your youngest brother comes here. 16One of you must go and get your brother. The rest of you will stay here in prison. We will see if you are telling the truth. If not, as surely as the king lives, you are spies." 17Then Joseph put them all in prison for three days.

18On the third day Joseph said to them, "I am a God-fearing man. Do this and I will let you live: 19If you are honest men, let one of your brothers stay here in prison while the rest of you go and carry grain back to feed your hungry families. 20Then bring your youngest brother back here to me. If you do this, I will know you are telling the truth, and you will not die."

The brothers agreed to this. 21They said to each other, "We are being punished for what we did to our brother. We saw his trouble, and he begged

us to save him, but we refused to listen. That is why we are in this trouble now."

22Then Reuben said to them, "I told you not to harm the boy, but you refused to listen to me. So now we are being punished for what we did to him."

23When Joseph talked to his brothers, he used an interpreter, so they did not know that Joseph understood what they were saying. 24Then Joseph left them and cried. After a short time he went back and spoke to them. He took Simeon and tied him up while the other brothers watched. 25Joseph told his servants to fill his brothers' bags with grain and to put the money the brothers had paid for the grain back in their bags. The servants were also to give them what they would need for their trip back home. And the servants did this.

26So the brothers put the grain on their donkeys and left. 27When they stopped for the night, one of the brothers opened his sack to get food for his donkey. Then he saw his money in the top of the sack. 28He said to the other brothers, "The money I paid for the grain has been put back. Here it is in my sack!"

The brothers were very frightened. They said to each other, "What has God done to us?"

The Brothers Return to Jacob

29The brothers went to their father Jacob in the land of Canaan and told him everything that had happened. 30They said, "The master of that land spoke unkindly to us. He accused us of spying on his country, 31but we told him that we were honest men, not spies. 32We told him that we were ten of twelve brothers—sons of one father. We said that one of our brothers was gone and that our youngest brother was with our father in Canaan.

33"Then the master of the land said to us, 'Here is a way I can know you are honest men: Leave one of your brothers with me, and take grain to feed your hungry families, and go. 34And bring your youngest brother to me so I will know you are not spies but honest men. Then I will give you back your brother whom you leave with me, and you can move about freely in our land.' "

35As the brothers emptied their sacks, each of them found his money in his sack. When they and their father saw it, they were afraid.

36Their father Jacob said to them, "You are robbing me of all my children. Joseph is gone, Simeon is gone, and now you want to take Benjamin away, too. Everything is against me."

37Then Reuben said to his father, "You may put my two sons to death if I don't bring Benjamin back to you. Trust him to my care, and I will bring him back to you."

Israel   Also called Jacob.

38But Jacob said, "I will not allow Benjamin to go with you. His brother is dead, and he is the only son left from my wife Rachel. I am afraid something terrible might happen to him during the trip to Egypt. Then I would be sad until the day I die."

The Brothers Go Back to Egypt

43 Still no food grew in the land of Canaan. 2When Jacob's family had eaten all the grain they had brought from Egypt, Jacob said to them, "Go to Egypt again and buy a little more grain for us to eat."

3But Judah said to Jacob, "The governor of that country strongly warned us, 'If you don't bring your brother back with you, you will not be allowed to see me.' 4If you will send Benjamin with us, we will go down and buy food for you. 5But if you refuse to send Benjamin, we will not go. The governor of that country warned us that we would not see him if we didn't bring Benjamin with us."

6Israeln said, "Why did you tell the man you had another brother? You have caused me a lot of trouble."

7The brothers answered, "He questioned us carefully about ourselves and our family. He asked us, 'Is your father still alive? Do you have another brother?' We just answered his questions. How could we know he would ask us to bring our other brother to him?"

8Then Judah said to his father Jacob, "Send Benjamin with me, and we will go at once so that we, you, and our children may live and not die. 9I will guarantee you that he will be safe, and I will be personally responsible for him. If I don't bring him back to you, you can blame me all my life. 10If we had not wasted all this time, we could have already made two trips."

11Then their father Jacob said to them, "If it has to be that way, then do this: Take some of the best foods in our land in your packs. Give them to the man as a gift: some balm,d some honey, spices, myrrh,d pistachio nuts, and almonds. 12Take twice as much money with you this time, and take back the money that was returned to you in your sacks last time. Maybe it was a mistake. 13And take Benjamin with you. Now leave and go to the man. 14I pray that God Almighty will cause the governor to be merciful to you and that he will allow Simeon and Benjamin to come back with you. If I am robbed of my children, then I am robbed of them!"

15So the brothers took the gifts. They also took twice as much money as they had taken the first time, and they took Benjamin. They hurried down to Egypt and stood before Joseph.

16When Joseph saw Benjamin with them, he said to the servant in charge of his house, "Bring those men into my house. Kill an animal and prepare a meal. Those men will eat with me today at noon." 17The servant did as Joseph told him and brought the men to Joseph's house.

18The brothers were afraid when they were brought to Joseph's house and thought, "We were brought here because of the money that was put in our sacks on the first trip. He wants to attack us, make us slaves, and take our donkeys." 19So the brothers went to the servant in charge of Joseph's house and spoke to him at the door of the house. 20They said, "Master, we came here once before to buy food. 21While we were going home, we stopped for the night and when we opened our sacks each of us found all his money in his sack. We brought that money with us to give it back to you. 22And we have brought more money to pay for the food we want to buy this time. We don't know who put that money in our sacks."

23But the servant answered, "It's all right. Don't be afraid. Your God, the God of your father, must have put the money in your sacks. I got the money you paid me for the grain last time." Then the servant brought Simeon out to them.

24The servant led the men into Joseph's house and gave them water, and they washed their feet. Then he gave their donkeys food to eat. 25The men prepared their gift to give to Joseph when he arrived at noon, because they had heard they were going to eat with him there.

26When Joseph came home, the brothers gave him the gift they had brought into the house and bowed down to the ground in front of him. 27Joseph asked them how they were doing. He said, "How is your aged father you told me about? Is he still alive?"

28The brothers answered, "Your servant, our father, is well. He is still alive." And they bowed low before Joseph to show him respect.

29When Joseph saw his brother Benjamin, who had the same mother as he, Joseph asked, "Is this your youngest brother you told me about?" Then he said to Benjamin, "God be good to you, my son!" 30Then Joseph hurried off because he had to hold back the tears when he saw his brother Benjamin. So Joseph went into his room and cried there. 31Then he washed his face and came out. He controlled himself and said, "Serve the meal."

32So they served Joseph at one table, his brothers at another table, and the Egyptians who ate with him at another table. This was because Egyptians did not like Hebrews and never ate with them. 33Joseph's brothers were seated in front of him in order of their ages, from oldest to youngest. They looked at each other because they

Israel Also called Jacob.

were so amazed. ³⁴Food from Joseph's table was taken to them, but Benjamin was given five times more food than the others. Joseph's brothers ate and drank freely with him.

Joseph Sets a Trap

44 Then Joseph gave a command to the servant in charge of his house. He said, "Fill the men's sacks with as much grain as they can carry, and put each man's money into his sack with the grain. ²Put my silver cup in the sack of the youngest brother, along with his money for the grain." The servant did what Joseph told him.

³At dawn the brothers were sent away with their donkeys. ⁴They were not far from the city when Joseph said to the servant in charge of his house, "Go after the men. When you catch up with them, say, 'Why have you paid back evil for good? ⁵The cup you have stolen is the one my master uses for drinking and for explaining dreams. You have done a very wicked thing!' "

⁶So the servant caught up with the brothers and said to them what Joseph had told him to say. ⁷But the brothers said to the servant, "Why do you say these things? We would not do anything like that! ⁸We brought back to you from the land of Canaan the money we found in our sacks. So surely we would not steal silver or gold from your master's house. ⁹If you find that silver cup in the sack of one of us, then let him die, and we will be your slaves."

¹⁰The servant said, "We will do as you say, but only the man who has taken the cup will become my slave. The rest of you may go free."

¹¹Then every brother quickly lowered his sack to the ground and opened it. ¹²The servant searched the sacks, going from the oldest brother to the youngest, and found the cup in Benjamin's sack. ¹³The brothers tore their clothes to show they were afraid. Then they put their sacks on the donkeys and returned to the city.

¹⁴When Judah and his brothers went back to Joseph's house, Joseph was still there, so the brothers bowed facedown on the ground before him. ¹⁵Joseph said to them, "What have you done? Didn't you know that a man like me can learn things by signs and dreams?"

¹⁶Judah said, "Master, what can we say? And how can we show we are not guilty? God has uncovered our guilt, so all of us will be your slaves, not just Benjamin."

¹⁷But Joseph said, "I will not make you all slaves! Only the man who stole the cup will be my slave. The rest of you may go back safely to your father."

¹⁸Then Judah went to Joseph and said, "Master, please let me speak plainly to you, and please don't be angry with me. I know that you are as powerful as the king of Egypt himself. ¹⁹When we

were here before, you asked us, 'Do you have a father or a brother?' ²⁰And we answered you, 'We have an old father. And we have a younger brother, who was born when our father was old. This youngest son's brother is dead, so he is the only one of his mother's children left alive, and our father loves him very much.' ²¹Then you said to us, 'Bring that brother to me. I want to see him.' ²²And we said to you, 'That young boy cannot leave his father, because if he leaves him, his father would die.' ²³But you said to us, 'If you don't bring your youngest brother, you will not be allowed to see me again.' ²⁴So we went back to our father and told him what you had said.

²⁵"Later, our father said, 'Go again and buy us a little more food.' ²⁶We said to our father, 'We cannot go without our youngest brother. Without our youngest brother, we will not be allowed to see the governor.' ²⁷Then my father said to us, 'You know that my wife Rachel gave me two sons. ²⁸When one son left me, I thought, "Surely he has been torn apart by a wild animal," and I haven't seen him since. ²⁹Now you want to take this son away from me also. But something terrible might happen to him, and I would be miserable until the day I die.' ³⁰Now what will happen if we go home to our father without our youngest brother? He is so important in our father's life that ³¹when our father sees the young boy is not with us, he will die. And it will be our fault. We will cause the great sorrow that kills our father.

³²"I gave my father a guarantee that the young boy would be safe. I said to my father, 'If I don't bring him back to you, you can blame me all my life.' ³³So now, please allow me to stay here and be your slave, and let the young boy go back home with his brothers. ³⁴I cannot go back to my father if the boy is not with me. I couldn't stand to see my father that sad."

Joseph Reveals Who He Is

45 Joseph could not control himself in front of his servants any longer, so he cried out, "Have everyone leave me." When only the brothers were left with Joseph, he told them who he was. ²Joseph cried so loudly that the Egyptians heard him, and the people in the king's palace heard about it. ³He said to his brothers, "I am Joseph. Is my father still alive?" But the brothers could not answer him, because they were very afraid of him.

⁴So Joseph said to them, "Come close to me." *When the brothers came close to him, he said to* them, "I am your brother Joseph, whom you sold as a slave to go to Egypt. ⁵Now don't be worried or angry with yourselves because you sold me here. God sent me here ahead of you to save people's lives. ⁶No food has grown on the land for two years now, and there will be five more years

without planting or harvest. ⁷So God sent me here ahead of you to make sure you have some descendants*ᵈ* left on earth and to keep you alive in an amazing way. ⁸So it was not you who sent me here, but God. God has made me the highest officer of the king of Egypt. I am in charge of his palace, and I am the master of all the land of Egypt.

⁹"So leave quickly and go to my father. Tell him, 'Your son Joseph says: God has made me master over all Egypt. Come down to me quickly. ¹⁰Live in the land of Goshen where you will be near me. Your children, your grandchildren, your flocks and herds, and all that you have will also be near me. ¹¹I will care for you during the next five years of hunger so that you and your family and all that you have will not starve.'

¹²"Now you can see for yourselves, and so can my brother Benjamin, that the one speaking to you is really Joseph. ¹³So tell my father about how powerful I have become in Egypt. Tell him about everything you have seen. Now hurry and bring him back to me." ¹⁴Then Joseph hugged his brother Benjamin and cried, and Benjamin cried also. ¹⁵And Joseph kissed all his brothers and cried

as he hugged them. After this, his brothers talked with him.

¹⁶When the king of Egypt and his officers learned that Joseph's brothers had come, they were very happy. ¹⁷So the king said to Joseph, "Tell your brothers to load their animals and go back to the land of Canaan ¹⁸and bring their father and their families back here to me. I will give them the best land in Egypt, and they will eat the best food we have here. ¹⁹Tell them to take some wagons from Egypt for their children and their wives and to bring their father back also. ²⁰Tell them not to worry about bringing any of their things with them, because we will give them the best of what we have in Egypt."

²¹So the sons of Israel did this. Joseph gave them wagons as the king had ordered and food for their trip. ²²He gave each brother a change of clothes, but he gave Benjamin five changes of clothes and about seven and one-half pounds of silver. ²³Joseph also sent his father ten donkeys loaded with the best things from Egypt and ten female donkeys loaded with grain, bread, and other food for his father on his trip back. ²⁴Then Joseph told his brothers to go. As they were leav-

---

A Violent Cycle

Spangler was a powerful gang leader in Cleveland, Ohio. He and his "homeboys" spent their days and nights partying with drugs and booze. The only times they interrupted their ongoing parties were to make drug deals or to "jam" a rival.

Spangler had everything. He was untouchable. Or so he thought. One day, an off-duty bus driver accidently bumped Spangler's Mercedes-Benz. Enraged that someone would dent his car, Spangler walked up and pumped four bullets into the man's face.

"Nobody does that to me," he howled.

But someone saw. And Spangler—who had killed dozens of Blood, Crip, Jamaican, and Colombian gang members as well as innocent bystanders—was arrested and charged with first-degree murder. For killing a man he didn't know. For minor damage to a car he didn't really care about.

Spangler's gang activity revolved around revenge and hurting countless people. In **Genesis 45:3–8**, Joseph also had a motive and opportunity for revenge. Read how he acted differently.

■ What differences do you see between the attitudes of Joseph and Spangler? How did their attitudes affect their responses?
■ What can you learn from Joseph about grabbing chances for revenge?

CONSIDER

■ looking through a school yearbook to find people who have done something to you out of revenge. Decide how you'll respond the next time they try to get you.
■ evaluating the role revenge plays in a murder-mystery on television. Decide ways that characters could break the destructive cycle of revenge.

FOR MORE, SEE . . .

■ Joshua 20:1–6 (p. 210)　　　■ Acts 7:51–60 (p. 1109)
■ Luke 6:27–36 (p. 1013)

ing, he said to them, "Don't quarrel on the way home."

25So the brothers left Egypt and went to their father Jacob in the land of Canaan. 26They told him, "Joseph is still alive and is the ruler over all the land of Egypt." Their father was shocked and did not believe them. 27But when the brothers told him everything Joseph had said, and when Jacob saw the wagons Joseph had sent to carry him back to Egypt, he felt better. 28Israel^n said, "Now I believe you. My son Joseph is still alive, and I will go and see him before I die."

Jacob Goes to Egypt

46 So Israel^n took all he had and started his trip. He went to Beersheba, where he offered sacrifices to the God of his father Isaac. 2During the night God spoke to Israel in a vision and said, "Jacob, Jacob."

And Jacob answered, "Here I am."

3Then God said, "I am God, the God of your father. Don't be afraid to go to Egypt, because I will make your descendants^d a great nation there. 4I will go to Egypt with you, and I will bring you out of Egypt again. Joseph's own hands will close your eyes when you die."

5Then Jacob left Beersheba. The sons of Israel loaded their father, their children, and their wives in the wagons the king of Egypt had sent. 6They also took their farm animals and everything they had gotten in Canaan. So Jacob went to Egypt with all his descendants— 7his sons and grandsons, his daughters and granddaughters. He took all his family to Egypt with him.

Jacob's Family

8Now these are the names of the children of Israel who went into Egypt (Jacob and his descendants^d).

Reuben was Jacob's first son. 9Reuben's sons were Hanoch, Pallu, Hezron, and Carmi.

10Simeon's sons were Jemuel, Jamin, Ohad, Jakin, Zohar, and Shaul (Simeon's son by a Canaanite woman).

11Levi's sons were Gershon, Kohath, and Merari.

12Judah's sons were Er, Onan, Shelah, Perez, and Zerah (but Er and Onan had died in the land of Canaan). Perez's sons were Hezron and Hamul.

13Issachar's sons were Tola, Puah, Jashub, and Shimron.

14Zebulun's sons were Sered, Elon, and Jahleel.

15These are the sons of Leah and Jacob born in Northwest Mesopotamia, in addition to his daughter Dinah. There were thirty-three persons in this part of Jacob's family.

16Gad's sons were Zephon, Haggi, Shuni, Ezbon, Eri, Arodi, and Areli.

17Asher's sons were Imnah, Ishvah, Ishvi, and Beriah, and their sister was Serah. Beriah's sons were Heber and Malkiel.

18These are Jacob's sons by Zilpah, the slave girl whom Laban gave to his daughter Leah. There were sixteen persons in this part of Jacob's family.

19The sons of Jacob's wife Rachel were Joseph and Benjamin. 20In Egypt, Joseph became the father of Manasseh and Ephraim by his wife Asenath, the daughter of Potiphera, priest of On.

21Benjamin's sons were Bela, Beker, Ashbel, Gera, Naaman, Ehi, Rosh, Muppim, Huppim, and Ard.

22These are the sons of Jacob by his wife Rachel. There were fourteen persons in this part of Jacob's family.

23Dan's son was Hushim.

24Naphtali's sons were Jahziel, Guni, Jezer, and Shillem.

25These are Jacob's sons by Bilhah, the slave girl whom Laban gave to his daughter Rachel. There were seven persons in this part of Jacob's family.

26So the total number of Jacob's direct descendants who went to Egypt was sixty-six, not counting the wives of Jacob's sons. 27Joseph had two sons born in Egypt, so the total number in the family of Jacob in Egypt was seventy.

Jacob Arrives in Egypt

28Jacob sent Judah ahead of him to see Joseph in Goshen. When Jacob and his people came into the land of Goshen, 29Joseph prepared his chariot and went to meet his father Israel in Goshen. As soon as Joseph saw his father, he hugged him, and cried there for a long time.

30Then Israel said to Joseph, "Now I am ready to die, because I have seen your face and I know you are still alive."

31Joseph said to his brothers and his father's family, "I will go and tell the king you are here. I will say, 'My brothers and my father's family have left the land of Canaan and have come here to me. 32They are shepherds and take care of farm animals, and they have brought their flocks and their herds and everything they own with them.' 33When the king calls you, he will ask, 'What work do you do?' 34This is what you should tell him: 'We, your servants, have taken care of farm animals all our lives. Our ancestors did the same thing.' Then the king will allow you to settle in the land of Goshen, away from the Egyptians because they don't like to be near shepherds."

Israel Also called Jacob.

Jacob Settles in Goshen

47 Joseph went in to the king and said, "My father and my brothers have arrived from Canaan with their flocks and herds and everything they own. They are now in the land of Goshen." [2]Joseph chose five of his brothers to introduce to the king.

[3]The king said to the brothers, "What work do you do?"

And they said to him, "We, your servants, are shepherds, just as our ancestors were." [4]They said to the king, "We have come to live in this land, because there is no grass in the land of Canaan for our animals to eat, and the hunger is terrible there. So please allow us to live in the land of Goshen."

[5]Then the king said to Joseph, "Your father and your brothers have come to you, [6]and you may choose any place in Egypt for them to live. Give your father and your brothers the best land; let them live in the land of Goshen. And if any of them are skilled shepherds, put them in charge of my sheep and cattle."

[7]Then Joseph brought in his father Jacob and introduced him to the king, and Jacob blessed the king.

[8]Then the king said to Jacob, "How old are you?"

[9]Jacob said to him, "My life has been spent wandering from place to place. It has been short and filled with trouble — only one hundred thirty years. My ancestors lived much longer than I." [10]Then Jacob blessed the king and left.

[11]Joseph obeyed the king and gave his father and brothers the best land in Egypt, near the city of Rameses. [12]And Joseph gave his father, his brothers, and everyone who lived with them the food they needed.

Joseph Buys Land for the King

[13]The hunger became worse, and since there was no food anywhere in the land, Egypt and Canaan became very poor. [14]Joseph collected all the money that was to be found in Egypt and Canaan. People paid for the grain they were buying, and he brought that money to the king's palace. [15]After some time, when the people in Egypt and Canaan had no money left, they went to Joseph and said, "Please give us food. Our money is gone, and if we don't eat, we will die here in front of you."

[16]Joseph answered, "Since you have no money, give me your farm animals, and I will give you food in return." [17]So people brought their farm animals to Joseph, and he gave them food in exchange for their horses, sheep, goats, cattle, and

donkeys. And he kept them alive by trading food for their farm animals that year.

[18]The next year the people came to Joseph and said, "You know we have no money left, and all our animals belong to you. We have nothing left except our bodies and our land. [19]Surely both we and our land will die here in front of you. Buy us and our land in exchange for food, and we will be slaves to the king, together with our land. Give us seed to plant so that we will live and not die, and the land will not become a desert."

[20]So Joseph bought all the land in Egypt for the king. Every Egyptian sold Joseph his field, because the hunger was very great. So the land became the king's, [21]and Joseph made the people slaves from one end of Egypt to the other. [22]The only land he did not buy was the land the priests owned. They did not need to sell their land because the king paid them for their work. So they had money to buy food.

[23]Joseph said to the people, "Now I have bought you and your land for the king, so I will give you seed and you can plant your fields. [24]At harvest time you must give one-fifth to the king. You may keep four-fifths for yourselves to use as seed for the field and as food for yourselves, your families, and your children."

[25]The people said, "You have saved our lives. If you like, we will become slaves of the king."

[26]So Joseph made a law in Egypt, which continues today: One-fifth of everything from the land belongs to the king. The only land the king did not get was the priests' land.

"Don't Bury Me in Egypt"

[27]The Israelites continued to live in the land of Goshen in Egypt. There they got possessions and had many children and grew in number.

[28]Jacob[n] lived in Egypt seventeen years, so he lived to be one hundred forty-seven years old. [29]When Israel knew he soon would die, he called his son Joseph to him and said to him, "If you love me, put your hand under my leg.[n] Promise me you will not bury me in Egypt. [30]When I die, carry me out of Egypt, and bury me where my ancestors are buried."

Joseph answered, "I will do as you say."

[31]Then Jacob said, "Promise me." And Joseph promised him that he would do this. Then Israel worshiped as he leaned on the top of his walking stick.

Blessings for Manasseh and Ephraim

48 Some time later Joseph learned that his father was very sick, so he took his two sons Manasseh and Ephraim and went to his fa-

---

Jacob Also called Israel.
put . . . leg This showed that a person would keep a promise.

ther. [2]When Joseph arrived, someone told Jacob,[n] "Your son Joseph has come to see you." Jacob was weak, so he used all his strength and sat up on his bed.

[3]Then Jacob said to Joseph, "God Almighty appeared to me at Luz in the land of Canaan and blessed me there. [4]He said to me, 'I will give you many children. I will make you the father of many peoples, and I will give your descendants[d] this land forever.' [5]Your two sons, who were born here in Egypt before I came, will be counted as my own sons. Ephraim and Manasseh will be my sons just as Reuben and Simeon are my sons. [6]But if you have other children, they will be your own, and their land will be part of the land given to Ephraim and Manasseh. [7]When I came from Northwest Mesopotamia, Rachel died in the land of Canaan, as we were traveling toward Ephrath. This made me very sad, and I buried her there beside the road to Ephrath." (Today Ephrath is Bethlehem.)

[8]Then Israel saw Joseph's sons and said, "Who are these boys?"

[9]Joseph said to his father, "They are my sons that God has given me here in Egypt."

Israel said, "Bring your sons to me so I may bless them."

[10]At this time Israel's eyesight was bad because he was old. So Joseph brought the boys close to him, and Israel kissed the boys and put his arms around them. [11]He said to Joseph, "I thought I would never see you alive again, and now God has let me see you and also your children."

SIDELIGHT: If you have older brothers and sisters and think they always get the best deal, take some comfort in Genesis 48:13–14. Though Israel blessed both Manasseh, the oldest, and Ephraim, the youngest, he crossed his hands and blessed Ephraim with his right hand. That made Ephraim's blessing more important.

---

[12]Then Joseph moved his sons off Israel's lap and bowed facedown to the ground. [13]He put Ephraim on his right side and Manasseh on his left. (So Ephraim was near Israel's left hand, and Manasseh was near Israel's right hand.) Joseph brought the boys close to Israel. [14]But Israel crossed his arms and put his right hand on the *head of Ephraim, who was younger. He put his* left hand on the head of Manasseh, the firstborn[d] son. [15]And Israel blessed Joseph and said,

"My ancestors Abraham and Isaac served our God,

and like a shepherd God has led me all my life.
[16]He was the Angel who saved me from all my troubles.
Now I pray that he will bless these boys.
May my name be known through these boys,
and may the names of my ancestors
Abraham and Isaac be known through them.
May they have many descendants[d]
on the earth."

[17]When Joseph saw that his father put his right hand on Ephraim's head, he didn't like it. So he took hold of his father's hand, wanting to move it from Ephraim's head to Manasseh's head. [18]Joseph said to his father, "You are doing it wrong, Father. Manasseh is the firstborn son. Put your right hand on his head."

[19]But his father refused and said, "I know, my son, I know. Manasseh will be great and have many descendants. But his younger brother will be greater, and his descendants will be enough to make a nation." [20]So Israel blessed them that day and said,

"When a blessing is given in Israel, they will say:
'May God make you like Ephraim and Manasseh.'"

In this way he made Ephraim greater than Manasseh.

[21]Then Israel said to Joseph, "Look at me; I am about to die. But God will be with you and will take you back to the land of your fathers. [22]I have given you something that I did not give your brothers—the land of Shechem that I took from the Amorite people with my sword and my bow."

Jacob Blesses His Sons

49 Then Jacob called his sons to him. He said, "Come here to me, and I will tell you what will happen to you in the future.

[2]"Come together and listen, sons of Jacob.
Listen to Israel, your father."

[3]"Reuben, my first son, you are my strength.
Your birth showed I could be a father.
You have the highest position among my sons,
and you are the most powerful.
[4]But you are uncontrolled like water,
so you will no longer lead your brothers.
This is because you got into your father's bed
and shamed me by having sexual relations
with my slave girl.

[5]"Simeon and Levi are brothers
who used their swords to do violence.

Jacob Also called Israel.

⁶I will not join their secret talks,
  and I will not meet with them to plan evil.
They killed men because they were angry,
  and they crippled oxen just for fun.
⁷May their anger be cursed, because it is too
    violent.
  May their violence be cursed, because it is
    too cruel.
I will divide them up among the tribes*d* of
    Jacob
  and scatter them through all the tribes of
    Israel.

⁸"Judah, your brothers will praise you.
  You will grab your enemies by the neck,
  and your brothers will bow down to you.
⁹Judah is like a young lion.
  You have returned from killing, my son.
Like a lion, he stretches out and lies down to
    rest,
  and no one is brave enough to wake him.
¹⁰Kings will come from Judah's family;
  someone from Judah will always be on the
    throne.
Judah will rule until Shiloh comes,
  and the nations will obey him.
¹¹He ties his donkey to a grapevine,
  his young donkey to the best branch.
He can afford to use wine to wash his clothes
  and the best wine to wash his robes.
¹²His eyes are dark like the color of wine,
  and his teeth are as white as the color of
    milk.

¹³"Zebulun will live near the sea.
  His shore will be a safe place for ships,
  and his land will reach as far as Sidon.

¹⁴"Issachar is like a strong donkey
  who lies down while carrying his load.
¹⁵When he sees his resting place is good
  and how pleasant his land is,
he will put his back to the load
  and become a slave.

¹⁶"Dan will rule his own people
  like the other tribes in Israel.
¹⁷Dan will be like a snake by the side of the
    road,
  a dangerous snake lying near the path.
That snake bites a horse's leg,
  and the rider is thrown off backward.

¹⁸LORD, I wait for your salvation.

¹⁹"Robbers will attack Gad,
  but he will defeat them and drive them
    away.

²⁰"Asher's land will grow much good food;
  he will grow food fit for a king.

²¹"Naphtali is like a female deer that runs free,
  that has beautiful fawns.

²²"Joseph is like a grapevine that produces
    much fruit,
  a healthy vine watered by a spring,
  whose branches grow over the wall.
²³Archers attack him violently
  and shoot at him angrily,
²⁴but he aims his bow well.
  His arms are made strong.
He gets his power from the Mighty God of
    Jacob
  and his strength from the Shepherd, the
    Rock*d* of Israel.
²⁵Your father's God helps you.
  God Almighty blesses you.
He blesses you with rain from above,
  with water from springs below,
with many babies born to your wives,
  and many young ones born to your animals.
²⁶The blessings of your father are greater
  than the blessings of the oldest mountains,
  greater than the good things of the
    long-lasting hills.
May these blessings rest on the head of
    Joseph,
  on the forehead of the one who was
    separated from his brothers.

²⁷"Benjamin is like a hungry wolf.
  In the morning he eats what he has caught,
  and in the evening he divides what he has
    taken."

²⁸These are the twelve tribes of Israel, and this
is what their father said to them. He gave each
son the blessing that was right for him. ²⁹Then
Israel gave them a command and said, "I am
about to die. Bury me with my ancestors in the
cave in the field of Ephron the Hittite. ³⁰That cave
is in the field of Machpelah east of Mamre in the
land of Canaan. Abraham bought the field and
cave from Ephron the Hittite for a burying place.
³¹Abraham and Sarah his wife are buried there.
Isaac and Rebekah his wife are buried there, and
I buried my wife Leah there. ³²The field and the
cave in it were bought from the Hittite people."
³³After Jacob finished talking to his sons, he lay
down. He put his feet back on the bed, took his
last breath, and died.

Jacob's Burial

50 When Jacob died, Joseph hugged his father and cried over him and kissed him.
²He commanded the doctors who served him to
prepare his father's body, so the doctors prepared
Jacob's body to be buried. ³It took the doctors
forty days to prepare his body (the usual time it
took). And the Egyptians had a time of sorrow for
Jacob that lasted seventy days.

4When this time of sorrow had ended, Joseph spoke to the king's officers and said, "If you think well of me, please tell this to the king: 5'When my father was near death, I made a promise to him that I would bury him in a cave in the land of Canaan, in a burial place that he cut out for himself. So please let me go and bury my father, and then I will return.'"

6The king answered, "Keep your promise. Go and bury your father."

7So Joseph went to bury his father. All the king's officers, the older leaders, and all the leading men of Egypt went with Joseph. 8Everyone who lived with Joseph and his brothers went with him, as well as everyone who lived with his father. They left only their children, their flocks, and their herds in the land of Goshen. 9They went with Joseph in chariots and on horses. It was a very large group.

10When they came to the threshing*d* floor of Atad, near the Jordan River, they cried loudly and bitterly for his father. Joseph's time of sorrow continued for seven days. 11The people that lived in Canaan saw the sadness at the threshing floor of Atad and said, "Those Egyptians are showing great sorrow!" So now that place is named Sorrow of the Egyptians.

12So Jacob's sons did as their father commanded. 13They carried his body to the land of Canaan and buried it in the cave in the field of Machpelah near Mamre. Abraham had bought this cave and field from Ephron the Hittite to use as a burial place. 14After Joseph buried his father, he returned to Egypt, along with his brothers and everyone who had gone with him to bury his father.

The Brothers Fear Joseph

15After Jacob died, Joseph's brothers said,

"What if Joseph is still angry with us? We did many wrong things to him. What if he plans to pay us back?" 16So they sent a message to Joseph that said, "Your father gave this command before he died. 17He said to us, 'You have done wrong and have sinned and done evil to Joseph. Tell Joseph to forgive you, his brothers.' So now, Joseph, we beg you to forgive our wrong. We are the servants of the God of your father." When Joseph received the message, he cried.

18And his brothers went to him and bowed low before him and said, "We are your slaves."

19Then Joseph said to them, "Don't be afraid. Can I do what only God can do? 20You meant to hurt me, but God turned your evil into good to save the lives of many people, which is being done. 21So don't be afraid. I will take care of you and your children." So Joseph comforted his brothers and spoke kind words to them.

22Joseph continued to live in Egypt with all his father's family. He died when he was one hundred ten years old. 23During Joseph's life Ephraim had children and grandchildren, and Joseph's son Manasseh had a son named Makir. Joseph accepted Makir's children as his own.

The Death of Joseph

24Joseph said to his brothers, "I am about to die, but God will take care of you. He will lead you out of this land to the land he promised to Abraham, Isaac, and Jacob." 25Then Joseph had the sons of Israel make a promise. He said, "Promise me that you will carry my bones with you out of Egypt."

26Joseph died when he was one hundred ten years old. Doctors prepared his body for burial, and then they put him in a coffin in Egypt.

EXODUS

Why Read This Book:

- Discover how God works in miraculous ways to set people free (Exodus 1—18).
- Learn guidelines for living as they are described in the Ten Commandments Exodus 20).
- Compare ancient worship practices with worship today (Exodus 25—31, 35—40).

Behind the Scenes:

"Free at last, free at last; thank God Almighty, we are free at last."

This spiritual celebrated freedom from slavery in the United States. And it became an important song in the civil rights struggle in the 1950s and 1960s in the United States. But the spiritual also could have been sung by the Israelites as they escaped from Egypt with Moses as their leader.

The Israelites had settled in Egypt about four hundred years earlier when Joseph arranged for them to be Egypt's guests (see Genesis 47:1–12, p. 53). But, in time, Egypt's rulers died, and the new rulers turned the Israelites into slaves. The Israelites longed for freedom from the horrible slavery.

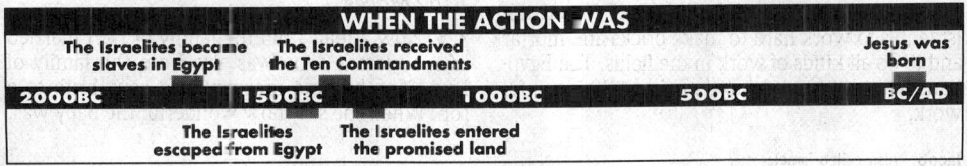

WHERE THE ACTION WAS

Mediterranean Sea

CANAAN

Possible location where the Israelites crossed the Red Sea or Sea of Reeds (Exodus 14:10–28).

GOSHEN Pithom

EGYPT

Rameses

Possible alternate routes for the Exodus.

The Egyptian king made the Israelite slaves build the cities of Pithom and Rameses (Exodus 1:11).

The traditional route of the Exodus.

Moses fled to the land of Midian after killing an Egyptian (Exodus 2:13–15).

SINAI

Possible site of Mt Sinai, where Moses received the Ten Commandments (Exodus 19:20–20:21).

MIDIAN

Note: Many of the places named in the book of Exodus are unknown. That's why scholars have different views of the route and where events took place.

WHEN THE ACTION WAS

The Israelites became slaves in Egypt	The Israelites received the Ten Commandments			Jesus was born
2000BC	1500BC	1000BC	500BC	BC/AD
	The Israelites escaped from Egypt	The Israelites entered the promised land		

**Behind the
Scenes** (cont.):

Exodus tells how God took the Hebrew people—descendants of Abraham—and shaped them into the free nation of Israel.

The book begins with the story of Moses being saved from slaughter. Rescued by the king's daughter, Moses grew up in the king's palace. When he became an adult, God called Moses to lead the Israelites to freedom.

Though filled with uncertainty, Moses answered God's call and negotiated with the Egyptian king. Again and again the king resisted, but God's miraculous power eventually convinced him to let Israel go. In joyous celebration, the Israelites left for the promised land, Canaan, only to be chased by the king's army. God's deliverance of Israel at the Red Sea is known as the Exodus.

Before reaching the promised land, however, the Israelites spent forty years in the wilderness. There they learned more about what God wanted them to do and be, as people and as a nation.

In Exodus 3:14, God reveals his name to Moses: I AM WHO I AM or Yahweh. It means "The One Who Is Always Present." And, indeed, God was always with Moses and the Israelites in the desert. And he is always with us today.

Jacob's Family Grows Strong

1 When Jacob[n] went to Egypt, he took his sons, and each son took his own family with him. These are the names of the sons of Israel: ²Reuben, Simeon, Levi, Judah, ³Issachar, Zebulun, Benjamin, ⁴Dan, Naphtali, Gad, and Asher. ⁵There was a total of seventy people who were descendants[d] of Jacob. Jacob's son Joseph was already in Egypt.

⁶Some time later, Joseph and his brothers died, along with all the people who had lived at that same time. ⁷But the people of Israel had many children, and their number grew greatly. They became very strong, and the country of Egypt was filled with them.

Trouble for the People of Israel

⁸Then a new king began to rule Egypt, who did not know who Joseph was. ⁹This king said to his people, "Look! The people of Israel are too many and too strong for us to handle! ¹⁰If we don't make plans against them, the number of their people will grow even more. Then if there is a war, they might join our enemies and fight us and escape from the country!"

¹¹So the Egyptians made life hard for the Israelites. They put slave masters over them, who forced the Israelites to build the cities Pithom and Rameses as supply centers for the king. ¹²But the harder the Egyptians forced the Israelites to work, the more the Israelites grew in number and spread out. So the Egyptians became very afraid of them ¹³and demanded even more of them. *¹⁴They made their lives bitter. They forced the Israelites to work hard to make bricks and mortar and to do all kinds of work in the fields. The Egyptians were not merciful to them in all their painful work.*

¹⁵Two Hebrew nurses, named Shiphrah and Puah, helped the Israelite women give birth to their babies. The king of Egypt said to the nurses, ¹⁶"When you are helping the Hebrew women give birth to their babies, watch! If the baby is a girl, let her live, but if it is a boy, kill him!" ¹⁷But the nurses feared God, so they did not do as the king told them; they let all the boy babies live. ¹⁸Then the king of Egypt sent for the nurses and said, "Why did you do this? Why did you let the boys live?"

> ✴ **SIDELIGHT:** Making bricks in Egypt was a slow process for the Israelites (Exodus 1:14). Egyptian records show that a person could make about sixty-five bricks a day. A modern brickmaker turns out about 3,500 bricks daily.

¹⁹The nurses said to him, "The Hebrew women are much stronger than the Egyptian women. They give birth to their babies before we can get there." ²⁰God was good to the nurses. And the Hebrew people continued to grow in number, so they became even stronger. ²¹Because the nurses feared God, he gave them families of their own. ²²So the king commanded all his people, "Every time a boy is born to the Hebrews, you must throw him into the Nile River, but let all the girl babies live."

Baby Moses

2 Now a man from the family of Levi married a woman who was also from the family of Levi. ²She became pregnant and gave birth to a son. When she saw how wonderful the baby was,

---

Jacob Also called Israel.

she hid him for three months. ³But after three months she was not able to hide the baby any longer, so she got a basket and covered it with tar so that it would float. She put the baby in the basket. Then she put the basket among the tall

stalks of grass at the edge of the Nile River. ⁴The baby's sister stood a short distance away to see what would happen to him.

⁵Then the daughter of the king of Egypt came to the river to take a bath, and her servant girls were walking beside the river. When she saw the basket in the tall grass, she sent her slave girl to get it. ⁶The king's daughter opened the basket and saw the baby boy. He was crying, so she felt sorry for him and said, "This is one of the Hebrew babies."

⁷Then the baby's sister asked the king's daughter, "Would you like me to go and find a Hebrew woman to nurse the baby for you?"

⁸The king's daughter said, "Go!" So the girl went and got the baby's own mother.

⁹The king's daughter said to the woman, "Take this baby and nurse him for me, and I will pay you." So the woman took her baby and nursed him. ¹⁰When the child grew older, the woman took him to the king's daughter, and she adopted

SUFFERING

Running for His Life

Sydney Maree felt like he didn't fit anywhere. A black in South Africa, he lived under harsh apartheid laws that restricted blacks in virtually all areas of life. He and his family could only live in black townships, and many things were off limits to them.

Sydney only felt at peace when he ran. Something about running gave him a sense of power in a world where he felt powerless because of unjust government policies. He'd run to school. He'd run more than a mile to the store. He'd run everywhere he went.

When he was sixteen, the high school track coach noticed Sydney's speed, and got him involved in track. Sydney trained tirelessly. "He was running for revenge," his trainer recalls, "running for liberation."

In 1976, his liberation began. He entered a major track meet in Port Elizabeth, South Africa, with the help of a white businessman. The only high schooler and the only black in the race, he won—and set a record for the fastest time ever by a high schooler.

Sydney's life changed that day. He became a national hero and then went to school in the United States. He set records running for Villanova University and joined the U.S. team in the 1984 Olympics.

The white businessman who helped Sydney begin racing in South Africa came to his college graduation. "Sydney started to tell me how he could never thank me enough," the supporter said. "I stopped him and said, 'No, it is I who must thank you.' Before I met him I'd only known blacks as people who did gardening for me. Now I know . . . that they too have goals and aspirations and can be like sons in my home."

Like Sydney, the Israelites faced extreme persecution as slaves in Egypt. Read about their situation in **Exodus 1:6—2:10**.

■ How was Sydney's world like the world of the enslaved Israelites?
■ How would you react if you faced the suffering the Israelites faced? How do you react to people suffering around you?

CONSIDER . . .

■ writing a story that describes a time you experienced suffering. Thank God for getting you through that tough time.
■ talking to someone who has been through tremendous suffering (such as a refugee or a war veteran). What helped him or her survive?

FOR MORE, SEE . . .

■ Psalm 57:1–11 (p. 515)   ■ 1 John 3:16–18 (p. 1319)
■ Philippians 4:14–19 (p. 1235)

the baby as her own son. The king's daughter named him Moses,[n] because she had pulled him out of the water.

Moses Tries to Help

[11]Moses grew and became a man. One day he visited his people and saw that they were forced to work very hard. He saw an Egyptian beating a Hebrew man, one of Moses' own people. [12]Moses looked all around and saw that no one was watching, so he killed the Egyptian and hid his body in the sand.

[13]The next day Moses returned and saw two Hebrew men fighting each other. He said to the one that was in the wrong, "Why are you hitting one of your own people?"

[14]The man answered, "Who made you our ruler and judge? Are you going to kill me as you killed the Egyptian?"

Moses was afraid and thought, "Now everyone knows what I did."

[15]When the king heard what Moses had done, he tried to kill him. But Moses ran away from the king and went to live in the land of Midian. There he sat down near a well.

Moses in Midian

[16]There was a priest in Midian who had seven daughters. His daughters went to that well to get water to fill the water troughs for their father's flock. [17]Some shepherds came and chased the girls away, but Moses defended the girls and watered their flock.

[18]When they went back to their father Reuel,[n] he asked them, "Why have you come home early today?"

[19]The girls answered, "The shepherds chased us away, but an Egyptian defended us. He got water for us and watered our flock."

[20]He asked his daughters, "Where is this man? Why did you leave him? Invite him to eat with us."

[21]Moses agreed to stay with Jethro, and he gave his daughter Zipporah to Moses to be his wife. [22]Zipporah gave birth to a son. Moses named him Gershom,[n] because Moses was a stranger in a land that was not his own.

[23]After a long time, the king of Egypt died. The people of Israel groaned, because they were forced to work very hard. When they cried for help, God heard them. [24]God heard their cries, and he remembered the agreement he had made with Abraham, Isaac, and Jacob. [25]He saw the troubles of the people of Israel, and he was concerned about them.

The Burning Bush

3 One day Moses was taking care of Jethro's flock. (Jethro was the priest of Midian and also Moses' father-in-law.) When Moses led the flock to the west side of the desert, he came to Sinai, the mountain of God. [2]There the angel of the LORD appeared to him in flames of fire coming out of a bush. Moses saw that the bush was on fire, but it was not burning up. [3]So he said, "I will go closer to this strange thing. How can a bush continue burning without burning up?"

[4]When the LORD saw Moses was coming to look at the bush, God called to him from the bush, "Moses, Moses!"

And Moses said, "Here I am."

[5]Then God said, "Do not come any closer. Take off your sandals, because you are standing on holy ground. [6]I am the God of your ancestors — the God of Abraham, the God of Isaac, and the God of Jacob." Moses covered his face because he was afraid to look at God.

[7]The LORD said, "I have seen the troubles my people have suffered in Egypt, and I have heard their cries when the Egyptian slave masters hurt them. I am concerned about their pain, [8]and I have come down to save them from the Egyptians. I will bring them out of that land and lead them to a good land with lots of room — a fertile land. It is the land of the Canaanites, Hittites, Amorites, Perizzites, Hivites, and Jebusites. [9]I have heard the cries of the people of Israel, and I have seen the way the Egyptians have made life hard for them. [10]So now I am sending you to the king of Egypt. Go! Bring my people, the Israelites, out of Egypt!"

[11]But Moses said to God, "I am not a great man! How can I go to the king and lead the Israelites out of Egypt?"

[12]God said, "I will be with you. This will be the proof that I am sending you: After you lead the people out of Egypt, all of you will worship me on this mountain."

[13]Moses said to God, "When I go to the Israelites, I will say to them, 'The God of your fathers sent me to you.' What if the people say, 'What is his name?' What should I tell them?"

[14]Then God said to Moses, "I AM WHO I AM.[n] When you go to the people of Israel, tell them, 'I AM sent me to you.' "

[15]God also said to Moses, "This is what you should tell the people: 'The LORD is the God of

---

Moses The name Moses sounds like the Hebrew word for "to pull out."
Reuel He was also called Jethro.
Gershom This name sounds like the Hebrew word meaning "a stranger there."
I . . . I AM The Hebrew words are like the name "Yahweh." This Hebrew name for God, usually called "LORD," shows that God always lives and is always with his people.

your ancestors — the God of Abraham, the God of Isaac, and the God of Jacob. He sent me to you.' This will always be my name, by which people from now on will know me.

16"Go and gather the older leaders and tell them this: 'The LORD, the God of your ancestors Abraham, Isaac, and Jacob, has appeared to me. He said, I care about you, and I have seen what has happened to you in Egypt. 17I promised I would take you out of your troubles in Egypt. I will lead you to the land of the Canaanites, Hittites, Amorites, Perizzites, Hivites, and Jebusites — a fertile land.'

18"The older leaders will listen to you. And then you and the older leaders of Israel will go to the king of Egypt and tell him, 'The LORD, the God of the Hebrews, appeared to us. Let us travel three days into the desert to offer sacrifices to the LORD our God.'

19"But I know that the king of Egypt will not let you go. Only a great power will force him to let you go, 20so I will use my great power against Egypt. I will strike Egypt with all the miracles[d] that will happen in that land. After I do that, he will let you go. 21I will cause the Egyptians to think well of the Israelites. So when you leave, they will give gifts to your people. 22Each woman should ask her Egyptian neighbor and any Egyptian woman living in her house for gifts — silver, gold, and clothing. You should put those gifts on your children when you leave Egypt. In this way you will take with you the riches of the Egyptians."

LEADERSHIP

Somebody Do Something!

In 1981 in the United States, 11,005 people between the ages of sixteen and twenty-one died in car accidents. Under normal circumstances, that statistic wouldn't have meant much to Robert Anastas, a hockey coach at Wayland Public School in Wayland, Massachusetts.

But two of those 11,005 young people had been on his hockey team. They were killed in a car accident involving a drunk driver. Robert was stunned. It doesn't have to be this way, he thought.

Robert knew nothing would change if no one did anything to combat the problem. So he started Students Against Driving Drunk (SADD) and has dedicated his life to combating the drunk driving problem. The organization works to alert students to the dangers of drinking and driving.

Under Robert's leadership, SADD has grown to a national organization with four million members and chapters in all fifty U.S. states and Canada. And Robert has received dozens of awards for battling this serious problem.

Robert saw a problem and became a leader in the fight to overcome it. In the same way, Moses learned about the Israelites' persecution in Egypt and followed God's call to lead them to freedom. Read about it in **Exodus 3:1–20.**

■ What similarities are there between Robert's call and Moses' call to leadership? What differences do you see?
■ Have you, like Moses, felt called by God to take leadership in fighting a particular problem? How have you responded?

C O N S I D E R . . .
■ watching the evening news and identifying leaders who are working to end suffering around the world. Pray for these leaders.
■ listing problems in your school, church, community, or country that you're concerned about. Then decide one area where your leadership can make a difference.

F O R   M O R E ,   S E E . . .

■ Psalm 22:1–11 (p. 493)   ■ Luke 4:16–21 (p. 1008)
■ Micah 2:6–13 (p. 863)

Proof for Moses

4 Then Moses answered, "What if the people of Israel do not believe me or listen to me? What if they say, 'The LORD did not appear to you'?"

2The LORD said to him, "What is that in your hand?"

Moses answered, "It is my walking stick."

3The LORD said, "Throw it on the ground."

So Moses threw it on the ground, and it became a snake. Moses ran from the snake, 4but the LORD said to him, "Reach out and grab the snake by its tail." When Moses reached out and took hold of the snake, it again became a stick in his hand. 5The LORD said, "This is so that the Israelites will believe that the LORD appeared to you. I am the God of their ancestors, the God of Abraham, the God of Isaac, and the God of Jacob."

6Then the LORD said to Moses, "Put your hand inside your coat." So Moses put his hand inside his coat. When he took it out, it was white with a skin disease.

7Then he said, "Now put your hand inside your coat again." So Moses put his hand inside his coat again. When he took it out, his hand was healthy again, like the rest of his skin.

8Then the LORD said, "If the people do not believe you or pay attention to the first miracle,*d* they may believe you when you show them this second miracle. 9After these two miracles, if they still do not believe or listen to you, take some water from the Nile River and pour it on the dry ground. The water will become blood when it touches the ground."

10But Moses said to the LORD, "Please, Lord, I have never been a skilled speaker. Even now, after talking to you, I cannot speak well. I speak slowly and can't find the best words."

11Then the LORD said to him, "Who made a person's mouth? And who makes someone deaf or not able to speak? Or who gives a person sight or blindness? It is I, the LORD. 12Now go! I will help you speak, and I will teach you what to say."

13But Moses said, "Please, Lord, send someone else."

14The LORD became angry with Moses and said, "Your brother Aaron, from the family of Levi, is a skilled speaker. He is already coming to meet you, and he will be happy when he sees you. 15You will speak to Aaron and tell him what to say. I will help both of you to speak and will teach *you what to do.* 16*Aaron will speak to the people* for you. You will tell him what God says, and he will speak for you. 17Take your walking stick with you, and use it to do the miracles."

Moses Returns to Egypt

18Moses went back to Jethro, his father-in-law, and said to him, "Let me go back to my people in Egypt. I want to see if they are still alive."

Jethro said to Moses, "Go! I wish you well."

19While Moses was still in Midian, the LORD said to him, "Go back to Egypt, because the men who wanted to kill you are dead now."

20So Moses took his wife and his sons, put them on a donkey, and started back to Egypt. He took with him the walking stick of God.

21The LORD said to Moses, "When you get back to Egypt, do all the miracles*d* I have given you the power to do. Show them to the king of Egypt. But I will make the king very stubborn, and he will not let the people go. 22Then say to the king, 'This is what the LORD says: Israel is my firstborn*d* son. 23I told you to let my son go so he may worship me. But you refused to let Israel go, so I will kill your firstborn son.' "

24As Moses was on his way to Egypt, he stopped at a resting place for the night. The LORD met him there and tried to kill him. 25But Zipporah took a flint knife and circumcised*d* her son. Taking the skin, she touched Moses' feet with it and said to him, "You are a bridegroom of blood to me." 26She said, "You are a bridegroom of blood," because she had to circumcise her son. So the LORD let Moses alone.

27Meanwhile the LORD said to Aaron, "Go out into the desert to meet Moses." When Aaron went, he met Moses at Sinai, the mountain of God, and kissed him. 28Moses told Aaron everything the LORD had said to him when he sent him to Egypt. He also told him about the miracles which the LORD had commanded him to do.

29Moses and Aaron gathered all the older leaders of the Israelites, 30and Aaron told them everything that the LORD had told Moses. Then Moses did the miracles for all the people to see, 31and the Israelites believed. When they heard that the LORD was concerned about them and had seen their troubles, they bowed down and worshiped him.

Moses and Aaron Before the King

5 After Moses and Aaron talked to the people, they went to the king of Egypt and said, "This is what the LORD, the God of Israel says: 'Let my people go so they may hold a feast for me in the desert.' "

2But the king of Egypt said, "Who is the LORD? Why should I obey him and let Israel go? I do not know the LORD, and I will not let Israel go."

3Then Aaron and Moses said, "The God of the Hebrews has met with us. Now let us travel three days into the desert to offer sacrifices to the LORD our God. If we don't do this, he may kill us with a disease or in war."

4But the king said to them, "Moses and Aaron, why are you taking the people away from their work? Go back to your jobs! ⁵There are very many Hebrews, and now you want them to quit working!"

⁶That same day the king gave a command to the slave masters and foremen. ⁷He said, "Don't give the people straw to make bricks as you used to do. Let them gather their own straw. ⁸But they must still make the same number of bricks as they did before. Do not accept fewer. They have become lazy, and that is why they are asking me, 'Let us go to offer sacrifices to our God.' ⁹Make these people work harder and keep them busy; then they will not have time to listen to the lies of Moses."

¹⁰So the slave masters and foremen went to the Israelites and said, "This is what the king says: I will no longer give you straw. ¹¹Go and get your own straw wherever you can find it. But you must make as many bricks as you made before." ¹²So the people went everywhere in Egypt looking for dry stalks to use for straw. ¹³The slave masters kept forcing the people to work harder. They said, "You must make just as many bricks as you did when you were given straw." ¹⁴The king's slave masters had made the Israelite foremen responsible for the work the people did. The Egyptian slave masters beat these men and asked them, "Why aren't you making as many bricks as you made in the past?"

¹⁵Then the Israelite foremen went to the king and complained, "Why are you treating us, your servants, this way? ¹⁶You give us no straw, but we are commanded to make bricks. Our slave masters beat us, but it is your own people's fault."

¹⁷The king answered, "You are lazy! You don't want to work! That is why you ask to leave here and make sacrifices to the LORD. ¹⁸Now, go back to work! We will not give you any straw, but you must make just as many bricks as you did before."

¹⁹The Israelite foremen knew they were in trouble, because the king had told them, "You must make just as many bricks each day as you did before." ²⁰As they were leaving the meeting with the king, they met Moses and Aaron, who were waiting for them. ²¹So they said to Moses and Aaron, "May the LORD punish you. You caused the king and his officers to hate us. You have given them an excuse to kill us."

Moses Complains to God

²²Then Moses returned to the LORD and said, "Lord, why have you brought this trouble on your people? Is this why you sent me here? ²³I went to the king and said what you told me to say, but ever since that time he has made the people suffer. And you have done nothing to save them."

6 Then the LORD said to Moses, "Now you will see what I will do to the king of Egypt. I will use my great power against him, and he will let

my people go. Because of my power, he will force them out of his country."

²Then God said to Moses, "I am the LORD. ³I appeared to Abraham, Isaac, and Jacob by the name God Almighty, but they did not know me by my name, the LORD. ⁴I also made my agreement with them to give them the land of Canaan. They lived in that land, but it was not their own. ⁵Now I have heard the cries of the Israelites, whom the Egyptians are treating as slaves, and I remember my agreement. ⁶So tell the people of Israel that I say to them, 'I am the LORD. I will save you from the hard work the Egyptians force you to do. I will make you free, so you will not be slaves to the Egyptians. I will free you by my great power, and I will punish the Egyptians terribly. ⁷I will make you my own people, and I will be your God. You will know that I am the LORD your God, the One who saves you from the hard work the Egyptians force you to do. ⁸I will lead you to the land that I promised to Abraham, Isaac, and Jacob, and I will give you that land to own. I am the LORD.'"

⁹So Moses told this to the Israelites, but they would not listen to him. They were discouraged, and their slavery was hard.

¹⁰Then the LORD said to Moses, ¹¹"Go tell the king of Egypt that he must let the Israelites leave his land."

¹²But Moses answered, "The Israelites will not listen to me, so surely the king will not listen to me either. I am not a good speaker."

¹³But the LORD spoke to Moses and Aaron and gave them orders about the Israelites and the king of Egypt. He commanded them to lead the Israelites out of Egypt.

Families of Israel

¹⁴These are the leaders of the families of Israel:

Israel's first son, Reuben, had four sons: Hanoch, Pallu, Hezron, and Carmi. These are the family groups of Reuben.

¹⁵Simeon's sons were Jemuel, Jamin, Ohad, Jakin, Zohar, and Shaul, the son of a Canaanite woman. These are the family groups of Simeon.

¹⁶Levi lived one hundred thirty-seven years. These are the names of his sons according to their family history: Gershon, Kohath, and Merari.

¹⁷Gershon had two sons, Libni and Shimei, with their families.

¹⁸Kohath lived one hundred thirty-three years. The sons of Kohath were Amram, Izhar, Hebron, and Uzziel.

¹⁹The sons of Merari were Mahli and Mushi. These are the family groups of Levi, according to their family history.

²⁰Amram married his father's sister Jochebed,

who gave birth to Aaron and Moses. Amram lived one hundred thirty-seven years.

21Izhar's sons were Korah, Nepheg, and Zicri. 22Uzziel's sons were Mishael, Elzaphan, and Sithri.

23Aaron married Elisheba, the daughter of Amminadab and the sister of Nahshon. Elisheba gave birth to Nadab, Abihu, Eleazar, and Ithamar. 24The sons of Korah were Assir, Elkanah, and Abiasaph. These are the family groups of the Korahites.

25Eleazar son of Aaron married a daughter of Putiel, and she gave birth to Phinehas.

These are the leaders of the family groups of the Levites.

26This was the Aaron and Moses to whom the LORD said, "Lead the people of Israel out of Egypt by their divisions." 27Aaron and Moses are the ones who talked to the king of Egypt and told him to let the Israelites leave Egypt.

God Repeats His Call to Moses

28The LORD spoke to Moses in the land of Egypt 29and said, "I am the LORD. Tell the king of Egypt everything I tell you."

30But Moses answered, "I am not a good speaker. The king will not listen to me."

7 The LORD said to Moses, "I have made you like God to the king of Egypt, and your brother Aaron will be like a prophet[d] for you. 2Tell Aaron your brother everything that I command you, and let him tell the king of Egypt to let the Israelites leave his country. 3But I will make the king stubborn. I will do many miracles[d] in Egypt, 4but he will still refuse to listen. So then I will punish Egypt terribly, and I will lead my divisions, my people the Israelites, out of that land. 5I will punish Egypt with my power, and I will bring the Israelites out of that land. Then they will know I am the LORD."

6Moses and Aaron did just as the LORD had commanded them. 7Moses was eighty years old and Aaron was eighty-three when they spoke to the king.

Aaron's Walking Stick Becomes a Snake

8The LORD said to Moses and Aaron, 9"Moses, when the king asks you to do a miracle,[d] tell Aaron to throw his walking stick down in front of the king, and it will become a snake."

10So Moses and Aaron went to the king as the LORD had commanded. Aaron threw his walking stick down in front of the king and his officers, and it became a snake.

11So the king called in his wise men and his magicians, and with their tricks the Egyptian magicians were able to do the same thing. 12They threw their walking sticks on the ground, and their sticks became snakes. But Aaron's stick

swallowed theirs. 13Still the king was stubborn and refused to listen to Moses and Aaron, just as the LORD had said.

The Water Becomes Blood

14Then the LORD said to Moses, "The king is being stubborn and refuses to let the people go. 15In the morning the king will go out to the Nile River. Go meet him by the edge of the river, and take with you the walking stick that became a snake. 16Tell him: The LORD, the God of the Hebrews, sent me to you. He said, 'Let my people go worship me in the desert.' Until now you have not listened. 17This is what the LORD says: 'This is how you will know that I am the LORD. I will strike the water of the Nile River with this stick in my hand, and the water will change into blood. 18Then the fish in the Nile will die, and the river will begin to stink. The Egyptians will not be able to drink the water from the Nile.'"

19The LORD said to Moses, "Tell Aaron: 'Take the walking stick in your hand and stretch your hand over the rivers, canals, ponds, and pools in Egypt.' The water will become blood everywhere in Egypt, both in wooden buckets and in stone jars."

20So Moses and Aaron did just as the LORD had commanded. In front of the king and his officers, Aaron raised his walking stick and struck the water in the Nile River. So all the water in the Nile changed into blood. 21The fish in the Nile died, and the river began to stink, so the Egyptians could not drink water from it. Blood was everywhere in the land of Egypt.

22Using their tricks, the magicians of Egypt did the same thing. So the king was stubborn and refused to listen to Moses and Aaron, just as the LORD had said. 23The king turned and went into his palace and ignored what Moses and Aaron had done. 24The Egyptians could not drink the water from the Nile, so all of them dug along the bank of the river, looking for water to drink.

The Frogs

25Seven days passed after the LORD changed the Nile River.

8 Then the LORD told Moses, "Go to the king of Egypt and tell him, 'This is what the LORD says: Let my people go to worship me. 2If you refuse, I will punish Egypt with frogs. 3The Nile River will be filled with frogs. They will come up *into your palace, into your bedroom, on your bed,* into the houses of your officers, and onto your people. They will come into your ovens and into your baking pans. 4The frogs will jump all over you, your people, and your officers.'"

5Then the LORD said to Moses, "Tell Aaron to hold his walking stick in his hand over the rivers, canals, and ponds. Make frogs come up out of the water onto the land of Egypt."

[6]So Aaron held his hand over all the waters of Egypt, and the frogs came up out of the water and covered the land of Egypt. [7]The magicians used their tricks to do the same thing, so even more frogs came up onto the land of Egypt.

SIDELIGHT: Lots of movies have been based on the Bible: The Ten Commandments, The Greatest Story Ever Told, David and Bathsheba. But what about the 1972 horror movie Frogs? Sounds an awful lot like Exodus 8:6–7, doesn't it?

---

[8]The king called for Moses and Aaron and said, "Pray to the LORD to take the frogs away from me and my people. I will let your people go to offer sacrifices to the LORD."

[9]Moses said to the king, "Please set the time when I should pray for you, your people, and your officers. Then the frogs will leave you and your houses and will remain only in the Nile."

[10]The king answered, "Tomorrow."

Moses said, "What you want will happen. By this you will know that there is no one like the LORD our God. [11]The frogs will leave you, your houses, your officers, and your people. They will remain only in the Nile."

[12]After Moses and Aaron left the king, Moses asked the LORD about the frogs he had sent to the king. [13]And the LORD did as Moses asked. The frogs died in the houses, in the yards, and in the fields. [14]The Egyptians put them in piles, and the whole country began to stink. [15]But when the king saw that they were free of the frogs, he became stubborn again. He did not listen to Moses and Aaron, just as the LORD had said.

The Gnats

[16]Then the LORD said to Moses, "Tell Aaron to raise his walking stick and strike the dust on the ground. Then everywhere in Egypt the dust will change into gnats." [17]They did this, and when Aaron raised the walking stick that was in his hand and struck the dust on the ground, everywhere in Egypt the dust changed into gnats. The gnats got on the people and animals. [18]Using their tricks, the magicians tried to do the same thing, but they could not make the dust change into gnats. The gnats remained on the people and animals. [19]So the magicians told the king that the power of God had done this. But the king was stubborn and refused to listen to them, just as the LORD had said.

The Flies

[20]The LORD told Moses, "Get up early in the morning and meet the king of Egypt as he goes out to the river. Tell him, 'This is what the LORD says: Let my people go so they can worship me. [21]If you don't let them go, I will send swarms of flies into your houses. The flies will be on you, your officers, and your people. The houses of Egypt will be full of flies, and they will be all over the ground, too. [22]But I will not treat the Israelites the same as the Egyptian people. There will not be any flies in the land of Goshen, where my people live. By this you will know that I, the LORD, am in this land. [23]I will treat my people differently from your people. This miracle[d] will happen tomorrow.' "

[24]So the LORD did as he had said, and great swarms of flies came into the king's palace and his officers' houses. All over Egypt flies were ruining the land. [25]The king called for Moses and Aaron and told them, "Offer sacrifices to your God here in this country."

[26]But Moses said, "It wouldn't be right to do that, because the Egyptians hate the sacrifices we offer to the LORD our God. If they see us offering sacrifices they hate, they will throw stones at us and kill us. [27]Let us make a three-day journey into the desert. We must offer sacrifices to the LORD our God there, as the LORD told us to do."

[28]The king said, "I will let you go so that you may offer sacrifices to the LORD your God in the desert, but you must not go very far away. Now go and pray for me."

[29]Moses said, "I will leave and pray to the LORD, and he will take the flies away from you, your officers, and your people tomorrow. But do not try to trick us again. Do not stop the people from going to offer sacrifices to the LORD."

[30]So Moses left the king and prayed to the LORD, [31]and the LORD did as he asked. He removed the flies from the king, his officers, and his people so that not one fly was left. [32]But the king became stubborn again and did not let the people go.

The Disease on the Farm Animals

9 Then the LORD told Moses, "Go to the king of Egypt and tell him, 'This is what the LORD, the God of the Hebrews, says: Let my people go to worship me. [2]If you refuse to let them go and continue to hold them, [3]the LORD will punish you. He will send a terrible disease on your farm animals that are in the fields. He will cause your horses, donkeys, camels, cattle, goats, and sheep to become sick. [4]But the LORD will treat Israel's animals differently from the animals of Egypt. None of the animals that belong to the Israelites will die. [5]The LORD has set tomorrow as the time he will do this in the land.' " ⁶The next day the LORD did as he promised. All the farm animals in Egypt died, but none of the animals belonging to Israelites died. ⁷The king sent people to see what had happened to the animals of Israel, and they found that not one of them had died. But the king was still stubborn and did not let the people go.

The Boils

⁸The LORD said to Moses and Aaron, "Fill your hands with ashes from a furnace. Moses, throw the ashes into the air in front of the king of Egypt. ⁹The ashes will spread like dust through all the land of Egypt. They will cause boils to break out and become sores on the skin of people and animals everywhere in the land."

¹⁰So Moses and Aaron took ashes from a furnace and went and stood before the king. Moses threw ashes into the air, which caused boils to break out and become sores on people and animals. ¹¹The magicians could not stand before Moses, because all the Egyptians had boils, even the magicians. ¹²But the LORD made the king stubborn, so he refused to listen to Moses and Aaron, just as the LORD had said.

The Hail

¹³Then the LORD said to Moses, "Get up early in the morning and go to the king of Egypt. Tell him, 'This is what the LORD, the God of the Hebrews, says: Let my people go to worship me. ¹⁴If you don't, this time I will punish you, your officers, and your people, with all my power. Then you will know there is no one in the whole land like me. ¹⁵By now I could have used my power and caused a terrible disease that would have destroyed you and your people from the earth. ¹⁶But I have let you live for this reason: to show you my power so that my name will be talked about in all the earth. ¹⁷You are still against my people and do not want to let them go. ¹⁸So at this time tomorrow, I will send a terrible hailstorm, the worst in Egypt since it became a nation. ¹⁹Now send for your animals and whatever you have in the fields, and bring them into a safe place. The hail will fall on every person or animal that is still in the fields. If they have not been brought in, they will die.' "
²⁰Some of the king's officers respected the word of the LORD and hurried to bring their slaves and animals inside. ²¹But others ignored the LORD's message and left their slaves and animals in the fields.

²²The LORD told Moses, "Raise your hand toward the sky. Then the hail will start falling in all the land of Egypt. It will fall on people, animals, and on everything that grows in the fields of Egypt." ²³When Moses raised his walking stick toward the sky, the LORD sent thunder and hail, and lightning flashed down to the earth. So he caused hail to fall upon the land of Egypt. ²⁴There was hail, and lightning flashed as it hailed — the worst hailstorm in Egypt since it had become a nation. ²⁵The hail destroyed all the people and animals that were in the fields in all the land of Egypt. It also destroyed everything that grew in the fields and broke all the trees in the fields. ²⁶The only place it did not hail was in the land of Goshen, where the Israelites lived.

²⁷The king sent for Moses and Aaron and told them, "This time I have sinned. The LORD is in the right, and I and my people are in the wrong. ²⁸Pray to the LORD. We have had enough of God's thunder and hail. I will let you go; you do not have to stay here any longer."

²⁹Moses told the king, "When I leave the city, I will raise my hands to the LORD in prayer, and the thunder and hail will stop. Then you will know that the earth belongs to the LORD. ³⁰But I know that you and your officers do not yet fear the LORD God."

³¹The flax was in bloom, and the barley had ripened, so these crops were destroyed. ³²But both wheat crops ripen later, so they were not destroyed.

³³Moses left the king and went outside the city. He raised his hands to the LORD, and the thunder and hail stopped. The rain also stopped falling to the ground. ³⁴When the king saw that the rain, hail, and thunder had stopped, he sinned again, and he and his officers became stubborn. ³⁵So the king became stubborn and refused to let the Israelites go, just as the LORD had said through Moses.

The Locusts

10 The LORD said to Moses, "Go to the king of Egypt. I have made him and his officers stubborn so I could show them my powerful miracles.ᵈ ²I also did this so you could tell your children and your grandchildren how I was hard on the Egyptians. Tell them about the miracles I did among them so that all of you will know that I am the LORD."

³So Moses and Aaron went to the king and told him, "This is what the LORD, the God of the Hebrews, says: 'How long will you refuse to be sorry for what you have done? Let my people go to worship me. ⁴If you refuse to let my people go, tomorrow I will bring locustsᵈ into your country. ⁵They will cover the land so that no one will be able to see the ground. They will eat anything that was left from the hailstorm and the leaves from every tree growing in the field. ⁶They will fill your palaces and all your officers' houses, as well as the houses of all the Egyptians. There will be more locusts than your fathers or ancestors have ever seen — more than there have been since people

began living in Egypt.' " Then Moses turned and walked away from the king.

[7]The king's officers asked him, "How long will this man make trouble for us? Let the Israelites go to worship the LORD their God. Don't you know that Egypt is ruined?"

[8]So Moses and Aaron were brought back to the king. He said to them, "Go and worship the LORD your God. But tell me, just who is going?"

[9]Moses answered, "We will go with our young and old people, our sons and daughters, and our flocks and herds, because we are going to have a feast to honor the LORD."

[10]The king said to them, "The LORD will really have to be with you if ever I let you and all of your children leave Egypt. See, you are planning something evil! [11]No! Only the men may go and worship the LORD, which is what you have been asking for." Then the king forced Moses and Aaron out of his palace.

[12]The LORD told Moses, "Raise your hand over the land of Egypt, and the locusts will come. They will spread all over the land of Egypt and will eat all the plants the hail did not destroy."

[13]So Moses raised his walking stick over the land of Egypt, and the LORD caused a strong wind to blow from the east. It blew across the land all that day and night, and when morning came, the east wind had brought the locusts. [14]Swarms of locusts covered all the land of Egypt and settled everywhere. There were more locusts than ever before or after, [15]and they covered the whole land so that it was black. They ate everything that was left after the hail—every plant in the field and all the fruit on the trees. Nothing green was left on any tree or plant anywhere in Egypt.

[16]The king quickly called for Moses and Aaron. He said, "I have sinned against the LORD your God and against you. [17]Now forgive my sin this time. Pray to the LORD your God, and ask him to stop this punishment that kills."

[18]Moses left the king and prayed to the LORD. [19]So the LORD changed the wind. He made a very strong wind blow from the west, and it blew the locusts away into the Red Sea.[d] Not one locust was left anywhere in Egypt. [20]But the LORD caused the king to be stubborn again, and he did not let the Israelites go.

The Darkness

[21]Then the LORD told Moses, "Raise your hand toward the sky, and darkness will cover the land of Egypt. It will be so dark you will be able to feel it." [22]Moses raised his hand toward the sky, and total darkness was everywhere in Egypt for three days. [23]No one could see anyone else, and no one could go anywhere for three days. But the Israelites had light where they lived.

[24]Again the king of Egypt called for Moses. He said, "All of you may go and worship the LORD. You may take your women and children with you, but you must leave your flocks and herds here."

[25]Moses said, "You must let us have animals to use as sacrifices and burnt offerings, because we have to offer them to the LORD our God. [26]So we must take our animals with us; not a hoof will be left behind. We have to use some of the animals to worship the LORD our God. We won't know exactly what we will need to worship the LORD until we get there."

[27]But the LORD made the king stubborn again, so he refused to let them go. [28]Then he told Moses, "Get out of here, and don't come again! The next time you see me, you will die."

[29]Then Moses told the king, "I'll do what you say. I will not come to see you again."

The Death of the Firstborn

11 Now the LORD had told Moses, "I have one more way to punish the king and the people of Egypt. After this, the king will send all of you away from Egypt. When he does, he will force you to leave completely. [2]Tell the men and women of Israel to ask their neighbors for things made of silver and gold." [3]The LORD had caused the Egyptians to respect the Israelites, and both the king's officers and the Egyptian people considered Moses to be a great man.

[4]So Moses said to the king, "This is what the LORD says: 'About midnight tonight I will go through all Egypt. [5]Every firstborn[d] son in the land of Egypt will die—from the firstborn son of the king, who sits on his throne, to the firstborn of the slave girl grinding grain. Also the firstborn farm animals will die. [6]There will be loud outcries everywhere in Egypt, worse than any time before or after this. [7]But not even a dog will bark at the Israelites or their animals.' Then you will know that the LORD treats Israel differently from Egypt. [8]All your officers will come to me. They will bow facedown to the ground before me and say, 'Leave and take all your people with you.' After that, I will leave." Then Moses very angrily left the king.

[9]The LORD had told Moses, "The king will not listen to you and Aaron so that I may do many miracles[d] in the land of Egypt." [10]Moses and Aaron did all these great miracles in front of the king. But the LORD made him stubborn, and the king would not let the Israelites leave his country.

The First Passover

12 The LORD spoke to Moses and Aaron in the land of Egypt: [2]"This month will be the beginning of months, the first month of the year for you. [3]Tell the whole community of Israel that on the tenth day of this month each man must get one lamb for the people in his house. 4If there are not enough people in his house to eat a whole lamb, he must share it with his closest neighbor, considering the number of people. There must be enough lamb for everyone to eat. 5The lamb must be a one-year-old male that has nothing wrong with it. This animal can be either a young sheep or a young goat. 6Take care of the animals until the fourteenth day of the month. On that day all the people of the community of Israel will kill them in the evening before dark. 7The people must take some of the blood and put it on the sides and tops of the doorframes of the houses where they eat the lambs. 8On this night they must roast the lamb over a fire. They must eat it with bitter herbs and bread made without yeast. 9Do not eat the lamb raw or boiled in water. Roast the whole lamb over a fire — with its head, legs, and inner organs. 10You must not leave any of it until morning, but if any of it is left over until morning, you must burn it with fire.

11"This is the way you must eat it: You must be fully dressed as if you were going on a trip. You must have your sandals on and your walking stick in your hand. You must eat it in a hurry; this is the LORD's Passover.*d*

12"That night I will go through the land of Egypt and kill all the firstborn*d* animals and people in the land of Egypt. I will also punish all the gods of Egypt. I am the LORD. 13But the blood will be a sign on the houses where you are. When I see the blood, I will pass over you. Nothing terrible will hurt you when I punish the land of Egypt.

14"You are always to remember this day and celebrate it with a feast to the LORD. Your descendants*d* are to honor the LORD with this feast from now on. 15For this feast you must eat bread made without yeast for seven days. On the first day, you are to remove all the yeast from your houses. No

GOD'S LOVE

Waiting for Miracles

When the children in George Müller's orphanage in Bristol, England, ate dinner that evening, they didn't know the food on their plates was the only food in the orphanage. No food or money was left for the next morning's breakfast. George prayed that something would arrive that evening, but nothing did. He went to bed, committing the need to God.

The next morning, George went out for his early morning walk and prayer. For some reason, he took a different route than usual, and a friend saw him. "I'm glad to see you," his friend said. "Please accept five pounds for the orphans."

"Thank you," George said graciously, never mentioning that the money would provide the kids' food for several days. "God bless you."

Because of his faith, George fed and housed hundreds of homeless kids in Bristol in the 1800s. But he never made public appeals for funds.

When the food ran out at the orphanage, George told no one but God. And, miraculously, God supplied it time and time again. When George was short on funds, only God knew. And the money arrived when George needed it.

George Müller would never have been able to help hundreds of orphans without God's love to provide for them. Similarly, the Israelites would never have escaped from Egypt without God's love to protect them. Read **Exodus 12:1–14** to see how God's love delivered them during the Passover.

■ What similarities do you see between God's provisions for George Müller's orphanages and his protection of the Israelites during the Passover?

■ Has God's love helped you through a situation you could never have survived on your own? How did the experience make you feel about God?

CONSIDER . . .

■ thanking God for his love that has delivered you in the past from tough situations.

■ writing on a card a tough situation you are experiencing. Put the card in a place where you will find it in a week or so to see how God helped you through that tough time.

FOR MORE, SEE . . .

■ Psalm 34 (p. 501)
■ Hosea 14:1–8 (p. 832)
■ Romans 5:1–11 (p. 1145)

one should eat any yeast for the full seven days of the feast, or that person will be cut off from Israel. ¹⁶You are to have holy meetings on the first and last days of the feast. You must not do any work on these days; the only work you may do is to prepare your meals. ¹⁷You must celebrate the Feast[d] of Unleavened Bread, because on this very day I brought your divisions of people out of Egypt. So all of your descendants must celebrate this day. This is a law that will last from now on. ¹⁸In the first month of the year you are to eat bread made without yeast, from the evening of the fourteenth day until the evening of the twenty-first day. ¹⁹For seven days there must not be any yeast in your houses. Anybody who eats yeast during this time, either an Israelite or non-Israelite, must be cut off from the community of Israel. ²⁰During this feast you must not eat anything made with yeast. You must eat only bread made without yeast wherever you live."

²¹Then Moses called all the older leaders of Israel together and told them, "Get the animals for your families and kill the lamb for the Passover. ²²Take a branch of the hyssop plant, dip it into the bowl filled with blood, and then wipe the blood on the sides and tops of the doorframes. No one may leave that house until morning. ²³When the LORD goes through Egypt to kill the Egyptians, he will see the blood on the sides and tops of the doorframes, and he will pass over that house. He will not let the one who brings death come into your houses and kill you.

²⁴"You must keep this command as a law for you and your descendants from now on. ²⁵Do this when you go to the land the LORD has promised to give you. ²⁶When your children ask you, 'Why are we doing these things?' ²⁷you will say, 'This is the Passover sacrifice to honor the LORD. When we were in Egypt, the LORD passed over the houses of Israel, and when he killed the Egyptians, he saved our homes.' " Then the people bowed down and worshiped the LORD. ²⁸They did just as the LORD commanded Moses and Aaron.

²⁹At midnight the LORD killed all the firstborn sons in the land of Egypt—from the firstborn of the king who sat on the throne to the firstborn of the prisoner in jail. Also, all the firstborn farm animals died. ³⁰The king, his officers, and all the Egyptians got up during the night because someone had died in every house. So there was a loud outcry everywhere in Egypt.

Israel Leaves Egypt

³¹During the night the king called for Moses and Aaron and said, "Get up and leave my people. You and your people may do as you have asked; go and worship the LORD. ³²Take all of your flocks and herds as you have asked, and go. And also bless me." ³³The Egyptians also asked the Israel-ites to hurry and leave, saying, "If you don't leave, we will all die!"

³⁴So the people took their dough before the yeast was added. They wrapped the bowls for making dough in clothing and carried them on their shoulders. ³⁵The Israelites did what Moses told them to do and asked their Egyptian neighbors for things made of silver and gold and for clothing. ³⁶The LORD caused the Egyptians to think well of them, and the Egyptians gave the people everything they asked for. So the Israelites took rich gifts from them.

³⁷The Israelites traveled from Rameses to Succoth. There were about six hundred thousand men walking, not including the women and children. ³⁸Many other people who were not Israel-ites went with them, as well as a large number of sheep, goats, and cattle. ³⁹The Israelites used the dough they had brought out of Egypt to bake loaves of bread without yeast. The dough had no yeast in it, because they had been rushed out of Egypt and had no time to get food ready for their trip.

⁴⁰The people of Israel had lived in Egypt for four hundred thirty years; ⁴¹on the very day the four hundred thirty years ended, the LORD's divisions of people left Egypt. ⁴²That night the LORD kept watch to bring them out of Egypt, and so on this same night the Israelites are to keep watch to honor the LORD from now on.

⁴³The LORD told Moses and Aaron, "Here are the rules for Passover:[d] No foreigner is to eat the Passover. ⁴⁴If someone buys a slave and circum-cises[d] him, the slave may eat the Passover. ⁴⁵But neither a person who lives for a short time in your country nor a hired worker may eat it.

⁴⁶"The meal must be eaten inside a house; take none of the meat outside the house. Don't break any of the bones. ⁴⁷The whole community of Israel must take part in this feast. ⁴⁸A foreigner who lives with you may share in the LORD's Passover if all the males in his house become circumcised. Then, since he will be like a citizen of Israel, he may share in the meal. But a man who is not cir-cumcised may not eat the Passover meal. ⁴⁹The same rules apply to an Israelite born in the country or to a foreigner living there."

⁵⁰So all the Israelites did just as the LORD had commanded Moses and Aaron. ⁵¹On that same day the LORD led the Israelites out of Egypt by their divisions.

The Law of the Firstborn

13 Then the LORD said to Moses, ²"Give every firstborn[d] male to me. Every firstborn male among the Israelites belongs to me, whether human or animal."

³Moses said to the people, "Remember this day, the day you left Egypt. You were slaves in

that land, but the LORD with his great power brought you out of it. You must not eat bread made with yeast. ⁴Today, in the month of Abib,*d* you are leaving Egypt. ⁵The LORD will lead you to the land of the Canaanites, Hittites, Amorites, Hivites, and Jebusites. This is the land he promised your ancestors he would give you, a fertile land. There you must celebrate this feast during the first month of every year. ⁶For seven days you must eat bread made without yeast, and on the seventh day there will be a feast to honor the LORD. ⁷So for seven days you must not eat any bread made with yeast. There must be no bread made with yeast anywhere in your land. ⁸On that day you should tell your son: 'We are having this feast because of what the LORD did for me when I came out of Egypt.' ⁹This feast will help you remember, like a mark on your hand or a reminder on your forehead. This feast will remind you to speak the LORD's teachings, because the LORD used his great power to bring you out of Egypt. ¹⁰So celebrate this feast every year at the right time.

¹¹"And when the LORD takes you into the land of the Canaanites, the land he promised to give you and your ancestors, ¹²you must give him every firstborn male. Also every firstborn male animal must be given to the LORD. ¹³Buy back every firstborn donkey by offering a lamb. But if you don't want to buy the donkey back, then break its neck. You must buy back from the LORD every firstborn of your sons.

¹⁴"From now on when your son asks you, 'What does this mean?' you will answer, 'With his great power, the LORD brought us out from Egypt, the land where we were slaves. ¹⁵The king of Egypt was stubborn and refused to let us leave. But the LORD killed every firstborn male in Egypt, both human and animal. That is why I sacrifice every firstborn male animal to the LORD, and that is why I buy back each of my firstborn sons from the LORD.' ¹⁶This feast is like a mark on your hand and a reminder on your forehead to help you remember that the LORD brought us out of Egypt with his great power."

The Way Out of Egypt

¹⁷When the king sent the people out of Egypt, God did not lead them on the road through the Philistine country, though that was the shortest way. God said, "If they have to fight, they might change their minds and go back to Egypt." ¹⁸So God led them through the desert toward the Red Sea.*d* The Israelites were dressed for fighting when they left the land of Egypt.

¹⁹Moses carried the bones of Joseph with him, because before Joseph died, he had made the Israelites promise to do this. He had said, "When God saves you, remember to carry my bones with you out of Egypt."

²⁰The Israelites left Succoth and camped at Etham, on the edge of the desert. ²¹The LORD showed them the way; during the day he went ahead of them in a pillar of cloud, and during the night he was in a pillar of fire to give them light. In this way they could travel during the day or night. ²²The pillar of cloud was always with them during the day, and the pillar of fire was always with them at night.

14 Then the LORD said to Moses, ²"Tell the Israelites to turn back to Pi Hahiroth and to camp between Migdol and the Red Sea. Camp across from Baal Zephon, on the shore of the sea. ³The king will think, 'The Israelites are lost, trapped by the desert.' ⁴I will make the king stubborn again so he will chase after them, but I will defeat the king and his army. This will bring honor to me, and the Egyptians will know that I am the LORD." The Israelites did just as they were told.

The King Chases the Israelites

⁵When the king of Egypt was told that the Israelites had left, he and his officers changed their minds about them. They said, "What have we done? We have let the Israelites leave. We have lost our slaves!" ⁶So the king prepared his war chariot and took his army with him. ⁷He took six hundred of his best chariots, together with all the other chariots of Egypt, each with an officer in it. ⁸The LORD made the king of Egypt stubborn, so he chased the Israelites, who were leaving victoriously. ⁹The Egyptians — with all the king's horses, chariot drivers, and army — chased the Israelites. They caught up with them while they were camped by the Red Sea,*d* near Pi Hahiroth and Baal Zephon.

¹⁰When the Israelites saw the king and his army coming after them, they were very frightened and cried to the LORD for help. ¹¹They said to Moses, "What have you done to us? Why did you bring us out of Egypt to die in the desert? There were plenty of graves for us in Egypt. ¹²We told you in Egypt, 'Let us alone; we will stay and serve the Egyptians.' Now we will die in the desert."

¹³But Moses answered, "Don't be afraid! Stand still and you will see the LORD save you today. You will never see these Egyptians again after today. ¹⁴You only need to remain calm; the LORD will fight for you."

¹⁵Then the LORD said to Moses, "Why are you crying out to me? Command the Israelites to start moving. ¹⁶Raise your walking stick and hold it over the sea so that the sea will split and the people can cross it on dry land. ¹⁷I will make the Egyptians stubborn so they will chase the Israelites, but I will be honored when I defeat the king and all of his chariot drivers and chariots. ¹⁸When

I defeat the king, his chariot drivers, and chariots, the Egyptians will know that I am the LORD."

¹⁹Now the angel of God that usually traveled in front of Israel's army moved behind them. Also, the pillar of cloud moved from in front of the people and stood behind them. ²⁰So the cloud came between the Egyptians and the Israelites. This made it dark for the Egyptians but gave light to the Israelites. So the cloud kept the two armies apart all night.

²¹Then Moses held his hand over the sea. All that night the LORD drove back the sea with a strong east wind, making the sea become dry ground. The water was split, ²²and the Israelites went through the sea on dry land, with a wall of water on their right and on their left.

²³Then all the king's horses, chariots, and chariot drivers followed them into the sea. ²⁴When morning came, the LORD looked down from the pillar of cloud and fire at the Egyptian army and made them panic. ²⁵He kept the wheels of the chariots from turning, making it hard to drive the chariots. The Egyptians shouted, "Let's get away from the Israelites! The LORD is fighting for them and against Egypt."

²⁶Then the LORD told Moses, "Hold your hand over the sea so that the water will come back over the Egyptians, their chariots, and chariot drivers." ²⁷So Moses raised his hand over the sea, and at dawn the sea returned to its place. The Egyptians tried to run from it, but the LORD swept them away into the sea. ²⁸The water returned, covering the chariots, chariot drivers, and all the king's army that had followed the Israelites into the sea. Not one of them survived.

²⁹But the Israelites crossed the sea on dry land, with a wall of water on their right and on their left. ³⁰So that day the LORD saved the Israelites from the Egyptians, and the Israelites saw the Egyptians lying dead on the seashore. ³¹When the Israelites saw the great power the LORD had used

---

A Place to Call Home

The hot August night made it too stuffy to sleep. Sharon McPherson-Mullins looked at her four children lying in the boxes in the back of her old car—the family's only home. She felt trapped in the world of homelessness with nowhere to go and no one to turn to.

"Oh God, my God," she cried and prayed silently. "Where are you, God? Have you forsaken me?" And she fell into a restless sleep.

For the next week, she went from shelter to shelter, hoping to find a place to live. One shelter took only children, and her four kids wanted to be with their mom. When a shelter finally had room for all of them, it still wasn't a home.

Then a Christian friend gave Sharon hope. She arranged for the family to rent a house without having to pay a deposit first—and the first month was free. "God has told me to help you," the owner explained.

The new home gave Sharon a freedom from poverty that she had never known. "As a family, we've never been more secure," she says. "God solved my homeless problem by using his people."

Sharon experienced new freedom from poverty and hopelessness as God worked through his people. The Israelites gained freedom from slavery in Egypt through Moses' leadership and God's work. Read about how they gained their freedom in **Exodus 14:19–31**.

- What feelings do you think Sharon would have if she read the story of the Israelites' new freedom? What parts would be most meaningful to her?
- As God led the Israelites to freedom, when has he freed you from a tough situation? How did you celebrate?

C O N S I D E R . . .
- finding someone in your school or church who's trapped by poverty, prejudice, or some other form of captivity. Talk to the person to find a way you can help him or her gain freedom.
- contacting a chapter of Habitat for Humanity in your area and volunteering to help build or repair homes for low-income people to help them escape from poverty.

F O R   M O R E ,   S E E . . .
- Exodus 15:1–11 (p. 72)
- John 8:31–38 (p. 1072)
- Galatians 5:1–15 (p. 1212)

against the Egyptians, they feared the LORD, and they trusted him and his servant Moses.

The Song of Moses

15 Then Moses and the Israelites sang this song to the LORD:

"I will sing to the LORD,
  because he is worthy of great honor.
He has thrown the horse and its rider
  into the sea.
²The LORD gives me strength and makes me
  sing;
  he has saved me.
He is my God,
  and I will praise him.
He is the God of my fathers,
  and I will honor him.
³The LORD is a warrior;
  the LORD is his name.
⁴The chariots and soldiers of the king of Egypt
  he has thrown into the sea.
The king's best officers
  are drowned in the Red Sea.ᵈ
⁵The deep waters covered them,
  and they sank to the bottom like a rock.
⁶Your right hand, LORD,
  is amazingly strong.
LORD, your right hand
  broke the enemy to pieces.
⁷In your great victory
  you destroyed those who were against you.
Your anger destroyed them,
  like fire burning straw.
⁸Just a blast of your breath,
  and the waters piled up.
The moving water stood like a wall;
  the deep waters became solid in the middle
    of the sea.

⁹"The enemy bragged,
  'I'll chase them and catch them.
I'll take all their riches;
  I'll take all I want.
I'll pull out my sword,
  and my hand will destroy them.'
¹⁰But you blew on them with your breath
  and covered them with the sea.
They sank like lead
  in the raging water.

¹¹"Are there any gods like you, LORD?
  There are no gods like you.
  You are wonderfully holy,
  amazingly powerful,
  a worker of miracles.ᵈ
¹²You reached out with your right hand,
  and the earth swallowed our enemies.

Marah This name means "bitter."

¹³You keep your loving promise
  and lead the people you have saved.
With your strength you will guide them
  to your holy place.

¹⁴"The other nations will hear this and tremble
  with fear;
  terror will take hold of the Philistines.
¹⁵The leaders of the tribesᵈ of Edom will be
  very frightened;
  the powerful men of Moab will shake with
    fear;
  the people of Canaan will lose all their
    courage.
¹⁶Terror and horror will fall on them.
When they see your strength,
  they will be as still as a rock.
They will be still until your people pass by,
  LORD.
They will be still until the people you have
  taken as your own pass by.
¹⁷You will lead your people and place them
  on your very own mountain,
  the place that you, LORD, made for yourself
    to live,
  the temple, Lord, that your hands have
    made.
¹⁸The LORD will be king forever!"

¹⁹The horses, chariot drivers, and chariots of the king of Egypt went into the sea, and the LORD covered them with water from the sea. But the Israelites walked through the sea on dry land. ²⁰Then Aaron's sister Miriam, a prophetess,ᵈ took a tambourineᵈ in her hand. All the women followed her, playing tambourines and dancing. ²¹Miriam told them:

"Sing to the LORD,
  because he is worthy of great honor;
he has thrown the horse and its rider
  into the sea."

Bitter Water Becomes Good

²²Moses led the Israelites away from the Red Seaᵈ into the Desert of Shur. They traveled for three days in the desert but found no water. ²³Then they came to Marah, where there was water, but they could not drink it because it was too bitter. (That is why the place was named Marah.ⁿ) ²⁴The people grumbled to Moses and asked, "What will we drink?"

²⁵So Moses cried out to the LORD, and the LORD showed him a tree. When Moses threw the tree into the water, the water became good to drink. There the LORD gave the people a rule and a law to live by, and there he tested their loyalty to him. ²⁶He said, "You must obey the LORD your God and do what he says is right. If you obey all

his commands and keep his rules, I will not bring on you any of the sicknesses I brought on the Egyptians. I am the Lord who heals you."

27Then the people traveled to Elim, where there were twelve springs of water and seventy palm trees. So the people camped there near the water.

The People Demand Food

16 The whole Israelite community left Elim and came to the Desert of Sin, which was between Elim and Sinai; they arrived there on the fifteenth day of the second month after they had left Egypt. 2Then the whole Israelite community grumbled to Moses and Aaron in the desert. 3They said to them, "It would have been better if the Lord had killed us in the land of Egypt. There we had meat to eat and all the food we wanted. But you have brought us into this desert to starve us to death."

4Then the Lord said to Moses, "I will cause food to fall like rain from the sky for all of you. Every day the people must go out and gather what they need for that day. I want to see if the people will do what I teach them. 5On the sixth day of each week, they are to gather twice as much as they gather on other days. Then they are to prepare it."

6So Moses and Aaron said to all the Israelites: "This evening you will know that the Lord is the one who brought you out of Egypt. 7Tomorrow morning you will see the glory of the Lord, because he has heard you grumble against him. We are nothing, so you are not grumbling against us, but against the Lord." 8And Moses said, "Each evening the Lord will give you meat to eat, and every morning he will give you all the bread you want, because he has heard you grumble against him. You are not grumbling against Aaron and

---

WORRYING

A Little Hope

Jimmy O'Neill, fifteen, has a lot to worry about. Born with cystic fibrosis, an inherited lung disease, he has been hospitalized five or six times a year since age six. Every day he takes twenty-five pills and spends twenty minutes in physical therapy.

Whenever he has a cold, he has to receive intravenous medication to fight off the infection. And if he feels a little sick, he immediately has to go to the hospital to see what's wrong. "My body is sort of like a car that everyone wants to keep in tip-top shape," he explains. As a result, he often misses fifty to sixty days of school each year.

Jimmy also has a future to worry about. "I have to realize that, no matter what, I'll never be totally independent," he says. "There's always going to have to be someone there for me."

Yet Jimmy doesn't worry. "There are some things in life you have choices about and there are things you don't," he explains. "God will take care of whatever is going to happen."

So instead of worrying, Jimmy has hope and faith in God. "You always have to have a little hope," he says, "because if you run out of that, there's nothing worth anything. You might as well give up right then and there."

Jimmy O'Neill has learned how faith helps overcome worries. In contrast, the Israelites in the desert worried about how to find food. Read **Exodus 16:2–15** to learn how God took care of their worries.

■ How does Jimmy's faith in God contrast with the Israelites' worries about how to survive?

■ What in the passage comforts you in an area of life that's had you worried lately?

            C O N S I D E R . .

■ asking someone with a disability how God has helped him or her overcome worries that come with the disability.

■ writing a list of your worries about the future. Then fold the sheet in half and write one of the Bible verses below on the back. Keep the sheet in your Bible as a reminder of God's promises.

F O R   M O R E ,   S E E . . .

■ Joshua 1:9 (p. 195)   ■ James 4:13–15 (p. 1298)
■ Luke 12:22–31 (p. 1028)

me, because we are nothing; you are grumbling against the LORD."

9Then Moses said to Aaron, "Speak to the whole community of the Israelites, and say to them, 'Meet together in the presence of the LORD, because he has heard your grumblings.' "

10While Aaron was speaking to the whole community of the Israelites, they looked toward the desert. There the glory of the LORD appeared in a cloud.

11The LORD said to Moses, 12"I have heard the grumblings of the people of Israel. So tell them, 'At twilight you will eat meat, and every morning you will eat all the bread you want. Then you will know I am the LORD your God.' "

13That evening quail came and covered the camp, and in the morning dew lay around the camp. 14When the dew was gone, thin flakes like frost were on the desert ground. 15When the Israelites saw it, they asked each other, "What is it?" because they did not know what it was.

So Moses told them, "This is the bread the LORD has given you to eat. 16The LORD has commanded, 'Each one of you must gather what he needs, about two quarts for every person in your family.' "

17So the people of Israel did this; some people gathered much, and some gathered little. 18Then they measured it. The person who gathered more did not have too much, nor did the person who gathered less have too little. Each person gathered just as much as he needed.

19Moses said to them, "Don't keep any of it to eat the next day." 20But some of the people did not listen to Moses and kept part of it to eat the next morning. It became full of worms and began to stink, so Moses was angry with those people.

21Every morning each person gathered as much food as he needed, but when the sun became hot, it melted away.

22On the sixth day the people gathered twice as much food — four quarts for every person. When all the leaders of the community came and told this to Moses, 23he said to them, "This is what the LORD commanded, because tomorrow is the Sabbath,d the LORD's holy day of rest. Bake what you want to bake, and boil what you want to boil today. Save the rest of the food until tomorrow morning."

24So the people saved it until the next morning, as Moses had commanded, and none of it began to stink or have worms in it. 25Moses told the people, "Eat the food you gathered yesterday. Today is a Sabbath, the LORD's day of rest; you will not find any out in the field today. 26You should gather the food for six days, but the seventh day

is a Sabbath day. On that day there will not be any food on the ground."

27On the seventh day some of the people went out to gather food, but they couldn't find any. 28Then the LORD said to Moses, "How long will you people refuse to obey my commands and teachings? 29Look, the LORD has made the Sabbath a day of rest for you. So on the sixth day he will give you enough food for two days, but on the seventh day each of you must stay where you are. Do not go anywhere." 30So the people rested on the seventh day.

31The people of Israel called the food manna.d It was like small white seeds and tasted like wafers made with honey.

32Then Moses said, "The LORD said, 'Save two quarts of this food for your descendants.d Then they can see the food I gave you to eat in the desert when I brought you out of Egypt.' "

33Moses told Aaron, "Take a jar and fill it with two quarts of manna. Then place it before the LORD, and save it for your descendants." 34So Aaron did what the LORD had commanded Moses. He put the jar of manna in front of the Agreement to keep it safe. 35The Israelites ate manna for forty years, until they came to the land where they settled — the edge of the land of Canaan. 36The measure they used for the manna was two quarts, or one-tenth of an ephah.n

Water from a Rock

17 The whole Israelite community left the Desert of Sin and traveled from place to place, as the LORD commanded. They camped at Rephidim, but there was no water there for the people to drink. 2So they quarreled with Moses and said, "Give us water to drink."

Moses said to them, "Why do you quarrel with me? Why are you testing the LORD?"

3But the people were very thirsty for water, so they grumbled against Moses. They said, "Why did you bring us out of Egypt? Was it to kill us, our children, and our farm animals with thirst?"

4So Moses cried to the LORD, "What can I do with these people? They are almost ready to stone me to death."

5The LORD said to Moses, "Go ahead of the people, and take some of the older leaders of Israel with you. Carry with you the walking stick that you used to strike the Nile River. Now go! 6I will stand in front of you on a rock at Mount Sinai. Hit that rock with the stick, and water will come out of it so that the people can drink." Moses did these things as the older leaders of Israel watched. 7He named that place Massah,n because the Israelites tested the LORD when they asked, "Is the

---

ephah An ephah was a measure that equaled twenty quarts.
Massah This name is the Hebrew word for "testing."

LORD with us or not?" He also named it Meribah,[n] because they quarreled.

The Amalekites Fight Israel

[8]At Rephidim the Amalekites came and fought the Israelites. [9]So Moses said to Joshua, "Choose some men and go and fight the Amalekites. Tomorrow I will stand on the top of the hill, holding the walking stick of God in my hands."

[10]Joshua obeyed Moses and went to fight the Amalekites, while Moses, Aaron, and Hur went to the top of the hill. [11]As long as Moses held his hands up, the Israelites would win the fight, but when Moses put his hands down, the Amalekites would win. [12]Later, when Moses' arms became tired, the men put a large rock under him, and he sat on it. Then Aaron and Hur held up Moses' hands — Aaron on one side and Hur on the other. They kept his hands steady until the sun went

down. [13]So Joshua defeated the Amalekites in this battle.

[14]Then the LORD said to Moses, "Write about this battle in a book so people will remember. And be sure to tell Joshua, because I will completely destroy the Amalekites from the earth."

[15]Then Moses built an altar and named it The LORD is my Banner. [16]Moses said, "I lifted my hands toward the LORD's throne. The LORD will fight against the Amalekites forever."

Meribah   This name is the Hebrew word for "quarrel."

SIDELIGHT: Ever do "the wave" at a sports event? You may not realize it, but Moses invented the cheer. Every time he lifted his arms, his "team" would start winning (Exodus 17:10–13).

PATIENCE

When the Going Gets Tough

The van was jammed with volleyballs, Frisbees, two guitars, a box of scissors, markers, string and glue, a big cooler, a water jug, eleven sweaty teenagers, and eleven backpacks crammed with shirts, shoes, and towels.

After a day of teaching crafts, songs, and Bible stories to children near Mexicali, Mexico, the teenagers were sunburned, dusty, and tired — and ready to head home.

But as they approached the border leaving Mexico, their hopes of being home soon evaporated into the hot summer air. Cars and trucks were backed up in a two-hour traffic jam.

As the young people roasted in the van without air conditioning, the sweat rolled down their faces, the exhaust fumes poured in, and everyone got hungry. The leaders figured that complaining, whining, and bickering would erupt any minute from impatient teenagers.

But then someone shouted, "I've got an idea," and pulled bread, peanut butter, and jelly from under the backpacks. "Let's make sandwiches." The fun began. Someone else passed around the water jug. And rather than getting upset when the jelly spilled, everyone laughed and helped clean up the sticky mess.

Caught in a frustrating situation, the van-load of teenagers pulled together and kept their patience. Read how the Israelites had a different reaction to their predicament in **Exodus 17:1–7**.

■ Do you think the teenagers could have been patient if their situation had been as serious as that of the Israelites?

■ What ideas from the Israelites' story can help you be patient when things aren't going your way?

CONSIDER...

■ counting to ten next time you're tempted to blow up instead of being patient.

■ trying a joke or a smile next time you're caught in a traffic jam or other uncontrollable predicament.

FOR MORE, SEE...

■ Proverbs 19:11 (p. 583)
■ Colossians 1:9–14 (p. 1233)
■ James 1:19 (p. 1294)

Jethro Visits Moses

18 Jethro, Moses' father-in-law, was the priest of Midian. He heard about everything that God had done for Moses and his people, the Israelites, and how the LORD had led the Israelites out of Egypt. [2]Now Moses had sent his wife Zipporah to Jethro, his father-in-law, [3]along with his two sons. The first son was named Gershom,[n] because when he was born, Moses said, "I am a stranger in a foreign country." [4]The other son was named Eliezer,[n] because when he was born, Moses said, "The God of my father is my help. He saved me from the king of Egypt."

[5]So Jethro, Moses' father-in-law, took Moses' wife and his two sons and went to Moses. He was camped in the desert near the mountain of God.

> ※ **SIDELIGHT:** The book of Exodus is quoted 250 times in the New Testament, making it the fourth-most-quoted book. Only Isaiah, Psalms, and Genesis are quoted more.

[6]Jethro had sent a message ahead to Moses that said, "I, Jethro, your father-in-law, am coming to you with your wife and her two sons."

[7]So Moses went out to meet his father-in-law and bowed down and kissed him. After the two men asked about each other's health, they went into Moses' tent. [8]Moses told his father-in-law everything the LORD had done to the king and the Egyptians to help Israel. He told about all the problems they had faced along the way and how the LORD had saved them.

[9]Jethro was very happy to hear all the good things the LORD had done for Israel when he had saved them from the Egyptians. [10]He said, "Praise the LORD. He has saved you from the Egyptians and their king, and he has saved the people from the power of the Egyptians. [11]Now I know the LORD is greater than all gods, because he did this to those who looked down on Israel." [12]Then Jethro, Moses' father-in-law, gave a whole burnt offering and other sacrifices to God. Aaron and all the older leaders of Israel came to Moses' father-in-law to eat the holy meal together before God.

[13]The next day Moses solved disagreements among the people, and the people stood around him from morning until night. [14]When Moses' father-in-law saw all that Moses was doing for the people, he asked, "What is all this you are doing for the people? Why are you the only one to solve

disagreements? All the people are standing around you from morning until night!"

[15]Then Moses said to his father-in-law, "It is because the people come to me for God's help in solving their disagreements. [16]When people have a disagreement, they come to me, and I decide who is right. I tell them God's laws and teachings."

[17]Moses' father-in-law said to him, "You are not doing this right. [18]You and the people who come to you will get too tired. This is too much work for you; you can't do it by yourself. [19]Now listen to me, and I will give you some advice. I want God to be with you. You must speak to God for the people and tell him about their disagreements. [20]Warn them about the laws and teachings, and teach them the right way to live and what they should do. [21]But choose some capable men from among the people—men who respect God, who can be trusted, and who will not change their decisions for money. Make these men officers over the people, to rule over groups of thousands, hundreds, fifties, and tens. [22]Let these officers solve the disagreements among the people all the time. They can bring the hard cases to you, but they can decide the simple cases themselves. That will make it easier for you, because they will share the work with you. [23]If you do this as God commands you, then you will be able to do your job, and all the people will go home with their disagreements solved."

[24]So Moses listened to his father-in-law and did everything he said. [25]He chose capable men from all the Israelites and made them leaders over the people; they were officers over groups of thousands, hundreds, fifties, and tens. [26]These officers solved disagreements among the people all the time. They brought the hard cases to Moses, but they decided the simple cases themselves.

[27]So Moses sent his father-in-law on his way, and Jethro went back to his own home.

Israel Camps at Sinai

19 Exactly three months after the Israelites had left Egypt, they reached the Desert of Sinai. [2]When they left Rephidim, they came to the Desert of Sinai and camped in the desert in front of the mountain. [3]Then Moses went up on the mountain to God. The LORD called to him from the mountain and said, "Say this to the family of Jacob, and tell the people of Israel: [4]'Every one of you has seen what I did to the people of Egypt. You saw how I carried you out of Egypt, as if on eagle's wings. And I brought you here to me. [5]So now if you obey me and keep my agreement, you will be my own possession, chosen

Gershom This name sounds like the Hebrew word for "a stranger there."
Eliezer This name sounds like the Hebrew words "My God is my help."

from all nations. Even though the whole earth is mine, ⁶you will be my kingdom of priests and a holy nation.' You must tell the Israelites these words."

⁷So Moses went down and called the older leaders of the people together. He told them all the words the LORD had commanded him to say. ⁸All the people answered together, "We will do everything he has said." Then Moses took their answer back to the LORD.

⁹And the LORD said to Moses, "I will come to you in a thick cloud and speak to you. The people will hear me speaking with you and will always trust you." Then Moses told the LORD what the people had said.

¹⁰The LORD said to Moses, "Go to the people and have them spend today and tomorrow preparing themselves. They must wash their clothes ¹¹and be ready by the day after tomorrow. On that day I, the LORD, will come down on Mount Sinai, and all the people will see me. ¹²But you must set a limit around the mountain that the people are not to cross. Tell them not to go up on the mountain and not to touch the foot of it. Anyone who touches the mountain must be put to death ¹³with stones or shot with arrows. No one is allowed to touch him. Whether it is a person or an animal, he will not live. But the trumpet will make a long blast, and only then may the people go up on the mountain."

FOLLOWING GOD

A Trusted Leader

The entire drama class snickered when it was announced: Judson Zinder would be the student director for the spring production of "How to Succeed in Business."

Judson Zinder? He was a tall, lanky, freckle-faced sophomore with a squeaky voice. The only reason classmates liked him was because he was a natural clown. He was hardly someone they would look up to.

But no matter. Mr. Hall would be directing, and having Judson as the assistant wouldn't hurt.

Then one evening the cast arrived for rehearsal to find Judson sitting in Mr. Hall's chair. "Mr. Hall is sick," Judson announced. "He'll be okay, but he won't be back for a couple of weeks."

Groans echoed across the stage. "There goes our big hit" someone onstage quipped. "Kiss that Tony Award good-bye." And everyone laughed. The rehearsal was a disaster. People joked with their lines, missed their entrances, and talked to Judson with mock respect.

Suddenly, Judson threw his clipboard on the stage in frustration. "Okay," he said. "I know I'm just a sophomore, and I know you guys don't think I can do this. But we've got to do it together—for Mr. Hall."

Surprised by his honesty, the cast started paying attention, and they discovered Judson was a natural at blocking and staging. In his quiet way, he turned a mediocre school play into a big success.

The cast members began following Judson when they realized he could lead them. The Israelites made a bigger commitment and trusted God because they had seen his work before. Read about their agreement to follow God in **Exodus 19:1–8**.

■ What similarities and differences do you see between Judson's speech to the cast and God's declaration to Moses? What parts of what they said provide the most motivation to follow them?

■ How does God's leadership of the Israelites give you faith that you too can follow God?

C O N S I D E R . . .

■ finding a calendar from the past month and writing ways God was with you through the month. Keep the calendar handy to remind you of God's guidance when you have trouble following him.

■ memorizing Exodus 19:4 to boost your faith when you're discouraged.

F O R   M O R E ,   S E E . . .

■ Jeremiah 2:1–11 (p. 692)
■ Ezekiel 16:59–63 (p. 774)

■ John 9:1–25 (p. 1073)

¹⁴After Moses went down from the mountain to the people, he made them prepare themselves for service to God, and they washed their clothes. ¹⁵Then Moses said to the people, "Be ready in three days. Do not have sexual relations during this time."

¹⁶On the morning of the third day, there was thunder and lightning with a thick cloud on the mountain. There was a very loud blast from a trumpet, and all the people in the camp trembled. ¹⁷Then Moses led the people out of the camp to meet God, and they stood at the foot of the mountain. ¹⁸Mount Sinai was covered with smoke, because the LORD came down on it in fire. The smoke rose from the mountain like smoke from a furnace, and the whole mountain shook wildly. ¹⁹The sound from the trumpet became louder. Then Moses spoke, and the voice of God answered him.

²⁰When the LORD came down on top of Mount Sinai, he called Moses to come up to the top of the mountain, and Moses went up. ²¹The LORD said to Moses, "Go down and warn the people that they must not force their way through to see me. If they do, many of them will die. ²²Even the priests, who may come near me, must first prepare themselves. If they don't, I, the LORD, will punish them."

²³Moses told the LORD, "The people cannot come up on Mount Sinai, because you yourself told us, 'Set a limit around the mountain, and set it apart as holy.' "

²⁴The LORD said to him, "Go down and bring Aaron up with you, but don't allow the priests or the people to force their way through. They must not come up to the LORD, or I will punish them."

²⁵So Moses went down to the people and told them these things.

The Ten Commandments

20 Then God spoke all these words: ²"I am the LORD your God, who brought you out of the land of Egypt where you were slaves.

³"You must not have any other gods except me.

⁴"You must not make for yourselves an idol that looks like anything in the sky above or on the earth below or in the water below the land. ⁵You must not worship or serve any idol, because I, the LORD your God, am a jealous God. If you hate me, I will punish your children, and even your grand-*children and great-grandchildren.* ⁶*But I show* kindness to thousands who love me and obey my commands.

⁷"You must not use the name of the LORD your God thoughtlessly; the LORD will punish anyone who misuses his name.

⁸"Remember to keep the Sabbath*ᵈ* holy. ⁹Work

and get everything done during six days each week, ¹⁰but the seventh day is a day of rest to honor the LORD your God. On that day no one may do any work: not you, your son or daughter, your male or female slaves, your animals, or the foreigners living in your cities. ¹¹The reason is that in six days the LORD made everything—the sky, the earth, the sea, and everything in them. On the seventh day he rested. So the LORD blessed the Sabbath day and made it holy.

¹²"Honor your father and your mother so that you will live a long time in the land that the LORD your God is going to give you.

¹³"You must not murder anyone.

¹⁴"You must not be guilty of adultery.*ᵈ*

¹⁵"You must not steal.

¹⁶"You must not tell lies about your neighbor.

¹⁷"You must not want to take your neighbor's house. You must not want his wife or his male or female slaves, or his ox or his donkey, or anything that belongs to your neighbor."

✸ **SIDELIGHT:** The Ten Commandments (Exodus 20:2–17) are twice as easy to find as most famous Bible passages. They're also listed in Deuteronomy 5:6–21 (p. 166), with only slight variations.

---

¹⁸When the people heard the thunder and the trumpet, and when they saw the lightning and the smoke rising from the mountain, they shook with fear and stood far away from the mountain. ¹⁹Then they said to Moses, "Speak to us yourself, and we will listen. But don't let God speak to us, or we will die."

²⁰Then Moses said to the people, "Don't be afraid, because God has come to test you. He wants you to respect him so you will not sin."

²¹The people stood far away from the mountain while Moses went near the dark cloud where God was. ²²Then the LORD told Moses to say these things to the Israelites: "You yourselves have seen that I talked with you from heaven. ²³You must not use gold or silver to make idols for yourselves; do not worship these gods in addition to me.

²⁴"Make an altar of dirt for me, and sacrifice on it your whole burnt offerings and fellowship offerings, your sheep and your cattle. Worship me in *every place that I choose, and I will come and* bless you. ²⁵If you use stones to make an altar for me, don't use stones that you have shaped with tools. When you use any tools on them, you make them unsuitable for use in worship. ²⁶And you must not go up to my altar on steps, or people will be able to see under your clothes."

Laws for Living

21 Then God said to Moses, "These are the laws for living that you will give to the Israelites:

²"If you buy a Hebrew slave, he will serve you for six years. In the seventh year you are to set him free, and he will have to pay nothing. ³If he is not married when he becomes your slave, he must leave without a wife. But if he is married when he becomes your slave, he may take his wife with him. ⁴If the slave's master gives him a wife, and she gives birth to sons or daughters, the woman and her children will belong to the master. When the slave is set free, only he may leave.

⁵"But if the slave says, 'I love my master, my wife and my children, and I don't want to go free,' ⁶then the slave's master must take him to God. The master is to take him to a door or doorframe and punch a hole through the slave's ear using a sharp tool. Then the slave will serve that master all his life.

⁷"If a man sells his daughter as a slave, the rules for setting her free are different from the rules for setting the male slaves free. ⁸If the master wanted to marry her but then decided he was not pleased

---

Following the Guidelines

"I just don't understand," Teresa Vasquez cried, sitting on her bed looking at the mail scattered around her. Three weeks earlier—right after Christmas—she'd written to colleges to begin applying for the fall. But her excitement dwindled as she opened each form letter.

"Dear student: Due to high interest last fall, we are out of catalogs. We will send you one when the new catalogs are available in April."

"Dear student: Our final date for admissions in the fall is January 10. Therefore, we will not be able to consider any more applications for this fall. We invite you to apply next year."

Even the schools that sent catalogs didn't sound too promising. First, several schools required four years of English in high school. She had quit English after her junior year because she didn't like the senior teacher. Then they wanted to know her Scholastic Aptitude Test (SAT) scores. She hadn't taken the test yet, and it wasn't being offered for another month.

She walked into the kitchen and slumped into a chair. "I don't get it," she complained to her dad. "Why do colleges have to have all these rules?"

"What would it be like if they didn't have rules?" her dad asked.

"Well, getting into college wouldn't be so hard," Teresa responded.

"If you didn't meet college entrance requirements, would you be able to keep up with college courses?" Dad continued.

"I guess not. But. . ."

"And what would have happened if you had started following the guidelines earlier?"

"Going to college would be a lot less hassle," Teresa finally admitted.

In the same way that following guidelines is necessary to get into college, following God's will is necessary to find meaning and purpose in life. Read the Ten Commandments in **Exodus 20:1—20** to learn what God requires of people.

- How does knowing a college's guidelines help students? How is that similar to knowing God's commandments?
- What do you think our world would be like if everyone followed the commandments in this passage?

C O N S I D E R . . .

- circling the commandment that's most difficult for you to follow. Then concentrate on following that commandment in the coming week.
- writing one key word from each commandment on a small card to keep in your purse or wallet as a reminder of God's will.

F O R   M O R E ,   S E E . . .

- Micah 6:6—8 (p. 866)
- Matthew 22:34—40 (p. 943)
- Romans 6:20—23 (p. 1148)

with her, he must let one of her close relatives buy her back. He has no right to sell her to foreigners, because he has treated her unfairly. ⁹If the man who bought her promises to let the woman marry his son, he must treat her as a daughter. ¹⁰If the man who bought her marries another woman, he must not keep his first wife from having food or clothing or sexual relations. ¹¹If he does not give her these three things, she may go free, and she owes him no money.

Laws About Injuries

¹²"Anyone who hits a person and kills him must be put to death. ¹³But if a person kills someone accidentally, God allowed that to happen, so the person must go to a place I will choose. ¹⁴But if someone plans and murders another person on purpose, put him to death, even if he has run to my altar for safety.

¹⁵"Anyone who hits his father or his mother must be put to death.

¹⁶"Anyone who kidnaps someone and either sells him as a slave or still has him when he is caught must be put to death.

¹⁷"Anyone who says cruel things to his father or mother must be put to death.

> ✳ **SIDELIGHT:** Did you know that "Honor your father and mother" is a two-part commandment? If you do, "you will live a long time." According to Israelite law, if you didn't honor them, you could be put to death (Exodus 21:17). And you thought being grounded was tough!

¹⁸"If two men argue, and one hits the other with a rock or with his fist, the one who is hurt but not killed might have to stay in bed. ¹⁹Later if he is able to get up and walk around outside with his walking stick, the one who hit him is not to be punished. But he must pay the injured man for the loss of his time, and he must support the injured man until he is completely healed.

²⁰"If a man beats his male or female slave with a stick, and the slave dies on the spot, the owner must be punished. ²¹But if the slave gets well after a day or two, the owner will not be punished since the slave belongs to him.

²²"Suppose two men are fighting and hit a pregnant woman, causing the baby to come out. If there is no further injury, the man who caused the accident must pay money—whatever amount the woman's husband says and the court allows. ²³But if there is further injury, then the punishment that must be paid is life for life, ²⁴eye for eye, tooth for tooth, hand for hand, foot for foot,

²⁵burn for burn, wound for wound, and bruise for bruise.

²⁶"If a man hits his male or female slave in the eye, and the eye is blinded, the man is to free the slave to pay for the eye. ²⁷If a master knocks out a tooth of his male or female slave, the man is to free the slave to pay for the tooth.

²⁸"If a man's bull kills a man or woman, you must kill that bull by throwing stones at it, and you should not eat the bull. But the owner of the bull is not guilty. ²⁹However, suppose the bull has hurt people in the past and the owner, though warned, did not keep it in a pen. Then if it kills a man or woman, the bull must be stoned to death, and the owner must also be put to death. ³⁰But if the family of the dead person accepts money, the one who owned the bull may buy back his life, but he must pay whatever is demanded. ³¹Use this same law if the bull kills a person's son or daughter. ³²If the bull kills a male or female slave, the owner must pay the master the price for a new slave, or twelve ounces of silver, and the bull must also be stoned to death.

³³"If a man takes the cover off a pit, or digs a pit and does not cover it, and another man's ox or donkey comes and falls into it, ³⁴the owner of the pit must pay the owner of the animal for the loss. The dead animal will belong to the one who pays.

³⁵"If a man's bull kills another man's bull, they must sell the bull that is alive. Both men will get half of the money and half of the bull that was killed. ³⁶But if a person's bull has hurt other animals in the past and the owner did not keep it in a pen, that owner must pay bull for bull, and the dead animal is his.

Property Laws

22 "If a man steals a bull or a sheep and kills or sells it, he must pay back five bulls for the one bull he stole and four sheep for the one sheep he stole.

²⁻⁴"The robber who is caught must pay back what he stole. If he owns nothing, he must be sold as a slave to pay for what he stole. If the stolen animal is found alive with the robber, he must give the owner two animals for every animal he stole, whether it was a bull, donkey, or sheep.

"If a thief is killed while breaking into a house at night, the one who killed him is not guilty of murder. But if this happens during the day, he is guilty of murder.

⁵"If a man lets his farm animal graze in his field or vineyard, and it wanders into another man's field or vineyard, the owner of the animal must pay back the loss from the best of his crop.

⁶"Suppose a man starts a fire that spreads through the thornbushes to his neighbor's field. If the fire burns his neighbor's growing grain or

grain that has been stacked, or if it burns his whole field, the person who started the fire must pay for what was burned.

⁷"Suppose a man gives his neighbor money or other things to keep for him and those things are stolen from the neighbor's house. If the thief is caught, he must pay back twice as much as he stole. ⁸But if the thief is never found, the owner of the house must make a promise before God that he has not stolen his neighbor's things.

⁹"Suppose two men disagree about who owns something—whether ox, donkey, sheep, clothing, or something else that is lost. If each says, 'This is mine,' each man must bring his case to God. God's judges will decide who is guilty, and that person must pay the other man twice as much as the object is worth.

¹⁰"Suppose a man asks his neighbor to keep his donkey, ox, sheep, or some other animal for him, and that animal dies, gets hurt, or is taken away, without anyone seeing what happened. ¹¹That neighbor must promise before the LORD that he did not harm or kill the other man's animal, and the owner of the animal must accept his promise made before God. The neighbor does not have to pay the owner for the animal. ¹²But if the animal was stolen from the neighbor, he must pay the owner for it. ¹³If wild animals killed it, the neighbor must bring the body as proof, and he will not have to pay for the animal that was killed.

¹⁴"If a man borrows an animal from his neighbor, and it gets hurt or dies while the owner is not there, the one who borrowed it must pay the owner for the animal. ¹⁵But if the owner is with the animal, the one who borrowed it does not have to pay. If the animal was rented, the rental price covers the loss.

Laws and Relationships

¹⁶"Suppose a man finds a woman who is not pledged to be married and has never had sexual relations with a man. If he tricks her into having sexual relations with him, he must give her family the payment to marry her, and she will become his wife. ¹⁷But if her father refuses to allow his daughter to marry him, the man must still give the usual payment for a bride who has never had sexual relations.

¹⁸"Put to death any woman who does evil magic.

¹⁹"Put to death anyone who has sexual relations with an animal.

²⁰"Destroy completely any person who makes a sacrifice to any god except the LORD.

²¹"Do not cheat or hurt a foreigner, because you were foreigners in the land of Egypt.

²²"Do not cheat a widow or an orphan. ²³If you do, and they cry out to me for help, I certainly will hear their cry. ²⁴And I will be very angry and kill

you in war. Then your wives will become widows, and your children will become orphans.

²⁵"If you lend money to one of my people who is poor, do not treat him as a moneylender would. Charge him nothing for using your money. ²⁶If your neighbor gives you his coat as a promise for the money he owes you, you must give it back to him by sunset, ²⁷because it is the only cover to keep his body warm. He has nothing else to sleep in. If he cries out to me for help, I will listen, because I am merciful.

²⁸"You must not speak against God or curse a leader of your people.

²⁹"Do not hold back your offering from the first of your harvest and the first wine that you make. Also, you must give me your firstborn*d* sons. ³⁰You must do the same with your bulls and your sheep. Let the firstborn males stay with their mothers for seven days, and on the eighth day you must give them to me.

³¹"You are to be my holy people. You must not eat the meat of any animal that has been killed by wild animals. Instead, give it to the dogs.

Laws About Fairness

23 "You must not tell lies. If you are a witness in court, don't help a wicked person by telling lies.

²"You must not do wrong just because everyone else is doing it. If you are a witness in court, you must not ruin a fair trial. You must not tell lies just because everyone else is. ³If a poor person is in court, you must not take his side just because he is poor

⁴"If you see your enemy's ox or donkey wandering away, you must return it to him. ⁵If you see that your enemy's donkey has fallen because its load is too heavy, do not leave it there. You must help your enemy get the donkey back on its feet.

⁶"You must not be unfair to a poor person when he is in court. ⁷You must not lie when you accuse someone in court. Never allow an innocent or honest person to be put to death as punishment, because I will not treat guilty people as if they were innocent.

⁸"You must not accept money from a person who wants you to lie in court, because such money will not let you see what is right. Such money makes good people tell lies.

⁹"You must not mistreat a foreigner. You know how it feels to be a foreigner, because you were foreigners in Egypt.

Laws for the Sabbath

¹⁰"For six years you are to plant and harvest crops on your land. ¹¹Then during the seventh year, do not plow or plant your land. If any food grows there, allow the poor people to have it, and let the wild animals eat what is left. You should

do the same with your vineyards and your orchards of olive trees.

12"You should work six days a week, but on the seventh day you must rest. This lets your ox and your donkey rest, and it also lets the slave born in your house and the foreigner be refreshed.

13"Be sure to do all that I have said to you. You must not even say the names of other gods; those names must not come out of your mouth.

Three Yearly Feasts

14"Three times each year you must hold a feast to honor me. 15You must celebrate the Feast*d* of Unleavened Bread in the way I commanded you. For seven days you must eat bread that is made without yeast at the set time during the month of Abib,*d* the month when you came out of Egypt. No one is to come to worship me without bringing an offering.

16"You must celebrate the Feast*d* of Weeks. Offer to God the first things you harvest from the crops you planted in your fields.

"You must celebrate the Feast*d* of Shelters in the fall, when you gather all the crops from your fields.

17"So three times during every year all your males must come to worship the LORD God.

18"You must not offer animal blood along with anything that has yeast in it.

"You must not save any of the fat from the sacrifice for the next day.

19"You must bring the best of the firstfruits*d* of your land to the Holy Tent*n* of the LORD your God.

"You must not cook a young goat in its mother's milk.

God Will Help Israel

20"I am sending an angel ahead of you, who will protect you as you travel. He will lead you to the place I have prepared. 21Pay attention to the angel and obey him. Do not turn against him; he will not forgive such turning against him because my power is in him. 22If you listen carefully to all he says and do everything that I tell you, I will be an enemy to your enemies. I will fight all who fight against you. 23My angel will go ahead of you and take you into the land of the Amorites, Hittites, Perizzites, Canaanites, Hivites, and Jebusites, and I will destroy them.

24"You must not bow down to their gods or worship them. You must not live the way those people live. You must destroy their idols, breaking into pieces the stone pillars they use in worship. 25If you worship the LORD your God, I will bless your bread and your water. I will take away sickness from you. 26None of your women will have

her baby die before it is born, and all women will have children. I will allow you to live long lives.

27"I will make your enemies afraid of me. I will confuse any people you fight against, and I will make all your enemies run away from you. 28I will send terror ahead of you that will force the Hivites, Canaanites, and Hittites out of your way. 29But I will not force all those people out in only one year. If I did, the land would become a desert and the wild animals would become too many for you. 30Instead, I will force those people out slowly, until there are enough of you to take over the land.

31"I will give you the land from the Red Sea to the Mediterranean Sea, and from the desert to the Euphrates River. I will give you power over the people who now live in the land, and you will force them out ahead of you. 32You must not make an agreement with those people or with their gods. 33You must not let them live in your land, or they will make you sin against me. If you worship their gods, you will be caught in a trap."

God and Israel Make Their Agreement

24 The LORD told Moses, "You, Aaron, Nadab, Abihu, and seventy of the older leaders of Israel must come up to me and worship me from a distance. 2Then Moses alone must come near me; the others must not come near. The rest of the people must not come up the mountain with Moses."

3Moses told the people all the LORD's words and laws for living. Then all of the people answered out loud together, "We will do all the things the LORD has said." 4So Moses wrote down all the words of the LORD. And he got up early the next morning and built an altar near the bottom of the mountain. He set up twelve stones, one stone for each of the twelve tribes*d* of Israel. 5Then Moses sent young Israelite men to offer whole burnt offerings and to sacrifice young bulls as fellowship offerings to the LORD. 6Moses put half of the blood of these animals in bowls, and he sprinkled the other half of the blood on the altar. 7Then he took the Book of the Agreement and read it so the people could hear him. And they said, "We will do everything that the LORD has said; we will obey."

8Then Moses took the blood from the bowls and sprinkled it on the people, saying, "This is the blood that begins the Agreement, the Agreement which the LORD has made with you about all these words."

9Moses, Aaron, Nadab, Abihu, and seventy of the older leaders of Israel went up the mountain 10and saw the God of Israel. Under his feet was a surface that looked as if it were paved with blue

Holy Tent Literally, "house of the LORD your God." See Exodus 25:9.

sapphire stones, and it was as clear as the sky! [11]These leaders of the Israelites saw God, but God did not destroy them. Then they ate and drank together.

God Promises Moses the Stone Tablets

[12]The LORD said to Moses, "Come up the mountain to me. Wait there, and I will give you two stone tablets. On these are the teachings and the commands I have written to instruct the people."

[13]So Moses and his helper Joshua set out, and Moses went up to Sinai, the mountain of God. [14]Moses said to the older leaders, "Wait here for us until we come back to you. Aaron and Hur are with you, and anyone who has a disagreement with others can take it to them."

Moses Meets with God

[15]When Moses went up on the mountain, the cloud covered it. [16]The glory of the LORD came down on Mount Sinai, and the cloud covered it for six days. On the seventh day the LORD called to Moses from inside the cloud. [17]To the Israelites the glory of the LORD looked like a fire burning on top of the mountain. [18]Then Moses went into the cloud and went higher up the mountain. He was on the mountain for forty days and forty nights.

Gifts for the Lord

25

The LORD said to Moses, [2]"Tell the Israelites to bring me gifts. Receive for me the gifts each person wants to give. [3]These are the gifts that you should receive from them: gold, silver, bronze; [4]blue, purple, and red thread; fine linen, goat hair; [5]sheepskins that are dyed red; fine leather; acacia wood; [6]olive oil to burn in the lamps; spices for sweet-smelling incense,[d] and the special olive oil poured on a person's head to make him a priest; [7]onyx stones, and other jewels to be put on the holy vest[d] and the chest covering.

[8]"The people must build a holy place for me so that I can live among them. [9]Build this Holy Tent[d] and everything in it by the plan I will show you.

The Ark of the Agreement

[10]"Use acacia wood and build an Ark[d] forty-five inches long, twenty-seven inches wide, and twenty-seven inches high. [11]Cover the Ark inside and out with pure gold, and put a gold strip all around it. [12]Make four gold rings for the Ark and attach them to its four feet, two rings on each side. [13]Then make poles from acacia wood and cover them with gold. [14]Put the poles through the rings on the sides of the Ark, and use these poles to carry it. [15]These poles must always stay in the rings of the Ark. Do not take them out. [16]Then put in the Ark the Agreement which I will make with you.

[17]"Then make a lid of pure gold for the Ark; this is the mercy seat.[d] Make it forty-five inches long and twenty-seven inches wide. [18]Then hammer gold to make two creatures with wings, and put one on each end of the lid. [19]Attach one creature on one end of the lid and the other creature on the other end. Make them to be one piece with the lid at the ends. [20]The creatures' wings should be spread upward, covering the lid, and the creatures are to face each other across the lid. [21]Put this lid on top of the Ark, and put in the Ark the Agreement which I will make with you. [22]I will meet with you there, above the lid between the two winged creatures on the Ark of the Agreement. There I will give you all my commands for the Israelites.

The Table

[23]"Make a table out of acacia wood, thirty-six inches long, eighteen inches wide, and twenty-seven inches high. [24]Cover it with pure gold, and put a gold strip around it. [25]Make a frame three inches high that stands up all around the edge, and put a gold strip around it. [26]Then make four gold rings. Attach them to the four corners of the table where the four legs are. [27]Put the rings close to the frame around the top of the table, because they will hold the poles for carrying it. [28]Make the poles out of acacia wood, cover them with gold, and carry the table with these poles. [29]Make the plates and bowls for the table, as well as the jars and cups, out of pure gold. They will be used for pouring out the drink offerings. [30]On this table put the bread that shows you are in my presence so that it is always there in front of me.

The Lampstand

[31]"Hammer pure gold to make a lampstand. Its base, stand, flower-like cups, buds, and petals must all be joined together in one piece. [32]The lampstand must have six branches going out from its sides—three on one side and three on the other. [33]Each branch must have three cups shaped like almond flowers on it. Each cup must have a bud and a petal. Each of the six branches going out from the lampstand must be the same. [34]And there must be four more cups made like almond flowers on the lampstand itself. These cups must also have buds and petals. [35]Put a bud under each pair of branches that goes out from the lampstand. Each of the six branches going out from the lampstand must be the same. [36]The branches, buds, and lampstand must be made of one piece, hammered out of pure gold.

[37]"Then make seven small oil lamps and put them on the lampstand so that they give light to the area in front of it. [38]The wick trimmers and trays must be made of pure gold. [39]Use seventy-five pounds of pure gold to make the lampstand

and everything with it. ⁴⁰Be very careful to make them by the plan I showed you on the mountain.

The Holy Tent

26 "Make for the Holy Tent^d ten curtains of fine linen and blue, purple, and red thread. Have a skilled craftsman sew designs of creatures with wings on the pieces of cloth. ²Make each curtain the same size — forty-two feet long and six feet wide. ³Sew five curtains together for one set, and sew the other curtains together for the second set. ⁴Make loops of blue cloth on the edge of the end curtain of one set, and do the same for the end curtain of the other set. ⁵Make fifty loops on the end curtain of the first set and fifty loops on the end curtain of the second set. These loops must be opposite each other. ⁶And make fifty gold hooks to join the two sets of curtains so that the Holy Tent is one piece.

⁷"Then make another tent that will cover the Holy Tent, using eleven curtains made from goat hair. ⁸All these curtains must be the same size — forty-five feet long and six feet wide. ⁹Sew five of the curtains together into one set. Then sew the other six curtains together into the second set. Fold the sixth curtain double over the front of the Tent. ¹⁰Make fifty loops down the edge of the end curtain of one set, and do the same for the end curtain of the other set. ¹¹Then make fifty bronze hooks and put them in the loops to join the tent together so that the covering is one piece. ¹²Let the extra half piece of cloth hang over the back of the Holy Tent. ¹³There will be eighteen inches hanging over the sides of the Holy Tent, to protect it. ¹⁴Make a covering for the Holy Tent from sheepskins colored red, and over that make a covering from fine leather.

¹⁵"Use acacia wood to make upright frames for the Holy Tent. ¹⁶Each frame must be fifteen feet long and twenty-seven inches wide, ¹⁷with two pegs side by side. Every frame must be made the same way. ¹⁸Make twenty frames for the south side of the Holy Tent. ¹⁹Each frame must have two silver bases to go under it, a peg fitting into each base. You must make forty silver bases for the frames. ²⁰Make twenty more frames for the north side of the Holy Tent ²¹and forty silver bases for them — two bases for each frame. ²²You must make six frames for the rear or west end of the Holy Tent ²³and two frames for each corner at the rear. ²⁴The two frames are to be doubled at the bottom and joined at the top with a metal ring. *Both corner frames must be made this way.* ²⁵So there will be a total of eight frames at the rear of the Tent, and there will be sixteen silver bases — two bases under each frame.

²⁶"Make crossbars of acacia wood to connect the upright frames of the Holy Tent. Make five crossbars to hold the frames together on one side

²⁷and five to hold the frames together on the other side. Also make five crossbars to hold the frames together on the west end, at the rear. ²⁸The middle crossbar is to be set halfway up the frames, and it is to run along the entire length of each side and rear. ²⁹Make gold rings on the sides of the frames to hold the crossbars, and cover the frames and the crossbars with gold. ³⁰Set up the Holy Tent by the plan shown to you on the mountain.

³¹"Make a curtain of fine linen and blue, purple, and red thread, and have a skilled craftsman sew designs of creatures with wings on it. ³²Hang the curtain by gold hooks on four posts of acacia wood that are covered with gold, and set them in four silver bases. ³³Hang the curtain from the hooks in the roof, and put the Ark^d of the Agreement containing the two stone tablets behind it. This curtain will separate the Holy Place from the Most Holy Place. ³⁴Put the lid on the Ark of the Agreement in the Most Holy Place.

³⁵"Outside the curtain, put the table on the north side of the Holy Tent. Put the lampstand on the south side of the Holy Tent across from the table.

The Entrance of the Holy Tent

³⁶"Then, for the entrance of the Tent,^d make a curtain with fine linen and blue, purple, and red thread. Someone who can sew well is to sew designs on it. ³⁷Make five posts of acacia wood covered with gold. Make gold hooks for them on which to hang the curtain, and make five bronze bases for them.

The Altar for Burnt Offerings

27 "Make an altar of acacia wood, four and one-half feet high. It should be square — seven and one-half feet long and seven and one-half feet wide. ²Make each of the four corners of the altar stick out like a horn, in such a way that the corners with their horns are all one piece. Then cover the whole altar with bronze.

³"Use bronze to make all the tools and dishes that will be used on the altar: the pots to remove the ashes, the shovels, the bowls for sprinkling blood, the meat forks, and the pans for carrying the burning wood. ⁴"Make a large bronze screen to hold the burning wood, and put a bronze ring at each of the four corners of it. ⁵Put the screen inside the altar, *under its rim, halfway up from the bottom.*

⁶"Make poles of acacia wood for the altar, and cover them with bronze. ⁷Put the poles through the rings on both sides of the altar to carry it. ⁸Make the altar out of boards and leave the inside hollow. Make it as you were shown on the mountain.

The Courtyard of the Holy Tent

9"Make a wall of curtains to form a courtyard around the Holy Tent.^d The south side should have a wall of fine linen curtains one hundred fifty feet long. ¹⁰Hang the curtain with silver hooks and bands on twenty bronze posts with twenty bronze bases. ¹¹The north side must also be one hundred fifty feet long. Hang its curtains on silver hooks and bands on twenty bronze posts with twenty bronze bases.

¹²"The west end of the courtyard must have a wall of curtains seventy-five feet long, with ten posts and ten bases on that wall. ¹³The east end of the courtyard must also be seventy-five feet long. ¹⁴On one side of the entry, there is to be a wall of curtains twenty-two and one-half feet long, held up by three posts on three bases. ¹⁵On the other side of the entry, there is also to be a wall of curtains twenty-two and one-half feet long, held up by three posts on three bases.

¹⁶"The entry to the courtyard is to be a curtain thirty feet wide, made of fine linen with blue, purple, and red thread. Someone who can sew well is to sew designs on it. It is to be held up by four posts on four bases. ¹⁷All the posts around the courtyard must have silver bands and hooks and bronze bases. ¹⁸The courtyard must be one hundred fifty feet long and seventy-five feet wide, with a wall of curtains around it seven and one-half feet high, made of fine linen. The bases in which the posts are set must be bronze. ¹⁹All the things used in the Holy Tent and all the tent pegs for the Holy Tent and the wall around the courtyard must be made of bronze.

Oil for the Lamp

²⁰"Command the people of Israel to bring you pure olive oil, made from pressed olives, to keep the lamps on the lampstand burning. ²¹Aaron and his sons must keep the lamps burning before the LORD from evening till morning. This will be in the Meeting Tent,^d outside the curtain which is in front of the Ark.^d The Israelites and their descendants^d must obey this rule from now on.

Clothes for the Priests

28 "Tell your brother Aaron to come to you, along with his sons Nadab, Abihu, Eleazar, and Ithamar. Separate them from the other Israelites to serve me as priests. ²Make holy clothes for your brother Aaron to give him honor and beauty. ³Tell all the skilled craftsmen to whom I have given wisdom to make special clothes for Aaron—clothes to show that he belongs to me so that he may serve me as a priest. ⁴These are the clothes they must make: a chest covering, a holy vest,^d an outer robe, a woven inner robe, a turban, and a cloth belt. The crafts-

men must make these holy clothes for your brother Aaron and his sons. Then they may serve me as priests. ⁵The craftsmen must use gold and blue, purple and red thread, and fine linen.

The Holy Vest

⁶"Use gold and blue, purple and red thread, and fine linen to make the holy vest;^d skilled craftsmen are to make it. ⁷At each top corner of this holy vest there will be a pair of shoulder straps tied together over each shoulder.

⁸"The craftsmen will very carefully weave a belt on the holy vest that is made with the same materials—gold and blue, purple and red thread, and fine linen.

⁹"Take two onyx stones and write the names of the twelve sons of Israel on them, ¹⁰six on one stone and six on the other. Write the names in order, from the oldest son to the youngest. ¹¹Carve the names of the sons of Israel on these stones in the same way a person carves words and designs on a seal.^d Put gold around the stones to hold them on the holy vest. ¹²Then put the two stones on the two straps of the holy vest as reminders of the twelve sons of Israel. Aaron is to wear their names on his shoulders in the presence of the LORD as reminders of the sons of Israel. ¹³Make two gold pieces to hold the stones ¹⁴and two chairs of pure gold, twisted together like a rope. Attach the chains to the two gold pieces that hold the stones.

The Chest Covering

¹⁵"Make a chest covering to help in making decisions. The craftsmen should make it as they made the holy vest,^d using gold and blue, purple and red thread, and fine linen. ¹⁶The chest covering must be square—nine inches long and nine inches wide—and folded double to make a pocket. ¹⁷Put four rows of beautiful gems on the chest covering: The first row must have a ruby, topaz, and yellow quartz; ¹⁸the second must have turquoise, a sapphire, and an emerald; ¹⁹the third must have a jacinth, an agate, and an amethyst; ²⁰the fourth must have a chrysolite, an onyx, and a jasper. Put gold around these jewels to attach them to the chest covering. ²¹There must be twelve jewels on the chest covering—one jewel for each of the names of the sons of Israel. Carve the name of one of the twelve tribes^d on each of the stones as you would carve a seal.^d

²²"Make chains of pure gold, twisted together like rope, for the chest covering. ²³Make two gold rings and put them on the two upper corners of the chest covering. ²⁴Attach the two gold chains to the two rings at the upper corners of the chest covering. ²⁵Attach the other ends of the two chains to the two gold pieces on the shoulder straps in the front of the holy vest.

²⁶"Make two gold rings and put them at the two lower corners of the chest covering, on the inside edge next to the holy vest. ²⁷Make two more gold rings and attach them to the bottom of the shoulder straps in the front of the holy vest. Put them close to the seam above the woven belt of the holy vest. ²⁸Join the rings of the chest covering to the rings of the holy vest with blue ribbon, connecting it to the woven belt so the chest covering will not swing out from the holy vest.

²⁹"When Aaron enters the Holy Place, he will wear the names of the sons of Israel over his heart, on the chest covering that helps in making decisions. This will be a continual reminder before the LORD. ³⁰And put the Urim and Thummim*ᵈ* inside the chest covering so that they will be on Aaron's heart when he goes before the LORD. They will help in making decisions for the Israelites. So Aaron will always carry them with him when he is before the LORD.

³¹"Make the outer robe to be worn under the holy vest, using only blue cloth. ³²Make a hole in the center for Aaron's head, with a woven collar around the hole so it will not tear. ³³Make balls like pomegranates*ᵈ* of blue, purple, and red thread, and hang them around the bottom of the

---

SIDELIGHT: Worried about being noisy at church? Priests in the Old Testament had the opposite problem; they worried about being too quiet. So they wore special robes with bells on the bottom hem (Exodus 28:33–34). The bells may have been there so the priests wouldn't go into God's presence unannounced.

---

outer robe with gold bells between them. ³⁴All around the bottom of the outer robe there should be a gold bell and a pomegranate ball, a gold bell and a pomegranate ball. ³⁵Aaron must wear this robe when he serves as priest. The ringing of the bells will be heard when he enters and leaves the Holy Place before the LORD so that Aaron will not die.

³⁶"Make a strip of pure gold and carve these words on it as you would carve a seal:*ᵈ* 'Holy to the LORD.' ³⁷Use blue ribbon to tie it to the turban; put it on the front of the turban. ³⁸Aaron must wear this on his forehead. In this way, he will be blamed if anything is wrong with the gifts of the Israelites. Aaron must always wear this on his head so the LORD will accept the gifts of the people.

³⁹"Make the woven inner robe of fine linen, and make the turban of fine linen also. Make the cloth belt with designs sewn on it. ⁴⁰Also make

woven inner robes, cloth belts, and headbands for Aaron's sons, to give them honor and beauty. ⁴¹Put these clothes on your brother Aaron and his sons, and pour olive oil on their heads to appoint them as priests. Make them belong to me so they may serve me as priests.

⁴²"Make for them linen underclothes to cover them from the waist to the upper parts of the legs. ⁴³Aaron and his sons must wear these underclothes when they enter the Meeting Tent*ᵈ* and anytime they come near the altar to serve as priests in the Holy Place. If they do not wear these clothes, they will be guilty of wrong, and they will die. This will be a law that will last from now on for Aaron and all his descendants.*ᵈ*

Appointing the Priests

29 "This is what you must do to appoint Aaron and his sons to serve me as priests. Take one young bull and two male sheep that have nothing wrong with them. ²Use fine wheat flour without yeast to make bread, cakes mixed with olive oil, and wafers brushed with olive oil. ³Put these in one basket, and bring them along with the bull and two male sheep. ⁴Bring Aaron and his sons to the entrance of the Meeting Tent*ᵈ* and wash them with water. ⁵Take the clothes and dress Aaron in the inner robe and the outer robe of the holy vest.*ᵈ* Then put on him the holy vest and the chest covering, and tie the holy vest on him with its skillfully woven belt. ⁶Put the turban on his head, and put the holy crown on the turban. ⁷Take the special olive oil and pour it on his head to make him a priest.

⁸"Then bring his sons and put the inner robes on them. ⁹Put the headbands on their heads, and tie cloth belts around their waists. Aaron and his descendants*ᵈ* will be priests in Israel, according to a rule that will continue from now on. This is how you will appoint Aaron and his sons as priests.

¹⁰"Bring the bull to the front of the Meeting Tent, and Aaron and his sons must put their hands on the bull's head. ¹¹Then kill the bull before the LORD at the entrance to the Meeting Tent. ¹²Use your finger to put some of the bull's blood on the corners of the altar, and then pour the blood that is left at the bottom of the altar. ¹³Take all the fat that covers the inner organs, as well as the best part of the liver, both kidneys, and the fat around them, and burn them on the altar. ¹⁴Take the bull's meat, skin, and intestines, and burn them outside the camp. This is an offering to take away sin.

¹⁵"Take one of the male sheep, and have Aaron and his sons put their hands on its head. ¹⁶Kill it, and take its blood and sprinkle it on all four sides of the altar. ¹⁷Then cut it into pieces and wash its inner organs and its legs, putting them with its head and its other pieces. ¹⁸Burn the whole sheep

on the altar; it is a burnt offering made by fire to the Lord. Its smell is pleasing to the Lord.

19"Take the other male sheep, and have Aaron and his sons put their hands on its head. 20Kill it and take some of its blood. Put the blood on the bottom of the right ears of Aaron and his sons and on the thumbs of their right hands and on the big toes of their right feet. Then sprinkle the rest of the blood against all four sides of the altar. 21Take some of the blood from the altar, and mix it with the special oil used in appointing priests. Sprinkle this on Aaron and his clothes and on his sons and their clothes. This will show that Aaron and his sons and their clothes are given to my service.

22"Then take the fat from the male sheep, the fat tail, and the fat that covers the inner organs. In addition, take the best part of the liver, both kidneys, and the fat around them, and the right thigh. (This is the male sheep to be used in appointing priests.)

23"Then take the basket of bread that you made without yeast, which you put before the Lord. From it take a loaf of bread, a cake made with olive oil, and a wafer. 24Put all of these in the hands of Aaron and his sons, and tell them to present them as an offering to the Lord. 25Then take them from their hands and burn them on the altar with the whole burnt offering. This is an offering made by fire to the Lord; its smell is pleasing to the Lord. 26Then take the breast of the male sheep used to appoint Aaron as priest, and present it before the Lord as an offering. This part of the animal will be your share. 27Set aside the breast and the thigh of the sheep that were used to appoint Aaron and his sons as priests. These parts belong to them. 28They are to be the regular share which the Israelites will always give to Aaron and his sons. It is the gift the Israelites must give to the Lord from their fellowship offerings.

29"The holy clothes made for Aaron will belong to his descendants so that they can wear these clothes when they are appointed as priests. 30Aaron's son, who will become high priest after Aaron, will come to the Meeting Tent to serve in the Holy Place. He is to wear these clothes for seven days.

31"Take the male sheep used to appoint priests and boil its meat in a place that is holy. 32Then at the entrance of the Meeting Tent, Aaron and his sons must eat the meat of the sheep and the bread that is in the basket. 33They should eat these offerings that were used to remove their sins and to make them holy when they were made priests. But no one else is to eat them, because they are holy things. 34If any of the meat from that sheep or any of the bread is left the next morning, it must be burned. It must not be eaten, because it is holy.

35"Do all these things that I commanded you to do to Aaron and his sons, and spend seven days appointing them. 36Each day you are to offer a bull to remove the sins of Aaron and his sons so they will be given for service to the Lord. Make the altar ready for service to the Lord, and pour oil on it to make it holy. 37Spend seven days making the altar ready for service to God and making it holy. Then the altar will become very holy, and anything that touches it must be holy.

The Daily Sacrifices

38"Every day from now on, offer on the altar two lambs that are one year old. 39Offer one lamb in the morning and the other in the evening before dark 40In the morning, when you offer the first lamb offer also two quarts of fine flour mixed with one quart of oil from pressed olives. Pour out a quart of wine as a drink offering. 41Offer the second lamb in the evening with the same grain offering and drink offering as you did in the morning. This is an offering made by fire to the Lord, and its smell is pleasing to him.

42"You must burn these things as an offering to the Lord every day, from now on, at the entrance of the Meeting Tent[d] before the Lord. When you make the offering, I, the Lord, will meet you there and speak to you. 43I will meet with the people of Israel there, and that place will be holy because of my glory.

44"So I will make the Meeting Tent and the altar holy; I will also make Aaron and his sons holy so they may serve me as priests. 45I will live with the people of Israel and be their God. 46And they will know that I am the Lord their God who led them out of Egypt so that I could live with them. I am the Lord their God.

The Altar for Burning Incense

30 "Make an altar out of acacia wood for burning incense.[d] 2Make it square— eighteen inches long and eighteen inches wide— and make it thirty-six inches high. The corners that stick out like horns must be one piece with the altar. 3Cover its top, its sides, and its corners with pure gold, and put a gold strip all around the altar. 4Make two gold rings beneath the gold strip on opposite sides of the altar, and slide poles through them to carry the altar. 5Make the poles from acacia wood and cover them with gold. 6Put the altar of incense in front of the curtain that is near the Ark[d] of the Agreement, in front of the lid that covers that Ark. There I will meet with you.

7"Aaron must burn sweet-smelling incense on the altar every morning when he comes to take care of the oil lamps. 8He must burn incense again in the evening when he lights the lamps, so incense will burn before the Lord every day from now on. 9Do not use this altar for offering any other incense, or burnt offering, or any kind of grain offering, or drink offering. [10]Once a year Aaron must make the altar ready for service to God by putting blood on its corners—the blood of the animal offered to remove sins. He is to do this once a year from now on. This altar belongs completely to the LORD's service."

The Tax for the Meeting Tent

[11]The LORD said to Moses, [12]"When you count the people of Israel, every person must buy back his life from the LORD so that no terrible things will happen to the people when you number them. [13]Every person who is counted must pay one-fifth of an ounce of silver. (This is set by using one-half of the Holy Place measure, which weighs two-fifths of an ounce.) This amount is a gift to the LORD. [14]Every person who is counted and is twenty years old or older must give this amount to the LORD. [15]A rich person must not give more than one-fifth of an ounce, and a poor person must not give less. You are paying this to the LORD to buy back your lives. [16]Gather from the people of Israel this money paid to buy back their lives, and spend it on things for the service in the Meeting Tent.[d] This payment will remind the LORD that the Israelites' lives have been bought back."

The Bronze Bowl

[17]The LORD said to Moses, [18]"Make a bronze bowl, on a bronze stand, for washing. Put the bowl and stand between the Meeting Tent[d] and the altar, and put water in the bowl. [19]Aaron and his sons must wash their hands and feet with the water from this bowl. [20]Each time they enter the Meeting Tent they must wash with water so they will not die. Whenever they approach the altar to serve as priests and offer a sacrifice to the LORD by fire, [21]they must wash their hands and their feet so they will not die. This is a rule which Aaron and his descendants[d] are to keep from now on."

Oil for Appointing

[22]Then the LORD said to Moses, [23]"Take the finest spices: twelve pounds of liquid myrrh,[d] half that amount (that is, six pounds) of sweet-smelling cinnamon, six pounds of sweet-smelling cane, [24]and twelve pounds of cassia.[d] Weigh all these by the Holy Place measure. Also take four quarts of olive oil, [25]and mix all these things like a perfume to make a holy olive oil. This special oil must be put on people and things to make them ready for service to God. [26]Put this oil on the Meeting Tent[d] and the Ark[d] of the Agreement, [27]on the table and all its dishes, on the lampstand and all its tools, and on the incense[d] altar. [28]Also, put the oil on the altar for burnt offerings and on all its tools, as well as on the bowl and the stand under the bowl. [29]You will prepare all these

things for service to God, and they will be very holy. Anything that touches these things must be holy.

[30]"Put the oil on Aaron and his sons to give them for service to me, that they may serve me as priests. [31]Tell the Israelites, 'This is to be my holy olive oil from now on. It is to be put on people and things to make them ready for service to God. [32]Do not pour it on the bodies of ordinary people, and do not make perfume the same way you make this oil. It is holy, and you must treat it as holy. [33]If anyone makes perfume like it or puts it on someone who is not a priest, that person must be cut off from his people.' "

Incense

[34]Then the LORD said to Moses, "Take these sweet-smelling spices: resin, onycha, galbanum, and pure frankincense.[d] Be sure that you have equal amounts of each. [35]Make incense[d] as a person who makes perfume would do. Add salt to it to keep it pure and holy. [36]Beat some of the incense into a fine powder, and put it in front of the Ark[d] of the Agreement in the Meeting Tent,[d] where I will meet with you. You must use this incense powder only for its very special purpose. [37]Do not make incense for yourselves the same way you make this incense. Treat it as holy to the LORD. [38]Whoever makes incense like this to use as perfume must be cut off from his people."

✳ SIDELIGHT: Kentucky Fried Chicken isn't the first company to have a secret recipe. In ancient Israel, priests had a secret recipe for the spices in the holy incense (Exodus 30:34–38). Three of the ingredients—resin, galbanum, and frankincense—were extracted from plants or trees. Onycha came from a shellfish in the Red Sea.

Bezalel and Oholiab Help

31 Then the LORD said to Moses, [2]"See, I have chosen Bezalel son of Uri from the tribe[d] of Judah. (Uri was the son of Hur.) [3]I have filled Bezalel with the Spirit[d] of God and have given him the skill, ability, and knowledge to do all kinds of work. [4]He is able to design pieces to be made from gold, silver, and bronze, [5]to cut jewels and put them in metal, to carve wood, and to do all kinds of work. [6]I have also chosen Oholiab son of Ahisamach from the tribe of Dan to work with Bezalel. I have given skills to all the craftsmen, and they will be able to make all these things I have commanded you: [7]the Meeting Tent,[d] the Ark[d] of the Agreement, the lid that covers the Ark, and everything in the Tent. ⁸This includes the table and everything on it, the pure gold lampstand and everything with it, the altar of incense,ᵈ ⁹the altar for burnt offerings and everything used with it, and the bowl and the stand under it. ¹⁰They will make the woven clothes and the holy clothes for Aaron and the clothes for his sons to wear when they serve as priests. ¹¹They will also make the special olive oil used in appointing people and things to the service of the LORD, and the sweet-smelling incense for the Holy Place.

"These workers will make all these things just as I have commanded you."

The Day of Rest

¹²Then the LORD said to Moses, ¹³"Tell the Israelites, 'You must keep the rules about my Sabbaths,ᵈ because they will be a sign between you and me from now on. In this way you will know that I, the LORD, make you holy.

¹⁴" 'Make the Sabbath a holy day. If anyone treats the Sabbath like any other day, that person must be put to death; anyone who works on the Sabbath day must be cut off from his people. ¹⁵There are six days for working, but the seventh day is a day of rest, a day holy for the LORD. Anyone who works during the Sabbath day must be put to death. ¹⁶The Israelites must remember the Sabbath day as an agreement between them and me that will continue from now on. ¹⁷The Sabbath day will be a sign between me and the Israelites forever, because in six days I, the LORD, made the sky and the earth. On the seventh day I did not work; I rested.' "

¹⁸When the LORD finished speaking to Moses on Mount Sinai, he gave him the two stone tablets with the Agreement written on them, written by the finger of God.

The People Make a Gold Calf

32 The people saw that a long time had passed and Moses had not come down from the mountain. So they gathered around Aaron and said, "Moses led us out of Egypt, but we don't know what has happened to him. Make us gods who will lead us."

²Aaron said to the people, "Take off the gold earrings that your wives, sons, and daughters are wearing, and bring them to me." ³So all the people took their gold earrings and brought them to Aaron. ⁴He took the gold from the people and formed it with a tool and made a statue of a calf. Then the people said, "Israel, these are your gods who brought you out of the land of Egypt!"

⁵When Aaron saw all this, he built an altar before the calf and announced, "Tomorrow there will be a special feast to honor the LORD." ⁶The people got up early the next morning and offered whole burnt offerings and fellowship offerings. They sat down to eat and drink, and then they got up and sinned sexually.

⁷Then the LORD said to Moses, "Go down from this mountain, because your people, the people you brought out of the land of Egypt, have ruined themselves. ⁸They have quickly turned away from the things I commanded them to do. They have made for themselves a calf covered with gold, and they have worshiped it and offered sacrifices to it. They have said, 'Israel, these are your gods who brought you out of Egypt.' "

⁹The LORD said to Moses, "I have seen these people, and I know that they are very stubborn. ¹⁰So now do not stop me. I am so angry with them that I am going to destroy them. Then I will make you and your descendantsᵈ a great nation."

¹¹But Moses begged the LORD his God and said, "LORD, don't let your anger destroy your people, whom you brought out of Egypt with your great power and strength. ¹²Don't let the people of Egypt say, 'The LORD brought the Israelites out of Egypt for an evil purpose. He planned to kill them in the mountains and destroy them from the earth.' So stop being angry, and don't destroy your people. ¹³Remember the men who served you—Abraham, Isaac, and Israel. You promised with an oath to them and said, 'I will make your descendants as many as the stars in the sky. I will give your descendants all this land that I have promised them, and it will be theirs forever.' "

¹⁴So the LORD changed his mind and did not destroy the people as he had said he might.

¹⁵Then Moses went down the mountain, and in his hands he had the two stone tablets with the Agreement on them. The commands were written on both sides of each stone, front and back. ¹⁶God himself had made the tablets, and God himself had written the commands on the tablets.

¹⁷When Joshua heard the sound of the people shouting, he said to Moses, "It sounds like war down in the camp."

¹⁸Moses answered:

"It is not a shout of victory;
  it is not a cry of defeat.
  It is the sound of singing that I hear."

¹⁹When Moses came close to the camp, he saw the gold calf and the dancing, and he became very angry. He threw down the stone tablets that he was carrying and broke them at the bottom of the mountain. ²⁰Then he took the calf that the people had made and melted it in the fire. He ground it into powder. Then he threw the powder into the water and forced the Israelites to drink it.

²¹Moses said to Aaron, "What did these people do to you? Why did you cause them to do such a terrible sin?"

²²Aaron answered, "Don't be angry, master. You know that these people are always ready to

do wrong. [23]The people said to me, 'Moses led us out of Egypt, but we don't know what has happened to him. Make us gods who will lead us.' [24]So I told the people, 'Take off your gold jewelry.' When they gave me the gold, I threw it into the fire and out came this calf!"

[25]Moses saw that the people were acting wildly. Aaron had let them get out of control and become fools in front of their enemies. [26]So Moses stood at the entrance to the camp and said, "Let anyone who wants to follow the LORD come to me." And all the people from the family of Levi gathered around Moses.

[27]Then Moses said to them, "The LORD, the God of Israel, says this: 'Every man must put on his sword and go through the camp from one end to the other. Each man must kill his brother, his friend, and his neighbor.' " [28]The people from the family of Levi obeyed Moses, and that day about three thousand of the Israelites died. [29]Then Moses said, "Today you have been given for service to the LORD. You were willing to kill your own sons and brothers, and God has blessed you for this."

[30]The next day Moses told the people, "You have done a terrible sin. But now I will go up to the LORD. Maybe I can do something so your sins will be removed." [31]So Moses went back to the LORD and said, "How terribly these people have sinned! They have made for themselves gods from gold. [32]Now, please forgive them of this sin. If you will not, then erase my name from the book in which you have written the names of your people."

[33]But the LORD told Moses, "I will erase from my book the names of the people who sin against

---

SIN

I Told You So

Tyrone Gilker carefully laid the extra pillows on his bed, fluffing them to make them look bigger. Then he covered them with the sheets and bedspread. "That should do it," he whispered as he shut off the light.

He tiptoed to the window and opened it carefully. Climbing out, he stretched his legs to reach the porch roof below, shimmied to the edge and climbed down the trellis, carefully avoiding the climbing roses.

Mark and Sandy were waiting in the Toyota around the corner. "No problem," Tyrone said, hopping into the back seat. "They'll never know I'm gone. Six Flags, here we come."

The three friends didn't plan to stay at the theme park too long, but they didn't want to completely miss the park's all-night extravaganza for graduating seniors. Tyrone had tried to get permission to go, but his parents wouldn't give him a later curfew. So he decided to go without them knowing.

It would have worked, except the trellis wasn't as strong as he had thought. When he returned home four hours later, his foot found a loose board, and he screamed, "Aaaaaaaaah!" as he tumbled into the roses.

When the light came on in his parents' room, Tyrone knew he was in trouble. What would happen now? he wondered as he sat on the lawn and waited for his dad to appear.

Tyrone knew what he was doing was wrong, but he did it anyway. Similarly, the Israelites knew they shouldn't build an idol to worship. Read **Exodus 32:1–14** to see what happened when they did it anyway.

■ What lesson might Tyrone have learned from the passage if he had read it before crawling out the window?

■ When have you, like the Israelites, doubted God's leadership and disobeyed him? What did you learn about trusting God from that experience?

CONSIDER . . .

■ praying that God will give you strength next time you're tempted to do something you know is wrong.

■ listening to popular songs on the radio to find out what things people trust instead of God. How is their misplaced trust sinful?

FOR MORE, SEE . . .

■ Deuteronomy 32:15–22 (p. 189)
■ 1 Kings 18:22–39 (p. 324)

■ Romans 6:1–7 (p. 1146)

me. [34]So now, go. Lead the people where I have told you, and my angel will lead you. When the time comes to punish, I will punish them for their sin."

[35]So the LORD caused terrible things to happen to the people because of what they did with the calf Aaron had made.

33

Then the LORD said to Moses, "You and the people you brought out of Egypt must leave this place. Go to the land that I promised with an oath to give to Abraham, Isaac, and Jacob when I said, 'I will give that land to your descendants.' [2]I will send an angel to lead you, and I will force these people out of the land: the Canaanites, Amorites, Hittites, Perizzites, Hivites, and Jebusites. [3]Go up to a fertile land. But I will not go with you, because I might destroy you on the way, since you are such a stubborn people."

[4]When the people heard this bad news, they became very sad, and none of them put on jewelry. [5]This was because the LORD had said to Moses, "Tell the Israelites, 'You are a stubborn people. If I were to go with you even for a moment, I would destroy you. So take off all your jewelry, and I will decide what to do with you.' " [6]So the people of Israel took off their jewelry at Mount Sinai.

The Meeting Tent

[7]Moses used to take a tent and set it up a long way outside the camp; he called it the "Meeting Tent."[d] Anyone who wanted to ask the LORD about something would go to the Meeting Tent outside the camp. [8]Whenever Moses went out to the Tent, all the people would rise and stand at the entrances of their tents, watching him until he entered the Meeting Tent. [9]When Moses went into the Tent, the pillar of cloud would always come down and stay at the entrance of the Tent while the LORD spoke with Moses. [10]Whenever the people saw the pillar of cloud at the entrance of the Tent, they stood and worshiped, each person at the entrance of his own tent.

[11]The LORD spoke to Moses face to face as a man speaks with his friend. Then Moses would return to the camp, but Moses' young helper, Joshua son of Nun, did not leave the Tent.

[12]Moses said to the LORD, "You have told me to lead these people, but you did not say whom you would send with me. You have said to me, 'I know you very well, and I am pleased with you.' [13]If I have truly pleased you, show me your plans so that I may know you and continue to please you. Remember that this nation is your people."

[14]The LORD answered, "I myself will go with you, and I will give you victory."

[15]Then Moses said to him, "If you yourself don't go with us, then don't send us away from this place. [16]If you don't go with us, no one will know that you are pleased with me and with your people. These people and I will be no different from any other people on earth."

[17]Then the LORD said to Moses, "I will do what you ask, because I know you very well, and I am pleased with you."

Moses Sees God's Glory

[18]Then Moses said, "Now, please show me your glory."

[19]The LORD answered, "I will cause all my goodness to pass in front of you, and I will announce my name, the LORD, so you can hear it. I will show kindness to anyone to whom I want to show kindness, and I will show mercy to anyone to whom I want to show mercy. [20]But you cannot see my face, because no one can see me and live.

[21]"There is a place near me where you may stand on a rock. [22]When my glory passes that place, I will put you in a large crack in the rock and cover you with my hand until I have passed by. [23]Then I will take away my hand, and you will see my back. But my face must not be seen."

Moses Gets New Stone Tablets

34

The LORD said to Moses, "Cut two more stone tablets like the first two, and I will write the same words on them that were on the first two stones which you broke. [2]Be ready tomorrow morning, and then come up on Mount Sinai. Stand before me there on the top of the mountain. [3]No one may come with you or even be seen any place on the mountain. Not even the flocks or herds may eat grass near that mountain."

[4]So Moses cut two stone tablets like the first ones. Then early the next morning he went up Mount Sinai, just as the LORD had commanded him, carrying the two stone tablets with him. [5]Then the LORD came down in the cloud and stood there with Moses, and the LORD called out his name the LORD.

[6]The LORD passed in front of Moses and said, "I am the LORD. The LORD is a God who shows mercy, who is kind, who doesn't become angry quickly, who has great love and faithfulness [7]and is kind to thousands of people. The LORD forgives people for evil, for sin, and for turning against him, but he does not forget to punish guilty people. He will punish not only the guilty people, but also their children, their grandchildren, their great-grandchildren, and their great-great-grandchildren."

[8]Then Moses quickly bowed to the ground and worshiped. [9]He said, "Lord, if you are pleased with me, please go with us. I know that these are stubborn people, but forgive our evil and our sin. Take us as your own people."

¹⁰Then the LORD said, "I am making this agreement with you. I will do miracles*ᵈ* in front of all your people — things that have never before been done for any other nation on earth — and the people with you will see my work. I, the LORD, will do wonderful things for you. ¹¹Obey the things I command you today, and I will force out the Amorites, Canaanites, Hittites, Perizzites, Hivites, and Jebusites ahead of you. ¹²Be careful that you don't make an agreement with the people who live in the land where you are going, because it will bring you trouble. ¹³Destroy their altars, break their stone pillars, and cut down their Asherah*ᵈ* idols. ¹⁴Don't worship any other god, because I, the LORD, the Jealous One, am a jealous God.

¹⁵"Be careful that you don't make an agreement with the people who live in that land. When they worship their gods, they will invite you to join them. Then you will eat their sacrifices. ¹⁶If you choose some of their daughters as wives for your sons and those daughters worship gods, they will lead your sons to do the same thing.

¹⁷"Do not make gods of melted metal.

¹⁸"Celebrate the Feast*ᵈ* of Unleavened Bread. For seven days you must eat bread made without yeast as I commanded you. Do this during the month I have chosen, the month of Abib,*ᵈ* because in that month you came out of Egypt.

¹⁹"The firstborn*ᵈ* of every mother belongs to me, including every firstborn male animal that is born in your flocks and herds. ²⁰You may buy back a donkey by paying for it with a lamb, but if you don't want to buy back a donkey, you must break its neck. You must buy back all your firstborn sons.

FORGIVENESS

Living With Consequences

Jay Jones had big plans for his life. When he graduated from high school, he would go to college to play basketball. He hoped to make it to the pros. If he didn't, he would go to law school and become a partner in his dad's firm.

Then Jay met Mindy at a school dance. They fell in love and became more and more involved. Even though they were Christians, they began having sex "because we love each other so much."

Several months passed. Then one day Mindy came to school sobbing. "I'm pregnant," she told Jay. "What am I going to do?"

As they talked—and cried—in the next few days, and faced up to their sin, they decided the best thing to do was to get married. They knew God would forgive them, but they also knew they would have to live with what they had done.

Jay quit the basketball team, dropped out of school, and started working at a fast-food restaurant to pay the doctor bills. He gave up his dream of playing pro basketball.

After the baby was born, Jay's life revolved around work and diapers. Sometimes he wanted to run away—to leave behind the stress and responsibility. But he didn't. Instead, he worked with Mindy to have the best possible family for their child.

By asking God's forgiveness, Jay and Mindy were able to keep going. But they had to live with what they had done. **Exodus 34:4–8** teaches that God forgives but doesn't take away the natural consequences of what we do.

■ How did God's forgiveness affect the way Jay and Mindy were able to work together to create their family? How might their relationship have been different if they hadn't sought God's forgiveness?

■ When have you asked for forgiveness but still had to live with the consequences of what you did? How did you feel?

C O N S I D E R . . .

■ making a chart that shows the consequences of a particular sin, such as premarital sex. Put the sin at the top and then list below it everything that might happen as a result. How does forgiveness affect the consequences?

■ asking God's forgiveness for something you have done, while also asking him to guide you as you deal responsibly with the consequences.

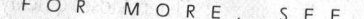

F O R   M O R E ,   S E E . . .

■ 2 Chronicles 6:24–31 (p. 390)
■ Psalm 51:1–13 (p. 511)

■ Luke 17:1–4 (p. 1039)

"No one is to come before me without a gift.

21"You must work for six days, but on the seventh day you must rest—even during the planting season and the harvest season.

22"Celebrate the Feast[d] of Weeks when you gather the first grain of the wheat harvest. And celebrate the Feast[d] of Shelters in the fall.

23"Three times each year all your males must come before the Lord God, the God of Israel. 24I will force out nations ahead of you and expand the borders of your land. You will go before the Lord your God three times each year, and at that time no one will try to take your land from you.

25"Do not offer the blood of a sacrifice to me with anything containing yeast, and do not leave any of the sacrifice of the Feast[d] of Passover until the next morning.

26"Bring the best first crops that you harvest from your ground to the Tent[d] of the Lord your God.

"You must not cook a young goat in its mother's milk."

27Then the Lord said to Moses, "Write down these words, because with these words I have made an agreement with you and Israel."

28Moses stayed there with the Lord forty days and forty nights, and during that time he did not eat food or drink water. And Moses wrote the words of the Agreement—the Ten Commandments—on the stone tablets.

The Face of Moses Shines

29Then Moses came down from Mount Sinai, carrying the two stone tablets of the Agreement in his hands. But he did not know that his face was shining because he had talked with the Lord. 30When Aaron and all the people of Israel saw that Moses' face was shining, they were afraid to go near him. 31But Moses called to them, so Aaron and all the leaders of the people returned to Moses, and he talked with them. 32After that, all the people of Israel came near him, and he gave them all the commands that the Lord had given him on Mount Sinai.

33When Moses finished speaking to the people, he put a covering over his face. 34Anytime Moses went before the Lord to speak with him, Moses took off the covering until he came out. Then Moses would come out and tell the Israelites what the Lord had commanded. 35They would see that Moses' face was shining. So he would cover his face again until the next time he went in to speak with the Lord.

Rules About the Sabbath

35

Moses gathered all the Israelite community together and said to them, "These are the things the Lord has commanded you to do. 2You are to work for six days, but the seventh day will be a holy day, a Sabbath[d] of rest to honor the Lord. Anyone who works on that day must be put to death. 3On the Sabbath day you must not light a fire in any of your houses."

4Moses said to all the Israelites, "This is what the Lord has commanded: 5From what you have, take an offering for the Lord. Let everyone who is willing bring this offering to the Lord: gold, silver, bronze, 6blue, purple and red thread, and fine linen, goat hair 7and male sheepskins that are colored red. They may also bring fine leather, acacia wood, 8olive oil for the lamps, spices for the special olive oil used for appointing priests and for the sweet-smelling incense,[d] 9onyx stones, and other jewels to be put on the holy vest[d] and chest covering of the priests.

10"Let all the skilled workers come and make everything the Lord commanded: 11the Holy Tent,[d] its outer tent and its covering, the hooks, frames, crossbars, posts, and bases; 12the Ark[d] of the Agreement, its poles, lid, and the curtain in front of it; 13the table, and its poles, all the things that go with the table, and the bread that shows we are in God's presence; 14the lamps and for the light and all the things that go with it, the lamps, and olive oil for the light; 15the altar of incense and its poles, the special oil and the sweet-smelling incense, the curtain for the entrance of the Meeting Tent; 16the altar of burnt offering and its bronze screen, its poles and all its tools, the bronze bowl and its base; 17the curtains around the courtyard, their posts and bases, and the curtain at the entry to the courtyard; 18the pegs of the Holy Tent and of the courtyard and their ropes; 19the special clothes that the priest will wear in the Holy Place. These are the holy clothes for Aaron the priest and his sons to wear when they serve as priests."

20Then all the people of Israel went away from Moses. 21Everyone who wanted to give came and brought a gift to the Lord for making the Meeting Tent, all the things in the Tent, and the special clothes. 22All the men and women who wanted to give brought gold jewelry of all kinds—pins, earrings, rings, and bracelets. They all presented their gold to the Lord. 23Everyone who had blue, purple, and red thread, and fine linen, and anyone who had goat hair or male sheepskins colored red or fine leather brought them to the Lord. 24Everyone who could give silver or bronze brought that as a gift to the Lord, and everyone who had acacia wood to be used in the work brought it. 25Every skilled woman used her hands to make the blue, purple, and red thread, and fine linen, and they brought what they had made. 26All the women who were skilled and wanted to help made thread of the goat hair. 27The leaders brought onyx stones and other jewels to put on the holy vest and chest covering for the priest.

²⁸They also brought spices and olive oil for the sweet-smelling incense, the special oil, and the oil to burn in the lamps. ²⁹All the men and women of Israel who wanted to help brought gifts to the LORD for all the work the LORD had commanded Moses and the people to do.

³⁰Then Moses said to the Israelites, "Look, the LORD has chosen Bezalel son of Uri the son of Hur, from the tribe*d* of Judah. ³¹The LORD has filled Bezalel with the Spirit*d* of God and has given him the skill, ability, and knowledge to do all kinds of work. ³²He is able to design pieces to be made of gold, silver, and bronze, ³³to cut stones and jewels and put them in metal, to carve wood, and to do all kinds of work. ³⁴Also, the LORD has given Bezalel and Oholiab, the son of Ahisamach from the tribe of Dan, the ability to teach others. ³⁵The LORD has given them the skill to do all kinds of work. They are able to cut designs in metal and stone. They can plan and sew designs in the fine linen with the blue, purple, and red thread. And

36 they are also able to weave things. ¹So Bezalel, Oholiab, and every skilled person will do the work the LORD has commanded, because he gave them the wisdom and understanding to do all the skilled work needed to build the Holy Tent."

²Then Moses called Bezalel, Oholiab, and all the other skilled people to whom the LORD had given skills, and they came because they wanted to help with the work. ³They received from Moses everything the people of Israel had brought as gifts to build the Holy Tent. The people continued to bring gifts each morning because they wanted to. ⁴So all the skilled workers left the work they were doing on the Holy Tent, ⁵and they said to Moses, "The people are bringing more than we need to do the work the LORD commanded."

⁶Then Moses sent this command throughout the camp: "No man or woman should make anything else as a gift for the Holy Tent." So the people were kept from giving more, ⁷because what they had was already more than enough to do all the work.

The Holy Tent

⁸Then the skilled workers made the Holy Tent.*d* They made the ten curtains of blue, purple, and red cloth, and they sewed designs of creatures with wings on the curtains. ⁹Each curtain was the same size — forty-two feet long and six feet wide. ¹⁰Five of the curtains were fastened together to make one set, and the other five were fastened together to make another set. ¹¹Then they made loops of blue cloth along the edge of the end curtain on the first set of five, and they did the same thing with the other set of five. ¹²There were fifty loops on one curtain and fifty loops on the other curtain, with the loops oppo-

site each other. ¹³They made fifty gold hooks to join the two curtains together so that the Holy Tent was joined together as one piece.

¹⁴Then the workers made another tent of eleven curtains made of goat hair, to put over the Holy Tent. ¹⁵All eleven curtains were the same size — forty-five feet long and six feet wide. ¹⁶The workers sewed five curtains together into one set and six together into another set. ¹⁷They made fifty loops along the edge of the outside curtain of one set and fifty loops along the edge of the outside curtain of the other set. ¹⁸Then they made fifty bronze rings to join the two sets of cloth together and make the tent one piece. ¹⁹They made two more coverings for the outer tent — one made of male sheepskins colored red and the other made of fine leather.

> ❋ **SIDELIGHT:** Goat hair was good material for building the Holy Tent (Exodus 36:14–19). When it's dry, it's open and airy, making it cooler inside. But when it rains, the goat hairs expand and keep out the moisture.

²⁰Then they made upright frames of acacia wood for the Holy Tent. ²¹Each frame was fifteen feet tall and twenty-seven inches wide, ²²and there were two pegs side by side on each one. Every frame of the Holy Tent was made this same way. ²³They made twenty frames for the south side of the Tent, ²⁴and they made forty silver bases that went under the twenty frames. There were two bases for every frame — one for each peg of each frame. ²⁵They also made twenty frames for the north side of the Holy Tent ²⁶and forty silver bases — two to go under each frame. ²⁷They made six frames for the rear or west end of the Holy Tent ²⁸and two frames for the corners at the rear of the Holy Tent. ²⁹These two frames were doubled at the bottom and joined at the top with a metal ring. They did this for each of these corners. ³⁰So there were eight frames and sixteen silver bases — two bases under each frame.

³¹Then they made crossbars of acacia wood to connect the upright frames of the Holy Tent. Five crossbars held the frames together on one side of the Tent, ³²and five held the frames together on the other side. Also, five crossbars held the frames together on the west end, at the rear of the Tent. ³³They made the middle crossbar run along the entire length of each side and rear of the Tent. It was set halfway up the frames. ³⁴They made gold rings on the sides of the frames to hold the crossbars, and they covered the frames and the crossbars with gold.

35Then they made the curtain of blue, purple, and red thread, and fine linen. A skilled craftsman sewed designs of creatures with wings on it. 36They made four posts of acacia wood for it and covered them with gold. Then they made gold hooks for the posts, as well as four silver bases in which to set the posts. 37For the entrance to the Tent, they made a curtain of blue, purple, and red thread, and fine linen. A person who sewed well sewed designs on it. 38Then they made five posts and hooks for it. They covered the tops of the posts and their bands with gold, and they made five bronze bases for the posts.

The Ark of the Agreement

37 Bezalel made the Ark*d* of acacia wood; it was forty-five inches long, twenty-seven inches wide, and twenty-seven inches high. 2He covered it, both inside and out, with pure gold, and he put a gold strip around it. 3He made four gold rings for it and attached them to its four feet, with two rings on each side. 4Then he made poles of acacia wood and covered them with gold. 5He put the poles through the rings on each side of the Ark to carry it. 6Then he made a lid of pure gold that was forty-five inches long and twenty-seven inches wide. 7Then Bezalel hammered gold to make two creatures with wings and attached them to each end of the lid. 8He made one creature on one end of the lid and the other creature on the other end. He attached them to the lid so that it would be one piece. 9The creatures' wings were spread upward, covering the lid, and the creatures faced each other across the lid.

The Table

10Then he made the table of acacia wood; it was thirty-six inches long, eighteen inches wide, and twenty-seven inches high. 11He covered it with pure gold and put a gold strip around it. 12He made a frame three inches high that stood up all around the edge, and he put a gold strip around it. 13Then he made four gold rings for the table and attached them to the four corners of the table where the four legs were. 14The rings were put close to the frame around the top of the table, because they held the poles for carrying it. 15The poles for carrying the table were made of acacia wood and were covered with gold. 16He made of pure gold all the things that were used on the table: the plates, bowls, cups, and jars used for pouring the drink offerings.

The Lampstand

17Then he made the lampstand of pure gold, hammering out its base and stand. Its flower-like cups, buds, and petals were joined together in one piece with the base and stand. 18Six branches

went out from the sides of the lampstand — three on one side and three on the other. 19Each branch had three cups shaped like almond flowers, and each cup had a bud and a petal. Each of the six branches going out from the lampstand was the same. 20There were four more cups shaped like almond flowers on the lampstand itself, each with its buds and petals. 21Three pairs of branches went out from the lampstand. A bud was under the place where each pair was attached to the lampstand. Each of the six branches going out from the lampstand was the same. 22The buds, branches, and lampstand were all one piece of pure, hammered gold. 23He made seven pure gold lamps for this lampstand, and he made pure gold wick trimmers and trays. 24He used about seventy-five pounds of pure gold to make the lampstand and all the things that go with it.

The Altar for Burning Incense

25Then he made the altar of incense*d* out of acacia wood. It was square — eighteen inches long and eighteen inches wide — and it was thirty-six inches high. Each corner that stuck out like a horn was joined into one piece with the altar. 26He covered the top and all the sides and the corners with pure gold, and he put gold trim around the altar. 27He made two gold rings and put them below the trim on opposite sides of the altar; these rings held the poles for carrying it. 28He made the poles of acacia wood and covered them with gold.

29Then he made the holy olive oil for appointing the priests and the pure, sweet-smelling incense. He made them like a person who mixes perfumes.

The Altar for Burnt Offerings

38 Then he built the altar for burnt offerings out of acacia wood. The altar was square — seven and one-half feet long and seven and one-half feet wide — and it was four and one-half feet high. 2He made each corner stick out like a horn so that the horns and the altar were joined together in one piece. Then he covered the altar with bronze. 3He made all the tools of bronze to use on the altar: the pots, shovels, bowls for sprinkling blood, meat forks, and pans for carrying the fire. 4He made a large bronze screen to hold the burning wood for the altar and put it inside the altar, under its rim, halfway up from the bottom. 5He made bronze rings to hold the poles for carrying the altar, and he put them at the four corners of the screen. 6Then he made poles of acacia wood and covered them with bronze. 7He put the poles through the rings on both sides of the altar, to carry it. He made the altar of boards and left the inside hollow.

The Bronze Bowl

⁸He made the bronze bowl for washing, and he built it on a bronze stand. He used the bronze from mirrors that belonged to the women who served at the entrance to the Meeting Tent.ᵈ

The Courtyard of the Holy Tent

⁹Then he made a wall of curtains to form a courtyard around the Holy Tent.ᵈ On the south side the curtains were one hundred fifty feet long and were made of fine linen. ¹⁰The curtains hung on silver hooks and bands, placed on twenty bronze posts with twenty bronze bases. ¹¹On the north side the wall of curtains was also one hundred fifty feet long, and it hung on silver hooks and bands on twenty posts with twenty bronze bases.

¹²On the west side of the courtyard, the wall of curtains was seventy-five feet long. It was held up by silver hooks and bands on ten posts with ten bases. ¹³The east side was also seventy-five feet long. ¹⁴On one side of the entry there was a wall of curtains twenty-two and one-half feet long, held up by three posts and three bases. ¹⁵On the other side of the entry there was also a wall of curtains twenty-two and one-half feet long, held up by three posts and three bases. ¹⁶All the curtains around the courtyard were made of fine linen. ¹⁷The bases for the posts were made of bronze. The hooks and the bands on the posts were made of silver, and the tops of the posts were covered with silver also. All the posts in the courtyard had silver bands.

¹⁸The curtain for the entry of the courtyard was made of blue, purple, and red thread, and fine linen, sewn by a person who could sew well. The curtain was thirty feet long and seven and one-half feet high, the same height as the curtains around the courtyard. ¹⁹It was held up by four posts and four bronze bases. The hooks and bands on the posts were made of silver, and the tops on the posts were covered with silver. ²⁰All the tent pegs for the Holy Tent and for the curtains around the courtyard were made of bronze.

²¹This is a list of the materials used to make the Holy Tent, where the Agreement is kept. Moses ordered the Levites to make this list, and Ithamar son of Aaron was in charge of keeping it. ²²Bezalel son of Uri, the son of Hur of the tribeᵈ of Judah, made everything the LORD commanded Moses. ²³Oholiab son of Ahisamach of the tribe of Dan helped him. He could cut designs into metal and stone; he was a designer and also skilled at sewing the blue, purple, and red thread, and fine linen.

²⁴The total amount of gold used to build the Holy Tent was presented to the LORD. It weighed over 2,000 pounds, as set by the Holy Place measure.

²⁵The silver was given by the members of the community who were counted. It weighed 7,550 pounds, as set by the Holy Place measure. ²⁶All the men twenty years old or older were counted. There were 603,550 men, and each man had to pay one-fifth of an ounce of silver, as set by the Holy Place measure. ²⁷Of this silver, 7,500 pounds were used to make the one hundred bases for the Holy Tent and for the curtain — 75 pounds of silver in each base. ²⁸They used 50 pounds of silver to make the hooks for the posts and to cover the tops of the posts and to make the bands on them.

²⁹The bronze which was presented to the LORD weighed about 5,000 pounds. ³⁰They used the bronze to make the bases at the entrance of the Meeting Tent, to make the altar and the bronze screen, and to make all the tools for the altar. ³¹This bronze was also used to make bases for the wall of curtains around the courtyard and bases for curtains at the entry to the courtyard, as well as to make the tent pegs for the Holy Tent and the curtains that surrounded the courtyard.

Clothes for the Priests

39 They used blue, purple, and red thread to make woven clothes for the priests to wear when they served in the Holy Place. They made the holy clothes for Aaron as the LORD had commanded Moses.

²They made the holy vestᵈ of gold, and blue, purple, and red thread, and fine linen. ³They hammered the gold into sheets and then cut it into long, thin strips. They worked the gold into the blue, purple, and red thread, and fine linen. This was done by skilled craftsmen. ⁴They made the shoulder straps for the holy vest, which were attached to the top corners of the vest and tied together over each shoulder. ⁵The skillfully woven belt was made in the same way; it was joined to the holy vest as one piece. It was made of gold, and blue, purple, and red thread, and fine linen, the way the LORD commanded Moses.

⁶They put gold around the onyx stones and then wrote the names of the sons of Israel on these gems, as a person carves words and designs on a seal.ᵈ ⁷Then they attached the gems on the shoulder straps of the holy vest, as reminders of the twelve sons of Israel. This was done just as the LORD had commanded Moses.

⁸The skilled craftsmen made the chest covering like the holy vest; it was made of gold, and blue, purple, and red thread, and fine linen. ⁹The chest covering was square — nine inches long and nine inches wide — and it was folded double to make a pocket. ¹⁰Then they put four rows of beautiful jewels on it: In the first row there was a ruby,

topaz, and a yellow quartz; [11]in the second there was a turquoise, a sapphire, and an emerald; [12]in the third there was a jacinth, an agate, and an amethyst; [13]in the fourth there was a chrysolite, an onyx, and a jasper. Gold was put around these jewels to attach them to the chest covering, [14]and the names of the sons of Israel were carved on these twelve jewels as a person carves a seal. Each jewel had the name of one of the twelve tribes[d] of Israel.

[15]They made chains of pure gold, twisted together like a rope, for the chest covering. [16]The workers made two gold pieces and two gold rings. They put the two gold rings on the two upper corners of the chest covering. [17]Then they put two gold chains in the two rings at the ends of the chest covering, [18]and they fastened the other two ends of the chains to the two gold pieces. They attached these gold pieces to the two shoulder straps in the front of the holy vest. [19]They made two gold rings and put them at the lower corners of the chest covering on the inside edge next to the holy vest. [20]They made two more gold rings on the bottom of the shoulder straps in front of the holy vest, near the seam, just above the woven belt of the holy vest. [21]They used a blue ribbon and tied the rings of the chest covering to the rings of the holy vest, connecting it to the woven belt. In this way the chest covering would not swing out from the holy vest. They did all these things the way the LORD commanded.

[22]Then they made the outer robe to be worn under the holy vest. It was woven only of blue cloth. [23]They made a hole in the center of the outer robe, with a woven collar sewn around it so it would not tear. [24]Then they made balls like pomegranates[d] of blue, purple, and red thread, and fine linen and hung them around the bottom of the outer robe. [25]They also made bells of pure gold and hung these around the bottom of the outer robe between the bells. [26]So around the bottom of the outer robe there was a bell and a pomegranate ball, a bell and a pomegranate ball. The priest wore this outer robe when he served as priest, just as the LORD had commanded Moses.

[27]They wove inner robes of fine linen for Aaron and his sons, [28]and they made turbans, headbands, and underclothes of fine linen. [29]Then they made the cloth belt of fine linen, and blue, purple, and red thread, and designs were sewn onto it, just as the LORD had commanded Moses.

[30]They made a strip of pure gold, which is the holy crown, and carved these words in the gold, as one might carve on a seal: "Holy to the LORD." [31]Then they tied this flat piece to the turban with a blue ribbon, as the LORD had commanded Moses.

[32]So all the work on the Meeting Tent[d] was finished. The Israelites did everything just as the LORD had commanded Moses. [33]Then they brought the Holy Tent to Moses: the Tent and all its furniture, hooks, frames, crossbars, posts, and bases; [34]the covering made of male sheepskins colored red, the covering made of fine leather, and the curtain that covered the entrance to the Most Holy[d] Place; [35]the Ark[d] of the Agreement, its poles and lid; [36]the table, all its containers, and the bread that showed they were in God's presence; [37]the pure gold lampstand with its lamps in a row, all its tools, and the olive oil for the light; [38]the gold altar, the special olive oil used for appointing priests, the sweet-smelling incense,[d] and the curtain that covered the entrance to the Tent; [39]the bronze altar and its screen, its poles and all its tools, the bowl and its stand; [40]the curtains for the courtyard with their posts and bases, the curtain that covered the entry to the courtyard, the cords, pegs, and all the things in the Meeting Tent. [41]They brought the clothes for the priests to wear when they served in the Holy Tent — the holy clothes for Aaron the priest and the clothes for his sons, which they wore when they served as priests.

[42]The Israelites had done all this work just as the LORD had commanded Moses. [43]Moses looked closely at all the work and saw they had done it just as the LORD had commanded. So Moses blessed them.

Setting Up the Holy Tent

40 Then the LORD said to Moses: [2]"On the first day of the first month, set up the Holy Tent,[d] which is the Meeting Tent. [3]Put the Ark[d] of the Agreement in it and hang the curtain in front of the Ark. [4]Bring in the table and arrange everything on the table that should be there. Then bring in the lampstand and set up its lamps. [5]Put the gold altar for burning incense[d] in front of the Ark of the Agreement, and put the curtain at the entrance to the Holy Tent.

[6]"Put the altar of burnt offerings in front of the entrance of the Holy Tent, the Meeting Tent. [7]Put the bowl between the Meeting Tent and the altar, and put water in it. [8]Set up the courtyard around the Holy Tent, and put the curtain at the entry to the courtyard.

[9]"Use the special olive oil and pour it on the Holy Tent and everything in it, in order to give the Tent and all that is in it for service to the LORD. They will be holy. [10]Pour the special oil on the altar for burnt offerings and on all its tools. Give the altar for service to God, and it will be very holy. [11]Then pour the special olive oil on the bowl and the base under it so that they will be given for service to God.

[12]"Bring Aaron and his sons to the entrance of the Meeting Tent, and wash them with water. [13]Then put the holy clothes on Aaron. Pour the

special oil on him, and give him for service to God so that he may serve me as a priest. [14]Bring Aaron's sons and put the inner robes on them. [15]Pour the special oil on them in the same way that you appointed their father as priest so that they may also serve me as priests. Pouring oil on them will make them a family of priests, they and their descendants[d] from now on." [16]Moses did everything that the LORD commanded him.

[17]So the Holy Tent was set up on the first day of the first month during the second year after they left Egypt. [18]When Moses set up the Holy Tent, he put the bases in place, and he put the frames on the bases. Next he put the crossbars through the rings of the frames and set up the posts. [19]After that, Moses spread the cloth over the Holy Tent and put the covering over it, just as the LORD commanded.

[20]Moses put the stone tablets that had the Agreement written on them into the Ark. He put the poles through the rings of the Ark and put the lid on it. [21]Next he brought the Ark into the Tent and hung the curtain to cover the Ark, just as the LORD commanded him.

[22]Moses put the table in the Meeting Tent on the north side of the Holy Tent in front of the curtain. [23]Then he put the bread on the table before the LORD, just as the LORD commanded him. [24]Moses put the lampstand in the Meeting Tent on the south side of the Holy Tent across from the table. [25]Then he put the lamps on the lampstand before the LORD, just as the LORD commanded him.

[26]Moses put the gold altar for burning incense in the Meeting Tent in front of the curtain. [27]Then he burned sweet-smelling incense on it, just as the LORD commanded him. [28]Then he hung the curtain at the entrance to the Holy Tent.

[29]He put the altar for burnt offerings at the entrance to the Holy Tent, the Meeting Tent, and offered a whole burnt offering and grain offerings on it, just as the LORD commanded him. [30]Moses put the bowl between the Meeting Tent and the altar for burnt offerings, and he put water in it for washing. [31]Moses, Aaron, and Aaron's sons used this water to wash their hands and feet. [32]They washed themselves every time they entered the Meeting Tent and every time they went near the altar for burnt offerings, just as the LORD commanded Moses.

[33]Then Moses set up the courtyard around the Holy Tent and the altar, and he put up the curtain at the entry to the courtyard. So Moses finished the work.

The Cloud over the Holy Tent

[34]Then the cloud covered the Meeting Tent,[d] and the glory of the LORD filled the Holy Tent. [35]Moses could not enter the Meeting Tent, because the cloud had settled on it, and the glory of the LORD filled the Holy Tent.

[36]When the cloud rose from the Holy Tent, the Israelites would begin to travel, [37]but as long as the cloud stayed on the Holy Tent, they did not travel. They stayed in that place until the cloud rose. [38]So the cloud of the LORD was over the Holy Tent during the day, and there was a fire in the cloud at night. So all the Israelites could see the cloud while they traveled.

LEVITICUS

**Why Read
This Book:**

■ Discover how worshiping God today is different than it used to be (Leviticus
1—7).
■ Learn ancient laws people followed to obey God (Leviticus 18—20).
■ Find out how people used to be punished for disobeying God's laws (Leviticus
24—26).

**Behind the
Scenes:**

If you were a boy in ancient Israel and your great-great-great-grandfather were
named Levi, you would be born with your career already planned. You would
know where to live, what to wear, and exactly how to do your job. That's because
the descendants of Levi—the Levites—were Israel's original priests. And Leviticus
was the manual they followed in leading people in worship.

The priests were the religious leaders in the Old Testament. They served God by
preparing sacrifices to God from the people. People offered sacrifices to thank God
and to ask for forgiveness for sins.

Priests were also responsible for maintaining the Meeting Place or tabernacle.
Many of the regulations in Leviticus deal with worship in the Meeting Tent—a
portable sanctuary used as the Israelites wandered in the wilderness after being
freed from slavery in Egypt. The worship regulations also applied to the Temple
when it was built in Jerusalem about three hundred fifty years later.

This book is sometimes difficult for us to follow. It's filled with detailed
(sometimes repulsive) instructions about animal sacrifices, building the Temple, and
celebrating various religious festivals. It also contains explicit guidelines for all
people about diet, sexuality, personal relationships, and other areas of life.

WHERE THE ACTION WAS

Where different worship acts took place in the Meeting Tent.

The priests kept
lamps burning on
gold lampstands
(Leviticus 24:1–4).

The Ark of the Agree-
ment, or Ark of the
Covenant, kept in the
Most Holy Place,
symbolized God's
presence. The high
priest entered this
sacred place only once
a year (Leviticus 16).

Twelve loaves of
bread were kept on
a golden table and
were eaten by the
priests at the end of
the week
(Leviticus 24:5–9).

The altar where the
Israelites offered burned
sacrifices to seek for-
giveness for their sins
(Leviticus 1–7).

WHEN THE ACTION WAS

Abraham lived	The Israelites escaped from Egypt	The Israelites wandered in the desert for forty years		Jesus was born
2000BC	**1500BC**	**1000BC**	**500BC**	**BC/AD**
	The Israelites became slaves in Egypt	The Israelites entered the promised land	The Temple was built in Jerusalem for worship	

Behind the Scenes (cont.): Many of the guidelines seem irrelevant to us today. But behind all the details are themes that help us understand what it means to follow God today. God wants a relationship with us, but we must first admit our sins and accept God's forgiveness. And God expects believers to live their lives in ways that are pleasing to him. As Leviticus 19:2 says: "I am the Lord your God. You must be holy because I am holy."

The Burnt Offering

1 The LORD called to Moses and spoke to him from the Meeting Tent,*d* saying, [2]"Tell the people of Israel: 'When you bring an offering to the LORD, bring as your offering an animal from the herd or flock.

[3]" 'If the offering is a whole burnt offering from the herd, it must be a male that has nothing wrong with it. The person must take the animal to the entrance of the Meeting Tent so that the LORD will accept the offering. [4]He must put his hand on the animal's head, and the LORD will accept it to remove the person's sin so he will belong to God. [5]He must kill the young bull before the LORD, and Aaron's sons, the priests, must bring its blood and sprinkle it on all sides of the altar at the entrance to the Meeting Tent. [6]After that he will skin the animal and cut it into pieces. [7]The priests, when they have put wood and fire on the altar, [8]are to lay the head, the fat, and other pieces on the wood that is on the fire of the altar. [9]The animal's inner organs and legs must be washed with water. Then the priest must burn all the animal's parts on the altar. It is a whole burnt offering, an offering made by fire, and its smell is pleasing to the LORD.

[10]" 'If the burnt offering is a sheep or a goat from the flock, it must be a male that has nothing wrong with it. [11]The person must kill the animal on the north side of the altar before the LORD, and Aaron's sons, the priests, must sprinkle its blood on all sides of the altar. [12]The person must cut the animal into pieces, and the priest must lay them, with the head and fat, on the wood that is on the fire of the altar. [13]The person must wash the animal's inner organs and legs with water, and then the priest must burn all its parts on the altar. It is a whole burnt offering, an offering made by fire, and its smell is pleasing to the LORD.

[14]" 'If the whole burnt offering for the LORD is a bird, it must be a dove or a young pigeon. [15]The priest will bring it to the altar and pull off its head, which he will burn on the altar; the bird's blood must be drained out on the side of the altar. [16]The priest must remove the bird's crop*n* and its contents and throw them on the east side of the altar, where the ashes are. [17]Then he must tear the bird open by its wings without dividing it into two

parts. He must burn the bird on the altar, on the wood which is on the fire. It is a whole burnt offering, an offering made by fire, and its smell is pleasing to the LORD.

The Grain Offering

2 " 'When anyone offers a grain offering to the LORD, it must be made from fine flour. The person must pour oil on it, put incense*d* on it, [2]and then take it to Aaron's sons, the priests. The priest must take a handful of the fine flour and oil and all the incense, and burn it on the altar as a memorial portion. It is an offering made by fire, and its smell is pleasing to the LORD. [3]The rest of the grain offering will belong to Aaron and the priests; it is a most holy part of the offerings made by fire to the LORD.

[4]" 'If you bring a grain offering that was baked in the oven, it must be made from fine flour. It may be loaves made without yeast and mixed with oil, or it may be wafers made without yeast that have oil poured over them. [5]If your grain offering is cooked on a griddle, it must be made, without yeast, of fine flour mixed with oil. [6]Crumble it and pour oil over it; it is a grain offering. [7]If your grain offering is cooked in a pan, it must be made from fine flour and oil. [8]Bring the grain offering made of these things to the LORD. Give it to the priest, and he will take it to the altar. [9]He will take out the memorial portion from the grain offering and burn it on the altar, as an offering made by fire. Its smell is pleasing to the LORD. [10]The rest of the grain offering belongs to Aaron and the priests. It is a most holy part of the offerings made to the LORD by fire.

[11]" 'Every grain offering you bring to the LORD must be made without yeast, because you must not burn any yeast or honey in an offering made by fire to the LORD. [12]You may bring yeast and honey to the LORD as an offering from the first harvest, but they must not be burned on the altar as a pleasing smell. [13]You must also put salt on all your grain offerings. Salt stands for your agreement with God that will last forever; do not leave it out of your grain offering. You must add salt to all your offerings.

[14]" 'If you bring a grain offering from the first harvest to the LORD, bring crushed heads of new

---

crop A small bag inside a bird's throat. When a bird eats, its food goes into this part first. There, the food is made soft before grain roasted in the fire. [15]Put oil and incense on it; it is a grain offering. [16]The priest will burn the memorial portion of the crushed grain and oil, with the incense on it. It is an offering by fire to the LORD.

The Fellowship Offering

3 " 'If a person's fellowship offering to the LORD is from the herd, it may be a male or female, but it must have nothing wrong with it. [2]The person must put his hand on the animal's head and kill it at the entrance to the Meeting Tent.[d] Then Aaron's sons, the priests, must sprinkle the blood on all sides of the altar. [3]From the fellowship offering he must make a sacrifice by fire to the LORD. He must offer the fat of the animal's inner organs (both the fat that is in them and that covers them), [4]both kidneys with the fat that is on them near the lower back muscle, and the best part of the liver, which he will remove with the kidneys. [5]Then the priests will burn these parts on the altar, on the whole burnt offering that is on the wood of the fire. It is an offering made by fire, and its smell is pleasing to the LORD.

[6]" 'If a person's fellowship offering to the LORD is a lamb or a goat, it may be a male or female, but it must have nothing wrong with it. [7]If he offers a lamb, he must bring it before the LORD [8]and put his hand on its head. Then he must kill the animal in front of the Meeting Tent, and the priests must sprinkle its blood on all sides of the altar. [9]From the fellowship offering the person must make a sacrifice by fire to the LORD. He must bring the fat, the whole fat tail cut off close to the backbone, the fat of the inner organs (both the fat that is in them and that covers them), [10]both kidneys with the fat that is on them, near the lower back muscle, and the best part of the liver, which he will remove with the kidneys. [11]Then the priest will burn these parts on the altar as food; it will be an offering made by fire to the LORD.

[12]" 'If a person's offering is a goat, he must offer it before the LORD [13]and put his hand on the its head. Then he must kill it in front of the Meeting Tent, and the priests must sprinkle its blood on all sides of the altar. [14]From this offering the person must make a sacrifice by fire to the LORD. He must offer all the fat of the goat's inner organs (both the fat that is in them and that covers them), [15]both kidneys with the fat that is on them near the lower back muscle, and the best part of the liver, which he will remove with the kidneys. [16]The priest will burn these parts on the altar as food. It is an offering made by fire, and its smell is pleasing to the LORD. All the fat belongs to the LORD. [17]" 'This law will continue for people from now on, wherever you live: You must not eat any fat or blood.' "

The Sin Offering

4 The LORD said to Moses, [2]"Tell the people of Israel this: 'When a person sins by accident and does some things the LORD has commanded not to be done, that person must do these things:

[3]" 'If the appointed priest sins so that he brings guilt on the people, then he must offer a young bull to the LORD, one that has nothing wrong with it, as a sin offering for the sin he has done. [4]He will bring the bull to the entrance of the Meeting Tent[d] in front of the LORD, put his hand on its head, and kill it before the LORD. [5]Then the appointed priest must bring some of the bull's blood into the Meeting Tent. [6]The priest is to dip his finger into the blood and sprinkle it seven times before the LORD in front of the curtain of the Most Holy Place. [7]The priest must also put some of the blood on the corners of the altar of incense[d] that stands before the LORD in the Meeting Tent. The rest of the blood he must pour out at the bottom of the altar of burnt offering, which is at the entrance of the Meeting Tent. [8]He must remove all the fat from the bull of the sin offering — the fat on and around the inner organs, [9]both kidneys with the fat that is on them near the lower back muscle, and the best part of the liver which he will remove with the kidneys. [10](He must do this in the same way the fat is removed from the bull of the fellowship offering.) Then the priest must burn the animal parts on the altar of burnt offering. [11]But the priest must carry off the skin of the bull and all its meat, along with the rest of the bull — its head, legs, intestines, and other inner organs. [12]He must take it outside the camp to the special clean[d] place where the ashes are poured out. He must burn it on a wood fire on the pile of ashes.

[13]" 'If the whole nation of Israel sins accidentally without knowing it and does something the LORD has commanded not to be done, they are guilty. [14]When they learn about the sin they have done, they must offer a young bull as a sin offering and bring it before the Meeting Tent. [15]The older leaders of the group of people must put their hands on the bull's head before the LORD, and it must be killed before the LORD. [16]Then the appointed priest must bring some of the bull's blood

into the Meeting Tent. ¹⁷Dipping his finger in the blood, he must sprinkle it seven times before the Lord in front of the curtain. ¹⁸Then he must put some of the blood on the corners of the altar that is before the Lord in the Meeting Tent. The priest must pour out the rest of the blood at the bottom of the altar of burnt offering, which is at the entrance to the Meeting Tent. ¹⁹He must remove all the fat from the animal and burn it on the altar; ²⁰he will do the same thing with this bull that he did with the first bull of the sin offering. In this way the priest removes the sins of the people so they will belong to the Lord and be forgiven. ²¹Then the priest must carry the bull outside the camp and burn it, just as he did with the first bull. This is the sin offering for the whole community.

²²" 'If a ruler sins by accident and does something the Lord his God has commanded must not be done, he is guilty. ²³When he learns about his sin, he must bring a male goat that has nothing wrong with it as his offering. ²⁴The ruler must put his hand on the goat's head and kill it in the place where they kill the whole burnt offering before the Lord; it is a sin offering. ²⁵The priest must take some of the blood of the sin offering on his finger and put it on the corners of the altar of burnt offering. He must pour out the rest of the blood at the bottom of the altar of burnt offering. ²⁶He must burn all the goat's fat on the altar in the same way he burns the fat of the fellowship offerings. In this way the priest removes the ruler's sin so he belongs to the Lord, and the Lord will forgive him.

²⁷" 'If any person in the community sins by accident and does something which the Lord has commanded must not be done, he is guilty. ²⁸When the person learns about his sin, he must bring a female goat that has nothing wrong with it as an offering for his sin. ²⁹He must put his hand on the animal's head and kill it at the place of the whole burnt offering. ³⁰Then the priest must take some of the goat's blood on his finger and put it on the corners of the altar of burnt offering. He must pour out the rest of the goat's blood at the bottom of the altar. ³¹Then the priest must remove all the goat's fat in the same way the fat is removed from the fellowship offerings. He must burn it on the altar as a smell pleasing to the Lord. In this way the priest will remove that person's sin so he will belong to the Lord, and the Lord will forgive him.

³²" '*If this person brings a lamb as his offering* for sin, he must bring a female that has nothing wrong with it. ³³He must put his hand on the animal's head and kill it as a sin offering in the place where the whole burnt offering is killed. ³⁴The priest must take some of the blood from the sin offering on his finger and put it on the corners of

the altar of burnt offering. He must pour out the rest of the lamb's blood at the bottom of the altar. ³⁵Then the priest must remove all the lamb's fat in the same way that the lamb's fat is removed from the fellowship offerings. He must burn the pieces on the altar on top of the offerings made by fire for the Lord. In this way the priest will remove that person's sins so he will belong to the Lord, and the Lord will forgive him.

Special Types of Accidental Sins

5 " 'If a person is ordered to tell in court what he has seen or what he knows and he does not tell the court, he is guilty of sin.

²" 'Or someone might touch something unclean,^d such as the dead body of an unclean wild animal or an unclean farm animal or an unclean crawling animal. Even if he does not know that he touched it, he will still be unclean and guilty of sin.

³" 'Someone might touch human uncleanness — anything that makes someone unclean — and not know it. But when he learns about it, he will be guilty.

⁴" 'Or someone might make a promise before the Lord without thinking. It might be a promise to do something bad or something good; it might be about anything. Even if he forgets about it, when he remembers, he will be guilty.

⁵" 'When anyone is guilty of any of these things, he must tell how he sinned. ⁶He must bring an offering to the Lord as a penalty for sin; it must be a female lamb or goat from the flock. The priest will perform the acts to remove that person's sin so he will belong to the Lord.

⁷" 'But if the person cannot afford a lamb, he must bring two doves or two young pigeons to the Lord as the penalty for his sin. One bird must be for a sin offering, and the other must be for a whole burnt offering. ⁸He must bring them to the priest, who will first offer the one for the sin offering. He will pull the bird's head from its neck, but he will not pull it completely off. ⁹He must sprinkle the blood from the sin offering on the side of the altar, and then he must pour the rest of the blood at the bottom of the altar; it is a sin offering. ¹⁰Then the priest must offer the second bird as a whole burnt offering, as the law says. In this way the priest will remove the person's sin so he will belong to the Lord, and the Lord will forgive him.

¹¹" 'If the person cannot afford two doves or *two pigeons, he must bring about two quarts of* fine flour as an offering for sin. He must not put oil or incense^d on the flour, because it is a sin offering. ¹²He must bring the flour to the priest. The priest will take a handful of the flour as a memorial offering and burn it on the altar on top of the offerings made by fire to the Lord; it is a

sin offering. [13]In this way the priest will remove the person's sins so he will belong to the Lord, and the Lord will forgive him. What is left of the sin offering belongs to the priest, like the grain offering.' "

The Penalty Offering

[14]The Lord said to Moses, [15]"If a person accidentally sins and does something against the holy things of the Lord, he must bring from the flock a male sheep that has nothing wrong with it. This will be his penalty offering to the Lord. Its value in silver must be correct as set by the Holy Place measure. It is a penalty offering. [16]That person must pay for the sin he did against the holy thing, adding one-fifth to its value. Then he must give it all to the priest. In this way the priest will remove the person's sin so he will belong to the Lord, by using the male sheep as the penalty offering. And the Lord will forgive the person.

[17]"If a person sins and does something the Lord has commanded not to be done, even if he does not know it, he is still guilty. He is responsible for his sin. [18]He must bring the priest a male sheep from the flock, one that has nothing wrong with it and that is worth the correct amount. It will be a penalty offering. Though the person sinned without knowing it, with this offering the priest will remove the sin so the person will belong to the Lord, and the Lord will forgive him. [19]The person is guilty of doing wrong, so he must give the penalty offering to the Lord."

6 The Lord said to Moses, [2]"A person might sin against the Lord by doing one of these sins: He might lie about what happened to something he was taking care of for someone else, or he might lie about a promise he made. He might steal something or cheat someone. [3]He might find something that had been lost and then lie about it. He might make a promise before the Lord about something and not mean it, or he might do some other sin. [4]If he does any of these things, he is guilty of sin. He must bring back whatever he stole or whatever he took by cheating. He must bring back the thing he took care of for someone else. He must bring back what he found and lied about [5]or what he made a false promise about. He must pay the full price plus an extra one-fifth of the value of what he took. He must give the money to the true owner on the day he brings his penalty offering. [6]He must bring his penalty to the priest—a male sheep from the flock, one that does not have anything wrong with it and that is worth the correct amount. It will be a penalty offering to the Lord. [7]Then the priest will perform the acts to remove that person's sin so he will belong to the Lord, and the Lord will forgive him for the sins that made him guilty."

The Whole Burnt Offering

[8]The Lord said to Moses, [9]"Give this command to Aaron and the priests: 'These are the teachings about the whole burnt offering: The burnt offering must stay on the altar all night until morning, and the altar's fire must be kept burning. [10]The priest must put on his linen robe and linen underclothes next to his body. Then he will remove the ashes from the burnt offering on the altar and put them beside the altar. [11]Then he must take off those clothes and put on others and carry the ashes outside the camp to a special clean[d] place. [12]But the fire must be kept burning on the altar; it must not be allowed to go out. The priest must put more firewood on the altar every morning, place the whole burnt offering on the fire, and burn the fat of the fellowship offerings. [13]The fire must be kept burning on the altar all the time; it must not go out.

The Grain Offering

[14]" 'These are the teachings about the grain offering: The priests must bring it to the Lord in front of the altar. [15]The priest must take a handful of fine flour, with the oil and all of the incense[d] on it, and burn the grain offering on the altar as a memorial offering to the Lord. Its smell is pleasing to him. [16]Aaron and the priests may eat what is left, but it must be eaten without yeast in a holy place. They must eat it in the courtyard of the Meeting Tent.[d] [17]It must not be cooked with yeast. I have given it as their share of the offerings made to me by fire; it is most holy, like the sin offering and the penalty offering. [18]Any male descendant[d] of Aaron may eat it as his share of the offerings made to the Lord by fire, and this will continue from now on. Whatever touches these offerings shall become holy.' "

[19]The Lord said to Moses, [20]"This is the offering Aaron and the priests must bring to the Lord on the day they appoint Aaron as high priest: They must bring two quarts of fine flour for a continual grain offering, half of it in the morning and half in the evening. [21]The fine flour must be mixed with oil and cooked on a griddle. Bring it when it is well mixed. Present the grain offering that is broken into pieces, and it will be a smell that is pleasing to the Lord. [22]One of the priests appointed to take Aaron's place as high priest must make the grain offering. It is a rule forever that the grain offering must be completely burned to the Lord. [23]Every grain offering made by a priest must be completely burned; it must not be eaten."

The Sin Offering

[24]The Lord said to Moses, [25]"Tell Aaron and the priests: These are the teachings about the sin

offering: The sin offering must be killed in front of the LORD in the same place the whole burnt offering is killed; it is most holy. 26The priest who offers the sin offering must eat it in a holy place, in the courtyard of the Meeting Tent.*d* 27Whatever touches the meat of the sin offering must be holy, and if the blood is sprinkled on any clothes, you must wash them in a holy place. 28The clay pot the meat is cooked in must be broken, or if a bronze pot is used, it must be scrubbed and rinsed with water. 29Any male in a priest's family may eat the offering; it is most holy. 30But if the blood of the sin offering is taken into the Meeting Tent and used to remove sin in the Holy Place, that sin offering must be burned with fire. It must not be eaten.

The Penalty Offering

7 " 'These are the teachings about the penalty offering, which is most holy: 2The penalty offering must be killed where the whole burnt offering is killed. Then the priest must sprinkle its blood on all sides of the altar. 3He must offer all the fat from the penalty offering—the fat tail, the fat that covers the inner organs, 4both kidneys with the fat that is on them near the lower back muscle, and the best part of the liver, which is to be removed with the kidneys. 5The priest must burn all these things on the altar as an offering made by fire to the LORD. It is a penalty offering. 6Any male in a priest's family may eat it. It is most holy, so it must be eaten in a holy place.

7" 'The penalty offering is like the sin offering in that the teachings are the same for both. The priest who offers the sacrifice to remove sins will get the meat for food. 8The priest who offers the burnt offering may also have the skin from it. 9Every grain offering that is baked in an oven, cooked on a griddle, or baked in a dish belongs to the priest who offers it. 10Every grain offering, either dry or mixed with oil, belongs to the priests, and all priests will share alike.

The Fellowship Offering

11" 'These are the teachings about the fellowship offering a person may offer to the LORD: 12If he brings the fellowship offering to show his thanks, he should also bring loaves of bread made without yeast that are mixed with oil, wafers made without yeast that have oil poured over them, and loaves of fine flour that are mixed with oil. *13He must also offer loaves of bread made* with yeast along with his fellowship offering, which he gives to show thanks. 14One of each kind of offering will be for the LORD; it will be given to the priest who sprinkles the blood of the fellowship offering. 15When the fellowship offering is given to thank the LORD, the meat from it

must be eaten the same day it is offered; none of it must be left until morning.

16" 'If a person brings a fellowship offering just to give a gift to God or because of a special promise to him, the sacrifice should be eaten the same day he offers it. If there is any left, it may be eaten the next day. 17If any meat from this sacrifice is left on the third day, it must be burned up. 18Any meat of the fellowship offering eaten on the third day will not be accepted, nor will the sacrifice count for the person who offered it. It will become unclean,*d* and anyone who eats the meat will be guilty of sin.

19" 'People must not eat meat that touches anything unclean; they must burn this meat with fire. Anyone who is clean may eat other meat. 20But if anyone is unclean and eats the meat from the fellowship offering that belongs to the LORD, he must be cut off from his people.

21" 'If anyone touches something unclean—uncleanness that comes from people, from an animal, or from some hated thing—touching it will make him unclean. If he then eats meat from the fellowship offering that belongs to the LORD, he must be cut off from his people.' "

22The LORD said to Moses, 23"Tell the people of Israel: 'You must not eat any of the fat from cattle, sheep, or goats. 24If an animal is found dead or torn by wild animals, you may use its fat for other things, but you must not eat it. 25If someone eats fat from an animal offering made by fire to the LORD, he must be cut off from his people. 26No matter where you live, you must not eat blood from any bird or animal. 27Anyone who eats blood must be cut off from his people.' "

The Priests' Share

28The LORD said to Moses, 29"Tell the people of Israel: 'If someone brings a fellowship offering to the LORD, he must give part of it as his sacrifice to the LORD. 30He must carry that part of the gift in his own hands as an offering made by fire to the LORD. He must bring the fat and the breast of the animal to the priest, to be presented to the LORD as the priests' share. 31Then the priest must burn the fat on the altar, but the breast of the animal will belong to Aaron and the priests. 32You must also give the right thigh from the fellowship offering to the priest as a gift; 33it will belong to the priest who offers the blood and fat of the fellowship offering. 34I have taken the breast and the thigh from the fellowship offerings of the Israel-*ites, and I have given these parts to Aaron and the* priests as their share for all time from the Israelites.' "

35This is the portion that belongs to Aaron and his sons from the offerings made by fire to the LORD. They were given this share on the day they were presented to the LORD as priests. 36On the day the LORD appointed the priests, he commanded Israel to give this share to them, and it is to be given to the priests as their share from now on.

37These are the teachings about the whole burnt offering, the grain offering, the sin offering, the penalty offering, the offering for the appointment of priests, and the fellowship offering. 38The LORD gave these teachings to Moses on Mount Sinai on the day he commanded the Israelites to bring their offerings to the LORD in the Sinai Desert.

Aaron and His Sons Appointed

8 The LORD said to Moses. 2"Bring Aaron and his sons and their clothes, the special olive oil used in appointing people and things to the service of the LORD, the bull of the sin offering and the two male sheep and the basket of bread made without yeast. 3Then gather the people together at the entrance to the Meeting Tent."d 4Moses did as the LORD commanded him, and the people met together at the entrance to the Meeting Tent.

5Then Moses spoke to the people and said, "This is what the LORD has commanded to be done." 6Bringing Aaron and his sons forward, Moses washed them with water. 7He put the inner robe on Aaron and tied the cloth belt around him. Then Moses put the outer robe on him and placed the holy vestd on him. He tied the skillfully woven belt around him so that the holy vest was tied to Aaron. 8Then Moses put the chest covering on him and put the Urim and the Thummimd in the chest covering. 9He also put the turban on Aaron's head. He put the strip of gold, the holy crown, on the front of the turban, as the LORD commanded him to do.

10Then Moses put the special oil on the Holy Tentd and everything in it, making them holy for the LORD. 11He sprinkled some oil on the altar seven times, sprinkling the altar and all its tools and the large bowl and its base. In this way he made them holy for the LORD. 12He poured some of the special oil on Aaron's head to make Aaron holy for the LORD. 13Then Moses brought Aaron's sons forward. He put the inner robes on them, tied cloth belts around them, and put headbands on them, as the LORD had commanded him.

14Then Moses brought the bull for the sin offering, and Aaron and his sons put their hands on its head. 15Moses killed the bull, took the blood, and with his finger put some of it on all the corners of the altar, to make it pure. Then he poured out the rest of the blood at the bottom of the altar. In this way he made it holy and ready for service to God. 16Moses took all the fat from the inner organs of the bull, the best part of the liver, and both kidneys with the fat that is on them, and he

burned them on the altar. 17But he took the bull's skin, its meat, and its intestines and burned them in a fire outside the camp, as the LORD had commanded him.

18Next Moses brought the male sheep of the burnt offering, and Aaron and his sons put their hands on its head. 19Then Moses killed it and sprinkled the blood on all sides of the altar. 20He cut the male sheep into pieces and burned the head, the pieces, and the fat. 21He washed the inner organs and legs with water and burned the whole sheep on the altar as a burnt offering made by fire to the LORD; its smell was pleasing to the LORD. Moses did these things as the LORD had commanded him.

22Then Moses brought the other male sheep, the one used in appointing Aaron and his sons as priests, and Aaron and his sons put their hands on its head. 23Then Moses killed the sheep and put some of its blood on the bottom of Aaron's right ear, some on the thumb of Aaron's right hand, and some on the big toe of his right foot. 24Then Moses brought Aaron's sons close to the altar. He put some of the blood on the bottom of their right ears, some on the thumbs of their right hands, and some on the big toes of their right feet. Then he sprinkled blood on all sides of the altar. 25He took the fat, the fat tail, all the fat on the inner organs, the best part of the liver, both kidneys with their fat, and the right thigh. 26From the basket of bread made without yeast that is put before the LORD each day, Moses took a loaf of bread, a loaf made with oil, and a wafer. He put these pieces of bread on the fat and right thigh of the male sheep. 27All these things he put in the hands of Aaron and his sons and presented them as an offering before the LORD. 28Then Moses took them from their hands and burned them on the altar on top of the burnt offering. So this was the offering for appointing Aaron and his sons as priests. It was an offering made by fire to the LORD, and its smell was pleasing to him. 29Moses also took the breast and presented it as an offering before the LORD. It was Moses' share of the male sheep used in appointing the priests, as the LORD had commanded him.

30Moses took some of the special oil and some of the blood which was on the altar, and he sprinkled them on Aaron and Aaron's clothes and on Aaron's sons and their clothes. In this way Moses made Aaron, his clothes, his sons, and their clothes holy for the LORD.

31Then Moses said to Aaron and his sons, "I gave you a command, saying, 'Aaron and his sons will eat these things.' So take the meat and basket of bread from the offering for appointing priests. Boil the meat at the door of the Meeting Tent, and eat it there with the bread. 32If any of the meat or bread is left, burn it. 33The time of appointing will last seven days; you must not go outside the entrance of the Meeting Tent until that time is up. Stay there until the time of your appointing is finished. ³⁴The LORD commanded the things that were done today to remove your sins so you will belong to him. ³⁵You must stay at the entrance of the Meeting Tent day and night for seven days. If you don't obey the LORD's commands, you will die. The LORD has given me these commands."

³⁶So Aaron and his sons did everything the LORD had commanded through Moses.

Aaron and His Sons Offer Sacrifices

9 On the eighth day after the time of appointing, Moses called for Aaron and his sons and for the older leaders of Israel. ²He said to Aaron, "Take a bull calf and a male sheep that have nothing wrong with them, and offer them to the LORD. The calf will be a sin offering, and the male sheep will be a whole burnt offering. ³Tell the people of Israel, 'Take a male goat for a sin offering and a calf and a lamb for a whole burnt offering; each must be one year old, and it must have nothing wrong with it. ⁴Also take a bull and a male sheep for fellowship offerings, along with a grain offering mixed with oil. Offer all these things to the LORD, because the LORD will appear to you today.' "

⁵So all the people came to the front of the Meeting Tent,ᵈ bringing the things Moses had commanded them to bring, and they stood before the LORD. ⁶Moses said, "You have done what the LORD commanded, so you will see the LORD's glory."

⁷Then Moses told Aaron, "Go to the altar and offer sin offerings and whole burnt offerings. Do this to remove your sins and the people's sins so you will belong to God. Offer the sacrifices for the people and perform the acts to remove their sins for them so they will belong to the LORD, as the LORD has commanded."

⁸So Aaron went to the altar and killed the bull calf as a sin offering for himself. ⁹Then his sons brought the blood to him, and he dipped his finger in the blood and put it on the corners of the altar. He poured out the rest of the blood at the bottom of the altar. ¹⁰Aaron took the fat, the kidneys, and the best part of the liver from the sin offering and burned them on the altar, in the way the LORD had commanded Moses. ¹¹The meat and skin he burned outside the camp.

¹²Then Aaron killed the animal for the whole burnt offering. His sons brought the blood to him, *and he sprinkled it on all sides of the altar.* ¹³As they gave him the pieces and head of the burnt offering, Aaron burned them on the altar. ¹⁴He also washed the inner organs and the legs of the burnt offering and burned them on top of the burnt offering on the altar.

¹⁵Then Aaron brought the offering that was for the people. He took the goat of the people's sin offering and killed it and offered it for the sin offering, just as he had done the first sin offering.

¹⁶Then Aaron brought the whole burnt offering and offered it in the way that the LORD had commanded. ¹⁷He also brought the grain offering to the altar. He took a handful of the grain and burned it on the altar, in addition to the morning's burnt offering.

¹⁸Aaron also killed the bull and the male sheep as the fellowship offerings for the people. His sons brought him the blood, and he sprinkled it on all sides of the altar. ¹⁹Aaron's sons also brought to Aaron the fat of the bull and the male sheep — the fat tail, the fat covering the inner organs, the kidneys, and the best part of the liver. ²⁰Aaron's sons put them on the breasts of the bull and the sheep. Then Aaron burned these fat parts on the altar. ²¹He presented the breasts and the right thigh before the LORD as the priests' share of the offering, as Moses had commanded.

²²Then Aaron lifted his hands toward the people and blessed them. When he had finished offering the sin offering, the burnt offering, and the fellowship offering, he stepped down from the altar.

²³Moses and Aaron went into the Meeting Tent. Then they came out and blessed the people, and the LORD's glory came to all the people. ²⁴Fire came out from the LORD and burned up the burnt offering and fat on the altar. When the people saw this, they shouted with joy and bowed facedown on the ground.

God Destroys Nadab and Abihu

10 Aaron's sons Nadab and Abihu took their pans for burning incense,ᵈ put fire in them, and added incense; but they did not use the special fire Moses had commanded them to use in the presence of the LORD. ²So fire came down from the LORD and destroyed Nadab and Abihu, and they died in front of the LORD. ³Then Moses said to Aaron, "This is what the LORD was speaking about when he said,

'I must be respected as holy
   by those who come near me;
before all the people
   I must be given honor.' "

So Aaron did not say anything about the death of his sons.

⁴Aaron's uncle Uzziel had two sons named Mishael and Elzaphan. Moses said to them, *"Come here and pick up your cousins' bodies,* Carry them outside the camp away from the front of the Holy Place." ⁵So Mishael and Elzaphan obeyed Moses and carried the bodies of Nadab and Abihu, still clothed in the special priest's inner robes, outside the camp.

⁶Then Moses said to Aaron and his other sons,

Eleazar and Ithamar, "Don't show sadness by tearing your clothes or leaving your hair uncombed. If you do, you will die, and the LORD will be angry with all the people. All the people of Israel, your relatives, may cry loudly about the LORD burning Nadab and Abihu, 7but you must not even leave the Meeting Tent.*d* If you go out of the entrance, you will die, because the LORD has appointed you to his service." So Aaron, Eleazar, and Ithamar obeyed Moses.

8Then the LORD said to Aaron. 9"You and your sons must not drink wine or beer when you go into the Meeting Tent. If you do, you will die. This law will continue from now on. 10You must keep what is holy separate from what is not holy; you must keep what is clean*d* separate from what is unclean. 11You must teach the people all the laws that the LORD gave to them through Moses."

12Moses said to Aaron and his remaining sons, Eleazar and Ithamar, "Eat the part of the grain offering that is left from the sacrifices offered by fire to the LORD, but do not add yeast to it. Eat it near the altar because it is most holy. 13You must eat it in a holy place, because this part of the offerings made by fire to the LORD belongs to you and your sons. I have been commanded to tell you this.

14"Also, you and your sons and daughters may eat the breast and thigh of the fellowship offering that was presented to the LORD. You must eat them in a clean place; they are your share of the fellowship offerings given by the Israelites. 15The people must bring the fat from their animals that was part of the offering made by fire, and they must present it to the LORD along with the thigh and the breast of the fellowship offering. They will be the regular share of the offerings for you and your children, as the LORD has commanded."

16Moses looked for the goat of the sin offering, but it had already been burned up. So he became very angry with Eleazar and Ithamar, Aaron's remaining sons. He said, 17"Why didn't you eat that goat in a holy place? It is most holy, and the LORD gave it to you to take away the guilt of the people, to remove their sins so they will belong to the LORD. 18You didn't bring the goat's blood inside the Holy Place. You were supposed to eat the goat in a holy place, as I commanded!"

19But Aaron said to Moses, "Today they brought their sin offering and burnt offering before the LORD, but these terrible things have still happened to me! Do you think the LORD would be any happier if I ate the sin offering today?" 20When Moses heard this, he was satisfied.

Rules About What May Be Eaten

11 The LORD said to Moses and Aaron, 2"Tell the Israelites this: 'These are the land animals you may eat: 3You may eat any animal that has split hoofs completely divided and that chews the cud.*d*

4" 'Some animals only chew the cud or only have split hoofs, and you must not eat them. The camel chews the cud but does not have a split hoof; it is unclean*d* for you. 5The rock badger chews the cud but does not have a split hoof; it is unclean for you. 6The rabbit chews the cud but does not have a split hoof; it is unclean for you. 7Now the pig has a split hoof that is completely divided, but it does not chew the cud; it is unclean for you. 8You must not eat the meat from these animals or even touch their dead bodies; they are unclean for you.

9" 'Of the animals that live in the sea or in a river, if the animal has fins and scales, you may eat it. 10But whatever lives in the sea or in a river and does not have fins and scales—including the things that fill the water and all other things that live in it—you should hate. 11You must not eat any meat from them or even touch their dead bodies, because you should hate them. 12You must hate any animal in the water that does not have fins and scales.

13" 'Also, these are the birds you are to hate. They are hateful and should not be eaten. You must not eat eagles, vultures, black vultures, 14kites, any kind of falcon, 15any kind of raven, 16horned owls, screech owls, sea gulls, any kind of hawk, 17little owls, cormorants, great owls, 18white owls, desert owls, ospreys, 19storks. any kind of heron, hoopoes, or bats.

20" 'Don't eat insects that have wings and walk on all four feet; they also are to be hated. 21" 'But you may eat certain insects that have wings and walk on four feet. You may eat those that have legs with joints above their feet so they can jump. 22These are the insects you may eat: all kinds of locusts, winged locusts, crickets, and grasshoppers. 23But all other insects that have wings and walk on four feet you are to hate. 24Those insects will make you unclean, and anyone who touches the dead body of one of these insects will become unclean until evening. 25Anyone who picks up one of these dead insects must wash his clothes and be unclean until evening.

26" 'Some animals have split hoofs, but the hoofs are not completely divided; others do not chew the cud. They are unclean for you, and anyone who touches the dead body of one of these animals will become unclean. 27Of all the animals that walk on four feet, the animals that walk on their paws are unclean for you. Anyone who touches the dead body of one of these animals will become unclean until evening. 28Anyone who picks up their dead bodies must wash his clothes and be unclean until evening; these animals are unclean for you.

29" 'These crawling animals are unclean for

you: moles, rats, all kinds of great lizards, [30]geckos, crocodiles, lizards, sand reptiles, and chameleons. [31]These crawling animals are unclean for you; anyone who touches their dead bodies will be unclean until evening.

SIDELIGHT: Ever have a craving for a leg o' lizard sandwich? If the Israelites did, they would have gone hungry. Their dietary laws forbade eating moles, rats, lizards, crocodiles, chameleons, and other slinky, slimy things (Leviticus 11:29–30). Many scholars believe this prohibition grew out of the fact that these animals transmitted diseases. Now there's a law we can live with!

---

[32]" 'If an unclean animal dies and falls on something, that item will also become unclean. This includes anything made from wood, cloth, leather, or rough cloth, regardless of its use. Whatever the animal falls on must be washed with water and be unclean until evening; then it will become clean again. [33]If the dead, unclean animal falls into a clay bowl, anything in the bowl will become unclean, and you must break the bowl. [34]If water from the unclean clay bowl gets on any food, that food will become unclean. [35]If any dead, unclean animal falls on something, it becomes unclean. If it is a clay oven or a clay baking pan, it must be broken into pieces. These things will be unclean; they are unclean for you. [36]" 'A spring or well that collects water will stay clean, but anyone who touches the dead body of any unclean animal will become unclean. [37]If a dead, unclean animal falls on a seed to be planted, that seed is still clean. [38]But if you put water on some seeds and a dead, unclean animal falls on them, they are unclean for you.

[39]" 'Also, if an animal which you use for food dies, anyone who touches its body will be unclean until evening. [40]Anyone who eats meat from this animal's dead body must wash his clothes and be unclean until evening. Anyone who picks up the animal's dead body must wash his clothes and be unclean until evening.

[41]" 'Every animal that crawls on the ground is to be hated; it must not be eaten. [42]You must not eat any of the animals that crawl on the ground, *including those that crawl on their stomachs, that* walk on all four feet, or on many feet. They are to be hated. [43]Do not make yourself unclean by these animals; you must not become unclean by them. [44]I am the LORD your God. Keep yourselves holy for me because I am holy. Don't make yourselves unclean with any of these crawling ani-

mals. [45]I am the LORD who brought you out of Egypt to be your God; you must be holy because I am holy.

[46]" 'These are the teachings about all of the cattle, birds, and other animals on earth, as well as the animals in the sea and those that crawl on the ground. [47]These teachings help people know the difference between unclean animals and clean animals; they help people know which animals may be eaten and which ones must not be eaten.' "

Rules for New Mothers

12 The LORD said to Moses, [2]"Tell the people of Israel this: 'If a woman gives birth to a son, she will become unclean[d] for seven days, as she is unclean during her monthly period. [3]On the eighth day the boy must be circumcised.[d] [4]Then it will be thirty-three days before she becomes clean from her loss of blood. She must not touch anything that is holy or enter the Holy Tent until her time of cleansing is finished. [5]But if she gives birth to a daughter, the mother will be unclean for two weeks, as she is unclean during her monthly period. It will be sixty-six days before she becomes clean from her loss of blood.

[6]" 'After she has a son or daughter and her days of cleansing are over, the new mother must bring certain sacrifices to the Meeting Tent.[d] She must give the priest at the entrance a year-old lamb for a burnt offering and a dove or young pigeon for a sin offering. [7]He will offer them before the LORD to make her clean so she will belong to the LORD again; then she will be clean from her loss of blood. These are the teachings for a woman who gives birth to a boy or girl.

[8]" 'If she cannot afford a lamb, she is to bring two doves or two young pigeons, one for a burnt offering and one for a sin offering. In this way the priest will make her clean so she will belong to the LORD again, and she will be clean.' "

Rules About Skin Diseases

13 The LORD said to Moses and Aaron, [2]"Someone might have on his skin a swelling or a rash or a bright spot. If the sore looks like a harmful skin disease, the person must be brought to Aaron the priest or to one of Aaron's sons, the priests. [3]The priest must look at the sore on the person's skin. If the hair in the sore has become white, and the sore seems deeper than the person's skin, it is a harmful skin disease. When he has finished looking at the person, the *priest must announce that the person is unclean.*

[4]"If there is a white spot on a person's skin, but the spot does not seem deeper than the skin, and if the hair from the spot has not turned white, the priest must separate that person from other people for seven days. [5]On the seventh day the priest must look at the person again. If he sees that the

sore has not changed and it has not spread on the skin, the priest must keep the person separated for seven more days. [6]On the seventh day the priest must look at the person again. If the sore has faded and has not spread on the skin, the priest must announce that the person is clean. The sore is only a rash. The person must wash his clothes, and he will become clean again.

[7]"But if the rash spreads again after the priest has announced him clean, the person must come again to the priest. [8]The priest must look at him, and if the rash has spread on the skin, the priest must announce that the person is unclean; it is a harmful skin disease.

[9]"If a person has a harmful skin disease, he must be brought to the priest, [10]and the priest must look at him. If there is a white swelling in the skin, and the hair has become white, and the skin looks raw in the swelling, [11]it is a harmful skin disease. It is one he has had for a long time. The priest must announce that the person is unclean. He will not need to separate that person from other people, because everyone already knows that the person is unclean.

[12]"If the skin disease spreads all over a person's body, covering his skin from his head to his feet, as far as the priest can see, the priest must look at the person's whole body. [13]If the priest sees that the disease covers the whole body and has turned all of the person's skin white, he must announce that the person is clean.

[14]"But when the person has an open sore, he is unclean. [15]When the priest sees the open sore, he must announce that the person is unclean. The open sore is not clean; it is a harmful skin disease. [16]If the open sore becomes white again, the person must come to the priest. [17]The priest must look at him, and if the sores have become white, the priest must announce that the person with the sores is clean. Then he will be clean.

[18]"Someone may have a boil on his skin that is healed. [19]If in the place where the boil was, there is a white swelling or a bright red spot, this place on the skin must be shown to the priest. [20]And the priest must look at it. If the spot seems deeper than the skin and the hair on it has become white, the priest must announce that the person is unclean. The spot is a harmful skin disease that has broken out from inside the boil. [21]But if the priest looks at the spot and there are no white hairs in it and the spot is not deeper than the skin and it has faded, the priest must separate the person from other people for seven days. [22]If the spot spreads on the skin, the priest must announce that the person is unclean; it is a disease that will spread. [23]But if the bright spot does not spread or change, it is only the scar from the old boil. Then the priest must announce that the person is clean.

[24]"When a person gets a burn on his skin, if the open sore becomes white or red, [25]the priest must look at it. If the white spot seems deeper than the skin and the hair at that spot has become white, it is a harmful skin disease. The disease has broken out in the burn, and the priest must announce that the person is unclean. It is a harmful skin disease. [26]But if the priest looks at the spot and there is no white hair in the bright spot, and the spot is no deeper than the skin and has faded, the priest must separate the person from other people for seven days. [27]On the seventh day the priest must look at him again. If the spot has spread on the skin, the priest must announce that the person is unclean. It is a harmful skin disease. [28]But if the bright spot has not spread on the skin but has faded, it is the swelling from the burn. The priest must announce that the person is clean, because the spot is only a scar from the burn.

[29]"When a man or a woman gets a sore on the scalp or on the chin, [30]a priest must look at the sore. If it seems deeper than the skin and the hair around it is thin and yellow, the priest must announce that the person is unclean. It is an itch, a harmful skin disease of the head or chin. [31]But if the priest looks at it and it does not seem deeper than the skin and there is no black hair in it, the priest must separate the person from other people for seven days. [32]On the seventh day the priest must look at the sore. If it has not spread, and there are no yellow hairs growing in it, and the sore does not seem deeper than the skin, [33]the person must shave himself, but he must not shave the sore place. The priest must separate that person from other people for seven more days. [34]On the seventh day the priest must look at the sore. If it has not spread on the skin and it does not seem deeper than the skin, the priest must announce that the person is clean. So the person must wash his clothes and become clean. [35]But if the sore spreads on the skin after the person has become clean, [36]the priest must look at him again. If the sore has spread on the skin, the priest doesn't need to look for the yellowish hair; the person is unclean. [37]But if the priest thinks the sore has stopped spreading, and black hair is growing in it, the sore has healed. The person is clean, and the priest must announce that he is clean.

[38]"When a man or a woman has white spots on the skin [39]a priest must look at them. If the spots on the skin are dull white, the disease is only a harmless rash. That person is clean.

[40]"When anyone loses hair from his head and is bald, he is clean. [41]If he loses hair from the front of his head and has a bald forehead, he is clean. [42]But if there is a red-white sore on his bald head or forehead, it is a skin disease breaking out in

those places. ⁴³A priest must look at that person. If the swelling of the sore on his bald head or forehead is red-white, like a skin disease that spreads, ⁴⁴that person has a skin disease. He is unclean. The priest must announce that the person is unclean because of the sore on his head.

⁴⁵"If a person has a skin disease that spreads, he must warn other people by shouting, 'Unclean, unclean!' His clothes must be torn at the seams, he must let his hair stay uncombed, and he must cover his mouth. ⁴⁶That person will be unclean the whole time he has the disease; he is unclean. He must live alone outside the camp.

Rules About Mildew

⁴⁷"Clothing might have mildew*ᵈ* on it. It might be clothing made of linen or wool ⁴⁸(either woven or knitted), or of leather, or something made from leather. ⁴⁹If the mildew in the clothing, leather, or woven or knitted material is green or red, it is a spreading mildew. It must be shown to the priest. ⁵⁰The priest must look at the mildew, and he must put that piece of clothing in a separate place for seven days. ⁵¹On the seventh day he must look at the mildew again. If the mildew has spread on the cloth (either woven or knitted) or the leather, no matter what the leather was used for, it is a mildew that destroys; it is unclean. ⁵²The priest must burn the clothing. It does not matter if it is woven or knitted, wool or linen, or made of leather, because the mildew is spreading. It must be burned.

⁵³"If the priest sees that the mildew has not spread in the cloth (either knitted or woven) or leather, ⁵⁴he must order the people to wash that piece of leather or cloth. Then he must separate the clothing for seven more days. ⁵⁵After the piece with the mildew has been washed, the priest must look at it again. If the mildew still looks the same, the piece is unclean,*ᵈ* even if the mildew has not spread. You must burn it in fire; it does not matter if the mildew is on one side or the other.

⁵⁶"But when the priest looks at that piece of leather or cloth, the mildew might have faded after the piece has been washed. Then the priest must tear the mildew out of the piece of leather or cloth (either woven or knitted). ⁵⁷But if the mildew comes back to that piece of leather or cloth (either woven or knitted), the mildew is spreading. And whatever has the mildew must be burned with fire. ⁵⁸When the cloth (either woven or knitted) or the leather is washed and the mildew is gone, it must be washed again; then it will be clean.

⁵⁹"These are the teachings about mildew on pieces of cloth (either woven or knitted) or leather, to decide if they are clean or unclean."

Rules for Cleansing from Skin Diseases

14 The Lord said to Moses, ²"These are the teachings for the time at which people who had a harmful skin disease are made clean.*ᵈ*

"The person shall be brought to the priest, ³and the priest must go outside the camp and look at the one who had the skin disease. If the skin disease is healed, ⁴the priest will command that two living, clean birds, a piece of cedar wood, a piece of red string, and a hyssop plant be brought for cleansing the person with the skin disease.

⁵"The priest must order one bird to be killed in a clay bowl containing fresh water. ⁶Then he will take the living bird, the piece of cedar wood, the red string, and the hyssop; all these he will dip into the blood of the bird that was killed over the fresh water. ⁷The priest will sprinkle the blood seven times on the person being cleansed from the skin disease. He must announce that the person is clean and then go to an open field and let the living bird go free.

⁸"The person to be cleansed must wash his clothes, shave off all his hair, and bathe in water. Then he will be clean and may go into the camp, though he must stay outside his tent for the first seven days. ⁹On the seventh day he must shave off all his hair — the hair from his head, his beard, his eyebrows, and the rest of his hair. He must wash his clothes and bathe his body in water, and he will be clean.

¹⁰"On the eighth day the person who had the skin disease must take two male lambs that have nothing wrong with them and a year-old female lamb that has nothing wrong with it. He must also take six quarts of fine flour mixed with oil for a grain offering and two-thirds of a pint of olive oil. ¹¹The priest who is to announce that the person is clean must bring him and his sacrifices before the Lord at the entrance of the Meeting Tent.*ᵈ* ¹²The priest will take one of the male lambs and offer it with the olive oil as a penalty offering; he will present them before the Lord as an offering. ¹³Then he will kill the male lamb in the holy place, where the sin offering and the whole burnt offering are killed. The penalty offering is like the sin offering — it belongs to the priest and it is most holy.

¹⁴"The priest will take some of the blood of the penalty offering and put it on the bottom of the right ear of the person to be made clean. He will also put some of it on the thumb of the person's right hand and on the big toe of the person's right foot. ¹⁵Then the priest will take some of the oil and pour it into his own left hand. ¹⁶He will dip a finger of his right hand into the oil that is in his left hand, and with his finger he will sprinkle some of the oil seven times before the Lord. ¹⁷The priest will put some oil from his hand on the

bottom of the right ear of the person to be made clean, some on the thumb of the person's right hand, and some on the big toe of the person's right foot. The oil will go on these places on top of the blood for the penalty offering. ¹⁸He will put the rest of the oil that is in his left hand on the head of the person to be made clean. In this way the priest will make that person clean so he can belong to the Lord again.

¹⁹"Next the priest will offer the sin offering to make that person clean so he can belong to the Lord again. After this the priest will kill the animal for the whole burnt offering, ²⁰and he will offer the burnt offering and grain offering on the altar. In this way he will make that person clean so he can belong to the Lord again.

²¹"But if the person is poor and unable to afford these offerings, he must take one male lamb for a penalty offering. It will be presented to the Lord to make him clean so he can belong to the Lord again. The person must also take two quarts of fine flour mixed with oil for a grain offering. He must also take two-thirds of a pint of olive oil ²²and two doves or two young pigeons, which he can afford. One bird is for a sin offering and the other for a whole burnt offering. ²³On the eighth day the person will bring them for his cleansing to the priest at the entrance of the Meeting Tent, before the Lord. ²⁴The priest will take the lamb for the penalty offering and the oil, and he will present them as an offering before the Lord. ²⁵Then he will kill the lamb of the penalty offering, take some of its blood, and put it on the bottom of the right ear of the person to be made clean. The priest will put some of this blood on the thumb of the person's right hand and some on the big toe of the person's right foot. ²⁶He will also pour some of the oil into his own left hand. ²⁷Then with a finger of his right hand, he will sprinkle some of the oil from his left hand seven times before the Lord. ²⁸The priest will take some of the oil from his hand and put it on the bottom of the right ear of the person to be made clean. He will also put some of it on the thumb of the person's right hand and some on the big toe of the person's right foot. The oil will go on these places on top of the blood from the penalty offering. ²⁹The priest must put the rest of the oil that is in his hand on the head of the person to be made clean, to make him clean so he can belong to the Lord again. ³⁰Then the priest will offer one of the doves or young pigeons, which the person can afford. ³¹He must offer one of the birds for a sin offering and the other for a whole burnt offering, along with the grain offering. In this way the priest will make the person clean so he can belong to the Lord again; he will become clean.

³²"These are the teachings for making a person clean after he has had a skin disease, if he

cannot afford the regular sacrifices for becoming clean."

Rules for Cleaning Mildew

³³The Lord also said to Moses and Aaron, ³⁴"I am giving the land of Canaan to your people. When they enter that land, if I cause mildew^d to grow in someone's house in that land, ³⁵the owner of that house must come and tell the priest. He should say, 'I have seen something like mildew in my house.' ³⁶Then the priest must order the people to empty the house before he goes in to look at the mildew. This is so he will not have to say that everything in the house is unclean.^d After this, the priest will go in to look at it. ³⁷He will look at the mildew, and if the mildew on the walls of the house is green or red and goes into the wall's surface, ³⁸he must go out and close up the house for seven days. ³⁹On the seventh day the priest must come back and check the house. If the mildew has spread on the walls of the house, ⁴⁰the priest must order the people to tear out the stones with the mildew on them. They should throw them away, at a certain unclean place outside the city. ⁴¹Then the priest must have all the inside of the house scraped. The people must throw away the plaster they scraped off the walls, at a certain unclean place outside the city. ⁴²Then the owner must put new stones in the walls, and he must cover the walls with new clay plaster.

⁴³"Suppose a person has taken away the old stones and plaster and put in new stones and plaster. If mildew again appears in his house, ⁴⁴the priest must come back and check the house again. If the mildew has spread in the house, it is a mildew that destroys things; the house is unclean. ⁴⁵Then the owner must tear down the house, remove all its stones, plaster, and wood, and take

---

SIDELIGHT: The bathroom's dirty, and it's your job to clean it. You're out of cleanser. What do you do? Leviticus 14:33–45 gives a detailed process for cleaning mildew. Of course, your parents may not like you tearing out all the mildewy bricks—or tearing down the house.

---

them to the unclean place outside the city. ⁴⁶Anyone who goes into that house while it is closed up will be unclean until evening. ⁴⁷Anyone who eats in that house or lies down there must wash his clothes.

⁴⁸"Suppose after new stones and plaster have been put in a house, the priest checks it again and the mildew has not spread. Then the priest will

announce that the house is clean, because the mildew is gone.

[49] "Then, to make the house clean, the priest must take two birds, a piece of cedar wood, a piece of red string, and a hyssop plant. [50]He will kill one bird in a clay bowl containing fresh water. [51]Then he will take the bird that is still alive, the cedar wood, the hyssop, and the red string, and he will dip them into the blood of the bird that was killed over the fresh water. The priest will sprinkle the blood on the house seven times. [52]He will use the bird's blood, the fresh water, the live bird, the cedar wood, the hyssop, and the red string to make the house clean. [53]He will then go to an open field outside the city and let the living bird go free. This is how the priest makes the house clean and ready for service to the Lord."

[54]These are the teachings about any kind of skin disease, [55]mildew on pieces of cloth or in a house, [56]swellings, rashes, or bright spots on the skin; [57]they help people decide when things are unclean and when they are clean. These are the teachings about all these kinds of diseases.

Rules About a Person's Body

15 The Lord also said to Moses and Aaron, [2]"Say to the people of Israel: 'When a fluid comes from a person's body, the fluid is unclean.[d] [3]It doesn't matter if the fluid flows freely or if it is blocked from flowing; the fluid will make him unclean. This is the way the fluid makes him unclean:

[4]" 'If the person who discharges the body fluid lies on a bed, that bed becomes unclean, and everything he sits on becomes unclean. [5]Anyone who touches his bed must wash his clothes and bathe in water, and the person will be unclean until evening. [6]Whoever sits on something that the person who discharges the fluid sat on must wash his clothes and bathe in water; he will be unclean until evening. [7]Anyone who touches the person who discharges the body fluid must wash his clothes and bathe in water; he will be unclean until evening.

[8]" 'If the person who discharges the body fluid spits on someone who is clean, that person must wash his clothes and bathe in water; he will be unclean until evening. [9]Everything on which the person who is unclean sits when riding will become unclean. [10]Anyone who touches something that was under him will be unclean until evening. And anyone who carries these things must wash *his clothes and bathe in water; he will be unclean* until evening.

[11]" 'If the person who discharges a body fluid has not washed his hands in water and touches another person, that person must wash his clothes

and bathe in water; he will be unclean until evening.

[12]" 'If a person who discharges a body fluid touches a clay bowl, that bowl must be broken. If he touches a wooden bowl, that bowl must be washed in water.

[13]" 'When a person who discharges a body fluid is made clean, he must count seven days for himself for his cleansing. He must wash his clothes and bathe his body in fresh water, and he will be clean. [14]On the eighth day he must take two doves or two young pigeons before the Lord at the entrance of the Meeting Tent.[d] He will give the two birds to the priest. [15]The priest will offer the birds, one for a sin offering and the other for a burnt offering. And the priest will make that person clean so he can belong to the Lord again.

[16]" 'If semen[n] goes out from a man, he must bathe in water; he will be unclean until evening. [17]If the fluid gets on any clothing or leather, it must be washed with water; it will be unclean until evening.

[18]" 'If a man has sexual relations with a woman and semen comes out, both people must bathe in water; they will be unclean until evening.

Rules About a Woman's Body

[19]" 'When a woman has her monthly period, she is unclean[d] for seven days; anyone who touches her will be unclean until evening. [20]Anything she lies on during this time will be unclean, and everything she sits on during this time will be unclean. [21]Anyone who touches her bed must wash his clothes and bathe in water; that person will be unclean until evening. [22]Anyone who touches something she has sat on must wash his clothes and bathe in water; that person will be unclean until evening. [23]It does not matter if the person touched the woman's bed or something she sat on; he will be unclean until evening.

[24]" 'If a man has sexual relations with a woman and her monthly period touches him, he will be unclean for seven days; every bed he lies on will be unclean.

[25]" 'If a woman has a loss of blood for many days and it is not during her regular monthly period, or if she continues to have a loss of blood after her regular period, she will be unclean, as she is during her monthly period. She will be unclean for as long as she continues to bleed. [26]Any bed she lies on during all the time of her bleeding will be like her bed during her regular *monthly period. Everything she sits on will be unclean,* as during her regular monthly period.

[27]" 'Whoever touches those things will be unclean and must wash his clothes and bathe in water; he will be unclean until evening. [28]When the

semen   A man's body fluid by which he can make a woman pregnant.

woman becomes clean from her bleeding, she must wait seven days, and after this she will be clean. 29Then on the eighth day she must take two doves or two young pigeons and bring them to the priest at the entrance of the Meeting Tent.*d* 30The priest must offer one bird for a sin offering and the other for a whole burnt offering. In this way the priest will make her clean so she can belong to the LORD again.

31" 'So you must warn the people of Israel to stay separated from things that make them unclean. If you don't warn the people, they might make my Holy Tent*d* unclean, and then they would have to die!' "

32These are the teachings for the person who discharges a body fluid and for the man who becomes unclean from semen*n* coming out of his body. 33These are the teachings for the woman who becomes unclean from her monthly period, for a man or woman who has a discharge, and for a man who becomes unclean by having sexual relations with a woman who is unclean.

The Day of Cleansing

16 Now two of Aaron's sons had died while offering incense*d* to the LORD, and after that time the LORD spoke to Moses. 2The LORD said to him, "Tell your brother Aaron that there are times when he cannot go behind the curtain into the Most Holy Place where the Ark*d* is. If he goes in when I appear in a cloud over the lid on the Ark, he will die.

3"This is how Aaron may enter the Most Holy Place: Before he enters, he must offer a bull for a sin offering and a male sheep for a whole burnt offering. 4He must put on the holy linen inner robe, with the linen underclothes next to his body. His belt will be the cloth belt, and he will wear the linen turban. These are holy clothes, so he must bathe his body in water before he puts them on.

5"Aaron must take from the people of Israel two male goats for a sin offering and one male sheep for a burnt offering. 6Then he will offer the bull for the sin offering for himself to remove sins from him and his family so they will belong to the LORD.

7"Next Aaron will take the two goats and bring them before the LORD at the entrance to the Meeting Tent.*d* 8He will throw lots*d* for the two goats — one will be for the LORD and the other for the goat that removes sin. 9Then Aaron will take the goat that was chosen for the LORD by throwing the lot, and he will offer it as a sin offering. 10The other goat, which was chosen by lot to remove the sin, must be brought alive before the LORD. The priest will use it to perform the acts

that remove Israel's sin so they will belong to the LORD. Then this goat will be sent out into the desert as a goat that removes sin.

11"Then Aaron will offer the bull as a sin offering for himself, to remove the sins from him and his family so they will belong to the LORD; he will kill the bull for the sin offering for himself. 12Then he must take a pan full of burning coals from the altar before the LORD and two handfuls of sweet incense that has been ground into powder. He must bring it into the room behind the curtain. 13He must put the incense on the fire before the LORD so that the cloud of incense will cover the lid on the Ark. Then when Aaron comes in, he will not die. 14Also, he must take some of the blood from the bull and sprinkle it with his finger on the front of the lid; with his finger he will sprinkle the blood seven times in front of the lid.

15"Then Aaron must kill the goat of the sin offering for the people and bring its blood into the room behind the curtain. He must do with the goat's blood as he did with the bull's blood. sprinkling it on the lid and in front of the lid. 16Because the people of Israel have been unclean,*d* Aaron will perform the acts to make the Most Holy Place ready for service to the LORD. Then it will be clean from the sins and crimes of the Israelites. He must also do this for the Meeting Tent, because it stays in the middle of unclean people. 17When Aaron makes the Most Holy Place ready for service to the LORD, no one is allowed in the Meeting Tent until he comes out. So Aaron will perform the acts to remove sins from himself, his family, and all the people of Israel, so they will belong to the LORD. 18Afterward he will go out to the altar that is before the LORD and will make it ready for service to the LORD. Aaron will take some of the bull's blood and some of the goat's blood and put it on the corners of the altar on all sides. 19Then, with his finger, he will sprinkle some of the blood on the altar seven times to make the altar holy for the LORD and clean from all the sins of the Israelites.

20"When Aaron has finished making the Most Holy Place, the Meeting Tent, and the altar ready for service to the LORD, he will offer the living goat. 21He will put both his hands on the head of the living goat, and he will confess over it all the sins and crimes of Israel. In this way Aaron will put the people's sins on the goat's head. Then he will send the goat away into the desert, and a man who has been appointed will lead the goat away. 22So the goat will carry on itself all the people's sins to a lonely place in the desert. The man who leads the goat will let it loose there.

23"Then Aaron will enter the Meeting Tent and take off the linen clothes he had put on before he

semen A man's body fluid by which he can make a woman pregnant.

went into the Most Holy Place; he must leave these clothes there. 24He will bathe his body in water in a holy place and put on his regular clothes. Then he will come out and offer the whole burnt offering for himself and for the people, to remove sins from himself and the people so they will belong to the LORD. 25Then he will burn the fat of the sin offering on the altar.

26"The person who led the goat, the goat to remove sins, into the desert must wash his clothes and bathe his body in water. After that, he may come back into the camp.

27"The bull and the goat for the sin offerings, whose blood was brought into the Most Holy Place to make it ready for service to the LORD, must be taken outside the camp; the animals' skins, bodies, and intestines will be burned in the fire. 28Then the one who burns them must wash his clothes and bathe his body in water. After that, he may come back into the camp.

29"This law will always continue for you: On the tenth day of the seventh month, you must not eat and you must not do any work. The travelers or foreigners living with you must not work either. 30It is on this day that the priests will make you clean so you will belong to the LORD again. All your sins will be removed. 31This is a very important day of rest for you, and you must not eat. This law will continue forever.

32"The priest appointed to take his father's place, on whom the oil was poured, will perform the acts for making things ready for service to the LORD. He must put on the holy linen clothes 33and make the Most Holy Place, the Meeting Tent, and the altar ready for service to the LORD. He must also remove the sins of the priests and all the people of Israel so they will belong to the LORD. 34That law for removing the sins of the Israelites so they will belong to the LORD will continue forever. You will do these things once a year."

So they did the things the LORD had commanded Moses.

Offering Sacrifices

17 The LORD said to Moses, 2"Speak to Aaron, his sons, and all the people of Israel. Tell them: 'This is what the LORD has commanded. 3If an Israelite kills an ox, a lamb, or a goat either inside the camp or outside it, 4when he should have brought the animal to the entrance of the Meeting Tent*d* as a gift to the LORD in front of the LORD's Holy Tent, he is guilty of *killing. He has killed, and he must be cut off from* the people. 5This rule is so people will bring their sacrifices, which they have been sacrificing in the open fields, to the LORD. They must bring those animals to the LORD at the entrance of the Meeting Tent; they must bring them to the priest and offer them as fellowship offerings. 6Then the

priest will sprinkle the blood from those animals on the LORD's altar near the entrance of the Meeting Tent. And he will burn the fat from those animals on the altar, as a smell pleasing to the LORD. 7They must not offer any more sacrifices to their goat idols, which they have chased like prostitutes.*d* These rules will continue for people from now on.'

8"Tell the people this: 'If any citizen of Israel or foreigner living with you offers a burnt offering or sacrifice, 9that person must take his sacrifice to the entrance of the Meeting Tent to offer it to the LORD. If he does not do this, he must be cut off from the people.

10" 'I will be against any citizen of Israel or foreigner living with you who eats blood. I will cut off that person from the people. 11This is because the life of the body is in the blood, and I have given you rules for pouring that blood on the altar to remove your sins so you will belong to the LORD. It is the blood that removes the sins, because it is life. 12So I tell the people of Israel this: "None of you may eat blood, and no foreigner living among you may eat blood."

13" 'If any citizen of Israel or foreigner living among you catches a wild animal or bird that can be eaten, that person must pour the blood on the ground and cover it with dirt. 14If blood is still in the meat, the animal's life is still in it. So I give this command to the people of Israel: "Don't eat meat that still has blood in it, because the animal's life is in its blood. Anyone who eats blood must be cut off."

15" 'If a person, either a citizen or a foreigner, eats an animal that died by itself or was killed by another animal, he must wash his clothes and bathe in water. He will be unclean until evening; then he will be clean. 16If he does not wash his clothes and bathe his body, he will be guilty of sin.' "

Rules About Sexual Relations

18 The LORD said to Moses, 2"Tell the people of Israel: 'I am the LORD your God. 3In the past you lived in Egypt, but you must not do what was done in that country. And you must not do as they do in the land of Canaan, where I am bringing you. Do not follow their customs. 4You must obey my rules and follow them. I am the LORD your God. 5Obey my laws and rules; a person who obeys them will live because of them. I am the LORD.

6" 'You must never have sexual relations with your close relatives. I am the LORD.

7" 'You must not shame your father by having sexual relations with your mother. She is your mother; do not have sexual relations with her. 8You must not have sexual relations with your father's wife; that would shame your father.

9" 'You must not have sexual relations with your sister, either the daughter of your father or your mother. It doesn't matter if she was born in your house or somewhere else.

10" 'You must not have sexual relations with your son's daughter or your daughter's daughter; that would bring shame on you.

11" 'If your father and his wife have a daughter, she is your sister. You must not have sexual relations with her.

12" 'You must not have sexual relations with your father's sister; she is your father's close relative. 13You must not have sexual relations with your mother's sister; she is your mother's close relative. 14You must not have sexual relations with the wife of your father's brother, because this would shame him. She is your aunt.

15" 'You must not have sexual relations with your daughter-in-law; she is your son's wife. Do not have sexual relations with her.

16" 'You must not have sexual relations with your brother's wife. That would shame your brother.

17" 'You must not have sexual relations with both a woman and her daughter. And do not have sexual relations with this woman's granddaughter, either the daughter of her son or her daughter; they are her close relatives. It is evil to do this.

18" 'While your wife is still living, you must not take her sister as another wife. Do not have sexual relations with her.

19" 'You must not go near a woman to have sexual relations with her during her monthly period, when she is unclean.*d*

20" 'You must not have sexual relations with your neighbor's wife and make yourself unclean with her.

21" 'You must not give any of your children to be sacrificed to Molech,*d* because this would show that you do not respect your God. I am the LORD.

22" 'You must not have sexual relations with a man as you would a woman. That is a hateful sin.

23" 'You must not have sexual relations with an animal and make yourself unclean with it. Also a woman must not have sexual relations with an animal; it is not natural.

24" 'Don't make yourself unclean by any of these wrong things. I am forcing nations out of their countries because they did these sins, and I am giving their land to you. 25The land has become unclean, and I punished it for its sins, so the land is throwing out those people who live there.

26" 'You must obey my laws and rules, and you must not do any of these hateful sins. These rules are for the citizens of Israel and for the people who live with you. 27The people who lived in the land before you did all these hateful things and made the land unclean. 28If you do these things,

you will also make the land unclean, and it will throw you out as it threw out the nations before you. 29Anyone who does these hateful sins must be cut off from the people. 30Keep my command not to do these hateful sins that were done by the people who lived in the land before you. Don't make yourself unclean by doing them. I am the LORD your God.' "

Other Laws

19 The LORD said to Moses, 2"Tell all the people of Israel: 'I am the LORD your God. You must be holy because I am holy.

3" 'You must respect your mother and father, and you must keep my Sabbaths.*d* I am the LORD your God.

4" 'Do not worship idols or make statues or gods for yourselves. I am the LORD your God.

5" 'When you sacrifice a fellowship offering to the LORD, offer it in such a way that will be accepted. You may eat it the same day you offer it or on the next day. But if any is left on the third day, you must burn it up. 7If any of it is eaten on the third day, it is unclean,*d* and it will not be accepted. 8Anyone who eats it then will be guilty of sin, because he did not respect the holy things that belong to the LORD. He must be cut off from the people.

9" 'When you harvest your crops on your land, do not harvest all the way to the corners of your fields. If grain falls onto the ground, don't gather it up. 10Don't pick all the grapes in your vineyards, and don't pick up the grapes that fall to the ground. You must leave those things for poor people and for people traveling through your country. I am the LORD your God.

SIDELIGHT: They may not have had government welfare programs to help the poor in Old Testament times, but the Israelites were careful to take care of the poor. Farmers were told to leave grain in their field so that poor people and travelers would have something to eat (Leviticus 19:9–10). The story of Ruth (Ruth 2:2–9, p. 240) illustrates a time when someone used this law that provides for outsiders.

11" 'You must not steal. You must not cheat people, and you must not lie to each other. 12You must not make a false promise by my name, or you will show that you don't respect your God. I am the LORD.

13" 'You must not cheat your neighbor or rob him. You must not keep a hired worker's salary all night until morning. ¹⁴You must not curse a deaf person or put something in front of a blind person to make him fall. But you must respect your God. I am the LORD.

¹⁵" 'Be fair in your judging. You must not show special favor to poor people or great people, but be fair when you judge your neighbor. ¹⁶You must not spread false stories against other people, and you must not do anything that would put your neighbor's life in danger. I am the LORD.

¹⁷" 'You must not hate your fellow citizen in your heart. If your neighbor does something wrong, tell him about it, or you will be partly to blame. ¹⁸Forget about the wrong things people do to you, and do not try to get even. Love your neighbor as you love yourself. I am the LORD.

¹⁹" 'Obey my laws. You must not mate two different kinds of cattle or sow your field with two different kinds of seed. You must not wear clothing made from two different kinds of material mixed together.

²⁰" 'If a man has sexual relations with a slave girl of another man, but this slave girl has not been bought or given her freedom, there must be punishment. But they are not to be put to death, because the woman was not free. ²¹The man must bring a male sheep as his penalty offering to the LORD at the entrance to the Meeting Tent.ᵈ ²²The priest will offer the sheep as a penalty offering before the LORD for the man's sin, to remove the sins of the man so he will belong to the LORD. Then he will be forgiven for his sin.

²³" 'In the future, when you enter your country, you will plant many kinds of trees for food. After planting a tree, wait three years before using its fruit. ²⁴In the fourth year the fruit from the tree will be the LORD's, a holy offering of praise to him. ²⁵Then in the fifth year, you may eat the fruit from

---

HONESTY

The Cover-Up

At first, Rick Johnson was reluctant. "I don't think it's a good idea to take this stuff from stores," he would tell his friends.

"It's no big deal," they would respond. "You're not taking much. Besides, they charge too much for this stuff."

Gradually, Rick joined the shoplifting sprees. Soon he was an expert.

Each time Rick brought something home, his parents would ask about it. "I bought it with my paper route money," he would lie. Or, "A friend gave it to me." Or, "I've had it for a long time."

He really didn't feel guilty about the lying or the shoplifting. "It was just a game—a challenge not to get caught," he recalls. "I thought I could ask God for forgiveness every time I took something, and God would wipe my slate clean again."

One day Rick let the truth slip. He gave his younger brother, Kevin, a stolen watch and bragged about how he had gotten it. Kevin told their parents, who made Rick return everything he had stolen—two hundred dollars worth.

At first Rick was angry with Kevin for telling, but soon he understood how telling the truth and getting caught were the best things that could have happened. Why? Because they made him realize he was wrong. And he never shoplifted again.

Rick finally understood that being honest is best for everyone, a point that's clear in **Leviticus 19:1–18**, particularly verses 11–16. Read God's commandments about getting along with other people.

■ Which verses in the passage would have helped Rick avoid shoplifting and lying? How did his dishonesty go against verse 18?

■ How could the honesty demanded in this passage help your relationships with people around you, and your relationship with God?

CONSIDER...
■ underlining the "do not" and "you must not" commands in the passage that are most difficult for you to follow.

■ *going to a friend or family member and "coming clean" on something you've lied or misled others about.*

FOR MORE, SEE...

■ Proverbs 11:1–3 (p. 576)
■ Matthew 5:33–37 (p. 915)

■ Acts 5:1–11 (p. 1104)

the tree. The tree will then produce more fruit for you. I am the LORD your God.

26" 'You must not eat anything with the blood in it.

" 'You must not try to tell the future by signs or black magic.

27" 'You must not cut the hair on the sides of your heads or cut the edges of your beard. 28You must not cut your body to show sadness for someone who died or put tattoo marks on yourselves. I am the LORD.

29" 'Do not dishonor your daughter by making her become a prostitute.ᶜ If you do this, the country will be filled with all kinds of sin.

30" 'Obey the laws about Sabbaths, and respect my Most Holy Place. I am the LORD.

31" 'Do not go to mediumsᵈ or fortune-tellers for advice, or you will become unclean. I am the LORD your God.

32" 'Show respect to old people; stand up in their presence. Show respect also to your God. I am the LORD.

33" 'Do not mistreat foreigners living in your country, 34but treat them just as you treat your own citizens. Love foreigners as you love yourselves, because you were foreigners one time in Egypt. I am the LORD your God.

35" 'Do not cheat when you measure the length or weight or amount of something. 36Your weights and balances should weigh correctly, with your weighing baskets the right size and your jars holding the right amount of liquid. I am the LORD your God. I brought you out of the land of Egypt.

37" 'Remember all my laws and rules, and obey them. I am the LORD.' "

Warnings About Various Sins

20 The LORD said to Moses, 2"You must also tell the people of Israel these things: 'If a person in your country gives one of his children to Molech,ᵈ that person must be killed. It doesn't matter if he is a citizen or a foreigner living in Israel; you must throw stones at him and kill him. 3I will be against him and cut him off from his people, because he gave his children to Molech. He showed that he did not respect my holy name, and he made my Holy Place unclean.ᵈ 4The people of the community might ignore that person and not kill the one who gave his children to Molech. 5But I will be against him and his family, and I will cut him off from his people. I will do this to anyone who follows him in being unfaithful to me by worshiping Molech.

6" 'I will be against anyone who goes to mediumsᵈ and fortune-tellers for advice, because that person is being unfaithful to me. So I will cut him off from his people.

7" 'Be my holy people. Be holy because I am

the LORD your God. 8Remember and obey my laws. I am the LORD, and I have made you holy.

9" 'Anyone who curses his father or mother must be put to death. He has cursed his father or mother, so he has brought his own death on himself.

Punishments for Sexual Sins

10" 'If a man has sexual relations with his neighbor's wife, both the man and the woman are guilty of adulteryᵈ and must be put to death. 11If a man has sexual relations with his father's wife, he has shamed his father, and both the man and his father's wife must be put to death. They have brought it on themselves.

12" 'If a man has sexual relations with his daughter-in-law, both of them must be put to death. What they have done is not natural. They have brought their own deaths on themselves.

13" 'If a man has sexual relations with another man as a man does with a woman, these two men have done a hateful sin. They must be put to death. They have brought it on themselves.

14" 'If a man has sexual relations with both a woman and her mother, this is evil. The people must burn that man and the two women in fire so that your people will not be evil.

15" 'If a man has sexual relations with an animal, he must be put to death. You must also kill the animal. 16If a woman approaches an animal and has sexual relations with it, you must kill the woman and the animal. They must be put to death. They have brought it on themselves.

17" 'It is shameful for a brother to marry his sister, the daughter of either his father or his mother, and to have sexual relations with her. In front of everyone they must both be cut off from their people. The man has shamed his sister, and he is guilty of sin.

18" 'If a man has sexual relations with a woman during her monthly period, both the woman and the man must be cut off from their people. They sinned because they showed the source of her blood.

19" 'Do not have sexual relations with your mother's sister or your father's sister, because that would shame a close relative. Both of you are guilty of this sin.

20" 'If a man has sexual relations with his uncle's wife, he has shamed his uncle. That man and his uncle's wife will die without children; they are guilty of sin.

21" 'It is unclean for a man to marry his brother's wife. That man has shamed his brother, and they will have no children.

22" 'Remember all my laws and rules, and obey them. I am leading you to your own land, and if you obey my laws and rules, that land will not throw you out. 23I am forcing out ahead of you the people who live there. Because they did all these sins, I have hated them. Do not live the way those people lived.

24" 'I have told you that you will get their land, which I will give to you as your very own; it is a fertile land. I am the LORD your God, and I have set you apart from other people and made you my own. 25So you must treat clean animals and birds differently from unclean animals and birds. Do not make yourselves unclean by any of these unclean birds or animals or things that crawl on the ground, which I have made unclean for you. 26So you must be holy to me because I, the LORD, am holy, and I have set you apart from other people to be my own.

27" 'A man or woman who is a medium*d* or a fortune-teller must be put to death. You must stone them to death; they have brought it on themselves.' "

How Priests Must Behave

21 The LORD said to Moses, "Tell these things to Aaron's sons, the priests: 'A priest must not make himself unclean*d* by touching a dead person. 2But if the dead person was one of his close relatives, he may touch him. The priest may make himself unclean if the dead person is his mother or father, son or daughter, brother or 3unmarried sister who is close to him because she has no husband. The priest may make himself unclean for her if she dies. 4But a priest must not make himself unclean if the dead person was only related to him by marriage.

5" 'Priests must not shave their heads, or shave off the edges of their beards, or cut their bodies. 6They must be holy to their God and show respect for God's name, because they present the offerings made by fire to the LORD, which is the food of their God. So they must be holy.

7" 'A priest must not marry an unclean prostitute*d* or a divorced woman, because he is holy to his God. 8Treat him as holy, because he offers up the food of your God. Think of him as holy; I am the LORD who makes you holy, and I am holy.

9" 'If a priest's daughter makes herself unclean by becoming a prostitute, she shames her father. She must be burned with fire.

10" 'The high priest, who was chosen from among his brothers, had the special olive oil poured on his head. He was also appointed to wear the priestly clothes. So he must not show his sadness by letting his hair go uncombed or tearing his clothes. 11He must not go into a house where there is a dead body. He must not make himself unclean, even if it is for his own father or mother. 12The high priest must not go out of the Holy Place, because if he does and becomes unclean,

he will make God's Holy Place unclean. The special oil used in appointing priests was poured on his head to separate him from the rest of the people. I am the LORD.

13" 'The high priest must marry a woman who is a virgin.*d* 14He must not marry a widow, a divorced woman, or a prostitute. He must marry a virgin from his own people 15so the people will respect his children as his own. I am the LORD. I have set the high priest apart for his special job.' "

16The LORD said to Moses, 17"Tell Aaron: 'If any of your descendants*d* have something wrong with them, they must never come near to offer the special food of their God. 18Anyone who has something wrong with him must not come near: blind men, crippled men, men with damaged faces, deformed men, 19men with a crippled foot or hand, 20hunchbacks, dwarfs, men who have something wrong with their eyes, men who have an itching disease or a skin disease, or men who have damaged sex glands.

21" 'If one of Aaron's descendants*d* has something wrong with him, he cannot come near to make the offerings made by fire to the LORD. He has something wrong with him; he cannot offer the food of his God. 22He may eat the most holy food and also the holy food. 23But he may not go through the curtain into the Most Holy Place, and he may not go near the altar, because he has something wrong with him. He must not make my Holy Place unfit. I am the LORD who makes these places holy.' "

24So Moses told these things to Aaron, Aaron's sons, and all the people of Israel.

22 The LORD said to Moses, 2"Tell Aaron and his sons: 'The people of Israel will give offerings to me. These offerings are holy, and they are mine, so you must respect them to show that you respect my holy name. I am the LORD. 3Say to them: If any one of your descendants*d* from now on is unclean*d* and comes near the offerings that the Israelites made holy for me, that person must be cut off from appearing before me. I am the LORD.

4" 'If one of Aaron's descendants has a harmful skin disease, or if he discharges a body fluid, he cannot eat the holy offerings until he becomes clean. He could also become unclean from touching a dead body, from his own semen, *n* 5from touching any unclean crawling animal, or from touching an unclean person (no matter what made the person unclean). 6Anyone who touches those things will become unclean until evening. That person must not eat the holy offerings unless he washes with water. 7He will be clean only after the sun goes down. Then he may eat the holy offerings; the offerings are his food.

---

semen A man's body fluid by which he can make a woman pregnant.

8" 'If a priest finds an animal that died by itself or that was killed by some other animal, he must not eat it. If he does, he will become unclean. I am the LORD.

9" 'If the priests keep all the rules I have given, they will not become guilty; if they are careful, they will not die. I am the LORD who has made them holy. 10Only people in a priest's family may eat the holy offering. A visitor staying with the priest or a hired worker must not eat it. 11But if the priest buys a slave with his own money, that slave may eat the holy offerings; slaves who were born in his house may also eat his food. 12If a priest's daughter marries a person who is not a priest, she must not eat any of the holy offerings. 13But if the priest's daughter becomes widowed or divorced, with no children to support her, and if she goes back to her father's house where she lived as a child, she may eat some of her father's food. But only people from a priest's family may eat this food.

14" 'If someone eats some of the holy offering by mistake, that person must pay back the priest for that holy food, adding another one-fifth of the price of that food.

15" 'When the Israelites give their holy offerings to the LORD, the priest must not treat these holy things as though they were not holy. 16The priests must not allow those who are not priests to eat the holy offerings. If they do, they cause the ones who eat the holy offerings to become guilty, and they will have to pay for it. I am the LORD, who makes them holy.' "

17The LORD said to Moses, 18"Tell Aaron and his sons and all the people of Israel: 'A citizen of Israel or a foreigner living in Israel might want to bring a whole burnt offering, either for some special promise he has made or for a special gift he wants to give to the LORD. 19If he does, he must bring a male animal that has nothing wrong with it — a bull, a sheep, or a goat — so it might be accepted for him. 20He must not bring an animal that has something wrong with it, or it will not be accepted for him.

21" 'If someone brings a fellowship offering to the LORD, either as payment for a special promise the person has made or as a special gift the person wants to give the LORD, it might be from the herd or from the flock. But it must be healthy, with nothing wrong with it, so that it will be accepted. 22You must not offer to the LORD any animal that is blind, that has broken bones or is crippled, that has running sores or any sort of skin disease. You must not offer any animals like these on the altar as an offering by fire to the LORD.

23" 'If an ox or lamb is smaller than normal or is not perfectly formed, you may give it as a special gift to the LORD; it will be accepted. But it will not be accepted as payment for a special promise you have made.

24" 'If an animal has bruised, crushed, torn, or cut sex glands, you must not offer it to the LORD. You must not do this in your own land, 25and you must not take such animals from foreigners as sacrifices to the LORD. Because the animals have been hurt in some way and have something wrong with them, they will not be accepted for you.' "

26The LORD said to Moses, 27"When an ox, a sheep, or a goat is born, it must stay seven days with its mother. But from the eighth day on, this animal will be accepted as a sacrifice by fire to the LORD. 28But you must not kill the animal and its mother on the same day, either an ox or a sheep.

29"If you want to offer some special offering of thanks to the LORD, you must do it in a way that pleases him. 30You must eat the whole animal that same day and not leave any of the meat for the next morning. I am the LORD.

31"Remember my commands and obey them; I am the LORD. 32Show respect for my holy name. You Israelites must remember that I am holy; I am the LORD, who has made you holy. 33I brought you out of Egypt to be your God. I am the LORD."

Special Holidays

23 The LORD said to Moses, 2"Tell the people of Israel: 'You will announce the LORD's appointed feasts as holy meetings. These are my special feasts.

The Sabbath

3" 'There are six days for you to work, but the seventh day will be a special day of rest. It is a day for a holy meeting; you must not do any work. It is a Sabbath[d] to the LORD in all your homes.

The Passover and Unleavened Bread

4" 'These are the LORD's appointed feasts, the holy meetings, which you will announce at the times set for them. 5The LORD's Passover[d] is on the fourteenth day of the first month, beginning at twilight. 6The Feast[d] of Unleavened Bread begins on the fifteenth day of the same month. You will eat bread made without yeast for seven days. 7On the first day of this feast you will have a holy meeting, and you must not do any work. 8For seven days you will bring an offering made by fire to the LORD. There will be a holy meeting on the seventh day, and on that day you must not do any regular work.' "

The First of the Harvest

9The LORD said to Moses, 10"Tell the people of Israel: 'You will enter the land I will give you and gather its harvest. At that time you must bring the first bundle of grain from your harvest to the priest. [11]The priest will present the bundle before the LORD, and it will be accepted for you; he will present the bundle on the day after the Sabbath.[d]

[12]" 'On the day when you present the bundle of grain, offer a male lamb, one year old, that has nothing wrong with it, as a burnt offering to the LORD. [13]You must also offer a grain offering—four quarts of fine flour mixed with olive oil as an offering made by fire to the LORD; its smell will be pleasing to him. You must also offer a quart of wine as a drink offering. [14]Until the day you bring your offering to your God, do not eat any new grain, roasted grain, or bread made from new grain. This law will always continue for people from now on, wherever you live.

The Feast of Weeks

[15]" 'Count seven full weeks from the morning after the Sabbath.[d] (This is the Sabbath that you bring the bundle of grain to present as an offering.) [16]On the fiftieth day, the first day after the seventh week, you will bring a new grain offering to the LORD. [17]On that day bring two loaves of bread from your homes to be presented as an offering. Use yeast and four quarts of flour to make those loaves of bread; they will be your gift to the LORD from the first wheat of your harvest.

[18]" 'Offer with the bread one young bull, two male sheep, and seven male lambs that are one year old and have nothing wrong with them. Offer them with their grain offerings and drink offerings, as a burnt offering to the LORD. They will be an offering made by fire, and the smell will be pleasing to the LORD. [19]You must also offer one male goat for a sin offering and two male, one-year-old lambs as a fellowship offering.

[20]" 'The priest will present the two lambs as an offering before the LORD, along with the bread from the first wheat of the harvest. They are holy to the LORD, and they will belong to the priest. [21]On that same day you will call a holy meeting; you must not do any work that day. This law will continue for you from now on, wherever you live.

[22]" 'When you harvest your crops on your land, do not harvest all the way to the corners of your field. If grain falls onto the ground, don't gather it up. Leave it for poor people and foreigners in your country. I am the LORD your God.' "

The Feast of Trumpets

[23]Again the LORD said to Moses, [24]"Tell the people of Israel: 'On the first day of the seventh *month you must have a special day of rest, a holy* meeting, when you blow the trumpet for a special time of remembering. [25]Do not do any work, and bring an offering made by fire to the LORD.' "

The Day of Cleansing

[26]The LORD said to Moses, [27]"The Day of Cleansing will be on the tenth day of the seventh month. There will be a holy meeting, and you will give up eating and bring an offering made by fire to the LORD. [28]Do not do any work on that day, because it is the Day of Cleansing. On that day the priests will go before the LORD and perform the acts to make you clean[d] so you will belong to the LORD.

[29]"Anyone who refuses to give up food on this day must be cut off from the people. [30]If anyone works on this day, I will destroy that person from among the people. [31]You must not do any work at all; this law will continue for people from now on wherever you live. [32]It will be a special day of rest for you, and you must not eat. You will start this special day of rest on the evening after the ninth day of the month, and it will continue from that evening until the next evening."

The Feast of Shelters

[33]Again the LORD said to Moses, [34]"Tell the people of Israel: 'On the fifteenth day of the seventh month is the Feast[d] of Shelters. This feast to the LORD will continue for seven days. [35]There will be a holy meeting on the first day; do not do any work. [36]You will bring an offering made by fire to the LORD each day for seven days. On the eighth day you will have another holy meeting, and you will bring an offering made by fire to the LORD. This will be a holy meeting; do not do any work.

[37](" 'These are the LORD's special feasts, when there will be holy meetings and when you bring offerings made by fire to the LORD. You will bring whole burnt offerings, grain offerings, sacrifices, and drink offerings—each at the right time. [38]These offerings are in addition to those for the LORD's Sabbath[d] days, in addition to offerings you give as payment for special promises, and in addition to special offerings you want to give to the LORD.)

[39]" 'So on the fifteenth day of the seventh month, after you have gathered in the crops of the land, celebrate the LORD's festival for seven days. You must rest on the first day and the eighth day. [40]On the first day you will take good fruit from the fruit trees, as well as branches from palm trees, poplars, and other leafy trees. You will celebrate before the LORD your God for seven days. [41]Celebrate this festival to the LORD for seven days each year. This law will continue from now on; you will celebrate it in the seventh month. [42]Live in *shelters for seven days. All the people born in Is-rael must live in shelters* [43]so that all your descendants[d] will know I made Israel live in *shelters* during the time I brought them out of Egypt. I am the LORD your God.' "

[44]So Moses told the people of Israel about all of the LORD's appointed feast days.

The Lampstand and the Holy Bread

24 The LORD said to Moses, [2]"Command the people of Israel to bring you pure oil from crushed olives. That oil is for the lamps so that these lamps may never go out. [3]Aaron will keep the lamps burning in the Meeting Tent[d] from evening until morning before the LORD; this is in front of the curtain of the Ark[d] of the Agreement. This law will continue from now on. [4]Aaron must always keep the lamps burning on the lampstands of pure gold before the LORD.

[5]"Take fine flour and bake twelve loaves of bread with it, using four quarts of flour for each loaf. [6]Put them in two rows on the golden table before the LORD, six loaves in each row. [7]Put pure incense[d] on each row as the memorial portion to take the place of the bread. It is an offering made by fire to the LORD. [8]Every Sabbath[d] day Aaron will put the bread in order before the LORD, as an agreement with the people of Israel that will continue forever. [9]That bread will belong to Aaron and his sons. They will eat it in a holy place, because it is a most holy part of the offerings made by fire to the LORD. That bread is their share forever."

The Man Who Cursed God

[10]Now there was a son of an Israelite woman and an Egyptian father who was walking among the Israelites. A fight broke out in the camp between him and an Israelite. [11]The son of the Israelite woman began cursing and speaking against the LORD, so the people took him to Moses. (The mother's name was Shelomith, the daughter of Debri from the family of Dan.) [12]The people held him as a prisoner while they waited for the LORD's command to be made clear to them.

[13]Then the LORD said to Moses, [14]"Take the one who spoke against me outside the camp. Then all the people who heard him must put their hands on his head, and all the people must throw stones at him and kill him. [15]Tell the people of Israel this: 'If anyone curses his God, he is guilty of sin. [16]Anyone who speaks against the LORD must be put to death; all the people must kill him by throwing stones at him. Foreigners must be punished just like the people born in Israel; if they speak against the LORD, they must be put to death.

[17]" 'Whoever kills another person must be put to death. [18]Whoever kills an animal that belongs to another person must give that person another animal to take its place. [19]And whoever causes an injury to a neighbor must receive the same kind of injury in return: [20]Broken bone for broken bone, eye for eye, tooth for tooth. Anyone who injures another person must be injured in the same way in return. [21]Whoever kills another person's animal must give that person another animal to take its place. But whoever kills another person must be put to death.

[22]" 'The law will be the same for the foreigner as for those from your own country. I am the LORD your God.' "

[23]Then Moses spoke to the people of Israel, and they took the person who had cursed outside the camp and killed him by throwing stones at him. So the people of Israel did as the LORD had commanded Moses.

The Time of Rest for the Land

25 The LORD said to Moses at Mount Sinai, [2]"Tell the people of Israel this: 'When you enter the land I will give you, let it have a special time of rest, to honor the LORD. [3]You may plant seed in your field for six years, and you may trim your vineyards for six years and bring in their fruits. [4]But during the seventh year, you must let the land rest. This will be a special time to honor the LORD. You must not plant seed in your field or trim your vineyards. [5]You must not cut the crops that grow by themselves after harvest, or gather the grapes from your vines that are not trimmed. The land will have a year of rest.

[6]" 'You may eat whatever the land produces during that year of rest. It will be food for your men and women servants, for your hired workers, and for the foreigners living in your country. [7]It will also be food for your cattle and the wild animals of your land. Whatever the land produces may be eaten.

The Year of Jubilee

[8]" 'Count off seven groups of seven years, or forty-nine years. During that time there will be seven years of rest for the land. [9]On the Day of Cleansing,[d] you must blow the horn of a male sheep; this will be on the tenth day of the seventh month. You must blow the horn through the whole country. [10]Make the fiftieth year a special year, and announce freedom for all the people living in your country. This time will be called Jubilee.[n] You will each go back to your own property, each to your own family and family group. [11]The fiftieth year will be a special time for you to celebrate. Don't plant seeds, or harvest the crops that grow by themselves, or gather grapes from the vines that are not trimmed. [12]That year is Jubilee; it will be a holy time for you. You may eat only the crops that come from the field. [13]In the year of Jubilee you each must go back to your own property.

[14]" 'If you sell your land to your neighbor, or if

Jubilee   This word comes from the Hebrew word for a horn of a male sheep.

you buy land from your neighbor, don't cheat each other. [15]If you want to buy your neighbor's land, count the number of years since the last Jubilee, and use that number to decide the right price. If your neighbor sells the land to you, count the number of years left for harvesting crops, and use that number to decide the right price. [16]If there are many years, the price will be high. But if there are only a few years, lower the price, because your neighbor is really selling only a few crops to you. [17]You must not cheat each other, but you must respect your God. I am the LORD your God.

[18]" 'Remember my laws and rules, and obey them so that you will live safely in the land. [19]The land will give good crops to you, and you will eat as much as you want and live safely in the land.

[20]" 'But you might ask, "If we don't plant seeds or gather crops, what will we eat the seventh year?" [21]I will send you such a great blessing during the sixth year that the land will produce enough crops for three years. [22]When you plant in the eighth year, you will still be eating from the old crop; you will eat the old crop until the harvest of the ninth year.

SIDELIGHT: If you have ever been sorry you gave something away, you would like the idea of the Year of Jubilee (Leviticus 25:8–22). To protect the poor and to ensure justice, the law said that all property had to be returned to its original owners after forty-nine years. Of course, after forty-nine years, that sweater you loaned to your best friend might not fit well!

Property Laws

[23]" 'The land really belongs to me, so you can't sell it for all time. You are only foreigners and travelers living for a while on my land. [24]People might sell their land, but it must always be possible for the family to get its land back. [25]If a person in your country becomes very poor and sells some land, then close relatives must come and buy it back. [26]If there is not a close relative to buy the land back, but if the person makes enough money to be able to buy it back, [27]the years must be counted since the land was sold. That number must be used to decide how much the first owner *should pay back the one who bought it. Then the land* will belong to the first owner again. [28]But if there is not enough money to buy it back, the one who bought it will keep it until the year of Jubilee.[d] During that celebration, the land will go back to the first owner's family.

[29]" 'If someone sells a home in a walled city, for

a full year after it is sold, the person has the right to buy it back. [30]But if the owner does not buy back the house before a full year is over, it will belong to the one who bought it and to his future sons. The house will not go back to the first owner at Jubilee. [31]But houses in small towns without walls are like open country; they can be bought back, and they must be returned to their first owner at Jubilee.

[32]" 'The Levites may always buy back their houses in the cities that belong to them. [33]If someone buys a house from a Levite, that house in the Levites' city will again belong to the Levites in the Jubilee. This is because houses in Levite cities belong to the people of Levi; the Israelites gave these cities to them. [34]Also the fields and pastures around the Levites' cities cannot be sold, because those fields belong to the Levites forever.

Rules for Slave Owners

[35]" 'If anyone from your country becomes too poor to support himself, help him to live among you as you would a stranger or foreigner. [36]Do not charge him any interest on money you loan to him, but respect your God; let the poor live among you. [37]Don't lend him money for interest, and don't try to make a profit from the food he buys. [38]I am the LORD your God, who brought you out of the land of Egypt to give the land of Canaan to you and to become your God.

[39]" 'If anyone from your country becomes very poor and sells himself as a slave to you, you must not make him work like a slave. [40]He will be like a hired worker and a visitor with you until the year of Jubilee.[d] [41]Then he may leave you, take his children, and go back to his family and the land of his ancestors. [42]This is because the Israelites are my servants, and I brought them out of slavery in Egypt. They must not become slaves again. [43]You must not rule this person cruelly, but you must respect your God.

[44]" 'Your men and women slaves must come from other nations around you; from them you may buy slaves. [45]Also you may buy as slaves children from the families of foreigners living in your land. These child slaves will belong to you, [46]and you may even pass them on to your children after you die; you can make them slaves forever. But you must not rule cruelly over your own people, the Israelites.

[47]" 'Suppose a foreigner or visitor among you *becomes rich. If someone in your country becomes so poor that he has to sell himself as a slave* to the foreigner living among you or to a member of the foreigner's family, [48]the poor person has the right to be bought back and become free. One of his relatives may buy him back: [49]His uncle, his uncle's son, or any one of his close relatives may

buy him back. Or, if he gets enough money, he may pay the money to free himself.

50" 'He and the one who bought him must count the time from when he sold himself up to the next year of Jubilee. Use that number to decide the price, because the person really only hired himself out for a certain number of years. 51If there are still many years before the year of Jubilee, the person must pay back a large part of the price. 52If there are only a few years left until Jubilee, the person must pay a small part of the first price. 53But he will live like a hired person with the foreigner every year; don't let the foreigner rule cruelly over him.

54" 'Even if no one buys him back, at the year of Jubilee, he and his children will become free. 55This is because the people of Israel are servants to me. They are my servants, whom I brought out of Egypt. I am the LORD your God.

Rewards for Obeying God

26 " 'Don't make idols for yourselves or set up statues or memorials. Don't put stone statues in your land to bow down to, because I am the LORD your God.

2" 'Remember my Sabbaths,*d* and respect my Holy Place. I am the LORD.

3" 'If you remember my laws and commands and obey them, 4I will give you rains at the right season; the land will produce crops, and the trees of the field will produce their fruit. 5Your threshing*d* will continue until the grape harvest, and your grape harvest will continue until it is time to plant. Then you will have plenty to eat and live safely in your land. 6I will give peace to your country; you will lie down in peace, and no one will make you afraid. I will keep harmful animals out of your country, and armies will not pass through it.

7" 'You will chase your enemies and defeat them, killing them with your sword. 8Five of you will chase a hundred men; a hundred of you will chase ten thousand men. You will defeat your enemies and kill them with your sword.

9" 'Then I will show kindness to you and let you have many children; I will keep my agreement with you. 10You will have enough crops to last for more than a year. When you harvest the new crops, you will have to throw out the old ones to make room for them. 11Also I will place my Holy Tent*d* among you, and I will not turn away from you. 12I will walk with you and be your God, and you will be my people. 13I am the LORD your God, who brought you out of Egypt, where you were slaves. I broke the heavy weights that were on your shoulders and let you walk proudly again.

Punishment for Not Obeying God

14" 'But if you do not obey me and keep all my commands, 15and if you turn away from my rules and hate my laws, refusing to obey all my commands, you have broken our agreement. 16As a result, I will do this to you: I will cause terrible things to happen to you. I will cause you to have disease and fever that will destroy your eyes and slowly kill you. You will not have success when you plant your seed, and your enemy will eat your crops. 17I will be against you, and your enemies will defeat you. These people who hate you will rule over you, and you will run away even when no one is chasing you.

18" 'If after all this you still do not obey me, I will punish you seven times more for your sins. 19I will break your great pride, and I will make the sky like iron and the earth like bronze.*n* 20You will work hard, but it will not help. Your land will not grow any crops, and your trees will not give their fruit.

21" 'If you still turn against me and refuse to obey me, I will beat you seven times harder. The more you sin, the more you will be punished. 22I will send wild animals to attack you, and they will take your children away from you and destroy your cattle. They will make you so few in number the roads will be empty.

23" 'If you don't learn your lesson after all these things, and if you still turn against me, 24I will also turn against you. I will punish you seven more times for your sins. 25You broke my agreement, and I will punish you. I will bring armies against you, and if you go into your cities for safety, I will cause diseases to spread among you so that your enemy will defeat you. 26There will be very little bread to eat; ten women will be able to cook all your bread in one oven. They will measure each piece of bread, and you will eat, but you will still be hungry.

27" 'If you still refuse to listen to me and still turn against me, 28I will show my great anger; I will punish you seven more times for your sins. 29You will eat the bodies of your sons and daughters. 30I will destroy your places where gods are worshiped and cut down your incense*d* altars. I will pile your dead bodies on the lifeless forms of your idols. I will hate you. 31I will destroy your cities and make your holy places empty, and I will not smell the pleasing smell of your offerings. 32I will make the land empty so that your enemies who come to live in it will be shocked at it. 33I will scatter you among the nations, and I will pull out my sword and destroy you. Your land will become empty, your cities a waste. 34When you are taken to your enemy's country, your land will finally get

---

sky ... bronze   This means the sky will give no rain and the earth will produce no crops.

its rest. It will enjoy its time of rest all the time it lies empty. [35]During the time the land is empty, it will have the rest you should have given it while you lived in it.

[36]" 'Those of you who are left alive will lose their courage in the land of their enemies. They will be frightened by the sound of a leaf being blown by the wind. They will run as if someone were chasing them with a sword, and they will fall even when no one is chasing them. [37]They will fall over each other, as if someone were chasing them with a sword, even though no one is chasing them. You will not be strong enough to stand up against your enemies. [38]You will die among other nations and disappear in your enemies' countries. [39]So those who are left alive will rot away in their enemies' countries because of their sins. They will also rot away because of their ancestors' sins.

There Is Always Hope

[40]" 'But maybe the people will confess their sins and the sins of their ancestors; maybe they will admit they turned against me and sinned against me, [41]which made me turn against them and send them into the land of their enemies. If these disobedient people are sorry for what they did and accept punishment for their sin, [42]I will remember my agreement with Jacob, my agreement with Isaac, and my agreement with Abraham, and I will remember the land. [43]The land will be left empty by its people, and it will enjoy its time of rest as it lies bare without them. Then those who are left alive will accept the punishment for their sins. They will learn that they were punished because they hated my laws and refused to obey my rules. [44]But even though this is true, I will not turn away from them when they are in the land of their enemies. I will not hate them so much that I completely destroy them and break my agreement with them, because I am the Lord their God. [45]For their good I will remember the agreement with their ancestors, whom I brought out of the land of Egypt so I could become their God; the other nations saw these things. I am the Lord.' "

[46]These are the laws, rules, and teachings the Lord made between himself and the Israelites through Moses at Mount Sinai.

Promises Are Important

27 The Lord said to Moses, [2]"Speak to the people of Israel and tell them: 'If someone makes a special promise to give a person as a servant to the Lord by paying a price that is the same value as that person, [3]the price for a man twenty to sixty years old is about one and one-fourth pounds of silver. (You must use the measure as set by the Holy Place.) [4]The price for a woman twenty to sixty years old is about twelve ounces of silver. [5]The price for a man five to twenty years old is about eight ounces of silver; for a woman it is about four ounces of silver. [6]The price for a baby boy one month to five years old is about two ounces of silver; for a baby girl the price is about one and one-half ounces of silver. [7]The price for a man sixty years old or older is about six ounces of silver; for a woman it is about four ounces of silver.

[8]" 'If anyone is too poor to pay the price, bring him to the priest, and the priest will set the price. The priest will decide how much money the person making the vow can afford to pay.

Gifts to the Lord

[9]" 'Some animals may be used as sacrifices to the Lord. If someone promises to bring one of these to the Lord, it will become holy. [10]That person must not try to put another animal in its place or exchange it, a good animal for a bad one, or a bad animal for a good one. If this happens, both animals will become holy.

[11]" 'Unclean[d] animals cannot be offered as sacrifices to the Lord, and if someone brings one of them to the Lord, that animal must be brought to the priest. [12]The priest will decide a price for the animal, according to whether it is good or bad; as the priest decides, that is the price for the animal. [13]If the person wants to buy back the animal, an additional one-fifth must be added to the price.

Value of a House

[14]" 'If a person gives a house as holy to the Lord, the priest must decide its value, according to whether the house is good or bad; as the priest decides, that is the price for the house. [15]But if the person who gives the house wants to buy it back, an additional one-fifth must be added to the price. Then the house will belong to that person again.

Value of Land

[16]" 'If a person gives some family property to the Lord, the value of the fields will depend on how much seed is needed to plant them. It will cost about one and one-fourth pounds of silver for each six bushels of barley seed needed. [17]If the person gives a field at the year of Jubilee,[d] its value will stay at what the priest has decided. [18]But if the person gives the field after the Jubilee, the priest must decide the exact price by counting the number of years to the next year of Jubilee. Then he will subtract that number from its value. [19]If the person who gave the field wants to buy it back, one-fifth must be added to that price, and the field will belong to the first owner again. [20]" 'If the person does not buy back the field, or if it is sold to someone else, the first person

cannot ever buy it back. ²¹When the land is released at the year of Jubilee, it will become holy to the LORD, like land specially given to him. It will become the property of the priests.

²²" 'If someone gives to the LORD a field he has bought, which is not a part of his family land, ²³the priest must count the years to the next Jubilee. He must decide the price for the land, and the price must be paid on that day. Then that land will be holy to the LORD. ²⁴At the year of Jubilee, the land will go back to its first owner, to the family who sold the land. ²⁵" 'You must use the measure as set by the Holy Place in paying these prices; it weighs two-fifths of an ounce.

Value of Animals

²⁶" 'If an animal is the first one born to its parent, it already belongs to the LORD, so people may not give it again. If it is a cow or a sheep, it is the LORD's. ²⁷If the animal is unclean,^d the person must buy it back for the price set by the priest, and the person must add one-fifth to that price. If

it is not bought back, the priest must sell it for the price he had decided.

²⁸" 'There is a special kind of gift that people set apart to give to the LORD; it may be a person, animal, or field from the family property. That gift cannot be bought back or sold. Every special kind of gift is most holy to the LORD.

²⁹" 'If anyone is given for the purpose of being destroyed, he cannot be bought back; he must be put to death.

³⁰" 'One-tenth of all crops belongs to the LORD, including the crops from fields and the fruit from trees. That one-tenth is holy to the LORD. ³¹If a person wants to get back that tenth, one-fifth must be added to its price.

³²" 'The priest will take every tenth animal from a person's herd or flock, and it will be holy to the LORD. ³³The owner should not pick out the good animals from the bad or exchange one animal for another. If that happens, both animals will become holy; they cannot be bought back.' "

³⁴These are the commands the LORD gave to Moses at Mount Sinai for the people of Israel.

NUMBERS

Why Read This Book:

- Learn what can happen when you don't trust God's power (Numbers 13—14).
- See that God plans to be good to his people (Numbers 22—24).
- Read about the first equal rights for women (Numbers 27:1–11).

Behind the Scenes:

The offense has just made a sensational play that put the team in easy scoring position—first down and goal to go. The coach sends in the next play. But in the huddle, the excited quarterback decides to change the play. The play fails miserably, and the quarterback gets sacked back at the forty-yard line. The discouraged team faces a long struggle.

The book of Numbers tells a similar story about a much more difficult situation. The Hebrew people had just been set free from slavery in Egypt and were headed to God's promised land. But they disobeyed God, and, as a result, spent forty difficult years wandering in a hot, hostile desert.

Numbers tells how God punished his people who had lost faith in themselves and in him. It emphasizes the importance of wholehearted trust in and obedience

WHERE THE ACTION WAS

Mediterranean Sea

Alternate northern routes suggested by some scholars.

Jericho

Dead Sea

CANAAN

EGYPT

MOAB

Numbers ends with the people on the Plains of Moab across from Jericho (Numbers 33:50).

Kadesh-Barnea

The Israelites may have spent up to thirty-eight years near Kadesh-Barnea, an oasis in the desert.

SINAI

Taberah

The route the Israelites may have traveled as they wandered in the desert for forty years.

ARABIAN DESERT

The possible location of Taberah, where God sent quail for the complaining Hebrew people to eat (Numbers 11).

Numbers begins with the people in the Desert of Sinai (Numbers 1:1).

WHEN THE ACTION WAS

Abraham lived	The Israelites escaped from Egypt	The Israelites wandered in the desert for forty years		Jesus was born
2000BC	1500BC	1000BC	500BC	BC/AD
	The Israelites became slaves in Egypt	The Israelites entered the promised land	The Temple was built in Jerusalem for worship	

Behind the Scenes (cont.): to God. And it shows how God patiently and persistently disciplines his stubborn children.

Numbers gets its name from the census taken near the beginning and end of the book. However, the book's original Hebrew name—"In the Desert" or "In the Wilderness"—more accurately describes it.

The People of Israel Are Counted

1 The LORD spoke to Moses in the Meeting Tent in the Desert of Sinai. This was on the first day of the second month in the second year after the Israelites left Egypt. He said to Moses: 2"You and Aaron must count all the people of Israel by families and family groups, listing the name of each man. 3You and Aaron must count every man twenty years old or older who will serve in the army of Israel, and list them by their divisions. 4One man from each tribe, the leader of his family, will help you. 5These are the names of the men who will help you:

from the tribe of Reuben — Elizur son of Shedeur;
6from the tribe of Simeon — Shelumiel son of Zurishaddai;
7from the tribe of Judah — Nahshon son of Amminadab;
8from the tribe of Issachar — Nethanel son of Zuar;
9from the tribe of Zebulun — Eliab son of Helon;
10from the tribe of Ephraim son of Joseph — Elishama son of Ammihud;
from the tribe of Manasseh son of Joseph — Gamaliel son of Pedahzur;
11from the tribe of Benjamin — Abidan son of Gideoni;
12from the tribe of Dan — Ahiezer son of Ammishaddai;
13from the tribe of Asher — Pagiel son of Ocran;
14from the tribe of Gad — Eliasaph son of Deuel;
15from the tribe of Naphtali — Ahira son of Enan."

16These were the men chosen from the people to be leaders of their tribes, the heads of Israel's family groups.

17Moses and Aaron took these men who had been picked 18and called all the people of Israel together on the first day of the second month. Then the people were listed by their families and family groups, and all the men who were twenty years old or older were listed by name. 19Moses did exactly what the LORD had commanded and listed the people while they were in the Desert of Sinai.

20The tribe of Reuben, the first son born to Israel, was counted; all the men twenty years old or older who were able to serve in the army were listed by name with their families and family groups. 21The tribe of Reuben totaled 46,500 men.

22The tribe of Simeon was counted; all the men twenty years old or older who were able to serve in the army were listed by name with their families and family groups. 23The tribe of Simeon totaled 59,300 men.

24The tribe of Gad was counted; all the men twenty years old or older who were able to serve in the army were listed by name with their families and family groups. 25The tribe of Gad totaled 45,650 men.

26The tribe of Judah was counted; all the men twenty years old or older who were able to serve in the army were listed by name with their families and family groups. 27The tribe of Judah totaled 74,600 men.

28The tribe of Issachar was counted; all the men twenty years old or older who were able to serve in the army were listed by name with their families and family groups. 29The tribe of Issachar totaled 54,400 men.

30The tribe of Zebulun was counted; all the men twenty years old or older who were able to serve in the army were listed by name with their families and family groups. 31The tribe of Zebulun totaled 57,400 men.

32The tribe of Ephraim, a son of Joseph, was counted: all the men twenty years old or older who were able to serve in the army were listed by name with their families and family groups. 33The tribe of Ephraim totaled 40,500 men.

34The tribe of Manasseh, also a son of Joseph, was counted; all the men twenty years old or older who were able to serve in the army were listed by name with their families and family groups. 35The tribe of Manasseh totaled 32,200 men.

36The tribe of Benjamin was counted; all the men twenty years old or older who were able to serve in the army were listed by name with their families and family groups. 37The tribe of Benjamin totaled 35,400 men.

38The tribe of Dan was counted; all the men twenty years old or older who were able to serve in the army were listed by name with their families and family groups. 39The tribe of Dan totaled 62,700 men.

40The tribe of Asher was counted; all the men

twenty years old or older who were able to serve in the army were listed by name with their families and family groups. 41The tribe of Asher totaled 41,500 men.

42The tribe of Naphtali was counted; all the men twenty years old or older who were able to serve in the army were listed by name with their families and family groups. 43The tribe of Naphtali totaled 53,400 men.

44Moses, Aaron, and the twelve leaders of Israel, one from each of the families, counted these men. 45Every man of Israel twenty years old or older who was able to serve in the army was counted and listed with his family. 46The total number of men was 603,550.

SIDELIGHT: Imagine the entire population of San Diego—more than two million—wandering through the Mojave Desert in Southern California. That would be about how many Israelites some scholars say escaped from Egypt and wandered in the desert, according to the figures in Numbers 1:45–46.

47The families from the tribe of Levi were not listed with the others, because 48the LORD had told Moses: 49"Do not count the tribe of Levi or include them with the other Israelites. 50Instead put the Levites in charge of the Holy Tent*d* of the Agreement and everything that is with it. They must carry the Holy Tent and everything in it, and they must take care of it and make their camp around it. 51Any time the Holy Tent is moved, the Levites must take it down, and any time it is set up, the Levites must do it. Anyone else who goes near the Holy Tent will be put to death. 52The Israelites will make their camps in separate divisions, each family near its flag. 53But the Levites must make their camp around the Holy Tent of the Agreement so that I will not be angry with the Israelites. The Levites will take care of the Holy Tent of the Agreement."

54So the Israelites did everything just as the LORD commanded Moses.

The Camp Arrangement

2 The LORD said to Moses and Aaron: 2"The Israelites should make their camps around the Meeting Tent,*d* but they should not camp too close to it. They should camp under their family flag and banners."

3The camp of Judah will be on the east side, where the sun rises, and they will camp by divisions there under their flag. The leader of the peo-

ple of Judah is Nahshon son of Amminadab. 4There are 74,600 men in his division.

5Next to them the tribe*d* of Issachar will camp. The leader of the people of Issachar is Nethanel son of Zuar. 6There are 54,400 men in his division.

7Next is the tribe of Zebulun. The leader of the people of Zebulun is Eliab son of Helon. 8There are 57,400 men in his division.

9There are a total of 186,400 men in the camps of Judah and its neighbors, in all their divisions. They will be the first to march out of camp.

10The divisions of the camp of Reuben will be on the south side, where they will camp under their flag. The leader of the people of Reuben is Elizur son of Shedeur. 11There are 46,500 men in his division.

12Next to them the tribe of Simeon will camp. The leader of the people of Simeon is Shelumiel son of Zurishaddai. 13There are 59,300 men in his division.

14Next is the tribe of Gad. The leader of the people of Gad is Eliasaph son of Deuel. 15There are 45,650 men in his division.

16There are a total of 151,450 men in the camps of Reuben and its neighbors, in all their divisions. They will be the second group to march out of camp.

17When the Levites march out with the Meeting Tent, they will be in the middle of the other camps. The tribes will march out in the same order as they camp, each in its place under its flag.

18The divisions of the camp of Ephraim will be on the west side, where they will camp under their flag. The leader of the people of Ephraim is Elishama son of Ammihud. 19There are 40,500 men in his division.

20Next to them the tribe of Manasseh will camp. The leader of the people of Manasseh is Gamaliel son of Pedahzur. 21There are 32,200 men in his division.

22Next is the tribe of Benjamin. The leader of the people of Benjamin is Abidan son of Gideoni. 23There are 35,400 men in his division.

24There are a total of 108,100 men in the camps of Ephraim and its neighbors, in all their divisions. They will be the third group to march out of camp.

25The divisions of the camp of Dan will be on the north side, where they will camp under their flag. The leader of the people of Dan is Ahiezer son of Ammishaddai. 26There are 62,700 men in his division.

27Next to them the tribe of Asher will camp. The leader of the people of Asher is Pagiel son of Ocran. 28There are 41,500 men in his division.

29Next is the tribe of Naphtali. The leader of the people of Naphtali is Ahira son of Enan. 30There are 53,400 men in his division.

[31]There are 157,600 men in the camps of Dan and its neighbors. They will be the last to march out of camp, and they will travel under their own flag.

[32]These are the Israelites who were counted by families. The total number of Israelites in the camps, counted by divisions, is 603,550. [33]Moses obeyed the Lord and did not count the Levites among the other people of Israel.

[34]So the Israelites obeyed everything the Lord commanded Moses. They camped under their flags and marched out by families and family groups.

Aaron's Family, the Priests

3 This is the family history of Aaron and Moses at the time the Lord talked to Moses on Mount Sinai.

[2]Aaron had four sons: Nadab, the oldest, Abihu, Eleazar, and Ithamar. [3]These were the names of Aaron's sons, who were appointed to serve as priests. [4]But Nadab and Abihu died in the presence of the Lord when they offered the wrong kind of fire before the Lord in the Desert of Sinai. They had no sons. So Eleazar and Ithamar served as priests during the lifetime of their father Aaron.

[5]The Lord said to Moses, [6]"Bring the tribe[d] of Levi and present them to Aaron the priest to help him. [7]They will help him and all the Israelites at the Meeting Tent,[d] doing the work in the Holy Tent. [8]The Levites must take care of everything in the Meeting Tent and serve the people of Israel by doing the work in the Holy Tent. [9]Give the Levites to Aaron and his sons; of all the Israelites, the Levites are given completely to him. [10]Appoint Aaron and his sons to serve as priests, but anyone else who comes near the holy things must be put to death."

[11]The Lord also said to Moses, [12]"I am choosing the Levites from all the Israelites to take the place of all the firstborn[d] children of Israel. The Levites will be mine, [13]because the firstborn are mine. When you were in Egypt, I killed all the firstborn children of the Egyptians and took all the firstborn of Israel to be mine, both animals and children. They are mine. I am the Lord."

[14]The Lord again said to Moses in the Desert of Sinai, [15]"Count the Levites by families and family groups. Count every male one month old or older." [16]So Moses obeyed the Lord and counted them all.

[17]Levi had three sons, whose names were Gershon, Kohath, and Merari.

[18]The Gershonite family groups were Libni and Shimei.

[19]The Kohathite family groups were Amram, Izhar, Hebron, and Uzziel.

[20]The Merarite family groups were Mahli and Mushi.

These were the family groups of the Levites.

[21]The family groups of Libni and Shimei belonged to Gershon; they were the Gershonite family groups. [22]The number that was counted was 7,500 males one month old or older. [23]The Gershonite family groups camped on the west side, behind the Holy Tent. [24]The leader of the families of Gershon was Eliasaph son of Lael. [25]In the Meeting Tent the Gershonites were in charge of the Holy Tent, its covering, the curtain at the entrance to the Meeting Tent, [26]the curtains in the courtyard, the curtain at the entry to the courtyard around the Holy Tent and the altar, the ropes, and all the work connected with these items.

[27]The family groups of Amram, Izhar, Hebron, and Uzziel belonged to Kohath; they were the Kohathite family groups. [28]They had 8,600 males one month old or older, and they were responsible for taking care of the Holy Place. [29]The Kohathite family groups camped south of the Holy Tent. [30]The leader of the Kohathite families was Elizaphan son of Uzziel. [31]They were responsible for the Ark,[d] the table, the lampstand, the altars, the tools of the Holy Place which they were to use, the curtain, and all the work connected with these items. [32]The main leader of the Levites was Eleazar son of Aaron, the priest, who was in charge of all those responsible for the Holy Place.

[33]The family groups of Mahli and Mushi belonged to Merari; they were the Merarite family groups. [34]The number that was counted was 6,200 males one month old or older. [35]The leader of the Merari families was Zuriel son of Abihail, and they were to camp north of the Holy Tent. [36]The Merarites were responsible for the frames of the Holy Tent, the braces, the posts, the bases, and all the work connected with these items. [37]They were also responsible for the posts in the courtyard around the Holy Tent and their bases, tent pegs, and ropes.

[38]Moses, Aaron, and his sons camped east of the Holy Tent, toward the sunrise, in front of the Meeting Tent. They were responsible for the Holy Place for the Israelites. Anyone else who came near the Holy Place was to be put to death.

[39]Moses and Aaron counted the Levite men by their families, as the Lord commanded, and there were 22,000 males one month old or older.

Levites Take the Place of the Firstborn Sons

[40]The Lord said to Moses, "Count all the firstborn[d] sons in Israel one month old or older, and list their names. [41]Take the Levites for me instead of the firstborn sons of Israel; take the animals of

the Levites instead of the firstborn animals from the rest of Israel. I am the LORD."

⁴²So Moses did what the LORD commanded and counted all the firstborn sons of the Israelites. ⁴³When he listed all the firstborn sons one month old or older, there were 22,273 names.

⁴⁴The LORD also said to Moses, ⁴⁵"Take the Levites instead of all the firstborn sons of the Israelites, and take the animals of the Levites instead of the animals of the other people. The Levites are mine. I am the LORD. ⁴⁶Since there are 273 more firstborn sons than Levites, ⁴⁷collect two ounces of silver for each of the 273 sons. Use the measure as set by the Holy Place, which is two-fifths of an ounce. ⁴⁸Give the silver to Aaron and his sons as the payment for the 273 Israelites."

⁴⁹So Moses collected the money for the people the Levites could not replace. ⁵⁰From the firstborn of the Israelites, he collected thirty-five pounds of silver, using the measure set by the Holy Place. ⁵¹Moses obeyed the command of the LORD and gave the silver to Aaron and his sons.

The Jobs of the Kohath Family

4 The LORD said to Moses and Aaron, ²"Count the Kohathites among the Levites by family groups and families. ³Count the men from thirty to fifty years old, all who come to serve in the Meeting Tent.*d*

⁴"The Kohathites are responsible for the most holy things in the Meeting Tent. ⁵When the Israelites are ready to move, Aaron and his sons must go into the Holy Tent, take down the curtain, and cover the Ark*d* of the Agreement with it. ⁶Over this they must put a covering made from fine leather, then spread the solid blue cloth over that, and put the poles in place.

⁷"Then they must spread a blue cloth over the table for the bread that shows a person is in God's presence. They must put the plates, pans, bowls, and the jars for drink offerings on the table; they must leave the bread that is always there on the table. ⁸Then they must put a red cloth over all of these things, cover everything with fine leather, and put the poles in place.

⁹"With a blue cloth they must cover the lampstand, its lamps, its wick trimmers, its trays, and all the jars for the oil used in the lamps. ¹⁰Then they must wrap everything in fine leather and put all these things on a frame for carrying them.

¹¹"They must spread a blue cloth over the gold altar, cover it with fine leather, and put the poles in place. ¹²"They must gather all the things used for serving in the Holy Place and wrap them in a blue cloth. Then they must cover that with fine leather and put these things on a frame for carrying them. ¹³"They must clean the ashes off the bronze altar and spread a purple cloth over it. ¹⁴They

must gather all the things used for serving at the altar—the pans for carrying the fire, the meat forks, the shovels, and the bowls—and put them on the bronze altar. Then they must spread a covering of fine leather over it and put the poles in place.

¹⁵"When the Israelites are ready to move, and when Aaron and his sons have covered the holy furniture and all the holy things, the Kohathites may go in and carry them away. In this way they won't touch the holy things and die. It is the Kohathites' job to carry the things that are in the Meeting Tent.

¹⁶"Eleazar son of Aaron, the priest, will be responsible for the Holy Tent and for everything in it, for all the holy things it has: the oil for the lamp, the sweet-smelling incense,*d* the continual grain offering, and the oil used to appoint priests and things to the LORD's service."

¹⁷The LORD said to Moses and Aaron, ¹⁸"Don't let the Kohathites be cut off from the Levites. ¹⁹Do this for the Kohathites so that they may go near the Most Holy Place and not die: Aaron and his sons must go in and show each Kohathite what to do and what to carry. ²⁰The Kohathites must not enter and look at the holy things, even for a second, or they will die."

The Jobs of the Gershon Family

²¹The LORD said to Moses, ²²"Count the Gershonites by families and family groups. ²³Count the men from thirty to fifty years old, all who have a job to do in the Meeting Tent.*d*

²⁴"This is what the Gershonite family groups must do and what they must carry. ²⁵They must carry the curtains of the Holy Tent,*d* the Meeting Tent, its covering, and its outer covering made from fine leather. They must also carry the curtains for the entrance to the Meeting Tent, ²⁶the curtains of the courtyard that goes around the Holy Tent and the altar, the curtain for the entry to the courtyard, the ropes, and all the things used with the curtains. They must do everything connected with these things. ²⁷Aaron and his sons are in charge of what the Gershonites do or carry; you tell them what they are responsible for carrying. ²⁸This is the work of the Gershonite family group at the Meeting Tent. Ithamar son of Aaron, the priest, will direct their work.

The Jobs of the Merari Family

²⁹"Count the Merarite families and family groups. ³⁰Count the men from thirty to fifty years old, all who work at the Meeting Tent.*d* ³¹It is their job to carry the following as they serve in the Meeting Tent: the frames of the Holy Tent, the crossbars, the posts, and bases, ³²in addition to the posts that go around the courtyard, their bases, tent pegs, ropes, and everything that is used with

the poles around the courtyard. Tell each man exactly what to carry. [33]This is the work the Merarite family group will do for the Meeting Tent. Ithamar son of Aaron, the priest, will direct their work."

The Levite Families

[34]Moses, Aaron, and the leaders of Israel counted the Kohathites by families and family groups, [35]the men from thirty to fifty years old who were to work at the Meeting Tent.[d] [36]There were 2,750 men in the family groups. [37]This was the total of the Kohath family groups who worked at the Meeting Tent, whom Moses and Aaron counted as the LORD had commanded Moses.

[38]Also, the Gershonite were counted by families and family groups, [39]the men from thirty to fifty years old who were given work at the Meeting Tent. [40]The families and family groups had 2,630 men. [41]This was the total of the Gershon family groups who worked at the Meeting Tent, whom Moses and Aaron counted as the LORD had commanded.

[42]Also, the men in the families and family groups of the Merari family were counted, [43]the men from thirty to fifty years old who were to work at the Meeting Tent. [44]The family groups had 3,200 men. [45]This was the total of the Merari family groups, whom Moses and Aaron counted as the LORD had commanded Moses.

[46]So Moses, Aaron, and the leaders of Israel counted all the Levites by families and family groups. [47]They counted the men from thirty to fifty who were given work at the Meeting Tent and who carried the Tent. [48]The total number of these men was 8,580. [49]Each man was counted as the LORD had commanded Moses; each man was given his work and told what to carry as the LORD had commanded Moses.

Rules About Cleanliness

5 The LORD said to Moses, [2]"Command the Israelites to send away from camp anyone with a harmful skin disease. Send away anyone who gives off body fluid or who has become unclean by touching a dead body. [3]Send both men and women outside the camp so that they won't spread the disease there, where I am living among you." [4]So Israel obeyed the LORD's command and sent those people outside the camp. They did just as the LORD had told Moses.

Paying for Doing Wrong

[5]The LORD said to Moses, [6]"Tell the Israelites: 'When a man or woman does something wrong to another person, that is really sinning against the LORD. That person is guilty [7]and must admit the wrong that has been done. The person must fully pay for the wrong that has been done, adding

one-fifth to it, and giving it to the person who was wronged. [8]But if that person is dead and does not have any close relatives to receive the payment, the one who did wrong owes the LORD and must pay the priest. In addition, the priest must sacrifice a male sheep to remove the wrong so that the person will belong to the LORD. [9]When an Israelite brings a holy gift, it should be given to the priest. [10]No one has to give these holy gifts, but if someone does give them, they belong to the priest.' "

Suspicious Husbands

[11]Then the LORD said to Moses, [12]"Tell the Israelites: 'A man's wife might be unfaithful to him [13]and have sexual relations with another man. Her sin might be kept hidden from her husband so that he does not know about the wrong she did. Perhaps no one saw it, and she wasn't caught. [14]But if her husband has feelings of jealousy and suspects she has sinned—whether she has or not— [15]he should take her to the priest. The husband must also take an offering for her of two quarts of barley flour. He must not pour oil or incense[d] on it, because this is a grain offering for jealousy, an offering of remembrance. It is to find out if she is guilty.

[16]" 'The priest will bring in the woman and make her stand before the LORD. [17]He will take some holy water in a clay jar, and he will put some dirt from the floor of the Holy Tent into the water. [18]The priest will make the woman stand before the LORD, and he will loosen her hair. He will hand her the offering of remembrance, the grain offering for jealousy; he will hold the bitter water that brings a curse. [19]The priest will make her take an oath and ask her, "Has another man had sexual relations with you? Have you been unfaithful to your husband? If you haven't, this bitter water that brings a curse won't hurt you. [20]But if you have been unfaithful to your husband and have had sexual relations with a man besides him"— [21]the priest will then put on her the curse that the oath will bring—"the LORD will make the people curse and reject you. He will make your stomach get big, and he will make your body unable to give birth to another baby. [22]This water that brings a curse will go inside you and make your body unable to give birth to another baby."

" 'The woman must say, "I agree."

[23]" 'The priest should write these curses on a scroll, wash the words off into the bitter water, [24]and make the woman drink the bitter water that brings a curse. If she is guilty, the water will make her sick. [25]Then the priest will take the grain offering for jealousy from her. He will present it before the LORD and bring it to the altar. [26]He will take a handful of the grain, which is a memorial offering, and burn it on the altar. After that he will

make the woman drink the water ²⁷to see if she is not pure and if she has sinned against her husband. When it goes into her, if her stomach gets big so that she is not able to have another baby, her people will reject her. ²⁸But if the woman has not sinned, she is pure. She is not guilty, and she will be able to have babies.

²⁹" 'So this is the teaching about jealousy. This is what to do when a woman does wrong and is unfaithful while she is married to her husband. ³⁰It also should be done if the man gets jealous because he suspects his wife. The priest will have her stand before the Lord, and he will do all these things, just as the teaching commands. ³¹In this way the husband can be proven correct, and the woman will suffer if she has done wrong.' "

Rules for the Nazirites

6 The Lord said to Moses, ²"Tell the Israelites: 'If men or women want to promise to belong to the Lord in a special way, they will be called Nazirites. ³During this time, they must not drink wine or beer, or vinegar made from wine or beer. They must not even drink grape juice or eat grapes or raisins. ⁴While they are Nazirites, they must not eat anything that comes from the grapevine, even the seeds or the skin.

⁵" 'During the time they have promised to belong to the Lord, they must not cut their hair. They must be holy until this special time is over. They must let their hair grow long. ⁶During their special time of belonging to the Lord, Nazirites must not go near a dead body. ⁷Even if their own father, mother, brother, or sister dies, they must not touch them, or they will become unclean.ᵈ They must still keep their promise to belong to God in a special way. ⁸While they are Nazirites, they belong to the Lord in a special way.

SIDELIGHT: What do you call a person who grows a beard, watches what he eats, and never cuts his hair? A Nazirite. Nazirites were men who took a special vow to dedicate their lives to God (Numbers 6:2–8). Samson, whose story is in Judges 13—16 (p. 229), was probably the most famous of these Nazirites.

---

⁹" 'If they are next to someone who dies suddenly, their hair, which was part of their promise, has been made unclean. So they must shave their head seven days later to be clean. ¹⁰Then on the eighth day, they must bring two doves or two young pigeons to the priest at the entrance to the Meeting Tent.ᵈ ¹¹The priest will offer one as a sin offering and the other as a burnt offering. This removes sin so they will belong to the Lord. (They had sinned because they were near a dead body.) That same day they will again promise to let their hair grow ¹²and give themselves to the Lord for another special time. They must bring a male lamb a year old as a penalty offering. The days of the special time before don't count, because they became unclean during their first special time.

¹³" 'This is the teaching for the Nazirites. When the promised time is over, they must go the entrance of the Meeting Tentᵈ ¹⁴and give their offerings to the Lord. They must offer a year-old male lamb that has nothing wrong with it, as a burnt offering, a year-old female lamb that has nothing wrong with it, as a sin offering, and a male sheep that has nothing wrong with it, for a fellowship offering. ¹⁵They must also bring the grain offerings and drink offerings that go with them. And they must bring a basket of bread made without yeast, loaves made with fine flour mixed with oil, and wafers made without yeast spread with oil.

¹⁶" 'The priest will give these offerings to the Lord and make the sin offering and the burnt offering. ¹⁷Then he will kill the male sheep as a fellowship offering to the Lord; along with it, he will present the basket of bread made without yeast, the grain offering, and the drink offering.

¹⁸" 'The Nazirites must go to the entrance of the Meeting Tent and shave off their hair that they grew for their promise. The hair will be put in the fire that is under the sacrifice of the fellowship offering.

¹⁹" 'After the Nazirites cut off their hair, the priest will give them a boiled shoulder from the male sheep. From the basket he will also give a loaf and a wafer, both made without yeast. ²⁰Then the priest will present them to the Lord. They are holy and belong to the priest. Also, he is to present the breast and the thigh from the male sheep. After that, the Nazirites may drink wine.

²¹" 'This is the teaching for the Nazirites who make a promise. Everyone who makes the Nazirite promise must give all of these gifts to the Lord. If they promised to do more, they must keep their promise, according to the teaching of the Nazirites.' "

The Priests' Blessings

²²The Lord said to Moses, ²³"Tell Aaron and his sons, 'This is how you should bless the Israelites. Say to them:
²⁴"May the Lord bless you and keep you.
²⁵May the Lord show you his kindness
    and have mercy on you.
²⁶May the Lord watch over you
    and give you peace." '
²⁷"So Aaron and his sons will bless the Israelites with my name, and I will bless them."

The Holy Tent

7 When Moses finished setting up the Holy Tent,*d* he gave it for service to the LORD by pouring olive oil on the Tent and on everything used in it. He also poured oil on the altar and all its tools to prepare them for service to the LORD. ²Then the leaders of Israel made offerings. These were the heads of the families, the leaders of each tribe*d* who counted the people. ³They brought to the LORD six covered carts and twelve oxen—each leader giving an ox, and every two leaders giving a cart. They brought these to the Holy Tent.

⁴The LORD said to Moses, ⁵"Accept these gifts from the leaders and use them in the work of the Meeting Tent. Give them to the Levites as they need them."

⁶So Moses accepted the carts and the oxen and gave them to the Levites. ⁷He gave two carts and four oxen to the Gershonites, which they needed for their work. ⁸Then Moses gave four carts and eight oxen to the Merarites, which they needed for their work. Ithamar son of Aaron, the priest, directed the work of all of them. ⁹Moses did not give any oxen or carts to the Kohathites, because

their job was to carry the holy things on their shoulders.

¹⁰When the oil was poured on the altar, the leaders brought their offerings to it to give it to the LORD's service; they presented them in front of the altar. ¹¹The LORD told Moses, "Each day one leader must bring his gift to make the altar ready for service to me."

¹²⁻⁸³Each of the twelve leaders brought these gifts. Each leader brought one silver plate that weighed about three and one-fourth pounds, and one silver bowl that weighed about one and three-fourths pounds. These weights were set by the Holy Place measure. The bowl and the plate were filled with fine flour mixed with oil for a grain offering. Each leader also brought a large gold dish that weighed about four ounces and was filled with incense.*d*

In addition, each of the leaders brought one young bull, one male sheep, and one male lamb a year old for a burnt offering; one male goat for a sin offering; and two oxen, five male sheep, five male goats, and five male lambs a year old for a fellowship offering.

On the first day Nahshon son of Amminadab

---

brought his gifts. He was the leader of the tribe of Judah.

On the second day Nethanel son of Zuar brought his gifts. He was the leader of the tribe of Issachar.

On the third day Eliab son of Helon brought his gifts. He was the leader of the tribe of Zebulun.

On the fourth day Elizur son of Shedeur brought his gifts. He was the leader of the tribe of Reuben.

On the fifth day Shelumiel son of Zurishaddai brought his gifts. He was the leader of the tribe of Simeon.

On the sixth day Eliasaph son of Deuel brought his gifts. He was the leader of the tribe of Gad.

On the seventh day Elishama son of Ammihud brought his gifts. He was the leader of the tribe of Ephraim.

On the eighth day Gamaliel son of Pedahzur brought his gifts. He was the leader of the tribe of Manasseh.

On the ninth day Abidan son of Gideoni brought his gifts. He was the leader of the tribe of Benjamin.

On the tenth day Ahiezer son of Ammishaddai brought his gifts. He was the leader of the tribe of Dan.

On the eleventh day Pagiel son of Ocran brought his gifts. He was the leader of the tribe of Asher.

On the twelfth day Ahira son of Enan brought his gifts. He was the leader of the tribe of Naphtali.

84So these were the gifts from the Israelite leaders when oil was poured on the altar and it was given for service to the LORD: twelve silver plates, twelve silver bowls, and twelve gold dishes. 85Each silver plate weighed about three and one-fourth pounds, and each bowl weighed about one and three-fourths pounds. All the silver plates and silver bowls together weighed about sixty pounds according to a weight set by the Holy Place measure. 86The twelve gold dishes filled with incense weighed four ounces each, according to the weight set by the Holy Place measure. Together the gold dishes weighed about three pounds. 87The total number of animals for the burnt offering was twelve bulls, twelve male sheep, and twelve male lambs a year old. There was also a grain offering, and there were twelve male goats for a sin offering. 88The total number of animals for the fellowship offering was twenty-four bulls, *sixty male sheep, sixty male goats, and sixty male* lambs a year old. All these offerings were for giving the altar to the service of the LORD after the oil had been poured on it.

89When Moses went into the Meeting Tent to speak with the LORD, he heard the LORD speaking to him. The voice was coming from between the two gold creatures with wings that were above the lid of the Ark*d* of the Agreement. In this way the LORD spoke with him.

The Lampstand

8 The LORD said to Moses, 2"Speak to Aaron and tell him, 'Put the seven lamps where they can light the area in front of the lampstand.' "

3Aaron did this, putting the lamps so they lighted the area in front of the lampstand; he obeyed the command the LORD gave Moses. 4The lampstand was made from hammered gold, from its base to the flowers. It was made exactly the way the LORD had showed Moses.

The Levites Are Given to God

5The LORD said to Moses, 6"Take the Levites away from the other Israelites and make them clean.*d* 7This is what you should do to make them clean: Sprinkle the cleansing water on them, and have them shave their bodies and wash their clothes so they will be clean. 8They must take a young bull and the grain offering of flour mixed with oil that goes with it. Then take a second young bull for a sin offering. 9Bring the Levites to the front of the Meeting Tent,*d* and gather all the Israelites around. 10When you bring the Levites before the LORD, the Israelites should put their hands on them.*n* 11Aaron will present the Levites before the LORD as an offering presented from the Israelites. Then the Levites will be ready to do the work of the LORD.

12"The Levites will put their hands on the bulls' heads—one bull will be a sin offering to the LORD, and the other will be a burnt offering, to remove the sins of the Levites so they will belong to the LORD. 13Make the Levites stand in front of Aaron and his sons and present the Levites as an offering to the LORD. 14In this way you must set apart the Levites from the other Israelites; the Levites will be mine.

15"Make the Levites pure, and present them as an offering so that they may come to work at the Meeting Tent. 16They will be given completely to me from the Israelites; I have taken them for myself instead of the firstborn*d* of every Israelite woman. 17All the firstborn in Israel—people or animals—are mine. When I killed all the firstborn in Egypt, I set the *firstborn in Israel aside for myself.* 18But I have taken the Levites instead of all the firstborn in Israel. 19From all the Israelites I have given the Levites to Aaron and his sons so that they may serve the Israelites at the Meeting Tent. They will help remove the Israelites' sins so

---

put . . . them   This showed that the people had a part in giving the Levites their special work they will belong to the LORD and so that no disaster will strike the Israelites when they approach the Holy Place."

²⁰So Moses, Aaron, and all the Israelites obeyed and did with the Levites what the LORD commanded Moses. ²¹The Levites made themselves clean and washed their clothes. Then Aaron presented them as an offering to the LORD. He also removed their sins so they would be pure. ²²After that, the Levites came to the Meeting Tent to work, and Aaron and his sons told them what to do. They did with the Levites what the LORD commanded Moses.

²³The LORD said to Moses, ²⁴"This command is for the Levites. Everyone twenty-five years old or older must come to the Meeting Tent, because they all have jobs to do there. ²⁵At the age of fifty, they must retire from their jobs and not work again. ²⁶They may help their fellow Levites with their work at the Meeting Tent, but they must not do the work themselves. This is the way you are to give the Levites their jobs."

The Passover Is Celebrated

9 The LORD spoke to Moses in the Desert of Sinai in the first month of the second year after the Israelites left Egypt. He said, ²"Tell the Israelites to celebrate the Passover*d* at the appointed time. ³That appointed time is the fourteenth day of this month at twilight; they must obey all the rules about it."

⁴So Moses told the Israelites to celebrate the Passover, ⁵and they did; it was in the Desert of Sinai at twilight on the fourteenth day of the first month. The Israelites did everything just as the LORD commanded Moses.

⁶But some of the people could not celebrate the Passover on that day because they were unclean*d* from touching a dead body. So they went to Moses and Aaron that day and ⁷said to Moses, "We are unclean because of touching a dead body. But why should we be kept from offering gifts to the LORD at this appointed time? Why can't we join the other Israelites?"

⁸Moses said to them, "Wait, and I will find out what the LORD says about you."

⁹Then the LORD said to Moses, ¹⁰"Tell the Israelites this: 'If you or your descendants*d* become unclean because of a dead body, or if you are away on a trip during the Passover, you must still celebrate the LORD's Passover. ¹¹But celebrate it at twilight on the fourteenth day of the second month. Eat the lamb with bitter herbs and bread made without yeast. ¹²Don't leave any of it until the next morning or break any of its bones. When you celebrate the Passover, follow all the rules. ¹³Anyone who is clean and is not away on a trip but does not eat the Passover must be cut off from the people. That person did not give an offering

to the LORD at the appointed time and must be punished for the sin.

¹⁴" 'Foreigners among you may celebrate the LORD's Passover, but they must follow all the rules. You must have the same rules for foreigners as you have for yourselves.' "

The Cloud Above the Tent

¹⁵On the day the Holy Tent,*d* the Tent of the Agreement, was set up, a cloud covered it. From dusk until dawn the cloud above the Tent looked like fire. ¹⁶The cloud stayed above the Tent, and at night it looked like fire. ¹⁷When the cloud moved from its place over the Tent, the Israelites moved, and wherever the cloud stopped, the Israelites camped. ¹⁸So the Israelites moved at the LORD's command, and they camped at his command. While the cloud stayed over the Tent, they remained camped. ¹⁹Sometimes the cloud stayed over the Tent for a long time, but the Israelites obeyed the LORD and did not move. ²⁰Sometimes the cloud was over it only a few days. At the LORD's command the people camped, and at his command they moved. ²¹Sometimes the cloud stayed only from dusk until dawn; when the cloud lifted the next morning, the people moved. When the cloud lifted, day or night, the people moved. ²²The cloud might stay over the Tent for two days, a month, or a year. As long as it stayed, the people camped, but when it lifted, they moved. ²³At the LORD's command the people camped, and at his command they moved. They obeyed the LORD's order that he commanded through Moses.

The Silver Trumpets

10 The LORD said to Moses, ²"Make two trumpets of hammered silver, and use them to call the people together and to march out of camp. ³When both trumpets are blown, the people should gather before you at the entrance to the Meeting Tent.*d* ⁴If you blow only one trumpet, the leaders, the heads of the family groups of Israel, should meet before you. ⁵When you loudly blow the trumpets, the tribes*d* camping on the east should move. ⁶When you loudly blow them again, the tribes camping on the south should move; the loud sound will tell them to move. ⁷When you want to gather the people, blow the trumpets, but don't blow them as loudly.

⁸"Aaron's sons, the priests, should blow the trumpets. This is a law for you and your descendants*d* from now on. ⁹When you are fighting an enemy who attacks you in your own land, blow the trumpets loudly. The LORD your God will take notice of you and will save you from your enemies. ¹⁰Also blow your trumpets at happy times and during your feasts and at New Moon*d* festivals. Blow them over your burnt offerings and fel-

lowship offerings, because they will help you remember your God. I am the LORD your God."

The Israelites Move Camp

[11]The cloud lifted from the Tent[d] of the Agreement on the twentieth day of the second month of the second year. [12]So the Israelites moved from the Desert of Sinai and continued until the cloud stopped in the Desert of Paran. [13]This was their first time to move, and they did it as the LORD had commanded Moses.

[14]The divisions from the camp of Judah moved first under their flag. Nahshon son of Amminadab was the commander. [15]Nethanel son of Zuar was over the division of the tribe[d] of Issachar. [16]Eliab son of Helon was over the division of the tribe of Zebulun. [17]Then the Holy Tent was taken down, and the Gershonites and Merarites, who carried it, moved next.

[18]Then came the divisions from the camp of Reuben under their flag, and Elizur son of Shedeur was the commander. [19]Shelumiel son of Zurishaddai was over the division of the tribe of Simeon. [20]Eliasaph son of Deuel was over the division of the tribe of Gad. [21]Then came the Kohathites, who carried the holy things; the Holy Tent was to be set up before they arrived.

[22]Next came the divisions from the camp of Ephraim under their flag, and Elishama son of Ammihud was the commander. [23]Gamaliel son of Pedahzur was over the division of the tribe of Manasseh, [24]and Abidan son of Gideoni was over the division of the tribe of Benjamin.

[25]The last ones were the rear guard for all the tribes. These were the divisions from the camp of Dan under their flag, and Ahiezer son of Ammishaddai was the commander. [26]Pagiel son of Ocran was over the division of the tribe of Asher; [27]Ahira son of Enan was over the division of the tribe of Naphtali. [28]This was the order the Israelite divisions marched in when they moved.

[29]Hobab was the son of Reuel the Midianite,[n] who was Moses' father-in-law. Moses said to Hobab, "We are moving to the land the LORD promised to give us. Come with us and we will be good to you, because the LORD has promised good things to Israel."

[30]But Hobab answered, "No, I will not go. I will go back to my own land where I was born."

[31]But Moses said, "Please don't leave us. You know where we can camp in the desert, and you can be our guide. [32]Come with us. We will share with you all the good things the LORD gives us."

[33]So they left the mountain of the LORD and traveled for three days. The Ark[d] of the LORD's Agreement went in front of the people for those three days, as they looked for a place to camp. [34]The LORD's cloud was over them during the day when they left their camp.

[35]When the Ark left the camp, Moses said,
"Rise up, LORD!
  Scatter your enemies:
  make those who hate you run from you."
[36]And when the Ark was set down, Moses said,
"Return, LORD,
  to the thousands of people of Israel."

Fire from the Lord

11 Now the people complained to the LORD about their troubles, and when he heard them, he became angry. Then fire from the LORD burned among the people at the edge of the camp. [2]The people cried out to Moses, and when he prayed to the LORD, the fire stopped burning. [3]So that place was called Taberah,[n] because the LORD's fire had burned among them.

Seventy Older Leaders Help Moses

[4]Some troublemakers among them wanted better food, and soon all the Israelites began complaining. They said, "We want meat! [5]We remember the fish we ate for free in Egypt. We also had cucumbers, melons, leeks, onions, and garlic. [6]But now we have lost our appetite; we never see anything but this manna!"

[7]The manna was like small white seeds. [8]The people would go to gather it, and then grind it in handmills, or crush it between stones. After they cooked it in a pot or made cakes with it, it tasted like bread baked with olive oil. [9]When the dew fell on the camp each night, so did the manna.

[10]Moses heard every family crying as they stood in the entrances of their tents. Then the LORD became very angry, and Moses got upset. [11]He asked the LORD, "Why have you brought me, your servant, this trouble? What have I done wrong that you made me responsible for all these people? [12]I am not the father of all these people, and I didn't give birth to them. So why do you make me carry them to the land you promised to our ancestors? Must I carry them in my arms as a nurse carries a baby? [13]Where can I get meat for all these people? They keep crying to me, 'We want meat!' [14]I can't take care of all these people alone. It is too much for me. [15]If you are going to continue doing this to me, then kill me now. If you care about me, put me to death, and then I won't have any more troubles."

[16]The LORD said to Moses, "Bring me seventy of Israel's older leaders, men that you know are leaders among the people. Bring them to the Meeting Tent,[d] and have them stand there with

---

Reuel the Midianite Also called Jethro.
Taberah This name means "burning."

you. [17]I will come down and speak with you there. I will take some of the Spirit[d] that is in you, and I will give it to them. They will help you care for the people so that you will not have to care for them alone.

[18]"Tell the people this: 'Make yourselves holy for tomorrow, and you will eat meat. You cried to the Lord, "We want meat! We were better off in Egypt!" So now the Lord will give you meat to eat. [19]You will eat it not for just one, two, five, ten, or even twenty days, [20]but you will eat that meat for a whole month. You will eat it until it comes out your nose, and you will grow to hate it. This is because you have rejected the Lord, who is with you. You have cried to him, saying, "Why did we ever leave Egypt?"'"

[21]Moses said, "Lord, here are six hundred thousand people standing around me, and you say, 'I will give them enough meat to eat for a month!' [22]If we killed all the flocks and herds, that would not be enough. If we caught all the fish in the sea, that would not be enough."

[23]But the Lord said to Moses, "Do you think I'm weak? Now you will see if I can do what I say."

[24]So Moses went out to the people and told them what the Lord had said. He gathered seventy of the older leaders together and had them stand around the Tent. [25]Then the Lord came down in the cloud and spoke to Moses. The Lord took some of the Spirit Moses had, and he gave it to the seventy leaders. With the Spirit in them, they prophesied,[d] but just that one time.

[26]Two men named Eldad and Medad were also listed as leaders, but they did not go to the Tent. They stayed in the camp, but the Spirit was also given to them, and they prophesied in the camp. [27]A young man ran to Moses and said, "Eldad and Medad are prophesying in the camp."

[28]Joshua son of Nun said, "Moses, my master, stop them!" (Ever since he was a young boy, Joshua had been Moses' assistant.)

[29]But Moses answered "Are you jealous for me? I wish all the Lord's people could prophesy. I wish the Lord would give his Spirit to all of them!" [30]Then Moses and the leaders of Israel went back to the camp.

The Lord Sends Quail

[31]The Lord sent a strong wind from the sea, and it blew quail into the area all around the camp. The quail were about three feet deep on the ground, and there were quail a day's walk in any direction. [32]But the people went out and gathered quail all that day, that night, and the next day. Everyone gathered at least sixty bushels, and they spread them around the camp. [33]But the

Lord became very angry, and he gave the people a terrible sickness that came while the meat was still in their mouths. [34]So the people named that place Kibroth Hattaavah,[n] because there they buried those who wanted other food.

[35]From Kibroth Hattaavah the people went to stay at Hazeroth.

> **SIDELIGHT:** If you get sick of Thanksgiving leftovers, imagine having one hundred eighty turkeys left! That's about how much quail the Israelites each gathered after complaining that God hadn't provided them with meat in the desert. No wonder they all got sick (Numbers 11:31–32).

Miriam and Aaron Speak Against Moses

12 Miriam and Aaron began to talk against Moses because of his Cushite wife (he had married a Cushite). [2]They said, "Is Moses the only one the Lord speaks through? Doesn't he also speak through us?" And the Lord heard this.

[3](Now Moses was very humble. He was the least proud person on earth.)

[4]So the Lord suddenly spoke to Moses, Aaron, and Miriam and said, "All three of you come to the Meeting Tent."[d] So they went. [5]The Lord came down in a pillar of cloud and stood at the entrance to the Tent. He called to Aaron and Miriam, and they both came near. [6]He said, "Listen to my words:

When a prophet[d] is among you,
    I, the Lord, will show myself to him in
        visions;
    I will speak to him in dreams.
[7]But this is not true with my servant Moses.
    I trust him to lead all my people.
[8]I speak face to face with him —
    clearly not with hidden meanings.
    He has even seen the form of the Lord.
You should be afraid
    to speak against my servant Moses."

[9]The Lord was very angry with them, and he left.

[10]When the cloud lifted from the Tent and Aaron turned toward Miriam, she was as white as snow; she had a skin disease. [11]Aaron said to Moses, "Please, my master, forgive us for our foolish sin. [12]Don't let her be like a baby who is born dead. (Sometimes a baby is born with half of its flesh eater away.)"

[13]So Moses cried out to the Lord, "God, please heal her!"

Kibroth Hattaavah This name in Hebrew means "graves of wanting."

14The LORD answered Moses, "If her father had spit in her face, she would have been shamed for seven days, so put her outside the camp for seven days. After that, she may come back." 15So Miriam was put outside of the camp for seven days, and the people did not move on until she came back.

16After that, the people left Hazeroth and camped in the Desert of Paran.

The Spies Explore Canaan

13 The LORD said to Moses, 2"Send men to explore the land of Canaan, which I will give to the Israelites. Send one leader from each tribe."*d*

3So Moses obeyed the LORD's command and sent the Israelite leaders out from the Desert of Paran. 4These are their names: from the tribe of Reuben, Shammua son of Zaccur; 5from the tribe of Simeon, Shaphat son of Hori; 6from the tribe of Judah, Caleb son of Jephunneh; 7from the tribe of Issachar, Igal son of Joseph; 8from the tribe of Ephraim, Hoshea son of Nun; 9from the tribe of Benjamin, Palti son of Raphu; 10from the tribe of Zebulun, Gaddiel son of Sodi; 11from the tribe of Manasseh (a tribe of Joseph), Gaddi son of Susi; 12from the tribe of Dan, Ammiel son of Gemalli; 13from the tribe of Asher, Sethur son of Michael; 14from the tribe of Naphtali, Nahbi son of Vophsi; 15from the tribe of Gad, Geuel son of Maki.

16These are the names of the men Moses sent to explore the land. (Moses gave Hoshea son of Nun the new name Joshua.)

17Moses sent them to explore Canaan and said, "Go through southern Canaan and then into the mountains. 18See what the land looks like. Are the people who live there strong or weak? Are there a few or many? 19What kind of land do they live in? Is it good or bad? What about the towns they live in—are they open like camps, or do they have walls? 20What about the soil? Is it fertile or poor? Are there trees there? Try to bring back some of the fruit from that land." (It was the season for the first grapes.)

21So they went up and explored the land, from the Desert of Zin all the way to Rehob by Lebo Hamath. 22They went through the southern area to Hebron, where Ahiman, Sheshai, and Talmai, the descendants*d* of Anak lived.*d* (The city of Hebron had been built seven years before Zoan in Egypt.) 23In the Valley of Eshcol, they cut off a branch of a grapevine that had one bunch of grapes on it and carried that branch on a pole between two of them. They also got some pomegranates*d* and figs. 24That place was called the Valley of Eshcol,*n* because the Israelites cut off the

bunch of grapes there. 25After forty days of exploring the land, the men returned to the camp.

26They came back to Moses and Aaron and all the Israelites at Kadesh, in the Desert of Paran. The men reported to them and showed everybody the fruit from the land. 27They told Moses, "We went to the land where you sent us, and it is a fertile land! Here is some of its fruit. 28But the people who live there are strong. Their cities are walled and very large. We even saw some Anakites there. 29The Amalekites live in the southern area; the Hittites, Jebusites, and Amorites live in the mountains; and the Canaanites live near the sea and along the Jordan River."

30Then Caleb told the people near Moses to be quiet, and he said, "We should certainly go up and take the land for ourselves. We can certainly do it."

31But the men who had gone with him said, "We can't attack those people; they are stronger than we are." 32And those men gave the Israelites a bad report about the land they explored, saying, "The land that we explored is too large to conquer. All the people we saw are very tall. 33We saw the Nephilim*d* people there. (The Anakites come from the Nephilim people.) We felt like grasshoppers, and we looked like grasshoppers to them."

The People Complain Again

14 That night all the people in the camp began crying loudly. 2All the Israelites complained against Moses and Aaron, and all the people said to them, "We wish we had died in Egypt or in this desert. 3Why is the LORD bringing us to this land to be killed with swords? Our wives and children will be taken away. We would be better off going back to Egypt." 4They said to each other, "Let's choose a leader and go back to Egypt."

5Then Moses and Aaron bowed facedown in front of all the Israelites gathered there. 6Joshua son of Nun and Caleb son of Jephunneh, who had explored the land, tore their clothes. 7They said to all of the Israelites, "The land we explored is very good. 8If the LORD is pleased with us, he will lead us into that land and give us that fertile land. 9Don't turn against the LORD! Don't be afraid of the people in that land! We will chew them up. They have no protection, but the LORD is with us. So don't be afraid of them."

10Then all the people talked about killing them *with stones. But the glory of the LORD appeared at the Meeting Tentd to all the Israelites.* 11The LORD said to Moses, "How long will these people ignore me? How long will they not believe me in spite of the miracles*d* I have done among them? 12I will give them a terrible sickness and get rid of

Eshcol   This name in Hebrew means "bunch."

them. But I will make you into a great nation that will be stronger than they are."

[13]Then Moses said to the Lord, "The Egyptians will hear about it! You brought these people from there by your great power, [14]and the Egyptians will tell this to those who live in this land. They have already heard about you, Lord. They know that you are with your people and that you were seen face to face. They know that your cloud stays over your people and that you lead your people with that cloud during the day and with fire at night. [15]If you put these people to death all at once, the nations who have heard about your power will say, [16]'The Lord was not able to bring them into the land he promised them. So he killed them in the desert.'

[17]"So show your strength now, Lord. Do what you said: [18]'The Lord doesn't become angry quickly, but he has great love. He forgives sin and law breaking. But the Lord never forgets to punish guilty people. When parents sin, he will also punish their children, their grandchildren, their great-grandchildren, and their great-great-grandchildren.' [19]By your great love, forgive these people's sin, just as you have forgiven them from the time they left Egypt until now."

[20]The Lord answered, "I have forgiven them as you asked. [21]But, as surely as I live and as surely as my glory fills the whole earth, I make this promise: [22]All these men saw my glory and the miracles I did in Egypt and in the desert, but they disobeyed me and tested me ten times. [23]So not one of them will see the land I promised to their ancestors. No one who rejected me will see that land. [24]But my servant Caleb thinks differently and follows me completely. So I will bring him into the land he has already seen, and his children will own that land. [25]Since the Amalekites and the Canaanites are living in the valleys, leave tomorrow and follow the desert road toward the Red Sea."

The Lord Punishes the People

[26]The Lord said to Moses and Aaron, [27]"How long will these evil people complain about me? I have heard the grumbling and complaining of these Israelites. [28]So tell them, 'This is what the Lord says. I heard what you said, and as surely as I live, I will do those very things to you: [29]You will die in this desert. Every one of you who is twenty years old or older and who was counted with the people — all of you who complained against me — will die. [30]Not one of you will enter the land where I promised you would live; only Caleb son of Jephunneh and Joshua son of Nun will go in. [31]You said that your children would be taken away, but I will bring them into the land to enjoy what you refused. [32]As for you, you will die in this desert. [33]Your children will be shepherds

here for forty years. Because you were not loyal, they will suffer until you lie dead in the desert. [34]For forty years you will suffer for your sins — a year for each of the forty days you explored the land. You will know me as your enemy.' [35]I, the Lord, have spoken, and I will certainly do these things to all these evil people who have come together against me. So they will all die here in this desert."

[36]The men Moses had sent to explore the land had returned and spread complaints among all the people. They had given a bad report about the land. [37]The men who gave a very bad report died; the Lord killed them with a terrible sickness. [38]Only two of the men who explored the land did not die — Joshua son of Nun and Caleb son of Jephunneh.

[39]When Moses told these things to all the Israelites, they were very sad. [40]Early the next morning they started to go toward the top of the mountains, saying, "We have sinned. We will go where the Lord told us."

[41]But Moses said, "Why are you disobeying the Lord's command? You will not win! [42]Don't go, because the Lord is not with you and you will be beaten by your enemies. [43]You will run into the Amalekites and Canaanites, who will kill you with swords. You have turned away from the Lord, so the Lord will not be with you."

[44]But they were proud. They went toward the top of the mountains, but Moses and the Ark[d] of the Agreement with the Lord did not leave the camp. [45]The Amalekites and the Canaanites who lived in those mountains came down and attacked the Israelites and beat them back all the way to Hormah.

Rules About Sacrifices

15 The Lord said to Moses, [2]"Speak to the Israelites and say to them, 'When you enter the land that I am giving you as a home, [3]give the Lord offerings made by fire. These may be from your herds or flocks, as a smell pleasing to the Lord. These may be burnt offerings or sacrifices for special promises, or as gifts to him, or as festival offerings. [4]The one who brings the offering shall also give the Lord a grain offering. It should be two quarts of fine flour mixed with one quart of olive oil. [5]Each time you offer a lamb as a burnt offering or sacrifice, also prepare a quart of wine as a drink offering.

[6]"'If you are giving a male sheep, also prepare a grain offering of four quarts of fine flour mixed with one and one-fourth quarts of olive oil. [7]Also prepare one and one-fourth quarts of wine as a drink offering. Its smell will be pleasing to the Lord.

[8]"'If you prepare a young bull as a burnt offering or sacrifice, whether it is for a special promise

or a fellowship offering to the Lord, ⁹bring a grain offering with the bull. It should be six quarts of fine flour mixed with two quarts of olive oil. ¹⁰Also bring two quarts of wine as a drink offering. This offering is made by fire, and its smell will be pleasing to the Lord. ¹¹Prepare each bull or male sheep, lamb or young goat this way. ¹²Do this for every one of the animals you bring.

¹³" 'All citizens must do these things in this way, and the smell of their offerings by fire will be pleasing to the Lord. ¹⁴From now on if foreigners who live among you want to make offerings by fire so the smell will be pleasing to the Lord, they must offer them the same way you do. ¹⁵The law is the same for you and for foreigners, and it will be from now on; you and the foreigners are alike before the Lord. ¹⁶The teachings and rules are the same for you and for the foreigners among you.' "

¹⁷The Lord said to Moses, ¹⁸"Tell the Israelites: 'You are going to another land, where I am taking you. ¹⁹When you eat the food there, offer part of it to the Lord. ²⁰Offer a loaf of bread from the first of your grain, which will be your offering from the threshing*d* floor. ²¹From now on offer to the Lord the first part of your grain.

²²" 'Now what if you forget to obey any of these commands the Lord gave Moses? ²³These are the Lord's commands given to you through Moses, which began the day the Lord gave them to you and will continue from now on. ²⁴If the people forget to obey one of these commands, all the people must offer a young bull as a burnt offering, a smell pleasing to the Lord. By law you must also give the grain offering and the drink offering with it, and you must bring a male goat as a sin offering.

²⁵" 'The priest will remove that sin for all the Israelites so they will belong to the Lord. They are forgiven, because they didn't know they were sinning. For the wrong they did they brought offerings to the Lord, an offering by fire and a sin offering. ²⁶So all of the people of Israel and the foreigners living among them will be forgiven. No one meant to do wrong.

²⁷" 'If just one person sins without meaning to, a year-old female goat must be brought for a sin offering. ²⁸The priest will remove the sin of the person who sinned accidentally. He will remove it before the Lord, and the person will be forgiven. ²⁹The same teaching is for everyone who *sins accidentally* — for those born Israelites and for foreigners living among you.

³⁰" 'But anyone who sins on purpose is against the Lord and must be cut off from the people, whether it is someone born among you or a foreigner. ³¹That person has turned against the Lord's word and has not obeyed his commands.

Such a person must surely be cut off from the others. He is guilty.' "

A Man Worked on the Sabbath

³²When the Israelites were still in the desert, they found a man gathering wood on the Sabbath*d* day. ³³Those who found him gathering wood brought him to Moses and Aaron and all the people. ³⁴They held the man under guard, because they did not know what to do with him. ³⁵Then the Lord said to Moses, "The man must surely die. All the people must kill him by throwing stones at him outside the camp." ³⁶So all the people took him outside the camp and stoned him to death, as the Lord commanded Moses.

The Tassels

³⁷The Lord said to Moses, ³⁸"Speak to the Israelites and tell them this: 'Tie several pieces of thread together and attach them to the corners of your clothes. Put a blue thread in each one of these tassels. Wear them from now on. ³⁹You will have these tassels to look at to remind you of all the Lord's commands. Then you will obey them and not be disloyal by following what your bodies and eyes want. ⁴⁰Then you will remember to obey all my commands, and you will be God's holy people. ⁴¹I am the Lord your God, who brought you out of Egypt to be your God. I am the Lord your God.' "

Korah, Dathan, Abiram, and On

16 Korah, Dathan, Abiram, and On turned against Moses. (Korah was the son of Izhar, the son of Kohath, the son of Levi; Dathan and Abiram were brothers, the sons of Eliab; and On was the son of Peleth; Dathan, Abiram, and On were from the tribe*d* of Reuben.) ²These men gathered two hundred fifty other Israelite men, well-known leaders chosen by the community, and challenged Moses. ³They came as a group to speak to Moses and Aaron and said, "You have gone too far. All the people are holy, every one of them, and the Lord is among them. So why do you put yourselves above all the people of the Lord?"

⁴When Moses heard this, he bowed facedown. ⁵Then he said to Korah and all his followers: "Tomorrow morning the Lord will show who belongs to him. He will bring the one who is holy near to him; he will bring to himself the person he chooses. ⁶So Korah, you and all your followers do this: Get some pans for burning incense.*d* ⁷Tomorrow put fire and incense in them and take them before the Lord. He will choose the man who is holy. You Levites have gone too far."

⁸Moses also said to Korah, "Listen, you Levites. ⁹The God of Israel has separated you from the rest of the Israelites. He brought you near to himself

to do the work in the LORD's Holy Tent*d* and to stand before all the Israelites and serve them. Isn't that enough? [10]He has brought you and all your fellow Levites near to himself, yet now you want to be priests. [11]You and your followers have joined together against the LORD. Your complaint is not against Aaron."

[12]Then Moses called Dathan and Abiram, the sons of Eliab, but they said, 'We will not come! [13]You have brought us out of a fertile land to this desert to kill us, and now you want to order us around. [14]You haven't brought us into a fertile land; you haven't given us any land with fields and vineyards. Will you put out the eyes of these men? No! We will not come!"

[15]Then Moses became very angry and said to the LORD, "Don't accept their gifts. I have not taken anything from them, not even a donkey, and I have not done wrong to any of them."

[16]Then Moses said to Korah, "You and all your followers must stand before the LORD tomorrow. And Aaron will stand there with you and them. [17]Each of you must take your pan and put incense in it; present these two hundred fifty pans before the LORD. You and Aaron must also present your pans." [18]So each man got his pan and put burning incense in it and stood with Moses and Aaron at the entrance to the Meeting Tent. [19]Korah gathered all his followers who were against Moses and Aaron, and they stood at the entrance to the Meeting Tent. Then the glory of the LORD appeared to everyone.

[20]The LORD said to Moses and Aaron, [21]"Move away from these men so I can destroy them quickly."

[22]But Moses and Aaron bowed facedown and cried out, "God, you are the God over the spirits of all people. Please don't be angry with this whole group. Only one man has really sinned."

[23]Then the LORD said to Moses, [24]"Tell everyone to move away from the tents of Korah, Dathan, and Abiram."

[25]Moses stood and went to Dathan and Abiram; the older leaders of Israel followed him. [26]Moses warned the people, "Move away from the tents of these evil men! Don't touch anything of theirs, or you will be destroyed because of their sins." [27]So they moved away from the tents of Korah, Dathan, and Abiram. Dathan and Abiram were standing outside their tents with their wives, children, and little babies.

[28]Then Moses said, "Now you will know that the LORD has sent me to do all these things; it was not my idea. [29]If these men die a normal death — the way men usually die — then the LORD did not really send me. [30]But if the LORD does something new, you will know they have insulted the LORD. The ground will open and swallow them. They will be buried alive and will go to the place of the dead, and everything that belongs to them will go with them."

[31]When Moses finished saying these things, the ground under the men split open. [32]The earth opened and swallowed them and all their families. All Korah's men and everything they owned went down. [33]They were buried alive, going to the place of the dead, and everything they owned went with them. Then the earth covered them. They died and were gone from the community. [34]The people of Israel around them heard their screams and ran away, saying, "The earth will swallow us, too!"

[35]Then a fire came down from the LORD and destroyed the two hundred fifty men who had presented the incense.

[36]The LORD said to Moses, [37]"Tell Eleazar son of Aaron, the priest, to take all the incense pans out of the fire. Have him scatter the coals a long distance away. But the incense pans are still holy. [38]Take the pans of these men who sinned and lost their lives and hammer them into flat sheets that will be used to cover the altar. They are holy, because they were presented to the LORD, and they will be a sign to the Israelites."

[39]So Eleazar the priest gathered all the bronze pans that had been brought by the men who were burned up. He had the pans hammered into flat sheets to put on the altar, [40]as the LORD had commanded him through Moses. These sheets were to remind the Israelites that only descendants*d* of Aaron should burn incense before the LORD. Anyone else would die like Korah and his followers.

Aaron Saves the People

[41]The next day all the Israelites complained against Moses and Aaron and said, "You have killed the LORD's people."

[42]When the people gathered to complain against Moses and Aaron, they turned toward the Meeting Tent,*d* and the cloud covered it. The glory of the LORD appeared. [43]Then Moses and Aaron went in front of the Meeting Tent.

[44]The LORD said to Moses, [45]"Move away from these people so I can destroy them quickly." So Moses and Aaron bowed facedown.

[46]Then Moses said to Aaron, "Get your pan, and put fire from the altar and incense*d* in it. Hurry to the people and remove their sin. The LORD is angry with them; the sickness has already started." [47]So Aaron did as Moses said. He ran to the middle of the people, where the sickness had already started among them. So Aaron offered the incense to remove their sin. [48]He stood between the dead and the living, and the sickness stopped there. [49]But 14,700 people died from that sickness, in addition to those who died because of Korah. [50]Then Aaron went back to Moses at the

entrance to the Meeting Tent. The terrible sickness had been stopped.

Aaron's Walking Stick Buds

17 The LORD said to Moses, [2]"Speak to the people of Israel and get twelve walking sticks from them — one from the leader of each tribe.[d] Write the name of each man on his stick, and [3]on the stick from Levi, write Aaron's name. There must be one stick for the head of each tribe. [4]Put them in the Meeting Tent[d] in front of the Ark[d] of the Agreement, where I meet with you. [5]I will choose one man whose walking stick will begin to grow leaves; in this way I will stop the Israelites from always complaining against you."

[6]So Moses spoke to the Israelites. Each of the twelve leaders gave him a walking stick — one from each tribe — and Aaron's walking stick was among them. [7]Moses put them before the LORD in the Tent of the Agreement.

[8]The next day, when Moses entered the Tent, he saw that Aaron's stick (which stood for the family of Levi) had grown leaves. It had even budded, blossomed, and produced almonds. [9]So Moses brought out to the Israelites all the walking sticks from the LORD's presence. They all looked, and each man took back his stick.

[10]Then the LORD said to Moses, "Put Aaron's walking stick back in front of the Ark of the Agreement. It will remind these people who are always turning against me to stop their complaining against me so they won't die." [11]So Moses obeyed what the LORD commanded him.

[12]The people of Israel said to Moses, "We are going to die! We are destroyed. We are all destroyed! [13]Anyone who even comes near the Holy Tent of the LORD will die. Will we all die?"

The Work of the Priests and Levites

18 The LORD said to Aaron, "You, your sons, and your family are now responsible for any wrongs done against the Holy Place; you and your sons are responsible for any wrongs done against the priests. [2]Bring with you your fellow Levites from your tribe,[d] and they will help you and your sons serve in the Tent[d] of the Agreement. [3]They are under your control, to do all the work that needs to be done in the Tent. But they must not go near the things in the Holy Place or near the altar. If they do, both you and they will *die.* [4]*They will join you in taking care of the Meeting Tent. They must do the work at the Tent, and no one else may come near you.*

[5]*You must take care of the Holy Place and the altar so that I won't become angry with the Israelites again.* [6]I myself chose your fellow Levites from among the Israelites as a gift given for you

to the LORD, to work at the Meeting Tent. [7]But only you and your sons may serve as priests. Only you may serve at the altar or go behind the curtain. I am giving you this gift of serving as a priest, and anyone else who comes near the Holy Place will be put to death."

[8]Then the LORD said to Aaron, "I myself make you responsible for the offerings given to me. All the holy offerings that the Israelites give to me, I give to you and your sons as your share, your continual portion. [9]Your share of the holy offerings is that part which is not burned. When the people bring me gifts as most holy offerings, whether they are grain or sin or penalty offerings, they will be set apart for you and your sons. [10]You must eat the offering in a most holy place. Any male may eat it, but you must respect it as holy.

[11]"I also give you the offerings the Israelites present to me. I give these to you and your sons and daughters as your continual share. Anyone in your family who is clean[d] may eat it.

[12]"And I give you all the best olive oil and all the best new wine and grain. This is what the Israelites give to me, the LORD, from the first crops they harvest. [13]When they bring to the LORD all the first things they harvest, they will be yours. Anyone in your family who is clean may eat these things.

[14]"Everything in Israel that is given to the LORD is yours. [15]The first one born to any family, whether people or animals, will be offered to the LORD. And that will be yours. But you must make a payment for every firstborn[d] child and every firstborn animal that is unclean. [16]When they are one month old, you must make a payment for them of two ounces of silver, as set by the Holy Place measure.

SIDELIGHT: Your parents may say you're priceless, but the ancient Hebrews knew exactly how much a baby was worth. Numbers 18:15–16 tells how parents had to offer their child to God and then buy it back for about two ounces of silver when the baby was a month old.

---

[17]"But you must not make a payment for the firstborn ox or sheep or goat. Those animals are *holy. Sprinkle their blood on the altar and burn* their fat as an offering made by fire. The smell is pleasing to the LORD. [18]But the meat will be yours, just as the breast that is presented and the right thigh will be yours. [19]Anything the Israelites present as holy gifts I, the LORD, give to you, your sons and daughters as your continual portion.

This is a lasting agreement of salt[n] before the LORD for you and your children forever."

[20]The LORD also said to Aaron, "You will not inherit any of the land, and you will not own any land among the other people. I will be yours. Out of all the Israelites, only you will inherit me.

[21]"When the people of Israel give me a tenth of what they make, I will give that tenth to the Levites. This is their payment for the work they do serving at the Meeting Tent. [22]But the other Israelites must never go near the Meeting Tent, or they will die for their sin. [23]Only the Levites should work in the Meeting Tent and be responsible for any sins against it. This is a rule from now on. The Levites will not inherit any land among the other Israelites, [24]but when the Israelites give a tenth of everything they make to me, I will give that tenth to the Levites as a reward. That is why I said about the Levites: 'They will not inherit any land among the Israelites.' "

[25]The LORD said to Moses, [26]"Speak to the Levites and tell them: 'You will receive a tenth of everything the Israelites make, which I will give to you. But you must give a tenth of that back to the LORD. [27]I will accept your offering just as much as I accept the offerings from others, who give new grain or new wine. [28]In this way you will present an offering to the LORD as the other Israelites do. When you receive a tenth from the Israelites, you will give a tenth of that to Aaron, the priest, as the LORD's share. [29]Choose the best and holiest part from what you are given as the portion you must give to the LORD.'

[30]"Say to the Levites 'When you present the best, it will be accepted as much as the grain and wine from the other people. [31]You and your families may eat all that is left anywhere, because it is your pay for your work in the Meeting Tent. [32]And if you always give the best part to the LORD, you will never be guilty If you do not sin against the holy offerings of the Israelites, you will not die.' "

The Offering for Cleansing

19 The LORD said to Moses and Aaron, [2]"These are the teachings that the LORD commanded. Tell the Israelites to get a young red cow that does not have anything wrong with it and that has never been worked. [3]Give the cow to Eleazar the priest; he will take it outside the camp and kill it. [4]Then Eleazar the priest must put some of its blood on his finger and sprinkle it seven times toward the front of the Meeting Tent.[d] [5]The whole cow must be burned while he watches; the skin, the meat, the blood, and the

intestines must all be burned. [6]Then the priest must take a cedar stick, a hyssop branch, and a red string and throw them onto the burning cow. [7]After the priest has washed himself and his clothes with water, he may come back into the camp, but he will be unclean[d] until evening. [8]The man who burns the cow must wash himself and his clothes in water; he will be unclean until evening.

[9]"Then someone who is clean will collect the ashes from the cow and put them in a clean place outside the camp. The Israelites will keep these ashes to use in the cleansing water, in a special ceremony to cleanse away sin. [10]The man who collected the cow's ashes must wash his clothes and be unclean until evening. This is a lasting rule for the Israelites and for the foreigners among them.

[11]"Those who touch a dead person's body will be unclean for seven days. [12]They must wash themselves with the cleansing water on the third day and on the seventh day; then they will be clean. But if they do not wash themselves on the third day and the seventh day, they cannot be clean. [13]If those who touch a dead person's body stay unclean and go to the LORD's Holy Tent, it becomes unclean; they must be cut off from Israel. If the cleansing water is not sprinkled on them, they are unclean and will stay unclean.

[14]"This is the teaching about someone who dies in a tent: Anyone in the tent or anyone who enters it will be unclean for seven days. [15]And every open jar or pot without a cover becomes unclean. [16]If anyone is outside and touches someone who was killed by a sword or who died a natural death, or if anyone touches a human bone or a grave, that person will be unclean for seven days.

[17]"So you must use the ashes from the burnt offering to make that person clean again. Pour fresh water over the ashes into a jar. [18]A clean person must take a hyssop branch and dip it into the water, and then he must sprinkle it over the Tent and all its objects. He must also sprinkle the people who were there, as well as anyone who touched a bone, or the body of someone who was killed, or a dead person, or a grave. [19]The person who is clean must sprinkle this water on the unclean people on the third day and on the seventh day. On the seventh day they will become clean. They must wash their clothes and take a bath, and they will be clean that evening. [20]If any who are unclean do not become clean, they must be cut off from the community. Since they were not sprinkled with the cleansing water, they stay unclean, and they could make the LORD's Holy Tent

---

agreement of salt The meaning is not clear, but Leviticus 2:13 says, "Salt stands for your agreement with God that will last forever."

unclean. ²¹This is a lasting rule. Those who sprinkle the cleansing water must also wash their clothes, and anyone who touches the water will be unclean until evening. ²²Anything an unclean person touches becomes unclean, and whoever touches it will be unclean until evening."

Moses Disobeys God

20 In the first month all the people of Israel arrived at the Desert of Zin, and they stayed at Kadesh. There Miriam died and was buried. ²There was no water for the people, so they came together against Moses and Aaron. ³They argued with Moses and said, "We should have died in front of the LORD as our brothers did. ⁴Why did you bring the LORD's people into this desert? Are we and our animals to die here? ⁵Why did you bring us from Egypt to this terrible place? It has no grain, figs, grapevines, or pomegranates,ᵈ and there's no water to drink!"

⁶So Moses and Aaron left the people and went to the entrance of the Meeting Tent.ᵈ There they bowed facedown, and the glory of the LORD appeared to them. ⁷The LORD said to Moses, ⁸"Take your walking stick, and you and your brother Aaron should gather the people. Speak to that rock in front of them so that its water will flow from it. When you bring the water out from that rock, give it to the people and their animals."

⁹So Moses took the stick from in front of the LORD, as he had said. ¹⁰Moses and Aaron gathered the people in front of the rock, and Moses said, "Now listen to me, you who turn against God! Do you want us to bring water out of this rock?" ¹¹Then Moses lifted his hand and hit the rock twice with his stick. Water began pouring out, and the people and their animals drank it.

¹²But the LORD said to Moses and Aaron, "Because you did not believe me, and because you did not honor me as holy before the people, you will not lead them into the land I will give them."

¹³These are the waters of Meribah,ⁿ where the Israelites argued with the LORD and where he showed them he was holy.

Edom Will Not Let Israel Pass

¹⁴From Kadesh, Moses sent messengers to the king of Edom. He said, "Your brothers, the Israelites, say to you: You know about all the troubles we have had, ¹⁵how our ancestors went down into Egypt and we lived there for many years. The people of Egypt were cruel to us and our ancestors, ¹⁶but when we cried out to the LORD, he heard us and sent us an angel to bring us out of Egypt.

"Now we are here at Kadesh, a town on the edge of your land. ¹⁷Please let us pass through your country. We will not touch any fields of grain or vineyards, and will not drink water from the wells. We will travel only along the king's road, not turning right or left until we have passed through your country."

¹⁸But the king of Edom answered: "You may not pass through here. If you try, I will come and meet you with swords."

¹⁹The Israelites answered: "We will go along the main road, and if we or our animals drink any of your water, we will pay for it. We only want to walk through. That's all."

²⁰But he answered: "You may not pass through here."

Then the Edomites went out to meet the Israelites with a large and powerful army. ²¹The Edomites refused to let them pass through their country, so the Israelites turned back.

Aaron Dies

²²All the Israelites moved from Kadesh to Mount Hor, ²³near the border of Edom. There the LORD said to Moses and Aaron, ²⁴"Aaron will die. He will not enter the land that I'm giving to the Israelites, because you both acted against my command at the waters of Meribah. ²⁵Take Aaron and his son Eleazar up on Mount Hor, ²⁶and take off Aaron's special clothes and put them on his son Eleazar. Aaron will die there; he will join his ancestors."

²⁷Moses obeyed the LORD's command. They climbed up Mount Hor, and all the people saw them go. ²⁸Moses took off Aaron's clothes and put them on Aaron's son Eleazar. Then Aaron died there on top of the mountain. Moses and Eleazar came back down the mountain, ²⁹and when all the people learned that Aaron was dead, everyone in Israel cried for him for thirty days.

War with the Canaanites

21 The Canaanite king of Arad lived in the southern area. When he heard that the Israelites were coming on the road to Atharim, he attacked them and captured some of them. ²Then the Israelites made this promise to the LORD: "If you will help us defeat these people, we will completely destroy their cities." ³The LORD listened to the Israelites, and he let them defeat the Canaanites. The Israelites completely destroyed the Canaanites and their cities, so the place was named Hormah.ⁿ

The Bronze Snake

⁴The Israelites left Mount Hor and went on the road toward the Red Sea, in order to go around

---

Meribah   This name in Hebrew means "argument."
Hormah   This name in Hebrew means "completely destroyed."

the country of Edom. But the people became impatient on the way ⁵and grumbled at God and Moses. They said, "Why did you bring us out of Egypt to die in this desert? There is no bread and no water, and we hate this terrible food!"

⁶So the LORD sent them poisonous snakes; they bit the people, and many of the Israelites died. ⁷The people came to Moses and said, "We sinned when we grumbled at you and the LORD. Pray that the LORD will take away these snakes." So Moses prayed for the people.

⁸The LORD said to Moses, "Make a bronze snake, and put it on a pole. When anyone who is bitten looks at it, that person will live." ⁹So Moses made a bronze snake and put it on a pole. Then when a snake bit anyone, that person looked at the bronze snake and lived.

The Journey to Moab

¹⁰The Israelites went and camped at Oboth. ¹¹They went from Oboth to Iye Abarim, in the desert east of Moab. ¹²From there they went and camped in the Zered Valley. ¹³From there they went and camped across the Arnon, in the desert just inside the Amorite country. The Arnon is the border between the Moabites and the Amorites. ¹⁴That is why the Book of the Wars of the LORD says:

". . . and Waheb in Suphah, and the ravines,
the Arnon, ¹⁵and the slopes of the ravines
that lead to the settlement of Ar.
These places are at the border of Moab."

¹⁶The Israelites went from there to Beer; a well is there where the LORD said to Moses, "Gather the people and I will give them water."

DISCOURAGEMENT

Specially Chosen

If there was anything Adrienne Rivera didn't want, it was attention. She felt self-conscious about her looks, and she was fairly sure no one really liked her.

Adrienne began having trouble with her right knee. Soon she could hardly walk on it, and nothing eased the pain. Finally, she went to a doctor.

She couldn't believe what the doctor found: a rare, cancerous tumor. And to save her life, he had to treat her with chemotherapy and then amputate her leg.

Amputate? Word spread fast through school. Adrienne—who avoided being in the spotlight—suddenly found herself the center of school gossip and the focus of curious stares. She hated it.

Adrienne was confused and angry. Was God punishing her? What had she done to deserve this?

Then one day during her chemo treatments, Adrienne was thinking about her three-in-a-million chance of getting this cancer. And a thought struck her. "Suppose God isn't punishing me? Suppose he chose me?"

Adrienne's new perspective gave her the courage to face surgery—and the world. During recovery, her shyness disappeared as she answered her classmates' questions and satisfied their curiosity.

With just one natural leg, she joined the school flag squad, swim team, and track team. Recently she started something she probably wouldn't have done with two legs: downhill competitive skiing. Now there's no stopping the girl who once had trouble standing on her own two feet.

Like Adrienne, the Israelites in the Bible faced a discouraging situation. Read how they dealt with discouragement in **Numbers 21:4–9**.

■ How were Adrienne's questions like the questions the Israelites asked? How did God provide hope and healing for Adrienne and the Israelites in the midst of discouragement?

■ When you're discouraged, how can this passage help your attitude?

CONSIDER . .

■ listing reasons you get discouraged. Then use a marker to write "But God . . ." boldly over each reason.

■ asking a friend, parent, or trusted adult for help if your discouragement is overwhelming.

FOR MORE, SEE . . .

■ Job 19:7–27(p. 463)
■ Psalm 56:1–13 (p. 514)

■ Romans 8:31–39 (p. 1152)

¹⁷Then the Israelites sang this song:
"Pour out water, well!
   Sing about it.
¹⁸Princes dug this well.
   Important men made it.
   With their scepters*d* and poles, they dug it."
The people went from the desert to Mattanah.
¹⁹From Mattanah they went to Nahaliel and on to
Bamoth. ²⁰From Bamoth they went to the valley
of Moab where the top of Mount Pisgah looks
over the desert.

Israel Kills Sihon and Og

²¹The Israelites sent messengers to Sihon, king
of the Amorites, saying, ²²"Let us pass through
your country. We will not go through any fields
of grain or vineyards, or drink water from the
wells. We will travel only along the king's road
until we have passed through your country."

²³But King Sihon would not let the Israelites
pass through his country. He gathered his whole
army together, and they marched out to meet Israel in the desert. At Jahaz they fought the Israelites. ²⁴Israel killed the king and captured his land
from the Arnon River to the Jabbok River. They
took the land as far as the Ammonite border,
which was strongly defended. ²⁵Israel captured all
the Amorite cities and lived in them, taking Heshbon and all the towns around it. ²⁶Heshbon was
the city where Sihon, the Amorite king, lived. In
the past he had fought with the king of Moab and
had taken all the land as far as the Arnon.

²⁷That is why the poets say:
"Come to Heshbon
   and rebuild it;
   rebuild Sihon's city.
²⁸A fire began in Heshbon;
   flames came from Sihon's city.
It destroyed Ar in Moab,
   and it burned the Arnon highlands.
²⁹How terrible for you, Moab!
   The people of Chemosh*d* are ruined.
His sons ran away
   and his daughters were captured
   by Sihon, king of the Amorites.
³⁰But we defeated those Amorites.
   We ruined their towns from Heshbon to
      Dibon,
   and we destroyed them as far as Nophah,
      near Medeba."

³¹So Israel lived in the land of the Amorites.
³²After Moses sent spies to the town of Jazer,
they captured the towns around it, forcing out the
Amorites who lived there.

³³Then the Israelites went up the road toward
Bashan. Og king of Bashan and his whole army
marched out to meet the Israelites, and they
fought at Edrei.
³⁴The Lord said to Moses, "Don't be afraid of

him. I will hand him, his whole army, and his
land over to you. Do to him what you did to Sihon, the Amorite king who lived in Heshbon."

³⁵So the Israelites killed Og and his sons and all
his army; no one was left alive. And they took his
land.

Balak Sends for Balaam

22 Then the people of Israel went to the
plains of Moab, and they camped near
the Jordan River across from Jericho.

²Balak son of Zippor saw everything the Israel-
ites had done to the Amorites. ³And Moab was
scared of so many Israelites; truly, Moab was terrified by them.

⁴The Moabites said to the older leaders of Mid-
ian, "These people will take everything around us
like an ox eating grass."

Balak son of Zippor was the king of Moab at
this time. ⁵He sent messengers to Balaam son of
Beor at Pethor, near the Euphrates River in his
native land. Balak said, "A nation has come out of
Egypt that covers the land. They have camped
next to me, ⁶and they are too powerful for me. So
come and put a curse on them. Maybe then I can
defeat them and make them leave the area. I
know that if you bless someone, the blessings happen, and if you put a curse on someone, it happens."

⁷The older leaders of Moab and Midian went
with payment in their hands. When they found
Balaam, they told him what Balak had said.

⁸Balaam said to them, "Stay here for the night,
and I will tell you what the Lord tells me." So the
Moabite leaders stayed with him.

⁹God came to Balaam and asked, "Who are
these men with you?"

¹⁰Balaam said to God, "The king of Moab, Ba-
lak son of Zippor, sent them to me with this message: ¹¹'A nation has come out of Egypt that covers the land. So come and put a curse on them,
and maybe I can fight them and force them out
of my land.'"

¹²But God said to Balaam, "Do not go with
them. Don't put a curse on those people, because
I have blessed them."

¹³The next morning Balaam awoke and said to
Balak's leaders, "Go back to your own country;
the Lord has refused to let me go with you."

¹⁴So the Moabite leaders went back to Balak
and said, "Balaam refused to come with us."

¹⁵So Balak sent other leaders — this time there
were more of them, and they were more impor-
tant. ¹⁶They went to Balaam and said, "Balak son
of Zippor says this: Please don't let anything stop
you from coming to me. ¹⁷I will pay you very well,
and I will do what you say. Come and put a curse
on these people for me."

¹⁸But Balaam answered Balak's servants, "King

Balak could give me his palace full of silver and gold, but I cannot disobey the LORD my God in anything, great or small. ¹⁹You stay here tonight as the other men did, and I will find out what more the LORD tells me.'

²⁰That night God came to Balaam and said, "These men have come to ask you to go with them. Go, but only do what I tell you."

Balaam's Donkey Speaks

²¹Balaam got up the next morning and put a saddle on his donkey. Then he went with the Moabite leaders. ²²But God became angry because Balaam went, so the angel of the LORD stood in the road to stop Balaam. Balaam was riding his donkey, and he had two servants with him. ²³When the donkey saw the angel of the LORD standing in the road with a sword in his hand, the donkey left the road and went into the field. Balaam hit the donkey to force her back on the road.

²⁴Later, the angel of the LORD stood on a narrow path between two vineyards, with walls on both sides. ²⁵Again the donkey saw the angel of the LORD, and she walked close to one wall, crushing Balaam's foot against it. So he hit her again.

²⁶The angel of the LORD went ahead again and stood at a narrow place, too narrow to turn left or right. ²⁷When the donkey saw the angel of the LORD, she lay down under Balaam. This made him so angry that he hit her with his stick. ²⁸Then the LORD made the donkey talk, and she said to Balaam, "What have I done to make you hit me three times?"

²⁹Balaam answered the donkey, "You have made me look foolish! I wish I had a sword in my hand! I would kill you right now!"

³⁰But the donkey said to Balaam, "I am your very own donkey, which you have ridden for years. Have I ever done this to you before?"

"No," Balaam said.

³¹Then the LORD let Balaam see the angel of the LORD, who was standing in the road with his sword drawn. Then Balaam bowed facedown on the ground.

³²The angel of the LORD asked Balaam, "Why have you hit your donkey three times? I have stood here to stop you, because what you are doing is wrong. ³³The donkey saw me and turned away from me three times. If she had not turned away, I would have killed you by now, but I would have let her live."

³⁴Then Balaam said to the angel of the LORD, "I have sinned; I did not know you were standing in the road to stop me. If I am wrong I will go back."

³⁵The angel of the LORD said to Balaam, "Go with these men, but say only what I tell you." So Balaam went with Balak's leaders.

³⁶When Balak heard that Balaam was coming, he went out to meet him at Ar in Moab, which was beside the Arnon, at the edge of his country. ³⁷Balak said to Balaam, "I had asked you before to come quickly. Why didn't you come to me? I am able to reward you well."

³⁸But Balaam answered, "I have come to you now, but I can't say just anything. I can only say what God tells me to say."

³⁹Then Balaam went with Balak to Kiriath Huzoth. ⁴⁰Balak offered cattle and sheep as a sacrifice and gave some meat to Balaam and the leaders with him

⁴¹The next morning Balak took Balaam to Bamoth Baal; from there he could see the edge of the Israelite camp.

Balaam's First Message

23 Balaam said to Balak, "Build me seven altars here, and prepare seven bulls and seven male sheep for me." ²Balak did what Balaam asked, and they offered a bull and a male sheep on each of the altars.

³Then Balaam said to Balak, "Stay here beside your burnt offering and I will go. If the LORD comes to me, I will tell you whatever he shows me." Then Balaam went to a higher place.

⁴God came to Balaam there, and Balaam said to him, "I have prepared seven altars, and I have offered a bull and a male sheep on each altar."

⁵The LORD told Balaam what he should say. Then the LORD said, "Go back to Balak and give him this message."

⁶So Balaam went back to Balak. Balak and all the leaders of Moab were still standing beside his burnt offering ⁷when Balaam gave them this message:

"Balak brought me here from Aram
　the king of Moab brought me from the
　eastern mountains.
Balak said, 'Come, put a curse on the people
　of Jacob for me.

Come, call down evil on the people of
Israel.'
8But God has not cursed them,
so I cannot curse them.
The LORD has not called down evil on them,
so I cannot call down evil on them.
9I see them from the top of the mountains;
I see them from the hills.
I see a people who live alone,
who think they are different from other
nations.
10No one can number the many people of
Jacob,
and no one can count a fourth of Israel.
Let me die like good men,
and let me end up like them!"
11Balak said to Balaam, "What have you done
to me? I brought you here to curse my enemies,
but you have only blessed them!"
12But Balaam answered, "I must say what the
LORD tells me to say."

Balaam's Second Message

13Then Balak said to him, "Come with me to
another place, where you can also see the people.
But you can only see part of them, not all of them.
Curse them for me from there." 14So Balak took
Balaam to the field of Zophim, on top of Mount
Pisgah. There Balak built seven altars and offered
a bull and a male sheep on each altar.

15So Balaam said to Balak, "Stay here by your
burnt offering, and I will meet with God over
there."

16So the LORD came to Balaam and told him
what to say. Then he said, "Go back to Balak and
say such and such."

17So Balaam went to Balak, where he and the
leaders of Moab were standing beside his burnt
offering. Balak asked him, "What did the LORD
say?"

18Then Balaam gave this message:
"Stand up, Balak, and listen.
Hear me, son of Zippor.
19God is not a human being, and he will not
lie.
He is not a human, and he does not change
his mind.
What he says he will do, he does.
What he promises, he makes come true.
20He told me to bless them,
so I cannot change the blessing.
21He has found no wrong in the people of
Jacob;
he saw no fault in Israel.
The LORD their God is with them,
and they praise their King.
22God brought them out of Egypt;
they are as strong as a wild ox.
23No tricks will work on the people of Jacob,

and no magic will work against Israel.
People now say about them,
'Look what God has done for Israel!'
24The people rise up like a lioness;
they get up like a lion.
Lions don't rest until they have eaten,
until they have drunk their enemies'
blood."
25Then Balak said to Balaam, "You haven't
cursed these people, so at least, don't bless
them!"
26Balaam answered Balak, "I told you before
that I can only do what the LORD tells me."

Balaam's Third Message

27Then Balak said to Balaam, "Come, I will take
you to another place. Maybe God will be pleased
to let you curse them from there." 28So Balak took
Balaam to the top of Peor, the mountain that
looks over the desert.

29Balaam told Balak, "Build me seven altars
here and prepare for me seven bulls and seven
male sheep." 30Balak did what Balaam asked, and
he offered a bull and a male sheep on each altar.

24 Balaam saw that the LORD wanted to
bless Israel, so he did not try to use any
magic but looked toward the desert. 2When Balaam saw the Israelites camped in their tribes,*d*
the Spirit*d* of God took control of him, 3and he
gave this message:
"This is the message of Balaam son of Beor,
the message of a man who sees clearly;
4this is the message of a man who hears the
words of God.
I see a vision from the Almighty,
and my eyes are open as I fall before him.
5Your tents are beautiful, people of Jacob!
So are your homes, Israel!
6Your tents spread out like valleys,
like gardens beside a river.
They are like spices planted by the LORD,
like cedar trees growing by the water.
7Israel's water buckets will always be full,
and their crops will have plenty of water.
Their king will be greater than Agag;
their kingdom will be very great.
8God brought them out of Egypt;
they are as strong as a wild ox.
They will defeat their enemies
and break their enemies' bones;
they will shoot them with arrows.
9Like a lion, they lie waiting to attack;
like a lioness, no one would be brave
enough to wake them.
Anyone who blesses you will be blessed,
and anyone who curses you will be
cursed."
10Then Balak was angry with Balaam, and he
pounded his fist. He said to Balaam, "I called you

here to curse my enemies, but you have continued to bless them three times. [11]Now go home! I said I would pay you well, but the Lord has made you lose your reward."

[12]Balaam said to Balak, "When you sent messengers to me, I told them, [13]'Balak could give me his palace filled with silver and gold, but I still cannot go against the Lord's commands. I could not do anything, good or bad, on my own, but I must say what the Lord says.' [14]Now I am going back to my own people, but I will tell you what these people will do to your people in the future."

Balaam's Final Message

[15]Then Balaam gave this message:
"This is the message of Balaam son of Beor,
    the message of a man who sees clearly;
[16]this is the message of a man who hears the
    words of God.
I know well the Most High God.
I see a vision from the Almighty,
    and my eyes are open as I fall before him.
[17]I see someone who will come some day,
    someone who will come, but not soon.
A star will come from Jacob;
    a ruler will rise from Israel.
He will crush the heads of the Moabites
    and smash the skulls of the sons of Sheth.
[18]Edom will be conquered;
    his enemy Edom will be conquered,
    but Israel will grow wealthy.
[19]A ruler will come from the descendants[d] of
    Jacob
    and will destroy those left in the city."

[20]Then Balaam saw Amalek and gave this message:
"Amalek was the most important nation,
    but Amalek will be destroyed at last."

[21]Then Balaam saw the Kenites and gave this message:
"Your home is safe,
    like a nest on a cliff.
[22]But you Kenites will be burned up;
    Assyria will keep you captive."

[23]Then Balaam gave this message:
"No one can live when God does this.
[24] Ships will sail from the shores of Cyprus
    and defeat Assyria and Eber,
    but they will also be destroyed."

[25]Then Balaam got up and returned home, and Balak also went on his way.

Israel Worships Baal at Peor

25 While the people of Israel were still camped at Acacia, the men began sinning sexually with Moabite women. [2]The women invited them to their sacrifices to their gods, and the Israelites ate food there and worshiped these gods. [3]So the Israelites began to worship Baal[d] of Peor, and the Lord was very angry with them.

[4]The Lord said to Moses, "Get all the leaders of the people and kill them in open daylight in the presence of the Lord. Then the Lord will not be angry with the people of Israel."

[5]So Moses said to Israel's judges, "Each of you must put to death your people who have become worshipers of Baal of Peor."

[6]Moses and the Israelites were gathered at the entrance to the Meeting Tent,[d] crying there. Then an Israelite man brought a Midianite woman to his brothers in plain sight of Moses and all the people. [7]Phinehas son of Eleazar, the son of Aaron, the priest, saw this, so he left the meeting and got his spear. [8]He followed the Israelite into his tent and drove his spear through both the Israelite man and the Midianite woman. Then the terrible sickness among the Israelites stopped. [9]This sickness had killed twenty-four thousand people.

[10]The Lord said to Moses, [11]"Phinehas son of Eleazar, the son of Aaron, the priest, has saved the Israelites from my anger. He hates sin as much as I do. Since he tried to save my honor among them, I will not kill them. [12]So tell Phinehas that I am making my peace agreement with him. [13]He and his descendants[d] will always be priests, because he had great concern for the honor of his God. He removed the sins of the Israelites so they would belong to God."

[14]The Israelite man who was killed with the Midianite woman was named Zimri son of Salu. He was the leader of a family in the tribe[d] of Simeon. [15]And the name of the Midianite woman who was put to death was Cozbi daughter of Zur, who was the chief of a Midianite family.

[16]The Lord said to Moses, [17]"The Midianites are your enemies, and you should kill them. [18]They have already made you their enemies, because they tricked you at Peor and because of their sister Cozbi, the daughter of a Midianite leader. She was the woman who was killed when the sickness came because the people sinned at Peor."

The People Are Counted

26 After the great sickness, the Lord said to Moses and Eleazar son of Aaron, the priest, [2]"Count all the people of Israel by families. Count all the men who are twenty years old or older who will serve in the army of Israel." [3]Moses and Eleazar the priest spoke to the people on the plains of Moab near the Jordan River, across from Jericho. They said, [4]"Count the men twenty years old or older, as the Lord commanded Moses."

Here are the Israelites who came out of Egypt:

5The tribe*d* of Reuben, the first son born to Israel, was counted. From Hanoch came the Hanochite family group; from Pallu came the Palluite family group; 6from Hezron came the Hezronite family group; from Carmi came the Carmite family group. 7These were the family groups of Reuben, and the total number of men was 43,730.

8The son of Pallu was Eliab, 9and Eliab's sons were Nemuel, Dathan, and Abiram. Dathan and Abiram were the leaders who turned against Moses and Aaron and followed Korah when he turned against the LORD. 10The earth opened up and swallowed them and Korah; they died at the same time the fire burned up the 250 men. This was a warning, 11but the children of Korah did not die.

12These were the family groups in the tribe of Simeon: From Nemuel came the Nemuelite family group; from Jamin came the Jaminite family group; from Jakin came the Jakinite family group; 13from Zerah came the Zerahite family group; from Shaul came the Shaulite family group. 14These were the family groups of Simeon, and the total number of men was 22,200.

15These were the family groups in the tribe of Gad: From Zephon came the Zephonite family group; from Haggi came the Haggite family group; from Shuni came the Shunite family group; 16from Ozni came the Oznite family group; from Eri came the Erite family group; 17from Arodi came the Arodite family group; from Areli came the Arelite family group. 18These were the family groups of Gad, and the total number of men was 40,500.

19Two of Judah's sons, Er and Onan, died in Canaan.

20These were the family groups in the tribe of Judah: From Shelah came the Shelanite family group; from Perez came the Perezite family group; from Zerah came the Zerahite family group. 21These were the family groups from Perez: From Hezron came the Hezronite family group; from Hamul came the Hamulite family group. 22These were the family groups of Judah, and the total number of men was 76,500.

23These were the family groups in the tribe of Issachar: From Tola came the Tolaite family group; from Puah came the Puite family group; 24from Jashub came the Jashubite family group; from Shimron came the Shimronite family group. 25These were the family groups of Issachar, and the total number of men was 64,300.

26These were the family groups in the tribe of Zebulun: From Sered came the Seredite family group; from Elon came the Elonite family group; from Jahleel came the Jahleelite family group. 27These were the family groups of Zebulun, and the total number of men was 60,500.

28These were the family groups of Joseph through Manasseh and Ephraim.

29These were the family groups of Manasseh: From Makir came the Makirite family group (Makir was the father of Gilead); from Gilead came the Gileadite family group. 30These were the family groups that came from Gilead: From Iezer came the Iezerite family group; from Helek came the Helekite family group; 31from Asriel came the Asrielite family group; from Shechem came the Shechemite family group; 32from Shemida came the Shemidaite family group; from Hepher came the Hepherite family group. 33(Zelophehad son of Hepher had no sons; he had only daughters, and their names were Mahlah, Noah, Hoglah, Milcah, and Tirzah.) 34These were the family groups of Manasseh, and the total number of men was 52,700.

35These were the family groups in the tribe of Ephraim: From Shuthelah came the Shuthelahite family group; from Beker came the Bekerite family group; from Tahan came the Tahanite family group. 36This was the family group from Shuthelah: From Eran came the Eranite family group. 37These were the family groups of Ephraim, and the total number of men was 32,500. These are the family groups that came from Joseph.

38These were the family groups in the tribe of Benjamin: From Bela came the Belaite family group; from Ashbel came the Ashbelite family group; from Ahiram came the Ahiramite family group; 39from Shupham came the Shuphamite family group; from Hupham came the Huphamite family group. 40These were the family groups from Bela through Ard and Naaman: From Ard came the Ardite family group; from Naaman came the Naamite family group. 41These were the family groups of Benjamin, and the total number of men was 45,600.

42This was the family group in the tribe of Dan: From Shuham came the Shuhamite family group. That was the family of Dan, 43and the total number of men in the Shuhamite family group of Dan was 64,400.

44These were the family groups in the tribe of Asher: From Imnah came the Imnite family group; from Ishvi came the Ishvite family group; from Beriah came the Beriite family group. 45These were the family groups that came from Beriah: From Heber came the Heberite family group; from Malkiel came the Malkielite family group. 46(Asher also had a daughter named Serah.) 47These were the family groups of Asher, and the total number of men was 53,400.

48These were the family groups in the tribe of Naphtali: From Jahzeel came the Jahzeelite family group; from Guni came the Gunite family group; 49from Jezer came the Jezerite family group; from Shillem came the Shillemite family group. 50These were the family groups of Naphtali, and the total number of men was 45,400.

⁵¹So the total number of the men of Israel was 601,730.

⁵²The LORD said to Moses, ⁵³"Divide the land among these people by the number of names. ⁵⁴A large tribe will get more land, and a small tribe will get less land; the amount of land each tribe gets will depend on the number of its people. ⁵⁵Divide the land by drawing lots,ᵈ and the land each tribe gets will be named for that tribe. ⁵⁶Divide the land between large and small groups by drawing lots."

⁵⁷The tribe of Levi was also counted. These were the family groups of Levi: From Gershon came the Gershonite family group; from Kohath came the Kohathite family group; from Merari came the Merarite family group. ⁵⁸These also were Levite family groups: the Libnite family group, the Hebronite family group, the Mahlite family group, the Mushite family group, and the Korahite family group. (Kohath was the ancestor of Amram, ⁵⁹whose wife was named Jochebed. She was from the tribe of Levi and she was born in Egypt. She and Amram had two sons, Aaron and Moses, and their sister Miriam. ⁶⁰Aaron was the father of Nadab, Abihu, Eleazar, and Ithamar. ⁶¹But Nadab and Abihu died because they made an offering before the LORD with the wrong kind of fire.)

⁶²The total number of male Levites one month old or older was 23,000. But these men were not counted with the other Israelites, because they were not given any of the land among the other Israelites.

⁶³Moses and Eleazar the priest counted all these people. They counted the Israelites on the plains of Moab across the Jordan River from Jericho. ⁶⁴Moses and Aaron the priest had counted the Israelites in the Desert of Sinai, but no one Moses counted on the plains of Moab was in the first counting. ⁶⁵The LORD had told the Israelites they would all die in the desert, and the only two left were Caleb son of Jephunneh and Joshua son of Nun.

Zelophehad's Daughters

27 Then the daughters of Zelophehad came near. Zelophehad was the son of Hepher, the son of Gilead, the son of Makir, the son of Manasseh. Zelophehad's daughters belonged to the family groups of Manasseh son of Joseph. The daughters' names were Mahlah, Noah, Hoglah, Milcah, and Tirzah. ²They went to the entrance of the Meeting Tentᵈ and stood before Moses, Eleazar the priest, the leaders, and all the people. They said, ³"Our father died in the desert. He was not one of Korah's followers who came together against the LORD, but he died because of his own

sin, and he had no sons. ⁴Our father's name will die out because he had no sons. Give us property among our father's relatives."

⁵So Moses brought their case to the LORD, ⁶and the LORD said to him, ⁷"The daughters of Zelophehad are right; they should certainly get what their father owned. Give them property among their father's relatives.

⁸"Tell the Israelites, 'If a man dies and has no son, then everything he owned should go to his daughter ⁹If he has no daughter, then everything he owned should go to his brothers. ¹⁰If he has no brothers, then everything he owned should go to his father's brothers. ¹¹And if his father had no brothers, then everything he owned should go to the nearest relative in his family group. This should be a rule among the people of Israel, as the LORD has given this command to Moses.' "

Joshua is the New Leader

¹²Then the LORD said to Moses, "Climb this mountain in the Abarim Mountains, and look at the land I have given to the Israelites. ¹³After you have seen it, you will die and join your ancestors as your brother Aaron did, ¹⁴because you both acted against my command in the Desert of Zin. You did not honor me as holy before the people at the waters of Meribah." (This was at Meribah in Kadesh in the Desert of Zin.)

¹⁵Moses said to the LORD, ¹⁶"The LORD is the God of the spirits of all people. May he choose a leader for these people, ¹⁷who will go in and out before them. He must lead them out like sheep and bring them in; the LORD's people must not be like sheep without a shepherd."

¹⁸So the LORD said to Moses, "Take Joshua son of Nun, because my Spiritᵈ is in him. Put your hand on him, ¹⁹and have him stand before Eleazar the priest and all the people. Then give him his orders as they watch. ²⁰Let him share your honor so that all the Israelites will obey him. ²¹He must stand before Eleazar the priest, and Eleazar will get advice from the LORD by using the Urim.ᵈ At his command all the Israelites will go out, and at his command they will all come in."

²²Moses did what the LORD told him. He took Joshua and had him stand before Eleazar the priest and all the people, ²³and he put his hands on him and gave him orders, just as the LORD had told him.

Daily Offerings

28 The LORD said to Moses, ²"Give this command to the Israelites. Tell them: 'Bring me food offerings made by fire, for a smell that is pleasing to me, and be sure to bring them at the right time.' ³Say to them, 'These are the offerings you must bring to the LORD: two male lambs, a year old, as a burnt offering each day.

They must have nothing wrong with them. 4Offer one lamb in the morning and the other lamb at twilight. 5Also bring a grain offering of two quarts of fine flour, mixed with one quart of oil from pressed olives. 6This is the daily burnt offering which began at Mount Sinai; its smell is pleasing to the LORD. 7Offer one quart of wine with each lamb as a drink offering; pour it out to the LORD at the Holy Place. 8Offer the second lamb at twilight. As in the morning, also give a grain offering and a drink offering. This offering is made by fire, and its smell is pleasing to the LORD.

Sabbath Offerings

9" 'On the Sabbath*d* day you must give two male lambs, a year old, that have nothing wrong with them. Also give a drink offering and a grain offering; the grain offering must be four quarts of fine flour mixed with olive oil. 10This is the burnt offering for every Sabbath, in addition to the daily burnt offering and drink offering.

Monthly Offerings

11" 'On the first day of each month bring a burnt offering to the LORD. This will be two young bulls, one male sheep, and seven male lambs a year old, and they must have nothing wrong with them. 12Give a grain offering with each bull of six quarts of fine flour mixed with olive oil. Also give a grain offering with the male sheep. It must be four quarts of fine flour mixed with olive oil. 13And give a grain offering with each lamb of two quarts of fine flour mixed with olive oil. This is a burnt offering, and its smell is pleasing to the LORD. 14The drink offering with each bull will be two quarts of wine, with the male sheep it will be one and one-third quarts, and with each lamb it will be one quart of wine. This is the burnt offering that must be offered each month of the year. 15Besides the daily burnt offerings and drink offerings, bring a sin offering of one goat to the LORD.

LEADERSHIP

Walking in My Own Footsteps

Clarence Mitchell was a legend. For twenty-nine years, he had been the chief lobbyist in Washington, D.C., for the National Association for the Advancement of Colored People (NAACP).

Using his knowledge of the law and his persuasive powers, he pushed legislators to pass laws to protect the rights of black people. Every civil rights law passed by Congress during the turbulent 1960s had his fingerprints on it.

Then, in 1978, he retired, and Althea T. L. Simmons took his place. For years, she had dedicated her life to studying and practicing civil rights law. And she had worked for twenty-five years honing her skills and knowledge.

Soon after she took the new position, she went to the White House to meet with U.S. President Jimmy Carter. "Miss Simmons," he said, "you've got some very big shoes to fill."

She responded: "Mr. President, nobody can fill Clarence Mitchell's shoes. I'll have to walk in my own footsteps."

As a leader, Clarence Mitchell left a legacy. Moses—one of the Israelites' greatest leaders—left a legacy by leading them out of captivity in Egypt. When he died, Joshua became the new leader with a new agenda. Read about the challenge he faced in **Numbers 27:12–23**.

■ How were Althea Simmons's years of experience and training similar to Joshua's forty years of preparation to become a leader?

■ In what ways that are described in the passage are you being prepared to become a leader in your school, church, or community?

CONSIDER . . .

■ asking your parent to list leadership skills, gifts, or qualities he or she would like to pass on to you. Then decide together ways for you to learn those skills.

■ *interviewing your pastor or another church leader about how he or she became a leader. Then write a short biography for the church newsletter.*

FOR MORE, SEE . . .

■ Judges 6:11–16 (p. 222)
■ John 21:15–22 (p. 1095)
■ 2 Timothy 2:1–7 (p. 1264)

The Passover

16" 'The Lord's Passover*d* will be on the fourteenth day of the first month. 17The Feast*d* of Unleavened Bread begins on the fifteenth day of that month. For seven days, you may eat only bread made without yeast. 18Have a holy meeting on the first day of the festival, and don't work that day. 19Bring to the Lord an offering made by fire, a burnt offering of two young bulls, one male sheep, and seven male lambs a year old. They must have nothing wrong with them. 20With each bull give a grain offering of six quarts of fine flour mixed with olive oil. With the male sheep it must be four quarts of fine flour mixed with oil. 21With each of the seven lambs, it must be two quarts of fine flour mixed with oil. 22Bring one goat as a sin offering, to remove your sins so you will belong to God. 23Bring these offerings in addition to the burnt offerings you give every morning. 24So bring food for the offering made by fire each day for seven days, for a smell that is pleasing to the Lord. Do it in addition to the daily burnt offering and its drink offering. 25On the seventh day have a holy meeting, and don't work that day.

The Feast of Weeks

26" 'On the day of firstfruits*d* when you bring new grain to the Lord during the Feast*d* of Weeks, have a holy meeting. Don't work that day. 27Bring this burnt offering to the Lord: two young bulls, one male sheep, and seven male lambs a year old. This smell is pleasing to the Lord. 28Also, with each bull give a grain offering of six quarts of fine flour mixed with oil. With the male sheep, it must be four quarts of flour, 29and with each of the seven lambs offer two quarts of flour. 30Offer one male goat to remove your sins so you will belong to God. 31Bring these offerings and their drink offerings in addition to the daily burnt offering and its grain offering. The animals must have nothing wrong with them.

The Feast of Trumpets

29 " 'Have a holy meeting on the first day of the seventh month, and don't work on that day. That is the day you blow the trumpets. 2Bring these burnt offerings as a smell pleasing to the Lord: one young bull, one male sheep, and seven male lambs a year old. They must have nothing wrong with them. 3With the bull give a grain offering of six quarts of fine flour mixed with oil. With the male sheep offer four quarts, 4and with each of the seven lambs offer two quarts. 5Offer one male goat for a sin offering to remove your sins so you will belong to God. 6These offerings are in addition to the monthly and daily burnt offerings. Their grain offerings and drink offerings must be done as you have been told. These offerings are made by fire to the Lord, and their smell is pleasing to him.

The Day of Cleansing

7" 'Have a holy meeting on the tenth day of the seventh month. On that day do not eat and do not work. 8Bring these burnt offerings as a smell pleasing to the Lord: one young bull, one male sheep, and seven male lambs a year old. They must have nothing wrong with them. 9With the bull give a grain offering of six quarts of fine flour mixed with oil. With the male sheep it must be four quarts, 10and with each of the seven lambs it must be two quarts. 11Offer one male goat as a sin offering. This will be in addition to the sin offering which removes your sins, the daily burnt offering with its grain offering, and the drink offerings.

The Feast of Shelters

12" 'Have a holy meeting on the fifteenth day of the seventh month, and do not work on that day. Celebrate a festival to the Lord for seven days. 13Bring these burnt offerings, made by fire, as a smell pleasing to the Lord: thirteen young bulls, two male sheep, and fourteen male lambs a year old. They must have nothing wrong with them. 14With each of the thirteen bulls offer a grain offering of six quarts of fine flour mixed with oil. With each of the two male sheep it must be four quarts, 15and with each of the fourteen lambs it must be two quarts. 16Offer one male goat as a sin offering in addition to the daily burnt offering with its grain and drink offerings.

17" 'On the second day of this festival give an offering of twelve bulls, two male sheep, and fourteen male lambs a year old. They must have nothing wrong with them. 18Bring the grain and drink offerings for the bulls, sheep, and lambs, according to the number required. 19Offer one male goat as a sin offering, in addition to the daily burnt offering with its grain and drink offerings.

20" 'On the third day offer eleven bulls, two male sheep, and fourteen male lambs a year old. They must have nothing wrong with them. 21Bring the grain and drink offerings for the bulls, sheep, and lambs, according to the number required. 22Offer one male goat as a sin offering, in addition to the daily burnt offering with its grain and drink offerings.

23" 'On the fourth day offer ten bulls, two male sheep, and fourteen male lambs a year old. They must have nothing wrong with them. 24Bring the grain and drink offerings for the bulls, sheep, and lambs, according to the number required. 25Offer one male goat as a sin offering, in addition to the daily burnt offering with its grain and drink offerings.

26" 'On the fifth day offer nine bulls, two male sheep, and fourteen male lambs a year old. They must have nothing wrong with them. ²⁷Bring the grain and drink offerings for the bulls, sheep, and lambs, according to the number required. ²⁸Offer one male goat as a sin offering, in addition to the daily burnt offering with its grain and drink offerings.

²⁹" 'On the sixth day offer eight bulls, two male sheep, and fourteen male lambs a year old. They must have nothing wrong with them. ³⁰Bring the grain and drink offerings for the bulls, sheep, and lambs, according to the number required. ³¹Offer one male goat as a sin offering, in addition to the daily burnt offering with its grain and drink offerings.

³²" 'On the seventh day offer seven bulls, two male sheep, and fourteen male lambs a year old. They must have nothing wrong with them. ³³Bring the grain and drink offerings for the bulls, sheep, and lambs, according to the number required. ³⁴Offer one male goat as a sin offering, in addition to the daily burnt offering with its grain and drink offerings.

³⁵" 'On the eighth day have a closing meeting, and do not work on that day. ³⁶Bring an offering made by fire, a burnt offering, as a smell pleasing to the LORD. Offer one bull, one male sheep, and seven male lambs a year old. They must have nothing wrong with them. ³⁷Bring the grain and drink offerings for the bull, the male sheep, and the lambs, according to the number required. ³⁸Offer one male goat as a sin offering, in addition to the daily burnt offering with its grain and drink offerings.

³⁹" 'At your festivals you should bring these to the LORD: your burnt offerings, grain offerings, drink offerings and fellowship offerings. These are in addition to other promised offerings and special gifts you want to give to the LORD.' "

⁴⁰Moses told the Israelites everything the LORD had commanded him.

Rules About Special Promises

30 Moses spoke with the leaders of the Israelite tribes.ᵈ He told them these commands from the LORD.

²"If a man makes a promise to the LORD or says he will do something special, he must keep his promise. He must do what he said. ³If a young woman still living at home makes a promise to the LORD or pledges to do something special, ⁴and if her father hears about the promise or pledge and says nothing, she must do what she promised. She *must keep her pledge.* ⁵*But if her father hears about the promise or pledge and does not allow it, then the promise or pledge does not have to be kept. Her father would not allow it, so the LORD will free her from her promise.*

⁶"If a woman makes a pledge or a careless promise and then gets married, ⁷and if her hus-

band hears about it and says nothing, she must keep her promise or the pledge she made. ⁸But if her husband hears about it and does not allow it, he cancels her pledge or the careless promise she made. The LORD will free her from keeping it.

⁹"If a widow or divorced woman makes a promise, she must do whatever she promised.

¹⁰"If a woman makes a promise or pledge while she is married, ¹¹and if her husband hears about it but says nothing and does not stop her, she must keep her promise or pledge. ¹²But if her husband hears about it and cancels it, she does not have to do what she said. Her husband has canceled it, so the LORD will free her from it. ¹³A woman's husband may make her keep or cancel any promise or pledge she has made. ¹⁴If he says nothing to her about it for several days, she must keep her promises. If he hears about them and says nothing, she must keep her promises. ¹⁵But if he cancels them long after he heard about them, he is responsible if she breaks her promise."

¹⁶These are commands that the LORD gave to Moses for husbands and wives, and for fathers with daughters living at home.

Israel Attacks the Midianites

31 The LORD spoke to Moses and said, ²"Pay back the Midianites for what they did to the Israelites; after that you will die."

³So Moses said to the people, "Get some men ready for war. The LORD will use them to pay back the Midianites. ⁴Send to war a thousand men from each of the tribesᵈ of Israel." ⁵So twelve thousand men got ready for war, a thousand men from each tribe. ⁶Moses sent those men to war; Phinehas son of Eleazar the priest was with them. He took with him the holy things and the trumpets for giving the alarm. ⁷They fought the Midianites as the LORD had commanded Moses, and they killed every Midianite man. ⁸Among those they killed were Evi, Rekem, Zur, Hur, and Reba, who were the five kings of Midian. They also killed Balaam son of Beor with a sword.

⁹The Israelites captured the Midianite women and children, and they took all their flocks, herds, and goods. ¹⁰They burned all the Midianite towns where they had settled and all their camps, ¹¹but they took all the people and animals and goods. ¹²Then they brought the captives, the animals, and the goods back to Moses and Eleazar the priest and all the Israelites. Their camp was on the plains of Moab near the Jordan River, across from Jericho.

¹³Moses, Eleazar the priest, and all the leaders of the people went outside the camp to meet them. ¹⁴Moses was angry with the army officers, the commanders over a thousand men, and those over a hundred men, who returned from war. ¹⁵He asked them, "Why did you let the women

live? 16They were the ones who followed Balaam's advice and turned the Israelites from the LORD at Peor. Then a terrible sickness struck the LORD's people. 17Kill all the Midianite boys, and kill all the Midianite women who have had sexual relations. 18But save for yourselves the girls who have not had sexual relations with a man.

19"All you men who killed anyone or touched a dead body must stay outside the camp for seven days. On the third and seventh days you and your captives must make yourselves clean.d 20You must clean all your clothes and anything made of leather, goat hair, or wood."

21Then Eleazar the priest said to the soldiers who had gone to war, "These are the teachings that the LORD gave to Moses: 22Put any gold, silver, bronze, iron, tin, or lead — 23anything that will not burn — into the fire, and then it will be clean. But also purify those things with the cleansing water. Then they will be clean. If something cannot stand the fire, wash it with the water. 24On the seventh day wash your clothes, and you will be clean. After that you may come into the camp."

Dividing the Goods

25The LORD said to Moses, 26"You, Eleazar the priest, and the leaders of the family groups should take a count of the goods, the men, and the animals that were taken. 27Then divide those possessions between the soldiers who went to war and the rest of the people. 28From the soldiers who went to war, take a tax for the LORD of one item out of every five hundred. This includes people, cattle, donkeys, or sheep. 29Take it from the soldiers' half, and give it to Eleazar the priest as the LORD's share. 30And from the people's half, take one item out of every fifty. This includes people, cattle, donkeys, sheep, or other animals. Give that to the Levites, who take care of the LORD's Holy Tent."d 31So Moses and Eleazar did as the LORD commanded Moses.

32There remained from what the soldiers had taken 675,000 sheep, 3372,000 cattle, 3461,000 donkeys, 35and 32,000 women who had not had sexual relations with a man. 36The soldiers who went to war got 337,000 sheep, 37and they gave 675 of them to the LORD. 38They got 36,000 cattle, and they gave 72 of them to the LORD. 39They got 30,500 donkeys, and they gave 61 of them to the LORD. 40They got 16,000 people, and they gave 32 of them to the LORD. 41Moses gave the LORD's share to Eleazar the priest, as the LORD had commanded him.

42Moses separated the people's half from the soldiers' half. 43The people got 337,500 sheep, 4436,000 cattle, 4530,500 donkeys, 46and 16,000 people. 47From the people's half Moses took one item out of every fifty for the LORD. This included

the animals and the people. Then he gave them to the Levites, who took care of the LORD's Holy Tent. This was what the LORD had commanded Moses.

48Then the officers of the army, the commanders of a thousand men and commanders of a hundred men, came to Moses. 49They told Moses, "We, your servants, have counted our soldiers under our command, and not one of them is missing. 50So we have brought the LORD a gift of the gold things that each of us found: arm bands, bracelets, signetd rings, earrings, and necklaces. These are to remove our sins so we will belong to the LORD."

51So Moses and Eleazar the priest took the gold from them, which had been made into all kinds of objects. 52The commanders of a thousand men and the commanders of a hundred men gave the LORD the gold, and all of it together weighed about 420 pounds; 53each soldier had taken something for himself. 54Moses and Eleazar the priest took the gold from the commanders of a thousand men and the commanders of a hundred men. Then they put it in the Meeting Tentd as a memorial before the LORD for the people of Israel.

The Tribes East of the Jordan

32 The people of Reuben and Gad had large flocks and herds. When they saw that the lands of Jazer and Gilead were good for the animals, 2they came to Moses, Eleazar the priest, and the leaders of the people. 3-4They said, "We, your servants, have flocks and herds. The LORD has captured for the Israelites a land that is good for animals — the land around Ataroth, Dibon, Jazer, Nimrah, Heshbon, Elealeh, Sebam, Nebo, and Beon. 5If it pleases you, we would like this land to be given to us. Don't make us cross the Jordan River."

6Moses told the people of Gad and Reuben, "Shall your brothers go to war while you stay behind? 7You will discourage the Israelites from going over to the land the LORD has given them. 8Your ancestors did the same thing. I sent them from Kadesh Barnea to look at the land. 9They went as far as the Valley of Eshcol, and when they saw the land, they discouraged the Israelites from going into the land the LORD had given them. 10The LORD became very angry that day and made this promise: 11'None of the people who came from Egypt and who are twenty years old or older will see the land that I promised to Abraham, Isaac, and Jacob. These people have not followed me completely. 12Only Caleb son of Jephunneh the Kenizzite and Joshua son of Nun followed the LORD completely.'

13"The LORD was angry with Israel, so he made them wander in the desert for forty years. Finally all the people who had sinned against the LORD died, [14]and now you are acting just like your ancestors! You sinful people are making the Lord even more angry with Israel. [15]If you quit following him, it will add to their stay in the desert, and you will destroy all these people."

[16]Then the Reubenites and Gadites came up to Moses and said, "We will build pens for our animals and cities for our children here. [17]Then our children will be in strong, walled cities, safe from the people who live in this land. Then we will prepare for war. We will help the other Israelites get their land, [18]and we will not return home until every Israelite has received his land. [19]We won't take any of the land west of the Jordan River; our part of the land is east of the Jordan."

[20]So Moses told them, "You must do these things. You must go before the Lord into battle [21]and cross the Jordan River armed, until the Lord forces out the enemy. [22]After the Lord helps us take the land, you may return home. You will have done your duty to the Lord and Israel, and you may have this land as your own.

[23]"But if you don't do these things, you will be sinning against the Lord; know for sure that you will be punished for your sin. [24]Build cities for your children and pens for your animals, but then you must do what you promised."

[25]The Gadites and Reubenites said to Moses, "We are your servants, and we will do what you, our master, command. [26]Our children, wives, and all our cattle will stay in the cities of Gilead, [27]but we, your servants, will prepare for battle. We will go over and fight for the Lord, as you, our master, have said."

[28]So Moses gave orders about them to Eleazar the priest, to Joshua son of Nun, and to the leaders of the tribes[d] of Israel. [29]Moses said to them, "If the Gadites and Reubenites prepare for battle and cross the Jordan River with you, to go before the Lord and help you take the land, give them the land of Gilead for their own. [30]But if they do not go over armed, they will not receive it; their land will be in Canaan with you."

[31]The Gadites and Reubenites answered, "We are your servants, and we will do as the Lord said. [32]We will cross over into Canaan and go before the Lord ready for battle. But our land will be east of the Jordan River."

[33]So Moses gave that land to the tribes of Gad, Reuben, and East Manasseh. (Manasseh was Joseph's son.) That land had been the kingdom of Sihon, king of the Amorites, and the kingdom of Og, king of Bashan, as well as all the cities and the land around them.

[34]The Gadites rebuilt the cities of Dibon, Ataroth, Aroer, [35]Atroth Shophan, Jazer, Jogbehah, [36]Beth Nimrah, and Beth Haran. These were strong, walled cities. And they built sheep pens. [37]The Reubenites rebuilt Heshbon, Elealeh, Kiriathaim, [38]Nebo, Baal Meon, and Sibmah. They renamed Nebo and Baal Meon when they rebuilt them.

[39]The descendants[d] of Makir son of Manasseh went and captured Gilead and forced out the Amorites who were there. [40]So Moses gave Gilead to the family of Makir son of Manasseh, and they settled there. [41]Jair son of Manasseh went out and captured the small towns there, and he called them the Towns of Jair. [42]Nobah went and captured Kenath and the small towns around it; then he named it Nobah after himself.

Israel's Journey from Egypt

33 These are the places the Israelites went as Moses and Aaron led them out of Egypt in divisions. [2]At the Lord's command Moses recorded the places they went, and these are the places they went.

[3]On the fifteenth day of the first month, the day after the Passover,[d] the Israelites left Rameses and marched out boldly in front of all the Egyptians. [4]The Egyptians were burying their firstborn[d] sons, whom the Lord had killed; the Lord showed that the gods of Egypt were false.

[5]The Israelites left Rameses and camped at Succoth.

[6]They left Succoth and camped at Etham, at the edge of the desert.

[7]They left Etham and went back to Pi Hahiroth, to the east of Baal Zephon, and camped near Migdol.

[8]They left Pi Hahiroth and walked through the sea into the desert. After going three days through the Desert of Etham, they camped at Marah.

[9]They left Marah and went to Elim; there were twelve springs of water and seventy palm trees where they camped.

[10]They left Elim and camped near the Red Sea.[d]

[11]They left the Red Sea and camped in the Desert of Sin.

[12]They left the Desert of Sin and camped at Dophkah.

[13]They left Dophkah and camped at Alush.

[14]They left Alush and camped at Rephidim, where the people had no water to drink.

[15]They left Rephidim and camped in the Desert of Sinai.

[16]They left the Desert of Sinai and camped at Kibroth Hattaavah.

[17]They left Kibroth Hattaavah and camped at Hazeroth.

[18]They left Hazeroth and camped at Rithmah.

[19]They left Rithmah and camped at Rimmon Perez.

[20]They left Rimmon Perez and camped at Libnah.

[21]They left Libnah and camped at Rissah.

[22]They left Rissah and camped at Kehelathah.

23They left Kehelathah and camped at Mount Shepher.

24They left Mount Shepher and camped at Haradah.

25They left Haradah and camped at Makheloth.

26They left Makheloth and camped at Tahath.

27They left Tahath and camped at Terah.

28They left Terah and camped at Mithcah.

29They left Mithcah and camped at Hashmonah.

30They left Hashmonah and camped at Moseroth.

31They left Moseroth and camped at Bene Jaakan.

32They left Bene Jaakan and camped at Hor Haggidgad.

33They left Hor Haggidgad and camped at Jotbathah.

34They left Jotbathah and camped at Abronah.

35They left Abronah and camped at Ezion Geber.

36They left Ezion Geber and camped at Kadesh in the Desert of Zin.

37They left Kadesh and camped at Mount Hor, on the border of Edom. 38Aaron the priest obeyed the LORD and went up Mount Hor. There he died on the first day of the fifth month in the fortieth year after the Israelites left Egypt. 39Aaron was 123 years old when he died on Mount Hor.

40The Canaanite king of Arad, who lived in the southern area of Canaan, heard that the Israelites were coming.

41The people left Mount Hor and camped at Zalmonah.

42They left Zalmonah and camped at Punon.

43They left Punon and camped at Oboth.

44They left Oboth and camped at Iye Abarim, on the border of Moab.

45They left Iye Abarim and camped at Dibon Gad.

46They left Dibon Gad and camped at Almon Diblathaim.

47They left Almon Diblathaim and camped in the mountains of Abarim, near Nebo.

48They left the mountains of Abarim and camped on the plains of Moab near the Jordan River across from Jericho. 49They camped along the Jordan on the plains of Moab, and their camp went from Beth Jeshimoth to Abel Acacia.

50On the plains of Moab by the Jordan River across from Jericho, the LORD spoke to Moses. He said, 51"Speak to the Israelites and tell them, 'When you cross the Jordan River and go into Canaan, 52force out all the people who live there. Destroy all of their carved statues and metal idols. Wreck all of their places of worship. 53Take over the land and settle there, because I have given this land to you to own. 54Throw lots*d* to divide up the land by family groups, giving larger por-

tions to larger family groups and smaller portions to smaller family groups. The land will be given as the lots decide; each tribe*d* will get its own land.

55" 'But if you don't force those people out of the land, they will bring you trouble. They will be like sharp hooks in your eyes and thorns in your sides. They will bring trouble to the land where you live. 56Then I will punish you as I had planned to punish them.' "

The Borders of Canaan

34 The LORD said to Moses, 2"Give this command to the people of Israel: 'You will soon enter Canaan and it will be yours. These shall be the borders: 3On the south you will get part of the Desert of Zin near the border of Edom. On the east side your southern border will start at the south end of the Dead Sea,*d* 4cross south of Scorpion Pass, and go through the Desert of Zin and south of Kadesh Barnea. Then it will go to Hazar Addar and over to Azmon. 5From Azmon it will go to the brook of Egypt, and it will end at the Mediterranean Sea.

6" 'Your western border will be the Mediterranean Sea.

7" 'Your northern border will begin at the Mediterranean Sea and go to Mount Hor. 8From Mount Hor it will go to Lebo Hamath, and on to Zedad. 9Then the border will go to Ziphron, and it will end at Hazar Enan. This will be your northern border.

10" 'Your eastern border will begin at Hazar Enan and go to Shepham. 11From Shepham the border will go east of Ain to Riblah and along the hills east of Lake Galilee. 12Then the border will go down along the Jordan River and end at the Dead Sea.

" 'These are the borders around your country.' "

13So Moses gave this command to the Israelites: "This is the land you will receive. Throw lots*d* to divide it among the nine and one-half tribes,*d* because the LORD commanded that it should be theirs. 14The tribes of Reuben, Gad, and East Manasseh have already received their land. 15These two and one-half tribes received land east of the Jordan River, across from Jericho."

16Then the LORD said to Moses, 17"These are the men who will divide the land: Eleazar the priest and Joshua son of Nun. 18Also take one leader from each tribe to help divide the land. 19These are the names of the leaders: from the tribe of Judah, Caleb son of Jephunneh; 20from the tribe of Simeon, Shemuel son of Ammihud; 21from the tribe of Benjamin, Elidad son of Kislon; 22from the tribe of Dan, Bukki son of Jogli; 23from the tribe of Manasseh son of Joseph, Hanniel son of Ephod; 24from the tribe of Ephraim son of Joseph, Kemuel son of Shiphtan; [25]from the tribe of Zebulun, Elizaphan son of Parnach; [26]from the tribe of Issachar, Paltiel son of Azzan; [27]from the tribe of Asher, Ahihud son of Shelomi; [28]from the tribe of Naphtali, Pedahel son of Ammihud."

[29]The LORD commanded these men to divide the land of Canaan among the Israelites.

The Levites' Towns

35 The LORD spoke to Moses on the plains of Moab across from Jericho by the Jordan River. He said, [2]"Command the Israelites to give the Levites cities to live in from the land they receive. Also give the Levites the pastureland around these cities. [3]Then the Levites will have cities where they may live and pastureland for their cattle, flocks, and other animals. [4]The pastureland you give the Levites will extend fifteen hundred feet from the city wall. [5]Also measure three thousand feet in each direction outside the city wall — three thousand feet east of the city, three thousand feet south of the city, three thousand feet west of the city, and three thousand feet north of the city, with the city in the center. This will be pastureland for the Levites' cities.

Cities of Safety

[6]"Six of the cities you give the Levites will be cities of safety.[d] A person who accidentally kills someone may run to one of those cities for safety. You must also give forty-two other cities to the Levites; [7]give the Levites a total of forty-eight cities and their pastures. [8]The larger tribes[d] of Israel must give more cities, and the smaller tribes must give fewer cities. Each tribe must give some of its cities to the Levites, but the number of cities they give will depend on the size of their land."

[9]Then the LORD said to Moses, [10]"Tell the Israelites these things: 'When you cross the Jordan River and go into Canaan, [11]you must choose cities to be cities of safety, so that a person who accidentally kills someone may run to them for safety. [12]There the person will be safe from the dead person's relative who has the duty of punishing the killer. He will not die before he receives a fair trial in court. [13]The six cities you give will be cities of safety. [14]Give three cities east of the Jordan River and three cities in Canaan as cities of safety. [15]These six cities will be places of safety for citizens of Israel, as well as for foreigners and other people living with you. Any of these people who accidentally kills someone may run to one of these cities.

[16]"'Anyone who uses an iron weapon to kill someone is a murderer. He must be put to death. [17]Anyone who takes a rock and kills a person with it is a murderer. He must be put to death. [18]Anyone who picks up a piece of wood and kills someone with it is a murderer. He must be put to

death. [19]A relative of the dead person must put the murderer to death; when they meet, the relative must kill the murderer. [20]A person might shove someone or throw something at someone and cause death. [21]Or a person might hit someone with his hand and cause death. If it were done from hate, the person is a murderer and must be put to death. A relative of the dead person must kill the murderer when they meet.

[22]"'But a person might suddenly shove someone, and not from hatred. Or a person might accidentally throw something and hit someone. [23]Or a person might drop a rock on someone he couldn't see and kill that person. There was no plan to hurt anyone and no hatred for the one who was killed. [24]If that happens, the community must judge between the relative of the dead person and the killer, according to these rules. [25]They must protect the killer from the dead person's relative, sending the killer back to the original city of safety, to stay there until the high priest dies (the high priest had the holy oil poured on him).

[26]"'Such a person must never go outside the limits of the city of safety. [27]If a relative of the dead person finds the killer outside the city, the relative may kill that person and not be guilty of murder. [28]The killer must stay in the city of safety until the high priest dies. After the high priest dies, the killer may go home.

SIDELIGHT: Today, if a person kills someone, a trial is held to determine guilt or innocence, and sentencing. In Old Testament times, such a person could be murdered. To protect people who accidentally killed, Numbers 35:6–28 tells of six cities of safety where someone could go to be safe from the victim's relatives. But if the killer left the city, the dead person's family could take revenge.

---

[29]"'These laws are for you from now on, wherever you live.

[30]"'If anyone kills a person, the murderer may be put to death only if there are witnesses. No one may be put to death with only one witness.

[31]"'Don't take money to spare the life of a murderer who should be put to death. A murderer must be put to death.

[32]"'If someone has run to a city of safety, don't take money to let the person go back home before the high priest dies.

[33]"'Don't let murder spoil your land. The only way to remove the sin of killing an innocent person is for the murderer to be put to death. [34]I am the LORD, and I live among the Israelites. I live in

that land with you, so do not spoil it with murder.' "

Land for Zelophehad's Daughters

36 The leaders of Gilead's family group went to talk to Moses and the leaders of the families of Israel. (Gilead was the son of Makir, the son of Manasseh, the son of Joseph.) [2]They said, "The LORD commanded you, our master, to give the land to the Israelites by throwing lots,[d] and the LORD commanded you to give the land of Zelophehad, our brother, to his daughters. [3]But if his daughters marry men from other tribes[d] of Israel, then that land will leave our family, and the people of the other tribes will get that land. So we will lose some of our land. [4]When the time of Jubilee[d] comes for the Israelites, their land will go to the tribes of the people they marry; their land will be taken away from us, the land we received from our fathers."

[5]Then Moses gave the Israelites this command from the LORD: "These men from the tribe of Joseph are right. [6]This is the LORD's command to Zelophehad's daughters: You may marry anyone you wish, as long as the person is from your own tribe. [7]In this way the Israelites' land will not pass from tribe to tribe, and each Israelite will keep the land in the tribe that belonged to his ancestors. [8]A woman who inherits her father's land may marry, but she must marry someone from her own tribe. In this way every Israelite will keep the land that belonged to his ancestors. [9]The land must not pass from tribe to tribe, and each Israelite tribe will keep the land it received from its ancestors."

[10]Zelophehad's daughters obeyed the LORD's command to Moses.

[11]So Zelophehad's daughters—Mahlah, Tirzah, Hogah, Milcah, and Noah—married their cousins, their father's relatives. [12]Their husbands were from the tribe of Manasseh son of Joseph, so their land stayed in their father's family group and tribe.

[13]These were the laws and commands that LORD gave to the Israelites through Moses on the plains of Moab by the Jordan River, across from Jericho.

DEUTERONOMY

Why Read This Book:

- Be reminded of all the good things God has done for his people (Deuteronomy 1—4).
- Find out what God requires of people because of his special relationship with them (Deuteronomy 5—28).
- See what God has in store for his people, when they do right and when they do wrong (Deuteronomy 29—30).

Behind the Scenes:

You've spent weeks reading books, listening to lectures, and doing homework. You've learned lots of important information that will help you in the future. Then the week before the big test, your teacher reviews what you've learned and urges you to remember everything that has happened.

The book of Deuteronomy is a lot like that last week of review. The Israelites had escaped from slavery in Egypt. But because they would not do God's will, they had to wander in the desert for forty years until they died, and their children

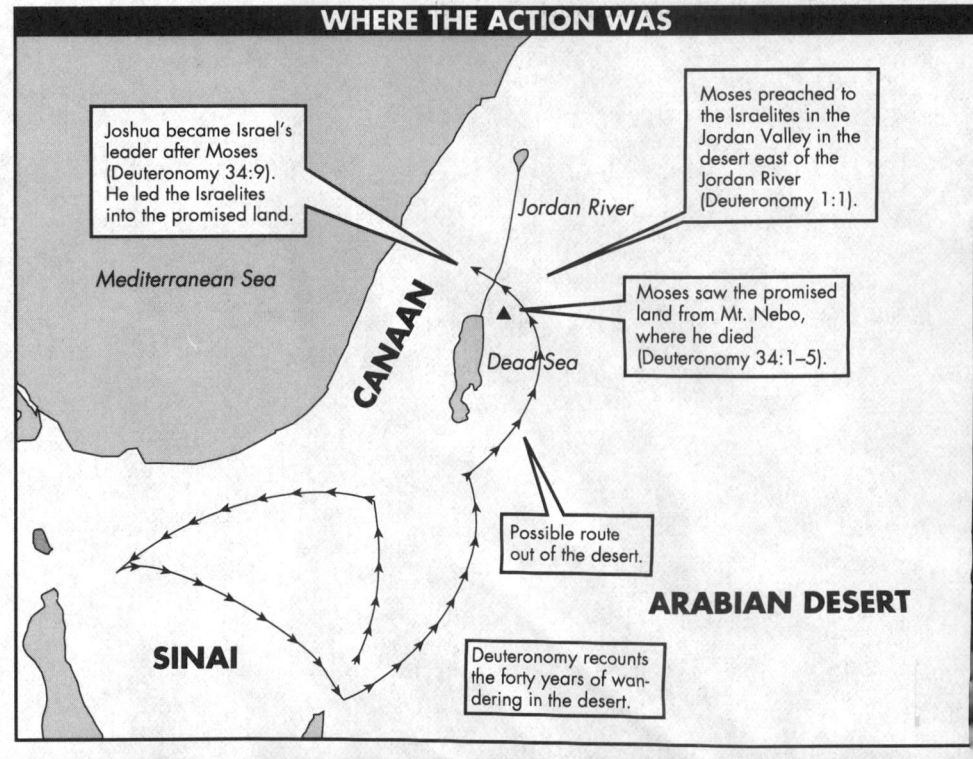

WHERE THE ACTION WAS

Joshua became Israel's leader after Moses (Deuteronomy 34:9). He led the Israelites into the promised land.

Moses preached to the Israelites in the Jordan Valley in the desert east of the Jordan River (Deuteronomy 1:1).

Jordan River

Mediterranean Sea

CANAAN

Dead Sea

Moses saw the promised land from Mt. Nebo, where he died (Deuteronomy 34:1–5).

Possible route out of the desert.

ARABIAN DESERT

SINAI

Deuteronomy recounts the forty years of wandering in the desert.

WHEN THE ACTION WAS

2000BC	1500BC		1000BC	500BC	BC/AD

The Israelites escaped from Egypt

Moses died on Mt. Nebo

Jesus was born

The Israelites wandered in the desert

Joshua led the Israelites into Canaan

Behind the Scenes (cont.):
took their places. In the desert, Moses, their leader, had received laws from God and had helped the new generation learn what it meant to be a nation that followed God.

Now the people were preparing for "finals week"—when they would enter the land of Canaan, the promised land. Just before his death, Moses gave the people three "review sessions" or sermons. He reminded them of what God had done for them, and he urged the people to keep God's commandments as they entered a new land with new temptations.

Deuteronomy means "second law" or "repetition of the law." It restates many of the laws the Israelites had received in the desert. But unlike other law books, it focuses more on why people should keep the laws, namely, out of gratitude for God's love.

Moses Talks to the Israelites

1 This is the message Moses gave to all the people of Israel in the desert east of the Jordan River. They were in the desert area near Suph, between Paran and the towns of Tophel, Laban, Hazeroth, and Dizahab.

²(The trip from Mount Sinai to Kadesh Barnea on the Mount Seir road takes eleven days.) ³Forty years after the Israelites had left Egypt, on the first day of the eleventh month, Moses told the people of Israel everything the LORD had commanded him to tell them. ⁴This was after the LORD had defeated Sihon and Og. Sihon was king of the Amorite people and lived in Heshbon. Og was king of Bashan and lived in Ashteroth and Edrei.

⁵Now the Israelites were east of the Jordan River in the land of Moab, and there Moses began to explain what God had commanded. He said:

⁶The LORD our God spoke to us at Mount Sinai and said, "You have stayed long enough at this mountain. ⁷Get ready, and go to the mountain country of the Amorites, and to all the places around there—the Jordan Valley, the mountains, the western hills, the southern area, the seacoast, the land of Canaan, and Lebanon. Go as far as the great river, the Euphrates. ⁸See, I have given you this land, so go in and take it for yourselves. The LORD promised it to your ancestors—Abraham, Isaac, and Jacob and their descendants."*d*

Moses Appoints Leaders

⁹At that time I said, "I am not able to take care of you by myself. ¹⁰The LORD your God has made you grow in number so that there are as many of you as there are stars in the sky. ¹¹I pray that the LORD, the God of your ancestors, will give you a thousand times more people and do all the wonderful things he promised. ¹²But I cannot take care of your problems, your troubles, and your arguments by myself. ¹³So choose some men from each tribe*d*—wise men who have understanding and experience—and I will make them leaders over you."

¹⁴And you said, "That's a good thing to do."

¹⁵So I took the wise and experienced leaders of your tribes, and I made them your leaders. I appointed commanders over a thousand people, over a hundred people, over fifty people, and over ten people and made them officers over your tribes. ¹⁶Then I told your leaders, "Listen to the arguments between your people. Judge fairly between two Israelites or between an Israelite and a foreigner. ¹⁷When you judge, be fair to everyone; don't act as if one person is more important than another, and don't be afraid of anyone, because your decision comes from God. Bring the hard cases to me, and I will judge them." ¹⁸At that time I told you everything you must do.

Spies Enter the Land

¹⁹Then, as the LORD our God commanded us, we left Mount Sinai and went toward the mountain country of the Amorite people. We went through that large and terrible desert you saw, and then we came to Kadesh Barnea. ²⁰I said to you, "You have now come to the mountain country of the Amorites, to the land the LORD our God will give us. ²¹Look, here it is! Go up and take it. The LORD, the God of your ancestors, told you to do this, so don't be afraid and don't worry."

²²Then all of you came to me and said, "Let's send men before us to spy out the land. They can come back and tell us about the way we should go and the cities we will find."

²³I thought that was a good idea, so I chose twelve of your men, one for each tribe.*d* ²⁴They left and went up to the mountains, and when they came to the Valley of Eshcol they explored it. ²⁵They took some of the fruit from that land and brought it down to us, saying, "It is a good land that the LORD our God is giving us."

Israel Refuses to Enter

²⁶But you refused to go. You would not obey the command of the LORD your God, ²⁷but grumbled in your tents, saying, "The LORD hates us. He brought us out of Egypt just to give us to the Amorites, who will destroy us. ²⁸Where can we go now? The spies we sent have made us afraid, because they said, 'The people there are stronger

and taller than we are. The cities are big, with walls up to the sky. And we saw the Anakites[d] there!' "

[29]Then I said to you, "Don't be frightened; don't be afraid of those people. [30]The LORD your God will go ahead of you and fight for you as he did in Egypt; you saw him do it. [31]And in the desert you saw how the LORD your God carried you, like one carries a child. And he has brought you safely all the way to this place."

[32]But you still did not trust the LORD your God, even though [33]he had always gone before you to find places for you to camp. In a fire at night and in a cloud during the day, he showed you which way to go.

[34]When the LORD heard what you said, he was angry and made an oath, saying, [35]"I promised a good land to your ancestors, but none of you evil people will see it. [36]Only Caleb son of Jephunneh will see it. I will give him and his descendants[d] the land he walked on, because he followed the LORD completely."

[37]Because of you, the LORD was also angry with me and said, "You won't enter the land either, [38]but your assistant, Joshua son of Nun, will enter it. Encourage him, because he will lead Israel to take the land for their own.

[39]"Your little children that you said would be captured, who do not know right from wrong at this time, will go into the land. I will give the land to them, and they will take it for their own. [40]But you must turn around and follow the desert road toward the Red Sea."

[41]Then you said to me, "We have sinned against the LORD, but now we will go up and fight, as the LORD our God commanded us." Then all of you put on weapons, thinking it would be easy to go into the mountains.

[42]But the LORD said to me, "Tell the people, 'You must not go up there and fight. I will not be with you, and your enemies will defeat you.' "

[43]So I told you, but you would not listen. You would not obey the LORD's command. You were proud, so you went on up into the mountains, [44]and the Amorites who lived in those mountains came out and fought you. They chased you like bees and defeated you from Edom to Hormah. [45]So you came back and cried before the LORD, but the LORD did not listen to you; he refused to pay attention to you. [46]So you stayed in Kadesh a long time.

Israel Wanders in the Desert

2 Then we turned around, and we traveled on the desert road toward the Red Sea, as the LORD had told me to do. We traveled through the mountains of Edom for many days.

[2]Then the LORD said to me, [3]"You have traveled through these mountains long enough. Turn north [4]and give the people this command: 'You will soon go through the land that belongs to your relatives, the descendants[d] of Esau who live in Edom. They will be afraid of you, but be very careful. [5]Do not go to war against them. I will not give you any of their land — not even a foot of it, because I have given the mountains of Edom to Esau as his own. [6]You must pay them in silver for any food you eat or water you drink.' "

[7]The LORD your God has blessed everything you have done; he has protected you while you traveled through this great desert. The LORD your God has been with you for the past forty years, and you have had everything you needed.

[8]So we passed by our relatives, the descendants of Esau who lived in Edom. We turned off the Jordan Valley road that comes from the towns of Elath and Ezion Geber and traveled along the desert road to Moab.

The Land of Ar

[9]Then the LORD said to me, "Don't bother the people of Moab. Don't go to war against them, because I will not give you any of their land as your own; I have given Ar to the descendants[d] of Lot as their own." [10](The Emites, who lived in Ar before, were strong people, and there were many of them. They were very tall, like the Anakites.[d] [11]The Emites were thought to be Rephaites,[d] like the Anakites, but the Moabite people called them Emites. [12]The Horites also lived in Edom before, but the descendants of Esau forced them out and destroyed them, taking their place as Israel did in the land the LORD gave them as their own.)

[13]And the LORD said to me, "Now get up and cross the Zered Valley." So we crossed the valley. [14]It had been thirty-eight years from the time we left Kadesh Barnea until we crossed the Zered Valley. By then, all the fighting men from that time had died, as the LORD had promised would happen. [15]The LORD continued to work against them to remove them from the camp until they were all dead.

[16]When the last of those fighting men had died, [17]the LORD said to me, [18]"Today you will pass by Ar, on the border of Moab. [19]When you come near the people of Ammon, don't bother them or go to war against them, because I will not give you any of their land as your own. I have given it to the descendants of Lot for their own."

[20](That land was also thought to be a land of the Rephaites, because those people used to live there, but the Ammonites called them Zamzummites. [21]They were strong people, and there were many of them; they were very tall, like the Anakites. The LORD destroyed the Zamzummites, and the Ammonites forced them out of the land and took their place. [22]The LORD did the same thing for the descendants of Esau, who lived in Edom,

when he destroyed the Horites. The Edomites forced them out of the land and took their place, and they l ve there to this day. 23The Cretan people came from Crete and destroyed the Avvites, who lived in towns all the way to Gaza; the Cretans destroyed them and took their place.)

Fighting the Amorites

24The LORD said, "Get up and cross the Arnon Ravine. See, I am giving you the power to defeat Sihon the Amorite, king of Heshbon, and I am giving you his land. So fight against him and begin taking his and. 25Today I will begin to make all the people in the world afraid of you. When they hear reports about you, they will shake with fear, and they will be terrified of you."

26I sent messengers from the desert of Kedemoth to Sihon king of Heshbon. They offered him peace, saying, 27"If you let us pass through your country, we will stay on the road and not turn right or left. 28We will pay you in silver for any food we eat or water we drink. We only want to walk through your country. 29The descendants*d* of Esau in Edom let us go through their land, and so did the Moabites in Ar. We want to cross the Jordan River into the land the LORD our God has given us." 30But Sihon king of Heshbon would not let us pass, because the LORD your God had made him stubborn. The LORD wanted you to defeat Sihon, and now this has happened.

31The LORD said to me, "See, I have begun to give Sihon and his country to you. Begin taking the land as your own."

32Then Sihon and all his army came out and fought us at Jahaz, 33but the LORD our God gave Sihon to us. We defeated him, his sons, and all his army. 34We captured all his cities at that time and completely destroyed them, as well as the men, women, and children. We left no one alive. 35But we kept the cattle and valuable things from the cities for ourselves. 36We defeated Aroer on the edge of the Arnon Ravine, and we defeated the town in the ravine, and even as far as Gilead. No town was too strong for us; the LORD our God gave us all of them. 37But you did not go near the land of the Ammonites, on the shores of the Jabbok River, or the towns in the mountains, as the LORD our God had commanded.

The Battle at Bashan

3 When we turned and went up the road toward Bashan, Og king of Bashan and all his army came out to fight us at Edrei. 2The LORD said to me, "Don't be afraid of Og, because I will hand him, his whole army, and his land over to you. Do to him what you did to Sihon king of the Amorites, who ru ed in Heshbon."

3So the LORD our God gave us Og king of Bashan and all his army; we defeated them and left

no one alive. 4Then we captured all of Og's cities, all sixty of them, and took the whole area of Argob, Og's kingdom in Bashan. 5All these were strong cities, with high walls and gates with bars. And there were also many small towns with no walls. 6We completely destroyed them, just like the cities of Sihon king of Heshbon. We killed all the men, women, and children, 7but we kept all the cattle and valuable things from the cities for ourselves.

8So at that time we took the land east of the Jordan River, from the Arnon Ravine to Mount Hermon, from these two Amorite kings. 9(Hermon is called Sirion by the Sidonian people, but The Amorites call it Senir.) 10We captured all the cities on the high plain and all of Gilead, and we took all of Bashan as far as Salecah and Edrei, towns in Og's kingdom of Bashan. 11(Only Og king of Bashan was left of the few Rephaites.*d* His bed was made of iron, and it was more than thirteen feet long and six feet wide! It is still in the Ammonite city of Rabbah.)

The Land Is Divided

12At that time we took this land to be our own. I gave the people of Reuben and Gad the land from Aroer by the Arnon Ravine, as well as half of the mountain country of Gilead and the cities in it. 13To the people of East Manasseh I gave the rest of Gilead and all of Bashan, the kingdom of Og. (The area of Argob in Bashan was called the land of the Rephaites.*d* 14Jair, a descendant*d* of Manasseh, took the whole area of Argob, all the way to the border of the Geshurites and Maacathites. So that land was named for Jair, and even today Bashan is called the Towns of Jair.) 15I gave Gilead to Makir. 16I gave the Reubenites and the Gadites the land that begins at Gilead and goes from the Arnon Ravine (the middle of the Arnon is the border) to the Jabbok River, which is the Ammonite border. 17The border on the west was the Jordan River in the Jordan Valley, and it goes from Lake Galilee to the Dead Sea*d* west of Mount Pisgah.

18At that time I gave you this command: "The LORD your God has given you this land as your own. Now your fighting men must take their weapons, and you must lead the other Israelites across the river. 19Your wives, your young children, and your cattle may stay here. I know you have many cattle, and they may stay here in the cities I have given you, 20until the LORD also gives your Israelite relatives a place to rest. They will receive the land the LORD your God has given them on the other side of the Jordan River. After that, you may each return to the land I have given you."

21Then I gave this command to Joshua: "You have seen for yourself all that the LORD your God has done to these two kings. The LORD will do the same thing to all the kingdoms where you are going. 22Don't be afraid of them, because the LORD your God will fight for you."

Moses Cannot Enter the Land

23Then I begged the LORD: 24"Lord GOD, you have begun to show me, your servant, how great you are. You have great strength, and no other god in heaven or on earth can do the powerful things you do. There is no other god like you. 25Please let me cross the Jordan River so that I may see the good land by the Jordan. I want to see the beautiful mountains and Lebanon."

26But the LORD was angry with me because of you, and he would not listen to me. The LORD said to me, "That's enough. Don't talk to me anymore about it. 27Climb to the top of Mount Pisgah and look west, north, south, and east. You can look at the land, but you will not cross the Jordan River. 28Appoint Joshua and help him be brave and strong. He will lead the people across the river and give them the land that they are to inherit, but you can only look at it." 29So we stayed in the valley opposite Beth Peor.

Moses Tells Israel to Obey

4 Now, Israel, listen to the laws and commands I will teach you. Obey them so that you will live and so that you will go over and take the land the LORD, the God of your ancestors, is giving to you. 2Don't add to these commands, and don't leave anything out, but obey the commands of the LORD your God that I give you.

3You have seen for yourselves what the LORD did at Baal Peor, how the LORD your God destroyed everyone among you who followed Baal*d* in Peor. 4But all of you who continued following the LORD your God are still alive today.

5Look, I have taught you the laws and rules the LORD my God commanded me. Now you can obey the laws in the land you are entering, in the land you will take. 6Obey these laws carefully, in order to show the other nations that you have wisdom and understanding. When they hear about these laws, they will say, "This great nation of Israel is wise and understanding." 7No other nation is as great as we are. Their gods do not come near them, but the LORD our God comes near when we pray to him. 8And no other nation has such good teachings and commands as those I am giving to you today.

9But be careful! Watch out and don't forget the things you have seen. Don't forget them as long as you live, but teach them to your children and grandchildren. 10Remember the day you stood before the LORD your God at Mount Sinai. He said to me, "Bring the people together so I can tell them what I have to say. Then they will respect me as long as they live in the land, and they will teach these things to their children." 11When you came and stood at the bottom of the mountain, it blazed with fire that reached to the sky, and black clouds made it very dark. 12The LORD spoke to you from the fire. You heard the sound of words, but you did not see him; there was only a voice. 13The LORD told you about his Agreement, the Ten Commandments. He told you to obey them, and he wrote them on two stone tablets. 14Then the LORD commanded me to teach you the laws and rules that you must obey in the land you will take when you cross the Jordan River.

Laws About Idols

15Since the LORD spoke to you from the fire at Mount Sinai, but you did not see him, watch yourselves carefully! 16Don't sin by making idols of any kind, and don't make statues — of men or women, 17of animals on earth or birds that fly in the air, 18of anything that crawls on the ground, or of fish in the water below. 19When you look up at the sky, you see the sun, moon, and stars, and everything in the sky. But don't bow down and worship them, because the LORD your God has made these things for all people everywhere. 20But the LORD brought you out of Egypt, which tested you like a furnace for melting iron, and he made you his very own people, as you are now.

21The LORD was angry with me because of you, and he swore that I would not cross the Jordan River to go into the good land the LORD your God is giving you as your own. 22I will die here in this land and not cross the Jordan, but you will soon go across and take that good land. 23Be careful. Don't forget the Agreement of the LORD your God that he made with you, and don't make any idols for yourselves, as the LORD your God has commanded you not to do. 24The LORD your God is a jealous God, like a fire that burns things up.

25Even after you have lived in the land a long time and have had children and grandchildren, don't do evil things. Don't make any kind of idol, and don't do what the LORD your God says is evil, because that will make him angry. 26If you do, I ask heaven and earth to speak against you this day that you will quickly be removed from this land that you are crossing the Jordan River to take. You will not live there long after that, but you will be completely destroyed. 27The LORD will scatter you among the other nations. Only a few of you will be left alive, and those few will be in other nations where the LORD will send you. 28There you will worship gods made by people, gods made of wood and stone, that cannot see, hear, eat, or smell. 29But even there you can look for the LORD your God, and you will find him if you look for him with your whole being. 30It will be hard when all these things happen to you. But after that you will come back to the Lord your God and obey him, [31]because the Lord your God is a merciful God. He will not leave you or destroy you. He will not forget the Agreement with your ancestors, which he swore to them.

The Lord Is Great

[32]Nothing like this has ever happened before! Look at the past, long before you were even born. Go all the way back to when God made humans on the earth, and look from one end of heaven to the other. Nothing like this has ever been heard of! [33]No other people have ever heard God speak from a fire and have still lived. But you have. [34]No other god has ever taken for himself one nation out of another. But the Lord your God did this for you in Egypt, right before your own eyes. He did it with tests, signs, miracles,[d] war, and great sights, by his great power and strength.

[35]He showed you things so you would know that the Lord is God, and there is no other God besides him. [36]He spoke to you from heaven to teach you. He showed you his great fire on earth, and you heard him speak from the fire. [37]Because the Lord loved your ancestors, he chose you, their descendants,[d] and he brought you out of Egypt himself by his great strength. [38]He forced nations out of their land ahead of you, nations that were bigger and stronger than you were. The Lord did this so he could bring you into their land and give it to you as your own, and this land is yours today.

[39]Know and believe today that the Lord is God. He is God in heaven above and on the earth below. There is no other god! [40]Obey his laws and commands that I am giving you today so that

---

things will go well for you and your children. Then you will live a long time in the land that the LORD your God is giving to you forever.

Cities of Safety

41Moses chose three cities east of the Jordan River, 42where a person who accidentally killed someone could go. If the person was not killed because of hatred, the murderer's life could be saved by running to one of these cities. 43These were the cities: Bezer in the desert high plain was for the Reubenites; Ramoth in Gilead was for the Gadites; and Golan in Bashan was for the Manassites.

The Laws Moses Gave

44These are the teachings Moses gave to the people of Israel. 45They are the rules, commands, and laws he gave them when they came out of Egypt. 46They were in the valley near Beth Peor, east of the Jordan River, in the land of Sihon. Sihon king of the Amorites ruled in Heshbon and was defeated by Moses and the Israelites as they came out of Egypt. 47The Israelites took his land and the land of Og king of Bashan, the two Amorite kings east of the Jordan River. 48This land went from Aroer, on the edge of the Arnon Ravine, to Mount Hermon. 49It included all the Jordan Valley east of the Jordan River, and it went as far as the Dead Sea*d* below Mount Pisgah.

The Ten Commandments

5 Moses called all the people of Israel together and said: Listen, Israel, to the commands and laws I am giving you today. Learn them and obey them carefully. 2The LORD our God made an Agreement with us at Mount Sinai. 3He did not make this Agreement with our ancestors, but he made it with us, with all of us who are alive here today. 4The LORD spoke to you face to face from the fire on the mountain. 5(At that time I stood between you and the LORD in order to tell you what the LORD said; you were afraid of the fire, so you would not go up on the mountain.) The LORD said:

6"I am the LORD your God; I brought you out of the land of Egypt where you were slaves.

7"You must not have any other gods except me.

8"You must not make for yourselves any idols or anything to worship that looks like something in the sky above or on the earth below or in the *water below the land.* 9*You must not worship or* serve any idol, because I, the LORD your God, am a jealous God. If people sin against me and hate me, I will punish their children, even their grandchildren and great-grandchildren. 10But I will be very kind for a thousand lifetimes to those who love me and obey my commands.

11"You must not use the name of the LORD your God thoughtlessly, because the LORD will punish anyone who uses his name in this way.

12"Keep the Sabbath*d* as a holy day, as the LORD your God has commanded you. 13You may work and get everything done during six days each week, 14but the seventh day is a day of rest to honor the LORD your God. On that day no one may do any work: not you, your son or daughter, your male or female slaves, your ox, your donkey, or any of your animals, or the foreigners living in your cities. That way your servants may rest as you do. 15Remember that you were slaves in Egypt and that the LORD your God brought you out of there by his great power and strength. So the LORD your God has commanded you to rest on the Sabbath day.

16"Honor your father and your mother as the LORD your God has commanded you. Then you will live a long time, and things will go well for you in the land that the LORD your God is going to give you.

17"You must not murder anyone.

18"You must not be guilty of adultery.*d*

19"You must not steal.

20"You must not tell lies about your neighbor.

21"You must not want to take your neighbor's wife. You must not want to take your neighbor's house or land, his male or female slaves, his ox or his donkey, or anything that belongs to your neighbor."

22The LORD spoke these commands to all of you on the mountain in a loud voice out of the fire, the cloud, and the deep darkness; he did not say anything else. Then he wrote them on two stone tablets, and he gave them to me.

23When you heard the voice from the darkness, as the mountain was blazing with fire, all your older leaders and leaders of your tribes*d* came to me. 24And you said, "The LORD our God has shown us his glory and majesty, and we have heard his voice from the fire. Today we have seen that a person can live even if God speaks to him. 25But now, we will die! This great fire will burn us up, and we will die if we hear the LORD our God speak anymore. 26No human being has ever heard the living God speaking from a fire and still lived, but we have. 27Moses, you go near and listen to everything the LORD our God says. Then you tell us what the LORD our God tells you, and we will listen and obey."

28The LORD heard what you said to me, and he said to me, "I have heard what the people said to you. Everything they said was good. 29I wish their hearts would always respect me and that they would always obey my commands so that things would go well for them and their children forever!

30"Go and tell the people to return to their

tents, ³¹but you stay here with me so that I may give you all the commands, rules, and laws that you must teach the people to obey in the land I am giving them as their own."

³²So be careful to do what the LORD your God has commanded you, and follow the commands exactly. ³³Live the way the LORD your God has commanded you so that you may live and have what is good and have a long life in the land you will take.

The Command to Love God

6 These are the commands, rules, and laws that the LORD your God told me to teach you to obey in the land you are crossing the Jordan River to take. ²You, your children, and your grandchildren must respect the LORD your God as long as you live. Obey all his rules and commands I give you so that you will live a long time. ³Listen, Israel, and carefully obey these laws. Then all will go well for you, and you will become a great nation in a fertile land, just as the LORD, the God of your ancestors, has promised you.

⁴Listen, people of Israel! The LORD our God is the only LORD. ⁵Love the LORD your God with all your heart, all your soul, and all your strength. ⁶Always remember these commands I give you today. ⁷Teach them to your children, and talk about them when you sit at home and walk along the road, when you lie down and when you get up. ⁸Write them down and tie them to your hands as a sign. Tie them on your forehead to remind you, ⁹and write them on your doors and gates.

> **S DELIGHT:** Deuteronomy 6:4–9 is as important to the Jews as the Lord's Prayer (Matthew 6:9–13, p. 918) is to Christians. The Deuteronomy passage is the basis for the Jewish Shema, which is recited morning and evening by many Jews. This classic declaration of faith is also recited just before death and in times of martyrdom.

¹⁰The LORD your God will bring you into the land he promised to your ancestors, to Abraham, Isaac, and Jacob, and he will give it to you. The land has large, growing cities you did not build, ¹¹houses full of good things you did not buy, wells you did not dig, and vineyards and olive trees you did not plant. You will eat as much as you want. ¹²But be careful! Do not forget the LORD, who

FOLLOWING GOD

Totally Committed

Joseph Clark, fifteen, was determined. So what if his 900-student high school had only thirty black students? He still believed the school should have a major, annual celebration to commemorate Martin Luther King, Jr.'s contribution to society.

School officials were reluctant. The school already had a black history program. But Joseph kept pushing and eventually succeeded in gaining approval for a special program for King's birthday. Then he planned the program and invited the speakers, who helped the students understand the leader's legacy.

But Joseph wasn't satisfied. He talked to his pastor about having a special worship service to honor Dr. King. With a little work, he convinced the minister too.

Joseph doesn't tire of his efforts. He's totally dedicated to promoting his black heritage. It's that kind of wholehearted commitment that God wants his people to have when following his will. Read **Deuteronomy 6:1–9** to learn about the importance of total commitment when following God.

■ How does Joseph's commitment to his cause compare to the commitment called for in the passage? What is similar?

■ How difficult is it for you to be completely dedicated to God as the passage challenges? How are you working on your commitment?

CONSIDER . . .

■ rewriting in your own words what Deuteronomy 6:5 means to you.

■ evaluating what area of your life is most difficult to give totally to God. Pray that God will give you the strength to commit that area to him.

FOR MORE, SEE . . .

■ Deuteronomy 10:12–22 (p. 171)
■ Luke 14:25–35 (p. 1034)
■ Philippians 3:12–16 (p. 1232)

brought you out of the land of Egypt where you were slaves.

¹³Respect the Lord your God. You must worship him and make your promises only in his name. ¹⁴Do not worship other gods as the people around you do, ¹⁵because the Lord your God is a jealous God. He is present with you, and if you worship other gods, he will become angry with you and destroy you from the earth. ¹⁶Do not test the Lord your God as you did at Massah. ¹⁷Be sure to obey the commands of the Lord your God and the rules and laws he has given you. ¹⁸Do what the Lord says is good and right so that things will go well for you. Then you may go in and take the good land the Lord promised to your ancestors. ¹⁹He will force all your enemies out as you go in, as the Lord has said.

²⁰In the future when your children ask you, "What is the meaning of the laws, commands, and rules the Lord our God gave us?" ²¹tell them, "We were slaves to the king of Egypt, but the Lord brought us out of Egypt by his great power. ²²The Lord showed us great and terrible signs and miracles,ᵈ which he did to Egypt, the king, and his whole family. ²³The Lord brought us out of Egypt to lead us here and to give us the land he promised our ancestors. ²⁴The Lord ordered us to obey all these commands and to respect the Lord our God so that we will always do well and stay alive, as we are today. ²⁵The right thing for us to do is this: Obey all these rules in the presence of the Lord our God, as he has commanded."

You Are God's People

7 The Lord your God will bring you into the land that you are entering and that you will have as your own. As you go in, he will force out these nations: the Hittites, Girgashites, Amorites, Canaanites, Perizzites, Hivites, and Jebusites—seven nations that are stronger than you. ²The Lord your God will hand these nations over to you, and when you defeat them, you must destroy them completely. Do not make a peace treaty with them or show them any mercy. ³Do not marry any of them, or let your daughters marry their sons, or let your sons marry their daughters. ⁴If you do, those people will turn your children away from me, to begin serving other gods. Then the Lord will be very angry with you, and he will quickly destroy you. ⁵This is what you must do to those people: Tear down their altars, smash their holy stone pillars, cut down their Asherahᵈ idols, and burn their idols in the fire. ⁶You are holy people who belong to the Lord your God. He has chosen you from all the people on earth to be his very own.

⁷The Lord did not care for you and choose you because there were many of you—you are the smallest nation of all. ⁸But the Lord chose you because he loved you, and he kept his promise to your ancestors. So he brought you out of Egypt by his great power and freed you from the land of slavery, from the power of the king of Egypt. ⁹So know that the Lord your God is God, the faithful God. He will keep his agreement of love for a thousand lifetimes for people who love him and obey his commands. ¹⁰But he will pay back those people who hate him. He will destroy them, and he will not be slow to pay back those who hate him. ¹¹So be careful to obey the commands, rules, and laws I give you today.

¹²If you pay attention to these laws and obey them carefully, the Lord your God will keep his agreement and show his love to you, as he promised your ancestors. ¹³He will love and bless you. He will make the number of your people grow; he will bless you with children. He will bless your fields with good crops and will give you grain, new wine, and oil. He will bless your herds with calves and your flocks with lambs in the land he promised your ancestors he would give you. ¹⁴You will be blessed more than any other people. Every husband and wife will have children, and all your cattle will have calves. ¹⁵The Lord will take away all disease from you; you will not have the terrible diseases that were in Egypt, but he will give them to all the people who hate you. ¹⁶You must destroy all the people the Lord your God hands over to you. Do not feel sorry for them, and do not worship their gods, or they will trap you.

¹⁷You might say to yourselves, "Because these nations are stronger than we are, we can't force them out." ¹⁸But don't be afraid of them. Remember what the Lord your God did to all of Egypt and its king. ¹⁹You saw for yourselves the troubles, signs, and miraclesᵈ he did, how the Lord's great power and strength brought you out of Egypt. The Lord your God will do the same thing to all the nations you now fear. ²⁰The Lord your God will also send terror among them so that even those who are alive and hiding from you will die. ²¹Don't be afraid of them, because the Lord your God is with you; he is a great God and people are afraid of him. ²²When the Lord your God forces those nations out of the land, he will do it little by little ahead of you. You won't be able to destroy them all at once; otherwise, the wild animals will grow too many in number. ²³But the Lord your God will hand those nations over to you, confusing them until they are destroyed. ²⁴The Lord will help you defeat their kings, and the world will forget who they were. No one will be able to stop you; you will destroy them all. ²⁵Burn up their idols in the fire. Do not wish for the silver and gold they have, and don't take it for yourselves, or you will be trapped by it. The Lord

your God hates it. ²⁶Do not bring one of those hateful things into your house, or you will be completely destroyed along with it. Hate and reject those things; they must be completely destroyed.

Remember the Lord

8 Carefully obey every command I give you today. Then you will live and grow in number, and you will enter and take the land the Lord promised your ancestors. ²Remember how the Lord your God has led you in the desert for these forty years, taking away your pride and testing you, because he wanted to know what was in your heart. He wanted to know if you would obey his commands. ³He took away your pride when he let you get hungry, and then he fed you with manna,ᵈ which neither you nor your ancestors had ever seen. This was to teach you that a person does not live by eating only bread, but by everything the Lord says. ⁴During these forty years, your clothes did not wear out, and your feet did not swell. ⁵Know in your heart that the Lord your God corrects you as a parent corrects a child.

⁶Obey the commands of the Lord your God, living as he has commanded you and respecting him. ⁷The Lord your God is bringing you into a good land, a land with rivers and pools of water, with springs that flow in the valleys and hills, ⁸a land that has wheat and barley, vines, fig trees, pomegranates,ᵈ olive oil, and honey. ⁹It is a land where you will have plenty of food, where you will have everything you need, where the rocks are iron, and where you can dig copper out of the hills.

¹⁰When you have all you want to eat, then praise the Lord your God for giving you a good land. ¹¹Be careful not to forget the Lord your God so that you fail to obey his commands, laws, and rules that I am giving to you today. ¹²When you

---

Remembering Love

Terrence Shaw, seventeen, bravely held back tears as he tossed a shovel of dirt into his mother's grave.

What would his family do now? He, his four younger brothers, and his dad had depended on their mom for everything. None of them knew how to cook, do laundry, or clean the house. And, making matters worse, his dad had been laid off from his job just a week before Mom's stroke.

After the burial, Terrence and his family went to the church where lunch was provided. Mrs. Hammer pulled Terrence aside. "I just spoke with your father, Terrence," she said. "Some of the women of the church want to help you and your brothers around the house. We'll be over tomorrow to do some cooking and cleaning."

Two women arrived the next morning and spent several hours in the home. And through the next month, different people came back. They patiently taught Terrence and the others how to cook meals, separate and wash the laundry, and clean the floors. Gradually, the family learned what it needed to cope without Mom.

Now a pastor, Terrence testifies: "I don't know what we would have done without our church family. Their love is what made me decide to become a minister. They helped make me what I am today."

Terrence has never forgotten how God provided for his family through the church. **Deuteronomy 8:10–18** reminds us never to forget that all good things come from God.

■ How does Terrence's choice to be a pastor show the spirit of thankfulness spoken of in this passage?
■ In what ways mentioned in the passage has God helped you? How have you expressed your thanks?

CONSIDER . . .

■ writing a list of everything you can think of that God has given you in the past month. Then thank God for something different every day in the next week.
■ taking a dessert or a meal to someone who's suffering as a way of saying thanks to God.

FOR MORE, SEE . . .

■ Psalm 77:11–20 (p. 527)
■ Psalm 92:1–5 (p. 536)
■ 2 Corinthians 9:6–15 (p. 1201)

eat all you want and build nice houses and live in them, [13]when your herds and flocks grow large and your silver and gold increase, when you have

more of everything, [14]then your heart will become proud. You will forget the LORD your God, who brought you out of the land of Egypt, where you were slaves. [15]He led you through the large and terrible desert that was dry and had no water, and that had poisonous snakes and stinging insects. He gave you water from a solid rock [16]and manna to eat in the desert. Manna was something your ancestors had never seen. He did this to take away your pride and to test you, so things would go well for you in the end. [17]You might say to yourself, "I am rich because of my own power and strength," [18]but remember the LORD your God! It is he who gives you the power to become rich, keeping the agreement he promised to your ancestors, as it is today.

[19]If you ever forget the LORD your God and follow other gods and worship them and bow down to them, I warn you today that you will be destroyed. [20]Just as the LORD destroyed the other nations for you, you can be destroyed if you do not obey the LORD your God.

The Lord Will Be with Israel

9 Listen, Israel. You will soon cross the Jordan River to go in and force out nations that are bigger and stronger than you. They have large cities with walls up to the sky. [2]The people there are Anakites,[d] who are strong and tall. You know about them, and you have heard it said: "No one can stop the Anakites." [3]But today remember that the LORD your God goes in before you to destroy them like a fire that burns things up. He will defeat them ahead of you, and you will force them out and destroy them quickly, just as the LORD has said.

[4]After the LORD your God has forced those nations out ahead of you, don't say to yourself, "The LORD brought me here to take this land because *I am so good." No! It is because these nations are* evil that the LORD will force them out ahead of you. [5]You are going in to take the land, not because you are good and honest, but because these nations are evil. That is why the LORD your God will force them out ahead of you, to keep his promise to your ancestors, to Abraham, Isaac, and

Jacob. [6]The LORD your God is giving you this good land to take as your own. But know this: It is not because you are good; you are a stubborn people.

Remember the Lord's Anger

[7]Remember this and do not forget it: You made the LORD your God angry in the desert. You would not obey the LORD from the day you left Egypt until you arrived here. [8]At Mount Sinai you made the LORD angry—angry enough to destroy you. [9]When I went up on the mountain to receive the stone tablets, the tablets with the Agreement the LORD had made with you, I stayed on the mountain for forty days and forty nights; I did not eat bread or drink water. [10]The LORD gave me two stone tablets, which God had written on with his own finger. On them were all the commands that the LORD gave to you on the mountain out of the fire, on the day you were gathered there.

[11]When the forty days and forty nights were over, the LORD gave me the two stone tablets, the tablets with the Agreement on them. [12]Then the LORD told me, "Get up and go down quickly from here, because the people you brought out from Egypt are ruining themselves. They have quickly turned away from what I commanded and have made an idol for themselves."

[13]The LORD said to me, "I have watched these people, and they are very stubborn! [14]Get away so that I may destroy them and make the whole world forget who they are. Then I will make another nation from you that will be bigger and stronger than they are."

[15]So I turned and came down the mountain that was burning with fire, and the two stone tablets with the Agreement were in my hands. [16]When I looked, I saw you had sinned against the LORD your God and had made an idol in the shape of a calf. You had quickly turned away from what the LORD had told you to do. [17]So I took the two stone tablets and threw them down, breaking them into pieces right in front of you.

[18]Then I again bowed facedown on the ground before the LORD for forty days and forty nights; I did not eat bread or drink water. You had sinned by doing what the LORD said was evil, and you made him angry. [19]I was afraid of the LORD's anger and rage, because he was angry enough with you to destroy you, but the LORD listened to me again. [20]And the LORD was angry enough with Aaron to destroy him, but then I prayed for Aaron, too. [21]I took that sinful calf idol you had made and *burned it in the fire. I crushed it into a powder,* like dust and threw the dust into a stream that flowed down the mountain.

[22]You also made the LORD angry at Taberah, Massah, and Kibroth Hattaavah.

[23]Then the LORD sent you away from Kadesh Barnea and said, "Go up and take the land I have

given you." But you rejected the command of the LORD your God. You did not trust him or obey him. [24]You have refused to obey the LORD as long as I have known you.

[25]The LORD had said he would destroy you, so I threw myself down in front of him for those forty days and forty nights. [26]I prayed to the LORD and said, "Lord GOD, do not destroy your people, your own people, whom you freed and brought out of Egypt by your great power and strength. [27]Remember your servants Abraham, Isaac, and Jacob. Don't look at how stubborn these people are, and don't look at their sin and evil. [28]Otherwise, Egypt will say, 'It was because the LORD was not able to take his people into the land he promised them, and it was because he hated them that he took them into the desert to kill them.' [29]But they are your people, LORD, your own people, whom you brought out of Egypt with your great power and strength."

New Stone Tablets

10 At that time the LORD said to me, "Cut two stone tablets like the first ones and come up to me on the mountain. Also make a wooden Ark.[d] [2]I will write on the tablets the same words that were on the first tablets, which you broke, and you will put the new tablets in the Ark."

[3]So I made the Ark out of acacia wood, and I cut out two stone tablets like the first ones. Then I went up on the mountain with the two tablets in my hands. [4]The LORD wrote the same things on these tablets he had written before—the Ten Commandments that he had told you on the mountain from the fire, on the day you were gathered there. And the LORD gave them to me. [5]Then I turned and came down the mountain; I put the tablets in the Ark I had made, as the LORD had commanded, and they are still there.

[6](The people of Israel went from the wells of the Jaakanites to Moserah. Aaron died there and was buried; his son Eleazar became priest in his place. [7]From Moserah they went to Gudgodah, and from Gudgodah they went to Jotbathah, a place with streams of water. [8]At that time the LORD chose the tribe[d] of Levi to carry the Ark of the Agreement with the LORD. They were to serve the LORD and to bless the people in his name, which they still do today. [9]That is why the Levites did not receive any land of their own; instead, they received the LORD himself as their gift, as the LORD your God told them.)

[10]I stayed on the mountain forty days and forty nights just like the first time, and the LORD listened to me this time also. He did not want to destroy you. [11]The LORD said to me, "Go and lead the people so that they will go in and take the land promised their ancestors."

What the Lord Wants You To Do

[12]Now Israel, this is what the LORD your God wants you to do: Respect the LORD your God, and do what he has told you to do. Love him. Serve the LORD your God with your whole being, [13]and obey the LORD's commands and laws that I am giving you today for your own good.

[14]The LORD owns the world and everything in it—the heavens, even the highest heavens, are his. [15]But the LORD cared for and loved your ancestors, and he chose you, their descendants,[d] over all the other nations, just as it is today. [16]Give yourselves completely to serving him, and do not be stubborn any longer. [17]The LORD your God is God of all gods and Lord of all lords. He is the great God who is strong and wonderful. He does not take sides, and he will not be talked into doing evil. [18]He helps orphans and widows, and he loves foreigners and gives them food and clothes. [19]You also must love foreigners, because you were foreigners in Egypt. [20]Respect the LORD your God and serve him. Be loyal to him and make your promises in his name. [21]He is the one you should praise; he is your God, who has done great and wonderful things for you, which you have seen with your own eyes. [22]There were only seventy of your ancestors when they went down to Egypt, and now the LORD your God has made you as many as the stars in the sky.

Great Things Israel Saw

11 Love the LORD your God and always obey his orders, rules, laws, and commands. [2]Remember today it was not your children who saw and felt the correction of the LORD your God. They did not see his majesty, his power, his strength, [3]or his signs and the things he did in Egypt to the king and his whole country. [4]They did not see what he did to the Egyptian army, its horses and chariots, when he drowned them in the Red Sea[d] as they were chasing you. The LORD ruined them forever. [5]They did not see what he did for you in the desert until you arrived here. [6]They did not see what he did to Dathan and Abiram, the sons of Eliab the Reubenite, when the ground opened up and swallowed them, their families, their tents, and everyone who stood with them in Israel. [7]It was you who saw all these great things the LORD has done.

[8]So obey all the commands I am giving you today so that you will be strong and can go in and take the land you are going to take as your own. [9]Then you will live a long time in the land that the LORD promised to give to your ancestors and their descendants,[d] a fertile land. [10]The land you are going to take is not like Egypt, where you were. There you had to plant your seed and water it, like a vegetable garden, by using your feet. [11]But

the land that you will soon cross the Jordan River to take is a land of hills and valleys, a land that drinks rain from heaven. [12]It is a land the LORD your God cares for. His eyes are on it continually, and he watches it from the beginning of the year to the end.

[13]If you carefully obey the commands I am giving you today and love the LORD your God and serve him with your whole being, [14]then he will send rain on your land at the right time, in the fall and spring, and you will be able to gather your grain, new wine, and oil. [15]He will put grass in the fields for your cattle, and you will have plenty to eat.

[16]Be careful, or you will be fooled and will turn away to serve and worship other gods. [17]If you do, the LORD will become angry with you and will shut the heavens so it will not rain. Then the land will not grow crops, and you will soon die in the good land the LORD is giving you. [18]Remember my words with your whole being. Write them down and tie them to your hands as a sign; tie

---

SIDELIGHT: If you have trouble remembering scripture passages, you are not alone. The Israelites apparently did too. So God told his people to write down his words and tie them to their hands so they wouldn't forget them (Deuteronomy 11:18). This approach might get cumbersome if you memorized the whole Bible!

---

them on your foreheads to remind you. [19]Teach them well to your children, talking about them when you sit at home and walk along the road, when you lie down and when you get up. [20]Write them on your doors and gates [21]so that both you and your children will live a long time in the land the LORD promised your ancestors, as long as the skies are above the earth.

[22]If you are careful to obey every command I am giving you to follow, and love the LORD your God, and do what he has told you to do, and are loyal to him, [23]then the LORD will force all those nations out of the land ahead of you, and you will take the land from nations that are bigger and stronger than you. [24]Everywhere you step will be yours. Your land will go from the desert to Lebanon and from the Euphrates River to the Mediterranean Sea. [25]No one will be able to stop you. The LORD your God will do what he promised and will make the people afraid everywhere you go.

[26]See, today I am letting you choose a blessing or a curse. [27]You will be blessed if you obey the commands of the LORD your God that I am giving you today. [28]But you will be cursed if you disobey

the commands of the LORD your God. So do not disobey the commands I am giving you today, and do not worship other gods you do not know. [29]When the LORD your God brings you into the land you will take as your own, you are to announce the blessings from Mount Gerizim and the curses from Mount Ebal. [30](These mountains are on the other side of the Jordan River, to the west, toward the sunset. They are near the great trees of Moreh in the land of the Canaanites who live in the Jordan Valley opposite Gilgal.) [31]You will soon cross the Jordan River to enter and take the land the LORD your God is giving you. When you take it over and live there, [32]be careful to obey all the commands and laws I am giving you today.

The Place for Worship

12 These are the commands and laws you must carefully obey in the land the LORD, the God of your ancestors, is giving you. Obey them as long as you live in the land. [2]When you inherit the lands of these nations, you must completely destroy all the places where they serve their gods, on high mountains and hills and under every green tree. [3]Tear down their altars, smash their holy stone pillars, and burn their Asherah[d] idols in the fire. Cut down their idols and destroy their names from those places.

[4]Don't worship the LORD your God that way, [5]but look for the place the LORD your God will choose — a place among your tribes[d] where he is to be worshiped. Go there, [6]and bring to that place your burnt offerings and sacrifices; bring a tenth of what you gain and your special gifts; bring what you have promised and the special gifts you want to give the LORD, and bring the first animals born to your herds and flocks.

[7]There you will be together with the LORD your God. There you and your families will eat, and you will enjoy all the good things for which you have worked, because the LORD your God has blessed you.

[8]Do not worship the way we have been doing today, each person doing what he thinks is right. [9]You have not yet come to a resting place, to the land the LORD your God will give you as your own. [10]But soon you will cross the Jordan River to live in the land the LORD your God is giving you as your own, where he will give you rest from all your enemies and you will live in safety. [11]Then the LORD your God will choose a place where he is to be worshiped. To that place you must bring everything I tell you: your burnt offerings and sacrifices, your offerings of a tenth of what you gain, your special gifts, and all your best things you promised to the LORD. [12]There rejoice before the LORD your God. Everyone should rejoice: you, your sons and daughters, your male and female

servants, and the Levites from your towns who have no land of their own. [13]Be careful that you don't sacrifice your burnt offerings just anywhere you please. [14]Offer them only in the place the Lord will choose. He will choose a place in one of your tribes, and there you must do everything I am commanding you.

[15]But you may kill your animals in any of your towns and eat as much of the meat as you want, as if it were a deer or a gazelle; this is the blessing the Lord your God is giving you. Anyone, clean[d] or unclean, may eat this meat, [16]but do not eat the blood. Pour it out on the ground like water. [17]Do not eat in your own towns what belongs to the Lord: one-tenth of your grain, new wine, or oil; the first animals born to your herds or flocks; whatever you have promised to give; the special gifts you want to give to the Lord, or any other gifts. [18]Eat these things when you are together with the Lord your God in the place the Lord your God chooses to be worshiped. Everyone must do this: you, your sons and daughters, your male and female servants, and the Levites from your towns. Rejoice in the Lord your God's presence about the things you have worked for. [19]Be careful not to forget the Levites as long as you live in the land.

[20]When the Lord your God enlarges your country as he has promised, and you want some meat so you say, "I want some meat," you may eat as much meat as you want. [21]If the Lord your God chooses a place where he is to be worshiped that is too far away from you, you may kill animals from your herds and flocks, which the Lord has given to you. I have commanded that you may do this. You may eat as much of them as you want in your own towns, [22]as you would eat gazelle or deer meat. Both clean and unclean people may eat this meat, [23]but be sure you don't eat the blood, because the life is in the blood. Don't eat the life with the meat. [24]Don't eat the blood, but pour it out on the ground like water. [25]If you don't eat it, things will go well for you and your children, because you will be doing what the Lord says is right.

[26]Take your holy things and the things you have promised to give, and go to the place the Lord will choose. [27]Present your burnt offerings on the altar of the Lord your God, both the meat and the blood. The blood of your sacrifices should be poured beside the altar of the Lord your God, but you may eat the meat. [28]Be careful to obey all the rules I am giving you so that things will always go well for you and your children, and you will be doing what the Lord your God says is good and right.

[29]You will enter the land and take it away from the nations that the Lord your God will destroy ahead of you. When you force them out and live in their land, [30]they will be destroyed for you, but be careful not to be trapped by asking about their gods. Don't say, "How do these nations worship? I will do the same." [31]Don't worship the Lord your God that way, because the Lord hates the evil way they worship their gods. They even burn their sons and daughters as sacrifices to their gods!

[32]Be sure to do everything I have commanded you. Do not add anything to it, and do not take anything away from it.

False Prophets

13 Prophets[d] or those who tell the future with dreams might come to you and say they will show you a miracle[d] or a sign. [2]The miracle or sign might even happen, and then they might say, "Let's serve other gods" (gods you have not known) "and let's worship them." [3]But you must not listen to those prophets or dreamers. The Lord your God is testing you, to find out if you love him with your whole being. [4]Serve only the Lord your God. Respect him, keep his commands, and obey him. Serve him and be loyal to him. [5]The prophets or dreamers must be killed, because they said you should turn against the Lord your God, who brought you out of Egypt and saved you from the land where you were slaves. They tried to turn you from doing what the Lord your God commanded you to do. You must get rid of the evil among you.

[6]Someone might try to lead you to serve other gods—it might be your brother, your son or daughter, the wife you love, or a close friend. The person might say, "Let's go and worship other gods." (These are gods that neither you nor your ancestors have known, [7]gods of the people who live around you, either nearby or far away, from one end of the land to the other.) [8]Do not give in to such people. Do not listen or feel sorry for them, and do not let them go free or protect them. [9]You must put them to death. You must be the first one to start to kill them, and then everyone else must join in. [10]You must throw stones at them until they die, because they tried to turn you away from the Lord your God, who brought you out of the land of Egypt, where you were slaves. [11]Then everyone in Israel will hear about this and be afraid, and no one among you will ever do such an evil thing again.

Cities to Destroy

[12]The Lord your God is giving you cities in which to live, and you might hear something about one of them. Someone might say [13]that evil people have moved in among you. And they might lead the people of that city away from God, saying, "Let's go and worship other gods." (These are gods you have not known.) [14]Then you must

ask about it, looking into the matter and checking carefully whether it is true. If it is proved that a hateful thing has happened among you, 15you must kill with a sword everyone who lives in that city. Destroy the city completely and kill everyone in it, as well as the animals, with a sword. 16Gather up everything those people owned, and put it in the middle of the city square. Then completely burn the city and everything they owned as a burnt offering to the LORD your God. That city should never be rebuilt; let it be ruined forever. 17Don't keep for yourselves any of the things found in that city, so the LORD will not be angry anymore. He will give you mercy and feel sorry for you, and he will make your nation grow larger, as he promised to your ancestors. 18You will have obeyed the LORD your God by keeping all his commands that I am giving to you today, and you will be doing what the LORD says is right.

God's Special People

14 You are the children of the LORD your God. When someone dies, do not cut yourselves or shave your heads to show your sadness. 2You are holy people, who belong to the LORD your God. He has chosen you from all the people on earth to be his very own.

3Do not eat anything the LORD hates. 4These are the animals you may eat: oxen, sheep, goats, 5deer, gazelle, roe deer, wild goats, ibex, antelope, and mountain sheep. 6You may eat any animal that has a split hoof and chews the cud,d 7but you may not eat camels, rabbits, or rock badgers. These animals chew the cud, but they do not have split hoofs, so they are uncleand for you. 8Pigs are also unclean for you; they have split hoofs, but they do not chew the cud. Do not eat their meat or touch their dead bodies.

9There are many things that live in the water. You may eat anything that has fins and scales, 10but do not eat anything that does not have fins and scales. It is unclean for you.

11You may eat any clean bird. 12But do not eat these birds: eagles, vultures, black vultures, 13red kites, falcons, any kind of kite, 14any kind of raven, 15horned owls, screech owls, sea gulls, any kind of hawk, 16little owls, great owls, white owls, 17desert owls, ospreys, cormorants, 18storks, any kind of heron, the hoopoes, or bats.

19All insects with wings are unclean for you; do not eat them. 20Other things with wings are clean, and you may eat them.

21Do not eat anything you find that is already dead. You may give it to a foreigner living in your town, and he may eat it, or you may sell it to a foreigner. But you are holy people, who belong to the LORD your God.

Do not cook a baby goat in its mother's milk.

Giving One-Tenth

22Be sure to save one-tenth of all your crops each year. 23Take it to the place the LORD your God will choose where he is to be worshiped.

> **SIDELIGHT:** If you've got a new recipe for goat meat boiled in goat's milk, don't try it. The cooking technique was forbidden in Deuteronomy 14:21—for a good reason. It was a practice associated with pagan worship.

There, where you will be together with the LORD, eat the tenth of your grain, new wine, and oil, and eat the animals born first to your herds and flocks. Do this so that you will learn to respect the LORD your God always. 24But if the place the LORD will choose to be worshiped is too far away and he has blessed you so much you cannot carry a tenth, 25exchange your one-tenth for silver. Then take the silver with you to the place the LORD your God shall choose. 26Use the silver to buy anything you wish—cattle, sheep, wine, beer, or anything you wish. Then you and your family will eat and celebrate there before the LORD your God. 27Do not forget the Levites in your town, because they have no land of their own among you.

28At the end of every third year, everyone should bring one-tenth of that year's crop and store it in your towns. 29This is for the Levites so they may eat and be full. (They have no land of their own among you.) It is also for strangers, orphans, and widows who live in your towns so that all of them may eat and be full. Then the LORD your God will bless you and all the work you do.

The Special Seventh Year

15 At the end of every seven years, you must tell those who owe you anything that they do not have to pay you back. 2This is how you must do it: Everyone who has loaned money must cancel the loan and not make a neighbor or relative pay it back. This is the LORD's time for canceling what people owe. 3You may make a foreigner pay what is owed to you, but you must not collect what another Israelite owes you. 4But there should be no poor people among you, because the LORD your God will richly bless you in the land he is giving you as your own. 5He will bless you if you obey the LORD your God completely, but you must be careful to obey all the commands I am giving you today. 6The LORD your God will bless you as he promised, and you will lend to other nations, but you will not need to borrow from them. You will rule over many nations, but none will rule over you.

[7]If there are poor among you, in one of the towns of the land the LORD your God is giving you, do not be selfish or greedy toward them. [8]But give freely to them, and freely lend them whatever they need. [9]Beware of evil thoughts. Don't think, "The seventh year is near, the year to cancel what people owe." You might be mean to the needy and not give them anything. Then they will complain to the LORD about you, and he will find you guilty of sin. [10]Give freely to the poor person, and do not wish that you didn't have to give. The LORD your God will bless your work and everything you touch. [11]There will always be poor people in the land, so I command you to give freely to your neighbors and to the poor and needy in your land.

Letting Slaves Go Free

[12]If one of your own people sells himself to you as a slave, whether it is a Hebrew man or woman, that person will serve you for six years. But in the seventh year you must let the slave go free. [13]When you let slaves go, don't send them away without anything. [14]Give them some of your flock, your grain, and your wine, giving to them as the LORD has given to you. [15]Remember that you were slaves in Egypt, and the LORD your God saved you. That is why I am commanding this to you today.

[16]But if your slave says to you, "I don't want to leave you," because he loves you and your family and has a good life with you, [17]stick an awl[n] through his ear into the door; he will be your slave for life. Also do this to a female slave.

[18]Do not think of it as a hard thing when you let your slaves go free. After all, they served you six years and did twice the work of a hired person. The LORD your God will bless you in everything you do.

Rules About Firstborn Animals

[19]Save all the first male animals born to your herds and flocks. They are for the LORD your God. Do not work the first calf born to your oxen, and do not cut off the wool from the first lamb born to your sheep. [20]Each year you and your family are to eat these animals in the presence of the LORD your God, in the place he will choose to be worshiped. [21]If an animal is crippled or blind or has something else wrong, do not sacrifice it to the LORD your God. [22]But you may eat that animal in your own town. Both clean[d] and unclean people may eat it, as they would eat a gazelle or a deer. [23]But don't eat its blood; pour it out on the ground like water.

The Passover

16 Celebrate the Passover[d] of the LORD your God during the month of Abib,[d] because it was during Abib that he brought you out of Egypt at night. [2]As the sacrifice for the Passover to the LORD your God, offer an animal from your flock or herd at the place the LORD will choose to be worshiped. [3]Do not eat it with bread made with yeast. But for seven days eat bread made without yeast, the bread of suffering, because you left Egypt in a hurry. So all your life you will remember the time you left Egypt. [4]There must be no yeast anywhere in your land for seven days. Offer the sacrifice on the evening of the first day, and eat all the meat before morning; do not leave it overnight.

[5]Do not offer the Passover sacrifice in just any town the LORD your God gives you, [6]but offer it in the place he will choose to be worshiped. Offer it in the evening as the sun goes down, which is when you left Egypt. [7]Roast the meat and eat it at the place the LORD your God will choose. The next morning go back to your tents. [8]Eat bread made without yeast for six days. On the seventh day have a special meeting for the LORD your God, and do not work that day.

The Feast of Weeks

[9]Count seven weeks from the time you begin to harvest the grain, [10]and then celebrate the Feast[d] of Weeks for the LORD your God. Bring an offering as a special gift to him, giving to him just as he has blessed you. [11]Rejoice before the LORD your God at the place he will choose to be worshiped. Everybody should rejoice: you, your sons and daughters, your male and female servants, the Levites in your town, the strangers, orphans, and widows living among you. [12]Remember that you were slaves in Egypt, and carefully obey all these laws.

The Feast of Shelters

[13]Celebrate the Feast[d] of Shelters for seven days, after you have gathered your harvest from the threshing[d] floor and winepress.[d] [14]Everybody should rejoice at your Feast: you, your sons and daughters, your male and female servants, the Levites, strangers, orphans, and widows who live in your towns. [15]Celebrate the Feast to the LORD your God for seven days at the place he will choose, because the LORD your God will bless all your harvest and all the work you do, and you will be completely happy.

[16]All your men must come before the LORD three times a year to the place he will choose. They must come at these times: the Feast[d] of Un-

---

awl A tool like a big needle with a handle at one end.

leavened Bread, the Feast[d] of Weeks, and the Feast of Shelters. No man should come before the LORD without a gift. [17]Each of you must bring a gift that will show how much the LORD your God has blessed you.

Judges for the People

[18]Appoint judges and officers for your tribes[d] in every town the LORD your God is giving you; they must judge the people fairly. [19]Do not judge unfairly or take sides. Do not let people pay you to make wrong decisions, because that kind of payment makes wise people seem blind, and it changes the words of good people. [20]Always do what is right so that you will live and always have the land the LORD your God is giving you.

God Hates Idols

[21]Do not set up a wooden Asherah[d] idol next to the altar you build for the LORD your God, [22]and do not set up holy stone pillars. The LORD your God hates them.

17 If an ox or sheep has something wrong with it, do not offer it as a sacrifice to the LORD your God. He would hate that.

[2]A man or woman in one of the towns the LORD gave you might be found doing something evil and breaking the Agreement. [3]That person may have served other gods and bowed down to them or to the sun or moon or stars of the sky, which I have commanded should not be done. [4]If someone has told you about it, you must look into the matter carefully. If it is true that such a hateful thing has happened in Israel, [5]take the man or woman who has done the evil thing to the city gates and throw stones at that person until he dies. [6]There must be two or three witnesses that it is true before the person is put to death; if there is only one witness, the person should not be put to death. [7]The witnesses must be the first to throw stones at the person, and then everyone else will follow. You must get rid of the evil among you.

Courts of Law

[8]Some cases that come before you, such as murder, quarreling, or attack, may be too difficult to judge. Take these cases to the place the LORD your God will choose. [9]Go to the priests who are Levites and to the judge who is on duty at that time. Ask them about the case, and they will decide. [10]You must follow the decision they give you *at the place the LORD your God will choose. Be careful to do everything they tell you.* [11]Follow the teachings they give you, and do whatever they decide, exactly as they tell you. [12]The person who does not show respect for the judge or priest who is there serving the LORD your God must be put to death. You must get rid of that evil from

Israel. [13]Then everyone will hear about this and will be afraid, and they will not show disrespect anymore.

Choosing a King

[14]When you enter the land the LORD your God is giving you, taking it as your own and living in it, you will say, "Let's appoint a king over us like the nations all around us." [15]Be sure to appoint over you the king the LORD your God chooses. He must be one of your own people. Do not appoint as your king a foreigner who is not a fellow Israelite. [16]The king must not have too many horses for himself, and he must not send people to Egypt to get more horses, because the LORD has told you, "Don't return that way again." [17]The king must not have many wives, or his heart will be led away from God. He must not have too much silver and gold.

[18]When he becomes king, he should write a copy of the teachings on a scroll for himself, a copy taken from the priests and Levites. [19]He should keep it with him all the time and read from it every day of his life. Then he will learn to respect the LORD his God, and he will obey all the teachings and commands. [20]He should not think he is better than his fellow Israelites, and he must not stop obeying the law in any way so that he and his descendants[d] may rule the kingdom for a long time.

Shares for Priests and Levites

18 The priests are from the tribe[d] of Levi, and that tribe will not receive a share of the land with the Israelites. They will eat the offerings made to the LORD by fire, which is their share. [2]They will not inherit any of the land like their brothers, but they will inherit the LORD himself, as he has promised them.

[3]When you offer a bull or sheep as a sacrifice, you must share with the priests, giving them the shoulder, the cheeks, and the inner organs. [4]Give them the first of your grain, new wine, and oil, as well as the first wool you cut from your sheep. [5]The LORD your God has chosen the priests and their descendants[d] out of all your tribes to stand and serve the LORD always.

[6]If a Levite moves from one of your towns anywhere in Israel where he lives and comes to the place the LORD will choose, because he wants to serve the LORD there, [7]he may serve the LORD his God. He will be like his fellow Levites who serve *there before the LORD.* [8]*They all will have an* equal share of the food. That is separate from what he has received from the sale of family possessions.

Do Not Follow Other Nations

[9]When you enter the land the LORD your God

is giving you, don't learn to do the hateful things the other nations do. ¹⁰Don't let anyone among you offer a son or daughter as a sacrifice in the fire. Don't let anyone use magic or witchcraft,ᵈ or try to explain the meaning of signs. ¹¹Don't let anyone try to control others with magic, and don't let them be mediumsᵈ or try to talk with the spirits of dead people. ¹²The LORD hates anyone who does these things. Because the other nations do these things, the LORD your God will force them out of the land ahead of you. ¹³But you must be innocent in the presence of the LORD your God.

The Lord's Special Prophet

¹⁴The nations you will force out listen to people who use magic and witchcraft,ᵈ but the LORD your God will not let you do those things. ¹⁵The LORD your God will give you a prophetᵈ like me, who is one of your own people. Listen to him. ¹⁶This is what you asked the LORD your God to do when you were gathered at Mount Sinai. You said, "Don't make us listen to the voice of the LORD our God again, and don't make us look at this terrible fire anymore, or we will die."

¹⁷So the LORD said to me, "What they have said is good. ¹⁸So I will give them a prophet like you, who is one of their own people. I will tell him what to say, and he will tell them everything I command. ¹⁹This prophet will speak for me; anyone who does not listen when he speaks will answer to me. ²⁰But if a prophet says something I did not tell him to say as though he were speaking

---

LEADERSHIP

Standing for Right

George Fox had a message from God, and he was not going to let anyone stop him from preaching it. In England in the 1600s, he urged people to listen to Christ, to be honest in business, and to be compassionate to the poor. Central to his message was the idea of religious liberty and that God worked through individual people, not just through the established church.

Though many people believed him and were converted, others opposed him. On many occasions, he was thrown down church steps or beaten. Once he was thrown into jail for six months. But he would not bend his beliefs and so got sentenced to six more months as a result. "Truth can live in the jails," he wrote. "Be valiant for Truth upon the earth and tread upon deceit."

Despite the government's efforts to stop him from challenging the official church, Fox's message got through to people because of his conviction and honesty. Within eight years of beginning his ministry, fifty thousand people had heard his message and had become followers. Young followers, known as "the valiant sixty," joined Fox in preaching at fairs, in markets, in fields, in jails, and in courts.

When he died in 1691, about one hundred thousand people had joined Fox's movement, which became known as the Society of Friends. Today the Friends (or Quakers) span the world, spreading a message of peace, holiness, service, and religious liberty.

George Fox's ministry had a long-term impact because his message was a true message from God. In his farewell speech, Moses urged the Israelites to listen carefully to prophets' messages to learn if they are true or not. Read **Deuteronomy 18:15–20** to see the guidelines he established.

■ In what ways did George Fox's message fit with the message of the prophets as described in this passage?
■ How can this passage help you evaluate messages you hear from people who have leadership roles?

CONSIDER . . .
■ choosing key words from this passage to make a checklist for evaluating leaders. Use it whenever you wonder whether to believe what someone tells you.
■ praying for Christian leaders around the world who sometimes have to risk their lives to speak God's truth.

FOR   MORE,   SEE . .
■ Jeremiah 37:1–21 (p. 734)   ■ Hebrews 11:32–40 (p. 1283)
■ Luke 4:23–30 (p. 1009)

for me, or if a prophet speaks in the name of other gods, that prophet must be killed."

²¹You might be thinking, "How can we know if a message is not from the LORD?" ²²If what a prophet says in the name of the LORD does not happen, it is not the LORD's message. That prophet was speaking his own ideas. Don't be afraid of him.

Cities of Safety

19 When the LORD your God gives you land that belongs to the other nations, nations that he will destroy, you will force them out and live in their cities and houses. ²Then choose three cities in the middle of the land the LORD your God is giving you as your own. ³Build roads to these cities, and divide the land the LORD is giving you into three parts so that someone who kills another person may run to these cities.

⁴This is the rule for someone who kills another person and runs to one of these cities in order to save his life. But the person must have killed a neighbor without meaning to, not out of hatred. ⁵For example, suppose someone goes into the forest with a neighbor to cut wood and swings an ax to cut down a tree. If the ax head flies off the handle, hitting and killing the neighbor, the one who killed him may run to one of these cities to save his life. ⁶Otherwise, the dead person's relative who has the duty of punishing a murderer might be angry and chase him. If the city is far away, the relative might catch and kill the person, even though he should not be killed because there was no intent to kill his neighbor. ⁷This is why I command you to choose these three cities.

⁸⁻⁹Carefully obey all these laws I'm giving you today. Love the LORD your God, and always do what he wants you to do. Then the LORD your God will enlarge your land as he promised your ancestors, giving you the whole land he promised to them. After that, choose three more cities of safety ¹⁰so that innocent people will not be killed in your land, the land that the LORD your God is giving you as your own. By doing this you will not be guilty of allowing the death of innocent people.

¹¹But if a person hates his neighbor and, after hiding and waiting, attacks and kills him and then runs to one of these cities for safety, ¹²the older leaders of his own city should send for the murderer. They should bring the person back from the city of safety and hand him over to the relative who has the duty of punishing the murderer. ¹³Show no mercy. You must remove from Israel the guilt of murdering innocent people so that things will go well for you.

¹⁴Do not move the stone that marks the border of your neighbor's land, which people long ago set in place. It marks what you inherit in the land the LORD your God is giving you as your own.

Rules About Witnesses

¹⁵One witness is not enough to accuse a person of a crime or sin. A case must be proved by two or three witnesses.

¹⁶If a witness lies and accuses a person of a crime, ¹⁷the two people who are arguing must stand in the presence of the LORD before the priests and judges who are on duty. ¹⁸The judges must check the matter carefully. The witness who is a liar, lying about a fellow Israelite, ¹⁹must be punished. He must be punished in the same way the other person would have been punished. You must get rid of the evil among you. ²⁰The rest of the people will hear about this and be afraid, and no one among you will ever do such an evil thing again. ²¹Show no mercy. A life must be paid for a life, an eye for an eye, a tooth for a tooth, a hand for a hand, a foot for a foot.

Laws for War

20 When you go to war against your enemies and you see horses and chariots and an army that is bigger than yours, don't be afraid of them. The LORD your God, who brought you out of Egypt, will be with you. ²The priest must come and speak to the army before you go into battle. ³He will say, "Listen, Israel! Today you are going into battle against your enemies. Don't lose your courage or be afraid. Don't panic or be frightened, ⁴because the LORD your God goes with you, to fight for you against your enemies and to save you."

⁵The officers should say to the army, "Has anyone built a new house but not given it to God? He may go home, because he might die in battle and someone else would get to give his house to God. ⁶Has anyone planted a vineyard and not begun to enjoy it? He may go home, because he might die in battle and someone else would enjoy his vineyard. ⁷Is any man engaged to a woman and not yet married to her? He may go home, because he might die in battle and someone else would marry

---

✹ **SIDELIGHT:** If the military had had chaplains in Old Testament times, they would not have performed many weddings for soldiers. That's because engaged men didn't have to serve in the military (Deuteronomy 20:7). And newly married men were exempt from military duty for a year (Deuteronomy 24:5, p. 181)!

---

her." ⁸Then the officers should also say, "Is anyone here afraid? Has anyone lost his courage? He may go home so that he will not cause others to lose their courage, too." ⁹When the officers finish speaking to the army, they should appoint commanders to lead it.

10When you march up to attack a city, first make them an offer of peace. 11If they accept your offer and open their gates to you, all the people of that city will become your slaves and work for you. 12But if they do not make peace with you and fight you in battle, you should surround that city. 13The LORD your God will give it to you. Then kill all the men with your swords, 14and you may take everything else in the city for yourselves. Take the women, children, and animals, and you may use these things the LORD your God gives you from your enemies. 15Do this to all the cities that are far away, that do not belong to the nations nearby.

16But leave nothing alive in the cities of the land the LORD your God is giving you. 17Completely destroy these people: the Hittites, Amorites, Canaanites, Perizzites, Hivites, and Jebusites, as the LORD your God has commanded. 18Otherwise, they will teach you what they do for their gods, and if you do these hateful things, you will sin against the LORD your God.

19If you surround and attack a city for a long time, trying to capture it, do not destroy its trees with an ax. You can eat the fruit from the trees, but do not cut them down. These trees are not the enemy, so don't make war against them. 20But you may cut down trees that you know are not fruit trees and use them to build devices to attack the city walls, until the city is captured.

A Person Found Murdered

21 Suppose someone is found murdered, lying in a field in the land the LORD your God is giving you as your own, and no one knows who killed the person. 2Your older leaders and judges should go to where the body was found, and they should measure how far it is to the nearby cities. 3The older leaders of the city nearest the body must take a young cow that has never worked or worn a yoke,*d* 4and they must lead her down to a valley that has never been plowed or planted, with a stream flowing through it. There they must break the young cow's neck. 5The priests, the sons of Levi, should come forward, because they have been chosen by the LORD your God to serve him and to give blessings in the LORD's name. They are the ones who decide cases of quarreling and attacks. 6Then all the older leaders of the city nearest the murdered person should wash their hands over the young cow whose neck was broken in the valley. 7They should declare: "We did not kill this person, and we did not see it happen. 8LORD, remove this sin from your people Israel, whom you have saved. Don't blame your people, the Israelites, for the murder of this innocent person." And so the murder will be paid for. 9Then you will have removed from yourselves the guilt of murdering an innocent person, because you will be doing what the LORD says is right.

Captive Women as Wives

10When you go to war against your enemies, the LORD will help you defeat them so that you will take them captive. 11If you see a beautiful woman among the captives and are attracted to her, you may take her as your wife. 12Bring her into your home, where she must shave her head and cut her nails 13and change the clothes she was wearing when you captured her. After she has lived in your house and cried for her parents for a month, you may marry her. You will be her husband, and she will be your wife. 14But if you are not pleased with her, you must let her go anywhere she wants. You must not sell her for money or make her a slave, because you have taken away her honor.

The Oldest Son

15A man might have two wives, one he loves and one he doesn't. Both wives might have sons by him. If the older son belongs to the wife he does not love, 16when that man wills his property to his sons, he must not give the son of the wife he loves what belongs to the older son, the son of the wife he does not love. 17He must agree to give the older son two shares of everything he owns, even though the older son is from the wife he does not love. That son was the first to prove his father could have children, so he has the rights that belong to the older son.

Sons Who Refuse to Obey

18If someone has a son who is stubborn, who turns against his father and mother and doesn't obey them or listen when they correct him, 19his parents must take him to the older leaders at the city gate. 20They will say to the leaders, "Our son is stubborn and turns against us. He will not obey us. He eats too much, and he is always drunk." 21Then all the men in his town must throw stones at him until he dies. Get rid of the evil among you, because then all the people of Israel will hear about this and be afraid.

Other Laws

22If someone is guilty of a sin worthy of death, he must be put to death and his body displayed on a tree. 23But don't leave his body hanging on the tree overnight; be sure to bury him that same day, because anyone whose body is displayed on a tree is cursed by God. You must not ruin the land the LORD your God is giving you as your own.

22 If you see your fellow Israelite's ox or sheep wandering away, don't ignore it. Take it back to its owner. [2]If the owner does not live close to you, or if you do not know who the owner is, take the animal home with you. Keep it until the owner comes looking for it; then give it back. [3]Do the same thing if you find a donkey or coat or anything someone lost. Don't just ignore it.

[4]If you see your fellow Israelite's donkey or ox fallen on the road, don't ignore it. Help the owner get it up.

[5]A woman must not wear men's clothes, and a man must not wear women's clothes. The LORD your God hates anyone who does that.

[6]If you find a bird's nest by the road, either in a tree or on the ground, and the mother bird is sitting on the young birds or eggs, do not take the mother bird with the young birds. [7]You may take the young birds, but you must let the mother bird go free. Then things will go well for you, and you will live a long time.

[8]When you build a new house, build a low wall around the edge of the roof[n] so you will not be guilty if someone falls off the roof.

[9]Don't plant two different kinds of seeds in your vineyard. Otherwise, both crops will be ruined.

[10]Don't plow with an ox and a donkey tied together.

[11]Don't wear clothes made of wool and linen woven together.

[12]Tie several pieces of thread together; then put these tassels on the four corners of your coat.

Marriage Laws

[13]If a man marries a girl and has sexual relations with her but then decides he does not like her, [14]he might talk badly about her and give her a bad name. He might say, "I married this woman, but when I had sexual relations with her, I did not find that she was a virgin."[d] [15]Then the girl's parents must bring proof that she was a virgin to the older leaders at the city gate. [16]The girl's father will say to the leaders, "I gave my daughter to this man to be his wife, but now he does not want her. [17]This man has told lies about my daughter. He has said, 'I did not find your daughter to be a virgin,' but here is the proof that my daughter was a virgin." Then her parents are to show the sheet to the city leaders, [18]and the leaders must take the man and punish him. [19]They must make him pay about two and one-half pounds of silver to the girl's father, because the man has given an Israelite virgin a bad name. The

girl will continue to be the man's wife, and he may not divorce her as long as he lives.

[20]But if the things the husband said about his wife are true, and there is no proof that she was a virgin, [21]the girl must be brought to the door of her father's house. Then the men of the town must put her to death by throwing stones at her. She has done a disgraceful thing in Israel by having sexual relations before she was married. You must get rid of the evil among you.

[22]If a man is found having sexual relations with another man's wife, both the woman and the man who had sexual relations with her must die. Get rid of this evil from Israel.

[23]If a man meets a virgin in a city and has sexual relations with her, but she is engaged to another man, [24]you must take both of them to the city gate and put them to death by throwing stones at them. Kill the girl, because she was in a city and did not scream for help. And kill the man for having sexual relations with another man's wife. You must get rid of the evil among you.

[25]But if a man meets an engaged girl out in the country and forces her to have sexual relations with him, only the man who had sexual relations with her must be put to death. [26]Don't do anything to the girl, because she has not done a sin worthy of death. This is like the person who attacks and murders a neighbor; [27]the man found the engaged girl in the country and she screamed, but no one was there to save her.

[28]If a man meets a virgin who is not engaged to be married and forces her to have sexual relations with him and people find out about it, [29]the man must pay the girl's father about one and one-fourth pounds of silver. He must also marry the girl, because he has dishonored her, and he may never divorce her for as long as he lives.

[30]A man must not marry his father's wife; he must not dishonor his father in this way.

The Lord's People

23 No man who has had part of his sex organ cut off may come into the meeting to worship the LORD.

[2]No one born to parents who were forbidden by law to marry may come into the meeting to worship the LORD. The descendants for ten generations may not come in either.

[3]No Ammonite or Moabite may come into the meeting to worship the LORD, and none of their *descendants for ten generations may come in.* [4]This is because the Ammonites and Moabites did not give you bread and water when you came out of Egypt. And they hired Balaam son of Beor, from

---

roof In Bible times houses were built with flat roofs. The roof was used for drying things such as flax and fruit. And it was used as an extra room, as a place for worship, and as a place to sleep in the summer.

Pethor in Northwest Mesopotamia, to put a curse on you. [5]But the Lord your God would not listen to Balaam. He turned the curse into a blessing for you, because the Lord your God loves you. [6]Don't wish for their peace or success as long as you live.

[7]Don't hate Edomites; they are your close relatives. Don't hate Egyptians, because you were foreigners in their country. [8]The great-grandchildren of these two peoples may come into the meeting to worship the Lord.

Keeping the Camp Clean

[9]When you are camped in time of war, keep away from unclean[d] things. [10]If a man becomes unclean during the night, he must go outside the camp and not come back. [11]But when evening comes, he must wash himself, and at sunset he may come back into the camp.

[12]Choose a place outside the camp where people may go to relieve themselves. [13]Carry a tent peg with you, and when you relieve yourself, dig a hole and cover up your dung. [14]The Lord your God moves around through your camp to protect you and to defeat your enemies for you, so the camp must be holy. He must not see anything unclean among you so that he will not leave you.

Other Laws

[15]If an escaped slave comes to you, do not hand over the slave to his master. [16]Let the slave live with you anywhere he likes, in any town he chooses. Do not mistreat him.

[17]No Israelite man or woman must ever become a temple prostitute.[d] [18]Do not bring a male or female prostitute's pay to the Temple[d] of the Lord your God to pay what you have promised to the Lord, because the Lord your God hates prostitution.

[19]If you loan your fellow Israelites money or food or anything else, don't make them pay back more than you loaned them. [20]You may charge foreigners, but not fellow Israelites. Then the Lord your God will bless everything you do in the land you are entering to take as your own.

[21]If you make a promise to give something to the Lord your God, do not be slow to pay it, because the Lord your God demands it from you. Do not be guilty of sin. [22]But if you do not make the promise, you will not be guilty. [23]You must do whatever you say you will do, because you chose to make the promise to the Lord your God.

[24]If you go into your neighbor's vineyard, you may eat as many grapes as you wish, but do not put any grapes into your basket. [25]If you go into your neighbor's grainfield, you may pick grain with your hands, but you must not cut down your neighbor's grain with your sickle.

24

[1]A man might marry a woman but later decide she doesn't please him because he has found something bad about her. He writes out divorce papers for her, gives them to her, and sends her away from his house. [2]After she leaves his house, she goes and marries another man, [3]but her second husband does not like her either. So he writes out divorce papers for her, gives them to her, and sends her away from his house. Or the second husband might die. [4]In either case, her first husband who divorced her must not marry her again, because she has become unclean.[d] The Lord would hate this. Don't bring this sin into the land the Lord your God is giving you as your own.

[5]A man who has just married must not be sent to war or be given any other duty. He should be free to stay home for a year to make his new wife happy.

[6]If someone owes you something, do not take his two stones for grinding grain—not even the upper one—in place of what he owes, because this is how the person makes a living.

[7]If someone kidnaps a fellow Israelite, either to make him a slave or sell him, the kidnapper must be killed. You must get rid of the evil among you.

[8]Be careful when someone has a skin disease. Do exactly what the priests, the Levites, teach you, being careful to do what I have commanded them. [9]Remember what the Lord your God did to Miriam on your way out of Egypt.

[10]When you make a loan to your neighbors, don't go into their homes to get something in place of it [11]Stay outside and let them go in and get what they promised you. [12]If a poor person gives you a coat to show he will pay the loan back, don't keep it overnight. [13]Give the coat back at sunset, because your neighbor needs that coat to sleep in, and he will be grateful to you. And the Lord your God will see that you have done a good thing.

[14]Don't cheat hired servants who are poor and needy, whether they are fellow Israelites or foreigners living in one of your towns. [15]Pay them each day before sunset, because they are poor and need the money. Otherwise, they may complain to the Lord about you, and you will be guilty of sin.

[16]Parents must not be put to death if their children do wrong, and children must not be put to death if their parents do wrong. Each person must die for his own sin.

[17]Do not be unfair to a foreigner or an orphan. Don't take a widow's coat to make sure she pays you back. [18]Remember that you were slaves in Egypt, and the Lord your God saved you from there. That is why I am commanding you to do this.

[19]When you are gathering your harvest in the

field and leave behind a bundle of grain, don't go back and get it. Leave it there for foreigners, orphans, and widows so that the LORD your God can bless everything you do. 20When you beat your olive trees to knock the olives off, don't beat the trees a second time. Leave what is left for foreigners, orphans, and widows. 21When you harvest the grapes in your vineyard, don't pick the vines a second time. Leave what is left for foreigners, orphans, and widows. 22Remember that you were slaves in Egypt; that is why I am commanding you to do this.

25 If two people have an argument and go to court, the judges will decide the case. They will declare one person right and the other guilty. 2If the guilty person has to be punished with a beating, the judge will make that person lie down and be beaten in front of him. The number of lashes should match the crime. 3But don't hit a person more than forty times, because more than that would disgrace him before others.

4When an ox is working in the grain, do not cover its mouth to keep it from eating.

5If two brothers are living together, and one of them dies without having a son, his widow must not marry someone outside her husband's family. Her husband's brother must marry her, which is his duty to her as a brother-in-law. 6The first son she has counts as the son of the dead brother so that his name will not be forgotten in Israel.

7But if a man does not want to marry his brother's widow, she should go to the older leaders at the town gate. She should say, "My brother-in-law will not carry on his brother's name in Israel. He refuses to do his duty for me."

SIDELIGHT: If you have a married brother, be glad if you like his wife. In Old Testament times, a man was supposed to marry his brother's wife if the brother died, to carry on his brother's name. If the man didn't want to marry her, she would publicly spit in his face, take off one of his sandals, and curse him (Deuteronomy 25:5–9).

8Then the older leaders of the town must call for the man and talk to him. But if he is stubborn and says, "I don't want to marry her," 9the woman must go up to him in front of the leaders. She must take off one of his sandals and spit in his face and say, "This is for the man who won't continue his brother's family!" 10Then that man's family shall be known in Israel as the Family of the Unsandaled.

11If two men are fighting and one man's wife comes to save her husband from his attacker, grabbing the attacker by his sex organs, 12you must cut off her hand. Show her no mercy.

13Don't carry two sets of weights with you, one heavy and one light. 14Don't have two different sets of measures in your house, one large and one small. 15You must have true and honest weights and measures so that you will live a long time in the land the LORD your God is giving you. 16The LORD your God hates anyone who is dishonest and uses dishonest measures.

17Remember what the Amalekites did to you when you came out of Egypt. 18When you were tired and worn out, they met you on the road and attacked all those lagging behind. They were not afraid of God. 19When the LORD your God gives you rest from all the enemies around you in the land he is giving you as your own, you shall destroy any memory of the Amalekites on the earth. Do not forget!

The First Harvest

26 When you go into the land the LORD your God is giving you as your own, to take it over and live in it, 2you must take some of the first harvest of crops that grow from the land the LORD your God is giving you. Put the food in a basket and go to the place where the LORD your God will choose to be worshiped. 3Say to the priest on duty at that time, "Today I declare before the LORD your God that I have come into the land the LORD promised our ancestors that he would give us." 4The priest will take your basket and set it down in front of the altar of the LORD your God. 5Then you shall announce before the LORD your God: "My father was a wandering Aramean. He went down to Egypt with only a few people, but they became a great, powerful, and large nation there. 6But the Egyptians were cruel to us, making us suffer and work very hard. 7So we prayed to the LORD, the God of our ancestors, and he heard us. When he saw our trouble, hard work, and suffering, 8the LORD brought us out of Egypt with his great power and strength, using great terrors, signs, and miracles.d 9Then he brought us to this place and gave us this fertile land. 10Now I bring part of the first harvest from this land that you, LORD, have given me." Place the basket before the LORD your God and bow down before him. 11Then you and the Levites and foreigners among you should rejoice, because the LORD your God has given good things to you and your family.

12Bring a tenth of all your harvest the third year (the year to give a tenth of your harvest). Give it to the Levites, foreigners, orphans, and widows so that they may eat in your towns and be full. 13Then say to the LORD your God, "I have taken out of my house the part of my harvest that belongs to God, and I have given it to the Levites, foreigners, orphans, and widows. I have done everything you commanded me; I have not broken your commands, and I have not forgotten any of them. ¹⁴I have not eaten any of the holy part while I was in sorrow. I have not removed any of it while I was unclean,ᵈ and I have not offered it for dead people. I have obeyed you, the LORD my God, and have done everything you commanded me. ¹⁵So look down from heaven, your holy home. Bless your people Israel and bless the land you have given us, which you promised to our ancestors—a fertile land."

Obey the Lord's Commands

¹⁶Today the LORD your God commands you to obey all these rules and laws; be careful to obey them with your whole being. ¹⁷Today you have said that the LORD is your God, and you have promised to do what he wants you to do—to keep his rules, commands, and laws. You have said you will obey him. ¹⁸And today the LORD has said that you are his very own people, as he has promised you. But you must obey his commands. ¹⁹He will make you greater than all the other nations he made. He will give you praise, fame, and honor, and you will be a holy people to the LORD your God, as he has said.

The Law Written on Stones

27 Then Moses, along with the older leaders of Israel, commanded the people, saying, "Keep all the commands I have given you today. ²Soon you will cross the Jordan River to go into the land the LORD your God is giving you. On that day set up some large stones and cover them with plaster. ³When you cross over, write all the words of these teachings on them. Then you may enter the land the LORD your God is giving you, a fertile land, just as the LORD, the God of your ancestors, promised. ⁴After you have crossed the Jordan River, set up these stones on Mount Ebal, as I command you today, and cover them with plaster. ⁵Build an altar of stones there to the LORD your God but don't use any iron tool to cut the stones; ⁶build the altar of the LORD your God with stones from the field. Offer burnt offerings on it to the LORD your God, ⁷and offer fellowship offerings there, and eat them and rejoice before the LORD your God. ⁸Then write clearly all the words of these teachings on the stones."

GIVING

Sharing With Joy

Jennie Meehl didn't realize what she was getting into when she agreed to go on a two-and-a-half-week mission trip to an orphanage in Mexico with her youth group.

"It was culture shock," she admits. For the first time ever, she realized how much she had been given in her life.

After returning home, Jennie couldn't get the kids in the orphanage out of her mind. So she went back—by herself. She traveled more than two thousand miles from Minnesota to spend her entire next summer helping the children in the orphanage. She bathed them, played games with them, fed them, and helped take care of them.

"It helped me realize the important things in life," she explains. "Sharing my love helped me grow."

Jennie had learned the importance of giving to God and others because of what God has given to us. "Help others," she challenges, "because the rewards are greater than you can imagine." Similarly, **Deuteronomy 26:5–11** challenged the Israelites to give to God because of all he had given them.

■ How does Jennie's story model the giving discussed in the passage?
■ What can you bring to God from your "first harvest" in thanks for the many things God gives you?

CONSIDER . . .

■ participating in a service project at your church as a way of giving back to God part of the love and time he has given you.
■ taking ten percent of the money in your purse or wallet and giving it to God.

FOR MORE, SEE . . .

■ Genesis 28:22 (p. 33)
■ Malachi 3:8–10 (p. 901)
■ Luke 11:42 (p. 1026)

Curses of the Law

⁹Then Moses and the Levites who were priests spoke to all Israel and said, "Be quiet, Israel. Listen! Today you have become the people of the LORD your God. ¹⁰Obey the LORD your God, and keep his commands and laws that I give you today."

¹¹That day Moses also gave the people this command:

¹²When you cross the Jordan River, these tribes*d* must stand on Mount Gerizim to bless the people: Simeon, Levi, Judah, Issachar, Joseph and Benjamin. ¹³And these tribes must stand on Mount Ebal to announce the curses: Reuben, Gad, Asher, Zebulun, Dan, and Naphtali.

¹⁴The Levites will say to all the people of Israel in a loud voice:

¹⁵"Anyone will be cursed who makes an idol or statue and secretly sets it up, because the LORD hates the idols people make."

Then all the people will say, "Amen!"

¹⁶"Anyone will be cursed who dishonors his father or mother."

Then all the people will say, "Amen!"

¹⁷"Anyone will be cursed who moves the stone that marks a neighbor's border."

Then all the people will say, "Amen!"

¹⁸"Anyone will be cursed who sends a blind person down the wrong road."

Then all the people will say, "Amen!"

¹⁹"Anyone will be cursed who is unfair to foreigners, orphans, or widows."

Then all the people will say, "Amen!"

²⁰"A man will be cursed who has sexual relations with his father's wife, because it is a dishonor to his father."

Then all the people will say, "Amen!"

²¹"Anyone will be cursed who has sexual relations with an animal."

Then all the people will say, "Amen!"

²²"A man will be cursed who has sexual relations with his sister, whether she is his father's daughter or his mother's daughter."

Then all the people will say, "Amen!"

²³"A man will be cursed who has sexual relations with his mother-in-law."

Then all the people will say, "Amen!"

²⁴"Anyone will be cursed who kills a neighbor secretly."

Then all the people will say, "Amen!"

²⁵"Anyone will be cursed who takes money to murder an innocent person."

Then all the people will say, "Amen!"

²⁶"Anyone will be cursed who does not agree with the words of these teachings and does not obey them."

Then all the people will say, "Amen!"

Blessings for Obeying

28 You must completely obey the LORD your God, and you must carefully follow all his commands I am giving you today. Then the LORD your God will make you greater than any other nation on earth. ²Obey the LORD your God so that all these blessings will come and stay with you:

³You will be blessed in the city and blessed in the country.

⁴Your children will be blessed, as well as your crops; your herds will be blessed with calves and your flocks with lambs.

⁵Your basket and your kitchen will be blessed.

⁶You will be blessed when you come in and when you go out.

⁷The LORD will help you defeat the enemies that come to fight you. They will attack you from one direction, but they will run from you in seven directions.

⁸The LORD your God will bless you with full barns, and he will bless everything you do. He will bless the land he is giving you.

⁹The LORD will make you his holy people, as he promised. But you must obey his commands and do what he wants you to do. ¹⁰Then everyone on earth will see that you are the LORD's people, and they will be afraid of you. ¹¹The LORD will make you rich: You will have many children, your animals will have many young, and your land will give good crops. It is the land that the LORD promised your ancestors he would give to you.

¹²The LORD will open up his heavenly storehouse so that the skies send rain on your land at the right time, and he will bless everything you do. You will lend to other nations, but you will not need to borrow from them. ¹³The LORD will make you like the head and not like the tail; you will be on top and not on bottom. But you must obey the commands of the LORD your God that I am giving you today, being careful to keep them. ¹⁴Do not disobey anything I command you today. Do exactly as I command, and do not follow other gods or serve them.

Curses for Disobeying

¹⁵But if you do not obey the LORD your God and carefully follow all his commands and laws I am giving you today, all these curses will come upon you and stay:

¹⁶You will be cursed in the city and cursed in the country.

¹⁷Your basket and your kitchen will be cursed.

¹⁸Your children will be cursed, as well as your crops; the calves of your herds and the lambs of your flocks will be cursed.

¹⁹You will be cursed when you go in and when you go out.

20The LORD will send you curses, confusion, and punishment in everything you do. You will be destroyed and suddenly ruined because you did wrong when you left him. 21The LORD will give you terrible diseases and destroy you from the land you are going to take. 22The LORD will punish you with disease, fever, swelling, heat, lack of rain, plant diseases, and mildew*d* until you die. 23The sky above will be like bronze,*n* and the ground below will be like iron. 24The LORD will turn the rain into dust and sand, which will fall from the skies until you are destroyed.

25The LORD will help your enemies defeat you. You will attack them from one direction, but you will run from them in seven directions. And you will become a thing of horror among all the kingdoms on earth. 26Your dead bodies will be food for all the birds and wild animals, and there will be no one to scare them away. 27The LORD will punish you with boils like those the Egyptians had. You will have bad growths, sores, and itches that can't be cured. 28The LORD will give you madness, blindness, and a confused mind. 29You will have to feel around in the daylight like a blind person. You will fail in everything you do. People will hurt you and steal from you every day, and no one will save you.

30You will be engaged to a woman, but another man will force her to have sexual relations with him. You will build a house, but you will not live in it. You will plant a vineyard, but you will not get its grapes. 31Your ox will be killed before your eyes, but you will not eat any of it. Your donkey will be taken away from you, and it will not be brought back. Your sheep will be given to your enemies, and no one will save you. 32Your sons and daughters will be given to another nation, and you will grow tired looking for them every day, but there will be nothing you can do. 33People you don't know will eat the crops your land and hard work have produced. You will be mistreated and abused all your life. 34The things you see will cause you to go mad. 35The LORD will give you sore boils on your knees and legs that cannot be cured, and they will go from the soles of your feet to the tops of your heads.

36The LORD will send you and your king away to a nation neither you nor your ancestors know, where you will serve other gods made of wood and stone. 37You will become a hated thing to the nations where the LORD sends you; they will laugh at you and make fun of you.

38You will plant much seed in your field, but your harvest will be small, because locusts*d* will eat the crop. 39You will plant vineyards and work hard in them, but you will not pick the grapes or drink the wine, because the worms will eat them.

40You will have olive trees in all your land, but you will not get any olive oil, because the olives will drop off the trees. 41You will have sons and daughters, but you will not be able to keep them, because they will be taken captive. 42Locusts will destroy all your trees and crops.

43The foreigners who live among you will get stronger and stronger, and you will get weaker and weaker. 44Foreigners will lend money to you, but you will not be able to lend to them. They will be like the head, and you will be like the tail.

45All these curses will come upon you. They will chase you and catch you and destroy you, because you did not obey the LORD your God and keep the commands and laws he gave you. 46The curses will be signs and miracles*d* to you and your descendants*d* forever. 47You had plenty of everything, but you did not serve the LORD your God with joy and a pure heart, 48so you will serve the enemies the LORD sends against you. You will be hungry, thirsty, naked, and poor, and the LORD will put a load on you until he has destroyed you.

The Curse of an Enemy Nation

49The LORD will bring a nation against you from far away, from the end of the world, and it will swoop down like an eagle. You won't understand their language, 50and they will look mean. They will not respect old people or feel sorry for the young. 51They will eat the calves from your herds and the harvest of your field, and you will be destroyed. They will not leave you any grain, new wine or oil, or any calves from your herds or lambs from your flocks. You will be ruined. 52That nation will surround and attack all your cities. You trust in your high, strong walls, but they will fall down. That nation will surround all your cities everywhere in the land the LORD your God is giving you.

53Your enemy will surround you. Those people will make you starve so that you will eat your own babies, the bodies of the sons and daughters the LORD your God gave you. 54Even the most gentle and kind man among you will become cruel to his brother, his wife whom he loves, and his children who are still alive. 55He will not even give them any of the flesh of his children he is eating, because it will be all he has left. Your enemy will surround you and make you starve in all your cities. 56The most gentle and kind woman among you, so gentle and kind she would hardly even walk on the ground, will be cruel to her husband whom she loves and to her son and daughter. 57She will give birth to a baby, but she will plan to eat the baby and what comes after the birth itself. She will eat them secretly while the

sky ... bronze   This means the sky will give no rain and the earth will produce no crops.

enemy surrounds the city. Those people will make you starve in all your cities.

58Be careful to obey everything in these teachings that are written in this book. You must respect the glorious and wonderful name of the LORD your God, 59or the LORD will give terrible diseases to you and your descendants.d You will have long and serious diseases, and long and miserable sicknesses. 60He will give you all the diseases of Egypt that you dread, and the diseases will stay with you. 61The LORD will also give you every disease and sickness not written in this Book of the Teachings, until you are destroyed. 62You people may have outnumbered the stars, but only a few of you will be left, because you did not obey the LORD your God. 63Just as the LORD was once happy with you and gave you good things and made you grow in number, so then the LORD will be happy to ruin and destroy you, and you will be removed from the land you are entering to take as your own.

64Then the LORD will scatter you among the nations — from one end of the earth to the other. There you will serve other gods of wood and stone, gods that neither you nor your ancestors have known. 65You will have no rest among those nations and no place that is yours. The LORD will make your mind worried, your sight weak, and your soul sad. 66You will live with danger and be afraid night and day. You will not be sure that you will live. 67In the morning you will say, "I wish it were evening," and in the evening you will say, "I wish it were morning." Terror will be in your heart, and the things you have seen will scare you. 68The LORD will send you back to Egypt in ships, even though I, Moses, said you would never go back to Egypt. And there you will try to sell yourselves as slaves to your enemies, but no one will buy you.

The Agreement in Moab

29 The LORD commanded Moses to make an agreement with the Israelites in Moab in addition to the agreement he had made with them at Mount Sinai. These are the words of that agreement.

2Moses called all the Israelites together and said to them:

You have seen everything the LORD did before your own eyes to the king of Egypt and to the king's leaders and to the whole country. 3With your own eyes you saw the great troubles, signs, and miracles.d 4But to this day the LORD has not given you a mind that understands; you don't really understand what you see with your eyes or hear with your ears. 5I led you through the desert for forty years, and during that time neither your clothes nor sandals wore out. 6You ate no bread and drank no wine or beer. This was so you

would understand that I am the LORD your God.

7When you came to this place, Sihon king of Heshbon and Og king of Bashan came out to fight us, but we defeated them. 8We captured their land and gave it to the tribesd of Reuben, Gad, and East Manasseh to be their own.

9You must carefully obey everything in this agreement so that you will succeed in everything you do. 10Today you are all standing here before the LORD your God — your leaders and important men, your older leaders, officers, and all the other men of Israel, 11your wives and children and the foreigners who live among you, who chop your wood and carry your water. 12You are all here to enter into an agreement and a promise with the LORD your God, an agreement the LORD your God is making with you today. 13This will make you today his own people. He will be your God, as he told you and as he promised your ancestors Abraham, Isaac, and Jacob. 14But I am not just making this agreement and its promises with you 15who are standing here before the LORD your God today, but also with those who are not here today.

16You know how we lived in Egypt and how we passed through the countries when we came here. 17You saw their hateful idols made of wood, stone, silver, and gold. 18Make sure no man, woman, family group, or tribe among you leaves the LORD our God to go and serve the gods of those nations. They would be to you like a plant that grows bitter, poisonous fruit.

19These are the kind of people who hear these curses but bless themselves, thinking, "We will be safe even though we continue doing what we want to do." Those people may destroy all of your land, both wet and dry. 20The LORD will not forgive them. His anger will be like a burning fire against those people, and all the curses written in this book will come on them. The LORD will destroy any memory of them on the earth. 21He will separate them from all the tribes of Israel for punishment. All the curses of the Agreement that are written in this Book of the Teachings will happen to them.

22Your children who will come after you, as well as foreigners from faraway lands, will see the disasters that come to this land and the diseases the LORD will send on it. They will say, 23"The land is nothing but burning cinders and salt. Nothing is planted, nothing grows, and nothing blooms. It is like Sodom and Gomorrah, and Admah and Zeboiim, which the LORD destroyed because he was very angry." 24All the other nations will ask, "Why has the LORD done this to the land? Why is he so angry?"

25And the answer will be, "It is because the people broke the Agreement of the LORD, the God of their ancestors, which he made with them when he brought them out of Egypt. 26They went and served other gods and bowed down to gods they did not even know. The Lord did not allow that, 27so he became very angry at the land and brought all the curses on it that are written in this book. 28Since the Lord became angry and furious with them, he took them out of their land and put them in another land where they are today."

29There are some things the Lord our God has kept secret, but there are some things he has let us know. These things belong to us and our children forever so that we will do everything in these teachings.

The Israelites Will Return

30 When all these blessings and curses I have described happen to you, and the Lord your God has sent you away to other nations, think about these things. 2Then you and your children will return to the Lord your God, and you will obey him with your whole being in everything I am commanding you today. 3Then the Lord your God will give you back your freedom. He will feel sorry for you, and he will bring you back again from the nations where he scat-

tered you. 4He may send you to the ends of the earth, but he will gather you and bring you back from there, 5back to the land that belonged to your ancestors. It will be yours. He will give you success, and there will be more of you than there were of your ancestors. 6The Lord your God will prepare you and your descendants*d* to love him with your whole being so that you will live. 7The Lord your God will put all these curses on your enemies, who hate you and are cruel to you. 8And you will again obey the Lord, keeping all his commands that I give you today. 9The Lord your God will make you successful in everything you do. You will have many children, your cattle will have many calves, and your fields will produce good crops, because the Lord will again be happy with you just as he was with your ancestors. 10But you must obey the Lord your God by keeping all his commands and rules that are written in this Book of the Teachings. You must return to the Lord your God with your whole being.

Choose Life or Death

11This command I give you today is not too

DECISION MAKING

Living With Deadlines

Wayne Holsten had never kissed a girl—until he met Karen Mills at youth camp. It was love at first sight. Karen and Wayne were good for each other, and they encouraged each other in their faith.

But there was Andrea to think about—Wayne's girlfriend back home. She was cynical about the church, and she made fun of Wayne's efforts to grow in his faith. Wayne decided he needed to end this unhealthy relationship.

When Wayne got back home at the end of July, he had mixed emotions. It was hard breaking away from the past. So he decided he would go back to his old girlfriend if he didn't get a letter from Karen by August 15.

Each day, he checked his mail. No letters. On August 15, he nervously flipped through the mail. Nothing.

So he called Andrea.

On August 16, Karen's letter came, but Wayne had already made his choice.

In the same way Wayne had to decide what to do, the Israelites had a choice to make in **Deuteronomy 30:11–20**. Theirs was a much more important choice: whether or not to follow God.

■ With this passage in mind, how would you advise Wayne if he came to you for advice about his dilemma?
■ What principles from this passage can help you make wise choices?

CONSIDER . . .

■ circling the things in the passage that God asks people to do. Underline the "not to do" items.
■ writing out an important decision you face. List all the pros and cons of your choices. Then circle any reasons that fit the scripture passage. Cross out any that contradict it. Your decision may be easier now.

FOR MORE, SEE . . .

■ Genesis 39:6–23 (p. 45)   ■ Matthew 25:1–13 (p. 953)
■ Joshua 24:14–15 (p. 214)

hard for you; it is not beyond what you can do. [12]It is not up in heaven. You do not have to ask, "Who will go up to heaven and get it for us so we can obey it and keep it?" [13]It is not on the other side of the sea. You do not have to ask, "Who will go across the sea and get it? Who will tell it to us so we can keep it?" [14]No, the word is very near you. It is in your mouth and in your heart so you may obey it.

[15]Look, today I offer you life and success, death and destruction. [16]I command you today to love the LORD your God, to do what he wants you to do, and to keep his commands, his rules, and his laws. Then you will live and grow in number, and the LORD your God will bless you in the land you are entering to take as your own.

[17]But if you turn away from the LORD and do not obey him, if you are led to bow and serve other gods, [18]I tell you today that you will surely be destroyed. And you will not live long in the land you are crossing the Jordan River to enter and take as your own.

[19]Today I ask heaven and earth to be witnesses. I am offering you life or death, blessings or curses. Now, choose life! Then you and your children may live. [20]To choose life is to love the LORD your God, obey him, and stay close to him. He is your life, and he will let you live many years in the land, the land he promised to give your ancestors Abraham, Isaac, and Jacob.

Joshua Takes Moses' Place

31 Then Moses went and spoke these words to all the Israelites: [2]"I am now one hundred twenty years old, and I cannot lead you anymore. The LORD told me I would not cross the Jordan River; [3]the LORD your God will lead you across himself. He will destroy those nations for you, and you will take over their land. Joshua will also lead you across, as the LORD has said. [4]The LORD will do to those nations what he did to Sihon and Og, the kings of the Amorites, when he destroyed them and their land. [5]The LORD will give those nations to you; do to them everything I told you. [6]Be strong and brave. Don't be afraid of them and don't be frightened, because the LORD your God will go with you. He will not leave you or forget you."

[7]Then Moses called Joshua and said to him in front of the people, "Be strong and brave, because you will lead these people into the land the LORD promised to give their ancestors, and help them take it as their own. [8]The LORD himself will go before you. He will be with you; he will not leave you or forget you. Don't be afraid and don't worry."

Moses Writes the Teachings

[9]So Moses wrote down these teachings and gave them to the priests and all the older leaders of Israel. (The priests are the sons of Levi, who carry the Ark[d] of the Agreement with the LORD.) [10-11]Then Moses commanded them: "Read these teachings for all Israel to hear at the end of every seven years, which is the year to cancel what people owe. Do it during the Feast[d] of Shelters, when all the Israelites will come to appear before the LORD your God and stand at the place he will choose. [12]Gather all the people: the men, women, children, and foreigners living in your towns so that they can listen and learn to respect the LORD your God and carefully obey everything in this law. [13]Since their children do not know this law, they must hear it. They must learn to respect the LORD your God for as long as they live in the land you are crossing the Jordan River to take for your own."

The Lord Calls Moses and Joshua

[14]The LORD said to Moses, "Soon you will die. Get Joshua and come to the Meeting Tent[d] so that I may command him." So Moses and Joshua went to the Meeting Tent.

[15]The LORD appeared at the Meeting Tent in a cloud; the cloud stood over the entrance of the Tent. [16]And the LORD said to Moses, "You will soon die. Then these people will not be loyal to me but will worship the foreign gods of the land they are entering. They will leave me, breaking the Agreement I made with them. [17]Then I will become very angry at them, and I will leave them. I will turn away from them, and they will be destroyed. Many terrible things will happen to them. Then they will say, 'It is because God is not with us that these terrible things are happening.' [18]I will surely turn away from them then, because they have done wrong and have turned to other gods.

[19]"Now write down this song and teach it to the Israelites. Then have them sing it, because it will be my witness against them. [20]When I bring them into the land I promised to their ancestors, a fertile land, they will eat as much as they want and get fat. Then they will turn to other gods and serve them. They will reject me and break my Agreement. [21]Then when many troubles and terrible things happen to them, this song will testify against them, because the song will not be forgotten by their descendants.[d] I know what they plan to do, even before I take them into the land I promised them." [22]So Moses wrote down the song that day, and he taught it to the Israelites.

[23]Then the LORD gave this command to Joshua son of Nun: "Be strong and brave, because you will lead the people of Israel to the land I promised them, and I will be with you."

[24]After Moses finished writing all the words of the teachings in a book, [25]he gave a command to

the Levites, who carried the Ark*d* of the Agreement with the Lord. 26He said, "Take this Book of the Teachings and put it beside the Ark of the Agreement with the Lord your God. It must stay

---

SIDELIGHT: Have you ever done a research paper and found that an important book is out of print? Bible scholars often have that problem. The Bible mentions several books that no longer exist. Deuteronomy 31:26 mentions the "Book of the Teachings." Others include: the "Book of the Wars of the Lord" (Numbers 21:14–15, p. 145), and the "Book of Jashar" (Joshua 10:13, p. 202).

---

there as a witness against you. 27I know how stubborn and disobedient you are. You have disobeyed the Lord while I am alive and with you, and you will disobey even more after I die! 28Gather all the older leaders of your tribes*d* and all your officers to me so that I may say these things for them to hear, and so that I may ask heaven and earth to testify against them. 29I know that after I die you will become completely evil. You will turn away from the commands I have given you. Terrible things will happen to you in the future when you do what the Lord says is evil, and you will make him angry with the idols you have made."

Moses' Song

30And Moses spoke this whole song for all the people of Israel to hear:

32 Hear, heavens, and I will speak.
Listen, earth, to what I say.
2My teaching will drop like rain;
my words will fall like dew.
They will be like showers on the grass;
they will pour down like rain on young plants.
3I will announce the name of the Lord.
Praise God because he is great!
4He is like a rock; what he does is perfect,
and he is always fair.
He is a faithful God who does no wrong,
who is right and fair.
5They have done evil against him.
To their shame they are no longer his children;
they are an evil and lying people.
6This is not the way to repay the Lord,
you foolish and unwise people.
He is your Father and Maker,
who made you and formed you.

7Remember the old days.
Think of the years already passed.
Ask your father and he will tell you;
ask your older leaders and they will inform you.
8God Most High gave the nations their lands,
dividing up the human race.
He set up borders for the people
and even numbered the Israelites.
9The Lord took his people as his share,
the people of Jacob as his very own.

10He found them in a desert,
a windy, empty land.
He surrounded them and brought them up,
guarding them as those he loved very much.
11He was like an eagle building its nest
that flutters over its young.
It spreads its wings to catch them
and carries them on its feathers.
12The Lord alone led them,
and there was no foreign god helping him.

13The Lord brought them to the heights of the land
and fed them the fruit of the fields.
He gave them honey from the rocks,
bringing oil from the solid rock.
14There were milk curds from the cows and
milk from the flock;
there were fat sheep and goats.
There were sheep and goats from Bashan
and the best of the wheat.
You drank the juice of grapes.

15Israel grew fat and kicked;
they were fat and full and firm.
They left the God who made them
and rejected the Rock*d* who saved them.
16They made God jealous with foreign gods
and angry with hateful idols.
17They made sacrifices to demons,*d* not God,
to gods they had never known,
new gods from nearby,
gods your ancestors did not fear.
18You left God who is the Rock, your Father,
and you forgot the God who gave you birth.

19The Lord saw this and rejected them;
his sons and daughters had made him angry.
20He said, "I will turn away from them
and see what will happen to them.
They are evil people,
unfaithful children.
21They used things that are not gods to make me jealous
and worthless idols to make me angry.

So I will use those who are not a nation to
make them jealous;
I will use a nation that does not understand
to make them angry.
22My anger has started a fire
that burns down to the place of the dead.
It will burn up the ground and its crops,
and it will set fire to the base of the
mountains.

23"I will pile troubles upon them
and shoot my arrows at them.
24They will be starved and sick,
destroyed by terrible diseases.
I will send them vicious animals
and gliding, poisonous snakes.
25In the streets the sword will kill;
in their homes there will be terror.
Young men and women will die,
and so will babies and gray-haired men.
26I will scatter them as I said,
and no one will remember them.
27But I didn't want their enemy to brag;
their enemy might misunderstand
and say, 'We have won!
The Lord has done none of this.' "

28Israel has no sense;
they do not understand.
29I wish they were wise and understood this;
I wish they could see what will happen to
them.
30One person cannot chase a thousand people,
and two people cannot fight ten thousand
unless their Rock has sold them,
unless the Lord has given them up.
31The rock of these people is not like our
Rock;
our enemies agree to that.
32Their vine comes from Sodom,
and their fields are like Gomorrah.
Their grapes are full of poison;
their bunches of grapes are bitter.
33Their wine is like snake poison,
like the deadly poison of cobras.

34"I have been saving this,
and I have it locked in my storehouses.
35I will punish those who do wrong; I will
repay them.
Soon their foot will slip,
because their day of trouble is near,
and their punishment will come quickly."

36The Lord will defend his people
and have mercy on his servants.
He will see that their strength is gone,
that nobody is left, slaves or free.
37Then he will say, "Where are their gods?
Where is the rock they trusted?

38Who ate the fat from their sacrifices,
and who drank the wine of their drink
offerings?
Let those gods come to help you!
Let them protect you!

39"Now you will see that I am the one God!
There is no god but me.
I send life and death;
I can hurt, and I can heal.
No one can escape from me.
40I raise my hand toward heaven and make this
promise:
As surely as I live forever,
41I will sharpen my flashing sword,
and I will take it in my hand to judge.
I will punish my enemies
and pay back those who hate me.
42My arrows will be covered with their blood;
my sword will eat their flesh.
The blood will flow from those who are
killed and the captives.
The heads of the enemy leaders will be cut
off."

43Be happy, nations, with his people,
because he will repay you for the blood of
his servants.
He will punish his enemies,
and he will remove the sin of his land and
people.

44Moses came with Joshua son of Nun, and
they spoke all the words of this song for the people to hear. 45When Moses finished speaking
these words to all Israel, 46he said to them: "Pay
careful attention to all the words I have said
to you today, and command your children to
obey carefully everything in these teachings.
47These should not be unimportant words for
you, but rather they mean life for you! By these
words you will live a long time in the land you
are crossing the Jordan River to take as your
own."

Moses Goes Up to Mount Nebo

48The Lord spoke to Moses again that same
day and said, 49"Go up the Abarim Mountains, to
Mount Nebo in the country of Moab, across from
Jericho. Look at the land of Canaan that I am giving to the Israelites as their own. 50On that mountain that you climb, you will die and join your
ancestors, just as your brother Aaron died on
Mount Hor and joined his ancestors. 51You both
sinned against me at the waters of Meribah Kadesh in the Desert of Zin, and you did not honor
me as holy there among the Israelites. 52So now
you will only look at the land from far away. You
will not enter the land I am giving the people of
Israel."

Moses Blesses the People

33 Moses, the man of God, gave this blessing to the Israelites before he died. [2]He said:

"The LORD came from Mount Sinai
and rose like the sun from Edom;
he showed his greatness from Mount Paran.
He came with thousands of angels
from the southern mountains.
[3]The LORD surely loves his people
and takes care of all those who belong to
him.
They bow down at his feet,
and they are taught by him.
[4]Moses gave us the teachings
that belong to the people of Jacob.
[5]The LORD became king of Israel
when the leaders of the people gathered,
when the tribes[d] of Israel came together.

[6]"Let the people of Reuben live and not die,
but let the people be few."

[7]Moses said this about the people of Judah:
"LORD, listen to Judah's prayer;
bring them back to their people.
They defend themselves with their hands.
Help them fight their enemies!"

[8]Moses said this about the people of Levi:
"LORD, your Thummim and Urim[d] belong
to Levi, whom you love.
LORD, you tested him at Massah
and argued with him at the waters of
Meribah.
[9]He said about his father and mother,
'I don't care about them.'
He did not treat his brothers as favorites
or give special favors to his children,
but he protected your word
and guarded your agreement.
[10]He teaches your laws to the people of Jacob
and your teachings to the people of Israel.

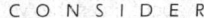

GOD'S POWER

Stronger Than Hatred

Andrew Casindola was livid. He had come to pick up his son Rob from church camp. While waiting for the last session to end, he had overheard his son telling other campers how he hated his dad because of abuse. But Christ had changed Rob's life that week. "And I know Christ can change my dad, too," he had concluded.

Andrew stormed to camp director Enoch Olson's office and verbally abused the director for what he had overheard.

Enoch calmed Andrew down and responded, "If your son is worse because of this camp experience, call me. I'll personally apologize. But, if your son is better, write to thank me."

Andrew picked up his son, still steaming with anger. The two drove silently in the car listening to the radio. About a hundred miles from camp, Rob's dad pulled into a rest area. As they looked at the view, Rob awkwardly put his arms around his dad and said, "Dad, I've hated you ever since I can remember. Will you forgive me?"

Two hours later, Enoch Olson found Rob's dad sitting at a picnic table back at the camp. "Christ made my son better," he told Enoch. "Can he do it in my life too?"

That day, Rob's dad began the long process of healing and recovery. It was not easy for either Rob or his dad to let go of the feelings of anger and hatred. But, in the process, they discovered God's power in the world and in their own lives. Read a description of God's power in **Deuteronomy 32:36—33:4**.

■ How might Rob's father have responded to this passage in the first part of the story? How might he have responded at the end?
■ What characteristic of God in the passage helps you understand God's power the most? What comfort do you gain from knowing that power?

C O N S I D E R . . .
■ confessing a way you've tried to escape from God (such as making decisions for selfish reasons), then letting God's power work in that area of your life.
■ sharing your faith in God's power with someone who has no hope.

F O R   M O R E ,   S E E . . .
■ Job 9:4–10 (p. 457)
■ Isaiah 46:8–12 (p. 664)
■ Ephesians 1.19–22 (p. 1218)

He burns incense[d] before you
and makes whole burnt offerings on your
altar.

[11]LORD, make them strong;
be pleased with the work they do.
Defeat those who attack them,
and don't let their enemies rise up again."

[12]Moses said this about the people of Benjamin:
"The LORD's loved ones will lie down in
safety,
because he protects them all day long.
The ones he loves rest with him."

[13]Moses said this about the people of Joseph:
"May the LORD bless their land with
wonderful dew from heaven,
with water from the springs below,
[14]with the best fruits that the sun brings,
and with the best fruits that the moon
brings.
[15]Let the old mountains give the finest crops,
and let the everlasting hills give the best
fruits.

[16]Let the full earth give the best fruits,
and let the LORD who lived in the burning
bush be pleased.
May these blessings rest on the head of
Joseph,
on the forehead of the one who was
blessed among his brothers.
[17]Joseph has the majesty of a firstborn[d] bull;
he is as strong as a wild ox.
He will stab other nations,
even those nations far away.
These are the ten thousands of Ephraim,
and these are the thousands of Manasseh."

[18]Moses said this about the people of Zebulun:
"Be happy when you go out, Zebulun,
and be happy in your tents, Issachar.
[19]They will call the people to the mountain,
and there they will offer the right sacrifices.
They will do well from all that is in the sea,
and they will do well from the treasures
hidden in the sand on the shore."

[20]Moses said this about the people of Gad:

DEATH

He's Gone

Cory Weskamp will never graduate from high school. He'll never have a date. He won't ever play in another band concert. He lost the battle to cancer before he turned sixteen. Cory didn't broadcast his illness. While some friends knew he was sick, they hadn't expected him to die.

The word rolled quickly down the halls of Goodrich Junior High. "Cory is dead." Students were stunned. Shocked. Afraid.

"I don't know what to think," said Ron, one of Cory's friends.

"It makes me look at life differently," Fred explained, worrying about his other friends getting sick. "Death could happen to anyone. It doesn't matter how old you are."

"It left an empty feeling knowing that I'd never be able to talk or laugh with him again," one student admitted. "I got scared."

Another shared, "I felt kind of sick. I didn't think someone of his age and strength would die."

When someone dies, people need time to grieve. When their great leader Moses died, the Israelites grieved for a long time. Read about how they dealt with Moses' death in **Deuteronomy 34:1–12**.

■ How do the students' statements about Cory's death compare to what the Israelites must have felt when Moses died?

■ When have you experienced the loss of someone you respected? How was that experience like the Israelites' experience when Moses died?

C O N S I D E R . . .

■ talking to a friend and a family member about times they've lost someone close. Ask what emotions they felt and how long they grieved.

■ comforting someone who's facing death or grieving by making a phone call, sending a card, visiting, or giving a hug.

F O R   M O R E ,   S E E . . .

■ 2 Samuel 1:17–27 (p. 245)
■ John 11:28–44 (p. 1077)
■ Revelation 21:1–4 (p. 1347)

"Praise God who gives Gad more land!
Gad lives there like a lion,
who tears off arms and heads.
21They chose the best land for themselves.
They received a large share, like that given
to an officer.
When the leaders of the people gathered,
the people of Gad did what the LORD said
was right,
and they judged Israel fairly."

22Moses said this about the people of Dan:
"Dan is like a lion's cub,
who jumps out of Bashan."

23Moses said this about the people of Naphtali:
"Naphtali enjoys special kindnesses,
and they are full of the LORD's blessings.
Take as your own the west and south."

24Moses said this about the people of Asher:
"Asher is the most blessed of the sons;
let him be his brothers' favorite.
Let him bathe his feet in olive oil.
25Your gates will have locks of iron and bronze,
and you will be strong as long as you live.

26"There is no one like the God of Israel,
who rides through the skies to help you,
who rides on the clouds in his majesty.
27The everlasting God is your place of safety,
and his arms will hold you up forever.
He will force your enemy out ahead of you,
saying, 'Destroy the enemy!'
28The people of Israel will lie down in safety.
Jacob's spring is theirs alone.
Theirs is a land full of grain and new wine,
where the skies drop their dew.
29Israel, you are blessed!
No one else is like you,
because you are a people saved by the
LORD.

He is your shield and helper,
your glorious sword.
Your enemies will be afraid of you,
and you will walk all over their holy
places."

Moses Dies

34 Then Moses climbed Mount Nebo from
the plains of Moab to the top of Mount
Pisgah, across from Jericho. From there the LORD
showed him all the land from Gilead to Dan, 2all
of Naphtali and the lands of Ephraim and Manasseh, all the land of Judah as far as the Mediterranean Sea, 3as well as the southern desert and
the whole Valley of Jericho up to Zoar. (Jericho is
called the city of palm trees.) 4Then the LORD said
to Moses "This is the land I promised to Abraham, Isaac, and Jacob when I said to them, 'I will
give this land to your descendants.'d I have let you
look at it, Moses, but you will not cross over
there."

5Then Moses, the servant of the LORD, died
there in Moab, as the LORD had said. 6He buried
Moses in Moab in the valley opposite Beth Peor,
but even today no one knows where his grave is.
7Moses was one hundred twenty years old when
he died. His eyes were not weak, and he was still
strong. 8The Israelites cried for Moses for thirty
days, staying in the plains of Moab until the time
of sadness was over.

9Joshua son of Nun was then filled with wisdom, because Moses had put his hands on him.
So the Israelites listened to Joshua, and they did
what the LORD had commanded Moses.

10There has never been another propheta in Israel like Moses. The LORD knew Moses face to
face 11and sent him to do signs and miraclesd in
Egypt—to the king, to all his officers, and to the
whole land of Egypt. 12Moses had great power,
and he did great and wonderful things for all the
Israelites to see.

JOSHUA

Why Read This Book:

- See how God leads people to victory when they are faithful (Joshua 1—12).
- Learn how God takes care of people's needs (Joshua 13—21).
- Be challenged to stay faithful to God (Joshua 22—24).

Behind the Scenes:

The book of Joshua could be a great script for an action-packed movie. It's filled with spies, surprise attacks, guerrilla warfare, courageous leaders, unusual battles, and victory celebrations.

The central hero is Joshua, a creative military mind with great organizational skills. But above all, he is absolutely loyal to and dependent on God.

The plot tells how the Israelites conquered land God promised to their ancestor Abram (Genesis 12:7, p. 15). Their parents had escaped from Egypt but had not followed God. So the whole generation that left Egypt had died in the desert, leaving the children—under Joshua's leadership—to cross the Jordan River and conquer the land of Canaan.

Canaan consisted of many independent cities, each with its own king and army,

WHERE THE ACTION WAS

Mediterranean Sea

ASHER
NAPHTALI
ZEBULUN
ISSACHAR
MANASSEH
EPHRAIM

The sun stood still at Gibeon so Joshua's forces could win the battle against five kings (Joshua 10).

Jordan River

GAD

The approximate place where the Israelites crossed the Jordan River into Canaan (Joshua 3).

Gibeon Jericho
DAN
BENJAMIN
REUBEN

JUDAH
SIMEON

Dead Sea

The Israelites conquered Jericho by marching around it and blowing trumpets (Joshua 6).

SINAI

The approximate areas divided among the tribes of Israel (Joshua 13—21).

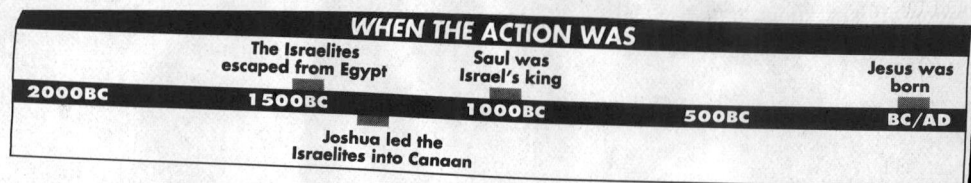

WHEN THE ACTION WAS

| 2000BC | The Israelites escaped from Egypt 1500BC | Saul was Israel's king 1000BC | 500BC | Jesus was born BC/AD |

Joshua led the Israelites into Canaan

and many had strong, high walls. So the Israelites had to defeat the cities one by one, beginning with the famous battle of Jericho (Joshua 6, p. 198).

Two major themes flow through Joshua. First, the book shows how God works through people to fulfill his purposes on earth. And it emphasizes the importance of loyally following God, depending on God's power in all things.

God's Command to Joshua

1 After Moses, the servant of the LORD, died, the LORD spoke to Joshua son of Nun, Moses' assistant. ²The LORD said, "My servant Moses is dead. Now you and all these people go across the Jordan River into the land I am giving to the Israelites. ³I promised Moses I would give you this land, so I will give you every place you go in the land. ⁴All the land from the desert in the south to Lebanon in the north will be yours. All the land from the great river, the Euphrates, in the east, to the Mediterranean Sea in the west will be yours, too, including the land of the Hittites. ⁵No one will be able to defeat you all your life. Just as I was with Moses, so I will be with you. I will not leave you or forget you.

> ✳ **SIDELIGHT:** The Hebrew name
> Joshua means "The Lord saves." It's a more famous name than you might think. When you translate it to English, it's Jesus.

⁶"Joshua, be strong and brave! You must lead these people so they can take the land that I promised their fathers I would give them. ⁷Be strong and brave. Be sure to obey all the teachings my servant Moses gave you. If you follow them exactly, you will be successful in everything you do. ⁸Always remember what is written in the Book of the Teachings. Study it day and night to be sure to obey everything that is written there. If you do this, you will be wise and successful in everything. ⁹Remember that I commanded you to be strong and brave. Don't be afraid, because the LORD your God will be with you everywhere you go."

Joshua's Orders to the People

¹⁰Then Joshua gave orders to the officers of the people: ¹¹"Go through the camp and tell the people, 'Get your supplies ready. Three days from now you will cross the Jordan River and take the land the LORD your God is giving you.' "

¹²Then Joshua said to the people of Reuben, Gad, and East Manasseh, ¹³"Remember what Moses, the servant of the LORD, told you. He said the LORD your God would give you rest and would

give you this land. ¹⁴Now the LORD has given you this land east of the Jordan River. Your wives, children, and animals may stay here, but your fighting men must dress for war and cross the Jordan River ahead of your brothers to help them. ¹⁵The LORD has given you a place to rest and will do the same for your brothers. But you must help them until they take the land the LORD their God is giving them. Then you may return to your own land east of the Jordan River, the land that Moses, the servant of the LORD, gave you."

¹⁶Then the people answered Joshua, "Anything you command us to do, we will do. Any place you send us, we will go. ¹⁷Just as we fully obeyed Moses, we will obey you. We ask only that the LORD your God be with you just as he was with Moses. ¹⁸Whoever refuses to obey your commands or turns against you will be put to death. Just be strong and brave!"

Spies Sent to Jericho

2 Joshua son of Nun secretly sent out two spies from Acacia and said to them, "Go and look at the land, particularly at the city of Jericho."

So the men went to Jericho and stayed at the house of a prostitute[d] named Rahab.

²Someone told the king of Jericho, "Some men from Israel have come here tonight to spy out the land."

³So the king of Jericho sent this message to Rahab: "Bring out the men who came to you and entered your house. They have come to spy out our whole land."

⁴But the woman had hidden the two men. She said, "They did come here, but I didn't know where they came from. ⁵In the evening, when it was time to close the city gate, they left. I don't know where they went, but if you go quickly, maybe you can catch them." ⁶(The woman had taken the men up to the roof[n] and had hidden them there under stalks of flax[d] that she had spread out.) ⁷So the king's men went out looking for the spies on the road that leads to the crossings of the Jordan River. The city gate was closed just after the king's men left the city.

⁸Before the spies went to sleep for the night, Rahab went up to the roof. ⁹She said to them, "I know the LORD has given this land to your people. You frighten us very much. Everyone living in this land is terribly afraid of you ¹⁰because we have

---

roof In Bible times houses were built with flat roofs. The roof was used for drying things such as flax and fruit. It was also used as an extra room, as a place for worship, and as a place to sleep in the summer.

heard how the LORD dried up the Red Sea[d] when you came out of Egypt. We have heard how you destroyed Sihon and Og, two Amorite kings who lived east of the Jordan. [11]When we heard this, we were very frightened. Now our men are afraid to fight you because the LORD your God rules the heavens above and the earth below! [12]So now, promise me before the LORD that you will show kindness to my family just as I showed kindness to you. Give me some proof that you will do this. [13]Allow my father, mother, brothers, sisters, and all of their families to live. Save us from death."

[14]The men agreed and said, "It will be our lives for your lives if you don't tell anyone what we are doing. When the LORD gives us the land, we will be kind and true to you."

[15]The house Rahab lived in was built on the city wall, so she used a rope to let the men down through a window. [16]She said to them, "Go into the hills so the king's men will not find you. Hide there for three days. After the king's men return, you may go on your way."

> ✳ **SIDELIGHT:** Rahab, the prostitute, could help the Israelite spies escape from the king because her house was built into the city wall (Joshua 2:15). It's another one of those stories about a beautiful girl from the wrong side of the wall!

[17]The men said to her, "You must do as we say. If not, we cannot be responsible for keeping this oath you have made us swear. [18]When we return

---

BIBLE STUDY

Where's Your Focus?

Gary Richards was appalled when he saw the tapes in his friend Tim Fellman's car. "How can you listen to this trash?" he asked as he read the sexually explicit and raunchy song titles.

"Give it a rest," Tim shot back. "These groups know music. Who cares about the words? Stop being a crusader."

The conversation came back to haunt Tim that Wednesday night in Bible study. The group read the Bible and tried to apply its principles to their lives. They focused on how being a Christian shapes your priorities and interests in life and how it affects everything you do.

Tim was challenged by the discussion and wanted to talk about it with Gary. On the way home from the Bible study, they talked about friendships and being honest. Then Gary asked, "What does all this say about your music, Tim? Can you listen to raunchy songs and read your Bible at the same time?"

Tim was steamed. "Sure I can!" he shouted, hoping Gary would back off. Which he did. They rode in silence until Tim dropped off Gary at home.

Two weeks later Gary found a note stuffed through the slot in his school locker. "You were right," it simply said. "The songs I liked and God's Word don't mix. I've changed to more positive music. Thanks."

Tim had discovered how focusing on God's Word can change your values and priorities. God gave Joshua the same advice, and it guided him to be successful as God's leader. Read the advice in **Joshua 1:6–9**.

■ How did studying the Bible help Tim learn more about what it means to follow God? How did it change the way he lived?

■ How has reading the Bible given you courage or success in the past? How can it guide you in a particular area of your life right now?

C O N S I D E R . . .

■ reading three or four devotions on a topic with which you're struggling right now. (See the devotion guide on page 11 for suggestions.) Discover how Bible study changes how you think and what you do.

✒ *writing Joshua 1:9 on a three-by-five card and carrying it in your pocket for a week or two. Glance at it occasionally to remind you God is with you.*

F O R   M O R E ,   S E E . . .

■ Deuteronomy 11:16–21 (p. 172)
■ Psalm 119:105–120 (p. 553)

■ Romans 15:4–6 (p. 1161)

to this land, you must tie this red rope in the window through which you let us down. Bring your father, mother, brothers, and all your family into your house. ¹⁹If anyone leaves your house and is killed, it is his own fault. We cannot be responsible for him. If anyone in your house is hurt, we will be responsible. ²⁰But if you tell anyone about this, we will be free from the oath you made us swear."

²¹Rahab answered, "I agree to this." So she sent them away, and they left. Then she tied the red rope in the window.

²²The men left and went into the hills where they stayed for three days. The king's men looked for them all along the road, but after three days, they returned to the city without finding them. ²³Then the two men started back. They left the hills and crossed the river and came to Joshua son of Nun and told him everything that had happened to them. ²⁴They said, "The LORD surely has given us all of the land. All the people in that land are terribly afraid of us."

Crossing the Jordan

3 Early the next morning Joshua and all the Israelites left Acacia. They traveled to the Jordan River and camped there before crossing it. ²After three days the officers went through the camp ³and gave orders to the people: "When you see the priests and Levites carrying the Ark*d* of the Agreement with the LORD your God, leave where you are and follow it. ⁴That way you will know which way to go since you have never been here before. But do not follow too closely. Stay about a thousand yards behind the Ark."

⁵Then Joshua told the people, "Make yourselves holy, because tomorrow the LORD will do amazing things among you."

⁶Joshua said to the priests, "Take the Ark of the Agreement and go ahead of the people." So the priests lifted the Ark and carried it ahead of the people.

⁷Then the LORD said to Joshua, "Today I will begin to make you great in the opinion of all the Israelites so the people will know I am with you just as I was with Moses. ⁸Tell the priests who carry the Ark of the Agreement to go to the edge of the Jordan River and stand in the water."

⁹Then Joshua said to the Israelites, "Come here and listen to the words of the LORD your God. ¹⁰Here is proof that the living God is with you and that he will force out the Canaanites, Hittites, Hivites, Perizzites, Girgashites, Amorites, and Jebusites. ¹¹The Ark of the Agreement with the Lord of the whole world will go ahead of you into the Jordan River. ¹²Now choose twelve men from among you, one from each of the twelve tribes*d* of Israel. ¹³The priests will carry the Ark of the LORD, the Master of the whole world, into the

Jordan ahead of you. When they step into the water, it will stop. The river will stop flowing and will stand up in a heap."

¹⁴So the people left the place where they had camped, and they followed the priests who carried the Ark of the Agreement across the Jordan River. ¹⁵During harvest the Jordan overflows its banks. When the priests carrying the Ark came to the edge of the river and stepped into the water, ¹⁶the water upstream stopped flowing. It stood up in a heap a great distance away at Adam, a town near Zarethan. The water flowing down to the Sea of Arabah (the Dead Sea*d*) was completely cut off. So the people crossed the river near Jericho. ¹⁷The priests carried the Ark of the Agreement with the LORD to the middle of the river and stood there on dry ground. They waited there while all the people of Israel walked across the Jordan River on dry land.

Rocks to Remind the People

4 After all the people had finished crossing the Jordan, the LORD said to Joshua, ²"Choose twelve men from among the people, one from each tribe.*d* ³Tell them to get twelve rocks from the middle of the river, from where the priests stood. Carry the rocks and put them down where you stay tonight."

⁴So Joshua chose one man from each tribe. Then he called the twelve men together ⁵and said to them, "Go out into the river where the Ark*d* of the LORD your God is. Each of you bring back one rock, one for each tribe of Israel, and carry it on your shoulder. ⁶They will be a sign among you. In the future your children will ask you, 'What do these rocks mean?' ⁷Tell them the water stopped flowing in the Jordan when the Ark of the Agreement with the LORD crossed the river. These rocks will always remind the Israelites of this."

⁸So the Israelites obeyed Joshua and carried twelve rocks from the middle of the Jordan River, one rock for each of the twelve tribes of Israel, just as the LORD had commanded Joshua. They carried the rocks with them and put them down where they made their camp. ⁹Joshua also put twelve rocks in the middle of the Jordan River where the priests had stood while carrying the Ark of the Agreement. These rocks are still there today.

¹⁰The priests carrying the Ark continued standing in the middle of the river until everything was done that the LORD had commanded Joshua to tell the people, just as Moses had told Joshua. The people hurried across the river. ¹¹After they finished crossing the river, the priests carried the Ark of the LORD to the other side as the people watched. ¹²The men from the tribes of Reuben, Gad, and East Manasseh obeyed what Moses had told them. They were dressed for war, and they

crossed the river ahead of the other people.
¹³About forty thousand soldiers prepared for war passed before the LORD as they marched across the river, going toward the plains of Jericho.

¹⁴That day the LORD made Joshua great in the opinion of all the Israelites. They respected Joshua all his life, just as they had respected Moses.

¹⁵Then the LORD said to Joshua, ¹⁶"Command the priests to bring the Ark of the Agreement out of the river."

¹⁷So Joshua commanded the priests, "Come up out of the Jordan."

¹⁸Then the priests carried the Ark of the Agreement with the LORD out of the river. As soon as their feet touched dry land, the water began flowing again. The river again overflowed its banks, just as it had before they crossed.

¹⁹The people crossed the Jordan on the tenth day of the first month and camped at Gilgal, east of Jericho. ²⁰They carried with them the twelve rocks taken from the Jordan, and Joshua set them up at Gilgal. ²¹Then he spoke to the Israelites: "In the future your children will ask you, 'What do these rocks mean?' ²²Tell them, 'Israel crossed the Jordan River on dry land. ²³The LORD your God caused the water to stop flowing until you finished crossing it, just as the LORD did to the Red Sea.ᵈ He stopped the water until we crossed it. ²⁴The LORD did this so all people would know he has great power and so you would always respect the LORD your God.' "

5 All the kings of the Amorites west of the Jordan and the Canaanite kings living by the Mediterranean Sea heard that the LORD dried up the Jordan River until the Israelites had crossed it. After that they were scared and too afraid to face the Israelites.

The Israelites Are Circumcised

²At that time the LORD said to Joshua, "Make knives from flint stones and circumciseᵈ the Israelites." ³So Joshua made knives from flint stones and circumcised the Israelites at Gibeath Haaraloth.

⁴This is why Joshua circumcised the men: After the Israelites left Egypt, all the men old enough to serve in the army died in the desert on the way out of Egypt. ⁵The men who had come out of Egypt had been circumcised, but none of those who were born in the desert on the trip from Egypt had been circumcised. ⁶The Israelites had moved about in the desert for forty years. During that time all the fighting men who had left Egypt had died because they had not obeyed the LORD. So the LORD swore they would not see the land he had promised their ancestors to give them, a fertile land. ⁷Their sons took their places. But none of the sons born on the trip from Egypt had

been circumcised, so Joshua circumcised them. ⁸After all the Israelites had been circumcised, they stayed in camp until they were healed.

⁹Then the LORD said to Joshua, "As slaves in Egypt you were ashamed, but today I have removed that shame." So Joshua named that place Gilgal, which it is still named today.

¹⁰The people of Israel were camped at Gilgal on the plains of Jericho. It was there, on the evening of the fourteenth day of the month, they celebrated the Passoverᵈ Feast. ¹¹The day after the Passover, the people ate food grown on that land: bread made without yeast and roasted grain. ¹²The day they ate this food, the mannaᵈ stopped coming. The Israelites no longer got the manna from heaven. They ate the food grown in the land of Canaan that year.

¹³Joshua was near Jericho when he looked up and saw a man standing in front of him with a sword in his hand. Joshua went to him and asked, "Are you a friend or an enemy?"

¹⁴The man answered, "I am neither. I have come as the commander of the LORD's army."

Then Joshua bowed facedown on the ground and asked, "Does my master have a command for me, his servant?"

¹⁵The commander of the LORD's army answered, "Take off your sandals, because the place where you are standing is holy." So Joshua did.

The Fall of Jericho

6 The people of Jericho were afraid because the Israelites were near. They closed the city gates and guarded them. No one went into the city, and no one came out.

²Then the LORD said to Joshua, "Look, I have given you Jericho, its king, and all its fighting men. ³March around the city with your army once a day for six days. ⁴Have seven priests carry trumpets made from horns of male sheep and have them march in front of the Ark.ᵈ On the seventh day march around the city seven times and have the priests blow the trumpets as they march. ⁵They will make one long blast on the trumpets. When you hear that sound, have all the people give a loud shout. Then the walls of the city will fall so the people can go straight into the city."

⁶So Joshua son of Nun called the priests together and said to them, "Carry the Ark of the Agreement. Tell seven priests to carry trumpets and march in front of it." ⁷Then Joshua ordered the people, "Now go! March around the city. The soldiers with weapons should march in front of the Ark of the Agreement with the LORD."

⁸When Joshua finished speaking to the people, the seven priests began marching before the LORD. They carried the seven trumpets and blew them as they marched. The priests carrying the

Ark of the Agreement with the LORD followed them. [9]Soldiers with weapons marched in front of the priests, and armed men walked behind the Ark. The priests were blowing their trumpets. [10]But Joshua had told the people not to give a war cry. He said, "Don't shout. Don't say a word until the day I tell you. Then shout." [11]So Joshua had the Ark of the LORD carried around the city one time. Then they went back to camp for the night.

[12]Early the next morning Joshua got up, and the priests carried the Ark of the LORD again. [13]The seven priests carried the seven trumpets and marched in front of the Ark of the LORD, blowing their trumpets. Soldiers with weapons marched in front of them, and other soldiers walked behind the Ark of the LORD. All this time the priests were blowing their trumpets. [14]So on the second day they marched around the city one time and then went back to camp. They did this every day for six days.

[15]On the seventh day they got up at dawn and marched around the city, just as they had on the days before. But on that day they marched around the city seven times. [16]The seventh time around the priests blew their trumpets. Then Joshua gave the command: "Now, shout! The LORD has given you this city! [17]The city and everything in it are to be destroyed as an offering to the LORD. Only Rahab the prostitute[d] and everyone in her house should remain alive. They must not be killed, because Rahab hid the two spies we sent out. [18]Don't take any of the things that are to be destroyed as an offering to the LORD. If you take them and bring them into our camp, you yourselves will be destroyed, and you will bring trouble to all of Israel. [19]All the silver and gold and things made from bronze and iron belong to the LORD and must be saved for him."

[20]When the priests blew the trumpets, the people shouted. At the sound of the trumpets and the people's shout, the walls fell, and everyone ran straight into the city. So the Israelites defeated that city. [21]They completely destroyed with the sword every living thing in the city — men and women, young and old, cattle, sheep, and donkeys.

[22]Joshua said to the two men who had spied out the land, "Go into the prostitute's house. Bring her out and bring out those who are with her, because of the promise you made to her." [23]So the two men went into the house and brought out Rahab, her father, mother, brothers, and all those with her. They put all of her family in a safe place outside the camp of Israel.

[24]Then Israel burned the whole city and everything in it, but they did not burn the things made from silver, gold, bronze, and iron. These were saved for the LORD. [25]Joshua saved Rahab the prostitute, her family, and all who were with her, because Rahab had helped the men he had sent to spy out Jericho. Rahab still lives among the Israelites today.

[26]Then Joshua made this oath:

"Anyone who tries to rebuild this city of
    Jericho
    will be cursed by the LORD.
The one who lays the foundation of this city
    will lose his oldest son,
and the one who sets up the gates
    will lose his youngest son."

[27]So the LORD was with Joshua, and Joshua became famous through all the land.

The Sin of Achan

7 But the Israelites did not obey the LORD. There was a man from the tribe[d] of Judah named Achan. (He was the son of Carmi and grandson of Zabdi, who was the son of Zerah.) Because Achan kept some of the things that were to be given to the LORD, the LORD became very angry at the Israelites.

[2]Joshua sent some men from Jericho to Ai, which was near Beth Aven, east of Bethel. He told them, "Go to Ai and spy out the area." So the men went to spy on Ai.

[3]Later they came back to Joshua and said, "There are only a few people in Ai, so we will not need all our people to defeat them. Send only two or three thousand men to fight. There is no need to send all of our people." [4]So about three thousand men went up to Ai, but the people of Ai beat them badly. [5]The people of Ai killed about thirty-six Israelites and then chased the rest from the city gate all the way down to the canyon, killing them as they went down the hill. When the Israelites saw this, they lost their courage.

[6]Then Joshua tore his clothes in sorrow. He bowed facedown on the ground before the Ark[d] of the LORD and stayed there until evening. The leaders of Israel did the same thing. They also threw dirt on their heads to show their sorrow. [7]Then Joshua said, "Lord GOD, you brought our

people across the Jordan River. Why did you bring us this far and then let the Amorites destroy us? We would have been happy to stay on the other side of the Jordan. [8]Lord, there is nothing I can say now. Israel has been beaten by the enemy. [9]The Canaanites and all the other people in this country will hear about this and will surround and kill us all! Then what will you do for your own great name?"

[10]The LORD said to Joshua, "Stand up! Why are you down on your face? [11]The Israelites have sinned; they have broken the agreement I commanded them to obey. They took some of the things I commanded them to destroy. They have stolen and lied and have taken those things for themselves. [12]That is why the Israelites cannot face their enemies. They turn away from the fight and run, because I have commanded that they be destroyed. I will not help you anymore unless you destroy everything as I commanded you.

[13]"Now go! Make the people holy. Tell them, 'Set yourselves apart to the LORD for tomorrow. The LORD, the God of Israel, says some of you are keeping things he commanded you to destroy. You will never defeat your enemies until you throw away those things.

[14]" 'Tomorrow morning you must be present with your tribes. The LORD will choose one tribe to stand alone before him. Then the LORD will choose one family group from that tribe to stand before him. Then the LORD will choose one family from that family group to stand before him, person by person. [15]The one who is keeping what should have been destroyed will himself be destroyed by fire. Everything he owns will be destroyed with him. He has broken the agreement with the LORD and has done a disgraceful thing among the people of Israel!' "

[16]Early the next morning Joshua led all of Israel to present themselves in their tribes, and the LORD chose the tribe of Judah. [17]So the family groups of Judah presented themselves, and the LORD then chose the family group of Zerah. When all the families of Zerah presented themselves, the family of Zabdi was chosen. [18]And Joshua told all the men in that family to present themselves. The LORD chose Achan son of Carmi. (Carmi was the son of Zabdi, who was the son of Zerah.)

[19]Then Joshua said to Achan, "My son, tell the truth. Confess to the LORD, the God of Israel. Tell me what you did, and don't try to hide anything from me."

[20]Achan answered, "It is true! I have sinned against the LORD, the God of Israel. This is what I did: [21]Among the things I saw was a beautiful coat from Babylonia and about five pounds of silver and more than one and one-fourth pounds of gold. I wanted these things very much for myself, so I took them. You will find them buried in the

ground under my tent, with the silver underneath."

[22]So Joshua sent men who ran to the tent and found the things hidden there, with the silver. [23]The men brought them out of the tent, took them to Joshua and all the Israelites, and spread them out on the ground before the LORD. [24]Then Joshua and all the people led Achan son of Zerah to the Valley of Trouble. They also took the silver, the coat, the gold, Achan's sons, daughters, cattle, donkeys, sheep, tent, and everything he owned. [25]Joshua said, "I don't know why you caused so much trouble for us, but now the LORD will bring trouble to you." Then all the people threw stones at Achan and his family until they died. Then the people burned them. [26]They piled rocks over Achan's body, and they are still there today. That is why it is called the Valley of Trouble. After this the LORD was no longer angry.

Ai Is Destroyed

8 Then the LORD said to Joshua, "Don't be afraid or give up. Lead all your fighting men to Ai. I will help you defeat the king of Ai, his people, his city, and his land. [2]You will do to Ai and its king what you did to Jericho and its king. Only this time you may take all the wealth and keep it for yourselves. Now tell some of your soldiers to set up an ambush behind the city."

[3]So Joshua led his whole army toward Ai. Then he chose thirty thousand of his best fighting men and sent them out at night. [4]Joshua gave them these orders: "Listen carefully. You must set up an ambush behind the city. Don't go far from it, but continue to watch and be ready. [5]I and the men who are with me will march toward the city, and the men in the city will come out to fight us, just as they did before. Then we will turn and run away from them. [6]They will chase us away from the city, thinking we are running away from them as we did before. When we run away, [7]come out from your ambush and take the city. The LORD your God will give you the power to win. [8]After you take the city, burn it. See to it! You have your orders."

[9]Then Joshua sent them to wait in ambush between Bethel and Ai, to the west of Ai. But Joshua stayed the night with his people.

[10]Early the next morning Joshua gathered his men together. He and the older leaders of Israel led them up to Ai. [11]All of the soldiers who were with Joshua marched up to Ai and stopped in front of the city and made camp north of it. There was a valley between them and the city. [12]Then Joshua chose about five thousand men and set them in ambush in the area west of the city between Bethel and Ai. [13]So the people took their positions; the main camp was north of the city,

and the other men were hiding to the west. That night Joshua went down into the valley.

14Now when the king of Ai saw the army of Israel, he and his people got up early the next morning and hurried out to fight them. They went out to a place east of the city, but the king did not know soldiers were waiting in ambush behind the city. 15Joshua and all the men of Israel let the army of Ai push them back. Then they ran toward the desert. 16The men in Ai were called to chase Joshua and his men, so they left the city and went after them. 17All the men of Ai and Bethel chased the army of Israel. The city was left open; not a man stayed to protect it.

18Then the LORD said to Joshua, "Hold your spear toward Ai, because I will give you that city." So Joshua held his spear toward the city of Ai. 19When the Israelites who were in ambush saw this, they quickly came out of their hiding place and hurried toward the city. They entered the city, took control of it, and quickly set it on fire.

20When the men of Ai looked back, they saw smoke rising from their city. At the same time the Israelites stopped running and turned against the men of Ai, who could not escape in any direction. 21When Joshua and all his men saw that the army had taken control of the city and saw the smoke rising from it, they stopped running and turned to fight the men of Ai. 22The men who were in ambush also came out of the city to help with the fight. So the men of Ai were caught between the armies of Israel. None of the enemy escaped. The Israelites fought until not one of the men of Ai was left alive, except 23the king of Ai, and they brought him to Joshua.

A Review of the Fighting

24During the fighting the army of Israel chased the men of Ai into the fields and desert and killed all of them. Then they went back to Ai and killed everyone there. 25All the people of Ai died that day, twelve thousand men and women. 26Joshua had held his spear toward Ai, as a sign to destroy the city, and did not draw it back until all the people of Ai were destroyed. 27The people of Israel kept for themselves the animals and the other things the people of Ai had owned, as the LORD had commanded Joshua to do.

28Then Joshua burned the city of Ai and made it a pile of ruins. And it is still like that today. 29Joshua hanged the king of Ai on a tree and left him there until evening. At sunset Joshua told his men to take the king's body down from the tree and to throw it down at the city gate. Then they covered it with a pile of rocks, which is still there today.

30Joshua built an altar for the LORD, the God of Israel, on Mount Ebal, as 31Moses, the LORD's servant, had commanded. Joshua built the altar as it was explained in the Book of the Teachings of Moses. It was made from uncut stones; no tool was ever used on them. On that altar the Israelites offered burnt offerings to the LORD and fellowship offerings. 32There Joshua wrote the teachings of Moses on stones for all the people of Israel to see. 33The older leaders, officers, judges, and all the Israelites were there; Israelites and non-Israelites were all standing around the Ark[d] of the Agreement with the LORD in front of the priests, the Levites who had carried the Ark. Half of the people stood in front of Mount Ebal, and half stood in front of Mount Gerizim. This was the way the LORD's servant Moses had earlier commanded the people to be blessed.

34Then Joshua read all the words of the teachings, the blessings and the curses, exactly as they were written in the Book of the Teachings. 35All the Israelites were gathered together—men, women, and children—along with the non-Israelites who lived among them. Joshua read every command that Moses had given.

The Gibeonite Trickery

9 All the kings west of the Jordan River heard about these things: the kings of the Hittites, Amorites, Canaanites, Perizzites, Hivites, and Jebusites. They lived in the mountains and on the western hills and along the whole Mediterranean Sea coast. 2So all these kings gathered to fight Joshua and the Israelites.

3When the people of Gibeon heard how Joshua had defeated Jericho and Ai, 4they decided to trick the Israelites. They gathered old sacks and old leather wine bags that were cracked and mended, and they put them on the backs of their donkeys. 5They put old sandals on their feet and wore old clothes, and they took some dry, moldy bread. 6Then they went to Joshua in the camp near Gilgal.

The men said to Joshua and the Israelites, "We have traveled from a faraway country. Make a peace agreement with us."

7The Israelites said to these Hivites, "Maybe you live near us. How can we make a peace agreement with you?"

8The Hivites said to Joshua, "We are your servants."

But Joshua asked, "Who are you? Where do you come from?"

9The men answered, "We are your servants who have come from a far country, because we heard of the fame of the LORD your God. We heard about what he has done and everything he did in Egypt. 10We heard that he defeated the two kings of the Amorites from the east side of the Jordan River—Sihon king of Heshbon and Og king of Bashan who ruled in Ashtaroth. 11So our older leaders and our people said to us, 'Take food for your journey and go and meet the Israelites. Tell them, "We are your servants. Make a peace agreement with us." '

12"Look at our bread. On the day we left home to come to you it was warm and fresh, but now it is dry and moldy. 13Look at our leather wine bags. They were new and filled with wine, but now they are cracked and old. Our clothes and sandals are worn out from the long journey."

14The men of Israel tasted the bread, but they did not ask the Lord what to do. 15So Joshua agreed to make peace with the Gibeonites and to let them live. And the leaders of the Israelites swore an oath to keep the agreement.

16Three days after they had made the agreement, the Israelites learned that the Gibeonites lived nearby. 17So the Israelites went to where they lived and on the third day came to their cities: Gibeon, Kephirah, Beeroth, and Kiriath Jearim. 18But the Israelites did not attack those cities, because they had made a promise to them before the Lord, the God of Israel.

All the Israelites grumbled against the leaders. 19But the leaders answered, "We have given our promise before the Lord, the God of Israel, so we cannot attack them now. 20This is what we must do. We must let them live. Otherwise, God's anger will be against us for breaking the oath we swore to them. 21So let them live, but they will cut wood and carry water for our people." So the leaders kept their promise to them.

22Joshua called for the Gibeonites and asked, "Why did you lie to us? Your land was near our camp, but you told us you were from a far country. 23Now, you will be placed under a curse to be our slaves. You will have to cut wood and carry water for the house of my God."

24The Gibeonites answered Joshua, "We lied to you because we were afraid you would kill us. We heard that the Lord your God commanded his servant Moses to give you all of this land and to kill all the people who lived in it. That is why we did this. 25Now you can decide what to do with us, whatever you think is right."

26So Joshua saved their lives by not allowing the Israelites to kill them, 27but he made the Gibeonites slaves. They cut wood and carried water for the Israelites, and they did it for the altar of the Lord — wherever he chose it to be. They are still doing this today.

The Sun Stands Still

10 At this time Adoni-Zedek king of Jerusalem heard that Joshua had defeated Ai and completely destroyed it, as he had also done to Jericho and its king. The king also learned that the Gibeonites had made a peace agreement with Israel and that they lived nearby. 2Adoni-Zedek and his people were very afraid because of this.

Gibeon was not a little town like Ai; it was a large city, as big as a city that had a king, and all its men were good fighters. 3So Adoni-Zedek king of Jerusalem sent a message to Hoham king of Hebron, Piram king of Jarmuth, Japhia king of Lachish, and Debir king of Eglon. He begged them, 4"Come with me and help me attack Gibeon, which has made a peace agreement with Joshua and the Israelites."

5Then these five Amorite kings — the kings of Jerusalem, Hebron, Jarmuth, Lachish, and Eglon — gathered their armies, went to Gibeon, surrounded it, and attacked it.

6The Gibeonites sent this message to Joshua in his camp at Gilgal: "Don't let us, your servants, be destroyed. Come quickly and help us! Save us! All the Amorite kings from the mountains have joined their armies and are fighting against us."

7So Joshua marched out of Gilgal with his whole army, including his best fighting men. 8The Lord said to Joshua, "Don't be afraid of those armies, because I will hand them over to you. None of them will be able to stand against you."

9Joshua and his army marched all night from Gilgal for a surprise attack. 10The Lord confused those armies when Israel attacked, so Israel defeated them in a great victory at Gibeon. They chased them along the road going up to Beth Horon and killed men all the way to Azekah and Makkedah. 11As they chased the enemy down the Beth Horon Pass to Azekah, the Lord threw large hailstones on them from the sky and killed them. More people were killed by the hailstones than by the Israelites' swords.

12On the day that the Lord gave up the Amorites to the Israelites, Joshua stood before all the people of Israel and said to the Lord:

"Sun, stand still over Gibeon.
  Moon, stand still over the Valley of
    Aijalon."

13So the sun stood still,
  and the moon stopped
    until the people defeated their enemies.

These words are written in the Book of Jashar. The sun stopped in the middle of the sky and waited to go down for a full day. 14That has never happened at any time before that day or since. That was the day the Lord listened to a human being. Truly the Lord was fighting for Israel!

15After this, Joshua and his army went back to the camp at Gilgal.

16During the fight the five kings ran away and hid in a cave near Makkedah, 17but someone found them hiding in the cave at Makkedah and told Joshua. 18So he said, "Cover the opening of the cave with large rocks. Put some men there to guard it, 19but don't stay there yourselves. Continue chasing the enemy and attacking them from behind. Don't let them get to their cities, because the LORD your God will hand them over to you."

20So Joshua and the Israelites killed the enemy, but a few were able to get back to their strong, walled cities. 21After the fighting, Joshua's men came back safely to him at Makkedah. No one was brave enough to say a word against the Israelites.

22Joshua said, "Move the rocks that are covering the opening of the cave and bring those five kings out to me." 23So Joshua's men brought the five kings out of the cave—the kings of Jerusalem, Hebron, Jarmuth, Lachish, and Eglon. 24When they brought the five kings out to him, he called for all his men. He said to the commanders of his army, "Come here! Put your feet on the necks of these kings." So they came close and put their feet on their necks.

25Joshua said to his men, "Be strong and brave! Don't be afraid, because I will show you what the LORD will do to the enemies you will fight in the future." 26Then Joshua killed the five kings and hung their bodies on five trees, where he left them until evening.

27At sunset Joshua told his men to take the bodies down from the trees. Then they threw them into the same cave where they had been hiding and covered the opening of the cave with large rocks, which are still there today.

28That day Joshua defeated Makkedah. He killed the king and completely destroyed all the people in that city as an offering to the LORD; no one was left alive. He did the same thing to the king of Makkedah that he had done to the king of Jericho.

Defeating Southern Cities

29Joshua and all the Israelites traveled from Makkedah to Libnah and attacked it. 30The LORD handed over the city and its king. They killed every person in the city; no one was left alive. And they did the same thing to that king that they had done to the king of Jericho.

31Then Joshua and all the Israelites left Libnah and went to Lachish, which they surrounded and attacked. 32The LORD handed over Lachish on the second day. The Israelites killed everyone in that city just as they had done to Libnah. 33During this same time Horam king of Gezer came to help Lachish, but Joshua also defeated him and his army; no one was left alive.

GOD'S POWER

In Just Fifteen Seconds

At 5:04 P.M. on October 17, 1989, the San Francisco area shook like Jell-O under the force of a major earthquake. The quake lasted just fifteen seconds, but it left massive devastation.
- 67 people were killed.
- 3,757 people were injured.
- 1,018 houses were destroyed.
- 366 businesses were destroyed.
- 1.4 million customers lost electricity.
- $6 billion in property damage was caused.
- 64,159 people sought shelter from the Red Cross.

If the earth stores up that much power for destruction, imagine God's power to do good in the world he created. Read **Joshua 10:5–14** to see how God used that power to give victory to Joshua and the Israelites.
- What similarities do you see between God's power in the passage and the effects of the earthquake? What is different about the two displays of power?
- Have you experienced God's power when you've been surrounded by enemies? How can you begin to trust God's power in a new way?

CONSIDER . . .
- throwing a quick celebration party when God's power gives you victory over problems you face. (Hint: The sun doesn't have to stop in the sky for God to be at work!)
- praying that God's power will be with you next time you feel you're being attacked by enemies.

FOR MORE, SEE . . .
- Exodus 14:19–31 (p. 71)
- 1 Kings 18:20–39 (p. 324)
- 1 Corinthians 1:18–31 (p. 1168)

34Then Joshua and all the Israelites went from Lachish to Eglon. They surrounded Eglon, attacked it, and 35captured it the same day. They killed all its people and completely destroyed everything in it as an offering to the LORD, just as they had done to Lachish.

36Then Joshua and the Israelites went from Eglon to Hebron and attacked it, 37capturing it and all the little towns near it. The Israelites killed everyone in Hebron; no one was left alive there. Just as they had done to Eglon, they completely destroyed the city and all its people as an offering to the LORD.

38Then Joshua and the Israelites went back to Debir and attacked it. 39They captured that city, its king, and all the little towns near it, completely destroying everyone in Debir as an offering to the LORD; no one was left alive there. Israel did to Debir and its king just as they had done to Libnah and its king, just as they had done to Hebron.

40So Joshua defeated all the kings of the cities of these areas: the mountains, southern Canaan, the western hills, and the slopes. The LORD, the God of Israel, had told Joshua to completely destroy all the people as an offering to the LORD, so he left no one alive in those places. 41Joshua captured all the cities from Kadesh Barnea to Gaza, and from Goshen to Gibeon. 42He captured all these cities and their kings on one trip, because the LORD, the God of Israel, was fighting for Israel.

43Then Joshua and all the Israelites returned to their camp at Gilgal.

Defeating Northern Kings

11 When Jabin king of Hazor heard about all that had happened, he sent messages to Jobab king of Madon, to the king of Shimron, and to the king of Acshaph. 2He sent messages to the kings in the northern mountains and also to the kings in the Jordan Valley south of Lake Galilee and in the western hills. He sent a message to the king of Naphoth Dor in the west 3and to the kings of the Canaanites in the east and in the west. He sent messages to the Amorites, Hittites, Perizzites, and Jebusites in the mountains. Jabin also sent one to the Hivites, who lived below Mount Hermon in the area of Mizpah. 4So the armies of all these kings came together with their horses and chariots. There were as many soldiers as grains of sand on the seashore.

5All of these kings met together at the waters *of Merom, joined their armies together into one* camp, and made plans to fight against the Israelites.

6Then the LORD said to Joshua, "Don't be afraid of them, because at this time tomorrow I will give them to you. You will cripple their horses and burn all their chariots."

7So Joshua and his whole army surprised the enemy by attacking them at the waters of Merom. 8The LORD handed them over to Israel. They chased them to Greater Sidon, Misrephoth Maim, and the Valley of Mizpah in the east. Israel fought until none of the enemy was left alive. 9Joshua did what the LORD said to do; he crippled their horses and burned their chariots.

10Then Joshua went back and captured the city of Hazor and killed its king. (Hazor had been the leader of all the kingdoms that fought against

> ☀ **SIDELIGHT:** Joshua's victory over Hazor was remarkable, considering that the city was huge for its day (Joshua 11:10). It had forty thousand residents, and its walls were about fifty feet high—about four to five stories. But despite the city's power, it was never rebuilt after Israel destroyed it.

Israel.) 11Israel killed everyone in Hazor, completely destroying them; no one was left alive. Then they burned Hazor itself.

12Joshua captured all of these cities, killed all of their kings, and completely destroyed everything in these cities. He did this just as Moses, the servant of the LORD, had commanded. 13But the Israelites did not burn any cities that were built on their mounds, except Hazor; only that city was

> ☀ **SIDELIGHT:** It's probably a good idea to clean your room from time to time. When war destroyed an ancient city, the people never cleaned away the rubble. They simply built on top of it. Before long, the cities looked like they were built on hills (Joshua 11:13). As many as five thousand of these hills (which archaeologists call "tells") exist today.

burned by Joshua. 14The people of Israel kept for themselves everything they found in the cities, including all the animals. But they killed all the people there; they left no one alive. 15Long ago the LORD had commanded his servant Moses to do this, and then Moses had commanded Joshua to *do it. Joshua did everything the LORD had commanded Moses.*

16So Joshua defeated all the people in the land. He had control of the mountains and the area of southern Canaan, all the areas of Goshen, the western hills, and the Jordan Valley. He controlled the mountains of Israel and all the hills near them. [17]Joshua controlled all the land from Mount Halak near Edom to Baal Gad in the Valley of Lebanon, below Mount Hermon. Joshua also captured all the kings in the land and killed them. [18]He fought against them for many years. [19]The people of only one city in all the land had made a peace agreement with Israel — the Hivites living in Gibeon. All the other cities were defeated in war. [20]The LORD made those people stubborn so they would fight against Israel and he could completely destroy them without mercy. This is what the LORD had commanded Moses to do.

[21]Now Joshua fought the Anakites[d] who lived in the mountains of Hebron, Debir, Anab, Judah, and Israel, and he completely destroyed them and their towns. [22]There were no Anakites left living in the land of the Israelites and only a few were left in Gaza, Gath, and Ashdod. [23]Joshua took control of all the land of Israel as the LORD had told Moses to do long ago. He gave the land to Israel, because he had promised it to them. Then Joshua divided the land among the tribes[d] of Israel, and there was peace in the land.

Kings Defeated by Israel

12 The Israelites took control of the land east of the Jordan River from the Arnon Ravine to Mount Hermon and all the land along the eastern side of the Jordan Valley. These lands belonged to the kings whom the Israelites defeated.

[2]Sihon king of the Amorites lived in the city of Heshbon and ruled the land from Aroer at the Arnon Ravine to the Jabbok River. His land started in the middle of the ravine, which was their border with the Ammonites. Sihon ruled over half the land of Gilead [3]and over the eastern side of the Jordan Valley from Lake Galilee to the Dead Sea.[d] And he ruled from Beth Jeshimoth south to the slopes of Pisgah.

[4]Og king of Bashan was one of the last of the Rephaites.[d] He ruled the land in Ashtaroth and Edrei. [5]He ruled over Mount Hermon, Salecah, and all the area of Bashan up to where the people of Geshur and Maacah lived. Og also ruled half the land of Gilead up to the border of Sihon king of Heshbon.

[6]The LORD's servant Moses and the Israelites defeated all these kings, and Moses gave that land to the tribes[d] of Reuben and Gad and to East Manasseh as their own.

[7]Joshua and the Israelites also defeated kings in the land west of the Jordan River. He gave the people the land and divided it among the twelve tribes to be their own. It was between Baal Gad in the Valley of Lebanon and Mount Halak near Edom. [8]This included the mountains, the western hills, the Jordan Valley, the slopes, the desert, and southern Canaan. This was the land where the

Hittites, Amorites, Canaanites, Perizzites, Hivites, and Jebusites had lived. The Israelites defeated the king of each of the following cities: [9]Jericho, Ai (near Bethel), [10]Jerusalem, Hebron, [11]Jarmuth, Lachish. [12]Eglon, Gezer, [13]Debir, Geder, [14]Hormah, Arad, [15]Libnah, Adullam, [16]Makkedah, Bethel, [17]Tappuah, Hepher, [18]Aphek, Lasharon, [19]Madon, Hazor, [20]Shimron Meron, Acshaph, [21]Taanach, Megiddo, [22]Kedesh, Jokneam in Carmel, [23]Dor (in Naphoth Dor), Goyim in Gilgal, and [24]Tirzah.

The total number of kings was thirty-one.

Land Still to Be Taken

13 When Joshua was very old, the LORD said to him, "Joshua, you have grown old, but there is still much land for you to take. [2]This is what is left: the regions of Geshur and of the Philistines; [3]the area from the Shihor River at the border of Egypt to Ekron in the north, which belongs to the Canaanites; the five Philistine leaders at Gaza, Ashdod, Ashkelon, Gath, and Ekron; the Avvites, [4]who live south of the Canaanite land; [5]the Gebalites, and the area of Lebanon east of Baal Gad below Mount Hermon to Lebo Hamath.

[6]"The Sidonians are living in the hill country from Lebanon to Misrephoth Maim, but I will force all of them out ahead of the Israelites. Be sure to remember this land when you divide the land among the Israelites, as I told you. [7]"Now divide the land among the nine tribes[d] and West Manasseh."

Dividing the Land

[8]East Manasseh and the tribes of Reuben and Gad had received their land. The LORD's servant Moses had given them the land east of the Jordan River. [9]Their land started at Aroer at the Arnon Ravine and continued to the town in the middle of the ravine, and it included the whole plain from Medeba to Dibon. [10]All the towns ruled by Sihon king of the Amorites, who ruled in the city of Heshbon, were in that land. The land continued to the area where the Ammonites lived. [11]Gilead was also there, as well as the area where the people of Geshur and Maacah lived, and all of Mount Hermon and Bashan as far as Salecah. [12]All the kingdom of Og king of Bashan was in the land. Og was one of the last of the Rephaites, and in the past he ruled in Ashtaroth and Edrei. Moses had defeated them and had taken their land. [13]Because the Israelites did not force out the people of Geshur and Maacah, they still live among the Israelites today.

[14]The tribe of Levi was the only one that did not get any land. Instead, they were given all the burned sacrifices made to the LORD, the God of Israel, as he had promised them.

15Moses had given each family group from the tribe of Reuben some land: 16Theirs was the land from Aroer near the Arnon Ravine to the town of Medeba, including the whole plain and the town in the middle of the ravine; 17Heshbon and all the towns on the plain: Dibon, Bamoth Baal, and Beth Baal Meon, 18Jahaz, Kedemoth, Mephaath, 19Kiriathaim, Sibmah, Zereth Shahar on the hill in the valley, 20Beth Peor, the hills of Pisgah, and Beth Jeshimoth. 21So that land included all the towns on the plain and all the area that Sihon king of the Amorites had ruled from the town of Heshbon. Moses had defeated him along with the leaders of the Midianites, including Evi, Rekem, Zur, Hur, and Reba. All these leaders fought together with Sihon and lived in that country. 22The Israelites killed many people during the fighting, including Balaam of Beor, who tried to use magic to tell the future. 23The land given to Reuben stopped at the shore of the Jordan River. So the land given to the family groups of Reuben included all these towns and their villages that were listed.

24This is the land Moses gave to the tribe of Gad, to all its family groups: 25the land of Jazar and all the towns of Gilead; half the land of the Ammonites that went as far as Aroer near Rabbah; 26the area from Heshbon to Ramath Mizpah and Betonim; the area from Mahanaim to the land of Debir; 27in the valley, Beth Haram, Beth Nimrah, Succoth, and Zaphon, the other land Sihon king of Heshbon had ruled east of the Jordan River and continuing to the end of Lake Galilee. 28All this land went to the family groups of Gad, including all these towns and their villages.

29This is the land Moses had given to East Manasseh. Half of all the family groups in the tribe of Manasseh were given this land: 30The land started at Mahanaim and included all of Bashan and the land ruled by Og king of Bashan; all the towns of Jair in Bashan, sixty cities in all; 31half of Gilead, Ashtaroth, and Edrei, the cities where Og king of Bashan had ruled. All this went to the family of Makir son of Manasseh, and half of all his sons were given this land.

32Moses had given this land to these tribes on the plains of Moab across the Jordan River east of Jericho. 33But Moses had given no land to the tribe of Levi because the LORD, the God of Israel, promised that he himself would be the gift for the Levites.

14 Eleazar the priest, Joshua son of Nun, and the leaders of all the tribes of Israel decided what land to give to the people in the land of Canaan. 2The LORD had commanded Moses long ago how he wanted the people to choose their land. The people of the nine-and-a-half tribes threw lotsd to decide which land they would re-

ceive. 3Moses had already given the two-and-a-half tribes their land east of the Jordan River. But the tribe of Levi was not given any land like the others. 4The sons of Joseph had divided into two tribes — Manasseh and Ephraim. The tribe of Levi was not given any land. It was given only some towns in which to live and pastures for its animals. 5The LORD had told Moses how to give the land to the tribes of Israel, and the Israelites divided the land.

Caleb's Land

6One day some men from the tribed of Judah went to Joshua at Gilgal. Among them was Caleb son of Jephunneh the Kenizzite. He said to Joshua, "You remember what the LORD said at Kadesh Barnea when he was speaking to the prophet Moses about you and me. 7Moses, the LORD's servant, sent me to look at the land where we were going. I was forty years old then. When I came back, I told Moses what I thought about the land. 8The other men who went with me frightened the people, but I fully believed the LORD would allow us to take the land. 9So that day Moses promised me, 'The land where you went will become your land, and your children will own it forever. I will give you that land because you fully believed in the LORD, my God.'

10"Now then, the LORD has kept his promise. He has kept me alive for forty-five years from the time he said this to Moses during the time we all wandered in the desert. Now here I am, eighty-five years old. 11I am still as strong today as I was the day Moses sent me out, and I am just as ready to fight now as I was then. 12So give me the mountain country the LORD promised me that day long ago. Back then you heard that the Anakited people lived there and the cities were large and well protected. But now with the LORD helping me, I will force them out, just as the LORD said."

13Joshua blessed Caleb son of Jephunneh and gave him the city of Hebron as his own. 14Hebron still belongs to the family of Caleb son of Jephunneh the Kenizzite because he had faith and obeyed the LORD, the God of Israel. 15(In the past it was called Kiriath Arba, named for Arba, the greatest man among the Anakites.)

After this there was peace in the land.

Land for Judah

15 The land that was given to the tribed of Judah was divided among all the family groups. It went all the way to the Desert of Zin in the far south, at the border of Edom.

2The southern border of Judah's land started at the south end of the Dead Sead 3and went south of Scorpion Pass to Zin. From there it passed to the south of Kadesh Barnea and continued past Hezron to Addar. From Addar it turned and went to Karka. ⁴It continued to Azmon, the brook of Egypt, and then to the Mediterranean Sea. This was the southern border.

⁵The eastern border was the shore of the Dead Sea, as far as the mouth of the Jordan River.

The northern border started at the bay of the sea at the mouth of the Jordan River. ⁶Then it went to Beth Hoglah and continued north of Beth Arabah to the stone of Bohan son of Reuben. ⁷Then the northern border went through the Valley of Achor to Debir where it turned toward the north and went to Gilgal. Gilgal is across from the road that goes through Adummim Pass, on the south side of the ravine. The border continued to the waters of En Shemesh and stopped at En Rogel. ⁸Then it went through the Valley of Ben Hinnom, next to the southern side of the Jebusite city (which is called Jerusalem). There the border went to the top of the hill on the west side of Hinnom Valley, at the northern end of the Valley of Giants. ⁹From there it went to the spring of the waters of Nephtoah and then it went to the cities near Mount Ephron. There it turned and went toward Baalah, which is called Kiriath Jearim. ¹⁰At Baalah the border turned west and went toward Mount Seir. It continued along the north side of Mount Jearim (also called Kesalon) and came to Beth Shemesh. From there it went past Timnah ¹¹to the hill north of Ekron. Then it turned toward Shikkeron and went past Mount Baalah and continued on to Jabneel, ending at the sea.

¹²The Mediterranean Sea was the western border. Inside these borders lived the family groups of Judah.

¹³The Lᴏʀᴅ had commanded Joshua to give Caleb son of Jephunneh part of the land in Judah, so he gave Caleb the town of Kiriath Arba, also called Hebron. (Arba was the father of Anak.ᵈ) ¹⁴Caleb forced out the three Anakite families living in Hebron: Sheshai, Ahiman, and Talmai, the descendantsᵈ of Anak. ¹⁵Then he left there and went to fight against the people living in Debir. (In the past Debir had been called Kiriath Sepher.) ¹⁶Caleb said, "I will give Acsah, my daughter, as a wife to the man who attacks and captures the city of Kiriath Sepher." ¹⁷Othniel son of Kenaz, Caleb's brother, captured the city, so Caleb gave his daughter Acsah to Othniel to be his wife. ¹⁸When Acsah came to Othniel, she told him to ask her father for a field.

So Acsah went to her father. When she got down from her donkey, Caleb asked her, "What do you want?"

¹⁹Acsah answered, "Do me a special favor. Since you have given me land in southern Canaan, also give me springs of water." So Caleb gave her the upper and lower springs.

²⁰The tribe of Judah got the land God had promised them. Each family group got part of the land.

²¹The tribe of Judah got all these towns in the southern part of Canaan near the border of Edom: Kabzeel, Eder, Jagur, ²²Kinah, Dimonah, Adadah, ²³Kedesh, Hazor, Ithnan, ²⁴Ziph, Telem, Bealoth, ²⁵Hazor Hadattah, Kerioth Hezron (also called Hazor), ²⁶Amam, Shema, Moladah, ²⁷Hazar Gaddah, Heshmon, Beth Pelet, ²⁸Hazar Shual, Beersheba, Biziothiah, ²⁹Baalah, Iim, Ezem, ³⁰Eltolad, Kesil, Hormah, ³¹Ziklag, Madmannah, Sansannah, ³²Lebaoth, Shilhim, Ain, and Rimmon. There were twenty-nine towns and their villages.

³³The tribe of Judah got these towns in the western hills: Eshtaol, Zorah, Ashnah, ³⁴Zanoah, En Gannim, Tappuah, Enam, ³⁵Jarmuth, Adullam, Socoh, Azekah, ³⁶Shaaraim, Adithaim, and Gederah (also called Gederothaim). There were fourteen towns and their villages.

³⁷Judah was also given these towns in the western hills: Zenan, Hadashah, Migdal Gad, ³⁸Dilean, Mizpah, Joktheel, ³⁹Lachish, Bozkath, Eglon, ⁴⁰Cabbon, Lahmas, Kitlish, ⁴¹Gederoth, Beth Dagon, Naamah, and Makkedah. There were sixteen towns and their villages.

⁴²Judah was also given these towns in the western hills: Libnah, Ether, Ashan, ⁴³Iphtah, Ashnah, Nezib, ⁴⁴Keilah, Aczib, and Mareshah. There were nine towns and their villages.

⁴⁵The tribe of Judah was also given these towns: Ekron and all the small towns and villages near it; ⁴⁶the area west of Ekron and all the villages and small towns near Ashdod; ⁴⁷Ashdod and the small towns and villages around it; the villages and small towns around Gaza as far as the brook of Egypt and along the coast of the Mediterranean Sea.

⁴⁸The tribe of Judah was also given these towns in the mountains: Shamir, Jattir, Socoh, ⁴⁹Dannah, Kiriath Sannah (also called Debir), ⁵⁰Anab, Eshtemoh, Anim, ⁵¹Goshen, Holon, and Giloh. There were eleven towns and their villages.

⁵²They were also given these towns in the mountains: Arab, Dumah, Eshan, ⁵³Janim, Beth Tappuah, Aphekah, ⁵⁴Humtah, Kiriath Arba (also called Hebron), and Zior. There were nine towns and their villages.

⁵⁵Judah was also given these towns in the mountains: Maon, Carmel, Ziph, Juttah, ⁵⁶Jezreel, Jokdeam, Zanoah, ⁵⁷Kain, Gibeah, and Timnah. There were ten towns and their villages.

⁵⁸They were also given these towns in the mountains: Halhul, Beth Zur, Gedor, ⁵⁹Maarath, Beth Anoth, and Eltekon. There were six towns and their villages.

⁶⁰The people of Judah were also given the two towns of Rabbah and Kiriath Baal (also called Kiriath Jearim) and their villages.

⁶¹Judah was given these towns in the desert:

Beth Arabah, Middin, Secacah, 62Nibshan, the City of Salt, and En Gedi. There were six towns and all their villages.

63The army of Judah was not able to force out the Jebusites living in Jerusalem, so the Jebusites still live among the people of Judah to this day.

Land for Ephraim and Manasseh

16 This is the land the tribe*d* of Joseph received. It started at the Jordan River near Jericho and continued to the waters of Jericho, just east of the city. The border went up from Jericho to the mountains of Bethel. 2Then it continued from Bethel (also called Luz) to the Arkite border at Ataroth. 3From there it went west to the border of the Japhletites and continued to the area of the Lower Beth Horon. Then it went to Gezer and ended at the sea.

4So Manasseh and Ephraim, sons of Joseph, received their land.

5This is the land that was given to the family groups of Ephraim: Their border started at Ataroth Addar in the east, went to Upper Beth Horon, 6and then to the sea. From Micmethath it turned eastward toward Taanath Shiloh and continued eastward to Janoah. 7Then it went down from Janoah to Ataroth and to Naarah. It continued until it touched Jericho and stopped at the Jordan River. 8The border went from Tappuah west to Kanah Ravine and ended at the sea. This is all the land that was given to each family group in the tribe of the Ephraimites. 9Many of the towns were actually within Manasseh's borders, but the people of Ephraim got those towns and their villages. 10The Ephraimites could not force the Canaanites to leave Gezer, so the Canaanites still live among the Ephraimites today, but they became slaves of the Ephraimites.

17 Then land was given to the tribe of Manasseh, Joseph's first son. Manasseh's first son was Makir, the father of Gilead. Makir was a great soldier, so the lands of Gilead and Bashan were given to his family. 2Land was also given to the other family groups of Manasseh — Abiezer, Helek, Asriel, Shechem, Hepher, and Shemida. These were all the other sons of Manasseh son of Joseph.

3Zelophehad was the son of Hepher, who was the son of Gilead, who was the son of Makir, who was the son of Manasseh. Zelophehad had no sons, but he had five daughters, named Mahlah, Noah, Hoglah, Milcah, and Tirzah. 4They went to *Eleazar the priest and to Joshua son of Nun and* all the leaders. They said, "The LORD told Moses to give us land like the men received." So Eleazar obeyed the LORD and gave the daughters some land, just like the brothers of their father. 5So the tribe of Manasseh had ten sections of land west of the Jordan River and two more sections, Gilead

and Bashan, on the east side of the Jordan River. 6The daughters of Manasseh received land just as the sons did. Gilead was given to the rest of the families of Manasseh.

7The lands of Manasseh were in the area between Asher and Micmethath, near Shechem. The border went south to the En Tappuah area, 8which belonged to Manasseh, except for the town of Tappuah. It was along the border of Manasseh's land and belonged to the sons of Ephraim. 9The border of Manasseh continued south to Kanah Ravine. The cities in this area of Manasseh belonged to Ephraim. Manasseh's border was on the north side of the ravine and went to the sea. 10The land to the south belonged to Ephraim, and the land to the north belonged to Manasseh. The Mediterranean Sea was the western border. The border touched Asher's land on the north and Issachar's land on the east.

11In the areas of Issachar and Asher, the people of Manasseh owned these towns: Beth Shan and its small towns; Ibleam and its small towns; the people who lived in Dor and its small towns; the people in Naphoth Dor and its small towns; the people who lived in Taanach and its small towns; the people in Megiddo and its small towns. 12Manasseh was not able to defeat those cities, so the Canaanites continued to live there. 13When the Israelites grew strong, they forced the Canaanites to work for them, although they did not force them to leave the land.

✲ **SIDELIGHT:** When we think of nations, we think of united territory. But when the Israelites conquered Canaan, they really only conquered parts of it at first. So they divided the land among the twelve tribes before they really controlled it (Joshua 17:11–13). Later, individual tribes would conquer cities to unite their areas.

14The people from the tribes of Joseph said to Joshua, "You gave us only one area of land, but we are many people. Why did you give us only one part of all the land the LORD gave his people?"

15And Joshua answered them, "If you have too many people, go up to the forest and make a place for yourselves to live there in the land of the Perizzites and the Rephaites.*d* The mountain country of Ephraim is too small for you."

16The people of Joseph said, "It is true. The mountain country of Ephraim is not enough for us, but the land where the Canaanites live is dangerous. They are skilled fighters. They have powerful weapons in Beth Shan and all the small towns in that area, and they are also in the Valley of Jezreel."

17Then Joshua said to the people of Joseph — to Ephraim and Manasseh, "There are many of you, and you have great power. You should be given more than one share of land. 18You also will have the mountain country. It is a forest, but you can cut down the trees and make it a good place to live. You will own all of it because you will force the Canaanites to leave the land even though they have powerful weapons and are strong."

The Rest of the Land Divided

18 All of the Israelites gathered together at Shiloh where they set up the Meeting Tent.d The land was now under their control. 2But there were still seven tribesd of Israel that had not yet received their land.

3So Joshua said to the Israelites: "Why do you wait so long to take your land? The LORD, the God of your ancestors, has given this land to you. 4Choose three men from each tribe, and I will send them out to study the land. They will describe in writing the land their tribe wants as its share, and then they will come back to me. 5They will divide the land into seven parts. The people of Judah will keep their land in the south, and the people of Joseph will keep their land in the north. 6You should describe the seven parts of land in writing and bring what you have written to me. Then I will throw lots in the presence of the LORD our God. 7But the Levites do not get any part of these lands, because they are priests, and their work is to serve the LORD. Gad, Reuben, and East Manasseh have received the land promised to them, which is east of the Jordan River. Moses, the servant of the LORD, gave it to them."

8So the men who were chosen to map the land started out. Joshua told them, "Go and study the land and describe it in writing. Then come back to me, and I will throw lots in the presence of the LORD here in Shiloh." 9So the men left and went into the land. They described in a scroll each town in the seven parts of the land. Then they came back to Joshua, who was still at the camp at Shiloh. 10There Joshua threw lots in the presence of the LORD to choose the lands that should be given to each tribe.

Land for Benjamin

11The first part of the land was given to the tribed of Benjamin. Each family group received some land between the land of Judah and the land of Joseph. This is the land chosen for Benjamin: 12The northern border started at the Jordan River and went along the northern edge of Jericho, and then it went west into the mountains. That boundary continued until it was just east of Beth Aven. 13From there it went south to Luz (also called Bethel) and then down to Ataroth Addar, which is on the hill south of Lower Beth Horon.

14At the hill to the south of Beth Horon, the border turned and went south near the western side of the hill. It went to Kiriath Baal (also called Kiriath Jearim), a town where people of Judah lived. This was the western border.

15The southern border started near Kiriath Jearim and went west to the waters of Nephtoah. 16Then it went down to the bottom of the hill, which was near the Valley of Ben Hinnom, on the north side of the Valley of Rephaim. The border continued down the Hinnom Valley just south of the Jebusite city to En Rogel. 17There it turned north and went to En Shemesh. It continued to Geliloth near the Adummim Pass. Then it went down to the great Stone of Bohan son of Reuben. 18The border continued to the northern part of Beth Arabah and went down into the Jordan Valley. 19From there it went to the northern part of Beth Hoglah and ended at the north shore of the Dead Sea,d where the Jordan River flows into the sea. This was the southern border.

20The Jordan River was the border on the eastern side. So this was the land given to the family groups of Benjamin with the borders on all sides.

21The family groups of Benjamin received these cities: Jericho, Beth Hoglah, Emek Keziz, 22Beth Arabah, Zemaraim, Bethel, 23Avvim, Parah, Ophrah, 24Kephar Ammoni, Ophni, and Geba. There were twelve towns and all their villages.

25The tribe of Benjamin also received Gibeon, Ramah, Beeroth, 26Mizpah, Kephirah, Mozah, 27Rekem Irpeel, Taralah, 28Zelah, Haeleph, the Jebusite city (Jerusalem), Gibeah, and Kiriath. There were fourteen towns and their villages. All these areas are the lands the family groups of Benjamin were given.

Land for Simeon

19 The second part of the land was given to the tribed of Simeon. Each family group received some of the land inside the area of Judah. 2They received Beersheba (also called Sheba), Moladah 3Hazar Shual, Balah, Ezem, 4Eltolad, Bethul, Hormah, 5Ziklag, Beth Marcaboth, Hazar Susah, 6Beth Lebaoth, and Sharuhen. There were thirteen towns and their villages.

7They received the towns of Ain, Rimmon, Ether, and Ashan, four towns and their villages. 8They also received all the very small areas with people living in them as far as Baalath Beer (this is the same as Ramah in southern Canaan). So these were the lands given to the family groups in the tribe of Simeon. 9The land of the Simeonites was taken from part of the land of Judah. Since Judah had much more land than they needed, the Simeonites received part of their land.

Land for Zebulun

¹⁰The third part of the land was given to the tribe*d* of Zebulun. Each family group of Zebulun received some of the land. The border of Zebulun went as far as Sarid. ¹¹Then it went west to Maralah and came near Dabbesheth and then near Jokneam. ¹²Then it turned to the east. It went from Sarid to the area of Kisloth Tabor and on to Daberath and to Japhia. ¹³It continued eastward to Gath Hepher and Eth Kazin, ending at Rimmon. There the border turned and went toward Neah. ¹⁴At Neah it turned again and went to the north to Hannathon and continued to the Valley of Iphtah El. ¹⁵Inside this border were the cities of Kattath, Nahalal, Shimron, Idalah, and Bethlehem. There were twelve towns and their villages.

¹⁶So these are the towns and the villages that were given to the family groups of Zebulun.

Land for Issachar

¹⁷The fourth part of the land was given to the tribe*d* of Issachar. Each family group of Issachar received some of the land. ¹⁸Their land included Jezreel, Kesulloth, Shunem, ¹⁹Hapharaim, Shion, Anaharath, ²⁰Rabbith, Kishion, Ebez, ²¹Remeth, En Gannim, En Haddah, and Beth Pazzez.

²²The border of their land touched the area called Tabor, Shahazumah, and Beth Shemesh and stopped at the Jordan River. There were sixteen towns and their villages.

²³These cities and towns were part of the land that was given to the family groups of Issachar.

Land for Asher

²⁴The fifth part of the land was given to the tribe*d* of Asher. Each family group of Asher received some of the land. ²⁵Their land included Helkath, Hali, Beten, Acshaph, ²⁶Allammelech, Amad, and Mishal.

The western border touched Mount Carmel and Shihor Libnath. ²⁷Then it turned east and went to Beth Dagon, touching Zebulun and the Valley of Iphtah El. Then it went north of Beth Emek and Neiel and passed north to Cabul. ²⁸From there it went to Abdon, Rehob, Hammon, and Kanah and continued to Greater Sidon. ²⁹Then the border went back south toward Ramah and continued to the strong, walled city of Tyre. There it turned and went toward Hosah, ending at the sea. This was in the area of Aczib, ³⁰Ummah, Aphek, and Rehob. There were *twenty-two towns and their villages.*

³¹These cities and their villages were part of the land that was given to the family groups of Asher.

Land for Naphtali

³²The sixth part of the land was given to the tribe*d* of Naphtali. Each family group of Naphtali received some of the land. ³³The border of their land started at the large tree in Zaanannim, which is near Heleph. Then it went through Adami Nekeb and Jabneel, as far as Lakkum, and ended at the Jordan River. ³⁴Then it went to the west through Aznoth Tabor and stopped at Hukkok. It went to the area of Zebulun on the south, Asher on the west, and Judah, at the Jordan River, on the east. ³⁵The strong, walled cities inside these borders were called Ziddim, Zer, Hammath, Rakkath, Kinnereth, ³⁶Adamah, Ramah, Hazor, ³⁷Kedesh, Edrei, En Hazor, ³⁸Iron, Migdal El, Horem, Beth Anath, and Beth Shemesh. There were nineteen towns and all their villages.

³⁹The towns and the villages around them were in the land that was given to the family groups of Naphtali.

Land for Dan

⁴⁰The seventh part of the land was given to the tribe*d* of Dan. Each family group of Dan received some of the land. ⁴¹Their land included Zorah, Eshtaol, Ir Shemesh, ⁴²Shaalabbin, Aijalon, Ithlah, ⁴³Elon, Timnah, Ekron, ⁴⁴Eltekeh, Gibbethon, Baalath, ⁴⁵Jehud, Bene Berak, Gath Rimmon, ⁴⁶Me Jarkon, Rakkon, and the area near Joppa.

⁴⁷(But the Danites had trouble taking their land. They went and fought against Leshem, defeated it, and killed the people who lived there. So the Danites moved into the town of Leshem and changed its name to Dan, because he was the father of their tribe.) ⁴⁸All of these towns and villages were given to the family groups of Dan.

Land for Joshua

⁴⁹After the leaders finished dividing the land and giving it to the different tribes,*d* the Israelites gave Joshua son of Nun his land also. ⁵⁰They gave Joshua the town he asked for, Timnath Serah in the mountains of Ephraim, just as the LORD commanded. He built up the town and lived there.

⁵¹So these lands were given to the different tribes of Israel. Eleazar the priest, Joshua son of Nun, and the leaders of each tribe divided up the land by lots at Shiloh. They met in the presence of the LORD at the entrance to the Meeting Tent.*d* Now they were finished dividing the land.

Cities of Safety

20 Then the LORD said to Joshua: ²"Tell the Israelites to choose the special cities of safety,*d* as I had Moses command you to do. ³If a *person kills someone accidentally and without* meaning to kill him, that person may go to a city of safety to hide. There the killer will be safe from the relative who has the duty of punishing a murderer.

⁴"When the killer runs to one of those cities, he must stop at the entrance gate, stand there, and

tell the leaders of the people what happened. Then that person will be allowed to enter the city and will be given a place to live among them. 5But if the one who is chasing him follows him to that city, the leaders of the city must not hand over the killer. It was an accident. He did not hate him beforehand or kill him on purpose. 6The killer must stay in the city until a court comes to a decision and until the high priest dies. Then he may go back home to the town from which he ran away."

7So the Israelites chose these cities to be cities of safety: Kedesh in Galilee in the mountains of Naphtali; Shechem in the mountains of Ephraim; Kiriath Arba (also called Hebron) in the mountains of Judah; 8Bezer on the east side of the Jordan River near Jericho in the desert in the land of Reuben; Ramoth in Gilead in the land of Gad; and Golan in Bashan in the land of Manasseh. 9Any Israelite or anyone living among them who killed someone accidentally was to be allowed to run to one of these cities of safety. There he would not be killed, before he was judged, by the relative who had the duty of punishing a murderer.

Towns for the Levites

21 The heads of the Levite families went to talk to Eleazar the priest, to Joshua son of Nun, and to the heads of the families of all the tribes*d* of Israel. 2At Shiloh in the land of Canaan, the heads of the Levite families said to them, "The LORD commanded Moses that you give us towns where we may live and pastures for our animals." 3So the Israelites obeyed this command of the LORD and gave the Levite people these towns and pastures for their own land: 4The Kohath family groups were part of the tribe of Levi. Some of the Levites in the Kohath family groups were from the family of Aaron the priest. To these Levites were given thirteen towns in the areas of Judah, Simeon, and Benjamin. 5The other family groups of Kohath were given ten towns in the areas of Ephraim, Dan, and West Manasseh.

6The people from the Gershon family groups were given thirteen towns in the land of Issachar, Asher, Naphtali, and the East Manasseh in Bashan.

7The family groups of Merari were given twelve towns in the areas of Reuben, Gad, and Zebulun.

8So the Israelites gave the Levites these towns and the pastures around them, just as the LORD had commanded Moses.

9These are the names of the towns that came from the lands of Judah and Simeon. 10The first choice of towns was given to the Kohath family groups of the Levites. 11They gave them Kiriath Arba, also called Hebron, and all its pastures in the mountains of Judah. (Arba was the father of

Anak.*d*) 12But the fields and the villages around Kiriath Arba had been given to Caleb son of Jephunneh.

13So they gave the city of Hebron to the descendants*d* of Aaron (Hebron was a city of safety*d*). They also gave them the towns of Libnah, 14Jattir, Eshtemoa, 15Holon, Debir, 16Ain, Juttah, and Beth Shemesh, and all the pastures around them. Nine towns were given from these two tribes.

17They also gave the people of Aaron these cities that belonged to the tribe of Benjamin: Gibeon, Geba, 18Anathoth, and Almon. They gave them these four towns and the pastures around them.

19So these thirteen towns with their pastures were given to the priests, who were from the family of Aaron.

20The other Kohathite family groups of the Levites were given these towns from the tribe of Ephraim: 21Shechem in the mountains of Ephraim (which was a city of safety), Gezer, 22Kibzaim, and Beth Horon. There were four towns and their pastures.

23The tribe of Dan gave them Eltekeh, Gibbethon, 24Aijalon, and Gath Rimmon. There were four towns and their pastures.

25West Manasseh gave them Taanach and Gath Rimmon and the pastures around these two towns.

26So these ten towns and the pastures around them were given to the rest of the Kohathite family groups.

27The Gershonite family groups of the Levite tribe were given these towns: East Manasseh gave them Golan in Bashan, which was a city of safety, and Be Eshtarah, and the pastures around these two towns.

28The tribe of Issachar gave them Kishion, Daberath, 29Jarmuth, and En Gannim, and the pastures around these four towns.

30The tribe of Asher gave them Mishal, Abdon, 31Helkath, and Rehob, and the pastures around these four towns.

32The tribe of Naphtali gave them Kedesh in Galilee (a city of safety), Hammoth Dor, and Kartan, and the pastures around these three towns.

33So the Gershonite family groups received thirteen towns and the pastures around them.

34The Merarite family groups (the rest of the Levites) were given these towns: The tribe of Zebulun gave them Jokneam, Kartah, 35Dimnah, and Nahalal, and the pastures around these four towns.

36The tribe of Reuben gave them Bezer, Jahaz, 37Kedemoth, and Mephaath, along with the pastures around these four towns.

38The tribe of Gad gave them Ramoth in Gilead (a city of safety), Mahanaim, 39Heshbon, and Jazer, and the pastures around these four towns.

40So the total number of towns given to the Merarite family groups was twelve.

41A total of forty-eight towns with their pastures in the land of Israel were given to the Levites. 42Each town had pastures around it.

43So the LORD gave the people all the land he had promised their ancestors. The people took the land and lived there. 44The LORD gave them peace on all sides, as he had promised their ancestors. None of their enemies defeated them; the LORD handed all their enemies over to them. 45He kept every promise he had made to the Israelites; each one came true.

Three Tribes Go Home

22 Then Joshua called a meeting of all the people from the tribes*d* of Reuben, Gad, and East Manasseh. 2He said to them, "You have done everything Moses, the LORD's servant, told you to do. You have also obeyed all my commands. 3For a long time you have supported the other Israelites. You have been careful to obey the commands the LORD your God gave you. 4The LORD your God promised to give the Israelites peace, and he has kept his promise. Now you may go back to your homes, to the land that Moses, the LORD's servant, gave you, on the east side of the Jordan River. 5But be careful to obey the teachings and laws Moses, the LORD's servant, gave you: to love the LORD your God and obey his commands, to continue to follow him and serve him the very best you can."

6Then Joshua said good-bye to them, and they left and went away to their homes. 7Moses had given the land of Bashan to East Manasseh. Joshua gave land on the west side of the Jordan River to West Manasseh. And he sent them to their homes and he blessed them. 8He said, "Go back to your homes and your riches. You have many animals, silver, gold, bronze, and iron, and many beautiful clothes. Also, you have taken many things from your enemies that you should divide among yourselves."

9So the people from the tribes of Reuben, Gad, and East Manasseh left the other Israelites at Shiloh in Canaan and went back to Gilead. It was their own land, given to them by Moses as the LORD had commanded.

10The people of Reuben, Gad, and East Manasseh went to Geliloth, near the Jordan River in the land of Canaan. There they built a beautiful altar. 11The other Israelites still at Shiloh heard about the altar these three tribes built at the border of Canaan at Geliloth, near the Jordan River on Israel's side. 12All the Israelites became very angry at these three tribes, so they met together and decided to fight them.

13The Israelites sent Phinehas son of Eleazar the priest to Gilead to talk to the people of Reuben, Gad, and East Manasseh. 14They also sent one leader from each of the ten tribes at Shiloh. Each of them was a leader of his family group of Israelites.

15These leaders went to Gilead to talk to the people of Reuben, Gad, and East Manasseh. They said: 16"All the Israelites ask you: 'Why did you turn against the God of Israel by building an altar for yourselves? You know that this is against God's law. 17Remember what happened at Peor? We still suffer today because of that sin, for which God made many Israelites very sick. 18And now are you turning against the LORD and refusing to follow him?

" 'If you don't stop what you're doing today, the LORD will be angry with everyone in Israel tomorrow. 19If your land is unclean,*d* come over into our land where the LORD's Tent is. Share it with us. But don't turn against the LORD and us by building another altar for the LORD our God. 20Remember how Achan son of Zerah refused to obey the command about what must be completely destroyed. That one man broke God's law, but all the Israelites were punished. Achan died because of his sin, but others also died.' "

21The people from Reuben, Gad, and East Manasseh answered, 22"The LORD is God of gods! The LORD is God of gods! God knows, and we want you to know also. If we have done something wrong, you may kill us. 23If we broke God's law, we ask the LORD himself to punish us. We did not build this altar to offer burnt offerings or grain and fellowship offerings.

24"We did not build it for that reason. We feared that some day your people would not accept us as part of your nation. Then they might say, 'You cannot worship the LORD, the God of Israel. 25The LORD made the Jordan River a border between us and you people of Reuben and Gad. You cannot worship the LORD.' So we feared that your children might make our children stop worshiping the LORD.

26"That is why we decided to build this altar. But it is not for burnt offerings and sacrifices. 27This altar is proof to you and us and to all our children who will come after us that we worship the LORD with our whole burnt offerings, grain, and fellowship offerings. This was so your children would not say to our children, 'You are not the LORD's.'

28"In the future if your children say that, our children can say, 'See the altar made by our ancestors. It is exactly like the LORD's altar, but we do not use it for sacrifices. It shows that we are part of Israel.'

29"Truly, we don't want to be against the LORD or to stop following him by building an altar for burnt offerings, grain offerings, or sacrifices. We know the only true altar to the LORD our God is in front of the Holy Tent.*d"*

30When Phinehas the priest and the ten leaders heard the people of Reuben, Gad, and East Manasseh, they were pleased. 31So Phinehas, son of Eleazar the priest, said, 'Now we know the LORD is with us and that you didn't turn against him. Now the Israelites will not be punished by the LORD."

32Then Phinehas and the leaders left the people of Reuben and Gad in Gilead and went back to Canaan where they told the Israelites what had happened. 33They were pleased and thanked God. So they decided not to fight the people of Reuben and Gad and destroy those lands.

34And the people of Reuben and Gad named the altar Proof That We Believe the LORD Is God.

✳ **SIDELIGHT:** It's okay to worship God anywhere, right? Well, that wasn't always the case. In Joshua's time, Israel only presented its sacrifices at the tabernacle. When three tribes built an altar by the Jordan River, other tribes thought they might sacrifice to a pagan god. They almost went to war, but talked out their differences instead (Joshua 22:9-34).

The Last Words of Joshua

23 The LORD gave Israel peace from their enemies around them. Many years passed, and Joshua grew very old. 2He called a meeting of all the older leaders, heads of families, judges, and officers of Israel. He said, "I am now very old. 3You have seen what the LORD has done to our enemies to help us. The LORD your God fought for you. 4Remember that your people have been given their land between the Jordan River and the Mediterranean Sea in the west, the land I promised to give you. 5The LORD your God will force out the people living there. The LORD will push them out ahead of you. And you will own the land, as he has promised you.

6"Be strong. You must be careful to obey everything commanded in the Book of the Teachings of Moses. Do exactly as it says. 7Don't become friends with the people living among us who are not Israelites. Don't say the names of their gods or make anyone swear by them. Don't serve or worship them. 8You must continue to follow the LORD your God, as you have done in the past.

9"The LORD has forced many great and powerful nations to leave ahead of you. No nation has been able to defeat you. 10With his help, one Israelite could defeat a thousand, because the LORD your God fights for you, as he promised to do.

11So you must be careful to love the LORD your God.

12"If you turn away from the way of the LORD and become friends with these people who are not part of Israel and marry them, 13the LORD your God will not help you defeat your enemies. They will be like traps for you, like whips on your back and thorns in your eyes, and none of you will be left in this good land the LORD your God has given you.

14"It's almost time for me to die. You know and fully believe that the LORD has done great things for you. You know that he has not failed to keep any of his promises. 15Every good promise that the LORD your God made has come true, and in the same way, his other promises will come true. He promised that evil will come to you and that he will destroy you from this good land that he gave you. 16This will happen if you don't keep your agreement with the LORD your God. If you go and serve other gods and worship them, the LORD will become very angry with you. Then none of you will be left in this good land he has given you."

24 Joshua gathered all the tribes*d* of Israel together at Shechem. He called the older leaders, heads of families, judges, and officers of Israel to stand before God.

2Then Joshua said to all the people, "Here's what the LORD, the God of Israel, says to you: 'A long time ago your ancestors lived on the other side of the Euphrates River. Terah, the father of Abraham and Nahor, worshiped other gods. 3But I, the LORD, took your ancestor Abraham from the other side of the river and led him through the land of Canaan. And I gave him many children, including his son Isaac. 4I gave Isaac two sons named Jacob and Esau. I gave the land around the mountains of Edom to Esau, but Jacob and his sons went down to Egypt. 5Then I sent Moses and Aaron to Egypt, where I brought many disasters on the Egyptians. Afterwards I brought you out. 6When I brought your ancestors out of Egypt, they came to the Red Sea,*d* and the Egyptians chased them with chariots and men on horses. 7So the people called out to the LORD. And I brought darkness between you and the Egyptians and made the sea to cover them. You yourselves saw what I did to the army of Egypt. After that, you lived in the desert for a long time.

8" 'Then I brought you to the land of the Amorites, east of the Jordan River. They fought against you, but I handed them over to you. I destroyed them before you, and you took control of that land. 9But the king of Moab, Balak son of Zippor, prepared to fight against the Israelites. The king sent for Balaam son of Beor to curse you, 10but I refused to listen to Balaam. So he asked for good things to happen to you! I saved you and brought you out of his power.

11" 'Then you crossed the Jordan River and came to Jericho, where the people of Jericho fought against you. Also, the Amorites, Perizzites, Canaanites, Hittites, Girgashites, Hivites, and Jebusites fought against you. But I handed them over to you. 12I sent terror ahead of you to force out two Amorite kings. You took the land without using swords and bows. 13I gave you that land where you did not have to work. I gave you cities that you did not have to build. And now you live in that land and in those cities, and you eat from vineyards and olive trees that you did not plant.' "

14Then Joshua said to the people, "Now respect the LORD and serve him fully and sincerely. Throw away the gods that your ancestors worshiped on the other side of the Euphrates River and in Egypt. Serve the LORD. 15But if you don't want to serve the LORD, you must choose for yourselves today whom you will serve. You may serve the gods that your ancestors worshiped when they lived on the other side of the Euphrates River, or you may serve the gods of the Amorites who lived in this land. As for me and my family, we will serve the LORD."

16Then the people answered, "We will never stop following the LORD to serve other gods! 17It was the LORD our God who brought our ancestors out of Egypt. We were slaves in that land, but the LORD did great things for us there. He brought us out and protected us while we traveled through other lands. 18Then he forced out all the people living in these lands, even the Amorites. So we will serve the LORD, because he is our God."

19Then Joshua said, "You are not able to serve the LORD, because he is a holy God and a jealous God. If you turn against him and sin, he will not forgive you. 20If you leave the LORD and serve other gods, he will send you great trouble. The LORD may have been good to you, but if you turn against him, he will destroy you."

21But the people said to Joshua, "No! We will serve the LORD."

22Then Joshua said, "You are your own witnesses that you have chosen to serve the LORD."

The people said, "Yes, we are."

23Then Joshua said, "Now throw away the gods that you have. Love the LORD, the God of Israel, with all your heart."

24Then the people said to Joshua, "We will serve the LORD our God, and we will obey him."

25On that day at Shechem Joshua made an agreement for the people. He made rules and laws for them to follow. 26Joshua wrote these things in the Book of the Teachings of God. Then he took a large stone and set it up under the oak tree near the LORD's Holy Tent.d

27Joshua said to all the people, "See this stone! It will remind you of what we did today. It was here the LORD spoke to us today. It will remind you of what happened so you will not turn against your God."

Joshua Dies

28Then Joshua sent the people back to their land.

29After that, Joshua son of Nun died at the age of one hundred ten. 30They buried him in his own land at Timnath Serah, in the mountains of Ephraim, north of Mount Gaash.

31The Israelites served the LORD during the lifetime of Joshua and during the lifetimes of the older leaders who lived after Joshua who had seen what the LORD had done for Israel.

SIDELIGHT: When Joseph's bones were buried (Joshua 24:32), the people didn't dig a grave as we do today. Rather, the bones were probably placed in a family cave or a tomb cut from rock, large enough for several family members.

Joseph Comes Home

32When the Israelites left Egypt, they carried the bones of Joseph with them. They buried them at Shechem, in the land Jacob had bought for a hundred pieces of silver from the sons of Hamor (Hamor was the father of Shechem). This land now belonged to Joseph's children.

33And Eleazar son of Aaron died and was buried at Gibeah in the mountains of Ephraim, which had been given to Eleazar's son Phinehas.

JUDGES

Why Read This Book:

■ See how God does not want his people to follow the crowd (Judges 1—2).
■ Discover how sin can capture people, but God can set them free if they ask for forgiveness (Judges 3—16).
■ Understand how people can become corrupt when they don't follow God (Judges 17—21).

Behind the Scenes:

Working in a fast food restaurant can be a disaster if the work isn't organized. Fries aren't ready when the burgers are done. The soft-serve ice cream runs empty. Customers receive the wrong orders. During the dinner-hour rush, lettuce can fly, mayonnaise can spill, and tempers can flare as each person tries frantically to catch up.

The chaos of an unorganized fast-food restaurant is similar to the chaos in Israel during the book of Judges. The last verse of the book summarizes what it was like: "In those days Israel did not have a king. Everyone did what seemed right" (Judges 21:25, p. 237).

Under the leadership of Joshua (see the book of Joshua, p. 195), the Israelites

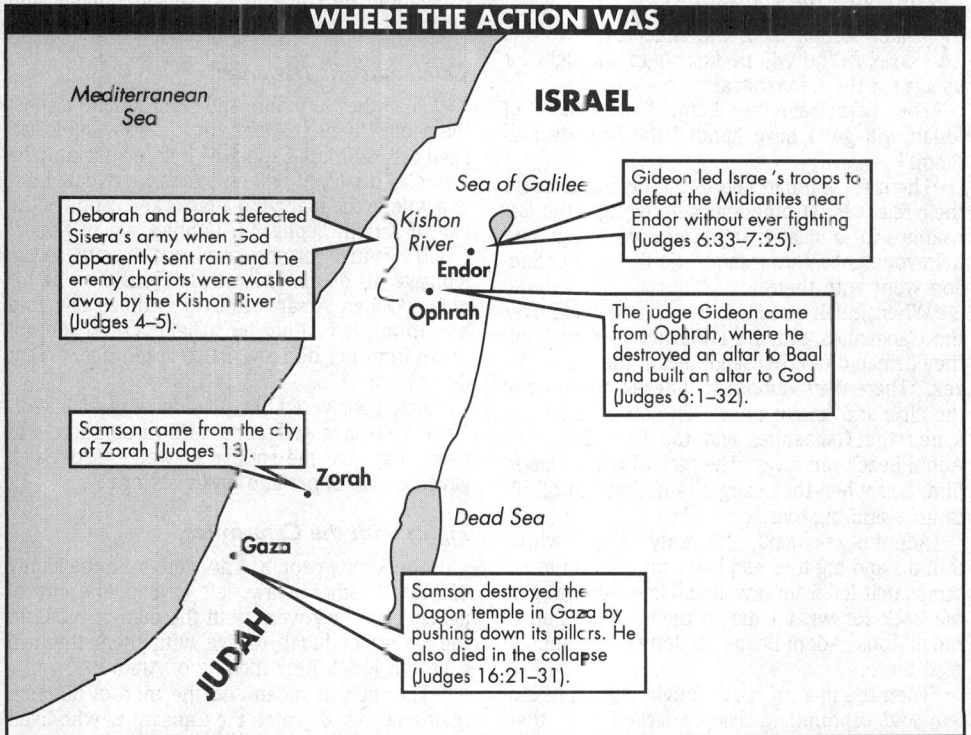

WHERE THE ACTION WAS

Mediterranean Sea

ISRAEL

Sea of Galilee

Kishon River

Deborah and Barak defected Sisera's army when God apparently sent rain and the enemy chariots were washed away by the Kishon River (Judges 4–5).

Gideon led Israel's troops to defeat the Midianites near Endor without ever fighting (Judges 6:33–7:25).

Endor

Ophrah

The judge Gideon came from Ophrah, where he destroyed an altar to Baal and built an altar to God (Judges 6:1–32).

Samson came from the city of Zorah (Judges 13).

Zorah

Dead Sea

Gaza

JUDAH

Samson destroyed the Dagon temple in Gaza by pushing down its pillars. He also died in the collapse (Judges 16:21–31).

WHEN THE ACTION WAS

	The Israelites escaped from Egypt	Saul was Israel's king		Jesus was born
2000BC	1500BC	1000BC	500BC	BC/AD
	Joshua led the Israelites into Canaan	The judges led the Israelites in times of trouble		

Behind the Scenes (cont.): had conquered major Canaanite cities and divided the land among the twelve Israelite tribes. But many Canaanites and other people still remained. They didn't believe in God, but worshiped idols and pagan gods.

These other people threatened the Israelites in two ways. First, they wanted the land back that the Israelites had taken away. So the Israelites constantly had to defend themselves. Second, the Israelites married Canaanites, which God had said not to do; then they accepted the Canaanites' religious practices, forgetting the true God.

Like workers in fast-food restaurants, the Israelites needed leaders to organize them and keep them on track. So in times of crisis, God chose different judges to bring the twelve tribes together to fight their enemies. These judges—such as Deborah, Samson, and Gideon—became national heroes for the Israelites.

Judges illustrates a common theme in the Old Testament. When a judge or leader was faithful to God, the people remained loyal to God and prospered. But when the judge died, the people sinned and were conquered. Then in their suffering, they confessed their sin, and God called a new judge to deliver them. This cycle continued for several generations.

Judges reminds us of the importance of always following God—and the dangers of ignoring God. At the same time, it shows that God is always willing to forgive us when we come back to him.

Judah Fights the Canaanites

1 After Joshua died, the Israelites asked the LORD, "Who will be first to go and fight for us against the Canaanites?"

²The LORD said to them, "The tribe*d* of Judah will go. I have handed the land over to them."

³The men of Judah said to the men of Simeon, their relatives, "Come and help us fight the Canaanites for our land. If you do, we will go and help you fight for your land." So the men of Simeon went with them.

⁴When Judah attacked, the LORD handed over the Canaanites and the Perizzites to them, and they defeated ten thousand men at the city of Bezek. ⁵There they found Adoni-Bezek, the ruler of the city, and fought him. The men of Judah defeated the Canaanites and the Perizzites, ⁶but Adoni-Bezek ran away. The men of Judah chased him, and when they caught him, they cut off his thumbs and big toes.

⁷Adoni-Bezek said, "Seventy kings whose thumbs and big toes had been cut off used to eat scraps that fell from my table. Now God has paid me back for what I did to them." The men of Judah took Adoni-Bezek to Jerusalem, and he died there.

⁸Then the men of Judah fought against Jerusalem and captured it. They attacked with their swords and burned the city.

⁹*Later, they went down to fight the Canaanites who lived in the mountains, in the dry country to the south, and in the western hills.* ¹⁰The men of Judah went to fight against the Canaanites in the city of Hebron (which used to be called Kiriath

Arba). And they defeated Sheshai, Ahiman, and Talmai.

Caleb and His Daughter

¹¹Then they left there and went to fight against the people living in Debir. (In the past Debir had been called Kiriath Sepher.) ¹²Before attacking the city, Caleb said, "I will give Acsah, my daughter, as a wife to the man who attacks and captures the city of Kiriath Sepher." ¹³Othniel son of Kenaz, Caleb's younger brother, captured the city, so Caleb gave his daughter Acsah to Othniel to be his wife. ¹⁴When Acsah came to Othniel, she told him to ask her father for a field. When she got down from her donkey, Caleb asked her, "What do you want?"

¹⁵Acsah answered him, "Do me a special favor. Since you have given me land in southern Canaan, also give me springs of water." So Caleb gave her the upper and lower springs.

Fights with the Canaanites

¹⁶The Kenite people, who were from the family of Moses' father-in-law, left Jericho, the city of palm trees. They went with the men of Judah to the Desert of Judah to live with them there in southern Judah near the city of Arad.

¹⁷The men of Judah and the men of Simeon, their relatives, defeated the Canaanites who lived in Zephath. They completely destroyed the city, *so they called it Hormah.ⁿ* ¹⁸*The men of Judah* captured Gaza, Ashkelon, Ekron, and the lands around them.

¹⁹The LORD was with the men of Judah. They took the land in the mountains, but they could

---

Hormah   Hormah sounds like the Hebrew word meaning "to destroy completely."

not force out the people living on the plain, because they had iron chariots. ²⁰As Moses had promised, Hebron was given to Caleb, and Caleb forced out the three sons of Anak.^d ²¹But the people of Benjamin could not make the Jebusite people leave Jerusalem. Since that time the Jebusites have lived with the Benjaminites in Jerusalem.

²²The men of Joseph went to fight against the city of Bethel, and the LORD was with them. ²³They sent some spies to Bethel (which used to be called Luz). ²⁴The spies saw a man coming out of the city and said to him, "Show us a way into the city, and we will be kind to you." ²⁵So the man showed them the way into the city. The men of Joseph attacked with swords the people in Bethel, but they let the man and his family go free. ²⁶He went to the land where the Hittites lived and built a city. He named it Luz, which is called even today.

²⁷There were Canaanites living in the cities of Beth Shan, Taanach, Dor, Ibleam, Megiddo, and the small towns around them. The people of Manasseh did not force those people out of their towns, because the Canaanites were determined to stay there. ²⁸Later, the Israelites grew strong and forced the Canaanites to work as slaves, but they did not make all the Canaanites leave their land. ²⁹The people of Ephraim did not force out all of the Canaanites living in Gezer. So the Canaanites continued to live in Gezer with the people of Ephraim. ³⁰The people of Zebulun did not force out the Canaanites living in the cities of Kitron and Nahalol. They stayed and lived with the people of Zebulun, but Zebulun made them work as slaves.

³¹The people of Asher did not force the Canaanites from the cities of Acco, Sidon, Ahlab, Aczib, Helbah, Aphek, and Rehob. ³²Since the people of Asher did not force them out, the Canaanites continued to live with them. ³³The people of Naphtali did not force out the people of the cities of Beth Shemesh and Beth Anath. So they continued to live with the Canaanites in those cities, and the Canaanites worked as slaves. ³⁴The Amorites forced the Danites back into the mountains and would not let them come down to live in the plain. ³⁵The Amorites were determined to stay in Mount Heres, Aijalon, and Shaalbim. But when the Israelites grew stronger, they made the Amorites work as slaves. ³⁶The land of the Amorites was from Scorpion Pass to Sela and beyond.

The Angel of the Lord at Bokim

2 The angel of the LORD went up from Gilgal to Bokim and said, "I brought you up from Egypt and led you to the land I promised to give your ancestors. I said, 'I will never break my

Bokim   This name means "crying."

agreement with you. ²But you must not make an agreement with the people who live in this land. You must destroy their altars.' But you did not obey me. How could you do this? ³Now I tell you, 'I will not force out the people in this land. They will be your enemies, and their gods will be a trap for you.' "

⁴After the angel gave Israel this message from the LORD, they cried loudly. ⁵So they named the place Bokim.ⁿ There they offered sacrifices to the LORD.

Joshua Dies

⁶Then Joshua sent the people back to their land. ⁷The people served the LORD during the lifetime of Joshua and during the lifetimes of the older leaders who lived after Joshua and who had seen what great things the LORD had done for Israel. ⁸Joshua son of Nun, the servant of the LORD, died at the age of one hundred ten. ⁹They buried him in his own land at Timnath Serah in the mountains of Ephraim, north of Mount Gaash.

The People Disobey

¹⁰After those people had died, their children grew up and did not know the LORD or what he had done for Israel. ¹¹So they did what the LORD said was wrong, and they worshiped the Baal^d

idols. ¹²They quit following the LORD, the God of their ancestors who had brought them out of Egypt. They began to worship the gods of the people who lived around them, and that made the LORD angry. ¹³The Israelites quit following the LORD and worshiped Baal and Ashtoreth.^d ¹⁴The LORD was angry with the people of Israel, so he handed them over to robbers who took their possessions. He let their enemies who lived around them defeat them; they could not protect themselves. ¹⁵When the Israelites went out to fight, they always lost, because the LORD was not with them. The LORD had sworn to them this would happen. So the Israelites suffered very much.

God Chooses Judges

[16]Then the LORD chose leaders called judges,[n] who saved the Israelites from the robbers. [17]But the Israelites did not listen to their judges. They

---

SIDELIGHT: Judges in the Old Testament wouldn't fit in well in today's court system. Instead of making judgments in court, the ancient judges were leaders in battle and heroes for the people (Judges 2:16). Imagine what that would do to our law schools!

---

were not faithful to God but worshiped other gods instead. Their ancestors had obeyed the LORD's commands, but they quickly turned away and did not obey. [18]When their enemies hurt them, the Israelites cried for help. So the LORD felt sorry for them and sent judges to save them from their enemies. The LORD was with those judges all their lives. [19]But when the judges died, the Israelites again sinned and worshiped other gods. They became worse than their ancestors. The Israelites were very stubborn and refused to change their evil ways.

[20]So the LORD became angry with the Israelites. He said, "These people have broken the agreement I made with their ancestors. They have not listened to me. [21]I will no longer defeat the nations who were left when Joshua died. [22]I will use them to test Israel, to see if Israel will keep the LORD's commands as their ancestors did." [23]In the past the LORD had permitted those nations to stay in the land. He did not quickly force them out or help Joshua's army defeat them.

3 These are the nations the LORD did not force to leave. He wanted to test the Israelites who had not fought in the wars of Canaan. [2](The only reason the LORD left those nations in the land was to teach the descendants[d] of the Israelites who had not fought in those wars how to fight.) [3]These are the nations: the five rulers of the Philistines, all the Canaanites, the people of Sidon, and the Hivites who lived in the Lebanon mountains from Mount Baal Hermon to Lebo Hamath. [4]Those nations were in the land to test the Israelites — to see if they would obey the commands the LORD had given to their ancestors by Moses.

[5]The people of Israel lived with the Canaanites, Hittites, Amorites, Perizzites, Hivites, and Jebusites. [6]The Israelites began to marry the daughters of those people, and they allowed their daughters to marry the sons of those people. Israel also served their gods.

Othniel, the First Judge

[7]The Israelites did what the LORD said was wrong. They forgot about the LORD their God and served the idols of Baal[d] and Asherah.[d] [8]So the LORD was angry with Israel and allowed Cushan-Rishathaim king of Northwest Mesopotamia to rule over the Israelites for eight years. [9]When Israel cried to the LORD, the LORD sent someone to save them. Othniel son of Kenaz, Caleb's younger brother, saved the Israelites. [10]The Spirit[d] of the LORD entered Othniel, and he became Israel's judge. When he went to war, the LORD handed over to him Cushan-Rishathaim king of Northwest Mesopotamia. [11]So the land was at peace for forty years. Then Othniel son of Kenaz died.

Ehud, the Judge

[12]Again the people of Israel did what the LORD said was wrong. So the LORD gave Eglon king of Moab power to defeat Israel because of the evil Israel did. [13]Eglon got the Ammonites and the Amalekites to join him. Then he attacked Israel and took Jericho, the city of palm trees. [14]So the people of Israel were ruled by Eglon king of Moab for eighteen years.

[15]When the people cried to the LORD, he sent someone to save them. He was Ehud, son of Gera from the people of Benjamin, who was left-handed. Israel sent Ehud to give Eglon king of Moab the payment he demanded. [16]Ehud made himself a sword with two edges, about eighteen inches long, and he tied it to his right hip under his clothes. [17]Ehud gave Eglon king of Moab the payment he demanded. Now Eglon was a very fat man. [18]After he had given Eglon the payment, Ehud sent away the people who had carried it. [19]When he passed the statues near Gilgal, he turned around and said to Eglon, "I have a secret message for you, King Eglon."

The king said, "Be quiet!" Then he sent all of his servants out of the room. [20]Ehud went to King Eglon, as he was sitting alone in the room above his summer palace.

Ehud said, "I have a message from God for you." As the king stood up from his chair, [21]Ehud reached with his left hand and took out the sword that was tied to his right hip. Then he stabbed the sword deep into the king's belly! [22]Even the handle sank in, and the blade came out his back. The *king's fat covered the whole sword, so Ehud left* the sword in Eglon. [23]Then he went out of the room and closed and locked the doors behind him.

[24]When the servants returned just after Ehud

---

judges They were not judges in courts of law, but leaders of the people in times of emergency.

left, they found the doors to the room locked. So they thought the king was relieving himself. 25They waited for a long time. Finally they became worried because he still had not opened the doors. So they got the key and unlocked them and saw their king lying dead on the floor!

26While the servants were waiting, Ehud had escaped. He passed by the statues and went to Seirah. 27When he reached the mountains of Ephraim he blew the trumpet. The people of Israel heard it and went down from the hills with Ehud leading them.

28He said to them, "Follow me! The LORD has helped you to defeat your enemies, the Moabites." So Israel followed Ehud and captured the crossings of the Jordan River. They did not allow the Moabites to cross the Jordan River. 29Israel killed about ten thousand strong and able men from Moab; not one escaped. 30So that day Moab was forced to be under the rule of Israel, and there was peace in the land for eighty years.

Shamgar, the Judge

31After Ehud, Shamgar son of Anath saved Israel. Shamgar killed six hundred Philistines with a sharp stick used to guide oxen.

Deborah, the Woman Judge

4 After Ehud died, the Israelites again did what the LORD said was wrong. 2So he let Jabin, a king of Canaan who ruled in the city of Hazor, defeat Israel. Sisera, who lived in Harosheth Haggoyim, was the commander of Jabin's army. 3Because he had nine hundred iron chariots and was very cruel to the people of Israel for twenty years, they cried to the LORD for help.

4A prophetess*d* named Deborah, the wife of Lappidoth, was judge of Israel at that time. 5Deborah would sit under the Palm Tree of Deborah, which was between the cities of Ramah and Bethel, in the mountains of Ephraim. And the people of Israel would come to her to settle their arguments.

6Deborah sent a message to Barak son of Abinoam. Barak lived in the city of Kedesh, which is in the area of Naphtali. Deborah said to Barak, "The LORD, the God of Israel, commands you: 'Go and gather ten thousand men of Naphtali and Zebulun and lead them to Mount Tabor. 7I will make Sisera, the commander of Jabin's army, and his chariots, and his army meet you at the Kishon River. I will hand Sisera over to you.' "

8Then Barak said to Deborah, "I will go if you

Pass the Paintbrush

Leonardo da Vinci was one of the greatest artists who has ever lived. In the late 1400s and early 1500s, this Italian genius was revered for his painting, sculpting, architecture, engineering, and inventing.

One day a student walked into da Vinci's studio to find the master working on a huge carvas. He had chosen the subject, planned the perspective, sketched the outline, and begun painting. Then, suddenly, he stopped and asked the student to finish the painting.

The student protested, saying he could never do justice to the great painter's work. He felt he was unworthy to complete such an important job.

Da Vinci cut him off. "Will not what I have done inspire you to do your best?" he asked.

In the same way that da Vinci hoped to encourage his student, Deborah wanted to motivate Barak and the Israelites in battle. Read how she challenged Barak in **Judges 4:4–16**.

■ How was da Vinci's challenge to the student similar to Deborah's challenge to Barak?

■ How can you use God's power to help you inspire others the way Deborah inspired Barak to overcome a challenge?

C O N S I D E R . . .

■ asking someone you admire for support to deal with a challenge you're facing.

■ sending a thank-you note to someone—a parent, a friend, someone at church—who has inspired you in your faith in recent months.

F O R   M O R E ,   S E E . . .

■ Judges 5:1–31 (p. 220)   ■ Hebrews 12:1–3 (p. 1289)
■ 1 Corinthians 1:10–17 (p. 1168)

will go with me, but if you won't go with me, I won't go."

9"Of course I will go with you," Deborah answered, "but you will not get credit for the victory. The LORD will let a woman defeat Sisera." So Deborah went with Barak to Kedesh. 10At Kedesh, Barak called the people of Zebulun and Naphtali together. From them, he gathered ten thousand men to follow him, and Deborah went with him also.

11Now Heber the Kenite had left the other Kenites, the descendants*d* of Hobab, Moses' brother-in-law. Heber had put up his tent by the great tree in Zaanannim, near Kedesh.

12When Sisera was told that Barak son of Abinoam had gone to Mount Tabor, 13Sisera gathered his nine hundred iron chariots and all the men with him, from Harosheth Haggoyim to the Kishon River.

14Then Deborah said to Barak, "Get up! Today is the day the LORD will hand over Sisera. The LORD has already cleared the way for you." So Barak led ten thousand men down Mount Tabor. 15As Barak approached, the LORD confused Sisera and his army and chariots. The LORD defeated them with the sword, but Sisera left his chariot and ran away on foot. 16Barak and his men chased Sisera's chariots and army to Harosheth Haggoyim. With their swords they killed all of Sisera's men; not one of them was left alive.

17But Sisera himself ran away to the tent where Jael lived. She was the wife of Heber, one of the Kenite family groups. Heber's family was at peace with Jabin king of Hazor. 18Jael went out to meet Sisera and said to him, "Come into my tent, master! Come in. Don't be afraid." So Sisera went into Jael's tent, and she covered him with a rug.

19Sisera said to Jael, "I am thirsty. Please give me some water to drink." So she opened a leather bag of milk and gave him a drink. Then she covered him up.

☀ SIDELIGHT: When Jael gave Sisera milk to drink, it probably wasn't ice cold (Judges 4:19). Because of the hot climate, people often curdled milk to preserve it. The nutritious result (known as kefir) is similar to yogurt. Unfortunately, you couldn't get it with strawberries and bananas mixed in.

20He said to her, "Go stand at the entrance to the tent. If anyone comes and asks you, 'Is anyone here?' say, 'No.' "

21But Jael, the wife of Heber, took a tent peg and a hammer and quietly went to Sisera. Since he was very tired, he was in a deep sleep. She hammered the tent peg through the side of Sisera's head and into the ground. And so Sisera died.

22At that very moment Barak came by Jael's tent, chasing Sisera. Jael went out to meet him and said, "Come. I will show you the man you are looking for." So Barak entered her tent, and there Sisera lay dead, with the tent peg in his head.

23On that day God defeated Jabin king of Canaan in the sight of Israel. 24Israel became stronger and stronger against Jabin king of Canaan until finally they destroyed him.

The Song of Deborah

5 On that day Deborah and Barak son of Abinoam sang this song:

2"The leaders led Israel.
　　The people volunteered to go to battle.
　　Praise the LORD!
3Listen, kings.
　　Pay attention, rulers!
I myself will sing to the LORD.
　　I will make music to the LORD, the God of Israel.

4"LORD, when you came from Edom,
　　when you marched from the land of Edom,
the earth shook,
　　the skies rained,
　　and the clouds dropped water.
5The mountains shook before the LORD, the God of Mount Sinai,
　　before the LORD, the God of Israel!

6"In the days of Shamgar son of Anath,
　　in the days of Jael, the main roads were empty.
Travelers went on the back roads.
7There were no warriors in Israel
　　until I, Deborah, arose,
　　until I arose to be a mother to Israel.
8At that time they chose to follow new gods.
　　Because of this, enemies fought us at our city gates.
No one could find a shield or a spear
　　among the forty thousand people of Israel.
9My heart is with the commanders of Israel.
　　They volunteered freely from among the people.
Praise the LORD!

10"*You who ride on white donkeys*
　　and sit on saddle blankets,
　　and you who walk along the road, listen!
11Listen to the sound of the singers
　　at the watering holes.
There they tell about the victories of the LORD,

the victories of the Lord's warriors in Israel.
Then the Lord's people went down to the city gates.

12"Wake up, wake up, Deborah!
Wake up, wake up, sing a song!
Get up, Barak!
Go capture your enemies, son of Abinoam!

13"Then those who were left came down to the important leaders.
The Lord's people came down to me with strong men.

14They came from Ephraim in the mountains of Amalek.
Benjamin was among the people who followed you.
From the family group of Makir, the commanders came down.
And from Zebulun came those who lead.

15The princes of Issachar were with Deborah.
The people of Issachar were loyal to Barak and followed him into the valley.
The Reubenites thought hard about what they would do.

16Why did you stay by the sheepfold?
Was it to hear the music played for your sheep?
The Reubenites thought hard about what they would do.

17The people of Gilead stayed east of the Jordan River.
People of Dan, why did you stay by the ships?
The people of Asher stayed at the seashore, at their safe harbors.

18But the people of Zebulun risked their lives, as did the people of Naphtali on the battlefield.

19"The kings came, and they fought.
At that time the kings of Canaan fought at Taanach, by the waters of Megiddo.
But they took away no silver or possessions of Israel.

20The stars fought from heaven;
from their paths, they fought Sisera.

21The Kishon River swept Sisera's men away, that old river, the Kishon River.
March on, my soul, with strength!

22Then the horses' hoofs beat the ground.
Galloping, galloping go Sisera's mighty horses.

23'May the town of Meroz be cursed,' said the angel of the Lord.
'Bitterly curse its people,
because they did not come to help the Lord.
They did not fight the strong enemy.'

24"May Jael, the wife of Heber the Kenite,
be blessed above all women who live in tents.

25Sisera asked for water,
but Jael gave him milk.
In a bowl fit for a ruler,
she brought him cream.

26Jael reached out and took the tent peg.
Her right hand reached for the workman's hammer.
She hit Sisera! She smashed his head!
She crushed and pierced the side of his head!

27At Jael's feet he sank.
He fell, and he lay there.
At her feet he sank. He fell.
Where Sisera sank, there he fell, dead.

28"Sisera's mother looked out through the window.
She looked through the curtains and cried out,
'Why is Sisera's chariot so late in coming?
Why are sounds of his chariots' horses delayed?'

29The wisest of her servant ladies answer her,
and Sisera's mother says to herself,

30'Surely they are robbing the people they defeated!
Surely they are dividing those things among themselves!
Each soldier is given a girl or two.
Maybe Sisera is taking pieces of dyed cloth.
Maybe they are even taking
pieces of dyed, embroidered cloth for the necks of the victors!'

31"Let all your enemies die this way, Lord!
But let all the people who love you
be as strong as the rising sun!"

Then there was peace in the land for forty years.

The Midianites Attack Israel

6 Again the Israelites did what the Lord said was wrong. So for seven years the Lord handed them over to Midian. 2Because the Midianites were very powerful and were cruel to Israel, the Israelites made hiding places in the mountains, in caves, and in safe places. 3Whenever the Israelites planted crops, the Midianites, Amalekites, and other peoples from the east would come and attack them. 4They camped in the land and destroyed the crops that the Israelites had planted as far away as Gaza. They left nothing for Israel to eat, and no sheep, cattle, or donkeys. 5The Midianites came with their tents and their animals like swarms of locusts[d] to ruin the land. There were so many people and camels they could not be counted. 6Israel became very

poor because of the Midianites, so they cried out to the LORD.

7When the Israelites cried out to the LORD against the Midianites, 8the LORD sent a prophet*d* to them. He said, "This is what the LORD, the God of Israel, says: I brought you out of Egypt, the land of slavery. 9I saved you from the Egyptians and from all those who were against you. I forced the Canaanites out of their land and gave it to you. 10Then I said to you, 'I am the LORD your God. Live in the land of the Amorites, but do not worship their gods.' But you did not obey me."

The Angel of the Lord Visits Gideon

11The angel of the LORD came and sat down under the oak tree at Ophrah that belonged to Joash, one of the Abiezrite people. Gideon, Joash's son, was separating some wheat from the chaff*d* in a winepress*d* to keep the wheat from the Midianites. 12The angel of the LORD appeared to Gideon and said, "The LORD is with you, mighty warrior!"

13Then Gideon said, "Sir, if the LORD is with us, why are we having so much trouble? Where are the miracles*d* our ancestors told us he did when the LORD brought them out of Egypt? But now he has left us and has handed us over to the Midianites."

14The LORD turned to Gideon and said, "Go with your strength and save Israel from the Midianites. I am the one who is sending you."

15But Gideon answered, "Lord, how can I save Israel? My family group is the weakest in Manasseh, and I am the least important member of my family."

16The LORD answered him, "I will be with you. It will seem as if the Midianites you are fighting are only one man."

17Then Gideon said to the LORD, "If you are pleased with me, give me proof that it is really you talking with me. 18Please wait here until I come back to you. Let me bring my offering and set it in front of you."

And the LORD said, "I will wait until you return."

19So Gideon went in and cooked a young goat, and with twenty quarts of flour, made bread without yeast. Then he put the meat into a basket and the broth into a pot. He brought them out and gave them to the angel under the oak tree.

20The angel of God said to Gideon, "Put the meat and the bread without yeast on that rock over there. Then pour the broth on them." And Gideon did as he was told. 21The angel of the LORD touched the meat and the bread with the end of the stick that was in his hand. Then fire jumped up from the rock and completely burned up the meat and the bread! And the angel of the LORD disappeared! 22Then Gideon understood he

had been talking to the angel of the LORD. So Gideon cried out, "Lord GOD! I have seen the angel of the LORD face to face!"

23But the LORD said to Gideon, "Calm down! Don't be afraid! You will not die!"

24So Gideon built an altar there to worship the LORD and named it The LORD Is Peace. It still stands at Ophrah, where the Abiezrites live.

Gideon Tears Down the Altar of Baal

25That same night the LORD said to Gideon, "Take the bull that belongs to your father and a second bull seven years old. Pull down your father's altar to Baal,*d* and cut down the Asherah*d* idol beside it. 26Then build an altar to the LORD your God with its stones in the right order on this high ground. Kill and burn a second bull on this altar, using the wood from the Asherah idol."

27So Gideon got ten of his servants and did what the LORD had told him to do. But Gideon was afraid that his family and the men of the city might see him, so he did it at night, not in the daytime.

28When the men of the city got up the next morning, they saw that the altar for Baal had been destroyed and that the Asherah idol beside it had been cut down! They also saw the altar Gideon had built and the second bull that had been sacrificed on it. 29The men of the city asked each other, "Who did this?"

After they asked many questions, someone told them, "Gideon son of Joash did this."

30So they said to Joash, "Bring your son out. He has pulled down the altar of Baal and cut down the Asherah idol beside it. He must die!"

31But Joash said to the angry crowd around him, "Are you going to take Baal's side? Are you going to defend him? Anyone who takes Baal's side will be killed by morning! If Baal is a god, let him fight for himself. It's his altar that has been pulled down." 32So on that day Gideon got the name Jerub-Baal, which means "let Baal fight against him," because Gideon pulled down Baal's altar.

Gideon Defeats Midian

33All the Midianites, the Amalekites, and other peoples from the east joined together and came across the Jordan River and camped in the Valley of Jezreel. 34But the Spirit*d* of the LORD entered Gideon, and he blew a trumpet to call the Abiezrites to follow him. 35He sent messengers to all of *Manasseh, calling them to follow him. He also* sent messengers to the people of Asher, Zebulun, and Naphtali. So they also went up to meet Gideon and his men.

36Then Gideon said to God, "You said you would help me save Israel. 37I will put some wool on the threshing*d* floor. If there is dew only on the wool but all of the ground is dry, then I will know that you will use me to save Israel, as you said." ³⁸And that is just what happened. When Gideon got up early the next morning and squeezed the wool, he got a full bowl of water from it.

³⁹Then Gideon said to God, "Don't be angry with me if I ask just one more thing. Please let me make one more test. Let only the wool be dry while the ground around it gets wet with dew." ⁴⁰That night God did that very thing. Just the wool was dry, but the ground around it was wet with dew.

7 Early in the morning Jerub-Baal (also called Gideon) and all his men set up their camp at the spring of Harod. The Midianites were camped north of them in the valley at the bottom of the hill called Moreh. ²Then the LORD said to Gideon, "You have too many men to defeat the Midianites. I don't want the Israelites to brag that they saved themselves. ³So now, announce to the people, 'Anyone who is afraid may leave Mount Gilead and go back home.'" So twenty-two thousand men returned home, but ten thousand remained.

⁴Then the LORD said to Gideon, "There are still too many men. Take the men down to the water, and I will test them for you there. If I say, 'This man will go with you, he will go. But if I say, 'That one will not go with you,' he will not go."

⁵So Gideon led the men down to the water. There the LORD said to him, "Separate them into those who drink water by lapping it up like a dog

Conquering Doubt

The ropes course was almost over. A one hundred-foot steel cable—a zip line—swung between two trees. Carol Berry was strapped into the harness fifty feet above the ground, in position to zoom down the line to a soft landing at the other end.

But she wasn't ready—at least not mentally.

Crossing the high beam had been scary enough. "Let me be last," she had pleaded. "I don't want to slow the group down." But everyone knew the real reason she wanted to wait was to build up her own confidence.

Now Carol faced the terrifying free fall down the zip line. Even I'll-go-first Kevin had hesitated. He had stood on the platform five minutes before he gave a horrifying scream and shot down the line. And, one by one, the rest of the group had followed and cheered.

Except Carol. She stood alone on the platform, crying. The group was silent, except for gentle encouragement. "You can do this, Carol. We know you can."

Fifteen minutes passed.

Suddenly, she stepped off the platform and whooshed down the line, so fast it took her breath away.

"I did it!" she shouted with joy when she landed on the ground. "I really did it!"

Carol's friends cheered her accomplishment. "I couldn't have done it without you guys," she finally said. "Thanks for reassuring me."

Just as Carol needed reassurance to help her conquer doubt, Gideon needed assurance that God would be with him as he led the Israelites into battle. Read how he got God's reassurance in **Judges 6:36—40.**

■ How was the group's confidence in Carol like God's patience with Gideon?

■ When have you wanted to "test" God before trusting him? What did you do? What happened?

CONSIDER. . .

■ writing on a sheet of paper a doubt you have about God or the world, then thinking about it through the week. Be alert for new insights as you read the Bible, talk with friends or a parent, or watch television. Whenever you have new insights, jot them down. Then evaluate what you have learned about doubt.

■ asking a friend or a parent to tell about a time he or she doubted God. Find out how that person dealt with the doubt and what you can learn from the experience.

FOR MORE, SEE. . .

■ Genesis 18:1–15 (p 19)   ■ John 20:24–29 (p. 1094)
■ Matthew 4:22–33 (p. 934)

and those who bend down to drink." ⁶There were three hundred men who used their hands to bring water to their mouths, lapping it as a dog does. All the rest got down on their knees to drink.

⁷Then the LORD said to Gideon, "Using the three hundred men who lapped the water, I will save you and hand Midian over to you. Let all the others go home." ⁸So Gideon sent the rest of Israel to their homes. But he kept three hundred men and took the jars and the trumpets of those who left.

Now the camp of Midian was in the valley below Gideon. ⁹That night the LORD said to Gideon, "Get up. Go down and attack the camp of the Midianites, because I will give them to you. ¹⁰But if you are afraid to go down, take your servant Purah with you. ¹¹When you come to the camp of Midian, you will hear what they are saying. Then you will not be afraid to attack the camp."

Gideon Is Encouraged

So Gideon and his servant Purah went down to the edge of the enemy camp. ¹²The Midianites, the Amalekites, and all the peoples from the east were camped in that valley. There were so many of them they seemed like locusts.ᵈ Their camels could not be counted because they were as many as the grains of sand on the seashore!

¹³When Gideon came to the enemy camp, he heard a man telling his friend about a dream. He was saying, "I dreamed that a loaf of barley bread rolled into the camp of Midian. It hit the tent so hard that the tent turned over and fell flat!"

¹⁴The man's friend said, "Your dream is about the sword of Gideon son of Joash, a man of Israel. God will hand Midian and the whole army over to him!"

¹⁵When Gideon heard about the dream and what it meant, he worshiped God. Then Gideon went back to the camp of Israel and called out to them, "Get up! The LORD has handed the army of Midian over to you!" ¹⁶Gideon divided the three hundred men into three groups. He gave each man a trumpet and an empty jar with a burning torch inside.

¹⁷Gideon told the men, "Watch me and do what I do. When I get to the edge of the camp, do what I do. ¹⁸Surround the enemy camp. When I and everyone with me blow our trumpets, you blow your trumpets, too. Then shout, 'For the LORD and for Gideon!' "

Midian Is Defeated

¹⁹So Gideon and the one hundred men with him came to the edge of the enemy camp just after they had changed guards. It was during the middle watch of the night. Then Gideon and his men blew their trumpets and smashed their jars. ²⁰All three groups of Gideon's men blew their trumpets and smashed their jars. They held the torches in their left hands and the trumpets in their right hands. Then they shouted, "A sword for the LORD and for Gideon!" ²¹Each of Gideon's men stayed in his place around the camp, but the Midianites began shouting and running to escape.

²²When Gideon's three hundred men blew their trumpets, the LORD made all the Midianites fight each other with their swords! The enemy army ran away to the city of Beth Shittah toward Zererah. They ran as far as the border of Abel Meholah, near the city of Tabbath. ²³Then men of Israel from Naphtali, Asher, and all of Manasseh were called out to chase the Midianites. ²⁴Gideon sent messengers through all the mountains of Ephraim, saying, "Come down and attack the Midianites. Take control of the Jordan River as far as Beth Barah before the Midianites can get to it."

So they called out all the men of Ephraim, who took control of the Jordan River as far as Beth Barah. ²⁵The men of Ephraim captured two princes of Midian named Oreb and Zeeb. They killed Oreb at the rock of Oreb and Zeeb at the winepressᵈ of Zeeb, and they continued chasing the Midianites. They brought the heads of Oreb and Zeeb to Gideon, who was east of the Jordan River.

8 The men of Ephraim asked Gideon, "Why did you treat us this way? Why didn't you call us when you went to fight against Midian?" They argued angrily with Gideon.

²But he answered them, "I have not done as well as you! The small part you did was better than all that my people of Abiezer did. ³God let you capture Oreb and Zeeb, the princes of Midian. How can I compare what I did with what you did?" When the men of Ephraim heard Gideon's answer, they were not as angry anymore.

Gideon Captures Two Kings

⁴When Gideon and his three hundred men came to the Jordan River, they were tired, but they chased the enemy across to the other side. ⁵Gideon said to the men of Succoth, "Please give my soldiers some bread because they are very tired. I am chasing Zebah and Zalmunna, the kings of Midian."

⁶But the leaders of Succoth said, "Why should we give your soldiers bread? You haven't caught Zebah and Zalmunna yet."

⁷Then Gideon said, "The LORD will surrender Zebah and Zalmunna to me. After that, I will whip your skin with thorns and briers from the desert."

⁸Gideon left Succoth and went to the city of Peniel and asked them for food. But the people of Peniel gave him the same answer as the people of Succoth. ⁹So Gideon said to the men of Peniel,

"After I win the victory, I will return and pull down this tower."

¹⁰Zebah and Zalmunna and their army were in the city of Karkor. About fifteen thousand men were left of the armies of the peoples of the east. Already one hundred twenty thousand soldiers had been killed. ¹¹Gideon went up the road of those who live in tents east of Nobah and Jogbehah, and he attacked the enemy army when they did not expect it. ¹²Zebah and Zalmunna, the kings of Midian, ran away, but Gideon chased and captured them and frightened away their army.

¹³Then Gideon son of Joash returned from the battle by the Pass of Heres. ¹⁴Gideon captured a young man from Succoth and asked him some questions. So the young man wrote down for Gideon the names of seventy-seven officers and older leaders of Succoth.

Gideon Punishes Succoth

¹⁵When Gideon came to Succoth, he said to the people of that city, "Here are Zebah and Zalmunna. You made fun of me by saying, 'Why should we give bread to your tired men? You have not caught Zebah and Zalmunna yet.' " ¹⁶So Gideon took the older leaders of the city and punished them with thorns and briers from the desert. ¹⁷He also pulled down the tower of Peniel and killed the people in that city.

¹⁸Gideon asked Zebah and Zalmunna, "What were the men like that you killed on Mount Tabor?"

They answered, "They were like you. Each one of them looked like a prince."

¹⁹Gideon said, "Those were my brothers, my mother's sons. As surely as the LORD lives, I would not kill you if you had spared them." ²⁰Then Gideon said to Jether, his oldest son, "Kill them." But Jether was only a boy and was afraid, so he did not take out his sword.

²¹Then Zebah and Zalmunna said to Gideon, "Come on. Kill us yourself. As the saying goes, 'It takes a man to do a man's job.' " So Gideon got up and killed Zebah and Zalmunna and took the decorations off their camels' necks.

Gideon Makes an Idol

²²The people of Israel said to Gideon, "You saved us from the Midianites. Now, we want you and your son and your grandson to rule over us."

²³But Gideon told them, "The LORD will be your ruler. I will not rule over you, nor will my son rule over you." ²⁴He said, "I want you to do this one thing for me. I want each of you to give me a gold earring from the things you took in the fighting." (The Ishmaelites[n] wore gold earrings.)

²⁵They said, "We will gladly give you what you want." So they spread out a coat, and everyone threw down an earring from what he had taken. ²⁶The gold earrings weighed about forty-three pounds. This did not count the decorations, necklaces, and purple robes worn by the kings of Midian, nor the chains from the camels' necks. ²⁷Gideon used the gold to make a holy vest, which he put in his hometown of Ophrah. But all the Israelites were unfaithful to God and worshiped it, so it became a trap for Gideon and his family.

> ✳ **SIDELIGHT:** People today wear earrings for decoration, but that has not always been the only reason. Three thousand years ago, people also wore earrings because they thought they had magical power—which may be one reason the Israelites took away the Ishmaelites' earrings in battle (Judges 8:23–27).

The Death of Gideon

²⁸So Midian was under the rule of Israel; they did not cause trouble anymore. And the land had peace for forty years, as long as Gideon was alive.

²⁹Gideon[n] son of Joash went to his home to live. ³⁰He had seventy sons of his own, because he had many wives. ³¹He had a slave woman[d] who lived in Shechem, and he had a son by her, whom he named Abimelech. ³²So Gideon son of Joash died at a good old age. He was buried in the tomb of Joash, his father, in Ophrah, where the Abiezrites live.

³³As soon as Gideon died, the people of Israel were again unfaithful to God and followed the Baals.[d] They made Baal-Berith their god. ³⁴The Israelites did not remember the LORD their God, who had saved them from all their enemies living all around them. ³⁵And they were not kind to the family of Jerub-Baal, also called Gideon, for all the good he had done for Israel.

Abimelech Becomes King

9 Abimelech son of Gideon[n] went to his uncles in the city of Shechem. He said to his uncles and all of his mother's family group, ²"Ask the leaders of Shechem, 'Is it better for the seventy sons of Gideon to rule over you or for one man to rule?' Remember, I am your relative."

³Abimelech's uncles spoke to all the leaders of Shechem about this. And they decided to follow Abimelech, because they said, "He is our relative." ⁴So the leaders of Shechem gave Abimelech

---

Ishmaelites Another name for the Midianites. See Genesis 37:25-28.
Gideon Also called Jerub-Baal.

about one and three-quarter pounds of silver from the temple of the god Baal-Berith. Abimelech used the silver to hire some worthless, reckless men, who followed him wherever he went. [5]He went to Ophrah, the hometown of his father, and murdered his seventy brothers, the sons of Gideon. He killed them all on one stone. But Gideon's youngest son, Jotham, hid from Abimelech and escaped. [6]Then all of the leaders of Shechem and Beth Millo gathered beside the great tree standing in Shechem. There they made Abimelech their king.

Jotham's Story

[7]When Jotham heard this, he went and stood on the top of Mount Gerizim. He shouted to the people: "Listen to me, you leaders of Shechem, so that God will listen to you! [8]One day the trees decided to appoint a king to rule over them. They said to the olive tree, 'You be king over us!' [9]"But the olive tree said, 'Men and gods are honored by my oil. Should I stop making it and go and sway over the other trees?' [10]"Then the trees said to the fig tree, 'Come and be king over us!' [11]"But the fig tree answered, 'Should I stop making my sweet and good fruit and go and sway over the other trees?' [12]"Then the trees said to the vine, 'Come and be king over us!' [13]"But the vine answered, 'My new wine makes men and gods happy. Should I stop making it and go and sway over the trees?' [14]"Then all the trees said to the thornbush, 'Come and be king over us.' [15]"But the thornbush said to the trees, 'If you really want to appoint me king over you, come and find shelter in my shade! But if not, let fire come out of the thornbush and burn up the cedars of Lebanon!' [16]"Now, were you completely honest and sincere when you made Abimelech king? Have you been fair to Gideon[n] and his family? Have you treated Gideon as you should? [17]Remember, my father fought for you and risked his life to save you from the power of the Midianites. [18]But now you have turned against my father's family and have killed his seventy sons on one stone. You have made Abimelech, the son of my father's slave girl, king over the leaders of Shechem just because he is your relative! [19]So then, if you have *been honest and sincere to Gideon and his family* today, be happy with Abimelech as your king. *And may he be happy with you!* [20]But if not, may fire come out of Abimelech and completely burn you leaders of Shechem and Beth Millo! Also may

fire come out of the leaders of Shechem and Beth Millo and burn up Abimelech!"

[21]Then Jotham ran away and escaped to the city of Beer. He lived there because he was afraid of his brother Abimelech.

Abimelech Fights Against Shechem

[22]Abimelech ruled Israel for three years. [23]Then God sent an evil spirit to make trouble between Abimelech and the leaders of Shechem so that the leaders of Shechem turned against him. [24]Abimelech had killed Gideon's[n] seventy sons, his own brothers, and the leaders of Shechem had helped him. So God sent the evil spirit to punish them. [25]The leaders of Shechem were against Abimelech then. They put men on the hilltops in ambush who robbed everyone going by. And Abimelech was told.

[26]A man named Gaal son of Ebed and his brothers moved into Shechem, and the leaders of Shechem trusted him. [27]They went out to the vineyards to pick grapes, and they squeezed the grapes. Then they had a feast in the temple of their god, where they ate and drank and cursed Abimelech. [28]Gaal son of Ebed said, "We are the men of Shechem. Who is Abimelech that we should serve him? Isn't he one of Gideon's sons, and isn't Zebul his officer? We should serve the men of Hamor, Shechem's father. Why should we serve Abimelech? [29]If you made me commander of these people, I would get rid of Abimelech. I would say to him, 'Get your army ready and come out to battle.' "

[30]Now when Zebul, the ruler of Shechem, heard what Gaal son of Ebed said, he was very angry. [31]He sent secret messengers to Abimelech, saying, "Gaal son of Ebed and Gaal's brothers have come to Shechem, and they are turning the city against you! [32]You and your men should get up during the night and hide in the fields outside the city. [33]As soon as the sun comes up in the morning, attack the city. When Gaal and his men come out to fight you, do what you can to them."

[34]So Abimelech and all his soldiers got up during the night and hid near Shechem in four groups. [35]Gaal son of Ebed went out and was standing at the entrance to the city gate. As he was standing there, Abimelech and his soldiers came out of their hiding places.

[36]When Gaal saw the soldiers, he said to Zebul, "Look! There are people coming down from the mountains!"

But Zebul said, "You are seeing the shadows of the mountains. The shadows just look like people."

[37]But again Gaal said, "Look, there are people coming down from the center of the land, and

Gideon   Also called Jerub-Baal.

there is a group coming from the fortune-tellers' tree!"

[38]Zebul said to Gaal, "Where is your bragging now? You said, 'Who is Abimelech that we should serve him?' You made fun of these men. Now go out and fight them."

[39]So Gaal led the men of Shechem out to fight Abimelech. [40]Abimelech and his men chased them, and many of Gaal's men were killed before they could get back to the city gate. [41]While Abimelech stayed at Arumah, Zebul forced Gaal and his brothers to leave Shechem.

[42]The next day the people of Shechem went out to the fields. When Abimelech was told about it, [43]he separated his men into three groups and hid them in the fields. When he saw the people coming out of the city, he jumped up and attacked them. [44]Abimelech and his group ran to the entrance gate to the city. The other two groups ran out to the people in the fields and struck them down. [45]Abimelech and his men fought the city of Shechem all day until they captured it and killed its people. Then he tore it down and threw salt[n] over the ruins.

The Tower of Shechem Burns

[46]When the leaders who were in the Tower of Shechem heard what had happened to Shechem, they gathered in the safest room of the temple of El Berith. [47]Abimelech heard that all the leaders of the Tower of Shechem had gathered there. [48]So he and all his men went up Mount Zalmon, near Shechem. Abimelech took an ax and cut some branches and put them on his shoulders. He said to all those with him, "Hurry! Do what I have done!" [49]So all those men cut branches and followed Abimelech and piled them against the safest room of the temple. Then they set them on fire and burned the people inside. So all the people who were at the Tower of Shechem also died — about a thousand men and women.

Abimelech's Death

[50]Then Abimelech went to the city of Thebez. He surrounded the city, attacked it, and captured it. [51]But inside the city was a strong tower, so all the men, women, and leaders of that city ran to the tower. When they got inside, they locked the door behind them. Then they climbed up to the roof of the tower. [52]Abimelech came to the tower to attack it. He approached the door of the tower to set it on fire, [53]but as he came near, a woman dropped a grinding stone on his head, crushing his skull.

[54]He quickly called to the officer who carried his armor and said, "Take out your sword and kill me. I don't want people to say, 'A woman killed Abimelech.' " So the officer stabbed Abimelech, and he died. [55]When the people of Israel saw Abimelech was dead, they all returned home.

[56]In that way God punished Abimelech for all the evil he had done to his father by killing his seventy brothers. [57]God also punished the men of Shechem for the evil they had done. So the curse spoken by Jotham, the youngest son of Gideon,[n] came true.

Tola, the Judge

10 After Abimelech died, another judge came to save Israel. He was Tola son of Puah, the son of Dodo. Tola was from the people of Issachar and lived in the city of Shamir in the mountains of Ephraim. [2]Tola was a judge for Israel for twenty-three years. Then he died and was buried in Shamir.

Jair, the Judge

[3]After Tola died, Jair from the region of Gilead became judge. He was a judge for Israel for twenty-two years. [4]Jair had thirty sons, who rode thirty donkeys. These thirty sons controlled thirty towns in Gilead, which are called the Towns of Jair to this day. [5]Jair died and was buried in the city of Kamon.

The Ammonites Trouble Israel

[6]Again the Israelites did what the LORD said was wrong. They worshiped Baal[d] and Ashtoreth,[d] the gods of Aram, Sidon, Moab, and Ammon, and the gods of the Philistines. The Israelites left the LORD and stopped serving him. [7]So the LORD was angry with them and handed them over to the Philistines and the Ammonites. [8]In the same year those people destroyed the Israelites who lived east of the Jordan River in the region of Gilead, where the Amorites lived. So the Israelites suffered for eighteen years. [9]The Ammonites then crossed the Jordan River to fight the people of Judah, Benjamin, and Ephraim, causing much trouble to the people of Israel. [10]So the Israelites cried out to the LORD, "We have sinned against you. We left our God and worshiped the Baal idols."

[11]The LORD answered the Israelites, "When the Egyptians, Amorites, Ammonites, Philistines, [12]Sidonians, Amalekites, and Maonites were cruel to you, you cried out to me, and I saved you. [13]But now you have left me again and have worshiped other gods. So I refuse to save you again. [14]You have chosen those gods. So go call to them for help. Let them save you when you are in trouble."

[15]But the people of Israel said to the LORD, "We

---

salt   The salt would keep crops from growing there.
Gideon   Also called Jerub-Baal.

have sinned. Do to us whatever you want, but please save us today!" [16]Then the Israelites threw away the foreign gods among them, and they worshiped the LORD again. So he felt sorry for them when he saw their suffering.

[17]The Ammonites gathered for war and camped in Gilead. The Israelites gathered and camped at Mizpah. [18]The leaders of the people of Gilead said, "Who will lead us to attack the Ammonites? He will become the head of all those who live in Gilead."

Jephthah Is Chosen as Leader

11 Jephthah was a strong soldier from Gilead. His father was named Gilead, and his mother was a prostitute.[d] [2]Gilead's wife had several sons. When they grew up, they forced Jephthah to leave his home, saying to him, "You will not get any of our father's property, because you are the son of another woman." [3]So Jephthah ran away from his brothers and lived in the land of Tob. There some worthless men began to follow him.

[4]After a time the Ammonites fought against Israel. [5]When the Ammonites made war against Israel, the older leaders of Gilead went to Jephthah to bring him back from Tob. [6]They said to him, "Come and lead our army so we can fight the Ammonites."

[7]But Jephthah said to them, "Didn't you hate me? You forced me to leave my father's house. Why are you coming to me now that you are in trouble?"

[8]The older leaders of Gilead said to Jephthah, "It is because of those troubles that we come to you now. Please come with us and fight against the Ammonites. You will be the ruler over everyone who lives in Gilead."

[9]Then Jephthah answered, "If you take me back to Gilead to fight the Ammonites and the LORD helps me win, I will be your ruler."

[10]The older leaders of Gilead said to him, "The LORD is listening to everything we are saying. We promise to do all that you tell us to do." [11]So Jephthah went with the older leaders of Gilead, and the people made him their leader and commander of their army. Jephthah repeated all of his words in front of the LORD at Mizpah.

Jephthah Sends Messengers to the Ammonite King

[12]Jephthah sent messengers to the king of the Ammonites, asking, "What have you got against Israel? Why have you come to attack our land?"

[13]The king of the Ammonites answered the messengers of Jephthah, "We are fighting Israel because you took our land when you came up from Egypt. You took our land from the Arnon

River to the Jabbok River to the Jordan River. Now give our land back to us peacefully."

[14]Jephthah sent the messengers to the Ammonite king again. [15]They said:

"This is what Jephthah says: Israel did not take the land of the people of Moab or Ammon. [16]When the Israelites came out of Egypt, they went into the desert to the Red Sea and then to Kadesh. [17]Israel sent messengers to the king of Edom, saying, 'Let the people of Israel go across your land.' But the king of Edom refused. We sent the same message to the king of Moab, but he also refused. So the Israelites stayed at Kadesh.

[18]"Then the Israelites went into the desert around the borders of the lands of Edom and Moab. Israel went east of the land of Moab and camped on the other side of the Arnon River, the border of Moab. They did not cross it to go into the land of Moab.

[19]"Then Israel sent messengers to Sihon king of the Amorites, king of the city of Heshbon, asking, 'Let the people of Israel pass through your land to go to our land.' [20]But Sihon did not trust the Israelites to cross his land. So he gathered all of his people and camped at Jahaz and fought with Israel.

[21]"But the LORD, the God of Israel, handed Sihon and his army over to Israel. All the land of the Amorites became the property of Israel. [22]So Israel took all the land of the Amorites from the Arnon River to the Jabbok River, from the desert to the Jordan River.

[23]"It was the LORD, the God of Israel, who forced out the Amorites ahead of the people of Israel. So do you think you can make them leave? [24]Take the land that your god Chemosh[d] has given you. We will live in the land the LORD our God has given us!

[25]"Are you any better than Balak son of Zippor, king of Moab? Did he ever quarrel or fight with the people of Israel? [26]For three hundred years the Israelites have lived in Heshbon and Aroer and the towns around them and in all the cities along the Arnon River. Why have you not taken these cities back in all that time? [27]I have not sinned against you, but you are sinning against me by making war on me. May the LORD, the Judge, decide whether the Israelites or the Ammonites are right."

[28]But the king of the Ammonites ignored this message from Jephthah.

Jephthah's Promise

[29]Then the Spirit[d] of the LORD entered Jephthah. Jephthah passed through Gilead and Manasseh and the city of Mizpah in Gilead to the land of the Ammonites. [30]Jephthah made a promise to the LORD, saying, "If you will hand over the Ammonites to me, [31]I will give you as a burnt offering

the first thing that comes out of my house to meet me when I return from the victory. It will be the LORD's."

³²Then Jephthah went over to fight the Ammonites, and the LORD handed them over to him. ³³In a great defeat Jephthah struck them down from the city of Aroer to the area of Minnith, and twenty cities as far as the city of Abel Keramim. So the Ammonites were defeated by the Israelites.

³⁴When Jephthah returned to his home in Mizpah, his daughter was the first one to come out to meet him, playing a tambourine*d* and dancing. She was his only child; he had no other sons or daughters. ³⁵When Jephthah saw his daughter, he tore his clothes to show his sorrow. He said, "My daughter! You have made me so sad because I made a promise to the LORD, and I cannot break it!"

³⁶Then his daughter said, "Father, you made a promise to the LORD. So do to me just what you promised, because the LORD helped you defeat your enemies, the Ammonites." ³⁷She also said, "But let me do one thing. Let me be alone for two months to go to the mountains. Since I will never marry, let me and my friends go and cry together."

³⁸Jephthah said, "Go." So he sent her away for two months. She and her friends stayed in the mountains and cried for her because she would never marry. ³⁹After two months she returned to her father, and Jephthah did to her what he had promised. Jephthah's daughter never had a husband.

From this came a custom in Israel that ⁴⁰every year the young women of Israel would go out for four days to remember the daughter of Jephthah from Gilead.

SIDELIGHT: Have you ever made a promise you later regretted? Judge Jephthah did. He promised to sacrifice the first thing that came out of his house after battle. Jephthah may have expected to see an animal, since houses in that day often included space for cattle. But when his only daughter appeared, he tore his clothes in sorrow (Judges 11:30–40).

Jephthah and Ephraim

12 The men of Ephraim called all their soldiers together and crossed the river to the town of Zaphon. They said to Jephthah, "Why didn't you call us to help you fight the Ammonites? We will burn your house down with you in it."

²Jephthah answered them, "My people and I fought a great battle against the Ammonites. I called you, but you didn't come to help me. ³When I saw that you would not help me, I risked my own life and went against the Ammonites. The LORD handed them over to me. So why have you come to fight against me today?"

⁴Then Jephthah called the men of Gilead together and fought the men of Ephraim. The men of Gilead struck them down because the Ephraimites had said, "You men of Gilead are nothing but deserters from Ephraim—living between Ephraim and Manasseh." ⁵The men of Gilead captured the crossings of the Jordan River that led to the country of Ephraim. A person from Ephraim trying to escape would say, "Let me cross the river." Then the men of Gilead would ask him, "Are you from Ephraim?" If he replied no, ⁶they would say to him, "Say the word 'Shibboleth.' " The men of Ephraim could not say that word correctly. So if the person from Ephraim said, "Sibboleth," the men of Gilead would kill him at the crossing. So forty-two thousand people from Ephraim were killed at that time.

⁷Jephthah was a judge for Israel for six years. Then Jephthah, the man from Gilead, died and was buried in a town in Gilead.

Ibzan, the Judge

⁸After Jephthah died, Ibzan from Bethlehem was a judge for Israel. ⁹He had thirty sons and thirty daughters. He let his daughters marry men who were not in his family group, and he brought thirty women who were not in his tribe*d* to be wives for his sons. Ibzan judged Israel for seven years. ¹⁰Then he died and was buried in Bethlehem.

Elon, the Judge

¹¹After Ibzan died, Elon from the tribe*d* of Zebulun was a judge for Israel. He judged Israel for ten years. ¹²Then Elon, the man of Zebulun, died and was buried in the city of Aijalon in the land of Zebulun.

Abdon, the Judge

¹³After Elon died, Abdon son of Hillel from the city of Pirathon was a judge for Israel. ¹⁴He had forty sons and thirty grandsons, who rode on seventy donkeys. He judged Israel for eight years. ¹⁵Then Abdon son of Hillel died and was buried in Pirathon in the land of Ephraim, in the mountains where the Amalekites lived.

The Birth of Samson

13 Again the people of Israel did what the LORD said was wrong. So he handed them over to the Philistines for forty years.

²There was a man named Manoah from the tribe*d* of Dan, who lived in the city of Zorah. He had a wife, but she could not have children. ³The angel of the LORD appeared to Manoah's wife and said, "You have not been able to have children, but you will become pregnant and give birth to a son. ⁴Be careful not to drink wine or beer or eat anything that is unclean,*d* ⁵because you will become pregnant and have a son. You must never cut his hair, because he will be a Nazirite,*d* given to God from birth. He will begin to save Israel from the power of the Philistines."

⁶Then Manoah's wife went to him and told him what had happened. She said, "A man from God came to me. He looked like an angel from God; his appearance was frightening. I didn't ask him where he was from, and he didn't tell me his name. ⁷But he said to me, 'You will become pregnant and will have a son. Don't drink wine or beer or eat anything that is unclean, because the boy will be a Nazirite to God from his birth until the day of his death.' "

⁸Then Manoah prayed to the LORD: "Lord, I beg you to let the man of God come to us again. Let him teach us what we should do for the boy who will be born to us."

⁹God heard Manoah's prayer, and the angel of God came to Manoah's wife again while she was sitting in the field. But her husband Manoah was not with her. ¹⁰So she ran to tell him, "He is here! The man who appeared to me the other day is here!"

¹¹Manoah got up and followed his wife. When he came to the man, he said, "Are you the man who spoke to my wife?"

The man said, "I am."

¹²So Manoah asked, "When what you say happens, what kind of life should the boy live? What should he do?"

¹³The angel of the LORD said, "Your wife must be careful to do everything I told her to do. ¹⁴She must not eat anything that grows on a grapevine, or drink any wine or beer, or eat anything that is unclean. She must do everything I have commanded her."

¹⁵Manoah said to the angel of the LORD, "We would like you to stay awhile so we can cook a young goat for you."

¹⁶The angel of the LORD answered, "Even if I stay awhile, I would not eat your food. But if you want to prepare something, offer a burnt offering to the LORD." (Manoah did not understand that *the man was really the angel of the LORD.*)

¹⁷Then Manoah asked the angel of the LORD, "What is your name? Then we will honor you when what you have said really happens."

¹⁸The angel of the LORD said, "Why do you ask my name? It is too amazing for you to understand." ¹⁹So Manoah sacrificed a young goat on a

rock and offered some grain as a gift to the LORD. Then an amazing thing happened as Manoah and his wife watched. ²⁰The flames went up to the sky from the altar. As the fire burned, the angel of the LORD went up to heaven in the flame. When Manoah and his wife saw that, they bowed facedown on the ground. ²¹The angel of the LORD did not appear to them again. Then Manoah understood that the man was really the angel of the LORD. ²²Manoah said, "We have seen God, so we will surely die."

²³But his wife said to him, "If the LORD wanted to kill us, he would not have accepted our burnt offering or grain offering. He would not have shown us all these things or told us all this."

²⁴So the woman gave birth to a boy and named him Samson. He grew, and the LORD blessed him. ²⁵The Spirit*d* of the LORD began to work in Samson while he was in the city of Mahaneh Dan, between the cities of Zorah and Eshtaol.

Samson's First Marriage

14 Samson went down to the city of Timnah where he saw a Philistine woman. ²When he returned home, he said to his father and mother, "I saw a Philistine woman in Timnah. I want you to get her for me so I can marry her."

³His father and mother answered, "Surely there is a woman from Israel you can marry. Do you have to marry a woman from the Philistines, who are not circumcised?"*d*

But Samson said, "Get that woman for me! She is the one I want!" ⁴(Samson's parents did not know that the LORD wanted this to happen because he was looking for a way to challenge the Philistines, who were ruling over Israel at this time.) ⁵Samson went down with his father and mother to Timnah, as far as the vineyard near there. Suddenly, a young lion came roaring toward Samson! ⁶The Spirit*d* of the LORD entered Samson with great power, and he tore the lion apart with his bare hands. For him it was as easy as tearing apart a young goat. But Samson did not tell his father or mother what he had done. ⁷Then he went down to the city and talked to the Philistine woman, and he liked her.

⁸Several days later Samson went back to marry her. On his way he went over to look at the body of the dead lion and found a swarm of bees and honey in it. ⁹Samson got some of the honey with his hands and walked along eating it. When he came to his parents, he gave some to them. They ate it, too, but Samson did not tell them he had taken the honey from the body of the dead lion.

¹⁰Samson's father went down to see the Philistine woman. And Samson gave a feast, as was the custom for the bridegroom. ¹¹When the people saw him, they sent thirty friends to be with him

Samson's Riddle

[12]Samson said to them, "Let me tell you a riddle. Try to find the answer during the seven days of the feast. If you can, I will give you thirty linen shirts and thirty changes of clothes. [13]But if you can't, you must give me thirty linen shirts and thirty changes of clothes."

So they said, "Tell us your riddle so we can hear it."

[14]Samson said,

"Out of the eater comes something to eat.
Out of the strong comes something sweet."

After three days, they had not found the answer.

[15]On the fourth[n] day they said to Samson's wife, "Did you invite us here to make us poor? Trick your husband into telling us the answer to the riddle. If you don't, we will burn you and everyone in your father's house."

[16]So Samson's wife went to him, crying, and said, "You hate me! You don't really love me! You told my people a riddle, but you won't tell me the answer."

Samson said, "I haven't even told my father or mother. Why should I tell you?"

[17]Samson's wife cried for the rest of the seven days of the feast. So he finally gave her the answer on the seventh day, because she kept bothering him. Then she told her people the answer to the riddle.

[18]Before sunset on the seventh day of the feast, the Philistine men had the answer. They came to Samson and said,

"What is sweeter than honey?
What is stronger than a lion?"

Then Samson said to them,

"If you had not plowed with my young cow,
you would not have solved my riddle!"

[19]Then the Spirit[d] of the Lord entered Samson and gave him great power. Samson went down to the city of Ashkelon and killed thirty of its men and took all that they had and gave the clothes to the men who had answered his riddle. Then he went to his father's house very angry. [20]And Samson's wife was given to his best man.

Samson Troubles the Philistines

15 At the time of the wheat harvest, Samson went to visit his wife, taking a young goat with him. He said, "I'm going to my wife's room," but her father would not let him go in.

[2]He said to Samson, "I thought you really hated your wife, so I gave her to your best man. Her younger sister is more beautiful. Take her instead."

[3]But Samson said to them, "This time no one will blame me for hurting you Philistines!" [4]So Samson went out and caught three hundred foxes. He took two foxes at a time, tied their tails together, and then tied a torch to the tails of each pair of foxes. [5]After he lit the torches, he let the foxes loose in the grainfields of the Philistines so that he burned up their standing grain, the piles of grain, their vineyards, and their olive trees.

[6]The Philistines asked, "Who did this?"

Someone told them, "Samson, the son-in-law of the man from Timnah, did because his father-in-law gave his wife to his best man."

So the Philistines burned Samson's wife and her father to death. [7]Then Samson said to the Philistines, "Since you did this, I won't stop until I pay you back!" [8]Samson attacked the Philistines and killed many of them. Then he went down and stayed in a cave in the rock of Etam.

[9]The Philistines went up and camped in the land of Judah, near a place named Lehi. [10]The men of Judah asked them, "Why have you come here to fight us?"

They answered, "We have come to make Samson our prisoner, to pay him back for what he did to our people."

[11]Then three thousand men of Judah went to the cave in the rock of Etam and said to Samson, "What have you done to us? Don't you know that the Philistines rule over us?"

Samson answered, "I only paid them back for what they did to me."

[12]Then they said to him, "We have come to tie you up and to hand you over to the Philistines."

Samson said to them, "Promise me you will not hurt me yourselves."

[13]The men from Judah said, "We agree. We will just tie you up and give you to the Philistines. We will not kill you." So they tied Samson with two new ropes and led him up from the cave in the rock. [14]When Samson came to the place named Lehi, the Philistines came to meet him, shouting for joy. Then the Spirit[d] of the Lord entered Samson and gave him great power. The ropes on him weakened like burned strings and fell off his hands! [15]Samson found the jawbone of

---

fourth   The Hebrew word is "seventh." Some old translations say "fourth," which fits the order of events better.

a dead donkey, took it, and killed a thousand men with it!

[16]Then Samson said,

"With a donkey's jawbone
I made donkeys out of them.
With a donkey's jawbone
I killed a thousand men!"

[17]When he finished speaking, he threw away the jawbone. So that place was named Ramath Lehi.[n]

[18]Samson was very thirsty, so he cried out to the LORD, "You gave me, your servant, this great victory. Do I have to die of thirst now? Do I have to be captured by people who are not circumcised?"[d] [19]Then God opened up a hole in the ground at Lehi, and water came out. When Samson drank, he felt better; he felt strong again. So he named that spring Caller's Spring, which is still in Lehi.

[20]Samson judged Israel for twenty years in the days of the Philistines.

Samson Goes to the City of Gaza

16 One day Samson went to Gaza and saw a prostitute[d] there. He went in to spend the night with her. [2]When the people of Gaza heard, "Samson has come here!" they surrounded the place and waited for him near the city gate all night. They whispered to each other, "When dawn comes, we will kill Samson!"

[3]But Samson only stayed with the prostitute until midnight. Then he got up and took hold of the doors and the two posts of the city gate and tore them loose, along with the bar. He put them on his shoulders and carried them to the top of the hill that faces the city of Hebron.

Samson and Delilah

[4]After this, Samson fell in love with a woman named Delilah, who lived in the Valley of Sorek. [5]The Philistine rulers went to Delilah and said, "Find out what makes Samson so strong. Trick him into telling how we can overpower him and capture him and tie him up. If you do this, each one of us will give you twenty-eight pounds of silver."

[6]So Delilah said to Samson, "Tell me why you are so strong. How can someone tie you up and capture you?"

[7]Samson answered, "Someone would have to tie me up with seven new bowstrings that have not been dried. Then I would be as weak as any other man."

[8]The Philistine rulers brought Delilah seven new bowstrings that had not been dried, and she tied Samson with them. [9]Some men were hiding in another room. Delilah said to him, "Samson, the Philistines are here!" But Samson broke the bowstrings like pieces of burned string. So the Philistines did not find out the secret of Samson's strength.

[10]Then Delilah said to Samson, "You made a fool of me. You lied to me. Now tell me how someone can tie you up."

[11]Samson said, "They would have to tie me with new ropes that have not been used before. Then I would become as weak as any other man."

[12]So Delilah took new ropes and tied Samson. Some men were hiding in another room. She called out to him, "Samson, the Philistines are here!" But he broke the ropes as easily as if they were threads.

[13]Then Delilah said to Samson, "Again you have made a fool of me. You lied to me. Tell me how someone can tie you up."

He said, "Using the loom,[n] weave the seven braids of my hair into the cloth, and tighten it with a pin. Then I will be as weak as any other man."

While Samson slept, Delilah wove the seven braids of his hair into the cloth. [14]Then she fastened it with a pin.

Again she said to him, "Samson, the Philistines are here!" Samson woke up and pulled out the pin and the loom with the cloth.

[15]Then Delilah said to him, "How can you say, 'I love you,' when you don't even trust me? This is the third time you have made a fool of me. You haven't told me the secret of your great strength."

[16]She kept bothering Samson about his secret day after day until he felt he was going to die!

[17]So he told her everything. He said, "I have never had my hair cut, because I have been set apart to God as a Nazirite[d] since I was born. If someone shaved my head, I would lose my strength and be as weak as any other man."

[18]When Delilah saw that he had told her everything sincerely, she sent a message to the Philistine rulers. She said, "Come back one more time, because he has told me everything." So the Philistine rulers came back to Delilah and brought the silver with them. [19]Delilah got Samson to sleep, lying in her lap. Then she called in a man to shave off the seven braids of Samson's hair. In this way she began to make him weak, and his strength left him.

[20]Then she said, "Samson, the Philistines are here!"

He woke up and thought, "I'll leave as I did before and shake myself free." But he did not know that the LORD had left him.

[21]Then the Philistines captured Samson and

Ramath Lehi This name means Jawbone Hill.
loom A machine for making cloth from thread.

tore out his eyes. They took him down to Gaza, where they put bronze chains on him and made him grind grain in the prison. ²²But his hair began to grow again.

⁂ **SIDELIGHT:** When Samson was forced to grind grain as a prisoner, the punishment was severe (Judges 16:21). The millstone he would have turned was probably made of limestone and was at least two feet across with a hole in the middle. Only large animals and extremely strong people could operate the grinding mills.

Samson Dies

²³The Philistine rulers gathered to celebrate and to offer a great sacrifice to their god Dagon.^d They said, "Our god has handed Samson our enemy over to us." ²⁴When the people saw him, they praised their god, saying,

"This man destroyed our country.
    He killed many of us!
But our god handed over
    our enemy to us."

²⁵While the people were enjoying the celebration, they said, "Bring Samson out to perform for us." So they brought Samson from the prison, and he performed for them. They made him stand between the pillars. ²⁶Samson said to the servant holding his hand, "Let me feel the pillars that hold up the temple so I can lean against them." ²⁷Now the temple was full of men and women. All the Philistine rulers were there, and about three thousand men and women were on the roofⁿ watching Samson perform. ²⁸Then Samson prayed to the LORD, "Lord GOD, remember me. God, please give me strength one more time so I can pay these Philistines back for putting out my two eyes!" ²⁹Then Samson turned to the two center pillars that supported the whole temple. He braced himself between the two pillars, with his right hand on one and his left hand on the other. ³⁰Samson said, "Let me die with these Philistines!" Then he pushed as hard as he could, causing the temple to fall on the rulers and all the people in it. So Samson killed more of the Philistines when he died than when he was alive.

³¹Samson's brothers and his whole family went down to get his body. They brought him back and buried him in the tomb of Manoah, his father, between the cities of Zorah and Eshtaol. Samson was a judge for the people of Israel for twenty years.

Micah's Idols

17 There was a man named Micah who lived in the mountains of Ephraim. ²He said to his mother, "I heard you speak a curse about the twenty-eight pounds of silver that were taken from you. I have the silver with me; I took it."

His mother said, "The LORD bless you, my son!"

³Micah gave the twenty-eight pounds of silver to his mother. Then she said, "I will give this silver to the LORD. I will have my son make an idol and a statue. So I will give the silver back to you."

⁴When he gave the silver back to his mother, she took about five pounds and gave it to a silversmith. With it he made an idol and a statue, which stood in Micah's house. ⁵Micah had a special holy place, and he made a holy vest^d and some household idols. Then Micah chose one of his sons to be his priest. ⁶At that time Israel did not have a king, so everyone did what seemed right.

⁷There was a young man who was a Leviteⁿ from the city of Bethlehem in Judah who was from the people of Judah. ⁸He left Bethlehem to look for another place to live, and on his way he came to Micah's house in the mountains of Ephraim. ⁹Micah asked him, "Where are you from?"

He answered, "I'm a Levite from Bethlehem in Judah. I'm looking for a place to live."

¹⁰Micah said to him, "Live with me and be my father and my priest. I will give you four ounces of silver each year and clothes and food." So the Levite went in. ¹¹He agreed to live with Micah and became like one of Micah's own sons. ¹²Micah made him a priest, and he lived in Micah's house. ¹³Then Micah said, "Now I know the LORD will be good to me, because I have a Levite as my priest."

Dan's Family Captures Laish

18 At that time Israel did not have a king. And at that time the tribe^d of Dan was still looking for a land where they could live, a land of their own. The Danites had not yet been given their own land among the tribes of Israel. ²So, from their family groups, they chose five soldiers from the cities of Zorah and Eshtaol to spy out and explore the land. They were told, "Go, explore the land."

They came to the mountains of Ephraim, to Mi-

---

roof In Bible times houses were built with flat roofs. The roof was used for drying things such as flax and fruit. And it was used as an extra room, as a place for worship, and as a place to sleep in the summer.

Levite The Levites were the only ones God had appointed as priests.

cah's house, where they spent the night. ³When they came near Micah's house, they recognized the voice of the young Levite. ⁿ So they stopped there and asked him, "Who brought you here? What are you doing here? Why are you here?"

⁴He told them what Micah had done for him, saying "He hired me. I am his priest."

⁵They said to him, "Please ask God if our journey will be successful."

⁶The priest said to them, "Go in peace. The LORD is pleased with your journey."

⁷So the five men left. When they came to the city of Laish, they saw that the people there lived in safety, like the people of Sidon. They thought they were safe and had plenty of everything. They lived a long way from the Sidonians and had no dealings with anyone else.

⁸When the five men returned to Zorah and Eshtaol, their relatives asked them, "What did you find?"

⁹They answered, "We have seen the land, and it is very good. We should attack them. Aren't you going to do something? Don't wait! Let's go and take that land! ¹⁰When you go, you will see there is plenty of land — plenty of everything! The people are not expecting an attack. Surely God has handed that land over to us!"

¹¹So six hundred Danites left Zorah and Eshtaol ready for war. ¹²On their way they set up camp near the city of Kiriath Jearim in Judah. That is why the place west of Kiriath Jearim is named Mahaneh Danⁿ to this day. ¹³From there they traveled on to the mountains of Ephraim. Then they came to Micah's house.

¹⁴The five men who had explored the land around Laish said to their relatives, "Do you know in one of these houses there are a holy vest,ᵈ household gods, an idol, and a statue? You know what to do." ¹⁵So they stopped at the Levite's house, which was also Micah's house, and greeted the Levite. ¹⁶The six hundred Danites stood at the entrance gate, wearing their weapons of war. ¹⁷The five spies went into the house and took the idol, the holy vest, the household idols, and the statue. The priest and the six hundred men armed for war stood by the entrance gate.

¹⁸When the spies went into Micah's house and took the image, the holy vest, the household idols, and the statue, the priest asked them, "What are you doing?"

¹⁹They answered, "Be quiet! Don't say a word. Come with us and be our father and priest. Is it better for you to be a priest for one man's house or for a tribe and family group in Israel?" ²⁰This made the priest happy. So he took the holy vest, the household idols, and the idol and went with

the Danites. ²¹They left Micah's house, putting their little children, their animals, and everything they owned in front of them.

²²When they had gone a little way from Micah's house, the men who lived near Micah were called out and caught up with them. ²³The men with Micah shouted at the Danites, who turned around and said to Micah, "What's the matter with you? Why have you been called out to fight?"

²⁴Micah answered, "You took my gods that I made and my priest. What do I have left? How can you ask me, 'What's the matter?' "

²⁵The Danites answered, "You should not argue with us. Some of our angry men might attack you, killing you and your family." ²⁶Then the Danites went on their way. Micah knew they were too strong for him, so he turned and went back home.

²⁷Then the Danites took what Micah had made and his priest and went on to Laish. They attacked those peaceful people and killed them with their swords and then burned the city. ²⁸There was no one to save the people of Laish. They lived too far from Sidon, and they had no dealings with anyone else. Laish was in a valley near Beth Rehob. The people of Dan rebuilt the city and lived there. ²⁹They changed the name of Laish to Dan, naming it for their ancestor Dan, one of the sons of Israel.

³⁰The people of Dan set up the idols in the city of Dan. Jonathan son of Gershom, Moses' son, and his sons served as priests for the tribe of Dan until the land was captured. ³¹The people of Dan set up the idols Micah had made as long as the Holy Tentᵈ of God was in Shiloh.

A Levite and His Servant

19 At that time Israel did not have a king. There was a Levite who lived in the faraway mountains of Ephraim. He had taken a slave womanᵈ from the city of Bethlehem in the land of Judah to live with him, ²but she was unfaithful to him. She left him and went back to her father's house in Bethlehem in Judah and stayed there for four months. ³Then her husband went to ask her to come back to him, taking with him his servant and two donkeys. When the Levite came to her father's house, she invited him to come in, and her father was happy to see him. ⁴The father-in-law, the young woman's father, asked him to stay. So he stayed for three days and ate, drank, and slept there.

⁵On the fourth day they got up early in the morning. The Levite was getting ready to leave, but the woman's father said to his son-in-law,

---

Levite   The Levites were the only ones God had appointed as priests.
Mahaneh Dan   This name means "the camp of Dan."

"Refresh yourself by eating something. Then go."
⁶So the two men sat down to eat and drink together. After that, the father said to him, "Please stay tonight. Relax and enjoy yourself." ⁷When the man got up to go, his father-in-law asked him to stay. So he stayed again that night. ⁸On the fifth day the man got up early in the morning to leave. The woman's father said, "Refresh yourself. Wait until this afternoon." So the two men ate together.

⁹When the Levite, his slave woman, and his servant got up to leave, the father-in-law, the young woman's father, said, "It's almost night. The day is almost gone. Spend the night here and enjoy yourself. Tomorrow morning you can get up early and go home." ¹⁰But the Levite did not want to stay another night. So he took his two saddled donkeys and his slave woman and traveled toward the city of Jebus (also called Jerusalem).

¹¹As the day was almost over, they came near Jebus. So the servant said to his master, "Let's stop at this city of the Jebusites, and spend the night here."

¹²But his master said, "No. We won't go inside a foreign city. Those people are not Israelites. We will go on to the city of Gibeah." ¹³He said, "Come on. Let's try to make it to Gibeah or Ramah so we can spend the night in one of those cities." ¹⁴So they went on. The sun went down as they came near Gibeah, which belongs to the tribe*d* of Benjamin. ¹⁵They stopped there to spend the night. They came to the public square of the city and sat down, but no one invited them home to spend the night.

¹⁶Finally, in the evening an old man came in from his work in the fields. His home was in the mountains of Ephraim, but now he was living in Gibeah. (The people of Gibeah were from the tribe of Benjamin.) ¹⁷He saw the traveler in the public square and asked, "Where are you going? Where did you come from?"

¹⁸The Levite answered, "We are traveling from Bethlehem in Judah to my home in the mountains of Ephraim. I have been to Bethlehem in Judah, but now I am going to the Holy Tent*d* of the Lord. No one has invited me to stay in his house. ¹⁹We already have straw and food for our donkeys and bread and wine for me, the young woman, and my servant. We don't need anything."

²⁰The old man said, "You are welcome to stay at my house. Let me give you anything you need, but don't spend the night in the public square." ²¹So the old man took the Levite into his house, and he fed their donkeys. They washed their feet and had something to eat and drink.

²²While they were enjoying themselves, some wicked men of the city surrounded the house and beat on the door. They shouted to the old man who owned the house, "Bring out the man who came to your house. We want to have sexual relations with him."

²³The owner of the house went outside and said to them, "No, my friends. Don't be so evil. This man is a guest in my house. Don't do this terrible thing! ²⁴Look, here are my daughter, who has never had sexual relations before, and the man's slave woman. I will bring them out to you now. Do anything you want with them, but don't do such a terrible thing to this man.'

²⁵But the men would not listen to him. So the Levite took his slave woman and sent her outside to them. They forced her to have sexual relations with them, and they abused her all night long. Then, at dawn, they let her go. ²⁶She came back to the house where her master was staying and fell down at the door and lay there until daylight.

²⁷In the morning when the Levite got up, he opened the door of the house and went outside to go on his way. But his slave woman was lying at the doorway of the house, with her hands on the doorsill. ²⁸The Levite said to her, "Get up; let's go." But she did not answer. So he put her on his donkey and went home.

²⁹When the Levite got home, he took a knife and cut his slave woman into twelve parts, limb by limb. Then he sent a part to each area of Israel. ³⁰Everyone who saw this said, "Nothing like this has ever happened before, not since the people of Israel came out of Egypt. Think about it. Tell us what to do."

The War Between Israel and Benjamin

20 So all the Israelites from Dan to Beersheba,*n* including the land of Gilead, joined together before the Lord in the city of Mizpah. ²The leaders of all the tribes*d* of Israel took their places in the meeting of the people of God. There were 400,000 soldiers with swords. ³(The people of Benjamin heard that the Israelites had gone up to Mizpah.) Then the Israelites said to the Levite, "Tell us how this evil thing happened."

⁴So the husband of the murdered woman answered, "My slave woman*d* and I came to Gibeah in Benjamin to spend the night. ⁵During the night the men of Gibeah came after me. They surrounded the house and wanted to kill me. They forced my slave woman to have sexual relations and she died. ⁶I took her and cut her into parts and sent one part to each area of Israel because the people of Benjamin did this wicked and terri-

---

Dan ... Beersheba Dan was the city farthest north in Israel. Beersheba was the city farthest south. So this means all the people of Israel.

ble thing in Israel. ⁷Now, all you Israelites, speak up. What is your decision?"

⁸Then all the people stood up at the same time, saying, "None of us will go home. Not one of us will go back to his house! ⁹Now this is what we will do to Gibeah. We will throw lots.ᵈ ¹⁰That way we will choose ten men from every hundred men from all the tribes of Israel, and we will choose a hundred men from every thousand, and a thousand men from every ten thousand. These will find supplies for the army. Then the army will go to the city of Gibeah of Benjamin to repay them for the terrible thing they have done in Israel." ¹¹So all the men of Israel were united and gathered against the city.

¹²The tribes of Israel sent men throughout the tribe of Benjamin demanding, "What is this evil thing some of your men have done? ¹³Hand over the wicked men in Gibeah so that we can put them to death. We must remove this evil from Israel."

But the Benjaminites would not listen to their fellow Israelites. ¹⁴The Benjaminites left their own cities and met at Gibeah to fight the Israelites. ¹⁵In only one day the Benjaminites got 26,000 soldiers together who were trained with swords. They also had 700 chosen men from Gibeah. ¹⁶Seven hundred of these trained soldiers were left-handed, each of whom could sling a stone at a hair and not miss!

✳ SIDELIGHT: Looking for a good left-handed pitcher for your baseball team? Check out Judges 20:16, which tells about the Benjaminite army that included seven hundred lefties who were such good aims they could hit a hair with a stone from a sling. They would probably be all-stars today.

---

¹⁷The Israelites, except for the Benjaminites, gathered 400,000 soldiers with swords.

¹⁸The Israelites went up to the city of Bethel and asked God, "Which tribe shall be first to attack the Benjaminites?"

The Lord answered, "Judah shall go first."

¹⁹The next morning the Israelites got up and made a camp near Gibeah. ²⁰The men of Israel went out to fight the Benjaminites and took their battle position at Gibeah. ²¹Then the Benjaminites came out of Gibeah and killed 22,000 Israelites during the battle that day. ²²⁻²³The Israelites went before the Lord and cried until evening. They asked the Lord, "Shall we go to fight our relatives, the Benjaminites, again?"

The Lord answered, "Go up and fight them."

The men of Israel encouraged each other. So they took the same battle positions they had taken the first day.

²⁴The Israelites came to fight the Benjaminites the second day. ²⁵The Benjaminites came out of Gibeah to attack the Israelites. This time, the Benjaminites killed 18,000 Israelites, all of whom carried swords.

²⁶Then the Israelites went up to Bethel. There they sat down and cried to the Lord and went without food all day until evening. They also brought burnt offerings and fellowship offerings to the Lord. ²⁷The Israelites asked the Lord a question. (In those days the Arkᵈ of the Agreement with God was there at Bethel. ²⁸A priest named Phinehas son of Eleazar, the son of Aaron, served before the Ark of the Agreement.) They asked, "Shall we go to fight our relatives, the Benjaminites, again, or shall we stop fighting?"

The Lord answered, "Go, because tomorrow I will hand them over to you."

²⁹Then the Israelites set up ambushes all around Gibeah. ³⁰They went to fight against the Benjaminites at Gibeah on the third day, getting into position for battle as they had done before. ³¹When the Benjaminites came out to fight them, the Israelites backed up and led the Benjaminites away from the city. The Benjaminites began to kill some of the Israelites as they had done before. About thirty Israelites were killed — some in the fields and some on the roads leading to Bethel and to Gibeah.

³²The Benjaminites said, "We are winning as before!"

But the Israelites said, "Let's run. Let's trick them into going farther away from their city and onto the roads."

³³All the Israelites moved from their places and got into battle positions at a place named Baal Tamar. Then the Israelites ran out from their hiding places west of Gibeah. ³⁴Ten thousand of the best trained soldiers from all of Israel attacked Gibeah. The battle was very hard. The Benjaminites did not know disaster was about to come to them. ³⁵The Lord used the Israelites to defeat the Benjaminites. On that day the Israelites killed 25,100 Benjaminites, all armed with swords. ³⁶Then the Benjaminites saw that they were defeated.

The Israelites had moved back because they were depending on the surprise attack they had set up near Gibeah. ³⁷The men in hiding rushed into Gibeah, spread out, and killed everyone in the city with their swords. ³⁸Now the Israelites had set up a signal with the men in hiding. The men in the surprise attack were to send up a cloud of smoke from the city. ³⁹Then the army of Israel turned around in the battle.

The Benjaminites had killed about thirty Israelites. They were saying, "We are winning, as in the first battle!" ⁴⁰But then a cloud of smoke began to rise from the city. The Benjaminites turned around and saw that the whole city was going up in smoke. ⁴¹Then the Israelites turned and began to fight. The Benjaminites were terrified because they knew that disaster was coming to them. ⁴²So the Benjaminites ran away from the Israelites toward the desert, but they could not escape the battle. And the Israelites who came out of the cities killed them. ⁴³They surrounded the Benjaminites and chased them and caught them in the area east of Gibeah. ⁴⁴So 18,000 brave Benjaminite fighters were killed. ⁴⁵The Benjaminites ran toward the desert to the rock of Rimmon, but the Israelites killed 5,000 Benjaminites along the roads. They chased them as far as Gidom and killed 2,000 more Benjaminites there.

⁴⁶On that day 25,000 Benjaminites were killed, all of whom had fought bravely with swords. ⁴⁷But 600 Benjaminites ran to the rock of Rimmon in the desert, where they stayed for four months. ⁴⁸Then the Israelites went back to the land of Benjamin and killed the people in every city and also the animals and everything they could find. And they burned every city they found.

Wives for the Men of Benjamin

21 At Mizpah the men of Israel had sworn, "Not one of us will let his daughter marry a man from the tribe*d* of Benjamin."

²The people went to the city of Bethel and sat before God until evening, crying loudly. ³They said, "LORD, God of Israel, why has this terrible thing happened to us so that one tribe of Israel is missing today?"

⁴Early the next day the people built an altar and put burnt offerings and fellowship offerings to God on it.

⁵Then the Israelites asked, "Did any tribe of Israel not come here to meet with us in the presence of the LORD?" They asked this question because they had sworn that anyone who did not meet with them at Mizpah would be killed.

⁶The Israelites felt sorry for their relatives, the Benjaminites. They said, "Today one tribe has been cut off from Israel. ⁷We swore before the LORD that we would not allow our daughters to marry a Benjaminite. How can we make sure that the remaining men of Benjamin will have wives?"

⁸Then they asked, "Which one of the tribes of Israel did not come here to Mizpah?" They found that no one from the city of Jabesh Gilead had

come. ⁹The people of Israel counted everyone, but there was no one from Jabesh Gilead.

¹⁰So the whole group of Israelites sent twelve thousand soldiers to Jabesh Gilead to kill the people with their swords, even the women and children.

¹¹"This is what you must do: Kill every man in Jabesh Gilead and every married woman." ¹²The soldiers found four hundred young unmarried women in Jabesh Gilead, so they brought them to the camp at Shiloh in Canaan.

¹³Then the whole group of Israelites sent a message to the men of Benjamin, who were at the rock of Rimmon, offering to make peace with them. ¹⁴So the men of Benjamin came back at that time. The Israelites gave them the women from Jabesh Gilead who had not been killed, but there were not enough women.

¹⁵The people of Israel felt sorry for the Benjaminites because the LORD had separated the tribes of Israel. ¹⁶The older leaders of the Israelites said, "The women of Benjamin have been killed. Where can we get wives for the men of Benjamin who are still alive? ¹⁷These men must have children to continue their families so a tribe in Israel will not die out. ¹⁸But we cannot allow our daughters to marry them, because we swore, 'Anyone who gives a wife to a man of Benjamin is cursed.' ¹⁹We have an idea! There is a yearly festival of the LORD at Shiloh, which is north of the city of Bethel, east of the road that goes from Bethel to Shechem, and south of the city of Lebonah."

²⁰So the older leaders told the men of Benjamin, "Go and hide in the vineyards. ²¹Watch for the young women from Shiloh to come out to join the dancing. Then run out from the vineyards and take one of the young Shiloh women and return to the land of Benjamin. ²²If their fathers or brothers come to us and complain, we will say: 'Be kind to the men of Benjamin. We did not get wives for Benjamin during the war, and you did not give the women to the men from Benjamin. So you are not guilty.' "

²³So that is what the Benjaminites did. While the young women were dancing, each man caught one of them, took her away, and married her. Then they went back to the land God had given them and rebuilt their cities and lived there.

²⁴Then the Israelites went home to their own tribes and family groups, to their own land that God had given them.

²⁵In those days Israel did not have a king. Everyone did what seemed right.

RUTH

Why Read This Book:
- See how relationships grow strong (Ruth 1—2).
- Discover the importance of keeping agreements (Ruth 3—4).

Behind the Scenes:

The story of Ruth would never have made the evening news. There are no wars, no twisted plots, no villains. In fact, much more "important" things were happening at the time. The story took place during the period of the judges (see Judges, p. 215), and Israel faced moral decline, foreign attacks and national chaos.

But in the midst of other seemingly important events, the Bible tells the simple, beautiful story of Ruth. It's a story of loyalty and faithfulness, a story of how ordinary people kept following God even when the nation of Israel was abandoning God.

The story opens in Moab, a non-Jewish area, where Naomi had gone to live. Her son had married a Moabite woman, Ruth. After only ten years, Ruth's husband died. Even though Naomi could have left Ruth, she took her in, and the two became close friends.

WHERE THE ACTION WAS

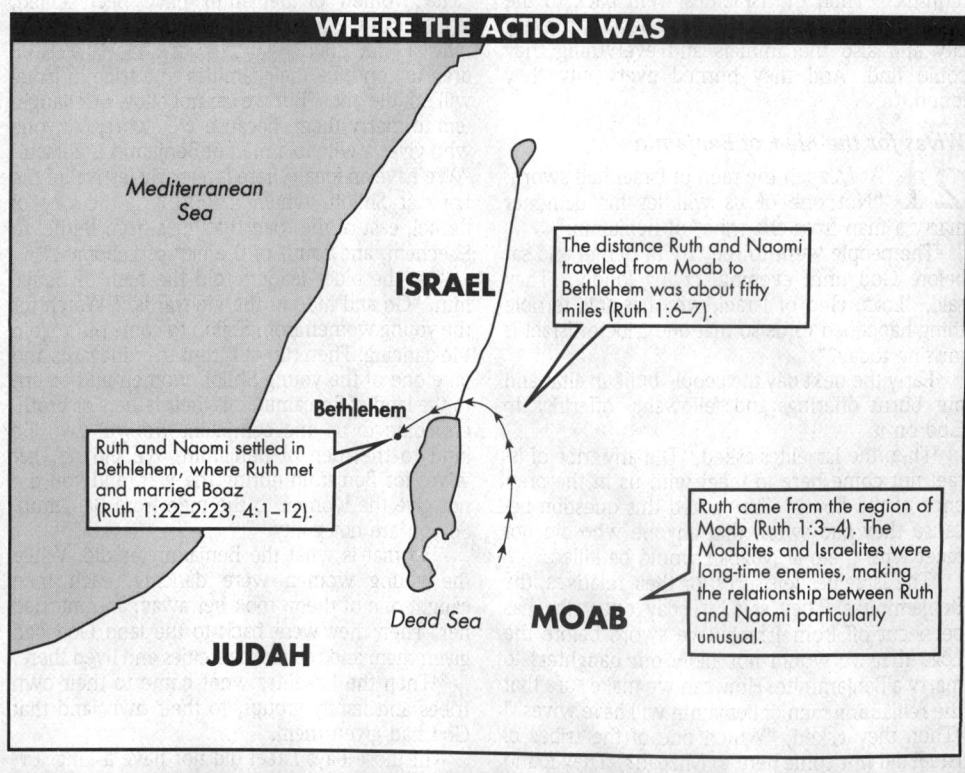

Mediterranean Sea

ISRAEL

The distance Ruth and Naomi traveled from Moab to Bethlehem was about fifty miles (Ruth 1:6–7).

Bethlehem

Ruth and Naomi settled in Bethlehem, where Ruth met and married Boaz (Ruth 1:22–2:23, 4:1–12).

Ruth came from the region of Moab (Ruth 1:3–4). The Moabites and Israelites were long-time enemies, making the relationship between Ruth and Naomi particularly unusual.

Dead Sea   MOAB

JUDAH

WHEN THE ACTION WAS

2000BC	1500BC	1000BC	500BC	BC/AD
	The Israelites escaped from Egypt	Saul was Israel's king		Jesus was born
	Joshua led the Israelites into Canaan	Ruth lived during the time of the judges		

Behind the Scenes (cont.): Then Ruth and Naomi moved to Israel, Naomi's homeland, where Ruth was a foreigner. There Ruth met Boaz, who married her so Ruth's family name could continue. Years later, one of Ruth's descendants, David, became the greatest king of Israel. Even more important, Ruth thus was included in the family of Jesus Christ (see Matthew 1:5, p. 906).

The story of Ruth emphasizes the importance of faithfulness and loyalty—of one person to another and to God. Each main character—Ruth, Naomi, Boaz—shows a loyalty beyond what's required.

The story also reminds us that we don't have to be famous or do great things to be important to God. What is most important to God is that people are faithful in whatever they do, whether or not they are famous.

1

¹⁻²Long ago when the judges[n] ruled Israel, there was a shortage of food in the land. So a man named Elimelech left the town of Bethlehem in Judah to live in the country of Moab with his wife and his two sons. His wife was named Naomi, and his two sons were named Mahlon and Kilion. They were Ephrathahites from Bethlehem in Judah. When they came to Moab, they settled there.

³Then Naomi's husband, Elimelech, died, and she was left with her two sons. ⁴These sons married women from Moab. One was named Orpah, and the other was named Ruth. Naomi and her sons had lived in Moab about ten years ⁵when Mahlon and Kilion also died. So Naomi was left alone without her husband or her two sons.

⁶While Naomi was in Moab, she heard that the Lord had come to help his people and had given them food again. So she and her daughters-in-law got ready to leave Moab and return home. ⁷Naomi and her daughters-in-law left the place where they had lived and started back to the land of Judah. ⁸But Naomi said to her two daughters-in-law, "Go back home, each of you to your own

judges They were not judges in courts of law, but leaders of the people in times of emergency.

FRIENDS

A Little Encouragement

Dean Agnew would lie awake nights waiting to hear the sound of a car driving up. When he did, he would run to the front door to unlock it. Then he would cry with fear as his stepfather stumbled in, reeking of alcohol.

Doors slammed. Dishes broke in the kitchen. And yelling—the horrible yelling at his mother—made Dean wish his alcoholic stepfather would die.

Dean might have gone crazy if it hadn't been for friends like Tom Kruger. Tom was a year older than Dean. The two laughed a lot together, and Tom, a mechanical wizard, taught Dean how to fix cars.

Whenever Tom gave Dean a ride somewhere, he would end the trip by saying, "Stay cool, guy." Dean knew he meant, "Hang in there."

Those were tough times for Dean, but he survived because of his friends—people like Tom.

Ruth and Naomi also faced tough times. Both lost their husbands, and Naomi also lost her only sons. But because of their friendship with each other, they made it through. Read about their relationship in **Ruth 1:1–19**.

■ How were Dean's and Ruth's situations made better by the friendships of Tom and Naomi?

■ How can Ruth's example help you be a more committed friend?

CONSIDER . . .

■ befriending a newcomer at school or someone with a different background from you

■ being a committed friend to someone who is facing tough times by letting him or her talk openly about the problems.

FOR MORE, SEE . . .

■ Leviticus 19:9–10 (p. 115)

■ 1 John 3:11–18 (p. 1318)

■ 1 Samuel 20:11–17 (p. 263)

mother's house. May the LORD be as kind to you as you have been to me and my sons who are now dead. ⁹May the LORD give you another happy home and a new husband."

When Naomi kissed the women good-bye, they began to cry out loud. ¹⁰They said to her, "No, we want to go with you to your people."

¹¹But Naomi said, "My daughters, return to your own homes. Why do you want to go with me? I cannot give birth to more sons to give you new husbands; ¹²go back, my daughters, to your own homes. I am too old to have another husband. Even if I told myself, 'I still have hope' and had another husband tonight, and even if I had more sons, ¹³should you wait until they were grown into men? Should you live for so many years without husbands? Don't do that, my daughters. My life is much too sad for you to share, because the LORD has been against me!"

¹⁴The women cried together out loud again. Then Orpah kissed her mother-in-law Naomi good-bye, but Ruth held on to her tightly.

¹⁵Naomi said to Ruth, "Look, your sister-in-law is going back to her own people and her own gods. Go back with her."

Ruth Stays with Naomi

¹⁶But Ruth said, "Don't beg me to leave you or to stop following you. Where you go, I will go. Where you live, I will live. Your people will be my people, and your God will be my God. ¹⁷And where you die, I will die, and there I will be buried. I ask the LORD to punish me terribly if I do not keep this promise: Not even death will separate us."

¹⁸When Naomi saw that Ruth had firmly made up her mind to go with her, she stopped arguing with her. ¹⁹So Naomi and Ruth went on until they came to the town of Bethlehem. When they entered Bethlehem, all the people became very excited. The women of the town said, "Is this really Naomi?"

²⁰Naomi answered the people, "Don't call me Naomi.ⁿ Call me Mara,ⁿ because the Almighty has made my life very sad. ²¹When I left, I had all I wanted, but now, the LORD has brought me home with nothing. Why should you call me Naomi when the LORD has spoken against me and the Almighty has given me so much trouble?"

²²So Naomi and her daughter-in-law Ruth, the Moabite, returned from Moab and arrived at Bethlehem at the beginning of the barley harvest.

Ruth Meets Boaz

2 Now Naomi had a rich relative named Boaz, from Elimelech's family.

Naomi This name means "happy" or "pleasant."
Mara This name means "bitter" or "sad."

²One day Ruth, the Moabite, said to Naomi, "I am going to the fields. Maybe someone will be kind enough to let me gather the grain he leaves behind."

Naomi said, "Go, my daughter."

³So Ruth went to the fields and gathered the grain that the workers cutting the grain had left behind. It just so happened that the field belonged to Boaz, from Elimelech's family.

⁴Soon Boaz came from Bethlehem and greeted his workers, "The LORD be with you!"

And the workers answered, "May the LORD bless you!"

⁵Then Boaz asked his servant in charge of the workers, "Whose girl is that?"

⁶The servant answered, "She is the young Moabite woman who came back with Naomi from the country of Moab. ⁷She said, 'Please let me follow the workers cutting grain and gather what they leave behind.' She came and has remained here, from morning until just now. She has stopped only a few moments to rest in the shelter."

⁸Then Boaz said to Ruth, "Listen, my daughter. Don't go to gather grain for yourself in another field. Don't even leave this field at all, but continue following closely behind my women workers. ⁹Watch to see into which fields they go to cut grain and follow them. I have warned the young men not to bother you. When you are thirsty, you may go and drink from the water jugs that the young men have filled."

¹⁰Then Ruth bowed low with her face to the ground and said to him, "I am not an Israelite. Why have you been so kind to notice me?"

¹¹Boaz answered her, "I know about all the help you have given your mother-in-law after your husband died. You left your father and mother and your own country to come to a nation where you did not know anyone. ¹²May the LORD reward you for all you have done. May your wages *be paid in full by the LORD, the God of Israel,* under whose wings you have come for shelter."

¹³Then Ruth said, "I hope I can continue to please you, sir. You have said kind and encourag-

ing words to me, your servant, though I am not one of your servants."

14At mealtime Boaz told Ruth, "Come here. Eat some of our bread and dip it in our sauce."

So Ruth sat down beside the workers. Boaz handed her some roasted grain, and she ate until she was full; she even had some food left over. 15When Ruth rose and went back to work, Boaz commanded his workers, "Let her gather even around the piles of cut grain. Don't tell her to go away. 16In fact, drop some full heads of grain for her from what you have in your hands, and let her gather them. Don't tell her to stop."

17So Ruth gathered grain in the field until evening. Then she separated the grain from the chaff,d and there was about one-half bushel of barley. 18Ruth carried the grain into town, and her mother-in-law saw how much she had gathered. Ruth also took out the food that was left over from lunch and gave it to Naomi.

19Naomi asked her, "Where did you gather all this grain today? Where did you work? Blessed be whoever noticed you!"

Ruth told her mother-in-law whose field she had worked in. She said, "The man I worked with today is named Boaz."

20Naomi told her daughter-in-law, "The LORD bless him! He continues to be kind to us — both the living and the dead!" Then Naomi told Ruth, "Boaz is one of our close relatives,n one who should take care of us."

21Then Ruth, the Moabite, said, "Boaz also told me, 'Keep close to my workers until they have finished my whole harvest.' "

22But Naomi said to her daughter-in-law Ruth, "It is better for you to continue working with his women workers. If you work in another field, someone might hurt you." 23So Ruth continued working closely with the workers of Boaz, gathering grain until the barley harvest and the wheat harvest were finished. And she continued to live with Naomi, her mother-in-law.

Naomi's Plan

3 Then Naomi, Ruth's mother-in-law, said to her, "My daughter. I must find a suitable home for you, one that will be good for you. 2Now Boaz, whose young women you worked with, is our close relative.n Tonight he will be working at the threshingd floor. 3Wash yourself, put on perfume, change your clothes, and go down to the threshing floor. But don't let him know you're there until he has finished his dinner. 4Watch him so you will know where he lies

down to sleep. When he lies down, go and lift the cover of his feetn and lie down. He will tell you what you should do."

5Then Ruth answered, "I will do everything you say."

6So Ruth went down to the threshing floor and did all her mother-in-law told her to do. 7After his evening meal, Boaz felt good and went to sleep lying beside the pile of grain. Ruth went to him quietly and lifted the cover from his feet and lay down.

8About midnight Boaz was startled and rolled over. There was a woman lying near his feet! 9Boaz asked, "Who are you?"

She said, "I am Ruth, your servant girl. Spread your cover over me, because you are a relative who is supposed to take care of me.' n

10Then Boaz said, "The LORD bless you, my daughter. This act of kindness is greater than the kindness you showed to Naomi in the beginning. You didn't look for a young man to marry, either rich or poor. 11Now, my daughter, don't be afraid. I will do everything you ask, because all the people in our town know you are a good woman. 12It is true that I am a relative who is to take care of you, but you have a closer relative than I. 13Stay here tonight, and in the morning we will see if he will take care of you. If he decides to take care of you, that is fine. But if he refuses, I will take care of you myself, as surely as the LORD lives. So stay here until morning."

14So Ruth stayed near his feet until morning but got up while it was still too dark to recognize anyone. Boaz thought, "People in town must not know that the woman came here to the threshingd floor." 15So Boaz said to Ruth, "Bring me your shawl and hold it open."

So Ruth held her shawl open, and Boaz poured six portions of barley into it. Boaz then put it on her head and went back to the city.

16When Ruth went back to her mother-in-law, Naomi asked, "How did you do, my daughter?"

Ruth told Naomi everything that Boaz did for her. 17She said, "Boaz gave me these six portions of barley, saying, 'You must not go home without a gift for your mother-in-law.' "

18Naomi answered, "Ruth, my daughter, wait here until you see what happens. Boaz will not rest until he has finished doing what he should do today."

Boaz Marries Ruth

4 Boaz went to the city gate and sat there until the close relative he had mentioned passed

---

close relatives   In Bible times the closest relative could marry a widow without children so she could have children. He would care for this family, but they and their property would not belong to him. They would belong to the dead husband.

lift ... feet   This showed Ruth was asking him to be her husband.

Spread ... me   By this, Ruth was asking Boaz to marry her.

by. Boaz called to him, "Come here, friend, and sit down." So the man came over and sat down. ²Boaz gathered ten of the older leaders of the city and told them, "Sit down here!" So they sat down.

³Then Boaz said to the close relative, "Naomi, who has come back from the country of Moab, wants to sell the piece of land that belonged to our relative Elimelech. ⁴So I decided to tell you about it: If you want to buy back the land, then buy it in front of the people who are sitting here and in front of the older leaders of my people. But if you don't want to buy it, tell me, because you are the only one who can buy it, and I am next after you."

The close relative answered, "I will buy back the land."

⁵Then Boaz explained, "When you buy the land from Naomi, you must also marry Ruth, the Moabite, the dead man's wife. That way, the land will stay in the dead man's name."

⁶The close relative answered, "I can't buy back the land. If I did, I might harm what I can pass on to my own sons. I cannot buy the land back, so buy it yourself."

> ☀ **SIDELIGHT:** "Proof of purchase" coupons like those on cereal boxes are nothing new. In the Old Testament, people gave away one sandal as a proof of purchase (Ruth 4:7). Today's coupon is a definite improvement—especially when the other person's feet are smaller than yours!

⁷Long ago in Israel when people traded or bought back something, one person took off his sandal and gave it to the other person. This was the proof of ownership in Israel.

MARRIAGE

Ask Her, John!

John Anderson and Kim Mayo were special youth leaders. John's energy and Kim's spiritual insight made them a dynamic team. Everyone could see how they complemented each other. They were natural together.

John and Kim joined a two-year Bible study program and found themselves together again. In the study, they talked often about the Bible and their growing faith.

The youth group kids began taunting John and Kim. "Hey John!" they would tease. "When are you going to open your eyes and ask Kim out?"

He would blush. She would smile.

Finally, John asked her for a date. And another. And another. For two years, the youth group enjoyed watching the two leaders fall in love.

"When are you going to pop the question?" kids would tease John.

"We really love each other," John would reply, "but getting married is a big commitment. . . . We don't want to rush it."

Six months later, the couple walked into the youth room beaming. Kim proudly displayed a beautiful ring on her left hand. The whole youth group cheered, knowing this marriage would last a lifetime. When Boaz married Ruth, he also committed himself to her, even though his commitment was different from John's. Read about how Boaz made a marriage commitment in **Ruth 4:7–17**.

■ How did Boaz show that his commitment to Ruth was strong? How is what he did similar to and different from a wedding ceremony today?

■ What can you learn from Boaz and Ruth about what's most important in choosing a spouse?

CONSIDER . . .

■ writing a list of characteristics you hope to find in a spouse if you marry. Then evaluate the list in light of your faith and your commitments.

■ asking a husband and wife you respect to explain how commitment holds their relationship together.

FOR MORE, SEE . . .

■ Genesis 29:15–30 (p. 34)
■ Matthew 19:6 (p. 941)

■ Ephesians 5:21–33 (p. 1225)

⁸So the close relative said to Boaz, "Buy the land yourself," and he took off his sandal.

⁹Then Boaz said to the older leaders and to all the people, "You are witnesses today. I am buying from Naomi everything that belonged to Elimelech and Kilion and Mahlon. ¹⁰I am also taking Ruth, the Moabite who was the wife of Mahlon, as my wife. I am doing this so her dead husband's property will stay in his name and his name will not be separated from his family and his hometown. You are witnesses today."

¹¹So all the people and older leaders who were at the city gate said, "We are witnesses. May the LORD make this woman, who is coming into your home, like Rachel and Leah, who had many children and built up the people of Israel. May you become powerful in the district of Ephrathah and famous in Bethlehem. ¹²As Tamar gave birth to Judah's son Perez, ⁿ may the LORD give you many children through Ruth. May your family be great like his."

¹³So Boaz took Ruth home as his wife and had sexual relations with her. The LORD let her become pregnant, and she gave birth to a son. ¹⁴The women told Naomi, "Praise the LORD who gave you this grandson. May he become famous in Israel. ¹⁵He will give you new life and will take care of you in your old age because of your daughter-in-law who loves you. She is better for you than seven sons, because she has given birth to your grandson."

¹⁶Naomi took the boy, held him in her arms, and cared for him. ¹⁷The neighbors gave the boy his name saying, "This boy was born for Naomi." They named him Obed. Obed was the father of Jesse, and Jesse was the father of David.

¹⁸This is the family history of Perez, the father of Hezron. ¹⁹Hezron was the father of Ram, who was the father of Amminadab. ²⁰Amminadab was the father of Nahshon, who was the father of Salmon. ²¹Salmon was the father of Boaz, who was the father of Obed. ²²Obed was the father of Jesse, and Jesse was the father of David.

Perez   One of Boaz's ancestors.

1 SAMUEL

Why Read This Book:

■ See how God uses great leaders (1 Samuel 1—7).
■ Discover what can happen when leaders don't obey God (1 Samuel 8—15).
■ Find out how God can unite a nation under a holy leader (1 Samuel 16—31).

Behind the Scenes:

After the American Revolution in the 1770s, the thirteen states were almost like independent countries. Each had its own laws, and they constantly bickered. Only after the country had a new constitution and a strong president, George Washington, did the states unite.

The Israelites in Samuel's time lived in a similar situation. They didn't have any central government or regular army. For about a hundred years, the tribes had come together only during crises.

But the Israelites lived in constant fear of the Philistines. This warlike nation with superior iron weapons controlled the fertile plains along the Mediterranean Sea and wanted to add to its territory. So the Philistines wanted to conquer the Israelites and take their land.

To survive, the independent tribes had to unite and stop the invaders. They

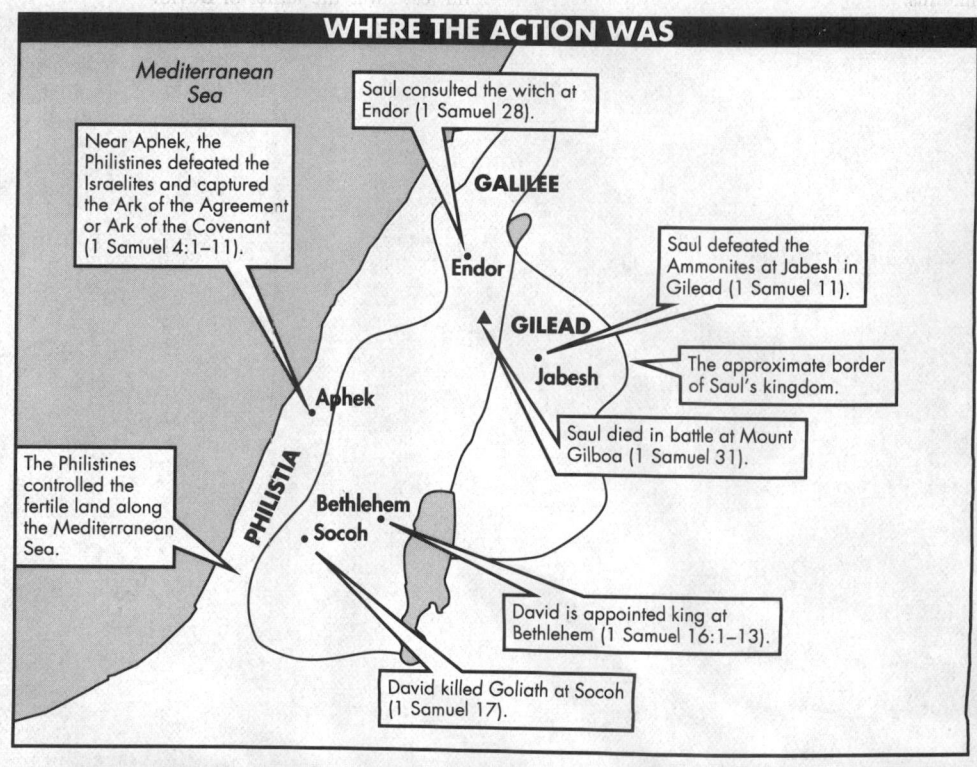

WHERE THE ACTION WAS

Mediterranean Sea

Saul consulted the witch at Endor (1 Samuel 28).

Near Aphek, the Philistines defeated the Israelites and captured the Ark of the Agreement or Ark of the Covenant (1 Samuel 4:1–11).

GALILEE

Endor

Saul defeated the Ammonites at Jabesh in Gilead (1 Samuel 11).

GILEAD

Jabesh

The approximate border of Saul's kingdom.

Aphek

PHILISTIA

Saul died in battle at Mount Gilboa (1 Samuel 31).

The Philistines controlled the fertile land along the Mediterranean Sea.

Bethlehem

Socoh

David is appointed king at Bethlehem (1 Samuel 16:1–13).

David killed Goliath at Socoh (1 Samuel 17).

WHEN THE ACTION WAS

| 2000BC | The Israelites escaped from Egypt | 1500BC | Saul was Israel's king | David was Israel's king | 1000BC | 500BC | Jesus was born | BC/AD |

Joshua led the Israelites into Canaan

Samuel served as Israel's last judge

Behind the Scenes (cont.):

needed a leader to unite them to stand up to the threat. That leader would be Samuel.

As it turned out, Samuel changed Israel's history. He stopped the Philistines from advancing, and, even more important, he appointed Israel's first two kings: King Saul and King David.

First Samuel contains some of the most thrilling stories in the Bible, including Saul's spectacular victories over the Philistines, David's battle with Goliath, David's friendship with Jonathan, and Saul's final days. Through all the stories, 1 Samuel shows the importance of having leaders who follow God.

Samuel's Birth

1 There was a man named Elkanah son of Jeroham from Ramathaim in the mountains of Ephraim. Elkanah was from the family of Zuph. (Jeroham was Elihu's son. Elihu was Tohu's son, and Tohu was the son of Zuph from the family group of Ephraim.) ²Elkanah had two wives named Hannah and Peninnah. Peninnah had children, but Hannah had none.

> **SIDELIGHT:** First and Second Samuel were originally one book. The prophet Samuel—after whom the books were named—doesn't even appear in 2 Samuel.

³Every year Elkanah left his town of Ramah and went up to Shiloh to worship the LORD All-Powerful and to offer sacrifices to him. Shiloh was where Hophni and Phinehas, the sons of Eli, served as priests of the LORD. ⁴When Elkanah offered sacrifices, he always gave a share of the meat to his wife Peninnah and to her sons and daughters. ⁵But Elkanah always gave a special share of the meat to Hannah, because he loved Hannah and because the LORD had kept her from having children. ⁶Peninnah would tease Hannah and upset her, because the LORD had made her unable to have children. ⁷This happened every year when they went up to the house of the LORD at Shiloh. Peninnah would upset Hannah until Hannah would cry and not eat anything. ⁸Her husband Elkanah would say to her, "Hannah, why are you crying and why won't you eat? Why are you sad? Don't I mean more to you than ten sons?"

⁹Once, after they had eaten their meal in Shiloh, Hannah got up. Now Eli the priest was sitting on a chair near the entrance to the LORD's house. ¹⁰Hannah was so sad that she cried and prayed to the LORD. ¹¹She made a promise, saying, "LORD All-Powerful, see how sad I am. Remember me and don't forget me. If you will give me a son, I will give him back to you all his life, and no one will ever cut his hair with a razor." [a]

¹²While Hannah kept praying, Eli watched her mouth. ¹³She was praying in her heart so her lips moved, but her voice was not heard. Eli thought she was drunk ¹⁴and said to her, "Stop getting drunk! Throw away your wine!"

¹⁵Hannah answered, "No, sir, I have not drunk any wine or beer. I am a deeply troubled woman, and I was telling the LORD about all my problems. ¹⁶Don't think I am an evil woman. I have been praying because I have many troubles and am very sad."

¹⁷Eli answered, "Go! I wish you well. May the God of Israel give you what you asked of him."

¹⁸Hannah said, "May I always please you." When she left and ate something, she was not sad anymore.

¹⁹Early the next morning Elkanah's family got up and worshiped the LORD. Then they went back home to Ramah. Elkanah had sexual relations with his wife Hannah, and the LORD remembered her. ²⁰So Hannah became pregnant, and in time she gave birth to a son. She named him Samuel, [n] saying, "His name is Samuel because I asked the LORD for him."

Hannah Gives Samuel to God

²¹Every year Elkanah went with his whole family to Shiloh to offer sacrifices and to keep the promise he had made to God. ²²But one time Hannah did not go with him. She told him, "When the boy is old enough to eat solid food, I will take him to Shiloh. Then I will give him to the LORD, and he will always live there."

²³Elkanah, Hannah's husband, said to her, "Do what you think is best. You may stay home until the boy is old enough to eat. May the LORD do what you have said." So Hannah stayed at home to nurse her son until he was old enough to eat.

²⁴When Samuel was old enough to eat, Hannah

---

cut ... razor People who made special promises not to cut their hair or to drink wine or beer were called Nazirites. These people gave a specific time in their lives, or sometimes their entire lives, to the Lord. See Numbers 6:1-5.
Samuel This name sounds like the Hebrew word for "God heard."

took him to the house of the LORD at Shiloh, along with a three-year-old bull, one-half bushel of flour, and a leather bag filled with wine. 25After they had killed the bull for the sacrifice, Hannah brought Samuel to Eli. 26She said to Eli, "As surely as you live, sir, I am the same woman who stood near you praying to the LORD. 27I prayed for this child, and the LORD answered my prayer and gave him to me. 28Now I give him back to the LORD. He will belong to the LORD all his life." And he worshiped the LORD there.

Hannah Gives Thanks

2 Hannah prayed:

"The LORD has filled my heart with joy;
I feel very strong in the LORD.
I can laugh at my enemies;
I am glad because you have helped me!

2"There is no one holy like the LORD.
There is no God but you;
there is no Rock[d] like our God.

3"Don't continue bragging,
don't speak proud words.
The LORD is a God who knows everything,
and he judges what people do.

4"The bows of warriors break,
but weak people become strong.
5Those who once had plenty of food now
must work for food,
but people who were hungry are hungry no
more.
The woman who could not have children
now has seven,
but the woman who had many children
now is sad.

6"The LORD sends death,
and he brings to life.
He sends people to the grave,
and he raises them to life again.
7The LORD makes some people poor,
and others he makes rich.
He makes some people humble,
and others he makes great.
8The LORD raises the poor up from the dust,
and he lifts the needy from the ashes.

BRAGGING

She Spoke Too Soon

Arlis Jordan was gorgeous. Stylish hair. Perfect complexion. Long eyelashes. Five-foot-five, one hundred eight pounds. Flawless figure. Everyone knew she was the best-looking girl at Westmont High.

Everyone, including Arlis. Whenever she had a chance, she would point out her own beauty and slam the "plain" girls. "Don't you care how you look?" she would chide if someone's hair wasn't carefully curled or if make-up didn't hide every blemish. "You really should take care of yourself . . . like I do."

When it was time for the Westmont Beauty Pageant, everyone knew Arlis would enter. And Arlis knew she would win. "Come on," she would sneer if someone questioned her. "Who in this city can give me any competition?"

As it turned out, Kris Jackson could. Kris entered the pageant because she wanted scholarship money for college. And though she wasn't as strikingly beautiful as Arlis, her vibrant personality and smile gave her the edge.

When Kris was crowned Miss Westmont, Arlis didn't even congratulate her. She burst into tears and stormed off the stage. "The judges are just stupid!" she cried, alone in the dressing room. "This whole thing is stupid!"

Arlis discovered how dangerous and humiliating bragging can be. Read **1 Samuel 2:1–10** to see what God thinks of braggers.
■ How does the passage describe what happened to Arlis? What does it say about Kris?
■ What caution about bragging do you see in the passage?

CONSIDER . . .
■ stopping yourself next time you're tempted to brag about a good grade, honor or public recognition. Instead, use your gifts to help others.
■ thanking God for the gifts you have, instead of bragging about them.

FOR MORE, SEE . . .
■ Proverbs 16:18–20 (p. 581)
■ Jeremiah 9:23–24 (p. 703)
■ Luke 1:46–55 (p. 1001)

He lets the poor sit with princes
and receive a throne of honor.

"The foundations of the earth belong to the
Lord,
and the Lord set the world upon them.
⁹He protects those who are loyal to him,
but evil people will be silenced in darkness.
Power is not the key to success.
¹⁰The Lord destroys his enemies;
he will thunder in heaven against them.
The Lord will judge all the earth.
He will give power to his king
and make his appointed king strong."

Eli's Evil Sons

¹¹Then Elkanah went home to Ramah, but the
boy continued to serve the Lord under Eli the
priest.

¹²Now Eli's sons were evil men; they did not
care about the Lord. ¹³This is what the priests
would normally do to the people: Every time
someone brought a sacrifice, the meat would be
cooked in a pot. The priest's servant would then
come carrying a fork that had three prongs. ¹⁴He
would plunge the fork into the pot or the kettle.
Whatever the fork brought out of the pot belonged to the priest. But this is how they treated
all the Israelites who came to Shiloh to offer sacrifices. ¹⁵Even before the fat was burned, the
priest's servant would come to the person offering
sacrifices and say, "Give the priest some meat to
roast. He won't accept boiled meat from you, only
raw meat."

¹⁶If the one who offered the sacrifice said, "Let
the fat be burned up first as usual, and then take
anything you want," the priest's servant would
answer, "No, give me the meat now. If you don't,
I'll take it by force."

¹⁷The Lord saw that the sin of the servants was
very great because they did not show respect for
the offerings made to the Lord.

Samuel Grows Up

¹⁸But Samuel obeyed the Lord. As a boy he
wore a linen holy vest.ᵈ ¹⁹Every year Samuel's
mother made a little coat for him and took it to
him when she went with her husband to Shiloh
for the sacrifice. ²⁰When Eli blessed Elkanah and
his wife, he would say, "May the Lord repay you
with children through Hannah to take the place
of the boy Hannah prayed for and gave back to the
Lord." Then Elkanah and Hannah would go
home. ²¹The Lord was kind to Hannah, so she
became the mother of three sons and two daughters. And the boy Samuel grew up serving the
Lord.

²²Now Eli was very old. He heard about everything his sons were doing to all the Israelites and

how his sons had sexual relations with the
women who served at the entrance to the Meeting Tent.ᵈ ²³Eli said to his sons, "Why do you do
these evil things that the people tell me about?
²⁴No, my sons. The Lord's people are spreading
a bad report about you. ²⁵If you sin against someone, God can help you. But if you sin against the
Lord himself, no one can help you!" But Eli's
sons would not listen to him, because the Lord
had decided to put them to death.

²⁶The boy Samuel grew physically. He pleased
the Lord and the people.

²⁷A man of God came to Eli and said, "This is
what the Lord says: 'I clearly showed myself to
the family of your ancestor Aaron when they were
slaves to the king of Egypt. ²⁸I chose them from
all the tribesᵈ of Israel to be my priests. I wanted
them to go up to my altar, to burn incense,ᵈ and
to wear the holy vest. I also let the family of your
ancestor have part of all the offerings sacrificed by
the Israelites. ²⁹So why don't you respect the sacrifices and gifts? You honor your sons more than
me. You grow fat on the best parts of the meat the
Israelites bring to me.'

³⁰"So the Lord, the God of Israel, says: 'I promised that your family and your ancestor's family
would serve me always.' But now the Lord says:
'This must stop! I will honor those who honor
me, but I will dishonor those who ignore me.
³¹The time is coming when I will destroy the
descendantsᵈ of both you and your ancestors. No
man will grow old in your family. ³²You will see
trouble in my house. No matter what good things
happen to Israel, there will never be an old man
in your family. ³³I will not totally cut off your family from my altar. But your eyes will cry and your
heart be sad, because all your descendants will
die.

³⁴" 'I will give you a sign. Both your sons,
Hophni and Phinehas, will die on the same day.
³⁵I will choose a loyal priest for myself who will
listen to me and do what I want. I will make his
family continue, and he will always serve before
my appointed king. ³⁶Then everyone left in your
family will come and bow down before him. They
will beg for a little money or a little food and say,
"Please give me a job as priest so I can have food
to eat." ' "

God Calls Samuel

3 The boy Samuel served the Lord under Eli.
In those days the Lord did not speak directly
to people very often; there were very few visions.

²Eli's eyes were so weak he was almost blind.
One night he was lying in bed. ³Samuel was also
in bed in the Lord's house, where the Arkᵈ of the
Agreement was. God's lamp was still burning.

⁴Then the LORD called Samuel, and Samuel answered, "I am here!" ⁵He ran to Eli and said, "I am here. You called me."

But Eli said, "I didn't call you. Go back to bed." So Samuel went back to bed.

⁶The LORD called again, "Samuel!"

Samuel again went to Eli and said, "I am here. You called me."

Again Eli said, "I didn't call you. Go back to bed."

⁷Samuel did not yet know the LORD, and the LORD had not spoken directly to him yet.

⁸The LORD called Samuel for the third time. Samuel got up and went to Eli and said, "I am here. You called me."

Then Eli realized the LORD was calling the boy. ⁹So he told Samuel, "Go to bed. If he calls you again, say, 'Speak, LORD. I am your servant and I am listening.' " So Samuel went and lay down in bed.

¹⁰The LORD came and stood there and called as he had before, "Samuel, Samuel!"

Samuel said, "Speak, LORD. I am your servant and I am listening."

¹¹The LORD said to Samuel, "Watch, I am going to do something in Israel that will shock those who hear about it. ¹²At that time I will do to Eli and his family everything I promised, from beginning to end. ¹³I told Eli I would punish his family always, because he knew his sons were evil. They acted without honor, but he did not stop them. ¹⁴So I swore to Eli's family, 'Your guilt will never be removed by sacrifice or offering.' "

¹⁵Samuel lay down until morning. Then he

FOLLOWING GOD

Did Someone Call?

From the time she learned to play the flute, Ramona Sanchez wanted to be a marching band director. She spent hours practicing flute and learning marching patterns for her high school band.

When Ramona wasn't practicing her music, she was working on the school newspaper or yearbook. She hadn't planned on doing them, but the yearbook adviser had asked her to be yearbook editor. Then the newspaper editor asked her to write features.

"I know you love music," her yearbook adviser told her, "but maybe you're overlooking your writing gifts."

Ramona dismissed the thought and kept concentrating on music. She regularly entered music competitions, hoping to get into a good music school. She did well in regional competitions, but never in state. However, when the yearbook was entered in state competition, it won first place.

"What's going on?" Ramona wondered, as she filled out applications for music schools. Her adviser's thoughts came to mind: "Maybe you're overlooking your writing gifts."

Ramona went to music school, but didn't do well. She didn't enjoy all the theory and hours of practice. To lift her spirits, she went to work at the college newspaper. Now that was fun!

After the first semester, she knew what she had to do. She dropped her music major and majored in English and communications. "It took me a while to figure out what to do," she recalls. "I'm glad I finally paid attention to the gifts God gave me."

It took several years for Ramona to understand how God wanted her to use her gifts. Similarly, Samuel didn't recognize God's call right away in **1 Samuel 3:1–20**. But by listening to the advice of Eli the priest, Samuel heard and followed God's call.

■ What signs did Ramona see that were similar to the calls Samuel heard?
■ When have you, like Samuel, had trouble knowing what God wanted you to do?

C O N S I D E R . . .

■ silently listening for God's direction when you pray.
■ asking someone you respect to help you figure out ways God might want you to follow him.

F O R   M O R E ,   S E E . . .

■ Isaiah 6:1–8 (p. 622)
■ Mark 1:16–20 (p. 964)

■ Acts 9:1–19 (p. 1112)

opened the doors of the house of the Lord. He was afraid to tell Eli about the vision, [16]but Eli called to him, "Samuel, my son!"

Samuel answered, "I am here."

[17]Eli asked, "What did the Lord say to you? Don't hide it from me. May God punish you terribly if you hide from me anything he said to you." [18]So Samuel told Eli everything and did not hide anything from him. Then Eli said, "He is the Lord. Let him do what he thinks is best."

[19]The Lord was with Samuel as he grew up; he did not let any of Samuel's messages fail to come true. [20]Then all Israel, from Dan to Beersheba,[n] knew Samuel was a true prophet[d] of the Lord. [21]And the Lord continued to show himself at Shiloh, and he showed himself to Samuel through his word.

4 So, news about Samuel spread through all of Israel.

The Philistines Capture the Ark of the Agreement

At that time the Israelites went out to fight the Philistines. The Israelites camped at Ebenezer and the Philistines at Aphek. [2]The Philistines went to meet the Israelites in battle. And as the battle spread, they defeated the Israelites, killing about four thousand soldiers on the battlefield. [3]When some Israelite soldiers went back to their camp, the older leaders of Israel asked, "Why did the Lord let the Philistines defeat us? Let's bring the Ark[d] of the Agreement with the Lord here from Shiloh and take it with us into battle. Then God will save us from our enemies."

[4]So the people sent men to Shiloh. They brought back the Ark of the Agreement with the Lord All-Powerful, who sits between the gold creatures with wings. Eli's two sons, Hophni and Phinehas, were there with the Ark.

[5]When the Ark of the Agreement with the Lord came into the camp, all the Israelites gave a great shout of joy that made the ground shake. [6]When the Philistines heard Israel's shout, they asked, "What's all this shouting in the Hebrew camp?"

Then the Philistines found out that the Ark of the Lord had come into the Hebrew camp. [7]They were afraid and said, "A god has come into the Hebrew camp! We're in trouble! This has never happened before! [8]How terrible it will be for us! Who can save us from these powerful gods? They are the ones who struck the Egyptians with all kinds of disasters in the desert. [9]Be brave, Philistines! Fight like men! In the past they were our

slaves. So fight like men, or we will become their slaves."

[10]So the Philistines fought hard and defeated the Israelites, and every Israelite soldier ran away to his own home. It was a great defeat for Israel, because thirty thousand Israelite soldiers were killed. [11]The Ark of God was taken by the Philistines, and Eli's two sons, Hophni and Phinehas, died.

[12]That same day a man from the tribe[d] of Benjamin ran from the battle. He tore his clothes and put dust on his head to show his great sadness. [13]When he arrived in Shiloh, Eli was by the side of the road. He was sitting there in a chair, watching, because he was worried about the Ark of God. When the Benjaminite entered Shiloh, he told the bad news. Then all the people in town cried loudly. [14]Eli heard the crying and asked, "What's all this noise?"

The Benjaminite ran to Eli and told him what had happened. [15]Eli was now ninety-eight years old, and he was blind. [16]The Benjaminite told him, "I have come from the battle. I ran all the way here today."

Eli asked, "What happened, my son?"

[17]The Benjaminite answered, "Israel ran away from the Philistines, and the Israelite army has lost many soldiers. Your two sons are both dead, and the Philistines have taken the Ark of God."

[18]When he mentioned the Ark of God, Eli fell backward off his chair. He fell beside the gate, broke his neck, and died, because he was old and fat. He had led Israel for forty years.

SIDELIGHT: Ever get yelled at fo leaning back in your chair? It's dangerous. You could fall over backwards. Eli did . . . and died (1 Samuel 4:18).

The Glory Is Gone

[19]Eli's daughter-in-law, the wife of Phinehas, was pregnant and was about to give birth. When she heard the news that the Ark[d] of God had been taken and that Eli, her father-in-law, and Phinehas, her husband, were both dead, she began to give birth to her child. The child was born, but the mother had much trouble in giving birth. [20]As she was dying, the women who helped her said, "Don't worry! You've given birth to a son!" But she did not answer or pay attention. [21]She named the baby Ichabod,[n] saying, "Israel's glory is gone." She said this because the Ark of God had been taken and her father-in-law and husband

---

Dan to Beersheba Dan was the city farthest north in Israel, and Beersheba was the city farthest south. So this means all the people of Israel.
Ichabod This name means "no glory."

were dead. ²²She said, "Israel's glory is gone, because the Ark of God has been taken away."

Trouble for the Philistines

5 After the Philistines had captured the Ark*d* of God, they took it from Ebenezer to Ashdod. ²They carried it into Dagon's*d* temple and put it next to Dagon. ³When the people of Ashdod rose early the next morning, they found that Dagon had fallen on his face on the ground before the Ark of the Lord. So they put Dagon back in his place. ⁴The next morning when they rose, they again found Dagon fallen on the ground before the Ark of the Lord. His head and hands had broken off and were lying in the doorway. Only his body was still in one piece. ⁵So, even today, Dagon's priests and others who enter his temple at Ashdod refuse to step on the doorsill.

⁶The Lord was hard on the people of Ashdod and their neighbors. He caused them to suffer and gave them growths on their skin. ⁷When the people of Ashdod saw what was happening, they said, "The Ark of the God of Israel can't stay with us. God is punishing us and Dagon our god." ⁸The people of Ashdod called all five Philistine kings together and asked them, "What should we do with the Ark of the God of Israel?"

The rulers answered, "Move the Ark of the God of Israel to Gath." So the Philistines moved it to Gath.

⁹But after they moved it to Gath, there was a great panic. The Lord was hard on that city also, and he gave both old and young people in Gath growths on their skin. ¹⁰Then the Philistines sent the Ark of God to Ekron.

But when it came into Ekron, the people of Ekron yelled, "Why are you bringing the Ark of the God of Israel to our city? Do you want to kill us and our people?" ¹¹So they called all the kings of the Philistines together and said, "Send the Ark of the God of Israel back to its place before it kills us and our people!" All the people in the city were struck with terror because God was so hard on them there. ¹²The people who did not die were troubled with growths on their skin. So the people of Ekron cried loudly to heaven.

The Ark of God Is Sent Home

6 The Philistines kept the Ark*d* of God in their land seven months. ²Then they called for their priests and magicians and said, "What *should we do with the Ark of the Lord? Tell us* how to send it back home!"

³The priests and magicians answered, "If you send back the Ark of the God of Israel, don't send it back empty. You must give a penalty offering. If you are then healed, you will know that it was because of the Ark that you had such trouble."

⁴The Philistines asked, "What kind of penalty offering should we send to Israel's God?"

They answered, "Make five gold models of the growths on your skin and five gold models of rats. The number of models must match the number of Philistine kings, because the same sickness has come on you and your kings. ⁵Make models of the growths and the rats that are ruining the country, and give honor to Israel's God. Then maybe he will stop being so hard on you, your gods, and your land. ⁶Don't be stubborn like the king of Egypt and the Egyptians. After God punished them terribly, they let the Israelites leave Egypt.

⁷"You must build a new cart and get two cows that have just had calves. These must be cows that have never had yokes*d* on their necks. Hitch the cows to the cart, and take the calves home, away from their mothers. ⁸Put the Ark of the Lord on the cart and the gold models for the penalty offering in a box beside the Ark. Then send the cart straight on its way. ⁹Watch the cart. If it goes toward Beth Shemesh in Israel's own land, the Lord has given us this great sickness. But if it doesn't, we will know that Israel's God has not punished us. Our sickness just happened by chance."

¹⁰The Philistines did what the priests and magicians said. They took two cows that had just had calves and hitched them to the cart, but they kept their calves at home. ¹¹They put the Ark of the Lord and the box with the gold rats and models of growths on the cart. ¹²Then the cows went straight toward Beth Shemesh. They stayed on the road, mooing all the way, and did not turn right or left. The Philistine kings followed the cows as far as the border of Beth Shemesh.

¹³Now the people of Beth Shemesh were harvesting their wheat in the valley. When they looked up and saw the Ark of the Lord, they were very happy. ¹⁴The cart came to the field belonging to Joshua of Beth Shemesh and stopped near a large rock. The people of Beth Shemesh chopped up the wood of the cart. Then they sacrificed the cows as burnt offerings to the Lord. ¹⁵The Levites took down the Ark of the Lord and the box that had the gold models, and they put both on the large rock. That day the people of Beth Shemesh offered whole burnt offerings and made sacrifices to the Lord. ¹⁶After the five Philistine kings saw this, they went back to Ekron the same day.

¹⁷The Philistines had sent these gold models of *the growths as penalty offerings to the Lord.* They sent one model for each Philistine town: Ashdod, Gaza, Ashkelon, Gath, and Ekron. ¹⁸And the Philistines also sent gold models of rats. The number of rats matched the number of towns belonging to the Philistine kings, including both strong, walled cities and country villages. The

large rock on which they put the Ark of the LORD is still there in the field of Joshua of Beth She-mesh.

¹⁹But some of the men of Beth Shemesh looked into the Ark of the LORD. So God killed seventy of them. The people of Beth Shemesh cried be-cause the LORD had struck them down. ²⁰They said, "Who can stand before the LORD, this holy God? Whom will he strike next?"

²¹Then they sent messengers to the people of Kiriath Jearim, saying, "The Philistines have brought back the Ark of the LORD. Come down and take it to your city."

7 The men of Kiriath Jearim came and took the Ark of the LORD to Abinadab's house on a hill. There they made Abinadab's son Eleazar holy for the LORD so he could guard the Ark of the LORD.

The Lord Saves the Israelites

²The Ark*d* stayed at Kiriath Jearim a long time — twenty years in all. And the people of Is-rael began to follow the LORD again. ³Samuel spoke to the whole group of Israel, saying, "If you're turning back to the LORD with all your hearts, you must remove your foreign gods and your idols of Ashtoreth.*d* You must give your-selves fully to the LORD and serve only him. Then he will save you from the Philistines."

⁴So the Israelites put away their idols of Baal*d* and Ashtoreth, and they served only the LORD.

⁵Samuel said, "All Israel must meet at Mizpah, and I will pray to the LORD for you." ⁶So the Israel-ites met together at Mizpah. They drew water from the ground and poured it out before the LORD and did not eat that day. They confessed, "We have sinned against the LORD." And Samuel served as judge of Israel at Mizpah.

⁷The Philistines heard the Israelites were meet-ing at Mizpah, so the Philistine kings came up to attack them. When the Israelites heard they were coming, they were afraid. ⁸They said to Samuel, "Don't stop praying to the LORD our God for us! Ask him to save us from the Philistines!" ⁹Then Samuel took a baby lamb and offered it to the LORD as a whole burnt offering. He called to the LORD for Israel's sake, and the LORD answered him.

¹⁰While Samuel was burning the offering, the Philistines came near to attack Israel. But the LORD thundered against them with loud thunder. They were so frightened they became confused. So the Israelites defeated the Philistines in battle. ¹¹The men of Israel ran out of Mizpah and chased the Philistines almost to Beth Car, killing the Phi-listines along the way.

Peace Comes to Israel

¹²After this happened Samuel took a stone and set it up between Mizpah and Shen. He named the stone Ebenezer,*n* saying, "The LORD has helped us to this point." ¹³So the Philistines were defeated and did not enter the Israelites' land again.

The LORD was against the Philistines all Sam-uel's life. ¹⁴Earlier the Philistines had taken towns from the Israelites, but the Israelites won them back, from Ekron to Gath. They also took back from the Philistines the lands near these towns. There was peace also between Israel and the Am-orites.

¹⁵Samuel continued as judge of Israel all his life. ¹⁶Every year he went from Bethel to Gilgal to Miz-pah and judged the Israelites in all these towns. ¹⁷But Samuel always went back to Ramah, where his home was. There he judged Israel and built an altar to the LORD.

Israel Asks for a King

8 When Samuel was old, he made his sons judges for Israel. ²His first son was named Joel, and his second son was named Abijah. Joel and Abijah were judges in Beersheba. ³But Sam-uel's sons did not live as he did. They tried to get money dishonestly, and they accepted money se-cretly to make wrong judgments.

⁴So all the older leaders came together and met Samuel at Ramah. ⁵They said to him, "You're old, and your sons don't live as you do. Give us a king to rule over us like all the other nations."

⁶When the older leaders said that, Samuel was not pleased. He prayed to the LORD, ⁷and the LORD told Samuel, "Listen to whatever the people say to you. They have not rejected you. They have rejected me from being their king. ⁸They are do-ing as they have always done. When I took them out of Egypt they left me and served other gods. They are doing the same to you. ⁹Now listen to the people, but warn them what the king who rules over them will do."

¹⁰So Samuel told those who had asked him for a king what the LORD had said. ¹¹Samuel said, "If you have a king ruling over you, this is what he will do: He will take your sons and make them serve with his chariots and his horses, and they will run in front of the king's chariot. ¹²The king will make some of your sons commanders over thousands or over fifties. He will make some of your other sons plow his ground and reap his har-vest. He will make others to make weapons of war and equipment for his chariots. ¹³He will take your daughters to make perfume and cook and bake for him. ¹⁴He will take your best fields, vine-

yards, and olive groves and give them to his servants. [15]He will take one-tenth of your grain and grapes and give it to his officers and servants. [16]He will take your male and female servants, your best cattle, and your donkeys and use them all for his own work. [17]He will take one-tenth of your flocks, and you yourselves will become his slaves. [18]When that time comes, you will cry out because of the king you chose. But the LORD will not answer you then."

[19]But the people would not listen to Samuel. They said, "No! We want a king to rule over us. [20]Then we will be the same as all the other nations. Our king will judge for us and go with us and fight our battles."

[21]After Samuel heard all that the people said, he repeated their words to the LORD. [22]The LORD answered, "You must listen to them. Give them a king."

Then Samuel told the people of Israel, "Go back to your towns."

Saul Looks for His Father's Donkeys

9 Kish, son of Abiel from the tribe[d] of Benjamin, was an important man. (Abiel was the son of Zeror, who was the son of Becorath, who was the son of Aphiah of Benjamin.) [2]Kish had a son named Saul, who was a fine young man. There was no Israelite better than he. Saul stood a head taller than any other man in Israel.

[3]Now the donkeys of Saul's father, Kish, were lost. So Kish said to Saul, his son, "Take one of the servants, and go and look for the donkeys." [4]Saul went through the mountains of Ephraim and the land of Shalisha, but he and the servant could not find the donkeys. They went into the land of Shaalim, but the donkeys were not there. They went through the land of Benjamin, but they still did not find them. [5]When they arrived in the area of Zuph, Saul said to his servant, "Let's go back or my father will stop thinking about the donkeys and will start worrying about us."

[6]But the servant answered, "A man of God is in this town. People respect him because everything he says comes true. Let's go into the town now. Maybe he can tell us something about the journey we have taken."

[7]Saul said to his servant, "If we go into the town, what can we give him? The food in our bags is gone. We have no gift to give him. Do we have anything?"

[8]Again the servant answered Saul. "Look, I have one-tenth of an ounce of silver. Give it to the man of God. Then he will tell us about our journey." [9](In the past, if someone in Israel wanted to ask something from God, he would say, "Let's go to the seer."[d] We call the person a prophet[d] today, but in the past he was called a seer.)

[10]Saul said to his servant, "That's a good idea. Come, let's go." So they went toward the town where the man of God was.

[11]As Saul and the servant were going up the hill to the town, they met some young women coming out to get water. Saul and the servant asked them, "Is the seer here?"

[12]The young women answered, "Yes, he's here. He's ahead of you. Hurry now. He has just come to our town today, because the people will offer a sacrifice at the place of worship. [13]As soon as you enter the town, you will find him before he goes up to the place of worship to eat. The people will not begin eating until the seer comes, because he must bless the sacrifice. After that, the guests will eat. Go now, and you should find him."

Saul Meets Samuel

[14]Saul and the servant went up to the town. Just as they entered it, they saw Samuel coming toward them on his way up to the place of worship.

[15]The day before Saul came, the LORD had told Samuel: [16]"About this time tomorrow I will send you a man from the land of Benjamin. Appoint him to lead my people Israel. He will save my people from the Philistines. I have seen the suffering of my people, and I have listened to their cry."

[17]When Samuel first saw Saul, the LORD said to Samuel, "This is the man I told you about. He will organize my people."

[18]Saul approached Samuel at the gate and said, "Please tell me where the seer's[d] house is."

[19]Samuel answered, "I am the seer. Go with me to the place of worship. Today you and your servant are to eat with me. Tomorrow morning I will answer all your questions and send you home. [20]Don't worry about the donkeys you lost three days ago, because they have been found. Soon all the wealth of Israel will belong to you and your family."

[21]Saul answered, "But I am from the tribe[d] of Benjamin, the smallest tribe in Israel. And my family group is the smallest in the tribe of Benjamin. Why are you saying such things?"

[22]Then Samuel took Saul and his servant into a large room and gave them a choice place at the table. About thirty guests were there. [23]Samuel said to the cook, "Bring the meat I gave you, the portion I told you to set aside."

[24]So the cook took the thigh and put it on the table in front of Saul. Samuel said, "This is the meat saved for you. Eat it, because it was set aside for you for this special time. As I said, 'I had invited the people.' " So Saul ate with Samuel that day.

[25]After they finished eating, they came down from the place of worship and went to the town.

Then Samuel talked with Saul on the roof[n] of his house. [26]At dawn they got up, and Samuel called to Saul on the roof. He said, "Get up, and I will send you on your way." So Saul got up and went out of the house with Samuel. [27]As Saul, his servant, and Samuel were getting near the edge of the city, Samuel said to Saul, "Tell the servant to go on ahead of us, but you stay, because I have a message from God for you."

Samuel Appoints Saul

10 Samuel took a jar of olive oil and poured it on Saul's head. He kissed Saul and said, "The LORD has appointed you to lead his people. [2]After you leave me today, you will meet two men near Rachel's tomb on the border of Benjamin at Zelzah. They will say to you, 'The donkeys you were looking for have been found. But now your father has stopped thinking about his donkeys and is worrying about you. He is asking, "What will I do about my son?" '

[3]"Then you will go on until you reach the big tree at Tabor. Three men on their way to worship God at Bethel will meet you there. One man will be carrying three goats. Another will be carrying three loaves of bread. And the third will have a leather bag full of wine. [4]They will greet you and offer you two loaves of bread, which you must accept. [5]Then you will go to Gibeah of God, where a Philistine camp is. When you approach this town, a group of prophets[d] will come down from the place of worship. They will be playing harps, tambourines,[d] flutes, and lyres,[d] and they will be prophesying. [6]Then the Spirit[d] of the LORD will rush upon you with power. You will prophesy with these prophets, and you will be changed into a different man. [7]After these signs happen, do whatever you find to do, because God will help you.

[8]"Go ahead of me to Gilgal. I will come down to you to offer whole burnt offerings and fellowship offerings. But you must wait seven days. Then I will come and tell you what to do."

Saul Made King

[9]When Saul turned to leave Samuel, God changed Saul's heart. All these signs came true that day. [10]When Saul and his servant arrived at Gibeah, Saul met a group of prophets.[d] The Spirit[d] of God rushed upon him, and he prophesied with the prophets. [11]When people who had known Saul before saw him prophesying with the prophets, they asked each other, "What has happened to Kish's son? Is even Saul one of the prophets?"

[12]A man who lived there said, "Who is the father of these prophets?" So this became a famous

saying: "Is even Saul one of the prophets?" [13]When Saul finished prophesying, he entered the place of worship.

[14]Saul's uncle asked him and his servant, "Where have you been?"

Saul said, "We were looking for the donkeys. When we couldn't find them, we went to talk to Samuel.'

[15]Saul's uncle asked, "Please tell me. What did Samuel say to you?"

[16]Saul answered, "He told us the donkeys had already been found." But Saul did not tell his uncle what Samuel had said about his becoming king.

[17]Samuel called all the people of Israel to meet with the LORD at Mizpah. [18]He said, "This is what the LORD, the God of Israel, says: 'I led Israel out of Egypt. I saved you from Egypt's control and from other kingdoms that were troubling you.' [19]But now you have rejected your God. He saves you from all your troubles and problems, but you said, 'No! We want a king to rule over us.' Now come, stand before the LORD in your tribes[d] and family groups."

[20]When Samuel gathered all the tribes of Israel, the tribe of Benjamin was picked. [21]Samuel had them pass by in family groups, and Matri's family was picked. Then he had each man of Matri's family pass by, and Saul son of Kish was picked. But when they looked for Saul, they could not find him. [22]They asked the LORD, "Has Saul come here yet?"

The LORD said, "Yes. He's hiding behind the baggage."

[23]So they ran and brought him out. When Saul stood among the people, he was a head taller than anyone else. [24]Then Samuel said to the people, "See the man the LORD has chosen. There is no one like him among all the people."

Then the people shouted, "Long live the king!"

※ SIDELIGHT: Even if you're shy, you could still be president. Saul, Israel's first king, was so shy that when the people tried to crown him, he hid in the baggage (Samuel 10:20–24).

---

[25]Samuel explained the rights and duties of the king and then wrote them in a book and put it before the LORD. Then he told the people to go to their homes.

[26]Saul also went to his home in Gibeah. God touched the hearts of certain brave men who

---

roof In Bible times houses were built with flat roofs. The roof was used for drying things such as flax and fruit. And it was used as an extra room, as a place for worship, and as a place to sleep in the summer.

went along with him. 27But some troublemakers said, "How can this man save us?" They disapproved of Saul and refused to bring gifts to him. But Saul kept quiet.

Nahash Troubles Jabesh Gilead

11 About a month later Nahash the Ammonite and his army surrounded the city of Jabesh in Gilead. All the people of Jabesh said to Nahash, "Make a treaty with us, and we will serve you."

2But he answered, "I will make a treaty with you only if I'm allowed to poke out the right eye of each of you. Then all Israel will be ashamed!"

3The older leaders of Jabesh said to Nahash, "Give us seven days to send messengers through all Israel. If no one comes to help us, we will give ourselves up to you."

4When the messengers came to Gibeah where Saul lived and told the people the news, they cried loudly. 5Saul was coming home from plowing the fields with his oxen when he heard the people crying. He asked, "What's wrong with the people that they are crying?" Then they told Saul what the messengers from Jabesh had said. 6When Saul heard their words, God's Spirit*d* rushed upon him with power, and he became very angry. 7So he took a pair of oxen and cut them into pieces. Then he gave the pieces of the oxen to messengers and ordered them to carry them through all the land of Israel.

The messengers said, "This is what will happen to the oxen of anyone who does not follow Saul and Samuel." So the people became very afraid of the LORD. They all came together as if they were

---

✺ **SIDELIGHT:** Modern military recruiters might not have much luck enlisting volunteers if they used Saul's methods in 1 Samuel 11:7. He cut two oxen into pieces and gave the pieces to messengers to carry around the country to mobilize people for war. (The act symbolized uniting all the people.) The approach worked for Saul; his army walloped the Ammonites (1 Samuel 11:11).

---

one person. 8Saul gathered the people together at Bezek. There were three hundred thousand men *from Israel and thirty thousand men from Judah.* 9They said to the messengers who had come, "Tell the people at Jabesh Gilead this: 'Before the day warms up tomorrow, you will be saved.' " So the messengers went and reported this to the people at Jabesh, and they were very happy. 10The people said to Nahash the Ammonite, "Tomorrow

we will come out to meet you. Then you can do anything you want to us."

11The next morning Saul divided his soldiers into three groups. At dawn they entered the Ammonite camp and defeated them before the heat of the day. The Ammonites who escaped were scattered; no two of them were still together.

12Then the people said to Samuel, "Who didn't want Saul as king? Bring them here and we will kill them!"

13But Saul said, "No! No one will be put to death today. Today the LORD has saved Israel!"

14Then Samuel said to the people, "Come, let's go to Gilgal. There we will again promise to obey the king." 15So all the people went to Gilgal, and there, before the LORD, the people made Saul king. They offered fellowship offerings to the LORD, and Saul and all the Israelites had a great celebration.

Samuel's Farewell Speech

12 Samuel said to all Israel, "I have done everything you wanted me to do and have put a king over you. 2Now you have a king to lead you. I am old and gray, and my sons are here with you. I have been your leader since I was young. 3Here I am. If I have done anything wrong, you must testify against me before the LORD and his appointed king. Did I steal anyone's ox or donkey? Did I hurt or cheat anyone? Did I ever secretly accept money to pretend not to see something wrong? If I did any of these things, I will make it right."

4The Israelites answered, "You have not cheated us, or hurt us, or taken anything unfairly from anyone."

5Samuel said to them, "The LORD is a witness to what you have said. His appointed king is also a witness today that you did not find anything wrong in me."

"He is our witness," they said.

6Then Samuel said to the people, "It is the LORD who chose Moses and Aaron and brought your ancestors out of Egypt. 7Now, stand there, and I will remind you of all the good things the LORD did for you and your ancestors.

8"After Jacob entered Egypt, his descendants*d* cried to the LORD for help. So the LORD sent Moses and Aaron, who took your ancestors out of Egypt and brought them to live in this place.

9"But they forgot the LORD their God. So he handed them over as slaves to Sisera, the com*mander of the army of Hazor, and as slaves to the* Philistines and the king of Moab. They all fought against your ancestors. 10Then your ancestors cried to the LORD and said, 'We have sinned. We have left the LORD and served the Baals*d* and the Ashtoreths.*d* But now save us from our enemies, and we will serve you.' 11So the LORD sent Gideon,[n] Barak, Jephthah, and Samuel. He saved you from your enemies around you, and you lived in safety. [12]But when you saw Nahash king of the Ammonites coming against you, you said, 'No! We want a king to rule over us!' — even though the LORD your God was your king. [13]Now here is the king you chose, the one you asked for. The LORD has put him over you. [14]You must honor the LORD and serve him. You must obey his word and not turn against his commands. Both you and the king ruling over you must follow the LORD your God. If you do, it will be well with you. [15]But if you don't obey the LORD, and if you turn against his commands, he will be against you. He will do to you what he did to your ancestors.

[16]"Now stand still and see the great thing the LORD will do before your eyes. [17]It is now the time of the wheat harvest.[n] I will pray for the LORD to send thunder and rain. Then you will know what an evil thing you did against the LORD when you asked for a king."

[18]Then Samuel prayed to the LORD, and that same day the LORD sent thunder and rain. So the people were very afraid of the LORD and Samuel. [19]They said to Samuel, "Pray to the LORD your God for us, your servants! Don't let us die! We've added to all our sins the evil of asking for a king."

[20]Samuel answered, "Don't be afraid. It's true that you did wrong, but don't turn away from the LORD. Serve the LORD with all your heart. [21]Idols are of no use, so don't worship them. They can't help you or save you. They are useless! [22]For his own sake, the LORD won't leave his people. Instead, he was pleased to make you his own people. [23]I will surely not stop praying for you, because that would be sinning against the LORD. I will teach you what is good and right. [24]You must honor the LORD and truly serve him with all your heart. Remember the wonderful things he did for you! [25]But if you are stubborn and do evil, he will sweep you and your king away."

13 Saul was thirty years old when he became king, and he was king over Israel forty-two years.[n] [2]Saul chose three thousand men from Israel. Two thousand men stayed with him at Micmash in the mountains of Bethel, and one thousand men stayed with Jonathan at Gibeah in Benjamin. Saul sent the other men in the army back home.

[3]Jonathan attacked the Philistine camp in Geba, and the other Philistines heard about it. Saul said, "Let the Hebrews hear what happened." So he told the men to blow trumpets through all the land of Israel. [4]All the Israelites heard the news. The men said, "Saul has defeated the Philistine camp. Now the Philistines will really hate us!" Then the Israelites were called to join Saul at Gilgal.

[5]The Philistines gathered to fight Israel with three thousand[n] chariots and six thousand men to ride in them. Their soldiers were as many as the grains of sand on the seashore. The Philistines went and camped at Micmash, which is east of Beth Aven. [6]When the Israelites saw that they were in trouble, they went to hide in caves and bushes, among the rocks, and in pits and wells. [7]Some Hebrews even went across the Jordan River to the land of Gad and Gilead.

But Saul stayed at Gilgal, and all the men in his army were shaking with fear. [8]Saul waited seven days, because Samuel had said he would meet him then. But Samuel did not come to Gilgal, and the soldiers began to leave.

[9]So Saul said, "Bring me the whole burnt offering and the fellowship offerings." Then Saul offered the whole burnt offering. [10]Just as he finished, Samuel arrived, and Saul went to greet him.

[11]Samuel asked, "What have you done?"

Saul answered, "I saw the soldiers leaving me, and you were not here when you said you would be. The Philistines were gathering at Micmash. [12]Then I thought, 'The Philistines will come against me at Gilgal, and I haven't asked for the LORD's approval.' So I forced myself to offer the whole burnt offering."

[13]Samuel said, "You acted foolishly! You haven't obeyed the command of the LORD your God. If you had obeyed him, the LORD would have made your kingdom continue in Israel always, [14]but now your kingdom will not continue. The LORD has looked for the kind of man he wants. He has appointed him to rule his people, because you haven't obeyed his command."

[15]Then Samuel left Gilgal and went to Gibeah in Benjamin. Saul counted the men who were still with him, and there were about six hundred.

Hard Times for Israel

[16]Saul and his son Jonathan and the soldiers with him stayed in Gibeah in the land of Benjamin. The Philistines made their camp at Micmash. [17]Three groups went out from the Philistine camp to make raids. One group went on the Ophrah road in the land of Shual. [18]The second group went on the Beth Horon road. The third group went on the border road that overlooks the Valley of Zeboim toward the desert.

Gideon Also called Jerub-Baal.
time . . . harvest This was a dry time in the summer when no rains fell.
Saul . . . years This is how the verse is worded in some early Greek copies. The Hebrew is not clear here.
three thousand Some Greek copies say three thousand. The Hebrew copies say thirty thousand.

¹⁹The whole land of Israel had no blacksmith because the Philistines had said, "The Hebrews might make swords and spears." ²⁰So all the Israelites had to go down to the Philistines to have their plows, hoes, axes, and sickles sharpened. ²¹The Philistine blacksmiths charged about one-fourth of an ounce of silver for sharpening plows and hoes. And they charged one-eighth of an ounce of silver for sharpening picks, axes, and the sticks used to guide oxen.

²²So when the battle came, the soldiers with Saul and Jonathan had no swords or spears. Only Saul and his son Jonathan had them.

⚜ **SIDELIGHT:** The Philistines were so threatening to the Israelites partly because they held a monopoly on iron weapons. Only Israelite royalty had spears or swords (1 Samuel 13:19–22), and they were probably smuggled in from other countries.

Israel Defeats the Philistines

²³A group from the Philistine army had gone out to the pass at Micmash.

14 One day Jonathan, Saul's son, said to the officer who carried his armor, "Come, let's go over to the Philistine camp on the other side." But Jonathan did not tell his father.

²Saul was sitting under a pomegranateᵈ tree at the threshingᵈ floor near Gibeah. He had about six hundred men with him. ³One man was Ahijah who was wearing the holy vest.ᵈ (Ahijah was a son of Ichabod's brother Ahitub. Ichabod was the son of Phinehas, the son of Eli, the LORD's priest in Shiloh.) No one knew Jonathan had left.

⁴There was a steep slope on each side of the pass that Jonathan planned to go through to reach the Philistine camp. The cliff on one side was named Bozez, and the cliff on the other side was named Seneh. ⁵One cliff faced north toward Micmash. The other faced south toward Geba.

⁶Jonathan said to his officer who carried his armor, "Come. Let's go to the camp of those men who are not circumcised.ᵈ Maybe the LORD will help us. The LORD can give us victory if we have many people, or just a few."

⁷The officer who carried Jonathan's armor said to him, "Do whatever you think is best. Go ahead. I'm with you."

⁸Jonathan said, "Then come. We will cross over to the Philistines and let them see us. ⁹If they say to us, 'Stay there until we come to you,' we will stay where we are. We won't go up to them. ¹⁰But if they say, 'Come up to us,' we will climb up, and the LORD will let us defeat them. This will be the sign for us."

¹¹When both Jonathan and his officer let the Philistines see them, the Philistines said, "Look! The Hebrews are crawling out of the holes they were hiding in!" ¹²The Philistines in the camp shouted to Jonathan and his officer, "Come up to us. We'll teach you a lesson!"

Jonathan said to his officer, "Climb up behind me, because the LORD has given the Philistines to Israel!" ¹³So Jonathan climbed up, using his hands and feet, and his officer climbed just behind him. Jonathan struck down the Philistines as he went, and his officer killed them as he followed behind him. ¹⁴In that first fight Jonathan and his officer killed about twenty Philistines over a half acre of ground.

¹⁵All the Philistine soldiers panicked — those in the camp and those in the raiding party. The ground itself shook! God had caused the panic.

¹⁶Saul's guards were at Gibeah in the land of Benjamin when they saw the Philistine soldiers running in every direction. ¹⁷Saul said to his army, "Check to see who has left our camp." When they checked, they learned that Jonathan and his officer were gone.

¹⁸So Saul said to Ahijah the priest, "Bring the Arkᵈ of God." (At that time it was with the Israelites.) ¹⁹While Saul was talking to the priest, the confusion in the Philistine camp was growing. Then Saul said to Ahijah, "Put your hand down!"

²⁰Then Saul gathered his army and entered the battle. They found the Philistines confused, striking each other with their swords! ²¹Earlier, there were Hebrews who had served the Philistines and had stayed in their camp, but now they joined the Israelites with Saul and Jonathan. ²²When all the Israelites hidden in the mountains of Ephraim heard that the Philistine soldiers were running away, they also joined the battle and chased the Philistines. ²³So the LORD saved the Israelites that day, and the battle moved on past Beth Aven.

Saul Makes Another Mistake

²⁴The men of Israel were miserable that day because Saul had made an oath for all of them. He had said, "No one should eat food before evening and before I finish defeating my enemies. If he does, he will be cursed!" So no Israelite soldier ate food.

²⁵Now the army went into the woods, where there was some honey on the ground. ²⁶They came upon some honey, but no one took any because they were afraid of the oath. ²⁷Jonathan had not heard the oath Saul had put on the army, so he dipped the end of his stick into the honey and lifted some out and ate it. Then he felt better. ²⁸Then one of the soldiers told Jonathan, "Your father made an oath for all the soldiers. He said any man who eats today will be cursed! That's why they are so weak."

29Jonathan said, "My father has made trouble for the land! See how much better I feel after just tasting a little of this honey! 30It would have been much better for the men to eat the food they took from their enemies today. We could have killed many more Philistines!"

31That day the Israelites defeated the Philistines from Micmash to Aijalon. After that, they were very tired. 32They had taken sheep, cattle, and calves from the Philistines. Now they were so hungry they killed the animals on the ground and ate them, without draining the blood from them! 33Someone said to Saul, "Look! The men are sinning against the LORD. They're eating meat without draining the blood from it!"

Saul said, "You have sinned! Roll a large stone over here now!" 34Then he said, "Go to the men and tell them that each person must bring his ox and sheep to me and kill it here and eat it. Don't sin against the LORD by eating meat without draining the blood from it."

That night everyone brought his animals and killed them there. 35Then Saul built an altar to the LORD. It was the first altar he had built to the LORD.

36Saul said, "Let's go after the Philistines tonight and rob them. We won't let any of them live!"

The men answered, "Do whatever you think is best."

But the priest said, "Let's ask God."

37So Saul asked God, "Should I chase the Philistines? Will you let us defeat them?" But God did not answer Saul at that time. 38Then Saul said to all the leaders of his army, "Come here. Let's find out what sin has been done today. 39As surely as the LORD lives who has saved Israel, even if my son Jonathan did the sin, he must die." But no one in the army spoke.

40Then Saul said to all the Israelites, "You stand on this side. I and my son Jonathan will stand on the other side."

The men answered, "Do whatever you think is best."

41Then Saul prayed to the LORD, the God of Israel, "Give me the right answer."

And Saul and Jonathan were picked; the other men went free. 42Saul said, "Now let us discover if it is I or Jonathan my son who is guilty." And Jonathan was picked.

43Saul said to Jonathan, "Tell me what you have done."

So Jonathan told Saul, "I only tasted a little honey from the end of my stick. And must I die now?"

44Saul said, "Jonathan, if you don't die, may God punish me terribly."

45But the soldiers said to Saul, "Must Jonathan die? Never! He is responsible for saving Israel today! As surely as the LORD lives, not even a hair of his head will fall to the ground! Today Jonathan fought against the Philistines with God's help!" So the army saved Jonathan, and he did not die.

46Then Saul stopped chasing the Philistines, and they went back to their own land.

Saul Fights Israel's Enemies

47When Saul became king over Israel, he fought against Israel's enemies all around. He fought Moab, the Ammonites, Edom, the king of Zobah, and the Philistines. Everywhere Saul went he defeated Israel's enemies. 48He fought bravely and defeated the Amalekites. He saved the Israelites from their enemies who had robbed them.

49Saul's sons were Jonathan, Ishvi, and Malki-Shua. His older daughter was named Merab, and his younger daughter was named Michal. 50Saul's wife was Ahinoam daughter of Ahimaaz. The commander of his army was Abner son of Ner, Saul's uncle. 51Saul's father Kish and Abner's father Ner were sons of Abiel.

52All Saul's life he fought hard against the Philistines. When he saw strong or brave men, he took them into his army.

Saul Rejected as King

15 Samuel said to Saul, "The LORD sent me to appoint you king over Israel. Now listen to his message. 2This is what the LORD All-Powerful says: 'When the Israelites came out of Egypt, the Amalekites tried to stop them from going to Canaan. So I will punish them. 3Now go, attack the Amalekites and destroy everything they own as an offering to the LORD. Don't let anything live. Put to death men and women, children and small babies, cattle and sheep, camels and donkeys.' "

4So Saul called the army together at Telaim. There were two hundred thousand foot soldiers and ten thousand men from Judah. 5Then Saul went to the city of Amalek and set up an ambush in the ravine. 6He said to the Kenites, "Go away. Leave the Amalekites so that I won't destroy you with them because you showed kindness to the Israelites when they came out of Egypt." So the Kenites moved away from the Amalekites.

7Then Saul defeated the Amalekites. He fought them all the way from Havilah to Shur, at the border of Egypt. 8He took King Agag of the Amalekites alive, but he killed all of Agag's army with the sword. 9Saul and the army let Agag live, along with the best sheep, fat cattle, and lambs. They let every good animal live, because they did not want to destroy them. But when they found an animal that was weak or useless, they killed it.

10Then the LORD spoke his word to Samuel: 11"I am sorry I made Saul king, because he has stopped following me and has not obeyed my commands." Samuel was upset, and he cried out to the LORD all night long.

¹²Early the next morning Samuel got up and went to meet Saul. But the people told Samuel, "Saul has gone to Carmel, where he has put up a monument in his own honor. Now he has gone down to Gilgal."

¹³When Samuel came to Saul, Saul said, "May the LORD bless you! I have obeyed the LORD's commands."

¹⁴But Samuel said, "Then why do I hear cattle mooing and sheep bleating?"

¹⁵Saul answered, "The soldiers took them from the Amalekites. They saved the best sheep and cattle to offer as sacrifices to the LORD your God, but we destroyed all the other animals."

¹⁶Samuel said to Saul, "Stop! Let me tell you what the LORD said to me last night."

Saul answered, "Tell me."

¹⁷Samuel said, "Once you didn't think much of yourself, but now you have become the leader of the tribes^d of Israel. The LORD appointed you to be king over Israel. ¹⁸And he sent you on a mission. He said, 'Go and destroy those evil people, the Amalekites. Make war on them until all of them are dead.' ¹⁹Why didn't you obey the LORD? Why did you take the best things? Why did you do what the LORD said was wrong?"

²⁰Saul said, "But I did obey the LORD. I did what the LORD told me to do. I destroyed all the Amalekites, and I brought back Agag their king. ²¹The soldiers took the best sheep and cattle to sacrifice to the LORD your God at Gilgal."

²²But Samuel answered,

"What pleases the LORD more:
burnt offerings and sacrifices
  or obedience to his voice?
It is better to obey than to sacrifice.
  It is better to listen to God than to offer the
     fat of sheep.
²³Disobedience is as bad as the sin of sorcery.^d
  Pride is as bad as the sin of worshiping
     idols.
You have rejected the LORD's command.
  Now he rejects you as king."

²⁴Then Saul said to Samuel, "I have sinned. I didn't obey the LORD's commands and your words. I was afraid of the people, and I did what they said. ²⁵Now, I beg you, forgive my sin. Come back with me so I may worship the LORD."

²⁶But Samuel said to Saul, "I won't go back with you. You rejected the LORD's command, and *now he rejects you as king of Israel.*"

²⁷As Samuel turned to leave, Saul caught his robe, and it tore. ²⁸Samuel said to him, "The LORD has torn the kingdom of Israel from you today and has given it to one of your neighbors who is better than you. ²⁹The LORD is the Eternal One of Israel. He does not lie or change his mind. He is not a

human being, so he does not change his mind.

³⁰Saul answered, "I have sinned. But please honor me in front of the older leaders of my people and in front of the Israelites. Come back with me so that I can worship the LORD your God." ³¹So Samuel went back with Saul, and Saul worshiped the LORD.

³²Then Samuel said, "Bring me King Agag of the Amalekites."

Agag came to Samuel in chains, but Agag thought, "Surely the threat of death has passed."

³³Samuel said to him, "Your sword made other mothers lose their children. Now your mother will have no children." And Samuel cut Agag to pieces before the LORD at Gilgal.

³⁴Then Samuel left and went to Ramah, but Saul went up to his home in Gibeah. ³⁵And Samuel never saw Saul again the rest of his life, but he was sad for Saul. And the LORD was very sorry he had made Saul king of Israel.

Samuel Goes to Bethlehem

16 The LORD said to Samuel, "How long will you continue to feel sorry for Saul? I have rejected him as king of Israel. Fill your container with olive oil and go. I am sending you to Jesse who lives in Bethlehem, because I have chosen one of his sons to be king."

²But Samuel said, "If I go, Saul will hear the news and will try to kill me."

The LORD said, "Take a young calf with you. Say, 'I have come to offer a sacrifice to the LORD.' ³Invite Jesse to the sacrifice. Then I will tell you what to do. You must appoint the one I show you."

⁴Samuel did what the LORD told him to do. When he arrived at Bethlehem, the older leaders of Bethlehem shook with fear. They met him and asked, "Are you coming in peace?"

⁵Samuel answered, "Yes, I come in peace. I have come to make a sacrifice to the LORD. Set yourselves apart to the LORD and come to the sacrifice with me." Then he set Jesse and his sons apart to the LORD, and he invited them to come to the sacrifice.

⁶When they arrived, Samuel saw Eliab, and he thought, "Surely the LORD has appointed this person standing here before him."

⁷But the LORD said to Samuel, "Don't look at how handsome Eliab is or how tall he is, because I have not chosen him. God does not see the same way people see. People look at the outside of a *person, but the LORD looks at the heart.*"

⁸Then Jesse called Abinadab and told him to pass by Samuel. But Samuel said, "The LORD has not chosen this man either." ⁹Then Jesse had Shammah pass by. But Samuel said, "No, the LORD has not chosen this one." ¹⁰Jesse had seven of his sons pass by Samuel. But Samuel said to

him, "The LORD has not chosen any of these."

¹¹Then he asked Jesse, "Are these all the sons you have?"

Jesse answered, "I still have the youngest son. He is out taking care of the sheep."

Samuel said, "Send for him. We will not sit down to eat until he arrives."

¹²So Jesse sent and had his youngest son brought in. He was a fine boy, tanned, and handsome.

The LORD said to Samuel, "Go, appoint him, because he is the one."

¹³So Samuel took the container of olive oil and poured it on Jesse's youngest son to appoint him in front of his brothers. From that day on, the LORD's Spirit*d* worked in David. Samuel then went back to Ramah.

David Serves Saul

¹⁴But the LORD's Spirit*d* had left Saul, and an evil spirit from the LORD troubled him.

¹⁵Saul's servants said to him, "See, an evil spirit from God is troubling you. ¹⁶Give us the command to look for someone who can play the harp. When the evil spirit from God troubles you, he will play, and you will feel better."

¹⁷So Saul said to his servants, "Find someone who can play well and bring him to me."

¹⁸One of the servants said, "I have seen a son of Jesse of Bethlehem play the harp. He is brave and courageous. He is a good speaker and handsome, and the LORD is with him."

¹⁹Then Saul sent messengers to Jesse, saying, "Send me your son David, who is with the sheep." ²⁰So Jesse loaded a donkey with bread, a leather bag full of wine, and a young goat, and he sent them with his son David to Saul.

²¹When David came to Saul, he began to serve him. Saul liked David and made him the officer who carried his armor. ²²Saul sent a message to Jesse, saying, "Let David stay and serve me because I like him."

²³When the evil spirit from God troubled Saul, David would take his harp and play. Then the evil

---

Bigger Isn't Always Better

"Too short."

That was the assessment of basketball coaches at Wilmer-Hutchins High School near Dallas. At five-foot-seven, Spud Webb didn't look like he was varsity basketball material.

But Spud thought they were wrong, and he played hard every day. He became the team's best passer, dribbler, and outside shooter.

Coaches at Midland Junior College told Spud the same thing: He was too short for the team. But Spud believed in himself and proved them wrong.

Coaches at North Carolina State also thought Spud was too short to play major-college ball. But Spud believed in himself, and he not only started for NC State, but he became an All-Atlantic Coast Conference player.

When Spud graduated, the sports commentators said he was too short to play in the National Basketball Association. But the Atlanta Hawks drafted him in 1985, and he proved the commentators wrong.

In a league where some players towered two feet above him, Spud's slashing, driving style made him one of the most feared guards in professional basketball.

Spud Webb became a superstar—despite people's predictions. Likewise, David became king of Israel, even though he wasn't the tallest, smartest, or strongest choice. Read why God chose him in **1 Samuel 16:1–13**.

■ What might have happened if Spud Webb and David had believed what others said?

■ What qualities did David have that you see in yourself?

CONSIDER . . .

■ identifying some good things about yourself that someone looking at you from the outside might not notice. Decide how you'll use those qualities to serve God.

■ finding out some good things that are hidden in someone who is unpopular at school or church, then encouraging him or her in those things.

FOR MORE, SEE . . .

■ Psalm 147:10–11 (p. 564)
■ Galatians 2:6 (p. 1207)
■ Ephesians 1:3–6 (p. 1217)

spirit would leave him, and Saul would feel better.

David and Goliath

17 The Philistines gathered their armies for war. They met at Socoh in Judah and camped at Ephes Dammim between Socoh and Azekah. ²Saul and the Israelites gathered in the Valley of Elah and camped there and took their positions to fight the Philistines. ³The Philistines controlled one hill while the Israelites controlled another. The valley was between them.

⁴The Philistines had a champion fighter from Gath named Goliath. He was about nine feet, four inches tall. He came out of the Philistine camp ⁵with a bronze helmet on his head and a coat of bronze armor that weighed about one hundred twenty-five pounds. ⁶He wore bronze protectors on his legs, and he had a bronze spear on his back. ⁷The wooden part of his larger spear was like a weaver's rod, and its blade weighed about fifteen pounds. The officer who carried his shield walked in front of him.

⁸Goliath stood and shouted to the Israelite soldiers, "Why have you taken positions for battle? I am a Philistine, and you are Saul's servants! Choose a man and send him to fight me. ⁹If he can fight and kill me, we will be your servants. But if I can kill him, you will be our servants." ¹⁰Then he said, "Today I stand and dare the army of Israel! Send one of your men to fight me!" ¹¹When Saul and the Israelites heard the Philistine's words, they were very scared.

¹²Now David was the son of Jesse, an Ephrathite from Bethlehem in Judah. Jesse had eight sons. In Saul's time Jesse was an old man. ¹³His three oldest sons followed Saul to the war. The first son was Eliab, the second was Abinadab, and the third was Shammah. ¹⁴David was the youngest. Jesse's three oldest sons followed Saul, ¹⁵but David went back and forth from Saul to Bethlehem, where he took care of his father's sheep.

¹⁶For forty days the Philistine came out every morning and evening and stood before the Israelite army.

¹⁷Jesse said to his son David, "Take this half bushel of cooked grain and ten loaves of bread to your brothers in the camp. ¹⁸Also take ten pieces

---

SERVICE

When People Can't Say Thanks

Rick Marty's friends couldn't believe he was taking a summer job at the nursing home after graduation. When he described his job, they gagged.

"I'll be working with eight Alzheimer's patients," he explained. "Waking them up. Changing their adult diapers. Taking them to breakfast. Feeding them."

And that's what he did for three months. Every day, he would wake people and get them ready for the day. And even though he was always there, they never recognized him. In fact, some would slap him and yell at him without any reason. And they never thanked him or even recognized all the work he did for them.

"How do you do it?" his amazed friends asked one Saturday night when the gang went out for pizza. "It sounds terrible."

"You have to realize what these people are going through," Rick said. "They're frustrated with themselves, not you. You just have to help them be as comfortable as they can be."

Rick had learned what it means to serve someone even when it's tough. David had similar experiences with service in a tough situation. Read about it in **1 Samuel 16:14—23**.

■ How does Rick's servant attitude compare with David's dedicated service to King Saul? Read 1 Samuel 18:10–11 (p. 262) to see what happened later. How does this information change your view of David's dedication?

■ When have you comforted someone who, like King Saul, could never express gratitude? How did you feel?

C O N S I D E R . . .

■ volunteering at a nursing home or day care center for people who need special help.

◀ writing a letter of encouragement to someone who is doing a thankless, but necessary, service.

F O R   M O R E ,   S E E . . .

■ Proverbs 11:24–25 (p. 577)
■ Matthew 10:5–8 (p. 922)

■ 2 Corinthians 1:3–7 (p. 1193)

of cheese to the commander and to your brothers. See how your brothers are and bring back some proof to show me that they are all right. ¹⁹Your brothers are with Saul and the army in the Valley of Elah, fighting against the Philistines."

²⁰Early in the morning David left the sheep with another shepherd. He took the food and left as Jesse had told him. When David arrived at the camp, the army was going out to their battle positions, shouting their war cry. ²¹The Israelites and Philistines were lining up their men to face each other in battle.

²²David left the food with the man who kept the supplies and ran to the battle line to talk to his brothers. ²³While he was talking with them, Goliath, the Philistine champion from Gath, came out. He shouted things against Israel as usual, and David heard him. ²⁴When the Israelites saw Goliath, they were very much afraid and ran away.

²⁵They said, "Look at this man! He keeps coming out to challenge Israel. The king will give much money to whoever kills him. He will also let whoever kills him marry his daughter. And his father's family will not have to pay taxes in Israel."

²⁶David asked the men who stood near him, "What will be done to reward the man who kills this Philistine and takes away the shame from Israel? Who does this uncircumcised[d] Philistine think he is? Does he think he can speak against the armies of the living God?"

²⁷The Israelites told David what would be done for the man who would kill Goliath.

²⁸When David's oldest brother Eliab heard David talking with the soldiers, he was angry with David. He asked David, "Why did you come here? Who's taking care of those few sheep of yours in the desert? I know you are proud and wicked at heart. You came down here just to watch the battle."

²⁹David asked, "Now what have I done wrong? Can't I even talk?" ³⁰When he turned to other people and asked the same questions, they gave him the same answer as before. ³¹Yet what David said was told to Saul, and he sent for David.

³²David said to Saul, "Don't let anyone be discouraged. I, your servant, will go and fight this Philistine!"

³³Saul answered, "You can't go out against this Philistine and fight him. You're only a boy. Goliath has been a warrior since he was a young man."

³⁴But David said to Saul, "I, your servant, have been keeping my father's sheep. When a lion or bear came and took a sheep from the flock, ³⁵I would chase it. I would attack it and save the sheep from its mouth. When it attacked me, I caught it by its fur and hit it and killed it. ³⁶I, your servant, have killed both a lion and a bear! This uncircumcised Philistine will be like them, because he has spoken against the armies of the living God. ³⁷The LORD who saved me from a lion and a bear will save me from this Philistine."

Saul said to David, "Go, and may the LORD be with you." ³⁸Saul put his own clothes on David. He put a bronze helmet on his head and dressed him in armor. ³⁹David put on Saul's sword and tried to walk around, but he was not used to all the armor Saul had put on him.

He said to Saul, "I can't go in this, because I'm not used to it." Then David took it all off. ⁴⁰He took his stick in his hand and chose five smooth stones from a stream. He put them in his shepherd's bag and grabbed his sling. Then he went to meet the Philistine.

⁴¹At the same time, the Philistine was coming closer to David. The man who held his shield walked in front of him. ⁴²When Goliath looked at David and saw that he was only a boy, tanned and handsome, he looked down on David with disgust. ⁴³He said, "Do you think I am a dog, that you come at me with a stick?" He used his gods' names to curse David. ⁴⁴He said to David, "Come here. I'll feed your body to the birds of the air and the wild animals!"

⁴⁵But David said to him, "You come to me using a sword and two spears. But I come to you in the name of the LORD All-Powerful, the God of the armies of Israel! You have spoken against him. ⁴⁶Today the LORD will hand you over to me, and I'll kill you and cut off your head. Today I'll feed the bodies of the Philistine soldiers to the birds of the air and the wild animals. Then all the world will know there is a God in Israel! ⁴⁷Everyone gathered here will know the LORD does not need swords or spears to save people. The battle belongs to him, and he will hand you over to us."

⁴⁸As Goliath came near to attack him, David ran quickly to meet him. ⁴⁹He took a stone from his bag, put it into his sling, and slung it. The stone hit the Philistine and went deep into his forehead, and Goliath fell facedown on the ground.

⁵⁰So David defeated the Philistine with only a sling and a stone. He hit him and killed him. He did not even have a sword in his hand. ⁵¹Then David ran and stood beside him. He took Goliath's sword out of its holder and killed him by cutting off his head.

When the Philistines saw that their champion was dead, they turned and ran. ⁵²The men of Israel and Judah shouted and chased the Philistines all the way to the entrance of the city of Gath and to the gates of Ekron.

The Philistines' bodies lay on the Shaaraim road as far as Gath and Ekron. ⁵³The Israelites returned after chasing the Philistines and robbed their camp. ⁵⁴David took Goliath's head to Jerusalem and put Goliath's weapons in his own tent.

⁵⁵When Saul saw David go out to meet Goliath, Saul asked Abner, commander of the army, "Abner, who is that young man's father?"

☀ **SIDELIGHT:** Slam-dunking would have been easy for Goliath. At nine-foot-four, his head would have been just a few inches below the basketball rim. But he was still no match for David, who was good at "long shots" (1 Samuel 17:41–54).

Abner answered, "As surely as you live, my king, I don't know."

⁵⁶The king said, "Find out whose son he is."

⁵⁷When David came back from killing Goliath, Abner brought him to Saul. David was still holding Goliath's head.

⁵⁸Saul asked him, "Young man, who is your father?"

David answered, "I am the son of your servant Jesse of Bethlehem."

Saul Fears David

18 When David finished talking with Saul, Jonathan felt very close to David. He loved David as much as he loved himself. ²Saul kept David with him from that day on and did not let him go home to his father's house. ³Jonathan made an agreement with David, because he loved David as much as himself. ⁴He took off his coat and gave it to David, along with his armor, including his sword, bow, and belt.

⁵Saul sent David to fight in different battles, and David was very successful. Then Saul put David over the soldiers, which pleased Saul's officers and all the other people.

⁶After David had killed the Philistine, he and the men returned home. Women came out from all the towns of Israel to meet King Saul. They sang songs of joy, danced, and played tambourines*d* and stringed instruments. ⁷As they played, they sang,

"Saul has killed thousands of his enemies,
  but David has killed tens of thousands."

⁸The women's song upset Saul, and he became very angry. He thought, "The women say David *has killed tens of thousands, but they say I have* killed only thousands. The only thing left for him to have is the kingdom!" ⁹So Saul watched David closely from then on, because he was jealous.

¹⁰The next day an evil spirit from God rushed upon Saul, and he prophesied*d* in his house. David was playing the harp as he usually did, but

Saul had a spear in his hand. ¹¹He threw the spear, thinking, "I'll pin David to the wall." But David escaped from him twice.

¹²The LORD was with David but had left Saul. So Saul was afraid of David. ¹³He sent David away and made him commander of a thousand soldiers. So David led them in battle. ¹⁴He had great success in everything he did because the LORD was with him. ¹⁵When Saul saw that David was very successful, he feared David even more. ¹⁶But all the people of Israel and Judah loved David because he led them well in battle.

Saul's Daughter Marries David

¹⁷Saul said to David, "Here is my older daughter Merab. I will let you marry her. All I ask is that you remain brave and fight the LORD's battles." Saul thought, "I won't have to kill David. The Philistines will do that."

¹⁸But David answered Saul, saying, "Who am I? My family is not important enough for me to become the king's son-in-law." ¹⁹So, when the time came for Saul's daughter Merab to marry David, Saul gave her instead to Adriel of Meholah.

²⁰Now Saul's other daughter, Michal, loved David. When they told Saul, he was pleased. ²¹He thought, "I will let her marry David. Then she will be a trap for him, and the Philistines will defeat him." So Saul said to David a second time, "You may become my son-in-law."

²²And Saul ordered his servants to talk with David in private and say, "Look, the king likes you. His servants love you. You should be his son-in-law."

²³Saul's servants said these words to David, but David answered, "Do you think it is easy to become the king's son-in-law? I am poor and unimportant."

²⁴When Saul's servants told him what David had said, ²⁵Saul said, "Tell David, 'The king doesn't want money for the bride. All he wants is a hundred Philistine foreskins to get even with his enemies.' " Saul planned to let the Philistines kill David.

²⁶When Saul's servants told this to David, he was pleased to become the king's son-in-law. ²⁷So he and his men went out and killed two hundred Philistines. David brought all their foreskins to Saul so he could be the king's son-in-law. Then Saul gave him his daughter Michal for his wife. ²⁸Saul saw that the LORD was with David and that *his daughter Michal loved David. ²⁹So he grew* even more afraid of David, and he was David's enemy all his life.

³⁰The Philistine commanders continued to go out to fight the Israelites, but every time, David was more skillful than Saul's officers. So he became famous.

Saul Tries to Kill David

19 Saul told his son Jonathan and all his servants to kill David, but Jonathan liked David very much. ²So he warned David, "My father Saul is looking for a chance to kill you. Watch out in the morning. Hide in a secret place. ³I will go out and stand with my father in the field where you are hiding, and I'll talk to him about you. Then I'll let you know what I find out."

⁴When Jonathan talked to Saul his father, he said good things about David. Jonathan said, "The king should do no wrong to your servant David since he has done nothing wrong to you. What he has done has helped you greatly. ⁵David risked his life when he killed Goliath the Philistine, and the LORD won a great victory for all Israel. You saw it and were happy. Why would you do wrong against David? He's innocent. There's no reason to kill him!"

⁶Saul listened to Jonathan and then made this promise: "As surely as the LORD lives, David won't be put to death."

⁷So Jonathan called to David and told him everything that had been said. He brought David to Saul, and David was with Saul as before.

⁸When war broke out again, David went out to fight the Philistines. He defeated them, and they ran away from him.

⁹But once again an evil spirit from the LORD rushed upon Saul as he was sitting in his house with his spear in his hand. David was playing the harp. ¹⁰Saul tried to pin David to the wall with his spear, but David jumped out of the way. So Saul's spear went into the wall, and David ran away that night.

¹¹Saul sent messengers to David's house to watch it and to kill him in the morning. But Michal, David's wife, warned him, saying, "Tonight you must run for your life. If you don't, you will be dead in the morning." ¹²So she let David down out of a window, and he ran away and escaped. ¹³Then Michal took an idol, laid it on the bed, covered it with clothes, and put goats' hair at its head.

¹⁴Saul sent messengers to take David prisoner, but Michal said, "He is sick."

¹⁵Saul sent them back to see David, saying, "Bring him to me on his bed so I can kill him."

¹⁶When the messengers entered David's house, they found just an idol on the bed with goats' hair on its head.

¹⁷Saul said to Michal, "Why did you trick me this way? You let my enemy go so he could run away!"

Michal answered Saul, "David told me if I did not help him escape, he would kill me."

¹⁸After David had escaped from Saul, he went to Samuel at Ramah and told him everything Saul had done to him. Then David and Samuel went to Naioth and stayed there. ¹⁹Saul heard that David was in Naioth at Ramah. ²⁰So he sent messengers to capture him. But they met a group of prophets prophesying, with Samuel standing there leading them. So the Spirit of God entered Saul's men, and they also prophesied.

²¹When Saul heard the news, he sent more messengers, but they also prophesied. Then he sent messengers a third time, but they also prophesied. ²²Finally, Saul himself went to Ramah, to the well at Secu. He asked, "Where are Samuel and David?"

The people answered, "In Naioth at Ramah."

²³When Saul went to Naioth at Ramah, the Spirit of God also rushed upon him. And he walked on, prophesying until he came to Naioth at Ramah. ²⁴He took off his robes and prophesied in front of Samuel. He lay that way all day and all night. That is why people ask, "Is even Saul one of the prophets?"

Jonathan Helps David

20 Then David ran away from Naioth in Ramah. He went to Jonathan and asked, "What have I done? What is my crime? How did I sin against your father? Why is he trying to kill me?"

²Jonathan answered, "No! You won't die! See, my father doesn't do anything great or small without first telling me. Why would he keep this from me? It's not true!"

³But David took an oath, saying, "Your father knows very well that you like me. He says to himself, 'Jonathan must not know about it, or he will tell David.' As surely as the LORD lives and as you live, I am only a step away from death."

⁴Jonathan said to David, "I'll do anything you want me to do."

⁵So David said, "Look, tomorrow is the New Moon festival. I am supposed to eat with the king, but let me hide in the field until the third evening. ⁶If your father notices I am gone, tell him, 'David begged me to let him go to his hometown of Bethlehem. Every year at this time his family group offers a sacrifice.' ⁷If your father says, 'Fine,' I am safe. But if he becomes angry, you will know that he wants to hurt me. ⁸Jonathan, be loyal to me, your servant. You have made an agreement with me before the LORD. If I am guilty, you may kill me yourself! Why hand me over to your father?"

⁹Jonathan answered, "No, never! If I learn that my father plans to hurt you, I will warn you!"

¹⁰David asked, "Who will let me know if your father answers you unkindly?"

¹¹Then Jonathan said, "Come, let's go out into the field." So the two of them went out into the field.

¹²Jonathan said to David, "I promise this before the LORD, the God of Israel: At this same time the day after tomorrow, I will find out how my father feels. If he feels good toward you, I will send word to you and let you know. ¹³But if my father plans to hurt you, I will let you know and send you away safely. May the LORD punish me terribly if I don't do this. And may the LORD be with you as he has been with my father. ¹⁴But show me the kindness of the LORD as long as I live so that I may not die. ¹⁵You must never stop showing your kindness to my family, even when the LORD has destroyed all your enemies from the earth."

¹⁶So Jonathan made an agreement with David. He said, "May the LORD hold David's enemies responsible." ¹⁷And Jonathan asked David to repeat his promise of love for him, because he loved David as much as he loved himself.

¹⁸Jonathan said to David, "Tomorrow is the New Moon festival. Your seat will be empty, so my father will miss you. ¹⁹On the third day go to the place where you hid when this trouble began. Wait by the rock Ezel. ²⁰On the third day I will shoot three arrows to the side of the rock as if I am shooting at a target. ²¹Then I will send a boy to find the arrows. If I say to him, 'The arrows are near you; bring them here,' you may come out of hiding. You are safe. As the LORD lives, there is no danger. ²²But if I say to the boy, 'Look, the arrows are beyond you,' you must go, because the LORD is sending you away. ²³Remember what we talked about. The LORD is a witness between you and me forever."

²⁴So David hid in the field. When the New Moon festival came, the king sat down to eat. ²⁵He sat where he always sat, near the wall. Jonathan sat across from him, and Abner sat next to Saul, but David's place was empty. ²⁶That day Saul said nothing. He thought, "Maybe something has happened to David so that he is unclean."ᵈ ²⁷But the next day was the second day of the month, and David's place was still empty. So Saul said to Jonathan, "Why hasn't the son of Jesse come to the feast yesterday or today?"

²⁸Jonathan answered, "David begged me to let him go to Bethlehem. ²⁹He said, 'Let me go, because our family has a sacrifice in the town, and my brother has ordered me to be there. Now if I am your friend, please let me go to see my brothers.' That is why he has not come to the king's table."

³⁰Then Saul became very angry with Jonathan. *He said, "You son of a wicked, worthless woman!* I know you are on the side of David son of Jesse! You bring shame on yourself and on your mother who gave birth to you. ³¹As long as Jesse's son lives, you will never be king or have a kingdom.

Now send for David and bring him to me. He must die!"

³²Jonathan asked his father, "Why should David be killed? What wrong has he done?" ³³Then Saul threw his spear at Jonathan, trying to kill him. So Jonathan knew that his father really wanted to kill David. ³⁴Jonathan was very angry and left the table. That second day of the month he refused to eat. He was ashamed of his father and upset over David.

³⁵The next morning Jonathan went out to the field to meet David as they had agreed. He had a young boy with him. ³⁶Jonathan said to the boy, "Run and find the arrows I shoot." When he ran, Jonathan shot an arrow beyond him. ³⁷The boy ran to the place where Jonathan's arrow fell, but Jonathan called, "The arrow is beyond you!" ³⁸Then he shouted, "Hurry! Go quickly! Don't stop!" The boy picked up the arrow and brought it back to his master. ³⁹(The boy knew nothing about what this meant; only Jonathan and David knew.) ⁴⁰Then Jonathan gave his weapons to the boy and told him, "Go back to town."

⁴¹When the boy left, David came out from the south side of the rock. He bowed facedown on the ground before Jonathan three times. Then David and Jonathan kissed each other and cried together, but David cried the most.

⁴²Jonathan said to David, "Go in peace. We have promised by the LORD that we will be friends. We said, 'The LORD will be a witness between you and me, and between our descendants'ᵈ always.' " Then David left, and Jonathan went back to town.

David Goes to See Ahimelech

21 David went to Nob to see Ahimelech the priest. Ahimelech shook with fear when he saw David, and he asked, "Why are you alone? Why is no one with you?"

²David answered him, "The king gave me a special order. He told me, 'No one must know what I am sending you to do or what I told you to do.' I told my men where to meet me. ³Now, what food do you have with you? Give me five loaves of bread or anything you find."

⁴The priest said to David, "I don't have any plain bread here, but I do have some holy bread.ⁿ You may eat it if your men have kept themselves from women."

⁵David answered, "No women have been near *us for days. My men always keep themselves* holy, even when we do ordinary work. And this is especially true when the work is holy."

⁶So the priest gave David the holy bread from the presence of God because there was no other.

holy bread   This was the bread that showed the people were in the presence of God. Normally only the priests ate this bread.

Each day the holy bread was replaced with hot bread.

⁷One of Saul's servants happened to be there that day. He had been held there before the LORD. He was Doeg the Edomite, the chief of Saul's shepherds.

⁸David asked Ahimelech, "Do you have a spear or sword here? The king's business was very important, so I left without my sword or any other weapon."

⁹The priest answered. "The sword of Goliath the Philistine, the one you killed in the Valley of Elah, is here. It is wrapped in a cloth behind the holy vest.ᵈ If you want it, you may take it. There's no other sword here but that one."

David said, "There is no other sword like it. Give it to me."

David Goes to Gath

¹⁰That day David ran away from Saul and went to Achish king of Gath. ¹¹But the servants of Achish said to him, "This is David, the king of the Israelites. He's the man they dance and sing about, saying:

'Saul has killed thousands of his enemies,
    but David has killed tens of thousands.' "

¹²David paid attention to these words and was very much afraid of Achish king of Gath. ¹³So he pretended to be crazy in front of Achish and his servants. While he was with them, he acted like a madman and clawed on the doors of the gate and let spit run down his beard.

¹⁴Achish said to his servants, "Look at the man! He's crazy! Why do you bring him to me? ¹⁵I have enough madmen. I don't need you to bring him here to act like this in front of me! Don't let him in my house!"

David at Adullam and Mizpah

22 David left Gath and escaped to the cave of Adullam. When his brothers and other relatives heard that he was there, they went to see him. ²Everyone who was in trouble, or who owed money, or who was unsatisfied gathered around David, and he became their leader. About four hundred men were with him.

³From there David went to Mizpah in Moab and spoke to the king of Moab. He said, "Please let my father and mother come and stay with you until I learn what God is going to do for me." ⁴So he left them with the king of Moab, and they stayed with him as long as David was hiding in the stronghold.ᵈ

⁵But the prophetᵈ Gad said to David, "Don't stay in the stronghold. Go to the land of Judah." So David left and went to the forest of Hereth.

Saul Destroys Ahimelech's Family

⁶Saul heard that David and his men had been seen. Saul was sitting under the tamarisk tree on the hill at Gibeah, and all his officers were standing around him. He had a spear in his hand. ⁷Saul said to them, "Listen, men of Benjamin! Do you think the son of Jesse will give all of you fields and vineyards? Will David make you commanders over thousands of men or hundreds of men? ⁸You have all made plans against me! No one tells me when my son makes an agreement with the son of Jesse! No one cares about me! No one tells me when my son has encouraged my servant to ambush me this very day!"

⁹Doeg the Edomite, who was standing there with Saul's officers, said, "I saw the son of Jesse. He came to see Ahimelech son of Ahitub at Nob. ¹⁰Ahimelech prayed to the LORD for David and gave him food and gave him the sword of Goliath the Philistine."

¹¹Then the king sent for the priest Ahimelech son of Ahitub and for all of Ahimelech's relatives who were priests at Nob. And they all came to the king. ¹²Saul said to Ahimelech, "Listen now, son of Ahitub."

Ahimelech answered, "Yes, master."

¹³Saul said, "Why are you and Jesse's son against me? You gave him bread and a sword! You prayed to God for him. David has turned against me and is waiting to attack me even now!"

¹⁴Ahimelech answered, "You have no other servant who is as loyal as David, your own son-in-law and captain of your bodyguards. Everyone in your house respects him. ¹⁵That was not the first time I prayed to God for David. Don't blame me or any of my relatives. I, your servant, know nothing about what is going on."

¹⁶But the king said, "Ahimelech, you and all your relatives must die!" ¹⁷Then he told the guards at his side, "Go and kill the priests of the LORD, because they are on David's side. They knew he was running away, but they didn't tell me."

But the king's officers refused to kill the priests of the LORD.

¹⁸Then the king ordered Doeg, "Go and kill the priests." So Doeg the Edomite went and killed the priests. That day he killed eighty-five men who wore the linen holy vest.ᵈ ¹⁹He also killed the peo-

ple of Nob, the city of the priests. With the sword he killed men, women, children, babies, cattle, donkeys, and sheep.

20But Abiathar, a son of Ahimelech, who was the son of Ahitub, escaped. He ran away and joined David. 21He told David that Saul had killed the Lord's priests. 22Then David told him, "Doeg the Edomite was there at Nob that day. I knew he would surely tell Saul. So I am responsible for the death of all your father's family. 23Stay with me. Don't be afraid. The man who wants to kill you also wants to kill me. You will be safe with me."

David Saves the People of Keilah

23 Someone told David, "Look, the Philistines are fighting against Keilah and stealing grain from the threshing floors."

2David asked the Lord, "Should I go and fight these Philistines?"

The Lord answered him, "Go. Attack them, and save Keilah."

3But David's men said to him, "We're afraid here in Judah. We will be more afraid if we go to Keilah where the Philistine army is."

4David again asked the Lord, and the Lord answered, "Go down to Keilah. I will help you defeat the Philistines." 5So David and his men went to Keilah and fought the Philistines and took their cattle. David killed many Philistines and saved the people of Keilah. 6(Now Abiathar son of Ahimelech had brought the holy vest with him when he came to David at Keilah.)

Saul Chases David

7Someone told Saul that David was now at Keilah. Saul said, "God has handed David over to me! He has trapped himself, because he has entered a town with gates and bars." 8Saul called all his army together for battle, and they prepared to go down to Keilah to attack David and his men.

9David learned Saul was making evil plans against him. So he said to Abiathar the priest, "Bring the holy vest." 10David prayed, "Lord, God of Israel, I have heard that Saul plans to come to Keilah to destroy the town because of me. 11Will the leaders of Keilah hand me over to Saul? Will Saul come down to Keilah, as I heard? Lord, God of Israel, tell me, your servant!"

The Lord answered, "Saul will come down."

12Again David asked, "Will the leaders of Keilah hand me and my men over to Saul?"

The Lord answered, "They will."

13So David and his six hundred men left Keilah and kept moving from place to place. When Saul found out that David had escaped from Keilah, he did not go there.

14David stayed in the desert hideouts and in the hills of the Desert of Ziph. Every day Saul looked for David, but the Lord did not surrender David to him.

15While David was at Horesh in the Desert of Ziph, he learned that Saul was coming to kill him. 16But Saul's son Jonathan went to David at Horesh and strengthened his faith in God. 17Jonathan told him, "Don't be afraid, because my father won't touch you. You will be king of Israel, and I will be second to you. Even my father Saul knows this." 18The two of them made an agreement before the Lord. Then Jonathan went home, but David stayed at Horesh.

19The people from Ziph went to Saul at Gibeah and told him, "David is hiding in our land. He's at the hideouts of Horesh, on the hill of Hakilah, south of Jeshimon. 20Now, our king, come down anytime you want. It's our duty to hand David over to you."

21Saul answered, "The Lord bless you for helping me. 22Go and learn more about him. Find out where he is staying and who has seen him there. I have heard that he is clever. 23Find all the hiding places he uses, and come back and tell me everything. Then I'll go with you. If David is in the area, I will track him down among all the families in Judah."

24So they went back to Ziph ahead of Saul. Now David and his men were in the Desert of Maon in the desert area south of Jeshimon. 25Saul and his men went to look for David, but David heard about it and went down to a rock and stayed in the Desert of Maon. When Saul heard that, he followed David into the Desert of Maon.

26Saul was going along one side of the mountain, and David and his men were on the other side. They were hurrying to get away from Saul, because Saul and his men were closing in on them. 27But a messenger came to Saul, saying, "Come quickly! The Philistines are attacking our land!" 28So Saul stopped chasing David and went to challenge the Philistines. That is why people call this place Rock of Parting. 29David also left the Desert of Maon and stayed in the hideouts of En Gedi.

David Shames Saul

24 After Saul returned from chasing the Philistines, he was told, "David is in the Desert of En Gedi." 2So he took three thousand chosen men from all Israel and began looking for David and his men near the Rocks of the Wild Goats.

3Saul came to the sheep pens beside the road. A cave was there, and he went in to relieve him-

Maon Some early Greek copies say "Maon." The Hebrew copies say "Paran."

self. Now David and his men were hiding far back in the cave. [4]The men said to David, "Today is the day the LORD spoke of when he said, 'I will give your enemy over to you. Do anything you want with him.' "

Then David crept up to Saul and quietly cut off a corner of Saul's robe. [5]Later David felt guilty because he had cut off a corner of Saul's robe. [6]He said to his men, "May the LORD keep me from doing such a thing to my master! Saul is the LORD's appointed king. I should not do anything against him, because he is the LORD's appointed king!" [7]David used these words to stop his men; he did not let them attack Saul. Then Saul left the cave and went his way.

[8]When David came out of the cave, he shouted to Saul, "My master and king!" Saul looked back, and David bowed facedown on the ground. [9]He said to Saul, "Why do you listen when people say, 'David wants to harm you'? [10]You have seen something with your own eyes today. The LORD put you in my power in the cave. They said I should kill you, but I was merciful. I said, 'I won't harm my master, because he is the LORD's appointed king.' [11]My father, look at this piece of your robe in my hand! I cut off the corner of your robe, but I didn't kill you. Now understand and know I am not planning any evil against you. I did nothing wrong to you, but you are hunting me to kill me. [12]May the LORD judge between us, and may he punish you for the wrong you have done to me! But I am not against you. [13]There is an old saying: 'Evil things come from evil people.' But I am not against you. [14]Whom is the king of Israel coming out against? Whom are you chasing? It's as if you are chasing a dead dog or a flea. [15]May the LORD be our judge and decide between you and me. May he support me and show that I am right. May he save me from you!"

[16]When David finished saying these words, Saul asked, "Is that your voice, David my son?" And he cried loudly. [17]He said, "You are a better man than I am. You have been good to me, but I have done wrong to you. [18]You told me what good things you did. The LORD handed me over to you, but you did not kill me. [19]If a person finds his enemy, he doesn't just send him on his way, does he? May the LORD reward you because you were good to me today. [20]I know you will surely be king, and you will rule the kingdom of Israel. [21]Now swear to me by the LORD that you will not kill my descendants[d] and that you won't wipe out my name from my father's family."

[22]So David made the promise to Saul. Then Saul went back home, and David and his men went up to their hideout.

Nabal Insults David

25 Now Samuel died, and all the Israelites met and had a time of sadness for him. Then they buried him at his home in Ramah.

David moved to the Desert of Maon.[n] [2]A man in Maon who had land at Carmel was very rich. He had three thousand sheep and a thousand goats. He was cutting the wool off his sheep at Carmel. [3]His name was Nabal, and he was a descendant[d] of Caleb. His wife was named Abigail. She was wise and beautiful, but Nabal was cruel and mean.

[4]While David was in the desert, he heard that Nabal was cutting the wool from his sheep. [5]So he sent ten young men and told them, "Go to Nabal at Carmel, and greet him for me. [6]Say to Nabal, 'May you and your family and all who belong to you have good health! [7]I have heard that you are cutting the wool from your sheep. When your shepherds were with us, we did not harm them. All the time your shepherds were at Carmel, we stole nothing from them. [8]Ask your servants, and they will tell you. We come at a happy time, so be kind to my young men. Please give anything you can find for them and for your son David.' "

[9]When David's men arrived, they gave the message to Nabal, but Nabal insulted them. [10]He answered them, "Who is David? Who is this son of Jesse? Many slaves are running away from their masters today! [11]I have bread and water, and I have meat that I killed for my servants who cut the wool. But I won't give it to men I don't know."

[12]David's men went back and told him all Nabal had said. [13]Then David said to them, "Put on your swords!" So they put on their swords, and David put on his also. About four hundred men went with David, but two hundred men stayed with the supplies.

[14]One of Nabal's servants said to Abigail, Nabal's wife, "David sent messengers from the desert to greet our master, but Nabal insulted them. [15]These men were very good to us. They did not harm us. They stole nothing from us during all the time we were out in the field with them. [16]Night and day they protected us. They were like a wall around us while we were with them caring for the sheep. [17]Now think about it, and decide what you can do. Terrible trouble is coming to our master and all his family. Nabal is such a wicked man that no one can even talk to him."

[18]Abigail hurried. She took two hundred loaves of bread, two leather bags full of wine, five cooked sheep, a bushel of cooked grain, a hundred cakes of raisins, and two hundred cakes of

---

Maon   Some early Greek copies say "Maon." The Hebrew copies say "Paran."

pressed figs and put all these on donkeys. [19]Then she told her servants, "Go on. I'll follow you." But she did not tell her husband.

[20]Abigail rode her donkey and came down toward the mountain hideout. There she met David and his men coming down toward her.

[21]David had just said, "It's been useless! I watched over Nabal's property in the desert. I made sure none of his sheep was missing. I did good to him, but he has paid me back with evil. [22]May God punish my enemies even more. I will not leave one of Nabal's men alive until morning."

[23]When Abigail saw David, she quickly got off her donkey and bowed facedown on the ground before him. [24]She fell at David's feet and said, "My master, let the blame be on me! Please let me talk to you. Listen to what I say. [25]My master, don't pay attention to this worthless man Nabal. He is like his name. His name means 'fool,' and he is truly a fool. But I, your servant, didn't see the men you sent. [26]The LORD has kept you from killing and punishing anyone. As surely as the LORD lives and as surely as you live, may your enemies become like Nabal! [27]I have brought a gift to you for the men who follow you. [28]Please forgive my wrong. The LORD will certainly let your family have many kings, because you fight his battles. As long as you live, may you do nothing bad. [29]Someone might chase you to kill you, but the LORD your God will keep you alive. He will throw away your enemies' lives as he would throw a stone from a sling. [30]The LORD will keep all his promises of good things for you. He will make you leader over Israel. [31]Then you won't feel guilty or troubled because you killed innocent people and punished them. Please remember me when the LORD brings you success."

[32]David answered Abigail, "Praise the LORD, the God of Israel, who sent you to meet me. [33]May you be blessed for your wisdom. You have kept me from killing or punishing people today. [34]As surely as the LORD, the God of Israel, lives, he has kept me from hurting you. If you hadn't come quickly to meet me, not one of Nabal's men would have lived until morning."

[35]Then David accepted Abigail's gifts. He told her, "Go home in peace. I have heard your words, and I will do what you have asked."

Nabal's Death

[36]When Abigail went back to Nabal, he was in the house, eating like a king. He was very drunk and in a good mood. So she told him nothing until the next morning. [37]In the morning when he was not drunk, his wife told him everything. His heart stopped, and he became like stone. [38]About ten days later the LORD struck Nabal and he died.

[39]When David heard that Nabal was dead, he said, "Praise the LORD! Nabal insulted me, but the LORD has supported me! He has kept me from doing wrong. The LORD has punished Nabal for his wrong."

Then David sent a message to Abigail, asking her to be his wife. [40]His servants went to Carmel and said to Abigail, "David sent us to take you so you can become his wife."

[41]Abigail bowed facedown on the ground and said, "I am your servant. I'm ready to serve you and to wash the feet of my master's servants." [42]Abigail quickly got on a donkey and went with David's messengers, with her five maids following her. And she became David's wife.

[43]David also had married Ahinoam of Jezreel. So they were both David's wives. [44]Saul's daughter Michal was also David's wife, but Saul had given her to Paltiel son of Laish, who was from Gallim.

David Shames Saul Again

26 The people of Ziph went to Saul at Gibeah and said to him, "David is hiding on the hill of Hakilah opposite Jeshimon."

[2]So Saul went down to the Desert of Ziph with three thousand chosen men of Israel to look for David there. [3]Saul made his camp beside the road on the hill of Hakilah opposite Jeshimon, but David stayed in the desert. When he heard Saul had followed him, [4]he sent out spies and learned for certain that Saul had come to Hakilah.

[5]Then David went to the place where Saul had camped. He saw where Saul and Abner son of Ner, the commander of Saul's army, were sleeping. Saul was sleeping in the middle of the camp with all the army around him.

[6]David asked Ahimelech the Hittite and Abishai son of Zeruiah, Joab's brother, "Who will go down into Saul's camp with me?"

Abishai answered, "I'll go with you."

[7]So that night David and Abishai went into Saul's camp. Saul was asleep in the middle of the camp with his spear stuck in the ground near his head. Abner and the army were sleeping around Saul. [8]Abishai said to David, "Today God has handed your enemy over to you. Let me pin Saul to the ground with my spear. I'll only have to do it once. I won't need to hit him twice."

[9]But David said to Abishai, "Don't kill Saul! No one can harm the LORD's appointed king and still be innocent! [10]As surely as the LORD lives, the LORD himself will punish Saul. Maybe Saul will die naturally, or maybe he will go into battle and be killed. [11]But may the LORD keep me from harming his appointed king! Take the spear and water jug that are near Saul's head. Then let's go."

[12]So David took the spear and water jug that were near Saul's head, and they left. No one saw

them or knew about it or woke up, because the LORD had put them sound asleep.

13David crossed over to the other side of the hill and stood on top of the mountain far from Saul's camp. They were a long way away from each other. 14David shouted to the army and to Abner son of Ner, "Won't you answer me, Abner?"

Abner answered, "Who is calling for the king? Who are you?"

15David said, "You're the greatest man in Israel. Isn't that true? Why didn't you guard your master the king? Someone came into your camp to kill your master the king! 16You have not done well. As surely as the LORD lives, you and your men should die. You haven't guarded your master, the LORD's appointed king. Look! Where are the king's spear and water jug that were near his head?"

17Saul knew David's voice. He said, "Is that your voice, David my son?"

David answered, "Yes, it is, my master and king." 18David also said, "Why are you chasing me, my master? What wrong have I done? What evil am I guilty of? 19My master and king, listen to me. If the LORD made you angry with me, let him accept an offering. But if people did it, may the LORD curse them! They have made me leave the land the LORD gave me. They have told me, 'Go and serve other gods.' 20Now don't let me die far away from the LORD's presence. The king of Israel has come out looking for a flea! You're just hunting a bird in the mountains!"

21Then Saul said, "I have sinned. Come back, David my son. Today you respected my life, so I will not try to hurt you. I have been very stupid and foolish."

22David answered, "Here is your spear. Let one of your young men come here and get it. 23The LORD rewards us for the things we do right and for our loyalty to him. The LORD handed you over to me today, but I wouldn't harm the LORD's appointed king. 24As I respected your life today, may the LORD also respect my life and save me from all trouble."

25Then Saul said to David, "You are blessed, my son David. You will do great things and succeed."

So David went on his way, and Saul went back home.

David Lives with the Philistines

27 But David thought to himself, "Saul will catch me someday. The best thing I can do is escape to the land of the Philistines. Then he will give up looking for me in Israel, and I can get away from him."

2So David and his six hundred men left Israel and went to Achish son of Maoch, king of Gath. 3David, his men, and their families made their home in Gath with Achish. David had his two wives with him—Ahinoam of Jezreel and Abigail of Carmel, the widow of Nabal. 4When Saul heard that David had run away to Gath, he stopped looking for him.

5Then David said to Achish, "If you are pleased with me, give me a place in one of the country towns where I can live. I don't need to live in the royal city with you."

6That day Achish gave David the town of Ziklag, and Ziklag has belonged to the kings of Judah ever since. 7David lived in the Philistine land a year and four months.

8David and his men raided the people of Geshur, Girzi, and Amalek. (These people had lived for a long time in the land that reached to Shur and Egypt.) 9When David fought them, he killed all the men and women and took their sheep, cattle, donkeys, camels, and clothes. Then he returned to Achish.

10Achish would ask David, "Where did you go raiding today?" And David would tell him that he had gone to the southern part of Judah, or Jerahmeel, or to the land of the Kenites. 11David never brought a man or woman alive to Gath. He thought, "If we bring people alive, they may tell Achish, 'This is what David really did.' " David did this all the time he lived in the Philistine land. 12So Achish trusted David and said to himself, "David's own people, the Israelites, now hate him very much. He will serve me forever."

Saul and the Witch of Endor

28 Later, the Philistines gathered their armies to fight against Israel. Achish said to David, "You understand that you and your men must join my army."

2David answered, "You will see for yourself what I, your servant, can do!"

Achish said, "Fine, I'll make you my permanent bodyguard."

3Now Samuel was dead, and all the Israelites had shown their sadness for him. They had buried Samuel in his hometown of Ramah.

And Saul had forced out the mediums*d* and fortune-tellers from the land.

4The Philistines came together and made camp at Shunem. Saul gathered all the Israelites and made camp at Gilboa. 5When he saw the Philistine army, he was afraid, and his heart pounded with fear. 6He prayed to the LORD, but the LORD did not answer him through dreams, Urim,*d* or prophets.*d* 7Then Saul said to his servants, "Find me a woman who is a medium*d* so I may go and ask her what will happen."

His servants answered, "There is a medium in Endor."

8Then Saul put on other clothes to disguise himself, and at night he and two of his men went to see the woman. Saul said to her, "Talk to a spirit for me. Bring up the person I name."

⁹But the woman said to him, "Surely you know what Saul has done. He has forced the mediums and fortune-tellers from the land. You are trying to trap me and get me killed."

¹⁰Saul made a promise to the woman in the name of the LORD. He said, "As surely as the LORD lives, you won't be punished for this."

¹¹The woman asked, "Whom do you want me to bring up?"

He answered, "Bring up Samuel."

¹²When the woman saw Samuel, she screamed. She said, "Why have you tricked me? You are Saul!"

¹³The king said to the woman, "Don't be afraid! What do you see?"

The woman said, "I see a spirit coming up out of the ground."

¹⁴Saul asked, "What does he look like?"

The woman answered, "An old man wearing a coat is coming up."

Then Saul knew it was Samuel, and he bowed facedown on the ground.

¹⁵Samuel asked Saul, "Why have you disturbed me by bringing me up?"

Saul said, "I am greatly troubled. The Philistines are fighting against me, and God has left me. He won't answer me anymore, either by prophets or in dreams. That's why I called for you. Tell me what to do."

¹⁶Samuel said, "The LORD has left you and has become your enemy. So why do you call on me? ¹⁷He has done what he said he would do — the things he said through me. He has torn the kingdom out of your hands and given it to one of your neighbors, David. ¹⁸You did not obey the LORD; you did not show the Amalekites how angry he was with them. That's why he has done this to you today. ¹⁹The LORD will hand over both Israel and you to the Philistines. Tomorrow you and your sons will be with me. The LORD will hand over the army of Israel to the Philistines."

²⁰Saul quickly fell flat on the ground and was afraid of what Samuel had said. He was also very weak because he had eaten nothing all that day and night.

²¹Then the woman came to Saul and saw that he was really frightened. She said, "Look, I, your servant, have obeyed you. I have risked my life and done what you told me to do. ²²Now please listen to me. Let me give you some food so you may eat and have enough strength to go on your way."

²³But Saul refused, saying, "I won't eat."

His servants joined the woman in asking him to eat, and he listened to them. So he got up from the ground and sat on the bed.

²⁴At the house the woman had a fat calf, which she quickly killed. She took some flour and mixed dough with her hands. Then she baked some bread without yeast. ²⁵She put the food before them, and they ate. That same night they got up and left.

David Goes Back to Ziklag

29 The Philistines gathered all their soldiers at Aphek. Israel camped by the spring at Jezreel. ²The Philistine kings were marching with their groups of a hundred and a thousand men. David and his men were marching behind Achish. ³The Philistine commanders asked, "What are these Hebrews doing here?"

Achish told them, "This is David. He served Saul king of Israel, but he has been with me for over a year now. I have found nothing wrong in David since the time he left Saul."

⁴But the Philistine commanders were angry with Achish and said, "Send David back to the city you gave him. He cannot go with us into battle. If he does, we'll have an enemy in our own camp. He could please his king by killing our own men. ⁵David is the one the Israelites dance and sing about, saying:

'Saul has killed thousands of his enemies,
　but David has killed tens of thousands.' "

⁶So Achish called David and said to him, "As surely as the LORD lives, you are loyal. I would be pleased to have you serve in my army. Since the day you came to me, I have found no wrong in you. But the other kings don't trust you. ⁷Go back in peace. Don't do anything to displease the Philistine kings."

⁸David asked, "What wrong have I done? What evil have you found in me from the day I came to you until now? Why can't I go fight your enemies, my lord and king?"

⁹Achish answered, "I know you are as good as an angel from God. But the Philistine commanders have said, 'David must not go with us into battle.' ¹⁰Early in the morning you and your master's servants should leave. Get up as soon as it is light and go."

¹¹So David and his men got up early in the morning and went back to the country of the Philistines. And the Philistines went up to Jezreel.

David's War with the Amalekites

30 On the third day, when David and his men arrived at Ziklag, he found that the Amalekites had raided southern Judah and Ziklag, attacking Ziklag and burning it. ²They captured the women and everyone, young and old, but they had not killed anyone. They had only taken them away.

³When David and his men came to Ziklag, they found the town had been burned and their wives,

sons, and daughters had been taken as prisoners. 4Then David and his army cried loudly until they were too weak to cry anymore. 5David's two

wives had also been taken—Ahinoam of Jezreel and Abigail the widow of Nabal from Carmel. 6The men in the army were threatening to kill David with stones, which greatly upset David. Each man was sad and angry because his sons and daughters had been captured, but David found strength in the LORD his God. 7David said to Abiathar the priest, "Bring me the holy vest."*d*

8Then David asked the LORD, "Should I chase the people who took our families? Will I catch them?"

The LORD answered, "Chase them. You will catch them, and you will succeed in saving your families."

9David and the six hundred men with him came to the Besor Ravine, where some of the men stayed. 10David and four hundred men kept up the chase. The other two hundred men stayed behind because they were too tired to cross the ravine.

11They found an Egyptian in a field and brought him to David. They gave the Egyptian some water to drink and some food to eat. 12And they gave him a piece of a fig cake and two clusters of raisins. Then he felt better, because he had not eaten any food or drunk any water for three days and nights.

13David asked him, "Who is your master? Where do you come from?"

He answered, "I'm an Egyptian, the slave of an Amalekite. Three days ago my master left me, because I was sick. 14We had raided the southern area of the Kerethites, the land of Judah, and the southern area of Caleb. We burned Ziklag, as well."

15David asked him, "Can you lead me to the people who took our families?"

He answered, "Yes, if you promise me before God that you won't kill me or give me back to my master. Then I will take you to them."

16So the Egyptian led David to the Amalekites. They were lying around on the ground, eating and drinking and celebrating with the things they had taken from the land of the Philistines and from Judah. 17David fought them from sunset until the evening of the next day. None of them escaped, except four hundred young men who rode off on their camels. 18David got his two wives back and everything the Amalekites had taken. 19Nothing was missing. David brought back everyone, young and old, sons and daughters. He recovered the valuable things and everything the Amalekites had taken. 20David took all the sheep and cattle, and his men made these animals go in front, saying, "They are David's prize."

21Then David came to the two hundred men who had been too tired to follow him, who had stayed at the Besor Ravine. They came out to meet David and the people with him. When he came near, David greeted the men at the ravine.

22But the evil men and troublemakers among those who followed David said, "Since these two hundred men didn't go with us, we shouldn't give them any of the things we recovered. Just let each man take his wife and children and go."

23David answered, "No, my brothers. Don't do that after what the LORD has given us. He has protected us and given us the enemy who attacked us. 24Who will listen to what you say? The share will be the same for the one who stayed with the supplies as for the one who went into battle. All will share alike." 25David made this an order and rule for Israel, which continues even today.

26When David arrived in Ziklag, he sent some of the things he had taken from the Amalekites to his friends, the leaders of Judah. He said, "Here is a present for you from the things we took from the LORD's enemies."

27David also sent some things to the leaders in Bethel, Ramoth in the southern part of Judah, Jattir, 28Aroer, Siphmoth, Eshtemoa, 29Racal, the cities of the Jerahmeelites and the Kenites, 30Hormah, Bor Ashan, Athach, 31Hebron, and to the people in all the other places where he and his men had been.

The Death of Saul

31 The Philistines fought against Israel, and the Israelites ran away from them. Many Israelites were killed on Mount Gilboa. 2The Philistines fought hard against Saul and his sons, killing his sons Jonathan, Abinadab, and Malki-Shua. 3The fighting was heavy around Saul. The archers shot him, and he was badly wounded. 4He said to the officer who carried his armor, "Pull out your sword and kill me. Then those uncircumcised*d* men won't make fun of me and kill me." But Saul's officer refused, because he was afraid. So Saul took his own sword and threw himself on it. 5When the officer saw that Saul was dead, he threw himself on his own sword, and he died with Saul. 6So Saul, his three sons, and the officer who carried his armor died together that day.

7When the Israelites who lived across the Jezreel Valley and those who lived across the Jordan River saw how the Israelite army had run away, and that Saul and his sons were dead, they left their cities and ran away. Then the Philistines came and lived there.

8The next day when the Philistines came to take all the valuable things from the dead soldiers, they found Saul and his three sons dead on Mount Gilboa. 9They cut off Saul's head and took off his armor. Then they sent messengers through all the land of the Philistines to tell the news in the temple of their idols and to their people. 10They put Saul's armor in the temple of the Ashtoreths*d* and hung his body on the wall of Beth Shan.

11When the people living in Jabesh Gilead heard what the Philistines had done to Saul, 12the brave men of Jabesh marched all night and came to Beth Shan. They removed the bodies of Saul and his sons from the wall of Beth Shan and brought them to Jabesh. There they burned the bodies. 13They took their bones and buried them under the tamarisk tree in Jabesh. Then the people of Jabesh gave up eating for seven days.

2 SAMUEL

Why Read This Book:

- Learn how leaders can encourage people to follow God (2 Samuel 1—6).
- Discover how God can use people for good in spite of their faults (2 Samuel 7—12).
- See how family problems can hurt leaders (2 Samuel 13—20).

Behind the Scenes:

War was inevitable. King Saul was dead. David—a popular hero among southern tribes—had the charisma and leadership skills needed in a king. But while David was being crowned king in Judah (the southern half of the nation), Saul's son Ish-Bosheth took control of the northern part of the kingdom, Israel.

It took seven and a half years of civil war, but David finally united the kingdom when Ish-Bosheth was murdered. Then with decisive and effective leadership, David began building the country to the height of its military and political power. The kingdom he established would last four hundred years.

David's power came from following God. But he wasn't perfect. In 2 Samuel, David commits adultery with Bathsheba and then has her husband killed so that

WHERE THE ACTION WAS

Outlined area is where the twelve tribes of Israel lived.

Mediterranean Sea

ARAM

ISRAEL

When he became king, David had the Ark of God moved from Baalah to Jerusalem (2 Samuel 6:1—2).

David's army defeated the Israelite forces of Absalom, David's son, in the forest of Ephraim (2 Samuel 18:6—8).

AMMON

• Baalah

Jerusalem •

David moved the capital of Israel to Jerusalem after he united the nation (2 Samuel 5:4—7).

Hebron •

Dead Sea

MOAB

David became king and started his rule in Hebron (2 Samuel 2:2—4).

EDOM

WHEN THE ACTION WAS

	The Israelites escaped from Egypt		Saul was Israel's king	David was Israel's king		Jesus was born
2000BC	**1500BC**		**1000BC**		**500BC**	**BC/AD**
		Joshua led the Israelites into Canaan		Samuel served as Israel's last judge		

Behind the Scenes (cont.): he can cover his sin and can marry her. We see David struggling with family problems that led to bloodshed and the death of his son Absalom.

Yet in the midst of his problems and sinfulness, David always tried to follow God. When God's prophet confronted him, he admitted his sin and sought forgiveness. When his family was torn apart, he asked for God's help. Because he relied on God, David became known as Israel's greatest king.

David's dramatic story reminds all people of the importance of following God and relying on God. Even when we fail, God is with us, ready to pick us up and give us another chance.

David Learns About Saul's Death

1 Now Saul was dead. After David had defeated the Amalekites, he returned to Ziklag and stayed there two days. ²On the third day a young man from Saul's camp came to Ziklag. To show his sadness, his clothes were torn and he had dirt on his head. He came and bowed facedown on the ground before David.

³David asked him, "Where did you come from?"

The man answered, "I escaped from the Israelite camp."

⁴David asked him, "What happened? Please tell me!"

The man answered, "The people have run away from the battle, and many of them have fallen and are dead. Saul and his son Jonathan are dead also."

⁵David asked him, "How do you know Saul and his son Jonathan are dead?"

⁶The young man answered, "I happened to be on Mount Gilboa. There I saw Saul leaning on his spear. The Philistine chariots and the men riding in them were coming closer to Saul. ⁷When he looked back and saw me, he called to me. I answered him, 'Here I am!'

⁸"Then Saul asked me, 'Who are you?'

"I told him, 'I am an Amalekite.'

⁹"Then Saul said to me, 'Please come here and kill me. I am badly hurt and am almost dead already.'

¹⁰"So I went over and killed him. He had been hurt so badly I knew he couldn't live. Then I took the crown from his head and the bracelet from his arm, and I have brought them here to you, my master."

¹¹Then David tore his clothes to show his sorrow, and all the men with him did also. ¹²They were very sad and cried and did not eat until evening. They cried for Saul and his son Jonathan and for all the people of the LORD and for all the Israelites who had died in the battle.

David Orders the Amalekite Killed

¹³David asked the young man who brought the report, "Where are you from?"

The young man answered, "I am the son of a foreigner, an Amalekite."

¹⁴David asked him, "Why were you not afraid to kill the LORD's appointed king?"

¹⁵Then David called one of his men and told him, "Go! Kill the Amalekite!" So the Israelite killed him. ¹⁶David had said to the Amalekite, "You are responsible for your own death. You confessed by saying, 'I have killed the LORD's appointed king.'"

David's Song About Saul and Jonathan

¹⁷David sang a funeral song about Saul and his son Jonathan, ¹⁸and he ordered that the people of Judah be taught this song. It is called "The Bow," and it is written in the Book of Jashar:

¹⁹"Israel, your leaders have been killed on the hills.
How the mighty have fallen in battle!
²⁰Don't tell it in Gath.
Don't announce it in the streets of Ashkelon.
If you do, the Philistine women will be happy.
The daughters of the Philistines will rejoice.

²¹"May there be no dew or rain on the mountains of Gilboa,
and may their fields produce no grain,
because there the mighty warrior's shield was dishonored.
Saul's shield will no longer be rubbed with oil.

✹ SIDELIGHT: Saul's shield (2 Samuel 1:21) would have been made of leather. If the shield was "no longer rubbed with oil," it would dry up, crack, and fall apart.

---

²²Jonathan's bow did not fail
to kill many soldiers.

Saul's sword did not fail
to wound many strong men.

23 "We loved Saul and Jonathan
and enjoyed them while they lived.
They are together even in death.
They were faster than eagles.
They were stronger than lions.

24 "You daughters of Israel, cry for Saul.
Saul clothed you with red dresses
and put gold decorations on them.

25 "How the mighty have fallen in battle!
Jonathan is dead on Gilboa's hills.
26 I cry for you, my brother Jonathan.
I enjoyed your friendship so much.
Your love to me was wonderful,
better than the love of women.

27 "How the mighty have fallen!
The weapons of war are gone."

David Is Made King of Judah

2 Later, David prayed to the LORD, saying, "Should I go up to any of the cities of Judah?"

The LORD said to David, "Go."

David asked, "Where should I go?"

The LORD answered, "To Hebron."

2 So David went up to Hebron with his two wives: Ahinoam from Jezreel and Abigail, the widow of Nabal from Carmel. 3 David also brought his men and their families, and they all made their homes in the cities of Hebron. 4 Then the men of Judah came to Hebron and appointed David king over Judah.

They told David that the men of Jabesh Gilead had buried Saul. 5 So David sent messengers to the men of Jabesh Gilead and said to them, "The LORD bless you. You have shown loyalty to your master Saul by burying him. 6 May the LORD now be loyal and true to you. I will also treat you well because you have done this. 7 Now be strong and

DEATH

A Tribute

Dennis Olson was the popular band teacher at Fridley Junior High. Not only did he patiently help students learn music, but he cared about each band member. He would send kids birthday cards and was sure to ask, "How're you doing?" if he heard one of them had been sick.

So the band sat silently as the principal explained. "I'm sorry to have to tell you that Mr. Olson was in a car accident yesterday. He's in serious—actually, critical—condition. We'll be getting a new teacher next week."

In the weeks that followed, band members sent cards and regularly visited Mr. Olson in the hospital as his condition got worse and worse.

Then Mr. Olson died, and the principal came back to the band class. "You all know about Mr. Olson," he began. "I talked to Mrs. Olson today, and she said her husband wanted this band to play at his funeral. Would you?"

The band members were willing, even though it meant extra practices. They wanted to do something to show their respect for their former teacher.

On the day of the funeral, band members played with tears in their eyes. Then they each filed past the casket and laid a white carnation on top. It was hard, but they were glad they had done it for Mr. Olson.

In **2 Samuel 1:17–27**, David also felt great loss when Saul and his son Jonathan—David's friend—died in battle. Read how David expressed his grief for these people he respected and loved.

■ How is David's song like the band's tribute at Mr. Olson's funeral?

■ When have you felt the grief that David expresses in the passage?

CONSIDER . . .

■ reading the obituaries in your newspaper, and praying each day for one family that has experienced a death.

■ making a scrapbook about deceased family members—so their memories will live on.

FOR MORE, SEE . . .

■ Deuteronomy 34:1–12 (p. 193)
■ Matthew 5:4 (p. 912)
■ Isaiah 61:1–3 (p. 680)

brave. Saul your master is dead, and the people of Judah have appointed me their king."

War Between Judah and Israel

⁸Abner son of Ner was the commander of Saul's army. Abner took Saul's son Ish-Bosheth to Mahanaim ⁹and made him king of Gilead, Ashuri, Jezreel, Ephraim, Benjamin, and all Israel. ¹⁰Saul's son Ish-Bosheth was forty years old when he became king over Israel, and he ruled two years. But the people of Judah followed David. ¹¹David was king in Hebron for seven years and six months.

¹²Abner son of Ner and the servants of Ish-Bosheth son of Saul left Mahanaim and went to Gibeon. ¹³Joab son of Zeruiah and David's men also went there and met Abner and Ish-Bosheth's men at the pool of Gibeon. Abner's group sat on one side of the pool; Joab's group sat on the other. ¹⁴Abner said to Joab, "Let the young men have a contest here."

Joab said, "Yes, let them have a contest."

¹⁵Then the men got up and were counted — twelve from the people of Benjamin for Ish-Bosheth son of Saul, and twelve from David's men. ¹⁶Each man grabbed the one opposite him by the head and stabbed him in the side with a knife. So the men fell down together. For that reason, that place in Gibeon is called the Field of Knives. ¹⁷That day there was a terrible battle, and David's men defeated Abner and the Israelites.

※ SIDELIGHT: The pool of Gibeon—where Saul's and David's armies fought—was a huge well (2 Samuel 2:8–17). Archaeologists have discovered what was probably the pool. It is thirty-seven feet in diameter, and has a seventy-nine-step winding stairway down to the water level, which is thirty-three feet below the ground.

Abner Kills Asahel

¹⁸Zeruiah's three sons, Joab, Abishai, and Asahel, were there. Now Asahel was a fast runner, as fast as a deer in the field. ¹⁹Asahel chased Abner, going straight toward him. ²⁰Abner looked back and asked, "Is that you, Asahel?"

Asahel said, "Yes, it is."

²¹Then Abner said to Asahel, "Turn to your right or left and catch one of the young men and take his armor." But Asahel refused to stop chasing him.

²²Abner again said to Asahel, "Stop chasing me! If you don't stop, I'll have to kill you! Then I won't be able to face your brother Joab again!"

²³But Asahel refused to stop chasing Abner. So using the back end of his spear, Abner stabbed Asahel in the stomach, and the spear came out of his back. Asahel died right there, and everyone stopped when they came to the place where Asahel's body lay.

²⁴But Joab and Abishai continued chasing Abner. As the sun was going down, they arrived at the hill of Ammah, near Giah on the way to the desert near Gibeon. ²⁵The men of Benjamin came to Abner, and all stood together at the top of the hill.

²⁶Abner shouted to Joab, "Must the sword kill forever? Surely you must know this will only end in sadness! Tell the people to stop chasing their own brothers!"

²⁷Then Joab said, "As surely as God lives, if you had not said anything, the people would have chased their brothers until morning." ²⁸Then Joab blew a trumpet, and his people stopped chasing the Israelites. They did not fight them anymore.

²⁹Abner and his men marched all night through the Jordan Valley. They crossed the Jordan River, and after marching all day, arrived at Mahanaim.

³⁰After he had stopped chasing Abner, Joab came back and gathered the people together. Asahel and nineteen of David's men were missing. ³¹But David's men had killed three hundred sixty Benjaminites who had followed Abner. ³²David's men took Asahel and buried him in the tomb of his father at Bethlehem. Then Joab and his men marched all night. The sun came up as they reached Hebron.

3 There was a long war between the people who supported Saul's family and those who supported David's family. The supporters of David's family became stronger and stronger, but the supporters of Saul's family became weaker and weaker.

David's Sons

²Sons were born to David at Hebron. The first was Amnon, whose mother was Ahinoam from Jezreel. ³The second son was Kileab, whose mother was Abigail, the widow of Nabal from Carmel. The third son was Absalom, whose mother was Maacah daughter of Talmai, the king of Geshur. ⁴The fourth son was Adonijah, whose mother was Haggith. The fifth son was Shephatiah, whose mother was Abital. ⁵The sixth son was Ithream, whose mother was Eglah, David's wife. These sons were born to David at Hebron.

Abner Joins David

⁶During the war between the supporters of Saul's family and the supporters of David's family, Abner made himself a main leader among the supporters of Saul.

⁷Saul once had a slave woman[d] named Rizpah, who was the daughter of Aiah. Ish-Bosheth said

to Abner, "Why did you have sexual relations with my father's slave woman?"

[8]Abner was very angry because of what Ish-Bosheth said, and he replied, "I have been loyal to Saul and his family and friends! I didn't hand you over to David. I am not a traitor working for Judah! But now you are saying I did something wrong with this woman! [9]May God help me if I don't join David! I will make sure that what the LORD promised does happen! [10]I will take the kingdom from the family of Saul and make David king of Israel and Judah, from Dan to Beersheba!"[n]

[11]Ish-Bosheth couldn't say anything to Abner, because he was afraid of him.

[12]Then Abner sent messengers to ask David, "Who is going to rule the land? Make an agreement with me, and I will help you unite all Israel."

[13]David answered, "Good! I will make an agreement with you, but I ask you one thing. I will not meet with you unless you bring Saul's daughter Michal to me." [14]Then David sent messengers to Saul's son Ish-Bosheth, saying, "Give me my wife Michal. She was promised to me, and I killed a hundred Philistines to get her."

[15]So Ish-Bosheth sent men to take Michal from her husband Paltiel son of Laish. [16]Michal's husband went with her, crying as he followed her to Bahurim. But Abner said to Paltiel, "Go back home." So he went home.

SIDELIGHT: If you feel like your parent interferes with your dating life, imagine how David felt. He married Saul's daughter, Michal (1 Samuel 18:20–29, p. 262). But when Saul got angry with David, he took back his daughter and gave her to someone else to marry (1 Samuel 25:44, p. 268). Later she returned to David as part of a political bargain (2 Samuel 3:12–16).

---

[17]Abner sent this message to the older leaders of Israel: "You have been wanting to make David your king. [18]Now do it! The LORD said of David, 'Through my servant David, I will save my people Israel from the Philistines and all their enemies.'"

[19]Abner also said these things to the people of Benjamin. He then went to Hebron to tell David what the Benjaminites and Israel wanted to do. [20]Abner came with twenty men to David at Hebron. There David prepared a feast for them. [21]Abner said to David, "My master and king, I will go and bring all the Israelites to you. Then they will make an agreement with you so you will rule over all Israel as you wanted." So David let Abner go, and he left in peace.

Abner's Death

[22]Just then Joab and David's men came from a battle, bringing many valuable things they had taken from the enemy. David had let Abner leave in peace, so he was not with David at Hebron. [23]When Joab and all his army arrived at Hebron, the army said to Joab, "Abner son of Ner came to King David, and David let him leave in peace."

[24]Joab came to the king and said, "What have you done? Abner came to you. Why did you let him go? Now he's gone. [25]You know Abner son of Ner! He came to trick you! He came to learn about everything you are doing!"

[26]After Joab left David, he sent messengers after Abner, and they brought him back from the well of Sirah. But David did not know this. [27]When Abner arrived at Hebron, Joab took him aside into the gateway. He acted as though he wanted to talk with Abner in private, but Joab stabbed him in the stomach, and Abner died. Abner had killed Joab's brother Asahel, so Joab killed Abner to pay him back.

[28]Later when David heard the news, he said, "My kingdom and I are innocent forever of the death of Abner son of Ner. The LORD knows this. [29]Joab and his family are responsible for this. May his family always have someone with sores or with a skin disease. May they always have someone who must lean on a crutch. May some of his family be killed in war. May they always have someone without food to eat."

[30](Joab and his brother Abishai killed Abner, because he had killed their brother Asahel in the battle at Gibeon.)

[31]Then David said to Joab and to all the people with Joab, "Tear your clothes and put on rough cloth to show how sad you are. Cry for Abner." King David himself followed the body of Abner. [32]They buried Abner in Hebron, and David and all the people cried at Abner's grave.

[33]King David sang this funeral song for Abner.

"Did Abner die like a fool?
[34] His hands were not tied.
His feet were not in chains.
He fell at the hands of evil men."

Then all the people cried again for Abner. [35]They came to encourage David to eat while it was still day. But he made a promise, saying, "May God punish me terribly if I eat bread or anything else before the sun sets!"

[36]All the people saw what happened, and they

Dan to Beersheba Dan was the city farthest north in Israel, and Beersheba was the city farthest south. So this means all the people of Israel.

agreed with what the king was doing, just as they agreed with everything he did. [37]That day all the people of Judah and Israel understood that David did not order the killing of Abner son of Ner.

[38]David said to his officers, "You know that a great man died today in Israel. [39]Even though I am the appointed king, I feel empty. These sons of Zeruiah are too much for me. May the LORD give them the punishment they should have."

Ish-Bosheth's Death

4 When Ish-Bosheth son of Saul heard that Abner had died at Hebron, he was shocked and all Israel became frightened. [2]Two men who were captains in Saul's army came to Ish-Bosheth. One was named Baanah, and the other was named Recab. They were the sons of Rimmon of Beeroth, who was a Benjaminite. (The town Beeroth belonged to the tribe[d] of Benjamin. [3]The people of Beeroth ran away to Gittaim, and they still live there as foreigners today.)

[4](Saul's son Jonathan had a son named Mephibosheth, who was crippled in both feet. He was five years old when the news came from Jezreel that Saul and Jonathan were dead. Mephibosheth's nurse had picked him up and run away. But as she hurried to leave, she dropped him, and now he was lame.)

[5]Recab and Baanah, sons of Rimmon from Beeroth, went to Ish-Bosheth's house in the afternoon while he was taking a nap. [6-7]They went into the middle of the house as if to get some wheat. Ish-Bosheth was lying on his bed in his bedroom. Then Recab and Baanah stabbed him in the stomach, killed him, cut off his head, and took it with them. They escaped and traveled all night through the Jordan Valley. [8]When they arrived at Hebron, they gave his head to David and said to the king, "Here is the head of Ish-Bosheth son of Saul, your enemy. He tried to kill you! Today the LORD has paid back Saul and his family for what they did to you!"

[9]David answered Recab and his brother Baanah, the sons of Rimmon of Beeroth, "As surely as the LORD lives, he has saved me from all trouble! [10]Once a man thought he was bringing me good news. When he told me, 'Saul is dead!' I seized him and killed him at Ziklag. That was the reward I gave him for his news! [11]So even more I must put you evil men to death because you have killed an innocent man on his own bed in his own house!"

[12]So David commanded his men to kill Recab and Baanah. They cut off the hands and feet of Recab and Baanah and hung them over the pool of Hebron. Then they took Ish-Bosheth's head and buried it in Abner's tomb at Hebron.

David Is Made King of Israel

5 Then all the tribes[d] of Israel came to David at Hebron and said to him, "Look, we are your own family. [2]Even when Saul was king, you were the one who led Israel in battle. The LORD said to you, 'You will be a shepherd for my people Israel. You will be their leader.' "

[3]So all the older leaders of Israel came to King David at Hebron, and he made an agreement with them in Hebron in the presence of the LORD. Then they poured oil on David to make him king over Israel.

[4]David was thirty years old when he became king, and he ruled forty years. [5]He was king over Judah in Hebron for seven years and six months, and he was king over all Israel and Judah in Jerusalem for thirty-three years.

[6]When the king and his men went to Jerusalem to attack the Jebusites who lived there, the Jebusites said to David, "You can't get inside our city. Even the blind and the crippled can stop you." They thought David could not enter their city. [7]But David did take the city of Jerusalem with its strong walls, and it became the City of David.

[8]That day David said to his men, "To defeat the Jebusites you must go through the water tunnel. Then you can reach those 'crippled' and 'blind' enemies. This is why people say, 'The blind and the crippled may not enter the palace.' "

[9]So David lived in the strong, walled city and called it the City of David. David built more buildings around it, beginning where the land was filled in. He also built more buildings inside the

---

✳ **SIDELIGHT:** Jerusalem wasn't very big by modern standards when King David captured it (2 Samuel 5:6–9). It covered only eleven acres—smaller than the thirteen-acre Superdome stadium in New Orleans, Louisiana.

---

city. [10]He became stronger and stronger, because the LORD God All-Powerful was with him.

[11]Hiram king of the city of Tyre sent messengers to David, along with cedar logs, carpenters, and stonecutters. They built a palace for David. [12]Then David knew that the LORD really had made him king of Israel and that the LORD had made his kingdom great because the LORD loved his people Israel.

[13]After he came from Hebron, David took for himself more slave women[d] and wives in Jerusalem. More sons and daughters were born to David. [14]These are the names of the sons born to

David in Jerusalem: Shammua, Shobab, Nathan, Solomon, [15]Ibhar, Elishua, Nepheg, Japhia, [16]Elishama, Eliada, and Eliphelet.

David Defeats the Philistines

[17]When the Philistines heard that David had been made king over Israel, all the Philistines went to look for him. But when David heard the news, he went down to the stronghold.[d] [18]The Philistines came and camped in the Valley of Rephaim. [19]David asked the Lord, "Should I attack the Philistines? Will you hand them over to me?"

The Lord said to David, "Go! I will certainly hand them over to you."

[20]So David went to Baal Perazim and defeated the Philistines there. David said, "Like a flood of water, the Lord has broken through my enemies in front of me." So David named the place Baal Perazim.[n] [21]The Philistines left their idols behind

at Baal Perazim, so David and his men carried them away.

[22]Once again the Philistines came and camped at the Valley of Rephaim. [23]When David prayed to the Lord, he answered, "Don't attack the Philistines from the front. Instead, go around and attack them in front of the balsam trees. [24]When you hear the sound of marching in the tops of the balsam trees act quickly. I, the Lord, will have gone ahead of you to defeat the Philistine army." [25]So David did what the Lord commanded. He defeated the Philistines and chased them all the way from Gibeon to Gezer.

The Ark Is Brought to Jerusalem

6 David again gathered all the chosen men of Israel — thirty thousand of them. [2]Then he and all his people went to Baalah in Judah[n] to bring back the Ark[d] of God. The Ark is called by the Name, the name of the Lord All-Powerful,

Baal Perazim This name means "the Lord breaks through."
Baalah in Judah Another name for Kiriath Jearim.

LEADERSHIP

Earned Respect

The other track team members didn't know what to think when Anne Cleveland walked into the locker room the first day of practice. She was a sophomore, and everyone else on the team was a junior or senior. "How's everybody doing?" she said cheerfully.

But as the other team members ran their warm-up laps, they couldn't ignore Anne's rhythmic stride and seemingly effortless pace. And by the end of the afternoon, they all knew this girl would fit in. She worked hard, did well and encouraged others.

Within weeks, Anne had become a star, setting the state record in the 400-meter dash. But when the school newspaper reporter asked her about it, she replied: "I'm glad the team did well. The whole team encouraged me in that race. We work hard together."

Anne never would take glory for her performance. And, gradually, the older girls began asking her for pointers. By the end of the season, the whole team had become one of the best in the state.

When it came to picking a captain for the next year, no one questioned whom to pick. Sure she was only a junior, and a senior usually led the team, but Anne was the team's natural leader.

Like Anne, David had proven his leadership skills for years. So when it came time to find a new king, he was a natural choice, even though he was young. Read how the country chose him in **2 Samuel 5:1–5**.

■ How did both Anne and David earn respect so that they were chosen as leaders? How did their humility help them both as leaders?
■ How can you, like David, work to earn respect so you can be a leader?

CONSIDER . . .
■ talking to a leader you respect about how he or she became a leader. Then put into practice one tip you learned.
■ working to be a team player at church, school and work, then watching to see what leadership role you might play.

FOR MORE, SEE . . .
■ Jeremiah 1:4–10 (p. 691)   ■ 1 Corinthians 3:5–9 (p. 1170)
■ Matthew 20:20–28 (p. 944)

whose throne is between the gold creatures with wings. [3]They put the Ark of God on a new cart and brought it out of Abinadab's house on the hill. Uzzah and Ahio, sons of Abinadab, led the new cart [4]which had the Ark of God on it. Ahio was walking in front of it. [5]David and all the Israelites were celebrating in the presence of the LORD. They were playing wooden instruments: lyres,[d] harps, tambourines,[d] rattles, and cymbals.

[6]When David's men came to the threshing[d] floor of Nacon, the oxen stumbled. So Uzzah reached out to steady the Ark of God. [7]The LORD was angry with Uzzah and killed him because of what he did. So Uzzah died there beside the Ark of God. [8]David was angry because the LORD had killed Uzzah. Now that place is called the Punishment of Uzzah.

[9]David was afraid of the LORD that day, and he said, "How can the Ark of the LORD come to me now?" [10]So David would not move the Ark of the LORD to be with him in Jerusalem. Instead, he took it to the house of Obed-Edom, a man from Gath. [11]The Ark of the LORD stayed in Obed-Edom's house for three months, and the LORD blessed Obed-Edom and all his family.

[12]The people told David, "The LORD has blessed the family of Obed-Edom and all that belongs to him, because the Ark of God is there." So David went and brought it up from Obed-Edom's house to Jerusalem with joy. [13]When the men carrying the Ark of the LORD had walked six steps, David sacrificed a bull and a fat calf. [14]Then David danced with all his might before the LORD. He had on a holy linen vest.[d] [15]David and all the Israelites shouted with joy and blew the trumpets as they brought the Ark of the LORD to the city.

[16]As the Ark of the LORD came into the city, Saul's daughter Michal looked out the window. When she saw David jumping and dancing in the presence of the LORD, she hated him.

[17]David put up a tent for the Ark of the LORD, and then the Israelites put it in its place inside the tent. David offered whole burnt offerings and fellowship offerings before the LORD. [18]When David finished offering the whole burnt offerings and the fellowship offerings, he blessed the people in the name of the LORD All-Powerful. [19]David gave a loaf of bread, a cake of dates, and a cake of raisins to every Israelite, both men and women. Then all the people went home.

[20]David went back to bless the people in his home, but Saul's daughter Michal came out to *meet him. She said,* "With what honor the king of Israel acted today! You took off your clothes in front of the servant girls of your officers like one who takes off his clothes without shame!"

[21]Then David said to Michal, "I did it in the presence of the LORD. The LORD chose me, not your father or anyone from Saul's family. The LORD appointed me to be over Israel. So I will celebrate in the presence of the LORD. [22]Maybe I will lose even more honor, and maybe I will be brought down in my own opinion, but the girls you talk about will honor me!"

[23]And Saul's daughter Michal had no children to the day she died.

David Wants to Build a Temple

7 King David was living in his palace, and the LORD had given him peace from all his enemies around him. [2]Then David said to Nathan the prophet,[d] "Look, I am living in a palace made of cedar wood, but the Ark[d] of God is in a tent!"

[3]Nathan said to the king, "Go and do what you really want to do, because the LORD is with you."

[4]But that night the LORD spoke his word to Nathan, [5]"Go and tell my servant David, 'This is what the LORD says: Will you build a house for me to live in? [6]From the time I brought the Israelites out of Egypt until now I have not lived in a house. I have been moving around all this time with a tent as my home. [7]As I have moved with the Israelites, I have never said to the tribes,[d] whom I commanded to take care of my people Israel, "Why haven't you built me a house of cedar?" '

[8]"You must tell my servant David, 'This is what the LORD All-Powerful says: I took you from the pasture and from tending the sheep and made you leader of my people Israel. [9]I have been with you everywhere you have gone and have defeated your enemies for you. I will make you as famous as any of the great people on the earth. [10]Also I will choose a place for my people Israel, and I will plant them so they can live in their own homes. They will not be bothered anymore. Wicked people will no longer bother them as they have in the past [11]when I chose judges for my people Israel. But I will give you peace from all your enemies. I also tell you that I will make your descendants[d] kings of Israel after you.

[12]" 'When you die and join your ancestors, I will make one of your sons the next king, and I will set up his kingdom. [13]He will build a house for me, and I will let his kingdom rule always. [14]I will be his father, and he will be my son. When he sins, I will use other people to punish him. They will be my whips. [15]I took away my love from Saul, whom I removed before you, but I will never stop loving your son. [16]But your family and your kingdom will continue always before me. *Your throne will last forever.*' "

[17]Nathan told *David everything God had said* in this vision.

David Prays to God

[18]Then King David went in and sat in front of the LORD. David said, "Lord GOD, who am I?

What is my family? Why did you bring me to this point? ¹⁹But even this is not enough for you, Lord GOD. You have also made promises about my future family. This is not normal, Lord GOD.

²⁰"What more can I say to you, Lord GOD, since you know me, your servant, so well! ²¹You have done this great thing because you said you would and because you wanted to, and you have let me know about it. ²²This is why you are great, Lord GOD! There is no one like you. There is no God except you. We have heard all this ourselves! ²³There is no nation like your people Israel. They are the only people on earth that God chose to be his own. You made your name well known. You did great and wonderful miracles[d] for them. You went ahead of them and forced other nations and their gods out of the land. You freed your people from slavery in Egypt. ²⁴You made the people of Israel your very own people forever, and, LORD, you are their God.

²⁵"Now, LORD God, keep the promise forever that you made about my family and me, your servant. Do what you have said. ²⁶Then you will be honored always, and people will say, 'The LORD All-Powerful is God over Israel!' And the family of your servant David will continue before you.

²⁷"LORD All-Powerful, the God of Israel, you have said to me, 'I will make your family great.' So I, your servant, am brave enough to pray to you. ²⁸Lord GOD, you are God, and your words are true. And you have promised these good things to me, your servant. ²⁹Please, bless my family. Let it continue before you always. Lord GOD, you have said so. With your blessing let my family always be blessed."

David Wins Many Wars

8 Later, David defeated the Philistines, conquered them, and took the city of Metheg Ammah.

²He also defeated the people of Moab. He made them lie on the ground, and then he used a rope to measure them. Those who were measured within two rope lengths were killed, but those who were within the next rope length were allowed to live. So the people of Moab became servants of David and gave him the payment he demanded.

³David also defeated Hadadezer son of Rehob, king of Zobah, as he went to take control again at the Euphrates River. ⁴David captured one thousand chariots, seven thousand men who rode in chariots, and twenty thousand foot soldiers. He crippled all but a hundred of the chariot horses.

THANKFULNESS

Unnoticed Gifts

If you have trouble thinking of things to thank God for, start with this list of things he has given you:

■ A defense against tiny bacteria and larger critters such as scorpions, fleas, and bugs.
■ Something to keep some things in while keeping other things out.
■ A radiator to cool you.
■ Padding that takes the shape of objects it touches.
■ Half a million transmitters that send messages through your body.
■ A unique pattern that identifies you.

All these things are in just one part of your body: your skin. Imagine how much else you have to be thankful for in your life and world!

David recognized the gifts God had given him and his family. Read his prayer of thanksgiving in **2 Samuel 7:18–29**.

■ Why does David say God gives good things? What is David's response?
■ What has God given you that reminds you of how important you are? How have you thanked God for that?

C O N S I D E R . . .

■ making a list of people and things for which you are most thankful. Thank God for each of these people or things this week, and call or write each person a thank-you message.
■ tracing your family tree back as far as you can. Then talk with your parent about the strengths and weaknesses of each generation. Pray that God will guide and bless you and future generations.

F O R   M O R E ,   S E E . . .

■ Psalm 98:1–9 (p. 538)　　　　　■ Colossians 1:9–13 (p. 1238)
■ Isaiah 63:7–9 (p. 683)

⁵Arameans from Damascus came to help Hadadezer king of Zobah, but David killed twenty-two thousand of them. ⁶Then David put groups of soldiers in Damascus in Aram. The Arameans became David's servants and gave him the payment he demanded. The LORD gave David victory everywhere he went.

⁷David took the shields of gold that had belonged to Hadadezer's officers and brought them to Jerusalem. ⁸David also took many things made of bronze from Tebah and Berothai, which had been cities under Hadadezer's control.

⁹Toi king of Hamath heard that David had defeated all the army of Hadadezer. ¹⁰So Toi sent his son Joram to greet and congratulate King David for defeating Hadadezer. (Hadadezer had been at war with Toi.) Joram brought items made of silver, gold, and bronze. ¹¹King David gave them to the LORD, along with the silver and gold he had taken from the other nations he had defeated. ¹²These nations were Edom, Moab, Ammon, Philistia, and Amalek. David also gave the LORD what he had taken from Hadadezer son of Rehob, king of Zobah.

¹³David was famous after he returned from defeating eighteen thousand Arameans in the Valley of Salt. ¹⁴He put groups of soldiers all over Edom, and all the Edomites became his servants. The LORD gave David victory everywhere he went.

¹⁵David was king over all Israel, and he did what was fair and right for all his people. ¹⁶Joab son of Zeruiah was commander over the army. Jehoshaphat son of Ahilud was the recorder. ¹⁷Zadok son of Ahitub and Abiathar son of Ahimelech were priests. Seraiah was the royal secretary. ¹⁸Benaiah son of Jehoiada was over the Kerethites and Pelethites. ⁿ And David's sons were priests.

David Helps Saul's Family

9 David asked, "Is anyone still left in Saul's family? I want to show kindness to that person for Jonathan's sake!"

²Now there was a servant named Ziba from Saul's family. So David's servants called Ziba to him. King David said to him, "Are you Ziba?"

He answered, "Yes, I am your servant."

³The king asked, "Is anyone left in Saul's family? I want to show God's kindness to that person."

Ziba answered the king, "Jonathan has a son still living who is crippled in both feet."

⁴The king asked Ziba, "Where is this son?"

Ziba answered, "He is at the house of Makir son of Ammiel in Lo Debar."

⁵Then King David had servants bring Jonathan's son from the house of Makir son of Ammiel

in Lo Debar. ⁶Mephibosheth, Jonathan's son, came before David and bowed facedown on the floor.

David said, "Mephibosheth!"

Mephibosheth said, "I am your servant."

⁷David said to him, "Don't be afraid. I will be kind to you for your father Jonathan's sake. I will give you back all the land of your grandfather Saul, and you will always eat at my table."

⁸Mephibosheth bowed to David again and said, "You are being very kind to me, your servant! And I am no better than a dead dog!"

⁹Then King David called Saul's servant Ziba. David said to him, "I have given your master's grandson everything that belonged to Saul and his family. ¹⁰You, your sons, and your servants will farm the land and harvest the crops. Then your family will have food to eat. But Mephibosheth, your master's grandson, will always eat at my table."

(Now Ziba had fifteen sons and twenty servants.) ¹¹Ziba said to King David, "I, your servant, will do everything my master, the king, commands me."

So Mephibosheth ate at David's table as if he were one of the king's sons. ¹²Mephibosheth had a young son named Mica. Everyone in Ziba's family became Mephibosheth's servants. ¹³Mephibosheth lived in Jerusalem, because he always ate at the king's table. And he was crippled in both feet.

War with the Ammonites and Arameans

10 When Nahash king of the Ammonites died, his son Hanun became king after him. ²David said, "Nahash was loyal to me, so I will be loyal to his son Hanun." So David sent his messengers to comfort Hanun about his father's death.

David's officers went to the land of the Ammonites. ³But the Ammonite leaders said to Hanun, their master, "Do you think David wants to honor your father by sending men to comfort you? No! David sent them to study the city and spy it out and capture it!" ⁴So Hanun arrested David's officers. To shame them he shaved off half their beards and cut off their clothes at the hips. Then he sent them away.

⁵When the people told David, he sent messengers to meet his officers because they were very ashamed. King David said, "Stay in Jericho until your beards have grown back. Then come home."

⁶The Ammonites knew that they had insulted David. So they hired twenty thousand Aramean foot soldiers from Beth Rehob and Zobah. They also hired the king of Maacah with a thousand men and twelve thousand men from Tob.

Kerethites and Pelethites These were probably special units of the army that were responsible for the king's safety, a kind of palace guard.

7When David heard about this, he sent Joab with the whole army. 8The Ammonites came out and prepared for battle at the city gate. The Arameans from Zobah and Rehob and the men from Tob and Maacah were out in the field by themselves.

9Joab saw that there were enemies both in front of him and behind him. So he chose some of the best soldiers of Israel and sent them out to fight the Arameans. 10Joab put the rest of the army under the command of Abishai, his brother. Then he sent them out to fight the Ammonites. 11Joab said to Abishai, "If the Arameans are too strong for me, you must help me. Or, if the Ammonites are too strong for you, I will help you. 12Be strong. We must fight bravely for our people and the cities of our God. The Lord will do what he thinks is right."

13Then Joab and the army with him went to attack the Arameans, and the Arameans ran away. 14When the Ammonites saw that the Arameans were running away, they also ran away from Abishai and went back to their city. So Joab returned from the battle with the Ammonites and came to Jerusalem.

15When the Arameans saw that Israel had defeated them, they came together into one big army. 16Hadadezer sent messengers to bring the Arameans from east of the Euphrates River, and they went to Helam. Their leader was Shobach, the commander of Hadadezer's army.

17When David heard about this, he gathered all the Israelites together. They crossed over the Jordan River and went to Helam. There the Arameans prepared for battle and attacked him. 18But the Arameans ran away from the Israelites. David killed seven hundred Aramean chariot drivers and forty thousand Aramean horsemen. He also killed Shobach, the commander of the Aramean army.

SIDELIGHT: If you wanted to shame a man in ancient Israel, you could shave off his beard. But if you did it, you had better be prepared for him to strike back in revenge. In 2 Samuel 10:1–19, a shaving party resulted in a war that took about 40,700 lives.

19When the kings who served Hadadezer saw that the Israelites had defeated them, they made peace with the Israelites and served them. And the Arameans were afraid to help the Ammonites again.

David Sins with Bathsheba

11 In the spring, when the kings normally went out to war, David sent out Joab, his servants, and all the Israelites. They destroyed the Ammonites and attacked the city of Rabbah. But David stayed in Jerusalem. 2One evening David got up from his bed and walked around on the roofn of his palace. While he was on the roof, he saw a woman bathing. She was very beautiful. 3So David sent his servants to find out who she was. A servant answered, "That woman is Bathsheba daughter of Eliam. She is the wife of Uriah the Hittite." 4So David sent messengers to bring Bathsheba to him. When she came to him, he had sexual relations with her. (Now Bathsheba had purified herself from her monthly period.) Then she went back to her house. 5But Bathsheba became pregnant and sent word to David, saying, "I am pregnant."

6So David sent a message to Joab: "Send Uriah the Hittite to me." And Joab sent Uriah to David. 7When Uriah came to him, David asked him how Joab was, how the soldiers were, and how the war was going. 8Then David said to Uriah, "Go home and rest."

So Uriah left the palace, and the king sent a gift to him. 9But Uriah did not go home. Instead, he slept outside the door of the palace as all the king's officers did.

10The officers told David, "Uriah did not go home."

Then David said to Uriah, "You came from a long trip. Why didn't you go home?"

11Uriah said to him, "The Arkd and the soldiers of Israel and Judah are staying in tents. My master Joab and his officers are camping out in the fields. It isn't right for me to go home to eat and drink and have sexual relations with my wife!"

12David said to Uriah, "Stay here today. Tomorrow I'll send you back to the battle." So Uriah stayed in Jerusalem that day and the next. 13Then David called Uriah to come to see him, so Uriah ate and drank with David. David made Uriah drunk, but he still did not go home. That evening Uriah again slept with the king's officers.

14The next morning David wrote a letter to Joab and sent it by Uriah. 15In the letter David wrote, "Put Uriah on the front lines where the fighting is worst and leave him there alone. Let him be killed in battle."

16Joab watched the city and saw where its strongest defenders were and put Uriah there. 17When the men of the city came out to fight against Joab, some of David's men were killed. And Uriah the Hittite was one of them.

18Then Joab sent David a complete account of

roof In Bible times houses were built with flat roofs. The roof was used for drying things such as flax and fruit. And it was used as an extra room, as a place for worship, and as a place to sleep in the summer.

the war. [19]Joab told the messenger, "Tell King David what happened in the war. [20]After you finish, the king may be angry and ask, 'Why did you go so near the city to fight? Didn't you know they would shoot arrows from the city wall? [21]Do you remember who killed Abimelech son of Jerub-Besheth?[n] It was a woman on the city wall. She threw a large stone for grinding grain on Abimelech and killed him there in Thebez. Why did you go so near the wall?' If King David asks that, tell him, 'Your servant Uriah the Hittite also died.' "

[22]The messenger left and went to David and told him everything Joab had told him to say. [23]The messenger told David, "The men of Ammon were winning. They came out and attacked us in the field, but we fought them back to the city gate. [24]The archers on the city wall shot at your servants, and some of your men were killed. Your servant Uriah the Hittite also died."

[25]David said to the messenger, "Say this to Joab: 'Don't be upset about this. The sword kills everyone the same. Make a stronger attack against the city and capture it.' Encourage Joab with these words."

[26]When Bathsheba heard that her husband was dead, she cried for him. [27]After she finished her time of sadness, David sent servants to bring her to his house. She became David's wife and gave birth to his son, but the LORD did not like what David had done.

David's Son Dies

12 The LORD sent Nathan to David. When he came to David, he said, "There were two men in a city. One was rich, but the other was poor. [2]The rich man had many sheep and cattle. [3]But the poor man had nothing except one little female lamb he had bought. The poor man fed the lamb, and it grew up with him and his

Jerub-Besheth   Another name for Gideon.

SEXUALITY

Risking Everything

Something about LaDonna King turned Allan Gentry's head. Maybe her figure. Maybe her playful smile. Maybe her piercing eyes. Whatever it was, Allan couldn't get her out of his mind.

After two weeks of nervous planning, he finally found the courage to ask her out. He did everything he could to impress her. He waxed his vintage Mustang and took her to the fanciest restaurant in town. He turned on his charm, making sure she knew how important he was.

After that first date, they kissed at the door. But over the next few weeks, Allan wanted more. Each time, he would try to go a little farther. Each time she would resist.

As their dizzying romance continued, Allan became more aggressive. LaDonna bravely continued to resist, but Allan applied even more pressure. "If you really loved me," he said, "you wouldn't make me stop."

"But I do love you, Allan," she replied.

"Well, I can't be sure unless you show me."

Frightened at the prospect of losing Allan, LaDonna finally gave in. Three months later, she discovered she was pregnant.

Out of her fear of losing Allan, she lost so much more.

Like LaDonna, David risked everything to have Bathsheba. And it nearly cost him everything. Read **2 Samuel 11:1–15** to see what happened.

■ How did Allan and David abuse their power? What choices did LaDonna and Bathsheba have?

■ What would you have done if you had been in David's situation? What about Bathsheba's?

CONSIDER . . .

■ writing on a small card three things you could say to someone who pressures you to have sex. Keep the card in your wallet or purse.

■ praying regularly that God will give you strength to resist sexual temptation.

FOR MORE, SEE . . .

■ 2 Samuel 12:1–14 (p. 284)
■ Matthew 5:27–30 (p. 914)

■ 1 Thessalonians 4:3–8 (p. 1247)

children. It shared his food and drank from his cup and slept in his arms. The lamb was like a daughter to him.

⁴"Then a traveler stopped to visit the rich man. The rich man wanted to feed the traveler, but he didn't want to take one of his own sheep or cattle. Instead, he took the lamb from the poor man and cooked it for his visitor."

⁵David became very angry at the rich man. He said to Nathan, "As surely as the LORD lives, the man who did this should die! ⁶He must pay for the lamb four times for doing such a thing. He had no mercy!"

⁷Then Nathan said to David, "You are the man! This is what the LORD, the God of Israel, says: 'I appointed you king of Israel and saved you from Saul. ⁸I gave you his kingdom and his wives. And I made you king of Israel and Judah. And if that had not been enough, I would have given you even more. ⁹So why did you ignore the LORD's command? Why did you do what he says is wrong? You killed Uriah the Hittite with the sword of the Ammonites and took his wife to be your wife! ¹⁰Now there will always be people in your family who will die by a sword, because you did not respect me; you took the wife of Uriah the Hittite for yourself!'

¹¹"This is what the LORD says: 'I am bringing trouble to you from your own family. While you watch, I will take your wives from you and give them to someone who is very close to you. He will have sexual relations with your wives, and everyone will know it. ¹²You had sexual relations with Bathsheba in secret, but I will do this so all the people of Israel can see it.'"

¹³Then David said to Nathan, "I have sinned against the LORD."

Nathan answered, "The LORD has taken away your sin. You will not die. ¹⁴But what you did caused the LORD's enemies to lose all respect for

---

SIN

Hidden Sins

■ It wasn't a big crash. Just a little nudge in the parking lot. From what Joni Snyder could tell, just the taillight was broken. She would get it fixed before her parents returned from their weekend getaway, and they would never know she had taken the Volvo without permission.
She didn't notice that the license plate was also bent.

■ When Terrence Ball's parents asked him if he smoked pot, he was furious. "Of course not!" he shouted. "Don't you trust me?"
But his parents could smell the smoke in his jean jacket.

■ It would be harmless. No one would know that Terri Walker's English term paper was just like Amy Woods's paper from four years ago. Amy had gotten an A on it, so Terri figured she could too—with a lot less work.
But she wasn't prepared when the teacher asked for an oral report too.

■ The lawn in front of the school looked like a moonscape. The tires had torn the sod so badly that the whole lawn would have to be replaced. The principal demanded that anyone who knew what had happened report it. Almost everyone knew it was Don Hunter and Gary Richards, the football stars. But no one said anything.

Just as people try to hide their sins today, David tried to hide his sin when he committed adultery with Bathsheba. But, as **2 Samuel 12:1–25** reveals, God saw the sin.

■ What might the prophet Nathan say to the teenagers who tried to hide their sins?

■ Just as David suffered the consequences of his sin, how have you suffered the consequences of something you've done wrong?

CONSIDER . . .

■ confessing to a parent or friend something you've done wrong but have kept hidden. Also confess it to God and accept his forgiveness.

■ being honest and open next time you're confronted about something you did. See how the approach affects what happens.

FOR   MORE,   SEE . . .

■ Psalm 51:1–13 (p. 511)   ■ 1 John 1:8–10 (p. 1316)
■ Isaiah 29:15–16 (p. 645)

him. For this reason the son who was born to you will die."

15Then Nathan went home. And the LORD caused the son of David and Bathsheba, Uriah's widow, to be very sick. 16David prayed to God for the baby. David refused to eat or drink. He went into his house and stayed there, lying on the ground all night. 17The older leaders of David's family came to him and tried to pull him up from the ground, but he refused to get up or to eat food with them.

18On the seventh day the baby died. David's servants were afraid to tell him that the baby was dead. They said, "Look, we tried to talk to David while the baby was alive, but he refused to listen to us. If we tell him the baby is dead, he may do something awful."

19When David saw his servants whispering, he knew that the baby was dead. So he asked them, "Is the baby dead?"

They answered, "Yes, he is dead."

20Then David got up from the floor, washed himself, put lotions on, and changed his clothes. Then he went into the LORD's house to worship. After that, he went home and asked for something to eat. His servants gave him some food, and he ate.

21David's servants said to him, "Why are you doing this? When the baby was still alive, you refused to eat and you cried. Now that the baby is dead, you get up and eat food."

22David said, "While the baby was still alive, I refused to eat, and I cried. I thought, 'Who knows? Maybe the LORD will feel sorry for me and let the baby live.' 23But now that the baby is dead, why should I go without food? I can't bring him back to life. Some day I will go to him, but he cannot come back to me."

24Then David comforted Bathsheba his wife. He slept with her and had sexual relations with her. She became pregnant again and had another son, whom David named Solomon. The LORD loved Solomon. 25The LORD sent word through Nathan the prophet*d* to name the baby Jedidiah,*n* because the LORD loved the child.

David Captures Rabbah

26Joab fought against Rabbah, a royal city of the Ammonites, and he was about to capture it. 27Joab sent messengers to David and said, "I have fought against Rabbah and have captured its water supply. 28Now bring the other soldiers together and attack this city. Capture it before I capture it myself and it is called by my name!"

29So David gathered all the army and went to Rabbah and fought against it and captured it. 30David took the crown off their king's head and

had it placed on his own head. That gold crown weighed about seventy-five pounds, and it had valuable gems in it. And David took many valuable things from the city. 31He also brought out the people of the city and forced them to work with saws, iron picks, and axes. He also made them build with bricks. David did this to all the Ammonite cities. Then David and all his army returned to Jerusalem.

Amnon and Tamar

13 David had a son named Absalom and a son named Amnon. Absalom had a beautiful sister named Tamar, and Amnon loved her. 2Tamar was a virgin.*d* Amnon made himself sick just thinking about her, because he could not find any chance to be alone with her.

3Amnon had a friend named Jonadab son of Shimeah, David's brother. Jonadab was a very clever man. 4He asked Amnon, "Son of the king, why do you look so sad day after day? Tell me what's wrong!"

Amnon told him, "I love Tamar, the sister of my half-brother Absalom."

5Jonadab said to Amnon, "Go to bed and act as if you are sick. Then your father will come to see you. Tell him, 'Please let my sister Tamar come in and give me food to eat. Let her make the food in front of me so I can watch and eat it from her hand.' "

6So Amnon went to bed and acted sick. When King David came in to see him, Amnon said to him, "Please let my sister Tamar come in. Let her make two of her special cakes for me while I watch. Then I will eat them from her hands."

7David sent for Tamar in the palace, saying, "Go to your brother Amnon's house and make some food for him." 8So Tamar went to her brother Amnon's house, and he was in bed. Tamar took some dough and pressed it together with her hands. She made some special cakes while Amnon watched. Then she baked them. 9Next she took the pan and served him, but he refused to eat.

He said to his servants, "All of you, leave me alone!" So they all left him alone. 10Amnon said to Tamar, "Bring the food into the bedroom so I may eat from your hand."

Tamar took the cakes she had made and brought them to her brother Amnon in the bedroom. 11She went to him so he could eat from her hands, but Amnon grabbed her. He said, "Sister, come and have sexual relations with me."

12Tamar said to him, "No, brother! Don't force me! This should never be done in Israel! Don't do this shameful thing! 13I could never get rid of my shame! And you will be like the shameful fools in

Jedidiah   This name means "loved by the LORD."

Israel! Please talk with the king, and he will let you marry me."

14But Amnon refused to listen to her. He was stronger than she was, so he forced her to have sexual relations with him. 15After that, Amnon hated Tamar. He hated her more than he had loved her before. Amnon said to her, "Get up and leave!"

16Tamar said to him, "No! Sending me away would be worse than what you've already done!"

But he refused to listen to her. 17He called his young servant back in and said, "Get this woman out of here and away from me! Lock the door after her." 18So his servant led her out of the room and bolted the door after her.

Tamar was wearing a special robe with long sleeves, because the king's virgin daughters wore this kind of robe. 19To show how upset she was, Tamar put ashes on her head and tore her special robe and put her hand on her head. Then she went away, crying loudly.

20Absalom, Tamar's brother, said to her, "Has Amnon, your brother, forced you to have sexual relations with him? For now, sister, be quiet. He is your half-brother. Don't let this upset you so much!" So Tamar lived in her brother Absalom's house and was sad and lonely.

21When King David heard the news, he was very angry. 22Absalom did not say a word, good or bad, to Amnon. But he hated Amnon for disgracing his sister Tamar.

Absalom's Revenge

23Two years later Absalom had some men come to Baal Hazor, near Ephraim, to cut the wool from his sheep. Absalom invited all the king's sons to come also. 24Absalom went to the king and said, "I have men coming to cut the wool. Please come with your officers and join me."

25King David said to Absalom, "No, my son. We won't all go, because it would be too much trouble for you." Although Absalom begged David, he would not go, but he did give his blessing.

26Absalom said, "If you don't want to come, then please let my brother Amnon come with us."

King David asked, "Why should he go with you?"

27Absalom kept begging David until he let Amnon and all the king's sons go with Absalom.

28Then Absalom instructed his servants, "Watch Amnon. When he is drunk, I will tell you, 'Kill Amnon.' Right then, kill him! Don't be afraid, because I have commanded you! Be strong and brave!" 29So Absalom's young men killed Amnon as Absalom commanded, but all of David's other sons got on their mules and escaped.

30While the king's sons were on their way, the news came to David, "Absalom has killed all of the king's sons! Not one of them is left alive!" 31King David tore his clothes and lay on the ground to show his sadness. All his servants standing nearby tore their clothes also.

32Jonadab son of Shimeah, David's brother, said to David, "Don't think all the young men, your sons, are killed. No, only Amnon is dead! Absalom has planned this ever since Amnon forced his sister Tamar to have sexual relations with him. 33My master and king, don't think that all of the king's sons are dead. Only Amnon is dead!"

34In the meantime Absalom had run away.

A guard standing on the city wall saw many people coming from the other side of the hill. 35So Jonadab said to King David, "Look, I was right! The king's sons are coming!"

36As soon as Jonadab had said this, the king's sons arrived, crying loudly. David and all his servants began crying also. 37David cried for his son every day.

But Absalom ran away to Talmai[n] son of Ammihud, the king of Geshur. 38After Absalom ran away to Geshur, he stayed there for three years. 39When King David got over Amnon's death, he missed Absalom greatly.

Joab Sends a Wise Woman to David

14 Joab son of Zeruiah knew that King David missed Absalom very much. 2So Joab sent messengers to Tekoa to bring a wise woman from there. He said to her, "Pretend to be very sad. Put on funeral clothes and don't put lotion on yourself. Act like a woman who has been crying many days for someone who died. 3Then go to the king and say these words." Then Joab told her what to say.

4So the woman from Tekoa spoke to the king. She bowed facedown on the ground to show respect and said, "My king, help me!"

5King David asked her, "What is the matter?"

The woman said, "I am a widow; my husband is dead. 6I had two sons. They were cut in the field fighting, and no one was there to stop them. So one son killed the other son. 7Now all the family group is against me. They said to me, 'Bring the son who killed his brother so we may kill him for killing his brother. That way we will also get rid of the one who would receive what belonged to his father.' My son is like the last spark of a fire. He is all I have left. If they kill him, my husband's name and property will be gone from the earth."

8Then the king said to the woman, "Go home. I will take care of this for you."

9The woman of Tekoa said to him, "Let the

Talmai He was Absalom's grandfather.

blame be on me and my father's family. My master and king, you and your throne are innocent."

10King David said, "Bring me anyone who says anything bad to you. Then he won't bother you again."

11The woman said, "Please promise in the name of the LORD your God. Then my relative who has the duty of punishing a murderer won't add to the destruction by killing my son."

David said, "As surely as the LORD lives, no one will hurt your son. Not one hair from his head will fall to the ground."

12The woman said, "Let me say something to you, my master and king."

The king said, "Speak."

13Then the woman said, "Why have you decided this way against the people of God? When you judge this way, you show that you are guilty for not bringing back your son who was forced to leave home. 14We will all die some day. We're like water spilled on the ground; no one can gather it back. But God doesn't take away life. Instead, he plans ways that those who have been sent away will not have to stay away from him! 15My master and king, I came to say this to you because the people have made me afraid! I thought, 'Let me talk to the king. Maybe he will do what I ask. 16Maybe he will listen. Perhaps he will save me from those who want to keep both me and my son from getting what God gave us.'

17"Now I say, 'May the words of my master the king give me rest. Like an angel of God, you know what is good and what is bad. May the LORD your God be with you!' "

18Then King David said, "Do not hide the truth. Answer me one question."

The woman said, "My master the king, please ask your question."

19The king said, "Did Joab tell you to say all these things?"

The woman answered, "As you live, my master the king, no one could avoid that question. You are right. Your servant Joab did tell me to say these things. 20Joab did it so you would see things differently. My master, you are wise like an angel of God who knows everything that happens on earth."

Absalom Returns to Jerusalem

21The king said to Joab, "Look, I will do what I promised. Bring back the young man Absalom."

22Joab bowed facedown on the ground and blessed the king. Then he said, "Today I know you are pleased with me, because you have done what I asked."

23Then Joab got up and went to Geshur and brought Absalom back to Jerusalem. 24But King

David said, "Absalom must go to his own house. He may not come to see me." So Absalom went to his own house and did not go to see the king.

25Absalom was greatly praised for his handsome appearance. No man in Israel was as handsome as he. No blemish was on him from his head to his foot. 26At the end of every year, Absalom would cut his hair, because it became too heavy. When he weighed it, it would weigh about five pounds by the royal measure.

27Absalom had three sons and one daughter. His daughter's name was also Tamar, and she was a beautiful woman.

28Absalom lived in Jerusalem for two full years without seeing King David. 29Then Absalom sent for Joab so he could send him to the king, but Joab would not come. Absalom sent a message a second time, but Joab still refused to come. 30Then Absalom said to his servants, "Look, Joab's field is next to mine, and he has barley growing there. Go burn it." So Absalom's servants set fire to Joab's field.

31Then Joab went to Absalom's house and said to him, "Why did your servants burn my field?"

32Absalom said to Joab, "I sent a message to you, asking you to come here. I wanted to send you to the king to ask him why he brought me home from Geshur. It would have been better for me to stay there! Now let me see the king. If I have sinned, he can put me to death!"

33So Joab went to the king and told him Absalom's words. Then the king called for Absalom. Absalom came and bowed facedown on the ground before the king, and the king kissed him.

Absalom Plans to Take David's Kingdom

15 After this, Absalom got a chariot and horses for himself and fifty men to run before him. 2Absalom would get up early and stand near the city gate.ⁿ Anyone who had a problem for the king to settle would come here. When someone came, Absalom would call out and say, "What city are you from?"

The person would answer, "I'm from one of the tribesᵈ of Israel."

3Then Absalom would say, "Look, your claims are right, but the king has no one to listen to you." 4Absalom would also say, "I wish someone would make me judge in this land! Then people with problems could come to me, and I could help them get justice."

5People would come near Absalom to bow to him. When they did, Absalom would reach out his hand and take hold of them and kiss them. 6Absalom did that to all the Israelites who came to King David for decisions. In this way, Absalom stole the hearts of all Israel.

city gate People came here to conduct business. Public meetings and court cases were also held here.

7After four years Absalom said to King David, "Please let me go to Hebron. I want to carry out my promise that I made to the LORD 8while I was living in Geshur in Aram. I said, 'If the LORD takes me back to Jerusalem, I will worship him in Hebron.'"

9The king said, "Go in peace."

So Absalom went to Hebron. 10But he sent secret messengers through all the tribes of Israel. They told the people, "When you hear the trumpets, say this: 'Absalom is the king at Hebron!'"

11Absalom had invited two hundred men to go with him. So they went from Jerusalem with him, but they didn't know what he was planning. 12While Absalom was offering sacrifices, he sent for Ahithophel, one of the people who advised David, to come from his hometown of Giloh. So Absalom's plans were working very well. More and more people began to support him.

13A messenger came to David, saying, "The Israelites are giving their loyalty to Absalom."

14Then David said to all his officers who were with him in Jerusalem, "We must leave quickly! If we don't, we won't be able to get away from Absalom. We must hurry before he catches us and destroys us and kills the people of Jerusalem."

15The king's officers said to him, "We will do anything you say."

16The king set out with everyone in his house, but he left ten slave women to take care of the palace. 17The king left with all his people following him, and they stopped at a house far away. 18All the king's servants passed by him — the Kerethites and Pelethites,n all those from Gath, and the six hundred men who had followed him.

19The king said to Ittai, a man from Gath, "Why are you also going with us? Turn back and stay with King Absalom because you are a foreigner. This is not your homeland. 20You joined me only a short time ago. Should I make you wander with us when I don't even know where I'm going? Turn back and take your brothers with you. May kindness and loyalty be shown to you."

21But Ittai said to the king, "As surely as the

LORD lives and as you live, I will stay with you, whether it means life or death."

22David said to Ittai, "Go, march on." So Ittai from Gath and all his people with their children marched on. 23All the people cried loudly as everyone passed by. King David crossed the Kidron Valley, and then all the people went on to the desert. 24Zadok and all the Levites with him carried the Arkd of the Agreement with God. They set it down, and Abiathar offered sacrifices until all the people had left the city.

25The king said to Zadok, "Take the Ark of God back into the city. If the LORD is pleased with me, he will bring me back and will let me see both it and Jerusalem again. 26But if the LORD says he is not pleased with me, I am ready. He can do what he wants with me."

27The king also said to Zadok the priest, "Aren't you a seer?d Go back to the city in peace and take your son Ahimaaz and Abiathar's son Jonathan with you 28I will wait near the crossings into the desert until I hear from you." 29So Zadok and Abiathar took the Ark of God back to Jerusalem and stayed there.

30David went up the Mount of Olives,d crying as he went. He covered his head and went barefoot. All the people with David covered their heads also and cried as they went. 31Someone told David, "Ahithophel is one of the people with Absalom who made secret plans against you."

So David prayed, "LORD, please make Ahithophel's advice foolish."

32When David reached the top of the mountain where people used to worship God, Hushai the Arkite came to meet him. Hushai's coat was torn, and there was dirt on his head to show how sad he was. 33David said to Hushai, "If you go with me, you will be just one more person for me to take care of. 34But if you return to the city, you can make Ahithophel's advice useless. Tell Absalom, 'I am your servant, my king. In the past I served your father, but now I will serve you.' 35The priests Zadok and Abiathar will be with you. Tell them everything you hear in the royal palace. 36Zadok's son Ahimaaz and Abiathar's son Jonathan are with them. Send them to tell me everything you hear." 37So David's friend Hushai entered Jerusalem just as Absalom arrived.

Ziba Meets David

16 When David had passed a short way over the top of the Mount of Olives,d Ziba, Mephibosheth's servant, met him. Ziba had a row of donkeys loaded with two hundred loaves of bread, one hundred cakes of raisins, one hundred cakes of figs, and leather bags full of wine.

Kerethites and Pelethites These were probably special units of the army that were responsible for the king's safety, a kind of palace guard.

[2]The king asked Ziba, "What are these things for?"

Ziba answered, "The donkeys are for your family to ride. The bread and cakes of figs are for the servants to eat. And the wine is for anyone to drink who might become weak in the desert."

[3]The king asked, "Where is Mephibosheth?"

Ziba answered him, "Mephibosheth is staying in Jerusalem because he thinks, 'Today the Israelites will give me my father's kingdom back to me!' "

[4]Then the king said to Ziba, "All right. Everything that belonged to Mephibosheth, I now give to you!"

Ziba said, "I bow to you. I hope I will always be able to please you."

Shimei Curses David

[5]As King David came to Bahurim, a man came out and cursed him. He was from Saul's family group, and his name was Shimei son of Gera. [6]He threw stones at David and his officers, but the people and soldiers gathered all around David. [7]Shimei cursed David, saying, "Get out, get out, you murderer, you troublemaker. [8]The Lord is punishing you for the people in Saul's family you killed! You took Saul's place as king, but now the Lord has given the kingdom to your son Absalom! Now you are ruined because you are a murderer!"

[9]Abishai son of Zeruiah said to the king, "Why should this dead dog curse you, the king? Let me go over and cut off his head!"

[10]But the king answered, "This does not concern you, sons of Zeruiah! If he is cursing me because the Lord told him to, who can question him?"

[11]David also said to Abishai and all his officers, "My own son is trying to kill me! This man is a Benjaminite and has more right to kill me! Leave him alone, and let him curse me because the Lord told him to do this. [12]Maybe the Lord will see my misery and repay me with something good for Shimei's curses today!"

[13]So David and his men went on down the road, but Shimei followed on the nearby hillside. He kept cursing David and throwing stones and dirt at him. [14]When the king and all his people arrived at the Jordan, they were very tired, so they rested there.

[15]Meanwhile, Absalom, Ahithophel, and all the Israelites arrived at Jerusalem. [16]David's friend *Hushai the Arkite* came to Absalom and said to him, *"Long live the king! Long live the king!"*

[17]Absalom asked, "Why are you not loyal to your friend David? Why didn't you leave Jerusalem with your friend?"

[18]Hushai said, "I belong to the one chosen by the Lord and by these people and everyone in Israel. I will stay with you. [19]In the past I served your father. So whom should I serve now? David's son! I will serve you as I served him."

Ahithophel's Advice

[20]Absalom said to Ahithophel, "Tell us what we should do."

[21]Ahithophel said, "Your father left behind some of his slave women[d] to take care of the palace. Have sexual relations with them. Then all Israel will hear that your father is your enemy, and all your people will be encouraged to give you more support." [22]So they put up a tent for Absalom on the roof[n] of the palace where everyone in Israel could see it. And Absalom had sexual relations with his father's slave women.

[23]At that time people thought Ahithophel's advice was as reliable as God's own word. Both David and Absalom thought it was that reliable.

17 Ahithophel said to Absalom, "Let me choose twelve thousand men and chase David tonight. [2]I'll catch him while he is tired and weak, and I'll frighten him so all his people will run away. But I'll kill only King David. [3]Then I'll bring everyone back to you. If the man you are looking for is dead, everyone else will return safely." [4]This plan seemed good to Absalom and to all the leaders of Israel.

[5]But Absalom said, "Now call Hushai the Arkite, so I can hear what he says." [6]When Hushai came to Absalom, Absalom said to him, "This is the plan Ahithophel gave. Should we follow it? If not, tell us."

[7]Hushai said to Absalom, "Ahithophel's advice is not good this time." [8]Hushai added, "You know your father and his men are strong. They are as angry as a bear that is robbed of its cubs. Your father is a skilled fighter. He won't stay all night with the army. [9]He is probably already hiding in a cave or some other place. If the first attack fails, people will hear the news and think, 'Absalom's followers are losing!' [10]Then even the men who are as brave as lions will be frightened, because all the Israelites know your father is a fighter. They know his men are brave!

[11]"This is what I suggest: Gather all the Israelites from Dan to Beersheba.[n] There will be as many people as grains of sand by the sea. Then you yourself must go into the battle. [12]We will go to David wherever he is hiding. We will fall on

---

roof In Bible times houses were built with flat roofs. The roof was used for drying things such as flax and fruit. And it was used as an extra room, as a place for worship, and as a place to sleep in the summer.
Dan to Beersheba Dan was the city farthest north in Israel, and Beersheba was the city farthest south. So this means all the people of Israel.

him as dew falls on the ground. We will kill him and all of his men so that no one will be left alive. [13]If David escapes into a city, all the Israelites will bring ropes to that city and pull it into the valley. Not a stone will be left!"

[14]Absalom and all the Israelites said, "The advice of Hushai the Arkite is better than that of Ahithophel." (The LORD had planned to destroy the good advice of Ahithophel so the LORD could bring disaster on Absalom.)

[15]Hushai told Zadok and Abiathar, the priests, what Ahithophel had suggested to Absalom and the older leaders of Israel. He also reported to them what he himself had suggested. Hushai said, [16]"Quickly! Send a message to David. Tell him not to stay tonight at the crossings into the desert but to cross over the Jordan River at once. If he crosses the river, he and all his people won't be destroyed."

[17]Jonathan and Ahimaaz were waiting at En Rogel. They did not want to be seen going into the city, so a servant girl would go out to them and give them messages. Then Jonathan and Ahimaaz would go and tell King David.

[18]But a boy saw Jonathan and Ahimaaz and told Absalom. So Jonathan and Ahimaaz left quickly and went to a man's house in Bahurim. He had a well in his courtyard, and they climbed down into it. [19]The man's wife spread a sheet over the opening of the well and covered it with grain. No one could tell that anyone was hiding there.

[20]Absalom's servants came to the woman at the house and asked, "Where are Ahimaaz and Jonathan?"

She said to them, "They have already crossed the brook."

Absalom's servants then went to look for Jonathan and Ahimaaz, but they could not find them. So they went back to Jerusalem.

[21]After Absalom's servants left, Jonathan and Ahimaaz climbed out of the well and went to tell King David. They said, "Hurry, cross over the river! Ahithophel has said these things against you!" [22]So David and all his people crossed the Jordan River. By dawn, everyone had crossed the Jordan.

[23]When Ahithophel saw that the Israelites did not accept his advice, he saddled his donkey and went to his hometown. He left orders for his family and property, and then he hanged himself. He died and was buried in his father's tomb.

War Between David and Absalom

[24]David arrived at Mahanaim. And Absalom and all his Israelites crossed over the Jordan River. [25]Absalom had made Amasa captain of the army instead of Joab. Amasa was the son of a man named Jether the Ishmaelite. Amasa's mother

was Abigail daughter of Nahash and sister of Zeruiah, Joab's mother. [26]Absalom and the Israelites camped in the land of Gilead.

[27]Shobi, Makir, and Barzillai were at Mahanaim when David arrived. Shobi son of Nahash was from the Ammonite town of Rabbah. Makir son of Ammiel was from Lo Debar, and Barzillai was from Rogelim in Gilead. [28]They brought beds, bowls, clay pots, wheat, barley, flour, roasted grain, beans, small peas, [29]honey, milk curds, sheep, and cheese made from cows' milk for David and his people. They said, "The people are hungry and tired and thirsty in the desert."

18
David counted his men and placed over them commanders of thousands and commanders of hundreds. [2]He sent the troops out in three groups. Joab commanded one-third of the men. Joab's brother Abishai son of Zeruiah commanded another third. And Ittai from Gath commanded the last third. King David said to them, "I will also go with you."

[3]But the men said, "You must not go with us! If we run away in the battle, Absalom's men won't care. Even if half of us are killed, Absalom's men won't care. But you're worth ten thousand of us! You can help us most by staying in the city."

[4]The king said to his people, "I will do what you think is best." So the king stood at the side of the gate as the army went out in groups of a hundred and a thousand.

[5]The king commanded Joab, Abishai, and Ittai, "Be gentle with young Absalom for my sake." Everyone heard the king's orders to the commanders about Absalom.

[6]David's army went out into the field against Absalom's Israelites, and they fought in the forest of Ephraim. [7]There David's army defeated the Israelites. Many died that day—twenty thousand men. [8]The battle spread through all the country, but that day more men died in the forest than in the fighting.

✴ **SIDELIGHT:** If you haven't gotten your hair cut lately, be careful. Absalom's long hair got caught in a tree when his mule rode under it, leaving Absalom hanging (2 Samuel 18:9). It's no wonder, either. He only cut it once a year when it became too heavy—weighing five pounds (2 Samuel 14:26)!

Absalom Dies

[9]Then Absalom happened to meet David's troops. As Absalom was riding his mule, it went under the thick branches of a large oak tree. Absa-

lom's head got caught in the tree, and his mule ran out from under him. So Absalom was left hanging above the ground.

¹⁰When one of the men saw it happen, he told Joab, "I saw Absalom hanging in an oak tree!"

¹¹Joab said to him, "You saw him? Why didn't you kill him and let him fall to the ground? I would have given you a belt and four ounces of silver!"

¹²The man answered, "I wouldn't touch the king's son even if you gave me twenty-five pounds of silver. We heard the king command you, Abishai, and Ittai, 'Be careful not to hurt young Absalom.' ¹³If I had killed him, the king would have found out, and you would not have protected me!"

¹⁴Joab said, "I won't waste time here with you!" Absalom was still alive in the oak tree, so Joab took three spears and stabbed him in the heart. ¹⁵Ten young men who carried Joab's armor also gathered around Absalom and struck him and killed him.

¹⁶Then Joab blew the trumpet, so the troops stopped chasing the Israelites. ¹⁷Then Joab's men took Absalom's body and threw it into a large pit in the forest and filled the pit with many stones. All the Israelites ran away to their homes.

¹⁸When Absalom was alive, he had set up a pillar for himself in the King's Valley. He said, "I have no son to keep my name alive." So he named the pillar after himself, and it is called Absalom's Monument even today.

¹⁹Ahimaaz son of Zadok said to Joab, "Let me run and take the news to King David. I'll tell him the LORD has saved him from his enemies."

²⁰Joab answered Ahimaaz, "No, you are not the one to take the news today. You may do it another time, but do not take it today, because the king's son is dead."

²¹Then Joab said to a man from Cush, "Go, tell the king what you have seen." The Cushite bowed to Joab and ran to tell David.

²²But Ahimaaz son of Zadok begged Joab again, "No matter what happens, please let me go along with the Cushite!"

Joab said, "Son, why do you want to carry the news? You won't get any reward."

²³Ahimaaz answered, "No matter what happens, I will run."

So Joab said to Ahimaaz, "Run!" Then Ahimaaz ran by way of the Jordan Valley and passed the Cushite.

²⁴David was sitting between the inner and outer gates of the city. The watchman went up to the roof of the gate by the walls, and as he looked up, he saw a man running alone. ²⁵He shouted the news to the king.

The king said, "If he is alone, he is bringing good news!"

The man came nearer and nearer to the city. ²⁶Then the watchman saw another man running, and he called to the gatekeeper, "Look! Another man is running alone!"

The king said, "He is also bringing good news!"

²⁷The watchman said, "I think the first man runs like Ahimaaz son of Zadok."

The king said, "Ahimaaz is a good man. He must be bringing good news!"

²⁸Then Ahimaaz called a greeting to the king. He bowed facedown on the ground before the king and said, "Praise the LORD your God! The LORD has defeated those who were against you, my king."

²⁹The king asked, "Is young Absalom all right?"

Ahimaaz answered, "When Joab sent me, I saw some great excitement, but I don't know what it was."

³⁰The king said, "Step over here and wait." So Ahimaaz stepped aside and stood there.

³¹Then the Cushite arrived. He said, "Master and king, hear the good news! Today the LORD has punished those who were against you!"

³²The king asked the Cushite, "Is young Absalom all right?"

The Cushite answered, "May your enemies and all who come to hurt you be like that young man!"

³³Then the king was very upset, and he went to the room over the city gate and cried. As he went, he cried out, "My son Absalom, my son Absalom! I wish I had died and not you. Absalom, my son, my son!"

Joab Scolds David

19 People told Joab, "Look, the king is sad and crying because of Absalom." ²David's army had won the battle that day. But it became a very sad day for all the people, because they heard that the king was very sad for his son. ³The people came into the city quietly that day. They were like an army that had been defeated in battle and had run away. ⁴The king covered his face and cried loudly, "My son Absalom! Absalom, my son, my son!"

⁵Joab went into the king's house and said, "Today you have shamed all your men. They saved your life and the lives of your sons, daughters, wives, and slave women.ᵈ ⁶You have shamed them because you love those who hate you, and you hate those who love you. Today you have made it clear that your commanders and men mean nothing to you. What if Absalom had lived and all of us were dead? I can see you would be pleased. ⁷Now go out and encourage your servants. I swear by the LORD that if you don't go out, no man will be left with you by tonight! That will be worse than all the troubles you have had from your youth until today."

⁸So the king went to the city gate. *n* When the news spread that the king was at the gate, everyone came to see him.

David Goes Back to Jerusalem

All the Israelites who had followed Absalom had run away to their homes. ⁹People in all the tribes*d* of Israel began to argue, saying, "The king saved us from the Philistines and our other enemies, but he left the country because of Absalom. ¹⁰We appointed Absalom to rule us, but now he has died in battle. We should make David the king again."

¹¹King David sent a message to Zadok and Abiathar, the priests, that said, "Speak to the older leaders of Judah. Say, 'Even in my house I have heard what all the Israelites are saying. So why are you the last tribe to bring the king back to his palace? ¹²You are my brothers, my own family. Why are you the last tribe to bring back the king?' ¹³And say to Amasa, 'You are part of my own family. May God punish me terribly if I don't make you commander of the army in Joab's place!' "

city gate　People came here to conduct business. Public meetings and court cases were also held here.

REBELLION

Donna's Diary

October 15—I got drunk last night. Again. I had to do something to ease the tensions at home. Mom and Dad keep hassling me about what I'm going to do with my life. Why won't they leave me alone? Why won't they let me grow up? I'm sixteen—old enough to make my own decisions.

I can't take it! The rules. The curfews. The restrictions. They're driving me crazy. Just tonight. Jerry called. When I told Mom and Dad, they blew up. "Why do you hang out with that scum?" Mom cried.

October 23—Mom and Dad caught me coming home drunk last night. I've never seen them so angry. So this morning they packed me into the car and brought me to this funny farm.

January 29—I just got out of the alcohol-abuse treatment program this week. I thought things would be better when I got home, but I was wrong. Mom and Dad watch me constantly. They're so paranoid I'll do something wrong again.

Well, I don't have to deal with this anymore. Jerry said I could move in with him. I think I will. Tomorrow it's good-bye to this place and hello to a new, free life.

April 18. It wasn't supposed to be this way. I mean, Jerry seemed like such a great guy. But I hadn't seen him angry—really angry. Like he was last night. Now the side of my face is swollen, and I can't open my left eye.

What can I do? He said he'd kill me if I told anyone. And, after last night, I believe him.

Should I tell Mom and Dad? We used to be so close. But, since I left home, I don't know. Would they help me? Do they still love me?

Does anyone really love me? What went wrong?

Donna's diary describes rebellion from a teenager's perspective. Read about rebellion from a parent's perspective in **2 Samuel 18:24—33**, where King David expresses deep pain at his son Absalom's rebellion when he learns about Absalom's death.

■ If Absalom had written a diary, what do you think he might have said to his father, King David?

■ When have you wanted to rebel against your parent or parents? What did you do? What happened?

C O N S I D E R . . .

■ praying for families that are torn apart by rebellion. Ask God to help the families communicate and come back together.

■ negotiating with your parents to decide together what to do if you feel overly restricted or stifled.

F O R   M O R E ,   S E E . . .

■ Hosea 11:1–11 (p. 831)

■ Ephesians 6:1–4 (p. 1225)

■ Luke 15:11–32 (p. 1035)

¹⁴David touched the hearts of all the people of Judah at once. They sent a message to the king that said, "Return with all your men." ¹⁵Then the king returned as far as the Jordan River. The men of Judah came to Gilgal to meet him and to bring him across the Jordan.

¹⁶Shimei son of Gera, a Benjaminite who lived in Bahurim, hurried down with the men of Judah to meet King David. ¹⁷With Shimei came a thousand Benjaminites. Ziba, the servant from Saul's family, also came, bringing his fifteen sons and twenty servants with him. They all hurried to the Jordan River to meet the king. ¹⁸The people went across the Jordan to help bring the king's family back to Judah and to do whatever the king wanted. As the king was crossing the river, Shimei son of Gera came to him and bowed face-down on the ground in front of the king. ¹⁹He said to the king, "My master, don't hold me guilty. Don't remember the wrong I did when you left Jerusalem! Don't hold it against me. ²⁰I know I have sinned. That is why I am the first person from Joseph's family to come down and meet you today, my master and king!"

²¹But Abishai son of Zeruiah said, "Shimei should die because he cursed you, the Lord's appointed king!"

²²David said, "This does not concern you, sons of Zeruiah! Today you're against me! No one will be put to death in Israel today. Today I know I am king over Israel!" ²³Then the king promised Shimei, "You won't die."

²⁴Mephibosheth, Saul's grandson, also went down to meet King David. Mephibosheth had not cared for his feet, cut his beard, or washed his clothes from the time the king had left Jerusalem until he returned safely. ²⁵When Mephibosheth came from Jerusalem to meet the king, the king asked him, "Mephibosheth, why didn't you go with me?"

²⁶He answered, "My master, my servant Ziba tricked me! I said to Ziba, 'I am crippled, so saddle a donkey. Then I will ride it so I can go with the king.' ²⁷But he lied about me to you. You, my master and king, are like an angel from God. Do what you think is good. ²⁸You could have killed all my grandfather's family. Instead, you put me with those people who eat at your own table. So I don't have a right to ask anything more from the king!"

²⁹The king said to him, "Don't say anything more. I have decided that you and Ziba will divide the land."

³⁰Mephibosheth said to the king, "Let Ziba take all the land now that my master the king has arrived safely home."

³¹Barzillai of Gilead came down from Rogelim to cross the Jordan River with the king. ³²Barzillai was a very old man, eighty years old. He had taken care of the king when David was staying at Mahanaim, because Barzillai was a very rich man. ³³David said to Barzillai, "Cross the river with me. Come with me to Jerusalem, and I will take care of you."

³⁴But Barzillai answered the king, "Do you know how old I am? Do you think I can go with you to Jerusalem? ³⁵I am eighty years old! I am too old to taste what I eat or drink. I am too old to hear the voices of men and women singers. Why should you be bothered with me? ³⁶I am not worthy of a reward from you, but I will cross the Jordan River with you. ³⁷Then let me go back so I may die in my own city near the grave of my father and mother. But here is Kimham, your servant. Let him go with you, my master and king. Do with him whatever you want."

³⁸The king answered, "Kimham will go with me. I will do for him anything you wish, and I will do anything for you that you wish." ³⁹The king kissed Barzillai and blessed him. Then Barzillai returned home, and the king and all the people crossed the Jordan.

⁴⁰When the king crossed over to Gilgal, Kimham went with him. All the troops of Judah and half the troops of Israel led David across the river.

⁴¹Soon all the Israelites came to the king and said to him, "Why did our relatives, the people of Judah, steal you away? Why did they bring you and your family across the Jordan River with your men?"

⁴²All the people of Judah answered the Israelites, "We did this because the king is our close relative. Why are you angry about it? We have not eaten food at the king's expense or taken anything for ourselves!"

⁴³The Israelites answered the people of Judah, "We have ten tribes in the kingdom, so we have more right to David than you do! But you ignored us! We were the first ones to talk about bringing our king back!"

But the people of Judah spoke even more unkindly than the people of Israel.

Sheba Leads Israel Away from David

20 It happened that a troublemaker named Sheba son of Bicri from the tribe*ᵈ* of Benjamin was there. He blew the trumpet and said:

"We have no share in David!
We have no part in the son of Jesse!
People of Israel, let's go home!"

²So all the Israelites left David and followed Sheba son of Bicri. But the people of Judah stayed with their king all the way from the Jordan River to Jerusalem.

³David came back to his palace in Jerusalem. He had left ten of his slave women*ᵈ* there to take care of the palace. Now he put them in a locked house. He gave them food, but he did not have

sexual relations with them. So they lived like widows until they died.

[4]The king said to Amasa, "Tell the men of Judah to meet with me in three days, and you must also be here." [5]So Amasa went to call the men of Judah together, but he took more time than the king had said.

[6]David said to Abishai, "Sheba son of Bicri is more dangerous to us than Absalom was. Take my men and chase him before he finds walled cities and escapes from us." [7]So Joab's men, the Kerethites and the Pelethites,[n] and all the soldiers went with Abishai. They went out from Jerusalem to chase Sheba son of Bicri.

[8]When Joab and the army came to the great rock at Gibeon, Amasa came out to meet them. Joab was wearing his uniform, and at his waist he wore a belt that held his sword in its case. As Joab stepped forward, his sword fell out of its case. [9]Joab asked Amasa, "Brother, is everything all right with you?" Then with his right hand he took Amasa by the beard to kiss him. [10]Amasa was not watching the sword in Joab's hand. So Joab pushed the sword into Amasa's stomach, causing Amasa's insides to spill onto the ground. Joab did not have to stab Amasa again; he was already dead. Then Joab and his brother Abishai continued to chase Sheba son of Bicri.

[11]One of Joab's young men stood by Amasa's body and said, "Everyone who is for Joab and David should follow Joab!" [12]Amasa lay in the middle of the road, covered with his own blood. When the young man saw that everyone was stopping to look at the body, he dragged it from the road, laid it in a field, and put a cloth over it. [13]After Amasa's body was taken off the road, all the men followed Joab to chase Sheba son of Bicri.

[14]Sheba went through all the tribes of Israel to Abel Beth Maacah. All the Berites also came together and followed him. [15]So Joab and his men came to Abel Beth Maacah and surrounded it. They piled dirt up against the city wall, and they began hacking at the walls to bring them down.

[16]But a wise woman shouted out from the city, "Listen! Listen! Tell Joab to come here. I want to talk to him!"

[17]So Joab came near her. She asked him, "Are you Joab?"

He answered, "Yes, I am."

Then she said, "Listen to what I say."

Joab said, "I'm listening."

[18]Then the woman said, "In the past people would say, 'Ask for advice at Abel,' and the problem would be solved. [19]I am one of the peaceful, loyal people of Israel. You are trying to destroy an important city of Israel. Why must you destroy what belongs to the LORD?"

[20]Joab answered, "I would prefer not to destroy or ruin anything! [21]That is not what I want. But there is a man here from the mountains of Ephraim, who is named Sheba son of Bicri. He has turned against King David. If you bring him to me, I will leave the city alone."

The woman said to Joab, "His head will be thrown over the wall to you."

[22]Then the woman spoke very wisely to all the people of the city. They cut off the head of Sheba son of Bicri and threw it over the wall to Joab. So he blew the trumpet, and the army left the city. Every man returned home, and Joab went back to the king in Jerusalem.

[23]Joab was commander of all the army of Israel. Benaiah son of Jehoiada led the Kerethites and Pelethites. [24]Adoniram was in charge of the men who were forced to do hard work. Jehoshaphat son of Ahilud was the recorder. [25]Sheva was the royal secretary. Zadok and Abiathar were the priests, [26]and Ira the Jairite was David's priest.

The Gibeonites Punish Saul's Family

21 [1]During the time David was king, there was a shortage of food that lasted for three years. So David prayed to the LORD.

The LORD answered, "Saul and his family of murderers are the reason for this shortage, because he killed the Gibeonites." [2](Now the Gibeonites were not Israelites; they were a group of Amorites who were left alive. The Israelites had promised not to hurt the Gibeonites, but Saul had tried to kill them, because he was eager to help the people of Israel and Judah.)

King David called the Gibeonites together and spoke to them. [3]He asked, "What can I do for you? How can I make up for the harm done so you can bless the LORD's people?"

[4]The Gibeonites said to David, "We cannot demand silver or gold from Saul or his family. And we don't have the right to kill anyone in Israel."

Then David asked, "What do you want me to do for you?"

[5]The Gibeonites said, "Saul made plans against us and tried to destroy all our people who are left in the land of Israel. [6]So bring seven of his sons to us. Then we will kill them and hang them on stakes in the presence of the LORD at Gibeah, the hometown of Saul, the LORD's chosen king."

The king said, "I will give them to you." [7]But the king protected Mephibosheth, the son of Jonathan, the son of Saul, because of the promise he had made to Jonathan in the LORD's name. [8]The

---

Kerethites and Pelethites   These were probably special units of the army that were responsible for the king's safety, a kind of palace guard.

king did take Armoni and Mephibosheth,[n] sons of Rizpah and Saul. (Rizpah was the daughter of Aiah.) And the king took the five sons of Saul's daughter Merab. (Adriel son of Barzillai the Meholathite was the father of Merab's five sons.) [9]David gave these seven sons to the Gibeonites. Then the Gibeonites killed them and hung them on stakes on a hill in the presence of the LORD. All seven sons died together. They were put to death during the first days of the harvest season at the beginning of barley harvest.

[10]Aiah's daughter Rizpah took the rough cloth that was worn to show sadness and put it on a rock for herself. She stayed there from the beginning of the harvest until the rain fell on her sons' bodies. During the day she did not let the birds of the sky touch her sons' bodies, and during the night she did not let the wild animals touch them.

[11]People told David what Aiah's daughter Rizpah, Saul's slave woman,[d] was doing. [12]Then David took the bones of Saul and Jonathan from the men of Jabesh Gilead. (The Philistines had hung the bodies of Saul and Jonathan in the public square of Beth Shan after they had killed Saul at Gilboa. Later the men of Jabesh Gilead had secretly taken them from there.) [13]David brought the bones of Saul and his son Jonathan from Gilead. Then the people gathered the bodies of Saul's seven sons who were hanged on stakes. [14]The people buried the bones of Saul and his son Jonathan at Zela in Benjamin in the tomb of Saul's father Kish. The people did everything the king commanded.

Then God answered the prayers for the land.

Wars with the Philistines

[15]Again there was war between the Philistines and Israel. David and his men went out to fight the Philistines, but David became tired. [16]Ishbi-Benob, one of the sons of Rapha,[d] had a bronze spearhead weighing about seven and one-half pounds and a new sword. He planned to kill David, [17]but Abishai son of Zeruiah killed the Philistine and saved David's life.

Then David's men made a promise to him, saying, "Never again will you go out with us to battle. If you were killed, Israel would lose its greatest leader."

[18]Later, at Gob, there was another battle with the Philistines. Sibbecai the Hushathite killed Saph, another one of the sons of Rapha.

[19]*Later, there was another battle at Gob with the Philistines. Elhanan son of Jaare-Oregim from Bethlehem killed Goliath*[n] *from Gath. His spear was as large as a weaver's rod.*

[20]At Gath another battle took place. A huge man was there; he had six fingers on each hand and six toes on each foot — twenty-four fingers and toes in all. This man also was one of the sons

> ✺ **SIDELIGHT:** One person in the Bible was not only big, but he had six toes on each foot and six fingers on each hand (2 Samuel 21:20). The extras probably came in handy in math class when counting numbers above twenty.

of Rapha. [21]When he challenged Israel, Jonathan son of Shimeah, David's brother, killed him. [22]These four sons of Rapha from Gath were killed by David and his men.

David's Song of Praise

22 David sang this song to the LORD when the LORD saved him from Saul and all his other enemies. [2]He said:

"The LORD is my rock, my protection, my Savior.
[3]My God is my rock.
   I can run to him for safety.
He is my shield and my saving strength,
   my defender and my place of safety.
The LORD saves me from those who want
   to harm me.
[4]I will call to the LORD, who is worthy of
   praise,
   and I will be saved from my enemies.

[5]"The waves of death came around me;
   the deadly rivers overwhelmed me.
[6]The ropes of death wrapped around me.
   The traps of death were before me.
[7]In my trouble I called to the LORD;
   I cried out to my God.
From his temple he heard my voice;
   my call for help reached his ears.

[8]"The earth trembled and shook.
   The foundations of heaven began to shake.
They trembled because the LORD was
   angry.
[9]Smoke came out of his nose,
   and burning fire came out of his mouth.
   Burning coals went before him.
[10]He tore open the sky and came down
   with dark clouds under his feet.
[11]*He rode a creature with wings and flew.*
   He raced on the wings of the wind.
[12]He made darkness his shelter,
   surrounded by fog and clouds.

Mephibosheth This is not Jonathan's son but another man with the same name.
Goliath In 1 Chronicles 20:5 he is called Lahmi brother of Goliath.

13Out of the brightness of his presence
  came flashes of lightning.
14The LORD thundered from heaven;
  the Most High raised his voice.
15He shot his arrows and scattered his enemies.
  His bolts of lightning confused them with
  fear.
16The LORD spoke strongly.
  The wind blew from his nose.
  Then the valleys of the sea appeared,
  and the foundations of the earth were seen.

17"The LORD reached down from above and
  took me;
  he pulled me from the deep water.
18He saved me from my powerful enemies,
  from those who hated me, because they
  were too strong for me.
19They attacked me at my time of trouble,
  but the LORD supported me.
20He took me to a safe place.
  Because he delights in me, he saved me.

21"The LORD spared me because I did what
  was right.
  Because I have not done evil, he has
  rewarded me.
22I have followed the ways of the LORD;
  I have not done evil by turning from my
  God.
23I remember all his laws
  and have not broken his rules.
24I am innocent before him;
  I have kept myself from doing evil.
25The LORD rewarded me because I did what
  was right,
  because I did what the LORD said was right.

26"LORD, you are loyal to those who are loyal,
  and you are good to those who are good.
27You are pure to those who are pure,
  but you are against those who are evil.
28You save the humble,
  but you bring down those who are proud.
29LORD, you give light to my lamp.
  The LORD brightens the darkness around
  me.
30With your help I can attack an army.
  With God's help I can jump over a wall.

31"The ways of God are without fault;
  the LORD's words are pure.
  He is a shield to those who trust him.
32Who is God? Only the LORD.
  Who is the Rock?d Only our God.
33God is my protection.
  He makes my way free from fault.
34He makes me like a deer that does not
  stumble;
  he helps me stand on the steep mountains.
35He trains my hands for battle

  so my arms can bend a bronze bow.
36You protect me with your saving shield.
  You have stooped to make me great.
37You give me a better way to live,
  so I ive as you want me to.
38I chased my enemies and destroyed them.
  I did not quit till they were destroyed.
39I destroyed and crushed them
  so they couldn't rise up again.
  They fell beneath my feet.
40You gave me strength in battle.
  You made my enemies bow before me.
41You made my enemies turn back,
  and destroyed those who hated me.
42They called for help,
  but no one came to save them.
  They called to the LORD,
  but he did not answer them.
43I beat my enemies into pieces,
  like dust on the ground.
  I poured them out and walked on them
  like mud in the streets.

44"You saved me when my people attacked me.
  You kept me as the leader of nations.
  People I never knew serve me.
45Foreigners obey me.
  As soon as they hear me, they obey me.
46They all become afraid
  and tremble in their hiding places.
47"The LORD lives!
  May my Rock be praised!
  Praise God, the Rock, who saves me!
48God gives me victory over my enemies
  and brings people under my rule.
49He frees me from my enemies.

"You set me over those who hate me.
  You saved me from cruel men.
50So I will praise you, LORD, among the
  nations.
  I will sing praises to your name.
51The LORD gives great victories to his king.
  He is loyal to his appointed king,
  to David and his descendantsd forever."

David's Last Words

23 These are the last words of David.
  This is the message of David son of
  Jesse.
  The man made great by the Most High God
  speaks.
  He is the appointed king of the God of Jacob;
  he is the sweet singer of Israel:

2"The LORD's Spiritd spoke through me,
  and his word was on my tongue.
3The God of Israel spoke;
  the Rockd of Israel said to me:

'Whoever rules fairly over people,
who rules with respect for God,
[4]is like the morning light at dawn,
like a morning without clouds.
He is like sunshine after a rain
that makes the grass sprout from the
ground.'

[5]"This is how God has cared for my family.
God made a lasting agreement with me,
right and sure in every way.
He will accomplish my salvation
and satisfy all my desires.

[6]"But all evil people will be thrown away like
thorns
that cannot be held in a hand.
[7]No one can touch them
except with a tool of iron or wood.
They will be thrown in the fire and burned
where they lie."

David's Army

[8]These are the names of David's warriors:
Josheb-Basshebeth, the Tahkemonite, was head of the Three.[n] He killed eight hundred men at one time.

[9]Next was Eleazar son of Dodai the Ahohite. Eleazar was one of the three soldiers who were with David when they challenged the Philistines. The Philistines were gathered for battle, and the Israelites drew back. [10]But Eleazar stayed where he was and fought the Philistines until he was so tired his hand stuck to his sword. The LORD gave a great victory for the Israelites that day. The troops came back after Eleazar had won the battle, but only to take weapons and armor from the enemy.

[11]Next there was Shammah son of Agee the Hararite. The Philistines came together to fight in a vegetable field. Israel's troops ran away from the Philistines, [12]but Shammah stood in the middle of the field and fought for it and killed the Philistines. And the LORD gave a great victory.

[13]Once, three of the Thirty, David's chief soldiers, came down to him at the cave of Adullam during harvest. The Philistine army had camped in the Valley of Rephaim. [14]At that time David

---

Three These were David's most powerful soldiers. See 1 Chronicles 11:11.

GOVERNMENT

Respected Leaders

Judge Bill Logue is a rare judge. He's respected by prosecuting attorneys and defense lawyers, by police officers and convicted felons alike. He knows the law, and his decisions are rarely overturned by a higher court.

Even with his back-breaking load of court cases, Judge Logue finds time each week to help underprivileged kids who have criminal records. He tutors them and helps them start constructive lives so he won't have to sentence them again.

Recently Judge Logue was stricken with throat cancer. Cards, letters, flowers and presents swamped the hospital. People from around the state wrote of their sympathy and prayers.

But nothing touched the judge as much as the fistful of letters he received from prisoners—prisoners he had sent to jail. "You helped me get my life back on track," they told him. "I'll never forget you. Thanks."

Judge Logue shows how God's followers can make a difference for good in government. When King David was dying, he celebrated how God had worked in his life for good. Read about it in **2 Samuel 23:1–7**.

■ How do verses 3 and 4 describe Judge Logue and other Christians like him who serve in government?

■ Do leaders today have the same opportunities to serve God as they did in David's time? How can you support and encourage them to do good?

CONSIDER . . .

■ praying that God will guide your country's leaders as they make important decisions.

✒ writing a letter to government officials to express your opinion on an important issue they are confronting.

FOR MORE, SEE . . .

■ Psalm 2:1–11 (p. 483)
■ Proverbs 16:10–15 (p. 581)
■ 1 Timothy 2:1–3 (p. 1256)

was in the stronghold,*d* and some of the Philistines were in Bethlehem.

15David had a strong desire for some water. He said, "Oh, I wish someone would get me water from the well near the city gate of Bethlehem!" 16So the three warriors broke through the Philistine army and took water from the well near the city gate of Bethlehem. Then they brought it to David, but he refused to drink it. He poured it out before the LORD, 17saying, "May the LORD keep me from drinking this water! It would be like drinking the blood of the men who risked their lives!" So David refused to drink it. These were the brave things that the three warriors did.

18Abishai, brother of Joab son of Zeruiah, was captain of the Three. Abishai fought three hundred soldiers with his spear and killed them. He became as famous as the Three 19and was more honored than the Three. He became their commander even though he was not one of them.

20Benaiah son of Jehoiada was a brave fighter from Kabzeel who did mighty things. He killed two of the best warriors from Moab. He also went down into a pit and killed a lion on a snowy day. 21Benaiah killed a large Egyptian who had a spear in his hand. Benaiah had a club, but he grabbed the spear from the Egyptian's hand and killed him with his own spear. 22These were the things Benaiah son of Jehoiada did. He was as famous as the Three. 23He received more honor than the Thirty, but he did not become a member of the Three. David made him leader of his bodyguards.

The Thirty Chief Soldiers

24The following men were among the Thirty:

Asahel brother of Joab;
Elhanan son of Dodo from Bethlehem;
25Shammah the Harodite;
Elika the Harodite;
26Helez the Paltite;
Ira son of Ikkesh from Tekoa;
27Abiezer the Anathothite;
Mebunnai the Hushathite;
28Zalmon the Ahohite;
Maharai the Netophathite;
29Heled son of Baanah the Netophathite;
Ithai son of Ribai from Gibeah in Benjamin;
30Benaiah the Pirathonite;
Hiddai from the ravines of Gaash;
31Abi-Albon the Arbathite;
Azmaveth the Barhumite;
32Eliahba the Shaalbonite;
the sons of Jashen;

Jonathan 33son of Shammah the Hararite;
Ahiam son of Sharar the Hararite;
34Eliphelet son of Ahasbai the Maacathite;
Eliam son of Ahithophel the Gilonite;
35Hezro the Carmelite;
Paarai the Arbite;
36Igal son of Nathan of Zobah;
the son of Hagri;
37Zelek the Ammonite;
Naharai the Beerothite, who carried the armor of Joab son of Zeruiah;
38Ira the Ithrite;
Gareb the Ithrite,
39and Uriah the Hittite.

There were thirty-seven in all.

David Counts His Army

24 The LORD was angry with Israel again, and he caused David to turn against the Israelites. He said, "Go, count the people of Israel and Judah."

2So King David said to Joab, the commander of the army, "Go through all the tribes*d* of Israel, from Dan to Beersheba,*n* and count the people. Then I will know how many there are."

3But Joab said to the king, "May the LORD your God give you a hundred times more people, and may my master the king live to see this happen. Why do you want to do this?"

4But the king commanded Joab and the commanders of the army, so they left the king to count the Israelites.

5After crossing the Jordan River, they camped near Aroer on the south side of the city in the ravine. They went through Gad and on to Jazer. 6Then they went to Gilead and the land of Tahtim Hodshi and to Dan Jaan and around to Sidon. 7They went to the strong, walled city of Tyre and to all the cities of the Hivites and Canaanites. Finally, they went to southern Judah, to Beersheba. 8After nine months and twenty days, they had gone through all the land. Then they came back to Jerusalem.

9Joab gave the list of the people to the king. There were eight hundred thousand men in Israel who could use the sword and five hundred thousand men in Judah.

10David felt ashamed after he had counted the people. He said to the LORD, "I have sinned greatly by what I have done. LORD, I beg you to forgive me, your servant, because I have been very foolish."

11When David got up in the morning, the LORD

Dan to Beersheba Dan was the city farthest north in Israel, and Beersheba was the city farthest south. So this means all the people of Israel.

spoke his word to Gad, who was a prophet[d] and David's seer.[d] [12]The LORD told Gad, "Go and tell David, 'This is what the LORD says: I offer you three choices. Choose one of them and I will do it to you.' "

[13]So Gad went to David and said to him, "Should three years of hunger come to you and your land? Or should your enemies chase you for three months? Or should there be three days of disease in your land? Think about it. Then decide which of these things I should tell the LORD who sent me."

[14]David said to Gad, "I am in great trouble. Let the LORD punish us, because the LORD is very merciful. Don't let my punishment come from human beings!"

[15]So the LORD sent a terrible disease on Israel. It began in the morning and continued until the chosen time to stop. From Dan to Beersheba seventy thousand people died. [16]When the angel raised his arm toward Jerusalem to destroy it, the LORD felt very sorry about the terrible things that had happened. He said to the angel who was destroying the people, "That is enough! Put down your arm!" The angel of the LORD was then by the threshing[d] floor of Araunah the Jebusite.

[17]When David saw the angel that killed the people, he said to the LORD, "I am the one who sinned and did wrong. These people only fol-lowed me like sheep. They did nothing wrong. Please punish me and my family."

[18]That day Gad came to David and said, "Go and build an altar to the LORD on the threshing floor of Araunah the Jebusite." [19]So David did what Gad told him to do, just as the LORD commanded.

[20]Araunah looked and saw the king and his servants coming to him. So he went out and bowed facedown on the ground before the king. [21]He said, "Why has my master the king come to me?"

David answered, "To buy the threshing floor from you so I can build an altar to the LORD. Then the terrible disease will stop."

[22]Araunah said to David, "My master and king, you may take anything you want for a sacrifice. Here are some oxen for the whole burnt offering and the threshing boards and the yokes[d] for the wood. [23]My king, I give everything to you." Araunah also said to the king, "May the LORD your God be pleased with you."

[24]But the king answered Araunah, "No, I will pay you for the land. I won't offer to the LORD my God burnt offerings that cost me nothing."

So David bought the threshing floor and the oxen for one and one-fourth pounds of silver. [25]He built an altar to the LORD there and offered whole burnt offerings and fellowship offerings. Then the LORD answered his prayer for the country, and the disease in Israel stopped.

1 KINGS

Why Read This Book:

- See how God blesses those who follow him (1 Kings 1—11).
- Recognize how faithfulness can help all parts of life (1 Kings 12—16).
- Discover what can happen to a country that turns away from God (1 Kings 17—22).

Behind the Scenes:

Imagine how history books would be different if they evaluated presidents and other world leaders based on whether they followed God. Their political, economic and military feats would only be important when they showed obedience to God. Which presidents, kings and leaders would be judged good? Which ones would be judged bad?

That's the kind of history we find in 1 and 2 Kings, which were one continuous book in the original text. The story begins with King David turning over the country to his son Solomon. Solomon inherited a strong and united nation, exploding with energy. Through political and economic maneuvering, Solomon made the country—and himself—rich and powerful.

Solomon seemed headed for greatness. But in the end, the writer says,

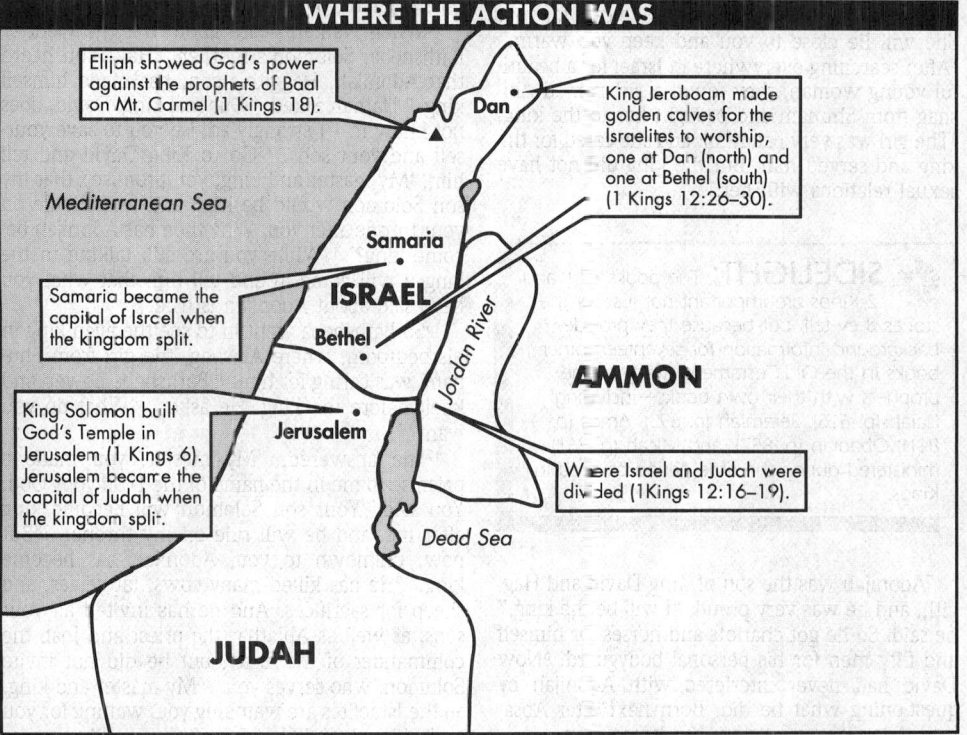

WHERE THE ACTION WAS

Elijah showed God's power against the prophets of Baal on Mt. Carmel (1 Kings 18).

King Jeroboam made golden calves for the Israelites to worship, one at Dan (north) and one at Bethel (south) (1 Kings 12:26–30).

Mediterranean Sea

Samaria became the capital of Israel when the kingdom split.

King Solomon built God's Temple in Jerusalem (1 Kings 6). Jerusalem became the capital of Judah when the kingdom split.

Where Israel and Judah were divided (1 Kings 12:16–19).

Dan

Samaria

ISRAEL

Bethel

Jordan River

AMMON

Jerusalem

Dead Sea

JUDAH

WHEN THE ACTION WAS

	Joshua led the Israelites into Canaan	The kingdom was split between Israel and Judah	Jerusalem fell to the Babylonians	Jesus was born
2000BC	**1500BC**	**1000BC**	**500BC**	**BC/AD**
	The Israelites escaped from Egypt	Solomon was Israel's king	The Northern Kingdom (Israel) fell to Assyria	

**Behind the
Scenes** (cont.):

"Solomon did what the Lord said was wrong and did not follow the Lord completely as his father David had done" (1 Kings 11:6, p. 315).

What happened? He began seeing the wealth and power as his own, not as gifts from God. Though he spent seven years building a beautiful temple for God (1 Kings 6), he spent thirteen years building his own palace. Soon his power and prestige became more important than following God. He began worshiping false gods.

The kingdom started to crumble. First it split between Israel (in the north) and Judah (in the south). Then one king after another didn't follow God, and the people suffered as a result. When kings did follow God, the people prospered. But by the end of 2 Kings, both kingdoms have been overthrown and the people taken away as slaves.

In telling about the rise and fall of good and bad kings, 1 Kings has a consistent theme: The longterm welfare of Israel and its people depended on obedience to God. And these stories remind us that—no matter what other forces are at play— God still works to accomplish his will in the world.

Adonijah Tries to Become King

1 At this time King David was very old, and although his servants covered him with blankets, he could not keep warm. ²They said to him, "We will look for a young woman to care for you. She will lie close to you and keep you warm." ³After searching everywhere in Israel for a beautiful young woman, they found a girl named Abishag from Shunam and brought her to the king. ⁴The girl was very beautiful, and she cared for the king and served him. But the king did not have sexual relations with her.

> ✳ **SIDELIGHT:** The books of 1 and 2 Kings are important not just for the stories they tell, but because they provide background information for seventeen other books in the Old Testament. Many of the prophets with their own books—including Isaiah (p. 616), Jeremiah (p. 690), Amos (p. 841), Obadiah (p. 852), and Micah (p. 861)— ministered during the time period covered in Kings.

⁵Adonijah was the son of King David and Haggith, and he was very proud. "I will be the king," he said. So he got chariots and horses for himself and fifty men for his personal bodyguard. ⁶Now David had never interfered with Adonijah by questioning what he did. Born next after Absalom, Adonijah was a very handsome man.

⁷Adonijah spoke with Joab son of Zeruiah and Abiathar the priest, and they agreed to help him. ⁸But Zadok the priest, Benaiah son of Jehoiada, Nathan the prophet,ᵈ Shimei, Rei, and King David's special guard did not join Adonijah.

⁹Then Adonijah killed some sheep, cows, and fat calves for sacrifices at the Stone of Zoheleth near the spring of Rogel. He invited all his brothers, the other sons of King David, to come, as well as all the men of Judah. ¹⁰But Adonijah did not invite Nathan the prophet, Benaiah, his father's special guard, or his brother Solomon.

¹¹When Nathan heard about this, he went to Bathsheba, Solomon's mother. "Have you heard that Adonijah, Haggith's son, has made himself king?" Nathan asked. "Our real king, David, does not know it. ¹²I strongly advise you to save yourself and your sons. ¹³Go to King David and tell him, 'My master and king, you promised that my son Solomon would be king and would rule on your throne after you. Why then has Adonijah become king?' ¹⁴While you are still talking to the king, I will come in and tell him that what you have said about Adonijah is true."

¹⁵So Bathsheba went in to see the aged king in his bedroom, where Abishag, the girl from Shunam, was caring for him. ¹⁶Bathsheba bowed and knelt before the king. He asked, "What do you want?"

¹⁷She answered, "My master, you made a promise to me in the name of the Lᴏʀᴅ your God. You said, 'Your son Solomon will become king after me, and he will rule on my throne.' ¹⁸But now, unknown to you, Adonijah has become king. ¹⁹He has killed many cows, fat calves, and sheep for sacrifices. And he has invited all your sons, as well as Abiathar the priest and Joab the commander of the army, but he did not invite Solomon, who serves you. ²⁰My master and king, all the Israelites are watching you, waiting for you to decide who will be king after you. ²¹As soon as you die, Solomon and I will be treated as criminals."

²²While Bathsheba was still talking with the king, Nathan the prophet arrived. ²³The servants told the king, "Nathan the prophet is here." So Nathan went to the king and bowed facedown on the ground before him.

24Nathan said, "My master and king, have you said that Adonijah will be the king after you and that he will rule on your throne? 25Today he has sacrificed many cows, fat calves, and sheep, and he has invited all your other sons, the commanders of the army, and Abiathar the priest. Right now they are eating and drinking with him. They are saying, 'Long live King Adonijah!' 26But he did not invite me, your own servant, or Zadok the priest, or Benaiah son of Jehoiada, or your son Solomon. 27Did you do this? Since we are your servants, why didn't you tell us who should be king after you?"

David Makes Solomon King

28Then the king said, "Tell Bathsheba to come in!" So she came in and stood before the king. 29Then the king made this promise, "The Lord has saved me from all trouble. As surely as he lives, 30I will do today what I have promised you in the name of the Lord, the God of Israel. I promised that your son Solomon would be king after me and rule on my throne in my place."

31Then Bathsheba bowed facedown on the ground and knelt before the king and said, "Long live my master King David!"

32Then King David said, "Tell Zadok the priest, Nathan the prophet,d and Benaiah son of Jehoiada to come in." When they came before the king, 33he said to them, "Take my servants with you and put my son Solomon on my own mule. Take him down to the spring called Gihon. 34There Zadok the priest and Nathan the prophet should pour olive oil on him and make him king over Israel. Blow the trumpet and shout, 'Long live King Solomon!' 35Then come back up here with him. He will sit on my throne and rule in my place, because he is the one I have chosen to be the ruler over Israel and Judah."

36Benaiah son of Jehoiada answered the king, "Amen! This is what the Lord, the God of my master, has declared! 37The Lord has always helped you, our king. May he also help Solomon and make King Solomon's throne an even greater throne than yours."

38So Zadok the priest, Nathan the prophet, and Benaiah son of Jehoiada left with the Kerethites and Pelethites.a They put Solomon on King David's mule and took him to the spring called Gihon. 39Zadok the priest took the container of olive oil from the Holy Tentd and poured the oil on Solomon's head to show he was the king. Then they blew the trumpet, and all the people shouted, "Long live King Solomon!" 40All the peo-

ple followed Solomon into the city. Playing flutes and shouting for joy, they made so much noise the ground shook.

41At this time Adonijah and all the guests with him were finishing their meal. When he heard the sound from the trumpet, Joab asked, "What does all that noise from the city mean?"

42While Joab was speaking, Jonathan son of Abiathar the priest arrived. Adonijah said, "Come in! You are an important man, so you must be bringing good news."

43But Jonathan answered, "No! Our master King David has made Solomon the new king. 44King David sent Zadok the priest, Nathan the prophet, Benaiah son of Jehoiada, and all the king's bodyguards with him, and they have put Solomon on the king's own mule. 45Then Zadok the priest and Nathan the prophet poured olive oil on Solomon at Gihon to make him king. After that they went into the city, shouting with joy. Now the whole city is excited, and that is the noise you hear. 46Solomon has now become the king. 47All the king's officers have come to tell King David that he has done a good thing. They are saying, 'May your God make Solomon even more famous than you and an even greater king than you.' " Jonathan continued, "And King David bowed down on his bed to worship God, 48saying, 'Bless the Lord, the God of Israel. Today he has made one of my sons the king and allowed me to see it.' "

49Then all of Adonijah's guests were afraid, and they left quickly and scattered. 50Adonijah was also afraid of Solomon, so he went and took hold of the corners of the altar.n 51Then someone told Solomon, "Adonijah is afraid of you, so he is at the altar, holding on to its corners. He says, 'Tell King Solomon to promise me today that he will not kill me.' "

52So Solomon answered, "Adonijah must show that he is a man of honor. If he does that, I promise he will not lose even a single hair from his head. But if he does anything wrong, he will die." 53Then King Solomon sent some men to get Adonijah. When he was brought from the altar, he came before King Solomon and bowed down. Solomon told him, "Go home."

The Death of David

2 Since it was almost time for David to die, he gave his son Solomon his last commands. 2David said, "My time to die is near. Be a good and strong leader. 3Obey the Lord your God. Follow him by obeying his demands, his commands,

---

Kerethites and Pelethites   These were probably special units of the army that were responsible for the king's safety, a kind of palace guard.

corners of the altar   If a person were innocent of a crime, he could run into the Holy Place where the altar was. If he held on to the corners of the altar, which looked like horns, he would be safe.

his laws, and his rules that are written in the teachings of Moses. If you do these things, you will be successful in all you do and wherever you go. ⁴And if you obey the LORD, he will keep the promise he made to me. He said: 'If your descendants*d* live as I tell them and have complete faith in me, a man from your family will always be king over the people of Israel.'

⁵"Also, you remember what Joab son of Zeruiah did to me. He killed the two commanders of Israel's armies: Abner son of Ner and Amasa son of Jether. He did this as if he and they were at war, although it was a time of peace. He put their blood on the belt around his waist and on his sandals on his feet. ⁶Punish him in the way you think is wisest, but do not let him die peacefully of old age.

⁷"Be kind to the children of Barzillai of Gilead, and allow them to eat at your table. They welcomed me when I ran away from your brother Absalom.

⁸"And remember, Shimei son of Gera, the Benjaminite, is here with you. He cursed me the day I went to Mahanaim. But when he came down to meet me at the Jordan River, I promised him before the LORD, 'Shimei, I will not kill you.' ⁹But

---

LEADERSHIP

The Measure of a Leader

During his lifetime, General Douglas MacArthur personified the best of America to millions of people. His determination and courage during the tumultuous years of World War II established him as a leading figure in world history. And his fairness as a military ruler of a conquered Japan made him a role model for all those who stood for justice and generosity.

But among all the general's great leadership achievements during those years, there was one achievement that towered above them all.

Douglas MacArthur had a son.

MacArthur spent the last years of his life in New England with his wife, Jean, and his son, Arthur. During that time, this great historical figure wrote a prayer that revealed what he believed was the true measure of leadership:

"Build me a son, O Lord, who will be strong enough to know when he is weak, and brave enough to face himself when he is afraid; one who will be proud and unbending in honest defeat, and humble and gentle in victory.

"Build me a son whose wishes will not take the place of deeds; a son who will know Thee . . . and that to know himself is the foundation stone of knowledge.

"Build me a son whose heart will be clear, whose goal will be high, a son who will master himself before he seeks to master other men; one who will reach into the future, yet never forget the past.

"And after all these things are his, add, I pray, enough of a sense of humor, so that he may always be serious, yet never take himself too seriously. Give him humility so that he may always remember the simplicity of true greatness, the open mind of true wisdom and the meekness of true strength.

"Then I, his father, will dare to whisper, 'I have not lived in vain.' "

For all his contributions to world events, General MacArthur believed the true measure of his leadership was in the raising of his son. King David was also a great leader who had dreams for his son's future. Read about David's wishes for Solomon in **1 Kings 2:1–12**.

■ What leadership traits did MacArthur and King David both show in their final days?

■ According to this passage, what responsibilities do we have to our leaders?

CONSIDER . . .

■ memorizing 1 Timothy 4:12.
■ *asking your father or youth pastor how you can become a better Christian leader at church and at school.*

FOR MORE, SEE . . .

■ Psalm 132:11–18 (p. 558)
■ John 16:4–15 (p. 1086)

■ 2 Timothy 4:1–5 (p. 1266)

you should not leave him unpunished. You are a wise man, and you will know what to do to him, but you must be sure he is killed."

¹⁰Then David died and was buried with his ancestors in Jerusalem. ¹¹He had ruled over Israel forty years — seven years in Hebron and thirty-three years in Jerusalem.

Solomon Takes Control as King

¹²Solomon became king after David, his father, and he was in firm control of his kingdom.

¹³At this time Adonijah son of Haggith went to Bathsheba, Solomon's mother. "Do you come in peace?" Bathsheba asked.

"Yes. This is a peaceful visit," Adonijah answered. ¹⁴"I have something to say to you."

"You may speak," she said.

¹⁵"You remember that at one time the kingdom was mine," Adonijah said. "All the people of Israel recognized me as their king, but things have changed. Now my brother is the king, because the LORD chose him. ¹⁶Now I have one thing to ask you; please do not refuse me."

Bathsheba answered, "What do you want?"

¹⁷"I know King Solomon will do anything you ask him," Adonijah continued. "Please ask him to give me Abishag the Shunammite to be my wife."

¹⁸"Very well," she answered. "I will speak to the king for you."

¹⁹So Bathsheba went to King Solomon to speak to him for Adonijah. When Solomon saw her, he stood up to meet her, then bowed down, and sat on the throne. He told some servants to bring another throne for his mother. Then she sat down at his right side.

²⁰Bathsheba said, "I have one small thing to ask you. Please do not refuse me."

"Ask, mother," the king answered. "I will not refuse you."

²¹So she said, "Allow Abishag the Shunammite to marry your brother Adonijah."

²²King Solomon answered his mother, "Why do you ask me to give him Abishag? Why don't you also ask for him to become the king since he is my older brother? Abiathar the priest and Joab son of Zeruiah would support him!"

²³Then King Solomon swore by the name of the LORD, saying, "May God punish me terribly if this doesn't cost Adonijah his life! ²⁴By the LORD who has given me the throne that belonged to my father David and who has kept his promise and given the kingdom to me and my people, Adonijah will die today!" ²⁵Then King Solomon gave orders to Benaiah son of Jehoiada, and he went and killed Adonijah.

²⁶King Solomon said to Abiathar the priest, "I

should kill you too, but I will allow you to go back to your fields in Anathoth. I will not kill you at this time, because you helped carry the Ark^d of the Lord GOD while marching with my father David. And I know you shared in all the hard times with him." ²⁷Then Solomon removed Abiathar from being the LORD's priest. This happened as the LORD had said it would, when he was speaking in Shiloh about the priest Eli and his descendants.^d

²⁸When Joab heard about what had happened, he was afraid. He had supported Adonijah but not Absalom. So Joab ran to the Tent^d of the LORD and took hold of the corners of the altar.ⁿ ²⁹Someone told King Solomon that Joab had run to the Tent of the LORD and was beside the altar. Then Solomon ordered Benaiah to go and kill him.

³⁰Benaiah went into the Tent of the LORD and said to Joab, "The king says, 'Come out!' "

But Joab answered, "No, I will die here."

So Benaiah went back to the king and told him what Joab had said. ³¹Then the king ordered Benaiah, "Do as he says! Kill him there and bury him. Then my family and I will be free of the guilt of Joab, who has killed innocent people. ³²Without my father knowing it, he killed two men who were much better than he was — Abner son of Ner, the commander of Israel's army, and Amasa son of Jether, the commander of Judah's army. So the LORD will pay him back for those deaths. ³³Joab and his family will be forever guilty for their deaths, but there will be peace from the LORD for David, his descendants, his family, and his throne forever."

³⁴So Benaiah son of Jehoiada killed Joab, and he was buried near his home in the desert. ³⁵The king then made Benaiah son of Jehoiada commander of the army in Joab's place. He also made Zadok the new high priest in Abiathar's place.

³⁶Next the king sent for Shimei. Solomon said to him, "Build a house for yourself in Jerusalem and live there. Don't leave the city. ³⁷The very day you leave and cross the Kidron Valley, someone will kill you, and it will be your own fault."

³⁸So Shimei answered the king, "I agree with what you say. I will do what you say, my master and king." So Shimei lived in Jerusalem for a long time.

³⁹But three years later two of Shimei's slaves ran away to Achish king of Gath, who was the son of Maacah. Shimei heard that his slaves were in Gath, ⁴⁰so he put his saddle on his donkey and went to Achish at Gath to find them. Then he brought them back from Gath.

⁴¹Someone told Solomon that Shimei had gone from Jerusalem to Gath and had returned. ⁴²So

---

corners of the altar If a person were innocent of a crime, he could run into the Holy Place where the altar was. If he held on to the corners of the altar, which looked like horns, he would be safe.

Solomon sent for Shimei and said, "I made you promise in the name of the LORD not to leave Jerusalem. I warned you if you went out anywhere you would die, and you agreed to what I said. ⁴³Why did you break your promise to the LORD and disobey my command?" ⁴⁴The king also said, "You know the many wrong things you did to my father David, so now the LORD will punish you for those wrongs. ⁴⁵But the LORD will bless me and make the rule of David safe before the LORD forever."

⁴⁶Then the king ordered Benaiah to kill Shimei, and he did. Now Solomon was in full control of his kingdom.

Solomon Asks for Wisdom

3 Solomon made an agreement with the king of Egypt by marrying his daughter and bringing her to Jerusalem. At this time Solomon was still building his palace and the Temple*d* of the LORD, as well as a wall around Jerusalem. ²The Temple for the worship of the LORD had not yet been finished, so people were still sacrificing at altars in many places of worship. ³Solomon showed he loved the LORD by following the commands his father David had given him, except many other places of worship were still used to offer sacrifices and to burn incense.*d*

⁴King Solomon went to Gibeon to offer a sacrifice, because it was the most important place of worship. He offered a thousand burnt offerings on that altar. ⁵While he was at Gibeon, the LORD appeared to him in a dream during the night. God said, "Ask for whatever you want me to give you."

⁶Solomon answered, "You were very kind to your servant, my father David. He obeyed you, and he was honest and lived right. You showed great kindness to him when you allowed his son to be king after him. ⁷LORD my God, now you have made me, your servant, king in my father's place. But I am like a little child; I don't know how to do what must be done. ⁸I, your servant, am here among your chosen people, and there are too many of them to count. ⁹I ask that you give me an obedient heart so I can rule the people in the right way and will know the difference between right and wrong. Otherwise, it is impossible to rule this great people of yours."

¹⁰The Lord was pleased that Solomon had asked this. ¹¹So God said to him, "You did not ask for a long life, or riches for yourself, or the death *of your enemies. Since you asked* for wisdom to make the right decisions, ¹²I will do what you asked. I will give you wisdom and understanding that is greater than anyone has had in the past or will have in the future. ¹³I will also give you what you did not ask for: riches and honor. During your life no other king will be as great as you. ¹⁴If

you follow me and obey my laws and commands, as your father David did, I will also give you a long life."

¹⁵After Solomon woke up from the dream, he went to Jerusalem. He stood before the Ark*d* of the Agreement with the Lord, where he made burnt offerings and fellowship offerings. After that, he gave a feast for all his leaders and officers.

Solomon Makes a Wise Decision

¹⁶One day two women who were prostitutes*d* came to Solomon. As they stood before him, ¹⁷one of the women said, "My master, this woman and I live in the same house. I gave birth to a baby while she was there with me. ¹⁸Three days later this woman also gave birth to a baby. No one else was in the house with us; it was just the two of us. ¹⁹One night this woman rolled over on her baby, and he died. ²⁰So she took my son from my bed during the night while I was asleep, and she carried him to her bed. Then she put the dead baby in my bed. ²¹The next morning when I got up to feed my baby, I saw that he was dead! When I looked at him more closely, I realized he was not my son."

²²"No!" the other woman cried. "The living baby is my son, and the dead baby is yours!"

But the first woman said, "No! The dead baby is yours, and the living one is mine!" So the two women argued before the king.

²³Then King Solomon said, "One of you says, 'My son is alive and your son is dead.' Then the other one says, 'No! Your son is dead and my son is alive.' "

²⁴The king sent his servants to get a sword. When they brought it to him, ²⁵he said, "Cut the living baby into two pieces, and give each woman half."

> ✺ SIDELIGHT: Many people have half-brothers or half-sisters these days because of stepfamilies. But Solomon suggested another approach: settling a dispute by cutting the baby in half and giving each mother a half (1 Kings 3:16–28). Scholars have found twenty-two similar stories of wisdom in other cultures of ancient times.

²⁶The real mother of the living child was full of love for her son. So she said to the king, "Please, my master, don't kill him! Give the baby to her!"

But the other woman said, "Neither of us will have him. Cut him into two pieces!"

²⁷Then King Solomon said, "Don't kill him. Give the baby to the first woman, because she is the real mother."

²³When the people of Israel heard about King Solomon's decision, they respected him very much. They saw he had wisdom from God to make the right decisions.

Solomon's Officers

4 King Solomon ruled over all Israel. ²These are the names of his leading officers:

Azariah son of Zadok was the priest;

³Elihoreph and Ahijah, sons of Shisha, recorded what happened in the courts;

Jehoshaphat son of Ahilud recorded the history of the people;

⁴Benaiah son of Jehoiada was commander of the army;

Zadok and Abiathar were priests;

⁵Azariah son of Nathan was in charge of the district governors;

Zabud son of Nathan was a priest and adviser to the king;

⁶Ahishar was responsible for everything in the palace;

Adoniram son of Abda was in charge of the labor force.

⁷Solomon placed twelve governors over the districts of Israel, who gathered food from their districts for the king and his family. Each governor was responsible for bringing food to the king one month of each year. ⁸These are the names of the twelve governors:

Ben-Hur was governor of the mountain country of Ephraim.

⁹Ben-Deker was governor of Makaz, Shaalbim, Beth Shemesh, and Elon Bethhanan.

¹⁰Ben-Hesed was governor of Arubboth, Socoh, and all the land of Hepher.

¹¹Ben-Abinadab was governor of Naphoth Dor. (He was married to Taphath, Solomon's daughter.)

¹²Baana son of Ahilud was governor of Taanach, Megiddo, and all of Beth Shan next to Zarethan. This was below Jezreel from Beth Shan to Abel Meholah across from Jokmeam.

¹³Ben-Geber was governor of Ramoth in Gilead. (He was governor of all the towns of Jair in Gilead. Jair was the son of Manasseh. Ben-Geber was also over the district of Argob in Bashan, which had sixty large, walled cities with bronze bars on their gates.)

¹⁴Ahinadab son of Iddo was governor of Mahanaim.

¹⁵Ahimaaz was governor of Naphtali. (He was married to Basemath, Solomon's daughter.)

¹⁶Baana son of Hushai was governor of Asher and Aloth.

¹⁷Jehoshaphat son of Paruah was governor of Issachar.

¹⁸Shimei son of Ela was governor of Benjamin.

¹⁹Geber son of Uri was governor of Gilead. Gilead had been the country of Sihon king of the Amorites and Og king of Bashan. But Geber was the only governor over this district.

Solomon's Kingdom

²⁰There were as many people in Judah and Israel as grains of sand on the seashore. The people ate, drank, and were happy. ²¹Solomon ruled over all the kingdoms from the Euphrates River to the land of the Philistines, as far as the border of Egypt. These countries brought Solomon the payments he demanded, and they were under his control all his life.

²²Solomon needed much food each day to feed himself and all the people who ate at his table: one hundred ninety-five bushels of fine flour, three hundred ninety bushels of grain, ²³ten cows that were fed on good grain, twenty cows that were raised in the fields, one hundred sheep, three kinds of deer, and fattened birds.

> ☀ **SIDELIGHT:** Each day it took thirty cattle (plus lots of other food) to feed all the people at Solomon's table (1 Kings 4:23). That would be about 120,000 Big Macs a day.

²⁴Solomon controlled all the countries west of the Euphrates River — the land from Tiphsah to Gaza. And he had peace on all sides of his kingdom. ²⁵During Solomon's life Judah and Israel, from Dan to Beersheba,ⁿ also lived in peace; all of his people were able to sit under their own fig trees and grapevines.

²⁶Solomon had four thousand stalls for his chariot horses and twelve thousand horses. ²⁷Each month one of the district governors gave King Solomon all the food he needed — enough for every person who ate at the king's table. The governors made sure he had everything he needed. ²⁸They also brought enough barley and straw for Solomon's chariot and work horses; each person brought this grain to the right place.

Solomon's Wisdom

²⁹God gave Solomon great wisdom so he could understand many things. His wisdom was as hard to measure as the grains of sand on the seashore. ³⁰His wisdom was greater than any wisdom of the

---

Dan to Beersheba Dan was the city farthest north in Israel, and Beersheba was the city farthest south. So this means all the people of Israel.

East, or any wisdom in Egypt. [31]He was wiser than anyone on earth. He was even wiser than Ethan the Ezrahite, as well as Heman, Calcol, and Darda — the three sons of Mahol. King Solomon became famous in all the surrounding countries. [32]During his life he spoke three thousand wise sayings and also wrote one thousand five songs. [33]He taught about many kinds of plants — everything from the great cedar trees of Lebanon to the weeds that grow out of the walls. He also taught about animals, birds, crawling things, and fish. [34]People from all nations came to listen to King Solomon's wisdom. The kings of all nations sent them to him, because they had heard of Solomon's wisdom.

Preparing to Build the Temple

5 Hiram, the king of Tyre, had always been David's friend. When Hiram heard that Solomon had been made king in David's place, he sent his messengers to Solomon. [2]Solomon sent this message back to King Hiram: [3]"You remember my father David had to fight many wars with the countries around him, so he was never able to build a temple for worshiping the LORD his God. David was waiting until the LORD allowed him to defeat all his enemies. [4]But now the LORD my God has given me peace on all sides of my country. I have no enemies now, and no danger threatens my people.

[5]"The LORD promised my father David, 'I will make your son king after you, and he will build a temple for worshiping me.' Now, I plan to build that temple for worshiping the LORD my God. [6]So send your men to cut down cedar trees for me from Lebanon. My servants will work with yours, and I will pay them whatever wages you decide. We don't have anyone who can cut down trees as well as the people of Sidon."

[7]When Hiram heard what Solomon asked, he was very happy. He said, "Praise the LORD today! He has given David a wise son to rule over this great nation!" [8]Then Hiram sent back this message to Solomon: "I received the message you sent, and I will give you all the cedar and pine trees you want. [9]My servants will bring them down from Lebanon to the sea. There I will tie them together and float them along the shore to the place you choose. Then I will separate the logs there, and you can take them away. In return it is my wish that you give food to all those who live with me." [10]So Hiram gave Solomon as much cedar and pine as he wanted. [11]And Solomon gave Hiram about one hundred twenty-five thousand bushels of wheat each year to feed the people who lived with him. Solomon also gave him about one hundred fifteen thousand gallons of pure olive oil every year.

[12]The LORD gave Solomon wisdom as he had

promised. And there was peace between Hiram and Solomon; these two kings made a treaty between themselves.

[13]King Solomon forced thirty thousand men of Israel to help in this work. [14]He sent a group of ten thousand men each month to Lebanon. Each group worked in Lebanon one month, then went home for two months. A man named Adoniram was in charge. [15]Solomon forced eighty thousand men to work in the hill country, cutting stone, and he had seventy thousand men to carry the stones. [16]There were also thirty-three hundred men who directed the workers. [17]King Solomon commanded them to cut large blocks of fine stone to be used for the foundation of the Temple.[d] [18]Solomon's and Hiram's builders and the men from Byblos carved the stones and prepared the stones and the logs for building the Temple.

Solomon Builds the Temple

6 Solomon began to build the Temple[d] four hundred eighty years after the people of Israel had left Egypt. This was during the fourth year of King Solomon's rule over Israel. It was the second month, the month of Ziv.

[2]The Temple was ninety feet long, thirty feet wide, and forty-five feet high. [3]The porch in front of the main room of the Temple was fifteen feet deep and thirty feet wide. This room ran along the front of the Temple itself. Its width was equal to that of the Temple. [4]The Temple also had windows that opened and closed. [5]Solomon also built some side rooms against the walls of the main room and the inner room of the Temple. He built rooms all around. [6]The rooms on the bottom floor were seven and one-half feet wide. Those on the middle floor were nine feet wide, and the rooms above them were ten and one-half feet wide. The Temple wall that formed the side of each room was thinner than the wall in the room below. These rooms were pushed against the Temple wall, but they did not have their main beams built into this wall.

[7]The stones were prepared at the same place where they were cut from the ground. Since these

stones were the only ones used to build the Temple, there was no noise of hammers, axes, or any other iron tools at the Temple.

> **SIDELIGHT:** Solomon's Temple was one of the largest structures in Israel at the time, but it wasn't very big by today's standards. It only had about twenty-seven hundred square feet of floor space—no larger than many good-sized homes today (1 Kings 6:2–38).

[8] The entrance to the lower rooms beside the Temple was on the south side. From there, stairs went up to the second-floor rooms. And from there, stairs went on to the third-floor rooms. [9] Solomon put a roof made from beams and cedar boards on the Temple. So he finished building the Temple [10] as well as the bottom floor that was beside the Temple. This bottom floor was seven and one-half feet high and was attached to the Temple by cedar beams.

[11] The LORD said to Solomon: [12] "If you obey all my laws and commands, I will do for you what I promised your father David. [13] I will live among the Israelites in this Temple, and I will never leave my people Israel."

[14] So Solomon finished building the Temple. [15] The inside walls were covered from floor to ceiling with cedar boards. The floor was made from pine boards. [16] A room thirty feet long was built in the back part of the Temple. This room, called the Most Holy Place, was separated from the rest of the Temple by cedar boards which reached from floor to ceiling. [17] The main room, the one in front of the Most Holy Place, was sixty feet long. [18] Everything inside the Temple was covered with cedar, which was carved with pictures of flowers and plants. A person could not see the stones of the wall, only the cedar.

[19] Solomon prepared the inner room at the back of the Temple to keep the Ark[d] of the Agreement with the LORD. [20] This inner room was thirty feet long, thirty feet wide, and thirty feet high. He covered this room with pure gold, and he also covered the altar of cedar. [21] He covered the inside of the Temple with pure gold, placing gold chains across the front of the inner room, which was also covered with gold. [22] So all the inside of the Temple, as well as the altar of the Most Holy Place, was covered with gold.

[23] Solomon made two creatures from olive wood and placed them in the Most Holy Place. Each creature was fifteen feet tall [24] and had two wings. Each wing was seven and one-half feet long, so it was fifteen feet from the end of one

wing to the end of the other. [25] The creatures were the same size and shape; [26] each was fifteen feet tall. [27] These creatures were put beside each other in the Most Holy Place with their wings spread out. One creature's wing touched one wall, and the other creature's wing touched the other wall with their wings touching each other in the middle of the room. [28] These two creatures were covered with gold.

[29] All the walls around the Temple were carved with pictures of creatures with wings, as well as palm trees and flowers. This was true for both the main room and the inner room. [30] The floors of both rooms were covered with gold.

> **SIDELIGHT:** Building Solomon's Temple would ruin any church's budget (1 Kings 6:21). According to one estimate, just the gold overlay in the Temple might be worth almost thirty-six billion dollars on today's gold market.

[31] Doors made from olive wood were placed at the entrance to the Most Holy Place. These doors had five-sided frames. [32] Creatures with wings, as well as palm trees and flowers, were also carved on the two olive wood doors that were covered with gold. The creatures and the palm trees on the doors were covered with gold as well. [33] At the entrance to the main room there was a square door frame made of olive wood. [34] Two doors were made from pine. Each door had two parts so the doors folded. [35] The doors were covered with pictures of creatures with wings, as well as palm trees and flowers. All of the carvings were covered with gold, which was evenly spread over them.

[36] The inner courtyard was enclosed by walls, which were made of three rows of cut stones and one row of cedar boards.

[37] Work began on the Temple in Ziv, the second month, during the fourth year Solomon was king over Israel. [38] The Temple was finished during the eleventh year he was king, in the eighth month, the month of Bul. It was built exactly as it was planned. Solomon had spent seven years building it.

Solomon's Palace

7 King Solomon also built a palace for himself; it took him thirteen years to finish it. [2] Built of cedars from the Forest of Lebanon, it was one hundred fifty feet long, seventy-five feet wide, and forty-five feet high. It had four rows of cedar columns which supported the cedar beams. [3] There were forty-five beams on the roof, with fifteen

beams in each row, and the ceiling was covered with cedar above the beams. [4]Windows were placed in three rows facing each other. [5]All the doors were square, and the three doors at each end faced each other.

[6]Solomon also built the porch that had pillars. This porch was seventy-five feet long and forty-five feet wide. Along the front of the porch was a roof supported by pillars.

[7]Solomon also built a throne room where he judged people, called the Hall of Justice. This room was covered with cedar from the floor to the ceiling. [8]The palace where Solomon lived was built like the Hall of Justice, and it was behind this hall. Solomon also built the same kind of palace for his wife, who was the daughter of the king of Egypt.

[9]All these buildings were made with blocks of fine stone. First they were carefully cut. Then they were trimmed with a saw in the front and back. These fine stones went from the foundations of the buildings to the top of the walls. Even the courtyard was made with blocks of stone. [10]The foundations were made with large blocks of fine stone, some as long as fifteen feet. Others were twelve feet long. [11]On top of these foundation stones were other blocks of fine stone and cedar beams. [12]The palace courtyard, the courtyard inside the Temple,[d] and the porch of the Temple were surrounded by walls. All of these walls had three rows of stone blocks and one row of cedar beams.

The Temple Is Completed Inside

[13]King Solomon sent to Tyre and had Huram brought to him. [14]Huram's mother was a widow from the tribe[d] of Naphtali. His father was from Tyre and had been skilled in making things from bronze. Huram was also very skilled and experienced in bronze work. So he came to King Solomon and did all the bronze work.

[15]He made two bronze pillars, each one twenty-seven feet tall and eighteen feet around. [16]He also made two bronze capitals[d] that were seven and one-half feet tall, and he put them on top of the pillars. [17]Then he made a net of seven chains for each capital, which covered the capitals on top of the two pillars. [18]He made two rows of bronze pomegranates[d] to go on the nets. These covered the capitals at the top of the pillars. [19]The capitals on top of the pillars in the porch were *shaped like lilies, and they were six feet tall.* [20]The capitals were on top of both pillars, above the bowl-shaped section and next to the nets. At that place there were two hundred pomegranates in rows all around the capitals. [21]Huram put these two bronze pillars at the porch of the Temple.[d] He named the south pillar He Establishes and the north pillar In Him Is Strength. [22]The capitals on

top of the pillars were shaped like lilies. So the work on the pillars was finished.

[23]Then Huram made from bronze a large round bowl, which was called the Sea. It was forty-five feet around, fifteen feet across, and seven and one-half feet deep. [24]Around the outer edge of the bowl was a rim. Under this rim were two rows of bronze plants which surrounded the bowl. There were ten plants every eighteen inches, and these plants were made in one piece with the bowl. [25]The bowl rested on the backs of twelve bronze bulls that faced outward from the center of the bowl. Three bulls faced north, three faced west, three faced south, and three faced east. [26]The sides of the bowl were four inches thick, and it held about eleven thousand gallons. The rim of the bowl was like the rim of a cup or like a lily blossom.

[27]Then Huram made ten bronze stands, each one six feet long, six feet wide, and four and one-half feet high. [28]The stands were made from square sides, which were put on frames. [29]On the sides were bronze lions, bulls, and creatures with wings. On the frames above and below the lions and bulls were designs of flowers hammered into the bronze. [30]Each stand had four bronze wheels with bronze axles. At the corners there were bronze supports for a large bowl, and the supports had designs of flowers. [31]There was a frame on top of the bowls, eighteen inches high above the bowls. The opening of the bowl was round, twenty-seven inches deep. Designs were carved into the bronze on the frame, which was square, not round. [32]The four wheels, placed under the frame, were twenty-seven inches high. The axles between the wheels were made as one piece with the stand. [33]The wheels were like a chariot's wheels. Everything on the wheels — the axles, rims, spokes, and hubs — were made of bronze.

[34]The four supports were on the four corners of each stand. They were made as one piece with the stand. [35]A strip of bronze around the top of each stand was nine inches deep. It was also made as one piece with the stand. [36]The sides of the stand and the frames were covered with carvings of creatures with wings, as well as lions, palm trees, and flowers. [37]This is the way Huram made the ten stands. The bronze for each stand was melted and poured into a mold, so all the stands were the same size and shape.

[38]*Huram also made ten bronze bowls, one* bowl for each of the ten stands. Each bowl was six feet across and could hold about two hundred thirty gallons. [39]Huram put five stands on the south side of the Temple and five on the north side. He put the large bowl in the southeast corner of the Temple. [40]Huram also made bowls, shovels, and small bowls.

So Huram finished all his work for King Solomon on the Temple of the LORD:

⁴¹two pillars;

two large bowls for the capitals on top of the pillars;

two nets to cover the two large bowls for the capitals on top of the pillars;

⁴²four hundred pomegranates for the two nets (there were two rows of pomegranates for each net covering the bowls for the capitals on top of the pillars);

⁴³ten stands with a bowl on each stand;

⁴⁴the large bowl with twelve bulls under it;

⁴⁵the pots, shovels, small bowls, and all the utensils for the Temple of the LORD.

Huram made everything King Solomon wanted from polished bronze. ⁴⁶The king had these things poured into clay molds that were made in the plain of the Jordan River between Succoth and Zarethan. ⁴⁷Solomon never weighed the bronze used to make these things, because there was too much to weigh. So the total weight of all the bronze was never known.

⁴⁸Solomon also made all the items for the Temple of the LORD:

the golden altar;

the golden table which held the bread that shows God's people are in his presence;

⁴⁹the lampstands of pure gold (five on the right side and five on the left side in front of the Most Holy Place);

the flowers, lamps, and tongs of gold;

⁵⁰the pure gold bowls, wick trimmers, small bowls, pans, and dishes used to carry coals;

the gold hinges for the doors of the Most Holy Place and the main room of the Temple.

⁵¹Finally the work King Solomon did for the Temple of the LORD was finished. Solomon brought in everything his father David had set apart for the Temple — silver, gold, and other articles. He put everything in the treasuries of the Temple of the LORD.

The Ark Is Brought into the Temple

8 King Solomon called for the older leaders of Israel, the heads of the tribes,ᵈ and the leaders of the families to come to him in Jerusalem. He wanted them to bring the Arkᵈ of the Agreement with the LORD from the older part of the city. ²So all the Israelites came together with King Solomon during the festival in the month of Ethanim, the seventh month.

³When all the older leaders of Israel arrived, the priests lifted up the Ark. ⁴They carried the Ark of the LORD, the Meeting Tent,ᵈ and the holy utensils; the priests and the Levites brought them up. ⁵King Solomon and all the Israelites gathered before the Ark and sacrificed so many sheep and cattle no one could count them all. ⁶Then the priests put the Ark of the Agreement with the LORD in its place inside the Most Holy Place in the Temple,ᶜ under the wings of the golden creatures. ⁷The wings of these creatures were spread out over the place for the Ark, covering it and its carrying poles. ⁸The carrying poles were so long that anyone standing in the Holy Place in front of the Most Holy Place could see the ends of the poles, but no one could see them from outside the Holy Place. The poles are still there today. ⁹The only things inside the Ark were two stone tabletsⁿ that Moses had put in the Ark at Mount Sinai. That was where the LORD made his agreement with the Israelites after they came out of Egypt.

¹⁰When the priests left the Holy Place, a cloud filled the Temple of the LORD. ¹¹The priests could not continue their work, because the Temple was filled with the glory of the LORD.

Solomon Speaks to the People

¹²Then Solomon said, "The LORD said he would live in a dark cloud. ¹³LORD, I have truly built a wonderful Templeᵈ for you — a place for you to live forever."

¹⁴While all the Israelites were standing there, King Solomon turned to them and blessed them. ¹⁵Then he said, "Praise the LORD, the God of Israel. He has done what he promised to my father David. The LORD said, ¹⁶'Since the time I brought my people Israel out of Egypt, I have not chosen a city in any tribeᵈ of Israel where a temple will be built for me. But I have chosen David to lead my people Israel.'

¹⁷"My father David wanted to build a temple for the LORD, the God of Israel. ¹⁸But the LORD said to my father David, 'It was good that you wanted to build a temple for me. ¹⁹But you are not the one to build it. Your son, who comes from your own body, is the one who will build my temple.'

²⁰"Now the LORD has kept his promise. I am the king now in place of David my father. Now I rule Israel as the LORD promised, and I have built the Temple for the LORD, the God of Israel. ²¹I have made a place there for the Ark, in which is the Agreement the LORD made with our ancestors when he brought them out of Egypt."

---

stone tablets They were the two tablets on which God wrote the Ten Commandments.

Solomon's Prayer

[22]Then Solomon stood facing the LORD's altar, and all the Israelites were standing behind him. He spread out his hands toward the sky [23]and said:

"LORD, God of Israel, there is no god like you in heaven above or on earth below. You keep your agreement of love with your servants who truly follow you. [24]You have kept the promise you made to your servant David, my father. You spoke it with your own mouth and finished it with your hands today. [25]Now LORD, God of Israel, keep the promise you made to your servant David, my father. You said, 'If your sons are careful to obey me as you have obeyed me, there will always be someone from your family ruling Israel.' [26]Now, God of Israel, please continue to keep that promise you made to your servant David, my father.

[27]"But, God, can you really live here on the earth? The sky and the highest place in heaven cannot contain you. Surely this house which I have built cannot contain you. [28]But please listen to my prayer and my request, because I am your servant. LORD my God, hear this prayer your servant prays to you today. [29]Night and day please watch over this Temple[d] where you have said, 'I will be worshiped there.' Hear the prayer I pray facing this Temple. [30]Hear my prayers and the prayers of your people Israel when we pray facing

---

PRAYER

Praying About Real Life

When seventeen-year-old Shelley Lundberg and her mom talked about Shelley's ex-boyfriend one evening, the conversation quickly escalated into a fight.

"LeRoy seems like such a nice young man, Shelley," Mom complained. "I really think you handled the whole thing wrong."

"I didn't ask your opinion, Mom. Thanks anyway." Shelley's words dripped with sarcasm. She felt as if she were about to explode.

"Now, just wait a minute, Miss. . . ."

"No, you wait a minute, Mother," Shelley's voice was strained with anger. "I'm tired of your constant meddling. I can't even put my shoes on without getting your approval first. I have a life, Mother. Why don't you let me live it by myself?"

Then Shelley stormed away. She didn't know or care what her mother thought—she just wanted to leave.

Shelley ended up at a nearby park for the next few hours. There, she discovered how much prayer can help. At first, she was angry with God. "Why does this stuff happen to me?" she asked God. "I shouldn't be having so much trouble with this! I'm a Christian." Shelley felt she should be able to deal with her family problems.

Soon, Shelley asked God to help her calm down. She sang a few worship songs, and she started feeling better. Once she had calmed down, Shelley asked God to help her understand her mom's side of the argument.

Shelley got home late, but in the morning, she and her mother apologized. That evening, they talked about how they could have dealt with their feelings better. And Shelley decided to talk to LeRoy. "It'll give me the chance to let him know I still care," she told her mom, smiling.

Shelley's relationship with her mom isn't perfect, but she knows she can turn to God in prayer for real-life issues like this one.

King Solomon also turned to God and prayed about real-life issues. Read his prayer after God's Temple was built in **1 Kings 8:22–30**.

■ What elements do Shelley's prayer and King Solomon's prayer have in common? What's different?

■ How does King Solomon's prayer compare with the kind of prayers you usually pray?

C O N S I D E R . . . .

■ listing all the concerns of your life on paper and then talking to God about each one.
■ offering to pray with others who are going through rough times.

F O R   M O R E ,   S E E . . .

■ 2 Samuel 22:1–51 (p. 296)
■ Luke 1:46–55 (p. 1001)

■ John 17:20–26 (p. 1089)

this place. Hear from your home in heaven, and when you hear, forgive us.

³¹"If someone wrongs another person, he will be brought to the altar in this Temple. If he swears an oath that he is not guilty, ³²then hear in heaven. Judge the case, punish the guilty, but declare that the innocent person is not guilty.

³³"When your people, the Israelites, sin against you, their enemies will defeat them. But if they come back to you and praise you and pray to you in this Temple, ³⁴then hear them in heaven. Forgive the sins of your people Israel, and bring them back to the land you gave to their ancestors.

³⁵"When they sin against you, you will stop the rain from falling on their land. Then they will pray, facing this place and praising you; they will stop sinning when you make them suffer. ³⁶When this happens, please hear their prayer in heaven, and forgive the sins of your servants, the Israelites. Teach them to do what is right. Then please send rain to this land you have given particularly to them.

³⁷"At times the land will become so dry that no food will grow, or a great sickness will spread among the people. Sometimes all the crops will be destroyed by locusts*d* or grasshoppers. Your people will be attacked in their cities by their enemy or will become sick. ³⁸When any of these things happen, the people will become truly sorry. If your people spread their hands in prayer toward this Temple, ³⁹then hear their prayers from your home in heaven. Forgive and treat each person as he should be treated because you know what is in a person's heart. Only you know what is in everyone's heart. ⁴⁰Then your people will respect you as long as they live in this land you gave to our ancestors.

⁴¹⁻⁴²"People who are not Israelites, foreigners from other lands, will hear about your greatness and power. They will come from far away to pray at this Temple. ⁴³Then hear from your home in heaven, and do whatever they ask you. Then people everywhere will know you and respect you, just as your people in Israel do. Then everyone will know I built this Temple as a place to worship you.

⁴⁴"When your people go out to fight their enemies along some road on which you send them, your people will pray to you, facing the city which you have chosen and the Temple I have built for you. ⁴⁵Then hear in heaven their prayers, and do what is right.

⁴⁶"Everyone sins, so your people will also sin against you. You will become angry with them and hand them over to their enemies. Their enemies will capture them and take them away to their countries far or near. ⁴⁷Your people will be sorry for their sins when they are held as prisoners in another country. They will be sorry and pray to

you in the land where they are held as prisoners, saying, 'We have sinned. We have done wrong and acted wickedly.' ⁴⁸They will truly turn back to you in the land of their enemies. They will pray to you, facing this land you gave their ancestors, this city you have chosen, and the Temple I have built for you. ⁴⁹Then hear their prayers from your home in heaven, and do what is right. ⁵⁰Forgive your people of all their sins and for turning against you. Make those who have captured them show them mercy. ⁵¹Remember, they are your special people. You brought them out of Egypt, as if you were pulling them out of a blazing furnace.

⁵²"Give your attention to my prayers and the prayers of your people Israel. Listen to them anytime they ask you for help. ⁵³You chose them from all the nations on earth to be your very own people. This is what you promised through Moses your servant when you brought our ancestors out of Egypt Lord Gᴏᴅ."

⁵⁴Solomon prayed this prayer to the Lᴏʀᴅ, kneeling in front of the altar with his arms raised toward heaven. When he finished praying, he got up. ⁵⁵Then, in a loud voice, he stood and blessed all the people of Israel, saying: ⁵⁶"Praise the Lᴏʀᴅ! He promised he would give rest to his people Israel, and he has given us rest. The Lᴏʀᴅ has kept all the good promises he gave through his servant Moses. ⁵⁷May the Lᴏʀᴅ our God be with us as he was with our ancestors. May he never leave us, ⁵⁸and may he turn us to himself so we will follow him. Let us obey all the laws and commands he gave our ancestors. ⁵⁹May the Lᴏʀᴅ our God remember this prayer day and night and do what is right for his servant and his people Israel day by day. ⁶⁰Then all the people of the world will know the Lᴏʀᴅ is the only true God. ⁶¹You must fully obey the Lᴏʀᴅ our God and follow all his laws and commands. Continue to obey in the future as you do now."

Sacrifices Are Offered

⁶²Then King Solomon and all Israel with him offered sacrifices to the Lᴏʀᴅ. ⁶³Solomon killed twenty-two thousand cattle and one hundred twenty thousand sheep as fellowship offerings. So the king and all the people gave the Temple*d* to the Lᴏʀᴅ

⁶⁴On that day King Solomon made holy the middle part of the courtyard which is in front of the Temple of the Lᴏʀᴅ. There he offered whole burnt offerings, grain offerings, and the fat of the fellowship offerings. He offered them in the courtyard, because the bronze altar before the Lᴏʀᴅ was too small to hold all the burnt offerings, the grain offerings, and the fat of the fellowship offerings.

⁶⁵Solomon and all the Israelites celebrated the other festival that came at that time. People came

from as far away as Lebo Hamath and the brook of Egypt. A great many people celebrated before the LORD for seven days, then seven more days, for a total of fourteen days. ⁶⁶On the following day Solomon sent the people home. They blessed the king as they went, happy because of all the good things the LORD had done for his servant David and his people Israel.

The Lord Appears to Solomon Again

9 Solomon finished building the Temple*d* of the LORD and his royal palace and everything he wanted to build. ²Then the LORD appeared to him again just as he had done before, in Gibeon. ³The LORD said to him: "I have heard your prayer and what you have asked me to do. You built this Temple, and I have made it a holy place. I will be worshiped there forever and will watch over it and protect it always.

⁴"But you must serve me as your father David did; he was fair and sincere. You must obey all I have commanded and keep my laws and rules. ⁵If you do, I will make your kingdom strong. This is the promise I made to your father David — that someone from his family would always rule Israel.

⁶"But you and your children must follow me and obey the laws and commands I have given you. You must not serve or worship other gods. ⁷If you do, I will force Israel to leave the land I have given them, and I will leave this Temple that I have made holy. All the nations will make fun of Israel and speak evil about them. ⁸If the Temple is destroyed, everyone who passes by will be shocked. They will make fun of you and ask, 'Why did the LORD do this terrible thing to this land and this Temple?' ⁹People will answer, 'This happened because they left the LORD their God. This was the God who brought their ancestors out of Egypt, but they decided to follow other gods. They worshiped and served those gods, so the LORD brought all this disaster on them.' "

Solomon's Other Achievements

¹⁰By the end of twenty years, King Solomon had built two buildings — the Temple*d* of the LORD and the royal palace. ¹¹At that time King Solomon gave twenty towns in Galilee to Hiram king of Tyre, because Hiram had helped with the buildings. Hiram had given Solomon all the cedar, pine, and gold he wanted. ¹²So Hiram traveled from Tyre to see the towns Solomon had given him, but when he saw them, he was not pleased. ¹³He asked, "What good are these towns you have given me, my brother?" So he named them the Land of Cabul,*n* and they are still called that today. ¹⁴Hiram had sent Solomon about nine thousand pounds of gold.

Cabul This name sounds like the Hebrew word for "worthless."

¹⁵This is the account of the forced labor Solomon used to build the Temple and the palace. He had them fill in the land and build the wall around Jerusalem. He also had them rebuild the cities of Hazor, Megiddo, and Gezer. ¹⁶(In the past the king of Egypt had attacked and captured Gezer. After burning it, he killed the Canaanites who lived there. Then he gave it as a wedding present to his daughter, who married Solomon. ¹⁷So Solomon rebuilt it.) He also built the cities of Lower Beth Horon ¹⁸and Baalath, as well as Tadmor, which is in the desert. ¹⁹King Solomon also built cities for storing grain and supplies and cities for his chariots and horses. He built whatever he wanted in Jerusalem, Lebanon, and everywhere he ruled.

²⁰There were other people in the land who were not Israelites — Amorites, Hittites, Perizzites, Hivites, and Jebusites. ²¹They were descendants*d* of people that the Israelites had not destroyed. Solomon forced them to work for him as slaves, as is still true today. ²²But Solomon did not make slaves of the Israelites. They were his soldiers, government leaders, officers, captains, chariot commanders, and drivers.

²³These were his most important officers over the work. There were five hundred fifty supervisors over the people who did the work on Solomon's projects.

²⁴The daughter of the king of Egypt moved from the old part of Jerusalem to the palace that Solomon had built for her. Then Solomon filled in the surrounding land.

²⁵Three times each year Solomon offered whole burnt offerings and fellowship offerings on the altar he had built for the LORD. He also burned incense*d* before the LORD. So he finished the work on the Temple.

²⁶King Solomon also built ships at Ezion Geber, a town near Elath on the shore of the Red Sea, in the land of Edom. ²⁷Hiram had skilled sailors, so he sent them to serve in these ships with Solomon's men. ²⁸The ships sailed to Ophir and brought back about thirty-two thousand pounds of gold to King Solomon.

The Queen of Sheba Visits Solomon

10 When the queen of Sheba heard about Solomon, she came to test him with hard questions. ²She traveled to Jerusalem with a large group of servants and camels carrying spices, jewels, and much gold. When she came to Solomon, she talked with him about all she had in mind, ³and Solomon answered all her questions. Nothing was too hard for him to explain to her. ⁴The queen of Sheba learned that Solomon was very wise. She saw the palace he had built, ⁵the food on his table, his many officers, the palace servants, and their good clothes. She saw the servants who served him at feasts and the whole burnt offerings he made in the Temple[d] of the LORD. All these things amazed her.

⁶So she said to King Solomon, "What I heard in my own country about your achievements and wisdom is true. ⁷I could not believe it then, but now I have come and seen it with my own eyes. I was not told even half of it! Your wisdom and wealth are much greater than I had heard. ⁸Your men and officers are very lucky, because in always serving you, they are able to hear your wisdom. ⁹Praise the LORD your God, who was pleased to make you king of Israel. The LORD has constant love for Israel, so he made you king to keep justice and to rule fairly."

¹⁰Then she gave the king about nine thousand pounds of gold and many spices and jewels. No one since that time has brought more spices than the queen of Sheba gave to King Solomon.

¹¹(Hiram's ships brought gold from Ophir, as well as much juniper wood and jewels. ¹²Solomon used the juniper wood to build supports for the Temple of the LORD and the palace, and to make harps and lyres[d] for the musicians. Such fine juniper wood has not been brought in or been seen since that time.)

¹³King Solomon gave the queen of Sheba everything she wanted and asked for, in addition to what he had already given her of his wealth. Then she and her servants returned to her own country.

Solomon's Wealth

¹⁴Every year King Solomon received about fifty thousand pounds of gold. ¹⁵Besides that, he also received gold from the traders and merchants, as well as from the kings of Arabia and governors of the land.

¹⁶King Solomon made two hundred large shields of hammered gold, each of which contained about seven and one-half pounds of gold. ¹⁷He also made three hundred smaller shields of hammered gold, each of which contained about four pounds of gold. The king put them in the Palace of the Forest of Lebanon.

¹⁸The king built a large throne of ivory and covered it with fine gold. ¹⁹The throne had six steps on it, and its back was round at the top. There were armrests on both sides of the chair, and each armrest had a lion beside it. ²⁰Twelve lions stood on the six steps, one lion at each end of each step. Nothing like this had ever been made for any other kingdom. ²¹All of Solomon's drinking cups, as well as the dishes in the Palace of the Forest of Lebanon, were made of pure gold. Nothing was made from silver, because silver was not valuable in Solomon's time.

²²King Solomon also had many trading ships at sea, along with Hiram's ships. Every three years the ships returned, bringing back gold, silver, ivory, apes, and baboons.

²³So Solomon had more riches and wisdom than all the other kings on earth. ²⁴People everywhere wanted to see King Solomon and listen to the wisdom God had given him. ²⁵Every year those who came brought gifts of silver and gold, clothes, weapons, spices, horses, and mules.

²⁶Solomon had fourteen hundred chariots and twelve thousand horses. He kept some in special cities for the chariots, and others he kept with him in Jerusalem. ²⁷In Jerusalem Solomon made silver as common as stones and cedar trees as common as the fig trees on the western hills. ²⁸He imported horses from Egypt and Kue. His traders bought them in Kue. ²⁹A chariot from Egypt cost about fifteen pounds of silver, and a horse cost nearly four pounds of silver. Solomon's traders also sold horses and chariots to all the kings of the Hittites and the Arameans.

Solomon's Many Wives

11 King Solomon loved many women who were not from Israel. He loved the daughter of the king of Egypt, as well as women of the Moabites, Ammonites, Edomites, Sidonians, and Hittites. ²The LORD had told the Israelites, "You must not marry people of other nations. If you do, they will cause you to follow their gods." But Solomon fell in love with these women. ³He had seven hundred wives who were from royal families and three hundred slave women[d] who gave birth to his children. His wives caused him to turn away from God. ⁴As Solomon grew old, his wives caused him to follow other gods. He did not follow the LORD completely as his father David had done. ⁵Solomon worshiped Ashtoreth,[d] the goddess of the people of Sidon, and Molech,[d] the hated god of the Ammonites. ⁶So Solomon did what the LORD said was wrong and did not follow the LORD completely as his father David had done.

⁷On a hill east of Jerusalem, Solomon built two places for worship. One was a place to worship Chemosh,[d] the hated god of the Moabites, and the other was a place to worship Molech, the hated god of the Ammonites. ⁸Solomon did the same thing for all his foreign wives so they could burn incense[d] and offer sacrifices to their gods.

⁹The LORD had appeared to Solomon twice, but the king turned away from following the LORD, the God of Israel. The LORD was angry with Solomon, ¹⁰because he had commanded Solomon not to follow other gods. But Solomon did not obey the LORD's command. ¹¹So the LORD said to Solomon, "Because you have chosen to break your agreement with me and have not obeyed my com-

mands, I will tear your kingdom away from you and give it to one of your officers. [12]But I will not take it away while you are alive because of my love for your father David. I will tear it away from your son when he becomes king. [13]I will not tear away all the kingdom from him, but I will leave him one tribe[d] to rule. I will do this because of David, my servant, and because of Jerusalem, the city I have chosen."

Solomon's Enemies

[14]The LORD caused Hadad the Edomite, a member of the family of the king of Edom, to become Solomon's enemy. [15]Earlier, David had defeated Edom. When Joab, the commander of David's army, went into Edom to bury the dead, he killed all the males. [16]Joab and all the Israelites stayed in Edom for six months and killed every male in Edom. [17]At that time Hadad was only a young boy, so he ran away to Egypt with some of his father's officers. [18]They left Midian and went to Paran, where they were joined by other men. Then they all went to Egypt to see the king, who gave Hadad a house, some food, and some land.

[19]The king liked Hadad so much he gave Hadad a wife—the sister of Tahpenes, the king's wife. [20]They had a son named Genubath. Queen Tahpenes brought him up in the royal palace with the king's own children.

[21]While he was in Egypt, Hadad heard that David had died and that Joab, the commander of the army, was dead also. So Hadad said to the king, "Let me go; I will return to my own country."

[22]"Why do you want to go back to your own country?" the king asked. "What haven't I given you here?"

"Nothing," Hadad answered, "but please, let me go."

[23]God also caused another man to be Solomon's enemy—Rezon son of Eliada. Rezon had run away from his master, Hadadezer king of Zobah. [24]After David defeated the army of Zobah, Rezon gathered some men and became the leader of a small army. They went to Damascus and settled there, and Rezon became king of Damascus. [25]Rezon ruled Aram, and he hated Israel. So he was an enemy of Israel all the time Solomon was alive. Both Rezon and Hadad made trouble for Israel.

[26]Jeroboam son of Nebat was one of Solomon's officers. He was an Ephraimite from the town of Zeredah, and he was the son of a widow named Zeruah. Jeroboam turned against the king.

[27]This is the story of how Jeroboam turned against the king. Solomon was filling in the land and repairing the wall of Jerusalem, the city of David, his father. [28]Jeroboam was a capable man, and Solomon saw that this young man was a good worker. So Solomon put him over all the workers from the tribes[d] of Ephraim and Manasseh.

[29]One day as Jeroboam was leaving Jerusalem, Ahijah, the prophet[d] from Shiloh, who was wearing a new coat, met him on the road. The two men were alone out in the country. [30]Ahijah took his new coat and tore it into twelve pieces. [31]Then he said to Jeroboam, "Take ten pieces of this coat for yourself. The LORD, the God of Israel, says: 'I will tear the kingdom away from Solomon and give you ten tribes. [32]But I will allow him to control one tribe. I will do this for the sake of my servant David and for Jerusalem, the city I have chosen from all the tribes of Israel. [33]I will do this because Solomon has stopped following me and has worshiped the Sidonian god Ashtoreth,[d] the Moabite god Chemosh,[d] and the Ammonite god Molech. Solomon has not obeyed me by doing what I said is right and obeying my laws and commands, as his father David did.

[34]"'But I will not take all the kingdom away from Solomon. I will let him rule all his life because of my servant David, whom I chose, who obeyed all my commands and laws. [35]But I will take the kingdom away from his son, and I will allow you to rule over the ten tribes. [36]I will allow Solomon's son to continue to rule over one tribe so that there will always be a descendant of David, my servant, in Jerusalem, the city where I chose to be worshiped. [37]But I will make you rule over everything you want. You will rule over all of Israel, [38]and I will always be with you if you do what I say is right. You must obey all my commands. If you obey my laws and commands as David did, I will be with you. I will make your family a lasting family of kings, as I did for David, and give Israel to you. [39]I will punish David's children because of this, but I will not punish them forever.' "

Solomon's Death

[40]Solomon tried to kill Jeroboam, but he ran away to Egypt, to Shishak king of Egypt, where he stayed until Solomon died.

[41]Everything else King Solomon did, and the wisdom he showed, is written in the book of the history of Solomon. [42]Solomon ruled in Jerusalem over all Israel for forty years. [43]Then he died and was buried in Jerusalem, the city of David, his father. And his son Rehoboam became king in his place.

Israel Turns Against Rehoboam

12 Rehoboam went to Shechem, where all the Israelites had gone to make him king. [2]Jeroboam son of Nebat was still in Egypt, where he had gone to escape from Solomon. When Jeroboam heard about Rehoboam being made king, he was living in Egypt. [3]After the people sent for him, he and the people went to Rehoboam and said to him, [4]"Your father forced us to work very hard. Now, make it easier for us, and don't make us work as hard as he did. Then we will serve you."

[5]Rehoboam answered, "Go away for three days, and then come back to me." So the people left.

[6]King Rehoboam asked the older leaders who had advised Solomon during his lifetime, "How do you think I should answer these people?"

[7]They said, "You should be like a servant to them today. If you serve them and give them a kind answer, they will serve you always."

[8]But Rehoboam rejected this advice. Instead, he asked the young men who had grown up with him and who served as his advisers. [9]Rehoboam asked them, "What is your advice? How should we answer these people who said, 'Don't make us work as hard as your father did'?"

[10]The young men who had grown up with him answered, "Those people said to you, 'Your father forced us to work very hard. Now make our work easier.' You should tell them, 'My little finger is bigger than my father's legs. [11]He forced you to work hard, but I will make you work even harder. My father beat you with whips, but I will beat you with whips that have sharp points.' "

[12]Rehoboam had told the people, "Come back to me in three days." So after three days Jeroboam and all the people returned to Rehoboam. [13]King Rehoboam spoke cruel words to them, because he had rejected the advice the older leaders had given him. [14]He followed the advice of the young men and said to the people, "My father forced you to work hard, but I will make you work even harder. My father beat you with whips, but I will beat you with whips that have sharp points." [15]So the king did not listen to the people. The LORD caused this to happen to keep the promise he had made to Jeroboam son of Nebat through Ahijah, a prophet from Shiloh.

[16]When all the Israelites saw that the new king refused to listen to them, they said to the king,

"We have no share in David!
We have no part in the son of Jesse!
People of Israel, let's go to our own homes!
Let David's son rule his own people!"

So the Israelites went home. [17]But Rehoboam still ruled over the Israelites who lived in the towns of Judah.

[18]Adoniram was in charge of the forced labor. When Rehoboam sent him to the people of Israel, they threw stones at him until he died. But King Rehoboam ran to his chariot and escaped to Jerusalem. [19]Since then, Israel has been against the family of David.

[20]When all the Israelites heard that Jeroboam had returned, they called him to a meeting and made him king over all Israel. Only the tribe[d] of Judah continued to follow the family of David.

[21]When Rehoboam arrived in Jerusalem, he gathered one hundred eighty thousand of the best soldiers from the tribes of Judah and Benjamin. As son of Solomon, Rehoboam wanted to fight the people of Israel to take back his kingdom.

✴ **SIDELIGHT:** When the kingdom was divided (1 Kings 12:16–19), Israel (the northern kingdom) was stronger economically, had more people, controlled major roads, and possessed the best land. Judah was smaller and had fewer resources. Yet Judah survived about one hundred fifty years longer than Israel. It didn't face as many attacks from hostile nations, and more of the kings followed God's leadership.

---

[22]But God spoke his word to Shemaiah, a man of God, saying, [23]"Speak to Solomon's son Rehoboam, the king of Judah, and to all the people of Judah and Benjamin and the rest of the people. Say to them, [24]'The LORD says you must not go to war against your brothers, the Israelites. Every one of you should go home, because I made all these things happen.' " So they obeyed the LORD's command and went home as the LORD had commanded.

[25]Then Jeroboam made Shechem in the mountains of Ephraim a very strong city, and he lived there. He also went to the city of Peniel and made it stronger.

Jeroboam Builds Golden Calves

[26]Jeroboam said to himself, "The kingdom will probably go back to David's family. [27]If the people continue going to the Temple[d] of the LORD in Jerusalem to offer sacrifices, they will want to be ruled again by Rehoboam. Then they will kill me and follow Rehoboam king of Judah."

[28]King Jeroboam asked for advice. Then he made two golden calves. "It is too long a journey for you to go to Jerusalem to worship," he said to the people. "Israel, here are your gods who brought you out of Egypt." [29]Jeroboam put one golden calf in the city of Bethel and the other in the city of Dan. [30]This became a very great sin, because the people traveled as far as Dan to worship the calf there.

[31]Jeroboam built temples on the places of worship. He also chose priests from all the people, not just from the tribe[d] of Levi. [32]And he started a new festival on the fifteenth day of the eighth month, just like the festival in Judah. During that time the king offered sacrifices on the altar, along

with sacrifices to the calves in Bethel he had made. He also chose priests in Bethel to serve at the places of worship he had made. [33]So Jeroboam chose his own time for a festival for the Israelites — the fifteenth day of the eighth month. During that time he offered sacrifices on the altar he had built in Bethel. He set up a festival for the Israelites and offered sacrifices on the altar.

The Man of God Speaks Against Bethel

13 The LORD commanded a man of God from Judah to go to Bethel. When he arrived, Jeroboam was standing by the altar to offer a sacrifice. [2]The LORD had commanded the man of God to speak against the altar. The man said, "Altar, altar, the LORD says to you: 'David's family will have a son named Josiah. The priests for the places of worship now make their sacrifices on you, but Josiah will sacrifice those priests on you. Human bones will be burned on you.'" [3]That same day the man of God gave proof that these things would happen. "This is the LORD's sign that this will happen," he said. "This altar will break apart, and the ashes on it will fall to the ground."

[4]When King Jeroboam heard what the man of God said about the altar in Bethel, the king raised his hand from the altar and pointed at the man. "Take him!" he said. But when the king said this, his arm was paralyzed, and he could not move it. [5]The altar also broke into pieces, and its ashes fell to the ground. This was the sign the LORD had told the man of God to give.

[6]Then the king said to the man of God, "Please pray to the LORD your God for me, and ask him to heal my arm."

So the man of God prayed to the LORD, and the king's arm was healed, becoming as it was before. [7]Then the king said to the man of God, "Please come home and eat with me, and I will give you a gift."

[8]But the man of God answered the king, "Even if you gave me half of your kingdom, I would not go with you. I will not eat or drink anything in this place. [9]The LORD commanded me not to eat or drink anything nor to return on the same road by which I came." [10]So he took a different road and did not return on the same road by which he had come to Bethel.

[11]Now an old prophet[d] was living in Bethel. His sons came and told him what the man of God had done there that day. They also told their father what he had said to King Jeroboam. [12]The father asked, "Which road did he use when he left?" So his sons showed him the road the man of God from Judah had taken. [13]Then the prophet told his sons to put a saddle on his donkey. So they saddled the donkey, and he left.

[14]He went after the man of God and found him sitting under an oak tree. The prophet asked, "Are you the man of God who came from Judah?"

The man answered, "Yes, I am."

[15]The prophet said, "Please come home and eat with me."

[16]"I can't go home with you," the man of God answered. "I can't eat or drink with you in this place. [17]The LORD said to me, 'Don't eat or drink anything there or return on the same road by which you came.'"

[18]Then the old prophet said, "But I also am a prophet like you." Then he told a lie. He said, "An angel from the LORD came to me and told me to bring you to my home. He said you should eat and drink with me." [19]So the man of God went to the old prophet's house, and he ate and drank with him there.

[20]While they were sitting at the table, the LORD spoke his word to the old prophet. [21]The old prophet cried out to the man of God from Judah, "The LORD said you did not obey him! He said you did not do what the LORD your God commanded you. [22]The LORD commanded you not to eat or drink anything in this place, but you came back and ate and drank. So your body will not be buried in your family grave."

[23]After the man of God finished eating and drinking, the prophet put a saddle on his donkey for him, and the man left. [24]As he was traveling home, a lion attacked and killed him. His body lay on the road, with the donkey and the lion standing nearby. [25]Some men who were traveling on that road saw the body and the lion standing nearby. So they went to the city where the old prophet lived and told what they had seen.

[26]The old prophet who had brought back the man of God heard what had happened. "It is the man of God who did not obey the LORD's command," he said. "So the LORD sent a lion to kill him, just as he said he would."

[27]Then the prophet said to his sons, "Put a saddle on my donkey," which they did. [28]The old prophet went out and found the body lying on the road, with the donkey and the lion still standing nearby. The lion had not eaten the body or hurt the donkey. [29]The prophet put the body on his donkey and carried it back to the city to have a time of sadness for him and to bury him. [30]The prophet buried the body in his own family grave, and they were sad for the man of God and said, "Oh, my brother."

[31]After the prophet buried the body, he said to his sons, "When I die, bury me in this same grave. Put my bones next to his. [32]Through him the LORD spoke against the altar at Bethel and against the places of worship in the towns of Samaria. What the LORD spoke through him will certainly come true."

[33]After this incident King Jeroboam did not stop

doing evil. He continued to choose priests for the places of worship from among all the people. Anyone who wanted to be a priest for the places of worship was allowed to be one. 34In this way the family of Jeroboam sinned, and this sin caused its ruin and destruction from the earth.

Jeroboam's Son Dies

14 At that time Jeroboam's son Abijah became very sick. 2So Jeroboam said to his wife, "Go to Shiloh to see the prophet*d* Ahijah. He is the one who said I would become king of Israel. But dress yourself so people won't know you are my wife. 3Take the prophet ten loaves of bread, some cakes, and a jar of honey. Then ask him what will happen to our son, and he will tell you." 4So the king's wife did as he said and went to Ahijah's home in Shiloh.

Now Ahijah was very old and blind. 5The Lord said to him, "Jeroboam's son is sick, and Jeroboam's wife is coming to ask you about him. When she arrives, she will pretend to be someone else." Then the Lord told Ahijah what to say.

6When Ahijah heard her walking to the door, he said, "Come in, wife of Jeroboam. Why are you pretending to be someone else? I have bad news for you. 7Go back and tell Jeroboam that this is what the Lord, the God of Israel, says: 'Jeroboam, I chose you from among all the people and made you the leader of my people Israel. 8I tore the kingdom away from David's family, and I gave it to you. But you are not like my servant David, who always obeyed my commands and followed me with all his heart. He did only what I said was right. 9But you have done more evil than anyone who ruled before you. You have quit following me and have made other gods and idols of metal. This has made me very angry, 10so I will soon bring disaster to your family. I will kill all the men in your family, both slaves and free men. I will destroy your family as completely as fire burns up manure. 11Anyone from your family who dies in the city will be eaten by dogs, and those who die in the fields will be eaten by the birds. The Lord has spoken.' "

12Then Ahijah said to Jeroboam's wife, "Go home now. As soon as you enter your city, your son will die, 13and all Israel will be sad for him and bury him. He is the only one of Jeroboam's family who will be buried, because he is the only one in the king's family who pleased the Lord, the God of Israel.

14"The Lord will put a new king over Israel, who will destroy Jeroboam's family, and this will happen soon. 15Then the Lord will punish Israel, which will be like grass moving in the water. The Lord will pull up Israel from this good land, the land he gave their ancestors. He will scatter Israel beyond the Euphrates River, because he is angry

with the people. They made the Lord angry when they set up idols to worship Asherah.*d* 16Jeroboam sinned, and then he made the people of Israel sin. So the Lord will let the people of Israel be defeated."

17Then Jeroboam's wife left and returned to Tirzah. As soon as she entered her home, the boy died. 18After they buried him, all Israel had a time of sadness for him, just as the Lord had said through his servant, the prophet Ahijah.

19Everything else Jeroboam did is written in the book of the history of the kings of Israel. He fought wars and continued to rule the people, 20serving as king for twenty-two years. Then he died, and his son Nadab became king in his place.

The Death of Rehoboam

21Solomon's son Rehoboam was forty-one years old when he became king of Judah. His mother was Naamah from Ammon. Rehoboam ruled in Jerusalem for seventeen years. (The Lord had chosen that city from all the land of Israel as the place where he would be worshiped.)

22The people of Judah did what the Lord said was wrong. Their sins made the Lord very angry, even more angry than he had been at their ancestors. 23The people built stone pillars and places to worship gods and Asherah*d* idols on every high hill and under every green tree. 24There were even male prostitutes*d* in the land. They acted like the people who had lived in the land before the Israelites. They had done many evil things, and God had taken the land away from them.

25During the fifth year Rehoboam was king, Shishak king of Egypt attacked Jerusalem. 26He took the treasures from the Temple*d* of the Lord and the king's palace. He took everything, even the gold shields Solomon had made. 27So King Rehoboam made bronze shields to put in their place and gave them to the commanders of the guards for the palace gates. 28Whenever the king went to the Temple of the Lord, the guards carried the shields. Later, they would put them back in the guardroom.

29Everything else King Rehoboam did is written in the book of the history of the kings of Judah. 30There was war between Rehoboam and Jeroboam the whole time. 31Rehoboam, son of Naamah from Ammon, died and was buried with his ancestors in Jerusalem, and his son Abijah became king in his place.

Abijah King of Judah

15 Abijah became king of Judah during the eighteenth year Jeroboam son of Nebat was king of Israel. 2Abijah ruled in Jerusalem for three years. His mother was Maacah daughter of Abishalom. 3He did all the same sins his father before him had done. Abijah was not faithful to

the Lord his God as David, his great-grandfather, had been. ⁴Because the Lord loved David, the Lord gave him a kingdom in Jerusalem and allowed him to have a son to be king after him. The Lord also kept Jerusalem safe. ⁵David always did what the Lord said was right and obeyed his commands all his life, except the one time when David sinned against Uriah the Hittite.

⁶There was war between Abijah and Jeroboam during Abijah's lifetime. ⁷Everything else Abijah did is written in the book of the history of the kings of Judah. During the time Abijah ruled, there was war between Abijah and Jeroboam. ⁸Abijah died and was buried in Jerusalem, and his son Asa became king in his place.

Asa King of Judah

⁹During the twentieth year Jeroboam was king of Israel, Asa became king of Judah. ¹⁰His grandmother's name was Maacah, the daughter of Abishalom. Asa ruled in Jerusalem for forty-one years.

¹¹Asa did what the Lord said was right, as his ancestor David had done. ¹²He forced the male prostitutes*d* at the worship places to leave the country. He also took away the idols that his ancestors had made. ¹³His grandmother Maacah had made a terrible Asherah*d* idol, so Asa removed her from being queen mother. He cut down that idol and burned it in the Kidron Valley. ¹⁴The places of worship to gods were not removed. Even so, Asa was faithful to the Lord all his life. ¹⁵Asa brought into the Temple*d* of the Lord the gifts he and his father had given: gold, silver, and utensils.

¹⁶There was war between Asa and Baasha king of Israel all the time they were kings. ¹⁷Baasha attacked Judah, and he made the town of Ramah strong so he could keep people from leaving or entering Judah, Asa's country.

¹⁸Asa took the rest of the silver and gold from the treasuries of the Temple of the Lord and his own palace and gave it to his officers. Then he sent them to Ben-Hadad son of Tabrimmon, who was the son of Hezion. Ben-Hadad was the king of Aram and ruled in the city of Damascus. Asa said, ¹⁹"Let there be a treaty between you and me as there was between my father and your father. I am sending you a gift of silver and gold. Break your treaty with Baasha king of Israel so he will leave my land."

²⁰Ben-Hadad agreed with King Asa, so he sent the commanders of his armies to attack the towns of Israel. They defeated the towns of Ijon, Dan, and Abel Beth Maacah, as well as all Galilee and the area of Naphtali. ²¹When Baasha heard about these attacks, he stopped building up Ramah and returned to Tirzah. ²²Then King Asa gave an order to all the people of Judah; everyone had to help. They carried away all the stones and wood Baasha

had been using in Ramah, and they used them to build up Geba and Mizpah in the land of Benjamin.

²³Everything else Asa did — his victories and the cities he built — is written in the book of the history of the kings of Judah. When he became old, he got a disease in his feet. ²⁴After Asa died, he was buried with his ancestors in Jerusalem, the city of David, his ancestor. Then Jehoshaphat, Asa's son, became king in his place.

Nadab King of Israel

²⁵Nadab son of Jeroboam became king of Israel during the second year Asa was king of Judah. Nadab was king of Israel for two years, ²⁶and he did what the Lord said was wrong. Jeroboam had led the people of Israel to sin, and Nadab sinned in the same way as his father Jeroboam.

²⁷Baasha son of Ahijah, from the tribe*d* of Issachar, made plans to kill Nadab. Nadab and all Israel were attacking the Philistine town of Gibbethon, so Baasha killed Nadab there. ²⁸This happened during Asa's third year as king of Judah, and Baasha became the next king of Israel.

Baasha King of Israel

²⁹As soon as Baasha became king, he killed all of Jeroboam's family, leaving no one in Jeroboam's family alive. He destroyed them all as the Lord had said would happen through his servant Ahijah from Shiloh. ³⁰King Jeroboam had sinned very much and had led the people of Israel to sin, so he made the Lord, the God of Israel, very angry.

³¹Everything else Nadab did is written in the book of the history of the kings of Israel. ³²There was war between Asa king of Judah and Baasha king of Israel all the time they ruled.

³³Baasha son of Ahijah became king of Israel during Asa's third year as king of Judah. Baasha ruled in Tirzah for twenty-four years, ³⁴and he did what the Lord said was wrong. Jeroboam had led the people of Israel to sin, and Baasha sinned in the same way as Jeroboam.

16 Jehu son of Hanani spoke the word of the Lord against King Baasha. ²The Lord said, "You were nothing, but I took you and made you a leader over my people Israel. But you have followed the ways of Jeroboam and have led my people Israel to sin. Their sins have made me angry, ³so, Baasha, I will soon destroy you and your family. I will do to you what I did to the family of Jeroboam son of Nebat. ⁴Anyone from your family who dies in the city will be eaten by dogs, and anyone from your family who dies in the fields will be eaten by birds."

⁵Everything else Baasha did and all his victories are written down in the book of the history of the kings of Israel. ⁶So Baasha died and was buried

in Tirzah, and his son Elah became king in his place.

7The LORD spoke his word against Baasha and his family through the prophet*d* Jehu son of Hanani. Baasha had done many things the LORD said were wrong, which made the LORD very angry. He did the same evil deeds that Jeroboam's family had done before him. The LORD also spoke against Baasha because he killed all of Jeroboam's family.

Elah King of Israel

8Elah son of Baasha became king of Israel during Asa's twenty-sixth year as king of Judah, and Elah ruled in Tirzah for two years.

9Zimri, one of Elah's officers, commanded half of Elah's chariots. Zimri made plans against Elah while the king was in Tirzah, getting drunk at Arza's home. (Arza was in charge of the palace at Tirzah.) 10Zimri went into Arza's house and killed Elah during Asa's twenty-seventh year as king of Judah. Then Zimri became king of Israel in Elah's place.

Zimri King of Israel

11As soon as Zimri became king, he killed all of Baasha's family, not allowing any of Baasha's family or friends to live. 12So Zimri destroyed all of Baasha's family just as the LORD had said it would happen through the prophet*d* Jehu. 13Baasha and his son Elah sinned and led the people of Israel to sin, and they made the LORD, the God of Israel, angry because of their worthless idols.

14Everything else Elah did is written in the book of the history of the kings of Israel.

15So during Asa's twenty-seventh year as king of Judah, Zimri became king of Israel and ruled in Tirzah seven days.

The army of Israel was camped near Gibbethon, a Philistine town. 16The men in the camp heard that Zimri had made secret plans against King Elah and had killed him. So that day in the camp they made Omri, the commander of the army, king over Israel. 17So Omri and all the Israelite army left Gibbethon and attacked Tirzah. 18When Zimri saw that the city had been captured, he went into the palace and set it on fire, burning the palace and himself with it. 19So Zimri died because he had sinned by doing what the LORD said was wrong. Jeroboam had led the people of Israel to sin, and Zimri sinned in the same way as Jeroboam.

20Everything else Zimri did and the story of how he turned against King Elah are written down in the book of the history of the kings of Israel.

Omri King of Israel

21The people of Israel were divided into two groups. Half of the people wanted Tibni son of Ginath to be king, while the other half wanted Omri. 22Omri's followers were stronger than the followers of Tibni son of Ginath, so Tibni died, and Omri became king.

23Omri became king of Israel during the thirty-first year Asa was king of Judah. Omri ruled Israel for twelve years, six of those years in the city of Tirzah. 24He bought the hill of Samaria from Shemer for about one hundred fifty pounds of silver. Omri built a city on that hill and called it Samaria after the name of its earlier owner, Shemer.

25But Omri did what the LORD said was wrong; he did more evil than all the kings who came before him. 26Jeroboam son of Nebat had led the people of Israel to sin, and Omri sinned in the same way as Jeroboam. The Israelites made the LORD, the God of Israel, very angry because they worshiped worthless idols.

27Everything else Omri did and all his successes are written in the book of the history of the kings of Israel. 28So Omri died and was buried in Samaria, and his son Ahab became king in his place.

SIDELIGHT: King Omri doesn't get much press in the Bible (1 Kings 16:23–28), but he probably was one of the most powerful leaders of the northern kingdom. According to other sources, he established a strong rule and conquered the Moabites, long-term enemies. But, the Bible says, "he did more evil than all the kings who came before him."

Ahab King of Israel

29Ahab son of Omri became king of Israel during Asa's thirty-eighth year as king of Judah, and Ahab ruled Israel in the city of Samaria for twenty-two years. 30More than any king before him, Ahab son of Omri did many things the LORD said were wrong. 31He sinned in the same ways as Jeroboam son of Nebat, but he did even worse things. He married Jezebel daughter of Ethbaal, the king of Sidon. Then Ahab began to serve Baal*d* and worship him. 32He built a temple in Samaria for worshiping Baal and put an altar there for Baal. 33Ahab also made an idol for worshiping Asherah.*d* He did more things to make the LORD, the God of Israel, angry than all the other kings before him.

34During the time of Ahab, Hiel from Bethel rebuilt the city of Jericho. It cost Hiel the life of Abiram, his oldest son, to begin work on the city, and it cost the life of Segub, his youngest son, to build the city gates. This happened just as the

LORD, speaking through Joshua son of Nun, said it would happen. [n]

Elijah Stops the Rain

17 Now Elijah the Tishbite was a prophet[d] from the settlers in Gilead. "I serve the LORD, the God of Israel," Elijah said to Ahab. "As surely as the LORD lives, no rain or dew will fall during the next few years unless I command it." [2]Then the LORD spoke his word to Elijah: [3]"Leave this place and go east and hide near Kerith Ravine east of the Jordan River. [4]You may drink from the stream, and I have commanded ravens to bring you food there." [5]So Elijah did what the LORD said; he went to Kerith Ravine, east of the Jordan, and lived there. [6]The birds brought Elijah bread and meat every morning and evening, and he drank water from the stream.

[7]After a while the stream dried up because there was no rain. [8]Then the LORD spoke his word to Elijah, [9]"Go to Zarephath in Sidon and live there. I have commanded a widow there to take care of you."

[10]So Elijah went to Zarephath. When he reached the town gate, he saw a widow gathering wood for a fire. Elijah asked her, "Would you bring me a little water in a cup so I may have a drink." [11]As she was going to get his water, Elijah said, "Please bring me a piece of bread, too."

[12]The woman answered, "As surely as the LORD your God lives, I have no bread. I have only a handful of flour in a jar and only a little olive oil in a jug. I came here to gather some wood so I

---

the LORD ... happen When Joshua destroyed Jericho, he said whoever rebuilt the city would lose his oldest and youngest sons. See Joshua 6:26.

HUNGER AND POVERTY

Letting God Use You

Jon Ralston went to help at the Rescue Mission mostly because someone asked him to go. He had never done anything like this in all of his fifteen years. But a friend asked him to help out this Sunday, and Jon couldn't think of any reason not to. So he went.

When they got there, Jon and his friends did simple tasks—preparing food, setting places, washing dishes, cleaning tables. "We just helped where we were needed," he says.

The Rescue Mission was run-down and dirty, Jon recalls. The people they served were dirty from the streets, and they didn't seem to appreciate what Jon and his friends were doing for them. Some of Jon's friends really didn't like it and didn't go back when they were asked to help out again.

But Jon went back. And he would go again.

"I'm needed there," he says. "And it's fun to give to people when you know they can't pay you back."

Jon was impressed with the staff at the Rescue Mission, too. They had a good attitude toward the people they served. "Even though the staff acts tough," Jon recalls, "they really care for the people who come there."

There's been hunger and poverty in the world almost since the beginning of time. God wants Christians—every Christian—to offer help and God's love to the poor and hungry. God even used the great prophet Elijah to help a widow and her son in **1 Kings 17:8—16**.

■ What's the difference between the widow in this passage and the people Jon helped? What motives did Jon have for helping the poor? What motives did Elijah have for helping the widow?

■ How does God keep the "jars of flour and jugs of oil" full for poor and hungry people today? What role can you play in providing food for hungry people?

CONSIDER . . .

■ skipping dinner tonight and spending that time praying for poor and hungry people.
■ following Jon's example by volunteering to work in a soup kitchen or a homeless shelter.

FOR MORE, SEE . . .

■ Exodus 16:1–15 (p. 73)
■ Mark 6:34–44 (p. 974)
■ John 6:30–35 (p. 1067)

could go home and cook our last meal. My son and I will eat it and then die from hunger."

13"Don't worry," Elijah said to her. "Go home and cook your food as you have said. But first make a small loaf of bread from the flour you have, and bring it to me. Then cook something for yourself and your son. 14The LORD, the God of Israel, says, 'That jar of flour will never be empty, and the jug will always have oil in it, until the day the LORD sends rain to the land.'"

15So the woman went home and did what Elijah told her to do. And the woman and her son and Elijah had enough food every day. 16The jar of flour and the jug of oil were never empty, just as the LORD, through Elijah, had promised.

Elijah Brings a Boy Back to Life

17Some time later the son of the woman who owned the house became sick. He grew worse and worse and finally stopped breathing. 18The woman said to Elijah, "Man of God, what have you done to me? Did you come here to remind me of my sin and to kill my son?"

19Elijah said to her, "Give me your son." Elijah took the boy from her, carried him upstairs, and laid him on the bed in the room where he was staying. 20Then he prayed to the LORD: "LORD my God, this widow is letting me stay in her house. Why have you done this terrible thing to her and caused her son to die?" 21Then Elijah lay on top of the boy three times. He prayed to the LORD, "LORD my God, let this boy live again!"

22The LORD answered Elijah's prayer; the boy began breathing again and was alive. 23Elijah carried the boy downstairs and gave him to his mother and said, "See! Your son is alive!"

24"Now I know you really are a man from God," the woman said to Elijah. "I know that the LORD truly speaks through you!"

Elijah Kills the Prophets of Baal

18 During the third year without rain, the LORD spoke his word to Elijah: "Go and meet King Ahab, and I will soon send rain." 2So Elijah went to meet Ahab.

By this time there was no food in Samaria. 3King Ahab sent for Obadiah, who was in charge of the king's palace. (Obadiah was a true follower of the LORD. 4When Jezebel was killing all the LORD's prophets,*d* Obadiah hid a hundred of them in two caves, fifty in one cave and fifty in another. He also brought them food and water.) 5Ahab said

---

SIN

What's the Connection?

"Oh, my back! Help, it hurts!"

When Jen Freeman hurt her back trying to push a car out of the snow, the doctor confined her to bed for a week. At the end of the week, Jen felt much better, so she went on a retreat she had signed up for two months earlier. Everything went fine until the third day, when Jen slipped on some ice. Then her back was worse than ever.

People helped Jen stand up and get around, and they brought things to her. Even more important, they prayed for her and comforted her. She began to talk about how difficult it was for her to rely on other people.

"I'm really independent," she said. "Relying on other people is hard for me, but here on the retreat, I have no choice. I can't even walk!"

God used Jen's injury to help her see how she was trying to isolate herself too much. Jen had to learn to rely on others.

In Old Testament times, most people believed illnesses were caused by sin. But that is not necessarily true. Read **1 Kings 17:17–24** to see how God used a boy's illness to show that Elijah was a man of God.

■ What connection is there between illness and sin for Jen and for the woman in the passage?

■ In what ways does God use illness, both in Bible times and today?

C O N S I D E R . . .

■ praying that God will use your next illness as a time of spiritual healing or renewal.

■ asking to visit a hospital with your pastor or a hospital chaplain so you can join in caring for the sick.

F O R   M O R E ,   S E E . . .

■ Deuteronomy 28:15–24 (p. 184)   ■ Acts 3:1–19 (p. 1100)
■ John 9:1–7 (p. 1073)

to Obadiah, "Let's check every spring and valley in the land. Maybe we can find enough grass to keep our horses and mules alive and not have to kill our animals." 6So each one chose a part of the country to search; Ahab went in one direction and Obadiah in another.

7While Obadiah was on his way, Elijah met him. Obadiah recognized Elijah, so he bowed down to the ground and said, "Elijah? Is it really you, master?"

8"Yes," Elijah answered. "Go tell your master that I am here."

9Then Obadiah said, "What wrong have I done for you to hand me over to Ahab like this? He will put me to death. 10As surely as the LORD your God lives, the king has sent people to every country to search for you. If the ruler said you were not there, Ahab forced the ruler to swear you could not be found in his country. 11Now you want me to go to my master and tell him, 'Elijah is here'? 12The Spirit*d* of the LORD may carry you to some other place after I leave. If I go tell King Ahab you are here, and he comes and doesn't find you, he will kill me! I have followed the LORD since I was a boy. 13Haven't you been told what I did? When Jezebel was killing the LORD's prophets, I hid a hundred of them, fifty in one cave and fifty in another. I brought them food and water. 14Now you want me to go and tell my master you are here? He will kill me!"

15Elijah answered, "As surely as the LORD All-Powerful lives, whom I serve, I will be seen by Ahab today."

16So Obadiah went to Ahab and told him where Elijah was. Then Ahab went to meet Elijah.

17When he saw Elijah, he asked, "Is it you — the biggest troublemaker in Israel?"

18Elijah answered, "I have not made trouble in Israel. You and your father's family have made all this trouble by not obeying the LORD's commands. You have gone after the Baals.*d* 19Now tell all Israel to meet me at Mount Carmel. Also bring the four hundred fifty prophets of Baal and the four hundred prophets of Asherah,*d* who eat at Jezebel's table."

20So Ahab called all the Israelites and those prophets to Mount Carmel. 21Elijah approached the people and said, "How long will you not decide between two choices? If the LORD is the true God, follow him, but if Baal is the true God, follow him!" But the people said nothing.

22Elijah said, "I am the only prophet of the LORD here, but there are four hundred fifty prophets of Baal. 23Bring two bulls. Let the prophets of Baal choose one bull and kill it and cut it into pieces. Then let them put the meat on the wood, but they are not to set fire to it. I will prepare the other bull, putting the meat on the wood but not setting fire to it. 24You prophets of Baal, pray to

your god, and I will pray to the LORD. The god who answers by setting fire to his wood is the true God."

All the people agreed that this was a good idea.

25Then Elijah said to the prophets of Baal, "There are many of you, so you go first. Choose a bull and prepare it. Pray to your god, but don't start the fire."

26So they took the bull that was given to them and prepared it. They prayed to Baal from morning until noon, shouting "Baal, answer us!" But there was no sound, and no one answered. They danced around the altar they had built.

27At noon Elijah began to make fun of them. "Pray louder!" he said. "If Baal really is a god, maybe he is thinking, or busy, or traveling! Maybe he is sleeping so you will have to wake him!" 28The prophets prayed louder, cutting themselves with swords and spears until their blood flowed, which was the way they worshiped. 29The afternoon passed, and the prophets continued to act like this until it was time for the evening sacrifice. But no voice was heard; Baal did not answer, and no one paid attention.

30Then Elijah said to all the people, "Now come to me." So they gathered around him, and Elijah rebuilt the altar of the LORD, which had been torn down. 31He took twelve stones, one stone for each of the twelve tribes,*d* the number of Jacob's sons. (The LORD changed Jacob's name to Israel.) 32Elijah used these stones to rebuild the altar in honor of the LORD. Then he dug a ditch around the altar that was big enough to hold about thirteen quarts of seed. 33Elijah put the wood on the altar, cut the bull into pieces, and laid the pieces on the wood. 34Then he said, "Fill four jars with water, and pour it on the meat and on the wood." Then Elijah said, "Do it again," and they did it again. Then he said, "Do it a third time," and they did it the third time. 35So the water ran off the altar and filled the ditch.

36At the time for the evening sacrifice, the prophet Elijah went near the altar. "LORD, you are the God of Abraham, Isaac, and Israel," he prayed. "Prove that you are the God of Israel and that I am your servant. Show these people that you commanded me to do all these things. [37]LORD, answer my prayer so these people will know that you, LORD, are God and that you will change their minds."

[38]Then fire from the LORD came down and burned the sacrifice, the wood, the stones, and the ground around the altar. It also dried up the water in the ditch. [39]When all the people saw this, they fell down to the ground, crying, "The LORD is God! The LORD is God!"

[40]Then Elijah said, "Capture the prophets of Baal! Don't let any of them run away!" The people captured all the prophets. Then Elijah led them down to the Kishon Valley, where he killed them.

The Rain Comes Again

[41]Then Elijah said to Ahab, "Now, go, eat, and drink, because a heavy rain is coming." [42]So King Ahab went to eat and drink. At the same time Elijah climbed to the top of Mount Carmel, where he bent down to the ground with his head between his knees.

[43]Then Elijah said to his servant, "Go and look toward the sea."

The servant went and looked. "I see nothing," he said.

Elijah told him to go and look again. This happened seven times. [44]The seventh time, the servant said, "I see a small cloud, the size of a human fist, coming from the sea."

Elijah told the servant, "Go to Ahab and tell him to get his chariot ready and go home now. Otherwise, the rain will stop him."

[45]After a short time the sky was covered with dark clouds. The wind began to blow, and soon a heavy rain began to fall. Ahab got in his chariot

---

☀ SIDELIGHT: For a short time, Elijah may have been the fastest runner in the world. Fearing the rain would start while he was on the mountain, Elijah received God's power and ran from Mt. Carmel to Jezreel—about ten miles—faster than the king's chariots (1 Kings 18:46). Some people will do anything to keep from getting their hair wet!

---

and started back to Jezreel. [46]The LORD gave his power to Elijah, who tightened his clothes around him and ran ahead of King Ahab all the way to Jezreel.

Elijah Runs Away

19 King Ahab told Jezebel everything Elijah had done and how Elijah had killed all the prophets[d] with a sword. [2]So Jezebel sent a messenger to Elijah, saying, "May the gods punish me terribly if by this time tomorrow I don't kill you just as you killed those prophets."

[3]When Elijah heard this, he was afraid and ran for his life, taking his servant with him. When they came to Beersheba in Judah, Elijah left his servant there. [4]Then Elijah walked for a whole day into the desert. He sat down under a bush and asked to die. "I have had enough, LORD," he prayed. "Let me die. I am no better than my ancestors." [5]Then he lay down under the tree and slept.

Suddenly an angel came to him and touched him. "Get up and eat," the angel said. [6]Elijah saw near his head a loaf baked over coals and a jar of water, so he ate and drank. Then he went back to sleep.

[7]Later the LORD's angel came to him a second time. The angel touched him and said, "Get up and eat. If you don't, the journey will be too hard for you." [8]So Elijah got up and ate and drank. The food made him strong enough to walk for forty days and nights to Mount Sinai, the mountain of God. [9]There Elijah went into a cave and stayed all night.

Then the LORD spoke his word to him: "Elijah! Why are you here?"

[10]He answered, "LORD God All-Powerful, I have always served you as well as I could. But the people of Israel have broken their agreement with you, destroyed your altars, and killed your prophets with swords. I am the only prophet left, and now they are trying to kill me, too."

[11]The LORD said to Elijah, "Go, stand in front of me on the mountain, and I will pass by you." Then a very strong wind blew until it caused the mountains to fall apart and large rocks to break in front of the LORD. But the LORD was not in the wind. After the wind, there was an earthquake, but the LORD was not in the earthquake. [12]After the earthquake, there was a fire, but the LORD was not in the fire. After the fire, there was a quiet, gentle sound. [13]When Elijah heard it, he covered his face with his coat and went out and stood at the entrance to the cave.

Then a voice said to him, "Elijah! Why are you here?"

[14]He answered, "LORD God All-Powerful, I have always served you as well as I could. But the people of Israel have broken their agreement with you, destroyed your altars, and killed your prophets with swords. I am the only prophet left, and now they are trying to kill me, too."

[15]The LORD said to him, "Go back on the road

that leads to the desert around Damascus. Enter that city, and pour olive oil on Hazael to make him king over Aram. [16]Then pour oil on Jehu son of Nimshi to make him king over Israel. Next, pour oil on Elisha son of Shaphat from Abel Meholah to make him a prophet in your place. [17]Jehu will kill anyone who escapes from Hazael's sword, and Elisha will kill anyone who escapes from Jehu's sword. [18]I have seven thousand people left in Israel who have never bowed down before Baal[d] and whose mouths have never kissed his idol."

Elisha Becomes a Prophet

[19]So Elijah left that place and found Elisha son of Shaphat plowing a field with a team of oxen. He owned twelve teams of oxen and was plowing with the twelfth team. Elijah came up to Elisha, took off his coat, and put it on Elisha. [20]Then Elisha left his oxen and ran to follow Elijah. "Let me kiss my father and my mother good-bye," Elisha said. "Then I will go with you."

Elijah answered, "Go back. It does not matter to me."

[21]So Elisha went back and took his pair of oxen and killed them. He used their wooden yoke[d] for a fire. Then he cooked the meat and gave it to the people. After they ate it, Elisha left and followed Elijah and became his helper.

LONELINESS

You Against the World

Cindy Barrington used to hang out with the popular crowd. That is, until one day on the school bus, when one of the guys got hold of a note that wasn't his. It belonged to Cindy's little sister Liz.

This guy decided to have some fun at Liz's expense. "Hey, listen to this everybody," Brad yelled. " 'Hey, Shannon, did you see that new guy at school yesterday? What a dream! We accidently bumped into each other in the hall, and he smiled at me. I almost died! I've got to find out his name. Signed, Liz.' "

"Hey, Liz," he added, "that was no 'accidental' bumping scene, now was it?" Everyone laughed. Liz shrunk in her seat.

As much as she wanted to go along with the popular crowd, Cindy couldn't let Brad hurt her sister like this.

"You know, I really pity you, Brad," Cindy said angrily. "I never knew you felt so bad about yourself that you'd stoop this low just for a laugh." Brad stopped laughing. "So why don't you just give me the note, Brad, and sit down. The real joke is on you."

The next day, the popular kids snubbed Cindy. They talked about her, loudly enough so she could hear, and they ignored her when she tried to talk. Cindy felt alone and lonely— all for standing up for what she believed was right.

Fortunately, her loneliness didn't last long. Soon, a few people told Cindy they were glad she stuck up for her sister. Before long, Cindy made new friends—kids she could be herself with. Cindy and Liz also grew closer together, and now they're better friends than ever.

After Elijah stood up for what he believed in and defeated the prophets of Baal, he thought he was alone against the world, too. But God showed Elijah there were other people on his side. Check out Elijah's conversation with God in **1 Kings 19:11–18**.

■ How did God show Elijah that he was with him, even when the situation seemed overwhelming? How did God show Cindy he was with her too?

■ How would you have reacted if you were in Elijah's place? Do you stand up for what is right, even when your beliefs go against the crowd? Why or why not?

CONSIDER . . .

■ taking a walk alone in a park and looking for the quiet ways God reveals himself.

■ reading this passage and the passages listed below the next time you feel lonely. Then write a letter to God that expresses your feelings.

FOR MORE, SEE . . .

■ Psalm 13:1–6 (p. 488)
■ Matthew 5:3–12 (p. 912)
■ Romans 11:1–5 (p. 1155)

Ben-Hadad and Ahab Go to War

20 Ben-Hadad king of Aram gathered together all his army. There were thirty-two kings with their horses and chariots who went with him and surrounded Samaria and attacked it. [2] The king sent messengers into the city to Ahab king of Israel.

This was his message: "Ben-Hadad says, [3] 'Your silver and gold belong to me, as well as the best of your wives and children.' "

[4] Ahab king of Israel answered, "My master and king, I agree to what you say. I and everything I have belong to you."

[5] Then the messengers came to Ahab again. They said, "Ben-Hadad says, 'I told you before that you must give me your silver and gold, your wives and your children. [6] About this time tomorrow I will send my men, who will search everywhere in your palace and in the homes of your officers. Whatever they want they will take and carry off.' "

[7] Then Ahab called a meeting of all the older leaders of his country. He said, "Ben-Hadad is looking for trouble. First he said I had to give him my wives, my children, my silver, and my gold, and I have not refused him."

[8] The older leaders and all the people said, "Don't listen to him or agree to this."

[9] So Ahab said to Ben-Hadad's messengers, "Tell my master the king: 'I will do what you said at first, but I cannot allow this second command.' " And King Ben-Hadad's men carried the message back to him.

[10] Then Ben-Hadad sent another message to Ahab: "May the gods punish me terribly if I don't completely destroy Samaria. There won't be enough left for each of my men to get a handful of dust!"

[11] Ahab answered, "Tell Ben-Hadad, 'The man who puts on his armor should not brag. It's the man who lives to take it off who has the right to brag.' "

[12] Ben-Hadad was drinking in his tent with the other rulers when the message came from Ahab. Ben-Hadad commanded his men to prepare to attack the city, and they moved into place for battle.

[13] At the same time a prophet[d] came to Ahab king of Israel. The prophet said, "Ahab, the LORD says to you, 'Do you see that big army? I will hand it over to you today so you will know I am the LORD.' "

[14] Ahab asked, "Who will you use to defeat them?"

The prophet answered, "The LORD says, 'The young officers of the district governors will defeat them.' "

Then the king asked, "Who will command the main army?"

The prophet answered, "You will."

[15] So Ahab gathered the young officers of the district governors, two hundred thirty-two of them. Then he called together the army of Israel, about seven thousand people in all.

[16] They marched out at noon, while Ben-Hadad and the thirty-two rulers helping him were getting drunk in their tents. [17] The young officers of the district governors attacked first. Ben-Hadad sent out scouts who told him that soldiers were coming from Samaria. [18] Ben-Hadad said, "They may be coming to fight, or they may be coming to ask for peace. In either case capture them alive."

[19] The young officers of the district governors led the attack, followed by the army of Israel. [20] Each officer of Israel killed the man who came against him. The men from Aram ran away as Israel chased them, but Ben-Hadad king of Aram escaped on a horse with some of his horsemen. [21] Ahab king of Israel led the army and destroyed the Arameans' horses and chariots. King Ahab thoroughly defeated the Aramean army.

[22] Then the prophet went to Ahab king of Israel and said, "The king of Aram will attack you again next spring. So go home now and strengthen your army and see what you need to do."

[23] Meanwhile the officers of Ben-Hadad king of Aram said to him, "The gods of Israel are mountain gods. Since we fought in a mountain area, Israel won. Let's fight them on the flat land, and then we will win. [24] This is what you should do. Don't allow the thirty-two rulers to command the armies, but put other commanders in their places. [25] Gather an army like the one that was destroyed and as many horses and chariots as before. We will fight the Israelites on flat land, and then we will win." Ben-Hadad agreed with their advice and did what they said.

[26] The next spring Ben-Hadad gathered the army of Aram and went up to Aphek to fight against Israel.

[27] The Israelites also had prepared for war. They marched out to meet the Arameans and camped opposite them. The Israelites looked like two small flocks of goats, but the Arameans covered the area.

[28] A man of God came to the king of Israel with this message: "The LORD says, 'The people of Aram say that I, the LORD, am a god of the mountains, not a god of the valleys. So I will allow you to defeat this huge army, and then you will know I am the LORD.' "

[29] The armies were camped across from each other for seven days. On the seventh day the battle began. The Israelites killed one hundred thousand Aramean soldiers in one day. [30] The rest of them ran away to the city of Aphek, where a city wall fell on twenty-seven thousand of them. Ben-Hadad also ran away to the city and hid in a room.

31His officers said to him, "We have heard that the kings of Israel are trustworthy. Let's dress in rough cloth to show our sadness, and wear ropes on our heads. Then we will go to the king of Israel, and perhaps he will let you live."

32So they dressed in rough cloth and wore ropes on their heads and went to the king of Israel. They said, "Your servant Ben-Hadad says, 'Please let me live.' "

Ahab answered, "Is he still alive? He is my brother."

33Ben-Hadad's men had wanted a sign from Ahab. So when Ahab called Ben-Hadad his brother, they quickly said, "Yes! Ben-Hadad is your brother."

Ahab said, "Bring him to me." When Ben-Hadad came, Ahab asked him to join him in the chariot.

34Ben-Hadad said to him, "Ahab, I will give you back the cities my father took from your father. And you may put shops in Damascus, as my father did in Samaria."

Ahab said, "If you agree to this, I will allow you to go free." So the two kings made a peace agreement. Then Ahab let Ben-Hadad go free.

A Prophet Speaks Against Ahab

35One prophet from one of the groups of prophets*d* told another, "Hit me!" He said this because the Lord had commanded it, but the other man refused. 36The prophet said, "You did not obey the Lord's command, so a lion will kill you as soon as you leave me." When the man left, a lion found him and killed him.

37The prophet went to another man and said, "Hit me, please!" So the man hit him and hurt him. 38The prophet wrapped his face in a cloth so no one could tell who he was. Then he went and waited by the road for the king. 39As Ahab king of Israel passed by, the prophet called out to him. "I went to fight in the battle," the prophet said. "One of our men brought an enemy soldier to me. Our man said, 'Guard this man. If he runs away, you will have to give your life in his place. Or, you will have to pay a fine of seventy-five pounds of silver.' 40But I was busy doing other things, so the man ran away."

The king of Israel answered, "You have already said what the punishment is. You must do what the man said."

41Then the prophet quickly took the cloth from his face. When the king of Israel saw him, he knew he was one of the prophets. 42The prophet said to the king, "This is what the Lord says: 'You freed the man I said should die, so your life will be taken instead of his. The lives of your people will also be taken instead of the lives of his people.' "

43Then King Ahab went back to his palace in Samaria, angry and upset.

> ✺ **SIDELIGHT:** Outside the Bible, the earliest mention of any Israelite king refers to King Ahab (1 Kings 20:1–43). An Assyrian monument commemorating a battle says Ahab contributed ten thousand soldiers and two thousand chariots to an alliance of countries that fought the Assyrians.

Ahab Takes Naboth's Vineyard

21 After these things had happened, this is what followed. A man named Naboth owned a vineyard in Jezreel, near the palace of Ahab king of Israel. 2One day Ahab said to Naboth, "Give me your vineyard. It is near my palace, and I want to make it into a vegetable garden. I will give you a better vineyard in its place, or, if you prefer, I will pay you what it is worth."

3Naboth answered, "May the Lord keep me from ever giving my land to you. It belongs to my family."

4Ahab went home angry and upset, because he did not like what Naboth from Jezreel had said. (Naboth had said, "I will not give you my family's land.") Ahab lay down on his bed, turned his face to the wall, and refused to eat.

5His wife, Jezebel, came in and asked him, "Why are you so upset that you refuse to eat?"

6Ahab answered, "I talked to Naboth, the man from Jezreel. I said, 'Sell me your vineyard, or, if you prefer, I will give you another vineyard for it.' But Naboth refused."

7Jezebel answered, "Is this how you rule as king over Israel? Get up, eat something, and cheer up. I will get Naboth's vineyard for you."

8So Jezebel wrote some letters, signed Ahab's name to them, and used his own seal*d* to seal them. Then she sent them to the older leaders and important men who lived in Naboth's town. 9The letter she wrote said: "Declare a day during which the people are to give up eating. Call the people together, and give Naboth a place of honor among them. 10Seat two troublemakers across from him, and have them say they heard Naboth speak against God and the king. Then take Naboth out of the city and kill him with stones."

11The older leaders and important men of Jezreel obeyed Jezebel's command, just as she wrote in the letters. 12They declared a special day on which the people were to give up eating. And they put Naboth in a place of honor before the people. 13Two troublemakers sat across from Naboth and said in front of everybody that they had heard him speak against God and the king. So the people carried Naboth out of the city and killed him with stones. ¹⁴Then the leaders sent a message to Jezebel, saying, "Naboth has been killed."

¹⁵When Jezebel heard that Naboth had been killed, she told Ahab, "Naboth of Jezreel is dead. Now you may go and take for yourself the vineyard he would not sell to you." ¹⁶When Ahab heard that Naboth of Jezreel was dead, he got up and went to the vineyard to take it for his own.

¹⁷At this time the Lord spoke his word to the prophet Elijah the Tishbite. The Lord said, ¹⁸"Go to Ahab king of Israel in Samaria. He is at Naboth's vineyard, where he has gone to take it as his own. ¹⁹Tell Ahab that I, the Lord, say to him, 'You have murdered Naboth and taken his land. So I tell you this: In the same place the dogs licked up Naboth's blood, they will also lick up your blood.' "

²⁰When Ahab saw Elijah, he said, "So you have found me, my enemy!"

Elijah answered, "Yes, I have found you. You have always chosen to do what the Lord says is wrong. ²¹So the Lord says to you, 'I will soon destroy you. I will kill you and every male in your family, both slave and free. ²²Your family will be like the family of King Jeroboam son of Nebat and like the family of King Baasha son of Ahijah. I will destroy you, because you have made me angry and have led the people of Israel to sin.'

²³"And the Lord also says, 'Dogs will eat the body of Jezebel in the city of Jezreel.'

²⁴"Anyone in your family who dies in the city will be eaten by dogs, and anyone who dies in the fields will be eaten by birds."

²⁵There was no one like Ahab who had chosen so often to do what the Lord said was wrong, because his wife Jezebel influenced him to do evil. ²⁶Ahab sinned terribly by worshiping idols, just as the Amorite people did. And the Lord had taken away their land and given it to the people of Israel.

²⁷After Elijah finished speaking, Ahab tore his clothes. He put on rough cloth, refused to eat, and even slept in the rough cloth to show how sad and upset he was.

²⁸The Lord spoke his word to Elijah the Tishbite: ²⁹"I see that Ahab is now sorry for what he has done. So I will not cause the trouble to come to him during his life, but I will wait until his son is king. Then I will bring this trouble to Ahab's family."

The Death of Ahab

22 For three years there was peace between Israel and Aram. ²During the third year Jehoshaphat king of Judah went to visit Ahab king of Israel.

³At that time Ahab asked his officers, "Do you remember that the king of Aram took Ramoth in Gilead from us? Why have we done nothing to get it back?" ⁴So Ahab asked King Jehoshaphat, "Will you go with me to fight at Ramoth in Gilead?"

"I will go with you," Jehoshaphat answered. "My soldiers are yours, and my horses are yours." ⁵Jehoshaphat also said to Ahab, "But first we should ask if this is the Lord's will."

⁶Ahab called about four hundred prophets[d] together and asked them, "Should I go to war against Ramoth in Gilead or not?"

They answered, "Go, because the Lord will hand them over to you."

⁷But Jehoshaphat asked, "Isn't there a prophet of the Lord here? Let's ask him what we should do."

⁸Then King Ahab said to Jehoshaphat, "There is one other prophet. We could ask the Lord through him, but I hate him. He never prophesies anything good about me, but something bad. He is Micaiah son of Imlah."

Jehoshaphat said, "King Ahab, you shouldn't say that!"

⁹So Ahab king of Israel told one of his officers to bring Micaiah to him at once.

¹⁰Ahab king of Israel and Jehoshaphat king of Judah had on their royal robes and were sitting on their thrones at the threshing[d] floor, near the entrance to the gate of Samaria. All the prophets were standing before them, speaking their messages. ¹¹Zedekiah son of Kenaanah had made some iron horns. He said to Ahab, "This is what the Lord says, 'You will use these horns to fight the Arameans until they are destroyed.' "

¹²All the other prophets said the same thing. "Attack Ramoth in Gilead and win, because the Lord will hand the Arameans over to you."

¹³The messenger who had gone to get Micaiah said to him, "All the other prophets are saying King Ahab will succeed. You should agree with them and give the king a good answer."

¹⁴But Micaiah answered, "As surely as the Lord lives, I can tell him only what the Lord tells me."

¹⁵When Micaiah came to Ahab, the king asked him, "Micaiah, should we attack Ramoth in Gilead or not?"

Micaiah answered, "Attack and win! The Lord will hand them over to you."

¹⁶But Ahab said to Micaiah, "How many times do I have to tell you to speak only the truth to me in the name of the Lord?"

¹⁷So Micaiah answered, "I saw the army of Israel scattered over the hills like sheep without a shepherd. The Lord said, 'They have no leaders. They should go home and not fight.' "

¹⁸Then Ahab king of Israel said to Jehoshaphat, "I told you! He never prophesies anything good about me, but only bad."

¹⁹But Micaiah said, "Hear the message from the

LORD: I saw the LORD sitting on his throne with his heavenly army standing near him on his right and on his left. 20The LORD said, 'Who will trick Ahab into attacking Ramoth in Gilead where he will be killed?'

"Some said one thing; some said another. 21Then one spirit came and stood before the LORD and said, 'I will trick him.'

22"The LORD asked, 'How will you do it?'

"The spirit answered, 'I will go to Ahab's prophets and make them tell lies.'

"So the LORD said, 'You will succeed in tricking him. Go and do it.' "

23Micaiah said, "Ahab, the LORD has made your prophets lie to you, and the LORD has decided that disaster should come to you."

24Then Zedekiah son of Kenaanah went up to Micaiah and slapped him in the face. Zedekiah said, "Has the LORD's spirit left me to speak through you?"

25Micaiah answered, "You will find out on the day you go to hide in an inside room."

26Then Ahab king of Israel ordered, "Take Micaiah and send him to Amon, the governor of the city, and to Joash, the king's son. 27Tell them I said to put this man in prison and give him only bread and water until I return safely from the battle."

28Micaiah said, "Ahab, if you come back safely from battle, the LORD has not spoken through me. Remember my words, all you people!"

29So Ahab king of Israel and Jehoshaphat king of Judah went to Ramoth in Gilead. 30King Ahab said to Jehoshaphat, "I will go into battle, but I will wear other clothes so no one will recognize me. But you wear your royal clothes." So Ahab wore other clothes and went into battle.

31The king of Aram had ordered his thirty-two chariot commanders, "Don't fight with anyone — important or unimportant — except the king of Israel." 32When these commanders saw Jehoshaphat, they thought he was certainly the king of Israel, so they turned to attack him. But Jehoshaphat began shouting. 33When they saw he was not King Ahab, they stopped chasing him.

34By chance, a soldier shot an arrow, but he hit Ahab king of Israel between the pieces of his armor. King Ahab said to his chariot driver, "Turn around and get me out of the battle, because I am hurt!" 35The battle continued all day. King Ahab was held up in his chariot and faced the Arameans. His blood flowed down to the bottom of the chariot. That evening he died. 36Near sunset a cry went out through the army of Israel: "Each man go back to his own city and land."

37In that way King Ahab died. His body was carried to Samaria and buried there. 38The men cleaned Ahab's chariot at a pool in Samaria where prostitutes*d* bathed, and the dogs licked his blood from the chariot. These things happened as the LORD had said they would.

39Everything else Ahab did is written in the book of the history of the kings of Israel. It tells about the palace Ahab built and decorated with ivory and the cities he built. 40So Ahab died, and his son Ahaziah became king in his place.

Jehoshaphat King of Judah

41Jehoshaphat son of Asa became king of Judah during Ahab's fourth year as king of Israel. 42Jehoshaphat was thirty-five years old when he became king, and he ruled in Jerusalem for twenty-five years. His mother's name was Azubah daughter of Shilhi. 43Jehoshaphat was good, like his father Asa, and he did what the LORD said was right. But Jehoshaphat did not destroy the places where gods were worshiped, so the people continued offering sacrifices and burning incense*d* there. 44Jehoshaphat was at peace with the king of Israel. 45Jehoshaphat fought many wars, and these wars and his successes are written in the book of the history of the kings of Judah. 46There were male prostitutes*d* still in the places of worship from the days of his father, Asa. So Jehoshaphat forced them to leave.

47During this time the land of Edom had no king; it was ruled by a governor.

48King Jehoshaphat built trading ships to sail to Ophir for gold. But the ships were wrecked at Ezion Geber, so they never set sail. 49Ahaziah son of Ahab went to help Jehoshaphat, offering to give Jehoshaphat some men to sail with his men, but Jehoshaphat refused.

50Jehoshaphat died and was buried with his ancestors in Jerusalem, the city of David, his ancestor. Then his son Jehoram became king in his place.

Ahaziah King of Israel

51Ahaziah son of Ahab became king of Israel in Samaria during Jehoshaphat's seventeenth year as king over Judah. Ahaziah ruled Israel for two years, 52and he did what the LORD said was wrong. He did the same evil his father Ahab, his mother Jezebel, and Jeroboam son of Nebat had done. All these rulers led the people of Israel into more sin. 53Ahaziah worshiped and served the god Baal,*d* and this made the LORD, the God of Israel, very angry. In these ways Ahaziah did what his father had done.

2 KINGS

Why Read This Book:

■ See how God uses leaders to encourage people to follow him (2 Kings 1—8).
■ Learn how unfaithfulness to God can destroy a nation (2 Kings 9—17).
■ Be encouraged that God keeps his promises even when people don't keep theirs (2 Kings 18—23).

Behind the Scenes:

The land was in shambles. The kingdom that David and Solomon built had split into Israel (in the north) and Judah (in the south), and both countries faced attack from the outside and unrest from within. Making matters worse, the people kept turning to the false god Baal for help, ignoring and forgetting the true God.

But even in this difficult situation, God hadn't forgotten his people. He sent the prophet Elisha to challenge them to turn back to God. Unlike his combative predecessor Elijah (1 Kings 16—19, p. 320) Elisha was more of a healer and comforter. He performed numerous miracles to ease people's pain (2 Kings 4), and he also performed miracles on behalf of the nation (2 Kings 5). He showed that

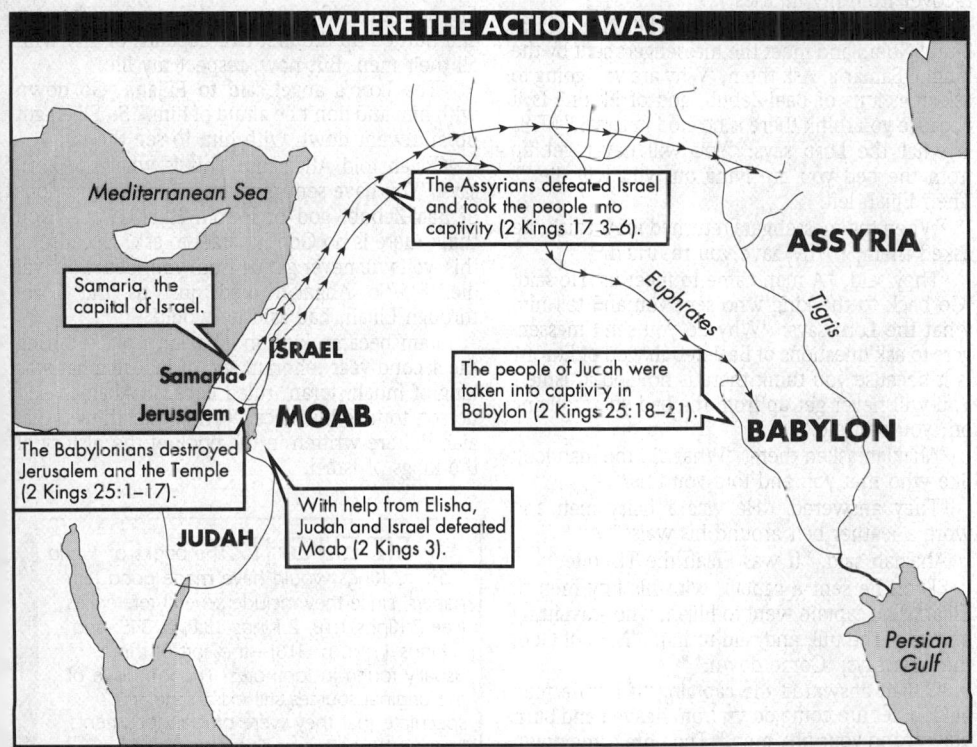

WHERE THE ACTION WAS

Mediterranean Sea

The Assyrians defeated Israel and took the people into captivity (2 Kings 17:3–6).

ASSYRIA

Samaria, the capital of Israel.

ISRAEL

Samaria

Jerusalem **MOAB**

The people of Judah were taken into captivity in Babylon (2 Kings 25:18–21).

BABYLON

The Babylonians destroyed Jerusalem and the Temple (2 Kings 25:1–17).

With help from Elisha, Judah and Israel defeated Moab (2 Kings 3).

JUDAH

Euphrates

Tigris

Persian Gulf

WHEN THE ACTION WAS

	Joshua led the Israelites into Canaan	The kingdom was split between Israel and Judah	Jerusalem fell to the Babylonians	Jesus was born
2000BC	**1500BC**	**1000BC**	**500BC**	**BC/AD**
		Saul was Israel's king	Elisha was a prophet in Israel	Israel fell to the Assyrians.

Behind the Scenes (cont.):

God hadn't given up on his people and would accept the Israelites if they would come back to him.

The northern kingdom did experience a brief revival under King Jeroboam II. But the overall decline continued, until Samaria—the northern capital—was destroyed and the people were taken into exile.

The southern kingdom also experienced some good years—under King Josiah, who repaired the Temple and led a religious revival in Judah. But in the end, Judah fell, the Temple was destroyed, and the Babylonians took the people into exile.

Despite the Israelites' unfaithfulness, God remained faithful. During this time he sent great prophets to call the people back to God. Even after Israel and Judah fell, God kept his promise to keep King David's descendants alive. And from those descendants eventually came Jesus.

Elijah and King Ahaziah

1 After Ahab died, Moab broke away from Israel's rule. ²Ahaziah fell down through the wooden bars in his upstairs room in Samaria and was badly hurt. He sent messengers and told them, "Go, ask Baal-Zebub, god of Ekron, if I will recover from my injuries."

³But the LORD's angel said to Elijah the Tishbite, "Go up and meet the messengers sent by the king of Samaria. Ask them, 'Why are you going to ask questions of Baal-Zebub, god of Ekron? Is it because you think there is no God in Israel?' ⁴This is what the LORD says: 'You will never get up from the bed you are lying on; you will die.'" Then Elijah left.

⁵When the messengers returned to Ahaziah, he asked them, "Why have you returned?"

⁶They said, "A man came to meet us. He said, 'Go back to the king who sent you and tell him what the LORD says: "Why do you send messengers to ask questions of Baal-Zebub, god of Ekron? Is it because you think there is no God in Israel? You will never get up from the bed you are lying on; you will die."'"

⁷Ahaziah asked them, "What did the man look like who met you and told you this?"

⁸They answered, "He was a hairy man and wore a leather belt around his waist."

Ahaziah said, "It was Elijah the Tishbite."

⁹Then he sent a captain with his fifty men to Elijah. The captain went to Elijah, who was sitting on top of the hill, and said to him, "Man of God, the king says, 'Come down!'"

¹⁰Elijah answered the captain, "If I am a man of God, let fire come down from heaven and burn up you and your fifty men." Then fire came down from heaven and burned up the captain and his fifty men.

¹¹Ahaziah sent another captain and fifty men to Elijah. The captain said to him, "Man of God, this is what the king says: 'Come down quickly!'"

¹²Elijah answered, "If I am a man of God, let fire come down from heaven and burn up you and your fifty men!" Then fire came down from heaven and burned up the captain and his fifty men.

¹³Ahaziah then sent a third captain with his fifty men. The third captain came and fell down on his knees before Elijah and begged, "Man of God, please respect my life and the lives of your fifty servants. ¹⁴See, fire came down from heaven and burned up the first two captains of fifty with all their men. But now, respect my life."

¹⁵The LORD's angel said to Elijah, "Go down with him and don't be afraid of him." So Elijah got up and went down with him to see the king.

¹⁶Elijah told Ahaziah, "This is what the LORD says: 'You have sent messengers to ask questions of Baal-Zebub, god of Ekron. Is it because you think there is no God in Israel to ask? Because of this, you will never get up from your bed; you will die.'" ¹⁷So Ahaziah died, just as the LORD, through Elijah, had said he would.

Joram became king in Ahaziah's place during the second year Jehoram son of Jehoshaphat was king of Judah. Joram ruled because Ahaziah had no son to take his place. ¹⁸The other things Ahaziah did are written in the book of the history of the kings of Israel.

✦ SIDELIGHT: The books of 1 and 2 Kings would have made good term papers, since they include several references (see 2 Kings 1:18, 2 Kings 13:8, p. 345, and 1 Kings 11:41, p. 316)—the sort of thing usually found in footnotes. Though none of the original sources still exist, scholars speculate that they were official documents kept in the palace or Temple.

Elijah Is Taken to Heaven

2 It was almost time for the LORD to take Elijah by a whirlwind up into heaven. While Elijah and Elisha were leaving Gilgal, ²Elijah said to Elisha, "Please stay here. The LORD has told me to go to Bethel."

SIDELIGHT: The prophets Elijah and Elisha had similar names but different styles. Elijah—whose name means "the Lord is my God"—preached judgment and repentance, and lived alone. Elisha—whose name means "the Lord is salvation"—stressed hope and grace, and lived among the people, especially the poor. Yet God used these two different people to accomplish his work.

But Elisha said, "As the LORD lives, and as you live, I won't leave you." So they went down to Bethel. [3]The groups of prophets at Bethel came out to Elisha and said to him, "Do you know the LORD will take your master away from you today?"

Elisha said, "Yes, I know, but don't talk about it."

[4]Elijah said to him, "Stay here, Elisha, because the LORD has sent me to Jericho."

But Elisha said, "As the LORD lives, and as you live, I won't leave you."

So they went to Jericho. [5]The groups of prophets at Jericho came to Elisha and said, "Do you know that the LORD will take your master away from you today?"

Elisha answered, "Yes, I know, but don't talk about it."

[6]Elijah said to Elisha, "Stay here. The LORD has sent me to the Jordan River."

Elisha answered, "As the LORD lives, and as you live I won't leave you."

So the two of them went on. [7]Fifty men of the groups of prophets came and stood far from where Elijah and Elisha were by the Jordan. [8]Elijah took off his coat, rolled it up, and hit the water. The water divided to the right and to the left, and Elijah and Elisha crossed over on dry ground.

FRIENDS

Saying Good-Bye

Laura Eggers remembers vividly when she first found out that her best friend, Micky, would be moving away. "I was staying the night at her house when she told me," Laura said. "And we cried."

"It was really hard, because we didn't know exactly when she'd be moving," she continued. Micky's father was being transferred, and his company couldn't say exactly when.

Laura explained, "We even got kind of distant at one point, drawing back to avoid the pain of separation. We recognized it before it got too far along, and we said, 'Wait a minute, what are we doing?'"

Laura and Micky spent as much time together as they could over the next few months. When Micky finally left, Laura felt sad, lonely, anxious, angry, even depressed. But the two friends were glad they had spent those last few months together.

And Laura is glad Micky and she are still friends, even though they are far away from each other.

In **2 Kings 2:1–12**, two other friends had to say good-bye. See how Elisha handled saying good-bye when it came time for Elijah to go to heaven.

■ What are the similarities between Laura and Micky's good-bye and Elijah and Elisha's good-bye?

■ Elijah promised Elisha a double share of his spirit when they said good-bye. What kinds of things has a friend left you when you've had to say good-bye?

C O N S I D E R . . .

■ what you would say to or do with a friend who was leaving—and say and do those things now, before you ever have to say good-bye.

■ watching the movie Brian's Song with friends and then discussing how to say good-bye to a friend.

F O R   M O R E ,   S E E . . .

■ Ruth 1:14–18 (p. 240)
■ 1 Samuel 20:41–42 (p. 264)
■ John 17:13–26 (p. 1089)

9After they had crossed over, Elijah said to Elisha, "What can I do for you before I am taken from you?"

Elisha said, "Leave me a double share of your spirit." *n*

10Elijah said, "You have asked a hard thing. But if you see me when I am taken from you, it will be yours. If you don't, it won't happen."

> ✹ **SIDELIGHT:** The prophet Elijah was whisked into heaven by a whirlwind, a chariot, and horses of fire—the first hot rod mentioned in the Bible (2 Kings 2:11). He is only one of two people mentioned in the Old Testament who never died. The other is Enoch (Genesis 5:24, p. 8).

11As they were walking and talking, a chariot and horses of fire appeared and separated Elijah from Elisha. Then Elijah went up to heaven in a whirlwind. 12Elisha saw it and shouted, "My father! My father! The chariots of Israel and their horsemen!" And Elisha did not see him anymore. Then Elisha grabbed his own clothes and tore them to show how sad he was.

13He picked up Elijah's coat that had fallen from him. Then he returned and stood on the bank of the Jordan. 14Elisha hit the water with Elijah's coat and said, "Where is the LORD, the God of Elijah?" When he hit the water, it divided to the right and to the left, and Elisha crossed over.

15The groups of prophets at Jericho were watching and said, "Elisha now has the spirit Elijah had." And they came to meet him, bowing down to the ground before him. 16They said to him, "There are fifty strong men with us. Please let them go and look for your master. Maybe the Spirit*d* of the LORD has taken Elijah up and set him down on some mountain or in some valley."

But Elisha answered, "No, don't send them."

17When the groups of prophets had begged Elisha until he couldn't refuse them anymore, he said, "Send them." So they sent fifty men who looked for three days, but they could not find him. 18Then they came back to Elisha at Jericho where he was staying. He said to them, "I told you not to go, didn't I?"

Elisha Makes the Water Pure

19The people of the city said to Elisha, "Look, master, this city is a nice place to live as you can see. But the water is so bad the land cannot grow crops."

20Elisha said, "Bring me a new bowl and put salt in it." So they brought it to him.

21Then he went out to the spring and threw the salt in it. He said, "This is what the LORD says: 'I have healed this water. From now on it won't cause death, and it won't keep the land from growing crops.' " 22So the water has been healed to this day just as Elisha had said.

Boys Make Fun of Elisha

23From there Elisha went up to Bethel. On the way some boys came out of the city and made fun of him. They said to him, "Go up too, you baldhead! Go up too, you baldhead!" 24Elisha turned around, looked at them, and put a curse on them in the name of the LORD. Then two mother bears came out of the woods and tore forty-two of the boys to pieces. 25Elisha went to Mount Carmel and from there he returned to Samaria.

> ✹ **SIDELIGHT:** If you like making fun of bald people, be careful. Some young men made fun of the prophet Elisha's baldness, and they got mauled by bears (2 Kings 2:23–25). Why was their teasing so bad? Elisha had shaved his head to show his role as a prophet of God, and they were jeering him to "go up" to heaven like Elijah. So they were really making fun of his faith.

War Between Israel and Moab

3 Joram son of Ahab became king over Israel at Samaria in Jehoshaphat's eighteenth year as king of Judah. And Joram ruled twelve years. 2He did what the LORD said was wrong, but he was not like his father and mother; he removed the stone pillars his father had made for Baal.*d* 3But he continued to sin like Jeroboam son of Nebat who had led Israel to sin. Joram did not stop doing these same sins.

4Mesha king of Moab raised sheep. He paid the king of Israel one hundred thousand lambs and the wool of one hundred thousand sheep. 5But when Ahab died, the king of Moab turned against the king of Israel. 6So King Joram went out from Samaria and gathered Israel's army. 7He also sent messengers to Jehoshaphat king of Judah. "The king of Moab has turned against me," he said. "Will you go with me to fight Moab?"

Jehoshaphat replied, "I will go with you. My soldiers and my horses are yours."

8Jehoshaphat asked, "Which way should we attack?"

Leave . . . spirit By law, the first son in a family would inherit a double share of his father's possessions. Elisha is asking to inherit a share of his master's power as his follower. He is not asking for twice as much power as Elijah had.

Joram answered, "Through the Desert of Edom."

9So the king of Israel went with the king of Judah and the king of Edom. After they had marched seven days, there was no more water for the army or for their animals that were with them. 10The king of Israel said, "This is terrible! The LORD has called us three kings together to hand us over to the Moabites!"

11But Jehoshaphat asked, "Is there a prophet*d* of the LORD here? We can ask the LORD through him."

An officer of the king of Israel answered, "Elisha son of Shaphat is here. He was Elijah's servant."

12Jehoshaphat said, 'He speaks the LORD's truth." So the king of Israel and Jehoshaphat and the king of Edom went down to see Elisha.

13Elisha said to the king of Israel, "I have nothing to do with you. Go to the prophets of your father and to the prophets of your mother!"

The king of Israel said to Elisha, "No, the LORD has called us three kings together to hand us over to the Moabites."

14Elisha said, "As surely as the LORD All-Powerful lives, whom I serve, I tell you the truth. I wouldn't even look at you or notice you if Jehoshaphat king of Judah were not here. I respect him. 15Now bring me someone who plays the harp."

While the harp was being played, the LORD gave Elisha power. 16Then Elisha said, "The LORD says to dig holes in the valley. 17The LORD says you won't see wind or rain, but the valley will be filled with water. Then you, your cattle, and your other animals can drink. 18This is easy for the LORD to do; he will also hand Moab over to you. 19You will destroy every strong, walled city and every important town. You will cut down every good tree and stop up all springs. You will ruin every good field with rocks."

20The next morning, about the time the sacrifice was offered, water came from the direction of Edom and filled the valley.

21All the Moabites heard that the kings had come up to fight against them. So they gathered everyone old enough to put on armor and waited at the border. 22But when the Moabites got up early in the morning, the sun was shining on the water. They saw the water across from them, and it looked as red as blood. 23Then they said, "This is blood! The kings must have fought and killed each other! Come, Moabites, let's take the valuables from the dead bodies!"

24When the Moabites came to the camp of Israel, the Israelites came out and fought them until they ran away. Then the Israelites went on into the land, killing the Moabites. 25They tore down the cities and threw rocks all over every good

field. They stopped up all the springs and cut down all the good trees. Kir Hareseth was the only city with its stones still in place, but the men with slingshots surrounded it and conquered it, too.

26When the king of Moab saw that the battle was too much for him, he took seven hundred men with swords to try to break through to the king of Edom. But they could not break through. 27Then the king of Moab took his oldest son, who would have been king after him, and offered him as a burnt offering on the wall. So there was great anger against the Israelites, who left and went back to their own land.

SIDELIGHT: If you judge prophets' power by the number of miracles they perform, Elisha was almost twice as powerful as his predecessor Elijah. The Bible tells of thirteen miracles Elisha performed (see 2 Kings 4—6 for examples), but only seven that Elijah performed. Miracles were important at that time to show that God was more powerful than the false god Baal.

A Widow Asks Elisha for Help

4 The wife of a man from the groups of prophets*d* said to Elisha, "Your servant, my husband, is dead. You know he honored the LORD. But now the man he owes money to is coming to take my two boys as his slaves!"

2Elisha answered, "How can I help you? Tell me, what do you have in your house?"

The woman said, "I don't have anything there except a pot of oil."

3Then Elisha said, "Go and get empty jars from all your neighbors. Don't ask for just a few. 4Then go into your house and shut the door behind you and your sons. Pour oil into all the jars, and set the full ones aside."

5So she left Elisha and shut the door behind her and her sons. As they brought the jars to her, she poured out the oil. 6When the jars were all full, she said to her son, "Bring me another jar."

But he said, "There are no more jars." Then the oil stopped flowing.

7She went and told Elisha. And the prophet said to her, "Go, sell the oil and pay what you owe. You and your sons can live on what is left."

The Shunammite Woman

8One day Elisha went to Shunem, where an important woman lived. She begged Elisha to stay and eat. So every time Elisha passed by, he stopped there to eat. 9The woman said to her husband, "I know that this is a holy man of God who passes by our house all the time. [10]Let's make a small room on the roof[n] and put a bed in the room for him. We can put a table, a chair, and a lampstand there. Then when he comes by, he can stay there."

[11]One day Elisha came to the woman's house. After he went to his room and rested, [12]he said to his servant Gehazi, "Call the Shunammite woman."

When the servant had called her, she stood in front of him. [13]Elisha had told his servant, "Now say to her, 'You have gone to all this trouble for us. What can I do for you? Do you want me to speak to the king or the commander of the army for you?' "

She answered, "I live among my own people."

[14]Elisha said to Gehazi, "But what can we do for her?"

He answered, "She has no son, and her husband is old."

[15]Then Elisha said to Gehazi, "Call her." When he called her, she stood in the doorway. [16]Then Elisha said, "About this time next year, you will hold a son in your arms."

The woman said, "No, master, man of God, don't lie to me, your servant!"

[17]But the woman became pregnant and gave birth to a son at that time the next year, just as Elisha had told her.

[18]The boy grew up and one day went out to his father, who was with the grain harvesters. [19]The boy said to his father, "My head! My head!"

The father said to his servant, "Take him to his mother!" [20]The servant took him to his mother, and he lay on his mother's lap until noon. Then he died. [21]So she took him up and laid him on Elisha's bed. Then she shut the door and left.

[22]She called to her husband, "Send me one of the servants and one of the donkeys. Then I can go quickly to the man of God and return."

[23]The husband said, "Why do you want to go to him today? It isn't the New Moon[d] or the Sabbath[d] day."

She said, "It will be all right."

[24]Then she saddled the donkey and said to her servant, "Lead on. Don't slow down for me unless I tell you." [25]So she went to Elisha, the man of God, at Mount Carmel.

When he saw her coming from far away, he said to his servant Gehazi, "Look, there's the Shunammite woman! [26]Run to meet her and ask, 'Are you all right? Is your husband all right? Is the boy all right?' "

She answered, "Everything is all right."

[27]Then she came to Elisha at the hill and grabbed his feet. Gehazi came near to pull her away, but Elisha said to him, "Leave her alone. She's very upset, and the LORD has not told me about it. He has hidden it from me."

[28]She said, "Master, did I ask you for a son? Didn't I tell you not to lie to me?"

[29]Then Elisha said to Gehazi, "Get ready. Take my walking stick in your hand and go quickly. If you meet anyone, don't say hello. If anyone greets you, don't respond. Lay my walking stick on the boy's face."

[30]The boy's mother said, "As surely as the LORD lives and as you live, I won't leave you!" So Elisha got up and followed her.

[31]Gehazi went on ahead and laid the walking stick on the boy's face, but the boy did not talk or move. Then Gehazi went back to meet Elisha. "The boy has not awakened," he said.

[32]When Elisha came into the house, the boy was lying dead on his bed. [33]Elisha entered the room and shut the door, so only he and the boy were in the room. Then he prayed to the LORD. [34]He went to the bed and lay on the boy, putting his mouth on the boy's mouth, his eyes on the boy's eyes, and his hands on the boy's hands. He stretched himself out on top of the boy. Soon the boy's skin became warm. [35]Elisha turned away and walked around the room. Then he went back and put himself on the boy again. The boy sneezed seven times and opened his eyes.

[36]Elisha called Gehazi and said, "Call the Shunammite!" So he did. When she came, Elisha said, "Pick up your son." [37]She came in and fell at Elisha's feet, bowing facedown to the floor. Then she picked up her son and went out.

Elisha and the Stew

[38]When Elisha returned to Gilgal, there was a shortage of food in the land. While the groups of prophets[d] were sitting in front of him, he said to his servant, "Put the large pot on the fire, and boil some stew for these men."

[39]One of them went out into the field to gather plants. Finding a wild vine, he picked fruit from the vine and filled his robe with it. Then he came and cut up the fruit into the pot. But they didn't know what kind of fruit it was. [40]They poured out the stew for the others to eat. When they began to eat it, they shouted, "Man of God, there's death in the pot!" And they could not eat it.

[41]Elisha told them to bring some flour. He threw it into the pot and said, "Pour it out for the people to eat." Then there was nothing harmful in the pot.

---

roof   In Bible times houses were built with flat roofs. The roof was used for drying things such as flax and fruit. And it was used as an extra room, as a place for worship, and as a place to sleep in the summer.

Elisha Feeds the People

⁴²A man from Baal Shalishah came to Elisha, bringing him twenty loaves of barley bread from the first harvest. He also brought fresh grain in his sack. Elisha said, "Give it to the people to eat."

⁴³Elisha's servant asked, "How can I feed a hundred people with so little?"

"Give the bread to the people to eat," Elisha said. "This is what the LORD says: 'They will eat and will have food left over.'" ⁴⁴After he gave it to them, the people ate and had food left over, as the LORD had said.

Naaman Is Healed

5 Naaman was commander of the army of the king of Aram. He was honored by his master, and he had much respect because the LORD used him to give victory to Aram. He was a mighty and brave man, but he had a skin disease.

²The Arameans had gone out to raid the Israelites and had taken a little girl as a captive. This little girl served Naaman's wife. ³She said to her mistress, "I wish my master would meet the prophet[d] who lives in Samaria. He would cure him of his disease."

⁴Naaman went to the king and told him what the girl from Israel had said. ⁵The king of Aram said, "Go ahead, and I will send a letter to the king of Israel." So Naaman left and took with him about seven hundred fifty pounds of silver, as well as one hundred fifty pounds of gold and ten changes of clothes. ⁶He brought the letter to the king of Israel, which read, "I am sending my servant Naaman to you so you can heal him of his skin disease."

⁷When the king of Israel read the letter, he tore his clothes to show how upset he was. He said, "I'm not God! I can't kill and make alive again! Why does this man send someone with a skin disease for me to heal? You can see that the king of Aram is trying to start trouble with me."

⁸When Elisha, the man of God, heard that the king of Israel had torn his clothes, he sent the king this message: "Why have you torn your clothes? Let Naaman come to me. Then he will know there is a prophet in Israel." ⁹So Naaman went with his horses and chariots to Elisha's house and stood outside the door.

¹⁰Elisha sent Naaman a messenger who said, "Go and wash in the Jordan River seven times.

SICKNESS

Take Your Medicine

Although the lightweight brace could be worn under her clothes, Allison Atkinson felt self-conscious about wearing it. She dreaded people's comments the first day she went to school with the "contraption." She thought everyone would notice it and make fun of her.

But if Allison didn't wear the brace, she would probably need to have surgery. Allison has a curvature of the spine known as scoliosis, a condition that can be stopped if she wears the back brace twenty-three hours a day during her growing years. Without the brace, the curvature can progress so that she will not be able to stand up straight.

Allison wore the brace. And as it turned out, no one noticed. "No one even knew I had it," she recalls.

That made the choice to wear the brace much easier. But it still seems like a nuisance. Every day over the past two years, Allison has had to choose: Will she wear her back brace or not?

Sometimes, people avoid medical treatment just because it's strange or embarrassing. But people won't get better if they don't follow the doctor's— or God's—orders. That was Naaman's predicament in **2 Kings 5:1–14**.

■ What does God have to do with Allison's and Naaman's medical treatments?

■ What kinds of things can keep God from working in our lives?

CONSIDER...

■ talking with someone at school who has to wear some kind of medical device and finding out how he or she feels about wearing it.

■ encouraging patients in a hospital to participate in God's healing processes by following doctor's orders.

FOR MORE, SEE...

■ Psalm 41 (p. 506)

■ Acts 3:1–10 (p. 1100)

■ John 9:1–11 (p. 1073)

Then your skin will be healed, and you will be clean."

¹¹Naaman became angry and left. He said, "I thought Elisha would surely come out and stand before me and call on the name of the LORD his God. I thought he would wave his hand over the place and heal the disease. ¹²The Abana and the Pharpar, the rivers of Damascus, are better than all the waters of Israel. Why can't I wash in them and become clean?" So Naaman went away very angry.

¹³Naaman's servants came near and said to him, "My father, if the prophet had told you to do some great thing, wouldn't you have done it? Doesn't it make more sense just to do it? After all, he only told you, 'Wash, and you will be clean.' " ¹⁴So Naaman went down and dipped in the Jordan seven times, just as Elisha had said. Then his skin became new again, like the skin of a child. And he was clean.

¹⁵Naaman and all his group returned to Elisha. He stood before Elisha and said, "Look, I now know there is no God in all the earth except in Israel. Now please accept a gift from me."

¹⁶But Elisha said, "As surely as the LORD lives whom I serve, I won't accept anything." Naaman urged him to take the gift, but he refused.

¹⁷Then Naaman said, "If you won't take the gift, then please give me some soil — as much as two of my mules can carry. From now on I'll not offer any burnt offering or sacrifice to any other gods but the LORD. ¹⁸But let the LORD pardon me for this: When my master goes into the temple of Rimmon[n] to worship, he leans on my arm. Then I must bow in that temple. May the LORD pardon me when I do that."

¹⁹Elisha said to him, "Go in peace."

Naaman left Elisha and went a short way. ²⁰Gehazi, the servant of Elisha the man of God, thought, "My master has not accepted what Naaman the Aramean brought. As surely as the LORD lives, I'll run after him and get something from him." ²¹So Gehazi went after Naaman.

When Naaman saw someone running after him, he got off the chariot to meet Gehazi. He asked, "Is everything all right?"

²²Gehazi said, "Everything is all right. My master has sent me. He said, 'Two young men from the groups of prophets in the mountains of Ephraim just came to me. Please give them seventy-five pounds of silver and two changes of clothes.' "

²³Naaman said, "Please take one hundred fifty pounds," and he urged Gehazi to take it. He tied one hundred fifty pounds of silver in two bags with two changes of clothes. Then he gave them to two of his servants to carry for Gehazi. ²⁴When they came to the hill, Gehazi took these things from Naaman's servants and put them in the house. Then he let Naaman's servants go, and they left.

²⁵When he came in and stood before his master, Elisha said to him, "Where have you been, Gehazi?"

"I didn't go anywhere," he answered.

²⁶But Elisha said to him, "My spirit was with you. I knew when the man turned from his chariot to meet you. This isn't a time to take money, clothes, olives, grapes, sheep, oxen, male servants, or female servants. ²⁷So Naaman's skin disease will come on you and your children forever." When Gehazi left Elisha, he had the disease and was as white as snow.

An Axhead Floats

6 The groups of prophets[d] said to Elisha, "The place where we meet with you is too small for us. ²Let's go to the Jordan River. There everyone can get a log, and let's build a place there to live."

Elisha said, "Go."

³One of them said, "Please go with us."

Elisha answered, "I will go," ⁴so he went with them. When they arrived at the Jordan, they cut down some trees. ⁵As one man was cutting down a tree, the head of his ax fell into the water. He yelled, "Oh, my master! I borrowed that ax!"

⁶Elisha asked, "Where did it fall?" The man showed him the place. Then Elisha cut down a stick and threw it into the water, and it made the iron head float. ⁷Elisha said, "Pick up the axhead." Then the man reached out and took it.

✳ **SIDELIGHT:** You've heard of a root beer float. How about an axhead float? You need an axhead, a river, and a prophet. The recipe is in 2 Kings 6:1–7.

Elisha and the Blinded Arameans

⁸The king of Aram was at war with Israel. He had a council meeting with his officers and said, "I will set up my camp in this place."

⁹Elisha, the man of God, sent a message to the king of Israel, saying, "Be careful! Don't pass that place, because the Arameans are going down there!"

¹⁰The king of Israel checked the place about which Elisha had warned him. Elisha warned him several times, so the king protected himself there.

¹¹The king of Aram was angry about this. He called his officers together and demanded, "Tell

---

temple of Rimmon   The place where the Aramean people worshiped the god Rimmon.

me who of us is working for the king of Israel."

¹²One of the officers said, "None, my master and king. It's Elisha, the prophet*d* from Israel. He can tell you what you speak in your bedroom."

¹³The king said, "Go and find him so I can send men and catch him."

The servants came back and reported, "He is in Dothan."

¹⁴Then the king sent horses, chariots, and many troops to Dothan. They arrived at night and surrounded the city.

¹⁵Elisha's servant got up early, and when he went out, he saw an army with horses and chariots all around the city. The servant said to Elisha, "Oh, my master, what can we do?"

¹⁶Elisha said, "Don't be afraid. The army that fights for us is larger than the one against us."

¹⁷Then Elisha prayed, "LORD, open my servant's eyes, and let him see."

The LORD opened the eyes of the young man, and he saw that the mountain was full of horses and chariots of fire all around Elisha.

¹⁸As the enemy came down toward Elisha, he prayed to the LORD, "Make these people blind." So he made the Aramean army blind, as Elisha had asked.

¹⁹Elisha said to them, "This is not the right road or the right city. Follow me and I'll take you to the man you are looking for." Then Elisha led them to Samaria.

²⁰After they entered Samaria, Elisha said, "LORD, open these men's eyes so they can see." So the LORD opened their eyes, and the Aramean army saw that they were inside the city of Samaria!

²¹When the king of Israel saw the Aramean army, he said to Elisha, "My father, should I kill them? Should I kill them?"

²²Elisha answered, "Don't kill them. You wouldn't kill people whom you captured with your sword and bow. Give them food and water, and let them eat and drink and then go home to their master." ²³So he prepared a great feast for the Aramean army. After they ate and drank, the king sent them away, and they went home to their master. The soldiers of Aram did not come anymore into the land of Israel.

A Shortage of Food

²⁴Later, Ben-Hadad king of Aram gathered his whole army and surrounded and attacked Samaria. ²⁵There was a shortage of food in Samaria. It was so bad that a donkey's head sold for about two pounds of silver, and half of a pint of dove's dung sold for about two ounces of silver.

²⁶As the king of Israel was passing by on the wall, a woman yelled out to him, "Help me, my master and king!"

²⁷The king said, "If the LORD doesn't help you,

how can I? Can I get help from the threshing*d* floor or from the winepress?"*d* ²⁸Then the king said to her, "What is your trouble?"

She answered, "This woman said to me, 'Give up your son so we can eat him today. Then we will eat my son tomorrow.' ²⁹So we boiled my son and ate him. Then the next day I said to her, 'Give up your son so we can eat him.' But she had hidden him."

³⁰When the king heard the woman's words, he tore his clothes in grief. As he walked along the wall, the people looked and saw he had on rough cloth under his clothes to show his sadness. ³¹He said, "May God punish me terribly if the head of Elisha son of Shaphat isn't cut off from his body today!"

³²The king sent a messenger to Elisha, who was sitting in his house with the older leaders. But before the messenger arrived, Elisha said to them, "See, this murderer is sending men to cut off my head. When the messenger arrives, shut the door and hold it; don't let him in. The sound of his master's feet is behind him."

³³Elisha was still talking with the leaders when the messenger arrived. The king said, "This trouble has come from the LORD. Why should I wait for the LORD any longer?"

7 Elisha said, "Listen to the LORD's word. This is what the LORD says: 'About this time tomorrow seven quarts of fine flour will be sold for two-fifths of an ounce of silver, and thirteen quarts of barley will be sold for two-fifths of an ounce of silver. This will happen at the gate of Samaria.' "

²Then the officer who was close to the king answered Elisha, "Even if the LORD opened windows in the sky, that couldn't happen."

Elisha said, "You will see it with your eyes, but you will not eat any of it."

³There were four men with a skin disease at the entrance to the city gate. They said to each other, "Why do we sit here until we die? ⁴There is no food in the city. So if we go into the city, we will die there. If we stay here, we will die. So let's go to the Aramean camp. If they let us live, we will live. If they kill us, we die."

⁵So they got up at twilight and went to the Aramean camp, but when they arrived, no one was there. ⁶The Lord had caused the Aramean army to hear the sound of chariots, horses, and a large army. They had said to each other, "The king of Israel has hired the Hittite and Egyptian kings to attack us!" ⁷So they got up and ran away in the twilight, leaving their tents, horses, and donkeys. They left the camp standing and ran for their lives.

⁸When the men with the skin disease came to the edge of the camp, they went into one of the tents and ate and drank. They carried silver, gold, and clothes out of the camp and hid them. Then

they came back and entered another tent. They carried things from this tent and hid them, also. ⁹Then they said to each other, "We're doing wrong. Today we have good news, but we are silent. If we wait until the sun comes up, we'll be discovered. Let's go right now and tell the people in the king's palace."

¹⁰So they went and called to the gatekeepers of the city. They said, "We went to the Aramean camp, but no one is there; we didn't hear anyone. The horses and donkeys were still tied up, and the tents were still standing." ¹¹Then the gatekeepers shouted out and told the people in the palace.

¹²The king got up in the night and said to his officers, "I'll tell you what the Arameans are doing to us. They know we are starving. They have gone out of the camp to hide in the field. They're saying, 'When the Israelites come out of the city, we'll capture them alive. Then we'll enter the city.'"

¹³One of his officers answered, "Let some men take five of the horses that are still left in the city. These men are like all the Israelites who are left; they are also about to die. Let's send them to see what has happened."

¹⁴So the men took two chariots with horses. The king sent them after the Aramean army, saying, "Go and see what has happened." ¹⁵The men followed the Aramean army as far as the Jordan River. The road was full of clothes and equipment that the Arameans had thrown away as they had hurriedly left. So the messengers returned and told the king. ¹⁶Then the people went out and took valuables from the Aramean camp. So seven quarts of fine flour were sold for two-fifths of an ounce of silver, and thirteen quarts of barley were sold for two-fifths of an ounce of silver, just as the LORD had said.

¹⁷The king chose the officer who was close to him to guard the gate, but the people trampled the officer to death. This happened just as Elisha had told the king when the king came to his house. ¹⁸He had said, "Thirteen quarts of barley and seven quarts of fine flour will each sell for two-fifths of an ounce of silver about this time tomorrow at the gate of Samaria."

¹⁹But the officer had answered, "Even if the LORD opened windows in the sky, that couldn't happen." And Elisha had told him, "You will see it with your eyes, but you won't eat any of it." ²⁰It happened to the officer just that way. The people trampled him in the gateway, and he died.

The Shunammite Regains Her Land

8 Elisha spoke to the woman whose son he had brought back to life. He said, "Get up and go with your family. Stay any place you can, because the LORD has called for a time without food that will last seven years." ²So the woman got up and did as the man of God had said. She left with her family, and they stayed in the land of the Philistines for seven years. ³After seven years she returned from the land of the Philistines and went to beg the king for her house and land. ⁴The king was talking with Gehazi, the servant of the man of God. The king had said, "Please tell me all the great things Elisha has done." ⁵Gehazi was telling the king how Elisha had brought a dead boy back to life. Just then the woman whose son Elisha had brought back to life came and begged the king for her house and land.

Gehazi said, "My master and king, this is the woman, and this is the son Elisha brought back to life."

⁶The king asked the woman, and she told him about it. Then the king chose an officer to help her. "Give the woman everything that is hers," the king said. "Give her all the money made from her land from the day she left until now."

Ben-Hadad Is Killed

⁷Then Elisha went to Damascus, where Ben-Hadad king of Aram was sick. Someone told him, "The man of God has arrived."

⁸The king said to Hazael, "Take a gift in your hand and go meet him. Ask the LORD through him if I will recover from my sickness."

⁹So Hazael went to meet Elisha, taking with him a gift of forty camels loaded with every good thing in Damascus. He came and stood before Elisha and said, "Your son Ben-Hadad king of Aram sent me to you. He asks if he will recover from his sickness."

¹⁰Elisha said to Hazael, "Go and tell Ben-Hadad, 'You will surely recover,' but the LORD has told me he will really die." ¹¹Hazael stared at Elisha until he felt ashamed. Then Elisha cried.

¹²Hazael asked, "Why are you crying, master?"

Elisha answered, "Because I know what evil you will do to the Israelites. You will burn their strong, walled cities with fire and kill their young men with swords. You will throw their babies to the ground and split open their pregnant women."

¹³Hazael said, "Am I a dog? How could I do such things?"

Elisha answered, "The LORD has shown me that you will be king over Aram."

¹⁴Then Hazael left Elisha and came to his master. Ben-Hadad said to him, "What did Elisha say to you?"

Hazael answered, "He told me that you will surely recover." ¹⁵But the next day Hazael took a blanket and dipped it in water. Then he put it over Ben-Hadad's face, and he died. So Hazael became king in Ben-Hadad's place.

Jehoram King of Judah

16While Jehoshaphat was king in Judah, Jehoram son of Jehoshaphat became king of Judah. This was during the fifth year Joram son of Ahab was king of Israel. 17Jehoram was thirty-two years old when he began to rule, and he ruled eight years in Jerusalem. 18He followed the ways of the kings of Israel, just as the family of Ahab had done, because he married Ahab's daughter. Jehoram did what the LORD said was wrong. 19But the LORD would not destroy Judah because of his servant David. The LORD had promised that one of David's descendants would always rule.

20In Jehoram's time Edom broke away from Judah's rule and chose their own king. 21So Jehoram and all his chariots went to Zair. The Edomites surrounded him and his chariot commanders. Jehoram got up and attacked the Edomites at night, but his army ran away to their tents. 22From then until now the country of Edom has fought against the rule of Judah. At the same time Libnah also broke away from Judah's rule.

23The other acts of Jehoram and all the things he did are written in the book of the history of the kings of Judah. 24Jehoram died and was buried with his ancestors in Jerusalem, and Jehoram's son Ahaziah ruled in his place.

25Ahaziah son of Jehoram became king of Judah during the twelfth year Joram son of Ahab was king of Israel. 26Ahaziah was twenty-two years old when he became king, and he ruled one year in Jerusalem. His mother's name was Athaliah, a granddaughter of Omri king of Israel. 27Ahaziah followed the ways of Ahab's family. He did what the LORD said was wrong, as Ahab's family had done, because he was a son-in-law to Ahab.

28Ahaziah went with Joram son of Ahab to Ramoth in Gilead, where they fought against Hazael king of Aram. The Arameans wounded Joram. 29So King Joram returned to Jezreel to heal from the wound he had received from the Arameans at Ramoth when he fought Hazael king of Aram. Ahaziah son of Jehoram king of Judah went down to visit Joram son of Ahab at Jezreel, because he had been wounded.

Jehu Is Chosen King

9 At the same time, Elisha the prophet[d] called a man from the groups of prophets. Elisha said, "Get ready, and take this small bottle of olive oil in your hand. Go to Ramoth in Gilead. 2When you arrive, find Jehu son of Jehoshaphat, the son of Nimshi. Go in and make Jehu get up from among his brothers, and take him to an inner room. 3Then take the bottle and pour the oil on Jehu's head and say, 'This is what the LORD says: I have appointed you king over Israel.' Then open the door and run away. Don't wait!"

4So the young man, the prophet, went to Ramoth in Gilead. 5When he arrived, he saw the officers of the army sitting together. He said, "Commander, I have a message for you."

Jehu asked, "For which one of us?"

The young man said, "For you, commander."

6Jehu got up and went into the house. Then the young prophet poured the olive oil on Jehu's head and said to him, "This is what the LORD, the God of Israel says: 'I have appointed you king over the LORD's people Israel. 7You must destroy the family of Ahab your master. I will punish Jezebel for the deaths of my servants the prophets and for all the LORD's servants who were murdered. 8All of Ahab's family must die. I will not let any male child in Ahab's family live in Israel, whether slave or free. 9I will make Ahab's family like the family of Jeroboam son of Nebat and like the family of Baasha son of Ahijah. 10The dogs will eat Jezebel at Jezreel, and no one will bury her.' "

Then the young prophet opened the door and ran away.

11When Jehu went back to his master's officers, one of them said to Jehu, "Is everything all right? Why did this crazy man come to you?"

Jehu answered, "You know the man and how he talks."

12They answered, "That's not true. Tell us."

Jehu said, "He said to me, 'This is what the LORD says: I have appointed you to be king over Israel.' "

13Then the officers hurried, and each man took off his own coat and put it on the stairs for Jehu. They blew the trumpet and shouted, "Jehu is king!"

Joram and Ahaziah Are Killed

14So Jehu son of Jehoshaphat, the son of Nimshi, made plans against Joram. Now Joram and all Israel had been defending Ramoth in Gilead from Hazael king of Aram. 15But King Joram had to return to Jezreel to heal from the injuries the Arameans had given him when he fought against Hazael king of Aram.

Jehu said, "If you agree with this, don't let anyone leave the city. They might tell the news in Jezreel." 16Then he got into his chariot and set out for Jezreel, where Joram was resting. Ahaziah king of Judah had gone down to see him.

17The lookout was standing on the watchtower in Jezreel when he saw Jehu's troops coming. He said, "I see some soldiers!"

Joram said, "Take a horseman and send him to meet them. Tell him to ask, 'Is all in order?' "

18The horseman rode out to meet Jehu, and he said, "This is what the king says: 'Is all in order?' "

Jehu said, "Why bother yourself with order? Come along behind me."

The lookout reported, "The messenger reached them, but he is not coming back."

¹⁹Then Joram sent out a second horseman. This rider came to Jehu's group and said, "This is what the king says: 'Is all in order?' "

Jehu answered, "Why bother yourself with order? Come along behind me."

²⁰The lookout reported, "The second man reached them, but he is not coming back. The man in the chariot is driving like Jehu son of Nimshi. He drives as if he were crazy!"

> **SIDELIGHT:** The first record of bad driving in the Bible is in 2 Kings 9:20. King Jehu was such a bad driver that people could recognize his chariot driving from a distance. They said he drove "as if he were crazy." But since he was king, he never got a ticket.

²¹Joram said, "Get my chariot ready." Then the servant got Joram's chariot ready. Joram king of Israel and Ahaziah king of Judah went out, each in his own chariot, to meet Jehu at the property of Naboth the Jezreelite.

²²When Joram saw Jehu, he said, "Is all in order, Jehu?"

Jehu answered, "There will never be any order as long as your mother Jezebel worships idols and uses witchcraft."*ᵈ*

²³Joram turned the horses to run away and yelled to Ahaziah, "It's a trick, Ahaziah!"

²⁴Then Jehu drew his bow and shot Joram between his shoulders. The arrow went through Joram's heart, and he fell down in his chariot.

²⁵Jehu ordered Bidkar, his chariot officer, "Pick up Joram's body, and throw it into the field of Naboth the Jezreelite. Remember when you and I rode together with Joram's father Ahab. The LORD made this prophecyᵈ against him: ²⁶'Yesterday I saw the blood of Naboth and his sons, says the LORD, so I will punish Ahab in his field, says the LORD.' Take Joram's body and throw it into the field, as the LORD has said."

²⁷When Ahaziah king of Judah saw this, he ran away toward Beth Haggan. Jehu chased him, saying, "Shoot Ahaziah, too!" Ahaziah was wounded in his chariot on the way up to Gur near Ibleam. He got as far as Megiddo but died there. ²⁸Ahaziah's servants carried his body in a chariot to Jerusalem and buried him with his ancestors in his tomb in Jerusalem. ²⁹(Ahaziah had become king over Judah in the eleventh year Joram son of Ahab was king.)

Death of Jezebel

³⁰When Jehu came to Jezreel, Jezebel heard about it. She put on her eye makeup and fixed her hair. Then she looked out the window. ³¹When Jehu entered the city gate, Jezebel said, "Have you come in peace, you Zimri,ⁿ you who killed your master?"

³²Jehu looked up at the window and said, "Who is on my side? Who?" Two or three servants looked out the window at Jehu. ³³He said to them, "Throw her down." So they threw Jezebel down, and the horses ran over her. Some of her blood splashed on the wall and on the horses.

> **SIDELIGHT:** When wicked Queen Jezebel put on make-up (2 Kings 9:30–33), it was probably quite elaborate. Women in those days used black eye liner, blue eye shadow, red lipstick and nail polish, powders, and perfume. None of it did much good, though, when she was thrown out the window and trampled by horses.

³⁴Jehu went into the house and ate and drank. Then he said, "Now see about this cursed woman. Bury her, because she is a king's daughter."

³⁵The men went to bury Jezebel, but they could not find her. They found only her skull, feet, and the palms of her hands. ³⁶When they came back and told Jehu, he said, "The LORD said this through his servant Elijah the Tishbite: 'The dogs will eat Jezebel at Jezreel. ³⁷Her body will be like manure on the field in the land at Jezreel. No one will be able to say that this is Jezebel.' "

Families of Ahab and Ahaziah Killed

10 Ahab had seventy sons in Samaria. Jehu wrote letters and sent them to Samaria to the officers and older leaders of Jezreel and to the guardians of the sons of Ahab. Jehu said, ²"You have your master's sons with you, and you have chariots, horses, a city with strong walls, and weapons. When you get this letter, ³choose the best and most worthy person among your master's sons, and make him king. Then fight for your master's family."

⁴But the officers and leaders of Jezreel were frightened. They said, "Two kings could not stand up to Jehu, so how can we?"

⁵The palace manager, the city governor, the leaders, and the guardians sent a message to Jehu. "We are your servants," they said. "We will do

Zimri   He was the man who killed Elah and the family of Baasha. Read 1 Kings 16:8-12.

everything you tell us to do. We won't make any man king, so do whatever you think is best."

⁶Then Jehu wrote a second letter, saying, "If you are on my side and will obey me, cut off the heads of your master's sons and come to me at Jezreel tomorrow about this time."

Now the seventy sons of the king's family were with the leading men of the city who were their guardians. ⁷When the leaders received the letter, they took the king's sons and killed all seventy of them. They put their heads in baskets and sent them to Jehu at Jezreel. ⁸The messenger came to Jehu and told him, "They have brought the heads of the king's sons."

Then Jehu said, "Lay the heads in two piles at the city gate until morning."

⁹In the morning, Jehu went out and stood before the people and said to them, "You are innocent. Look, I made plans against my master and killed him. But who killed all these? ¹⁰You should know that everything the LORD said about Ahab's family will come true. The LORD has spoken through his servant Elijah, and the LORD has done what he said." ¹¹So Jehu killed everyone of Ahab's family in Jezreel who was still alive. He also killed all Ahab's leading men, close friends, and priests. No one who had helped Ahab was left alive.

¹²Then Jehu left and went to Samaria by way of the road to Beth Eked of the Shepherds. ¹³There Jehu met some relatives of Ahaziah king of Judah. Jehu asked, "Who are you?"

They answered, "We are relatives of Ahaziah. We have come down to get revenge for the families of the king and the king's mother."

¹⁴Then Jehu said, "Take them alive!" So they captured Ahaziah's relatives alive and killed them at the well near Beth Eked—forty-two of them. Jehu did not leave anyone alive.

¹⁵After Jehu left there, he met Jehonadab son of Recab, who was also on his way to meet Jehu. Jehu greeted him and said, "Are you as good a friend to me as I am to you?"

Jehonadab answered, "Yes, I am."

Jehu said, "If you are, then give me your hand." So Jehonadab gave him his hand, and Jehu pulled him into the chariot. ¹⁶"Come with me," Jehu said. "You can see how strong my feelings are for the LORD." So Jehu had Jehonadab ride in his chariot.

¹⁷When Jehu came to Samaria, he killed all of Ahab's family in Samaria. He destroyed all those who were left, just as the LORD had told Elijah it would happen.

Baal Worshipers Killed

¹⁸Then Jehu gathered all the people together and said to them, "Ahab served Baal[d] a little, but Jehu will serve Baal much. ¹⁹Now call for me all

Baal's prophets and priests and all the people who worship Baal. Don't let anyone miss this meeting, because I have a great sacrifice for Baal. Anyone who is not there will not live." But Jehu was tricking them so he could destroy the worshipers of Baal. ²⁰He said, "Prepare a holy meeting for Baal." So they announced the meeting. ²¹Then Jehu sent word through all Israel, and all the worshipers of Baal came; not one stayed home. They came into the temple of Baal, and the temple was filled from one side to the other.

²²Jehu said to the man who kept the robes, "Bring out robes for all the worshipers of Baal." After he brought out robes for them, ²³Jehu and Jehonadab son of Recab went into the temple of Baal. Jehu said to the worshipers of Baal, "Look around, and make sure there are no servants of the LORD with you. Be sure there are only worshipers of Baal." ²⁴Then the worshipers of Baal went in to offer sacrifices and burnt offerings.

Jehu had eighty men waiting outside. He had told them, "Don't let anyone escape. If you do, you must pay with your own life."

²⁵As soon as Jehu finished offering the burnt offering, he ordered the guards and the captains, "Go in and kill the worshipers of Baal. Don't let anyone come out." So the guards and captains killed the worshipers of Baal with the sword and threw their bodies out. Then they went to the inner rooms of the temple ²⁶and brought out the pillars of the temple of Baal and burned them. ²⁷They tore down the stone pillar of Baal, as well as the temple of Baal. And they made it into a sewage pit, as it is today.

²⁸So Jehu destroyed Baal worship in Israel, ²⁹but he did not stop doing the sins Jeroboam son of Nebat had done. Jeroboam had led Israel to sin by worshiping the golden calves in Bethel and Dan.

³⁰The LORD said to Jehu, "You have done well in obeying what I said was right. You have done to the family of Ahab as I wanted. Because of this, your descendants[d] as far as your great-great-grandchildren will be kings of Israel." ³¹But Jehu was not careful to follow the teachings of the LORD, the God of Israel, with all his heart. He did not stop doing the same sins Jeroboam had done, by which he had led Israel to sin.

³²At that time the LORD began to make Israel smaller. Hazael defeated the Israelites in all the land of Israel, ³³taking all the land of the Jordan known as the land of Gilead. (It was the region of Gad, Reuben, and Manasseh.) He took land from Aroer by the Arnon Ravine through Gilead to Bashan.

³⁴The other things Jehu did—everything he did and all his victories—are recorded in the book of the history of the kings of Israel. ³⁵Jehu died and was buried in Samaria, and his son Jehoahaz be-

came king in his place. 36Jehu was king over Israel in Samaria for twenty-eight years.

Athaliah and Joash

11 When Ahaziah's mother, Athaliah, saw that her son was dead, she killed all the royal family. 2But Jehosheba, King Jehoram's daughter and Ahaziah's sister, took Joash, Ahaziah's son. She stole him from among the other sons of the king who were about to be murdered. She put Joash and his nurse in a bedroom to hide him from Athaliah, so he was not killed. 3He hid with her in the Temple*d* of the LORD for six years. During that time Athaliah ruled the land.

> **SIDELIGHT:** It may seem like a modern idea to have a woman as president, but one woman, Athaliah, ruled Judah for seven years (2 Kings 11:1–3). She didn't get her position by popular vote!

4In the seventh year Jehoiada sent for the commanders of groups of a hundred men, as well as the Carites.*n* He brought them together in the Temple of the LORD and made an agreement with them. There, in the Temple of the LORD, he made them promise loyalty, and then he showed them the king's son. 5He commanded them, "This is what you must do. A third of you who go on duty on the Sabbath*d* will guard the king's palace. 6A third of you will be at the Sur Gate, and another third will be at the gate behind the guard. This way you will guard the Temple. 7The two groups who go off duty on the Sabbath must protect the Temple of the LORD for the king. 8All of you must stand around the king, each man with his weapons in his hand. If anyone comes near, kill him. Stay close to the king when he goes out and when he comes in."

9The commanders over a hundred men obeyed everything Jehoiada the priest had commanded. Each one took his men who came on duty on the Sabbath and those who went off duty on the Sabbath, and they came to Jehoiada the priest. 10He gave the commanders the spears and shields that had belonged to King David and that were kept in the Temple of the LORD.

Joash Becomes King

11Then each guard took his place with his weapons in his hand. There were guards from the south side of the Temple*d* to the north side. They stood by the altar and the Temple and around the

king. 12Jehoiada brought out the king's son and put the crown on him and gave him a copy of the agreement. They appointed him king and poured olive oil on him. Then they clapped their hands and said, "Long live the king!"

13When Athaliah heard the noise of the guards and the people, she went to them at the Temple of the LORD. 14She looked, and there was the king, standing by the pillar, as the custom was. The officers and trumpeters were standing beside him, and all the people of the land were very happy and were blowing trumpets. Then Athaliah tore her clothes and screamed, "Traitors! Traitors!"

15Jehoiada the priest gave orders to the commanders of a hundred men, who led the army. He said, "Surround her with soldiers and kill with a sword anyone who follows her." He commanded this because he had said, "Don't put Athaliah to death in the Temple of the LORD." 16So they caught her when she came to the horses' entrance near the palace. There she was put to death.

17Then Jehoiada made an agreement between the LORD and the king and the people that they would be the LORD's special people. He also made an agreement between the king and the people. 18All the people of the land went to the temple of Baal*d* and tore it down, smashing the altars and idols. They also killed Mattan, the priest of Baal, in front of the altars.

Then Jehoiada the priest placed guards at the Temple of the LORD. 19He took with him the commanders of a hundred men and the Carites, the royal bodyguards, as well as the guards and all the people of the land. Together they took the king out of the Temple of the LORD and went into the palace through the gate of the guards. Then the king sat on the royal throne. 20So all the people of

> **SIDELIGHT:** If anyone asked Joash if he had "grown up in the church" he could have easily said yes. In fact, he was hidden in the Temple for six years to keep from getting killed. At age seven, he became the youngest king in the Bible (2 Kings 11:1–3, 21).

the land were very happy, and Jerusalem had peace, because Athaliah had been put to death with the sword at the palace.

21Joash was seven years old when he became king.

Carites This was probably a special unit of the army that was responsible for the king's safety, a kind of palace guard similar to the Kerethites and the Pelethites.

12

Joash became king of Judah in Jehu's seventh year as king of Israel, and he ruled for forty years in Jerusalem. His mother's name was Zibiah, and she was from Beersheba. [2]Joash did what the LORD said was right as long as Jehoiada the priest taught him. [3]But the places where gods were worshiped were not removed; the people still made sacrifices and burned incense[d] there.

Joash Repairs the Temple

[4]Joash said to the priests, "Take all the money brought as offerings to the Temple[d] of the LORD. This includes the money each person owes in taxes and the money each person promises or brings freely to the LORD. [5]Each priest will take the money from the people he serves. Then the priests must repair any damage they find in the Temple."

[6]But by the twenty-third year Joash was king, the priests still had not repaired the Temple. [7]So King Joash called for Jehoiada the priest and the other priests and said to them, "Why aren't you repairing the damage of the Temple? Don't take any more money from the people you serve, but hand over the money for the repair of the Temple." [8]The priests agreed not to take any more money from the people and not to repair the Temple themselves.

[9]Jehoiada the priest took a box and made a hole in the top of it. Then he put it by the altar, on the right side as the people came into the Temple of the LORD. The priests guarding the doorway put all the money brought to the Temple of the LORD into the box. [10]Each time the priests saw that the box was full of money, the king's royal secretary and the high priest came. They counted the money that had been brought to the Temple of the LORD, and they put it into bags. [11]Next they weighed the money and gave it to the people in charge of the work on the Temple. With it they paid the carpenters and the builders who worked on the Temple of the LORD, [12]as well as the bricklayers and stonecutters. They also used the money to buy timber and cut stone to repair the damage of the Temple of the LORD. It paid for everything.

[13]The money brought into the Temple of the LORD was not used to make silver cups, wick trimmers, bowls, trumpets, or gold or silver vessels. [14]They paid the money to the workers, who used it to repair the Temple of the LORD. [15]They did not demand to know how the money was spent, because the workers were honest. [16]The money from the penalty offerings and sin offerings was not brought into the Temple of the LORD, because it belonged to the priests.

Joash Saves Jerusalem

[17]About this time Hazael king of Aram attacked Gath and captured it. Then he went to attack Jerusalem. [18]Joash king of Judah took all the holy things given by his ancestors, the kings of Judah—Jehoshaphat, Jehoram, and Ahaziah. He also took his own holy things as well as the gold that was found in the treasuries of the Temple[d] of the LORD and the gold from the palace. Joash sent all this treasure to Hazael king of Aram, who turned away from Jerusalem.

[19]Everything else Joash did is written in the book of the history of the kings of Judah. [20]His officers made plans against him and killed him at Beth Millo on the road down to Silla. [21]The officers who killed him were Jozabad son of Shimeath and Jehozabad son of Shomer. Joash was buried with his ancestors in Jerusalem, and Amaziah, his son, became king in his place.

Jehoahaz King of Israel

13

Jehoahaz son of Jehu became king over Israel in Samaria during the twenty-third year Joash son of Ahaziah was king of Judah. Jehoahaz ruled seventeen years, [2]and he did what the LORD said was wrong. Jehoahaz did the same sins Jeroboam son of Nebat had done. Jeroboam had led Israel to sin, and Jehoahaz did not stop doing these same sins. [3]So the LORD was angry with Israel and handed them over to Hazael king of Aram and his son Ben-Hadad for a long time.

[4]Then Jehoahaz begged the LORD, and the LORD listened to him. The LORD had seen the troubles of Israel; he saw how terribly the king of Aram was treating them. [5]He gave Israel a man to save them, and they escaped from the Arameans. The Israelites then lived in their own homes as they had before, [6]but they still did not stop doing the same sins that the family of Jeroboam had done. He had led Israel to sin, and they continued doing those sins. The Asherah[d] idol also was left standing in Samaria.

[7]Nothing was left of Jehoahaz's army except fifty horsemen, ten chariots, and ten thousand foot soldiers. The king of Aram had destroyed them and made them like chaff.[d]

[8]Everything else Jehoahaz did and all his victories are written in the book of the history of the kings of Israel. [9]Jehoahaz died and was buried in Samaria, and his son Jehoash became king in his place.

Jehoash King of Israel

[10]Jehoash son of Jehoahaz became king of Israel in Samaria during Joash's thirty-seventh year as king of Judah. Jehoash ruled sixteen years, [11]and he did what the LORD said was wrong. He did not

stop doing the same sins Jeroboam son of Nebat had done. Jeroboam had led Israel to sin, and Jehoash continued to do the same thing. [12]Everything else he did and all his victories, including his war against Amaziah king of Judah, are written in the book of the history of the kings of Israel. [13]Jehoash died, and Jeroboam took his place on the throne. Jehoash was buried in Samaria with the kings of Israel.

The Death of Elisha

[14]At this time Elisha became sick. Before he died, Jehoash king of Israel went to Elisha and cried for him. Jehoash said, "My father, my father! The chariots of Israel and their horsemen!" [15]Elisha said to Jehoash, "Take a bow and arrows." So he took a bow and arrows. [16]Then Elisha said to him, "Put your hand on the bow." So Jehoash put his hand on the bow. Then Elisha put his hands on the king's hands. [17]Elisha said, "Open the east window." So Jehoash opened the window. Then Elisha said, "Shoot," and Jehoash shot. Elisha said, "The Lord's arrow of victory over Aram! You will defeat the Arameans at Aphek until you destroy them."

[18]Elisha said, "Take the arrows." So Jehoash took them. Then Elisha said to him, "Strike the ground." So Jehoash struck the ground three times and stopped. [19]The man of God was angry with him. "You should have struck five or six times!" Elisha said. "Then you would have struck Aram until you had completely destroyed it. But now you will defeat it only three times."

[20]Then Elisha died and was buried.

At that time groups of Moabites would rob the land in the springtime. [21]Once as some Israelites were burying a man, suddenly they saw a group of Moabites coming. The Israelites threw the dead man into Elisha's grave. When the man touched Elisha's bones, the man came back to life and stood on his feet.

War with Aram

[22]During all the days Jehoahaz was king, Hazael king of Aram troubled Israel. [23]But the Lord was kind to the Israelites; he had mercy on them and helped them because of his agreement with Abraham, Isaac, and Jacob. To this day he has never wanted to destroy them or reject them.

[24]When Hazael king of Aram died, his son Ben-Hadad became king in his place. [25]During a war Hazael had taken some cities from Jehoahaz, Jehoash's father. Now Jehoash took back those cities from Hazael's son Ben-Hadad. He defeated Ben-Hadad three times and took back the cities of Israel.

Amaziah King of Judah

14 Amaziah son of Joash became king of Judah during the second year Jehoash son of Jehoahaz was king of Israel. [2]Amaziah was twenty-five years old when he became king, and he ruled twenty-nine years in Jerusalem. His mother was named Jehoaddin, and she was from Jerusalem. [3]Amaziah did what the Lord said was right. He did everything his father Joash had done, but he did not do as his ancestor David had done. [4]The places where gods were worshiped were not removed, so the people still sacrificed and burned incense[d] there.

[5]As soon as Amaziah took control of the kingdom, he executed the officers who had murdered his father the king. [6]But he did not put to death the children of the murderers because of the rule written in the Book of the Teachings of Moses. The Lord had commanded: "Parents must not be put to death when their children do wrong, and children must not be put to death when their parents do wrong. Each must die for his own sins." [n]

[7]In battle Amaziah killed ten thousand Edomites in the Valley of Salt. He also took the city of Sela. He called it Joktheel, as it is still called today.

[8]Amaziah sent messengers to Jehoash son of Jehoahaz, the son of Jehu, king of Israel. They said, "Come, let's meet face to face."

[9]Then Jehoash king of Israel answered Amaziah king of Judah, "A thornbush in Lebanon sent a message to a cedar tree in Lebanon. It said, 'Let your daughter marry my son.' But then a wild animal from Lebanon came by, walking on and crushing the thornbush. [10]You have defeated Edom, but you have become proud. Stay at home and brag. Don't ask for trouble, or you and Judah will be defeated."

[11]But Amaziah would not listen, so Jehoash king of Israel went to attack. He and Amaziah king of Judah faced each other in battle at Beth Shemesh in Judah. [12]Israel defeated Judah, and every man of Judah ran away to his home. [13]At Beth Shemesh Jehoash king of Israel captured Amaziah king of Judah. (Amaziah was the son of Joash, who was the son of Ahaziah.) Jehoash went up to Jerusalem and broke down the wall of Jerusalem from the Gate of Ephraim to the Corner Gate, which was about six hundred feet. [14]He took all the gold and silver and all the utensils in the Temple[d] of the Lord, and he took the treasuries of the palace and some hostages. Then he returned to Samaria.

[15]The other acts of Jehoash and his victories, including his war against Amaziah king of Judah, are written in the book of the history of the kings of Israel. [16]Jehoash died and was buried in Sa-

---

"Parents . . . sins." See Deuteronomy 24:16.

maria with the kings of Israel, and his son Jeroboam became king in his place.

[17]Amaziah son of Joash, the king of Judah, lived fifteen years after the death of Jehoash son of Jehoahaz, the king of Israel. [18]The other things Amaziah did are written in the book of the history of the kings of Judah. [19]The people in Jerusalem made plans against him. So he ran away to the town of Lachish, but they sent men after him to Lachish and killed him. [20]They brought his body back on horses, and he was buried with his ancestors in Jerusalem, in the city of David.

[21]Then all the people of Judah made Uzziah[n] king in place of his father Amaziah. Uzziah was sixteen years old. [22]He rebuilt the town of Elath and made it part of Judah again after Amaziah died.

Jeroboam King of Israel

[23]Jeroboam son of Jehoash became king of Israel in Samaria during the fifteenth year Amaziah was king of Judah. (Amaziah was the son of Joash.) Jeroboam ruled for forty-one years, [24]and he did what the LORD said was wrong. Jeroboam son of Nebat had led Israel to sin, and Jeroboam son of Jehoash did not stop doing the same sins. [25]Jeroboam won back Israel's border from Lebo Hamath to the Dead Sea.[d] This happened as the LORD, the God of Israel, had said through his servant Jonah son of Amittai, the prophet[d] from Gath Hepher. [26]The LORD had seen how the Israelites, both slave and free, were suffering terribly. No one was left who could help Israel. [27]The LORD had not said he would completely destroy Israel from the world, so he saved the Israelites through Jeroboam son of Jehoash.

[28]Everything else Jeroboam did is written down — all his victories and how he won back from Judah the towns of Damascus and Hamath for Israel. All this is written in the book of the history of the kings of Israel. [29]Jeroboam died and was buried with his ancestors, the kings of Israel. Jeroboam's son Zechariah became king in his place.

Uzziah King of Judah

15 Uzziah[n] son of Amaziah became king of Judah during Jeroboam's twenty-seventh year as king of Israel. [2]Uzziah was sixteen years old when he became king, and he ruled fifty-two years in Jerusalem. His mother was named Jecoliah, and she was from Jerusalem. [3]He did what the LORD said was right, just as his father Amaziah had done. [4]But the places where gods were worshiped were not removed, so the people still made sacrifices and burned incense[d] there.

[5]The LORD struck Uzziah with a skin disease,

which he had until the day he died. So he had to live in a separate house. Jotham, the king's son, was in charge of the palace, and he governed the people of the land.

[6]All the other things Uzziah did are written in the book of the history of the kings of Judah. [7]Uzziah died and was buried near his ancestors in Jerusalem, and his son Jotham became king in his place.

Zechariah King of Israel

[8]Zechariah son of Jeroboam was king over Israel in Samaria. He ruled for six months during Uzziah's[n] thirty-eighth year as king of Judah. [9]Zechariah did what the LORD said was wrong, just as his ancestors had done. Jeroboam son of Nebat had led the people of Israel to sin, and Zechariah did not stop doing the same sins.

[10]Shallum son of Jabesh made plans against Zechariah and killed him in front of the people. Then Shallum became king in his place. [11]The other acts of Zechariah are written in the book of the history of the kings of Israel. [12]The LORD had told Jehu: "Your sons down to your great-great-grandchildren will be kings of Israel," and the LORD's word came true.

Shallum King of Israel

[13]Shallum son of Jabesh became king during Uzziah's thirty-ninth year as king of Judah. Shallum ruled for a month in Samaria. [14]Then Menahem son of Gadi came up from Tirzah to Samaria and attacked Shallum son of Jabesh in Samaria. He killed him and became king in Shallum's place.

[15]The other acts of Shallum and his secret plans are written in the book of the history of the kings of Israel.

Menahem King of Israel

[16]Menahem started out from Tirzah and attacked Tiphsah, destroying the city and the area nearby. This was because the people had refused to open the city gate for him. He defeated them and ripped open all their pregnant women.

[17]Menahem son of Gadi became king over Israel during Uzziah's thirty-ninth year as king of Judah. Menahem ruled ten years in Samaria, [18]and he did what the LORD said was wrong. Jeroboam son of Nebat had led Israel to sin, and all the time Menahem was king, he did not stop doing the same sins.

[19]Pul king of Assyria came to attack the land. Menahem gave him about seventy-four thousand pounds of silver so Pul would support him and make his hold on the kingdom stronger. [20]Menahem taxed Israel to pay about one and one-fourth

Uzziah Also called Azariah.

pounds of silver to each soldier of the king of Assyria. So the king left and did not stay in the land. [21]Everything else Menahem did is written in the book of the history of the kings of Israel. [22]Then Menahem died, and his son Pekahiah became king in his place.

Pekahiah King of Israel

[23]Pekahiah son of Menahem became king over Israel in Samaria during Uzziah's[n] fiftieth year as king of Judah. Pekahiah ruled two years, [24]and he did what the LORD said was wrong. Jeroboam son of Nebat had led Israel to sin, and Pekahiah did not stop doing the same sins.

[25]Pekah son of Remaliah was one of Pekahiah's captains, and he made plans against Pekahiah. He took fifty men of Gilead with him and killed Pekahiah, as well as Argob and Arieh, in the palace at Samaria. Then Pekah became king in Pekahiah's place.

[26]Everything else Pekahiah did is written in the book of the history of the kings of Israel.

Pekah King of Israel

[27]Pekah son of Remaliah became king over Israel in Samaria during Uzziah's[n] fifty-second year as king of Judah. Pekah ruled twenty years, [28]and he did what the LORD said was wrong. Jeroboam son of Nebat had led Israel to sin, and Pekah did not stop doing the same sins.

[29]Tiglath-Pileser[n] was king of Assyria. He attacked while Pekah was king of Israel, capturing the cities of Ijon, Abel Beth Maacah, Janoah, Kedesh, and Hazor. He also captured Gilead and Galilee and all the land of Naphtali and carried the people away to Assyria. [30]Then Hoshea son of Elah made plans against Pekah son of Remaliah and attacked and killed him. Then Hoseah became king in Pekah's place during the twentieth year Jotham son of Uzziah was king.

[31]Everything else Pekah did is written in the book of the history of the kings of Israel.

Jotham King of Judah

[32]Jotham son of Uzziah became king of Judah during the second year Pekah son of Remaliah was king of Israel. [33]Jotham was twenty-five years old when he became king, and he ruled sixteen years in Jerusalem. His mother's name was Jerusha daughter of Zadok. [34]Jotham did what the LORD said was right, just as his father Uzziah had done. [35]But the places where gods were worshiped were not removed, and the people still made sacrifices and burned incense[d] there. Jotham rebuilt the Upper Gate of the Temple[d] of the LORD.

[36]The other things Jotham did while he was king are written in the book of the history of the kings of Judah. [37]At that time the LORD began to send Rezin king of Aram and Pekah son of Remaliah against Judah. [38]Jotham died and was buried with his ancestors in Jerusalem, the city of David, his ancestor. Then Jotham's son Ahaz became king in his place.

Ahaz King of Judah

16 Ahaz was the son of Jotham king of Judah. Ahaz became king of Judah in the seventeenth year Pekah son of Remaliah was king of Israel. [2]Ahaz was twenty years old when he became king, and he ruled sixteen years in Jerusalem. Unlike his ancestor David, he did not do what the LORD his God said was right. [3]Ahaz did the same things the kings of Israel had done. He even made his son pass through fire. He did the same hateful sins as the nations had done whom the LORD had forced out of the land ahead of the Israelites. [4]Ahaz offered sacrifices and burned incense[d] at the places where gods were worshiped, on the hills, and under every green tree.

[5]Rezin king of Aram and Pekah son of Remaliah, the king of Israel, came up to attack Jerusalem. They surrounded Ahaz but could not defeat him. [6]At that time Rezin king of Aram took back the city of Elath for Aram, and he forced out all the people of Judah. Then Edomites moved into Elath, and they still live there today.

[7]Ahaz sent messengers to Tiglath-Pileser king of Assyria, saying, "I am your servant and your friend. Come and save me from the king of Aram and the king of Israel, who are attacking me." [8]Ahaz took the silver and gold that was in the Temple[d] of the LORD and in the treasuries of the palace, and he sent these as a gift to the king of Assyria. [9]So the king of Assyria listened to Ahaz. He attacked Damascus and captured it and sent all its people away to Kir. And he killed Rezin.

[10]Then King Ahaz went to Damascus to meet Tiglath-Pileser king of Assyria. Ahaz saw an altar at Damascus, and he sent plans and a pattern of this altar to Uriah the priest. [11]So Uriah the priest built an altar, just like the plans King Ahaz had sent him from Damascus. Uriah finished the altar before King Ahaz came back from Damascus. [12]When the king arrived from Damascus, he saw the altar and went near and offered sacrifices on it. [13]He burned his burnt offerings and grain offerings and poured out his drink offering. He also sprinkled the blood of his fellowship offerings on the altar.

[14]Ahaz moved the bronze altar that was before the LORD at the front of the Temple. It was be-

Uzziah　Also called Azariah.
Tiglath-Pileser　Also called Pul.

tween Ahaz's altar and the Temple of the Lord, but he put it on the north side of his altar. [15]King Ahaz commanded Uriah the priest, "On the large altar burn the morning burnt offering, the evening grain offering, the king's burnt offering and grain offering, and the whole burnt offering, the grain offering, and the drink offering for all the people of the land. Sprinkle on the altar all the blood of the burnt offering and of the sacrifice. But I will use the bronze altar to ask questions of God." [16]So Uriah the priest did everything as King Ahaz commanded him.

[17]Then King Ahaz took off the side panels from the bases and removed the washing bowls from the top of the bases. He also took the large bowl, which was called the Sea, off the bronze bulls that held it up, and he put it on a stone base. [18]Ahaz took away the platform for the royal throne, which had been built at the Temple of the Lord. He also took away the outside entrance for the king. He did these things because of the king of Assyria.

[19]The other things Ahaz did as king are written in the book of the history of the kings of Judah. [20]Ahaz died and was buried with his ancestors in Jerusalem, and Ahaz's son Hezekiah became king in his place.

Hoshea, Last King of Israel

17 Hoshea son of Elah became king over Israel during Ahaz's twelfth year as king of Judah. Hoshea ruled in Samaria nine years. [2]He did what the Lord said was wrong, but he was not as bad as the kings of Israel who had ruled before him.

[3]Shalmaneser king of Assyria came to attack Hoshea. Hoshea had been Shalmaneser's servant and had made the payments to Shalmaneser that he had demanded. [4]But the king of Assyria found out that Hoshea had made plans against him by sending messengers to So, the king of Egypt. Hoshea had also stopped giving Shalmaneser the payments, which he had paid every year in the past. For that, the king put Hoshea in prison. [5]Then the king of Assyria came and attacked all the land of Israel. He surrounded Samaria and attacked it for three years. [6]He defeated Samaria in the ninth year Hoshea was king, and he took the Israelites away to Assyria. He settled them in Halah, in Gozan on the Habor River, and in the cities of the Medes.

Israelites Punished for Sin

[7]All these things happened because the Israelites had sinned against the Lord their God. He had brought them out of Egypt and had rescued them from the power of the king of Egypt, but the Israelites had honored other gods. [8]They lived like the nations the Lord had forced out of the land ahead of them. They lived as their evil kings had shown them, [9]secretly sinning against the Lord their God. They built places to worship gods in all their cities, from the watchtower to the strong, walled city. [10]They put up stone pillars to gods and Asherah[d] idols on every high hill and under every green tree. [11]The Israelites burned incense[d] everywhere gods were worshiped, just as the nations who lived there before them had done, whom the Lord had forced out of the land. The Israelites did wicked things that made the Lord angry. [12]They served idols when the Lord had said, "You must not do this." [13]The Lord used every prophet[d] and seer[d] to warn Israel and Judah. He said, "Stop your evil ways and obey my commands and laws. Follow all the teachings that I commanded your ancestors, the teachings that I gave you through my servants the prophets."

[14]But the people would not listen. They were stubborn, just as their ancestors had been who did not believe in the Lord their God. [15]They rejected the Lord's laws and the agreement he had made with their ancestors. And they refused to listen to his warnings. They worshiped useless idols and became useless themselves. They did what the nations around them did, which the Lord had warned them not to do.

[16]The people rejected all the commands of the Lord their God. They molded statues of two calves, and they made an Asherah idol. They worshiped all the stars of the sky and served Baal.[d] [17]They made their sons and daughters pass through fire and tried to find out the future by magic and witchcraft.[d] They always chose to do what the Lord said was wrong, which made him angry. [18]Because he was very angry with the people of Israel, he removed them from his presence. Only the tribe[d] of Judah was left.

Judah Is Also Guilty

[19]But even Judah did not obey the commands of the Lord their God. They did what the Israelites had done, [20]so the Lord rejected all the people of Israel. He punished them and let others destroy them; he threw them out of his presence. [21]When the Lord separated them from the family of David, the Israelites made Jeroboam son of Nebat their king. Jeroboam led the Israelites away from the Lord and led them to sin greatly. [22]So they continued to do all the sins Jeroboam did. They did not stop doing these sins [23]until the Lord removed the Israelites from his presence, just as he had said through all his servants the prophets.[d] So the Israelites were taken out of their land to Assyria, and they have been there to this day.

The Beginning of the Samaritan People

24The king of Assyria brought people from Babylon, Cuthah, Avva, Hamath, and Sepharvaim and put them in the cities of Samaria to replace the Israelites. These people took over Samaria and lived in the cities. 25At first they did not worship the Lord, so he sent lions among them which killed some of them. 26The king of Assyria was told, "You sent foreigners into the cities of Samaria who do not know the law of the god of the land. This is why he has sent lions among them. The lions are killing them because they don't know what the god wants."

27Then the king of Assyria commanded, "Send back one of the priests you took away. Let him live there and teach the people what the god wants." 28So one of the priests who had been carried away from Samaria returned to live in Bethel. And he taught the people how to honor the Lord.

29But each nation made gods of its own and put them in the cities where they lived and in the temples where gods were worshiped. These temples had been built by the Samaritans. 30The people from Babylon made Succoth Benoth their god. The people from Cuthah worshiped Nergal. The people of Hamath worshiped Ashima. 31The Avvites worshiped Nibhaz and Tartak. The Sepharvites burned their children in the fire, sacrificing them to Adrammelech and Anammelech, the gods of Sepharvaim. 32They also honored the Lord, but they chose priests for the places where gods were worshiped. The priests were chosen from among themselves, and they made sacrifices for the people. 33The people honored the Lord but also served their own gods, just as the nations did from which they had been brought. 34Even today they do as they did in the past. They do not worship the Lord nor obey his rules and commands. They do not obey the teachings or the commands of the Lord, which he gave to the children of Jacob, whom he had named Israel. 35The Lord had made an agreement with them and had commanded them, "Do not honor other gods. Do not bow down to them or worship them or offer sacrifices to them. 36Worship the Lord who brought you up out of the land of Egypt with great power and strength. Bow down to him and offer sacrifices to him. 37Always obey the rules, orders, teachings, and commands he wrote for you. Do not honor other gods. 38Do not forget the agreement I made with you, and do not honor other gods. 39Instead worship the Lord your God, who will save you from all your enemies."

40But the Israelites did not listen. They kept on doing the same things they had done before. 41So these nations honored the Lord but also worshiped their idols, and their children and grandchildren still do as their ancestors did.

Hezekiah King of Judah

18 Hezekiah son of Ahaz king of Judah became king during the third year Hoshea son of Elah was king of Israel. 2Hezekiah was twenty-five years old when he became king, and he ruled twenty-nine years in Jerusalem. His mother's name was Abijah daughter of Zechariah. 3Hezekiah did what the Lord said was right, just as his ancestor David had done. 4He removed the places where gods were worshiped. He smashed the stone pillars and cut down the Asherah[d] idols. Also the Israelites had been burning incense[d] to Nehushtan, the bronze snake Moses had made. But Hezekiah broke it into pieces.

5Hezekiah trusted in the Lord, the God of Israel. There was no one like him among all the kings of Judah, either before him or after him. 6Hezekiah was loyal to the Lord and did not stop following him; he obeyed the commands the Lord had given Moses. 7And the Lord was with Hezekiah, so he had success in everything he did. He turned against the king of Assyria and stopped serving him. 8Hezekiah defeated the Philistines all the way to Gaza and its borders, including the watchtowers and the strong, walled cities.

The Assyrians Capture Samaria

9Shalmaneser king of Assyria surrounded Samaria and attacked it in the fourth year Hezekiah was king. This was the seventh year Hoshea son of Elah was king of Israel. 10After three years the Assyrians captured Samaria. This was in the sixth year Hezekiah was king, which was Hoshea's ninth year as king of Israel. 11The king of Assyria took the Israelites away to Assyria and settled them in Halah, in Gozan on the Habor River, and in the cities of the Medes. 12This happened because they did not obey the Lord their God. They broke his agreement and did not obey all that Moses, the Lord's servant, had commanded. They would not listen to the commands or do them.

Assyria Attacks Judah

13During Hezekiah's fourteenth year as king, Sennacherib king of Assyria attacked all the strong, walled cities of Judah and captured them. 14Then Hezekiah king of Judah sent a message to the king of Assyria at Lachish. He said, "I have done wrong. Leave me alone, and I will pay anything you ask." So the king of Assyria made Hezekiah pay about twenty-two thousand pounds of silver and two thousand pounds of gold. 15Hezekiah gave him all the silver that was in the Temple[d] of the Lord and in the palace treasuries. 16Hezekiah stripped all the gold that covered the doors and doorposts of the Temple of the Lord. Hezekiah had put gold on these doors himself, but he gave it all to the king of Assyria.

[17]The king of Assyria sent out his supreme commander, his chief officer, and his field commander. They went with a large army from Lachish to King Hezekiah in Jerusalem. When they came near the waterway from the upper pool on the road where people do their laundry, they stopped. [18]They called for the king, so the king sent Eliakim, Shebna, and Joah out to meet them. Eliakim son of Hilkiah was the palace manager, Shebna was the royal secretary, and Joah son of Asaph was the recorder

[19]The field commander said to them, "Tell Hezekiah this:

" 'The great king, the king of Assyria, says: What can you trust in now? [20]You say you have battle plans and power for war, but your words mean nothing. Whom are you trusting for help so that you turn against me? [21]Look, you are depending on Egypt to help you, but Egypt is like a splintered walking stick. If you lean on it for help, it will stab your hand and hurt you. The king of Egypt will hurt all those who depend on him. [22]You might say, "We are depending on the Lord our God," but Hezekiah destroyed the Lord's altars and the places of worship. Hezekiah told Judah and Jerusalem, "You must worship only at this one altar in Jerusalem."

[23]" 'Now make an agreement with my master, the king of Assyria: I will give you two thousand horses if you can find enough men to ride them. [24]You cannot defeat one of my master's least important officers, so why do you depend on Egypt to give you chariots and horsemen? [25]I have not come to attack and destroy this place without an order from the Lord. The Lord himself told me to come to this country and destroy it.' "

[26]Then Eliakim son of Hilkiah, Shebna, and Joah said to the field commander, "Please speak to us in the Aramaic language. We understand it. Don't speak to us in Hebrew, because the people on the city wall can hear you."

[27]"No," the commander said, "my master did not send me to tell these things only to you and your king. He sent me to speak also to those people sitting on the wall who will have to eat their own dung and drink their own urine like you."

[28]Then the commander stood and shouted loudly in the Hebrew language, "Listen to what the great king, the king of Assyria, says! [29]The king says you should not let Hezekiah fool you, because he can't save you from my power. [30]Don't let Hezekiah talk you into trusting the Lord by saying, 'The Lord will surely save us. This city won't be handed over to the king of Assyria.'

[31]"Don't listen to Hezekiah. The king of Assyria says, 'Make peace with me and come out of the city to me. Then everyone will be free to eat the fruit from his own grapevine and fig tree and to drink water from his own well. [32]After that I will come and take you to a land like your own—a land with grain and new wine, bread and vineyards, olives, and honey. Choose to live and not to die!'

"Don't listen to Hezekiah. He is fooling you when he says, 'The Lord will save us.' [33]Has a god of any other nation saved his people from the power of the king of Assyria? [34]Where are the gods of Hamath and Arpad? Where are the gods of Sepharvaim, Hena, and Ivvah? They did not save Samaria from my power. [35]Not one of all the gods of these countries has saved his people from me. Neither can the Lord save Jerusalem from my power."

[36]The people were silent. They didn't answer the commander at all, because King Hezekiah had ordered, Don't answer him."

[37]Then Eliakim, Shebna, and Joah tore their clothes to show how upset they were. (Eliakim son of Hilkiah was the palace manager, Shebna was the royal secretary, and Joah son of Asaph was the recorder.) The three men went to Hezekiah and told him what the field commander had said.

☀ **SIDELIGHT:** The Assyrians' attack on Jerusalem led by Sennacherib isn't recorded only in the Bible (2 Kings 8:13–37). Archaeologists have found "Sennacherib's Prism," which gives the invaders' view of the situation. Another source tells how a plague of mice attacked Sennacherib's army to make the Assyrians retreat.

Jerusalem Will Be Saved

19 When King Hezekiah heard the message, he tore his clothes and put on rough cloth to show how sad he was. Then he went into the Temple[d] of the Lord. [2]Hezekiah sent Eliakim, the palace manager, and Shebna, the royal secretary, and the older priests to Isaiah. They were all wearing rough cloth when they came to Isaiah the prophet,[d] the son of Amoz. [3]They told Isaiah, "This is what Hezekiah says: Today is a day of sorrow and punishment and disgrace, as when a child should be born, but the mother is not strong enough to give birth to it. [4]The king of Assyria sent his field commander to make fun of the living God. Maybe the Lord your God will hear what the commander said and will punish him for it. So pray for the few of us who are left alive."

[5]When Hezekiah's officers came to Isaiah, [6]he said to them, "Tell your master this: The Lord

says, 'Don't be afraid of what you have heard. Don't be frightened by the words the servants of the king of Assyria have spoken against me. 7Listen! I am going to put a spirit in the king of Assyria. He will hear a report that will make him return to his own country, and I will cause him to die by the sword there.'"

8The field commander heard that the king of Assyria had left Lachish. When he went back, he found the king fighting against the city of Libnah.

9The king received a report that Tirhakah, the Cushite king of Egypt, was coming to attack him. When the king of Assyria heard this, he sent messengers to Hezekiah, saying, 10"Tell Hezekiah king of Judah: Don't be fooled by the god you trust. Don't believe him when he says Jerusalem will not be handed over to the king of Assyria. 11You have heard what the kings of Assyria have done. They have completely defeated every country, so do not think you will be saved. 12Did the gods of those people save them? My ancestors destroyed them, defeating the cities of Gozan, Haran, and Rezeph, and the people of Eden living in Tel Assar. 13Where are the kings of Hamath and Arpad? Where are the kings of Sepharvaim, Hena, and Ivvah?"

Hezekiah Prays to the Lord

14When Hezekiah received the letter from the messengers and read it, he went up to the Temple*d* of the Lord. He spread the letter out before the Lord 15and prayed to the Lord: "Lord, God of Israel, whose throne is between the gold creatures with wings, only you are God of all the kingdoms of the earth. You made the heavens and the earth. 16Hear, Lord, and listen. Open your eyes, Lord, and see. Listen to the words Sennacherib has said to insult the living God. 17It is true, Lord, that the kings of Assyria have destroyed these countries and their lands. 18They have thrown the gods of these nations into the fire, but they were only wood and rock statues that people made. So the kings have destroyed them. 19Now, Lord our God, save us from the king's power so that all the kingdoms of the earth will know that you, Lord, are the only God."

God Answers Hezekiah

20Then Isaiah son of Amoz sent a message to Hezekiah that said, "This is what the Lord, the God of Israel, says: I have heard your prayer to me about Sennacherib king of Assyria. 21This is what the Lord has said against Sennacherib:
'The people of Jerusalem
    hate you and make fun of you.
The people of Jerusalem
    laugh at you as you run away.
22You have insulted me and spoken against me;
    you have raised your voice against me.

You have a proud look on your face,
    which is against me, the Holy One of
        Israel.
23You have sent your messengers to insult the
        Lord.
    You have said, "With my many chariots
I have gone to the tops of the mountains,
    to the highest mountains of Lebanon.
I have cut down its tallest cedars
    and its best pine trees.
I have gone to its farthest places
    and to its best forests.
24I have dug wells in foreign countries
    and drunk water there.
By the soles of my feet,
    I have dried up all the rivers of Egypt."

25" 'King of Assyria, surely you have heard.
    Long ago I, the Lord, planned these things.
Long ago I designed them,
    and now I have made them happen.
I allowed you to turn those strong, walled
        cities
    into piles of rocks.
26The people in those cities were weak;
    they were frightened and put to shame.
They were like grass in the field,
    like tender, young grass,
like grass on the housetop
    that is burned by the wind before it can
        grow.

27" 'I know when you rest,
    when you come and go,
    and how you rage against me.
28Because you rage against me,
    and because I have heard your proud
        words,
I will put my hook in your nose
    and my bit in your mouth.
Then I will force you to leave my country
    the same way you came.'

29"Then the Lord said, 'Hezekiah, I will give you this sign:
This year you will eat the grain that grows
        wild,
    and the second year you will eat what
        grows wild from that.
But in the third year, plant grain and harvest
        it.
    Plant vineyards and eat their fruit.
30Some of the people in the family of Judah
        will escape.
Like plants that take root,
    they will grow strong and have many
        children.
31A few people will come out of Jerusalem
        alive;
    a few from Mount Zion*d* will live.

The strong love of the Lord All-Powerful
will make this happen.'

32"So this is what the Lord says about the king
of Assyria:

'He will not enter this city
or even shoot an arrow here.
He will not fight against it with shields
or build a ramp to attack the city walls.
33He will return to his country the same way
he came,
and he will not enter this city,'
says the Lord.
34'I will defend and save this city
for my sake and for the sake of David, my
servant.' "

35That night the angel of the Lord went out
and killed one hundred eighty-five thousand men
in the Assyrian camp. When the people got up
early the next morning, they saw all the dead bodies. 36So Sennacherib king of Assyria left and went
back to Nineveh and stayed there.

37One day as Sennacherib was worshiping in
the temple of his god Nisroch, his sons Adrammelech and Sharezer killed him with a sword. Then
they escaped to the land of Ararat. So Sennacherib's son Esarhaddon became king of Assyria.

Hezekiah's Illness

20 At that time Hezekiah became so sick he
almost died. The prophet⁴ Isaiah son of
Amoz went to see him and told him, "This is
what the Lord says: Make arrangements because
you are not going to live, but die."

2Hezekiah turned toward the wall and prayed
to the Lord, 3"Lord, please remember that I have
always obeyed you. I have given myself completely to you and have done what you said was
right." Then Hezekiah cried loudly.

4Before Isaiah had left the middle courtyard,
the Lord spoke his word to Isaiah: 5"Go back and
tell Hezekiah, the leader of my people: 'This is
what the Lord, the God of your ancestor David,
says: I have heard your prayer and seen your
tears, so I will heal you. Three days from now you
will go up to the Temple of the Lord. 6I will add
fifteen years to your life. I will save you and this
city from the king of Assyria; I will protect the city
for my sake and for the sake of my servant David.' "

7Then Isaiah said, "Make a paste from figs." So
they made it and put it on Hezekiah's boil, and he
got well.

8Hezekiah had asked Isaiah, "What will be the
sign that the Lord will heal me and that I will go
up to the Temple of the Lord on the third day?"
9Isaiah said, "The Lord will do what he says.
This is the sign from the Lord to show you: Do

you want the shadow to go forward ten steps or
back ten steps?"
10Hezekiah answered, "It's easy for the shadow
to go forward ten steps. Instead, let it go back ten
steps."
11Then Isaiah the prophet called to the Lord,
and the Lord brought the shadow ten steps back
up the stairway of Ahaz that it had gone down.

Messengers from Babylon

12At that time Merodach-Baladan son of Baladan was king of Babylon. He sent letters and a gift
to Hezekiah, because he had heard that Hezekiah
was sick. 13Hezekiah listened to the messengers,
so he showed them what was in his storehouses:
the silver, gold, spices, expensive perfumes, his
swords and shields, and all his wealth. He showed
them everything in his palace and his kingdom.

14Then Isaiah the prophet⁴ went to King Hezekiah and asked him, "What did these men say?
Where did they come from?"
Hezekiah said, "They came from a faraway
country—from Babylon."
15So Isaiah asked him, "What did they see in
your palace?"
Hezekiah said, "They saw everything in my palace. I showed them all my wealth."
16Then Isaiah said to Hezekiah, "Listen to the
words of the Lord: 17'In the future everything in
your palace and everything your ancestors have
stored up until this day will be taken away to Babylon. Nothing will be left,' says the Lord. 18Some
of your own children, those who will be born to
you, will be taken away. And they will become
servants in the palace of the king of Babylon.' "
19Hezekiah told Isaiah, "These words from the
Lord are good." He said this because he thought,
"There will be peace and security in my lifetime."
20Everything else Hezekiah did—all his victories, his work on the pool, his work on the tunnel
to bring water into the city—is written in the

✺ SIDELIGHT: The tunnel King
Hezekiah dug to provide water for
Jerusalem during the Assyrian siege (2 Kings
20:20) was cut through 1,748 feet of solid
limestone—almost 200 feet longer than the
longest span of Brooklyn Bridge in New York
City. An inscription on "Hezekiah's Tunnel"
says workers started digging at each end and
met in the middle. People still walk through
the tunnel today.

---

book of the history of the kings of Judah. 21Then
Hezekiah died, and his son Manasseh became
king in his place.

Manasseh King of Judah

21 Manasseh was twelve years old when he became king, and he was king fifty-five years in Jerusalem. His mother's name was Hephzibah. ²He did what the LORD said was wrong. He

---

> ☀ **SIDELIGHT:** The longest reign in the Bible was that of Manasseh. He reigned fifty-five years (2 Kings 21:1). That would be about like Franklin D. Roosevelt being U.S. president still. Despite his long rule, Manasseh was considered one of the most evil kings of Judah (2 Chronicles 33:9, p. 411). The king with the shortest reign was Zimri (1 Kings 16:15, p. 321), who lasted only seven days!

---

did the hateful things the other nations had done — the nations that the LORD had forced out of the land ahead of the Israelites. ³Manasseh's father, Hezekiah, had destroyed the places where gods were worshiped, but Manasseh rebuilt them. He built altars for Baal,ᵈ and he made an Asherahᵈ idol as Ahab king of Israel had done. Manasseh also worshiped all the stars of the sky and served them. ⁴The LORD had said about the Temple,ᵈ "I will be worshiped in Jerusalem," but Manasseh built altars in the Temple of the LORD. ⁵He built altars to worship the stars in the two courtyards of the Temple of the LORD. ⁶He made his own son pass through fire. He practiced magic and told the future by explaining signs and dreams, and he got advice from mediumsᵈ and fortune-tellers. He did many things the LORD said were wrong, which made the LORD angry.

⁷Manasseh carved an Asherah idol and put it in the Temple. The LORD had said to David and his son Solomon about the Temple, "I will be worshiped forever in this Temple and in Jerusalem, which I have chosen from all the tribesᵈ of Israel. ⁸I will never again make the Israelites wander out of the land I gave their ancestors. But they must obey everything I have commanded them and all the teachings my servant Moses gave them." ⁹But the people did not listen. Manasseh led them to do more evil than the nations the LORD had destroyed ahead of the Israelites.

¹⁰The LORD said through his servants the prophets,ᵈ ¹¹"Manasseh king of Judah has done these hateful things. He has done more evil than the Amorites before him. He also has led Judah to sin with his idols. ¹²So this is what the LORD, the God of Israel, says: 'I will bring so much trouble on Jerusalem and Judah that anyone who hears about it will be shocked. ¹³I will stretch the measuring line of Samaria over Jerusalem, and the

plumb lineᵈ used against Ahab's family will be used on Jerusalem. I will wipe out Jerusalem as a person wipes a dish and turns it upside down. ¹⁴I will throw away the rest of my people who are left. I will give them to their enemies, and they will be robbed by all their enemies, ¹⁵because my people did what I said was wrong. They have made me angry from the day their ancestors left Egypt until now.' "

¹⁶Manasseh also killed many innocent people, filling Jerusalem from one end to the other with their blood. This was besides the sin he led Judah to do; he led Judah to do what the LORD said was wrong.

¹⁷The other things Manasseh did as king, even the sin he did, are written in the book of the history of the kings of Judah. ¹⁸Manasseh died and was buried in the garden of his own palace, the garden of Uzza. Then Manasseh's son Amon became king in his place.

Amon King of Judah

¹⁹Amon was twenty-two years old when he became king, and he was king for two years in Jerusalem. His mother's name was Meshullemeth daughter of Haruz, who was from Jotbah. ²⁰Amon did what the LORD said was wrong, as his father Manasseh had done. ²¹He lived in the same way his father had lived: he worshiped the idols his father had worshiped, and he bowed down before them. ²²Amon rejected the LORD, the God of his ancestors, and did not follow the ways of the LORD.

²³Amon's officers made plans against him and killed him in his palace. ²⁴Then the people of the land killed all those who had made plans to kill King Amon, and they made his son Josiah king in his place.

²⁵Everything else Amon did is written in the book of the history of the kings of Judah. ²⁶He was buried in his grave in the garden of Uzza, and his son Josiah became king in his place.

Josiah King of Judah

22 Josiah was eight years old when he became king, and he ruled thirty-one years in Jerusalem. His mother's name was Jedidah daughter of Adaiah, who was from Bozkath. ²Josiah did what the LORD said was right. He lived as his ancestor David had lived, and he did not stop doing what was right.

³In Josiah's eighteenth year as king, he sent Shaphan to the Templeᵈ of the LORD. Shaphan son of Azaliah, the son of Meshullam, was the royal secretary. Josiah said, ⁴"Go up to Hilkiah the high priest, and have him empty out the money the gatekeepers have gathered from the people. This is the money they have brought into the Temple of the LORD. ⁵Have him give the money

to the supervisors of the work on the Temple of the LORD. They must pay the workers who repair the Temple of the LORD — [6]the carpenters, builders, and bricklayers. Also use the money to buy timber and cut stone to repair the Temple. [7]They do not need to report how they use the money given to them, because they are working honestly."

The Book of the Teachings Is Found

[8]Hilkiah the high priest said to Shaphan the royal secretary, "I've found the Book of the Teachings in the Temple[d] of the LORD." He gave it to Shaphan, who read it.

[9]Then Shaphan the royal secretary went to the king and reported to Josiah, "Your officers have paid out the money that was in the Temple of the LORD. They have given it to the workers and supervisors at the Temple." [10]Then Shaphan the royal secretary told the king, "Hilkiah the priest has given me a book." And Shaphan read from the book to the king.

[11]When the king heard the words of the Book of the Teachings, he tore his clothes to show how upset he was. [12]He gave orders to Hilkiah the priest, Ahikam son of Shaphan, Acbor son of Micaiah, Shaphan the royal secretary, and Asaiah the king's servant. These were the orders: [13]"Go and ask the LORD about the words in the book that was found. Ask for me, for all the people, and for all Judah. The LORD's anger is burning against us, because our ancestors did not obey the words of this book; they did not do all the things written for us to do."

[14]So Hilkiah the priest, Ahikam, Acbor, Shaphan, and Asaiah went to talk to Huldah the prophetess.[d] She was the wife of Shallum son of Tikvah, the son of Harhas, who took care of the king's clothes. Huldah lived in Jerusalem, in the new area of the city.

[15]She said to them, "This is what the LORD, the God of Israel, says: Tell the man who sent you to me, [16]'This is what the LORD says: I will bring trouble to this place and to the people living here, as it is written in the book which the king of Judah has read. [17]The people of Judah have left me and have burned incense[d] to other gods. They have made me angry by all that they have done. My anger burns against this place like a fire, and it will not be put out.' [18]Tell the king of Judah, who sent you to ask the LORD, 'This is what the LORD, the God of Israel, says about the words you heard: [19]When you heard my words against this place and its people, you became sorry for what you had done and humbled yourself before me. I said they would be cursed and would be destroyed. You tore your clothes to show how upset you were, and you cried in my presence. This is why I have heard you, says the LORD. [20]So I will

let you die, and you will be buried in peace. You won't see all the trouble I will bring to this place.' "

So they took her message back to the king.

The People Hear the Agreement

23 Then the king gathered all the older leaders of Judah and Jerusalem together. [2]He went up to the Temple[d] of the LORD, and all the people from Judah and Jerusalem went with him. The priests, prophets,[d] and all the people — from the least important to the most important — went with him. He read to them all the words of the Book of the Agreement that was found in the Temple of the LORD. [3]The king stood by the pillar and made an agreement in the presence of the LORD to follow the LORD and obey his commands, rules, and laws with his whole being, and to obey the words of the agreement written in this book. Then all the people promised to obey the agreement.

Josiah Destroys the Places for Idol Worship

[4]The king commanded Hilkiah the high priest and the priests of the next rank and the gatekeepers to bring out of the Temple[d] of the LORD everything made for Baal,[d] Asherah,[d] and all the stars of the sky. Then Josiah burned them outside Jerusalem in the open country of the Kidron Valley and carried their ashes to Bethel. [5]The kings of Judah had chosen priests for these gods. These priests burned incense[u] in the places where gods were worshiped in the cities of Judah and the towns around Jerusalem. They burned incense to Baal, the sun, the moon, the planets, and all the stars of the sky. But Josiah took those priests away. [6]He removed the Asherah idol from the Temple of the LORD and took it outside Jerusalem to the Kidron Valley, where he burned it and beat it into dust. Then he threw the dust on the graves of the common people. [7]He also tore down the houses of the male prostitutes[d] who were in the Temple of the LORD, where the women did weaving for Asherah.

[8]King Josiah brought all the false priests from the cities of Judah. He ruined the places where gods were worshiped, where the priests had burned incense, from Geba to Beersheba. He destroyed the places of worship at the entrance to the Gate of Joshua, the ruler of the city, on the left side of the city gate. [9]The priests at the places where gods were worshiped were not allowed to serve at the LORD's altar in Jerusalem. But they could eat bread made without yeast with their brothers.

[10]Josiah ruined Topheth, in the Valley of Ben Hinnom, so no one could sacrifice his son or daughter to Molech.[d] [11]Judah's kings had placed

horses at the front door of the Temple of the LORD in the courtyard near the room of Nathan-Melech, an officer. These horses were for the worship of the sun. So Josiah removed them and burned the chariots that were for sun worship also.

[12]The kings of Judah had built altars on the roof[n] of the upstairs room of Ahaz. Josiah broke down these altars and the altars Manasseh had made in the two courtyards of the Temple of the LORD. Josiah smashed them to pieces and threw their dust into the Kidron Valley. [13]King Josiah ruined the places where gods were worshiped east of Jerusalem, south of the Mount of Olives.[n] Solomon king of Israel had built these places. One was for Ashtoreth,[d] the hated goddess of the Sidonians. One was for Chemosh,[d] the hated god of Moab. And one was for Molech, the hated god of the Ammonites. [14]Josiah smashed to pieces the stone pillars they worshiped, and he cut down the Asherah idols. Then he covered the places with human bones.

[15]Josiah also broke down the altar at Bethel — the place of worship made by Jeroboam son of Nebat, who had led Israel to sin. Josiah burned that place, broke the stones of the altar into pieces, then beat them into dust. He also burned the Asherah idol. [16]When he turned around, he saw the graves on the mountain. He had the bones taken from the graves, and he burned them on the altar to ruin it. This happened as the LORD had said it would through the man of God.

[17]Josiah asked, "What is that monument I see?"

The people of the city answered, "It's the grave of the man of God who came from Judah. This prophet announced the things you have done against the altar of Bethel."

[18]Josiah said, "Leave the grave alone. No one may move this man's bones." So they left his bones and the bones of the prophet who had come from Samaria.

[19]The kings of Israel had built temples for worshiping gods in the cities of Samaria, which had caused the LORD to be angry. Josiah removed all those temples and did the same things as he had done at Bethel. [20]He killed all the priests of those places of worship; he killed them on the altars and burned human bones on the altars. Then he went back to Jerusalem.

Josiah Celebrates the Passover

[21]The king commanded all the people, "Celebrate the Passover[d] to the LORD your God as it is written in this Book of the Agreement." [22]The Passover had not been celebrated like this since the judges led Israel. Nor had one like it happened while there were kings of Israel and kings of Judah. [23]This Passover was celebrated to the LORD in Jerusalem in the eighteenth year of King Josiah's rule.

[24]Josiah destroyed the mediums,[d] fortunetellers, house gods, and idols. He also destroyed all the hated gods seen in the land of Judah and Jerusalem. This was to obey the words of the teachings written in the book Hilkiah the priest had found in the Temple[d] of the LORD.

[25]There was no king like Josiah before or after him. He obeyed the LORD with all his heart, soul, and strength, following all the Teachings of Moses.

[26]Even so, the LORD did not stop his strong and terrible anger. His anger burned against Judah because of all Manasseh had done to make him angry. [27]The LORD said, "I will send Judah out of my sight, as I have sent Israel away. I will reject Jerusalem, which I chose. And I will take away the Temple about which I said, 'I will be worshiped there.'"

[28]Everything else Josiah did is written in the book of the history of the kings of Judah.

[29]While Josiah was king, Neco king of Egypt went to help the king of Assyria at the Euphrates River. King Josiah marched out to fight against Neco, but at Megiddo, Neco faced him and killed him. [30]Josiah's servants carried his body in a chariot from Megiddo to Jerusalem and buried him in his own grave. Then the people of Judah chose Josiah's son Jehoahaz and poured olive oil on him to make him king in his father's place.

Jehoahaz King of Judah

[31]Jehoahaz was twenty-three years old when he became king, and he was king in Jerusalem for three months. His mother's name was Hamutal, who was the daughter of Jeremiah from Libnah. [32]Jehoahaz did what the LORD said was wrong, just as his ancestors had done.

[33]King Neco took Jehoahaz prisoner at Riblah in the land of Hamath so that Jehoahaz could not rule in Jerusalem. Neco made the people of Judah pay about seventy-five hundred pounds of silver and about seventy-five pounds of gold. [34]King Neco made Josiah's son Eliakim the king in place of Josiah his father. Then Neco changed Eliakim's name to Jehoiakim. But Neco took Jehoahaz to Egypt, where he died. [35]Jehoiakim gave King Neco the silver and gold he demanded. Jehoiakim taxed the land and took silver and gold from the people of the land to give to King Neco. Each person had to pay his share.

---

roof In Bible times houses were built with flat roofs. The roof was used for drying things such as flax and fruit. And it was used as an extra room, as a place for worship, and as a place to sleep in the summer.
Mount of Olives Literally, "The Mountain of Ruin."

Jehoiakim King of Judah

³⁶Jehoiakim was twenty-five years old when he became king, and he was king in Jerusalem for eleven years. His mother's name was Zebidah daughter of Pedaiah, who was from Rumah. ³⁷Jehoiakim did what the LORD said was wrong, just as his ancestors had done.

24 While Jehoiakim was king, Nebuchadnezzar king of Babylon attacked the land of Judah. So Jehoiakim became Nebuchadnezzar's servant for three years. Then he turned against Nebuchadnezzar and broke away from his rule. ²The LORD sent raiding parties from Babylon, Aram, Moab, and Ammon against Jehoiakim to destroy Judah. This happened as the LORD had said it would through his servants the prophets.ᵈ

³The LORD commanded this to happen to the people of Judah, to remove them from his presence, because of all the sins of Manasseh. ⁴He had killed many innocent people and had filled Jerusalem with their blood. And the LORD would not forgive these sins.

⁵The other things that happened while Jehoiakim was king and all he did are written in the book of the history of the kings of Judah. ⁶Jehoiakim died, and his son Jehoiachin became king in his place.

⁷The king of Egypt did not leave his land again, because the king of Babylon had captured all that belonged to the king of Egypt, from the brook of Egypt to the Euphrates River.

Jehoiachin King of Judah

⁸Jehoiachin was eighteen years old when he became king, and he was king three months in Jerusalem. His mother's name was Nehushta daughter of Elnathan from Jerusalem. ⁹Jehoiachin did what the LORD said was wrong, just as his father had done.

¹⁰At that time the officers of Nebuchadnezzar king of Babylon came up to Jerusalem. When they reached the city, they attacked it. ¹¹Nebuchadnezzar himself came to the city while his officers were attacking it. ¹²Jehoiachin king of Judah surrendered to the king of Babylon, along with Jehoiachin's mother, servants, older leaders, and officers. So Nebuchadnezzar made Jehoiachin a prisoner in the eighth year he was king of Babylon. ¹³Nebuchadnezzar took all the treasures from the Templeᵈ of the LORD and from the palace. He cut up all the gold objects Solomon king of Israel had made for the Temple of the LORD. This happened as the LORD had said it would. ¹⁴Nebuchadnezzar took away all the people of Jerusalem, including all the leaders, all the wealthy people, and all the craftsmen and metal workers.

There were ten thousand prisoners in all. Only the poorest people in the land were left. ¹⁵Nebuchadnezzar carried away Jehoiachin to Babylon, as well as the king's mother and his wives, the officers, and the leading men of the land. They were taken captive from Jerusalem to Babylon. ¹⁶The king of Babylon also took all seven thousand soldiers, who were strong and able to fight in war, and about a thousand craftsmen and metal workers. Nebuchadnezzar took them as prisoners to Babylon. ¹⁷Then he made Mattaniah, Jehoiachin's uncle, king in Jehoiachin's place. He also changed Mattaniah's name to Zedekiah.

Zedekiah King of Judah

¹⁸Zedekiah was twenty-one years old when he became king, and he was king in Jerusalem for eleven years. His mother's name was Hamutal daughter of Jeremiahⁿ from Libnah. ¹⁹Zedekiah did what the LORD said was wrong, just as Jehoiakim had done. ²⁰All this happened in Jerusalem and Judah because the LORD was angry with them. Finally, he threw them out of his presence.

The Fall of Jerusalem

Zedekiah turned against the king of Babylon.

25 Nebuchadnezzar king of Babylon marched against Jerusalem with his whole army during Zedekiah's ninth year as king, on the tenth day of the tenth month. He made a camp around the city and piled dirt against the city walls to attack it. ²The city was under attack until Zedekiah's eleventh year as king. ³By the ninth day of the fourth month, the hunger was terrible in the city. There was no food for the people to eat. ⁴Then the city was broken into, and the whole army ran away at night through the gate between the two walls by the king's garden. While the Babylonians were still surrounding the city, Zedekiah and his men ran away toward the Jordan Valley. ⁵But the Babylonian army chased King Zedekiah and caught up with him in the plains of Jericho. All of his army was scattered from him, ⁶so they captured Zedekiah and took him to the king of Babylon at Riblah. There he passed sentence on Zedekiah. ⁷They killed Zedekiah's sons as he watched. Then they put out his eyes and put bronze chains on him and took him to Babylon.

⁸Nebuzaradan was the commander of the king's special guards. This officer of the king of Babylon came to Jerusalem on the seventh day of the fifth month, in Nebuchadnezzar's nineteenth year as king of Babylon. ⁹Nebuzaradan set fire to the Templeᵈ of the LORD and the palace and all the houses of Jerusalem. Every important building was burned.

ⁿeremiah   This is not the prophet Jeremiah, but a different man with the same name.

[10]The whole Babylonian army, led by the commander of the king's special guards, broke down the walls around Jerusalem. [11]Nebuzaradan, the commander of the guards, captured the people left in Jerusalem, those who had surrendered to the king of Babylon, and the rest of the people. [12]But the commander left behind some of the poorest people of the land to take care of the vineyards and fields.

[13]The Babylonians broke up the bronze pillars, the bronze stands, and the large bronze bowl, which was called the Sea, in the Temple of the LORD. Then they carried the bronze to Babylon. [14]They also took the pots, shovels, wick trimmers, dishes, and all the bronze objects used to serve in the Temple. [15]The commander of the king's special guards took away the pans for carrying hot coals, the bowls, and everything made of pure gold or silver. [16]There were two pillars and the large bronze bowl and the movable stands which Solomon had made for the Temple of the LORD. There was so much bronze that it could not be weighed. [17]Each pillar was about twenty-seven feet high. The bronze capital[d] on top of the pillar was about four and one-half feet high. It was decorated with a net design and bronze pomegranates[d] all around it. The other pillar also had a net design and was like the first pillar.

Judah Is Taken Prisoner

[18]The commander of the guards took some prisoners — Seraiah the chief priest, Zephaniah the priest next in rank, and the three doorkeepers. [19]Of the people who were still in the city, he took the officer in charge of the fighting men, as well as five people who advised the king. He took the royal secretary who selected people for the army and sixty other men who were in the city. [20]Nebuzaradan, the commander, took all these people and brought them to the king of Babylon at Rib-

lah. [21]There at Riblah, in the land of Hamath, the king had them killed. So the people of Judah were led away from their country as captives.

Gedaliah Becomes Governor

[22]Nebuchadnezzar king of Babylon left some people in the land of Judah. He appointed Gedaliah son of Ahikam, the son of Shaphan, as governor.

[23]The army captains and their men heard that the king of Babylon had made Gedaliah governor, so they came to Gedaliah at Mizpah. They were Ishmael son of Nethaniah, Johanan son of Kareah, Seraiah son of Tanhumeth the Netophathite, Jaazaniah son of the Maacathite, and their men. [24]Then Gedaliah promised these army captains and their men, "Don't be afraid of the Babylonian officers. Live in the land and serve the king of Babylon, and everything will go well for you."

[25]In the seventh month Ishmael son of Nethaniah, son of Elishama from the king's family, came with ten men and killed Gedaliah. They also killed the men of Judah and Babylon who were with Gedaliah at Mizpah. [26]Then all the people, from the least important to the most important, along with the army leaders, ran away to Egypt, because they were afraid of the Babylonians.

Jehoiachin Is Set Free

[27]Jehoiachin king of Judah was held in Babylon for thirty-seven years. In the thirty-seventh year Evil-Merodach became king of Babylon, and he let Jehoiachin out of prison on the twenty-seventh day of the twelfth month. [28]Evil-Merodach spoke kindly to Jehoiachin and gave him a seat of honor above the seats of the other kings who were with him in Babylon. [29]So Jehoiachin put away his prison clothes. For the rest of his life, he ate at the king's table. [30]Every day, for as long as Jehoiachin lived, the king gave him an allowance.

1 CHRONICLES

Why Read This Book:

■ See God's faithfulness traced through history (1 Chronicles 1—9).
■ Find out how David's relationship with God affected every area of his life (1 Chronicles 10—29).

Behind the Scenes:

In 1976, Alex Haley's book (and, later, TV mini-series), Roots, swept North America. People were entranced with the story Haley reconstructed of his ancestors' capture in Africa, of their being sold as slaves, and of their living on plantations with sometimes-brutal owners. Suddenly thousands of people began looking for their own "roots"—their own sense of where they had come from.

The books of 1 and 2 Chronicles (which were originally one book) are like the book Roots. They were written hundreds of years after the events to tell the Israelites where they had come from. The Israelites had been exiles—prisoners of war—in Babylon, where they had been taken because they did not follow God. They had returned to Jerusalem and were rebuilding their city, their history, and their lives.

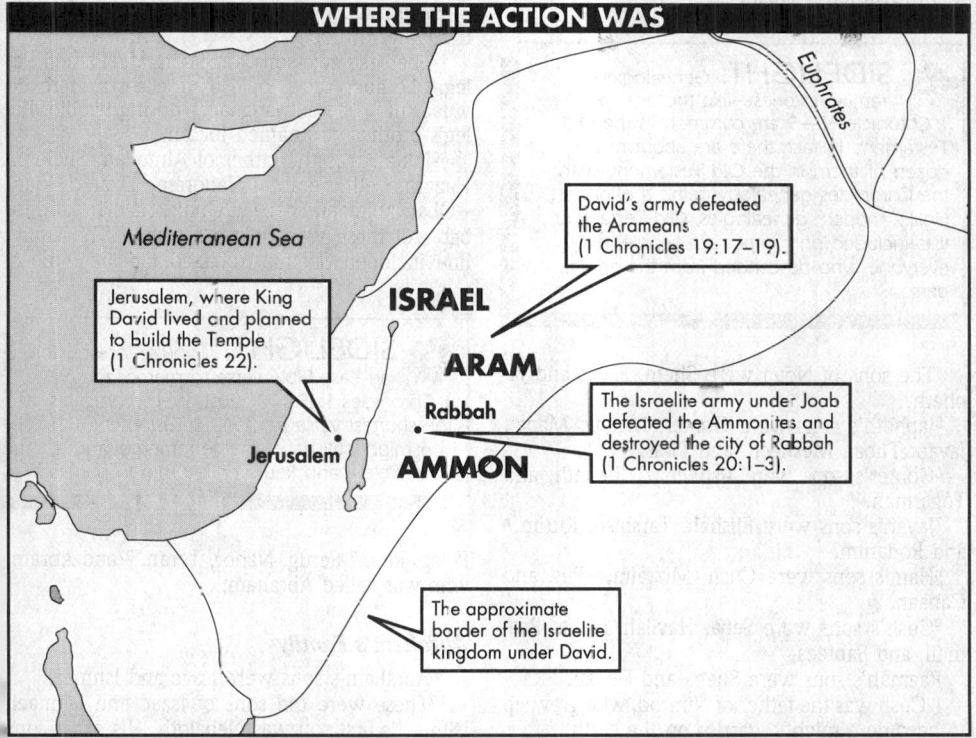

WHERE THE ACTION WAS

Euphrates

Mediterranean Sea

David's army defeated the Arameans (1 Chronicles 19:17-19).

Jerusalem, where King David lived and planned to build the Temple (1 Chronicles 22).

ISRAEL

ARAM

Rabbah

Jerusalem

The Israelite army under Joab defeated the Ammonites and destroyed the city of Rabbah (1 Chronicles 20:1-3).

AMMON

The approximate border of the Israelite kingdom under David.

WHEN THE ACTION WAS

Solomon was Israel's king		People returned to Jerusalem from exile	1 and 2 Chronicles were written		Jesus was born
1000BC	**750BC**	**500BC**		**250BC**	**BC/AD**
David was Israel's king	The Northern Kingdom (Israel) fell to Assyria	The Southern Kingdom (Judah) fell to Babylon			

Behind the Scenes (cont.):

First Chronicles was written to inspire these Israelites to return not only to Jerusalem but also to God. To do this, the author traced Israel's family roots and then told the story of the nation's greatest ruler, King David. Throughout the book one message is clear: The nation's success is directly linked to the people's relationship with God.

The two books of Chronicles weren't written to give a precise history of the Israelites. For example, the stories of David and Solomon are idealized here, leaving out some of the negative stories found in 1 and 2 Samuel (p. 245 and p. 274), and in 1 and 2 Kings (p. 302 and p. 332), which cover the same time period.

Instead, 1 and 2 Chronicles were written to point out how God had guided people in the past and to remind readers—including us—of the importance of following God.

From Adam to Abraham

1 Adam was the father of Seth. Seth was the father of Enosh. Enosh was the father of Kenan. ²Kenan was the father of Mahalalel. Mahalalel was the father of Jared. Jared was the father of Enoch. ³Enoch was the father of Methuselah. Methuselah was the father of Lamech, and Lamech was the father of Noah.

> ✳ **SIDELIGHT:** Genealogies— family histories—like the one in 1 Chronicles 1—9 are common in the Old Testament. In fact, there are about two dozen of them in the Old Testament, with the Chronicles genealogy being the longest. Unlike modern genealogies, Old Testament lists included only important people, not everyone who descended from the original person.

⁴The sons of Noah were Shem, Ham, and Japheth.

⁵Japheth's sons were Gomer, Magog, Madai, Javan, Tubal, Meshech, and Tiras.

⁶Gomer's sons were Ashkenaz, Riphath, and Togarmah.

⁷Javan's sons were Elishah, Tarshish, Kittim,ⁿ and Rodanim.

⁸Ham's sons were Cush, Mizraim,ⁿ Put, and Canaan.

⁹Cush's sons were Seba, Havilah, Sabta, Raamah, and Sabteca.

Raamah's sons were Sheba and Dedan.

¹⁰Cush was the father of Nimrod, who grew up to become a mighty warrior on the earth.

¹¹Mizraim was the father of the Ludites, Anamites, Lehabites, and Naphtuhites, ¹²Pathrusites, Casluhites, and Caphtorites. (The Philistines came from the Casluhites.)

¹³Canaan's first child was Sidon. He was also the father of the Hittites, ¹⁴Jebusites, Amorites, Girgashites, ¹⁵Hivites, Arkites, Sinites, ¹⁶Arvadites, Zemarites, and Hamathites.

¹⁷Shem's sons were Elam, Asshur, Arphaxad, Lud, and Aram.

Aram's sons were Uz, Hul, Gether, and Meshech.

¹⁸Arphaxad was the father of Shelah, who was the father of Eber.

¹⁹Eber had two sons. One son was named Peleg,ⁿ because the people on the earth were divided into different languages during his life. Peleg's brother was named Joktan.

²⁰Joktan was the father of Almodad, Sheleph, Hazarmaveth, Jerah, ²¹Hadoram, Uzal, Diklah, ²²Obal, Abimael, Sheba, ²³Ophir, Havilah, and Jobab. All these were Joktan's sons. ²⁴The family line included Shem, Arphaxad, Shelah, ²⁵Eber,

> ✳ **SIDELIGHT:** If you're looking for an easy Bible verse to memorize, try 1 Chronicles 1:25. With just three words, it's the shortest verse in the Old Testament. But you might still have trouble remembering it; Eber, Peleg, and Reu aren't common names.

Peleg, Reu, ²⁶Serug, Nahor, Terah, ²⁷and Abram, who was called Abraham.

Abraham's Family

²⁸Abraham's sons were Isaac and Ishmael.

²⁹These were the sons of Isaac and Ishmael. Ishmael's first son was Nebaioth. His other sons were Kedar, Adbeel, Mibsam, ³⁰Mishma, Dumah, Massa, Hadad, Tema, ³¹Jetur, Naphish, and Kedemah. These were Ishmael's sons. ³²Keturah, Abraham's slave woman,ᵈ gave birth to

---

Kittim His descendants were the people of Cyprus.
Mizraim This is another name for Egypt.
Peleg This name sounds like the Hebrew word for "divided."

Zimran, Jokshan, Medan, Midian, Ishbak, and Shuah.

Jokshan's sons were Sheba and Dedan.

33Midian's sons were Ephah, Epher, Hanoch, Abida, and Eldaah. All these were descendants[d] of Keturah.

34Abraham was the father of Isaac, and Isaac's sons were Esau and Israel.

35Esau's sons were Eliphaz, Reuel, Jeush, Jalam, and Korah.

36Eliphaz's sons were Teman, Omar, Zepho, Gatam, Kenaz, Timna, and Amalek.

37Reuel's sons were Nahath, Zerah, Shammah, and Mizzah.

The Edomites from Seir

38Seir's sons were Lotan, Shobal, Zibeon, Anah, Dishon, Ezer, and Dishan.

39Lotan's sons were Hori and Homam, and his sister was Timna.

40Shobal's sons were Alvan, Manahath, Ebal, Shepho, and Onam.

Zibeon's sons were Aiah and Anah.

41Anah's son was Dishon.

Dishon's sons were Hemdan, Eshban, Ithran, and Keran.

42Ezer's sons were Bilhan, Zaavan, and Akan. Dishan's sons were Uz and Aran.

The Kings of Edom

43These kings ruled in Edom before there were kings in Israel. Bela son of Beor was king of Edom, and his city was named Dinhabah.

44When Bela died, Jobab son of Zerah became king. He was from Bozrah.

45When Jobab died, Husham became king. He was from the land of the Temanites.

46When Husham died, Hadad son of Bedad became king, and his city was named Avith. Hadad defeated Midian in the country of Moab.

47When Hadad died, Samlah became king. He was from Masrekah.

48When Samlah died, Shaul became king. He was from Rehoboth by the river.

49When Shaul died, Baal-Hanan son of Acbor became king.

50When Baal-Hanan died, Hadad became king, and his city was named Pau. Hadad's wife was named Mehetabel, and she was the daughter of Matred, who was the daughter of Me-Zahab. 51Then Hadad died.

The leaders of the family groups of Edom were Timna, Alvah, Jetheth, 52Oholibamah, Elah, Pinon, 53Kenaz, Teman, Mibzar, 54Magdiel, and Iram. These were the leaders of Edom.

Israel's Family

2 The sons of Israel[n] were Reuben, Simeon, Levi, Judah, Issachar, Zebulun, 2Dan, Joseph, Benjamin, Naphtali, Gad, and Asher.

Judah's Family

3Judah's sons were Er, Onan, and Shelah. A Canaanite woman, the daughter of Shua, was their mother. Judah's first son, Er, did what the LORD said was wicked, so the LORD put him to death. 4Judah's daughter-in-law Tamar gave birth to Perez and Zerah. Judah was the father, so Judah had five sons.

5Perez's sons were Hezron and Hamul.

6Zerah had five sons: Zimri, Ethan, Heman, Calcol, and Darda.

7Carmi's son was Achan, who caused trouble for Israel because he took things that had been given to the LORD to be destroyed.

8Ethan's son was Azariah.

9Hezron's sons were Jerahmeel, Ram, and Caleb.

10Ram was Amminadab's father, and Amminadab was Nashon's father. Nahshon was the leader of the people of Judah. 11Nahshon was the father of Salmon, who was the father of Boaz. 12Boaz was the father of Obed, and Obed was the father of Jesse.

13Jesse's first son was Eliab. His second son was Abinadab, his third was Shimea, 14his fourth was Nethanel, his fifth was Raddai, 15his sixth was Ozem, and his seventh son was David. 16Their sisters were Zeruiah and Abigail. Zeruiah's three sons were Abishai, Joab, and Asahel. 17Abigail was the mother of Amasa, and his father was Jether, an Ishmaelite.

Caleb's Family

18Caleb son of Hezron had children by his wife Azubah and by Jerioth. Caleb and Azubah's sons were Jesher, Shobab, and Ardon. 19When Azubah died, Caleb married Ephrath. They had a son named Hur, 20who was the father of Uri, who was the father of Bezalel.

21Later, when Hezron was sixty years old, he married the daughter of Makir, Gilead's father. Hezron had sexual relations with Makir's daughter, and she had a son named Segub. 22Segub was the father of Jair. Jair controlled twenty-three cities in the country of Gilead. 23(But Geshur and Aram captured the Towns of Jair, as well as Kenath and the small towns around it—sixty towns in all.) All these were descendants[d] of Makir, the father of Gilead.

24After Hezron died in Caleb Ephrathah, his

Israel   Another name for Jacob.

wife Abijah had his son, named Ashhur. Ashhur became the father of Tekoa.

Jerahmeel's Family

25Hezron's first son was Jerahmeel. Jerahmeel's sons were Ram, Bunah, Oren, Ozem, and Ahijah. Ram was Jerahmeel's first son. 26Jerahmeel had another wife, named Atarah. She was the mother of Onam.

27Jerahmeel's first son, Ram, had sons. They were Maaz, Jamin, and Eker.

28Onam's sons were Shammai and Jada. Shammai's sons were Nadab and Abishur.

29Abishur's wife was named Abihail, and their sons were Ahban and Molid.

30Nadab's sons were Seled and Appaim. Seled died without having children.

31Appaim's son was Ishi, who became the father of Sheshan. Sheshan was the father of Ahlai.

32Jada was Shammai's brother, and Jada's sons were Jether and Jonathan. Jether died without having children.

33Jonathan's sons were Peleth and Zaza. These were Jerahmeel's descendants.d

34Sheshan did not have any sons, only daughters. He had a servant from Egypt named Jarha. 35Sheshan let his daughter marry his servant Jarha, and she had a son named Attai.

36Attai was the father of Nathan. Nathan was the father of Zabad. 37Zabad was the father of Ephlal. Ephlal was the father of Obed. 38Obed was the father of Jehu. Jehu was the father of Azariah. 39Azariah was the father of Helez. Helez was the father of Eleasah. 40Eleasah was the father of Sismai. Sismai was the father of Shallum. 41Shallum was the father of Jekamiah, and Jekamiah was the father of Elishama.

Caleb's Family

42Caleb was Jerahmeel's brother. Caleb's first son was Mesha. Mesha was the father of Ziph, and his son Mareshah was the father of Hebron. 43Hebron's sons were Korah, Tappuah, Rekem, and Shema. 44Shema was the father of Raham, who was the father of Jorkeam. Rekem was the father of Shammai. 45Shammai was the father of Maon, and Maon was the father of Beth Zur.

46Caleb's slave womand was named Ephah, and she was the mother of Haran, Moza, and Gazez. Haran was the father of Gazez.

47Jahdai's sons were Regem, Jotham, Geshan, Pelet, Ephah, and Shaaph.

48Caleb had another slave woman named Maacah. She was the mother of Sheber, Tirhanah, 49Shaaph, and Sheva. Shaaph was the father of Madmannah. Sheva was the father of Macbenah and Gibea. Caleb's daughter was Acsah.

50-51These were Caleb's descendants:d Caleb's son Hur was the first son of his mother Ephrathah. Hur's sons were Shobal, Salma, and Hareph. Shobal was the father of Kiriath Jearim. Salma was the father of Bethlehem. And Hareph was the father of Beth Gader.

52Shobal was the father of Kiriath Jearim. Shobal's descendants were Haroeh, half the Manahathites, 53and the family groups of Kiriath Jearim: the Ithrites, Puthites, Shumathites, and Mishraites. The Zorathites and the Eshtaolites came from the Mishraite people.

54Salma's descendants were Bethlehem, the Netophathites, Atroth Beth Joab, half the Manahathites, and the Zorites. 55His descendants included the families who lived at Jabez, who wrote and copied important papers. They were called the Tirathites, Shimeathites, and Sucathites and were from the Kenite family group who came from Hammath. He was the father of the people living in Recab.

David's Family

3 These are David's sons who were born in Hebron. The first was Amnon, whose mother was Ahinoam from Jezreel. The second son was Daniel, whose mother was Abigail from Carmel. 2The third son was Absalom, whose mother was Maacah daughter of Talmai, the king of Geshur. The fourth son was Adonijah, whose mother was Haggith. 3The fifth son was Shephatiah, whose mother was Abital. The sixth son was Ithream, whose mother was Eglah. 4These six sons of David were born to him in Hebron, where David ruled for seven and one-half years.

David ruled in Jerusalem thirty-three years. 5These were his children who were born in Jerusalem: Shammua, Shobab, Nathan, and Solomon — the four children of David and Bathsheba, Ammiel's daughter. 6-8David's other nine children were Ibhar, Elishua, Eliphelet, Nogah, Nepheg, Japhia, Elishama, Eliada, and Eliphelet. 9These were all of David's sons, except for those born to his slave women.d David also had a daughter named Tamar.

The Kings of Judah

10Solomon's son was Rehoboam. Rehoboam's son was Abijah. Abijah's son was Asa. Asa's son was Jehoshaphat. 11Jehoshaphat's son was Jehoram. Jehoram's son was Ahaziah. Ahaziah's son was Joash. 12Joash's son was Amaziah. Amaziah's son was Azariah. Azariah's son was Jotham. 13Jotham's son was Ahaz. Ahaz's son was Hezekiah. Hezekiah's son was Manasseh. 14Manasseh's son was Amon, and Amon's son was Josiah.

15These were Josiah's sons: His first son was Johanan, his second was Jehoiakim, his third was Zedekiah, and his fourth was Shallum.

[16]Jehoiakim was followed by Jehoiachin, and he was followed by Zedekiah.

David's Descendants After the Babylonian Captivity

[17]Jehoiachin was taken as a prisoner. His sons were Shealtiel, [18]Malkiram, Pedaiah, Shenazzar, Jekamiah, Hoshama, and Nedabiah.

[19]Pedaiah's sons were Zerubbabel and Shimei. Zerubbabel's sons were Meshullam and Hananiah, and their sister was Shelomith. [20]Zerubbabel also had five other sons: Hashubah, Ohel, Berekiah, Hasadiah, and Jushab-Hesed.

[21]Hananiah's descendants[d] were Pelatiah and Jeshaiah, and the sons of Rephaiah, Arnan, Obadiah, and Shecaniah.

[22]Shecaniah's son was Shemaiah. Shemaiah's sons were Hattush, Igal, Bariah, Neariah, and Shaphat. There were six in all.

[23]Neariah had three sons: Elioenai, Hizkiah, and Azrikam.

[24]Elioenai had seven sons: Hodaviah, Eliashib, Pelaiah, Akkub, Johanan, Delaiah, and Anani.

Other Family Groups of Judah

4 Judah's descendants[d] were Perez, Hezron, Carmi, Hur, and Shobal.

[2]Reaiah was Shobal's son. Reaiah was the father of Jahath, and Jahath was the father of Ahumai and Lahad. They were the family groups of the Zorathite people.

[3-4]Hur was the oldest son of Caleb and his wife Ephrathah. Hur was the leader of Bethlehem. His three sons were Etam, Penuel, and Ezer. Etam's sons were Jezreel, Ishma, and Idbash. They had a sister named Hazzelelponi. Penuel was the father of Gedor, and Ezer was the father of Hushah.

[5]Tekoa's father was Ashhur. Ashhur had two wives named Helah and Naarah.

[6]The sons of Ashhur and Naarah were Ahuzzam, Hepher, Temeni, and Haahashtari. These were the descendants of Naarah.

[7]Helah's sons were Zereth, Zohar, Ethnan, [8]and Koz. Koz was the father of Anub, Hazzobebah, and the Aharhel family group. Aharhel was the son of Harum.

[9]There was a man named Jabez, who was respected more than his brothers. His mother named him Jabez[n] because she said, "I was in much pain when I gave birth to him." [10]Jabez prayed to the God of Israel, "Please do good things for me and give me more land. Stay with me, and don't let anyone hurt me. Then I won't have any pain." And God did what Jabez had asked.

[11]Kelub, Shuhah's brother, was the father of Mehir. Mehir was the father of Eshton. [12]Eshton was the father of Beth Rapha, Paseah, and Tehinnah. Tehinnah was the father of the people from the town of Nahash. These people were from Recah.

[13]The sons of Kenaz were Othniel and Seraiah. Othniel's sons were Hathath and Meonothai. [14]Meonothai was the father of Ophrah.

Seraiah was the father of Joab. Joab was the ancestor of the people from Craftsmen's Valley, named that because the people living there were craftsmen.

> ✸ **SIDELIGHT:** Have you ever wondered where Sears gets its tools? Maybe from Joab's descendants. They all lived in Craftsmen's Valley (1 Chronicles 4:14).

---

[15]Caleb was Jephunneh's son. Caleb's sons were Iru, Elah, and Naam. Elah's son was Kenaz.

[16]Jehallelel's sons were Ziph, Ziphah, Tiria, and Asarel.

[17-18]Ezrah's sons were Jether, Mered, Epher, and Jalon. Mered married Bithiah, the daughter of the king of Egypt. The children of Mered and Bithiah were Miriam, Shammai, and Ishbah. Ishbah was the father of Eshtemoa. Mered also had a wife from Judah, who gave birth to Jered, Heber, and Jekuthiel. Jered became the father of Gedor. Heber became the father of Soco. And Jekuthiel became the father of Zanoah.

[19]Hodiah's wife was Naham's sister. The sons of Hodiah's wife were Eshtemoa and the father of Keilah. Keilah was from the Garmite people, and Eshtemoa was from the Maacathite people.

[20]Shimon's sons were Amnon, Rinnah, Ben-Hanan, and Tilon.

Ishi's sons were Zoheth and Ben-Zoheth.

[21-22]Shelah was Judah's son. Shelah's sons were Er, Laadah, Jokim, the men from Cozeba, Joash, and Saraph. Er was the father of Lecah. Laadah was the father of Mareshah and the family groups of linen workers at Beth Ashbea. Joash and Saraph ruled in Moab and Jashubi Lehem. The writings about this family are very old. [23]These sons of Shelah were potters. They lived in Netaim and Gederah and worked for the king.

Simeon's Children

[24]Simeon's sons were Nemuel, Jamin, Jarib, Zerah, and Shaul. [25]Shaul's son was Shallum. Shallum's son was Mibsam. Mibsam's son was Mishma.

[26]Mishma's son was Hammuel. Hammuel's son was Zaccur. Zaccur's son was Shimei. [27]Shimei

---

Jabez This name in Hebrew sounds like the word for "pain."

had sixteen sons and six daughters, but his brothers did not have many children, so there were not as many people in their family group as there were in Judah.

[28]Shimei's children lived in Beersheba, Moladah, Hazar Shual, [29]Bilhah, Ezem, Tolad, [30]Bethuel, Hormah, Ziklag, [31]Beth Marcaboth, Hazar Susim, Beth Biri, and Shaaraim. They lived in these cities until David became king. [32]The five villages near these cities were Etam, Ain, Rimmon, Token, and Ashan. [33]There were also other villages as far away as Baalath. This is where they lived. And they wrote the history of their family.

[34-38]The men in this list were leaders of their family groups: Meshobab, Jamlech, Joshah son of Amaziah, Joel, Jehu son of Joshibiah (Joshibiah was the son of Seraiah, who was the son of Asiel), Elioenai, Jaakobah, Jeshohaiah, Asaiah, Adiel, Jesimiel, Benaiah, and Ziza. (Ziza was the son of Shiphi, who was the son of Allon. Allon was the son of Jedaiah, who was the son of Shimri. And Shimri was the son of Shemaiah.)

These families grew very large. [39]They went outside the city of Gedor to the east side of the valley to look for pasture for their flocks. [40]They found good pastures with plenty of grass, and the land was open country and peaceful and quiet. Ham's descendants[d] had lived there in the past. [41]These men who were listed came to Gedor while Hezekiah was king of Judah. They fought against the Hamites, destroying their tents, and also against the Meunites who lived there, and completely destroyed them. So there are no Meunites there even today. Then these men began to live there, because there was pasture for their flocks. [42]Ishi's sons, Pelatiah, Neariah, Rephaiah, and Uzziel, led five hundred of the Simeonites and attacked the people living in the mountains of Edom. [43]They killed the few Amalekites who were still alive. From that time until now these Simeonites have lived in Edom.

Reuben's Children

5 Reuben was Israel's first son. Reuben should have received the special privileges of the oldest son, but he had sexual relations with his father's slave woman.[d] So those special privileges were given to Joseph's sons. (Joseph was a son of Israel.) In the family history Reuben's name is not listed as the first son. [2]Judah became stronger than his brothers, and a leader came from his family. But Joseph's family received the privileges that belonged to the oldest son. [3]Reuben was Israel's first son. Reuben's sons were Hanoch, Pallu, Hezron, and Carmi.

[4]These were the children of Joel: Shemaiah was Joel's son. Gog was Shemaiah's son. Shimei was Gog's son. [5]Micah was Shimei's son. Reaiah was Micah's son. Baal was Reaiah's son. [6]Beerah

was Baal's son. Beerah was a leader of the tribe[d] of Reuben. Tiglath-Pileser king of Assyria captured him and took him away.

[7]Joel's brothers and all his family groups are listed just as they are written in their family histories: Jeiel was the first, then Zechariah, [8]and Bela. (Bela was the son of Azaz. Azaz was the son of Shema, and Shema was the son of Joel.) They lived in the area of Aroer all the way to Nebo and Baal Meon. [9]Bela's people lived to the east — as far as the edge of the desert, which is beside the Euphrates River — because they had too many cattle for the land of Gilead.

[10]When Saul was king, Bela's people fought a war against the Hagrite people and defeated them. Then Bela's people lived in the tents that had belonged to the Hagrites in all the area east of Gilead.

Gad's Children

[11]The people from the tribe[d] of Gad lived near the Reubenites. The Gadites lived in the area of Bashan all the way to Salecah. [12]Joel was the main leader, Shapham was second, and then Janai and Shaphat were leaders in Bashan.

[13]The seven relatives in their families were Michael, Meshullam, Sheba, Jorai, Jacan, Zia, and Eber. [14]They were the descendants[d] of Abihail. Abihail was Huri's son. Huri was Jaroah's son. Jaroah was Gilead's son. Gilead was Michael's son. Michael was Jeshishai's son. Jeshishai was Jahdo's son, and Jahdo was the son of Buz. [15]Ahi was Abdiel's son, and Abdiel was Guni's son. Ahi was the leader of their family.

[16]The Gadites lived in Gilead, Bashan and the small towns around it, and on all the pasturelands in the Plain of Sharon all the way to the borders.

[17]All these names were written in the family history of Gad during the time Jotham was king of Judah and Jeroboam was king of Israel.

Soldiers Skilled in War

[18]There were forty-four thousand seven hundred sixty soldiers from the tribes[d] of Reuben and Gad and East Manasseh who carried shields and swords and bows. They were skilled in war. [19]They started a war against the Hagrites and the people of Jetur, Naphish, and Nodab. [20]The men from the tribes of Manasseh, Reuben, and Gad prayed to God during the war, asking him to help them. So he helped them because they trusted *him. He handed over to them the Hagrites and all* those who were with them. [21]They took the animals that belonged to the Hagrites: fifty thousand camels, two hundred fifty thousand sheep, and two thousand donkeys. They also captured one hundred thousand people. [22]Many Hagrites were killed because God helped the people of Reuben,

Gad, and Manasseh. Then they lived there until Babylon captured them and took them away.

East Manasseh

23There were many people in East Manasseh, and they lived in the area of Bashan all the way to Baal Hermon, Senir, and Mount Hermon. 24These were the family leaders: Epher, Ishi, Eliel, Azriel, Jeremiah, Hodaviah, and Jahdiel. They were all strong, brave, and famous men, and leaders in their families. 25But they sinned against the God that their ancestors had worshiped. They began worshiping the gods of the people in that land, and those were the people God was destroying. 26So the God of Israel made Pul king of Assyria want to go to war. (Pul was also called Tiglath-Pileser.) He captured the people of Reuben, Gad, and East Manasseh, and he took them away to Halah, Habor, Hara, and near the Gozan River. They have lived there from that time until this day.

Levi's Children

6 Levi's sons were Gershon, Kohath, and Merari.

2Kohath's sons were Amram, Izhar, Hebron, and Uzziel. 3Amram's children were Aaron, Moses, and Miriam.

Aaron's sons were Nadab, Abihu, Eleazar, and Ithamar. 4Eleazar was the father of Phinehas. Phinehas was the father of Abishua. 5Abishua was the father of Bukki. Bukki was the father of Uzzi. 6Uzzi was the father of Zerahiah. Zerahiah was the father of Meraioth. 7Meraioth was the father of Amariah. Amariah was the father of Ahitub. 8Ahitub was the father of Zadok. Zadok was the father of Ahimaaz. 9Ahimaaz was the father of Azariah. Azariah was the father of Johanan. 10Johanan was the father of Azariah. (Azariah was a priest in the Temple[d] Solomon built in Jerusalem.) 11Azariah was the father of Amariah. Amariah was the father of Ahitub. 12Ahitub was the father of Zadok. Zadok was the father of Shallum. 13Shallum was the father of Hilkiah. Hilkiah was the father of Azariah. 14Azariah was the father of Seraiah, and Seraiah was the father of Jehozadak.

15Jehozadak was forced to leave his home when the LORD sent Judah and Jerusalem into captivity under the control of Nebuchadnezzar.

16Levi's sons were Gershon, Kohath, and Merari.

17The names of Gershon's sons were Libni and Shimei.

18Kohath's sons were Amram, Izhar, Hebron, and Uzziel.

19Merari's sons were Mahli and Mushi.

This is a list of the family groups of Levi, listed by the name of the father of each group.

20Gershon's son was Libni. Libni's son was Jehath. Jehath's son was Zimmah. 21Zimmah's son was Joah. Joah's son was Iddo. Iddo's son was Zerah. And Zerah's son was Jeatherai.

22Kohath's son was Amminadab. Amminadab's son was Korah. Korah's son was Assir. 23Assir's son was Elkanah. Elkanah's son was Ebiasaph. Ebiasaph's son was Assir. 24Assir's son was Tahath. Tahath's son was Uriel. Uriel's son was Uzziah, and Uzziah's son was Shaul.

25Elkanah's sons were Amasai and Ahimoth. 26Ahimoth's son was Elkanah. Elkanah's son was Zophai. Zophai's son was Nahath. 27Nahath's son was Eliab. Eliab's son was Jeroham. Jeroham's son was Elkanah, and Elkanah's son was Samuel.

28Samuel's sons were Joel, the first son, and Abijah, the second son.

29Merari's son was Mahli. Mahli's son was Libni. Libni's son was Shimei. Shimei's son was Uzzah. 30Uzzah's son was Shimea. Shimea's son was Haggiah, and Haggiah's son was Asaiah.

The Temple Musicians

31David chose some people to be in charge of the music in the house of the LORD. They began their work after the Ark[d] of the Agreement was put there. 32They served by making music at the Holy Tent[d] (also called the Meeting Tent), and they served until Solomon built the Temple[d] of the LORD in Jerusalem. They followed the rules for their work.

SIDELIGHT: According to 1 Chronicles 6:31–32, King David may have started the first professional Jerusalem Philharmonic Orchestra and Chorus to lead music in the Temple. Today the musicians would probably go on strike: First Chronicles 9:33 says they were on duty "day and night."

33These are the musicians and their sons:

From Kohath's family there was Heman the singer. Heman was Joel's son. Joel was Samuel's son. 34Samuel was Elkanah's son. Elkanah was Jeroham's son. Jeroham was Eliel's son. Eliel was Toah's son. 35Toah was Zuph's son. Zuph was Elkanah's son. Elkanah was Mahath's son. Mahath was Amasai's son. 36Amasai was Elkanah's son. Elkanah was Joel's son. Joel was Azariah's son. Azariah was Zephaniah's son. 37Zephaniah was Tahath's son. Tahath was Assir's son. Assir was Ebiasaph's son. Ebiasaph was Korah's son. 38Korah was Izhar's son. Izhar was Kohath's son. Kohath was Levi's son. Levi was Israel's son.

39There was Heman's helper Asaph, whose group stood by Heman's right side. Asaph was

Berekiah's son. Berekiah was Shimea's son. [40]Shimea was Michael's son. Michael was Baaseiah's son. Baaseiah was Malkijah's son. [41]Malkijah was Ethni's son. Ethni was Zerah's son. Zerah was Adaiah's son. [42]Adaiah was Ethan's son. Ethan was Zimmah's son. Zimmah was Shimei's son. [43]Shimei was Jahath's son. Jahath was Gershon's son, and Gershon was Levi's son.

[44]Merari's family were the helpers of Heman and Asaph, and they stood by Heman's left side. In this group was Ethan son of Kishi. Kishi was Abdi's son. Abdi was Malluch's son. [45]Malluch was Hashabiah's son. Hashabiah was Amaziah's son. Amaziah was Hilkiah's son. [46]Hilkiah was Amzi's son. Amzi was Bani's son. Bani was Shemer's son. [47]Shemer was Mahli's son. Mahli was Mushi's son. Mushi was Merari's son, and Merari was Levi's son.

[48]The other Levites served by doing their own special work in the Holy Tent, the house of God. [49]Aaron and his descendants[d] offered the sacrifices on the altar of burnt offering and burned the incense on the altar of incense. They offered the sacrifices that removed the Israelites' sins so they could belong to God. They did all the work in the Most Holy Place and followed all the laws that Moses, God's servant, had commanded.

[50]These were Aaron's sons: Eleazar was Aaron's son. Phinehas was Eleazar's son. Abishua was Phinehas' son. [51]Bukki was Abishua's son. Uzzi was Bukki's son. Zerahiah was Uzzi's son. [52]Meraioth was Zerahiah's son. Amariah was Meraioth's son. Ahitub was Amariah's son. [53]Zadok was Ahitub's son, and Ahimaaz was Zadok's son.

Land for the Levites

[54]These are the places where Aaron's descendants[d] lived. His descendants from the Kohath family group received the first share of the land. [55]They were given the city of Hebron in Judah and the pastures around it, [56]but the fields farther from the city and the villages near Hebron were given to Caleb son of Jephunneh. [57]So the descendants of Aaron were given Hebron, one of the cities of safety.[n] They also received the towns and pastures of Libnah, Jattir, Eshtemoa, [58]Hilen, Debir, [59]Ashan, Juttah, and Beth Shemesh. [60]They also received these towns and pastures from the tribe of Benjamin: Gibeon, Geba, Alemeth, and Anathoth.

The Kohath family groups received a total of thirteen towns.

[61]The rest of the Kohath family group was given ten towns from the family groups of West Manasseh. The towns were chosen by throwing lots.[d]

[62]The Gershon family group received thirteen towns from the tribes of Issachar, Asher, Naphtali, and the part of Manasseh living in Bashan.

[63]The Merari family group received twelve towns from the tribes of Reuben, Gad, and Zebulun. Those towns were chosen by throwing lots.

[64]So the Israelites gave these towns and their pastures to the Levites. [65]The towns from the tribes of Judah, Simeon, and Benjamin, which were named, were chosen by throwing lots.

[66]Some of the Kohath family groups received towns and pastures from the tribe of Ephraim. [67]They received Shechem, one of the cities of safety, with its pastures in the mountains of Ephraim. They also received the towns and pastures of Gezer, [68]Jokmeam, Beth Horon, [69]Aijalon, and Gath Rimmon.

[70]The rest of the people in the Kohath family group received the towns of Aner and Bileam and their pastures from West Manasseh.

[71]From East Manasseh, the Gershon family received the towns and pastures of Golan in Bashan and Ashtaroth.

[72-73]From the tribe of Issachar, the Gershon family received the towns and pastures of Kedesh, Daberath, Ramoth, and Anem.

[74-75]From the tribe of Asher, the Gershon family received the towns and pastures of Mashal, Abdon, Hukok, and Rehob.

[76]From the tribe of Naphtali, the Gershon family received the towns and pastures of Kedesh in Galilee, Hammon, and Kiriathaim.

[77]The rest of the Levites, the people from the Merari family, received from the tribe of Zebulun the towns and pastures of Jokneam, Kartah, Rimmono, and Tabor.

[78-79]From the tribe of Reuben, the Merari family received the towns and pastures of Bezer in the desert, Jahzah, Kedemoth, and Mephaath. (The tribe of Reuben lived east of the Jordan River, across from Jericho.)

[80-81]From the tribe of Gad, the Merari family received the towns and pastures of Ramoth in Gilead, Mahanaim, Heshbon, and Jazer.

Issachar's Children

7 Issachar had four sons: Tola, Puah, Jashub, and Shimron.

[2]Tola's sons were Uzzi, Rephaiah, Jeriel, Jahmai, Ibsam, and Samuel, and they were leaders of their families. In the family history of Tola's descendants,[d] twenty-two thousand six hundred men were listed as fighting men during the time David was king.

[3]Uzzi's son was Izrahiah.

Izrahiah's sons were Michael, Obadiah, Joel,

---

cities of safety A person who had accidentally killed someone could go to one of the six cities of safety to receive protection and a fair trial.

and Isshiah. All five of them were leaders. [4]Their family history shows they had thirty-six thousand men ready to serve in the army, because they had many wives and children.

[5]The records of the family groups of Issachar show there were eighty-seven thousand fighting men.

Benjamin's Children

[6]Benjamin had three sons: Bela, Beker, and Jediael.

[7]Bela had five sons: Ezbon, Uzzi, Uzziel, Jerimoth, and Iri, and they were leaders of their families. Their family history shows they had twenty-two thousand thirty-four fighting men.

[8]Beker's sons were Zemirah, Joash, Eliezer, Elioenai, Omri, Jeremoth, Abijah, Anathoth, and Alemeth. They all were Beker's sons. [9]Their family history listed the family leaders and twenty thousand two hundred fighting men.

[10]Jediael's son was Bilhan.

Bilhan's sons were Jeush, Benjamin, Ehud, Kenaanah, Zethan, Tarshish, and Ahishahar. [11]All these sons of Jediael were leaders of their families. They had seventeen thousand two hundred fighting men ready to serve in the army.

[12]The Shuppites and Huppites were descendants[d] of Ir, and the Hushites were descendants of Aher.

Naphtali's Children

[13]Naphtali's sons were Jahziel, Guni, Jezer, and Shillem. They were Bilhah's grandsons.

Manasseh's Children

[14]These are Manasseh's descendants.[d] Manasseh had an Aramean slave woman,[d] who was the mother of Asriel and Makir. Makir was Gilead's father. [15]Makir took a wife from the Huppites and Shuppites. His sister was named Maacah. His second son was named Zelophehad, and he had only daughters. [16]Makir's wife Maacah had a son whom she named Peresh. Peresh's brother was named Sheresh. Sheresh's sons were Ulam and Rakem.

[17]Ulam's son was Bedan.

These were the sons of Gilead, who was the son of Makir. Makir was Manasseh's son. [18]Makir's sister Hammoleketh gave birth to Ishhod, Abiezer, and Mahlah.

[19]The sons of Shemida were Ahian, Shechem, Likhi, and Aniam.

Ephraim's Children

[20]These are the names of Ephraim's descendants.[d] Ephraim's son was Shuthelah. Shuthelah's son was Bered. Bered's son was Tahath. Tahath's son was Eleadah. Eleadah's son was Tahath. [21]Tahath's son was Zabad. Zabad's son was Shuthelah.

Ezer and Elead went to Gath to steal cows and sheep and were killed by some men who grew up in that city. [22]Their father Ephraim cried for them many days, and his family came to comfort him. [23]Then he had sexual relations with his wife again. She became pregnant and gave birth to a son whom Ephraim named Beriah[n] because of the trouble that had happened to his family. [24]Ephraim's daughter was Sheerah. She built Lower Beth Horon, Upper Beth Horon, and Uzzen Sheerah.

[25]Rephah was Ephraim's son. Resheph was Rephah's son. Telah was Resheph's son. Tahan was Telah's son. [26]Ladan was Tahan's son. Ammihud was Ladan's son. Elishama was Ammihud's son. [27]Nun was Elishama's son, and Joshua was the son of Nun.

[28]Ephraim's descendants lived in these lands and towns: Bethel and the villages near it, Naaran on the east, Gezer and the villages near it on the west, and Shechem and the villages near it. These villages went all the way to Ayyah and its villages. [29]Along the borders of Manasseh's land were the towns of Beth Shan, Taanach, Megiddo, and Dor, and the villages near them. The descendants of Joseph son of Israel lived in these towns.

Asher's Children

[30]Asher's sons were Imnah, Ishvah, Ishvi, and Beriah. Their sister was Serah.

[31]Beriah's sons were Heber and Malkiel. Malkiel was Birzaith's father.

[32]Heber was the father of Japhlet, Shomer, Hotham, and their sister Shua.

[33]Japhlet's sons were Pasach, Bimhal, and Ashvath. They were Japhlet's children.

[34]Japhlet's brother was Shomer. Shomer's sons were Rohgah, Hubbah, and Aram.

[35]Shomer's brother was Hotham. Hotham's sons were Zophah, Imna, Shelesh, and Amal.

[36]Zophah's sons were Suah, Harnepher, Shual, Beri, Imrah, [37]Bezer, Hod, Shamma, Shilshah, Ithran, and Beera.

[38]Jether's sons were Jephunneh, Pispah, and Ara.

[39]Ulla's sons were Arah, Hanniel, and Rizia.

[40]All these men were descendants of Asher and leaders of their families. They were powerful warriors and outstanding leaders. Their family history lists that they had twenty-six thousand soldiers ready to serve in the army.

The Family History of King Saul

8 Benjamin was the father of Bela, his first son. Ashbel was his second son, Aharah was his

---

Beriah   This name sounds like the Hebrew word for "trouble."

third, ²Nohah was his fourth, and Rapha was his fifth son.

³Bela's sons were Addar, Gera, Abihud, ⁴Abishua, Naaman, Ahoah, ⁵Gera, Shephuphan, and Huram.

⁶These were the descendants*d* of Ehud and leaders of their families in Geba. They were forced to move to Manahath. ⁷Ehud's descendants were Naaman, Ahijah, and Gera. Gera forced them to leave. He was the father of Uzza and Ahihud.

⁸⁻¹¹Shaharaim and his wife Hushim had sons named Abitub and Elpaal. In Moab, Shaharaim divorced his wives Hushim and Baara. Shaharaim and his wife Hodesh had these sons: Jobab, Zibia, Mesha, Malcam, Jeuz, Sakia, and Mirmah. They were leaders of their families.

¹²⁻¹³Elpaal's sons were Eber, Misham, Shemed, Beriah, and Shema. Shemed built the towns of Ono and Lod and the villages around them. Beriah and Shema were leaders of the families living in Aijalon, and they forced out the people who lived in Gath.

¹⁴Beriah's sons were Ahio, Shashak, Jeremoth, ¹⁵Zebadiah, Arad, Eder, ¹⁶Michael, Ishpah, and Joha.

¹⁷Elpaal's sons were Zebadiah, Meshullam, Hizki, Heber, ¹⁸Ishmerai, Izliah, and Jobab.

¹⁹Shimei's sons were Jakim, Zicri, Zabdi, ²⁰Elienai, Zillethai, Eliel, ²¹Adaiah, Beraiah, and Shimrath.

²²Shashak's sons were Ishpan, Eber, Eliel, ²³Abdon, Zicri, Hanan, ²⁴Hananiah, Elam, Anthothijah, ²⁵Iphdeiah, and Penuel.

²⁶Jeroham's sons were Shamsherai, Shehariah, Athaliah, ²⁷Jaareshiah, Elijah, and Zicri.

²⁸The family histories show that all these men were leaders of their families and lived in Jerusalem.

²⁹Jeiel lived in the town of Gibeon, where he was the leader. His wife was named Maacah. ³⁰Jeiel's first son was Abdon. His other sons were Zur, Kish, Baal, Ner, Nadab, ³¹Gedor, Ahio, Zeker, ³²and Mikloth. Mikloth was the father of Shimeah. These sons also lived near their relatives in Jerusalem.

³³Ner was the father of Kish. Kish was the father of Saul, and Saul was the father of Jonathan, Malki-Shua, Abinadab, and Esh-Baal.

³⁴Jonathan's son was Merib-Baal, who was the father of Micah.

³⁵Micah's sons were Pithon, Melech, Tarea, *and Ahaz. ³⁶Ahaz was the father of Jehoaddah. Jehoaddah* was the father of Alemeth, Azmaveth, and Zimri. Zimri was the father of Moza. ³⁷Moza was the father of Binea. Raphah was Binea's son. Eleasah was Raphah's son, and Azel was Eleasah's son.

³⁸Azel had six sons: Azrikam, Bokeru, Ishmael,

Sheariah, Obadiah, and Hanan. All these were Azel's sons.

³⁹Azel's brother was Eshek. Eshek's first son was Ulam, his second was Jeush, and Eliphelet was his third. ⁴⁰Ulam's sons were mighty warriors and good archers. They had many sons and grandsons—one hundred fifty of them in all.

All these men were Benjamin's descendants.

9 The names of all the people of Israel were listed in their family histories, and those family histories were put in the book of the kings of Israel.

The People in Jerusalem

The people of Judah were captured and forced to go to Babylon, because they were not faithful to God. ²The first people to come back and live in their own lands and towns were some Israelites, priests, Levites, and Temple*d* servants.

³People from the tribes*d* of Judah, Benjamin, Ephraim, and Manasseh lived in Jerusalem. This is a list of those people.

⁴There was Uthai son of Ammihud. (Ammihud was Omri's son. Omri was Imri's son. Imri was Bani's son. Bani was a descendant*d* of Perez, and Perez was Judah's son.)

⁵Of the Shilonite people there were Asaiah and his sons. Asaiah was the oldest son in his family.

⁶Of the Zerahite people there were Jeuel and other relatives of Zerah. There were six hundred ninety of them in all.

⁷From the tribe of Benjamin there was Sallu son of Meshullam. (Meshullam was Hodaviah's son, and Hodaviah was Hassenuah's son.) ⁸There was also Ibneiah son of Jeroham and Elah son of Uzzi. (Uzzi was Micri's son.) And there was Meshullam son of Shephatiah. (Shephatiah was Reuel's son, and Reuel was Ibnijah's son.) ⁹The family history of Benjamin lists nine hundred fifty-six people living in Jerusalem, and all these were leaders of their families.

¹⁰Of the priests there were Jedaiah, Jehoiarib, Jakin, and ¹¹Azariah son of Hilkiah. (Hilkiah was Meshullam's son. Meshullam was Zadok's son. Zadok was Meraioth's son. Meraioth was Ahitub's son. Ahitub was the officer responsible for the Temple of God.) ¹²As there was Adaiah son of Jeroham. (Jeroham was Pashhur's son, and Pashhur was Malkijah's son.) And there was Maasai son of Adiel. (Adiel was Jahzerah's son. Jahzerah was Meshullam's son. Meshullam was Me-*shillemith's son, and Meshillemith was Immer's* son.) ¹³There were one thousand seven hundred sixty priests. They were leaders of their families, and they were responsible for serving in the Temple of God.

¹⁴Of the Levites there was Semaiah son of Hasshub. (Hasshub was Azrikam's son, and Azrikam

was Hashabiah's son. Hashabiah was from the family of Merari.) ¹⁵There were also Bakbakkar, Heresh, Galal, and Mattaniah son of Mica. (Mica was Zicri's son, and Zicri was Asaph's son.) ¹⁶There was also Obadiah son of Shemaiah. (Shemaiah was Galal's son, and Galal was Jeduthun's son.) And there was Berekiah son of Asa. (Asa was the son of Elkanah, who lived in the villages of the Netophathites.)

¹⁷Of the gatekeepers there were Shallum, Akkub, Talmon, Ahiman, and their relatives. Shallum was their leader. ¹⁸These gatekeepers from the tribe of Levi still stand next to the King's Gate on the east side of the city. ¹⁹Shallum was Kore's son. Kore was Ebiasaph's son, and Ebiasaph was Korah's son. Shallum and his relatives from the family of Korah were gatekeepers and were responsible for guarding the gates of the Temple. Their ancestors had also been responsible for guarding the entrance to the Temple of the LORD. ²⁰In the past Phinehas, Eleazar's son, was in charge of the gatekeepers, and the LORD was with Phinehas. ²¹Zechariah son of Meshelemiah was the gatekeeper at the entrance to the Temple.

²²In all, two hundred twelve men were chosen to guard the gates, and their names were written in their family histories in their villages. David and Samuel the seer*d* chose these men because they were dependable. ²³The gatekeepers and their descendants had to guard the gates of the Temple of the LORD. (The Temple took the place of the Holy Tent.*d* ²⁴There were gatekeepers on all four sides of the Temple: east, west, north, and south. ²⁵The gatekeepers' relatives who lived in the villages had to come and help them at times. Each time they came they helped the gatekeepers for seven days. ²⁶Because they were dependable, four gatekeepers were made the leaders of all the gatekeepers. They were Levites, and they were responsible for the rooms and treasures in the Temple of God. ²⁷They stayed up all night guarding the Temple of God, and they opened it every morning.

²⁸Some of the gatekeepers were responsible for the utensils used in the Temple services. They counted these utensils when people took them out and when they brought them back. ²⁹Other gatekeepers were chosen to take care of the furniture and utensils in the Holy Place. They also took care of the flour, wine, oil, incense,*d* and spices, ³⁰but some of the priests took care of mixing the spices. ³¹There was a Levite named Mattithiah who was dependable and had the job of baking the bread used for the offerings. He was the first son of Shallum, who was from the family of Korah. ³²Some of the gatekeepers from the Kohath family had the job of preparing the special bread that was put on the table every Sabbath*d* day. ³³Some of the Levites were musicians in the Temple. The leaders of these families stayed in the rooms of the Temple. Since they were on duty day and night, they did not do other work in the Temple.

> ☀ **SIDELIGHT:** If being a gatekeeper sounds like a cushy job, read 1 Chronicles 9:28–32 before applying. The Temple gatekeepers were probably priests who washed dishes, kept inventory, baked bread, and mixed spices.

³⁴These are the leaders of the Levite families. Their names were listed in their family histories, and they lived in Jerusalem.

The Family History of King Saul

³⁵Jeiel lived in the town of Gibeon, where he was the leader. His wife was named Maacah. ³⁶Jeiel's first son was Abdon. His other sons were Zur, Kish, Baal, Ner, Nadab, ³⁷Gedor, Ahio, Zechariah, and Mikloth. ³⁸Mikloth was Shimeam's father. Jeiel's family lived near their relatives in Jerusalem.

³⁹Ner was Kish's father. Kish was Saul's father. Saul was the father of Jonathan, Malki-Shua, Abinadab, and Esh-Baal.

⁴⁰Jonathan's son was Merib-Baal, who was the father of Micah.

⁴¹Micah's sons were Pithon, Melech, Tahrea, and Ahaz. ⁴²Ahaz was Jadah's father. Jadah was the father of Alemeth, Azmaveth, and Zimri. Zimri was Moza's father. ⁴³Moza was Binea's father. Rephaiah was Binea's son. Eleasah was Rephaiah's son, and Azel was Eleasah's son.

⁴⁴Azel had six sons: Azrikam, Bokeru, Ishmael, Sheariah, Obadiah, and Hanan. They were Azel's sons.

The Death of King Saul

10 The Philistines fought against Israel, and the Israelites ran away from them. Many Israelites were killed on Mount Gilboa. ²The Philistines fought hard against Saul and his sons, killing his sons Jonathan, Abinadab, and Malki-Shua. ³The fighting was heavy around Saul, and the archers shot him with their arrows and wounded him.

⁴Then Saul said to the officer who carried his armor, "Pull out your sword and stab me. If you don't, these Philistines who are not circumcised will come and hurt me." But Saul's officer refused, because he was afraid. So Saul took his own sword and threw himself on it. ⁵When the officer saw that Saul was dead, he threw himself on his own sword and died. ⁶So Saul and three of his sons died; all his family died together.

[7]When the Israelites living in the valley saw that their army had run away and that Saul and his sons were dead, they left their towns and ran away. Then the Philistines came and settled in them.

[8]The next day when the Philistines came to strip the dead soldiers, they found Saul and his sons dead on Mount Gilboa. [9]The Philistines stripped Saul's body and took his head and his armor. Then they sent messengers through all their country to tell the news to their idols and to their people. [10]The Philistines put Saul's armor in the temple of their idols and hung his head in the temple of Dagon.[d]

[11]All the people in Jabesh Gilead heard what the Philistines had done to Saul. [12]So the brave men of Jabesh went and got the bodies of Saul and his sons and brought them to Jabesh. They buried their bones under the large tree in Jabesh. Then the people of Jabesh gave up eating for seven days.

[13]Saul died because he was not faithful to the LORD and did not obey the LORD. He even went to a medium[d] and asked her for advice [14]instead of asking the LORD. This is why the LORD put Saul to death and gave the kingdom to Jesse's son David.

David Becomes King

11 Then the people of Israel came to David at the town of Hebron and said, "Look, we are your own family. [2]Even when Saul was king, you were the one who led Israel in battle. The LORD your God said to you, 'You will be the shepherd for my people Israel. You will be their leader.' "

[3]So all the older leaders of Israel came to King David at Hebron. He made an agreement with them in Hebron in the presence of the LORD. Then they poured oil on David to make him king over Israel. The LORD had promised through Samuel that this would happen.

David Captures Jerusalem

[4]David and all the Israelites went to the city of Jerusalem. At that time Jerusalem was called Jebus, and the people living there were named Jebusites. [5]They said to David, "You can't get inside our city." But David did take the city of Jerusalem with its strong walls, and it became the City of David.

[6]David had said, "The person who leads the attack against the Jebusites will become the commander over all my army." Joab son of Zeruiah led the attack, so he became the commander of the army.

[7]Then David made his home in the strong,

walled city, which is why it was named the City of David. [8]David rebuilt the city, beginning where the land was filled in and going to the wall that was around the city. Joab repaired the other parts of the city. [9]David became stronger and stronger, and the LORD All-Powerful was with him.

David's Mighty Warriors

[10]This is a list of the leaders over David's warriors who helped make David's kingdom strong. All the people of Israel also supported David's kingdom. These heroes and all the people of Israel made David king, just as the LORD had promised.

[11]This is a list of David's warriors:

Jashobeam was from the Hacmonite people. He was the head of the Three,[n] David's most powerful soldiers. He used his spear to fight three hundred men at one time, and he killed them all.

[12]Next was Eleazar, one of the Three. Eleazar was Dodai's son from the Ahohite people. [13]Eleazar was with David at Pas-Dammim when the Philistines came there to fight. There was a field of barley at that place. The Israelites ran away from the Philistines, [14]but they stopped in the middle of that field and fought for it and killed the Philistines. The LORD gave them a great victory.

[15]Once, three of the Thirty, David's chief soldiers, came down to him at the rock by the cave near Adullam. At the same time the Philistine army had camped in the Valley of Rephaim. [16]At that time David was in a stronghold,[d] and some of the Philistines were in Bethlehem. [17]David had a strong desire for some water. He said, "Oh, I wish someone would get me water from the well near the city gate of Bethlehem!" [18]So the Three broke through the Philistine army and took water from the well near the city gate in Bethlehem. Then they brought it to David, but he refused to drink it. He poured it out before the LORD, [19]saying, "May God keep me from drinking this water! It would be like drinking the blood of the men who risked their lives to bring it to me!" So David refused to drink it.

These were the brave things that the three warriors did.

[20]Abishai brother of Joab was the captain of the Three. Abishai fought three hundred soldiers with his spear and killed them. He became as famous as the Three [21]and was more honored than the Three. He became their commander even though he was not one of them.

[22]Benaiah son of Jehoiada was a brave fighter from Kabzeel who did mighty things. He killed two of the best warriors from Moab. He also went down into a pit and killed a lion on a snowy day. [23]Benaiah killed an Egyptian who was about seven and one-half feet tall and had a spear as

---

Three   Or maybe "Thirty." These were David's most powerful soldiers. See 2 Samuel 23:8.

large as a weaver's rod. Benaiah had a club, but he grabbed the spear from the Egyptian's hand and killed him with his own spear. ²⁴These were the things Benaiah son of Jehoiada did. He was as famous as the Three. ²⁵He received more honor than the Thirty, but he did not become a member of the Three. David made him leader of his bodyguards.

The Thirty Chief Soldiers

²⁶These were also mighty warriors:
Asahel brother of Joab;
Elhanan son of Dodo from Bethlehem;
²⁷Shammoth the Harorite;
Helez the Pelonite;
²⁸Ira son of Ikkesh from Tekoa;
Abiezer the Anathothite;
²⁹Sibbecai the Hushathite;
Ilai the Ahohite;
³⁰Maharai the Netophathite;
Heled son of Baanah the Netophathite;
³¹Ithai son of Ribai from Gibeah in Benjamin;
Benaiah the Pirathonite;
³²Hurai from the ravines of Gaash;
Abiel the Arbathite;
³³Azmaveth the Baharumite;
Eliahba the Shaalbonite;
³⁴the sons of Hashem the Gizonite;
Jonathan son of Shagee the Hararite;
³⁵Ahiam son of Sacar the Hararite;
Eliphal son of Ur;
³⁶Hepher the Mekerathite;
Ahijah the Pelonite;
³⁷Hezro the Carmelite;
Naarai son of Ezbai;
³⁸Joel brother of Nathan;
Mibhar son of Hagri;
³⁹Zelek the Ammonite;
Naharai the Berothite, the officer who carried the armor for Joab son of Zeruiah;
⁴⁰Ira the Ithrite;
Gareb the Ithrite;
⁴¹Uriah the Hittite;
Zabad son of Ahlai;
⁴²Adina son of Shiza the Reubenite, who was the leader of the Reubenites, and his thirty soldiers;
⁴³Hanan son of Maacah;
Joshaphat the Mithnite;
⁴⁴Uzzia the Ashterathite;
Shama and Jeiel sons of Hotham the Aroerite;
⁴⁵Jediael son of Shimri;
Joha, Jediael's brother, the Tizite;
⁴⁶Eliel the Mahavite;
Jeribai and Joshaviah, Elnaam's sons;
Ithmah the Moabite;
⁴⁷Eliel, Obed, and Jaasiel the Mezobaites.

Warriors Join David

12 These were the men who came to David at Ziklag when David was hiding from Saul son of Kish. They were among the warriors who helped David in battle. ²They came with bows for weapons and could use either their right or left hands to shoot arrows or to sling rocks. They were Saul's relatives from the tribe*ᵈ* of Benjamin. ³Ahiezer was their leader, and there was Joash. (Ahiezer and Joash were sons of Shemaah, who was from the town of Gibeah.) There were also Jeziel and Pelet, the sons of Azmaveth. There were Beracah and Jehu from the town of Anathoth. ⁴And there was Ishmaiah from the town of Gibeon; he was one of the Thirty. In fact, he was the leader of the Thirty. There were Jeremiah, Jahaziel, Johanan, and Jozabad from Gederah. ⁵There were Eluzai, Jerimoth, Bealiah, and Shemariah. There was Shephatiah from Haruph. ⁶There were Elkanah, Isshiah, Azarel, Joezer, and Jashobeam from the family group of Korah. ⁷And there were Joelah and Zebadiah, the sons of Jeroham, from the town of Gedor.

⁸Part of the people of Gad joined David at his stronghold*ᵈ* in the desert. They were brave warriors trained for war and skilled with shields and spears. They were as fierce as lions and as fast as gazelles*ᵈ* over the hills.

⁹Ezer was the leader of Gad's army, and Obadiah was second in command. Eliab was third, ¹⁰Mishmannah was fourth, Jeremiah was fifth, ¹¹Attai was sixth, Eliel was seventh, ¹²Johanan was eighth, Elzabad was ninth, ¹³Jeremiah was tenth, and Macbannai was eleventh in command.

¹⁴They were the commanders of the army from Gad. The least of these leaders was in charge of a hundred soldiers, and the greatest was in charge of a thousand. ¹⁵They crossed the Jordan River and chased away the people living in the valleys, to the east and to the west. This happened in the first month of the year when the Jordan floods the valley.

¹⁶Other people from the tribes*ᵈ* of Benjamin and Judah also came to David at his stronghold. ¹⁷David went out to meet them and said to them, "If you have come peacefully to help me, I welcome you. Join me. But if you have come to turn me over to my enemies, even though I have done nothing wrong, the God of our fathers will see this and punish you."

¹⁸Then the Spirit*ᵈ* entered Amasai, the leader of the Thirty, and he said:

"We belong to you, David.
   We are with you, son of Jesse.
Success, success to you.
   Success to those who help you,
   because your God helps you."

So David welcomed these men and made them leaders of his army.

[19]Some of the men from Manasseh also joined David when he went with the Philistines to fight Saul. But David and his men did not really help the Philistines. After talking about it, the Philistine leaders decided to send David away. They said, "If David goes back to his master Saul, we will be killed." [20]These are the men from Manasseh who joined David when he went to Ziklag: Adnah, Jozabad, Jediael, Michael, Jozabad, Elihu, and Zillethai. Each of them was a leader of a thousand men from Manasseh. [21]All these men of Manasseh were brave soldiers, and they helped David fight against groups of men who went around the country robbing people. These soldiers became commanders in David's army. [22]Every day more men joined David, and his army became large, like the army of God.

Others Join David at Hebron

[23]These are the numbers of the soldiers ready for battle who joined David at Hebron. They came to help turn the kingdom of Saul over to David, just as the LORD had said.

[24]There were sixty-eight hundred men with their weapons from Judah. They carried shields and spears.

[25]There were seventy-one hundred men from Simeon. They were warriors ready for war.

[26]There were forty-six hundred men from Levi. [27]Jehoiada, a leader from Aaron's family, was in that group. There were thirty-seven hundred with him. [28]Zadok was also in that group. He was a strong young warrior, and with him came twenty-two leaders from his family.

[29]There were three thousand men from Benjamin, who were Saul's relatives. Most of them had remained loyal to Saul's family until then.

[30]There were twenty thousand eight hundred men from Ephraim. They were brave warriors and were famous men in their own family groups.

[31]There were eighteen thousand men from West Manasseh. Each one was especially chosen to make David king.

[32]There were two hundred leaders from Issachar. They knew what Israel should do, and they knew the right time to do it. Their relatives were with them and under their command.

[33]There were fifty thousand men from Zebulun. They were trained soldiers and knew how to use every kind of weapon of war. They followed David completely.

[34]There were one thousand officers from Naphtali. They had thirty-seven thousand soldiers with them who carried shields and spears.

[35]There were twenty-eight thousand six hundred men from Dan, who were ready for war.

[36]There were forty thousand trained soldiers from Asher, who were ready for war.

[37]There were one hundred twenty thousand soldiers from the east side of the Jordan River from the people of Reuben, Gad, and East Manasseh. They had every kind of weapon.

[38]All these fighting men were ready to go to war. They came to Hebron fully agreed to make David king of all Israel. All the other Israelites also agreed to make David king. [39]They spent three days there with David, eating and drinking, because their relatives had prepared food for them. [40]Also, their neighbors came from as far away as Issachar, Zebulun, and Naphtali, bringing food on donkeys, camels, mules, and oxen. They brought much flour, fig cakes, raisins, wine, oil, cows, and sheep, because the people of Israel were very happy.

Bringing Back the Ark

13 David talked with all the officers of his army, the commanders of a hundred men and the commanders of a thousand men. [2]Then David called the people of Israel together and said, "If you think it is a good idea, and if it is what the LORD our God wants, let's send a message. Let's tell our fellow Israelites in all the areas of Israel and the priests and Levites living with them in their towns and pastures to come and join us. [3]Let's bring the Ark[d] of our God back to us. We did not use it to ask God for help while Saul was king." [4]All the people agreed with David, because they all thought it was the right thing to do.

[5]So David gathered all the Israelites, from the Shihor River in Egypt to Lebo Hamath, to bring the Ark of God back from the town of Kiriath Jearim. [6]David and all the Israelites with him went to Baalah of Judah, which is Kiriath Jearim, to get the Ark of God the LORD. God's throne is between the golden, winged creatures on the Ark, and the Ark is called by his name.

[7]The people carried the Ark of God from Abinadab's house on a new cart, and Uzzah and Ahio guided it. [8]David and all the Israelites were celebrating in the presence of God. With all their strength they were singing and playing lyres,[d] harps, tambourines,[d] cymbals, and trumpets.

[9]When David's men came to the threshing[d] floor of Kidon, the oxen stumbled, and Uzzah reached out his hand to steady the Ark. [10]The LORD was angry with Uzzah and killed him, because he had touched the Ark. So Uzzah died there in the presence of God.

[11]David was angry because the LORD had punished Uzzah in his anger. Now that place is called The Punishment of Uzzah.

[12]David was afraid of God that day and asked, "How can I bring the Ark of God home to me?" [13]So David did not take the Ark with him to Jeru-

salem. Instead, he took it to the house of Obed-Edom who was from Gath. [14]The Ark of God stayed with Obed-Edom's family in his house for three months, and the LORD blessed Obed-Edom's family and everything he owned.

David's Kingdom Grows

14 Hiram king of the city of Tyre sent messengers to David. He also sent cedar logs, bricklayers, and carpenters to build a palace for David. [2]Then David knew that the LORD really had made him king of Israel and that he had made his kingdom great. The LORD did this because he loved his people Israel.

[3]David married more women in Jerusalem and had more sons and daughters. [4]These are the names of David's children born in Jerusalem: Shammua, Shobab, Nathan, Solomon, [5]Ibhar, Elishua, Elpelet, [6]Nogah, Nepheg, Japhia, [7]Elishama, Beeliada, and Eliphelet.

David Defeats the Philistines

[8]When the Philistines heard that David had been made king of all Israel, they went to look for him. But David heard about it and went out to fight them. [9]The Philistines had attacked and robbed the people in the Valley of Rephaim. [10]David asked God, "Should I go and attack the Philistines? Will you hand them over to me?"

The LORD answered him, "Go, I will hand them over to you."

[11]So David and his men went up to the town of Baal Perazim and defeated the Philistines. David said, "Like a flood of water, God has broken through my enemies by using me." So that place was named Baal Perazim.[n] [12]The Philistines had left their idols there, so David ordered his men to burn them.

[13]Soon the Philistines attacked the people in the valley again. [14]David prayed to God again, and God answered him, saying, "Don't attack the Philistines from the front. Instead, go around them and attack them in front of the balsam trees. [15]When you hear the sound of marching in the tops of the balsam trees, then attack. I, God, will have gone out before you to defeat the Philistine army." [16]David did as God commanded, and he and his men defeated the Philistine army all the way from Gibeon to Gezer.

[17]So David became famous in all the countries, and the LORD made all nations afraid of him.

The Ark Is Brought to Jerusalem

15 David built houses for himself in Jerusalem. Then he prepared a place for the Ark[d] of God, and he set up a tent for it. [2]David said, "Only the Levites may carry the Ark of God.

The LORD chose them to carry the Ark of the LORD and to serve him forever."

[3]David called all the people of Israel to come to Jerusalem. He wanted to bring the Ark of the LORD to the place he had made for it. [4]David called together the descendants[d] of Aaron and the Levites. [5]There were one hundred twenty people from Kohath's family group, with Uriel as their leader. [6]There were two hundred twenty people from Merari's family group, with Asaiah as their leader. [7]There were one hundred thirty people from Gershon's family group, with Joel as their leader. [8]There were two hundred people from Elizaphan's family group, with Shemaiah as their leader. [9]There were eighty people from Hebron's family group, with Eliel as their leader. [10]And there were one hundred twelve people from Uzziel's family group, with Amminadab as their leader.

[11]Then David asked the priests Zadok and Abiathar and these Levites to come to him: Uriel, Asaiah, Joel, Shemaiah, Eliel, and Amminadab. [12]David said to them, "You are the leaders of the families of Levi. You and the other Levites must give yourselves for service to the LORD. Bring up the Ark of the LORD, the God of Israel, to the place I have made for it. [13]The last time we did not ask the LORD how to carry it. You Levites didn't carry it, so the LORD our God punished us."

[14]Then the priests and Levites prepared themselves for service to the LORD so they could carry the Ark of the LORD, the God of Israel. [15]The Levites used special poles to carry the Ark of God on their shoulders, as Moses had commanded, just as the LORD had said they should.

[16]David told the leaders of the Levites to appoint their brothers as singers to play their lyres,[d] harps, and cymbals and to sing happy songs.

[17]So the Levites appointed Heman and his relatives Asaph and Ethan. Heman was Joel's son. Asaph was Berekiah's son. And Ethan, from the Merari family group, was Kushaiah's son. [18]There was also a second group of Levites: Zechariah, Jaaziel, Shemiramoth, Jehiel, Unni, Eliab, Benaiah, Maaseiah, Mattithiah, Eliphelehu, Mikneiah, Obed-Edom, and Jeiel. They were the Levite guards.

[19]The singers Heman, Asaph, and Ethan played bronze cymbals. [20]Zechariah, Jaaziel, Shemiramoth, Jehiel, Unni, Eliab, Maaseiah, and Benaiah played the lyres. [21]Mattithiah, Eliphelehu, Mikneiah, Obed-Edom, Jeiel, and Azaziah played the harps. [22]The Levite leader Kenaniah was in charge of the singing, because he was very good at it.

[23]Berekiah and Elkanah were two of the guards for the Ark of the Agreement. [24]The priests Shebaniah, Joshaphat, Nethanel, Amasai, Zechariah, Be-

---

Baal Perazim   This name means "the Lord breaks through."

naiah, and Eliezer had the job of blowing trumpets in front of the Ark of God. Obed-Edom and Jehiah were also guards for the Ark.

25David, the leaders of Israel, and the commanders of a thousand soldiers went to get the Ark of the Agreement with the Lord. They all went to bring the Ark from Obed-Edom's house with great joy. 26Because God helped the Levites who carried the Ark of the Agreement with the Lord, they sacrificed seven bulls and seven male sheep. 27All the Levites who carried the Ark, and Kenaniah, the man in charge of the singing, and all the singers wore robes of fine linen. David also wore a robe of fine linen and a holy vest*d* of fine linen. 28So all the people of Israel brought up the Ark of the Agreement with the Lord. They shouted, blew horns and trumpets, and played cymbals, lyres, and harps.

29As the Ark of the Agreement with the Lord entered Jerusalem, Saul's daughter Michal watched from a window. When she saw King David dancing and celebrating, she hated him.

16 They brought the Ark of God and put it inside the tent that David had set up for it. Then they offered burnt offerings and fellowship offerings to God. 2When David had finished giving the burnt offerings and fellowship offerings, he blessed the people in the name of the Lord. 3He gave a loaf of bread, some dates, and raisins to every Israelite man and woman.

4Then David appointed some of the Levites to serve before the Ark of the Lord. They had the job of leading the worship and giving thanks and praising the Lord, the God of Israel. 5Asaph, who played the cymbals, was the leader. Zechariah was second to him. The other Levites were Jaaziel, Shemiramoth, Jehiel, Mattithiah, Eliab, Benaiah, Obed-Edom, and Jeiel. They played the lyres and harps. 6Benaiah and Jahaziel were priests who blew the trumpets regularly before the Ark of the Agreement with God. 7That day David first gave Asaph and his relatives the job of singing praises to the Lord.

David's Song of Thanks

8Give thanks to the Lord and pray to him.
Tell the nations what he has done.
9Sing to him; sing praises to him.
Tell about all his miracles.*d*
10Be glad that you are his;
let those who seek the Lord be happy.
11Depend on the Lord and his strength;
always go to him for help.
12Remember the miracles he has done,
his wonders, and his decisions.
13You are the descendants*d* of his servant,
Israel;
you are the children of Jacob, his chosen
people.

14He is the Lord our God.
His laws are for all the world.
15He will keep his agreement forever;
he will keep his promises always.
16He will keep the agreement he made with
Abraham
and the promise he made to Isaac.
17He made it a law for the people of Jacob;
he made it an agreement with Israel to last
forever.
18He said, "I will give the land of Canaan to
you,
to belong to you."

19Then God's people were few in number,
and they were strangers in the land.
20They went from one nation to another,
from one kingdom to another.
21But he did not let anyone hurt them;
he warned kings not to harm them.
22He said, "Don't touch my chosen people,
and don't harm my prophets."*d*

23Sing to the Lord, all the earth.
Every day tell how he saves us.
24Tell the nations about his glory;
tell all peoples the miracles he does.
25The Lord is great; he should be praised.
He should be respected more than all the
gods.
26All the gods of the nations are only idols,
but the Lord made the skies.
27He has glory and majesty;
he has power and joy in his Temple.*d*

28Praise the Lord, all nations on earth.
Praise the Lord's glory and power;
29 praise the glory of the Lord's name.
Bring an offering and come to him.
Worship the Lord because he is holy.
30Tremble before him, everyone on earth.
The earth is set, and it cannot be moved.
31Let the skies rejoice and the earth be glad.
Let people everywhere say, "The Lord is
king!"
32Let the sea and everything in it shout;
let the fields and everything in them
rejoice.
33Then the trees of the forest will sing
for joy before the Lord.
They will sing because he is coming to
judge the world.

34Thank the Lord because he is good.
His love continues forever.
35Say to him, "Save us, God our Savior,
and bring us back and save us from other
nations.
Then we will thank you
and will gladly praise you."
36Praise the Lord, the God of Israel.

He always was and always will be.

All the people said "Amen" and praised the LORD.

³⁷Then David left Asaph and the other Levites there in front of the Ark^d of the Agreement with the LORD. They were to serve there every day. ³⁸David also left Obed-Edom and sixty-eight other Levites to serve with them. Hosah and Obed-Edom son of Jeduthun were guards.

³⁹David left Zadok the priest and the other priests who served with him in front of the Tent of the LORD at the place of worship in Gibeon. ⁴⁰Every morning and evening they offered burnt offerings on the altar of burnt offerings, following the rules written in the Teachings of the LORD, which he had given Israel. ⁴¹With them were Heman and Jeduthun and other Levites. They were chosen by name to sing praises to the LORD because his love continues forever. ⁴²Heman and Jeduthun also had the job of playing the trumpets and cymbals and other musical instruments when songs were sung to God. Jeduthun's sons guarded the gates.

⁴³Then all the people left. Each person went home, and David also went home to bless the people in his home.

God's Promise to David

17 When David moved into his palace, he said to Nathan the prophet, "Look, I am living in a palace made of cedar, but the Ark^d of the Agreement with the LORD sits in a tent."

²Nathan said to David, "Do what you want to do, because God is with you."

³But that night God spoke his word to Nathan, saying, ⁴"Go and tell David my servant, 'This is what the LORD says: You are not the person to build a house for me to live in. ⁵From the time I brought Israel out of Egypt until now I have not lived in a house. I have moved from one tent site to another and from one place to another. ⁶As I have moved with the Israelites to different places, I have never said to the leaders, whom I commanded to take care of my people, "Why haven't you built me a house of cedar?" '

⁷"Now, tell my servant David: 'This is what the LORD All-Powerful says: I took you from the pasture and from tending the sheep and made you king of my people Israel. ⁸I have been with you everywhere you have gone. I have defeated your enemies for you. I will make you as famous as any of the great people on the earth. ⁹I will choose a place for my people Israel, and I will plant them so they can live in their own homes. They will not be bothered anymore. Wicked people will no longer hurt them as they have in the past ¹⁰when I chose judges for my people Israel. I will defeat all your enemies.

" 'I tell you that the LORD will make your descendants^d kings of Israel after you. ¹¹When you die and join your ancestors, I will make one of your sons the new king, and I will set up his kingdom. ¹²He will build a house for me, and I will let his kingdom rule always. ¹³I will be his father, and he will be my son. I took away my love from Saul, who ruled before you, but I will never stop loving your son. ¹⁴I will put him in charge of my house and kingdom forever. His family will rule forever.' "

¹⁵Nathan told David everything God had said in this vision.

David Prays to God

¹⁶Then King David went in and sat in front of the LORD. David said, "LORD God, who am I? What is my family? Why did you bring me to this point? ¹⁷But that was not enough for you, God. You have also made promises about my future family. LORD God, you have treated me like a very important person.

¹⁸"What more can I say to you for honoring me, your servant? You know me so well. ¹⁹LORD, you have done this wonderful thing for my sake and because you wanted to. You have made known all these great things.

²⁰"There is no one like you, LORD. There is no God except you. We have heard all this ourselves! ²¹There is no nation like your people Israel. They are the only people on earth that God chose to be his own. You made your name well known by the great and wonderful things you did for them. You went ahead of them and forced other nations out of the land. You freed your people from slavery in Egypt. ²²You made the people of Israel your very own people forever, and, LORD, you are their God.

²³"LORD, keep the promise forever that you made about my family and me, your servant. Do what you have said. ²⁴Then you will be honored always, and people will say, 'The LORD All-Powerful, the God over Israel, is Israel's God!' And the family of your servant David will continue before you.

²⁵"My God, you have told me that you would make my family great. So I, your servant, am brave enough to pray to you. ²⁶LORD, you are God, and you have promised these good things to me, your servant. ²⁷You have chosen to bless my family. Let it continue before you always. LORD, you have blessed my family, so it will always be blessed."

David Defeats Nations

18 Later, David defeated the Philistines, conquered them, and took the city of Gath and the small towns around it.

²He also defeated the people of Moab. So the

people of Moab became servants of David and gave him the payment he demanded.

³David also defeated Hadadezer king of Zobah all the way to the town of Hamath as he tried to spread his kingdom to the Euphrates River. ⁴David captured one thousand of his chariots, seven thousand men who rode in chariots, and twenty thousand foot soldiers. He crippled all but a hundred of the chariot horses.

⁵Arameans from Damascus came to help Hadadezer king of Zobah, but David killed twenty-two thousand of them. ⁶Then David put groups of soldiers in Damascus in Aram. The Arameans became David's servants and gave him the payments he demanded. So the LORD gave David victory everywhere he went.

⁷David took the shields of gold that had belonged to Hadadezer's officers and brought them to Jerusalem. ⁸David also took many things made of bronze from Tebah and Cun, which had been cities under Hadadezer's control. Later, Solomon used this bronze to make things for the Temple:*d* the large bronze bowl, which was called the Sea, the pillars, and other bronze utensils.

⁹Toi king of Hamath heard that David had defeated all the army of Hadadezer king of Zobah. ¹⁰So Toi sent his son Hadoram to greet and congratulate King David for defeating Hadadezer. (Hadadezer had been at war with Toi.) Hadoram brought items made of gold, silver, and bronze. ¹¹King David gave them to the LORD, along with the silver and gold he had taken from these nations: Edom, Moab, the Ammonites, the Philistines, and Amalek.

¹²Abishai son of Zeruiah killed eighteen thousand Edomites in the Valley of Salt. ¹³David put groups of soldiers in Edom, and all the Edomites became his servants. The LORD gave David victory everywhere he went.

David's Important Officers

¹⁴David was king over all of Israel, and he did what was fair and right for all his people. ¹⁵Joab son of Zeruiah was commander over the army. Jehoshaphat son of Ahilud was the recorder. ¹⁶Zadok son of Ahitub and Abiathar son of Ahimelech were priests. Shavsha was the royal secretary. ¹⁷Benaiah son of Jehoiada was over the Kerethites and Pelethites.ⁿ And David's sons were important officers who served at his side.

War with the Ammonites and Arameans

19 When Nahash king of the Ammonites died, his son became king after him. ²David said, "Nahash was loyal to me, so I will be loyal to his son Hanun." So David sent messengers to comfort Hanun about his father's death.

David's officers went to the land of the Ammonites to comfort Hanun. ³But the Ammonite leaders said to Hanun, "Do you think David wants to honor your father by sending men to comfort you? No! David sent them to study the land and capture it and spy it out." ⁴So Hanun arrested David's officers. To shame them he shaved their beards and cut off their clothes at the hips. Then he sent them away.

⁵When the people told David what had happened to his officers, he sent messengers to meet them, because they were very ashamed. King David said, "Stay in Jericho until your beards have grown back. Then come home."

⁶The Ammonites knew that they had insulted David. So Hanun and the Ammonites sent about seventy-four thousand pounds of silver to hire chariots and chariot drivers from Northwest Mesopotamia, Aram Maacah, and Zobah. ⁷The Ammonites hired thirty-two thousand chariots and the king of Maacah and his army. So they came and set up camp near the town of Medeba. The Ammonites themselves came out of their towns and got ready for battle.

⁸When David heard about this, he sent Joab with the whole army. ⁹The Ammonites came out and prepared for battle at the city gate. The kings who had come to help were out in the field by themselves.

¹⁰Joab saw that there were enemies both in front of him and behind him. So he chose some of the best soldiers of Israel and sent them out to fight the Arameans. ¹¹Joab put the rest of the army under the command of Abishai, his brother. Then they went out to fight the Ammonites. ¹²Joab said to Abishai, "If the Arameans are too strong for me, you must help me. Or, if the Ammonites are too strong for you, I will help you. ¹³Be strong. We must fight bravely for our people and the cities of our God. The LORD will do what he thinks is right."

¹⁴Then Joab and the army with him went to attack the Arameans, and the Arameans ran away. ¹⁵When the Ammonites saw that the Arameans were running away, they also ran away from Joab's brother Abishai and went back to their city. So Joab went back to Jerusalem.

¹⁶When the Arameans saw that Israel had defeated them, they sent messengers to bring other Arameans from east of the Euphrates River. Their leader was Shophach, the commander of Hadadezer's army.

¹⁷When David heard about this, he gathered all the Israelites, and they crossed over the Jordan River. He prepared them for battle, facing the Ara-

---

Kerethites and Pelethites These were probably special units of the army that were responsible for the king's safety, a kind of palace guard.

means. The Arameans fought with him, [18]but they ran away from the Israelites. David killed seven thousand Aramean chariot drivers and forty thousand Aramean foot soldiers. He also killed Shophach, the commander of the Aramean army.

[19]When those who served Hadadezer saw that the Israelites had defeated them, they made peace with David and served him. So the Arameans refused to help the Ammonites again.

SIDELIGHT: Ecclesiastes 3:1 (p. 600) says, "There is a time for everything." Apparently the right time for war in the Old Testament was springtime (1 Chronicles 20:1). Kings would go to war right after the spring harvest when there wasn't much to do on the farm and when the soldiers could live off the land.

Joab Destroys the Ammonites

20 In the spring, the time of year when kings normally went out to battle, Joab led out the army of Israel. But David stayed in Jerusalem. The army of Israel destroyed the land of Ammon and went to the city of Rabbah and attacked it. [2]David took the crown off the head of their king,[n] and had it placed on his own head. That gold crown weighed about seventy-five pounds, and it had valuable gems in it. And David took many valuable things from the city. [3]He also brought out the people of the city and forced them to work with saws, iron picks, and axes. David did this to all the Ammonite cities. Then David and all his army returned to Jerusalem.

Philistine Giants Are Killed

[4]Later, at Gezer, war broke out with the Philistines. Sibbecai the Hushathite killed Sippai, who was one of the descendants[d] of the Rephaites.[d] So those Philistines were defeated.

[5]Later, there was another battle with the Philistines. Elhanan son of Jair killed Lahmi, the brother of Goliath, who was from the town of Gath. His spear was as large as a weaver's rod.

[6]At Gath another battle took place. A huge man was there; he had six fingers on each hand and six toes on each foot — twenty-four fingers and toes in all. This man also was one of the sons of Rapha.[d] [7]When he spoke against Israel, Jonathan son of Shimea, David's brother, killed him.

[8]These descendants of Rapha from Gath were killed by David and his men.

David Counts the Israelites

21 Satan was against Israel, and he caused David to count the people of Israel. [2]So David said to Joab and the commanders of the troops, "Go and count all the Israelites from Beersheba to Dan.[n] Then tell me so I will know how many there are."

[3]But Joab said, "May the LORD give the nation a hundred times more people. My master the king, all the Israelites are your servants. Why do you want to do this, my master? You will make Israel guilty of sin."

[4]But the king commanded Joab, so Joab left and went through all Israel. Then he returned to Jerusalem. [5]Joab gave the list of the people to David. There were one million one hundred thousand men in all of Israel who could use the sword, and there were four hundred seventy thousand men in Judah who could use the sword. [6]But Joab did not count the tribes[d] of Levi and Benjamin, because he didn't like King David's order. [7]David had done something God had said was wrong, so God punished Israel.

[8]Then David said to God, "I have sinned greatly by what I have done! Now, I beg you to forgive me, your servant, because I have been very foolish."

[9]The LORD said to Gad, who was David's seer,[d] [10]"Go and tell David, 'This is what the LORD says: I offer you three choices. Choose one of them and I will do it.' "

[11]So Gad went to David and said to him, "This is what the LORD says: 'Choose for yourself [12]three years of hunger. Or choose three months of running from your enemies as they chase you with their swords. Or choose three days of punishment from the LORD, in which a terrible disease will spread through the country. The angel of the LORD will go through Israel destroying the people.' Now, David, decide which of these things I should tell the LORD who sent me."

[13]David said to Gad, "I am in great trouble. Let the LORD punish me, because the LORD is very merciful. Don't let my punishment come from human beings."

[14]So the LORD sent a terrible disease on Israel, and seventy thousand people died. [15]God sent an angel to destroy Jerusalem, but when the angel started to destroy it, the LORD saw it and felt very sorry about the terrible things that had happened. So he said to the angel who was destroying, "That is enough! Put down your arm!" The angel of the LORD was then standing at the threshing[d] floor of Araunah the Jebusite.

[16]David looked up and saw the angel of the

---

their king Or, "Milcom," the god of the Ammonite people.
Beersheba to Dan Beersheba was the city farthest south in Israel. Dan was the city farthest north. So this means all the people of Israel.

LORD in the sky, holding his sword drawn and pointed at Jerusalem. Then David and the older leaders bowed facedown on the ground. They were wearing rough cloth to show their grief. [17]David said to God, "I am the one who sinned and did wrong. I gave the order for the people to be counted. These people only followed me like sheep. They did nothing wrong. LORD my God, please punish me and my family, but stop the terrible disease that is killing your people."

[18]Then the angel of the LORD told Gad to tell David that he should build an altar to the LORD on the threshing floor of Araunah the Jebusite. [19]So David did what Gad told him to do, in the name of the LORD.

[20]Araunah was separating the wheat from the straw. When he turned around, he saw the angel. Araunah's four sons who were with him hid. [21]David came to Araunah, and when Araunah saw him, he left the threshing floor and bowed facedown on the ground before David.

[22]David said to him, "Sell me your threshing floor so I can build an altar to the LORD here. Then the terrible disease will stop. Sell it to me for the full price."

[23]Araunah said to David, "Take this threshing floor. My master the king, do anything you want. Look, I will also give you oxen for the whole burnt offerings, the threshing boards for the wood, and wheat for the grain offering. I give everything to you."

[24]But King David answered Araunah, "No, I will pay the full price for the land. I won't take anything that is yours and give it to the LORD. I won't offer a burnt offering that costs me nothing."

[25]So David paid Araunah about fifteen pounds of gold for the place. [26]David built an altar to the LORD there and offered whole burnt offerings and fellowship offerings. David prayed to the LORD, and he answered him by sending down fire from heaven on the altar of burnt offering. [27]Then the LORD commanded the angel to put his sword back into its holder.

[28]When David saw that the LORD had answered him on the threshing floor of Araunah, he offered sacrifices there. [29]The Holy Tent[d] that Moses made while the Israelites were in the desert and the altar of burnt offerings were in Gibeon at the place of worship. [30]But David could not go to the Holy Tent to speak with God, because he was *afraid of the angel of the LORD and his sword.*

22 David said, "The Temple[d] of the LORD God and the altar for Israel's burnt offerings will be built here."

David Makes Plans for the Temple

[2]So David ordered all foreigners living in Israel to gather together. From that group David chose stonecutters to cut stones to be used in building the Temple[d] of God. [3]David supplied a large amount of iron to be used for making nails and hinges for the gate doors. He also supplied more bronze than could be weighed, [4]and he supplied more cedar logs than could be counted. Much of the cedar had been brought to David by the people from Sidon and Tyre.

[5]David said, "We should build a great Temple for the LORD, which will be famous everywhere for its greatness and beauty. But my son Solomon is young. He hasn't yet learned what he needs to know, so I will prepare for the building of it." So David got many of the materials ready before he died.

[6]Then David called for his son Solomon and told him to build the Temple for the LORD, the God of Israel. [7]David said to him, "My son, I wanted to build a temple for worshiping the LORD my God. [8]But the LORD spoke his word to me, 'David, you have killed many people. You have fought many wars. You cannot build a temple for worship to me, because you have killed many people. [9]But, you will have a son, a man of peace and rest. I will give him rest from all his enemies around him. His name will be Solomon,[n] and I will give Israel peace and quiet while he is king. [10]Solomon will build a temple for worship to me. He will be my son, and I will be his father. I will make his kingdom strong; someone from his family will rule Israel forever.' "

[11]David said, "Now, my son, may the LORD be with you. May you build a temple for the LORD your God, as he said you would. [12]He will make you the king of Israel. May the LORD give you wisdom and understanding so you will be able to obey the teachings of the LORD your God. [13]Be careful to obey the rules and laws the LORD gave Moses for Israel. If you obey them, you will have success. Be strong and brave. Don't be afraid or discouraged.

[14]"Solomon, I have worked hard getting many of the materials for building the Temple of the LORD. I have supplied about seven and one-half million pounds of gold, about seventy-five million pounds of silver, so much bronze and iron it cannot be weighed, and wood and stone. You may add to them. [15]You have many workmen—stonecutters, bricklayers, carpenters, and people skilled *in every kind of work.* [16]They are skilled in working with gold, silver, bronze, and iron. You have more craftsmen than can be counted. Now begin the work, and may the LORD be with you."

Solomon This name sounds like the Hebrew word for "peace."

¹⁷Then David ordered all the leaders of Israel to help his son Solomon. ¹⁸David said to them, "The LORD your God is with you. He has given you rest from our enemies. He has handed over to me the people living around us. The LORD and his people are in control of this land. ¹⁹Now give yourselves completely to obeying the LORD your God. Build the holy place of the LORD God; build the Temple for worship to the LORD. Then bring the Ark^d of the Agreement with the LORD and the holy items that belong to God into the Temple."

The Levites

23

After David had lived long and was old, he made his son Solomon the new king of Israel. ²David gathered all the leaders of Israel, along with the priests and Levites. ³He counted the Levites who were thirty years old and older. In all, there were thirty-eight thousand Levites. ⁴David said, "Of these, twenty-four thousand Levites will direct the work of the Temple^d of the LORD, six thousand Levites will be officers and judges, ⁵four thousand Levites will be gatekeepers, and four thousand Levites will praise the LORD with musical instruments I made for giving praise."

⁶David separated the Levites into three groups that were led by Levi's three sons: Gershon, Kohath, and Merari.

The People of Gershon

⁷From the people of Gershon, there were Ladan and Shimei.

⁸Ladan had three sons. His first son was Jehiel, and his other sons were Zetham and Joel.

⁹Shimei's sons were Shelomoth, Haziel, and Haran. These three sons were leaders of Ladan's families. ¹⁰Shimei had four sons: Jahath, Ziza, Jeush, and Beriah. ¹¹Jahath was the first son, and Ziza was the second son. But Jeush and Beriah did not have many children, so they were counted as if they were one family.

The People of Kohath

¹²Kohath had four sons: Amram, Izhar, Hebron, and Uzziel.

¹³Amram's sons were Aaron and Moses. Aaron and his descendants^d were chosen to be special forever. They were chosen to prepare the holy things for the LORD's service, to offer sacrifices before the LORD, and to serve him as priests. They were to give blessings in his name forever.

¹⁴Moses was the man of God, and his sons were counted as part of the tribe^d of Levi. ¹⁵Moses' sons were Gershom and Eliezer. ¹⁶Gershom's first son was Shubael. ¹⁷Eliezer's first son was Rehabiah. Eliezer had no other sons, but Rehabiah had many sons.

¹⁸Izhar's first son was Shelomith.

¹⁹Hebron's first son was Jeriah, his second was Amariah, his third was Jahaziel, and his fourth was Jekameam.

²⁰Uzziel's first son was Micah and his second was Isshiah.

The People of Merari

²¹Merari's sons were Mahli and Mushi. Mahli's sons were Eleazar and Kish. ²²Eleazar died without sons; he had only daughters. Eleazar's daughters married their cousins, the sons of Kish. ²³Mushi's three sons were Mahli, Eder, and Jerimoth.

The Levites' Work

²⁴These were Levi's descendants^d listed by their families. They were the leaders of families. Each person who was twenty years old or older was listed. They served in the LORD's Temple.^d

²⁵David had said, "The LORD, the God of Israel, has given rest to his people. He has come to live in Jerusalem forever. ²⁶So the Levites don't have to carry the Holy Tent^d or any of the things used in its services anymore." ²⁷David's last instructions were to count the Levites who were twenty years old and older.

²⁸The Levites had the job of helping Aaron's descendants in the service of the Temple of the LORD. They cared for the Temple courtyard and side rooms, and they made all the holy things pure. Their job was to serve in the Temple of God. ²⁹They were responsible for putting the holy bread on the table, for the flour in the grain offerings, for the bread made without yeast, for the baking and mixing, and for the measuring. ³⁰The Levites also stood every morning and gave thanks and praise to the LORD. They also did this every evening. ³¹The Levites offered all the burnt offerings to the LORD on the special days of rest, at the New Moon^d festivals, and at all appointed feasts. They served before the LORD every day. They were to follow the rules for how many Levites should serve each time. ³²So the Levites took care of the Meeting Tent and the Holy Place. And they helped their relatives, Aaron's descendants, with the services at the Temple of the LORD.

The Groups of the Priests

24

These were the groups of Aaron's sons: Aaron's sons were Nadab, Abihu, Eleazar, and Ithamar. ²But Nadab and Abihu died before their father did, and they had no sons. So Eleazar and Ithamar served as the priests. ³David, with the help of Zadok, a descendant^d of Eleazar, and Ahimelech, a descendant of Ithamar, separated their family groups into two different groups. Each group had certain duties. ⁴There were more leaders from Eleazar's family than from Ithamar's—sixteen leaders from Eleazar's family and eight leaders from Ithamar's family.

⁵Men were chosen from Eleazar's and Ithamar's families by throwing lots.ᵈ Some men from each family were chosen to be in charge of the Holy Place, and some were chosen to serve as priests.

⁶Shemaiah son of Nethanel, from the tribeᵈ of Levi, was the secretary. He recorded the names of those descendants in front of King David, the officers, Zadok the priest, Ahimelech son of Abiathar, and the leaders of the families of the priests and Levites. The work was divided by lots among the families of Eleazar and Ithamar. The following men with their groups were chosen.

⁷The first one chosen was Jehoiarib. The second was Jedaiah. ⁸The third was Harim. The fourth was Seorim. ⁹The fifth was Malkijah. The sixth was Mijamin. ¹⁰The seventh was Hakkoz. The eighth was Abijah. ¹¹The ninth was Jeshua. The tenth was Shecaniah. ¹²The eleventh was Eliashib. The twelfth was Jakim. ¹³The thirteenth was Huppah. The fourteenth was Jeshebeab. ¹⁴The fifteenth was Bilgah. The sixteenth was Immer. ¹⁵The seventeenth was Hezir. The eighteenth was Happizzez. ¹⁶The nineteenth was Pethahiah. The twentieth was Jehezkel. ¹⁷The twenty-first was Jakin. The twenty-second was Gamul. ¹⁸The twenty-third was Delaiah. The twenty-fourth was Maaziah.

¹⁹These were the groups chosen to serve in the Temple of the LORD. They obeyed the rules given them by Aaron, just as the LORD, the God of Israel, had commanded him.

The Other Levites

²⁰These are the names of the rest of Levi's descendants:ᵈ

Shubael was a descendant of Amram, and Jehdeiah was a descendant of Shubael.

²¹Isshiah was the first son of Rehabiah.

²²From the Izhar family group, there was Shelomoth, and Jahath was a descendant of Shelomoth.

²³Hebron's first son was Jeriah, Amariah was his second, Jahaziel was his third, and Jekameam was his fourth.

²⁴Uzziel's son was Micah. Micah's son was Shamir. ²⁵Micah's brother was Isshiah, and Isshiah's son was Zechariah.

²⁶Merari's descendants were Mahli and Mushi. Merari's son was Jaaziah. ²⁷Jaaziah son of Merari had sons named Shoham, Zaccur, and Ibri. ²⁸Mahli's son was Eleazar, but Eleazar did not have any sons.

²⁹Kish's son was Jerahmeel.

³⁰Mushi's sons were Mahli, Eder, and Jerimoth.

These are the Levites, listed by their families. ³¹They were chosen for special jobs by throwing lotsᵈ in front of King David, Zadok, Ahimelech, the leaders of the families of the priests, and the Levites. They did this just as their relatives, the priests, Aaron's descendants, had done. The families of the oldest brother and the youngest brother were treated the same.

> ☀ **SIDELIGHT:** It might seem strange if your pastor started singing during a sermon. But 1 Chronicles 25:1 describes people who were chosen to preach—and play harps, lyres, and cymbals. The cymbals must have helped if the sermon got boring.

The Music Groups

25 David and the commanders of the army chose some of the sons of Asaph, Heman, and Jeduthun to preach and play harps, lyres,ᵈ and cymbals. Here is a list of the men who served in this way:

²Asaph's sons who served were Zaccur, Joseph, Nethaniah, and Asarelah. King David chose Asaph to preach, and Asaph directed his sons.

³Jeduthun's sons who served were Gedaliah, Zeri, Jeshaiah, Shimei, Hashabiah, and Mattithiah. There were six of them, and Jeduthun directed them. He preached and used a harp to give thanks and praise to the LORD.

⁴Heman's sons who served were Bukkiah, Mattaniah, Uzziel, Shubael, Jerimoth, Hananiah, Hanani, Eliathah, Giddalti, Romamti-Ezer, Joshbekashah, Mallothi, Hothir, and Mahazioth. ⁵All these were sons of Heman, David's seer.ᵈ God promised to make Heman strong, so Heman had many sons. God gave him fourteen sons and three daughters. ⁶Heman directed all his sons in making music for the Templeᵈ of the LORD with cymbals, lyres, and harps; that was their way of serving in the Temple of God. King David was in charge of Asaph, Jeduthun, and Heman. ⁷These men and their relatives were trained and skilled in making music for the LORD. There were two hundred eighty-eight of them. ⁸Everyone threw lotsᵈ to choose the time his family was to serve at the Temple. The young and the old, the teacher and the student, had to throw lots.

⁹First, the lot fell to Joseph, from the family of Asaph.

Second, twelve men were chosen from Gedaliah, his sons and relatives.

¹⁰Third, twelve men were chosen from Zaccur, his sons and relatives.

¹¹Fourth, twelve men were chosen from Izri, his sons and relatives.

¹²Fifth, twelve men were chosen from Nethaniah, his sons and relatives.

¹³Sixth, twelve men were chosen from Bukkiah, his sons and relatives.

¹⁴Seventh, twelve men were chosen from Jesarelah, his sons and relatives.

¹⁵Eighth, twelve men were chosen from Jeshaiah, his sons and relatives.

¹⁶Ninth, twelve men were chosen from Mattaniah, his sons and relatives.

¹⁷Tenth, twelve men were chosen from Shimei, his sons and relatives.

¹⁸Eleventh, twelve men were chosen from Azarel, his sons and relatives.

¹⁹Twelfth, twelve men were chosen from Hashabiah, his sons and relatives.

²⁰Thirteenth, twelve men were chosen from Shubael, his sons and relatives.

²¹Fourteenth, twelve men were chosen from Mattithiah, his sons and relatives.

²²Fifteenth, twelve men were chosen from Jerimoth, his sons and relatives.

²³Sixteenth, twelve men were chosen from Hananiah, his sons and relatives.

²⁴Seventeenth, twelve men were chosen from Joshbekashah, his sons and relatives.

²⁵Eighteenth, twelve men were chosen from Hanani, his sons and relatives.

²⁶Nineteenth, twelve men were chosen from Mallothi, his sons and relatives.

²⁷Twentieth, twelve men were chosen from Eliathah, his sons and relatives.

²⁸Twenty-first, twelve men were chosen from Hothir, his sons and relatives.

²⁹Twenty-second, twelve men were chosen from Giddalti, his sons and relatives.

³⁰Twenty-third, twelve men were chosen from Mahazioth, his sons and relatives.

³¹Twenty-fourth, twelve men were chosen from Romamti-Ezer, his sons and relatives.

The Gatekeepers

26 These are the groups of the gatekeepers. From the family of Korah, there was Meshelemiah son of Kore, who was from Asaph's family. ²Meshelemiah had sons. Zechariah was his first son, Jediael was second, Zebadiah was third, Jathniel was fourth, ³Elam was fifth, Jehohanan was sixth, and Eliehoenai was seventh.

⁴Obed-Edom had sons. Shemaiah was his first son, Jehozabad was second, Joah was third, Sacar was fourth, Nethanel was fifth, ⁵Ammiel was sixth, Issachar was seventh, and Peullethai was eighth. God blessed Obed-Edom with children.

⁶Obed-Edom's son Shemaiah also had sons. They were leaders in their father's family because they were capable men. ⁷Shemaiah's sons were Othni, Rephael, Obed, Elzabad, Elihu, and Semakiah. Elihu, and Semakiah were skilled workers. ⁸All these were Obed-Edom's descendants.ᵈ They and their sons and relatives were capable men and strong workers. Obed-Edom had sixty-two descendants in all.

⁹Meshelemiah had sons and relatives who were skilled workers. In all, there were eighteen.

¹⁰From the Merari family, Hosah had sons. Shimri was chosen to be in charge. Although he was not the oldest son, his father chose him to be in charge. ¹¹Hilkiah was his second son, Tabaliah was third, and Zechariah was fourth. In all, Hosah had thirteen sons and relatives.

¹²These were the leaders of the groups of gatekeepers, and they served in the Templeᵈ of the Lord. Their relatives also worked in the Temple. ¹³By throwing lots,ᵈ each family chose a gate to guard. Young and old threw lots.

¹⁴Meshelemiah was chosen by lot to guard the East Gate. Then lots were thrown for Meshelemiah's son Zechariah. He was a wise counselor and was chosen for the North Gate. ¹⁵Obed-Edom was chosen for the South Gate, and Obed-Edom's sons were chosen to guard the storehouse. ¹⁶Shuppim and Hosah were chosen for the West Gate and the Shalleketh Gate on the upper road.

Guards stood side by side with guards. ¹⁷Six Levites stood guard every day at the East Gate; four Levites stood guard every day at the North Gate; four Levites stood guard every day at the South Gate; and two Levites at a time guarded the storehouse. ¹⁸There were two guards at the western court and four guards on the road to the court.

¹⁹These were the groups of the gatekeepers from the families of Korah and Merari.

Other Leaders

²⁰Other Levites were responsible for guarding the treasuries of the Templeᵈ of God and for the places where the holy items were kept.

²¹Ladan was Gershon's son and the ancestor of several family groups. Jehiel was a leader of one of the family groups. ²²His sons were Zetham and Joel his brother, and they were responsible for the treasuries of the Temple of the Lord.

²³Other leaders were chosen from the family groups of Amram, Izhar, Hebron, and Uzziel. ²⁴Shubael, the descendantᵈ of Gershom, who was Moses' son, was the leader responsible for the treasuries. ²⁵These were Shubael's relatives from Eliezer: Eliezer's son Rehabiah, Rehabiah's son Jeshaiah, Jeshaiah's son Joram, Joram's son Zicri, and Zicri's son Shelomith. ²⁶Shelomith and his relatives were responsible for everything that had been collected for the Temple by King David, by the heads of families, by the commanders of a thousand men and of a hundred men, and by other army commanders. ²⁷They also gave some of the things they had taken in wars to be used in repairing the Temple of the Lord. ²⁸Shelomith and his relatives took care of all the holy items. Some had been given by Samuel the seer,ᵈ Saul

son of Kish, Abner son of Ner, and Joab son of Zeruiah.

²⁹Kenaniah was from the Izhar family. He and his sons worked outside the Temple as officers and judges in different places in Israel.

³⁰Hashabiah was from the Hebron family. He and his relatives were responsible for the Lord's work and the king's business in Israel west of the Jordan River. There were seventeen hundred skilled men in Hashabiah's group. ³¹The history of the Hebron family shows that Jeriah was their leader. In David's fortieth year as king, the records were searched, and some capable men of the Hebron family were found living at Jazer in Gilead. ³²Jeriah had twenty-seven hundred relatives who were skilled men and leaders of families. King David gave them the responsibility of directing the tribes*d* of Reuben, Gad, and East Manasseh in God's work and the king's business.

Army Divisions

27 This is the list of the Israelites who served the king in the army. Each division was on duty one month each year. There were leaders of families, commanders of a hundred men, commanders of a thousand men, and other officers. Each division had twenty-four thousand men.

²Jashobeam son of Zabdiel was in charge of the first division for the first month. There were twenty-four thousand men in his division. ³Jashobeam, one of the descendants*d* of Perez, was leader of all the army officers for the first month.

⁴Dodai, from the Ahohites, was in charge of the division for the second month. Mikloth was a leader in the division. There were twenty-four thousand men in Dodai's division.

⁵The third commander, for the third month, was Benaiah son of Jehoiada the priest. There were twenty-four thousand men in his division. ⁶He was the Benaiah who was one of the Thirty*n* soldiers. Benaiah was a brave warrior who led those men. Benaiah's son Ammizabad was in charge of Benaiah's division.

⁷The fourth commander, for the fourth month, was Asahel, the brother of Joab. Later, Asahel's son Zebadiah took his place as commander. There were twenty-four thousand men in his division.

⁸The fifth commander, for the fifth month, was Shamhuth, from Izrah's family. There were twenty-four thousand men in his division.

⁹The sixth commander, for the sixth month, was Ira son of Ikkesh from the town of Tekoa. There were twenty-four thousand men in his division.

¹⁰The seventh commander, for the seventh month, was Helez. He was from the Pelonites and a descendant of Ephraim. There were twenty-four thousand men in his division.

¹¹The eighth commander, for the eighth month, was Sibbecai. He was from Hushah and was from Zerah's family. There were twenty-four thousand men in his division.

¹²The ninth commander, for the ninth month, was Abiezer. He was from Anathoth in Benjamin. There were twenty-four thousand men in his division.

¹³The tenth commander, for the tenth month, was Maharai. He was from Netophah and was from Zerah's family. There were twenty-four thousand men in his division.

¹⁴The eleventh commander, for the eleventh month, was Benaiah. He was from Pirathon in Ephraim. There were twenty-four thousand men in his division.

¹⁵The twelfth commander, for the twelfth month, was Heldai. He was from Netophah and was from Othniel's family. There were twenty-four thousand men in his division.

Leaders of the Tribes

¹⁶These were the leaders of the tribes*d* of Israel. Eliezer son of Zicri was over the tribe of Reuben. Shephatiah son of Maacah was over the tribe of Simeon. ¹⁷Hashabiah son of Kemuel was over the tribe of Levi. Zadok was over the people of Aaron. ¹⁸Elihu, one of David's brothers, was over the tribe of Judah. Omri son of Michael was over the tribe of Issachar. ¹⁹Ishmaiah son of Obadiah was over the tribe of Zebulun. Jerimoth son of Azriel was over the tribe of Naphtali. ²⁰Hoshea son of Azaziah was over the tribe of Ephraim. Joel son of Pedaiah was over West Manasseh. ²¹Iddo son of Zechariah was over East Manasseh. Jaasiel son of Abner was over the tribe of Benjamin. ²²Azarel son of Jeroham was over the tribe of Dan.

These were the leaders of the tribes of Israel.

²³The Lord had promised to make the Israelites as many as the stars in the sky. So David only counted the men who were twenty years old and older. ²⁴Joab son of Zeruiah began to count the people, but he did not finish. God became angry with Israel for counting the people, so the number of the people was not put in the history book about King David's rule.

The King's Directors

²⁵Azmaveth son of Adiel was in charge of the royal storehouses.

Jonathan son of Uzziah was in charge of the storehouses in the country, towns, villages, and towers.

²⁶Ezri son of Kelub was in charge of the field workers who farmed the land.

Thirty These were David's most powerful soldiers. See 2 Samuel 23:28.

²⁷Shimei, from the town of Ramah, was in charge of the vineyards.

Zabdi, from Shapham, was in charge of storing the wine that came from the vineyards.

²⁸Baal-Hanan, from Geder, was in charge of the olive trees and sycamore trees in the western hills.

Joash was in charge of storing the olive oil.

²⁹Shitrai, from Sharon, was in charge of the herds that fed in the Plain of Sharon.

Shaphat son of Adlai was in charge of the herds in the valleys.

³⁰Obil, an Ishmaelite, was in charge of the camels.

Jehdeiah, from Meronoth, was in charge of the donkeys.

³¹Jaziz, from the Hagrites, was in charge of the flocks.

All these men were the officers who took care of King David's property.

³²Jonathan was David's uncle, and he advised David. Jonathan was a wise man and a teacher of the law. Jehiel son of Hacmoni took care of the king's sons. ³³Ahithophel advised the king. Hushai, from the Arkite people, was the king's friend. ³⁴Jehoiada and Abiathar later took Ahithophel's place in advising the king. Jehoiada was Benaiah's son. Joab was the commander of the king's army.

David's Plans for the Temple

28 David commanded all the leaders of Israel to come to Jerusalem. There were the leaders of the tribes,ᵈ commanders of the divisions serving the king, commanders of a thousand men and of a hundred men, leaders who took care of the property and animals that belonged to the king and his sons, men over the palace, the powerful men, and all the brave warriors.

²King David stood up and said, "Listen to me, my relatives and my people. I wanted to build a place to keep the Arkᵈ of the Agreement with the LORD. I wanted it to be God's footstool. So I made plans to build a temple. ³But God said to me, 'You must not build a temple for worshiping me, because you are a soldier and have killed many people.'

⁴"But the LORD, the God of Israel, chose me from my whole family to be king of Israel forever. He chose the tribe of Judah to lead, and from the people of Judah, he chose my father's family. From that family God was pleased to make me king of Israel. ⁵The LORD has given me many sons, and from those sons he has chosen Solomon to be the new king of Israel. Israel is the LORD's kingdom. ⁶The LORD said to me, 'Your son Solomon will build my Templeᵈ and its courtyards. I have chosen Solomon to be my son, and I will be his father. ⁷He is obeying my laws and commands

now. If he continues to obey them, I will make his kingdom strong forever.' "

⁸David said, "Now, in front of all Israel, the assembly of the LORD, and in the hearing of God, I tell you these things: Be careful to obey all the commands of the LORD your God. Then you will keep this good land and pass it on to your descendantsᵈ forever.

⁹"And you, my son Solomon, accept the God of your father. Serve him completely and willingly, because the LORD knows what is in everyone's mind. He understands everything you think. If you go to him for help, you will get an answer. But if you turn away from him, he will leave you forever. ¹⁰Solomon, you must understand this. The LORD has chosen you to build the Temple as his holy place. Be strong and finish the job."

¹¹Then David gave his son Solomon the plans for building the Temple and the courtyard around the Temple. They included its buildings, its storerooms, its upper rooms, its inside rooms, and the place where the people's sins were removed. ¹²David gave him plans for everything he had in mind: the courtyards around the LORD's Temple and all the rooms around it, the Temple treasuries, and the treasuries of the holy items used in the Temple. ¹³David gave Solomon directions for the groups of the priests and Levites. David told him about all the work of serving in the Temple of the LORD and about the items to be used in the Temple service ¹⁴that were made of gold or silver. David told Solomon how much gold or silver should be used to make each thing. ¹⁵David told him how much gold to use for each gold lampstand and its lamps and how much silver to use for each silver lampstand and its lamps. The different lampstands were to be used where needed. ¹⁶David told how much gold should be used for each table that held the holy bread and how much silver should be used for the silver tables. ¹⁷He told how much pure gold should be used to make the forks, bowls, and pitchers and how much gold should be used to make each gold dish. He told how much silver should be used to make each silver dish ¹⁸and how much pure gold should be used for the altar of incense.ᵈ He also gave Solomon the plans for the chariot of the golden creatures that spread their wings over the Arkᵈ of the Agreement with the LORD.

¹⁹David said, "All these plans were written with the LORD guiding me. He helped me understand everything in the plans."

²⁰David also said to his son Solomon, "Be strong and brave, and do the work. Don't be afraid or discouraged, because the LORD God, my God, is with you. He will not fail you or leave you until all the work for the Temple of the LORD is finished. ²¹The groups of the priests and Levites are ready for all the work on the Temple of God.

Every skilled worker is ready to help you with all the work. The leaders and all the people will obey every command you give."

Gifts for Building the Temple

29 King David said to all the Israelites who were gathered, "God chose my son Solomon, who is young and hasn't yet learned what he needs to know, but the work is important. This palace is not for people; it is for the LORD God. ²I have done my best to prepare for building the Temple*ᵈ* of God. I have given gold for the things made of gold and silver for the things made of silver. I have given bronze for the things made of bronze and iron for the things made of iron. I have given wood for the things made of wood and onyx for the settings. I have given turquoise gems of many different colors, valuable stones, and white marble. I have given much of all these things. ³I have already given this for the Temple, but now I am also giving my own treasures of gold and silver, because I really want the Temple of my God to be built. ⁴I have given about two hundred twenty thousand pounds of pure gold from Ophir and about five hundred twenty thousand pounds of pure silver. They will be used to cover the walls of the buildings ⁵and for all the gold and silver

work. Skilled men may use the gold and silver to make things for the Temple. Now, who is ready to give himself to the service of the LORD today?"

⁶The family leaders and the leaders of the tribes of Israel, the commanders of a thousand men and of a hundred men, and the leaders responsible for the king's work gave their valuable things. ⁷They donated about three hundred eighty thousand pounds of gold, about seven hundred fifty thousand pounds of silver, about one million three hundred fifty thousand pounds of bronze, and about seven million five hundred thousand pounds of iron to the Temple of God. ⁸People who had valuable gems gave them to the treasury of the Temple of the LORD, and Jehiel, from the Gershon family, took care of the valuable gems. ⁹The leaders gave willingly and completely to the LORD. The people rejoiced to see their leaders give so gladly, and King David was also very happy.

David's Prayer

¹⁰David praised the LORD in front of all the people who were gathered. He said:
"We praise you, LORD,
  God of our father Israel.
 We praise you forever and ever.
¹¹LORD, you are great and powerful.

THANKFULNESS

A Letter to Dad

Jody Pearson was twenty when she moved to another state to work for the summer. While she was away she wrote this letter.

Dear Dad,

Lately I've thought of you often and wanted to thank you for many things! I guess I've started seeing the simple things you and Mom taught us. The basics—like manners and respect—but also contentment with what we have, finding joy in each other, listening, forgiving, and understanding! You taught us that those things not only make life flow more smoothly, but they also show Jesus to the world. Now I understand!

Dad, I miss being able to share things with you. You always listen and understand. Thank you for all your time, love, and care. You've planted many seeds. I know I'll be reaping from this garden for a lifetime!

Love, Jody

Jody showed her appreciation for her father through a letter. In **1 Chronicles 29:10–13**, King David thanked his heavenly father for all he had done for Israel.

■ How are Jody's letter and David's prayer alike?
■ How can you, like David, express your praise to God?

C O N S I D E R . . .
■ writing a poem expressing your thanks to God for something.
■ sending a card to thank someone for something he or she has done for you.

F O R   M O R E ,   S E E . . .
■ Psalm 100 (p. 539)
■ Ephesians 1:15–16 (p. 1218)
■ Revelation 7:9–12 (p. 1337)

You have glory, victory, and honor.
Everything in heaven and on earth belongs
to you.
The kingdom belongs to you, LORD;
you are the ruler over everything.
12Riches and honor come from you.
You rule everything.
You have the power and strength
to make anyone great and strong.
13Now, our God, we thank you
and praise your glorious name.

14"These things did not really come from me
and my people.
Everything comes from you;
we have given you back what you gave us.
15We are like foreigners and strangers,
as our ancestors were.
Our time on earth is like a shadow.
There is no hope.
16LORD our God, we have gathered all this
to build your Temple for worship to you.
But everything has come from you;
everything belongs to you.
17I know, my God, that you test people's
hearts.
You are happy when people do what is
right.
I was happy to give all these things,
and I gave with an honest heart.
Your people gathered here are happy to give
to you,
and I rejoice to see their giving.
18LORD, you are the God of our ancestors,
the God of Abraham, Isaac, and Jacob.
Make your people want to serve you always,
and make them want to obey you.
19Give my son Solomon a desire to serve you.
Help him always obey your commands,
laws, and rules.
Help him build the Temple
for which I have prepared."

20Then David said to all the people who were
gathered, "Praise the LORD your God." So they all
praised the LORD, the God of their ancestors, and
they bowed to the ground to give honor to the
LORD and the king.

Solomon Becomes King

21The next day the people sacrificed to the
LORD. They offered burnt offerings to him of a
thousand bulls, a thousand male sheep, and a
thousand male lambs. They also brought drink offerings. Many sacrifices were made for all the people of Israel. 22That day the people ate and drank
with much joy, and the LORD was with them.

And they made David's son Solomon king for
the second time. They poured olive oil on Solomon to appoint him king in the presence of the
LORD. And they poured oil on Zadok to appoint
him as priest. 23Then Solomon sat on the LORD's
throne as king and took his father David's place.
Solomon was very successful, and all the people
of Israel obeyed him. 24All the leaders and soldiers
and King David's sons accepted Solomon as king
and promised to obey him. 25The LORD made Solomon great before all the Israelites and gave Solomon much honor. No king of Israel before Solomon had such honor.

David's Death

26David son of Jesse was king over all Israel.
27He had ruled over Israel forty years—seven
years in Hebron and thirty-three years in Jerusalem. 28David died when he was old. He had lived
a good, long life and had received many riches
and honors. His son Solomon became king after
him.

29Everything David did as king, from beginning
to end, is recorded in the records of Samuel the
seer,d the records of Nathan the prophet, and the
records of Gad the seer. 30Those writings tell what
David did as king of Israel. They tell about his
power and what happened to him and to Israel
and to all the kingdoms around them.

2 CHRONICLES

Why Read This Book:

- See how following God can unite people and help them prosper (2 Chronicles 1—9).
- Learn what can happen when people turn away from God (2 Chronicles 10—36).

Behind the Scenes:

If God offered to grant you a wish, what would you request? Popularity? Lots of money? Good looks? Fame? A new sports car?

Second Chronicles begins with such a situation. Solomon had inherited Israel from his father, David, and God promised to give him whatever he asked for. Instead of asking for wealth or military power, Solomon requested wisdom to govern Israel the way God wanted it governed. His wish was granted. Second Chronicles describes a glorious, prosperous and peaceful reign for Solomon. Central to Solomon's grandeur was the spectacular Temple he built for God in Jerusalem. (See the introduction to 1 Kings for the rest of the story.)

Unfortunately, the nation struggled after Solomon's death. First a civil war divided Israel into two kingdoms. The North—keeping the name Israel—rejected rule by David's descendants and chose its own king. The South—adopting the name Judah—kept David's descendants in power but had trouble maintaining a relationship with God.

Picking up where 1 Chronicles left off, 2 Chronicles traces the history of the Israelites after King David, beginning with the united kingdom under Solomon and then focusing on Judah after the kingdom divided. The story is similar to the accounts in 1 and 2 Kings (p. 301 and p. 331).

Second Chronicles continues the message of 1 Chronicles, since they were originally one book (see 1 Chronicles introduction, p. 359). The writer is retelling the history of Israel and Judah as a reminder and warning that the nation's success is directly linked to its relationship with God.

WHERE THE ACTION WAS

Temple of Solomon

Only priests entered The Most Holy Place. Its walls were covered with gold (2 Chronicles 3:8).

Side rooms used for storage (see 1 Kings 6:5, p. 308).

A bronze altar was used for sacrifices (2 Chronicles 4:1).

The first nine chapters of 2 Chronicles revolve around Solomon and his efforts to build the Temple in Jerusalem.

The Temple was about ninety feet long (2 Chronicles 3:3).

People entered the Temple through this porch (2 Chronicles 3:4).

Two pillars in front of the Temple were about fifty-two feet tall (2 Chronicles 3:15).

A bronze bowl, called the Sea, was used for ceremonial washing (2 Chronicles 4:2–6).

WHEN THE ACTION WAS

Solomon was Israel's king		People returned to Jerusalem from exile	1 and 2 Chronicles were written	Jesus was born
1000BC	**750BC**	**500BC**	**250BC**	**BC/AD**
David was Israel's king	The Northern Kingdom (Israel) fell to Assyria	The Southern Kingdom (Judah) fell to Babylon		

Solomon Asks for Wisdom

1 Solomon, David's son, became a powerful king, because the LORD his God was with him and made him very great.

²Solomon spoke to all the people of Israel — the commanders of a hundred men and of a thousand men, the judges, every leader in all Israel, and the leaders of the families. ³Then Solomon and all the people with him went to the place of worship at the town of Gibeon. God's Meeting Tent,*d* which Moses the LORD's servant had made in the desert, was there. ⁴David had brought the Ark*d* of God from Kiriath Jearim to Jerusalem, where he had made a place for it and had set up a tent for it. ⁵The bronze altar that Bezalel son of Uri, who was the son of Hur, had made was in Gibeon in front of the Holy Tent. So Solomon and the people worshiped there. ⁶Solomon went up to the bronze altar in the presence of the LORD at the Meeting Tent and offered a thousand burnt offerings on it.

⁷That night God appeared to Solomon and said to him, "Ask for whatever you want me to give you."

⁸Solomon answered, "You have been very kind to my father David, and you have made me king in his place. ⁹Now, LORD God, may your promise to my father David come true. You have made me king of a people who are as many as the dust of the earth. ¹⁰Now give me wisdom and knowledge so I can lead these people in the right way, because no one can rule them without your help."

¹¹God said to Solomon, "You have not asked for wealth or riches or honor, or for the death of your enemies, or for a long life. But since you have asked for wisdom and knowledge to lead my people, over whom I have made you king, ¹²I will give you wisdom and knowledge. I will also give you more wealth, riches, and honor than any king who has lived before you or any who will live after you."

¹³Then Solomon left the place of worship, the Meeting Tent, at Gibeon and went back to Jerusalem. There King Solomon ruled over Israel.

Solomon's Wealth

¹⁴Solomon had fourteen hundred chariots and twelve thousand horses. He kept some in special cities for the chariots, and others he kept with him in Jerusalem. ¹⁵In Jerusalem Solomon made silver and gold as plentiful as stones and cedar trees as plentiful as the fig trees on the western hills. ¹⁶He imported horses from Egypt and Kue; his traders bought them in Kue. ¹⁷They imported chariots from Egypt for about fifteen pounds of silver apiece, and horses cost nearly four pounds of silver apiece. Then they sold the horses and chariots to all the kings of the Hittites and the Arameans.

Solomon Prepares for the Temple

2 Solomon decided to build a temple*d* as a place to worship the LORD and also a palace for himself. ²He chose seventy thousand men to carry loads, eighty thousand men to cut stone in the hill country, and thirty-six hundred men to direct the workers.

³Solomon sent this message to Hiram king of the city of Tyre: "Help me as you helped my father David by sending him cedar logs so he could build himself a palace to live in. ⁴I will build a temple for worshiping the LORD my God, and I will give this temple to him. There we will burn sweet-smelling spices in his presence. We will continually set out the holy bread in God's presence. And we will burn sacrifices every morning and evening, on Sabbath*d* days and New Moons,*d* and on the other feast days commanded by the LORD our God. This is a rule for Israel to obey forever.

⁵"The temple I build will be great, because our God is greater than all gods. ⁶But no one can really build a house for our God. Not even the highest of heavens can hold him. How then can I build a temple for him except as a place to burn sacrifices to him?

⁷"Now send me a man skilled in working with gold, silver, bronze, and iron, and with purple, red, and blue thread. He must also know how to make engravings. He will work with my skilled craftsmen in Judah and Jerusalem, whom my father David chose.

⁸"Also send me cedar, pine, and juniper logs from Lebanon. I know your servants are experienced at cutting down the trees in Lebanon, and my servants will help them. ⁹Send me a lot of wood, because the temple I am going to build will be large and wonderful. ¹⁰I will give your servants who cut the wood one hundred twenty-five thousand bushels of wheat, one hundred twenty-five thousand bushels of barley, one hundred fifteen thousand gallons of wine, and one hundred fifteen thousand gallons of oil."

¹¹Then Hiram king of Tyre answered Solomon with this letter: "Solomon, because the LORD loves his people, he chose you to be their king." ¹²Hiram also said: "Praise the LORD, the God of Israel, who made heaven and earth! He has given King David a wise son, one with wisdom and understanding, who will build a temple for the LORD and a palace for himself.

¹³"I will send you a skilled and wise man named Huram-Abi. ¹⁴His mother was from the people of Dan, and his father was from Tyre. Huram-Abi is skilled in working with gold, silver, bronze, iron, stone, and wood, and with purple, blue, and red thread, and expensive linen. He is skilled in making engravings and can make any

design you show him. He will help your craftsmen and the craftsmen of your father David.

15"Now send my servants the wheat, barley, oil, and wine you promised. 16We will cut as much wood from Lebanon as you need and will bring it on rafts by sea to Joppa. Then you may carry it to Jerusalem."

17Solomon counted all the foreigners living in Israel. (This was after the time his father David had counted the people.) There were one hundred fifty-three thousand six hundred foreigners in the country. 18Solomon chose seventy thousand of them to carry loads, eighty thousand of them to cut stone in the mountains, and thirty-six hundred of them to direct the workers and to keep the people working.

☀ SIDELIGHT: Mount Moriah, where Solomon built the Temple (2 Chronicles 3:1), is a highly sacred spot for modern-day Christians, Jews and Muslims. It is traditionally where Abraham offered his son Isaac as a sacrifice (Genesis 22:2, p. 25) and where Gad came to David (2 Samuel 24:18, p. 300). The Dome of the Rock, a Muslim shrine, has occupied this traditional spot since the seventh century A.D.

Solomon Builds the Temple

3 Then Solomon began to build the Temple*d* of the LORD in Jerusalem on Mount Moriah. This was where the LORD had appeared to David, Solomon's father. Solomon built the Temple on the place David had prepared on the threshing*d* floor of Araunah the Jebusite. 2Solomon began building in the second month of the fourth year he ruled Israel.

3Solomon used these measurements for building the Temple of God. It was ninety feet long and thirty feet wide, using the old measurement. 4The porch in front of the main room of the Temple was thirty feet long and thirty feet high.

He covered the inside of the porch with pure gold. 5He put panels of pine on the walls of the main room and covered them with pure gold. Then he put designs of palm trees and chains in the gold. 6He decorated the Temple with gems and gold from Parvaim.*n* 7He put gold on the Temple's ceiling beams, doorposts, walls, and doors, and he carved creatures with wings on the walls.

8Then he made the Most Holy Place. It was thirty feet long and thirty feet wide, as wide as the Temple. He covered its walls with about forty-six

thousand pounds of pure gold. 9The gold nails weighed over a pound. He also covered the upper rooms with gold.

10He made two creatures with wings for the Most Holy Place and covered them with gold. 11The wings of the gold creatures were thirty feet across. One wing of one creature was seven and one-half feet long and touched the Temple wall. The creature's other wing was also seven and one-half feet long, and it touched a wing of the second creature. 12One wing of the second creature touched the other side of the room and was also seven and one-half feet long. The second creature's other wing touched the first creature's wing, and it was also seven and one-half feet long. 13Together, the creatures' wings were thirty feet across. The creatures stood on their feet, facing the main room.

14He made the curtain of blue, purple, and red thread, and expensive linen, and he put designs of creatures with wings in it.

15He made two pillars to stand in front of the Temple. They were about fifty-two feet tall, and the capital*d* of each pillar was over seven feet tall. 16He made a net of chains and put them on the tops of the pillars. He made a hundred pomegranates*d* and put them on the chains. 17Then he put the pillars up in front of the Temple. One pillar stood on the south side, the other on the north. He named the south pillar He Establishes and the north pillar In Him Is Strength.

Things for the Temple

4 He made a bronze altar thirty feet long, thirty feet wide, and fifteen feet tall. 2Then he made from bronze a large round bowl, which was called the Sea. It was forty-five feet around, fifteen feet across, and seven and one-half feet deep. 3There were carvings of bulls under the rim of the bowl—ten bulls every eighteen inches. They were in two rows and were made in one piece with the bowl.

4The bowl rested on the backs of twelve bronze bulls that faced outward from the center of the bowl. Three bulls faced north, three faced west, three faced south, and three faced east. 5The sides of the bowl were four inches thick, and it held about seventeen thousand five hundred gallons. The rim of the bowl was like the rim of a cup or like a lily blossom.

6He made ten smaller bowls and put five on the south side and five on the north. They were for washing the animals for the burnt offerings, but the large bowl was for the priests to wash in.

7He made ten lampstands of gold, following the plans. He put them in the Temple,*d* five on the south side and five on the north.

Parvaim There was much gold there. It may have been in the country of Ophir.

[8]He made ten tables and put them in the Temple, five on the south side and five on the north. And he used gold to make a hundred other bowls.

[9]He also made the priests' courtyard and the large courtyard. He made the doors that opened to the courtyard and covered them with bronze. [10]Then he put the large bowl in the southeast corner of the Temple.

[11]Huram also made bowls, shovels, and small bowls. So he finished his work for King Solomon on the Temple of God:

[12]two pillars;

two large bowls for the capitals on top of the pillars;

two nets to cover the two large bowls for the capitals on top of the pillars;

[13]four hundred pomegranates[d] for the two nets (there were two rows of pomegranates for each net covering the bowls for the capitals on top of the pillars);

[14]the stands with a bowl on each stand;

[15]the large bowl with twelve bulls under it;

[16]the pots, shovels, forks, and all the things to go with them.

All the things that Huram-Abi made for King Solomon for the Temple of the Lord were made of polished bronze. [17]The king had these things poured into clay molds that were made in the plain of the Jordan River between Succoth and Zarethan. [18]Solomon had so many things made that the total weight of all the bronze was never known.

[19]Solomon also made all the things for God's Temple: the golden altar; tables which held the bread that shows God's people are in his presence; [20]the lampstands and their lamps of pure gold, to burn in front of the Most Holy Place as planned; [21]the flowers, lamps, and tongs of pure gold; [22]the pure gold wick trimmers, small bowls, pans, and dishes used to carry coals, the gold doors for the Temple, and the inside doors of the Most Holy Place and of the main room.

5 Finally all the work Solomon did for the Temple of the Lord was finished. He brought in everything his father David had set apart for the Temple — all the silver and gold and other articles. And he put everything in the treasuries of God's Temple.

The Ark Is Brought into the Temple

[2]Solomon called for the older leaders of Israel, the heads of the tribes,[d] and the leaders of the families to come to him in Jerusalem. He wanted them to bring the Ark[d] of the Agreement with the Lord from the older part of the city. [3]So all the Israelites came together with the king during the festival in the seventh month.

[4]When all the older leaders of Israel arrived, the Levites lifted up the Ark. [5]They carried the Ark of the Agreement, the Meeting Tent,[d] and the holy utensils in it; the priests and the Levites brought them up. [5]King Solomon and all the Israelites gathered before the Ark of the Agreement and sacrificed so many sheep and bulls no one could count them.

[7]Then the priests put the Ark of the Agreement with the Lord in its place inside the Most Holy Place in the Temple,[d] under the wings of the

> **SIDELIGHT:** Imagine having worship services on the church lawn outside your sanctuary. That's what the ancient Israelites did. The Temple was considered God's house, which was symbolized by putting the Ark of the Agreement in it (2 Chronicles 5:2, 7). It wasn't really a place to gather for worship or study. They had assemblies outside the Temple.

golden creatures. [8]The wings of these creatures were spread out over the place for the Ark, covering it and its carrying poles. [9]The carrying poles were so long that anyone standing in the Holy Place in front of the Most Holy Place could see the ends of the poles. But no one could see them from outside the Holy Place. The poles are still there today. [10]The only things inside the Ark were two stone tablets[n] that Moses had put in the Ark at Mount Sinai. That was where the Lord made his agreement with the Israelites after they came out of Egypt.

[11]Then all the priests left the Holy Place. (All the priests from each group had made themselves ready to serve the Lord.) [12]All the Levite musicians — Asaph, Heman, Jeduthun, and all their sons and relatives — stood on the east side of the altar. They were dressed in white linen and played cymbals, harps, and lyres.[d] With them were one hundred twenty priests who blew trumpets. [13]Those who blew the trumpets and those who sang together sounded like one person as they praised and thanked the Lord. They sang as others played their trumpets, cymbals, and other instruments. They praised the Lord with this song:

"He is good;

his love continues forever."

Then the Temple of the Lord was filled with a cloud. [14]The priests could not continue their

---

stone tablets They were the two stone tablets on which God wrote the Ten Commandments.

work because of the cloud, because the LORD's glory filled the Temple of God.

Solomon Speaks to the People

6 Then Solomon said, "The LORD said he would live in the dark cloud. [2]LORD, I have built a wonderful Temple for you—a place for you to live forever."

[3]While all the Israelites were standing there, King Solomon turned to them and blessed them. [4]Then he said, "Praise the LORD, the God of Israel. He has done what he promised to my father David. The LORD said, [5]'Since the time I brought my people out of Egypt, I have not chosen a city in any tribe[d] of Israel where a temple[d] will be built for me. I did not choose a man to lead my people Israel. [6]But now I have chosen Jerusalem as the place I am to be worshiped, and I have chosen David to lead my people Israel.'

[7]"My father David wanted to build a temple for the LORD, the God of Israel. [8]But the LORD said to my father David, 'It was good that you wanted to build a temple for me. [9]But you are not the one to build it. Your son, who comes from your own body, is the one who will build my temple.'

[10]"Now the LORD has kept his promise. I am the king now in place of David my father. Now I rule Israel as the LORD promised, and I have built the Temple for the LORD, the God of Israel. [11]There I have put the Ark,[d] in which is the Agreement the LORD made with the Israelites."

Solomon's Prayer

[12]Then Solomon stood facing the LORD's altar, and all the Israelites were standing behind him. He spread out his hands. [13]He had made a bronze platform seven and one-half feet long, seven and one-half feet wide, and seven and one-half feet high, and he had placed it in the middle of the outer courtyard. Solomon stood on the platform. Then he kneeled in front of all the people of Israel gathered there, and he spread out his hands toward the sky. [14]He said, "LORD, God of Israel, there is no god like you in heaven or on earth. You keep your agreement of love with your servants who truly follow you. [15]You have kept the promise you made to your servant David, my father. You spoke it with your own mouth and finished it with your hands today.

[16]"Now, LORD, God of Israel, keep the promise you made to your servant David, my father. You said, 'If your sons are careful to obey my teachings as you have obeyed, there will always be someone from your family ruling Israel.' [17]Now, LORD, God of Israel, please continue to keep that promise you made to your servant.

[18]"But, God, can you really live here on the earth with people? The sky and the highest place in heaven cannot contain you. Surely this house which I have built cannot contain you. [19]But please listen to my prayer and my request, because I am your servant. LORD my God, hear this prayer your servant prays to you. [20]Day and night please watch over this Temple where you have said you would be worshiped. Hear the prayer I pray facing this Temple. [21]Hear my prayers and the prayers of your people Israel when we pray facing this place. Hear from your home in heaven, and when you hear, forgive us.

[22]"If someone wrongs another person, he will be brought to the altar in this Temple. If he swears an oath that he is not guilty, [23]then hear in heaven. Judge the case, punish the guilty, but declare that the innocent person is not guilty.

[24]"When your people, the Israelites, sin against you, their enemies will defeat them. But if they come back to you and praise you and pray to you in this Temple, [25]then listen from heaven. Forgive the sin of your people Israel, and bring them back to the land you gave to them and their ancestors.

[26]"When they sin against you, you will stop the rain from falling on their land. Then they will pray, facing this place and praising you; they will stop sinning when you make them suffer. [27]When this happens, hear their prayer in heaven, and forgive the sins of your servants, the Israelites. Teach them to do what is right. Then please send rain to this land you have given particularly to them.

[28]"At times the land will get so dry that no food will grow, or a great sickness will spread among the people. Sometimes the crops will be destroyed by locusts[d] or grasshoppers. Your people will be attacked in their cities by their enemies, or will become sick. [29]When any of these things happens, the people will become truly sorry. If your people spread their hands in prayer toward this Temple, [30]then hear their prayers from your home in heaven. Forgive and treat each person as he should be treated because you know what is in a person's heart. Only you know what is in people's hearts. [31]Then the people will respect and obey you as long as they live in this land you gave our ancestors.

[32]"People who are not Israelites, foreigners from other lands, will hear about your greatness and power. They will come from far away to pray at this Temple. [33]Then hear from your home in heaven, and do whatever they ask you. Then people everywhere will know you and respect you, just as your people Israel do. Then everyone will know that I built this Temple as a place to worship you.

[34]"When your people go out to fight their enemies along some road on which you send them, your people will pray to you, facing this city which you have chosen and the Temple I have built for you. [35]Then hear in heaven their prayers, and do what is right.

36"Everyone sins, so your people will also sin against you. You will become angry with them and will hand them over to their enemies. Their enemies will capture them and take them away to a country far or near. 37Your people will be sorry for their sins when they are held as prisoners in another country. They will be sorry and pray to you in the land where they are held as prisoners, saying, 'We have sinned. We have done wrong and acted wickedly.' 38They will truly turn back to you in the land where they are captives. They will pray, facing this land you gave their ancestors, this city you have chosen, and the Temple I have built for you. 39Then hear their prayers from your home in heaven and do what is right. Forgive your people who have sinned against you.

40"Now, my God, look at us. Listen to the prayers we pray in this place.

41Now, rise, LORD God, and come to your resting place.

Come with the Ark^d of the Agreement that shows your strength.

Let your priests receive your salvation, LORD God,

and may your holy people be happy because of your goodness.

42LORD God, do not reject your appointed one. Remember your love for your servant David."

The Temple Is Given to the Lord

7 When Solomon finished praying, fire came down from the sky and burned up the burnt offering and the sacrifices. The LORD's glory filled the Temple.^{d} 2The priests could not enter the Temple of the LORD, because the LORD's glory filled it. 3When all the people of Israel saw the fire come down from heaven and the LORD's glory on the Temple, they bowed down on the pavement with their faces to the ground. They worshiped and thanked the LORD, saying,

"He is good;

his love continues forever."

4Then King Solomon and all the people offered sacrifices to the LORD. 5King Solomon offered a sacrifice of twenty-two thousand cattle and one hundred twenty thousand sheep. So the king and all the people gave the Temple to God. 6The priests stood ready to do their work. The Levites also stood with the instruments of the LORD's music that King David had made for praising the LORD. The priests and Levites were saying, "His love continues forever." The priests, who stood across from the Levites, blew their trumpets, and all the Israelites were standing.

7Solomon made holy the middle part of the courtyard, which is in front of the Temple of the LORD. There he offered whole burnt offerings and the fat of the fellowship offerings. He offered them in the courtyard, because the bronze altar he had made could not hold the burnt offerings, grain offerings, and fat.

8Solomon and all the Israelites celebrated the festival for seven days. There were many people, and they came from as far away as Lebo Hamath and the brook of Egypt. 9For seven days they celebrated giving the altar for the worship of God. Then they celebrated the festival for seven days. On the eighth day they had a meeting. 10On the twenty-third day of the seventh month Solomon sent the people home, full of joy. They were happy because the LORD had been so good to David, Solomon, and his people Israel.

The Lord Appears to Solomon

11Solomon finished the Temple^d of the LORD and his royal palace. He had success in doing everything he planned in the Temple of the LORD and his own palace. 12Then the LORD appeared to Solomon at night and said to him, "I have heard your prayer and have chosen this place for myself to be a Temple for sacrifices.

13"I may stop the sky from sending rain. I may command the locusts^d to destroy the land. I may send sicknesses to my people. 14Then if my people, who are called by my name, are sorry for what they have done, if they pray and obey me and stop their evil ways, I will hear them from heaven. I will forgive their sin, and I will heal their land. 15Now I will see them, and I will listen to the prayers prayed in this place. 16I have chosen this Temple and made it holy. So I will be worshiped there forever. Yes, I will always watch over it and love it.

17"But you must serve me as your father David did. You must obey all I have commanded and keep my laws and rules. 18If you do, I will make your kingdom strong. This is the agreement I made with your father David, saying, 'Someone from your family will always rule in Israel.'

19"But you must follow me and obey the laws and commands I have given you. You must not serve or worship other gods. 20If you do, I will take the Israelites out of my land, the land I have given them, and I will leave this Temple that I have made holy. All the nations will make fun of it and speak evil about it. 21This Temple is honored now, but then, everyone who passes by will be shocked. They will ask, 'Why did the LORD do this terrible thing to this land and this Temple?' 22People will answer, 'This happened because they left the LORD, the God of their ancestors, the God who brought them out of Egypt. They decided to follow other gods and worshiped and served them, so he brought all this disaster on them.' "

Solomon's Other Achievements

8 By the end of twenty years, Solomon had built the Temple*d* of the LORD and the royal palace. ²Solomon rebuilt the towns that Hiram had given him, and Solomon sent Israelites to live in them. ³Then he went to Hamath Zobah and captured it. ⁴Solomon also built the town of Tadmor in the desert, and he built all the towns in Hamath as towns for storing grain and supplies. ⁵He rebuilt the towns of Upper Beth Horon and Lower Beth Horon, protecting them with strong walls, gates, and bars in the gates. ⁶He also rebuilt the town of Baalath. And he built all the other towns for storage and all the cities for his chariots and horses. He built all he wanted in Jerusalem, Lebanon, and everywhere he ruled.

⁷There were other people in the land who were not Israelites — the Hittites, Amorites, Perizzites, Hivites, and Jebusites. ⁸They were descendants*d* of the people that the Israelites had not destroyed. Solomon forced them to be slave workers, as is still true today. ⁹But Solomon did not make slaves of the Israelites. They were his soldiers, chief captains, commanders of his chariots, and his chariot drivers. ¹⁰These were his most important officers. There were two hundred fifty of them to direct the people.

¹¹Solomon brought the daughter of the king of Egypt from the older part of Jerusalem to the palace he had built for her. Solomon said, "My wife must not live in King David's palace, because the places where the Ark*d* of the Agreement has been are holy."

¹²Then Solomon offered burnt offerings to the LORD on the altar he had built for the LORD in front of the Temple porch. ¹³He offered sacrifices every day as Moses had commanded. They were offered on the Sabbath*d* days, New Moons,*d* and the three yearly feasts — the Feast*d* of Unleavened Bread, the Feast of Weeks, and the Feast of Shelters. ¹⁴Solomon followed his father David's instructions and chose the groups of priests for their service and the Levites to lead the praise and to help the priests do their daily work. And he chose the gatekeepers by their groups to serve at each gate, as David, the man of God, had commanded. ¹⁵They obeyed all of Solomon's commands to the priests and Levites, as well as his commands about the treasuries.

¹⁶All Solomon's work was done as he had said from the day the foundation of the Temple of the LORD *was begun, until it was finished. So the Temple was finished.*

¹⁷Then Solomon *went to the towns of Ezion Geber and Elath near the Red Sea*d* in the land of Edom. ¹⁸Hiram sent ships to Solomon that were commanded by his own men, who were skilled sailors. Hiram's men went with Solomon's men to* Ophir and brought back about thirty-four thousand pounds of gold to King Solomon.

The Queen of Sheba Visits

9 When the queen of Sheba heard about Solomon's fame, she came to Jerusalem to test him with hard questions. She had a large group of servants with her and camels carrying spices, jewels, and much gold. When she came to Solomon, she talked with him about all she had in mind, ²and Solomon answered all her questions. Nothing was too hard for him to explain to her. ³The queen of Sheba saw that Solomon was very wise. She saw the palace he had built, ⁴the food on his table, his many officers, the palace servants and their good clothes, the servants who served Solomon his wine and their good clothes. She saw the whole burnt offerings he made in the Temple*d* of the LORD. All these things amazed her.

⁵So she said to King Solomon, "What I heard in my own country about your achievements and wisdom is true. ⁶I did not believe it then, but now I have come and seen it with my own eyes. I was not told even half of your great wisdom! You are much greater than I had heard. ⁷Your men and officers are very lucky, because in always serving you, they are able to hear your wisdom. ⁸Praise the LORD your God who was pleased to make you king. He has put you on his throne to rule for the LORD your God, because your God loves the people of Israel and supports them forever. He has made you king over them to keep justice and to rule fairly."

⁹Then she gave the king about nine thousand pounds of gold and many spices and jewels. No one had ever given such spices as the queen of Sheba gave to King Solomon.

¹⁰Hiram's men and Solomon's men brought gold from Ophir, juniper wood, and jewels. ¹¹King Solomon used the juniper wood to build steps for the Temple of the LORD and the palace and to make lyres*d* and harps for the musicians. No one in Judah had ever seen such beautiful things as these.

¹²King Solomon gave the queen of Sheba everything she wanted and asked for, even more than she had brought to him. Then she and her servants returned to her own country.

Solomon's Wealth

¹³Every year King Solomon received about fifty thousand pounds of gold. ¹⁴Besides that, he also *received gold from traders and merchants. All the kings of Arabia and the governors of the land also* brought gold and silver.

¹⁵King Solomon made two hundred large shields of hammered gold, each of which contained about seven and one-half pounds of hammered gold. ¹⁶He also made three hundred

smaller shields of hammered gold, each of which contained about four pounds of gold. The king put them in the Palace of the Forest of Lebanon.

[17]The king built a large throne of ivory and covered it with pure gold. [18]The throne had six steps on it and a gold footstool. There were armrests on both sides of the chair, and each armrest had a lion beside it. [19]Twelve lions stood on the six steps, one lion at each end of each step. Nothing like this had ever been made for any other kingdom. [20]All of Solomon's drinking cups, as well as the dishes in the Palace of the Forest of Lebanon, were made of pure gold. In Solomon's time people did not think silver was valuable.

[21]King Solomon had many ships that he sent out to trade, with Hiram's men as the crews. Every three years the ships returned, bringing back gold, silver, ivory, apes, and baboons.

[22]King Solomon had more riches and wisdom than all the other kings on earth. [23]All the kings of the earth wanted to see Solomon and listen to the wisdom God had given him. [24]Year after year everyone who came brought gifts of silver and gold, clothes, weapons, spices, horses, and mules.

[25]Solomon had four thousand stalls for horses and chariots and he had twelve thousand horses. He kept some in special cities for the chariots, and others he kept with him in Jerusalem. [26]Solomon ruled over all the kingdoms from the Euphrates River to the land of the Philistines, as far as the border of Egypt. [27]In Jerusalem the king made silver as common as stones and cedar trees as plentiful as the fig trees on the western hills. [28]Solomon imported horses from Egypt and all other countries.

Solomon's Death

[29]Everything else Solomon did, from the beginning to the end, is written in the records of Nathan the prophet,[d] and in the prophecy of Ahijah the Shilonite, and in the visions of Iddo the seer,[d] who wrote about Jeroboam, Nebat's son. [30]Solomon ruled in Jerusalem over all Israel for forty years. [31]Then Solomon died and was buried in Jerusalem, the city of David, his father. And Solomon's son Rehoboam became king in his place.

Israel Turns Against Rehoboam

10 Rehoboam went to Shechem, where all the Israelites had gone to make him king. [2]Jeroboam son of Nebat was in Egypt, where he had gone to escape from King Solomon. When Jeroboam heard about Rehoboam being made king, he returned from Egypt. [3]After the people sent for him, he and the people went to Rehoboam and said to him, [4]"Your father forced us to work very hard. Now, make it easier for us, and don't make us work as he did. Then we will serve you."

[5]Rehoboam answered, "Come back to me in three days." So the people left.

SIDELIGHT: Second Chronicles 10—36 is a lot like a Reader's Digest condensed version of 1 and 2 Kings (p. 301 and p. 331). In 2 Chronicles, the material on the divided kingdom takes up twenty-seven chapters, but Kings devotes thirty-six chapters to the same period.

---

[6]King Rehoboam asked the older leaders who had advised Solomon during his lifetime, "How do you think I should answer these people?"

[7]They answered, "Be kind to these people. If you please them and give them a kind answer, they will serve you always."

[8]But Rehoboam rejected this advice. Instead, he asked the young men who had grown up with him and who served as his advisers. [9]Rehoboam asked them, "What is your advice? How should we answer these people who said, 'Don't make us work as hard as your father did'?"

[10]The young men who had grown up with him answered, "The people said to you, 'Your father forced us to work very hard. Now make our work easier.' You should tell them, 'My little finger is bigger than my father's legs. [11]He forced you to work hard, but I will make you work even harder. My father beat you with whips, but I will beat you with whips that have sharp points.'"

[12]Rehoboam had told the people, "Come back to me in three days." So after three days Jeroboam and all the people returned to Rehoboam. [13]King Rehoboam spoke cruel words to them, because he had rejected the advice of the older leaders. [14]He followed the advice of the young men and said, "My father forced you to work hard, but I will make you work even harder. My father beat you with whips, but I will beat you with whips that have sharp points." [15]So the king did not listen to the people. God caused this to happen so that the LORD could keep the promise he had made to Jeroboam son of Nebat through Ahijah, a prophet[d] from Shiloh.

[16]When all the Israelites saw that the king refused to listen to them, they said to the king,

"We have no share in David!
We have no part in the son of Jesse!
People of Israel, let's go to our own homes!
Let David's son rule his own people."

So all the Israelites went home. [17]But Rehoboam still ruled over the Israelites who lived in the towns of Judah.

[18]Adoniram was in charge of the forced labor. When Rehoboam sent him to the people, they

threw stones at him until he died. But King Rehoboam ran to his chariot and escaped to Jerusalem. ¹⁹Since then, Israel has been against the family of David.

11 When Rehoboam arrived in Jerusalem, he gathered one hundred eighty thousand of the best soldiers from Judah and Benjamin. He wanted to fight Israel to take back his kingdom. ²But the LORD spoke his word to Shemaiah, a man of God, saying, ³"Speak to Solomon's son Rehoboam, the king of Judah, and to all the Israelites living in Judah and Benjamin. Say to them, ⁴'The LORD says you must not go to war against your brothers. Every one of you should go home, because I made all these things happen.' " So they obeyed the LORD's command and turned back and did not attack Jeroboam.

Rehoboam Makes Judah Strong

⁵Rehoboam lived in Jerusalem and built strong cities in Judah to defend it. ⁶He built up the cities of Bethlehem, Etam, Tekoa, ⁷Beth Zur, Soco, Adullam, ⁸Gath, Mareshah, Ziph, ⁹Adoraim, Lachish, Azekah, ¹⁰Zorah, Aijalon, and Hebron. These were strong, walled cities in Judah and Benjamin. ¹¹When Rehoboam made those cities strong, he put commanders and supplies of food, oil, and wine in them. ¹²Also, Rehoboam put shields and spears in all the cities and made them very strong. Rehoboam kept the people of Judah and Benjamin under his control.

¹³The priests and the Levites from all over Israel joined Rehoboam. ¹⁴The Levites even left their pasturelands and property and came to Judah and Jerusalem, because Jeroboam and his sons refused to let them serve as priests to the LORD. ¹⁵Jeroboam chose his own priests for the places of worship and for the goat and calf idols he had made. ¹⁶There were people from all the tribes*d* of Israel who wanted to obey the LORD, the God of Israel. So they went to Jerusalem with the Levites to sacrifice to the LORD, the God of their fathers. ¹⁷These people made the kingdom of Judah strong, and they supported Solomon's son Rehoboam for three years. During this time they lived the way David and Solomon had lived.

Rehoboam's Family

¹⁸Rehoboam married Mahalath, the daughter of Jerimoth and Abihail. Jerimoth was David's son, and Abihail was the daughter of Eliab, Jesse's son. ¹⁹Mahalath gave Rehoboam these sons: Jeush, Shemariah, and Zaham. ²⁰Then Rehoboam married Absalom's daughter Maacah, and she gave Rehoboam these children: Abijah, Attai, Ziza, and Shelomith. ²¹Rehoboam loved Maacah more than his other wives and slave women.*d* Rehoboam had eighteen wives and sixty slave women and was the father of twenty-eight sons and sixty daughters. ²²Rehoboam chose Abijah son of Maacah to be the leader of his own brothers, because he planned to make Abijah king. ²³Rehoboam acted wisely. He spread his sons through all the areas of Judah and Benjamin, sending them to every strong, walled city. He gave plenty of supplies to his sons, and he also found wives for them.

Shishak Attacks Jerusalem

12 After Rehoboam's kingdom was set up and he became strong, he and the people of Judah stopped obeying the teachings of the LORD. ²During the fifth year Rehoboam was king, Shishak king of Egypt attacked Jerusalem, because Rehoboam and the people were unfaithful to the LORD. ³Shishak had twelve hundred chariots and sixty thousand horsemen. He brought troops of Libyans, Sukkites, and Cushites from Egypt with him, so many they couldn't be counted. ⁴Shishak captured the strong, walled cities of Judah and came as far as Jerusalem.

⁵Then Shemaiah the prophet*d* came to Rehoboam and the leaders of Judah who had gathered in Jerusalem because they were afraid of Shishak. Shemaiah said to them, "This is what the LORD says: 'You have left me, so now I will leave you to face Shishak alone.' "

⁶Then the leaders of Judah and King Rehoboam were sorry for what they had done. They said, "The LORD does what is right."

⁷When the LORD saw they were sorry for what they had done, the LORD spoke his word to Shemaiah, saying, "The king and the leaders are sorry. So I will not destroy them but will save them soon. I will not use Shishak to punish Jerusalem in my anger. ⁸But the people of Jerusalem will become Shishak's servants so they may learn that serving me is different than serving the kings of other nations."

⁹Shishak king of Egypt attacked Jerusalem and took the treasures from the Temple*d* of the LORD and the king's palace. He took everything, even the gold shields Solomon had made. ¹⁰So King Rehoboam made bronze shields to take their place and gave them to the commanders of the guards for the palace gates. ¹¹Whenever the king went to the Temple of the LORD, the guards went with him, carrying the shields. Later, they would put them back in the guardroom.

¹²When Rehoboam was sorry for what he had done, the LORD held his anger back and did not fully destroy Rehoboam. There was some good in Judah.

¹³King Rehoboam made himself a strong king in Jerusalem. He was forty-one years old when he became king, and he was king in Jerusalem for seventeen years. Jerusalem is the city that the

LORD chose from all the tribes[d] of Israel in which he was to be worshiped. Rehoboam's mother was Naamah from the country of Ammon. [14]Rehoboam did evil because he did not want to obey the LORD.

[15]The things Rehoboam did as king, from the beginning to the end, are written in the records of Shemaiah the prophet and Iddo the seer,[d] in the family histories. There were wars between Rehoboam and Jeroboam all the time they ruled. [16]Rehoboam died and was buried in Jerusalem, and his son Abijah became king in his place.

Abijah King of Judah

13 Abijah became the king of Judah during the eighteenth year Jeroboam was king of Israel. [2]Abijah ruled in Jerusalem for three years. His mother was Maacah daughter of Uriel from the town of Gibeah.

And there was war between Abijah and Jeroboam. [3]Abijah led an army of four hundred thousand capable soldiers into battle, and Jeroboam prepared to fight him with eight hundred thousand capable soldiers.

[4]Abijah stood on Mount Zemaraim in the mountains of Ephraim and said, "Jeroboam and all Israel, listen to me! [5]You should know that the LORD, the God of Israel, gave David and his sons the right to rule Israel forever by an agreement of salt. [6]But Jeroboam son of Nebat, one of the officers of Solomon, David's son, turned against his master. [7]Then worthless, evil men joined Jeroboam against Rehoboam, Solomon's son. He was young and didn't know what to do, so he could not stop them.

[8]"Now you people are making plans against the LORD's kingdom, which belongs to David's sons. There are many of you, and you have the gold calves Jeroboam made for you as gods. [9]You have thrown out the Levites and the LORD's priests, Aaron's sons. You have chosen your own priests as people in other countries do. Anyone who comes with a young bull and seven male sheep can become a priest of idols that are not gods.

[10]"But as for us, the LORD is our God; we have not left him. The priests who serve the LORD are Aaron's sons, and the Levites help them. [11]They offer burnt offerings and sweet-smelling incense[d] to the LORD every morning and evening. They put the bread on the special table in the Temple.[d] And they light the lamps on the gold lampstand every evening. We obey the command of the LORD our God, but you have left him. [12]God himself is with us as our ruler. His priests blow the trumpet to call us to war against you. Men of Israel, don't fight against the LORD, the God of your ancestors, because you won't succeed."

[13]But Jeroboam had sent some troops to sneak behind Judah's army. So while Jeroboam was in front of Judah's army, Jeroboam's soldiers were behind them. [14]When the soldiers of Judah turned around, they saw Jeroboam's army attacking both in front and back. So they cried out to the LORD, and the priests blew the trumpets. [15]Then the men of Judah gave a battle cry. When they shouted, God caused Jeroboam and the army of Israel to run away from Abijah and the army of Judah. [16]When the army of Israel ran away from the men of Judah, God handed them over to Judah. [17]Abijah's army struck Israel so that five hundred thousand of Israel's best men were killed. [18]So at that time the people of Israel were defeated. And the people of Judah won, because they depended on the LORD, the God of their ancestors.

[19]Abijah's army chased Jeroboam's army and captured from him the towns of Bethel, Jeshanah, and Ephron, and the small villages near them. [20]Jeroboam never became strong again while Abijah was alive. The LORD struck Jeroboam, and he died.

[21]But Abijah became strong. He married fourteen women and was the father of twenty-two sons and sixteen daughters. [22]Everything else Abijah did—what he said and what he did—is recorded in the writings of the prophet Iddo.

14 Abijah died and was buried in Jerusalem. His son Asa became king in his place, and there was peace in the country for ten years during Asa's time.

Asa King of Judah

[2]Asa did what the LORD his God said was good and right. [3]He removed the foreign altars and the places where gods were worshiped. He smashed the stone pillars that honored other gods, and he tore down the Asherah[d] idols. [4]Asa commanded the people of Judah to follow the LORD, the God of their ancestors, and to obey his teachings and commandments. [5]He also removed the places where gods were worshiped and the incense altars from every town in Judah. So the kingdom had peace while Asa was king. [6]Asa built strong, walled cities in Judah during the time of peace. He had no war in these years, because the LORD gave him peace.

[7]Asa said to the people of Judah, "Let's build up these towns and put walls around them. Let's make towers, gates, and bars in the gates. This country is ours, because we have obeyed the LORD our God. We have followed him, and he has given us peace all around." So they built and had success.

[8]Asa had an army of three hundred thousand men from Judah and two hundred eighty thousand men from Benjamin. The men from Judah carried large shields and spears. The men from

Benjamin carried small shields and bows and arrows. All of them were brave fighting men.

⁹Then Zerah from Cush came out to fight them with an enormous army and three hundred chariots. They came as far as the town of Mareshah.

---

¹⁰So Asa went out to fight Zerah and prepared for battle in the Valley of Zephathah at Mareshah.

¹¹Asa called out to the LORD his God, saying, "LORD, only you can help weak people against the strong. Help us, LORD our God, because we depend on you. We fight against this enormous army in your name. LORD, you are our God. Don't let anyone win against you."

¹²So the LORD defeated the Cushites when Asa's army from Judah attacked them, and the Cushites ran away. ¹³Asa's army chased them as far as the town of Gerar. So many Cushites were killed that the army could not fight again; they were crushed by the LORD and his army. Asa and his army carried many valuable things away from the enemy. ¹⁴They destroyed all the towns near Gerar, because the people living in these towns were afraid of the LORD. Since these towns had many valuable things, Asa's army took them away. ¹⁵Asa's army also attacked the camps where the shepherds lived and took many sheep and camels. Then they returned to Jerusalem.

Asa's Changes

15 The Spirit*d* of God entered Azariah son of Oded. ²Azariah went to meet Asa and said, "Listen to me, Asa and all you people of Judah and Benjamin. The LORD is with you when you are with him. If you obey him, you will find him, but if you leave him, he will leave you. ³For a long time Israel was without the true God and without a priest to teach them and without the teachings. ⁴But when they were in trouble, they turned to the LORD, the God of Israel. They looked for him and found him. ⁵In those days no one could travel safely. There was much trouble in all the nations. ⁶One nation would destroy another nation, and one city would destroy another city, because God troubled them with all kinds of distress. ⁷But you should be strong. Don't give up, because you will get a reward for your good work."

⁸Asa felt brave when he heard these words and the message from Azariah son of Oded the prophet.*d* So he removed the hateful idols from all of Judah and Benjamin and from the towns he had captured in the hills of Ephraim. He repaired the LORD's altar that was in front of the porch of the Temple*d* of the LORD.

⁹Then Asa gathered all the people from Judah and Benjamin and from the tribes*d* of Ephraim, Manasseh, and Simeon who were living in Judah. Many people came to Asa even from Israel, because they saw that the LORD, Asa's God, was with him.

¹⁰Asa and these people gathered in Jerusalem in the third month of the fifteenth year of Asa's rule. ¹¹At that time they sacrificed to the LORD seven hundred bulls and seven thousand sheep and goats from the valuable things Asa's army had taken from their enemies. ¹²Then they made an agreement to obey the LORD, the God of their ancestors, with their whole being. ¹³Anyone who refused to obey the LORD, the God of Israel, was to be killed. It did not matter if that person was important or unimportant, a man or woman. ¹⁴Then Asa and the people made a promise before the LORD, shouting with a loud voice and blowing trumpets and sheep's horns. ¹⁵All the people of Judah were happy about the promise, because they had promised with all their heart. They looked for God and found him. So the LORD gave them peace in all the country.

¹⁶King Asa also removed Maacah, his grandmother, from being queen mother, because she had made a terrible Asherah*d* idol. Asa cut down that idol, smashed it into pieces, and burned it in the Kidron Valley. ¹⁷But the places of worship to gods were not removed from Judah. Even so, Asa was faithful all his life.

¹⁸Asa brought into the Temple of God the gifts he and his father had given: silver, gold, and utensils.

¹⁹There was no more war until the thirty-fifth year of Asa's rule.

Asa's Last Years

16 In the thirty-sixth year of Asa's rule, Baasha king of Israel attacked Judah. He made the town of Ramah strong so he could keep people from leaving or entering Judah, Asa's country.

²Asa took silver and gold from the treasuries of the Temple*d* of the LORD and out of his own palace. Then he sent it with messengers to Ben-Hadad king of Aram, who lived in Damascus. Asa said, ³"Let there be a treaty between you and me as there was between my father and your father. I am sending you silver and gold. Break your treaty with Baasha king of Israel so he will leave my land."

⁴Ben-Hadad agreed with King Asa and sent the commanders of his armies to attack the towns of Israel. They defeated the towns of Ijon, Dan, and

Abel Beth Maacah, and all the towns in Naphtali where treasures were stored. ⁵When Baasha heard about this, he stopped building up Ramah and left his work. ⁶Then King Asa brought all the people of Judah to Ramah, and they carried away the rocks and wood that Baasha had used. And they used them to build up Geba and Mizpah.

⁷At that time Hanani the seer*ᵈ* came to Asa king of Judah and said to him, "You depended on the king of Aram to help you and not on the LORD your God. So the king of Aram's army escaped from you. ⁸The Cushites and Libyans had a large and powerful army and many chariots and horsemen. But you depended on the LORD to help you, so he handed them over to you. ⁹The LORD searches all the earth for people who have given themselves completely to him. He wants to make them strong. Asa, you did a foolish thing, so from now on you will have wars."

¹⁰Asa was angry with Hanani the seer because of what he had said; he was so angry that he put Hanani in prison. And Asa was cruel to some of the people at the same time.

¹¹Everything Asa did as king, from the beginning to the end, is written in the book of the kings of Judah and Israel. ¹²In the thirty-ninth year of his rule, Asa got a disease in his feet. Though his disease was very bad, he did not ask for help from

> **SIDELIGHT:** Did King Asa have one of the world's first cases of athlete's foot (2 Chronicles 16:12)? Probably not. He may have had dropsy, which makes the feet swell like a tumor. Or the phrase may be a polite way to say he had a venereal disease.

the LORD, but only from the doctors. ¹³Then Asa died in the forty-first year of his rule. ¹⁴The people buried Asa in the tomb he had made for himself in Jerusalem. They laid him on a bed filled with spices and different kinds of mixed perfumes, and they made a large fire to honor him.

Jehoshaphat King of Judah

17 Jehoshaphat, Asa's son, became king of Judah in his place. Jehoshaphat made Judah strong so they could fight against Israel. ²He put troops in all the strong, walled cities of Judah, in the land of Judah, and in the towns of Ephraim that his father Asa had captured.

³The LORD was with Jehoshaphat, because he lived as his ancestor David had lived when he first became king. Jehoshaphat did not ask for help

from the Baal*ᵈ* idols, ⁴but from the God of his father. He obeyed God's commands and did not live as the people of Israel lived. ⁵The LORD made Jehoshaphat a strong king over Judah. All the people of Judah brought gifts to Jehoshaphat, so he had much wealth and honor. ⁶He wanted very much to obey the LORD. He also removed the places for worshiping gods and the Asherah*ᵈ* idols from Judah.

⁷During the third year of his rule, Jehoshaphat sent his officers to teach in the towns of Judah. These officers were Ben-Hail, Obadiah, Zechariah, Nethanel, and Micaiah. ⁸Jehoshaphat sent with them these Levites: Shemaiah, Nethaniah, Zebadiah, Asahel, Shemiramoth, Jehonathan, Adonijah, Tobijah, and Tob-Adonijah. He also sent the priests Elishama and Jehoram. ⁹These leaders, Levites, and priests taught the people in Judah. They took the Book of the Teachings of the LORD and went through all the towns of Judah and taught the people.

¹⁰The nations near Judah were afraid of the LORD, so they did not start a war against Jehoshaphat. ¹¹Some of the Philistines brought gifts and silver to Jehoshaphat as he demanded. Some Arabs brought him flocks: seventy-seven hundred sheep and seventy-seven hundred goats.

¹²Jehoshaphat grew more and more powerful. He built strong, walled cities and towns for storing supplies in Judah. ¹³He kept many supplies in the towns of Judah, and he kept trained soldiers in Jerusalem. ¹⁴These soldiers were listed by families. From the families of Judah, these were the commanders of groups of a thousand men: Adnah was the commander of three hundred thousand soldiers; ¹⁵Jehohanan was the commander of two hundred eighty thousand soldiers; ¹⁶Amasiah was the commander of two hundred thousand soldiers. Amasiah son of Zicri had volunteered to serve the LORD.

¹⁷These were the commanders from the families of Benjamin: Eliada, a brave soldier, had two hundred thousand soldiers who used bows and shields. ¹⁸And Jehozabad had one hundred eighty thousand men armed for war.

¹⁹All these soldiers served King Jehoshaphat. The king also put other men in the strong, walled cities through all of Judah.

Micaiah Warns King Ahab

18 Jehoshaphat had much wealth and honor, and he made an agreement with King Ahab through marriage.*ⁿ* ²A few years later Jehoshaphat went to visit Ahab in Samaria. Ahab sacrificed many sheep and cattle as a great feast to honor Jehoshaphat and the people with him. He encouraged Jehoshaphat to attack Ramoth in

---

agreement . . . through marriage Jehoshaphat's son Jehoram married Athaliah, Ahab's daughter. See 2 Chronicles 21:6.

Gilead. ³Ahab king of Israel asked Jehoshaphat king of Judah, "Will you go with me to attack Ramoth in Gilead?"

Jehoshaphat answered, "I will go with you, and my soldiers are yours. We will join you in the battle." ⁴Jehoshaphat also said to Ahab, "But first we should ask if this is the Lᴏʀᴅ's will."

⁵So King Ahab called four hundred prophets[d] together and asked them, "Should we go to war against Ramoth in Gilead or not?"

They answered, "Go, because God will hand them over to you."

⁶But Jehoshaphat asked, "Isn't there a prophet of the Lᴏʀᴅ here? Let's ask him what we should do."

⁷Then King Ahab said to Jehoshaphat, "There is one other prophet. We could ask the Lᴏʀᴅ through him, but I hate him. He never prophesies anything good about me, but always something bad. He is Micaiah son of Imlah."

Jehoshaphat said, "King Ahab, you shouldn't say that!"

⁸So Ahab king of Israel told one of his officers to bring Micaiah to him at once.

⁹Ahab king of Israel and Jehoshaphat king of Judah had on their royal robes and were sitting on their thrones at the threshing[d] floor, near the entrance to the gate of Samaria. All the prophets were standing before them speaking their messages. ¹⁰Zedekiah son of Kenaanah had made some iron horns. He said to Ahab, "This is what the Lᴏʀᴅ says: 'You will use these horns to fight the Arameans until they are destroyed.'"

¹¹All the other prophets said the same thing, "Attack Ramoth in Gilead and win, because the Lᴏʀᴅ will hand the Arameans over to you."

¹²The messenger who had gone to get Micaiah said to him, "All the other prophets are saying King Ahab will win. You should agree with them and give the king a good answer."

¹³But Micaiah answered, "As surely as the Lᴏʀᴅ lives, I can tell him only what my God says."

¹⁴When Micaiah came to Ahab, the king asked him, "Micaiah, should we attack Ramoth in Gilead or not?"

Micaiah answered, "Attack and win! They will be handed over to you."

¹⁵But Ahab said to Micaiah, "How many times do I have to tell you to speak only the truth to me in the name of the Lᴏʀᴅ?"

¹⁶So Micaiah answered, "I saw the army of Israel scattered over the hills like sheep without a shepherd. The Lᴏʀᴅ said, 'They have no leaders. They should go home and not fight.'"

¹⁷Then Ahab king of Israel said to Jehoshaphat, "I told you! He never prophesies anything good about me, but only bad."

¹⁸But Micaiah said, "Hear the message from the Lᴏʀᴅ: I saw the Lᴏʀᴅ sitting on his throne with his heavenly army standing on his right and on his left. ¹⁹The Lᴏʀᴅ said, 'Who will trick King Ahab of Israel into attacking Ramoth in Gilead where he will be killed?'

"Some said one thing; some said another. ²⁰Then one spirit came and stood before the Lᴏʀᴅ and said, 'I will trick him.'

"The Lᴏʀᴅ asked, 'How will you do it?'

²¹"The spirit answered, 'I will go to Ahab's prophets and make them tell lies.'

"So the Lᴏʀᴅ said, 'You will succeed in tricking him. Go and do it.'"

²²Micaiah said, "Ahab, the Lᴏʀᴅ has made your prophets lie to you, and the Lᴏʀᴅ has decided that disaster should come to you."

²³Then Zedekiah son of Kenaanah went up to Micaiah and slapped him in the face. Zedekiah said, "Has the Lᴏʀᴅ's Spirit[d] left me to speak through you?"

²⁴Micaiah answered, "You will find out on the day you go to hide in an inside room."

²⁵Then Ahab king of Israel ordered, "Take Micaiah and send him to Amon, the governor of the city, and to Joash, the king's son. ²⁶Tell them I said to put this man in prison and give him only bread and water until I return safely from the battle."

²⁷Micaiah said, "Ahab, if you come back safely from the battle, the Lᴏʀᴅ has not spoken through me. Remember my words, all you people!"

Ahab Is Killed

²⁸So Ahab king of Israel and Jehoshaphat king of Judah went to Ramoth in Gilead. ²⁹King Ahab said to Jehoshaphat, "I will go into battle, but I will wear other clothes so no one will recognize me. But you wear your royal clothes." So Ahab wore other clothes, and they went into battle.

³⁰The king of Aram ordered his chariot commanders, "Don't fight with anyone—important or unimportant—except the king of Israel." ³¹When these commanders saw Jehoshaphat, they thought he was the king of Israel, so they turned to attack him. But Jehoshaphat began shouting, and the Lᴏʀᴅ helped him. God made the chariot commanders turn away from Jehoshaphat. ³²When they saw he was not King Ahab, they stopped chasing him.

³³By chance, a soldier shot an arrow which hit Ahab king of Israel between the pieces of his armor. King Ahab said to his chariot driver, "Turn around and get me out of the battle, because I am hurt!" ³⁴The battle continued all day. King Ahab held himself up in his chariot and faced the Arameans until evening. Then he died at sunset.

19 Jehoshaphat king of Judah came back safely to his palace in Jerusalem. ²Jehu son of Hanani, a seer,[d] went out to meet him and said to the king, "Why did you help evil people? Why do you love those who hate the LORD? That is the reason the LORD is angry with you. ³But there is some good in you. You took the Asherah*d* idols out of this country, and you have tried to obey God."

Jehoshaphat Chooses Judges

⁴Jehoshaphat lived in Jerusalem. He went out again to be with the people, from Beersheba to the mountains of Ephraim, and he turned them back to the LORD, the God of their ancestors. ⁵Jehoshaphat appointed judges in all the land, in each of the strong, walled cities of Judah. ⁶Jehoshaphat said to them, "Watch what you do, because you are not judging for people but for the LORD. He will be with you when you make a decision. ⁷Now let each of you fear the LORD. Watch what you do, because the LORD our God wants people to be fair. He wants all people to be treated the same, and he doesn't want decisions influenced by money."

⁸And in Jerusalem Jehoshaphat appointed some of the Levites, priests, and leaders of Israelite families to be judges. They were to decide cases about the law of the LORD and settle problems between the people who lived in Jerusalem. ⁹Jehoshaphat commanded them, "You must always serve the LORD completely, and you must fear him. ¹⁰Your people living in the cities will bring you cases about killing, about the teachings, commands, rules, or some other law. In all these cases you must warn the people not to sin against the LORD. If you don't, he will be angry with you and your people. But if you warn them, you won't be guilty.

¹¹"Amariah, the leading priest, will be over you in all cases about the LORD. Zebadiah son of Ishmael, a leader in the tribe*d* of Judah, will be over you in all cases about the king. Also, the Levites will serve as officers for you. Have courage. May the LORD be with those who do what is right."

Jehoshaphat Faces War

20 Later the Moabites, Ammonites, and some Meunites came to start a war with Jehoshaphat. ²Messengers came and told Jehoshaphat, "A large army is coming against you from Edom, from the other side of the Dead Sea.*d* They are already in Hazazon Tamar!" (Hazazon Tamar is also called En Gedi.) ³Jehoshaphat was afraid, so he decided to ask the LORD what to do. He announced that no one in Judah should eat during this special time of prayer to God. ⁴The people of Judah came together to ask the LORD for help; they came from every town in Judah.

⁵The people of Judah and Jerusalem met in front of the new courtyard in the Temple*d* of the LORD. Then Jehoshaphat stood up, ⁶and he said,

"LORD, God of our ancestors, you are the God in heaven. You rule over all the kingdoms of the nations. You have power and strength, so no one can stand against you. ⁷Our God, you forced out the people who lived in this land as your people Israel moved in. And you gave this land forever to the descendants*d* of your friend Abraham. ⁸They lived in this land and built a Temple for you. They said, ⁹'If trouble comes upon us, or war, punishment, sickness, or hunger, we will stand before you and before this Temple where you have chosen to be worshiped. We will cry out to you when we are in trouble. Then you will hear and save us.'

¹⁰"But now here are men from Ammon, Moab, and Edom. You wouldn't let the Israelites enter their lands when the Israelites came from Egypt. So the Israelites turned away and did not destroy them. ¹¹But see how they repay us for not destroying them! They have come to force us out of your land, which you gave us as our own. ¹²Our God, punish those people. We have no power against this large army that is attacking us. We don't know what to do, so we look to you for help."

¹³All the men of Judah stood before the LORD with their babies, wives, and children. ¹⁴Then the Spirit*d* of the LORD entered Jahaziel. (Jahaziel was Zechariah's son. Zechariah was Benaiah's son. Benaiah was Jeiel's son, and Jeiel was Mattaniah's son.) Jahaziel, a Levite and a descendant of Asaph, stood up in the meeting. ¹⁵He said, "Listen to me, King Jehoshaphat and all you people living in Judah and Jerusalem. The LORD says this to you: 'Don't be afraid or discouraged because of this large army. The battle is not your battle, it is God's. ¹⁶Tomorrow go down there and fight those people. They will come up through the Pass of Ziz. You will find them at the end of the ravine that leads to the Desert of Jeruel. ¹⁷You won't need to fight in this battle. Just stand strong in your places, and you will see the LORD save you. Judah and Jerusalem, don't be afraid or discouraged, because the LORD is with you. So go out against those people tomorrow.' "

¹⁸Jehoshaphat bowed facedown on the ground. All the people of Judah and Jerusalem bowed down before the LORD and worshiped him. ¹⁹Then some Levites from the Kohathite and Korahite people stood up and praised the LORD, the God of Israel, with very loud voices.

²⁰Jehoshaphat's army went out into the Desert of Tekoa early in the morning. As they were starting out, Jehoshaphat stood and said, "Listen to me, people of Judah and Jerusalem. Have faith in the LORD your God, and you will stand strong. Have faith in his prophets,*d* and you will succeed." ²¹Jehoshaphat listened to the people's advice. Then he chose men to be singers to the LORD, to praise him because he is holy and won-

derful. As they marched in front of the army, they said,

"Thank the LORD,
because his love continues forever."

22As they began to sing and praise God, the LORD set ambushes for the people of Ammon, Moab, and Edom who had come to attack Judah. And they were defeated. 23The Ammonites and Moabites attacked the Edomites, destroying them completely. After they had killed the Edomites, they killed each other.

24When the men from Judah came to a place where they could see the desert, they looked at the enemy's large army. But they only saw dead bodies lying on the ground; no one had escaped. 25When Jehoshaphat and his army came to take their valuables, they found many supplies, much clothing, and other valuable things. There was more than they could carry away; there was so much it took three days to gather it all. 26On the fourth day Jehoshaphat and his army met in the Valley of Beracah and praised the LORD. That is why that place has been called the Valley of Beracah[n] to this day.

27Then Jehoshaphat led all the men from Judah and Jerusalem back to Jerusalem. The LORD had made them happy because their enemies were defeated. 28They entered Jerusalem with harps, lyres,[d] and trumpets and went to the Temple of the LORD.

29When all the kingdoms of the lands around them heard how the LORD had fought Israel's enemies, they feared God. 30So Jehoshaphat's kingdom was not at war. His God gave him peace from all the countries around him.

Jehoshaphat's Rule Ends

31Jehoshaphat ruled over the country of Judah. He was thirty-five years old when he became king, and he ruled in Jerusalem for twenty-five years. His mother's name was Azubah daughter of Shilhi. 32Jehoshaphat was good like his father Asa, and he did what the LORD said was right. 33But the places where gods were worshiped were not removed, and the people did not really want to follow the God of their ancestors.

34The other things Jehoshaphat did as king, from the beginning to the end, are written in the records of Jehu son of Hanani, which are in the book of the kings of Israel.

35Later, Jehoshaphat king of Judah made a treaty with Ahaziah king of Israel, which was a wrong thing to do. 36Jehoshaphat agreed with Ahaziah to build trading ships, which they built in the town of Ezion Geber. 37Then Eliezer son of Dodavahu from the town of Mareshah spoke

against Jehoshaphat. He said, "Jehoshaphat, because you joined with Ahaziah, the LORD will destroy what you have made." The ships were wrecked so they could not sail out to trade.

21 Jehoshaphat died and was buried with his ancestors in Jerusalem, the city of David. Then his son Jehoram became king in his place. 2Jehoram's brothers were Azariah, Jehiel, Zechariah, Azariahu, Michael, and Shephatiah. They were the sons of Jehoshaphat king of Judah. 3Jehoshaphat gave his sons many gifts of silver, gold, and valuable things, and he gave them strong, walled cities in Judah. But Jehoshaphat gave the kingdom to Jehoram, because he was the first son.

Jehoram King of Judah

4When Jehoram took control of his father's kingdom, he killed all his brothers with a sword and also killed some of the leaders of Judah. 5He was thirty-two years old when he began to rule, and he ruled eight years in Jerusalem. 6He followed in the ways of the kings of Israel, just as the family of Ahab had done, because he married Ahab's daughter. Jehoram did what the LORD said was wrong. 7But the LORD would not destroy David's family because of the agreement he had made with David. He had promised that one of David's descendants[d] would always rule.

8In Jehoram's time, Edom broke away from Judah's rule and chose their own king. 9So Jehoram went to Edom with all his commanders and chariots. The Edomites surrounded him and his chariot commanders, but Jehoram got up and attacked the Edomites at night. 10From then until now the country of Edom has fought against the rule of Judah. At the same time the people of Libnah also broke away from Jehoram because Jehoram left the LORD, the God of his ancestors.

11Jehoram also built places to worship gods on the hills in Judah. He led the people of Jerusalem to sin, and he led the people of Judah away from the LORD. 12Then Jehoram received this letter from Elijah the prophet:

This is what the LORD, the God of your ancestor David, says, "Jehoram, you have not lived as your father Jehoshaphat lived and as Asa king of Judah lived. 13But you have lived as the kings of Israel lived, leading the people of Judah and Jerusalem to sin against God, as Ahab and his family did. You have killed *your brothers, and they were better* than you. 14So now the LORD is about to punish your people, your children, wives, and everything you own. 15You will have a terrible disease in your intestines that will

---

Beracah This name means "blessing" or "praise."

become worse every day. Finally it will cause your intestines to come out."

16The LORD caused the Philistines and the Arabs who lived near the Cushites to be angry with Jehoram. 17So the Philistines and Arabs attacked Judah and carried away all the wealth of Jehoram's palace, as well as his sons and wives. Only Jehoram's youngest son, Ahaziah, was left.

18After these things happened, the LORD gave Jehoram a disease in his intestines that could not be cured. 19After he was sick for two years, Jehoram's intestines came out because of the disease, and he died in terrible pain. The people did not make a fire to honor Jehoram as they had done for his ancestors.

20Jehoram was thirty-two years old when he became king, and he ruled eight years in Jerusalem. No one was sad when he died. He was buried in Jerusalem, but not in the graves for the kings.

Ahaziah King of Judah

22 The people of Jerusalem chose Ahaziah, Jehoram's youngest son, to be king in his place. The robbers who had come with the Arabs to attack Jehoram's camp had killed all of Jehoram's older sons. So Ahaziah began to rule Judah. 2Ahaziah was twenty-two years old when he became king, and he ruled one year in Jerusalem. His mother's name was Athaliah, a granddaughter of Omri. 3Ahaziah followed the ways of Ahab's family, because his mother encouraged him to do wrong. 4Ahaziah did what the LORD said was wrong, as Ahab's family had done. They gave advice to Ahaziah after his father died, and their bad advice led to his death. 5Following their advice, Ahaziah went with Joram son of Ahab to Ramoth in Gilead, where they fought against Hazael king of Aram. The Arameans wounded Joram. 6So Joram returned to Jezreel to heal from the wounds he received at Ramoth when he fought Hazael king of Aram.

Ahaziah son of Jehoram and king of Judah went down to visit Joram son of Ahab at Jezreel because he had been wounded.

7God caused Ahaziah's death when he went to visit Joram. Ahaziah arrived and went out with Joram to meet Jehu son of Nimshi, whom the LORD had appointed to destroy Ahab's family. 8While Jehu was punishing Ahab's family, he found the leaders of Judah and the sons of Ahaziah's relatives who served Ahaziah, and Jehu killed them all. 9Then Jehu looked for Ahaziah. Jehu's men caught him hiding in Samaria, so they brought him to Jehu. Then they killed and buried him. They said, "Ahaziah is a descendant*d* of Jehoshaphat, and Jehoshaphat obeyed the LORD with all his heart." No one in Ahaziah's family had the power to take control of the kingdom of Judah.

Athaliah and Joash

10When Ahaziah's mother, Athaliah, saw that her son was dead, she killed all the royal family in Judah. 11But Jehosheba, King Jehoram's daughter, took Joash, Ahaziah's son. She stole him from among the other sons of the king who were going to be murdered and put him and his nurse in a bedroom. So Jehosheba, who was King Jehoram's daughter and Ahaziah's sister and the wife of Jehoiada the priest, hid Joash so Athaliah could not kill him. 12He hid with them in the Temple*d* of God for six years. During that time Athaliah ruled the land.

23 In the seventh year Jehoiada decided to do something. He made an agreement with the commanders of the groups of a hundred men: Azariah son of Jeroham, Ishmael son of Jehohanan, Azariah son of Obed, Maaseiah son of Adaiah, and Elishaphat son of Zicri. 2They went around in Judah and gathered the Levites from all the towns, and they gathered the leaders of the families of Judah. Then they went to Jerusalem. 3All the people together made an agreement with the king in the Temple of God.

Jehoiada said to them, "The king's son will rule, as the LORD promised about David's descendants.*d* 4Now this is what you must do: You priests and Levites go on duty on the Sabbath.*d* A third of you will guard the doors. 5A third of you will be at the king's palace, and a third of you will be at the Foundation Gate. All the other people will stay in the courtyards of the Temple of the LORD. 6Don't let anyone come into the Temple of the LORD except the priests and Levites who serve. They may come because they have been made ready to serve the LORD, but all the others must do the job the LORD has given them. 7The Levites must stay near the king, each man with his weapon in his hand. If anyone tries to enter the Temple, kill him. Stay close to the king when he goes in and when he goes out."

Joash Becomes King

8The Levites and all the people of Judah obeyed

everything Jehoiada the priest had commanded. He did not excuse anyone from the groups of the priests. So each commander took his men who came on duty on the Sabbath with those who went off duty on the Sabbath. ⁹Jehoiada gave the commanders of a hundred men the spears and the large and small shields that had belonged to King David and that were kept in the Temple of God. ¹⁰Then Jehoiada told the men where to stand, each man with his weapon in his hand. There were guards from the south side of the Temple to the north side. They stood by the altar and the Temple and around the king.

¹¹Jehoiada and his sons brought out the king's son and put the crown on him and gave him a copy of the agreement. Then they appointed him king and poured olive oil on him and shouted, "Long live the king!"

¹²When Athaliah heard the noise of the people running and praising the king, she went to them at the Temple of the Lord. ¹³She looked, and there was the king standing by his pillar at the entrance. The officers and the trumpeters were standing beside him, and all the people of the land were happy and blowing trumpets. The singers were playing musical instruments and leading praises. Then Athaliah tore her clothes and screamed, "Traitors! Traitors!"

¹⁴Jehoiada the priest sent out the commanders of a hundred men, who led the army. He said, "Surround her with soldiers and take her out of the Temple area. Kill with a sword anyone who follows her." He had said, "Don't put Athaliah to death in the Temple of the Lord." ¹⁵So they caught her when she came to the entrance of the Horse Gate near the palace. There they put her to death.

¹⁶Then Jehoiada made an agreement with the people and the king that they would be the Lord's special people. ¹⁷All the people went to the temple of Baalᵈ and tore it down, smashing the altars and idols. They killed Mattan, the priest of Baal, in front of the altars.

¹⁸Then Jehoiada chose the priests, who were Levites, to be responsible for the Temple of the Lord. David had given them duties in the Temple of the Lord. They were to offer the burnt offerings to the Lord as the Teachings of Moses commanded, and they were to offer them with much joy and singing as David had commanded. ¹⁹Jehoiada put guards at the gates of the Temple of the Lord so that anyone who was uncleanᵈ in any way could not enter.

²⁰Jehoiada took with him the commanders of a hundred men, the important men, the rulers of the people, and all the people of the land to take the king out of the Temple of the Lord. They went through the Upper Gate into the palace, and then they seated the king on the throne. ²¹So all the people of the land were very happy, and Jerusalem had peace, because Athaliah had been put to death with the sword.

Joash Repairs the Temple

24 Joash was seven years old when he became king, and he ruled forty years in Jerusalem. His mother's name was Zibiah, and she was from Beersheba. ²Joash did what the Lord said was right as long as Jehoiada the priest was alive. ³Jehoiada chose two wives for Joash, and Joash had sons and daughters.

⁴Later, Joash decided to repair the Templeᵈ of the Lord. ⁵He called the priests and the Levites together and said to them, "Go to the towns of Judah and gather the money all the Israelites have to pay every year. Use it to repair the Temple of your God. Do this now." But the Levites did not hurry.

⁶So King Joash called for Jehoiada the leading priest and said to him, "Why haven't you made the Levites bring in from Judah and Jerusalem the tax money that Moses, the Lord's servant, and the people of Israel used for the Holy Tent?"ᵈ

⁷In the past the sons of wicked Athaliah had broken into the Temple of God and used its holy things for worshiping the Baalᵈ idols.

⁸King Joash commanded that a box for contributions be made. They put it outside, at the gate of the Temple of the Lord. ⁹Then the Levites made an announcement in Judah and Jerusalem, telling people to bring to the Lord the tax money Moses, the servant of God, had made the Israelites give while they were in the desert. ¹⁰All the officers and people were happy to bring their money, and they put it in the box until the box was full. ¹¹When the Levites would take the box to the king's officers, they would see that it was full of money. Then the king's royal secretary and the leading priest's officer would come and take out the money and return the box to its place. They did this often and gathered much money. ¹²King Joash and Jehoiada gave the money to the people who worked on the Temple of the Lord. And they hired stoneworkers and carpenters to repair the Temple of the Lord. They also hired people to work with iron and bronze to repair the Temple.

¹³The people worked hard, and the work to repair the Temple went well. They rebuilt the Temple of God to be as it was before, but even stronger. ¹⁴When the workers finished, they brought the money that was left to King Joash and Jehoiada. They used that money to make utensils for the Temple of the Lord, utensils for the service in the Temple and for the burnt offerings, and bowls and other utensils from gold and silver. Burnt offerings were given every day in the Temple of the Lord while Jehoiada was alive.

15Jehoiada grew old and lived many years. Then he died when he was one hundred thirty years old. 16Jehoiada was buried in Jerusalem with the kings, because he had done much good in Judah for God and his Temple.

Joash Does Evil

17After Jehoiada died, the officers of Judah came and bowed down to King Joash, and he listened to them. 18The king and these leaders stopped worshiping in the Temple*d* of the LORD, the God of their ancestors. Instead, they began to worship the Asherah*d* idols and other idols. Because they did wrong, God was angry with the people of Judah and Jerusalem. 19Even though the LORD sent prophets*d* to the people to turn them back to him and even though the prophets warned them, they refused to listen.

20Then the Spirit*d* of God entered Zechariah son of Jehoiada the priest. Zechariah stood before the people and said, "This is what God says: 'Why do you disobey the LORD's commands? You will not be successful. Because you have left the LORD, he has also left you.' "

21But the king and his officers made plans against Zechariah. At the king's command they threw stones at him in the courtyard of the Temple of the LORD until he died. 22King Joash did not remember Jehoiada's kindness to him, so Joash killed Zechariah, Jehoiada's son. Before Zechariah died, he said, "May the LORD see what you are doing and punish you."

23At the end of the year, the Aramean army came against Joash. They attacked Judah and Jerusalem, killed all the leaders of the people, and sent all the valuable things to their king in Damascus. 24The Aramean army came with only a small group of men, but the LORD handed over to them a very large army from Judah, because the people of Judah had left the LORD, the God of their ancestors. So Joash was punished. 25When the Arameans left, Joash was badly wounded. His own officers made plans against him because he had killed Zechariah son of Jehoiada the priest. So they killed Joash in his own bed. He died and was bur-

---

REBELLION

This Is My Life

"Eleven p.m. No exceptions."

"Eleven? But I'm sixteen! Everyone's gonna laugh at me! Nobody has to be home that early!"

Mitch Rayburn couldn't believe his parents were so unfair. Maybe he had ignored their rules lately, but he was old enough to run his own life.

"I'm leaving!" he yelled and stormed out of the house. After spending the night with a friend, he came home, hoping his parents would be good and worried.

But his dad didn't yell or ask questions. He simply took away Mitch's car keys.

Not to be beaten, Mitch took his life savings of four hundred dollars and bought an old car. It was in bad shape, but he defiantly drove it home. Now what could his parents do?

That night Mitch decided to go cruising in his "new" car. He put the key in the ignition. Nothing happened. And Mitch didn't have any money for repairs. The car sat on the street until the police towed it away.

Mitch never saw his car or his four hundred dollars again. And he didn't drive the family car for two months.

By rebelling against his parents, Mitch lost money and privileges. Read **2 Chronicles 24:17–25** to learn how King Joash's rebellion against God affected his life.

■ What were common factors in Mitch's and Joash's rebellion?

■ Joash's rebellion against God resulted in a murder. If you've ever rebelled against God, what has been a result of that rebellion?

C O N S I D E R . . .

■ evaluating your own life for signs of rebellion against God and then working on ways to get rid of the rebellion.

■ visiting a jail or juvenile detention center and telling inmates that God can forgive them.

F O R   M O R E ,   S E E . . .

■ Proverbs 1:8–9 (p. 568)   ■ 1 Peter 2:13–25 (p. 1304)
■ Romans 3:9–20 (p. 1142)

ied in Jerusalem but not in the graves of the kings.

²⁶The officers who made plans against Joash were Jozabad and Jehozabad. Jozabad was the son of Shimeath, a woman from Ammon. And Jehozabad was the son of Shimrith, a woman from Moab. ²⁷The story of Joash's sons, the great propheciesᵈ against him, and how he repaired the Temple of God are written in the book of the kings. Joash's son Amaziah became king in his place.

Amaziah King of Judah

25 Amaziah was twenty-five years old when he became king, and he ruled for twenty-nine years in Jerusalem. His mother's name was Jehoaddin, and she was from Jerusalem. ²Amaziah did what the Lord said was right, but he did not really want to obey him. ³As soon as Amaziah took strong control of the kingdom, he executed the officers who had murdered his father the king. ⁴But Amaziah did not put to death their children. He obeyed what was written in the Book of Moses, where the Lord commanded, "Parents must not be put to death when their children do wrong, and children must not be put to death when their parents do wrong. Each must die for his own sins."ⁿ

⁵Amaziah gathered the people of Judah together. He grouped all the people of Judah and Benjamin by families, and he put commanders over groups of a thousand and over groups of a hundred. He counted the men who were twenty years old and older. In all there were three hundred thousand soldiers ready to fight and skilled with spears and shields. ⁶Amaziah also hired one hundred thousand soldiers from Israel for about seventy-five hundred pounds of silver. ⁷But a man of God came to Amaziah and said, "My king, don't let the army of Israel go with you. The Lord is not with Israel or the people from the tribeᵈ of Ephraim. ⁸You can make yourself strong for war, but God will defeat you. He has the power to help you or to defeat you."

⁹Amaziah said to the man of God, "But what about the seventy-five hundred pounds of silver I paid to the Israelite army?"

The man of God answered, "The Lord can give you much more than that."

¹⁰So Amaziah sent the Israelite army back home to Ephraim. They were very angry with the people of Judah and went home angry.

¹¹Then Amaziah became very brave and led his army to the Valley of Salt in the country of Edom. There Amaziah's army killed ten thousand Edomites. ¹²The army of Judah also captured ten thousand and took them to the top of a cliff and threw them off so that they split open.

¹³At the same time the Israelite troops that Amaziah had not let fight in the war were robbing towns in Judah. From Samaria to Beth Horon they killed three thousand people and took many valuable things.

¹⁴When Amaziah came home after defeating the Edomites, he brought back the idols they worshiped and started to worship them himself. He bowed down to them and offered sacrifices to them. ¹⁵The Lord was very angry with Amaziah, so he sent a prophetᵈ to him who said, "Why have you asked their gods for help? They could not even save their own people from you!"

¹⁶As the prophet spoke, Amaziah said to him, "We never gave you the job of advising the king. Stop, or you will be killed."

The prophet stopped speaking except to say, "I know that God has decided to destroy you because you have done this. You did not listen to my advice."

¹⁷Amaziah king of Judah talked with those who advised him. Then he sent a message to Jehoash son of Jehoahaz, who was the son of Jehu king of Israel. Amaziah said to Jehoash, "Come, let's meet face to face."

¹⁸Then Jehoash king of Israel answered Amaziah king of Judah, "A thornbush in Lebanon sent a message to a cedar tree in Lebanon. It said, 'Let your daughter marry my son.' But then a wild animal from Lebanon came by, walking on and crushing the thornbush. ¹⁹You say to yourself that you have defeated Edom, but you have become proud, and you brag. But you stay at home! Don't ask for trouble, or you and Judah will be defeated."

²⁰But Amaziah would not listen. God caused this to happen so that Jehoash would defeat Judah, because Judah asked for help from the gods of Edom. ²¹So Jehoash king of Israel went to attack. He and Amaziah king of Judah faced each other in battle at Beth Shemesh in Judah. ²²Israel defeated Judah, and every man of Judah ran away to his home. ²³At Beth Shemesh Jehoash king of Israel captured Amaziah king of Judah. (Amaziah was the son of Joash, who was the son of Ahaziah.) Then Jehoash brought him to Jerusalem. Jehoash broke down the wall of Jerusalem, from the Gate of Ephraim to the Corner Gate, about six hundred feet. ²⁴He took all the gold and silver and all the utensils from the Templeᵈ of God that Obed-Edom had taken care of. He also took the treasures from the palace and some hostages. Then he returned to Samaria.

²⁵Amaziah son of Joash, the king of Judah, lived fifteen years after the death of Jehoash son of Jehoahaz, the king of Israel. ²⁶The other things Amaziah did as king, from the beginning to the end,

---

"Parents ... sins." See Deuteronomy 24:16.

are written in the book of the kings of Judah and Israel. [27]When Amaziah stopped obeying the Lord, the people in Jerusalem made plans against him. So he ran away to the town of Lachish, but they sent men after him to Lachish and killed him. [28]They brought his body back on horses, and he was buried with his ancestors in Jerusalem, the city of David.

Uzziah King of Judah

26 Then all the people of Judah made Uzziah[n] king in place of his father Amaziah. Uzziah was sixteen years old. [2]He rebuilt the town of Elath and made it part of Judah again after Amaziah died.

[3]Uzziah was sixteen years old when he became king, and he ruled fifty-two years in Jerusalem. His mother's name was Jecoliah, and she was

---

☀ **SIDELIGHT:** Wouldn't it be nice if everyone obeyed your slightest command? Uzziah must have felt that way when he became king at age sixteen (2 Chronicles 26:3). Do you suppose his first decree was to outlaw homework?

---

from Jerusalem. [4]He did what the Lord said was right, just as his father Amaziah had done. [5]Uzziah obeyed God while Zechariah was alive, because he taught Uzziah how to respect and obey God. And as long as Uzziah obeyed the Lord, God gave him success.

[6]Uzziah fought a war against the Philistines. He tore down the walls around their towns of Gath, Jabneh, and Ashdod and built new towns near Ashdod and in other places among the Philistines. [7]God helped Uzziah fight the Philistines, the Arabs living in Gur Baal, and the Meunites. [8]Also, the Ammonites made the payments Uzziah demanded. He was very powerful, so his name became famous all the way to the border of Egypt.

[9]Uzziah built towers in Jerusalem at the Corner Gate, the Valley Gate, and where the wall turned, and he made them strong. [10]He also built towers in the desert and dug many wells, because he had many cattle on the western hills and in the plains. He had people who worked his fields and vineyards in the hills and in the fertile lands, because he loved the land.

[11]Uzziah had an army of trained soldiers. They were counted and put in groups by Jeiel the royal secretary and Maaseiah the officer. Hananiah, one of the king's commanders, was their leader. [12]There were twenty-six hundred leaders over the

soldiers. [13]They were in charge of an army of three hundred seven thousand five hundred men who fought with great power to help the king against the enemy. [14]Uzziah gave his army shields, spears, helmets, armor, bows, and stones for their slings. [15]In Jerusalem Uzziah made devices that were invented by clever men. These devices on the towers and corners of the city walls were used to shoot arrows and large rocks. So Uzziah became famous in faraway places, because he had much help until he became powerful.

☀ **SIDELIGHT:** Modern military experts debate whether their weapons are offensive or defensive. But ancient city walls (2 Chronicles 26:15) served both purposes. Massive in size, the walls offered a strong defense against battering and invasion. They also gave people on the walls an offensive position from which to drop rocks, shoot arrows, or pour hot oil on attackers.

---

[16]But when Uzziah became powerful, his pride led to his ruin. He was unfaithful to the Lord his God; he went into the Temple[d] of the Lord to burn incense[d] on the altar for incense. [17]Azariah and eighty other brave priests who served the Lord followed Uzziah into the Temple. [18]They told him he was wrong and said to him, "You don't have the right to burn incense to the Lord. Only the priests, Aaron's descendants,[d] should burn the incense, because they have been made holy. Leave this holy place. You have been unfaithful, and the Lord God will not honor you for this."

[19]Uzziah was standing beside the altar for incense in the Temple of the Lord, and in his hand was a pan for burning incense. He was very angry with the priests. As he was standing in front of the priests, a skin disease broke out on his forehead. [20]Azariah, the leading priest, and all the other priests looked at him and saw the skin disease on his forehead. So they hurried him out of the Temple. Uzziah also rushed out, because the Lord was punishing him. [21]So King Uzziah had the skin disease until the day he died. He had to live in a separate house and could not enter the Temple of the Lord. His son Jotham was in charge of the palace, and he governed the people of the land.

[22]The other things Uzziah did as king, from beginning to end, were written down by the prophet Isaiah son of Amoz. [23]Uzziah died and was buried near his ancestors in a graveyard that

---

Uzziah Also called Azariah.

belonged to the kings. This was because people said, "He had a skin disease." And his son Jotham became king in his place.

Jotham King of Judah

27 Jotham was twenty-five years old when he became king, and he ruled sixteen years in Jerusalem. His mother's name was Jerusha daughter of Zadok. ²Jotham did what the LORD said was right, just as his father Uzziah had done. But Jotham did not enter the Temple*d* of the LORD to burn incense*d* as his father had. But the people continued doing wrong. ³Jotham rebuilt the Upper Gate of the Temple of the LORD, and he added greatly to the wall at Ophel. ⁴He also built towns in the hill country of Judah, as well as walled cities and towers in the forests. ⁵Jotham also fought the king of the Ammonites and defeated them. So each year for three years they gave Jotham about seventy-five hundred pounds of silver, about sixty-two thousand bushels of wheat, and about sixty-two thousand bushels of barley. ⁶Jotham became powerful, because he always obeyed the LORD his God.

⁷The other things Jotham did while he was king and all his wars are written in the book of the kings of Israel and Judah. ⁸Jotham was twenty-five years old when he became king, and he ruled sixteen years in Jerusalem. ⁹Jotham died and was buried in Jerusalem, the city of David. Then Jotham's son Ahaz became king in his place.

Ahaz King of Judah

28 Ahaz was twenty years old when he became king, and he ruled sixteen years in Jerusalem. Unlike his ancestor David, he did not do what the LORD said was right. ²Ahaz did the same things the kings of Israel had done. He made metal idols to worship Baal.*d* ³He burned incense*d* in the Valley of Ben Hinnom and made his children pass through the fire. He did the same hateful sins as the nations had done whom the LORD had forced out of the land ahead of the Israelites. ⁴Ahaz offered sacrifices and burned incense at the places where gods were worshiped, and on the hills, and under every green tree.

⁵So the LORD his God handed over Ahaz to the king of Aram. The Arameans defeated Ahaz and took many people of Judah as prisoners to Damascus.

He also handed over Ahaz to Pekah king of Israel, and Pekah's army killed many soldiers of Ahaz. ⁶*The army of Pekah son of Remaliah killed one hundred twenty thousand brave soldiers from Judah in one day. Pekah defeated them because they had left the LORD, the God of their ancestors.* ⁷Zicri, a warrior from Ephraim, killed King Ahaz's son Maaseiah. He also killed Azrikam, the officer in charge of the palace, and Elkanah, who was

second in command to the king. ⁸The Israelite army captured two hundred thousand of their own relatives. They took women, sons and daughters, and many valuable things from Judah and carried them back to Samaria. ⁹But a prophet*d* of the LORD named Oded was there. He met the Israelite army when it returned to Samaria and said to them, "The LORD, the God of your ancestors, handed Judah over to you, because he was angry with those people. But God has seen the cruel way you killed them. ¹⁰Now you plan to make the people of Judah and Jerusalem your slaves, but you also have sinned against the LORD your God. ¹¹Now listen to me. Send back your brothers and sisters whom you captured, because the LORD is very angry with you."

¹²Then some of the leaders in Ephraim—Azariah son of Jehohanan, Berekiah son of Meshillemoth, Jehizkiah son of Shallum, and Amasa son of Hadlai—met the Israelite soldiers coming home from war. ¹³They warned the soldiers, "Don't bring the prisoners from Judah here. If you do, we will be guilty of sin against the LORD, and that will make our sin and guilt even worse. Our guilt is already so great that he is angry with Israel."

¹⁴So the soldiers left the prisoners and valuable things in front of the officers and people there. ¹⁵The leaders who were named took the prisoners and gave those who were naked the clothes that the Israelite army had taken. They gave the prisoners clothes, sandals, food, drink, and medicine. They put the weak prisoners on donkeys and took them back to their families in Jericho, the city of palm trees. Then they returned home to Samaria.

¹⁶⁻¹⁷At that time the Edomites came again and attacked Judah and carried away prisoners. So King Ahaz sent to the king of Assyria for help. ¹⁸The Philistines also robbed the towns in the western hills and in southern Judah. They captured the towns of Beth Shemesh, Aijalon, Gederoth, Soco, Timnah, and Gimzo, and the villages around them. Then the Philistines lived in those towns. ¹⁹The LORD brought trouble on Judah because Ahaz their king led the people of Judah to sin, and he was unfaithful to the LORD. ²⁰Tiglath-Pileser king of Assyria came to Ahaz, but he gave Ahaz trouble instead of help. ²¹Ahaz took some valuable things from the Temple*d* of the LORD, from the palace, and from the princes, and he gave them to the king of Assyria, but it did not help.

²²During Ahaz's troubles he was even more unfaithful to the LORD. ²³He offered sacrifices to the gods of the people of Damascus, who had defeated him. He thought, "The gods of the kings of Aram helped them. If I offer sacrifices to them, they will help me also." But this brought ruin to Ahaz and all Israel.

²⁴Ahaz gathered the things from the Temple of

God and broke them into pieces. Then he closed the doors of the Temple of the LORD. He made altars and put them on every street corner in Jerusalem. 25In every town in Judah, Ahaz made places for burning sacrifices to worship other gods. So he made the LORD, the God of his ancestors, very angry.

26The other things Ahaz did as king, from beginning to end, are written in the book of the kings of Judah and Israel. 27Ahaz died and was buried in the city of Jerusalem, but not in the graves of the kings of Israel. Ahaz's son Hezekiah became king in his place.

Hezekiah Purifies the Temple

29 Hezekiah was twenty-five years old when he became king, and he ruled twenty-nine years in Jerusalem. His mother's name was Abijah daughter of Zechariah. 2Hezekiah did what the LORD said was right, just as his ancestor David had done.

3Hezekiah opened the doors of the Temple*d* of the LORD and repaired them in the first month of the first year he was king. 4Hezekiah brought in the priests and Levites and gathered them in the courtyard on the east side of the Temple. 5Hezekiah said, "Listen to me, Levites. Make yourselves ready for the LORD's service, and make holy the Temple of the LORD, the God of your ancestors. Remove from the Temple everything that makes it impure. 6Our ancestors were unfaithful to God and did what the LORD said was wrong. They left the LORD and stopped worshiping at the Temple where he lives. They rejected him. 7They shut the doors of the porch of the Temple, and they let the fire go out in the lamps. They stopped burning incense*d* and offering burnt offerings in the holy place to the God of Israel. 8So the LORD became very angry with the people of Judah and Jerusalem, and he punished them. Other people are frightened and shocked by what he did to them. So they insult the people of Judah. You know these things are true. 9That is why our ancestors were killed in battle and our sons, daughters, and wives were taken captive. 10Now I, Hezekiah, have decided to make an agreement with the LORD, the God of Israel, so he will not be angry with us anymore. 11My sons, don't waste any more time. The LORD chose you to stand before him, to serve him, to be his servants, and to burn incense to him."

12These are the Levites who started to work. From the Kohathite family there were Mahath son of Amasai and Joel son of Azariah. From the Merarite family there were Kish son of Abdi and Azariah son of Jehallelel. From the Gershonite family there were Joah son of Zimmah and Eden son of Joah. 13From Elizaphan's family there were Shimri and Jeiel. From Asaph's family there were Zechariah and Mattaniah. 14From Heman's family there were Jehiel and Shimei. From Jeduthun's family there were Shemaiah and Uzziel.

15These Levites gathered their brothers together and made themselves holy for service in the Temple. Then they went into the Temple of the LORD to purify it. They obeyed the king's command that had come from the LORD. 16When the priests went into the Temple of the LORD to purify it, they took out all the unclean*d* things they found in the Temple of the LORD and put them in the Temple courtyard. Then the Levites took these things out to the Kidron Valley. 17Beginning on the first day of the first month, they made the Temple holy for the LORD's service. On the eighth day of the month, they came to the porch of Temple, and for eight more days they made the Temple of the LORD holy. So they finished on the sixteenth day of the first month.

18Then they went to King Hezekiah and said, "We have purified the entire Temple of the LORD, the altar for burnt offerings and its utensils, and the table for the holy bread and all its utensils. 19When Ahaz was king, he was unfaithful to God and removed some things from the Temple. But we have put them back and made them holy for the LORD. They are now in front of the LORD's altar."

20Early the next morning King Hezekiah gathered the leaders of the city and went up to the Temple of the LORD. 21They brought seven bulls, seven male sheep, seven lambs, and seven male goats. These animals were an offering to remove the sin of the people and the kingdom of Judah and to make the Temple ready for service to God. King Hezekiah commanded the priests, the descendants*d* of Aaron, to offer these animals on the LORD's altar. 22So the priests killed the bulls and sprinkled their blood on the altar. They killed the sheep and sprinkled their blood on the altar. Then they killed the lambs and sprinkled their blood on the altar. 23Then the priests brought the male goats for the sin offering before the king and the people there. After the king and the people put their hands on the goats, 24the priests killed them. With the goats' blood they made an offering on the altar to remove the sins of the Israelites so they would belong to God. The king had said that the burnt offering and sin offering should be made for all Israel.

25King Hezekiah put the Levites in the Temple of the LORD with cymbals, harps, and lyres,*d* as David, Gad, and Nathan had commanded. (Gad was the king's seer,*d* and Nathan was a prophet.*d*) This command came from the LORD through his prophets. 26So the Levites stood ready with David's instruments of music, and the priests stood ready with their trumpets.

27Then Hezekiah gave the order to sacrifice the

burnt offering on the altar. When the burnt offering began, the singing to the LORD also began. The trumpets were blown, and the musical instruments of David king of Israel were played. ²⁸All the people worshiped, the singers sang, and the trumpeters blew their trumpets until the burnt offering was finished.

²⁹When the sacrifices were completed, King Hezekiah and everyone with him bowed down and worshiped. ³⁰King Hezekiah and his officers ordered the Levites to praise the LORD, using the words David and Asaph the seer had used. So they praised God with joy and bowed down and worshiped.

³¹Then Hezekiah said, "Now that you people of Judah have given yourselves to the LORD, come near to the Temple of the LORD. Bring sacrifices and offerings, to show thanks to him." So the people brought sacrifices and thank offerings, and anyone who was willing also brought burnt offerings. ³²For burnt offerings they brought a total of seventy bulls, one hundred male sheep, and two hundred lambs; all these animals were sacrificed as burnt offerings to the LORD. ³³The holy offerings totaled six hundred bulls and three thousand sheep and goats. ³⁴There were not enough priests to skin all the animals for the burnt offerings. So their relatives the Levites helped them until the work was finished and other priests could be made holy. The Levites had been more careful to make themselves holy for the LORD's service than the priests. ³⁵There were many burnt offerings along with the fat of fellowship offerings and drink offerings. So the service in the Temple of the LORD began again. ³⁶And Hezekiah and the people were very happy that God had made it happen so quickly for his people.

The Passover Celebration

30 King Hezekiah sent messages to all the people of Israel and Judah, and he wrote letters to the people of Ephraim and Manasseh. Hezekiah invited all these people to come to the Temple*d* of the LORD in Jerusalem to celebrate the Passover*d* for the LORD, the God of Israel. ²King Hezekiah, his officers, and all the people in Jerusalem agreed to celebrate the Passover in the second month. ³They could not celebrate it at the normal time, because not enough priests had made themselves ready to serve the LORD, and the people had not yet gathered in Jerusalem. ⁴This plan satisfied King Hezekiah and all the people. ⁵So they made an announcement everywhere in Israel, from Beersheba to Dan,*n* telling the people to come to Jerusalem to celebrate the Passover for the LORD, the God of Israel. For a long time most of the people had not celebrated the Passover as the law commanded. ⁶At the king's command, the messengers took letters from him and his officers all through Israel and Judah. This is what the letters said:

People of Israel, return to the LORD, the God of Abraham, Isaac, and Israel. Then God will return to you who are still alive, who have escaped from the kings of Assyria. ⁷Don't be like your ancestors or your relatives. They turned against the LORD, the God of their ancestors, so he caused other people to be disgusted with them. You know this is true. ⁸Don't be stubborn as your ancestors were, but obey the LORD willingly. Come to the Temple, which he has made holy forever. Serve the LORD your God so he will not be angry with you. ⁹Come back to the LORD. Then the people who captured your relatives and children will be kind to them and will let them return to this land. The LORD your God is kind and merciful. He will not turn away from you if you return to him.

¹⁰The messengers went to every town in Ephraim and Manasseh, and all the way to Zebulun, but the people laughed at them and made fun of them. ¹¹But some men from Asher, Manasseh, and Zebulun were sorry for what they had done and went to Jerusalem. ¹²And God united all the people of Judah in obeying King Hezekiah and his officers, because their command had come from the LORD.

¹³In the second month a large crowd came together in Jerusalem to celebrate the Feast*d* of Unleavened Bread. ¹⁴The people removed the altars and incense*d* altars to gods in Jerusalem and threw them into the Kidron Valley.

¹⁵They killed the Passover lamb on the fourteenth day of the second month. The priests and the Levites were ashamed, so they made themselves holy and brought burnt offerings into the Temple of the LORD. ¹⁶They took their regular places in the Temple as the Teachings of Moses, the man of God, commanded. The Levites gave the blood of the sacrifices to the priests, who sprinkled it on the altar. ¹⁷Since many people in the crowd had not made themselves holy, the Levites killed the Passover lambs for everyone who was not clean.*d* The Levites made each lamb holy for the LORD. ¹⁸⁻¹⁹Although many people from Ephraim, Manasseh, Issachar, and Zebulun had not purified themselves for the feast, they ate the Passover even though it was against the law. So Hezekiah prayed for them, saying, "LORD, you are good. You are the LORD, the God of our ancestors.

Beersheba to Dan Dan was the city farthest north in Israel, and Beersheba was the city farthest south. So this means all the people of Israel.

Please forgive all those who try to obey you even if they did not make themselves clean as the rules of the Temple command." [20]The Lord listened to Hezekiah's prayer, and he healed the people. [21]The Israelites in Jerusalem celebrated the Feast of Unleavened Bread for seven days with great joy to the Lord. The Levites and priests praised the Lord every day with loud music. [22]Hezekiah encouraged all the Levites who showed they understood well how to do their service for the Lord. The people ate the feast for seven days, offered fellowship offerings, and praised the Lord, the God of their ancestors.

[23]Then all the people agreed to stay seven more days, so they celebrated with joy for seven more days. [24]Hezekiah king of Judah gave one thousand bulls and seven thousand sheep to the people. The officers gave one thousand bulls and ten thousand sheep to the people. Many priests made themselves holy. [25]All the people of Judah, the priests, the Levites, those who came from Israel, the foreigners from Israel, and the foreigners living in Judah were very happy. [26]There was much joy in Jerusalem, because there had not been a celebration like this since the time of Solomon son of David and king of Israel. [27]The priests and Levites stood up and blessed the people, and God heard them because their prayer reached heaven, his holy home.

The Collection for the Priests

31 When the Passover[d] celebration was finished, all the Israelites in Jerusalem went out to the towns of Judah. There they smashed the stone pillars used to worship gods. They cut down the Asherah[d] idols and destroyed the altars and places for worshiping gods in all of Judah, Benjamin, Ephraim, and Manasseh. After they had destroyed all of them, the Israelites returned to their own towns and homes.

[2]King Hezekiah appointed groups of priests and Levites for their special duties. They were to offer burnt offerings and fellowship offerings, to worship, and to give thanks and praise at the gates of the Lord's house. [3]Hezekiah gave some of his own animals for the burnt offerings, which were given every morning and evening, on Sabbath[d] days, during New Moons,[d] and at other feasts commanded in the Lord's Teachings. [4]Hezekiah commanded the people living in Jerusalem to give the priests and Levites the portion that belonged to them. Then the priests and Levites could give all their time to the Lord's Teachings. [5]As soon as the king's command went out to the Israelites, they gave freely of the first portion of their grain, new wine, oil, honey, and everything they grew in their fields. They brought a large amount, one-tenth of everything. [6]The people of Israel and Judah who lived in Judah also brought one-tenth of their cattle and sheep and one-tenth of the holy things that were given to the Lord their God, and they put all of them in piles. [7]The people began the piles in the third month and finished in the seventh month. [8]When Hezekiah and his officers came and saw the piles, they praised the Lord and his people, the people of Israel. [9]Hezekiah asked the priests and Levites about the piles. [10]Azariah, the leading priest from Zadok's family, answered Hezekiah, "Since the people began to bring their offerings to the Temple[d] of the Lord, we have had plenty to eat and plenty left over, because the Lord has blessed his people. So we have all this left over."

[11]Then Hezekiah commanded the priests to prepare the storerooms in the Temple of the Lord. So this was done. [12]Then the priests brought in the offerings and the things given to the Lord and one-tenth of everything the people had given. Conaniah the Levite was in charge of these things, and his brother Shimei was second to him. [13]Conaniah and his brother Shimei were over these supervisors: Jehiel, Azaziah, Nahath, Asahel, Jerimoth, Jozabad, Eliel, Ismakiah, Mahath, and Benaiah. King Hezekiah and Azariah the officer in charge of the Temple of God had chosen them.

[14]Kore son of Imnah the Levite was in charge of the special gifts the people wanted to give to God. He was responsible for giving out the contributions made to the Lord and the holy gifts. Kore was the guard at the East Gate. [15]Eden, Miniamin, Jeshua, Shemaiah, Amariah, and Shecaniah helped Kore in the towns where the priests lived. They gave from what was collected to the other groups of priests, both young and old.

[16]From what was collected, these men also gave to the males three years old and older who had their names in the Levite family histories. They were to enter the Temple of the Lord for their daily service, each group having its own responsibilities. [17]The priests were given their part of the collection, by families, as listed in the family histories. The Levites twenty years old and older were given their part of the collection, based on their responsibilities and their groups. [18]The Levites' babies, wives, sons, and daughters also got part of the collection. This was done for all the Levites who were listed in the family histories, because they always kept themselves ready to serve the Lord.

[19]Some of Aaron's descendants,[d] the priests, lived on the farmlands near the towns or in the towns. Men were chosen by name to give part of the collection to these priests. All the males and those named in the family histories of the Levites received part of the collection.

[20]This is what King Hezekiah did in Judah. He did what was good and right and obedient before

the LORD his God. [21]Hezekiah tried to obey God in his service of the Temple of God, and he tried to obey God's teachings and commands. He gave himself fully to his work for God. So he had success.

Assyria Attacks Judah

32 After Hezekiah did all these things to serve the LORD, Sennacherib king of Assyria came and attacked Judah. He and his army surrounded and attacked the strong, walled cities, hoping to take them for himself. [2]Hezekiah knew that Sennacherib had come to Jerusalem to attack it. [3]So Hezekiah and his officers and army commanders decided to cut off the water from the springs outside the city. So the officers and commanders helped Hezekiah. [4]Many people came and cut off all the springs and the stream that flowed through the land. They said, "The king of Assyria will not find much water when he comes here." [5]Then Hezekiah made Jerusalem stronger. He rebuilt all the broken parts of the wall and put towers on it. He also built another wall outside the first one and strengthened the area that was filled in on the east side of the old part of Jerusalem. He also made many weapons and shields.

[6]Hezekiah put army commanders over the people and met with them at the open place near the city gate. Hezekiah encouraged them, saying, [7]"Be strong and brave. Don't be afraid or worried because of the king of Assyria or his large army. There is a greater power with us than with him. [8]He only has men, but we have the LORD our God to help us and to fight our battles." The people were encouraged by the words of Hezekiah king of Judah.

SIDELIGHT: The Assyrian attack on Lachish (2 Chronicles 32:9) was horrible for its citizens. Archaeologists have found the bones of fifteen hundred bodies in a pit there, a sign of the terrible siege.

---

[9]After this King Sennacherib of Assyria and all his army surrounded and attacked Lachish. Then he sent his officers to Jerusalem with this message for King Hezekiah of Judah and all the people of Judah in Jerusalem:

[10]Sennacherib king of Assyria says this: "You have nothing to trust in to help you. It is no use for you to stay in Jerusalem under attack. [11]Hezekiah says to you, 'The LORD our God will save us from the king of Assyria,' but he is fooling you. If you stay in Jerusalem, you will die from hunger and thirst. [12]Hezekiah himself removed your LORD's places of worship and altars. He told you people of Judah and Jerusalem that you must worship and burn incense[d] on only one altar.

[13]"You know what my ancestors and I have done to all the people in other nations. The gods of those nations could not save their people from my power. [14]My ancestors destroyed those nations; none of their gods could save them from me. So your god cannot save you from my power. [15]Do not let Hezekiah fool you or trick you, and do not believe him. No god of any nation or kingdom has been able to save his people from me or my ancestors. Your god is even less able to save you from me."

[16]Sennacherib's officers said worse things against the LORD God and his servant Hezekiah. [17]King Sennacherib also wrote letters insulting the LORD, the God of Israel. They spoke against him, saying, "The gods of the other nations could not save their people from me. In the same way Hezekiah's god won't be able to save his people from me." [18]Then the king's officers shouted in Hebrew, calling out to the people of Jerusalem who were on the city wall. The officers wanted to scare the people away so they could capture Jerusalem. [19]They spoke about the God of Jerusalem as though he were like the gods the people of the world worshiped, which are made by human hands.

[20]King Hezekiah and the prophet[d] Isaiah son of Amoz prayed to heaven about this. [21]Then the LORD sent an angel who killed all the soldiers, leaders, and officers in the camp of the king of Assyria. So the king went back to his own country in disgrace. When he went into the temple of his god, some of his own sons killed him with a sword.

[22]So the LORD saved Hezekiah and the people in Jerusalem from Sennacherib king of Assyria and from all other people. He took care of them on every side. [23]Many people brought gifts for the LORD to Jerusalem, and they also brought valuable gifts to King Hezekiah of Judah. From then on all the nations respected Hezekiah.

Hezekiah Dies

[24]At that time Hezekiah became so sick he almost died. When he prayed to the LORD, the LORD spoke to him and gave him a sign.[n] [25]But Hezekiah did not thank God for his kindness, because he was so proud. So the LORD was angry with him and the people of Judah and Jerusalem.

---

sign See Isaiah 38:1-8. It tells the story about the sign and how the Lord gave Hezekiah fifteen more years to live.

²⁶But later Hezekiah and the people of Jerusalem were sorry and stopped being proud, so the Lᴏʀᴅ did not punish them while Hezekiah was alive.

²⁷Hezekiah had many riches and much honor. He made treasuries for his silver, gold, gems, spices, shields, and other valuable things. ²⁸He built storage buildings for grain, new wine, and oil and stalls for all the cattle and pens for the sheep. ²⁹He also built many towns. He had many flocks and herds, because God had given Hezekiah much wealth.

³⁰It was Hezekiah who cut off the upper pool of the Gihon spring and made those waters flow straight down to the west side of the older part of Jerusalem. And Hezekiah was successful in everything he did. ³¹But one time the leaders of Babylon sent messengers to Hezekiah, asking him about a strange sign ⁿ that had happened in the land. When they came, God left Hezekiah alone to test him so he could know everything that was in Hezekiah's heart. ⁿ

³²Hezekiah's love for God and the other things he did as king are written in the vision of the prophet ᵈ Isaiah son of Amoz. This is in the book of the kings of Judah and Israel. ³³Hezekiah died and was buried on a hill, where the graves of David's ancestors are. All the people of Judah and Jerusalem honored Hezekiah when he died, and his son Manasseh became king in his place.

Manasseh King of Judah

33 Manasseh was twelve years old when he became king, and he was king for fifty-five years in Jerusalem. ²He did what the Lᴏʀᴅ said was wrong. He did the hateful things the nations had done — the nations that the Lᴏʀᴅ had forced out of the land ahead of the Israelites. ³Manasseh's father, Hezekiah, had torn down the places where gods were worshiped, but Manasseh rebuilt them. He also built altars for the Baal ᵈ gods, and he made Asherah ᵈ idols and worshiped all the stars of the sky and served them. ⁴The Lᴏʀᴅ had said about the Temple, ᵈ "I will be worshiped in Jerusalem forever," but Manasseh built altars in the Temple of the Lᴏʀᴅ. ⁵He built altars to worship the stars in the two courtyards of the Temple of the Lᴏʀᴅ. ⁶He made his children pass through fire in the Valley of Ben Hinnom. He practiced magic and witchcraft ᵈ and told the future by explaining signs and dreams. He got advice from mediums ᵈ and fortune-tellers. He did many things the Lᴏʀᴅ said were wrong, which made the Lᴏʀᴅ angry.

⁷Manasseh carved an idol and put it in the Temple of God. God had said to David and his son Solomon about the Temple, "I will be worshiped

forever in this Temple and in Jerusalem, which I have chosen from all the tribes ᵈ of Israel. ⁸I will never again make the Israelites leave the land I gave to their ancestors. But they must obey everything I have commanded them in all the teachings, rules, and commands I gave them through Moses." ⁹But Manasseh led the people of Judah and Jerusalem to do wrong. They did more evil than the nations the Lᴏʀᴅ had destroyed ahead of the Israelites.

¹⁰The Lᴏʀᴅ spoke to Manasseh and his people, but they did not listen. ¹¹So the Lᴏʀᴅ brought the king of Assyria's army commanders to attack Judah. They captured Manasseh, put hooks in him, placed bronze chains on his hands, and took him to Babylon. ¹²As Manasseh suffered, he begged the Lᴏʀᴅ his God for help and humbled himself before the God of his ancestors. ¹³When Manasseh prayed, the Lᴏʀᴅ heard him and had pity on him. So the Lᴏʀᴅ let him return to Jerusalem and to his kingdom. Then Manasseh knew that the Lᴏʀᴅ is the true God.

¹⁴After that happened, Manasseh rebuilt the outer wall of Jerusalem and made it higher. It was in the valley on the west side of the Gihon spring and went to the entrance of the Fish Gate and around the hill of Ophel. Then he put commanders in all the strong, walled cities in Judah.

¹⁵Manasseh removed the idols of other nations, including the idol in the Temple of the Lᴏʀᴅ. He removed all the altars he had built on the Temple hill and in Jerusalem and threw them out of the city. ¹⁶Then he set up the Lᴏʀᴅ's altar and sacrificed on it fellowship offerings and offerings to show thanks to God. Manasseh commanded all the people of Judah to serve the Lᴏʀᴅ, the God of Israel. ¹⁷The people continued to offer sacrifices at the places of worship, but their sacrifices were only to the Lᴏʀᴅ their God. ¹⁸The other things Manasseh did as king, his prayer to his God, and what the seers ᵈ said to him in the name of the Lᴏʀᴅ, the God of Israel — all are recorded in the book of the history of the kings of Israel. ¹⁹Manasseh's prayer and God's pity for him, his sins, his unfaithfulness, the places he built for worshiping gods and the Asherah ᵈ idols before he humbled himself — all are written in the book of the seers. ²⁰Manasseh died and was buried in his palace. Then Manasseh's son Amon became king in his place.

Amon King of Judah

²¹Amon was twenty-two years old when he became king, and he was king for two years in Jerusalem. ²²He did what the Lᴏʀᴅ said was wrong, as his father Manasseh had done. Amon wor-

---

sign See Isaiah 38:1-8. It tells the story about the sign and how the Lord gave Hezekiah fifteen more years to live.
God . . . heart See 2 Kings 20:12-19.

shiped and offered sacrifices to all the carved idols Manasseh had made. 23Amon did not humble himself before the LORD as his father Manasseh had done. Instead, Amon sinned even more.

24King Amon's officers made plans against him and killed him in his palace. 25Then the people of the land killed all those who had made plans to kill King Amon, and they made his son Josiah king in his place.

Josiah King of Judah

34 Josiah was eight years old when he became king, and he ruled thirty-one years in Jerusalem. 2He did what the LORD said was right. He lived as his ancestor David had lived, and he did not stop doing what was right.

3In his eighth year as king while he was still young, Josiah began to obey the God of his ancestor David. In his twelfth year as king, Josiah began to remove from Judah and Jerusalem the gods, the places for worshiping gods, the Asherah*d* idols, and the wooden and metal idols. 4The people tore down the altars for the Baal*d* gods as Josiah directed. Then Josiah cut down the incense*d* altars that were above them. He broke up the Asherah idols and the wooden and metal idols and beat them into powder. Then he sprinkled the powder on the graves of the people who had offered sacrifices to these gods. 5He burned the bones of their priests on their own altars. So Josiah removed idol worship from Judah and Jerusalem, 6and from the towns in the areas of Manasseh, Ephraim, and Simeon all the way to Naphtali, and in the ruins near these towns. 7Josiah broke down the altars and Asherah idols and beat the idols into powder. He cut down all the incense altars in all of Israel. Then he went back to Jerusalem.

SIDELIGHT: The "places" or "high places" where people worshiped false gods weren't necessarily hills or mountains (2 Chronicles 34:3–7). They were sacred platforms on which idols stood. The only way to get people to stop worshiping at them was to destroy them completely as King Josiah did.

8In Josiah's eighteenth year as king, he made Judah and the Temple*d* pure again. He sent Shaphan son of Azaliah, Maaseiah the city leader, and Joah son of Joahaz the recorder to repair the Temple of the LORD, the God of Josiah. 9These men went to Hilkiah the high priest and gave him the money the Levite gatekeepers had gathered from the people of Manasseh, Ephraim, and all the Israelites who were left alive, and also from all the

people of Judah, Benjamin, and Jerusalem. This is the money they had brought into the Temple of God. 10Then the Levites gave it to the supervisors of the work on the Temple of the LORD, and they paid the workers who rebuilt and repaired the Temple. 11They gave money to carpenters and builders to buy cut stone and wood. The wood was used to rebuild the buildings and to make beams for them, because the kings of Judah had let the buildings fall into ruin. 12The men did their work well. Their supervisors were Jahath and Obadiah, who were Levites from the family of Merari, and Zechariah and Meshullam, who were from the family of Kohath. These Levites were all skilled musicians. 13They were also in charge of the workers who carried loads and all the other workers. Some Levites worked as secretaries, officers, and gatekeepers.

SIDELIGHT: If you don't think secretaries are important, read 2 Chronicles 34:13, which tells that the Levites served as honored secretaries in the Temple. Do you think they had to take a typing test?

The Book of the Teachings Is Found

14The Levites brought out the money that was in the Temple*d* of the LORD. As they were doing this, Hilkiah the priest found the Book of the LORD's Teachings that had been given through Moses. 15Hilkiah said to Shaphan the royal secretary, "I've found the Book of the Teachings in the Temple of the LORD!" Then he gave it to Shaphan.

16Shaphan took the book to the king and reported to Josiah, "Your officers are doing everything you told them to do. 17They have paid out the money that was in the Temple of the LORD and have given it to the supervisors and the workers." 18Then Shaphan the royal secretary told the king, "Hilkiah the priest has given me a book." And Shaphan read from the book to the king.

19When the king heard the words of the Teachings, he tore his clothes to show how upset he was. 20He gave orders to Hilkiah, Ahikam son of Shaphan, Acbor son of Micaiah, Shaphan the royal secretary, and Asaiah, the king's servant. These were the orders: 21"Go and ask the LORD about the words in the book that was found. Ask for me and for the people who are left alive in Israel and Judah. The LORD is very angry with us, because our ancestors did not obey the LORD's word; they did not do everything this book says to do."

22So Hilkiah and those the king sent with him went to talk to Huldah the prophetess.*d* She was the wife of Shallum son of Tikvah, the son of Harhas, who took care of the king's clothes. Huldah lived in Jerusalem, in the new area of the city.

23She said to them, "This is what the LORD, the God of Israel, says: Tell the man who sent you to me, 24'This is what the LORD says: I will bring trouble to this place and to the people living here. I will bring all the curses that are written in the book that was read to the king of Judah. 25The people of Judah have left me and have burned incense[d] to other gods. They have made me angry by all the evil things they have made. So I will punish them in my anger, which will not be put out.' 26Tell the king of Judah, who sent you to ask the LORD, 'This is what the LORD, the God of Israel, says about the words you heard: 27When you heard my words against this place and its people, you became sorry for what you had done and you humbled yourself before me. You tore your clothes to show how upset you were, and you cried in my presence. This is why I have heard you, says the LORD. 28So I will let you die and be buried in peace. You won't see all the trouble I will bring to this place and the people living here.' "

So they took her message back to the king.

29Then the king gathered all the older leaders of Judah and Jerusalem together. 30He went up to the Temple of the LORD, and all the people from Judah and from Jerusalem went with him. The priests, the Levites, and all the people — from the most important to the least important — went with him. He read to them all the words in the Book of the Agreement that was found in the Temple of the LORD. 31The king stood by his pillar and made an agreement in the presence of the LORD to follow the LORD and obey his commands, rules, and laws with his whole being and to obey the words of the agreement written in this book. 32Then Josiah made all the people in Jerusalem and Benjamin promise to accept the agreement. So the people of Jerusalem obeyed the agreement of God, the God of their ancestors.

33And Josiah threw out the hateful idols from all the land that belonged to the Israelites. He led everyone in Israel to serve the LORD their God. While Josiah lived, the people obeyed the LORD, the God of their ancestors.

Josiah Celebrates the Passover

35 King Josiah celebrated the Passover[d] to the LORD in Jerusalem. The Passover lamb was killed on the fourteenth day of the first month. 2Josiah chose the priests to do their duties, and he encouraged them as they served in the Temple[d] of the LORD. 3The Levites taught the Israelites and were made holy for service to the LORD. Josiah said to them, "Put the Holy Ark[d] in the Temple that David's son Solomon, the king of Is-

rael, built. Do not carry it from place to place on your shoulders anymore. Now serve the LORD your God and his people Israel. 4Prepare yourselves by your family groups for service, and do the jobs that King David and his son Solomon gave you to do.

5"Stand in the holy place with a group of the Levites for each family group of the people. 6Kill the Passover lambs, and make yourselves holy to the LORD. Prepare the lambs for your relatives, the people of Israel, as the LORD through Moses commanded us to do."

7Josiah gave the Israelites thirty thousand sheep and goats to kill for the Passover sacrifices, and he gave them three thousand cattle. They were all his own animals.

8Josiah's officers also gave willingly to the people, the priests, and the Levites. Hilkiah, Zechariah, and Jehiel, the officers in charge of the Temple, gave the priests twenty-six hundred lambs and goats and three hundred cattle for Passover sacrifices. 9Conaniah, his brothers Shemaiah and Nethanel, and Hashabiah, Jeiel, and Jozabad gave the Levites five thousand sheep and goats and five hundred cattle for Passover sacrifices. These men were leaders of the Levites.

10When everything was ready for the Passover service, the priests and Levites went to their places, as the king had commanded. 11The Passover lambs were killed. Then the Levites skinned the animals and gave the blood to the priests, who sprinkled it on the altar. 12Then they gave the animals for the burnt offerings to the different family groups so the burnt offerings could be offered to the LORD as was written in the book of Moses. They also did this with the cattle. 13The Levites roasted the Passover sacrifices over the fire as they were commanded, and they boiled the holy offerings in pots, kettles, and pans. Then they quickly gave the meat to the people. 14After this was finished, the Levites prepared meat for themselves and for the priests, the descendants[d] of Aaron. The priests worked until night, offering the burnt offerings and burning the fat of the sacrifices.

15The Levite singers from Asaph's family stood in the places chosen for them by King David, Asaph, Heman, and Jeduthun, the king's seer.[d] The gatekeepers at each gate did not have to leave their places, because their fellow Levites had prepared everything for them for the Passover.

16So everything was done that day for the worship of the LORD, as King Josiah commanded. The Passover was celebrated, and the burnt offerings were offered on the LORD's altar. 17The Israelites who were there celebrated the Passover and the Feast[d] of Unleavened Bread for seven days. 18The Passover had not been celebrated like this in Israel since the prophet[d] Samuel was alive. None of the kings of Israel had ever celebrated a Passover like it was celebrated by King Josiah, the priests, the Levites, the people of Judah and Israel who were there, and the people of Jerusalem. ¹⁹This Passover was celebrated in the eighteenth year Josiah was king.

The Death of Josiah

²⁰After Josiah did all this for the Temple,*ᵈ* Neco king of Egypt led an army to attack Carchemish, a town on the Euphrates River. And Josiah marched out to fight against Neco. ²¹But Neco sent messengers to Josiah, saying, "King Josiah, there should not be war between us. I did not come to fight you, but my enemies. God told me to hurry, and he is on my side. So don't fight God, or he will destroy you."

²²But Josiah did not go away. He wore different clothes so no one would know who he was. Refusing to listen to what Neco said at God's command, Josiah went to fight on the plain of Megiddo. ²³In the battle King Josiah was shot by

---

☀ SIDELIGHT: If you want to buy a house on the plain of Megiddo (2 Chronicles 35:22), expect to pay high "war insurance." This plain may be one of the bloodiest battlegrounds in the world. Archaeologists have uncovered twenty cities—one on top of the other—that have been destroyed at this site.

---

archers. He told his servants, "Take me away because I am badly wounded." ²⁴So they took him out of his chariot and put him in another chariot and carried him to Jerusalem. There he died and was buried in the graves where his ancestors were buried. All the people of Judah and Jerusalem were very sad because he was dead.

²⁵Jeremiah wrote some sad songs about Josiah. Even to this day all the men and women singers remember and honor Josiah with these songs. It became a custom in Israel to sing these songs that are written in the collection of sad songs.

²⁶⁻²⁷The other things Josiah did as king, from beginning to end, are written in the book of the kings of Israel and Judah. It tells how he loved what was written in the LORD's teachings.

Jehoahaz King of Judah

36 The people of Judah chose Josiah's son Jehoahaz and made him king in Jerusalem in his father's place.

²Jehoahaz was twenty-three years old when he became king, and he was king in Jerusalem for three months. ³Then King Neco of Egypt removed Jehoahaz from being king in Jerusalem. Neco

made the people of Judah pay about seventy-five hundred pounds of silver and about seventy-five pounds of gold. ⁴The king of Egypt made Jehoahaz's brother Eliakim the king of Judah and Jerusalem and changed his name to Jehoiakim. But Neco took his brother Jehoahaz to Egypt.

Jehoiakim King of Judah

⁵Jehoiakim was twenty-five years old when he became king, and he was king in Jerusalem for eleven years. He did what the LORD his God said was wrong. ⁶King Nebuchadnezzar of Babylon attacked Judah, captured Jehoiakim, put bronze chains on him, and took him to Babylon. ⁷Nebuchadnezzar removed some of the things from the Temple*ᵈ* of the LORD, took them to Babylon, and put them in his own palace.

⁸The other things Jehoiakim did as king, the hateful things he did, and everything he was guilty of doing, are written in the book of the kings of Israel and Judah. And Jehoiakim's son Jehoiachin became king in his place.

Jehoiachin King of Judah

⁹Jehoiachin was eighteen years old when he became king of Judah, and he was king in Jerusalem for three months and ten days. He did what the LORD said was wrong. ¹⁰In the spring King Nebuchadnezzar sent for Jehoiachin and brought him and some valuable treasures from the Temple*ᵈ* of the LORD to Babylon. Then Nebuchadnezzar made Jehoiachin's uncle Zedekiah the king of Judah and Jerusalem.

Zedekiah King of Judah

¹¹Zedekiah was twenty-one years old when he became king of Judah, and he was king in Jerusalem for eleven years. ¹²Zedekiah did what the LORD his God said was wrong. The prophet*ᵈ* Jeremiah spoke messages from the LORD, but Zedekiah did not obey. ¹³Zedekiah turned against King Nebuchadnezzar, who had forced him to swear in God's name to be loyal to him. But Zedekiah became stubborn and refused to obey the LORD, the God of Israel. ¹⁴Also, all the leaders of the priests and the people of Judah became more wicked, following the evil example of the other nations. The LORD had made the Temple*ᵈ* in Jerusalem holy, but the leaders made it unholy.

The Fall of Jerusalem

¹⁵The LORD, the God of their ancestors, sent *prophetsᵈ again and again to warn his people,* because he had pity on them and on his Temple. ¹⁶But they made fun of God's prophets and hated God's messages. They refused to listen to the prophets until, finally, the LORD became so angry with his people that he could not be stopped. ¹⁷So God brought the king of Babylon to attack them.

The king killed the young men even when they were in the Temple. He had no mercy on the young men or women, the old men or those who were sick. God handed all of them over to Nebuchadnezzar. [18]Nebuchadnezzar carried away to Babylon all the things from the Temple of God, both large and small, and all the treasures from the Temple of the LORD and from the king and his officers. [19]Nebuchadnezzar and his army set fire to God's Temple and broke down Jerusalem's wall and burned all the palaces. They took or destroyed every valuable thing in Jerusalem.

[20]Nebuchadnezzar took captive to Babylon the people who were left alive, and he forced them to be slaves for him and his descendants.[d] They remained there as slaves until the Persian kingdom defeated Babylon. [21]And so what the LORD had told Israel through the prophet Jeremiah happened: The country was an empty wasteland for seventy years to make up for the years of Sabbath rest[n] that the people had not kept.

[22]In the first year Cyrus was king of Persia, the LORD had Cyrus send an announcement to his whole kingdom. This happened so the LORD's message spoken by Jeremiah would come true. He wrote:

[23]This is what Cyrus king of Persia says:

The LORD, the God of heaven, has given me all the kingdoms of the earth, and he has appointed me to build a Temple for him at Jerusalem in Judah. Now may the LORD your God be with all of you who are his people. You are free to go to Jerusalem.

Sabbath rest The Law said that every seventh year the land was not to be farmed. See Leviticus 25:1-7.

ANGER

One Mad Mom

Cari Lightner was only thirteen years old when a drunk driver swerved off the road and killed her.

When the police arrested the driver, they discovered he had been arrested many times before for drunk driving. Still, they told Cari's mother, Candy, that this man would probably go free. There were no laws that could keep him in jail.

How could someone kill her daughter and go free? In her anger, Candy declared to friends, "I'm going to start an organization." She created Mothers Against Drunk Drivers (MADD), a group that would work to pass tough laws that would punish drunk drivers. And the work paid off. Within five years, every state in the United States had made its drunk-driving laws more strict.

MADD has made people aware of the problem of drinking and driving, and its efforts have saved lives.

Candy Lightner and the thousands of MADD members put their anger to work and brought about change. In **2 Chronicles 36:14–21**, you can see changes that occurred when God became angry with his people.

■ What part did anger play in Candy's—and God's—actions?
■ Based on this passage, what kinds of things make God angry?

CONSIDER . . .

■ writing your congressional representative about an issue you think needs to be changed.
■ thinking of one issue that makes you angry and then doing three specific things to change the situation.

FOR MORE, SEE . . .

■ Exodus 32:19–35 (p. 89)
■ Psalm 103:8 (p. 540)
■ Luke 19:45–48 (p. 1045)

EZRA

Why Read This Book:

- See how God uses world events to help his people (Ezra 1).
- Learn how to trust God in the face of opposition (Ezra 4—6).
- Examine the cost of compromising beliefs (Ezra 7—10).

Behind the Scenes:

If you have moved from one community to another, you know what it's like to visit the old community. Nothing seems the same. Trees look larger, buildings older and people different. Everything seems a little familiar, but it's also very different. It's no longer home.

The people of Judah had been gone from Israel for seventy years, captives of the Babylonian Empire. The Persians had then conquered Babylon and let the captives go home. The Jews could return to Jerusalem and worship their God. What a cause for celebration!

But things were different now. The people were different. Now they were called Jews, not Israelites. Many of them spoke primarily Aramaic, not the old Hebrew. They used to be rural people; now they were urban people.

Their world was different too. Instead of being an independent nation, the returning Jews were more like a religious community. The people who had stayed behind resented the exiles for wanting their land back. And Jerusalem, which the Babylonians had destroyed, lay in ruins. So, despite the excitement, home wasn't like they left it. There was work to do.

The books of Ezra and Nehemiah (p. 427), which were originally one book, tell the story of these returning exiles. In general, the books focus on the rebuilding of the Temple (Ezra 1—7), the preserving of the faith (Ezra 8—10), and the rebuilding of Jerusalem's walls (Nehemiah).

Through it all, we often see people wanting to give up. We see leaders

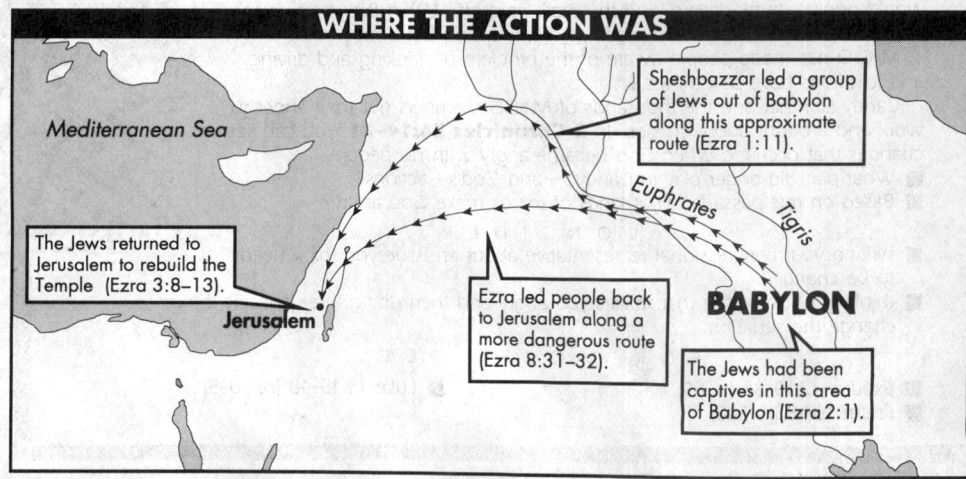

WHERE THE ACTION WAS

Mediterranean Sea

Sheshbazzar led a group of Jews out of Babylon along this approximate route (Ezra 1:11).

Euphrates

Tigris

The Jews returned to Jerusalem to rebuild the Temple (Ezra 3:8–13).

Jerusalem

Ezra led people back to Jerusalem along a more dangerous route (Ezra 8:31–32).

BABYLON

The Jews had been captives in this area of Babylon (Ezra 2:1).

WHEN THE ACTION WAS

	The Northern Kingdom (Israel) fell to Assyria	Jews began returning to Jerusalem from exile	Ezra returned to Jerusalem from exile		Jesus was born
1000BC	**750BC**		**500BC**	**250BC**	**BC/AD**
David was Israel's king		People of Judah taken into exile in Babylon	Nehemiah returned to Jerusalem from exile		

Behind the | challenging them and renewing their energy. And we see the people's faithfulness
Scenes (cont.): | even when the obstacles seem impossible. Their story can be a comfort and a
| challenge to help us stick with our faith in tough times.

Cyrus Helps the Captives Return

1 In the first year Cyrus was king of Persia, the LORD caused Cyrus to send an announcement to his whole kingdom and to put it in writing. This happened so the LORD's message spoken by Jeremiah would come true. He wrote:

²This is what Cyrus king of Persia says:

The LORD, the God of heaven, has given all the kingdoms of the earth to me, and he has appointed me to build a Temple[d] for him at Jerusalem in Judah. ³May God be with all of you who are his people. You are free to go to Jerusalem in Judah and build the Temple of the LORD, the God of Israel, who is in Jerusalem. ⁴Those who stay behind, wherever they live, should support those who want to go. Give them silver and gold, supplies and cattle, and special gifts for the Temple of God in Jerusalem.

> **SIDELIGHT:** King Cyrus's decree granting religious freedom to the Jews apparently wasn't a special privilege for them alone (Ezra 1:4). Archaeologists have unearthed The Cyrus Cylinder, which reveals that Cyrus's policy extended to all people who had been taken captive by Babylon.

⁵Then the family leaders of Judah and Benjamin and the priests and Levites got ready to go to Jerusalem — everyone God had caused to want to go to Jerusalem to build the Temple of the LORD. ⁶All their neighbors helped them, giving them things made of silver and gold, along with supplies, cattle, valuable gifts, and special gifts for the Temple. ⁷Also, King Cyrus brought out the bowls and pans that belonged to the Temple of the LORD, which Nebuchadnezzar had taken from Jerusalem and put in the temple of his own god. ⁸Cyrus king of Persia had Mithredath the treasurer bring them and count them out for Sheshbazzar, the prince of Judah.

⁹He listed thirty gold dishes, one thousand silver dishes, twenty-nine pans, ¹⁰thirty gold bowls, four hundred ten matching silver bowls, and one thousand other pieces.

¹¹There was a total of fifty-four hundred pieces of gold and silver. Sheshbazzar brought all these things along when the captives went from Babylon to Jerusalem.

The Captives Who Returned

2 These are the people of the area who returned from captivity, whom Nebuchadnezzar king of Babylon had taken away to Babylon.

> **SIDELIGHT:** When Cyrus sent the Jews back to Jerusalem, he had them take thirty gold dishes, one thousand silver dishes, twenty-nine silver pans, thirty gold bowls, and four hundred ten silver bowls (Ezra 1:9) — valuables that had been taken from the Temple in Jerusalem by King Nebuchadnezzar when he destroyed it (2 Kings 25:8–17, p. 357). Hope he sent a dishwasher, too!

They returned to Jerusalem and Judah, each going back to his own town. ²These people returned with Zerubbabel, Jeshua, Nehemiah, Seraiah, Reelaiah, Mordecai, Bilshan, Mispar, Bigvai, Rehum, and Baanah.

These are the people from Israel: ³the descendants[d] of Parosh — 2,172; ⁴the descendants of Shephatiah — 372; ⁵the descendants of Arah — 775; ⁶the descendants of Pahath-Moab (through the family of Jeshua and Joab) — 2,812; ⁷the descendants of Elam — 1,254; ⁸the descendants of Zattu — 945; ⁹the descendants of Zaccai — 760; ¹⁰the descendants of Bani — 642; ¹¹the descendants of Bebai — 623; ¹²the descendants of Azgad — 1,222; ¹³the descendants of Adonikam — 666; ¹⁴the descendants of Bigvai — 2,056; ¹⁵the descendants of Adin — 454; ¹⁶the descendants of Ater (through the family of Hezekiah) — 98; ¹⁷the descendants of Bezai — 323; ¹⁸the descendants of Jorah — 112; ¹⁹the descendants of Hashum — 223; ²⁰the descendants of Gibbar — 95.

²¹These are the people from the towns: of Bethlehem — 123; ²²of Netophah — 56; ²³of Anathoth — 128; ²⁴of Azmaveth — 42; ²⁵of Kiriath Jearim, Kephirah, and Beeroth — 743; ²⁶of Ramah and Geba — 621; ²⁷of Micmash — 122; ²⁸of Bethel and Ai — 223; ²⁹of Nebo — 52; ³⁰of Magbish — 156; ³¹of the other town of Elam — 1,254; ³²of Harim — 320; ³³of Lod, Hadid and Ono — 725; ³⁴of Jericho — 345; ³⁵of Senaah — 3,630.

³⁶These are the priests: the descendants of Jedaiah (through the family of Jeshua) — 973; ³⁷the descendants of Immer — 1,052; ³⁸the descendants of Pashhur — 1,247; ³⁹the descendants of Harim — 1,017.

⁴⁰These are the Levites: the descendants of Jeshua and Kadmiel (through the family of Hodaviah) — 74.

⁴¹These are the singers: the descendants of Asaph — 128.

⁴²These are the gatekeepers of the Temple:*d* the descendants of Shallum, Ater, Talmon, Akkub, Hatita, and Shobai — 139.

⁴³These are the Temple servants: the descendants of Ziha, Hasupha, Tabbaoth, ⁴⁴Keros, Siaha, Padon, ⁴⁵Lebanah, Hagabah, Akkub, ⁴⁶Hagab, Shalmai, Hanan, ⁴⁷Giddel, Gahar, Reaiah, ⁴⁸Rezin, Nekoda, Gazzam, ⁴⁹Uzza, Paseah, Besai, ⁵⁰Asnah, Meunim, Nephussim, ⁵¹Bakbuk, Hakupha, Harhur, ⁵²Bazluth, Mehida, Harsha, ⁵³Barkos, Sisera, Temah, ⁵⁴Neziah, and Hatipha.

⁵⁵These are the descendants of the servants of Solomon: the descendants of Sotai, Hassophereth, Peruda, ⁵⁶Jaala, Darkon, Giddel, ⁵⁷Shephatiah, Hattil, Pokereth-Hazzebaim, and Ami.

⁵⁸The Temple servants and the descendants of the servants of Solomon numbered 392.

⁵⁹Some people came to Jerusalem from the towns of Tel Melah, Tel Harsha, Kerub, Addon, and Immer, but they could not prove that their ancestors came from Israel. ⁶⁰They were the descendants of Delaiah, Tobiah, and Nekoda — 652.

⁶¹Also these priests: the descendants of Hobaiah, Hakkoz, and Barzillai, who had married a daughter of Barzillai from Gilead and was called by her family name.

⁶²These people searched for their family records but could not find them. So they could not be priests, because they were thought to be unclean. ⁶³The governor ordered them not to eat any of the food offered to God until a priest had settled this matter by using the Urim and Thummim.*d*

> ✷ **SIDELIGHT:** Not all the Jews returned from exile when the Persians let them leave (Ezra 2:1–2). According to Babylonian records, some Jews had become prominent bankers, business people, and government officials in Babylon.

⁶⁴The total number of those who returned was 42,360. ⁶⁵This is not counting their 7,337 male and female servants and the 200 male and female singers they had with them. ⁶⁶They had 736 horses, 245 mules, ⁶⁷435 camels, and 6,720 donkeys.

⁶⁸When they arrived at the Temple of the Lord in Jerusalem, some of the leaders of families gave offerings to rebuild the Temple of God on the same site as before. ⁶⁹They gave as much as they could to the treasury to rebuild the Temple — about 1,100 pounds of gold, about 6,000 pounds of silver, and 100 pieces of clothing for the priests.

⁷⁰All the Israelites settled in their hometowns. The priests, Levites, singers, gatekeepers, and Temple servants, along with some of the other people, settled in their own towns as well.

Rebuilding the Altar

3 In the seventh month, after the Israelites were settled in their hometowns, they met together in Jerusalem. ²Then Jeshua son of Jozadak and his fellow priests joined Zerubbabel son of Shealtiel and began to build the altar of the God of Israel where they could offer burnt offerings, just as it is written in the Teachings of Moses, the man of God. ³Even though they were afraid of the people living around them, they built the altar where it had been before. And they offered burnt offerings on it to the Lord morning and evening. ⁴Then, to obey what was written, they celebrated the Feast*d* of Shelters. They offered the right number of sacrifices for each day of the festival. ⁵After the Feast of Shelters, they had regular sacrifices every day, as well as sacrifices for the New Moon*d* and all the festivals commanded by the Lord. Also there were special offerings brought as gifts to the Lord. ⁶On the first day of the seventh month they began to bring burnt offerings to the Lord, but the foundation of the Lord's Temple*d* had not yet been laid.

Rebuilding the Temple

⁷Then they gave money to the bricklayers and carpenters. They also gave food, wine, and oil to the cities of Sidon and Tyre so they would float cedar logs from Lebanon to the seacoast town of Joppa. Cyrus king of Persia had given permission for this.

⁸In the second month of the second year after their arrival at the Temple*d* of God in Jerusalem, Zerubbabel son of Shealtiel, Jeshua son of Jozadak, their fellow priests and Levites, and all who had returned from captivity to Jerusalem began to work. They chose Levites twenty years old and older to be in charge of the building of the Temple of the Lord. ⁹These men were in charge of the work of building the Temple of God: Jeshua and his sons and brothers; Kadmiel and his sons who were the descendants of Hodaviah; and the sons of Henadad and their sons and brothers. They were all Levites.

¹⁰The builders finished laying the foundation of the Temple of the Lord. Then the priests, dressed in their robes, stood with their trumpets, and the Levites, the sons of Asaph, stood with their cymbals. They all took their places and praised the Lord just as David king of Israel had said to do.

[11]With praise and thanksgiving, they sang to the LORD:

"He is good;
    his love for Israel continues forever."

And then all the people shouted loudly, "Praise the LORD! The foundation of his Temple has been laid." [12]But many of the older priests, Levites, and family leaders who had seen the first Temple cried when they saw the foundation of this Temple. Most of the other people were shouting with joy. [13]The people made so much noise it could be heard far away, and no one could tell the difference between the joyful shouting and the sad crying.

Enemies of the Rebuilding

4 When the enemies of the people of Judah and Benjamin heard that the returned captives were building a Temple[d] for the LORD, the God of Israel, [2]they came to Zerubbabel and the leaders of the families. The enemies said, "Let us help you build, because we are like you and want to worship your God. We have been offering sacrifices to him since the time of Esarhaddon king of Assyria, who brought us here."

[3]But Zerubbabel, Jeshua, and the leaders of Israel answered, "You will not help us build a Temple to our God. We will build it ourselves for the LORD, the God of Israel, as King Cyrus, the king of Persia, commanded us to do."

[4]Then the people around them tried to discourage the people of Judah by making them afraid to build. [5]Their enemies hired others to delay the building plans during the time Cyrus was king of Persia. And it continued to the time Darius was king of Persia.

More Problems for the Builders

[6]When Xerxes first became king, those enemies wrote a letter against the people of Judah and Jerusalem.

[7]When Artaxerxes became king of Persia, Bishlam, Mithredath, Tabeel, and those with them wrote a letter to Artaxerxes. It was written in the Aramaic language and translated.

[8]Rehum the governor and Shimshai the governor's secretary wrote a letter against Jerusalem to Artaxerxes the king. It said:

[9]This letter is from Rehum the governor, Shimshai the secretary, and their fellow workers — the judges and important officers over the men who came from Tripolis, Persia, Erech, and Babylon, the Elamite people of Susa, [10]and those whom the great and honorable Ashurbanipal forced out of their countries and settled in the city of Samaria and in other places of the Trans-Euphrates.

[11](This is a copy of the letter they sent to Artaxerxes.)

To King Artaxerxes.
From your servants who live in Trans-Euphrates.

[12]King Artaxerxes, you should know that the Jewish people who came to us from you have gone to Jerusalem to rebuild that evil city that refuses to obey. They are fixing the walls and repairing the foundations of the buildings. [13]Now, King Artaxerxes, you should know that if Jerusalem is built and its walls are fixed, Jerusalem will not pay taxes of any kind. Then the amount of money your government collects will be less. [14]Since we must be loyal to the government, we don't want to see the king dishonored. So we are writing to let the king know. [15]We suggest you search the records of the kings who ruled before you. You will find out that the city of Jerusalem refuses to obey and makes trouble for kings and areas controlled by Persia. Since long ago it has been a place where disobedience has started. That is why it was destroyed. [16]We want you to know, King Artaxerxes, that if this city is rebuilt and its walls fixed, you will be left with nothing in Trans-Euphrates.

[17]King Artaxerxes sent this answer:

To Rehum the governor and Shimshai the secretary, to all their fellow workers living in Samaria, and to those in other places in Trans-Euphrates.

Greetings.

[18]The letter you sent to us has been translated and read to me. [19]I ordered the records to be searched, and it was done. We found that Jerusalem has a history of disobedience to kings and has been a place of problems and trouble. [20]Jerusalem has had powerful kings who have ruled over the whole area of Trans-Euphrates, and taxes of all kinds have

SIDELIGHT: The Old Testament was originally written in Hebrew, right? Well, not all of it. Ezra 4:8—6:18 and 7:12–26 were written in Aramaic, which was the language Jesus would speak centuries later. Three other Old Testament passages were also written in Aramaic (Genesis 31:47, p. 37; Jeremiah 10:11, p. 703; and Daniel 2:4—7:28 p. 807).

been paid to them. ²¹Now, give an order for those men to stop work. The city of Jerusalem will not be rebuilt until I say so. ²²Make sure you do this, because if they continue, it will hurt the government.

²³A copy of the letter that King Artaxerxes sent was read to Rehum and Shimshai the secretary and the others. Then they quickly went to the Jewish people in Jerusalem and forced them to stop building.

²⁴So the work on the Temple⁴ of God in Jerusalem stopped until the second year Darius was king of Persia.

Tattenai's Letter to Darius

5 The prophets Haggai and Zechariah, a descendant of Iddo, prophesied to the Jewish people in Judah and Jerusalem in the name of the God of Israel, who was over them. ²Then Zerubbabel son of Shealtiel and Jeshua son of Jozadak started working again to rebuild the Temple⁴ of God in Jerusalem. And the prophets of God were there, helping them.

³At that time Tattenai, the governor of Trans-Euphrates, and Shethar-Bozenai, and their fellow workers went to the Jewish people and asked, "Who gave you permission to rebuild this Temple and fix these walls?" ⁴They also asked, "What are the names of the men working on this building?" ⁵But their God was watching over the older leaders of the Jewish people. The builders were not stopped until a report could go to King Darius and his written answer could be received.

⁶This is a copy of the letter that was sent to King Darius by Tattenai, the governor of Trans-Euphrates, Shethar-Bozenai, and the other important officers of Trans-Euphrates. ⁷This is what was said in the report they sent to him:

To King Darius.

Greetings. May you have peace.

⁸King Darius, you should know that we went to the district of Judah where the Temple of the great God is. The people are building that Temple with large stones, and they are putting timbers in the walls. They are working very hard and are building very fast.

⁹We asked their older leaders, "Who gave you permission to rebuild this Temple and these walls?" ¹⁰We also asked for their names, and we wrote down the names of their leaders so you would know who they are.

¹¹This is the answer they gave to us: "We are the servants of the God of heaven and earth. We are rebuilding the Temple that a great king of Israel built and finished many years ago. ¹²But our ancestors made the God of heaven angry, so he handed them over to Nebuchadnezzar king of Babylon, who destroyed this Temple and took the people to Babylon as captives.

¹³"Later, in the first year Cyrus was king of Babylon, he gave a special order for this Temple to be rebuilt. ¹⁴Cyrus brought out from the temple in Babylon the gold and silver bowls and pans that came from the Temple of God. Nebuchadnezzar had taken them from the Temple in Jerusalem and had put them in the temple in Babylon.

"Then King Cyrus gave them to Sheshbazzar, his appointed governor. ¹⁵Cyrus said to him, 'Take these gold and silver bowls and pans, and put them back in the Temple in Jerusalem and rebuild the Temple of God where it was.' ¹⁶So Sheshbazzar came and laid the foundations of the Temple of God in Jerusalem. From that day until now the work has been going on, but it is not yet finished."

¹⁷Now, if the king wishes, let a search be made in the royal records of Babylon. See if King Cyrus gave an order to rebuild this Temple in Jerusalem. Then let the king write us and tell us what he has decided.

The Order of Darius

6 So King Darius gave an order to search the records kept in the treasury in Babylon. ²A scroll was found in Ecbatana, the capital city of Media. This is what was written on it:

Note:

³King Cyrus gave an order about the Temple⁴ of God in Jerusalem in the first year he was king. This was the order:

"Let the Temple be rebuilt as a place to present sacrifices. Let its foundations be laid; it should be ninety feet high and ninety feet wide. ⁴It must have three layers of large stones and then one layer of timbers. The costs should be paid from the king's treasury. ⁵The gold and silver utensils from the Temple of God should be put back in their places. Nebuchadnezzar took them from the Temple in Jerusalem and brought them to Babylon, but they are to be put back in the Temple of God in Jerusalem."

⁶Now then, Tattenai, governor of Trans-Euphrates, Shethar-Bozenai, and all the officers of that area, stay away from there. ⁷Do not bother the work on that Temple of God. Let the governor of the Jewish people and the older Jewish leaders rebuild this Temple where it was before.

⁸Also, I order you to do this for those older leaders of the Jewish people who are build-

ing this Temple: The cost of the building is to be fully paid from the royal treasury, from taxes collected from Trans-Euphrates. Do this so the work will not stop. [9]Give those people anything they need—young bulls, male sheep, or lambs for burnt offerings to the God of heaven, or wheat, salt, wine, or olive oil. Give the priests in Jerusalem anything they ask for every day without fail. [10]Then they may offer sacrifices pleasing to the God of heaven, and they may pray for the life of the king and his sons.

[11]Also, I give this order: If anyone changes this order, a wood beam is to be pulled from his house and driven through his body. Because of his crime, make his house a pile of

---

SIDELIGHT: King Darius didn't like his orders to be questioned. If you changed what he said, a wooden beam was to be taken from your house and driven through your body (Ezra 6:11). According to other sources, Darius impaled three thousand Babylonians when he captured their city.

---

ruins. [12]God has chosen Jerusalem as the place he is to be worshiped. May he punish any king or person who tries to change this order and destroy this Temple.

I, Darius, have given this order. Let it be obeyed quickly and carefully.

Completion of the Temple

[13]So, Tattenai, the governor of Trans-Euphrates, Shethar-Bozenai, and their fellow workers carried out King Darius' order quickly and carefully. [14]The older Jewish leaders continued to build and were successful because of the preaching of Haggai the prophet[d] and Zechariah, a descendant of Iddo. They finished building the Temple[d] as the God of Israel had commanded and as kings Cyrus, Darius, and Artaxerxes of Persia had ordered. [15]The Temple was finished on the third day of the month of Adar in the sixth year Darius was king.

[16]Then the people of Israel celebrated and gave the Temple to God to honor him. Everybody was happy: the priests, the Levites, and the rest of the Jewish people who had returned from captivity. [17]They gave the Temple to God by offering a hundred bulls, two hundred male sheep, and four hundred lambs as sacrifices. And as an offering to forgive the sins of all Israel, they offered twelve male goats, one goat for each tribe[d] in Israel.

[18]Then they put the priests and the Levites into their separate groups. Each group had a certain time to serve God in the Temple at Jerusalem as it is written in the Book of Moses.

The Passover Is Celebrated

[19]The Jewish people who returned from captivity celebrated the Passover[d] on the fourteenth day of the first month. [20]The priests and Levites had made themselves clean.[d] Then the Levites killed the Passover lambs for all the people who had returned from captivity, for their relatives the priests, and for themselves. [21]So all the people of Israel who returned from captivity ate the Passover lamb. So did the people who had given up the unclean ways of their non-Jewish neighbors in order to worship the LORD, the God of Israel. [22]For seven days they celebrated the Feast[d] of Unleavened Bread in a very joyful way. The LORD had made them happy by changing the mind of the king of Assyria so that he helped them in the work on the Temple of the God of Israel.

Ezra Comes to Jerusalem

7 After these things[n] during the rule of Artaxerxes king of Persia, Ezra came up from Babylon. Ezra was the son of Seraiah, the son of Azariah, the son of Hilkiah, [2]the son of Shallum, the son of Zadok, the son of Ahitub, [3]the son of Amariah, the son of Azariah, the son of Meraioth, [4]the son of Zerahiah, the son of Uzzi, the son of Bukki, [5]the son of Abishua, the son of Phinehas, the son of Eleazar, the son of Aaron the high priest. [6]This Ezra came to Jerusalem from Babylon. He was a teacher and knew well the Teachings of Moses that had been given by the LORD, the God of Israel. Ezra received everything he asked for from the king, because the LORD his God was helping him. [7]In the seventh year of King Artaxerxes more Israelites came to Jerusalem. Among them were priests, Levites, singers, gatekeepers, and Temple[d] servants.

[8]Ezra arrived in Jerusalem in the fifth month of Artaxerxes' seventh year as king. [9]Ezra had left Babylon on the first day of the first month, and he arrived in Jerusalem on the first day of the fifth

---

SIDELIGHT: Ezra's journey from Babylon to Jerusalem was about nine hundred miles—about the distance from Chicago to Dallas. But because there were no freeways in the Near East, the trip took about four months (Ezra 7:9).

After these things There is a time period of about sixty years between chapters six and seven.

month, because God was helping him. ¹⁰Ezra had worked hard to know and obey the Teachings of the LORD and to teach his rules and commands to the Israelites.

SIDELIGHT: Ezra is known as the "Father of Judaism" for his role in preserving the faith (Ezra 7:10). Tradition credits him with dictating from memory ninety-four books (including twenty-four in the Old Testament) that might otherwise have been lost or burned during the Exile.

Artaxerxes' Letter to Ezra

¹¹King Artaxerxes had given a letter to Ezra, a priest and teacher who taught about the commands and laws the LORD gave Israel. This is a copy of the letter:

¹²From Artaxerxes, king of kings, to Ezra the priest, a teacher of the Law of the God of heaven.

Greetings.
¹³Now I give this order: Any Israelite in my kingdom who wishes may go with you to Jerusalem, including priests and Levites. ¹⁴Ezra, you are sent by the king and the seven people who advise him to ask how Judah and Jerusalem are obeying the Law of your God, which you are carrying with you. ¹⁵Also take with you the silver and gold that the king and those who advise him have given freely to the God of Israel, whose Temple*d* is in Jerusalem. ¹⁶Also take the silver and gold you receive from the area of Babylon. Take the offerings the Israelites and their priests have given as gifts for the Temple of your God in Jerusalem. ¹⁷With this money buy bulls, male sheep, and lambs, and the grain offerings and drink offerings that go with those sacrifices. Then sacrifice them on the altar in the Temple of your God in Jerusalem.

¹⁸You and your fellow Jews may spend the silver and gold left over as you want and as God wishes. ¹⁹Take to the God of Jerusalem all the utensils for worship in the Temple of your God, ²⁰which we have given you. Use the royal treasury to pay for anything else *you need for the Temple of your God.*

²¹Now I, King Artaxerxes, give this order to all the men in charge of the treasury of Trans-Euphrates: Give Ezra, a priest and a teacher of the Law of the God of heaven, whatever he asks for. ²²Give him up to seventy-five hundred pounds of silver, six hundred bushels of wheat, six hundred gallons of wine, and six hundred gallons of olive oil. And give him as much salt as he wants. ²³Carefully give him whatever the God of heaven wants for the Temple of the God of heaven. We do not want God to be angry with the king and his sons. ²⁴Remember, you must not make these people pay taxes of any kind: priests, Levites, singers, gatekeepers, Temple servants, and other workers in this Temple of God.

²⁵And you, Ezra, use the wisdom you have from your God to choose judges and lawmakers to rule the Jewish people of Trans-Euphrates. They know the laws of your God, and you may teach anyone who does not know them. ²⁶Whoever does not obey the law of your God or of the king must be punished. He will be killed, or sent away, or have his property taken away, or be put in jail.

²⁷Praise the LORD, the God of our ancestors. He caused the king to want to honor the Temple of the LORD in Jerusalem. ²⁸The LORD has shown me, Ezra, his love in the presence of the king, those who advise the king, and the royal officers. Because the LORD my God was helping me, I had courage, and I gathered the leaders of Israel to return with me.

Leaders Who Returned with Ezra

8 These are the leaders of the family groups and those who were listed with them who came back with me from Babylon during the rule of King Artaxerxes.

²From the descendants*d* of Phinehas: Gershom.
From the descendants of Ithamar: Daniel.
From the descendants of David: Hattush ³of the descendants of Shecaniah.
From the descendants of Parosh: Zechariah, with one hundred fifty men.
⁴From the descendants of Pahath-Moab: Eliehoenai son of Zerahiah, with two hundred men.
⁵From the descendants of Zattu: Shecaniah son of Jahaziel, with three hundred men.
⁶From the descendants of Adin: Ebed son of Jonathan, with fifty men.
⁷From the descendants of Elam: Jeshaiah son of Athaliah, with seventy men.
⁸From the descendants of Shephatiah: Zeba-*diah son of Michael, with eighty men.*
⁹From the descendants of Joab: Obadiah son of Jehiel, with two hundred eighteen men.
¹⁰From the descendants of Bani: Shelomith son of Josiphiah, with one hundred sixty men.
¹¹From the descendants of Bebai: Zechariah son of Bebai, with twenty-eight men.

¹²From the descendants of Azgad: Johanan son of Hakkatan, with one hundred ten men.

¹³From the descendants of Adonikam, these were the last ones: Eliphelet, Jeuel, and Shemaiah, with sixty men.

¹⁴From the descendants of Bigvai: Uthai and Zaccur, with seventy men.

The Return to Jerusalem

¹⁵I called all those people together at the canal that flows toward Ahava, where we camped for three days. I checked all the people and the priests, but I did not find any Levites. ¹⁶So I called these leaders: Eliezer, Ariel, Shemaiah, Elnathan, Jarib, Elnathan, Nathan, Zechariah, and Meshullam. And I called Joiarib and Elnathan, who were teachers. ¹⁷I sent these men to Iddo, the leader at Casiphia, and told them what to say to Iddo and his relatives, who are the Temple*d* servants in Casiphia. I sent them to bring servants to us for the Temple*d* of our God. ¹⁸Our God was helping us, so Iddo's relatives gave us Sherebiah, a wise man from the descendants of Mahli son of Levi, who was the son of Israel. And they brought Sherebiah's sons and brothers, for a total of eighteen men. ¹⁹And they brought to us Hashabiah and Jeshaiah from the descendants of Merari, and his brothers and nephews. In all there were twenty men. ²⁰They also brought two hundred twenty of the Temple servants, a group David and the officers had set up to help the Levites. All of those men were listed by name.

²¹There by the Ahava Canal, I announced we would all give up eating and humble ourselves before our God. We would ask God for a safe trip for ourselves, our children, and all our possessions. ²²I was ashamed to ask the king for soldiers and horsemen to protect us from enemies on the road. We had said to the king, "Our God helps everyone who obeys him, but he is very angry with all who reject him." ²³So we gave up eating and prayed to our God about our trip, and he answered our prayers.

²⁴Then I chose twelve of the priests who were leaders, Sherebiah, Hashabiah, and ten of their relatives. ²⁵I weighed the offering of silver and gold and the utensils given for the Temple of our God, and I gave them to the twelve priests I had chosen. The king, the people who advised him, his officers, and all the Israelites there with us had given these things for the Temple. ²⁶I weighed out and gave them about fifty thousand pounds of silver, about seventy-five hundred pounds of silver objects, and about seventy-five hundred pounds of gold. ²⁷I gave them twenty gold bowls that weighed about nineteen pounds and two fine pieces of polished bronze that were as valuable as gold.

²⁸Then I said to the priests, "You and these

utensils belong to the LORD for his service. The silver and gold are gifts to the LORD, the God of your ancestors. ²⁹Guard these things carefully. In Jerusalem, weigh them in front of the leading priests, Levites, and the leaders of the family groups of Israel in the rooms of the Temple of the LORD." ³⁰So the priests and Levites accepted the silver, the gold, and the utensils that had been weighed to take them to the Temple of our God in Jerusalem.

³¹On the twelfth day of the first month we left the Ahava Canal and started toward Jerusalem. Our God helped us and protected us from enemies and robbers along the way. ³²Finally we arrived in Jerusalem where we rested three days.

³³On the fourth day we weighed out the silver, the gold, and the utensils in the Temple of our God. We handed them to the priest Meremoth son of Uriah. Eleazar son of Phinehas was with him, as were the Levites Jozabad son of Jeshua and Noadiah son of Binnui. ³⁴We checked everything by number and by weight, and the total weight was written down.

³⁵Then the captives who returned made burnt offerings to the God of Israel. They sacrificed twelve bulls for all Israel, ninety-six male sheep, and seventy-seven lambs. For a sin offering there were twelve male goats. All this was a burnt offering to the LORD. ³⁶They took King Artaxerxes' orders to the royal officers and to the governors of Trans-Euphrates. Then these men gave help to the people and the Temple of God.

Ezra's Prayer

9 After these things had been done, the leaders came to me and said, "Ezra, the Israelites, including the priests and Levites, have not kept themselves separate from the people around us. Those neighbors do evil things, as the Canaanites, Hittites, Perizzites, Jebusites, Ammonites, Moabites, Egyptians, and Amorites did. ²The Israelite men and their sons have married these women. They have mixed the people who belong to God with the people around them. The leaders and officers of Israel have led the rest of the Israelites to do this unfaithful thing."

³When I heard this, I angrily tore my robe and coat, pulled hair from my head and beard, and sat down in shock. ⁴Everyone who trembled in fear at the word of the God of Israel gathered around me because of the unfaithfulness of the captives who had returned. I sat there in shock until the evening sacrifice.

⁵At the evening sacrifice I got up from where I had shown my shame. My robe and coat were torn, and I fell on my knees with my hands spread out to the LORD my God. ⁶I prayed,

"My God, I am too ashamed and embarrassed to lift up my face to you, my God, because our sins are so many. They are higher than our heads. Our guilt even reaches up to the sky. [7]From the days of our ancestors until now, our guilt has been great. Because of our sins, we, our kings, and our priests have been punished by the sword and captivity. Foreign kings have taken away our things and shamed us, even as it is today.

> ✺ **SIDELIGHT:** When Ezra got upset, he tore his clothes and pulled hair out of his head and beard—the only person to do that in the Bible (Ezra 9:3). Nehemiah had a less painful approach—for him, at least. He pulled out the hair of people at whom he was angry (Nehemiah 13:25, p. 440).

[8]"But now, for a short time, the LORD our God has been kind to us. He has let some of us come back from captivity and has let us live in safety in his holy place. And so our God gives us hope and a little relief from our slavery. [9]Even though we are slaves, our God has not left us. He caused the kings of Persia to be kind to us and has given us new life. We can rebuild the Temple[d] and repair its ruins. And he has given us a wall to protect us in Judah and Jerusalem.

[10]"But now, our God, what can we say after you have done all this? We have disobeyed your commands [11]that you gave through your servants the prophets.[d] You said, 'The land you are entering to own is ruined; the people living there have spoiled it by the evil they do. Their evil filled the land with uncleanness[d] from one end to the other. [12]So do not let your daughters marry their sons, and do not let their daughters marry your sons. Do not wish for their peace or success. Then you will be strong and eat the good things of the land. Then you can leave this land to your descendants[d] forever.'

[13]"What has happened to us is our own fault. We have done evil things, and our guilt is great. But you, our God, have punished us less than we deserve; you have left a few of us alive. [14]We should not again break your commands by allowing marriages with these wicked people. If we did, you would get angry enough to destroy us, and none of us would be left alive. [15]LORD, God of Israel, by your goodness a few of us are left

FORGIVENESS

An Unexpected Visitor

"The Pope has been shot!" These words echoed throughout the world on May 13, 1981. Pope John Paul II had been shot in the stomach by Mehmet Ali Agca.

It took hours of surgery and weeks of painful rehabilitation for the Pope to regain his health. Yet he survived and returned to his duties. The terrorist was captured and imprisoned. It seemed the end of a near-fatal story.

But it wasn't.

Less than three years after the shooting, the Pope visited Agca in Rome's Rebibbia prison. Sitting in Agca's cell, John Paul held Agca's hand and spoke softly with him for twenty minutes.

What did the Pope say to the man who had tried to kill him? "I spoke to him as a brother whom I have pardoned, and who has my complete trust. . . . I was able to meet my assailant and repeat to him the pardon I gave him immediately."

Pope John Paul II showed love to Mehmet Ali Agca by forgiving him.

Ezra 9:1–9 tells how God showed love to his people by forgiving them.
- Did Agca or the Israelites deserve the love and forgiveness they received? Why or why not?
- When has God forgiven you when you felt you didn't deserve it?

C O N S I D E R . . .
- making a list of people who have offended you and then forgiving them in the same way God has forgiven you.
- doing one loving thing for someone who has been hard for you to love.

F O R   M O R E ,   S E E . . .
- Isaiah 1:18–20 (p. 618)
- Matthew 6:9–15 (p. 918)
- Romans 5:6–11 (p. 1145)

alive today. We admit that we are guilty and none of us should be allowed to stand before you."

The People Confess Sin

10 As Ezra was praying and confessing and crying and throwing himself down in front of the Temple,*d* a large group of Israelite men, women, and children gathered around him who were also crying loudly. ²Then Shecaniah son of Jehiel the Elamite said to Ezra, "We have been unfaithful to our God by marrying women from the peoples around us. But even so, there is still hope for Israel. ³Now let us make an agreement before our God. We will send away all these women and their children as you and those who respect the commands of our God advise. Let it be done to obey God's Teachings. ⁴Get up, Ezra. You are in charge, and we will support you. Have courage and do it."

⁵So Ezra got up and made the priests, Levites, and all the people of Israel promise to do what was suggested; and they promised. ⁶Then Ezra left the Temple and went to the room of Jehohanan son of Eliashib. While Ezra was there, he did not eat or drink, because he was still sad about the unfaithfulness of the captives who had returned.

⁷They sent an order in Judah and Jerusalem for all the captives who had returned to meet together in Jerusalem. ⁸Whoever did not come to Jerusalem within three days would lose his property and would no longer be a member of the community of the returned captives. That was the decision of the officers and older leaders.

⁹So within three days all the people of Judah and Benjamin gathered in Jerusalem. It was the twentieth day of the ninth month. All the people were sitting in the open place in front of the Temple and were upset because of the meeting and because it was raining. ¹⁰Ezra the priest stood up and said to them, "You have been unfaithful and have married non-Jewish women. You have made Israel more guilty. ¹¹Now, confess it to the LORD, the God of your ancestors. Do his will and separate yourselves from the people living around you and from your non-Jewish wives."

¹²Then the whole group answered Ezra with a loud voice, "Ezra, you're right! We must do what you say. ¹³But there are many people here, and it's the rainy season. We can't stand outside, and this problem can't be solved in a day or two, because we have sinned badly. ¹⁴Let our officers make a decision for the whole group. Then let everyone in our towns who has married a non-Jewish woman meet with the older leaders and judges of each town at a planned time, until the hot anger of our God turns away from us." ¹⁵Only Jonathan son of Asahel, Jahzeiah son of Tikvah,

Meshullam, and Shabbethai the Levite were against the plan.

¹⁶So the returned captives did what was suggested. Ezra the priest chose men who were leaders of the family groups and named one from each family division. On the first day of the tenth month they sat down to study each case. ¹⁷By the first day of the first month, they had finished with all the men who had married non-Jewish women.

Those Guilty of Marrying Non-Jewish Women

¹⁸These are the descendants*d* of the priests who had married foreign women:

From the descendants of Jeshua son of Jozadak and Jeshua's brothers: Maaseiah, Eliezer, Jarib, and Gedaliah. ¹⁹(They all promised to divorce their wives, and each one brought a male sheep from the flock as a penalty offering.)

²⁰From the descendants of Immer: Hanani and Zebadiah.

²¹From the descendants of Harim: Maaseiah, Elijah, Shemaiah, Jehiel, and Uzziah.

²²From the descendants of Pashhur: Elioenai, Maaseiah, Ishmael, Nethanel, Jozabad, and Elasah.

²³Among the Levites: Jozabad, Shimei, Kelaiah (also called Kelita), Pethahiah, Judah, and Eliezer.

²⁴Among the singers: Eliashib.

Among the gatekeepers: Shallum, Telem, and Uri.

²⁵And among the other Israelites, these married non-Jewish women:

From the descendants of Parosh: Ramiah, Izziah, Malkijah, Mijamin, Eleazar, Malkijah, and Benaiah.

²⁶From the descendants of Elam: Mattaniah, Zechariah, Jehiel, Abdi, Jeremoth, and Elijah.

²⁷From the descendants of Zattu: Elioenai, Eliashib, Mattaniah, Jeremoth, Zabad, and Aziza.

²⁸From the descendants of Bebai: Jehohanan, Hananiah, Zabbai, and Athlai.

²⁹From the descendants of Bani: Meshullam, Malluch, Adaiah, Jashub, Sheal, and Jeremoth.

³⁰From the descendants of Pahath-Moab: Adna, Kelal, Benaiah, Maaseiah, Mattaniah, Bezalel, Binnui, and Manasseh.

³¹From the descendants of Harim: Eliezer, Ishijah, Malkijah, Shemaiah, Shimeon, ³²Benjamin, Malluch, and Shemariah.

³³From the descendants of Hashum: Mattenai, Mattattah, Zabad, Eliphelet, Jeremai, Manasseh, and Shimei.

³⁴From the descendants of Bani: Maadai, Amram, Uel, ³⁵Benaiah, Bedeiah, Keluhi, ³⁶Vaniah, Meremoth, Eliashib, ³⁷Mattaniah, Mattenai, and Jaasu.

³⁸From the descendants of Binnui: Shimei,

³⁹Shelemiah, Nathan, Adaiah, ⁴⁰Macnadebai, Shashai, Sharai, ⁴¹Azarel, Shelemiah, Shemariah, ⁴²Shallum, Amariah, and Joseph.

⁴³From the descendants of Nebo: Jeiel, Mattithiah, Zabad, Zebina, Jaddai, Joel, and Benaiah.

⁴⁴All these men had married non-Jewish women, and some of them had children by these wives.

NEHEMIAH

Why Read This Book:

■ Understand the importance of acting on what you believe (Nehemiah 1—5).
■ Recognize how serving God sometimes means standing against those who don't serve him (Nehemiah 6—7).
■ See the life-changing effects of believing God's word (Nehemiah 8—13).

Behind the Scenes:

Imagine a member of the president's cabinet leaving that prestigious office to trek on foot across a desert to rebuild a city destroyed one hundred forty years earlier.

That's about what Nehemiah did. He held a high office in the kingdom of Persia, which ruled virtually all of the Near East. He had power, prestige, and money.

Unlike many leaders in biblical times, whose high positions led them away from God, Nehemiah was not happy in his high office. He had heard about his own people, the Jews, struggling to rebuild the walls around Jerusalem. Ezra (see p. 416) had rebuilt the Temple and started religious reforms. But the city wall lay in ruin, leaving the city vulnerable to attackers.

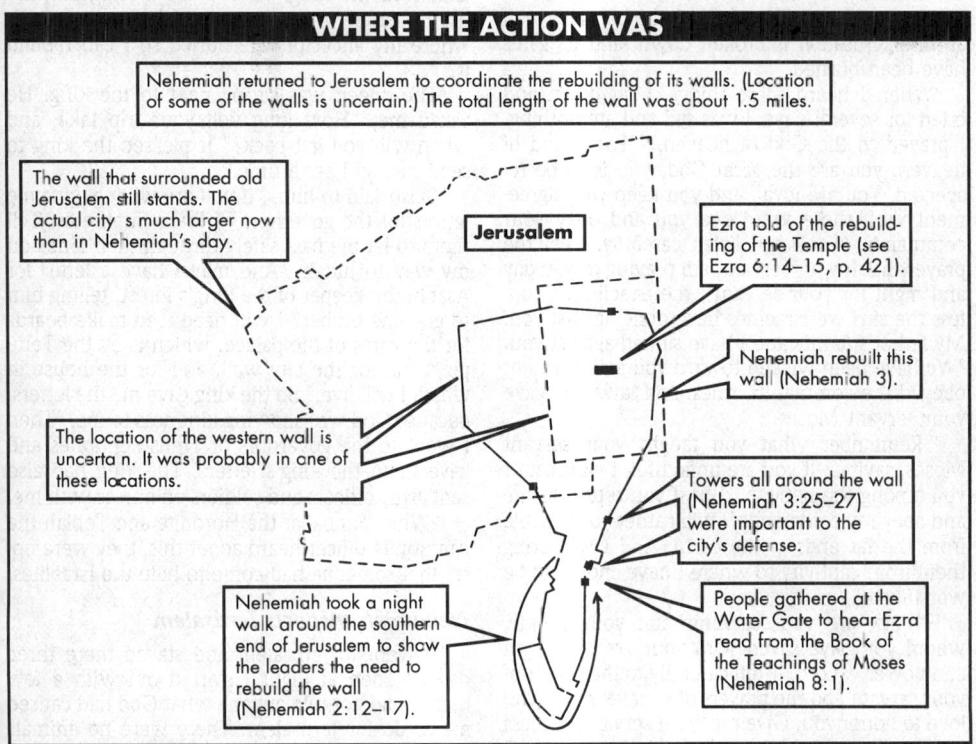

WHERE THE ACTION WAS

Nehemiah returned to Jerusalem to coordinate the rebuilding of its walls. (Location of some of the walls is uncertain.) The total length of the wall was about 1.5 miles.

Jerusalem

The wall that surrounded old Jerusalem still stands. The actual city is much larger now than in Nehemiah's day.

Ezra told of the rebuilding of the Temple (see Ezra 6:14–15, p. 421).

Nehemiah rebuilt this wall (Nehemiah 3).

The location of the western wall is uncertain. It was probably in one of these locations.

Towers all around the wall (Nehemiah 3:25–27) were important to the city's defense.

Nehemiah took a night walk around the southern end of Jerusalem to show the leaders the need to rebuild the wall (Nehemiah 2:12–17).

People gathered at the Water Gate to hear Ezra read from the Book of the Teachings of Moses (Nehemiah 8:1).

WHEN THE ACTION WAS

	The Northern Kingdom (Israel) fell to Assyria	Jews began returning to Jerusalem from exile	Ezra returned to Jerusalem from exile		Jesus was born
1000BC	**750BC**	**500BC**		**250BC**	**BC/AD**
David was Israel's king		People of Judah taken into exile in Babylon	Nehemiah returned to Jerusalem from exile		

So Nehemiah asked for a change of assignment and was appointed governor of Jerusalem. He returned to the city to rally the people to rebuild the walls. Once the walls were up, he returned to his duties. But when religious corruption started, he returned to Jerusalem for a second term as governor.

The book of Nehemiah tells the story of this great leader. Parts of it (such as Nehemiah 1—7) read like a private journal, showing the joys and frustrations of trying to lead the people. Reading the book gives us a glimpse of a great leader. Nehemiah's organizational skills, prayer life, dependence on God, and commitment to justice shine as an example for everyone.

Nehemiah's Prayer

1 These are the words of Nehemiah son of Hacaliah.

In the month of Kislev in the twentieth year,[n] I, Nehemiah, was in the capital city of Susa. [2]One of my brothers named Hanani came with some other men from Judah. I asked them about Jerusalem and the Jewish people who lived through the captivity.

[3]They answered me, "Those who are left from the captivity are back in Judah, but they are in much trouble and are full of shame. The wall around Jerusalem is broken down, and its gates have been burned."

[4]When I heard these things, I sat down and cried for several days. I was sad and ate nothing. I prayed to the God of heaven, [5]"LORD, God of heaven, you are the great God who is to be respected. You are loyal, and you keep your agreement with those who love you and obey your commands. [6]Look and listen carefully. Hear the prayer that I, your servant, am praying to you day and night for your servants, the Israelites. I confess the sins we Israelites have done against you. My father's family and I have sinned against you. [7]We have been wicked toward you and have not obeyed the commands, rules, and laws you gave your servant Moses.

[8]"Remember what you taught your servant Moses, saying, 'If you are unfaithful, I will scatter you among the nations. [9]But if you return to me and obey my commands, I will gather your people from the far ends of the earth. And I will bring them from captivity to where I have chosen to be worshiped.'

[10]"They are your servants and your people, whom you have saved with your great strength and power. [11]Lord, listen carefully to the prayer of your servant and the prayers of your servants who love to honor you. Give me, your servant, success today; allow this king to show kindness to me."

I was the one who served wine to the king.

Nehemiah Is Sent to Jerusalem

2 It was the month of Nisan in the twentieth year Artaxerxes was king. He wanted some wine, so I took some and gave it to the king. I had not been sad in his presence before. [2]So the king said, "Why does your face look sad even though you are not sick? Your heart must be sad."

Then I was very afraid. [3]I said to the king, "May the king live forever! My face is sad because the city where my ancestors are buried lies in ruins, and its gates have been destroyed by fire."

[4]Then the king said to me, "What do you want?"

First I prayed to the God of heaven. [5]Then I answered the king, "If you are willing and if I have pleased you, send me to the city in Judah where my ancestors are buried so I can rebuild it."

[6]The queen was sitting next to the king. He asked me, "How long will your trip take, and when will you get back?" It pleased the king to send me, so I set a time.

[7]I also said to him, "If you are willing, give me letters for the governors of Trans-Euphrates. Tell them to let me pass safely through their lands on my way to Judah. [8]And may I have a letter for Asaph, the keeper of the king's forest, telling him to give me timber? I will need it to make boards for the gates of the palace, which is by the Temple,[d] and for the city wall, and for the house in which I will live." So the king gave me the letters, because God was showing kindness to me. [9]Then I went to the governors of Trans-Euphrates and gave them the king's letters. The king had also sent army officers and soldiers on horses with me.

[10]When Sanballat the Horonite and Tobiah the Ammonite officer heard about this, they were upset that someone had come to help the Israelites.

Nehemiah Inspects Jerusalem

[11]I went to Jerusalem and stayed there three days. [12]Then at night I started out with a few men. I had not told anyone what God had caused me to do for Jerusalem. There were no animals with me except the one I was riding,

[13]*I went out at night through the Valley Gate. I rode toward the Dragon Well and the Trash Gate, inspecting the walls of Jerusalem that had been broken down and the gates that had been destroyed by fire.* [14]Then I rode on toward the

twentieth year This is probably referring to the twentieth year King Artaxerxes I ruled Persia.

Fountain Gate and the King's Pool, but there was not enough room for the animal I was riding to pass through. [15]So I went up the valley at night, inspecting the wall. Finally, I turned and went back in through the Valley Gate. [16]The guards did not know where I had gone or what I was doing. I had not yet said anything to the Jewish people, the priests, the important men, the officers, or any of the others who would do the work.

[17]Then I said to them, "You can see the trouble we have here. Jerusalem is a pile of ruins, and its gates have been burned. Come, let's rebuild the wall of Jerusalem so we won't be full of shame any longer." [8]I also told them how God had been kind to me and what the king had said to me. Then they answered, "Let's start rebuilding." So they began to work hard.

[19]But when Sanballat the Horonite, Tobiah the Ammonite officer, and Geshem the Arab heard about it, they made fun of us and laughed at us. They said, "What are you doing? Are you turning against the king?"

[20]But I answered them, "The God of heaven will give us success. We, his servants, will start rebuilding, but you have no share, claim, or memorial in Jerusalem."

Builders of the Wall

3 Eliashib the high priest and his fellow priests went to work and rebuilt the Sheep Gate. They gave it to the Lord's service and set its doors in place. They worked as far as the Tower of the Hundred and gave it to the Lord's service. Then they went on to the Tower of Hananel. [2]Next to them, the men of Jericho built part of the wall, and Zaccur son of Imri built next to them.

[3]The sons of Hassenaah rebuilt the Fish Gate, laying its boards and setting its doors, bolts, and bars in place. [4]Meremoth son of Uriah, the son of Hakkoz, made repairs next to them. Meshullam son of Berekiah, the son of Meshezabel, made repairs next to Meremoth. And Zadok son of Baana made repairs next to Meshullam. [5]The men from Tekoa made repairs next to them, but the leading men of Tekoa would not work under their supervisors.

[6]Joiada son of Paseah and Meshullam son of Besodeiah repaired the Old Gate. They laid its boards and set its doors, bolts, and bars in place. [7]Next to them, Melatiah from Gibeon, other men from Gibeon and Mizpah, and Jadon from Meronoth made repairs. These places were ruled by the governor of Trans-Euphrates. [8]Next to them, Uzziel son of Harhaiah, a goldsmith, made repairs. And next to him, Hananiah, a perfume maker, made repairs. These men rebuilt Jerusalem as far as the Broad Wall. [9]The next part of the wall was

repaired by Rephaiah son of Hur, the ruler of half of the district of Jerusalem. [10]Next to him, Jedaiah son of Harumaph made repairs opposite his own house. And next to him, Hattush son of Hashabneiah made repairs. [11]Malkijah son of Harim and Hasshub son of Pahath-Moab repaired another part of the wall and the Tower of the Ovens. [12]Next to them Shallum son of Hallohesh, the ruler of half of the district of Jerusalem, and his daughters made repairs.

SIDELIGHT: Did you know that women held construction jobs in Old Testament times? Check out Nehemiah 3:12.

---

[13]Hanun and the people of Zanoah repaired the Valley Gate, rebuilding it and setting its doors, bolts, and bars in place. They also repaired the five hundred yards of the wall to the Trash Gate.

[14]Malkijah son of Recab, the ruler of the district of Beth Hakkerem, repaired the Trash Gate. He rebuilt that gate and set its doors, bolts, and bars in place.

[15]Shallun son of Col-Hozeh, the ruler of the district of Mizpah, repaired the Fountain Gate. He rebuilt it, put a roof over it, and set its doors, bolts, and bars in place. He also repaired the wall of the Pool of Siloam next to the King's Garden all the way to the steps that went down from the older part of the city. [16]Next to Shallun was Nehemiah[n] son of Azbuk, the ruler of half of the district of Beth Zur. He made repairs opposite the tombs of David and as far as the man-made pool and the House of the Heroes.

[17]Next to him, the Levites made repairs, working under Rehum son of Bani. Next to him, Hashabiah, the ruler of half of the district of Keilah, for his district. [18]Next to him, Binnui son of Henadad and his Levites made repairs. Binnui was the ruler of the other half of the district of Keilah. [19]Next to them, Ezer son of Jeshua, the ruler of Mizpah, repaired another part of the wall. He worked across from the way up to the armory, as far as the bend. [20]Next to him, Baruch son of Zabbai worked hard on the wall that went from the bend to the entrance to the house of Eliashib, the high priest. [21]Next to him, Meremoth son of Uriah, the son of Hakkoz, repaired the wall that went from the entrance to Eliashib's house to the far end of it.

[22]Next to him worked the priests from the surrounding area. [23]Next to them, Benjamin and Hasshub made repairs in front of their own house. Next to them, Azariah son of Maaseiah, the son

---

Nehemiah This is a different Nehemiah than the one who wrote this book.

of Ananiah, made repairs beside his own house. 24Next to him, Binnui son of Henadad repaired the wall that went from Azariah's house to the bend and on to the corner. 25Palal son of Uzai worked across from the bend and by the tower on the upper palace, which is near the courtyard of the king's guard. Next to Palal, Pedaiah son of Parosh made repairs. 26The Temple*d* servants who lived on the hill of Ophel made repairs as far as a point opposite the Water Gate. They worked toward the east and the tower that extends from the palace. 27Next to them, the people of Tekoa repaired the wall from the great tower that extends from the palace to the wall of Ophel.

28The priests made repairs above the Horse Gate, each working in front of his own house. 29Next to them, Zadok son of Immer made repairs across from his own house. Next to him, Shemaiah son of Shecaniah, the guard of the East Gate, made repairs. 30Next to him, Hananiah son of Shelemiah, and Hanun, the sixth son of Zalaph, made repairs on another part of the wall. Next to them, Meshullam son of Berekiah made repairs across from where he lived. 31Next to him, Malkijah, one of the goldsmiths, made repairs. He worked as far as the house of the Temple servants and the traders, which is across from the Inspection Gate, and as far as the room above the corner of the wall. 32The goldsmiths and the traders made repairs between the room above the corner of the wall and the Sheep Gate.

Those Against the Rebuilding

4 When Sanballat heard we were rebuilding the wall, he was very angry, even furious. He made fun of the Jewish people. 2He said to his friends and those with power in Samaria, "What are these weak Jews doing? Will they rebuild the wall? Will they offer sacrifices? Can they finish it in one day? Can they bring stones back to life from piles of trash and ashes?"

3Tobiah the Ammonite, who was next to Sanballat, said, "If a fox climbed up on the stone wall they are building, it would break it down."

4I prayed, "Hear us, our God. We are hated.

Turn the insults of Sanballat and Tobiah back on their own heads. Let them be captured and stolen like valuables. 5Do not hide their guilt or take away their sins so that you can't see them, because they have insulted the builders."

6So we rebuilt the wall to half its height, because the people were willing to work.

7But Sanballat, Tobiah, the Arabs, the Ammonites, and the people from Ashdod were very angry when they heard that the repairs to Jerusalem's walls were continuing and that the holes in the wall were being closed. 8So they all made plans to come to Jerusalem and fight and stir up trouble. 9But we prayed to our God and appointed guards to watch for them day and night.

10The people of Judah said, "The workers are getting tired. There is so much trash we cannot rebuild the wall."

11And our enemies said, "The Jews won't know or see anything until we come among them and kill them and stop the work."

12Then the Jewish people who lived near our enemies came and told us ten times, "Everywhere you turn, the enemy will attack us." 13So I put people behind the lowest places along the wall — the open places — and I put families together with their swords, spears, and bows. 14Then I looked around and stood up and said to the important men, the leaders, and the rest of the people: "Don't be afraid of them. Remember the Lord, who is great and powerful. Fight for your brothers, your sons and daughters, your wives, and your homes."

15Then our enemies heard that we knew about their plans and that God had ruined their plans. So we all went back to the wall, each to his own work.

16From that day on, half my people worked on the wall. The other half was ready with spears, shields, bows, and armor. The officers stood in back of the people of Judah 17who were building the wall. Those who carried materials did their work with one hand and carried a weapon with the other. 18Each builder wore his sword at his side as he worked. The man who blew the trumpet to warn the people stayed next to me.

19Then I said to the important men, the leaders, and the rest of the people, "This is a very big job. We are spreading out along the wall so that we are far apart. 20Wherever you hear the sound of the trumpet, assemble there. Our God will fight for us."

21*So we continued to work with half the men* holding spears from sunrise till the stars came out. 22At that time I also said to the people, "Let every man and his helper stay inside Jerusalem at night. They can be our guards at night and workmen during the day." 23Neither I, my brothers, my workers, nor the guards with me ever took off our clothes. Each person carried his weapon even when he went for water.

Nehemiah Helps Poor People

5 The men and their wives complained loudly against their fellow Jews. [2]Some of them were saying, "We have many sons and daughters in our families. To eat and stay alive, we need grain."

[3]Others were saying, "We are borrowing money against our fields, vineyards, and homes to get grain because there is not much food."

[4]And still others were saying, "We are borrowing money to pay the king's tax on our fields and vineyards. [5]We are just like our fellow Jews, and our sons are like their sons. But we have to sell our sons and daughters as slaves. Some of our daughters have already been sold. But there is nothing we can do, because our fields and vineyards already belong to other people."

[6]When I heard their complaints about these things, I was very angry. [7]After I thought about it, I accused the important people and the leaders, "You are charging your own brothers too much interest." So I called a large meeting to deal with them. [8]I said to them, "As much as possible, we have bought freedom for our fellow Jews who had been sold to foreigners. Now you are selling your fellow Jews to us!" The leaders were quiet and had nothing to say.

[9]Then I said, "What you are doing is not right. Don't you fear God? Don't let our foreign enemies shame us. [10]I, my brothers, and my men are also lending money and grain to the people. But stop charging them so much for this. [11]Give back their fields, vineyards, olive trees, and houses right now. Also give back the extra amount you charged — the hundredth part of the money, grain, new wine, and oil."

[12]They said, "We will give it back and not demand anything more from them. We will do as you say."

Then I called for the priests, and I made the important men and leaders take an oath to do what they had said. [13]Also I shook out the folds of my robe and said, "In this way may God shake out everyone who does not keep his promise. May God shake him out of his house and out of

---

HUNGER AND POVERTY

A Blanket of Love

Eleven-year-old Trevor Ferrell learned there were people living on the streets of Philadelphia—not far from his suburban home. Curious, he talked his parents into taking him downtown. There Trevor got out of the car and gave a homeless person a blanket.

When Trevor returned home, he searched for extra blankets and clothing, and he convinced his parents to take him downtown again and again to deliver such items. He talked to people at his church, and they donated food, clothing, and even a van to take things to the homeless.

Soon Trevor was in the newspapers, on television, even meeting the President of the United States! Trevor wanted to tell others what they could do to help those in need.

Now there is a home in Philadelphia called "Trevor's Place." People can live and be fed there. Trevor Ferrell began by giving a little of himself and was able to challenge others to do the same.

"One person can make a difference," Trevor says. "Just do what you can and follow your heart."

Nehemiah was also a person who made a difference for the poor. See how he helped them in **Nehemiah 5:1–11**.

■ How did Nehemiah use his political power as governor of Judah to help the poor? How were Trevor's actions like Nehemiah's?

■ How can you, like Trevor and Nehemiah, help people who are hungry?

CONSIDER . . .

■ helping low-income people in your community by giving nonperishable food to a food bank that distributes supplies to people in need.

■ encouraging your government to take care of the needs of the poor by joining a Christian organization such as Bread for the World (801 Rhode Island Ave., NE, Washington, DC 20018).

FOR MORE, SEE . . .

■ Deuteronomy 15:7–8 (p. 175)   ■ James 2:1–9 (p. 1294)

■ Matthew 25:31–46 (p. 954)

the things that are his. Let that person be shaken out and emptied!"

Then the whole group said, "Amen," and they praised the LORD. So the people did what they had promised.

14I was appointed governor in the land of Judah in the twentieth year of King Artaxerxes' rule. I was governor of Judah for twelve years, until his thirty-second year. During that time neither my brothers nor I ate the food that was allowed for a governor. 15But the governors before me had placed a heavy load on the people. They took about one pound of silver from each person, along with food and wine. The governors' helpers before me also controlled the people, but I did not do that, because I feared God. 16I worked on the wall, as did all my men who were gathered there. We did not buy any fields.

17Also, I fed one hundred fifty Jewish people and officers at my table, as well as those who came from the nations around us. 18This is what was prepared every day: one ox, six good sheep, and birds. And every ten days there were all kinds of wine. But I never demanded the food that was due a governor, because the people were already working very hard.

19Remember to be kind to me, my God, for all the good I have done for these people.

More Problems for Nehemiah

6 Then Sanballat, Tobiah, Geshem the Arab, and our other enemies heard that I had rebuilt the wall and that there was not one gap in it. But I had not yet set the doors in the gates. 2So Sanballat and Geshem sent me this message: "Come, Nehemiah, let's meet together in Kephirim on the plain of Ono."

But they were planning to harm me. 3So I sent messengers to them with this answer: "I am doing a great work, and I can't come down. I don't want the work to stop while I leave to meet you." 4Sanballat and Geshem sent the same message to me four times, and each time I sent back the same answer.

5The fifth time Sanballat sent his helper to me with the message, and in his hand was an unsealed letter. 6This is what was written:

A report is going around to all the nations, and Geshem says it is true, that you and the Jewish people are planning to turn against the king and that you are rebuilding the wall. They say you are going to be their king 7and that you have appointed prophets*d* to announce in Jerusalem: "There is a king of Judah!" The king will hear about this. So come, let's discuss this together.

8So I sent him back this answer: "Nothing you are saying is really happening. You are just making it up in your own mind."

9Our enemies were trying to scare us, thinking, "They will get too weak to work. Then the wall will not be finished."

But I prayed, "God, make me strong."

10One day I went to the house of Shemaiah son of Delaiah, the son of Mehetabel. Shemaiah had to stay at home. He said, "Nehemiah, let's meet in the Temple*d* of God. Let's go inside the Temple and close the doors, because men are coming at night to kill you."

11But I said, "Should a man like me run away? Should I run for my life into the Temple? I will not go." 12I knew that God had not sent him but that Tobiah and Sanballat had paid him to prophesy against me. 13They paid him to frighten me so I would do this and sin. Then they could give me a bad name to shame me.

14I prayed, "My God, remember Tobiah and Sanballat and what they have done. Also remember the prophetess Noadiah and the other prophets who have been trying to frighten me."

SIDELIGHT: Building the wall around Jerusalem took only fifty-two days (Nehemiah 6:15). But some archaeologists believe the wall would have been stronger if Nehemiah had slowed down some. Portions of the wall that have been uncovered show signs of the hasty construction. But Nehemiah might not have been able to slow down (see Nehemiah 4:15–18, p. 430)!

The Wall Is Finished

15The wall of Jerusalem was completed on the twenty-fifth day of the month of Elul. It took fifty-two days to rebuild. 16When all our enemies heard about it and all the nations around us saw it, they were shamed. They then understood that the work had been done with the help of our God.

17Also in those days the important men of Judah sent many letters to Tobiah, and he answered them. 18Many Jewish people had promised to be faithful to Tobiah, because he was the son-in-law of Shecaniah son of Arah. And Tobiah's son Jehohanan had married the daughter of Meshullam son of Berekiah. 19These important men kept telling me about the good things Tobiah was doing, and then they would tell Tobiah what I said about him. So Tobiah sent letters to frighten me.

7 After the wall had been rebuilt and I had set the doors in place, the gatekeepers, singers, and Levites were chosen. 2I put my brother Ha-

nani, along with Hananiah, the commander of the palace, in charge of Jerusalem. Hananiah was honest and feared God more than most people. [3]I said to them. "The gates of Jerusalem should not be opened until the sun is hot. While the gatekeepers are still on duty, have them shut and bolt the doors. Appoint people who live in Jerusalem as guards, and put some at guard posts and some near their own houses."

The Captives Who Returned

[4]The city was large and roomy, but there were few people in it, and the houses had not yet been rebuilt. [5]Then my God caused me to gather the important men, the leaders, and the common people so I could register them by families. I found the family history of those who had returned first. This is what I found written there:

[6]These are the people of the area who returned from captivity, whom Nebuchadnezzar king of Babylon had taken away. They returned to Jerusalem and Judah, each going back to his own town. [7]These people returned with Zerubbabel, Jeshua, Nehemiah, Azariah, Raamiah, Nahamani, Mordecai, Bilshan, Mispereth, Bigvai, Nehum, and Baanah.

These are the people from Israel: [8]the descendants[d] of Parosh—2,172; [9]the descendants of Shephatiah—372; [10]the descendants of Arah—652; [11]the descendants of Pahath-Moab (through the family of Jeshua and Joab)—2,818; [12]the descendants of Elam—1,254; [13]the descendants of Zattu—845; [14]the descendants of Zaccai—760; [15]the descendants of Binnui—648; [16]the descendants of Bebai—628; [17]the descendants of Azgad—2,322; [18]the descendants of Adonikam—667 [19]the descendants of Bigvai—2,067; [20]the descendants of Adin—655; [21]the descendants of Ater (through Hezekiah)—98; [22]the descendants of Hashum—328; [23]the descendants of Bezai—324; [24]the descendants of Hariph—112; [25]the descendants of Gibeon—95.

[26]These are the people from the towns of Bethlehem and Netophah—188; [27]of Anathoth—128; [28]of Beth Azmaveth—42; [29]of Kiriath Jearim, Kephirah, and Beeroth—743; [30]of Ramah and Geba—621; [31]of Micmash—122; [32]of Bethel and Ai—123; [33]of the other Nebo—52;

[34]of the other Elam—1,254; [35]of Harim—320; [36]of Jericho—345; [37]of Lod, Hadid, and Ono—721; [38]of Senaah—3,930.

[39]These are the priests: the descendants of Jedaiah (through the family of Jeshua)—973; [40]the descendants of Immer—1,052; [41]the descendants of Pashhur—1,247; [42]the descendants of Harim—1,017.

[43]These are the Levites: the descendants of Jeshua (through Kadmiel through the family of Hodaviah)—74.

[44]These are the singers: the descendants of Asaph—148.

[45]These are the gatekeepers: the descendants of Shallum, Ater, Talmon, Akkub, Hatita, and Shobai—138.

[46]These are the Temple[d] servants: the descendants of Ziha, Hasupha, Tabbaoth, [47]Keros, Sia, Padon, [48]Lebana, Hagaba, Shalmai, [49]Hanan, Giddel, Gahar, [50]Reaiah, Rezin, Nekoda, [51]Gazzam, Uzza, Paseah, [52]Besai, Meunim, Nephussim, [53]Bakbuk, Hakupha, Harhur, [54]Bazluth, Mehida, Harsha, [55]Barkos, Sisera, Temah, [56]Neziah, and Hatipha.

[57]These are the descendants of the servants of Solomon: the descendants of Sotai, Sophereth, Perida, [58]Jaala, Darkon, Giddel, [59]Shephatiah, Hattil, Pokereth-Hazzebaim, and Amon.

[60]The Temple servants and the descendants of the servants of Solomon totaled 392 people.

[61]Some people came to Jerusalem from the towns of Tel Melah, Tel Harsha, Kerub, Addon, and Immer, but they could not prove that their ancestors came from Israel. Here are their names and their number: [62]the descendants of Delaiah, Tobiah, and Nekoda—642.

[63]And these priests could not prove that their ancestors came from Israel: the descendants of Hobaiah, Hakkoz, and Barzillai. (He had married a daughter of Barzillai from Gilead and was called by her family name.)

[64]These people searched for their family records, but they could not find them. So they could not be priests, because they were thought to be unclean.[d] [65]The governor ordered them not to eat any of the holy food until a priest settled this matter by using the Urim and Thummim.[d]

[66]The total number of those who returned was 42,360. [67]This is not counting their 7,337 male and female servants and the 245 male and female singers with them. [68]They had 736 horses, 245 mules, [69]435 camels, and 6,720 donkeys.

[70]Some of the family leaders gave to the work. The governor gave to the treasury about 19 pounds of gold, 50 bowls, and 530 pieces of clothing for the priests. [71]Some of the family leaders gave about 375 pounds of gold and about 2,660 pounds of silver to the treasury for the work. [72]The total of what the other people gave was

about 375 pounds of gold, about 2,250 pounds of silver, and 67 pieces of clothing for the priests. [73]So these people all settled in their own towns: the priests, the Levites, the gatekeepers, the singers, the Temple servants, and all the other people of Israel.

Ezra Reads the Teachings

By the seventh month the Israelites were settled in their own towns.

8 All the people of Israel gathered together in the square by the Water Gate. They asked Ezra the teacher to bring out the Book of the Teachings of Moses, which the LORD had given to Israel.

[2]So on the first day of the seventh month, Ezra the priest brought out the Teachings for the crowd. Men, women, and all who could listen and understand had gathered. [3]At the square by the Water Gate Ezra read the Teachings out loud from early morning until noon to the men, women, and everyone who could listen and understand. All the people listened carefully to the Book of the Teachings.

[4]Ezra the teacher stood on a high wooden platform that had been built just for this time. On his right were Mattithiah, Shema, Anaiah, Uriah, Hilkiah, and Maaseiah. And on his left were Pedaiah, Mishael, Malkijah, Hashum, Hashbaddanah, Zechariah, and Meshullam.

[5]Ezra opened the book in full view of everyone, because he was above them. As he opened it, all the people stood up. [6]Ezra praised the LORD, the great God, and all the people held up their hands and said, "Amen! Amen!" Then they bowed down and worshiped the LORD with their faces to the ground.

[7]These Levites explained the Teachings to the people as they stood there: Jeshua, Bani, Sherebiah, Jamin, Akkub, Shabbethai, Hodiah, Maaseiah, Kelita, Azariah, Jozabad, Hanan, and Pelaiah. [8]They read from the Book of the Teachings of God and explained what it meant so the people understood what was being read.

[9]Then Nehemiah the governor, Ezra the priest and teacher, and the Levites who were teaching said to all the people, "This is a holy day to the LORD your God. Don't be sad or cry." All the people had been crying as they listened to the words of the Teachings.

[10]Nehemiah said, "Go and enjoy good food and sweet drinks. Send some to people who have none, because today is a holy day to the Lord. Don't be sad, because the joy of the LORD will make you strong."

[11]The Levites helped calm the people, saying, "Be quiet, because this is a holy day. Don't be sad."

[12]Then all the people went away to eat and drink, to send some of their food to others, and to celebrate with great joy. They finally understood what they had been taught.

[13]On the second day of the month, the leaders of all the families, the priests, and the Levites met with Ezra the teacher. They gathered to study the words of the Teachings. [14]This is what they found written in the Teachings: The LORD commanded through Moses that the people of Israel were to live in shelters during the feast of the seventh month. [15]The people were supposed to preach this message and spread it through all their towns and in Jerusalem: "Go out into the mountains, and bring back branches from olive and wild olive trees, myrtle trees, palms, and shade trees. Make shelters with them, as it is written."

[16]So the people went out and got tree branches. They built shelters on their roofs, [n] in their courtyards, in the courtyards of the Temple, [d] in the square by the Water Gate, and in the square next to the Gate of Ephraim. [17]The whole group that had come back from captivity built shelters and lived in them. The Israelites had not done this since the time of Joshua son of Nun. And they were very happy.

[18]Ezra read to them every day from the Book of the Teachings, from the first day to the last. The people of Israel celebrated the feast for seven days, and then on the eighth day the people gathered as the law said.

Israel Confesses Sins

9 On the twenty-fourth day of that same month, the people of Israel gathered. They did not eat, and they wore rough cloth and put dust on their heads to show their sadness. [2]Those people whose ancestors were from Israel had separated themselves from all foreigners. They stood and confessed their sins and their ancestors' sins. [3]For a fourth of the day they stood where they were and read from the Book of the Teachings of the LORD their God. For another fourth of the day they confessed their sins and worshiped the LORD their God. [4]These Levites were standing on the stairs: Jeshua, Bani, Kadmiel, Shebaniah, Bunni, Sherebiah, Bani, and Kanani. They called out to the LORD their God with loud voices. [5]Then these Levites spoke: Jeshua, Kadmiel, Bani, Hashabneiah, Sherebiah, Hodiah, Shebaniah, and Pethahiah. They said, "Stand up and praise the LORD your God, who lives forever and ever."

---

roofs In Bible times houses were built with flat roofs. The roof was used for drying things such as flax and fruit. And it was used as an extra room, as a place for worship, and as a place to sleep in the summer.

The People's Prayer

"Blessed be your wonderful name.
It is more wonderful than all blessing and
praise.
⁶You are the only LORD.
You made the heavens, even the highest
heavens,
with all the stars.
You made the earth and everything on it,
the seas and everything in them;
you give life to everything.
The heavenly army worships you.

⁷"You are the LORD,
the God who chose Abram
and brought him out of Ur in Babylonia
and named him Abraham.
⁸You found him faithful to you,
so you made an agreement with him
to give his descendants*d* the land of the
Canaanites,
Hittites, Amorites,
Perizzites, Jebusites, and Girgashites.
You have kept your promise,
because you do what is right.

⁹"You saw our ancestors suffering in Egypt
and heard them cry out at the Red Sea.*d*
¹⁰You did signs and miracles*d* against the king
of Egypt,
and against all his officers and all his
people,
because you knew how proud they were.
You became as famous as you are today.
¹¹You divided the sea in front of our ancestors;
they walked through on dry ground.
But you threw the people chasing them into
the deep water,
like a stone thrown into mighty waters.
¹²You led our ancestors with a pillar of cloud
by day
and with a pillar of fire at night.
It lit the way
they were supposed to go.
¹³You came down to Mount Sinai
and spoke from heaven to our ancestors.
You gave them fair rules and true teachings,
good orders and commands.
¹⁴You told them about your holy Sabbath*d*
and gave them commands, orders, and
teachings
through your servant Moses.
¹⁵When they were hungry, you gave them
bread from heaven.
When they were thirsty, you brought them
water from the rock.
You told them to enter and take over
the land you had promised to give them.

¹⁶"But our ancestors were proud and stubborn

and did not obey your commands.
¹⁷They refused to listen;
they forgot the miracles*d* you did for them.
So they became stubborn and turned against
you,
choosing a leader to take them back to
slavery.
But you are a forgiving God.
You are kind and full of mercy.
You do not become angry quickly, and you
have great love.
So you did not leave them.
¹⁸Our ancestors even made an idol of a calf for
themselves.
They said, 'This is your god, Israel,
who brought you up out of Egypt.'
They spoke against you.

¹⁹"You have great mercy,
so you did not leave them in the desert.
The pillar of cloud guided them by day,
and the pillar of fire led them at night,
lighting the way they were to go.
²⁰You gave your good Spirit*d* to teach them.
You gave them manna*d* to eat
and water when they were thirsty.
²¹You took care of them for forty years in the
desert;
they needed nothing.
Their clothes did not wear out,
and their feet did not swell.

²²"You gave them kingdoms and nations;
you gave them more land.
They took over the country of Sihon king of
Heshbon
and the country of Og king of Bashan.
²³You made their children as many as the stars
in the sky,
and you brought them into the land
that you told their fathers to enter and take
over.
²⁴So their children went into the land and took
over.
The Canaanites lived there, but you
defeated them for our ancestors.
You handed over to them the Canaanites,
their kings, and the people of the land.
Our ancestors could do what they wanted
with them.
²⁵They captured strong, walled cities and fertile
land.
They took over houses full of good things,
wells that were already dug,
vineyards, olive trees, and many fruit trees.
They ate until they were full and grew fat;
they enjoyed your great goodness.

²⁶"But they were disobedient and turned
against you

and ignored your teachings.
Your prophets*d* warned them to come back to
you,
but they killed those prophets
and spoke against you.
27So you handed them over to their enemies,
and their enemies treated them badly.
But in this time of trouble our ancestors cried
out to you,
and you heard from heaven.
You had great mercy
and gave them saviors who saved them
from the power of their enemies.
28But as soon as they had rest,
they again did what was evil.
So you left them to their enemies
who ruled over them.
When they cried out to you again,
you heard from heaven.
Because of your mercy, you saved them
again and again.
29You warned them to return to your
teachings,
but they were proud and did not obey your
commands.
If someone obeys your laws, he will live,
but they sinned against your laws.
They were stubborn, unwilling, and
disobedient.
30You were patient with them for many years
and warned them by your Spirit through
the prophets,
but they did not pay attention.
So you handed them over to other
countries.
31But because your mercy is great, you did not
kill them all or leave them.
You are a kind and merciful God.

32"And so, our God, you are the great and
mighty and wonderful God.
You keep your agreement of love.
Do not let all our trouble seem unimportant
to you.
This trouble has come to us, to our kings and
our leaders,
to our priests and prophets,
to our ancestors and all your people
from the days of the kings of Assyria
until today.
33You have been fair in everything that has
happened to us;
you have been loyal, but we have been
wicked.
34Our kings, leaders, priests, and ancestors did
not obey your teachings;
they did not pay attention to the commands
and warnings you gave them.

35Even when our ancestors were living in their
kingdom,
enjoying all the good things you had given
them,
enjoying the land that was fertile and full of
room,
they did not stop their evil ways.

36"Look, we are slaves today
in the land you gave our ancestors.
They were to enjoy its fruit and its good
things,
but look, we are slaves here.
37The land's great harvest belongs to the kings
you have put over us
because of our sins.
Those kings rule over us and our cattle as
they please,
so we are in much trouble.

The People's Agreement

38"Because of all this, we are making an agreement in writing, and our leaders, Levites, and
priests are putting their seals*d* on it."

10 These are the men who sealed the agreement:
Nehemiah the governor, son of Hacaliah.
2Zedekiah, Seraiah, Azariah, Jeremiah, 3Pash-
hur, Amariah, Malkijah, 4Hattush, Shebaniah,
Malluch, 5Harim, Meremoth, Obadiah, 6Daniel,
Ginnethon, Baruch, 7Meshullam, Abijah, Mijamin, 8Maaziah, Bilgai, and Shemaiah. These
are the priests.
9These are the Levites who sealed it: Jeshua
son of Azaniah, Binnui of the sons of Henadad,
Kadmiel, 10and their fellow Levites: Shebaniah,
Hodiah, Kelita, Pelaiah, Hanan, 11Mica, Rehob,
Hashabiah, 12Zaccur, Sherebiah, Shebaniah, 13Ho-
diah, Bani, and Beninu.
14These are the leaders of the people who
sealed the agreement: Parosh, Pahath-Moab,
Elam, Zattu, Bani, 15Bunni, Azgad, Bebai, 16Ado-
nijah, Bigvai, Adin, 17Ater, Hezekiah, Azzur,
18Hodiah, Hashum, Bezai, 19Hariph, Anathoth,
Nebai, 20Magpiash, Meshullam, Hezir, 21Me-
shezabel, Zadok, Jaddua, 22Pelatiah, Hanan, Anaiah, 23Hoshea, Hananiah, Hasshub, 24Hallohesh,
Pilha, Shobek, 25Rehum, Hashabnah, Maaseiah,
26Ahiah, Hanan, Anan, 27Malluch, Harim, and Baanah.
28The rest of the people took an oath. They
were the priests, Levites, gatekeepers, singers,
Temple*d* servants, all those who separated themselves from foreigners to keep the Teachings of
God, and also their wives and their sons and
daughters who could understand. 29They joined
their fellow Israelites and their leading men in taking an oath, which was tied to a curse in case they

broke the oath. They promised to follow the Teachings of God, which they had been given through Moses the servant of God, and to obey all the commands, rules, and laws of the LORD our God.

30They said:

We promise not to let our daughters marry foreigners nor to let our sons marry their daughters. 31Foreigners may bring goods or grain to sell on the Sabbath,d but we will not buy on the Sabbath or any holy day. Every seventh year we will not plant, and that year we will forget all that people owe us.

32We will be responsible for the commands to pay for the service of the Temple of our God. We will give an eighth of an ounce of silver each year. 33It is for the bread that is set out on the table; the regular grain offerings and burnt offerings; the offerings on the Sabbaths, New Moond festivals, and special feasts; the holy offerings; the offerings to remove the sins of the Israelites so they will belong to God; and for the work of the Temple of our God.

34We, the priests, the Levites, and the people, have thrown lotsd to decide at what time of year each family must bring wood to the Temple. The wood is for burning on the altar of the LORD our God, and we will do this as it is written in the Teachings.

35We also will bring the first fruits from our crops and the first fruits of every tree to the Temple each year.

36We will bring to the Temple our firstbornd sons and cattle and the firstborn of our herds and flocks, as it is written in the Teachings. We will bring them to the priests who are serving in the Temple.

37We will bring to the priests at the storerooms of the Temple the first of our ground meal, our offerings, the fruit from all our trees, and our new wine and oil. And we will bring a tenth of our crops to the Levites, who will collect these things in all the towns where we work. 38A priest of Aaron's family must be with the Levites when they receive the tenth of the people's crops. The Levites must bring a tenth of all they receive to the Temple of our God to put in the storerooms of the treasury. 39The people of Israel and the Levites are to bring to the storerooms the gifts of grain, new wine, and oil. That is where the utensils for the Temple are kept and where the priests who are serving, the gatekeepers, and singers stay.

We will not ignore the Temple of our God.

New People Move into Jerusalem

11 The leaders of Israel lived in Jerusalem. But the rest of the people threw lotsd to choose one person out of every ten to come and live in Jerusalem, the holy city. The other nine could stay in their own cities. 2The people blessed those who volunteered to live in Jerusalem.

3These are the area leaders who lived in Jerusalem. (Some people lived on their own land in the cities of Judah. These included Israelites, priests, Levites, Temple servants, and descendantsd of Solomon's servants. 4Others from the families of Judah and Benjamin lived in Jerusalem.)

These are the descendants of Judah who moved into Jerusalem. There was Athaiah son of Uzziah. (Uzziah was the son of Zechariah, the son of Amariah. Amariah was the son of Shephatiah, the son of Mahalalel. Mahalalel was a descendant of Perez.) 5There was also Maaseiah son of Baruch. (Baruch was the son of Col-Hozeh, the son of Hazaiah. Hazaiah was the son of Adaiah, the son of Joiarib. Joiarib was the son of Zechariah, a descendant of Shelah.) 6All the descendants of Perez who lived in Jerusalem totaled 468 men. They were soldiers.

7These are descendants of Benjamin who moved into Jerusalem. There was Sallu son of Meshullam. (Meshullam was the son of Joed. the son of Pedaiah. Pedaiah was the son of Kolaiah, the son of Maaseiah. Maaseiah was the son of Ithiel, the son of Jeshaiah.) 8Following him were Gabbai and Sallai, for a total of 928 men. 9Joel son of Zicri was appointed over them, and Judah son of Hassenuah was second in charge of the new area of the city.

10These are the priests who moved into Jerusalem. There was Jedaiah son of Joiarib, Jakin, 11and Seraiah son of Hilkiah, the supervisor in the Temple. (Hilkiah was the son of Meshullam, the son of Zadok. Zadok was the son of Meraioth, the son of Ahitub.) 12And there were others with them who did the work for the Temple. All together there were 822 men. Also there was Adaiah son of Jeroham. (Jeroham was the son of Pelaliah, the son of Amzi. Amzi was the son of Zechariah, the son of Pashhur. Pashhur was the son of Malkijah.) 13And there were family heads with him. All together there were 242 men. Also there was Amashsai son of Azarel. (Azarel was the son of Ahzai, the son of Meshillemoth. Meshillemoth was the son of Immer.) 14And there were brave men with Amashsai. All together there were 128 men. Zabdiel son of Haggedolim was appointed over them.

15These are the Levites who moved into Jerusalem. There was Shemaiah son of Hasshub. (Hasshub was the son of Azrikam, the son of Hashabiah. Hashabiah was the son of Bunni.) 16And there were Shabbethai and Jozabad, two of the leaders of the Levites who were in charge of the work outside the Temple. [17]There was Mattaniah son of Mica. (Mica was the son of Zabdi, the son of Asaph.) Mattaniah was the director who led the people in thanksgiving and prayer. There was Bakbukiah, who was second in charge over his fellow Levites. And there was Abda son of Shammua. (Shammua was the son of Galal, the son of Jeduthun.) [18]All together 284 Levites lived in the holy city of Jerusalem.

[19]The gatekeepers who moved into Jerusalem were Akkub, Talmon, and others with them. There was a total of 172 men who guarded the city gates.

[20]The other Israelites, priests, and Levites lived on their own land in all the cities of Judah.

[21]The Temple servants lived on the hill of Ophel, and Ziha and Gishpa were in charge of them.

[22]Uzzi son of Bani was appointed over the Levites in Jerusalem. (Bani was the son of Hashabiah, the son of Mattaniah. Mattaniah was the son of Mica.) Uzzi was one of Asaph's descendants, who were the singers responsible for the service of the Temple. [23]The singers were under the king's orders, which regulated them day by day.

[24]Pethahiah son of Meshezabel was the king's spokesman. (Meshezabel was a descendant of Zerah, the son of Judah.)

[25]Some of the people of Judah lived in villages with their surrounding fields. They lived in Kiriath Arba and its surroundings, in Dibon and its surroundings, in Jekabzeel and its surroundings, [26]in Jeshua, Moladah, Beth Pelet, [27]Hazar Shual, Beersheba and its surroundings, [28]in Ziklag and Meconah and its surroundings, [29]in En Rimmon, Zorah, Jarmuth, [30]Zanoah, Adullam and their villages, in Lachish and the fields around it, and in Azekah and its surroundings. So they settled from Beersheba all the way to the Valley of Hinnom.

[31]The descendants of the Benjaminites from Geba lived in Micmash, Aija, Bethel and its surroundings, [32]in Anathoth, Nob, Ananiah, [33]Hazor, Ramah, Gittaim, [34]Hadid, Zeboim, Neballat, [35]Lod, Ono, and in the Valley of the Craftsmen.

[36]Some groups of the Levites from Judah settled in the land of Benjamin.

Priests and Levites

12 These are the priests and Levites who returned with Zerubbabel son of Shealtiel and with Jeshua. There were Seraiah, Jeremiah, Ezra, [2]Amariah, Malluch, Hattush, [3]Shecaniah, Rehum, Meremoth, [4]Iddo, Ginnethon, Abijah, [5]Mijamin, Moadiah, Bilgah, [6]Shemaiah, Joiarib, Jedaiah, [7]Sallu, Amok, Hilkiah, and Jedaiah. They were the leaders of the priests and their relatives in the days of Jeshua.

[8]The Levites were Jeshua, Binnui, Kadmiel, Sherebiah, Judah, and Mattaniah. Mattaniah and his relatives were in charge of the songs of thanksgiving. [9]Bakbukiah and Unni, their relatives, stood across from them in the services.

[10]Jeshua was the father of Joiakim. Joiakim was the father of Eliashib. Eliashib was the father of Joiada. [11]Joiada was the father of Jonathan, and Jonathan was the father of Jaddua.

[12]In the days of Joiakim, these priests were the leaders of the families of priests: Meraiah, from Seraiah's family; Hananiah, from Jeremiah's family; [13]Meshullam, from Ezra's family; Jehohanan, from Amariah's family; [14]Jonathan, from Malluch's family; Joseph, from Shecaniah's family; [15]Adna, from Harim's family; Helkai, from Meremoth's family; [16]Zechariah, from Iddo's family; Meshullam, from Ginnethon's family; [17]Zicri, from Abijah's family; Piltai, from Miniamin's and Moadiah's families; [18]Shammua, from Bilgah's family; Jehonathan, from Shemaiah's family; [19]Mattenai, from Joiarib's family; Uzzi, from Jedaiah's family; [20]Kallai, from Sallu's family; Eber, from Amok's family; [21]Hashabiah, from Hilkiah's family; and Nethanel, from Jedaiah's family.

[22]The leaders of the families of the Levites and the priests were written down in the days of Eliashib, Joiada, Johanan, and Jaddua, while Darius the Persian was king. [23]The family leaders among the Levites were written down in the history book, but only up to the time of Johanan son of Eliashib. [24]The leaders of the Levites were Hashabiah, Sherebiah, Jeshua son of Kadmiel, and their relatives. Their relatives stood across from them and gave praise and thanksgiving to God. One group answered the other group, as David, the man of God, had commanded.

[25]These were the gatekeepers who guarded the storerooms next to the gates: Mattaniah, Bakbukiah, Obadiah, Meshullam, Talmon, and Akkub. [26]They served in the days of Joiakim son of Jeshua, the son of Jozadak. They also served in the days of Nehemiah the governor and Ezra the priest and teacher.

The Wall of Jerusalem

[27]When the wall of Jerusalem was offered as a gift to God, they asked the Levites to come from wherever they lived to Jerusalem to celebrate with joy the gift of the wall. They were to celebrate with songs of thanksgiving and with the music of cymbals, harps, and lyres.[d] [28]They also brought together singers from all around Jerusalem, from the Netophathite villages, [29]from Beth Gilgal, and from the areas of Geba and Azmaveth. The singers had built villages for themselves around Jerusalem. [30]The priests and Levites made themselves pure, and they also made the people, the gates, and the wall of Jerusalem pure.

31I had the leaders of Judah go up on top of the wall, and I appointed two large choruses to give thanks. One chorus went to the right on top of the wall, toward the Trash Gate. 32Behind them went Hoshaiah and half the leaders of Judah. 33Azariah, Ezra, Meshullam, 34Judah, Benjamin, Shemaiah, and Jeremiah also went. 35Some priests with trumpets also went, along with Zechariah son of Jonathan. (Jonathan was the son of Shemaiah, the son of Mattaniah. Mattaniah was the son of Micaiah, the son of Zaccur. Zaccur was the son of Asaph.) 36Zechariah's relatives also went. They were Shemaiah, Azarel, Milalai, Gilalai, Maai, Nethanel, Judah, and Hanani. These men played the musical instruments of David, the man of God, and Ezra the teacher walked in front of them. 37They went from the Fountain Gate straight up the steps to the highest part of the wall by the older part of the city. They went on above the house of David to the Water Gate on the east.

38The second chorus went to the left, while I followed them on top of the wall with half the people. We went from the Tower of the Ovens to the Broad Wall, 39over the Gate of Ephraim to the Old Gate and the Fish Gate, to the Tower of Hananel and the Tower of the Hundred. We went as far as the Sheep Gate and stopped at the Gate of the Guard.

40The two choruses took their places at the Temple.d Half of the leaders and I did also. 41These priests were there with their trumpets: Eliakim, Maaseiah, Miniamin, Micaiah, Elioenai, Zechariah, and Hananiah. 42These people were also there: Maaseiah, Shemaiah, Eleazar, Uzzi, Jehohanan, Malkijah, Elam, and Ezer. The choruses sang, led by Jezrahiah. 43The people offered many sacrifices that day and were happy because God had given them great joy. The women and children were happy. The sound of happiness in Jerusalem could be heard far away.

SIDELIGHT: When the Jews dedicated the completed wall around Jerusalem (Nehemiah 12:27–43), they didn't cut a ribbon or break a bottle of champagne. They probably offered an animal sacrifice and sprinkled blood or holy water on the wall.

44At that time the leaders appointed men to be in charge of the storerooms. These rooms were for the gifts, the first fruits, and the ten percent that the people brought. The Teachings said they should bring a share for the priests and Levites from the fields around the towns. The people of Judah were happy to do this for the priests and Levites who served. 45They performed the service of their God in making things pure. The singers and gatekeepers also did their jobs, as David had commanded his son Solomon. 46Earlier, in the time of David and Asaph, there was a leader of the singers and of the songs of praise and thanksgiving to God. 47So it was in the days of Zerubbabel and Nehemiah. All the people of Israel gave something to the singers and gatekeepers, and they also set aside part for the Levites. Then the Levites set aside part for the descendantsd of Aaron.

Foreign People Are Sent Away

13 On that day they read the Book of Moses to the people, and they found that it said no Ammonite or Moabite should ever be allowed in the meeting to worship. 2The Ammonites and Moabites had not welcomed the Israelites with food and water. Instead, they had hired Balaam to put a curse on Israel. (But our God turned the curse into a blessing.) 3When the people heard this teaching, they separated all foreigners from Israel.

Nehemiah Returns to Jerusalem

4Before that happened, Eliashib the priest, who was in charge of the Templed storerooms, was friendly with Tobiah. 5Eliashib let Tobiah use one of the large storerooms. Earlier it had been used for grain offerings, incense,d the utensils, and the tenth offerings of grain, new wine, and olive oil that belonged to the Levites, singers, and gatekeepers. It had also been used for gifts for the priests.

6I was not in Jerusalem when this happened. I had gone back to Artaxerxes king of Babylon in the thirty-second year he was king. Finally I asked the king to let me leave. 7When I returned to Jerusalem, I found out the evil Eliashib had done by letting Tobiah have a room in the Temple courtyard. 8I was very upset at this, so I threw all of Tobiah's goods out of the room. 9I ordered the rooms to be purified, and I brought back the utensils for God's Temple, the grain offerings, and the incense.d

10Then I found out the people were not giving the Levites their shares. So the Levites and singers who served had gone back to their own farms. 11I argued with the officers, saying, "Why haven't you taken care of the Temple?" Then I gathered the Levites and singers and put them back at their places.

12All the people of Judah then brought to the storerooms a tenth of their crops, new wine, and olive oil. 13I put these men in charge of the storerooms: Shelemiah the priest, Zadok the teacher, and Pedaiah a Levite. I made Hanan son of Zaccur, the son of Mattaniah, their helper. Everyone knew they were honest men. They gave out the portions that went to their relatives.

¹⁴Remember me, my God, for this. Do not ignore my love for the Temple and its service.

¹⁵In those days I saw people in Judah working in the winepresses*d* on the Sabbath*d* day. They were bringing in grain and loading it on donkeys. And they were bringing loads of wine, grapes, and figs into Jerusalem on the Sabbath day. So I warned them about selling food on that day. ¹⁶People from the city of Tyre who were living in Jerusalem brought in fish and other things and sold them there on the Sabbath day to the people of Judah. ¹⁷I argued with the important men of Judah and said to them, "What is this evil thing you are doing? You are ruining the Sabbath day. ¹⁸This is just what your ancestors did. So our God did terrible things to us and this city. Now you are making him even more angry at Israel by ruining the Sabbath day."

¹⁹So I ordered that the doors be shut at sunset before the Sabbath and not be opened until the Sabbath was over. I put my servants at the gates so no load could come in on the Sabbath. ²⁰Once or twice traders and sellers of all kinds of goods spent the night outside Jerusalem. ²¹So I warned them, "Why are you spending the night by the wall? If you do it again, I will force you away." After that, they did not come back on the Sabbath. ²²Then I ordered the Levites to purify themselves and to guard the city gates to make sure the Sabbath remained holy.

Remember me, my God, for this. Have mercy on me because of your great love.

²³In those days I saw men of Judah who had married women from Ashdod, Ammon, and Moab. ²⁴Half their children were speaking the language of Ashdod or some other place, and they couldn't speak the language of Judah. ²⁵I argued with those people, put curses on them, hit some of them, and pulled out their hair. I forced them to make a promise to God, saying, "Do not let your daughters marry the sons of foreigners, and do not take the daughters of foreigners as wives for your sons or yourselves. ²⁶Foreign women made King Solomon of Israel sin. There was never a king like him in any of the nations. God loved Solomon and made him king over all Israel, but foreign women made him sin. ²⁷And now you are not obedient when you do this evil thing. You are unfaithful to our God when you marry foreign wives."

²⁸Joiada was the son of Eliashib the high priest. One of Joiada's sons married a daughter of Sanballat the Horonite, so I sent him away from me.

²⁹Remember them, my God, because they made the priesthood unclean*d* and the agreement of the priests and Levites unclean.

³⁰So I purified them of everything that was foreign. I appointed duties for the priests and Levites, giving each man his own job. ³¹I also made sure wood was brought for the altar at regular times and that the first fruits were brought.

Remember me, my God; be kind to me.

ESTHER

Why Read This Book:

- Recognize God's work in life's circumstances (Esther 1—2).
- Discover how an obedient person can have a major impact in the world (Esther 4—10).

Behind the Scenes:

How do you respond in a crisis? Does your fear make you freeze up so you can't do anything to help? Or do you reveal heroic strength and skill—far more than you would normally have?

Esther faced a tough situation. She might be able to save thousands of Jewish lives by stopping the decree of King Xerxes to exterminate all the Jews in the Persian Empire. But if she tried, she could lose her own life. Would she "freeze up," or would she take heroic action? This book tells how Esther responded.

The story begins when King Xerxes dumped Queen Vashti because she wouldn't obey him. Four years later, the king picked a new queen, Esther, not knowing that she was a Jew.

Then the plot thickens. Esther's cousin, Mordecai, refused to bow down to Haman, a court official. Haman became furious and convinced the king to order the killing of all the Jews. Through a messenger, Mordecai told Esther about the death decree and convinced her to use her influence to stop the order. Esther agreed, saying: "I will go to the king, even though it is against the law, and if I die, I die" (Esther 4:16). So she went to the king to plead for the Jews, including herself. She succeeded. Then Haman was executed and Mordecai honored.

Esther is one of the most unusual books in the Bible. In some ways, it's a "secular" book; nowhere does it mention God, worship, prayer, or other religious

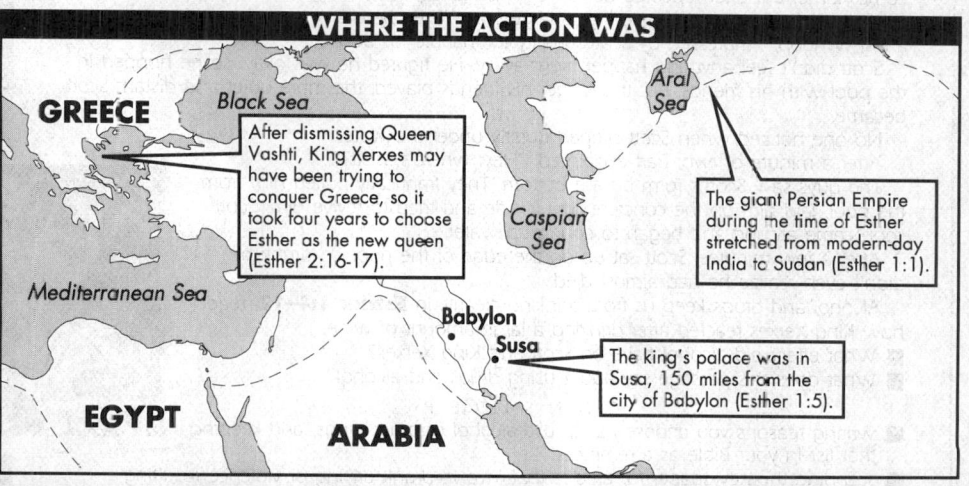

WHERE THE ACTION WAS

GREECE

Black Sea

After dismissing Queen Vashti, King Xerxes may have been trying to conquer Greece, so it took four years to choose Esther as the new queen (Esther 2:16-17).

Mediterranean Sea

Aral Sea

The giant Persian Empire during the time of Esther stretched from modern-day India to Sudan (Esther 1:1).

Caspian Sea

Babylon
Susa

The king's palace was in Susa, 150 miles from the city of Babylon (Esther 1:5).

EGYPT

ARABIA

WHEN THE ACTION WAS

	The Northern Kingdom (Israel) fell to Assyria	Jews began returning to Jerusalem from exile when Persia conquered Babylon		Jesus was born
1000BC	**750BC**	**500BC**	**250BC**	**BC/AD**
David was Israel's king		The Southern Kingdom (Judah) fell to Babylon	King Xerxes ruled Persia and the story of Esther took place during this time	

ESTHER 1   442

Behind the   practices. Yet God's protection is clear throughout. The number of "coincidences" in
Scenes (cont.): the book illustrate that God's hand is at work in events, even when we don't
               realize it.

Queen Vashti Disobeys the King

1 This is what happened during the time of King Xerxes, the king who ruled the one hundred twenty-seven states from India to Cush. ²In those days King Xerxes ruled from his capital city of Susa. ³In the third year of his rule, he gave a banquet for all his important men and royal offi-cers. The army leaders from the countries of Persia and Media and the important men from all Xerxes' empire were there.

⁴The banquet lasted one hundred eighty days. All during that time King Xerxes was showing off the great wealth of his kingdom and his own great riches and glory. ⁵When the one hundred eighty

---

DRUGS AND ALCOHOL

Under the Influence

"I wonder what it's like to drown," Scott Walters mused aloud. He quietly exhaled, then slipped under the water in his backyard pool.

Scott was in junior high when he began sampling drinks from his father's liquor cabinet. No one in the family seemed to notice or care, so he continued to drink occasionally—in small amounts.

One afternoon several of Scott's friends came over to swim. Scott began to brag about his free access to the family liquor cabinet.

"My family lets me drink whenever I want to," Scott claimed. "In fact, my dad and I drink together all the time."

"You're lying," scowled Bart, one of Scott's friends. "Your dad doesn't let you drink."

"What do you know?" countered Scott. "You've probably never had anything stronger than milk."

"Okay, then," Bart said, "prove it. Prove to us that you drink."

Scott didn't really want to drink right then, because he never knew when his dad would come home. But after repeated dares from his friends, Scott went to the liquor cabinet and poured a little from each bottle into a large glass. Then he drank it all. Scott's friends let out a big "whoop," impressed by Scott's ability to "handle his booze."

Scott didn't feel anything happen right away. He figured he was okay, so he hopped in the pool with his friends. But the longer his friends played, the more quiet and distant Scott became.

No one noticed when Scott slipped quietly under the water.

After a minute or two, Bart exclaimed, "Hey, where's Scott?"

The guys saw Scott's form on the bottom. They frantically pulled him from the pool, laid him on the concrete on his side and tried to revive him. Scott soon came around and began to cough up water.

After a few minutes, Scott sat up on the edge of the pool, so drunk he didn't even realize he had almost died.

Alcohol and drugs keep us from thinking clearly. In **Esther 1:4–12**, read how King Xerxes reacted after drinking a large amount of wine.

■ What effect did alcohol have on Scott and King Xerxes?
■ What does this passage say about using drugs and alcohol?

C O N S I D E R . . .

■ writing reasons you choose not to use alcohol or other drugs, and keeping that list in your Bible as a reminder.
■ scanning the newspaper for articles that involve drunk driving or violence resulting from drug or alcohol use; then consider asking God to help the people in each of those situations.

F O R   M O R E ,   S E E . . .

■ Proverbs 23:29–35 (p. 588)
■ Galatians 5:19–23 (p. 1213)

■ Ephesians 5:15–18 (p. 1224)

days were over, the king gave another banquet. It was held in the courtyard of the palace garden for seven days, and it was for everybody in the palace

at Susa, from the greatest to the least. 6The courtyard had fine white curtains and purple drapes that were tied to silver rings on marble pillars by white and purple cords. And there were gold and silver couches on a floor set with tiles of white marble, shells, and gems. 7Wine was served in gold cups of various kinds. And there was plenty of the king's wine, because he was very generous. 8The king commanded that the guests be permitted to drink as much as they wished. He told the wine servers to serve each person what he wanted.

9Queen Vashti also gave a banquet for the women in the royal palace of King Xerxes.

10On the seventh day of the banquet, King Xerxes was very happy, because he had been drinking much wine. He gave a command to the seven eunuchs*d* who served him—Mehuman, Biztha, Harbona, Bigtha, Abagtha, Zethar, and Carcas. 11He commanded them to bring him Queen Vashti, wearing her royal crown. She was to come to show her beauty to the people and important men, because she was very beautiful. 12The eunuchs told Queen Vashti about the king's command, but she refused to come. Then the king became very angry; his anger was like a burning fire.

13It was a custom for the king to ask advice from experts about law and order. So King Xerxes

spoke with the wise men who would know the right thing to do. 14The wise men the king usually talked to were Carshena, Shethar, Admatha, Tarshish, Meres, Marsena, and Memucan, seven of the important men of Persia and Media. These seven had special privileges to see the king and had the highest rank in the kingdom. 15The king asked them, "What does the law say must be done to Queen Vashti? She has not obeyed the command of King Xerxes, which the eunuchs took to her."

16Then Memucan said to the king and the other important men, "Queen Vashti has not done wrong to the king alone. She has also done wrong to all the important men and all the people in all the empire of King Xerxes. 17All the wives of the important men of Persia and Media will hear about the queen's actions. Then they will no longer honor their husbands. They will say, 'King Xerxes commanded Queen Vashti to be brought to him, but she refused to come.' 18Today the wives of the important men of Persia and Media have heard about the queen's actions. So they will speak in the same way to their husbands, and there will be no end to disrespect and anger.

19"So, our king, if it pleases you, give a royal order, and let it be written in the laws of Persia and Media, which cannot be changed. The law should say Vashti is never again to enter the presence of King Xerxes. Also let the king give her place as queen to someone who is better than she is. 20And let the king's order be announced everywhere in his enormous kingdom. Then all the women will respect their husbands, from the greatest to the least."

21The king and his important men were happy with this advice, so King Xerxes did as Memucan suggested. 22He sent letters to all the states of the kingdom in the writing of each state and in the language of each group of people. These letters announced that each man was to be the ruler of his own family.

Esther Is Made Queen

2 Later, when King Xerxes was not so angry, he remembered Vashti and what she had done and his order about her. 2Then the king's personal servants suggested, "Let a search be made for beautiful young girls for the king. 3Let the king choose supervisors in every state of his kingdom to bring every beautiful young girl to the palace at Susa. They should be taken to the women's quarters and put under the care of Hegai, the king's eunuch*d* in charge of the women. And let beauty treatments be given to them. 4Then let the girl who most pleases the king become queen in place of Vashti." The king liked this idea, so he did as they said.

5Now there was a Jewish man in the palace of

Susa whose name was Mordecai son of Jair. Jair was the son of Shimei, the son of Kish. Mordecai was from the tribe*d* of Benjamin, [6]which had been taken captive from Jerusalem by Nebuchadnezzar king of Babylon. They were part of the group taken into captivity with Jehoiachin king of Judah. [7]Mordecai had a cousin named Hadassah, who had no father or mother, so Mordecai took care of her. Hadassah was also called Esther, and she had a very pretty figure and face. Mordecai had adopted her as his own daughter when her father and mother died.

[8]When the king's command and order had been heard, many girls had been brought to the palace in Susa and put under the care of Hegai. Esther was also taken to the king's palace and put under the care of Hegai, who was in charge of the women. [9]Esther pleased Hegai, and he liked her. So Hegai quickly began giving Esther her beauty treatments and special food. He gave her seven servant girls chosen from the king's palace. Then he moved her and her seven servant girls to the best part of the women's quarters.

[10]Esther did not tell anyone about her family or who her people were, because Mordecai had told her not to. [11]Every day Mordecai walked back and forth near the courtyard where the king's women lived to find out how Esther was and what was happening to her.

[12]Before a girl could take her turn with King Xerxes, she had to complete twelve months of beauty treatments that were ordered for the women. For six months she was treated with oil and myrrh*d* and for six months with perfumes and cosmetics. [13]Then she was ready to go to the king. Anything she asked for was given to her to take with her from the women's quarters to the king's

---

SIDELIGHT: If you think your sister takes too long in the bathroom, just be glad she isn't Esther. It took Esther a year of beauty treatments to get ready for the king (Esther 2:12–13).

---

palace. [14]In the evening she would go to the king's palace, and in the morning she would return to another part of the women's quarters. There she would be placed under the care of Shaashgaz, the king's eunuch in charge of the slave women.*d* The girl would not go back to the king again unless he was pleased with her and asked for her by name.

[15]The time came for Esther daughter of Abihail, Mordecai's uncle, who had been adopted by Mordecai, to go to the king. She asked for only what Hegai suggested she should take. (Hegai was the king's eunuch who was in charge of the women.) Everyone who saw Esther liked her. [16]So Esther was taken to King Xerxes in the royal palace in the tenth month, the month of Tebeth, during Xerxes' seventh year as king.

[17]And the king was pleased with Esther more than with any of the other girls. He liked her more than any of the other girls, so he put a royal crown on her head and made her queen in place of Vashti. [18]Then the king gave a great banquet for Esther and invited all his important men and royal officers. He announced a holiday for all the empire and had the government give away gifts.

Mordecai Discovers an Evil Plan

[19]Now Mordecai was sitting at the king's gate when the girls were gathered the second time. [20]Esther still had not told anyone about her family or who her people were, just as Mordecai had commanded her. She obeyed Mordecai just as she had done when she was under his care.

[21]Now Bigthana and Teresh were two of the king's officers who guarded the doorway. While Mordecai was sitting at the king's gate, they became angry and began to make plans to kill King Xerxes. [22]But Mordecai found out about their plans and told Queen Esther. Then Esther told the king how Mordecai had discovered the evil plan. [23]When the report was investigated, it was found to be true, and the two officers who had planned to kill the king were hanged. All this was written down in the daily court record in the king's presence.

Haman Plans to Destroy the Jewish People

3 After these things happened, King Xerxes honored Haman son of Hammedatha the Agagite. He gave him a new rank that was higher than all the important men. [2]All the royal officers at the king's gate would bow down and kneel before Haman, as the king had ordered. But Mordecai would not bow down or show him honor.

[3]Then the royal officers at the king's gate asked Mordecai, "Why don't you obey the king's command?" [4]And they said this to him every day. When he did not listen to them, they told Haman about it. They wanted to see if Haman would accept Mordecai's behavior because Mordecai had told them he was Jewish.

[5]When Haman saw that Mordecai would not bow down to him or honor him, he became very angry. [6]He thought of himself as too important to *try to kill only Mordecai. He had been told who* the people of Mordecai were, so he looked for a way to destroy all of Mordecai's people, the Jews, in all of Xerxes' kingdom.

[7]It was in the first month of the twelfth year of King Xerxes' rule — the month of Nisan. Pur (that is, the lot*d*) was thrown before Haman to choose

a day and a month. So the twelfth month, the month of Adar, was chosen.

8Then Haman said to King Xerxes, "There is a certain group of people scattered among the other people in all the states of your kingdom. Their customs are different from those of all the other people, and they do not obey the king's laws. It is not right for you to allow them to continue living in your kingdom. 9If it pleases the king, let an order be given to destroy those people. Then I will pay seven hundred fifty thousand pounds of silver to those who do the king's business, and they will put it into the royal treasury."

10So the king took his signet*d* ring off and gave it to Haman son of Hammedatha, the Agagite, the enemy of the Jewish people. 11Then the king said to Haman, "The money and the people are yours. Do with them as you please."

12On the thirteenth day of the first month, the royal secretaries were called, and they wrote out all of Haman's orders. They wrote to the king's governors and to the captains of the soldiers in each state and to the important men of each group of people. The orders were written in the writing of each state and in the language of each people. They were written in the name of King Xerxes and sealed with his signet ring. 13Letters were sent by messengers to all the king's empire ordering them to destroy, kill, and completely wipe out all the Jewish people. That meant young and old, women and little children, too. It was to happen on a single day — the thirteenth day of the twelfth month, which was Adar. And they could take everything the Jewish people owned. 14A copy of the order was given out as a law in every state so all the people would be ready for that day.

15The messengers set out, hurried by the king's command, as soon as the order was given in the palace at Susa. The king and Haman sat down to drink, but the city of Susa was in confusion.

Mordecai Asks Esther to Help

4 When Mordecai heard about all that had been done, he tore his clothes, put on rough cloth and ashes, and went out into the city crying loudly and painfully. 2But Mordecai went only as far as the king's gate, because no one was allowed to enter that gate dressed in rough cloth. 3As the king's order reached every area, there was great sadness and loud crying among the Jewish people. They gave up eating and cried out loud, and many of them lay down on rough cloth and ashes to show how sad they were.

4When Esther's servant girls and eunuchs*d* came to her and told her about Mordecai, she was very upset and afraid. She sent clothes for Mordecai to put on instead of the rough cloth, but he would not wear them. 5Then Esther called for Hathach, one of the king's eunuchs chosen by the king to serve her. Esther ordered him to find out what was bothering Mordecai and why.

6So Hathach went to Mordecai, who was in the city square in front of the king's gate. 7Mordecai told Hathach everything that had happened to him, and he told Hathach about the amount of money Haman had promised to pay into the king's treasury for the killing of the Jewish people. 8Mordecai also gave him a copy of the order to kill the Jewish people, which had been given in Susa. He wanted Hathach to show it to Esther and to tell her about it. And Mordecai told him to order Esther to go into the king's presence to beg for mercy and to plead with him for her people.

9Hathach went back and reported to Esther everything Mordecai had said. 10Then Esther told Hathach to tell Mordecai, 11"All the royal officers and people of the royal states know that no man or woman may go to the king in the inner courtyard without being called. There is only one law about this: Anyone who enters must be put to death unless the king holds out his gold scepter.*d* Then that person may live. And I have not been called to go to the king for thirty days."

12Esther's message was given to Mordecai. 13Then Mordecai sent back word to Esther: "Just because you live in the king's palace, don't think that out of all the Jewish people you alone will escape. 14If you keep quiet at this time, someone else will help and save the Jewish people, but you and your father's family will all die. And who knows, you may have been chosen queen for just such a time as this."

15Then Esther sent this answer to Mordecai: 16"Go and get all the Jewish people in Susa together. For my sake, give up eating; do not eat or drink for three days, night and day. I and my servant girls will also give up eating. Then I will go to the king, even though it is against the law, and if I die, I die."

17So Mordecai went away and did everything Esther had told him to do.

Esther Speaks to the King

5 On the third day Esther put on her royal robes and stood in the inner courtyard of the king's palace, facing the king's hall. The king was sitting on his royal throne in the hall, facing the doorway. 2When the king saw Queen Esther standing in the courtyard, he was pleased. He held out to her the gold scepter*d* that was in his hand, so Esther went forward and touched the end of it.

3The king asked, "What is it, Queen Esther? What do you want to ask me? I will give you as much as half of my kingdom."

4Esther answered, "My king, if it pleases you, come today with Haman to a banquet that I have prepared for him."

⁵Then the king said, "Bring Haman quickly so we may do what Esther asks."

SIDELIGHT: If you're afraid to go talk to someone in authority over you, imagine how Esther must have felt about going to the king (Esther 5:1–2). Frequent political assassinations at that time made security around a king extremely tight, and anyone—including the queen—who approached the king without being invited could be in danger of being killed.

So the king and Haman went to the banquet Esther had prepared for them. ⁶As they were drinking wine, the king said to Esther, "Now, what are you asking for? I will give it to you. What is it you want? I will give you as much as half of my kingdom."

⁷Esther answered, "This is what I want and what I ask for. ⁸My king, if you are pleased with me and if it pleases you, give me what I ask for and do what I want. Come with Haman tomorrow to the banquet I will prepare for you. Then I will answer your question about what I want."

Haman's Plans Against Mordecai

⁹Haman left the king's palace that day happy and content. But when he saw Mordecai at the king's gate and saw that Mordecai did not stand up or tremble with fear before him, Haman became very angry with Mordecai. ¹⁰But he controlled his anger and went home.

Then Haman called together his friends and his wife, Zeresh. ¹¹He told them how wealthy he was and how many sons he had. He also told them all the ways the king had honored him and how the king had placed him higher than his important men and his royal officers. ¹²He also said, "I'm the only person Queen Esther invited to come with the king to the banquet she gave. And tomorrow

---

HEROES

Risky Business

"They were chasing a little boy, about ten years old. They caught up with him, and one of them took his gun and bashed the child's head in. They killed him."

Those are the words of Giorgio Perlasca, who witnessed this murder in Hungary in 1944. It was World War II, and the Nazis were killing the Jews, regardless of their age. Perlasca couldn't sit back and watch this happen.

Although he was Italian, Perlasca was able to get a passport to Hungary that identified him as a Spaniard. Because of Spain's close ties with Germany, he could masquerade as a top Spanish diplomat and help save the Jews.

For three months, Perlasca distributed letters to all the Jews he could find. The letters stated that the Jews had been granted the protection of the Spanish government. When he saw Jews being herded onto trains, headed for death, he confronted the Nazis and ordered them to return the people to him. He housed more than five thousand Jews in eleven apartment buildings where he hung Spain's flag to protect the occupants.

Historians estimate Perlasca helped save more than ten thousand people before his cover was blown when Spain cut off diplomatic relations with Hungary at the end of 1944.

Giorgio Perlasca heroically risked his own life to save the lives of others. Queen Esther also put her life on the line for the Jews. Read her story in **Esther 4:9–16**.

■ What risks did both Perlasca and Esther take to save the Jews?
■ We may not all have the chance to save thousands of people from dying, but we can still make a difference. How can you be a hero for God?

CONSIDER . . .
■ making a hero sandwich and sharing it with someone who is a hero to you.
■ who your heroes are and how well they measure up to the standards of Esther. Then decide if you need to change heroes.

FOR MORE, SEE . . .
■ Exodus 14:5–31 (p. 70)
■ Joshua 2:1–22 (p. 195)
■ Hebrews 11:29–40 (p. 1288)

also the queen has asked me to be her guest with the king. [13]But all this does not really make me happy when I see that Jew Mordecai sitting at the king's gate."

[14]Then Haman's wife, Zeresh, and all his friends said, "Have a seventy-five foot platform built, and in the morning ask the king to have Mordecai hanged on it. Then go to the banquet with the king and be happy." Haman liked this suggestion, so he ordered the platform to be built.

Mordecai Is Honored

6 That same night the king could not sleep. So he gave an order for the daily court record to be brought in and read to him. [2]It was found recorded that Mordecai had warned the king about Bigthana and Teresh, two of the king's officers who guarded the doorway and who had planned to kill the king.

[3]The king asked, "What honor and reward have been given to Mordecai for this?"

The king's personal servants answered, "Nothing has been done for Mordecai."

[4]The king said, "Who is in the courtyard?" Now Haman had just entered the outer court of the king's palace. He had come to ask the king about hanging Mordecai on the platform he had prepared.

[5]The king's personal servants said, "Haman is standing in the courtyard."

The king said, "Bring him in."

[6]So Haman came in. And the king asked him, "What should be done for a man whom the king wants very much to honor?"

And Haman thought to himself, "Whom would the king want to honor more than me?" [7]So he answered the king, "This is what you could do for the man you want very much to honor. [8]Have the servants bring a royal robe that the king himself has worn. And also bring a horse with a royal crown on its head, a horse that the king himself has ridden. [9]Let the robe and the horse be given to one of the king's most important men. Let the servants put the robe on the man the king wants to honor, and let them lead him on the horse through the city streets. As they are leading him, let them announce: 'This is what is done for the man whom the king wants to honor!' "

[10]The king commanded Haman, "Go quickly. Take the robe and the horse just as you have said, and do all this for Mordecai the Jew who sits at the king's gate. Do not leave out anything you have suggested."

[11]So Haman took the robe and the horse, and he put the robe on Mordecai. Then he led him on horseback through the city streets, announcing before Mordecai: "This is what is done for the man whom the king wants to honor!"

[12]Then Mordecai returned to the king's gate, but Haman hurried home with his head covered, because he was embarrassed and ashamed. [13]He told his wife, Zeresh, and all his friends everything that had happened to him.

Haman's wife and the men who gave him advice said, "You are starting to lose power to Mordecai. Since he is a Jew, you cannot win against him. You will surely be ruined." [14]While they were still talking, the king's eunuchs[d] came to Haman's house and made him hurry to the banquet Esther had prepared.

Haman Is Hanged

7 So the king and Haman went in to eat with Queen Esther. [2]As they were drinking wine on the second day, the king asked Esther again, "What are you asking for? I will give it to you. What is it you want? I will give you as much as half of my kingdom."

[3]Then Queen Esther answered, "My king, if you are pleased with me, and if it pleases you, let me live. This is what I ask. And let my people live, too. This is what I want. [4]My people and I have been sold to be destroyed, to be killed and completely wiped out. If we had been sold as male and female slaves, I would have kept quiet, because that would not be enough of a problem to bother the king."

[5]Then King Xerxes asked Queen Esther, "Who is he, and where is he? Who has done such a thing?"

[6]Esther said, "Our enemy and foe is this wicked Haman!"

Then Haman was filled with terror before the king and queen. [7]The king was very angry, so he got up, left his wine, and went out into the palace garden. But Haman stayed inside to beg Queen Esther to save his life. He could see that the king had already decided to kill him.

> ※ **SIDELIGHT:** Going to the palace garden to cool off was probably a good idea for the angry king (Esther 7:7). The palace at Susa was the king's winter palace because it was warmer than the government headquarters in Persepolis.

[8]When the king returned from the palace garden to the banquet hall, he saw Haman falling on the couch where Esther was lying. The king said, "Will he even attack the queen while I am in the house?"

As soon as the king said that, servants came in and covered Haman's face. [9]Harbona, one of the eunuchs[d] there serving the king, said, "Look, a seventy-five foot platform stands near Haman's house. This is the one Haman had prepared for Mordecai, who gave the warning that saved the king."

The king said, "Hang Haman on it!" [10]So they hanged Haman on the platform he had prepared for Mordecai. Then the king was not so angry anymore.

> **SIDELIGHT:** The execution planned by Haman for Mordecai, but carried out by the king on Haman (Esther 7:8–10), probably wouldn't have been a hanging in the modern sense. It probably involved impaling him on a sharp stake and then hanging the body in the city for display. Romans adapted this method to develop execution on crosses.

The King Helps the Jewish People

8 That same day King Xerxes gave Queen Esther everything Haman, the enemy of the Jewish people, had left when he died. And Mordecai came in to see the king, because Esther had told the king how he was related to her. [2]Then the king took off his signet[d] ring that he had taken back from Haman, and he gave it to Mordecai. Esther put Mordecai in charge of everything Haman left when he died.

[3]Once again Esther spoke to the king. She fell at the king's feet and cried and begged him to stop the evil plan that Haman the Agagite had planned against the Jews. [4]The king held out the gold scepter[d] to Esther. So Esther got up and stood in front of him.

[5]She said, "My king, if you are pleased with me, and if it pleases you to do this, if you think it is the right thing to do, and if you are happy with me, let an order be written to cancel the letters Haman wrote. Haman the Agagite sent messages to destroy all the Jewish people in all of your kingdom. [6]I could not stand to see that terrible thing happen to my people. I could not stand to see my family killed."

[7]King Xerxes answered Queen Esther and Mordecai the Jew, "Because Haman was against the Jewish people, I have given his things to Esther, and my soldiers have hanged him. [8]Now, in the king's name, write another order to the Jewish people as it seems best to you. Then seal the order with the king's signet[d] ring, because no letter written in the king's name and sealed with his signet ring can be canceled."

[9]At that time the king's secretaries were called. This was the twenty-third day of the third month, which is Sivan. The secretaries wrote out all of Mordecai's orders to the Jews, to the governors, to the captains of the soldiers in each state, and to the important men of the one hundred twenty-seven states that reached from India to Cush. They wrote in the writing of each state and in the language of each people. They also wrote to the Jewish people in their own writing and language.

> **SIDELIGHT:** The longest verse in the Bible is Esther 8:9. It's eighty-eight words long.

[10]Mordecai wrote orders in the name of King Xerxes and sealed the letters with the king's signet ring. Then he sent the king's orders by messengers on fast horses, horses that were raised just for the king.

[11]These were the king's orders: The Jewish people in every city have the right to gather together to protect themselves. They may destroy, kill, and completely wipe out the army of any state or people who attack them. And they are to do the same to the women and children of that army. They may also take by force the property of their enemies. [12]The one day set for the Jewish people to do this in all the empire of King Xerxes was the thirteenth day of the twelfth month, the month of Adar. [13]A copy of the king's order was to be sent out as a law in every state. It was to be made known to the people of every nation living in the kingdom so the Jewish people would be ready on that set day to strike back at their enemies.

[14]The messengers hurried out, riding on the royal horses, because the king commanded those messengers to hurry. And the order was also given in the palace at Susa.

> **SIDELIGHT:** They may not have had overnight mail, but the Persians had an excellent postal system to deliver Mordecai's letter (Esther 8:10). The Persian Empire was organized into twenty satrapies (or provinces), which were connected by efficient mail service begun by King Cyrus around 535 B.C.

[15]Mordecai left the king's presence wearing royal clothes of blue and white and a large gold crown. He also had a purple robe made of the best linen. And the people of Susa shouted for joy. [16]It was a time of happiness, joy, gladness, and honor for the Jewish people. [17]As the king's order went to every state and city, there was joy and gladness

among the Jewish people. In every state and city to which the king's order went, they were having feasts and celebrating. And many people through all the empire became Jews, because they were afraid of the Jewish people.

Victory for the Jewish People

9 The order the king had commanded was to be done on the thirteenth day of the twelfth month, the month of Adar. That was the day the enemies of the Jewish people had hoped to defeat them, but that was changed. So the Jewish people themselves defeated those who hated them. ²The Jews met in their cities in all the empire of King Xerxes in order to attack those who wanted to harm them. No one was strong enough to fight against them, because all the other people living in the empire were afraid of them. ³All the important men of the states, the governors, captains of the soldiers, and the king's officers helped the Jewish people, because they were afraid of Mordecai. ⁴Mordecai was very important in the king's palace. He was famous in all the empire, because he was becoming a leader of more and more people.

⁵And, with their swords, the Jewish people defeated all their enemies, killing and destroying them. And they did what they wanted with those people who hated them. ⁶In the palace at Susa, they killed and destroyed five hundred men. ⁷They also killed: Parshandatha, Dalphon, Aspatha, ⁸Poratha, Adalia, Aridatha, ⁹Parmashta, Arisai, Aridai, and Vaizatha, ¹⁰the ten sons of Haman, son of Hammedatha, the enemy of the Jewish people. But the Jewish people did not take their belongings.

¹¹On that day the number killed in the palace at Susa was reported to the king. ¹²The king said to Queen Esther, "The Jewish people have killed and destroyed five hundred people in the palace at Susa, and they have also killed Haman's ten sons. What have they done in the rest of the king's empire! Now what else are you asking? I will do it! What else do you want? It will be done!"

¹³Esther answered, "If it pleases the king, give the Jewish people who are in Susa permission to do again tomorrow what the king ordered for today. And let the bodies of Haman's ten sons be hanged on the platform."

¹⁴So the king ordered that it be done. A law was given in Susa, and the bodies of the ten sons of Haman were hanged. ¹⁵The Jewish people in Susa came together on the fourteenth day of the month of Adar. They killed three hundred people in Susa, but they did not take their belongings.

¹⁶At that same time, all the Jewish people in the king's empire also met to protect themselves and get rid of their enemies. They killed seventy-five thousand of those who hated them, but they did not take their belongings. ¹⁷This happened on the thirteenth day of the month of Adar. On the fourteenth day they rested and made it a day of joyful feasting.

The Feast of Purim

¹⁸But the Jewish people in Susa met on the thirteenth and fourteenth days of the month of Adar. Then they rested on the fifteenth day and made it a day of joyful feasting.

¹⁹This is why the Jewish people who live in the country and small villages celebrate on the fourteenth day of the month of Adar. It is a day of joyful feasting and a day for exchanging gifts.

²⁰Mordecai wrote down everything that had happened. Then he sent letters to all the Jewish people in all the empire of King Xerxes, far and near. ²¹He told them to celebrate every year on the fourteenth and fifteenth days of the month of Adar, ²²because that was when the Jewish people got rid of their enemies. They were also to celebrate it as the month their sadness was turned to joy and their crying for the dead was turned into celebration. He told them to celebrate those days as days of joyful feasting and as a time for giving food to each other and presents to the poor.

²³So the Jewish people agreed to do what Mordecai had written to them, and they agreed to hold the celebration every year. ²⁴Haman son of Hammedatha, the Agagite, was the enemy of all the Jewish people. He had made an evil plan against the Jewish people to destroy them, and he had thrown the Pur (that is, the lot[d]) to choose a day to ruin and destroy them. ²⁵But when the king learned of the evil plan, he sent out written orders that the evil plans Haman had made against the Jewish people would be used against him. And those orders said that Haman and his sons should be hanged on the platform. ²⁶So these days were called Purim, which comes from the word "Pur" (the lot). Because of everything written in this letter and what they had seen and what happened to them, ²⁷the Jewish people set up this custom. They and their descendants[f] and all those who join them are always to celebrate these two days every year. They should do it in the right way and at the time Mordecai had ordered them in the letter. ²⁸These two days should be remembered and celebrated from now on in every family, in every state, and in every city. These days of Purim should always be celebrated by the Jewish people, and their descendants should always remember to celebrate them, too.

²⁹So Queen Esther daughter of Abihail, along with Mordecai the Jew, wrote this second letter about Purim. Using the power they had, they wrote to prove the first letter was true. ³⁰And Mordecai sent letters to all the Jewish people in

the one hundred twenty-seven states of the kingdom of Xerxes, writing them a message of peace and truth. [31]He wrote to set up these days of Purim at the chosen times. Mordecai the Jew and

> ### SIDELIGHT: Looking for a reason to celebrate? Try the Feast of Purim, a joyous occasion Jews celebrate each year in February or March with parties, giftgiving and aid to the poor. The book of Esther describes the traditional beginning of this two-day festival (Esther 9:18–32).

Queen Esther had sent out the order for the Jewish people, just as they had set up things for themselves and their descendants: On these two days

the people should give up eating and cry loudly. [32]Esther's letter set up the rules for Purim, and they were written down in the records.

The Greatness of Mordecai

10 King Xerxes demanded taxes everywhere, even from the cities on the seacoast. [2]And all the great things Xerxes did by his power and strength are written in the record books of the kings of Media and Persia. Also written in those record books are all the things done by Mordecai, whom the king made great. [3]Mordecai the Jew was second in importance to King Xerxes, and he was the most important man among the Jewish people. His fellow Jews respected him very much, because he worked for the good of his people and spoke up for the safety of all the Jewish people.

JOB

- Learn patience from someone who is suffering unfairly (Job 1:21—2:10; 16; 19).
- Realize it's okay to question God (Job 10, 13, 23).
- See how God is always there, even when he doesn't seem to be (Job 38—42).

**Behind the
Scenes:**

Why do good people suffer? Why do bad people seem to get away with everything? How can God love us if he lets bad things happen to us? If you have ever asked those questions, you are not alone. For centuries, people have asked them and struggled with them.

The book of Job addresses those questions as it tells about Job, an upright and wealthy man. Like others of his day, he believed that all of his blessings were the result of his goodness. He accepted traditional answers to life's questions.

Then his life fell apart. He lost everything—his family, his health, and his belongings. Life wasn't supposed to work out this way. In his pain, he angrily cried out to God, "Why do innocent people suffer?"

Four friends made matters worse by telling Job the same old thing: God

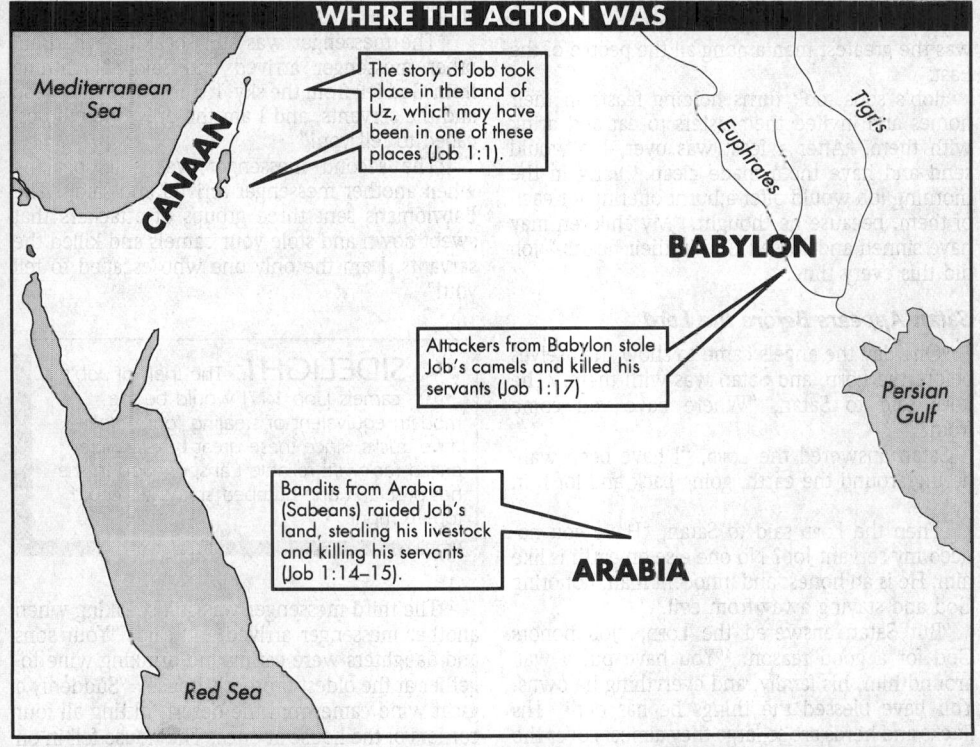

WHERE THE ACTION WAS

Mediterranean
Sea

CANAAN

The story of Job took place in the land of Uz, which may have been in one of these places (Job 1:1).

Euphrates

Tigris

BABYLON

Attackers from Babylon stole Job's camels and killed his servants (Job 1:17)

Persian
Gulf

Bandits from Arabia (Sabeans) raided Job's land, stealing his livestock and killing his servants (Job 1:14—15).

ARABIA

Red Sea

WHEN THE ACTION WAS

Abraham lived	Joseph was sold into slavery				Jesus was born
2000BC	**1500BC**	**1000BC**	**500BC**		**BC/AD**
The story of Job was set around this time	The Israelites escaped from Egypt				

Behind the Scenes (cont.): rewards the righteous and punishes sinners (Job 3—37). Job sincerely believed he was innocent, but he couldn't explain the suffering. He felt betrayed by God. Yet he patiently kept his faith in God and waited for God's answers to his questions.

Job and his friends never settled their debate. Suddenly God appeared on the scene through a storm, in chapters 38—41. He didn't answer Job, though he did speak to him. God reminded Job that his greatness and wisdom are beyond human understanding. Job then realized that it wasn't his place to try to understand God. Instead, he was to follow God faithfully no matter what happened.

People continue to struggle with why good people suffer. The book of Job tells us it's okay to ask God tough questions. It also challenges us to remain faithful in spite of suffering. In the end, we can trust in God's goodness, justice, and wisdom—even when we can't see it ourselves.

Job, the Good Man

1 A man named Job lived in the land of Uz. He was an honest and innocent man; he honored God and stayed away from evil. ²Job had seven sons and three daughters. ³He owned seven thousand sheep, three thousand camels, five hundred teams of oxen, and five hundred female donkeys. He also had a large number of servants. He was the greatest man among all the people of the East.

⁴Job's sons took turns holding feasts in their homes and invited their sisters to eat and drink with them. ⁵After a feast was over, Job would send and have them made clean.ᵈ Early in the morning Job would offer a burnt offering for each of them, because he thought, "My children may have sinned and cursed God in their hearts." Job did this every time.

Satan Appears Before the Lord

⁶One day the angels came to show themselves before the Lord, and Satan was with them. ⁷The Lord said to Satan, "Where have you come from?"

Satan answered the Lord, "I have been wandering around the earth, going back and forth in it."

⁸Then the Lord said to Satan, "Have you noticed my servant Job? No one else on earth is like him. He is an honest and innocent man, honoring God and staying away from evil."

⁹But Satan answered the Lord, "Job honors God for a good reason. ¹⁰You have put a wall around him, his family, and everything he owns. You have blessed the things he has done. His flocks and herds are so large they almost cover the land. ¹¹But reach out your hand and destroy everything he has, and he will curse you to your face."

¹²The Lord said to Satan, "All right, then. Everything Job has is in your power, but you must not touch Job himself." Then Satan left the Lord's presence.

¹³One day Job's sons and daughters were eating and drinking wine together at the oldest brother's house. ¹⁴A messenger came to Job and said, "The oxen were plowing and the donkeys were eating grass nearby, ¹⁵when the Sabeans attacked and carried them away. They killed the servants with swords, and I am the only one who escaped to tell you!"

¹⁶The messenger was still speaking when another messenger arrived and said, "Lightning from God fell from the sky. It burned up the sheep and the servants, and I am the only one who escaped to tell you!"

¹⁷The second messenger was still speaking when another messenger arrived and said, "The Babylonians sent three groups of attackers that swept down and stole your camels and killed the servants. I am the only one who escaped to tell you!"

> ✸ **SIDELIGHT:** The theft of Job's camels (Job 1:17) would be the modern equivalent of stealing four-wheel-drive trucks, since these great beasts were prized for swift, reliable transportation in the hot desert. A one-humped speedster could top 10 mph!

¹⁸The third messenger was still speaking when another messenger arrived and said, "Your sons and daughters were eating and drinking wine together at the oldest brother's house. ¹⁹Suddenly a great wind came from the desert, hitting all four corners of the house at once. The house fell in on *the young people, and they are all dead. I am the* only one who escaped to tell you!"

²⁰When Job heard this, he got up and tore his robe and shaved his head to show how sad he was. Then he bowed down to the ground to worship God. ²¹He said:

"I was naked when I was born,

and I will be naked when I die.
The LORD gave these things to me,
  and he has taken them away.
Praise the name of the LORD."
22In all this Job did not sin or blame God.

Satan Appears Before the Lord Again

2 On another day the angels came to show
   themselves before the LORD, and Satan was
with them again. 2The LORD said to Satan,
"Where have you come from?"

Satan answered the LORD, "I have been wandering around the earth, going back and forth in it."

3Then the LORD said to Satan, "Have you noticed my servant Job? No one else on earth is like him. He is an honest and innocent man, honoring God and staying away from evil. You caused me to ruin him for no good reason, but he continues to be without blame."

4"One skin for another!" Satan answered. "A man will give all he has to save his own life. 5But reach out your hand and destroy his flesh and bones, and he will curse you to your face."

6The LORD said to Satan, "All right, then. Job is in your power, but you may not take his life."

7So Satan left the LORD's presence. He put painful sores on Job's body, from the top of his head to the soles of his feet. 8Job took a piece of broken pottery to scrape himself, and he sat in ashes in misery.

9Job's wife said to him, "Why are you trying to stay innocent? Curse God and die!"

10Job answered, "You are talking like a foolish woman. Should we take only good things from God and not trouble?" In spite of all this Job did not sin in what he said.

Job's Three Friends Come to Help

11Now Job had three friends: Eliphaz the Temanite, Bildad the Shuhite, and Zophar the Naamathite. When these friends heard about Job's troubles, they agreed to meet and visit him. They wanted to show their concern and to comfort him. 12They saw Job from far away, but he looked so different they almost didn't recognize him. They began to cry loudly and tore their robes and put dirt on their heads to show how sad they were. 13Then they sat on the ground with Job seven days and seven nights. No one said a word to him because they saw how much he was suffering.

Job Curses His Birth

3 After seven days Job cried out and cursed the
   day he had been born, 2saying:

3"Let the day I was born be destroyed,
  and the night it was said, 'A boy is born!'

4Let that day turn to darkness.
  Don't let God care about it.
  Don't let light shine on it.
5Let darkness and gloom have that day.
  Let a cloud hide it.
  Let thick darkness cover its light.
6Let thick darkness capture that night.
  Don't count it among the days of the year
  or put it in any of the months.
7Let that night be empty,
  with no shout of joy to be heard.
8Let those who curse days curse that day.
  Let them prepare to wake up the sea
      monster Leviathan.d
9Let that day's morning stars never appear;
  let it wait for daylight that never comes.
  Don't let it see the first light of dawn,
10because it allowed me to be born
  and did not hide trouble from my eyes.

11"Why didn't I die as soon as I was born?
  Why didn't I die when I came out of the
      womb?
12Why did my mother's knees receive me,
  and my mother's breasts feed me?
13If they had not been there,
  I would be lying dead in peace;
  I would be asleep and at rest
14with kings and wise men of the earth
  who built places for themselves that are
      now ruined.
15I would be asleep with rulers
  who filled their houses with gold and silver.
16Why was I not buried like a child born dead,
  like a baby who never saw the light of day?
17In the grave the wicked stop making trouble,
  and the weary workers are at rest.
18In the grave there is rest for the captives
  who no longer hear the shout of the slave
      driver.
19People great and small are in the grave,
  and the slave is freed from his master.

20"Why is light given to those in misery?
  Why is life given to those who are so
      unhappy?
21They want to die, but death does not come.
  They search for death more than for hidden
      treasure.
22They are very happy
  when they get to the grave.
23They cannot see where they are going.
  God has hidden the road ahead.
24I make sad sounds as I eat;
  my groans pour out like water.
25Everything I feared and dreaded
  has happened to me.
26I have no peace or quietness.
  I have no rest, only trouble."

Eliphaz Speaks

4 Then Eliphaz the Temanite answered:

2"If someone tried to speak with you,
would you be upset?
I cannot keep from speaking.
3Think about the many people you have
taught
and the weak hands you have made strong.
4Your words have comforted those who fell,
and you have strengthened those who
could not stand.
5But now trouble comes to you, and you are
discouraged;
trouble hits you, and you are terrified.
6You should have confidence because you
respect God;
you should have hope because you are
innocent.

7"Remember that the innocent will not die;
honest people will never be destroyed.
8I have noticed that people who plow evil
and plant trouble, harvest it.
9God's breath destroys them,
and a blast of his anger kills them.
10Lions may roar and growl,
but when the teeth of a strong lion are
broken,
11that lion dies of hunger.
The cubs of the mother lion are scattered.

12"A word was brought to me in secret,
and my ears heard a whisper of it.
13It was during a nightmare
when people are in deep sleep.
14I was trembling with fear;
all my bones were shaking.
15A spirit glided past my face,
and the hair on my body stood on end.
16The spirit stopped,
but I could not see what it was.
A shape stood before my eyes,
and I heard a quiet voice.
17It said, 'Can a human be more right than
God?
Can a person be pure before his maker?
18God does not trust his angels;
he blames them for mistakes.
19So he puts even more blame on people who
live in clay houses, *n*
whose foundations are made of dust,
who can be crushed like a moth.
20Between *dawn and sunset many people are*
broken to pieces;
without being noticed, they die and are
gone forever.
21The ropes of their tents are pulled up,

and they die without wisdom.'

5 "Call if you want to, Job, but no one will
answer you.
You can't turn to any of the holy ones.
2Anger kills the fool,
and jealousy slays the stupid.
3I have seen a fool succeed,
but I cursed his home immediately.
4His children are far from safety
and are crushed in court with no defense.
5The hungry eat his harvest,
even taking what grew among the thorns,
and thirsty people want his wealth.
6Hard times do not come up from the ground,
and trouble does not grow from the earth.
7People produce trouble
as surely as sparks fly upward.

8"But if I were you, I would call on God
and bring my problem before him.
9God does wonders that cannot be
understood;
he does so many miracles*d* they cannot be
counted.
10He gives rain to the earth
and sends water on the fields.
11He makes the humble person important
and lifts the sad to places of safety.
12He ruins the plans of those who trick others
so they have no success.
13He catches the wise in their own clever traps
and sweeps away the plans of those who
try to trick others.
14Darkness covers them up in the daytime;
even at noon they feel around in the dark.
15God saves the needy from their lies
and from the harm done by powerful
people.
16So the poor have hope,
while those who are unfair are silenced.

17"The one whom God corrects is happy,
so do not hate being corrected by the
Almighty.
18God hurts, but he also bandages up;
he injures, but his hands also heal.
19He will save you from six troubles;
even seven troubles will not harm you.
20God will buy you back from death in times of
hunger,
and in battle he will save you from the
sword.
21*You will be protected from the tongue that*
strikes like a whip,
and you will not be afraid when destruction
comes.
22You will laugh at destruction and hunger,

clay houses This is probably talking about people's bodies.

and you will not fear the wild animals,
23because you will have an agreement with the
  stones in the field,
  and the wild animals will be at peace with
  you.
24You will know that your tent is safe,
  because you will check the things you own
  and find nothing missing.
25You will know that you will have many
  children,
  and your descendants*d* will be like the grass
  on the earth.
26You will come to the grave with all your
  strength,
  like bundles of grain gathered at the right
  time.
27"We have checked this, and it is true,
  so hear it and decide what it means to
  you."

Job Answers Eliphaz

6 Then Job answered:

2"I wish my suffering could be weighed
  and my misery put on scales.
3My sadness would be heavier than the sand
  of the seas.
  No wonder my words seem careless.
4The arrows of the Almighty are in me;
  my spirit drinks in their poison;
  God's terrors are gathered against me.

☀ SIDELIGHT: You may have
  never called God "King of the Hill,"
but the characters in Job did. "God Almighty"
is the translation of a Hebrew name that
literally means "Lord of the Mountain" (for
example, Job 6:4).

5A wild donkey does not bray when it has
  grass to eat,
  and an ox is quiet when it has feed.
6Tasteless food is not eaten without salt,
  and there is no flavor in the white of an
  egg.
7I refuse to touch it;
  such food makes me sick.

8"How I wish that I might have what I ask for
  and that God would give me what I hope
  for.
9How I wish God would crush me
  and reach out his hand to destroy me.
10Then I would have this comfort
  and be glad even in this unending pain,
  because I would know I did not reject the
  words of the Holy One.

11"I do not have the strength to wait.
  There is nothing to hope for,
  so why should I be patient?
12I do not have the strength of stone;
  my flesh is not bronze.
13I have no power to help myself,
  because success has been taken away from
  me.

14"They say, 'A man's friends should be kind to
  him when he is in trouble,
  even if he stops fearing the Almighty.'
15But my brothers cannot be counted on.
  They are like streams that do not always
  flow,
  streams that sometimes run over.
16They are made dark by melting ice
  and rise with melting snow.
17But they stop flowing in the dry season;
  they disappear when it is hot.
18Travelers turn away from their paths
  and go into the desert and die.
19The groups of travelers from Tema look for
  water,
  and the traders of Sheba look hopefully.
20They are upset because they had been sure;
  when they arrive, they are disappointed.
21You also have been no help.
  You see something terrible, and you are
  afraid.
22I have never said, 'Give me a gift.
  Use your wealth to pay my debt.
23Save me from the enemy's power.
  Buy me back from the clutches of cruel
  people.'

24"Teach me, and I will be quiet.
  Show me where I have been wrong.
25Honest words are painful,
  but your arguments prove nothing.
26Do you mean to correct what I say?
  Will you treat the words of a troubled man
  as if they were only wind?
27You would even gamble for orphans
  and would trade away your friend.

28"But now please look at me.
  I would not lie to your face.
29Change your mind; do not be unfair;
  think again, because my innocence is being
  questioned.
30What I am saying is not wicked;
  I can tell the difference between right and
  wrong.

7 "People have a hard task on earth,
  and their days are like those of a laborer.
2They are like a slave wishing for the evening
  shadows,
  like a laborer waiting to be paid.

³But I am given months that are empty,
and nights of misery have been given to
me.
⁴When I lie down, I think, 'How long until I
get up?'
The night is long, and I toss until dawn.
⁵My body is covered with worms and scabs,
and my skin is broken and full of sores.

⁶"My days go by faster than a weaver's tool,
and they come to an end without hope.
⁷Remember, God, that my life is only a
breath.
My eyes will never see happy times again.
⁸Those who see me now will see me no
more;
you will look for me, but I will be gone.
⁹As a cloud disappears and is gone,
people go to the grave and never return.
¹⁰They will never come back to their houses
again,
and their places will not know them
anymore.

¹¹"So I will not stay quiet;
I will speak out in the suffering of my
spirit.
I will complain because I am so unhappy.
¹²I am not the sea or the sea monster.
So why have you set a guard over me?
¹³Sometimes I think my bed will comfort me
or that my couch will stop my complaint.
¹⁴Then you frighten me with dreams
and terrify me with visions.
¹⁵My throat prefers to be choked;
my bones welcome death.
¹⁶I hate my life; I don't want to live forever.
Leave me alone, because my days have no
meaning.

¹⁷"Why do you make people so important
and give them so much attention?
¹⁸You examine them every morning
and test them every moment.
¹⁹Will you never look away from me
or leave me alone even long enough to
swallow?

DEPRESSION

Stirring Up Life

Mandy Lewis sat beside the swirling river that ran through town. Her fright and hurt had changed into a deadly heaviness. It stifled her. It dulled all hope.

Only last week everything had seemed okay. Then Josh McKinley dumped her—just put his arm around her best friend and took off. It nearly killed Mandy. How could he . . . when he said he loved her? And how could Sheila?

Mandy tried to talk to her mom, but the whole house was a constant battlefield, everyone yelling at each other. Her stepdad was out of work and there wasn't enough money to go around.

The water invited her into its depths. It offered an easy way out. Then she would never have to hurt again.

"Can I sit here with you?"

Mandy looked up at a tall girl. She had seen her a few times at school, always by herself, but self-assured, at ease.

"If you want."

"I'm nobody to you, but . . . I know what happened, and I care." The girl sat down. "I've been there. And even though it doesn't seem possible now, things will get better. Just hang in there, okay?"

Mandy looked into the girl's brown eyes. Their sincerity stirred life inside Mandy.

Like Mandy, Job felt overwhelmed by a sense of loss and depression. Read his story in **Job 7:1–8**.
■ How does Mandy's depression compare with Job's?
■ When you feel like Job did in verses 3 and 7, what do you need most?

CONSIDER
■ talking to a trusted friend about a problem that's getting you down.
➧ organizing a peer counseling program at your church or school. Talk to your youth pastor or school counselor for ideas.

FOR MORE, SEE
■ Psalm 139:1–24 (p. 561)
■ 2 Corinthians 1:3–7 (p. 1193)
■ Philippians 2:1–4 (p. 1230)

²⁰If I have sinned, what have I done to you,
   you watcher of humans?
Why have you made me your target?
Have I become a heavy load for you?
²¹Why don't you pardon my wrongs
   and forgive my sins?
I will soon lie down in the dust of death.
Then you will search for me, but I will be
   no more."

Bildad Speaks to Job

8 Then Bildad the Shuhite answered:

²"How long will you say such things?
Your words are no more than wind.
³God does not twist justice;
   the Almighty does not make wrong what is
      right.
⁴Your children sinned against God,
   and he punished them for their sins.
⁵But you should ask God for help
   and pray to the Almighty for mercy.
⁶If you are good and honest,
   he will stand up for you
   and bring you back where you belong.
⁷Where you began will seem unimportant,
   because your future will be so successful.

⁸"Ask old people;
   find out what their ancestors learned,
⁹because we were only born yesterday and
      know nothing.
Our days on earth are only a shadow.
¹⁰Those people will teach you and tell you
   and speak about what they know.
¹¹Papyrus^d plants cannot grow where there is
      no swamp,
   and reeds cannot grow tall without water.
¹²While they are still growing and not yet cut,
   they will dry up quicker than grass.
¹³That is what will happen to those who forget
      God;
   the hope of the wicked will be gone.
¹⁴What they hope in is easily broken;
   what they trust is like a spider's web.
¹⁵They lean on the spider's web, but it breaks.
They grab it, but it does not hold up.
¹⁶They are like well-watered plants in the
      sunshine
   that spread their roots all through the
      garden.
¹⁷They wrap their roots around a pile of rocks
   and look for a place among the stones.
¹⁸But if a plant is torn from its place,
   then that place rejects it and says, 'I never
      saw you.'
¹⁹Now joy has gone away;
   other plants grow up from the same dirt.

²⁰"Surely God does not reject the innocent
   or give strength to those who do evil.
²¹God will yet fill your mouth with laughter
   and your lips with shouts of joy.
²²Your enemies will be covered with shame,
   and the tents of the wicked will be gone."

Job Answers Bildad

9 Then Job answered:

²"Yes, I know that this is true,
but how can anyone be right in the
      presence of God?
³Someone might want to argue with God,
   but no one could answer God,
   not one time out of a thousand.
⁴God's wisdom is deep, and his power is
      great;
   no one can fight him without getting hurt.
⁵God moves mountains without anyone
      knowing it
   and turns them over when he is angry.
⁶He shakes the earth out of its place
   and makes its foundations tremble.
⁷He commands the sun not to shine
   and shuts off the light of the stars.
⁸He alone stretches out the skies
   and walks on the waves of the sea.
⁹It is God who made the Bear, Orion, and the
      Pleiadesⁿ
   and the groups of stars in the southern sky.
¹⁰He does wonders that cannot be understood;
   he does so many miracles^d they cannot be
      counted.
¹¹When he passes me, I cannot see him;
   when he goes by me, I do not recognize
      him.
¹²If he snatches something away, no one can
      stop him
   or say to him, 'What are you doing?'
¹³God will not hold back his anger.
Even the helpers of the monster Rahab^d lie
      at his feet in fear.
¹⁴So how can I argue with God,
   or even find words to argue with him?
¹⁵Even if I were right, I could not answer him;
   I could only beg God, my Judge, for mercy.
¹⁶If I called to him and he answered,
   I still don't believe he would listen to me.
¹⁷He would crush me with a storm
   and multiply my wounds for no reason.
¹⁸He would not let me catch my breath
   but would overwhelm me with misery.
¹⁹When it comes to strength, God is stronger
      than I;
   when it comes to justice, no one can
      accuse him.

Bear ... Pleiades   Names of well-known groups of stars.

²⁰Even if I were right, my own mouth would
say I was wrong;
if I were innocent, my mouth would say I
was guilty.
²¹"I am innocent,
but I don't care about myself.
I hate my own life.
²²It is all the same. That is why I say,
'God destroys both the innocent and the
guilty.'
²³If the whip brings sudden death,
God will laugh at the suffering of the
innocent.
²⁴When the land falls into the hands of evil
people,
he covers the judges' faces so they can't
see it.
If it is not God who does this, then who is
it?

²⁵"My days go by faster than a runner;
they fly away without my seeing any joy.
²⁶They glide past like paper boats.
They attack like eagles swooping down to
feed.
²⁷Even though I say, 'I will forget my
complaint;
I will change the look on my face and
smile,'
²⁸I still dread all my suffering.
I know you will hold me guilty.
²⁹I have already been found guilty,
so why should I struggle for no reason?
³⁰I might wash myself with soap
and scrub my hands with strong soap,
³¹but you would push me into a dirty pit,
and even my clothes would hate me.

³²"God is not a man like me, so I cannot
answer him.
We cannot meet each other in court.
³³I wish there were someone to make peace
between us,
someone to decide our case.
³⁴Maybe he could remove God's punishment
so his terror would no longer frighten me.
³⁵Then I could speak without being afraid,
but I am not able to do that.

10 "I hate my life,
so I will complain without holding
back;
I will speak because I am so unhappy.
²I will say to God: Do not hold me guilty,
but tell me what you have against me.
³Does it make you happy to trouble me?
Don't you care about me, the work of your
hands?
Are you happy with the plans of evil
people?

⁴Do you have human eyes
that see as we see?
⁵Are your days like the days of humans,
and your years like our years?
⁶You look for the evil I have done
and search for my sin.
⁷You know I am not guilty,
but no one can save me from your power.

⁸"Your hands shaped and made me.
Do you now turn around and destroy me?
⁹Remember that you molded me like a piece
of clay.
Will you now turn me back into dust?
¹⁰You formed me inside my mother
like cheese formed from milk.
¹¹You dressed me with skin and flesh;
you sewed me together with bones and
muscles.
¹²You gave me life and showed me kindness,
and in your care you watched over my life.

¹³"But in your heart you hid other plans.
I know this was in your mind.
¹⁴If I sinned, you would watch me
and would not let my sin go unpunished.
¹⁵How terrible it will be for me if I am guilty!
Even if I am right, I cannot lift my head.
I am full of shame
and experience only pain.
¹⁶If I hold up my head, you hunt me like a lion
and again show your terrible power against
me.
¹⁷You bring new witnesses against me
and increase your anger against me.
Your armies come against me.

¹⁸"So why did you allow me to be born?
I wish I had died before anyone saw me.
¹⁹I wish I had never lived,
but had been carried straight from birth to
the grave.
²⁰The few days of my life are almost over.
Leave me alone so I can have a moment of
joy.
²¹Soon I will leave; I will not return
from the land of darkness and gloom,
²²the land of darkest night,
from the land of gloom and confusion,
where even the light is darkness."

Zophar Speaks to Job

11 Then Zophar the Naamathite answered:
²"Should these words go unanswered?
Is this talker in the right?
³Your lies do not make people quiet;
people should correct you when you make
fun of God.
⁴You say, 'My teachings are right,
and I am clean^d in God's sight.'

⁵I wish God would speak
and open his lips against you
⁶and tell you the secrets of wisdom,
because wisdom has two sides.
Know this: God has even forgotten some of
your sin.

⁷"Can you understand the secrets of God?
Can you search the limits of the Almighty?
⁸His limits are higher than the heavens;
you cannot reach them!
They are deeper than the grave;
you cannot understand them!
⁹His limits are longer than the earth
and wider than the sea.

¹⁰"If God comes along and puts you in prison
or calls you into court, no one can stop
him.
¹¹God knows who is evil,
and when he sees evil, he takes note of it.
¹²A fool cannot become wise
any more than a wild donkey can be born
tame.

¹³"You must give your whole heart to him
and hold out your hands to him for help.
¹⁴Put away the sin that is in your hand;
let no evil remain in your tent.
¹⁵Then you can lift up your face without
shame,
and you can stand strong without fear.
¹⁶You will forget your trouble
and remember it only as water gone by.
¹⁷Your life will be as bright as the noonday
sun,
and darkness will seem like morning.
¹⁸You will feel safe because there is hope;
you will look around and rest in safety.
¹⁹You will lie down, and no one will scare you.
Many people will want favors from you.
²⁰But the wicked will not be able to see,
so they will not escape.
Their only hope will be to die."

Job Answers Zophar

12 Then Job answered:

²"You really think you are the only
wise people
and that when you die, wisdom will die
with you!
³But my mind is as good as yours;
you are not better than I am.
Everyone knows all these things.
⁴My friends all laugh at me
when I call on God and expect him to
answer me;
they laugh at me even though I am right
and innocent!

⁵Those who are comfortable don't care that
others have trouble;
they think it right that those people should
have troubles.
⁶The tents of robbers are not bothered,
and those who make God angry are safe.
They have their god in their pocket.

⁷"But ask the animals, and they will teach
you,
or ask the birds of the air, and they will tell
you.
⁸Speak to the earth, and it will teach you,
or let the fish of the sea tell you.
⁹Every one of these knows
that the hand of the Lᴏʀᴅ has done this.
¹⁰The life of every creature
and the breath of all people are in God's
hand.
¹¹The ear tests words
as the tongue tastes food.
¹²Older people are wise,
and long life brings understanding.

¹³"But only God has wisdom and power,
good advice and understanding.
¹⁴What he tears down cannot be rebuilt;
anyone he puts in prison cannot be let out.
¹⁵If God holds back the waters, there is no
rain;
if he lets the waters go, they flood the land.
¹⁶He is strong and victorious;
both the one who fools others and the one
who is fooled belong to him.
¹⁷God leads the wise away as captives
and turns judges into fools.
¹⁸He takes off chains that kings put on
and puts a garment on their bodies.
¹⁹He leads priests away naked
and destroys the powerful.
²⁰He makes trusted people be silent
and takes away the wisdom of older
leaders.
²¹He brings disgrace on important people
and takes away the weapons of the strong.
²²He uncovers the deep things of darkness
and brings dark shadows into the light.
²³He makes nations great and then destroys
them;
he makes nations large and then scatters
them.
²⁴He takes understanding away from the
leaders of the earth
and makes them wander through a pathless
desert.
²⁵They feel around in darkness with no light;
he makes them stumble like drunks.

13 "Now my eyes have seen all this;
my ears have heard and understood it.

2What you know, I also know.
  You are not better than I am.
3But I want to speak to the Almighty
  and to argue my case with God.
4But you smear me with lies.
  You are worthless doctors, all of you!
5I wish you would just stop talking;
  then you would really be wise!
6Listen to my argument,
  and hear the pleading of my lips.
7You should not speak evil in the name of
    God;
  you cannot speak God's truth by telling lies.
8You should not unfairly choose his side
    against mine;
  you should not argue the case for God.
9You will not do well if he examines you;
  you cannot fool God as you might fool
    humans.
10God would surely scold you
  if you unfairly took one person's side.
11His bright glory would scare you,
  and you would be very much afraid of him.
12Your wise sayings are worth no more than
    ashes,
  and your arguments are as weak as clay.

13"Be quiet and let me speak.
  Let things happen to me as they will.
14Why should I put myself in danger
  and take my life in my own hands?
15Even if God kills me, I have hope in him;
  I will still defend my ways to his face.
16This is my salvation.
  The wicked cannot come before him.
17Listen carefully to my words;
  let your ears hear what I say.
18See, I have prepared my case,
  and I know I will be proved right.
19No one can accuse me of doing wrong.
  If someone can, I will be quiet and die.

20"God, please just give me these two things,
  and then I will not hide from you:
21Take your punishment away from me,
  and stop frightening me with your terrors.
22Then call me, and I will answer,
  or let me speak, and you answer.
23How many evil things and sins have I done?
  Show me my wrong and my sin.
24Don't hide your face from me;
  don't think of me as your enemy.
25Don't punish a leaf that is blown by the
    wind;
  don't chase after straw.
26You write down cruel things against me
  and make me suffer for my boyhood sins.
27You put my feet in chains
  and keep close watch wherever I go.
  You even mark the soles of my feet.

28"Everyone wears out like something rotten,
  like clothing eaten by moths.

14 "All of us born to women
     live only a few days and have lots of
       trouble.
2We grow up like flowers and then dry up
    and die.
  We are like a passing shadow that does not
    last.
3Lord, do you need to watch me like this?
  Must you bring me before you to be
    judged?
4No one can bring something clean from
    something dirty.
5Our time is limited.
  You have given us only so many months to
    live
  and have set limits we cannot go beyond.
6So look away from us and leave us alone
  until we put in our time like a laborer.

7"If a tree is cut down,
  there is hope that it will grow again
  and will send out new branches.
8Even if its roots grow old in the ground,
  and its stump dies in the dirt,
9at the smell of water it will bud
  and put out new shoots like a plant.
10But we die, and our bodies are laid in the
    ground;
  we take our last breath and are gone.
11Water disappears from a lake,
  and a river loses its water and dries up.
12In the same way, we lie down and do not
    rise again;
  we will not get up or be awakened
  until the heavens disappear.

13"I wish you would hide me in the grave;
  hide me until your anger is gone.
  I wish you would set a time
    and then remember me!
14If a person dies, will he live again?
  All my days are a struggle;
  I will wait until my change comes.
15You will call, and I will answer you;
  you will desire the creature your hands
    have made.
16Then you will count my steps,
  but you will not keep track of my sin.
17My wrongs will be closed up in a bag,
  and you will cover up my sin.

18"A mountain washes away and crumbles;
  and a rock can be moved from its place.
19Water washes over stones and wears them
    down,
  and rushing waters wash away the dirt.
  In the same way, you destroy my hope.
20You defeat a person forever, and he is gone;

you change his appearance and send him
away.
²¹His sons are honored, but he does not know
it;
his sons are disgraced, but he does not
see it.
²²He only feels the pain of his body
and feels sorry for himself."

Eliphaz Answers Job

15 Then Eliphaz the Temanite answered:
²"A wise person would not answer
with empty words
or fill his stomach with the hot east wind.
³He would not argue with useless words
or make speeches that have no value.
⁴But you even destroy respect for God
and limit the worship of him.
⁵Your sin teaches your mouth what to say;
you use words to trick others.
⁶It is your own mouth, not mine, that shows
you are wicked;
your own lips testify against you.

⁷"You are not the first man ever born;
you are not older than the hills.
⁸You did not listen in on God's secret council.
But you limit wisdom to yourself.
⁹You don't know any more than we know.
You don't understand any more than we
understand.
¹⁰Old people with gray hair are on our side;
they are even older than your father.

> ✳ **SIDELIGHT:** While adults may
> try to hide their age today, growing
> old was a mark of dignity and respect in the
> Old Testament. That's why Eliphaz supported
> his argument by saying people with gray hair
> were on his side (Job 15:10).

¹¹Is the comfort God gives you not enough for
you,
even when words are spoken gently to
you?
¹²Has your heart carried you away from God?
Why do your eyes flash with anger?
¹³Why do you speak out your anger against
God?
Why do these words pour out of your
mouth?

¹⁴"How can anyone be pure?
How can someone born to a woman be
good?
¹⁵God places no trust in his holy ones,

and even the heavens are not pure in his
eyes.
¹⁶How much less pure is one who is terrible
and rotten
and drinks up evil as if it were water!

¹⁷"Listen to me, and I will tell you about it;
I will tell you what I have seen.
¹⁸These are things wise men have told;
their fathers told them, and they have
hidden nothing.
¹⁹(The land was given to their fathers only,
and no foreigner lived among them.)
²⁰The wicked suffer pain all their lives;
the cruel suffer during all the years saved
up for them.
²¹Terrible sounds fill their ears,
and when things seem to be going well,
robbers attack them.
²²Evil people give up trying to escape from the
darkness;
it has been decided that they will die by
the sword.
²³They wander around and will become food
for vultures.
They know darkness will soon come.
²⁴Worry and suffering terrify them;
they overwhelm them, like a king ready to
attack,
²⁵because they shake their fists at God
and try to get their own way against the
Almighty.
²⁶They stubbornly charge at God
with thick, strong shields.

²⁷"Although the faces of the wicked are thick
with fat,
and their bellies are fat with flesh,
²⁸they will live in towns that are ruined,
in houses where no one lives,
which are crumbling into ruins.
²⁹The wicked will no longer get rich,
and the riches they have will not last;
the things they own will no longer spread
over the land.
³⁰They will not escape the darkness.
A flame will dry up their branches;
God's breath will carry the wicked away.
³¹The wicked should not fool themselves by
trusting what is useless.
If they do, they will get nothing in return.
³²Their branches will dry up before they finish
growing
and will never turn green.
³³They will be like a vine whose grapes are
pulled off before they are ripe,
like an olive tree that loses its blossoms.
³⁴People without God can produce nothing.
Fire will destroy the tents of those who
take money to do evil,

³⁵who plan trouble and give birth to evil,
  whose hearts plan ways to trick others."

Job Answers Eliphaz

16 Then Job answered:
  ²"I have heard many things like these.
  You are all painful comforters!
³Will your long-winded speeches never end?
  What makes you keep on arguing?
⁴I also could speak as you do
  if you were in my place.
 I could make great speeches against you
  and shake my head at you.
⁵But, instead, I would encourage you,
  and my words would bring you relief.

⁶"Even if I speak, my pain is not less,
  and if I don't speak, it still does not go
    away.
⁷God, you have surely taken away my strength
  and destroyed my whole family.
⁸You have made me thin and weak,
  and this shows I have done wrong.
⁹God attacks me and tears me with anger;
  he grinds his teeth at me;
  my enemy stares at me with his angry eyes.
¹⁰People open their mouths to make fun of me
  and hit my cheeks to insult me.
  They join together against me.
¹¹God has turned me over to evil people
  and has handed me over to the wicked.
¹²Everything was fine with me,
  but God broke me into pieces;
  he held me by the neck and crushed me.
 He has made me his target;
¹³   his archers surround me.
 He stabs my kidneys without mercy;
  he spills my blood on the ground.
¹⁴Again and again God attacks me;
  he runs at me like a soldier.

¹⁵"I have sewed rough cloth over my skin to
    show my sadness
  and have buried my face in the dust.
¹⁶My face is red from crying;
  I have dark circles around my eyes.
¹⁷Yet my hands have never done anything
    cruel,
  and my prayer is pure.

¹⁸"Earth, please do not cover up my blood.
  Don't let my cry ever stop being heard!
¹⁹Even now I have one who speaks for me in
    heaven;
  the one who is on my side is high above.
²⁰The one who speaks for me is my friend.
  My eyes pour out tears to God.
²¹He begs God on behalf of a human
  as a person begs for his friend.

²²"Only a few years will pass
  before I go on the journey of no return.

17 My spirit is broken;
  the days of my life are almost gone.
 The grave is waiting for me.
²Those who laugh at me surround me;
  I watch them insult me.

³"God, make me a promise.
  No one will make a pledge for me.
⁴You have closed their minds to
    understanding.
  Do not let them win over me.
⁵A person might speak against his friends for
    money,
  but if he does, the eyes of his children go
    blind.

⁶"God has made my name a curse word;
  people spit in my face.
⁷My sight has grown weak because of my
    sadness,
  and my body is as thin as a shadow.
⁸Honest people are upset about this;
  innocent people are upset with those who
    do wrong.
⁹But those who do right will continue to do
    right,
  and those whose hands are not dirty with
    sin will grow stronger.

¹⁰"But, all of you, come and try again!
  I do not find a wise person among you.
¹¹My days are gone, and my plans have been
    destroyed,
  along with the desires of my heart.
¹²These men think night is day;
  when it is dark, they say, 'Light is near.'
¹³If the only home I hope for is the grave,
  if I spread out my bed in darkness,
¹⁴if I say to the grave, 'You are my father,'
  and to the worm, 'You are my mother' or
    'You are my sister,'
¹⁵where, then, is my hope?
  Who can see any hope for me?
¹⁶Will hope go down to the gates of death?
  Will we go down together into the dust?"

Bildad Answers Job

18 Then Bildad the Shuhite answered:
  ²"When will you stop these speeches?
  Be sensible, and then we can talk.
³You think of us as cattle,
  as if we are stupid.
⁴You tear yourself to pieces in your anger.
  Should the earth be vacant just for you?
  Should the rocks move from their places?

⁵"The lamp of the wicked will be put out,

and the flame in their lamps will stop
   burning.
⁶The light in their tents will grow dark,
   and the lamps by their sides will go out.
⁷Their strong steps will grow weak;
   they will fall into their own evil traps.
⁸Their feet will be caught in a net
   when they walk into its web.
⁹A trap will catch them by the heel
   and hold them tight.
¹⁰A trap for them is hidden on the ground,
   right in their path.
¹¹Terrible things startle them from every side
   and chase them at every step.
¹²Hunger takes away their strength,
   and disaster is at their side.
¹³Disease eats away parts of their skin;
   death gnaws at their arms and legs.
¹⁴They are torn from the safety of their tents
   and dragged off to Death, the King of
      Terrors.
¹⁵Their tents are set on fire,
   and sulfur is scattered over their homes.
¹⁶Their roots dry up below ground,
   and their branches die above ground.
¹⁷People on earth will not remember them;
   their names will be forgotten in the land.
¹⁸They will be driven from light into darkness
   and chased out of the world.
¹⁹They have no children or descendants*d*
   among their people,
   and no one will be left alive where they
      once lived.
²⁰People of the west will be shocked at what
   has happened to them,
   and people of the east will be very
      frightened.
²¹Surely this is what will happen to the
   wicked;
   such is the place of one who does not
      know God."

Job Answers Bildad

19 Then Job answered:

²"How long will you hurt me
   and crush me with your words?
³You have insulted me ten times now
   and attacked me without shame.
⁴Even if I have sinned,
   it is my worry alone.
⁵If you want to make yourselves look better
      than I,
   you can blame me for my suffering.
⁶Then know that God has wronged me
   and pulled his net around me.

⁷"I shout, 'I have been wronged!'
   But I get no answer.

I scream for help
   but I get no justice.
⁸God has blocked my way so I cannot pass;
   he has covered my paths with darkness.
⁹He has taken away my honor
   and removed the crown from my head.
¹⁰He beats me down on every side until I am
      gone;
   he destroys my hope like a fallen tree.
¹¹His anger burns against me,
   and he treats me like an enemy.
¹²His armies gather;
   they prepare to attack me.
   They camp around my tent.

¹³"God has made my brothers my enemies,
   and my friends have become strangers.
¹⁴My relatives have gone away,
   and my friends have forgotten me.
¹⁵My guests and my female servants treat me
      like a stranger;
   they look at me as if I were a foreigner.
¹⁶I call for my servant, but he does not answer,
   even when I beg him with my own mouth.
¹⁷My wife can't stand my breath,
   and my own family dislikes me.
¹⁸Even the little boys hate me
   and talk about me when I leave.
¹⁹All my close friends hate me;
   even those I love have turned against me.
²⁰I am nothing but skin and bones;
   I have escaped by the skin of my teeth.
²¹Pity me, my friends, pity me,
   because the hand of God has hit me.
²²Why do you chase me as God does?
   Haven't you hurt me enough?

²³"How I wish my words were written down,
   written on a scroll.
²⁴I wish they were carved with an iron pen
      into lead,
   or carved into stone forever.
²⁵I know that my Defender lives,
   and in the end he will stand upon the
      earth.
²⁶Even after my skin has been destroyed,
   in my flesh I will see God.
²⁷I will see him myself;
   I will see him with my very own eyes.
   How my heart wants that to happen!

²⁸"If you say, 'We will continue to trouble
      Job,
   because the problem lies with him,'
²⁹you should be afraid of the sword yourselves.
   God's anger will bring punishment by the
      sword.
   Then you will know there is judgment."

Zophar Answers

20 Then Zophar the Naamathite answered:

2"My troubled thoughts cause me to answer,
because I am very upset.
3You correct me and I am insulted,
but I understand how to answer you.

4"You know how it has been for a long time,
ever since people were first put on the earth.
5The happiness of evil people is brief,
and the joy of the wicked lasts only a moment.
6Their pride may be as high as the heavens,
and their heads may touch the clouds,
7but they will be gone forever, like their own dung.
People who knew them will say, 'Where are they?'
8They will fly away like a dream
and not be found again;
they will be chased away like a vision in the night.
9Those who saw them will not see them again;
the places where they lived will see them no more.
10Their children will have to pay back the poor,
and they will have to give up their wealth.
11They had the strength of their youth in their bones,
but it will lie with them in the dust of death.

12"Evil may taste sweet in their mouths,
and they may hide it under their tongues.
13They cannot stand to let go of it;
they keep it in their mouths.
14But their food will turn sour in their stomachs,
like the poison of a snake inside them.
15They have swallowed riches, but they will spit them out;
God will make them vomit their riches up.
16They will suck the poison of snakes,
and the snake's fangs will kill them.

17They will not admire the sparkling streams
or the rivers flowing with honey and cream.
18They must give back what they worked for without eating it;
they will not enjoy the money they made from their trading,
19because they troubled the poor and left them with nothing.
They have taken houses they did not build.

20"Evil people never lack an appetite,
and nothing escapes their selfishness.
21But nothing will be left for them to eat;
their riches will not continue.
22When they still have plenty, trouble will catch up to them,
and great misery will come down on them.
23When the wicked fill their stomachs,
God will send his burning anger against them,
and blows of punishment will fall on them like rain.
24The wicked may run away from an iron weapon,
but a bronze arrow will stab them.
25They will pull the arrows out of their backs
and pull the points out of their livers.
Terrors will come over them;
26   total darkness waits for their treasure.
A fire not fanned by people will destroy them
and burn up what is left of their tents.
27The heavens will show their guilt,
and the earth will rise up against them.
28A flood will carry their houses away,
swept away on the day of God's anger.
29This is what God plans for evil people;
this is what he has decided they will receive."

Job Answers Zophar

21 Then Job answered:

2"Listen carefully to my words,
and let this be the way you comfort me.
3Be patient while I speak.
After I have finished, you may continue to make fun of me.

4"My complaint is not just against people;
I have reason to be impatient.
5Look at me and be shocked;
put your hand over your mouth in shock.
6*When I think about this, I am terribly afraid*
and my body shakes.
7Why do evil people live a long time?
They grow old and become more powerful.
8They see their children around them;
they watch them grow up.
9Their homes are safe and without fear;

God does not punish them.
10Their bulls never fail to mate;
their cows have healthy calves.
11They send out their children like a flock;
their little ones dance about.
12They sing to the music of tambourines*d* and
harps,
and the sound of the flute makes them
happy.
13Evil people enjoy successful lives
and then go peacefully to the grave.
14They say to God, 'Leave us alone!
We don't want to know your ways.
15Who is the Almighty that we should serve
him?
What would we gain by praying to him?'
16The success of the wicked is not their own
doing.
Their way of thinking is different from
mine.
17Yet how often are the lamps of evil people
turned off?
How often does trouble come to them?
How often do they suffer God's angry
punishment?
18How often are they like straw in the wind
or like chaff*d* that is blown away by a
storm?
19It is said, 'God saves up a person's
punishment for his children.'
But God should punish the wicked
themselves so they will know it.
20Their eyes should see their own destruction,
and they should suffer the anger of the
Almighty.
21They do not care about the families they
leave behind
when their lives have come to an end.

22"No one can teach knowledge to God;
he is the one who judges even the most
important people.
23One person dies while he still has all his
strength,
feeling completely safe and comfortable.
24His body was well fed,
and his bones were strong and healthy.
25But another person dies with an unhappy
heart,
never enjoying any happiness.
26They are buried next to each other,
and worms cover them both.

27"I know very well your thoughts
and your plans to wrong me.
28You ask about me, 'Where is this great man's
house?
Where are the tents where the wicked
live?'
29Have you never asked those who travel?

Have you never listened to their stories?
30On the day of God's anger and punishment,
it is the wicked who are spared.
31Who will accuse them to their faces?
Who will pay them back for the evil they
have done?
32They are carried to their graves,
and someone keeps watch over their tombs.
33The dirt in the valley seems sweet to them.
Everybody follows after them,
and many people go before them.

34"So how can you comfort me with this
nonsense?
Your answers are only lies!"

Eliphaz Answers

22 Then Eliphaz the Temanite answered:

2"Can anyone be of real use to God?
Can even a wise person do him good?
3Does it help the Almighty for you to be
good?
Does he gain anything if you are innocent?
4Does God punish you for respecting him?
Does he bring you into court for this?
5No! It is because your evil is without limits
and your sins have no end.
6You took your brothers' things for a debt they
didn't owe;
you took clothes from people and left them
naked.
7You did not give water to tired people,
and you kept food from the hungry.
8You were a powerful man who owned land;
you were honored and lived in the land.
9But you sent widows away empty-handed,
and you mistreated orphans.
10That is why traps are all around you
and sudden danger frightens you.
11That is why it is so dark you cannot see
and a flood of water covers you.

12"God is in the highest part of heaven.
See how high the highest stars are!
13But you ask, 'What does God know?
Can he judge us through the dark clouds?
14Thick clouds cover him so he cannot see us
as he walks around high up in the sky.'
15Are you going to stay on the old path
where evil people walk?
16They were carried away before their time
was up,
and their foundations were washed away by
a flood.
17They said to God, 'Leave us alone!
The Almighty can do nothing to us.'
18But it was God who filled their houses with
good things.

Their way of thinking is different from
mine.

¹⁹"Good people can watch and be glad;
the innocent can laugh at them and say,
²⁰'Surely our enemies are destroyed,
and fire burns up their wealth.'

²¹"Obey God and be at peace with him;
this is the way to happiness.
²²Accept teaching from his mouth,
and keep his words in your heart.
²³If you return to the Almighty, you will be
blessed again.
So remove evil from your house.
²⁴Throw your gold nuggets into the dust
and your fine gold among the rocks in the
ravines.
²⁵Then the Almighty will be your gold
and the best silver for you.
²⁶You will find pleasure in the Almighty,
and you will look up to him.
²⁷You will pray to him, and he will hear you,
and you will keep your promises to him.
²⁸Anything you decide will be done,
and light will shine on your ways.
²⁹When people are made humble and you say,
'Have courage,'
then the humble will be saved.
³⁰Even a guilty person will escape
and be saved because your hands are
clean."*d*

Job Answers

23 Then Job answered:

²"My complaint is still bitter today.
I groan because God's heavy hand is on
me.
³I wish I knew where to find God
so I could go to where he lives.
⁴I would present my case before him
and fill my mouth with arguments.
⁵I would learn how he would answer me
and would think about what he would say.
⁶Would he not argue strongly against me?
No, he would really listen to me.
⁷Then an honest person could present his case
to God,
and I would be saved forever by my judge.

⁸"If I go to the east, God is not there;
if I go to the west, I do not see him.
⁹*When he is at work in the north, I catch no
sight of him;*
when he turns to the south, I cannot see
him.
¹⁰But God knows the way that I take,
and when he has tested me, I will come
out like gold.

¹¹My feet have closely followed his steps;
I have stayed in his way;
I did not turn aside.
¹²I have never left the commands he has
spoken;
I have treasured his words more than my
own.

¹³"But he is the only God.
Who can come against him?
He does anything he wants.
¹⁴He will do to me what he said he would do,
and he has many plans like this.
¹⁵That is why I am frightened of him;
when I think of this, I am afraid of him.
¹⁶God has made me afraid;
the Almighty terrifies me.
¹⁷But I am not hidden by the darkness,
by the thick darkness that covers my face.

24 "I wish the Almighty would set a time
for judging.
Those who know God do not see such a
day.
²Wicked people take other people's land;
they steal flocks and take them to new
pastures.
³They chase away the orphan's donkey
and take the widow's ox when she has no
money.
⁴They push needy people off the path;
all the poor of the land hide from them.
⁵The poor become like wild donkeys in the
desert
who go about their job of finding food.
The desert gives them food for their
children.
⁶They gather hay and straw in the fields
and pick up leftover grapes from the
vineyard of the wicked.
⁷They spend the night naked, because they
have no clothes,
nothing to cover themselves in the cold.
⁸They are soaked from mountain rains
and stay near the large rocks because they
have no shelter.
⁹The fatherless child is grabbed from its
mother's breast;
they take a poor mother's baby to pay for
what she owes.
¹⁰So the poor go around naked without any
clothes;
they carry bundles of grain but still go
hungry;
¹¹they crush olives to get oil
and grapes to get wine, but they still go
thirsty.
¹²Dying people groan in the city,
and the injured cry out for help,
but God accuses no one of doing wrong.

¹³"Those who fight against the light
do not know God's ways
or stay in his paths.
¹⁴When the day is over, the murderers get up
to kill the poor and needy.
At night they go about like thieves.
¹⁵Those who are guilty of adultery*d* watch for
the night,
thinking, 'No one will see us,'
and they keep their faces covered.
¹⁶In the dark, evil people break into houses.
In the daytime they shut themselves up in
their own houses,
because they want nothing to do with the
light.
¹⁷Darkness is like morning to all these evil
people
who make friends with the terrors of
darkness.

¹⁸"They are like foam floating on the water.
Their part of the land is cursed;
no one uses the road that goes by their
vineyards.
¹⁹As heat and dryness quickly melt the snow,
so the grave quickly takes away the sinners.
²⁰Their mothers forget them,
and worms will eat their bodies.
They will not be remembered,
so wickedness is broken in pieces like a
stick.
²¹These evil people abuse women who cannot
have children
and show no kindness to widows.
²²But God drags away the strong by his power.
Even though they seem strong, they do not
know how long they will live.
²³God may let these evil people feel safe,
but he is watching their ways.
²⁴For a little while they are important, and
then they die;
they are laid low and buried like everyone
else;
they are cut off like the heads of grain.
²⁵If this is not true, who can prove I am
wrong?
Who can show that my words are worth
nothing?"

Bildad Answers

25 Then Bildad the Shuhite answered:

²"God rules and he must be honored;
he set up order in his high heaven.
³No one can count God's armies.
His light shines on all people.
⁴So no one can be good in the presence of
God,
and no one born to a woman can be pure.
⁵Even the moon is not bright

and the stars are not pure in his eyes.
⁶People are much less! They are like insects.
They are only worms!"

Job Answers Bildad

26 Then Job answered:

²"You are no help to the helpless!
You have not aided the weak!
³Your advice lacks wisdom!
You have shown little understanding!
⁴Who has helped you say these words?
And where did you get these ideas?

⁵"The spirits of the dead tremble,
those who are beneath and in the waters.
⁶Death is naked before God;
destruction is uncovered before him.
⁷God stretches the northern sky out over
empty space
and hangs the earth on nothing.
⁸He wraps up the waters in his thick clouds,
but the clouds do not break under their
weight.
⁹He covers the face of the moon,
spreading his clouds over it.
¹⁰He draws the horizon like a circle on the
water
at the place where light and darkness meet.
¹¹Heaven's foundations shake
when he thunders at them.
¹²With his power he quiets the sea;
by his wisdom he destroys Rahab,*d* the sea
monster.
¹³He breathes, and the sky clears.
His hand stabs the fleeing snake.
¹⁴And these are only a small part of God's
works.
We only hear a small whisper of him.
Who could understand God's thundering
power?"

27 And Job continued speaking:

²"As surely as God lives, who has
taken away my rights,
the Almighty, who has made me unhappy,
³as long as I am alive
and God's breath of life is in my nose,
⁴my lips will not speak evil,
and my tongue will not tell a lie.
⁵I will never agree you are right;
until I die, I will never stop saying I am
innocent.
⁶I will insist that I am right; I will not back
down.
My conscience will never bother me.

⁷"Let my enemies be like evil people,
my foes like those who are wrong.

8What hope do the wicked have when they
die,
when God takes their life away?
9God will not listen to their cries
when trouble comes to them.
10They will not find joy in the Almighty,
even though they call out to God all the
time.

11"I will teach you about the power of God
and will not hide the ways of the Almighty.
12You have all seen this yourselves.
So why are we having all this talk that
means nothing?

13"Here is what God has planned for evil
people,
and what the Almighty will give to cruel
people:
14They may have many children, but the sword
will kill them.
Their children who are left will never have
enough to eat.
15Then they will die of disease and be buried,
and the widows will not even cry for them.
16The wicked may heap up silver like piles of
dirt
and have so many clothes they are like
piles of clay.
17But good people will wear what evil people
have gathered,
and the innocent will divide up their
silver.
18The houses the wicked build are like a
spider's web,
like a hut that a guard builds.
19The wicked are rich when they go to bed,
but they are rich for the last time;
when they open their eyes, everything is
gone.
20Fears come over them like a flood,
and a storm snatches them away in the
night.
21The east wind will carry them away, and
then they are gone,
because it sweeps them out of their place.
22The wind will hit them without mercy
as they try to run away from its power.
23It will be as if the wind is clapping its hands;
it will whistle at them as they run from
their place.

28 "There are mines where people dig
silver
and places where gold is made pure.
2Iron is taken from the ground,
and copper is melted out of rocks.
3Miners bring lights
and search deep into the mines
for ore in thick darkness.

4Miners dig a tunnel far from where people
live,
where no one has ever walked;
they work far from people, swinging and
swaying from ropes.
5Food grows on top of the earth,
but below ground things are changed as if
by fire.
6Sapphires are found in rocks,
and gold dust is also found there.
7No hawk knows that path;
the falcon has not seen it.
8Proud animals have not walked there,
and no lions cross over it.
9Miners hit the rocks of flint
and dig away at the bottom of the
mountains.
10They cut tunnels through the rock
and see all the treasures there.
11They search for places where rivers begin
and bring things hidden out into the light.

12"But where can wisdom be found,
and where does understanding live?
13People do not understand the value of
wisdom;
it cannot be found among those who are
alive.
14The deep ocean says, 'It's not in me;'
the sea says, 'It's not in me.'
15Wisdom cannot be bought with gold,
and its cost cannot be weighed in silver.
16Wisdom cannot be bought with fine gold
or with valuable onyx or sapphire gems.
17Gold and crystal are not as valuable as
wisdom,
and you cannot buy it with jewels of gold.
18Coral and jasper are not worth talking about,
and the price of wisdom is much greater
than rubies.
19The topaz from Cush cannot compare to
wisdom;
it cannot be bought with the purest gold.

20"So where does wisdom come from,
and where does understanding live?
21It is hidden from the eyes of every living
thing,
even from the birds of the air.
22The places of destruction and death say,
'We have heard reports about it.'
23Only God understands the way to wisdom,
and he alone knows where it lives,
24because he looks to the farthest parts of the
earth
and sees everything under the sky.
25When God gave power to the wind
and measured the water,
26when he made rules for the rain
and set a path for a thunderstorm to follow,

²⁷then he locked at wisdom and decided its
      worth;
  he set wisdom up and tested it.
²⁸Then he said to humans,
    'The fear of the Lord is wisdom;
    to stay away from evil is understanding.' "

Job Continues

29 Job continued to speak:

²"How I wish for the months that
      have passed
  and the days when God watched over me.
³God's lamp shined on my head,
    and I walked through darkness by his light.
⁴I wish for the days when I was strong,
    when God's close friendship blessed my
      house.
⁵The Almighty was still with me,
    and my children were all around me.
⁶It was as if my path were covered with
      cream
    and the rocks poured out olive oil for me.

⁷I would go to the city gate
    and sit in the public square.
⁸When the young men saw me, they would
      step aside,
    and the old men would stand up in respect.
⁹The leading men stopped speaking
    and covered their mouths with their hands.
¹⁰The voices of the important men were quiet,
    as if their tongues stuck to the roof of their
      mouths.
¹¹Anyone who heard me spoke well of me,
    and those who saw me praised me,
¹²because I saved the poor who called out
    and the orphan who had no one to help.
¹³The dying person blessed me,
    and I made the widow's heart sing.
¹⁴I put on right living as if it were clothing;
    I wore fairness like a robe and a turban.
¹⁵I was eyes for the blind
    and feet for the lame.
¹⁶I was like a father to needy people,
    and I took the side of strangers who were
      in trouble.

DECISION MAKING

To Fly or Not

Sixteen-year-old Neil stared at the model plane on his desk. He had loved planes all his life. Every penny he earned went for flying lessons, but now he wasn't sure if he ever wanted to fly.

The day before, Neil had watched helplessly as a friend's plane crashed before his eyes. He had rushed to the plane to try to help, but the crash was fatal. Neil could still feel his friend's head in his lap; he remembered his dying breath. What now? Should he go on with his own flying plans? He didn't want to die too.

For two days Neil sat in his bedroom. He analyzed the risks, struggled through his fears and dreams, and recalled the conflicting advice given to him. "Follow your dream!" "Dreams are worthless when you're dead!" He didn't know what to do.

Then he took out an old Sunday school notebook he had made. On its cover was a picture of Jesus; inside he had listed qualities of the Savior—"He was sinless"; "He championed the poor"; "He was unselfish"; "He was close to God." Neil studied them closely and then closed his eyes in thanksgiving and made his choice. "Mom," he said, "I hope you and Dad understand, but with God's help, I must go on flying."

Neil Armstrong's decision that day would eventually take him to the moon, to become the first human on its surface.

Neil learned that wisdom in making decisions is sometimes tough to find, as the writer said in **Job 28:20–28**.

■ How did Neil and the writer of Job find wisdom?
■ If wisdom is as difficult to find as verse 21 states, how do you find it?

                    C O N S I D E R . . .
■ asking God to give you wisdom concerning an important relationship in your life.
■ listing the pros and cons of decisions you must make soon. Pray that God will guide you.

              F O R   M O R E ,   S E E . . .
■ Deuteronomy 30:11–20 (p. 187)   ■ Matthew 26:36–45 (p. 957)
■ Joshua 24:14–15 (p. 214)

17I broke the fangs of evil people
and snatched the captives from their teeth.

18"I thought, 'I will live for as many days as
there are grains of sand,
and I will die in my own house.
19My roots will reach down to the water.
The dew will lie on the branches all night.
20New honors will come to me continually,
and I will always have great strength.'

21"People listened to me carefully
and waited quietly for my advice.
22After I finished speaking, they spoke no more.
My words fell very gently on their ears.
23They waited for me as they would for rain
and drank in my words like spring rain.
24I smiled at them when they doubted,
and my approval was important to them.
25I chose the way for them and was their
leader.
I lived like a king among his army,
like a person who comforts sad people.

30 "But now men who are younger
than I
make fun of me.
I would not have even let their fathers
sit with my sheep dogs.
2What use did I have for their strength
since they had lost their strength to work?
3They were thin from hunger
and wandered the dry and ruined land at
night.
4They gathered desert plants among the brush
and ate the root of the broom tree.
5They were forced to live away from people;
people shouted at them as if they were
thieves.
6They lived in dried up streambeds,
in caves, and among the rocks.
7They howled like animals among the bushes
and huddled together in the brush.
8They are worthless people without names
and were forced to leave the land.

9"Now they make fun of me with songs;
my name is a joke among them.
10They hate me and stay far away from me,
but they do not mind spitting in my face.
11God has taken away my strength and made
me suffer,
so they attack me with all their anger.
12On my right side they rise up like a mob.
They lay traps for my feet
and prepare to attack me.
13They break up my road
and work to destroy me,
and no one helps me.
14They come at me as if through a hole in the
wall,

and they roll in among the ruins.
15Great fears overwhelm me.
They blow my honor away as if by a great
wind,
and my safety disappears like a cloud.

16"Now my life is almost over;
my days are full of suffering.
17At night my bones ache;
gnawing pains never stop.
18In his great power God grabs hold of my
clothing
and chokes me with the collar of my coat.
19He throws me into the mud,
and I become like dirt and ashes.

20"I cry out to you, God, but you do not
answer;
I stand up, but you just look at me.
21You have turned on me without mercy;
with your powerful hand you attacked me.
22You snatched me up and threw me into the
wind
and tossed me about in the storm.
23I know you will bring me down to death,
to the place where all living people must
go.

24"Surely no one would hurt a ruined man
when he cries for help in his time of
trouble.
25I cried for those who were in trouble;
I have been very sad for poor people.
26But when I hoped for good, only evil came to
me;
when I looked for light, darkness came.
27I never stop being upset;
days of suffering are ahead of me.
28I have turned black, but not by the sun.
I stand up in public and cry for help.
29I have become a brother to wild dogs
and a friend to ostriches.
30My skin has become black and peels off,
as my body burns with fever.
31My harp is tuned to sing a sad song,
and my flute is tuned to moaning.

31 "But I made an agreement with my
eyes
not to look with desire at a girl.
2What has God above promised for people?
What has the Almighty planned from on
high?
3*It is ruin for evil people*
and disaster for those who do wrong.
4God sees my ways
and counts every step I take.

5"If I have been dishonest
or lied to others,
6then let God weigh me on honest scales.

Then he will know I have done nothing
    wrong.
7If I have turned away from doing what is
    right,
    or my heart has been led by my eyes to do
    wrong,
    or my hands have been made unclean,*d*
8then let other people eat what I have
    planted,
    and let my crops be plowed up.

9"If I have desired another woman
    or have waited at my neighbor's door for
    his wife,
10then let my wife grind another man's grain,
    and let other men have sexual relations
    with her.
11That would be shameful,
    a sin to be punished.
12It is like a fire that burns and destroys;
    all I have done would be plowed up.

13"If I have been unfair to my male and female
    slaves
    when they had a complaint against me,
14how could I tell God what I did?
    What will I answer when he asks me to
    explain what I've done?
15God made me in my mother's womb, and he
    also made them;
    the same God formed both of us in our
    mothers' wombs.

16"I have never refused the appeals of the poor
    or let widows give up hope while looking
    for help.
17I have not kept my food to myself
    but have given it to the orphans.
18Since I was young, I have been like a father
    to the orphans.
    From my birth I guided the widows.
19I have not let anyone die for lack of clothes
    or let a needy person go without a coat.
20That person's heart blessed me,
    because I warmed him with the wool of
    my sheep.
21I have never hurt an orphan
    even when I knew I could win in court.
22If I have, then let my arm fall off my
    shoulder
    and be broken at the joint.
23I fear destruction from God,
    and I fear his majesty, so I could not do
    such things.

24"I have not put my trust in gold
    or said to pure gold, 'You are my security.'
25I have not celebrated my great wealth
    or the riches my hands had gained.
26I have not thought about worshiping the sun
    in its brightness

nor admired the moon moving in glory
27so that my heart was pulled away from God.
    My hand has never offered the sun and
    moon a kiss of worship.
28If I had, these also would have been sins to
    be punished,
    because I would have been unfaithful to
    God.

29"I have not been happy when my enemy fell
    or laughed when he had trouble.
30I have not let my mouth sin
    by cursing my enemy's life.
31The men of my house have always said,
    'Everyone has eaten all he wants of Job's
    food.'
32No stranger ever had to spend the night in
    the street,
    because I always let travelers stay in my
    home.
33I have not hidden my sin as others do,
    secretly keeping my guilt to myself.
34I was not so afraid of the crowd
    that I kept quiet and stayed inside
    because I feared being hated by other
    families.

35("How I wish a court would hear my case!
    Here I sign my name to show I have told
    the truth.
    Now let the Almighty answer me;
    let the one who accuses me write it down.
36I would wear the writing on my shoulder;
    I would put it on like a crown.
37I would explain to God every step I took,
    and I would come near to him like a
    prince.)

38"If my land cries out against me
    and its plowed rows are not wet with tears,
39if I have taken the land's harvest without
    paying
    or have broken the spirit of those who
    worked the land,
40then let thorns come up instead of wheat,
    and let weeds come up instead of barley."

The words of Job are finished.

Elihu Speaks

32 These three men stopped trying to answer Job, because he was so sure he was right. 2But Elihu son of Barakel the Buzite, from the family of Ram, became very angry with Job, because Job claimed he was right instead of God. 3Elihu was also angry with Job's three friends who had no answer to show that Job was wrong, yet continued to blame him. 4Elihu had waited before speaking to Job, because the three friends were older than he was. 5But when Elihu saw that the three men had nothing more to say, he became very angry.

⁶So Elihu son of Barakel the Buzite said this:

"I am young,
and you are old.
That is why I was afraid
to tell you what I know.
⁷I thought, 'Older people should speak,
and those who have lived many years
should teach wisdom.'
⁸But it is the spirit in a person,
the breath of the Almighty, that gives
understanding.
⁹It is not just older people who are wise;
they are not the only ones who understand
what is right.
¹⁰So I say, listen to me.
I too will tell you what I know.
¹¹I waited while you three spoke,
and listened to your explanations.
While you looked for words to use,
¹² I paid close attention to you.
But not one of you has proved Job wrong;
none of you has answered his arguments.
¹³Don't say, 'We have found wisdom;
only God will show Job to be wrong, not
people.'
¹⁴Job has not spoken his words against me,
so I will not use your arguments to answer
Job.

¹⁵"These three friends are defeated and have
no more to say;
words have failed them.
¹⁶Now they are standing there with no answers
for Job.
Now that they are quiet, must I wait to
speak?
¹⁷No, I too will speak
and tell what I know.
¹⁸I am full of words,
and the spirit in me causes me to speak.
¹⁹I am like wine that has been bottled up;
I am ready to burst like a new leather wine
bag.
²⁰I must speak so I will feel relief;
I must open my mouth and answer.
²¹I will be fair to everyone
and not flatter anyone.
²²I don't know how to flatter,
and if I did, my Maker would quickly take
me away.

33 "Now, Job, listen to my words.
Pay attention to everything I say.
²I open my mouth
and am ready to speak.
³My words come from an honest heart,
and I am sincere in saying what I know.

⁴The Spirit*d* of God created me,
and the breath of the Almighty gave me
life.
⁵Answer me if you can;
get yourself ready and stand before me.
⁶I am just like you before God;
I too am made out of clay.
⁷Don't be afraid of me;
I will not be hard on you.

⁸"But I heard what you have said;
I heard every word.
⁹You said, 'I am pure and without sin;
I am innocent and free from guilt.
¹⁰But God has found fault with me;
he considers me his enemy.
¹¹He locks my feet in chains
and closely watches everywhere I go.'

¹²"But I tell you, you are not right in saying
this,
because God is greater than we are.
¹³Why do you accuse God
of not answering anyone?
¹⁴God does speak—sometimes one way and
sometimes another—
even though people may not understand it.
¹⁵He speaks in a dream or a vision of the night
when people are in a deep sleep,
lying on their beds.
¹⁶He speaks in their ears
and frightens them with warnings
¹⁷to turn them away from doing wrong
and to keep them from being proud.
¹⁸God does this to save a person from death,
to keep him from dying.
¹⁹A person may be corrected while in bed in
great pain;
he may have continual pain in his very
bones.
²⁰He may be in such pain that he even hates
food,
even the very best meal.
²¹His body becomes so thin there is almost
nothing left of it,
and his bones that were hidden now stick
out.
²²He is near death,
and his life is almost over.

²³"But there may be an angel to speak for
him,
one out of a thousand, who will tell him
what to do.
²⁴The angel will beg for mercy and say:
'Save him from death.
I have found a way to pay for his life.'
²⁵Then his body is made new like a child's.
It will return to the way it was when he
was young.

²⁶That person will pray to God, and God will
listen to him.
He will see God's face and will shout with
happiness.
And God will set things right for him again.
²⁷Then he will say to others,
'I sinned and twisted what was right,
but I did not receive the punishment I
should have received.
²⁸God bought my life back from death,
and I will continue to enjoy life.'

²⁹"God does all these things to a person
two or even three times
³⁰so he won't die as punishment for his sins
and so he may still enjoy life.

³¹"Job, pay attention and listen to me;
be quiet, and I will speak.
³²If you have anything to say, answer me;
speak up, because I want to prove you
right.
³³But if you have nothing to say, then listen to
me;
be quiet, and I will teach you wisdom."

34

Then Elihu said:
²"Hear my words, you wise men;
listen to me, you who know a lot.
³The ear tests words
as the tongue tastes food.
⁴Let's decide for ourselves what is right,
and let's learn together what is good.

⁵"Job says, I am not guilty,
and God has refused me a fair trial.
⁶Instead of getting a fair trial,
I am called a liar.
I have been seriously hurt,
even though I have not sinned.'
⁷There is no other man like Job;
he takes insults as if he were drinking
water.
⁸He keeps company with those who do evil
and spends time with wicked men,
⁹because he says, 'It is no use
to try to please God.'

¹⁰"So listen to me, you who can understand.
God can never do wrong!
It is impossible for the Almighty to do evil.
¹¹God pays a person back for what he has done
and gives him what his actions deserve.
¹²Truly God will never do wrong;
the Almighty will never twist what is right.
¹³No one chose God to rule over the earth
or put him in charge of the whole world.
¹⁴If God should decide
to take away life and breath,
¹⁵then everyone would die together
and turn back into dust.

¹⁶"If you can understand, hear this;
listen to what I have to say.
¹⁷Can anyone govern who hates what is right?
How can you blame God who is both fair
and powerful?
¹⁸God is the one who says to kings, 'You are
worthless,'
or to important people, 'You are evil.'
¹⁹He is not nicer to princes than other people,
nor kinder to rich people than poor people,
because he made them all with his own
hands.
²⁰They can die in a moment, in the middle of
the night.
They are struck down, and then they pass
away;
powerful people die without help.

²¹"God watches where people go;
he sees every step they take.
²²There is no dark place or deep shadow
where those who do evil can hide from
him.
²³He does not set a time
for people to come before him for judging.
²⁴Without asking questions, God breaks
powerful people into pieces
and puts others in their place.
²⁵Because God knows what people do,
he defeats them in the night, and they are
crushed.
²⁶He punishes them for the evil they do
so that everyone else can watch,
²⁷because they stopped following God
and did not care about any of his ways.
²⁸The cry of the poor comes to God;
he hears the cry of the needy.
²⁹But if God keeps quiet, who can blame him?
If he hides his face, who can see him?
God still rules over both nations and persons
alike.
³⁰ He keeps the wicked from ruling
and from trapping others.

³¹"But suppose someone says to God,
'I am guilty, but I will not sin anymore.
³²Teach me what I cannot see.
If I have done wrong, I will not do it
again.'
³³So, Job, should God reward you as you want
when you refuse to change?
You must decide, not I,
so tell me what you know.

³⁴"Those who understand speak,
and the wise who hear me say,
³⁵'Job speaks without knowing what is true;
his words show he does not understand.'
³⁶I wish Job would be tested completely,
because he answered like an evil man!

37Job now adds to his sin by turning against
　　God.
He claps his hands in protest,
　　speaking more and more against God."

35

Then Elihu said:
2"Do you think this is fair?
You say, 'God will show that I am right,'
3but you also ask, 'What's the use?
I don't gain anything by not sinning.'

4"I will answer you
　　and your friends who are with you.
5Look up at the sky
　　and see the clouds so high above you.
6If you sin, it does nothing to God;
　　even if your sins are many, they do nothing
　　　to him.
7If you are good, you give nothing to God;
　　he receives nothing from your hand.
8Your evil ways only hurt a man like yourself,
　　and the good you do only helps other
　　　human beings.

9"People cry out when they are in trouble;
　　they beg for relief from powerful people.
10But no one asks, 'Where is God, my Maker,
　　who gives us songs in the night,
11who makes us smarter than the animals of
　　the earth
　　and wiser than the birds of the air?'
12God does not answer evil people when they
　　cry out,
　　because the wicked are proud.
13God does not listen to their useless begging;
　　the Almighty pays no attention to them.
14He will listen to you even less
　　when you say that you do not see him,
　　that your case is before him,
　　that you must wait for him,
15　　that his anger never punishes,
　　and that he doesn't notice evil.
16So Job is only speaking nonsense,
　　saying many words without knowing what
　　is true."

Elihu's Speech Continues

36

Elihu continued:
2"Listen to me a little longer, and I
　　will show you
　　that there is more to be said for God.
3What I know comes from far away.
　　I will show that my Maker is right.
4You can be sure that my words are not false;
　　one who really knows is with you.

5"God is powerful, but he does not hate
　　people;
　　he is powerful and sure of what he wants
　　to do.

6He will not keep evil people alive,
　　but he gives the poor their rights.
7He always watches over those who do right;
　　he sets them on thrones with kings
　　and they are honored forever.
8If people are bound in chains,
　　or if trouble, like ropes, ties them up,
9God tells them what they have done,
　　that they have sinned in their pride.
10God makes them listen to his warning
　　and commands them to change from doing
　　evil.
11If they obey and serve him,
　　the rest of their lives will be successful,
　　and the rest of their years will be happy.
12But if they do not listen,
　　they will die by the sword,
　　and they will die without knowing why.

13"Those who have wicked hearts hold on to
　　anger.
Even when God punishes them, they do
　　not cry for help.
14They die while they are still young,
　　and their lives end in disgrace.
15But God saves those who suffer through their
　　suffering;
　　he gets them to listen through their pain.

16"God is gently calling you from the jaws of
　　trouble
　　to an open place of freedom
　　where he has set your table full of the best
　　food.
17But now you are being punished like the
　　wicked;
　　you are getting justice.
18Be careful! Don't be led away from God by
　　riches;
　　don't let much money turn you away.
19Neither your wealth nor all your great
　　strength
　　will keep you out of trouble.
20Don't wish for the night
　　when people are taken from their homes.
21Be careful not to turn to evil,
　　which you seem to want more than
　　suffering.

22"God is great and powerful;
　　no other teacher is like him.
23No one has planned his ways for him;
　　no one can say to God, 'You have done
　　wrong.'
24Remember to praise his work,
　　about which people have sung.
25Everybody has seen it;
　　people look at it from far off.
26God is so great, greater than we can
　　understand!

No one knows how old he is.

27"He evaporates the drops of water from the earth
and turns them into rain.
28The rain then pours down from the clouds,
and showers fall on people.
29No one understands how God spreads out the clouds
or how he sends thunder from where he lives.
30Watch how God scatters his lightning around him,
lighting up the deepest parts of the sea.
31This is the way God governs the nations;
this is how he gives us enough food.
32God fills his hands with lightning
and commands it to strike its target.
33His thunder announces the coming storm,
and even the cattle know it is near.

37 "At the sound of his thunder, my heart pounds
as if it will jump out of my chest.
2Listen! Listen to the thunder of God's voice
and to the rumbling that comes from his mouth.
3He turns his lightning loose under the whole sky
and sends it to the farthest parts of the earth.
4After that you can hear the roar
when he thunders with a great sound.
He does not hold back the flashing
when his voice is heard.
5God's voice thunders in wonderful ways;
he does great things we cannot understand.
6He says to the snow, 'Fall on the earth,'
and to the shower, 'Be a heavy rain.'
7With it, he stops everyone from working
so everyone knows it is the work of God.
8The animals take cover from the rain
and stay in their dens.
9The storm comes from where it was stored;
the cold comes with the strong winds.
10The breath of God makes ice,
and the wide waters become frozen.
11He fills the clouds with water
and scatters his lightning through them.
12At his command they swirl around
over the whole earth,
doing whatever he commands.
13He uses the clouds to punish people
or to water his earth and show his love.

14"Job, listen to this:
Stop and notice God's miracles.*d*
15Do you know how God controls the clouds
and makes his lightning flash?

16Do you know how the clouds hang in the sky?
Do you know the miracles of God, who knows everything?
17You suffer in your clothes
when the land is silenced by the hot, south wind.
18You cannot stretch out the sky like God
and make it look as hard as polished bronze.
19Tell us what we should say to him;
we cannot get our arguments ready because
we do not have enough understanding.
20Should God be told that I want to speak?
Would a person ask to be swallowed up?
21No one can look at the sun
when it is bright in the sky
after the wind has blown all the clouds away.
22God comes out of the north in golden light,
in overwhelming greatness.
23The Almighty is too high for us to reach.
He has great strength;
he is always right and never punishes unfairly.
24That is why people honor him;
he does not respect those who say they are wise."

The Lord Questions Job

38 Then the Lord answered Job from the storm. He said:

2"Who is this that makes my purpose unclear
by saying things that are not true?
3Be strong like a man!
I will ask you questions,
and you must answer me.
4Where were you when I made the earth's foundation?
Tell me, if you understand.
5Who marked off how big it should be?
Surely you know!
Who stretched a ruler across it?
6What were the earth's foundations set on,
or who put its cornerstone*d* in place

SIDELIGHT: Ancient cultures envisioned the earth resting on everything from pillars to sea turtles (Job 38:4–6). Everyone probably sleeps a little better since Isaac Newton discovered gravity.

7while the morning stars sang together
and all the angels shouted with joy?
8"Who shut the doors to keep the sea in

when it broke through and was born,
⁹when I made the clouds like a coat for the
sea
and wrapped it in dark clouds,
¹⁰when I put limits on the sea
and put its doors and bars in place,
¹¹when I said to the sea, 'You may come this
far, but no farther;
this is where your proud waves must stop'?

¹²"Have you ever ordered the morning to
begin,
or shown the dawn where its place was
¹³in order to take hold of the earth by its edges
and shake evil people out of it?
¹⁴At dawn the earth changes like clay being
pressed by a seal;*ᵈ*
the hills and valleys stand out like folds in
a coat.
¹⁵Light is not given to evil people;
their arm is raised to do harm, but it is
broken.

¹⁶"Have you ever gone to where the sea begins
or walked in the valleys under the sea?
¹⁷Have the gates of death been opened to you?
Have you seen the gates of the deep
darkness?
¹⁸Do you understand how wide the earth is?
Tell me, if you know all these things.

¹⁹"What is the path to light's home,
and where does darkness live?
²⁰Can you take them to their places?
Do you know the way to their homes?
²¹Surely you know, if you were already born
when all this happened!
Have you lived that many years?

²²"Have you ever gone into the storehouse of
the snow
or seen the storehouses for hail,
²³which I save for times of trouble,
for days of war and battle?
²⁴Where is the place from which light comes?
Where is the place from which the east
winds blow over the earth?
²⁵Who cuts a waterway for the heavy rains
and sets a path for the thunderstorm?
²⁶Who waters the land where no one lives,
the desert that has no one in it?
²⁷Who sends rain to satisfy the empty land
so the grass begins to grow?
²⁸*Does the rain have a father?*
Who is father to the drops of dew?
²⁹Who is the mother of the ice?
Who gives birth to the frost from the sky
³⁰when the water becomes hard as stone,
and even the surface of the ocean is
frozen?

³¹"Can you tie up the stars of the Pleiades
or loosen the ropes of the stars in Orion?
³²Can you bring out the stars on time
or lead out the stars of the Bear with its
cubs?
³³Do you know the laws of the sky
and understand their rule over the earth?

³⁴"Can you shout an order to the clouds
and cover yourself with a flood of water?
³⁵Can you send lightning bolts on their way?
Do they come to you and say, 'Here we
are'?
³⁶Who put wisdom inside the mind
or understanding in the heart?
³⁷Who has the wisdom to count the clouds?
Who can pour water from the jars of the
sky
³⁸when the dust becomes hard
and the clumps of dirt stick together?

³⁹"Do you hunt food for the female lion
to satisfy the hunger of the young lions
⁴⁰while they lie in their dens
or hide in the bushes waiting to attack?
⁴¹Who gives food to the birds
when their young cry out to God
and wander about without food?

39 "Do you know when the mountain
goats give birth?
Do you watch when the deer gives birth to
her fawn?
²Do you count the months until they give
birth
and know the right time for them to give
birth?
³They lie down, their young are born,
and then the pain of giving birth is over.
⁴Their young ones grow big and strong in the
wild country.
Then they leave their homes and do not
return.

⁵"Who let the wild donkey go free?
Who untied its ropes?
⁶I am the one who gave the donkey the desert
as its home;
I gave it the desert lands as a place to live.
⁷The wild donkey laughs at the confusion in
the city,
and it does not hear the drivers shout.
⁸It roams the hills looking for pasture,
looking for anything green to eat.

⁹"Will the wild ox agree to serve you
and stay by your feeding box at night?
¹⁰Can you hold it to the plowed row with a
harness
so it will plow the valleys for you?

11Will you depend on the wild ox for its great
  strength
    and leave your heavy work for it to do?
12Can you trust the ox to bring in your grain
    and gather it to your threshing*d* floor?

13"The wings of the ostrich flap happily,
    but they are not like the feathers of the
      stork.
14The ostrich lays its eggs on the ground
    and lets them warm in the sand.
15It does not stop to think that a foot might
      step on them and crush them;
    it does not care that some animal might
      walk on them.
16The ostrich is cruel to its young, as if they
      were not even its own.
    It does not care that its work is for nothing,
17because God did not give the ostrich
      wisdom;
    God did not give it a share of good sense.
18But when the ostrich gets up to run, it is so
      fast
    that it laughs at the horse and its rider.

19"Job, are you the one who gives the horse its
      strength
    or puts a flowing mane on its neck?
20Do you make the horse jump like a locust?*d*
    It scares people with its proud snorting.
21It paws wildly, enjoying its strength,
    and charges into battle.
22It laughs at fear and is afraid of nothing;
    it does not run away from the sword.
23The bag of arrows rattles against the horse's
      side,
    along with the flashing spears and swords.
24With great excitement, the horse races over
      the ground;
    and it cannot stand still when it hears the
      trumpet.
25When the trumpet blows, the horse snorts,
      'Aha!'
    It smells the battle from far away;
    it hears the shouts of commanders and the
      battle cry.

26"Is it through your wisdom that the hawk
      flies
    and spreads its wings toward the south?
27Are you the one that commands the eagle to
      fly
    and build its nest so high?
28It lives on a high cliff and stays there at
      night;
    the rocky peak is its protected place.
29From there it looks for its food;
    its eyes can see it from far away.

30Its young eat blood,
    and where there is something dead, the
      eagle is there."

40 The LORD said to Job:
  2"Will the person who argues with the
      Almighty correct him?
    Let the person who accuses God answer
      him."

3Then Job answered the LORD:
4"I am not worthy; I cannot answer you
      anything,
    so I will put my hand over my mouth.
5I spoke one time, but I will not answer
      again;
    I even spoke two times, but I will say
      nothing more."

6Then the LORD spoke to Job from the storm:
7"Be strong, like a man!
    I will ask you questions,
    and you must answer me.
8Would you say that I am unfair?
    Would you blame me to make yourself look
      right?
9Are you as strong as God?
    Can your voice thunder like his?
10If so, then decorate yourself with glory and
      beauty;
    dress in honor and greatness as if they were
      clothing.
11Let your great anger punish;
    look at the proud and bring them down.
12Look at the proud and make them humble.
    Crush the wicked wherever they are.
13Bury them all in the dirt together;
    cover their faces in the grave.
14If you can do that, then I myself will praise
      you,
    because you are strong enough to save
      yourself.

15"Look at the behemoth,*n*
    which I made just as I made you.
    It eats grass like an ox.
16Look at the strength it has in its body;
    the muscles of its stomach are powerful.
17Its tail is like a cedar tree;
    the muscles of its thighs are woven
      together.
18Its bones are like tubes of bronze;
    its legs are like bars of iron.
19It is one of the first of God's works,
    but its Maker can destroy it.
20The hills, where the wild animals play,
    provide food for it.
21It lies under the lotus plants,
    hidden by the tall grass in the swamp.

behemoth   A large land animal. It could refer to the hippopotamus, the elephant, or a monster.

22The lotus plants hide it in their shadow;
the poplar trees by the streams surround it.
23If the river floods, it will not be afraid;
it is safe even if the Jordan River rushes to
its mouth.
24Can anyone blind its eyes and capture it?
Can anyone put hooks in its nose?

41 "Can you catch the leviathan*ⁿ* on a
fishhook
or tie its tongue down with a rope?
2Can you put a cord through its nose
or a hook in its jaw?
3Will it keep begging you for mercy
and speak to you with gentle words?
4Will it make an agreement with you
and let you take it as your slave for life?
5Can you make a pet of the leviathan as you
would a bird
or put it on a leash for your girls?
6Will traders try to bargain with you for it?
Will they divide it up among the
merchants?
7Can you stick darts all over its skin
or fill its head with fishing spears?
8If you put one hand on it,
you will never forget the battle,
and you will never do it again!
9There is no hope of defeating it;
just seeing it overwhelms people.
10No one is brave enough to make it angry,
so who would be able to stand up against
me?
11No one has ever given me anything that I
must pay back,
because everything under the sky belongs
to me.

12"I will speak about Leviathan's arms and
legs,
its great strength and well-formed body.
13No one can tear off its outer hide
or poke through its double armor.
14No one can force open its great jaws;
they are filled with frightening teeth.
15It has rows of shields on its back
that are tightly sealed together.
16Each shield is so close to the next one
that no air can go between them.
17They are joined strongly to one another;
they hold on to each other and cannot be
separated.
18When it snorts, flashes of light are thrown
out,
and its eyes look like the light at dawn.
19Flames blaze from its mouth;
sparks of fire shoot out.
20Smoke pours out of its nose,

leviathan Possibly a crocodile or a sea monster.

as if coming from a large pot over a hot
fire.
21Its breath sets coals on fire,
and flames come out of its mouth.
22There is great strength in its neck.
People are afraid and run away.
23The folds of its skin are tightly joined;
they are set and cannot be moved.
24Its chest is as hard as a rock,
even as hard as a grinding stone.
25The powerful fear its terrible looks
and draw back in fear as it moves.
26The sword that hits it does not hurt it,
nor the arrows, darts, and spears.
27It treats iron as if it were straw
and bronze metal as if it were rotten wood.
28It does not run away from arrows;
stones from slings are like chaff*ᵈ* to it.
29Clubs feel like pieces of straw to it,
and it laughs when they shake a spear at it.
30The underside of its body is like broken
pieces of pottery.
It leaves a trail in the mud like a threshing*ᵈ*
board.
31It makes the deep sea bubble like a boiling
pot;
it stirs up the sea like a pot of oil.
32When it swims, it leaves a shining path in
the water
that makes the sea look as if it had white
hair.
33Nothing else on earth is equal to it;
it is a creature without fear.
34It looks down on all those who are too
proud;
it is king over all proud creatures."

Job Answers the Lord

42 Then Job answered the Lord:
2"I know that you can do all things
and that no plan of yours can be ruined.
3You asked, 'Who is this that made my
purpose unclear by saying things that
are not true?'
Surely I spoke of things I did not
understand;
I talked of things too wonderful for me to
know.

4You said, 'Listen now, and I will speak.
I will ask you questions,
and you must answer me.'
5My ears had heard of you before,
but now my eyes have seen you.
6So now I hate myself;
I will change my heart and life.
I will sit in the dust and ashes."

End of the Story

[7]After the LORD had said these things to Job, he said to Eliphaz the Temanite, "I am angry with you and your two friends, because you have not said what is right about me, as my servant Job did. [8]Now take seven bulls and seven male sheep, and go to my servant Job, and offer a burnt offering for yourselves. My servant Job will pray for you, and I will listen to his prayer. Then I will not punish you for being foolish. You have not said what is right about me, as my servant Job did." [9]So Eliphaz the Temanite, Bildad the Shuhite, and Zophar the Naamathite did as the LORD said, and the LORD listened to Job's prayer.

[10]After Job had prayed for his friends, the LORD gave him success again. The LORD gave Job twice as much as he had owned before. [11]Job's brothers and sisters came to his house, along with everyone who had known him before, and they all ate with him there. They comforted him and made him feel better about the trouble the LORD had brought on him, and each one gave Job a piece of silver and a gold ring.

> ✸ **SIDELIGHT:** If unusual names were a source of pride, Job's daughters must have been downright arrogant. Their Hebrew names in Job 42:14 translate "dove," "cinnamon," and "container of eyeshadow."

[12]The LORD blessed the last part of Job's life even more than the first part. Job had fourteen thousand sheep, six thousand camels, a thousand teams of oxen, and a thousand female donkeys. [13]Job also had seven sons and three daughters. [14]He named the first daughter Jemimah, the sec-

---

FOLLOWING GOD

His Presence

"There came into my soul . . . a sense of the glory of the divine being; a new sense, quite different from anything I had ever experienced before."

Jonathan Edwards (1703–1758)

Edwards followed God by devoting his life to proclaiming and defending the gospel as one of the leaders of the Great Awakening in New England.

"Down in my deep well, shrouded with blackness, feeling helpless and devoid of hope, I cried out for help. Now, at last, I was ready to go to any length to achieve sobriety. And God heard my cry and answered." "Michael"

"Michael" felt God's presence in his time of need and began the long road to recovery from alcoholism through Alcoholics Anonymous. He follows God day-by-day as a pastor who helps others recover from alcoholism.

"At this moment I feel something 'let go' inside and lo, God is here! It is a heart-melting 'here-ness,' a lovely whispering of father to child."

Frank Laubauch (1884–1970)

Laubauch became a missionary and developed a world-wide method of teaching people to read.

The experience of God's presence led these three to act on their faith. Job was also changed as he experienced God's presence. Read **Job 42:1–6**.

■ How does Job's reaction to meeting God compare to these three people's sense of God's presence with them? How is it different?
■ How would your faith change if you suddenly sensed God's presence, as in verses 4 and 5?

C O N S I D E R . . .

■ praying for God to give you a clear picture of what he wants you to do for him.
■ writing down what you value most, why you value it, and how your feelings about it would change if you considered it a loan from God.

F O R   M O R E ,   S E E . . .

■ 1 Kings 19:11–13 (p. 325)
■ Psalm 63:1–8 (p. 518)

■ Acts 9:3–19 (p. 1112)

ond daughter Keziah, and the third daughter Keren-Happuch. ¹⁵There were no other women in all the land as beautiful as Job's daughters. And their father Job gave them land to own along with their brothers.

¹⁶After this, Job lived one hundred forty years. He lived to see his children, grandchildren, great-grandchildren, and great-great-grandchildren. ¹⁷Then Job died; he was old and had lived many years.

PSALMS

Why Read This Book:

- ■ Be inspired to express your feelings through songs about tough and joyful situations (such as Psalms 4, 27, 55, 147).
- ■ Improve your prayer life by following the many models of prayer in the Psalms (such as Psalms 6, 32, 51, 102, 130, 143).
- ■ Learn to praise and worship God through songs of praise (such as Psalms 8, 47, 81, 84, 108, 150).

Behind the Scenes:

If you flip through a church hymnbook, you see lots of different songs. Some are upbeat; others are meditative. Some are for special occasions; others can be used almost any time. Some are favorites; others you barely know. Different hymns were written by different authors at different times.

The book of Psalms is a lot like a church hymnbook. In fact, it was the hymnbook for Jews and Christians for many centuries. Each psalm is really a song for worship. And, like modern hymnbooks, Psalms contains a wide variety of songs that express many different emotions—joy, sadness, celebration, loneliness and many others. Different psalms were written by different people over several centuries, so the book is rich with diversity.

MUSIC IN THIS SONGBOOK

Because Psalms is a songbook, it mentions a variety of instruments that were used in Old Testament times.

The lyre, a stringed instrument with two arms similar to a harp, was often used to accompany singing (Psalm 33:2).

The sheep's or ram's horn was made by heating and shaping the animal's hollow horn (Psalm 98:6). It could play only two or three notes.

Cymbals in the Bible were made of bronze and were only about four to six inches in diameter (Psalm 150:5).

The trumpet was a straight instrument made of metal that had a range of only four or five notes (Psalm 150:3).

WHEN THE ACTION WAS

2000BC	1500BC	1000BC	500BC	BC/AD
	King David ruled Israel and almost half the psalms refer to him		Judah fell to the Babylonians	Jesus was born
	The Israelites escaped from Egypt		Jews began returning to Jerusalem from exile	Final collection of psalms was probably completed

Behind the Scenes (cont.):

The New Testament quotes from Psalms more than it quotes from any other book in the Old Testament, with the exception of Isaiah. Psalms is also the longest book of the Bible and contains some of the most popular reading in the Bible. Through these poetic words we can better understand our own hearts' longings to be close to God.

Book 1

Two Ways to Live

1 Happy are those who don't listen to the wicked,
who don't go where sinners go,
who don't do what evil people do.
²They love the Lord's teachings,
and they think about those teachings day and night.

³They are strong, like a tree planted by a river.
The tree produces fruit in season,
and its leaves don't die.
Everything they do will succeed.

⁴But wicked people are not like that.
They are like chaff*ᵈ* that the wind blows away.
⁵So the wicked will not escape God's punishment.

PEER PRESSURE

The K. C. Kid

K. C. Bennett was a riot. He could make more weird sounds, contort his face into more outrageous expressions and do more imitations than almost any other seventeen-year-old. He was so thin he could do tricks with his shoulder blades. People couldn't stop laughing when he tried playing "Chopsticks" on the piano with them!

And K. C. was friendly. He seemed to relate to everyone. When the group stopped at a fast-food restaurant, in less than two minutes he would be charming the girl working the cash register and entertaining children three tables away.

K. C. was great to have in the church youth group. Sure, he didn't always pay attention when the pastor preached (he wasn't the only one), and there were times he turned a serious discussion into a joke. But he was a nice guy who treated people well.

In fact, K. C. fit in too well—everywhere. With the church kids, he was a great group member. Responsible. Upbeat. Moral. But when he was with the guys in his neighborhood, he fit in just as well—maybe better. Vandalism. Skipping school. Trouble with police. Drinking. Drugs. More trouble with police.

As hard as people at church tried, they couldn't keep K. C. in the group. In his senior year, he spent less and less time with church friends as his life spiraled down to the level of the neighborhood crowd. Eventually, he was gone.

Through the next ten years, K. C.'s life was a series of broken relationships, bouts with alcohol and drug abuse, and lost jobs. He regularly partied with some of the guys from the old neighborhood. K. C. still fit in.

K. C. never understood the danger of the wrong kind of peer pressure described in **Psalm 1**.

■ What might the psalmist say if he were writing a letter to K. C. today?
■ What does this psalm tell you to do about negative peer pressure?

CONSIDER . . .
■ planning to do something with a friend who will have a positive spiritual impact on you.
■ writing your own psalm (a song or a poem) that expresses your desire to do God's will rather than follow the crowd.

FOR MORE, SEE . . .
■ Genesis 26:1–11 (p. 30)
■ 2 Corinthians 6:14–18 (p. 1199)
■ Hebrews 10:24–25 (p. 1286)

Sinners will not worship with God's
people.
6This is because the Lord takes care of his
people,
but the wicked will be destroyed.

SIDELIGHT: The book of Psalms
is actually made up of five separate
books (see heading above chapter 1). Psalms
1—41 are Book One. Psalms 42—72 are
Book Two. Psalms 73—89 are Book Three.
Psalms 90—106 are Book Four. And Psalms
107—150 are Book Five. Each "book" may
have been collected at a different time.

The Lord's Chosen King

2 Why are the nations so angry?
Why are the people making useless
plans?
2The kings of the earth prepare to fight,
and their leaders make plans together
against the Lord
and his appointed one.
3They say, "Let's break the chains that hold us
back
and throw off the ropes that tie us down."

4But the one who sits in heaven laughs;
the Lord makes fun of them.
5Then the Lord warns them
and frightens them with his anger.
6He says, "I have appointed my own king
to rule in Jerusalem on my holy mountain,
Zion."

7Now I will tell you what the Lord has
declared:
He said to me, "You are my son.
Today I have become your father.
8If you ask me, I will give you the
nations;
all the people on earth will be yours.
9You will rule over them with an iron
rod.
You will break them into pieces like
pottery."

10So, kings, be wise;
rulers, learn this lesson.
11Obey the Lord with great fear.
Be happy, but tremble.
12Show that you are loyal to his son,
or you will be destroyed by his
anger,
because he can quickly become angry.
But happy are those who trust him for
protection.

A Morning Prayer

David sang this when he ran away
from his son Absalom.

3 Lord, I have many enemies!
Many people have turned against me.
2Many are saying about me,
"God won't rescue him." *Selah*d

3But, Lord, you are my shield,
my wonderful God who gives me courage.
4I will pray to the Lord,
and he will answer me from his holy
mountain. *Selah*

5I can lie down and go to sleep,
and I will wake up again,
because the Lord gives me strength.
6Thousands of troops may surround me,
but I am not afraid.

7Lord, rise up!
My God, come save me!
You have struck my enemies on the cheek;
you have broken the teeth of the wicked.
8The Lord can save his people.
Lord, bless your people. *Selah*

An Evening Prayer

For the director of music. With stringed instruments.
A psalm of David.

4 Answer me when I pray to you,
my God who does what is right.
Make things easier for me when I am in
trouble.
Have mercy on me and hear my prayer.

2People, how long will you turn my honor
into shame?
How long will you love what is false and
look for new lies? *Selah*d
3You know that the Lord has chosen for
himself those who are loyal to him.
The Lord listens when I pray to him.
4When you are angry, do not sin.
Think about these things quietly
as you go to bed. *Selah*

SIDELIGHT: The way citizens in
Bible times showed their loyalty to
royalty (Psalm 2:12) was by kissing the feet of
the king or prince.

5Do what is right as a sacrifice to the Lord
and trust the Lord.

6Many people ask,
"Who will give us anything good?"

LORD, be kind to us.
⁷But you have made me very happy,
  happier than they are,
  even with all their grain and new wine.
⁸I go to bed and sleep in peace,
  because, LORD, only you keep me safe.

A Morning Prayer for Protection

For the director of music. For flutes. A psalm of David.

5 LORD, listen to my words.
  Understand my sadness.
²Listen to my cry for help, my King and my
    God,
  because I pray to you.
³LORD, every morning you hear my voice.

Every morning, I tell you what I need,
  and I wait for your answer.

⁴You are not a God who is pleased with the
    wicked;
  you do not live with those who do evil.
⁵Those people who make fun of you cannot
    stand before you.
  You hate all those who do evil.
⁶You destroy liars;
  the LORD hates those who kill and trick
    others.

⁷Because of your great love,
  I can come into your Temple.ᵈ
Because I fear and respect you,
  I can worship in your holy Temple.

ANGER

He Lost His Grip

The school paper's sports headline said it all: "Tom Harley Loses Tennis Tournament With a Smash."

Tom read the biting article and then let out a sigh. He had felt so dumb for letting his anger get to him at the tournament that day. But the deed was done. Nothing could repair his tennis racket. He had hurled the stringed beast at the fence in a spark of rage. And his brand new racket abruptly met the fence post.

"C'mon, Tom," his partner, Jim, had whispered intensely. "Relax. Your temper's gonna throw this match for us."

"I'm fine," Tom had snapped. "Where's your extra racket?"

They probably would have lost anyway, but Tom was still mad about having to play with a racket he was unfamiliar with. They only won three games in the next two sets.

The coach didn't say a word that day, but Tom could tell he was furious. The next week at practice, he made Tom and Jim do extra "hate drills."

"Any doubles team with enough extra energy to waste on destroying tennis rackets," Coach said, "can surely handle a little extra running." So the twosome painfully ran the width of six tennis courts, frontward and backward, again and again.

And then there was the teasing from Tom's teammates.

"Hey, Tantrum Tom, fought off any attacking fence posts lately?"

"So, Tom, how many tennis rackets have you bought this month?"

Even with all this abuse, Tom hadn't learned his lesson. It took several more temper tantrums and broken rackets for him to learn the simple truth that anger wasn't going to make him play better tennis, or improve his life in any way!

Anger can sometimes be constructive. But, the psalmist reminds us how destructive anger can become. He warns us in **Psalm 4**, "When you are angry, do not sin." Hold on to the racket!

■ Do you think throwing a tennis racket in a fit of anger is a sin? Why or why not?

■ How can you avoid doing wrong things when you're angry?

CONSIDER...

■ seeking forgiveness from someone you've sinned against because of your anger.

■ *picturing the place or situation in which you get the angriest, and asking God to help you stay calm the next time you're there.*

FOR MORE, SEE...

■ Exodus 32 (p. 89)
■ Mark 11:15–19 (p. 995)

■ Ephesians 4:26–27 (p. 1224)

8Lord, since I have many enemies,
    show me the right thing to do.
    Show me clearly how you want me to live.

9My enemies' mouths do not tell the truth;
    in their hearts they want to destroy others.
    Their throats are like open graves;
    they use their tongues for telling lies.
10God, declare them guilty!
    Let them fall into their own traps.
    Send them away because their sins are many;
    they have turned against you.

11But let everyone who trusts you be happy;
    let them sing glad songs forever.
    Protect those who love you
    and who are happy because of you.
12Lord, you bless those who do what is right;
    you protect them like a soldier's shield.

A Prayer for Mercy in Troubled Times

For the director of music. With stringed instruments.
Upon the sheminith.d A psalm of David.

6 Lord, don't correct me when you are
    angry;
    don't punish me when you are very angry.
2Lord, have mercy on me because I am weak.
    Heal me, Lord, because my bones ache.
3I am very upset.
    Lord, how long will it be?

4Lord, return and save me;
    save me because of your kindness.
5Dead people don't remember you;
    those in the grave don't praise you.

6I am tired of crying to you.
    Every night my bed is wet with tears;
    my bed is soaked from my crying.
7My eyes are weak from so much crying;
    they are weak from crying about my
    enemies.

8Get away from me, all you who do evil,
    because the Lord has heard my crying.
9The Lord has heard my cry for help;
    the Lord will answer my prayer.
10All my enemies will be ashamed and
    troubled.
    They will turn and suddenly leave in
    shame.

A Prayer for Fairness

A shiggaiond of David which he sang to the Lord
about Cush, from the tribe of Benjamin.

7 Lord my God, I trust in you for
    protection.
    Save me and rescue me
    from those who are chasing me.
2Otherwise, like a lion they will tear me apart.

They will rip me to pieces, and no one can
    save me.

3Lord my God, what have I done?
    Have my hands done something wrong?
4Have I done wrong to my friend
    or stolen without reason from my enemy?
5If I have, let my enemy chase me and
    capture me.
    Let him trample me into the dust
    and bury me in the ground.   Selahd

6Lord, rise up in your anger;
    stand up against my enemies' anger.
    Get up and demand fairness.
7Gather the nations around you
    and rule them from above.
8Lord, judge the people.
    Lord, defend me because I am right,
    because I have done no wrong, God Most
    High.

9God, you do what is right.
    You know our thoughts and feelings.
    Stop those wicked actions done by evil
    people,
    and help those who do what is right.

10God protects me like a shield;
    he saves those whose hearts are right.
11God judges by what is right,
    and God is always ready to punish the
    wicked.
12If they do not change their lives,
    God will sharpen his sword;
    he will string his bow and take aim.
13He has prepared his deadly weapons;
    he has made his flaming arrows.

14There are people who think up evil
    and plan trouble and tell lies.
15They dig a hole to trap others,
    but they will fall into it themselves.
16They will get themselves into trouble;
    the violence they cause will hurt only
    themselves.

17I praise the Lord because he does what is
    right.
    I sing praises to the Lord Most High.

The Lord's Greatness

For the director of music. On the gittith.d
A psalm of David.

8 Lord our Lord,
    your name is the most wonderful name in
    all the earth!
    It brings you praise in heaven above.
2You have taught children and babies
    to sing praises to you
    because of your enemies.
    And so you silence your enemies

and destroy those who try to get even.

³I look at your heavens,
   which you made with your fingers.
I see the moon and stars,
   which you created.
⁴But why are people important to you?
   Why do you take care of human beings?
⁵You made them a little lower than the
      angels
   and crowned them with glory and honor.
⁶You put them in charge of everything you
      made.
   You put all things under their control:
⁷all the sheep, the cattle,
   and the wild animals,
⁸the birds in the sky,

the fish in the sea,
   and everything that lives under water.

⁹Lᴏʀᴅ our Lord,
   your name is the most wonderful name in
      all the earth!

Thanksgiving for Victory

For the director of music. To the tune of "The Death
of the Son." A psalm of David.

9 I will praise you, Lᴏʀᴅ, with all my heart.
   I will tell all the miracles*ᵈ* you have done.
²I will be happy because of you;
   God Most High, I will sing praises to your
      name.

³My enemies turn back;

SELF-ESTEEM

A Speck?

   When you look up in the sky at night, it's easy to see that the Earth is little more than a tiny speck in a giant universe. And within our solar system are nine planets, each of them unique and wonderful.

   Mercury, the closest planet to the sun, is still 36 million miles from the sun. Venus, the next closest planet, is just a little smaller than the Earth and is covered by a layer of clouds that hide its surface.

   Next beyond Earth is Mars, which is like a red desert of rock, sand, and soil. Jupiter, the largest planet, comes next. Its diameter is eleven times that of Earth. Saturn is next and is the last planet we can see with an unaided eye. The next planet, Uranus, is 1.8 billion miles from the sun. Beyond it are Neptune and Pluto, which have eccentric rotation patterns, so they sometimes switch places, making Pluto closer to the sun than Neptune.

   It's kind of overwhelming, isn't it? It makes us seem so insignificant.

   But wait!

   Mercury's temperature can reach 780 degrees. Clouds on Venus drip pure sulphuric acid. The atmosphere on Mars is like car exhaust. A mixture of sulphur and phosphorus make Jupiter like a giant match head, ready to ignite.

   On Saturn, raindrops are liquified methane gas. Uranus is covered in radioactive smog. One hemisphere of Neptune will not see sunlight until the year 2030. And Pluto is frozen solid.

   Makes you think God cares specially for us on Earth, doesn't it?

   When the psalmist looked to the heavens in **Psalm 8**, he, too, was overwhelmed and felt insignificant. But he recognized how special the Earth and its people are to God.

■ How do these scientific facts about the solar system relate to the message of Psalm 8?

■ Do you ever struggle with the thought that God values you and finds you important? What's the message of Psalm 8 for you?

C O N S I D E R . . .

■ listing the different ways you strive to feel important and comparing them to the reasons you believe that God truly values you. The Bible passages listed under "For More, See" can get you started.

■ *doing something special for yourself—such as going to a fun athletic event or buying yourself flowers—as a way of recognizing how special you are to God!*

F O R   M O R E ,   S E E . . .

■ Genesis 1:26–31 (p. 3)
■ John 3:16–17 (p. 1062)

■ Romans 5:6–8 (p. 1145)

they are overwhelmed and die because of
you.
⁴You have heard my complaint;
you sat on your throne and judged by what
was right.
⁵You spoke strongly against the foreign nations
and destroyed the wicked;
you wiped out their names forever and
ever.
⁶The enemy is gone forever.
You destroyed their cities;
no one even remembers them.

⁷But the Lord rules forever.
He sits on his throne to judge,
⁸and he will judge the world in fairness;
he will decide what is fair for the nations.
⁹The Lord defends those who suffer;
he defends them in times of trouble.
¹⁰Those who know the Lord trust him,
because he will not leave those who come
to him.

¹¹Sing praises to the Lord who is king on
Mount Zion.ᵈ
Tell the nations what he has done.
¹²He remembers who the murderers are;
he will not forget the cries of those who
suffer.
¹³Lord, have mercy on me.
See how my enemies hurt me.
Do not let me go through the gates of
death.
¹⁴Then, at the gates of Jerusalem, I will praise
you;
I will rejoice because you saved me.

¹⁵The nations have fallen into the pit they dug.
Their feet are caught in the nets they laid.
¹⁶The Lord has made himself known by his
fair decisions;
the wicked get trapped by what they do.

Higgaion.ᵈ Selahᵈ

¹⁷Wicked people will go to the grave,
and so will all those who forget God.
¹⁸But those who have troubles will not be
forgotten.
The hopes of the poor will never die.

¹⁹Lord, rise up and judge the nations.
Don't let people think they are strong.
²⁰Teach them to fear you, Lord.
The nations must learn that they are only
human.
Selah

A Complaint About Evil People

10
Lord, why are you so far away?
Why do you hide when there is
trouble?
²Proudly the wicked chase down those who
suffer.

Let them be caught in their own traps.
³They brag about the things they want.
They bless the greedy but hate the Lord.
⁴The wicked people are too proud.
They do not look for God;
there is no room for God in their thoughts.
⁵They always succeed.
They are far from keeping your laws;
they make fun of their enemies.
⁶They say to themselves, "Nothing bad will
ever happen to me;
I will never be ruined."
⁷Their mouths are full of curses, lies, and
threats;
they use their tongues for sin and evil.
⁸They hide near the villages.
They look for innocent people to kill;
they watch in secret for the helpless.
⁹They wait in hiding like a lion.
They wait to catch poor people;
they catch the poor in nets.
¹⁰The poor are thrown down and crushed;
they are defeated because the others are
stronger.
¹¹The wicked think, "God has forgotten us.
He doesn't see what is happening."

¹²Lord, rise up and punish the wicked.
Don't forget those who need help.
¹³Why do wicked people hate God?
They say to themselves, "God won't punish
us."
¹⁴Lord, surely you see these cruel and evil
things;
look at them and do something.
People in trouble look to you for help.
You are the one who helps the orphans.
¹⁵Break the power of wicked people.
Punish them for the evil they have done.

¹⁶The Lord is King forever and ever.
Destroy from your land those nations that
do not worship you.
¹⁷Lord, you have heard what the poor people
want.
Do what they ask, and listen to them.
¹⁸Protect the orphans and put an end to
suffering
so they will no longer be afraid of evil
people.

Trust in the Lord

For the director of music. Of David.

11
I trust in the Lord for protection.
So why do you say to me,
"Fly like a bird to your mountain.
²Like hunters, the wicked string their
bows;
they set their arrows on the bowstrings.

They shoot from dark places
   at those who are honest.
3When all that is good falls apart,
   what can good people do?"

4The LORD is in his holy temple;
   the LORD sits on his throne in heaven.
He sees what people do;
   he keeps his eye on them.
5The LORD tests those who do right,
   but he hates the wicked and those who
     love to hurt others.
6He will send hot coals and burning sulfur on
   the wicked.
A whirlwind is what they will get.

✺ SIDELIGHT: You would want
an air-conditioned tent if the
whirlwind of Psalm 11:6 blew in. Called a
sirocco, this hot desert wind could blow for
days, killing most vegetation.

7The LORD does what is right, and he loves
   justice,
so honest people will see his face.

A Prayer Against Liars

For the director of music. Upon the sheminith.*d*
A psalm of David.

12 Save me, LORD, because the good
    people are all gone;
no true believers are left on earth.
2Everyone lies to his neighbors;
   they say one thing and mean another.

3The LORD will stop those flattering
   lips
and cut off those bragging tongues.
4They say, "Our tongues will help us win.
   We can say what we wish; no one is our
     master."

5But the LORD says,
 "I will now rise up,
   because the poor are being hurt.
Because of the moans of the helpless,
   I will give them the help they want."
6The LORD's words are pure,
   like silver purified by fire,
 like silver purified seven times over.

7LORD, you will keep us safe;
   you will always protect us from such
    people.
8But the wicked are all around us;
   everyone loves what is wrong.

A Prayer for God to Be Near

For the director of music. A psalm of David.

13 How long will you forget me, LORD?
    Forever?
How long will you hide from me?
2How long must I worry
   and feel sad in my heart all day?
How long will my enemy win over me?

3LORD, look at me.
   Answer me, my God;
   tell me, or I will die.
4Otherwise my enemy will say, "I have won!"
   Those against me will rejoice that I've been
    defeated.

5I trust in your love.
   My heart is happy because you saved me.
6I sing to the LORD
   because he has taken care of me.

The Unbelieving Fool

For the director of music. Of David.

14 Fools say to themselves,
    "There is no God."
Fools are evil and do terrible things;
   there is no one who does anything good.

2The LORD looked down from heaven on all
   people
to see if anyone understood,
   if anyone was looking to God for help.
3But all have turned away.
   Together, everyone has become evil.
There is no one who does anything good,
   not even one.

4Don't the wicked understand?
   They destroy my people as if they were
    eating bread.
They do not ask the LORD for help.
5But the wicked are filled with terror,
   because God is with those who do what is
    right.
6The wicked upset the plans of the poor,
   but the LORD will protect them.

7I pray that victory will come to Israel from
   Mount Zion!*d*
May the LORD bring them back.
Then the people of Jacob will rejoice,
   and the people of Israel will be glad.

What the Lord Demands

A psalm of David.

15 LORD, who may enter your Holy
    Tent?*d*
Who may live on your holy mountain?

²Only those who are innocent
and who do what is right.
Such people speak the truth from their hearts
³ and do not tell lies about others.
They do no wrong to their neighbors
and do not gossip.
⁴They do not respect hateful people
but honor those who honor the LORD.
They keep their promises to their neighbors,
even when it hurts.
⁵They do not charge interest on money they
lend
and do not take money to hurt innocent
people.

Whoever does all these things will never be
destroyed.

The Lord Takes Care of His People

A miktam*d* of David.

16 Protect me, God,
because I trust in you.
²I said to the LORD, "You are my Lord.

Every good thing I have comes from you."
³As for the godly people in the world,
they are the wonderful ones I enjoy.
⁴But those who turn to idols
will have much pain.
I will not offer blood to those idols
or even speak their names.

⁵No, the LORD is all I need.
He takes care of me.
⁶My share in life has been pleasant;
my part has been beautiful.

⁷I praise the LORD because he advises me.
Even at night, I feel his leading.
⁸I keep the LORD before me always.
Because he is close by my side,
I will not be hurt.
⁹So I rejoice and am glad.
Even my body has hope,
¹⁰because you will not leave me in the grave.
You will not let your holy one rot.
¹¹You will teach me how to live a holy life.
Being with you will fill me with joy;

DOUBT

She Loves Me?

Mark Donigan nearly died emotionally while dating Sharon. She was his first real girlfriend. He really didn't understand how this "falling in love" stuff worked.

Mark just knew that sometimes when he saw Sharon, she was absolutely in love with him—that big smile, sparkling eyes, tight handhold. Other times, it was like she could barely stand him—no eye contact, nothing to say, arms folded, nothing but frowns.

About the time Mark's friends would convince him to break up, she would write a wonderful note, bake him some cookies, or do some other nice thing that convinced him she really did love him.

Doubt took its toll on Mark. One day up and the next down. One day she loved him; the next day she seemed distant. Finally, after about six months of roller-coaster emotions, Mark ended his relationship with Sharon.

The breakup hurt, but deep down Mark was relieved. He finally realized that real love doesn't turn on and off unpredictably.

Mark doubted Sharon's love because her actions seemed inconsistent. In the same way, David's circumstances became so difficult that he began to wonder whether God loved him. But there was no break in this relationship. Read **Psalm 13** to discover the different conclusion David reached.

■ Why, based on this psalm, could David be so confident in God's love? How is this different from Mark's doubts about Sharon's love?

■ When was the last time you doubted God's love for you? How did you work through your doubt?

CONSIDER...

■ starting a special prayer time for the relationship in your life that gives you the most doubts.

■ writing a letter to "Mr. Doubt," letting him know how you plan to handle him with God's help.

FOR MORE, SEE...

■ Jeremiah 1:4–10 (p. 691)
■ John 20:24–29 (p. 1094)

■ Romans 4:18–25 (p. 1145)

at your right hand I will find pleasure
forever.

A Prayer for Protection

A prayer of David.

17 Lord, hear me begging for fairness;
listen to my cry for help.
Pay attention to my prayer,
because I speak the truth.
²You will judge that I am right;
your eyes can see what is true.
³You have examined my heart;
you have tested me all night.
You questioned me without finding anything
wrong;
I have not sinned with my mouth.
⁴I have obeyed your commands,
so I have not done what evil people do.
⁵I have done what you told me;
I have not failed.

⁶I call to you, God,
and you answer me.
Listen to me now,
and hear what I say.
⁷Your love is wonderful.

By your power you save those who trust
you
from their enemies.
⁸Protect me as you would protect your own
eye.
Hide me under the shadow of your wings.
⁹Keep me from the wicked who attack me,
from my enemies who surround me.
¹⁰They are selfish
and brag about themselves.
¹¹They have chased me until they have
surrounded me.
They plan to throw me to the ground.
¹²They are like lions ready to kill;
like lions, they sit in hiding.

¹³Lord, rise up, face the enemy, and throw
them down.
Save me from the wicked with your
sword.
¹⁴Lord, save me by your power
from those whose reward is in this life.
They have plenty of food.
They have many sons
and leave much money to their children.

¹⁵Because I have lived right, I will see your
face.

REVENGE

Hate Stealer

I can't remember his name. I'm really not sure how old he was. I can hardly remember his face. His broken English was tough to understand. But, I've never forgotten his story.

Before being baptized, this Vietnamese refugee stood before our church to tell how Jesus Christ had changed his life. He spoke of the horrors of war—of escape through jungles and rivers and over the border into Thailand, of hunger and near starvation in overcrowded camps, and of the joy of coming to America.

But above all his captivating stories, one part of his testimony left a lasting impression on me.

"Brothers and sisters," he said. "I came to America alone, and I came with much hatred in my heart. But when Jesus came into my heart, he stole my hate away. Now I can say that I love even my enemies."

David faced circumstances similar to this Vietnamese refugee. Read **Psalm 17** to find David's response to his enemies.

■ What did David have in common with this Vietnamese refugee? How were their responses to their enemies different?

■ How can you leave matters in God's hands—as David did—when you are treated unfairly?

CONSIDER . . .

■ praying for someone who has treated you unfairly and whom you consider to be an "enemy."

■ listing ways the world would be different if people and nations would turn away from revenge. Then pray for world peace—starting in your own home and school.

FOR MORE, SEE . . .

■ 1 Samuel 24 (p. 266)
■ Matthew 5:38–48 (p. 915)
■ Romans 12:14–21 (p. 1158)

When I wake up, I will see your likeness
and be satisfied.

A Song of Victory

For the director of music. By the LORD's servant,
David. David sang this song to the LORD when the
LORD had saved him from Saul and
all his other enemies.

18 I love you, LORD. You are my
strength.

2 The LORD is my rock, my protection, my
Savior.
My God is my rock.
I can run to him for safety.
He is my shield and my saving strength, my
defender.
3 I will call to the LORD, who is worthy of
praise,
and I will be saved from my enemies.

4 The ropes of death came around me;
the deadly rivers overwhelmed me.
5 The ropes of death wrapped around me.
The traps of death were before me.
6 In my trouble I called to the LORD.
I cried out to my God for help.
From his temple he heard my voice;
my call for help reached his ears.

7 The earth trembled and shook.
The foundations of the mountains began to
shake.
They trembled because the LORD was
angry.
8 Smoke came out of his nose,
and burning fire came out of his mouth.
Burning coals went before him.
9 He tore open the sky and came down
with dark clouds under his feet.
10 He rode a creature with wings and flew.
He raced on the wings of the wind.
11 He made darkness his covering, his shelter
around him,
surrounded by fog and clouds.
12 Out of the brightness of his presence came
clouds
with hail and lightning.
13 The LORD thundered from heaven;
the Most High raised his voice,
and there was hail and lightning.
14 He shot his arrows and scattered his enemies.
His many bolts of lightning confused them
with fear.
15 LORD, you spoke strongly.
The wind blew from your nose.
Then the valleys of the sea appeared,
and the foundations of the earth were
seen.

16 The LORD reached down from above and
took me;
he pulled me from the deep water.
17 He saved me from my powerful enemies,
from those who hated me, because they
were too strong for me.
18 They attacked me at my time of trouble,
but the LORD supported me.
19 He took me to a safe place.
Because he delights in me, he saved me.

20 The LORD spared me because I did what was
right.
Because I have not done evil, he has
rewarded me.
21 I have followed the ways of the LORD;
I have not done evil by turning away from
my God.
22 I remember all his laws
and have not broken his rules.
23 I am innocent before him;
I have kept myself from doing evil.
24 The LORD rewarded me because I did what
was right,
because I did what the LORD said was right.

25 LORD, you are loyal to those who are loyal,
and you are good to those who are good.
26 You are pure to those who are pure,
but you are against those who are bad.
27 You save the humble,
but you bring down those who are proud.
28 LORD, you give light to my lamp.
My God brightens the darkness around me.
29 With your help I can attack an army.
With God's help I can jump over a wall.

30 The ways of God are without fault.
The LORD's words are pure.
He is a shield to those who trust him.
31 Who is God? Only the LORD.
Who is the Rock?d Only our God.
32 God is my protection.
He makes my way free from fault.
33 He makes me like a deer that does not
stumble;
he helps me stand on the steep mountains.
34 He trains my hands for battle
so my arms can bend a bronze bow.
35 You protect me with your saving shield.
You support me with your right hand.
You have stooped to make me great.
36 You give me a better way to live,
so I live as you want me to.
37 I chased my enemies and caught them.
I did not quit until they were destroyed.
38 I crushed them so they couldn't rise up
again.
They fell beneath my feet.
39 You gave me strength in battle.

You made my enemies bow before me.
⁴⁰You made my enemies turn back,
and I destroyed those who hated me.
⁴¹They called for help,
but no one came to save them.
They called to the LORD,
but he did not answer them.
⁴²I beat my enemies into pieces, like dust in
the wind.
I poured them out like mud in the streets.

⁴³You saved me when the people attacked me.
You made me the leader of nations.
People I never knew serve me.
⁴⁴As soon as they hear me, they obey me.
Foreigners obey me.
⁴⁵They all become afraid
and tremble in their hiding places.

⁴⁶The LORD lives!
May my Rock be praised.
Praise the God who saves me!
⁴⁷God gives me victory over my enemies
and brings people under my rule.
⁴⁸He saves me from my enemies.

You set me over those who hate me.
You saved me from cruel men.
⁴⁹So I will praise you, LORD, among the
nations.
I will sing praises to your name.
⁵⁰The LORD gives great victories to his king.
He is loyal to his appointed king,
to David and his descendants*d* forever.

God's Works and Word

For the director of music. A psalm of David.

19 The heavens tell the glory of God,
and the skies announce what his
hands have made.
²Day after day they tell the story;
night after night they tell it again.
³They have no speech or words;
they have no voice to be heard.
⁴But their message goes out through all the
world;
their words go everywhere on earth.
The sky is like a home for the sun.
⁵ The sun comes out like a bridegroom from
his bedroom.
It rejoices like an athlete eager to run a
race.
⁶*The sun rises at one end of the sky
and follows its path to the other end.*
Nothing hides from its heat.

⁷The teachings of the LORD are perfect;
they give new strength.
The rules of the LORD can be trusted;
they make plain people wise.

⁸The orders of the LORD are right;
they make people happy.
The commands of the LORD are pure;
they light up the way.
⁹Respect for the LORD is good;
it will last forever.
The judgments of the LORD are true;
they are completely right.
¹⁰They are worth more than gold,
even the purest gold.
They are sweeter than honey,
even the finest honey.
¹¹By them your servant is warned.
Keeping them brings great reward.

¹²People cannot see their own mistakes.
Forgive me for my secret sins.
¹³Keep me from the sins of pride;
don't let them rule me.
Then I can be pure
and innocent of the greatest of sins.

¹⁴I hope my words and thoughts please you.
LORD, you are my Rock,*d* the one who
saves me.

A Prayer for the King

For the director of music. A psalm of David.

20 May the LORD answer you in times of
trouble.
May the God of Jacob protect you.
²May he send you help from his Temple*d*
and support you from Mount Zion.*d*
³May he remember all your offerings
and accept all your sacrifices.   *Selah*d
⁴May he give you what you want
and make all your plans succeed,
⁵and we will shout for joy when you succeed,
and we will raise a flag in the name of our
God.
May the LORD give you all that you ask for.

⁶Now I know the LORD helps his appointed
king.
He answers him from his holy heaven
and saves him with his strong right hand.
⁷Some trust in chariots, others in horses,
but we trust the LORD our God.
⁸They are overwhelmed and defeated,
but we march forward and win.
⁹LORD, save the king!
Answer us when we call for help.

Thanksgiving for the King

For the director of music. A psalm of David.

21 LORD, the king rejoices because of
your strength;
he is so happy when you save him!
²You gave the king what he wanted

and did not refuse what he asked for.   *Selah*[d]
[3]You put good things before him
and placed a gold crown on his head.
[4]He asked you for life,
and you gave it to him,
so his years go on and on.
[5]He has great glory because you gave him victories;
you gave him honor and praise.
[6]You always gave him blessings;
you made him glad because you were with him.
[7]The king truly trusts the LORD.
Because God Most High always loves him,
he will not be overwhelmed.
[8]Your hand is against all your enemies;
those who hate you will feel your power.
[9]When you appear,
you will burn them as in a furnace.

In your anger you will swallow them up,
and fire will burn them up.
[10]You will destroy their families from the earth;
their children will not live.
[11]They made evil plans against you,
but their traps won't work.
[12]You will make them turn their backs
when you aim your arrows at them.
[13]Be supreme, LORD, in your power.
We sing and praise your greatness.

The Prayer of a Suffering Man

For the director of music. To the tune of "The Doe of Dawn." A psalm of David.

22 My God, my God, why have you rejected me?
You seem far from saving me,
far from the words of my groaning.

You'll Make It

Life began for Trisha Jones when she was seventeen years old. At summer camp she was introduced to Jesus Christ for the first time.

"I felt a mixture of relief and joy," says Trisha. "Relief, because I'd come to camp with my life in turmoil—I had destructive habits and relationships that just weren't right. And joy, because I really believed all things could be new for me as a Christian."

But with her joy over becoming a Christian, Trisha secretly wondered if it would last.

"I had so many problems," she recalls. "And even with Jesus in my life, I knew they weren't all just going to go away. I wasn't sure I was strong enough to make it through."

Returning home, Trisha wasn't in the camp's beautiful surroundings anymore. And the temptations she had given in to so many times before were back in full force.

"I couldn't believe so many things could go wrong in one week," Trisha says. "I had a major emotional letdown just from being away from the new friends I'd met at camp. My old friends pressured me to do the things I used to, and when I said no, they rejected me. And before the week was over, I'd failed to keep my commitment to Christ several times."

However, Trisha also started studying the Bible—sometimes joyfully and sometimes out of duty. And spending time with God through his Word helped Trisha learn about following Christ and encouraged her to do what was right. As she grew closer to Christ, it became easier to resist the temptations.

Trisha discovered how the Bible could help her change to be more like Christ. Read **Psalm 19** to discover how God's Word made a big difference in David's life!

■ What does David say about God's Word—referred to as "the Lord's teachings," his "rules," his "commands"—in Psalm 19 that would have helped Trisha in those early days?
■ How can you apply the truth in Psalm 19 to your life this week?

CONSIDER...
■ highlighting or underlining a verse in this psalm that has special meaning for you.
■ finding a friend who will meet with you once a week to study the Bible.

FOR MORE, SEE...
■ Psalm 119:1–48 (p. 550)
■ John 14:23–24 (p. 1085)
■ 2 Timothy 3:14–17 (p. 1266)

²My God, I call to you during the day,
  but you do not answer.
I call at night;
  I am not silent.

³You sit as the Holy One.
  The praises of Israel are your throne.
⁴Our ancestors trusted you;
  they trusted, and you saved them.
⁵They called to you for help
  and were rescued.
They trusted you
  and were not disappointed.

⁶But I am like a worm instead of a man.
  People make fun of me and hate me.
⁷Those who look at me laugh.
  They stick out their tongues and shake
    their heads.
⁸They say, "Turn to the Lord for help.
  Maybe he will save you.
If he likes you,
  maybe he will rescue you."

⁹You had my mother give birth to me.
  You made me trust you
    while I was just a baby.
¹⁰I have leaned on you since the day I was
    born;
  you have been my God since my mother
    gave me birth.
¹¹So don't be far away from me.
  Now trouble is near,
    and there is no one to help.
¹²People have surrounded me like angry bulls.
  Like the strong bulls of Bashan, they are on
    every side.

SIDELIGHT: Travelers through
the region of Bashan, northeast of
Galilee, might have needed professional
bodyguards. In addition to "strong bulls"
(Psalm 22:12), Bashan was notorious for fierce
lions and giant people.

¹³Like hungry, roaring lions
  they open their mouths at me.
¹⁴My strength is gone,
  like water poured out onto the ground,
  and my bones are out of joint.
My heart is like wax;
  it has melted inside me.
¹⁵My strength has dried up like a clay pot,
  and my tongue sticks to the top of my
    mouth.

You laid me in the dust of death.
¹⁶Evil people have surrounded me;
  like dogs they have trapped me.
  They have bitten my arms and legs.
¹⁷I can count all my bones;
  people look and stare at me.
¹⁸They divided my clothes among them,
  and they threw lots[d] for my clothing.

¹⁹But, Lord, don't be far away.
  You are my strength; hurry to help
    me.
²⁰Save me from the sword;
  save my life from the dogs.
²¹Rescue me from the lion's mouth;
  save me from the horns of the bulls.

²²Then I will tell my fellow Israelites about
    you;
  I will praise you in the public meeting.
²³Praise the Lord, all you who respect him.
  All you descendants[d] of Jacob, honor
    him;
  fear him, all you Israelites.
²⁴He does not ignore those in trouble.
  He doesn't hide from them
    but listens when they call out to him.
²⁵Lord, I praise you in the great meeting of
    your people;
  these worshipers will see me do what I
    promised.
²⁶Poor people will eat until they are full;
  those who look to the Lord will praise
    him.
  May your hearts live forever!
²⁷People everywhere will remember
  and will turn to the Lord.
All the families of the nations
  will worship him
²⁸because the Lord is King,
  and he rules the nations.

²⁹All the powerful people on earth will eat and
    worship.
  Everyone will bow down to him,
    all who will one day die.
³⁰The people in the future will serve him;
  they will always be told about the Lord.
³¹They will tell that he does what is right.
  People who are not yet born
    will hear what God has done.

SIDELIGHT: Psalm 23 has
always been one of the favorite, most-
quoted passages in the Old Testament. The
early Christian church sang this song when
people were baptized.

The Lord the Shepherd

A psalm of David.

23 The LORD is my shepherd;
I have everything I need.
2He lets me rest in green pastures.
He leads me to calm water.
3He gives me new strength.
He leads me on paths that are right
for the good of his name.
4Even if I walk through a very dark valley,
I will not be afraid,
because you are with me.
Your rod and your walking stick[n] comfort
me.
5You prepare a meal for me
in front of my enemies.
You pour oil on my head;[n]
you fill my cup to overflowing.
6Surely your goodness and love will be with
me
all my life,
and I will live in the house of the LORD
forever.

A Welcome for God into the Temple

A psalm of David.

24 The earth belongs to the LORD, and
everything in it—
the world and all its people.
2He built it on the waters
and set it on the rivers.

walking stick The stick a shepherd uses to guide and protect his sheep.
pour oil ... head This can mean that God gave him great wealth and blessed him.

HAPPINESS

Heart Strokes

Joe Castillo taught science at an inner-city high school in Kansas City. Some of the students were rough. He often had to break up fights. A student pulled a gun on him once, and knives were as common as notebooks.

But it didn't matter. Joe loved his students and did all he could to make science come alive for them. He would sell gum between classes to raise money for lab equipment the school district couldn't afford. He organized a clothes drive so his students could have winter coats. Most of his students loved him because they understood how much he cared. That's just the way he was.

When Joe had a stroke, it devastated his students. With incredible sadness, they watched him fight death every day. He lost many of his motor skills. He couldn't walk without a cane, and his speech began to slur. Many cried the day the principal told them the doctors wouldn't let Joe teach anymore. He had persevered ten months longer than the doctors thought he possibly could.

When students visited Joe in the hospital, they would go to his room sad. But when they would leave, they would be happy.

"I went to encourage him, and I left encouraged," one of Joe's seniors said. "Joe had me laughing so hard I almost forgot I was in the hospital. I don't know how anyone can be so happy in a place like that."

Despite awful pain, Joe held onto the truth that David declared in **Psalm 23**.

■ What phrase in Psalm 23 best describes the reason for Joe's happiness despite such terrible circumstances?

■ How can you make the truths of Psalm 23 the foundation for your happiness?

CONSIDER . . .

■ taking a personal inventory of the sources of your happiness, by writing as many responses as you can to this phrase: "Happiness, for me, is . . ."

■ taking a walk and talking to God about a "dark valley" you're going through right now.

FOR MORE, SEE . . .

■ Psalm 100 (p. 539)
■ Matthew 5:1–12 (p. 912)

■ Philippians 4:4–7 (p. 1234)

³Who may go up on the mountain of the
    LORD?
  Who may stand in his holy Temple?*d*
⁴Only those with clean hands and pure hearts,
    who have not worshiped idols,
    who have not made promises in the name
        of a false god.
⁵They will receive a blessing from the LORD;
    the God who saves them will declare them
        right.
⁶They try to follow God;
    they look to the God of Jacob for help.
                                    *Selah**d*

⁷Gates, open all the way.
  Open wide, aged doors
  so the glorious King will come in.
⁸Who is this glorious King?
  The LORD, strong and mighty.
  The LORD, the powerful warrior.
⁹Gates, open all the way.
  Open wide, aged doors
  so the glorious King will come in.
¹⁰Who is this glorious King?
  The LORD All-Powerful —
  he is the glorious King.   *Selah*

A Prayer for God to Guide

Of David.

25 LORD, I give myself to you;
    ² my God, I trust you.
  Do not let me be disgraced;
    do not let my enemies laugh at me.
³No one who trusts you will be disgraced,
    but those who sin without excuse will be
        disgraced.

⁴LORD, tell me your ways.
  Show me how to live.
⁵Guide me in your truth,
    and teach me, my God, my Savior.
  I trust you all day long.
⁶LORD, remember your mercy and love
    that you have shown since long ago.
⁷Do not remember the sins
    and wrong things I did when I was young.
  But remember to love me always
    because you are good, LORD.

⁸The LORD is good and right;
    he points sinners to the right way.
⁹*He shows those who are humble how to do*
        right,
    and he teaches them his ways.
¹⁰All the LORD's ways are loving and true
    for those who follow the demands of his
        agreement.

¹¹For the sake of your name, LORD,
    forgive my many sins.
¹²Are there those who respect the LORD?
    He will point them to the best way.
¹³They will enjoy a good life,
    and their children will inherit the land.
¹⁴The LORD tells his secrets to those who
        respect him;
    he tells them about his agreement.
¹⁵My eyes are always looking to the LORD for
        help.
    He will keep me from any traps.
¹⁶Turn to me and have mercy on me,
    because I am lonely and hurting.
¹⁷My troubles have grown larger;
    free me from my problems.
¹⁸Look at my suffering and troubles,
    and take away all my sins.
¹⁹Look at how many enemies I have!
    See how much they hate me!
²⁰Protect me and save me.
    I trust you, so do not let me be disgraced.
²¹My hope is in you,
    so may goodness and honesty guard
        me.
²²God, save Israel from all their troubles!

The Prayer of an Innocent Believer

Of David.

26 LORD, defend me because I have lived
    an innocent life.
  I have trusted the LORD and never doubted.
²LORD, try me and test me;
    look closely into my heart and mind.
³I see your love,
    and I live by your truth.
⁴I do not spend time with liars,
    nor do I make friends with those who hide
        their sin.
⁵I hate the company of evil people,
    and I won't sit with the wicked.
⁶I wash my hands to show I am innocent,
    and I come to your altar, LORD.
⁷I raise my voice in praise
    and tell of all the miracles*d* you have
        done.
⁸LORD, I love the Temple*d* where you
        live,
    where your glory is.
⁹Do not kill me with those sinners
    or take my life with those murderers.
¹⁰Evil is in their hands,
    and they do wrong for money.
¹¹But I have lived an innocent life,
    so save me and have mercy on me.
¹²I stand in a safe place.
  LORD, I praise you in the great meeting.

A Song of Trust in God

Of David.

27 The LORD is my light and the one
who saves me.
I fear no one.
The LORD protects my life;
I am afraid of no one.
²Evil people may try to destroy my body.
My enemies and those who hate me attack
me,
but they are overwhelmed and defeated.
³If an army surrounds me,
I will not be afraid.
If war breaks out,
I will trust the LORD.

⁴I ask only one thing from the LORD.

This is what I want:
Let me live in the LORD's house
all my life.
Let me see the LORD's beauty
and look with my own eyes at his Temple.*d*
⁵During danger he will keep me safe in his
shelter.
He will hide me in his Holy Tent,*d*
or he will keep me safe on a high
mountain.
⁶My head is higher than my enemies around
me.
I will offer joyful sacrifices in his Holy Tent.
I will sing and praise the LORD.

⁷LORD, hear me when I call;
have mercy and answer me.
⁸My heart said of you, "Go, worship him."

FEAR

An Antidote for Fear

Dr. Martin Luther King, Jr., a minister, was one of the foremost spokespeople for the civil rights movement that began in the United States in the 1950s. He risked his life and career around the country participating in nonviolent protests and preaching equality for all people. He was arrested many times and received numerous threats on his life before he was assassinated in 1968.

One Monday evening after a particularly tension-packed week, King spoke at a mass meeting. "I attempted to convey an overt impression of strength and courage," he said. "although I was inwardly depressed and fear-stricken."

After his talk, Mother Pollard—an elderly woman who had been instrumental in early civil rights victories—came to the front of the church and called, "Come here, son." King embraced her warmly as usual, but she wasn't going to let him move on just yet.

"Something is wrong with you. You didn't talk strong tonight."

"Oh, no Mother Pollard, nothing is wrong," King assured her. "I'm feeling as fine as ever."

"Now you can't fool me," she said. "I knows something is wrong. Is it that we ain't doing things to please you? Or is it that the white folks is bothering you? I done told you we is with you all the way. But even if we ain't with you, God's gonna take care of you."

"Since that dreary night, I have known very few quiet days," King later said. "But as the years have unfolded, the eloquently simple words of Mother Pollard have come back again and again to give light and peace and guidance to my troubled soul."

As you read **Psalm 27**, you'll find David expressing the same eloquently simple truth. He too found that the best antidote to fear is knowing "God's gonna take care of you."

■ What verses from Psalm 27 might have inspired Mother Pollard's assurance to Martin Luther King, Jr.?
■ What verse brings you the most assurance to face a fearful situation?

C O N S I D E R . . .

■ memorizing the verse from Psalm 27 that you most want to remember the next time you are afraid.
■ asking friends from school and church how they handle fear.

F O R   M O R E ,   S E E . . .

■ 1 Kings 9:1–18 (p. 325)
■ Luke 8:22–25 (p. 1017)
■ 1 John 4:17–18 (p. 1319)

So I come to worship you, LORD.
9Do not turn away from me.
Do not turn your servant away in
        anger;
you have helped me.
Do not push me away or leave me
        alone,
God, my Savior.
10If my father and mother leave me,
the LORD will take me in.
11LORD, teach me your ways,
and guide me to do what is right
because I have enemies.
12Do not hand me over to my enemies,
because they tell lies about me
and say they will hurt me.

13I truly believe
I will live to see the LORD's goodness.
14Wait for the LORD's help.
Be strong and brave,
and wait for the LORD's help.

A Prayer in Troubled Times

Of David.

28 LORD, my Rock,*d* I call out to you for
help.
Do not be deaf to me.
If you are silent,
I will be like those in the grave.
2Hear the sound of my prayer,
when I cry out to you for help.
I raise my hands
toward your Most Holy Place.
3Don't drag me away with the wicked,
with those who do evil.
They say "Peace" to their neighbors,
but evil is in their hearts.
4Pay them back for what they have done,
for their evil deeds.
Pay them back for what they have done;
give them their reward.
5They don't understand what the LORD has
        done
or what he has made.
So he will knock them down
and not lift them up.

6Praise the LORD,
because he heard my prayer for help.
7The LORD is my strength and shield.
I trust him, and he helps me.
I am very happy,
and I praise him with my song.
8The LORD is powerful;
he gives victory to his chosen one.
9Save your people
and bless those who are your own.
Be their shepherd and carry them forever.

God in the Thunderstorm

A psalm of David.

29 Praise the LORD, you angels;
praise the LORD's glory and power.
2Praise the LORD for the glory of his name;
worship the LORD because he is holy.

3The LORD's voice is heard over the sea.
The glorious God thunders;
the LORD thunders over the ocean.
4The LORD's voice is powerful;
the LORD's voice is majestic.
5The LORD's voice breaks the trees;
the LORD breaks the cedars of Lebanon.

> ✹ **SIDELIGHT:** God's power was
> indeed great to break the cedars of
> Lebanon (Psalm 29:5). These trees grew
> seventy to eighty feet tall, with trunks
> sometimes more than twelve feet in
> diameter. Imagine how many strings of lights
> you would need to decorate one of those for
> Christmas!

6He makes the land of Lebanon dance like a
        calf
and Mount Hermon jump like a baby bull.
7The LORD's voice makes the lightning flash.
8The LORD's voice shakes the desert;
the LORD shakes the Desert of Kadesh.
9The LORD's voice shakes the oaks
and strips the leaves off the trees.
In his Temple*d* everyone says, "Glory to
        God!"

10The LORD controls the flood.
The LORD will be King forever.
11The LORD gives strength to his people;
the LORD blesses his people with peace.

Thanksgiving for Escaping Death

A psalm of David. A song for giving
the Temple*d* to the LORD.

30 I will praise you, LORD,
because you rescued me.
You did not let my enemies laugh at me.
2LORD, my God, I prayed to you,
and you healed me.
3You lifted me out of the grave;
you spared me from going down to the
place of the dead.

4Sing praises to the LORD, you who belong to
        him;
praise his holy name.
5His anger lasts only a moment,

but his kindness lasts for a lifetime.
Crying may last for a night,
  but joy comes in the morning.

6When I felt safe, I said,
  "I will never fear."
7LORD, in your kindness you made my
  mountain safe.
But when you turned away, I was
  frightened.

8I called to you, LORD,
  and asked you to have mercy on me.
9I said, "What good will it do if I die
  or if I go down to the grave?
Dust cannot praise you;
  it cannot speak about your truth.
10LORD, hear me and have mercy on me.
  LORD, help me."

11You changed my sorrow into dancing.
  You took away my clothes of sadness,
  and clothed me in happiness.
12I will sing to you and not be silent.
  LORD, my God, I will praise you forever.

A Prayer of Faith in Troubled Times

For the director of music. A psalm of David.

31 LORD, I trust in you;
  let me never be disgraced.
  Save me because you do what is right.
2Listen to me
  and save me quickly.
Be my rock of protection,
  a strong city to save me.
3You are my rock and my protection.
  For the good of your name, lead me and
  guide me.

DEPRESSION

The Wall Came Tumbling Down

On August 13, 1961, at 2:30 A.M., with floodlights to illuminate their work and soldiers to ensure no interruptions, engineering crews began sinking posts in the pavement of Berlin. Then they attached massive sheets of barbed wire.

Many thought it was a farce, but from that middle-of-the-night beginning, the Berlin Wall was built. It divided families, friends and nations. About ten thousand East Germans attempted to cross the wall in the next twenty-nine years, by tunneling, driving, flying, even blasting. At least 191 died trying.

The best-known "defector," Peter Fechter, was shot down by border guards in front of photographers and TV crews in 1962. Countless others were imprisoned for attempting to cross the wall.

Nothing portrayed the division of an entire country more dramatically than the Berlin Wall. And nothing else so well symbolized the broken people of this war-torn territory.

On November 17, 1989, Egon Krenz, the premier of East Germany, ordered the wall torn down. In no time, sledge hammers wielded by East and West Berliners broke through, opening the way for millions to cross back and forth in one joyous parade. No papers were checked. Even the border guards fought to keep from smiling.

"The wall is gone!" the people chanted. "The wall is gone." From both sides of the city they climbed atop undamaged portions of the ten-foot structure, laughing, crying, embracing, singing, and dancing.

When David was delivered from his enemies, he expressed the same joyous feeling in his prayer, "You changed my sorrow into dancing." Read **Psalm 30** to find out how your sorrow and depression can be turned to joy.

■ How was the destruction of the Berlin Wall like David's deliverance from his enemies?

■ What "walls" of sorrow and depression need to be broken down by God in your life? What sorrow in your life would you like God to turn into dancing?

C O N S I D E R . . .

■ expressing thanks to people you turn to when you're depressed.
■ planning a personal "party" complete with your favorite dessert to celebrate a victory God has gained in your life.

F O R M O R E , S E E . . .

■ Isaiah 61:3 (p. 681)   ■ Luke 15:11–32 (p. 1035)
■ Jonah 2 (p. 857)

⁴Set me free from the trap they set for me,
 because you are my protection.
⁵I give you my life.
 Save me, LORD, God of truth.

⁶I hate those who worship false gods.
 I trust only in the LORD.
⁷I will be glad and rejoice in your love,
 because you saw my suffering;
 you knew my troubles.
⁸You have not handed me over to my enemies
 but have set me in a safe place.

⁹LORD, have mercy, because I am in misery.
 My eyes are weak from so much crying,
 and my whole being is tired from grief.
¹⁰My life is ending in sadness,
 and my years are spent in crying.
 My troubles are using up my strength,
 and my bones are getting weaker.
¹¹Because of all my troubles, my enemies hate
 me,
 and even my neighbors look down on me.
 When my friends see me,
 they are afraid and run.
¹²I am like a piece of a broken pot.
 I am forgotten as if I were dead.
¹³I have heard many insults.
 Terror is all around me.
 They make plans against me
 and want to kill me.

¹⁴LORD, I trust you.
 I have said, "You are my God."
¹⁵My life is in your hands.
 Save me from my enemies
 and from those who are chasing me.
¹⁶Show your kindness to me, your servant.
 Save me because of your love.
¹⁷LORD, I called to you,
 so do not let me be disgraced.
 Let the wicked be disgraced
 and lie silent in the grave.
¹⁸With pride and hatred
 they speak against those who do right.
 So silence their lying lips.

¹⁹How great is your goodness
 that you have stored up for those who fear
 you,
 that you have given to those who trust you.
 You do this for all to see.
²⁰You protect them by your presence
 from what people plan against them.
 You shelter them from evil words.
²¹Praise the LORD.
 His love to me was wonderful
 when my city was attacked.
²²In my distress, I said,
 "God cannot see me!"
 But you heard my prayer

when I cried out to you for help.
²³Love the LORD, all you who belong to him.
 The LORD protects those who truly believe,
 but he punishes the proud as much as they
 have sinned.
²⁴All you who put your hope in the LORD
 be strong and brave.

It Is Better to Confess Sin

A maskil*d* of David.

32 Happy is the person
 whose sins are forgiven,
 whose wrongs are pardoned.
²Happy is the person
 whom the LORD does not consider guilty
 and in whom there is nothing false.

³When I kept things to myself,
 I felt weak deep inside me.
 I moaned all day long.
⁴Day and night you punished me.
 My strength was gone as in the summer
 heat.   *Selah d*
⁵Then I confessed my sins to you
 and didn't hide my guilt.
 I said, "I will confess my sins to the LORD,"
 and you forgave my guilt.   *Selah*

⁶For this reason, all who obey you
 should pray to you while they still can.
 When troubles rise like a flood,
 they will not reach them.
⁷You are my hiding place.
 You protect me from my troubles
 and fill me with songs of salvation.   *Selah*

⁸The LORD says, "I will make you wise and
 show you where to go.
 I will guide you and watch over you.
⁹So don't be like a horse or donkey,
 that doesn't understand.
 They must be led with bits and reins,
 or they will not come near you."

¹⁰Wicked people have many troubles,
 but the LORD's love surrounds those who
 trust him.
¹¹Good people, rejoice and be happy in the
 LORD.
 Sing all you whose hearts are right.

Praise God Who Creates and Saves

33 Sing to the LORD, you who do what is
 right;
 honest people should praise him.
²Praise the LORD on the harp;
 make music for him on a ten-stringed lyre.*d*
³Sing a new song to him;
 play well and joyfully.

⁴God's word is true,
and everything he does is right.
⁵He loves what is right and fair;
the LORD's love fills the earth.

⁶The sky was made at the LORD's command.
By the breath from his mouth, he made all
the stars.
⁷He gathered the water of the sea into a heap.
He made the great ocean stay in its place.
⁸All the earth should worship the LORD;
the whole world should fear him.
⁹He spoke, and it happened.
He commanded, and it appeared.
¹⁰The LORD upsets the plans of nations;
he ruins all their plans.
¹¹But the LORD's plans will stand forever;
his ideas will last from now on.
¹²Happy is the nation whose God is the LORD,
the people he chose for his very own.
¹³The LORD looks down from heaven
and sees every person.
¹⁴From his throne he watches
all who live on earth.
¹⁵He made their hearts
and understands everything they do.
¹⁶No king is saved by his great army.
No warrior escapes by his great strength.
¹⁷Horses can't bring victory;
they can't save by their strength.
¹⁸But the LORD looks after those who fear him,
those who put their hope in his love.
¹⁹He saves them from death
and spares their lives in times of hunger.
²⁰So our hope is in the LORD.
He is our help, our shield to protect us.
²¹We rejoice in him,
because we trust his holy name.
²²LORD, show your love to us
as we put our hope in you.

✸ **SIDELIGHT:** Have you ever
made an acrostic in which you use
each letter of a word to start a new word or
phrase? Some psalms (such as Psalms 34, 37,
111 and 146) use this structure. In Hebrew,
each unit of those psalms begins with a
successive letter of the alphabet.

Praise God Who Judges and Saves

David's song from the time he acted crazy so
Abimelech would send him away, and David did leave.

34 I will praise the LORD at all times;
his praise is always on my lips.
²My whole being praises the LORD.
The poor will hear and be glad.

³Glorify the LORD with me,
and let us praise his name together.

⁴I asked the LORD for help, and he answered
me.
He saved me from all that I feared.
⁵Those who go to him for help are happy,
and they are never disgraced.
⁶This poor man called, and the LORD heard
him
and saved him from all his troubles.
⁷The angel of the LORD camps around those
who fear God,
and he saves them.

⁸Examine and see how good the LORD is.
Happy is the person who trusts him.
⁹You who belong to the LORD, fear him!
Those who fear him will have everything
they need.
¹⁰Even lions may get weak and hungry,
but those who look to the LORD will have
every good thing.
¹¹Children, come and listen to me.
I will teach you to worship the LORD.
¹²You must do these things
to enjoy life and have many happy days.
¹³You must not say evil things,
and you must not tell lies.
¹⁴Stop doing evil and do good.
Look for peace and work for it.

¹⁵The LORD sees the good people
and listens to their prayers.
¹⁶But the LORD is against those who do evil;
he makes the world forget them.
¹⁷The LORD hears good people when they cry
out to him,
and he saves them from all their troubles.
¹⁸The LORD is close to the brokenhearted,
and he saves those whose spirits have been
crushed.

¹⁹People who do what is right may have many
problems,
but the LORD will solve them all.
²⁰He will protect their very bones;
not one of them will be broken.
²¹Evil will kill the wicked;
those who hate good people will be judged
guilty.
²²But the LORD saves his servants' lives;
no one who trusts him will be judged
guilty.

A Prayer for Help

Of David.

35 LORD, battle with those who battle
with me.
Fight against those who fight against me.

2Pick up the shield and armor.
Rise up and help me.
3Lift up your spears, both large and small,
against those who chase me.
Tell me, "I will save you."

4Make those who want to kill me
be ashamed and disgraced.
Make those who plan to harm me
turn back and run away.
5Make them like chaff*d* blown by the wind
as the angel of the LORD forces them away.
6Let their road be dark and slippery
as the angel of the LORD chases them.
7For no reason they spread out their net to
trap me;
for no reason they dug a pit for me.
8So let ruin strike them suddenly.
Let them be caught in their own nets;
let them fall into the pit and die.
9Then I will rejoice in the LORD;
I will be happy when he saves me.
10Even my bones will say,
"LORD, who is like you?
You save the weak from the strong,
the weak and poor from robbers."

11Men without mercy stand up to testify.
They ask me things I do not know.
12They repay me with evil for the good I have
done,
and they make me very sad.
13Yet when they were sick, I put on clothes of
sadness
and showed my sorrow by going without
food.
But my prayers were not answered.
14 I acted as if they were my friends or
brothers.
I bowed in sadness as if I were crying for my
mother.
15But when I was in trouble, they gathered and
laughed;
they gathered to attack before I knew it.
They insulted me without stopping.
16They made fun of me and were cruel to me
and ground their teeth at me in anger.

17Lord, how long will you watch this happen?
Save my life from their attacks;
save me from these people who are like
lions.
18I *will praise you* in the great meeting.
I *will* praise you among crowds of people.
19Do not let my enemies laugh at me;
they hate me for no reason.
Do not let them make fun of me;
they have no cause to hate me.
20Their words are not friendly
but are lies about peace-loving people.

21They speak against me
and say, "Aha! We saw what you did!"
22LORD, you have been watching. Do not keep
quiet.
Lord, do not leave me alone.
23Wake up! Come and defend me!
My God and Lord, fight for me!
24LORD my God, defend me with your justice.
Don't let them laugh at me.
25Don't let them think, "Aha! We got what we
wanted!"
Don't let them say, "We destroyed him."
26Let them be ashamed and embarrassed,
because they were happy when I hurt.
Cover them with shame and disgrace,
because they thought they were better than
I was.
27May my friends sing and shout for joy.
May they always say, "Praise the greatness
of the LORD,
who loves to see his servants do well."
28I will tell of your goodness
and will praise you every day.

Wicked People and a Good God

For the director of music. Of David,
the servant of the LORD.

36 Sin speaks to the wicked in their
hearts.
They have no fear of God.
2They think too much of themselves
so they don't see their sin and hate it.
3Their words are wicked lies;
they are no longer wise or good.
4At night they make evil plans;
what they do leads to nothing good.
They don't refuse things that are evil.

5LORD, your love reaches to the heavens,
your loyalty to the skies.
6Your goodness is as high as the mountains.
Your justice is as deep as the great ocean.
LORD, you protect both people and animals.
7God, your love is so precious!
You protect people in the shadow of your
wings.
8They eat the rich food in your house,
and you let them drink from your river of
pleasure.
9You are the giver of life.
Your light lets us enjoy life.

10Continue to love those who know *you*
and to do good to those who are good.
11Don't let proud people attack me
and the wicked force me away.
12Those who do evil have been defeated.
They are overwhelmed;
they cannot do evil any longer.

God Will Reward Fairly

Of David.

37 Don't be upset because of evil people.
Don't be jealous of those who do
wrong,
²because like the grass, they will soon dry up.
Like green plants, they will soon die away.

³Trust the LORD and do good.
Live in the land and feed on truth.
⁴Enjoy serving the LORD,
and he will give you what you want.
⁵Depend on the LORD;
trust him, and he will take care of you.
⁶Then your goodness will shine like the sun,
and your fairness like the noonday sun.

⁷Wait and trust the LORD.
Don't be upset when others get rich
or when someone else's plans succeed.
⁸Don't get angry.
Don't be upset; it only leads to trouble.
⁹Evil people will be sent away,

but those who trust the LORD will inherit
the land.
¹⁰In a little while the wicked will be no more.
You may look for them, but they will be
gone.
¹¹People who are not proud will inherit the
land
and will enjoy complete peace.

¹²The wicked make evil plans against good
people.
They grind their teeth at them in anger.
¹³But the Lord laughs at the wicked,
because he sees that their day is coming.
¹⁴The wicked draw their swords
and bend their bows
to kill the poor and helpless,
to kill those who are honest.
¹⁵But their swords will stab their own hearts,
and their bows will break.

¹⁶It is better to have little and be right
than to have much and be wrong.
¹⁷The power of the wicked will be broken,

JEALOUSY

The Donald

During the 1980s, Donald Trump was one of the most-admired and most-envied men alive. His fortune grew from $100 million in 1982 to at least $1.7 billion in 1989. He claimed that his worth was closer to $5 billion. He bought an airline and named it after himself. He built hotels and casinos and named many of them after himself. He bought one of the finest yachts in the world and then decided to build one twice as nice. He had a beautiful wife, Ivana. His best-selling book, Trump: The Art of the Deal, drew in would-be entrepreneurs looking for words of financial wisdom.

People thought Trump was arrogant and greedy, but many still envied him. Who wouldn't want to be in his shoes?

In late 1989 and throughout 1990 Trump's fortune plummeted. He wasn't exactly in the poor house, still claiming to be worth around $500 million. But with all his debts, the threat of bankruptcy loomed. He left Ivana and filed for divorce. Many claimed he was estranged from his children, especially Donald, Jr.

Suddenly, few were saying they wanted to be like "The Donald." He became the butt of jokes. He symbolized the ruin of wasteful greed. Those who had envied him most now gloated most happily at his downfall.

If people had read and heeded **Psalm 37**, they would not have been jealous of Trump. Check out the psalmist's advice to people concerning the rich or the wicked.

■ What verse in Psalm 37 best applies to the Donald Trump story?
■ What should you do when you feel jealous of someone who gets ahead?

C O N S I D E R . . .
■ listing at least twenty reasons why being jealous of anyone, especially people who do wrong, is senseless.
■ talking to your parent or youth minister about why you feel jealous and how you can overcome those feelings.

F O R   M O R E ,   S E E . . .
■ Proverbs 24: –2 (p. 588)   ■ James 1:9–11 (p. 1294)
■ Matthew 6:19–24 (p. 918)

but the LORD supports those who do right.
18The LORD watches over the lives of the
innocent,
and their reward will last forever.
19They will not be ashamed when trouble
comes.
They will be full in times of hunger.
20But the wicked will die.
The LORD's enemies will be like the flowers
of the fields;
they will disappear like smoke.
21The wicked borrow and don't pay back,
but those who do right give freely to
others.
22Those whom the LORD blesses will inherit the
land,
but those he curses will be sent away.

23When a person's steps follow the LORD,
God is pleased with his ways.
24If he stumbles, he will not fall,
because the LORD holds his hand.

25I was young, and now I am old,
but I have never seen good people left
helpless
or their children begging for food.
26Good people always lend freely to others,
and their children are a blessing.

27Stop doing evil and do good,
so you will live forever.
28The LORD loves justice
and will not leave those who worship him.
He will always protect them,
but the children of the wicked will die.
29Good people will inherit the land
and will live in it forever.

30A good person speaks with wisdom,
and he says what is fair.
31The teachings of his God are in his heart,
so he does not fail to keep them.
32The wicked watch for good people
so that they may kill them.
33But the LORD will not take away his
protection
or let good people be judged guilty.

34Wait for the LORD's help
and follow him.
He will honor you and give you the land,
and you will see the wicked sent away.

35I saw a wicked and cruel man
who looked strong like a healthy tree in
good soil.
36But he died and was gone;
I looked for him, but he couldn't be found.

37Think of the innocent person,
and watch the honest one.

The man who has peace
will have children to live after him.
38But sinners will be destroyed;
in the end the wicked will die.

39The LORD saves good people;
he is their strength in times of trouble.
40The LORD helps them and saves them;
he saves them from the wicked,
because they trust in him for protection.

A Prayer in Time of Sickness

A psalm of David to remember.

38 LORD, don't correct me when you are
angry.
Don't punish me when you are furious.
2Your arrows have wounded me,
and your hand has come down on me.
3My body is sick from your punishment.
Even my bones are not healthy because of
my sin.
4My guilt has overwhelmed me;
like a load it weighs me down.

5My sores stink and become infected
because I was foolish.
6I am bent over and bowed down;
I am sad all day long.
7I am burning with fever,
and my whole body is sore.
8I am weak and faint.
I moan from the pain I feel.

9Lord, you know everything I want;
my cries are not hidden from you.
10My heart pounds, and my strength is gone.
I am losing my sight.
11Because of my wounds, my friends and
neighbors avoid me,
and my relatives stay far away.
12Some people set traps to kill me.
Those who want to hurt me plan trouble;
all day long they think up lies.

13I am like a deaf man; I cannot hear.
Like a mute, I cannot speak.
14I am like a person who does not hear,
who has no answer to give.
15I trust you, LORD.
You will answer, my Lord and God.
16I said, "Don't let them laugh at me
or brag when I am defeated."
17I am about to die,
and I cannot forget my pain.
18I confess my guilt;
I am troubled by my sin.
19My enemies are strong and healthy,
and many hate me for no reason.
20They repay me with evil for the good I did.
They lie about me because I try to do good.

²¹LORD, don't leave me;
    my God, don't go away.
²²Quickly come and help me,
    my Lord and Savior.

Life Is Short

For the director of music. For Jeduthun.
A psalm of David.

39 I said, "I will be careful how I act
    and will not sin by what I say.
I will be careful what I say
    around wicked people."
²So I kept very quiet.
    I didn't even say anything good,
    but I became even more upset.
³I became very angry inside,
    and as I thought about it, my anger burned.
    So I spoke:
⁴"LORD, tell me when the end will come
    and how long I will live.
    Let me know how long I have.
⁵You have given me only a short life;
    my lifetime is like nothing to you.
    Everyone's life is only a breath.   *Selah*ᵈ
⁶People are like shadows moving about.
    All their work is for nothing;
    they collect things but don't know who will
        get them.

⁷"So, Lord, what hope do I have?
    You are my hope.
⁸Save me from all my sins.
    Don't let wicked fools make fun of me.
⁹I am quiet; I do not open my mouth,
    because you are the one who has done
        this.
¹⁰Quit punishing me;
    your beating is about to kill me.
¹¹You correct and punish people for their sins;
    like a moth, you destroy what they love.
    Everyone's life is only a breath.   *Selah*

¹²"LORD, hear my prayer,
    and listen to my cry.
    Do not ignore my tears.
I am like a visitor with you.
    Like my ancestors, I'm only here a short
        time.
¹³Leave me alone so I can be happy
    before I leave and am no more."

Praise and Prayer for Help

For the director of music. A psalm of David.

40 I waited patiently for the LORD.
    He turned to me and heard my cry.
²He lifted me out of the pit of destruction,
    out of the sticky mud.

He stood me on a rock
    and made my feet steady.
³He put a new song in my mouth,
    a song of praise to our God.
Many people will see this and worship
        him.
    Then they will trust the LORD.

⁴Happy is the person
    who trusts the LORD,
who doesn't turn to those who are proud
    or to those who worship false gods.
⁵LORD my God, you have done many
        miracles.ᵈ
    Your plans for us are many.
If I tried to tell them all,
    there would be too many to count.

⁶You do not want sacrifices and offerings.
    But you have made a hole in my ear
    to show that my body and life are yours.
You do not ask for burnt offerings
    and sacrifices to take away sins.
⁷Then I said, "Look, I have come.
    It is written about me in the book.
⁸My God, I want to do what you want.
    Your teachings are in my heart."

⁹I will tell about your goodness in the great
        meeting of your people.
    LORD, you know my lips are not silent.
¹⁰I do not hide your goodness in my heart;
    I speak about your loyalty and salvation.
I do not hide your love and truth
    from the people in the great meeting.

¹¹LORD, do not hold back your mercy from me;
    let your love and truth always protect me.
¹²Troubles have surrounded me;
    there are too many to count.
My sins have caught me
    so that I cannot see a way to escape.
I have more sins than hairs on my head,
    and I have lost my courage.

¹³Please, LORD, save me.
    Hurry, LORD, to help me.
¹⁴People are trying to kill me.
    Shame them and disgrace them.
People want to hurt me.
    Let them run away in disgrace.
¹⁵People are making fun of me.
    Let them be shamed into silence.
¹⁶But let those who follow you
    be happy and glad.
They love you for saving them.
    May they always say, "Praise the LORD!"

¹⁷Lord, because I am poor and helpless,
    please remember me.
You are my helper and savior.
    My God, do not wait.

A Prayer in Time of Sickness

For the director of music. A psalm of David.

41 Happy is the person who thinks about the poor.
When trouble comes, the LORD will save him.
²The LORD will protect him and spare his life
and will bless him in the land.
He will not let his enemies take him.
³The LORD will give him strength when he is sick,
and he will make him well again.

⁴I said, "LORD, have mercy on me.
Heal me, because I have sinned against you."
⁵My enemies are saying evil things about me.
They say, "When will he die and be forgotten?"
⁶Some people come to see me,
but they lie.

They just come to get bad news.
Then they go and gossip.
⁷All my enemies whisper about me
and think the worst about me.
⁸They say, "He has a terrible disease.
He will never get out of bed again."
⁹My best and truest friend, who ate at my table,
has even turned against me.

¹⁰LORD, have mercy on me.
Give me strength so I can pay them back.
¹¹Because my enemies do not defeat me,
I know you are pleased with me.
¹²Because I am innocent, you support me
and will let me be with you forever.

¹³Praise the LORD, the God of Israel.
He has always been,
and he will always be.
Amen and amen.

GOD'S POWER

Against All Odds

It was June 18, 1940, one of Britain's grimmest historical moments. Nazi Germany had already wiped out the French army—one of the largest in the world—in forty days. Joseph Stalin of Russia had signed a nonaggression pact with Hitler. The United States was still officially neutral in what became World War II. Hitler's air force, the Luftwaffe, was mercilessly pounding London and the English countryside.

Germany had more than eleven hundred fighter planes and fifteen hundred light bombers facing fewer than seven hundred British Spitfires and Hurricanes. Before the Battle of Britain was over, forty-five thousand in London alone were killed or injured.

Sir Winston Churchill—a great leader for Britain during those dark years—was never known as a particularly religious man. But during the darkest hours of the battle, something in him seemed to understand that only God could save his country from the Nazi pounding: "If the Almighty God in his mercy should lighten or shorten our labors and the torment of all mankind, all his servants will be thankful. Let God defend the right; heed the call of duty and honor, and see that our policy and conduct are upon the highest level, and that honor should be our guide."

Against all odds, the British prevailed.

King David also called on God to save him from his enemies. Nowhere is David's cry for help expressed more strongly than in **Psalm 40**.

■ How do you think Churchill would have responded to verses 1 through 3 if he had read them while Germany was bombing London?

■ If you were writing a modern version of Psalm 40, what tough situations from your own life and the world would you include?

C O N S I D E R . . .

■ praying for God's deliverance in what you believe is the world's most pressing crisis.
■ scanning news reports of current world crises and looking for references to dependence on God for help.

F O R   M O R E ,   S E E . . .

■ Exodus 14:5–31 (p. 70)
■ Daniel 6 (p. 813)

■ 2 Peter 1:3–4 (p. 1311)

Book 2

Wishing to Be Near God

For the director of music. A maskil[d]
of the sons of Korah.

42 As a deer thirsts for streams of water,
so I thirst for you, God.
2I thirst for the living God.
When can I go to meet with him?
3Day and night, my tears have been my food.
People are always saying,
"Where is your God?"
4When I remember these things,
I speak with a broken heart.
I used to walk with the crowd
and lead them to God's Temple[d]
with songs of praise.

5Why am I so sad?
Why am I so upset?
I should put my hope in God
and keep praising him,
my Savior and 6my God.

I am very sad.
So I remember you where the Jordan River
begins,
near the peaks of Hermon and Mount Mizar.
7Troubles have come again and again,
sounding like waterfalls.
Your waves are crashing all around me.
8The LORD shows his true love every day.
At night I have a song,
and I pray to my living God.
9I say to God, my Rock,[a]
"Why have you forgotten me?
Why am I sad
and troubled by my enemies?"
10My enemies' insults make me feel
as if my bones were broken.
They are always saying,
"Where is your God?"

11Why am I so sad?
Why am I so upset?
I should put my hope in God
and keep praising him,
my Savior and my God.

A Prayer for Protection

43 God, defend me.
Argue my case against those who
don't follow you.
Save me from liars and those who do evil.
2God, you are my strength.
Why have you rejected me?
Why am I sad
and troubled by my enemies?
3Send me your light and truth
to guide me.

Let them lead me to your holy mountain,
to where you live.
4Then I will go to the altar of God,
to God who is my joy and happiness.
I will praise you with a harp,
God, my God.

5Why am I so sad?
Why am I so upset?
I should put my hope in God
and keep praising him,
my Savior and my God.

A Prayer for Help

For the director of music. A maskil[d]
of the sons of Korah.

44 God, we have heard about you.
Our ancestors told us
what you did in their days,
in days long ago.
2With your power you forced the nations out
of the land
and placed our ancestors here.
You destroyed those other nations,
but you made our ancestors grow strong.
3It wasn't their swords that took the land.
It wasn't their power that gave them
victory.
But it was your great power and strength.
You were with them because you loved
them.

4My God, you are my King.
Your commands led Jacob's people to
victory.
5With your help we pushed back our enemies.
In your name we trampled those who came
against us.
6I don't trust my bow to help me,
and my sword can't save me.
7You saved us from our foes,
and you made our enemies ashamed.
8We will praise God every day;
we will praise your name forever.　　Selah[d]

9But you have rejected us and shamed us.
You don't march with our armies anymore.
10You let our enemies push us back,
and those who hate us have taken our
wealth.
11You gave us away like sheep to be eaten
and have scattered us among the nations.
12You sold your people for nothing
and made no profit on the sale.

13You made us a joke to our neighbors;
those around us laugh and make fun of us.
14You made us a joke to the other nations;
people shake their heads.
15I am always in disgrace,

and I am covered with shame.
[16]My enemy is getting even
with insults and curses.

[17]All these things have happened to us,
but we have not forgotten you
or failed to keep our agreement with you.
[18]Our hearts haven't turned away from you,
and we haven't stopped following you.
[19]But you crushed us in this place where wild
dogs live,
and you covered us with deep darkness.

[20]If we had forgotten our God
or lifted our hands in prayer to foreign
gods,
[21]God would have known,
because he knows what is in our hearts.
[22]But for you we are in danger of death all the
time.
People think we are worth no more than
sheep to be killed.

[23]Wake up, Lord! Why are you sleeping?
Get up! Don't reject us forever.
[24]Why do you hide from us?
Have you forgotten our pain and troubles?

[25]We have been pushed down into the dirt;
we are flat on the ground.
[26]Get up and help us.
Because of your love, save us.

A Song for the King's Wedding

For the director of music. To the tune of "Lilies."
A maskil.[d] A love song of the sons of Korah.

45 Beautiful words fill my mind.
I am speaking of royal things.
My tongue is like the pen of a skilled
writer.

[2]You are more handsome than anyone,
and you are an excellent speaker,
so God has blessed you forever.
[3]Put on your sword, powerful warrior.
Show your glory and majesty.
[4]In your majesty win the victory
for what is true and right.
Your power will do amazing things.
[5]Your sharp arrows will enter
the hearts of the king's enemies.
Nations will be defeated before you.
[6]God, your throne will last forever and ever.
You will rule your kingdom with fairness.
[7]You love right and hate evil,
so God has chosen you from among your
friends;
he has set you apart with much joy.
[8]Your clothes smell like myrrh,[d] aloes,[d] and
cassia.[d]
From palaces of ivory

music comes to make you happy.
[9]Kings' daughters are among your honored
women.
Your bride stands at your right side
wearing gold from Ophir.

> ✳ **SIDELIGHT:** King Solomon
> could have made a giant wedding
> ring for the bride in Psalm 45:9. He received
> thirty-two thousand pounds of gold from the
> Arabian regions of Ophir! (See 1 Kings 9:28,
> p. 314.)

[10]Listen to me, daughter; look and pay
attention.
Forget your people and your father's family.
[11]The king loves your beauty.
Because he is your master, you should obey
him.
[12]People from the city of Tyre have brought a
gift.
Wealthy people will want to meet you.

[13]The princess is very beautiful.
Her gown is woven with gold.
[14]In her beautiful clothes she is brought to the
king.
Her bridesmaids follow behind her,
and they are also brought to him.
[15]They come with happiness and joy;
they enter the king's palace.

[16]You will have sons to replace your fathers.
You will make them rulers through all the
land.
[17]I will make your name famous from now on,
so people will praise you forever and ever.

God Protects His People

For the director of music. By alamoth.[d] A psalm of
the sons of Korah.

46 God is our protection and our
strength.
He always helps in times of trouble.
[2]So we will not be afraid even if the earth
shakes,
or the mountains fall into the sea,
[3]even if the oceans roar and foam,
or the mountains shake at the raging sea.
Selah[d]

[4]There is a river that brings joy to the city of
God,
the holy place where God Most High lives.
[5]God is in that city, and so it will not be
shaken.
God will help her at dawn.

⁶Nations tremble and kingdoms shake.
   God shouts and the earth crumbles.

⁷The Lord All-Powerful is with us;
   the God of Jacob is our defender.   *Selah*

⁸Come and see what the Lord has done,
   the amazing things he has done on the
      earth.
⁹He stops wars everywhere on the earth.
   He breaks all bows and spears
   and burns up the chariots with fire.
¹⁰God says, "Be quiet and know that I am
      God.
   I will be supreme over all the nations;
   I will be supreme in the earth."

¹¹The Lord All-Powerful is with us;
   the God of Jacob is our defender.   *Selah*

God, the King of the World

For the director of music. A psalm
of the sons of Korah.

47 Clap your hands, all you people.
     Shout to God with joy.
²The Lord Most High is wonderful.
   He is the great King over all the earth!
³He defeated nations for us
   and put them under our control.
⁴He chose the land we would inherit.
   We are the children of Jacob, whom he
      loved.   *Selah*ᵈ

⁵God has risen with a shout of joy;
   the Lord has risen as the trumpets
      sounded.
⁶Sing praises to God. Sing praises.
   Sing praises to our King. Sing praises.
⁷God is King of all the earth,
   so sing a song of praise to him.
⁸God is King over the nations.
   God sits on his holy throne.
⁹The leaders of the nations meet
   with the people of the God of Abraham,
   because the leaders of the earth belong to
      God.
   He is supreme.

Jerusalem, the City of God

A psalm of the sons of Korah.

48 The Lord is great; he should be
     praised
   in the city of our God, on his holy
      mountain.
²It is high and beautiful
   and brings joy to the whole world.
Mount Zionᵈ is like the high mountains of
      the north;
   it is the city of the Great King.

³God is within its palaces;
   he is known as its defender.
⁴Kings joined together
   and came to attack the city.
⁵But when they saw it, they were amazed.
   They ran away in fear.
⁶Fear took hold of them;
   they hurt like a woman having a baby.
⁷You destroyed the large trading ships
   with an east wind.

⁸First we heard
   and now we have seen
   that God will always keep his city safe.
   It is the city of the Lord All-Powerful,
   the city of our God.   *Selah*ᵈ

⁹God, we come into your Templeᵈ
   to think about your love.
¹⁰God, your name is known everywhere;
   all over the earth people praise you.
   Your right hand is full of goodness.
¹¹Mount Zion is happy
   and all the towns of Judah rejoice,
   because your decisions are fair.

¹²Walk around Jerusalem
   and count its towers.
¹³Notice how strong they are.
   Look at the palaces.
   Then you can tell your children about
      them.
¹⁴This God is our God forever and ever.
   He will guide us from now on.

Trusting Money Is Foolish

For the director of music. A psalm
of the sons of Korah.

49 Listen to this, all you nations;
     listen, all you who live on earth.
²Listen, both great and small,
   rich and poor together.
³What I say is wise,
   and my heart speaks with understanding.
⁴I will pay attention to a wise saying;
   I will explain my riddle on the harp.

⁵Why should I be afraid of bad days?
   Why should I fear when evil men surround
      me?
⁶They trust in their money
   and brag about their riches.
⁷No one can buy back the life of another.
   No one can pay God for his own life,
⁸because the price of a life is high.
   No payment is ever enough.
⁹Do people live forever?
   Don't they all face death?

¹⁰See, even wise people die.
   Fools and stupid people also die

and leave their wealth to others.
[11]Their graves will always be their homes.
They will live there from now on,
even though they named places after
themselves.
[12]Even rich people do not live forever;
like the animals, people die.

[13]This is what will happen to those who trust
in themselves
and to their followers who believe them.
Selah[d]
[14]Like sheep, they must die,

and death will be their shepherd.
Honest people will rule over them in the
morning,
and their bodies will rot in a grave far from
home.
[15]But God will save my life
and will take me from the grave.　　Selah

[16]Don't be afraid of rich people
because their houses are more beautiful.
[17]They don't take anything to the grave;
their wealth won't go down with
them.

WORSHIP

Clapping, Shouting, Singing

"Okay, then, it's a date," Mike Frazier said over the phone. "I'll meet you guys at the church at 6:00."

Five guys from Mike's youth group had wanted to go to a Christian rock concert in the Chicago area. All five were enthusiastic Christians and diehard rock 'n' roll fanatics. As their youth minister, Mike encouraged their interest and offered to take them.

The night was going to be super. Great friends. A Christian band that played great music. Nothing could spoil the plans for the evening. Except . . .

One of the guys, Tony Murelli, showed up with his dad, Bart, who didn't attend church. That made Mike nervous.

"What are you up to tonight?" Mike asked Bart.

"I decided to come to the concert," he responded.

Gulp. Tony's dad looked like he would be more comfortable watching a Lawrence Welk rerun. Mike wondered how Bart's attitude toward his son being a part of a church group would be affected by a high-decibel concert.

Mike didn't enjoy the concert nearly as much as he thought he would. He was too busy trying to watch everyone's reactions.

The guys? They loved it. They never sat down. They praised God all evening—stomping their feet, clapping their hands, and singing.

Tony's dad? Hard to tell. That is, until after the concert when, with his ears still ringing, Mike heard these amazing words:

"Frankly, Mike, I've wondered what Tony has been getting into, with all the time he spends at your church. I wanted to see one of your activities for myself."

Uh, oh.

"And I want you to know I've never been as impressed with a group of young people as I was tonight. That band, the kids, the way they expressed themselves—you can tell they really believe in something good."

What Bart observed was a group of Christians following the advice of the psalmist in **Psalm 47**. Read about how you too should lift praise to God.

■ If Tony's dad were to read Psalm 47, what insight might he gain about his son's attitude toward God?

■ What can you start doing in your time alone with God to follow the psalmist's call to "clap your hands," "shout to God with joy," and "sing praises"?

C O N S I D E R . . .

■ asking other Christians whom you respect how they build worship into their lives.
■ finding Christian tapes you can use in your devotion times to help you joyfully worship God.

F O R　M O R E ,　S E E . . .
■ 1 Chronicles 16:7–36 (p. 374)
■ Isaiah 6:1–4 (p. 622)
■ Revelation 7:9–17 (p. 1337)

18Even though they were praised when they
were alive—
and people may praise you when you
succeed—
19they will go to where their ancestors are.
They will never see light again.
20Rich people with no understanding
are just like animals that die.

God Wants True Worship

A psalm of Asaph.

50 The God of gods, the LORD, speaks.
He calls the earth from the rising to
the setting sun.
2God shines from Jerusalem,
whose beauty is perfect.
3Our God comes, and he will not be silent.
A fire burns in front of him,
and a powerful storm surrounds him.
4He calls to the sky above and to the earth
that he might judge his people.
5He says, "Gather around, you who worship
me,
who have made an agreement with me,
using a sacrifice."
6God is the judge,
and even the skies say he is right.   *Selah*ᵈ

7God says, "My people, listen to me;
Israel, I will testify against you.
I am God, your God.
8I do not scold you for your sacrifices.
You always bring me your burnt offerings.
9But I do not need bulls from your stalls
or goats from your pens,
10because every animal of the forest is already
mine.
The cattle on a thousand hills are mine.
11I know every bird on the mountains,
and every living thing in the fields is mine.
12If I were hungry, I would not tell you,
because the earth and everything in it are
mine.
13I don't eat the meat of bulls
or drink the blood of goats.
14Give an offering to show thanks to God.
Give God Most High what you have
promised.
15Call to me in times of trouble.
I will save you, and you will honor me."

16But God says to the wicked,
"Why do you talk about my laws?
Why do you mention my agreement?
17You hate my teachings
and turn your back on what I say.
18When you see a thief, you join him.
You take part in adultery.ᵈ

19You don't stop your mouth from speaking
evil,
and your tongue makes up lies.
20You speak against your brother
and lie about your mother's son.
21I have kept quiet while you did these things,
so you thought I was just like you.
But I will scold you
and accuse you to your face.
22"Think about this, you who forget God.
Otherwise, I will tear you apart,
and no one will save you.
23Those people honor me
who bring me offerings to show thanks.
And I, God, will save those who do that."

A Prayer for Forgiveness

For the director of music. A psalm of David when the
prophetᵈ Nathan came to David after David's
sin with Bathsheba.

51 God, be merciful to me
because you are loving.
Because you are always ready to be merciful,
wipe out all my wrongs.
2Wash away all my guilt
and make me clean again.

3I know about my wrongs,
and I can't forget my sin.
4You are the only one I have sinned against;
I have done what you say is wrong.
You are right when you speak
and fair when you judge.
5I was brought into this world in sin.
In sin my mother gave birth to me.

6You want me to be completely truthful,
so teach me wisdom.
7Take away my sin, and I will be clean.
Wash me, and I will be whiter than snow.
8Make me hear sounds of joy and gladness;
let the bones you crushed be happy again.
9Turn your face from my sins
and wipe out all my guilt.

10Create in me a pure heart, God,
and make my spirit right again.
11Do not send me away from you
or take your Holy Spiritᵈ away from me.
12Give me back the joy of your salvation.
Keep me strong by giving me a willing
spirit.
13Then I will teach your ways to those who do
wrong,
and sinners will turn back to you.

14God, save me from the guilt of murder,
God of my salvation,
and I will sing about your goodness.

¹⁵Lord, let me speak
  so I may praise you.
¹⁶You are not pleased by sacrifices, or I would
  give them.
  You don't want burnt offerings.
¹⁷The sacrifice God wants is a broken spirit.
  God, you will not reject a heart that is
  broken and sorry for sin.

¹⁸Do whatever good you wish for Jerusalem.
  Rebuild the walls of Jerusalem.
¹⁹Then you will be pleased with right sacrifices
  and whole burnt offerings,
  and bulls will be offered on your altar.

God Will Punish the Proud

For the director of music. A maskil^d of David. When
Doeg the Edomite came to Saul and said to him,
"David is in Ahimelech's house."

52 Mighty warrior, why do you brag
  about the evil you do?
  God's love will continue forever.
²You think up evil plans.
  Your tongue is like a sharp razor,
  making up lies.
³You love wrong more than right
  and lies more than truth.   *Selah*^{d}

SEXUALITY

Whiter Than Snow

Kimberly Johnson didn't understand what was happening to her.

She stood in church while the minister led the congregation in a benediction. But Kimberly felt weird. Her heart was racing, her eyes were welling up with tears. All she could think of was kneeling right there on the floor and asking God to help her.

One of the youth workers, Jan, noticed that Kimberly looked upset and approached her after the service.

"What's the matter, Kim?" Jan asked. But Kimberly started to cry and couldn't answer. Jan took her by the arm and led her to a corner, where they sat down together.

After a few minutes, Kimberly could finally talk.

"God could never love me," Kimberly said. "I've done too much to hurt him. I'm not worth it."

"Why do you think God doesn't love you?" Jan asked.

With more tears, Kimberly told Jan how she had been physically and sexually abused by an uncle when she was nine. At age thirteen she was sexually active with numerous guys and often dated guys four and five years older than she was.

"It's almost as if the last five years have been a bad dream and tonight somebody woke me up," she said.

"God does love you, Kimberly," Jan said confidently. "I'd like to pray with you for God to show you the special love he has for you."

As Kimberly and Jan prayed, something happened to Kimberly that radically changed her life. She understood the simple message about God's forgiveness, and believed it. Without reservation, she embraced God's healing and cleansing power.

"I came to church feeling like a tramp," she told Jan after they prayed. "But now I feel like God has made me clean again."

Kimberly grasped what David also understood when he prayed: "Take away my sin, and I will be clean. Wash me, and I will be whiter than snow." Read the rest of David's prayer for forgiveness in **Psalm 51**.

■ According to this psalm, what else does Kimberly need for God to do in her life? (See especially verses 10, 12.)

■ What verse from Psalm 51 best expresses your desire for God to forgive you for your sin—sexual or otherwise?

 C O N S I D E R . . . .

■ praying that God will give you the strength to stay away from sexual sin.
■ writing a verse from Psalm 51 on paper and keeping it with you as a reminder that God has forgiven you and can keep you from sin in the days ahead.

 F O R   M O R E ,   S E E . . .

■ 2 Samuel 11—12:14 (p. 283)
■ John 8:1–11 (p. 1070)

■ 1 Corinthians 6:12–20 (p. 1174)

⁴You love words that bite
and tongues that lie.

⁵But God will ruin you forever.
He will grab you and throw you out of
your tent;
he will tear you away from the land of the
living.   *Selah*
⁶Those who do right will see this and fear
God.
They will laugh at you and say,
⁷"Look what happened to the man
who did not depend on God
but depended on his money.
He grew strong by his evil plans."

⁸But I am like an olive tree
growing in God's Temple.*d*
I trust God's love
forever and ever.
⁹God, I will thank you forever for what you
have done.
With those who worship you, I will trust
you because you are good.

The Unbelieving Fool

For the director of music. By mahalath.*d*
A maskil*d* of David.

53 Fools say to themselves,
"There is no God."
Fools are evil and do terrible things;
none of them does anything good.

²God looked down from heaven on all
people
to see if anyone was wise,
if anyone was looking to God for
help.
³But all have turned away.
Together, everyone has become
evil;
none of them does anything good.
Not a single person.

⁴Don't the wicked understand?
They destroy my people as if they were
eating bread.
They do not ask God for help.
⁵The wicked are filled with terror
where there had been nothing to fear.
God will scatter the bones of your
enemies.
You will defeat them,
because God has rejected them.

⁶I pray that victory will come to Israel from
Mount Zion!*d*
May God bring them back.
Then the people of Jacob will rejoice,
and the people of Israel will be glad.

A Prayer for Help

For the director of music. With stringed instruments. A
maskil*d* of David when the Ziphites went to Saul and
said, "We think David is hiding among our people."

54 God, save me because of who you are.
By your strength show that I am
innocent.

SIDELIGHT: Feeling down?
Then praise God! That's the attitude of
even the saddest psalms, which are called
"laments." These laments (such as Psalms
54—61) show individuals and the nation of
Israel praying in times of crisis. Of all the
types of psalms, the lament is most common.

---

²Hear my prayer, God;
listen to what I say.
³Strangers turn against me,
and cruel men want to kill me.
They do not care about God.   *Selah*d

⁴See, God will help me;
the Lord will support me.
⁵Let my enemies be punished with their own
evil.
Destroy them because you are loyal to me.

⁶I will offer a sacrifice as a special gift to you.
I will thank you, Lord, because you are
good.
⁷You have saved me from all my troubles,
and I have seen my enemies defeated.

A Prayer About a False Friend

For the director of music. With stringed instruments.
A maskil*d* of David.

55 God, listen to my prayer
and do not ignore my cry for help.
²Pay attention to me and answer me.
I am troubled and upset
³by what the enemy says
and how the wicked look at me.
They bring troubles down on me,
and in anger they attack me.

⁴I am frightened inside;
the terror of death has attacked me.
⁵I am scared and shaking,
and terror grips me.
⁶I said, "I wish I had wings like a dove.
Then I would fly away and rest.
⁷I would wander far away
and stay in the desert.   *Selah*d
⁸I would hurry to my place of escape,
far away from the wind and storm."

9Lord, destroy and confuse their words,
  because I see violence and fighting in the
    city.
10Day and night they are all around its walls,
  and evil and trouble are everywhere
    inside.
11Destruction is everywhere in the city;
  trouble and lying never leave its streets.

12It was not an enemy insulting me.
  I could stand that.
 It was not someone who hated me.
  I could hide from him.
13But it is you, a person like me,
  my companion and good friend.
14We had a good friendship
  and walked together to God's Temple.d

15Let death take away my enemies.
  Let them die while they are still young
  because evil lives with them.
16But I will call to God for help,
  and the LORD will save me.
17Morning, noon, and night I am troubled and
    upset,
  but he will listen to me.
18Many are against me,
  but he keeps me safe in battle.
19God who lives forever

will hear me and punish them.   *Selah*
 But they will not change;
  they do not fear God.

20The one who was my friend attacks his
    friends
  and breaks his promises.
21His words are slippery like butter,
  but war is in his heart.
 His words are smoother than oil,
  but they cut like knives.

22Give your worries to the LORD,
  and he will take care of you.
 He will never let good people down.
23But, God, you will bring down
  the wicked to the grave.
 Murderers and liars will live
  only half a lifetime.
 But I will trust in you.

Trusting God for Help

For the director of music. To the tune of "The Dove in
the Distant Oak." A miktam*d* of David when the
Philistines captured him in Gath.

56 God, be merciful to me because
     people are chasing me;
  the battle has pressed me all day long.

FRIENDS

Betrayed

Gail Miller and Breck Peterson had been going out for well over a year. Deep down, Breck hoped that someday, probably after college, they would get married. But, just days before the beginning of their senior year in high school, Gail broke up with him.

Breck struggled to cope with the loss. His mind whirled as he tried to think of what to say and how to get Gail to change her mind.

Breck's best friend, Rick Leo, knew Breck was having a hard time, but Rick asked Gail out himself. Gail and Rick dated off and on for several months. They never really hit it off, and things ended quietly.

Breck's friendship with Rick, on the other hand, was ripped apart like a ship in a raging storm. Breck had never felt so betrayed. He found it hard to talk to Rick because every conversation reminded him of Gail—and Rick's betrayal.

Like Breck, many people know how it hurts to be betrayed by a friend.
Read **Psalm 55** to discover David's anguish over a friend who betrayed him.
■ Why was betrayal by a friend so hard for Breck and David to take?
■ How can David's advice in verse 22 help you when you feel betrayed by a friend?

C O N S I D E R . . .
■ asking God for forgiveness if you've betrayed a friend, or asking God to help you forgive a friend who's betrayed you.
■ trying to reconcile a relationship that has been ruined by betrayal, by having a heart-to-heart talk.

F O R   M O R E ,   S E E . . .
■ I Samuel 20 (p. 263)
■ Proverbs 17:9 (p. 582)
■ John 15:12–17 (p. 1085)

²My enemies have chased me all day;
  there are many proud people fighting me.
³When I am afraid,
  I will trust you.
⁴I praise God for his word.
  I trust God, so I am not afraid.
  What can human beings do to me?

⁵All day long they twist my words;
  all their evil plans are against me.
⁶They wait. They hide.
  They watch my steps,
  hoping to kill me.
⁷God, do not let them escape;
  punish the foreign nations in your anger.
⁸You have recorded my troubles.
  You have kept a list of my tears.
  Aren't they in your records?

⁹On the day I call for help, my enemies will
    be defeated.
  I know that God is on my side.
¹⁰I praise God for his word to me;
  I praise the LORD for his word.
¹¹I trust in God. I will not be afraid.
  What can people do to me?

¹²God, I must keep my promises to you.
  I will give you my offerings to thank you,
¹³because you have saved me from death.
  You have kept me from being defeated.
So I will walk with God
  in light among the living.

A Prayer in Troubled Times

For the director of music. To the tune of "Do Not
Destroy." A miktam*d* of David when he escaped from
Saul in the cave.

57 Be merciful to me, God; be merciful
      to me
because I come to you for protection.
Let me hide under the shadow of your wings
  until the trouble has passed.

²I cry out to God Most High,
  to the God who does everything for me.
³He sends help from heaven and saves me.
  He punishes those who chase me.   *Selah*d
  God sends me his love and truth.

⁴Enemies, like lions, are all around me;
  I must lie down among them.
Their teeth are like spears and arrows,
  their tongues as sharp as swords.

⁵God is supreme over the skies;
  his majesty covers the earth.

⁶They set a trap for me.
  I am very worried.
They dug a pit in my path,
  but they fell into it themselves.   *Selah*

⁷My heart is steady, God; my heart is steady.
  I will sing and praise you.
⁸Wake up, my soul.
  Wake up, harp and lyre!d
  I will wake up the dawn.
⁹Lord, I will praise you among the nations;
  I will sing songs of praise about you to all
    the nations.
¹⁰Your great love reaches to the skies,
  your truth to the clouds.
¹¹God, you are supreme above the skies.
  Let your glory be over all the earth.

Unfair Judges

For the director of music. To the tune of "Do Not
Destroy." A miktam*d* of David.

58 Do you rulers really say what is right?
      Do you judge people fairly?
²No, in your heart you plan evil;
  you think up violent crimes in the land.
³From birth, evil people turn away from God;
  they wander off and tell lies as soon as they
    are born.
⁴They are like poisonous snakes,
  like deaf cobras that stop up their ears
⁵so they cannot hear the music of the snake
    charmer
  no matter how well he plays.

⁶God, break the teeth in their mouths!
  Tear out the fangs of those lions, LORD!
⁷Let them disappear like water that flows
    away.
  Let them be cut short like a broken arrow.
⁸Let them be like snails that melt as they
    move.
  Let them be like a child born dead who
    never saw the sun.
⁹His anger will blow them away alive
  faster than burning thorns can heat a pot.
¹⁰Good people will be glad when they see him
    get even.
  They will wash their feet in the blood of
    the wicked.
¹¹Then people will say,
  "There really are rewards for doing what is
    right.
  There really is a God who judges the
    world."

A Prayer for Protection

For the director of music. To the tune of "Do Not
Destroy." A miktam*d* of David when Saul sent men to
watch David's house to kill him.

59 God, save me from my enemies.
      Protect me from those who come
against me.

²Save me from those who do evil
and from murderers.

³Look, men are waiting to ambush
me.
Cruel men attack me,
but I have not sinned or done wrong,
LORD.
⁴I have done nothing wrong, but they are
ready to attack me.
Wake up to help me, and look.
⁵You are the LORD God All-Powerful, the God
of Israel.
Arise and punish those people.
Do not give those traitors any mercy. *Selah*ᵈ

⁶They come back at night.
Like dogs they growl and roam around the
city.
⁷Notice what comes from their mouths.
Insults come from their lips,
because they say, "Who's listening?"
⁸But, LORD, you laugh at them;
you make fun of all of them.

⁹God, my strength, I am looking to you,
because God is my defender.
¹⁰My God loves me, and he goes in front of
me.
He will help me defeat my enemies.
¹¹Lord, our protector, do not kill them, or my
people will forget.
With your power scatter them and defeat
them.
¹²They sin by what they say;
they sin with their words.
They curse and tell lies,
so let their pride trap them.
¹³Destroy them in your anger;
destroy them completely!
Then they will know
that God rules over Israel
and to the ends of the earth. *Selah*

¹⁴They come back at night.
Like dogs they growl
and roam around the city.
¹⁵They wander about looking for food,
and they howl if they do not find
enough.
¹⁶But I will sing about your strength.
In the morning I will sing about your
love.
You are my defender,
my place of safety in times of trouble.
¹⁷God, my strength, I will sing praises to
you.
God, my defender, you are the God who
loves me.

A Prayer After a Defeat

For the director of music. To the tune of "Lily of the
Agreement." A miktamᵈ of David. For teaching. When
David fought the Arameans of Northwest Mesopotamia
and Zobah, and when Joab returned and defeated
twelve thousand Edomites at the Valley of Salt.

60 God, you have rejected us and
scattered us.
You have been angry, but please come back
to us.
²You made the earth shake and crack.
Heal its breaks because it is shaking.
³You have given your people trouble.
You made us unable to walk straight, like
people drunk with wine.
⁴You have raised a banner to gather those
who fear you.
Now they can stand up against the enemy.
*Selah*ᵈ
⁵Answer us and save us by your power
so the people you love will be rescued.

⁶God has said from his Temple,ᵈ
"When I win, I will divide Shechem
and measure off the Valley of Succoth.
⁷Gilead and Manasseh are mine.
Ephraim is like my helmet.
Judah holds my royal scepter.ᵈ
⁸Moab is like my washbowl.
I throw my sandals at Edom.
I shout at Philistia."

⁹Who will bring me to the strong, walled city?
Who will lead me to Edom?
¹⁰God, surely you have rejected us;
you do not go out with our armies.
¹¹Help us fight the enemy.
Human help is useless,
¹²but we can win with God's help.
He will defeat our enemies.

A Prayer for Protection

For the director of music. With stringed instruments.
Of David.

61 God, hear my cry;
listen to my prayer.
²I call to you from the ends of the earth
when I am afraid.
Carry me away to a high mountain.
³You have been my protection,
like a strong tower against my enemies.

⁴Let me live in your Holy Tentᵈ forever.
Let me find safety in the shelter of your
wings. *Selah*ᵈ
⁵God, you have heard my promises.
You have given me what belongs to those
who fear you.
⁶Give the king a long life;

let him live many years.
⁷Let him rule in the presence of God forever.
Protect him with your love and truth.
⁸Then I will praise your name forever,
and every day I will keep my promises.

Trust Only in God

For the director of music. For Jeduthun.
A psalm of David.

62 I find rest in God;
only he can save me.
²He is my rock and my salvation.
He is my defender;
I will not be defeated.
³How long will you attack someone?
Will all of you kill that person?
Who is like a leaning wall, like a fence
ready to fall?
⁴They are planning to make that person fall.
They enjoy telling lies.
With their mouths they bless,
but in their hearts they curse.   *Selah*ᵈ

⁵I find rest in God;
only he gives me hope.
⁶He is my rock and my salvation.
He is my defender;
I will not be defeated.
⁷My honor and salvation come from God.
He is my mighty rock and my protection.

⁸People, trust God all the time.
Tell him all your problems,
because God is our protection.   *Selah*

⁹The least of people are only a breath,
and even the greatest are just a lie.
On the scales, they weigh nothing;
together they are only a breath.
¹⁰Do not trust in force.
Stealing is of no use.
Even if you gain more riches,
don't put your trust in them.

¹¹God has said this,
and I have heard it over and over:
God is strong.

WORRYING

Geronimo-o-o-o!

Seven friends made plans to drive to the small municipal airport in southern Indiana. But only Larry Cramer and Pete Sanchez ended up going. As they drove to the terminal, Larry joked about the "chickens" who didn't show up. The two of them were calm, cool, and confident about their first experience with sky diving.

For two and a half hours that morning they learned about taking that first jump from an airplane. As Pete and Larry listened to the instructor, it got tougher and tougher to stay calm, cool, and confident. They heard about every potential jump catastrophe imaginable. By the time they finished their tumbling drills and headed for the little Cessna 150, Pete was worried. Real worried.

"The flight master warned us not to look down," he says. "I did anyway. Farm houses look tiny at three thousand feet. Yes, I was worried. I had planned to shout 'Geronimo-o-o-o' when I jumped, but I could barely talk. The worst moment was leaning forward from the plane to position my foot on the wing brace.

"But when the flight master yelled to jump, I jumped. And seconds later, all my worry was replaced by an unbelievable calm as my chute opened and I slowly floated three thousand feet to the ground."

David had a fail-proof "parachute" to rescue him from the worries he faced. He describes his "parachute" in **Psalm 62**.
■ How is David's trust in God like a sky diver's trust in a parachute?
■ How would your life change if you replaced the first word of verse 8 with your name and really believed what the psalmist has to say?

C O N S I D E R . . .
■ memorizing a verse from Psalm 62 that will help you cope with worry.
■ listing the things in your life that act as "parachutes" to relieve your worries and praying for God to become your ultimate parachute in life.

F O R   M O R E ,   S E E . . .
■ Proverbs 3:5–6 (p. 570)   ■ Philippians 4:6–8 (p. 1234)
■ Matthew 6:25–34 (p. 918)

¹²The Lord is loving.
You reward people for what they have
done.

Wishing to Be Near God

A psalm of David when he was in the desert of Judah.

63 God, you are my God.
I search for you.
I thirst for you
like someone in a dry, empty land
where there is no water.
²I have seen you in the Temple*d*
and have seen your strength and glory.
³Because your love is better than life,
I will praise you.
⁴I will praise you as long as I live.
I will lift up my hands in prayer to your
name.
⁵I will be content as if I had eaten the best
foods.
My lips will sing, and my mouth will praise
you.

⁶I remember you while I'm lying in bed;
I think about you through the night.
⁷You are my help.
Because of your protection, I sing.
⁸I stay close to you;
you support me with your right hand.

⁹Some people are trying to kill me,
but they will go down to the grave.
¹⁰They will be killed with swords
and eaten by wild dogs.
¹¹But the king will rejoice in his God.
All who make promises in his name will
praise him,
but the mouths of liars will be shut.

A Prayer Against Enemies

For the director of music. A psalm of David.

64 God, listen to my complaint.
I am afraid of my enemies;
protect my life from them.
²Hide me from those who plan wicked
things,
from that gang who does evil.
³They sharpen their tongues like swords
and shoot bitter words like arrows.
⁴From their hiding places they shoot at
innocent people;
they shoot suddenly and are not afraid.
⁵They encourage each other to do wrong.
They talk about setting traps,
thinking no one will see them.
⁶They plan wicked things and say,

"We have a perfect plan."
The mind of human beings is hard to
understand.

⁷But God will shoot them with arrows;
they will suddenly be struck down.
⁸Their own words will be used against
them.
All who see them will shake their
heads.
⁹Then everyone will fear God.
They will tell what God has done,
and they will learn from what he has
done.
¹⁰Good people will be happy in the LORD
and will find protection in him.
Let everyone who is honest praise the
LORD.

A Hymn of Thanksgiving

For the director of music. A psalm of David. A song.

65 God, you will be praised in Jerusalem.
We will keep our promises to you.
²You hear our prayers.
All people will come to you.
³Our guilt overwhelms us,
but you forgive our sins.
⁴Happy are the people you choose
and invite to stay in your court.
We are filled with good things in your house,
your holy Temple.*d*

⁵You answer us in amazing ways,
God our Savior.
People everywhere on the earth
and beyond the sea trust you.
⁶You made the mountains by your strength;
you are dressed in power.
⁷You stopped the roaring seas,
the roaring waves,
and the uproar of the nations.
⁸Even those people at the ends of the earth
fear your miracles.*d*
You are praised from where the sun rises to
where it sets.

⁹You take care of the land and water it;
you make it very fertile.
The rivers of God are full of water.
Grain grows because you make it grow.
¹⁰You send rain to the plowed fields;
you fill the rows with water.
You soften the ground with rain,
and then you bless it with crops.
¹¹You give the year a good harvest,
and you load the wagons with many crops.
¹²The desert is covered with grass
and the hills with happiness.

¹³The pastures are full of flocks,
and the valleys are covered with grain.
Everything shouts and sings for joy.

Praise God for What He Has Done

For the director of music. A song. A psalm.

66 Everything on earth, shout with joy to
God!
²Sing about his glory!
Make his praise glorious!
³Say to God, 'Your works are amazing!
Because your power is great,
your enemies fall before you.
⁴All the earth worships you
and sings praises to you.
They sing praises to your name." *Selah*ᵈ

⁵Come and see what God has done,
the amazing things he has done for
people.
⁶He turned the sea into dry land.
The people crossed the river on foot.
So let us rejoice because of what he did.
⁷He rules forever with his power.
He keeps his eye on the nations,
so people should not turn against him. *Selah*

⁸You people, praise our God;
loudly sing his praise.
⁹He protects our lives
and does not let us be defeated.
¹⁰God, you have tested us;
you have purified us like silver.
¹¹You let us be trapped
and put a heavy load on us.
¹²You let our enemies walk on our heads.
We went through fire and flood,
but you brought us to a place with good
things.

¹³I will come to your Templeᵈ with burnt
offerings.
I will give you what I promised,
¹⁴ things I promised when I was in trouble.
¹⁵I will bring you offerings of fat animals,
and I will offer sheep, bulls, and goats. *Selah*

¹⁶All of you who fear God, come and listen,
and I will tell you what he has done for
me.
¹⁷I cried out to him with my mouth
and praised him with my tongue.
¹⁸If I had known of any sin in my heart,
the Lord would not have listened to me.
¹⁹But God has listened;
he has heard my prayer.
²⁰Praise God,
who did not ignore my prayer
or hold back his love from me.

Everyone Should Praise God

For the director of music. With stringed instruments.
A psalm. A song.

67 God, have mercy on us and bless us
and show us your kindness *Selah*ᵈ
²so the world will learn your ways,
and all nations will learn that you can save.

³God, the people should praise you;
all people should praise you.
⁴The nations should be glad and sing
because you judge people fairly.
You guide all the nations on earth. *Selah*
⁵God, the people should praise you;
all people should praise you.

⁶The land has given its crops.
God, our God, blesses us.
⁷God blesses us
so people all over the earth will fear him.

Praise God Who Saved the Nation

For the director of music. A psalm of David. A song.

68 Let God rise up and scatter his
enemies;
let those who hate him run away from
him.
²Blow them away as smoke
is driven away by the wind.
As wax melts before a fire,
let the wicked be destroyed before God.
³But those who do right should be glad
and should rejoice before God;
they should be happy and glad.

⁴Sing to God; sing praises to his name.
Prepare the way for him
who rides through the desert,
whose name is the LORD.
Rejoice before him.
⁵God is in his holy Temple.ᵈ
He is a father to orphans,
and he defends the widows.

✹ **SIDELIGHT:** Israelite con artists
should have known better than to
bother orphans and widows, two groups of
people who had a special place in God's
heart (Psalm 68:5). Look up the nasty penalty
for cheating the defenseless in Exodus 22:22–
24, p. 81.

---

⁶God gives the lonely a home.
He leads prisoners out with joy,
but those who turn against God will live in
a dry land.

⁷God, you led your people out
  when you marched through the desert.

  *Selah*ᵈ

⁸The ground shook
  and the sky poured down rain
before God, the God of Mount Sinai,
  before God, the God of Israel.
⁹God, you sent much rain;
  you refreshed your tired land.
¹⁰Your people settled there.
  God, in your goodness
  you took care of the poor.

¹¹The Lord gave the command,
  and a great army told the news:
¹²"Kings and their armies run away.
  In camp they divide the wealth taken in
    war.
¹³Those who stayed by the campfires
  will share the riches taken in battle."
¹⁴The Almighty scattered kings
  like snow on Mount Zalmon.

¹⁵The mountains of Bashan are high;
  the mountains of Bashan have many
    peaks.
¹⁶Why do you mountains with many peaks
  look with envy

on the mountain that God chose for his
    home?
  The LORD will live there forever.
¹⁷God comes with millions of chariots;
  the Lord comes from Mount Sinai to his
    holy place.
¹⁸When you went up to the heights,
  you led a parade of captives.
  You received gifts from the people,
  even from those who turned against you.
  And the LORD God will live there.

¹⁹Praise the Lord, God our Savior,
  who helps us every day.   *Selah*
²⁰Our God is a God who saves us;
  the LORD God saves us from death.

²¹God will crush his enemies' heads,
  the hairy skulls of those who continue to
    sin.
²²The Lord said, "I will bring the enemy back
    from Bashan;
  I will bring them back from the depths of
    the sea.
²³Then you can stick your feet in their blood,
  and your dogs can lick their share."

²⁴God, people have seen your victory march;
  God my King marched into the holy place.

LONELINESS

On the Road Again

"Sometimes I think we're Gypsies," Rebekah confesses, describing the way her family has moved seven times in four years. "When your father's in the air force, you get used to it."
  She laughs, but it sounds forced, and she looks away. There's a sadness in her voice, and she seems a little scared.
  "You know, it's not that easy leaving friends and making new ones. When you're new, it helps a lot if people come up and introduce themselves," she says softly. "Or ask you to go to a club or church group meeting with them, or just to get a Coke. Loneliness must be one of the worst feelings in the world."
  Everyone feels lonely sometimes. But, like Rebekah, we all have a home with God no matter how alone we may feel. Read **Psalm 68:1–10** to find God's assurance that he gives the lonely a place to belong.
  ■ How do you think Rebekah would define the word "home" in this psalm?
  ■ When you're feeling lonely, what sort of "home" do you think faith in God's love can help you build?

C O N S I D E R . . .
  ■ organizing a "Welcome Wagon" of kids to greet newcomers to your school or church.
  ■ widening your circle of friends by making a list of talents God has given you, including personality traits, such as a sense of humor or the ability to listen, and using the list to guide you to new clubs and activities.

F O R   M O R E ,   S E E . . .
  ■ Job 19:13–27 (p. 463)
  ■ Matthew 28:18–20 (p. 962)   ■ 2 Timothy 4:16–18 (p. 1268)

²⁵The singers are in front and the instruments
are behind.
In the middle are the girls with the
tambourines.*d*
²⁶Praise God in the meeting place;
praise the LORD in the gathering of Israel.
²⁷There is the smallest tribe,*d* Benjamin, leading
them.
And there are the leaders of Judah with
their group.
There also are the leaders of Zebulun and
of Naphtali.

²⁸God, order up your power;
show the mighty power you have used for
us before.
²⁹Kings will bring their wealth to you,
to your Temple in Jerusalem.
³⁰Punish Egypt, the beast in the tall grass along
the river.
Punish the leaders of nations, those bulls
among the cows.
Defeated, they will bring you their silver.
Scatter those nations that love war.
³¹Messengers will come from Egypt;
the people of Cush will pray to God.

³²Kingdoms of the earth, sing to God;
sing praises to the Lord.   *Selah*
³³Sing to the one who rides through the skies,
which are from long ago.
He speaks with a thundering voice.
³⁴Announce that God is powerful.
He rules over Israel,
and his power is in the skies.
³⁵God, you are wonderful in your Temple.
The God of Israel gives his people strength
and power.

Praise God!

A Cry for Help

For the director of music. To the tune of "Lilies."
A psalm of David.

69 God, save me,
because the water has risen to my
neck.
²I'm sinking down into the mud,
and there is nothing to stand on.
I am in deep water,
and the flood covers me.
³I am tired from calling for help;
my throat is sore.
My eyes are tired from waiting
for God to help me.
⁴There are more people who hate me for no
reason than hairs on my head;
powerful enemies want to destroy me for
no reason.
They make me pay back

what I did not steal.
⁵God, you know what I have done wrong;
I cannot hide my guilt from you.
⁶Lord GOD All-Powerful,
do not let those who hope in you be
ashamed because of me.
God of Israel,
do not let your worshipers be disgraced
because of me.
⁷For you, I carry this shame,
and my face is covered with disgrace.
⁸I am like a stranger to my closest relatives
and a foreigner to my mother's children.
⁹My strong love for your Temple*d* completely
controls me.
When people insult you, it hurts me.
¹⁰When I cry and go without food,
they make fun of me.
¹¹When I wear clothes of sadness,
they joke about me.
¹²They make fun of me in public places,
and the drunkards make up songs about
me.

¹³But I pray to you, LORD, for favor.
God, because of your great love, answer me.
You are truly able to save.
¹⁴Pull me from the mud,
and do not let me sink.
Save me from those who hate me
and from the deep water.
¹⁵Do not let the flood drown me
or the deep water swallow me
or the grave close its mouth over me.
¹⁶LORD, answer me because your love is so
good.
Because of your great kindness, turn to me.
¹⁷Do not hide from me, your servant.
I am in trouble. Hurry to help me!
¹⁸Come near and save me;
rescue me from my enemies.

¹⁹You see my shame and disgrace.
You know all my enemies and what they
have said.
²⁰Insults have broken my heart
and left me weak.
I looked for sympathy, but there was none;
I found no one to comfort me.
²¹They put poison in my food
and gave me vinegar to drink.

²²Let their own feasts cause their ruin;
let their feasts trap them and pay them
back.
²³Let their eyes be closed so they cannot see
and their backs be forever weak from
troubles.
²⁴Pour your anger out on them;
let your anger catch up with them.

25May their place be empty;
  leave no one to live in their tents.
26They chase after those you have hurt,
  and they talk about the pain of those you
    have wounded.
27Charge them with crime after crime,
  and do not let them have anything good.
28Wipe their names from the book of life,
  and do not list them with those who do
    what is right.

29I am sad and hurting.
  God, save me and protect me.

30I will praise God in a song
  and will honor him by giving thanks.
31That will please the LORD more than offering
  him cattle,

more than sacrificing a bull with horns and
    hoofs.
32Poor people will see this and be glad.
  Be encouraged, you who worship
    God.
33The LORD listens to those in need
  and does not look down on captives.

34Heaven and earth should praise him,
  the seas and everything in them.
35God will save Jerusalem
  and rebuild the cities of Judah.
  Then people will live there and own the
    land.
36 The descendantsd of his servants will inherit
    that land,
  and those who love him will live there.

FRIENDS

Everyone Welcome (Almost)

Everybody was surprised when Max Chezik showed up in Sunday school class. Shocked
might be a better word.
  "Somebody guard the collection plate," Jeanie Hackle whispered, and the rest of the
class stifled giggles. Max had been suspended three times for breaking into lockers at
school.
  After announcements, the kids gathered in the sanctuary for group singing. Max lagged
behind in the classroom. When the group returned ten minutes later, the class collection
plate was empty. Every penny of the $6.47 was gone. Max Chezik had even stolen from
God!
  No one said anything, but the kids were obviously angry. What a total jerk, Jeanie
thought. I hope he never shows his face around here again.
  Then after class, something happened that made everyone stop dead in their tracks.
Randy Jenks put his arm across Max's skinny shoulders as he was walking out.
  He said, "Max, we enjoyed having you this morning, and we want you to come back
next week."
  What? Are you crazy, Randy? the kids' looks seemed to say.
  "Thanks," said Max. "I'll try."
  Everyone thought Randy had lost his brain. But the next week, Max came!
And everyone watched as he gave a crumpled ten dollar bill.
  Randy smiled. No one knew if that was Max's own money, or God's with
interest. And no one really seemed to care anymore. He had shown what
was most important—accepting Max as he was without judging him.
  Like Randy, King David knew the dangers of judging people harshly. Read
Psalm 69:6–15 to see how David coped when others judged him.
■ Which verses in this psalm describe Max?
■ Based on this passage, what will you do the next time you're judged
  unfairly? How about the next time you're tempted to judge someone else?

                    C O N S I D E R . . . .
■ making friends with others who are often shunned by the "in" crowd.
■ making a list of all the people you've made negative judgments about and then asking
  God to forgive you.

            F O R   M O R E ,   S E E . . .
■ Leviticus 19:15–18 (p. 116)
■ Matthew 7:1–5 (p. 918)   ■ Romans 2:1–16 (p. 1141)

A Cry for God to Help Quickly

For the director of music. A psalm of David. To help people remember.

70 God, come quickly and save me.
LORD, hurry to help me.
[2]Let those who are trying to kill me
be ashamed and disgraced.
Let those who want to hurt me
run away in disgrace.
[3]Let those who make fun of me
stop because of their shame.
[4]But let all those who worship you
rejoice and be glad.
Let those who love your salvation
always say, "Praise the greatness of God."
[5]I am poor and helpless;
God, hurry to me.
You help me and save me.
LORD, do not wait.

An Old Person's Prayer

71 In you, LORD, is my protection.
Never let me be ashamed.
[2]Because you do what is right, save and
rescue me;
listen to me and save me.
[3]Be my place of safety
where I can always come.
Give the command to save me,
because you are my rock and my strong,
walled city.
[4]My God, save me from the power of the
wicked
and from the hold of evil and cruel people.
[5]LORD, you are my hope.
LORD, I have trusted you since I was
young.
[6]I have depended on you since I was born;
you helped me even on the day of my
birth.
I will always praise you.

[7]I am an example to many people,
because you are my strong protection.
[8]I am always praising you;
all day long I honor you.
[9]Do not reject me when I am old;
do not leave me when my strength is gone.
[10]My enemies make plans against me,
and they meet together to kill me.
[11]They say, "God has left him.
Go after him and take him,
because no one will save him."

[12]God, don't be far off.
My God, hurry to help me.
[13]Let those who accuse me
be ashamed and destroyed.
Let those who are trying to hurt me

be covered with shame and disgrace.
[14]But I will always have hope
and will praise you more and more.
[15]I will tell how you do what is right.
I will tell about your salvation all day long,
even though it is more than I can tell.
[16]I will come and tell about your powerful
works, Lord GOD.
I will remind people that only you do what
is right.

[17]God, you have taught me since I was young.
To this day I tell about the miracles[d] you
do.
[18]Even though I am old and gray,
do not leave me, God.
I will tell the children about your power;
I will tell those who live after me about
your might.

[19]God, your justice reaches to the skies.
You have done great things;
God, there is no one like you.
[20]You have given me many troubles and bad
times,
but you will give me life again.
When I am almost dead,
you will keep me alive.
[21]You will make me greater than ever,
and you will comfort me again.

[22]I will praise you with the harp.
I trust you, my God.
I will sing to you with the lyre,[d]
Holy One of Israel.
[23]I will shout for joy when I sing praises to
you.
You have saved me.
[24]I will tell about your justice all day long.
And those who want to hurt me
will be ashamed and disgraced.

A Prayer for the King

Of Solomon.

72 God, give the king your good
judgment
and the king's son your goodness.
[2]Help him judge your people fairly
and decide what is right for the poor.
[3]Let there be peace on the mountains
and goodness on the hills for the people.
[4]Help him be fair to the poor
and save the needy
and punish those who hurt them.

[5]May they respect you as long as the sun
shines
and as long as the moon glows.
[6]Let him be like rain on the grass,
like showers that water the earth.

⁷Let goodness be plentiful while he lives.
  Let peace continue as long as there is a
    moon.

⁸Let his kingdom go from sea to sea,
  and from the Euphrates River to the ends
    of the earth.
⁹Let the people of the desert bow down to
    him,
  and make his enemies lick the dust.
¹⁰Let the kings of Tarshish and the faraway
    lands
  bring him gifts.
  Let the kings of Sheba and Seba
  bring their presents to him.
¹¹Let all kings bow down to him
  and all nations serve him.

¹²He will help the poor when they cry out
  and will save the needy when no one else
    will help.
¹³He will be kind to the weak and poor,
  and he will save their lives.
¹⁴He will save them from cruel people who try
    to hurt them,

because their lives are precious to
  him.

¹⁵Long live the king!
  Let him receive gold from Sheba.
  Let people always pray for him
  and bless him all day long.
¹⁶Let the fields grow plenty of grain
  and the hills be covered with crops.
  Let the land be as fertile as Lebanon,
  and let the cities grow like the grass in a
    field.
¹⁷Let the king be famous forever;
  let him be remembered as long as the sun
    shines.
  Let the nations be blessed because of him,
  and may they all bless him.

¹⁸Praise the LORD God, the God of Israel,
  who alone does such miracles.ᵈ
¹⁹Praise his glorious name forever.
  Let his glory fill the whole world.
        Amen and amen.

²⁰This ends the prayers of David son of Jesse.

HUNGER AND POVERTY

One Friend at a Time

When a few of her friends signed up to help at the Springfield community Salvation Army one Saturday, Jill Christy went along grudgingly.

"I figured you couldn't really change things for poor people in our town," she remembers. "It was just too big a problem."

About midday, Jill was straightening the sweater racks when Carolyn Harper came in with her three small children.

"I was really shocked," Jill recalls. "Carolyn seemed to be about my age."

Jill asked Carolyn if she needed any help.

"I need skirts and blouses," Carolyn whispered, sounding embarrassed. "The employment lady says she's found a good job for me that'll get us off welfare. If . . . you know . . . I can . . . well . . . look okay for an office."

Jill's heart ached for Carolyn. She quickly realized Carolyn needed a friend—someone to understand—as much as she needed clothes. Along with skirts, blouses, and shoes, Jill gave a listening ear, a smile and a little of her heart that afternoon.

Jill has never been the same since that encounter. Like the writer of **Psalm 72**, Jill realized the importance of dealing compassionately with people in need.

■ In what ways is Jill doing what the psalmist suggests?
■ The psalmist uses the term "fair." How can you become more fair in your attitudes and actions toward needy people in your community?

        C O N S I D E R . . .
■ setting aside the same amount of money you've spent on "fun" this week and giving that amount to a hunger project.
■ volunteering at a local clothes distribution center or food pantry.

        F O R   M O R E ,   S E E . . .
■ Deuteronomy 14:28–29 (p. 174)
■ Proverbs 14:31 (p. 580)
■ 2 Corinthians 9:6–11 (p. 1201)

Book 3

Should the Wicked Be Rich?

A psalm of Asaph.

73 God is truly good to Israel,
to those who have pure hearts.
²But I had almost stopped believing;
I had almost lost my faith
³because I was jealous of proud people.
I saw wicked people doing well.

⁴They are not suffering;
they are healthy and strong.
⁵They don't have troubles like the rest of us;
they don't have problems like other people.
⁶They wear pride like a necklace
and put on violence as their clothing.
⁷They are looking for profits
and do not control their selfish desires.
⁸They make fun of others and speak evil;
proudly they speak of hurting others.
⁹They brag to the sky.
They say that they own the earth.
¹⁰So their people turn to them
and give them whatever they want.
¹¹They say, "How can God know?
What does God Most High know?"
¹²These people are wicked,
always at ease, and getting richer.
¹³So why have I kept my heart pure?
Why have I kept my hands from doing
wrong?
¹⁴I have suffered all day long;
I have been punished every morning.

¹⁵God, if I had decided to talk like this,
I would have let your people down.
¹⁶I tried to understand all this,
but it was too hard for me to see
¹⁷until I went to the Temple*d* of God.
Then I understood what will happen to
them.
¹⁸You have put them in danger;
you cause them to be destroyed.
¹⁹They are destroyed in a moment;
they are swept away by terrors.
²⁰It will be like waking from a dream.
Lord, when you rise up, they will
disappear.

²¹When my heart was sad
and I was angry,
²²I was senseless and stupid.
I acted like an animal toward you.
²³But I am always with you;
you have held my hand.
²⁴You guide me with your advice,
and later you will receive me in honor.

²⁵I have no one in heaven but you;
I want nothing on earth besides you.
²⁶My body and my mind may become weak,
but God is my strength.
He is mine forever.

²⁷Those who are far from God will die;
you destroy those who are unfaithful.
²⁸But I am close to God, and that is good.
The Lord God is my protection.
I will tell all that you have done.

A Nation in Trouble Prays

*A maskil*d* of Asaph.*

74 God, why have you rejected us for so
long?
Why are you angry with us, the sheep of
your pasture?
²Remember the people you bought long ago.
You saved us, and we are your very own.
After all, you live on Mount Zion.*d*
³Make your way through these old ruins;
the enemy wrecked everything in the
Temple.*d*

⁴Those who were against you shouted in your
meeting place
and raised their flags there.
⁵They came with axes raised
as if to cut down a forest of trees.
⁶They smashed the carved panels
with their axes and hatchets.
⁷They burned your Temple to the ground;
they have made the place where you live
unclean.*d*
⁸They thought, "We will completely crush
them!"
They burned every place where God was
worshiped in the land.
⁹We do not see any signs.
There are no more prophets,
and no one knows how long this will last.
¹⁰God, how much longer will the enemy make
fun of you?
Will they insult you forever?
¹¹Why do you hold back your power?
Bring your power out in the open and
destroy them!

¹²God, you have been our king for a long time.
You bring salvation to the earth.
¹³You split open the sea by your power
and broke the heads of the sea monster.
¹⁴You smashed the heads of the monster
Leviathan*d*
and gave him to the desert creatures as
food.

¹⁵You opened up the springs and streams
and made the flowing rivers run dry.
¹⁶Both the day and the night are yours;
you made the sun and the moon.
¹⁷You set all the limits on the earth;
you created summer and winter.

¹⁸LORD, remember how the enemy insulted
you.
Remember how those foolish people made
fun of you.
¹⁹Do not give us, your doves, to those wild
animals.
Never forget your poor people.
²⁰Remember the agreement you made with us,
because violence fills every dark corner of
this land.
²¹Do not let your suffering people be disgraced.
Let the poor and helpless praise you.

²²God, arise and defend yourself.
Remember the insults that come from those
foolish people all day long.
²³Don't forget what your enemies said;
don't forget their roar as they rise against
you always.

God the Judge

For the director of music. To the tune of "Do Not
Destroy." A psalm of Asaph. A song.

75 God, we thank you;
we thank you because you are near.
We tell about the miracles*d* you do.

²You say, "I set the time for trial,
and I will judge fairly.
³The earth with all its people may shake,
but I am the one who holds it steady.   *Selah*d
⁴I say to those who are proud, 'Don't brag,'
and to the wicked, 'Don't show your
power.
⁵Don't try to use your power against heaven.
Don't be stubborn.' "

⁶No one from the east or the west
or the desert can judge you.
⁷God is the judge;
he judges one person as guilty and another
as innocent.
⁸The LORD holds a cup of anger in his hand;
it is full of wine mixed with spices.
He pours it out even to the last drop,
and the wicked drink it all.

⁹I will tell about this forever;
I will sing praise to the God of Jacob.
¹⁰He will take all power away from the
wicked,
but the power of good people will grow.

The God Who Always Wins

For the director of music. With stringed instruments.
A psalm of Asaph. A song.

76 People in Judah know God;
his fame is great in Israel.
²His Tent*d* is in Jerusalem;
his home is on Mount Zion.*d*
³There God broke the flaming arrows,
the shields, the swords, and the weapons of
war.   *Selah*d

⁴God, how wonderful you are!
You are more splendid than the hills full of
animals.
⁵The brave soldiers were stripped
as they lay asleep in death.
Not one warrior
had the strength to stop it.
⁶God of Jacob, when you spoke strongly,
horses and riders fell dead.
⁷You are feared;
no one can stand against you when you are
angry.
⁸From heaven you gave the decision,
and the earth was afraid and silent.
⁹God, you stood up to judge
and to save the needy people of the earth.
Selah
¹⁰People praise you for your anger against evil.
Those who live through your anger are
stopped from doing more evil.
¹¹Make and keep your promises to the LORD
your God.
From all around, gifts should come to the
God we worship.
¹²God breaks the spirits of great leaders;
the kings on earth fear him.

Remembering God's Help

For the director of music. For Jeduthun.
A psalm of Asaph.

77 I cry out to God;
I call to God, and he will hear me.
²I look for the Lord on the day of trouble.
All night long I reach out my hands,
but I cannot be comforted.
³When I remember God, I become upset;
when I think, I become afraid.   *Selah*d

⁴You keep my eyes from closing.
I am too upset to say anything.
⁵I keep thinking about the old days,
the years of long ago.
⁶At night I remember my songs.
I think and I ask myself:
⁷"Will the Lord reject us forever?
Will he never be kind to us again?
⁸Is his love gone forever?

Has he stopped speaking for all time?
⁹Has God forgotten mercy?
Is he too angry to pity us?"   *Selah*
¹⁰Then I say "This is what makes me sad:
For years the power of God Most High was
with us."

¹¹I remember what the LORD did;
I remember the miracles*d* you did long
ago.
¹²I think about all the things you did
and consider your deeds.

¹³God, your ways are holy.
No god is as great as our God.
¹⁴You are the God who does miracles;
you have shown people your power.
¹⁵By your power you have saved your people,
the descendants*d* of Jacob and Joseph.   *Selah*

¹⁶God, the waters saw you;
they saw you and became afraid;
the deep waters shook with fear.
¹⁷The clouds poured down their rain.
The sky thundered.
Your lightning flashed back and forth like
arrows.
¹⁸Your thunder sounded in the whirlwind.
Lightning lit up the world.
The earth trembled and shook.
¹⁹You made a way through the sea
and paths through the deep waters,
but your footprints were not seen.
²⁰You led your people like a flock
by using Moses and Aaron.

God Saved Israel from Egypt

A maskil*d* of Asaph.

78 My people, listen to my teaching;
listen to what I say.
²I will speak using stories;
I will tell secret things from long ago.
³We have heard them and known them
by what our ancestors have told us.
⁴We will not keep them from our children;
we will tell those who come later
about the praises of the LORD.
We will tell about his power
and the miracles*d* he has done.

⁵The LORD made an agreement with Jacob
and gave the teachings to Israel,
which he commanded our ancestors
to teach to their children.
⁶Then their children would know them,
even their children not yet born.
And they would tell their children.
⁷So they would all trust God
and would not forget what he had done
but would obey his commands.

⁸They would not be like their ancestors
who were stubborn and disobedient.
Their hearts were not loyal to God,
and they were not true to him.

⁹The men of Ephraim had bows for weapons,
but they ran away on the day of battle.
¹⁰They didn't keep their agreement with God
and refused to live by his teachings.
¹¹They forgot what he had done
and the miracles he had shown them.
¹²He did miracles while their ancestors
watched,
in the fields of Zoan in Egypt.
¹³He divided the Red Sea*d* and led them
through.
He made the water stand up like a wall.
¹⁴He led them with a cloud by day
and by the light of a fire by night.
¹⁵He split the rocks in the desert
and gave them more than enough water, as
if from the deep ocean.
¹⁶He brought streams out of the rock
and caused water to flow down like rivers.

¹⁷But the people continued to sin against him;
in the desert they turned against God Most
High.
¹⁸They decided to test God
by asking for the food they wanted.
¹⁹Then they spoke against God,
saying, "Can God prepare food in the
desert?
²⁰When he hit the rock, water poured out
and rivers flowed down.
But can he give us bread also?
Will he provide his people with meat?"
²¹When the LORD heard them, he was very
angry.
His anger was like fire to the people of
Jacob;
his anger grew against the people of Israel.
²²They had not believed God
and had not trusted him to save them.
²³But he gave a command to the clouds above
and opened the doors of heaven.
²⁴He rained manna*d* down on them to eat;
he gave them grain from heaven.
²⁵So they ate the bread of angels.
He sent them all the food they could eat.
²⁶He sent the east wind from heaven
and led the south wind by his power.
²⁷He rained meat on them like dust.
The birds were as many as the sand of the
sea.
²⁸He made the birds fall inside the camp,
all around the tents.
²⁹So the people ate and became very full.
God had given them what they wanted.
³⁰While they were still eating,

and while the food was still in their
mouths,
³¹God became angry with them.
He killed some of the healthiest of them;
he struck down the best young men of
Israel.

³²But they kept on sinning;
they did not believe even with the miracles.
³³So he ended their days without meaning
and their years in terror.
³⁴Anytime he killed them, they would look to
him for help;
they would come back to God and follow
him.
³⁵They would remember that God was their
Rock,ᵈ
that God Most High had saved them.
³⁶But their words were false,
and their tongues lied to him.
³⁷Their hearts were not really loyal to God;
they did not keep his agreement.
³⁸Still God was merciful.
He forgave their sins
and did not destroy them.
Many times he held back his anger
and did not stir up all his anger.
³⁹He remembered that they were only human,
like a wind that blows and does not come
back.

⁴⁰They turned against God so often in the
desert
and grieved him there.
⁴¹Again and again they tested God
and brought pain to the Holy One of Israel.
⁴²They did not remember his power
or the time he saved them from the enemy.
⁴³They forgot the signs he did in Egypt
and his wonders in the fields of Zoan.
⁴⁴He turned their rivers to blood
so no one could drink the water.
⁴⁵He sent flies that bit the people.
He sent frogs that destroyed them.
⁴⁶He gave their crops to grasshoppers
and what they worked for to locusts.ᵈ
⁴⁷He destroyed their vines with hail
and their sycamore trees with sleet.
⁴⁸He killed their animals with hail
and their cattle with lightning.
⁴⁹He showed them his hot anger.
He sent his strong anger against them,
his destroying angels.
⁵⁰He found a way to show his anger.
He did not keep them from dying
but let them die by a terrible disease.
⁵¹God killed all the firstbornᵈ sons in Egypt,
the oldest son of each family of Ham.ⁿ

⁵²But God led his people out like sheep
and he guided them like a flock through
the desert.
⁵³He led them to safety so they had nothing to
fear,
but their enemies drowned in the sea.
⁵⁴So God brought them to his holy land,
to the mountain country he took with his
own power.
⁵⁵He forced out the other nations,
and he had his people inherit the land.
He let the tribesᵈ of Israel settle there in
tents.

⁵⁶But they tested God
and turned against God Most High;
they did not keep his rules.
⁵⁷They turned away and were disloyal just like
their ancestors.
They were like a crooked bow that does
not shoot straight.
⁵⁸They made God angry by building places to
worship gods;
they made him jealous with their idols.
⁵⁹When God heard them, he became very
angry
and rejected the people of Israel completely.
⁶⁰He left his dwelling at Shiloh,
the Tent where he lived among the people.
⁶¹He let the Ark,ᵈ his power, be captured;
he let the Ark, his glory, be taken by
enemies.
⁶²He let his people be killed;
he was very angry with his children.
⁶³The young men died by fire,
and the young women had no one to
marry.
⁶⁴Their priests fell by the sword,
but their widows were not allowed to cry.

⁶⁵Then the Lord got up as if he had been
asleep;
he awoke like a man who had been drunk
with wine.
⁶⁶He struck down his enemies
and disgraced them forever.
⁶⁷But God rejected the family of Joseph;
he did not choose the tribe of Ephraim.
⁶⁸Instead, he chose the tribe of Judah
and Mount Zion,ᵈ which he loves.
⁶⁹And he built his Templeᵈ high like the
mountains.
Like the earth, he built it to last forever.
⁷⁰He chose David to be his servant
and took him from the sheep pens.
⁷¹He brought him from tending the sheep
so he could lead the flock, the people of
Jacob,

Ham The people in Egypt were descendants of Ham, one of Noah's sons. See Genesis 10:6.

his own people, the people of Israel.
72And David led them with an innocent heart
and guided them with skillful hands.

The Nation Cries for Jerusalem

A psalm of Asaph.

79

God, nations have come against your
chosen people.
They have ruined your holy Temple.*d*
They have turned Jerusalem into ruins.
2They have given the bodies of your servants
as food to the wild birds.
They have given the bodies of those who
worship you to the wild animals.
3They have spilled blood like water all around
Jerusalem.
No one was left to bury the dead.
4We are a joke to the other nations;
they laugh and make fun of us.

5Lord, how long will this last?
Will you be angry forever?
How long will your jealousy burn like a
fire?
6Be angry with the nations that do not know
you
and with the kingdoms that do not honor
you.
7They have gobbled up the people of Jacob
and destroyed their land.
8Don't punish us for our past sins.
Show your mercy to us soon,
because we are helpless!
9God our Savior, help us
so people will praise you.
Save us and forgive our sins
so people will honor you.
10Why should the nations say,
"Where is their God?"
Tell the other nations in our presence
that you punish those who kill your
servants.
11Hear the moans of the prisoners.
Use your great power
to save those sentenced to die.

12Repay those around us seven times over
for their insults to you, Lord.
13We are your people, the sheep of your flock.
We will thank you always;
forever and ever we will praise you.

A Prayer to Bring Israel Back

For the director of music. To the tune of "Lilies of the
Agreement." A psalm of Asaph.

80

Shepherd of Israel, listen to us.
You lead the people of Joseph like a
flock.

You sit on your throne between the gold
creatures with wings.
Show your greatness 2to the people of
Ephraim, Benjamin, and Manasseh.
Use your strength,
and come to save us.

3God, take us back.
Show us your kindness so we can be
saved.

4Lord God All-Powerful,
how long will you be angry
at the prayers of your people?
5You have fed your people with tears;
you have made them drink many tears.
6You made those around us fight over us,
and our enemies make fun of us.

7God All-Powerful, take us back.
Show us your kindness so we can be
saved.

8You brought us out of Egypt as if we were a
vine.
You forced out other nations and planted us
in the land.
9You cleared the ground for us.
Like a vine, we took root and filled the
land.
10We covered the mountains with our shade.
We had limbs like the mighty cedar tree.
11Our branches reached the Mediterranean
Sea,
and our shoots went to the Euphrates
River.

12So why did you pull down our walls?
Now everyone who passes by steals from
us.
13Like wild pigs they walk over us;
like wild animals they feed on us.

14God All-Powerful, come back.
Look down from heaven and see.
Take care of us, your vine.
15 You planted this shoot with your own
hands
and strengthened this child.
16Now it is cut down and burned with fire;
you destroyed us by your angry looks.
17With your hand,
strengthen the one you have chosen for
yourself.
18Then we will not turn away from you.
Give us life again, and we will call to you
for help.

19Lord God All-Powerful, take us back.
Show us your kindness so we can be
saved.

A Song for a Holiday

For the director of music. By the gittith.[d]
A psalm of Asaph.

81 Sing for joy to God, our strength;
shout out loud to the God of Jacob.
[2]Begin the music. Play the tambourines.[d]
Play pleasant music on the harps and
lyres.[d]
[3]Blow the trumpet at the time of the New
Moon,[d]
when the moon is full, when our feast
begins.

> ✳ **SIDELIGHT:** The sheep's horn
> was used like a trumpet (Psalm 81:3).
> It is the only ancient instrument mentioned in
> the Bible that's still used in Jewish
> synagogues. It's made by heating and
> shaping the animal's hollow horn.

[4]This is the law for Israel;
it is the command of the God of Jacob.
[5]He gave this rule to the people of Joseph
when they went out of the land of Egypt.

I heard a language I did not know, saying:

[6]"I took the load off their shoulders;
I let them put down their baskets.
[7]When you were in trouble, you called, and I
saved you.
I answered you with thunder.
I tested you at the waters of Meribah. *Selah*[d]
[8]My people, listen. I am warning you.
Israel, please listen to me!
[9]You must not have foreign gods;
you must not worship any false god.
[10]I, the LORD, am your God,
who brought you out of Egypt.
Open your mouth and I will feed
you.

[11]"But my people did not listen to me;
Israel did not want me.
[12]So I let them go their stubborn way
and follow their own advice.
[13]I wish my people would listen to me;
I wish Israel would live my way
[14]Then I would quickly defeat their enemies
and turn my hand against their foes.
[15]Those who hate the LORD would bow before
him.
Their punishment would continue
forever.
[16]But I would give you the finest wheat
and fill you with honey from the
rocks."

CELEBRATING

Shout Out Loud!

Imagine . . .
- ■ Christmas without Christmas carols
- ■ a wedding without the "Wedding March"
- ■ a football game without a band
- ■ Graduation without "Pomp and Circumstance"

Now for a really hard one. Imagine turning a year older without a group of friends and relatives singing "Happy Birthday"!

Pretty dismal, huh?

People have used music to celebrate life's joys for generations, dating all the way back to ancient writings such as the Psalms. **Psalm 81:1–10** calls people to shout and "sing for joy to God, our strength" for God's goodness and gifts.

- ■ Why do you think the psalmist included a variety of methods for celebrating?
- ■ What way of celebrating God do you enjoy most?

CONSIDER . . .
- ■ putting a simple prayer to music and singing it to God.
- ■ learning a new song or joining a music group to find new ways to worship God.

FOR MORE, SEE . . .
- ■ 1 Chronicles 13:6–8 (p. 372)
- ■ Psalm 149 (p. 565)
- ■ Ephesians 5:15–20 (p. 1224)

A Cry for Justice

A psalm of Asaph.

82 God is in charge of the great meeting;
he judges among the "gods."

²He says, "How long will you defend evil
people?
How long will you show greater kindness
to the wicked?   *Selah*[d]

³Defend the weak and the orphans;
defend the rights of the poor and suffering.

⁴Save the weak and helpless;
free them from the power of the wicked.

⁵"You know nothing. You don't understand.
You walk in the dark,
while the world is falling apart.

⁶I said, 'You are "gods."
You are all sons of God Most High.'

⁷But you will die like any other person;
you will fall like all the leaders."

⁸God, come and judge the earth,
because you own all the nations.

A Prayer Against the Enemies

A song. A psalm of Asaph.

83 God, do not keep quiet;
God, do not be silent or still.

²Your enemies are making noises;
those who hate you are getting ready to
attack.

³They are making secret plans against your
people;
they plot against those you love.

⁴They say, "Come, let's destroy them as a
nation.
Then no one will ever remember the name
'Israel.' "

⁵They are united in their plan.
These have made an agreement against
you:

⁶the families of Edom and the Ishmaelites,
Moab and the Hagrites,

⁷the people of Byblos, Ammon, Amalek,
Philistia, and Tyre.

⁸Even Assyria has joined them
to help Ammon and Moab, the
descendants[d] of Lot.   *Selah*[d]

⁹God, do to them what you did to Midian,
what you did to Sisera and Jabin at the
Kishon River.

¹⁰They died at Endor,
and their bodies rotted on the ground.

¹¹Do to their important leaders what you did to
Oreb and Zeeb.
Do to their princes what you did to Zebah
and Zalmunna.

¹²They said, "Let's take for ourselves

the pasturelands that belong to God."

¹³My God, make them like tumbleweed,
like chaff[d] blown away by the wind.

¹⁴Be like a fire that burns a forest
or like flames that blaze through the hills.

¹⁵Chase them with your storm,
and frighten them with your wind.

¹⁶Cover them with shame.
Then people will look for you, LORD.

¹⁷Make them afraid and ashamed forever.
Disgrace them and destroy them.

¹⁸Then they will know that you are the LORD,
that only you are God Most High over all
the earth.

SIDELIGHT: Psalms 84 and 122—among others—were "songs for the road" or pilgrim songs. Three times a year, faithful Jews packed up the family camel and traveled to Jerusalem to celebrate, singing along the way (see Deuteronomy 16:16, p. 175).

Wishing to Be in the Temple

For the director of music. On the gittith.[d] A psalm
of the sons of Korah.

84 LORD All-Powerful,
how lovely is your Temple![d]

²I want more than anything
to be in the courtyards of the LORD's
Temple.
My whole being wants
to be with the living God.

³The sparrows have found a home,
and the swallows have nests.
They raise their young near your altars,
LORD All-Powerful, my King and my God.

⁴Happy are the people who live at your
Temple;
they are always praising you.   *Selah*[d]

⁵Happy are those whose strength comes from
you,
who want to travel to Jerusalem.

⁶As they pass through the Valley of Baca,
they make it like a spring.
The autumn rains fill it with pools of water.

⁷The people get stronger as they go,
and everyone meets with God in Jerusalem.

⁸LORD God All-Powerful, hear my prayer;
God of Jacob, listen to me.   *Selah*

⁹God, look at our shield;
be kind to your appointed king.

¹⁰One day in the courtyards of your Temple is
better

than a thousand days anywhere else.
I would rather be a doorkeeper in the
Temple of my God
than live in the homes of the wicked.
11The LORD God is like a sun and shield;
the LORD gives us kindness and honor.
He does not hold back anything good
from those whose lives are innocent.
12LORD All-Powerful,
happy are the people who trust you!

A Prayer for the Nation

For the director of music. A psalm
of the sons of Korah.

85 LORD, you have been kind to your
land;
you brought back the people of Jacob.
2You forgave the guilt of the people
and covered all their sins. *Selah*[d]
3You stopped all your anger;
you turned back from your strong anger.

4God our Savior, bring us back again.
Stop being angry with us.
5Will you be angry with us forever?
Will you stay angry from now on?
6Won't you give us life again?
Your people would rejoice in you.

7LORD, show us your love,
and save us.

8I will listen to God the LORD.
He has ordered peace for those who
worship him.
Don't let them go back to foolishness.
9God will soon save those who respect him,
and his glory will be seen in our land.
10Love and truth belong to God's people;
goodness and peace will be theirs.
11On earth people will be loyal to God,
and God's goodness will shine down from
heaven.
12The LORD will give his goodness,
and the land will give its crops.
13Goodness will go before God
and prepare the way for him.

A Cry for Help

A prayer of David.

86 LORD, listen to me and answer me.
I am poor and helpless.
2Protect me, because I worship you.
My God, save me, your servant who trusts
in you.
3Lord, have mercy on me,
because I have called to you all day.

WORSHIP

Happy Are Those

Su Ling admits that for years she took her church for granted. "It was a place to meet my friends on Sunday morning. We'd share the back pew and sometimes write notes to each other on the offering envelopes especially when the sermon got boring."

But then Su's grandmother died, and the sadness that settled into Su seemed endless. Grandma had been her best friend—the only person Su felt loved her without reservation. Now, Su felt a hole inside where that wonderful, happy love had been.

"I went to the church alone one night when I couldn't stop crying," Su recalls, "and when I prayed in the empty sanctuary, I felt suddenly calm. I realized God was there, waiting for me. I could tell because I felt surrounded again by the same kind of special love I'd always felt with Grandma. Now, I feel God close to me every time I pray or worship wherever I am."

Su Ling learned the special joy of living in God's presence. The writer of **Psalm 84** knew that same joy. Read about how he yearned to live in God's presence "in the courtyards of the Lord's Temple."

■ To which verses of this psalm might Su Ling relate?
■ What do you experience in your church that helps you worship?

C O N S I D E R . . .

🔥 shocking the pastor by sitting in the front of the sanctuary one Sunday.
■ finding a special time to go into your church to pray quietly, alone with God.

F O R   M O R E ,   S E E . . .

■ 1 Chronicles 16:25–29 (p. 374)   ■ John 4:19–26 (p. 1063)
■ Psalm 132:7–9 (p. 558)

⁴Give happiness to me, your servant,
  because I give my life to you, Lord.
⁵Lord, you are kind and forgiving
  and have great love for those who call to
  you.
⁶LORD, hear my prayer,
  and listen when I ask for mercy.
⁷I call to you in times of trouble,
  because you will answer me.

⁸Lord, there is no god like you
  and no works like yours.
⁹Lord, all the nations you have made
  will come and worship you.
  They will honor you.
¹⁰You are great and you do miracles.ᵈ
  Only you are God.

¹¹LORD, teach me what you want me to do,
  and I will live by your truth.
Teach me to respect you completely.
¹²Lord, my God, I will praise you with all my
  heart,
  and I will honor your name forever.
¹³You have great love for me.
  You have saved me from death.

¹⁴God, proud men are attacking me;
  a gang of cruel men is trying to kill me.
  They do not respect you.
¹⁵But Lord, you are a God who shows mercy
  and is kind.
  You don't become angry quickly.
  You have great love and faithfulness.
¹⁶Turn to me and have mercy.
  Give me, your servant, strength.
  Save me, the son of your female servant.
¹⁷Show me a sign of your goodness.
  When my enemies look, they will be
  ashamed.
  You, LORD, have helped me and comforted
  me.

God Loves Jerusalem

A song. A psalm of the sons of Korah.

87 The LORD built Jerusalem on the holy
mountain.
² He loves its gates
  more than any other place in Israel.
³City of God,
  wonderful things are said about you.   *Selah*ᵈ
⁴God says, "I will put Egypt and Babylonia
  on the list of nations that know me.
People from Philistia, Tyre, and Cush
  will be born there."

⁵They will say about Jerusalem,
  "This one and that one were born there.
  God Most High will strengthen her."

⁶The LORD will keep a list of the nations.
  He will note, "This person was born there."
                                        Selah

⁷They will dance and sing,
  "All good things come from Jerusalem."

A Sad Complaint

A song. A psalm of the sons of Korah. For the director
of music. By the mahalath leannoth.ᵈ A maskilᵈ
of Heman the Ezrahite.

88 LORD, you are the God who saves me.
I cry out to you day and night.
²Receive my prayer,
  and listen to my cry.

³My life is full of troubles,
  and I am nearly dead.
⁴They think I am on the way to my grave.
  I am like a man with no strength.
⁵I have been left as dead,
  like a body lying in a grave
  whom you don't remember anymore,
  cut off from your care.
⁶You have brought me close to death;
  I am almost in the dark place of the dead.
⁷You have been very angry with me;
  all your waves crush me.   *Selah*ᵈ
⁸You have taken my friends away from me
  and have made them hate me.
I am trapped and cannot escape.
⁹ My eyes are weak from crying.
  LORD, I have prayed to you every day;
  I have lifted my hands in prayer to you.

¹⁰Do you show your miraclesᵈ for the dead?
  Do their spirits rise up and praise you?   *Selah*
¹¹Will your love be told in the grave?
  Will your loyalty be told in the place of
  death?
¹²Will your miracles be known in the dark
  grave?
  Will your goodness be known in the land
  of forgetfulness?

¹³But, LORD, I have called out to you for help;
  every morning I pray to you.
¹⁴LORD, why do you reject me?
  Why do you hide from me?
¹⁵I have been weak and dying since I was
  young.
  I suffer from your terrors, and I am
  helpless.
¹⁶You have been angry with me,
  and your terrors have destroyed me.
¹⁷They surround me daily like a flood;
  they are all around me.
¹⁸You have taken away my loved ones and
  friends.
  Darkness is my only friend.

A Song About God's Loyalty

A maskil[d] of Ethan the Ezrahite.

89 I will always sing about the Lord's love;
I will tell of his loyalty from now on.
²I will say, "Your love continues forever;
your loyalty goes on and on like the sky."
³You said, "I made an agreement with the man of my choice;
I made a promise to my servant David.
⁴I told him, 'I will make your family continue forever.
Your kingdom will go on and on.' "   Selah[d]

⁵Lord, the heavens praise you for your miracles[d]
and for your loyalty in the meeting of your holy ones.
⁶Who in heaven is equal to the Lord?
None of the angels is like the Lord.
⁷When the holy ones meet, it is God they fear.
He is more frightening than all who surround him.
⁸Lord God All-Powerful, who is like you?
Lord, you are powerful and completely trustworthy.
⁹You rule the mighty sea
and calm the stormy waves.
¹⁰You crushed the sea monster Rahab;[d]
by your power you scattered your enemies.
¹¹The skies and the earth belong to you.
You made the world and everything in it.
¹²You created the north and the south.
Mount Tabor and Mount Hermon sing for joy at your name.
¹³Your arm has great power.
Your hand is strong; your right hand is lifted up.
¹⁴Your kingdom is built on what is right and fair.
Love and truth are in all you do.

¹⁵Happy are the people who know how to praise you.
Lord, let them live in the light of your presence.
¹⁶In your name they rejoice
and continually praise your goodness.
¹⁷You are their glorious strength,
and in your kindness you honor our king.
¹⁸Our king, our shield, belongs to the Lord,
to the Holy One of Israel.

¹⁹Once, in a vision, you spoke
to those who worship you.
You said, "I have given strength to a warrior;
I have raised up a young man from my people.

²⁰I have found my servant David;
I appointed him by pouring holy oil on him.
²¹I will steady him with my hand
and strengthen him with my arm.
²²No enemy will make him give forced payments,
and wicked people will not defeat him.
²³I will crush his enemies in front of him;
I will defeat those who hate him.
²⁴My loyalty and love will be with him.
Through me he will be strong.
²⁵I will give him power over the sea
and control over the rivers.
²⁶He will say to me, 'You are my father,
my God, the Rock,[d] my Savior.'
²⁷I will make him my firstborn[d] son,
the greatest king on earth.
²⁸My love will watch over him forever,
and my agreement with him will never end.
²⁹I will make his family continue,
and his kingdom will last as long as the skies.

³⁰"If his descendants[d] reject my teachings
and do not follow my laws,
³¹if they ignore my demands
and disobey my commands,
³²then I will punish their sins with a rod
and their wrongs with a whip.
³³But I will not hold back my love from David,
nor will I stop being loyal.
³⁴I will not break my agreement
nor change what I have said.
³⁵I have promised by my holiness,
I will not lie to David.
³⁶His family will go on forever.
His kingdom will last before me like the sun.
³⁷It will continue forever, like the moon,
like a dependable witness in the sky."   Selah

³⁸But now you have refused and rejected your appointed king.
You have been angry with him.
³⁹You have abandoned the agreement with your servant
and thrown his crown to the ground.
⁴⁰You have torn down all his city walls;
you have turned his strong cities into ruins.
⁴¹Everyone who passes by steals from him.
His neighbors insult him.
⁴²You have given strength to his enemies
and have made them all happy.
⁴³You have made his sword useless;
you did not help him stand in battle.
⁴⁴You have kept him from winning
and have thrown his throne to the ground.
⁴⁵You have cut his life short

and covered him with shame.   *Selah*

⁴⁶Lord, how long will this go on?
  Will you ignore us forever?
  How long will your anger burn like a fire?
⁴⁷Remember how short my life is.
  Why did you create us? For nothing?
⁴⁸What person alive will not die?
  Who can escape the grave?   *Selah*

⁴⁹Lord, where is your love from times past,
  which in your loyalty you promised to
    David?
⁵⁰Lord, remember how they insulted your
    servant;
  remember how I have suffered the insults
    of the nations.
⁵¹Lord, remember how your enemies insulted
    you
  and how they insulted your appointed king
    wherever he went.

⁵²Praise the Lord forever!
  Amen and amen.

Book 4

God Is Eternal, and We Are Not

A prayer of Moses, the man of God.

90 Lord, you have been our home
         since the beginning.
²Before the mountains were born
  and before you created the earth and the
    world,
  you are God.
  You have always been, and you will always
    be.

³You turn people back into dust.
  You say, "Go back into dust, human
    beings."
⁴To you, a thousand years
  is like the passing of a day,
  or like a few hours in the night.
⁵While people sleep, you take their lives.
  They are like grass that grows up in the
    morning.
⁶In the morning they are fresh and new,
  but by evening they dry up and die.

⁷We are destroyed by your anger;
  we are terrified by your hot anger.
⁸You have put the evil we have done right in
    front of you;
  you clearly see our secret sins.
⁹All our days pass while you are angry.
  Our years end with a moan.
¹⁰Our lifetime is seventy years
  or, if we are strong, eighty years.
  But the years are full of hard work and pain.

They pass quickly, and then we are gone.

¹¹Who knows the full power of your anger?
  Your anger is as great as our fear of you
    should be.
¹²Teach us how short our lives really are
  so that we may be wise.

¹³Lord, how long before you return
  and show kindness to your servants?
¹⁴Fill us with your love every morning.
  Then we will sing and rejoice all our lives.
¹⁵We have seen years of trouble.
  Now give us as much joy as you gave us
    sorrow.
¹⁶Show your servants the wonderful things you
    do;
  show your greatness to their children.
¹⁷Lord our God, treat us well.
  Give us success in what we do;
  yes, give us success in what we do.

Safe in the Lord

91 Those who go to God Most High for
         safety
  will be protected by the Almighty.
²I will say to the Lord, "You are my place of
    safety and protection.
  You are my God and I trust you."

³God will save you from hidden traps
  and from deadly diseases.
⁴He will cover you with his feathers,
  and under his wings you can hide.
  His truth will be your shield and protection.
⁵You will not fear any danger by night
  or an arrow during the day.
⁶You will not be afraid of diseases that come
    in the dark
  or sickness that strikes at noon.
⁷At your side one thousand people may die,
  or even ten thousand right beside you,
  but you will not be hurt.
⁸You will only watch
  and see the wicked punished.

⁹The Lord is your protection;
  you have made God Most High your place
    of safety.
¹⁰Nothing bad will happen to you;
  no disaster will come to your home.
¹¹He has put his angels in charge of you
  to watch over you wherever you go.
¹²They will catch you in their hands
  so that you will not hit your foot on a rock.
¹³You will walk on lions and cobras;
  you will step on strong lions and snakes.

¹⁴The Lord says, "Whoever loves me, I will
    save.
  I will protect those who know me.

¹⁵They will call to me, and I will answer them.
  I will be with them in trouble;
  I will rescue them and honor them.
¹⁶I will give them a long, full life,
  and they will see how I can save."

Thanksgiving for God's Goodness

A psalm. A song for the Sabbath^d day.

92 It is good to praise you, LORD,
  to sing praises to God Most High.
²It is good to tell of your love in the morning
  and of your loyalty at night.
³It is good to praise you with the ten-stringed
  lyre^d
  and with the soft-sounding harp.

⁴LORD, you have made me happy by what you
    have done;
  I will sing for joy about what your hands
    have done.
⁵LORD, you have done such great things!
  How deep are your thoughts!
⁶Stupid people don't know these things,
  and fools don't understand.
⁷Wicked people grow like the grass.
  Evil people seem to do well,
  but they will be destroyed forever.
⁸But, LORD, you will be honored forever.

⁹LORD, surely your enemies,
  surely your enemies will be destroyed,
  and all who do evil will be scattered.
¹⁰But you have made me as strong as an ox.
  You have poured fine oils on me.
¹¹When I looked, I saw my enemies;
  I heard the cries of those who are against
    me.

¹²But good people will grow like palm trees;
  they will be tall like the cedars of Lebanon.
¹³Like trees planted in the Temple of the LORD,
  they will grow strong in the courtyards of
    our God.
¹⁴When they are old, they will still produce
    fruit;
  they will be healthy and fresh.
¹⁵They will say that the LORD is good.
  He is my Rock,^d and there is no wrong in
    him.

The Majesty of the Lord

93 The LORD is king. He is clothed in
  majesty.
The LORD is clothed in majesty
  and armed with strength.
The world is set,
  and it cannot be moved.
²LORD, your kingdom was set up long ago;
  you are everlasting.

³LORD, the seas raise,
  the seas raise their voice.
  The seas raise up their pounding waves.
⁴The sound of the water is loud;
  the ocean waves are powerful,
  but the LORD above is much greater.

⁵LORD, your laws will stand forever.
  Your Temple^d will be holy forevermore.

God Will Pay Back His Enemies

94 The LORD is a God who punishes.
  God, show your greatness and punish!
²Rise up, Judge of the earth,
  and give the proud what they deserve.
³How long will the wicked be happy?
  How long, LORD?

⁴They are full of proud words;
  those who do evil brag about what they
    have done.
⁵LORD, they crush your people
  and make your children suffer.
⁶They kill widows and foreigners
  and murder orphans.
⁷They say, "The LORD doesn't see;
  the God of Jacob doesn't notice."

⁸You stupid ones among the people, pay
    attention.
  You fools, when will you understand?
⁹Can't the creator of ears hear?
  Can't the maker of eyes see?
¹⁰Won't the one who corrects nations punish
    you?
  Doesn't the teacher of people know
    everything?
¹¹The LORD knows what people think.
  He knows their thoughts are just a puff of
    wind.

¹²LORD, those you correct are happy;
  you teach them from your law.
¹³You give them rest from times of trouble
  until a pit is dug for the wicked.
¹⁴The LORD won't leave his people
  nor give up his children.
¹⁵Judgment will again be fair,
  and all who are honest will follow it.

¹⁶Who will help me fight against the wicked?
  Who will stand with me against those who
    do evil?
¹⁷If the LORD had not helped me,
  I would have died in a minute.
¹⁸I said, "I am about to fall,"
  but, LORD, your love kept me safe.
¹⁹I was very worried,
  but you comforted me and made me happy.

²⁰Crooked leaders cannot be your friends.
  They use the law to cause suffering.

21They join forces against people who do right
and sentence to death the innocent.
22But the LORD is my defender;
my God is the rock of my protection.
23God will pay them back for their sins
and will destroy them for their evil.
The LORD our God will destroy them.

A Call to Praise and Obedience

95 Come, let's sing for joy to the LORD.
Let's shout praises to the Rock*d* who
saves us.
2Let's come to him with thanksgiving.
Let's sing songs to him,
3because the LORD is the great God,
the great King over all gods.
4The deepest places on earth are his,
and the highest mountains belong to him.
5The sea is his because he made it,
and he created the land with his own
hands.

6Come, let's worship him and bow down.
Let's kneel before the LORD who made us,
7because he is our God
and we are the people he takes care of
and the sheep that he tends.

Today listen to what he says:
8 "Do not be stubborn, as your ancestors
were at Meribah,
as they were that day at Massah in the
desert.
9There your ancestors tested me
and tried me even though they saw what I
did.
10I was angry with those people for forty years.
I said, 'They are not loyal to me
and have not understood my ways.'
11I was angry and made a promise,
'They will never enter my rest.' "

Praise for the Lord's Glory

96 Sing to the LORD a new song;
sing to the LORD, all the earth.
2Sing to the LORD and praise his name;
every day tell how he saves us.
3Tell the nations of his glory;
tell all peoples the miracles*d* he does,

4because the LORD is great; he should be
praised at all times.
He should be honored more than all the
gods,
5because all the gods of the nations are only
idols,
but the LORD made the heavens.
6The LORD has glory and majesty;
he has power and beauty in his Temple.*d*

7Praise the LORD, all nations on earth;
praise the LORD's glory and power.
8Praise the glory of the LORD's name.
Bring an offering and come into his Temple
courtyards.
9Worship the LORD because he is holy.
Tremble before him, everyone on earth.
10Tell the nations, "The LORD is king."
The earth is set, and it cannot be moved.
He will judge the people fairly.
11Let the skies rejoice and the earth be glad;
let the sea and everything in it shout.
12 Let the fields and everything in them
rejoice.
Then all the trees of the forest will sing for
joy
13 before the LORD, because he is coming.
He is coming to judge the world;
he will judge the world with fairness
and the peoples with truth.

A Hymn About the Lord's Power

97 The LORD is king. Let the earth
rejoice;
faraway lands should be glad.
2Thick, dark clouds surround him.
His kingdom is built on what is right and
fair.
3A fire goes before him
and burns up his enemies all around.
4His lightning lights up the world;
when the people see it, they tremble.
5The mountains melt like wax before the
LORD,
before the Lord of all the earth.
6The heavens tell about his goodness,
and all the people see his glory.

7Those who worship idols should be ashamed;
they brag about their gods.
All the gods should worship the LORD.
8When Jerusalem hears this, she is glad,
and the towns of Judah rejoice.
They are happy because of your judgments,
LORD.
9You are the LORD Most High over all the
earth;
you are supreme over all gods.

10People who love the LORD hate evil.
The LORD watches over those who follow
him
and frees them from the power of the
wicked.
11Light shines on those who do right;
joy belongs to those who are honest.
12Rejoice in the LORD, you who do right.
Praise his holy name.

The Lord of Power and Justice

A psalm.

98 Sing to the LORD a new song,
because he has done miracles.[d]
By his right hand and holy arm
he has won the victory.
2 The LORD has made known his power to
save;
he has shown the other nations his victory
for his people.
3 He has remembered his love
and his loyalty to the people of Israel.
All the ends of the earth have seen
God's power to save.

4 Shout with joy to the LORD, all the earth;
burst into songs and make music.
5 Make music to the LORD with harps,
with harps and the sound of singing.
6 Blow the trumpets and the sheep's horns;
shout for joy to the LORD the King.

7 Let the sea and everything in it shout;
let the world and everyone in it sing.
8 Let the rivers clap their hands;
let the mountains sing together for joy.
9 Let them sing before the LORD,

because he is coming to judge the world.
He will judge the world fairly;
he will judge the peoples with fairness.

The Lord, the Fair and Holy King

99 The LORD is king.
Let the peoples shake with fear.
He sits between the gold creatures with
wings.
Let the earth shake.
2 The LORD in Jerusalem is great;
he is supreme over all the peoples.
3 Let them praise your name;
it is great, holy and to be feared.

4 The King is powerful and loves justice.
LORD, you made things fair;
you have done what is fair and right
for the people of Jacob.
5 Praise the LORD our God,
and worship at the Temple,[d] his footstool.
He is holy.

6 Moses and Aaron were among his priests,
and Samuel was among his worshipers.
They called to the LORD,
and he answered them.
7 He spoke to them from the pillar of cloud.

EVIL

Taking a Stand

When Ron Daly dozed off during math class, Rose giggled like everybody else. But Ron didn't stir when Ms. Shaster called on him ten minutes later. And he still didn't stir when she shook his shoulder, hard. The class laughter turned to panic and an ambulance was called. He was revived in the hospital several hours later, just barely.

Rose went to the hospital that evening to see how Ron was. He looked exhausted—pale, weak, and depressed—and Rose was amazed at how close Ron had come to death.

"Until I'd seen the effects of a drug overdose up close like that, I just thought of cocaine as a bad habit—gross, sure, but no big deal," Rose says. She got involved the next week in the school's anti-drug campaign.

"Ron's a good friend," Rose adds, "and now I know his habit is evil—a killer! Because I care about Ron, I have to hate his addiction."

"People who love the Lord hate evil," says the writer of **Psalm 97**. Read the passage for more of the psalmist's reflections on evil.

■ Rose decided to take a stand against evil. What does the psalmist say about people who go out of their way to do what's right, like Rose?
■ In what areas of your life do you need to take a stand against evil?

C O N S I D E R . . .
■ writing a definition of "evil" based on Psalm 97 and carrying that definition in your pocket or purse this week to increase your awareness of the evil around you.
✒ talking with an adult friend about an addiction you cannot break.

F O R   M O R E ,   S E E . . .
■ Proverbs 22:1–5, 8 (p. 586)   ■ Colossians 3:1–14 (p. 1241)
■ Isaiah 5 (p. 621)

They kept the rules and laws he gave them.

8Lord our God, you answered them.
  You showed them that you are a forgiving
    God,
  but you punished them for their wrongs.
9Praise the Lord our God,
  and worship at his holy mountain,
  because the Lord our God is holy.

A Call to Praise the Lord

A psalm of thanks.

100 Shout to the Lord, all the earth.
  2 Serve the Lord with joy;
come before him with singing.
3Know that the Lord is God.
  He made us, and we belong to him;
  we are his people, the sheep he tends.

4Come into his city with songs of thanksgiving
  and into his courtyards with songs of praise.
  Thank him and praise his name.
5The Lord is good. His love is forever,
  and his loyalty goes on and on.

A Promise to Rule Well

A psalm of David.

101 I will sing of your love and
  fairness;
Lord, I will sing praises to you.
2I will be careful to live an innocent life.
  When will you come to me?

I will live an innocent life in my house.
3 I will not look at anything wicked.
I hate those who turn against you;
  they will not be found near me.
4Let those who want to do wrong stay away
    from me;
  I will have nothing to do with evil.
5If anyone secretly says things against his
    neighbor,
  I will stop him.
I will not allow people
  to be proud and look down on others.

6I will look for trustworthy people
  so I can live with them in the land.
Only those who live innocent lives
  will be my servants.
7No one who is dishonest will live in my
    house;
  no liars will stay around me.
8Every morning I will destroy the wicked in
    the land.
  I will rid the Lord's city of people who do
    evil.

A Cry for Help

A prayer of a person who is suffering when he is
discouraged and tells the Lord his complaints.

102 Lord, listen to my prayer;
  let my cry for help come to you.
2Do not hide from me
  in my time of trouble.
Pay attention to me.
  When I cry for help, answer me quickly.

3My life is passing away like smoke,
  and my bones are burned up with fire.
4My heart is like grass
  that has been cut and dried.
  I forget to eat.
5Because of my grief,
  my skin hangs on my bones.
6I am like a desert owl,
  like an owl living among the ruins.
7I lie awake.
  I am like a lonely bird on a housetop.
8All day long enemies insult me;
  those who make fun of me use my name as
    a curse.
9I eat ashes for food,
  and my tears fall into my drinks.
10Because of your great anger,
  you have picked me up and thrown me
    away.
11My days are like a passing shadow;
  I am like dried grass.

12But, Lord, you rule forever,
  and your fame goes on and on.
13You will come and have mercy on Jerusalem,
  because the time has now come to be kind
    to her;
  the right time has come.
14Your servants love even her stones;
  they even care about her dust.
15Nations will fear the name of the Lord,
  and all the kings on earth will honor you.

> **SIDELIGHT:** If you repeat
> yourself too much, just tell people
> you're making up Hebrew poetry. One
> characteristic of this poetry—called
> parallelism—was that two consecutive lines
> would each say essentially the same thing in
> a different way. (For example, see Psalm
> 101:7.)

16The Lord will rebuild Jerusalem;
  there his glory will be seen.
17He will answer the prayers of the needy;
  he will not reject their prayers.

¹⁸Write these things for the future
so that people who are not yet born will
praise the LORD.
¹⁹The LORD looked down from his holy place
above;
from heaven he looked down at the earth.
²⁰He heard the moans of the prisoners,
and he freed those sentenced to die.
²¹The name of the LORD will be heard in
Jerusalem;
his praise will be heard there.
²²People will come together,
and kingdoms will serve the LORD.

²³God has made me tired of living;
he has cut short my life.
²⁴So I said, "My God, do not take me in the
middle of my life.
Your years go on and on.
²⁵In the beginning you made the earth,
and your hands made the skies.
²⁶They will be destroyed, but you will remain.
They will all wear out like clothes.
And, like clothes, you will change them
and throw them away.
²⁷But you never change,
and your life will never end.

²⁸Our children will live in your presence,
and their children will remain with you."

Praise to the Lord of Love

Of David.

103 My whole being, praise the LORD;
all my being, praise his holy name.
²My whole being, praise the LORD
and do not forget all his kindnesses.
³He forgives all my sins
and heals all my diseases.
⁴He saves my life from the grave
and loads me with love and mercy.
⁵He satisfies me with good things
and makes me young again, like the eagle.

⁶The LORD does what is right and fair
for all who are wronged by others.
⁷He showed his ways to Moses
and his deeds to the people of Israel.
⁸The LORD shows mercy and is kind.
He does not become angry quickly, and he
has great love.
⁹He will not always accuse us,
and he will not be angry forever.
¹⁰He has not punished us as our sins should be
punished;

GOD'S LOVE

Easy to Take for Granted

It's invisible—easy to take for granted.
Your hand will go right through it.
It combines with practically everything, and if it didn't, life couldn't exist. It's a part of hundreds of thousands of things we use daily, and it makes up two-thirds of your body . . . nine-tenths of the oceans . . . one-fifth of the air you breathe.
Try living without it. You can't. Nothing can.
It's invisible. You take it for granted and never think about it because it's everywhere.
You guessed it—it's oxygen.
In many ways, God's love is like oxygen. They're both invisible, and they're both everywhere.
But God's love is even more essential than oxygen for life. The writer of **Psalm 103** knew the importance of God's love for living.

■ What phrases in this psalm reflect God's active, aggressive love for us?
■ How is God's love alive in the attitudes and actions of people you know?

C O N S I D E R . . .

■ thinking about what God has done in your life and writing two-word sentences combining the noun "He . . . ." and an active, descriptive verb, such as "He strengthens" or "He listens."
■ choosing three ways you can become more active in showing God's love to others, starting this week.

F O R   M O R E ,   S E E . . .

■ Genesis 1:26–31 (p. 3)
■ Proverbs 3:11–12 (p. 570)

■ John 3:16–21 (p. 1062)

he has not repaid us for the evil we have
done.

¹¹As high as the sky is above the earth,
so great is his love for those who respect
him.

¹²He has taken our sins away from us
as far as the east is from west.

¹³The LORD has mercy on those who respect
him,
as a father has mercy on his children.

¹⁴He knows how we were made;
he remembers that we are dust.

¹⁵Human life is like grass;
we grow like a flower in the field.

¹⁶After the wind blows, the flower is gone,
and there is no sign of where it was.

¹⁷But the LORD's love for those who respect
him
continues forever and ever,
and his goodness continues to their
grandchildren

¹⁸and to those who keep his agreement
and who remember to obey his orders.

¹⁹The LORD has set his throne in heaven,
and his kingdom rules over everything.

²⁰You who are his angels, praise the LORD.
You are the mighty warriors who do what
he says
and who obey his voice.

²¹You, his armies, praise the LORD;
you are his servants who do what he
wants.

²²Everything the LORD has made
should praise him in all the places he rules.
My whole being, praise the LORD.

Praise to God Who Made the World

104 My whole being, praise the LORD.
LORD my God, you are very great.
You are clothed with glory and majesty;
² you wear light like a robe.
You stretch out the skies like a tent.

³ You build your room above the clouds.
You make the clouds your chariot,
and you ride on the wings of the wind.

⁴You make the winds your messengers,
and flames of fire are your servants.

⁵You built the earth on its foundations
so it can never be moved.

⁶You covered the earth with oceans;
the water was above the mountains.

⁷But at your command, the water rushed
away.
When you thundered your orders, it
hurried away.

⁸The mountains rose; the valleys sank.

The water went to the places you made for
it.

⁹You set borders for the seas that they cannot
cross,
so water will never cover the earth again.

¹⁰You make springs pour into the ravines;
they flow between the mountains.

¹¹They water all the wild animals;
the wild donkeys come there to drink.

¹²Wild birds make nests by the water;
they sing among the tree branches.

¹³You water the mountains from above.
The earth is full of the things you made.

¹⁴You make the grass for cattle
and vegetables for the people.
You make food grow from the earth.

¹⁵You give us wine that makes happy hearts
and olive oil that makes our faces shine.
You give us bread that gives us strength.

¹⁶The LORD's trees have plenty of water;
they are the cedars of Lebanon, which he
planted.

¹⁷The birds make their nests there;
the stork's home is in the fir trees.

¹⁸The high mountains belong to the wild goats.
The rocks are hiding places for the badgers.

¹⁹You made the moon to mark the seasons,
and the sun always knows when to set.

²⁰You make it dark, and it becomes night.
Then all the wild animals creep around.

²¹The lions roar as they attack.
They look to God for food.

²²When the sun rises, they leave
and go back to their dens to lie down.

²³Then people go to work
and work until evening.

²⁴LORD, you have made many things;
with your wisdom you made them all.
The earth is full of your riches.

²⁵Look at the sea, so big and wide,
with creatures large and small that cannot
be counted.

²⁶Ships travel over the ocean,
and there is the sea monster Leviathan,*d*
which you made to play there.

²⁷All these things depend on you
to give them their food at the right time.

²⁸When you give it to them,
they gather it up.
When you open your hand,
they are filled with good food.

²⁹When you turn away from them,
they become frightened.
When you take away their breath,
they die and turn to dust.

³⁰When you breathe on them,
they are created,

and you make the land new again.

31May the glory of the LORD be forever.
  May the LORD enjoy what he has made.
32He just looks at the earth, and it shakes.
  He touches the mountains, and they smoke.

33I will sing to the LORD all my life;
  I will sing praises to my God as long as I
    live.
34May my thoughts please him;
  I am happy in the LORD.
35Let sinners be destroyed from the earth,
  and let the wicked live no longer.

My whole being, praise the LORD.
  Praise the LORD.

God's Love for Israel

105 Give thanks to the LORD and pray
to him.
Tell the nations what he has done.
2Sing to him; sing praises to him.
  Tell about all his miracles.*d*
3Be glad that you are his;
  let those who seek the LORD be happy.
4Depend on the LORD and his strength;
  always go to him for help.
5Remember the miracles he has done;
  remember his wonders and his decisions.
6You are descendants*d* of his servant Abraham,
  the children of Jacob, his chosen people.
7He is the LORD our God.
  His laws are for all the world.

8He will keep his agreement forever;
  he will keep his promises always.
9He will keep the agreement he made with
    Abraham
  and the promise he made to Isaac.
10He made it a law for the people of Jacob;
  he made it an agreement with Israel to last
    forever.
11The LORD said, "I will give you the land of
    Canaan,
  and it will belong to you."

12Then God's people were few in number.
  They were strangers in the land.
13They went from one nation to another,
  from one kingdom to another.
14But the LORD did not let anyone hurt them;
  he warned kings not to harm them.
15He said, "Don't touch my chosen people,
  and don't harm my prophets."*d*

16God ordered a time of hunger in the land,
  and he destroyed all the food.

17Then he sent a man ahead of them —
  Joseph, who was sold as a slave.
18They put chains around his feet
  and an iron ring around his neck.
19Then the time he had spoken of came,
  and the LORD's words proved that Joseph
    was right.
20The king of Egypt sent for Joseph and freed
    him;
  the ruler of the people set him free.
21He made him the master of his house;
  Joseph was in charge of his riches.
22He could order the princes as he wished.
  He taught the older men to be wise.
23Then his father Israel came to Egypt;
  Jacob*n* lived in Egypt.*n*
24The LORD made his people grow in number,
  and he made them stronger than their
    enemies.
25He caused the Egyptians to hate his people
  and to make plans against his servants.
26Then he sent his servant Moses,
  and Aaron, whom he had chosen.
27They did many signs among the Egyptians
  and worked wonders in Egypt.
28The LORD sent darkness and made the land
    dark,
  but the Egyptians turned against what he
    said.
29So he changed their water into blood
  and made their fish die.
30Then their country was filled with frogs,
  even in the bedrooms of their rulers.
31The LORD spoke and flies came,
  and gnats were everywhere in the country.
32He made hail fall like rain
  and sent lightning through their land.
33He struck down their grapevines and fig
    trees,
  and he destroyed every tree in the country.
34He spoke and grasshoppers came;
  the locusts*d* were too many to count.
35They ate all the plants in the land
  and everything the earth produced.
36The LORD also killed all the firstborn*d* sons in
    the land,
  the oldest son of each family.

37Then he brought his people out,
  and they carried with them silver and gold.
  Not one of his people stumbled.
38The Egyptians were glad when they left,
  because the Egyptians were afraid of them.
39The LORD covered them with a cloud
  and lit up the night with fire.
40When they asked, he brought them quail

Jacob Also called Israel.
Egypt Literally, "the land of Ham." Also in verse 27. The people in Egypt were descendants of Ham, one of Noah's sons.
See Genesis 10:6.

and filled them with bread from heaven.
41God split the rock, and water flowed out;
    it ran like a river through the desert.
42He remembered his holy promise
    to his servant Abraham.

43So God brought his people out with joy,
    his chosen ones with singing.
44He gave them lands of other nations,
    so they received what others had worked
        for.
45This was so they would keep his orders
    and obey his teachings.

Praise the LORD!

Israel's Failure to Trust God

106
Praise the LORD!
Thank the LORD because he is
good.
His love continues forever.
2No one can tell all the mighty things the
    LORD has done;
    no one can speak all his praise.
3Happy are those who do right,
    who do what is fair at all times.

4LORD, remember me when you are kind to
    your people;
    help me when you save them.
5Let me see the good things you do for your
    chosen people.
    Let me be happy along with your happy
        nation;
    let me join your own people in praising
        you.

6We have sinned just as our ancestors did.
    We have done wrong; we have done evil.
7Our ancestors in Egypt
    did not learn from your miracles.d
    They did not remember all your kindnesses,
    so they turned against you at the Red Sea.d
8But the LORD saved them for his own sake,
    to show his great power.
9He commanded the Red Sea, and it dried up.
    He led them through the deep sea as if it
        were a desert.
10He saved them from those who hated them.
    He saved them from their enemies.
11and the water covered their foes.
    Not one of them escaped.
12Then the people believed what the LORD
        said,
    and they sang praises to him.

13But they quickly forgot what he had done;
    they did not wait for his advice.
14They became greedy for food in the desert,

and they tested God there.
15So he gave them what they wanted,
    but he also sent a terrible disease among
        them.

16The people in the camp were jealous of
        Moses
    and of Aaron, the holy priest of the LORD.
17Then the ground opened up and swallowed
        Dathan
    and closed over Abiram's group.
18A fire burned among their followers,
    and flames burned up the wicked.

19The people made a gold calf at Mount Sinai
    and worshiped a metal statue.
20They exchanged their glorious God
    for a statue of a bull that eats grass.
21They forgot the God who saved them,
    who had done great things in Egypt,
22who had done miracles in Egyptn
    and amazing things by the Red Sea.
23So God said he would destroy them.
    But Moses, his chosen one, stood before
        him
    and stopped God's anger from destroying
        them.

24Then they refused to go into the beautiful
        land of Canaan;
    they did not believe what God promised.
25They grumbled in their tents
    and did not obey the LORD.
26So he swore to them
    that they would die in the desert.
27He said their children would be killed by
        other nations
    and that they would be scattered among
        other countries.

28They joined in worshiping Baald at Peor
    and ate meat that had been sacrificed to
        lifeless statues.
29They made the LORD angry by what they did,
    so many people became sick with a terrible
        disease.
30But Phinehas prayed to the LORD,
    and the disease stopped.
31Phinehas did what was right,
    and it will be remembered from now on.

32The people also made the LORD angry at
        Meribah,
    and Moses was in trouble because of them.
33The people turned against the Spiritd of God,
    so Moses spoke without stopping to think.
34The people did not destroy the other nations
    as the LORD had told them to do.
35Instead, they mixed with the other nations

Egypt Literally, "the land of Ham." The people in Egypt were descendants of Ham, one of Noah's sons. See Genesis 10:6.

and learned their customs.
36They worshiped other nations' idols
　　and were trapped by them.
37They even killed their sons and daughters
　　as sacrifices to demons.*d*
38They killed innocent people,
　　their own sons and daughters,
　as sacrifices to the idols of Canaan.
　　So the land was made unholy by their
　　　blood.
39The people became unholy by their sins;
　　they were unfaithful to God in what they
　　　did.

40So the LORD became angry with his people
　　and hated his own children.
41He handed them over to other nations
　　and let their enemies rule over them.
42Their enemies were cruel to them
　　and kept them under their power.
43The LORD saved his people many times,
　　but they continued to turn against him.
　　So they became even more wicked.

44But God saw their misery
　　when he heard their cry.
45He remembered his agreement with them,
　　and he felt sorry for them because of his
　　　great love.
46He caused them to be pitied
　　by those who held them captive.

47LORD our God, save us
　　and bring us back from other nations.
　Then we will thank you
　　and will gladly praise you.

48Praise the LORD, the God of Israel.
　　He always was and always will be.
　Let all the people say, "Amen!"

　Praise the LORD!

Book 5

God Saves from Many Dangers

107 Thank the LORD because he is
good.
　His love continues forever.
2That is what those whom the LORD has saved
　　should say.
　He has saved them from the enemy
3and has gathered them from other lands,
　　from east and west, north and south.

4Some people had wandered in the desert
　　lands:
　They found no city in which to live.
5They were hungry and thirsty,
　　and they were discouraged.
6In their misery they cried out to the LORD,
　　and he saved them from their troubles.

7He led them on a straight road
　　to a city where they could live.
8Let them give thanks to the LORD for his love
　　and for the miracles*d* he does for people.
9He satisfies the thirsty
　　and fills up the hungry.

10Some sat in gloom and darkness;
　　they were prisoners suffering in chains.
11They had turned against the words of God
　　and had refused the advice of God Most
　　　High.
12So he broke their pride by hard work.
　　They stumbled, and no one helped.
13In their misery they cried out to the LORD,
　　and he saved them from their troubles.
14He brought them out of their gloom and
　　　darkness
　　and broke their chains.
15Let them give thanks to the LORD for his love
　　and for the miracles he does for people.
16He breaks down bronze gates
　　and cuts apart iron bars.

17Some fools turned against God
　　and suffered for the evil they did.
18They refused to eat anything,
　　so they almost died.
19In their misery they cried out to the LORD,
　　and he saved them from their troubles.
20God gave the command and healed them,
　　so they were saved from dying.
21Let them give thanks to the LORD for his love
　　and for the miracles he does for people.
22Let them offer sacrifices to thank him.
　　With joy they should tell what he has
　　　done.

23Others went out to sea in ships
　　and did business on the great oceans.
24They saw what the LORD could do,
　　the miracles he did in the deep oceans.
25He spoke, and a storm came up,
　　which blew up high waves.
26The ships were tossed as high as the sky and
　　　fell low to the depths.
　　The storm was so bad that they lost their
　　　courage.
27They stumbled and fell like people who were
　　　drunk.
　　They did not know what to do.
28In their misery they cried out to the LORD,
　　and he saved them from their troubles.
29He stilled the storm
　　and calmed the waves.
30They were happy that it was quiet,
　　and God guided them to the port they
　　　wanted.
31Let them give thanks to the LORD for his love
　　and for the miracles he does for people.

[32]Let them praise his greatness in the meeting
of the people;
let them praise him in the meeting of the
older leaders.

[33]He changed rivers into a desert
and springs of water into dry ground.
[34]He made fertile land salty,
because the people there did evil.
[35]He changed the desert into pools of water
and dry ground into springs of water.
[36]He had the hungry settle there
so they could build a city in which to live.
[37]They planted seeds in the fields and
vineyards,
and they had a good harvest.
[38]God blessed them, and they grew in number.
Their cattle did not become fewer.

[39]Because of disaster, troubles, and sadness,
their families grew smaller and weaker.
[40]He showed he was displeased with their
leaders
and made them wander in a pathless
desert.
[41]But he lifted the poor out of their suffering
and made their families grow like flocks of
sheep.
[42]Good people see this and are happy,
but the wicked say nothing.

[43]Whoever is wise will remember these things
and will think about the love of the LORD.

A Prayer for Victory

A song. A psalm of David.

108

God, my heart is steady.
I will sing and praise you with all
my being.
[2]Wake up, harp and lyre![d]
I will wake up the dawn.
[3]LORD, I will praise you among the nations;
I will sing songs of praise about you to all
the nations.
[4]Your great love reaches to the skies,
your truth to the heavens.
[5]God, you are supreme above the skies.
Let your glory be over all the earth.

[6]Answer us and save us by your power
so the people you love will be rescued.
[7]God has said from his Temple,[d]
"When I win, I will divide Shechem
and measure off the Valley of Succoth.
[8]Gilead and Manasseh are mine.
Ephraim is like my helmet.
Judah holds my royal scepter.[d]
[9]Moab is like my washbowl.
I throw my sandals at Edom.
I shout at Philistia."

[10]Who will bring me to the strong, walled
city?
Who will lead me to Edom?
[11]God, surely you have rejected us;
you do not go out with our armies.
[12]Help us fight the enemy.
Human help is useless,
[13]but we can win with God's help.
He will defeat our enemies.

> **SIDELIGHT:** Not all the psalms
> are positive and upbeat. Psalm 109, for
> example, sounds downright nasty. Verses 6–
> 20 are written in the form of ancient Near
> Eastern curses, which were said to try to
> speed justice upon enemies and guilty
> people. A curse was intended to go into
> effect only if the person was guilty (see
> Numbers 5:18–28, p. 131, and Deuteronomy
> 27:15–26, p. 184).

A Prayer Against an Enemy

For the director of music. A psalm of David.

109

God, I praise you.
Do not be silent.
[2]Wicked people and liars have spoken against
me;
they have told lies about me.
[3]They have said hateful things about me
and attack me for no reason.
[4]They attacked me, even though I loved them
and prayed for them.
[5]I was good to them, but they repay me with
evil.
I loved them, but they hate me in return.

[6]They say about me, "Have an evil person
work against him,
and let an accuser stand against him.
[7]When he is judged, let him be found guilty,
and let even his prayers show his guilt.
[8]Let his life be cut short,
and let another man replace him as leader.
[9]Let his children become orphans
and his wife a widow.
[10]Make his children wander around, begging
for food.
Let them be forced out of the ruins in
which they live.
[11]Let the people to whom he owes money take
everything he owns,
and let strangers steal everything he has
worked for.
[12]Let no one show him love
or have mercy on his orphaned children.
[13]Let all his descendants[d] die

and be forgotten by those who live after
him.
¹⁴Lord, remember how wicked his ancestors
were,
and don't let the sins of his mother be
wiped out.
¹⁵Lord, always remember their sins.
Then make people forget about them
completely.

¹⁶"He did not remember to be loving.
He hurt the poor, the needy, and those
who were sad
until they were nearly dead.
¹⁷He loved to put curses on others,
so let those same curses fall on him.
He did not like to bless others,
so do not let good things happen to him.
¹⁸He cursed others as often as he wore
clothes.
Cursing others filled his body and his
life,
like drinking water and using olive oil.
¹⁹So let curses cover him like clothes
and wrap around him like a belt."
²⁰May the Lord do these things to those who
accuse me,
to those who speak evil against me.

²¹But you, Lord God,
be kind to me so others will know you are
good.
Because your love is good, save me.
²²I am poor and helpless
and very sad.
²³I am dying like an evening shadow;
I am shaken off like a locust.ᵈ
²⁴My knees are weak from hunger,
and I have grown thin.
²⁵My enemies insult me;
they look at me and shake their heads.

²⁶Lord my God, help me;
because you are loving, save me.
²⁷Then they will know that your power has
done this;
they will know that you have done it,
Lord.
²⁸They may curse me, but you bless me.
They may attack me, but they will be
disgraced.
Then I, your servant, will be glad.
²⁹Let those who accuse me be disgraced
and covered with shame like a coat.

³⁰I will thank the Lord very much;
I will praise him in front of many people.
³¹He defends the helpless
and saves them from those who accuse
them.

The Lord Appoints a King

A psalm of David.

110 The Lord said to my Lord,
"Sit by me at my right side
until I put your enemies under your
control."
²The Lord will enlarge your kingdom beyond
Jerusalem,
and you will rule over your enemies.
³Your people will join you on your day of
battle.
You have been dressed in holiness from
birth;
you have the freshness of a child.

⁴The Lord has made a promise
and will not change his mind.
He said, "You are a priest forever,
a priest like Melchizedek."

⁵The Lord is beside you to help you.
When he becomes angry, he will crush
kings.
⁶He will judge those nations, filling them with
dead bodies;
he will defeat rulers all over the world.
⁷The king will drink from the brook on the
way.
Then he will be strengthened.

Praise the Lord's Goodness

111 Praise the Lord!
I will thank the Lord with all my
heart
in the meeting of his good people.
²The Lord does great things;
those who enjoy them seek them.
³What he does is glorious and splendid,
and his goodness continues forever.
⁴His miraclesᵈ are unforgettable.
The Lord is kind and merciful.
⁵He gives food to those who fear him.
He remembers his agreement forever.
⁶He has shown his people his power
when he gave them the lands of other
nations.

⁷Everything he does is good and fair;
all his orders can be trusted.
⁸They will continue forever.
They were made true and right.
⁹He sets his people free.
He made his agreement everlasting.
He is holy and wonderful.

¹⁰Wisdom begins with respect for the Lord;
those who obey his orders have good
understanding.
He should be praised forever.

Honest People Are Blessed

112
Praise the LORD!

Happy are those who respect the LORD,
who want what he commands.
2Their descendants[d] will be powerful in the
land;
the children of honest people will be
blessed.
3Their houses will be full of wealth and riches,
and their goodness will continue forever.
4A light shines in the dark for honest people,
for those who are merciful and kind and
good.
5It is good to be merciful and generous.
Those who are fair in their business
6will never be defeated.
Good people will always be remembered.
7They won't be afraid of bad news;
their hearts are steady because they trust
the LORD.
8They are confident and will not be afraid;
they will look down on their enemies.
9They give freely to the poor.
The things they do are right and will
continue forever.
They will be given great honor.

10The wicked will see this and become angry;
they will grind their teeth in anger and
then disappear.
The wishes of the wicked will come to
nothing.

SIDELIGHT: When Jesus and
his disciples sang on the night Judas
betrayed Jesus (Matthew 26:30, p. 957), they
probably sang Psalms 113—114 or Psalms
115—118. These songs were customarily
sung during the Passover, which was being
celebrated at the time.

Praise for the Lord's Kindness

113
Praise the LORD!

Praise him, you servants of the
LORD;
praise the name of the LORD.
2The LORD's name should be praised
now and forever.
3The LORD's name should be praised
from where the sun rises to where it sets.
4The LORD is supreme over all the nations;
his glory reaches to the skies.

HONESTY

Slow But Sure

Almost everyone cheated in Mrs. Yount's algebra class. It was just so incredibly easy. The
three class "brains" were generous with whispered answers on tests and would lend
homework papers for copying. Mrs. Yount didn't seem to catch on, or else she ignored it,
not knowing how to put a stop to it.

Chuck Cameron didn't believe in cheating, though. He plugged along,
doing his own work, pulling B's or B-'s. That's why everybody was surprised
when he got the best math college entrance test scores of anybody at
Marshall High—even better than the "brains"—and was accepted into a top-
rate college.

"How did you do it, Chuck?" asked one of the brains from algebra.
"I just knew the stuff," Chuck said with a smile. "I learned it, slowly but
surely."

Honesty carries its own rewards today, just as it did in ancient times.
Psalm 112 talks about many of those rewards.
■ How would the phrase 'fair in their business" in verse 5 apply to Chuck?
■ What are ways honesty can keep you "steady" (verse 7) as you go about
your business at school, work, and home?

C O N S I D E R . . .
■ rewriting this psalm using your own words and applying it to your own circumstances.
■ committing to God never to cheat in school.

F O R   M O R E ,   S E E . . .
■ 1 Samuel 12:1–5 (p. 254)
■ Isaiah 33:15–17 (p. 649)
■ Colossians 3:9–10 (p. 1241)

⁵No one is like the Lord our God,
who rules from heaven,
⁶who bends down to look
at the skies and the earth.
⁷The Lord lifts the poor from the dirt
and takes the helpless from the ashes.
⁸He seats them with princes,
the princes of his people.
⁹He gives children to the woman who has none
and makes her a happy mother.

Praise the Lord!

God Brought Israel from Egypt

114 When the Israelites went out of Egypt,
the people of Jacob left that foreign country.
²Then Judah became God's holy place;
Israel became the land he ruled.

³The Red Sea*d* looked and ran away;
the Jordan River turned back.
⁴The mountains danced like sheep
and the hills like little lambs.
⁵Sea, why did you run away?
Jordan, why did you turn back?
⁶Mountains, why did you dance like sheep?
Hills, why did you dance like little lambs?

⁷Earth, shake with fear before the Lord,
before the God of Jacob.
⁸He turned a rock into a pool of water,
a hard rock into a spring of water.

The One True God

115 It does not belong to us, Lord.
The glory belongs to you
because of your love and loyalty.

²Why do the nations ask,
"Where is their God?"
³Our God is in heaven.
He does what he pleases.
⁴Their idols are made of silver and gold,
the work of human hands.
⁵They have mouths, but they cannot speak.
They have eyes, but they cannot see.
⁶They have ears, but they cannot hear.
They have noses, but they cannot smell.
⁷They have hands, but they cannot feel.
They have feet, but they cannot walk.
No sounds come from their throats.
⁸People who make idols will be like them,
and so will those who trust them.

⁹Family of Israel, trust the Lord;
he is your helper and your protection.
¹⁰Family of Aaron, trust the Lord;
he is your helper and your protection.

¹¹You who respect the Lord should trust him;
he is your helper and your protection.

¹²The Lord remembers us and will bless us.
He will bless the family of Israel;
he will bless the family of Aaron.
¹³The Lord will bless those who respect him,
from the smallest to the greatest.

¹⁴May the Lord give you success,
and may he give you and your children success.
¹⁵May you be blessed by the Lord,
who made heaven and earth.

¹⁶Heaven belongs to the Lord,
but he gave the earth to people.
¹⁷Dead people do not praise the Lord;
those in the grave are silent.
¹⁸But we will praise the Lord
now and forever.

Praise the Lord!

Thanksgiving for Escaping Death

116 I love the Lord,
because he listens to my prayers for help.
²He paid attention to me,
so I will call to him for help as long as I live.
³The ropes of death bound me,
and the fear of the grave took hold of me.
I was troubled and sad.
⁴Then I called out the name of the Lord.
I said, "Please, Lord, save me!"

⁵The Lord is kind and does what is right;
our God is merciful.
⁶The Lord watches over the foolish;
when I was helpless, he saved me.
⁷I said to myself, "Relax,
because the Lord takes care of you."
⁸Lord, you saved me from death.
You stopped my eyes from crying;
you kept me from being defeated.
⁹So I will walk with the Lord
in the land of the living.
¹⁰I believed, so I said,
"I am completely ruined."
¹¹In my distress I said,
"All people are liars."

¹²What can I give the Lord
for all the good things he has given to me?
¹³I will lift up the cup of salvation,
and I will pray to the Lord.
¹⁴I will give the Lord what I promised
in front of all his people.

¹⁵The death of one that belongs to the Lord
is precious in his sight.

[16]Lord, I am your servant;
I am your servant and the son of your
female servant.
You have freed me from my chains.
[17]I will give you an offering to show thanks to
you,
and I will pray to the Lord.
[18]I will give the Lord what I promised
in front of all his people,
[19]in the Temple[d] courtyards
in Jerusalem.

Praise the Lord!

A Hymn of Praise

117

All you nations, praise the Lord.
All you people, praise him
[2]because the Lord loves us very much,
and his truth is everlasting.

Praise the Lord!

Thanksgiving for Victory

118

Thank the Lord because he is
good.
His love continues forever.
[2]Let the people of Israel say,
"His love continues forever."
[3]Let the family of Aaron say,
"His love continues forever."
[4]Let those who respect the Lord say,
"His love continues forever."

[5]I was in trouble, so I called to the Lord.
The Lord answered me and set me free.
[6]I will not be afraid, because the Lord is with
me.

SIDELIGHT: The shortest chapter in the Bible—Psalm 117—is long on praise. The psalmist encourages the whole world to make music to God, which would make the Guinness Book of World Records for the Largest Community Sing-a-Long.

THANKFULNESS

Thanks, But No Thanks

Kyle Pierce is a polite guy. He's always careful to say "no, thank you" when he turns down the supper his mother makes, choosing instead a few fast-food tacos.

Kyle isn't interested in fitness, but when someone invites him to jog or shoot some baskets he always remembers his manners. "No, thanks," he says.

Recently, his girlfriend, Cora, got the same polite response when she urged him to attend a seminar to help him kick his smoking habit.

"Not interested," he said, then smiled. "But thanks."

"Don't you dare use that word with me!" she fumed.

"What word?" Kyle asked, innocently.

"The word 'thanks'! God's given you good health, and you choose to blow it away with lousy nutrition, no exercise, and nicotine. You're obviously not thankful at all!"

Cora's outburst made Kyle stop, think, and begin to make changes. For instance, he and Cora have taken up playing tennis together. And when someone offers him a cigarette now, he declines—politely, of course.

The writer of **Psalm 116** was also in a potentially life-threatening situation, and God saved him. Read the psalmist's heart-felt words to discover the kind of thankful heart God wants.

■ How would you use this psalm to advise Kyle about his attitude and actions?

■ In what areas of your own life are you making choices that say "thanks, but no thanks," to God?

CONSIDER . . .

■ listing all the things you're thankful for.

■ keeping track of all your "no thank you's" for a week and seeing what they say about your lifestyle choices.

FOR MORE, SEE . . .

■ 1 Chronicles 29:10–20 (p. 384)
■ Colossians 3:12–17 (p. 1232)

■ 1 Thessalonians 5:16–18 (p. 1249)

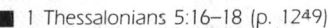

People can't do anything to me.
7The LORD is with me to help me,
so I will see my enemies defeated.
8It is better to trust the LORD
than to trust people.
9It is better to trust the LORD
than to trust princes.

10All the nations surrounded me,
but I defeated them in the name of the
LORD.
11They surrounded me on every side,
but with the LORD's power I defeated them.
12They surrounded me like a swarm of bees,
but they died as quickly as thorns burn.
By the LORD's power, I defeated them.
13They chased me until I was almost defeated,
but the LORD helped me.
14The LORD gives me strength and a song.
He has saved me.

15Shouts of joy and victory
come from the tents of those who do right:
"The LORD has done powerful things."
16The power of the LORD has won the victory;
with his power the LORD has done mighty
things.

17I will not die, but live,
and I will tell what the LORD has done.
18The LORD has taught me a hard lesson,
but he did not let me die.

19Open for me the Temple*d* gates.
Then I will come in and thank the LORD.
20This is the LORD's gate;
only those who are good may enter through
it.
21LORD, I thank you for answering me.
You have saved me.

22The stone that the builders rejected
became the cornerstone.*d*
23The LORD did this,
and it is wonderful to us.
24This is the day that the LORD has made.
Let us rejoice and be glad today!

25Please, LORD, save us;
please, LORD, give us success.
26God bless the one who comes in the name of
the LORD.
We bless all of you from the Temple of the
LORD.
27The LORD is God,
and he has shown kindness to us.
With branches in your hands, join the feast.
Come to the corners of the altar.

28You are my God, and I will thank you;
you are my God, and I will praise your
greatness.

29Thank the LORD because he is good.
His love continues forever.

> ☀ **SIDELIGHT:** "Ah, your eyes,
> your lips, your regulations!" You've
> probably never written a love song to a book
> of laws, but the writer of Psalm 119 did. The
> longest chapter in the Bible serenades God's
> commandments—probably as written in
> Genesis through Deuteronomy.

The Word of God

119 Happy are those who live pure
lives,
who follow the LORD's teachings.
2Happy are those who keep his rules,
who try to obey him with their whole
heart.
3They don't do what is wrong;
they follow his ways.
4LORD, you gave your orders
to be obeyed completely.
5I wish I were more loyal
in obeying your demands.
6Then I would not be ashamed
when I study your commands.
7When I learned that your laws are fair,
I praised you with an honest heart.
8I will obey your demands,
so please don't ever leave me.

9How can a young person live a pure life?
By obeying your word.
10With all my heart I try to obey you.
Don't let me break your commands.
11I have taken your words to heart
so I would not sin against you.
12LORD, you should be praised.
Teach me your demands.
13My lips will tell about
all the laws you have spoken.
14I enjoy living by your rules
as people enjoy great riches.
15I think about your orders
and study your ways.
16I enjoy obeying your demands,
and I will not forget your word.

17Do good to me, your servant, so I can live,
so I can obey your word.
18Open my eyes to see
the miracles*d* in your teachings.
19I am a stranger on earth.
Do not hide your commands from me.
20I wear myself out with desire
for your laws all the time.
21You scold proud people;

those who ignore your commands are
cursed.
22Don't let me be insulted and hated
because I keep your rules.
23Even if princes speak against me,
I, your servant, will think about your
demands.
24Your rules give me pleasure;
they give me good advice.
25I am about to die.
Give me life, as you have promised.
26I told you about my life, and you answered
me.
Teach me your demands.
27Help me understand your orders.
Then I will think about your miracles.
28I am sad and tired.
Make me strong again as you have
promised.
29Don't let me be dishonest;
have mercy on me by helping me obey
your teachings.
30I have chosen the way of truth;
I have obeyed your laws.
31I hold on to your rules.
LORD, do not let me be disgraced.
32I will quickly obey your commands,
because you have made me happy.

33LORD, teach me your demands,
and I will keep them until the end.
34Help me understand, so I can keep your
teachings,
obeying them with all my heart.
35Lead me in the path of your commands,
because that makes me happy.
36Make me want to keep your rules
instead of wishing for riches.
37Keep me from looking at worthless things.
Let me live by your word.
38Keep your promise to me, your servant,
so you will be respected.
39Take away the shame I fear,
because your laws are good.
40How I want to follow your orders.
Give me life because of your goodness.

41LORD, show me your love,
and save me as you have promised.
42I have an answer for people who insult me,
because I trust what you say.
43Never keep me from speaking your truth,
because I depend on your fair laws.
44I will obey your teachings
forever and ever.
45So I will live in freedom,
because I want to follow your orders.
46I will discuss your rules with kings

FOLLOWING GOD

To Live in Freedom

Reward posters offered large sums of money for her capture, dead or alive. Though she
was barely five feet tall and subject to fainting spells because of a head injury inflicted by
an owner when she was younger, many regarded her as extremely dangerous. Some even
called her "the devil."

But others, many others, called her "Moses." She had, after all, led more
than two hundred men, women, and children out of slavery to freedom in
Canada via the Underground Railroad.

Her real name was Harriet Tubman, and in the years just before America's
Civil War in the 1800s, she risked her life repeatedly to return to the South
and guide escaped slaves to freedom in the North.

In **Psalm 119:33–48**, the psalmist yearns for guidance to "live in
freedom," as so many slaves did long ago. As the slaves depended on Harriet
Tubman, the psalmist depended on God to show him the way.

■ Which verses of the passage would Harriet Tubman have identified with?
■ According to this passage, how can God set you free?

C O N S I D E R . . .
■ writing what total freedom means to you and what you think God would
say it means.
■ becoming a "Moses" to someone else by helping him or her overcome an enslaving
problem, such as drug abuse or a negative attitude.

F O R   M O R E ,   S E E . . .
■ Joshua 1:8–9 (p. 195)   ■ Romans 6:15–23 (p. 1147)
■ John 8:34–47 (p. 1072)

and will not be ashamed.
⁴⁷I enjoy obeying your commands,
which I love.
⁴⁸I praise your commands, which I love,
and I think about your demands.

⁴⁹Remember your promise to me, your servant;
it gives me hope.
⁵⁰When I suffer, this comforts me:
Your promise gives me life.
⁵¹Proud people always make fun of me,
but I do not reject your teachings.
⁵²I remember your laws from long ago,
and they comfort me, LORD.
⁵³I become angry with wicked people
who do not keep your teachings.
⁵⁴I sing about your demands
wherever I live.
⁵⁵LORD, I remember you at night,
and I will obey your teachings.
⁵⁶This is what I do:
I follow your orders.

⁵⁷LORD, you are my share in life;
I have promised to obey your words.
⁵⁸I prayed to you with all my heart.
Have mercy on me as you have promised.
⁵⁹I thought about my life,
and I decided to follow your rules.
⁶⁰I hurried and did not wait
to obey your commands.
⁶¹Wicked people have tied me up,
but I have not forgotten your teachings.
⁶²In the middle of the night, I get up to thank
you
because your laws are right.
⁶³I am a friend to everyone who fears you,
to anyone who obeys your orders.
⁶⁴LORD, your love fills the earth.
Teach me your demands.

⁶⁵You have done good things for your servant,
as you have promised, LORD.
⁶⁶Teach me wisdom and knowledge
because I trust your commands.
⁶⁷Before I suffered, I did wrong,
but now I obey your word.
⁶⁸You are good, and you do what is good.
Teach me your demands.
⁶⁹Proud people have made up lies about me,
but I will follow your orders with all my
heart.
⁷⁰Those people have no feelings,
but I love your teachings.
⁷¹It was good for me to suffer
so I would learn your demands.
⁷²Your teachings are worth more to me
than thousands of pieces of gold and silver.

⁷³You made me and formed me with your
hands.

Give me understanding so I can learn your
commands.
⁷⁴Let those who respect you rejoice when they
see me,
because I put my hope in your word.
⁷⁵LORD, I know that your laws are right
and that it was right for you to punish me.
⁷⁶Comfort me with your love,
as you promised me, your servant.
⁷⁷Have mercy on me so that I may live.
I love your teachings.
⁷⁸Make proud people ashamed because they
lied about me.
But I will think about your orders.
⁷⁹Let those who respect you return to me,
those who know your rules.
⁸⁰Let me obey your demands perfectly
so I will not be ashamed.

⁸¹I am weak from waiting for you to save me,
but I hope in your word.
⁸²My eyes are tired from looking for your
promise.
When will you comfort me?
⁸³Even though I am like a wine bag going up
in smoke,
I do not forget your demands.
⁸⁴How long will I live?
When will you judge those who are hurting
me?
⁸⁵Proud people have dug pits to trap me.
They have nothing to do with your
teachings.
⁸⁶All of your commands can be trusted.
Liars are hurting me. Help me!
⁸⁷They have almost put me in the grave,
but I have not rejected your orders.
⁸⁸Give me life by your love
so I can obey your rules.

⁸⁹LORD, your word is everlasting;
it continues forever in heaven.
⁹⁰Your loyalty will go on and on;
you made the earth, and it still stands.
⁹¹All things continue to this day because of
your laws,
because all things serve you.
⁹²If I had not loved your teachings,
I would have died from my sufferings.
⁹³I will never forget your orders,
because you have given me life by them.
⁹⁴I am yours. Save me.
I want to obey your orders.
⁹⁵Wicked people are waiting to destroy me,
but I will think about your rules.
⁹⁶Everything I see has its limits,
but your commands have none.

⁹⁷How I love your teachings!
I think about them all day long.

98Your commands make me wiser than my
enemies,
because they are mine forever.
99I am wiser than all my teachers,
because I think about your rules.
100I have more understanding than the older
leaders,
because I follow your orders.
101I have avoided every evil way
so I could obey your word.
102I haven't walked away from your laws,
because you yourself are my teacher.
103Your promises are sweet to me,
sweeter than honey in my mouth!
104Your orders give me understanding,
so I hate lying ways.

105Your word is like a lamp for my feet
and a light for my path.
106I will do what I have promised
and obey your fair laws.
107I have suffered for a long time.
LORD, give me life by your word.
108LORD, accept my willing praise
and teach me your laws.
109My life is always in danger,
but I haven't forgotten your teachings.
110Wicked people have set a trap for me,
but I haven't strayed from your orders.
111I will follow your rules forever,
because they make me happy.
112I will try to do what you demand
forever, until the end.

113I hate disloyal people,
but I love your teachings.
114You are my hiding place and my shield;
I hope in your word.
115Get away from me, you who do evil,
so I can keep my God's commands.
116Support me as you promised so I can live.
Don't let me be embarrassed because of my
hopes.
117Help me, and I will be saved.
I will always respect your demands.
118You reject those who ignore your demands,
because their lies mislead them.
119You throw away the wicked of the world
like trash.
So I will love your rules.
120I shake in fear of you;
I respect your laws.

121I have done what is fair and right.
Don't leave me to those who wrong me.
122Promise that you will help me, your servant.
Don't let proud people wrong me.
123My eyes are tired from looking for your
salvation
and for your good promise.

124Show your love to me, your servant,
and teach me your demands.
125I am your servant. Give me wisdom
so I can understand your rules.
126LORD, it is time for you to do something,
because people have disobeyed your
teachings.
127I love your commands
more than the purest gold.
128I respect all your orders,
so I hate lying ways.

129Your rules are wonderful.
That is why I keep them.
130Learning your words gives wisdom
and understanding for the foolish.
131I am nearly out of breath.
I really want to learn your commands.
132Look at me and have mercy on me
as you do for those who love you.
133Guide my steps as you promised;
don't let any sin control me.
134Save me from harmful people
so I can obey your orders.
135Show your kindness to me, your servant.
Teach me your demands.
136Tears stream from my eyes,
because people do not obey your teachings.

137LORD, you do what is right,
and your laws are fair.
138The rules you commanded are right
and completely trustworthy.
139I am so upset I am worn out,
because my enemies have forgotten your
words.
140Your promises are proven,
so I, your servant, love them.
141I am unimportant and hated,
but I have not forgotten your orders.
142Your goodness continues forever,
and your teachings are true.
143I have had troubles and misery,
but I love your commands.
144Your rules are always good.
Help me understand so I can live.

145LORD, I call to you with all my heart.
Answer me, and I will keep your demands.
146I call to you.
Save me so I can obey your rules.
147I wake up early in the morning and cry out.
I hope in your word.
148I stay awake all night
so I can think about your promises.
149Listen to me because of your love;
LORD, give me life by your laws.
150Those who love evil are near,
but they are far from your teachings.

151But, Lord, you are also near,
and all your commands are true.
152Long ago I learned from your rules
that you made them to continue forever.

153See my suffering and rescue me,
because I have not forgotten your
teachings.
154Argue my case and save me.
Let me live by your promises.
155Wicked people are far from being saved,
because they do not want your demands.
156Lord, you are very kind;
give me life by your laws.
157Many enemies are after me,
but I have not rejected your rules.
158I see those traitors, and I hate them,
because they do not obey what you
say.
159See how I love your orders.
Lord, give me life by your love.
160Your words are true from the start,
and all your laws will be fair forever.

161Leaders attack me for no reason,
but I fear your law in my heart.
162I am as happy over your promises
as if I had found a great treasure.
163I hate and despise lies,
but I love your teachings.
164Seven times a day I praise you
for your fair laws.
165Those who love your teachings will find true
peace,
and nothing will defeat them.
166I am waiting for you to save me, Lord.
I will obey your commands.
167I obey your rules,
and I love them very much.
168I obey your orders and rules,
because you know everything I do.

169Hear my cry to you, Lord.
Let your word help me understand.
170Listen to my prayer;
save me as you promised.
171Let me speak your praise,
because you have taught me your demands.
172Let me sing about your promises,
because all your commands are fair.
173Give me your helping hand,
because I have chosen your commands.
174I want you to save me, Lord.
I love your teachings.
175Let me live so I can praise you,
and let your laws help me.
176I have wandered like a lost sheep.
Look for your servant, because I have not
forgotten your commands.

A Prayer of Someone Far from Home

A psalm for going up to worship.

120 When I was in trouble, I called to
the Lord,
and he answered me.
2Lord, save me from liars
and from those who plan evil.

3You who plan evil, what will God do to you?
How will he punish you?
4He will punish you with the sharp arrows of
a warrior
and with burning coals of wood.

5How terrible it is for me to live in the land of
Meshech,
to live among the people of Kedar.
6I have lived too long
with people who hate peace.
7When I talk peace,
they want war.

The Lord Guards His People

A song for going up to worship.

121 I look up to the hills,
but where does my help come
from?
2My help comes from the Lord,
who made heaven and earth.

3He will not let you be defeated.
He who guards you never sleeps.
4He who guards Israel
never rests or sleeps.
5The Lord guards you.
The Lord is the shade that protects you
from the sun.
6The sun cannot hurt you during the day,
and the moon cannot hurt you at night.
7The Lord will protect you from all dangers;
he will guard your life.
8The Lord will guard you as you come and
go,
both now and forever.

Happy People in Jerusalem

A song for going up to worship. Of David.

122 I was happy when they said to
me,
"Let's go to the Temple*d* of the Lord."
2Jerusalem, we are standing
at your gates.

3Jerusalem is built as a city
with the buildings close together.
4The tribes*d* go up there,
the tribes who belong to the Lord.

It is the rule in Israel
  to praise the LORD at Jerusalem.
[5]There the descendants[d] of David
  set their thrones to judge the people.

[6]Pray for peace in Jerusalem:
  "May those who love her be safe.
[7]May there be peace within her walls
  and safety within her strong towers."
[8]To help my relatives and friends,
  I say, "Let Jerusalem have peace."
[9]For the sake of the Temple of the LORD our
    God,
  I wish good for her.

A Prayer for Mercy

A song for going up to worship.

123 LORD, I look upward to you,
  you who live in heaven.
[2]Slaves depend on their masters,
  and a female servant depends on her
    mistress.
In the same way, we depend on the LORD
  our God;
  we wait for him to show us mercy.

[3]Have mercy on us, LORD. Have mercy on
  us,
  because we have been insulted.
[4]We have suffered many insults from lazy
  people
  and much cruelty from the proud.

The Lord Saves His People

A song for going up to worship. Of David.

124 What if the LORD had not been on
  our side?
(Let Israel repeat this.)
[2]What if the LORD had not been on our side
  when we were attacked?
[3]When they were angry with us,
  they would have swallowed us alive.
[4]They would have been like a flood drowning
  us;
  they would have poured over us like a
    river.
[5] They would have swept us away like a
  mighty stream.

[6]Praise the LORD,
  who did not let them chew us up.
[7]We escaped like a bird
  from the hunter's trap.
The trap broke,
  and we escaped.
[8]Our help comes from the LORD,
  who made heaven and earth.

God Protects Those Who Trust Him

A song for going up to worship.

125 Those who trust the LORD are like
  Mount Zion,[d]
which sits unmoved forever.
[2]As the mountains surround Jerusalem,
  the LORD surrounds his people
  now and forever.

[3]The wicked will not rule
  over those who do right.
If they did, the people who do right
  might use their power to do evil.

[4]LORD, be good to those who are good,
  whose hearts are honest.
[5]But, LORD, when you remove those who do
  evil,
  also remove those who stop following you.

Let there be peace in Israel.

Lord, Bring Your People Back

A song for going up to worship.

126 When the LORD brought the
  prisoners back to Jerusalem,
it seemed as if we were dreaming.
[2]Then we were filled with laughter,
  and we sang happy songs.
Then the other nations said,
  "The LORD has done great things for them."
[3]The LORD has done great things for us,
  and we are very glad.

[4]LORD, return our prisoners again,
  as you bring streams to the desert.
[5]Those who cry as they plant crops
  will sing at harvest time.
[6]Those who cry
  as they carry out the seeds
will return singing
  and carrying bundles of grain.

All Good Things Come from God

A song for going up to worship. Of Solomon.

127 If the LORD doesn't build the
  house,
the builders are working for nothing.
If the LORD doesn't guard the city,
  the guards are watching for nothing.
[2]It is no use for you to get up early
  and stay up late,
working for a living.
  The LORD gives sleep to those he loves.
[3]Children are a gift from the LORD;
  babies are a reward.
[4]Children who are born to a young man
  are like arrows in the hand of a warrior.

⁵Happy is the man
  who has his bag full of arrows.
They will not be defeated
  when they fight their enemies at the city
    gate.

The Happy Home

A song for going up to worship.

128 Happy are those who respect the LORD
and obey him.
²You will enjoy what you work for,
  and you will be blessed with good
    things.
³Your wife will give you many children,
  like a vine that produces much fruit.
Your children will bring you much good,
  like olive branches that produce many
    olives.
⁴This is how the man who respects the
  LORD
  will be blessed.
⁵May the LORD bless you from Mount Zion;ᵈ

may you enjoy the good things of Jerusalem
  all your life.
⁶May you see your grandchildren.

Let there be peace in Israel.

A Prayer Against the Enemies

A song for going up to worship.

129 They have treated me badly all my life.
(Let Israel repeat this.)
²They have treated me badly all my life,
  but they have not defeated me.
³Like farmers plowing, they plowed over my
    back,
  making long wounds.
⁴But the LORD does what is right;
  he has set me free from those wicked
    people.

⁵Let those who hate Jerusalem
  be turned back in shame.
⁶Let them be like the grass on the roof
  that dries up before it has grown.

FAMILY

A Father's Love

"Where to first: burgers or the mall?" Jo Carasco called to Rosa Martinez over the music on the radio.

"Let's go to Fast Jack's for burgers!" Rosa called back. "It'll be crawling with cute guys."

They both laughed as Jo looked down to turn the radio up a notch. That's the last thing she remembers clearly—before the spin and the sickening jolt as the car turned on its side and then slammed to a stop against a concrete divider.

"I saw the stop sign, but it was too late to stop," Jo remembers. "When Rosa and I crawled out my window and I knew we were both okay, my next thought was, Dad will kill us! The hardest thing I ever had to do was call him from the police station to tell him I had just totaled his car."

But her father didn't even ask for details about the car. Over and over, while Jo clutched the phone and sobbed, he only asked for assurance that she and Rosa were okay.

"How can he love me like that?" she still asks today, four years later. "I'll tell you one thing. That love convinced me to drive differently. I try to live up to it."

Jo's father cared for his family. God cares about families too. Read **Psalm 127** to discover God's unselfish, protective love for families.

■ According to verse 1, what's the danger of trying to build a family without God's guidance?

■ How can you help make God a more prominent part of your family?

CONSIDER . . .
■ stopping activities in your life that make your parents worry.
✎ writing and signing an agreement with your parents that makes God the central focus of your family.

FOR MORE, SEE . . .
■ Joshua 24:14–15 (p. 214)
■ 2 Corinthians 6:14–18 (p. 1199)
■ Ephesians 5:21—6:4 (p. 1225)

7There is not enough of it to fill a hand
or to make into a bundle to fill one's arms.
8Let those who pass by them not say,
"May the Lᴏʀᴅ bless you.
We bless you by the power of the
Lᴏʀᴅ."

A Prayer for Mercy

A song for going up to worship.

130 Lᴏʀᴅ, I am in great trouble,
so I call out to you.
2Lord, hear my voice;
listen to my prayer for help.
3Lᴏʀᴅ, if you punished people for all their
sins,

no one would be left, Lord.
4But you forgive us,
so you are respected.

5I wait for the Lᴄʀᴅ to help me,
and I trust his word.
6I wait for the Lord to help me
more than night watchmen wait for the
dawn,
more than night watchmen wait for the
dawn.

7People of Israel, put your hope in the
Lᴏʀᴅ
because he is loving
and able to save.
8He will save Israel
from all their sins.

SIN

What Harm?

Sarah Furstie guessed it was stealing, in a way at least. But what choice did she have? Mr. Tanhover, the band director, had talked her into taking a solo to contests, but her flute was old and unreliable. It sounded more like a tin pipe than a flute when she played it.

Ann Filburgh, on the other hand, had a new, top-of-the-line flute that made each note sound like liquid silver. Ann didn't like other people playing her instrument, but what would be the harm if Sarah just switched the flutes in their cases the day before the contest?

For days Sarah agonized over her decision but finally decided, right or wrong, she just had to do it. She was nearly sick with nerves as she sneaked into the deserted band room the day before the contest, but the actual switch was easy. Nobody was anywhere around to see her.

Sarah played her solo for the judges the next day. Ann's flute sounded lovely, but Sarah made lots of dumb mistakes. Her fingers felt like rubber. She couldn't concentrate.

Afterward, she found Ann warming up for the band's contest number, using, of course, Sarah's old tin-pipe flute. As Sarah sat down in her own second-chair place beside Ann's first-chair spot, Ann stopped playing and turned to face her.

"Are you ready to trade back?" Ann asked quietly. Sarah heard, or thought she heard, hurt and anger in Ann's voice.

"Ann, I'm so sorry," Sarah whispered, her face burning. "I'm so ashamed. I just feel sick, and have all day."

Ann looked in Sarah's eyes for a long minute and then smiled. "Let's just forget it happened," she said. "It's okay. Really."

But Sarah knew it wasn't okay. Not quite. Ann had forgiven her, but it would be harder for Sarah to forgive herself. She had let herself down.

People like Sarah have always faced temptation, and sometimes they've given in. **Psalm 130** shows the need for forgiveness of these sins.

■ What might the psalmist advise Sarah to do next in her situation?
■ What temptations do you face that you need to ask God to help you sort out?

C O N S I D E R . . .

■ writing on a slip of paper the major temptations you face today and then asking God each week to help you overcome them.
■ apologizing to someone for something you did that hurt him or her.

F O R   M O R E ,   S E E . . .

■ Isaiah 44:22–23 (p. 663)   ■ 1 Corinthians 15:1–5 (p. 1187)
■ Jeremiah 31:31–34 (p. 727)

Childlike Trust in the Lord

A song for going up to worship. Of David.

131 Lord, my heart is not proud;
I don't look down on others.
I don't do great things,
and I can't do miracles.*d*
²But I am calm and quiet,
like a baby with its mother.
I am at peace, like a baby with its mother.

³People of Israel, put your hope in the Lord
now and forever.

In Praise of the Temple

A song for going up to worship.

132 Lord, remember David
and all his suffering.
²He made an oath to the Lord,
a promise to the Mighty God of Jacob.
³He said, "I will not go home to my house,
or lie down on my bed,
⁴or close my eyes,
or let myself sleep
⁵until I find a place for the Lord.
I want to provide a home for the Mighty
God of Jacob."

⁶We heard about the Ark*d* in Bethlehem.
We found it at Kiriath Jearim.
⁷Let's go to the Lord's house.
Let's worship at his footstool.
⁸Rise, Lord, and come to your resting place;
come with the Ark that shows your
strength.
⁹May your priests do what is right.
May your people sing for joy.

¹⁰For the sake of your servant David,
do not reject your appointed king.
¹¹The Lord made a promise to David,
a sure promise that he will not take back.
He promised, "I will make one of your
descendants*d*
rule as king after you.
¹²If your sons keep my agreement
and the rules that I teach them,
then their sons after them will rule
on your throne forever and ever."

¹³The Lord has chosen Jerusalem;
he wants it for his home.
¹⁴He says, "This is my resting place forever.
Here is where I want to stay.
¹⁵I will bless her with plenty;
I will fill her poor with food.
¹⁶I will cover her priests with salvation,
and those who worship me will really sing
for joy.

¹⁷"I will make a king come from the family of
David.
I will provide my appointed one
descendants*d* to rule after him.
¹⁸I will cover his enemies with shame,
but his crown will shine."

The Love of God's People

A song for going up to worship. Of David.

133 It is good and pleasant
when God's people live together in
peace!
²It is like perfumed oil poured on the priest's
head
and running down his beard.
It ran down Aaron's beard
and on to the collar of his robes.
³It is like the dew of Mount Hermon
falling on the hills of Jerusalem.
There the Lord gives his blessing
of life forever.

SIDELIGHT: The night servants
in the Temple (Psalm 134:1) were the
security guards of their day. They kept the
keys to the Temple gates and made sure the
furnishings didn't "walk off." (See
1 Chronicles 9:22, p. 369.)

Temple Guards, Praise the Lord

A song for going up to worship.

134 Praise the Lord, all you servants
of the Lord,
you who serve at night in the Temple*d* of
the Lord.
²Raise your hands in the Temple
and praise the Lord.

³May the Lord bless you from Mount Zion,*d*
he who made heaven and earth.

The Lord Saves, Idols Do Not

135 Praise the Lord!
Praise the name of the Lord;
praise him, you servants of the Lord,
²you who stand in the Lord's Temple*d*
and in the Temple courtyards.
³Praise the Lord, because he is good;
sing praises to him, because it is pleasant.

⁴The Lord has chosen the people of Jacob for
himself;
he has chosen the people of Israel for his
very own.
⁵I know that the Lord is great.

Our Lord is greater than all the gods.
⁶The LORD does what he pleases,
in heaven and on earth,
in the seas and the deep oceans.
⁷He brings the clouds from the ends of the
earth.
He sends the lightning with the rain.
He brings out the wind from his
storehouses.

⁸He destroyed the firstborn*d* sons in Egypt
the firstborn of both people and animals.
⁹He did many signs and miracles*d* in Egypt
against the king and his servants.
¹⁰He defeated many nations
and killed powerful kings:
¹¹Sihon king of the Amorites,
Og king of Bashan,
and all the kings of Canaan.
¹²Then he gave their land as a gift,
a gift to his people, the Israelites.

¹³LORD, your name is everlasting;
LORD, you will be remembered forever.
¹⁴The LORD defends his people
and has mercy on his servants.

¹⁵The idols of other nations are made of silver
and gold,
the work of human hands.
¹⁶They have mouths, but they cannot speak.
They have eyes, but they cannot see.
¹⁷They have ears, but they cannot hear.
They have no breath in their mouths.
¹⁸People who make idols will be like them,
and so will those who trust them.

¹⁹Family of Israel, praise the LORD.
Family of Aaron, praise the LORD.
²⁰Family of Levi, praise the LORD.
You who respect the LORD should praise
him.
²¹You people of Jerusalem, praise the LORD on
Mount Zion.*d*
Praise the LORD!

God's Love Continues Forever

136 Give thanks to the LORD because
he is good.
His love continues forever.
²Give thanks to the God of gods.
His love continues forever.
³Give thanks to the Lord of lords.
His love continues forever.

⁴Only he can do great miracles.*d*
His love continues forever.
⁵With his wisdom he made the skies.
His love continues forever.
⁶He spread out the earth on the seas.
His love continues forever.

⁷He made the sun and the moon.
His love continues forever.
⁸He made the sun to rule the day.
His love continues forever.
⁹He made the moon and stars to rule the
night.
His love continues forever.

¹⁰He killed the firstborn*d* sons of the Egyptians.
His love continues forever.
¹¹He brought the people of Israel out of Egypt.
His love continues forever.
¹²He did it with his great power and strength.
His love continues forever.
¹³He parted the water of the Red Sea.*d*
His love continues forever.
¹⁴He brought the Israelites through the middle
of it.
His love continues forever.
¹⁵But the king of Egypt and his army drowned
in the Red Sea.
His love continues forever.

¹⁵He led his people through the desert.
His love continues forever.
¹⁷He defeated great kings.
His love continues forever.
¹⁸He killed powerful kings.
His love continues forever.
¹⁹He defeated Sihon king of the Amorites.
His love continues forever.
²⁰He defeated Og king of Bashan.
His love continues forever.
²¹He gave their land as a gift.
His love continues forever.
²²It was a gift to his servants, the Israelites.
His love continues forever.

²³He remembered us when we were in trouble.
His love continues forever.
²⁴He freed us from our enemies.
His love continues forever.
²⁵He gives food to every living creature.
His love continues forever.

²⁶Give thanks to the God of heaven.
His love continues forever.

Israelites in Captivity

137 By the rivers in Babylon we sat
and cried
when we remembered Jerusalem.
²On the poplar trees nearby
we hung our harps.
³Those who captured us asked us to sing;
our enemies wanted happy songs.
They said, "Sing us a song about
Jerusalem!"

⁴But we cannot sing songs about the LORD
while we are in this foreign country!

⁵Jerusalem, if I forget you,
  let my right hand lose its skill.
⁶Let my tongue stick to the roof of my
    mouth
  if I do not remember you,
  if I do not think about Jerusalem
  as my greatest joy.

⁷LORD, remember what the Edomites did
  on the day Jerusalem fell.
They said, "Tear it down!
  Tear it down to its foundations!"

⁸People of Babylon, you will be destroyed.
  The people who pay you back for what you
    did to us will be happy.
⁹They will grab your babies
  and throw them against the rocks.

A Hymn of Thanksgiving

A psalm of David.

138 LORD, I will thank you with all my
heart;
I will sing to you before the gods.
²I will bow down facing your holy Temple,ᵈ

and I will thank you for your love and
  loyalty.
You have made your name and your word
  greater than anything.
³On the day I called to you, you answered
  me.
You made me strong and brave.

⁴LORD, let all the kings of the earth praise you
  when they hear the words you speak.
⁵They will sing about what the LORD has
  done,
because the LORD's glory is great.

⁶Though the LORD is supreme,
  he takes care of those who are humble,
  but he stays away from the proud.
⁷LORD, even when I have trouble all around
  me,
you will keep me alive.
When my enemies are angry,
  you will reach down and save me by your
    power.
⁸LORD, you do everything for me.
LORD, your love continues forever.
Do not leave us, whom you made.

LONELINESS

Left, But Not Forgotten

Somvilay's family came to America as refugees, and Somvilay will never forget the way his mother sat silently in the ship on the way to the new country, endlessly weaving small Laotian luck charms from delicate thread. Her eyes were downcast.

"I was the first in my family to learn English," Somvilay says proudly. "I learn in school. Now, after six years, all in my family know American speech, American ways. Well . . . somewhat."

Somvilay smiles with a shrug that reveals that Americans can still seem strange, with unfamiliar customs, styles and ways of thinking.

"Sometimes it is lonely," Somvilay confesses. "I miss my village in Laos, the people, my friends. America is different, not like home. I feel alone here."

Psalm 137:1—6 expresses the loneliness Somvilay and his family must sometimes feel as strangers in a strange land. Read the passage to see how the psalmist dealt with his loneliness as he expressed the Israelites' feelings as captives in a foreign land.

■ In what ways are you like Somvilay and the psalmist? In what ways are you different?

■ How can you overcome lonely feelings when it seems you're isolated—as if in a foreign country?

C O N S I D E R . . .

■ listing the names of everyone who cares about you and then writing each one a thank-you note for his or her love and loyalty.

 calling a trusted friend to talk about your loneliness and discussing ways to deal with it.

F O R   M O R E ,   S E E . . .

■ Leviticus 19:33–34 (p. 117)
■ Philippians 2:25–30 (p. 1231)
■ Hebrews 13:1–2 (p. 1290)

God Knows Everything

For the director of music. A psalm of David.

139 Lord, *you have* examined me
and know all about me.
²You know when I sit down and when I get
up.
You know my thoughts before I think
them.
³You know where I go and where I lie down.
You know thoroughly everything I do.
⁴Lord, even before I say a word,
you already know it.
⁵You are all around me — in front and in
back —
and have put your hand on me.
⁶Your knowledge is amazing to me;
it is more than I can understand.

⁷Where can I go to get away from your
Spirit?*ᵈ*
Where can I run from you?
⁸If I go up to the heavens, you are there.
If I lie down in the grave, you are there.
⁹If I rise with the sun in the east
and settle in the west beyond the sea,
¹⁰even there you would guide me.
With your right hand you would hold me.

¹¹I could say, "The darkness will hide me.
Let the light around me turn into night."
¹²But even the darkness is not dark to you.
The night is as light as the day;
darkness and light are the same to you.

¹³You made my whole being;
you formed me in my mother's body.
¹⁴I praise you because you made me in an
amazing and wonderful way.
What you have done is wonderful.
I know this very well.
¹⁵You saw my bones being formed
as I took shape in my mother's body.
When I was put together there,
¹⁶ you saw my body as it was formed.
All the days planned for me
were written in your book
before I was one day old.

¹⁷God, your thoughts are precious to me.
They are so many!
¹⁸If I could count them,
they would be more than all the grains of
sand.
When I wake up,
I am still with you.

¹⁹God, I wish you would kill the wicked!
Get away from me, you murderers!
²⁰They say evil things about you.
Your enemies use your name thoughtlessly.

²¹Lord, I hate those who hate you;
I hate those who rise up against you.
²²I feel only hate for them;
they are my enemies.

²³God, examine me and know my heart;
test me and know my nervous thoughts.
²⁴See if there is any bad thing in me.
Lead me on the road to everlasting life.

A Prayer for Protection

For the director of music. A psalm of David.

140 Lord, rescue me from evil people;
protect me from cruel people
²who make evil plans,
who always start fights.
³They make their tongues sharp as a snake's;
their words are like snake poison.　　Selahᵈ

⁴Lord, guard me from the power of wicked
people;
protect me from cruel people
who plan to trip me up.
⁵The proud hid a trap for me.
They spread out a net beside the road;
they set traps for me.　　Selah

⁶I said to the Lord, "You are my God."
Lord, listen to my prayer for help.
⁷Lord God, my mighty savior,
you protect me in battle.
⁸Lord, do not give the wicked what they
want.
Don't let their plans succeed,
or they will become proud.　　Selah

⁹Those around me have planned trouble.
Now let it come to them.
¹⁰Let burning coals fall on them.
Throw them into the fire
or into pits from which they cannot escape.
¹¹Don't let liars settle in the land.
Let evil quickly hunt down cruel people.

¹²I know the Lord will get justice for the poor
and will defend the needy in court.
¹³Good people will praise his name;
honest people will live in his presence.

A Prayer Not to Sin

A psalm of David.

141 Lord, I call to you. Come quickly.
Listen to me when I call to you.
²Let my prayer be like incense*ᵈ* placed before
you,
and my praise like the evening sacrifice.

³Lord, help me control my tongue;
help me be careful about what I say.
⁴Take away my desire to do evil

or to join others in doing wrong.
Don't let me eat tasty food
  with those who do evil.

[5] If a good person punished me, that would be
    kind.
  If he corrected me, that would be like
    perfumed oil on my head.
  I shouldn't refuse it.
  But I pray against those who do evil.
[6] Let their leaders be thrown down the cliffs.
  Then people will know that I have spoken
    correctly:
[7] "The ground is plowed and broken up.
  In the same way, our bones have been
    scattered at the grave."

[8] GOD, I look to you for help.
  I trust in you, LORD. Don't let me die.
[9] Protect me from the traps they set for me
  and from the net that evil people have
    spread.
[10] Let the wicked fall into their own nets,
  but let me pass by safely.

A Prayer for Safety

A maskil[d] of David when he was in the cave.
A prayer.

142
  I cry out to the LORD;
  I pray to the LORD for mercy.
[2] I pour out my problems to him;
  I tell him my troubles.
[3] When I am afraid,
  you, LORD, know the way out.
  In the path where I walk,
  a trap is hidden for me.
[4] Look around me and see.
  No one cares about me.
  I have no place of safety;
  no one cares if I live.

[5] LORD, I cry out to you.
  I say, "You are my protection.
  You are all I want in this life."
[6] Listen to my cry,
  because I am helpless.
  Save me from those who are chasing me,
  because they are too strong for me.
[7] Free me from my prison,
  and then I will praise your name.
  Then good people will surround me,
  because you have taken care of me.

A Prayer Not to Be Killed

A psalm of David.

143
  LORD, hear my prayer;
  listen to my cry for mercy.
Answer me
  because you are loyal and good.

[2] Don't judge me, your servant,
  because no one alive is right before you.
[3] My enemies are chasing me;
  they crushed me to the ground.
  They made me live in darkness
    like those long dead.
[4] I am afraid;
  my courage is gone.

[5] I remember what happened long ago;
  I consider everything you have done.
  I think about all you have made.
[6] I lift my hands to you in prayer.
  As a dry land needs rain, I thirst for you.
                                            Selah[d]

[7] LORD, answer me quickly,
  because I am getting weak.
  Don't turn away from me,
  or I will be like those who are dead.
[8] Tell me in the morning about your love,
  because I trust you.
  Show me what I should do,
  because my prayers go up to you.
[9] LORD, save me from my enemies;
  I hide in you.
[10] Teach me to do what you want,
  because you are my God.
  Let your good Spirit[d]
  lead me on level ground.

[11] LORD, let me live
  so people will praise you.
  In your goodness
  save me from my troubles.
[12] In your love defeat my enemies.
  Destroy all those who trouble me,
  because I am your servant.

A Prayer for Victory

Of David.

144
  Praise the LORD, my Rock,[d]
  who trains me for war,
  who trains me for battle.
[2] He protects me like a strong, walled city, and
    he loves me.
  He is my defender and my Savior,
  my shield and my protection.
  He helps me keep my people under control.

[3] LORD, why are people important to you?
  Why do you even think about human
    beings?
[4] People are *like a breath*;
  their lives are like passing shadows.

[5] LORD, tear open the sky and come down.
  Touch the mountains so they will smoke.
[6] Send the lightning and scatter my enemies.
  Shoot your arrows and force them away.

⁷Reach down from above.
  Save me and rescue me out of this sea of
    enemies,
  from these foreigners.
⁸They are liars;
  they are dishonest.

⁹God, I will sing a new song to you;
  I will play to you on the ten-stringed harp.
¹⁰You give victory to kings.
  You save your servant David from cruel
    swords.
¹¹Save me, rescue me from these foreigners.
  They are liars; they are dishonest.

¹²Let our sons in their youth
  grow like plants.
  Let our daughters be
    like the decorated stones in the Temple.*d*
¹³Let our barns be filled
  with crops of all kinds.
  Let our sheep in the fields have
    thousands and tens of thousands of lambs.
¹⁴ Let our cattle be strong.
  Let no one break in.
  Let there be no war,
    no screams in our streets.

¹⁵Happy are those who are like this;
  happy are the people whose God is the
    Lord.

SIDELIGHT: If you're looking for
something new to pray before each
meal, try Psalm 145. This psalm is still recited
in the morning, at noon and in the evening
in Jewish synagogues. A fourth-century rabbi
believed that reciting the psalm three times a
day would assure one a place in the world
to come.

Praise to God the King

A psalm of praise. Of David.

145
¹I praise your greatness, my God
  the King;
  I will praise you forever and ever.
²I will praise you every day;
  I will praise you forever and ever.
³The Lord is great and worthy of our praise;
  no one can understand how great he is.

⁴Parents will tell their children what you have
    done.
  They will retell your mighty acts,
⁵wonderful majesty, and glory.
  And I will think about your miracles.*d*

⁶They will tell about the amazing things you
    do,
  and I will tell how great you are.
⁷They will remember your great goodness
  and will sing about your fairness.
⁸The Lord is kind and shows mercy.
  He does not become angry quickly but is
    full of love.
⁹The Lord is good to everyone;
  he is merciful to all he has made.
¹⁰Lord, everything you have made will praise
    you;
  those who belong to you will bless you.
¹¹They will tell about the glory of your
    kingdom
  and will speak about your power.
¹²Then everyone will know the mighty things
    you do
  and the glory and majesty of your kingdom.
¹³Your kingdom will go on and on,
  and you will rule forever.

The Lord will keep all his promises;
  he is loyal to all he has made.
¹⁴The Lord helps those who have been
    defeated
  and takes care of those who are in trouble.
¹⁵All living things look to you for food,
  and you give it to them at the right time.
¹⁶You open your hand,
  and you satisfy all living things.

¹⁷Everything the Lord does is right.
  He is loyal to all he has made.
¹⁸The Lord is close to everyone who prays to
    him,
  to all who truly pray to him.
¹⁹He gives those who respect him what they
    want.
  He listens when they cry, and he saves
    them.
²⁰The Lord protects everyone who loves him,
  but he will destroy the wicked.

²¹I will praise the Lord.
  Let everyone praise his holy name forever.

Praise God Who Helps the Weak

146
Praise the Lord!
  My whole being, praise the Lord.
²I will praise the Lord all my life;
  I will sing praises to my God as long as I
    live.

³Do not put your trust in princes
  or other people, who cannot save you.
⁴When people die, they are buried.
  Then all of their plans come to an end.
⁵Happy are those who are helped by the God
    of Jacob.

Their hope is in the Lᴏʀᴅ their God.
⁶He made heaven and earth,
  the sea and everything in it.
  He remains loyal forever.
⁷He does what is fair for those who have been
    wronged.
  He gives food to the hungry.
  The Lᴏʀᴅ sets the prisoners free.
8 The Lᴏʀᴅ gives sight to the blind.
  The Lᴏʀᴅ lifts up people who are in trouble.
  The Lᴏʀᴅ loves those who do right.
⁹The Lᴏʀᴅ protects the foreigners.
  He defends the orphans and widows,
  but he blocks the way of the wicked.

¹⁰The Lᴏʀᴅ will be King forever.
  Jerusalem, your God is everlasting.

Praise the Lᴏʀᴅ!

Praise God Who Helps His People

147 Praise the Lᴏʀᴅ!
  It is good to sing praises to our
God;
  it is good and pleasant to praise him.

²The Lᴏʀᴅ rebuilds Jerusalem;
  he brings back the captured Israelites.
³He heals the brokenhearted
  and bandages their wounds.

⁴He counts the stars
  and names each one.
⁵Our Lord is great and very powerful.
  There is no limit to what he knows.
⁶The Lᴏʀᴅ defends the humble,
  but he throws the wicked to the ground.

⁷Sing praises to the Lᴏʀᴅ;
  praise our God with harps.
⁸He fills the sky with clouds
  and sends rain to the earth
  and makes grass grow on the hills.
⁹He gives food to cattle
  and to the little birds that call.

¹⁰He does not enjoy the strength of a horse
  or the strength of a man.
¹¹The Lᴏʀᴅ is pleased with those who respect
  him,
  with those who trust his love.

¹²Jerusalem, praise the Lᴏʀᴅ;

HUNGER AND POVERTY

The Numbers Tell the Story

Suppose you were sitting in a classroom of thirty people and that your classroom represented the world. How would your classroom "world" look? Check it out:

- Only two of you would live to age seventy-four.
- Seventeen of you would make less than six hundred dollars a year.
- Two of you would be so malnourished that your growth would be stunted.
- Ten of you would suffer some form of nutritional deficiency.
- Only fifteen of you would have access to clean drinking water.
- One of you would control 80 percent of the farmland.
- Only six of you would live in safe, sturdy homes.

Startling, isn't it? According to Worldwatch Institute, about 1.2 billion people live today without sufficient food, clothing, and shelter to meet their basic needs. Though North Americans tend to think of hunger as a Third World problem, statistics show that nearly 20 percent of Americans live below the poverty level, with that percentage even higher among children.

God wants to use the church to protect and help the less fortunate. Read **Psalm 146** to find out more about God's promises to people in need.

- The psalmist says the Lord "loves those who do right." What does this phrase mean with respect to helping the poor?
- How can you join with God in helping the "orphans and widows" in your community?

CONSIDER . . .

- keeping a jar by the washing machine and putting all your family's loose change into it. Give this to your church to help the disadvantaged.
- volunteering your time and energy to help repair the homes of the less fortunate.

FOR MORE, SEE . . .

- Psalm 140:12–13 (p. 561)
- Matthew 25:31–46 (p. 954)
- 2 Corinthians 9:7–9 (p. 1201)

Jerusalem, praise your God.
¹³He makes your city gates strong
and blesses your children inside.
¹⁴He brings peace to your country
and fills you with the finest grain.

¹⁵He gives a command to the earth,
and it quickly obeys him.
¹⁶He spreads the snow like wool
and scatters the frost like ashes.
¹⁷He throws down hail like rocks.
No one can stand the cold he sends.
¹⁸Then he gives a command, and it melts.
He sends the breezes, and the waters flow.

¹⁹He gave his word to Jacob,
his laws and demands to Israel.
²⁰He didn't do this for any other nation.
They don't know his laws.

Praise the LORD!

The World Should Praise the Lord

148 Praise the LORD!
Praise the LORD from the skies.
Praise him high above the earth.
²Praise him, all you angels.
Praise him, all you armies of heaven.
³Praise him, sun and moon.
Praise him, all you shining stars.
⁴Praise him, highest heavens
and you waters above the sky.
⁵Let them praise the LORD,
because they were created by his
command.
⁶He put them in place forever and ever;
he made a law that will never change.

⁷Praise the LORD from the earth,
you large sea animals and all the oceans,
⁸lightning and hail, snow and mist,
and stormy winds that obey him,
⁹mountains and all hills,
fruit trees and all cedars,
¹⁰wild animals and all cattle,
crawling animals and birds,
¹¹kings of the earth and all nations,
princes and all rulers of the earth,
¹²young men and women,
old people and children.

¹³Praise the LORD,
because he alone is great.
He is more wonderful than heaven and
earth.

¹⁴God has given his people a king.
He should be praised by all who belong to
him;
he should be praised by the Israelites, the
people closest to his heart.

Praise the LORD!

Praise the God of Israel

149 Praise the LORD!
Sing a new song to the LORD;
sing his praise in the meeting of his people.

²Let the Israelites be happy because of God,
their Maker.
Let the people of Jerusalem rejoice because
of their King.
³They should praise him with dancing.
They should sing praises to him with
tambourines*d* and harps.
⁴The LORD is pleased with his people;
he saves the humble.
⁵Let those who worship him rejoice in his
glory.
Let them sing for joy even in bed!

⁶Let them shout his praise
with their two-edged swords in their hands.
⁷They will punish the nations
and defeat the people.
⁸They will put those kings in chains
and those important men in iron bands.
⁹They will punish them as God has written.
God is honored by all who worship him.

Praise the LORD!

Praise the Lord with Music

150 Praise the LORD!
Praise God in his Temple;*d*
praise him in his mighty heaven.
²Praise him for his strength;
praise him for his greatness.
³Praise him with trumpet blasts;
praise him with harps and lyres.*d*
⁴Praise him with tambourines*d* and dancing;
praise him with stringed instruments and
flutes.
⁵Praise him with loud cymbals;
praise him with crashing cymbals.
⁶Let everything that breathes praise the LORD.

Praise the LORD!

WORSHIP

Time Out!

Tara Donagie often takes time out to worship, especially when something good happens in her life, as when she makes a new friend, finds a notebook that's been lost, or even gets over the flu.

Sometimes, she uses her guitar to praise God with a song.

"Especially if some friends are around and we're all celebrating," Tara says. "We may sing a couple of songs, laugh because we feel so good, and maybe say a prayer together."

Late last spring, things got really hectic. Tara began forgetting to take time out to worship God. "I lost my ability to be thankful in the shuffle of final exams and looking for a summer job," she says.

But that didn't last long.

"I couldn't handle it," Tara confesses. "Without taking time out to worship God, I took everything in my life for granted. I didn't feel thankful. This sounds weird, but the good stuff just didn't feel as good without the celebration."

Tara understood the unique blessings that come from worshiping God. **Psalm 150** expresses much of what Tara feels as she worships.

■ How is Tara's attitude like the psalmist's in this passage?

■ Why do you think it is good to practice worshiping and thanking God? What happens to our attitude if we don't?

C O N S I D E R . . .

■ writing a list of items beginning with the phrase "Praise the Lord for . . ."
■ keeping a diary of "blessings" so you won't get busy and forget to praise God and celebrate the things he gives you.

F O R   M O R E ,   S E E . . .

■ 1 Chronicles 23:1–5 (p. 379)
■ Psalm 147 (p. 564)

■ Luke 2:8–14 (p. 1003)

PROVERBS

Why Read This Book:

■ Discover life's basic goal (Proverbs 2:1–15).
■ Find clear guidance on right and wrong (Proverbs 3, 10–23).
■ Learn how to be wise instead of foolish (Proverbs 4, 6, 8, 9, 24).

Behind the Scenes:

If you like "quotable quotes" or bumper sticker slogans, you'll love Proverbs. Unlike other books of the Bible, Proverbs is mostly a collection of one- and two-line sayings on various everyday subjects—family life, work, money, getting along with others, honesty and many more. These sayings represent the heart of important truths about life and relationships. This is the wisdom of God for every day.

The book is filled with sharp phrases, dramatic contrasts, and vivid scenes from everyday life. A chapter may deal with dozens of different subjects (for example, see chapter 14). Because of their short, catchy style, these proverbs are easy to memorize. Other parts of Proverbs are longer, unified poems about wisdom, which is personified as a woman (see Proverbs 1:20–33).

Proverbs is divided into eight main sections. It begins with an introduction on wisdom (Proverbs 1—9), then has six collections of sayings by various "wise men" (Proverbs 10—31:9). It concludes with an acrostic poem on a perfect wife (Proverbs 31:10–31). Many scholars note that the perfect wife fulfills the virtues described in the rest of the book.

Collected hundreds of years ago to teach young people principles for life, Proverbs can still help guide us to make smart choices. And though many parts of Proverbs don't explicitly mention God, the sayings were gathered to help us follow God in everything we do.

WHEN THE ACTION WAS				
	Jerusalem fell to the Babylonians	Jews began returning to Jerusalem from exile		Jesus was born
1000BC	750BC	500BC	250BC	BC/AD
Solomon ruled Israel and many proverbs are attributed to him		Proverbs was probably put into its final form		

The Importance of Proverbs

1 These are the wise words of Solomon son of David, king of Israel.

²They teach wisdom and self-control;
they will help you understand wise words.

SIDELIGHT: Proverbs—short, catchy sayings—aren't found just in the book of Proverbs. They were a common type of writing in ancient times, and Jesus used them regularly in his teaching. See some examples in Matthew 6:21 (p. 918) and Matthew 7:13 (p. 919).

---

³They will teach you how to be wise and self-controlled
and will teach you to do what is honest and fair and right.
⁴They make the uneducated smarter
and give knowledge and sense to the young.
⁵Wise people can also listen and learn;
even smart people can find good advice in these words.
⁶Then anyone can understand wise words and stories,
the words of the wise and their riddles.

⁷Knowledge begins with respect for the LORD,
but fools hate wisdom and self-control.

Warnings Against Evil

⁸My child, listen to your father's teaching
and do not forget your mother's advice.
⁹Their teaching will be like flowers in your hair
or a necklace around your neck.

¹⁰My child, if sinners try to lead you into sin,
do not follow them.
¹¹They will say, "Come with us.
Let's ambush and kill someone;
let's attack some innocent people just for fun.
¹²Let's swallow them alive, as death does;
let's swallow them whole, as the grave does.
¹³We will take all kinds of valuable things
and fill our houses with stolen goods.
¹⁴Come join us,
and we will share with you stolen goods."
¹⁵My child, do not go along with them;
do not do what they do.
¹⁶They are eager to do evil
and are quick to kill.
¹⁷It is useless to spread out a net
right where the birds can see it.

¹⁸But sinners will fall into their own traps;
they will only catch themselves!
¹⁹All greedy people end up this way;
greed kills selfish people.

Wisdom Speaks

²⁰Wisdom is like a woman shouting in the street;
she raises her voice in the city squares.
²¹She cries out in the noisy street
and shouts at the city gates:
²²"You fools, how long will you be foolish?
How long will you make fun of wisdom
and hate knowledge?
²³If only you had listened when I corrected you,
I would have told you what's in my heart;
I would have told you what I am thinking.
²⁴I called, but you refused to listen;
I held out my hand, but you paid no attention.
²⁵You did not follow my advice
and did not listen when I corrected you.
²⁶So I will laugh when you are in trouble.
I will make fun when disaster strikes you,
²⁷when disaster comes over you like a storm,
when trouble strikes you like a whirlwind,
when pain and trouble overwhelm you.

²⁸"Then you will call to me,
but I will not answer.
You will look for me,
but you will not find me.
²⁹It is because you rejected knowledge
and did not choose to respect the LORD.
³⁰You did not accept my advice,
and you rejected my correction.
³¹So you will get what you deserve;
you will get what you planned for others.
³²Fools will die because they refuse to listen;
they will be destroyed because they do not care.
³³But those who listen to me will live in safety
and be at peace, without fear of injury."

Rewards of Wisdom

2 My child, listen to what I say
and remember what I command you.
²Listen carefully to wisdom;
set your mind on understanding.
³Cry out for wisdom,
and beg for understanding.
⁴Search for it like silver,
and hunt for it like hidden treasure.
⁵Then you will understand respect for the LORD,
and you will find that you know God.
⁶Only the LORD gives wisdom;
he gives knowledge and understanding.

⁷He stores up wisdom for those who are
honest.
Like a shield he protects the innocent.
⁸He makes sure that justice is done,
and he protects those who are loyal to him.

⁹Then you will understand what is honest and
fair
and what is the good and right thing to do.
¹⁰Wisdom will come into your mind,
and knowledge will be pleasing to you.
¹¹Good sense will protect you;
understanding will guard you.
¹²It will keep you from the wicked,
from those whose words are bad,
¹³who don't do what is right
but what is evil.
¹⁴They enjoy doing wrong
and are happy to do what is crooked and
evil.
¹⁵What they do is wrong,

and their ways are dishonest.

¹⁶It will save you from the unfaithful wife
who tries to lead you into adulteryᵈ with
pleasing words.
¹⁷She leaves the husband she married when
she was young.
She ignores the promise she made before
God.
¹⁸Her house is on the way to death;
those who took that path are now all dead.
¹⁹No one who goes to her comes back
or walks the path of life again.

²⁰But wisdom will help you be good
and do what is right.
²¹Those who are honest will live in the land,
and those who are innocent will remain in
it.
²²But the wicked will be removed from the
land,
and the unfaithful will be thrown out of it.

SCHOOL

Stunned Into Action

Over the past three years, Kelly Hunt had come to respect and trust Mr. Hudson. Sometimes she would pop into his office to share good news or ask advice about her classes or boyfriend. Other times she would share an orange with him as they walked across campus. Always, he cared—and listened.

But today she sat in his office, watching a worried Mr. Hudson collect his thoughts.

Finally, he spoke. "Kelly, I'm concerned about you. Let me tell you what I see." Mr. Hudson leaned forward in his chair. "Your grades are falling. You've dropped your old friends and taken up with another group—one that's on the fringe of trouble. And I've heard you talking about dropping out of school."

Kelly swallowed.

"In your eyes I see rebellion and fear. Something has control of you. How about talking to your folks about it?"

Kelly walked out of the office, stunned. If wise, objective, Mr. Hudson thought she had a problem, then she must have one. She had been fooling herself about her drinking—she could admit that now. Kelly decided she didn't want to destroy her whole future by messing up at school.

A few days later Kelly sat down with her parents and told them she needed help. That was her first step on her way to recovery.

Kelly was rewarded for staying in school and following Mr. Hudson's wisdom. **Proverbs 2:1–10** describes the rewards wisdom and education bring.

■ According to this passage, what things had to happen before Kelly received wisdom's reward?
■ What rewards, described in these verses, would you like to have?

CONSIDER . . .

■ copying different verses from the scripture passage onto your class notebooks.
■ talking to a teacher you consider wise and asking for tips on how to get more out of your education.

FOR MORE, SEE . . .

■ 1 Kings 3:4–15 (p. 306)
■ Colossians 2:1–4 (p. 1240)
■ James 1:5–8 (p. 1294)

Advice to Children

3 My child, do not forget my teaching,
but keep my commands in mind.
²Then you will live a long time,
and your life will be successful.

³Don't ever forget kindness and truth.
Wear them like a necklace.
Write them on your heart as if on a tablet.
⁴Then you will be respected
and will please both God and people.

⁵Trust the LORD with all your heart,
and don't depend on your own
understanding.
⁶Remember the LORD in all you do,
and he will give you success.

⁷Don't depend on your own wisdom.
Respect the LORD and refuse to do wrong.
⁸Then your body will be healthy,
and your bones will be strong.

⁹Honor the LORD with your wealth
and the firstfruits*d* from all your crops.
¹⁰Then your barns will be full,
and your wine barrels will overflow with
new wine.

¹¹My child, do not reject the LORD's discipline,
and don't get angry when he corrects you.
¹²The LORD corrects those he loves,
just as parents correct the child they delight
in.

¹³Happy is the person who finds wisdom,
the one who gets understanding.
¹⁴Wisdom is worth more than silver;
it brings more profit than gold.
¹⁵Wisdom is more precious than rubies;
nothing you could want is equal to it.
¹⁶With her right hand wisdom offers you a long
life,
and with her left hand she gives you riches
and honor.
¹⁷Wisdom will make your life pleasant
and will bring you peace.
¹⁸As a tree produces fruit, wisdom gives life to
those who use it,
and everyone who uses it will be happy.

¹⁹The LORD made the earth, using his wisdom.
He set the sky in place, using his
understanding.
²⁰With his knowledge, he made springs flow
into rivers
and the clouds drop rain on the earth.

²¹My child, hold on to wisdom and good sense.
Don't let them out of your sight.
²²They will give you life

and beauty like a necklace around your
neck.
²³Then you will go your way in safety,
and you will not get hurt.
²⁴When you lie down, you won't be afraid;
when you lie down, you will sleep in
peace.
²⁵You won't be afraid of sudden trouble;
you won't fear the ruin that comes to the
wicked,
²⁶because the LORD will keep you safe.
He will keep you from being trapped.

²⁷Whenever you are able,
do good to people who need help.
²⁸If you have what your neighbor asks for,
don't say, "Come back later.
I will give it to you tomorrow."
²⁹Don't make plans to hurt your neighbor
who lives nearby and trusts you.
³⁰Don't accuse a person for no good reason;
don't accuse someone who has not harmed
you.
³¹Don't be jealous of those who use violence,
and don't choose to be like them.
³²The LORD hates those who do wrong,
but he is a friend to those who are honest.
³³The LORD will curse the evil person's house,
but he will bless the home of those who do
right.
³⁴The LORD laughs at those who laugh at him,
but he gives grace to those who are not
proud.
³⁵Wise people will receive honor,
but fools will be disgraced.

Wisdom Is Important

4 My children, listen to your father's
teaching;
pay attention so you will understand.
²What I am telling you is good,
so do not forget what I teach you.
³When I was a young boy in my father's
house
and like an only child to my mother,
⁴my father taught me and said,
"Hold on to my words with all your heart.
Keep my commands and you will live.
⁵Get wisdom and understanding.
Don't forget or ignore my words.
⁶Hold on to wisdom, and it will take care of
you.
Love it, and it will keep you safe.
⁷Wisdom is the most important thing; so get
wisdom.
If it costs everything you have, get
understanding.
⁸Treasure wisdom, and it will make you great;
hold on to it, and it will bring you honor.

⁹It will be like flowers in your hair
and like a beautiful crown on your head."

¹⁰My child, listen and accept what I say.
Then you will have a long life.
¹¹I am guiding you in the way of wisdom,
and I am leading you on the right path.
¹²Nothing will hold you back;
you will not be overwhelmed.
¹³Always remember what you have been
taught,
and don't let go of it.
Keep all that you have learned;
it is the most important thing in life.
¹⁴Don't follow the ways of the wicked;
don't do what evil people do.
¹⁵Avoid their ways, and don't follow them.
Stay away from them and keep on going,
¹⁶because they cannot sleep until they do evil.
They cannot rest until they harm someone.
¹⁷They feast on wickedness and cruelty
as if they were eating bread and drinking
wine.
¹⁸The way of the good person is like the light
of dawn,
growing brighter and brighter until full
daylight.
¹⁹But the wicked walk around in the dark;
they can't even see what makes them
stumble.

²⁰My child, pay attention to my words;
listen closely to what I say.
²¹Don't ever forget my words;
keep them always in mind.
²²They are the key to life for those who find
them;
they bring health to the whole body.
²³Be careful what you think,
because your thoughts run your life.
²⁴Don't use your mouth to tell lies;
don't ever say things that are not true.
²⁵Keep your eyes focused on what is right,
and look straight ahead to what is good.
²⁶Be careful what you do,
and always do what is right.
²⁷Don't turn off the road of goodness;
keep away from evil paths.

Warning About Adultery

5 My son, pay attention to my wisdom;
listen to my words of understanding.
²Be careful to use good sense,
and watch what you say.
³The words of another man's wife may seem
sweet as honey;
they may be as smooth as olive oil.
⁴But in the end she will bring you sorrow,
causing you pain like a two-edged sword.

⁵She is on the way to death;
her steps are headed straight to the grave.
⁶She gives little thought to life.
She doesn't even know that her ways are
wrong.

⁷Now, my sons, listen to me,
and don't ignore what I say.
⁸Stay away from such a woman.
Don't even go near the door of her house,
⁹or you will give your riches to others,
and the best years of your life will be given
to someone cruel.
¹⁰Strangers will enjoy your wealth,
and what you worked so hard for will go to
someone else.
¹¹You will groan at the end of your life
when your health is gone.
¹²Then you will say, "I hated being told what
to do!
I would not listen to correction!
¹³I would not listen to my teachers
or pay attention to my instructors.
¹⁴I came close to being completely ruined
in front of a whole group of people."

¹⁵Be faithful to your own wife,
just as you drink water from your own
well.
¹⁶Don't pour your water in the streets;
don't give your love to just any woman.
¹⁷These things are yours alone
and shouldn't be shared with strangers.
¹⁸Be happy with the wife you married when
you were young.
She gives you joy, as your fountain gives
you water.
¹⁹She is as lovely and graceful as a deer.
Let her love always make you happy;
let her love always hold you captive.
²⁰My son, don't be held captive by a woman
who takes part in adultery.*d*
Don't hug another man's wife.

²¹The LORD sees everything you do,
and he watches where you go.
²²An evil man will be caught in his wicked
ways;
the ropes of his sins will tie him up.
²³He will die because he does not control
himself,
and he will be held captive by his
foolishness.

Dangers of Being Foolish

6 My child, be careful about giving a
guarantee for somebody else's loan,
about promising to pay what someone else
owes.
²You might get trapped by what you say;

you might be caught by your own words.
³My child, if you have done this and are
    under your neighbor's control,
    here is how to get free.
Don't be proud. Go to your neighbor
    and beg to be free from your promise.
⁴Don't go to sleep
    or even rest your eyes,
⁵but free yourself like a deer running from a
    hunter,
    like a bird flying away from a trapper.

⁶Go watch the ants, you lazy person.
    Watch what they do and be wise.
⁷Ants have no commander,
    no leader or ruler,
⁸but they store up food in the summer
    and gather their supplies at harvest.
⁹How long will you lie there, you lazy person?
    When will you get up from sleeping?
¹⁰You sleep a little; you take a nap.
    You fold your hands and lie down to rest.
¹¹So you will be as poor as if you had been
    robbed;
    you will have as little as if you had been
    held up.

SIDELIGHT: Sleeping until noon
would be a no-no for the writer of
Proverbs 6:6–11. The book of Proverbs
constantly blasts laziness and warns that lazy
people will end up poor. Yet it doesn't say all
poor people are lazy. Read the other side of
the story in Proverbs 13:23 (p. 579) and
Proverbs 22:1–2, 22–23 (p. 586).

---

¹²Some people are wicked and no good.
    They go around telling lies,
¹³winking with their eyes, tapping with their
    feet,
    and making signs with their fingers.
¹⁴They make evil plans in their hearts
    and are always starting arguments.
¹⁵So trouble will strike them in an instant;
    suddenly they will be so hurt no one can
    help them.

¹⁶There are six things the LORD hates.
    There are seven things he cannot stand:
¹⁷   a proud look,
    a lying tongue,
    hands that kill innocent people,
¹⁸   a mind that thinks up evil plans,
    feet that are quick to do evil,
¹⁹   a witness who lies,
    and someone who starts arguments
    among families.

Warning About Adultery

²⁰My son, keep your father's commands,
    and don't forget your mother's teaching.
²¹Keep their words in mind forever
    as though you had them tied around your
    neck.
²²They will guide you when you walk.
    They will guard you when you sleep.
    They will speak to you when you are
    awake.
²³These commands are like a lamp;
    this teaching is like a light.
    And the correction that comes from them
    will help you have life.
²⁴They will keep you from sinful women
    and from the pleasing words of another
    man's unfaithful wife.
²⁵Don't desire her because she is beautiful.
    Don't let her capture you by the way she
    looks at you.
²⁶A prostitute*d* will treat you like a loaf of
    bread,
    and a woman who takes part in adultery*d*
    may cost you your life.
²⁷You cannot carry hot coals against your
    chest
    without burning your clothes,
²⁸and you cannot walk on hot coals
    without burning your feet.
²⁹The same is true if you have sexual relations
    with another man's wife.
    Anyone who does so will be punished.

³⁰People don't hate a thief
    when he steals because he is hungry.
³¹But if he is caught, he must pay back seven
    times what he stole,
    and it may cost him everything he owns.
³²A man who takes part in adultery has no
    sense;
    he will destroy himself.
³³He will be beaten up and disgraced,
    and his shame will never go away.
³⁴Jealousy makes a husband very angry,
    and he will have no pity when he gets
    revenge.
³⁵He will accept no payment for the wrong;
    he will take no amount of money.

The Woman of Adultery

7 My son, remember what I say,
    and treasure my commands.
²Obey my commands, and you will live,
    Guard my teachings as you would your
    own eyes.
³Remind yourself of them;
    write them on your heart as if on a tablet.
⁴Treat wisdom as a sister,
    and make understanding your closest friend.

⁵Wisdom and understanding will keep you
away from adultery,*d*
away from the unfaithful wife and her
pleasing words.

⁶Once while I was at the window of my
house
I looked out through the shutters
⁷and saw some foolish, young men.
I noticed one of them had no wisdom.
⁸He was walking down the street near the
corner
on the road leading to her house.
⁹It was the twilight of the evening;
the darkness of the night was just
beginning.
¹⁰Then the woman approached him,
dressed like a prostitute*d*
and planning to trick him.
¹¹She was loud and stubborn
and never stayed at home.
¹²She was always out in the streets or in the
city squares,
waiting around on the corners of the
streets.
¹³She grabbed him and kissed him.
Without shame she said to him,
¹⁴"I made my fellowship offering and took
some of the meat home.
Today I have kept my special promises.
¹⁵So I have come out to meet you;
I have been looking for you and have found
you.
¹⁶I have covered my bed
with colored sheets from Egypt.
¹⁷I have made my bed smell sweet
with myrrh,*d* aloes,*d* and cinnamon.
¹⁸Come, let's make love until morning.
Let's enjoy each other's love.
¹⁹My husband is not home;
he has gone on a long trip.
²⁰He took a lot of money with him
and won't be home for weeks."
²¹By her clever words she made him give in;
by her pleasing words she led him into
doing wrong.
²²All at once he followed her,
like an ox led to the butcher,
like a deer caught in a trap
²³ and shot through the liver with an arrow.
Like a bird caught in a trap,
he didn't know what he did would kill
him.

²⁴Now, my sons, listen to me;
pay attention to what I say.
²⁵Don't let yourself be tricked by such a
woman;
don't go where she leads you.
²⁶She has ruined many good men,

and many have died because of her.
²⁷Her house is on the road to death,
the road that leads down to the grave.

Listen to Wisdom

8 Wisdom calls to you like someone
shouting;
understanding raises her voice.
²On the hilltops along the road
and at the crossroads, she stands calling.
³Beside the city gates,
at the entrances into the city, she calls out:
⁴"Listen, everyone, I'm calling out to you;
I am shouting to all people.
⁵You who are uneducated, be smarter.
You who are foolish, get understanding.
⁶Listen, because I have important things to
say,
and what I tell you is right.
⁷What I say is true,
I refuse to speak evil.
⁸Everything I say is honest;
nothing I say is crooked or false.
⁹People with good sense know what I say is
true;
and those with knowledge know my words
are right.
¹⁰Choose my teachings instead of silver,
and knowledge rather than the finest gold.
¹¹Wisdom is more precious than rubies.
Nothing you could want is equal to it.

¹²"I am wisdom, and I am smart.
I also have knowledge and good sense.
¹³If you respect the LORD, you will also hate
evil.
I hate pride and bragging,
evil ways and lies.
¹⁴I have good sense and advice,
and I have understanding and power.
¹⁵I help kings to govern
and rulers to make fair laws.
¹⁶Princes use me to lead,
and so do all important people who judge
fairly.
¹⁷I love those who love me,
and those who seek me find me.
¹⁸Riches and honor are mine to give.
So are wealth and lasting success.
¹⁹What I give is better than the finest gold,
better than the purest silver.
²⁰I do what is right
and follow the path of justice.
²¹I give wealth to those who love me,
filling their houses with treasures.

²²"I, wisdom, was with the LORD when he
began his work,
long before he made anything else.
²³I was created in the very beginning,

even before the world began.
²⁴I was born before there were oceans,
  or springs overflowing with water,
²⁵before the hills were there,
  before the mountains were put in place.
²⁶God had not made the earth or fields,
  not even the first dust of the earth.
²⁷I was there when God put the skies in place,
  when he stretched the horizon over the
    oceans,
²⁸when he made the clouds above
  and put the deep underground springs in
    place.
²⁹I was there when he ordered the sea
  not to go beyond the borders he had set.
  I was there when he laid the earth's
    foundation.
³⁰ I was like a child by his side.
  I was delighted every day,
  enjoying his presence all the time,
³¹enjoying the whole world,
  and delighted with all its people.
³²"Now, my children, listen to me,
  because those who follow my ways are
    happy.
³³Listen to my teaching, and you will be wise;
  do not ignore it.

³⁴Happy are those who listen to me,
  watching at my door every day,
  waiting at my open doorway.
³⁵Those who find me find life,
  and the LORD will be pleased with them.
³⁶Those who do not find me hurt themselves.
  Those who hate me love death."

Being Wise or Foolish

9 Wisdom has built her house;
  she has made its seven columns;
²She has prepared her food and wine;
  she has set her table.
³She has sent out her servant girls,
  and she calls out from the highest place in
    the city.
⁴She says to those who are uneducated,
  "Come in here, you foolish people!
⁵Come and eat my food
  and drink the wine I have prepared.
⁶Stop your foolish ways, and you will
    live;
  take the road of understanding.
⁷"If you correct someone who makes fun of
    wisdom, you will be insulted.
  If you correct an evil person, you will get
    hurt.

CREATION

Moment of Wonder

Waves on the Sea of Cortez rolled under Marty Stypes's kayak. One crested behind her and broke, spewing foam over her back. Panic gripped her. She leaned into the wind, paddling hard. Her muscles ached. Why had she taken this wilderness course?

The answer echoed within her, "to test myself, to get back in touch with God." But where was he?

When she rounded the rocky point, stillness surrounded her. Sunlight broke through the clouds, sparkling into the turquoise depths of the protected cove. Marty rested her paddle and looked beneath her. Sea fans waved their purple lace. Yellow fish darted. She leaned back and gazed at the horizon. Pelicans skimmed inches above the water.

Suddenly the sea split beside her. A dolphin arched high, then dove, circling her. She sucked in her breath, overcome with wonder.

"Lord, oh Lord, you're everywhere!"

The voice of Wisdom, in Proverbs, speaks about the joy in observing God's creation. Read about it in **Proverbs 8:22–31**.

■ What might Wisdom's voice say to Marty from this passage?
■ Where do you most strongly sense God's presence? Why?

CONSIDER . . .

■ searching for the tiny forms of God's creation as you walk across a yard or a vacant lot, and thanking God for them.
■ finding a special place in nature where you can go regularly to be with God.

FOR MORE, SEE . . .

■ Psalm 104:1–35 (p. 541)
■ Luke 8:22–26 (p. 1017)
■ Revelation 4:11 (p. 1335)

⁸Do not correct those who make fun of
    wisdom, or they will hate you.
But correct the wise, and they will love
    you.
⁹Teach the wise, and they will become even
    wiser;
teach good people, and they will learn even
    more.

¹⁰"Wisdom begins with respect for the Lord,
    and understanding begins with knowing the
    Holy One.
¹¹If you live wisely, you will live a long time;
    wisdom will add years to your life.
¹²The wise person is rewarded by wisdom,
    but whoever makes fun of wisdom will
    suffer for it."

¹³Foolishness is like a loud woman;
    she does not have wisdom or knowledge.
¹⁴She sits at the door of her house
    at the highest place in the city.
¹⁵She calls out to those who are passing by,
    who are going along, minding their own
    business.

¹⁶She says to those who are uneducated,
    "Come in here, you foolish people!
¹⁷Stolen water is sweeter,
    and food eaten in secret tastes better."
¹⁸But these people don't know that everyone
    who goes there dies,
    that her guests end up deep in the grave.

> ※ **SIDELIGHT:** Two sections of
> Proverbs (Proverbs 10:1–22:16 and
> 25:1–29:27, p. 589) are attributed to
> Solomon, the king who was said to have
> spoken three thousand wise sayings (1 Kings
> 4:32–34, p. 308).

The Wise Words of Solomon

10 These are the wise words of Solomon:

A wise son makes his father happy,
but a foolish son makes his mother sad.

²Riches gotten by doing wrong have no value,
but right living will save you from death.

SCHOOL

Crossroads

Chad Monroe's cane tapped from side to side, sweeping across the sidewalk. He
approached a street intersection, but veered left. As his cane tip struck metal, he stopped.
    "Mr. Wright? Where am I?" he called.
    Chad's mobility instructor from the school for the blind stood at a safe distance,
observing Chad's cane technique.
    "What have you hit?" he asked. "Listen to the sound of it. Feel it."
    Chad swung his cane again, turning his head as he listened to the metallic ring. "It's a
car." He felt its fender.
    "Good. Get back on the walk, and cross the street." The instructor tensed.
Would Chad follow what he had been taught? Or would he step in the path
of a car?
    Trucks raced in front of Chad. "I'm scared!"
    "Listen for the parallel traffic to start. You can do it," the instructor said.
    Finally, Chad stepped into the crosswalk. The instructor let out a relieved
breath; Chad had picked the right time.
    Proverbs 9:8–12 describes the rewards for a wise student who learns
from a good teacher, as Chad did.
■ According to this passage, where does true wisdom begin?
■ How have you been rewarded by wisdom at school, as mentioned in
    verse 12?

CONSIDER . . .
■ telling a teacher whom you admire how he or she has helped you in life.
■ offering to tutor classmates who are having trouble in school so you can pass on to
    others what your teachers have taught you.

FOR MORE, SEE . . .
■ Psalm 16:5–11 (p. 489)   ■ John 7:14–18 (p. 1069)
■ Daniel 1:3–18 (p. 807)

³The Lord does not let good people go
hungry,
but he keeps evil people from getting what
they want.

⁴A lazy person will end up poor,
but a hard worker will become rich.

⁵Those who gather crops on time are wise,
but those who sleep through the harvest
are a disgrace.

⁶Good people will have rich blessings,
but the wicked will be overwhelmed by
violence.

⁷Good people will be remembered as a
blessing,
but evil people will soon be forgotten.

⁸The wise do what they are told,
but a talkative fool will be ruined.

⁹The honest person will live in safety,
but the dishonest will be caught.

¹⁰A wink may get you into trouble,
and foolish talk will lead to your ruin.

¹¹The words of a good person give life, like a
fountain of water,
but the words of the wicked contain
nothing but violence.

¹²Hatred stirs up trouble,
but love forgives all wrongs.

¹³Smart people speak wisely,
but people without wisdom should be
punished.

¹⁴The wise don't tell everything they know,
but the foolish talk too much and are
ruined.

¹⁵Having lots of money protects the rich,
but having no money destroys the poor.

¹⁶Good people are rewarded with life,
but evil people are paid with punishment.

¹⁷Whoever accepts correction is on the way to
life,
but whoever ignores correction will lead
others away from life.

¹⁸Whoever hides hate is a liar.
Whoever tells lies is a fool.

¹⁹*If you talk a lot, you are sure to sin;*
if you are wise, you will keep quiet.

²⁰The words of a good person are like pure
silver,
but an evil person's thoughts are worth
very little.

²¹Good people's words will help many others,

but fools will die because they don't have
wisdom.

²²The Lord's blessing brings wealth,
and no sorrow comes with it.

²³A foolish person enjoys doing wrong,
but a person with understanding enjoys
doing what is wise.

²⁴Evil people will get what they fear most,
but good people will get what they want
most.

²⁵A storm will blow the evil person away,
but a good person will always be safe.

²⁶A lazy person affects the one he works for
like vinegar on the teeth or smoke in the
eyes.

²⁷Whoever respects the Lord will have a long
life,
but the life of an evil person will be cut
short.

²⁸A good person can look forward to happiness,
but an evil person can expect nothing.

²⁹The Lord will protect good people
but will ruin those who do evil.

³⁰Good people will always be safe,
but evil people will not remain in the land.

³¹A good person says wise things,
but a liar's tongue will be stopped.

³²Good people know the right thing to say,
but evil people only tell lies.

11 The Lord hates dishonest scales,
but he is pleased with honest weights.

✺ **SIDELIGHT:** Since they didn't
have digital scales in Bible times,
people had to use stones and metal objects
to figure out how heavy something was
before buying or selling it. They probably
used hand-held scales and put the
merchandise on one side and the weight on
the other. Proverbs 11:1 warns against using
inaccurate scales to cheat someone.

---

²Pride leads only to shame;
it is wise to be humble.

³Good people will be guided by honesty;
dishonesty will destroy those who are not
trustworthy.

⁴Riches will not help when it's time to die,
but right living will save you from death.

5The goodness of the innocent makes life
easier,
but the wicked will be destroyed by their
wickedness.

6Doing right brings freedom to honest people,
but those who are not trustworthy will be
caught by their own desires.

7When the wicked die, hope dies with them;
their hope in riches will come to nothing.

8The good person is saved from trouble;
it comes to the wicked instead.

9With words an evil person can destroy a
neighbor,
but a good person will escape by being
smart.

10When good people succeed, the city is happy.
When evil people die, there are shouts of
joy.

11Good people bless and build up their city,
but the wicked can destroy it with their
words.

12People without good sense find fault with
their neighbors,
but those with understanding keep quiet.

13Gossips can't keep secrets,
but a trustworthy person can.

14Without leadership a nation falls,
but lots of good advice will save it.

15Whoever guarantees to pay somebody else's
loan will suffer.
It is safer to avoid such promises.

16A kind woman gets respect,
but cruel men get only wealth.

17Kind people do themselves a favor,
but cruel people bring trouble on
themselves

18An evil person really earns nothing,
but a good person will surely be rewarded.

19Those who are truly good will live,
but those who chase after evil will die.

20The LORD hates those with evil hearts
but is pleased with those who are innocent.

21Evil people will certainly be punished,
but those who do right will be set free.

22A beautiful woman without good sense
is like a gold ring in a pig's snout.

23Those who do right only wish for good,
but the wicked can expect to be defeated
by God's anger.

24Some people give much but get back even
more.
Others don't give what they should and
end up poor.

25Whoever gives to others will get richer;
those who help others will themselves be
helped.

26People curse those who keep all the grain,
but they bless the one who is willing to sell
it.

27Whoever looks for good will find kindness,
but whoever looks for evil will find trouble.

28Those who trust in riches will be ruined,
but a good person will be healthy like a
green leaf.

29Whoever brings trouble to his family
will be left with nothing but the wind.
A fool will be a servant to the wise.

30A good person gives life to others;
the wise person teaches others how to live.

31Good people will be rewarded on earth,
and the wicked and the sinners will be
punished.

12 Anyone who loves learning accepts
correction,
but a person who hates being corrected is
stupid.

2The LORD is pleased with a good person,
but he will punish anyone who plans evil.

3Doing evil brings no safety at all,
but a good person has safety and security.

4A good wife is like a crown for her husband,
but a disgraceful wife is like a disease in his
bones.

5The plans that good people make are fair,
but the advice of the wicked will trick you.

6The wicked talk about killing people,
but the words of good people will save
them.

7Wicked people die and they are no more,
but a good person's family continues.

8The wisdom of the wise wins praise,
but there is no respect for the stupid.

9A person who is not important but has a
servant is better off
than someone who acts important but has
no food.

10Good people take care of their animals,
but even the kindest acts of the wicked are
cruel.

¹¹Those who work their land will have plenty
of food,
    but the one who chases empty dreams is
not wise.

¹²The wicked want what other evil people have
stolen,
    but good people want to give what they
have to others.

¹³Evil people are trapped by their evil talk,
    but good people stay out of trouble.

¹⁴People will be rewarded for what they say,
    and they will also be rewarded for what
they do.

¹⁵Fools think they are doing right,
    but the wise listen to advice.

¹⁶Fools quickly show that they are upset,
    but the wise ignore insults.

¹⁷An honest witness tells the truth,
    but a dishonest witness tells lies.

¹⁸Careless words stab like a sword,
    but wise words bring healing.

¹⁹Truth will continue forever,
    but lies are only for a moment.

²⁰Those who plan evil are full of lies,
    but those who plan peace are happy.

²¹No harm comes to a good person,
    but an evil person's life is full of trouble.

²²The Lord hates those who tell lies
    but is pleased with those who keep their
promises.

²³Wise people keep what they know to
themselves,
    but fools can't keep from showing how
foolish they are.

²⁴Hard workers will become leaders,
    but those who are lazy will be slaves.

²⁵Worry is a heavy load,
    but a kind word cheers you up.

²⁶Good people take advice from their friends,
    but an evil person is easily led to do wrong.

²⁷The lazy catch no food to cook,
    but a hard worker will have great wealth.

²⁸Doing what is right is the way to life,
    but there is another way that leads to
death.

13 Wise children take their parents'
advice,
but whoever makes fun of wisdom won't
listen to correction.

²People will be rewarded for what they say,
    but those who can't be trusted want only
violence.

³Those who are careful about what they say
protect their lives,
    but whoever speaks without thinking will
be ruined.

⁴The lazy will not get what they want,
    but those who work hard will.

⁵Good people hate what is false,
    but the wicked do shameful and disgraceful
things.

⁶Doing what is right protects the honest
person,
    but doing evil ruins the sinner.

⁷Some people pretend to be rich but really
have nothing.
    Others pretend to be poor but really are
wealthy.

⁸The rich may have to pay a ransom for their
lives,
    but the poor will face no such danger.

⁹Good people can look forward to a bright
future,
    but the future of the wicked is like a flame
going out.

¹⁰Pride only leads to arguments,
    but those who take advice are wise.

¹¹Money that comes easily disappears quickly,
    but money that is gathered little by little
will grow.

¹²It is sad not to get what you hoped for.
    But wishes that come true are like eating
fruit from the tree of life.

¹³Those who reject what they are taught will
pay for it,
    but those who obey what they are told will
be rewarded.

¹⁴The teaching of a wise person gives life.
    It is like a fountain that can save people
from death.

¹⁵People with good understanding will be well
liked,
    but the lives of those who are not
trustworthy are hard.

¹⁶Every wise person acts with good sense,
    but fools show how foolish they are.

¹⁷A wicked messenger brings nothing but
trouble,
    but a trustworthy one makes everything
right.

18A person who refuses correction will end up
poor and disgraced,
but the one who accepts correction will be
honored.

19It is so good when wishes come true,
but fools hate to stop doing evil.

20Spend time with the wise and you will
become wise,
but the friends of fools will suffer.

21Trouble always comes to sinners,
but good people enjoy success.

22Good people leave their wealth to their
grandchildren,
but a sinner's wealth is stored up for good
people.

23A poor person's field might produce plenty of
food,
but others often steal it away.

24If you do not punish your children, you don't
love them,
but if you love your children, you will
correct them.

25Good people have enough to eat,
but the wicked will go hungry.

14 A wise woman strengthens her family,
but a foolish woman destroys hers by
what she does.

2People who live good lives respect the LORD,
but those who live evil lives don't.

3Fools will be punished for their proud words,
but the words of the wise will protect
them.

4When there are no oxen, no food is in the
barn.
But with a strong ox, much grain can be
grown.

✳ SIDELIGHT: In ancient times,
oxen were more valuable to the
Israelites than a stereo is to a teenager
(Proverbs 14:4). These great beasts were used
to plow, tread corn, and pull carts. They even
had a day off on the Sabbath (Exodus 23:12,
p. 82).

5A truthful witness does not lie,
but a false witness tells nothing but lies.

6Those who make fun of wisdom look for it
and do not find it,

but knowledge comes easily to those with
understanding.

7Stay away from fools,
because they can't teach you anything.

8A wise person will understand what to do,
but a foolish person is dishonest.

9Fools don't care if they sin,
but honest people work at being right.

10No one else can know your sadness,
and strangers cannot share your joy.

11The wicked person's house will be destroyed,
but a good person's tent will still be
standing.

12Some people think they are doing right,
but in the end it leads to death.

13Someone who is laughing may be sad inside,
and joy may end in sadness.

14Evil people will be paid back for their evil
ways,
and good people will be rewarded for their
good ones.

15Fools will believe anything,
but the wise think about what they do.

16Wise people are careful and stay out of
trouble,
but fools are careless and quick to act.

17Someone with a quick temper does foolish
things,
but someone with understanding remains
calm.

18Fools are rewarded with nothing but more
foolishness,
but the wise are rewarded with knowledge.

19Evil people will bow down to those who are
good;
the wicked will bow down at the door of
those who do right.

20The poor are rejected, even by their
neighbors,
but the rich have many friends.

21It is a sin to hate your neighbor,
but being kind to the needy brings
happiness.

22Those who make evil plans will be ruined,
but those who plan to do good will be
loved and trusted.

23Those who work hard make a profit,
but those who only talk will be poor.

24Wise people are rewarded with wealth,
but fools only get more foolishness.

²⁵A truthful witness saves lives,
but a false witness is a traitor.

²⁶Those who respect the LORD will have
security,
and their children will be protected.

²⁷Respect for the LORD gives life.
It is like a fountain that can save people
from death.

²⁸A king is honored when he has many people
to rule,
but a prince is ruined if he has none.

²⁹Patient people have great understanding,
but people with quick tempers show their
foolishness.

³⁰Peace of mind means a healthy body,
but jealousy will rot your bones.

³¹Whoever mistreats the poor insults their
Maker,
but whoever is kind to the needy honors
God.

³²The wicked are ruined by their own evil,
but those who do right are protected even
in death.

³³Wisdom lives in those with understanding,
and even fools recognize it.

³⁴Doing what is right makes a nation great,
but sin will bring disgrace to any people.

³⁵A king is pleased with a wise servant,
but he will become angry with one who
causes him shame.

15 A gentle answer will calm a person's
anger,
but an unkind answer will cause more
anger.

²Wise people use knowledge when they speak,
but fools pour out foolishness.

³The LORD's eyes see everything;
he watches both evil and good people.

⁴As a tree gives fruit, healing words give life,
but dishonest words crush the spirit.

⁵Fools reject their parents' correction,
but anyone who accepts correction is wise.

⁶Much wealth is in the houses of good people,
but evil people get nothing but trouble.

⁷Wise people use their words to spread
knowledge,
but there is no knowledge in the thoughts
of fools.

⁸The LORD hates the sacrifice that the wicked
offer,

but he likes the prayers of honest people.

⁹The LORD hates what evil people do,
but he loves those who do what is right.

¹⁰The person who quits doing what is right will
be punished,
and the one who hates to be corrected will
die.

¹¹The LORD knows what is happening in the
world of the dead,
so he surely knows the thoughts of the
living.

¹²Those who make fun of wisdom don't like to
be corrected;
they will not ask the wise for advice.

¹³Happiness makes a person smile,
but sadness can break a person's spirit.

¹⁴People with understanding want more
knowledge,
but fools just want more foolishness.

¹⁵Every day is hard for those who suffer,
but a happy heart is like a continual feast.

¹⁶It is better to be poor and respect the LORD
than to be wealthy and have much trouble.

¹⁷It is better to eat vegetables with those who
love you
than to eat meat with those who hate you.

¹⁸People with quick tempers cause trouble,
but those who control their tempers stop a
quarrel.

¹⁹A lazy person's life is like a patch of thorns,
but an honest person's life is like a smooth
highway.

²⁰A wise son makes his father happy,
but a foolish son disrespects his mother.

²¹A person without wisdom enjoys being
foolish,
but someone with understanding does what
is right.

²²Plans fail without good advice,
but they succeed with the advice of many
others.

²³People enjoy giving good advice.
Saying the right word at the right time is so
pleasing.

²⁴Wise people's lives get better and better.
They avoid whatever would cause their
death.

²⁵The LORD will tear down the proud person's
house,
but he will protect the widow's property.

26The LORD hates evil thoughts
but is pleased with kind words.

27Greedy people bring trouble to their families,
but the person who can't be paid to do
wrong will live.

28Good people think before they answer,
but the wicked simply pour out evil.

29The LORD does not listen to the wicked,
but he hears the prayers of those who do
right.

30Good news makes you feel better.
Your happiness will show in your eyes.

31If you listen to correction to improve your
life,
you will live among the wise.

32Those who refuse correction hate themselves,
but those who accept correction gain
understanding.

33Respect for the LORD will teach you wisdom.
If you want to be honored, you must be
humble.

16 People may make plans in their minds,
but only the LORD can make them
come true

2You may believe you are doing right,
but the LORD will judge your reasons.

3Depend on the LORD in whatever you do,
and your plans will succeed.

4The LORD makes everything go as he pleases.
He has even prepared a day of disaster for
evil people.

5The LORD hates those who are proud.
They will surely be punished.

6Love and truth bring forgiveness of sin.
By respecting the LORD you will avoid evil.

7When people live so that they please the
LORD,
even their enemies will make peace with
them.

8It is better to be poor and right
than to be wealthy and dishonest.

9People may make plans in their minds,
but the LORD decides what they will do.

10The words of a king are like a message from
God,
so his decisions should be fair.

11The LORD wants honest balances and scales;
all the weights are his work.

12Kings hate those who do wrong,
because governments only continue if they
are fair.

13Kings like honest people;
they value someone who speaks the truth.

14An angry king can put someone to death,
so a wise person will try to make him
happy.

15A smiling king can give people life;
his kindness is like a spring shower.

16It is better to get wisdom than gold,
and to choose understanding rather than
silver!

17Good people stay away from evil.
By watching what they do, they protect
their lives.

18Pride will destroy a person;
a proud attitude leads to ruin.

19It is better to be humble and be with those
who suffer
than to share stolen property with the
proud.

20Whoever listens to what is taught will
succeed,
and whoever trusts the LORD will be happy.

21The wise are known for their understanding.
Their pleasant words make them better
teachers.

22Understanding is like a fountain which gives
life to those who use it,
but foolishness brings punishment to fools.

23Wise people's minds tell them what to say,
and that helps them be better teachers.

24Pleasant words are like a honeycomb,
making people happy and healthy.

25Some people think they are doing right,
but in the end it leads to death.

26The workers' hunger helps them,
because their desire to eat makes them
work.

27Useless people make evil plans,
and their words are like a burning fire.

28A useless person causes trouble,
and a gossip ruins friendships.

29Cruel people trick their neighbors
and lead them to do wrong.

30Someone who winks is planning evil,
and the one who grins is planning
something wrong.

31Gray hair is like a crown of honor;

it is earned by living a good life.

32Patience is better than strength.
Controlling your temper is better than
capturing a city.

33People throw lots*d* to make a decision,
but the answer comes from the LORD.

17 It is better to eat a dry crust of bread
in peace
than to have a feast where there is
quarreling.

2A wise servant will rule over the master's
disgraceful child
and will even inherit a share of what the
master leaves his children.

3A hot furnace tests silver and gold,
but the LORD tests hearts.

4Evil people listen to evil words.
Liars pay attention to cruel words.

5Whoever mistreats the poor insults their
Maker;
whoever enjoys someone's trouble will be
punished.

6Old people are proud of their grandchildren,
and children are proud of their parents.

7Fools should not be proud,
and rulers should not be liars.

8Some people think they can pay others to do
anything they ask.
They think it will work every time.

9Whoever forgives someone's sin makes a
friend,
but gossiping about the sin breaks up
friendships.

10A wise person will learn more from a
warning
than a fool will learn from a hundred
lashings.

11Disobedient people look only for trouble,
so a cruel messenger will be sent against
them.

12It is better to meet a bear robbed of her cubs
than to meet a fool doing foolish things.

13Whoever gives evil in return for good
will always have trouble at home.

14Starting a quarrel is like a leak in a dam,
so stop it before a fight breaks out.

15The LORD hates both of these things:
freeing the guilty and punishing the
innocent.

16It won't do a fool any good to try to buy
wisdom,
because he doesn't have the ability to be
wise.

17A friend loves you all the time,
and a brother helps in time of trouble.

18It is not wise to promise
to pay what your neighbor owes.

19Whoever loves to argue loves to sin.
Whoever brags a lot is asking for trouble.

20A person with an evil heart will find no
success,
and the person whose words are evil will
get into trouble.

21It is sad to have a foolish child;
there is no joy in being the parent of a fool.

22A happy heart is like good medicine,
but a broken spirit drains your strength.

23When the wicked accept money to do wrong
there can be no justice.

24The person with understanding is always
looking for wisdom,
but the mind of a fool wanders everywhere.

25A foolish son makes his father sad
and causes his mother great sorrow.

26It is not good to punish the innocent
or to beat leaders for being honest.

27The smart person says very little,
and one with understanding stays calm.

28Even fools seem to be wise if they keep
quiet;
if they don't speak, they appear to
understand.

18 Unfriendly people are selfish
and hate all good sense.

2Fools do not want to understand anything.
They only want to tell others what they
think.

3Do something evil, and people won't like
you.
Do something shameful, and they will make
fun of you.

4Spoken words can be like deep water,
but *wisdom is like a flowing stream.*

5It is not good to honor the wicked
or to be unfair to the innocent.

6The words of fools start quarrels.
They make people want to beat them.

7The words of fools will ruin them;

their own words will trap them.

8The words of a gossip are like tasty bits of
　food.
　People like to gobble them up.

9A person who doesn't work hard
　is just like someone who destroys things.

10The LORD is like a strong tower;
　those who do right can run to him for
　safety.

11Rich people trust their wealth to protect
　them.
　They think it is like the high walls of a city.

12Proud people will be ruined,
　but the humble will be honored.

13Anyone who answers without listening
　is foolish and confused.

14The will to live can get you through sickness,
　but no one can live with a broken spirit.

15The mind of a person with understanding
　gets knowledge;
　the wise person listens to learn more.

16Taking a gift to an important man
　will help get you in to see him.

17The person who tells one side of a story
　seems right,
　until someone else comes and asks
　questions.

18Throwing lots*d* can settle arguments
　and keep the two sides from fighting.

19A brother who has been insulted is harder to
　win back than a walled city,
　and arguments separate people like the
　barred gates of a palace.

20People will be rewarded for what they say;
　they will be rewarded by how they speak.

21What you say can mean life or death.
　Those who speak with care will be
　rewarded.

22When a man finds a wife, he finds something
　good.
　It shows that the LORD is pleased with him.

23The poor beg for mercy,
　but the rich give rude answers.

24Some friends may ruin you,
　but a real friend will be more loyal than a
　brother.

19 It is better to be poor and honest
　　than to be foolish and tell lies.

2Enthusiasm without knowledge is not good.

If you act too quickly, you might make a
　mistake.

3People's own foolishness ruins their lives,
　but in their minds they blame the LORD.

4Wealthy people are always finding more
　friends,
　but the poor lose all theirs.

5A witness who lies will not go free;
　liars will never escape.

6Many people want to please a leader,
　and everyone is friends with those who
　give gifts.

7Poor people's relatives avoid them;
　even their friends stay far away.
　They run after them, begging,
　but they are gone.

8Those who get wisdom do themselves a
　favor,
　and those who love learning will succeed.

9A witness who lies will not go free,
　liars will die.

10A fool should not live in luxury.
　A slave should not rule over princes.

11Smart people are patient;
　they will be honored if they ignore insults.

12An angry king is like a roaring lion,
　but his kindness is like the dew on the
　grass.

13A foolish son will ruin his father,
　and a quarreling wife is like dripping water.

SIDELIGHT: When we think of
dripping water, we most often think of
a leaking faucet. But the dripping water of
Proverbs 19:13 was much more annoying. It
probably referred to a leaking roof. In Bible
times, homes were made of mud and had
flat roofs. With good care, roofs stayed pretty
watertight, but leaky roofs were a common
problem—and the source of many jokes.

14Houses and wealth are inherited from
　parents,
　but a wise wife is a gift from the LORD.

15Lazy people sleep a lot,
　and idle people will go hungry.

16Those who obey the commands protect
　themselves,
　but those who are careless will die.

17Being kind to the poor is like lending to the LORD;
he will reward you for what you have done.

18Correct your children while there is still hope;
do not let them destroy themselves.

19People with quick tempers will have to pay for it.
If you help them out once, you will have to do it again.

20Listen to advice and accept correction,
and in the end you will be wise.

21People can make all kinds of plans,
but only the LORD's plan will happen.

22People want others to be loyal,
so it is better to be poor than to be a liar.

23Those who respect the LORD will live
and be satisfied, unbothered by trouble.

24Though the lazy person puts his hand in the dish,
he won't lift the food to his mouth.

25Whip those who make fun of wisdom, and perhaps foolish people will gain some wisdom.
Correct those with understanding, and they will gain knowledge.

26A son who robs his father and sends away his mother
brings shame and disgrace on himself.

27Don't stop listening to correction, my child,
or you will forget what you have already learned.

28An evil witness makes fun of fairness,
and wicked people love what is evil.

29People who make fun of wisdom will be punished,
and the backs of foolish people will be beaten.

20 Wine and beer make people loud and uncontrolled;
it is not wise to get drunk on them.

2An angry king is like a roaring lion.
Making him angry may cost you your life.

3Foolish people are always fighting,
but avoiding quarrels will bring you honor.

4Lazy farmers don't plow when they should;
they expect a harvest, but there is none.

5People's thoughts can be like a deep well,
but someone with understanding can find the wisdom there.

6Many people claim to be loyal,
but it is hard to find a trustworthy person.

7The good people who live honest lives
will be a blessing to their children.

8When a king sits on his throne to judge,
he knows evil when he sees it.

9No one can say, "I am innocent;
I have never done anything wrong."

10The LORD hates both these things:
dishonest weights and dishonest measures.

11Even children are known by their behavior;
their actions show if they are innocent and good.

12The LORD has made both these things:
ears to hear and eyes to see.

13If you love to sleep, you will be poor.
If you stay awake, you will have plenty of food.

14Buyers say, "This is bad. It's no good."
Then they go away and brag about what they bought.

15There is gold and plenty of rubies,
but only a few people speak with knowledge.

16Take the coat of someone who promises to pay a stranger's debts,
and keep it until he pays what the stranger owes.

17Stolen food may taste sweet at first,
but later it will feel like a mouth full of gravel.

18Get advice if you want your plans to work.
If you go to war, get the advice of others.

19Gossips can't keep secrets,
so avoid people who talk too much.

20Those who curse their father or mother
will be like a light going out in darkness.

21Wealth inherited quickly in the beginning
will do you no good in the end.

22Don't say, "I'll pay you back for the wrong you did."
Wait for the LORD, and he will make things right.

23The LORD hates dishonest weights,
and dishonest scales do not please him.

24The LORD decides what a person will do;

no one understands what his life is all
about.

25It's dangerous to promise something to God
too quickly.
After you've thought about it, it may be too
late.

26A wise king sorts out the evil people,
and he punishes them as they deserve.

27The LORD looks deep inside people
and searches through their thoughts.

28Loyalty and truth keep a king in power;
he continues to rule if he is loyal.

29Young men glory in their strength,
and old men are honored for their gray
hair.

30Hard punishment will get rid of evil,
and whippings can change an evil heart.

21 The LORD can control a king's mind as
he controls a river;
he can direct it as he pleases.

2You may believe you are doing right,
but the LORD judges your reasons.

3Doing what is right and fair
is more important to the LORD than
sacrifices.

4Proud looks, proud thoughts,
and evil actions are sin.

5The plans of hard-working people earn a
profit,
but those who act too quickly become
poor.

6Wealth that comes from telling lies
vanishes like a mist and leads to death.

7The violence of the wicked will destroy
them,
because they refuse to do what is right.

8Guilty people live dishonest lives,
but honest people do right.

9It is better to live in a corner on the roof[n]
than inside the house with a quarreling
wife.

10Evil people only want to harm others.
Their neighbors get no mercy from them.

11If you punish those who make fun of
wisdom, a foolish person may gain
some wisdom.
But if you teach the wise, they will get
knowledge.

12God, who is always right, watches the house
of the wicked
and brings ruin on every evil person.

13Whoever ignores the poor when they cry for
help
will also cry for help and not be answered.

14A secret gift will calm an angry person;
a present given in secrecy will quiet great
anger.

15When justice is done, good people are happy,
but evil people are ruined.

16Whoever does not use good sense
will end up among the dead.

17Whoever loves pleasure will become poor;
whoever loves wine and perfume will never
be rich.

18Wicked people will suffer instead of good
people,
and those who cannot be trusted will suffer
instead of those who do right.

19It is better to live alone in the desert
than with a quarreling and complaining
wife.

20Wise people's houses are full of the best
foods and olive oil,
but fools waste everything they have.

21Whoever tries to live right and be loyal
finds life, success, and honor.

22A wise person can defeat a city full of
warriors
and tear down the defenses they trust in.

23Those who are careful about what they say
keep themselves out of trouble.

24People who act with stubborn pride
are called "proud," "bragger," and
"mocker."

25Lazy people's desire for sleep will kill them,
because they refuse to work.
26All day long they wish for more,
but good people give without holding back.

27The LORD hates sacrifices brought by evil
people,
particularly when they offer them for the
wrong reasons.

28A lying witness will be forgotten,
but a truthful witness will speak on.

29Wicked people are stubborn,

---

roof In Bible times houses were built with flat roofs. The roof was used for drying things such as flax and fruit. And it was
used as an extra room, as a place for worship, and as a place to sleep in the summer.

but good people think carefully about what they do.

³⁰There is no wisdom, understanding, or advice that can succeed against the LORD.

³¹You can get the horses ready for battle, but it is the LORD who gives the victory.

22 Being respected is more important than having great riches.
To be well thought of is better than silver or gold.

²The rich and the poor are alike in that the LORD made them all.

³The wise see danger ahead and avoid it, but fools keep going and get into trouble.

⁴Respecting the LORD and not being proud will bring you wealth, honor, and life.

⁵Evil people's lives are like paths covered with thorns and traps.
People who guard themselves don't have such problems.

⁶Train children how to live right, and when they are old, they will not change.

⁷The rich rule over the poor, and borrowers are servants to lenders.

⁸Those who plan evil will receive trouble. Their cruel anger will come to an end.

⁹Generous people will be blessed,

FAMILY

Trust

"Whirr, whirr, whirr, whirr!"

No, not a speeding ticket! Tanya Parker thought. At the worst possible time, too.

Tanya pulled over and waited for the police officer to come to the window. Tanya almost felt like crying. She had been planning to drive to an out-of-town concert this weekend, but getting a speeding ticket would jeopardize her concert plans—if her parents knew. As the police officer handed her the pink slip, she decided it would be better to tell Mom and Dad about the ticket after the concert. Then she returned home and kept quiet.

That night Tanya tossed and turned. Her parents had always trusted her to tell the truth. Finally, around midnight, she got up and went to her older brother to ask his advice. He was still up listening to music.

Tanya told him what had happened and then asked what he thought.

"You'd better tell them," he said. "They'll find out, and then you'll really be in trouble!"

The next morning at breakfast, Tanya spilled the whole story to her parents. She told them about the ticket, and how bad she felt about it, and how she had struggled about telling them.

Disappointment clouded their eyes.

"I don't like the thought of your speeding in our car," Dad said firmly.

"I know, Dad. I'm sorry," Tanya said. "I'll never do it again."

Mom and Dad left the room for a few minutes to talk. Then they returned.

"You have to pay the fine," Mom said and then paused. "And if you agree never to speed again, we won't take away your driving privileges."

"And you can still drive to the concert," Dad added with a grin.

Thrilled, Tanya determined never to betray her parents' trust. And she kept that promise.

Read how **Proverbs 22:1–9** reflects Tanya's family values of honesty and generosity.

■ Which verse in this passage best summarizes Tanya's story?
■ What would you pay to gain your family's respect and trust? As much as is stated in verse 1?

C O N S I D E R . . .

■ talking with a parent about building trust in your relationship.
■ writing on a card four things you can do to build your family's trust in you. Post it where only you can see it.

F O R   M O R E ,   S E E . . .

■ Genesis 4:1–12 (p. 7)
■ Genesis 45:1–11 (p. 50)
■ 2 Timothy 3:14–15 (p. 1266)

because they share their food with the poor.

10Get rid of the one who makes fun of wisdom.
Then fighting, quarrels, and insults will stop.

11Whoever loves pure thoughts and kind words will have even the king as a friend.

12The LORD guards knowledge,
but he destroys false words.

13The lazy person says, "There's a lion outside! I might get killed out in the street!"

14The words of an unfaithful wife are like a deep trap.
Those who make the LORD angry will get caught by them.

15Every child is full of foolishness,
but punishment can get rid of it.

16Whoever gets rich by mistreating the poor, and gives presents to the wealthy, will become poor.

Other Wise Sayings

17Listen carefully to what wise people say;
pay attention to what I am teaching you.
18It will be good to keep these things in mind
so that you are ready to repeat them.
19I am teaching them to you now
so that you will put your trust in the LORD.
20I have written thirty sayings for you,
which give knowledge and good advice.
21I am teaching you true and reliable words
so that you can give true answers to anyone who asks.

22Do not abuse poor people because they are poor,
and do not take away the rights of the needy in court.
23The LORD will defend them in court
and will take the life of those who take away their rights.

24Don't make friends with quick-tempered people
or spend time with those who have bad tempers.
25If you do, you will be like them.
Then you will be in real danger.

26Don't promise to pay what someone else owes,
and don't guarantee anyone's loan.
27If you cannot pay the loan,
your own bed may be taken right out from under you.

28Don't move an old stone that marks a border,
because those stones were set up by your ancestors.

29Do you see people skilled in their work?
They will work for kings, not for ordinary people.

23 If you sit down to eat with a ruler,
notice the food that is in front of you.
2Control yourself
if you have a big appetite.
3Don't be greedy for his fine foods,
because that food might be a trick.

4Don't wear yourself out trying to get rich;
be wise enough to control yourself.
5Wealth can vanish in the wink of an eye.
It can seem to grow wings
and fly away like an eagle.

6Don't eat the food of selfish people;
don't be greedy for their fine foods.
7Selfish people are always worrying
about how much the food costs.
They tell you, "Eat and drink,"
but they don't really mean it.
8You will throw up the little you have eaten,
and you will have wasted your kind words.

9Don't speak to fools;
they will only ignore your wise words.

10Don't move an old stone that marks a border,
and don't take fields that belong to orphans.
11God, their defender, is strong;
he will take their side against you.

12Remember what you are taught,
and listen carefully to words of knowledge.

13Don't fail to punish children.
If you spank them, they won't die.
14If you spank them,
you will save them from death.

15My child, if you are wise,
then I will be happy.
16I will be so pleased
if you speak what is right.

17Don't envy sinners,
but always respect the LORD.
18Then you will have hope for the future,
and your wishes will come true.

19Listen, my child, and be wise.
Keep your mind on what is right.
20Don't drink too much wine
or eat too much food.
21Those who drink and eat too much become poor.

They sleep too much and end up wearing
rags.

22Listen to your father, who gave you life,
and do not forget your mother when she is
old.
23Learn the truth and never reject it.
Get wisdom, self-control, and
understanding.
24The father of a good child is very happy;
parents who have wise children are glad
because of them.
25Make your father and mother happy;
give your mother a reason to be glad.

26My son, pay attention to me,
and watch closely what I do.
27A prostitute*d* is as dangerous as a deep pit,
and an unfaithful wife is like a narrow well.
28They ambush you like robbers
and cause many men to be unfaithful to
their wives.

29Who has trouble? Who has pain?
Who fights? Who complains?
Who has unnecessary bruises?
Who has bloodshot eyes?
30It is people who drink too much wine,
who try out all different kinds of strong
drinks.
31Don't stare at the wine when it is red,
when it sparkles in the cup,
when it goes down smoothly.
32Later it bites like a snake
with poison in its fangs.
33Your eyes will see strange sights,
and your mind will be confused.
34You will feel dizzy as if you're in a storm on
the ocean,
as if you're on top of a ship's sails.
35You will think, "They hit me, but I'm not
hurt.
They beat me up, but I don't remember it.
I wish I could wake up.
Then I would get another drink."

24 Don't envy evil people
or try to be friends with them.
2Their minds are always planning violence,
and they always talk about making trouble.

3It takes wisdom to have a good family,
and it takes understanding to make it
strong.
4*It takes knowledge to fill a home*
with rare and beautiful treasures.

5Wise people have great power,
and those with knowledge have great
strength.
6So you need advice when you go to war.

If you have lots of good advice, you will
win.

7Foolish people cannot understand wisdom.
They have nothing to say in a discussion.

8Whoever makes evil plans
will be known as a troublemaker.
9Making foolish plans is sinful,
and making fun of wisdom is hateful.

10If you give up when trouble comes,
it shows that you are weak.

11Save those who are being led to their death;
rescue those who are about to be killed.
12If you say, "We don't know anything about
this,"
God, who knows what's in your mind, will
notice.
He is watching you, and he will know.
He will reward each person for what he
has done.

13My child, eat honey because it is good.
Honey from the honeycomb tastes sweet.
14In the same way, wisdom is pleasing to you.
If you find it, you have hope for the future,
and your wishes will come true.

15Don't be wicked and attack a good family's
house;
don't rob the place where they live.
16Even though good people may be bothered
by trouble seven times, they are never
defeated,
but the wicked are overwhelmed by
trouble.

17Don't be happy when your enemy is
defeated;
don't be glad when he is overwhelmed.
18The LORD will notice and be displeased.
He may not be angry with them anymore.

19Don't envy evil people,
and don't be jealous of the wicked.
20An evil person has nothing to hope for;
the wicked will die like a flame that is put
out.

21My child, respect the LORD and the king.
Don't join those people who refuse to obey
them.
22The LORD and the king will quickly destroy
such people.
Those two can cause great disaster!

More Words of Wisdom
23These are also sayings of the wise:

It is not good to take sides when you are the
judge.
24Don't tell the wicked that they are innocent;

people will curse you, and nations will hate
you.
25 But things will go well if you punish the
guilty,
and you will receive rich blessings.

26 An honest answer is as pleasing
as a kiss on the lips.

27 First, finish your outside work
and prepare your fields.
After that, you can build your house.

28 Don't testify against your neighbor for no
good reason.
Don't say things that are false.
29 Don't say, "I'll get even;
I'll do to him what he did to me."

30 I passed by a lazy person's field
and by the vineyard of someone with no
sense.
31 Thorns had grown up everywhere.
The ground was covered with weeds,
and the stone walls had fallen down.
32 I thought about what I had seen;
I learned this lesson from what I saw.
33 You sleep a little; you take a nap.
You fold your hands and lie down to rest.
34 Soon you will be as poor as if you had been
robbed;
you will have as little as if you had been
held up.

More Wise Sayings of Solomon

25 These are more wise sayings of Solomon,
copied by the men of Hezekiah king of
Judah.

2 God is honored for what he keeps secret.
Kings are honored for what they can
discover.

3 No one can measure the height of the skies
or the depth of the earth.
So also no one can understand the mind of
a king.

SIDELIGHT: Need a good brain
teaser to fool your friends? Proverbs is
filled with ancient riddles (see Proverbs 25:2–
3, for example). Unfortunately, the punch
lines have lost some of their luster over the
years and in the translation, so they are not
as intriguing as they used to be.

---

4 Remove the scum from the silver,
so the silver can be used by the silversmith.

5 Remove wicked people from the king's
presence;
then his government will be honest and last
a long time.

6 Don't brag to the king
and act as if you are great.
7 It is better for him to give you a higher
position
than to bring you down in front of the
prince.

Because of something you have seen,
8 do not quickly take someone to court.
What will you do later
when your neighbor proves you wrong?

9 If you have an argument with your neighbor,
don't tell other people what was said.
10 Whoever hears it might shame you,
and you might not ever be respected again.

11 The right word spoken at the right time
is as beautiful as gold apples in a silver
bowl.

12 A wise warning to someone who will listen
is as valuable as gold earrings or fine gold
jewelry.

13 Trustworthy messengers refresh those who
send them,
like the coolness of snow in the
summertime.

14 People who brag about gifts they never give
are like clouds and wind that give no rain.

15 With patience you can convince a ruler,
and a gentle word can get through to the
hard-headed.

16 If you find honey, don't eat too much,
or it will make you throw up.
17 Don't go to your neighbor's house too often;
too much of you will make him hate you.

18 When you lie about your neighbors,
it hurts them as much as a club, a sword,
or a sharp arrow.

19 Trusting unfaithful people when you are in
trouble
is like eating with a broken tooth or
walking with a crippled foot.

20 Singing songs to someone who is sad
is like taking away his coat on a cold day
or pouring vinegar on soda.

21 If your enemy is hungry, feed him.
If he is thirsty, give him a drink.
22 Doing this will be like pouring burning coals
on his head,
and the LORD will reward you.

23As the north wind brings rain,
telling gossip brings angry looks.

24It is better to live in a corner on the roof[n]
than inside the house with a quarreling
wife.

25Good news from a faraway place
is like a cool drink when you are tired.

26A good person who gives in to evil
is like a muddy spring or a dirty well.

27It is not good to eat too much honey,
nor does it bring you honor to brag about
yourself.

28Those who do not control themselves
are like a city whose walls are broken
down.

26 It shouldn't snow in summer or rain
at harvest.
Neither should a foolish person ever be
honored.

2Curses will not harm someone who is
innocent;

they are like sparrows or swallows that fly
around and never land.

3Whips are for horses, and harnesses are for
donkeys,
so paddles are good for fools.

4Don't give fools a foolish answer,
or you will be just like them.

5But answer fools as they should be answered,
or they will think they are really wise.

6Sending a message by a foolish person
is like cutting off your feet or drinking
poison.

7A wise saying spoken by a fool
is as useless as the legs of a crippled
person.

8Giving honor to a foolish person
is like tying a stone in a slingshot.

9A wise saying spoken by a fool
is like a thorn stuck in the hand of a
drunk.

---

roof In Bible times houses were built with flat roofs. The roof was used for drying things such as flax and fruit. And it was
used as an extra room, as a place for worship, and as a place to sleep in the summer.

BRAGGING

All Puffed Up

Porcupine puffer fish dart in and out of coral reefs as they feed. Their pale brown color
blends magically with the buff coral. But let a predator, such as a barracuda, threaten them,
and they immediately become defensive. They pump water into themselves, almost
doubling their size. They inflate into spine-covered balls. The attacker usually retreats,
unwilling to swallow such large, thorny creatures.

However, when they puff up, human predators can spot them. These
floating curiosities are worth a lot of money. Once netted and brought to the
surface, puffer fish inflate themselves with air. In that condition they die. Then
they are dried and eventually hung on walls or heaped on shelves of coastal
curio shops.

People who brag and boast are like spiny puffers. Take in what **Proverbs
25:6–7** says about puffed-up people.

■ What are the puffer fish and the "braggart" in this passage trying to hide?
■ In what situations are you tempted to exaggerate your knowledge,
abilities, or material possessions? What might happen to you if you didn't
pretend to be "great" as this passage directs?

C O N S I D E R . . .
■ writing on a ribbon three things you're tempted to brag about. Then tie the
ribbon to your keychain or purse as a reminder not to brag.
■ writing a note to at least three people you admire for not being "people-pleasers,"
telling how you admire that quality in them.

F O R   M O R E .   S E E . . .
■ Daniel 4:28–37 (p. 811)
■ Mark 9:33–35 (p. 980)
■ Luke 18:9–14 (p. 1041)

¹⁰Hiring a foolish person or anyone just passing
by
is like an archer shooting at just anything.

¹¹A fool who repeats his foolishness
is like a dog that goes back to what it has
thrown up.

¹²There is more hope for a foolish person
than for those who think they are wise.

¹³The lazy person says, "There's a lion in the
road!
There's a lion in the streets!"

¹⁴Like a door turning back and forth on its
hinges,
the lazy person turns over and over in bed.

¹⁵Lazy people may put their hands in the dish,
but they are too tired to lift the food to
their mouths.

¹⁶The lazy person thinks he is wiser
than seven people who give sensible
answers.

¹⁷Interfering in someone else's quarrel as you
pass by
is like grabbing a dog by the ears.

¹⁸Like a madman shooting
deadly, burning arrows
¹⁹is the one who tricks a neighbor
and then says, "I was just joking."

²⁰Without wood, a fire will go out,
and without gossip, quarreling will stop.

²¹Just as charcoal and wood keep a fire going,
a quarrelsome person keeps an argument
going.

²²The words of a gossip are like tasty bits of
food;
people like to gobble them up.

²³Kind words from a wicked mind
are like a shiny coating on a clay pot.

²⁴Those who hate you may try to fool you with
their words,
but in their minds they are planning evil.

²⁵People's words may be kind, but don't
believe them,
because their minds are full of evil
thoughts.

²⁶Lies can hide hate,
but the evil will be plain to everyone.

²⁷Whoever digs a pit for others will fall into it.
Whoever tries to roll a boulder down on
others will be crushed by it.

²⁸Liars hate the people they hurt,
and false praise can ruin others.

27 Don't brag about tomorrow;
you don't know what may happen
then.

²Don't praise yourself. Let someone else do it.
Let the praise come from a stranger and not
from your own mouth.

³Stone is heavy, and sand is weighty,
but a complaining fool is worse than either.

⁴Anger is cruel and destroys like a flood,
but no one can put up with jealousy!

⁵It is better to correct someone openly
than to have love and not show it.

⁶The slap of a friend can be trusted to help
you,
but the kisses of an enemy are nothing but
lies.

⁷When you are full, not even honey tastes
good,
but when you are hungry, even something
bitter tastes sweet.

⁸A person who leaves his home
is like a bird that leaves its nest.

⁹The sweet smell of perfume and oils is
pleasant,
and so is good advice from a friend.

SIDELIGHT: If you don't like
taking baths, slap on some extra after-
shave or perfume. Water was usually scarce
in Israel in Old Testament times, and that's
what people did. No wonder putting on oil
and perfume made people happy (Proverbs
27:9). It probably made everyone nearby even
happier!

---

¹⁰Don't forget your friend or your parent's
friend.
Don't always go to your family for help
when trouble comes.
A neighbor close by is better than a family
far away.

¹¹Be wise, my child, and make me happy.
Then I can respond to any insult.

¹²The wise see danger ahead and avoid it,
but fools keep going and get into trouble.

¹³Take the coat of someone who promises to
pay a stranger's loan,
and keep it until he pays what the stranger
owes.

¹⁴If you loudly greet your neighbor early in the
morning,
he will think of it as a curse.

¹⁵A quarreling wife is as bothersome
as a continual dripping on a rainy day.
¹⁶Stopping her is like stopping the wind
or trying to grab oil in your hand.

¹⁷As iron sharpens iron,
so people can improve each other.

¹⁸Whoever tends a fig tree gets to eat its fruit,
and whoever takes care of his master will
receive honor.

¹⁹As water reflects your face,
so your mind shows what kind of person
you are.

²⁰People will never stop dying and being
destroyed,
and they will never stop wanting more than
they have.

²¹A hot furnace tests silver and gold,
and people are tested by the praise they
receive.

²²Even if you ground up a foolish person like
grain in a bowl,
you couldn't remove the foolishness.

²³Be sure you know how your sheep are doing,
and pay attention to the condition of your
cattle.
²⁴Riches will not go on forever,
nor do governments go on forever.
²⁵Bring in the hay, and let the new grass
appear.
Gather the grass from the hills.
²⁶Make clothes from the lambs' wool,
and sell some goats to buy a field.
²⁷There will be plenty of goat's milk
to feed you and your family
and to make your servant girls healthy.

28 Evil people run even though no one is
chasing them,
but good people are as brave as a lion.

²When a country is lawless, it has one ruler
after another;
but when it is led by a man with
understanding and knowledge, it
continues strong.

³*Rulers who mistreat the poor*
are like a hard rain that destroys the crops.

⁴Those who disobey what they have been
taught praise the wicked,
but those who obey what they have been
taught are against them.

⁵Evil people do not understand justice,
but those who follow the LORD understand
it completely.

⁶It is better to be poor and innocent
than to be rich and wicked.

⁷Children who obey what they have been
taught are smart,
but friends of troublemakers disgrace their
parents.

⁸Some people get rich by overcharging others,
but their wealth will be given to those who
are kind to the poor.

⁹If you refuse to obey what you have been
taught,
your prayers will not be heard.

¹⁰Those who lead good people to do wrong
will be ruined by their own evil,
but the innocent will be rewarded with
good things.

¹¹Rich people may think they are wise,
but the poor with understanding will prove
them wrong.

¹²When good people triumph, there is great
happiness,
but when the wicked get control,
everybody hides.

¹³If you hide your sins, you will not succeed.
If you confess and reject them, you will
receive mercy.

¹⁴Those who are always respectful will be
happy,
but those who are stubborn will get into
trouble.

¹⁵A wicked ruler is as dangerous to poor people
as a roaring lion or a charging bear.

¹⁶A ruler without wisdom will be cruel,
but the one who refuses to take dishonest
money will rule a long time.

¹⁷Don't help those who are guilty of murder;
let them run until they die.

¹⁸Innocent people will be kept safe,
but those who are dishonest will suddenly
be ruined.

¹⁹Those who work their land will have plenty
of food,
but the ones who chase empty dreams
instead will end up poor.

²⁰A truthful person will have many blessings,
but those eager to get rich will be
punished.

²¹It is not good for a judge to take sides,

but some will sin for only a piece of bread.

22Selfish people are in a hurry to get rich
and do not realize they soon will be poor.

23Those who correct others will later be liked
more than those who give false praise.

24Whoever robs his father or mother
and says, "It's not wrong,"
is just like someone who destroys things.

25A greedy person causes trouble,
but the one who trusts the LORD will
succeed.

26Those who trust in themselves are foolish,
but those who live wisely will be kept safe.

27Whoever gives to the poor will have
everything he needs,
but the one who ignores the poor will
receive many curses.

28When the wicked get control, everybody
hides,
but when they die, good people do well.

29 Whoever is stubborn after being
corrected many times
will suddenly be hurt beyond cure.

2When good people do well, everyone is
happy,
but when evil people rule, everyone groans.

3Those who love wisdom make their parents
happy,
but friends of prostitutes*d* waste their
money.

4If a king is fair, he makes his country strong,
but if he takes gifts dishonestly, he tears his
country down.

5Those who give false praise to their neighbors
are setting a trap for them.

6Evil people are trapped by their own sin,
but good people can sing and be happy.

7Good people care about justice for the poor,
but the wicked are not concerned.

8People who make fun of wisdom cause
trouble in a city,
but wise people calm anger down.

9When a wise person takes a foolish person to
court,
the fool only shouts or laughs, and there is
no peace.

10Murderers hate an honest person
and try to kill those who do right.

11Foolish people lose their tempers,
but wise people control theirs.

12If a ruler pays attention to lies,
all his officers will become wicked.

13The poor person and the cruel person are
alike
in that the LORD gave eyes to both of them.

14If a king judges poor people fairly,
his government will continue forever.

15Correction and punishment make children
wise,
but those left alone will disgrace their
mother.

16When there are many wicked people, there is
much sin,
but those who do right will see them
destroyed.

17Correct your children, and you will be proud;
they will give you satisfaction.

18Where there is no word from God, people
are uncontrolled,
but those who obey what they have been
taught are happy.

19Words alone cannot correct a servant,
because even if he understands, he won't
respond.

20Do you see people who speak too quickly?
There is more hope for a foolish person
than for them.

21If you spoil your servants when they are
young,
they will bring you grief later on.

22An angry person causes trouble;
a person with a quick temper sins a lot.

23Pride will ruin people,
but those who are humble will be honored.

24Partners of thieves are their own worst
enemies.
If they have to testify in court, they are
afraid to say anything.

25Being afraid of people can get you into
trouble,
but if you trust the LORD, you will be safe.

26Many people want to speak to a ruler,
but justice comes only from the LORD.

27Good people hate those who are dishonest,
and the wicked hate those who are honest.

Wise Words from Agur

30 These are the words of Agur son of Ja-
keh.

This is his message to Ithiel and Ucal:

2"I am the most stupid person there is,
and I have no understanding.
3I have not learned to be wise,
and I don't know much about God, the
Holy One.
4Who has gone up to heaven and come back
down?
Who can hold the wind in his hand?
Who can gather up the waters in his coat?
Who has set in place the ends of the earth?
What is his name or his son's name?
Tell me, if you know!

5"Every word of God is true.
He guards those who come to him for
safety.
6Do not add to his words,
or he will correct you and prove you are a
liar.

7"I ask two things from you, LORD.
Don't refuse me before I die.
8Keep me from lying and being dishonest.
And don't make me either rich or poor;
just give me enough food for each day.
9If I have too much, I might reject you
and say, 'I don't know the LORD.'
If I am poor, I might steal
and disgrace the name of my God.

10"Do not say bad things about servants to
their masters,
or they will curse you, and you will suffer
for it.

11"Some people curse their fathers
and do not bless their mothers.
12Some people think they are pure,
but they are not really free from evil.
13Some people have such a proud look!
They look down on others.
14Some people have teeth like swords;
their jaws seem full of knives.
They want to remove the poor from the earth
and the needy from the land.

15"Greed has two daughters
named 'Give' and 'Give.'
There are three things that are never
satisfied,
really four that never say, 'I've had
enough!':
16the cemetery, the childless mother,
the land that never gets enough rain,
and fire that never says, 'I've had enough!'

17"If you make fun of your father
and refuse to obey your mother,
the birds of the valley will peck out your
eyes,
and the vultures will eat them.

18"There are three things that are too hard for
me,
really four I don't understand:
19the way an eagle flies in the sky,
the way a snake slides over a rock,
the way a ship sails on the sea,
and the way a man and a woman fall in
love.

20"This is the way of a woman who takes part
in adultery:*d*
She acts as if she had eaten and washed
her face;
she says, 'I haven't done anything wrong.'

21"There are three things that make the earth
tremble,
really four it cannot stand:
22a servant who becomes a king,
a foolish person who has plenty to eat,
23a hated woman who gets married,
and a maid who replaces her mistress.

24"There are four things on earth that are
small,
but they are very wise:
25Ants are not very strong,
but they store up food in the summer.
26Rock badgers are not very powerful,
but they can live among the rocks.
27Locusts*d* have no king,
but they all go forward in formation.
28Lizards can be caught in the hand,
but they are found even in kings' palaces.

29"There are three things that strut proudly,
really four that walk as if they were
important:
30a lion, the proudest animal,
which is strong and runs from nothing,
31a rooster, a male goat,
and a king when his army is around him.

32"If you have been foolish and proud,
or if you have planned evil, shut your
mouth.
33Just as stirring milk makes butter,
and twisting noses makes them bleed,
so stirring up anger causes trouble."

Wise Words of King Lemuel

31 These are the words of King Lemuel, the
message his mother taught him:

2"My son, I gave birth to you.
You are the son I prayed for.
3Don't waste your strength on women
or your time on those who ruin kings.

4"Kings should not drink wine, Lemuel,
and rulers should not desire beer.
5If they drink, they might forget the law

and keep the needy from getting their rights.
⁶Give beer to people who are dying
and wine to those who are sad.
⁷Let them drink and forget their need
and remember their misery no more.

⁸"Speak up for those who cannot speak for themselves;
defend the rights of all those who have nothing.
⁹Speak up and judge fairly,
and defend the rights of the poor and needy."

The Good Wife

¹⁰It is hard to find a good wife,
because she is worth more than rubies.
¹¹Her husband trusts her completely.
With her, he has everything he needs.
¹²She does him good and not harm
for as long as she lives.
¹³She looks for wool and flax
and likes to work with her hands.

¹⁴She is like a trader's ship,
bringing food from far away.
¹⁵She gets up while it is still dark
and prepares food for her family
and feeds her servant girls.
¹⁶She inspects a field and buys it.
With money she earned, she plants a vineyard.
¹⁷She does her work with energy,
and her arms are strong.
¹⁸She knows that what she makes is good.
Her lamp burns late into the night.

SIDELIGHT: The "good wife" of Proverbs 31:10–31 would have been a "supermom" centuries before that term was common. Not only did she do everything around the house; she also farmed (verse 16), worked in manufacturing (verse 24), and did volunteer work (verse 20). Makes you wonder what her husband did!

MARRIAGE

Like Great-Grandmother

Tracy Bilmer stood in her great-grandmother's wedding dress, watching her mother fit the new sleeves into place. "I'm scared."

"Of what, sweetie?"

"Marriage." Tracy stared into the mirror. "I'm scared of being an adult. Of being responsible for building a new life with Chris."

"I know." Her mother pushed back her hair. "But follow your great-grandmother's example. She built a grand life for herself and her husband."

Her mother smiled, remembering. "She helped clear the Colorado homestead, bore babies, worked beside my granddad in the fields, set her children's broken bones, canned a thousand jars of food each summer, sewed clothes, and prayed beside her children's beds each night. And through it all she was a loving lady. She and Granddad truly loved each other, and they made a great team. As Granddad lay dying, after sixty-six years of marriage, he said she was still his angel."

"Funny, she seems modern—a working woman, besides being a wife and mother," Tracy said.

"Loving determination, that's what she had. That and her faith in God."

The good wife in Proverbs also possessed some of the great-grandmother's qualities. Read **Proverbs 31:10–31**.

■ In what ways is the great-grandmother like the wife described in this passage?
■ Which qualities, listed in these verses, do you most want in your life?

C O N S I D E R . . .

■ looking for qualities of a godly wife or husband at your church, then asking God to help you build those qualities in yourself so you will be a godly spouse if you marry.
■ asking couples you admire for their secret of a successful marriage.

F O R   M O R E ,   S E E . . .

■ Ruth 3—4 (p. 241)
■ Ephesians 5:21–33 (p. 1225)
■ 1 Peter 3:1–7 (p. 1306)

[19]She makes thread with her hands
and weaves her own cloth.
[20]She welcomes the poor
and helps the needy.
[21]She does not worry about her family when it
snows,
because they all have fine clothes to keep
them warm.
[22]She makes coverings for herself;
her clothes are made of linen and other
expensive material.
[23]Her husband is known at the city meetings,
where he makes decisions as one of the
leaders of the land.
[24]She makes linen clothes and sells them
and provides belts to the merchants.
[25]She is strong and is respected by the people.

She looks forward to the future with
joy.
[26]She speaks wise words
and teaches others to be kind.
[27]She watches over her family
and never wastes her time.
[28]Her children speak well of her.
Her husband also praises her,
[29]saying, "There are many fine women,
but you are better than all of them."
[30]Charm can fool you, and beauty can trick
you,
but a woman who respects the LORD
should be praised.
[31]Give her the reward she has earned;
she should be praised in public for what
she has done.

ECCLESIASTES

Why Read This Book:

■ See the results of living a variety of lifestyles (Ecclesiastes 1—2).
■ Find companionship when bad things happen (Ecclesiastes 4—5).
■ Explore the problem of injustice and the mystery of God (Ecclesiastes 9—10).
■ Accept and enjoy life as God has given it (Ecclesiastes 3, 6, 11—12).

Behind the Scenes:

What brings happiness? What gives life meaning? People look in all kinds of places for answers to these questions.

Some people spend their lives making money to buy happiness. Then they die feeling empty and lonely.

Other people work hard on the job, hoping to find a way to leave a lasting impression on the world. Then they die, and people forget them.

Some people study and learn all they can in a quest for knowledge and understanding. Yet the world still holds mysteries they can't understand.

Other people spend all their time on the "party scene," trying to have fun and feel good. But afterward, life seems hollow and purposeless.

The writer of Ecclesiastes—often called the Preacher or the Teacher—walked down all these paths looking for happiness. Yet he never found it. Life was too complex and contradictory to understand through simple formulas. Good people suffered. Bad people prospered. It didn't make sense.

The book of Ecclesiastes contains the Teacher's thoughts about life and its meaning. Sometimes he seems skeptical and cynical, because nothing in life seems meaningful (Ecclesiastes 1:2 and 12:8). Sometimes he says God is so distant we can't know him (Ecclesiastes 5:2).

Yet Ecclesiastes also gives insight and comfort on several levels.

■ First, the book affirms the importance of exploring and reflecting on what it means to follow God. Not only does Ecclesiastes remind us it's okay to ask tough questions, but the author's arguments can help us think through those questions.

■ Second, the author's philosophical thoughts show the emptiness of life without God. True wisdom and meaning can't be found with human effort; they are gifts from God.

■ Third, the author believes life is worth living, even with its problems. He urges people to grab onto and enjoy the good things God gives us.

■ Finally, the author affirms that God is in control—even when we can't see his work. "Honor God and obey his commands," he urges, "because this is all people must do" (Ecclesiastes 12:13).

WHEN THE ACTION WAS

	Jerusalem fell to the Babylonians	Jews began returning to Jerusalem from exile		Jesus was born
1000BC	**750BC**	**500BC**	**250BC**	**BC/AD**
King Solomon ruled Israel and many people believe he wrote Ecclesiastes		Ecclesiastes may have been written		

1 These are the words of the Teacher, a son of David, king in Jerusalem.
²The Teacher says,
"Useless! Useless!
Completely useless!
Everything is useless."

³What do people really gain
from all the hard work they do here on earth?

Things Never Change

⁴People live, and people die,
but the earth continues forever.
⁵The sun rises, the sun sets,
and then it hurries back to where it rises again.
⁶The wind blows to the south;
it blows to the north.

It blows from one direction and then another. Then it turns around and repeats the same pattern, going nowhere.

> ✳ **SIDELIGHT:** The title of Ecclesiastes is, itself, a mystery. It's translated from the Hebrew word "Qoheleth," but no one is sure what it means. Some scholars think it might be a proper name; others say it means "The Preacher," "The Teacher," or "Speaker." But still others think it could mean "The Arguer," which captures the book's content well!

⁷All the rivers flow to the sea,
but the sea never becomes full.
⁸Everything is boring,

DISCOURAGEMENT

Failure Turned Around

Charles sat on the steps in misery. He watched his classmates pass by him as if he were invisible. The yearbook committee rejection note in his hands branded him "First Class Loser"—a label he had worn many times. He had hoped this time would be different. He had hoped that his one ability, cartooning, would help promote him from his self-imposed "loser" status. But the note unceremoniously crushed his hopes.

"The yearbook committee has decided not to use your submission this year. Thank you for submitting your material."

Why should he be surprised? Failure slugged him regularly. He recounted his blunders:
■ An F in Latin
■ An F in Algebra
■ Failed every class in the 8th grade
■ A klutz in sports
■ Last place in the school golf tournament and its consolation match
■ Too scared to ask any girl out on a date

With a resigned sigh, Charles turned toward home. He believed nothing was ever going to change for him.

He continued to create imaginary worlds on paper, unable to stop drawing. Repeatedly, through the years, his cartoons were rejected. Then one day he created a character like himself—a habitual failure.

And Charlie Brown was born.

In Ecclesiastes, the writer is discouraged because he feels like nothing ever changes, just as Charles Schulz once did. But Schulz later created the famous Peanuts comic strip. Read **Ecclesiastes 1:2–11**.
■ Which of these verses best describe Charles's feelings?
■ Which verses best describe you when you're discouraged?

C O N S I D E R . . .
■ identifying your strongest interest and writing yourself a promise to develop it to the fullest.
■ asking a friend this week to encourage you by telling you what positive qualities he or she sees in you.

F O R   M O R E ,   S E E . . .
■ Isaiah 43:18–21 (p. 660)
■ Matthew 6:25–27 (p. 918)
■ Romans 15:1–7 (p. 1161)

so boring that you don't even want to talk
　　about it.
Words come again and again to our ears,
　　but we never hear enough,
　　nor can we ever really see all we want to
　　　　see.
9All things continue the way they have been
　　since the beginning.
　　What has happened will happen again;
　　there is nothing new here on earth.
10Someone might say,
　　"Look, this is new,"
　　but really it has always been here.
　　It was here before we were.
11People don't remember what happened long
　　ago,
　　and in the future people will not remember
　　　what happens now.
　　Even later, other people will not remember
　　　what was done before them.

Does Wisdom Bring Happiness?

12I, the Teacher, was king over Israel in Jerusalem. 13I decided to use my wisdom to learn about
everything that happens on earth. I learned that
God has given us terrible things to face. 14I looked
at everything done on earth and saw that it is all
useless, like chasing the wind.

15If something is crooked,
　　you can't make it straight.
　　If something is missing,
　　you can't say it is there.

16I said to myself, "I have become very wise
and am now wiser than anyone who ruled Jerusalem before me. I know what wisdom and knowledge really are." 17So I decided to find out about
wisdom and knowledge and also about foolish
thinking, but this turned out to be like chasing the
wind.

18With much wisdom comes much
　　disappointment;
　　the person who gains more knowledge also
　　gains more sorrow.

Does "Having Fun" Bring Happiness?

2 I said to myself, "I will try having fun. I will
　enjoy myself." But I found that this is also
useless. 2It is foolish to laugh all the time, and
having fun doesn't accomplish anything. 3I decided to cheer myself up with wine while my
mind was still thinking wisely. I wanted to find a
way to enjoy myself and see what was good for
people to do during their few days of life.

Does Hard Work Bring Happiness?

4Then I did great things: I built houses and
planted vineyards for myself. 5I made gardens and

parks, and I planted all kinds of fruit trees in them.
6I made pools of water for myself and used them
to water my growing trees. 7I bought male and
female slaves, and slaves were also born in my
house. I had large herds and flocks, more than
anyone in Jerusalem had ever had before. 8I also
gathered silver and gold for myself, treasures from
kings and other areas. I had male and female singers and all the women a man could ever want. 9I
became very famous, even greater than anyone
who had lived in Jerusalem before me. My wisdom helped me in all this.

10Anything I saw and wanted, I got for myself;
　　I did not miss any pleasure I desired.
　　I was pleased with everything I did,
　　and this pleasure was the reward for all my
　　　hard work.
11But then I looked at what I had done,
　　and I thought about all the hard work.
　　Suddenly I realized it was useless, like
　　　chasing the wind.
　　There is nothing to gain from anything we
　　　do here on earth.

> ✸ **SIDELIGHT:** The Teacher
> mentions hard work more than thirty
> times in Ecclesiastes (for example, Ecclesiastes
> 2:4–11). Yet he considers it useless activity
> apart from God. Maybe he should have
> joined Workaholics Anonymous.

Maybe Wisdom Is the Answer

12Then I began to think again about being
　　wise,
　　and also about being foolish and doing
　　　crazy things.
　　But after all, what more can anyone do?
　　He can't do more than what the other king
　　　has already done.
13I saw that being wise is certainly better than
　　being foolish,
　　just as light is better than darkness.
14Wise people see where they are going,
　　but fools walk around in the dark.
　　Yet I saw that
　　both wise and foolish people end the same
　　　way.

15I thought to myself,
　　"What happens to a fool will happen to me,
　　　too,
　　so what is the reward for being wise?"
　　I said to myself,
　　"Being wise is also useless."
16The wise person and the fool
　　will both die,

and no one will remember either one for long.
In the future, both will be forgotten.

Is There Real Happiness in Life?

[17]So I hated life. It made me sad to think that everything here on earth is useless, like chasing the wind. [18]I hated all the things I had worked for here on earth, because I must leave them to someone who will live after me. [19]Someone else will control everything for which I worked so hard here on earth, and I don't know if he will be wise or foolish. This is also useless. [20]So I became sad about all the hard work I had done here on earth. [21]People can work hard using all their wisdom, knowledge, and skill, but they will die, and other people will get the things for which they worked. They did not do the work, but they will get everything. This is also unfair and useless. [22]What do people get for all their work and struggling here on earth? [23]All of their lives their work is full of pain and sorrow, and even at night their minds don't rest. This is also useless.

[24]The best that people can do is eat, drink, and enjoy their work. I saw that even this comes from God, [25]because no one can eat or enjoy life without him. [26]If people please God, God will give them wisdom, knowledge, and joy. But sinners will get only the work of gathering and storing wealth that they will have to give to the ones who please God. So all their work is useless, like chasing the wind.

There Is a Time for Everything

3 There is a time for everything,
  and everything on earth has its special
    season.
[2]There is a time to be born
  and a time to die.
There is a time to plant
  and a time to pull up plants.
[3]There is a time to kill
  and a time to heal.
There is a time to destroy
  and a time to build.
[4]There is a time to cry
  and a time to laugh.
There is a time to be sad
  and a time to dance.
[5]There is a time to throw away stones

HAPPINESS

In the Here and Now

At dawn Jay Norris lay in his lakeside tent and replayed the state track meet in his head. He was running the 3200-meter race, pushing toward the finish line. His only chance for an athletic scholarship was riding on the finish. He had to place in the top three.

He came in seventh.

"Jay, pancakes on!" Uncle Carl called from the campfire. Uncle Carl had always been there for him, ever since Dad had left. He crawled out and joined Uncle Carl.

"I want to tell you something, boy," Uncle Carl said, serving Jay's plate. "You lost that race . . . that's life." He looked straight at Jay. "The point is—God has given you legs to enjoy running with."

"So?"

"I'm talking about enjoying the moment—the feel of your feet in your shoes, the pounding of your shoes on the track, and the tingle in your arms and legs!" He grinned at Jay. "Now, that's living."

Uncle Carl's words didn't mean much to Jay then. But over the years they've shaped the way he looks at life. Now he strives to enjoy what God's given to him.

The writer of Ecclesiastes tried to find happiness in the middle of loss also.
Read **Ecclesiastes 2:18–26**.

■ How does Uncle Carl's advice compare with the advice in Ecclesiastes?
■ How can you apply the advice in the passage to your life this week?

            C O N S I D E R . . .
■ focusing only on your body sensations while washing the car, or eating or exercising.
■ going for a walk in the woods and then recording in a journal all the fun moments you experienced.

      F O R   M O R E ,   S E E . . .
■ Psalm 16:7–11 (p. 489)
■ Luke 12:22–31 (p. 1028)
        ■ 2 Corinthians 4:7–9 (p. 1195)

and a time to gather them.
There is a time to hug
and a time not to hug.
6There is a time to look for something
and a time to stop looking for it.
There is a time to keep things
and a time to throw things away.
7There is a time to tear apart
and a time to sew together.
There is a time to be silent
and a time to speak.
8There is a time to love
and a time to hate.
There is a time for war
and a time for peace.

God Controls His World

9Do people really gain anything from their work? 10I saw the hard work God has given people to do. 11God has given them a desire to know the future. He does everything just right and on time, but people can never completely understand what he is doing. 12So I realize that the best thing for them is to be happy and enjoy themselves as long as they live. 13God wants all people to eat and drink and be happy in their work, which are gifts from God. 14I know that everything God does will continue forever. People cannot add anything to what God has done, and they cannot take anything away from it. God does it this way to make people respect him.

15What happens now has happened in the past,
and what will happen in the future has
happened before.
God makes the same things happen again
and again.

Unfairness on Earth

16I also saw this here on earth:
Where there should have been justice, there
was evil;
where there should have been right, there
was wrong.
17I said to myself,
God has planned a time for every thing and
every action,
so he will judge both good people and bad.

18I decided that God leaves it the way it is to test people and to show them they are just like

---

SADNESS

Death Watch

Derek Grimm's grandfather lay quietly in his bed at home, shriveled to the bone by Parkinson's disease.

Derek held his calloused hand and whispered. "I love you, Gramps."

"I love you too," the old man whispered back, barely able to talk.

Tears sprang to Derek's eyes. "What will I do without you?"

"Remember our good times." The old man closed his eyes. "Enjoy your life . . . and follow the Lord."

"I don't want to let you go," Derek began to cry.

"It's all right," Gramps said. "It's my time to go. God knows what he's doing."

Derek fought back tears as he watched his grandfather struggle to breathe.

"Will you play 'Take My Hand, Precious Lord'? It soothes me," Gramps asked.

Derek sat at the piano in the next room and played the song Gramps had heard so many times before. Derek's heart broke with each note. But there was also a distant joy for the times he and Gramps had shared and the fact that the pain would finally end.

Even the sadness of death can be seen as a natural part of life, according to **Ecclesiastes 3:1–13**.
■ Where in these verses are there words like Gramps spoke?
■ How do these verses help you cope with sadness?

CONSIDER . . .
■ writing an example for each of the "times" listed in the passage.
■ looking through family photos and remembering times like those listed in Ecclesiastes.

FOR MORE, SEE . . .
■ Psalm 88 p. 533
■ Philippians 3:4–7 (p 1232)
■ Romans 5 3–5 (p 1145)

animals. [19]The same thing happens to animals and to people; they both have the same breath, so they both die. People are no better off than the animals, because everything is useless. [20]Both end up the same way; both came from dust and both will go back to dust. [21]Who can be sure that the human spirit goes up to God and that the spirit of an animal goes down into the ground? [22]So I saw that the best thing people can do is to enjoy their work, because that is all they have. No one can help another person see what will happen in the future.

Is It Better to Be Dead?

4 Again I saw all the people who were mistreated here on earth.
I saw their tears
    and that they had no one to comfort them.
Cruel people had all the power,
    and there was no one to comfort those they
        hurt.
[2]I decided that the dead
    are better off than the living.
[3]But those who have never been born
    are better off still;
they have not seen the evil
    that is done here on earth.

Why Work So Hard?

[4]I realized the reason people work hard and try to succeed: They are jealous of each other. This, too, is useless, like chasing the wind.

[5]Some say it is foolish to fold your hands and
        do nothing,
    because you will starve to death.
[6]Maybe so, but I say it is better to be content
    with what little you have.
Otherwise, you will always be struggling for
        more,
    and that is like chasing the wind.

[7]Again I saw something here on earth that
        was useless:
[8]I saw a man who had no family,
    no son or brother.
He always worked hard
    but was never satisfied with what he had.
He never asked himself, "For whom am I
        working so hard?
Why don't I let myself enjoy life?"
This also is very sad and useless.

Friends and Family Give Strength

[9]Two people are better than one,
    because they get more done by working
        together.
[10]If one falls down,
    the other can help him up.

But it is bad for the person who is alone and
        falls,
    because no one is there to help.
[11]If two lie down together, they will be warm,
    but a person alone will not be warm.
[12]An enemy might defeat one person,
    but two people together can defend
        themselves;
a rope that is woven of three strings is hard
        to break.

Fame and Power Are Useless

[13]A poor but wise boy is better than a foolish but old king who doesn't listen to advice. [14]A boy became king. He had been born poor in the kingdom and had even gone to prison before becoming king. [15]I watched all the people who live on earth follow him and make him their king. [16]Many followed him at first, but later, they did not like him, either. So fame and power are useless, like chasing the wind.

Be Careful About Making Promises

5 Be careful when you go to worship at the Temple.[d] It is better to listen than to offer foolish sacrifices without even knowing you are doing wrong.

[2]Think before you speak,
    and be careful about what you say to God.
God is in heaven,
    and you are on the earth,
    so say only a few words to God.
[3]The saying is true: Bad dreams come from
        too much worrying,
    and too many words come from foolish
        people.

[4]If you make a promise to God, don't be slow to keep it. God is not happy with fools, so give God what you promised. [5]It is better not to promise anything than to promise something and not do it. [6]Don't let your words cause you to sin, and don't say to the priest at the Temple, "I didn't mean what I promised." If you do, God will become angry with your words and will destroy everything you have worked for. [7]Many useless promises are like so many dreams; they mean nothing. You should respect God.

> ☀ **SIDELIGHT:** Making a promise in biblical times (Ecclesiastes 5:4–7) was more like signing an important legal contract (such as a marriage license) today. Once you made a promise, you couldn't really get out of it.

Officers Cheat Each Other

8In some places you will see poor people mistreated. Don't be surprised when they are not treated fairly or given their rights. One officer is cheated by a higher officer who in turn is cheated by even higher officers. 9The wealth of the country is divided up among them all. Even the king makes sure he gets his share of the profits.

Wealth Cannot Buy Happiness

10Whoever loves money
    will never have enough money;
Whoever loves wealth
    will not be satisfied with it.
    This is also useless.
11The more wealth people have,
    the more friends they have to help spend it.
So what do people really gain?
    They gain nothing except to look at their
        riches.
12Those who work hard sleep in peace;
    it is not important if they eat little or much.
But rich people worry about their wealth
    and cannot sleep.

13I have seen real misery here on earth:
Money saved is a curse to its owners.
14   They lose it all in a bad deal
and have nothing to give to their children.
15People come into this world with nothing,
    and when they die they leave with nothing.
In spite of all their hard work,
    they leave just as they came.
16This, too, is real misery:
They leave just as they came.
    So what do they gain from chasing the
        wind?
17All they get are days full of sadness and
        sorrow,
    and they end up sick, defeated, and angry.

Enjoy Your Life's Work

18I have seen what is best for people here on earth. They should eat and drink and enjoy their work, because the life God has given them on earth is short. 19God gives some people the ability to enjoy the wealth and property he gives them, as well as the ability to accept their state in life and enjoy their work. 20They do not worry about how short life is, because God keeps them busy with what they love to do.

6 I have seen something else wrong here on earth that causes serious problems for people. 2God gives great wealth, riches, and honor to some people; they have everything they want. But God does not let them enjoy such things; a stranger enjoys them instead. This is useless and very wrong. 3A man might have a hundred children and live a long time, but what good is it if

he can't enjoy the good God gives him or have a proper burial? I say a baby born dead is better off than he is. 4A baby born dead is useless. It returns to darkness without even a name. 5That baby never saw the sun and never knew anything, but it finds more rest than that man. 6Even if he lives two thousand years, he doesn't enjoy the good God gives him. Everyone is going to the same place.

7People work just to feed themselves,
    but they never seem to get enough to eat.
8In this way a wise person
    is no better off than a fool.
Then, too, it does a poor person little good
    to know how to get along in life.
9It is better to see what you have
    than to want more.
Wanting more is useless—
    like chasing the wind.

Who Can Understand God's Plan?

10Whatever happens was planned long ago.
    Everyone knows what people are like.
No one can argue with God,
    who is stronger than anyone.
11The more you say,
    the more useless it is.
    What good does it do?

12People have only a few useless days of life on the earth; their short life passes like a shadow. Who knows what is best for them while they live? Who can tell them what the future will bring?

Some Benefits of Serious Thinking

7 It is better to have respect than good
    perfume.
The day of death is better than the day of
        birth.
2It is better to go to a funeral
    than to a party.
We all must die,
    and everyone living should think about this.
3Sorrow is better than laughter,
    and sadness has a good influence on you.
4A wise person thinks about death,
    but a fool thinks only about having a good
        time.
5It is better to be criticized by a wise person
    than to be praised by a fool.
6The laughter of fools
    is like the crackling of thorns in a cooking
        fire.
    Both are useless.

7Even wise people are fools
    if they let money change their thinking.

8It is better to finish something
    than to start it.

It is better to be patient
    than to be proud.
⁹Don't become angry quickly,
    because getting angry is foolish.

¹⁰Don't ask, "Why was life better in the 'good
    old days'?"
    It is not wise to ask such questions.

¹¹Wisdom is better when it comes with money.
    They both help those who are alive.
¹²Wisdom is like money:
    they both help.
    But wisdom is better,
    because it can save whoever has it.

¹³Look at what God has done:
    No one can straighten what he has bent.
¹⁴When life is good, enjoy it.
    But when life is hard, remember:
    God gives good times and hard times,
    and no one knows what tomorrow will
    bring.

It Is Impossible to Be Truly Good

¹⁵In my useless life I have seen both of these:
    I have seen good people die in spite of their
    goodness
    and evil people live a long time in spite of
    their evil.
¹⁶Don't be too right,
    and don't be too wise.
    Why destroy yourself?
¹⁷Don't be too wicked,
    and don't be foolish.
    Why die before your time?
¹⁸It is good to grab the one and not let go of
    the other;
    those who honor God will hold them both.

¹⁹Wisdom makes a person stronger
    than ten leaders in a city.

²⁰Surely there is not a good person on earth
    who always does good and never sins.

²¹Don't listen to everything people say,
    or you might hear your servant insulting
    you.
²²You know that many times
    you have insulted others.

²³I used wisdom to test all these things.
    I wanted to be wise,
    but it was too hard for me.
²⁴I cannot understand why things are as they
    are.
    It is too hard for anyone to understand.
²⁵I studied and tried very hard to find wisdom,
    to find some meaning for everything.
    I learned that it is foolish to be evil,
    and it is crazy to act like a fool.

²⁶I found that some women are worse than
    death
    and are as dangerous as traps.
    Their love is like a net,
    and their arms hold men like chains.
    A man who pleases God will be saved from
    them,
    but a sinner will be caught by them.

²⁷The Teacher says, "This is what I learned:
    I added all these things together
    to find some meaning for everything.
²⁸While I was searching,
    I did not find one man among the
    thousands I found.
    Nor did I find a woman among all these.
²⁹One thing I have learned:
    God made people good,
    but they have found all kinds of ways to be
    bad."

Obey the King

8 No one is like the wise person
    who can understand what things mean.
    Wisdom brings happiness;
    it makes sad faces happy.

²Obey the king's command, because you made
a promise to God. ³Don't be too quick to leave the
king. Don't support something that is wrong, because the king does whatever he pleases. ⁴What
the king says is law; no one tells him what to do.

⁵Whoever obeys the king's command will be
    safe.
    A wise person does the right thing at the
    right time.
⁶There is a right time and a right way for
    everything,
    yet people often have many troubles.
⁷They do not know what the future holds,
    and no one can tell them what will
    happen.
⁸No one can control the wind
    or stop his own death.
    No soldier is released in times of war,
    and evil does not set free those who do
    evil.

Justice, Rewards, and Punishment

⁹I saw all of this as I considered all that is done
here on earth. Sometimes men harm those they
control. ¹⁰I saw the funerals of evil people who
used to go in and out of the holy place. They were
honored in the same towns where they had done
evil. This is useless, too.

¹¹When evil people are not punished right
away, it makes others want to do evil, too.
¹²Though a sinner might do a hundred evil things
and might live a long time, I know it will be better

for those who honor God. [13]I also know it will not go well for evil people, because they do not honor God. Like a shadow, they will not last. [14]Sometimes something useless happens on earth. Bad things happen to good people, and good things happen to bad people. I say that this is also useless. [15]So I decided it was more important to enjoy life. The best that people can do here on earth is to eat, drink, and enjoy life, because these joys will help them do the hard work God gives them here on earth.

We Cannot Understand All God Does

[16]I tried to understand all that happens on earth. I saw how busy people are, working day and night and hardly ever sleeping. [17]I also saw all that God has done. Nobody can understand what God does here on earth. No matter how hard people try to understand it, they cannot. Even if wise people say they understand, they cannot; no one can really understand it.

Is Death Fair?

9 I thought about all this and tried to understand it. I saw that God controls good people and wise people and what they do, but no one knows if they will experience love or hate.

[2]Good and bad people end up the same—
　those who are right and those who are
　　wrong,
those who are good and those who are evil,
　those who are clean and those who are
　　unclean,
　those who sacrifice and those who do not.
The same things happen to a good person
　as happen to a sinner,
to a person who makes promises to God
　and to one who does not.

[3]This is something wrong that happens here on earth: What happens to one happens to all. So people's minds are full of evil and foolish thoughts while they live. After that, they join the dead. [4]But anyone still alive has hope; even a live dog is better off than a dead lion!

[5]The living know they will die,
　but the dead know nothing.
Dead people have no more reward,
　and people forget them.
[6]After people are dead,
　they can no longer love or hate or envy.
They will never again share
　in what happens here on earth.

Enjoy Life While You Can

[7]So go eat your food and enjoy it;
　drink your wine and be happy,
because that is what God wants you to do.

[8]Put on nice clothes
　and make yourself look good.

[9]Enjoy life with the wife you love. Enjoy all the useless days of this useless life God has given you here on earth, because it is all you have. So enjoy the work you do here on earth. [10]Whatever work you do, do your best, because you are going to the grave, where there is no working, no planning, no knowledge, and no wisdom.

✴ SIDELIGHT: Like most ancient Jews, the Teacher believed that death brought only "the grave" (Ecclesiastes 9:10). The Hebrew word "Sheol" referred to a silent, gloomy, mysterious world where the early Jews believed that departed spirits went. The idea of heaven is more appealing, don't you think?

Time and Chance

[11]I also saw something else here on earth:
The fastest runner does not always win the
　race,
　the strongest soldier does not always win
　　the battle,
the wisest does not always have food,
　the smartest does not always become
　　wealthy,
　and the talented one does not always
　　receive praise.
Time and chance happen to everyone.
[12]No one knows what will happen next.
Like a fish caught in a net,
　or a bird caught in a trap,
people are trapped by evil
　when it suddenly falls on them.

Wisdom Does Not Always Win

[13]I also saw something wise here on earth that impressed me. [14]There was a small town with only a few people in it. A great king fought against it and put his armies all around it. [15]Now there was a poor but wise man in the town who used his wisdom to save his town. But later on, everyone forgot about him. [16]I still think wisdom is better than strength. But those people forgot about the poor man's wisdom and stopped listening to what he said.

[17]The quiet words of a wise person are better
　than the shouts of a foolish ruler.
[18]Wisdom is better than weapons of war,
　but one sinner can destroy much good.

10 Dead flies can make even perfume stink.

In the same way, a little foolishness can
spoil wisdom.
2The heart of the wise leads to right,
but the heart of a fool leads to wrong.
3Even in the way fools walk along the road,
they show they are not wise;
they show everyone how stupid they are.
4Don't leave your job
just because your boss is angry with you.
Remaining calm solves great problems.

5There is something else wrong that happens
here on earth.
It is the kind of mistake rulers make:
6Fools are given important positions
while gifted people are given lower ones;
7I have seen servants ride horses
while princes walk like servants on foot.
8Anyone who digs a pit might fall into it;
anyone who knocks down a wall might be
bitten by a snake;
9anyone who moves boulders might be hurt
by them;
and anyone who cuts logs might be harmed
by them.
10A dull ax means
harder work.
Being wise will make it easier.
11If a snake bites the tamer before it is tamed,
what good is the tamer?

12The words of the wise bring them praise,
but the words of a fool will destroy them.
13A fool begins by saying foolish things
and ends by saying crazy and wicked
things.
14A fool talks too much.
No one knows the future,
and no one can tell what will happen after
death.

15Work wears fools out;
they don't even know how to get home.

The Value of Work

16How terrible it is for a country whose king is
a child
and whose leaders eat all morning.
17How lucky a country is whose king comes
from a good family,
whose leaders eat only at mealtime
and for strength, not to get drunk.
18If someone is lazy, the roof will begin to fall.
If he doesn't fix it, the house will leak.

19A party makes you feel good,
wine makes you feel happy,
and money buys anything.

20Don't make fun of the king,

and don't make fun of rich people, even in
your bedroom.
A little bird might carry your words;
a bird might fly and tell what you said.

Boldly Face the Future

11 Invest what you have,
because after a while you will get a
return.
2Invest what you have in several different
businesses,
because you don't know what disasters
might happen.

3If clouds are full of rain,
they will shower on the earth.
A tree can fall to the north or south,
but it will stay where it falls.
4Those who wait for perfect weather
will never plant seeds;
those who look at every cloud
will never harvest crops.

5You don't know where the wind will blow,
and you don't know how a baby grows
inside the mother.
In the same way, you don't know what God
is doing,
or how he created everything.
6Plant early in the morning,
and work until evening,
because you don't know if this or that will
succeed.
They might both do well.

Serve God While You Are Young

7Sunshine is sweet;
it is good to see the light of day.
8People ought to enjoy every day of their lives,
no matter how long they live.
But they should also remember this:
You will be dead a long time.
Everything that happens then is useless.
9Young people, enjoy yourselves while you are
young;
be happy while you are young.
Do whatever your heart desires,
whatever you want to do.
But remember that God will judge you
for everything you do.
10Don't worry,
and forget the troubles of your body,
because youth and childhood are useless.

The Problems of Old Age

12 Remember your Creator
while you are young,
before the days of trouble come
and the years when you say,
"I find no pleasure in them."

²When you get old,
  the light from the sun, moon, and stars will
    grow dark;
  the rain clouds will never seem to go away.
³At that time your arms will shake
  and your legs will become weak.
Your teeth will fall out so you cannot chew,
  and your eyes will not see clearly.
⁴Your ears will be deaf to the noise in the
    streets,
  and you will barely hear the millstone
    grinding grain.
You'll wake up when a bird starts singing,
  but you will barely hear singing.
⁵You will fear high places
  and will be afraid to go for a walk.
Your hair will become white like the flowers
    on an almond tree.
You will limp along like a grasshopper
  when you walk.
  Your appetite will be gone.
Then you will go to your everlasting home,
  and people will go to your funeral.

⁶Soon your life will snap like a silver chain
  or break like a golden bowl.
You will be like a broken pitcher at a spring,
  or a broken wheel at a well.
⁷You will turn back into the dust of the earth
    again,
  but your spirit will return to God who gave
    it.

⁸Everything is useless!

The Teacher says that everything is useless.

Conclusion: Honor God

⁹The Teacher was very wise and taught the
people what he knew. He very carefully thought
about, studied, and set in order many wise teachings. ¹⁰The Teacher looked for just the right
words to write what is dependable and true.

SIDELIGHT: When the
homework piles up, quote the last part
of Ecclesiastes 12:12. Maybe someone will
take pity on you. The words "my son" were
a common way for teachers to address pupils
in Old Testament times.

---

¹¹Words from wise people are like sharp sticks
used to guide animals. They are like nails that
have been driven in firmly. Altogether they are
wise teachings that come from one Shepherd.
¹²So be careful, my son, about other teachings.
People are always writing books, and too much
study will make you tired.

¹³Now, everything has been heard,
  so I give my final advice:
Honor God and obey his commands,
  because this is all people must do.
¹⁴God will judge everything,
  even what is done in secret,
  the good and the evil.

SONG OF SOLOMON

■ Identify with lovers' longing for each other (Song of Solomon 1—2).
■ Celebrate true love and affection for a lover (Song of Solomon 3—5).
■ Watch true love develop into commitment (Song of Solomon 6—8).

Behind the Scenes:

Romance. We read about it, dream about it, and fantasize about it. We each hope that someone wonderful will choose us, marry us, share passionate, lasting love with us. But we don't expect to find much about this kind of romance in the Bible.

That's what's so surprising about the Song of Solomon, also known as Song of Songs. Using graphic imagery and language, this unusual book in the Bible celebrates God's gifts of love and sexuality. It appears to tell about a king and a shepherd both pursuing a beautiful peasant woman. Through poetry, the book shows admiration, yearning for love, physical attractiveness and dedicated commitment.

Scholars have debated the Song of Solomon for centuries—beginning before Jesus was born. They suggest several possible ways to interpret this unusual book:

■ Symbolic—The book has a hidden or symbolic religious meaning about the relationship between God and Israel or between Christ and the church. Beneath the pictures of physical love lies the spiritual truth that God loves us completely.
■ Literal—The book is what it appears to be: Love songs about a beautiful courtship between a man and a woman. Thus these poems affirm a place for beautiful expressions of human love within our faith.
■ Dramatic—The book is a drama about sexual love. The songs were written to be sung or performed by two to four actors and a chorus. The drama may have been performed as entertainment during weddings.

Whatever your view on the book's purpose, Song of Solomon should be treasured, because it gives beautiful images of committed love—both physical and spiritual—and celebrates human love as a gift from God.

WHEN THE ACTION WAS

1000BC	750BC		500BC	250BC	BC/AD
	Jerusalem fell to the Babylonians	Jews began returning to Jerusalem from exile			Jesus was born

King Solomon ruled and may have written Song of Solomon

1
Solomon's Greatest Song.

The Woman Speaks to the Man She Loves

²Kiss me with the kisses of your mouth,
　because your love is better than wine.

> **SIDELIGHT:** Song of Solomon is also known as the "Song of Songs." Repeating the word meant it was great. So this book could be called "Greatest Song" or "Most Beautiful Song." Wonder if it made the top ten?

---

³The smell of your perfume is pleasant,
　and your name is pleasant like expensive
　　perfume.
　That's why the young women love you.
⁴Take me with you; let's run together.
　The king takes me into his rooms.

Friends Speak to the Man

　We will rejoice and be happy with you;
　we praise your love more than wine.
　With good reason, the young women love
　　you.

The Woman Speaks

⁵I'm dark but lovely,
　women of Jerusalem,
　dark like the tents of Kedar,
　like the curtains of Solomon.
⁶Don't look at how dark I am,
　at how dark the sun has made me.
　My brothers were angry with me
　and made me tend the vineyards,
　so I haven't tended my own vineyard!
⁷Tell me, you whom I love,
　where do you feed your sheep?
　Where do you let them rest at noon?
　Why should I look for you near your friend's
　　sheep,
　like a woman who wears a veil?[n]

The Man Speaks to the Woman

⁸You are the most beautiful of women.
　Surely you know to follow the sheep
　and feed your young goats
　　near the shepherds' tents.
⁹My darling, you are like a mare
　among the king's stallions.
¹⁰Your cheeks are beautiful with ornaments,
　and your neck with jewels.

¹¹We will make for you gold earrings
　with silver hooks.

The Woman Speaks

¹²The smell of my perfume spreads out
　to the king on his couch.
¹³My lover is like a bag of myrrh[d]
　that lies all night between my
　　breasts.
¹⁴My lover is like a bunch of flowers
　from the vineyards at En Gedi.

> **SIDELIGHT:** Ancient lovers didn't have designer perfumes, but they were still into being attractive to others. Women wore sachets of fragrance around their necks (Song of Solomon 1:12–14), while men splashed perfume on their beards and robes.

The Man Speaks

¹⁵My darling, you are beautiful!
　Oh, you are beautiful,
　and your eyes are like doves.

The Woman Answers the Man

¹⁶You are so handsome, my lover,
　and so pleasant!
　Our bed is the grass.
¹⁷Cedar trees form our roof;
　our ceiling is made of juniper wood.

The Woman Speaks Again

2
I am a rose in the Plain of Sharon,
a lily in the valleys.

The Man Speaks Again

²Among the young women, my darling
　is like a lily among thorns!

The Woman Answers

³Among the young men, my lover
　is like an apple tree in the woods!
　I enjoy sitting in his shadow;
　his fruit is sweet to my taste.
⁴He brought me to the banquet room,
　and his banner over me is love.
⁵Strengthen me with raisins,
　and refresh me with apples,
　because I am weak with love.
⁶My lover's left hand is under my
　　head,
　and his right arm holds me tight.

** eil**　This was the way a prostitute usually dressed.

The Woman Speaks to the Friends

[7]Women of Jerusalem, promise me
   by the gazelles[d] and the deer
not to awaken
   or excite my feelings of love
   until it is ready.

The Woman Speaks Again

[8]I hear my lover's voice.
   Here he comes jumping across the
      mountains,
   skipping over the hills.
[9]My lover is like a gazelle[d] or a young deer.
   Look, he stands behind our wall
peeking through the windows,
   looking through the blinds.
[10]My lover spoke and said to me,
   "Get up, my darling;
   let's go away, my beautiful one.
[11]Look, the winter is past;
   the rains are over and gone.
[12]Blossoms appear through all the land.
   The time has come to sing;
   the cooing of doves is heard in our land.
[13]There are young figs on the fig trees,
   and the blossoms on the vines smell sweet.
Get up, my darling;
   let's go away, my beautiful one."

The Man Speaks

[14]My beloved is like a dove hiding in the
      cracks of the rock,
   in the secret places of the cliff.
Show me your face,
   and let me hear your voice.
Your voice is sweet,
   and your face is lovely.
[15]Catch the foxes for us —
   the little foxes that ruin the vineyards
   while they are in blossom.

The Woman Speaks

[16]My lover is mine, and I am his.
   He feeds among the lilies
[17]until the day dawns
   and the shadows disappear.
Turn, my lover.
   Be like a gazelle[d] or a young deer
   on the mountain valleys.

The Woman Dreams

3 At night on my bed,
   I looked for the one I love;
   I looked for him, but I could not find him.
[2]I got up and went around the city,
   in the streets and squares,
   looking for the one I love.

LOVE

Am I Really in Love?

Test yourself to discover whether you're really in love.

"I love you if . . ." I value your uniqueness. I freely give my joy, interests, knowledge, understanding, humor and sadness to you. I give you freedom to be true to yourself. I am happy to be with you most of the time. I really like, trust and respect you. I want our relationship to be permanent. I focus on your personality, not just sexual feelings. I care about your pleasure and well-being as much as my own. I feel like I "belong" to you. Our relationship has deepened during the past six months.

When we're really in love, we can honestly answer "yes" to these questions. The lovers in Song of Solomon are enthralled with each other. Read **Song of Solomon 2:10–17**.

■ Which of the conditions above do you think apply to the couple in this passage?

■ Based on this passage and the checklist, what would your checklist be for knowing if you are in love?

C O N S I D E R . . .

■ talking to a couple you know who have a strong relationship, and asking them what makes their marriage so strong.

■ *making a list of action-oriented goals based on the passage that you can use when* you're in a special relationship that you want to grow.

F O R   M O R E ,   S E E . . .

■ Hosea 3 (p. 825)
■ John 15:9–17 (p. 1085)

■ 1 John 4:7–21 (p. 1319)

I looked for him. but I could not find him.
3The watchmen found me as they patrolled
   the city,
so I asked, "Have you seen the one I
   love?"
4As soon as I had left them,
   I found the one I love.
I held him and would not let him go
until I brought him to my mother's house,
   to the room where I was born.

The Woman Speaks to the Friends

5Women of Jerusalem, promise me
   by the gazelles*d* and the deer
not to awaken
   or excite my feelings of love
   until it is ready.
6Who is this coming out of the desert
   like a cloud of smoke?
Who is this that smells like myrrh,*d* incense,*d*
   and other spices?
7Look, it's Solomon's couch*n*
   with sixty soldiers around it,
   the finest soldiers of Israel.
8These soldiers all carry swords
   and have been trained in war.
Every man wears a sword at his side
   and is ready for the dangers of the night.
9King Solomon had a couch made for himself
   of wood from Lebanon.
10He made its posts of silver
   and its braces of gold.
The seat was covered with purple cloth
   that the women of Jerusalem wove with
   love.
11Women of Jerusalem, go out and see King
   Solomon.
   He is wearing the crown his mother put on
   his head
on his wedding day,
   when his heart was happy!

The Man Speaks to the Woman

4 How beautiful you are, my darling!
   Oh, you are beautiful!
Your eyes behind your veil are like doves.
   Your hair is like a flock of goats streaming
   down Mount Gilead.
2Your teeth are white like newly sheared
   sheep
just coming from their bath.
Each one has a twin,
   and none of them is missing.
3Your lips are like red silk thread,
   and your mouth is lovely.
Your cheeks behind your veil

are like slices of a pomegranate.*d*
4Your neck is like David's tower,
   built with rows of stones.
A thousand shields hang on its walls;
   each shield belongs to a strong soldier.
5Your breasts are like two fawns,
   like twins of a gazelle,*d*
   feeding among the lilies.
6Until the day dawns
   and the shadows disappear,
I will go to that mountain of myrrh*d*
   and to that hill of incense.*d*
7My darling, everything about you is beautiful,
   and there is nothing at all wrong with you.

> **SIDELIGHT:** The poem in Song
> of Solomon 4:1–7 contains
> comparisons that may seem gross to us
> today, but they were quite appealing in
> ancient times. . . . Honest!

8Come with me from Lebanon, my bride.
   Come with me from Lebanon,
from the top of Mount Amana,
   from the tops of Mount Senir and Mount
   Hermon.
Come from the lions' dens
   and from the leopards' hills.
9My sister, my bride,
   you have thrilled my heart;
you have thrilled my heart
   with a glance of your eyes,
   with one sparkle from your necklace.
10Your love is so sweet, my sister, my bride.
   Your love is better than wine,
   and your perfume smells better than any
   spice.
11My bride, your lips drip honey;
   honey and milk are under your tongue.
   Your clothes smell like the cedars of
   Lebanon.
12My sister, my bride, you are like a garden
   locked up,
   like a walled-in spring, a closed-up fountain.
13Your limbs are like an orchard
   of pomegranates with all the best fruit,
filled with flowers and nard,*d*
14nard and saffron,*d* calamus,*d* and cinnamon,
   with trees of incense, myrrh, and aloes*d*—
   all the best spices.
15You are like a garden fountain—
   a well of fresh water
   flowing down from the mountains of
   Lebanon.

couch   Something like a bed carried by slaves on which the king lay or sat while traveling.

The Woman Speaks

¹⁶Awake, north wind.
  Come, south wind.
Blow on my garden,
  and let its sweet smells flow out.
Let my lover enter the garden
  and eat its best fruits.

The Man Speaks

5 I have entered my garden, my sister, my
  bride.
I have gathered my myrrh*d* with my spice.
I have eaten my honeycomb and my honey.
I have drunk my wine and my milk.

The Friends Speak

Eat, friends, and drink;
  yes, drink deeply, lovers.

The Woman Dreams

²I sleep, but my heart is awake.
  I hear my lover knocking.
"Open to me, my sister, my darling,

my dove, my perfect one.
My head is wet with dew,
  and my hair with the dampness of the
    night."
³I have taken off my garment
  and don't want to put it on again.
I have washed my feet
  and don't want to get them dirty again.
⁴My lover put his hand through the opening,
  and I felt excited inside.
⁵I got up to open the door for my lover.
  Myrrh*d* was dripping from my hands
and flowing from my fingers,
  onto the handles of the lock.
⁶I opened the door for my lover,
  but my lover had left and was gone.
When he spoke, he took my breath away.
I looked for him, but I could not find him;
  I called for him, but he did not answer.
⁷The watchmen found me
  as they patrolled the city.
They hit me and hurt me;
  the guards on the wall took away my veil.
⁸Promise me, women of Jerusalem,

SEXUALITY

How Far?

Sherry Loomis leaned into Greg's muscular arms. His masculine scent, heightened by cologne, aroused a hunger in her. They kissed, again and again. Tonight her parents were gone, leaving them alone in the house.

"You're everything I want," Greg breathed. His hands moved over her eagerly. "Please," he urged.

Sherry pulled away. "I'm not sure . . ."

"I love you." He smiled, his eyes dark with passion.

The door bell rang. After straightening her clothes, Sherry opened the door and found her best friend standing there. Friends from church waited in the car.

"We're going out for pizza. Want to go with us?" Beth asked. Sherry took a deep breath; she was disappointed, yet relieved. "Yeah." She turned toward Greg. "Let's go with them, okay?"

The passion that Sherry and Greg feel is described in **Song of Solomon 5:2–6**. Although passion is a normal part of a love relationship, God has reserved it for marriage, because only a marriage agreement has the power to sustain the kind of intimacy that comes from passion.

■ How is Sherry's experience like that of the woman in the passage?
■ Sherry stopped short of going "all the way" with Greg. What are good reasons for you not to have sex until you're married?

C O N S I D E R . . .

■ writing on a secret card exactly how far you'll go physically with a casual date, your boyfriend or girlfriend, and the person you're engaged to. Keep the card in your Bible as a promise to yourself and to God.
■ *controlling the temptation to "go too far" by dating in groups, avoiding alcohol, and staying away from secluded areas.*

F O R   M O R E ,   S E E . . .

■ Genesis 2:24–25 (p. 4)
■ 1 Thessalonians 4:3–8 (p. 1247)

■ 1 John 1:9 (p. 1316)

if you find my lover,
tell him I am weak with love.

The Friends Answer the Woman

⁹How is your lover better than other lovers,
most beautiful of women?
How is your lover better than other lovers?
Why do you want us to promise this?

The Woman Answers the Friends

¹⁰My lover is healthy and tan,
the best of ten thousand men.
¹¹His head is like the finest gold;
his hair is wavy and black like a raven.
¹²His eyes are like doves
by springs of water.
They seem to be bathed in cream
and are set like jewels.
¹³His cheeks are like beds of spices;
they smell like mounds of perfume.
His lips are like lilies
flowing with myrrh.ᵈ
¹⁴His hands are like gold hinges,
filled with jewels.
His body is like shiny ivory
covered with sapphires.
¹⁵His legs are like large marble posts,
standing on bases of fine gold.
He is like a cedar of Lebanon,
like the finest of the trees.
¹⁶His mouth is sweet to kiss,
and I desire him very much.
Yes, daughters of Jerusalem,
this is my lover
and my friend.

The Friends Speak to the Woman

6 Where has your lover gone,
most beautiful of women?
Which way did your lover turn?
We will look for him with you.

The Woman Answers the Friends

²My lover has gone down to his garden,
to the beds of spices,
to feed in the gardens
and to gather lilies.
³I belong to my lover,
and my lover belongs to me.
He feeds among the lilies.

The Man Speaks to the Woman

⁴My darling, you are as beautiful as the city of
Tirzah,
as lovely as the city of Jerusalem,
like an army flying flags.
⁵Turn your eyes from me,
because they excite me too much.
Your hair is like a flock of goats

streaming down Mount Gilead.
⁶Your teeth are white like sheep
just coming from their bath;
each one has a twin,
and none of them is missing.
⁷Your cheeks behind your veil
are like slices of a pomegranate.ᵈ

✳ SIDELIGHT: You might not say
your sweetheart has "fruity" cheeks,
but that was a compliment in ancient times
(Song of Solomon 6:7). The pomegranate is a
small, red fruit that's especially refreshing in a
hot climate like Israel's (Song of Solomon 8:2,
p. 614). The round fruit is filled with pulp
and seeds, somewhat like the inside of an
orange in texture.

---

⁸There may be sixty queens and eighty slave
womenᵈ
and so many girls you cannot count them,
⁹but there is only one like my dove, my
perfect one.
She is her mother's only daughter,
the brightest of the one who gave her birth.
The young women saw her and called her
happy;
the queens and the slave women also
praised her.

The Young Women Praise the Woman

¹⁰Who is that young woman
that shines out like the dawn?
She is as pretty as the moon,
as bright as the sun,
as wonderful as an army flying flags.

The Man Speaks

¹¹I went down into the orchard of nut trees
to see the blossoms of the valley,
to look for buds on the vines,
to see if the pomegranateᵈ trees had
bloomed.
¹²Before I realized it, my desire for you made
me feel
like a prince in a chariot.

The Friends Call to the Woman

¹³Come back, come back, woman of Shulam.
Come back, come back,
so we may look at you!

The Woman Answers the Friends

Why do you want to look at the woman of
Shulam
as you would at the dance of two armies?

The Man Speaks to the Woman

7 Your feet are beautiful in sandals,
you daughter of a prince.
Your round thighs are like jewels
shaped by an artist.
²Your navel is like a round drinking cup
always filled with wine.
Your stomach is like a pile of wheat
surrounded with lilies.
³Your breasts are like two fawns,
like twins of a gazelle.*d*
⁴Your neck is like an ivory tower.
Your eyes are like the pools in Heshbon
near the gate of Bath Rabbim.
Your nose is like the mountain of Lebanon
that looks down on Damascus.
⁵Your head is like Mount Carmel,
and your hair is like purple cloth;
the king is captured in its folds.
⁶You are beautiful and pleasant;
my love, you are full of delights.
⁷You are tall like a palm tree,
and your breasts are like its bunches of
fruit.
⁸I said, "I will climb up the palm tree
and take hold of its fruit."
Let your breasts be like bunches of grapes,
the smell of your breath like apples,
⁹   and your mouth like the best wine.

The Woman Speaks to the Man

Let this wine go down sweetly for my lover;
may it flow gently past the lips and teeth.
¹⁰I belong to my lover,
and he desires only me.
¹¹Come, my lover,
let's go out into the country
and spend the night in the fields.
¹²Let's go early to the vineyards
and see if the buds are on the vines.
Let's see if the blossoms have already opened
and if the pomegranates*d* have bloomed.
There I will give you my love.
¹³The mandrake flowers give their sweet smell,
and all the best fruits are at our gates.
I have saved them for you, my lover,
the old delights and the new.

✹ **SIDELIGHT:** The mandrake
flower (Song of Solomon 7:13) not
*only gave a sweet smell but was also
thought to arouse sexual desire. The yellow-
red fruit was also thought to increase fertility
(see Genesis 30:14–16, p. 35). No wonder it
was called the "love apple"!*

---

8 I wish you were like my brother
who fed at my mother's breasts.
If I found you outside,
I would kiss you,
and no one would look down on me.
²I would lead you and bring you
to my mother's house;
she is the one who taught me.
I would give you a drink of spiced wine
from my pomegranates.

The Woman Speaks to the Friends

³My lover's left hand is under my head,
and his right arm holds me tight.
⁴Women of Jerusalem,
promise not to awaken
or excite my feelings of love
until it is ready.

The Friends Speak

⁵Who is this coming out of the desert,
leaning on her lover?

The Man Speaks to the Woman

I woke you under the apple tree
where you were born;
there your mother gave birth to you.
⁶Put me like a seal on your heart,
like a seal on your arm.
Love is as strong as death;
jealousy is as strong as the grave.
Love bursts into flames
and burns like a hot fire.
⁷Even much water cannot put out the flame of
love;
floods cannot drown love.
If a man offered everything in his house for
love,
people would totally reject it.

The Woman's Brothers Speak

⁸We have a little sister,
and her breasts are not yet grown.
What should we do for our sister
on the day she becomes engaged?
⁹If she is a wall,
we will put silver towers on her.
If she is a door,
we will protect her with cedar boards.

The Woman Speaks

¹⁰I am a wall,
and my breasts are like towers.
So I was to him,
as one who brings happiness.
¹¹Solomon had a vineyard at Baal Hamon.

He rented the vineyards for others to
tend,
and everyone who rented had to pay
twenty-five pounds of silver for the fruit.
¹²But my own vineyard is mine to give.

> ⁂ **SIDELIGHT:** If girls think their
> brothers are overprotective today,
> imagine how they would have felt in biblical
> times (Song of Solomon 8:8–9). Brothers were
> responsible for a sister until marriage, so they
> kept other men from taking advantage of her
> innocence. They would probably ride in the
> back seat on her dates today!

Solomon, the twenty-five pounds of silver
are for you,
and five pounds are for those who tend the
fruit.

The Man Speaks to the Woman

¹³You who live in the gardens,
my friends are listening for your voice;
let me hear it.

The Woman Speaks to the Man

¹⁴Hurry, my lover,
be like a gazelle[d]
or a young deer
on the mountains where spices grow.

ISAIAH

Why Read This Book:

- See how God works through world events to bring people to himself (Isaiah 1—35).
- Discover what can happen when people trust in things other than God (Isaiah 36—39).
- Be assured that God is working in the world, even when life seems hopeless (Isaiah 40—66).

Behind the Scenes:

Isaiah could have had a simple life in Judah. He was probably well-educated and may have been a priest. He knew "movers and shakers" in Jerusalem, including the king.

But Isaiah saw trouble brewing, and the Lord called him to be a prophet. Though his country had been peaceful and prosperous under King Uzziah's leadership (see 2 Chronicles 26:1—23, p. 405), Isaiah could tell the good situation was changing. God would have him speak out!

First, he watched as the Assyrians conquered neighboring Israel and threatened

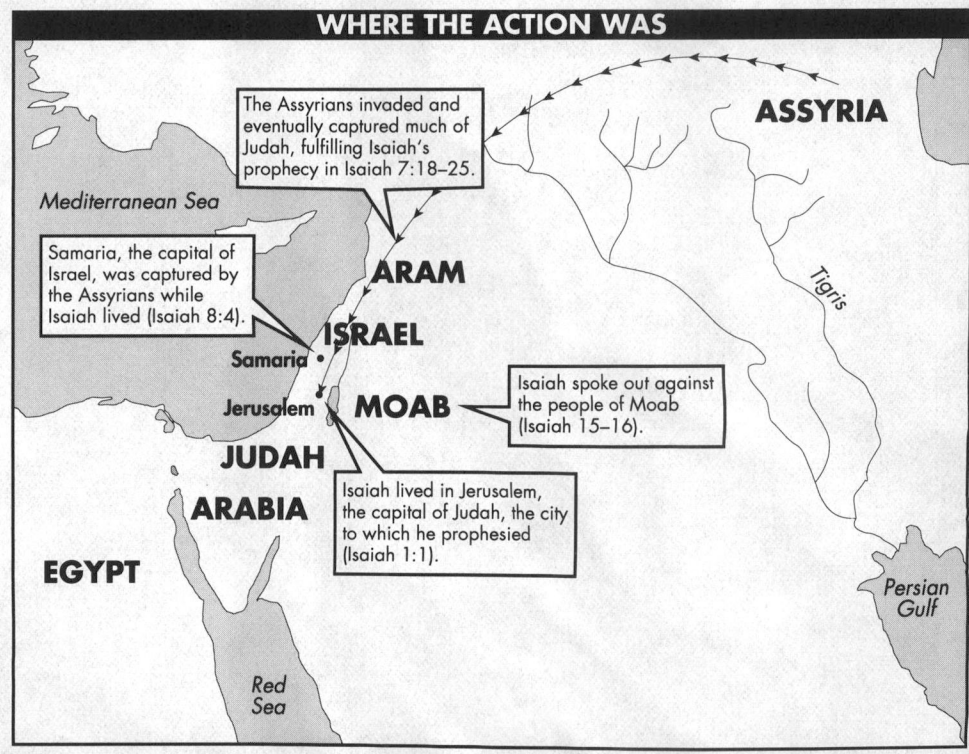

WHERE THE ACTION WAS

The Assyrians invaded and eventually captured much of Judah, fulfilling Isaiah's prophecy in Isaiah 7:18—25.

Samaria, the capital of Israel, was captured by the Assyrians while Isaiah lived (Isaiah 8:4).

Isaiah spoke out against the people of Moab (Isaiah 15—16).

Isaiah lived in Jerusalem, the capital of Judah, the city to which he prophesied (Isaiah 1:1).

ASSYRIA

Mediterranean Sea

ARAM

ISRAEL

Samaria

Jerusalem

MOAB

JUDAH

ARABIA

EGYPT

Red Sea

Tigris

Persian Gulf

WHEN THE ACTION WAS

	Isaiah began his prophetic ministry	The Northern Kingdom (Israel) fell to Assyria			Jesus was born
1000BC	**750BC**		**500BC**	**250BC**	**BC/AD**
Saul was Israel's king	The kingdom was split between Israel and Judah		The Southern Kingdom (Judah) fell to Babylon		

Behind the Scenes (cont.): Judah. The king of Judah was tempted to form military alliances to protect the nation; Isaiah believed Judah should rely on God instead.

Second, while people paid lip service to God, they didn't really follow him. Instead, they took advantage of the poor.

The book of Isaiah has two distinct parts:

Chapters 1—39 deal with events in the eighth century before Christ, when Judah was independent but constantly threatened by the Assyrians. During this time, the prophet blasted out against the rich and powerful who neglected and oppressed the poor. And he challenged the nation not to rely on military power to defend itself, but to rely on God.

Chapters 40—66 zoom forward to about two hundred years later, when the Persian Empire controlled Judah. After being in exile, the Jews were trying to rebuild their lives. Through this section, the prophet constantly comforts the people, assuring them that the past, present, and future are all in God's hands. God's presence and love gave them hope.

Isaiah's message of hope points to a time when God would deliver his people through God's suffering servant (Isaiah 52—57). Since New Testament times, Christians have believed these promises were fulfilled in the coming of Jesus Christ, who suffered and died for the sins of the world. (For example, see Isaiah 53.)

---

1 This is the vision Isaiah son of Amoz saw about what would happen to Judah and Jerusalem. Isaiah saw these things while Uzziah, Jotham, Ahaz, and Hezekiah were kings of Judah.

> ✹ **SIDELIGHT:** The book of Isaiah is quoted more in the New Testament than any other book—and more than all the other prophetic books combined. The New Testament refers to Isaiah one hundred fifty times and actually quotes it fifty times.

God's Case Against His Children

²Heaven and earth, listen,
  because the LORD is speaking:
"I raised my children and helped them grow up,
  but they have turned against me.
³An ox knows its master,
  and a donkey knows where its owner feeds it,
but the people of Israel do not know me;
  my people do not understand."

⁴How terrible! Israel is a nation of sin,
  a people loaded down with guilt,
a group of children doing evil,
  children who are full of evil.
They have left the LORD;
  they hate God, the Holy One of Israel,
  and have turned away from him as if he were a stranger.

⁵Why should you continue to be punished?
  Why do you continue to turn against him?

Your whole head is hurt,
  and your whole heart is sick.
⁶There is no healthy spot
  from the bottom of your foot to the top of your head;
  you are covered with wounds, hurts, and open sores
that are not cleaned and covered,
  and no medicine takes away the pain.

⁷Your land is ruined;
  your cities have been burned with fire.
While you watch,
  your enemies are stealing everything from your land;
  it is ruined like a country destroyed by enemies.
⁸Jerusalem is left alone
  like an empty shelter in a vineyard,
like a hut left in a field of melons,
  like a city surrounded by enemies.
⁹The LORD All-Powerful
  allowed a few of our people to live.
  Otherwise we would have been completely destroyed
like the cities of Sodom and Gomorrah.

¹⁰Jerusalem, your rulers are like those of Sodom,
  and your people are like those of Gomorrah.
Hear the word of the LORD;
  listen to the teaching of our God!
¹¹The LORD says,
  "I do not want all these sacrifices.
I have had enough of your burnt sacrifices
  of male sheep and fat from fine animals.

I am not pleased
  by the blood of bulls, lambs, and goats.
12You come to meet with me,
  but who asked you to do
  all this running in and out of my Temple's*d*
    rooms?
13Don't continue bringing me worthless
    sacrifices!
  I hate the incense*d* you burn.
  I can't stand your New Moons,*d* Sabbaths,*d*
    and other feast days;
  I can't stand the evil you do in your holy
    meetings.
14I hate your New Moon feasts
  and your other yearly feasts.
  They have become a heavy weight on me,
    and I am tired of carrying it.
15When you raise your arms to me in prayer,
  I will refuse to look at you.
  Even if you say many prayers,
    I will not listen to you,
  because your hands are full of blood.
16Wash yourselves and make yourselves clean.*d*
    Stop doing the evil things I see you do.
  Stop doing wrong.
    Learn to do good.
  Seek justice.
    Punish those who hurt others.
  Help the orphans.
    Stand up for the rights of widows."

18The LORD says,
  "Come, let us talk about these things.
  Though your sins are like scarlet,
    they can be as white as snow.
  Though your sins are deep red,
    they can be white like wool.
19If you become willing and obey me,
    you will eat good crops from the land.
20But if you refuse to obey and if you turn
    against me,
  you will be destroyed by your enemies'
    swords."
  The LORD himself said these things.

Jerusalem Is Not Loyal to God

21The city of Jerusalem once followed the
    LORD,
  but she is no longer loyal to him.
  She used to be filled with fairness;
    people there lived the way God wanted.
  But now, murderers live there.
22Jerusalem, you have become like the scum
    left when silver is purified;
  you are like wine mixed with water.
23Your rulers are rebels
  and friends of thieves.
  They all accept money for doing wrong,
    and they are paid to cheat people.

They don't seek justice for the orphans
  or listen to the widows' needs.
24So the Lord GOD All-Powerful,
  the Mighty One of Israel, says:
  "You, my enemies, will not cause me any
    more trouble.
  I will pay you back for what you did.
25I will turn against you
  and clean away all your wrongs as if with
    soap;
  I will take all the worthless things out of
    you.
26I will bring back judges as you had long ago;
  your counselors will be like those you had
    in the beginning.
  Then you will be called the City That Is
    Right with God,
  the Loyal City."

27By doing what is fair,
  Jerusalem will be free again.
  By doing what is right,
    her people who come back to the LORD
    will have freedom.
28But sinners and those who turn against him
    will be destroyed;
  those who have left the LORD will die.

29"You will be ashamed,
  because you have worshiped gods under
    the oak trees.
  You will be disgraced,
    because you have worshiped idols in your
    gardens.
30You will be like an oak whose leaves are
    dying
  or like a garden without water.
31Powerful people will be like small, dry pieces
    of wood,
  and their works will be like sparks.
  They will burn together,
    and no one will be able to put out that
    fire."

The Message About Jerusalem

2 Isaiah son of Amoz saw this message about
  Judah and Jerusalem:
2In the last days
  the mountain on which the LORD's Temple*d*
    stands
  will become the most important of all
    mountains.
  It will be raised above the hills,
    and people from all nations will come
    streaming to it.
3Many nations will come and say,
  "Come, let us go up to the mountain of the
    LORD,
  to the Temple of the God of Jacob.

Then God will teach us his ways,
and we will obey his teachings."
His teachings will go out from Jerusalem;
the message of the LORD will go out from
Jerusalem.
⁴He will settle arguments among the nations
and will make decisions for many nations.
Then they will make their swords into plows
and their spears into hooks for trimming
trees.
Nations will no longer fight other nations,
nor will they train for war anymore.
⁵Come, family of Jacob,
and let us follow the way of the LORD.

A Terrible Day Is Coming

⁶LORD, you have left your people,
the family of Jacob,
because they have become filled with wrong
ideas from people in the East.
They try to tell the future like the
Philistines,

and they have completely accepted those
foreign ideas.
⁷Their land has been filled with silver and
gold;
there are a great many treasures there.
Their land has been filled with horses;
there are many chariots there.
⁸Their land is full of idols.
The people worship these idols they made
with their own hands
and shaped with their own fingers.
⁹People will not be proud any longer
but will bow low with shame.
God, do not forgive them.

¹⁰Go into the caves of the cliffs;
dig holes and hide in the ground
from the anger of the LORD
and from his great power!
¹¹Proud people will be made humble,
and they will bow low with shame.
At that time only the LORD will still be
praised.

PEACE

Sibling Rivalry

Almost anything can make Jason and Rick Lewis argue:
"You're supposed to help me take out the garbage."
"Dad told you to do it!"
"No, Dad told us to do it!"
"I did it yesterday!"
"You never do it."
"Just drop it, okay? I'll do it later!"
Sometimes the Lewis home sounds like a war zone in the Middle East.
Despite their fighting, Jason and Rick love each other and stand up for each other.
Anytime someone begins to argue with one of the brothers, the other will immediately lend
support.

Jason and Rick argue about little things, but they are bonded together
when it comes to big things such as love, loyalty and support. One reason for
their closeness is their shared family name, which lets them know they're part
of something that will last no matter how they feel. They're family.

Jason and Rick still argue even though they deeply love each other. But
according to **Isaiah 2:1–5**, one day God will settle all our arguments, strife
and struggles forever.
■ According to this passage, what's the only way true peace—at home or in
the world—can be achieved?
■ How does this passage's picture of God challenge you to make peace in
your family? church? school? world?

CONSIDER . . .
■ reestablishing ties with someone you used to be friends with.
■ writing a prayer to God for peace in your home, school, city, nation, and world. Listen
for one way God might use you to bring about that peace.

FOR MORE, SEE . . .
■ Isaiah 60:15–20 (p. 680)   ■ 1 Thessalonians 5:12–18 (p. 1249)
■ John 14:27–29 (p. 1085)

12The LORD All-Powerful has a certain day
  planned
    when he will punish the proud and those
      who brag,
    and they will no longer be important.
13He will bring down the tall cedar trees from
  Lebanon
    and the great oak trees of Bashan,
14all the tall mountains
    and the high hills,
15every tall tower
    and every high, strong wall,
16all the trading ships
    and the beautiful ships.
17At that time proud people will be made
  humble,
    and they will bow low with shame.
  At that time only the LORD will be praised,
18 but all the idols will be gone.

19People will run to caves in the rocky cliffs
    and will dig holes and hide in the ground
  from the anger of the LORD
    and his great power,
    when he stands to shake the earth.
20At that time people will throw away
    their gold and silver idols,
  which they made for themselves to worship;
    they will throw them away to the bats and
      moles.
21Then the people will hide in caves
    and cracks in the rocks
  from the anger of the LORD
    and his great power,
    when he stands to shake the earth.

22You should stop trusting in people to save
    you,
  because people are only human;
  they aren't able to help you.

God Will Punish Judah and Jerusalem

3 Understand this:
  The Lord GOD All-Powerful
  will take away everything Judah and
    Jerusalem need—
    all the food and water,
2the heroes and great soldiers,
  the judges and prophets,*d*
people who do magic and older leaders,
3the military leaders and government leaders,
  the counselors, the skilled craftsmen, and
    those who try to tell the future.
4The LORD says, "I will cause young boys to
    be your leaders,
  and foolish children will rule over you.
5People will be against each other; everyone
    will be against his neighbor.

Young people will not respect older people,
  and common people will not respect
    important people."
6At that time a man will grab one of his
  brothers
    from his own family and say,
  "You have a coat, so you will be our leader.
  These ruins will be under your control."
7But that brother will stand up and say,
  "I cannot help you,
  because I do not have food or clothes in my
    house.
  You will not make me your leader."
8This will happen because Jerusalem has
    stumbled,
    and Judah has fallen.
  The things they say and do are against the
    LORD;
    they turn against him.
9The look on their faces shows they are guilty;
  like the people of Sodom, they are proud of
    their sin.
  They don't care who sees it.
  How terrible it will be for them,
  because they have brought much trouble on
    themselves.

10Tell those who do what is right that things
    will go well for them,
  because they will receive a reward for what
    they do.
11But how terrible it will be for the wicked!
  They will be punished for all the wrong
    they have done.
12Children treat my people cruelly,
    and women rule over them.
  My people, your guides lead you in the
    wrong way
    and turn you away from what is right.

13The LORD takes his place in court
    and stands to judge the people.
14The LORD presents his case
    against the older leaders and other leaders
      of his people:
  "You have burned the vineyard.
    Your houses are full of what you took from
      the poor.
15What gives you the right to crush my people
    and grind the faces of the poor into the
      dirt?"
  The Lord GOD All-Powerful says this.

A Warning to Women of Jerusalem

16The LORD says,
  "The women of Jerusalem are proud.
  They walk around with their heads held
    high,

and they flirt with their eyes.
They take quick, short steps,
making noise with their ankle bracelets."
¹⁷So the Lord will put sores on the heads of
those women in Jerusalem,
and he will make them lose their hair.

¹⁸At that time the Lord will take away everything that makes them proud: their beautiful ankle bracelets, their headbands, their necklaces
shaped like the moon, ¹⁹their earrings, bracelets,
and veils, ²⁰their scarves, ankle chains, the cloth
belts worn around their waists, their bottles of
perfume, and charms, ²¹their signet* rings, nose
rings, ²²their fine robes, capes, shawls, and
purses, ²³their mirrors, linen dresses, turbans, and
long shawls.

²⁴Instead of wearing sweet-smelling perfume,
they will stink.
Instead of fine cloth belts, they will wear
the ropes of captives.
Instead of having their hair fixed in fancy
ways, they will be bald.
Instead of fine clothes, they will wear
clothes of sadness.
Instead of being beautiful, they will wear
the brand of a captive.
²⁵At that time your men will be killed with
swords,
and your heroes will die in war.
²⁶There will be crying and sadness near the
city gates.
Jerusalem will be like a woman who has
lost everything and sits on the ground.

4 At that time seven women
will grab one man
and say, "We will eat our own bread
and make our own clothes,
but please marry us!
Please, take away our shame."

The Branch of the Lord

²At that time the Lord's branch will be very
beautiful and great. The people still living in Israel
will be proud of what the land grows. ³Those who
are still living in Jerusalem will be called holy;
their names are recorded among the living in Jerusalem. ⁴The Lord will wash away the filth from
the women of Jerusalem. He will wash the blood-
stains out of Jerusalem and clean the city with the
spirit of fairness and the spirit of fire. ⁵Then the
Lord will cover Mount Zion and the people who
meet there with a cloud of smoke during the day
and with a bright, flaming fire at night. There will
be a covering over every person. ⁶This covering
will protect the people from the heat of the sun
and will provide a safe place to hide from the
storm and rain.

Israel, the Lord's Vineyard

5 Now I will sing for my friend a song about
his vineyard.
My friend had a vineyard
on a hill with very rich soil.
²He dug and cleared the field of stones
and planted the best grapevines there.
He built a tower in the middle of it
and cut out a winepress* as well.
He hoped good grapes would grow there,
but only bad ones grew.

³My friend says, "You people living in
Jerusalem,
and you people of Judah,
judge between me and my vineyard.
⁴What more could I have done for my
vineyard
than I have already done?
Although I expected good grapes to grow,
why were there only bad ones?
⁵Now I will tell you
what I will do to my vineyard:
I will remove the hedge,
and it will be burned.
I will break down the stone wall,
and it will be walked on.
⁶I will ruin my field.
It will not be trimmed or hoed,
and weeds and thorns will grow there.
I will command the clouds
not to rain on it."

⁷The vineyard belonging to the Lord
All-Powerful
is the nation of Israel;
the garden that he loves
is the people of Judah.
He looked for justice, but there was only
killing.
He hoped for right living, but there were
only cries of pain.

⁸How terrible it will be for you who add more
houses to your houses
and more fields to your fields
until there is no room left for other people.
Then you are left alone in the land.

⁹The Lord All-Powerful said this to me:
"The fine houses will be destroyed;
the large and beautiful houses will be left
empty.
¹⁰At that time a ten-acre vineyard will make
only six gallons of wine,
and ten bushels of seed will grow only half
a bushel of grain."

¹¹How terrible it will be for people who rise
early in the morning
to look for strong drink,

who stay awake late at night,
becoming drunk with wine.
¹²At their parties they have lyres,*d* harps,
tambourines,*d* flutes, and wine.
They don't see what the LORD has done
or notice the work of his hands.
¹³So my people will be captured and taken
away,
because they don't really know me.
All the great people will die of hunger,
and the common people will die of thirst.
¹⁴So the place of the dead wants more and
more people,
and it opens wide its mouth.
Jerusalem's important people and common
people will go down into it,
with their happy and noisy ones.
¹⁵So the common people and the great people
will be brought down;
those who are proud will be humbled.
¹⁶The LORD All-Powerful will receive glory by
judging fairly;
the holy God will show himself holy by
doing what is right.
¹⁷Then the sheep will go anywhere they want,
and lambs will feed on the land that rich
people once owned.

¹⁸How terrible it will be for those people!
They pull their guilt and sins behind them
as people pull wagons with ropes.
¹⁹They say, "Let God hurry;
let him do his work soon
so we may see it.
Let the plan of the Holy One of Israel happen
soon
so that we will know what it is."

²⁰How terrible it will be for people who call
good things bad
and bad things good,
who think darkness is light
and light is darkness,
who think sour is sweet
and sweet is sour.

²¹How terrible it will be for people who think
they are wise
and believe they are clever.

²²How terrible it will be for people who are
famous for drinking wine
and are champions at mixing drinks.
²³*They take money to set the guilty free*
and don't allow good people to be judged
fairly.
²⁴They will be destroyed
just as fire burns straw or dry grass.
They will be destroyed
like a plant whose roots rot

and whose flower dies and blows away like
dust.
They have refused to obey the teachings of
the LORD All-Powerful
and have hated the message from the Holy
God of Israel.
²⁵So the LORD has become very angry with his
people,
and he has raised his hand to punish them.
Even the mountains are frightened.
Dead bodies lie in the streets like garbage.

But the LORD is still angry;
his hand is still raised to strike down the
people.

²⁶He raises a banner for the nations far away.
He whistles to call those people from the
ends of the earth.
Look! The enemy comes quickly!
²⁷Not one of them becomes tired or falls down.
Not one of them gets sleepy and falls
asleep.
Their weapons are close at hand,
and their sandal straps are not broken.
²⁸Their arrows are sharp,
and all of their bows are ready to shoot.
The horses' hoofs are hard as rocks,
and their chariot wheels move like a
whirlwind.
²⁹Their shout is like the roar of a lion;
it is loud like a young lion.
They growl as they grab their captives.
There is no one to stop them from taking
their captives away.
³⁰On that day they will roar
like the waves of the sea.
And when people look at the land,
they will see only darkness and pain;
all light will become dark in this thick
cloud.

Isaiah Becomes a Prophet

6 In the year that King Uzziah died, I saw the
Lord sitting on a very high throne. His long
robe filled the Temple.*d* ²Heavenly creatures of
fire stood above him. Each creature had six
wings: It used two wings to cover its face, two
wings to cover its feet, and two wings for flying.
³Each creature was calling to the others:
"Holy, holy, holy is the LORD All-Powerful.
His glory fills the whole earth."
⁴Their calling caused the frame around the door
to shake, as the Temple filled with smoke.
⁵I said, "Oh, no! I will be destroyed. I am not
pure, and I live among people who are not pure,
but I have seen the King, the LORD All-Powerful."
⁶One of the heavenly creatures used a pair of
tongs to take a hot coal from the altar. Then he
flew to me with the hot coal in his hand. ⁷The

creature touched my mouth with the hot coal and said, "Look, your guilt is taken away, because this hot coal has touched your lips. Your sin is taken away."

[8]Then I heard the Lord's voice, saying, "Whom can I send? Who will go for us?"

So I said, "Here I am. Send me!"

[9]Then the Lord said, "Go and tell this to the people:

'You will listen and listen, but you will not understand.
You will look and look, but you will not learn.'
[10]Make the minds of these people dumb.
Shut their ears. Cover their eyes.
Otherwise, they might really understand what they see with their eyes
and hear with their ears.
They might really understand in their minds and come back to me and be healed."

SIDELIGHT:

Isaiah is a hot book! It includes thirty-two references to fire, including Isaiah 6:6–7. Throughout the Bible, fire is a common symbol of God's presence, action, and judgment. See, for example, Genesis 15:17 (p. 17), Exodus 13:21–32 (p. 70), Acts 2:3 (p. 1098), Hebrews 12:29 (p. 1290), and Revelation 2:18 (p. 1334).

WORSHIP

Understanding God's Heart

When John Wesley was rescued from a blazing house as a child, he was convinced God had saved him for a purpose. As he grew up in eighteenth-century England, he applied all his energy toward accomplishing God's will for his life. While studying at Oxford University, John led a group of men known as the Holy Club. They met for Bible study and prayer, and cared for the sick, poor and imprisoned. Not long after completing his work at the university, John and his brother, Charles, sailed to America to spread Christ's message to native Americans.

John had good intentions but still felt like a failure. He knew God had given him a purpose in life, but he couldn't seem to carry it out. He needed to know and experience God's heart before he could offer it to anyone else. John and Charles returned to England discouraged and disillusioned. "I went to America to convert the Indians," John said. "But, oh, who shall convert me?"

Then something wonderful happened. On May 24, 1738, John attended a Christian meeting in London, and his life was changed. In his journal, John described what happened.

"I felt my heart strangely warmed," he wrote. "I felt I did trust in Christ, Christ alone for salvation; and an assurance was given to me that he had taken away my sins, even mine, and saved me from the law of sin and death."

John Wesley became one of the most influential men in the history of Christianity. During the fifty-two years following that experience in 1738, he preached over forty thousand sermons and traveled over two hundred thousand miles, sharing the message of Christ with hundreds of thousands.

John needed to understand and worship God before trying to serve him. The prophet Isaiah had a similar experience that launched his ministry. Read about Isaiah's encounter with God in **Isaiah 6:1–8**:

■ Why did both John Wesley and Isaiah need to understand God's heart and worship him before they could adequately serve God?

■ According to this passage, what do you know about God's character?

CONSIDER . . .

■ asking God to reveal himself to you the way he did to Isaiah or to John Wesley.

■ writing a poem or song of worship to God, praising him for the qualities about him that you know are true.

FOR MORE, SEE . . .

■ 2 Chronicles 29:18–36 (p. 407)

■ Revelation 19:1–9 (p. 1345)

■ Psalm 50 (p. 511)

11Then I asked, "Lord, how long should I do this?"

He answered,

"Until the cities are destroyed
and the people are gone,
until there are no people left in the houses,
until the land is destroyed and left empty.
12The LORD will send the people far away,
and the land will be left empty.
13One-tenth of the people will be left in the
land,
but it will be destroyed again.
These people will be like an oak tree
whose stump is left when the tree is
chopped down.
The people who remain will be like a
stump that will sprout again."

Trouble with Aram

7 Now Ahaz was the son of Jotham, who was the son of Uzziah. When Ahaz was king of Judah, Rezin king of Aram and Pekah son of Remaliah, the king of Israel, went up to Jerusalem to fight against it. But they were not able to defeat the city.

2Ahaz king of Judah received a message saying, "The armies of Aram and Israel n have joined together."

When Ahaz heard this, he and the people were frightened. They shook with fear like trees of the forest blown by the wind.

3Then the LORD told Isaiah, "You and your son Shear-Jashub n should go and meet Ahaz at the place where the water flows into the upper pool, on the road where people do their laundry. 4Tell Ahaz, 'Be careful. Be calm and don't worry. Don't let those two men, Rezin and Pekah son of Remaliah, scare you. Don't be afraid of their anger or Aram's anger, because they are like two barely burning sticks that are ready to go out. 5They have made plans against you, saying, 6"Let's fight against Judah and tear it apart. We will divide the land for ourselves and make the son of Tabeel the new king of Judah." 7But I, the Lord GOD, say,

" 'Their plan will not succeed;
it will not happen,
8because Aram is led by the city of Damascus,
and Damascus is led by its weak king,
Rezin.
Within sixty-five years Israel will no longer be
a nation.
9Israel is led by the city of Samaria,
and Samaria is led by its weak king, the
son of Remaliah.

If your faith is not strong,
you will not have strength enough to
last.' "

Immanuel — God Is with Us

10Then the LORD spoke to Ahaz again, saying, 11"Ask for a sign from the LORD your God to prove to yourself that these things are true. It may be a sign from as deep as the place of the dead or as high as the heavens."

12But Ahaz said, "I will not ask for a sign or test the LORD."

13Then Isaiah said, "Ahaz, descendant d of David, listen carefully! Isn't it bad enough that you wear out the patience of people? Do you also have to wear out the patience of my God? 14The Lord himself will give you a sign: The virgin n will be pregnant. She will have a son, and she will name him Immanuel. n 15He will be eating milk curds and honey when he learns to reject what is evil and to choose what is good. 16You are afraid of the kings of Israel and Aram now. But before the child learns to choose good and reject evil, the lands of Israel and Aram will be empty. 17The LORD will bring troubled times to you, your people, and to the people of your father's family. They will be worse than anything that has happened since Israel separated from Judah. The LORD will bring the king of Assyria to fight against you.

18"At that time the LORD will whistle for the Egyptians, and they will come like flies from Egypt's faraway streams. He will call for the Assyrians, and they will come like bees. 19These enemies will camp in the deep ravines and in the cliffs, by the thornbushes and watering holes. 20The Lord will hire Assyria and use it like a razor to punish Judah. It will be as if the Lord is shaving the hair from Judah's head and legs and removing Judah's beard.

21"At that time a person will be able to keep only one young cow and two sheep alive. 22There will be only enough milk for that person to eat milk curds. All who remain in the land will go back to eating just milk curds and honey. 23In this land there are now vineyards that have a thousand grapevines, which are worth about twenty-five pounds of silver. But these fields will become full of weeds and thorns. 24The land will become wild and useful only as a hunting ground. 25People once worked and grew food on these hills, but at that time people will not go there, because the land will be filled with weeds and thorns. Only sheep and cattle will go to those places."

Israel Literally, "Ephraim." Isaiah often uses "Ephraim" to mean all of Israel.
Shear-Jashub This name means "a part of the people will come back."
virgin The Hebrew word means "a young woman." Often this meant a girl who was not married and had not yet had sexual relations with anyone.
Immanuel This name means "God is with us."

Assyria Will Come Soon

8 The LORD told me, "Take a large scroll and write on it with an ordinary pen: 'Maher-Shalal-Hash-Baz.' ²I will gather some men to be reliable witnesses: Uriah the priest and Zechariah son of Jeberekiah."

³Then I went to the prophetess,*d* and she became pregnant and had a son. The LORD told me, "Name the boy Maher-Shalal-Hash-Baz,*n* ⁴because the king of Assyria will take away all the wealth and possessions of Damascus and Samaria before the boy learns to say 'my father' or 'my mother.' "

⁵Again the LORD spoke to me, saying,
⁶"These people refuse to accept
   the slow-moving waters of the pool of
      Shiloah
and are terrified of Rezin
   and Pekah son of Remaliah.
⁷So I, the Lord, will bring

the king of Assyria and all his power
   against them,
like a powerful flood of water from the
   Euphrates River.
The Assyrians will be like water rising over
   the banks of the river,
flowing over the land.
⁸That water will flow into Judah and pass
   through it,
rising to Judah's throat.
Immanuel, this army will spread its wings
   like a bird
until it covers your whole country."

⁹Be broken, all you nations,
   and be smashed to pieces.
Listen, all you faraway countries.
   Prepare for battle and be smashed to
      pieces!
   Prepare for battle and be smashed to
      pieces!

Maher-Shalal-Hash-Baz This name means "there will soon be looting and stealing."

DOUBT

Having Confidence

Jon Krause had a problem talking with girls.

While it seemed all of Jon's friends in high school had steady girlfriends, he couldn't even approach a girl without breaking out in a cold sweat. It was bad enough being a freshman in a new school, without also having to suffer the embarrassment of a glistening forehead and sweaty palms.

One night, Jon sought comfort and advice from his older brother, Mike. "I guess I'll never have a girlfriend," Jon confessed. "I just don't know what to say to girls. I'm not like the other guys. All of them have girlfriends."

"That's ridiculous," Mike said flatly. "Those guys don't have anything you haven't got. You've just got to believe in yourself. Take a risk. It's much easier to talk to girls after that first conversation."

Jon went to his room to think and pray about what Mike said. That night, he asked God to help him see himself the way God does. He prayed for God to help him develop confidence.

Two months later Jon began going steady with Diane.

Jon needed help from God to ease his doubts and build his confidence. In **Isaiah 7:10–16**, King Ahaz also needed God's help to ease his doubts.

■ What do King Ahaz and Jon have in common?
■ Why do you sometimes hesitate to ask God for something, even if you feel you really need it?

C O N S I D E R . . .

■ listing ways God could help you ease your doubt about him or any situation in your life and then asking him to give you that help.
■ asking your parent or youth pastor about ways you can overcome specific doubts in your life.

F O R   M O R E ,   S E E . . .

■ Judges 6:11–24 (p. 222)
■ Matthew 14:22–33 (p. 934)
■ James 1:6–8 (p. 1294)

¹⁰Make your plans for the fight,
    but they will be defeated.
Give orders to your armies,
    but they will be useless,
because God is with us.

Warnings to Isaiah

¹¹The LORD spoke to me with his great power and warned me not to follow the lead of the rest of the people. He said,
¹²"People are saying that others make plans
        against them,
    but you should not believe them.
Don't be afraid of what they fear;
    do not dread those things.
¹³But remember that the LORD All-Powerful is
        holy.
    He is the one you should fear;
    he is the one you should dread.
¹⁴Then he will be a place of safety for you.
    But for the two families of Israel,
he will be like a stone that causes people to
        stumble,
    like a rock that makes them fall.
He will be like a trap for the people of
        Jerusalem,
    and he will catch them in his trap.
¹⁵Many people will fall over this rock.
    They will fall and be broken;
    they will be trapped and caught."

¹⁶Make an agreement.
    Seal up the teaching while my followers are
        watching.
¹⁷I will wait for the LORD to help us,
    the LORD who is ashamed of the family of
        Israel.
I will wait for him.

¹⁸I am here, and with me are the children the LORD has given me. We are signs and proofs for the people of Israel from the LORD All-Powerful, who lives on Mount Zion.ᵈ
¹⁹Some people say, "Ask the mediumsᵈ and fortune-tellers, who whisper and mutter, what to do." But I tell you that people should ask their God for help. Why should people who are still alive ask something from the dead? ²⁰You should follow the teachings and the agreement with the LORD. The mediums and fortune-tellers do not speak the word of the LORD, so their words are worth nothing.
²¹People will wander through the land troubled and hungry. When they become hungry, they will become angry and will look up and curse their king and their God. ²²They will look around them at their land and see only trouble, darkness, and awful gloom. And they will be forced into the darkness.

A New Day Is Coming

9 But suddenly there will be no more gloom for the land that suffered. In the past God made the lands of Zebulun and Naphtali hang their heads in shame, but in the future those lands will be made great. They will stretch from the road along the Mediterranean Sea to the land beyond the Jordan River and north to Galilee, the land of people who are not Israelites.

²Before those people lived in darkness,
    but now they have seen a great light.
They lived in a dark land,
    but a light has shined on them.
³God, you have caused the nation to grow
    and made the people happy.
And they have shown their happiness to you,
    like the joy during harvest time,
like the joy of people
    taking what they have won in war.
⁴Like the time you defeated Midian,
    you have taken away their heavy load
and the heavy pole from their backs
    and the rod the enemy used to punish
        them.
⁵Every boot that marched in battle
    and every uniform stained with blood
    has been thrown into the fire.
⁶A child has been born to us;
    God has given a son to us.
He will be responsible for leading the
        people.
His name will be Wonderful Counselor,
        Powerful God,
    Father Who Lives Forever, Prince of Peace.
⁷Power and peace will be in his kingdom
    and will continue to grow forever.
He will rule as king on David's throne
    and over David's kingdom.
He will make it strong
    by ruling with justice and goodness
    from now on and forever.
The LORD All-Powerful will do this
    because of his strong love for his people.

God Will Punish Israel

⁸The Lord sent a message against the people
        of Jacob;
    it says that God will judge Israel.
⁹Then everyone in Israel, even the leaders in
        Samaria,
    will know that God has sent it.
Those people are proud and brag by saying,
¹⁰"These bricks have fallen,
    but we will build again with cut stones.
These small trees have been chopped down,
    but we will put great cedars there."
¹¹But the LORD has brought the enemies of
        Rezin against them;

he has stirred up their enemies against
   them.
¹²The Arameans came from the east
   and the Philistines from the west,
and they ate up Israel with their armies.

But the LORD was still angry;
   his hand was still raised to punish the
   people.

¹³But the people did not return to the one who
   had struck them;
   they did not follow the LORD All-Powerful.
¹⁴So the LORD cut off Israel's head and tail,
   taking away both the branch and stalk in
   one day.
¹⁵The older leaders and important men were
   the head,
   and the prophets* who speak lies were the
   tail.
¹⁶Those who led the people led them in the
   wrong direction,
   and those who followed them were
   destroyed.
¹⁷So the Lord is not happy with the young
   people,

nor will he show mercy to the orphans and
   widows.
All the people are separated from God and
   are very evil;
   they all speak lies.

But the LORD is still angry;
   his hand is still raised to strike down the
   people.

¹⁸Evil is like a small fire.
   First, it burns weeds and thorns.
Next, it burns the larger bushes in the forest,
   and they all go up in a column of smoke.
¹⁹The LORD All-Powerful is angry,
   so the land will be burned.
The people are like fuel for the fire;
   no one will try to save his brother or sister.
²⁰People will grab something on the right,
   but they will still be hungry.
They will eat something on the left,
   but they will not be filled.
Then they will each turn and eat their own
   children.
²¹The people of Manasseh will fight against the
   people of Ephraim,

JUSTICE

She Died in a Box

Rebecca Smith grew up enjoying the pine trees and fresh smells of spring in Virginia.
One of thirteen children, Rebecca excelled in school and graduated as valedictorian of her
class at the prestigious Hampton Institute.

Forty-three years later, Rebecca died from overexposure to the cold on a New York City
street in January. She was living in a rug-covered cardboard box on the corner of Tenth
Avenue and West Seventeenth Street. Few people on the city streets knew anything about
her besides her name. She was considered by many to be a "crazy" or a throw-away.

What happened to Rebecca in those forty-three years? Years earlier, she
had been hospitalized for schizophrenia and underwent involuntary shock
therapy. For twenty years, she was in and out of hospitals and was often put
on strong medication. Because of her state of mind, she failed to go to
necessary interviews, and she lost her public assistance and benefits. In the
end, through no fault of her own, she lived and died on the streets.

In our world, thousands of people experience the kind of injustice Rebecca
experienced. But the Bible tells of a time when a child will rule with
"goodness and fair judgment." Read about this promised time in **Isaiah
9:1–7**.

■ Isaiah says people then lived in darkness. How does that apply now to
   people like Rebecca? What is the "light" Isaiah talks about?
■ What's one area of your life that needs God's light?

                         C O N S I D E R . . .
■ praying for God to intervene in a bad situation you're concerned about.
■ scanning the newspaper for examples of injustice and then writing down ideas for
   what can be done to solve the problems.

               F O R   M O R E ,   S E E . . .

■ Psalm 82 (p. 531)   ■ 1 Corinthians 6:9–11 (p. 1173)
■ John 5:30 (p. 1056)

and Ephraim will fight against Manasseh.
Then both of them will turn against Judah.

But the Lord is still angry;
his hand is still raised to strike down the
people.

10 How terrible it will be for those who
make unfair laws,
and those who write laws that make life
hard for people.
2They are not fair to the poor,
and they rob my people of their rights.
They allow people to steal from widows
and to take from orphans what really
belongs to them.
3How will you explain the things you have
done?
What will you do when your destruction
comes from far away?
Where will you run for help?
Where will you hide your riches then?
4You will have to bow down among the
captives
or fall down among the dead bodies.

But the Lord is still angry;
his hand is still raised to strike down the
people.

God Will Punish Assyria

5God says, "How terrible it will be for the
king of Assyria.
I use him like a rod to show my anger;
in anger I use Assyria like a club.
6I send it to fight against a nation that is
separated from God.
I am angry with those people,
so I command Assyria to fight against them,
to take their wealth from them,
to trample them down like dirt in the
streets.
7But Assyria's king doesn't understand that I
am using him;
he doesn't know he is a tool for me.
He only wants to destroy other people
and to defeat many nations.
8The king of Assyria says to himself,
'All of my commanders are like kings.
9The city Calno is like the city Carchemish.
The city Hamath is like the city Arpad.
The city Samaria is like the city Damascus.
10I defeated those kingdoms that worship idols,
and those idols were more than the idols of
Jerusalem and Samaria.
11As I defeated Samaria and her idols,
I will also defeat Jerusalem and her idols.' "

12When the Lord finishes doing what he
planned to Mount Zion*d* and Jerusalem, he will
punish Assyria. The king of Assyria is very proud,
and his pride has made him do these evil things,
so God will punish him. 13The king of Assyria says
this:
"By my own power I have done these things;
by my wisdom I have defeated many
nations.
I have taken their wealth,
and, like a mighty one, I have taken their
people.
14I have taken the riches of all these people,
like a person reaching into a bird's nest.
I have taken these nations,
like a person taking eggs.
Not one raised a hand
or opened its mouth to stop me."

15An ax is not better than the person who
swings it.
A saw is not better than the one who uses
it.
A stick cannot control the person who picks
it up.
A club cannot pick up the person!
16So the Lord God All-Powerful
will send a terrible disease upon Assyria's
soldiers.
The strength of Assyria will be burned up
like a fire burning until everything is gone.

SIDELIGHT: When the Assyrian
army rolled into town, the locals could
count on disaster (Isaiah 10:12–16). The
Assyrians were known for flattening cities
with battering rams, shooting defenders from
mobile archery towers, and skinning survivors
alive.

17God, the Light of Israel, will be like a fire;
the Holy One will be like a flame.
He will be like a fire
that suddenly burns the weeds and thorns.
18The fire burns away the great trees and rich
farmlands,
destroying everything.
It will be like a sick person who wastes
away.
19The trees left standing will be so few
that even a child could count them.

20At that time some people will be left alive in
Israel
from the family of Jacob.
They will not continue to depend
on the person who defeated them.
They will learn truly to depend on the Lord,
the Holy One of Israel.
21Those who are left alive in Jacob's family

will again follow the powerful God.
²²Israel, your people are many,
like the grains of sand by the sea.
But only a few of them will be left alive to
return to the LORD.
God has announced that he will destroy the
land
completely and fairly.
²³The Lord GOD All-Powerful will certainly
destroy this land,
as he has announced.

²⁴This is what the Lord GOD All-Powerful says:
"My people living in Jerusalem,
don't be afraid of the Assyrians,
who beat you with a rod
and raise a stick against you, as Egypt did.
²⁵After a short time my anger against you will
stop,
and then I will turn my anger to destroying
them."

²⁶Then the LORD All-Powerful will beat the
Assyrians with a whip
as he defeated Midian at the rock of Oreb.
He will raise his stick over the waters
as he did in Egypt.
²⁷Then the troubles that Assyria puts on you
will be removed,
and the load they make you carry
will be taken away.

Assyria Invades Israel

²⁸The army of Assyria will enter near Aiath.
Its soldiers will walk through Migron.
They will store their food in Micmash.
²⁹The army will go over the pass.
The soldiers will sleep at Geba.
The people of Ramah will be afraid,
and the people at Gibeah of Saul will run
away.
³⁰Cry out, Bath Gallim!
Laishah, listen!
Poor Anathoth!
³¹The people of Madmenah are running away;
the people of Gebim are hiding.
³²This day the army will stop at Nob.
They will shake their fist at Mount Zion,^d
at the hill of Jerusalem.

³³Watch! The Lord GOD All-Powerful
with his great power will chop them down
like a great tree.
Those who are great will be cut down;
those who are important will fall to the
ground.
³⁴He will cut them down
as a forest is cut down with an ax.

And the great trees of Lebanon
will fall by the power of the Mighty One.

The King of Peace Is Coming

11 A new branch will grow
from a stump of a tree;
so a new king will come
from the family of Jesse.ⁿ
²The Spirit^d of the LORD will rest upon that
king.
The Spirit will give him wisdom and
understanding, guidance and power.
The Spirit will teach him to know and
respect the LORD.
³This king will be glad to obey the LORD.
He will not judge by the way things look
or decide by what he hears.
⁴But he will judge the poor honestly;
he will be fair in his decisions for the poor
people of the land.
At his command evil people will be punished,
and by his words the wicked will be put to
death.
⁵Goodness and fairness will give him strength,
like a belt around his waist.

⁶Then wolves will live in peace with lambs,
and leopards will lie down to rest with
goats.
Calves, lions, and young bulls will eat
together,
and a little child will lead them.
⁷Cows and bears will eat together in peace.
Their young will lie down to rest together.
Lions will eat hay as oxen do.
⁸A baby will be able to play near a cobra's
hole,
and a child will be able to put his hand
into the nest of a poisonous snake.

> **SIDELIGHT:** Until God fully sets
> up the peaceful, new kingdom, you'll
> want to steer clear of the cobra (Isaiah 11:8).
> Some varieties of this snake—which can
> grow up to six feet long—spit venom into
> their victims' eyes.

⁹They will not hurt or destroy each other
on all my holy mountain,
because the earth will be full of the
knowledge of the LORD,
as the sea is full of water.

¹⁰At that time the new king from the family of
Jesse will stand as a banner for all peoples. The

Jesse King David's father.

nations will come together around him, and the place where he lives will be filled with glory. ¹¹At that time the Lord will again reach out and take his people who are left alive in Assyria, North Egypt, South Egypt, Cush, Elam, Babylonia, Hamath, and all the islands of the sea.

¹²God will raise a banner as a sign for all
nations,
and he will gather the people of Israel who
were forced from their country.
He will gather the scattered people of Judah
from all parts of the earth.
¹³At that time Israel will not be jealous
anymore,
and Judah will have no more enemies.

Israel will not be jealous of Judah,
and Judah will not hate Israel.
¹⁴But Israel and Judah will attack the Philistines
on the west.
Together they will take the riches from the
people of the east.
They will conquer Edom and Moab,
and the people of Ammon will be under
their control.
¹⁵The LORD will dry up
the Red Sea*d* of Egypt.
He will wave his arm over the Euphrates
River
and dry it up with a scorching wind.
He will divide it into seven small rivers

FUTURE

Assurance of Hope

Desmond Tutu is a small man with a big laugh. He bounces into rooms like a joyful elf who simultaneously puts others at ease and captures their attention. His eyes sparkle behind his gold-rimmed glasses. And his hands gesture wildly as he speaks about the issues that motivate his life in South Africa—God, Christianity, humanity and apartheid (the government system that denies basic rights to anyone who is not white).

Tutu has been leading his people in the war against apartheid for many years. Progress is slow. Yet he is convinced that he—and his people— will win. His confidence isn't based on political scheming or the possibility of civil war. His confidence is based on God. Tutu has a vision for a future free of racism and injustice in South Africa. He has shared his vision with kings, presidents and other leaders, all with the hope of creating a better future for his people.

"What we are looking for is not driving white people into the sea. What we are looking for is a new society where we are saying . . . 'Hey, let's go hand-in-hand together, black and white, into this glorious future that God opened up for us in this wonderful land so that we together—black and white—can walk tall and know that we count not because of the color of our skin, but we count because we are each creatures of infinite value made in the image of God.'

"What chance does the South African government stand?" asks Tutu. "There is just no hope for them. And they really ought to listen to us when we say, 'We are asking you to join the winning side.' When we say we are on the winning side, it isn't that God is on our side because we are good; it is because he is that kind of God."

Desmond Tutu is confident of the future because he believes in God's faithfulness and power to deliver those who cry to him. The writer of **Isaiah 11:1–10** also looks hopefully to the future, for God has promised a time in the future when peace will reign on the earth.
■ How is Desmond Tutu's view of the future like Isaiah's in this passage? How is it different?
■ How does this passage apply to your future?

CONSIDER . . .
■ writing all the dreams you have for your future and then committing them *each to God.*
■ choosing one goal you have for your future and committing yourself to achieve that goal this year.

FOR MORE, SEE . . .
■ Psalm 42 (p. 507)
■ Luke 19:11–27 (p. 1091)
■ 1 John 3:1–3 (p. 1318)

so that people can walk across them
with their sandals on.
16So God's people who are left alive
will have a way to leave Assyria,
just like the time the Israelites
came out of Egypt.

A Song of Praise to God

12 At that time you will say:
"I praise you, Lord!
You were angry with me,
but you are not angry with me now!
You have comforted me.
2God is the one who saves me;
I will trust him and not be afraid.
The Lord, the Lord gives me strength and
makes me sing.
He has saved me.'
3You will receive your salvation with joy
as you would draw water from a well.

4At that time you will say,
"Praise the Lord and worship him.
Tell everyone what he has done
and how great he is.
5Sing praise to the Lord, because he has
done great things.
Let all the world know what he has
done.

6Shout and sing for joy, you people of
Jerusalem,
because the Holy One of Israel does great
things before your eyes."

God's Message to Babylon

13 God showed Isaiah son of Amoz this
message about Babylon:
2Raise a flag on the bare mountain.
Call out to the men.
Raise your hand to signal them
to enter through the gates for important
people.
3I myself have commanded those people
whom I have separated as mine.
I have called those warriors to carry out my
anger.
They rejoice and are glad to do my will.

4Listen to the loud noise in the mountains,
the sound of many people.
Listen to the noise among the kingdoms,
the sound of nations gathering together.
The Lord All-Powerful is calling
his army together for battle.
5This army is coming from a faraway land,
from the edge of the horizon.
In anger the Lord is using this army like a
weapon

ETERNAL LIFE

Safe Under the Falls

From a distance, Niagara Falls is a spectacular sight. But up close, it can be terrifying. Millions of gallons of water rush over the cliff, falling one hundred sixty feet with tremendous force. Anyone caught in the falls would die instantly from the crushing impact on the jagged rocks below.

But with the help of guides, visitors can put on rubber suits and carefully make their way behind the falls. With water roaring and spraying just a few feet away, they can stand in a particular spot known as the Cave of the Winds and be perfectly safe.

Sometimes life can seem like the crushing pressure of Niagara Falls. But, as **Isaiah 12** promises, we can trust God to save and protect us with his gift of eternal life.

■ What similarities are there between the Cave of the Winds and God's promise of eternal life?

■ How does reading this passage give you assurance of God's gift when you are surrounded by troubles?

CONSIDER . . .

■ blowing up a balloon and writing on it reasons you have to celebrate God's gift of eternal life. Keep the balloon in your room as a reminder.

■ following Isaiah 12:4 by telling a non-Christian friend about the joy you have found in God's love, comfort, and salvation.

FOR MORE, SEE . . .

■ Micah 7:7–9 (p. 868)   ■ 2 Peter 1:3–11 (p. 1311)
■ John 3:1–16 (p. 1061)

to destroy the whole country.

⁶Cry, because the LORD's day of judging is
near;
the Almighty is sending destruction.
⁷People will be weak with fear,
and their courage will melt away.
⁸Everyone will be afraid.
Pain and hurt will grab them;
they will hurt like a woman giving birth to
a baby.
They will look at each other in fear,
with their faces red like fire.

God's Judgment Against Babylon

⁹Look, the LORD's day of judging is coming—
a terrible day, a day of God's anger.
He will destroy the land
and the sinners who live in it.
¹⁰The stars will not show their light;
the skies will be dark.
The sun will grow dark as it rises,
and the moon will not give its light.
¹¹The LORD says, "I will punish the world for
its evil
and wicked people for their sins.
I will cause proud people to lose their pride,
and I will destroy the pride of those who
are cruel to others.
¹²People will be harder to find than pure gold;
there will be fewer people than there is fine
gold in Ophir.
¹³I will make the sky shake,
and the earth will be moved from its place
by the anger of the LORD All-Powerful
at the time of his burning anger.
¹⁴"Then the people from Babylon will run away
like hunted deer
or like sheep who have no shepherd.
Everyone will turn back to his own people;
each will run back to his own land.
¹⁵Everyone who is captured will be killed;
everyone who is caught will be killed with
a sword.
¹⁶Their little children will be beaten to death in
front of them.
Their houses will be robbed
and their wives raped.

¹⁷"Look, I will cause the armies of Media to
attack Babylon.
They do not care about silver
or delight in gold.
¹⁸Their soldiers will shoot the young men with
arrows;
they will show no mercy on children,
nor will they feel sorry for little ones.
¹⁹Babylon is the most beautiful of all kingdoms,
and the Babylonians are very proud of it.

But God will destroy it
like Sodom and Gomorrah.
²⁰No one will ever live there
or settle there again.
No Arab will put a tent there;
no shepherd will bring sheep there.
²¹Only desert animals will live there,
and their houses will be full of wild dogs.
Owls will live there,
and wild goats will leap about in the
houses.
²²Wolves will howl within the strong walls,
and wild dogs will bark in the beautiful
buildings.
The end of Babylon is near;
its time is almost over."

Israel Will Return Home

14 The LORD will show mercy to the people
of Jacob, and he will again choose the
people of Israel. He will settle them in their own
land. Then non-Israelite people will join the Israelites and will become a part of the family of Jacob.
²Nations will take the Israelites back to their land.
Then those men and women from the other na-
tions will become slaves to Israel in the LORD's
land. In the past the Israelites were their slaves,
but now the Israelites will defeat those nations
and rule over them.

The King of Babylon Will Fall

³The LORD will take away the Israelites' hard
work and will comfort them. They will no longer
have to work hard as slaves. ⁴On that day Israel
will sing this song about the king of Babylon:
The cruel king who ruled us is finished;
his angry rule is finished!
⁵The LORD has broken the scepter^d of evil
rulers
and taken away their power.
⁶The king of Babylon struck people in anger
again and again.
He ruled nations in anger
and continued to hurt them.
⁷But now, the whole world rests and is quiet.
Now the people begin to sing.
⁸Even the pine trees are happy,
and the cedar trees of Lebanon rejoice.
They say, "The king has fallen,
so no one will ever cut us down again."

⁹The place of the dead is excited
to meet you when you come.
It wakes the spirits of the dead,
the leaders of the world.
It makes kings of all nations
stand up from their thrones to greet you.
¹⁰All these leaders will make fun of you
and will say,

"Now you are weak, as we are.
Now you are just like us."
11Your pride has been sent down to the place
of the dead.
The music from your harps goes with it.
Flies are spread out like your bed beneath
you,
and worms cover your body like a blanket.

12King of Babylon, morning star, you have
fallen from heaven,
even though you were as bright as the
rising sun!
In the past all the nations on earth bowed
down before you,
but now you have been cut down.
13You told yourself,
"I will go up to heaven.
I will put my throne
above God's stars.
I will sit on the mountain of the gods,
on the slopes of the sacred mountain.
14I will go up above the tops of the clouds.
I will be like God Most High."
15But you were brought down to the grave,
to the deep places where the dead are.

16Those who see you stare at you.
They think about what has happened to
you
and say, "Is this the same man who caused
great fear on earth,
who shook the kingdoms,
17who turned the world into a desert,
who destroyed its cities,
who captured people in war
and would not let them go home?"

18Every king of the earth has been buried with
honor,
each in his own grave.
19But you are thrown out of your grave,
like an unwanted branch.
You are covered by bodies
that died in battle,
by bodies to be buried in a rocky pit.
You are like a dead body other soldiers
walk on.
20 You will not be buried with those bodies,
because you ruined your own country
and killed your own people.
The children of evil people
will never be mentioned again.

21Prepare to kill his children,
because their father is guilty.
They will never again take control of the
earth;
they will never again fill the world with
their cities.

22The LORD All-Powerful says this:
"I will fight against those people;
I will destroy Babylon and its people,
its children and their descendants,"[d] says
the LORD.
23"I will make Babylon fit only for owls
and for swamps.
I will sweep Babylon as with a broom of
destruction,"
says the LORD All-Powerful.

God Will Punish Assyria

24The LORD All-Powerful has made this promise:
"These things will happen exactly as I
planned them;
they will happen exactly as I set them up.
25I will destroy the king of Assyria in my
country;
I will trample him on my mountains.
He placed a heavy load on my people,
but that weight will be removed.

26"This is what I plan to do for all the earth.
And this is the hand that I have raised over
all nations."
27When the LORD All-Powerful makes a plan,
no one can stop it.
When the LORD raises his hand to punish
people,
no one can stop it.

God's Message to Philistia

28This message was given in the year that King
Ahaz died:
29Country of Philistia, don't be happy
that the king who struck you is now dead.
He is like a snake that will give birth to
another dangerous snake.
The new king will be like a quick,
dangerous snake to bite you.
30Even the poorest of my people will be able to
eat safely,
and people in need will be able to lie down
in safety.
But I will kill your family with hunger,
and all your people who are left will die.

31People near the city gates, cry out!
Philistines, be frightened,
because a cloud of dust comes from the
north.
It is an army, full of men ready to fight.
32What shall we tell the messengers from
Philistia?
Say that the LORD has made Jerusalem
strong
and that his poor people will go there for
safety.

God's Message to Moab

15 This is a message about Moab:
In one night armies took the wealth
from Ar in Moab,
and it was destroyed.
In one night armies took the wealth from Kir
in Moab,
and it was destroyed.

SIDELIGHT: Even though the Moabites (Isaiah 15:1) were distant cousins of the Israelites, the two groups had been enemies ever since Moses tried to enter Canaan about seven hundred years before Isaiah (Judges 11:17, p. 228).

---

[2]The people of Dibon go to the places of
worship to cry.
The people of Moab cry for the cities of
Nebo and Medeba.
Every head and beard has been shaved to
show how sad Moab is.
[3]In the streets they wear rough cloth to show
their sadness.
On the roofs[n] and in the public squares,
they are crying loudly.
[4]People in the cities Heshbon and Elealeh cry
out loud.
You can hear their voices far away in the
city Jahaz.
Even the soldiers are frightened;
they are shaking with fear.

[5]My heart cries with sorrow for Moab.
Its people run away to Zoar for safety;
they run to Eglath Shelishiyah.
People are going up the mountain road to
Luhith,
crying as they go.
People are going on the road to Horonaim,
crying over their destruction.
[6]But the water of Nimrim has dried up.
The grass has dried up,
and all the plants are dead;
nothing green is left.
[7]So the people gather up what they have
saved
and carry it across the Ravine of the
Poplars.
[8]Crying is heard everywhere in Moab.
Their crying is heard as far away as the city
Eglaim;
it is heard as far away as Beer Elim.
[9]The water of the city Dibon is full of blood,

and I, the LORD, will bring even more
troubles to Dibon.
A few people living in Moab have escaped
the enemy,
but I will send lions to kill them.

16 Send the king of the land
the payment he demands.
Send a lamb from Sela through the desert
to the mountain of Jerusalem.
[2]The women of Moab
try to cross the river Arnon
like little birds
that have fallen from their nest.

[3]They say: "Help us.
Tell us what to do.
Protect us from our enemies
as shade protects us from the noon sun.
Hide us, because we are running for safety!
Don't give us to our enemies.
[4]Let those of us who were forced out of Moab
live in your land.
Hide us from our enemies."

The robbing of Moab will stop.
The enemy will be defeated;
those who hurt others will disappear from
the land.
[5]Then a new loyal king will come;
this faithful king will be from the family of
David.
He will judge fairly
and do what is right.

[6]We have heard that the people of Moab are
proud
and very conceited.
They are very proud and angry,
but their bragging means nothing.
[7]So the people of Moab will cry;
they will all be sad.
They will moan and groan
for the raisin cakes they had in Kir
Hareseth.
[8]But the fields of Heshbon and the vines of
Sibmah cannot grow grapes;
foreign rulers have destroyed the
grapevines.
The grapevines once spread as far as the city
of Jazer and into the desert;
they had spread as far as the sea.
[9]I cry with the people of Jazer
for the grapevines of Sibmah.
I will cry with the people of Heshbon and
Elealeh.
There will be no shouts of joy,

---

roofs In Bible times houses were built with flat roofs. The roof was used for drying things such as flax and fruit. And it was used as an extra room, as a place for worship, and as a place to sleep in the summer.

because there will be no harvest or ripe
fruit.

[10]There will be no joy and happiness in the
orchards
and no songs or shouts of joy in the
vineyards.
No one makes wine in the winepresses,[d]
because I have put an end to shouts of joy.

[11]My heart cries for Moab like a harp playing a
funeral song;
I am very sad for Kir Hareseth.

[12]The people of Moab will go to their places of
worship
and will try to pray.
But when they go to their temple to pray,
they will not be able.

[13]Earlier the LORD said these things about
Moab. [14]Now the LORD says, "In three years all
those people and what they take pride in will be
hated. (This is three years as a hired helper would
count time.) There will be a few people left, but
they will be weak."

God's Message to Aram

17 This is a message about Damascus:
"The city of Damascus will be
destroyed;
only ruins will remain.

[2]People will leave the cities of Aroer.
Flocks will wander freely in those empty
towns,
and there will be no one to bother them.

[3]The strong, walled cities of Israel will be
destroyed.
The government in Damascus will end.
Those left alive of Aram will be
like the glory of Israel," says the LORD
All-Powerful.

[4]"At that time Israel's wealth will all be gone.
Israel will be like someone who has lost
much weight from sickness.

[5]That time will be like the grain harvest in the
Valley of Rephaim.
The workers cut the wheat.
Then they cut the heads of grain from the
plants
and collect the grain.

[6]That time will also be like the olive harvest,
when a few olives are left.
Two or three olives are left in the top
branches.
Four or five olives are left on full
branches," says the LORD, the God of
Israel.

[7]At that time people will look to God, their
Maker;
their eyes will see the Holy One of Israel.

[8]They will not trust the altars they have made,
nor will they trust what their hands have
made,
not even the Asherah[d] idols
and altars.

[9]In that day all their strong cities will be empty.
They will be like the cities the Hivites and the
Amorites left when the Israelites came to take the
land. Everything will be ruined.

[10]You have forgotten the God who saves you;
you have not remembered that God is your
place of safety.
You plant the finest grapevines
and grapevines from faraway places.

[11]You plant your grapevines one day and try to
make them grow,
and the next day you make them blossom.
But at harvest time everything will be dead;
a sickness will kill all the plants.

[12]Listen to the many people!
Their crying is like the noise from the sea.
Listen to the nations!
Their crying is like the crashing of great
waves.

[13]The people roar like the waves,
but when God speaks harshly to them, they
will run away.
They will be like chaff[d] on the hills being
blown by the wind,
or like tumbleweeds blown away by a
storm.

[14]At night the people will be very frightened.
Before morning, no one will be left.
So our enemies will come to our land,
but they will become nothing.

God's Message to Cush

18 How terrible it will be for the land
beyond the rivers of Cush.
It is filled with the sound of wings.

[2]That land sends messengers across the sea;
they go on the water in boats made of
reeds.

Go, quick messengers,
to a people who are tall and
smooth-skinned,
who are feared everywhere.
They are a powerful nation that defeats other
nations.
Their land is divided by rivers.

[3]All you people of the world, look!
Everyone who lives in the world, look!
You will see a banner raised on a mountain.
You will hear a trumpet sound.

[4]The LORD said to me,
"I will quietly watch from where I live,

like heat in the sunshine,
   like the dew in the heat of harvest time."
5The time will come, after the flowers have
   bloomed and before the harvest,
when new grapes will be budding and
   growing.
The enemy will cut the plants with knives;
   he will cut down the vines and take them
   away.
6They will be left for the birds of the
   mountains
and for the wild animals.
Birds will feed on them all summer,
   and wild animals will eat them that
   winter."

7At that time a gift will be brought to the
   LORD All-Powerful
from the people who are tall and
   smooth-skinned,
who are feared everywhere.
They are a powerful nation that defeats other
   nations.
Their land is divided by rivers.
These gifts will be brought to the place of the
   LORD All-Powerful,
to Mount Zion.*d*

God's Message to Egypt

19 This is a message about Egypt:
   Look, the LORD is coming on a fast
   cloud
to enter Egypt.
The idols of Egypt will tremble before him,
   and Egypt's courage will melt away.

2The LORD says, "I will cause the Egyptians to
   fight against themselves.
People will fight with their relatives;
   neighbors will fight neighbors;
   cities will fight cities;
   kingdoms will fight kingdoms.
3The Egyptians will be afraid,
   and I will ruin their plans.
They will ask advice from their idols and
   spirits of the dead,
from their mediums*d* and fortune-tellers."
4The Lord GOD All-Powerful says,
"I will hand Egypt over to a hard master,
   and a powerful king will rule over them."

5The sea will become dry,
   and the water will disappear from the Nile
   River.
6The canals will stink;
   the streams of Egypt will decrease and dry
   up.
All the water plants will rot;
7 all the plants along the banks of the Nile
   will die.

Even the planted fields by the Nile
   will dry up, blow away, and disappear.
8The fishermen, all those who catch fish from
   the Nile,
will groan and cry;
those who fish in the Nile will be sad.
9All the people who make cloth from flax will
   be sad,
and those who weave linen will lose
   hope.
10Those who weave cloth will be broken.
   All those who work for money will be sad.

11The officers of the city of Zoan are fools;
   the wise men who advise the king of Egypt
   give wrong advice.
How can you say to him, 'I am wise'?
   How can you say, 'I am from the old family
   of the kings'?
12Egypt, where are your wise men?
   Let them show you
what the LORD All-Powerful has planned for
   Egypt.
13The officers of Zoan have been fooled;
   the leaders of Memphis have believed false
   things.
So the leaders of Egypt
   lead that nation the wrong way.
14The LORD has made the leaders confused.
   They have led Egypt to wander in the
   wrong ways,
like drunk people stumbling in their own
   vomit.
15There is nothing Egypt can do;
   no one there can help.

16In that day the Egyptians will be like women. They will be afraid of the LORD All-Powerful, because he will raise his hand to strike them down. 17The land of Judah will bring fear to Egypt. Anyone there who hears the name Judah will be afraid, because the LORD All-Powerful has planned terrible things for them. 18At that time five cities in Egypt will speak Hebrew, the language of Canaan, and they will promise to be loyal to the LORD All-Powerful. One of these cities will be named the City of Destruction. 19At that time there will be an altar for the LORD in the middle of Egypt and a monument to the LORD at the border of Egypt. 20This will be a sign and a witness to the LORD All-Powerful in the land of Egypt. When the people cry to the LORD for help, he will send someone to save and defend them. He will rescue them from those who hurt them.

21So the LORD will show himself to the Egyptians, and then they will know he is the LORD. They will worship God and offer many sacrifices. They will make promises to the LORD and will keep them. 22The LORD will punish the Egyptians, but then he will heal them. They will come back to the LORD, and he will listen to their prayers and heal them.

²³At that time there will be a highway from Egypt to Assyria, and the Assyrians will go to Egypt, and the Egyptians will go to Assyria. The Egyptians and Assyrians will worship God together. ²⁴At that time Israel, Assyria, and Egypt will join together, which will be a blessing for the earth. ²⁵The LORD All-Powerful will bless them, saying, "Egypt, you are my people. Assyria, I made you. Israel, I own you. You are all blessed!"

※ SIDELIGHT: Sargon, an Assyrian king during Isaiah's time (Isaiah 20:1), was not only a powerful military leader, but must have also been quite a scholar. He built the oldest library archaeologists have discovered, where twenty-five hundred books were found. Of course, that's a small number compared to modern libraries, which can have several million books.

Assyria Will Defeat Egypt and Cush

20 Sargon king of Assyria sent a military commander to Ashdod to attack that city. So the commander attacked and captured it. ²Then the LORD spoke through Isaiah son of Amoz, saying, "Take the rough cloth off your body, and take your sandals off your feet." So Isaiah obeyed and walked around naked and barefoot.

³Then the LORD said, "Isaiah my servant has walked around naked and barefoot for three years as a sign against Egypt and Cush. ⁴The king of Assyria will carry away prisoners from Egypt and Cush. Old people and young people will be led away naked and barefoot, with their buttocks bare. So the Egyptians will be shamed. ⁵People who looked to Cush for help will be afraid, and those who were amazed by Egypt's glory will be shamed. ⁶People who live near the sea will say, 'Look at those countries. We trusted them to help us. We ran to them so they would save us from the king of Assyria. So how will we be able to escape?'"

God's Message to Babylon

21 This is a message about the Desert by the Sea:*ⁿ*
Disaster is coming from the desert
    like wind blowing in the south.
    It is coming from a terrible country.
²I have seen a terrible vision.
    I see traitors turning against you

and people taking your wealth.

Elam, attack the people!
    Media, surround the city and attack it!
    I will bring an end to the pain the city
        causes.

³I saw those terrible things, and now I am in
        pain;
    my pains are like the pains of giving birth.
What I hear makes me very afraid;
    what I see causes me to shake with fear.
⁴I am worried,
    and I am shaking with fear.
My pleasant evening
    has become a night of fear.

⁵They set the table;
    they spread the rugs;
    they eat and drink.
Leaders, stand up.
    Prepare the shields for battle!

⁶The Lord said to me,
    "Go, place a lookout for the city
        and have him report what he sees.
⁷If he sees chariots and teams of horses,
        donkeys, or camels,
    he should pay very close attention."

⁸Then the lookout called out,
    "My master, each day I stand in the
        watchtower watching;
    every night I have been on guard.
⁹Look, I see a man coming in a chariot
    with a team of horses."
The man gives back the answer,
    "Babylon has fallen. It has fallen!
All the statues of her gods
    lie broken on the ground."

¹⁰My people are crushed like grain on the
        threshing*ᵈ* floor.
    My people, I tell you what I have heard
from the LORD All-Powerful,
    from the God of Israel.

God's Message to Edom

¹¹This is a message about Dumah:*ⁿ*
Someone calls to me from Edom,
    "Watchman, how much of the night is left?
    Watchman, how much longer will it be
        night?"
¹²The watchman answers,
    "Morning is coming, but then night will
        come again.
    If you have something to ask,
        then come back and ask."

Desert by the Sea Probably Babylon.
Dumah Another name for Edom.

God's Message to Arabia

13This is a message about Arabia:
A group of traders from Dedan
spent the night near some trees in
Arabia.
14 They gave water to thirsty travelers;
the people of Tema gave food
to those who were escaping.
15They were running from swords,
from swords ready to kill,
from bows ready to shoot,
from a hard battle.

16This is what the Lord said to me: "In one year
all the glory of the country of Kedar will be gone.
(This is a year as a hired helper counts time.) 17At
that time only a few of the archers, the soldiers of
Kedar, will be left alive." The LORD, the God of
Israel, has spoken.

God's Message to Jerusalem

22 This is a message about the Valley of
Vision:*n*
What is wrong with you people?
Why are you on your roofs?*n*
2This city was a very busy city,
full of noise and wild parties.
Now your people have been killed,
but not with swords,
nor did they die in battle.
3All your leaders ran away together,
but they have been captured without using
a bow.
All you who were captured
tried to run away before the enemy came.
4So I say, "Don't look at me.
Let me cry loudly.
Don't hurry to comfort me
about the destruction of Jerusalem."
5The Lord GOD All-Powerful has chosen a
special day
of riots and confusion.
People will trample each other in the Valley
of Vision.
The city walls will be knocked down,
and the people will cry out to the
mountain.
6The soldiers from Elam will gather their
arrows
and their chariots and men on horses.
Kir will prepare their shields.
7Your nicest valleys will be filled with chariots.
Horsemen will be ordered to guard the
gates of the city.
8 The walls protecting Judah will fall.

At that time the people of Jerusalem
depended on
the weapons kept at the Palace of the
Forest.
9You saw that the walls of Jerusalem
had many cracks that needed repairing.
You stored up water in the lower pool.
10You counted the houses of Jerusalem,
and you tore down houses to repair the
walls with their stones.
11You made a pool between the two walls
to save water from the old pool,
but you did not trust the God who made
these things;
you did not respect the One who planned
them long ago.

12The Lord GOD All-Powerful told the people
to cry and be sad,
to shave their heads and wear rough cloth.
13But look, the people are happy
and are having wild parties.
They kill the cattle and the sheep;
they eat the food and drink the wine.
They say, "Let us eat and drink,
because tomorrow we will die."

14The LORD All-Powerful said to me: "You people will die before this guilt is forgiven." The Lord
GOD All-Powerful said this.

God's Message to Shebna

15This is what the Lord GOD All-Powerful says:
"Go to this servant Shebna,
the manager of the palace.
16Say to him, 'What are you doing here?
Who said you could cut out a tomb for
yourself here?
Why are you preparing your tomb in a high
place?
Why are you carving out a tomb from the
rock?
17Look, mighty one! The LORD will throw you
away.
He will take firm hold of you
18and roll you tightly into a ball
and throw you into another country.
There you will die,
and there your fine chariots will remain.
You are a disgrace to your master's house.
19I will force you out of your important job,
and you will be thrown down from your
important place.'

20"At that time I will call for my servant Eliakim
son of Hilkiah. 21I will take your robe and put it
on him and give him your belt. I will hand over

Valley of Vision This probably means a valley near Jerusalem.
roofs In Bible times houses were built with flat roofs. The roof was used for drying things such as flax and fruit. And it was
used as an extra room, as a place for worship, and as a place to sleep in the summer.

to him the important job you have, and he will be like a father to the people of Jerusalem and the family of Judah. ²²I will put the key to the house of David around his neck. If he opens a door, no one will be able to close it; if he closes a door, no one will be able to open it. ²³He will be like an honored chair in his father's house. I will make him strong like a peg that is hammered into a strong board. ²⁴All the honored and important things of his family will depend on him; all the adults and little children will depend on him. They will be like bowls and jars hanging on him.

²⁵"At that time," says the LORD All-Powerful, "the peg hammered into the strong board will weaken. It will break and fall, and everything hanging on it will be destroyed." The LORD says this.

God's Message to Lebanon

23 This is a message about Tyre:
You trading ships, cry!
The houses and harbor of Tyre are
destroyed.
This news came to the ships
from the land of Cyprus.
²Be silent, you who live on the island of Tyre;
you merchants of Sidon, be silent.
Sailors have made you rich.
³They traveled the sea to bring grain from
Egypt;
the sailors of Tyre brought grain from the
Nile Valley
and sold it to other nations.

⁴Sidon, be ashamed.
Strong city of the sea, be ashamed, because
the sea says:
"I have not felt the pain of giving birth;
I have not reared young men or women."
⁵Egypt will hear the news about Tyre,
and it will make Egypt hurt with sorrow.

⁶You ships should return to Tarshish.
You people living near the sea should be
sad.
⁷Look at your once happy city!
Look at your old, old city!
People from that city have traveled
far away to live.
⁸Who planned Tyre's destruction?
Tyre made others rich.
Its merchants were treated like princes,
and its traders were greatly respected.
⁹It was the LORD All-Powerful who planned
this.
He decided to make these proud people
unimportant;
he decided to disgrace those who were
greatly respected.
¹⁰Go through your land, people of Tarshish,

like the Nile goes through Egypt.
There is no harbor for you now!
¹¹The LORD has stretched his hand over the sea
and made its kingdoms tremble.
He commands that Canaan's
strong, walled cities be destroyed.
¹²He said, "Sidon, you will not rejoice any
longer,
because you are destroyed.
Even if you cross the sea to Cyprus,
you will not find a place to rest."
¹³Look at the land of the Babylonians;
it is not a country now.
Assyria has made it a place for wild animals.
Assyria built towers to attack it;
the soldiers took all the treasures from its
cities,
and they turned it into ruins.
¹⁴So be sad, you trading ships,
because your strong city is destroyed.

¹⁵At that time people will forget about Tyre for seventy years, which is the length of a king's life. After seventy years, Tyre will be like the prostitute^d in this song:

¹⁶"Oh woman, you are forgotten.
Take your harp and walk through the city.
Play your harp well. Sing your song often.
Then people will remember you."

¹⁷After seventy years the LORD will deal with Tyre, and it will again have trade. It will be like a prostitute for all the nations of the earth. ¹⁸The profits will be saved for the LORD. Tyre will not keep the money she earns but will give them to the people who serve the LORD, so they will have plenty of food and nice clothes.

The Lord Will Punish the World

24 Look! The LORD will destroy the earth
and leave it empty;
he will ruin the surface of the land and
scatter its people.
²At that time the same thing will happen to
everyone:
to common people and priests,
to slaves and masters,
to women slaves and their women masters,
to buyers and sellers,
to those who borrow and those who lend,
to bankers and those who owe the bank.
³The earth will be completely empty.
The wealth will all be taken,
because the LORD has commanded it.
⁴The earth will dry up and die;
the world will grow weak and die;
the great leaders in this land will become
weak.
⁵The people of the earth have ruined it,
because they do not follow God's teachings

or obey God's laws
  or keep their agreement with God that was
    to last forever.
⁶So a curse will destroy the earth.
  The people of the world are guilty,
  so they will be burned up;
  only a few will be left.
⁷The new wine will be bad, and the
    grapevines will die.
  People who were happy will be sad.
⁸The happy music of the tambourines*d* will
    end.
  The happy sounds of wild parties will stop.
  The joyful music from the harps will end.
⁹People will no longer sing while they drink
    their wine.
  The beer will taste bitter to those who
    drink it.
¹⁰The ruined city will be empty,
  and people will hide behind closed doors.
¹¹People in the streets will ask for wine,
  but joy will have turned to sadness;
  all the happiness will have left.
¹²The city will be left in ruins,
  and its gates will be smashed to pieces.
¹³This is what will happen all over the earth
  and to all the nations.
  The earth will be like an olive tree after the
    harvest
  or like the few grapes left on a vine after
    harvest.

¹⁴The people shout for joy.
  From the west they praise the greatness of
    the LORD.
¹⁵People in the east, praise the LORD.
  People in the islands of the sea,
  praise the name of the LORD, the God of
    Israel.
¹⁶We hear songs from every part of the earth
  praising God, the Righteous One.

  But I said, "I am dying! I am dying!
  How terrible it will be for me!
  Traitors turn against people;
  with their dishonesty, they turn against
    people."
¹⁷There are terrors, holes, and traps
  for the people of the earth.
¹⁸Anyone who tries to escape from the sound
    of terror
  will fall into a hole.
  Anyone who climbs out of the hole
    will be caught in a trap.
  The clouds in the sky will pour out rain,
    and the foundations of the earth will
      shake.
¹⁹The earth will be broken up;
  the earth will split open;
  the earth will shake violently.

²⁰The earth will stumble around like someone
    who is drunk;
  it will shake like a hut in a storm.
  Its sin is like a heavy weight on its back;
  it will fall and never rise again.

²¹At that time the LORD will punish
  the powers in the sky above
  and the rulers on earth below.
²²They will be gathered together
  like prisoners thrown into a dungeon;
  they will be shut up in prison.
  After much time they will be punished.
²³The moon will be embarrassed,
  and the sun will be ashamed,
  because the LORD All-Powerful will rule as
    king
  on Mount Zion*d* in Jerusalem.
  Jerusalem's leaders will see his greatness.

A Song of Praise to God

25 LORD, you are my God.
  I honor you and praise you,
because you have done amazing things.
  You have always done what you said you
    would do;
  you have done what you planned long ago.
²You have made the city a pile of rocks
  and have destroyed her walls.
  The city our enemies built with strong walls
    is gone;
  it will never be built again.
³People from powerful nations will honor you;
  cruel people from strong cities will fear
    you.
⁴You protect the poor;
  you protect the helpless when they are in
    danger.
  You are like a shelter from storms,
  like shade that protects them from the heat.
  The cruel people attack
  like a rainstorm beating against the wall,
⁵ like the heat in the desert.
  But you, God, stop their violent attack.
  As a cloud cools a hot day,
  you silence the songs of those who have no
    mercy.

God's Banquet for His Servants

⁶The LORD All-Powerful will prepare a feast
  on this mountain for all people.
  It will be a feast with all the best food and
    wine,
  the finest meat and wine.
⁷On this mountain God will destroy
  the veil that covers all nations,
  the veil that stretches over all peoples;
⁸ he will destroy death forever.

The Lord God will wipe away every tear
from every face.
He will take away the shame of his people
from the earth.
The Lord has spoken.

⁹At that time people will say,
"Our God is doing this!
We have waited for him, and he has come to
save us.
This is the Lord. We waited for him,
so we will rejoice and be happy when he
saves us."
¹⁰The Lord will protect Jerusalem,
but he will crush our enemy Moab
like straw that is trampled down in the
manure.
¹¹They will spread their arms in it
like a person who is swimming.

But God will bring down their pride,
and all the clever things they have made
will mean nothing.

SIDELIGHT: Lawn care services may be new, but fertilizer has been around for a long time. The ancient Israelite farmers would mix together straw and manure to make fertilizer (Isaiah 25:10). If they were around today, those farmers could sell their produce at all-organic stores.

---

¹²Moab's high walls protect them,
but God will destroy these walls.
He will throw them down to the ground,
even to the dust.

DEATH

Bittersweet

Jacob Blevins was a rebel. He didn't like church or the kids who went there. But something inside him kept drawing him to the youth group. Perhaps it was the way the kids treated each other. They truly cared. Or perhaps it was just the fun events.

For whatever reason, Jacob came to the harvest hayride. He arrived early and walked quietly around the church. He talked to a few people, but mostly kept to himself.

Just before the hayride trailer took off, Jacob saw Kellie, a girl he knew—and liked— from school. Jacob knew she was a Christian, and wondered whether she would talk to him. Despite his fears, he plopped down beside her on the front of one side of the trailer, and they took off.

Jacob and Kellie had a great time. They talked and laughed, and even wrestled playfully in the hay.

Then it happened. Kellie just suddenly wasn't there. There was no scream, no sound at all. It was like a weird dream, but Jacob couldn't wake himself up. He sat stunned as the trailer came to an abrupt halt.

Kellie was dead. While she and Jacob were wrestling, her foot had gotten caught in the trailer wheel. The turning of the wheel pulled her off the trailer, and under the tire.

Jacob struggled to get over the pain of that night. But through the months that followed, he developed a relationship with God that remains strong. Jacob knows he'll never see Kellie again in this lifetime. But now that he knows Christ, he's assured that he'll see her again . . . in heaven.

Isaiah 25:6–9 describes how God will destroy death and bring all his people together at the end of time. Read the passage to see what Jacob and Kellie's reunion will be like.

■ Verse 7 describes death as a "veil." How is death like a "veil" separating Jacob and Kellie?
■ According to this passage, why should we not fear death?

CONSIDER . . .
■ writing all the positive things about someone you love who has died and then looking at your list every time you feel sad about that person's death.
■ spending time with someone you know who has lost someone he or she loved.

FOR MORE, SEE . . .
■ Psalm 23 (p. 495)
■ 1 Corinthians 15:50–57 (p. 1189)
■ 1 Thessalonians 4:13–18 (p. 1248)

A Song of Praise to God

26 At that time people will sing this song in Judah:

We have a strong city.
God protects us with its strong walls and
defenses.
²Open the gates,
and the good people will enter,
those who follow God.
³You, LORD, give true peace
to those who depend on you,
because they trust you.
⁴So, trust the LORD always,
because he is our Rock^d forever.
⁵He will destroy the proud city,
and he will punish the people living there.
He will bring that high city down to the
ground
and throw it down into the dust.
⁶Then those who were hurt by the city will
walk on its ruins;
those who were made poor by the city will
trample it under their feet.

⁷The path of life is level for those who are
right with God;
LORD, you make the way of life smooth for
those people.
⁸But, LORD, we are waiting
for your way of justice.
Our souls want to remember
you and your name.
⁹My soul wants to be with you at night,
and my spirit wants to be with you at the
dawn of every day.
When your way of justice comes to the land,
people of the world will learn the right way
of living.
¹⁰Evil people will not learn to do good
even if you show them kindness.
They will continue doing evil, even if they
live in a good world;
they never see the LORD's greatness.
¹¹LORD, you are ready to punish those people,
but they do not see that.
Show them your strong love for your people.
Then those who are evil will be ashamed.
Burn them in the fire
you have prepared for your enemies.
¹²LORD, all our success is because of what you
have done,
so give us peace.
¹³LORD, our God, other masters besides you
have ruled us,
but we honor only you.
¹⁴Those masters are now dead;
their ghosts will not rise from death.
You punished and destroyed them
and erased any memory of them.

¹⁵LORD, you multiplied the number of your
people;
you multiplied them and brought honor to
yourself.
You made the borders of the land wide.
¹⁶LORD, people remember you when they are
in trouble;
they say quiet prayers to you when you
punish them.
¹⁷LORD, when we are with you,
we are like a woman giving birth to a
baby;
she cries and has pain from the birth.
¹⁸In the same way, we had pain.
We gave birth, but only to wind.
We don't bring salvation to the land
or make new people for the world.
¹⁹Your people have died, but they will live
again;
their bodies will rise from death.
You who lie in the ground,
wake up and be happy!
The dew covering you is like the dew of a
new day;
the ground will give birth to the dead.

Judgment: Reward or Punishment

²⁰My people, go into your rooms
and shut your doors behind you.
Hide in your rooms for a short time
until God's anger is finished.
²¹The LORD will leave his place
to punish the people of the world for their
sins.
The earth will show the blood of the people
who have been killed;
it will not cover the dead any longer.

27 At that time the LORD will punish
Leviathan,^d the gliding snake.
He will punish Leviathan, the coiled
snake,
with his great and hard and powerful
sword.
He will kill the monster in the sea.

²At that time
people will sing about the pleasant
vineyard.
³"I, the LORD, will care for that vineyard;
I will water it at the right time.
No one will hurt it,
because I will guard it day and night.
⁴I am not angry.
If anyone builds a wall of thornbushes in
war,
I will march to it and burn it.
⁵But if anyone comes to me for safety
and wants to make peace with me,
he should come and make peace with me."

⁶In the days to come, the people of Jacob will
   be like a plant with good roots;
  Israel will grow like a plant beginning to
   bloom.
  Then the world will be filled with their
   children.

The Lord Will Send Israel Away

⁷The Lord has not hurt his people as he hurt
   their enemies.
  his people have not been killed like those
   who tried to kill them.
⁸He will settle his argument with Israel by
   sending it far away.
  Like a hot desert wind, he will drive it
   away.
⁹This is how Israel's guilt will be forgiven;
   this is how its sins will be taken away:
  Israel will crush the rocks of the altar to dust,
  and no statues or altars will be left standing
   for the Asherah*d* idols.
¹⁰At that time the strong, walled city will be
   empty
   like a desert.
  Calves will eat grass there.
  They will lie down there
   and eat leaves from the branches.
¹¹The limbs will become dry and break off,
   so women will use them for firewood.
  The people refuse to understand,
   so God will not comfort them;
   their Maker will not be kind to them.
¹²At that time the Lord will begin gathering his
people one by one from the Euphrates River to the
brook of Egypt. He will separate them from others
as grain is separated from chaff.*d* ¹³Many of my
people are now lost in Assyria. Some have run
away to Egypt. But at that time a great trumpet
will be blown, and all those people will come and
worship the Lord on that holy mountain in Jerusalem.

Warnings to Israel

28 How terrible it will be for Samaria, the
pride of Israel's drunken people!
  That beautiful crown of flowers is just a
   dying plant
  set on a hill above a rich valley where
   drunkards live.
²Look, the Lord has someone who is strong
   and powerful.
  Like a storm of hail and strong wind,
  like a sudden flood of water pouring over the
   country,
  he will throw Samaria down to the ground.
³That city, the pride of Israel's drunken
   people,
  will be trampled underfoot.

⁴That beautiful crown of flowers is just a
   dying plant
  set on a hill above a rich valley.
  That city will be like the first fig of summer.
  Anyone who sees it
   quickly picks it and eats it.

⁵At that time the Lord All-Powerful
   will be like a beautiful crown,
  like a wonderful crown of flowers
   for his people who are left alive.
⁶Then he will give wisdom to the judges who
   must decide cases
  and strength to those who battle at the city
   gate.
⁷But now those leaders are drunk with wine;
   they stumble from drinking too much beer.
  The priests and prophets*d* are drunk with
   beer
  and are filled with wine.
  They stumble from too much beer.
  The prophets are drunk when they see
   their visions;
  the judges stumble when they make their
   decisions.
⁸Every table is covered with vomit,
   so there is not a clean place anywhere.

⁹The Lord is trying to teach the people a
   lesson;
  he is trying to make them understand his
   teachings.
  But the people are like babies too old for
   breast milk,
  like those who no longer nurse at their
   mother's breast.
¹⁰So they make fun of the Lord's prophet and
   say:
  "A command here, a command there.
  A rule here, a rule there.
  A little lesson here, a little lesson there."
¹¹So the Lord will use strange words and
   foreign languages
   to speak to these people.
¹²God said to them,
  "Here is a place of rest;
   let the tired people come and rest.
  This is the place of peace."
  But the people would not listen.
¹³So the words of the Lord will be,
  "A command here, a command there.
  A rule here, a rule there.
  A little lesson here, a little lesson there."
  They will fall back and be defeated;
   they will be trapped and captured.

¹⁴So listen to the Lord's message, you who
   brag,
  you leaders in Jerusalem.

¹⁵You say, "We have made an agreement with
    death;
we have a contract with death.
When terrible punishment passes by,
    it won't hurt us.
Our lies will keep us safe,
    and our tricks will hide us."

¹⁶Because of these things, this is what the Lord
GOD says:
"I will put a stone in the ground in
    Jerusalem,
a tested stone.
Everything will be built on this important and
    precious rock.
Anyone who trusts in it will never be
    disappointed.
¹⁷I will use justice as a measuring line
    and goodness as the standard.
The lies you hide behind will be destroyed as
    if by hail.
They will be washed away as if in a flood.
¹⁸Your agreement with death will be erased;
    your contract with death will not help you.
When terrible punishment comes,
    you will be crushed by it.
¹⁹Whenever punishment comes, it will take
        you away.
It will come morning after morning;
    it will defeat you by day and by night.
Those who understand this punishment will
    be terrified."

²⁰You will be like the person who tried to sleep
    on a bed that was too short
and with a blanket that was too narrow
    to wrap around himself.
²¹The LORD will fight as he did at Mount
    Perazim.
He will be angry as he was in the Valley of
    Gibeon.
He will do his work, his strange work.
He will finish his job, his strange job.
²²Now, you must not make fun of these things,
    or the ropes around you will become
        tighter.
The Lord GOD All-Powerful has told me
    how the whole earth will be destroyed.

The Lord Punishes Fairly

²³Listen closely to what I tell you;
    listen carefully to what I say.
²⁴A farmer does not plow his field all the time;
    he does not go on working the soil.
²⁵He makes the ground flat and smooth.
Then he plants the dill and scatters the
    cumin.
He plants the wheat in rows,
    the barley in its special place,

and other wheat as a border around the
    field.
²⁶His God teaches him
    and shows him the right way.
²⁷A farmer doesn't use heavy boards to crush
    dill;
he doesn't use a wagon wheel to crush
    cumin.
He uses a small stick to break open the dill,
    and with a stick he opens the cumin.
²⁸The grain is ground to make bread.
People do not ruin it by crushing it forever.
The farmer separates the wheat from the
    chaff*ᵈ* with his cart,
but he does not let his horses grind it.
²⁹This lesson also comes from the LORD
    All-Powerful,
who gives wonderful advice, who is very
    wise.

Warnings to Jerusalem

29 How terrible it will be for you,
    Jerusalem,
    the city where David camped.
Your festivals have continued
    year after year.
²I will attack Jerusalem,
    and that city will be filled with sadness and
        crying.
It will be like an altar to me.
³I will put armies all around you, Jerusalem;
    I will surround you with towers
    and with devices to attack you.
⁴You will be pulled down and will speak from
        the ground;
I will hear your voice rising from the
    ground.
It will sound like the voice of a ghost;
    your words will come like a whisper from
        the dirt.

⁵Your many enemies will become like fine
    dust;
the many cruel people will be like chaff*ᵈ*
    that is blown away.
Everything will happen very quickly.
⁶ The LORD All-Powerful will come
with thunder, earthquakes, and great noises,
    with storms, strong winds, and a fire that
        destroys.
⁷Then all the nations that fight against
    Jerusalem
    will be like a dream;
all the nations that attack her
    will be like a vision in the night.
⁸They will be like a hungry man who dreams
        he is eating,
but when he awakens, he is still hungry.

They will be like a thirsty man who dreams
>   he is drinking,
>   but when he awakens, he is still weak and
>   thirsty.
> It will be the same way with all the nations
>   who fight against Mount Zion.[d]

⁹Be surprised and amazed.
>   Blind yourselves so that you cannot see.
> Become drunk, but not from wine.
>   Trip and fall, but not from beer.
¹⁰The Lord has made you go into a deep sleep.
>   He has closed your eyes. (The prophets are
>   your eyes.)
>   He has covered your heads. (The seers[d] are
>   your heads.)

¹¹This vision is like the words of a book that is closed and sealed. You may give the book to someone who can read and tell that person to read it. But he will say, "I can't read the book, because it is sealed." ¹²Or you may give the book to someone who cannot read and tell him to read it. But he will say, "I don't know how to read."

¹³The Lord says:
> "These people say they love me;
>   they show honor to me with words,
>   but their hearts are far from me.
> The honor they show me
>   is nothing but human rules.
¹⁴So I will continue to amaze these people
>   by doing more and more miracles.[d]
> Their wise men will lose their wisdom;
>   their wise men will not be able to
>   understand."

Warnings About Other Nations

¹⁵How terrible it will be for those who try
>   to hide things from the Lord
> and who do their work in darkness.
>   They think no one will see them or know
>   what they do.
¹⁶You are confused.
>   You think the clay is equal to the potter.
> You think that an object can tell the one who
>   made it,
>   "You didn't make me."
> This is like a pot telling its maker,
>   "You don't know anything."

A Better Time Is Coming

¹⁷In a very short time, Lebanon will become
>   rich farmland,
> and the rich farmland will seem like a
>   forest.
¹⁸At that time the deaf will hear the words in a
>   book.
> Instead of having darkness and gloom, the
>   blind will see.

¹⁹The Lord will make the poor people happy;
>   they will rejoice in the Holy One of Israel.
²⁰Then the people without mercy will come to
>   an end;
>   those who do not respect God will
>   disappear.
> Those who enjoy doing evil will be gone:
²¹those who lie about others in court,
>   those who trap people in court,
>   those who lie and take justice from
>   innocent people in court.

²²This is what the Lord who set Abraham free says to the family of Jacob:
> "Now the people of Jacob will not be
>   ashamed
> or disgraced any longer.
²³When they see all their children,
>   the children I made with my hands,
> they will say my name is holy.
>   They will agree that the Holy One of Jacob
>   is holy,
>   and they will respect the God of Israel.
²⁴People who do wrong will now understand.
>   Those who complain will accept being
>   taught."

Warnings to the Stubborn Nation

30 The Lord said,
> "How terrible it will be for these
>   stubborn children.
> They make plans, but they don't ask me to
>   help them.
> They make agreements with other nations,
>   without asking my Spirit.[d]
> They are adding more and more sins to
>   themselves.
²They go down to Egypt for help
>   without asking me about it first.
> They hope they will be saved by the king of
>   Egypt;
>   they want Egypt to protect them.
³But hiding in Egypt will bring you only
>   shame;
>   Egypt's protection will only disappoint you.
⁴Your officers have gone to Zoan,
>   and your messengers have gone to Hanes,
⁵but they will be put to shame,
>   because Egypt is useless to them.
> It will give no help and will be of no use;
>   it will cause them only shame and
>   embarrassment."

God's Message to Judah

⁶This is a message about the animals in southern Judah:
> Southern Judah is a dangerous place
>   full of lions and lionesses,
>   poisonous snakes and darting snakes.

The messengers travel through there with
their wealth on the backs of donkeys
and their treasure on the backs of camels.
They carry them to a nation that cannot help
them,
7 to Egypt whose help is useless.
So I call that country Rahab*d* the Do-Nothing.

8Now write this on a sign for the people,
write this on a scroll,
so that for the days to come
this will be a witness forever.
9These people are like children who lie and
refuse to obey;
they refuse to listen to the Lord's
teachings.
10They tell the seers,*d*
"Don't see any more visions!"
They say to the prophets,*d*
"Don't tell us the truth!
Say things that will make us feel good;
see only good things for us.
11Stop blocking our path.
Get out of our way.
Stop telling us
about God, the Holy One of Israel."

12So this is what the Holy One of Israel says:
"You people have refused to accept this
message
and have depended on cruelty and lies to
help you.
13You are guilty of these things.
So you will be like a high wall with cracks
in it
that falls suddenly and breaks into small
pieces.
14You will be like a clay jar that breaks,
smashed into many pieces.
Those pieces will be too small
to take coals from the fire
or to get water from a well."

15This is what the Lord God, the Holy One of
Israel, says:
"If you come back to me and trust me, you
will be saved.
If you will be calm and trust me, you will
be strong."
But you don't want to do that.
16You say, "No, we need horses to run away
on."
So you will run away on horses.
You say, "We will ride away on fast horses."
So those who chase you will be fast.
17One enemy will make threats,
and a thousand of your men will run
away.
Five enemies will make threats,
and all of you will run from them.

You will be left alone like a flagpole on a
hilltop,
like a banner on a hill.
18The Lord wants to show his mercy to you.
He wants to rise and comfort you.
The Lord is a fair God,
and everyone who waits for his help will be
happy.

The Lord Will Help His People

19You people who live on Mount Zion*d* in Jerusalem will not cry anymore. The Lord will hear
your crying, and he will comfort you. When he
hears you, he will help you. 20The Lord has given
you sorrow and hurt like the bread and water you
ate every day. He is your teacher; he will not continue to hide from you, but you will see your
teacher with your own eyes. 21If you go the
wrong way — to the right or to the left — you will
hear a voice behind you saying, "This is the right
way. You should go this way." 22You have statues
covered with silver and gold, but you will ruin
them for further use. You will throw them away
like filthy rags and say, "Go away!"

23At that time the Lord will send rain for the
seeds you plant in the ground, and the ground
will grow food for you. The harvest will be rich
and great, and you will have plenty of food in the
fields for your animals. 24Your oxen and donkeys
that work the soil will have all the food they need.
You will have to use shovels and pitchforks to
spread all their food. 25Every mountain and hill
will have streams filled with water. These things
will happen after many people are killed and the
towers are pulled down. 26At that time the light
from the moon will be bright like the sun, and the
light from the sun will be seven times brighter
than now, like the light of seven days. These
things will happen when the Lord bandages his
broken people and heals the hurts he gave them.

27Look! The Lord comes from far away.
His anger is like a fire with thick clouds of
smoke.
His mouth is filled with anger,
and his tongue is like a burning fire.
28His breath is like a rushing river,
which rises to the throat.
He will judge the nations as if he is sifting
them through the strainer of
destruction.
He will place in their mouths a bit that will
lead them the wrong way.
29You will sing happy songs
as on the nights you begin a festival.
You will be happy like people listening to
flutes
as they come to the mountain of the Lord,
to the Rock*d* of Israel.

30The LORD will cause all people to hear his
great voice
and to see his powerful arm come down
with anger,
like a great fire that burns everything,
like a great storm with much rain and hail.

31Assyria will be afraid when it hears the voice
of the LORD,
because he will strike Assyria with a rod.
32When the LORD punishes Assyria with a rod,
he will beat them to the music of
tambourines*d* and harps;
he will fight against them with his mighty
weapons.
33Topheth*n* has been made ready for a long
time;
it is ready for the king.
It was made deep and wide
with much wood and fire.
And the LORD's breath will come
like a stream of burning sulfur and set it on
fire.

Warnings About Relying on Egypt

31 How terrible it will be for those
people who go down to Egypt for
help.
They think horses will save them.
They think their many chariots
and strong horsemen will save them.
But they don't trust God, the Holy One of
Israel,
or ask the LORD for help.
2But he is wise and can bring them disaster.
He does not change his warnings.
He will rise up and fight against the evil
people
and against those who try to help evil
people.
3The Egyptians are only people and are not
God.
Their horses are only animals and are not
spirit.
The LORD will stretch out his arm,
and the one who helps will stumble,

and the people who wanted help will fall.
All of them will be destroyed together.

4The LORD says this to me:
"When a lion or a lion's cub kills an animal
to eat,
it stands over the dead animal and roars.
A band of shepherds
may be assembled against it,
but the lion will not be afraid of their yelling
or upset by their noise.
So the LORD All-Powerful will come down
to fight on Mount Zion*d* and on its hill.
5The LORD All-Powerful will defend Jerusalem
like birds flying over their nests.
He will defend and save it;
he will 'pass over' and save Jerusalem."

6You children of Israel, come back to the God
you fought against. 7The time is coming when
each of you will stop worshiping idols of gold and
silver, which you sinned by making.

8"Assyria will be defeated by a sword, but not
the sword of a person;
Assyria will be destroyed, but not by a
person's sword.
Assyria will run away from the sword of God,
but its young men will be caught and made
slaves.
9They will panic, and their protection will be
destroyed
Their commanders will be terrified when
they see God's battle flag,"
says the LORD,
whose fire is in Jerusalem
and whose furnace is in Jerusalem.

A Good Kingdom Is Coming

32 A king will rule in a way that brings
justice,
and leaders will make fair decisions.
2Then each ruler will be like a shelter from
the wind,
like a safe place in a storm,
like streams of water in a dry land,
like a cool shadow from a large rock in a
hot land.
3People will look to the king for help,
and they will truly listen to what he says.
4People who are now worried will be able to
understand.
Those who cannot speak clearly now will
then be able to speak clearly and
quickly.
5Fools will not be called great,
and people will not respect the wicked.
6A fool says foolish things,

Topheth Gehenna; the Valley of Hinnom. Here people burned the bodies of criminals and animals, along with garbage.

and in his mind he plans evil.
A fool does things that are wicked,
and he says wrong things about the LORD.
A fool does not feed the hungry
or let thirsty people drink water.
⁷The wicked person uses evil like a tool.
He plans ways to take everything from the
poor.
He destroys the poor with lies,
even when the poor person is in the right.
⁸But a good leader plans to do good,
and those good things make him a good
leader.

Hard Times Are Coming

⁹You women who are calm now,
stand up and listen to me.
You women who feel safe now,
hear what I say.
¹⁰You women feel safe now,
but after one year you will be afraid.
There will be no grape harvest
and no summer fruit to gather.
¹¹Women, you are calm now, but you should
shake with fear.
Women, you feel safe now, but you should
tremble.
Take off your nice clothes
and put rough cloth around your waist to
show your sadness.
¹²Beat your breasts in grief, because the fields
that were pleasant are now empty.
Cry, because the vines that once had fruit
now have no more grapes.
¹³Cry for the land of my people,
in which only thorns and weeds now grow.
Cry for the city that once was happy
and for all the houses that once were filled
with joy.
¹⁴The palace will be empty;
people will leave the noisy city.
Strong cities and towers will be empty.
Wild donkeys will love to live there, and
sheep will go there to eat.

Things Will Get Better

¹⁵This will continue until God pours his Spirit*d*
from above upon us.
Then the desert will be like a fertile field
and the fertile field like a forest.
¹⁶Justice will be found even in the desert,
and fairness will be found in the fertile
fields.
¹⁷That fairness will bring peace,
and it will bring calm and safety forever.
¹⁸My people will live in peaceful places
and in safe homes
and in calm places of rest.
¹⁹Hail will destroy the forest,

and the city will be completely destroyed.
²⁰But you will be happy as you plant seeds
near every stream
and as you let your cattle and donkeys
wander freely.

Warnings to Assyria and Promises to God's People

33 How terrible it will be for you who
destroy others
but have not been destroyed yet.
How terrible it will be for you, traitor,
whom no one has turned against yet.
When you stop destroying,
others will destroy you.
When you stop turning against others,
they will turn against you.

²LORD, be kind to us.
We have waited for your help.
Give us strength every morning.
Save us when we are in trouble.
³Your powerful voice makes people run away
in fear;
your greatness causes the nations to run
away.
⁴Like locusts,*d* your enemies will take away
the things you stole in war.
Like locusts rushing about, they will take
your wealth.
⁵The LORD is very great, and he lives in a high
place.
He fills Jerusalem with fairness and justice.
⁶He will be your safety.
He is full of salvation, wisdom, and
knowledge.
Respect for the LORD is the greatest
treasure.

⁷See, brave men are crying out in the streets;
those who tried to bring peace are crying
loudly.
⁸There is no one on the roads,
no one walking in the paths.
People have broken the agreements they
made.
They refuse to believe the proof from
witnesses.
No one respects other people.
⁹The land is sick and dying;
Lebanon is ashamed and dying.
The Plain of Sharon is dry like the desert,
and the trees of Bashan and Carmel are
dying.

¹⁰The LORD says, "Now, I will stand up
and show my greatness.
Now, I will become important to the
people.
¹¹You people do useless things

that are like hay and straw.
A destructive wind will burn you like fire.
¹²People will be burned until their bones
become like lime;
they will burn quickly like dry
thornbushes.'

¹³You people in faraway lands, hear what I
have done.
You people who are near me, learn about
my power.
¹⁴The sinners in Jerusalem are afraid;
those who are separated from God shake
with fear.
They say, "Can any of us live through this
fire that destroys?
Who can live near this fire that burns on
and on?"
¹⁵A person who does what is right
and speaks what is right,
who refuses to take money unfairly,
who refuses to take money to hurt others,
who does not listen to plans of murder,
who refuses to think about evil—
¹⁶this is the kind of person who will be safe.
He will be protected as he would be in a
high, walled city
He will always have bread,
and he will not run out of water.
¹⁷Your eyes will see the king in his beauty.
You will see the land that stretches far
away.
¹⁸You will think about the terror of the past:
"Where is that officer?
Where is the one who collected the taxes?
Where is the officer in charge of our
defense towers?"
¹⁹No longer will you see those proud people
from other countries,
whose strange language you couldn't
understand.

God Will Protect Jerusalem

²⁰Look at Jerusalem, the city of our festivals.
Look at Jerusalem, that beautiful place of
rest.
It is like a tent that will never be moved;
the pegs that hold her in place will never
be pulled up,
and her ropes will never be broken.
²¹There the LORD will be our Mighty One.
That land is a place with streams and wide
rivers,
but there will be no enemy boats on those
rivers;
no powerful ship will sail on them.
²²This is because the LORD is our judge.
The LORD makes our laws.
The LORD is our king.

He will save us.
²³You sailors from other lands, hear:
The ropes on your boats hang loose.
The mast is not held firm.
The sails are not spread open.
Then your great wealth will be divided.
There will be so much wealth that even
the crippled people will carry off a
share.
²⁴No one living in Jerusalem will say, "I am
sick."
The people who live there will have their
sins forgiven.

God Will Punish His Enemies

34 All you nations, come near and listen.
Pay attention, you peoples!
The earth and all the people in it should
listen,
the world and everything in it.
²The LORD is angry with all the nations;
he is angry with their armies.
He will destroy them and kill them all.
³Their bodies will be thrown outside.
The stink will rise from the bodies,
and the blood will flow down the
mountains.
⁴The sun, moon, and stars will dissolve,
and the sky will be rolled up like a scroll.
The stars will fall
like dead leaves from a vine
or dried-up figs from a fig tree.
⁵The LORD's sword in the sky is covered with
blood.
It will cut through Edom
and destroy those people as an offering to
the LORD.
⁶The LORD's sword will be covered with
blood;
it will be covered with fat,
with the blood from lambs and goats,
with the fat from the kidneys of sheep.
This is because the LORD decided there will
be a sacrifice in Bozrah
and much killing in Edom.
⁷The oxen will be killed,
and the cattle and the strong bulls.
The land will be filled with their blood,
and the dirt will be covered with their fat.

⁸The LORD has chosen a time for punishment.
He has chosen a year when people must
pay for the wrongs they did to
Jerusalem.
⁹Edom's rivers will be like hot tar.
Its dirt will be like burning sulfur.
Its land will be like burning tar.
¹⁰The fires will burn night and day;
the smoke will rise from Edom forever.

Year after year that land will be empty;
no one will ever travel through that land
again.
11Birds and small animals will own that land,
and owls and ravens will live there.
God will make it an empty wasteland;
it will have nothing left in it.
12The important people will have no one left to
rule them;
the leaders will all be gone.
13Thorns will take over the strong towers,
and wild bushes will grow in the walled
cities.
It will be a home for wild dogs
and a place for owls to live.
14Desert animals will live with the hyenas,
and wild goats will call to their friends.
Night animals will live there
and find a place of rest.
15Owls will nest there and lay eggs.
When they hatch open, the owls will
gather their young under their wings.

Hawks will gather
with their own kind.

16Look at the LORD's scroll and read what is
written there:
None of these will be missing;
none will be without its mate.
God has given the command,
so his Spirit*d* will gather them together.
17God has divided the land among them,
and he has given them each their portion.
So they will own that land forever
and will live there year after year.

God Will Comfort His People

35 The desert and dry land will become
happy;
the desert will be glad and will produce
flowers.
Like a flower, 2it will have many blooms.
It will show its happiness, as if it were
shouting with joy.

DEPRESSION

Positive

"Are you sure you did the test right?" asked Jan Dempsy as she gently coaxed the
instruction sheet out of Sheila Burk's trembling hand. "Each one of these home kits is
different, and you have to follow the directions just so." Jan began to read the instructions.
Sheila stood shaking as the tears ran silently down her blushed cheeks. She could barely
muster a reply.
"I've taken this test three times, and it's the same every time." Sheila's voice began to
crack. "I'm pregnant. I'm going to have a baby. But I don't want a baby . . . not now. I'm
only sixteen years old. Jan, I'm so afraid, and so sad. Why did this have to happen to me?"
Sheila walked across the room and collapsed into the old brown chair that had
comforted her so many times when she was a little girl. But there was no comfort in that
chair now.
With no words left, Jan quietly sat down next to Sheila, put her arms
around her and began to pray.
Sheila's sin may cause her to face many bouts with depression, but God
can help her. Read **Isaiah 35** to discover the comfort God can bring for
Sheila and others who turn to him.
■ If you could talk to Sheila, which verses of Isaiah 35 would you use to
encourage her?
■ Think about how you feel when you're depressed. What does Isaiah 35
say to you about your depression?

C O N S I D E R . . .
■ suggesting that your Sunday school teacher put a box marked "Teenage
Problems" in your Sunday school room, and encouraging class members to
submit, anonymously, any situations they are having problems with. Spend time each
week discussing the problems and finding biblical solutions.
■ talking to a trusted friend about the cause of your depression.

F O R   M O R E ,   S E E . . .
■ Job 19:7–27 (p. 463)
■ Psalm 88 (p. 533)
■ 2 Corinthians 1:3–5 (p. 1193)

It will be beautiful like the forest of Lebanon,
  as beautiful as the hill of Carmel and the
    Plain of Sharon.
Everyone will see the glory of the LORD
  and the splendor of our God.

³Make the weak hands strong
  and the weak knees steady.
⁴Say to people who are frightened,
  "Be strong. Don't be afraid.
Look, your God will come,
  and he will punish your enemies.
He will make them pay for the wrongs they
    did,
  but he will save you."

⁵Then the blind people will see again,
  and the deaf will hear.
⁶Crippled people will jump like deer,
  and those who can't talk now will shout
    with joy.
Water will flow in the desert,
  and streams will flow in the dry land.
⁷The burning desert will have pools of water,
  and the dry ground will have springs.
Where wild dogs once lived,
  grass and water plants will grow.
⁸A road will be there;
  this highway will be called "The Road to
    Being Holy."
Evil people will not be allowed to walk on
    that road;
  only good people will walk on it.
  No fools will go on it.
⁹No lions will be there,
  nor will dangerous animals be on that road.
  They will not be found there.
That road will be for the people God saves;
¹⁰ the people the LORD has freed will return
    there.
They will enter Jerusalem with joy,
  and their happiness will last forever.
Their gladness and joy will fill them
    completely,
  and sorrow and sadness will go far away.

The Assyrians Invade Judah

36 During Hezekiah's fourteenth year as king, Sennacherib king of Assyria attacked all the strong, walled cities of Judah and captured them. ²The king of Assyria sent out his field commander with a large army from Lachish to King Hezekiah in Jerusalem. When the commander came near the waterway from the upper pool on the road where people do their laundry, he stopped. ³Eliakim, Shebna, and Joah went out to meet him. Eliakim son of Hilkiah was the palace manager, Shebna was the royal secretary, and Joah son of Asaph was the recorder.

⁴The field commander said to them, "Tell Hezekiah this:

" 'The great king, the king of Assyria, says: What can you trust in now? ⁵You say you have battle plans and power for war, but your words mean nothing. Whom are you trusting for help so that you turn against me? ⁶Look, you are depending on Egypt to help you, but Egypt is like a splintered walking stick. If you lean on it for help, it will stab your hand and hurt you. The king of Egypt will hurt all those who depend on him. ⁷You might say, "We are depending on the LORD our God," but Hezekiah destroyed the LORD's altars and the places of worship. Hezekiah told Judah and Jerusalem, "You must worship only at this one altar."

⁸" 'Now make an agreement with my master, the king of Assyria: I will give you two thousand horses if you can find enough men to ride them. ⁹You cannot defeat one of my master's least important officers, so why do you depend on Egypt to give you chariots and horsemen? ¹⁰I have not come to attack and destroy this country without an order from the LORD. The LORD himself told me to come to this country and destroy it.' "

¹¹Then Eliakim, Shebna, and Joah said to the field commander, "Please speak to us in the Aramaic language. We understand it. Don't speak to us in Hebrew, because the people on the city wall can hear you."

¹²But the commander said, "My master did not send me to tell these things only to you and your king. He sent me to speak also to those people sitting on the wall who will have to eat their own dung and drink their own urine like you."

¹³Then the commander stood and shouted loudly in the Hebrew language, "Listen to what the great king, the king of Assyria says, ¹⁴The king says you should not let Hezekiah fool you, because he can't save you. ¹⁵Don't let Hezekiah talk you into trusting the LORD by saying, 'The LORD will surely save us. This city won't be handed over to the king of Assyria.'

¹⁶"Don't listen to Hezekiah. The king of Assyria says, 'Make peace with me, and come out of the city to me. Then everyone will be free to eat the fruit from his own grapevine and fig tree and to drink water from his own well. ¹⁷After that I will come and take you to a land like your own—a land with grain and new wine, bread and vineyards.'

¹⁸"Don't let Hezekiah fool you, saying, 'The LORD will save us.' Has a god of any other nation saved his people from the power of the king of Assyria? ¹⁹Where are the gods of Hamath and Arpad? Where are the gods of Sepharvaim? They did not save Samaria from my power. ²⁰Not one of all the gods of these countries has saved his people

from me. Neither can the LORD save Jerusalem from my power."

²¹The people were silent. They didn't answer the commander at all, because King Hezekiah had ordered, "Don't answer him."

²²Then Eliakim, Shebna, and Joah tore their clothes to show how upset they were. (Eliakim son of Hilkiah was the palace manager, Shebna was the royal secretary, and Joah son of Asaph was the recorder.) The three men went to Hezekiah and told him what the field commander had said.

Hezekiah Asks God to Help

37 When King Hezekiah heard the message, he tore his clothes and put on rough cloth to show how sad he was. Then he went into the Temple*d* of the LORD. ²Hezekiah sent Eliakim, the palace manager, and Shebna, the royal secretary, and the older priests to Isaiah. They were all wearing rough cloth when they came to Isaiah the prophet,*d* the son of Amoz. ³They told Isaiah, "This is what Hezekiah says: Today is a day of sorrow and punishment and disgrace, as when a child should be born, but the mother is not strong enough to give birth to it. ⁴The king of Assyria sent his field commander to make fun of the living God. Maybe the LORD your God will hear what the commander said and will punish him for it. So pray for the few of us who are left alive."

⁵When Hezekiah's officers came to Isaiah, ⁶he said to them, "Tell your master this: The LORD says, 'Don't be afraid of what you have heard. Don't be frightened by the words the servants of the king of Assyria have spoken against me. ⁷Listen! I am going to put a spirit in the king of Assyria. He will hear a report that will make him return to his own country, and I will cause him to die by the sword there.' "

⁸The field commander heard that the king of Assyria had left Lachish. When he went back, he found the king fighting against the city of Libnah.

⁹The king received a report that Tirhakah, the Cushite king of Egypt, was coming to attack him. When the king of Assyria heard this, he sent messengers to Hezekiah, saying, ¹⁰"Tell Hezekiah king of Judah: Don't be fooled by the god you trust. Don't believe him when he says Jerusalem will not be handed over to the king of Assyria. ¹¹You have heard what the kings of Assyria have done. They have completely defeated every country, so do not think you will be saved. ¹²Did the gods of those people save them? My ancestors destroyed them, defeating the cities of Gozan, Haran, and Rezeph, and the people of Eden living in Tel Assar. ¹³Where are the kings of Hamath and Arpad? Where are the kings of Sepharvaim, Hena, and Ivvah?"

Hezekiah Prays to the Lord

¹⁴When Hezekiah received the letter from the messengers and read it, he went up to the Temple*d* of the LORD. He spread the letter out before the LORD ¹⁵and prayed to the LORD: ¹⁶"LORD All-Powerful, you are the God of Israel, whose throne is between the gold creatures with wings, only you are God of all the kingdoms of the earth. You made the heavens and the earth. ¹⁷Hear, LORD, and listen. Open your eyes, LORD, and see. Listen to all the words Sennacherib has said to insult the living God.

¹⁸"It is true, LORD, that the kings of Assyria have destroyed all these countries and their lands. ¹⁹They have thrown the gods of these nations into the fire, but they were only wood and rock statues that people made. So the kings have destroyed them. ²⁰Now, LORD our God, save us from the king's power so that all the kingdoms of the earth will know that you, LORD, are the only God."

The Lord Answers Hezekiah

²¹Then Isaiah son of Amoz sent a message to Hezekiah that said, "This is what the LORD, the God of Israel, says: 'You prayed to me about Sennacherib king of Assyria. ²²So this is what the LORD has said against Sennacherib:

The people of Jerusalem
   hate you and make fun of you;
the people of Jerusalem
   laugh at you as you run away.
²³You have insulted me and spoken against me;
   you have raised your voice against me.
You have a proud look on your face,
   which is against me, the Holy One of
    Israel!
²⁴You have sent your messengers to insult the
   Lord.
You have said, "With my many chariots
I have gone to the tops of the mountains,
   to the highest mountains of Lebanon.
I have cut down its tallest cedars
   and its best pine trees.
I have gone to its greatest heights
   and its best forests.
²⁵I have dug wells in foreign countries
   and drunk water there.
By the soles of my feet,
   I have dried up all the rivers of Egypt."

²⁶" 'King of Assyria, surely you have heard.
   Long ago I, the LORD, planned these things.
Long ago I designed them,
   and now I have made them happen.
I allowed you to turn those strong, walled
   cities
   into piles of rocks.
²⁷The people in those cities were weak;
   they were frightened and put to shame.

They were like grass in the field,
　　like tender, young grass,
　like grass on the housetop
　　　that is burned by the wind before it can
　　　　grow.

28 " 'I know when you rest,
　　when you come and go,
　　and how you rage against me.
29 Because you rage against me,
　　and because I have heard your proud
　　　　words,
　I will put my hook in your nose
　　and my bit in your mouth.
　Then I will force you to leave my country
　　the same way you came.'

30 "Then the LORD said, 'Hezekiah, I will give
you this sign:
　This year you will eat the grain that grows
　　　wild,
　　and the second year you will eat what
　　　grows wild from that.
　But in the third year, plant grain and harvest
　　it.
　Plant vineyards and eat their fruit.
31 Some of the people in the family of Judah
　　will escape.
　Like plants that take root,
　　they will grow strong and have many
　　　children.
32 A few people will come out of Jerusalem
　　　alive;
　　a few from Mount Zion[d] will live.
　The strong love of the LORD All-Powerful
　　will make this happen.'

33 "So this is what the LORD says about the king
of Assyria:
　'He will not enter this city
　　or even shoot an arrow here.
　He will not fight against it with shields
　　or build a ramp to attack the city walls.
34 He will return to his country the same way
　　　he came,
　　and he will not enter this city,'
　says the LORD.
35 'I will defend and save this city
　　for my sake and for David, my servant.' "

36 Then the angel of the LORD went out and
killed one hundred eighty-five thousand men in
the Assyrian camp. When the people got up early
the next morning, they saw all the dead bodies.
37 So Sennacherib king of Assyria left and went
back to Nineveh and stayed there. 38 One day as Sennacherib was worshiping in
the temple of his god Nisroch, his sons Adram-
melech and Sharezer killed him with a sword.
Then they escaped to the land of Ararat. So Sennacherib's son Esarhaddon became king of
Assyria.

Hezekiah's Illness

38 At that time Hezekiah became very sick;
he was almost dead. The prophet[d] Isaiah
son of Amoz went to see him and told him, "This
is what the LORD says: Make arrangements, because you are not going to live, but die."

2 Hezekiah turned toward the wall and prayed
to the LORD, 3 "LORD, please remember that I have
always obeyed you. I have given myself completely to you and have done what you said was
right." Then Hezekiah cried loudly.

4 Then the LORD spoke his word to Isaiah: 5 "Go
to Hezekiah and tell him: 'This is what the LORD,
the God of your ancestor David, says: I have
heard your prayer and seen your tears. So I will
add fifteen years to your life. 6 I will save you and
this city from the king of Assyria; I will defend this
city.

7 " 'The LORD will do what he says. This is the
sign from the LORD to show you: 8 The sun has
made a shadow go down the stairway of Ahaz,
but I will make it go back ten steps.' " So the
shadow made by the sun went back up the ten
steps it had gone down.

9 After Hezekiah king of Judah got well, he
wrote this song:
10 I said, "I am in the middle of my life.
　　Do I have to go through the gates of death?
　　Will I have the rest of my life taken away
　　　from me?"
11 I said, "I will not see the LORD
　　in the land of the living again.
　I will not again see the people
　　who live on the earth.
12 Like a shepherd's tent,
　　my home has been pulled down and taken
　　　from me.
　I am finished
　　like the cloth a weaver rolls up and cuts
　　　from the loom.[n]
　In one day you brought me to this end.
13 All night I cried loudly.
　　Like a lion, he crushed all my bones.
　　In one day you brought me to this end.
14 I cried like a bird
　　and moaned like a dove.
　My eyes became tired as I looked to the
　　　heavens.
　　Lord, I have troubles. Please help me."

15 What can I say?

---

loom　A machine for making cloth from thread.

The Lord told me what would happen and
  then made it happen.
I have had these troubles in my soul,
  so now I will be humble all my life.
16Lord, because of you, people live.
  Because of you, my spirit also lives;
  you made me well and let me live.
17It was for my own good
  that I had such troubles.
Because you love me very much,
  you did not let me die
but threw my sins
  far away.
18People in the place of the dead cannot praise
  you;
  those who have died cannot sing praises to
  you;
  those who die don't trust you
  to help them.
19The people who are alive are the ones who
  praise you.
  They praise you as I praise you today.
A father should tell his children
  that you provide help.

20The LORD saved me,
  so we will play songs on stringed
  instruments
in the Temple of the LORD
  all the days of our lives.

21Then Isaiah said, "Make a paste from figs and
put it on Hezekiah's boil. Then he will get well."
22Hezekiah then asked Isaiah, "What will be the
sign? What will show that I will go up to the Tem-
ple^d of the LORD?"

Messengers from Babylon

39 At that time Merodach-Baladan son of
  Baladan was king of Babylon. He sent
letters and a gift to Hezekiah, because he had
heard that Hezekiah had been sick and was
now well. 2Hezekiah was pleased and showed
the messengers what was in his storehouses:
the silver, gold, spices, expensive perfumes,
his swords and shields, and all his wealth. He
showed them everything in his palace and in
his kingdom.

3Then Isaiah the prophet^d went to King Hezekiah and asked him, "What did these men say?
Where did they come from?"

Hezekiah said, "They came from a faraway
country—from Babylon."

4So Isaiah asked him, "What did they see in
your palace?"

Hezekiah said, "They saw everything in my palace. I showed them all my wealth."

5Then Isaiah said to Hezekiah: "Listen to the
words of the LORD All-Powerful: 6'In the future
everything in your palace and everything your ancestors have stored up until this day will be taken
away to Babylon. Nothing will be left,' says the
LORD. 7Some of your own children, those who
will be born to you, will be taken away, and they
will become servants in the palace of the king of
Babylon."

8Hezekiah told Isaiah, "These words from the
LORD are good." He said this because he thought,
"There will be peace and security in my life-
time."

Israel's Punishment Will End

40 Your God says,
  "Comfort, comfort my people.
2Speak kindly to the people of Jerusalem
  and tell them
that their time of service is finished,
  that they have paid for their sins,
that the LORD has punished Jerusalem
  twice for every sin they did."

3This is the voice of one who calls
  out:
"Prepare in the desert
  the way for the LORD.
Make a straight road in the dry lands
  for our God.
4Every valley should be raised up,
  and every mountain and hill should be
  made flat.
The rough ground should be made level,
  and the rugged ground should be made
  smooth.
5Then the glory of the LORD will be shown,
  and all people together will see it.
The LORD himself said these things."

6A voice says, "Cry out!"
  Then I said, "What shall I cry out?"

"Say all people are like the grass,
  and all their glory is like the flowers of the
  field.
7The grass dies and the flowers fall
  when the breath of the LORD blows on
  them.
Surely the people are like grass.

⁸The grass dies and the flowers fall,
 but the word of our God will live forever."
⁹Jerusalem, you have good news to tell.
 Go up on a high mountain.
Jerusalem, you have good news to tell.
 Shout out loud the good news.
Shout it out and don't be afraid.
 Say to the towns of Judah,
 "Here is your God."
¹⁰Look, the Lord GOD is coming with power
 to rule all the people.
Look, he will bring reward for his people;
 he will have their payment with him.
¹¹He takes care of his people like a shepherd.
 He gathers them like lambs in his arms
 and carries them close to him.
He gently leads the mothers of the lambs.

God Is Supreme

¹²Who has measured the oceans in the palm of
 his hand?
 Who has used his hand to measure the
 sky?

Who has used a bowl to measure all the dust
 of the earth
 and scales to weigh the mountains and
 hills?
¹³Who has known the mind of the LORD
 or been able to give him advice?
¹⁴Whom did he ask for help?
 Who taught him the right way?
Who taught him knowledge
 and showed him the way to understanding?

¹⁵The nations are like one small drop in a
 bucket;
 they are no more than the dust on his
 measuring scales.
To him the islands are no more than fine
 dust on his scales.
¹⁶All the trees in Lebanon are not enough for
 the altar fires,
 and all the animals in Lebanon are not
 enough for burnt offerings.
¹⁷Compared to the LORD all the nations are
 worth nothing;
 to him they are less than nothing.

---

¹⁸Can you compare God to anything?
Can you compare him to an image of
anything?
¹⁹An idol is formed by a craftsman,
and a goldsmith covers it with gold
and makes silver chains for it.
²⁰A poor person cannot buy those expensive
statues,
so he finds a tree that will not rot.
Then he finds a skilled craftsman
to make it into an idol that will not fall
over.

²¹Surely you know. Surely you have heard.
Surely from the beginning someone told
you.
Surely you understand how the earth was
created.
²²God sits on his throne above the circle of the
earth,
and compared to him, people are like
grasshoppers.
He stretches out the skies like a piece of
cloth
and spreads them out like a tent to sit
under.
²³He makes rulers unimportant
and the judges of this world worth nothing.
²⁴They are like plants that are placed in the
ground,
like seeds that are planted.
As soon as they begin to grow strong,
he blows on them and they die,
and the wind blows them away like chaff.*d*

²⁵God, the Holy One, says, "Can you compare
me to anyone?
Is anyone equal to me?"
²⁶Look up to the skies.
Who created all these stars?
He leads out the army of heaven one by one
and calls all the stars by name.
Because he is strong and powerful,
not one of them is missing.

²⁷People of Jacob, why do you complain?
People of Israel, why do you say,
"The LORD does not see what happens to
me;
he does not care if I am treated fairly"?
²⁸Surely you know.
Surely you have heard.
The LORD is the God who lives forever,
who created all the world.
He does not become tired or need to rest.
No one can understand how great his
wisdom is.
²⁹He gives strength to those who are tired
and more power to those who are weak.
³⁰Even children become tired and need to rest,

and young people trip and fall.
³¹But the people who trust the LORD will
become strong again.
They will rise up as an eagle in the sky;
they will run and not need rest;
they will walk and not become tired.

The Lord Will Help Israel

41 The LORD says, "Faraway countries,
listen to me.
Let the nations become strong.
Come to me and speak;
we will meet together to decide who is
right.

²"Who caused the one to come from the east?
Who gives him victories everywhere he
goes?
The one who brought him gives nations over
to him
and defeats kings.
He uses his sword, and kings become like
dust.
He uses his bow, and they are blown away
like chaff.*d*
³He chases them and is never hurt,
going places he has never been before.
⁴Who caused this to happen?
Who has controlled history since the
beginning?
I, the LORD, am the one. I was here at the
beginning,
and I will be here when all things are
finished."

⁵All you faraway places, look and be afraid;
all you places far away on the earth, shake
with fear.
Come close and listen to me.
⁶ The workers help each other
and say to each other, "Be strong!"
⁷The craftsman encourages the goldsmith,
and the workman who smooths the metal
with a hammer encourages the one
who shapes the metal.
He says, "This metal work is good."
He nails the statue to a base so it can't fall
over.

Only the Lord Can Save Us

⁸The LORD says, "People of Israel, you are my
servants.
People of Jacob, I chose you.
You are from the family of my friend
Abraham.
⁹I took you from places far away on the earth
and called you from a faraway country.
I said, 'You are my servants.'
I have chosen you and have not turned
against you.

¹⁰So don't worry, because I am with you.
Don't be afraid, because I am your God.
I will make you strong and will help you;
I will support you with my right hand that
saves you.

¹¹"All those people who are angry with you
will be ashamed and disgraced.
Those who are against you
will disappear and be lost.
¹²You will look for your enemies,
but you will not find them.
Those who fought against you
will vanish completely.
¹³I am the LORD your God,
who holds your right hand,
and I tell you, 'Don't be afraid.
I will help you.'
¹⁴You few people of Israel who are left,
do not be afraid even though you are weak
as a worm.
I myself will help you," says the LORD.
"The one who saves you is the Holy One
of Israel.
¹⁵Look, I have made you like a new threshing[d]
board
with many sharp teeth.
So you will walk on mountains and crush
them;
you will make the hills like chaff.[d]
¹⁶You will throw them into the air, and the
wind will carry them away;
a windstorm will scatter them.
Then you will be happy in the LORD;
you will be proud of the Holy One of
Israel.

¹⁷"The poor and needy people look for water,
but they can't find any.
Their tongues are dry with thirst.
But I, the LORD, will answer their prayers;
I, the God of Israel, will not leave them to
die.
¹⁸I will make rivers flow on the dry hills
and springs flow through the valleys.
I will change the desert into a lake of water
and the dry land into fountains of water.
¹⁹I will make trees grow in the desert —
cedars, acacia, myrtle, and olive trees.
I will put pine, fir, and cypress trees
growing together in the desert.
²⁰People will see these things and understand;
they will think carefully about these things
and learn
that the LORD's power did this,
that the Holy One of Israel made these
things."

The Lord Challenges False Gods

²¹The LORD says, "Present your case."
The King of Jacob says, "Tell me your
arguments.
²²Bring in your idols to tell us
what is going to happen.
Have them tell us what happened in the
beginning.
Then we will think about these things,
and we will know how they will turn out.
Or tell us what will happen in the future.
²³ Tell us what is coming next
so we will believe that you are gods.
Do something, whether it is good or bad,
and make us afraid.
²⁴You gods are less than nothing;
you can't do anything.
Those who worship you should be hated.

²⁵"I have brought someone to come out of the
north.[n]
I have called by name a man from the east,
and he knows me.
He walks on kings as if they were mud,
just as a potter walks on the clay.
²⁶Who told us about this before it happened?
Who told us ahead of time so we could
say, 'He was right'?
None of you told us anything;
none of you told us before it happened;
no one heard you tell about it.
²⁷I, the LORD, was the first one to tell
Jerusalem that the people were coming
home.
I sent a messenger to Jerusalem with the
good news.
²⁸I look at the idols, but there is not one that
can answer.
None of them can give advice;
none of them can answer my questions.
²⁹Look, all these idols are false.
They cannot do anything;
they are worth nothing.

The Lord's Special Servant

42 "Here is my servant, the one I
support.
He is the one I chose, and I am pleased
with him.
I have put my Spirit[d] upon him,
and he will bring justice to all nations.
²He will not cry out or yell
or speak loudly in the streets.
³He will not break a crushed blade of grass
or put out even a weak flame.
He will truly bring justice;
⁴ he will not lose hope or give up

---

someone . . . north This probably means Cyrus, a king of Persia.

until he brings justice to the world.
And people far away will trust his
teachings."

⁵God, the LORD, said these things.
He created the skies and stretched them out.
He spread out the earth and everything on
it.
He gives life to all people on earth,
to everyone who walks on the earth.
⁶The LORD says, "I, the LORD, called you to do
right,
and I will hold your hand
and protect you.
You will be the sign of my agreement with
the people,
a light to shine for all people.
⁷You will help the blind to see.
You will free those who are in prison,

and you will lead those who live in
darkness out of their prison.

⁸"I am the LORD. That is my name.
I will not give my glory to another;
I will not let idols take the praise that
should be mine.
⁹The things I said would happen have
happened,
and now I tell you about new things.
Before those things happen,
I tell you about them."

A Song of Praise to the Lord

¹⁰Sing a new song to the LORD;
sing his praise everywhere on the earth.
Praise him, you people who sail on the
seas and you animals who live in
them.

SERVICE

Called to Compassion

Claudia was blind, autistic, and in pain. Put in an institution when she was young, Claudia was angry and withdrawn. She would scream, eat her clothes, and refuse to cooperate with others.

Now Claudia is fifteen. She is still blind, and she is still autistic. She cannot really communicate with people. But now she is peaceful, loving, and trusting. What has changed?

When she was nine or ten, Claudia became part of a l'Arche community in Honduras. The love, compassion, and care she experienced in this Christian community helped her discover inner peace.

Founded by Canadian-born Jean Vanier, more than seventy l'Arche (which means "the Ark" in French) communities around the world are home to handicapped people who are forgotten or rejected by their society. For about thirty years, Vanier has given his life to these "little people," as he calls them.

For Vanier, his work is his ministry in Christ's name. "When we love others," Vanier says, "we can walk with them and share their pain. . . . I believe that Jesus is calling us to be men and women of compassion, to walk with people in their pain. . . . And then we discover how the pain and the cross are intimately linked with the joy of the resurrection."

Through his work with mentally handicapped people around the world, Jean Vanier lives a life that reflects the spirit of **Isaiah 42:1–9**, which promises a special servant who would lead the people—a promise that was fulfilled in Jesus Christ.

■ What parallels are there between the ministry of Jean Vanier and the description in the passage?
■ How can you follow in the footsteps of the special servant described in the passage?

CONSIDER . . .

■ giving a few hours of your free time to work with mentally or physically handicapped people in your community. Afterwards, talk with a parent, friend, or trusted adult about the experience.
■ reaching out to someone in need even when it may be inconvenient for you.

FOR MORE, SEE . . .

■ Deuteronomy 11:13–15 (p. 172)
■ 1 Samuel 3:1–10 (p. 247)
■ 1 Corinthians 9:19–23 (p. 1178)

Praise him, you people living in faraway
  places.
[11]The deserts and their cities should praise him.
  The settlements of Kedar should praise him.
  The people living in Sela should sing for joy;
  they should shout from the mountaintops.
[12]They should give glory to the LORD.
  People in faraway lands should praise him.
[13]The LORD will march out like a strong
    soldier;
  he will be excited like a man ready to fight
  a war.
He will shout out the battle cry
  and defeat his enemies.

[14]The LORD says, "For a long time I have said
    nothing;
  I have been quiet and held myself back.
  But now I will cry out
    and strain like a woman giving birth to a
    child.
[15]I will destroy the hills and mountains
  and dry up all their plants.
I will make the rivers become dry land
  and dry up the pools of water.
[16]Then I will lead the blind along a way they
    never knew;
  I will guide them along paths they have not
    known.
I will make the darkness become light for
    them,
  and the rough ground smooth.
These are the things I will do;
  I will not leave my people.
[17]But those who trust in idols,
  who say to their statues,
  'You are our gods'
  will be rejected in disgrace.

Israel Refused to Listen to the Lord

[18]"You who are deaf, hear me.
  You who are blind, look and see.
[19]No one is more blind than my servant Israel
  or more deaf than the messenger I send.
No one is more blind than the person I own
  or more blind than the servant of the LORD.
[20]Israel, you have seen much, but you have not
    obeyed.
  You hear, but you refuse to listen."
[21]The LORD made his teachings wonderful,
  because he is good.
[22]These people have been defeated and robbed.
  They are trapped in pits
  or locked up in prison.
Like robbers, enemies have taken them away,
  and there is no one to save them.
Enemies carried them off,
  and no one said, "Bring them back."
[23]Will any of you listen to this?

Will you listen carefully in the future?
[24]Who let the people of Jacob be carried off?
  Who let robbers take Israel away?
The LORD allowed this to happen,
  because we sinned against him.
We did not live the way he wanted us to live
  and did not obey his teaching.
[25]So he became very angry with us
  and brought terrible wars against us.
It was as if the people of Israel had fire all
    around them,
  but they didn't know what was happening.
It was as if they were burning,
  but they didn't pay any attention.

God Is Always with His People

43 Now this is what the LORD says.
He created you, people of Jacob;
he formed you, people of Israel.
He says, "Don't be afraid, because I have
    saved you.
  I have called you by name, and you are
    mine.
[2]When you pass through the waters, I will be
    with you.
  When you cross rivers, you will not drown.
When you walk through fire, you will not be
    burned,
  nor will the flames hurt you.
[3]This is because I, the LORD, am your God,
  the Holy One of Israel, your Savior.
I gave Egypt to pay for you,
  and I gave Cush and Seba to make you
    mine.
[4]Because you are precious to me,
  because I give you honor and love you,
I will give other people in your place;
  I will give other nations to save your life.
[5]Don't be afraid, because I am with you.
  I will bring your children from the east
  and gather you from the west.
[6]I will tell the north: Give my people to me.
  I will tell the south: Don't keep my people
    in prison.
Bring my sons from far away
  and my daughters from faraway places.
[7]Bring to me all the people who are mine,
  whom I made for my glory,
  whom I formed and made."

Judah Is God's Witness

[8]Bring out the people who have eyes but don't
    see
  and those who have ears but don't hear.
[9]All the nations gather together,
  and all the people come together.
Which of their gods said this would happen?
  Which of their gods can tell what happened
    in the beginning?

Let them bring their witnesses to prove they
    were right.
Then others will say, "It is true."
¹⁰The LORD says, "You are my witnesses
    and the servant I chose.
I chose you so you would know and believe
    me,
so you would understand that I am the true
    God.
There was no God before me,
    and there will be no God after me.
¹¹I myself am the LORD;
    I am the only Savior.
¹²I myself have spoken to you, saved you, and
    told you these things.
It was not some foreign god among you.
You are my witnesses, and I am God,"
    says the LORD.
¹³ "I have always been God.
No one can save people from my power;
    when I do something, no one can change
    it."

¹⁴This is what the LORD, who saves you,
    the Holy One of Israel, says:
"I will send armies to Babylon for you,
    and I will knock down all its locked gates.
The Babylonians will shout their cries of
    sorrow.
¹⁵I am the LORD, your Holy One,
    the Creator of Israel, your King."

God Will Save His People Again

¹⁶This is what the LORD says.
He is the one who made a road through
    the sea
    and a path through rough waters.
¹⁷He is the one who defeated the chariots and
    horses
    and the mighty armies.
They fell together and will never rise again.
    They were destroyed as a flame is put out.
¹⁸The LORD says, "Forget what happened
    before,
    and do not think about the past.

SIN

Taking the Weight Off

Miriam Arkin didn't want to be in Sunday school. Lately, she felt distant from God. As she entered the classroom, her teacher handed her paper and a pencil.

"Write down whatever's bothering you," Sarah Evans said, "mistakes you've made or worries you have."

Miriam watched other kids working on their lists. She thought about the party she had gone to two weeks earlier. To fit in, she had let the other kids talk her into drinking several beers. Then she made out with this popular guy she didn't even really like. The whole experience made her feel cheap, like she wasn't worthy of anyone's respect. She started writing: "acting wild," "going further than I wanted to."

"When we give our problems to God, he makes the weight lighter," Sarah said, after everyone finished. She passed a metal wastebasket around the circle, and Miriam dropped her list in quickly. Sarah struck a match and set fire to the lists. As Miriam watched her list of sins burning, she felt God's love within her "burn away" the hurt of the sins she had committed. She took a deep breath and felt relieved for the first time in days. She realized that by admitting her mistakes to God she felt closer to him. Maybe she could start over now.

Sin keeps people from being what God wants them to be. **Isaiah 43:16–25** reminds us that God is willing to forgive sin so we can be close to him.
■ How would Miriam have reacted to reading this passage?
■ Which verses in this passage help you understand God's forgiveness of your sin?

CONSIDER . . .
■ making a list of sins you've committed recently. Ask God to forgive you for each sin. Then burn the list in a metal trash can outside.
■ giving God a thank-you present because he forgives you. Choose a gift God would appreciate, such as something for the needy, a gift to your church, or a time commitment from you.

FOR MORE, SEE . . .
■ Psalm 32:1–7 (p. 500)
■ Micah 7:18–20 (p. 868)
■ Romans 3:23–26 (p. 1143)

¹⁹Look at the new thing I am going to do.
    It is already happening. Don't you see it?
I will make a road in the desert
    and rivers in the dry land.
²⁰Even the wild animals will be thankful to
        me—
    the wild dogs and owls.
They will honor me when I put water in the
        desert
    and rivers in the dry land
to give water to my people, the ones I chose.
²¹ The people I made
    will sing songs to praise me.

²²"People of Jacob, you have not called to me;
    people of Israel, you have become tired of
        me.
²³You have not brought me your sacrifices of
        sheep
    nor honored me with your sacrifices.
I did not weigh you down with sacrifices to
        offer
    or make you tired with incense*d* to burn.
²⁴So you did not buy incense for me;
    you did not freely bring me fat from your
        sacrifices.

Instead you have weighed me down with
    your many sins;
you have made me tired of your many
    wrongs.

²⁵"I, I am the One who forgives all your sins,
    for my sake;
I will not remember your sins.
²⁶But you should remind me.
    Let's meet and decide what is right.
    Tell what you have done and show you are
        right.
²⁷Your first father sinned,
    and your leaders have turned against me.
²⁸So I will make your holy rulers unholy.
    I will bring destruction on the people of
        Jacob,
    and I will let Israel be insulted."

The Lord Is the Only God

44 The LORD says, "People of Jacob, you
    are my servants. Listen to me!
People of Israel, I chose you."
²This is what the LORD says, who made you,
    who formed you in your mother's body,
    who will help you:

SELF-ESTEEM

Are You Okay?

Take a simple quiz to measure your self-esteem. After each situation, decide whether your self-esteem rises, falls, or stays the same.
1. Your parent wakes you with a hug, calling you a dream of a teenager.
2. Your parent wakes you, complaining about the state of your room. Terms like "slob" and "pigpen" fly.
3. You miss the school bus.
4. The person you want to date drives by and offers you a ride.
5. You get an A on your term paper.
6. You get a C— on your math test.
7. You want to be in the upcoming school play, but your name is not on the cast list when it is posted.
How did your self-esteem do? Did you balance the good and bad with a healthy dose of self-respect? Or, did you end up in the dumps?
Life brings ups and downs that affect self-esteem, but God offers a better way to see ourselves. Read **Isaiah 44:1—8** to learn how God wants us to feel about who we are.

■ What does the passage say to someone whose self-esteem is based on life's ups and downs?
■ How does belonging to God affect how you feel about yourself?

C O N S I D E R . . .

■ making a list of what you like about yourself. For each item suggest one way you could use this characteristic to serve God.
■ asking your youth pastor for advice on how to boost your self-esteem.

F O R   M O R E ,   S E E . . .

■ Deuteronomy 7:6—9 (p. 168)   ■ 1 Peter 2:9—10 (p. 1303)
■ Psalm 139:1—16 (p. 561)

"People of Jacob, my servants, don't be
    afraid.
Israel, I chose you.
³I will pour out water for the thirsty land
    and make streams flow on dry land.
I will pour out my Spirit^d into your children
    and my blessing on your descendants.
⁴Your children will grow like a tree in the
        grass,
    like poplar trees growing beside streams of
        water.
⁵One person will say, 'I belong to the LORD,'
    and another will use the name Jacob.
Another will sign his name 'I am the LORD's,'
    and another will use the name Israel."

⁶The LORD, the king of Israel,
    is the LORD All-Powerful, who saves Israel.
This is what he says: "I am the beginning
        and the end.
I am the only God.
⁷Who is a god like me?
    That god should come and prove it.
Let him tell and explain all that has happened
        since I set up my ancient people.
He should also tell what will happen in the
        future.
⁸Don't be afraid! Don't worry!
I have always told you what will happen.
You are my witnesses.
    There is no other God but me.
    I know of no other Rock;^d I am the only
        One."

Idols Are Useless

⁹Some people make idols, but they are worth
        nothing.
People treasure them, but they are useless.
Those people are witnesses for the statues,
    but those people cannot see.
They know nothing, so they will be
        ashamed.
¹⁰Who made these gods?
    Who made these useless idols?
¹¹The workmen who made them will be
        ashamed,
    because they are only human.
If they all would come together,
    they would all be ashamed and afraid.

¹²One workman uses tools to heat iron,
    and he works over hot coals.
With his hammer he beats the metal and
        makes a statue,
    using his powerful arms.
But when he becomes hungry, he loses his
        power.
If he does not drink water, he becomes
        tired.

¹³Another workman uses a line and a compass
    to draw on the wood.
Then he uses his chisels to cut a statue
    and his calipers to measure the statue.
In this way, the workman makes the wood
        look exactly like a person,
    and this statue of a person sits in the
        house.
¹⁴He cuts down cedars
    or cypress or oak trees.
Those trees grew by their own power in the
        forest.
Or he plants a pine tree, and the rain
    makes it grow.
¹⁵Then he burns the tree.
    He uses some of the wood for a fire to
        keep himself warm.
He also starts a fire to bake his bread.
But he uses part of the wood to make a god,
    and then he worships it!
He makes the idol and bows down to it!
¹⁶The man burns half of the wood in the fire.
    He uses the fire to cook his meat,
    and he eats the meat until he is full.
He also burns the wood to keep himself
        warm. He says,
    "Good! Now I am warm. I can see because
        of the fire's light."
¹⁷But he makes a statue from the wood that is
        left and calls it his god.
He bows down to it and worships it.
He prays to it and says,
    "You are my god. Save me!"
¹⁸Those people don't know what they are
        doing. They don't understand!
    It is as if their eyes are covered so they
        can't see.
Their minds don't understand.
¹⁹They have not thought about these things;
    they don't understand.
They have never thought to themselves,
    "I burned half of the wood in the fire
    and used the hot coals to bake my bread.
I cooked and ate my meat.
And I used the wood that was left to make
        this hateful thing.
I am worshiping a block of wood!"
²⁰He doesn't know what he is doing;
    his confused mind leads him the wrong
        way.
He cannot save himself
    or say, "This statue I am holding is a false
        god."

The Lord Is the True God

²¹"People of Jacob, remember these things!
People of Israel, remember you are my
        servants.
I made you, and you are my servants.

So Israel, I will not forget you.
22I have swept away your sins like a big cloud;
    I have removed your sins like a cloud that
        disappears into the air.
Come back to me because I saved you."

23Skies, sing for joy because the LORD did great
        things!
    Earth, shout for joy, even in your deepest
        parts!
Sing, you mountains, with thanks to God.
    Sing, too, you trees in the forest!
The LORD saved the people of Jacob!
    He showed his glory when he saved Israel.
24This is what the LORD says, who saved you,
    who formed you in your mother's body:
"I, the LORD, made everything,
    stretching out the skies by myself
    and spreading out the earth all alone.
25I show that the lying prophets'd signs are
        false;
    I make fools of those who do magic.
I confuse even wise men;
    they think they know much, but I make
        them look foolish.
26I make the messages of my servants come
        true;
    I make the advice of my messengers come
        true.
I say to Jerusalem,
    'People will live in you again!'
I say to the towns of Judah,
    'You will be built again!'
I say to Jerusalem's ruins,
    'I will repair you.'
27I tell the deep waters, 'Become dry!
    I will make your streams become dry!'
28I say of Cyrus,n 'He is my shepherd
    and will do all that I want him to do.
He will say to Jerusalem, "You will be built
        again!"
He will tell the Temple,d "Your foundations
    will be rebuilt." ' "

God Chooses Cyrus to Free Israel

45 This is what the LORD says to Cyrus,
    his appointed king:
"I hold your right hand
    and will help you defeat nations
    and take away other kings' power.
I will open doors for you
    so city gates will not stop you.
2I will go before you
    and make the mountains flat.
I will break down the bronze gates of the
        cities
    and cut through their iron bars.

3I will give you the wealth that is stored away
    and the hidden riches
so you will know I am the LORD,
    the God of Israel, who calls you by name.
4I do these things for my servants, the people
        of Jacob,
    and for my chosen people, the Israelites.
Cyrus, I call you by name,
    and I give you a title of honor even though
        you don't know me.
5I am the LORD. There is no other God;
    I am the only God.
I will make you strong,
    even though you don't know me,
6so that everyone will know
    there is no other God.
From the east to the west they will know
    I alone am the LORD.
7I made the light and the darkness.
    I bring peace, and I cause troubles.
    I, the LORD, do all these things.

8"Sky above, make victory fall like rain;
    clouds, pour down victory.
Let the earth receive it,
    and let salvation grow,
and let victory grow with it.
    I, the LORD, have created it.

9"How terrible it will be for those who argue
        with the God who made them.
    They are like a piece of broken pottery
        among many pieces.
The clay does not ask the potter,
    'What are you doing?'
The thing that is made doesn't say to its
        maker,
    'You have no hands.'
10How terrible it will be for the child who says
        to his father,
    'Why are you giving me life?'
How terrible it will be for the child who says
        to his mother,
    'Why are you giving birth to me?' "

11This is what the LORD,
    the Holy One of Israel, and its Maker, says:
"You ask me about what will happen.
    You question me about my children.
    You give me orders about what I have
        made.
12I made the earth
    and all the people living on it.
With my own hands I stretched out the skies,
    and I commanded all the armies in the sky.
13I will bring Cyrus to do good things,
    and I will make his work easy.
He will rebuild my city

Cyrus A king of Persia who ruled from about 550-530 B.C.

and set my people free
without any payment or reward.
The LORD All-Powerful says this."

14The LORD says,
"The goods made in Egypt and Cush
and the tall people of Seba
will come to you
and will become yours.
The Sabeans will walk behind you,
coming along in chains.
They will bow down before you
and pray to you, saying,
'God is with you,
and there is no other God.' "

15God and Savior of Israel,
you are a God that people cannot see.
16All the people who make idols will be put to
great shame;
they will go off together in disgrace.
17But Israel will be saved by the LORD,
and that salvation will continue forever.
Never again will Israel be put to shame.

18The LORD created the heavens.
He is the God who formed the earth and
made it.
He did not want it to be empty,
but he wanted life on the earth.
This is what the LORD says:
"I am the LORD. There is no other God.
19I did not speak in secret
or hide my words in some dark place.
I did not tell the family of Jacob
to look for me in empty places.
I am the LORD, and I speak the truth;
I say what is right.

20"You people who have escaped from other
nations,
gather together and come before me;
come near together.
People who carry idols of wood don't know
what they are doing.
They pray to a god who cannot save them.
21Tell these people to come to me.
Let them talk about these things together.
Who told you long ago that this would
happen?
Who told about it long ago?
I, the LORD, said these things.
There is no other God besides me.
I am the only good God. I am the Savior.
There is no other God.

22"All people everywhere,
follow me and be saved.
I am God. There is no other God.
23I will make a promise by my own power,
and my promise is true;

what I say will not be changed.
I promise that everyone will bow before me
and will promise to follow me.
24People will say about me, 'Goodness and
power
come only from the LORD.' "
Everyone who has been angry with him
will come to him and be ashamed.
25But with the LORD's help, the people of Israel
will be found to be good,
and they will praise him.

False Gods Are Useless

46 Beld and Nebod bow down.
Their idols are carried by animals.
The statues are only heavy loads that must be
carried;
they only make people tired.
2These gods will all bow down.
They cannot save themselves
but will all be carried away like prisoners.

3"Family of Jacob, listen to me!
All you people from Israel who are still
alive, listen!
I have carried you since you were born;
I have taken care of you from your birth.
4Even when you are old, I will be the same.
Even when your hair has turned gray, I will
take care of you.
I made you and will take care of you.
I will carry you and save you.

5"Can you compare me to anyone?
No one is equal to me or like me.
6Some people are rich with gold
and weigh their silver on the scales.
They hire a goldsmith, and he makes it into a
god.
Then they bow down and worship it.
7They put it on their shoulders and carry it.
They set it in its place, and there it stands;
it cannot move from its place.
People may yell at it, but it cannot answer.
It cannot save them from their troubles.

8"Remember this, and do not forget it!
Think about these things, you who turn
against God.
9Remember what happened long ago.

Remember that I am God, and there is no
other God.
I am God, and there is no one like me.
¹⁰From the beginning I told you what would
happen in the end.
A long time ago I told you things that have
not yet happened.
When I plan something, it happens.
What I want to do, I will do.
¹¹I am calling a man from the east to carry out
my plan;
he will come like a hawk from a country
far away.
I will make what I have said come true;
I will do what I have planned.
¹²Listen to me, you stubborn people,
who are far from what is right.
¹³I will soon do the things that are right.
I will bring salvation soon.
I will save Jerusalem
and bring glory to Israel."

God Will Destroy Babylon

47 The Lord says, "City of Babylon,
go down and sit in the dirt.
People of Babylon, sit on the ground.
You are no longer the ruler.
You will no longer be called
tender or beautiful.
² You must use large stones to grind grain
into flour.
Remove your veil and your nice skirts.
Uncover your legs and cross the rivers.
³People will see your nakedness;
they will see your shame.
I will punish you;
I will punish every one of you."

⁴Our Savior is named the Lord All-Powerful;
he is the Holy One of Israel.

⁵"Babylon, sit in darkness and say nothing.
You will no longer be called the queen of
kingdoms.
⁶I was angry with my people,
so I rejected those who belonged to me.
I gave them to you,
but you showed them no mercy.
You even made the old people
work very hard.
⁷You said, 'I will live forever
as the queen.'
But you did not think about these things
or consider what would happen.

⁸"Now, listen, you lover of pleasure.
You think you are safe.
You tell yourself,
'I am the only important person.
I will never be a widow

or lose my children.'
⁹Two things will happen to you suddenly, in a
single day.
You will lose your children and your
husband.
These things will truly happen to you,
in spite of all your magic,
in spite of your powerful tricks.
¹⁰You do evil things, but you feel safe
and say, 'No one sees what I do.'
Your wisdom and knowledge
have fooled you.
You say to yourself,
'I am God, and no one is equal to me.'
¹¹But troubles will come to you,
and you will not know how to stop them.
Disaster will fall on you,
and you will not be able to keep it away.
You will be destroyed quickly;
you will not even see it coming.

¹²"Keep on using your tricks
and doing all your magic
that you have used since you were young.
Maybe they will help you;
maybe you will be able to scare someone.
¹³You are tired of the advice you have
received.
So let those who study the sky —
those who tell the future by looking at the
stars and the new moons —
let them save you from what is about to
happen to you.
¹⁴But they are like straw;
fire will quickly burn them up.
They cannot save themselves
from the power of the fire.
They are not like coals that give warmth
nor like a fire that you may sit beside.
¹⁵You have worked with these people,
and they have been with you since you
were young,
but they will not be able to help you.
Everyone will go his own way,
and there will be no one left to save you."

God Controls the Future

48 The Lord says, "Family of Jacob, listen
to me.
You are called Israel,
and you come from the family of Judah.
You swear by the Lord's name
and praise the God of Israel,
but you are not honest or sincere.
²You call yourselves people of the holy city,
and you depend on the God of Israel,
who is named the Lord All-Powerful.
³Long ago I told you what would happen.
I said these things and made them known;

suddenly I acted, and these things
   happened.
⁴I knew you were stubborn;
   your neck was like an iron muscle,
   and your head was like bronze.
⁵So a long time ago I told you about these
      things;
   I told you about them before they
      happened
so you couldn't say, 'My idols did this,
   and my wooden and metal statues made
      these things happen.'

⁶"You heard and saw everything that
      happened,
   so you should tell this news to others.
Now I will tell you about new things,
   hidden things that you don't know yet.
⁷These things are happening now, not long
      ago;
   you have not heard about them before
      today.
So you cannot say, 'We already knew about
      that.'
⁸But you have not heard me; you have not
      understood.
   Even long ago you did not listen to me.
I knew you would surely turn against me;
   you have fought against me since you were
      born.
⁹But for my own sake I will be patient.
   People will praise me for not becoming
      angry
   and destroying you.
¹⁰I have made you pure, but not by fire, as
      silver is made pure.
   I have purified you by giving you troubles.
¹¹I do this for myself, for my own sake.
   I will not let people speak evil against me,
   and I will not let some god take my glory.

Israel Will Be Free

¹²"People of Jacob, listen to me.
   People of Israel, I have called you to be my
      people.
I am God;
   I am the beginning and the end.
¹³I made the earth with my own hands.
   With my right hand I spread out the skies.
When I call them,
   they come together before me."

¹⁴All of you, come together and listen.
   None of the gods said these things would
      happen.
The LORD has chosen someone
   to attack the Babylonians;

him This probably refers to Cyrus king of Persia.

he will carry out his wishes against
   Babylon.

¹⁵"I have spoken; I have called him. ⁿ
   I have brought him, and I will make him
      successful.
¹⁶Come to me and listen to this.
   From the beginning I have spoken openly.
   From the time it began, I was there."

Now, the Lord GOD
   has sent me with his Spirit.ᵈ

¹⁷This is what the LORD, who saves you,
   the Holy One of Israel, says:
"I am the LORD your God,
   who teaches you to do what is good,
   who leads you in the way you should go.
¹⁸If you had obeyed me,
   you would have had peace like a
      full-flowing river.
   Good things would have flowed to you like
      the waves of the sea.
¹⁹You would have had many children,
   as many as the grains of sand.
They would never have died out
   nor been destroyed."

²⁰My people, leave Babylon!
   Run from the Babylonians!
Tell this news with shouts of joy to the
      people;
   spread it everywhere on earth.
Say, "The LORD has saved his servants, the
      people of Jacob."
²¹They did not become thirsty when he led
      them through the deserts.
   He made water flow from a rock for them.
He split the rock,
   and water flowed out.

²²"There is no peace for evil people," says the
   LORD.

God Calls His Special Servant

49

All of you people in faraway places,
   listen to me.
Listen, all you nations far away.
Before I was born, the LORD called me to
      serve him.
   The LORD named me while I was still in
      my mother's body.
²He made my tongue like a sharp sword.
   He hid me in the shadow of his hand.
He made me like a sharp arrow.
   He hid me in the holder for his arrows.
³He told me, "Israel, you are my servant.
   I will show my glory through you."
⁴But I said, "I have worked hard for nothing;

I have used all my power, but I did nothing
useful.
But the Lord will decide what my work is
worth;
God will decide my reward."
⁵The Lord made me in the body of my
mother
to be his servant,
to lead the people of Jacob back to him
so that Israel might be gathered to him.
The Lord will honor me,
and I will get my strength from my God.
⁶Now he told me,
"You are an important servant to me
to bring back the tribes*d* of Jacob,
to bring back the people of Israel who are
left alive.
But, more importantly, I will make you a
light for all nations
to show people all over the world the way
to be saved."

⁷The Lord who saves you
is the Holy One of Israel.
He speaks to the one who is hated by the
people,
to the servant of rulers.
This is what he says: "Kings will see you and
stand to honor you;
great leaders will bow down before you,
because the Lord can be trusted.
He is the Holy One of Israel, who has
chosen you."

The Day of Salvation

⁸This is what the Lord says:
"At the right time I will hear your prayers.
On the day of salvation I will help you.
I will protect you,
and you will be the sign of my agreement
with the people.
You will bring back the people to the land
and give the land that is now ruined back
to its owners.
⁹You will tell the prisoners, 'Come out of your
prison.'
You will tell those in darkness, 'Come into
the light.'
The people will eat beside the roads,
and they will find food even on bare hills.
¹⁰They will not be hungry or thirsty.

What Will You Do?

"Instead of spending spring break on the ski slopes this year, we're going on a mission trip to Mexico!" The new youth minister looked at a sea of blank faces.

"But we always go skiing," they responded.

Nevertheless, at spring break a caravan headed for Mexico, packed with supplies and the California teenagers who were willing to try something new. They arrived just in time to overwhelm a tiny, Spanish-speaking congregation that was meeting for worship.

"We didn't think you'd really come," said the Mexican pastor. When the crew translated their desire to help build or fix whatever was needed, the pastor cried.

"You are an answer to prayer," he told them. "We've been praying that we could build a church, and here you are." What started out as something to fill spring break became part of God's mission in the world.

God has a purpose for his people, even when they are not sure what it is. Listen for the purpose God has for you in **Isaiah 49:1–13**.

■ What might Isaiah have said to the California group as it planned its spring break?
■ How does this passage encourage you as you make decisions about what to do with your life?

C O N S I D E R . . .

■ rewriting Isaiah 49:1–13 in your own words, emphasizing how each verse might apply to God's will for you.
■ asking your parent or youth pastor to pray for you to discover God's will for your future.

F O R   M O R E ,   S E E . . .

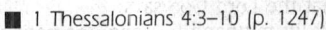

■ 1 Chronicles 29:17–18 (p. 385)   ■ 1 Thessalonians 4:3–10 (p. 1247)
■ Romans 12:1–2 (p. 1157)

Neither the hot sun nor the desert wind
will hurt them.
The God who comforts them will lead them
and guide them by springs of water.
¹¹I will make my mountains into roads,
and the roads will be raised up.
¹²Look, people are coming to me from far
away,
from the north and from the west,
from Aswan in southern Egypt."

¹³Heavens and earth, be happy.
Mountains, shout with joy,
because the LORD comforts his people
and will have pity on those who suffer.

Jerusalem and Her Children

¹⁴But Jerusalem said, "The LORD has left me;
the Lord has forgotten me."

¹⁵The LORD answers, "Can a woman forget the
baby she nurses?
Can she feel no kindness for the child to
which she gave birth?
Even if she could forget her children,
I will not forget you.
¹⁶See, I have written your name on my hand.
Jerusalem, I always think about your walls.
¹⁷Your children will soon return to you,
and the people who defeated you and
destroyed you will leave.
¹⁸Look up and look around you.
All your children are gathering to return to
you."
The LORD says, "As surely as I live,
your children will be like jewels
that a bride wears proudly.

¹⁹"You were destroyed and defeated,
and your land was made useless.
But now you will have more people than the
land can hold,
and those people who destroyed you will
be far away.
²⁰Children were born to you while you were
sad,
but they will say to you,
'This place is too small for us.
Give us a bigger place to live.'
²¹Then you will say to yourself,
'Who gave me all these children?
I was sad and lonely,
defeated and separated from my people.
So who reared these children?
I was left all alone.
Where did all these children come from?' "

²²This is what the Lord GOD says:
"See, I will lift my hand to signal the nations;
I will raise my banner for all the people to
see.

Then they will bring your sons back to you in
their arms,
and they will carry your daughters on their
shoulders.
²³Kings will teach your children,
and daughters of kings will take care of
them.
They will bow down before you
and kiss the dirt at your feet.
Then you will know I am the LORD.
Anyone who trusts in me will not be
disappointed."

²⁴Can the wealth a soldier wins in war be
taken away from him?
Can a prisoner be freed from a powerful
soldier?
²⁵This is what the LORD says:
"The prisoners will be taken from the strong
soldiers.
What the soldiers have taken will be saved.
I will fight your enemies,
and I will save your children.
²⁶I will force those who trouble you to eat
their own flesh.
Their own blood will be the wine that
makes them drunk.
Then everyone will know
I, the LORD, am the One who saves you;
I am the Powerful One of Jacob who saves
you."

Israel Was Punished for Its Sin

50 This is what the LORD says:
"People of Israel, you say I divorced
your mother.
Then where is the paper that proves it?
Or do you think I sold you
to pay a debt?
Because of the evil things you did, I sold you.
Because of the times she turned against me,
your mother was sent away.
²I came home and found no one there;
I called, but no one answered.
Do you think I am not able to save you?
Do I not have the power to save you?
Look, I need only to shout and the sea
becomes dry.
I change rivers into a desert,
and their fish rot because there is no water;
they die of thirst.
³I can make the skies dark;
I can make them black like clothes of
sadness."

God's Servant Obeys

⁴The Lord GOD gave me the ability to teach
so that I know what to say to make the
weak strong.

Every morning he wakes me.
He teaches me to listen like a student.
5The Lord GOD helps me learn,
and I have not turned against him
nor stopped following him.
6I offered my back to those who beat me.
I offered my cheeks to those who pulled
my beard.
I won't hide my face from them
when they make fun of me and spit
at me.
7The Lord GOD helps me,
so I will not be ashamed.
I will be determined,
and I know I will not be disgraced.
8He shows that I am innocent, and he is close
to me.
So who can accuse me?
If there is someone, let us go to court
together.
If someone wants to prove I have done
wrong,
he should come and tell me.
9Look! It is the Lord GOD who helps me.
So who can prove me guilty?

Look! All those who try will become useless
like old clothes;
moths will eat them.

10Who among you fears the LORD
and obeys his servant?
That person may walk in the dark
and have no light.
Then let him trust in the LORD
and depend on his God.
11But instead, some of you want to light your
own fires
and make your own light.
So, go, walk in the light of your fires,
and trust your own light to guide you.
But this is what you will receive from me:
You will lie down in a place of pain.

Jerusalem Will Be Saved

51 The LORD says, "Listen to me,
those of you who try to live right and
follow the LORD.
Look at the rock from which you were cut;
look at the stone quarry from which you
were dug.

REVENGE

Different Strength

Tex, Pueblo, and Goat were leaders of Chicago street gangs. They grew up surrounded by poverty, poor schools and violence. Striking out with violence was their way to be recognized.

A black leader took interest in these boys. He listened to their stories and persuaded them to try nonviolence as a way to be seen and heard.

So in 1966, carloads of Chicago gang members drove to Mississippi to participate in their first nonviolent demonstration, a Freedom March. The marchers were treated unfairly; they were attacked with tear gas. But the experience changed the lives of these young men and women. They realized that nonviolence was a better way to respond.

Back in Chicago the gangs marched again. During this march a brick was hurled at the demonstrators. Goat jumped up and protected a woman from the brick by catching it with his bare hands. Instead of hurling it back, he continued marching peacefully.

Revenge harms the person who seeks it. **Isaiah 50:4—9** explains how God has a better way to handle tough situations.

■ How was the gang members' new attitude similar to Isaiah's in this passage?
■ How can this scripture help you when you're tempted to get even with those who have done you wrong?

CONSIDER . . .
■ listing ways people try to get revenge for something and then making a second list of positive things you could do when confronted with an unfair situation.
■ inviting someone who has wronged you to an activity that you or your group is planning. Include this person as you would a good friend.

FOR MORE, SEE . . .

■ Leviticus 19:17–18 (p. 116)   ■ Romans 12:17–21 (p. 1158)
■ Matthew 5:38–48 (p. 915)

²Look at Abraham, your ancestor,
and Sarah, who gave birth to your
ancestors.
Abraham had no children when I called him,
but I blessed him and gave him many
descendants.*d*
³So the LORD will comfort Jerusalem;
he will show mercy to those who live in
her ruins.
He will change her deserts into a garden like
Eden;
he will make her empty lands like the
garden of the LORD.
People there will be very happy;
they will give thanks and sing songs.

⁴"My people, listen to me;
my nation, pay attention to me.
I will give the people my teachings,
and my decisions will be like a light to all
people.
⁵I will soon show that I do what is right.
I will soon save you.
I will use my power and judge all nations.
All the faraway places are waiting for me;
they wait for my power to help them.
⁶Look up to the heavens.
Look around you at the earth below.
The skies will disappear like clouds of smoke.
The earth will become useless like old
clothes,
and its people will die like flies.
But my salvation will continue forever,
and my goodness will never end.

⁷"You people who know what is right should
listen to me;
you people who follow my teachings should
hear what I say.
Don't be afraid of the evil things people say,
and don't be upset by their insults.
⁸Moths will eat those people as if they were
clothes,
and worms will eat them as if they were
wool.
But my goodness will continue forever,
and my salvation will continue from now
on."

⁹Wake up, wake up, and use your strength,
powerful LORD.
Wake up as you did in the old times,
as you did a long time ago.
*With your own power, you cut Rahab*d *into
pieces*
and killed that sea monster.
¹⁰You dried up the sea
and the waters of the deep ocean.
You made the deepest parts of the sea into a
road

for your people to cross over and be saved.
¹¹The people the LORD has freed will return
and enter Jerusalem with joy.
Their happiness will last forever.
They will have joy and gladness,
and all sadness and sorrow will be gone far
away.

✺ **SIDELIGHT:** When Isaiah 51:9
talks about cutting Rahab into little
pieces, it's not referring to a person named
Rahab. Rather, it refers to a sea monster of
chaos that, according to an old legend, God
killed in battle when he created the world.
That's why the name was a put-down when
it was used to refer to Egypt in Isaiah 30:7
(p. 646).

---

¹²The LORD says, "I am the one who comforts
you.
So why should you be afraid of people,
who die?
Why should you fear people who die like
the grass?
¹³Have you forgotten the LORD who made you,
who stretched out the skies
and made the earth?
Why are you always afraid
of those angry people who trouble you
and who want to destroy?
But where are those angry people now?
¹⁴ People in prison will soon be set free;
they will not die in prison,
and they will have enough food.
¹⁵I am the LORD your God,
who stirs the sea and makes the waves
roar.
My name is the LORD All-Powerful.
¹⁶I will give you the words I want you to say.
I will cover you with my hands and protect
you.
I made the heavens and the earth,
and I say to Jerusalem, 'You are my
people.' "

God Punished Israel

¹⁷Awake! Awake!
Get up, Jerusalem.
The LORD was very angry with you;
your punishment was like wine in a
cup.
The LORD made you drink that wine;
you drank the whole cup until you
stumbled.
¹⁸Jerusalem had many people,
but there was not one to lead her.

Of all the people who grew up there,
no one was there to guide her.
[19]Troubles came to you two by two,
but no one will feel sorry for you.
There was ruin and disaster, great hunger
and fighting.
No one can comfort you.
[20]Your people have become weak.
They fall down and lie on every street
corner,
like animals caught in a net.
They have felt the full anger of the LORD
and have heard God's angry shout.

[21]So listen to me, poor Jerusalem,
you who are drunk but not from wine.
[22]Your God will defend his people.
This is what the LORD your God says:
"The punishment I gave you is like a cup of
wine.
You drank it and could not walk straight.

But I am taking that cup of my anger away
from you,
and you will never be punished by my
anger again.
[23]I will now give that cup of punishment to
those who gave you pain,
who told you,
'Bow down so we can walk over you.'
They made your back like dirt for them to
walk on;
you were like a street for them to travel
on."

Jerusalem Will Be Saved

52 Wake up, wake up, Jerusalem!
Become strong!
Be beautiful again,
holy city of Jerusalem.
The people who do not worship God and
who are not pure

FREEDOM

Tearing Down the Walls

Angela Baxter looked like she had stepped out of the pages of Glamour magazine. She
never went anywhere unless her outfit and makeup were perfect. As she walked up the
stairs at Jackson Street Chapel, however, she looked out of place. "Excuse me," she
mumbled to a group of street people around the doorway, "I'm here to volunteer." She
heard snickers as she walked inside.

Gradually, over a period of months, as she worked several hours weekly at the chapel,
Angela became a fixture there. She worked in the clothes closet. She planned after-school
children's programs and visited with senior adults. She made a difference.

At the end of her visits, Angela would spend a few minutes alone in the sanctuary.
Hanging at the front was a banner that pictured a crumbling wall and the words, "Tearing
Down Walls." Here at the chapel, rich and poor, young and old, black and white became
friends. The love of Jesus Christ and the freedom he offers tore down the barriers that
usually come between people. She would glance at her clothes—usually a
comfortable sweatshirt, jeans, and well-worn shoes. She would remember the
walls that were there when she had first come to Jackson Street in her
expensive outfits.

Maybe I've found freedom too, she thought, freedom to see what's most
important.

God wants to set people free from anything that keeps them from serving
him. Read about the freedom God offers in **Isaiah 52:1–10**.

■ How is Angela's story like Jerusalem's story in this passage?
■ What things hold you back and keep you from the freedom Isaiah talks
about in this passage?

C O N S I D E R . . .

■ writing down things in your life that might keep you from following Christ
and then asking God to free you from those obstacles.
■ sharing your time, talent, or money with an organization that helps the needy. Plan an
activity for which you could volunteer, or organize an offering or fund-raiser.

F O R   M O R E ,   S E E . . .

■ Psalm 118:5–17 (p. 549)
■ John 8:31–36 (p. 1072)
■ Romans 6:15–23 (p. 1147)

will not enter you again.

²Jerusalem, you once were a prisoner.
  Now shake off the dust and stand up.
Jerusalem, you once were a prisoner.
  Now free yourself from the chains around
    your neck.
³This is what the LORD says:
  "You were not sold for a price,
    so you will be saved without cost."
⁴This is what the Lord GOD says:
  "First my people went down to Egypt
    to live.
  Later Assyria made them slaves.

⁵"Now see what has happened," says the
    LORD.
  "Another nation has taken away my people
    for nothing.
This nation who rules them makes fun of
    me," says the LORD.
  "All day long they speak against me.
⁶This has happened so my people will know
    who I am,
  and so, on that future day, they will know
that I am the one speaking to them.
  It will really be me."

⁷How beautiful is the person
  who comes over the mountains to bring
    good news,
who announces peace
  and brings good news,
  who announces salvation
and says to Jerusalem,
  "Your God is King."
⁸Listen! Your guards are shouting.
  They are all shouting for joy!
They all will see with their own eyes
  when the LORD returns to Jerusalem.
⁹Jerusalem, your buildings are destroyed now,
  but shout and rejoice together,
because the LORD has comforted his people.
  He has saved Jerusalem.
¹⁰The LORD will show his holy power
  to all the nations.
Then everyone on earth
  will see the salvation of our God.

¹¹You people, leave, leave; get out of Babylon!
  Touch nothing that is unclean.*d*
You men who carry the LORD's things used
    in worship,
  leave there and make yourselves pure.
¹²*You will not be forced to leave Babylon*
    quickly;
  you will not be forced to run away,
because the LORD will go before you,
  and the God of Israel will guard you from
    behind.

The Lord's Suffering Servant

¹³The LORD says, "See, my servant will act
    wisely.
  People will greatly honor and respect him.
¹⁴Many people were shocked when they saw
    him.
  His appearance was so changed he did not
    look like a man;
  his form was changed so much they could
    barely tell he was human.
¹⁵But now he will surprise many nations.
  Kings will be amazed and shut their
    mouths.
They will see things they had not been told
    about him,
  and they will understand things they had
    not heard."

53 Who would have believed what we
      heard?
Who saw the LORD's power in this?
²He grew up like a small plant before the
    LORD,
  like a root growing in a dry land.
He had no special beauty or form to make us
    notice him;
  there was nothing in his appearance to
    make us desire him.
³He was hated and rejected by people.
  He had much pain and suffering.
People would not even look at him.
  He was hated, and we didn't even notice
    him.

⁴But he took our suffering on him
  and felt our pain for us.
We saw his suffering
  and thought God was punishing him.
⁵But he was wounded for the wrong we did;
  he was crushed for the evil we did.
The punishment, which made us well, was
    given to him,
  and we are healed because of his wounds.
⁶We all have wandered away like sheep;
  each of us has gone his own way.
But the LORD has put on him the punishment
  for all the evil we have done.

⁷He was beaten down and punished,
  but he didn't say a word.
He was like a lamb being led to be killed.
  He was quiet, as a sheep is quiet while *its*
    wool is being cut;
  he never opened his mouth.
⁸Men took him away roughly and unfairly.
  He died without children to continue his
    family.
He was put to death;
  he was punished for the sins of my people.

⁹He was buried with wicked men,
and he died with the rich.
He had done nothing wrong,
and he had never lied.

¹⁰But it was the Lᴏʀᴅ who decided
to crush him and make him suffer.
The Lᴏʀᴅ made his life a penalty offering,
but he will still see his descendants*d* and live
a long life.
He will complete the things the Lᴏʀᴅ
wants him to do.
¹¹"After his soul suffers many things,
he will see life and be satisfied.
My good servant will make many people
right with God;
he will carry away their sins.
¹²For this reason I will make him a great man
among people,
and he will share in all things with those
who are strong.
He willingly gave his life
and was treated like a criminal.
But he carried away the sins of many people
and asked forgiveness for those who
sinned."

People Will Return to Jerusalem

54 The Lᴏʀᴅ says, "Sing, Jerusalem.
You are like a woman who never gave
birth to children.
Start singing and shout for joy.
You never felt the pain of giving birth,
but you will have more children
than the woman who has a husband.
²Make your tent bigger;
stretch it out and make it wider.
Do not hold back.
Make the ropes longer
and its stakes stronger,
³because you will spread out to the right and
to the left.
Your children will take over other nations,
and they will again live in cities that once
were destroyed.

⁴'Don't be afraid, because you will not be
ashamed.
Don't be embarrassed, because you will not
be disgraced.
You will forget the shame you felt earlier;
you will not remember the shame you felt
when you lost your husband.

JESUS CHRIST

What Love Looks Like

Robert Nichols was an MK, a missionary kid; his parents served in South Asia. Sitting around a table with American friends one night, he and some friends started talking about missions and how to know whether a person was "cut out" to be a missionary. Robert thought about his parents. He knew the commitment and love it took to be effective for Christ.

"It takes love to do missions," Robert stated. "And do you know what love looks like?

"Once I watched my dad hold a man's diseased feet in his hands," Robert continued. "The feet were swollen and full of pus, but he wasn't afraid to touch him, because he cared for that person. His only concern was loving that man like Jesus does. That's the kind of love I want to have."

Because of Jesus' deep love for us, he experienced extreme pain and suffering. **Isaiah 52:13—53:12** is a prophetic picture of this servant of God, the Son of God.

■ How was the love of Robert's father for the sick man like the love of God's servant in this passage?

■ What kind of suffering could you face as God's servant today?

CONSIDER . . .

■ writing a description of how Jesus might live today. What would he wear? How would he spend his time? With whom would he associate? Where would he go?

■ "adopting" a person who serves God through missions work, ministry, or some kind of service by writing a note of appreciation, praying for the work he or she does, or offering your assistance.

FOR MORE, SEE . . .

■ Isaiah 11:1–10 (p. 629)
■ John 1:1–18 (p. 1058)

■ Philippians 2:1–11 (p. 1230)

⁵The God who made you is like your
     husband.
His name is the LORD All-Powerful.
The Holy One of Israel is the one who saves
     you.
He is called the God of all the earth.
⁶You were like a woman whose husband left
     her,
     and you were very sad.
You were like a wife who married young
     and then her husband left her.
But the LORD called you to be his,"
     says your God.
⁷God says, "I left you for a short time,
     but with great kindness I will bring you
     back again.
⁸I became very angry
     and hid from you for a time,
     but I will show you mercy with kindness
     forever,"
     says the LORD who saves you.

⁹The LORD says, "This day is like the time of
     Noah to me.
I promised then that I would never flood
     the world again.
In the same way, I promise I will not be
     angry with you
     or punish you again.
¹⁰The mountains may disappear,
     and the hills may come to an end,
     but my love will never disappear;
     my promise of peace will not come to an
     end,"
     says the LORD who shows mercy to you.

¹¹"You poor city. Storms have hurt you,
     and you have not been comforted.
But I will rebuild you with turquoise stones,
     and I will build your foundations with
     sapphires.
¹²I will use rubies to build your walls
     and shining jewels for the gates
     and precious jewels for all your outer walls.
¹³All your children will be taught by the LORD,
     and they will have much peace.
¹⁴I will build you using fairness.
You will be safe from those who would hurt
     you,
     so you will have nothing to fear.
Nothing will come to make you afraid.
¹⁵I will not send anyone to attack you,
     and you will defeat those who do attack
     you.

¹⁶"See, I made the blacksmith.
He fans the fire to make it hotter,
     and he makes the kind of tool he wants.
In the same way I have made the destroyer
     to destroy.

¹⁷ So no weapon that is used against you will
     defeat you.
You will show that those who speak against
     you are wrong.
These are the good things my servants
     receive.
Their victory comes from me," says the
     LORD.

God Gives What Is Good

55 The LORD says, "All you who are
     thirsty,
come and drink.
Those of you who do not have money,
     come, buy and eat!
Come buy wine and milk
     without money and without cost.
²Why spend your money on something that is
     not real food?
Why work for something that doesn't really
     satisfy you?
Listen closely to me, and you will eat what is
     good;
     your soul will enjoy the rich food that
     satisfies.
³Come to me and listen;
     listen to me so you may live.
I will make an agreement with you that will
     last forever.
I will give you the blessings I promised to
     David.
⁴I made David a witness of my power for all
     nations,
     a ruler and commander of many nations.
⁵You will call for nations that you don't yet
     know.
And these nations that do not know you
     will run to you
because of the LORD your God,
     because of the Holy One of Israel who
     honors you."

⁶So you should look for the LORD before it is
     too late;
     you should call to him while he is near.
⁷The wicked should stop doing wrong,
     and they should stop their evil thoughts.
They should return to the LORD so he may
     have mercy on them.
They should come to our God, because he
     will freely forgive them.

⁸The LORD says, "My thoughts are not like
     your thoughts.
Your ways are not like my ways.
⁹Just as the heavens are higher than the earth,
     so are my ways higher than your ways
     and my thoughts higher than your
     thoughts.
¹⁰Rain and snow fall from the sky

and don't return without watering the
ground.
They cause the plants to sprout and grow,
making seeds for the farmer
and bread for the people.
¹¹The same thing is true of the words I speak.
They will not return to me empty.
They make the things happen that I want to
happen,
and they succeed in doing what I send
them to do.

¹²"So you will go out with joy
and be led out in peace.
The mountains and hills will burst into song
before you,
and all the trees in the fields will clap their
hands.
¹³Large cypress trees will grow where
thornbushes were.
Myrtle trees will grow where weeds were.
These things will be a reminder of the LORD's
promise,
and this reminder will never be destroyed."

SIDELIGHT: Replacing
thornbushes with myrtle would require
more than a little plant food (Isaiah 55:13).
Thornbushes and weeds (or briars) are
scraggly desert plants that survive with little
nourishment. The myrtle is an evergreen
shrub that grows along rivers and streams,
and it symbolizes peace, joy, generosity, and
justice—which fits the prophet's vision for the
future.

All Nations Will Obey the Lord

56 This is what the LORD says:
"Give justice to all people,
and do what is right,
because my salvation will come to you soon.
Soon everyone will know that I do what is
right.
²The person who obeys the law about the
Sabbath
will be blessed,
and the person who does no evil
will be blessed."

³Foreigners who have joined the LORD should
not say,
"The LORD will not accept me with his
people."
The eunuch should not say,
"Because I cannot have children, the LORD
will not accept me."
⁴This is what the LORD says:

"The eunuchs should obey the law about the
Sabbath
and do what I want
and keep my agreement.
⁵If they do, I will make their names
remembered
within my Temple and its walls.
It will be better for them than children.
I will give them a name that will last forever,
that will never be forgotten.
⁶Foreigners will join the LORD
to worship him and love him,
to serve him,
to obey the law about the Sabbath,
and to keep my agreement.
⁷I will bring these people to my holy
mountain
and give them joy in my house of prayer.
The offerings and sacrifices
they place on my altar will please me,
because my Temple will be called
a house for prayer for people from all
nations."
³The Lord GOD says—
he who gathers the Israelites that were
forced to leave their country:
"I will bring together other people
to join those who are already gathered."

Israel's Leaders Are Evil

⁹All you animals of the field,
all you animals of the forest, come to eat.
¹⁰The leaders who are to guard the people are
blind;
they don't know what they are doing.
All of them are like quiet dogs
that don't know how to bark.
They lie down and dream
and love to sleep.
¹¹They are like hungry dogs
that are never satisfied.
They are like shepherds
who don't know what they are doing.
They all have gone their own way;
all they want to do is satisfy themselves.
¹²They say, "Come, let's drink some wine;
let's drink all the beer we want.
And tomorrow we will do this again,
or, maybe we will have an even better
time."

Israel Does Not Follow God

57 Those who are right with God may
die,
but no one pays attention.
Good people are taken away,
but no one understands.
Those who do right are being taken away
from evil

2 and are given peace.
Those who live as God wants
  find rest in death.

3 "Come here, you magicians!
  Come here, you sons of prostitutes[d] and
    those who take part in adultery![d]
4 Of whom are you making fun?
  Whom are you insulting?
  At whom do you stick out your tongue?
You turn against God,
  and you are liars.
5 You have sexual relations under every green
    tree
  to worship your gods.
You kill children in the ravines
  and sacrifice them in the rocky places.
6 You take the smooth rocks from the ravines
  as your portion.
You pour drink offerings on them to worship
    them,
  and you give grain offerings to them.
Do you think this makes me want to show
    you mercy?
7 You make your bed on every hill and
    mountain,
  and there you offer sacrifices.
8 You have hidden your idols
  behind your doors and doorposts.
You have left me, and you have uncovered
    yourself.
  You have pulled back the covers and
    climbed into bed.
You have made an agreement with those
    whose beds you love,
  and you have looked at their nakedness.
9 You use your oils and perfumes
  to look nice for Molech.[d]
You have sent your messengers to faraway
    lands;
  you even tried to send them to the place of
    the dead.
10 You were tired from doing these things,
  but you never gave up.
You found new strength,
  so you did not quit.

11 "Whom were you so afraid of
  that you lied to me?
You have not remembered me
  or even thought about me.
I have been quiet for a long time.
  Is that why you are not afraid of me?
12 *I will tell about your 'goodness' and what*
    you do,
  and those things will do you no good.
13 When you cry out for help,
  let the gods you have gathered help you.
The wind will blow them all away;
  just a puff of wind will take them away.

But the person who depends on me will
    receive the land
  and own my holy mountain."

The Lord Will Save His People

14 Someone will say, "Build a road! Build a
    road! Prepare the way!
  Make the way clear for my people."
15 And this is the reason: God lives forever and
    is holy.
  He is high and lifted up.
He says, "I live in a high and holy place,
  but I also live with people who are sad and
    humble.
I give new life to those who are humble
  and to those whose hearts are broken.
16 I will not accuse forever,
  nor will I always be angry,
because then human life would grow weak.
  Human beings, whom I created, would die.
17 I was angry because they were dishonest in
    order to make money.
I punished them and turned away from
    them in anger,
  but they continued to do evil.
18 I have seen what they have done, but I will
    heal them.
I will guide them and comfort them and
    those who felt sad for them.
  They will all praise me.
19 I will give peace, real peace, to those far and
    near,
  and I will heal them," says the LORD.
20 But evil people are like the angry sea,
  which cannot rest,
  whose waves toss up waste and mud.
21 "There is no peace for evil people," says my
    God.

How to Honor God

58 The LORD says, "Shout out loud. Don't
    hold back.
  Shout out loud like a trumpet.
Tell my people what they have done against
    their God;
  tell the family of Jacob about their sins.
2 They still come every day looking for me
  and want to learn my ways.
They act just like a nation that does *what is*
    right,
  that obeys the commands of its God.
They ask me to judge them fairly,
  They want God to be near them.
3 They say, 'To honor you we had special days
    when we gave up eating,
  but you didn't see.
We humbled ourselves to honor you,
  but you didn't notice.' "

But the LORD says, "You do what pleases
    yourselves on these special days,
and you are unfair to your workers.
⁴On these special days when you do not eat,
    you argue and fight
and hit each other with your fists.
You cannot do these things as you do
    now
and believe your prayers are heard in
    heaven.
⁵This kind of special day is not what I want.
    This is not the way I want people to be
    sorry for what they have done.
I don't want people just to bow their heads
    like a plant
and wear rough cloth and lie in ashes to
    show their sadness.
This is what you do on your special days
    when you do not eat,
but do you think this is what the LORD
    wants?
⁶"I will tell you the kind of special day I
    want:

Free the people you have put in prison
    unfairly
and undo their chains.
Free those to whom you are unfair
    and stop their hard labor.
⁷Share your food with the hungry
    and bring poor, homeless people into your
    own homes.
When you see someone who has no clothes,
    give him yours,
and don't refuse to help your own relatives.
⁸Then your light will shine like the dawn,
    and your wounds will quickly heal.
Your God will walk before you,
    and the glory of the LORD will protect you
    from behind.
⁹Then you will call out, and the LORD will
    answer.
You will cry out, and he will say, 'Here I
    am.'

"If you stop making trouble for others,
    if you stop using cruel words and pointing
    your finger at others,

HYPOCRISY

Are You for Real?

The bus was packed with everything, except servant attitudes. Compact disc players and hairspray were more important than the Bible Club materials crumpled under the seats. Efforts to work on club lessons were half-hearted.

"We'll help later," some in the group groaned, 'it's just too hot right now."

Attitudes didn't improve much that missions week. While teenagers talked about Jesus' love, they rarely showed love to any of the children. "Jesus is your friend," Sam Cooper told the boys and girls during his turn to tell the story. But after the story, he left their circle and joined his own friends under a tree.

On the last Bible Club day, the teenagers brought cameras. "Matt, get our picture," yelled Kristy Land, surrounded by her friends. Seven-year-old Bobby grinned and jumped into the pose.

"Not you," Kristy smiled, pushing him out of camera range. Embarrassed, Bobby walked away. He guessed God's love was just a story they told.

The Bible says that many people pretend to serve God when they are only pleasing themselves. Read **Isaiah 58:3–9a** to discover what God wants from his people.

■ If the teenagers had used this passage as a guide, how might their week have been different?

■ If the passage were addressed to you, how would you change the way you show love to God?

CONSIDER . . .

■ confessing to God a time when you treated someone unkindly. Ask God to help you find a way to make amends for your actions.

■ choosing a person you often overlook and having an Appreciation Day for him or her. Volunteer your time, write a note, or make something special.

FOR MORE, SEE . . .

■ Micah 6:6–8 (p. 866)

■ Matthew 23:23–26 (p. 949)

■ James 1:22–27 (p. 1294)

¹⁰if you feed those who are hungry
    and take care of the needs of those who
        are troubled,
then your light will shine in the darkness,
    and you will be bright like sunshine at
        noon.
¹¹The LORD will always lead you.
    He will satisfy your needs in dry lands
    and give strength to your bones.
You will be like a garden that has much
        water,
    like a spring that never runs dry.
¹²Your people will rebuild the old cities that
        are now in ruins;
    you will rebuild their foundations.
You will be known for repairing the broken
        places
    and for rebuilding the roads and houses.

¹³"You must obey God's law about the
        Sabbath*ᵈ*
    and not do what pleases yourselves on that
        holy day.
You should call the Sabbath a joyful day
    and honor it as the LORD's holy day.
You should honor it by not doing whatever
        you please
    nor saying whatever you please on that day.
¹⁴Then you will find joy in the LORD,
    and I will carry you to the high places
        above the earth.
    I will let you eat the crops of the land your
        ancestor Jacob had."
The LORD has said these things.

The Evil That People Do

59 Surely the LORD's power is enough to
    save you.
    He can hear you when you ask him for
        help.
²It is your evil that has separated
    you from your God.
Your sins cause him to turn away from you,
    so he does not hear you.
³With your hands you have killed others,
    and with your fingers you have done
        wrong.
With your lips you have lied,
    and with your tongue you say evil things.
⁴People take each other to court unfairly,
    and no one tells the truth in arguing his
        case.
They accuse each other falsely and tell lies.
    They cause trouble and create more evil.
⁵They hatch evil like eggs from poisonous
        snakes.
    If you eat one of those eggs, you will die,
    and if you break one open, a poisonous
        snake comes out.

People tell lies as they would spin a spider's
        web.
⁶ The webs they make cannot be used for
        clothes;
    you can't cover yourself with those webs.
The things they do are evil,
    and they use their hands to hurt others.
⁷They eagerly run to do evil,
    and they are always ready to kill innocent
        people.
They think evil thoughts.
    Everywhere they go they cause ruin and
        destruction.
⁸They don't know how to live in peace,
    and there is no fairness in their lives.
They are dishonest.
    Anyone who lives as they live will never
        have peace.

Israel's Sin Brings Trouble

⁹Fairness has gone far away;
    goodness is nowhere to be found.
We wait for the light, but there is only
        darkness now.
    We hope for a bright light, but all we have
        is darkness.
¹⁰We are like the blind feeling our way along a
        wall.
    We feel our way as if we had no eyes.
In the brightness of day we trip as if it were
        night.
    We are like dead men among the strong.
¹¹All of us growl like the bears.
    We call out sadly like the doves.
We look for justice, but there isn't any.
    We want to be saved, but salvation is far
        away.
¹²We have done many wrong things against
        our God;
    our sins show we are wrong.
We know we have turned against God;
    we know the evil things we have done:
¹³sinning and rejecting the LORD,
    turning away from our God,
planning to hurt others and to disobey God,
    planning and speaking lies.
¹⁴So we have driven away justice,
    and we have kept away from what is right.
Truth is not spoken in the streets;
    what is honest is not allowed to enter the
        city.
¹⁵Truth cannot be found anywhere,
    and people who refuse to do evil are
        attacked.

The LORD looked and could not find any
        justice,
    and he was displeased.

¹⁶He could not find anyone to help the people,
and he was surprised that there was no one
to help.
So he used his own power to save the
people;
his own goodness gave him strength.
¹⁷He covered himself with goodness like armor.
He put the helmet of salvation on his head.
He put on the clothes of punishment
and wrapped himself in the coat of his
strong love.
¹⁸The Lord will pay back his enemies for what
they have done.
He will show his anger to those who were
against him;
he will punish the people in faraway places
as they deserve.
¹⁹Then people from the west will fear the
Lord,
and people from the east will fear his glory.
The Lord will come quickly like a
fast-flowing river,
driven by the breath of the Lord.

²⁰"Then a Savior will come to Jerusalem

and to the people of Jacob who have
turned from sin,"
says the Lord.

²¹The Lord says, "This is my agreement with
these people: My Spirit^d and my words that I give
you will never leave you or your children or your
grandchildren, now and forever."

Jerusalem Will Be Great

60 "Jerusalem, get up and shine, because
your light has come,
and the glory of the Lord shines on you.
²Darkness now covers the earth;
deep darkness covers her people.
But the Lord shines on you,
and people see his glory around you.
³Nations will come to your light;
kings will come to the brightness of your
sunrise.

⁴"Look around you.
People are gathering and coming to you.
Your sons are coming from far away,
and your daughters are coming with them.

SHARING FAITH

How Can I Tell You?

Dona Smith usually ate lunch on a park bench by the White House. She loved her
summer job as a subway attendant: the work, the subway, and the city. Each noon she
wrote about her experiences in a notebook.

"Lord," she wrote one day, "how can I tell Matt about you?" She thought of the
employee she had befriended. With no family, Matt was used to street life and had never
been to church. Dona talked with him everyday. While she knew a lot about him, she had
never said much about herself. She had never said, "I'm a Christian."

"He needs to know," she wrote. "Help me know what to say and the time
to say it."

That afternoon Matt stopped by her desk. He asked, "Why do you smile so
much? You just always seem so happy." Dona's faith had shown before she
said anything. Her opportunity was obvious.

"You've told me about your life," she began. "Let me tell you about mine."
When the conversation was over, Matt agreed to visit Dona's church and
spend a Sunday with her family.

When people reflect God's light, they draw others to God. See in **Isaiah
60:1–6** how God shines on his followers to make them witnesses.
■ How does this passage apply to Dona's situation?
■ How can you reflect the kind of light Isaiah describes?

CONSIDER . . .
■ using a permanent marker to write on a light bulb words that describe how
you might show God's love to others. Place the light in your bedroom.
■ keeping a prayer journal for one month. Write about situations where you could be
God's light.

FOR   MORE,   SEE . . .
■ Isaiah 9:2–7 (p. 626)   ■ Colossians 4:5–6 (p. 1243)
■ Mark 16:15–20 (p. 997)

⁵When you see them, you will shine with
     happiness;
  you will be excited and full of joy,
because the wealth of the nations across the
     seas will be given to you;
  the riches of the nations will come to you.
⁶Herds of camels will cover your land,
  young camels from Midian and Ephah.
People will come from Sheba
  bringing gold and incense,ᵈ
  and they will sing praises to the LORD.

SIDELIGHT: The promise to
Jerusalem that people from Sheba
would come to Jerusalem to worship was
quite an impressive promise (Isaiah 60:6).
Sheba was at least fourteen hundred miles
away—across the desert of present-day Saudi
Arabia. Years earlier, the queen of Sheba had
visited King Solomon and seen all his wealth
(1 Kings 10:1–13, p. 314).

---

⁷All the sheep from Kedar will be given to
     you;
  the sheep from Nebaioth will be brought to
     you.
They will be pleasing sacrifices on my altar,
  and I will make my beautiful Templeᵈ more
     beautiful.

⁸"The people are returning to you like clouds,
  like doves flying to their nests.
⁹People in faraway lands are waiting for me.
  The great trading ships will come first,
bringing your children from faraway lands,
  and with them silver and gold.
This will honor the LORD your God,
  the Holy One of Israel,
  who does wonderful things for you.

¹⁰"Jerusalem, foreigners will rebuild your walls,
  and their kings will serve you.
When I was angry, I hurt you,
  but now I want to be kind to you and
     comfort you.
¹¹Your gates will always be open;
  they will not be closed day or night
so the nations can bring their wealth to you,
  and their kings will be led to you.
¹²The nation or kingdom that doesn't serve you
     will be destroyed;
  it will be completely ruined.

¹³"The great trees of Lebanon will be given to
     you;
  its pine, fir, and cypress trees together.
You will use them to make my Temple
     beautiful,

and I will give much honor to this place
  where I rest my feet.
¹⁴The people who have hurt you will bow
     down to you;
  those who hated you will bow down at
     your feet.
They will call you The City of the LORD,
  Jerusalem, city of the Holy One of Israel.

¹⁵"You have been hated and left empty
  with no one passing through.
But I will make you great from now on;
  you will be a place of happiness forever and
     ever.
¹⁶You will be given what you need from the
     nations,
  like a child drinking milk from its mother.
Then you will know that it is I, the LORD,
  who saves you.
You will know that the Powerful One of
     Jacob protects you.
¹⁷I will bring you gold in place of bronze,
  silver in place of iron,
bronze in place of wood,
  iron in place of rocks.
I will change your punishment into peace,
  and you will be ruled by what is right.
¹⁸There will be no more violence in your
     country;
  it will not be ruined or destroyed.
You will name your walls Salvation
  and your gates Praise.
¹⁹The sun will no longer be your light during
     the day
  nor will the brightness from the moon be
     your light,
because the LORD will be your light forever,
  and your God will be your glory.
²⁰Your sun will never set again,
  and your moon will never be dark,
because the LORD will be your light forever,
  and your time of sadness will end.
²¹All of your people will do what is right.
  They will receive the earth forever.
They are the plant I have planted,
  the work of my own hands
  to show my greatness.
²²The smallest family will grow to a thousand.
  The least important of you will become a
     powerful nation.
I am the LORD,
  and when it is time, I will make these
  things happen quickly."

The Lord's Message of Freedom

61 The Lord GOD has put his Spiritᵈ in
me,
because the LORD has appointed me to tell
  the good news to the poor.

He has sent me to comfort those whose
hearts are broken,
to tell the captives they are free,
and to tell the prisoners they are released.
²He has sent me to announce the time when
the LORD will show his kindness
and the time when our God will punish
evil people.
He has sent me to comfort all those who are
sad
³ and to help the sorrowing people of
Jerusalem.
I will give them a crown to replace their
ashes,
and the oil of gladness to replace their
sorrow,
and clothes of praise to replace their spirit
of sadness.
Then they will be called Trees of Goodness,

trees planted by the LORD to show his
greatness.
⁴They will rebuild the old ruins
and restore the places destroyed long ago.
They will repair the ruined cities
that were destroyed for so long.
⁵My people, foreigners will come to tend your
sheep.
People from other countries will tend your
fields and vineyards.
⁶You will be called priests of the LORD;
you will be named the servants of our
God.
You will have riches from all the nations on
earth,
and you will take pride in them.
⁷Instead of being ashamed, my people will
receive twice as much wealth.

Chasing the Blues Away

Are you ever sad or depressed? You're not alone:
■ Twenty percent of all American teenagers report feeling emotionally empty, while
another 20 percent feel confused most of the time.
■ Sixty-one percent of teenagers feel extremely sad or depressed at least ten times during
their teenage years.
■ More than 50 percent of kids "worry a lot" about getting a bad report card, being in a
plane crash, being in a car accident, or experiencing the death of a parent.
■ More than 30 percent of high school students have experienced moderate or severe
levels of symptoms of depression.
How do people get rid of the blues once they have them? Here are the top seven
coping techniques most teenagers use:
1. listening to music
2. thinking of a solution by yourself
3. daydreaming
4. watching television
5. swearing
6. going shopping
7. going to a video arcade

There are lots of ways—both good and bad—to ease the weight of
depression, but their benefits are almost always short-lived. God offers a way
to get rid of the blues. Hear of the hope offered to depressed people in
Isaiah 61:1–11.
■ What's the difference between the way people try to escape their trouble
and the way God suggests in this passage?
■ How can these words of Isaiah help you when you feel depressed?

CONSIDER . . .

■ listing all the things that make you sad and then thanking God that he can
turn sadness into joy.
■ making a new list of coping techniques based on the Bible passage and then doing
one of them this week.

FOR MORE, SEE . . .

■ Psalm 42 (p. 507)
■ Romans 8:18–28 (p. 1151)
■ 2 Corinthians 4:7–18 (p. 1210)

Instead of being disgraced, they will be
    happy because of what they receive.
They will receive a double share of the land,
    so their happiness will continue forever.
8"I, the LORD, love justice.
    I hate stealing and everything that is
        wrong.
I will be fair and give my people what they
    should have,
    and I will make an agreement with them
        that will continue forever.
9Everyone in all nations will know the
    children of my people,
    and their children will be known among
        the nations.
Anyone who sees them will know
    that they are people the LORD has blessed."

10The LORD makes me very happy;
    all that I am rejoices in my God.
He has covered me with clothes of salvation
    and wrapped me with a coat of goodness,
    like a bridegroom dressed for his wedding,

like a bride dressed in jewels.
11The earth causes plants to grow,
    and a garden causes the seeds planted in it
        to grow.
In the same way the Lord GOD will make
    goodness and praise
    come from all the nations.

New Jerusalem

62 Because I love Jerusalem, I will
    continue to speak for her;
for Jerusalem's sake I will not stop speaking
until her goodness shines like a bright light,
    until her salvation burns bright like a flame.
2Jerusalem, the nations will see your goodness,
    and all kings will see your glory.
Then you will have a new name,
    which the LORD himself will give you.
3You will be like a beautiful crown in the
    LORD's hand,
    like a king's crown in your God's hand.
4You will never again be called the People
    that God Left,

PATIENCE

He's Still at Work

Barbara Davis heard crying, but didn't see anyone. Finally, she spotted Maggie Howard leaning against the back wall of the chapel, feet under the last pew.

"I'm tired of my life," Maggie cried. "I'm tired of nothing working out. I'll never find anyone to be with. I'll never be the person everyone at church expects me to be." For the moment, she only saw the things she wasn't.

Barbara saw her friend differently. She remembered what Maggie was like a year before, when she first came to the youth group. She was only interested in getting rowdy and causing trouble. Barbara could see that this life, given to God, was growing. Maggie read the Bible now, and really tried to absorb what was said at youth meetings. Barbara sat next to Maggie and held her close. They cried together a few minutes and then Barbara spoke. "Be patient," she said, "and keep praying. Good things are happening."

Growing spiritually takes time. Find encouragement to keep working at it in **Isaiah 62:1–12**.

■ How is Barbara's advice to Maggie similar to Isaiah's words to God's people?
■ According to these verses, why do you need both prayer and patience in your Christian life?

                    C O N S I D E R . . .
■ writing a description of the person you hope to be five years from now. Include qualities you want to have. Keep this in your Bible and pray that God will help you grow.
■ designing a step-by-step "Patience Program" to use during times when you're impatient. Include scriptures on patience (such as 1 Thessalonians 5:12–14, p. 1249 and James 5:7–8, p. 1299), the benefits of waiting, and a list of things to pray about and do in the meantime.

            F O R   M O R E ,   S E E . . .
■ Psalm 37:3–9 (p. 503)
■ Luke 18:1–8 (p. 1041)
                            ■ Romans 5:3–5 (p. 1145)

nor your land the Land that God
    Destroyed.
You will be called the People God Loves,
    and your land will be called the Bride of
    God,
because the LORD loves you.
    And your land will belong to him as a bride
    belongs to her husband.
5As a young man marries a woman,
    so your children will marry your land.
As a man rejoices over his new wife,
    so your God will rejoice over you.

6Jerusalem, I have put guards on the walls to
    watch.
    They must not be silent day or night.
You people who remind the LORD of your
    needs in prayer
should never be quiet.
7You should not stop praying to him until he
    builds up Jerusalem
    and makes it a city all people will praise.

8The LORD has made a promise,
    and by his power he will keep his promise.
He said, "I will never again give your grain
    as food to your enemies.
I will not let your enemies drink the new
    wine
    that you have worked to make.
9The person who gathers food will eat it,
    and he will praise the LORD.
The person who gathers the grapes will drink
    the wine
    in the courts of my Temple."d

10Go through, go through the gates!
    Make the way ready for the people.
Build up, build up the road!
    Move all the stones off the road.
Raise the banner as a sign for the people.

11The LORD is speaking
    to all the faraway lands:
"Tell the people of Jerusalem,
    'Look, your Savior is coming.
He is bringing your reward to you;
    he is bringing his payment with him.' "
12His people will be called the Holy People,
    the Saved People of the LORD,
and Jerusalem will be called the City God
    Wants,
    the City God Has Not Rejected.

The Lord Judges His People

63 Who is this coming from Edom,
    from the city of Bozrah, dressed in
    red?
Who is this dressed in fine clothes
    and marching forward with his great
    power?

He says, "I, the LORD, speak what is right.
    I have the power to save you."

2Someone asks, "Why are your clothes bright
    red
    as if you had walked on the grapes to make
    wine?"

3The LORD answers, "I have walked in the
    winepressd alone,
    and no one among the nations helped me.
I was angry and walked on the nations
    and crushed them because of my anger.
Blood splashed on my clothes,
    and I stained all my clothing.
4I chose a time to punish people,
    and the time has come for me to save.
5I looked around, but I saw no one to help
    me.
    I was surprised that no one supported me.
So I used my own power to save my people;
    my own anger supported me.
5While I was angry, I walked on the nations.
    In my anger I punished them
    and poured their blood on the ground."

The Lord's Kindness to His People

7I will tell about the LORD's kindness
    and praise him for everything he has done.
I will praise the LORD for the many good
    things he has given us
    and for his goodness to the people of Israel.
He has shown great mercy to us
    and has been very kind to us.
3He said, "These are my people;
    my children will not lie to me."
    So he saved them.
9When they suffered, he suffered also.
    He sent his own angel to save them.
Because of his love and kindness, he saved
    them.
    Since long ago he has picked them up and
    carried them.
10But they turned against him
    and made his Holy Spiritd very sad.
So he became their enemy,
    and he fought against them.

11But then his people remembered what
    happened long ago,
    in the days of Moses and the Israelites with
    him.
Where is the LORD who brought the people
    through the sea,
    with the leaders of his people?
Where is the one
    who put his Holy Spirit among them,
12who led Moses by the right hand
    with his wonderful power,
who divided the water before them

to make his name famous forever,
13who led the people through the deep waters?
Like a horse walking through a desert,
the people did not stumble.
14Like cattle that go down to the valley,
the Spirit of the LORD gave the people a
place to rest.
LORD, that is the way you led your people,
and by this you won for yourself wonderful
fame.

A Prayer for Help

15LORD, look down from the heavens and see;
look at us from your wonderful and holy
home in heaven.
Where is your strong love and power?
Why are you keeping your love and mercy
from us?
16You are our father.
Abraham doesn't know we are his children,
and Israel doesn't recognize us.
LORD, you are our father.
You are called "the one who has always
saved us."

17LORD, why are you making us wander from
your ways?
Why do you make us stubborn so that we
don't honor you?
For our sake come back to us,
your servants, who belong to you.
18Your people had your Temple*d* for a while,
but now our enemies have walked on your
holy place and crushed it.
19We have become like people you never ruled
over,
like those who have never worn your
name.

64 Tear open the skies and come down
to earth
so that the mountains will tremble before
you.
2Like a fire that burns twigs,
like a fire that makes water boil,
let your enemies know who you are.
Then all nations will shake with fear when
they see you.
3You have done amazing things we did not
expect.

SUFFERING

In Sickness and in Health

The dresses, tuxes, and flowers were beautiful. On this fine day, Marshall Younger and Stephanie Eubank promised their love to each other for life. Guests released helium balloons when the couple left the church. It was a gorgeous wedding.

But just hours after the decorations were gone, the groom came down with the flu. In the middle of the night Stephanie went to find medication for Marshall. She stayed up all night caring for him.

When Marshall felt better, they watched a video of their wedding. They heard the words "in sickness and in health" and started laughing.

"I didn't realize how soon I'd be tested on that promise," said Stephanie. "Maybe what happened to us is a better picture of a good marriage than any wedding picture—feeling what the other one feels, taking care of each other no matter what."

Just as Stephanie shared in Marshall's sickness, God is so close to his people that he hurts when they hurt. Read about how he cares in **Isaiah 63:7–9**.

■ Why do you think God chooses to hurt when his people hurt?
■ According to the passage, what are ways you can know God cares for you when you're hurting?

CONSIDER . . .

■ designing a "first-aid" plan to help hurting people. List things you could give to care for people in pain, such as visits, prayers, cards and food.
■ filling a one-month calendar with names of people, groups and countries that experience suffering. For example, the homeless, Ethiopia or a cerebral palsy victim you know. Write a different name, group or country on each day of the month, and use this as a prayer calendar.

FOR MORE, SEE . . .

■ Psalm 103:1–14 (p. 540)
■ John 11:28–44 (p. 1077)
■ Hebrews 13:1–3 (p. 1290)

You came down, and the mountains
  trembled before you.
⁴From long ago no one has ever heard of a
    God like you.
  No one has ever seen a God besides you,
  who helps the people who trust you.
⁵You help those who enjoy doing good,
  who remember how you want them to live.
 But you were angry because we sinned.
  For a long time we disobeyed,
  so how can we be saved?
⁶All of us are dirty with sin.
  All the right things we have done are like
    filthy pieces of cloth.
 All of us are like dead leaves,
  and our sins, like the wind, have carried us
    away.
⁷No one worships you
  or even asks you to help us.
 That is because you have turned away
    from us
  and have let our sins destroy us.

⁸But Lord, you are our father.
  We are like clay, and you are the potter;
  your hands made us all.
⁹Lord, don't continue to be angry with us;

don't remember our sins forever.
 Please, look at us,
  because we are your people.
¹⁰Your holy cities are empty like the desert.
  Jerusalem is like a desert;
  it is destroyed.
¹¹ Our ancestors worshiped you
    in our holy and wonderful Temple,
  but now it has been burned with fire,
    and all our precious things have been
      destroyed.
¹²When you see these things, will you hold
      yourself back from helping us, Lord?
  Will you be silent and punish us beyond
    what we can stand?

All People Will Learn About God

65 The Lord says, "I made myself known
  to people who were not looking for
  me.
 I was found by those who were not asking
    me for help.
 I said, 'Here I am. Here I am,'
  to a nation that was not praying to me.
²All day long I stood ready to accept
  people who turned against me,

FOLLOWING GOD

Where Am I?

Stay calm. Don't worry—yet, Tessa Gore said to herself as she walked. After half an hour on the Ridgecrest Mountain she knew she was lost. Why did I come alone? She remembered how she'd wanted time to think, away from the noise of her group's cabin.

Don't panic, she thought, biting her lip. She had never felt lost before. She kept watching for landmarks and listening for sounds that seemed familiar. After wandering for almost an hour, she sat on a log and began to cry.

"Lord, help me out of here," she prayed.

In the distance she heard faint laughter and conversation. She wasn't completely alone! She followed the sounds until she found other campers—and the way home.

"Next time I go for a walk," she told her friends later, "I'll take a guide or a map—or both!"

The scripture describes how lost we feel when we're not following God. Hear what life is like without God in **Isaiah 63:16—64:8**.

■ How is being physically lost similar to wandering away from God, like the Israelites in the passage?

■ When have you wandered from God as the Israelites did?

CONSIDER . . .

■ creating a timeline of your life that highlights times you followed God and times you felt lost. Then ask God to help you follow him more.

■ packing a survival kit to use as you follow God. Include a list of people you could call when you run into trouble, a Bible, a Christian songbook, a journal, and a pen.

FOR MORE, SEE . . .

■ Psalm 25 (p. 496)
■ Jeremiah 18:1–10 (p. 711)

■ John 14:1–14 (p. 1083)

but the way they continue to live is not
  good;
they do anything they want to do.
³Right in front of me
  they continue to do things that make me
    angry.
  They offer sacrifices to their gods in their
    gardens,
  and they burn incense*d* on altars of brick.
⁴They sit among the graves
  and spend their nights waiting to get
    messages from the dead.
  They eat the meat of pigs,
  and their pots are full of soup made from
    meat that is wrong to eat.
⁵But they tell others, 'Stay away, and don't
    come near me.
  I am too holy for you.'
These people are like smoke in my nose.
  Like a fire that burns all the time, they
    continue to make me angry.

⁶"Look, it is written here before me.
  I will not be quiet; instead, I will repay you
    in full.
  I will punish you for what you have done.
⁷I will punish you for your sins and your
    ancestors' sins,"
  says the LORD.
  "They burned incense to gods on the
    mountains
  and shamed me on those hills.
  So I will punish them as they should be
    punished
  for what they did."

⁸This is what the LORD says:
  "When there is juice left in the grapes,
    people do not destroy them,
  because they know there is good left in
    them.
  So I will do the same thing to my servants—
    I will not completely destroy them.
⁹I will leave some of the children of Jacob,
    and some of the people of Judah will
      receive my mountain.
  I will choose the people who will live there;
    my servants will live there.
¹⁰Then the Plain of Sharon will be a field for
    flocks,
  and the Valley of Achor will be a place for
    herds to rest.
  They will be for the people who want to
    follow me.

¹¹"But as for you who left the LORD,
  who forgot about my holy mountain,
who worship the god Luck,
  who hold religious feasts for the god Fate,

¹²I decide your fate, and I will punish you with
    my sword.
  You will all be killed,
  because I called you, but you refused to
    answer.
  I spoke to you, but you wouldn't listen.
  You did the things I said were evil
    and chose to do things that displease me."

¹³So this is what the Lord GOD says:
  "My servants will eat,
    but you evil people will be hungry.
  My servants will drink,
    but you evil people will be thirsty.
  My servants will be happy,
    but you evil people will be shamed.
¹⁴My servants will shout for joy
    because of the goodness of their hearts,
  but you evil people will cry,
    because you will be sad.
  You will cry loudly, because your spirits
    will be broken.
¹⁵Your names will be like curses to my
    servants,
  and the Lord GOD will put you to death.
  But he will call his servants by another
    name.
¹⁶People in the land who ask for blessings
    will ask for them from the faithful God.
  And people in the land who make a promise
    will promise in the name of the faithful
      God,
  because the troubles of the past will be
    forgotten.
  I will make those troubles go away.

A New Time Is Coming

¹⁷"Look, I will make new heavens and a new
    earth,
  and people will not remember the past
    or think about those things.
¹⁸My people will be happy forever
    because of the things I will make.
  I will make a Jerusalem that is full of joy,
    and I will make her people a delight.
¹⁹Then I will rejoice over Jerusalem
    and be delighted with my people.
  There will never again be heard in that city
    the sounds of crying and sadness.
²⁰There will never be a baby from that city
    who lives only a few days.
And there will never be an older person
  who doesn't have a long life.
A person who lives a hundred years will be
    called young,
  and a person who dies before he is a
    hundred will be thought of as a sinner.

21In that city those who build houses will live
there.

Those who plant vineyards will get to eat
their grapes.

22No more will one person build a house and
someone else live there.

One person will not plant a garden and
someone else eat its fruit.

My people will live a long time,
as trees live long.

My chosen people will live there
and enjoy the things they make.

23They will never again work for nothing.

They will never again give birth to children
who die young.

All my people will be blessed by the Lord;
they and their children will be blessed.

24I will provide for their needs before they ask,
and I will help them while they are still
asking for help.

25Wolves and lambs will eat together in peace.

Lions will eat hay like oxen,
and a snake on the ground will not hurt
anyone.

They will not hurt or destroy each other
on all my holy mountain,"

says the Lord.

The Lord Will Judge All Nations

66 This is what the Lord says:
"Heaven is my throne,
and the earth is my footstool.

So do you think you can build a house for me?
Do I need a place to rest?

2My hand made all things.

All things are here because I made them,"
says the Lord.

"These are the people I am pleased with:
those who are not proud or stubborn
and who fear my word.

3But those people who kill bulls as a sacrifice
to me
are like those who kill people.

Those who kill sheep as a sacrifice
are like those who break the necks of dogs.

Those who give me grain offerings
are like those who offer me the blood of
pigs.[n]

Those who burn incense[d]
are like those who worship idols.

These people choose their own ways, not
mine,
and they love the terrible things they do.

4So I will choose their punishments,
and I will punish them with what they fear
most.

This is because I called to them, but they did
not listen.

I spoke to them, but they did not hear me.

They did things I said were evil;
they chose to do things I did not like."

5You people who obey the words of the Lord,
listen to what he says:
"Your brothers hated you
and turned against you because you
followed me.

Your brothers said, 'Let the Lord be honored
so we may see you rejoice,'
but they will be punished.

6Listen to the loud noise coming from the
city;
hear the noise from the Temple.[d]

It is the Lord punishing his enemies,
giving them the punishment they should
have.

7"A woman does not give birth before she
feels the pain;
she does not give birth to a son before the
pain starts.

8No one has ever heard of that happening;
no one has ever seen that happen.

In the same way no one ever saw a country
begin in one day;
no one has ever heard of a new nation
beginning in one moment.

But Jerusalem will give birth to her children
just as soon as she feels the birth pains.

9In the same way I will not cause pain
without allowing something new to be
born," says the Lord.

"If I cause you the pain,
I will not stop you from giving birth to
your new nation," says your God.

10'Jerusalem, rejoice.

All you people who love Jerusalem, be
happy.

Those of you who felt sad for Jerusalem
should now feel happy with her.

11You will take comfort from her and be
satisfied,
as a child is nursed by its mother.

You will receive her good things
and enjoy her wealth."

12This is what the Lord says:

"I will give her peace that will flow to her
like a river.

The wealth of the nations will come to her
like a river overflowing its banks.

Like babies you will be nursed and held in
my arms
and bounced on my knees.

---

dogs . . . pigs God did not want his people to offer dogs and pigs as sacrifices because they were unclean animals.

[13]I will comfort you
    as a mother comforts her child.
    You will be comforted in Jerusalem."

[14]When you see these things, you will be
    happy,
    and you will grow like the grass.
The LORD's servants will see his power,
    but his enemies will see his anger.
[15]Look, the LORD is coming with fire
    and his armies with clouds of dust.
He will punish those people with his anger;
    he will punish them with flames of fire.
[16]The LORD will judge the people with fire,
    and he will destroy many people with his
      sword;
    he will kill many people.

[17]"These people make themselves holy and pure to go to worship their gods in their gardens. Following each other into their special gardens, they eat the meat of pigs and rats and other hateful things. But they will all be destroyed together," says the LORD. [18]"I know they have evil thoughts and do evil

things, so I am coming to punish them. I will gather all nations and all people, and they will come together and see my glory.

> **SIDELIGHT:** Isaiah is the "Bible-in-miniature." It has sixty-six chapters—as compared to sixty-six biblical books. Both Isaiah and the Bible end with "new heavens and the new earth" (Isaiah 66:22 and Revelation 21:1, p. 1347).

[19]"I will put a mark on some of the people, and I will send some of these saved people to the nations: to Tarshish, Libya, Lud (the land of archers), Tubal, Greece, and all the faraway lands. These people have never heard about what I have done nor seen my glory. So the saved people will tell the nations about my glory. [20]And they will bring all your fellow Israelites from all nations to my holy mountain in Jerusalem. Your fellow Israelites will come on horses, donkeys, and camels and in chariots and wagons. They will be like the

GOD'S LOVE

You'll Always Be My Baby

She was usually on the phone. "Come by and pick up diapers," she would say. Or, "I'll meet you at the emergency room in ten minutes." Stacks of baby clothes and cribs lined the walls of her office.

Susan Brown directed the Infant Resource Center in Louisville, Kentucky. Located near a cluster of hospitals, the center ministered to "rock-bottom poor" mothers, often in their teens. Many times the women had nothing to put their babies in when they came home from the hospital, and often they used dresser drawers for cribs. Sometimes poor prenatal care meant the babies needed emergency treatment after birth.

Susan loved the teenagers and their babies as a good mother would. She gave them basic supplies and information. She spent hours in doctors' offices and hospitals, holding the hands of scared mothers. As she cared for these women, she told them about God's love.

A new mother needs more than baby clothes and supplies. She needs the strength that comes from Christ. Susan Brown made a difference by offering young mothers that kind of strength.

God loves his people as a mother loves her children. **Isaiah 66:10–14** describes God's love and care for us.

■ How did Susan demonstrate the love this passage describes?
■ In what ways does God comfort and care for you?

C O N S I D E R . . . .

■ writing a thank-you note to someone who has shown you the kind of love this passage describes.
◀ writing a description of the "perfect" parent and then thanking God for being a perfect parent to you.

F O R   M O R E ,   S E E . . . .
■ Deuteronomy 32:9–12 (p. 189)
■ Hosea 11:1–4 (p. 831)
    ■ 1 John 4:7–10 (p. 1319)

grain offerings that the people bring in clean containers to the Temple," says the LORD. 21"And I will choose even some of these people to be priests and Levites," says the LORD.

22"I will make new heavens and the new earth, which will last forever," says the LORD. "In the same way, your names and your children will always be with me. 23All people will come to worship me every Sabbath[d] and every New Moon,"[d] says the LORD. 24"They will go out and see the dead bodies of the people who sinned against me. The worms that eat them will never die, and the fires that burn them will never stop, and everyone will hate to see those bodies."

JEREMIAH

Why Read This Book:

- Learn responsibilities that come with belonging to God (Jeremiah 1—25).
- See God's continuing love for people even when they have sinned (Jeremiah 26—36).
- Find hope even in times of suffering (Jeremiah 37—45).

Behind the Scenes:

The nation of Judah was like a child caught in the crossfire between warring inner-city gangs. Like gangs fighting over turf, three world powers were fighting for control of the area we call the Near East. The Assyrians had been in control for quite a while, but the Egyptians and Babylonians would each take power within Jeremiah's lifetime. And Judah was caught in the middle.

But Judah was not like an innocent victim. Judah had stopped following God and was forming partnerships with pagan nations to try to protect itself. The people needed a word from God, and Jeremiah became the one whom God would use to proclaim that word—a word that Judah did not want to hear.

Jeremiah warned the people of Judah that they needed to obey God and rely

WHERE THE ACTION WAS

Babylon became the dominant power in the region when it captured the Assyrian capital of Nineveh.

Most of the people of Jerusalem were taken into exile in Babylon when Jerusalem was captured by the Babylonians (Jeremiah 52:1–30).

Nineveh

Euphrates

Tigris

Mediterranean Sea

Jeremiah spent most of his life and ministry in Jerusalem.

Jerusalem

BABYLON

The border of the Babylonian Empire in Jeremiah's time.

Jeremiah was taken into exile in Egypt, where he died (Jeremiah 43:4–7).

EGYPT

Persian Gulf

Red Sea

ARABIAN DESERT

WHEN THE ACTION WAS

	The Northern Kingdom (Israel) fell to Assyria	Jeremiah began his ministry	The Jews began returning from exile		Jesus was born
1000BC	**750BC**		**500BC**	**250BC**	**BC/AD**
The kingdom was split between Israel and Judah	King Josiah began reforms in Judah	Jerusalem was destroyed by the Babylonians			

Behind the
Scenes (cont.): on him. He condemned the false prophets and emphasized the need to repent and seek a personal relationship with God.

Jeremiah's tough message wasn't easy to accept—for Jeremiah or for the people of Judah. At first, Jeremiah was reluctant even to take the job (Jeremiah 1:6). He was abused, ridiculed, exiled to Egypt, and, in the end, possibly killed for what he said. The pain he faced and the pain he saw his people experiencing saddened him.

His book—which was dictated to his secretary Baruch (Jeremiah 36:4)—is sometimes difficult to follow. The poems (or oracles) aren't arranged in logical order. Events jump back and forth in history. To get a better feel for the historical events surrounding the book, read either 2 Kings 23—24 (p. 355) or 2 Chronicles 34—36 (p. 412).

Through poems, stories, and object lessons, the book of Jeremiah shows the personal struggles, depression, and anger Jeremiah experienced during his career. But through it all, Jeremiah continued doing the tough job he had been given. And even when he felt like giving up, he remembered that God would stand by him and comfort him.

Jeremiah was faithful to God's call—even when it was unpopular. And he was honest with God and faithful to God, even in the midst of his doubts, frustrations, and anger. His life can be a valuable model for us today.

---

1 These are the words of Jeremiah son of Hilkiah. He belonged to the family of priests who lived in the town of Anathoth in the land of Benjamin. ²The LORD spoke his word to Jeremiah during the thirteenth year that Josiah son of Amon was king of Judah. ³The LORD also spoke to Jeremiah while Jehoiakim son of Josiah was king of Judah and during the eleven years that Zedekiah son of Josiah was king of Judah. In the fifth month of his last year, the people of Jerusalem were taken away as captives.

The Lord Calls Jeremiah

⁴The LORD spoke his word to me, saying:
⁵"Before I made you in your mother's womb,
   I chose you.
Before you were born, I set you apart for a
   special work.
I appointed you as a prophet*d* to the
   nations."

⁶Then I said, "But Lord GOD, I don't know how to speak. I am only a boy."

SIDELIGHT: Jeremiah was probably about twenty years old when he began his ministry (Jeremiah 1:6). Josiah was only eight when he became king—and sixteen when he began to follow God. Youth power!

---

⁷But the LORD said to me, "Don't say, 'I am only a boy.' You must go everywhere I send you, and you must say everything I tell you to say.

⁸Don't be afraid of anyone, because I am with you to protect you," says the LORD.

⁹Then the LORD reached out his hand and touched my mouth. He said to me, "See, I am putting my words in your mouth. ¹⁰Today I have put you in charge of nations and kingdoms. You will pull up and tear down, destroy and overthrow, build up and plant."

Jeremiah Sees Two Visions

¹¹The LORD spoke his word to me, saying: "Jeremiah, what do you see?"

I answered, "I see a stick of almond wood."

¹²The LORD said to me, "You have seen correctly, because I am watching to make sure my words come true."

¹³The LORD spoke his word to me again: "What do you see?"

I answered, "I see a pot of boiling water, tipping over from the north."

¹⁴The LORD said to me, "Disaster will come from the north and strike all the people who live in this country. ¹⁵In a short time I will call all of the people in the northern kingdoms," said the LORD.

"Those kings will come and set up their
      thrones
   near the entrance of the gates of Jerusalem.
They will attack all the city walls around
      Jerusalem
   and all the cities in Judah.
¹⁶And I will announce my judgments against
      my people
   because of their evil in turning away from
      me.
They offered sacrifices to other gods

and worshiped idols they had made with their own hands.

¹⁷"Jeremiah, get ready. Stand up and tell them everything I command you to say. Don't be afraid of the people, or I will give you good reason to be afraid of them. ¹⁸Today I am going to make you a strong city, an iron pillar, a bronze wall. You will be able to stand against everyone in the land: Judah's kings, officers, priests, and the people of the land. ¹⁹They will fight against you, but they will not defeat you, because I am with you to protect you!" says the LORD.

Israel Turns from God

2 The LORD spoke his word to me, saying: ²"Go and speak to the people of Jerusalem, saying: This is what the LORD says:
'I remember how faithful you were to me
    when you were a young nation.
You loved me like a young bride.
You followed me through the desert,

a land that had never been planted.
³The people of Israel were holy to the LORD,
    like the first fruits from his harvest.
Those who tried to hurt Israel were judged
    guilty.
Disasters struck them,' " says the LORD.

⁴Hear the word of the LORD, family of Jacob,
    all you family groups of Israel.
⁵This is what the LORD says:
"I was fair to your ancestors,
    so why did they turn away from me?
Your ancestors worshiped useless idols
    and became useless themselves.
⁶Your ancestors didn't say,
    'Where is the LORD who brought us out of
    Egypt?
He led us through the desert,
    through a dry and rocky land,
through a dark and dangerous land.
    He led us where no one travels or lives.'
⁷I brought you into a fertile land

SELF-ESTEEM

The New Kid in the Group

As the newest member of the theater group, Adam Sanchez felt a little intimidated. There were good actors in the group. Plus, Adam was afraid that friendships—and cliques—had already formed and that he would be an outsider.

On top of that, people in theater learn to be very honest with their feelings, even blunt. Adam feared someone would criticize him and tell him he was a lousy actor. What if he didn't measure up?

But Adam's fears evaporated as he got involved. The group figured out pretty quickly that Adam was a good actor. People accepted him at first because of his talent, and later they accepted him as a good friend too.

Adam was a little shy about sharing his friendship with God with his newfound friends. Before long, however, he found himself in deep conversations about faith with people who hadn't really given God much thought. He invited them to church, and some went.

Although he started as an intimidated newcomer, with God's help Adam discovered his own value to the group and to God. As a result, he grew as a respected leader and a faithful witness.

Jeremiah was a young man when God first called him. Read how God responded to Jeremiah's fears and lack of self-esteem, in **Jeremiah 1:4–10**.

■ Why were both Adam and Jeremiah at first fearful of what they had to do?

■ When you sense that God wants you to do something, how do your feelings and thoughts compare to young Jeremiah's?

CONSIDER...

■ writing verses 6–8 on a piece of paper and carrying it with you for times you need a confidence boost.

◢ giving three friends a self-esteem boost this week by telling them each a reason you like or respect them.

FOR MORE, SEE...
■ Isaiah 6:1–8 (p. 622)
■ Galatians 1:1–20 (p. 1206)
■ 1 Timothy 4:12–16 (p. 1259)

so you could eat its fruit and produce.
But you came and made my land unclean;[d]
you made it a hateful place.
[8]The priests didn't ask,
'Where is the LORD?'
The people who know the teachings didn't
know me.
The leaders turned against me.
The prophets[d] prophesied in the name of
Baal[d]
and worshiped useless idols.

[9]"So now I will again tell what I have against
you," says the LORD.
"And I will tell what I have against your
grandchildren.
[10]Go across the sea to the island of Cyprus and
see.
Send someone to the land of Kedar to look
closely.
See if there has ever been anything like
this.
[11]Has a nation ever exchanged its gods?
(Of course, its gods are not really gods at
all.)
But my people have exchanged their glorious
God
for idols worth nothing.
[12]Skies, be shocked at the things that have
happened
and shake with great fear!" says the LORD.
[13]"My people have done two evils:
They have turned away from me,
the spring of living water.
And they have dug their own wells,
which are broken wells that cannot hold
water.
[14]Have the people of Israel become slaves?
Have they become like someone who was
born a slave?
Why were they taken captive?
[15]Enemies have roared like lions at Israel;
they have growled at Israel.
They have destroyed the land of Israel.
The cities of Israel lie in ruins,
and all the people have left.
[16]The men from the cities of Memphis and
Tahpanhes
have disgraced you by shaving the top of
your head.
[17]Haven't you brought this on yourselves
by turning away from the LORD your God
when he was leading you in the right
way?
[18]It did not help to go to Egypt
and drink from the Shihor River.
It did not help to go to Assyria
and drink from the Euphrates River.
[19]Your evil will bring punishment to you,

and the wrong you have done will teach
you a lesson.
Think about it and understand
that it is a terrible evil to turn away from the
LORD your God.
It is wrong not to fear me,"
says the Lord GOD All-Powerful.

[20]"Long ago you refused to obey me as an ox
breaks its yoke.[d]
You broke the ropes I used to hold you
and said, 'I will not serve you!'
In fact, on every high hill
and under every green tree
you lay down as a prostitute.[d]
[21]But I planted you as a special vine,
as a very good seed.
How then did you turn
into a wild vine that grows bad fruit?
[22]Although you wash yourself with cleanser
and use much soap,
I can still see the stain of your guilt," says
the Lord GOD.
[23]"How can you say to me, 'I am not guilty.
I have not worshiped the Baal[d] idols'?
Look at the things you did in the valley.
Think about what you have done.
You are like a she-camel in mating season
that runs from place to place.
[24]You are like a wild donkey that lives in the
desert
and sniffs the wind at mating time.
At that time who can hold her back?
Any male who chases her will easily catch
her;
at mating time, it is easy to find her.
[25]Don't run until your feet are bare
or until your throat is dry.
But you say, 'It's no use!
I love those other gods,
and I must chase them!'

[26]"A thief is ashamed when someone catches
him stealing.
In the same way, the family of Israel is
ashamed —
they, their kings, their officers,
their priests, and their prophets.
[27]They say to things of wood, 'You are my
father,'
and to idols of stone, 'You gave birth to
me.'
Those people won't look at me;
they have turned their backs to me.
But when they get into trouble, they say,
'Come and save us!'
[28]Where are the idols you made for yourselves?
Let them come and save you
when you are in trouble!
People of Judah, you have as many idols

as you have towns!

29"Why do you complain to me?
All of you have turned against me," says
the LORD.
30"I punished your people, but it did not help.
They didn't come back when they were
punished.
With your swords you killed your prophets
like a hungry lion.

31"People of Judah, pay attention to the word
of the LORD:
Have I been like a desert to the people of
Israel
or like a dark and dangerous land?
Why do my people say, 'We are free to
wander.
We won't come to you anymore'?
32A young woman does not forget her jewelry,
and a bride does not forget the decorations
for her dress.
But my people have forgotten me
for more days than can be counted.
33You really know how to chase after love.
Even the worst women can learn evil ways
from you.
34Even on your clothes you have the blood
of poor and innocent people,
but they weren't thieves you caught
breaking in.
You do all these things,
35 but you say, 'I am innocent.
God is not angry with me.'
But I will judge you guilty of lying,
because you say, 'I have not sinned.'
36It is so easy for you to change your mind.
Even Egypt will let you down,
as Assyria let you down.
37You will eventually leave that place
with your hands on your head, like
captives.
You trusted those countries,
but you will not be helped by them,
because the LORD has rejected them.

Judah Is Unfaithful

3 "If a man divorces his wife
and she leaves him and marries another
man,
should her first husband come back to her
again?
If he went back to her, wouldn't the land
become completely unclean?d
But you have acted like a prostituted with
many lovers,
and now you want to come back to me?"
says the LORD.
2"Look up to the bare hilltops, Judah.

Is there any place where you have not been
a prostitute?
You have sat by the road waiting for lovers,
like an Arab in the desert.
You made the land unclean,
because you did evil and were like a
prostitute.
3So the rain has not come,
and there have not been any spring rains.
But your face still looks like the face of a
prostitute.
You refuse even to be ashamed of what you
did.

SIDELIGHT: If you're planning a
barbecue in the Middle East, most of
the year you don't have to worry about
getting rained out. Almost all the rain falls
during spring (May) and fall (October). Since
crops depended on this rain, good rains were
considered a sign of God's blessing, and a
lack of rain was considered a curse (Jeremiah
3:3).

4Now you are calling to me,
'My father, you have been my friend since
I was young.
5Will you always be angry at me?
Will your anger last forever?'
Judah, you said this,
but you did as much evil as you could!"

Judah and Israel Are like Sisters

6When King Josiah was ruling Judah, the LORD
said to me, "Did you see what unfaithful Israel
did? She was like a prostituted with her idols on
every hill and under every green tree. 7I said to
myself, 'Israel will come back to me after she does
this evil,' but she didn't come back. And Israel's
wicked sister Judah saw what she did. 8Judah saw
that I divorced unfaithful Israel because of her
adultery,d but that didn't make Israel's wicked sister Judah afraid. She also went out and acted like
a prostitute! 9And she didn't care that she was
acting like a prostitute. So she made her country
uncleand and was guilty of adultery, because she
worshiped idols made of stone and wood. 10Is-
rael's wicked sister didn't even come back to me
with her whole heart, but only pretended," says
the LORD.

11The LORD said to me, "Unfaithful Israel had
a better excuse than wicked Judah. 12Go and
speak this message toward the north:
'Come back, unfaithful people of Israel,' says
the LORD.
'I will stop being angry at you,

because I am full of mercy,' says the Lord.
'I will not be angry with you forever.
¹³All you have to do is admit your sin —
that you turned against the Lord your God
and worshiped gods under every green tree
and didn't obey me,' " says the Lord.

¹⁴"Come back to me, you unfaithful children,"
says the Lord, "because I am your master. I will
take one person from every city and two from every
family group, and I will bring you to Jerusalem. ¹⁵Then I will give you new rulers who will
be faithful to me, who will lead you with knowledge and understanding. ¹⁶In those days there
will be many of you in the land," says the Lord.
"At that time people will no longer say, 'I remember the Ark*d* of the Agreement.' They won't think
about it anymore or remember it or miss it or
make another one. ¹⁷At that time people will call
Jerusalem The Throne of the Lord, and all nations will come together in Jerusalem to show respect to the Lord. They will not follow their stubborn, evil hearts anymore. ¹⁸In those days the
family of Judah will join the family of Israel. They
will come together from a land in the north to the
land I gave their ancestors.

¹⁹"I, the Lord, said,
'How happy I would be to treat you as my
own children
and give you a pleasant land,
a land more beautiful than that of any other
nation.'
I thought you would call me 'My Father'
and not turn away from me.
²⁰But like a woman who is unfaithful to her
husband,
family of Israel, you have been unfaithful to
me," says the Lord.

²¹You can hear crying on the bare hilltops.
It is the people of Israel crying and praying
for mercy.
They have become very evil
and have forgotten the Lord their God.

²²"Come back to me, you unfaithful children,
and I will forgive you for being unfaithful."

"Yes, we will come to you,
because you are the Lord our God.
²³It was foolish to worship idols on the hills
and on the mountains.
Surely the salvation of Israel
comes from the Lord our God.
²⁴Since our youth, shameful gods have eaten
up in sacrifice
everything our ancestors worked for —
their flocks and herds,
their sons and daughters.
²⁵Let us lie down in our shame,
and let our disgrace cover us like a blanket.

We have sinned against the Lord our God,
both we and our ancestors.
From our youth until now,
we have not obeyed the Lord our God."

4 "If you will return, Israel,
then return to me," says the Lord.
"If you will throw away your idols that I
hate,
then don't wander away from me.
²If you say when you make a promise,
'As surely as the Lord lives,'
and you can say it in a truthful, honest,
and right way,
then the nations will be blessed by him,
and they will praise him for what he has
done."

³This is what the Lord says to the people of
Judah and to Jerusalem:
"Plow your unplowed fields,
and don't plant seeds among thorns.
⁴Give yourselves to the service of the Lord,
and decide to obey him,
people of Judah and people of Jerusalem.
If you don't, my anger will spread among you
like a fire,
and no one will be able to put it out,
because of the evil you have done.

Trouble from the North

⁵"Announce this message in Judah and say it
in Jerusalem:
'Blow the trumpet throughout the country!'
Shout out loud and say,
'Come together!
Let's all escape to the strong, walled cities!'
⁶Raise the signal flag toward Jerusalem!
Run for your lives, and don't wait,
because I am bringing disaster from the
north.
There will be terrible destruction."

⁷A lion has come out of his den;
a destroyer of nations has begun to march.
He has left his home
to destroy your land.
Your towns will be destroyed
with no one left to live in them.
⁸So put on rough cloth,
show how sad you are, and cry loudly.
The terrible anger of the Lord
has not turned away from us.

⁹"When this happens," says the Lord,
"the king and officers will lose their
courage.
The priests will be terribly afraid,
and the prophets*d* will be shocked!"

¹⁰Then I said, "Lord God, you have tricked the
people of Judah and Jerusalem. You said, 'You will

have peace,' but now the sword is pointing at our throats!"

¹¹At that time this message will be given to Judah and Jerusalem: "A hot wind blows from the bare hilltops of the desert toward the LORD's people. It is not a gentle wind to separate grain from chaff.*d* ¹²I feel a stronger wind than that. Now even I will announce judgments against the people of Judah."

¹³Look! The enemy rises up like a cloud,
    and his chariots come like a tornado.
His horses are faster than eagles.
    How terrible it will be for us! We are
        ruined!
¹⁴People of Jerusalem, clean the evil from your
        hearts so that you can be saved.
Don't continue making evil plans.
¹⁵A voice from Dan makes an announcement
    and brings bad news from the mountains of
        Ephraim.
¹⁶"Report this to the nations.
    Spread this news in Jerusalem:
'Invaders are coming from a faraway country,
    shouting words of war against the cities of
        Judah.
¹⁷The enemy has surrounded Jerusalem as men
        guard a field,
    because Judah turned against me,' " says
        the LORD.
¹⁸"The way you have lived and acted
    has brought this trouble to you.
This is your punishment.
    How terrible it is!
    The pain stabs your heart!"

Jeremiah's Cry

¹⁹Oh, how I hurt! How I hurt!
    I am bent over in pain.
Oh, the torture in my heart!
    My heart is pounding inside me.
I cannot keep quiet,
    because I have heard the sound of the
        trumpet.
    I have heard the shouts of war.
²⁰Disaster follows disaster;
    the whole country has been destroyed.
My tents are destroyed in only a moment.
    My curtains are torn down quickly.
²¹How long must I look at the war flag?
    How long must I listen to the war
        trumpet?

²²The LORD says, "My people are foolish.
    They do not know me.
They are stupid children;
    they don't understand.
They are skillful at doing evil,
    but they don't know how to do good."

Disaster Is Coming

²³I looked at the earth,
    and it was empty and had no shape.
I looked at the sky,
    and its light was gone.
²⁴I looked at the mountains,
    and they were shaking.
All the hills were trembling.
²⁵I looked, and there were no people.
    Every bird in the sky had flown away.
²⁶I looked, and the good, rich land had become
        a desert.
All its towns had been destroyed
    by the LORD and his great anger.

²⁷This is what the LORD says:
"All the land will be ruined,
    but I will not completely destroy it.
²⁸So the people in the land will cry loudly,
    and the sky will grow dark,
because I have spoken and will not change
        my mind.
    I have made a decision, and I will not
        change it."

²⁹At the sound of the horsemen and the
        archers,
    all the people in the towns run away.
They hide in the thick bushes
    and climb up into the rocks.
All of the cities of Judah are empty;
    no one lives in them.
³⁰Judah, you destroyed nation, what are you
        doing?
    Why do you put on your finest dress
    and decorate yourself with gold jewelry?
Why do you put color around your eyes?
    You make yourself beautiful, but it is all
        useless.
Your lovers hate you;
    they want to kill you.

³¹I hear a cry like a woman having a baby,
    distress like a woman having her first child.
It is the sound of Jerusalem gasping for
        breath.
    She lifts her hands in prayer and says,
"Oh! I am about to faint
    before my murderers!"

No One Is Right

5 The LORD says, "Walk up and down the
    streets of Jerusalem.
Look around and discover these things.
    Search the public squares of the city.
If you can find one person who does honest
        things,
    who searches for the truth,
    I will forgive this city.

²Although the people say, 'As surely as the
  LORD lives!'
  they don't really mean it."

³LORD, don't you look for truth in people?
  You struck the people of Judah,
    but they didn't feel any pain.
  You crushed them,
    but they refused to learn what is right.
  They became more stubborn than a rock;
    they refused to turn back to God.
⁴But I thought,
  "These are only the poor, foolish people.
  They have not learned the way of the LORD
    and what their God wants them to do.
⁵So I will go to the leaders of Judah
    and talk to them.
  Surely they understand the way of the LORD
    and know what God wants them to do."
  But even the leaders had all joined together
    to break away from the LORD;
    they had broken their ties with him.
⁶So a lion from the forest will attack them.
  A wolf from the desert will kill them.
  A leopard is waiting for them near their
    towns.
    It will tear to pieces anyone who comes out
      of the city,
  because the people of Judah have sinned
    greatly.
  They have wandered away from the LORD
    many times.

⁷The LORD said, "Tell me why I should forgive
    you.
  Your children have left me
    and have made promises to idols that are
      not gods at all.
  I gave your children everything they needed,
    but they still were like an unfaithful wife to
      me.
  They spent much time in houses of
    prostitutes.ᵈ
⁸They are like well-fed horses filled with
    sexual desire;
    each one wants another man's wife.
⁹Shouldn't I punish the people of Judah for
    doing these things?" says the LORD.
  "Shouldn't I give a nation such as this the
    punishment it deserves?

¹⁰"Go along and cut down Judah's vineyards,
    but do not completely destroy them.
  Cut off all her people as if they were
    branches,
  because they do not belong to the LORD.
¹¹The families of Israel and Judah
  have been completely unfaithful to me,"
    says the LORD.

¹²Those people have lied about the LORD

and said, "He will not do anything to us!
  Nothing bad will happen to us!
  We will never see war or hunger!
¹³The prophetsᵈ are like an empty wind;
  the word of God is not in them.
  Let the bad things they say happen to
    them."

¹⁴So this is what the LORD God All-Powerful
says:
  "The people said I would not punish them.
  So, the words I give you will be like fire,
    and these people will be like wood that it
      burns up.
¹⁵Listen, family of Israel," says the LORD,
  "I will soon bring a nation from far away to
    attack you.
  It is an old nation that has lasted a long time.
  The people there speak a language you do
    not know;
    you cannot understand what they say.
¹⁶Their arrows bring death.
  All their people are strong warriors.
¹⁷They will eat your crops and your food.
  They will eat your sons and daughters.
  They will eat your flocks and herds.
  They will eat your grapes and figs.
  They will destroy with their swords
    the strong, walled cities you trust.

¹⁸"Yet even then," says the LORD, "I will not
destroy you completely. ¹⁹When the people of Judah ask, 'Why has the LORD our God done all
these terrible things to us?' then give them this
answer: 'You have left the LORD and served foreign idols in your own land. So now you will
serve foreigners in a land that does not belong to
you.'

²⁰"Announce this message to the family of
    Jacob,
  and tell it to the nation of Judah:
²¹Hear this message, you foolish people who
    have no sense.
  They have eyes, but they don't really see.
  They have ears, but they don't really listen.
²²Surely you are afraid of me," says the LORD.
  "You should shake with fear in my
    presence.
  I am the one who made the beaches to be a
    border for the sea,
    a border the water can never go past.
  The waves may pound the beach, but they
    can't win over it.
  They may roar, but they cannot go beyond
    it.
²³But the people of Judah are stubborn and
    have turned against me.
  They have turned aside and gone away
    from me.

24They do not say to themselves,
  'We should fear the LORD our God,
who gives us autumn and spring rains in
    their seasons,
  who makes sure we have the harvest at the
    right time.'
25But your evil has kept away both rain and
    harvest.
  Your sins have kept you from enjoying good
    things.
26There are wicked men among my people.
  Like those who make nets for catching
    birds,
  they set their traps to catch people.
27Like cages full of birds,
  their houses are full of lies.
They have become rich and powerful.
28 They have grown big and fat.
  There is no end to the evil things they do.
  They won't plead the case of the orphan
  or help the poor be judged fairly.
29Shouldn't I punish the people of Judah for
    doing these things?" says the LORD.
  "Shouldn't I give a nation such as this the
    punishment it deserves?

30"A terrible and shocking thing
  has happened in the land of Judah:
31The prophets speak lies,
  and the priests take power into their own
    hands,
and my people love it this way.
  But what will you do when the end comes?

Jerusalem Is Surrounded

6 "Run for your lives, people of Benjamin!
  Run away from Jerusalem!
Blow the war trumpet in the town of Tekoa!
  Raise the warning flag over the town of
    Beth Hakkerem!
Disaster is coming from the north;
  terrible destruction is coming to you.
2Jerusalem, I will destroy you,
  you who are fragile and gentle.
3Shepherds with their flocks will come against
    Jerusalem.
  They will set up their tents all around her,
  each shepherd taking care of his own
    section."
4They say, "Get ready to fight against
    Jerusalem!
  Get up! We will attack at noon!
  But it is already getting late;
  the evening shadows are growing long.
5So get up! We will attack at night.
  We will destroy the strong towers of
    Jerusalem!"

6This is what the LORD All-Powerful says:
"Cut down the trees around Jerusalem,

and build an attack ramp to the top of its
    walls.
This city must be punished.
  Inside it is nothing but slavery.
7Jerusalem pours out her evil
  as a well pours out its water.
The sounds of violence and destruction are
    heard within her.
  I can see the sickness and hurts of
    Jerusalem.
8Listen to this warning, Jerusalem,
  or I will turn my back on you
and make your land an empty desert
  where no one can live."

9This is what the LORD All-Powerful says:
"Gather the few people of Israel who are left
    alive,
  as you would gather the last grapes on a
    grapevine.
Check each vine again,
  like someone who gathers grapes."

10To whom can I speak? Whom can I warn?
  Who will listen to me?
The people of Israel have closed ears,
  so they cannot hear my warnings.
They don't like the word of the LORD;
  they don't want to listen to it!
11But I am full of the anger of the LORD,
  and I am tired of holding it in.

"Pour out my anger on the children who play
    in the street
  and on the young men gathered together.
A husband and his wife will both be caught
    in his anger,
  as will the very old.
12Their houses will be turned over to others,
  along with their fields and wives,
because I will raise my hand
  and punish the people of Judah," says the
    LORD.
13"Everyone, from the least important to the
    greatest,
  is greedy for money.
Even the prophetsd and priests
  all tell lies.
14They tried to heal my people's serious injuries
  as if they were small wounds.
They said, 'It's all right, it's all right.'
  But really, it is not all right.
15They should be ashamed of the terrible way
    they act,
  but they are not ashamed at all.
They don't even know how to blush about
    their sins.
So they will fall, along with everyone else.
  They will be thrown to the ground when I
    punish them," says the LORD.

16This is what the Lord says:
"Stand where the roads cross and look.
Ask where the old way is,
where the good way is, and walk on it.
If you do, you will find rest for yourselves.
But they have said, 'We will not walk on
the good way.'
17I set watchmen over you
and told you, 'Listen for the sound of the
war trumpet!'
But they said, 'We will not listen.'
18So listen, all you nations,
and pay attention, you witnesses.
Watch what I will do to the people of
Judah.
19Hear this, people of the earth:
I am going to bring disaster to the people of
Judah
because of the evil they plan.
They have not listened to my messages
and have rejected my teachings.
20Why do you bring me offerings of incense[d]
from the land of Sheba?
Why do you bring me sweet-smelling cane
from a faraway land?
Your burnt offerings will not be accepted;
your sacrifices do not please me."

21So this is what the Lord says:
"I will put problems in front of Judah.
Fathers and sons will stumble over them
together.
Neighbors and friends will die."

22This is what the Lord says:
"Look, an army is coming
from the land of the north;
a great nation is coming
from the far sides of the earth.
23The soldiers carry bows and spears.
They are cruel and show no mercy.
They sound like the roaring ocean
when they ride their horses.
That army is coming lined up for battle,
ready to attack you, Jerusalem."

24We have heard the news about that army
and are helpless from fear.
We are gripped by our pain,
like a woman having a baby.
25Don't go out into the fields
or walk down the roads,
because the enemy has swords.
There is terror on every side.
26My people, put on rough cloth
and roll in the ashes to show how sad you
are.
Cry loudly for those who are dead,
as if your only son were dead,
because the destroyer

will soon come against us.

27"Jeremiah, I have made you like a worker
who tests metal,
and my people are like the ore.
You must observe their ways
and test them.
28All my people have turned against me and
are stubborn.
They go around telling lies about others.
They are like bronze and iron
that became covered with rust.
They all act dishonestly.
29The fire is fanned to make it hotter,
but the lead does not melt.
The pure metal does not come out;
the evil is not removed from my people.
30My people will be called rejected silver,
because the Lord has rejected them."

Jeremiah's Temple Message

7 This is the word that the Lord spoke to Jeremiah: 2"Stand at the gate of the Temple[d] and preach this message there:

" 'Hear the word of the Lord, all you people of the nation of Judah! All you who come through these gates to worship the Lord, listen to this message! 3This is what the Lord All-Powerful, the God of Israel, says: Change your lives and do what is right! Then I will let you live in this place. 4Don't trust the lies of people who say, "This is the Temple of the Lord. This is the Temple of the Lord. This is the Temple of the Lord!" 5You must change your lives and do what is right. Be fair to each other. 6You must not be hard on strangers, orphans, and widows. Don't kill innocent people in this place! Don't follow other gods, or they will ruin your lives. 7If you do these things, I will let you live in this land that I gave to your ancestors to keep forever.

8" 'But look, you are trusting lies, which is useless. 9Will you steal and murder and be guilty of adultery?[d] Will you falsely accuse other people? Will you burn incense[d] to the god Baal[d] and follow other gods you have not known? 10If you do that, do you think you can come before me and stand in this place where I have chosen to be worshiped? Do you think you can say, "We are safe!" when you do all these hateful things? 11This place where I have chosen to be worshiped is nothing more to you than a hideout for robbers. I have been watching you, says the Lord.

12" 'You people of Judah, go now to the town of Shiloh, where I first made a place to be worshiped. See what I did to it because of the evil things the people of Israel had done. 13You people of Judah have done all these evil things too, says the Lord. I spoke to you again and again, but you did not listen to me. I called you, but you did not answer. [14]So I will destroy the place where I have chosen to be worshiped in Jerusalem. You trust in that place, which I gave to you and your ancestors, but I will destroy it just as I destroyed Shiloh. [15]I will push you away from me just as I pushed away your relatives, the people of Israel!'

[16]"As for you, Jeremiah, don't pray for these people. Don't cry out for them or ask anything for them or beg me to help them, because I will not listen to you. [17]Don't you see what they are doing in the towns of Judah and in the streets of Jerusalem? [18]The children gather wood, and the fathers use the wood to make a fire. The women make the dough for cakes of bread, and they offer them to the Queen Goddess.[d] They pour out drink offerings to other gods to make me angry. [19]But I am not the one the people of Judah are really hurting, says the LORD. They are only hurting themselves and bringing shame upon themselves.

[20]" 'So this is what the Lord GOD says: I will pour out my anger on this place, on people and animals, on the trees in the field and the crops in the ground. My anger will be like a hot fire that no one can put out.

Obedience Is More than Sacrifice

[21]" 'This is what the LORD All-Powerful, the God of Israel, says: Offer burnt offerings along with your other sacrifices, and eat the meat yourselves! [22]When I brought your ancestors out of Egypt, I did not speak to them and give them commands only about burnt offerings and sacrifices. [23]I also gave them this command: Obey me, and I will be your God and you will be my people. Do all that I command so that good things will happen to you. [24]But your ancestors did not listen or pay attention to me. They were stubborn and did whatever their evil hearts wanted. They went backward, not forward. [25]Since the day your ancestors left Egypt, I have sent my servants, the prophets, again and again to you. [26]But your ancestors did not listen or pay attention to me. They were very stubborn and did more evil than their ancestors.'

[27]"Jeremiah, you will tell all these things to the people of Judah, but they will not listen to you. You will call to them, but they will not answer you. [28]So say to them, 'This is the nation that has not obeyed the LORD its God. These people do

---

FOLLOWING GOD

No Exceptions

As one of ten prefects in her private school, Amy Harmon represents the student body to the administration. She considers her office an honor and privilege, and she tries to keep the trust of both teachers and students.

Other prefects are not as conscientious as Amy. Because of their special status, they know they can bend—even break—the school rules, and get away with it. Past prefects have been caught drinking and cheating—serious violations at Amy's school.

"Some lied their way out, and others have gotten off easy because they were prefects," she says. They see their prefect title not as an honor, but as a license to break school rules.

Like the prefects who abuse their privilege, the people in Jerusalem in Jeremiah's time thought their special status allowed them to do whatever they wanted. In **Jeremiah 7:1–15**, the prophet warns the people not to use title or status as an excuse for not following God.

■ How are the other prefects' actions like the actions of the people described in the passage? How is Amy's commitment like the commitment God wants?

■ In the passage, God tells the people how they must change their lives to follow him. If God were to speak to you through Jeremiah today, what might he ask you to change?

CONSIDER . . .

■ listing some of the common excuses people use for not following God's commands. Then commit yourself to not using those excuses yourself.

■ taking an honest inventory of what needs to change in your life. Then seek out people, groups, or programs to support your efforts to change.

FOR MORE, SEE . . .

■ 1 Kings 9:1–9 (p. 314)
■ Luke 3:7–9 (p. 1006)
■ John 8:31–47 (p. 1072)

nothing when I correct them. They do not tell the truth; it has disappeared from their lips.

The Valley of Killing

²⁹" 'Cut off your hair and throw it away. Go up to the bare hilltop and cry out, because the LORD has rejected these people. He has turned his back on them, and in his anger will punish them. ³⁰The people of Judah have done what I said was evil, says the LORD. They have set up their hateful idols in the place where I have chosen to be worshiped and have made it unclean.^d ³¹The people of Judah have built places of worship at Topheth in the Valley of Ben Hinnom. There they burned their own sons and daughters as sacrifices, something I never commanded. It never even entered my mind. ³²So, I warn you. The days are coming, says the LORD, when people will not call this place Topheth or the Valley of Ben Hinnom anymore. They will call it the Valley of Killing. They will bury the dead in Topheth until there is no room to bury anyone else. ³³Then the bodies of the dead will become food for the birds of the sky and for the wild animals. There will be no one left alive to chase them away. ³⁴I will end the happy sounds of the bride and bridegroom. There will be no happy sounds in the cities of Judah or in the streets of Jerusalem, because the land will become an empty desert!

8 " 'The LORD says: At that time they will remove from their tombs the bones of Judah's kings and officers, priests and prophets,^d and the people of Jerusalem. ²The bones will be spread on the ground under the sun, moon, and stars that the people loved and served and went after and searched for and worshiped. No one will gather up the bones and bury them. So they will be like dung thrown on the ground. ³I will force the people of Judah to leave their homes and their land. Those of this evil family who are not dead will wish they were, says the LORD All-Powerful.'

Sin and Punishment

⁴"Say to the people of Judah: 'This is what the LORD says:
When people fall down, don't they get up
    again?
  And when someone goes the wrong way,
    doesn't he turn back?
⁵Why, then, have the people of Jerusalem
    gone the wrong way
  and not turned back?
They believe their own lies
  and refuse to turn around and come back.
⁶I have listened to them very carefully,
  but they do not say what is right.
They do not feel sorry about their wicked
    ways,
  saying, "What have I done?"

Each person goes his own way,
  like a horse charging into a battle.
⁷Even the birds in the sky
  know the right times to do things.
The storks, doves, swifts, and thrushes
  know when it is time to migrate.
But my people don't know
  what the LORD wants them to do.

⁸" 'You keep saying, "We are wise,
  because we have the teachings of the
    LORD."
But actually, those who explain the Scriptures
  have written lies with their pens.
⁹These wise men refused to listen to the word
    of the LORD,
  so they are not really wise at all.
They will be ashamed.
  They will be shocked and trapped.
¹⁰So I will give their wives to other men
  and their fields to new owners.
Everyone, from the least important to the
    greatest,
  is greedy for money.
Even the prophets^d and priests
  all tell lies.
¹¹They tried to heal my people's serious injuries
  as if they were small wounds.
They said, "It's all right, it's all right."
  But really, it is not all right.
¹²They should be ashamed of the terrible way
    they act,
  but they are not ashamed at all.
  They don't even know how to blush about
    their sins.
So they will fall, along with everyone else.
  They will be thrown to the ground when I
    punish them, says the LORD.

¹³" 'I will take away their crops, says the LORD.
  There will be no grapes on the vine
and no figs on the fig tree.
  Even the leaves will dry up and die.
I will take away what I gave them.' "

¹⁴"Why are we just sitting here?
  Let's get together!
We have sinned against the LORD,
  so he has given us poisoned water to drink.
Come, let's run to the strong, walled cities.
  The LORD our God has decided that we
    must die,
  so let's die there.
¹⁵We hoped to have peace,
  but nothing good has come.
We hoped for a time when he would heal
    us,
  but only terror has come.
¹⁶From the land of Dan,
  the snorting of the enemy's horses is heard.

The ground shakes from the neighing of
their large horses.
They have come and destroyed
the land and everything in it,
the city and all who live there."

17"Look! I am sending poisonous snakes to
attack you.
These snakes cannot be charmed,
and they will bite you," says the LORD.

Jeremiah's Sadness

18God, you are my comfort when I am very
sad
and when I am afraid.
19Listen to the sound of my people.
They cry from a faraway land:
"Isn't the LORD still in Jerusalem?
Isn't Jerusalem's king still there?"

But God says, "Why did the people make me
angry by worshiping idols,
useless foreign idols?"

20And the people say, "Harvest time is over;
summer has ended,
and we have not been saved."

21Because my people are crushed, I am
crushed.
I cry loudly and am afraid for them.
22Isn't there balm*d* in the land of Gilead?
Isn't there a doctor there?
So why aren't the hurts of my people healed?

> ✸ **SIDELIGHT:** The "balm of
> Gilead" (Jeremiah 8:22) was a gummy
> substance taken from bushes in an area east
> of the Jordan River. As early as Genesis 37:25
> (p. 43), when Joseph was sold to traders
> from Gilead, it was famous for its fragrant
> healing powers. But was it "no-sting, no-
> stain"?

9 I wish my head were like a spring of
water
and my eyes like a fountain of tears!
Then I could cry day and night
for my people who have been killed.
2I wish I had a place in the desert—
a house where travelers spend the night—
so I could leave my people.
I could go away from them,
because they are all unfaithful to God;
they are all turning against him.

Judah's Failures

3"They use their tongues like a bow,
shooting lies from their mouths like arrows.
Lies, not truth,
have grown strong in the land.
They go from one evil thing to another.
They do not know who I am," says the
LORD.
4"Watch out for your friends,
and don't trust your own relatives,
because every relative is a cheater,
and every friend tells lies about you.
5Everyone lies to his friend,
and no one speaks the truth.
The people of Judah have taught their
tongues to lie.
They have become tired from sinning.
6Jeremiah, you live in the middle of lies.
With their lies the people refuse to know
me," says the LORD.

7So this is what the LORD All-Powerful says:
"I will test the people of Judah as a person
tests metal in a fire.
I have no other choice,
because my people have sinned.
8Their tongues are like sharp arrows.
Their mouths speak lies.
Everyone speaks nicely to his neighbor,
but he is secretly planning to attack him.
9Shouldn't I punish the people for doing this?"
says the LORD.
"Shouldn't I give a nation like this the
punishment it deserves?"

10I, Jeremiah, will cry loudly for the mountains
and sing a funeral song for the empty fields.
They are empty, and no one passes through.
The mooing of cattle cannot be heard.
The birds have flown away,
and the animals are gone.

11"I, the LORD, will make the city of Jerusalem
a heap of ruins,
a home for wild dogs.
I will destroy the cities of Judah
so no one can live there."

12What person is wise enough to understand
these things? Is there someone who has been
taught by the LORD who can explain them? Why
was the land ruined? Why has it been made like
an empty desert where no one goes?

13The LORD answered, "It is because Judah quit
following my teachings that I gave them. They
have not obeyed me or done what I told them to
do. 14Instead, they were stubborn and followed
the Baals,*d* as their ancestors taught them to do.
15So this is what the LORD All-Powerful, the God
of Israel, says: "I will soon make the people of
Judah eat bitter food and drink poisoned water.
16I will scatter them through other nations that
they and their ancestors never knew about. I will

chase the people of Judah with the sword until they are all killed."

[17]This is what the LORD All-Powerful says:
"Now, think about these things!
Call for the women who cry at funerals to
  come.
Send for those women who are good at
  that job.
[18]Let them come quickly
  and cry loudly for us.
Then our eyes will fill with tears,
  and streams of water will flow from our
  eyelids.
[19]The sound of loud crying is heard from
  Jerusalem:
  'We are truly ruined!
  We are truly ashamed!
We must leave our land,
  because our houses are in ruins.' "

[20]Now, women of Judah, listen to the word of
  the LORD;
  open your ears to hear the words of his
  mouth.
Teach your daughters how to cry loudly.
Teach one another a funeral song.
[21]Death has climbed in through our windows
  and has entered our strong cities.
Death has taken away our children who play
  in the streets
  and the young men who meet in the city
  squares.

[22]Say, "This is what the LORD says:
'The dead bodies of people will lie
  in the open field like dung.
They will lie like grain a farmer has cut,
  but there will be no one to gather them.' "

[23]This is what the LORD says:
"The wise must not brag about their wisdom.
  The strong must not brag about their
  strength.
The rich must not brag about their money.
[24]But if someone wants to brag, let him brag
  that he understands and knows me.
Let him brag that I am the LORD,
  and that I am kind and fair,
  and that I do things that are right on earth.
This kind of bragging pleases me," says the
  LORD.

[25]The LORD says, "The time is coming when I will punish all those who are circumcised[d] only in the flesh: [26]the people of Egypt, Judah, Edom, Ammon, Moab, and the desert people who cut their hair short. The men in all those countries are not circumcised. And the whole family of Israel does not give itself to serving me."

The Lord and the Idols

10 Family of Israel, listen to what the LORD says to you. [2]This is what he says:
"Don't live like the people from other
  nations,
  and don't be afraid of special signs in the
  sky,
even though the other nations are afraid of
  them.
[3]The customs of other people are worth
  nothing.
Their idols are just wood cut from the
  forest,
shaped by a worker with his chisel.
[4]They decorate their idols with silver and gold.
  With hammers and nails they fasten them
  down
so they won't fall over.
[5]Their idols are like scarecrows in melon
  fields;
  they cannot talk.
Since they cannot walk,
  they must be carried.
Do not be afraid of those idols,
  because they can't hurt you,
  and they can't help you either."

[6]LORD, there is no one like you.
  You are great,
  and your name is great and powerful.
[7]Everyone should respect you, King of the
  nations;
  you deserve respect.
Of all the wise people among the nations
  and in all the kingdoms,
  none of them is as wise as you.
[8]Those wise people are stupid and foolish.
  Their teachings come from worthless
  wooden idols.
[9]Hammered silver is brought from Tarshish
  and gold from Uphaz,
so the idols are made by craftsmen and
  goldsmiths.
They put blue and purple clothes on the
  idols.
All these things are made by skilled
  workers.
[10]But the LORD is the only true God.
  He is the only living God, the King forever.
The earth shakes when he is angry,
  and the nations cannot stand up to his
  anger.

[11]"Tell them this message: 'These gods did not make heaven and earth; they will be destroyed and disappear from heaven and earth.' "

[12]God made the earth by his power.
  He used his wisdom to build the world

and his understanding to stretch out the
skies.
13When he thunders, the waters in the skies
roar.
He makes clouds rise in the sky all over the
earth.
He sends lightning with the rain
and brings out the wind from his
storehouses.

14People are so stupid and know so little.
Goldsmiths are made ashamed by their
idols,
because those statues are only false gods.
They have no breath in them.
15They are worth nothing; people make fun of
them.
When they are judged, they will be
destroyed.
16But God, who is Jacob's Portion,*d* is not like
the idols.
He made everything,
and he chose Israel to be his special people.
The LORD All-Powerful is his name.

Destruction Is Coming

17Get everything you own and prepare to leave,
you people who are trapped by your
enemies.
18This is what the LORD says:
"At this time I will throw out the people
who live in this land.
I will bring trouble to them
so that they may be captured."

19How terrible it will be for me because of my
injury.
My wound cannot be healed.
Yet I told myself,
"This is my sickness; I must suffer through
it."
20My tent is ruined,
and all its ropes are broken.
My children have gone away and left me.
No one is left to put up my tent again
or to set up a shelter for me.
21The shepherds are stupid
and don't ask the LORD for advice.
So they do not have success,
and all their flocks are scattered and lost.
22Listen! The news is coming.
A loud noise comes from the north
to make the towns of Judah an empty desert
and a home for wild dogs!

Jeremiah's Prayer

23LORD, I know that a person's life doesn't
really belong to him.
No one can control his own life.
24LORD, correct me, but be fair.

Don't punish me in your anger,
or you will destroy me.
25Pour out your anger on other nations
that do not know you
and do not pray to you.
Those nations have destroyed Jacob's family.
They have eaten him up completely
and destroyed his homeland.

The Agreement Is Broken

11 These are the words that the LORD spoke
to Jeremiah: 2"Listen to the words of this
agreement and tell them to the people of Judah
and those living in Jerusalem. 3Tell them this is
what the LORD, the God of Israel, says: 'Cursed
is the person who does not obey the words of this
agreement 4that I made with your ancestors when
I brought them out of Egypt. Egypt was like a furnace for melting iron!' I told them, 'Obey me and
do everything I command you. Then you will be
my people, and I will be your God. 5Then I will
keep the promise I made to your ancestors to give
them a fertile land.' And you are living in that
country today."

I answered, "Amen, LORD."

6The LORD said to me, "Announce*d* this message in the towns of Judah and in the streets of
Jerusalem: 'Listen to the words of this agreement
and obey them. 7I warned your ancestors to obey
me when I brought them out of Egypt. I have
warned them again and again to this very day:
"Obey me!" 8But your ancestors did not listen to
me. They were stubborn and did what their own
evil hearts wanted. So I made all the curses of this
agreement come upon them. I commanded them
to obey the agreement, but they did not.' "

9Then the LORD said to me, "I know the people
of Judah and those living in Jerusalem have made
secret plans. 10They have gone back to the same
sins their ancestors did. Their ancestors refused to
listen to my message and followed and worshiped
other gods instead. The families of Israel and Judah have broken the agreement I made with their
ancestors. 11So this is what the LORD says: 'I will
soon bring a disaster on the people of Judah which
they will not be able to escape. They will cry to
me for help, but I will not listen to them. 12The
people living in the towns of Judah and the city
of Jerusalem will pray to their idols to whom they
burn incense.*d* But those idols will not be able to
help when disaster comes. 13Look, people of Judah, you have as many idols as there are towns in
Judah. You have built as many altars to burn incense to that shameful god Baal*d* as there are
streets in Jerusalem.'

14"As for you, Jeremiah, don't pray for these
people or cry out for them or ask anything for
them. I will not listen when they call to me in the
time of their trouble.

15"What is my beloved Judah doing in my
Temple*d*
when she makes many evil plans?
Do you think animal sacrifices will stop
your punishment?
When you do your evil, then you are happy."
16The Lord called you "a leafy olive tree,
with beautiful fruit and shape."
But with the roar of a strong storm
he will set that tree on fire,
and its branches will be burned up.

17The Lord All-Powerful, who planted you, has
announced that disaster will come to you. This is
because the families of Israel and Judah have done
evil and have made him angry by burning incense
to Baal.

Evil Plans Against Jeremiah

18The Lord showed me that men were making
plans against me. Because he showed me what
they were doing, I knew they were against me.
19Before this, I was like a gentle lamb waiting to
be butchered. I did not know they had made
plans against me, saying:
"Let us destroy the tree and its fruit.
Let's kill him so people will forget him."
20But, Lord All-Powerful, you are a fair judge.
You know how to test peoples' hearts and
minds.
I have told you what I have against them.
So let me see you give them the
punishment they deserve.

21So the Lord speaks about the men from Anathoth who plan to kill Jeremiah and say, "Don't
prophesy*d* in the name of the Lord, or we will kill
you!" 22So this is what the Lord All-Powerful
says: "I will soon punish the men from Anathoth.
Their young men will die in war. Their sons and
daughters will die from hunger. 23No one from
the city of Anathoth will be left alive, because I
will cause a disaster to happen to them that year."

Jeremiah's First Complaint

12 Lord, when I bring my case to you,
you are always right.
But I want to ask you about the justice you
give.
Why are evil people successful?
Why do dishonest people have such easy
lives?
2You have put the evil people here
like plants with strong roots.
They grow and produce fruit.
With their mouths they speak well of you,
but their hearts are really far away from
you.
3But you know my heart, Lord.

You see me and test my thoughts about
you.
Drag the evil people away like sheep to be
butchered.
Set them aside for the day of killing.
4How much longer will the land stay dried up
and the grass in every field be dead?
The animals and birds in the land have died,
because the people are evil.
Yes, they are even saying,
"God does not see what happens to us."

> **SIDELIGHT:** How would you
> like to have a complaint named after
> you? Jeremiah's protesting to God (Jeremiah
> 12:1-4) made its way into the dictionary as a
> "jeremiad"—"a lamentation or tale of woe."

The Lord's Answer to Jeremiah

5"If you get tired while racing against people,
how can you race against horses?
If you stumble in a country that is safe,
what will you do in the thick thornbushes
along the Jordan River?
6Even your own brothers and members of
your own family
are making plans against you.
They are crying out against you.
Don't trust them,
even when they say nice things to you!

7"I have left Israel;
I have left my people.
I have given the people I love
over to their enemies.
8My people have become to me
like a lion in the forest.
They roar at me,
so I hate them.
9My people have become to me
like a speckled bird attacked on all sides by
hawks.
Go, gather the wild animals.
Bring them to get something to eat.
10Many shepherds have ruined my vineyards
and trampled the plants in my field.
They have turned my beautiful field
into an empty desert.
11They have turned my field into a desert
that is wilted and dead.
The whole country is an empty desert,
because no one who lives there cares.
12Many soldiers have marched over those
barren hills.
The Lord is using the armies to punish that
land

from one end to the other.
No one is safe.
13The people have planted wheat,
but they have harvested only thorns.
They have worked hard until they were very
tired,
but they have nothing for all their work.
They are ashamed of their poor harvest,
because the LORD's terrible anger has
caused this."

14This is what the LORD said to me: "Here is what I will do to all my wicked neighbors who take the land I gave my people Israel. I will pull them up and throw them out of their land. And I will pull up the people of Judah from among them. 15But after I pull them up, I will feel sorry for them again. I will bring each person back to his own property and to his own land. 16I want them to learn their lessons well. In the past they taught my people to swear by Baal's*d* name. But if they will now learn to swear by my name, saying 'As surely as the LORD lives . . .' I will allow them to rebuild among my people. 17But if a nation will not listen to my message, I will pull it up completely and destroy it," says the LORD.

Jeremiah's Linen Belt

13 This is what the LORD said to me: "Go and buy a linen belt and put it around your waist. Don't let the belt get wet."

2So I bought a linen belt, just as the LORD told me, and put it around my waist. 3Then the LORD spoke his word to me a second time: 4"Take the belt you bought and are wearing, and go to Perath. Hide the belt there in a crack in the rocks." 5So I went to Perath and hid the belt there, just as the LORD told me.

6Many days later the LORD said to me, "Now go to Perath and get the belt I told you to hide there." 7So I went to Perath and dug up the belt and took it from where I had hidden it. But now it was ruined; it was good for nothing.

8Then the LORD spoke his word to me. 9This is what the LORD said: "In the same way I will ruin the pride of the people of Judah and the great pride of Jerusalem. 10These evil people refuse to listen to my warnings. They stubbornly do only what they want to do, and they follow other gods to serve and worship them. So they will become like this linen belt—good for nothing. 11As a belt is wrapped tightly around a person's waist, I *wrapped the families of Israel and Judah around* me," says the LORD. "I did that so they would be my people and bring fame, praise, and honor to me. But my people would not listen.

Warnings About Leather Wine Bags

12"Say to them: 'This is what the LORD, the

God of Israel, says: All leather bags for holding wine should be filled with wine.' People will say to you: 'Of course, we know all wine bags should be filled with wine.' 13Then you will say to them,

'This is what the LORD says: I will make everyone in this land like a drunken person—the kings who sit on David's throne, the priests and the prophets,*d* and all the people who live in Jerusalem. 14I will make them smash against one another, fathers and sons alike, says the LORD. I will not feel sorry or have pity on them or show mercy that would stop me from destroying them.' "

Threat of Slavery

15Listen and pay attention.
Don't be too proud,
because the LORD has spoken to you.
16Give glory to the LORD your God
before he brings darkness
and before you slip and fall
on the dark hills.
You hope for light,
but he will turn it into thick darkness;
he will change it into deep gloom.
17If you don't listen to him,
I will cry secretly
because of your pride.
I will cry painfully,
and my eyes will overflow with tears,
because the LORD's people will be captured.

18Tell this to the king and the queen mother:
"Come down from your thrones,
because your beautiful crowns
have fallen from your heads."
19The cities of southern Judah are locked up,
and no one can open them.
All Judah will be taken as captives to a
foreign land;
they will be carried away completely.

20Jerusalem, look up and see
the people coming from the north.
Where is the flock God gave you to care for,
the flock you bragged about?
21What will you say when they appoint as your
heads
those you had thought were your friends?
Won't you have much pain and trouble,

like a woman giving birth to a baby?
22You might ask yourself,
    "Why has this happened to me?"
It happened because of your many sins.
    Because of your sins, your skirt was torn off
    and your body has been treated badly.
23Can a person from Cush change the color of
        his skin?
    Can a leopard change his spots?
In the same way, Jerusalem, you cannot
        change and do good,
    because you are accustomed to doing evil.

24"I will scatter you like chaff[d] that is blown
        away by the desert wind.
25This is what will happen to you;
    this is your part in my plans," says the
        LORD.
"Because you forgot me
    and trusted in false gods,
26I will pull your skirts up over your face
    so everyone will see your shame.
27I have seen the terrible things you have
        done:
    your acts of adultery[d] and your snorting,
    your prostitution,[d]
    your hateful acts
        on the hills and in the fields.
How terrible it will be for you, Jerusalem.
    How long will you continue being
        unclean?"[d]

A Time Without Rain

14 These are the words that the LORD spoke
to Jeremiah about the time when there
was no rain:
2"The nation of Judah cries as if someone has
        died,
    and her cities are very sad.
They are distressed over the land.
    A cry goes up to God from Jerusalem.
3The important men send their servants to get
        water.
    They go to the wells,
    but they find no water.
So they return with empty jars.
    They are ashamed and embarrassed
    and cover their heads in shame.
4The ground is dry and cracked open,
    because no rain falls on the land.
The farmers are upset and sad,
    so they cover their heads in shame.
5Even the mother deer in the field
    leaves her newborn fawn to die,
    because there is no grass.
6Wild donkeys stand on the bare hills
    and sniff the wind like wild dogs.
But their eyes go blind,
    because there is no food."

7We know that we suffer because of our sins.
    LORD, do something to help us for the good
        of your name.
We have left you many times;
    we have sinned against you.
8God, the Hope of Israel,
    you have saved Israel in times of trouble.
Why are you like a stranger in the land,
    or like a traveler who only stays one night?
9Why are you like someone who has been
        attacked by surprise,
    like a warrior who is not able to save
        anyone?
But you are among us, LORD,
    and we are called by your name
    so don't leave us without help!

10This is what the LORD says about the people
of Judah:
"They really love to wander from me;
    they don't stop themselves from leaving
        me.
So now the LORD will not accept them.
    He will now remember the evil they do
    and will punish them for their sins."

11Then the LORD said, "Don't pray for good
things to happen to the people of Judah. 12Even if
they give up eating, I will not listen to their
prayers. Even if they offer burnt offerings and
grain offerings to me, I will not accept them. Instead, I will destroy the people of Judah with war,
hunger, and terrible diseases."

13But I said, "Oh, Lord GOD, the prophets[d]
keep telling the people, 'You will not suffer from
an enemy's sword or from hunger. I, the LORD,
will give you peace in this land.'"

14Then the LORD said to me, "Those prophets
are prophesying lies in my name. I did not send
them or appoint them or speak to them. They
have been prophesying false visions, idolatries,
worthless magic, and their own wishful thinking.
15So this is what I say about the prophets who are
prophesying in my name. I did not send them.
They say, 'No enemy will attack this country with
swords. There will never be hunger in this land.'
So those prophets will die from hunger and from
an enemy's sword. 16And the people to whom the
prophets speak will be thrown into the streets of
Jerusalem. There they will die from hunger and
from an enemy's sword. And no one will be there
to bury them, or their wives, or their sons, or their
daughters. I will punish them.

17"Jeremiah, speak this message to the people
of Judah:
'Let my eyes be filled with tears
    night and day, without stopping.
My people have received a terrible blow;
    they have been hurt badly.
18If I go into the country,

I see people killed by swords.
If I go into the city,
  I see much sickness, because the people
    have no food.
Both the priests and the prophets
  have been taken to a foreign land.' "

¹⁹Lord, have you completely rejected the
    nation of Judah?
  Do you hate Jerusalem?
Why have you hurt us so badly
  that we cannot be made well again?
We hoped for peace,
  but nothing good has come.
We looked for a time of healing,
  but only terror came.
²⁰Lord, we admit that we are wicked
  and that our ancestors did evil things.
  We have sinned against you.
²¹For your sake, do not hate us.
  Do not take away the honor from your
    glorious throne.
Remember your agreement with us,
  and do not break it.
²²Do foreign idols have the power to bring
    rain?
  Does the sky itself have the power to send
    down showers?
No, it is you, Lord our God.
  You are our only hope,
  because you are the one who made all
    these things.

15 Then the Lord said to me: "I would not
feel sorry for the people of Judah even if
Moses and Samuel prayed for them. Send them
away from me! Tell them to go! ²When they ask
you, 'Where will we go?' tell them: 'This is what
the Lord says:
Those who are meant to die
  will die.
Those who are meant to die in war
  will die in war.
Those who are meant to die from hunger
  will die from hunger.
Those who are meant to be taken captive
  will be taken captive.'

³"I will send four kinds of destroyers against
them," says the Lord. "I will send war to kill,
dogs to drag the bodies away, and the birds of the
air and wild animals to eat and destroy the bodies.
⁴I will make the people of Judah hated by everyone on earth because of what Manasseh did in
Jerusalem. (Manasseh son of Hezekiah was king
of the nation of Judah.)

⁵"Who will feel sorry for you, Jerusalem?
  Who will be sad and cry for you?
  Who will go out of his way to ask how you
    are?

⁶Jerusalem, you have left me," says the Lord.
  "You keep going farther and farther away,
  so I have taken hold of you and destroyed
    you.
  I was tired of holding back my anger.
⁷I have separated the people of Judah with my
    pitchfork
  and scattered them at the city gates of the
    land.
My people haven't changed their ways.
  So I have destroyed them
  and taken away their children.
⁸There are more widows than grains of sand
    in the sea.
I brought a destroyer at noontime
  against the mothers of the young men of
    Judah.
I suddenly brought pain and fear
  on the people of Judah.
⁹When the enemy attacked, a woman with
    seven sons felt faint because they would
    all die.
She became weak and unable to breathe.
Her bright day became dark from sadness.
  She felt shame and disgrace.
And everyone else left alive in Judah
  I will hand over to the enemies, too!" says
    the Lord.

Jeremiah's Second Complaint

¹⁰Mother, I am sorry that you gave birth to me
  since I must accuse and criticize the whole
    land.
I have not loaned or borrowed anything,
  but everyone curses me.
¹¹The Lord said,
  "I have saved you for a good reason.
I have made your enemies beg you
  in times of disaster and trouble.
¹²No one can smash a piece of iron or bronze
  that comes from the north.
¹³Your wealth and treasures
  I will give to others free of charge,
  because the people of Judah have sinned
    throughout the country.
¹⁴I will make you slaves to your enemies
  in a land you have never known.
My anger is like a hot fire,
  and it will burn against you."

¹⁵Lord, you understand.
  Remember me and take care of me.
Punish for me those who are hurting me.
Don't destroy me while you remain patient
    with them.
  Think about the shame I suffer for you.
¹⁶Your words came to me, and I listened
    carefully to them.

Your words made me very happy,
because I am called by your name,
LORD God All-Powerful.
[17]I never sat with the crowd
as they laughed and had fun.
I sat by myself, because you were there,
and you filled me with anger at the evil
around me.
[18]I don't understand why my pain has no end.
I don't understand why my injury is not
cured or healed.
Will you be like a brook that goes dry?
Will you be like a spring that stops flowing?

> ☀ **SIDELIGHT:** Reading Jeremiah is
> like cracking open a diary full of
> private anguish and loud weeping (for
> example, see Jeremiah 15:10–18 and 20:7–18,
> p. 713). No wonder Jeremiah became known
> as the "weeping prophet."

[19]So this is what the LORD says:
"If you change your heart and return to me, I
will take you back.
Then you may serve me.
And if you speak things that have worth,
not useless words,
then you may speak for me.
Let the people of Judah turn to you,
but you must not change and be like them.
[20]I will make you as strong as a wall to this
people,
as strong as a wall of bronze.
They will fight against you,
but they will not defeat you,
because I am with you.
I will rescue you and save you," says the
LORD.
[21]"I will save you from these wicked people
and rescue you from these cruel people."

The Day of Disaster

16 Then the LORD spoke his word to me:
[2]"You must not get married or have sons
or daughters in this place."

[3]The LORD says this about the sons and daughters born in this land and their mothers and fathers: [4]"They will die of terrible diseases, and no one will cry for them or bury them. Their bodies will lie on the ground like dung. They will die in war, or they will starve to death. Their bodies will be food for the birds of the sky and for the wild animals."

[5]So this is what the LORD says: "Jeremiah, do not go into a house where there is a funeral meal. Do not go there to cry for the dead or to show your sorrow for them, because I have taken back my blessing, my love, and my pity from these people," says the LORD. [6]"Important people and common people will die in the land of Judah. No one will bury them or cry for them or cut himself or shave his head to show sorrow for them. [7]No one will bring food to comfort those who are crying for the dead. No one will offer a drink to comfort someone whose mother or father has died.

[8]"Do not go into a house where the people are having a feast to sit down to eat and drink, [9]because this is what the LORD All-Powerful, the God of Israel, says: I will soon stop the sounds of joy and gladness and the happy sounds of brides and bridegrooms in this place. This will happen during your lifetime.

[10]"When you tell the people of Judah these things, they will ask you, 'Why has the LORD said these terrible things to us? What have we done wrong? What sin have we done against the LORD our God?' [11]"Then say to them: 'This is because your ancestors quit following me,' says the LORD. 'And they followed other gods and served and worshiped them. Your ancestors left me and quit obeying my teaching. [12]But you have done even more evil than your ancestors. You are very stubborn and do only what you want to do; you have not obeyed me. [13]So I will throw you out of this country and send you into a land that you and your ancestors never knew. There you can serve other gods day and night, because I will not help you or show you any favors.'

[14]"People say, 'As surely as the LORD lives, who brought the people of Israel out of Egypt . . .' But the time is coming," says the LORD, "when people will not say this anymore. [15]They will say instead, 'As surely as the LORD lives, who brought the Israelites from the northern land and from all the countries where he had sent them . . .' And I will bring them back to the land I gave to their ancestors.

[16]"I will soon send for many fishermen to come to this land," says the LORD. "And they will catch the people of Judah. After that, I will send for many hunters to come to this land. And they will hunt the people of Judah on every mountain and hill and in the cracks of the rocks. [17]I see everything they do. They cannot hide from me the things they do; their sin is not hidden from my eyes. [18]I will pay back the people of Judah twice for every one of their sins, because they have made my land unclean.[d] They have filled my country with their hateful idols."

¹⁹LORD, you are my strength and my
    protection,
  my safe place in times of trouble.
The nations will come to you from all over
    the world
  and say, "Our ancestors had only false
    gods,
  useless idols that didn't help them.
²⁰Can people make gods for themselves?
  They will not really be gods!"

²¹The LORD says, "So I will teach those who
    make idols.
  This time I will teach them
    about my power and my strength.
  Then they will know
    that my name is the LORD.

Judah's Guilty Heart

17 "The sin of the people of Judah is
    written with an iron tool.
  Their sins were cut with a hard point into
    the stone that is their hearts.
  Their sins were cut into the corners of their
    altars.
²Even their children remember
    their altars to idols and their Asherah^d idols
  beside the green trees

and on the high hills.
³My mountain in the open country
  and your wealth and treasures
  I will give away to other people.
  I will give away the places of worship in
    your country,
  because you sinned by worshiping there.
⁴You will lose the land I gave you,
  and it is your own fault.
  I will let your enemies take you as their
    slaves
  to a land you have never known.
This is because you have made my anger
    burn like a hot fire,
  and it will burn forever."

Trusting in Humans or God

⁵This is what the LORD says:
"A curse is placed on those who trust other
    people,
  who depend on humans for strength,
  who have stopped trusting the LORD.
⁶They are like a bush in a desert
    that grows in a land where no one lives,
  a hot and dry land with bad soil.
  They don't know about the good things God
    can give.

DECISION MAKING

What Do You Believe?

The book Walden Two tells about scientists who pulled a trick on some sheep. First, they fenced them in with an electrified wire. The sheep figured out pretty quickly that they should stay away from the wire.

Then the scientists replaced the wire with a piece of string. Not knowing the difference, the sheep stayed away from the string too. They even taught their young to stay away from the string. The young sheep believed that the string was dangerous, because that's what the older sheep taught them.

Humans may not believe in electrified string, but we surely listen to a lot of things other people tell us. God warns us to put our trust in him, not in other people. He used Jeremiah to warn the people of Israel to trust in him and not be led astray by other people. Read about it in **Jeremiah 17:5–8**.

■ How are the sheep in the experiment like the people described in this passage?

■ According to this passage, how should you evaluate others' advice so that you don't end up hurting yourself and others?

CONSIDER . . .

■ listening to your favorite radio station and writing down the messages you hear in several songs. Do you trust those messages?

■ keeping a list this week of the messages you hear about yourself from your friends (for example, "you're pretty," "you're a clown," "you're strange") and deciding if you agree with those messages.

FOR MORE, SEE . . .

■ Exodus 32:1–35 (p. 89)
■ Psalm 146:3–6 (p. 563)
■ 2 Corinthians 11:12–15 (p. 1202)

7"But the person who trusts in the LORD will
be blessed.
The LORD will show him that he can be
trusted.
8He will be strong, like a tree planted near
water
that sends its roots by a stream.
It is not afraid when the days are hot;
its leaves are always green.
It does not worry in a year when no rain
comes;
it always produces fruit.

9"More than anything else, a person's mind is
evil
and cannot be healed.
No one truly understands it.
10But I, the LORD, look into a person's heart
and test the mind.
So I can decide what each one deserves;
I can give each one the right payment for
what he does."

11Like a bird hatching an egg it did not lay,
so are the people who get rich by cheating.
When their lives are half finished, they will
lose their riches.
At the end of their lives, it will be clear
they were fools.

12From the beginning, our Temple*d* has been
honored
as a glorious throne for God.
13LORD, hope of Israel,
those who leave you will be shamed.
People who quit following the LORD will be
like a name written in the dust,
because they have left the LORD, the spring
of living water.

Jeremiah's Third Complaint

14LORD, heal me, and I will truly be healed.
Save me, and I will truly be saved.
You are the one I praise.
15The people of Judah keep asking me,
"Where is the word from the LORD?
Let's see that message come true!"

16LORD, I didn't run away from being the
shepherd you wanted.
I didn't want the terrible day to come.
You know everything I have said;
you see all that is happening.
17Don't be a terror to me.
I run to you for safety in times of trouble.
18Make those who are hurting me be ashamed,
but don't bring shame to me.
Let them be terrified,
but keep me from terror.
Bring the day of disaster on my enemies.
Destroy them, and destroy them again.

Keeping the Sabbath Holy

19This is what the LORD said to me: "Go and
stand at the People's Gate of Jerusalem, where
the kings of Judah go in and out. And then go to
all the other gates of Jerusalem. 20Say to them
there: 'Hear the word of the LORD, kings of Judah,
all you people of Judah, and all who live in Jerusalem, who come through these gates into the city.
21This is what the LORD says: Be careful not to
carry a load on the Sabbath*d* day or bring it
through the gates of Jerusalem. 22Don't take a
load out of your houses on the Sabbath or do any
work on that day. But keep the Sabbath as a holy
day, as I commanded your ancestors. 23But your
ancestors did not listen or pay attention to me.
They were very stubborn and did not listen. I punished them, but it didn't do any good. 24But you
must be careful to obey me, says the LORD. You
must not bring a load through the gates of Jerusalem on the Sabbath, but you must keep the Sabbath as a holy day and not do any work on that
day.

25" 'If you obey this command, kings who sit on
David's throne will come through the gates of Jerusalem with their officers. They will come riding
in chariots and on horses, along with the people
of Judah and Jerusalem. And the city of Jerusalem
will have people living in it forever. 26People will
come to Jerusalem from the villages around it,
from the towns of Judah, from the land of Benjamin, from the western hills, from the mountains,
and from southern Judah. They will all bring to
the Temple*d* of the LORD burnt offerings, sacrifices, grain offerings, incense,*d* and offerings to
show thanks to God. 27But you must obey me and
keep the Sabbath day as a holy day. You must not
carry any loads into Jerusalem on the Sabbath. If
you don't obey me, I will start a fire at the gates
of Jerusalem, and it will burn until it burns even
the strong towers. And it will not be put out.' "

The Potter and the Clay

18 This is the word the LORD spoke to Jeremiah: 2"Go down to the potter's house,
and I will give you my message there." 3So I went
down to the potter's house and saw him working
at the potter's wheel. 4He was using his hands to
make a pot from clay, but something went wrong
with it. So he used that clay to make another pot
the way he wanted it to be.

5Then the LORD spoke his word to me: 6"Family of Israel, can't I do the same thing with you?"
says the LORD. "You are in my hands like the clay
in the potter's hands. 7There may come a time
when I will speak about a nation or a kingdom
that I will pull up by its roots or that I will pull
down to destroy it. 8But if the people of that nation stop doing the evil they have done, I will

change my mind and not carry out my plans to bring disaster to them. ⁹There may come another time when I will speak about a nation that I will build up and plant. ¹⁰But if I see it doing evil by not obeying me, I will change my mind and not carry out my plans to do good for them.

SIDELIGHT: The potter (Jeremiah 18:1–4) had an important job in the ancient world. Pottery was preferred over leather or baskets, because it lasted longer, held liquids better, and protected things from animals and insects. Even broken pottery was useful. People etched notes on it because leather and papyrus—the paper of the day—were too expensive.

---

¹¹"So, say this to the people of Judah and those who live in Jerusalem: 'This is what the LORD says: I am preparing disaster for you and making plans against you. So stop doing evil. Change your ways and do what is right.' ¹²But the people of Judah will answer, 'It won't do any good to try! We will continue to do what we want. Each of us will do what his stubborn, evil heart wants!' "

¹³So this is what the LORD says:
"Ask the people in other nations this
    question:
'Have you ever heard anything like this?'
The people of Israel have done a horrible
    thing.
¹⁴The snow on the mountains of Lebanon
    never melts from the rocks.
Its cool, flowing streams
    do not dry up.
¹⁵But my people have forgotten me.
    They burn incense to worthless idols
and have stumbled in what they do
    and in the old ways of their ancestors.
They walk along back roads
    and on poor highways.
¹⁶So Judah's country will become an empty
    desert.
    People will not stop making fun of it.
They will shake their heads as they pass by;
    they will be shocked at how the country
        was destroyed.
¹⁷Like a strong east wind,
    I will scatter them before their enemies.
At that awful time they will not see me
    coming to help them;
    they will see me leaving."

Jeremiah's Fourth Complaint

¹⁸Then the people said, "Come, let's make

plans against Jeremiah. Surely the teaching of the law by the priest will not be lost. We will still have the advice from the wise men and the words of the prophets.ᵈ So let's ruin him by telling lies about him. We won't pay attention to anything he says."

¹⁹LORD, listen to me.
    Listen to what my accusers are saying!
²⁰Good should not be paid back with evil,
    but they have dug a pit in order to kill me.
Remember that I stood before you
    and asked you to do good things for these
        people
    and to turn your anger away from them.
²¹So now, let their children starve,
    and let their enemies kill them with
        swords.
Let their wives lose their children and
    husbands.
    Let the men from Judah be put to death
    and the young men be killed with swords
        in battle.
²²Let them cry out in their houses
    when you bring an enemy against them
        suddenly.
Let all this happen, because my enemies have
    dug a pit to capture me
    and have hidden traps for my feet.
²³LORD, you know
    about all their plans to kill me.
Don't forgive their crimes
    or erase their sins from your mind.
Make them fall from their places;
    punish them while you are angry.

Judah Is like a Broken Jar

19 This is what the LORD said to me: "Go and buy a clay jar from a potter. ²Take some of the older leaders of the people and the priests, and go out to the Valley of Ben Hinnom, near the front of the Potsherd Gate. There speak the words I tell you. ³Say, 'Kings of Judah and people of Jerusalem, listen to this message from the LORD. This is what the LORD All-Powerful, the God of Israel, says: I will soon bring a disaster on this place that will amaze and frighten everyone who hears about it. ⁴The people of Judah have quit following me. They have made this a place for foreign gods. They have burned sacrifices to other gods that neither they, nor their ancestors, nor the kings of Judah had ever known before. They filled this place with the blood of innocent people. ⁵They have built places on hilltops to worship Baal,ᵈ where they burn their children in the fire to Baal. That is something I did not command or speak about; it never even entered my mind. ⁶Now people call this place the Valley of Ben Hinnom or Topheth, but the days are coming, says the LORD, when people will call it the Valley of Killing.

7" 'At this place I will ruin the plans of the people of Judah and Jerusalem. The enemy will chase them, and I will have them killed with swords. I will make their dead bodies food for the birds and wild animals. 8I will completely destroy this city. People will make fun of it and shake their heads when they pass by. They will be shocked when they see how the city was destroyed. 9An enemy army will surround the city and will not let anyone go out to get food. I will make the people so hungry that they will eat the bodies of their own sons and daughters, and then they will begin to eat each other.'

10"While the people with you are watching, break that jar. 11Then say this: 'The LORD All-Powerful says: I will break this nation and this city just as someone breaks a clay jar that cannot be put back together again. The dead people will be buried here in Topheth, because there is no other place for them. 12This is what I will do to these people and to this place, says the LORD. I will make this city like Topheth. 13The houses in Jerusalem and the king's palaces will become as unclean*d* as this place, Topheth, because the people worshiped gods on the roofs*n* of their houses. They worshiped the stars and burned incense*d* to honor them and gave drink offerings to gods.' "

14When Jeremiah left Topheth where the LORD had sent him to prophesy,*d* he went to the LORD's Temple,*d* stood in the courtyard, and said to all the people: 15"This is what the LORD All-Powerful, the God of Israel, says: 'I will soon bring disaster to Jerusalem and the villages around it, as I said I would. This will happen because the people are very stubborn and do not listen at all to what I say.' "

Pashhur Will Be Captured

20 Pashhur son of Immer was a priest and the highest officer in the Temple*d* of the LORD. When he heard Jeremiah prophesying*d* in the Temple courtyard, 2he had Jeremiah the prophet beaten. And he locked Jeremiah's hands and feet between large blocks of wood at the Upper Gate of Benjamin of the LORD's Temple. 3The next day when Pashhur took Jeremiah out of the blocks of wood, Jeremiah said to him, "The LORD's name for you is not Pashhur. Now his name for you is Terror on Every Side. 4This is what the LORD says: 'I will soon make you a terror to yourself and to all your friends. You will watch enemies killing your friends with swords. And I will give all the people of Judah to the king of Babylon, who will take them away as captives to

Babylon and then will kill them with swords. 5I will give all the wealth of this city to its enemies — its goods, its valuables, and the treasures of the kings of Judah. The enemies will carry all those valuables off to Babylon. 6And Pashhur, you and everyone in your house will be taken captive. You will be forced to go to Babylon, where you will die and be buried, you and your friends to whom you have prophesied lies.' "

Jeremiah's Fifth Complaint

7LORD, you tricked me, and I was fooled.
    You are stronger than I am, so you won.
I have become a joke;
    everyone makes fun of me all day long.
8Every time I speak, I shout.
    I am always shouting about violence and
        destruction.
I tell the people about the message I received
        from the LORD,
    but this only brings me insults.
The people make fun of me all day long.
9Sometimes I say to myself,
    "I will forget about the LORD.
I will not speak anymore in his name."
But then his message becomes like a burning
        fire inside me,
    deep within my bones.
I get tired of trying to hold it inside of me,
    and finally, I cannot hold it in.
10I hear many people whispering about me:
    "Terror on every side!
Tell on him! Let's tell the rulers about
        him."
My friends are all just waiting for me to
        make some mistake.
    They are saying,
"Maybe we can trick him
    so we can defeat him
    and pay him back."

11But the LORD is with me like a strong
        warrior,
    so those who are chasing me will trip and
        fall;
    they will not defeat me.
They will be ashamed because they have
        failed,
    and their shame will never be forgotten.

12LORD All-Powerful, you test good people;
    you look deeply into the heart and mind of
        a person.
I have told you my arguments against these
        people,
    so let me see you give them the
        punishment they deserve.

---

roofs In Bible times houses were built with flat roofs. The roof was used for drying things such as flax and fruit; and it was used as an extra room, as a place for worship, and as a place to sleep in the summer.

¹³Sing to the Lord!
    Praise the Lord!
He saves the life of the poor
    from the power of the wicked.

Jeremiah's Sixth Complaint

¹⁴Let there be a curse on the day I was born;
    let there be no blessing on the day when
        my mother gave birth to me.
¹⁵Let there be a curse on the man
    who brought my father the news:
    "You have a son!"
    This made my father very glad.
¹⁶Let that man be like the towns
    the Lord destroyed without pity.
Let him hear loud crying in the morning
    and battle cries at noon,
¹⁷because he did not kill me before I was born.
    Then my mother would have been my
        grave;
    she would have stayed pregnant forever.
¹⁸Why did I have to come out of my mother's
        body?
    All I have known is trouble and sorrow,
    and my life will end in shame.

God Rejects King Zedekiah's Request

21 This is the word that the Lord spoke to Jeremiah. It came when Zedekiah king of Judah sent Pashhur son of Malkijah and the priest Zephaniah son of Maaseiah to Jeremiah. ²They said, "Ask the Lord for us what will happen, because Nebuchadnezzar king of Babylon is attacking us. Maybe the Lord will do miracles*d* for us as he did in the past so Nebuchadnezzar will stop attacking us and leave."

³But Jeremiah answered them, "Tell King Zedekiah this: ⁴'Here is what the Lord, the God of Israel, says: You have weapons of war in your hands to defend yourselves against the king of Babylon and the Babylonians, who are all around the city wall. But I will make those weapons useless. Soon I will bring them into the center of this city. ⁵In my anger, my very great anger, I myself will fight against you with my great power and strength. ⁶I will kill everything living in Jerusalem—both people and animals. They will die from terrible diseases. ⁷Then, says the Lord, I'll hand over Zedekiah king of Judah, his officers, and the people in Jerusalem who do not die from the terrible diseases or battle or hunger, to Nebuchadnezzar king of Babylon. I will let those win *who want to kill the people of Judah, so the peo*ple of Judah and Jerusalem will be killed in war. Nebuchadnezzar will not show any mercy or pity or feel sorry for them!'

⁸"Also tell this to the people of Jerusalem: 'This is what the Lord says: I will let you choose to live or die. ⁹Anyone who stays in Jerusalem will die in war or from hunger or from a terrible disease. But anyone who goes out of Jerusalem and surrenders to the Babylonians who are attacking you will live. Anyone who leaves the city will save his life as if it were a prize won in war. ¹⁰I have decided to make trouble for this city and not to help it, says the Lord. I will give it to the king of Babylon, and he will burn it with fire.'

¹¹"Say to Judah's royal family: 'Hear the word of the Lord. ¹²Family of David, this is what the Lord says:

You must judge people fairly every morning.
    Save the person who has been robbed
    from the power of his attacker.
If you don't, I will become very angry.
    My anger will be like a fire that no one can
        put out,
    because you have done evil things.

¹³" 'Jerusalem, I am against you,
    you who live on top of the mountain
    over this valley, says the Lord.
You say, "No one can attack us
    or come into our strong city."
¹⁴But I will give you the punishment you
        deserve, says the Lord.
    I will start a fire in your forests
    that will burn up everything around you!' "

Judgment Against Evil Kings

22 This is what the Lord says: "Go down to the palace of the king of Judah and prophesy*d* this message there: ²'Hear the word of the Lord, king of Judah, who rules from David's throne. You and your officers, and your people who come through these gates, listen! ³This is what the Lord says: Do what is fair and right. Save the one who has been robbed from the power of his attacker. Don't mistreat or hurt the foreigners, orphans, or widows. Don't kill innocent people here. ⁴If you carefully obey these commands, kings who sit on David's throne will come through the gates of this palace with their officers and people, riding in chariots and on horses. ⁵But if you don't obey these commands, says the Lord, I swear by my own name that this king's palace will become a ruin.' "

⁶This is what the Lord says about the palace where the king of Judah lives:

"You are tall like the forests of Gilead,
    like the mountaintops of Lebanon.
But I will truly make you into a desert,
    into towns where no one lives.
⁷I will send men to destroy the palace,
    each with his weapons.
They will cut up your strong, beautiful cedar
        beams
    and throw them into the fire.

⁸"People from many nations will pass by this

city and ask each other, 'Why has the LORD done such a terrible thing to Jerusalem, this great city?' ⁹And the answer will be: 'Because the people of Judah quit following the agreement with the LORD their God. They worshiped and served other gods.' "

Judgment Against Jehoahaz

¹⁰Don't cry for the dead king or be sad about him.
But cry painfully for the king who is being taken away,
because he will never return
or see his homeland again.

¹¹This is what the LORD says about Jehoahaz son of Josiah who became king of Judah after his father died and who has left this place: "He will never return. ¹²He will die where he has been taken captive, and he will not see this land again."

Judgment Against Jehoiakim

¹³"How terrible it will be for one who builds his palace by doing evil,
who cheats people so he can build its upper rooms.
He makes his own people work for nothing and does not pay them.
¹⁴He says, 'I will build a great palace for myself with large upper rooms.'
So he builds it with large windows
and uses cedar wood for the walls,
which he paints red.

¹⁵"Does having a lot of cedar in your house make you a great king?
Your father was satisfied to have food and drink.
He did what was right and fair,
so everything went well for him.
¹⁶He helped those who were poor and needy,
so everything went well for him.
That is what it means to know God,"
says the LORD.
¹⁷"But you only look for and think about what you can get dishonestly.
You are even willing to kill innocent people to get it.
You feel free to hurt people and to steal from them."

¹⁸So this is what the LORD says to Jehoiakim son of Josiah king of Judah:
"The people of Judah will not cry when Jehoiakim dies,
saying: 'Oh, my brother,' or 'Oh, my sister.'
They will not cry for him, saying:
'Oh, master,' or 'Oh, my king.'
¹⁹They will bury him like a donkey,
dragging his body away

and throwing it outside the gates of Jerusalem.

²⁰"Judah, go up to Lebanon and cry out.
Let your voice be heard in Bashan.
Cry out from Abarim,
because all your friends are destroyed!
²¹Judah, when you were successful, I warned you,
but you said, 'I won't listen.'
You have acted like this since you were young;
you have not obeyed me.
²²Like a storm, my punishment will blow all your shepherds away
and send your friends into captivity.
Then you will really be ashamed and disgraced
because of all the wicked things you did.
²³King, you live in your palace,
cozy in your rooms of cedar.
But when your punishment comes, how you will groan
like a woman giving birth to a baby!

Judgment upon Jehoiachin

²⁴"As surely as I live," says the LORD, "Jehoiachin son of Jehoiakim king of Judah, even if you were a signet*d* ring on my right hand, I would still pull you off. ²⁵I will hand you over to Nebuchadnezzar king of Babylon and to the Babylonians — those people you fear because they want to kill you. ²⁶I will throw you and your mother into another country. Neither of you was born there, but both of you will die there. ²⁷They will want to come back, but they will never be able to return."

²⁸Jehoiachin is like a broken pot someone threw away;
he is like something no one wants.
Why will Jehoiachin and his children be thrown out
and sent into a foreign land?
²⁹Land, land, land of Judah,
hear the word of the LORD!
³⁰This is what the LORD says:
"Write this down in the record about Jehoiachin:
He is a man without children,
a man who will not be successful in his lifetime.
And none of his descendants will be successful;
none will sit on the throne of David
or rule in Judah."

The Evil Leaders of Judah

23 "How terrible it will be for the leaders of Judah, who are scattering and destroying my people," says the LORD.

²They are responsible for the people, so the LORD, the God of Israel, says to them: "You have scattered my people and forced them away and not taken care of them. So I will punish you for the evil things you have done," says the LORD. ³"I sent my people to other countries, but I will gather those who are left alive and bring them back to their own country. Then they will have many children and grow in number. ⁴I will place new leaders over my people, who will take care of them. And my people will not be afraid or terrified again, and none of them will be lost," says the LORD.

The Good Branch Will Come

⁵"The days are coming," says the LORD,
  "when I will raise up a good branch in
    David's family.
He will be a king who will rule in a wise
    way;
  he will do what is fair and right in the
    land.
⁶In his time Judah will be saved,
  and Israel will live in safety.
This will be his name:

The LORD Does What Is Right.
⁷"So the days are coming," says the LORD, "when people will not say again: 'As surely as the LORD lives, who brought Israel out of Egypt . . .' ⁸But people will say something new: 'As surely as the LORD lives, who brought the descendants of Israel from the land of the north and from all the countries where he had sent them away. . .' Then the people of Israel will live in their own land."

False Prophets Will Be Punished

⁹A message to the prophets:ᵈ
My heart is broken.
  All my bones shake.
I'm like someone who is drunk,
  like someone who has been overcome with
    wine.
This is because of the LORD
  and his holy words.
¹⁰The land of Judah is full of people who are
    guilty of adultery.ᵈ
Because of this, the LORD cursed the land.
It has become a very sad place,
  and the pastures have dried up.
The people are evil

LEADERSHIP

Who'll Pay for It?

Stephanie Fishkin had nothing to do with the senior class prank that caused damages of about fourteen hundred dollars to a small park on school grounds. She didn't destroy the park's cherry tree, break the branches off the hackberry tree, or saw through the split-rail fence. But it was her picture that appeared on the front page of the "Denver Post" with the news account of the vandalism.

Why? Because as senior class president, Stephanie was responsible for answering to the press. She and the other class officers also had the responsibility to pay for the damage out of the class treasury. They had planned to donate those funds to Denver Children's Hospital or to a scholarship fund.

Ironically, the park had been built as a memorial to a student who died in 1974. The student's parents spent at least ten thousand dollars of their own money to build the park. This family, at the very least, deserved an apology. Whose responsibility was that?

Most class presidents consider that position to be an honor. But being a leader, Stephanie found out, also carries responsibility. In Judah, God held the leaders responsible for misguiding his people. See what God has to say to them in **Jeremiah 23:1–6.**

■ Why do you think Stephanie and the leaders of Judah were held accountable for the things happening around them?
■ What are some ways you can serve as a leader for God's people?

            C O N S I D E R . . .
■ helping your family by taking responsibility for a household chore without being asked,
■ offering your leadership in your school or church for a project that needs to be done, and then responsibly completing it.

          F O R   M O R E ,   S E E . . .
■ Micah 3:9–12 (p. 864)
■ Matthew 23:13–36 (p. 949)
                            ■ 2 Peter 2:1–3 (p. 1311)

and use their power in the wrong way.

11"Both the prophets and the priests live as if
there were no God.
I have found them doing evil things even in
my own Temple,"*d* says the LORD.
12"So they will be in danger.
They will be forced into darkness
where they will be defeated.
I will bring disaster on them
in the year I punish them," says the LORD.

13"I saw the prophets of Samaria
do something wrong.
Those prophets prophesied by Baal*d*
and led my people Israel away.
14And I have seen the prophets of Jerusalem
do terrible things.
They are guilty of adultery
and live by lies.
They encourage evil people to keep on doing
evil,
so the people don't stop sinning.
All of those people are like the city of Sodom.
The people of Jerusalem are like the city of
Gomorrah to me!"

15So this is what the LORD All-Powerful says
about the prophets:
"I will make those prophets eat bitter food
and drink poisoned water,
because the prophets of Jerusalem spread
wickedness
through the whole country."

16This is what the LORD All-Powerful says:
"Don't pay attention to what those prophets
are saying to you.
They are trying to fool you.
They talk about visions their own minds
made up,
not about visions from me.
17They say to those who hate me:
'The LORD says: You will have peace.'
They say to all those who are stubborn and
do as they please:
'Nothing bad will happen to you.'
18But none of these prophets has stood in the
meeting of angels
to see or hear the message of the LORD.
None of them has paid close attention to
his message.
19Look, the punishment from the LORD
will come like a storm.
His anger will be like a hurricane.
It will come swirling down on the heads of
those wicked people.
20The LORD's anger will not stop
until he finishes what he plans to do.
When that day is over,
you will understand this clearly.

21I did not send those prophets,
but they ran to tell their message.
I did not speak to them,
but they prophesied anyway.
22But if they had stood in the meeting of
angels,
they would have told my message to my
people.
They would have turned the people from
their evil ways
and from doing evil.

23"I am a God who is near," says the LORD.
"I am also a God who is far away."
24"No one can hide
where I cannot see him," says the LORD.
"I fill all of heaven and earth," says the
LORD.

25"I have heard the prophets who prophesy lies
in my name. They say, 'I have had a dream! I have
had a dream!' 26How long will this continue in the
minds of these lying prophets? They prophesy
from their own wishful thinking. 27They are trying to make the people of Judah forget me by telling each other these dreams. In the same way,
their ancestors forgot me and worshiped Baal. 28Is
straw the same thing as wheat?" says the LORD.
"If a prophet wants to tell about his dreams, let
him! But let the person who hears my message
speak it truthfully! 29Isn't my message like a
fire?" says the LORD. "Isn't it like a hammer that
smashes a rock?

30"So I am against the false prophets," says the
LORD. "They keep stealing words from each other
and say they are from me. 31I am against the false
prophets," says the LORD. "They use their own
words and pretend it is a message from me. 32I am
against the prophets who prophesy false dreams,"
says the LORD. "They mislead my people with
their lies and false teachings! I did not send them
or command them to do anything for me. They
can't help the people of Judah at all," says the
LORD.

The Sad Message from the Lord

33"Suppose the people of Judah, a prophet,*d* or
a priest asks you: 'Jeremiah, what is the message
from the LORD?' You will answer them and say,
'You are a heavy load to the LORD, and I will
throw you down, says the LORD.' 34A prophet or
a priest or one of the people might say, 'This is a
message from the LORD.' That person has lied, so
I will punish him and his whole family. 35This is
what you will say to each other: 'What did the
LORD answer?' or 'What did the LORD say?' 36But
you will never again say, 'The message of the
LORD,' because the only message you speak is
your own words. You have changed the words of
our God, the living God, the LORD All-Powerful.

³⁷This is how you should speak to the prophets: 'What answer did the Lord give you?' or 'What did the Lord say?' ³⁸But don't say, 'The message from the Lord.' If you use these words, this is what the Lord says: Because you called it a 'message from the Lord,' though I told you not to use those words, ³⁹I will pick you up and throw you away from me, along with Jerusalem, which I gave to your ancestors and to you. ⁴⁰And I will make a disgrace of you forever; your shame will never be forgotten."

The Good and Bad Figs

24 Nebuchadnezzar king of Babylon captured Jehoiachin son of Jehoiakim and king of Judah, his officers, and all the craftsmen and metalworkers of Judah. He took them away from Jerusalem and brought them to Babylon. It was then that the Lord showed me two baskets of figs arranged in front of the Temple*ᵈ* of the Lord. ²One of the baskets had very good figs in it, like figs that ripen early in the season. But the other basket had figs too rotten to eat.

³The Lord said to me, "What do you see, Jeremiah?"

I answered, "I see figs. The good figs are very good, but the rotten figs are too rotten to eat."

⁴Then the Lord spoke his word to me: ⁵"This is what the Lord, the God of Israel, says: 'I sent the people of Judah out of their country to live in the country of Babylon. I think of those people as good, like these good figs. ⁶I will look after them and bring them back to the land of Judah. I will not tear them down, but I will build them up. I will not pull them up, but I will plant them so they can grow. ⁷I will make them want to know me, that I am the Lord. They will be my people, and I will be their God, because they will return to me with their whole hearts.

⁸" 'But the bad figs are too rotten to eat.' So this is what the Lord says: 'Zedekiah king of Judah, his officers, and all the people from Jerusalem who are left alive, even those who live in Egypt, will be like those rotten figs. ⁹I will make those people hated as an evil people by all the kingdoms of the earth. People will make fun of them and tell

---

HONESTY

Slow to Heal

After placing second at the regional karate tournament, Dan McCarty got an invitation to nationals. But one week before the trip, he tore the ligaments in his ankle and ended up in a cast.

Still, nothing would stop Dan. He convinced his parents to let him make the trip anyway, promising just to watch the tournament. Once on his way, he told his karate instructor that the doctor had put him in a cast only as a precaution. He said he had both his doctor's and parents' permission to participate. Since it was a removable cast, he took it off when he got to the tournament and competed. He even won a few matches.

Although the cast was back on when he got home, his parents figured out what he had done by the way he talked about the competition. They felt angry and betrayed!

Dan paid for his scheme: His ankle healed much more slowly than it would have. Luckily, the ankle wasn't permanently damaged.

Dan falsely used the authority of his doctor and parents to back up his lies to his instructor. In a similar way, false prophets appealed to God's authority to back up their lies in **Jeremiah 23:23–30**.

■ Why were Dan's karate instructor and the people in the passage quick to accept lies?

■ When people say, "Honest to God!" do you believe their story more than you would have otherwise? Why or why not?

C O N S I D E R . . .

■ tracking down the source of a rumor you've heard at school and finding out how much is true.

■ Mark Twain's humorous thought on lying: "If you tell the truth you don't have to remember anything." Think of a time you've lied. Then make a list of all the other lies you had to tell to support it.

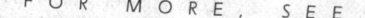

F O R   M O R E ,   S E E . . .

■ Psalm 139:1–18 (p. 561)
■ Matthew 5:33–37 (p. 915)
■ 1 John 4:1–6 (p. 1319)

jokes about them and point fingers at them and curse them everywhere I scatter them. ¹⁰I will send war, hunger, and disease against them. I will attack them until they have all been killed. Then they will no longer be in the land I gave to them and their ancestors.' "

SIDELIGHT: If you have trouble figuring out all the oracles, history, and stories in the book of Jeremiah, read a summary of his ministry in Jeremiah 25. This may be the first "Reader's Digest Condensed Book."

A Summary of Jeremiah's Preaching

25 This is the message that came to Jeremiah concerning all the people of Judah. It came in the fourth year that Jehoiakim son of Josiah was king of Judah and the first year Nebuchadnezzar was king of Babylon. ²This is the message Jeremiah the prophet*ᵈ* spoke to all the people of Judah and Jerusalem:

³The LORD has spoken his word to me again and again for these past twenty-three years. I have been a prophet since the thirteenth year of Josiah son of Amon king of Judah. I have spoken messages from the LORD to you from that time until today, but you have not listened. ⁴The LORD has sent all his servants the prophets to you over and over again, but you have not listened or paid any attention to them. ⁵Those prophets have said, "Stop your evil ways. Stop doing what is wrong so you can stay in the land that the LORD gave to you and your ancestors to live in forever. ⁶Don't follow other gods to serve them or to worship them. Don't make me, the LORD, angry by worshiping idols that are the work of your own hands, or I will punish you."

⁷"But you people of Judah did not listen to me," says the LORD. "You made me angry by worshiping idols that were the work of your own hands, so I punished you."

⁸So this is what the LORD All-Powerful says: "Since you have not listened to my messages, ⁹I will send for all the peoples of the north," says the LORD, "along with my servant Nebuchadnezzar king of Babylon. I will bring them all against Judah, those who live there, and all the nations around you, too. I will completely destroy all those countries and leave them in ruins forever. People will be shocked when they see how badly I have destroyed those countries. ¹⁰I will bring an end to the sounds of joy and happiness, the sounds of brides and bridegrooms, and the sound of people grinding meal. And I will take away the light of the lamp. ¹¹That whole area will be an empty desert, and these nations will be slaves of the king of Babylon for seventy years.

¹²"But when the seventy years have passed, I will punish the king of Babylon and his entire nation for their evil," says the LORD. "I will make that land a desert forever. ¹³I will make happen all the terrible things I said about Babylonia — everything Jeremiah prophesied about all those foreign nations, the warnings written in this book. ¹⁴Even the Babylonians will have to serve many nations and many great kings. I will give them the punishment they deserve for all their own hands have done."

Judgment on the Nations

¹⁵The LORD, the God of Israel, said this to me: "My anger is like the wine in a cup. Take it from my hand and make all the nations, to whom I am sending you, drink all of my anger from this cup. ¹⁶They will drink my anger and stumble about and act like madmen because of the war I am going to send among them."

¹⁷So I took the cup from the LORD's hand and went to those nations and made them drink from it. ¹⁸I served this wine to the people of Jerusalem and the towns of Judah, and the kings and officers of Judah, so they would become a ruin. Then people would be shocked and would insult them and speak evil of them. And so it has been to this day. ¹⁹I also made these people drink of the LORD's anger: the king of Egypt, his servants, his officers, all his people, ²⁰and all the foreigners there; all the kings of the land of Uz; all the kings of the Philistines (the kings of the cities of Ashkelon, Gaza, Ekron, and the people left at Ashdod); ²¹the people of Edom, Moab, and Ammon; ²²all the kings of Tyre and Sidon; all the kings of the coastal countries to the west; ²³the people of Dedan and Tema and Buz; all who cut their hair short; ²⁴all the kings of Arabia; and the kings of the people who live in the desert; ²⁵all the kings of Zimri, Elam, and Media; ²⁶and all the kings of the north, near and far, one after the other. I made all the kingdoms on earth drink from the cup of the LORD's anger, but the king of Babylon will drink from this cup after all the others.

²⁷"Then say to them, 'This is what the LORD All-Powerful, the God of Israel, says: Drink this cup of my anger. Get drunk from it and vomit. Fall down and don't get up because of the war I am sending among you!'

²⁸"If they refuse to take the cup from your hand and drink, say to them, 'The LORD All-Powerful says this: You must drink from this cup. ²⁹Look! I am already bringing disaster on Jerusalem, the city that is called by my name. Do you think you will not be punished? You will be punished! I am sending war on all the people of the earth, says the LORD All-Powerful.'

³⁰"You, Jeremiah, will prophesy*d* against them with all these words. Say to them:

'The LORD will roar from heaven
    and will shout from his Holy Temple.*d*
He will roar loudly against his land.
He will shout like people who walk on grapes
        to make wine;
he will shout against all who live on the
    earth.
³¹The noise will spread all over the earth,
    because the LORD will accuse all the
    nations.
He will judge and tell what is wrong with all
    people,
and he will kill the evil people with a
    sword,' " says the LORD.

³²This is what the LORD All-Powerful says:
"Disasters will soon spread
    from nation to nation.
They will come like a powerful storm
    from the faraway places on earth."

³³At that time those killed by the LORD will reach from one end of the earth to the other. No one will cry for them or gather up their bodies and bury them. They will be left lying on the ground like dung.

³⁴Cry, you leaders! Cry out loud!
    Roll around in the dust, leaders of the
        people!
It is now time for you to be killed.
    You will fall and be scattered,
    like pieces of a broken jar.
³⁵There will be no place for the leaders to
    hide;
    they will not escape.
³⁶I hear the sound of the leaders shouting.
    I hear the leaders of the people crying
        loudly,
    because the LORD is destroying their land.
³⁷Those peaceful pastures will be like an empty
    desert,
    because the LORD is very angry.
³⁸Like a lion, he has left his den.
    Their land has been destroyed
because of the terrible war he brought,
    because of his fierce anger.

Jeremiah's Lesson at the Temple

26 This message came from the LORD soon after Jehoiakim son of Josiah became *king of Judah.* ²This is what the LORD said: "Jeremiah, stand in the courtyard of the Temple*d* of the LORD. Give this message to all the people of the towns of Judah who are coming to worship at the Temple of the LORD. Tell them everything I tell you to say; don't leave out a word. ³Maybe they will listen and stop their evil ways. If they will, I

will change my mind about bringing on them the disaster that I am planning because of the evil they have done. ⁴Say to them: 'This is what the LORD says: You must obey me and follow my teachings that I gave you. ⁵You must listen to what my servants the prophets*d* say to you. I have sent them to you again and again, but you did not listen. ⁶If you don't obey me, I will destroy my Temple in Jerusalem as I destroyed my Holy Tent*d* at Shiloh. When I do, people all over the world will curse Jerusalem.' "

⁷The priests, the prophets, and all the people heard Jeremiah speaking these words in the Temple of the LORD. ⁸When Jeremiah finished speaking everything the LORD had commanded him to say, the priests, prophets, and all the people grabbed Jeremiah. They said, "You must die! ⁹How dare you prophesy in the name of the LORD that this Temple will be destroyed like the one at Shiloh! How dare you say that Jerusalem will become a desert without anyone to live in it!" And all the people crowded around Jeremiah in the Temple of the LORD.

¹⁰Now when the officers of Judah heard about what was happening, they came out of the king's palace and went up to the Temple of the LORD and took their places at the entrance of the New Gate. ¹¹Then the priests and prophets said to the officers and all the other people, "Jeremiah should be killed. He prophesied against Jerusalem, and you heard him yourselves."

¹²Then Jeremiah spoke these words to all the officers of Judah and all the other people: "The LORD sent me to say everything you have heard about this Temple and this city. ¹³Now change your lives and start doing good and obey the LORD your God. Then he will change his mind and not bring on you the disaster he has told you about. ¹⁴As for me, I am in your power. Do to me what you think is good and right. ¹⁵But be sure of one thing. If you kill me, you will be guilty of killing an innocent person. You will make this city and everyone who lives in it guilty, too! The LORD truly sent me to you to give you this message."

¹⁶Then the officers and all the people said to the priests and the prophets, "Jeremiah must not be killed. What he told us comes from the LORD our God."

¹⁷Then some of the older leaders of Judah stood up and said to all the people, ¹⁸"Micah, from the city of Moresheth, was a prophet during the time Hezekiah was king of Judah. Micah said to all the people of Judah, 'This is what the LORD All-Powerful says:

Jerusalem will be plowed like a field.
    It will become a pile of rocks,
    and the hill where the Temple stands will
        be covered with bushes.'
¹⁹"Hezekiah king of Judah and the people of

Judah did not kill Micah. You know that Hezekiah feared the Lord and tried to please the Lord. So the Lord changed his mind and did not bring on Judah the disaster he had promised. If we hurt Jeremiah, we will bring a terrible disaster on ourselves!"

[20](Now there was another man who prophesied in the name of the Lord. His name was Uriah son of Shemaiah from the city of Kiriath Jearim. He preached the same things against Jerusalem and the land of Judah that Jeremiah did. [21]When King Jehoiakim, all his army officers, and all the leaders of Judah heard Uriah preach, King Jehoiakim wanted to kill Uriah. But Uriah heard about it and was afraid. So he escaped to Egypt. [22]Then King Jehoiakim sent Elnathan son of Acbor and some other men to Egypt, [23]and they brought Uriah back from Egypt. Then they took him to King Jehoiakim, who had Uriah killed with a sword. His body was thrown into the burial place where poor people are buried.)

[24]Ahikam son of Shaphan supported Jeremiah.

So Ahikam did not hand Jeremiah over to be killed by the people.

Nebuchadnezzar Is Made Ruler

27 The Lord spoke his word to Jeremiah soon after Zedekiah son of Josiah was made king of Judah. [2]This is what the Lord said to me: "Make a yoke[d] out of straps and poles, and put it on the back of your neck. [3]Then send messages to the kings of Edom, Moab, Ammon, Tyre, and Sidon by their messengers who have come to Jerusalem to see Zedekiah king of Judah. [4]Tell them to give this message to their masters: 'The Lord All-Powerful, the God of Israel, says: "Tell your masters: [5]I made the earth, its people, and all its animals with my great power and strength. I can give the earth to anyone I want. [6]Now I have given all these lands to Nebuchadnezzar king of Babylon, my servant. I will make even the wild animals obey him. [7]All nations will serve Nebuchadnezzar and his son and grandson. Then the time will come for Babylon to be defeated, and

---

many nations and great kings will make Babylon their servant.

8" ' "But if some nations or kingdoms refuse to serve Nebuchadnezzar king of Babylon and refuse to be under his control, I will punish them with war, hunger, and terrible diseases, says the LORD. I will use Nebuchadnezzar to destroy them. 9So don't listen to your false prophets,*d* those who use magic to tell the future, those who explain dreams, the mediums,*d* or magicians. They all tell you, 'You will not be slaves to the king of Babylon.' 10They are telling you lies that will cause you to be taken far from your homeland. I will force you to leave your homes, and you will die in another land. 11But the nations who put themselves under the control of the king of Babylon and serve him I will let stay in their own country, says the LORD. The people from those nations will live in their own land and farm it." ' "

12I gave the same message to Zedekiah king of Judah. I said, "Put yourself under the control of the king of Babylon and serve him, and you will live. 13Why should you and your people die from war, hunger, or disease, as the LORD said would happen to those who do not serve the king of Babylon? 14But the false prophets are saying, 'You will never be slaves to the king of Babylon.' Don't listen to them because they are prophesying lies to you! 15'I did not send them,' says the LORD. 'They are prophesying lies and saying the message is from me. So I will send you away, Judah. And you and those prophets who prophesy to you will die.' "

16Then I, Jeremiah, said to the priests and all the people, "This is what the LORD says: Those false prophets are saying, 'The Babylonians will soon return what they took from the Temple*d* of the LORD.' Don't listen to them! They are prophesying lies to you. 17Don't listen to those prophets. But serve the king of Babylon, and you will live. There is no reason for you to cause Jerusalem to become a ruin. 18If they are prophets and have the message from the LORD, let them pray to the LORD All-Powerful. Let them ask that the items which are still in the Temple of the LORD and in the king's palace and in Jerusalem not be taken away to Babylon.

19"This is what the LORD All-Powerful says about those items left in Jerusalem: the pillars, the large bronze bowl, which is called the Sea, the stands that can be moved, and other things. 20Nebuchadnezzar king of Babylon did not take *these away when he took as captives Jehoiachin* son of Jehoiakim king of Judah and all the other important people from Judah and Jerusalem to Babylon. 21This is what the LORD All-Powerful, the God of Israel, says about the items left in the Temple of the LORD and in the king's palace and in Jerusalem: 22'All of them will also be taken to Babylon. And they will stay there until the day I go to get them,' says the LORD. 'Then I will bring them back and return them to this place.' "

The False Prophet Hananiah

28 It was in that same year, in the fifth month of Zedekiah's fourth year as king of Judah, soon after he began to rule. The prophet*d* Hananiah son of Azzur, from the town of Gibeon, spoke to me in the Temple*d* of the LORD in front of the priests and all the people. He said: 2"The LORD All-Powerful, the God of Israel, says: 'I have broken the yoke*d* the king of Babylon has put on Judah. 3Before two years are over, I will bring back everything that Nebuchadnezzar king of Babylon took to Babylon from the LORD's Temple. 4I will also bring back Jehoiachin son of Jehoiakim king of Judah and all the other captives from Judah who went to Babylon,' says the LORD. 'So I will break the yoke the king of Babylon put on Judah.' "

5Then the prophet Jeremiah spoke to the prophet Hananiah in front of the priests and all the people who were standing in the Temple*d* of the LORD. 6He said, "Amen! Let the LORD really do that! May the LORD make the message you prophesy come true. May he bring back here everything from the LORD's Temple and all the people who were taken as captives to Babylon.

7"But listen to what I am going to say to you and all the people. 8There were prophets long before we became prophets, Hananiah. They prophesied that war, hunger, and terrible diseases would come to many countries and great kingdoms. 9But if a prophet prophesies that we will have peace and that message comes true, he can be recognized as one truly sent by the LORD."

10Then the prophet Hananiah took the yoke off Jeremiah's neck and broke it. 11Hananiah said in front of all the people, "This is what the LORD says: 'In the same way I will break the yoke of Nebuchadnezzar king of Babylon. He put that yoke on all the nations of the world, but I will break it before two years are over.' " After Hananiah had said that, Jeremiah left the Temple.

12The LORD spoke his word to Jeremiah after the prophet Hananiah had broken the yoke off of the prophet Jeremiah's neck. 13The LORD said, "Go and tell Hananiah, 'This is what the LORD says: You have broken a wooden yoke, but I will make a yoke of iron in its place! 14The LORD All-Powerful, the God of Israel, says: I will put a yoke of iron on the necks of all these nations to make them serve Nebuchadnezzar king of Babylon, and they will be slaves to him. I will even give Nebuchadnezzar control over the wild animals.' "

15Then the prophet Jeremiah said to the prophet Hananiah, "Listen, Hananiah! The LORD did not send you, and you have made the people of Judah trust in lies. [16]So this is what the LORD says: 'Soon I will remove you from the earth. You will die this year, because you taught the people to turn against the LORD.' "

[17]Hananiah died in the seventh month of that same year.

A Letter to the Captives in Babylon

29 This is the letter that Jeremiah the prophet[d] sent from Jerusalem to the older leaders who were among the captives, the priests, and the prophets. He sent it to all the other people Nebuchadnezzar had taken as captives from Jerusalem to Babylon. [2](This letter was sent after all these people were taken away: Jehoiachin the king and the queen mother; the officers and leaders of Judah and Jerusalem; and the craftsmen and metalworkers from Jerusalem.) [3]Zedekiah king of Judah sent Elasah son of Shaphan and Gemariah son of Hilkiah to Babylon to Nebuchadnezzar king of Babylon. So Jeremiah gave them this letter to carry to Babylon:

[4]This is what the LORD All-Powerful, the God of Israel, says to all those people I sent away from Jerusalem as captives to Babylon: [5]"Build houses and settle in the land. Plant gardens and eat the food they grow. [6]Get married and have sons and daughters. Find wives for your sons, and let your daughters be married so they also may have sons and daughters. Have many children in Babylon; don't become fewer in number. [7]Also do good things for the city where I sent you as captives. Pray to the LORD for the city where you are living, because if good things happen in the city, good things will happen to you also." [8]The LORD All-Powerful, the God of Israel, says: "Don't let the prophets among you and the people who do magic fool you. Don't listen to their dreams. [9]They are prophesying lies to you, saying that their message is from me. But I did not send them," says the LORD.

[10]This is what the LORD says: "Babylon will be powerful for seventy years. After that time I will come to you, and I will keep my promise to bring you back to Jerusalem. [11]I say this because I know what I am planning for you," says the LORD. "I have good plans for you, not plans to hurt you. I will give you hope and a good future. [12]Then you will call my name. You will come to me and pray to me, and I will listen to you. [13]You will search for me. And when you search for me with all your heart, you will find me! [14]I will let you find me," says the LORD. "And I will bring you back from your captivity. I forced you to leave this place, but I will gather you from all the nations, from the places I have sent you as captives," says the LORD. "And I will bring you back to this place."

[15]You might say, "The LORD has given us prophets here in Babylon."

[16]But the LORD says this about the king who is sitting on David's throne now and all the other people still in Jerusalem, your relatives who did not go as captives to Babylon with you. [17]The LORD All-Powerful says: "I will soon send war, hunger, and terrible diseases against those still in Jerusalem. I will make them like bad figs that are too rotten to eat. [18]I will chase them with war, hunger, and terrible diseases. I will make them hated by all the kingdoms of the earth. People will curse them and be shocked and will use them as a shameful example wherever I make them go. [19]This is because they have not listened to my message," says the LORD. "I sent my message to them again and again through my servants, the prophets, but they did not listen," says the LORD.

[20]You captives, whom I forced to leave Jerusalem and go to Babylon, listen to the message from the LORD. [21]The LORD All-Powerful, the God of Israel, says this about Ahab son of Kolaiah and Zedekiah son of Maaseiah: "These two men have been prophesying lies to you, saying that their message is from me. But soon I will hand over those two prophets to Nebuchadnezzar king of Babylon, and he will kill them in front of you. [22]Because of them, all the captives from Judah in Babylon will use this curse: 'May the LORD treat you like Zedekiah and Ahab, whom the king of Babylon burned in the fire.' [23]They have done evil things among the people of Israel. They are guilty of adultery[d] with their neighbors' wives. They have also spoken lies and said those lies were a message from me. I did not tell them to do that. I know what they have done; I am a witness to it," says the LORD.

[24]Also give a message to Shemaiah from the Nehelamite family. [25]The LORD All-Powerful, the God of Israel, says: "Shemaiah, you sent letters in your name to all the people in Jerusalem, to the priest Zephaniah son of Maaseiah, and to all the priests. [26]You said to Zephaniah, 'The LORD has made you priest in place of Jehoiada. You are to be in charge of the Temple[d] of the LORD. You should arrest any madman who acts like a prophet. Lock his hands and feet between wooden blocks, and put iron rings around his neck. [27]Now Jeremiah from Anathoth is acting like a prophet. So why haven't you arrested him? [28]Jeremiah has sent this message to us in Babylon:

You will be there for a long time, so build houses and settle down. Plant gardens and eat what they grow.' "

29Zephaniah the priest read the letter to Jeremiah the prophet. 30Then the LORD spoke his word to Jeremiah: 31"Send this message to all the captives in Babylon: 'This is what the LORD says about Shemaiah the Nehelamite: Shemaiah has prophesied to you, but I did not send him. He has made you believe a lie. 32So the LORD says, I will soon punish Shemaiah the Nehelamite and his family. He will not see the good things I will do for my people, says the LORD. None of his family will be left alive among the people, because he has taught the people to turn against me.' "

✳ **SIDELIGHT:** Though most of Jeremiah is bad news, chapters 30 to 33 are good news. These chapters have been called the "Book of Consolation" or the "Little Book of Comfort" because of their message of hope.

Promises of Hope

30 These are the words that the LORD spoke to Jeremiah. 2The LORD, the God of Israel, said: "Jeremiah, write in a book all the words I have spoken to you. 3The days will come when I will bring Israel and Judah back from captivity," says the LORD. "I will return them to the land I gave their ancestors, and they will own it!" says the LORD.

4The LORD spoke this message about the people of Israel and Judah: 5This is what the LORD said:
"We hear people crying from fear.
They are afraid; there is no peace.
6Ask this question, and consider it:
A man cannot have a baby.
So why do I see every strong man
holding his stomach in pain like a woman having a baby?
Why is everyone's face turning white like a dead man's face?
7This will be a terrible day!
There will never be another time like this.
This is a time of great trouble for the people of Jacob,
but they will be saved from it."

8The LORD All-Powerful says, "At that time
I will break the yoke*d* from their necks
and tear off the ropes that hold them.
Foreign people will never again make my people slaves.
9They will serve the LORD their God

and David their king,
whom I will send to them.
10"So people of Jacob, my servants, don't be afraid.
Israel, don't be frightened," says the LORD.
"I will soon save you from that faraway place where you are captives.
I will save your family from that land.
The people of Jacob will be safe and have peace again;
there will be no enemy to frighten them.
11I am with you and will save you,"
says the LORD.
"I will completely destroy all those nations where I scattered you,
but I will not completely destroy you.
I will punish you fairly,
but I will still punish you."

12This is what the LORD said:
"You people have a wound that cannot be cured;
your injury will not heal.
13There is no one to argue your case
and no cure for your sores.
So you will not be healed.
14All those nations who were your friends have forgotten you.
They don't care about you.
I have hurt you as an enemy would.
I punished you very hard,
because your guilt was so great
and your sins were so many.
15Why are you crying out about your injury?
There is no cure for your pain.
I did these things to you because of your great guilt,
because of your many sins.
16But all those nations that destroyed you will now be destroyed.
All your enemies will become captives in other lands.
Those who stole from you will have their own things stolen.
Those who took things from you in war will have their own things taken.
17I will bring back your health
and heal your injuries," says the LORD,
"because other people forced you away.
They said about you, 'No one cares about Jerusalem!' "

18This is what the LORD said:
"I will soon make the tents of Jacob's people as they used to be,
and I will have pity on Israel's houses.
The city will be rebuilt on its hill of ruins,
and the king's palace will stand in its proper place.

¹⁹People in those places will sing songs of
praise.
There will be the sound of laughter.
I will give them many children
so their number will not be small.
I will bring honor to them
so no one will look down on them.
²⁰Their descendants*d* will be as they were in
the old days.
I will set them up as a strong people before
me,
and I will punish the nations who have hurt
them.
²¹One of their own people will lead them;
their ruler will come from among them.
He will come near to me when I invite him.
Who would dare to come to me
uninvited?" says the LORD.
²²"So you will be my people,
and I will be your God."

²³Look! It is a storm from the LORD!

He is angry and has gone out to punish the
people.
Punishment will come like a storm
crashing down on the evil people.
²⁴The LORD will stay angry
until he finishes punishing the people.
He will stay angry
until he finishes the punishment he
planned.
When that day comes,
you will understand this.

The New Israel

31 The LORD says, "At that time I will be
God of all Israel's family groups, and
they will be my people."
²This is what the LORD says:
"The people who were not killed by the
enemy's sword
found help in the desert.
I came to give rest to Israel."

CELEBRATING

Remembering Matt

Matt Floyd, seventeen, finished writing his talk for the upcoming retreat and attended a planning meeting on Sunday, but he never gave his talk. Three days later, while hiking in the mountains, Matt lost his footing and fell to his death.

Matt's death shocked the other retreat team members. But over the next few weeks, they pulled together and learned how to celebrate even in the face of tragedy. They attended Matt's funeral and celebrated the seventeen years of life God had granted him. They celebrated the gift of Matt's fun-loving friendship that each of them had experienced.

Then they went on with the retreat, introducing other teenagers to the God whom Matt knew. Matt's talk was read at the time he was scheduled to give it. Kids cried as they listened to his words and remembered his voice. Some of the team members wore woven-yarn rings to remind them of Matt's friendship. At the end of the weekend, they offered those rings to God.

"When Matt died we thought about canceling the retreat," said one of the planning team members. "But I'm glad we didn't. God brought us closer together and helped us celebrate the blessings Matt had brought us."

Matt's friends learned that even in the midst of tragedies, we can celebrate God's goodness. Read how God encourages celebration—in hard times as well as good ones—in **Jeremiah 31:1–17**.

■ What role does God play in the celebrations for Matt and the ones described in the passage?
■ How do these celebrations compare to your ideas about celebrating?

CONSIDER...

■ celebrating something God has done for you the next time you are going through a tough situation.
■ writing your thoughts and memories of a relative or friend who has died, celebrating what that person meant to you.

FOR MORE, SEE...

■ Nehemiah 8:9–12 (p. 434)
■ Psalm 150 (p. 565)

■ Luke 1:68–79 (p. 1002)

3And from far away the LORD appeared to his
people and said,
"I love you people
    with a love that will last forever.
That is why I have continued
    showing you kindness.
4People of Israel, I will build you up again,
    and you will be rebuilt.
You will pick up your tambourines*d* again
    and dance with those who are joyful.
5You will plant vineyards again
    on the hills around Samaria.
The farmers will plant them
    and enjoy their fruit.
6There will be a time when watchmen in the
    mountains of Ephraim shout this
    message:
    'Come, let's go up to Jerusalem to worship
    the LORD our God!' "

7This is what the LORD says:
"Be happy and sing for the people of Jacob.
    Shout for Israel, the greatest of the nations.
Sing your praises and shout this:
    'LORD, save your people,
    those who are left alive from the nation of
    Israel!'
8Look, I will soon bring Israel from the
    country in the north,
and I will gather them from the faraway
    places on earth.
Some of the people are blind and crippled.
    Some of the women are pregnant, and
    some are ready to give birth.
A great many people will come back.
9They will be crying as they come,
    but they will pray as I bring them back.
I will lead those people by streams of water
    on an even road where they will not
    stumble.
I am Israel's father,
    and Israel is my firstborn*d* son.

10"Nations, listen to the message from the
    LORD.
Tell this message in the faraway lands by
    the sea:
    'The one who scattered the people of Israel
    will bring them back,
and he will watch over his people like a
    shepherd.'
11The LORD will pay for the people of Jacob
    and will buy them back from people
    stronger than they were.
12The people of Israel will come to the high
    points of Jerusalem
    and shout for joy.
Their faces will shine with happiness about
    all the good things from the LORD:

the grain, new wine, oil, young sheep, and
    young cows.
They will be like a garden that has plenty of
    water,
    and they will not be troubled anymore.
13Then young women of Israel will be happy
    and dance,
    the young men and old men also.
I will change their sadness into happiness;
    I will give them comfort and joy instead of
    sadness.
14The priests will have more than enough
    sacrifices,
    and my people will be filled with the good
    things I give them!" says the LORD.

15This is what the LORD says:
"A voice was heard in Ramah
    of painful crying and deep sadness:
Rachel crying for her children.
    She refused to be comforted,
    because her children are dead!"

16But this is what the LORD says:
"Stop crying;
    don't let your eyes fill with tears.
You will be rewarded for your work!" says
    the LORD.
    "The people will return from their enemy's
    land.
17So there is hope for you in the future," says
    the LORD.
    "Your children will return to their own
    land.

18"I have heard Israel moaning:
    'LORD, you punished me, and I have
    learned my lesson.
I was like a calf that had never been
    trained.
Take me back so that I may come back.
    You truly are the LORD my God.
19LORD, after I wandered away from you,
    I changed my heart and life.
After I understood,
    I beat my breast with sorrow.
I was ashamed and disgraced,
    because I suffered for the foolish things I
    did when I was young.'

20"You know that Israel is my dear son,
    The child I love.
Yes, I often speak against Israel,
    but I still remember *him.*
I love him very much,
    and I want to comfort him," says the LORD.

21"People of Israel, fix the road signs.
    Put up signs to show you the way home.
Watch the road.

Pay attention to the road on which you
travel.
People of Israel, come home,
come back to your towns.
²²You are an unfaithful daughter.
How long will you wander before you
come home?
The LORD has made something new happen
in the land:
A woman will go seeking a man."

²³The LORD All-Powerful, the God of Israel,
says: "I will again do good things for the people
of Judah. At that time the people in the land of
Judah and its towns will again use these words:
'May the LORD bless you, home of what is good,
holy mountain.' ²⁴People in all the towns of Judah
will live together in peace. Farmers and those
who move around with their flocks will live together in peace. ²⁵I will give rest and strength to
those who are weak and tired."

²⁶After hearing that, I, Jeremiah, woke up and
looked around. My sleep had been very pleasant.

²⁷The LORD says, "The time is coming when I
will help the families of Israel and Judah and their
children and animals to grow. ²⁸In the past I
watched over Israel and Judah, to pull them up
and tear them down, to destroy them and bring
them disaster. But now I will watch over them to
build them up and make them strong," says the
LORD.

²⁹"At that time people will no longer say:
'The parents have eaten sour grapes,
and that caused the children to grind their
teeth from the sour taste.'
³⁰Instead, each person will die for his own sin; the
person who eats sour grapes will grind his own
teeth.

The New Agreement

³¹"Look, the time is coming," says the LORD,
"when I will make a new agreement
with the people of Israel
and the people of Judah.
³²It will not be like the agreement
I made with their ancestors

PROMISES

Changing Lives

Aristides Alvarado, twenty, is a junior at Rensselaer Polytechnic Institute in upstate New
York. But when he was a sixth grader, most people who knew him gave him less than a
50 percent chance of graduating from high school.

Fortunately, "most people" didn't include Eugene M. Lang.

Lang is a wealthy businessman, in fact, a millionaire. A few years ago, he returned to his
elementary school—Public School 121 in East Harlem, New York—now one of the poorest
schools in the United States. He promised the sixty-one sixth-graders, including Aristides,
that if they graduated from high school he would pay for their college education.

Lang is keeping that promise. He helped those students through their junior and senior
high school years, paying for workshops, cultural trips, even tutors to help them stay in
school. About one-half of the original sixty-one is in college, and their
education is being paid for through Lang's "I Have a Dream" Foundation.

The students, who call themselves "Dreamers," are deeply grateful that
Lang is keeping his promise. "Mr. Lang was one of the first people who took
a personal interest in me and made me look at my life in a different way,"
says Aristides. "I know I'm going to make it. And someday I'll be big—real
big—and pay the tuition for my class of dreamers."

Lang and his friends aren't the only ones keeping promises these days.
Read about God's promises in **Jeremiah 31:27–37**.

■ What effects might Lang's or God's promises have on the people
involved?

■ What choices must you make to receive the benefits of God's promises?

C O N S I D E R . . .

■ reading Jesus' teaching in the Beatitudes (Matthew 5:1–12, p. 0000). Imagine Jesus
using your name in his promises for believers.

■ keeping a promise you've neglected.

F O R   M O R E ,   S E E . . .

■ Lamentations 3:22–25 (p. 757) ■ John 2:18–22 (p. 1060)
■ Matthew 7:7–11 (p. 919)

when I took them by the hand
　　to bring them out of Egypt.
I was a husband to them,
　　but they broke that agreement," says the
　　　Lord.
33"This is the agreement I will make
　　with the people of Israel at that time," says
　　　the Lord:
"I will put my teachings in their minds
　　and write them on their hearts.
I will be their God,
　　and they will be my people.
34People will no longer have to teach their
　　　neighbors and relatives
　　to know the Lord,
because all people will know me,
　　from the least to the most important," says
　　　the Lord.
"I will forgive them for the wicked things
　　they did,
　　and I will not remember their sins
　　anymore."

The Lord Will Never Leave Israel

35The Lord makes the sun shine in the day
　　and the moon and stars to shine at night.
He stirs up the sea so that its waves crash on
　　　the shore.
The Lord All-Powerful is his name.
This is what the Lord says:
36"Only if these laws should ever fail,"
　　says the Lord,
"will Israel's descendants*d* ever stop
　　being a nation before me."

37This is what the Lord says:
"Only if people can measure the sky above
　　and learn the secrets of the earth below,
will I reject all the descendants of Israel
　　because of what they have done," says the
　　　Lord.

The New Jerusalem

38The Lord says, "The time is coming when
Jerusalem will be rebuilt for me—everything
from the Tower of Hananel to the Corner Gate.
39The measuring line will stretch from the Corner
Gate straight to the hill of Gareb. Then it will turn
to the place named Goah. 40The whole valley
where dead bodies and ashes are thrown, and all
the terraces out to the Kidron Valley on the east
as far as the corner of the Horse Gate—all that
area will be holy to the Lord. The city of Jerusalem will never again be torn down or destroyed."

Jeremiah Buys a Field

32 This is the word the Lord spoke to Jeremiah in the tenth year Zedekiah was
king of Judah, which was the eighteenth year of

Nebuchadnezzar. 2At that time the army of the
king of Babylon was surrounding Jerusalem. Jeremiah the prophet was under arrest in the courtyard of the guard, which was at the palace of the
king of Judah.

3Zedekiah king of Judah had put Jeremiah in
prison there. Zedekiah had asked, "Why have you
prophesied*d* the things you have?" (Jeremiah had
said, "This is what the Lord says: 'I will soon
hand the city of Jerusalem over to the king of Babylon, and he will capture it. 4Zedekiah king of Judah will not escape from the Babylonian army,
but he will surely be handed over to the king of
Babylon. And he will speak to the king of Babylon
face to face and see him with his own eyes. 5The
king will take Zedekiah to Babylon, where he will
stay until I have punished him,' says the Lord. 'If
you fight against the Babylonians, you will not
succeed.' ")

6While Jeremiah was in prison, he said, "The
Lord spoke this word to me: 7Your cousin Hanamel, son of your uncle Shallum, will come to you
soon. Hanamel will say to you, 'Jeremiah, you are
my nearest relative, so buy my field near the town
of Anathoth. It is your right and your duty to buy
that field.'

8"Then it happened just as the Lord had said.
My cousin Hanamel came to me in the courtyard
of the guard and said to me, 'Buy for yourself my
field near Anathoth in the land of Benjamin. It is
your right and duty to buy it and own it.' So I
knew this was a message from the Lord.

9"I bought the field at Anathoth from my
cousin Hanamel, weighing out seven ounces of
silver for him. 10I signed the record and sealed it
and had some people witness it. I also weighed
out the silver on the scales. 11Then I took both
copies of the record of ownership—the one that
was sealed that had the demands and limits of
ownership, and the one that was not sealed.
12And I gave them to Baruch son of Neriah, the
son of Mahseiah. My cousin Hanamel, the other
witnesses who signed the record of ownership, and many Jews sitting in the courtyard of
the guard saw me give the record of ownership
to Baruch.

13"With all the people watching, I told Baruch,
14'This is what the Lord All-Powerful, the God of
Israel, says: Take both copies of the record of
ownership—the sealed copy and the copy that
was not sealed—and put them in a clay jar so
they will last a long time. 15This is what the Lord
All-Powerful, the God of Israel, says: In the future
my people will once again buy houses and fields
for grain and vineyards in the land of Israel.'

16"After I gave the record of ownership to Baruch son of Neriah, I prayed to the Lord, 17Oh,
Lord God, you made the skies and the earth with
your very great power. There is nothing too hard

for you to do. [18]You show love and kindness to thousands of people, but you also bring punishment to children for their parents' sins. Great and powerful God, your name is the LORD All-Powerful. [19]You plan and do great things. You see everything that people do, and you reward people for the way they live and for what they do. [20]You did miracles[d] and wonderful things in the land of Egypt. You have continued doing them in Israel and among the other nations even until today. So you have become well known. [21]You brought your people, the Israelites, out of Egypt using signs and miracles and your great power and strength. You brought great terror on everyone. [22]You gave them this land that you promised to their ancestors long ago, a fertile land. [23]They came into this land and took it for their own, but they did not obey you or follow your teachings. They did not do everything you commanded. So you made all these terrible things happen to them.

[24]"Look! The enemy has surrounded the city and has built roads to the top of the walls to capture it. Because of war, hunger, and terrible diseases, the city will be handed over to the Babylonians who are attacking it. You said this would happen, and now you see it is happening. [25]But now, Lord GOD, you tell me, 'Buy the field with silver and call in witnesses.' You tell me this while the Babylonian army is ready to capture the city."

[26]Then the LORD spoke this word to Jeremiah: [27]"I am the LORD, the God of every person on the earth. Nothing is impossible for me. [28]So this is what the LORD says: I will soon hand over the city of Jerusalem to the Babylonian army and to Nebuchadnezzar king of Babylon, who will capture it. [29]The Babylonian army is already attacking the city of Jerusalem. They will soon enter it and start a fire to burn down the city and its houses. The people of Jerusalem offered sacrifices to Baal[d] on the roofs[n] of those same houses and poured out drink offerings to other idols to make me angry. [30]From their youth, the people of Israel and Judah have done only the things I said were wrong. They have made me angry by worshiping idols made with their own hands," says the LORD. [31]"From the day Jerusalem was built until now, this city has made me angry, so angry that I must remove it from my sight. [32]I will destroy it, because of all the evil the people of Israel and Judah have done. The people, their kings and officers, their priests and prophets, all the people of Judah, and the people of Jerusalem have made me angry. [33]They turned their backs to me, not their faces. I tried to teach them again and again, but they wouldn't listen or learn. [34]They put their hateful idols in the place where I have chosen to be worshiped, so they made it unclean.[d] [35]In the Valley of Ben Hinnom they built places to worship Baal so they could burn their sons and daughters as sacrifices to Molech.[d] But I never commanded them to do such a hateful thing. It never entered my mind that they would do such a thing and cause Judah to sin.

[36]"You are saying, 'Because of war, hunger, and terrible diseases, the city will be handed over to the king of Babylon.' But the LORD, the God of Israel, says about Jerusalem: [37]I forced the people of Israel and Judah to leave their land, because I was furious and very angry with them. But soon I will gather them from all the lands where I forced them to go, and I will bring them back to this place, where they may live in safety. [38]The people of Israel and Judah will be my people, and I will be their God. [39]I will make them truly want to be one people with one goal. They will truly want to worship me all their lives, for their own good and for the good of their children after them. [40]"I will make an agreement with them that will last forever. I will never turn away from them; I will always do good to them. I will make them want to respect me so they will never turn away from me. [41]I will enjoy doing good to them. And with my whole being I will surely plant them in this land and make them grow."

[42]This is what the LORD says: "I have brought this great disaster to the people of Israel and Judah. In the same way I will bring the good things that I promise to do for them. [43]You are saying, 'This land is an empty desert, without people or animals. It has been handed over to the Babylonians.' But in the future, people will again buy fields in this land. [44]They will use their money to buy fields. They will sign and seal their agreements and call in witnesses. They will again buy fields in the land of Benjamin, in the area around Jerusalem, in the towns of Judah and in the mountains, in the western hills, and in southern Judah. I will make everything as good for them as it once was," says the LORD.

The Promise of the Lord

33 While Jeremiah was still locked up in the courtyard of the guards, the LORD spoke his word to him a second time: [2]"These are the words of the LORD, who made the earth, shaped it, and gave it order, whose name is the LORD: [3]'Judah, pray to me, and I will answer you. I will tell you important secrets you have never heard before.' [4]This is what the LORD, the God of Israel, says about the houses in Jerusalem and the royal

---

roofs   In Bible times houses were built with flat roofs. The roof was used for drying things such as flax and fruit. And it was used as an extra room, as a place for worship, and as a place to sleep in the summer.

palaces of Judah that have been torn down to be used in defense of the attack by the Babylonian army: 5'Some people will come to fight against the Babylonians. They will fill these houses with the bodies of people I killed in my hot anger. I have turned away from this city because of all the evil its people have done.

6" 'But then I will bring health and healing to the people there. I will heal them and let them enjoy great peace and safety. 7I will bring Judah and Israel back from captivity and make them strong countries as in the past. 8They sinned against me, but I will wash away that sin. They did evil and turned away from me, but I will forgive them. 9Then 'Jerusalem' will be to me a name that brings joy! And people from all nations of the earth will praise it when they hear about the good things I am doing there. They will be surprised and shocked at all the good things and the peace I will bring to Jerusalem.'

10"You are saying, 'Our country is an empty desert, without people or animals.' But this is what the LORD says: It is now quiet in the streets of Jerusalem and in the towns of Judah, without people or animals, but it will be noisy there soon! 11There will be sounds of joy and gladness and the happy sounds of brides and bridegrooms. There will be the sounds of people bringing to the Tem-

pled of the LORD their offerings of thanks to the LORD. They will say,
'Praise the LORD All-Powerful,
   because the LORD is good!
   His love continues forever!'
They will say this because I will again do good things for Judah, as I did in the beginning," says the LORD.

12This is what the LORD All-Powerful says: "This place is empty now, without people or animals. But there will be shepherds in all the towns of Judah and pastures where they let their flocks rest. 13Shepherds will again count their sheep as the sheep walk in front of them. They will count them in the mountains and in the western hills, in southern Judah and the land of Benjamin, and around Jerusalem and the other towns of Judah!" says the LORD.

The Good Branch

14The LORD says, "The time is coming when I will do the good thing I promised to the people of Israel and Judah.
15In those days and at that time,
   I will make a good branch sprout from
      David's family.
   He will do what is fair and right in the
      land.

FUTURE

Will Peace Ever Come?

"The atomic bomb is another weapon in the arsenal of righteousness." —Harry S Truman, U.S. president
   "The atomic age is here to stay—but are we?" —Bennett Cerf, publisher
   "The way to win an atomic war is to make certain it never starts." —Omar Bradley, U.S. Army general
   "There is no evil in the atom—only in men's souls." —Adlai Stevenson, statesman
   The future can seem uncertain and dangerous, and the spread of nuclear weapons adds to that uncertainty. But, even in difficult times, God keeps his promises. Read one of God's promises for the future in **Jeremiah 33:14—16**.
■ God promises a Savior in the passage. Do you think that promise includes being saved from nuclear weapons and war? Why or why not?
■ How does your future look? How does faith in Christ affect the way you look at your future?

C O N S I D E R . . .
■ each day asking God to guide some part of your future. For example, Monday: Who will I marry? Tuesday: What career should I choose?
◢ writing one paragraph on how you would like to be remembered after your death. Choose one thing to do this week to help you toward your goals.

F O R   M O R E ,   S E E . . .
■ Genesis 9:8–17 (p. 11)
■ Matthew 6:25–34 (p. 918)
■ Acts 1:6–11 (p. 1098)

¹⁶At that time Judah will be saved,
and the people of Jerusalem will live in
safety.
The branch will be named:
The LORD Does What Is Right."

¹⁷This is what the LORD says: "Someone from
David's family will always sit on the throne of the
family of Israel. ¹⁸And there will always be priests
from the family of Levi. They will always stand
before me to offer burnt offerings and grain offerings and sacrifices to me."

¹⁹The LORD spoke his word to Jeremiah, saying: ²⁰"This is what the LORD says: I have an
agreement with day and night that they will always come at the right times. If you could change
that agreement, ²¹only then could you change my
agreement with David and Levi. Only then would
my servant David not have a descendant*d* ruling
as king on David's throne. And only then would
the family of Levi not be priests serving me in the
Temple.*d* ²²But I will give many descendants to
my servant David and to the family group of Levi
who serve me in the Temple. They will be as
many as the stars in the sky that no one can
count. They will be as many as the grains of sand
on the seashore that no one can measure."

²³The LORD spoke his word to Jeremiah, saying: ²⁴"Jeremiah, have you heard what the people
are saying? They say: 'The LORD turned away
from the two families of Israel and Judah that he
chose.' Now they don't think of my people as a
nation anymore!"

²⁵This is what the LORD says: "If I had not
made my agreement with day and night, and if
I had not made the laws for the sky and
earth, ²⁶only then would I turn away from
Jacob's descendants. And only then would I not
let the descendants of David my servant rule over
the descendants of Abraham, Isaac, and Jacob.
But I will be kind to them and cause good
things to happen to them again."

A Warning to Zedekiah

34 The LORD spoke his word to Jeremiah
when Nebuchadnezzar king of Babylon
was fighting against Jerusalem and all the towns
around it. Nebuchadnezzar had with him all his
army and the armies of all the kingdoms and peoples he ruled. ²This is what the LORD, the God of
Israel, said: "Jeremiah, go to Zedekiah king of Judah and tell him: 'This is what the LORD says: I
will soon hand the city of Jerusalem over to the
king of Babylon, and he will burn it down! ³You
will not escape from the king of Babylon; you will
surely be captured and handed over to him. You
will see the king of Babylon with your own eyes,
and he will talk to you face to face. And you will
go to Babylon. ⁴But, Zedekiah king of Judah, listen

to the promise of the LORD. This is what the LORD
says about you: You will not be killed with a
sword. ⁵You will die in a peaceful way. As people
made funeral fires to honor your ancestors, the
kings who ruled before you, so people will make
a funeral fire to honor you. They will cry for you
and sadly say, "Ah, master!" I myself make this
promise to you, says the LORD.' "

⁶So Jeremiah the prophet*d* gave this message to
Zedekiah in Jerusalem. ⁷This was while the army
of the king of Babylon was fighting against Jerusalem and the cities of Judah that had not yet
been taken—Lachish and Azekah. These were
the only strong, walled cities left in the land of
Judah.

Slaves Are Mistreated

⁸The LORD spoke his word to Jeremiah. This
was after King Zedekiah had made an agreement
with all the people in Jerusalem to free all the
Hebrew slaves. ⁹Everyone was supposed to free
his Hebrew slaves, both male and female. No one
was to keep a fellow Jew as a slave. ¹⁰All the officers and all the people accepted this agreement;
they agreed to free their male and female slaves
and no longer keep them as slaves. So all the
slaves were set free. ¹¹But after that, the people
who had slaves changed their minds. So they took
back the people they had set free and made them
slaves again.

¹²Then the LORD spoke his word to Jeremiah:
¹³"This is what the LORD, the God of Israel, says:
I brought your ancestors out of Egypt where they
were slaves and made an agreement with them.
¹⁴I said to your ancestors: 'At the end of every
seven years, each one of you must set his Hebrew
slaves free. If a fellow Hebrew has sold himself to
you, you must let him go free after he has served
you for six years.' But your ancestors did not listen or pay attention to me. ¹⁵A short time ago you
changed your hearts and did what I say is right.
Each of you gave freedom to his fellow Hebrews who were slaves. And you even made an
agreement before me in the place where I have
chosen to be worshiped. ¹⁶But now you have
changed your minds. You have shown you
do not honor me. Each of you has taken back
the male and female slaves you had set free,
and you have forced them to become your
slaves again.

¹⁷"So this is what the LORD says: You have not
obeyed me. You have not given freedom to your
fellow Hebrews, neither relatives nor friends. But
now I will give freedom, says the LORD, to war,
to terrible diseases, and to hunger. I will make
you hated by all the kingdoms of the earth. ¹⁸I will
hand over the men who broke my agreement,
who have not kept the promises they made before

me. They cut a calf into two pieces before me and walked between the pieces.[n] [19]These people made the agreement before me by walking between the pieces of the calf: the leaders of Judah and Jerusalem, the officers of the court, the priests, and all the people of the land. [20]So I will hand them over to their enemies and to everyone who wants to kill them. Their bodies will become food for the birds of the air and for the wild animals of the earth. [21]I will hand Zedekiah king of Judah and his officers over to their enemies, and to everyone who wants to kill them, and to the army of the king of Babylon, even though they have left Jerusalem. [22]I will give the order, says the LORD, to bring the Babylonian army back to Jerusalem. It will fight against Jerusalem, capture it, set it on fire, and burn it down. I will destroy the towns in Judah so that they become ruins where no one lives!"

The Recabite Family Obeys God

35 When Jehoiakim son of Josiah was king of Judah, the LORD spoke his word to Jeremiah, saying: [2]"Go to the family of Recab. Invite them to come to one of the side rooms of the Temple[d] of the LORD, and offer them wine to drink."

[3]So I went to get Jaazaniah son of Jeremiah,[n] the son of Habazziniah. And I gathered all of Jaazaniah's brothers and sons and the whole family of the Recabites together. [4]Then I brought them into the Temple of the LORD. We went into the room of the sons of Hanan son of Igdaliah, who was a man of God. The room was next to the one where the officers stay and above the room of Maaseiah son of Shallum, the doorkeeper in the Temple. [5]Then I put some bowls full of wine and some cups before the men of the Recabite family. And I said to them, "Drink some wine."

[6]But the Recabite men answered, "We never drink wine. Our ancestor Jonadab son of Recab gave us this command: 'You and your descendants[d] must never drink wine. [7]Also you must never build houses, plant seeds, or plant vineyards, or do any of those things. You must live only in tents. Then you will live a long time in the land where you are wanderers.' [8]So we Recabites have obeyed everything Jonadab our ancestor commanded us. Neither we nor our wives, sons, or daughters ever drink wine. [9]We never build houses in which to live, or own fields or vineyards, or plant crops. [10]We have lived in tents and have obeyed everything our ancestor Jonadab commanded us. [11]But when Nebuchadnezzar king of Babylon attacked Judah, we said to each other, 'Come, we must enter Jerusalem so we can

escape the Babylonian army and the Aramean army.' So we have stayed in Jerusalem."

[12]Then the LORD spoke his word to Jeremiah: [13]"This is what the LORD All-Powerful, the God of Israel, says: Jeremiah, go and tell the men of Judah and the people of Jerusalem: 'You should learn a lesson and obey my message,' says the LORD. [14]'Jonadab son of Recab ordered his descendants not to drink wine, and that command has been obeyed. Until today they have obeyed their ancestor's command; they do not drink wine. But I, the LORD, have given you messages again and again, but you did not obey me. [15]I sent all my servants the prophets to you again and again, saying, "Each of you must stop doing evil. You must change and be good. Do not follow other gods to serve them. If you obey me, you will live in the land I have given to you and your ancestors." But you have not listened to me or paid attention to my message. [16]The descendants of Jonadab son of Recab obeyed the commands their ancestor gave them, but the people of Judah have not obeyed me.'

[17]"So the LORD God All-Powerful, the God of Israel, says: 'I will soon bring every disaster I said would come to Judah and to everyone living in Jerusalem. I spoke to those people, but they refused to listen. I called out to them, but they did not answer me.' "

[18]Then Jeremiah said to the Recabites, "This is what the LORD All-Powerful, the God of Israel, says: 'You have obeyed the commands of your ancestor Jonadab and have followed all of his teachings; you have done everything he commanded.' [19]So this is what the LORD All-Powerful, the God of Israel, says: 'There will always be a descendant of Jonadab son of Recab to serve me.' "

Jehoiakim Burns Jeremiah's Scroll

36 The LORD spoke this word to Jeremiah during the fourth year that Jehoiakim son of Josiah was king of Judah: [2]"Get a scroll. Write on it all the words I have spoken to you about Israel and Judah and all the nations. Write everything from when I first spoke to you, when Josiah was king, until now. [3]Maybe the family of Judah will hear what disasters I am planning to bring on them and will stop doing wicked things. Then I would forgive them for the sins and the evil things they have done."

[4]So Jeremiah called for Baruch son of Neriah. Jeremiah spoke the messages the LORD had given him, and Baruch wrote those messages on the scroll. [5]Then Jeremiah commanded Baruch, "I cannot go to the Temple[d] of the LORD. I must stay

They . . . pieces. This showed that the men were willing to be killed, like this animal, if they did not keep their agreement.
Jeremiah Not the prophet Jeremiah, but a different man with the same name.

here. ⁶So I want you to go to the Temple of the LORD on a day when the people are giving up eating. Read from the scroll to all the people of Judah who come into Jerusalem from their towns. Read the messages from the LORD, which are the words you wrote on the scroll as I spoke them to you.

> ### ☀ SIDELIGHT: Baruch was
> Jeremiah's secretary and friend who recorded the prophet's thoughts on scrolls made from treated animal skins (Jeremiah 36:4). Baruch was an important citizen of Jerusalem and probably served as a royal clerk. That made working with Jeremiah an occupational hazard, since Jeremiah was rarely on the king's good side.

⁷Perhaps they will ask the LORD to help them. Perhaps each one will stop doing wicked things, because the LORD has announced that he is very angry with them." ⁸So Baruch son of Neriah did everything Jeremiah the prophet*ᵈ* told him to do. In the LORD's Temple he read aloud the scroll that had the LORD's messages written on it.

⁹In the ninth month of the fifth year that Jehoiakim son of Josiah was king, a special time to give up eating was announced. All the people of Jerusalem and everyone who had come into Jerusalem from the towns of Judah were supposed to give up eating to honor the LORD. ¹⁰At that time Baruch read to all the people there the scroll containing Jeremiah's words. He read the scroll in the Temple of the LORD in the room of Gemariah son of Shaphan, a royal secretary. That room was in the upper courtyard at the entrance of the New Gate of the Temple.

¹¹Micaiah son of Gemariah, the son of Shaphan, heard all the messages from the LORD that were on the scroll. ¹²Micaiah went down to the royal secretary's room in the king's palace where all of the officers were sitting: Elishama the royal secretary; Delaiah son of Shemaiah; Elnathan son of Acbor; Gemariah son of Shaphan; Zedekiah son of Hananiah; and all the other officers. ¹³Micaiah told those officers everything he had heard Baruch read to the people from the scroll.

¹⁴Then the officers sent a man named Jehudi son of Nethaniah to Baruch. (Nethaniah was the son of Shelemiah, who was the son of Cushi.) Jehudi said to Baruch, "Bring the scroll that you read to the people and come with me."

So Baruch son of Neriah took the scroll and went with Jehudi to the officers. ¹⁵Then the officers said to Baruch, "Please sit down and read the scroll to us."

So Baruch read the scroll to them. ¹⁶When the officers heard all the words, they became afraid and looked at each other. They said to Baruch, 'We must certainly tell the king about these words." ¹⁷Then the officers asked Baruch, "Tell us, please, where did you get all these words you wrote on the scroll? Did you write down what Jeremiah said to you?"

¹⁸"Yes," Baruch answered. "Jeremiah spoke them all to me, and I wrote them down with ink on this scroll."

¹⁹Then the officers said to Baruch, "You and Jeremiah must go and hide, and don't tell anyone where you are."

²⁰The officers put the scroll in the room of Elishama the royal secretary. Then they went to the king in the courtyard and told him all about the scroll. ²¹So King Jehoiakim sent Jehudi to get the scroll. Jehudi brought the scroll from the room of Elishama the royal secretary and read it to the king and to all the officers who stood around the king. ²²It was the ninth month of the year, so King Jehoiakim was sitting in the winter apartment. There was a fire burning in a small firepot in front of him. ²³After Jehudi had read three or four columns, the king cut those columns off of the scroll with a penknife and threw them into the firepot. Finally, the whole scroll was burned in the fire. ²⁴King Jehoiakim and his servants heard everything that was said, but they were not frightened! They did not tear their clothes to show their sorrow. ²⁵Elnathan, Delaiah, and Gemariah even tried to talk King Jehoiakim out of burning the scroll, but he would not listen to them. ²⁶Instead, the king ordered Jerahmeel son of the king, Seraiah son of Azriel, and Shelemiah son of Abdeel to arrest Baruch the secretary and Jeremiah the prophet. But the LORD had hidden them.

> ### ☀ SIDELIGHT: If you've ever
> written a long, difficult report in school, you know how scary it can be to have the teacher grade it. Imagine how Jeremiah felt when the king, after hearing what Jeremiah had written, cut up and burned his scroll (Jeremiah 36:20–26). Jeremiah didn't give up, though. He wrote an even longer book to replace the burned one (Jeremiah 36:27–32).

²⁷So King Jehoiakim burned the scroll where Baruch had written all the words Jeremiah had spoken to him. Then the LORD spoke his word to Jeremiah: ²⁸"Get another scroll. Write all the words on it that were on the first scroll that Jehoiakim king of Judah burned up. ²⁹Also say this to Jehoiakim king of Judah: 'This is what the LORD

says: You burned up that scroll and said, "Why, Jeremiah, did you write on it 'the king of Babylon will surely come and destroy this land and the people and animals in it'?" ³⁰So this is what the LORD says about Jehoiakim king of Judah: Jehoiakim's descendants*d* will not sit on David's throne. When Jehoiakim dies, his body will be thrown out on the ground. It will be left out in the heat of the day and in the cold frost of the night. ³¹I will punish Jehoiakim and his children and his servants, because they have done evil things. I will bring disasters upon them and upon all the people in Jerusalem and Judah — everything I promised but which they refused to hear.' "

³²So Jeremiah took another scroll and gave it to Baruch son of Neriah, his secretary. As Jeremiah spoke, Baruch wrote on the scroll the same words that were on the scroll Jehoiakim king of Judah had burned in the fire. And many similar words were added to the second scroll.

Jeremiah in Prison

37 Nebuchadnezzar king of Babylon had appointed Zedekiah son of Josiah to be king of Judah. Zedekiah took the place of Jehoiachin son of Jehoiakim. ²But Zedekiah, his servants, and the people of Judah did not listen to the words the LORD had spoken through Jeremiah the prophet.*d*

³Now King Zedekiah sent Jehucal son of Shelemiah and the priest Zephaniah son of Maaseiah with a message to Jeremiah the prophet. This was the message: "Jeremiah, please pray to the LORD our God for us."

⁴At that time Jeremiah had not yet been put into prison. So he was free to go anywhere he wanted. ⁵The army of the king of Egypt had marched from Egypt toward Judah. Now the Babylonian army had surrounded the city of Jerusalem. When they heard about the Egyptian army marching toward them, the Babylonian army left Jerusalem.

⁶The LORD spoke his word to Jeremiah the prophet: ⁷"This is what the LORD, the God of Israel, says: Jehucal and Zephaniah, I know Zedekiah king of Judah sent you to seek my help. Tell this to King Zedekiah: 'The army of the king of Egypt came here to help you, but they will go back to Egypt. ⁸After that,' the Babylonian army will return and attack Jerusalem and capture it and burn it down.'

⁹"This is what the LORD says: People of Jerusalem, do not fool yourselves. Don't say, 'The Babylonian army will surely leave us alone.' They will not! ¹⁰Even if you defeated all of the Babylonian army that is attacking you and there were only a few injured men left in their tents, they would come from their tents and burn down Jerusalem!" ¹¹So the Babylonian army left Jerusalem to fight

the army of the king of Egypt. ¹²Now Jeremiah tried to travel from Jerusalem to the land of Benjamin to get his share of the property that belonged to his family. ¹³When Jeremiah got to the Benjamin Gate of Jerusalem, the captain in charge of the guards arrested him. The captain's name was Irijah son of Shelemiah son of Hananiah. Irijah said, "You are leaving us to join the Babylonians!"

¹⁴But Jeremiah said to Irijah, "That's not true! I am not leaving to join the Babylonians." Irijah refused to listen to Jeremiah, so he arrested Jeremiah and took him to the officers of Jerusalem. ¹⁵Those rulers were very angry with Jeremiah and beat him. Then they put him in jail in the house of Jonathan the royal secretary, which had been made into a prison. ¹⁶So those people put Jeremiah into a cell in a dungeon, and Jeremiah was there for a long time.

¹⁷Then King Zedekiah sent for Jeremiah and had him brought to the palace. Zedekiah asked him in private, "Is there any message from the LORD?"

Jeremiah answered, "Yes, there is. Zedekiah, you will be handed over to the king of Babylon." ¹⁸Then Jeremiah said to King Zedekiah, "What crime have I done against you or your officers or the people of Jerusalem? Why have you thrown me into prison? ¹⁹Where are your prophets that prophesied this message to you: 'The king of Babylon will not attack you or this land of Judah?' ²⁰But now, my master, king of Judah, please listen to me, and please do what I ask of you. Do not send me back to the house of Jonathan the royal secretary, or I will die there!"

²¹So King Zedekiah gave orders for Jeremiah to be put under guard in the courtyard of the guard and to be given bread each day from the street of the bakers until there was no more bread in the city. So he stayed under guard in the courtyard of the guard.

Jeremiah Is Thrown into a Well

38 Shephatiah son of Mattan, Gedaliah son of Pashhur, Jehucal son of Shelemiah, and Pashhur son of Malkijah heard what Jeremiah was telling all the people. He said: ²"This is what the LORD says: 'Everyone who stays in Jerusalem will die from war, or hunger, or terrible diseases. But everyone who surrenders to the Babylonian army will live; they will escape with their lives and live.' ³And this is what the LORD says: 'This city of Jerusalem will surely be handed over to the army of the king of Babylon. He will capture this city!' "

⁴Then the officers said to the king, "Jeremiah must be put to death! He is discouraging the soldiers who are still in the city, and all the people, by what he is saying to them. He does not want good to happen to us; he wants to ruin us."

⁵King Zedekiah said to them, "Jeremiah is in your control. I cannot do anything to stop you." ⁶So the officers took Jeremiah and put him into the well of Malkijah, the king's son, which was in the courtyard of the guards. The officers used ropes to lower Jeremiah into the well, which did not have any water in it, only mud. And Jeremiah sank down into the mud.

SIDELIGHT: Talk about being "the pits"! Jeremiah's "well of a jail" (Jeremiah 38:6) was a muddy cistern, a plastered hole in the ground that could have been twenty feet deep. It was originally used as a water supply.

---

⁷But Ebed-Melech, a Cushite and a servant in the palace, heard that the officers had put Jeremiah into the well. As King Zedekiah was sitting at the Benjamin Gate, ⁸Ebed-Melech left the palace and went to the king. Ebed-Melech said to him, ⁹"My master and king, these rulers have acted in an evil way. They have treated Jeremiah the prophet badly. They have thrown him into a well and left him there to die! When there is no more bread in the city, he will starve to death." ¹⁰Then King Zedekiah commanded Ebed-Melech the Cushite, "Take thirty men from the palace and lift Jeremiah the prophet out of the well before he dies."

¹¹So Ebed-Melech took the men with him and went to a room under the storeroom in the palace. He took some old rags and worn-out clothes from that room. Then he let those rags down with some ropes to Jeremiah in the well. ¹²Ebed-Melech the Cushite said to Jeremiah, "Put these old rags and worn-out clothes under your arms to be pads for the ropes." So Jeremiah did as Ebed-Melech said. ¹³The men pulled Jeremiah up with the ropes and lifted him out of the well. And Jeremiah stayed under guard in the courtyard of the guard.

Zedekiah Questions Jeremiah

¹⁴Then King Zedekiah sent someone to get Jeremiah the prophet*d* and bring him to the third entrance to the Temple*d* of the Lord. The king said to Jeremiah, "I am going to ask you something. Do not hide anything from me, but tell me everything honestly."

¹⁵Jeremiah said to Zedekiah, "If I give you an answer, you will surely kill me. And even if I give you advice, you will not listen to me."

¹⁶But King Zedekiah made a secret promise to Jeremiah, "As surely as the Lord lives who has given us breath and life, I will not kill you. And I promise not to hand you over to the officers who want to kill you."

¹⁷Then Jeremiah said to Zedekiah, "This is what the Lord God All-Powerful, the God of Israel, says: 'If you surrender to the officers of the king of Babylon, your life will be saved. Jerusalem will not be burned down, and you and your family will live. ¹⁸But if you refuse to surrender to the officers of the king of Babylon, Jerusalem will be handed over to the Babylonian army, and they will burn it down. And you yourself will not escape from them.' "

¹⁹Then King Zedekiah said to Jeremiah, "I'm afraid of some Jews who have already gone over to the side of the Babylonian army. If the Babylonians hand me over to them, they will treat me badly."

²⁰But Jeremiah answered, "The Babylonians will not hand you over to the Jews. Obey the Lord by doing what I tell you. Then things will go well for you, and your life will be saved. ²¹But if you refuse to surrender to the Babylonians, the Lord has shown me what will happen. ²²All the women left in the palace of the king of Judah will be brought out and taken to the important officers of the king of Babylon. Your women will make fun of you with this song:

'Your good friends misled you
  and were stronger than you.
While your feet were stuck in the mud,
  they left you.'

²³"All your wives and children will be brought out and given to the Babylonian army. You yourself will not even escape from them. You will be taken prisoner by the king of Babylon, and Jerusalem will be burned down."

²⁴Then Zedekiah said to Jeremiah, "Do not tell anyone that I have been talking to you, or you will die. ²⁵If the officers find out I talked to you, they will come to you and say, 'Tell us what you said to King Zedekiah and what he said to you. Don't keep any secrets from us. If you don't tell us everything, we will kill you.' ²⁶If they ask you, tell them, 'I was begging the king not to send me back to Jonathan's house to die.' "

²⁷All the officers did come to question Jeremiah. So he told them everything the king had ordered him to say. Then the officers said no more to Jeremiah, because no one had heard what Jeremiah and the king had discussed.

²⁸So Jeremiah stayed under guard in the courtyard of the guard until the day Jerusalem was captured.

The Fall of Jerusalem

39 This is how Jerusalem was captured: Nebuchadnezzar king of Babylon marched against Jerusalem with his whole army and surrounded the city to attack it. This was during the tenth month of the ninth year Zedekiah was king of Judah. [2]This lasted until the ninth day of the fourth month in Zedekiah's eleventh year. Then the city wall was broken through. [3]And all these officers of the king of Babylon came into Jerusalem and sat down at the Middle Gate: Nergal-Sharezer of the district of Samgar; Nebo-Sarsekim, a chief officer; Nergal-Sharezer, an important leader; and all the other important officers.

[4]When Zedekiah king of Judah and all his soldiers saw them, they ran away. They left Jerusalem at night and went out from the king's garden. They went through the gate that was between the two walls and then headed toward the Jordan Valley. [5]But the Babylonian army chased them and caught up with Zedekiah in the plains of Jericho. They captured him and took him to Nebuchadnezzar king of Babylon, who was at the town of Riblah in the land of Hamath. There Nebuchadnezzar passed his sentence on Zedekiah. [6]At Riblah the king of Babylon killed Zedekiah's sons and all the important officers of Judah as Zedekiah watched. [7]Then he put out Zedekiah's eyes. He put bronze chains on Zedekiah and took him to Babylon.

[8]The Babylonians set fire to the palace and to the houses of the people, and they broke down the walls around Jerusalem. [9]Nebuzaradan, commander of the king's special guards, took the people left in Jerusalem, those captives who had surrendered to him earlier, and the rest of the people of Jerusalem, and he took them all away to Babylon. [10]But Nebuzaradan, commander of the guard, left some of the poorest people of Judah behind. They owned nothing, but that day he gave them vineyards and fields.

�֎ **SIDELIGHT:** The eighteen-month siege of Jerusalem by the Babylonians was a grueling experience for Jeremiah (Jeremiah 39:1–10). Lamentations 4 (p. 758) describes the horrible conditions, including starvation and cannibalism.

---

[11]Nebuchadnezzar king of Babylon had given these orders about Jeremiah through Nebuzaradan, commander of the guard: [12]"Find Jeremiah and take care of him. Do not hurt him, but do for *him whatever he asks you.*" [13]*So Nebuchadnez-*zar sent these men for Jeremiah: Nebuzaradan, commander of the guards; Nebushazban, a chief officer; Nergal-Sharezer, an important leader; and all the other officers of the king of Babylon. [14]They had Jeremiah taken out of the courtyard of the guard. Then they turned him over to Gedaliah son

of Ahikam son of Shaphan, who had orders to take Jeremiah back home. So they took him home, and he stayed among the people left in Judah.

[15]While Jeremiah was guarded in the courtyard, the LORD spoke his word to him: [16]"Jeremiah, go and tell Ebed-Melech the Cushite this message: 'This is what the LORD All-Powerful, the God of Israel, says: Very soon I will make my words about Jerusalem come true through disaster, not through good times. You will see everything come true with your own eyes. [17]But I will save you on that day, Ebed-Melech, says the LORD. You will not be handed over to the people you fear. [18]I will surely save you, Ebed-Melech. You will not die from a sword, but you will escape and live. This will happen because you have trusted in me, says the LORD.' "

Jeremiah Is Set Free

40 The LORD spoke his word to Jeremiah after Nebuzaradan, commander of the guards, had set Jeremiah free at the city of Ramah. He had found Jeremiah in Ramah bound in chains with all the captives from Jerusalem and Judah who were being taken away to Babylon. [2]When commander Nebuzaradan found Jeremiah, Nebuzaradan said to him, "The LORD your God announced this disaster would come to this place. [3]And now the LORD has done everything he said he would do. This disaster happened because the people of Judah sinned against the LORD and did not obey him. [4]But today I am freeing you from the chains on your wrists. If you want to, come with me to Babylon, and I will take good care of you. But if you don't want to come, then don't. Look, the whole country is open to you. Go wherever you wish." [5]Before Jeremiah turned to leave, Nebuzaradan said, "Or go back to Gedaliah son of Ahikam, the son of Shaphan. The king of Babylon has chosen him to be governor over the towns of Judah. Go and live with Gedaliah among the people, or go anywhere you want."

Then Nebuzaradan gave Jeremiah some food and a present and let him go. [6]So Jeremiah went to Gedaliah son of Ahikam at Mizpah and stayed with him there. He lived among the people who were left behind in Judah.

The Short Rule of Gedaliah

[7]Some officers and their men from the army of Judah were still out in the open country. They *heard that the king of Babylon had put Gedaliah* son of Ahikam in charge of the people who were left in the land: the men, women, and children who were the poorest. They were the ones who were not taken to Babylon as captives. [8]So these soldiers came to Gedaliah at Mizpah: Ishmael son of Nethaniah, Johanan and Jonathan sons of Ka-

reah, Seraiah son of Tanhumeth, the sons of Ephai the Netophathite, Jaazaniah son of the Maacathite, and their men.

⁹Gedaliah son of Ahikam, the son of Shaphan, made a promise to them, saying, "Do not be afraid to serve the Babylonians. Stay in the land and serve the king of Babylon. Then everything will go well for you. ¹⁰I myself will live in Mizpah and will speak for you before the Babylonians who come to us here. Harvest the wine, the summer fruit, and the oil, and put what you harvest in your storage jars. Live in the towns you control."

¹¹The Jews in Moab, Ammon, Edom, and other countries also heard that the king of Babylon had left a few Jews alive in the land. And they heard the king of Babylon had chosen Gedaliah as governor over them. (Gedaliah was the son of Ahikam, the son of Shaphan.) ¹²When the people of Judah heard this news, they came back to Judah from all the countries where they had been scattered. They came to Gedaliah at Mizpah and gathered a large harvest of wine and summer fruit.

¹³Johanan son of Kareah and all the army officers of Judah still in the open country came to Gedaliah at Mizpah. ¹⁴They said to him, "Don't you know that Baalis king of the Ammonite people wants you dead? He has sent Ishmael son of Nethaniah to kill you." But Gedaliah son of Ahikam did not believe them.

¹⁵Then Johanan son of Kareah spoke to Gedaliah in private at Mizpah. He said, "Let me go and kill Ishmael son of Nethaniah. No one will know anything about it. We should not let Ishmael kill you. Then all the Jews gathered around you would be scattered to different countries again, and the few people of Judah who are left alive would be lost."

¹⁶But Gedaliah son of Ahikam said to Johanan son of Kareah, "Do not kill Ishmael! The things you are saying about Ishmael are not true."

41 In the seventh month Ishmael son of Nethaniah and ten of his men came to Gedaliah son of Ahikam at Mizpah. (Nethaniah was the son of Elishama.) Now Ishmael was a member of the king's family and had been one of the officers of the king of Judah. While they were eating a meal with Gedaliah at Mizpah, ²Ishmael and his ten men got up and killed Gedaliah son of Ahikam, the son of Shaphan, with a sword. (Gedaliah was the man the king of Babylon had chosen as governor over Judah.) ³Ishmael also killed all the Jews and the Babylonian soldiers who were there with Gedaliah at Mizpah.

⁴The day after Gedaliah was murdered, before anyone knew about it, ⁵eighty men came to Mizpah bringing grain offerings and incense*d* to the Temple*d* of the LORD. Those men from Shechem,

Shiloh, and Samaria had shaved off their beards, torn their clothes, and cut themselves. ⁶Ishmael son of Nethaniah went out from Mizpah to meet them, crying as he walked. When he met them, he said, "Come with me to meet Gedaliah son of Ahikam." ⁷So they went into Mizpah. Then Ishmael son of Nethaniah and his men killed seventy of them and threw the bodies into a deep well. ⁸But the ten men who were left alive said to Ishmael, "Don't kill us! We have wheat and barley and oil and honey that we have hidden in a field." So Ishmael let them live and did not kill them with the others. ⁹Now the well where he had thrown all the bodies had been made by King Asa as a part of his defenses against Baasha king of Israel. But Ishmael son of Nethaniah put dead bodies in it until it was full.

¹⁰Ishmael captured all the other people in Mizpah: the king's daughters and all the other people who were left there. They were the ones whom Nebuzaradan commander of the guard had chosen Gedaliah son of Ahikam to take care of. So Ishmael son of Nethaniah captured those people, and he started to cross over to the country of the Ammonites.

¹ Johanan son of Kareah and all his army officers with him heard about all the evil things Ishmael son of Nethaniah had done. ¹²So they took their men and went to fight Ishmael son of Nethaniah and caught him near the big pool of water at Gibeon. ¹³When the captives Ishmael had taken saw Johanan and the army officers, they were glad. ¹⁴So all the people Ishmael had taken captive from Mizpah turned around and ran to Johanan son of Kareah. ¹⁵But Ishmael son of Nethaniah and eight of his men escaped from Johanan and ran away to the Ammonites.

¹⁶So Johanan son of Kareah and all his army officers saved the captives that Ishmael son of Nethaniah had taken from Mizpah after he murdered Gedaliah son of Ahikam. Among those left alive were soldiers, women, children, and palace officers. And Johanan brought them back from the town of Gibeon.

The Escape to Egypt

¹⁷-¹⁸Johanan and the other army officers were afraid of the Babylonians. Since the king of Babylon had chosen Gedaliah son of Ahikam to be governor of Judah but Ishmael son of Nethaniah had murdered him, Johanan was afraid that the Babylonians would be angry. So they decided to run away to Egypt. On the way they stayed at Geruth Kimham, near the town of Bethlehem.

42 While there, Johanan son of Kareah and Jezaniah son of Hoshaiah went to Jeremiah the prophet.*d* All the army officers and all

---

shaved . . . themselves   The men did this to show they were sad about the Temple in Jerusalem being destroyed.

the people, from the least important to the greatest, went along, too. ²They said to him, "Jeremiah, please listen to what we ask. Pray to the LORD your God for all the people left alive from the family of Judah. At one time there were many of us, but you can see that there are few of us now. ³So pray that the LORD your God will tell us where we should go and what we should do."

⁴Then Jeremiah the prophet answered, "I understand what you want me to do. I will pray to the LORD your God as you have asked. I will tell you everything he says and not hide anything from you."

⁵Then the people said to Jeremiah, "May the LORD be a true and loyal witness against us if we don't do everything the LORD your God sends you to tell us. ⁶It does not matter if we like the message or not. We will obey the LORD our God, to whom we are sending you. We will obey what he says so good things will happen to us."

⁷Ten days later the LORD spoke his word to Jeremiah. ⁸Then Jeremiah called for Johanan son of Kareah, the army officers with him, and all the other people, from the least important to the greatest. ⁹Jeremiah said to them, "You sent me to ask the LORD for what you wanted. This is what the God of Israel says: ¹⁰'If you will stay in Judah, I will build you up and not tear you down. I will plant you and not pull you up, because I am sad about the disaster I brought on you. ¹¹Now you fear the king of Babylon, but don't be afraid of him. Don't be afraid of him,' says the LORD, 'because I am with you. I will save you and rescue you from his power. ¹²I will be kind to you, and he will also treat you with mercy and let you stay in your land.'

¹³"But if you say, 'We will not stay in Judah,' you will disobey the LORD your God. ¹⁴Or you might say, 'No, we will go and live in Egypt. There we will not see war, or hear the trumpets of war, or be hungry.' ¹⁵If you say that, listen to the message of the LORD, you who are left alive from Judah. This is what the LORD All-Powerful, the God of Israel, says: 'If you make up your mind to go and live in Egypt, these things will happen: ¹⁶You are afraid of war, but it will find you in the land of Egypt. And you are worried about hunger, but it will follow you into Egypt, and you will die there. ¹⁷Everyone who goes to live in Egypt will die in war or from hunger or terrible disease. No one who goes to Egypt will live; no one will escape the terrible things I will bring to them.'

¹⁸"This is what the LORD All-Powerful, the God of Israel, says: 'I showed my anger against the people of Jerusalem. In the same way I will show my anger against you when you go to Egypt. Other nations will speak evil of you. People will be shocked by what will happen to you. You will become a curse word, and people will insult you. And you will never see Judah again.'

¹⁹"You who are left alive in Judah, the LORD has told you, 'Don't go to Egypt.' Be sure you understand this; I warn you today ²⁰that you are making a mistake that will cause your deaths. You sent me to the LORD your God, saying, 'Pray to the LORD our God for us. Tell us everything the LORD our God says, and we will do it.' ²¹So today I have told you, but you have not obeyed the LORD your God in all that he sent me to tell you. ²²So now be sure you understand this: You want to go to live in Egypt, but you will die there by war, hunger, or terrible diseases."

43 So Jeremiah finished telling the people the message from the LORD their God; he told them everything the LORD their God had sent him to tell them.

²Azariah son of Hoshaiah, Johanan son of Kareah, and some other men were too proud. They said to Jeremiah, "You are lying! The LORD our God did not send you to say, 'You must not go to Egypt to live there.' ³Baruch son of Neriah is causing you to be against us. He wants you to hand us over to the Babylonians so they can kill us or capture us and take us to Babylon."

⁴So Johanan, the army officers, and all the people disobeyed the LORD's command to stay in Judah. ⁵But Johanan son of Kareah and the army officers led away those who were left alive from Judah. They were the people who had run away from the Babylonians to other countries but then had come back to live in Judah. ⁶They led away the men, women, and children, and the king's daughters. Nebuzaradan commander of the guard had put Gedaliah son of Ahikam son of Shaphan in charge of those people. Johanan also took Jeremiah the prophet[d] and Baruch son of Neriah. ⁷These people did not listen to the LORD. So they all went to Egypt to the city of Tahpanhes.

SIDELIGHT: Tahpanhes (Jeremiah 43:7) was an Egyptian border fortress in the delta area of the Nile River. It would be the first city that refugees from Israel would reach when they entered Egypt.

---

⁸In Tahpanhes the LORD spoke his word to Jeremiah: ⁹"Take some large stones. Bury them in the clay in the brick pavement in front of the king of Egypt's palace in Tahpanhes. Do this while the Jews are watching you. ¹⁰Then say to them, 'This is what the LORD All-Powerful, the God of Israel, says: I will soon send for my servant, Nebuchad-

nezzar king of Babylon. I will set his throne over these stones I have buried, and he will spread his covering for shade above them. [11]He will come here and attack Egypt. He will bring death to those who are supposed to die. He will make prisoners of those who are to be taken captive, and he will bring war to those who are to be killed with a sword. [12]Nebuchadnezzar will set fire to the temples of the gods of Egypt and burn them. And he will take the idols away as captives. As a shepherd wraps himself in his clothes, so Nebuchadnezzar will wrap Egypt around him. Then he will safely leave Egypt. [13]He will destroy the stone pillars in the temple of the sun god in Egypt, and he will burn down the temples of the gods of Egypt.' "

Disaster in Egypt

44 Jeremiah received a message from the Lord for all the Jews living in Egypt — in the cities of Migdol, Tahpanhes, Memphis, and in southern Egypt. This was the message: [2]"The Lord All-Powerful, the God of Israel, says: You saw all the terrible things I brought on Jerusalem and the towns of Judah, which are ruins today with no one living in them. [3]It is because the people who lived there did evil. They made me angry by burning incense[d] and worshiping other gods that neither they nor you nor your ancestors ever knew. [4]I sent all my servants, the prophets,[d] to you again and again. By them I said to you, 'Don't do this terrible thing that I hate.' [5]But they did not listen or pay attention. They did not stop doing evil things and burning incense to other gods. [6]So I showed my great anger against them. I poured out my anger in the towns of Judah and the streets of Jerusalem so they are only ruins and piles of stones today.

[7]"Now the Lord All-Powerful, the God of Israel, says: Why are you doing such great harm to yourselves? You are cutting off the men and women, children and babies from the family of Judah, leaving yourselves without anyone from the family of Judah. [8]Why do you want to make me angry by making idols? Why do you burn incense to the gods of Egypt, where you have come to live? You will destroy yourselves. Other nations will speak evil of you and make fun of you. [9]Have you forgotten about the evil things your ancestors did? And have you forgotten the evil the kings and queens of Judah did? Have you forgotten about the evil you and your wives did? These things were done in the country of Judah and in the streets of Jerusalem. [10]Even to this day the people of Judah are still too proud. They have not learned to respect me or to follow my teachings. They have not obeyed the laws I gave you and your ancestors.

[11]"So this is what the Lord All-Powerful, the God of Israel, says: I am determined to bring disasters on you. I will destroy the whole family of Judah. [12]The few who were left alive from Judah were determined to go to Egypt and settle there, but they will all die in Egypt. They will be killed in war or die from hunger. From the least important to the greatest, they will be killed in war or die from hunger. Other nations will speak evil about them. People will be shocked by what has happened to them. They will become a curse word, and people will insult them. [13]I will punish those people who have gone to live in Egypt, just as I punished Jerusalem, using swords, hunger, and terrible diseases. [14]Of the people of Judah who were left alive and have gone to live in Egypt, none will escape my punishment. They want to return to Judah and live there, but none of them will live to return to Judah, except a few people who will escape."

[15]A large group of the people of Judah who lived in southern Egypt were meeting together. Among them were many women of Judah who were burning incense to other gods, and their husbands knew it. All these people said to Jeremiah, [16]"We will not listen to the message from the Lord that you spoke to us. [17]We promised to make sacrifices to the Queen Goddess,[d] and we will certainly do everything we promised. We will burn incense and pour out drink offerings to worship her, just as we, our ancestors, kings, and officers did in the towns of Judah and in the streets of Jerusalem. At that time we had plenty of food and were successful, and nothing bad happened to us. [18]But since we stopped making sacrifices to the Queen Goddess and stopped pouring out drink offerings to her, we have had great problems. Our people have also been killed in war and by hunger."

[19]The women said, "Our husbands knew what we were doing. We had their permission to burn incense to the Queen Goddess and to pour out drink offerings to her. Our husbands knew we were making cakes that looked like her and were pouring out drink offerings to her."

[20]Then Jeremiah spoke to all the people — men and women — who answered him. [21]He said to them, "The Lord remembered that you and your ancestors, kings and officers, and the people of the land burned incense in the towns of Judah and in the streets of Jerusalem. He remembered and thought about it. [22]Then he could not be patient with you any longer. He hated the terrible things you did. So he made your country an empty desert, where no one lives. Other people curse that country. And so it is today. [23]All this happened because you burned incense to other gods. You sinned against the Lord. You did not obey him or follow his teachings or the laws he gave you. You did not keep your part of the agreement

with him. So this disaster has happened to you. It is there for you to see."

24Then Jeremiah said to all those men and women, "People of Judah who are now in Egypt, hear the word of the LORD: 25The LORD All-Powerful, the God of Israel, says: You and your wives did what you said you would do. You said, 'We will certainly keep the promises we made. We promised to make sacrifices to the Queen Goddess and to pour out drink offerings to her.' So, go ahead. Do the things you promised, and keep your promises. 26But hear the word of the LORD. Listen, all you Jews living in Egypt. The LORD says, 'I have sworn by my great name: The people of Judah now living in Egypt will never again use my name to make promises. They will never again say in Egypt, "As surely as the Lord GOD lives. . ." 27I am watching over them, not to take care of them, but to hurt them. The Jews who live in Egypt will die from swords or hunger until they are all destroyed. 28A few will escape being killed by the sword and will come back to Judah from Egypt. Then, of the people of Judah who came to live in Egypt, those who are left alive will know if my word or their word came true. 29I will give you a sign that I will punish you here in Egypt,' says the LORD. 'When you see it happen, you will know that my promises to hurt you will really happen.' 30This is what the LORD says: 'Hophra king of Egypt has enemies who want to kill him. Soon I will hand him over to his enemies just as I handed Zedekiah king of Judah over to Nebuchadnezzar king of Babylon, who wanted to kill him.' "

A Message to Baruch

45 It was the fourth year that Jehoiakim son of Josiah was king of Judah. Jeremiah the prophet[d] told these things to Baruch son of Neriah, and Baruch wrote them on a scroll: 2"This is what the LORD, the God of Israel, says to you, Baruch: 3You have said, 'How terrible it is for me! The LORD has given me sorrow along with my pain. I am tired because of my suffering and cannot rest.' "

4The LORD said, "Say this to Baruch: 'This is what the LORD says: I will soon tear down what I have built, and I will pull up what I have planted everywhere in Judah. 5Baruch, you are looking for great things for yourself. Don't look for them, because I will bring disaster on all the people, says the LORD. You will have to go many places, but I will let you escape alive wherever you go.' "

Messages to the Nations

46 The LORD spoke this word to Jeremiah the prophet[d] about the nations:

2This message is to Egypt. It is about the army of Neco king of Egypt, which was defeated at the city of Carchemish on the Euphrates River by Nebuchadnezzar king of Babylon. This was in the fourth year that Jehoiakim son of Josiah was king of Judah. This is the LORD's message to Egypt:

3"Prepare your shields, large and small,
  and march out for battle!
4Harness the horses
  and get on them!
Go to your places for battle
  and put on your helmets!
Polish your spears.
  Put on your armor!
5What do I see?
  That army is terrified,
and the soldiers are running away.
  Their warriors are defeated.
They run away quickly
  without looking back.
  There is terror on every side!" says the
    LORD.
6"The fast runners cannot run away;
  the strong soldiers cannot escape.
They stumble and fall
  in the north, by the Euphrates River.
7Who is this, rising up like the Nile River,
  like strong, fast rivers?
8Egypt rises up like the Nile River,
  like strong, fast rivers.
Egypt says, 'I will rise up and cover the
    earth.
I will destroy cities and the people in
    them!'
9Horsemen, charge into battle!
  Chariot drivers, drive hard!
March on, brave soldiers—
  soldiers from the countries of Cush and Put
    who carry shields,
  soldiers from Lydia who use bows.

10"But that day belongs to the Lord GOD
    All-Powerful.
At that time he will give those people the
    punishment they deserve.
The sword will kill until it is finished,
  until it satisfies its thirst for their blood.
The Lord GOD All-Powerful will offer a
    sacrifice
  in the land of the north, by the Euphrates
    River.

11"Go up to Gilead and get some balm,[d]
  people of Egypt!
You have prepared many medicines,
  but they will not work;
  you will not be healed.
12The nations have heard of your shame,
  and your cries fill all the earth.
One warrior has run into another;
  both of them have fallen down together!"

¹³This is the message the LORD spoke to Jeremiah the prophet*d* about Nebuchadnezzar king of Babylon's coming to attack Egypt:
¹⁴"Announce this message in Egypt, and preach it in Migdol.

Preach it also in the cities of Memphis and Tahpanhes:
'Get ready for war,
because the battle is all around you.'
¹⁵Egypt, why were your warriors killed?
They could not stand because the LORD pushed them down.
¹⁶They stumbled again and again
and fell over each other.
They said, 'Get up. Let's go back
to our own people and our homeland.
We must get away from our enemy's sword!'
¹⁷In their homelands those soldiers called out,
'The king of Egypt is only a lot of noise.
He missed his chance for glory!'"

¹⁸The King's name is the LORD All-Powerful.
He says, "As surely as I live,
a powerful leader will come.
He will be like Mount Tabor among the mountains,
like Mount Carmel by the sea.
¹⁹People of Egypt, pack your things
to be taken away as captives,
because Memphis will be destroyed.
It will be a ruin, and no one will live there.

²⁰"Egypt is like a beautiful young cow,
but a horsefly is coming
from the north to attack her.
²¹The hired soldiers in Egypt's army
are like fat calves,
because even they all turn and run away together;
they do not stand strong against the attack.
Their time of destruction is coming;
they will soon be punished.
²²Egypt is like a hissing snake that is trying to escape.
The enemy comes closer and closer.
They come against Egypt with axes
like men who cut down trees.
²³They will chop down Egypt's army
as if it were a great forest," says the LORD.
"There are more enemy soldiers than locusts;*d*
there are too many to count.
²⁴The people of Egypt will be ashamed.
They will be handed over to the enemy
from the north."

²⁵The LORD All-Powerful, the God of Israel, says: "Very soon I will punish Amon, the god of the city of Thebes. And I will punish Egypt, her kings, her gods, and the people who depend on the king. ²⁶I will hand those people over to their enemies, who want to kill them. I will give them to Nebuchadnezzar king of Babylon and his officers. But in the future, Egypt will live in peace as it once did," says the LORD.

A Message to Israel

²⁷"People of Jacob, my servants, don't be afraid;
don't be frightened, Israel.
I will surely save you from those faraway places
and your children from the lands where they are captives.
The people of Jacob will have peace and safety again,
and no one will make them afraid.
²⁸People of Jacob, my servants, do not be afraid,
because I am with you," says the LORD.
"I will completely destroy the many different nations
where I scattered you.
But I will not completely destroy you.
I will punish you fairly,
but I will not let you escape your punishment."

A Message to the Philistines

47 Before the king of Egypt attacked the city of Gaza, the LORD spoke his word to Jeremiah the prophet.*d* This message is to the Philistine people.

²This is what the LORD says:
"See, the enemy is gathering in the north like rising waters.
They will become like an overflowing stream
and will cover the whole country like a flood,
even the towns and the people living in them.
Everyone living in that country
will cry for help;
the people will cry painfully.
³They will hear the sound of the running horses
and the noisy chariots
and the rumbling chariot wheels.
Parents will not help their children to safety,
because they will be too weak to help.
⁴The time has come
to destroy all the Philistines.
It is time to destroy all who are left alive
who could help the cities of Tyre and Sidon.
The LORD will soon destroy the Philistines,
those left alive from the island of Crete.

⁵The people from the city of Gaza will be sad
and shave their heads.
The people from the city of Ashkelon will
be made silent.
Those left alive from the valley,
how long will you cut yourselves? [n]

⁶"You cry, 'Sword of the LORD,
how long will you keep fighting?
Return to your holder.
Stop and be still.'
⁷But how can his sword rest
when the LORD has given it a command?
He has ordered it
to attack Ashkelon and the seacoast."

A Message to Moab

48 This message is to the country of Moab.
This is what the LORD All-Powerful, the
God of Israel, says:
"How terrible it will be for the city of Nebo,
because it will be ruined.
The town of Kiriathaim will be disgraced and
captured;
the strong city will be disgraced and
shattered.
²Moab will not be praised again.
Men in the town of Heshbon plan Moab's
defeat.
They say, 'Come, let us put an end to that
nation!'
Town of Madmen, [n] you will also be
silenced.
The sword will chase you.
³Listen to the cries from the town of
Horonaim,
cries of much confusion and destruction.
⁴Moab will be broken up.
Her little children will cry for help.
⁵Moab's people go up the path to the town of
Luhith,
crying loudly as they go.
On the road down to Horonaim,
cries of pain and suffering can be heard.
⁶Run! Run for your lives!
Go like a bush being blown through the
desert.
⁷You trust in the things you do and in your
wealth,
so you also will be captured.
The god Chemosh [d] will go into captivity
and his priests and officers with him.
⁸The destroyer will come against every town;
not one town will escape.
The valley will be ruined,

and the high plain will be destroyed,
as the LORD has said.
⁹Give wings to Moab,
because she will surely leave her land.
Moab's towns will become empty,
with no one to live in them.
¹⁰A curse will be on anyone who doesn't do
what the LORD says,
and a curse will be on anyone who holds
back his sword from killing.

¹¹"The people of Moab have never known
trouble.
They are like wine left to settle;
they have never been poured from one jar to
another.
They have not been taken into captivity.
So they taste as they did before,
and their smell has not changed.
¹²A time is coming," says the LORD,
"When I will send people to pour you from
your jars.
They will empty Moab's jars
and smash her jugs.
¹³The people of Israel trusted that god in the
town of Bethel,
and they were ashamed when there was no
help.
In the same way Moab will be ashamed of
their god Chemosh.

¹⁴"You cannot say, 'We are warriors!
We are brave men in battle!'
¹⁵The destroyer of Moab and her towns has
arrived.
Her best young men will be killed!" says
the King,
whose name is the LORD All-Powerful.
¹⁶"The end of Moab is near,
and she will soon be destroyed.
¹⁷All you who live around Moab,
all you who know her, cry for her.
Say, 'The ruler's power is broken;
Moab's power and glory are gone.'

¹⁸"You people living in the town of Dibon,
come down from your place of honor
and sit on the dry ground,
because the destroyer of Moab has come
against you.
And he has destroyed your strong, walled
cities.
¹⁹You people living in the town of Aroer,
stand next to the road and watch.
See the man running away and the woman
escaping.
Ask them, 'What happened?'

---

sad and . . . yourselves The people did these things to show their sadness.
Madmen This name sounds like the Hebrew word for "be silenced."

²⁰Moab is filled with shame, because she is
    ruined.
  Cry, Moab, cry out!
Announce at the Arnon River
  that Moab is destroyed.
²¹People on the high plain have been punished.
  Judgment has come to these towns:
  Holon, Jahzah, and Mephaath;
²² Dibon, Nebo, and Beth Diblathaim;
²³ Kiriathaim, Beth Gamul, and Beth Meon;
²⁴ Kerioth and Bozrah.
  Judgment has come to all the towns of
    Moab, far and near.
²⁵Moab's strength has been cut off,
  and its arm broken!" says the LORD.

²⁶"The people of Moab thought they were
    greater than the LORD,
  so punish them until they act as if they are
    drunk.
  Moab will fall and roll around in its own
    vomit,
  and people will even make fun of it.
²⁷Moab, you made fun of Israel.
  Israel was caught in the middle of a gang of
    thieves.
  When you spoke about Israel,
  you shook your head and acted as if you
    were better than it.
²⁸People in Moab, leave your towns empty
  and go live among the rocks.
Be like a dove that makes its nest
  at the entrance of a cave.

²⁹"We have heard that the people of Moab are
    proud,
    very proud.
  They are proud, very proud,
  and in their hearts they think they are
    important."
³⁰The LORD says,
  "I know Moab's great pride, but it is
    useless.
  Moab's bragging accomplishes nothing.
³¹So I cry sadly for Moab,
  for everyone in Moab.
  I moan for the people from the town of Kir
    Hareseth.
³²I cry with the people of the town of Jazer
  for you, the grapevines of the town of
    Sibmah.
  In the past your vines spread all the way to
    the sea,
  as far as the sea of Jazer.
But the destroyer has taken over
  your fruit and grapes.

³³Joy and happiness are gone
  from the large, rich fields of Moab.
  I have stopped the flow of wine from the
    winepresses.ᵈ
  No one walks on the grapes with shouts of
    joy.
  There are shouts,
  but not shouts of joy.

³⁴"Their crying can be heard from Moabite
    towns,
  from Heshbon to Elealeh and Jahaz.
  It can be heard from Zoar as far away as
    Horonaim and Eglath Shelishiyah.
  Even the waters of Nimrim are dried up.
³⁵I will stop Moab
  from making burnt offerings at the places of
    worship
  and from burning incenseᵈ to their gods,"
    says the LORD.

³⁶"My heart cries sadly for Moab like a flute
    playing a funeral song.
  It cries like a flute for the people from Kir
    Hareseth.
  The money they made has all been taken
    away.
³⁷Every head has been shaved
  and every beard cut off.
Everyone's hands are cut,
  and everyone wears rough cloth around his
    waist.ⁿ

> ⚙ **SIDELIGHT:** If you meet
> someone with a scraggly beard or
> long hair, don't assume he's just a scruffy
> guy. Maybe he read Jeremiah 48:37, which
> says that clipped beards and shaved heads
> were signs of disgrace and defeat. Don't tell
> that to any hair stylists!

³⁸People are crying on every roofⁿ in Moab
  and in every public square.
  There is nothing but sadness,
  because I have broken Moab
  like a jar no one wants," says the LORD.
³⁹"Moab is shattered! The people are crying!
  Moab turns away in shame!
People all around her make fun of her.
  The things that happened fill them with
    great fear."

⁴⁰This is what the LORD says:

Every head . . . waist. The people did these things to show their sadness for those who had died.
roof In Bible times houses were built with flat roofs. The roof was used for drying things such as flax and fruit. And it was
  used as an extra room, as a place for worship, and as a place to sleep in the summer.

"Look! Someone is coming, like an eagle
diving down from the sky
and spreading its wings over Moab.
⁴¹The towns of Moab will be captured,
and the strong, walled cities will be
defeated.
At that time Moab's warriors will be
frightened,
like a woman who is having a baby.
⁴²The nation of Moab will be destroyed,
because they thought they were greater
than the LORD.
⁴³Fear, deep pits, and traps wait for you,
people of Moab," says the LORD.
⁴⁴"People will run from fear,
but they will fall into the pits.
Anyone who climbs out of the pits
will be caught in the traps.
I will bring the year of punishment to Moab,"
says the LORD.

⁴⁵"People have run from the powerful enemy
and have gone to Heshbon for safety.
But fire started in Heshbon;
a blaze has spread from the hometown of
Sihon king of Moab.
It burned up the leaders of Moab
and destroyed those proud people.
⁴⁶How terrible it is for you, Moab!
The people who worship Chemosh have
been destroyed.
Your sons have been taken captive,
and your daughters have been taken away.

⁴⁷"But in days to come,
I will make good things happen again to
Moab," says the LORD.

This ends the judgment on Moab.

A Message to Ammon

49 This message is to the Ammonite people.
This is what the LORD says:
"Do you think that Israel has no children?
Do you think there is no one to take the
land when the parents die?
If that were true, why did Molech*d* take
Gad's land
and why did Molech's people settle in
Gad's towns?"
²The LORD says,
"The time will come when I will make
Rabbah,
the capital city of the Ammonites, hear the
battle cry.
It will become a hill covered with ruins,
and the towns around it will be burned.
Those people forced Israel out of that land,
but now Israel will force them out!" says
the LORD.

³"People in the town of Heshbon, cry sadly
because the town of Ai is destroyed!
Those who live in Rabbah, cry out!
Put on your rough cloth to show your
sadness, and cry loudly.
Run here and there for safety inside the
walls,
because Molech will be taken captive
and his priests and officers with him.
⁴You brag about your valleys
and about the fruit in your valleys.
You are like an unfaithful child
who believes his treasures will save him.
You think, 'Who would attack me?'
⁵I will soon bring terror on you
from everyone around you,"
says the Lord GOD All-Powerful.
"You will all be forced to run away,
and no one will be able to gather you.

⁶"But the time will come
when I will make good things happen to
the Ammonites again,"
says the LORD.

A Message to Edom

⁷This message is to Edom. This is what the
LORD All-Powerful says:
"Is there no more wisdom in the town of
Teman?
Can the wise men of Edom no longer give
good advice?
Have they lost their wisdom?
⁸You people living in the town of Dedan,
run away and hide in deep caves,
because I will bring disaster on the people of
Esau.
It is time for me to punish them.
⁹If workers came and picked the grapes from
your vines,
they would leave a few grapes behind.
If robbers came at night,
they would steal only enough for
themselves.
¹⁰But I will strip Edom bare.
I will find all their hiding places,
so they will not be able to hide from me.
The children, relatives, and neighbors will
die,
and Edom will be no more.
¹¹Leave the orphans, and I will take care of
them.
Your widows also can trust in me."

¹²This is what the LORD says: "Some people did
not deserve to be punished, but they had to drink
from the cup of suffering anyway. People of
Edom, you deserve to be punished, so you will
not escape punishment. You must certainly drink
from the cup of suffering." ¹³The LORD says, "I

swear by my own name that the city of Bozrah will become a pile of ruins! People will be shocked by what happened there. They will insult that city and speak evil of it. And all the towns around it will become ruins forever."

[14]I have heard a message from the LORD.
A messenger has been sent among the nations, saying,
"Gather your armies to attack it!
Get ready for battle!"
[15]"Soon I will make you the smallest of nations,
and you will be greatly hated by everyone.
[16]Edom, you frightened other nations,
but your pride has fooled you.
You live in the hollow places of the cliff
and control the high places of the hills.
Even if you build your home as high as an eagle's nest,
I will bring you down from there," says the LORD.
[17]"Edom will be destroyed.
People who pass by will be shocked to see the destroyed cities,
and they will be amazed at all her injuries.
[18]Edom will be destroyed like the cities of Sodom and Gomorrah
and the towns around them," says the LORD.
"No one will live there!
No one will stay in Edom."

[19]"Like a lion coming up from the thick bushes near the Jordan River
to attack a strong pen for sheep,
I will suddenly chase Edom from its land.
Who is the one I have chosen to do this?
There is no one like me,
no one who can take me to court.
None of their leaders can stand up against me."

[20]So listen to what the LORD has planned to do against Edom.
Listen to what he has decided to do to the people in the town of Teman.
He will surely drag away the young ones of Edom.
Their hometowns will surely be shocked at what happens to them.
[21]At the sound of Edom's fall, the earth will shake.
Their cry will be heard all the way to the Red Sea.
[22]The LORD is like an eagle swooping down
and spreading its wings over the city of Bozrah.

At that time Edom's soldiers will become very frightened,
like a woman having a baby.

A Message to Damascus

[23]This message is to the city of Damascus:
"The towns of Hamath and Arpad are put to shame,
because they have heard bad news.
They are discouraged.
They are troubled like the tossing sea.
[24]The city of Damascus has become weak.
The people want to run away;
they are ready to panic.
The people feel pain and suffering,
like a woman giving birth to a baby.
[25]Damascus was a city of my joy.
Why have the people not left that famous city yet?
[26]Surely the young men will die in the city squares,
and all her soldiers will be killed at that time," says the LORD All-Powerful.
[27]"I will set fire to the walls of Damascus,
and it will completely burn the strong cities of King Ben-Hadad."

A Message to Kedar and Hazor

[28]This message is to the tribe[d] of Kedar and the kingdoms of Hazor, which Nebuchadnezzar king of Babylon defeated. This is what the LORD says:
"Go and attack the people of Kedar,
and destroy the people of the East.
[29]Their tents and flocks will be taken away.
Their belongings will be carried off—
their tents, all their goods, and their camels.
Men will shout to them,
'Terror on every side!'
[30]"Run away quickly!
People in Hazor, find a good place to hide!" says the LORD.
"Nebuchadnezzar king of Babylon has made plans against you
and wants to defeat you.
[31]"Get up! Attack the nation that is comfortable,
that is sure no one will defeat it," says the LORD.
"It does not have gates or fences to protect it.
Its people live alone.
[32]The enemy will steal their camels
and their large herds of cattle as war prizes.
I will scatter the people who cut their hair short to every part of the earth,
and I will bring disaster on them from everywhere," says the LORD.

33"The city of Hazor will become a home for
wild dogs;
it will be an empty desert forever.
No one will live there,
and no one will stay in it."

A Message to Elam

34Soon after Zedekiah became king of Judah,
the LORD spoke this word to Jeremiah the
prophet.*d* This message is to the nation of Elam.
35This is what the LORD All-Powerful says:
"I will soon break Elam's bow,
its greatest strength.
36I will bring the four winds against Elam
from the four corners of the skies.
I will scatter its people everywhere the four
winds blow;
its captives will go to every nation.
37I will terrify Elam in front of their enemies,
who want to destroy them.
I will bring disaster to Elam
and show them how angry I am!" says the
LORD.
"I will send a sword to chase Elam
until I have killed them all.
38I will set up my throne in Elam to show that
I am king,
and I will destroy its king and its officers!"
says the LORD.

39"But I will make good things happen to Elam
again
in the future," says the LORD.

A Message to Babylon

50 This is the message the LORD spoke to
Babylon and the Babylonian people
through Jeremiah the prophet.*d*
2"Announce this to the nations.
Lift up a banner and tell them.
Speak the whole message and say:
'Babylon will be captured.
The god Bel*d* will be put to shame,
and the god Marduk*d* will be afraid.
Babylon's gods will be put to shame,
and her idols will be afraid!'
3A nation from the north will attack Babylon
and make it like an empty desert.
No one will live there;
both people and animals will run away."

4The LORD says, "At that time
the people of Israel and Judah will come
together.
They will cry and look for the LORD their
God.
5Those people will ask how to go to Jerusalem
and will start in that direction.
They will come and join themselves to the
LORD.

They will make an agreement with him
that will last forever,
an agreement that will never be forgotten.

6"My people have been like lost sheep.
Their leaders have led them in the wrong
way
and made them wander around in the
mountains and hills.
They forgot where their resting place was.
7Whoever saw my people hurt them.
And those enemies said, 'We did nothing
wrong.'
Those people sinned against the LORD, their
true resting place,
the God their fathers trusted.'

8"Run away from Babylon,
and leave the land of the Babylonians.
Be like the goats that lead the flock.
9I will soon bring against Babylon
many great nations from the north.
They will take their places for war against it,
and it will be captured by people from the
north.
Their arrows are like trained soldiers
who do not return from war with empty
hands.
10The enemy will take all the wealth from the
Babylonians.
Those enemy soldiers will get all they
want," says the LORD.

11"Babylon, you are excited and happy,
because you took my land.
You dance around like a young cow in the
grain.
Your laughter is like the neighing of male
horses.
12Your mother will be very ashamed;
the woman who gave birth to you will be
disgraced.
Soon Babylonia will be the least important of
all the nations.
She will be an empty, dry desert.
13Because of the LORD's anger,
no one will live there.
She will be completely empty.
Everyone who passes by Babylon will be
shocked.
They will shake their heads when they see
all her injuries.

14"Take your positions for war against Babylon,
all you soldiers with bows.
Shoot your arrows at Babylon! Do not save
any of them,
because Babylon has sinned against the
LORD.
15Soldiers around Babylon, shout the war cry!

Babylon has surrendered, her towers have
fallen,
and her walls have been torn down.
The Lord is giving her people the
punishment they deserve.
You nations should give her what she
deserves;
do to her what she has done to others.
16Don't let the people from Babylon plant their
crops
or gather the harvest.
The soldiers treated their captives cruelly.
Now, let everyone go back home.
Let everyone run to his own country.

17"The people of Israel are like a flock of sheep
that are scattered
from being chased by lions.
The first lion to eat them up
was the king of Assyria.
The last lion to crush their bones
was Nebuchadnezzar king of Babylon."

18So this is what the Lord All-Powerful, the
God of Israel, says:
"I will punish the king of Babylon and his
country
as I punished the king of Assyria.
19But I will bring the people of Israel back to
their own pasture.
They will eat on Mount Carmel and in
Bashan.
They will eat and be full
on the hills of Ephraim and Gilead."
20The Lord says,
"At that time people will try to find Israel's
guilt,
but there will be no guilt.
People will try to find Judah's sins,
but no sins will be found,
because I will leave a few people alive from
Israel and Judah,
and I will forgive their sins.

21"Attack the land of Merathaim.
Attack the people who live in Pekod.
Chase them, kill them, and completely
destroy them.
Do everything I commanded you!" says the
Lord.

22"The noise of battle can be heard all over the
country;
it is the noise of much destruction.
23Babylon was the hammer of the whole earth,
but how broken and shattered that hammer
is now.
It is truly the most ruined
of all the nations.
24Babylon, I set a trap for you,
and you were caught before you knew it.

You fought against the Lord,
so you were found and taken prisoner.
25The Lord has opened up his storeroom
and brought out the weapons of his anger,
because the Lord God All-Powerful has work
to do
in the land of the Babylonians.
26Come against Babylon from far away.
Break open her storehouses of grain.
Pile up her dead bodies like heaps of grain.
Completely destroy Babylon
and do not leave anyone alive.
27Kill all the young men in Babylon;
let them be killed like animals.
How terrible it will be for them, because the
time has come for their defeat;
it is time for them to be punished.
28Listen to the people running to escape the
country of Babylon!
They are telling Jerusalem
how the Lord our God is punishing Babylon
as it deserves
for destroying his Temple.*d*

29"Call for the archers
to come against Babylon.
Tell them to surround the city,
and let no one escape.
Pay her back for what she has done;
do to her what she has done to other
nations.
Babylon acted with pride against the Lord,
the Holy One of Israel.
30So her young men will be killed in her
streets.
All her soldiers will die on that day," says
the Lord.
31"Babylon, you are too proud, and I am
against you,"
says the Lord God All-Powerful.
'The time has come
for you to be punished.
32Proud Babylon will stumble and fall,
and no one will help her get up.
I will start a fire in her towns,
and it will burn up everything around her."

33This is what the Lord All-Powerful says:
"The people of Israel
and Judah are slaves.
The enemy took them as prisoners
and won't let them go.
34But God is strong and will buy them back.
His name is the Lord All-Powerful.
He will surely defend them with power
so he can give rest to their land.
But he will not give rest to those living in
Babylon."

35The Lord says,

"Let a sword kill the people living in Babylon
and her officers and wise men!
36Let a sword kill her false prophets,*d*
and they will become fools.
Let a sword kill her warriors,
and they will be full of terror.
37Let a sword kill her horses and chariots
and all the soldiers hired from other
countries!
Then they will be like frightened women.
Let a sword attack her treasures,
so they will be taken away.
38Let a sword attack her waters
so they will be dried up.
She is a land of idols,
and the people go crazy with fear over
them.

39"Desert animals and hyenas will live there,
and owls will live there,
but no people will ever live there again.
She will never be filled with people again.
40God completely destroyed the cities of Sodom
and Gomorrah
and the towns around them," says the
LORD.
"In the same way no people will live in
Babylon,
and no human being will stay there.

41"Look! An army is coming from the north.
A powerful nation and many kings
are coming together from all around the
world.
42Their armies have bows and spears.
The soldiers are cruel and have no mercy.
As the soldiers come riding on their horses,
the sound is loud like the roaring sea.
They stand in their places, ready for battle.
They are ready to attack you, city of
Babylon.
43The king of Babylon heard about those
armies,
and he became helpless with fear.
Distress has gripped him.
His pain is like that of a woman giving
birth to a baby.

44"Like a lion coming up from the thick bushes
near the Jordan River
to attack a strong pen for sheep,
I will suddenly chase the people of Babylon
from their land.
Who is the one I have chosen to do this?
There is no one like me,
no one who can take me to court.
None of their leaders can stand up against
me."

45So listen to what the LORD has planned to do
against Babylon.

Listen to what he has decided to do to the
people in the city of Babylon.
He will surely drag away the young ones of
Babylon.
Their hometowns will surely be shocked at
what happens to them.
46At the sound of Babylon's capture, the earth
will shake.
People in all nations will hear Babylon's cry
of distress.

51 This is what the LORD says:
"I will soon cause a destroying wind
to blow
against Babylon and the Babylonian people.
2I will send foreign people to destroy Babylon
like a wind that blows chaff*d* away.
They will destroy the land.
Armies will surround the city
when the day of disaster comes upon her.
3Don't let the Babylonian soldiers prepare their
bows to shoot.
Don't even let them put on their armor.
Don't feel sorry for the young men of
Babylon,
but completely destroy her army.
4They will be killed in the land of the
Babylonians
and will die in her streets.
5The Lord GOD All-Powerful
did not leave Israel and Judah,
even though they were completely guilty
in the presence of the Holy One of Israel.
6"Run away from Babylon
and save your lives!
Don't stay and be killed because of
Babylon's sins.
It is time for the LORD to punish Babylon;
he will give Babylon the punishment she
deserves.
7Babylon was like a gold cup in the LORD's
hand
that made the whole earth drunk.
The nations drank Babylon's wine,
so they went crazy.
8Babylon has suddenly fallen and been broken.
Cry for her!
Get balm*d* for her pain,
and maybe she can be healed.

9"Foreigners in Babylon say, 'We tried to heal
Babylon,
but she cannot be healed.
So let us leave her and each go to his own
country.
Babylon's punishment is as high as the sky;
it reaches to the clouds.'

10"The people of Judah say, 'The LORD has
shown us to be right.
Come, let us tell in Jerusalem

what the Lord our God has done.'

11"Sharpen the arrows!
  Pick up your shields!
The Lord has stirred up the kings of the
    Medes,
because he wants to destroy Babylon.
The Lord will punish them as they deserve
  for destroying his Temple.[d]
12Lift up a banner against the walls of Babylon!
  Bring more guards.
Put the watchmen in their places,
  and get ready for a secret attack!
The Lord will certainly do what he has
    planned
  and what he said he would do against the
    people of Babylon.
13People of Babylon, you live near much water
  and are rich with many treasures,
but your end as a nation has come.
  It is time to stop you from robbing other
    nations.
14The Lord All-Powerful has promised in his
    own name:
  'Babylon, I will surely fill you with so many
    enemy soldiers they will be like a
    swarm of locusts.[d]
  They will stand over you and shout their
    victory.'

15"The Lord made the earth by his power.
  He used his wisdom to build the world
  and his understanding to stretch out the
    skies.
16When he thunders, the waters in the skies
    roar.
  He makes clouds rise in the sky all over the
    earth.
  He sends lightning with the rain
  and brings out the wind from his
    storehouses.

17"People are so stupid and know so little.
  Goldsmiths are made ashamed by their
    idols,
because those statues are only false gods.
  They have no breath in them.
18They are worth nothing; people make fun of
    them.
  When they are judged, they will be
    destroyed.
19But God, who is Jacob's Portion,[d] is not like
    the idols.
  He made everything,
and he chose Israel to be his special people.
  The Lord All-Powerful is his name.

20"You are my war club,
  my battle weapon.
I use you to smash nations.
  I use you to destroy kingdoms.

21I use you to smash horses and riders.
  I use you to smash chariots and drivers.
22I use you to smash men and women.
  I use you to smash old people and young
    people.
  I use you to smash young men and young
    women.
23I use you to smash shepherds and flocks.
  I use you to smash farmers and oxen.
  I use you to smash governors and officers.

24"But I will pay back Babylon and all the Babylonians for all the evil things they did to Jerusalem in your sight," says the Lord.

25The Lord says,
  "Babylon, you are a destroying mountain,
  and I am against you.
  You have destroyed the whole land.
  I will put my hand out against you.
  I will roll you off the cliffs,
  and I will make you a burned-out
    mountain.
26People will not find any rocks in Babylon big
    enough for cornerstones.[d]
  People will not take any rocks from
    Babylon to use for the foundation of a
    building,
  because your city will be just a pile of ruins
    forever," says the Lord.

27"Lift up a banner in the land!
  Blow the trumpet among the nations!
Get the nations ready for battle against
    Babylon.
  Call these kingdoms of Ararat, Minni, and
    Ashkenaz to fight against her.
Choose a commander to lead the army
    against Babylon.
  Send so many horses that they are like a
    swarm of locusts.
28Get the nations ready for battle against
    Babylon—
  the kings of the Medes,
their governors and all their officers,
  and all the countries they rule.
29The land shakes and moves in pain,
  because the Lord will do what he has
    planned to Babylon.
He will make Babylon an empty desert,
  where no one will live.
30Babylon's warriors have stopped fighting.
  They stay in their protected cities.
Their strength is gone,
  and they have become like frightened
    women.
Babylon's houses are burning.
  The bars of her gates are broken.
31One messenger follows another;
  messenger follows messenger.

They announce to the king of Babylon
that his whole city has been captured.
32The river crossings have been captured,
and the swamplands are burning.
All of Babylon's soldiers are terribly afraid."

33This is what the LORD All-Powerful, the God
of Israel, says:
"The city of Babylon is like a threshing*d* floor,
where people crush the grain at harvest
time.
The time to harvest Babylon is coming
soon."

34"Nebuchadnezzar king of Babylon has
defeated and destroyed us.
In the past he took our people away,
and we became like an empty jar.
He was like a giant snake that swallowed us.
He filled his stomach with our best things.
Then he spit us out.
35Babylon did terrible things to hurt us.
Now let those things happen to Babylon,"
say the people of Jerusalem.
"The people of Babylon killed our people.
Now let them be punished for what they
did," says Jerusalem.

36So this is what the LORD says:
"I will soon defend you, Judah,
and make sure that Babylon is punished.
I will dry up Babylon's sea
and make her springs become dry.
37Babylon will become a pile of ruins,
a home for wild dogs.
People will be shocked by what happened
there.
No one will live there anymore.
38Babylon's people roar like young lions;
they growl like baby lions.
39While they are stirred up,
I will give a feast for them
and make them drunk.
They will shout and laugh.
And they will sleep forever and never wake
up!" says the LORD.
40"I will take the people of Babylon to be
killed.
They will be like lambs,
like sheep and goats waiting to be killed.

41"How Babylon has been defeated!
The pride of the whole earth has been
taken captive.
People from other nations are shocked at
what happened to Babylon,
and the things they see make them afraid.
42The sea has risen over Babylon;
its roaring waves cover her.
43Babylon's towns are ruined and empty.
It has become a dry, desert land,

a land where no one lives.
People do not even travel through Babylon.
44I will punish the god Bel*d* in Babylon.
I will make him spit out what he has
swallowed.
Nations will no longer come to Babylon;
even the wall around the city will fall.

45"Come out of Babylon, my people!
Run for your lives!
Run from the LORD's great anger.
46Don't lose courage;
rumors will spread through the land, but
don't be afraid.
One rumor comes this year, and another
comes the next year.
There will be rumors of terrible fighting in
the country,
of rulers fighting against rulers.
47The time will surely come
when I will punish the idols of Babylon,
and the whole land will be disgraced.
There will be many dead people lying all
around.
48Then heaven and earth and all that is in
them
will shout for joy about Babylon.
They will shout because the army comes
from the north
to destroy Babylon," says the LORD.

49"Babylon must fall, because she killed people
from Israel.
She killed people from everywhere on
earth.
50You who have escaped being killed with
swords,
leave Babylon! Don't wait!
Remember the LORD in the faraway land
and think about Jerusalem."

51"We people of Judah are disgraced,
because we have been insulted.
We have been shamed,
because strangers have gone into
the holy places of the LORD's Temple!"*d*

52So the LORD says, "The time is coming soon
when I will punish the idols of Babylon.
Wounded people will cry with pain
all over that land.
53Even if Babylon grows until she touches the
sky,
and even if *she makes her highest cities*
strong,
I will send people to destroy her," says the
LORD.

54"Sounds of people crying are heard in
Babylon.
Sounds of people destroying things

are heard in the land of the Babylonians.
55The Lord is destroying Babylon
and making the loud sounds of the city
become silent.
Enemies come roaring in like ocean waves.
The roar of their voices is heard all around.
56The army has come to destroy Babylon.
Her soldiers have been captured,
and their bows are broken,
because the Lord is a God who punishes
people for the evil they do.
He gives them the full punishment they
deserve.
57I will make Babylon's rulers and wise men
drunk,
and her governors, officers, and soldiers,
too.
Then they will sleep forever and never wake
up," says the King,
whose name is the Lord All-Powerful.

58This is what the Lord All-Powerful says:
"Babylon's thick wall will be completely
pulled down
and her high gates burned.
The people will work hard, but it won't help;
their work will only become fuel for the
flames!"

A Message to Babylon

59This is the message that Jeremiah the
prophet*d* gave to the officer Seraiah son of Neriah,
who was the son of Mahseiah. Seraiah went to
Babylon with Zedekiah king of Judah in the fourth
year Zedekiah was king of Judah. His duty was to
arrange the king's food and housing on the trip.
60Jeremiah had written on a scroll all the terrible
things that would happen to Babylon, all these
words about Babylon. 61Jeremiah said to Seraiah,
"As soon as you come to Babylon, be sure to read
this message so all the people can hear you.
62Then say, 'Lord, you have said that you will
destroy this place so that no people or animals will
live in it. It will be an empty ruin forever.' 63After
you finish reading this scroll, tie a stone to it and
throw it into the Euphrates River. 64Then say, 'In
the same way Babylon will sink and will not rise
again because of the terrible things I will make
happen here. Her people will fall.' "
The words of Jeremiah end here.

The Fall of Jerusalem

52 Zedekiah was twenty-one years old
when he became king, and he was king
in Jerusalem for eleven years. His mother's name
was Hamutal daughter of Jeremiah, *n* and she was
from Libnah. 2Zedekiah did what the Lord said

was wrong, just as Jehoiakim had done. 3All this
happened in Jerusalem and Judah because the
Lord was angry with them. Finally, he threw
them out of his presence.
Zedekiah turned against the king of Babylon.
4Then Nebuchadnezzar king of Babylon marched
against Jerusalem with his whole army. They
made a camp around the city and built devices all
around the city walls to attack it. This happened
on Zedekiah's ninth year, tenth month, and tenth
day as king. 5And the city was under attack until
Zedekiah's eleventh year as king.
6By the ninth day of the fourth month, the hunger
was terrible in the city; there was no food for
the people to eat. 7Then the city wall was broken
through, and the whole army of Judah ran away
at night. They left the city through the gate between
the two walls by the king's garden. Even
though the Babylonians were surrounding the
city, Zedekiah and his men headed toward the
Jordan Valley.
8But the Babylonian army chased King Zedekiah
and caught him in the plains of Jericho. All
of his army was scattered from him. 9So the Babylonians
captured Zedekiah and took him to the
king of Babylon at the town of Riblah in the land
of Hamath. There he passed sentence on Zedekiah.
10At Riblah the king of Babylon killed Zedekiah's
sons as he watched. The king also killed
all the officers of Judah. 11Then he put out Zedekiah's
eyes, and put bronze chains on him, and
took him to Babylon. And the king kept Zedekiah
in prison there until the day he died.
12Nebuzaradan, commander of the king's special
guards and servant of the king of Babylon,
came to Jerusalem on the tenth day of the fifth
month. This was in Nebuchadnezzar's nineteenth
year as king of Babylon. 13Nebuzaradan set fire to
the Temple*d* of the Lord, the palace, and all the
houses of Jerusalem; every important building
was burned. 14The whole Babylonian army, led by
the commander of the king's special guards, broke
down all the walls around Jerusalem. 15Nebuzaradan,
the commander of the king's special guards,
took captive some of the poorest people, those
who were left in Jerusalem, those who had surrendered
to the king of Babylon, and the skilled
craftsmen who were left in Jerusalem. 16But Nebuzaradan
left behind some of the poorest people
of the land to take care of the vineyards and fields.
17The Babylonians broke into pieces the bronze
pillars, the bronze stands, and the large bronze
bowl, called the Sea, which were in the Temple
of the Lord. Then they carried all the bronze
pieces to Babylon. 18They also took the pots, shovels,
wick trimmers, bowls, dishes, and all the
bronze objects used to serve in the Temple. 19The

Jeremiah　This is not the prophet Jeremiah but a different man with the same name.

commander of the king's special guards took away bowls, pans for carrying hot coals, large bowls, pots, lampstands, pans, and bowls used for drink offerings. He took everything that was made of pure gold or silver.

20There was so much bronze that it could not be weighed: two pillars, the large bronze bowl called the Sea with the twelve bronze bulls under it, and the movable stands, which King Solomon had made for the Temple of the LORD.

21Each of the pillars was about twenty-seven feet high, eighteen feet around, and hollow inside. The wall of each pillar was three inches thick. 22The bronze capital*d* on top of the one pillar was about seven and one-half feet high. It was decorated with a net design and bronze pomegranates*d* all around it. The other pillar also had pomegranates and was like the first pillar. 23There were ninety-six pomegranates on the sides of the pillars. There was a total of a hundred pomegranates above the net design.

> ✴ **SIDELIGHT:** If you think allowances are just for kids, read Jeremiah 52:34, which tells about an allowance for King Jehoiachin. Archaeologists have uncovered actual records that show the allowances the king and his family received.

24The commander of the king's special guards took as prisoners Seraiah the chief priest, Zepha-niah the priest next in rank, and the three door-keepers. 25He also took from the city the officer in charge of the soldiers, seven people who advised the king, the royal secretary who selected people for the army, and sixty other men from Judah who were in the city when it fell. 26Nebuzaradan, the commander, took these people and brought them to the king of Babylon at the town of Riblah. 27There at Riblah, in the land of Hamath, the king had them killed.

So the people of Judah were led away from their country as captives. 28This is the number of the people Nebuchadnezzar took away as captives: in the seventh year, 3,023 Jews; 29in Nebuchadnezzar's eighteenth year, 832 people from Jerusalem; 30in Nebuchadnezzar's twenty-third year, Nebuzaradan, commander of the king's special guards, took 745 Jews as captives.

In all 4,600 people were taken captive.

Jehoiachin Is Set Free

31Jehoiachin king of Judah was in prison in Babylon for thirty-seven years. The year Evil-Merodach became king of Babylon he let Jehoiachin king of Judah out of prison. He set Jehoiachin free on the twenty-fifth day of the twelfth month. 32Evil-Merodach spoke kindly to Jehoiachin and gave him a seat of honor above the seats of the other kings who were with him in Babylon. 33So Jehoiachin put away his prison clothes, and for the rest of his life, he ate at the king's table. 34Every day the king of Babylon gave Jehoiachin an allowance. This lasted as long as he lived, until the day Jehoiachin died.

LAMENTATIONS

Why Read This Book:
- Find ways to express grief to God (Lamentations 1—2).
- Learn about taking responsibility for choices and consequences (Lamentations 3—4).
- Be encouraged to turn to God in times of trouble (Lamentations 5).

Behind the Scenes:

All of Jerusalem was in ruins.
Babylonians had surrounded the city and then burned it to the ground.
Children, women and men had been killed.
Desolation was everywhere.
Everything the Jews had known and loved was gone.
Full of sorrow, the five poems in Lamentations were written.
Grief is evident in each of the poems.
Hope shines through only toward the end of the book.
In future years, people read the book in times of sorrow.
Jews read it each year in August to remember the Temple's destruction and to repent of their sins.

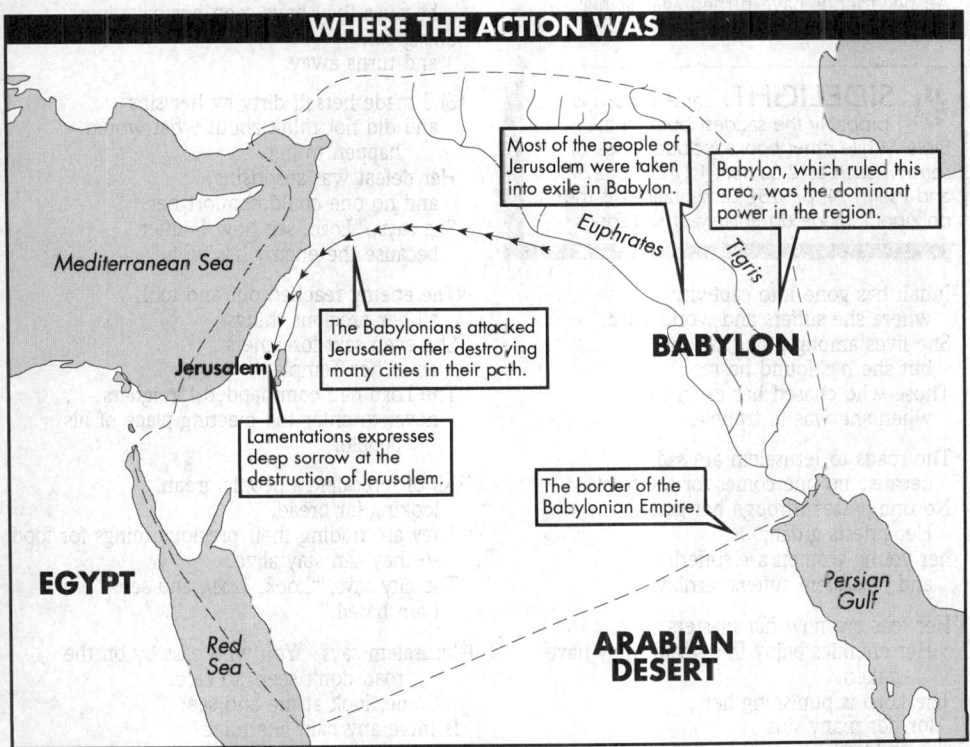

WHERE THE ACTION WAS

Most of the people of Jerusalem were taken into exile in Babylon.

Babylon, which ruled this area, was the dominant power in the region.

Mediterranean Sea

Euphrates

Tigris

The Babylonians attacked Jerusalem after destroying many cities in their path.

Jerusalem

BABYLON

Lamentations expresses deep sorrow at the destruction of Jerusalem.

The border of the Babylonian Empire.

EGYPT

Persian Gulf

Red Sea

ARABIAN DESERT

WHEN THE ACTION WAS

	The Northern Kingdom (Israel) fell to Assyria	The Jews began returning from exile		Jesus was born
1000BC	**750BC**	**500BC**	**250BC**	**BC/AD**
The kingdom was split between Israel and Judah	Jerusalem was destroyed by the Babylonians	The poems in Lamentations were written		

Behind the
Scenes (cont.):   Knowing God's love can help through times of crisis like this.
Like the lines above, each stanza in the five poems in Lamentations begins with
a different consecutive letter of the Hebrew alphabet—twenty-two letters in all. Of
course, we can't see the structure in English, because the translated words are
different. But the ancient Hebrews understood that the poems expressed their
sorrow from beginning to end, "from A to Z."

Jerusalem Cries over Her Loss

1 Jerusalem once was full of people,
but now the city is empty.
Jerusalem once was a great city among the
nations,
but now she*n* is like a widow.
She was like a queen of all the other cities,
but now she is a slave.

²She cries loudly at night,
and tears are on her cheeks.
There is no one to comfort her;
all who loved her are gone.
All her friends have turned against her
and are now her enemies.

³Judah has gone into captivity
where she suffers and works hard.
She lives among other nations,
but she has found no rest.
Those who chased her caught her
when she was in trouble.

⁴The roads to Jerusalem are sad,
because no one comes for the feasts.
No one passes through her gates.
Her priests groan,
her young women are suffering,
and Jerusalem suffers terribly.

⁵Her foes are now her masters.
Her enemies enjoy the wealth they have
taken.
The LORD is punishing her
for her many sins.
Her children have gone away
as captives of the enemy.

⁶The beauty of Jerusalem
has gone away.
Her rulers are like deer
that cannot find food.

They are weak
and run from the hunters.

⁷Jerusalem is suffering and homeless.
She remembers all the good things
from the past.
But her people were defeated by the enemy,
and there was no one to help her.
When her enemies saw her,
they laughed to see her ruined.

⁸Jerusalem sinned terribly,
so she has become unclean.*d*
Those who honored her now hate her,
because they have seen her nakedness.
She groans
and turns away.

⁹She made herself dirty by her sins
and did not think about what would
happen to her.
Her defeat was surprising,
and no one could comfort her.
She says, "LORD, see how I suffer,
because the enemy has won."

¹⁰The enemy reached out and took
all her precious things.
She even saw foreigners
enter her Temple.*d*
The LORD had commanded foreigners
never to enter the meeting place of his
people.

¹¹All of Jerusalem's people groan,
looking for bread.
They are trading their precious things for food
so they can stay alive.
The city says, "Look, LORD, and see.
I am hated."

¹²Jerusalem says, "You who pass by on the
road don't seem to care.
Come, look at me and see:
Is there any pain like mine?
Is there any pain like that he has caused
me?
The LORD has punished me
on the day of his great anger.

¹³"He sent fire from above
that went down into my bones.

---

she In this poem the city of Jerusalem is described as a woman.

He stretched out a net for my feet
    and turned me back.
He made me so sad and lonely
    that I am weak all day.

14"He has noticed my sins;
    they are tied together by his hands;
they hang around my neck.
    He has turned my strength into weakness.
The Lord has handed me over
    to those who are stronger than I.

15"The Lord has rejected
    all my mighty men inside my walls.
He brought an army against me
    to destroy my young men.
As if in a winepress,*d* the Lord has crushed
    the capital city of Judah.

16"I cry about these things;
    my eyes overflow with tears.
There is no one near to comfort me,
    no one who can give me strength again.
My children are left sad and lonely,
    because the enemy has won."

17Jerusalem reaches out her hands,
    but there is no one to comfort her.
The Lord commanded the people of Jacob
    to be surrounded by their enemies.
Jerusalem is now unclean
    like those around her.

18Jerusalem says, "The Lord is right,
    but I refused to obey him.
Listen, all you people,
    and look at my pain.
My young women and men
    have gone into captivity.

19"I called out to my friends,
    but they turned against me.
My priests and my older leaders
    have died in the city
while looking for food
    to stay alive.

20"Look at me, Lord. I am upset
    and greatly troubled.
My heart is troubled,
    because I have been so stubborn.
Out in the streets, the sword kills;
    inside the houses, death destroys.

21"People have heard my groaning,
    and there is no one to comfort me.
All my enemies have heard of my trouble,
    and they are happy you have done this to
      me.
Now bring that day you have announced
    so that my enemies will be like me.

22"Look at all their evil.

Do to them what you have done to me
    because of all my sins.
I groan over and over again,
    and I am afraid."

The Lord Destroyed Jerusalem

2 Look how the Lord in his anger
    has brought Jerusalem to shame.
He has thrown down the greatness of Israel
    from the sky to the earth;
he did not remember the Temple,*d* his
      footstool,
    on the day of his anger.

2The Lord swallowed up without mercy
    all the houses of the people of Jacob;
in his anger he pulled down
    the strong places of Judah.
He threw her kingdom and its rulers
    down to the ground in dishonor.

3In his anger he has removed
    all the strength of Israel;
he took away his power from Israel
    when the enemy came.
He burned against the people of Jacob like a
      flaming fire
    that burns up everything around it.

4Like an enemy, he prepared to shoot his
      bow,
    and his hand was against us.
Like an enemy, he killed
    all the good-looking people;
he poured out his anger like fire
    on the tents of Jerusalem.

5The Lord was like an enemy;
    he swallowed up Israel.
He swallowed up all her palaces
    and destroyed all her strongholds.*d*
He has caused more moaning and groaning
    for Judah.

6He cut down his Temple like a garden;
    he destroyed the meeting place.
The Lord has made Jerusalem forget
    the set feasts and Sabbath*d* days.
He has rejected the king and the priest
    in his great anger.

7The Lord has rejected his altar
    and abandoned his Temple.
He has handed over to the enemy
    the walls of Jerusalem's palaces.
Their uproar in the Lord's Temple
    was like that of a feast day.

8The Lord planned to destroy
    the wall around Jerusalem.
He measured the wall

and did not stop himself from destroying it.
He made the walls and defenses sad;
    together they have fallen.

⁹Jerusalem's gates have fallen to the ground;
    he destroyed and smashed the bars of the
        gates.
Her king and her princes are among the
        nations.
The teaching of the Lord has stopped,
and the prophets*d* do not have
    visions from the Lord.

¹⁰The older leaders of Jerusalem
    sit on the ground in silence.
They throw dust on their heads
    and put on rough cloth to show their
        sadness.
The young women of Jerusalem
    bow their heads to the ground in sorrow.

¹¹My eyes have no more tears,
    and I am sick to my stomach.
I feel empty inside,
    because my people have been destroyed.
Children and babies are fainting
    in the streets of the city.

¹²They ask their mothers,
    "Where is the grain and wine?"
They faint like wounded soldiers
    in the streets of the city
    and die in their mothers' arms.

¹³What can I say about you, Jerusalem?
    What can I compare you to?
What can I say you are like?
    How can I comfort you, Jerusalem?
Your ruin is as deep as the sea.
    No one can heal you.

¹⁴Your prophets saw visions,
    but they were false and worth nothing.
They did not point out your sins
    to keep you from being captured.
They preached what was false
    and led you wrongly.

¹⁵All who pass by on the road
    clap their hands at you;
they make fun of Jerusalem
    and shake their heads.
They ask, "Is this the city that people called
    the most beautiful city,
    the happiest place on earth?"

¹⁶All your enemies open their mouths
    to speak against you.
They make fun and grind their teeth in
        anger.
They say, "We have swallowed you up.
This is the day we were waiting for!
We have finally seen it happen."

¹⁷The Lord has done what he planned;
    he has kept his word
    that he commanded long ago.
He has destroyed without mercy,
    and he has let your enemies laugh at you.
He has strengthened your enemies.

¹⁸The people cry out to the Lord.
    Wall of Jerusalem,
let your tears flow
    like a river day and night.
Do not stop
    or let your eyes rest.

¹⁹Get up, cry out in the night,
    even as the night begins.
Pour out your heart like water
    in prayer to the Lord.
Lift up your hands in prayer to him
    for the life of your children
who are fainting with hunger
    on every street corner.

²⁰Jerusalem says: "Look, Lord, and see
    to whom you have done this.
Women eat their own babies,
    the children they have cared for.
Priests and prophets are killed
    in the Temple of the Lord.

²¹"People young and old
    lie outside on the ground.
My young women and young men
    have been killed by the sword.
You killed them on the day of your anger;
    you killed them without mercy.

²²"You invited terrors to come against me on
        every side,
    as if you were inviting them to a feast.
No one escaped or remained alive
    on the day of the Lord's anger.
My enemy has killed
    those I cared for and brought up."

The Meaning of Suffering

3 I am a man who has seen the suffering
    that comes from the rod of the Lord's
        anger.
²He led me
    into darkness, not light.
³He turned his hand against me
    again and again, all day long.

⁴*He wore out my flesh and skin*
    and broke my bones.
⁵He surrounded me with sadness
    and attacked me with grief.
⁶He made me sit in the dark,
    like those who have been dead a long time.

⁷He shut me in so I could not get out;

he put heavy chains on me.
⁸I cry out and beg for help,
but he ignores my prayer.
⁹He blocked my way with a stone wall
and led me in the wrong direction.

¹⁰He is like a bear ready to attack me,
like a lion in hiding.
¹¹He led me the wrong way and let me stray
and left me without help.
¹²He prepared to shoot his bow
and made me the target for his arrows.

¹³He shot me in the kidneys
with the arrows from his bag.
¹⁴I was a joke to all my people,
who make fun of me with songs all day
long.
¹⁵The LORD filled me with misery;
he made me drunk with suffering.

¹⁶He broke my teeth with gravel
and trampled me into the dirt.
¹⁷I have no more peace.
I have forgotten what happiness is.
¹⁸I said, "My strength is gone,
and I have no hope in the LORD."

¹⁹LORD, remember my suffering and my misery,

my sorrow and trouble.
²⁰Please remember me
and think about me.
²¹But I have hope
when I think of this:

²²The LORD's love never ends;
his mercies never stop.
²³They are new every morning;
LORD, your loyalty is great.
²⁴I say to myself, "The LORD is mine,
so I hope in him."

²⁵The LORD is good to those who hope in him,
to those who seek him.
²⁶It is good to wait quietly
for the LORD to save.
²⁷It is good for someone to work hard
while he is young.

²⁸He should sit alone and be quiet;
the LORD has given him hard work to do.
²⁹He should bow down to the ground;
maybe there is still hope.
³⁰He should let anyone slap his cheek;
he should be filled with shame.

³¹The Lord will not reject
his people forever.

SUFFERING

Lord, Remember Me

After dating for seven months, Brad, seventeen, and Angie, sixteen, broke up. "It was a really hard breakup," Brad remembers. "Part of me didn't want to do it, and part did."

For about three months afterward, Brad was severely depressed. "Angie was a source of energy for me," he explains. "After the breakup, I'd think about her and sigh and wonder why it had to happen."

Brad felt pretty bad sometimes, but he didn't blame God for what happened. In fact, he believes God got him through the loss, even if God's guidance wasn't clear. And he believes God's love came through his parents and friends, who listened as he shared his feelings. "What kept me going," he remembers, "was knowing that whatever happens, happens for the best."

Even though Brad was going through a tough time, he sensed God was with him. Read how the writer of **Lamentations 3:1–24** expresses a much greater disappointment and pain.

■ If Brad wrote a poem about his breakup, what would be the similarities and differences between Brad's poem and this passage?
■ What does God's love have to do with times of suffering, both in biblical times and today?

C O N S I D E R . . .
■ watching an old comedy routine, such as one from Laurel and Hardy. Sometimes laughter gives perspective to difficult times.
■ volunteering to serve on phone hot lines, in a shelter, or with another group that helps people through crises.

F O R   M O R E ,   S E E . . .
■ 2 Kings 24:18—25:21 (p. 357)
■ Psalm 22 (p. 493)
■ 2 Corinthians 12:7–10 (p. 1203)

³²Although he brings sorrow,
      he also has mercy and great love.
³³He does not like to punish people
      or make them sad.

³⁴He sees if any prisoner of the earth
      is crushed under his feet;
³⁵he sees if someone is treated unfairly
      before the Most High God;
³⁶the Lord sees
      if someone is cheated in his case in court.

³⁷Nobody can speak and have it happen
      unless the Lord commands it.
³⁸Both bad and good things
      come by the command of the Most High
         God.
³⁹No one should complain
      when he is punished for his sins.

⁴⁰Let us examine and see what we have done
      and then return to the LORD.
⁴¹Let us lift up our hands and pray from our
         hearts
      to God in heaven:
⁴²"We have sinned and turned against you,
      and you have not forgiven us.

⁴³"You wrapped yourself in anger and chased
         us;
      you killed us without mercy.
⁴⁴You wrapped yourself in a cloud,
      and no prayer could get through.
⁴⁵You made us like scum and trash
      among the other nations.

⁴⁶"All of our enemies
      open their mouths and speak against us.
⁴⁷We have been frightened and fearful,
      ruined and destroyed."
⁴⁸Streams of tears flow from my eyes,
      because my people are destroyed.

⁴⁹My tears flow continually,
      without stopping,
⁵⁰until the LORD looks down
      and sees from heaven.
⁵¹I am sad when I see
      what has happened to all the women of my
         city.

⁵²Those who are my enemies for no reason
      hunted me like a bird.
⁵³They tried to kill me in a pit;
      they threw stones at me.
⁵⁴*Water came up over my head,*
      and I said, "I am going to die."
⁵⁵I called out to you, LORD,
      from the bottom of the pit.
⁵⁶You heard me calling, "Do not close your
         ears
      and ignore my gasps and shouts."

⁵⁷You came near when I called to you;
      you said, "Don't be afraid."

⁵⁸Lord, you have taken my case
      and given me back my life.
⁵⁹LORD, you have seen how I have been
         wronged.
      Now judge my case for me.
⁶⁰You have seen how my enemies took revenge
         on me
      and made evil plans against me.

⁶¹LORD, you have heard their insults
      and all their evil plans against me.
⁶²The words and thoughts of my enemies
      are against me all the time.
⁶³Look! In everything they do
      they make fun of me with songs.

⁶⁴Pay them back, LORD,
      for what they have done.
⁶⁵Make them stubborn,
      and put your curse on them.
⁶⁶Chase them in anger, LORD,
      and destroy them from under your heavens.

※ SIDELIGHT: Because only priests were allowed to enter the Most Holy Place in the Temple, the Babylonian trampling of the Temple (Lamentations 4:1) was difficult to cope with. In fact, the Temple's destruction was even more tragic to the devout Jew than the devastation in the rest of Jerusalem.

The Attack on Jerusalem

4 See how the gold has lost its shine,
      how the pure gold has dulled!
The stones of the Temple* are scattered
      at every street corner.

²The precious people of Jerusalem
      were more valuable than gold,
but now they are thought of as clay jars
      made by the hands of a potter.

³Even wild dogs give their milk
      to feed their young,
but my people are cruel
      like ostriches in the desert.

⁴The babies are so thirsty
      their tongues stick to the roofs of their
         mouths.
Children beg for bread,
      but no one gives them any.

⁵Those who once ate fine foods
      are now starving in the streets.
People who grew up wearing nice clothes

now pick through trash piles.

⁶My people have been punished
　　more than Sodom was.
Sodom was destroyed suddenly,
　　and no hands reached out to help her.

⁷Our princes were purer than snow,
　　and whiter than milk.
Their bodies were redder than rubies;
　　they looked like sapphires.

⁸But now they are blacker than coal,
　　and no one recognizes them in the streets.
Their skin hangs on their bones;
　　it is as dry as wood.

⁹Those who were killed in the war were
　　　　better off
　　than those killed by hunger.
They starve in pain and die,
　　because there is no food from the field.

¹⁰With their own hands kind women
　　cook their own children.
They became food
　　when my people were destroyed.

¹¹The LORD turned loose all of his anger;
　　he poured out his strong anger.
He set fire to Jerusalem,
　　burning it down to the foundations.

¹²Kings of the earth and people of the world
　　could not believe
that enemies and foes
　　could enter the gates of Jerusalem.

¹³It happened because her prophetsᵈ sinned
　　and her priests did evil.
They killed in the city
　　those who did what was right.

¹⁴They wandered in the streets
　　as if they were blind.
They were dirty with blood,
　　so no one would touch their clothes.

¹⁵"Go away! You are unclean,"ᵈ people shouted
　　　　at them.
　　"Get away! Get away! Don't touch us!"
So they ran away and wandered.
　　Even the other nations said, "Don't stay
　　　　here."

¹⁶The LORD himself scattered them
　　and did not look after them anymore.
No one respects the priests
　　or honors the older leaders.

¹⁷Also, our eyes grew tired,
　　looking for help that never came.
We kept watch from our towers
　　for a nation to save us.

¹⁸Our enemies hunted us,
　　so we could not even walk in the streets.
Our end is near. Our time is up.
　　Our end has come.

¹⁹Those who chased us
　　were faster than eagles in the sky.
They ran us into the mountains
　　and ambushed us in the desert.

²⁰The LORD's appointed king, who was our
　　　　very breath,
　　was caught in their traps.
We had said about him, "We will be
　　　　protected by him
　　among the nations."

²¹Be happy and glad, people of Edom,
　　you who live in the land of Uz.
The cup of God's anger will come to you;
　　then you will get drunk and go naked.

²²Your punishment is complete, Jerusalem.
　　He will not send you into captivity again.
But the LORD will punish the sins of Edom;
　　he will uncover your evil.

A Prayer to the Lord

5 Remember, LORD, what happened to us.
　　Look and see our disgrace.
²Our land has been turned over to strangers;
　　our houses have been given to foreigners.
³We are like orphans with no father;
　　our mothers are like widows.
⁴We have to buy the water we drink;
　　we must pay for the firewood.
⁵Those who chase after us want to catch us
　　　　by the neck.
　　We are tired and find no rest.
⁶We made an agreement with Egypt
　　and with Assyria to get enough food.
⁷Our ancestors sinned against you, but they
　　　　are gone;
　　now we suffer because of their sins.
⁸Slaves have become our rulers,
　　and no one can save us from them.
⁹We risk our lives to get our food;
　　we face death in the desert.
¹⁰Our skin is hot like an oven;
　　we burn with starvation.
¹¹The enemy abused the women of Jerusalem
　　and the girls in the cities of Judah.
¹²Princes were hung by the hands;
　　they did not respect our older leaders.
¹³The young men ground grain at the mill,
　　and boys stumbled under loads of wood.
¹⁴The older leaders no longer sit at the city
　　　　gates;
　　the young men no longer sing.
¹⁵We have no more joy in our hearts;
　　our dancing has turned to sadness.

¹⁶The crown has fallen from our head.
How terrible it is because we sinned.
¹⁷Because of this we are afraid,
and now our eyes are dim.
¹⁸Mount Zion*ᵈ* is empty,
and wild dogs wander around it.

¹⁹But you rule forever, LORD.

You will be King from now on.
²⁰Why have you forgotten us for so long?
Have you left us forever?
²¹Bring us back to you, LORD, and we will
return.
Make our days as they were before,
²²or have you completely rejected us?
Are you so angry with us?

EZEKIEL

Why Read This Book:

- ■ Be encouraged by God's extraordinary efforts to call his people back to himself (Ezekiel 1—24).
- ■ Take comfort in the promises God made through the prophet Ezekiel (Ezekiel 33—48).

Behind the Scenes:

"PROPHET SEES UFO!" the headline would have screamed if tabloid newspapers had been around in Ezekiel's time.

The story would reveal how Ezekiel, the prophet, saw the sky opening up, glowing lights in the sky, fire, and something like glowing metal in the middle of a cloud. Then, the story would continue, the prophet saw creatures—creatures who, the writer suggests, were probably aliens.

Finally—and this was the best part—a voice above the creatures boomed out. When Ezekiel looked up, he saw an amazing throne. It was all so powerful he was knocked off his feet.

But the prophet didn't see a UFO. The prophet saw a vision of God, as described in the first chapter of Ezekiel.

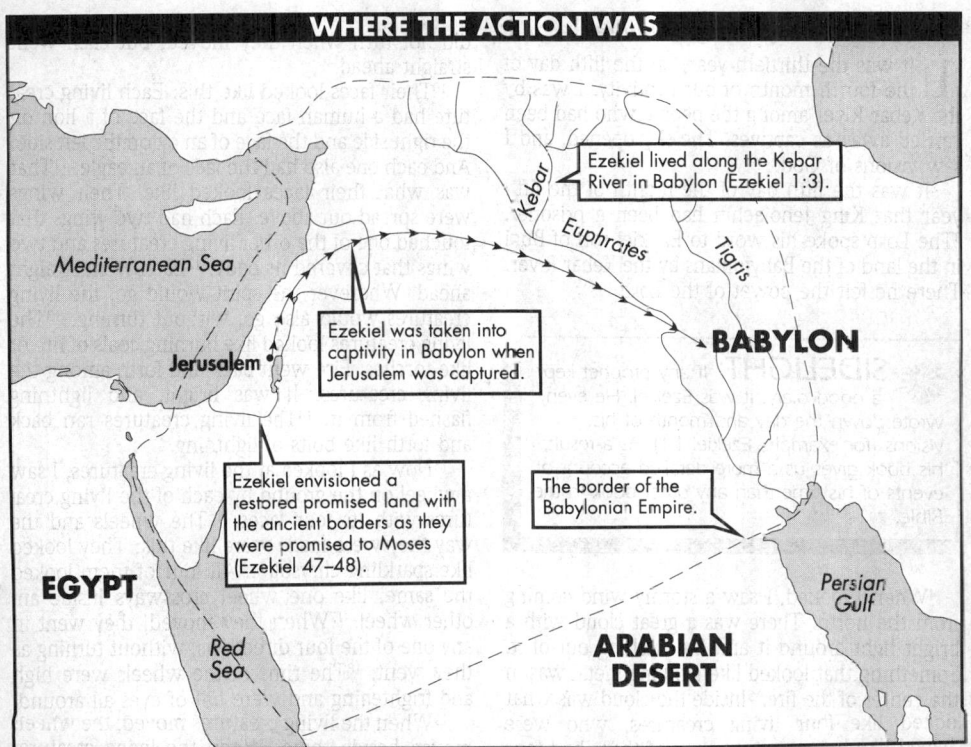

WHERE THE ACTION WAS

Ezekiel lived along the Kebar River in Babylon (Ezekiel 1:3).

Ezekiel was taken into captivity in Babylon when Jerusalem was captured.

Ezekiel envisioned a restored promised land with the ancient borders as they were promised to Moses (Ezekiel 47–48).

The border of the Babylonian Empire.

Mediterranean Sea

Jerusalem

BABYLON

EGYPT

Red Sea

ARABIAN DESERT

Persian Gulf

Kebar

Euphrates

Tigris

WHEN THE ACTION WAS

1000BC	750BC	500BC	250BC	BC/AD
The kingdom was split between Israel and Judah	Ezekiel began his ministry in exile in Babylon	The Jews began returning from exile		Jesus was born
	The Northern Kingdom (Israel) fell to Assyria	Jerusalem was totally destroyed by the Babylonians		

This unusual book is filled with such stories. Ezekiel lived during the most difficult time in the Old Testament. Jerusalem had been destroyed, and the people—including Ezekiel—had been taken into exile, mostly in Babylon. The people couldn't understand what had happened to their beloved, holy city. Had God abandoned them?

Through visions, strange actions, and symbolic language, the prophet interpreted what had happened to the city and his people. First, he told how the people of Judah got themselves into trouble by refusing to listen to earlier prophets or to follow God. So God had used the invading Babylonians to punish the people.

Yet God had not abandoned his chosen people, Ezekiel insisted. Because of God's love and trustworthiness, he would restore the city to them and renew his relationship with them. They would respond to his gift by returning to him. At that point, God would again comfort his people.

As Ezekiel describes his dreams and visions, it's sometimes hard to understand the prophet's underlying message. In fact, from the beginning scholars have been stumped by the specific meanings of passages.

But beneath all the unusual language, poetry, and imagery is a consistent message that still has meaning for us today: Through everything, God wants people to "know that I am the Lord God"—a phrase that's repeated more than sixty times through the book.

Ezekiel's Vision of Living Creatures

1 It was the thirtieth year, on the fifth day of the fourth month of our captivity. I was by the Kebar River among the people who had been carried away as captives. The sky opened, and I saw visions of God.

²It was the fifth day of the month of the fifth year that King Jehoiachin had been a prisoner. ³The LORD spoke his word to Ezekiel son of Buzi in the land of the Babylonians by the Kebar River. There he felt the power of the LORD.

⁴When I looked, I saw a stormy wind coming from the north. There was a great cloud with a bright light around it and fire flashing out of it. Something that looked like glowing metal was in the center of the fire. ⁵Inside the cloud was what looked like four living creatures, who were shaped like humans, ⁶but each of them had four *faces and four wings. Their legs were straight.* Their feet were like a calf's hoofs and sparkled like polished bronze. ⁸The living creatures had human hands under their wings on their four sides. All four of them had faces and wings, ⁹and their wings touched each other. The living creatures did not turn when they moved, but each went straight ahead.

¹⁰Their faces looked like this: Each living creature had a human face and the face of a lion on the right side and the face of an ox on the left side. And each one also had the face of an eagle. ¹¹That was what their faces looked like. Their wings were spread out above. Each had two wings that touched one of the other living creatures and two wings that covered its body. ¹²Each went straight ahead. Wherever the spirit would go, the living creatures would also go, without turning. ¹³The living creatures looked like burning coals of fire or like torches. Fire went back and forth among the living creatures. It was bright, and lightning flashed from it. ¹⁴The living creatures ran back and forth like bolts of lightning.

¹⁵Now as I looked at the living creatures, I saw a wheel on the ground by each of the living creatures with its four faces. ¹⁶The wheels and the way they were made were like this: They looked like sparkling chrysolite. All four of them looked the same, like one wheel crossways inside another wheel. ¹⁷When they moved, they went in any one of the four directions, without turning as they went. ¹⁸The rims of the wheels were high and frightening and were full of eyes all around.

¹⁹When the living creatures moved, the wheels moved beside them. When the living creatures *were lifted up from the ground, the wheels also* were lifted up. ²⁰Wherever the spirit would go, the living creatures would go. And the wheels were lifted up beside them, because the spirit of the living creatures was in the wheels. ²¹When the living creatures moved, the

wheels moved. When the living creatures stopped, the wheels stopped. And when the living creatures were lifted from the ground, the wheels were lifted beside them, because the spirit of the living creatures was in the wheels.

22Now, over the heads of the living creatures was something like a dome that sparkled like ice and was frightening. 23And under the dome the wings of the living creatures were stretched out straight toward one another. Each living creature also had two wings covering its body. 24I heard the sound of their wings, like the roaring sound of the sea, as they moved. It was like the voice of God Almighty, a roaring sound like a noisy army. When the living creatures stopped, they lowered their wings.

25A voice came from above the dome over the heads of the living creatures. When the living creatures stopped, they lowered their wings. 26Now above the dome there was something that looked like a throne. It looked like a sapphire gem. And on the throne was a shape like a human. 27Then I noticed that from the waist up the shape looked like glowing metal with fire inside. From the waist down it looked like fire, and a bright light was all around. 28The surrounding glow looked like the rainbow in the clouds on a rainy day. It seemed to look like the glory of the LORD. So when I saw it, I bowed facedown on the ground and heard a voice speaking.

The Lord Speaks to Ezekiel

2 He said to me, "Human, stand up on your feet so I may speak with you." 2While he spoke to me, the Spirit*d* entered me and put me on my feet. Then I heard the LORD speaking to me.

3He said, "Human, I am sending you to the people of Israel. That nation has turned against me and broken away from me. They and their ancestors have sinned against me until this very day. 4I am sending you to people who are stubborn and who do not obey. You will say to them, 'This is what the Lord GOD says.' 5They may listen, or they may not, since they are a people who have turned against me. But they will know that a prophet*d* has been among them. 6You, human, don't be afraid of the people or their words. Even though they may be like thorny branches and stickers all around you, and though you may feel like you live with poisonous insects, don't be afraid. Don't be afraid of their words or their looks, because they are a people who turn against me. 7But speak my words to them. They may listen, or they may not, because they turn against me. 8But you, human, listen to what I say to you. Don't turn against me as those people do. Open your mouth and eat what I am giving you."

9Then I looked and saw a hand stretched out to me, and a scroll was in it. 10He opened the scroll in front of me. Funeral songs, sad writings, and words about troubles were written on the front and back.

3 Then the LORD said to me, "Human, eat what you find; eat this scroll. Then go and speak to the people of Israel." 2So I opened my mouth, and he gave me the scroll to eat.

3He said to me, "Human, eat this scroll which I am giving you, and fill your stomach with it." Then I ate it, and it was as sweet as honey in my mouth.

SIDELIGHT: You've eaten gummy bears, right? How about "Gummy Scrolls"? Ezekiel tried them and said they tasted like honey—even though they were full of gloomy messages (Ezekiel 3:1–3). For Ezekiel, eating God's message symbolized accepting God's mission to tell the news to the Jews.

4Then he said to me, "Human, go to the people of Israel, and speak my words to them. 5You are not being sent to people whose speech you can't understand, whose language is difficult. You are being sent to Israel. 6You are not being sent to many nations whose speech you can't understand, whose language is difficult, whose words you cannot understand. If I had sent you to them, they would have listened to you. 7But the people of Israel will not be willing to listen to you, because they are not willing to listen to me. Yes, all the people of Israel are stubborn and will not obey. 8See, I now make you as stubborn and as hard as they are. 9I am making you as hard as a diamond, harder than stone. Don't be afraid of them or be frightened by them, though they are a people who turn against me."

10Also, he said to me, "Human, believe all the words I will speak to you, and listen carefully to them. 11Then go to the captives, your own people, and say to them, 'The Lord GOD says this.' Tell them this whether they listen or not."

12Then the Spirit lifted me up, and I heard a loud rumbling sound behind me, saying, "Praise the glory of the LORD in heaven." 13I heard the wings of the living creatures touching each other and the sound of the wheels by them. It was a loud rumbling sound. 14So the Spirit lifted me up and took me away. I was unhappy and angry, and I felt the great power of the LORD. 15I came to the captives from Judah, who lived by the Kebar River at Tel Abib. I sat there seven days where these people lived, feeling shocked.

Israel's Warning

¹⁶After seven days the LORD spoke his word to me again. He said, ¹⁷"Human, I now make you a watchman for Israel. Any time you hear a word from my mouth, warn them for me. ¹⁸When I say to the wicked, 'You will surely die,' you must warn them so they may live. If you don't speak out to warn the wicked to stop their evil ways, they will die in their sin. But I will hold you responsible for their death. ¹⁹If you warn the wicked and they do not turn from their wickedness or their evil ways, they will die because of their sin. But you will have saved your life.

²⁰"Again, those who do right may turn away from doing good and do evil. If I make something bad happen to them, they will die. Because you have not warned them, they will die because of their sin, and the good they did will not be remembered. But I will hold you responsible for their deaths. ²¹But if you have warned those good people not to sin, and they do not sin, they will surely live, because they believed the warning. And you will have saved your life."

²²Then I felt the power of the LORD there. He said to me, "Get up and go out to the plain. There I will speak to you." ²³So I got up and went out to the plain. I saw the glory of the LORD standing there, like the glory I saw by the Kebar River, and I bowed facedown on the ground.

²⁴Then the Spirit^d entered me and made me stand on my feet. He spoke to me and said, "Go, shut yourself up in your house. ²⁵As for you, human, the people will tie you up with ropes so that you will not be able to go out among them. ²⁶Also, I will make your tongue stick to the roof of your mouth so you will be silent. You will not be able to argue with the people, even though they turn against me. ²⁷But when I speak to you, I will open your mouth, and you will say to them, 'The Lord GOD says this.' Those who will listen, let them listen. Those who refuse, let them refuse, because they are a people who turn against me.

The Map of Jerusalem

4 "Now, human, get yourself a brick, put it in front of you, and draw a map of Jerusalem on it. ²Then surround it with an army. Build battle works against the city and a dirt road to the top of the city walls. Set up camps around it, and put heavy logs in place to break down the walls. ³Then get yourself an iron plate and set it up like an iron wall between you and the city. Turn your face toward the city as if to attack it and then attack. This is a sign to Israel.

⁴"Then lie down on your left side, and take the guilt of Israel on yourself. Their guilt will be on you for the number of days you lie on your left side. ⁵I have given you the same number of days

---

HONESTY

The Whole Truth

Jessica knew she was in trouble when the car skidded and slid on the wet road, hitting the curb hard enough to ruin a front wheel. Even though no one was hurt, the disabled car would not move.

When she got home, Jessica told her parents what had happened. She admitted having seven people in her compact car, and driving faster than the speed limit. Then she described the damage.

"What I didn't tell them was that a friend was driving my car," she says.

Jessica's paying for the damage now with money from her part-time job. She's afraid that if she tells her parents the whole truth, she will slide into even more trouble. Jessica's parents might appreciate her honesty and not punish her more severely. God, too, appreciates honesty. He expects it even when it may cause more trouble than keeping silent. He demanded that Ezekiel tell the people the whole truth in **Ezekiel 3:16–21**.

■ Why might it be difficult for Jessica or Ezekiel to be completely honest?

■ How can you be honest with a friend who is doing something wrong and still preserve the friendship?

C O N S I D E R . . .

■ warning a friend about something he or she is doing that's wrong.

■ discussing with your friends when, if ever, it's okay to tell white lies.

F O R   M O R E ,   S E E . . .

■ Genesis 3:1–9 (p. 4)

■ 2 Samuel 12:1–14 (p. 284)

■ Acts 5:1–11 (p. 1104)

as the years of the people's sin. So you will have the guilt of Israel's sin on you for three hundred ninety days.

6"After you have finished these three hundred ninety days, lie down a second time, on your right side. You will then have the guilt of Judah on you. I will give it to you for forty days, a day for each year of their sin. 7Then you will look toward Jerusalem, which is being attacked. With your arm bare, you will prophesy*d* against Jerusalem. 8I will put ropes on you so you cannot turn from one side to the other until you have finished the days of your attack on Jerusalem.

9"Take wheat, barley, beans, small peas, and millet seeds, and put them in one bowl, and make them into bread for yourself. You will eat it the three hundred ninety days you lie on your side. 10You will eat eight ounces of food every day at set times. 11You will drink about two-thirds of a quart of water every day at set times. 12Eat your food as you would eat a barley cake, baking it over human dung where the people can see." 13Then the LORD said, "In the same way Israel will eat unclean*d* food among the nations where I force them to go."

14But I said, "No, Lord GOD! I have never been made unclean. From the time I was young until now I've never eaten anything that died by itself or was torn by animals. Unclean meat has never entered my mouth."

15"Very well," he said. "Then I will give you cow's dung instead of human dung to use for your fire to bake your bread."

16He also said to me, "Human, I am going to cut off the supply of bread to Jerusalem. They will eat the bread that is measured out to them, and they will worry as they eat. They will drink water that is measured out to them, and they will be in shock as they drink it. 17This is because bread and water will be hard to find. The people will be shocked at the sight of each other, and they will become weak because of their sin.

Ezekiel Cuts His Hair

5 "Now, human, take a sharp sword, and use it like a barber's razor to shave your head and beard. Then take scales and weigh and divide the hair. 2Burn one-third with fire in the middle of the city when the days of the attack on Jerusalem are over. Then take one-third and cut it up with the knife all around the city. And scatter one-third to the wind. This is how I will chase them with a sword. 3Also take a few of these hairs and tie them in the folds of your clothes. 4Take a few more and throw them into the fire and burn them up. From there a fire will spread to all the people of Israel.

5"This is what the Lord GOD says: This is Jerusalem. I have put her at the center of the nations with countries all around her. 6But she has refused to obey my laws and has been more evil than the nations. She has refused to obey my rules, even more than nations around her. The people of Jerusalem have rejected my laws and have not lived by my rules.

7"So this is what the Lord GOD says: You have caused more trouble than the nations around you. You have not followed my rules or obeyed my laws. You have not even obeyed the laws of the nations around you.

8"So this is what the Lord GOD says: I myself am against you, and I will punish you as the nations watch. 9I will do things among you that I have not done before and that I will never do anything like again, because you do the things I hate. 10So parents among you will eat their children, and children will eat their parents. I will punish you and will scatter to the winds all who are left alive. 11So the Lord GOD says: You have made my Temple*d* unclean*d* with all your evil idols and the hateful things you do. Because of this, as surely as I live, I will cut you off. I will have no pity, and I will show no mercy. 12A third of you will die by disease or be destroyed by hunger inside your walls. A third will fall dead by the sword outside your walls. And a third I will scatter in every direction as I chase them with a sword. 13Then my anger will come to an end. I will use it up against them, and then I will be satisfied. Then they will know that I, the LORD, have spoken. After I have carried out my anger against them, they will know how strongly I felt.

14"I will make you a ruin and a shame among

the nations around you, to be seen by all who pass by. ¹⁵Then the nations around you will shame you and make fun of you. You will be a warning and a terror to them. This will happen when I punish you in my great anger. I, the Lord, have spoken. ¹⁶I will send a time of hunger to destroy you, and then I will make your hunger get even worse, and I will cut off your supply of food. ¹⁷I will send a time of hunger and wild animals against you, and they will kill your children. Disease and death will sweep through your people, and I will bring the sword against you to kill you. I, the Lord, have spoken."

Prophecies Against the Mountains

6 Again the Lord spoke his word to me, saying: ²"Human, look toward the mountains of Israel, and prophesy*d* against them. ³Say, 'Mountains of Israel, listen to the word of the Lord God. The Lord God says this to the mountains, the hills, the ravines, and the valleys: I will bring a sword against you, and I will destroy your places of idol worship. ⁴Your altars will be destroyed and your incense*d* altars broken down. Your people will be killed in front of your idols. ⁵I will lay the dead bodies of the Israelites in front of their idols, and I will scatter your bones around your altars. ⁶In all the places you live, cities will become empty. The places of idol worship will be ruined; your altars will become lonely ruins. Your idols will be broken and brought to an end. Your incense altars will be cut down, and the things you made will be wiped out. ⁷Your people will be killed and fall among you. Then you will know that I am the Lord.

⁸" 'But I will leave some people alive; some will not be killed by the nations when you are scattered among the foreign lands. ⁹Then those who have escaped will remember me, as they live among the nations where they have been taken as captives. They will remember how I was hurt because they were unfaithful to me and turned away from me and desired to worship their idols. They will hate themselves because of the evil things they did that I hate. ¹⁰Then they will know that I am the Lord. I did not bring this terrible thing on them for no reason.

¹¹" 'This is what the Lord God says: Clap your hands, stamp your feet, and groan because of all the hateful, evil things the people of Israel have done. They will die by war, hunger, and disease. ¹²The person who is far away will die by disease. The one who is nearby will die in war. The person who is still alive and has escaped these will die from hunger. So I will carry out my anger on them. ¹³Their people will lie dead among their idols around the altars, on every high hill, on all the mountain tops, and under every green tree and leafy oak — all the places where they offered

sweet-smelling incense to their idols. Then you will know that I am the Lord. ¹⁴I will use my power against them to make the land empty and wasted from the desert to Diblah, wherever they live. Then they will know that I am the Lord.' "

Ezekiel Tells of the End

7 Again the Lord spoke his word to me, saying: ²"Human, the Lord God says this to the land of Israel: An end! The end has come on the

four corners of the land. ³Now the end has come for you, and I will send my anger against you. I will judge you for the way you have lived, and I will make you pay for all your actions that I hate. ⁴I will have no pity on you; I will not hold back punishment from you. Instead, I will make you pay for the way you have lived and for your actions that I hate. Then you will know that I am the Lord.

⁵"This is what the Lord God says: Disaster on top of disaster is coming. ⁶The end has come! The end has come! It has stirred itself up against you! Look! It has come! ⁷Disaster has come for you who live in the land! The time has come; the day of confusion is near. There will be no happy shouting on the mountains. ⁸Soon I will pour out my anger against you; I will carry out my anger against you. I will judge you for the way you have lived and will make you pay for everything you have done that I hate. ⁹I will show no pity, and I will not hold back punishment. I will pay you back for the way you have lived and the things you have done that I hate. Then you will know that I am the Lord who punishes.

¹⁰"Look, the day is here. It has come. Disaster has come, violence has grown, and there is more pride than ever. ¹¹Violence has grown into a weapon for punishing wickedness. None of the people will be left — none of that crowd, none of their wealth, and nothing of value. ¹²The time has come; the day has arrived. Don't let the buyer be happy or the seller be sad, because my burning anger is against the whole crowd. ¹³Sellers will not return to the land they have sold as long as they live, because the vision against all that crowd will not be changed. Because of their sins, they will not save their lives. ¹⁴They have blown the trumpet, and everything is ready.

But no one is going to the battle, because my anger is against all that crowd.

15"The sword is outside, and disease and hunger are inside. Whoever is in the field will die by the sword. Hunger and disease will destroy those in the city. 16Those who are left alive and who escape will be on the mountains, moaning like doves of the valleys about their own sin. 17All hands will hang weakly with fear, and all knees will become weak as water. 18They will put on rough cloth to show how sad they are. They will tremble all over with fear. Their faces will show their shame, and all their heads will be shaved. 19The people will throw their silver into the streets, and their gold will be like trash. Their silver and gold will not save them from the Lord's anger. It will not satisfy their hunger or fill their stomachs, because it caused them to fall into sin. 20They were proud of their beautiful jewelry and used it to make their idols and their evil statues, which I hate. So I will turn their wealth into trash. 21I will give it to foreigners as loot from war and to the most evil people in the world as treasure, and they will dishonor it. 22I will also turn away from the people of Israel, and they will dishonor my treasured place. Then robbers will enter and dishonor it.

23"Make chains for captives, because the land is full of bloody crimes and the city is full of violence. 24So I will bring the worst of the nations to take over the people's houses. I will also end the pride of the strong, and their holy places will be dishonored. 25When the people are suffering greatly, they will look for peace, but there will be none. 26Disaster will come on top of disaster, and rumor will be added to rumor. Then they will try to get a vision from a prophet;*d* the teachings of God from the priest and the advice from the older leaders will be lost. 27The king will cry greatly, the prince will give up hope, and the hands of the people who own land will shake with fear. I will punish them for the way they have lived. The way they have judged others is the way I will judge them. Then they will know that I am the Lord."

Ezekiel's Vision of Jerusalem

8 It was the sixth year, on the fifth day of the sixth month of our captivity. I was sitting in my house with the older leaders of Judah in front of me. There I felt the power of the Lord God. 2I looked and saw something that looked like a human. From the waist down it looked like fire, and from the waist up it looked like bright glowing metal. 3It stretched out the shape of a hand and caught me by the hair on my head. The Spirit*d*

lifted me up between the earth and the sky. He took me in visions of God to Jerusalem, to the entrance to the north gate of the inner courtyard of the Temple.*d* In the courtyard was the idol that caused God to be jealous. 4I saw the glory of the God of Israel there, as I had seen on the plain.

5Then he said to me, "Human, now look toward the north." So I looked up toward the north, and in the entrance north of the gate of the altar was the idol that caused God to be jealous.

6He said to me, "Human, do you see what they are doing? Do you see how many hateful things the people of Israel are doing here that drive me far away from my Temple? But you will see things more hateful than these."

7Then he brought me to the entry of the courtyard. When I looked, I saw a hole in the wall. 8He said to me, "Human, dig through the wall." So I dug through the wall and saw an entrance.

9Then he said to me, "Go in and see the hateful, evil things they are doing here." 10So I entered and looked, and I saw every kind of crawling thing and hateful beast and all the idols of the people of Israel, carved on the wall all around. 11Standing in front of these carvings and idols were seventy of the older leaders of Israel and Jaazaniah son of Shaphan. Each man had his pan for burning incense*d* in his hand, and a sweet-smelling cloud of incense was rising.

12Then he said to me, "Human, have you seen what the older leaders of Israel are doing in the dark? Have you seen each man in the room of his own idol? They say, 'The Lord doesn't see us. The Lord has left the land.'" 13He also said to me, "You will see even more hateful things that they are doing."

14Then he brought me to the entrance of the north gate of the Temple of the Lord, where I saw women sitting and crying for Tammuz.*n* 15He said to me, "Do you see, human? You will see things even more hateful than these."

16Then he brought me into the inner courtyard of the Temple. There I saw about twenty-five men at the entrance to the Temple of the Lord, between the porch and the altar. With their backs turned to the Temple of the Lord, they faced east and were worshiping the sun in the east.

17He said to me, "Do you see, human? Is it unimportant that the people of Judah are doing the hateful things they have done here? They have filled the land with violence and made me continually angry. Look, they are insulting me every way they can. 18So I will act in anger. I will have no pity, nor will I show mercy. Even if they shout in my ears, I won't listen to them."

Tammuz   Tammuz was a god in Babylon. Every year people thought this god died when the plants died. After they cried for him, they believed he came back to life and the plants lived again.

Vision of the Angels

9 Then he shouted with a loud voice in my ears, "You who are chosen to punish this city, come near with your weapon in your hand." [2]Then six men came from the direction of the upper gate, which faces north, each with his powerful weapon in his hand. Among them was a man dressed in linen with a writing case at his side. The men went in and stood by the bronze altar. [3]Then the glory of the God of Israel went up from above the creatures with wings, where it had been, to the place in the Temple[d] where the door opened. He called to the man dressed in linen who had the writing case at his side. [4]He said to the man, "Go through Jerusalem and put a mark on the foreheads of the people who groan and cry about all the hateful things being done among them."

✸ **SIDELIGHT:** The mark of Ezekiel 9:4 was the taw, the last letter of the Hebrew alphabet. This is one I.D. you wouldn't want to be without; those in the vision without the mark were killed.

---

[5]As I listened, he said to the other men, "Go through the city behind the man dressed in linen and kill. Don't pity anyone, and don't show mercy. [6]Kill and destroy old men, young men and women, little children, and older women, but don't touch any who have the mark on them. Start at my Temple." So they started with the older leaders who were in front of the Temple. [7]Then he said to them, "Make the Temple unclean,[d] and fill the courtyards with those who have been killed. Go out!" So the men went out and killed the people in the city. [8]While the men were killing the people, I was left alone. I bowed facedown on the ground and I cried out, "Oh, Lord God! Will you destroy everyone left alive in Israel when you turn loose your anger on Jerusalem?"

[9]Then he said to me, "The sin of the people of Israel and Judah is very great. The land is filled with people who murder, and the city is full of people who are not fair. The people say, 'The Lord has left the land, and the Lord does not see.' [10]But I will have no pity, nor will I show mercy. I will bring their evil back on their heads." [11]Then the man dressed in linen with the writing case at his side reported, "I have done just as you commanded me."

The Coals of Fire

10 Then I looked and saw in the dome above the heads of the living creatures something like a sapphire gem which looked like a throne. [2]The Lord said to the man dressed in linen, "Go in between the wheels under the living creatures, fill your hands with coals of fire from between the living creatures, and scatter the coals over the city."

As I watched, the man with linen clothes went in. [3]Now the living creatures were standing on the south side of the Temple[d] when the man went in. And a cloud filled the inner courtyard. [4]Then the glory of the Lord went up from the living creatures and stood over the door of the Temple. The Temple was filled with the cloud, and the courtyard was full of the brightness from the glory of the Lord. [5]The sound of the wings of the living creatures was heard all the way to the outer courtyard. It was like the voice of God Almighty when he speaks.

[6]When the Lord commanded the man dressed in linen, "Take fire from between the wheels, from between the living creatures," the man went in and stood by a wheel. [7]One living creature put out his hand to the fire that was among them, took some of the fire, and put it in the hands of the man dressed in linen. Then the man took the fire and went out.

The Wheels and the Creatures

[8]Something that looked like a human hand could be seen under the wings of the living creatures. [9]I saw the four wheels by the living creatures, one wheel by each living creature. The wheels looked like shining chrysolite. [10]All four wheels looked alike: Each looked like a wheel crossways inside another wheel. [11]When the wheels moved, they went in any of the directions that the four living creatures faced. The wheels did not turn about, and the living creatures did not turn their bodies as they went. [12]All their bodies, their backs, their hands, their wings, and the wheels were full of eyes all over. Each of the four living creatures had a wheel. [13]I heard the wheels being called "whirling wheels." [14]Each living creature had four faces. The first face was the face of a creature with wings. The second face was a human face, the third was the face of a lion, and the fourth was the face of an eagle.

[15]Then the living creatures flew up. They were the same living creatures I had seen by the Kebar River. [16]When the living creatures moved, the wheels moved beside them. When the living creatures lifted their wings to fly up from the ground, the wheels did not leave their place beside them. [17]When the living creatures stopped, the wheels stopped. When the creatures went up, the wheels went up also, because the spirit of the living creatures was in the wheels.

[18]Then the glory of the Lord left the door of the Temple[d] and stood over the living creatures. [19]As

I watched, the living creatures spread their wings and flew up from the ground, with the wheels beside them. They stood where the east gate of the Temple of the LORD opened, and the glory of the God of Israel was over them.

20These were the living creatures I had seen under the God of Israel by the Kebar River. I knew they were called cherubim.d 21Each one had four faces and four wings, and under their wings were things that looked like human hands. 22Their faces looked the same as the ones I had seen by the Kebar River. They each went straight ahead.

Prophecies Against Evil Leaders

11 The Spirite lifted me up and brought me to the front gate of the Templed of the LORD, which gate faces east. I saw twenty-five men where the gate opens, among them Jaazaniah son of Azzur and Pelatiah son of Benaiah, who were leaders of the people. 2Then the LORD said to me, "Human, these are the men who plan evil and give wicked advice in this city of Jerusalem. 3They say, 'It is almost time for us to build houses. This city is like a cooking pot, and we are like the best meat.' 4So prophesyd against them, prophesy, human."

5Then the Spirit of the LORD entered me and told me to say: "This is what the LORD says: You have said these things, people of Israel, and I know what you are thinking. 6You have killed many people in this city, filling its streets with their bodies.

7"So this is what the Lord GOD says: Those people you have killed and left in the middle of the city are like the best meat, and this city is like the cooking pot. But I will force you out of the city. 8You have feared the sword, but I will bring a sword against you, says the Lord GOD. 9I will force you out of the city and hand you over to strangers and punish you. 10You will die by the sword. I will punish you at the border of Israel so you will know that I am the LORD. 11This city will not be your cooking pot, and you will not be the best meat in the middle of it. I will punish you at the border of Israel. 12Then you will know that I am the LORD. You did not live by my rules or obey my laws. Instead, you did the same things as the nations around you."

13As I prophesied, Pelatiah son of Benaiah died. Then I bowed facedown on the ground and shouted with a loud voice, "Oh no, Lord GOD! Will you completely destroy the Israelites who are left alive?"

Promise to Those Remaining

14The LORD spoke his word to me, saying, 15"Human, the people still in Jerusalem have spoken about your own relatives and all the people of Israel who are captives with you, saying, 'They are far from the LORD. This land has been given to us as our property.'

16"So say, 'This is what the Lord GOD says: I sent the people far away among the nations and scattered them among the countries. But for a little while I have become a Templed to them in the countries where they have gone.'

17"So say: 'This is what the Lord GOD says: I will gather you from the nations and bring you together from the countries where you have been scattered. Then I will give you back the land of Israel.'

18"When they come to this land, they will remove all the evil idols and all the hateful images. 19I will give them a desire to respect me completely, and I will put inside them a new way of thinking. I will take out the stubborn heart of stone from their bodies, and I will give them an obedient heart of flesh. 20Then they will live by my rules and obey my laws and keep them. They will be my people, and I will be their God. 21But those who want to serve their evil statues and hateful idols, I will pay back for their evil ways, says the Lord GOD."

Ezekiel's Vision Ends

22Then the living creatures lifted their wings with the wheels beside them, and the glory of the God of Israel was above them. 23The glory of the LORD went up from inside Jerusalem and stopped on the mountain on the east side of the city. 24The Spiritd lifted me up and brought me to the captives who had been taken from Judah to Babylonia. This happened in a vision given by the Spirit of God, and then the vision I had seen ended. 25And I told the captives from Judah all the things the LORD had shown me.

Ezekiel Moves Out

12 Again the LORD spoke his word to me, saying: 1"Human, you are living among a people who refuse to obey. They have eyes to see, but they do not see, and they have ears to hear, but they do not hear, because they are a people who refuse to obey.

3"So, human, pack your things as if you will be taken away captive, and walk away like a captive in the daytime with the people watching. Move from your place to another with the people watching. Maybe they will understand, even though they are a people who refuse to obey. 4During the day when the people are watching, bring out the things you would pack as captive. At evening, with the people watching, leave your place like those who are taken away as captives from their country. 5Dig a hole through the wall while they watch, and bring your things out through it. 6Lift them onto your shoulders with the people watching, and carry them out in the dark. Cover your face so you cannot see the ground, because I have made you a sign to the people of Israel."

⁷I did these things as I was commanded. In the daytime I brought what I had packed as if I were being taken away captive. Then in the evening I dug through the wall with my hands. I brought my things out in the dark and carried them on my shoulders as the people watched.

⁸Then in the morning the LORD spoke his word to me, saying: ⁹"Human, didn't Israel, who refuses to obey, ask you, 'What are you doing?'

¹⁰"Say to them, 'This is what the Lord GOD says: This message is about the king in Jerusalem and all the people of Israel who live there.' ¹¹Say, 'I am a sign to you.'

"The same things I have done will be done to the people in Jerusalem. They will be taken away from their country as captives. ¹²The king among them will put his things on his shoulder in the dark and will leave. The people will dig a hole through the wall to bring him out. He will cover his face so he cannot see the ground. ¹³But I will spread my net over him, and he will be caught in my trap. Then I will bring him to Babylon in the land of the Babylonians. He will not see that land, but he will die there. ¹⁴All who are around the king—his helpers and all his army—I will scatter in every direction, and I will chase them with a sword.

¹⁵"They will know that I am the LORD when I scatter them among the nations and spread them among the countries. ¹⁶But I will save a few of them from the sword and from hunger and disease. Then they can tell about their hateful actions among the nations where they go. Then they will know that I am the LORD."

The Lesson of Ezekiel's Shaking

¹⁷The LORD spoke his word to me, saying: ¹⁸"Human, tremble as you eat your food, and shake with fear as you drink your water. ¹⁹Then say to the people of the land: 'This is what the Lord GOD says about the people who live in Jerusalem in the land of Israel: They will eat their food with fear and drink their water in shock, because their land will be stripped bare because of the violence of the people who live in it. ²⁰The cities where people live will become ruins, and the land will become empty. Then you will know that I am the LORD.' "

The Visions Will Come True

²¹The LORD spoke his word to me, saying: ²²"Human, what is this saying you have in the land of Israel: 'The days go by and every vision comes to nothing'? ²³So say to them, 'This is what the Lord GOD says: I will make them stop saying this, and nobody in Israel will use this saying anymore.' But tell them, 'The time is near when every vision will come true. ²⁴There will be no more false visions or pleasing propheciesᵈ inside the nation of Israel, ²⁵but I, the LORD, will speak. What I say will be done, and it will not be delayed. You refuse to obey, but in your time I will say the word and do it, says the Lord GOD.' "

²⁶The LORD spoke his word to me, saying: ²⁷"Human, the people of Israel are saying, 'The vision that Ezekiel sees is for a time many years from now. He is prophesying about times far away.'

²⁸"So say to them: 'The Lord GOD says this: None of my words will be delayed anymore. What I have said will be done, says the Lord GOD.' "

Ezekiel Speaks Against False Prophets

13 The LORD spoke his word to me, saying: ²"Human, prophesyᵈ against the prophets of Israel. Say to those who make up their own prophecies: 'Listen to the word of the LORD. ³This is what the Lord GOD says: How terrible it will be for the foolish prophets who follow their own ideas and have not seen a vision from me! ⁴People of Israel, your prophets have been like wild dogs hunting to kill and eat among ruins. ⁵Israel is like a house in ruins, but you have not gone up into the broken places or repaired the wall. So how can Israel hold back the enemy in the battle on the LORD's day of judging? ⁶Your prophets see false visions and prophesy lies. They say, "This is the message of the LORD," when the LORD has not sent them. But they still hope their words will come true. ⁷You said, "This is the message of the LORD," but that is a false vision. Your prophecies are lies, because I have not spoken.

⁸" 'So this is what the Lord GOD says: Because you prophets spoke things that are false and saw visions that do not come true, I am against you, says the Lord GOD. ⁹I will punish the prophets who see false visions and prophesy lies. They will have no place among my people. Their names will not be written on the list of the people of Israel, and they will not enter the land of Israel. Then you will know that I am the Lord GOD.

¹⁰" 'It is because they lead my people the wrong way by saying, "Peace!" when there is no peace. When the people build a weak wall, the prophets cover it with whitewash to make it look strong. ¹¹So tell those who cover a weak wall with *whitewash that it will fall down.* Rain will pour down, hailstones will fall, and a stormy wind will break the wall down. ¹²When the wall has fallen, people will ask you, "Where is the whitewash you used on the wall?"

¹³" 'So this is what the Lord GOD says: I will break the wall with a stormy wind. In my anger

rain will pour down, and hailstones will destroy the wall. 14I will tear down the wall on which you put whitewash. I will level it to the ground so that people will see the wall's foundation. And when the wall falls, you will be destroyed under it. Then you will know that I am the LORD. 15So I will carry out my anger on the wall and against those who covered it with whitewash. Then I will tell you, "The wall is gone, and those who covered it with whitewash are gone. 16The prophets of Israel who prophesy to Jerusalem and who see visions of peace for the city, when there is no peace, will be gone, says the Lord GOD." '

False Women Prophets

17"Now, human, look toward the women among your people who make up their own prophecies.d Prophesy against them. 18Say, 'This is what the Lord GOD says: How terrible it will be for women who sew magic charms on their wrists and make veils of every length to trap people! You ruin the lives of my people but try to save your own lives. 19For handfuls of barley and pieces of bread, you have dishonored me among my people. By lying to my people, who listen to lies, you have killed people who should not die, and you have kept alive those who should not live.

20" 'So this is what the Lord GOD says: I am against your magic charms, by which you trap people as if they were birds. I will tear those charms off your arms, and I will free those people you have trapped like birds. 21I will also tear off your veils and save my people from your hands. They will no longer be trapped by your power. Then you will know that I am the LORD. 22By your lies you have caused those who did right to be sad, when I did not make them sad. And you have encouraged the wicked not to stop being wicked, which would have saved their lives. 23So you will not see false visions or prophesy anymore, and I will save my people from your power so you will know that I am the LORD.' "

Stop Worshiping Idols

14 Some of the older leaders of Israel came to me and sat down in front of me. 2Then the LORD spoke his word to me, saying: 3"Human, these men want to worship idols. They put up evil things that cause people to sin. Should I allow them to ask me for help? 4So speak to them and tell them, 'This is what the Lord GOD says: When any of the people of Israel want to worship idols and put up evil things that cause people to sin and then come to the prophet,d I, the LORD, will answer them myself for worshiping idols. 5Then I will win back my people Israel, who have left me because of all their idols.'

6"So say to the people of Israel, 'This is what the Lord GOD says: Change your hearts and lives, and stop worshiping idols. Stop doing all the things I hate. 7Any of the Israelites or foreigners in Israel can separate themselves from me by wanting to worship idols or by putting up the things that cause people to sin. Then if they come to the prophet to ask me questions, I, the LORD, will answer them myself. 8I will reject them. I will make them a sign and an example, and I will separate them from my people. Then you will know that I am the LORD.

9" 'But if the prophet is tricked into giving a prophecy, it is because I, the LORD, have tricked that prophet to speak. Then I will use my power against him and destroy him from among my people Israel. 10The prophet will be as guilty as the one who asks him for help; both will be responsible for their guilt. 11Then the nation of Israel will not leave me anymore or make themselves uncleand anymore with all their sins. They will be my people, and I will be their God, says the Lord GOD.' "

☀ **SIDELIGHT:** If Ezekiel's mother were living, she might have washed his mouth out with soap when he talked about pagan idols (Ezekiel 14:1–11). His term for these idols literally means "dung balls" or "animal dung." Ezekiel uses the term thirty-nine times, but it only appears nine times in the rest of the Old Testament.

Jerusalem Will Not Be Spared

12The LORD spoke his word to me, saying: 13"Human, if the people of a country sin against me by not being loyal, I will use my power against them. I will cut off their supply of food and send a time of hunger, destroying both people and animals. 14Even if three great men like Noah, Daniel, and Job were in that country, their goodness could save only themselves, says the Lord GOD.

15"Or I might send wild animals into that land, leaving the land empty and without children. Then no one would pass through it because of the animals. 16As surely as I live, says the Lord GOD, even if Noah, Daniel, and Job were in the land, they could not save their own sons or daughters. They could save only themselves, but that country would become empty.

17"Or I might bring a war against that country. I might say, 'Let a war be fought in that land,' in this way destroying its people and its animals. 18As surely as I live, says the Lord GOD, even if those three men were in the land, they could not save their sons or daughters. They could save only themselves.

19"Or I might cause a disease to spread in that

country. I might pour out my anger against it, destroying and killing people and animals. 20As surely as I live, says the Lord God, even if Noah, Daniel, and Job were in the land, they could not save their son or daughter. They could save only themselves because they did what was right.

21"This is what the Lord God says: My plans for Jerusalem are much worse! I will send my four terrible punishments against it — war, hunger, wild animals, and disease — to destroy its people and animals. 22But some people will escape; some sons and daughters will be led out. They will come out to you, and you will see what happens to people who live as they did. Then you will be comforted after the disasters I have brought against Jerusalem, after all the things I have brought against it. 23You will be comforted when you see what happens to them for living as they did, because you will know there was a good reason for what I did to Jerusalem, says the Lord God."

Story of the Vine

15 The Lord spoke his word to me, saying: 2"Human, is the wood of the vine better than the wood of any tree in the forest? 3Can wood be taken from the vine to make anything? Can you use it to make a peg on which to hang something? 4If the vine is thrown into the fire for fuel, and the fire burns up both ends and starts to burn the middle, is it useful for anything? 5When the vine was whole, it couldn't be made into anything. When the fire has burned it completely, it certainly cannot be made into anything."

6So this is what the Lord God says: "Out of all the trees in the forest, I have given the wood of the vine as fuel for fire. In the same way I have given up the people who live in Jerusalem 7and will turn against them. Although they came through one fire, fire will still destroy them. When I turn against them, you will know that I am the Lord. 8So I will make the land empty, because the people have not been loyal, says the Lord God."

The Lord's Kindness to Jerusalem

16 The Lord spoke his word to me, saying: 2"Human, tell Jerusalem about her hateful actions. 3Say, 'This is what the Lord God says to Jerusalem: Your beginnings and your ancestors were in the land of the Canaanites. Your father was an Amorite, and your mother was a Hittite. 4On the day you were born, your cord*a* was not cut. You were not washed with water to clean you. You were not rubbed with salt or wrapped in cloths. 5No one felt sorry enough for you to do any of these things for you. No, you

were thrown out into the open field, because you were hated on the day you were born.

6" 'When I passed by and saw you kicking about in your blood, I said to you, "Live!" 7I made you grow like a plant in the field. You grew up and became tall and became like a beautiful jewel. Your breasts formed, and your hair grew, but you were naked and without clothes.

8" 'Later when I passed by you and looked at you, I saw that you were old enough for love. So I spread my robe over you and covered your nakedness. I also made a promise to you and entered into an agreement with you so that you became mine, says the Lord God.

9" 'Then I bathed you with water, washed all the blood off of you, and put oil on you. 10I put beautiful clothes made with needlework on you and put sandals of fine leather on your feet. I wrapped you in fine linen and covered you with silk. 11I put jewelry on you: bracelets on your arms, a necklace around your neck, 12a ring in your nose, earrings in your ears, and a beautiful crown on your head. 13So you wore gold and silver. Your clothes were made of fine linen, silk, and beautiful needlework. You ate fine flour, honey, and olive oil. You were very beautiful and became a queen. 14Then you became famous among the nations, because you were so beautiful. Your beauty was perfect, because of the glory I gave you, says the Lord God.

Jerusalem Becomes a Prostitute

15" 'But you trusted in your beauty. You became a prostitute,*d* because you were so famous. You had sexual relations with anyone who passed by. 16You took some of your clothes and made your places of worship colorful. There you carried on your prostitution. These things should not happen; they should never occur. 17You also took your beautiful jewelry, made from my gold and silver I had given you, and you made for yourselves male idols so you could be a prostitute with them. 18Then you took your clothes with beautiful needlework and covered the idols. You gave my oil and incense*d* as an offering to them. 19Also, you took the bread I gave you, the fine flour, oil,

cord The umbilical cord that gives the unborn baby food and air from its mother.

and honey I gave you to eat, and you offered them before the gods as a pleasing smell. This is what happened, says the Lord God.

20" 'But your sexual sins were not enough for you. You also took your sons and daughters who were my children, and you sacrificed them to the idols as food. 21You killed my children and offered them up in fire to the idols. 22While you did all your hateful acts and sexual sins, you did not remember when you were young, when you were naked and had no clothes and were left in your blood.

23" 'How terrible! How terrible it will be for you, says the Lord God. After you did all these evil things, 24you built yourself a place to worship gods. You made for yourself a place of worship in every city square. 25You built a place of worship at the beginning of every street. You made your beauty hateful, offering your body for sex to anyone who passed by, so your sexual sins became worse and worse. 26You also had sexual relations with the Egyptians, who were your neighbors and partners in sexual sin. Your sexual sins became even worse, and they caused me to be angry. 27So then, I used my power against you and took away some of your land. I let you be defeated by those who hate you, the Philistine women, who were ashamed of your evil ways. 28Also, you had sexual relations with the Assyrians, because you could not be satisfied. Even though you had sexual relations with them, you still were not satisfied. 29You did many more sexual sins in Babylonia, the land of traders, but even this did not satisfy you.

30" 'Truly your will is weak, says the Lord God. You do all the things a stubborn prostitute does. 31You built your place to worship gods at the beginning of every street, and you made places of worship in every city square. But you were not like a prostitute when you refused to accept payment.

32" 'You are a wife who is guilty of adultery.d You desire strangers instead of your husband. 33Men pay prostitutes, but you pay all your lovers to come to you. And they come from all around for sexual relations. 34So you are different from other prostitutes. No man asks you to be a prostitute, and you pay money instead of having money paid to you. Yes, you are different.

The Prostitute Is Judged

35" 'So, prostitute,d hear the word of the Lord. 36This is what the Lord God says: You showed your nakedness to other countries. You uncovered your body in your sexual sins with them as your lovers and with all your hateful idols. You killed your children and offered their blood to your idols. 37So I will gather all your lovers with whom you found pleasure. Yes, I will gather all those you loved and those you hated. I will gather

them against you from all around, and I will strip you naked in front of them so they can see your nakedness. 38I will punish you as women guilty of adulteryd or as murderers are punished. I will put you to death because I am angry and jealous. 39I will also hand you over to your lovers. They will tear down your places of worship and destroy other places where you worship gods. They will tear off your clothes and take away your jewelry, leaving you naked and bare. 40They will bring a crowd against you to throw stones at you and to cut you into pieces with their swords. 41They will burn down your houses and will punish you in front of many women. I will put an end to your sexual sins, and you will no longer pay your lovers. 42Then I will rest from my anger against you, and I will stop being jealous. I will be quiet and not angry anymore.

43" 'Because you didn't remember when you were young, but have made me angry in all these ways, I will repay you for what you have done, says the Lord God. Didn't you add sexual sins to all your other acts which I hate?

44" 'Everyone who uses wise sayings will say this about you: "The daughter is like her mother." 45You are like your mother, who hated her husband and children. You are also like your sisters, who hated their husbands and children. Your mother was a Hittite, and your father was an Amorite. 46Your older sister is Samaria, who lived north of you with her daughters; your younger sister is Sodom, who lived south of you with her daughters. 47You not only followed their ways and did the hateful things they did, but you were soon worse than they were in all your ways. 48As surely as I live, says the Lord God, this is true. Your sister Sodom and her daughters never did what you and your daughters have done.

49" 'This was the sin of your sister Sodom: She and her daughters were proud and had plenty of food and lived in great comfort, but she did not help the poor and needy. 50So Sodom and her daughters were proud and did things I hate in front of me. So I got rid of them when I saw what they did. 51Also, Samaria did not do half the sins you do; you have done more hateful things than they did. So you make your sisters look good because of all the hateful things you have done. 52You will suffer disgrace, because you have provided an excuse for your sisters. They are better than you are. Your sins were even more terrible than theirs. Feel ashamed and suffer disgrace, because you made your sisters look good.

53" 'But I will give back to Sodom and her daughters the good things they once had. I will give back to Samaria and her daughters the good things they once had. And with them I will also give back the good things you once had 54so you may suffer disgrace and feel ashamed for all the things you have done. You even gave comfort to your sisters in their sins. [55]Your sisters, Sodom with her daughters and Samaria with her daughters, will return to what they were before. You and your daughters will also return to what you were before. [56]You humiliated your sister Sodom when you were proud, [57]before your evil was uncovered. And now the Edomite women and their neighbors humiliate you. Even the Philistine women humiliate you. Those around you hate you. [58]This is your punishment for your terrible sins and for actions that I hate, says the Lord.

God Keeps His Promises

[59]" 'This is what the Lord God says: I will do to you what you have done. You hated and broke the agreement you promised to keep. [60]But I will remember my agreement I made with you when you were young, and I will make an agreement that will continue forever with you. [61]Then you will remember what you have done and feel ashamed when you receive your sisters — both your older and your younger sisters. I will give them to you like daughters, but not because they share in my agreement with you. [62]I will set up my agreement with you, and you will know that I am the Lord. [63]You will remember what you did and feel ashamed. You will not open your mouth again because of your shame, when I forgive you for all the things you have done, says the Lord God.' "

The Eagle and the Vine

17 The Lord spoke his word to me, saying: [2]"Human, give a riddle and tell a story to the people of Israel. [3]Say, 'This is what the Lord God says: A giant eagle with big wings and long feathers of many different colors came to Lebanon and took hold of the top of a cedar tree. [4]He pulled off the top branch and brought it to a land of traders, where he planted it in a city of traders.

[5]" 'The eagle took some seed from the land and planted it in a good field near plenty of water. He planted it to grow like a willow tree. [6]It sprouted and became a low vine that spread over the ground. The branches turned toward the eagle, but the roots were under the eagle. So the seed became a vine, and its branches grew, sending out leaves.

[7]" 'But there was another giant eagle with big wings and many feathers. The vine then bent its roots toward this eagle. It sent out its branches from the area where it was planted toward the eagle so he could water it. [8]It had been planted in a good field by plenty of water so it could grow branches and give fruit. It could have become a fine vine.'

[9]"Say to them, 'This is what the Lord God says: The vine will not continue to grow. The first eagle will pull up the vine's roots and strip off its fruit. Then the vine and all its new leaves will dry up and die. It will not take a strong arm or many people to pull the vine up by its roots. [10]Even if it is planted again, it will not continue to grow. It will completely dry up and die when the east wind hits it in the area where it grew.' "

Zedekiah Against Nebuchadnezzar

[11]Then the Lord spoke his word to me, saying: [12]"Say now to the people who refuse to obey: 'Do you know what these things mean?' Say: 'The king of Babylon came to Jerusalem and took the king and important men of Jerusalem and brought them to Babylon. [13]Then he took a member of the family of the king of Judah and made an agreement with him, forcing him to take an oath. The king also took away the leaders of Judah [14]to make the kingdom weak so it would not be strong again. Then the kingdom of Judah could continue only by keeping its agreement with the king of Babylon. [15]But the king of Judah turned against the king of Babylon by sending his messengers to Egypt and asking them for horses and many soldiers. Will the king of Judah succeed? Will the one who does such things escape? He cannot break the agreement and escape.

[16]" 'As surely as I live, says the Lord God, he will die in Babylon, in the land of the king who made him king of Judah. The king of Judah hated his promise to the king of Babylon and broke his agreement with him. [17]The king of Egypt with his mighty army and many people will not help the king of Judah in the war. The Babylonians will build devices to attack the cities and to kill many people. [18]The king of Judah showed that he hated the promise by breaking the agreement. He promised to support Babylon, but he did all these things. So he will not escape.

[19]" 'So this is what the Lord God says: As surely as I live, this is true: I will pay back the king of Judah for hating my promise and breaking my agreement. [20]I will spread my net over him, and he will be caught in my trap. Then I will bring him to Babylon, where I will punish him for the unfaithful acts he did against me. [21]All the best of his soldiers who escape will die by the sword, and those who live will be scattered to every wind. Then you will know that I, the Lord, have spoken.

[22]" 'This is what the Lord God says: I myself will also take a young branch from the top of a cedar tree, and I will plant it. I will cut off a small twig from the top of the tree's young branches, and I will plant it on a very high mountain. [23]I will plant it on the high mountain of Israel. Then it will grow branches and give fruit and become a great cedar tree. Birds of every kind will build nests in it and live in the shelter of the tree's

branches. ²⁴Then all the trees in the countryside will know that I am the Lᴏʀᴅ. I bring down the high tree and make the low tree tall. I dry up the green tree and make the dry tree grow. I am the Lᴏʀᴅ. I have spoken, and I will do it.' "

God Is Fair

18 The Lᴏʀᴅ spoke his word to me, saying: ²"What do you mean by using this saying about the land of Israel:

'The parents have eaten sour grapes,
  and that caused the children to grind their
    teeth from the sour taste'?

³"As surely as I live, says the Lord Gᴏᴅ, this is true: You will not use this saying in Israel anymore. ⁴Every living thing belongs to me. The life of the parent is mine, and the life of the child is mine. The person who sins is the one who will die.

⁵"Suppose a person is good and does what is fair and right. ⁶He does not eat at the mountain places of worship. He does not look to the idols of Israel for help. He does not have sexual relations with his neighbor's wife or with a woman during her time of monthly bleeding. ⁷He does not mistreat anyone but returns what was given as a promise for a loan. He does not rob other people. He gives bread to the hungry and clothes to those who have none. ⁸He does not lend money to get too much interest or profit. He keeps his hand from doing wrong. He judges fairly between one person and another. ⁹He lives by my rules and obeys my laws faithfully. Whoever does these things is good and will surely live, says the Lord Gᴏᴅ.

¹⁰"But suppose this person has a wild son who murders people and who does any of these other things. ¹¹(But the father himself has not done any of these things.) This son eats at the mountain places of worship. He has sexual relations with his neighbor's wife. ¹²He mistreats the poor and needy. He steals and refuses to return what was promised for a loan. He looks to idols for help. He does things which I hate. ¹³He lends money for too much interest and profit. Will this son live? No, he will not live! He has done all these hateful things, so he will surely be put to death. He will be responsible for his own death.

¹⁴"Now suppose this son has a son who has seen all his father's sins, but after seeing them does not do those things. ¹⁵He does not eat at the mountain places of worship. He does not look to the idols of Israel for help. He does not have sexual relations with his neighbor's wife. ¹⁶He does not mistreat anyone or keep something promised for a loan or steal. He gives bread to the hungry and clothes to those who have none. ¹⁷He keeps his hand from doing wrong. He does not take too much interest or profit when he lends money. He obeys my laws and lives by my rules. He will not die for his father's sin; he will surely live. ¹⁸But his father took other people's money unfairly and robbed his brother and did what was wrong among his people. So he will die for his own sin.

¹⁹"But you ask, 'Why is the son not punished for the father's sin?' The son has done what is fair and right. He obeys all my rules, so he will surely live. ²⁰The person who sins is the one who will die. A child will not be punished for a parent's sin, and a parent will not be punished for a child's sin. Those who do right will enjoy the results of their own goodness; evil people will suffer the results of their own evil.

²¹"But suppose the wicked stop doing all the sins they have done and obey all my rules and do what is fair and right. Then they will surely live; they will not die. ²²Their sins will be forgotten. Because they have done what is right they will live. ²³I do not really want the wicked to die, says the Lord Gᴏᴅ. I want them to stop their bad ways and live.

²⁴"But suppose good people stop doing good and do wrong and do the same hateful things the wicked do. Will they live? All their good acts will be forgotten, because they became unfaithful. They have sinned, so they will die because of their sins.

²⁵"But you say, 'What the Lord does isn't fair.' Listen, people of Israel. I am fair. It is what you do that is not fair! ²⁶When good people stop doing good and do wrong, they will die because of it. They will die, because they did wrong. ²⁷When the wicked stop being wicked and do what is fair and right, they will save their lives. ²⁸Because they thought about it and stopped doing all the sins they had done, they will surely live; they will not die. ²⁹But the people of Israel still say, 'What the Lord does isn't fair.' People of Israel, I am fair. It is what you do that is not fair.

³⁰"So I will judge you, people of Israel; I will judge each of you by what you do, says the Lord Gᴏᴅ. Change your hearts and stop all your sinning so sin will not bring your ruin. ³¹Get rid of all the sins you have done, and get for yourselves a new heart and a new way of thinking. Why do you want to die, people of Israel? ³²I do not want anyone to die, says the Lord Gᴏᴅ, so change your hearts and lives so you may live.

A Sad Song for Israel

19 "Sing a funeral song for the leaders of Israel. ²Say:

'Your mother was like a female lion.
She lay down among the young lions.
  She had many cubs.
³When she brought up one of her cubs,
  he became a strong lion.
He learned to tear the animals he hunted,

and he ate people.
4The nations heard about him.
   He was trapped in their pit,
and they brought him with hooks
   to the land of Egypt.

5" 'The mother lion waited and saw
   that there was no hope for her cub.
So she took another one of her cubs
   and made him a strong lion.
6This cub roamed among the lions.
   He was now a strong lion.
He learned to tear the animals he hunted,
   and he ate people.
7He tore down their strong places
   and destroyed their cities.
The land and everything in it
   were terrified by the sound of his roar.
8Then the nations came against him
   from areas all around,
and they spread their net over him.
   He was trapped in their pit.
9Then they put him into a cage with chains
   and brought him to the king of Babylon.
They put him into prison
   so his roar could not be heard again
   on the mountains of Israel.

10" 'Your mother was like a vine in your
      vineyard,
   planted beside the water.
The vine had many branches and gave much
      fruit,
   because there was plenty of water.
11The vine had strong branches,
   good enough for a king's scepter.d
The vine became tall
   among the thick branches.
And it was seen, because it was tall
   with many branches.
12But it was pulled up by its roots in anger
   and thrown down to the ground.
The east wind dried it up.
   Its fruit was torn off.
Its strong branches were broken off
   and burned up.
13Now the vine is planted in the desert,
   in a dry and thirsty land.
14Fire spread from the vine's main branch,
   destroying its fruit.
There is not a strong branch left on it
   that could become a scepter for a king.'

This is a funeral song; it is to be used as a funeral
song."

Israel Has Refused God

20 It was the seventh year of our captivity,
in the fifth month, on the tenth day of
the month. Some of the older leaders of Israel

came to ask about the LORD and sat down in front
of me.
   2The LORD spoke his word to me, saying: 3"Human, speak to the older leaders of Israel and say
to them: 'This is what the Lord GOD says: Did
you come to ask me questions? As surely as I live,
I will not let you ask me questions.'
   4"Will you judge them? Will you judge them,
human? Let them know the hateful things their
ancestors did. 5Say to them: 'This is what the
Lord GOD says: When I chose Israel, I made a
promise to the descendantsd of Jacob. I made myself known to them in Egypt, and I promised
them, "I am the LORD your God." 6At that time
I promised them I would bring them out of Egypt
into a land I had found for them, a fertile land, the
best land in the world. 7I said to them, "Each one
of you must throw away the hateful idols you
have seen and liked. Don't make yourselves uncleand with the idols of Egypt. I am the LORD your
God."
   8" 'But they turned against me and refused to
listen to me. They did not throw away the hateful
idols which they saw and liked; they did not give
up the idols of Egypt. Then I decided to pour out
my anger against them while they were still in
Egypt. 9But I acted for the sake of my name so it
would not be dishonored in full view of the nations where the Israelites lived. I made myself
known to the Israelites with a promise to bring
them out of Egypt while the nations were watching. 10So I took them out of Egypt and brought
them into the desert. 11I gave them my rules and
told them about my laws, by which people will
live if they obey them. 12I also gave them my Sab-
bathsd to be a sign between us so they would
know that I am the LORD who made them holy.
   13" 'But in the desert Israel turned against me.
They did not follow my rules, and they rejected
my laws, by which people will live if they obey
them. They dishonored my Sabbaths. Then I decided to pour out my anger against them and destroy them in the desert. 14But I acted for the sake
of my name so it would not be dishonored in full
view of the nations who watched as I had brought
the Israelites out of Egypt. 15And in the desert I
swore to the Israelites that I would not bring them
into the land I had given them. It is a fertile land,
the best land in the world. 16This was because
they rejected my laws and did not follow my
rules. They dishonored my Sabbaths and wanted
to worship their idols. 17But I had pity on them.
I did not destroy them or put an end to them in
the desert. 18I said to their children in the desert,
"Don't live by the rules of your parents, or obey
their laws. Don't make yourselves unclean with
their idols. 19I am the LORD your God. Live by my
rules, obey my laws, and follow them. 20Keep my
Sabbaths holy, and they will be a sign between me

and you. Then you will know that I am the LORD your God."

21" 'But the children turned against me. They did not live by my rules, nor were they careful to obey my laws, by which people will live if they obey them. They dishonored my Sabbaths. So I decided to pour out my anger against them in the desert. 22But I held back my anger. I acted for the sake of my name so it would not be dishonored in full view of the nations who watched as I brought the Israelites out. 23And in the desert I swore to the Israelites that I would scatter them among the nations and spread them among the countries, 24because they had not obeyed my laws. They had rejected my rules and dishonored my Sabbaths and worshiped the idols of their parents. 25I also allowed them to follow rules that were not good and laws by which they could not live. 26I let the Israelites make themselves unclean by the gifts they brought to their gods when they sacrificed their first children in the fire. I wanted to terrify them so they would know that I am the LORD.'

27"So, human, speak to the people of Israel. Say to them, 'This is what the Lord GOD says: Your ancestors spoke against me by being unfaithful to me in another way 28When I had brought them into the land I promised to give them, they saw every high hill and every leafy tree. There they offered their sacrifices to gods. They brought offerings that made me angry and burned their incense*d* and poured out their drink offerings. 29Then I said to them: What is this high place where you go to worship?' " (It is still called High Place today.)

30"So say to the people of Israel: 'This is what the Lord GOD says: Are you going to make yourselves unclean as your ancestors did? Are you going to be unfaithful and desire their hateful idols? 31When you offer your children as gifts and sacrifice them in the fire, you are making yourselves unclean with all your idols even today. So, people of Israel, should I let you ask me questions? As surely as I live, says the Lord GOD, I will not accept questions from you.

32" 'What you want will not come true. You say, "We want to be like the other nations, like the people in other lands. We want to worship idols made of wood and stone." 33As surely as I live, says the Lord GOD, I will use my great power and strength and anger to rule over you. 34I will bring you out from the foreign nations. With my great power and strength and anger I will gather you from the lands where you are scattered. 35I will bring you among the nations as I brought your ancestors into the desert with Moses. There I will judge you face to face. 36I will judge you the same way I judged your ancestors in the desert of the land of Egypt, says the Lord GOD. 37I will

count you like sheep and will bring you into line with my agreement. 38I will get rid of those who refuse to obey me and who turn against me. I will bring them out of the land where they are now living, but they will never enter the land of Israel. Then you will know that I am the LORD.

39" 'This is what the Lord GOD says: People of Israel, go serve your idols for now. But later you will listen to me; you will not continue to dishonor my holy name with your gifts and gods. 40On my holy mountain, the high mountain of Israel, all Israel will serve me in the land, says the Lord GOD. There I will accept you. There I will expect your offerings, the first harvest of your offerings, and all your holy gifts. 41I will accept you like the pleasing smell of sacrifices when I bring you out from the foreign nations and gather you from the lands where you are scattered. Then through you I will show how holy I am so the nations will see. 42When I bring you into the land of Israel, the land I promised your ancestors, you will know that I am the LORD. 43There you will remember everything you did that made you unclean, and then you will hate yourselves for all the evil things you have done. 44I will deal with you for the sake of my name, not because of your evil ways or unclean actions. Then you will know I am the LORD, people of Israel, says the Lord GOD.' "

Babylon, the Lord's Sword

45Now the LORD spoke his word to me, saying: 46"Human, look toward the south. Prophesy*d* against the south and against the forest of the southern area. 47Say to that forest: 'Hear the word of the LORD. This is what the Lord GOD says: I am ready to start a fire in you that will destroy all your green trees and all your dry trees. The flames that burn will not be put out. Every face from south to north will feel their heat. 48Then all the people will see that I, the LORD, have started the fire. It will not be put out.' "

49Then I said, "Ah, Lord GOD! The people are saying about me, 'He is only telling stories.' "

21 Then the LORD spoke his word to me, saying: 2"Human, look toward Jerusalem and speak against the holy place. Prophesy*d* against the land of Israel. 3Say to Israel: 'This is what the LORD says: I am against you. I will pull my sword out of its holder, and I will cut off from you both the wicked and those who do right. 4Because I am going to cut off the wicked and those who do right, my sword will come out from its holder and attack all people from south to north. 5Then all people will know that I, the LORD, have pulled my sword out from its holder. My sword will not go back in again.'

6"So, human, groan with breaking heart and great sadness. Groan in front of the people.

7When they ask you, 'Why are you groaning?' you will say, 'Because of what I have heard is going to happen. When it happens, every heart will melt with fear, and all hands will become weak. Everyone will be afraid; all knees will become weak as water. Look, it is coming, and it will happen, says the Lord GOD.' "

8The LORD spoke his word to me, saying: 9"Human, prophesy and say, 'This is what the Lord says:

A sword, a sword,
    made sharp and polished.
10It is made sharp for the killing.
    It is polished to flash like lightning.
" 'You are not happy about this horrible punishment by the sword. But my son Judah, you did not change when you were only beaten with a rod.
11The sword should be polished.
    It is meant to be held in the hand.
It is made sharp and polished,
    ready for the hand of a killer.
12Shout and yell, human,
    because the sword is meant for my people,
    for all the rulers of Israel.
They will be killed by the sword,
    along with my people.
    So beat your chest in sadness.
13" 'The test will come. And Judah, who is hated by the armies of Babylon, will not last, says the Lord GOD.'

14"So, human, prophesy
    and clap your hands.
Let the sword strike
    two or three times.
It is a sword meant for killing,
    a sword meant for much killing.
This sword surrounds the people to be
    killed.
15Their hearts will melt with fear,
    and many people will die.
I have placed the killing sword
    at all their city gates.
Oh! The sword is made to flash like
    lightning.
    It is held, ready for killing.
16Sword, cut on the right side;
    then cut on the left side.
    Cut anywhere your blade is turned.
17I will also clap my hands
    and use up my anger.
    I, the LORD, have spoken."

Jerusalem to Be Destroyed

18The LORD spoke his word to me, saying: 19"Human, mark two roads that the king of Babylon and his sword can follow. Both of these roads will start from the same country. And make signs where the road divides and one way goes toward the city. 20Mark one sign to show the road he can take with his sword to Rabbah in the land of the Ammonites. Mark the other sign to show the road to Judah and Jerusalem, which is protected with strong walls. 21The king of Babylon has come to where the road divides, and he is using magic. He throws lots*d* with arrows and asks questions of his family idols. He looks at the liver of a sacrificed

> **✺ SIDELIGHT:** Using arrows to predict the future (Ezekiel 21:21) was a favorite Babylonian divination (magic trick) to help make decisions—as some people use tarot cards, tea leaves, and horoscopes today. The person would shake the arrows and then throw them on the ground. Their formation would tell what to do.

animal to learn where he should go. 22The lot in his right hand tells him to go to Jerusalem. It tells him to use logs to break down the city gates, to shout the battle cry and give the order to kill, and to build a dirt road to the top of the walls and devices to attack the walls. 23The people of Jerusalem have made agreements with other nations to help them fight Babylon. So they will think this prediction is wrong, but it is really proof of their sin, and they will be captured.

24"So this is what the Lord GOD says: 'You have shown how sinful you are by turning against the LORD. Your sins are seen in all the things you do. Because of this proof against you, you will be taken captive by the enemy.

25" 'You unclean*d* and evil leader of Israel, you will be killed! The time of your final punishment has come. 26This is what the Lord GOD says: Take off the royal turban, and remove the crown. Things will change. Those who are important now will be made unimportant, and those who are unimportant now will be made important. 27A ruin! A ruin! I will make it a ruin! This place will not be rebuilt until the one comes who has a right to be king. Then I will give him that right.'

The Punishment of Ammon

28"And you, human, prophesy*d* and say: 'This is what the Lord GOD says about the people of Ammon and their insults:

A sword, a sword
    is pulled out of its holder.
It is polished to kill and destroy,
    to flash like lightning!
29Prophets*d* see false visions about you
    and prophesy lies about you.
The sword will be put on the necks

of these unclean^d and evil people.
Their day of judging has come;
　　the time of final punishment has come.
³⁰Put the sword back in its holder.
　I will judge you
in the place where you were created,
　in the land where you were born.
³¹I will pour out my anger against you
　and blast you with the fire of my anger.
I will hand you over to cruel men,
　experts in destruction.
³²You will be like fuel for the fire;
　you will die in the land.
You will not be remembered,
　because I, the LORD, have spoken.' "

The Sins of Jerusalem

22 The LORD spoke his word to me, saying: ²"And you, human, will you judge? Will you judge the city of murderers? Then tell her about all her hateful acts. ³You are to say: 'This is what the Lord GOD says: You are a city that kills those who come to live there. You make yourself unclean^d by making idols. ⁴You have become guilty of murder and have become unclean by your idols which you have made. So you have brought your time of punishment near; you have come to the end of your years. That is why I have made you a shame to the nations and why all lands laugh at you. ⁵Those near and those far away laugh at you with your bad name, you city full of confusion.

⁶" 'Jerusalem, see how each ruler of Israel in you has been trying to kill people. ⁷The people in you hate their fathers and mothers. They mistreat the foreigners in you and wrong the orphans and widows in you. ⁸You hate my holy things and dishonor my Sabbaths.^d ⁹The men in you tell lies to cause the death of others. The people in you eat food offered to idols at the mountain places of worship, and they take part in sexual sins. ¹⁰The men in you have sexual relations with their fathers' wives and with women who are unclean, during their time of monthly bleeding. ¹¹One man in you does a hateful act with his neighbor's wife, while another has shamefully made his daughter-in-law unclean sexually. And another forces his half sister to have sexual relations with him. ¹²The people in you take money to kill others. You take unfair interest and profits and make profits by mistreating your neighbor. And you have forgotten me, says the Lord GOD.

¹³" 'So, Jerusalem, I will shake my fist at you for stealing money and for murdering people. ¹⁴Will you still be brave and strong when I punish you? I, the LORD, have spoken, and I will act. ¹⁵I will scatter you among the nations and spread you through the countries. That is how I will get rid of your uncleanness. ¹⁶But you, yourself, will be

dishonored in the sight of the nations. Then you will know that I am the LORD.' "

Israel Is Worthless

¹⁷The LORD spoke his word to me, saying: ¹⁸"Human, the people of Israel have become useless like scum to me. They are like the copper, tin, iron, and lead left in the furnace when silver is purified. ¹⁹So this is what the Lord GOD says: 'Because you have become useless like scum, I am going to put you together inside Jerusalem. ²⁰People put silver, copper, iron, lead, and tin together inside a furnace to melt them down in a blazing fire. In the same way I will gather you in my hot anger and put you together in Jerusalem and melt you down. ²¹I will put you together and make you feel the heat of my anger. You will be melted down inside Jerusalem. ²²As silver is melted in a furnace, you will be melted inside the city. Then you will know that I, the LORD, have poured out my anger on you.' "

Sins of the People

²³The LORD spoke his word to me, saying: ²⁴"Human, say to the land, 'You are a land that has not had rain or showers when God is angry.' ²⁵Like a roaring lion that tears the animal it has caught, Israel's rulers make evil plans. They have destroyed lives and have taken treasure and valuable things. They have caused many women to become widows. ²⁶Israel's priests do cruel things to my teachings and do not honor my holy things. They make no difference between holy and unholy things, and they teach there is no difference between clean^d and unclean things. They do not remember my Sabbaths,^d so I am dishonored by them. ²⁷Like wolves tearing a dead animal, Jerusalem's leaders have killed people for profit. ²⁸And the prophets^d try to cover this up by false visions and by lying messages. They say, 'This is what the Lord GOD says' when the LORD has not spoken. ²⁹The people cheat others and steal. They hurt people who are poor and needy. They cheat foreigners and do not treat them fairly.

³⁰"I looked for someone to build up the walls and to stand before me where the walls are broken to defend these people so I would not have to destroy them. But I could not find anyone. ³¹So I let them see my anger. I destroyed them with an anger that was like fire because of all the things they have done, says the Lord GOD."

Samaria and Jerusalem

23 The LORD spoke his word to me, saying: ²"Human, a woman had two daughters. ³While they were young, they went to Egypt and became prostitutes.^d They let men touch and hold their breasts. ⁴The older girl was named Oholah, and her sister was named Oholibah. They became my wives and had sons and daughters. Oholah is Samaria, and Oholibah is Jerusalem.[n]

5"While still my wife, Samaria had sexual relations with other men. She had great sexual desire for her lovers, men from Assyria. The Assyrians were warriors and 6wore blue uniforms. They were all handsome young captains and lieutenants riding on horseback. 7Samaria became a prostitute for all the important men in Assyria and made herself unclean[d] with all the idols of everyone she desired. 8She continued the prostitution she began in Egypt. When she was young, she had slept with men, and they touched her breasts and had sexual relations with her.

9"So I handed her over to her lovers, the Assyrians, that she wanted so badly. 10They stripped her naked and took away her sons and daughters. Then they killed her with a sword. Women everywhere began talking about how she had been punished.

11"Her sister Jerusalem saw what happened, but she became worse than her sister in her sexual desire and prostitution. 12She also desired the Assyrians, who were all soldiers in beautiful uniforms — handsome young captains and lieutenants riding horses. 13I saw that both girls were alike; both were prostitutes.

14"But Jerusalem went even further. She saw carvings of Babylonian men on a wall. They wore red 15and had belts around their waists and turbans on their heads. They all looked like chariot officers born in Babylonia. 16When she saw them, she wanted to have sexual relations with them and sent messengers to them in Babylonia. 17So these Babylonian men came and had sexual relations with her and made her unclean. After that, she became sick of them. 18But she continued her prostitution so openly that everyone knew about it. And I finally became sick of her, as I had her sister. 19But she remembered how she was a young prostitute in Egypt, so she took part in even more prostitution. 20She wanted men who behaved like animals in their sexual desire. 21In the same way you desired to do the sinful things you had done in Egypt. There men touched and held your young breasts.

God's Judgment on Jerusalem

22"So, Jerusalem, this is what the Lord God says: You are tired of your lovers. So now I will make them angry with you and have them attack you from all sides. 23Men from Babylon and all Babylonia and men from Pekod, Shoa, and Koa will attack you. All the Assyrians will attack you: handsome young captains and lieutenants, all of them important men and all riding horses.

24Those men will attack with great armies and with their weapons, chariots, and wagons. They will surround you with large and small shields and with helmets. And I will give them the right to punish you, and they will give you their own kind of punishment. 25Then you will see how strong my anger can be when they punish you in their anger. They will cut off your noses and ears. They will take away your sons and daughters, and those who are left will be burned. 26They will take off your clothes and steal your jewelry. 27I will put a stop to the sinful life you began when you were in Egypt so that you will not desire it or remember Egypt anymore.

28"This is what the Lord God says: You became tired of your lovers, but I am going to hand you over to those men you now hate. 29They will treat you with hate and take away everything you worked for, leaving you empty and naked. Everyone will know about the sinful things you did. Your sexual sins 30have brought this on you. You have had sexual relations with the nations and made yourselves unclean[d] by worshiping their idols. 31You did the same things your sister did, so you will get the same punishment, like a bitter cup to drink.

32"This is what the Lord God says:

You will drink the same cup your sister did,
　and that cup is deep and wide.
Everyone will make fun of you,
　because the cup is full.
33It will make you miserable and drunk.
It is the cup of fear and ruin.
It is the cup of your sister Samaria.
34You will drink everything in it,
　and then you will smash it
　and tear at your breasts.
I have spoken, says the Lord God.

35"So this is what the Lord God says: You have forgotten me and turned your back on me. So you will be punished for your sexual sins."

Judgment on Samaria and Jerusalem

36The Lord said to me: "Human, will you judge Samaria and Jerusalem, showing them their hateful acts? 37They are guilty of adultery[d] and murder. They have taken part in adultery with their idols. They even offered our children as sacrifices in the fire to be food for these idols. 38They have also done this to me: They made my Temple[d] unclean[d] at the same time they dishonored my Sabbaths.[d] 39They sacrificed their children to their idols. Then they entered my Temple at that very time to dishonor it. That is what they did inside my Temple!

40"They even sent for men from far away, who

came after a messenger was sent to them. The two sisters bathed themselves for them, painted their eyes, and put on jewelry. ⁴¹They sat on a fine bed with a table set before it, on which they put my incense*d* and my oil.

⁴²"There was the noise of a reckless crowd in the city. Common people gathered, and drunkards were brought from the desert. They put bracelets on the wrists of the two sisters and beautiful crowns on their heads. ⁴³Then I said about the one who was worn out by her acts of adultery, 'Let them continue their sexual sins with her. She is nothing but a prostitute.'*d* ⁴⁴They kept going to her as they would go to a prostitute. So they continued to go to Samaria and Jerusalem, these shameful women. ⁴⁵But men who do right will punish them as they punish women who take part in adultery and who murder people, because they are guilty of adultery and murder.

⁴⁶"This is what the Lord God says: Bring together a mob against Samaria and Jerusalem, and hand them over to be frightened and robbed. ⁴⁷Let the mob kill them by throwing stones at them, and let them cut them down with their swords. Let them kill their sons and daughters and burn their houses down.

⁴⁸"So I will put an end to sexual sins in the land. Then all women will be warned, and they will not do the sexual sins you have done. ⁴⁹You will be punished for your sexual sins and the sin of worshiping idols. Then you will know that I am the Lord God."

The Pot and the Meat

24 The Lord spoke his word to me in the ninth year of our captivity, in the tenth month, on the tenth day of the month. He said: ²"Human, write down today's date, this very date. The king of Babylon has surrounded Jerusalem this very day. ³And tell a story to the people who refuse to obey me. Say to them: 'This is what the Lord God says:

Put on the pot; put it on
   and pour water in it.
⁴Put in the pieces of meat,
   the best pieces — the legs and the shoulders.
Fill it with the best bones.
⁵ Take the best of the flock,
   and pile wood under the pot.
   Boil the pieces of meat
      until even the bones are cooked.

⁶ 'This is what the Lord God says:
How terrible it will be for the city of
      murderers!
   How terrible it will be for the rusty pot
      whose rust will not come off!
Take the meat out of it, piece by piece.
   Don't choose any special piece.

⁷" 'The blood from her killings is still in the
      city.
   She poured the blood on the bare rock.
She did not pour it on the ground
   where dust would cover it.
⁸To stir up my anger and revenge,
   I put the blood she spilled on the bare rock
   so it will not be covered.

⁹ 'So this is what the Lord God says:
How terrible it will be for the city of
      murderers!
   I myself will pile the wood high for
      burning.
¹⁰Pile up the wood
   and light the fire.
Finish cooking the meat.
   Mix in the spices,
   and let the bones burn.
¹¹Then set the empty pot on the coals
   so it may become hot and its copper sides
      glow.
The dirty scum stuck inside it may then melt
   and its rust burn away.
¹²But efforts to clean the pot have failed.
   Its heavy rust cannot be removed,
   even in the fire.

¹³" 'By your sinful action you have become unclean.*d* I wanted to cleanse you, but you are still unclean. You will never be cleansed from your sin until my anger against you is carried out.

¹⁴ 'I, the Lord, have spoken. The time has come for me to act. I will not hold back punishment or feel pity or change my mind. I will judge you by your ways and actions, says the Lord God.' "

The Death of Ezekiel's Wife

¹⁵Then the Lord spoke his word to me, saying: ¹⁶"Human, I am going to take your wife from you, the woman you look at with love. She will die suddenly, but you must not be sad or cry loudly for her or shed any tears. ¹⁷Groan silently; do not cry loudly for the dead. Tie on your turban, and put your sandals on your feet. Do not cover your face, and do not eat the food people eat when they are sad about a death."

¹⁸So I spoke to the people in the morning, and my wife died in the evening. The next morning I did as I had been commanded.

¹⁹Then the people asked me, "Tell us, what do the things you are doing mean for us?"

²⁰Then I said to them, "The Lord spoke his word to me. He said, ²¹Say to the people of Israel, This is what the Lord God says: I am going to dishonor my Temple.*d* You think it gives you strength. You are proud of it, and you look at it with love and tenderness. But your sons and daughters that you left behind in Jerusalem will

fall dead by the sword. [22]When that happens, you are to act as I have: you are not to cover your face, and you are not to eat the food people eat when they are sad about a death. [23]Your turbans must stay on your heads, and your sandals on your feet. You must not cry loudly, but you must rot away in your sins and groan to each other. [24]So Ezekiel is to be an example for you. You must do all the same things he did. When all this happens, you will know that I am the Lord God.'

SIDELIGHT: If God had allowed Ezekiel to grieve for his wife, there would have been no flowers or nice funeral clothes. Under normal circumstances, the prophet would have gone barefoot, worn sackcloth, and sprinkled ashes on his head. To learn why he did none of them read Ezekiel 24:15–24.

---

[25]"And as for you, human, this is how it will be. I will take away the Temple that gives them strength and joy, that makes them proud. They look at it with love, and it makes them happy. And I will take away their sons and daughters also. [26]At that time a person who escapes will come to you with information for you to hear. [27]At that very time your mouth will be opened. You will speak and be silent no more. So you will be a sign for them, and they will know that I am the Lord."

Prophecy Against Ammon

25 The Lord spoke his word to me, saying: [2]"Human, look toward the people of Ammon and prophesy[d] against them. [3]Say to them, 'Hear the word of the Lord God. This is what the Lord God says: You were glad when my Temple[d] was dishonored, when the land of Israel was ruined, and when the people of Judah were taken away as captives. [4]So I am going to give you to the people of the East to be theirs. They will set up their camps among you and make their homes among you. They will eat your fruit and drink your milk. [5]I will make the city of Rabbah a pasture for camels and the land of Ammon a resting place for sheep. Then you will know that I am the Lord. [6]This is what the Lord God says: You have clapped your hands and stamped your feet; you *have laughed about all the insults you made* against the land of Israel. [7]So I will use my power against you. I will give you to the nations as if you were treasures taken in war. I will wipe you out of the lands so you will no longer be a nation, and I will destroy you. Then you will know that I am the Lord.'

Prophecy Against Moab and Edom

[8]"This is what the Lord God says: 'Moab and Edom say, "The people of Judah are like all the other nations." [9]So I am going to take away the cities that protect Moab's borders, the best cities in that land: Beth Jeshimoth, Baal Meon, and Kiriathaim. [10]Then I will give Moab, along with the Ammonites, to the people of the East as their possession. Then, along with the Ammonites, Moab will not be a nation anymore. [11]So I will punish the people of Moab, and they will know that I am the Lord.'

Prophecy Against Edom

[12]"This is what the Lord God says: 'Edom took revenge on the people of Judah, and the Edomites became guilty because of it. [13]So this is what the Lord God says: I will use my power against Edom, killing every human and animal in it. And I will destroy Edom all the way from Teman to Dedan as they die in battle. [14]I will use my people Israel to take revenge on Edom. So the Israelites will do to Edom what my hot anger demands. Then the Edomites will know what my revenge feels like, says the Lord God.'

Prophecy Against Philistia

[15]"This is what the Lord God says: 'The Philistines have taken revenge with hateful hearts. Because of their strong hatred, they have tried to destroy Judah. [16]So this is what the Lord God says: I will use my power against the Philistines. I will kill the Kerethites, and I will destroy those people still alive on the coast of the Mediterranean Sea. [17]I will punish them in my anger and do great acts of revenge to them. They will know that I am the Lord when I take revenge on them.' "

Prophecy Against Tyre

26 It was the eleventh year of our captivity, on the first day of the month. The Lord spoke his word to me, saying: [2]"Human, the city of Tyre has spoken against Jerusalem: 'The city that traded with the nations is destroyed. Now we can be the trading center. Since the city of Jerusalem is ruined, we can make money.' [3]So this is what the Lord God says: I am against you, Tyre. I will bring many nations against you, like the sea beating its waves on your island shores. [4]They will destroy the walls of Tyre and pull down her *towers. I will also scrape away her ruins and make* her a bare rock. [5]Tyre will be an island where fishermen dry their nets. I have spoken, says the Lord God. The nations will steal treasures from Tyre. [6]Also, her villages on the shore across from the island will be destroyed by war. Then they will know that I am the Lord.

Nebuchadnezzar to Attack Tyre

7"This is what the Lord God says: I will bring a king from the north against Tyre. He is Nebuchadnezzar king of Babylon, the greatest king, with his horses, chariots, horsemen, and a great army. 8He will fight a battle and destroy your villages on the shore across from the island. He will set up devices to attack you. He will build a road of earth to the top of the walls. He will raise his shields against you. 9He will bring logs to pound through your city walls, and he will break down your towers with his iron bars. 10His horses will be so many that they will cover you with their dust. Your walls will shake at the noise of horsemen, wagons, and chariots. The king of Babylon will enter your city gates as men enter a city where the walls are broken through. 11The hoofs of his horses will run over your streets. He will kill your army with the sword, and your strong pillars will fall down to the ground. 12Also, his men will take away your riches and will steal the things you sell. They will break down your walls and destroy your nice houses. They will throw your stones, wood, and trash into the sea. 13So I will stop your songs; the music of your harps will not be heard anymore. 14I will make you a bare rock, and you will be a place for drying fishing nets. You will not be built again, because I, the Lord, have spoken, says the Lord God.

15"This is what the Lord God says to Tyre: The people who live along the seacoast will shake with fear when they hear about your defeat. Those of you who are injured and dying will groan. 16Then all the leaders of the seacoast will get down from their thrones, take off their beautiful needlework clothes, and show how afraid they are. They will sit on the ground and tremble all the time. When they see you, they will be shocked. 17They will begin singing a funeral song about you and will say to you:

'Tyre, you famous city, you have been destroyed!
    You have lost your sea power!
You and your people
    had great power on the seas.
You made everyone around you
    afraid of you.
18Now the people who live by the coast tremble,
    now that you have fallen.
The islands of the sea
    are afraid because you have been defeated.'

19"This is what the Lord God says: I will make you an empty city, like cities that have no people living in them. I will bring the deep ocean waters over you, and the Mediterranean Sea will cover

you. 20At that time I will send you down to the place of the dead to join those who died long ago. I will make you live with the dead below the earth in places that are like old ruins. You will not come back from there or have any place in the world of the living again. 21Other people will be afraid of what happened to you, and it will be the end of you. People will look for you, but they will never find you again, says the Lord God."

A Funeral Song for Tyre

27 The Lord spoke his word to me, saying: 2"Human, sing a funeral song for the city of Tyre. 3Speak to Tyre, which has ports for the Mediterranean Sea and is a place for trade for the people of many lands along the seacoast. 'This is what the Lord God says:

Tyre, you have said,
    "I am like a beautiful ship."
4You were at home on the high seas.
    Your builders made your beauty perfect.
5They made all your boards
    of fir trees from Mount Hermon.
They took a cedar tree from Lebanon
    to make a ship's mast for you.
6They made your oars
    from oak trees from Bashan.
They made your deck
    from cypress trees from the coast of Cyprus
    and set ivory into it.
7Your sail of linen with designs sewed on it
    came from Egypt
    and became like a flag for you.
Your cloth shades over the deck were blue
    and purple
    and came from the island of Cyprus.
8Men from Sidon and Arvad used oars to row you.
    Tyre, your skilled men were the sailors on your deck.
9Workers of Byblos were with you,
    putting caulk[n] in your ship's seams.
All the ships of the sea and their sailors
    came alongside to trade with you.

10" 'Men of Persia, Lydia, and Put

---

caulk Something like tar put between the boards of a ship to make it waterproof

were warriors in your navy
and hung their shields and helmets on your
    sides.
They made you look beautiful.
¹¹Men of Arvad and Cilicia
guarded your city walls all around.
Men of Gammad
were in your watchtowers
and hung their shields around your walls.
    They made your beauty perfect.

¹²" 'People of Tarshish became traders for you
because of your great wealth. They traded your
goods for silver, iron, tin, and lead.

¹³" 'People of Greece, Tubal, and Meshech became merchants for you. They traded your goods
for slaves and items of bronze.

¹⁴" 'People of Beth Togarmah traded your
goods for work horses, war horses, and mules.

¹⁵" 'People of Rhodes became merchants for
you, selling your goods on many coastlands. They
brought back ivory tusks and valuable black wood
as your payment.

¹⁶" 'People of Aram became traders for you, because you had so many good things to sell. They
traded your goods for turquoise, purple cloth,
cloth with designs sewed on, fine linen, coral, and
rubies.

¹⁷" 'People of Judah and Israel became merchants for you. They traded your goods for wheat
from Minnith, and for honey, olive oil, and balm.ᵈ

¹⁸⁻¹⁹" 'People of Damascus became traders for
you because you have many good things and great
wealth. They traded your goods for wine from
Helbon, wool from Zahar, and barrels of wine
from Izal. They received wrought iron, cassia,ᵈ
and sugar cane in payment for your good things.

²⁰" 'People of Dedan became merchants for
you, trading saddle blankets for riding.

²¹" 'People of Arabia and all the rulers of Kedar
became traders for you. They received lambs,
male sheep, and goats in payment for you.

²²" 'The merchants of Sheba and Raamah became merchants for you. They traded your goods
for all the best spices, valuable gems, and gold.

²³" 'People of Haran, Canneh, Eden, and the
traders of Sheba, Asshur, and Kilmad became
merchants for you. ²⁴They were paid with the
best clothes, blue cloth, cloth with designs sewed
on, carpets of many colors, and tightly wound
ropes.

²⁵" 'Trading ships
    carried the things you sold.
You were like a ship full of heavy cargo
    in the middle of the sea.
²⁶The men who rowed you
    brought you out into the high seas,
but the east wind broke you to pieces
    in the middle of the sea.

²⁷Your wealth, your trade, your goods,
    your seamen, your sailors, your workers,
your traders, your warriors,
    and everyone else on board
sank into the sea
    on the day your ship was wrecked.
²⁸The people on the shore shake with fear
    when your sailors cry out.
²⁹All the men who row
    leave their ships;
the seamen and the sailors of other ships
    stand on the shore.
³⁰They cry loudly about you;
    they cry very much.
They throw dust on their heads
    and roll in ashes to show they are sad.
³¹They shave their heads for you,
    and they put on rough cloth to show they
        are upset.
They cry and sob for you;
    they cry loudly.
³²And in their loud crying
    they sing a funeral song for you:
"No one was ever destroyed like Tyre,
    surrounded by the sea."
³³When the goods you traded went out over
        the seas,
    you met the needs of many nations.
With your great wealth and goods,
    you made kings of the earth rich.
³⁴But now you are broken by the sea
    and have sunk to the bottom.
Your goods and all the people on board
    have gone down with you.
³⁵All those who live along the shore
    are shocked by what happened to you.
Their kings are terribly afraid,
    and their faces show their fear.
³⁶The traders among the nations hiss at
        you.
    You have come to a terrible end,
    and you are gone forever.' "

Prophecy Against the King of Tyre

28 The Lord spoke his word to me, saying:
²"Human, say to the ruler of Tyre: 'This
is what the Lord God says:
Because you are proud,
    you say, "I am a god.
I sit on the throne of a god
    in the middle of the seas."
You think you are as wise as a god,
    but you are a human, not a god.
³You think you are wiser than Daniel.
    You think you can find out all secrets.
⁴Through your wisdom and understanding
    you have made yourself rich.
You have gained gold and silver
    and have saved it in your storerooms.

⁵Through your great skill in trading,
  you have made your riches grow.
You are too proud
  because of your riches.

⁶" 'So this is what the Lord GOD says:
You think you are wise
  like a god,
⁷but I will bring foreign people against you,
  the cruelest nation.
They will pull out their swords
  and destroy all that your wisdom has built,
  and they will dishonor your greatness.
⁸They will kill you;
  you will die a terrible death
  like those who are killed at sea.
⁹While they are killing you,
  you will not be able to say anymore, "I am
    a god."
You will be only a human, not a god,
  when your murderers kill you.
¹⁰You will die like an unclean⁴ person;
  foreigners will kill you.

I have spoken, says the Lord GOD.' "

¹¹The LORD spoke his word to me, saying:
¹²"Human, sing a funeral song for the king of
Tyre. Say to him: 'This is what the Lord GOD
says:
You were an example of what was perfect,
  full of wisdom and perfect in beauty.
¹³You had a wonderful life,
  as if you were in Eden, the garden of God.
Every valuable gem was on you:
  ruby, topaz, and emerald,
  yellow quartz, onyx, and jasper,
  sapphire, turquoise, and chrysolite.
Your jewelry was made of gold.
  It was prepared on the day you were
    created.
¹⁴I appointed a living creature to guard you.
  I put you on the holy mountain of God.
You walked among the gems that shined
  like fire.
¹⁵Your life was right and good
  from the day you were created,
  until evil was found in you.
¹⁶Because you traded with countries far away,
  you learned to be cruel, and you sinned.
So I threw you down in disgrace from the
    mountain of God.
And the living creature who guarded you
  forced you out from among the gems that
    shined like fire.
¹⁷You became too proud
  because of your beauty.
You ruined your wisdom
  because of your greatness.
I threw you down to the ground.

Your example taught a lesson to other
    kings.
¹³You dishonored your places of worship
  through your many sins and dishonest
    trade.
So I set on fire the place where you lived,
  and the fire burned you up.
I turned you into ashes on the ground
  for all those watching to see.
¹⁹All the nations who knew you
  are shocked about you.
Your punishment was so terrible,
  and you are gone forever.' "

Prophecy Against Sidon

²⁰The LORD spoke his word to me, saying:
²¹"Human, look toward the city of Sidon and
prophesy⁴ against her. ²²Say: 'This is what the
Lord GOD says:
I am against you, Sidon,
  and I will show my glory among you.
People will know that I am the LORD
  when I have punished Sidon;
  I will show my holiness by defeating her.
²³I will send diseases to Sidon,
  and blood will flow in her streets.
Those who are wounded in Sidon will fall
    dead,
  attacked from all sides.
Then they will know that I am the LORD.

God Will Help Israel

²⁴ 'No more will neighboring nations be like
thorny branches or sharp stickers to hurt Israel.
Then they will know that I am the Lord GOD.
²⁵ 'This is what the Lord GOD says: I will
gather the people of Israel from the nations where
they are scattered. I will show my holiness when
the nations see what I do for my people. Then
they will live in their own land — the land I gave
to my servant Jacob. ²⁶They will live safely in the
land and will build houses and plant vineyards.
They will live in safety after I have punished all
the nations around who hate them. Then they
will know that I am the LORD their God.' "

Prophecy Against Egypt

29 It was the tenth year of our captivity, in
the tenth month, on the twelfth day of
the month. The LORD spoke his word to me, saying: ²"Human, look toward the king of Egypt, and
prophesy⁴ against all Egypt. ³Say: 'This
is what the Lord GOD says:
I am against you, king of Egypt.
  You are like a great crocodile that lies in
    the Nile River.
You say, "The Nile is mine;
  I made it for myself."
⁴But I will put hooks in your jaws,

and I will make the fish of the Nile stick to
    your sides.
I will pull you up out of your rivers,
    with all the fish sticking to your sides.
⁵I will leave you in the desert,
    you and all the fish from your rivers.
You will fall onto the ground;
    you will not be picked up or buried.
I have given you to the wild animals
    and to the birds of the sky for food.
⁶Then all the people who live in Egypt will know
that I am the Lord.

" 'Israel tried to lean on you for help, but you
were like a crutch made out of a weak stalk of
grass. ⁷When their hands grabbed you, you splintered and tore open their shoulders. When they
leaned on you, you broke and made all their backs
twist.

⁸" 'So this is what the Lord God says: I will
cause an enemy to attack you and kill your people
and animals. ⁹Egypt will become an empty desert.
Then they will know that I am the Lord.

" 'Because you said, "The Nile River is mine,
and I have made it," ¹⁰I am against you and your
rivers. I will destroy the land of Egypt and make
it an empty desert from Migdol in the north to
Aswan in the south, all the way to the border of
Cush. ¹¹No person or animal will walk through it,
and no one will live in Egypt for forty years. ¹²I
will make the land of Egypt the most deserted
country of all. Her cities will be the most deserted of all ruined cities for forty years. I will scatter the Egyptians among the nations, spreading
them among the countries.

¹³" 'This is what the Lord God says: After forty
years I will gather Egypt from the nations where
they have been scattered. ¹⁴I will bring back the
Egyptian captives and make them return to southern Egypt, to the land they came from. They will
become a weak kingdom there. ¹⁵It will be the
weakest kingdom, and it will never again rule
other nations. I will make it so weak it will never
again rule over the nations. ¹⁶The Israelites will
never again depend on Egypt. Instead, Egypt's
punishment will remind the Israelites of their sin
in turning to Egypt for help. Then they will know
that I am the Lord God.' "

Egypt Is Given to Babylon

¹⁷It was the twenty-seventh year of our captivity, in the first month, on the first day of the
month. The Lord spoke his word to me, saying:
¹⁸"Human, Nebuchadnezzar king of Babylon
made his army fight hard against Tyre. Every soldier's head was rubbed bare, and every shoulder
was rubbed raw. But Nebuchadnezzar and his
army gained nothing from fighting Tyre. ¹⁹So this
is what the Lord God says: I will give the land of
Egypt to Nebuchadnezzar king of Babylon. He

will take away Egypt's people and its wealth and
its treasures as pay for his army. ²⁰I am giving
Nebuchadnezzar the land of Egypt as a reward for
working hard for me, says the Lord God.

²¹"At that time I will make Israel grow strong
again, and I will let you, Ezekiel, speak to them.
Then they will know that I am the Lord."

Egypt Will Be Punished

30 The Lord spoke his word to me, saying:
²"Human, prophesy*d* and say, 'This is
what the Lord God says:
    Cry and say,
        "The terrible day is coming."
³The day is near;
    the Lord's day of judging is near.
It is a cloudy day
    and a time when the nations will be
        judged.
⁴An enemy will attack Egypt,
    and Cush will tremble with fear.
When the killing begins in Egypt,
    her wealth will be taken away,
    and her foundations will be torn down.

⁵Cush, Put, Lydia, Arabia, Libya, and some of my
people who had made an agreement with Egypt
will fall dead in war.
    ⁶" 'This is what the Lord says:
Those who fight on Egypt's side will fall.
    The power she is proud of will be lost.
The people in Egypt will fall dead in war
    from Migdol in the north to Aswan in the
        south,
    says the Lord God.
⁷They will be the most deserted lands.
    Egypt's cities will be the worst of cities that
        lie in ruins.
⁸Then they will know that I am the Lord
    when I set fire to Egypt
    and when all those nations on her side are
        crushed.

⁹" 'At that time I will send messengers in ships
to frighten Cush, which now feels safe. The people of Cush will tremble with fear when Egypt is
punished. And that time is sure to come.
    ¹⁰" 'This is what the Lord God says:
I will destroy great numbers of people in
        Egypt
    through the power of Nebuchadnezzar king
        of Babylon.
¹¹Nebuchadnezzar and his army,
    the cruelest army of any nation,
    will be brought in to destroy the land.
They will pull out their swords against Egypt
    and will fill the land with those they kill.
¹²I will make the streams of the Nile River
    become dry land,
    and then I will sell the land to evil people.

I will destroy the land and everything in it
  through the power of foreigners.

I, the LORD, have spoken.

Egypt's Idols Are Destroyed

13" 'This is what the Lord GOD says:
I will destroy the idols
  and take away the statues of gods from the
    city of Memphis.
There will no longer be a leader in Egypt,
  and I will spread fear through the land of
    Egypt.
14I will make southern Egypt empty
  and start a fire in Zoan
  and punish Thebes.
15And I will pour out my anger against
    Pelusium,
  the strong place of Egypt.
I will destroy great numbers of people in
    Thebes.
16I will set fire to Egypt.
  Pelusium will be in great pain.
The walls of Thebes will be broken open,
  and Memphis will have troubles every day.
17The young men of Heliopolis and Bubastis
  will fall dead in war,
  and the people will be taken away as
    captives.
18In Tahpanhes the day will be dark
  when I break Egypt's power.
  Then she will no longer be proud of her
    power.
A cloud will cover Egypt,
  and her villages will be captured and taken
    away.
19So I will punish Egypt,
  and they will know I am the LORD.' "

Egypt Becomes Weak

20It was in the eleventh year of our captivity, in
the first month, on the seventh day of the month.
The LORD spoke his word to me, saying: 21"Human, I have broken the powerful arm of the king
of Egypt. It has not been tied up, so it will not get
well. It has not been wrapped with a bandage, so
it will not be strong enough to hold a sword in
war. 22So this is what the Lord GOD says: I am
against the king of Egypt. I will break his arms,
both the strong arm and the broken arm, and I
will make the sword fall from his hand. 23I will
scatter the Egyptians among the nations, spreading them among the countries. 24I will make the
arms of the king of Babylon strong and put my
sword in his hand. But I will break the arms of the
king of Egypt. Then when he faces the king of
Babylon, he will cry out in pain like a dying person. 25So I will make the arms of the king of Babylon strong, but the arms of the king of Egypt will

fall. Then people will know that I am the LORD
when I put my sword into the hand of the king
of Babylon and he uses it in war against Egypt.
26Then I will scatter the Egyptians among the nations, spreading them among the countries. Then
they will know that I am the LORD."

A Cedar Tree

31 It was in the eleventh year of our captiv-
    ity, in the third month, on the first day
of the month. The LORD spoke his word to me,
saying: 2"Human, say to the king of Egypt and his
people:
  'No one is like you in your greatness.
3Assyria was once like a cedar tree in Lebanon
  with beautiful branches that shaded the
    forest.
It was very tall;
  its top was among the clouds.
4Much water made the tree grow;
  the deep springs made it tall.
Rivers flowed
  around the bottom of the tree
and sent their streams
  to all other trees in the countryside.
5So the tree was taller
  than all the other trees in the countryside.
Its limbs became long and big
  because of so much water.
6All the birds of the sky
  made their nests in the tree's limbs.
And all the wild animals
  gave birth under its branches.
All great nations
  lived in the tree's shade.
7So the tree was great and beautiful,
  with its long branches,
  because its roots reached down to much
    water.
8The cedar trees in the garden of God
  were not as great as it was.
The pine trees
  did not have such great limbs.
The plane trees
  did not have such branches.
No tree in the garden of God
  was as beautiful as this tree.
9I made it beautiful
  with many branches,
and all the trees of Eden in the garden of
    God
  wanted to be like it.

10" 'So this is what the Lord GOD says: The tree
grew tall. Its top reached the clouds, and it became proud of its height. 11So I handed it over to
a mighty ruler of the nations for him to punish it.
Because it was evil, I got rid of it. 12The cruelest
foreign nation cut it down and left it. The tree's

branches fell on the mountains and in all the valleys, and its broken limbs were in all the ravines of the land. All the nations of the earth left the shade of that tree. ¹³The birds of the sky live on the fallen tree. The wild animals live among the tree's fallen branches. ¹⁴So the trees that grow by the water will not be proud to be tall; they will not put their tops among the clouds. None of the trees that are watered well will grow that tall, because they all are meant to die and go under the ground. They will be with people who have died and have gone down to the place of the dead.

¹⁵" 'This is what the Lord GOD says: On the day when the tree went down to the place of the dead, I made the deep springs cry loudly. I covered them and held back their rivers, and the great waters stopped flowing. I dressed Lebanon in black to show her sadness about the great tree, and all the trees in the countryside were sad about it. ¹⁶I made the nations shake with fear at the sound of the tree falling when I brought it down to the place of the dead. It went to join those who have gone down to the grave. Then all the trees of Eden and the best trees of Lebanon, all the well-watered trees, were comforted in the place of the dead below the earth. ¹⁷These trees had also gone down with the great tree to the place of the dead. They joined those who were killed in war and those among the nations who had lived under the great tree's shade.

¹⁸" 'So no tree in Eden is equal to you, Egypt, in greatness and honor, but you will go down to join the trees of Eden in the place below the earth. You will lie among unclean*d* people, with those who were killed in war.

" 'This is about the king of Egypt and all his people, says the Lord GOD.' "

A Funeral Song

32 It was in the twelfth year of our captivity, in the twelfth month, on the first day of the month. The LORD spoke his word to me, saying: ²"Human, sing a funeral song about the king of Egypt. Say to him:
'You are like a young lion among the nations.
You are like a crocodile in the seas.
You splash around in your streams
and stir up the water with your feet,
making the rivers muddy.

³" 'This is what the Lord GOD says:
I will spread my net over you,
and I will use a large group of people
to pull you up in my net.
⁴Then I will throw you on the land
dropping you onto the ground.
I will let the birds of the sky rest on you
and all the animals of the earth eat you
until they are full.

⁵I will scatter your flesh on the mountains
and fill the valleys with what is left of you.
⁶I will drench the land with your flowing
blood
as far as the mountains,
and the ravines will be full of your flesh.
⁷When I make you disappear,
I will cover the sky and make the stars
dark.
I will cover the sun with a cloud,
and the moon will not shine.
⁸I will make all the shining lights in the sky
become dark over you;
I will bring darkness over your land,
says the Lord GOD.
⁹I will cause many people to be afraid
when I bring you as a captive into other
nations,
to lands you have not known.
¹⁰I will cause many people to be shocked about
you.
Their kings will tremble with fear because
of you
when I swing my sword in front of them.
They will shake every moment
on the day you fall;
each king will be afraid for his own life.

¹¹" 'So this is what the Lord GOD says:
The sword of the king of Babylon
will attack you.
¹²I will cause your people to fall
by the swords of mighty soldiers,
the most terrible in the world.
They will destroy the pride of Egypt
and all its people.
¹³I will also destroy all Egypt's cattle
which live alongside much water.
The foot of a human will not stir the water,
and the hoofs of cattle will not muddy it
anymore.
¹⁴So I will let the Egyptians' water become
clear.
I will cause their rivers to run as smoothly
as olive oil,
says the Lord GOD.
¹⁵When I make the land of Egypt empty
and take everything that is in the land,
when I destroy all those who live in Egypt,
then they will know that I am the LORD.'

¹⁶"This is the funeral song people will sing for Egypt. The women of the nations will sing it; they *will sing a funeral song for Egypt and all its* people, says the Lord GOD."

Egypt to Be Destroyed

¹⁷It was in the twelfth year of our captivity, on the fifteenth day of the month. The LORD spoke his word to me, saying: ¹⁸"Human, cry for the

people of Egypt. Bring down Egypt, together with the women of the powerful nations; bring them down to the place of the dead below the earth to join those who go to the place of the dead. ¹⁹Say to them: 'Are you more beautiful than others? Go lie down in death with those who are unclean.'^d ²⁰The Egyptians will fall among those killed in war. The sword is ready; the enemy will drag Egypt and all her people away. ²¹From the place of the dead the leaders of the mighty ones will speak about the king of Egypt and the nations which help him: 'The unclean, those killed in war, have come down here and lie dead.'

²²"Assyria and all its army lie dead there. The graves of their soldiers are all around. All were killed in war, ²³and their graves were put in the deepest parts of the place of the dead. Assyria's army lies around its grave. When they lived on earth, they frightened people, but now all of them have been killed in war.

²⁴"The nation of Elam is there with all its army around its grave. All of them were killed in war. They had frightened people on earth and were unclean, so they went down to the lowest parts of the place of the dead. They must carry their shame with those who have gone down to the place of the dead. ²⁵A bed has been made for Elam with all those killed in war. The graves of her soldiers are all around her. All Elam's people are unclean, killed in war. They frightened people when they lived on earth, but now they must carry their shame with those who have gone down to the place of the dead. Their graves are with the rest who were killed.

²⁶"Meshech and Tubal are there with the graves of all their soldiers around them. All of them are unclean and have been killed in war. They also frightened people when they lived on earth. ²⁷But they are not buried with the other soldiers who were killed in battle long ago, those who went with their weapons of war to the place of the dead. These soldiers had their swords laid under their heads and their shields on their bodies. These mighty soldiers used to frighten people when they lived on earth.

²⁸"You, king of Egypt, will be broken and lie among those who are unclean, who were killed in war.

²⁹"Edom is there also, with its kings and all its leaders. They were mighty, but now they lie in death with those killed in war, with those who are unclean, with those who have gone down to the place of the dead.

³⁰"All the rulers of the north and all the Sidonians are there. Their strength frightened people, but they have gone down in shame with those who were killed. They are unclean, lying with those killed in war. They carry their shame with those who have gone down to the place of the dead.

³¹"The king of Egypt and his army will see these who have been killed in war. Then he will be comforted for all his soldiers killed in war, says the Lord God. ³²I made people afraid of the king of Egypt while he lived on earth. But he and all his people will lie among those who are unclean, who were killed in war, says the Lord God."

Ezekiel Is Watchman for Israel

33 The Lord spoke his word to me, saying: ²"Human, speak to your people and say to them: 'Suppose I bring a war against a land. The people of the land may choose one of their men and make him their watchman. ³When he sees the enemy coming to attack the land, he will blow the trumpet and warn the people. ⁴If they hear the sound of the trumpet but do nothing, the enemy will come and kill them. They will be responsible for their own deaths. ⁵They heard the sound of the trumpet but didn't do anything. So they are to blame for their own deaths. If they had done something, they would have saved their own lives. ⁶But if the watchman sees the enemy coming to attack and does not blow the trumpet, the people will not be warned. Then if the enemy comes and kills any of them, they have died because of their own sin. But I will punish the watchman for their deaths.'

⁷"You, human, are the one I have made a watchman for Israel. If you hear a word from my mouth, you must warn them for me. ⁸Suppose I say to the wicked: 'Wicked people, you will surely die,' but you don't speak to warn the wicked to stop doing evil. Then they will die because they were sinners, but I will punish you for their deaths. ⁹But if you warn the wicked to stop doing evil and they do not stop, they will die because they were sinners. But you have saved your life.

¹⁰"So you, human, say to Israel: 'You have said: Surely our law-breaking and sins are hurting us. They will kill us. What can we do so we will live?' ¹¹Say to them: 'The Lord God says: As surely as I live, I do not want any who are wicked to die. I want them to stop doing evil and live. Stop! Stop your wicked ways! You don't want to die, do you, people of Israel?'

¹²"Human, say to your people: 'The goodness of those who do right will not save them when they sin. The evil of wicked people will not cause them to be punished if they stop doing it. If good people sin, they will not be able to live by the good they did earlier.' ¹³If I tell good people, "You will surely live," they might think they have done enough good and then do evil. Then none of the good things they did will be remembered. They will die because of the evil they have done. ¹⁴Or,

if I say to the wicked people, "You will surely die," they may stop sinning and do what is right and honest. ¹⁵For example, they may return what somebody gave them as a promise to repay a loan, or pay back what they stole. If they live by the rules that give life and do not sin, then they will surely live, and they will not die. ¹⁶They will not be punished for any of their sins. They now do what is right and fair, so they will surely live.

¹⁷"Your people say: 'The way of the Lord is not fair.' But it is their own ways that are not fair. ¹⁸When the good people stop doing good and do evil, they will die for their evil. ¹⁹But when the wicked stop doing evil and do what is right and fair, they will live. ²⁰You still say: 'The way of the Lord is not fair.' Israel, I will judge all of you by your own ways."

The Fall of Jerusalem Explained

²¹It was in the twelfth year of our captivity, on the fifth day of the tenth month. A person who had escaped from Jerusalem came to me and said, "Jerusalem has been captured." ²²Now I had felt the power of the Lord on me the evening before. He had made me able to talk again before this person came to me. I could speak; I was not without speech anymore.

²³Then the Lord spoke his word to me, saying: ²⁴"Human, people who live in the ruins in the land of Israel are saying: 'Abraham was only one person, yet he was given the land as his own. Surely the land has been given to us, who are many, as our very own.' ²⁵So say to them: 'This is what the Lord God says: You eat meat with the blood still in it, you ask your idols for help, and you murder people. Should you then have the land as your very own? ²⁶You depend on your sword and do terrible things which I hate. Each of you has sexual relations with his neighbor's wife. So should you have the land?'

²⁷"Say to them: 'This is what the Lord God says: As surely as I live, those who are among the city ruins in Israel will be killed in war. I will cause those who live in the country to be eaten by wild animals. People hiding in the strongholds*d* and caves will die of disease. ²⁸I will make the land an empty desert. The people's pride in the land's power will end. The mountains of Israel will become empty so that no one will pass through them. ²⁹They will know that I am the Lord when I make the land an empty desert because of the things they have done that I hate.'

³⁰"But as for you, human, your people are talking about you by the walls and in the doorways of houses. They say to each other: 'Come now, and hear the message from the Lord.' ³¹So they come to you in crowds as if they were really ready to listen. They sit in front of you as if they were

my people and hear your words, but they will not obey them. With their mouths they tell me they love me, but their hearts desire their selfish profits. ³²To your people you are nothing more than a singer who sings love songs and has a beautiful voice and plays a musical instrument well. They hear your words, but they will not obey them.

³³"When this comes true, and it surely will happen, then the people will know that a prophet*d* has been among them."

The Leaders Are like Shepherds

34 The Lord spoke his word to me, saying: ²"Human, prophesy*d* against the leaders of Israel, who are like shepherds. Prophesy and say to them: 'This is what the Lord God says: How terrible it will be for the shepherds of Israel who feed only themselves! Why don't the shepherds feed the flock? ³You eat the milk curds, and you clothe yourselves with the wool. You kill the fat sheep, but you do not feed the flock. ⁴You have not made the weak strong. You have not healed the sick or put bandages on those that were hurt. You have not brought back those who strayed away or searched for the lost. But you have ruled the sheep with cruel force. ⁵The sheep were scattered, because there was no shepherd, and they became food for every wild animal. ⁶My flock wandered over all the mountains and on every high hill. They were scattered all over the face of the earth, and no one searched or looked for them.

⁷"'So, you shepherds, hear the word of the Lord. This is what the Lord God says: ⁸As surely as I live, my flock has been caught and eaten by all the wild animals, because the flock has no shepherd. The shepherds did not search for my flock. No, they fed themselves instead of my flock. ⁹So, you shepherds, hear the word of the Lord. ¹⁰This is what the Lord God says: I am against the shepherds. I will blame them for what has happened to my sheep and will not let them tend the flock anymore. Then the shepherds will stop feeding themselves, and I will take my flock from their mouths so they will no longer be their food.

¹¹"'This is what the Lord God says: I, myself,

will search for my sheep and take care of them. ¹²As a shepherd takes care of his scattered flock when it is found, I will take care of my sheep. I will save them from all the places where they were scattered on a cloudy and dark day. ¹³I will bring them out from the nations and gather them from the countries. I will bring them to their own land and pasture them on the mountains of Israel, in the ravines, and in all the places where people live in the land. ¹⁴I will feed them in a good pasture, and they will eat grass on the high mountains of Israel. They will lie down on good ground where they eat grass, and they will eat in rich grassland on the mountains of Israel. ¹⁵I will feed my flock and lead them to rest, says the Lord God. ¹⁶I will search for the lost, bring back those that strayed away, put bandages on those that were hurt, and make the weak strong. But I will destroy those sheep that are fat and strong. I will tend the sheep with fairness.

¹⁷" 'This is what the Lord God says: As for you, my flock, I will judge between one sheep and another, between the male sheep and the male goats. ¹⁸Is it not enough for you to eat grass in the good land? Must you crush the rest of the grass with your feet? Is it not enough for you to drink clear water? Must you make the rest of the water muddy with your feet? ¹⁹Must my flock eat what you crush, and must they drink what you make muddy with your feet?

²⁰" 'So this is what the Lord God says to them: I, myself, will judge between the fat sheep and the thin sheep. ²¹You push with your side and with your shoulder, and you knock down all the weak sheep with your horns until you have forced them away. ²²So I will save my flock; they will not be hurt anymore. I will judge between one sheep and another. ²³Then I will put over them one shepherd, my servant David. He will feed them and tend them and be their shepherd. ²⁴Then I,

Abused Privileges

Jenny Carlsen felt honored to be selected for the Vocal Ensemble, a special choir at her school. The group was invited to compete at the state music conference, held at a hotel. After the performance, the judges raved and gave the group top honors. Jenny felt proud to be a member of the group.

The choir director gave the singers some free time before returning home. Many of them felt pretty rowdy. How could they have fun?

First, they tried monopolizing the elevators and escalators. Jenny joined in.

They began shouting and screaming, disrupting others who had come for the conference. Jenny did too.

Some invaded the hotel pharmacy, where one member was kicked out after fooling around with a pair of crutches. Others dumped ash trays on the floor.

Finally, the hotel manager demanded to see the director. When the director learned what was going on, she discontinued the Vocal Ensemble on the spot. "I gave you free time as a reward for performing well," she said angrily, "but you selfishly violated my trust and other people's rights."

Now Jenny is not so proud to have been a part of the Ensemble. "It's a memory that you wish wasn't a memory," she says.

Like the members of the Vocal Ensemble, God's people receive special honors and privileges. When God promised special gifts for his people in **Ezekiel 34:11–24**, he also warned them not to selfishly abuse them.

■ What do this passage and Jenny's story have to say about selfishness?
■ What gifts has God given you that you must be careful not to selfishly abuse?

CONSIDER...
■ drawing four circles on a sheet of paper, one each for family, time, money, and friends. In each circle, list one way you can be less selfish this coming week, and then do all four ideas.
■ asking forgiveness from someone whose trust you've broken or with whom you've acted selfishly.

FOR MORE, SEE...
■ Exodus 16:11–21 (p. 74)   ■ 1 Corinthians 11:20–22 (p. 1181)
■ Mark 12:1–12 (p. 987)

the LORD, will be their God, and my servant David will be a ruler among them. I, the LORD, have spoken.

25" 'I will make an agreement of peace with my sheep and will remove harmful animals from the land. Then the sheep will live safely in the desert and sleep in the woods. 26I will bless them and let them live around my hill. I will cause the rains to come when it is time; there will be showers to bless them. 27Also the trees in the countryside will give their fruit, and the land will give its harvest. And the sheep will be safe on their land. Then they will know that I am the LORD when I break the bars of their captivity and save them from the power of those who made them slaves. 28They will not be led captive by the nations again. The wild animals will not eat them, but they will live safely, and no one will make them afraid. 29I will give them a place famous for its good crops, so they will no longer suffer from hunger in the land. They will not suffer the insults of other nations anymore. 30Then they will know that I, the LORD their God, am with them. The nation of Israel will know that they are my people, says the Lord GOD. 31You, my human sheep, are the sheep I care for, and I am your God, says the Lord GOD.' "

Prophecy Against Edom

35 The LORD spoke his word to me, saying: 2"Human, look toward Edom and prophesy*d* against it. 3Say to it: 'This is what the Lord GOD says: I am against you, Edom. I will stretch out my hand against you and make you an empty desert. 4I will destroy your cities, and you will become empty. Then you will know that I am the LORD.

5" 'You have always been an enemy of Israel. You let them be defeated in war when they were in trouble at the time of their final punishment. 6So the Lord GOD says, as surely as I live, I will let you be murdered. Murder will chase you. Since you did not hate murdering people, murder will chase you. 7I will make Edom an empty ruin and destroy everyone who goes in or comes out of it. 8I will fill its mountains with those who are killed. Those killed in war will fall on your hills, in your valleys, and in all your ravines. 9I will make you a ruin forever; no one will live in your cities. Then you will know that I am the LORD.

10" 'You said, "These two nations, Israel and Judah, and these two lands will be ours. We will take them for our own." But the LORD was there. 11So this is what the Lord GOD says: As surely as I live, I will treat you just as you treated them. You were angry and jealous because you hated them. So I will punish you and show the Israelites who I am. 12Then you will know that I, the LORD, have heard all your insults against the mountains of Israel. You said, "They have been ruined. They

have been given to us to eat." 13You have not stopped your proud talk against me. I have heard you. 14This is what the Lord GOD says: All the earth will be happy when I make you an empty ruin. 15You were happy when the land of Israel was ruined, but I will do the same thing to you. Mount Seir and all Edom, you will become an empty ruin. Then you will know that I am the LORD.' "

Israel to Come Home

36 "Human, prophesy*d* to the mountains of Israel and say: 'Mountains of Israel, hear the word of the LORD. 2This is what the Lord GOD says: The enemy has said about you, "Now the old places to worship gods have become ours." ' 3So prophesy and say: 'This is what the Lord GOD says: They have made you an empty ruin and have crushed you from all around. So you became a possession of the other nations. People have talked and whispered against you. 4So, mountains of Israel, hear the word of the Lord GOD. The Lord GOD speaks to the mountains, hills, ravines, and valleys, to the empty ruins and abandoned cities that have been robbed and laughed at by the other nations. 5This is what the Lord GOD says: I speak in hot anger against the other nations. I speak against the people of Edom, who took my land for themselves with joy and with hate in their hearts. They forced out the people and took their pastureland.' 6So prophesy about the land of Israel and say to the mountains, hills, ravines, and valleys: 'This is what the Lord GOD says: I speak in my jealous anger, because you have suffered the insults of the nations. 7So this is what the Lord GOD says: I promise that the nations around you will also have to suffer insults.

8" 'But you, mountains of Israel, will grow branches and fruit for my people, who will soon come home. 9I am concerned about you; I am on your side. You will be plowed, and seed will be planted in you. 10I will increase the number of people who live on you, all the people of Israel. The cities will have people living in them, and the ruins will be rebuilt. 11I will increase the number of people and animals living on you. They will grow and have many young. You will have people living on you as you did before, and I will make you better off than at the beginning. Then you will know that I am the LORD. 12I will cause my people Israel to walk on you and own you, and you will belong to them. You will never again take their children away from them.

13" 'This is what the Lord GOD says: People say about you, "You eat people and take children from your nation." 14But you will not eat people anymore or take away the children, says the Lord GOD. 15I will not make you listen to insults from the nations anymore; you will not suffer shame from them anymore. You will not cause your nation to fall anymore, says the Lord God.' "

The Lord Acts for Himself

[16]The Lord spoke his word to me again, saying: [17]"Human, when the nation of Israel was living in their own land, they made it unclean[d] by their ways and the things they did. Their ways were like a woman s uncleanness in her time of monthly bleeding. [18]So I poured out my anger against them, because they murdered in the land and because they made the land unclean with their idols. [19]I scattered them among the nations, and they were spread through the countries. I punished them for how they lived and what they did. [20]They dishonored my holy name in the nations where they went. The nations said about them: 'These are the people of the Lord, but they had to leave the land which he gave them.' [21]But I had concern for my holy name, which the nation of Israel had dishonored among the nations where they went.

[22]"So say to the people of Israel, 'This is what the Lord God says: Israel, I am going to act, but not for your sake. I will do something to help my holy name, which you have dishonored among the nations where you went. [23]I will prove the holiness of my great name, which has been dishonored among the nations. You have dishonored it among these nations, but the nations will know that I am the Lord when I prove myself holy before their eyes, says the Lord God.

[24]" 'I will take you from the nations and gather you out of all the lands and bring you back into your own land. [25]Then I will sprinkle clean water on you, and you will be clean. I will cleanse you from all your uncleanness and your idols. [26]Also, I will teach you to respect me completely, and I will put a new way of thinking inside you. I will take out the stubborn hearts of stone from your bodies, and I will give you obedient hearts of flesh. [27]I will put my Spirit[d] inside you and help you live by my rules and carefully obey my laws. [28]You will live in the land I gave to your ancestors, and you will be my people, and I will be your God. [29]So I will save you from all your uncleanness. I will command the grain to come and grow; I will not allow a time of hunger to hurt you. [30]I will increase the harvest of the field so you will never again suffer shame among the nations because of hunger. [31]Then you will remember your evil ways and actions that were not good, and you will hate yourselves because of your sins and your terrible acts that I hate. [32]I want you to know that I am not going to do this for your sake, says the Lord God. Be ashamed and embarrassed about your ways, Israel.

[33]" 'This is what the Lord God says: This is what will happen on the day I cleanse you from all your sins: I will cause the cities to have people living in them again, and the destroyed places will be rebuilt. [34]The empty land will be plowed so it will no longer be a ruin for everyone who passes by to see. [35]They will say, "This land was ruined, but now it has become like the garden of Eden. The cities were destroyed, empty, and ruined, but now they are protected and have people living in them." [36]Then those nations still around you will know that I, the Lord, have rebuilt what was destroyed and have planted what was empty. I, the Lord, have spoken, and I will do it.'

[37]"This is what the Lord God says: I will let myself be asked by the people of Israel to do this for them again: I will make their people grow in number like a flock. [38]They will be as many as the flocks brought to Jerusalem during her holy feasts. Her ruined cities will be filled with flocks of people. Then they will know that I am the Lord."

The Vision of Dry Bones

37 I felt the power of the Lord on me, and he brought me out by the Spirit[d] of the Lord and put me down in the middle of a valley. It was full of bones. [2]He led me around among the bones, and I saw that there were many bones in the valley and that they were very dry. [3]Then he asked me, "Human, can these bones live?"

I answered, "Lord God, only you know."

[4]He said to me, "Prophesy[d] to these bones and say to them, 'Dry bones, hear the word of the Lord. [5]This is what the Lord God says to the bones: I will cause breath to enter you so you will come to life. [6]I will put muscles on you and flesh on you and cover you with skin. Then I will put breath in you so you will come to life. Then you will know that I am the Lord.' "

[7]So I prophesied as I was commanded. While I prophesied, there was a noise and a rattling. The bones came together, bone to bone. [8]I looked and saw muscles come on the bones, and flesh grew, and skin covered the bones. But there was no breath in them.

[9]Then he said to me, "Prophesy to the wind.[n] Prophesy, human, and say to the wind, 'This is what the Lord God says: Wind, come from the four winds, and breathe on these people who were killed so they can come back to life.' " [10]So I prophesied as the Lord commanded me. And the breath came into them, and they came to life and stood on their feet, a very large army.

[11]Then he said to me, "Human, these bones are like all the people of Israel. They say, 'Our bones are dried up, and our hope has gone. We are destroyed.' [12]So, prophesy and say to them, 'This is

---

wind This Hebrew word could also mean "breath" or "spirit."

what the Lord GOD says: My people, I will open your graves and cause you to come up out of your graves. Then I will bring you into the land of Israel. 13My people, you will know that I am the LORD when I open your graves and cause you to come up from them. 14And I will put my Spirit inside you, and you will come to life. Then I will put you in your own land. And you will know that I, the LORD, have spoken and done it, says the LORD.' "

Judah and Israel Back Together

15The LORD spoke his word to me, saying, 16"Human, take a stick and write on it, 'For Judah and all the Israelites with him.' Then take another stick and write on it, 'The stick of Ephraim, for Joseph and all the Israelites with him.' 17Then join them together into one stick so they will be one in your hand.

18"When your people say to you, 'Explain to us what you mean by this,' 19say to them, 'This is what the Lord GOD says: I will take the stick for Joseph and the tribes*d* of Israel with him, which is in the hand of Ephraim, and I will put it with the stick of Judah. I will make them into one stick, and they will be one in my hand.' 20Hold the sticks on which you wrote these names in your hand so the people can see them. 21Say to the people, 'This is what the Lord GOD says: I am going to take the people of Israel from among the nations where they have gone. I will gather them from all around and bring them into their own land. 22I will make them one nation in the land, on the mountains of Israel. One king will rule all of them. They will never again be two nations; they will not be divided into two kingdoms anymore. 23They will not continue to make themselves unclean*d* by their idols, their statues of gods

DISCOURAGEMENT

God Is Here

Todd Petracek thought his relationship with Erin Chatham was over. First, he had acted like a jerk by often teasing her past the point of it being funny. Then he wouldn't apologize. Worse, he wouldn't even admit he had done anything wrong. Each time they talked, things seemed to get worse.

Finally, confused and hurt, Erin told Todd she hated him. She said she didn't think she could ever respect or trust him again.

By the time Todd got home that night, he wondered if they would ever speak again. He did the only thing he could think to do in such a discouraging situation: He prayed. Todd asked God to help him with what was left of his friendship with Erin.

Todd believes God answered his prayer. He believes God helped Erin call him the next night, to ask if they could get together and talk. And God helped Erin and Todd both see the situation more clearly.

They realized that Todd was afraid of getting too close to Erin, since they would soon be leaving for colleges three thousand miles apart. So he had acted as he did as a way of pulling away from her.

God helped Todd to be sorry for his actions, and he helped Erin to forgive Todd. Now, they are good friends, at peace with each other.

When a situation seems discouraging, there's still hope in God. In time, and with prayer, God will use your discouragements to help you grow and to help you know him better. That's the lesson God taught Todd and Erin. It's also the lesson in **Ezekiel 37:1–14**.

■ What are the similarities between God's actions with Todd and Erin and God's actions in this passage?

■ In what ways might God respond to your prayers in times that seem hopeless?

CONSIDER . . .

■ calling someone who is discouraged and inviting him or her out for a Coke.

■ writing "I can do all things through Christ, because he gives me strength" (Philippians *4:13, p. 1235) on credit-card size pieces of paper. Then have them laminated. Keep* one for yourself, and give others to discouraged people.

FOR MORE, SEE . . .

■ Psalm 121 (p. 554)
■ John 11:1–44 (p. 1076)
■ Ephesians 2:1–10 (p. 1219)

which I hate, or by their sins. I will save them from all the ways they sin and turn against me, and I will make them clean. Then they will be my people, and I will be their God.

²⁴" 'My servant David will be their king, and they will all have one shepherd. They will live by my rules and obey my laws. ²⁵They will live on the land I gave to my servant Jacob, the land in which your ancestors lived. They will all live on the land forever: they, their children, and their grandchildren. David my servant will be their king forever. ²⁶I will make an agreement of peace with them, an agreement that continues forever. I will put them in their land and make them grow in number. Then I will put my Temple[d] among them forever. ²⁷The place where I live will be with them. I will be their God, and they will be my people. ²⁸When my Temple is among them forever, the nations will know that I, the Lord, make Israel holy.' "

Prophecy Against Gog

38 The Lord spoke his word to me, saying, ²"Human, look toward Gog of the land of Magog, the chief ruler of the nations of Meshech and Tubal. Prophesy[d] against him ³and say, 'The Lord God says this: I am against you, Gog,

> ✹ **SIDELIGHT:** Gog and Magog sound like they might be creatures from a strange horror movie (Ezekiel 38:2). Actually, they are the names of an unknown king and nation hostile to Israel. Wonder if their soldiers looked like giant lizards?

chief ruler of Meshech and Tubal. ⁴I will turn you around and put hooks in your jaws. And I will bring you out with all your army, horses, and horsemen, all of whom will be dressed in beautiful uniforms. They will be a large army with large and small shields and all having swords. ⁵Persia, Cush, and Put will be with them, all of them having shields and helmets. ⁶There will also be Gomer with all its troops and the nation of Togarmah from the far north with all its troops — many nations with you.

⁷" 'Be prepared. Be prepared, you and all the armies that have come together to make you their commander. ⁸After a long time you will be called for service. After those years you will come into a land that has been rebuilt from war. The people in the land will have been gathered from many nations to the mountains of Israel, which were empty for a long time. These people were brought out from the nations, and they will all be living in safety. ⁹You will come like a storm. You, all your

troops, and the many nations with you will be like a cloud covering the land.

¹⁰" 'This is what the Lord God says: At that time ideas will come into your mind, and you will think up an evil plan. ¹¹You will say, "I will march against a land of towns without walls. I will attack those who are at rest and live in safety. All of them live without city walls or gate bars or gates. ¹²I will capture treasures and take loot. I will turn my power against the rebuilt ruins that now have people living in them. I will attack these people who have been gathered from the nations, who have become rich with farm animals and property, who live at the center of the world." ¹³Sheba, Dedan, and the traders of Tarshish, with all its villages, will say to you, "Did you come to capture treasure? Did you bring your troops together to take loot? Did you bring them to carry away silver and gold and to take away farm animals and property?" '

¹⁴"So prophesy, human, and say to Gog, 'This is what the Lord God says: Now that my people Israel are living in safety, you will know about it. ¹⁵You will come with many people from your place in the far north. You will have a large group with you, a mighty army, all riding on horses. ¹⁶You will attack my people Israel like a cloud that covers the land. This will happen in the days to come when I bring you against my land. Gog, then the nations will know me when they see me prove how holy I am in what I do through you.

¹⁷" 'This is what the Lord God says: You are the one about whom I spoke in past days. I spoke through my servants, the prophets of Israel, who prophesied for many years that I would bring you against them. ¹⁸This is what will happen: On the day Gog attacks the land of Israel, I will become very angry, says the Lord God. ¹⁹With jealousy and great anger I tell you that at that time there will surely be a great earthquake in Israel. ²⁰The fish of the sea, the birds of the sky, the wild animals, everything that crawls on the ground, and all the people on the earth will shake with fear before me. Also the mountains will be thrown down, the cliffs will fall, and every wall will fall to the ground. ²¹Then I will call for a war against Gog on all my mountains, says the Lord God. Everyone's sword will attack the soldier next to him. ²²I will punish Gog with disease and death. I will send a heavy rain with hailstones and burning sulfur on Gog, his army, and the many nations with him. ²³Then I will show how great I am. I will show my holiness, and I will make myself known to the many nations that watch. Then they will know that I am the Lord.'

The Death of Gog and His Army

39 "Human, prophesy[d] against Gog and say, 'This is what the Lord God says: I am against you, Gog, chief ruler of Meshech and Tubal. [2]I will turn you around and lead you. I will bring you from the far north and send you to attack the mountains of Israel. [3]I will knock your bow out of your left hand and throw down your arrows from your right hand. [4]You, all your troops, and the nations with you will fall dead on the mountains of Israel. I will let you be food for every bird that eats meat and for every wild animal. [5]You will lie fallen on the ground, because I have spoken, says the Lord God. [6]I will send fire on Magog and those who live in safety on the coastlands. Then they will know that I am the Lord.

[7]" 'I will make myself known among my people Israel, and I will not let myself be dishonored anymore. Then the nations will know that I am the Lord, the Holy One in Israel. [8]It is coming! It will happen, says the Lord God. The time I talked about is coming.

[9]" 'Then those who live in the cities of Israel will come out and make fires with the enemy's weapons. They will burn them, both large and small shields, bows and arrows, war clubs, and spears. They will use the weapons to burn in their fires for seven years. [10]They will not need to take wood from the field or chop firewood from the forests, because they will make fires with the weapons. In this way they will take the treasures of those who took their treasures; they will take the loot of those who took their loot, says the Lord God.

[11]" 'At that time I will give Gog a burial place in Israel, in the Valley of the Travelers, east of the Dead Sea.[d] It will block the road for travelers. Gog and all his army will be buried there, so people will call it The Valley of Gog's Army.

[12]" 'The people of Israel will be burying them for seven months to make the land clean[d] again. [13]All the people in the land will bury them, and they will be honored on the day of my victory, says the Lord God.

[14]" 'The people of Israel will choose men to work through the land to make it clean. Along with others, they will bury Gog's soldiers still lying dead on the ground. After the seven months are finished, they will still search. [15]As they go through the land, anyone who sees a human bone is to put a marker by it. The sign will stay there until the gravediggers bury the bone in The Valley of Gog's Army. [16]A city will be there named Hamonah. So they will make the land clean again.'

[17]"Human, this is what the Lord God says: Speak to every kind of bird and wild animal: 'Come together, come! Come together from all around to my sacrifice, a great sacrifice which I will prepare for you on the mountains of Israel. Eat flesh and drink blood! [18]You are to eat the flesh of the mighty and drink the blood of the rulers of the earth as if they were fat animals from Bashan: male sheep, lambs, goats, and bulls. [19]You are to eat and drink from my sacrifice which I have prepared for you, eating fat until you are full and drinking blood until you are drunk. [20]At my table you are to eat until you are full of horses and riders, mighty men and all kinds of soldiers,' says the Lord God.

[21]"I will show my glory among the nations. All the nations will see my power when I punish them. [22]From that time onward the people of Israel will know that I am the Lord their God. [23]The nations will know Israel was taken away captive because they turned against me. So I turned away from them and handed them over to their enemies until all of them died in war. [24]Because of their uncleanness[d] and their sins, I punished them and turned away from them.

[25]"So this is what the Lord God says: Now I will bring the people of Jacob back from captivity, and I will have mercy on the whole nation of Israel. I will not let them dishonor me. [26]The people will forget their shame and how they rejected me when they live again in safety on their own land with no one to make them afraid. [27]I will bring the people back from other lands and gather them from the lands of their enemies. So I will use my people to show many nations that I am holy. [28]Then my people will know that I am the Lord their God, because I sent them into captivity among the nations, but then I brought them back to their own land, leaving no one behind. [29]I will not turn away from them anymore, because I will put my Spirit[d] into the people of Israel, says the Lord God."

SIDELIGHT: Ezekiel's final vision is packed with measurements for a restored temple in Jerusalem (chapters 40–48). Its total floor space was about eight hundred sixty-one square feet, which is about the size of three large bedrooms today.

The New Temple

40 It was the twenty-fifth year of our captivity, at the beginning of the year, on the tenth day of the month. It was in the fourteenth year after Jerusalem was captured. On that same day I felt the power of the Lord, and he brought me to Jerusalem. [2]In the visions of God he brought me to the land of Israel and put me down on a very high mountain. On the south of the mountain there were some buildings that looked like a city. [3]He took me closer to the buildings, and I saw a man who looked as if he were made of bronze, standing in the gateway. He had a cord made of linen and a stick in his hand, both for measuring. [4]The man said to me, "Human, look with your eyes and hear with your ears. Pay attention to all that I will show you, because that's why you have been brought here. Tell the people of Israel all that you see."

The East Gateway

[5]I saw a wall that surrounded the Temple[d] area. The measuring stick in the man's hand was ten and one-half feet long. So the man measured the wall, which was ten and one-half feet thick and ten and one-half feet high.

[6]Then the man went to the east gateway. He went up its steps and measured the opening of the gateway. It was ten and one-half feet deep. [7]The rooms for the guards were ten and one-half feet long and ten and one-half feet wide. The walls that came out between the guards' rooms were about nine feet thick. The opening of the gateway next to the porch that faced the Temple was ten and one-half feet deep.

[8]Then the man measured the porch of the gateway. [9]It was about fourteen feet deep, and its side walls were three and one-half feet thick. The porch of the gateway faced the Temple.

[10]On each side of the east gateway were three rooms, which measured the same on each side. The walls between each room were the same thickness. [11]The man measured the width of the entrance to the gateway, which was seventeen and one-half feet wide. The width of the gate was about twenty-three feet. [12]And there was a low wall about twenty-one inches high in front of each room. The rooms were ten and one-half feet on each side. [13]The man measured the gateway from the roof of one room to the roof of the opposite room. It was about forty-four feet from one door to the opposite door. [14]The man also measured the porch, which was about thirty-five feet wide. The courtyard was around the porch. [15]From the front of the outer side of the gateway to the front of the porch of the inner side of the gateway was eighty-seven and one-half feet. [16]The rooms and porch had small windows on both sides. The windows were narrower on the side facing the gateway. Carvings of palm trees were on each side wall of the rooms.

The Outer Courtyard

[17]Then the man brought me into the outer courtyard where I saw rooms and a pavement of stones all around the court. Thirty rooms were along the edge of the paved walkway. [18]The pavement ran alongside the gates and was as deep as the gates were wide. This was the lower pavement. [19]Then the man measured from the outer wall to the inner wall. The outer court between

these two walls was one hundred seventy-five feet on the east and on the north.

The North Gateway

[20]The man measured the length and width of the north gateway leading to the outer courtyard. [21]Its three rooms on each side, its inner walls, and its porch measured the same as the first gateway. It was eighty-seven and one-half feet long and forty-four feet wide. [22]Its windows, porch, and carvings of palm trees measured the same as the east gateway. Seven steps went up to the gateway, and the gateway's porch was at the inner end. [23]The inner courtyard had a gateway across from the northern gateway like the one on the east. The man measured it and found it was one hundred seventy-five feet from inner gateway to outer gateway.

The South Gateway

[24]Then the man led me south where I saw a gateway facing south. He measured its inner walls and its porch, and they measured the same as the other gateways. [25]The gateway and its porch had windows all around like the other gateways. It was eighty-seven and one-half feet long and forty-four feet wide. [26]Seven steps went up to this gateway. Its porch was at the inner end, and it had carvings of palm trees on its inner walls. [27]The inner courtyard had a gateway on its south side. The man measured from gate to gate on the south side, which was one hundred seventy-five feet.

The Inner Courtyard

[28]Then the man brought me through the south gateway into the inner courtyard. The inner south gateway measured the same as the gateways in the outer wall. [29]The inner south gateway's rooms, inner walls, and porch measured the same as the gateways in the outer wall. There were windows all around the gateway and its porch. The gateway was eighty-seven and one-half feet long and forty-four feet wide. [30]Each porch of each inner gateway was about forty-four feet long and about nine feet wide. [31]The inner south gateway's porch faced the outer courtyard. Carvings of palm trees were on its side walls, and its stairway had eight steps.

[32]The man brought me into the inner courtyard on the east side. He measured the inner east gateway, and it was the same as the other gateways. [33]The inner east gateway's rooms, inside walls, and porch measured the same as the other gateways. Windows were all around the gateway and its porch. The inner east gateway was eighty-seven and one-half feet long and forty-four feet wide. [34]Its porch faced the outer courtyard. Carvings of palm trees were on its inner walls on each side, and its stairway had eight steps.

35Then the man brought me to the inner north gateway. He measured it, and it was the same as the other gateways. 36Its rooms, inner walls, and porch measured the same as the other gateways. There were windows all around the gateway, which was eighty-seven and one-half feet long and forty-four feet wide. 37Its porch faced the outer courtyard. Carvings of palm trees were on its inner walls on each side, and its stairway had eight steps.

Rooms for Preparing Sacrifices

38There was a room with a door that opened onto the porch of the inner north gateway. In this room the priests washed animals for the burnt offerings. 39There were two tables on each side of the porch, on which animals for burnt offerings, sin offerings, and penalty offerings were killed. 40Outside, by each side wall of the porch, at the entrance to the north gateway, were two more tables. 41So there were four tables inside the gateway, and four tables outside. In all there were eight tables on which the priests killed animals for sacrifices. 42There were four tables made of cut stone for the burnt offering. These tables were about three feet long, three feet wide, and about two feet high. On these tables the priests put their tools which they used to kill animals for burnt offerings and the other sacrifices. 43Double shelves three inches wide were put up on all the walls. The flesh for the offering was put on the tables.

The Priests' Rooms

44There were two rooms in the inner courtyard. One was beside the north gateway and faced south. The other room was beside the south gateway and faced north. 45The man said to me, "The room which faces south is for the priests who serve in the Temple*d* area, 46while the room that faces north is for the priests who serve at the altar. This second group of priests are descendants*d* of Zadok, the only descendants of Levi who can come near the LORD to serve him."

47The man measured the inner courtyard. It was a square — one hundred seventy-five feet long and one hundred seventy-five feet wide. The altar was in front of the Temple.

The Temple Porch

48The man brought me to the porch of the Temple*d* and measured each side wall of the porch. *Each was about nine feet thick. The doorway was* twenty-four and one-half feet wide. The side walls of the doorway were each about five feet wide. 49The porch was thirty-five feet long and twenty-one feet wide, with ten steps leading up to it. Pillars were by the side walls, one on each side of the entrance.

The Holy Place of the Temple

41 The man brought me to the Holy Place and measured its side walls, which were each ten and one-half feet thick. 2The entrance was seventeen and one-half feet wide. The walls alongside the entrance were each about nine feet wide. The man measured the Holy Place, which was seventy feet long and thirty-five feet wide.

3Then the man went inside and measured the side walls of the next doorway. Each was three and one-half feet thick. The doorway was ten and one-half feet wide, and the walls next to it were each more than twelve feet thick. 4Then the man measured the room at the end of the Holy Place. It was thirty-five feet long and thirty-five feet wide. The man said to me, "This is the Most Holy Place."

5Then the man measured the wall of the Temple,*d* which was ten and one-half feet thick. There were side rooms seven feet wide all around the Temple. 6The side rooms were on three different stories, each above the other, with thirty rooms on each story. All around the Temple walls there were ledges for the side rooms. The upper rooms rested on the ledges but were not attached to the Temple walls. 7The side rooms around the Temple were wider on each higher story, so rooms were wider on the top story. A stairway went up from the lowest story to the highest through the middle story.

8I also saw that the Temple had a raised base all around. Its edge was the foundation for the side rooms, and it was ten and one-half feet thick. 9The outer wall of the side rooms was about nine feet thick. There was an open area between the side rooms of the Temple 10and some other rooms. It was thirty-five feet wide and went all around the Temple. 11The side rooms had doors which led to the open area around the outside of the Temple. One door faced north, and the other faced south. The open area was about nine feet wide all around.

12The building facing the private area at the west side was one hundred twenty-two and one-half feet wide. The wall around the building was about nine feet thick and one hundred fifty-seven and one-half feet long.

13Then the man measured the Temple. It was one hundred seventy-five feet long. The private area, including the building and its walls, was in all one hundred seventy-five feet long. 14Also the *front of the Temple and the private area on its east* side were one hundred seventy-five feet wide.

15The man measured the length of the building facing the private area on the west side, and it was one hundred seventy-five feet from one wall to the other.

The Holy Place, the Most Holy Place, and the

outer porch [16]had wood panels on the walls. By the doorway, the Temple had wood panels on the walls. The wood covered all the walls from the floor up to the windows, [17]up to the part of the wall above the entrance.

All the walls inside the Most Holy Place and the Holy Place, and on the outside, in the porch, [18]had carvings of creatures with wings and palm trees. A palm tree was between each carved creature, and every creature had two faces. [19]One was a human face looking toward the palm tree on one side. The other was a lion's face looking toward the palm tree on the other side. They were carved all around the Temple walls. [20]From the floor to above the entrance, palm trees and creatures with wings were carved. The walls of the Holy Place [21]had square doorposts. In front of the Most Holy Place was something that looked like [22]an altar of wood. It was more than five feet high and three feet wide. Its corners, base, and sides were wood. The man said to me, "This is the table that is in the presence of the LORD." [23]Both the Holy Place and the Most Holy Place had double doors. [24]Each of the doors had two pieces that would swing open. [25]Carved on the doors of the Holy Place were palm trees and creatures with wings, like those carved on the walls. And there was a wood roof over the front Temple porch. [26]There were windows and palm trees on both side walls of the porch. The side rooms of the Temple were also covered by a roof over the stairway.

The Priests' Rooms

42 Then the man led me north out into the outer courtyard and to the rooms across from the private area and the building. [2]These rooms on the north side were one hundred seventy-five feet long and eighty-seven and one-half feet wide. [3]There was thirty-five feet of the inner courtyard between them and the Temple. On the other side, they faced the stone pavement of the outer courtyard. The rooms were built in three stories like steps and had balconies. [4]There was a path on the north side of the rooms, which was seventeen and one-half feet wide and one hundred seventy-five feet long. Doors led into the rooms from this path. [5]The top rooms were narrower, because the balconies took more space from them. The rooms on the first and second stories of the building were wider. [6]The rooms were on three stories. They did not have pillars like the pillars of the courtyards. So the top rooms were farther back than those on the first and second stories. [7]There was a wall outside parallel to the rooms and to the outer courtyard. It ran in front of the rooms for eighty-seven and one-half feet. [8]The row of rooms along the outer courtyard was eighty-seven and one-half feet long, and the

rooms that faced the Temple were about one hundred seventy-five feet long. [9]The lower rooms had an entrance on the east side so a person could enter them from the outer courtyard, [10]at the start of the wall beside the courtyard.

There were rooms on the south side, which were across from the private area and the building. [11]These rooms had a path in front of them. They were like the rooms on the north with the same length and width and the same doors. [12]The doors of the south rooms were like the doors of the north rooms. There was an entrance at the open end of a path beside the wall, so a person could enter at the east end.

[13]The man said to me, "The north and south rooms across from the private area are holy rooms. There the priests who go near the LORD will eat the most holy offerings. There they will put the most holy offerings: the grain offerings, sin offerings, and the penalty offerings, because the place is holy. [14]The priests who enter the Holy Place must leave their serving clothes there before they go into the outer courtyard, because these clothes are holy. After they put on other clothes, they may go to the part of the Temple area which is for the people."

Outside the Temple Area

[15]When the man finished measuring inside the Temple[d] area, he brought me out through the east gateway. He measured the area all around. [16]The man measured the east side with the measuring stick; it was eight hundred seventy-five feet by the measuring stick. [17]He measured the north side; it was eight hundred seventy-five feet by the measuring stick. [18]He measured the south side; it was eight hundred seventy-five feet by the measuring stick. [19]He went around to the west side; it measured eight hundred seventy-five feet by the measuring stick. [20]So he measured the Temple area on all four sides. The Temple area had a wall all around it that was eight hundred seventy-five feet long and eight hundred seventy-five feet wide. It separated what was holy from that which was not holy.

The Lord Among His People

43 Then the man led me to the outer east gateway, [2]and I saw the glory of the God of Israel coming from the east. It sounded like the roar of rushing water, and its brightness made the earth shine. [3]The vision I saw was like the vision I had seen when the LORD came to destroy the city and also like the vision I had seen by the Kebar River. I bowed facedown on the ground. [4]The glory of the LORD came into the Temple[d] area through the east gateway.

[5]Then the Spirit[d] picked me up and brought me into the inner courtyard. There I saw the LORD's

glory filling the Temple. ⁶As the man stood at my side, I heard someone speaking to me from inside the Temple. ⁷The voice from the Temple said to me, "Human, this is my throne and the place where my feet rest. I will live here among the Israelites forever. The people of Israel will not make my holy name unclean*d* again. Neither the people nor their kings will make it unclean with their sexual sins or with the dead bodies of their kings. ⁸The kings made my name unclean by putting their doorway next to my doorway, and their doorpost next to my doorpost so only a wall separated me from them. When they did their acts that I hate, they made my holy name unclean, and so I destroyed them in my anger. ⁹Now let them stop their sexual sins and take the dead bodies of their kings far away from me. Then I will live among them forever.

¹⁰"Human, tell the people of Israel about the Temple so they will be ashamed of their sins. Let them think about the plan of the Temple. ¹¹If they are ashamed of all they have done, let them know the design of the Temple and how it is built. Show them its exits and entrances, all its designs, and also all its rules and teachings. Write the rules as they watch so they will obey all the teachings and rules about the Temple. ¹²This is the teaching about the Temple: All the area around the top of the mountain is most holy. This is the teaching about the Temple.

The Altar

¹³"These are the measurements of the altar, using the measuring stick. The altar's gutter is twenty-one inches high and twenty-one inches wide, and its rim is about nine inches around its edge. And the altar is this tall: ¹⁴From the ground up to the lower ledge, it measures three and one-half feet. It is twenty-one inches wide. It measures seven feet from the smaller ledge to the larger ledge and is twenty-one inches wide. ¹⁵The place where the sacrifice is burned on the altar is seven feet high, with its four corners shaped like horns and reaching up above it. ¹⁶It is square, twenty-one feet long and twenty-one feet wide. ¹⁷The upper ledge is also square, twenty-four and one-half feet long and twenty-four and one-half feet wide. The rim around the altar is ten and one-half inches wide, and its gutter is twenty-one inches wide all around. Its steps are on the east side."

¹⁸Then the man said to me, "Human, this is what the Lord GOD says: These are the rules for the altar. When it is built, use these rules to offer burnt offerings and to sprinkle blood on it. ¹⁹You must give a young bull as a sin offering to the priests, the Levites who are from the family of Zadok and who come near me to serve me, says the Lord GOD. ²⁰Take some of the bull's blood and put it on the four corners of the altar, on the four corners of the ledge, and all around the rim. This is how you will make the altar pure and ready for God's service. ²¹Then take the bull for the sin offering and burn it in the proper place in the Temple*d* area, outside the Temple building.

²²"On the second day offer a male goat that has nothing wrong with it for a sin offering. The priests will make the altar pure and ready for God's service as they did with the young bull. ²³When you finish making the altar pure and ready, offer a young bull and a male sheep from the flock, which have nothing wrong with them. ²⁴You must offer them in the presence of the LORD, and the priests are to throw salt on them and offer them as a burnt offering to the LORD.

²⁵"You must prepare a goat every day for seven days as a sin offering. Also, the priests must prepare a young bull and male sheep from the flock, which have nothing wrong with them. ²⁶For seven days the priests are to make the altar pure and ready for God's service. Then they will give the altar to God. ²⁷After these seven days, on the eighth day, the priests must offer your burnt offerings and your fellowship offerings on the altar. Then I will accept you, says the Lord GOD."

The Outer East Gate

44 Then the man brought me back to the outer east gateway of the Temple*d* area, but the gate was shut. ²The LORD said to me, "This gate will stay shut; it will not be opened. No one may enter through it, because the LORD God of Israel has entered through it. So it must stay shut. ³Only the ruler himself may sit in the gateway to eat a meal in the presence of the LORD. He must enter through the porch of the gateway and go out the same way."

⁴Then the man brought me through the outer north gate to the front of the Temple. As I looked, I saw the glory of the LORD filling the Temple of the LORD, and I bowed facedown on the ground. ⁵The LORD said to me, "Human, pay attention. Use your eyes to see, and your ears to hear. See and hear everything I tell you about all the rules and teachings of the Temple of the LORD. Pay attention to the entrance to the Temple and to all the exits from the Temple area. ⁶Then speak to those who refuse to obey. Say to the people of Israel, 'This is what the Lord GOD says: Stop doing all your acts that I hate, Israel! ⁷You brought foreigners into my Holy Place who were not circumcised*d* in the flesh and had not given themselves to serving me. You dishonored my Temple when you offered me food, fat, and blood. You broke my agreement by all the things you did that I hate. ⁸You did not take care of my holy things yourselves but put foreigners in charge of my Temple. ⁹This is what the Lord GOD says: Foreigners who are not circumcised in flesh and who

do not give themselves to serving me may not enter my Temple. Not even a foreigner living among the people of Israel may enter.

10" 'But the Levites who stopped obeying me when Israel left me and who followed their idols must be punished for their sin. 11These Levites are to be servants in my Holy Place. They may guard the gates of the Temple and serve in the Temple area. They may kill the animals for the burnt offering and the sacrifices for the people. They may stand before the people to serve them. 12But these Levites helped the people worship their idols and caused the people of Israel to fall, so I make this promise: They will be punished for their sin, says the Lord God. 13They will not come near me to serve as priests, nor will they come near any of my holy things or the most holy offerings. But they will be made ashamed of the things they did that I hate. 14I will put them in charge of taking care of the Temple area, all the work that must be done in it.

15" 'But the priests who are Levites and descendants*d* of Zadok took care of my Holy Place when Israel left me, so they may come near to serve me. They may stand in my presence to offer me the fat and blood of the animals they sacrifice, says the Lord God. 16They are the only ones who may enter my Holy Place. Only they may come near my table to serve me and take care of the things I gave them to do.

17" 'When they enter the gates of the inner courtyard, they must wear linen robes. They must not wear wool to serve at the gates of the inner courtyard or in the Temple. 18They will wear linen turbans on their heads and linen underclothes. They will not wear anything that makes them perspire. 19When they go out into the outer courtyard to the people, they must take off their serving clothes before they go. They must leave these clothes in the holy rooms and put on other clothes. Then they will not let their holy clothes hurt the people.

20" 'They must not shave their heads or let their hair grow long but must keep the hair of their heads trimmed. 21None of the priests may drink wine when they enter the inner courtyard. 22The priests must not marry widows or divorced women. They may marry only virgins*d* from the people of Israel or widows of priests. 23They must teach my people the difference between what is holy and what is not holy. They must help my people know what is unclean*d* and what is clean.

24" 'In court they will act as judges. When they judge, they will follow my teachings. They must obey my laws and my rules at all my special feasts and keep my Sabbaths*d* holy.

25" 'They must not go near a dead person, making themselves unclean.*d* But they are allowed to make themselves unclean if the dead person is

their father, mother, son, daughter, brother, or a sister who has not married. 26After a priest has been made clean again, he must wait seven days. 27Then he may go into the inner courtyard to serve in the Temple, but he must offer a sin offering for himself, says the Lord God.

28" 'These are the rules about the priests and their property: They will have me instead of property. You will not give them any land to own in Israel; I am what they will own. 29They will eat the grain offerings, sin offerings, and penalty offerings. Everything Israel gives to me will be theirs. 30The best fruits of all the first harvests and all the special gifts offered to me will belong to the priests. You will also give to the priests the first part of your grain that you grind and so bring a blessing on your family. 31The priests must not eat any bird or animal that died a natural death or one that has been torn by wild animals.

The Land Is Divided

45 " 'When you divide the land for the Israelite tribes*d* by throwing lots,*d* you must give a part of the land to belong to the Lord. It will be about seven miles long and about six miles wide; all of this land will be holy. 2From this land, an area eight hundred seventy-five feet square will be for the Temple.*d* There will be an open space around the Temple that is eighty-seven and one-half feet wide. 3In the holy area you will measure a part about seven miles long and three miles wide, and in it will be the Most Holy Place. 4This holy part of the land will be for the priests who serve in the Temple, who come near to the Lord to serve him. It will be a place for the priests' houses and for the Temple. 5Another area about seven miles long and more than three miles wide will be for the Levites, who serve in the Temple area. It will belong to them so they will have cities in which to live.

6" 'You must give the city an area that is about one and one-half miles wide and about seven miles long, along the side of the holy area. It will belong to all the people of Israel.

7" 'The ruler will have land on both sides of the holy area and the city. On the west of the holy area, his land will reach to the Mediterranean Sea. On the east of the holy area, his land will reach to the eastern border. It will be as long as the land given to each tribe. 8Only this land will be the ruler's property in Israel. So my rulers will not be cruel to my people anymore, but they will let each tribe in the nation of Israel have its share of the land.

9" 'This is what the Lord God says: You have gone far enough, you rulers of Israel! Stop being cruel and hurting people, and do what is right and fair. Stop forcing my people out of their homes, says the Lord God. 10You must have honest scales, an honest dry measurement and an honest liquid measurement. [11]The dry measure and the liquid measure will be the same: The liquid measure will always be a tenth of a homer, [n] and the ephah will always be a tenth of a homer. The measurement they follow will be the homer. [12]The shekel [n] will be worth twenty gerahs, and a mina will be worth sixty shekels.

Offerings and Holy Days

[13]" 'This is the gift you should offer: a sixth of an ephah from every homer of wheat, and a sixth of an ephah from every homer of barley. [14]The amount of oil you are to offer is a tenth of a bath from each cor. (Ten baths make a homer and also make a cor.) [15]You should give one sheep from each flock of two hundred from the watering places of Israel. All these are to be offered for the grain offerings, burnt offerings, and fellowship offerings to remove sins so you will belong to God, says the Lord God. [16]All people in the land will give this special offering to the ruler of Israel. [17]It will be the ruler's responsibility to supply the burnt offerings, grain offerings, and drink offerings. These offerings will be given at the feasts, at the New Moons, [d] on the Sabbaths, [d] and at all the other feasts of Israel. The ruler will supply the sin offerings, grain offerings, and fellowship offerings to pay for the sins of Israel.

[18]" 'This is what the Lord God says: On the first day of the first month take a young bull that has nothing wrong with it. Use it to make the Temple [d] pure and ready for God's service. [19]The priest will take some of the blood from this sin offering and put it on the doorposts of the Temple, on the four corners of the ledge of the altar, and on the posts of the gate to the inner courtyard. [20]You will do the same thing on the seventh day of the month for anyone who has sinned by accident or without knowing it. This is how you make the Temple pure and ready for God's service.

Passover Feast Offerings

[21]" 'On the fourteenth day of the first month you will celebrate the Feast [d] of Passover. It will be a feast of seven days when you eat bread made without yeast. [22]On that day the ruler must offer a bull for himself and for all the people of the land as a sin offering. [23]During the seven days of the feast he must offer seven bulls and seven male sheep that have nothing wrong with them. They *will be burnt offerings to the Lord, which the* ruler will offer every day of the seven days of the feast. He must also offer a male goat every day as a sin offering. [24]The ruler must give as a grain

offering one-half bushel for each bull and one-half bushel for each sheep. He must give a gallon of olive oil for each half bushel.

[25]" 'Beginning on the fifteenth day of the seventh month, when you celebrate the Feast [d] of Shelters, the ruler will supply the same things for seven days: the sin offerings, burnt offerings, grain offerings, and the olive oil.

Rules for Worship

46 " 'This is what the Lord God says: The east gate of the inner courtyard will stay shut on the six working days, but it will be opened on the Sabbath [d] day and on the day of the New Moon. [d] [2]The ruler will enter from outside through the porch of the gateway and stand by the gatepost, while the priests offer the ruler's burnt offering and fellowship offering. The ruler will worship at the entrance of the gateway, and then he will go out. But the gate will not be shut until evening. [3]The people of the land will worship at the entrance of that gateway in the presence of the Lord on the Sabbaths and New Moons. [4]This is the burnt offering the ruler will offer to the Lord on the Sabbath day: six male lambs that have nothing wrong with them and a male sheep that has nothing wrong with it. [5]He must give a half-bushel grain offering with the male sheep, but he may give as much grain offering with the lambs as he pleases. He must also give a gallon of olive oil for each half bushel of grain. [6]On the day of the New Moon he must offer a young bull that has nothing wrong with it. He must also offer six lambs and a male sheep that have nothing wrong with them. [7]The ruler must give a half-bushel grain offering with the bull and one-half bushel with the male sheep. With the lambs, he may give as much grain as he pleases. But he must give a gallon of olive oil for each half bushel of grain. [8]When the ruler enters, he must go in through the porch of the gateway, and he must go out the same way.

[9]" 'When the people of the land come into the Lord's presence at the special feasts, those who enter through the north gate to worship must go out through the south gate. Those who enter through the south gate must go out through the north gate. They must not return the same way they entered; everyone must go out the opposite way. [10]The ruler will go in with the people when they go in and go out with them when they go *out.*

[11]" 'At the feasts and regular times of worship one-half bushel of grain must be offered with a young bull, and one-half bushel of grain must be

---

homer   The Hebrew word means "donkey-load." It measured about five dry bushels or one hundred seventy-five liquid quarts.
So an ephah was about one-half bushel, and a bath was about eighteen quarts.
shekel   In Ezekiel's time a shekel weighed about two-fifths of an ounce.

offered with a male sheep. But with an offering of lambs, the ruler may give as much grain as he pleases. He should give a gallon of olive oil for each half bushel of grain. [12]The ruler may give an offering as a special gift to the LORD; it may be a burnt offering or fellowship offering. When he gives it to the LORD, the inner east gate is to be opened for him. He must offer his burnt offering or his fellowship offering as he does on the Sabbath[d] day. Then he will go out, and the gate will be shut after he has left.

[13]" 'Every day you will give a year-old lamb that has nothing wrong with it for a burnt offering to the LORD. Do it every morning. [14]Also, you must offer a grain offering with the lamb every morning. For this you will give three and one-third quarts of grain and one and one-third quarts of olive oil, to make the fine flour moist, as a grain offering to the LORD. This is a rule that must be kept from now on. [15]So you must always give the lamb, together with the grain offering and the olive oil, every morning as a burnt offering.

Rules for the Ruler

[16]" 'This is what the Lord GOD says: If the ruler gives a gift from his land to any of his sons, that land will belong to the son and then to the son's children. It is their property passed down from their family. [17]But if the ruler gives a gift from his land to any of his servants, that land will belong to the servant only until the year of freedom. Then the land will go back to the ruler. Only the ruler's sons may keep a gift of land from the ruler. [18]The ruler must not take any of the people's land, forcing them out of their land. He must give his sons some of his own land so my people will not be scattered out of their own land.' "

The Special Kitchens

[19]The man led me through the entrance at the side of the gateway to the priests' holy rooms that face north. There I saw a place at the west end. [20]The man said to me, "This is where the priests will boil the meat of the penalty offering and sin offering and bake the grain offering. Then they will not need to bring these holy offerings into the outer courtyard, because that would hurt the people."

[21]Then the man brought me out into the outer courtyard and led me to its four corners. In each corner of the courtyard was a smaller courtyard. [22]Small courtyards were in the four corners of the courtyard. Each small courtyard was the same size, seventy feet long and fifty-two and one-half feet wide. [23]A stone wall was around each of the four small courtyards, and places for cooking were built in each of the stone walls. [24]The man said to me, "These are the kitchens where those

who work in the Temple[d] will boil the sacrifices offered by the people."

The River from the Temple

47

The man led me back to the door of the Temple,[d] and I saw water coming out from under the doorway and flowing east. (The Temple faced east.) The water flowed down from the south side wall of the Temple and then south of the altar. [2]The man brought me out through the outer north gate and led me around outside to the outer east gate. I found the water coming out on the south side of the gate.

[3]The man went toward the east with a line in his hand and measured about one-third of a mile. Then he led me through water that came up to my ankles. [4]The man measured about one-third of a mile again and led me through water that came up to my knees. Then he measured about one-third of a mile again and led me through water up to my waist. [5]The man measured about one-third of a mile again, but it was now a river that I could not cross. The water had risen too high; it was deep enough for swimming; it was a river that no one could cross. [6]The man asked me, "Human, do you see this?"

Then the man led me back to the bank of the river. [7]As I went back, I saw many trees on both sides of the river. [8]The man said to me, "This water will flow toward the eastern areas and go down into the Jordan Valley. When it enters the Dead Sea,[d] it will become fresh. [9]Everywhere the river goes, there will be many fish. Wherever this water goes the Dead Sea will become fresh, and so where the river goes there will be many living things. [10]Fishermen will stand by the Dead Sea. From En Gedi all the way to En Eglaim there will be places to spread fishing nets. There will be many kinds of fish in the Dead Sea, as many as in

> ※ **SIDELIGHT:** In its current state, the Dead Sea is hardly a healthy habitat for the "many kinds of fish" that Ezekiel sees in his vision (Ezekiel 47:8–10). The surface of this body of water is 1,294 feet below sea level, and 25 percent of the sea is minerals—making it the saltiest and most uninhabitable sea in the world. It would take a true miracle for water to become fresh when it left the Dead Sea.

the Mediterranean Sea. [11]But its swamps and marshes will not become fresh; they will be left for salt. [12]All kinds of fruit trees will grow on both banks of the river, and their leaves will not dry and die. The trees will have fruit every month, because the water for them comes from the Temple. The fruit from the trees will be used for food, and their leaves for medicine."

Borders of the Land

¹³This is what the Lord GOD says: "These are the borders of the land to be divided among the twelve tribes*d* of Israel. Joseph will have two parts of land. ¹⁴You will divide the land equally. I promised to give it to your ancestors, so this land will belong to you as family property.

¹⁵"This will be the border line of the land: "On the north side it will start at the Mediterranean Sea. It will go through Hethlon, toward Lebo Hamath and on to the towns of Zedad, ¹⁶Berothah, and Sibraim on the border between Damascus and Hamath. Then it will go on to the town of Hazer Hatticon on the border of the country of Hauran. ¹⁷So the border line will go from the Mediterranean Sea east to the town of Hazar Enan, where the land belonging to Damascus and Hamath lies on the north side. This will be the north side of the land.

¹⁸"On the east side the border runs south from a point between Hauran and Damascus. It will go along the Jordan between Gilead and the land of Israel and will continue to the town of Tamar on the Dead Sea.*d* This will be the east side of the land.

¹⁹"On the south side the border line will go east from Tamar all the way to the waters of Meribah Kadesh. Then it will run along the brook of Egypt to the Mediterranean Sea. This will be the south side of the land.

²⁰"On the west side the Mediterranean Sea will be the border line up to a place across from Lebo Hamath. This will be the west side of your land.

²¹"You will divide this land among the tribes of Israel. ²²You will divide it as family property for yourselves and for the foreigners who live and have children among you. You are to treat these foreigners the same as people born in Israel; they are to share the land with the tribes of Israel. ²³In whatever tribe the foreigner lives, you will give him some land," says the Lord GOD.

Dividing the Land

48 "These are the areas of the tribes*d* named here: Dan will have one share at the northern border. It will go from the sea through Hethlon to Lebo Hamath, all the way to Hazar Enan, where Damascus lies to the north. It *will stop there next to Hamath. This will be Dan's* northern border from the east side to the Mediterranean Sea on the west side.

²"South of Dan's border, Asher will have one share. It will go from the east side to the west side.

³"South of Asher's border, Naphtali will have

one share. It will go from the east side to the west side.

⁴"South of Naphtali's border, Manasseh will have one share. It will go from the east side to the west side.

⁵"South of Manasseh's border, Ephraim will have one share. It will go from the east side to the west side.

⁶"South of Ephraim's border, Reuben will have one share. It will go from the east side to the west side.

⁷"South of Reuben's border, Judah will have one share. It will go from the east side to the west side.

⁸"South of Judah's border will be the holy area which you are to give. It will be about seven miles wide and as long and wide as one of the tribes' shares. It will run from the east side to the west side. The Temple*d* will be in the middle of this area.

⁹"The share which you will give the LORD will be about seven miles long and three miles wide. ¹⁰The holy area will be divided among these people. The priests will have land about seven miles long on the north and south sides, and three miles wide on the west and east sides. The Temple of the LORD will be in the middle of it. ¹¹This land is for the priests who are given the holy duty of serving the LORD. They are the descendants*d* of Zadok who did my work and did not leave me when Israel and the Levites left me. ¹²They will have as their share a very holy part of the holy portion of the land. It will be next to the land of the Levites.

¹³"Alongside the land for the priests, the Levites will have a share about seven miles long and three miles wide; its full length will be about seven miles and its full width about three miles. ¹⁴The Levites are not to sell or trade any of this land. They are not to let anyone else own any of this best part of the land, because it belongs to the LORD.

City Property

¹⁵"The rest of the area will be about one and one-half miles wide and seven miles long. It will not be holy but will belong to the city and be used for homes and pastures. The city will be in the middle of it. ¹⁶These are the city's measurements: the north side will be about one mile, the south side about one mile, the east side about one mile, and the west side about one mile. ¹⁷*The city's land for pastures will be about* four hundred thirty-seven feet on the north, four hundred thirty-seven feet on the south, four hundred thirty-seven feet on the east, and four hundred thirty-seven feet on the west. ¹⁸Along the long side of the holy area there will be left three miles on the east and three miles on the west. It

will be used to grow food for the city workers. [19]The city workers from all the tribes[d] of Israel will farm this land. [20]This whole area will be square, seven miles by seven miles. You shall give to the LORD the holy share along with the city property.

[21]"Land that is left over on both sides of the holy area and city property will belong to the ruler. That land will extend east of the holy area to the eastern border and west of it to the Mediterranean Sea. Both of these areas run the length of the lands of the tribes, and they belong to the ruler. The holy area with the Holy Place of the Temple[d] will be in the middle. [22]The Levites' land and the city property will be in the middle of the lands belonging to the ruler. Those lands will be between Judah's border and Benjamin's border.

The Other Tribes' Land

[23]"Here is what the rest of the tribes will receive: Benjamin will have one share. It will go from the east side to the Mediterranean Sea on the west side.

[24]"South of Benjamin's land, Simeon will have one share. It will go from the east side to the west side.

[25]"South of Simeon's land, Issachar will have one share. It will go from the east side to the west side.

[26]"South of Issachar's land, Zebulun will have one share. It will go from the east side to the west side.

[27]"South of Zebulun's land, Gad will have one share. It will go from the east side to the west side.

[28]"The southern border of Gad's land will go east from Tamar on the Dead Sea[d] to the waters of Meribah Kadesh. Then it will run along the brook of Egypt to the Mediterranean Sea.

[29]"This is the land you will divide among the tribes of Israel to be their shares," says the Lord GOD.

The Gates of the City

[30]"These will be the outside borders of the city: The north side will measure more than one mile. [31]There will be three gates facing north: Reuben's Gate, Judah's Gate, and Levi's Gate, named for the tribes[d] of Israel.

[32]"The east side will measure more than one mile. There will be three gates facing east: Joseph's Gate, Benjamin's Gate, and Dan's Gate.

[33]"The south side will measure more than one mile. There will be three gates facing south: Simeon's Gate, Issachar's Gate, and Zebulun's Gate.

[34]"The west side will measure more than one mile. There will be three gates facing west: Gad's Gate, Asher's Gate, and Naphtali's Gate.

[35]"The city will measure about six miles around. From then on the name of the city will be The LORD Is There."

DANIEL

Why Read This Book:

■ Find courage to stand against pressure to compromise your beliefs (Daniel 1—6).

■ Be assured that God works through history to fulfill his purposes (Daniel 7—12).

Behind the Scenes:

After moving to a new town, he quickly became popular. People respected him. Then he started getting pressured to compromise—to do things he knew were wrong. Saying no would have been easier if the people pressuring him weren't so important. He had to please them, didn't he?

It sounds like something that could happen today, right? But it's a story set twenty-five hundred years ago. Daniel had been dragged off to Babylon (modern-day Iraq) when the empire conquered Judah. Because of Daniel's ability to interpret dreams, the king chose him to be an important adviser.

But Daniel's career took a downward turn when he resisted the pressure to set aside his faith and worship the king. Because he wouldn't give in, he was sent to die in a den of lions, but God's power protected him. Through everything, Daniel remained faithful to God.

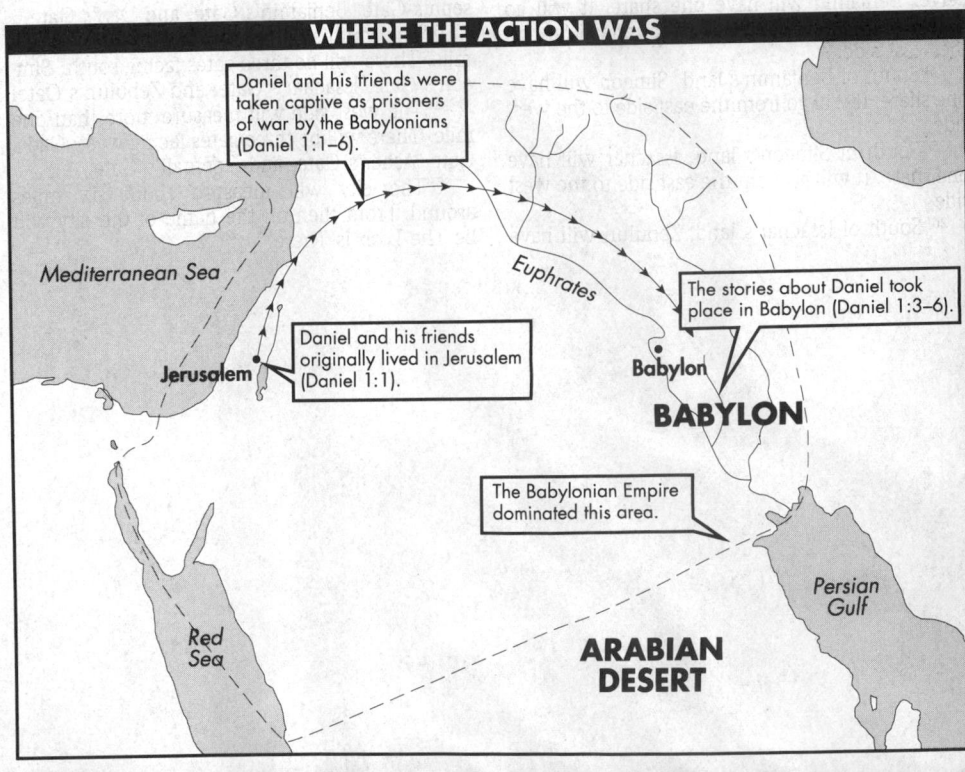

WHERE THE ACTION WAS

Daniel and his friends were taken captive as prisoners of war by the Babylonians (Daniel 1:1–6).

Daniel and his friends originally lived in Jerusalem (Daniel 1:1).

The stories about Daniel took place in Babylon (Daniel 1:3–6).

The Babylonian Empire dominated this area.

Mediterranean Sea

Euphrates

Jerusalem

Babylon

BABYLON

Red Sea

Persian Gulf

ARABIAN DESERT

WHEN THE ACTION WAS

	The Northern Kingdom (Israel) fell to Assyria	The Southern Kingdom (Judah) fell, and Daniel was taken to Babylon		Jesus was born
1000BC	**750BC**	**500BC**	**250BC**	**BC/AD**
David was Israel's king		People began returning to Jerusalem from Babylon		

Behind the Scenes (cont.): The book of Daniel has two parts. In the first part (chapters 1—6), we read the heroic story of Daniel and his friends. Then chapters 7—12 consist of Daniel's unusual visions that include strange symbols and heavenly messengers that proclaim God's Word.

Though parts of Daniel are difficult to understand, the book's underlying message is consistent: God is in control of history. Even when things get rough and we are under pressure, we can know that God is working to protect his people and advance his purposes in the world. We, like Daniel, should rely on God and remain faithful to God, no matter what happens.

Daniel Taken to Babylon

1 During the third year that Jehoiakim was king of Judah, Nebuchadnezzar king of Babylon came to Jerusalem and surrounded it with his army. ²The Lord allowed Nebuchadnezzar to capture Jehoiakim king of Judah. Nebuchadnezzar also took some of the things from the Temple[d] of God, which he carried to Babylonia and put in the temple of his gods.

³Then King Nebuchadnezzar ordered Ashpenaz, his chief officer, to bring some of the Israelite men into his palace. He wanted them to be from important families, including the family of the king of Judah. ⁴King Nebuchadnezzar wanted only young Israelite men who had nothing wrong with them. They were to be handsome and well educated, capable of learning and understanding, and able to serve in his palace. Ashpenaz was to teach them the language and writings of the Babylonians. ⁵The king gave the young men a certain amount of food and wine every day, just like the food he ate. The young men were to be trained for three years, and then they would become servants of the king of Babylon. ⁶Among those young men were Daniel, Hananiah, Mishael, and Azariah from the people of Judah.

SIDELIGHT: In Old Testament times, names had important meanings. All four of the Israelites' names in Daniel 1:6 included syllables meaning God (El) or the Lord God (Yah). So these faithful men probably weren't excited when they were given Babylonian names, some of which included the names of false gods.

---

⁷Ashpenaz, the chief officer, gave them Babylonian names. Daniel's new name was Belteshazzar, Hananiah's was Shadrach, Mishael's was Meshach, and Azariah's was Abednego.

⁸Daniel decided not to eat the king's food or drink his wine because that would make him unclean.[d] So he asked Ashpenaz for permission not to make himself unclean in this way.

⁹God made Ashpenaz, the chief officer, want to be kind and merciful to Daniel, ¹⁰but Ashpenaz said to Daniel, "I am afraid of my master, the king. He ordered me to give you this food and drink. If you begin to look worse than other young men your age, the king will see this. Then he will cut off my head because of you."

¹¹Ashpenaz had ordered a guard to watch Daniel, Hananiah, Mishael, and Azariah. ¹²Daniel said to the guard, "Please give us this test for ten days: Don't give us anything but vegetables to eat and water to drink. ¹³After ten days compare how we look with how the other young men look who eat the king's food. See for yourself and then decide how you want to treat us, your servants."

¹⁴So the guard agreed to test them for ten days. ¹⁵After ten days they looked healthier and better fed than all the young men who ate the king's food. ¹⁶So the guard took away the king's special food and wine, feeding them vegetables instead.

¹⁷God gave these four young men wisdom and the ability to learn many things that people had written and studied. Daniel could also understand visions and dreams.

¹⁸At the end of the time set for them by the king, Ashpenaz brought all the young men to King Nebuchadnezzar. ¹⁹The king talked to them and found that none of the young men were as good as Daniel, Hananiah, Mishael, and Azariah. So those four young men became the king's servants. ²⁰Every time the king asked them about something important, they showed much wisdom and understanding. They were ten times better than all the fortune-tellers and magicians in his kingdom! ²¹So Daniel continued to be the king's servant until the first year Cyrus was king.

Nebuchadnezzar's Dream

2 During Nebuchadnezzar's second year as king, he had dreams that bothered him and kept him awake at night. ²So the king called for his fortune-tellers, magicians, wizards, and wise men, because he wanted them to tell him what he had dreamed. They came in and stood in front of the king.

³Then the king said to them, "I had a dream that bothers me, and I want to know what it means."

⁴The wise men answered the king in the Ara-

maic language, "O king, live forever! Please tell us, your servants, your dream. Then we will tell you what it means."

⁵King Nebuchadnezzar said to them, "I meant what I said. You must tell me the dream and what it means. If you don't, I will have you torn apart, and I will turn your houses into piles of stones. ⁶But if you tell me my dream and its meaning, I will reward you with gifts and great honor. So tell me the dream and what it means."

⁷Again the wise men said to the king, "Tell us, your servants, the dream, and we will tell you what it means."

⁸King Nebuchadnezzar answered, "I know you are trying to get more time, because you know that I meant what I said. ⁹If you don't tell me my dream, you will be punished. You have all agreed to tell me lies and wicked things, hoping things will change. Now, tell me the dream so that I will know you can tell me what it really means!"

¹⁰The wise men answered the king, saying, "No one on earth can do what the king asks! No great and powerful king has ever asked the fortune-tellers, magicians, or wise men to do this; ¹¹the king is asking something that is too hard. Only the gods could tell the king this, but the gods do not live among people."

¹²When the king heard their answer, he became very angry. He ordered that all the wise men of Babylon be killed. ¹³So King Nebuchadnezzar's order to kill the wise men was announced, and men were sent to look for Daniel and his friends to kill them.

¹⁴Arioch, the commander of the king's guards, was going to kill the wise men of Babylon. But Daniel spoke to him with wisdom and skill, ¹⁵saying, "Why did the king order such a terrible punishment?" Then Arioch explained everything to Daniel. ¹⁶So Daniel went to King Nebuchadnezzar and asked for an appointment so that he could tell the king what his dream meant.

¹⁷Then Daniel went to his house and explained the whole story to his friends Hananiah, Mishael, and Azariah. ¹⁸Daniel asked his friends to pray that the God of heaven would show them mercy and help them understand this secret so he and his friends would not be killed with the other wise men of Babylon.

¹⁹During the night God explained the secret to Daniel in a vision. Then Daniel praised the God of heaven. ²⁰Daniel said:

"Praise God forever and ever,
    because he has wisdom and power.
²¹He changes the times and seasons of the
    year.
He takes away the power of kings
    and gives their power to new kings.
He gives wisdom to those who are wise
    and knowledge to those who understand.

²²He makes known secrets that are deep and
    hidden;
he knows what is hidden in darkness,
    and light is all around him.
²³I thank you and praise you, God of my
    ancestors,
because you have given me wisdom and
    power.
You told me what we asked of you;
    you told us about the king's dream."

The Meaning of the Dream

²⁴Then Daniel went to Arioch, the man King Nebuchadnezzar had chosen to kill the wise men of Babylon. Daniel said to him, "Don't put the wise men of Babylon to death. Take me to the king, and I will tell him what his dream means."

²⁵Very quickly Arioch took Daniel to the king and said, "I have found a man among the captives from Judah who can tell the king what his dream means."

²⁶The king asked Daniel, who was also called Belteshazzar, "Are you able to tell me what I dreamed and what it means?"

²⁷Daniel answered, "No wise man, magician, or fortune-teller can explain to the king the secret he has asked about. ²⁸But there is a God in heaven who explains secret things, and he has shown King Nebuchadnezzar what will happen at a later time. This is your dream, the vision you saw while lying on your bed: ²⁹O king, as you were lying there, you thought about things to come. God, who can tell people about secret things, showed you what is going to happen. ³⁰God also told this secret to me, not because I have greater wisdom than any other living person, but so that you may know what it means. In that way you will understand what went through your mind.

³¹"O king, in your dream you saw a huge, shiny, and frightening statue in front of you. ³²The head of the statue was made of pure gold. Its chest and arms were made of silver. Its stomach and the upper part of its legs were made of bronze. ³³The lower part of the legs were made of iron, while its feet were made partly of iron and partly of baked clay. ³⁴While you were looking at the statue, you saw a rock cut free, but no human being touched the rock. It hit the statue on its feet of iron and clay and smashed them. ³⁵Then the iron, clay, bronze, silver, and gold broke to pieces at the same time. They became like chaff*d* on a threshing*d* floor in the summertime; the wind blew them away, and there was nothing left. Then the rock that hit the statue became a very large mountain that filled the whole earth.

³⁶"That was your dream. Now we will tell the king what it means. ³⁷O king, you are the greatest king. God of heaven has given you a kingdom, power, strength, and glory. ³⁸Wherever people,

wild animals, and birds live, God made you ruler over them. King Nebuchadnezzar, you are the head of gold on that statue.

³⁹"Another kingdom will come after you, but it will not be as great as yours. Next a third kingdom, the bronze part, will rule over the earth. ⁴⁰Then there will be a fourth kingdom, strong as iron. In the same way that iron crushes and smashes things to pieces, the fourth kingdom will smash and crush all the other kingdoms.

⁴¹"You saw that the statue's feet and toes were partly baked clay and partly iron. That means the fourth kingdom will be a divided kingdom. It will have some of the strength of iron in it, just as you saw iron was mixed with clay. ⁴²The toes of the statue were partly iron and partly clay. So the fourth kingdom will be partly strong like iron and partly breakable like clay. ⁴³You saw the iron mixed with clay, but iron and clay do not hold together. In the same way the people of the fourth kingdom will be a mixture, but they will not be united as one people.

⁴⁴"During the time of those kings, the God of heaven will set up another kingdom that will never be destroyed or given to another group of people. This kingdom will crush all the other kingdoms and bring them to an end, but it will continue forever.

⁴⁵"King Nebuchadnezzar, you saw a rock cut from a mountain, but no human being touched it. The rock broke the iron, bronze, clay, silver, and gold to pieces. In this way the great God showed you what will happen. The dream is true, and you can trust this explanation."

⁴⁶Then King Nebuchadnezzar fell facedown on the ground in front of Daniel. The king honored him and commanded that an offering and incense*d* be presented to him. ⁴⁷Then the king said to Daniel, "Truly I know your God is the greatest of all gods, the Lord of all the kings. He tells people about things they cannot know. I know this is true, because you were able to tell these secret things to me."

⁴⁸Then the king gave Daniel many gifts plus an important position in his kingdom. Nebuchadnezzar made him ruler over the whole area of Babylon and put him in charge of all the wise men of Babylon. ⁴⁹Daniel asked the king to make Shadrach, Meshach, and Abednego leaders over the area of Babylon, so the king did as Daniel asked. Daniel himself became one of the people who stayed at the royal court.

The Gold Idol and Blazing Furnace

3 King Nebuchadnezzar made a gold statue ninety feet high and nine feet wide and set it up on the plain of Dura in the area of Babylon.

²Then he called for the leaders: the governors, assistant governors, captains of the soldiers, people who advised the king, keepers of the treasury, judges, rulers, and all other officers in his kingdom. He wanted them to come to the special service for the statue he had set up. ³So they all came for the special service and stood in front of the statue that King Nebuchadnezzar had set up. ⁴Then the man who made announcements for the king said in a loud voice, "People, nations, and those of every language, this is what you are commanded to do: ⁵When you hear the sound of the horns, flutes, lyres,*d* zithers,*n* harps, pipes, and all the other musical instruments, you must bow down and worship the gold statue that King Nebuchadnezzar has set up. ⁶Anyone who doesn't bow down and worship will immediately be thrown into a blazing furnace."

⁷Now people, nations, and those who spoke every language were there. When they heard the sound of the horns, flutes, lyres, zithers, pipes, and all the other musical instruments, they bowed down and worshiped the gold statue King Nebuchadnezzar had set up.

⁸Then some Babylonians came up to the king and began speaking against the men of Judah. ⁹They said to King Nebuchadnezzar, "O king, live forever! ¹⁰O king, you gave a command that everyone who heard the horns, lyres, zithers, harps, pipes, and all the other musical instruments would have to bow down and worship the gold statue. ¹¹Anyone who wouldn't do this was to be thrown into a blazing furnace. ¹²O king, there are some men of Judah whom you made officers in the area of Babylon that did not pay attention to your order. Their names are Shadrach, Meshach, and Abednego. They do not serve your gods and do not worship the gold statue you have set up."

¹³Nebuchadnezzar became very angry and called for Shadrach, Meshach, and Abednego. When they were brought to the king, ¹⁴Nebuchadnezzar said, "Shadrach, Meshach, and Abednego, is it true that you do not serve my gods nor worship the gold statue I have set up? ¹⁵In a moment you will again hear the sound of the horns, flutes, lyres, zithers, harps, pipes, and all the other musical instruments. If you bow down and worship the statue I made, that will be good. But if you do not worship it, you will immediately be thrown into the blazing furnace. What god will be able to save you from my power then?"

¹⁶Shadrach, Meshach, and Abednego answered the king, saying, "Nebuchadnezzar, we do not need to defend ourselves to you. ¹⁷If you throw us into the blazing furnace, the God we serve is able to save us from the furnace. He will save us from your power, O king. ¹⁸But even if God does not

---

zithers Musical instruments with thirty to forty strings.

save us, we want you, O king, to know this: We will not serve your gods or worship the gold statue you have set up."

¹⁹Then Nebuchadnezzar was furious with Shadrach, Meshach, and Abednego, and he changed his mind. He ordered the furnace to be heated seven times hotter than usual. ²⁰Then he commanded some of the strongest soldiers in his army to tie up Shadrach, Meshach, and Abednego and throw them into the blazing furnace.

²¹So Shadrach, Meshach, and Abednego were tied up and thrown into the blazing furnace while still wearing their robes, trousers, turbans, and other clothes. ²²The king's command was very strict, and the furnace was made so hot that the flames killed the strong soldiers who threw Shadrach, Meshach, and Abednego into the furnace. ²³Firmly tied, Shadrach, Meshach, and Abednego fell into the blazing furnace.

²⁴Then King Nebuchadnezzar was so surprised that he jumped to his feet. He asked the men who advised him, "Didn't we tie up only three men and throw them into the fire?"

They answered, "Yes, O king."

²⁵The king said, "Look! I see four men walking around in the fire. They are not tied up, and they are not burned. The fourth man looks like a son of the gods."

²⁶Then Nebuchadnezzar went to the opening of the blazing furnace and shouted, "Shadrach, Meshach, and Abednego, come out! Servants of the Most High God, come here!"

So Shadrach, Meshach, and Abednego came out of the fire. ²⁷When they came out, the governors, assistant governors, captains of the soldiers, and royal advisers crowded around them and saw that the fire had not harmed their bodies. Their hair was not burned, their robes were not burned, and they didn't even smell like smoke!

SIDELIGHT: We can hope that Shadrach, Meshach, and Abednego weren't wearing any jewelry when they were thrown into the blazing furnace (Daniel 3:16–27). The furnace would have been one used to smelt metals. Archaeologists have uncovered this kind of furnace, which is about nine feet in diameter.

---

²⁸Then Nebuchadnezzar said, "Praise the God of Shadrach, Meshach, and Abednego. Their God has sent his angel and saved his servants from the fire! These three men trusted their God and refused to obey my command. They were willing to die rather than serve or worship any god other than their own. ²⁹So I now give this command:

Anyone from any nation or language who says anything against the God of Shadrach, Meshach, and Abednego will be torn apart and have his house turned into a pile of stones. No other god can save his people like this." ³⁰Then the king promoted Shadrach, Meshach, and Abednego in the area of Babylon.

Nebuchadnezzar's Dream of a Tree

4 King Nebuchadnezzar sent this letter to the people, nations, and those who speak every language in all the world:

I wish you peace and great wealth!

²The Most High God has done miracles[d] and wonderful things for me that I am happy to tell you about.

³His wonderful acts are great,
and his miracles are mighty.
His kingdom goes on forever,
and his rule continues from now on.

⁴I, Nebuchadnezzar, was happy and successful at my palace, ⁵but I had a dream that made me afraid. As I was lying on my bed, I saw pictures and visions in my mind that alarmed me. ⁶So I ordered all the wise men of Babylon to come to me and tell me what my dream meant. ⁷The fortune-tellers, magicians, and wise men came, and I told them about the dream. But they could not tell me what it meant.

⁸Finally, Daniel came to me. (I called him Belteshazzar to honor my god, because the spirit of the holy gods is in him.) I told my dream to him. ⁹I said, "Belteshazzar, you are the most important of all the fortune-tellers. I know that the spirit of the holy gods is in you, so there is no secret that is too hard for you to understand. This was what I dreamed; tell me what it means. ¹⁰These are the visions I saw while I was lying in my bed: I looked, and there in front of me was a tree standing in the middle of the earth. And it was very tall. ¹¹The tree grew large and strong. The top of the tree touched the sky and could be seen from anywhere on earth. ¹²The leaves of the tree were beautiful. It had plenty of good fruit on it, enough food for everyone. The wild animals found shelter under the tree, and the birds lived in its branches. Every animal ate from it.

¹³"As I was looking at those things in the vision while lying on my bed, I saw an observer, a holy angel coming down from heaven. ¹⁴He spoke very loudly and said, 'Cut down the tree and cut off its branches. Strip off its leaves and scatter its fruit. Let the animals under the tree run away, and let the

birds in its branches fly away. [15]But leave the stump and its roots in the ground with a band of iron and bronze around it; let it stay in the field with the grass around it.

" 'Let the man become wet with dew, and let him live among the animals and plants of the earth. [16]Let him not think like a human any longer, but let him have the mind of an animal for seven years.

[17]" 'The observers gave this command; the holy ones declared the sentence. This is so all people may know that the Most High God rules over every kingdom on earth. God gives those kingdoms to anyone he wants, and he chooses people to rule them who are not proud.'

[18]"That is what I, King Nebuchadnezzar, dreamed. Now Belteshazzar,[n] tell me what the dream means. None of the wise men in my kingdom can explain it to me, but you can, because the spirit of the holy gods is in you."

Daniel Explains the Dream

[19]Then Daniel, who was called Belteshazzar, was very quiet for a while, because his understanding of the dream frightened him. So the king said, "Belteshazzar, do not let the dream or its meaning make you afraid."

Then Belteshazzar answered, "My master, I wish the dream were about your enemies, and I wish its meaning were for those who are against you! [20]You saw a tree in your dream that grew large and strong. Its top touched the sky, and it could be seen from all over the earth. [21]Its leaves were beautiful, and it had plenty of fruit for everyone to eat. It was a home for the wild animals, and its branches were nesting places for the birds. [22]O king, you are that tree! You have become great and powerful, like the tall tree that touched the sky. Your power reaches to the far parts of the earth.

[23]"O king, you saw an observer, a holy angel, coming down from heaven who said, 'Cut down the tree and destroy it. But leave the stump and its roots in the ground with a band of iron and bronze around it; leave it in the field with the grass. Let him become wet with dew and live like a wild animal for seven years.'

[24]"This is the meaning of the dream, O king. The Most High God has commanded these things to happen to my master the king: [25]You will be forced away from people to live among the wild animals. People will feed you grass like an ox, and dew from the sky will make you wet. Seven years will pass, and then you will learn this lesson: The Most High God is ruler over every kingdom on earth, and he gives those kingdoms to anyone he chooses.

[26]"Since the stump of the tree and its roots were left in the ground, your kingdom will be given back to you when you learn that one in heaven rules your kingdom. [27]So, O king, please accept my advice. Stop sinning and do what is right. Stop doing wicked things and be kind to the poor. Then you might continue to be successful."

The King's Dream Comes True

[28]All these things happened to King Nebuchadnezzar. [29]Twelve months later as he was walking on the roof[n] of his palace in Babylon, [30]he said, "I have built this great Babylon as my royal home. I built it by my power to show my glory and my majesty."

[31]The words were still in his mouth when a voice from heaven said, "King Nebuchadnezzar, these things will happen to you: Your royal power has been taken away from you. [32]You will be forced away from people. You will live with the wild animals and will be fed grass like an ox. Seven years will pass before you learn this lesson: The Most High God rules over every kingdom on earth and gives those kingdoms to anyone he chooses."

[33]Immediately the words came true. Nebuchadnezzar was forced to go away from people, and he began eating grass like an ox. He became wet from dew. His hair grew long like the feathers of an eagle, and his nails grew like the claws of a bird.

SIDELIGHT: The power-hungry, grass-chomping King Nebuchadnezzar may have suffered from pica, an unnatural craving for unusual objects (Daniel 4:33). It's the same word used for pregnant women who crave clay or paint!

---

[34]At the end of that time, I, Nebuchadnezzar, looked up toward heaven, and I could think normally again! Then I gave praise to the Most High God; I gave honor and glory to him who lives forever.

Belteshazzar Another name for Daniel.
roof In Bible times houses were built with flat roofs. The roof was used for drying things such as flax and fruit. And it was used as an extra room, as a place for worship, and as a place to sleep in the summer.

God's rule is forever,
  and his kingdom continues for all
    time.
35People on earth
  are not truly important.
God does what he wants
  with the powers of heaven
  and the people on earth.
No one can stop his powerful hand
  or question what he does.

36At that time I could think normally again, and God gave back my great honor and power and returned the glory to my kingdom. The people who advised me and the royal family came to me for help again. I became king again and was even greater and more powerful than before. 37Now I, Nebuchadnezzar, give praise and honor and glory to the King of heaven. Everything he does is right and fair, and he is able to make proud people humble.

The Writing on the Wall

5 King Belshazzar gave a big banquet for a thousand royal guests and drank wine with them. 2As Belshazzar was drinking his wine, he gave orders to bring the gold and silver cups that his ancestor Nebuchadnezzar had taken from the Temple*d* in Jerusalem. This was so the king, his royal guests, his wives, and his slave women*d* could drink from those cups. 3So they brought the gold cups that had been taken from the Temple of God in Jerusalem. And the king and his royal guests, his wives, and his slave women drank from them. 4As they were drinking, they praised their gods, which were made from gold, silver, bronze, iron, wood, and stone.

5Suddenly the fingers of a person's hand appeared and began writing on the plaster of the wall, near the lampstand in the royal palace. The king watched the hand as it wrote.

6King Belshazzar was very frightened. His face turned white, his knees knocked together, and he could not stand up because his legs were too weak. 7The king called for the magicians, wise men, and wizards of Babylon and said to them, "Anyone who can read this writing and explain it will receive purple clothes fit for a king and a gold chain around his neck. And I will make that person the third highest ruler in the kingdom."

8Then all the king's wise men came in, but they *could not read the writing or tell the king what* it meant. 9King Belshazzar became even more afraid, and his face became even whiter. His royal guests were confused.

10Then the king's mother, who had heard the voices of the king and his royal guests, came into the banquet room. She said, "O king, live forever!

Don't be afraid or let your face be white with fear! 11There is a man in your kingdom who has the spirit of the holy gods. In the days of your father, this man showed understanding, knowledge, and wisdom like the gods. Your father, King Nebuchadnezzar, put this man in charge of all the wise men, fortune-tellers, magicians, and wizards. 12The man I am talking about is named Daniel, whom the king named Belteshazzar. He was very smart and had knowledge and understanding. He could explain dreams and secrets and could answer very hard problems. Call for Daniel. He will tell you what the writing on the wall means."

13So they brought Daniel to the king, and the king asked, "Is your name Daniel? Are you one of the captives my father the king brought from Judah? 14I have heard that the spirit of the gods is in you, and that you are very smart and have knowledge and extraordinary understanding. 15The wise men and magicians were brought to me to read this writing and to explain what it means, but they could not explain it. 16I have heard that you are able to explain what things mean and can find the answers to hard problems. Read this writing on the wall and explain it to me. If you can, I will give you purple clothes fit for a king and a gold chain to wear around your neck. And you will become the third highest ruler in the kingdom."

17Then Daniel answered the king, "You may keep your gifts for yourself, or you may give those rewards to someone else. But I will read the writing on the wall for you and will explain to you what it means.

18"O king, the Most High God made your father Nebuchadnezzar a great, important, and powerful king. 19Because God made him important, all the people, nations, and those who spoke every language were very frightened of Nebuchadnezzar. If he wanted someone to die, he killed that person. If he wanted someone to live, he let that person live. Those he wanted to promote, he promoted. Those he wanted to be less important, he made less important.

20"But Nebuchadnezzar became too proud and stubborn, so he was taken off his royal throne. His glory was taken away. 21He was forced away from people, and his mind became like the mind of an animal. He lived with the wild donkeys and was fed grass like an ox and became wet with dew. These things happened to him until he learned his lesson: The Most High God rules over every kingdom on earth, and he sets anyone he chooses over those kingdoms.

22"Belshazzar, you already knew these things, because you are a descendant*d* of Nebuchadnezzar. Still you have not been sorry for what you have done. 23Instead, you have set yourself against the Lord of heaven. You ordered the drinking cups from the Temple of the Lord to be brought to you. Then you and your royal guests, your wives, and your slave women drank wine from them. You praised the gods of silver, gold, bronze, iron, wood, and stone that are not really gods; they cannot see or hear or understand anything. You did not honor God, who has power over your life and everything you do. ²⁴So God sent the hand that wrote on the wall.

²⁵"These are the words that were written on the wall: 'Mene, mene, tekel, and parsin.'

²⁶"This is what the words mean: Mene: God has counted the days until your kingdom will end. ²⁷Tekel: You have been weighed on the scales and found not good enough. ²⁸Parsin: Your kingdom is being divided and will be given to the Medes and the Persians."

²⁹Then Belshazzar gave an order for Daniel to be dressed in purple clothes and to have a gold chain put around his neck. And it was announced that Daniel was the third highest ruler in the kingdom. ³⁰That very same night Belshazzar, king of the Babylonian people, was killed. ³¹So Darius the Mede became the new king when he was sixty-two years old.

Daniel and the Lions

6 Darius thought it would be a good idea to choose one hundred twenty governors who would rule his kingdom. ²He chose three men as supervisors over those governors, and Daniel was one of the supervisors. The supervisors were to ensure that the governors did not try to cheat the king. ³Daniel showed that he could do the work better than the other supervisors and governors, so the king planned to put Daniel in charge of the whole kingdom. ⁴Because of this, the other supervisors and governors tried to find reasons to accuse Daniel about his work in the government. But they could not find anything wrong with him or any reason to accuse him, because he was trustworthy and not lazy or dishonest. ⁵Finally these men said, "We will never find any reason to accuse Daniel unless it is about the law of his God."

⁶So the supervisors and governors went as a group to the king and said: "King Darius, live forever! ⁷The supervisors, assistant governors, governors, the people who advise you, and the captains of the soldiers have all agreed that you should make a new law for everyone to obey: For the next thirty days no one should pray to any god or human except to you, O king. Anyone who doesn't obey will be thrown into the lions' den. ⁸Now, O king, make the law and sign your name to it so that it cannot be changed, because then it will be a law of the Medes and Persians and cannot be canceled." ⁹So King Darius signed the law.

¹⁰Even though Daniel knew that the new law had been written, he went to pray in an upstairs room in his house, which had windows that opened toward Jerusalem. Three times each day Daniel would kneel down to pray and thank God, just as he always had done.

¹¹Then those men went as a group and found Daniel praying and asking God for help. ¹²So they went to the king and talked to him about the law he had made. They said, "Didn't you sign a law that says no one may pray to any god or human except you, O king? Doesn't it say that anyone who disobeys during the next thirty days will be thrown into the lions' den?"

The king answered, "Yes, that is the law, and the laws of the Medes and Persians cannot be canceled."

¹³Then they said to the king, "Daniel, one of the captives from Judah, is not paying attention to you, O king, or to the law you signed. Daniel still prays to his God three times every day." ¹⁴The king became very upset when he heard this. He wanted to save Daniel, and he worked hard until sunset trying to think of a way to save him.

¹⁵Then those men went as a group to the king. They said, "Remember, O king, the law of the Medes and Persians says that no law or command given by the king can be changed."

¹⁶So King Darius gave the order, and Daniel was brought in and thrown into the lions' den. The king said to Daniel, "May the God you serve all the time save you!" ¹⁷A big stone was brought and placed over the opening of the lions' den. Then the king used his signet^d ring and the rings of his royal officers to put special seals^d on the rock. This ensured that no one would move the rock and bring Daniel out. ¹⁸Then King Darius went back to his palace. He did not eat that night, he did not have any entertainment brought to him, and he could not sleep.

¹⁹The next morning King Darius got up at dawn and hurried to the lions' den. ²⁰As he came near the den, he was worried. He called out to Daniel, "Daniel, servant of the living God! Has your God that you always worship been able to save you from the lions?"

²¹Daniel answered, "O king, live forever! ²²My God sent his angel to close the lions' mouths. They have not hurt me, because my God knows

I am innocent. I never did anything wrong to you, O king."

²³King Darius was very happy and told his servants to lift Daniel out of the lions' den. So they lifted him out and did not find any injury on him, because Daniel had trusted in his God.

²⁴Then the king commanded that the men who had accused Daniel be brought to the lions' den. They, their wives, and their children were thrown into the den. The lions grabbed them before they hit the floor of the den and crushed their bones.

²⁵Then King Darius wrote a letter to all people and all nations, to those who spoke every language in the world:

I wish you great peace and wealth.

²⁶I am making a new law for people in every part of my kingdom. All of you must fear and respect the God of Daniel.

Daniel's God is the living God;
he lives forever.
His kingdom will never be destroyed,
and his rule will never end.
²⁷God rescues and saves people
and does mighty miracles*d*
in heaven and on earth.
He is the one who saved Daniel
from the power of the lions.

²⁸So Daniel was successful during the time Darius was king and when Cyrus the Persian was king.

Daniel's Dream about Four Animals

7 In Belshazzar's first year as king of Babylon, Daniel had a dream. He saw visions as he was lying on his bed, and he wrote down what he had dreamed.

²Daniel said: "I saw my vision at night. In the vision the wind was blowing from all four directions, which made the sea very rough. ³I saw four huge animals come up from the sea, and each animal was different from the others.

⁴"The first animal looked like a lion, but had wings like an eagle. I watched this animal until its wings were torn off. It was lifted from the ground so that it stood up on two feet like a human, and it was given the mind of a human.

⁵Then I saw a second animal before me that looked like a bear. It was raised up on one of its sides and had three ribs in its mouth between its teeth. It was told, 'Get up and eat all the meat you want!'

⁶"After that, I looked, and there before me was another animal. This animal looked like a leopard with four wings on its back that looked like a bird's wings. This animal had four heads and was given power to rule.

⁷"After that, in my vision at night I saw in front

of me a fourth animal that was cruel, terrible, and very strong. It had large iron teeth. It crushed and ate what it killed, and then it walked on whatever was left. This fourth animal was different from any animal I had seen before, and it had ten horns.

⁸"While I was thinking about the horns, another horn grew up among them. It was a little horn with eyes like a human's eyes. It also had a mouth, and the mouth was bragging. The little horn pulled out three of the other horns.

⁹"As I looked,
thrones were put in their places,
and God, who has been alive forever, sat
on his throne.
His clothes were white like snow,
and the hair on his head was white like
wool.
His throne was made from fire,
and the wheels of his throne were blazing
with fire.
¹⁰A river of fire was flowing
from in front of him.
Many thousands of angels were serving him,
and millions of angels stood before him.
Court was ready to begin,
and the books were opened.

¹¹"I kept on looking because the little horn was bragging. I kept watching until finally the fourth animal was killed. Its body was destroyed, and it was thrown into the burning fire. ¹²(The power and rule of the other animals had been taken from them, but they were permitted to live for a certain period of time.)

¹³"In my vision at night I saw in front of me someone who looked like a human being coming on the clouds in the sky. He came near God, who has been alive forever, and he was led to God. ¹⁴He was given authority, glory, and the strength of a king. People of every tribe,*d* nation, and language will serve him. His rule will last forever, and his kingdom will never be destroyed.

The Meaning of the Dream

¹⁵"I, Daniel, was worried. The visions that went through my mind frightened me. ¹⁶I came near one of those standing there and asked what all this meant.

"So he told me and explained to me what these things meant: ¹⁷'The four great animals are four kingdoms that will come from the earth. ¹⁸But the holy people who belong to the Most High God will receive the power to rule and will have the power to rule forever, from now on.'

¹⁹"Then I wanted to know what the fourth animal meant, because it was different from all the others. It was very terrible and had iron teeth and bronze claws. It was the animal that crushed and ate what it killed and then walked on whatever

and newer than the other. [4]I watched the sheep charge to the west, the north, and the south. No animal could stand before him, and none could save another animal from his power. He did whatever he wanted and became very powerful.

[5]While I was watching this, I saw a male goat come from the west. This goat had one large horn between his eyes that was easy to see. He crossed over the whole earth so fast that his feet hardly touched the ground.

[6]In his anger the goat charged the sheep with the two horns that I had seen standing by the canal. [7]I watched the angry goat attack the sheep and break the sheep's two horns. The sheep was not strong enough to stop it. The goat knocked the sheep to the ground and then walked all over him. No one was able to save the sheep from the goat, [8]so the male goat became very great. But when he was strong, his big horn broke off and four horns grew in place of the one big horn. Those four horns pointed in four different directions and were easy to see.

[9]Then a little horn grew from one of those four horns, and it became very big. It grew to the south, the east, and toward the beautiful land of Judah. [10]That little horn grew until it reached to the sky. It even threw some of the army of heaven to the ground and walked on them! [11]That little horn set itself up as equal to God, the Commander of heaven's armies. It stopped the daily sacrifices that were offered to him, and the Temple,[d] the place where people worshiped him, was pulled down. [12]Because there was a turning away from God, the people stopped the daily sacrifices. Truth was thrown down to the ground, and the horn was successful in everything it did.

[13]Then I heard a holy angel speaking. Another holy angel asked the first one, "How long will the things in this vision last — the daily sacrifices, the turning away from God that brings destruction, the Temple[d] being pulled down, and the army of heaven being walked on?"

[14]The angel said to me, "This will happen for twenty-three hundred evenings and mornings. Then the holy place will be repaired."

[15]I, Daniel, saw this vision and tried to understand what it meant. In it I saw someone who looked like a man standing near me. [16]And I heard a man's voice calling from the Ulai Canal: "Gabriel, explain the vision to this man."

[17]Gabriel came to where I was standing. When he came close to me, I was very afraid and bowed facedown on the ground. But Gabriel said to me, "Human being, understand that this vision is about the time of the end."

[18]While Gabriel was speaking, I fell into a deep sleep with my face on the ground. Then he touched me and lifted me to my feet. [19]He said, "Now, I will explain to you what will happen in the time of God's anger. Your vision was about the set time of the end.

[20]"You saw a male sheep with two horns, which are the kings of Media and Persia. [21]The male goat is the king of Greece, and the big horn between its eyes is the first king. [22]The four horns that grew in the place of the broken horn are four kingdoms. Those four kingdoms will come from the nation of the first king, but they will not be as strong as the first king.

[23]"When the end comes near for those kingdoms, a bold and cruel king who tells lies will come. This will happen when many people have turned against God. [24]This king will be very powerful, but his power will not come from himself. He will cause terrible destruction and will be successful in everything he does. He will destroy powerful people and even God's holy people. [25]This king will succeed by using lies and force. He will think that he is very important. He will destroy many people without warning; he will try to fight even the Prince of princes! But that cruel king will be destroyed, and not by human power. [26]"The vision that has been shown to you about these evenings and mornings is true. But seal up the vision, because those things won't happen for a long time."

> ✲ **SIDELIGHT:** When Daniel was told to seal the vision (Daniel 8:26), it probably involved writing it on a scroll, then rolling up the scroll, tying it shut, and fastening the ties with clay. The clay was then imprinted with a ring or stamp with a special seal or emblem on it. Then all the documents were placed in clay jars for safekeeping.

[27]I, Daniel, became very weak and was sick for several days after that vision. Then I got up and went back to work for the king, but I was very upset about the vision. I didn't understand what it meant.

Daniel's Prayer

9 These things happened during the first year Darius son of Xerxes was king over Babylon. He was a descendant[d] of the Medes. [2]During Darius' first year as king, I, Daniel, was reading the Scriptures.[d] I saw that the LORD told Jeremiah that Jerusalem would be empty ruins for seventy years.

[3]Then I turned to the Lord God and prayed and asked him for help. I did not eat any food. To show my sadness, I put on rough cloth and sat in ashes. [4]I prayed to the LORD my God and told him

about all of our sins. I said, "Lord, you are a great God who causes fear and wonder. You keep your agreement of love with all who love you and obey your commands.

5"But we have sinned and done wrong. We have been wicked and turned against you, your commands, and your laws. 6We did not listen to your servants, the prophets, who spoke for you to our kings, our leaders, our ancestors, and all the people of the land.

7"Lord, you are good and right, but we are full of shame today—the people of Judah and Jerusalem, all the people of Israel, those near and far whom you scattered among many nations because they were not loyal to you. 8LORD, we are all ashamed. Our kings and leaders and our fathers are ashamed, because we have sinned against you.

9"But, Lord our God, you show us mercy and forgive us even though we have turned against you. 10We have not obeyed the LORD our God or the teachings he gave us through his servants, the prophets. 11All the people of Israel have disobeyed your teachings and have turned away, refusing to obey you. So you brought on us the curses and promises of punishment written in the Teachings of Moses, the servant of God, because we sinned against you.

12"You said these things would happen to us and our leaders, and you made them happen; you brought on us a great disaster. Nothing has ever been done on earth like what was done to Jerusalem. 13All this disaster came to us just as it is written in the Teachings of Moses. But we have not pleaded with the LORD our God. We have not stopped sinning. We have not paid attention to your truth. 14The LORD was ready to bring the disaster on us, and he did it because the LORD our God is right in everything he does. But we still did not obey him.

15"Lord our God, you used your power and brought us out of Egypt. Because of that, your name is known even today. But we have sinned and have done wrong. 16Lord, you do what is right, but please do not be angry with Jerusalem, your city on your holy hill. Because of our sins and the evil things done by our ancestors, people all around insult and make fun of Jerusalem and your people.

17"Now, our God, hear the prayers of your servant. Listen to my prayer for help, and for your sake do good things for your holy place that is in ruins. 18My God, pay attention and hear me. Open your eyes and see all the terrible things that have happened to us. See how our lives have been ruined and what has happened to the city that is called by your name. We do not ask these things because we are good; instead, we ask because of your mercy. 19Lord, listen! Lord, forgive! Lord,

hear us and do something! For your sake, don't wait, because your city and your people are called by your name."

Gabriel's Explanation

20While I was saying these things in my prayer to the LORD, my God, confessing my sins and the sins of the people of Israel and praying for God's holy hill, 21Gabriel came to me. (I had seen him in my last vision.) He came flying quickly to me about the time of the evening sacrifice, while I was still praying. 22He taught me and said to me, "Daniel, I have come to give you wisdom and to help you understand. 23When you first started praying, an answer was given, and I came to tell you, because God loves you very much. So think about the message and understand the vision.

24"God has ordered four hundred ninety years for your people and your holy city for these reasons: to stop people from turning against God; to put an end to sin; to take away evil; to bring in goodness that continues forever; to bring about the vision and prophecy;*d* and to appoint a most holy place.

25"Learn and understand these things. A command will come to rebuild Jerusalem. The time from this command until the appointed leader comes will be forty-nine years and four hundred thirty-four years. Jerusalem will be rebuilt with streets and a trench filled with water around it, but it will be built in times of trouble. 26After the four hundred thirty-four years the appointed leader will be killed; he will have nothing. The people of the leader who is to come will destroy the city and the holy place. The end of the city will come like a flood, and war will continue until the end. God has ordered that place to be completely destroyed. 27That leader will make firm an agreement with many people for seven years. He will stop the offerings and sacrifices after three and one-half years. A destroyer will do terrible things until the ordered end comes to the destroyed city."

Daniel's Vision of a Man

10 During Cyrus' third year as king of Persia, Daniel, whose name was Belteshazzar, received a vision about a great war. It was a true message that Daniel understood.

2At that time I, Daniel, had been very sad for three weeks. 3I did not eat any fancy food or meat, or drink any wine, or use any perfumed oil for three weeks.

4On the twenty-fourth day of the first month, I was standing beside the great Tigris River. 5While standing there, I looked up and saw a man dressed in linen clothes with a belt of fine gold wrapped around his waist. 6His body was like shiny yellow quartz. His face was bright like lightning, and his eyes were like fire. His arms and legs were shiny like polished bronze, and his voice sounded like the roar of a crowd.

7I, Daniel, was the only person who saw the vision. The men with me did not see it, because they were so frightened that they ran away and hid. 8So I was left alone, watching this great vision. I lost my strength, my face turned white like a dead person, and I was helpless. 9Then I heard the man in the vision speaking. As I listened, I fell into a deep sleep with my face on the ground.

10Then a hand touched me and set me on my hands and knees. I was so afraid that I was shaking. 11The man in the vision said to me, "Daniel, God loves you very much. Think carefully about the words I will speak to you, and stand up, because I have been sent to you." When he said this, I stood up, but I was still shaking.

12Then the man said to me, "Daniel, do not be afraid. Some time ago you decided to get understanding and to humble yourself before your God. Since that time God has listened to you, and I have come because of your prayers. 13But the prince of Persia has been fighting against me for twenty-one days. Then Michael, one of the most important angels, came to help me, because I had been left there with the king of Persia. 14Now I have come to explain to you what will happen to your people, because the vision is about a time in the future."

15While he was speaking to me, I bowed facedown and could not speak. 16Then one who looked like a man touched my lips, so I opened my mouth and started to speak. I said to the one standing in front of me, "Master, I am upset and afraid because of what I saw in the vision. I feel helpless. 17Master, how can I, your servant, talk with you? My strength is gone, and it is hard for me to breathe."

18The one who looked like a man touched me again and gave me strength. 19He said, "Daniel, don't be afraid. God loves you very much. Peace be with you. Be strong now; be courageous."

When he spoke to me, I became stronger and said, "Master, speak, since you have given me strength."

20Then he said, "Daniel, do you know why I have come to you? Soon I must go back to fight against the prince of Persia. When I go, the prince of Greece will come, 21but I must first tell you what is written in the Book of Truth. No one stands with me against these enemies except Michael, the angel ruling over your people.

11 In the first year that Darius the Mede was king, I stood up to support Michael in his fight against the prince of Persia.

Kingdoms of the South and North

2"Now then, Daniel, I tell you the truth: Three more kings will rule in Persia, and then a fourth king will come. He will be much richer than all the kings of Persia before him and will use his riches to get power. He will stir up everyone against the kingdom of Greece. 3Then a mighty king will come, who will rule with great power and will do anything he wants. 4After that king has come, his kingdom will be broken up and divided out toward the four parts of the world. His kingdom will not go to his descendants,d and it will not have the power that he had, because his kingdom will be pulled up and given to other people.

5"The king of the South will become strong, but one of his commanders will become even stronger. He will begin to rule his own kingdom with great power. 6Then after a few years, a new friendship will develop. The daughter of the king of the South will marry the king of the North in order to bring peace. But she will not keep her power, and his family will not last. She, her husband, her child, and those who brought her to that country will be killed.

7"But a person from her family will become king of the South and will attack the armies of the king of the North. He will go into that king's strong, walled city and will fight and win. 8He will take their gods, their metal idols, and their valuable things made of silver and gold back to Egypt. Then he will not bother the king of the North for a few years. 9Next, the king of the North will attack the king of the South, but he will be beaten back to his own country.

10"The sons of the king of the North will prepare for war. They will get a large army together that will move through the land very quickly, like a powerful flood. Later, that army will come back and fight all the way to the strong, walled city of the king of the South. 11Then the king of the South will become very angry and will march out to fight against the king of the North. The king of the North will have a large army, but he will lose the battle, 12and the soldiers will be carried away. The king of the South will then be very proud and will kill thousands of soldiers from the northern army, but he will not continue to be successful. 13The king of the North will gather another army, larger than the first one. After several years he will attack with a large army and many weapons.

14"In those times many people will be against the king of the South. Some of your own people who love to fight will turn against the king of the South, thinking it is time for God's promises to come true. But they will fail. 15Then the king of the North will come. He will build ramps to the tops of the city walls and will capture a strong, walled city. The southern army will not have the power to fight back; even their best soldiers will not be strong enough to stop the northern army.

16So the king of the North will do whatever he wants; no one will be able to stand against him. He will gain power and control in the beautiful land of Israel and will have the power to destroy it. 17The king of the North will decide to use all his power to fight against the king of the South, but he will make a peace agreement with the king of the South. The king of the North will give one of his daughters as a wife to the king of the South so that he can defeat him. But those plans will not succeed or help him. 18Then the king of the North will turn his attention to cities along the coast of the Mediterranean Sea and will capture them. But a commander will put an end to the pride of the king of the North, turning his pride back on him. 19After that happens the king of the North will go back to the strong, walled cities of his own country, but he will lose his power. That will be the end of him.

20"The next king of the North will send out a tax collector so he will have plenty of money. In a few years that ruler will be killed, although he will not die in anger or in a battle.

21"That ruler will be followed by a very cruel and hated man, who will not have the honor of being from a king's family. He will attack the kingdom when the people feel safe, and he will take power by lying to the people. 22He will sweep away in defeat large and powerful armies and even a prince who made an agreement. 23Many nations will make agreements with that cruel and hated ruler, but he will lie to them. He will gain much power, but only a few people will support him. 24The richest areas will feel safe, but that cruel and hated ruler will attack them. He will succeed where his ancestors did not. He will rob the countries he defeats and will give those things to his followers. He will plan to defeat and destroy strong cities, but he will be successful for only a short time.

25"That very cruel and hated ruler will have a large army that he will use to stir up his strength and courage. He will attack the king of the South. The king of the South will gather a large and very powerful army and prepare for war. But the people who are against him will make secret plans, and the king of the South will be defeated. 26People who were supposed to be his good friends will try to destroy him. His army will be swept away in defeat; many of his soldiers will be killed in battle. 27Those two kings will want to hurt each other. They will sit at the same table and lie to each other, but it will not do either one any good, because God has set a time for their end to come. 28The king of the North will go back to his own country with much wealth. Then he will decide to go against the holy agreement. He will take action and then return to his own country.

29"At the right time the king of the North will attack the king of the South again, but this time he will not be successful as he was before. 30Ships from the west will come and fight against the king of the North, so he will be afraid. Then he will return and show his anger against the holy agreement. He will be good to those who have stopped obeying the holy agreement.

31"The king of the North will send his army to make the Temple*d* in Jerusalem unclean.*d* They will stop the people from offering the daily sacrifice, and then they will set up the destroying terror. 32The king of the North will tell lies and cause those who have not obeyed God to be ruined. But those who know God and obey him will be strong and fight back.

33"Those who are wise will help the others understand what is happening. But they will be killed with swords, or burned, or taken captive, or robbed of their homes and possessions. These things will continue for many days. 34When the wise ones are suffering, they will get a little help, but many who join the wise ones will not help them in their time of need. 35Some of the wise ones will be killed. But the hard times must come so they can be made stronger and purer and without faults until the time of the end comes. Then, at the right time, the end will come.

The King Who Praises Himself

36"The king of the North will do whatever he wants. He will brag about himself and praise himself and think he is even better than a god. He will say things against the God of gods that no one has ever heard. And he will be successful until all the bad things have happened. Then what God has planned to happen will happen. 37The king of the North will not care about the gods his ancestors worshiped or the god that women worship. He won't care about any god. Instead, he will make himself more important than any god. 38The king of the North will worship power and strength, which his ancestors did not worship. He will honor the god of power with gold and silver, expensive jewels and gifts. 39That king will attack strong, walled cities with the help of a foreign god. He will give much honor to the people who join him, making them rulers in charge of many other people. And he will make them pay him for the land they rule.

40"At the time of the end, the king of the South will fight a battle against the king of the North. The king of the North will attack with chariots, soldiers on horses, and many large ships. He will invade many countries and sweep through their lands like a flood. 41The king of the North will attack the beautiful land of Judah. He will defeat many countries, but Edom, Moab, and the leaders of Ammon will be saved from him. 42The king of the North will show his power in many countries;

Egypt will not escape. 43The king will get treasures of gold and silver and all the riches of Egypt. The Libyan and Nubian people will obey him. 44But the king of the North will hear news from the east and the north that will make him afraid and angry. He will go to destroy completely many nations. 45He will set up his royal tents between the sea and the beautiful mountain where the holy Temple*d* is built. But, finally, his end will come, and no one will help him.

The Time of the End

12 "At that time Michael, the great prince who protects your people, will stand up. There will be a time of much trouble, the worst time since nations have been on earth, but your people will be saved. Everyone whose name is written in God's book will be saved. 2Many people who have already died will live again. Some

of them will wake up to have life forever, but some will wake up to find shame and disgrace

---

SIDELIGHT: Rise and shine! Daniel 12:2 is the clearest reference in the Old Testament to the resurrection of the dead. Another possible reference is found in Isaiah 26:19 (p. 642).

---

forever. 3The wise people will shine like the brightness of the sky. Those who teach others to live right will shine like stars forever and ever.

4"But you, Daniel, close up the book and seal it. These things will happen at the time of the end. Many people will go here and there to find true knowledge."

ETERNAL LIFE

Going the Distance

At the age of nineteen, Canadian Terry Fox lost his right leg to cancer. After the amputation, he became a discouraged and bitter young man. He assumed he was stuck in a wheelchair forever and felt cheated out of the "normal" things in life.

Trying to provide some motivation, Terry's former basketball coach showed him an article about a one-legged man who competed in the New York Marathon. The article ignited a sense of challenge in Terry. "If he can do it, so can I," Terry thought.

Gradually, Terry began to set goals for himself and decided to take more control of his life. He began to build his body and find ways to run with an artificial limb. He perfected the stride that came to be called the "Fox Trot." He was soon running frequently and feeling good about his life.

On April 12, 1980, Terry started his "marathon of hope," a solo run across Canada to raise money for cancer research. Four and one-half months later, after covering 3,317 miles and raising twenty-four million dollars, he had to stop. The cancer had spread to his lungs. Terry was hospitalized, and pneumonia set in. He died at the age of twenty-two.

Terry remains a dramatic symbol of hope and courage to Canada and to the world. "I wanted to show people that just because they are disabled, it's not the end," he said.

His memory will live for many, many years.

All of us need more of that kind of hope and courage. Read about the rewards in **Daniel 12:1–3** for those who trust in God for strength to go the distance.

■ What hope and encouragement would Terry have found in this passage as he struggled to complete his transcontinental trek?
■ If you were to be remembered forever, how would you like to be remembered?

C O N S I D E R . . .
■ completing this sentence as many ways as possible: "When I think of eternal life, I imagine . . . ."
■ drawing a star and writing the name of a person you respect on it (see verse 3) and then thanking God for that person each day this week.

F O R   M O R E ,   S E E . . .
■ Ezekiel 37:1–14 (p. 793)
■ Mark 13:1–12 (p. 989)
■ 1 Corinthians 15:12–28 (p. 1187)

[5]Then I, Daniel, looked, and saw two other men. One was standing on my side of the river, and the other was standing on the far side. [6]The man who was dressed in linen was standing over the water in the river. One of the two men spoke to him and asked, "How long will it be before these amazing things come true?"

[7]The man dressed in linen, who stood over the water, raised his hands toward heaven. And I heard him swear by the name of God who lives forever, "It will be for three and one-half years. The power of the holy people will finally be broken, and then all these things will come true."

[8]I heard the answer, but I did not really understand, so I asked, "Master, what will happen after all these things come true?"

[9]He answered, "Go your way, Daniel. The message is closed up and sealed until the time of the end. [10]Many people will be made clean,[a] pure, and spotless, but the wicked will continue to be wicked. Those wicked people will not understand these things, but the wise will understand them.

[11]"The daily sacrifice will be stopped. Then, after 1,290 days from that time, the destroying terror will be set up. [12]Those who wait for the end of the 1,335 days will be happy.

[13]"As for you, Daniel, go your way until the end. You will get your rest, and at the end you will rise to receive your reward."

HOSEA

Why Read This Book:
- Discover how strong God's love is (Hosea 1—3).
- Learn what can happen when people turn from God (Hosea 6—10).
- Find assurance in God's love and forgiveness (Hosea 11—14).

Behind the Scenes:

Imagine God telling someone to marry a prostitute. Then imagine that man remaining faithful to his bride even after she returned to her old job.

As improbable as that situation may sound, it is what happened in the book of Hosea. The prophet Hosea married Gomer, a prostitute. She was unfaithful to him, yet he continued to love her and forgive her. Even though her unfaithfulness hurt him, Hosea never stopped loving his unfaithful wife.

Hosea's life symbolized God's relationship to Israel. God had tried to build a relationship with the Israelites. But time after time, the Israelites had turned to other "lovers"—other gods. Yet God's love wouldn't let Israel go.

Hosea preached in the Northern Kingdom (Israel) in the eighth century B.C. It was a time of prosperity, so the people didn't listen to him. But years of immorality

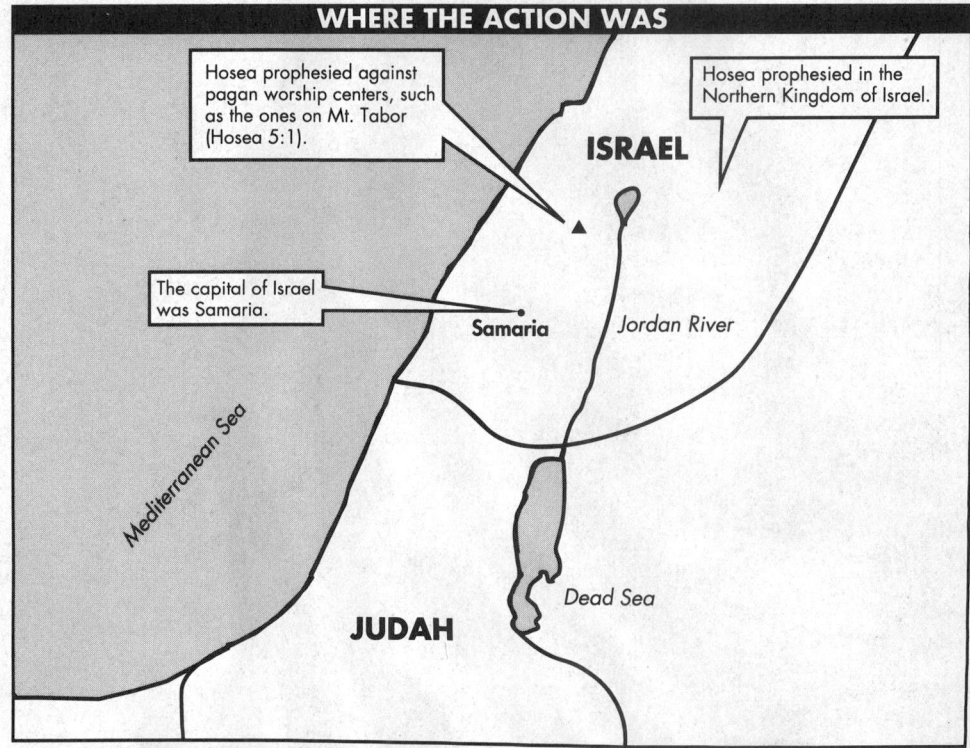

WHERE THE ACTION WAS

Hosea prophesied against pagan worship centers, such as the ones on Mt. Tabor (Hosea 5:1).

Hosea prophesied in the Northern Kingdom of Israel.

ISRAEL

The capital of Israel was Samaria.

Samaria

Jordan River

Mediterranean Sea

Dead Sea

JUDAH

WHEN THE ACTION WAS

The kingdom was split between Israel and Judah	Hosea ministered in Israel	The Jews began returning from exile		Jesus was born
1000BC	**750BC**	**500BC**	**250BC**	**BC/AD**
Saul was Israel's king	The Northern Kingdom (Israel) fell to Assyria	The Southern Kingdom (Judah) fell to Babylon		

Behind the and unfaithfulness followed, leading to Israel's destruction in 722 B.C. by the
Scenes (cont.): Assyrians.

The book of Hosea tells the story of a prophet's pleading with the people to
stop turning away from God and to recognize God's everlasting and tender love.
Through the prophet, God says, "I want faithful love. . . . I want people to know
me. . . ." (Hosea 6:6). This central message in Hosea is a message for all time!

---

1 The LORD spoke his word to Hosea son of
Beeri during the time that Uzziah, Jotham,
Ahaz, and Hezekiah were kings of Judah and Jero-
boam son of Jehoash was king of Israel.

Hosea's Wife and Children

2When the LORD began speaking through Hosea, the LORD said to him, "Go, and marry an unfaithful woman and have unfaithful children,
because the people in this country have
been completely unfaithful to the LORD." 3So
Hosea married Gomer daughter of Diblaim, and
she became pregnant and gave birth to Hosea's
son.

4The LORD said to Hosea, "Name him Jezreel,
because soon I will punish the family of Jehu for
the people they killed at Jezreel. In the future I
will put an end to the kingdom of Israel 5and
break the power of Israel's army in the Valley of
Jezreel."

6Gomer became pregnant again and gave birth
to a daughter. The LORD said to Hosea, "Name
her Lo-Ruhamah,n because I will not pity Israel
anymore, nor will I forgive them. 7But I will show
pity to the people of Judah. I will save them, but
not by using bows or swords, horses or horsemen,
or weapons of war. I, the LORD their God, will
save them."

8After Gomer had stopped nursing Lo-
Ruhamah, she became pregnant again and gave
birth to another son. 9The LORD said, "Name him
Lo-Ammi,n because you are not my people, and
I am not your God.

God's Promise to Israel

10"But the number of the Israelites will become
like the grains of sand of the sea, which no one
can measure or count. They were called, 'You are
not my people,' but later they will be called 'children of the living God.' 11The people of Judah and
Israel will join together again and will choose one
leader for themselves. They will come up from
the land, because the day of Jezreeln will be truly
great.

2 "You are to call your brothers, 'my people,'
and your sisters, 'you have been shown pity.'

God Speaks About Israel

2"Plead with your mother.n
Accuse her, because she is no longer my
wife,
and I am no longer her husband.
Tell her to stop acting like a prostitute,d
to stop behaving like an unfaithful wife.
3If she refuses, I will strip her naked
and leave her bare like the day she was
born.
I will make her dry like a desert,
like a land without water,
and I will kill her with thirst.
4I will not take pity on her children,
because they are the children of a
prostitute.
5Their mother has acted like a prostitute;
the one who became pregnant with them
has acted disgracefully.
She said, 'I will chase after my lovers,n
who give me my food and water,
wool and flax, wine and olive oil.'
6So I will block her road with thornbushes;
I will build a wall around her
so she cannot find her way.
7She will run after her lovers,
but she won't catch them.
She will look for them,
but she won't find them.

SIDELIGHT: If you've been
teased because your parents gave you
an unusual name, imagine how Jezreel, Lo-
Ruhamah, and Lo-Ammi felt (Hosea 1:4–9).
Their names meant, respectively, "God
plants," "not pitied," and "not my people."

Lo-Ruhamah This name in Hebrew means "not pitied."
Lo-Ammi This name in Hebrew means "not my people."
Jezreel This name in Hebrew means "God plants."
mother Refers to the nation of Israel here.
lovers Refers to the nations surrounding Israel, who led Israel to worship false gods.

Then she will say, 'I will go back to my first
    husband,[n]
because life was better then for me than it
    is now.'
[8]But she does not know that I was the one
    who gave her grain, new wine, and oil.
I gave her much silver and gold,
    but she used it for Baal.[d]

[9]"So I will come back and take away my grain
    at harvest time
and my new wine when it is ready.
I will take back my wool and linen
    that covered her nakedness.
[10]So I will show her nakedness to her
    lovers,
    and no one will save her from me.
[11]I will put an end to all her celebrations:
    her yearly festivals, her New Moon[d]
    festivals, and her Sabbaths.[d]
I will stop all of her special feasts.

[12]I will destroy her vines and fig trees,
    which she said were her pay from her
    lovers.
I will turn them into a forest,
    and wild animals will eat them.
[13]I will punish her for all the times
    she burned incense[d] to the Baals.
She put on her rings and jewelry
    and went chasing after her lovers,
but she forgot me!"
    says the LORD.

[14]"So I am going to attract her;
    I will lead her into the desert
    and speak tenderly to her.
[15]There I will give her back her vineyards,
    and I will make the Valley of Trouble a
    door of hope.
There she will respond as when she was
    young,
    as when she came out of Egypt."

husband   Refers to God here.

Going to the Desert

Sometimes it was so difficult to think clearly back home. Danny Washington had grown up in the noise, clamor, and confusion of inner-city Philadelphia. Similar confusion filled his own life. Arrested for a series of minor crimes, Danny was assigned to a juvenile delinquent treatment program.

Now here he was on a mountain ridge in West Virginia, participating in a wilderness challenge course—nineteen days of mountain living. The course had been frustrating so far. His feelings of frustration and anger from the inner city followed him. He had snapped at the advisers because of the cold and the rain, the long days of hiking with backpacks, and getting lost. Why couldn't he ever just relax and handle the situation? Why did he always feel so angry and out of control?

Sitting under the quiet, star-filled sky, Danny tried to sort out his feelings of failure by talking with Bob, his group adviser. They talked about thoughts and fears for a long time. Then Bob said, "If there were just one gift I could give you, it'd be the gift of peace—the peace that begins with accepting yourself as loved by God."

Tears welled in Danny's eyes. In the silence of the wilderness, Danny felt the quiet peace and acceptance of God for the first time.

Sometimes following God requires us to leave our usual surroundings and go to a quiet place to hear his message. In **Hosea 2:14–20** read how God would become more real in the wilderness.

■ How is God's message to Israel similar to the one that Danny heard?
■ How does the passage's theme compare with your own ideas of what it means to follow God?

CONSIDER . . .
■ taking a long walk by yourself and listening for ways God wants you to serve him.
■ serving God through a quiet act of kindness, such as listening to someone without interrupting, or donating your time and money to a ministry you support.

FOR   MORE,   SEE . . .
■ Exodus 3:1–6 (p. 60)
■ Matthew 4:1–11 (p. 910)
■ Luke 9:28–36 (p. 1019)

16The Lord says, "In the future she will call me 'my husband';
no longer will she call me 'my baal.'[n]
17I will never let her say the names of Baal again;
people won't use their names anymore.
18At that time I will make an agreement for them
with the wild animals, the birds, and the crawling things.
I will smash from the land
the bow and the sword and the weapons of war,
so my people will live in safety.
19And I will make you my promised bride forever.
I will be good and fair;
I will show you my love and mercy.
20I will be true to you as my promised bride,
and you will know the Lord.

21"At that time I will speak to you," says the Lord.
"I will speak to the skies,
and they will give rain to the earth.
22The earth will produce grain, new wine, and oil;
much will grow because my people are called Jezreel.[n]
23I will plant my people in the land,
and I will show pity to the one I had called 'not shown pity.'
I will say, 'You are my people'
to those I had called 'not my people.'
And they will say to me, 'You are our God.' "

SIDELIGHT: Hosea's wife, Gomer, probably wasn't an ordinary prostitute (Hosea 3:1). Most likely she was a cult prostitute—or cult priestess—in the temples of the false god Baal. The Baal religion included a variety of fertility rites thought to bring rain and a bountiful harvest.

Hosea Buys a Wife

3 The Lord said to me again, "Go, show your love to a woman loved by someone else, who has been unfaithful to you. In the same way the Lord loves the people of Israel, even though they worship other gods and love to eat the raisin cakes."[n]

2So I bought her for six ounces of silver and ten bushels of barley. 3Then I told her, "You must wait for me for many days. You must not be a prostitute,[d] and you must not have sexual relations with any other man. I will act the same way toward you."

4In the same way Israel will live many days without a king or leader, without sacrifices or holy stone pillars, and without the holy vest[d] or an idol. 5After this, the people of Israel will return to the Lord their God and follow him, and the king from David's family. In the last days they will turn in fear to the Lord, and he will bless them.

The Lord's Word Against Israel

4 People of Israel, listen to the Lord's message.
The Lord has this
against you who live in the land:
"The people are not true, not loyal to God,
nor do those who live in the land even know him.
2Cursing, lying, killing, stealing and adultery[d]
are everywhere.
One murder follows another.
3Because of this the land dries up,
and all its people are dying.
Even the wild animals and the birds of the air
and the fish of the sea are dying.

God's Case Against the Priests

4"No one should accuse
or blame another person.
Don't blame the people, you priests,
when they quarrel with you.
5You will be ruined in the day,
and your prophets[d] will be ruined with you in the night.
I will also destroy your mother.[n]
6My people will be destroyed,
because they have no knowledge.
You have refused to learn,
so I will refuse to let you be priests to me.
You have forgotten the teachings of your God,
so I will forget your children.
7The more priests there are,
the more they sin against me.
I will take away their honor
and give them shame.
8Since the priests live off the sin offerings of the people,

---

baal　Another Hebrew word for husband, but it was the same word as the god Baal.
Jezreel　This name in Hebrew means "God plants."
raisin cakes　This food was eaten in the feasts that honored false gods.
mother　Here "mother" refers to the nation of Israel.

they want the people to sin more and
more.
[9]The priests are as wrong as the people,
and I will punish them both for what they
have done.
I will repay them for the wrong they have
done.

[10]"They will eat
but not have enough;
they will have sexual relations with the
prostitutes,[d]
but they will not have children,
because they have left the LORD
to give themselves to [11]prostitution,
to old and new wine,
which take away their ability to understand.

God's Case Against the People

[12]"My people ask wooden idols for advice;
they ask those sticks of wood to advise
them!
Like prostitutes, they have chased after other
gods
and have left their own God.
[13]They make sacrifices on the tops of the
mountains.
They burn offerings on the hills,
under oaks, poplars, and other trees,
because their shade is nice.
So your daughters become prostitutes,
and your daughters-in-law are guilty of
adultery.[d]

[14]"But I will not punish your daughters
for becoming prostitutes,
nor your daughters-in-law
for their sins of adultery.
I will not punish them,
because the men have sexual relations with
prostitutes
and offer sacrifices with the temple
prostitutes.
A foolish people will be ruined.

[15]"Israel, you act like a prostitute,
but do not be guilty toward the LORD.
Don't go to Gilgal
or go up to Beth Aven.[n]
Don't make promises,
saying, 'As surely as the LORD lives . . .'
[16]The people of Israel are stubborn
like a stubborn young cow.
Now the LORD will feed them
like lambs in the open country.
[17]The Israelites have chosen to worship idols,
so leave them alone.
[18]When they finish their drinking,

they completely give themselves to being
prostitutes;
they love these disgraceful ways.
[19]They will be swept away as if by a
whirlwind,
and their sacrifices will bring them only
shame.

God's Word Against the Leaders

5 "Listen, you priests.
Pay attention, people of Israel.
Listen, royal family,
because you will all be judged.
You have been like a trap at Mizpah
and like a net spread out at Mount Tabor.
[2]You have done many evil things,
so I will punish you all.
[3]I know all about the people of Israel;
what they have done is not hidden from
me.
Now that Israel acts like a prostitute,[d]
it has made itself unclean.[d]

[4]"They will not give up their deeds
and return to their God.
They are determined to be unfaithful to me;
they do not know the LORD.
[5]Israel's pride testifies against them.
The people of Israel will stumble because of
their sin,
and the people of Judah will stumble with
them.
[6]They will come to worship the LORD,
bringing their flocks and herds,
but they will not be able to find him,
because he has left them.
[7]They have not been true to the LORD;
they are children who do not belong to
him.
So their false worship
will destroy them and their land.

[8]"Blow the horn in Gibeah
and the trumpet in Ramah.
Give the warning at Beth Aven,
and be first into battle, people of Benjamin.
[9]Israel will be ruined
on the day of punishment.
To the tribes[d] of Israel
I tell the truth.
[10]The leaders of Judah are like those
who steal other people's land.
I will pour my punishment over them
like a flood of water.
[11]Israel is crushed by the punishment,
because it decided to follow idols.
[12]I am like a moth to Israel,
like a rot to the people of Judah.

Gilgal . . . Beth Aven Cities in Israel where people worshiped false gods.

13"When Israel saw its illness
  and Judah saw its wounds,
Israel went to Assyria for help
  and sent to the great king of Assyria.
But he cannot heal you
  or cure your wounds.
14I will be like a lion to Israel,
  like a young lion to Judah.
I will attack them
  and tear them to pieces.
I will drag them off,
  and no one will be able to save them.
15Then I will go back to my place

until they suffer for their guilt and turn
  back to me.
In their trouble they will look for me."

The People Are Not Faithful

6 "Come, let's go back to the LORD.
  He has hurt us, but he will heal us.
He has wounded us, but he will bandage
  our wounds.
2In two days he will put new life in us;
  on the third day he will raise us up
so that we may live in his presence 3and
  know him.

FOLLOWING GOD

Shape Up or Ship Out

Even as a child, Nadja Salerno-Sonnenberg was a "natural" on the violin. Nadja could play the most difficult violin music as easily as most people breathe or sleep. She made her official concert debut with the Philadelphia Orchestra at the age of ten.

"When I was young I was very talented. I still am, but I rode on that talent for such a long time," Nadja says.

"At age fourteen, I'd walk on stage and whip off the Carmen Fantasy as if I were Heifetz, because I had the ability in my fingers. At sixteen, I was still kind of whipping it off. At seventeen or eighteen, I walked on stage and stumbled all over it. I finally realized how difficult it was to play the violin." So, incredibly, Nadja abandoned her instrument while already a student at Juilliard School of Music.

Her teacher at Juilliard, Dorothy DeLay, had previously taught some of the world's best violinists. She grew angry with Nadja's "going through the motions" and her mediocre effort. When Nadja began showing up for lessons without her violin, Dorothy told her to shape up or ship out. "She was threatening to throw me out of class," says Nadja. "I was petrified."

Jolted out of her complacency, Nadja followed her teacher's demand: intense, dedicated practice. She entered the prestigious Naumburg Competition. "I was like a horse with blinders on. My goal was to make the finals so that everybody would know I was still out there," she says.

Everybody watched in awe as, at age twenty, she played her way to becoming the youngest first-prize winner in the competition's history. She's gone on to perform for astonished audiences at sold-out concerts around the world.

Just as Nadja once "went through the motions" of violin lessons, the people in Hosea's time were "going through the motions" of faith. Instead of following God, they paid him token attention with ritualistic animal sacrifices. God, through Hosea, shares his anger about this dull, ho-hum faith. Read what God does want in **Hosea 6:1–6.**

■ Why did Nadja's teacher and God become angry with empty efforts?
■ How would your life change if you more intensely followed God's desire that you love him faithfully? How might your church be different? your world?

C O N S I D E R . . .

■ making two columns on a sheet of paper, one headed by "Dull, dead faith" and the other by "God-following faith." List as many activities as you can think of that fit each category. Pick one from the God-following column and do it.
■ spending more time each day in prayer and reading the Bible to get to know God.

F O R   M O R E ,   S E E . . .

■ Micah 6:8 (p. 866)   ■ Colossians 3:12–17 (p. 1241)
■ Matthew 22:34–40 (p. 948)

Let's try to learn about the LORD;
    He will come to us as surely as the dawn
        comes.
He will come to us like rain,
    like the spring rain that waters the
        ground."

4The LORD says, "Israel, what should I do
    with you?
Judah, what should I do with you?
Your faithfulness is like a morning mist,
    like the dew that goes away early in the
        day.
5I have warned you by my prophets[d]
    that I will kill you and destroy you.
My justice comes out like bright light.
6I want faithful love
    more than I want animal sacrifices.
I want people to know me
    more than I want burnt offerings.
7But they have broken the agreement as Adam
    did;
    they have been unfaithful to me.
8Gilead is a city of people who do evil;
    their footprints are bloody.
9The priests are like robbers waiting to attack
        people;
    they murder people on the road to
        Shechem[n]
    and do wicked things.
10I have seen horrible things in Israel.
Look at Israel's prostitution;[d]
    Israel has become unclean.[d]

11"Judah, I have set a harvest time for you
    when I will make the lives of my people
        good again.

7 When I heal Israel,
    Israel's sin will go away,
and so will Samaria's evil.

"They cheat a lot!
    Thieves break into houses,
    and robbers are in the streets.
2It never enters their minds
    that I remember all their evil deeds.
The bad things they do are all around them;
    they are right in front of me.

Israel's Evil Kings

3"They make the king happy with their
        wickedness;
    their rulers are glad with their lies.
4But all of them are traitors.
    They are like an oven heated by a baker.
While he mixes the dough,
    he does not need to stir up the fire.

Shechem A city of safety where people could go for protection.

5The kings get so drunk they get sick every
        day.
The rulers become crazy with wine;
    they make agreements with those who do
        not know the true God.
6They burn like an oven;
    their hearts burn inside them.
All night long their anger is low,
    but when morning comes, it becomes a
        roaring fire.
7All these people are as hot as an oven;
    they burn up their rulers.
All their kings fall,
    and no one calls on me.

Israel and the Other Nations

8"Israel mixes with other nations;
    he is like a pancake cooked only on one
        side.
9Foreign nations have eaten up his strength,
    but he doesn't know it.
Israel is weak and feeble, like an old man,
    but he doesn't know it.
10Israel's pride will cause their defeat;
    they will not turn back to the LORD their
        God
    or look to him for help in all this.
11Israel has become like a pigeon—
    easy to fool and stupid.
First they call to Egypt for help.
    Then they run to Assyria.
12When they go, I will catch them in a net,
    I will bring them down like birds from the
        sky;
    I will punish them countless times for their
        evil.
13How terrible for them because they left me!
    They will be destroyed, because they
        turned against me.
I want to save them,
    but they have spoken lies against me.
14They do not call to me from their hearts.
They just lie on their beds and cry.
They come together to ask for grain and new
        wine,
    but they really turn away from me.

[15]Though I trained them and gave them
  strength,
  they have made evil plans against me.
[16]They did not turn to the Most High God.
  They are like a loose bow that can't
    shoot.
Because their leaders brag about their
  strength,
  they will be killed with swords,
and the people in Egypt
  will laugh at them.

Israel Has Trusted Wrong Things

8 "Put the trumpet to your lips and give the
  warning!
  The enemy swoops down on the LORD's
    people like an eagle.
The Israelites have broken my agreement
  and have turned against my teachings.
[2]They cry out to me,
  'Our God, we in Israel know you!'
[3]But Israel has rejected what is good,
  so the enemy will chase them.
[4]They chose their own kings
  without asking my permission.
They chose their own leaders,
  people I did not know.
They made their silver and gold into idols,
  and for all this they will be destroyed.
[5]I hate the calf-shaped idol of Israel!
  I am very angry with the people.
How long will they remain unclean?[d]
[6]The idol is something a craftsman made;
  it is not God.
Israel's calf-shaped idol
  will surely be smashed to pieces.

[7]"Israel's foolish plans are like planting the
    wind,
  but they will harvest a storm.
Like a stalk with no head of grain,
  it produces nothing.
Even if it produced something,
  other nations would eat it.
[8]Israel is eaten up;
  the people are mixed among the other
    nations
  and have become useless to me.
[9]Israel is like a wild donkey all by itself.
  They have run to Assyria;
  They have hired other nations to protect
    them.
[10]Although Israel is mixed among the nations,
  I will gather them together.
They will become weaker and weaker
  as they suffer under the great king of
    Assyria.

[11]"Although Israel built more altars to remove
    sin,
  they have become altars for sinning.
[12]I have written many teachings for them,
  but they think the teachings are strange
    and foreign.
[13]The Israelites offer sacrifices to me as gifts
  and eat the meat,
but the LORD is not pleased with them.
  He remembers the evil they have done,
and he will punish them for their sins.
  They will be slaves again as they were in
    Egypt.
[14]Israel has forgotten their Maker and has built
    palaces;
  Judah has built many strong, walled cities.
But I will send fire on their cities
  and destroy their strong buildings."

Israel's Punishment

9 Israel, do not rejoice;
  don't shout for joy as the other nations
    do.
  You have been like a prostitute[d] against your
    God.
  You love the pay of prostitutes on every
    threshing[d] floor.
[2]But the threshing floor and the winepress will
    not feed the people,
  and there won't be enough new wine.
[3]The people will not stay in the LORD's land.
  Israel will return to being captives as they
    were in Egypt,
  and in Assyria they will eat food that they
    are not allowed to eat.
[4]The Israelites will not give offerings of wine
    to the LORD;
  they will not give him sacrifices.
Their sacrifices will be like food that is eaten
    at a funeral;
  it is unclean,[d] and everyone who eats it
    becomes unclean.
Their food will only satisfy their hunger;
  they cannot sacrifice it in the Temple.[d]
[5]What will you do then on the day of feasts
  and on the day of the LORD's festival?
[6]Even if the people are not destroyed,
  Egypt will capture them;
  Memphis[n] will bury them.
Weeds will grow over their silver treasures,
  and thorns will drive them out of their
    tents.
[7]The time of punishment has come,
  the time to pay for sins.
  Let Israel know this:
You think the prophet[d] is a fool,
  and you say the spiritual person is crazy.

Memphis A city in Egypt famous for its tombs.

You have sinned very much,
and your hatred is great.
[8]Is Israel a watchman?
Are God's people prophets?
Everywhere Israel goes, traps are set for him.
He is an enemy in God's house.
[9]The people of Israel have gone deep into sin
as the people of Gibeah[n] did.
The Lord will remember the evil things they
have done,
and he will punish their sins.

[10]"When I found Israel,
it was like finding grapes in the desert.
Your ancestors were like
finding the first figs on the fig tree.
But when they came to Baal Peor,
they began worshiping an idol,
and they became as hateful as the thing
they worshiped.
[11]Israel's glory will fly away like a bird;
there will be no more pregnancy, no more
births, no more getting pregnant.
[12]But even if the Israelites bring up children,
I will take them all away.
How terrible it will be for them
when I go away from them!
[13]I have seen Israel, like Tyre,
given a pleasant place.
But the people of Israel will soon bring out
their children to be killed."
[14]LORD, give them what they should have.
What will you give them?
Make their women unable to have
children;
give them dried-up breasts that cannot feed
their babies.

[15]"The Israelites were very wicked in Gilgal,
so I have hated them there.
Because of the sinful things they have done,
I will force them to leave my land.
I will no longer love them;
their leaders have turned against me.
[16]Israel is beaten down;
its root is dying, and it has no fruit.
If they have more children,
I will kill the children they love."

[17]God will reject them,
because they have not obeyed him;
they will wander among the nations.

Israel Will Pay for Sin

10 Israel is like a large vine
that produced plenty of fruit.
As the people became richer,

they built more altars for idols.
As their land became better,
they put up better stone pillars to honor
gods.
[2]Their heart was false,
and now they must pay for their guilt.
The LORD will break down their altars;
he will destroy their holy stone pillars.

[3]Then they will say, "We have no king,
because we didn't honor the LORD.
As for the king,
he couldn't do anything for us."
[4]They make many false promises
and agreements which they don't keep.
So people sue each other in court;
they are like poisonous weeds growing in a
plowed field.
[5]The people from Israel are worried about
the calf-shaped idol at Beth Aven.
The people will cry about it,
and the priests will cry about it.
They used to shout for joy about its glory,
[6]but it will be carried off to Assyria
as a gift to the great king.
Israel will be disgraced,
and the people will be ashamed for not
obeying.
[7]Israel will be destroyed;
its king will be like a chip of wood floating
on the water.
[8]The places of false worship will be destroyed,
the places where Israel sins.
Thorns and weeds will grow up
and cover their altars.
Then they will say to the mountains, "Cover
us!"
and to the hills, "Fall on us!"

[9]"Israel, you have sinned since the time of
Gibeah,[n]
and the people there have continued
sinning.
But war will surely overwhelm them in
Gibeah,
because of the evil they have done there.
[10]When I am ready,
I will come to punish them.
Nations will come together against them,
and they will be punished for their double
sins.
[11]Israel is like a well-trained young cow
that likes to thresh[d] grain.
I will put a yoke[d] on her neck
and make her work hard in the field.
Israel will plow,
and Judah will break up the ground.

Gibeah The sins of the people of Gibeah caused a civil war. See Judges 19-21.

12I said, 'Plant goodness,
   harvest the fruit of loyalty,
   plow the new ground of knowledge.
Look for the Lord until he comes
   and pours goodness on you like water.'
13But you have plowed evil
   and harvested trouble;
   you have eaten the fruit of your lies.
Because you have trusted in your own power
   and your many soldiers,
14your people will hear the noise of battle,
   and all your strong, walled cities will be
     destroyed.
It will be like the time King Shalman
   destroyed Beth Arbel in battle,
   when mothers and their children were
     bashed to death.
15The same will happen to you, people of
     Bethel,
   because you did so much evil.
When the sun comes up,
   the king of Israel will die.

God's Love for Israel

11 "When Israel was a child, I loved him,
   and I called my son out of Egypt.
2But when I called the people of Israel,
   they went away from me.
They offered sacrifices to the Baals*d*
   and burned incense*d* to the idols.
3It was I who taught Israel to walk,
   and I took them by the arms,
but they did not understand
   that I had healed them.
4I led them with cords of human kindness,
   with ropes of love.
I lifted the yoke*d* from their neck
   and bent down and fed them.

5"The Israelites will become captives again, as
     they were in Egypt,
   and Assyria will become their king,
   because they refuse to turn back to God.
6War will sweep through their cities
   and will destroy them
   and kill them because of their wicked
     plans.
7My people have made up their minds
   to turn away from me.
The prophets*d* call them to turn to me,
   but none of them honors me at all.

8"Israel, how can I give you up?
   How can I give you away, Israel?
I don't want to make you like Admah
   or treat you like Zeboiim.*n*
My heart beats for you,
   and my love for you stirs up my pity.

9"I won't punish you in my anger,
   and I won't destroy Israel again.
I am God and not a human;
   I am the Holy One, and I am among you.
   I will not come against you in anger.
10They will go after the Lord,
   and he will roar like a lion.
When he roars,
   his children will hurry to him from the
     west.
11They will come swiftly
   like birds from Egypt
   and like doves from Assyria.
I will settle them again in their homes,"
   says the Lord.

The Lord Is Against Israel

12Israel has surrounded me with lies;
   the people have made evil plans.
And Judah turns against God,
   the faithful Holy One.

12 What Israel does is as useless as
     chasing the wind;
he chases the east wind all day.
They tell more and more lies
   and do more and more violence.
They make agreements with Assyria,
   and they send a gift of olive oil to Egypt.
2The Lord also has some things against Judah.
   He will punish Israel for what they have
     done;
   he will give them what they deserve.
3Their ancestor Jacob held on to his brother's
     heel
while the two of them were being born.
When he grew to be a man,
   he wrestled with God.
4When Jacob wrestled with the angel and
     won,
   he cried and asked for his blessing.
Later, God met with him at Bethel
   and spoke with him there.
5It was the Lord God All-Powerful;
   the Lord is his great name.
6You must return to your God;
   love him, do what is just,
   and always trust in him as your God.

7The merchants use dishonest scales;
   they like to cheat people.
8Israel said, "I am rich! I am someone with
     power!"
All their money will do them no good
   because of the sins they have done.

9"But I am the Lord your God,
   who brought you out of Egypt.
I will make you live in tents again

Admah ... Zeboiim Two other cities destroyed when God destroyed Sodom and Gomorrah.

as you used to do on worship days.
[10]I spoke to the prophets[d]
  and gave them many visions;
  through them, I taught my lessons to you."

[11]The people of Gilead are evil,
    worth nothing.
  Though people sacrifice bulls at Gilgal,
    their altars will become like piles of stone
    in a plowed field.
[12]Your ancestor Jacob fled to Northwest
        Mesopotamia
    where he worked to get a wife;
  he tended sheep to pay for her.
[13]Later the LORD used a prophet
    to bring Jacob's descendants[d] out of Egypt;
  he used a prophet
    to take care of the Israelites.
[14]But the Israelites made the Lord angry when
        they killed other people,
    and they deserve to die for their crimes.
  The Lord will make them pay
    for the disgraceful things they have done.

The Final Word Against Israel

13 People used to fear the tribe[d] of
    Ephraim;
  they were important people in Israel.
  But they sinned by worshiping Baal,[d]
    so they must die.
[2]But they still keep on sinning more and
        more.
  They make idols of their silver,
    idols that are cleverly made,
    the work of a craftsman.
  Yet the people of Israel say to each other,
    "Kiss those calf idols and sacrifice to them."
[3]So those people will be like the morning
        mist;
    they will disappear like the morning dew.
  They will be like chaff[d] blown from the
        threshing[d] floor,
    like smoke going out a window.

[4]"I, the LORD, have been your God
    since you were in the land of Egypt.
  You should have known no other God except
        me.
  I am the only one who saves.
[5]I cared for them in the desert
    where it was hot and dry.
[6]I gave them food, and they became full and
        satisfied.
  But then they became too proud and forgot
        me.
[7]That is why I will be like a lion to them,
    like a leopard waiting by the road.
[8]*I will attack like a bear robbed of her cubs,*
    ripping their bodies open.
  I will devour them like a lion

and tear them apart like a wild animal.
[9]"Israel, I will destroy you.
    Who will be your helper then?
[10]What good is your king?
    Can he save you in any of your towns?
  What good are your leaders?
    You said, 'Give us a king and leaders.'
[11]So I gave you a king, but only in anger,
    and I took him away in my great anger.
[12]The sins of Israel are on record,
    stored away, waiting for punishment.
[13]The pain of birth will come for him,
    but he is like a foolish baby
    who won't come out of its mother's womb.

✻ **SIDELIGHT:** Childbirth was
  much more dangerous in Old
Testament times than it is today in most
places (Hosea 13:13). Many a woman died
during childbirth because she couldn't deliver
her child.

---

[14]Will I save them from the place of the dead?
    Will I rescue them from death?
  Where is your sickness, death?
    Where is your pain, place of death?
  I will show them no mercy.
[15]Israel is doing well among the nations,
    but the LORD will send a wind from the
        east,
  coming from the desert,
    that will dry up his springs and wells of
        water.
  He will destroy from their treasure houses
    everything of value.
[16]The nation of Israel will be ruined,
    because it fought against God.
  The people of Israel will die in war;
    their children will be torn to pieces,
    and their pregnant women will be ripped
        open."

Israel Returns to God

14 Israel, return to the LORD your God,
    because your sins have made you fall.
[2]Come back to the LORD
    and say these words to him:
  "Take away all our sin
    and kindly receive us,
  and we will keep the promises we made to
        you.
[3]Assyria cannot save us,
    nor will we trust in our horses.
  We will not say again, 'Our gods,'
    to the things our hands have made.
  You show mercy to orphans."

⁴The LORD says,
 "I will forgive them for leaving me
   and will love them freely,
   because I am not angry with them
     anymore.
⁵I will be like the dew to Israel,
   and they will blossom like a lily.
 Like the cedar trees in Lebanon,
   their roots will be firm.
⁶They will be like spreading branches,
   like the beautiful olive trees
 and the sweet-smelling cedars in Lebanon.
⁷The people of Israel will again live under my
     protection.
 They will grow like the grain,

they will bloom like a vine,
   and they will be as famous as the wine of
     Lebanon.
⁸Israel, have nothing to do with idols.
   I, the LORD, am the one who answers your
     prayers and watches over you.
 I am like a green pine tree;
   your blessings come from me."

⁹A wise person will know these things,
   and an understanding person will take them
     to heart.
 The LORD's ways are right.
   Good people live by following them,
   but those who turn against God die
     because of them.

JOEL

Why Read This Book:

■ See how forgiveness begins with a change of heart (Joel 2).
■ Hear Joel announce a new life for the faithful (Joel 3).

Behind the Scenes:

In the 1930s, the United States was devastated by the Great Depression. Crops died in the "dust bowls." People lost their jobs. The whole nation was in trouble. People who lived through those years will never forget them.

Judah faced a similar catastrophe, except its land was attacked by locusts. These insects destroyed all vegetation, attacking fields, trees, and vineyards. The swarms turned farmland into desert. The people had never seen anything like it.

The prophet Joel interpreted what was happening to the land as a sign of God's judgment on the people. He called them to repent for turning away from God. In the end, Joel predicted, God's judgment would be much worse than a plague of locusts if the people didn't turn back to God. Restoration and blessing would come only if the people turned back to God.

We don't know much about the prophet Joel, but his central message is a message for all time: God will judge those who oppose him and will bless those who follow him.

WHEN THE ACTION WAS

Saul was Israel's king	Possible time of Joel's life	The Northern Kingdom (Israel) fell to Assyria	Jews began returning from exile		Jesus was born
1000BC	750BC		500BC	250BC	BC/AD
The kingdom was split between Israel and Judah		The Southern Kingdom (Judah) fell to Babylon			

Locusts Destroy the Crops

1 The LORD spoke his word to Joel son of Pethuel:

²Older leaders, listen to this message.
Listen to me, all you who live in the
land.
Nothing like this has ever happened during
your lifetime
or during your ancestors' lifetimes.

> **SIDELIGHT:** The name Joel is
> common in the Old Testament (Joel
> 1:1). Twelve other people share this name
> (for examples, see 1 Samuel 8:2, p. 251, and
> Nehemiah 11:9, p. 437). The name means
> "The Lord is God" or "The Lord is my God."

³Tell your children about these things,
let your children tell their children,
and let your grandchildren tell their
children.
⁴What the cutting locusts have left,
the swarming locusts have eaten;
what the swarming locusts have left,
the hopping locusts have eaten,
and what the hopping locusts have
left,
the destroying locusts[n] have eaten.

⁵Drunks, wake up and cry!
All you people who drink wine, cry!
Cry because your wine
has been taken away from your mouths.
⁶A powerful nation has come into my land
with too many soldiers to count.
It has teeth like a lion,
jaws like a female lion.
⁷It has made my grapevine a waste
and made my fig tree a stump.
It has stripped all the bark off my trees
and left the branches white.

⁸Cry as a young woman cries
when the man she was going to marry has
died.

> **SIDELIGHT:** The locust invasion
> described in Joel 1 wasn't a unique
> event. As recently as 1915 and 1930, the
> Middle East has been ravaged by plagues of
> these insects.

⁹There will be no more grain or drink
offerings
to offer in the Temple[d] of the LORD.
Because of this, the priests,
the servants of the LORD, are sad.
¹⁰The fields are ruined;
the ground is dried up.
The grain is destroyed,
the new wine is dried up,
and the olive oil runs out.
¹¹Be sad, farmers.
Cry loudly, you who grow grapes.
Cry for the wheat and the barley.
Cry because the harvest of the field is lost.
¹²The vines have become dry,
and the fig trees are dried up.
The pomegranate[d] trees, the date palm trees,
the apple trees —
all the trees in the field have died.
And the happiness of the people has died,
too.
¹³Priests, put on your rough cloth and cry to
show your sadness.
Servants of the altar, cry out loud.
Servants of my God,
keep your rough cloth on all night to show
your sadness.
Cry because there will be no more grain or
drink offerings
to offer in the Temple of your God.
¹⁴Call for a day when no one eats food!
Tell everyone to stop work!
Bring the older leaders
and everyone who lives in the land
to the Temple of the LORD your God,
and cry out to the LORD.
¹⁵What a terrible day it will be!
The LORD's day of judging is near,
when punishment will come
like a destroying attack from the Almighty.

¹⁶Our food is taken away
while we watch.
Joy and happiness are gone
from the Temple of our God.
¹⁷Though we planted fig seeds,
they lie dry and dead in the dirt.
The barns are empty and falling down.
The storerooms for grain have been broken
down,
because the grain has dried up.
¹⁸The animals are groaning!
The herds of cattle wander around
confused,
because they have no grass to eat;
even the flocks of sheep suffer.

---

cutting . . . locusts These are different names for an insect like a large grasshopper. The locust can quickly destroy trees,
plants, and crops, and in this destruction Joel sees a warning. God will cause this type of destruction when he punishes
his people.

¹⁹LORD, I am calling to you for help,
because fire has burned up the open
pastures,
and flames have burned all the trees in the
field.
²⁰Wild animals also need your help.
The streams of water have dried up,
and fire has burned up the open pastures.

The Coming Day of Judgment

2 Blow the trumpet in Jerusalem;
shout a warning on my holy mountain.
Let all the people who live in the land shake
with fear,
because the LORD's day of judging is
coming;
it is near.
²It will be a dark, gloomy day,
cloudy and black.
Like the light at sunrise,

a great and powerful army will spread over
the mountains.
There has never been anything like it before,
and there will never be anything like it
again.

³In front of them a fire destroys;
in back of them a flame burns.
The land in front of them is like the garden
of Eden;
the land behind them is like an empty
desert.
Nothing will escape from them.
⁴They look like horses,
and they run like war horses.
⁵It is like the noise of chariots
rumbling over the tops of the mountains,
like the noise of a roaring fire
burning dry stalks.
They are like a powerful army lined up for
battle.

GOD'S POWER

The Big Blast

For one hundred twenty-three years Mount St. Helens slept quietly. Whenever geologists
looked down the throat of the Washington volcano, all they found were ash and ice. Then,
on March 20, 1980, earthquakes shook the area. Within a week the volcano began spewing
steam and ash into the air.

At first, people were frightened. But as weeks went by and nothing happened, they
grew accustomed to living next to an active volcano. They got tired of hearing warnings of
possible disaster. In fact, a carnival-like attitude prevailed, and the volcano's small eruptions
became a source of entertainment.

On May 18, Mount St. Helens was rattled by another series of earthquakes. This time a
huge section of the northern slope came crashing down the mountain. Two minutes later,
the mountain exploded. The explosion, heard two hundred miles away, was louder and
more powerful than an atomic bomb. A billowing cloud of ash shot more than twelve
miles into the air. More than one hundred eighty-five square miles of forest
land were leveled. Hundreds of thousands of trees vaporized, clouds of gray
ash filled the air, and the land was left barren.

The predicted eruption had come.

Like many of the people who scoffed at the predictions of Mount St.
Helens's eruption, most of the people in Joel's time paid little attention to the
prophet's warnings that the Lord's judgment was soon to come. Read how
the prophet describes God's warnings in **Joel 2:1–2**.

■ Why do you think many of the people living near Mount St. Helens and
those who heard Joel's prophecy of God's power didn't believe the
warnings?

■ What warning signs should you be paying attention to?

CONSIDER

■ riding a bicycle and viewing God's power in nature as you ride.
◢ reading Revelation (p. 1331) and comparing John's visions of God's power to the ones
in Joel.

FOR MORE, SEE . . .

■ Psalm 98 (p. 538)
■ Matthew 12:33–37 (p. 929)
■ 2 Peter 3:1–13 (p. 1313)

⁶When they see them, nations shake with fear,
  and everyone's face becomes pale.

⁷They charge like soldiers;
  they climb over the wall like warriors.
They all march straight ahead
  and do not move off their path.
⁸They do not run into each other,
  because each walks in line.
They break through all efforts to stop them
  and keep coming.
⁹They run into the city.
  They run at the wall
and climb into the houses,
  entering through windows like thieves.

SIDELIGHT: The Israelites couldn't keep the locusts out of their houses (Joel 2:9), because they didn't have screens or glass windows. Instead, their windows had wooden latticework in them. I would check in the sheets before climbing into bed, wouldn't you?

---

¹⁰Before them, earth and sky shake.
  The sun and the moon become dark,
  and the stars stop shining.
¹¹The LORD shouts out orders
  to his army.
His army is very large!
  Those who obey him are very strong!
The LORD's day of judging
  is an overwhelming and terrible day.
  No one can stand up against it!

Change Your Hearts

¹²The LORD says, "Even now, come back to me
    with all your heart.
  Go without food, and cry and be sad."

¹³Tearing your clothes is not enough to show
      you are sad;
  let your heart be broken.
Come back to the LORD your God,
  because he is kind and shows mercy.
He doesn't become angry quickly,
  and he has great love.
He can change his mind about doing harm.
¹⁴Who knows? Maybe he will turn back to you
  and leave behind a blessing for you.
Grain and drink offerings belong to the LORD
    your God.

¹⁵Blow the trumpet in Jerusalem;
  call for a day when no one eats food.
  Tell everyone to stop work.
¹⁶Bring the people together
  and make the meeting holy for the LORD.

Bring together the older leaders,
  as well as the children,
  and even babies that still feed at their
      mothers' breasts.
The bridegroom should come from his room,
  the bride from her bedroom.
¹⁷The priests, the LORD's servants, should cry
  between the altar and the entrance to the
      Temple.ᵈ
They should say, "LORD, have mercy on your
    people.
Don't let them be put to shame;
  don't let other nations make fun of them.
Don't let people in other nations ask,
  'Where is their God?'"

The Lord Restores the Land

¹⁸Then the LORD became concerned about his
    land
  and felt sorry for his people.
¹⁹He said to them:
  "I will send you grain, new wine, and olive
    oil,
  so that you will have plenty.
No more will I shame you
  among the nations.
²⁰I will force the army from the north to leave
    your land
  and go into a dry, empty land.
Their soldiers in front will be forced into the
    Dead Sea,ᵈ
  and those in the rear into the
      Mediterranean Sea.
Their bodies will rot and stink.
  The LORD has surely done a wonderful
      thing!"

²¹Land, don't be afraid;
  be happy and full of joy,
  because the LORD has done a wonderful
      thing.
²²Wild animals, don't be afraid,
  because the open pastures have grown
      grass.
The trees have given fruit;
  the fig trees and the grapevines have grown
      much fruit.
²³So be happy, people of Jerusalem;
  be joyful in the LORD your God.
Because he does what is right,
  he has brought you rain;
he has sent the fall rain
  and the spring rain for you, as before.
²⁴And the threshingᵈ floors will be full of grain;
  the barrels will overflow with new wine
      and olive oil.

The Lord Speaks

²⁵"Though I sent my great army against you—

those swarming locusts and hopping locusts,
the destroying locusts and the cutting
locusts[n] that ate your crops—
I will pay you back
for those years of trouble.
26Then you will have plenty to eat
and be full.
You will praise the name of the LORD your
God,
who has done miracles[d] for you.
My people will never again be shamed.
27Then you will know that I am among the
people of Israel,
that I am the LORD your God,
and there is no other God.
My people will never be shamed again.

28"After this,
I will pour out my Spirit[d] on all kinds of
people.

Your sons and daughters will prophesy,[d]
your old men will dream dreams,
and your young men will see visions.
29At that time I will pour out my Spirit
also on male slaves and female
slaves.
30I will show miracles
in the sky and on the earth:
blood, fire, and thick smoke.
31The sun will become dark,
the moon red as blood,
before the overwhelming and terrible day of
the LORD comes.
32Then anyone who calls on the LORD
will be saved,
because on Mount Zion[d] and in Jerusalem
there will be people who will be saved,
just as the LORD has said.
Those left alive after the day of punishment
are the people whom the LORD called.

swarming . . . locusts These are different names for an insect like a large grasshopper. The locust can quickly destroy trees, plants, and crops, and in this destruction, Joel sees a warning. God will cause this type of destruction when he punishes his people.

FORGIVENESS

Change of Heart

When their only son was killed by a drunk driver, Frank and Elizabeth Morris had just one wish: revenge. "We wanted him dead," Mrs. Morris admits, talking about the killer.

Tommy Pigage pleaded guilty to the charge and was sent to jail. The Morrises were angry at the court for not punishing him more severely. In time, however, they realized their bitterness stopped them from getting on with their lives. They decided to visit Tommy in jail.

Tommy expressed deep remorse for killing their son and admitted that he deserved his punishment. The Morrises were moved by his sensitivity and honesty. "I didn't want my son's death to be totally in vain," Mrs. Morris says. "And in my heart I know that if he could, my son would tell us to forgive Tommy."

The Morrises' decision to forgive not only freed them from their bitterness, but also started a change in Tommy's life. He quit drinking and turned to God. The Morrises continue to visit Tommy regularly and support him in his struggle with alcoholism. "The accident already wiped out one very special life. I don't want to see it waste Tommy's life, too," Mrs. Morris says.

The giving and receiving of forgiveness is necessary for living in Christ. To change their lives, the Morrises needed to forgive—and Tommy needed their forgiveness. Read **Joel 2:12–19** for God's plea for people to change their hearts.

■ How is the Morrises' (and Tommy's) change of heart similar to what God required of the people in Joel's time?
■ Is forgiveness the same thing as fairness? Why or why not?

CONSIDER . . .

■ making a paper heart and listing on it people you need to forgive. Ask God to help *you forgive them.*
■ taking the risk of asking forgiveness from someone you've hurt.

FOR MORE, SEE . . .

■ Psalm 51 (p. 511)
■ Matthew 5:21–26 (p. 913)
■ Luke 13:1–5 (p. 1030)

Punishment for Judah's Enemies

3 "In those days and at the time,
    when I will make things better for Judah
        and Jerusalem,
²I will gather all the nations together
    and bring them down into the Valley
        Where the Lord Judges.
    There I will judge them,
because those nations scattered my own
        people Israel
    and forced them to live in other nations.
They divided up my land
³   and threw lots*d* for my people.
They traded boys for prostitutes,*d*
    and they sold girls to buy wine to drink.

⁴"Tyre and Sidon and all of you regions of Philistia! What did you have against me? Were you punishing me for something I did, or were you doing something to hurt me? I will very quickly do to you what you have done to me. ⁵You took my silver and gold, and you put my precious treasures in your temples. ⁶You sold the people of Judah and Jerusalem to the Greeks so that you could send them far from their land.

⁷"You sent my people to that faraway place, but I will get them and bring them back, and I will do to you what you have done to them. ⁸I will sell your sons and daughters to the people of Judah, and they will sell them to the Sabean people far away." The Lord said this.

God Judges the Nations

⁹Announce this among the nations:
    Prepare for war!
  Wake up the soldiers!
    Let all the men of war come near and
        attack.
¹⁰Make swords from your plows,
    and make spears from your hooks for
        trimming trees.
  Let even the weak person say,
    "I am a soldier."
¹¹All of you nations, hurry,

CREATION

Trashed Out

Marion Stoddart and her family watched their nice neighborhood on the Nashua River in Groton, Massachusetts, become a dumping ground for industrial waste and trash. Once beautiful, the river bank was scattered with litter, discarded appliances, and abandoned cars. The river smelled like a sewer.

Finally, Marion realized she could either move away or rescue the Nashua River, which was so polluted that people said it was "too thick to pour and too thin to plow." She organized other concerned residents in the community to reclaim the river.

They showed labor unions, business leaders, and politicians how everyone would benefit from making the river "fishable and swimmable." They even got the governor's attention by giving him a bottle of filthy river water to keep on his desk until the Nashua was clean again. Slowly, the various users of the river did their part to stop polluting and to clean up the mess, due in large part to Mrs. Stoddart's group. Mrs. Stoddart says it is possible for ordinary people to reclaim their world for good.

"You don't have to be real smart to make a difference," she says. "You just have to persuade the people with power, the people who care, and be really committed, persistent, and honest."

It is not God's will that we trash his creation. In **Joel 2:21–27** read of God's desire for the land's health and vitality.

- How does Mrs. Stoddart's crusade for the Nashua River compare to God's will for the land in Joel?
- From your reading of the passage, what do you think is God's will for the way we are to use the earth?

CONSIDER . . .

- choosing one way today to show God's love for creation by reducing the amount of trash you create.
- leading a group from your school or church in cleaning up a riverbank, a public park, or a lake shore where you live.

FOR MORE, SEE . . .

- Genesis 1 (p. 2)
- Luke 12:22–31 (p. 1028)
- Psalm 104 (p. 541)

and come together in that place.
Lord, send your soldiers
    to gather the nations.

12"Wake up, nations,
    and come to attack in the Valley Where the
        Lord Judges.
There I will sit to judge
    all the nations on every side.
13Swing the cutting tool,
    because the harvest is ripe.
Come, walk on them as you would walk on
        grapes to get their juice,
    because the winepress*d* is full
    and the barrels are spilling over,
because these people are so evil!"

14There are huge numbers of people
    in the Valley of Decision,*n*
because the Lord's day of judging is near
    in the Valley of Decision.
15The sun and the moon will become dark,
    and the stars will stop shining.
16The Lord will roar like a lion from
        Jerusalem;
    his loud voice will thunder from that city,
    and the sky and the earth will shake.
But the Lord will be a safe place for his
        people,
    a strong place of safety for the people of
        Israel.

17"Then you will know that I, the Lord your
        God,
    live on my holy Mount Zion.*d*
Jerusalem will be a holy place,
    and strangers will never even go through it
        again.

A New Life Promised for Judah

18"On that day wine will drip from the
        mountains,
    milk will flow from the hills,
    and water will run through all the ravines
        of Judah.
A fountain will flow from the Temple*d* of the
        Lord
    and give water to the valley of acacia
        trees.
19But Egypt will become empty,
    and Edom an empty desert,
because they were cruel to the people of
        Judah.
    They killed innocent people in that land.
20But there will always be people living in
        Judah,
    and people will live in Jerusalem from now
        on.
21Egypt and Edom killed my people,
    so I will definitely punish them."

The Lord lives in Jerusalem!

Valley of Decision This is like the name Valley Where the Lord Judges in 3:2 and 3:12.

AMOS

Why Read This Book:

■ Read of the Lord's punishment for injustice (Amos 1—2).
■ Be warned about vanity and self-centeredness (Amos 6).
■ See the Lord's reaction to those who oppress the poor (Amos 8).

Behind the Scenes:

Amos was one angry farmer! All around him were smug, satisfied people. The nation was prosperous and secure. Surely God was on Israel's side. So why was Amos angry?

Because underneath the veneer of prosperity was religious and moral corruption. People had acquired their wealth by stepping on the poor. They relied on military might instead of God. Their worship was superficial. In short, they had forgotten what it meant to follow God.

Though he lived in the southern kingdom of Judah, Amos preached to the people of Israel in the north. He took his strong, uncompromising message straight to the religious authorities of his day. Instead of listening to him, they threw him out. Sometimes the truth is hard to hear.

In the same way Amos challenged the Israelites to reconsider their priorities, he

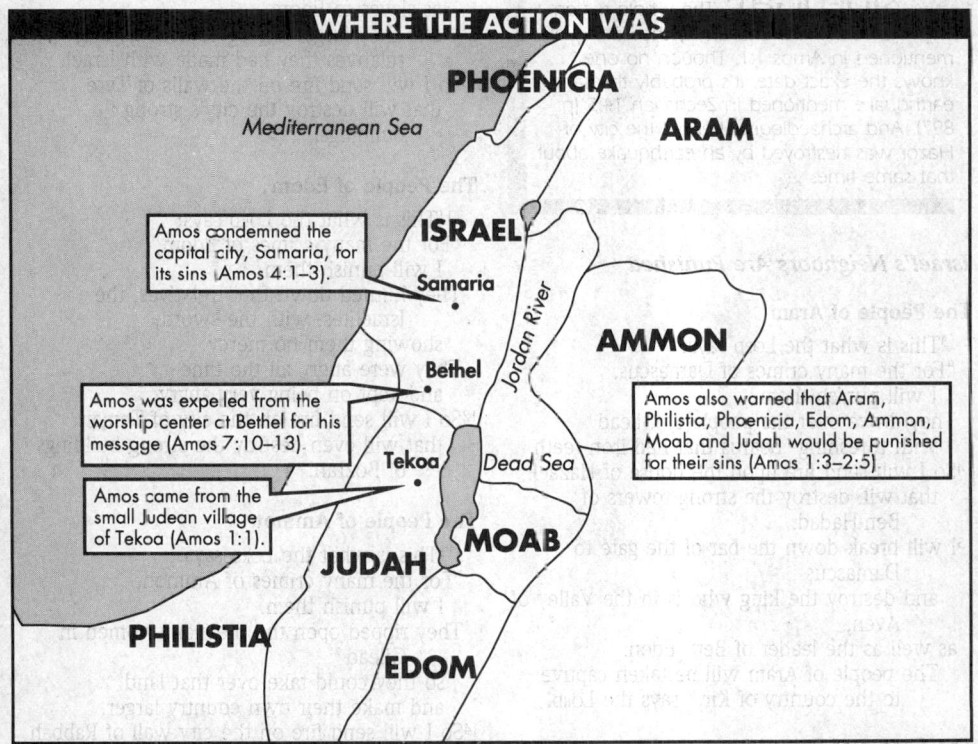

WHERE THE ACTION WAS

PHOENICIA

Mediterranean Sea

ARAM

ISRAEL

Amos condemned the capital city, Samaria, for its sins (Amos 4:1–3).

Samaria

Jordan River

AMMON

Bethel

Amos was expelled from the worship center at Bethel for his message (Amos 7:10–13).

Tekoa

Dead Sea

Amos also warned that Aram, Philistia, Phoenicia, Edom, Ammon, Moab and Judah would be punished for their sins (Amos 1:3–2:5).

Amos came from the small Judean village of Tekoa (Amos 1:1).

MOAB

JUDAH

PHILISTIA

EDOM

WHEN THE ACTION WAS

The kingdom was split between Israel and Judah	Amos prophesied to Israel		The Jews began returning from exile		Jesus was born
1000BC	**750BC**		**500BC**	**250BC**	**BC/AD**
Saul was Israel's king	The Northern Kingdom (Israel) fell to Assyria	The Southern Kingdom (Judah) fell to Babylon			

challenges us. In the climax to his book, he reminds us what God wants from us: "Let justice flow like a river, and let goodness flow like a stream that never stops" (Amos 5:24).

---

1 These are the words of Amos, one of the shepherds from the town of Tekoa. He saw this vision about Israel two years before the earthquake. It was at the time Uzziah was king of Judah and Jeroboam son of Jehoash was king of Israel.

²Amos said,

"The LORD will roar from Jerusalem;
  he will send his voice from Jerusalem.
The pastures of the shepherds will become dry,
  and even the top of Mount Carmel will dry up."

> ✹ **SIDELIGHT:** The whole region of Israel was shaken by the earthquake mentioned in Amos 1:1. Though no one knows the exact date, it's probably the same earthquake mentioned in Zechariah 14:5 (p. 897). And archaeologists believe the city of Hazor was destroyed by an earthquake about that same time.

Israel's Neighbors Are Punished

The People of Aram

³This is what the LORD says:
"For the many crimes of Damascus,
  I will punish them.
They drove over the people of Gilead
  with threshing*d* boards that had iron teeth.
⁴So I will send fire upon the house of Hazael
  that will destroy the strong towers of Ben-Hadad.
⁵I will break down the bar of the gate to Damascus
  and destroy the king who is in the Valley of Aven,
as well as the leader of Beth Eden.
  The people of Aram will be taken captive
  to the country of Kir," says the LORD.

The People of Philistia

⁶This is what the LORD says:
"For the many crimes of Gaza,
  I will punish them.
They sold all the people of one area

as slaves to Edom.
⁷So I will send a fire on the walls of Gaza
  that will destroy the city's strong buildings.
⁸I will destroy the king of the city of Ashdod,
  as well as the leader of Ashkelon.
Then I will turn against the people of the city of Ekron,
  and the last of the Philistines will die," says the Lord GOD.

The People of Phoenicia

⁹This is what the LORD says:
"For the many crimes of Tyre,
  I will punish them.
They sold all the people of one area
  as slaves to Edom,
  and they forgot the agreement among relatives they had made with Israel.
¹⁰So I will send fire on the walls of Tyre
  that will destroy the city's strong buildings."

The People of Edom

¹¹This is what the LORD says:
"For the many crimes of Edom,
  I will punish them.
They hunted down their relatives, the Israelites, with the sword,
  showing them no mercy.
They were angry all the time
  and kept on being very angry.
¹²So I will send fire on the city of Teman
  that will even destroy the strong buildings of Bozrah." *n*

The People of Ammon

¹³This is what the LORD says:
"For the many crimes of Ammon,
  I will punish them.
They ripped open the pregnant women in Gilead
  so they could take over that land
  and make their own country larger.
¹⁴So I will send fire on the city wall of Rabbah
  that will destroy its strong buildings.
It will come during a day of battle,
  during a stormy day with strong winds.
¹⁵Then their king and leaders will be taken captive;

Teman ... Bozrah Since Teman was in northern Edom and Bozrah was in southern Edom, this means the whole country will be destroyed.

they will all be taken away together," says
the LORD.

The People of Moab

2 This is what the LORD says:
"For the many crimes of Moab,
I will punish them.
They burned the bones of the king of Edom
into lime.
²So I will send fire on Moab
that will destroy the strong buildings of the
city of Kerioth.
The people of Moab will die in a great noise,
in the middle of the sounds of war and
trumpets.
³So I will bring an end to the king of Moab,
and I will kill all its leaders with him," says
the LORD.

The People of Judah

⁴This is what the LORD says:
"For the many crimes of Judah,
I will punish them.
They rejected the teachings of the LORD
and did not keep his commands;
they followed the same gods
as their ancestors had followed.
⁵So I will send fire on Judah,
and it will destroy the strong buildings of
Jerusalem."

Israel Is Punished

⁶This is what the LORD says:
"For the many crimes of Israel,
I will punish them.
For silver, they sell people who have done
nothing wrong;
they sell the poor to buy a pair of sandals.
⁷They walk on poor people as if they were
dirt,
and they refuse to be fair to those who are
suffering.
Fathers and sons have sexual relations with
the same woman,
and so they ruin my holy name.
⁸As they worship at their altars,
they lie down on clothes taken from the
poor.
They fine people,
and with that money they buy wine to
drink in the house of their god.
⁹"But it was I who destroyed the Amorites
before them,
who were tall like cedar trees and as strong
as oaks—
I destroyed them completely.
¹⁰It was I who brought you from the land of
Egypt

and led you for forty years through the
desert
so I could give you the land of the
Amorites.
¹¹I made some of your children to be prophets*d*
and some of your young people to be
Nazirites.*d*
People of Israel, isn't this true?" says the
LORD.
¹²"But you made the Nazirites drink wine
and told the prophets not to prophesy.
¹³Now I will make you get stuck,
as a wagon loaded with grain gets stuck.
¹⁴No one will escape, not even the fastest
runner.
Strong people will not be strong enough;
warriors will not be able to save
themselves.
¹⁵Soldiers with bows and arrows will not stand
and fight,
and even fast runners will not get away;
soldiers on horses will not escape alive.
¹⁶At that time even the bravest warriors
will run away without their armor," says
the LORD.

Warning to Israel

3 Listen to this word that the LORD has spoken
against you, people of Israel, against the
whole family he brought out of Egypt.
²"I have chosen only you
out of all the families of the earth,
so I will punish you
for all your sins."

³Two people will not walk together
unless they have agreed to do so.
⁴A lion in the forest does not roar
unless it has caught an animal;
it does not growl in its den
when it has caught nothing.
⁵A bird will not fall into a trap
where there is no bait;
the trap will not spring shut
if there is nothing to catch.
⁶When a trumpet blows a warning in a city,
the people tremble.
When trouble comes to a city,
the LORD has caused it.
⁷Before the Lord GOD does anything,
he tells his plans to his servants the
prophets.*d*
⁸The lion has roared!
Who wouldn't be afraid?
The Lord GOD has spoken.
Who will not prophesy?

⁹Announce this to the strong buildings of
Ashdod
and to the strong buildings of Egypt:

"Come to the mountains of Samaria,
where you will see great confusion
and people hurting others."

10"The people don't know how to do what is
right," says the LORD.
"Their strong buildings are filled with
treasures they took by force from
others."

11So this is what the Lord GOD says:
"An enemy will take over the land
and pull down your strongholds;[d]
he will take the treasures out of your strong
buildings."

12This is what the LORD says:
"A shepherd might save from a lion's mouth
only two leg bones or a scrap of an ear of
his sheep.
In the same way only a few Israelites in
Samaria will be saved—
people who now sit on their beds
and on their couches."

13"Listen and be witnesses against the family of
Jacob," says the Lord GOD, the God All-Powerful.

14"When I punish Israel for their sins,
I will also destroy the altars at Bethel.
The corners of the altar will be cut off,
and they will fall to the ground.
15I will tear down the winter house,
together with the summer house.
The houses decorated with ivory will be
destroyed,
and the great houses will come to an end,"
says the LORD.

Israel Will Not Return

4 Listen to this message, you cows of
Bashan[n] on the Mountain of Samaria.
You take things from the poor
and crush people who are in need.
Then you command your husbands,
"Bring us something to drink!"
2The Lord GOD has promised this:
"Just as surely as I am a holy God,

the time will come
when you will be taken away by hooks,
and what is left of you with fishhooks.
3You will go straight out of the city
through holes in the walls,
and you will be thrown on the garbage
dump," says the LORD.

4"Come to the city of Bethel and sin;
come to Gilgal and sin even more.
Offer your sacrifices every morning,
and bring one-tenth of your crops every
three days.
5Offer bread made with yeast as a sacrifice to
show your thanks,
and brag about the special offerings you
bring,
because this is what you love to do,
Israelites," says the Lord GOD.

6"I did not give you any food in your cities,
and there was not enough to eat in any of
your towns,
but you did not come back to me," says
the LORD.
7"I held back the rain from you
three months before harvest time.
Then I let it rain on one city
but not on another.
Rain fell on one field,
but another field got none and dried up.
8People weak from thirst went from town to
town for water,
but they could not get enough to drink.
Still you did not come back to me," says
the LORD.
9"I made your crops die from disease and
mildew.[d]
When your gardens and your vineyards got
larger,
locusts[d] ate your fig and olive trees.
But still you did not come back to me,"
says the LORD.
10"I sent disasters against you,
as I did to Egypt.
I killed your young men with swords,
and your horses were taken from you.
I made you smell the stink from all the dead
bodies,
but still you did not come back to me,"
says the LORD.
11"I destroyed some of you
as I destroyed Sodom and Gomorrah.
You were like a burning stick pulled from a
fire,
but still you did not come back to me,"
says the LORD.

Bashan Amos compares the rich, lazy women of Samaria to well-fed cows from Bashan, a place known for its rich animal
pastures.

12"So this is what I will do to you, Israel;
  because I will do this to you,
  get ready to meet your God, Israel."

13He is the one who makes the mountains
  and creates the wind
  and makes his thoughts known to people.
He changes the dawn into darkness
  and walks over the mountains of the earth.
  His name is the LORD God All-Powerful.

Israel Needs to Repent

5 Listen to this funeral song that I sing about
  you, people of Israel.
2"The young girl Israel has fallen,
  and she will not rise up again.
She was left alone in her own land,
  and there is no one to help her up."

3This is what the Lord GOD says:
"If a thousand soldiers leave a city,
  only a hundred will return;
if a hundred soldiers leave a city,
  only ten will return."

4This is what the LORD says to the nation of
Israel:
"Come to me and live.
5 But do not look in Bethel
or go to Gilgal,
  and do not go down to Beersheba.
The people of Gilgal will be taken away as
    captives,
  and Bethel will become nothing."
6Come to the LORD and live,
  or he will move like fire against the
    descendantsd of Joseph.
The fire will burn Bethel,
  and there will be no one to put it out.
7You turn justice upside down,
  and you throw on the ground what is right.

8God is the one who made the star groups
    Pleiades and Orion;
  he changes darkness into the morning light,
  and the day into dark night.
He calls for the waters of the sea
  to pour out on the earth.
  The LORD is his name.
9He destroys the protected city;
  he ruins the strong, walled city.

10You hate those who speak in court against
    evil,
  and you can't stand those who tell the
    truth.
11You walk on poor people,
  forcing them to give you grain.
You have built fancy houses of cut stone,
  but you will not live in them.
You have planted beautiful vineyards,
but you will not drink the wine from them.
12I know your many crimes,
  your terrible sins.
You hurt people who do right,
  you take money to do wrong,
  and you keep the poor from getting justice
    in court.
13In such times the wise person will keep
    quiet,
  because it is a bad time.

14Try to do good, not evil,
  so that you will live,
  and the LORD God All-Powerful will be with
    you
  just as you say he is.
15Hate evil and love good;
  be fair in the courts.
Maybe the LORD God All-Powerful will be
    kind
  to the people of Joseph who are left alive.

16This is what the Lord, the LORD God All-
Powerful, says:
"People will be crying in all the streets;
  they will be saying, 'Oh, no!' in the public
    places.
They will call the farmers to come and weep
  and will pay people to cry out loud for
    them.
17People will be crying in all the vineyards,
  because I will pass among you to punish
    you," says the LORD.

SIDELIGHT: The people in
Amos's time expected "the day of the
LORD" to be a sunny picnic, but Amos
countered with a dark vision of inescapable
terror (Amos 5:18–19). You can run, but you
can't hide!

The Lord's Day of Judging

18How terrible it will be for you who want
    the LORD's day of judging to come.
Why do you want that day to come?
  It will bring darkness for you, not light.
19It will be like someone who runs from a lion
    and meets a bear,
  or like someone who goes into his house
    and puts his hand on the wall,
    and then is bitten by a snake.
20So the LORD's day of judging will bring
    darkness, not light;
  it will be very dark, not light at all.

21The LORD says, "I completely hate your
    feasts;

I cannot stand your religious meetings.
22If you offer me burnt offerings and grain offerings,
I won't accept them.
You bring your best fellowship offerings of fattened cattle,
but I will ignore them.
23Take the noise of your songs away from me!
I won't listen to the music of your harps.
24But let justice flow like a river,
and let goodness flow like a stream that never stops.

25"People of Israel, you did not bring me sacrifices and offerings
while you traveled in the desert for forty years.
26You have carried with you
your king, the god Sakkuth,
and Kaiwan your idol,
and the star gods you have made.

27So I will send you away as captives beyond Damascus,"
says the LORD, whose name is the God All-Powerful.

Israel Will Be Destroyed

6 How terrible it will be for those who have an easy life in Jerusalem,
for those who feel safe living on Mount Samaria.
You think you are the important people of the best nation in the world;
the Israelites come to you for help.
2Go look at the city of Calneh,
and from there go to the great city Hamath;
then go down to Gath of the Philistines.
You are no better than these kingdoms.
Your land is no larger than theirs.

HYPOCRISY

Empty Words

In her high school, Shannon Smith usually hung around with a close group of five or six girls. One of the fringe members of the group, Joanna, was a common topic of conversation when she wasn't around. Even though Joanna could be fun, the group didn't really like her.

When Joanna was with the other girls, they always acted friendly. But after she left, they would go back to talking about her. "We all did it," Shannon says. "We were nice to her when she was around but destroyed her behind her back. It was kind of a habit to talk bad about her."

After a while, Shannon realized the group was being hypocritical. "You really couldn't tell whether or not we liked Joanna," she says. "I began to feel funny about the way we were treating her."

Shannon soon realized she couldn't believe much of what the group said. Their words were often empty. So Shannon left the group. What do they say about me now that I'm not around? she wonders.

Just as Shannon's group was hypocritical in saying one thing but doing another, the people in Amos's time participated in Temple worship, but behaved in ways opposite to God's desires. In **Amos 5:18–24**, the people of Israel are rebuked because their sinful actions didn't match their pious words.

■ What was hypocritical about the way the group treated Joanna and the way the people worshiped God in the passage?
■ How do you think God's desire for justice, as expressed in the passage, applies to your own worship?

CONSIDER . . .
■ keeping a list of times you have been hypocritical—when your actions were different from your beliefs. Pray for integrity and offer the list to God.
■ calling your friends' attention to their mistreatment of someone else, but doing so in a Christian manner.

FOR MORE, SEE . . .
■ Psalm 62 (p. 517)
■ Matthew 6:2–6 (p. 917)
■ Luke 13:10–17 (p. 1031)

³You put off the day of punishment,
  but you bring near the day when you can
    do evil to others.
⁴You lie on beds decorated with ivory
  and stretch out on your couches.
You eat tender lambs
  and fattened calves.
⁵You make up songs on your harps,
  and, like David, you compose songs on
    musical instruments.
⁶You drink wine by the bowlful
  and use the best perfumed lotions.
But you are not sad over the ruin of Israel,
⁷so you will be some of the first ones taken as
    slaves.
  Your feasting and lying around will come to
    an end.

⁸The Lord GOD made this promise; the LORD
God All-Powerful says:
"I hate the pride of the Israelites,
  and I hate their strong buildings,
so I will let the enemy take the city
  and everything in it."

⁹At that time there might be only ten people
left alive in just one house, but they will also die.
¹⁰When the relatives come to get the bodies to
take them outside, one of them will call to the
other and ask, 'Are there any other dead bodies
with you?"

That person will answer, "No."

Then the one who asked will say, "Hush! We
must not say the name of the LORD."

¹¹The LORD has given the command;
  the large house will be broken into
    pieces,
  and the small house into bits.
¹²Horses do not run on rocks,
  and people do not plow rocks with
    oxen.
But you have changed fairness into
    poison;
  you have changed what is right into
    a bitter taste.
¹³You are happy that the town of Lo Debar
    was captured,

SELF-ESTEEM

It's What's Inside

Brandon Edwards had been selling balloons all afternoon. A little boy suddenly appeared across the street and watched him intently for at least thirty minutes. Finally the boy spoke, "Hey, Mister, do you think the green balloons can fly as high as the other balloons?"

"Of course," said Brandon, not paying him much attention.

After several minutes, the young boy asked, "Hey, Mister, do you think the red balloons can fly as high as the other balloons?"

"Of course," Brandon replied.

A few minutes passed and the boy asked, "Hey, Mister, how about the black balloons? Do you think the black balloons can fly as high as the other balloons?"

Brandon walked across the street to the boy, gave him a balloon, and said, "It's not the color of the balloon that makes it fly. It's what's inside the balloon that makes it fly."

It's "what's inside" that makes us "fly" in our relationship with God. Read **Amos 6:1–7** to see why God rebukes Israel for ignoring the source of real worth and value.

■ How was the distorted self-esteem of the people in the passage like the boy's belief that colors affect balloon aerodynamics?

■ How much do the images of materialism in the passage reflect your own values and self-esteem or your feelings of security?

C O N S I D E R . . .

■ listing the values—not the material things—that would improve your self-esteem and then doing one thing today to grow in the one value you believe is most important.

■ joining a peer ministry or peer counseling group to help others (and yourself) grow in good self-esteem.

F O R   M O R E ,   S E E . . .

■ Proverbs 22:1–4 (p. 566)   ■ James 4:1–6 (p. 1297)
■ Philippians 2:1–4 (p. 1230)

and you say, "We have taken Karnaim[n] by our own strength."

[14]The LORD God All-Powerful says,
"Israel, I will bring a nation against you
that will make your people suffer from Lebo
   Hamath in the north
to the valley south of the Dead Sea."[d]

The Vision of Locusts

7 This is what the Lord GOD showed me: He was forming a swarm of locusts,[d] after the king had taken his share of the first crop and the second crop had just begun growing. [2]When the locusts ate all the crops in the country, I said, "Lord GOD, forgive us. How could Israel live through this? It is too small already!"

[3]So the LORD changed his mind about this. "It will not happen," said the LORD.

The Vision of Fire

[4]This is what the Lord GOD showed me: The Lord GOD was calling for fire to come down like rain. It burned up the deep water and was going to burn up the land. [5]Then I cried out, "Lord GOD, stop! How could Israel live through this? It is too small already."

[6]So the LORD changed his mind about this too. "It will not happen," said the Lord GOD.

The Vision of the Plumb Line

[7]This is what he showed me: The Lord stood by a straight wall, with a plumb line[d] in his hand. [8]The LORD said to me, "Amos, what do you see?"

I said, "A plumb line."

Then the Lord said, "See, I will put a plumb line among my people Israel to show how crooked they are. I will not look the other way any longer.

[9]"The places where Isaac's descendants[d]
   worship will be destroyed,
Israel's holy places will be turned into
   ruins,
and I will attack King Jeroboam's family
   with the sword."

Amaziah Speaks Against Amos

[10]Amaziah, a priest at Bethel, sent this message to Jeroboam king of Israel: "Amos is making evil plans against you with the people of Israel. He has been speaking so much that this land can't hold all his words. [11]This is what Amos has said:
'Jeroboam will die by the sword,
and the people of Israel will be taken as
   captives
out of their own country.' "

[12]Then Amaziah said to Amos, "Seer,[d] go back right now to Judah. Do your prophesying[d] and earn your living there, [13]but don't prophesy anymore here at Bethel. This is the king's holy place, and it is the nation's temple."

[14]Then Amos answered Amaziah, "I do not make my living as a prophet, nor am I a member of a group of prophets. I make my living as a shepherd, and I take care of sycamore trees. [15]But the

---

✦ **SIDELIGHT:** When Amos said he took care of sycamore trees (Amos 7:14)—which bore figs—he did more than pick their fruit once a year. To ensure good fruit from these trees, the farmer had to slit the top of each fig as it grew.

LORD took me away from tending the flock and said to me, 'Go, prophesy to my people Israel.' [16]So listen to the LORD's word. You tell me,
'Don't prophesy against Israel,
   and stop prophesying against the
      descendants of Isaac.'

[17]"Because you have said this, the LORD says:
'Your wife will become a prostitute[d] in the
   city,
and your sons and daughters will be killed
   with swords.
Other people will measure your land and
   divide it among themselves,
and you will die in a foreign country.
The people of Israel will definitely be taken
   from their own land as captives.' "

The Vision of Ripe Fruit

8 This is what the Lord GOD showed me: a basket of summer fruit. [2]He said to me, "Amos, what do you see?"

I said, "A basket of summer fruit."

Then the LORD said to me, "An end[n] has come for my people Israel, because I will not overlook their sins anymore.

[3]"On that day the palace songs will become funeral songs," says the Lord GOD. "There will be dead bodies thrown everywhere! Silence!"

[4]Listen to me, you who walk on helpless
   people,
you who are trying to destroy the poor
   people of this country, saying,
[5]"When will the New Moon[d] festival be over
   so we can sell grain?
When will the Sabbath[d] be over
   so we can bring out wheat to sell?

Lo Debar ... Karnaim These were cities in Israel that the Israelites had captured in war.
end The Hebrew word for "end" sounds like the Hebrew word for "summer fruit."

We can charge them more
  and give them less,
  and we can change the scales to cheat the
    people.
⁶We will buy poor people for silver,
  and needy people for the price of a pair of
    sandals.
  We will even sell the wheat that was swept
    up from the floor."

⁷The LORD has sworn by his name, the Pride of
Jacob, "I will never forget everything that these
people did.
⁸The whole land will shake because of it,
  and everyone who lives in the land will cry
    for those who died.

The whole land will rise like the Nile;
  it will be shaken, and then it will fall
    like the Nile River in Egypt."

⁹The Lord GOD says:
"At that time I will cause the sun to go
    down at noon
  and make the earth dark on a bright day.
¹⁰I will change your festivals into days of crying
    for the dead,
  and all your songs will become songs of
    sadness.
I will make all of you wear rough cloth to
    show your sadness;
  I will make you shave your heads as
    well.

Making a Difference

By most measures, Robert Hayes was set for life. Graduating near the top of his law
school class at New York University, he landed a six-figure salary with an elite Wall Street
law firm. He was on the way to becoming a partner which would have paid him three
hundred thousand dollars to nine hundred thousand dollars a year for the rest of his life.
  The only problem with his fast-track career was the morning walk to the subway. He
began noticing "the assorted bums sleeping in doorways and begging for handouts."
Gradually, he says, he started talking with the people, asking them how they ended up on
the streets. He "got curious and then got angry," as he describes it, when he learned how
tens of thousands of New Yorkers barely survived day-to-day, bounced from one filthy
shelter to another.
  He visited all sorts of shelters, flophouses and organizations struggling to help the
homeless. His law firm allowed him time to sue the state to do more for the homeless. In
time he founded the New York Coalition for the Homeless and then the National Coalition
for the Homeless.
  Hayes came to realize that his life's work wasn't in Wall Street; it was with the people of
the streets. "I realized what I wanted to do in life," he says. "So I did it." He resigned from
his firm, leaving behind wealth and prestige, to become a lawyer for the homeless in a tiny
office with flickering fluorescent lights.
  "You achieve a balance in life," he says to people now. "You don't have to
become Mother Teresa, but you can decide to make less and have the
freedom to help people, and to make a difference."
  Robert Hayes's reaction to the mistreatment of the homeless is a lot like
Amos's reaction to how the Israelites treated the poor, as described in **Amos
8:4–8**.

■ How are Robert Hayes's actions different from the unjust ones God
  condemns in the passage?
■ What oppression of the poor as described by Amos do you see in your
  town or city?

C O N S I D E R . . .
■ learning about the homeless people near you, and then volunteering your
  time to organizations that help them.
■ donating to an organization that helps homeless people, such as the National Coalition
  for the Homeless (1621 Connecticut Ave. NW, Suite 400, Washington, DC 20009).

F O R   M O R E ,   S E E . . .
■ Psalm 146 (p. 563)   ■ Luke 16:19–31 (p. 1038)
■ Isaiah 32:1–5 (p. 647)

I will make it like a time of crying for the
        death of an only son,
    and its end like the end of an awful day."

11The Lord GOD says: "The days are coming
    when I will cause a time of hunger in the
    land.
The people will not be hungry for bread or
        thirsty for water,
    but they will be hungry for words from the
        LORD.
12They will wander from the Mediterranean
        Sea to the Dead Sea,*d*
    from the north to the east.
They will search for the word of the LORD,
    but they won't find it.
13At that time the beautiful young women and
        the young men
    will become weak from thirst.
14They make promises by the idol in Samaria
    and say, 'As surely as the god of Dan
        lives . . . '
    and, 'As surely as the god of Beersheba*n*
        lives, we promise . . . '
So they will fall
    and never get up again."

Israel Will Be Destroyed

9 I saw the Lord standing by the altar, and he
    said:
"Smash the top of the pillars
    so that even the bottom of the doors will
        shake.
Make the pillars fall on the people's heads;
    anyone left alive I will kill with a sword.
Not one person will get away;
    no one will escape.
2If they dig down as deep as the place of the
        dead,
    I will pull them up from there.
If they climb up into heaven,
    I will bring them down from there.
3If they hide at the top of Mount Carmel,
    I will find them and take them away.
If they try to hide from me at the bottom of
        the sea,
    I will command a snake to bite them.

SIDELIGHT: If you were looking
for a good place to hide, Mt. Carmel
would be an excellent choice (Amos 9:3). It's
a wooded mountain filled with honeycomb-
like caves, and it juts out over the
Mediterranean Sea. Yet it's still not a good
enough hiding place to escape from God.

4If they are captured and taken away by their
        enemies,
    I will command the sword to kill them.
I will keep watch over them,
    but I will keep watch to give them trouble,
        not to do them good."

5The Lord GOD All-Powerful touches the land,
    and the land shakes.
Then everyone who lives in the land cries
        for the dead.
The whole land rises like the Nile River
    and falls like the river of Egypt.
6The LORD builds his upper rooms above the
        skies;
    he sets their foundations on the earth.
He calls for the waters of the sea
    and pours them out on the land.
    The LORD is his name.

7The LORD says,
"Israel, you are no different to me than the
        people of Cush.
I brought Israel out of the land of Egypt,
    and the Philistines from Crete,
    and the Arameans from Kir.
8I, the Lord GOD, am watching the sinful
        kingdom Israel.
I will destroy it
    from off the earth,
but I will not completely destroy
    Jacob's descendants,"*d* says the LORD.
9"I am giving the command
    to scatter the nation of Israel among all
        nations.
It will be like someone shaking grain through
        a strainer,
    but not even a tiny stone falls through.
10All the sinners among my people
    will die by the sword—
those who say,
    'Nothing bad will happen to us.'

The Lord Promises to Restore Israel

11"The kingdom of David is like a fallen tent,
    but in that day I will set it up again
        and mend its broken places.
I will rebuild its ruins
    as it was before.
12Then Israel will take over what is left of
        Edom
    and the other nations that belong to me,"
says the LORD,
    who will make it happen.

13The LORD says, "The time is coming when
        there will be all kinds of food.

Dan . . . Beersheba Dan was the city farthest north in Israel, and Beersheba was the city farthest south.

People will still be harvesting crops
  when it's time to plow again.
People will still be taking the juice from
  grapes
  when it's time to plant again.
Wine will drip from the mountains
  and pour from the hills.
14I will bring my people Israel back from
  captivity;

they will build the ruined cities again,
  and they will live in them.
They will plant vineyards and drink the wine
  from them;
  they will plant gardens and eat their fruit.
15I will plant my people on their land,
  and they will not be pulled out again
  from the land which I have given them,"
  says the LORD your God.

OBADIAH

Why Read This Book:
- Learn what can happen to a nation that's filled with false pride (Obadiah 2–8).
- See how the righteous will be victorious (Obadiah 17–21).

Behind the Scenes:

If you think you've seen real rivalries on the basketball court or football field, you haven't seen real rivalries. Israel vs. Edom—now that's a real rivalry!

Even though they were close neighbors, these two countries had been rivals for hundreds of years. They fought over control of trade routes. Then when Israel was sacked by major empires, Edom not only didn't help but actually shared in the war booty! All this from a nation of people who were actually related to Israel. Esau, the father of the Edomites, was the brother of Jacob (who was also called Israel). (See Genesis 25:30, p. 30.)

Into the middle of this rivalry steps the prophet Obadiah. He describes God's anger at Edom for not helping oppressed people and for rejoicing over the Israelites' misfortune. And he predicts that Edom will be destroyed for its sinfulness, and the nation of Israel will have the final victory.

Obadiah's message was more than a motivational talk at a pep rally for the

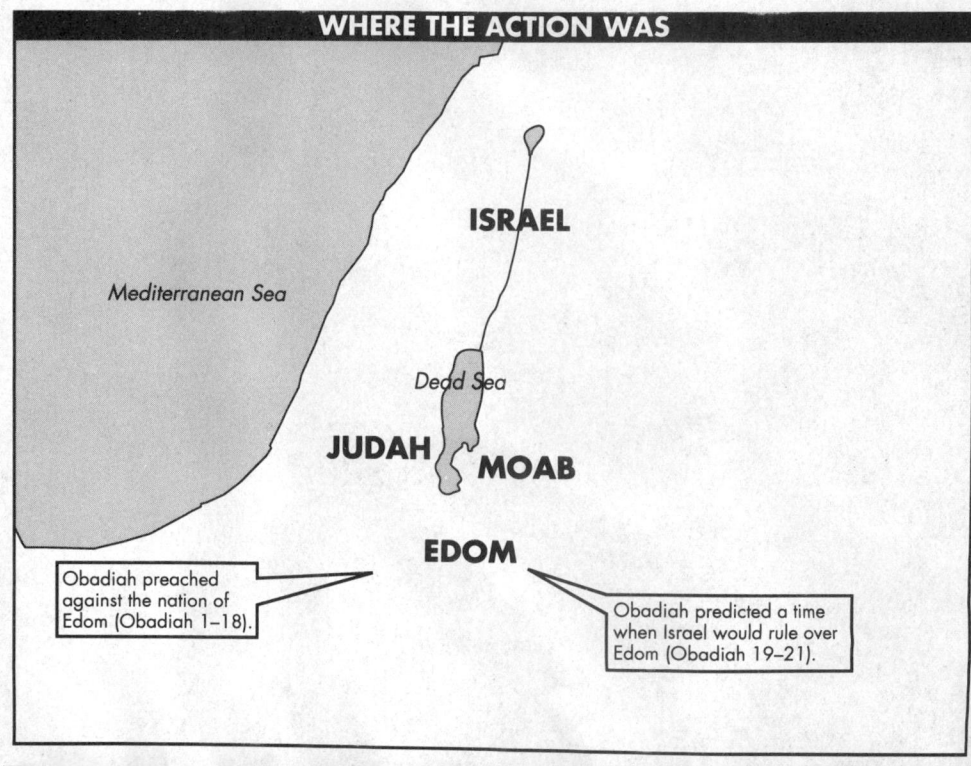

WHERE THE ACTION WAS

Mediterranean Sea

ISRAEL

Dead Sea

JUDAH

MOAB

EDOM

Obadiah preached against the nation of Edom (Obadiah 1–18).

Obadiah predicted a time when Israel would rule over Edom (Obadiah 19–21).

WHEN THE ACTION WAS

1000BC		750BC		500BC		250BC		BC/AD
	Obadiah may have lived		Obadiah may have lived	The Jews began returning from exile				Jesus was born
Saul was Israel's king		The Northern Kingdom (Israel) fell to Assyria		The Southern Kingdom (Judah) fell to Babylon				

Behind the Scenes (cont.): Israelites. At times, it was harsh and full of revenge. God will correct the injustice by bringing down the Edomites, Obadiah said. His message reminds us to care for the weak around us and to keep hopeful even when we feel overwhelmed and beaten down. God will be victorious in the end!

The shortest book in the Old Testament, Obadiah only has one chapter. So its verses are numbered without chapter markings.

The Lord Will Punish the Edomites

¹This is the vision of Obadiah.

This is what the Lord God says about Edom: *ⁿ*
We have heard a message from the Lord.
A messenger has been sent among the
   nations, saying,

"Attack! Let's go attack Edom!"

The Lord Speaks to the Edomites

²"Soon I will make you the smallest of
   nations.
You will be greatly hated by everyone.
³Your pride has fooled you,

Edom   The Edomites were the people who came from Esau, Jacob's twin brother. They were enemies of the Israelites.

SIN

Laughing at Others' Troubles

"What am I doing here?" Dan Gallager kept asking himself. About the last place he expected to be during his summer vacation was knee-deep in water and mud far from home. But that's exactly where he was, digging a trench for a water line.

Dan was in Appalachia with his youth group, repairing homes for the poor. "I knew in my mind that I was doing the right thing. But I was tired and wet, and I had just ruined my best pair of basketball shoes," Dan says.

The house was run-down, but it was home to a family of seven. In addition to the water line, the house needed siding, paint, and a new porch. While the other young people worked on the building, Dan dug the trench for the water pipe.

"What's wrong with this lazy family, anyway?" Dan thought to himself. "I began to wonder why they didn't just fix all of this themselves. How could they live without running water?" He started making sarcastic jokes to the other workers about the people who lived there.

As the group finished for the day and prepared to go back to their host church for dinner, the mother of the family, Mrs. Hoffman, came out of the house to talk to Dan. She was carrying a new pair of basketball shoes. "I saw how your sneakers got ruined today," she said to Dan. "These look to be about your size. I'd appreciate it if you would take them. Thanks for all you're doing for us."

Dan just stood there, feeling guilty about the cruel words he had spoken and thought. As he got in the van to leave, he wondered who was really helping whom.

Our actions and words don't go unnoticed. Read in **Obadiah 12–14** how the Lord reacts to those who laugh at people's troubles.

■ How is Dan's attitude toward the Appalachian family similar to the sin of laughing at others' troubles described in the passage?
■ How do you usually feel about yourself after laughing at someone's troubles or problems?

C O N S I D E R . . .
■ saying a word of encouragement to a family member who has had a hard day.
■ befriending a student at your school who is often laughed at or picked on.

F O R   M O R E ,   S E E . . .
■ Proverbs 19:17 (p. 584)
■ John 8:1–11 (p. 1070)
■ Galatians 6:1–6 (p. 1213)

you who live in the hollow places of the
cliff.
Your home is up high,
you who say to yourself,
'No one can bring me down to the
ground.'
[4]Even if you fly high like the eagle
and make your nest among the stars,
I will bring you down from there," says the
LORD.
[5]"You will really be ruined!
If thieves came to you,
if robbers came by night,
they would steal only enough for
themselves.
If workers came and picked the grapes from
your vines,
they would leave a few behind.
[6]But you, Edom, will really lose everything!
People will find all your hidden treasures!

SIDELIGHT: Some people hide
their money under mattresses, but the
Edomites reportedly squirreled their wealth in
the red cliffs south of the Dead Sea where
they lived (Obadiah 6). Obadiah mentions
"treasures" on an average of every seventh
verse.

---

[7]All the people who are your friends
will force you out of the land.
The people who are at peace with you
will trick you and defeat you.
Those who eat your bread with you now
are planning a trap for you,
and you will not notice it."

[8]The LORD says, "On that day
I will surely destroy the wise people from
Edom,
and those with understanding from the
mountains of Edom.
[9]Then, city of Teman, your best warriors will
be afraid,
and everyone from the mountains of Edom
will be killed.
[10]You did violence to your relatives, the
Israelites,
so you will be covered with shame
and destroyed forever.
[11]You stood aside without helping
while strangers carried Israel's treasures
away.
When foreigners entered Israel's city gate

and threw lots[d] to decide what part of
Jerusalem they would take,
you were like one of them.

Commands That Edom Broke

[12]"Edom, do not laugh at your brother Israel in
his time of trouble
or be happy about the people of Judah when
they are destroyed.
Do not brag when cruel things are done to
them.
[13]Do not enter the city gate of my people
in their time of trouble
or laugh at their problems
in their time of trouble.
Do not take their treasures
in their time of trouble.
[14]Do not stand at the crossroads
to destroy those who are trying to escape.
Do not capture those who escape alive and
turn them over to their enemy
in their time of trouble.

The Nations Will Be Judged

[15]"The LORD's day of judging is coming soon
to all the nations.
The same evil things you did to other people
will happen to you;
they will come back upon your own head.
[16]Because you drank in my Temple,[d]
all the nations will drink on and on.
They will drink and drink
until they disappear.
[17]But on Mount Zion[d] some will escape the
judgment,
and it will be a holy place.
The people of Jacob will take back their land
from those who took it from them.
[18]The people of Jacob will be like a fire
and the people of Joseph[n] like a flame.
But the people of Esau[n] will be like dry
stalks.
The people of Jacob will set them on fire
and burn them up.
There will be no one left of the people of
Esau."
This will happen because the LORD has said
it.

[19]Then God's people will regain southern Judah
from Edom;
they will take back the mountains of Edom.
They will take back the western hills
from the Philistines.
They will regain the lands of Ephraim and
Samaria,

---

people of Jacob . . . Joseph The people who came from Jacob and Joseph, or the Israelites.
people of Esau The people who came from Esau, or the Edomites.

and Benjamin will take over Gilead.

²⁰People from Israel who once were forced to
leave their homes
will take the land of the Canaanites,
all the way to Zarephath.
People from Judah who once were forced to
leave Jerusalem and live in Sepharad

will take back the cities of southern Judah.

²¹Powerful warriors will go up on Mount
Zion,
where they will rule the people living on
Edom's mountains.
And the kingdom will belong to the
LORD.

JONAH

Why Read This Book:
- Discover truth in a story of a prophet who was reluctant to do what God wanted him to do (Jonah 1—2).
- See that God's love and mercy are for all the world (Jonah 3—4).

Behind the Scenes:

Being chosen to be a leader or to fill an office is always a great honor. But you probably wouldn't last long in the position if you simply basked in the glow of being chosen. You would have to fulfill the tasks and responsibilities—some that you might not like—that come with the honor.

The Jews had been chosen by God to be his special people. Through history, God had guided and protected them. But what responsibilities for the rest of the world did that honor include? Should God's people shut off the world, focusing on their gifts from God? Or should they take the story of God's love to the rest of the world?

The story of Jonah addressed this dilemma. God called the prophet Jonah to go preach at Nineveh, the heathen capital of Assyria. Not wanting to preach to non-Jewish people—especially pagans whose cruelty and barbaric actions were widely known—Jonah went the opposite direction. Like many Israelites, he enjoyed God's mercy on Israel but wanted all enemies to be destroyed.

God wouldn't let Jonah off from his mission, though. Through a storm and a big fish, God got Jonah's attention and turned him around. Reluctantly, Jonah went to Nineveh and preached, and the whole city turned to God. But Jonah wasn't happy. He went to sulk and complain about God sparing the Ninevites from destruction.

God responded with a message that's at the heart of the book: "Shouldn't I show concern for the great city Nineveh, which has people who do not know right from wrong . . . ?" (Jonah 4:11).

Jonah's story reminds all God's followers that no one has a "corner" on God.

WHERE THE ACTION WAS

Black Sea

SPAIN
Tarshish

ITALY

Jonah was sent to the city of Nineveh (Jonah 1:2). Later he actually went there (Jonah 3:3).

Nineveh

AFRICA

Mediterranean Sea

Joppa

Jonah sailed for Tarshish, which was probably here in modern-day Spain (Jonah 1:3).

Instead of going east across land to Nineveh, Jonah boarded a ship at Joppa to go west to Tarshish (Jonah 1:3).

Red Sea

WHEN THE ACTION WAS

The kingdom was split between Israel and Judah	The prophet Jonah lived	The Jews began returning from exile		Jesus was born
1000BC	**750BC**	**500BC**	**250BC**	**BC/AD**
Saul was Israel's king	The Northern Kingdom (Israel) fell to Assyria	The Southern Kingdom (Judah) fell to Babylon		

Behind the   God wants his people to tell others about his love. As Jesus said in Luke 5:32 (p.
Scenes (cont.):   1012), "I have not come to invite good people but sinners to change their hearts
and lives."

God Calls and Jonah Runs

1 The LORD spoke his word to Jonah son of Amittai: [2]"Get up, go to the great city of Nineveh, and preach against it, because I see the evil things they do."

[3]But Jonah got up to run away from the LORD by going to Tarshish. He went to the city of Joppa, where he found a ship that was going to the city of Tarshish. Jonah paid for the trip and went aboard, planning to go to Tarshish to run away from the LORD.

> **SIDELIGHT:** The name Jonah (Jonah 1:1) means "dove," which may have been a traditional symbol for the nation of Israel (see Psalm 74:19–21, p. 526).

[4]But the LORD sent a great wind on the sea, which made the sea so stormy that the ship was in danger of breaking apart. [5]The sailors were afraid, and each man cried to his own god. They began throwing the cargo from the ship into the sea to make the ship lighter.

But Jonah had gone down far inside the ship to lie down, and he fell fast asleep. [6]The captain of the ship came and said, "Why are you sleeping? Get up and pray to your god! Maybe your god will pay attention to us, and we won't die!"

[7]Then the men said to each other, "Let's throw lots[d] to see who caused these troubles to happen to us."

When they threw lots, the lot showed that the trouble had happened because of Jonah. [8]Then they said to him, "Tell us, who caused our trouble? What is your job? Where do you come from? What is your country? Who are your people?"

[9]Then Jonah said to them, "I am a Hebrew. I fear the LORD, the God of heaven, who made the sea and the land."

[10]The men were very afraid, and they asked Jonah, "What terrible thing did you do?" (They knew he was running away from the LORD because he had told them.)

[11]Since the wind and the waves of the sea were becoming much stronger, they said to him, "What should we do to you to make the sea calm down for us?"

[12]Jonah said to them, "Pick me up, and throw me into the sea, and then it will calm down. I know it is my fault that this great storm has come on you."

[13]Instead, the men tried to row the ship back to the land, but they could not, because the sea was becoming more stormy.

Jonah's Punishment

[14]So the men cried to the LORD, "LORD, please don't let us die because of this man's life; please don't think we are guilty of killing an innocent person. LORD, you have caused all this to happen; you wanted it this way." [15]So they picked up Jonah and threw him into the sea, and the sea became calm. [16]Then they began to fear the LORD very much; they offered a sacrifice to the LORD and made promises to him.

[17]The LORD caused a big fish to swallow Jonah, and Jonah was inside the fish three days and three nights.

> **SIDELIGHT:** Being swallowed by a big fish may have been a bit of divine comedy (Jonah 1:17). In an ancient kind of writing known as cuneiform the name Nineveh may have been represented by a box with a fish inside.

2 While Jonah was inside the fish, he prayed to the LORD his God and said,
[2]"When I was in danger,
    I called to the LORD,
    and he answered me.
I was about to die,
    so I cried to you,
    and you heard my voice.
[3]You threw me into the sea,
    down, down into the deep sea.
The water was all around me,
    and your powerful waves flowed over me.
[4]I said, 'I was driven out of your presence,
    but I hope to see your Holy Temple[d] again.'
[5]The waters of the sea closed around my
        throat.
    The deep sea was all around me;
    seaweed was wrapped around my head.
[6]When I went down to where the mountains
        of the sea start to rise,
    I thought I was locked in this prison
        forever,
but you saved me from the pit of death,
    LORD my God.

7"When my life had almost gone,
  I remembered the LORD.
I prayed to you,
  and you heard my prayers in your Holy
    Temple.

8"People who worship useless idols
  give up their loyalty to you.
9But I will praise and thank you
  while I give sacrifices to you,
  and I will keep my promises to you.
Salvation comes from the LORD!"

10Then the LORD spoke to the fish, and the fish
threw up Jonah onto the dry land.

God Calls and Jonah Obeys

3 The LORD spoke his word to Jonah again and
said, 2"Get up, go to the great city Nineveh,
and preach to it what I tell you to say."

3So Jonah obeyed the LORD and got up and
went to Nineveh. It was a very large city; just to
walk across it took a person three days. 4After Jonah had entered the city and walked for one day,
he preached to the people, saying, "After forty
days, Nineveh will be destroyed!"

5The people of Nineveh believed God. They announced that they would stop eating for a while,

and they put on rough cloth to show their sadness. All the people in the city did this, from the
most important to the least important.

6When the king of Nineveh heard this news, he
got up from his throne, took off his robe, and covered himself with rough cloth and sat in ashes to
show how upset he was.

SIDELIGHT: The rough cloth the
king put on when he heard about
Nineveh's sins would make polyester feel like
fine silk (Jonah 3:6). It was probably made of
scratchy goat hair. Wearing it next to the skin
virtually guaranteed discomfort. It was the
common clothing to wear during times of
repentance or mourning.

7He sent this announcement through Nineveh:

By command of the king and his important
men: No person or animal, herd or flock,
will be allowed to taste anything. Do not let
them eat food or drink water. 8But every person and animal should be covered with
rough cloth, and people should cry loudly to

THANKFULNESS

A Simple Thank You

When she was three years old, Lisa Greene was pulled from the flames engulfing her
home in Brooklyn, New York. She spent three months in a hospital, where she recovered
from severe burns.

Fourteen years later, as her high school graduation approached, she decided to track
down the firefighter who saved her life. With the fire department's help she located Lt.
Marvin Bunch, who had retired to Las Vegas. Lisa invited him to her
graduation so she could thank him.

"I always wanted to thank him personally, and I wanted to show him that
it really was worthwhile saving my life," Lisa explains. "I have a future—I'm
going to college—and it's all because of him." Moved by her gratitude, Lt.
Bunch returned to New York to share Lisa's happiness.

Jonah, too, experienced being saved from a life-threatening situation. Read
of Jonah's thankfulness to God in **Jonah 2:2–9**.
■ How was Lisa's experience similar to Jonah's?
■ When was the last time you thanked God for saving you?

C O N S I D E R . . .
■ drawing a "wheel of thankfulness" (a circle with pie-shaped wedges),
  writing the things you're thankful to God for in the spaces. Offer a prayer
  thanking God for them.
◀ giving a small present as "thanks" to someone who has helped you through a difficult
  time.

F O R   M O R E ,   S E E . . .
■ Psalm 65 (p. 518)
■ Luke 17:11–19 (p. 1040)
■ 1 Thessalonians 5:12–18 (p. 1249)

God. Everyone must turn away from evil living and stop doing harm all the time. 9Who knows? Maybe God will change his mind. Maybe he will stop being angry, and then we will not die.

10When God saw what the people did, that they stopped doing evil, he changed his mind and did not do what he had warned. He did not punish them.

God's Mercy Makes Jonah Angry

4 But this made Jonah very unhappy, and he became angry. 2He prayed to the LORD, "When I was still in my own country this is what I said would happen, and that is why I quickly ran away to Tarshish. I knew that you are a God who is kind and shows mercy. You don't become angry quickly, and you have great love. I knew you would choose not to cause harm. 3So now I ask you, LORD, please kill me. It is better for me to die than to live."

4Then the LORD said, "Do you think it is right for you to be angry?"

5Jonah went out and sat down east of the city. There he made a shelter for himself and sat in the shade, waiting to see what would happen to the

---

FORGIVENESS

Personal Peace

By 1938, when eighteen-year-old Joseph Mavsar left home to study for the ministry, he had heard many sermons about forgiveness. In a few years, however, he would know how hard it would become to live out those sermons.

In 1941, Italy invaded Yugoslavia and occupied Joseph's village. The family's troubles increased when his father, a respected leader, refused to join the local Communist resistance.

The family gathered for Christmas, 1942. Two days later, the Communists attacked the house and killed Joseph's parents, four of his brothers and his only sister. Joseph and his twelve-year-old brother, Bill, jumped from a second-floor window and fled to the woods. The Communists burned the others' bodies and stole the family's property.

Just two brothers of the large family survived the war.

Joseph came to the United States in 1948 as a minister. He amazed some and shocked others as he preached forgiveness for the war crimes. Although he wanted the truth of the crimes against his family to be known, he still preached forgiveness.

As the twenty-fifth anniversary of his ordination approached, however, Joseph still struggled to personally forgive the people who had killed his family and taken all its possessions. Then a cousin in Yugoslavia wrote to Joseph, telling him that some of the killers were haunted by what they had done. "Come back and make peace with them," the cousin wrote.

Joseph returned to his village and found one of the Communists living in his father's house. "As I shook this man's hand and told him I forgave him," Joseph remembers, "he thanked me over and over, and said it was the best day of his life."

In his old age, Joseph continued to preach forgiveness. "In life we cannot be happy unless we're able to forgive," he said. "We must forgive, no matter how painful the hurt."

He knows what he's talking about.

Sometimes offenses seem too great to ever be forgiven. Read in **Jonah 3:1–10** how the Lord forgives the people of Nineveh for their many sins.

■ Jonah did not want to forgive Nineveh (Jonah 4:1). How do Joseph and Jonah differ in their willingness to forgive?

■ Have you ever found it difficult to forgive someone, even though it was necessary for your own peace of mind?

CONSIDER . . .

■ forgiving someone who has hurt you, even though it's difficult to do.

■ making the first move to restore a damaged relationship within your family or peers.

FOR MORE, SEE . . .

■ Joel 2:12–19 (p. 837)   ■ Acts 10:43 (p. 1115)

■ Luke 23:26–34 (p. 1053)

city. ⁶The Lᴏʀᴅ made a plant grow quickly up over Jonah, which gave him shade and helped him to be more comfortable. Jonah was very pleased to have the plant. ⁷But the next day when the sun rose, God sent a worm to attack the plant so that it died.

⁸As the sun rose higher in the sky, God sent a very hot east wind to blow, and the sun became so hot on Jonah's head that he became very weak and wished he were dead. He said, "It is better for me to die than to live."

⁹But God said to Jonah, "Do you think it is right for you to be angry about the plant?"

Jonah answered, "It is right for me to be angry! I am so angry I could die!"

¹⁰And the Lᴏʀᴅ said, "You are so concerned for that plant even though you did nothing to make it grow. It appeared one day, and the next day it died. ¹¹Then shouldn't I show concern for the great city Nineveh, which has more than one hundred twenty thousand people who do not know right from wrong, and many animals, too?"

MICAH

Why Read This Book:

■ See God's judgment on a nation that didn't follow him (Micah 1—2).
■ Find out what happens when leaders' actions are unjust (Micah 3).
■ Be encouraged by God's promise for the future (Micah 7).

Behind the Scenes:

Everything was falling apart, but no one seemed to notice. And when people were confronted with their problems, they just rolled their eyes, unwilling to listen to a message that seemed so farfetched.

That was the prophet Micah's situation. When he started preaching in Judah, its northern neighbor, Israel, was about to be conquered by the Assyrians. And, he believed, the same fate awaited Judah because of its injustice to the poor and its immoral leadership.

The book of Micah is a collection of Micah's sermons about God's punishment of Judah. Yet Micah also saw hope and redemption in the future. Because of God's mercy, Micah said, God would reclaim the Israelites and establish a kingdom of eternal peace.

The heart of Micah's message summarized what most of the prophets called

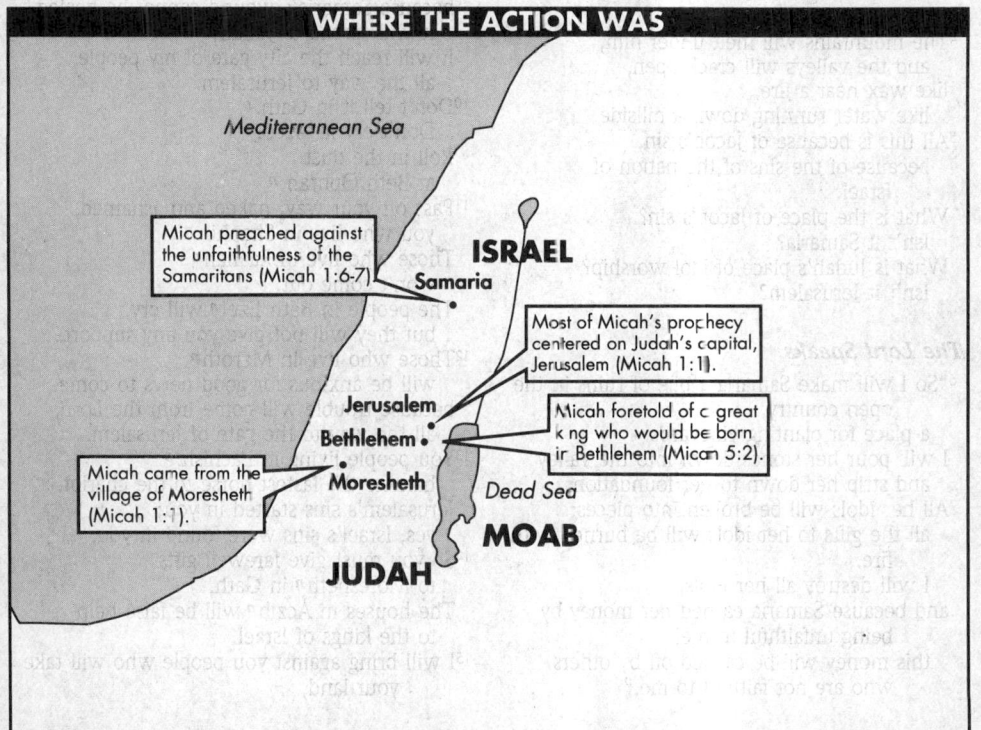

WHERE THE ACTION WAS

Mediterranean Sea

Micah preached against the unfaithfulness of the Samaritans (Micah 1:6-7)

ISRAEL

Samaria

Most of Micah's prophecy centered on Judah's capital, Jerusalem (Micah 1:1).

Jerusalem

Bethlehem

Micah foretold of a great king who would be born in Bethlehem (Micah 5:2).

Micah came from the village of Moresheth (Micah 1:1).

Moresheth

Dead Sea

MOAB

JUDAH

WHEN THE ACTION WAS

The kingdom was split between Israel and Judah	Micah prophesied in Jerusalem	The Jews began returning from exile		Jesus was born
1000BC	**750BC**	**500BC**	**250BC**	**BC/AD**
Saul was Israel's king	The Northern Kingdom (Israel) fell to Assyria	The Southern Kingdom (Judah) fell to Babylon		

Behind the Scenes (cont.):
people to do: "The Lord has told you, human, what is good; he has told you what he wants from you: to do what is right to other people, love being kind to others, and live humbly, obeying your God" (Micah 6:8). It's a message that's just as relevant today as it was more than twenty-five hundred years ago.

Samaria and Israel to Be Punished

1 During the time that Jotham, Ahaz, and Hezekiah were kings of Judah, the word of the LORD came to Micah, who was from Moresheth. He saw these visions about Samaria and Jerusalem.

²Hear this, all you nations;
  listen, earth and all you who live on
    it.
The Lord GOD will be a witness against
    you,
  the Lord from his Holy Temple.*d*
³See, the LORD is coming out of his place;
  he is coming down to walk on the tops of
    the mountains.
⁴The mountains will melt under him,
  and the valleys will crack open,
like wax near a fire,
  like water running down a hillside.
⁵All this is because of Jacob's sin,
  because of the sins of the nation of
    Israel.
What is the place of Jacob's sin?
  Isn't it Samaria?
What is Judah's place of idol worship?
  Isn't it Jerusalem?

The Lord Speaks

⁶"So I will make Samaria a pile of ruins in the
    open country,
  a place for planting vineyards.
I will pour her stones down into the valley
  and strip her down to her foundations.
⁷All her idols will be broken into pieces;
  all the gifts to her idols will be burned with
    fire.
I will destroy all her idols,
and because Samaria earned her money by
    being unfaithful to me,
  this money will be carried off by others
    who are not faithful to me."

✹ **SIDELIGHT:** Micah has sometimes been called the "wailing prophet," based on Micah 1:8. He's not the only one who went "barefoot and naked" to make a point. Isaiah attracted attention the same way, in Isaiah 20:2–4 (p. 637).

Micah's Great Sadness

⁸I will moan and cry because of this evil,
  going around barefoot and naked.
I will cry loudly like the wild dogs
  and make sad sounds like the owls do,
⁹because Samaria's wound cannot be healed.
  It will spread to Judah;
it will reach the city gate of my people,
  all the way to Jerusalem.
¹⁰Don't tell it in Gath.*n*
  Don't cry in Acco.*n*
Roll in the dust
  at Beth Ophrah.*n*
¹¹Pass on your way, naked and ashamed,
  you who live in Shaphir.*n*
Those who live in Zaanan*n*
  won't come out.
The people in Beth Ezel*n* will cry,
  but they will not give you any support.
¹²Those who live in Maroth*n*
  will be anxious for good news to come,
because trouble will come from the LORD,
  all the way to the gate of Jerusalem.
¹³You people living in Lachish,*n*
  harness the fastest horse to the chariot.
Jerusalem's sins started in you;
  yes, Israel's sins were found in you.
¹⁴So you must give farewell gifts
  to Moresheth*n* in Gath.
The houses in Aczib*n* will be false help
  to the kings of Israel.
¹⁵I will bring against you people who will take
    your land,

Gath This name sounds like the Hebrew word for "tell."
Acco This name sounds like the Hebrew word for "cry."
Beth Ophrah This name means "house of dust."
Shaphir This name means "beautiful."
Zaanan This name sounds like the Hebrew word for "come out."
Beth Ezel This name means "house by the side of another," suggesting help or support.
Maroth This name sounds like the Hebrew word for "sad" or "miserable."
Lachish This name sounds like the Hebrew word for "horses."
Moresheth This may be a play on the word "engaged," referring to a farewell gift to a bride.
Aczib This name means "lie" or "trick."

you who live in Mareshah.*n*
The glory of Israel
will go in to Adullam.
¹⁶Cut off your hair to show you are sad
for the children you love.
Make yourself bald like the eagle,
because your children will be taken away
to a foreign land.

The Evil Plans of People

2 How terrible it will be for people who
plan wickedness,
who lie on their beds and make evil plans.
When the morning light comes, they do what
they planned,
because they have the power to do so.
²They want fields, so they take them;
they want houses, so they take them away.
They cheat people to get their houses;
they rob them even of their property.

³That is why the LORD says:
"Look, I am planning trouble against such
people,
and you won't be able to save yourselves.
You will no longer walk proudly,
because it will be a terrible time.
⁴At that time people will make fun of you
and sing this sad song about you:
'We are completely ruined;
the LORD has taken away my people's land.
Yes, he has taken it away from me
and divided our fields among our
enemies!' "
⁵So you will have no one from the LORD's
people
to throw lots*d* to divide the land.

Micah Is Asked Not to Prophesy

⁶The prophets say, "Don't prophesy*d* to us!
Don't prophesy about these things!
Nothing to make us feel bad will happen!"
⁷But I must say this, people of Jacob:
The LORD is becoming angry about what
you have done.
My words are welcome
to the person who does what is right.
⁸But you are fighting against my people like an
enemy.
You take the coats from people who pass
by;
you rob them of their safety;
you plan war.
⁹You've forced the women of my people
from their nice houses;
you've taken my glory
from their children forever.

¹⁰Get up and leave.
This is not your place of rest anymore.
You have made this place unclean,*d*
and it is doomed to destruction.
¹¹But you people want a false prophet
who will tell you nothing but lies.
You want one who promises to prophesy
good things for you
if you give him wine and beer.
He's just the prophet for you.

The Lord Promises to Rescue His People

¹²"Yes, people of Jacob, I will bring all of you
together;
I will bring together all those left alive in
Israel.
I will put them together like sheep in a pen,
like a flock in its pasture;
the place will be filled with many people.
¹³Someone will open the way and lead the
people out.
The people will break through the gate and
leave the city where they were held
captive.
Their king will go out in front of them,
and the LORD will lead them."

The Leaders of Israel Are Guilty of Evil

3 Then I said,
"Listen, leaders of the people of Jacob;
listen, you rulers of the nation of Israel.
You should know how to decide cases fairly,
² but you hate good and love evil.
You skin my people alive
and tear the flesh off their bones.
³You eat my people's flesh
and skin them and break their bones;
you chop them up like meat for the pot,
like meat in a cooking pan.
⁴They will cry to the LORD,
but he won't answer them.
At that time he will hide his face from them,
because what they have done is evil."

⁵The LORD says this about the prophets*d* who
teach his people the wrong way of living:
"If these prophets are given food to eat,
they shout, 'Peace!'
But if someone doesn't give them what they
ask for,
they call for a holy war against that person.
⁶So it will become like night for them,
without visions.
It will become dark for them, without any
way to tell the future.
The sun is about to set for the prophets;
their day will become dark.

Mareshah   This name sounds like the Hebrew word for a person who captures other cities and lands.

7The seers[d] will be ashamed;
   the people who see the future will be
      embarrassed.
Yes, all of them will cover their mouths,
   because there will be no answer from
      God."

Micah Is an Honest Prophet of God

8But I am filled with power,
   with the Spirit[d] of the LORD,
   and with justice and strength,
to tell the people of Jacob how they have
      turned against God,
   and the people of Israel how they have
      sinned.
9Leaders of Jacob and rulers of Israel,
   listen to me,
you who hate fairness
   and twist what is right.
10You build Jerusalem by murdering people;
   you build it with evil.
11Its judges take money
   to decide who wins in court.
Its priests only teach for pay,
   and its prophets[d] only look into the future
      when they get paid.
But they lean on the LORD and say,
   "The LORD is here with us,
   so nothing bad will happen to us."
12Because of you,
   Jerusalem will be plowed like a field.
The city will become a pile of rocks,
   and the hill on which the Temple[d] stands
      will be covered with bushes.

The Mountain of the Lord

4 In the last days
   the mountain on which the LORD's
      Temple[d] stands
   will become the most important of all
      mountains.
It will be raised above the hills,
   and people from other nations will come
      streaming to it.
2Many nations will come and say,
   "Come, let us go up to the mountain of the
      LORD,
   to the Temple of the God of Jacob,
so that he can teach us his ways,
   and we can obey his teachings."
His teachings will go out from Jerusalem,
   the word of the LORD from that city.
3The Lord will judge many nations;
   he will make decisions about strong nations
      that are far away.

They will hammer their swords into plow
      blades
   and their spears into hooks for trimming
      trees.
Nations will no longer raise swords against
      other nations;
   they will not train for war anymore.
4Everyone will sit under his own vine and fig
      tree,
   and no one will make them afraid,
   because the LORD All-Powerful has said it.
5All other nations may follow their own gods,
   but we will follow the LORD our God
      forever and ever.

6The LORD says, "At that time,
I will gather the crippled;
   I will bring together those who were sent
      away,
   those whom I caused to have trouble.
7I will keep alive those who were crippled,
   and I will make a strong nation of those
      who were sent away.
The LORD will be their king in Mount Zion[d]
   from now on and forever.
8And you, watchtower of the flocks,[n] hill of
      Jerusalem,
   to you will come the kingdom as in the
      past.
Jerusalem, the right to rule will come again
   to you."

Why the Israelites Must Go to Babylon

9Now, why do you cry so loudly?
   Is your king gone?
Have you lost your helper,
   so that you are in pain, like a woman
      trying to give birth?
10People of Jerusalem, strain and be in pain.
   Be like a woman trying to give birth,
because now you must leave the city
   and live in the field.
You will go to Babylon,
   but you will be saved from that place.
The LORD will go there
   and buy you back from your enemies.

11But now many nations
   have come to fight against you,
saying, "Let's destroy Jerusalem.
   We will look at her and be glad we have
      defeated her."
12But they don't know
   what the LORD is thinking;
they don't understand his plan.
   He has gathered them like bundles of grain
      to the threshing[d] floor.

watchtower . . . flocks This probably means a part of Jerusalem. The leaders would be like shepherds in a tower watching
their sheep.

¹³"Get up and beat them, people of Jerusalem.
   I will make you strong as if you had horns
      of iron
and hoofs of bronze.
   You will beat many nations into small
      pieces
and give their wealth to the Lord,
   their treasure to the Lord of all the
      earth."

5 So, strong city, gather your soldiers
     together,
because we are surrounded and attacked.
They will hit the leader of Israel
   in the face with a club.

※ **SIDELIGHT:** The book of Micah
has been important to Christians, partly
because of Micah 5:2. Matthew 2:6 (p. 907)
says this prophecy was fulfilled when Jesus
was born in Bethlehem.

The Ruler to Be Born in Bethlehem

²"But you, Bethlehem Ephrathah,
   though you are too small to be among the
      army groups from Judah,
from you will come one who will rule Israel
      for me.
He comes from very old times,
   from days long ago."

³The Lord will give up his people
   until the one who is having a baby gives
      birth;
then the rest of his relatives will return
   to the people of Israel.
⁴At that time the ruler of Israel will stand
   and take care of his people
with the Lord's strength
   and with the power of the name of the
     Lord his God.
The Israelites will live in safety,
   because his greatness will reach all over the
     earth.
⁵ He will bring peace.

LEADERSHIP

A Leader Who Overcame

He grew up in the country, an area so rural that he had to study on his own because it was too far to travel to the nearest school. In fact, by the time he was an adult, his total official schooling amounted to no more than one year. His parents were uneducated; his mother was unable to read or write.

His family wasn't rich, so he had to stay around the homestead with his brothers and sisters to help keep up the farm. Because of his limited traveling, he knew very little of the world outside of Illinois until he was eighteen years old.

Small town, no schooling, unfamiliar with the world. With a background like that, you might not expect this person to become one of the greatest leaders in U.S. history: Abraham Lincoln.

There's more to being a leader than where you were brought up, whether you're rich, or whom you know. Lincoln was a good leader because of his wisdom, honesty, and trustworthiness. People felt confident under his leadership. Read **Micah 5:2–4** to find out about another world leader born in the "backwoods" town of Bethlehem in Judah.

■ What similarities are there between Abraham Lincoln and Jesus? What differences are there?
■ Which obstacles might keep a person from becoming a leader? Which obstacles are possible for a leader to overcome?

C O N S I D E R . . .

■ choosing two leadership qualities you admire and developing those qualities in yourself.
■ getting involved with underprivileged children and encouraging them to overcome obstacles.

F O R   M O R E ,   S E E . . .

■ Exodus 4:10–17 (p. 62)
■ Matthew 2:1–6 (p. 907)
■ Titus 1:5–9 (p. 1270)

Rescue and Punishment

Assyria will surely come into our country
    and walk over our large buildings.
We will set up seven shepherds,
    eight leaders of the people.
6They will destroy the Assyrians with their
    swords;
they will conquer the land of Assyria with
    their swords drawn.
They will rescue us from the Assyrians when
    they come into our land,
when they walk over our borders.

7Then the people of Jacob who are left alive
    will be to other people
like dew from the LORD
    or rain on the grass—
it does not wait for human beings;
    it does not pause for any person.
8Those of Jacob's people who are left alive
    will be scattered among many nations and
    peoples.
They will be like a lion among the animals of
    the forest,
like a young lion in a flock of sheep:
As it goes, it jumps on them
    and tears them to pieces,
    and no one can save them.
9So you will raise your fist in victory over
    your enemies,
    and all your enemies will be destroyed.

10The LORD says, "At that time,
    I will take your horses from you
    and destroy your chariots.
11I will destroy the cities in your country
    and tear down all your defenses.
12I will take away the magic charms you use
    so you will have no more fortune-tellers.
13I will destroy your statues of gods
    and the stone pillars you worship
so that you will no longer worship
    what your hands have made.
14I will tear down Asherah^d idols from you
    and destroy your cities.
15In my anger and rage,
    I will pay back the nations that have not
    listened."

The Lord's Case

6 Now hear what the LORD says:
    "Get up; plead your case in front of the
    mountains;
let the hills hear your story.
2Mountains, listen to the LORD's legal case.
    Foundations of the earth, listen.
The LORD has a legal case against his people,
    and he will accuse Israel."

3He says, "My people, what did I do to you?
    How did I make you tired of me?
    Tell me.
4I brought you from the land of Egypt
    and freed you from slavery;
    I sent Moses, Aaron, and Miriam to you.
5My people, remember
    the evil plans of Balak king of Moab
    and what Balaam son of Beor told Balak.
Remember what happened from Acacia to
    Gilgal
    so that you will know the LORD does what
    is right!"

6You say, "What can I bring with me
    when I come before the LORD,
    when I bow before God on high?
Should I come before him with burnt
    offerings,
    with year-old calves?
7Will the LORD be pleased with a thousand
    male sheep?
Will he be pleased with ten thousand rivers
    of oil?
Should I give my first child for the evil I have
    done?
Should I give my very own child for my
    sin?"
8The LORD has told you, human, what is
    good;
    he has told you what he wants from you:
to do what is right to other people,
    love being kind to others,
    and live humbly, obeying your God.

9The voice of the LORD calls to the city,
    and the wise person honors him.
So pay attention to the rod of punishment;
    pay attention to the One who threatens to
    punish.
10Are there still in the wicked house
    wicked treasures
    and the cursed false measure?
11Can I forgive people who cheat others
    with wrong weights and scales?
12The rich people of the city
    do cruel things.
Its people tell lies;
    they do not tell the truth.
13As for me, I will make you sick.
    I will attack you, ruining you because of
    your sins.
14You will eat, but you won't become full;
    you will still be hungry and empty.
You will store up, *but save nothing,*
    and what you store up, the sword will
    destroy.
15You will plant,
    but you won't harvest.

You will step on your olives,
but you won't get any oil from them.
You will crush the grapes,
but you will not drink the new wine.
16This is because you obey the laws of King
Omri
and do all the things that Ahab's family
does;
you follow their advice.
So I will let you be destroyed.
The people in your city will be laughed at,
and other nations will make fun of you.

The Evil That People Do

7 Poor me! I am like a hungry man,
and all the summer fruit has been
picked —

there are no grapes left to eat,
none of the early figs I love.
2All of the faithful people are gone;
there is not one good person left in this
country.
Everyone is waiting to kill someone;
everyone is trying to trap someone
else.
3With both hands they are doing evil.
Rulers ask for money,
and judges' decisions are bought for a
price.
Rich people tell what they want,
and they get it.
4Even the best of them is like a thornbush;
the most honest of them is worse than a
prickly plant.

SERVICE

Not Just Lip Service

Monika Tirrell's life was pretty protected and carefree. She went to a private school in a Chicago suburb. Although she had gone on several ministry projects, she had never gotten involved in ministry on a consistent basis.

Until her private college's "Day of Prayer." As her work project for the day, she chose a one-day, clean-up crew at the Chicago Gospel League, a shelter for battered and homeless women. When Monika first entered the shelter, she felt as though the women would not accept her and would say to themselves, "Who do you think you are, anyway?"

But after that first visit, Monika and a few friends decided to help out at Gospel League regularly. They promised to return to the shelter every Saturday morning to do whatever was needed.

Monika knew that a few hours a week probably would not make a huge difference in the women's daily hardships. But Monika and her friends wanted to try.

Monika began leading a Bible study and focused on something the women had little of: security. "They couldn't be secure in anything—spouse, home, family, job," Monika said. "Even Gospel League was just a temporary shelter."

Through the Bible studies, Monika encouraged the women to share their experiences and prayer concerns. The women opened up and showed Monika more of what their lives were like. After the studies, Monika and the other volunteers stayed to talk individually with the residents.

Monika readily admits that while the Bible studies did the Gospel League women some good, the entire experience had a more definite long-term effect on her. Monika now wants to commit her life to living with and helping the poor and needy.

Through volunteering at the shelter, Monika learned what it means to serve God. Read **Micah 6:1–8** to see what God said to the Israelites about what it means to serve and follow him.

■ How did Monika fulfill what God says he wants from people in verse 8?
■ How can you fulfill verse 8 in your own life?

C O N S I D E R . . .
■ being kind to others by saying one kind thing to someone each day.
■ learning about helping professions such as social worker, minister, doctor or counselor.
Pray about whether God would have you invest your life in helping others.

F O R   M O R E ,   S E E . . .
■ Ecclesiastes 12:13–14 (p. 607)
■ Mark 9:33–37 (p. 980)
■ Ephesians 2:4–10 (p. 1219)

The day that your watchmen [n] warned you
about has come.
Now they will be confused.
[5]Don't believe your neighbor
or trust a friend.
Don't say anything,
even to your wife.
[6]A son will not honor his father,
a daughter will turn against her mother,
and a daughter-in-law will be against her
mother-in-law;
a person's enemies will be members of his
own family.

The Lord's Kindness

[7]Israel says, "I will look to the LORD for help.
I will wait for God to save me;
my God will hear me.
[8]Enemy, don't laugh at me.
I have fallen, but I will get up again.
I sit in the shadow of trouble now,
but the LORD will be a light for me.
[9]I sinned against the LORD,
so he was angry with me,
but he will defend my case in court.
He will bring about what is right for me.
Then he will bring me out into the light,
and I will see him set things right.
[10]Then my enemies will see this,
and they will be ashamed,
those who said to me,
'Where is the LORD your God?'
I will look down on them.
They will get walked on, like mud in the
street."

Israel Will Return

[11]The time will come when your walls will be
built again,
when your country will grow.
[12]At that time your people will come back to
you
from Assyria and the cities of Egypt,
and from Egypt to the Euphrates River,
and from sea to sea and mountain to
mountain.
[13]The earth will be ruined for the people who
live in it
because of their deeds.

A Prayer to God

[14]So shepherd your people with your stick;
tend the flock of people who belong to
you.
That flock now lives alone in the forest
in the middle of a garden land.
Let them feed in Bashan and Gilead
as in days long ago.

[15]"As in the days when I brought you out of
Egypt,
I will show them miracles." [d]

[16]When the nations see those miracles,
they will no longer brag about their power.
They will put their hands over their mouths,
refusing to listen.
[17]They will crawl in the dust like a snake,
like insects crawling on the ground.
They will come trembling from their holes to
the LORD our God
and will turn in fear before you.
[18]There is no God like you.
You forgive those who are guilty of sin;
you don't look at the sins of your people
who are left alive.
You will not stay angry forever,
because you enjoy being kind.
[19]You will have mercy on us again;
you will conquer our sins.
You will throw away all our sins
into the deepest part of the sea.

> ✳ SIDELIGHT: Micah's name
> means, "Who is like God?" He
> answers the question in Micah 7:18–19. No
> one is. In fact, the Lord is so great he tosses
> our darkest sins into the ocean. Since the
> Middle Ages, Orthodox Jews have visited a
> river or other body of water on the Jewish
> New Year and repeated verse 19 three times
> while tossing bread crumbs on the water.

[20]You will be true to the people of Jacob,
and you will be kind to the people of
Abraham
as you promised to our ancestors long
ago.

---

watchmen Another name for prophets. The prophets were like guards who stood on a city's wall and watched for trouble
coming from far away.

NAHUM

Why Read This Book:

- Discover how God can become angry when people don't follow him (Nahum 1).
- See how God's justice is victorious in the end (Nahum 2—3).

Behind the Scenes:

Think of the most powerful force in all the universe. Now imagine that force being angry. Scary, isn't it?

Nineveh—the capital of Assyria—heated God's anger to a boiling point. The Assyrians had captured and destroyed Israel. For about two hundred and fifty years, the brutal Assyrians had attacked and persecuted Israel and Judah. As a result, the city of Nineveh had come to symbolize everything evil.

The prophet Nahum announced the downfall of Nineveh, using a series of poems to convey his message. In these poems, we see God's anger at unrighteousness, and we see the wickedness of this city. Compare the book of Nahum to the book of Jonah (p. 856), which also focuses on Nineveh. The comparison gives you a better sense of the many dimensions of God's personality. And in both books, we're reminded that God's strength extends to the whole world.

WHERE THE ACTION WAS

ASSYRIA

Nineveh

At the height of its power, Assyria controlled much of the known world.

Through the whole book, Naham blasted the city of Nineveh, the capital of Assyria, for its sins.

Mediterranean Sea

Assyria had destroyed the city of Samaria and captured Israel.

ISRAEL

Samaria

Nahum probably lived in Judah.

JUDAH

Euphrates

Tigris

BABYLON

Nahum predicted that Babylon would destroy Nineveh, which it did (Nahum 2:1).

WHEN THE ACTION WAS

	Nahum preached against Nineveh, the Assyrian capital	The Jews began returning from exile		Jesus was born
1000BC	**750BC**	**500BC**	**250BC**	**BC/AD**
Saul was Israel's king	The Northern Kingdom (Israel) fell to Assyria	The Babylonians destroyed the city of Nineveh		

1 This is the message for the city of Nineveh. [n] This is the book of the vision of Nahum, who was from the town of Elkosh.

The Lord Is Angry with Nineveh

2The LORD is a jealous God who punishes;
  the LORD punishes and is filled with anger.
The LORD punishes those who are against
    him,
  and he stays angry with his enemies.
3The LORD does not become angry quickly,
  and his power is great.
The LORD will not let the guilty go
    unpunished.

Where the LORD goes, there are whirlwinds
    and storms,
  and the clouds are the dust beneath his
    feet.
4He speaks to the sea and makes it dry;
  he dries up all the rivers.
The areas of Bashan and Carmel dry up,
  and the flowers of Lebanon dry up.
5The mountains shake in front of him,
  and the hills melt.
The earth trembles when he comes;
  the world and all who live in it shake with
    fear.
6No one can stay alive when he is angry;
  no one can survive his strong anger.

Nineveh   The capital city of the country of Assyria. Nahum uses Nineveh to stand for all of Assyria.

ANGER

Jealous Anger

After ten years of marriage and three kids, Trent Davis's commitment to his family began
to wane. He started spending more time at the plant, and he was distant whenever he
was home. Finally, he told his wife, Cami, that he had been having an affair for more than
a year. He was confused, he said, and guilt-ridden. He didn't expect Cami to forgive him,
and even if she did, he wasn't sure he wanted the marriage to continue.

Cami was crushed. Their marriage had seemed so stable. Although they had fought
more lately, Trent had always seemed to be a good father and husband.

Emotions flooded Cami. Sadness. Fear. Confusion. But, most of all, anger. She wanted to
hurt the woman who had intruded into her family. "I hate her," Cami cried. "If I see her, I'll
probably kill her—and maybe Trent too."

But Cami knew that wasn't the answer. So she prayed, and as she prayed, she believed
God wanted her to hold her family together. Cami channeled her anger into saving her
family.

She told Trent she loved him; she demanded that he cut off contact with the other
woman; and she moved out of the house until Trent could decide also that his family was
worth fighting for.

One month later, Trent went to Cami. He told her he wanted his family
more than anything. He told her he needed God back in his life. And he told
her the affair was over.

Trent and Cami have spent the past two years rebuilding their family with
God's help.

God restored Trent and Cami's family because Cami channeled her jealous
anger for good. Read **Nahum 1:2–6** to find out how God uses his jealous
anger against his enemies.

■ How is God's jealous anger like Cami's? How is it different?
■ What are some other ways jealous anger can have good results? What are
  its dangers?

CONSIDER . . .

■ defining positive jealous anger and negative jealous anger. Include in your
  definitions the difference between the two.
◀ asking your parents or other married adults how they have seen jealous anger in their
  relationship have positive or negative results.

FOR MORE, SEE . . .

■ Hosea 11:1–11 (p. 831)
■ Jonah 4:1–11 (p. 859)
■ John 2:12–16 (p. 1060)

His anger is poured out like fire;
the rocks are smashed by him.

[7]The Lord is good,
giving protection in times of trouble.
He knows who trusts in him.
[8]But like a rushing flood,
he will completely destroy Nineveh;
he will chase his enemies until he kills
them.

SIDELIGHT: New York City is
called "the Big Apple" because it is a
place where so much power, action, glamor,
and tradition are centered. Nineveh was the
"Big Apple" of Nahum's day—a fast-lane city
surrounded by a seven-and-a-half-mile-long
wall with fifteen gates. It also was
surrounded by a 150-foot-wide moat. The
party's over, though. A few mounds are all
that remain of the city.

---

[9]The Lord will completely destroy
anyone making plans against him.
Trouble will not come a second time.
[10]Those people will be like tangled thorns
or like people drunk from their wine;
they will be burned up quickly like dry
weeds.
[11]Someone has come from Nineveh
who makes evil plans against the Lord
and gives wicked advice.

[12]This is what the Lord says:
"Although Assyria is strong and has many
people,
it will be defeated and brought to an
end.
Although I have made you suffer, Judah,
I will make you suffer no more.
[13]Now I will free you from their control
and tear away your chains."

[14]The Lord has given you this command,
Nineveh:
"You will not have descendants[d] to carry
on your name.
I will destroy the idols and metal images
that are in the temple of your gods.
I will make a grave for you,
because you are wicked."

[15]Look, there on the hills,
someone is bringing good news!
He is announcing peace!

Celebrate your feasts, people of Judah,
and give your promised sacrifices to God.
The wicked will not come to attack you
again;
they have been completely destroyed.

Nineveh Will Be Defeated

2 The destroyer[n] is coming to attack you,
Nineveh.
Guard the defenses.
Watch the road.
Get ready.
Gather all your strength!
[2]Destroyers have destroyed God's people
and ruined their vines,
but the Lord will bring back Jacob's
greatness
like Israel's greatness.

[3]The shields of his soldiers are red;
the army is dressed in red.
The metal on the chariots flashes like fire
when they are ready to attack;
their horses are excited.
[4]The chariots race through the streets
and rush back and forth through the city
squares.
They look like torches;
they run like lightning.

[5]He[n] calls his officers,
but they stumble on the way.
They hurry to the city wall,
and the shield is put into place.
[6]The river gates are thrown open,
and the palace is destroyed.
[7]It has been announced that the people of
Nineveh
will be captured and carried away.
The slave girls moan like doves
and beat their breasts, because they are sad.
[8]Nineveh is like a pool,
and now its water is draining away.
"Stop! Stop!" the people yell,
but no one turns back.
[9]Take the silver!
Take the gold!
There is no end to the treasure—
piles of wealth of every kind.
[10]Nineveh is robbed, ruined, and destroyed.
The people lose their courage, and their
knees knock.
Stomachs ache, and everyone's face grows
pale.

[11]Where is the lions'[n] den
and the place where they feed their young?

---

destroyer The Babylonians, the Scythians, and the Medes destroyed Nineveh.
He This probably means the king of Assyria.
lions' The symbol of Assyria was the lion.

Where did the lion, lioness, and cubs go
without being afraid?
¹²The lion killed enough for his cubs,
enough for his mate.
He filled his cave with the animals he
caught;
he filled his den with meat he had killed.

¹³"I am against you, Nineveh,"
says the LORD All-Powerful.
"I will burn up your chariots in smoke,
and the sword will kill your young lions.
I will stop you from hunting down others
on the earth,
and your messengers' voices
will no longer be heard."

It Will Be Terrible for Nineveh

3 How terrible it will be for the city that
has killed so many.
It is full of lies
and goods stolen from other countries.
It is always killing somebody.
²Hear the sound of whips
and the noise of the wheels.
Hear horses galloping
and chariots bouncing along!
³Horses are charging,
swords are shining,
spears are gleaming!
Many are dead;
their bodies are piled up—
too many to count.
People stumble over the dead bodies.

✷ **SIDELIGHT:** The wartime cruelty
of the Assyrians (Nahum 3:3) would
have been similar to the terrible things that
happened to the Jewish people in World
War II. One Assyrian king bragged of building
pyramids of chopped-off heads outside the
enemy's city. Other kings stacked corpses like
firewood near the conquered city's gates.

---

⁴The city was like a prostitute;ᵈ
she was charming and a lover of magic.
She made nations slaves with her
prostitutionᵈ
and her witchcraft.ᵈ

⁵"I am against you, Nineveh," says the LORD
All-Powerful.
"I will pull your dress up over your face
and show the nations your nakedness
and the kingdoms your shame.

Thebes A great city in Egypt.

⁶I will throw filthy garbage on you
and make a fool of you.
I will make people stare at you.
⁷Everyone who sees you will run away and
say,
'Nineveh is in ruins. Who will cry for her?'
Nineveh, where will I find anyone to
comfort you?"

⁸You are no better than Thebes,ⁿ
who sits by the Nile River
with water all around her.
The river was her defense;
the waters were like a wall around her.
⁹Cush and Egypt gave her endless strength;
Put and Libya supported her.
¹⁰But Thebes was captured
and went into captivity.
Her small children were beaten to death
at every street corner.
Lotsᵈ were thrown for her important men,
and all of her leaders were put in chains.

¹¹Nineveh, you will be drunk, too.
You will hide;
you will look for a place safe from the
enemy.
¹²All your defenses are like fig trees with ripe
fruit.
When the tree is shaken, the figs fall into
the mouth of the eater.
¹³Look at your soldiers.
They are all women!
The gates of your land
are wide open for your enemies;
fire has burned the bars of your gates.

¹⁴Get enough water before the long war
begins.
Make your defenses strong!
Get mud,
mix clay,
make bricks!
¹⁵There the fire will burn you up.
The sword will kill you;
like grasshoppers eating crops, the battle
will completely destroy you.
Grow in number like hopping locusts;ᵈ
grow in number like swarming locusts!
¹⁶Your traders are more than the stars in the
sky,
but like locusts, they strip the land and
then fly away.
¹⁷Your guards are like locusts.
Your officers are like swarms of locusts
that hang on the walls on a cold day.
When the sun comes up, they fly away,
and no one knows where they have gone.

18King of Assyria, your rulers are asleep;
   your important men lie down to rest.
Your people have been scattered on the
      mountains,
   and there is no one to bring them back.

19Nothing can heal your wound;
   your injury will not heal.
Everyone who hears about you applauds,
   because everyone has felt your endless
      cruelty.

HABAKKUK

Why Read This Book:

■ Listen to what God says about why wicked people prosper (Habakkuk 1—2).
■ Learn the importance of waiting patiently for God (Habakkuk 3).

Behind the Scenes:

Sometimes it's hard to understand what God is doing in the world. Bad people seem to do great while good people suffer. Is God absent? Isn't he in control? Doesn't he have the power to control things? Or is God not a righteous God?

The prophet Habakkuk had those tough questions, and he wasn't afraid to ask them directly to God. His book takes the form of a question-and-answer session with God. Habakkuk asks the questions, and then God, through visions, gives answers:

Habakkuk: God, why don't you deliver your people from injustice?
God: Be patient. I've got it under control. The evil people will be punished.
Habakkuk: Why do you wait silently while wicked people destroy other people?
God: Justice will come. Live faithfully, and you will be rewarded.

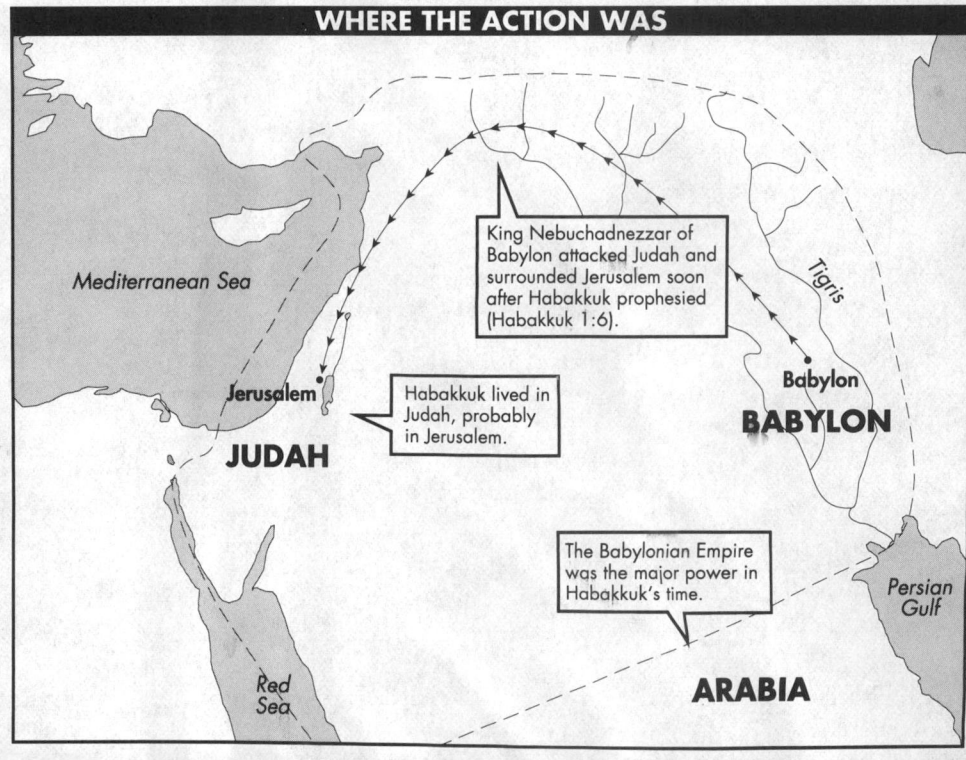

WHERE THE ACTION WAS

Mediterranean Sea

King Nebuchadnezzar of Babylon attacked Judah and surrounded Jerusalem soon after Habakkuk prophesied (Habakkuk 1:6).

Tigris

Jerusalem

Habakkuk lived in Judah, probably in Jerusalem.

JUDAH

Babylon

BABYLON

The Babylonian Empire was the major power in Habakkuk's time.

Red Sea

Persian Gulf

ARABIA

WHEN THE ACTION WAS

The kingdom was split between Israel and Judah

Habakkuk lived

The Jews began returning from exile

Jesus was born

1000BC	750BC	500BC	250BC	BC/AD

Saul was Israel's king

Habakkuk's prophecy was fulfilled when Babylon attacked Jerusalem

Behind the Scenes (cont.):

This short book is filled with comfort for people who suffer unjustly and for those who have trouble finding meaning in life. Not only does the prophet take honest questions to God, but the answers convince him that God is faithful and powerful.

"I will still be glad in the Lord," Habakkuk concludes. "I will rejoice in God my Savior. The Lord God is my strength" (Habakkuk 3:18–19a). It's a reassuring message of faith and hope for all people who see life as meaningless or who suffer unjustly.

---

1 This is the message Habakkuk the prophet received.*d*

Habakkuk Complains

²Lord, how long must I ask for help
  and you ignore me?
I cry out to you about violence,
  but you do not save us!
³Why do you make me see wrong things
and make me look at trouble?
People are destroying things and hurting
  others in front of me;
they are arguing and fighting.
⁴So the teachings are weak,
  and justice never comes.
Evil people gain while good people
  lose;
the judges no longer make fair decisions.

DISCOURAGEMENT

Is There Hope?

Bill Evans had volunteered to stay all night at the homeless shelter, hoping he would be able to make a difference, hoping conditions might somehow change, hoping to feel needed and useful.

The only thing Bill felt as he left the old building, though, was discouragement. As he left the shelter, he was glad to be free from the smell of old clothes, the sight of loneliness, and the sounds of sadness.

He knew one thing: This type of service wasn't for him. He felt he wasn't helpful and could do no good. Why do anything?

As Bill opened his car door, he prayed, "God, why don't you do something?"

Bill thought of how the men in the shelter would accept anything—stale food, old clothing, a heartless handshake—and accept it with thanks and gratitude.

"They settle for so little, but they need so much," Bill said to himself.

Then it hit Bill almost as an answer to his questioning prayer. The poor were so open for gifts; they would be the most happy and pleased to receive God's gift of grace and eternal life.

"It's no wonder, God," Bill thought, "that you came to the poor and needy. They are the most accepting and grateful of all."

Like Bill, Habakkuk felt discouraged. And like Bill, Habakkuk turned to God with his discouragement. Read about Habakkuk's discouragement in **Habakkuk 1:1–3**.

■ How was Habakkuk's response to discouragement similar to Bill's? How was it different?

■ If Habakkuk were alive today, what things might he complain to God about? How might God answer those complaints?

C O N S I D E R . . .

■ listing the complaints you make to God when you're discouraged. Keep the list with you for a week and then review it to see how God may have answered the questions.

■ volunteering your time to spend a day with a young child and encouraging the child with positive words.

F O R   M O R E ,   S E E . . .

■ Zephaniah 3:14–18 (p. 884)
■ Luke 6:20–26 (p. 1012)
■ Romans 8:31–39 (p. 1152)

The Lord Answers

5"Look at the nations!
Watch them and be amazed and shocked.
I will do something in your lifetime
    that you won't believe even when you are
        told about it.

SIDELIGHT: We know hardly anything about the prophet Habakkuk, but his name may give us a clue (Habakkuk 1:1). It means "embracer" or "a garden plant." Makes you wonder if he was a couch potato!

6I will use the Babylonians,
    those cruel and wild people
who march across the earth
    and take lands that don't belong to them.
7They scare and frighten people.
    They do what they want to do
    and are good only to themselves.
8Their horses are faster than leopards
    and quicker than wolves at sunset.
Their horse soldiers attack quickly;
    they come from places far away.
They attack quickly, like an eagle swooping
        down for food.
9 They all come to fight.
Nothing can stop them.
    Their prisoners are as many as the grains of
        sand.
10They laugh at kings
    and make fun of rulers.
They laugh at all the strong, walled cities
    and build dirt piles to the top of the walls
        to capture them.
11Then they leave like the wind and move on.
    They are guilty of worshiping their own
        strength."

Habakkuk Complains Again

12LORD, you live forever,
    my God, my holy God.
    We will not die.
LORD, you have chosen the Babylonians to
        punish people;
    our Rock,ᵈ you picked them to punish.
13Your eyes are too good to look at evil;
    you cannot stand to see those who do
        wrong.
So how can you put up with those evil
        people?
    How can you be quiet when the wicked
        swallow up people who are better than
        they are?
14You treat people like fish in the sea,

like sea animals without a leader.
15The enemy brings them in with hooks.
    He catches them in his net
and drags them in his fishnet.
    So he rejoices and sings for joy.

SIDELIGHT: Wearing nose jewelry may be fashionable at different times, but people probably wouldn't be attracted to the "hooks" mentioned in Habakkuk 1:15. The verse may refer to the Assyrian practice of leading prisoners of war by a rope that was attached to a hook pierced through the nose or lower lip.

16The enemy offers sacrifices to his net
    and burns incenseᵈ to worship it,
because it lets him live like the rich
    and enjoy the best food.
17Will he keep on taking riches with his net?
    Will he go on destroying people without
        showing mercy?

2 I will stand like a guard to watch
    and place myself at the tower.
I will wait to see what he will say to me;
    I will wait to learn how God will answer
        my complaint.

The Lord Answers

2The LORD answered me:
"Write down the vision;
    write it clearly on clay tablets
    so whoever reads it can run to tell others.
3It is not yet time for the message to come
        true,
    but that time is coming soon;
    the message will come true.
It may seem like a long time,
    but be patient and wait for it,
because it will surely come;
    it will not be delayed.
4The evil nation is very proud of itself;
    it is not living as it should.
    But those who are right with God will live
        by trusting in him.

5"Just as wine can trick a person,
    those who are too proud will not last,
because their desire is like a grave's desire for
        death,
    and like death they always want more.
They gather other nations for themselves
    and collect for themselves all the countries.
6But all the nations the Babylonians have hurt
        will laugh at them.
They will make fun of the Babylonians

and say, 'How terrible it will be for the one
that steals many things.
How long will that nation get rich by
forcing others to pay them?'

⁷"One day the people from whom you have
taken money will turn against you.
They will realize what is happening and
make you shake with fear.
Then they will take everything you
have.
⁸Because you have stolen from many nations,
those who are left will take much from
you.
This is because you have killed many people,
destroying countries and cities and everyone
in them.

⁹"How terrible it will be for the nation that
becomes rich by doing wrong,
thinking they will live in a safe place
and escape harm.
¹⁰Because you have made plans to destroy
many people,
you have made your own houses ashamed
of you.
Because of it, you will lose your lives.

¹¹The stones of the walls will cry out against
you,
and the boards that support the roof will
agree that you are wrong.

¹²'How terrible it will be for the nation that
kills people to build a city,
that wrongs others to start a town.
¹³The Lord All-Powerful will send fire
to destroy what those people have built;
all the nations' work will be for nothing.
¹⁴Then, just as water covers the sea,
people everywhere will know the Lord's
glory.

¹⁵"How terrible for the nation that makes its
neighbors drink,
pouring from the jug of wine until they are
drunk
so that it can look at their naked bodies.
¹⁶You Babylonians will be filled with disgrace,
not respect.
It's your turn to drink and fall to the
ground like a drunk person.
The cup of anger from the Lord's right hand
is coming around to you.
You will receive disgrace, not respect.

PATIENCE

Pumping Iron

Push. Squeeze. Pump. Pain.

These are just a few of the things Matt Davis goes through each day as he works out with weights at the gym. All that pumping and breathing and clanging and lifting get tiring after a while. Matt has not only had to struggle with moving weights around, but he's had difficulty moving his schedule around to make room for the daily two-hour workout.

You would think that as tired as Matt gets each day he would be bulging with muscles. Not yet. Oh, he's seen improvement. That's what keeps him going. But Matt looks around the gym at other guys and realizes he has a long way to go to get his body to its full potential.

Every now and then Matt considers taking a shortcut in his training. He's struggling with the temptation of turning to steroids—drugs that could boost his muscle growth—or quitting his training totally. Every now and then Matt finds his patience wearing thin. He wants results fast.

Habakkuk felt a similar struggle with patience as he waited for God to take action against God's enemies. Read about God's answer in **Habakkuk 2:1–4**.

■ How is Matt's struggle with patience similar to Habakkuk's?
■ When have you been impatient like Habakkuk and Matt?

C O N S I D E R . . .

■ writing things that you are impatient about and committing yourself to be patient as you wait for God to work them out.
■ carrying a small, tablet-shaped stone in your pocket or purse to remind you to be patient and trust God.

F O R   M O R E ,   S E E . . .

■ Job 38:1–15 (p. 475)　　　　　　■ James 5:7–8 (p. 1299)
■ Hebrews 6:10–12 (p 1281)

¹⁷You hurt many people in Lebanon,
    but now you will be hurt.
You killed many animals there,
    and now you must be afraid
because of what you did
    to that land, those cities, and the people
        who lived in them.

The Message About Idols

¹⁸"An idol does no good, because a human
        made it;
    it is only a statue that teaches lies.
The one who made it expects his own work
        to help him,
    but he makes idols that can't even speak!
¹⁹How terrible it will be for the one who says
        to a wooden statue, 'Come to life!'
How terrible it will be for the one who
        says to a silent stone, 'Get up!'
It cannot tell you what to do.
    It is only a statue covered with gold and
        silver;
    there is no life in it.
²⁰The LORD is in his Holy Temple;[d]
    all the earth should be silent in his
        presence."

Habakkuk's Prayer

3 This is the prayer of Habakkuk the prophet,[d]
    on shigionoth.[d]

²LORD, I have heard the news about you;
    I am amazed at what you have done.
LORD, do great things once again in our time;
    make those things happen again in our own
        days.
Even when you are angry,
    remember to be kind.

³God is coming from Teman;
    the Holy One comes from Mount Paran.[n]

                                        Selah[d]
His glory covers the skies,
    and his praise fills the earth.
⁴He is like a bright light.
    Rays of light shine from his hand,
    and there he hides his power.
⁵Sickness goes before him,
    and disease follows behind him.
⁶He stands and shakes the earth.
    He looks, and the nations shake with fear.
The mountains, which stood for ages, break
    into pieces;

the old hills fall down.
    God has always done this.

⁷I saw that the tents of Cushan were in
        trouble
    and that the tents of Midian trembled.
⁸LORD, were you angry at the rivers,
    or were you angry at the streams?
Were you angry with the sea
    when you rode your horses and chariots of
        victory?[n]
⁹You uncovered your bow
    and commanded many arrows to be
        brought to you.   Selah
You split the earth with rivers.
¹⁰ The mountains saw you and shook with
        fear.
    The rushing water flowed.
    The sea made a loud noise,
    and its waves rose high.
¹¹The sun and moon stood still in the sky;
    they stopped when they saw the flash of
        your flying arrows
    and the gleam of your shining spear.
¹²In anger you marched on the earth;
    in anger you punished the nations.
¹³You came out to save your people,
    to save your chosen one.
You crushed the leader of the wicked ones
    and took everything he had, from head to
        toe.   Selah
¹⁴With the enemy's own spear you stabbed the
        leader of his army.
    His soldiers rushed out like a storm to
        scatter us.
They were happy
    as they were robbing the poor people in
        secret.
¹⁵But you marched through the sea with your
        horses,
    stirring the great waters.

¹⁶I hear these things, and my body trembles;
    my lips tremble when I hear the sound.
My bones feel weak,
    and my legs shake.

But I will wait patiently for the day of
        disaster
    that will come to the people who attack us.
¹⁷Fig trees may not grow figs,
    and there may be no grapes on the vines.
There may be no olives growing
    and no food growing in the fields.

Teman ... Paran God is seen as again coming from the direction of Mount Sinai. He came from Sinai when he rescued his
    people from Egypt.
sea ... victory This is probably talking about the Israelites crossing the Red Sea.

There may be no sheep in the
    pens
and no cattle in the barns.
¹⁸But I will still be glad in the LORD;
    I will rejoice in God my Savior.
¹⁹The Lord GOD is my strength.

He makes me like a deer that does not
    stumble
so I can walk on the steep mountains.

For the director of music. On my stringed instruments.

ZEPHANIAH

Why Read This Book:

■ Discover what moral corruption can do to people (Zephaniah 1—2).
■ Hear the promise of God's comfort for the faithful (Zephaniah 3).

Behind the Scenes:

Have you ever had a really lousy day—so lousy that you were glad to go to bed to get it over with? When you woke up the next morning, you were determined to start out fresh, and you did everything you could to make sure the next day would be better.

In a sense, the people of Judah had just had a lousy hundred years. Their land had been controlled by the Assyrians. But now they had gained independence. They were ready to start a new day—to rebuild their nation and start over. King Josiah would lead them to new political strength.

But the people needed religious renewal as well. Domination by foreign powers had brought with it foreign customs and pagan gods. The Canaanite religion, Baalism, flourished in the country.

The prophet Zephaniah saw the corruption in the land and warned the people

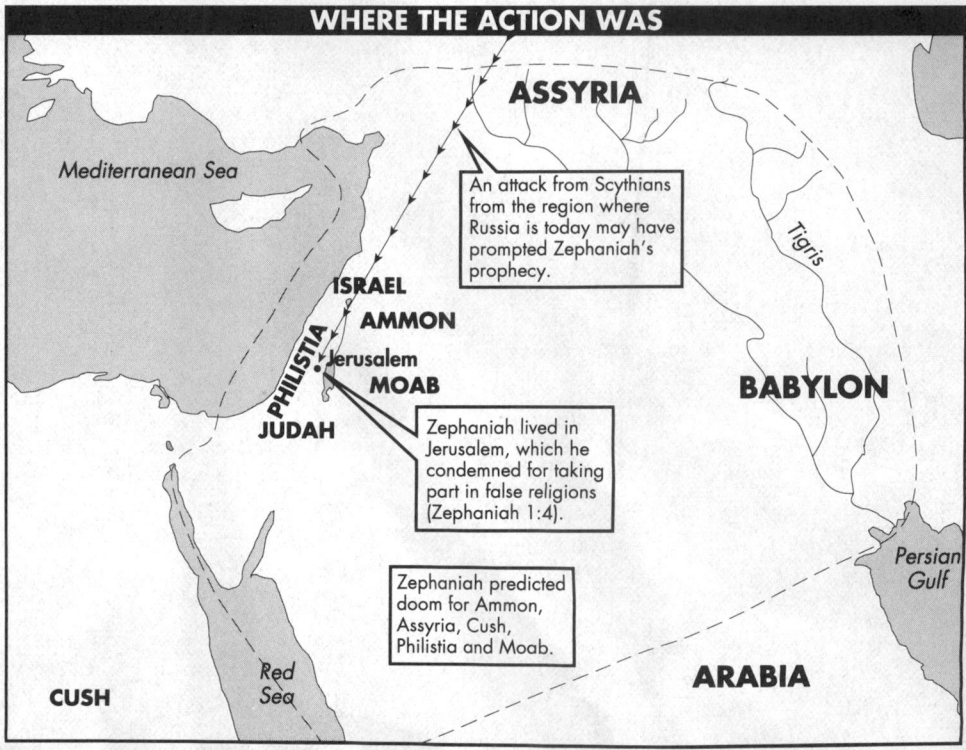

WHERE THE ACTION WAS

ASSYRIA

Mediterranean Sea

An attack from Scythians from the region where Russia is today may have prompted Zephaniah's prophecy.

Tigris

ISRAEL

AMMON

PHILISTIA

Jerusalem

MOAB

BABYLON

JUDAH

Zephaniah lived in Jerusalem, which he condemned for taking part in false religions (Zephaniah 1:4).

Zephaniah predicted doom for Ammon, Assyria, Cush, Philistia and Moab.

Persian Gulf

CUSH

Red Sea

ARABIA

WHEN THE ACTION WAS

The kingdom was split between Israel and Judah	Zephaniah prophesied in Judah	The Jews began returning from exile		Jesus was born
1000BC	750BC	500BC	250BC	BC/AD
Saul was Israel's king	The Northern Kingdom (Israel) fell to Assyria	The Southern Kingdom (Judah) fell to Babylon		

Behind the Scenes (cont.):

to change. As a prophet in Jerusalem, his ministry was probably influential in getting King Josiah to institute widespread religious reform based on the book of Deuteronomy (p. 160).

Zephaniah's message to the people was that God would judge Judah for turning away from him. The book is filled with terrifying images of doom and punishment on "the Lord's day of judging" (Zephaniah 1:14). But the book ends on a positive note, describing a time when people would return to God and the nation would be restored.

The book of Zephaniah has a message that's similar to that of many prophets: Disaster will ultimately come for those who turn away from God. But God will build a new, lasting relationship with those who repent and serve him faithfully.

---

1 This is the word of the Lord that came through Zephariah while Josiah son of Amon was king of Judah. Zephaniah was the son of Cushi, who was the son of Gedaliah. Gedaliah was the son of Amariah, who was the son of Hezekiah.

The Lord's Judgment

²"I will sweep away everything
from the earth," says the Lord.
³"I will sweep away the people and animals;
I will destroy the birds in the air
and the fish of the sea.
I will ruin the evil people,
and I will remove human beings from the
earth," says the Lord.

The Future of Judah

⁴"I will punish Judah
and all the people living in Jerusalem.
I will remove from this place
all signs of Baal,^d the false priests, and the
other priests.
⁵I will destroy those who worship
the stars from the roofs,ⁿ
and those who worship and make promises
by both the Lord and the god Molech,^d

> **SIDELIGHT:** The false religion of Baalism included numerous terrible practices, including human sacrifices, temple prostitution, and astrology. Making matters worse, the Israelites often tried to mix these false religions with true religion—and practice them both at the same time (Zephaniah 1:4–5)!

---

⁶and those who turned away from the Lord,
and those who quit following the Lord and
praying to him for direction.
⁷Be silent before the Lord God,

because the Lord's day for judging people
is coming soon.
The Lord has prepared a sacrifice;
he has made holy his invited guests.
⁸On the day of the Lord's sacrifice,
I, the Lord, will punish the princes and the
king's sons
and all those who wear foreign clothes.
⁹On that day I will punish those who worship
Dagon,^d
those who hurt others and tell lies in the
temples of their gods.

¹⁰"On that day," says the Lord,
"a cry will be heard at the Fish Gate.
A wail will come from the new area of the
city,
and a loud crash will echo from the hills.
¹¹Cry, you people living in the market area,
because all the merchants will be dead;
all the silver traders will be gone.
¹²At that time I, the Lord, will search
Jerusalem with lamps.
I will punish those who are satisfied with
themselves,
who think, 'The Lord won't help us or
punish us.'
¹³Their wealth will be stolen
and their houses destroyed.
They may build houses,
but they will not live in them.
They may plant vineyards,
but they will not drink any wine from
them.

The Lord's Day of Judging

¹⁴"The Lord's day of judging is coming soon;
it is near and coming fast.
The cry will be very sad on the day of the
Lord;
even soldiers will cry.
¹⁵That day will be a day of anger,
a day of terror and trouble.

---

roofs In Bible times houses were built with flat roofs. The roof was used for drying things such as flax and fruit. And it was used as an extra room, as a place for worship, and as a place to sleep in the summer.

a day of destruction and ruin,
    a day of darkness and gloom,
    a day of clouds and blackness,
16a day of alarms and battle cries.
    'Attack the strong, walled cities!
    Attack the corner towers!'
17I will make life hard on the people;
    they will walk around like the blind,
    because they have sinned against the
        LORD.
Their blood will be poured out like dust,
    and their insides will be dumped like
        trash.
18On the day that God will show his anger,
    neither their silver nor gold will save them.
The LORD's anger will be like a fire
    that will burn up the whole world;
suddenly he will bring an end, yes, an end
    to everyone on earth."

The Lord Asks People to Change

2 Gather together, gather,
    you unwanted people.
2Do it before it's too late,
    before you are blown away like chaff,*d*
before the LORD's terrible anger reaches you,
    before the day of the LORD's anger comes
        to you.
3Come to the LORD, all you who are not
        proud,
    who obey his laws.
Do what is right. Learn to be humble.
    Maybe you will escape
    on the day the LORD shows his anger.

Philistia Will Be Punished

4No one will be left in the city of Gaza,
    and the city of Ashkelon will be destroyed.
Ashdod will be empty by noon,

MONEY

Look Where It Got Them

Who, in 1923, was:
- president of the United States' largest steel company?
- president of the largest gas company?
- president of the New York Stock Exchange?
- the greatest wheat speculator in America?
- the "Great Bear" of Wall Street?

In their day, these people made lots of money. They would have been considered the most successful men in the world. But look at what became of these "successful" moneybags:

- The president of the largest steel company, Charles Schwab, died penniless.
- The president of the largest gas company, Howard Hopson, went insane.
- The president of the New York Stock Exchange, Richard Whitney, was released from prison to die at home.
- Arthur Cutten, the greatest wheat speculator, died overseas— penniless and homeless.
- Mr. C. Rivermore, the "Great Bear" of Wall Street, committed suicide.

Although these men had wealth and worldly success, their "kingdom" fell. They had based their lives and priorities on money, and money couldn't meet all their needs.

God wanted the people in Zephaniah's day to base their lives and priorities on much more than money. Read **Zephaniah 1:7–18** to learn more about God's directions and the limitations of money.

- How are the men's lives in this story like the lives of the people in this passage?
- According to the Bible passage, what will happen to those who trust in money and riches?

CONSIDER . . .

- giving some of your money and prized possessions to someone less fortunate.
- keeping track of the money you spend this week and evaluating whether your spending is pleasing to God.

FOR MORE, SEE . . .

- Ecclesiastes 7:11–12 (p. 604)
- Matthew 6:19–34 (p. 918)
- Mark 10:17–31 (p. 982)

and the people of Ekron will be chased
away.
⁵How terrible it will be for you who live by
the Mediterranean Sea,
you Philistines!
The word of the LORD is against you,
Canaan, land of the Philistines.

"I will destroy you
so that no one will be left."
⁶The land by the Mediterranean Sea, in which
you live,
will become pastures, fields for shepherds,
and pens for sheep.
⁷It will belong to the descendants*d* of Judah
who are left alive.
There they will let their sheep eat grass.
At night they will sleep
in the houses of Ashkelon.
The LORD their God will pay attention to
them
and will make their life good again.

Moab and Ammon Will Be Punished

⁸"I have heard the insults of the country of
Moab
and the threats of the people of Ammon.
They have insulted my people
and have taken their land."
⁹So the LORD All-Powerful, the God of Israel,
says,
"As surely as I live,
Moab will be destroyed like Sodom,
and Ammon will be destroyed like
Gomorrah*n*—
a heap of weeds, a pit of salt,
and a ruin forever.
Those of my people who are left alive will
take whatever they want from them;
those who are left from my nation will take
their land."

¹⁰This is what Moab and Ammon get for being
proud,
because they insulted and made fun of the
people of the LORD All-Powerful.
¹¹The LORD will frighten them,
because he will destroy all the gods of the
earth.
Then everyone in faraway places
will worship him wherever they are.

Cush and Assyria Will Be Destroyed

¹²"You Cushites also
will be killed by my sword."
¹³Then the LORD will turn against the north
and destroy Assyria.
He will make Nineveh

a ruin as dry as a desert.
¹⁴Flocks and herds will lie down there,
and all wild animals.
The owls and crows will sit
on the stone pillars.
The owl will hoot through the windows,
trash will be in the doorways,
and the wooden boards of the buildings
will be gone.

✳ **SIDELIGHT:** The nation of Cush
(Zephaniah 2:12–14) is modern-day
Ethiopia. By pairing Assyria and Cush in this
passage, the prophet shows the broadness of
God's judgment, since the two nations were
in the extreme north and south of the known
world at that time.

---

¹⁵This is the happy and safe city
that thinks there is no one else as strong as
it is.
But what a ruin it will be,
a place where wild animals live.
All those who pass by will make fun
and shake their fists.

Jerusalem Will Be Punished

3 How terrible for the wicked, stubborn city
of Jerusalem,
which hurts its own people.
²It obeys no voice;
it can't be taught to do right.
It doesn't trust the LORD;
it doesn't worship its God.
³Its officers are like roaring lions.
Its rulers are like hungry wolves that attack
in the evening,
and in the morning nothing is left of those
they attacked.
⁴Its prophets*d* are proud;
they are people who cannot be trusted.
Its priests don't respect holy things;
they break God's teachings.
⁵But the LORD is good, and he is there in that
city.
He does no wrong.
Every morning he governs the people fairly;
every day he can be trusted.
But evil people are not ashamed of what
they do.

⁶"I have destroyed nations;
their towers were ruined.
I made their streets empty
so no one goes there anymore.

Sodom . . . Gomorrah   Two cities God destroyed because the people were so evil.

Their cities are ruined;
no one lives there at all.
⁷I said, 'Surely now Jerusalem will respect me
and will accept my teaching.'
Then the place where they lived would not
be destroyed,
and I would not have to punish them.
But they were still eager
to do evil in everything they did.
⁸Just wait," says the LORD.
"Some day I will stand up as a witness.
I have decided that I will gather nations
and assemble kingdoms.
I will pour out my anger on them,
all my strong anger.
My anger will be like fire
that will burn up the whole world.

A New Day for God's People

⁹"Then I will give the people of all nations
pure speech
so that all of them will speak the name of
the LORD
and worship me together.
¹⁰People will come from where the Nile River
begins;

my scattered people will come with gifts for
me.
¹¹Then Jerusalem will not be ashamed
of the wrongs done against me,
because I will remove from this city
those who like to brag;
there will never be any more proud people
on my holy mountain in Jerusalem.
¹²But I will leave in the city
the humble and those who are not proud,
and they will trust in the LORD.
¹³Those who are left alive in Israel won't do
wrong
or tell lies;
they won't trick people with their words.
They will eat and lie down
with no one to make them afraid."

A Happy Song

¹⁴Sing, Jerusalem.
Israel, shout for joy!
Jerusalem, be happy
and rejoice with all your heart.
¹⁵The LORD has stopped punishing you;
he has sent your enemies away.
The King of Israel, the LORD, is with you;

HAPPINESS

Glad You're Here . . . Finally

Jim felt terribly out of place. Everyone at the party knew everybody. Except Jim. He
knew no one. And no one knew him. Jim was sure everyone was staring, wondering why
he even came. He looked at the front door constantly, hoping someone he knew would
walk in.

Finally Jim could take no more. He reached for his coat and started
walking to the front door. As he stepped outside, he heard a familiar voice
call from the street.

"Jim! Sorry I'm late. I stopped by to get Janet and the others. How's the
party?"

Jim's eyes brightened as he recognized Terry and five other friends.

"Fine! The party's great . . . now that you're here."

Jim learned that good friends can add to happiness. Find out how a
trustworthy friend brought happiness to Israel in **Zephaniah 3:14—18**.
■ What made Jim and the people in this passage happy?
■ How is having God with us the same as having a close friend with us?
How is it different?

C O N S I D E R . . .

■ rereading the scripture passage with your own name in place of
"Jerusalem," "Israel," and "you."
■ writing a poem about a close friend or family member who makes you happy and
then sending the poem to that person.

F O R   M O R E ,   S E E . . .

■ Psalm 146 (p. 563)
■ Proverbs 16:20 (p. 581)
■ John 16:16—24 (p. 1087)

you will never again be afraid of being
  harmed.
16On that day Jerusalem will be told,
  "Don't be afraid, city of Jerusalem.
  Don't give up.
17The LORD your God is with you;
  the mighty One will save you.
He will rejoice over you.
  You will rest in his love;
  he will sing and be joyful about you."

18"I will take away the sadness planned for
  you,
  which would have made you very ashamed.

19At that time I will punish
  all those who harmed you.
I will save my people who cannot walk
  and gather my people who have been
  thrown out.
I will give them praise and honor
  in every place where they were shamed.
20At that time I will gather you;
  at that time I will bring you back home.
I will give you honor and praise
  from people everywhere
when I make things go well again for you,
  as you will see with your own eyes," says
  the LORD.

HAGGAI

Why Read This Book:

- Understand the importance of focusing on God's priorities instead of our own desires (Haggai 1).
- See the excitement of working together for God's glory (Haggai 2).

Behind the Scenes:

If you've ever moved, you know what it's like to get settled. You have to find your way around the neighborhood. You have to make new friends. You have to settle into a job or a school. In short, you stay busy getting your new life together.

The Jewish people were in that kind of situation. They had just returned to Judah after being captives in Babylon. They were caught up in planting crops, repairing homes, and earning a living.

But something was missing. While the Jews were enjoying their new freedom in their nice homes, God's Temple lay in ruins. So the people were permitted to return from Persia to rebuild the Temple. God sent the prophet Haggai to show the Jews that their priorities were wrong, that they were being selfish and materialistic.

Building the Temple was important for the Jews, not so they would have a place to worship, but as a symbol of God's leadership and lordship in the nation. It was the "place" of God's personal contact with his people. Haggai believed the completed Temple would bring hope to a people who were depressed and struggling.

Haggai's ministry involved motivating people to complete God's Temple, which had been started almost twenty years earlier. He was successful, too; within three weeks, the people had started work on the Temple again. And four years later, the Temple was complete.

Though we don't face the challenge of building a Temple in Jerusalem, the book of Haggai still has important reminders for us. It reminds us to keep our

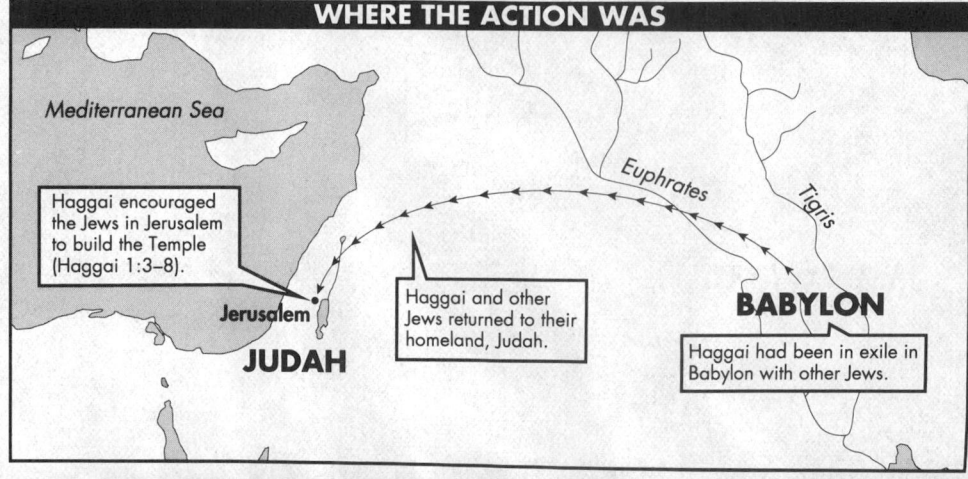

WHERE THE ACTION WAS

Mediterranean Sea

Haggai encouraged the Jews in Jerusalem to build the Temple (Haggai 1:3–8).

Jerusalem

JUDAH

Haggai and other Jews returned to their homeland, Judah.

Euphrates

Tigris

BABYLON

Haggai had been in exile in Babylon with other Jews.

WHEN THE ACTION WAS

The kingdom was split between Israel and Judah

The Jews began returning from exile

The rebuilt Temple was completed

Jesus was born

1000BC · 750BC · 500BC · 250BC · BC/AD

Saul was Israel's king

The Southern Kingdom (Judah) fell to Babylon

Haggai began to preach

Behind the Scenes (cont.): priorities straight. And it reminds us to make God the center of our lives—just as the Temple was the center of life for the Jewish people.

It Is Time to Build the Temple

1 The prophet[d] Haggai spoke the word of the LORD to Zerubbabel son of Shealtiel, the governor of Judah, and to Joshua son of Jehozadak, the high priest. This message came in the second year that Darius was king, on the first day of the sixth month:

2"This is what the LORD All-Powerful says: 'The people say the right time has not come to rebuild the Temple[d] of the LORD.' "

3Then Haggai the prophet spoke the word of the LORD: 4"Is it right for you to be living in fancy houses while the Temple is still in ruins?"

5This is what the LORD All-Powerful says: "Think about what you have done. 6You have planted much, but you harvest little. You eat, but you do not become full. You drink, but you are still thirsty. You put on clothes, but you are not warm enough. You earn money, but then you lose it all as if you had put it into a purse full of holes."

7This is what the LORD All-Powerful says: "Think about what you have done. 8Go up to the mountains, bring back wood, and build the Temple. Then I will be pleased with it and be hon-ored," says the LORD. 9"You look for much, but you find little. When you bring it home, I destroy it. Why?" asks the LORD All-Powerful. "Because you all work hard for your own houses while my house is still in ruins! 10Because of what you have done, the sky holds back its rain and the ground

> **SIDELIGHT:** The warning of a dry time that would ruin the harvest was scary, since the Jews depended on the crops to survive (Haggai 1:11). The olive tree, for example, was used for food, fuel, medicine, and anointing oil. Plus it was used in sacrifices and for building furniture. Olive trees covered the countryside, even growing on rocky hillsides.

holds back its crops. 11I have called for a time without rain on the land, and on the mountains, and on the grain, the new wine, the olive oil, the plants which the earth produces, the people, the farm animals, and all the work of your hands."

PRIORITIES

The Way to Bee

It has no single home of its own. It makes nothing for itself. Yet the bee constantly works from one flower to another, gathering nectar on its legs and carrying it back to the hive.

The other bees—all with their own tasks—work the nectar into food, building the hive and feeding the queen.

Because the bee's main concern is the hive and its community, all other needs are taken care of—food, shelter, family, and job. Through working together, bees create a strong community with their main priority in place: the survival of the hive.

Through the prophet Haggai, God also spoke about priorities. Read **Haggai 1:5–11** to find out what God says about priorities.
- How is God asking the people of Israel to be like bees?
- What might God be telling you to make your top priority?

C O N S I D E R . . .
- pledging to give one-tenth of all the money you make this year to your church.
- asking your pastor for ways to help around the church building and gathering a group of friends to help do those things.

F O R   M O R E ,   S E E . . .
- Genesis 25:27–34 (p. 30)
- Matthew 13:44–46 (p. 932)
- Matthew 19:16–26 (p. 942)

¹²Zerubbabel son of Shealtiel and Joshua son of Jehozadak, the high priest, and all the rest of the people who were left alive obeyed the Lord their God and the message from Haggai the prophet, because the Lord their God had sent him. And the people feared the Lord.

¹³Haggai, the Lord's messenger, gave the Lord's message to the people, saying, "The Lord says, 'I am with you.' " ¹⁴The Lord stirred up Zerubbabel son of Shealtiel, the governor of Judah, and Joshua son of Jehozadak, the high priest, and all the rest of the people who were left alive. So they came and worked on the Temple of their God, the Lord All-Powerful. ¹⁵They began on the twenty-fourth day of the sixth month in the second year Darius was king.

The Beauty of the Temple

2 On the twenty-first day of the seventh month, the Lord spoke his word through Haggai the prophet,*d* saying, ²"Speak to Zerubbabel son of Shealtiel, governor of Judah, and to Joshua son of Jehozadak, the high priest, and to the rest of the people who are left alive. Say, ³'Do any of you remember how great the Temple*d* was before it was destroyed? What does it look like now? Doesn't it seem like nothing to you?' ⁴But the Lord says, 'Zerubbabel, be brave. Also, Joshua son of Jehozadak, the high priest, be brave. And all you people who live in the land, be brave,' says the Lord. 'Work, because I am with you,' says the Lord All-Powerful. ⁵'I made a promise to you when you came out of Egypt, and my Spirit*d* is still with you. So don't be afraid.'

⁶"This is what the Lord All-Powerful says: 'In a short time I will once again shake the heavens and the earth, the sea and the dry land. ⁷I will shake all the nations, and they will bring their wealth. Then I will fill this Temple with glory,' says the Lord All-Powerful. ⁸'The silver is mine, and the gold is mine,' says the Lord All-Powerful. ⁹'The new Temple will be greater than the one before,' says the Lord All-Powerful. 'And in this place I will give peace,' says the Lord All-Powerful."

¹⁰On the twenty-fourth day of the ninth month in the second year Darius was king, the Lord spoke his word to Haggai the prophet, saying, ¹¹"This is what the Lord All-Powerful says: 'Ask the priests for a teaching. ¹²Suppose a person carries in the fold of his clothes some meat made holy for the Lord. If that fold touches bread, cooked food, wine, olive oil, or some other food, will that be made holy?' "

The priests answered, "No."

¹³Then Haggai said, "A person who touches a dead body will become unclean.*d* If he touches any of these foods, will it become unclean, too?"

The priests answered, "Yes, it would become unclean."

¹⁴Then Haggai answered, "The Lord says, 'This is also true for the people of this nation. They are unclean, and everything they do with their hands is unclean to me. Whatever they offer at the altar is also unclean.

¹⁵" 'Think about this from now on! Think about how it was before you started laying stones on top of stones to build the Temple of the Lord. ¹⁶A person used to come to a pile of grain expecting to find twenty basketfuls, but there were only ten. And a person used to come to the wine vat to take out fifty jarfuls, but only twenty were there. ¹⁷I destroyed your work with diseases, mildew,*d* and hail, but you still did not come back to me,' says the Lord. ¹⁸'It is the twenty-fourth day of the ninth month, the day in which the people finished working on the foundation of the Temple of the Lord. From now on, think about these things: ¹⁹Do you have seeds for crops still in the barn? Your vines, fig trees, pomegranates,*d* and olive trees have not given fruit yet. But from now on I will bless you!' "

The Lord Makes a Promise to Zerubbabel

²⁰Then the Lord spoke his word a second time to Haggai on the twenty-fourth day of the month. He said, ²¹"Tell Zerubbabel, the governor of Judah, 'I am going to shake the heavens and the earth. ²²I will destroy the foreign kingdoms and take away the power of the kingdoms of the nations. I will destroy the chariots and their riders. The horses will fall with their riders, as people kill each other with swords.' ²³The Lord All-Powerful says, 'On that day I will take you, Zerubbabel son of Shealtiel, my servant,' says the Lord, 'and I will make you important like my signet*d* ring, because I have chosen you!' says the Lord All-Powerful."

ZECHARIAH

Why Read This Book:

- Be challenged to follow God and do his will (Zechariah 1—8).
- Find encouragement in knowing a glorious, peaceful future awaits God's people (Zechariah 9—14).

Behind the Scenes:

When you work on something, you like to see results. You want to know that your hard work will be worth the time and energy you've invested.

The people of Israel also wanted to see results when they started rebuilding their Temple. They wanted to know they would be blessed for what they were doing.

The prophet Zechariah was there to assure them and encourage them. Like his colleague Haggai (p. 886), who ministered during the same time, Zechariah believed completing the Temple would be the first step for bringing God's kingdom to earth.

Zechariah's encouragement came in a series of visions about the Temple (Zechariah 1:7—6:8). Each vision in the first part of the book shows activity between heaven and earth. They each show a world that's changing, and they have a universal theme—that God is bigger than the Temple or Judah. Through each vision, Zechariah encourages the people to rebuild the Temple and to focus on following God so they will be ready for the coming of God's kingdom.

The second part of Zechariah (chapters 9—14) has a different focus. It concentrates on the coming kingdom of God instead of the Temple. In the coming age, the wicked will be destroyed and the righteous will be saved. This new kingdom will focus on justice, kindness, and mercy rather than rituals of religion.

The book of Zechariah has been treasured by Christians because many of its images of the Messiah (such as the Prince of Peace, Zechariah 9:9-10), foreshadow Jesus Christ's life and ministry. Just as Zechariah offered encouragement, hope, and joy to the people of his day, the book offers encouragement, hope, and joy to us today.

WHEN THE ACTION WAS				
Saul was Israel's king	The Northern Kingdom (Israel) fell to Assyria	Jews began returning from exile		Jesus was born
1000BC	750BC	500BC	250BC	BC/AD
The kingdom was split between Israel and Judah	The Southern Kingdom (Judah) fell to Babylon	Zechariah had his visions		

The Lord Calls His People Back

1 In the eighth month of the second year Darius was king, the LORD spoke his word to the prophet^d Zechariah son of Berekiah, who was the son of Iddo. The LORD said, ²"The LORD was very angry with your ancestors. ³So tell the people: This is what the LORD All-Powerful says: 'Return to me, and I will return to you,' says the

---

LORD All-Powerful. ⁴Don't be like your ancestors. In the past the prophets said to them: This is what the LORD All-Powerful says: 'Stop your evil ways and evil actions.' But they wouldn't listen or pay attention to me, says the LORD. ⁵Your ancestors are dead, and those prophets didn't live forever. ⁶I commanded my words and laws to my servants the prophets, and they preached to your ancestors, who returned to me. They said, 'The LORD All-Powerful did as he said he would. He punished us for the way we lived and for what we did.' "

The Vision of the Horses

⁷It was on the twenty-fourth day of the eleventh month, which is the month of Shebat, in Darius's second year as king. The LORD spoke his word to the prophet^d Zechariah son of Berekiah, who was the son of Iddo.

⁸During the night I had a vision. I saw a man riding a red horse. He was standing among some myrtle trees in a ravine, with red, brown, and white horses behind him.

⁹I asked, "What are these, sir?"

The angel who was talking with me answered, "I'll show you what they are."

¹⁰Then the man standing among the myrtle trees explained, "They are the ones the LORD sent through all the earth."

¹¹Then they spoke to the LORD's angel, who was standing among the myrtle trees. They said, "We have gone through all the earth, and everything is calm and quiet."

¹²Then the LORD's angel asked, "LORD All-Powerful, how long will it be before you show

mercy to Jerusalem and the cities of Judah? You have been angry with them for seventy years now." ¹³So the LORD answered the angel who was talking with me, and his words were comforting and good.

¹⁴Then the angel who was talking to me said to me, "Announce this: This is what the LORD All-Powerful says: 'I have a strong love for Jerusalem. ¹⁵And I am very angry with the nations that feel so safe. I was only a little angry at them, but they made things worse.'

¹⁶"So this is what the LORD says: 'I will return to Jerusalem with mercy. My Temple^d will be rebuilt,' says the LORD All-Powerful, 'and the measuring line will be used to rebuild Jerusalem.'

¹⁷"Also announce: This is what the LORD All-Powerful says: 'My towns will be rich again. The LORD will comfort Jerusalem again, and I will again choose Jerusalem.' "

The Vision of the Horns

¹⁸Then I looked up and saw four animal horns. ¹⁹I asked the angel who was talking with me, "What are these?"

He said, "These are the horns that scattered the people of Judah, Israel, and Jerusalem."

²⁰Then the LORD showed me four craftsmen. ²¹I asked, "What are they coming to do?"

He answered, "They have come to scare and throw down the horns. These horns scattered the people of Judah so that no one could even lift up his head. These horns stand for the nations that attacked the people of Judah and scattered them."

The Vision of the Measuring Line

2 Then I looked up and saw a man holding a line for measuring things. ²I asked him, "Where are you going?"

He said to me, "I am going to measure Jerusalem, to see how wide and how long it is."

³Then the angel who was talking with me left, and another angel came out to meet him. ⁴The second angel said to him, "Run and tell that young man, 'Jerusalem will become a city without walls, because there will be so many people and cattle in it. ⁵I will be a wall of fire around it,' says the LORD. 'And I will be the glory within it.'

⁶"Oh no! Oh no! Run away from Babylon, because I have scattered you like the four winds of heaven," says the LORD.

⁷"Oh no, Jerusalem! Escape, you who live right in Babylon." ⁸This is what the LORD All-Powerful says: "After he has honored me and sent me against the nations who took your possessions — because whoever touches you hurts what is precious to me — ⁹I will shake my hand against them so that their slaves will rob them."

Then you will know that the LORD All-Powerful sent me.

10"Shout and be glad, Jerusalem. I am coming, and I will live among you," says the LORD. 11"At that time people from many nations will join with the LORD and will become my people. Then I will live among you, and you will know that the LORD All-Powerful has sent me to you. 12The LORD will take Judah as his own part of the holy land, and Jerusalem will be his chosen city again. 13Be silent, everyone, in the presence of the LORD. He is coming out of the holy place where he lives."

The Vision of the High Priest

3 Then he showed me Joshua, the high priest, standing in front of the LORD's angel. And Satan was standing by Joshua's right side to accuse him. 2The LORD said to Satan, "The LORD says no to you, Satan! The LORD who has chosen Jerusalem says no to you! This man was like a burning stick pulled from the fire."

3Joshua was wearing dirty clothes and was standing in front of the angel. 4The angel said to those standing in front of him, "Take off those dirty clothes."

Then the angel said to Joshua, "Look, I have taken away your sin from you, and I am giving you beautiful, fine clothes."

5Then I said, "Put a clean turban on his head." So they put a clean turban on his head and dressed him while the LORD's angel stood there.

6Then the LORD's angel said to Joshua, 7"This is what the LORD All-Powerful says: 'If you do as I tell you and serve me, you will be in charge of my Temple[d] and my courtyards. And I will let you be with these angels who are standing here.

8" 'Listen, Joshua, the high priest, and your friends who are sitting in front of you. They are symbols of what will happen. I am going to bring my servant called the Branch. 9Look, I put this stone in front of Joshua, a stone with seven sides. I will carve a message on it,' says the LORD All-Powerful. 'And in one day I will take away the sin of this land.'

10"The LORD All-Powerful says, 'In that day, each of you will invite your neighbor to sit under your own grapevine and under your own fig tree.' "

The Vision of the Lampstand

4 Then the angel who was talking with me returned and woke me up as if I had been asleep. 2He asked me, "What do you see?"

I said, "I see a solid gold lampstand with a bowl at the top. And there are seven lamps and also seven places for wicks. 3There are two olive trees by it, one on the right of the bowl and the other on the left."

4I asked the angel who talked with me, "Sir, what are these?"

5The angel said, "Don't you know what they are?"

"No, sir," I said.

6Then he told me, "This is the word of the LORD to Zerubbabel: 'You will not succeed by your own strength or power, but by my Spirit,'[d] says the LORD All-Powerful.

7"Who are you, big mountain? In front of Zerubbabel you will become flat land, and he will bring out the topmost stone, shouting, 'It's beautiful! It's beautiful!' "

8Then the LORD spoke his word to me again, saying, 9"Zerubbabel has laid the foundation of this Temple,[d] and he will complete it. Then you will know that the LORD All-Powerful has sent me to you.

10"The people should not think that small beginnings are unimportant. They will be happy when they see Zerubbabel with tools, building the Temple.

"(These are the seven eyes of the LORD, which look back and forth across the earth.)"

11Then I asked the angel, "What are the two olive trees on the right and left of the lampstand?"

12I also asked him, "What are the two olive branches beside the two gold pipes, from which the olive oil flows to the lamps?"

13He answered, "Don't you know what they are?"

"No, sir," I said.

14So he said, "They are symbols of the two who have been appointed to serve the LORD of all the earth."

�֍ **SIDELIGHT:** Though the flying scroll of Zechariah 5 had impressive dimensions, it doesn't hold the record. Archaeologists have discovered scrolls that would stretch almost half the length of a football field. Try fitting one of those textbooks into your locker!

The Vision of the Flying Scroll

5 I looked up again and saw a flying scroll. 2The angel asked me, "What do you see?"

I answered, "I see a flying scroll, thirty feet long and fifteen feet wide."

3And he said to me, "This is the curse that will go all over the land. One side says every thief will be taken away. The other side says everyone who makes false promises will be taken away. 4The LORD All-Powerful says, 'I will send it to the houses of thieves and to those who use my name to make false promises. The scroll will stay in that person's house and destroy it with its wood and stones.' "

The Vision of the Woman

⁵Then the angel who was talking with me came forward and said to me, "Look up and see what is going out."

⁶"What is it?" I asked.

He answered, "It is a measuring basket going out." He also said, "It is a symbol of the people's sins in all the land."

⁷Then the lid made of lead was raised, and there was a woman sitting inside the basket. ⁸The angel said, "The woman stands for wickedness." Then he pushed her back into the basket and put the lid back down.

⁹Then I looked up and saw two women going out with the wind in their wings. Their wings were like those of a stork, and they lifted up the basket between earth and the sky.

¹⁰I asked the angel who was talking with me, "Where are they taking the basket?"

¹¹"They are going to Babylonia to build a temple for it," he answered. "When the temple is ready, they will set the basket there in its place."

The Vision of the Four Chariots

6 I looked up again and saw four chariots going out between two mountains, mountains of bronze. ²Red horses pulled the first chariot. Black horses pulled the second chariot. ³White horses pulled the third chariot, and strong, spotted horses pulled the fourth chariot. ⁴I asked the angel who was talking with me, "What are these, sir?"

⁵He said, "These are the four spirits of heaven. They have just come from the presence of the Lord of the whole world. ⁶The chariot pulled by the black horses will go to the land of the north. The white horses will go to the land of the west, and the spotted horses will go to the land of the south."

⁷When the powerful horses went out, they were eager to go through all the earth. So he said, "Go through all the earth," and they did.

⁸Then he called to me, "Look, the horses that went north have caused my spirit to rest in the land of the north."

A Crown for Joshua

⁹The Lord spoke his word to me, saying, ¹⁰"Take silver and gold from Heldai, Tobijah, and Jedaiah, who were captives in Babylon. Go that same day to the house of Josiah son of Zephaniah, who came from Babylon. ¹¹Make the silver and gold into a crown, and put it on the head of Joshua son of Jehozadak, the high priest. ¹²Tell him this is what the Lord All-Powerful says: 'A man whose name is the Branch will branch out

from where he is, and he will build the Temple[d] of the Lord. ¹³One man[n] will build the Temple of the Lord, and the other[n] will receive honor. One man will sit on his throne and rule, and the other will be a priest on his throne. And these two men will work together in peace.' ¹⁴The crown will be kept in the Temple of the Lord to remind Heldai, Tobijah, Jedaiah, and Josiah son of Zephaniah. ¹⁵People living far away will come and build the Temple of the Lord. Then you will know the Lord All-Powerful has sent me to you. This will happen if you completely obey the Lord your God."

SIDELIGHT: Going without food for religious reasons is called "fasting" (Zechariah 7). Like Zechariah, Jesus considered faithfulness to God more important than fasting (Matthew 6:16–18, p. 918). Anybody hungry?

The People Should Show Mercy

7 In the fourth year Darius was king, on the fourth day of the ninth month, which is called Kislev, the Lord spoke his word to Zechariah. ²The city of Bethel sent Sharezer, Regem-Melech, and their men to ask the Lord a question. ³They went to the prophets[d] and priests who were at the Temple[d] of the Lord All-Powerful. The men said, "For years in the fifth month of each year we have shown our sadness and gone without food. Should we continue to do this?"

⁴The Lord All-Powerful spoke his word to me, saying, ⁵"Tell the priests and the people in the land: 'For seventy years you went without food and cried in the fifth and seventh months, but that was not really for me. ⁶And when you ate and drank, it was really for yourselves. ⁷The Lord used the earlier prophets to say the same thing, when Jerusalem and the surrounding towns were at peace and wealthy, and people lived in the southern area and the western hills.' "

⁸And the Lord spoke his word to Zechariah again, saying, ⁹"This is what the Lord All-Powerful says: 'Do what is right and true. Be kind and merciful to each other. ¹⁰Don't hurt widows and orphans, foreigners or the poor; don't even think of doing evil to somebody else.'

¹¹"But they refused to pay attention; they were stubborn and did not want to listen anymore. ¹²They made their hearts as hard as rock and would not listen to the teachings of the Lord All-Powerful. And they would not hear the words he

---

One man This probably refers to Zerubbabel.
other This probably refers to Joshua.

sent by his Spirit through the earlier prophets. So the LORD All-Powerful became very angry.

13" 'When I called to them, they would not listen. So when they called to me, I would not listen,' says the LORD All-Powerful. 14'I scattered them like a hurricane to other countries they did not know. This good land was left so ruined behind them that no one could live there. They had made the desired land a ruin.' "

The Lord Will Bless Jerusalem

8 The LORD All-Powerful spoke his word, saying, 2This is what the LORD All-Powerful says: "I have a very strong love for Jerusalem. My strong love for her is like a fire burning in me."

3This is what the LORD says: "I will return to Jerusalem and live in it. Then it will be called the City of Truth, and the mountain of the LORD All-Powerful will be called the Holy Mountain."

4This is what the LORD All-Powerful says: "Old men and old women will again sit along Jerusalem's streets, each carrying a cane because of age. 5And the streets will be filled with boys and girls playing."

6This is what the LORD All-Powerful says: "Those who are left alive then may think it is too difficult to happen, but it is not too difficult for me," says the LORD All-Powerful. 7This is what the LORD All-Powerful says: "I will save my people from countries in the east and west. 8I will bring them back, and they will live in Jerusalem. They will be my people, and I will be their good and loyal God."

9This is what the LORD All-Powerful says: "Work hard, you who are hearing these words today. The prophets spoke these words when the foundation was laid for the house of the LORD All-Powerful, for the building of the Temple.d 10Before that time there was no money to hire people or animals. People could not safely come and go because of the enemies; I had turned everyone against his neighbor. 11But I will not do to these people who are left what I did in the past," says the LORD All-Powerful.

12"They will plant their seeds in peace, their grapevines will have fruit, the ground will give good crops, and the sky will send rain. I will give all this to the people who are left alive. 13Judah and Israel, your names have been used as curses in other nations. But I will save you, and you will become a blessing. So don't be afraid; work hard."

14This is what the LORD All-Powerful says: "When your ancestors made me angry, I planned to punish you. I did not change my mind," says the LORD All-Powerful. 15"But now I will do something different. I am planning to do good to Jerusalem and Judah. So don't be afraid. 16These are the things you should do: Tell each other the truth. In the courts judge with truth and complete fairness. 17Do not make plans to hurt your neighbors, and don't love false promises. I hate all these things," says the LORD.

18The LORD All-Powerful spoke his word to me again. 19This is what the LORD All-Powerful says: "The special days when you give up eating in the fourth, fifth, seventh, and tenth months will become good, joyful, happy feasts in Judah. But you must love truth and peace."

20This is what the LORD All-Powerful says: "Many people from many cities will still come to Jerusalem. 21People from one city will go and say to those from another city, 'We are going to pray to the LORD and to ask the LORD All-Powerful for help. Come and go with us.' 22Many people and powerful nations will come to worship the LORD All-Powerful in Jerusalem and to pray to the LORD for help."

23This is what the LORD All-Powerful says: "At that time, ten men from different countries will come and take hold of a Judean by his coat. They will say to him, 'Let us go with you, because we have heard that God is with you.' "

Punishment on Israel's Enemies

9 This message is the word of the LORD.

The message is against the land of
Hadrach
and the city of Damascus.
The tribesd of Israel and all people
belong to the LORD.
2The message is also against the city of
Hamath, on the border,
and against Tyre and Sidon, with their skill.
3Tyre has built a strong wall for herself.
She has piled up silver like dust
and gold like the mud in the streets.
4But the Lord will take away all she has
and destroy her power on the sea.
That city will be destroyed by fire.
5The city of Ashkelon will see it and be afraid.
The people of Gaza will shake with fear,
and the people of Ekron will lose hope.
No king will be left in Gaza,
and no one will live in Ashkelon anymore.
6Foreigners will live in Ashdod,
and I will destroy the pride of the
Philistines.
7I will stop them from drinking blood
and from eating forbidden food.
Those left alive will belong to God.
They will be leaders in Judah,
and Ekron will become like the Jebusites.
8I will protect my Templed
from armies who would come or go.
No one will hurt my people again,
because now I am watching them.

The King Is Coming

9Rejoice greatly, people of Jerusalem!
   Shout for joy, people of Jerusalem!
Your king is coming to you.
   He does what is right, and he saves.
   He is gentle and riding on a donkey,
   on the colt of a donkey.

❋ **SIDELIGHT:** The limousine of
the ancient world was a white
warhorse. But Zechariah pictures the future
king of Jerusalem on a donkey—the biblical
equivalent of an economy car (Zechariah 9:9;
see also Matthew 21:5, p. 944).

10I will take away the chariots from Ephraim
   and the horses from Jerusalem.
The bows used in war will be broken.
The king will talk to the nations about peace.
His kingdom will go from sea to sea,
   and from the Euphrates River to the ends
   of the earth.

11As for you, because of the blood of the
   agreement with you
   I will set your prisoners free from the
   waterless pit.
12You prisoners who have hope,
   return to your place of safety.
Today I am telling you
   that I will give you back twice as much as
   before.
13I will use Judah like a bow
   and Ephraim like the arrows.
Jerusalem, I will use your men
   to fight the men of Greece.
I will use you like a warrior's sword.

14Then the Lord will appear above them,
   and his arrows will shoot like lightning.
The Lord God will blow the trumpet,
   and he will march in the storms of the
   south.
15The Lord All-Powerful will protect them;
   they will destroy the enemy with slingshots.
They will drink and shout like drunk men.
   They will be filled like a bowl
   used for sprinkling blood at the corners of
   the altar.
16On that day the Lord their God will save
   them
as if his people were sheep.
They will shine in his land
   like jewels in a crown.
17They will be so pretty and beautiful.
   The young men will grow strong on the
   grain

and the young women on new wine.

The Lord's Promises

10 Ask the Lord for rain during the
springtime rains.
The Lord is the one who makes the
   clouds.
He sends the showers
   and gives everyone green fields.
2Idols tell lies;
   fortune-tellers see false visions
and tell about false dreams.
The comfort they give is worth nothing.
So the people are like lost sheep.
   They are abused, because there is no
   shepherd.

3The Lord says, "I am angry at my shepherds,
   and I will punish the leaders.
I, the Lord All-Powerful, care
   for my flock, the people of Judah.
I will make them like my proud war
   horses.
4From Judah will come the cornerstone,*d*
   and the tent peg,
   the battle bow,
   and every ruler.
5Together they will be like soldiers
   marching to battle through muddy streets.
The Lord is with them,
   so they will fight and defeat the horsemen.

6"I will strengthen the people of Judah
   and save the people of Joseph.
I will bring them back,
   because I care about them.
It will be as though
   I had never left them,
because I am the Lord their God,
   and I will answer them.
7The people of Ephraim will be strong like
   soldiers;
   they will be glad as when they have drunk
   wine.
Their children will see it and rejoice;
   they will be happy in the Lord.
8I will call my people
   and gather them together.
I will save them,
   and they will grow in number as they grew
   in number before.
9I have scattered them among the nations,
   but in those faraway places, they will
   remember me.
They and their children will live and
   return.
10I will bring them back from the land of Egypt
   and gather them from Assyria.
I will bring them to Gilead and Lebanon
   until there isn't enough room for them all.

11They will come through the sea of trouble.
The waves of the sea will be calm,
and the Nile River will dry up.
I will defeat Assyria's pride
and destroy Egypt's power over other
countries.
12I will make my people strong,
and they will live as I say," says the LORD.

11 Lebanon, open your gates
so fire may burn your cedar trees. n
2Cry, pine trees, because the cedar has fallen,
because the tall trees are ruined.
Cry, oaks in Bashan,
because the mighty forest has been cut
down.
3Listen to the shepherds crying
because their rich pastures are destroyed.
Listen to the lions roaring
because the lovely land of the Jordan River
is ruined.

The Two Shepherds

4This is what the LORD my God says: "Feed the
flock that are about to be killed. 5Their buyers kill
them and are not punished. Those who sell them
say, 'Praise the LORD, I am rich.' Even the shepherds don't feel sorry for their sheep. 6I don't feel
sorry anymore for the people of this country,"
says the LORD. "I will let everyone be under the
power of his neighbor and king. They will bring
trouble to the country, and I will not save anyone
from them."

7So I fed the flock about to be killed, particularly the weakest ones. Then I took two sticks; I
called one Pleasant and the other Union, and I fed
the flock. 8In one month I got rid of three shepherds. The flock did not pay attention to me, and
I got impatient with them. 9I said, "I will no
longer take care of you like a shepherd. Let those
that are dying die, and let those that are to be
destroyed be destroyed. Let those that are left eat
each other."

10Then I broke the stick named Pleasant to
break the agreement God made with all the nations. 11That day it was broken. The weak ones in
the flock who were watching me knew this message was from the LORD.

12Then I said, "If you want to pay me, pay me.
If not, then don't." So they paid me thirty pieces
of silver.

13The LORD said to me, "Throw the money to
the potter." That is how little they thought I was
worth. n So I took the thirty pieces of silver and
threw them to the potter in the Temple d of the
LORD.

14Then I broke the second stick, named Union,
to break the brotherhood between Judah and Israel.

15Then the LORD said to me, "Get the things
used by a foolish shepherd again, 16because I am
going to get a new shepherd for the country. He
will not care for the dying sheep, or look for the
young ones, or heal the injured ones, or feed the
healthy. But he will eat the best sheep and tear off
their hoofs.

17"How terrible it will be for the useless
shepherd
who abandoned the flock.
A sword will strike his arm and his right eye.
His arm will lose all its strength,
and his right eye will go blind."

Jerusalem Will Be Saved

12 This message is the word of the LORD to
Israel. This is what the LORD says, who
stretched out the skies, and laid the foundations
of the earth, and put the human spirit within: 2"I
will make Jerusalem like a cup of poison to the
nations around her. They will come and attack
Jerusalem and Judah. 3One day all the nations on
earth will come together to attack Jerusalem, but
I will make it like a heavy rock; anyone who tries
to move it will get hurt. 4At that time I will confuse every horse and cause its rider to go crazy,"
says the LORD. "I will watch over Judah, but I will
blind all the horses of the enemies. 5Then the
leaders of Judah will say to themselves, 'The people of Jerusalem are strong, because the LORD All-
Powerful is their God.'

6"At that time I will make the leaders of Judah
like a fire burning a stack of wood or like a fire
burning straw. They will destroy all the people
around them left and right. But the people of Jerusalem will remain safe.

7"The LORD will save the homes of Judah first
so that the honor given to David's family and to
the people of Jerusalem won't be greater than the
honor given to Judah. 8At that time the LORD will
protect the people in Jerusalem. Then even the
weakest of them will be strong like David. And
the family of David will be like God, like an angel
of the LORD in front of them. 9At that time I will
go to destroy all the nations that attack Jerusalem.

Crying for the One They Stabbed

10"I will pour out on David's family and the
people in Jerusalem a spirit of kindness and
mercy. They will look at me, the one they have
stabbed, and they will cry like someone crying
over the death of an only child. They will be as

---

trees   In this poem, trees, bushes, and animals stand for leaders of countries around Judah.
worth   This was a small amount. It was about the price paid for a slave.

sad as someone who has lost a firstborn*d* son. [11]At that time there will be much crying in Jerusalem, like the crying for Hadad Rimmon in the plain of Megiddo. [12]The land will cry, each family by itself: the family of David by itself and their wives by themselves, the family of Nathan by itself and their wives by themselves, [13]the family of Levi by itself and their wives by themselves, the family of Shimei by itself and their wives by themselves, [14]and all the rest of the families by themselves and their wives by themselves.

13 "At that time a fountain will be open for David's descendants*d* and for the people of Jerusalem to cleanse them of their sin and uncleanness."

[2]The Lord All-Powerful says, "At that time I will get rid of the names of the idols from the land; no one will remember them anymore. I will also remove the prophets*d* and unclean*d* spirits from the land. [3]If a person continues to prophesy, his own father and mother, the ones who gave birth to him, will tell him, 'You have told lies using the Lord's name, so you must die.' When he prophesies, his own father and mother who gave birth to him will stab him.

[4]"At that time the prophets will be ashamed of their visions and prophecies. They won't wear the prophet's clothes made of hair to trick people. [5]Each of them will say, 'I am not a prophet. I am a farmer and have been a farmer since I was young.' [6]But someone will ask, 'What are the deep cuts on your body?' And each will answer, 'I was hurt at my friend's house.'

> ❋ **SIDELIGHT:** If false prophets tried to get new jobs, they would have had trouble hiding their previous occupation. The deep cuts on their bodies (Zechariah 13:6) were probably self-inflicted while they were prophesying.

The Shepherd Is Killed

[7]"Sword, hit the shepherd.
   Attack the man who is my friend,"
   says the Lord All-Powerful.
"Kill the shepherd,
   and the sheep will scatter,
   and I will punish the little ones."

SADNESS

Stabbed in the Back

Youth leader Denise McNeil felt cheated and abused by her youth group. After returning from a recent retreat, she discovered that one of the older teenagers had bought and supplied liquor for the kids on the trip. All the kids knew about the alcohol, but no one had told Denise.

When the group returned home, the word got out. Parents called Denise the next day, asking how such a thing could happen.

Denise had no idea how it had happened. That was what made it so embarrassing. She thought she knew the group. Now she wasn't so sure. She had trusted the kids. Now she could make no promises.

Denise spent the next month talking to all the kids who were on the retreat. She shared her anger, pain, and sadness. She also showed the group she still loved them. Then she worked—against heavy opposition—to plan another youth retreat, one that could be done right.

When the kids saw how much Denise cared for them and how they had abused her trust in them, they felt sad and sorry. The sadness they felt was much like the sadness described in **Zechariah 12:7–10**.

■ How did Denise's youth group act like the people described in verse 10?
■ According to this passage, how does God feel when we disobey?

C O N S I D E R . . . .
■ listening carefully to a friend the next time he or she is sad.
■ rewriting Zechariah 12:7–9, substituting your own name for "the people of Judah," "the people in Jerusalem," and "the family of David." Read the passage to yourself when you're down.

F O R   M O R E ,   S E E . . . .
■ Job 2:11–13 (p. 453)
■ Mark 15:33–34 (p. 995)
■ Luke 19:41–44 (p. 1045)

8The LORD says, "Two-thirds of the people
through all the land will die. They will be
gone,
and one-third will be left.
9The third that is left I will test with fire,
purifying them like silver,
testing them like gold.
Then they will call on me,
and I will answer them.
I will say, 'You are my people,'
and they will say, 'The LORD is our God.' "

The Day of Punishment

14 The LORD's day of judging is coming
when the wealth you have taken will be
divided among you.

2I will bring all the nations together to fight Jerusalem. They will capture the city and rob the
houses and attack the women. Half the people
will be taken away as captives, but the rest of the
people won't be taken from the city.

3Then the LORD will go to war against those
nations; he will fight as in a day of battle. 4On that
day he will stand on the Mount of Olives,*d* east of
Jerusalem. The Mount of Olives will split in two,
forming a deep valley that runs east and west.
Half the mountain will move toward the north,
and half will move toward the south. 5You will
run through this mountain valley to the other
side, just as you ran from the earthquake when
Uzziah was king of Judah. Then the LORD my God
will come and all the holy ones with him.

6On that day there will be no light, cold, or
frost. 7There will be no other day like it, and the
LORD knows when it will come. There will be no
day or night; even at evening it will still be light.

8At that time fresh water will flow from Jerusalem. Half of it will flow east to the Dead Sea,*d* and
half will flow west to the Mediterranean Sea. It
will flow summer and winter.

9Then the LORD will be king over the whole
world. At that time there will be only one LORD,
and his name will be the only name.

10All the land south of Jerusalem from Geba to
Rimmon will be turned into a plain. Jerusalem
will be raised up, but it will stay in the same place.
The city will reach from the Benjamin Gate and
to the First Gate to the Corner Gate, and from the
Tower of Hananel to the king's winepresses.*d*
11People will live there, and it will never be destroyed again. Jerusalem will be safe.

12But the LORD will bring a terrible disease on
the nations that fought against Jerusalem. Their
flesh will rot away while they are still standing up.
Their eyes will rot in their sockets, and their
tongues will rot in their mouths. 13At that time
the LORD will cause panic. Everybody will grab his
neighbor, and they will attack each other. 14The
people of Judah will fight in Jerusalem. And the
wealth of the nations around them will be collected — much gold, silver, and clothes. 15A similar disease will strike the horses, mules, camels,
donkeys, and all the animals in the camps.

16All of those left alive of the people who came
to fight Jerusalem will come back to Jerusalem
year after year to worship the King, the LORD All-
Powerful, and to celebrate the Feast*d* of Shelters.
17Anyone from the nations who does not go to
Jerusalem to worship the King, the LORD All-
Powerful, will not have rain fall on his land. 18If
the Egyptians do not go to Jerusalem, they will
not have rain. Then the LORD will send them the
same terrible disease he sent the other nations
that did not celebrate the Feast of Shelters. 19This
will be the punishment for Egypt and any nation
which does not go to celebrate the Feast of Shelters.

20At that time the horses' bells will have written on them: HOLY TO THE LORD. The cooking pots
in the Temple*d* of the LORD will be like the holy
altar bowls. 21Every pot in Jerusalem and Judah
will be holy to the LORD All-Powerful, and everyone who offers sacrifices will be able to take food
from them and cook in them. At that time there
will not be any buyers or sellers in the Temple of
the LORD All-Powerful.

MALACHI

Why Read This Book:

■ Learn how to be loyal when things are tough (Malachi 1—2).
■ Claim God's promise in the midst of discouragement (Malachi 3).

Behind the Scenes:

Everything was supposed to be better now. The Jewish people returned to Jerusalem from exile, excited by the promises of Haggai (p. 886) and Zechariah (p. 889) about the coming of God's kingdom. But many years had passed, and life seemed about like it had been—if not worse.

The community was still poor. Droughts and locusts continually ruined crops. Families were falling apart by divorce and adultery. The poor were being abused. And, worst of all, people had forgotten their faith. They just went through the motions of worshiping God.

In short, times were hard and God seemed far away. Why even try? the people seemed to say. They were upset and impatient. It seemed that God had not carried through with his part of the agreement.

Enter Malachi, whose name means "my messenger." He pointed out how the country's priests were abusing or neglecting their God-given responsibilities. Their failure, the prophet said, was the main reason things hadn't gotten any better. The prophet then challenged people to return to their faith. Then, at the time of judgment, the faithful would receive God's blessing.

When things don't go as we expect or hope, it's easy to think God has let us down. And it's easy to relax our faith. But the book of Malachi urges us to stay strong. God loves us and is faithful, even when we can't see him working. We can have courage and hope in knowing that, in the end, God has a great future for all who follow him.

WHEN THE ACTION WAS			
Saul was Israel's king	The Northern Kingdom (Israel) fell to Assyria	Jews began returning from exile	Jesus was born
1000BC	750BC	500BC	250BC	BC/AD
The kingdom was split between Israel and Judah		The Southern Kingdom (Judah) fell to Babylon	Malachi ministered in Jerusalem	

1

This message is the word of the LORD given to Israel through Malachi.

God Loves Israel

²The LORD said, "I have loved you."

But you ask, "How have you loved us?"

The LORD said, "Esau and Jacob were brothers. I loved Jacob, ³but I hated Esau. I destroyed his mountain country and left his land to the wild dogs of the desert."

⁴The people of Edom might say, "We were destroyed, but we will go back and rebuild the ruins."

But the LORD All-Powerful says, "If they rebuild them, I will destroy them. People will say, 'Edom is a wicked country. The LORD is always angry with the Edomites.' ⁵You will see these things with your own eyes. And you will say, 'The LORD is great, even outside the borders of Israel!' "

The Priests Don't Respect God

⁶The LORD All-Powerful says, "A child honors his father, and a servant honors his master. I am a father, so why don't you honor me? I am a master, so why don't you respect me? You priests do not respect me.

"But you ask, 'How have we shown you disrespect?'

⁷"You have shown it by bringing unclean*d* food to my altar.

"But you ask, 'What makes it unclean?'

"It is unclean because you don't respect the altar of the LORD. ⁸When you bring blind animals as sacrifices, that is wrong. When you bring crippled and sick animals, that is wrong. Try giving them to your governor. Would he be pleased with you? He wouldn't accept you," says the LORD All-Powerful.

⁹"Now ask God to be kind to you, but he won't accept you with such offerings," says the LORD All-Powerful.

¹⁰"I wish one of you would close the Temple*d* doors so that you would not light useless fires on my altar! I am not pleased with you and will not accept your gifts," says the LORD All-Powerful. ¹¹"From the east to the west I will be honored among the nations. Everywhere they will bring incense*d* and clean offerings to me, because I will be honored among the nations," says the LORD All-Powerful.

¹²"But you don't honor me. You say about the Lord's altar, 'It is unclean, and the food has no worth.' ¹³You say, 'We are tired of doing this,' and you sniff at it in disgust," says the LORD All-Powerful.

"And you bring hurt, crippled, and sick animals as gifts. You bring them as gifts, but I won't accept them from you," says the LORD. ¹⁴"The person who cheats will be cursed. He has a male animal in his flock and promises to offer it, but then he offers to the Lord an animal that has something wrong with it. I am a great king," says the LORD All-Powerful, "and I am feared by all the nations.

Rules for Priests

2

"Priests, this command is for you. ²Listen to me. Pay attention to what I say. Honor my name," says the LORD All-Powerful. "If you don't, I will send a curse on you and on your blessings. I have already cursed them, because you don't pay attention to what I say.

³"I will punish your descendants.*d* I will smear your faces with the animal insides left from your feasts, and you will be thrown away with it. ⁴Then you will know that I am giving you this command so my agreement with Levi will continue," says the LORD All-Powerful. ⁵"My agreement for priests was with the tribe*d* of Levi. I promised them life and peace so they would honor me. And they did honor me and fear me. ⁶They taught the true teachings and spoke no lies. With peace and honesty they did what I said they should do, and they kept many people from sinning.

⁷"A priest should teach what he knows, and people should learn the teachings from him, because he is the messenger of the LORD All-Powerful. ⁸But you priests have stopped obeying me. With your teachings you have caused many people to do wrong. You have broken the agreement with the tribe*d* of Levi!" says the LORD All-Powerful. ⁹"You have not been careful to do what I say, but instead you take sides in court cases. So I have caused you to be hated and disgraced in front of everybody."

Judah Was Not Loyal to God

¹⁰We all have the same father; the same God made us. So why do people break their promises to each other and show no respect for the agreement our ancestors made with God? ¹¹The people of Judah have broken their promises. They have done something God hates in Israel and Jerusalem: The people of Judah did not respect the Temple*d* that the LORD loves, and the men of Judah married women who worship foreign gods. ¹²Whoever does this might bring offerings to the LORD All-Powerful, but the LORD will still cut that person off from the community of Israel.

¹³This is another thing you do. You cover the Lord's altar with your tears. You cry and moan, because he does not accept your offerings and is not pleased with what you bring. ¹⁴You ask, "Why?" It is because the LORD sees how you treated the wife you married when you were young. You broke your promise to her, even though she was your partner and you had an

agreement with her. [15]God made husbands and wives to become one body and one spirit for his purpose — so they would have children who are true to God.

So be careful, and do not break your promise to the wife you married when you were young. [16]The LORD God of Israel says, "I hate divorce. And I hate people who do cruel things as easily as they put on clothes," says the LORD All-Powerful. So be careful. And do not break your trust.

The Special Day of Judging

[17]You have tired the LORD with your words.

You ask, "How have we tired him?"

You did it by saying, "The LORD thinks anyone who does evil is good, and he is pleased with them." Or you asked, "Where is the God who is fair?"

3 The LORD All-Powerful says, "I will send my messenger, who will prepare the way for me. Suddenly, the Lord you are looking for will come to his Temple;[d] the messenger of the agree-

ment, whom you want, will come." [2]No one can live through that time; no one can survive when he comes. He will be like a purifying fire and like laundry soap. [3]Like someone who heats and purifies silver, he will purify the Levites and make them pure like gold and silver. Then they will bring offerings to the LORD in the right way. [4]And the LORD will accept the offerings from Judah and Jerusalem, as it was in the past. [5]The LORD All-Powerful says, "Then I will come to you and judge you. I will be quick to testify against those who take part in evil magic, adultery,[d] and lying under oath, those who cheat workers of their pay and who cheat widows and orphans, those who are unfair to foreigners, and those who do not respect me.

Stealing from God

[6]"I the LORD do not change. So you descendants[d] of Jacob have not been destroyed. [7]Since the time of your ancestors, you have disobeyed my rules and have not kept them. Return to me,

---

GOD'S POWER

The Power of Right

Laura Frey, the senior class president, had a remarkable power over the students at her school. The whole gymnasium could be full, and all Laura needed to do to quiet things down was to stand up, look out over the crowd, and wait. Within a minute the whole gym would be quiet.

Where did Laura get her power?

Ask her fellow students:

"I trust her. If she says she's going to do something, she always does her best to do it."

Ask her teachers:

"She's truthful and honest. She owns up to her mistakes and will always try to do better. She even helps others through their mistakes."

Ask her friends' parents:

"I like her sincerity. Laura will listen to my daughter if she has a problem. She's a good friend who's there for others."

People had no reason to doubt Laura and countless reasons to admire her.

As you get to know God, you'll discover a God who has the ultimate powerful qualities of trust, honesty, and sincerity. Read **Malachi 3:1–4** about the promised "messenger" of God whose power is like a purifying fire. This "messenger" is the promised Messiah, the Son of God.

■ How much greater is God's power in Malachi than that of leaders like Laura?

■ What area of your life needs the purifying power of God?

C O N S I D E R . . .

■ choosing one of the symbols of God's power from the passage (matches, laundry soap, silver, or gold) and keeping it in your room as a reminder of God's power.

◗ wearing something gold or silver every day this week to remind you to pray for God's purifying power in your life.

F O R   M O R E ,   S E E . . .

■ Psalm 51:10–13 (p. 511)
■ Isaiah 25:1–5 (p. 640)
■ Revelation 21:1–8 (p. 1347)

and I will return to you," says the LORD All-Powerful.

"But you ask, 'How can we return?'

8"Should a person rob God? But you are robbing me.

"You ask, 'How have we robbed you?'

"You have robbed me in your offerings and the tenth of your crops. 9So a curse is on you, because the whole nation has robbed me. 10Bring to the storehouse a full tenth of what you earn so there will be food in my house. Test me in this," says the LORD All-Powerful. "I will open the windows of heaven for you and pour out all the blessings

vines before they are ready to pick," says the LORD All-Powerful. 12"All the nations will call you blessed, because you will have a pleasant country," says the LORD All-Powerful.

The Lord's Promise of Mercy

13The LORD says, "You have said terrible things about me.

'But you ask, 'What have we said about you?'

14"You have said, 'It is useless to serve God. It did no good to obey his laws and to show the LORD All-Powerful that we were sorry for what we did. 15So we say that proud people are happy. Evil people succeed. They challenge God and get away with it.' "

16Then those who honored the LORD spoke with each other, and the LORD listened and heard them. The names of those who honored the LORD and respected him were written in his presence in a book to be remembered.

17The LORD All-Powerful says, "They belong to me; on that day they will be my very own. As a parent shows mercy to his child who serves him, I will show mercy to my people. 18You will again see the difference between good and evil people, between those who serve God and those who don't.

you need. 11I will stop the insects so they won't eat your crops. The grapes won't fall from your

---

SIN

Unfair Acquisitions

It didn't seem fair to Alicia Hall. She needed a new dress just as much as Donna Sims. She wanted the cassette tapes just as much as Donna. She liked chocolate just as much as Donna. She even wanted a new car stereo just as much as Donna.

But unlike Donna, she wasn't willing to steal and cheat to get them.

It wasn't fair.

Alicia sometimes hoped that Donna would get caught shoving a tape into her purse or wearing a new dress out of a store or lying to her insurance company about the "theft" of her old car stereo.

But Alicia didn't stay honest just because she was afraid of being caught. She was honest because she knew it was the right thing to do. She knew that others were hurt by Donna's stealing and lies. Alicia also knew that God would not approve of Donna's dishonesty.

Dishonesty will separate you from God. Read **Malachi 4:1–2** to find out how God will deal with those who do evil things and those who honor God.

■ According to the scripture, what punishment awaits dishonest and greedy people like Donna?
■ How can you honor God and receive the goodness and healing he promises in this passage?

CONSIDER . . .

■ confronting any friends who shoplift.
■ returning to their rightful owners any items you've stolen.

FOR MORE, SEE . . .

■ Genesis 3 (p. 4)   ■ 1 John 4:1–6 (p. 1319)
■ 1 Corinthians 3:12–15 (p. 1171)

The Day of the Lord's Judging

4 "There is a day coming that will burn like a hot furnace, and all the proud and evil people will be like straw. On that day they will be completely burned up so that not a root or branch will be left," says the LORD All-Powerful. ²"But for you who honor me, goodness will shine on you like the sun, with healing in its rays. You will jump around, like well-fed calves. ³Then you will crush the wicked like ashes under your feet on the day I will do this," says the LORD All-Powerful.

⁴"Remember the teaching of Moses my servant, those laws and rules I gave to him on Mount Sinai for all the Israelites.

⁵"But I will send you Elijah the prophet*a* before that great and terrifying day of the LORD's judging. ⁶Elijah will help parents love their children and children love their parents. Otherwise, I will come and put a curse on the land."

NEW
TESTAMENT

MATTHEW

Why Read This Book:

- Learn how Jesus filled the role of the Messiah—the Savior whose coming was anticipated in the Old Testament (Matthew 1—3).
- Find guidelines for living (Matthew 5—7).
- Understand Jesus' power as shown through many miracles and stories (Matthew 8—20).
- See what happened to Jesus that led to his death and resurrection (Matthew 21—28).

Behind the Scenes:

When candidates announce they are running for political office, the press begins a flurry of investigation. Reporters check the candidate's background and experience. Where is he from? What's her family like? Is he trustworthy? Has she done what she says she's done?

The book of Matthew is something like stories about new candidates. This Gospel digs into Jesus' background. It tells his relationship to the Jewish faith—how he fulfills Old Testament prophecies about a Messiah or Savior. That's why the book quotes Old Testament passages more than any other book in the New

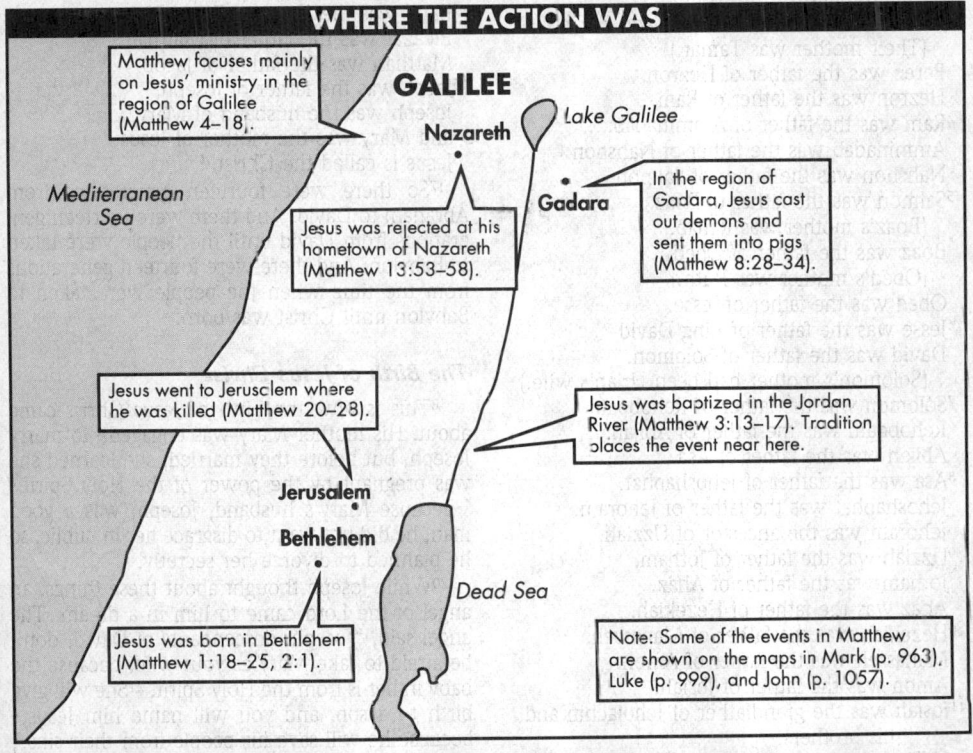

WHERE THE ACTION WAS

Matthew focuses mainly on Jesus' ministry in the region of Galilee (Matthew 4–18).

GALILEE

Lake Galilee

Nazareth

Jesus was rejected at his hometown of Nazareth (Matthew 13:53–58).

Mediterranean Sea

Gadara

In the region of Gadara, Jesus cast out demons and sent them into pigs (Matthew 8:28–34).

Jesus went to Jerusalem where he was killed (Matthew 20–28).

Jesus was baptized in the Jordan River (Matthew 3:13–17). Tradition places the event near here.

Jerusalem

Bethlehem

Dead Sea

Jesus was born in Bethlehem (Matthew 1:18–25, 2:1).

Note: Some of the events in Matthew are shown on the maps in Mark (p. 963), Luke (p. 999), and John (p. 1057).

WHEN THE ACTION WAS

Jesus was born	Jesus was crucified, rose from the dead, and went to heaven	Paul began his missionary work	Fire destroyed Rome	
BC/AD	**25AD**	**50AD**	**75AD**	**100AD**
	Jesus began his ministry		Romans destroyed the Temple in Jerusalem	

Behind the Scenes (cont.): Testament. And because the Jews expected a political messiah to establish a kingdom on earth, this book emphasizes Jesus' teachings about what his kingdom would be like.

The book of Matthew uses a straightforward, biographical approach to tell stories of Jesus' life and teachings. It begins by telling about his birth (chapters 1—2), then focuses on his ministry, primarily around Lake Galilee, where he grew up (chapters 3—18). Then the book moves to tell about events in Jerusalem that ultimately led to Jesus' death (chapters 19—27). The book concludes with Jesus' resurrection and last instructions to his disciples (chapter 28).

Matthew is a good source for examining what Jesus did and said while he was on earth. By reading it, we learn what Jesus expects of us if we intend to follow him.

The Family History of Jesus

1 This is the family history of Jesus Christ. He came from the family of David, and David came from the family of Abraham.

2 Abraham was the father[n] of Isaac.
Isaac was the father of Jacob.
Jacob was the father of Judah and his brothers.
3 Judah was the father of Perez and Zerah. (Their mother was Tamar.)
Perez was the father of Hezron.
Hezron was the father of Ram.
4 Ram was the father of Amminadab.
Amminadab was the father of Nahshon.
Nahshon was the father of Salmon.
5 Salmon was the father of Boaz. (Boaz's mother was Rahab.)
Boaz was the father of Obed. (Obed's mother was Ruth.)
Obed was the father of Jesse.
6 Jesse was the father of King David.
David was the father of Solomon. (Solomon's mother had been Uriah's wife.)
7 Solomon was the father of Rehoboam.
Rehoboam was the father of Abijah.
Abijah was the father of Asa.
8 Asa was the father of Jehoshaphat.
Jehoshaphat was the father of Jehoram.
Jehoram was the ancestor of Uzziah.
9 Uzziah was the father of Jotham.
Jotham was the father of Ahaz.
Ahaz was the father of Hezekiah.
10 Hezekiah was the father of Manasseh.
Manasseh was the father of Amon.
Amon was the father of Josiah.
11 Josiah was the grandfather of Jehoiachin and his brothers. (This was at the time that the people were taken to Babylon.)
12 After they were taken to Babylon:

Jehoiachin was the father of Shealtiel.
Shealtiel was the grandfather of Zerubbabel.
13 Zerubbabel was the father of Abiud.
Abiud was the father of Eliakim.
Eliakim was the father of Azor.
14 Azor was the father of Zadok.
Zadok was the father of Akim.
Akim was the father of Eliud.
15 Eliud was the father of Eleazar.
Eleazar was the father of Matthan.
Matthan was the father of Jacob.
16 Jacob was the father of Joseph.
Joseph was the husband of Mary, and Mary was the mother of Jesus. Jesus is called the Christ.[d]

17 So there were fourteen generations from Abraham to David. And there were fourteen generations from David until the people were taken to Babylon. And there were fourteen generations from the time when the people were taken to Babylon until Christ was born.

The Birth of Jesus Christ

18 This is how the birth of Jesus Christ came about. His mother Mary was engaged[n] to marry Joseph, but before they married, she learned she was pregnant by the power of the Holy Spirit.[d] 19 Because Mary's husband, Joseph, was a good man, he did not want to disgrace her in public, so he planned to divorce her secretly.

20 While Joseph thought about these things, an angel of the Lord came to him in a dream. The angel said, "Joseph, descendant[d] of David, don't be afraid to take Mary as your wife, because the baby in her is from the Holy Spirit. 21 She will give birth to a son, and you will name him Jesus,[n] because he will save his people from their sins."

22 All this happened to bring about what the Lord had said through the prophet:[d] 23 "The virgin[d] will be pregnant. She will have a son, and

---

father "Father" in Jewish lists of ancestors can sometimes mean grandfather or more distant relative.
engaged For the Jewish people an engagement was a lasting agreement, which could only be broken by a divorce. If a bride was unfaithful, it was considered adultery, and she could be put to death.
Jesus The name Jesus means "salvation."

they will name him Immanuel,"[n] which means "God is with us."

24When Joseph woke up, he did what the Lord's angel had told him to do. Joseph took Mary as his wife, 25but he did not have sexual relations with her until she gave birth to the son. And Joseph named him Jesus.

Wise Men Come to Visit Jesus

2 Jesus was born in the town of Bethlehem in Judea during the time when Herod was king. When Jesus was born, some wise men from the east came to Jerusalem. 2They asked, "Where is the baby who was born to be the king of the Jews? We saw his star in the east and have come to worship him."

3When King Herod heard this, he was troubled, as well as all the people in Jerusalem. 4Herod called a meeting of all the leading priests and teachers of the law and asked them where the Christ[d] would be born. 5They answered, "In the town of Bethlehem in Judea. The prophet[d] wrote about this in the Scriptures:[d]

6'But you, Bethlehem, in the land of Judah,
    are important among the tribes[d] of Judah.
A ruler will come from you

"The virgin ... Immanuel"   Quotation from Isaiah 7:14.

Taking a Stand

As a young man in Germany, Martin Luther feared he wasn't good enough for God. He even became a monk, hoping to avoid God's anger. Luther tested the patience of other monks as he beat himself with whips and slept without a blanket in the frigid German winter. He confessed every tiny thought or deed, just in case it might be evil.

Regardless of his quirks, Luther grew as a highly skilled Bible professor. But he still felt spiritually distressed by his fear of an angry, judging God. While preparing lectures on the Psalms and later on Paul's letter to the Romans, he discovered something that would change his life: He couldn't earn God's approval. God loved him as he was! He knew now that God really loved him, no matter how unlovable he was. He was happy for the first time in his life. He began teaching and preaching his newfound faith, and criticizing many church policies of the day.

Predictably, the religious authorities disapproved. A long-standing rewards system required people to earn their salvation. The authorities gave Luther a clear choice. Take back everything he had written and said, or be kicked out of the church, lose his job and perhaps lose his life.

Luther had to choose between following God and going along with the system. At a dramatic trial before several authorities, he looked at his accusers and said, "Here I stand. I can do no other."

He was thrown out of the church, and he had to hide in a remote castle from would-be assassins. Yet, his view of a loving God instead of a punishing one ignited the flame that grew into a bonfire of church reform in the sixteenth century.

In **Matthew 1:18–25**, Joseph, like Luther, had to choose between following God and taking the easy way out.

■ What factors might have made both Luther's and Joseph's decisions difficult?

■ Do you ever find yourself facing a situation in which following God looks like the most difficult way? What direction or comfort does this Bible story give you?

C O N S I D E R . . .

■ writing out a tough decision you're now facing. Based on what you have read in the passage, list your options for following God, and choose.

■ encouraging friends who are facing hard choices to follow God's direction, although it may seem difficult.

F O R   M O R E ,   S E E . . .

■ Exodus 3:1–15 (p. 60)   ■ 1 Timothy 4:6–10 (p 1258)
■ Luke 2:1–7 (p. 1003)

who will be like a shepherd for my people Israel.' "

Micah 5:2

7Then Herod had a secret meeting with the wise men and learned from them the exact time they first saw the star. 8He sent the wise men to Bethlehem, saying, "Look carefully for the child. When you find him, come tell me so I can worship him too."

9After the wise men heard the king, they left. The star that they had seen in the east went before them until it stopped above the place where the child was. 10When the wise men saw the star, they were filled with joy. 11They came to the house where the child was and saw him with his mother, Mary, and they bowed down and wor-shiped him. They opened their gifts and gave him treasures of gold, frankincense,*d* and myrrh.*d* 12But God warned the wise men in a dream not to go back to Herod, so they returned to their own country by a different way.

Jesus' Parents Take Him to Egypt

13After they left, an angel of the Lord came to Joseph in a dream and said, "Get up! Take the child and his mother and escape to Egypt, because Herod is starting to look for the child so he can kill him. Stay in Egypt until I tell you to return." 14So Joseph got up and left for Egypt during the night with the child and his mother. 15And Joseph stayed in Egypt until Herod died. This happened

---

WORSHIP

Enjoying God's Gifts

Sean Sutcliffe hated Sunday mornings. "Sunday meant church, and that meant boring," he said. He felt boredom start with the first note of the organ, and steadily suffered as worship went on. The best part to him was driving out of the church parking lot on the way to lunch.

"Much of what happened there just didn't seem important," he said. "We sang a few old songs, read a few scriptures, listened to somebody talk for thirty minutes—how did any of that really worship God?"

The only thing that kept Sean's interest in church was the youth group. One Sunday evening, the group gathered at a nearby lake. They started a campfire, and somebody played soft guitar while everyone watched a spectacular sunset. Sean sat in silence, enjoying the sunset's reflection on the still lake, until the last pink streak faded in the sky. "That's the most beautiful thing I've ever seen," he said.

Caroline McGee overheard him. She had been sitting so quietly he hadn't noticed her. She asked him, "Do you think God hears us when we say things like that? Do you think God likes it when we enjoy a sunset?"

"Yeah," Sean replied. Then suddenly something "clicked" for Sean about worship. "Maybe part of worship is enjoying something God made," he said. "To watch a sunset, or a butterfly, or the rain, and to be thankful that God had such good taste. Am I right?"

The next time he worshiped at church, he looked around at the people. Many of their faces wore the same expression of awe Sean had felt at the lake. Maybe this feeling of "wow!" is worship, he thought. It isn't the motions you go through. It's when you see or hear or remember things so good that you have to catch your breath, and then thank and praise God for them.

In **Matthew 2:1–12**, read about the "wow!" the wise men must have felt when they saw and worshiped the infant Jesus.

■ In what ways might the wise men have felt as Sean did while he watched the sunset?

■ When have you experienced a sense of "wow!" in worship, either in or out of church?

C O N S I D E R . . . .

■ noticing the ways your church worships God and finding out the meaning of each part of the service.

➤ visiting a few other churches with your family or friends, and seeing what each church does differently.

F O R   M O R E ,   S E E . . .

■ Psalm 19:1–6 (p. 492)
■ Luke 9:28–36 (p. 1019)

■ Revelation 4:1–11 (p. 1335)

to bring about what the Lord had said through the prophet:*d* "I called my son out of Egypt." *n*

Herod Kills the Baby Boys

16When Herod saw that the wise men had tricked him, he was furious. So he gave an order to kill all the baby boys in Bethlehem and in the surrounding area who were two years old or younger. This was in keeping with the time he learned from the wise men. 17So what God had said through the prophet*d* Jeremiah came true:

18"A voice was heard in Ramah
  of painful crying and deep sadness:
Rachel crying for her children.
  She refused to be comforted,
  because her children are dead."   *Jeremiah 31:15*

Joseph and Mary Return

19After Herod died, an angel of the Lord spoke to Joseph in a dream while he was in Egypt. 20The angel said, "Get up! Take the child and his mother and go to the land of Israel, because the

"I called . . . Egypt." Quotation from Hosea 11:1.

Going to a Safe Place

White journalist Donald Woods openly opposed the South African government's cruel policies toward its black people. In the early 1970s, Woods began to publish a newspaper that chronicled the government's repressive actions.

Woods befriended several leaders in the black liberation movement, including Steve Biko; and he grew even more committed to freedom for blacks. In spite of government and police warnings, Woods refused to turn his back on his friends.

The political situation soon worsened in South Africa. The police stepped up arrests of black leaders, who were later found tortured and often dead. In 1977, Steve Biko was arrested. Woods worked furiously for his friend's release, but faced unbending opposition from officials.

When Woods personally discovered the dead body of his tortured friend, he blasted the official explanation that Biko's death was accidental. While questioning the doctor who had determined the cause of Biko's death, Woods heard the doctor tearfully admit to falsifying the autopsy report. Woods, in his raging grief, openly accused the government of murdering Biko. South Africa's response was to arrest Woods.

After Woods was held under house arrest for three months, his friends in the liberation movement devised a plan for him to escape from the country. After escaping the guards, he crossed the country disguised as a priest. Along the way, sympathizers risked their lives to see him safely along. But he finally made it to the bordering country of Lesotho.

Woods's family also escaped and joined him in Lesotho. They moved to England, where Woods wrote the story of South Africa's cruelty. If he had not been able to escape, his story and Steve Biko's would not have been told. Because of changes in South Africa, Woods has been able to return. His story—and others like it—directly influenced these changes.

Joseph, Mary, and Jesus also had to flee from their country so Jesus could grow up and fulfill God's purpose for him. Read their story in **Matthew 2:13–23**.

■ Why did Joseph and Mary and Donald Woods temporarily leave their homes instead of facing their persecutors?
■ Have you ever had to leave a "comfort zone" in your life to follow God? What happened?

C O N S I D E R . . .

■ watching the movie Cry Freedom (about Donald Woods) and talking about whether God's freedom is similar or different, and why.
■ looking up the word freedom in the dictionary, and then defining "Christian freedom" in your own words.

F O R   M O R E ,   S E E . . .

■ Exodus 12:31–50 (p. 69)   ■ Galatians 5:13–15 (p. 1212)
■ John 8:31–36 (p. 1072)

people who were trying to kill the child are now dead."

21So Joseph took the child and his mother and went to Israel. 22But he heard that Archelaus was now king in Judea since his father Herod had died. So Joseph was afraid to go there. After being warned in a dream, he went to the area of Galilee, 23to a town called Nazareth, and lived there. And so what God had said through the prophets[d] came true: "He will be called a Nazarene." [n]

The Work of John the Baptist

3 About that time John the Baptist[d] began preaching in the desert area of Judea. 2John said, "Change your hearts and lives because the kingdom of heaven is near." 3John the Baptist is the one Isaiah the prophet[d] was talking about when he said:

"This is a voice of one
who calls out in the desert:
'Prepare the way for the Lord.
Make the road straight for him.' "   *Isaiah 40:3*

4John's clothes were made from camel's hair, and he wore a leather belt around his waist. For food, he ate locusts[d] and wild honey. 5Many people came from Jerusalem and Judea and all the area around the Jordan River to hear John. 6They confessed their sins, and he baptized them in the Jordan River.

7Many of the Pharisees[d] and Sadducees[d] came to the place where John was baptizing people. When John saw them, he said, "You are all snakes! Who warned you to run away from God's coming punishment? 8Do the things that show you really have changed your hearts and lives. 9And don't think you can say to yourselves, 'Abraham is our father.' I tell you that God could make children for Abraham from these rocks. 10The ax is now ready to cut down the trees, and every tree

that does not produce good fruit will be cut down and thrown into the fire. [n]

11"I baptize you with water to show that your hearts and lives have changed. But there is one coming after me who is greater than I am, whose sandals I am not good enough to carry. He will baptize you with the Holy Spirit[d] and fire. 12He will come ready to clean the grain, separating the good grain from the chaff.[d] He will put the good part of the grain into his barn, but he will burn the chaff with a fire that cannot be put out." [n]

Jesus Is Baptized by John

13At that time Jesus came from Galilee to the Jordan River and wanted John to baptize him. 14But John tried to stop him, saying, "Why do you come to me to be baptized? I need to be baptized by you!"

15Jesus answered, "Let it be this way for now. We should do all things that are God's will." So John agreed to baptize Jesus.

16As soon as Jesus was baptized, he came up out of the water. Then heaven opened, and he saw God's Spirit[d] coming down on him like a dove. 17And a voice from heaven said, "This is my Son, whom I love, and I am very pleased with him."

The Temptation of Jesus

4 Then the Spirit[d] led Jesus into the desert to be tempted by the devil. 2Jesus ate nothing for forty days and nights. After this, he was very hungry. 3The devil came to Jesus to tempt him, saying, "If you are the Son of God, tell these rocks to become bread."

4Jesus answered, "It is written in the Scriptures,[d] 'A person does not live by eating only bread, but by everything God says.' " [n]

Nazarene   A person from the city of Nazareth, a name probably meaning "branch" (see Isaiah 11:1).
The ax . . . fire.   This means that God is ready to punish his people who do not obey him.
He will . . . out.   This means that Jesus will come to separate good people from bad people, saving the good and punishing the bad.
'A person . . . says.'   Quotation from Deuteronomy 8:3.

⁵Then the devil led Jesus to the holy city of Jerusalem and put him on a high place of the Temple.ᵈ ⁶The devil said, "If you are the Son of God, jump down, because it is written in the Scriptures:

'He has put his angels in charge of you.
They will catch you in their hands
so that you will not hit your foot on a
rock.' "   *Psalm 91:11-12*

⁷Jesus answered him, "It also says in the Scriptures, 'Do not test the Lord your God.' "ⁿ

⁸Then the devil led Jesus to the top of a very high mountain and showed him all the kingdoms of the world and all their splendor. ⁹The devil said, 'If you will bow down and worship me, I will give you all these things."

¹⁰Jesus said to the devil, "Go away from me, Satan! It is written in the Scriptures, 'You must worship the Lord your God and serve only him.' "ⁿ

¹¹So the devil left Jesus, and angels came and took care of him.

'Do ... God.' Quotation from Deuteronomy 6:16.
'You ... him.' Quotation from Deuteronomy 6:13.

GOD'S WILL

God's Surprises

It was February, and time to begin rehearsals for Wheeler High School's senior play. Trina Cook eagerly auditioned for a part, convinced she would make the cast. But when the list was posted, Trina couldn't find her name on it.

She tried to hide her disappointment as she walked toward her last class of the day. Mr. Hendon, the director, caught up with her. "Trina," he said, "I meant to talk to you before the names were posted. We know you would have worked hard and done a good job for us. But you've had a lot of honors already, so we decided to let some of the others have a chance. I hope you're not too disappointed."

"Thanks, Mr. Hendon," she answered. "Thanks for explaining it to me." She still felt sad, but she didn't want him to know. In a way, she understood what he was saying.

A week later, Trina cringed as sharp pains shot through her stomach. Soon she was in the hospital, recovering from an emergency appendectomy. Mr. Hendon came to visit her. "It's a good thing you didn't put me in the senior play," she said. "You'd be looking for a replacement now."

A few weeks later, the missions committee at Trina's church decided to produce a drama about a woman who had spent her life in missions efforts. By this time Trina had regained her strength. She was chosen to play the leading role.

At every rehearsal, the cast prayed that God would use their efforts through the play to touch someone's heart.

Trina had no idea that she would be the one whose heart would be touched. On the evening of the performance, she committed her life to God's service and went on to be a missionary.

Disappointments, closed doors, and unexpected events often lead to surprises of God's will for our lives. Just as Trina was surprised by her road to a missionary career, John the Baptist was surprised to learn that God's will was for him to baptize the Messiah, instead of vice versa. You'll find the story of Jesus' baptism in **Matthew 3:13–17**.

■ Why were both John the Baptist and Trina surprised by God's will?
■ How has God used ironic or unusual circumstances in your life to do his will? How did you respond in those situations?

C O N S I D E R . . .

■ writing a list of prayer concerns. As you pray, follow each with, "We know that in everything God works for the good of those who love him" (Romans 8:28, p. 1151).
■ thinking of unexpected events that have happened to you in the last month, and how God might be leading you. Then act on one of those leads.

F O R   M O R E ,   S E E . . .

■ Isaiah 55:8–11 (p. 674)   ■ 1 Corinthians 1:18–25 (p. 1168)
■ Luke 3:1–20 (p. 1005)

Jesus Begins Work in Galilee

12When Jesus heard that John had been put in prison, he went back to Galilee. 13He left Nazareth and went to live in Capernaum, a town near Lake Galilee, in the area near Zebulun and Naphtali. 14Jesus did this to bring about what the prophet*d* Isaiah had said:
15"Land of Zebulun and land of Naphtali
   along the sea,
beyond the Jordan River.
   This is Galilee where the non-Jewish people
   live.
16These people who live in darkness
   will see a great light.
They live in a place covered with the
   shadows of death,
   but a light will shine on them."   *Isaiah 9:1-2*

Jesus Chooses Some Followers

17From that time Jesus began to preach, saying, "Change your hearts and lives, because the kingdom of heaven is near."

18As Jesus was walking by Lake Galilee, he saw two brothers, Simon (called Peter) and his brother Andrew. They were throwing a net into the lake because they were fishermen. 19Jesus said, "Come follow me, and I will make you fish for people." 20So Simon and Andrew immediately left their nets and followed him.

21As Jesus continued walking by Lake Galilee, he saw two other brothers, James and John, the sons of Zebedee. They were in a boat with their father Zebedee, mending their nets. Jesus told them to come with him. 22Immediately they left the boat and their father, and they followed Jesus.

Jesus Teaches and Heals People

23Jesus went everywhere in Galilee, teaching in the synagogues,*d* preaching the Good News*d* about the kingdom of heaven, and healing all the people's diseases and sicknesses. 24The news about Jesus spread all over Syria, and people brought all the sick to him. They were suffering from different kinds of diseases. Some were in great pain, some had demons,*d* some were epileptics,*n* and some were paralyzed. Jesus healed all of them. 25Many people from Galilee, the Ten Towns,*n* Jerusalem, Judea, and the land across the Jordan River followed him.

Jesus Teaches the People

5 When Jesus saw the crowds, he went up on a hill and sat down. His followers came to him, 2and he began to teach them, saying:

3"Those people who know they have great
   spiritual needs are happy,
   because the kingdom of heaven belongs to
   them.
4Those who are sad now are happy,
   because God will comfort them.
5Those who are humble are happy,
   because the earth will belong to them.
6Those who want to do right more than
   anything else are happy,
   because God will fully satisfy them.
7Those who show mercy to others are happy,
   because God will show mercy to them.
8Those who are pure in their thinking are
   happy,
   because they will be with God.
9Those who work to bring peace are happy,
   because God will call them his children.
10Those who are treated badly for doing good
   are happy,
   because the kingdom of heaven belongs to
   them.
11"People will insult you and hurt you. They will lie and say all kinds of evil things about you because you follow me. But when they do, you will be happy. 12Rejoice and be glad, because you have a great reward waiting for you in heaven. People did the same evil things to the prophets*d* who lived before you.

You Are like Salt and Light

13"You are the salt of the earth. But if the salt loses its salty taste, it cannot be made salty again. It is good for nothing, except to be thrown out and walked on.

14"You are the light that gives light to the world. A city that is built on a hill cannot be hidden. 15And people don't hide a light under a bowl. They put it on a lampstand so the light shines for all the people in the house. 16In the same way, you should be a light for other people. Live so that they will see the good things you do and will praise your Father in heaven.

The Importance of the Law

17"Don't think that I have come to destroy the law of Moses or the teaching of the prophets.*d* I have not come to destroy them but to bring about what they said. 18I tell you the truth, nothing will disappear from the law until heaven and earth are gone. Not even the smallest letter or the smallest part of a letter will be lost until everything has happened. 19Whoever refuses to obey any command and teaches other people not to obey that

epileptics People with a disease that causes them sometimes to lose control of their bodies and maybe faint, shake strongly, or not be able to move.
Ten Towns In Greek, called "Decapolis." It was an area east of Lake Galilee that once had ten main towns.

command will be the least important in the kingdom of heaven. But whoever obeys the commands and teaches other people to obey them will be great in the kingdom of heaven. ²⁰I tell you that if you are no more obedient than the teachers of the law and the Pharisees,*d* you will never enter the kingdom of heaven.

Jesus Teaches About Anger

²¹"You have heard that it was said to our people long ago, 'You must not murder anyone.*n*

Anyone who murders another will be judged.' ²²But I tell you, if you are angry with a brother or sister,*n* you will be judged. If you say bad things to a brother or sister, you will be judged by the council. And if you call someone a fool, you will be in danger of the fire of hell.

²³"So when you offer your gift to God at the altar, and you remember that your brother or sister has something against you, ²⁴leave your gift there at the altar. Go and make peace with that person, and then come and offer your gift.

You . . . anyone.   Quotation from Exodus 20:13; Deuteronomy 5:17.
brother . . . sister   Although the Greek text reads "brother" here and throughout this book, Jesus' words were meant for the entire church, including men and women.

HAPPINESS

The Secret of Real Happiness

Young Francesco had it all: money, friends, power. His father was one of the wealthiest businessmen in the city-state of Assisi, in twelfth-century Italy. Francesco partied away his teenage years, often carousing in the streets until dawn.

But something was missing. When the parties ended, he felt depressed.

To try to find happiness and purpose, Francesco trained to be a knight. At twenty-one, he gallantly rode off to war against the neighboring city-state of Perugia. After a disastrous battlefield decision, he and his soldiers were taken prisoners. In a dungeon Francesco caught a fever that almost killed him. The enemy released him, and he somehow stumbled back to Assisi. He had left as a proud knight; he returned as a sad, sick failure.

These experiences made Francesco reexamine his life. He spent days in prayer, poring over Jesus' Sermon on the Mount in Matthew 5—7. He saw a chance for genuine happiness by following Jesus' teachings about storing treasures in heaven instead of on earth, not worrying about tomorrow, and trusting God. He began to run through meadows, singing like the birds and flinging his arms open to embrace the wind and sun. He gave away all his possessions and lived in caves because he didn't want to be burdened with "things." He traded his expensive clothing for a shepherd's robe.

His relationships with other people changed too. For the first time, he was happy. He spent his days helping the poor, homeless, and disabled. He went to the local leper colony and embraced people who had once nauseated him. He attracted several friends who shared his poverty and worked beside him, ministering to the poor of their community.

Francesco was named St. Francis shortly after his death, and remains one of the most beloved of all Christians. Eight hundred years later, people still seek the secret to the happiness St. Francis of Assisi found.

One of the passages that changed Francesco's life was **Matthew 5:1–12**. Read how Jesus' secret to happiness transformed St. Francis's life.

■ What do you find in Jesus' words that could so powerfully change Francesco's depression to happiness?

■ How does Jesus' secret for happiness compare to what you've been taught about happiness?

C O N S I D E R . . .

■ looking at the "things" in your bedroom that make you happy and asking yourself which of them would make Jesus happy.

■ writing each verse of this passage on a separate card, and then putting a different one on your mirror for eight days.

F O R   M O R E ,   S E E . . .

■ Psalm 4 (p. 483)
■ Luke 6:17–49 (p. 1012)

■ John 15:5–11 (p. 1085)

25"If your enemy is taking you to court, become friends quickly, before you go to court. Otherwise, your enemy might turn you over to the judge, and the judge might give you to a guard to put you in jail. 26I tell you the truth, you will not leave there until you have paid everything you owe.

Jesus Teaches About Sexual Sin

27"You have heard that it was said, 'You must not be guilty of adultery.' [n] 28But I tell you that if anyone looks at a woman and wants to sin sexually with her, in his mind he has already done that sin with the woman. 29If your right eye causes you

to sin, take it out and throw it away. It is better to lose one part of your body than to have your whole body thrown into hell. 30If your right hand causes you to sin, cut it off and throw it away. It is better to lose one part of your body than for your whole body to go into hell.

Jesus Teaches About Divorce

31"It was also said, 'Anyone who divorces his wife must give her a written divorce paper.' [n] 32But I tell you that anyone who divorces his wife forces her to be guilty of adultery. [d] The only reason for a man to divorce his wife is if she has sexual relations with another man. And anyone

'You ... adultery.'   Quotation from Exodus 20:14; Deuteronomy 5:18.
'Anyone ... divorce paper.'   Quotation from Deuteronomy 24:1.

SHARING FAITH

Salt and Light

Brett Clanton's image of a homeless person had always been of a bag lady rummaging through dumpsters. He was afraid of poor people. And he was a little scared as he and his youth group traveled to San Antonio, Texas, to help in a homeless shelter for a week.

Brett and the other young people spent their days with homeless families—serving food, helping them find clothing, reading the Bible with them, playing with their children. By the end of the week the image of the faceless bag lady was gone from Brett's mind. These people were now his friends.

The group went to the city's famous river walk on their last evening of the trip, and they saw street people along the way. "I saw a man asleep on a bench, and I started to make a wide path to avoid him, and I suddenly realized that I knew him!" Brett later told the church. "I knew his name, where he was from—and I wasn't afraid. Then I realized that all homeless people have names and home towns, and that becoming homeless could happen to any of us."

One Wednesday evening the young people shared their experiences with the whole church. The next day, several of the adults from Brett's church attended a meeting of more than thirty-five area ministers. These adults had been so moved by the young people's stories that they shared them with leaders from the other churches.

The truth that Brett and the others had learned in San Antonio had spread from a few teenagers to an entire church, and then to a gathering of area ministers. The group now sponsors a task force on local poverty and hunger. The young people energized the task force members to respond to poverty in their community.

Brett discovered the contagious power of being the salt of the earth and light of the world as Jesus describes in **Matthew 5:13–16**. Jesus promises that when faith is shared, things change.

■ How did Brett's youth group act as salt and light in San Antonio and in their home town?

■ How can you be "salt and light" in your world, as Jesus describes in the passage?

CONSIDER . . .

■ telling someone you know about your faith this week.
■ choosing two people you know who seem most like "salt and light" and asking them what they've learned as they have shared their faith.

FOR MORE, SEE . . .

■ Isaiah 9:2–7 (p. 626)
■ 2 Corinthians 4:1–6 (p. 1194)

■ 1 John 1:5–6 (p. 1316)

who marries that divorced woman is guilty of adultery.

Make Promises Carefully

33"You have heard that it was said to our people long ago, 'Don't break your promises, but keep the promises you make to the Lord.' *n* 34But I tell you, never swear an oath. Don't swear an oath using the name of heaven, because heaven is God's throne. 35Don't swear an oath using the name of the earth, because the earth belongs to God. Don't swear an oath using the name of Jeru-salem, because that is the city of the great King. 36Don't even swear by your own head, because you cannot make one hair on your head become white or black. 37Say only yes if you mean yes, and no if you mean no. If you say more than yes or no, it is from the Evil One.

Don't Fight Back

38"You have heard that it was said, 'An eye for an eye, and a tooth for a tooth.' *n* 39But I tell you, don't stand up against an evil person. If someone slaps you on the right cheek, turn to him the other

'Don't ... Lord.'   This refers to Leviticus 19:12; Numbers 30:2; Deuteronomy 23:21.
'An eye ... tooth.'   Quotation from Exodus 21:24; Leviticus 24:20; Deuteronomy 19:21.

ANGER

Beating the Bully

Life wasn't going well for twelve-year-old Keith Jenkins. His parents had recently divorced, and he and his mom had moved from their farm to a nearby city. Keith felt alone in his new school, which seemed huge. But now there was another problem. Another student, Brian, had threatened to beat up Keith after school. And he meant it.

After the last bell on Thursday, Keith tried to slip out of school without being seen. He wanted to get home quickly. As he turned a corner, Brian was waiting for him.

Keith's heart pounded with fear. Brian attacked and landed blow after blow. Keith tried to fight back, but Brian was several years older and much stronger. After a few minutes of a one-sided fight, Brian left his victim lying on the sidewalk. Keith got up slowly and walked the rest of the way home. At the front door, his mother saw his torn clothes, his bloody face and hands. Keith told what happened and asked, "Mom, why are people like that? Why does Brian like to hurt other people?"

"I don't know, honey," she answered. "It doesn't make sense. There must be something wrong with him." Keith knew that she was upset, though she was trying to hide her anger toward Brian.

Later that evening, Keith looked at his reflection in the hall mirror. His face was already puffy and purple. He looked at his mom and said, "I look pretty weird, don't I?"

She laughed, and then he began to laugh. "You've certainly looked better," she said, with a sad smile. "How do you feel?"

"Sore," he said. "And a little scared. But you know what? I'm not really mad at Brian. What you said about there being something wrong—I think there is. I thought I'd hate him. But I don't. I feel kind of sorry for him. I don't think anybody likes him. Maybe that's why he does those things."

Jesus offers several ways to respond when we're angered and hurt by others. In **Matthew 5:17–26**, read how Jesus might have reacted in Keith's situation.

■ Did Keith react in the way Jesus commands? Why or why not?
■ If Brian had beaten you up, how would you have handled your anger and hurt? What are some ways to handle the situation according to the passage?

CONSIDER . . .
■ watching how some TV characters handle their anger. What would happen in the real world if people handled their anger in those ways?
■ making peace with someone with whom you have a conflict before the next time you attend worship.

FOR MORE, SEE . . .

■ Proverbs 15:1 (p. 580)   ■ Ephesians 4:17–32 (p. 1223)
■ Matthew 5:38–48 (p. 915)

cheek also. [40]If someone wants to sue you in court and take your shirt, let him have your coat also.

Love your neighbor   Quotation from Leviticus 19:18.

[41]If someone forces you to go with him one mile, go with him two miles. [42]If a person asks you for something, give it to him. Don't refuse to give to someone who wants to borrow from you.

Love All People

[43]"You have heard that it was said, 'Love your neighbor[n] and hate your enemies.' [44]But I say to you, love your enemies. Pray for those who hurt you. [45]If you do this, you will be true children of your Father in heaven. He causes the sun to rise on good people and on evil people, and he sends rain to those who do right and to those who do wrong. [46]If you love only the people who love

SEXUALITY

A Special Gift

Anna Bradley, thirteen, felt her life turning upside down. Her body was changing so fast she couldn't figure out what was happening. Along with the physical changes, she had new feelings she didn't understand.

A couple of years earlier, she didn't even like being around boys. Now she was fascinated by them. Especially Larry. He was so cute! She hung around outside the science lab just to see him when he came out. When he said "hi" to her in the hall, she felt like she was melting inside. "What's going on here?" she asked herself. "What's happening to me?"

She finally got the courage to ask her youth leader, Deanna.

"You're beginning to change from a young girl into a young woman," Deanna said.

"You mean my feelings—these desires—aren't bad?"

"How could they be bad if God put them there? But God also expects you to use this gift wisely."

"But what will the kids at school say if I tell them I want to stay a virgin until I marry? What will boys say if I go on a date with them?"

"You can tell them this is your decision, and that's all there is to it. If they're your friends, they'll respect your decision."

"What about the waiting part? Will it be hard to control myself all that time?"

"You can do it. People can control themselves—although some may not think they can, and many simply don't want to. But it's possible, and it'll be worth it. You'll discover how God's gift of sexuality is so wonderful in a committed marriage relationship."

Jesus considered sexuality a special gift from God. As such he spoke of the serious consequence of sex being used outside of marriage. **Matthew 5:27–37** has some rather harsh things to say about specific sexual behaviors. Read the passage and think about what Anna might think as she reads it.

■ How does Deanna's advice relate to Jesus' teaching in the passage?

■ Why do you think Jesus took sexual relations so seriously?

C O N S I D E R . . .

■ talking about sexuality with a parent or an adult whom you trust. Write your questions first if that's helpful. Be honest about your feelings.

✐ organizing a discussion group at your church—perhaps a panel with adults and youth—on issues involving sexuality and teenagers.

F O R   M O R E ,   S E E . . .

■ Genesis 1:26–28 (p. 3)

■ Song of Solomon 2:1–17 (p. 609)

■ 1 Corinthians 7:1–15 (p. 1174)

you, you will get no reward. Even the tax collectors do that. 47And if you are nice only to your friends, you are no better than other people. Even those who don't know God are nice to their friends. 48So you must be perfect, just as your Father in heaven is perfect.

Jesus Teaches About Giving

6 "Be careful! When you do good things, don't do them in front of people to be seen by them. If you do that, you will have no reward from your Father in heaven.

2"When you give to the poor, don't be like the hypocrites.*d* They blow trumpets in the synagogues*d* and on the streets so that people will see them and honor them. I tell you the truth, those hypocrites already have their full reward. 3So when you give to the poor, don't let anyone know what you are doing. 4Your giving should be done in secret. Your Father can see what is done in secret, and he will reward you.

Jesus Teaches About Prayer

5"When you pray, don't be like the hypocrites.*d*

PEACE

The Second Mile

Tracy Collins pulled her car into the driveway and groaned when she saw that the front door was ajar. "Not again!" she fumed. She knew her apartment had been robbed for the third time.

When the police arrived, they helped her take inventory of what was missing. "Not that there was much left to take," she said. "He really cleaned me out the first time."

The police were virtually positive who the thief was. After the previous burglary, one of the officers had let the name slip: Tim O'Conner. They recognized his "style." A warrant for his arrest had been issued months earlier.

Tracy worked in an inner-city mission distributing food and clothing to needy people. Among the volunteers were adults placed on probation for nonviolent crimes. Instead of going to jail, they were required to provide community service.

Several weeks after the third burglary, Tracy interviewed a new probationer, filling out a form that would record the hours worked. "What's your name?" she asked, her pen ready on the correct line.

"Tim O'Conner," he said.

Tracy choked, and looked into the young man's eyes. He sat calmly, waiting for the next question. He was well-dressed, well-groomed, and had good manners. She shook her head as if to clear it, and turned the document back to the first page, searching for the line that would tell her why he had been convicted. "Burglary of a habitation," it read.

"Is something wrong?" he asked in a polite voice.

"He has no idea I'm one of his victims," she thought angrily. Then her anger turned into compassion as she wondered what made him break into other people's homes. "No," she answered. "Let's finish this form."

After they finished the interview, Tim was given an assignment. "Thanks," he said. "I'm glad the judge sent me here."

"So am I," Tracy said.

Tracy was surprised when she didn't feel like striking back at Tim. Then she realized Jesus' words in **Matthew 5:38–48** must have helped her handle her anger in a peaceful manner.

■ In light of the passage, do you think Tracy did the right thing?
■ Does "turning the other cheek" mean that Jesus wants people to walk all over your rights? Why or why not?

CONSIDER . . .
■ listing the "normal" ways for handling conflicts, and then listing the "cheek-turning," peaceful ways next to them. Promise yourself to "turn the other cheek" the next time a conflict arises.
■ walking away from a fight or keeping your cool in an argument in the future.

FOR MORE, SEE . . .
■ Psalm 37 (p. 503)   ■ Colossians 3:12–13 (p. 1241)
■ Luke 6:27–36 (p. 1013)

They love to stand in the synagogues[d] and on the street corners and pray so people will see them. I tell you the truth, they already have their full reward. 6When you pray, you should go into your room and close the door and pray to your Father who cannot be seen. Your Father can see what is done in secret, and he will reward you.

SIDELIGHT: Jews in Jesus' day had plenty of opportunities to give to people in need, which could lead to the problems Jesus talked about in Matthew 6:1–4. Jerusalem had a "chamber of secrets" where people quietly left gifts. Then the needy could slip in unnoticed and claim goods without embarrassment.

7"And when you pray, don't be like those people who don't know God. They continue saying things that mean nothing, thinking that God will hear them because of their many words. 8Don't be like them, because your Father knows the things you need before you ask him. 9So when you pray, you should pray like this:

'Our Father in heaven,
may your name always be kept holy.
10May your kingdom come
and what you want be done,
here on earth as it is in heaven.
11Give us the food we need for each day.
12Forgive us for our sins,
just as we have forgiven those who sinned
against us.
13And do not cause us to be tempted,
but save us from the Evil One.'

14Yes, if you forgive others for their sins, your Father in heaven will also forgive you for your sins. 15But if you don't forgive others, your Father in heaven will not forgive your sins.

Jesus Teaches About Worship

16"When you give up eating,[n] don't put on a sad face like the hypocrites.[d] They make their faces look sad to show people they are giving up eating. I tell you the truth, those hypocrites already have their full reward. 17So when you give up eating, comb your hair and wash your face. 18Then people will not know that you are giving up eating, but your Father, whom you cannot see, will see you. Your Father sees what is done in secret, and he will reward you.

God Is More Important than Money

19"Don't store treasures for yourselves here on earth where moths and rust will destroy them and thieves can break in and steal them. 20But store your treasures in heaven where they cannot be destroyed by moths or rust and where thieves cannot break in and steal them. 21Your heart will be where your treasure is.

22"The eye is a light for the body. If your eyes are good, your whole body will be full of light. 23But if your eyes are evil, your whole body will be full of darkness. And if the only light you have is really darkness, then you have the worst darkness.

24"No one can serve two masters. The person will hate one master and love the other, or will follow one master and refuse to follow the other. You cannot serve both God and worldly riches.

Don't Worry

25"So I tell you, don't worry about the food or drink you need to live, or about the clothes you need for your body. Life is more than food, and the body is more than clothes. 26Look at the birds in the air. They don't plant or harvest or store food in barns, but your heavenly Father feeds them. And you know that you are worth much more than the birds. 27You cannot add any time to your life by worrying about it.

28"And why do you worry about clothes? Look at how the lilies in the field grow. They don't work or make clothes for themselves. 29But I tell you that even Solomon with his riches was not dressed as beautifully as one of these flowers. 30God clothes the grass in the field, which is alive today but tomorrow is thrown into the fire. So you can be even more sure that God will clothe you. Don't have so little faith! 31Don't worry and say, 'What will we eat?' or 'What will we drink?' or 'What will we wear?' 32The people who don't know God keep trying to get these things, and your Father in heaven knows you need them. 33The thing you should want most is God's kingdom and doing what God wants. Then all these other things you need will be given to you. 34So don't worry about tomorrow, because tomorrow will have its own worries. Each day has enough trouble of its own.

Be Careful About Judging Others

7 "Don't judge other people, or you will be judged. 2You will be judged in the same way that you judge others, and the amount you give to others will be given to you.

3"Why do you notice the little piece of dust in your friend's eye, but you don't notice the big piece of wood in your own eye? 4How can you say

give up eating This is called "fasting." The people would give up eating for a special time of prayer and worship to God. It was also done to show sadness and disappointment.

to your friend, 'Let me take that little piece of dust out of your eye'? Look at yourself! You still have that big piece of wood in your own eye. [5]You hypocrite![d] First, take the wood out of your own eye. Then you will see clearly to take the dust out of your friend's eye.

[6]"Don't give holy things to dogs, and don't throw your pearls before pigs. Pigs will only trample on them, and dogs will turn to attack you.

Ask God for What You Need

[7]"Ask, and God will give to you. Search, and you will find. Knock, and the door will open for you. [8]Yes, everyone who asks will receive. Everyone who searches will find. And everyone who knocks will have the door opened.

[9]"If your children ask for bread, which of you would give them a stone? [10]Or if your children ask for a fish, would you give them a snake? [11]Even though you are bad, you know how to give good gifts to your children. How much more your heavenly Father will give good things to those who ask him!

The Most Important Rule

[12]"Do to others what you want them to do to you. This is the meaning of the law of Moses and the teaching of the prophets.[d]

The Way to Heaven Is Hard

[13]"Enter through the narrow gate. The gate is wide and the road is wide that leads to hell, and many people enter through that gate. [14]But the gate is small and the road is narrow that leads to true life. Only a few people find that road.

WORRYING

Sweating It Out

Jason Taylor stood at the coach's door, staring a long time at the recently posted roster. There it was: His name was on the list. He had made the junior varsity basketball team. Jason let out a deep sigh of relief and offered a silent thanks to God.

Anxiety was Jason's trademark. He worried about everything. In the two-day waiting period between tryouts and team roster, Jason couldn't sleep, concentrate on school, or eat much of anything. These worries were added to his stress of being a new kid in school. His family had moved from Georgia to Seattle over the summer.

His new friend Marc, seeing Jason staring at the roster, came over and shared Jason's happy time. "I knew you'd make it," Marc said, slapping him on the back. "Congratulations!"

Jason shook his head. "Since seventh grade," he said, "I had been looking forward to going to Stone Mountain High. Coach Wilson said I had a good chance of making junior varsity there this year. But then Dad told us we'd have to move here to Seattle because of his transfer to the new branch office. I didn't think I'd have a chance to make the team here. I've been sweating it out all summer. It even made me get off to a bad start on my grades."

"I told you there wasn't anything to worry about," Marc said.

"Easy for you to say," Jason thought. Suddenly a new worry hit Jason: "What if I'm not good enough to start?"

People today worry about many things, as did the people in Jesus' earthly ministry. He reminded them often not to worry. Read Jesus' practical teachings about worrying in **Matthew 6:25–34**.

■ How could the analogy of the birds and flowers apply to Jason's life? How are the two kinds of worry different?

■ If God doesn't want you to use time for worrying, how does he want you to use it?

CONSIDER . . .

■ taking ten to fifteen minutes to watch a bird. Why do you think Jesus saw birds as examples of how you could live?

■ listing some things you're worried about. Analyze each item on the list and decide if it's something you can change or something you should leave in God's hands.

FOR MORE, SEE . . .

■ Psalm 46 (p. 508)   ■ Philippians 4:5–7 (p. 1234)

■ Luke 10:41–42 (p. 1024)

People Know You by Your Actions

15"Be careful of false prophets.*d* They come to you looking gentle like sheep, but they are really dangerous like wolves. 16You will know these people by what they do. Grapes don't come from thornbushes, and figs don't come from thorny weeds. 17In the same way, every good tree produces good fruit, but a bad tree produces bad fruit. 18A good tree cannot produce bad fruit, and a bad tree cannot produce good fruit. 19Every tree that does not produce good fruit is cut down and thrown into the fire. 20In the same way, you will know these false prophets by what they do.

21"Not all those who say that I am their Lord will enter the kingdom of heaven. The only people who will enter the kingdom of heaven are those who do what my Father in heaven wants. 22On the last day many people will say to me, 'Lord, Lord, we spoke for you, and through you we forced out demons*d* and did many miracles.'*d* 23Then I will tell them clearly, 'Get away from me, you who do evil. I never knew you.'

Two Kinds of People

24"Everyone who hears my words and obeys them is like a wise man who built his house on rock. 25It rained hard, the floods came, and the winds blew and hit that house. But it did not fall, because it was built on rock. 26Everyone who hears my words and does not obey them is like a foolish man who built his house on sand. 27It rained hard, the floods came, and the winds blew and hit that house, and it fell with a big crash."

28When Jesus finished saying these things, the people were amazed at his teaching, 29because he did not teach like their teachers of the law. He taught like a person who had authority.

Jesus Heals a Sick Man

8 When Jesus came down from the hill, great crowds followed him. 2Then a man with a skin disease came to Jesus. The man bowed down before him and said, "Lord, you can heal me if you will."

3Jesus reached out his hand and touched the man and said, "I will. Be healed!" And immediately the man was healed from his disease. 4Then Jesus said to him, "Don't tell anyone about this. But go and show yourself to the priest*n* and offer

show . . . priest   The law of Moses said a priest must say when a Jewish person with a skin disease was well.

CULTS

Deadly Deception

Malaya is home for a species of praying mantis that's made a career of looking like a flower. But this "flower" kills unsuspecting bugs.

Pink, petal-like structures flank its spindly legs. Part of its green thorax simulates the stem of an orchid. A few brown markings here and there make it look slightly wilted. When a soft breeze blows, the mantis even simulates the flower's gentle, swaying motion.

But this unusual insect is as deadly as it is beautiful. If a butterfly mistakes the mantis for an orchid, the mantis strikes with frightful speed and captures the butterfly in pink, vice-like forelegs.

Like butterflies, Christians need to be aware that not everything is as it appears. Many cults may look appealing, just as the praying mantis looks like an orchid to an unsuspecting butterfly. Learn how you can watch out for this kind of deception in **Matthew 7:15-29**.

■ How is a butterfly captured by a praying mantis like those who build their houses on the sand?

■ Who are some modern-day "false prophets" or groups you have heard of or been contacted by? How might Jesus react to them?

CONSIDER . . .

■ praying for ways to resist the temptations of cults, and then investing time to grow in *your faith in Christ.*

■ praying for those caught in cults, and sharing your faith with non-Christians.

FOR MORE, SEE . . .

■ 1 Kings 18:1-40 (p. 323)
■ Mark 13:14-23 (p. 990)

■ 2 Peter 2:1-22 (p. 1311)

the gift Moses commanded[n] for people who are made well. This will show the people what I have done."

Jesus Heals a Soldier's Servant

[5]When Jesus entered the city of Capernaum, an army officer came to him, begging for help. [6]The officer said, "Lord, my servant is at home in bed. He can't move his body and is in much pain."

[7]Jesus said to the officer, "I will go and heal him."

[8]The officer answered, "Lord, I am not worthy for you to come into my house. You only need to command it, and my servant will be healed. [9]I, too, am a man under the authority of others, and I have soldiers under my command. I tell one soldier, 'Go,' and he goes. I tell another soldier, 'Come,' and he comes. I say to my servant, 'Do this,' and my servant does it.

[10]When Jesus heard this, he was amazed. He said to those who were following him, "I tell you the truth, this is the greatest faith I have found, even in Israel. [11]Many people will come from the east and from the west and will sit and eat with Abraham, Isaac, and Jacob in the kingdom of heaven. [12]But those people who should be in the kingdom will be thrown outside into the darkness, where people will cry and grind their teeth with pain."

[13]Then Jesus said to the officer, "Go home. Your servant will be healed just as you believed he would." And his servant was healed that same hour.

Jesus Heals Many People

[14]When Jesus went to Peter's house, he saw that Peter's mother-in-law was sick in bed with a fever. [15]Jesus touched her hand, and the fever left her. Then she stood up and began to serve Jesus. [16]That evening people brought to Jesus many who had demons.[d] Jesus spoke and the demons left them, and he healed all the sick. [17]He did these things to bring about what Isaiah the prophet[d] had said:

"He took our suffering on him
   and carried our diseases."   *Isaiah 53:4*

People Want to Follow Jesus

[18]When Jesus saw the crowd around him, he told his followers to go to the other side of the lake. [19]Then a teacher of the law came to Jesus and said, "Teacher, I will follow you any place you go."

[20]Jesus said to him, "The foxes have holes to live in, and the birds have nests, but the Son of Man[d] has no place to rest his head."

[21]Another man, one of Jesus' followers, said to him, "Lord, first let me go and bury my father."

[22]But Jesus told him, "Follow me, and let the people who are dead bury their own dead."

Jesus Calms a Storm

[23]Jesus got into a boat, and his followers went with him. [24]A great storm arose on the lake so that waves covered the boat, but Jesus was sleeping. [25]His followers went to him and woke him, saying, "Lord, save us! We will drown!"

[26]Jesus answered, "Why are you afraid? You don't have enough faith." Then Jesus got up and gave a command to the wind and the waves, and it became completely calm.

[27]The men were amazed and said, "What kind of man is this? Even the wind and the waves obey him!"

Jesus Heals Two Men with Demons

[28]When Jesus arrived at the other side of the lake in the area of the Gadarene[n] people, two men who had demons[d] in them met him. These men lived in the burial caves and were so dangerous that people could not use the road by those caves. [29]They shouted, "What do you want with us, Son of God? Did you come here to torture us before the right time?"

[30]Near that place there was a large herd of pigs feeding. [31]The demons begged Jesus, "If you make us leave these men, please send us into that herd of pigs."

[32]Jesus said to them, "Go!" So the demons left the men and went into the pigs. Then the whole herd rushed down the hill into the lake and were drowned. [33]The herdsmen ran away and went into town, where they told about all of this and what had happened to the men who had demons. [34]Then the whole town went out to see Jesus. When they saw him, they begged him to leave their area.

Jesus Heals a Paralyzed Man

9 Jesus got into a boat and went back across the lake to his own town. [2]Some people brought to Jesus a man who was paralyzed and lying on a mat. When Jesus saw the faith of these people, he said to the paralyzed man, "Be encouraged, young man. Your sins are forgiven."

[3]Some of the teachers of the law said to themselves, "This man speaks as if he were God. That is blasphemy!"[n]

[4]Knowing their thoughts, Jesus said, "Why are

Moses commanded   Read about this in Leviticus 14:1-32.
Gadarene   From Gadara, an area southeast of Lake Galilee.
blasphemy   Saying things against God or not showing respect for God.

you thinking evil thoughts? [5]Which is easier: to say, 'Your sins are forgiven,' or to tell him, 'Stand up and walk'? [6]But I will prove to you that the Son of Man[d] has authority on earth to forgive sins." Then Jesus said to the paralyzed man, "Stand up, take your mat, and go home." [7]And the man stood up and went home. [8]When the people saw this, they were amazed and praised God for giving power like this to human beings.

Jesus Chooses Matthew

[9]When Jesus was leaving, he saw a man named Matthew sitting in the tax collector's booth. Jesus said to him, "Follow me," and he stood up and followed Jesus.

[10]As Jesus was having dinner at Matthew's house, many tax collectors and "sinners" came and ate with Jesus and his followers. [11]When the Pharisees[d] saw this, they asked Jesus' followers,

"Why does your teacher eat with tax collectors and sinners?"

[12]When Jesus heard them, he said, "It is not the healthy people who need a doctor, but the sick.

> ## SIDELIGHT: As a tax collector,
> Matthew was hardly Mr. Popularity (Matthew 9:9–13). He could tax you for crossing a bridge—and also tax your cart, its axle, and the engine (or donkey). And you thought toll roads were bad!

[13]Go and learn what this means: 'I want kindness more than I want animal sacrifices.'[n] I did not come to invite good people but to invite sinners."

'I want . . . sacrifices.'   Quotation from Hosea 6:6.

NON-CHRISTIANS

How to Win Friends

Carlos Trujillo thought he had found a simple solution to negative peer influence: just avoid non-Christians. But then he got a job at a fast-food restaurant.

Because he was a team worker, Carlos often helped others finish their work. One day he helped Todd, another worker, wipe off the last table before their shift ended.

"Thanks for your help, Carlos," Todd said. "I've really got to hustle tonight because I have to study for a huge chemistry exam tomorrow. Mrs. Stafford's tests are really tough."

"You take chemistry from Mrs. Stafford, too?" Carlos asked. "Why don't we study together?"

Todd and Carlos spent two hours at the library reviewing for the test. Although he later learned that Todd had never been inside a church, Carlos discovered they had a lot in common. "Maybe," Carlos thought, "God has a good reason for Todd and me to be friends."

Over time, Carlos began to reach out in friendship to other non-Christians. His initial fear of how non-Christians would be a bad influence on him quickly disappeared. In fact, he discovered that many of his non-Christian friends were hungry for the truth of Christ.

In **Matthew 9:9–13**, Jesus chose to eat with Matthew, a tax collector, and other "sinners." This action raised pious eyebrows among the religious leaders. Read Jesus' response to their criticism.

■ Why might the Pharisees have agreed with Carlos's initial plan to avoid non-Christians?

■ What do these verses say to you about reaching non-Christians in your world?

CONSIDER . . . .

■ inviting someone at school or at work to attend church with you, or bringing that person to your next youth group outing.

■ taking time this week to establish a relationship with a non-Christian or unchurched friend.

FOR MORE, SEE . . .

■ Isaiah 56:1–8 (p. 675)
■ Luke 12:8–9 (p. 1027)

■ James 2:14–26 (p. 1295)

Jesus' Followers Are Criticized

[14]Then the followers of John[n] came to Jesus and said, "Why do we and the Pharisees[d] often give up eating for a certain time,[n] but your followers don't?"

[15]Jesus answered, "The friends of the bridegroom are not sad while he is with them. But the time will come when the bridegroom will be taken from them, and then they will give up eating.

[16]"No one sews a patch of unshrunk cloth over a hole in an old coat. If he does, the patch will shrink and pull away from the coat, making the hole worse. [17]Also, people never pour new wine into old leather bags. Otherwise, the bags will break, the wine will spill, and the wine bags will be ruined. But people always pour new wine into new wine bags. Then both will continue to be good."

Jesus Gives Life to a Dead Girl and Heals a Sick Woman

[18]While Jesus was saying these things, a leader of the synagogue[d] came to him. He bowed down before Jesus and said, "My daughter has just died. But if you come and lay your hand on her, she will live again." [19]So Jesus and his followers stood up and went with the leader.

[20]Then a woman who had been bleeding for twelve years came behind Jesus and touched the edge of his coat. [21]She was thinking, "If I can just touch his clothes, I will be healed."

[22]Jesus turned and saw the woman and said, "Be encouraged, dear woman. You are made well because you believed." And the woman was healed from that moment on.

[23]Jesus continued along with the leader and went into his house. There he saw the funeral musicians and many people crying. [24]Jesus said, "Go away. The girl is not dead, only asleep." But the people laughed at him. [25]After the crowd had been thrown out of the house, Jesus went into the girl's room and took hold of her hand, and she stood up. [26]The news about this spread all around the area.

Jesus Heals More People

[27]When Jesus was leaving there, two blind men followed him. They cried out, "Have mercy on us, Son of David!"[d]

[28]After Jesus went inside, the blind men went with him. He asked the men, "Do you believe that I can make you see again?"

They answered, "Yes, Lord."

[29]Then Jesus touched their eyes and said, "Because you believe I can make you see again, it will happen." [30]Then the men were able to see. But Jesus warned them strongly, saying, "Don't tell anyone about this." [31]But the blind men left and spread the news about Jesus all around that area.

[32]When the two men were leaving, some people brought another man to Jesus. This man could not talk because he had a demon[d] in him. [33]After Jesus forced the demon to leave the man, he was able to speak. The crowd was amazed and said, "We have never seen anything like this in Israel."

[34]But the Pharisees[d] said, "The prince of demons is the one that gives him power to force demons out."

[35]Jesus traveled through all the towns and villages, teaching in their synagogues,[d] preaching the Good News[d] about the kingdom, and healing all kinds of diseases and sicknesses. [36]When he saw the crowds, he felt sorry for them because they were hurting and helpless, like sheep without a shepherd. [37]Jesus said to his followers, "There are many people to harvest but only a few workers to help harvest them. [38]Pray to the Lord, who owns the harvest, that he will send more workers to gather his harvest."[n]

Jesus Sends Out His Apostles

10 Jesus called his twelve followers together and gave them authority to drive out evil spirits and to heal every kind of disease and sickness. [2]These are the names of the twelve apostles:[d] Simon (also called Peter) and his brother Andrew; James son of Zebedee, and his brother John; [3]Philip and Bartholomew; Thomas and Matthew, the tax collector; James son of Alphaeus, and Thaddaeus; [4]Simon the Zealot[d] and Judas Iscariot, who turned against Jesus.

[5]Jesus sent out these twelve men with the following order: "Don't go to the non-Jewish people or to any town where the Samaritans[d] live. [6]But go to the people of Israel, who are like lost sheep. [7]When you go, preach this: 'The kingdom of heaven is near.' [8]Heal the sick, raise the dead to life again, heal those who have skin diseases, and force demons[d] out of people. I give you these powers freely, so help other people freely. [9]Don't carry any money with you — gold or silver or copper. [10]Don't carry a bag or extra clothes or sandals or a walking stick. Workers should be given what they need.

[11]"When you enter a city or town, find some

John John the Baptist, who preached to people about Christ's coming (Matthew 3, Luke 3).

give up ... time This is called "fasting." The people would give up eating for a special time of prayer and worship to God. It was also done to show sadness and disappointment.

"There are ... harvest." As a farmer sends workers to harvest the grain, Jesus sends his followers to bring people to God.

worthy person there and stay in that home until you leave. ¹²When you enter that home, say, 'Peace be with you.' ¹³If the people there welcome you, let your peace stay there. But if they don't welcome you, take back the peace you wished for them. ¹⁴And if a home or town refuses to welcome you or listen to you, leave that place and shake its dust off your feet.[n] ¹⁵I tell you the truth, on the Judgment Day it will be better for the towns of Sodom and Gomorrah[n] than for the people of that town.

Jesus Warns His Apostles

¹⁶"Listen, I am sending you out like sheep among wolves. So be as smart as snakes and as innocent as doves. ¹⁷Be careful of people, because they will arrest you and take you to court and whip you in their synagogues.[d] ¹⁸Because of me you will be taken to stand before governors and kings, and you will tell them and the non-Jewish people about me. ¹⁹When you are arrested, don't worry about what to say or how to say it. At that time you will be given the things to say. ²⁰It will not really be you speaking but the Spirit of your Father speaking through you.

²¹"Brothers will give their own brothers to be killed, and fathers will give their own children to be killed. Children will fight against their own

shake . . . feet. A warning. It showed that they had rejected these people.
Sodom and Gomorrah Two cities that God destroyed because the people were so evil.

SICKNESS

Giving the World Friends

Rebecca Smathers, a high school junior, dances, walks, and runs. No big deal for most of us—but for Rebecca those abilities prove God's power. For not long ago, she was almost completely paralyzed.

In her freshman year, Rebecca felt her muscles slowly becoming numb. She started avoiding golf and softball practices. Play rehearsals caused excruciating pain. Her mother finally took her to a doctor, and Rebecca was admitted to the hospital that same day.

A spinal tap confirmed she had Guillain Barr Syndrome, a rare condition in which a virus attacks the nervous system, causing paralysis in all of the motor functions. Although she began various drug and physical treatments, Rebecca's condition worsened. "The syndrome spread, and I could no longer sit upright in bed by myself," she recalls.

Doctors gave her little chance for recovery. However, Rebecca believes the care and prayers of others made the difference. "My spirits have been strengthened because of the love from family and friends," Rebecca says. "Daily I received phone calls, cards, and flowers. My room was crowded with friends every day. It was a time for fellowship and support, not only for me, but also for my family and friends."

The doctors continued treatment, and Rebecca slowly recovered.

"Some people say the Lord doesn't give us answers we can see or touch, yet we all see and touch our family and friends," Rebecca says. "The Lord answered my prayers with a family who stroked my hair and sat next to me day and night while I lay motionless.

"The Lord brought me friends who told me, 'You will get better, because I'm praying for you.' I thank God for the answers he's given me."

Rebecca's doctors were amazed at the healing power of faith. Yet **Matthew 9:35—10:8** tells how Jesus commissioned the disciples to heal the sick.

■ How well did the people who prayed and stayed with Rebecca follow Jesus' commission to the apostles?

■ Why does God care not only about your physical health, but also your spiritual health?

CONSIDER . . .

 doing one activity this week to better your health and well-being.
■ visiting someone in a hospital or nursing home and praying with him or her.

FOR MORE, SEE . . .

■ 2 Kings 20:1–11 (p. 327)
■ Psalm 30:2–3 (p. 498)   ■ Luke 18:35–43 (p. 1043)

parents and have them put to death. 22All people will hate you because you follow me, but those people who keep their faith until the end will be saved. 23When you are treated badly in one city, run to another city. I tell you the truth, you will not finish going through all the cities of Israel before the Son of Man*d* comes.

24"A student is not better than his teacher, and a servant is not better than his master. 25A student should be satisfied to become like his teacher; a servant should be satisfied to become like his master. If the head of the family is called Beelzebul,*d* then the other members of the family will be called worse names!

Fear God, Not People

26"So don't be afraid of those people, because everything that is hidden will be shown. Everything that is secret will be made known. 27I tell you these things in the dark, but I want you to tell them in the light. What you hear whispered in your ear you should shout from the housetops. 28Don't be afraid of people, who can kill the body but cannot kill the soul. The only one you should fear is the one who can destroy the soul and the body in hell. 29Two sparrows cost only a penny, but not even one of them can die without your Father's knowing it. 30God even knows how many hairs are on your head. 31So don't be afraid. You are worth much more than many sparrows.

Tell People About Your Faith

32"All those who stand before others and say they believe in me, I will say before my Father in heaven that they belong to me. 33But all who stand before others and say they do not believe in me, I will say before my Father in heaven that they do not belong to me.

34"Don't think that I came to bring peace to the earth. I did not come to bring peace, but a sword.

SELF-ESTEEM

Playing Your Part

The second-period algebra test had been a disaster for Charlene Markham. Then she had slipped and fallen in the hallway in front of two dozen other students. As she sat in sixth-period band practice, her mind was everywhere except on the sheets of music.

"Sometimes I wonder if my being here at Springbrook High makes any difference at all," she thought as the band music filled the room. "It's like the flutists' part in this medley. All you can hear are the trumpets and trombones, anyway."

As an experiment, Charlene raised the flute to her lips but only pretended to play. "See," she thought after the piece, "no one even noticed."

Just before the bell rang, Mr. Westmore, the band director, instructed the students to put away their instruments. Then he asked Charlene to stay after the bell.

"Why didn't you play in the Sousa medley?" he asked.

Charlene was stunned that he knew what she had done. She didn't answer him. "Charlene," he said kindly, yet firmly, "we need every part in a piece of music to make it complete. The director looks for everyone to be playing his or her part."

Somehow Charlene felt better knowing she had been missed. "Maybe I have a part to play after all," she thought. Learn what Jesus says about your importance in **Matthew 10:24–33**.

■ How does the Bible passage speak to Charlene's feelings of worthlessness?
■ How does knowing that God loves you affect your feelings about yourself?

C O N S I D E R . . .
■ investing thirty minutes today in an activity for your own growth, health and well-being.
■ listing all of the "sections" in God's "band" (the church) you can think of, such as pastors, leaders, choirs and so forth. Pick the one section that you're most interested in, and volunteer to "play" in it.

F O R   M O R E ,   S E E . . .
■ Psalm 8:3–9 (p. 486)   ■ 1 Corinthians 12:12–31 (p. 1182)
■ Romans 5:1–11 (p. 1145)

35I have come so that
'a son will be against his father,
    a daughter will be against her mother,
a daughter-in-law will be against her
    mother-in-law.
36 A person's enemies will be members of his
    own family.'   *Micah 7:6*
37"Those who love their father or mother more
than they love me are not worthy to be my followers. Those who love their son or daughter more
than they love me are not worthy to be my followers. 38Whoever is not willing to carry the cross
and follow me is not worthy of me. 39Those who
try to hold on to their lives will give up true life.
Those who give up their lives for me will hold on
to true life. 40Whoever accepts you also accepts
me, and whoever accepts me also accepts the One
who sent me. 41Whoever meets a prophet*d* and
accepts him will receive the reward of a prophet.
And whoever accepts a good person because that
person is good will receive the reward of a good
person. 42Those who give one of these little ones
a cup of cold water because they are my followers
will truly get their reward."

Jesus and John the Baptist

11 After Jesus finished telling these things
to his twelve followers, he left there
and went to the towns in Galilee to teach and
preach.
2John the Baptist*d* was in prison, but he heard
about what Christ was doing. So John sent some
of his followers to Jesus. 3They asked him, "Are
you the One who is to come, or should we wait
for someone else?"
4Jesus answered them, "Go tell John what you
hear and see: 5The blind can see, the crippled can
walk, and people with skin diseases are healed.
The deaf can hear, the dead are raised to life, and
the Good News*d* is preached to the poor. 6Those
who do not stumble in their faith because of me
are blessed."
7As John's followers were leaving, Jesus began
talking to the people about John. Jesus said,
"What did you go out into the desert to see? A
reed*n* blown by the wind? 8What did you go out
to see? A man dressed in fine clothes? No, those
who wear fine clothes live in kings' palaces. 9So

reed It means that John was not ordinary or weak like grass blown by the wind.

Doing the Right Thing

Dad appeared in Marcia Sloan's bedroom doorway. "What's all this I hear about you
going to a Christian college next year?" he asked.
    This was the moment she had been dreading. "It's true, Dad. That's what I've decided."
    "Ever since you started going to that church, you've been getting weird ideas," he said.
"If you want to go to medical school, you'll need the quality of education that you can get
at a state school."
    Then he dropped the ultimatum: "If you go to that Christian college, don't
look to us for financial support."
    Marcia's father kept his promise. But Marcia firmly believed that the
Christian college was God's will for her.
    Marcia's freshman year in college was difficult. Because she had to pay her
own tuition, she worked several hours part-time in the evenings. But she kept
going, knowing she had made a smart choice.
    Jesus cautioned that following him would not always be easy. Read in
Matthew 10:34—42 about the difficult choices Christians may face.
■ How was Marcia's predicament like that described in the passage?
■ What does this passage say about your priorities in your family and in
    other areas of life?

CONSIDER . . .
■ giving encouragement to a Christian friend whose parents are not believers.
◤ taking your mom or dad out for dessert after dinner one night this week, and talking
    with them about your goals and priorities.

FOR MORE, SEE . . .
■ Genesis 22:1–18 (p. 25)
■ Exodus 20:12 (p. 78)   ■ 1 John 3:1–3 (p. 1318)

why did you go out? To see a prophet?[d] Yes, and I tell you, John is more than a prophet. [10]This was written about him:

'I will send my messenger ahead of you,
who will prepare the way for you.' *Malachi 3:1*

[11]I tell you the truth, John the Baptist is greater than any other person ever born, but even the least important person in the kingdom of heaven is greater than John. [12]Since the time John the Baptist came until now, the kingdom of heaven has been going forward in strength, and people have been trying to take it by force. [13]All the prophets and the law of Moses told about what would happen until the time John came. [14]And if you will believe what they said, you will believe that John is Elijah, whom they said would come. [15]You people who can hear me, listen!

[16]"What can I say about the people of this time? What are they like? They are like children sitting in the marketplace, who call out to each other,

[17]'We played music for you, but you did not dance;

we sang a sad song, but you did not cry.'

[18]John came and did not eat or drink like other people. So people say, 'He has a demon.'[d] [19]The Son of Man[d] came, eating and drinking, and people say, 'Look at him! He eats too much and drinks too much wine, and he is a friend of tax collectors and sinners.' But wisdom is proved to be right by what it does."

Jesus Warns Unbelievers

[20]Then Jesus criticized the cities where he did most of his miracles,[d] because the people did not change their lives and stop sinning. [21]He said, "How terrible for you, Korazin! How terrible for you, Bethsaida! If the same miracles I did in you had happened in Tyre and Sidon,[n] those people would have changed their lives a long time ago. They would have worn rough cloth and put ashes

Tyre and Sidon　Towns where wicked people lived.

The Faith Difference

Next time friends ask you, "Does your faith make a difference?" remember these statistics about teenagers in the United States*:

1. Teenagers who have never used illegal drugs—61 percent of regular churchgoers, versus 39 percent of nonchurchgoers.

2. Teenagers who have never had sexual intercourse—61 percent of regular churchgoers, versus 35 percent of nonchurchgoers.

3. Teenagers who believe in a personal God—87 percent of regular churchgoers, versus 64 percent of nonchurchgoers.

4. Teenagers who read the Bible weekly—58 percent of regular churchgoers, versus 17 percent of nonchurchgoers.

5. Teenagers who plan to go to college—57 percent of regular churchgoers, versus 33 percent of nonchurchgoers.

Faith isn't a "heady" thing. It's something that affects everything we do. As the statistics above illustrate, a committed faith makes a visible, real difference in the way we live. In **Matthew 11:2–11** the followers of John the Baptist asked Jesus whether he was the Christ. Read how he responded.

■ Why is faith a powerful force in the miracles of Jesus as well as the behavior of regular churchgoers?

■ What difference does faith make in your own life? Have you seen the signs of God's work that are listed in the passage?

CONSIDER . . . .

■ surveying your own behavior in comparison to the statistics. How well did you fit the categories?

■ drawing up your own survey and interviewing both churchgoers and nonchurchgoers. Share your results with others at church and school.

FOR MORE, SEE . . .

■ Judges 6:11–24 (p. 222)　　　　■ James 5:13–18 (p. 1299)
■ Luke 13:1–9 (p. 1030)

*Eugene C. Roehlkepartain ed., The Youth Ministry Resource Book; (Loveland, CO: Group Books, 1988).

on themselves to show they had changed. [22]But I tell you, on the Judgment Day it will be better for Tyre and Sidon than for you. [23]And you, Capernaum, [n] will you be lifted up to heaven? No, you will be thrown down to the depths. If the miracles I did in you had happened in Sodom, [n] its people would have stopped sinning, and it would still be a city today. [24]But I tell you, on the Judgment Day it will be better for Sodom than for you."

Jesus Offers Rest to People

[25]At that time Jesus said, "I praise you, Father, Lord of heaven and earth, because you have hidden these things from the people who are wise and smart. But you have shown them to those who are like little children. [26]Yes, Father, this is what you really wanted.

[27]"My Father has given me all things. No one knows the Son, except the Father. And no one knows the Father, except the Son and those whom the Son chooses to tell.

[28]"Come to me, all of you who are tired and have heavy loads, and I will give you rest. [29]Accept my teachings and learn from me, because I am gentle and humble in spirit, and you will find rest for your lives. [30]The teaching that I ask you to accept is easy; the load I give you to carry is light."

Jesus Is Lord of the Sabbath

12 At that time Jesus was walking through some fields of grain on a Sabbath[d] day. His followers were hungry, so they began to pick the grain and eat it. [2]When the Pharisees[d] saw this, they said to Jesus, "Look! Your followers are doing what is unlawful to do on the Sabbath day."

[3]Jesus answered, "Have you not read what David did when he and the people with him were hungry? [4]He went into God's house, and he and those with him ate the holy bread, which was lawful only for priests to eat. [5]And have you not read in the law of Moses that on every Sabbath day the priests in the Temple[d] break this law about the Sabbath day? But the priests are not wrong for doing that. [6]I tell you that there is something here that is greater than the Temple.

Korazin . . . Bethsaida . . . Capernaum   Towns by Lake Galilee where Jesus preached to the people.
Sodom   A city that God destroyed because the people were so evil.

WORRYING

Making It Through Your Day

Why did everyone else seem to have such a carefree life? Stacy Campbell wondered.

For more than a year her mother had been threatening to leave her father. Her school counselor told her she would have to raise her grades in physics and math if she ever wanted to take engineering in college. While other students received allowances, Stacy worked long hours at a "lousy" part-time job. And Grandma Campbell had just gone into a nursing home because she couldn't care for herself anymore.

Stacy usually fell into bed after midnight. But she often had trouble going to sleep. Even in her sleep she couldn't find rest; the day's problems crept into her dreams.

But then one evening she stumbled across a way to unwind at day's end. She began to spend a little time reading her Bible and praying just before going to bed. In time, this habit helped to settle her down, set her mind at peace and place her day's troubles in God's care.

Jesus offered ways to cope with the stresses of life. Read about his promise in **Matthew 11:25–30**.

■ What truth in this passage did Stacy stumble upon?
■ What kinds of stresses do you have that you can take to Jesus?

CONSIDER . . .

■ writing a thank-you note to Jesus for helping you cope with problems.
■ setting aside ten minutes a day for one week for Bible reading and prayer. Perhaps begin by reading a psalm (p. 482) and a chapter of Proverbs (p. 568) each day. Many of the psalms are prayers you can use.

FOR MORE, SEE . . .

■ Psalm 4 (p. 483)
■ Luke 11:5–13 (p. 1024)

■ Jude 24–25 (p. 1330)

[7]The Scripture[d] says, 'I want kindness more than I want animal sacrifices.'[n] You don't really know what those words mean. If you understood them, you would not judge those who have done nothing wrong.

[8]"So the Son of Man[d] is Lord of the Sabbath day."

SIDELIGHT: It was hard not to break Sabbath laws in Jesus' day (Matthew 12:1–8). The Pharisees believed thirty-nine different actions violated Sabbath laws. You couldn't take a trip, light a fire, get a drink, or pick up anything that weighed more than two figs. How much does a TV remote control weigh?

Jesus Heals a Man's Hand

[9]Jesus left there and went into their synagogue,[d] [10]where there was a man with a crippled hand. They were looking for a reason to accuse Jesus, so they asked him, "Is it right to heal on the Sabbath[d] day?"[n]

[11]Jesus answered, "If any of you has a sheep, and it falls into a ditch on the Sabbath day, you will help it out of the ditch. [12]Surely a human being is more important than a sheep. So it is lawful to do good things on the Sabbath day."

[13]Then Jesus said to the man with the crippled hand, "Hold out your hand." The man held out his hand, and it became well again, like the other hand. [14]But the Pharisees[d] left and made plans to kill Jesus.

Jesus Is God's Chosen Servant

[15]Jesus knew what the Pharisees[d] were doing, so he left that place. Many people followed him, and he healed all who were sick. [16]But Jesus warned the people not to tell who he was. [17]He did these things to bring about what Isaiah the prophet[d] had said:

[18]"Here is my servant whom I have chosen.
I love him, and I am pleased with him.
I will put my Spirit[d] upon him,
    and he will tell of my justice to all people.
[19]He will not argue or cry out;
    no one will hear his voice in the streets.
[20]He will not break a crushed blade of grass
    or put out even a weak flame
until he makes justice win the victory.
[21] In him will the non-Jewish people find
        hope."
                                        Isaiah 42:1-4

Jesus' Power Is from God

[22]Then some people brought to Jesus a man who was blind and could not talk, because he had a demon.[d] Jesus healed the man so that he could talk and see. [23]All the people were amazed and said, "Perhaps this man is the Son of David!"[d]

[24]When the Pharisees[d] heard this, they said, "Jesus uses the power of Beelzebul,[d] the ruler of demons, to force demons out of people."

[25]Jesus knew what the Pharisees were thinking, so he said to them, "Every kingdom that is divided against itself will be destroyed. And any city or family that is divided against itself will not continue. [26]And if Satan forces out himself, then Satan is divided against himself, and his kingdom will not continue. [27]You say that I use the power of Beelzebul to force out demons. If that is true, then what power do your people use to force out demons? So they will be your judges. [28]But if I use the power of God's Spirit[d] to force out demons, then the kingdom of God has come to you.

[29]"If anyone wants to enter a strong person's house and steal his things, he must first tie up the strong person. Then he can steal the things from the house.

[30]"Whoever is not with me is against me. Whoever does not work with me is working against me. [31]So I tell you, people can be forgiven for every sin and everything they say against God. But whoever speaks against the Holy Spirit will not be forgiven. [32]Anyone who speaks against the Son of Man[d] can be forgiven, but anyone who speaks against the Holy Spirit will not be forgiven, now or in the future.

People Know You by Your Words

[33]"If you want good fruit, you must make the tree good. If your tree is not good, it will have bad fruit. A tree is known by the kind of fruit it produces. [34]You snakes! You are evil people, so how can you say anything good? The mouth speaks the things that are in the heart. [35]Good people have good things in their hearts, and so they say good things. But evil people have evil in their hearts, so they say evil things. [36]And I tell you that on the Judgment Day people will be responsible for every careless thing they have said. [37]The words you have said will be used to judge you. Some of your words will prove you right, but some of your words will prove you guilty."

The People Ask for a Miracle

[38]Then some of the Pharisees[d] and teachers of the law answered Jesus, saying, "Teacher, we want to see you work a miracle[d] as a sign."

[39]Jesus answered, "Evil and sinful people are

'I . . . sacrifices.'   Quotation from Hosea 6:6.
"Is it right . . . day?"   It was against Jewish law to work on the Sabbath day.

the ones who want to see a miracle for a sign. But no sign will be given to them, except the sign of the prophet[d] Jonah. [40]Jonah was in the stomach of the big fish for three days and three nights. In the same way, the Son of Man[d] will be in the grave three days and three nights. [41]On the Judgment Day the people from Nineveh[n] will stand up with you people who live now, and they will show that you are guilty. When Jonah preached to them, they were sorry and changed their lives. And I tell you that someone greater than Jonah is here. [42]On the Judgment Day, the Queen of the South[n] will stand up with you people who live today. She will show that you are guilty, because she came from far away to listen to Solomon's wise teaching. And I tell you that someone greater than Solomon is here.

People Today Are Full of Evil

[43]"When an evil spirit comes out of a person, it travels through dry places, looking for a place to rest, but it doesn't find it. [44]So the spirit says, 'I will go back to the house I left.' When the spirit comes back, it finds the house still empty, swept clean, and made neat. [45]Then the evil spirit goes out and brings seven other spirits even more evil than it is, and they go in and live there. So the person has even more trouble than before. It is the same way with the evil people who live today."

Jesus' True Family

[46]While Jesus was talking to the people, his mother and brothers stood outside, trying to find a way to talk to him. [47]Someone told Jesus, "Your mother and brothers are standing outside, and they want to talk to you."

[48]He answered, "Who is my mother? Who are my brothers?" [49]Then he pointed to his followers and said, "Here are my mother and my brothers. [50]My true brother and sister and mother are those who do what my Father in heaven wants."

A Story About Planting Seed

13 That same day Jesus went out of the house and sat by the lake. [2]Large crowds gathered around him, so he got into a boat and sat down, while the people stood on the shore. [3]Then Jesus used stories to teach them many things. He said: "A farmer went out to plant his seed. [4]While he was planting, some seed fell by the road, and the birds came and ate it all up. [5]Some seed fell on rocky ground, where there wasn't much dirt. That seed grew very fast, because the ground was not deep. [6]But when the sun rose, the plants dried up, because they did not have deep roots. [7]Some other seed fell among thorny weeds, which grew and choked the good plants. [8]Some other seed fell on good ground where it grew and produced a crop. Some plants made a hundred times more, some made sixty times more, and some made thirty times more. [9]You people who can hear me, listen."

Why Jesus Used Stories to Teach

[10]The followers came to Jesus and asked, "Why do you use stories to teach the people?"

[11]Jesus answered, "You have been chosen to know the secrets about the kingdom of heaven, but others cannot know these secrets. [12]Those who have understanding will be given more, and they will have all they need. But those who do not have understanding, even what they have will be taken away from them. [13]This is why I use stories to teach the people: They see, but they don't really see. They hear, but they don't really hear or understand. [14]So they show that the things Isaiah said about them are true:

'You will listen and listen, but you will not understand.
You will look and look, but you will not learn.
[15]For the minds of these people have become stubborn.
They do not hear with their ears,
and they have closed their eyes.
Otherwise they might really understand
what they see with their eyes
and hear with their ears.
They might really understand in their minds
and come back to me and be healed.'
Isaiah 6:9-10

[16]But you are blessed, because you see with your eyes and hear with your ears. [17]I tell you the truth, many prophets[d] and good people wanted to see the things that you now see, but they did not see them. And they wanted to hear the things that you now hear, but they did not hear them.

Jesus Explains the Seed Story

[18]"So listen to the meaning of that story about the farmer. [19]What is the seed that fell by the road? That seed is like the person who hears the message about the kingdom but does not understand it. The Evil One comes and takes away what was planted in that person's heart. [20]And what is the seed that fell on rocky ground? That seed is like the person who hears the teaching and quickly accepts it with joy. [21]But he does not let the teaching go deep into his life, so he keeps it

---

Nineveh The city where Jonah preached to warn the people. Read Jonah 3.
Queen of the South The Queen of Sheba. She traveled a thousand miles to learn God's wisdom from Solomon. Read 1 Kings 10:1-13.

only a short time. When trouble or persecution comes because of the teaching he accepted, he quickly gives up. ²²And what is the seed that fell among the thorny weeds? That seed is like the person who hears the teaching but lets worries about this life and the temptation of wealth stop that teaching from growing. So the teaching does not produce fruit*ⁿ* in that person's life. ²³But what is the seed that fell on the good ground? That seed is like the person who hears the teaching and understands it. That person grows and produces fruit, sometimes a hundred times more, sometimes sixty times more, and sometimes thirty times more."

A Story About Wheat and Weeds

²⁴Then Jesus told them another story: "The kingdom of heaven is like a man who planted good seed in his field. ²⁵That night, when everyone was asleep, his enemy came and planted weeds among the wheat and then left. ²⁶Later, the wheat sprouted and the heads of grain grew, but the weeds also grew. ²⁷Then the man's servants came to him and said, 'You planted good seed in your field. Where did the weeds come from?' ²⁸The man answered, 'An enemy planted weeds.' The servants asked, 'Do you want us to pull up the weeds?' ²⁹The man answered, 'No, because when you pull up the weeds, you might also pull up the wheat. ³⁰Let the weeds and the wheat grow together until the harvest time. At harvest time I will tell the workers, "First gather the weeds and tie them together to be burned. Then gather the wheat and bring it to my barn." ' "

Stories of Mustard Seed and Yeast

³¹Then Jesus told another story: "The kingdom of heaven is like a mustard seed that a man planted in his field. ³²That seed is the smallest of all seeds, but when it grows, it is one of the largest garden plants. It becomes big enough for the wild birds to come and build nests in its branches."

³³Then Jesus told another story: "The kingdom of heaven is like yeast that a woman took and hid in a large tub of flour until it made all the dough rise."

³⁴Jesus used stories to tell all these things to the

---

produce fruit   To produce fruit means to have in your life the good things God wants.

Tuned In

One beautiful spring morning, an experienced hiker was walking with a friend down Fifth Avenue in Manhattan. The streets rumbled with the sounds of weekday rush-hour traffic. Suddenly the hiker stopped. "Listen," he said. "I hear a cricket."

"That's nonsense!" his friend scoffed. "Why do you think you hear a lowly cricket in all this downtown uproar?"

"I'm sure I do," the hiker said. "Watch this." He pulled a dime from his pocket and dropped it on the pavement. Almost all of the people nearby stopped at the sound of the coin hitting the concrete.

"All of us are tuned to certain things," the hiker said to his friend. "Our ears hear what they are tuned to. Mine happen to be tuned to crickets."

In a similar way we need to be open to God's word. Jesus said we need "eyes to see" and "ears to hear" before we can tune in to the gospel. Read how to gain a new view of your faith in **Matthew 13:1–23**.

■ How was the hiker's hearing the cricket like the ability to hear Jesus' message?

■ Why do you think Jesus compares following God to being the "good ground" for the seed of faith?

C O N S I D E R . . .

■ looking around your room or yard as if you've never seen it before. What do you see, hear or feel that's gone unnoticed? Then do the same process at your church. How can you follow God in ways you may not have noticed?

■ listing three specific things you can do in the next week to better see and hear ways to follow God.

F O R   M O R E ,   S E E . . .

■ 1 Samuel 3:1–21 (p. 247)   ■ 1 Corinthians 13:8–13 (p. 1184)

■ Isaiah 42:18–20 (p. 659)

people; he always used stories to teach them. [35]This is as the prophet[d] said:

"I will speak using stories;
   I will tell things that have been secret since
      the world was made."   *Psalm 78:2*

Jesus Explains About the Weeds

[36]Then Jesus left the crowd and went into the house. His followers came to him and said, "Explain to us the meaning of the story about the weeds in the field."

[37]Jesus answered, "The man who planted the good seed in the field is the Son of Man.[d] [38]The field is the world, and the good seed are all of God's children who belong to the kingdom. The weeds are those people who belong to the Evil One. [39]And the enemy who planted the bad seed is the devil. The harvest time is the end of the world, and the workers who gather are God's angels.

[40]"Just as the weeds are pulled up and burned in the fire, so it will be at the end of the world. [41]The Son of Man will send out his angels, and they will gather out of his kingdom all who cause sin and all who do evil. [42]The angels will throw them into the blazing furnace, where the people will cry and grind their teeth with pain. [43]Then the good people will shine like the sun in the kingdom of their Father. You people who can hear me, listen.

Stories of a Treasure and a Pearl

[44]"The kingdom of heaven is like a treasure hidden in a field. One day a man found the treasure, and then he hid it in the field again. He was so happy that he went and sold everything he owned to buy that field.

[45]"Also, the kingdom of heaven is like a man looking for fine pearls. [46]When he found a very valuable pearl, he went and sold everything he had and bought it.

A Story of a Fishing Net

[47]"Also, the kingdom of heaven is like a net that was put into the lake and caught many different kinds of fish. [48]When it was full, the fishermen pulled the net to the shore. They sat down and put all the good fish in baskets and threw away the bad fish. [49]It will be this way at the end of the world. The angels will come and separate the evil people from the good people. [50]The angels will throw the evil people into the blazing furnace, where people will cry and grind their teeth with pain."

SIN

A Crafty Enemy

Life in the Arctic would be pretty safe for a ringed seal if it weren't for its enemy the polar bear.

This crafty predator probably uses more strategies than any other animal in capturing and killing its prey. It may spend thirty minutes in the water approaching a resting seal on an ice floe, surfacing silently to see where the prey is and then submerging again. It may drift like a small harmless iceberg to within striking distance, and then explode from the water so suddenly and ferociously that the seal has no time to react.

When it's stalking on the ice, the polar bear slithers along on its chest and forelegs. It will build mounds of snow to hide behind while it waits at the edge of a breathing hole. It can surface in the seal's den and catch it sleeping there. Or it can dive so quickly into the den from above that the seal cannot escape.

We, too, must be wary of a crafty enemy. You can read about the enemy in Jesus' parable of the wheat and weeds in **Matthew 13:24–30**.

■ How are the polar bear's tactics similar to the enemy's in the passage?
■ How can you be prepared for the traps of the enemy in your life?

C O N S I D E R . . .

■ separating the forms of entertainment that you enjoy into categories of "wheat" and "weeds." Consider giving up one (or more) of the "weeds."
◀ looking up references to "Satan" and "devil" in the "Dictionary with Topical Concordance" at the back of this Bible (p. 1350). Share what you learn with friends.

F O R   M O R E ,   S E E . . .

■ Genesis 3:1–9 (p. 4)
■ Hebrews 3:12–14 (p. 1279)
■ 1 Peter 5:8–9 (p. 1308)

⁵¹Jesus asked his followers, "Do you understand all these things?"

They answered, "Yes, we understand."

⁵²Then Jesus said to them, "So every teacher of the law who has been taught about the kingdom of heaven is like the owner of a house. He brings out both new things and old things he has saved."

Jesus Goes to His Hometown

⁵³When Jesus finished teaching with these stories, he left there. ⁵⁴He went to his hometown and taught the people in the synagogue,ᵈ and they were amazed. They said, "Where did this man get this wisdom and this power to do miracles?ᵈ ⁵⁵He is just the son of a carpenter. His mother is Mary, and his brothers are James, Joseph, Simon, and Judas. ⁵⁶And all his sisters are here with us. Where then does this man get all these things?" ⁵⁷So the people were upset with Jesus.

But Jesus said to them, "A prophetᵈ is honored everywhere except in his hometown and in his own home."

⁵⁸So he did not do many miracles there because they had no faith.

How John the Baptist Was Killed

14 At that time Herod, the ruler of Galilee, heard the reports about Jesus. ²So he said to his servants, "Jesus is John the Baptist,ᵈ who has risen from the dead. That is why he can work these miracles."ᵈ

³Sometime before this, Herod had arrested John, tied him up, and put him into prison. Herod did this because of Herodias, who had been the wife of Philip, Herod's brother. ⁴John had been telling Herod, "It is not lawful for you to be married to Herodias." ⁵Herod wanted to kill John, but he was afraid of the people, because they believed John was a prophet.ᵈ

⁶On Herod's birthday, the daughter of Herodias danced for Herod and his guests, and she pleased him. ⁷So he promised with an oath to give her anything she wanted. ⁸Herodias told her daughter what to ask for, so she said to Herod, "Give me the head of John the Baptist here on a platter." ⁹Although King Herod was very sad, he had made a promise, and his dinner guests had heard him. So Herod ordered that what she asked for be

---

HAPPINESS

Real Treasure

When seventeen-year-old Derek Green bought his first car—a "previously owned" model—he expected to hit the road and leave his problems in the dust.

The car, Derek expected, would give him more time to do as he pleased. It would get him out of the house and away from his parents' fighting all the time. It would surely improve his standing with girls.

But only a week later, with three friends in the car, a fan belt broke on the way to a football game.

One month later, he had to buy two new tires.

Now he discovered, twenty miles from home, that the radiator was leaking. As the traffic swished past on the freeway, Derek and his friend Phil sat in the front seat of the car, watching the steam rise from under the hood.

"I always looked forward to owning my own car," Derek said. "But sometimes I feel as if the car owns me."

Derek learned an ageless truth that the more things we acquire, the more they use our time and energy. Possessions rarely bring the happiness expected, and often bring just the opposite. The Bible talks often about the spiritual kingdom and the only true happiness. Read three of Jesus' parables on the kingdom in **Matthew 13:44–52**.

■ What are the differences between Derek's car and the "treasure hidden in a field" mentioned in the passage?
■ What is the true value of the things you treasure?

C O N S I D E R . . .

■ praying that God will help you value the things in life that truly last.
■ interviewing an elderly Christian about the things that have meant the most in his or her lifetime.

F O R   M O R E ,   S E E . . .

■ Ecclesiastes 3:1–8 (p. 600)
■ Philippians 4:4–9 (p. 1234)
■ Revelation 3:14–22 (p. 1335)

done. [10]He sent soldiers to the prison to cut off John's head. [11]And they brought it on a platter and gave it to the girl, and she took it to her mother. [12]John's followers came and got his body and buried it. Then they went and told Jesus.

More than Five Thousand Fed

[13]When Jesus heard what had happened to John, he left in a boat and went to a lonely place by himself. But the crowds heard about it and followed him on foot from the towns. [14]When he arrived, he saw a great crowd waiting. He felt sorry for them and healed those who were sick.

[15]When it was evening, his followers came to him and said, "No one lives in this place, and it is already late. Send the people away so they can go to the towns and buy food for themselves."

[16]But Jesus answered, "They don't need to go away. You give them something to eat."

[17]They said to him, "But we have only five loaves of bread and two fish."

[18]Jesus said, "Bring the bread and the fish to me." [19]Then he told the people to sit down on the grass. He took the five loaves and the two fish and, looking to heaven, he thanked God for the food. Jesus divided the bread and gave it to his followers, who gave it to the people. [20]All the people ate and were satisfied. Then the followers filled twelve baskets with the leftover pieces of food. [21]There were about five thousand men there who ate, not counting women and children.

SIDELIGHT: The fish mentioned in Matthew 14:17–21 may have referred to the small, sardine-like fish that were plentiful in Lake Galilee. The poor usually ate this fish with barley bread.

Jesus Walks on the Water

[22]Immediately Jesus told his followers to get into the boat and go ahead of him across the lake. He stayed there to send the people home. [23]After he had sent them away, he went by himself up into the hills to pray. It was late, and Jesus was there alone. [24]By this time, the boat was already far away from land. It was being hit by waves, because the wind was blowing against it.

[25]Between three and six o'clock in the morning, Jesus came to them, walking on the water. [26]When his followers saw him walking on the water, they were afraid. They said, "It's a ghost!" and cried out in fear.

[27]But Jesus quickly spoke to them, "Have courage! It is I. Do not be afraid."

[28]Peter said, "Lord, if it is really you, then command me to come to you on the water."

[29]Jesus said, "Come."

And Peter left the boat and walked on the water to Jesus. [30]But when Peter saw the wind and the waves, he became afraid and began to sink. He shouted, "Lord, save me!"

[31]Immediately Jesus reached out his hand and caught Peter. Jesus said, "Your faith is small. Why did you doubt?"

[32]After they got into the boat, the wind became calm. [33]Then those who were in the boat worshiped Jesus and said, "Truly you are the Son of God!"

[34]When they had crossed the lake, they came to shore at Gennesaret. [35]When the people there recognized Jesus, they told people all around there that Jesus had come, and they brought all their sick to him. [36]They begged Jesus to let them touch just the edge of his coat, and all who touched it were healed.

Obey God's Law

15 Then some Pharisees[d] and teachers of the law came to Jesus from Jerusalem. They asked him, [2]"Why don't your followers obey the unwritten laws which have been handed down to us? They don't wash their hands before they eat."

[3]Jesus answered, "And why do you refuse to obey God's command so that you can follow your own teachings? [4]God said, 'Honor your father and your mother,'[n] and 'Anyone who says cruel things to his father or mother must be put to death.'[n] [5]But you say a person can tell his father or mother, 'I have something I could use to help you, but I have given it to God already.' [6]You teach that person not to honor his father or his mother. You rejected what God said for the sake of your own rules. [7]You are hypocrites![d] Isaiah was right when he said about you:

[8]'These people show honor to me with words,
    but their hearts are far from me.
[9]Their worship of me is worthless.
    The things they teach are nothing but
        human rules.' "   *Isaiah 29:13*

[10]After Jesus called the crowd to him, he said, "Listen and understand what I am saying. [11]It is not what people put into their mouths that makes them unclean.[d] It is what comes out of their mouths that makes them unclean."

[12]Then his followers came to him and asked, "Do you know that the Pharisees are angry because of what you said?"

'Honor ... mother.' Quotation from Exodus 20:12; Deuteronomy 5:16.
'Anyone ... death.' Quotation from Exodus 21:17.

13Jesus answered, "Every plant that my Father in heaven has not planted himself will be pulled up by the roots. 14Stay away from the Pharisees; they are blind leaders. And if a blind person leads a blind person, both will fall into a ditch."

15Peter said, "Explain the example to us."

16Jesus said, "Do you still not understand? 17Surely you know that all the food that enters the mouth goes into the stomach and then goes out of the body. 18But what people say with their mouths comes from the way they think; these are the things that make people unclean. 19Out of the mind come evil thoughts, murder, adultery,*d* sexual sins, stealing, lying, and speaking evil of others. 20These things make people unclean; eating with unwashed hands does not make them unclean."

Jesus Helps a Non-Jewish Woman

21Jesus left that place and went to the area of Tyre and Sidon. 22A Canaanite woman from that area came to Jesus and cried out, "Lord, Son of David,*d* have mercy on me! My daughter has a demon,*d* and she is suffering very much."

23But Jesus did not answer the woman. So his followers came to Jesus and begged him, "Tell the woman to go away. She is following us and shouting."

24Jesus answered, "God sent me only to the lost sheep, the people of Israel."

25Then the woman came to Jesus again and bowed before him and said, "Lord, help me!"

26Jesus answered, "It is not right to take the children's bread and give it to the dogs."

FEAR

The Handicap

Curt Ryan was "cool." Nothing seemed to unnerve him. That's why the youth group was surprised when he strongly objected to the idea of a weekend service retreat at a home for mentally and physically disabled people.

"Why don't you like the idea?" someone asked.

"It's stupid, that's all!" Curt said.

"Are you scared, or what?" someone else asked.

"Yeah, right," Curt responded sarcastically.

The group decided to go ahead, and planned the retreat. Curt grudgingly went along, and kept up his "cool" veneer. But inside, Curt was afraid of the people at the home. He coped with his fear by avoiding any contact with residents.

But he couldn't avoid the dance. Curt walked in late and leaned against a wall in a dark corner. Sally, one of the residents, saw him and rushed up in her wheelchair. She tugged at his arm. "Dance with me," she pleaded.

He pretended he had not heard her.

"Please dance with me," she persisted. "Please?"

Reluctantly, Curt agreed. Although he felt awkward at first, Curt's fears soon faded. He discovered Sally was fun. She had a sharp wit. Sally actually made Curt feel comfortable.

"I was scared," he admitted later. "I didn't know what to expect. Then I saw the love and care these people give. They are just like me. I am the one who was handicapped."

Like Curt's fear of the residents, Peter, one of Jesus' disciples, often suffered from fear. Read how he was afraid to walk on water in **Matthew 14:22–33**.

■ How are Curt's and Peter's reactions to fear similar?

■ Would you have stayed in the boat or gotten out to walk on the water? Why?

                    C O N S I D E R . . .

■ dividing a piece of paper equally. On the left side list fears. On the right side list ways to overcome fears. Share it with a friend. Pray for one another.

■ taking a step this week in overcoming one of your fears. For example, if you're shy, go up to someone at school or church and introduce yourself.

             F O R   M O R E ,   S E E . . .

■ Psalm 27 (p. 497)   ■ 1 Corinthians 2:1–5 (p. 1168)

■ Mark 4:35–41 (p. 972)

²⁷The woman said, "Yes, Lord, but even the dogs eat the crumbs that fall from their masters' table."

²⁸Then Jesus answered, "Woman, you have great faith! I will do what you asked." And at that moment the woman's daughter was healed.

Jesus Heals Many People

²⁹After leaving there, Jesus went along the shore of Lake Galilee. He went up on a hill and sat there.

³⁰Great crowds came to Jesus, bringing with them the lame, the blind, the crippled, those who could not speak, and many others. They put them at Jesus' feet, and he healed them. ³¹The crowd was amazed when they saw that people who could not speak before were now able to speak. The crippled were made strong. The lame could walk, and the blind could see. And they praised the God of Israel for this.

More than Four Thousand Fed

³²Jesus called his followers to him and said, "I feel sorry for these people, because they have already been with me three days, and they have nothing to eat. I don't want to send them away hungry. They might faint while going home."

³³His followers asked him, "How can we get enough bread to feed all these people? We are far away from any town."

³⁴Jesus asked, "How many loaves of bread do you have?"

They answered, "Seven, and a few small fish."

³⁵Jesus told the people to sit on the ground. ³⁶He took the seven loaves of bread and the fish and gave thanks to God. Then he divided the food and gave it to his followers, and they gave it to the people. ³⁷All the people ate and were satisfied. Then his followers filled seven baskets with the leftover pieces of food. ³⁸There were about four thousand men there who ate, besides women and children. ³⁹After sending the people home, Jesus got into the boat and went to the area of Magadan.

The Leaders Ask for a Miracle

16 The Pharisees*d* and Sadducees*d* came to Jesus, wanting to trick him. So they asked him to show them a miracle*d* from God.

²Jesus answered, "At sunset you say we will

PERSISTENCE

Go for the Gold

In 1972 Mark Spitz was an Olympic hero. He competed in seven swimming events, won seven gold medals, and set seven world records. Spitz remains a legend.

Almost twenty years later, Spitz is attempting a comeback. He wants to compete again in the Olympics, hoping to beat his time in the 100-meter butterfly. That time would have placed him eighth in the 1988 Olympics.

It takes persistence to prepare for competition. Spitz admits the closest he's been to water since his 1972 accomplishments is in the shower or his son's wading pool.

Why do it? "I just want to see if I can," Spitz says. "God gifted me with a certain talent and ability. You've got to get hungry if you want to prove something. I'm hungry to prove myself."

His coach believes in Spitz. "If anyone can do it, Mark can," he says. "He's a winner, a master competitor."

In a way similar to Spitz's dedication to his swimming dream, a woman pursued Jesus to heal her daughter. Read **Matthew 15:21–28** to see how she showed great persistence and faith.

■ How is Spitz's persistence similar to the mother's in the passage?
■ When have you been persistent like the mother? What happened?

C O N S I D E R . . .
■ looking for examples of persistent people in newspapers or on television. What qualities do they possess? Write five of those qualities on a card. Tape it to your mirror as a reminder.
■ setting a realistic goal for a project or task you've been putting off. Share it with a friend and ask him or her to help you reach your goal.

F O R   M O R E ,   S E E . . .
■ Ruth 1:1–18 (p. 239)
■ Mark 5:25–34 (p. 972)
■ Ephesians 6:10–20 (p. 1226)

have good weather, because the sky is red. ³And in the morning you say that it will be a rainy day, because the sky is dark and red. You see these signs in the sky and know what they mean. In the same way, you see the things that I am doing now, but you don't know their meaning. ⁴Evil and sinful people ask for a miracle as a sign, but they will not be given any sign, except the sign of Jonah." ⁿ Then Jesus left them and went away.

Guard Against Wrong Teachings

⁵Jesus' followers went across the lake, but they had forgotten to bring bread. ⁶Jesus said to them, "Be careful! Beware of the yeast of the Pharisees*d* and the Sadducees."*d*

⁷His followers discussed the meaning of this, saying, "He said this because we forgot to bring bread."

⁸Knowing what they were talking about, Jesus asked them, "Why are you talking about not having bread? Your faith is small. ⁹Do you still not understand? Remember the five loaves of bread that fed the five thousand? And remember that you filled many baskets with the leftovers? ¹⁰Or the seven loaves of bread that fed the four thousand and the many baskets you filled then also? ¹¹I was not talking to you about bread. Why don't you understand that? I am telling you to beware of the yeast of the Pharisees and the Sadducees." ¹²Then the followers understood that Jesus was not telling them to beware of the yeast used in bread but to beware of the teaching of the Pharisees and the Sadducees.

Peter Says Jesus Is the Christ

¹³When Jesus came to the area of Caesarea Philippi, he asked his followers, "Who do people say the Son of Man*d* is?"

¹⁴They answered, "Some say you are John the Baptist.*d* Others say you are Elijah, and still others say you are Jeremiah or one of the prophets."*d*

¹⁵Then Jesus asked them, "And who do you say I am?"

¹⁶Simon Peter answered, "You are the Christ,*d* the Son of the living God."

¹⁷Jesus answered, "You are blessed, Simon son of Jonah, because no person taught you that. My Father in heaven showed you who I am. ¹⁸So I tell you, you are Peter. ⁿ On this rock I will build my church, and the power of death will not be able to defeat it. ¹⁹I will give you the keys of the kingdom of heaven; the things you don't allow on earth will be the things that God does not allow, and the things you allow on earth will be the things that God allows." ²⁰Then Jesus warned his followers not to tell anyone he was the Christ.

Jesus Says that He Must Die

²¹From that time on Jesus began telling his followers that he must go to Jerusalem, where the older Jewish leaders, the leading priests, and the teachers of the law would make him suffer many things. He told them he must be killed and then be raised from the dead on the third day.

²²Peter took Jesus aside and told him not to talk like that. He said, "God save you from those things, Lord! Those things will never happen to you!"

²³Then Jesus said to Peter, "Go away from me, Satan! ⁿ You are not helping me! You don't care about the things of God, but only about the things people think are important."

²⁴Then Jesus said to his followers, "If people want to follow me, they must give up the things they want. They must be willing even to give up their lives to follow me. ²⁵Those who want to save their lives will give up true life, and those who give up their lives for me will have true life. ²⁶It is worth nothing for them to have the whole world if they lose their souls. They could never pay enough to buy back their souls. ²⁷The Son of Man*d* will come again with his Father's glory and with his angels. At that time, he will reward them for what they have done. ²⁸I tell you the truth, some people standing here will see the Son of Man coming with his kingdom before they die."

Jesus Talks with Moses and Elijah

17 Six days later, Jesus took Peter, James, and John, the brother of James, up on a high mountain by themselves. ²While they watched, Jesus' appearance was changed; his face became bright like the sun, and his clothes became white as light. ³Then Moses and Elijah ⁿ appeared to them, talking with Jesus.

⁴Peter said to Jesus, "Lord, it is good that we

---

sign of Jonah   Jonah's three days in the fish are like Jesus' three days in the tomb. The story about Jonah is in the book of Jonah.
Peter   The Greek name "Peter," like the Aramaic name "Cephas," means "rock."
Satan   Name for the devil, meaning "the enemy." Jesus means that Peter was talking like Satan.
Moses and Elijah   Two of the most important Jewish leaders in the past. Moses had given them the law, and Elijah was an important prophet.

are here. If you want, I will put up three tents here — one for you, one for Moses, and one for Elijah."

SIDELIGHT: When Peter suggested camping out in Matthew 17:4, he may have been thinking about the annual Feast of Shelters. During this harvest festival, Jews from everywhere came to Jerusalem and built shelters or booths in the streets and town square—anywhere with a little space. It made for bad traffic jams, but was cheaper than staying in a hotel.

⁵While Peter was talking, a bright cloud covered them. A voice came from the cloud and said, "This is my Son, whom I love, and I am very pleased with him. Listen to him!"

⁶When his followers heard the voice, they were so frightened they fell to the ground. ⁷But Jesus went to them and touched them and said, "Stand up. Don't be afraid." ⁸When they looked up, they saw Jesus was now alone.

⁹As they were coming down the mountain, Jesus commanded them not to tell anyone about what they had seen until the Son of Man*ᵈ* had risen from the dead.

¹⁰Then his followers asked him, "Why do the teachers of the law say that Elijah must come first?"

¹¹Jesus answered, "They are right to say that Elijah is coming and that he will make everything the way it should be. ¹²But I tell you that Elijah has already come, and they did not recognize him. They did to him whatever they wanted to do. It will be the same with the Son of Man; those same people will make the Son of Man suffer." ¹³Then the followers understood that Jesus was talking about John the Baptist.*ᵈ*

Jesus Heals a Sick Boy

¹⁴When Jesus and his followers came back to the crowd, a man came to Jesus and bowed before

FAITH

T-e-a-c-h-e-r

A fever left Helen Keller blind and deaf at birth. She was imprisoned in a dark, silent world.

In 1887, when Helen was seven, Anne Sullivan, herself partially blind, became Helen's teacher. Anne had great vision and hope. She believed Helen held untapped and unseen abilities.

Months passed with very little progress, but Anne still believed.

Then, finally, Anne witnessed the results of faith. Helen was playing at the water pump. Anne finger-spelled "w-a-t-e-r" into her free hand. Anne wrote in her journal, "The word coming so close upon the sensation of cold water rushing over her hand seemed to startle her. A new light came into her face. She understood! Then turning around she asked my name. I spelled "T-e-a-c-h-e-r."

Thanks to Anne's faith, Helen's dark, lonely life opened wide to the light of communication and learning. Helen graduated with honors from Radcliffe College, and went on to a distinguished career as an educator, speaker and author. Helen and "Teacher" were lifelong companions.

"Teacher's" faith brought Helen out of darkness and into light. In **Matthew 16:13–20**, read how Jesus had faith in Peter, even when Peter wasn't sure of his own faith.

■ How was Anne's and Helen's friendship similar to Jesus' and Peter's?
■ Anne's faith enabled her to teach Helen. Peter's faith helped him become a church leader. What does your faith help you do?

C O N S I D E R . . .

■ helping young children grow in their faith by volunteering to help one Sunday in the church nursery, Sunday school or vacation church school.
■ writing a Haiku poem that expresses faith. A Haiku poem has three lines. The first and third lines each have seven syllables. The middle line has five.

F O R   M O R E ,   S E E . . .

■ Nehemiah 9:6–8 (p. 435)
■ Mark 8:27–38 (p. 979)
■ Hebrews 11 (p. 1287)

him. [15]The man said, "Lord, have mercy on my son. He has epilepsy[n] and is suffering very much, because he often falls into the fire or into the water. [16]I brought him to your followers, but they could not cure him."

[17]Jesus answered, "You people have no faith, and your lives are all wrong. How long must I put up with you? How long must I continue to be patient with you? Bring the boy here." [18]Jesus commanded the demon[d] inside the boy. Then the demon came out, and the boy was healed from that time on.

[19]The followers came to Jesus when he was alone and asked, "Why couldn't we force the demon out?"

[20]Jesus answered, "Because your faith is too small. I tell you the truth, if your faith is as big as a mustard seed, you can say to this mountain, 'Move from here to there,' and it will move. All things will be possible for you." [21] [n]

Jesus Talks About His Death

[22]While Jesus' followers were gathering in Galilee, he said to them, "The Son of Man[d] will be handed over to people, [23]and they will kill him. But on the third day he will be raised from the dead." And the followers were filled with sadness.

Jesus Talks About Paying Taxes

[24]When Jesus and his followers came to Capernaum, the men who collected the Temple[d] tax came to Peter. They asked, "Does your teacher pay the Temple tax?"

[25]Peter answered, "Yes, Jesus pays the tax."

Peter went into the house, but before he could speak, Jesus said to him, "What do you think? The kings of the earth collect different kinds of taxes. But who pays the taxes — the king's children or others?"

[26]Peter answered, "Other people pay the taxes."

Jesus said to Peter, "Then the children of the king don't have to pay taxes. [27]But we don't want to upset these tax collectors. So go to the lake and fish. After you catch the first fish, open its mouth and you will find a coin. Take that coin and give it to the tax collectors for you and me."

Who Is the Greatest?

18 At that time the followers came to Jesus and asked, "Who is greatest in the kingdom of heaven?"

[2]Jesus called a little child to him and stood the child before his followers. [3]Then he said, "I tell you the truth, you must change and become like little children. Otherwise, you will never enter the kingdom of heaven. [4]The greatest person in the kingdom of heaven is the one who makes himself humble like this child.

[5]"Whoever accepts a child in my name accepts me. [6]If one of these little children believes in me, and someone causes that child to sin, it would be better for that person to have a large stone tied around the neck and be drowned in the sea. [7]How terrible for the people of the world because of the things that cause them to sin. Such things will happen, but how terrible for the one who causes them to happen! [8]If your hand or your foot causes you to sin, cut it off and throw it away. It is better for you to lose part of your body and live forever than to have two hands and two feet and be thrown into the fire that burns forever. [9]If your eye causes you to sin, take it out and throw it away. It is better for you to have only one eye and live forever than to have two eyes and be thrown into the fire of hell.

A Lost Sheep

[10]"Be careful. Don't think these little children are worth nothing. I tell you that they have angels in heaven who are always with my Father in heaven. [11] [n]

[12]"If a man has a hundred sheep but one of the sheep gets lost, he will leave the other ninety-nine on the hill and go to look for the lost sheep. [13]I tell you the truth, he is happier about that one sheep than about the ninety-nine that were never lost. [14]In the same way, your Father in heaven does not want any of these little children to be lost.

When a Person Sins Against You

[15]"If your fellow believer sins against you, go and tell him in private what he did wrong. If he listens to you, you have helped that person to be your brother or sister again. [16]But if he refuses to listen, go to him again and take one or two other people with you. 'Every case may be proved by two or three witnesses.' [n] [17]If he refuses to listen to them, tell the church. If he refuses to listen to the church, then treat him like a person who does not believe in God or like a tax collector.

[18]"I tell you the truth, the things you don't allow on earth will be the things God does not allow. And the things you allow on earth will be the things that God allows.

[19]"Also, I tell you that if two of you on earth

---

epilepsy A disease that causes a person sometimes to lose control of his body and maybe faint, shake strongly, or not be able to move.

Verse 21 Some Greek copies add verse 21: "That kind of spirit comes out only if you use prayer and give up eating."

Verse 11 Some Greek copies add verse 11: "The Son of Man came to save lost people."

'Every ... witnesses.' Quotation from Deuteronomy 19:15.

agree about something and pray for it, it will be done for you by my Father in heaven. ²⁰This is true because if two or three people come together in my name, I am there with them."

An Unforgiving Servant

²¹Then Peter came to Jesus and asked, "Lord, when my fellow believer sins against me, how many times must I forgive him? Should I forgive him as many as seven times?"

²²Jesus answered, "I tell you, you must forgive him more than seven times. You must forgive him even if he does wrong to you seventy-seven times.

²³"The kingdom of heaven is like a king who decided to collect the money his servants owed him. ²⁴When the king began to collect his money, a servant who owed him several million dollars was brought to him. ²⁵But the servant did not

have enough money to pay his master, the king. So the master ordered that everything the servant owned should be sold, even the servant's wife and children. Then the money would be used to pay the king what the servant owed.

²⁶"But the servant fell on his knees and begged, 'Be patient with me, and I will pay you everything I owe.' ²⁷The master felt sorry for his servant and told him he did not have to pay it back. Then he let the servant go free.

²⁸"Later, that same servant found another servant who owed him a few dollars. The servant grabbed him around the neck and said, 'Pay me the money you owe me!'

²⁹"The other servant fell on his knees and begged him, 'Be patient with me, and I will pay you everything I owe.'

³⁰"But the first servant refused to be patient. He

FRIENDS

I Hate You!

"What's going on?" Dad asked Suzanne, his fourteen-year-old daughter. "I was outside the house and heard your screaming."

"I hate her!" Suzanne yelled. "How could Vicki do this to me?" Suzanne Hinton and Vicki Linder had grown up together. As kids they had played with Barbie dolls and built tree forts. They had walked to school together and shared lunches. In middle school they were still friends.

Then Jean Lawlor moved to town. Jean caused trouble. To Suzanne it seemed Jean enjoyed setting Suzanne and Vicki against each other.

Dad listened as Suzanne alternated between crying and telling him what was going on. Jean had told Vicki that Suzanne was interested in Todd, Vicki's boyfriend. Jean later told Vicki that Suzanne had asked Todd out on a date, which wasn't true. Suzanne and Vicki had just argued on the phone, screaming at each other before Vicki slammed down the receiver.

"Can you believe it?" Suzanne wailed. "Vicki believed Jean—not me! I hate Jean! And Vicki! They betrayed me!"

"Sounds like you have a major conflict," Dad said.

"It's their fault!" Suzanne cried.

"The issue is: What are you going to do?" Dad said.

Sooner or later, conflict will erupt in most friendships. Jesus taught his followers several guidelines for dealing with conflict. Read **Matthew 18:15–20** and see how Suzanne, Vicki, and Jean might find ways to settle their differences.

■ If Suzanne follows Jesus' teachings, what can she do to resolve her conflict with Vicki and Jean?

■ How might Jesus' prescription for dealing with conflict help you in your friendships?

C O N S I D E R . . .

■ making a list of friends with whom you have conflicts. Pray daily for strength to help you deal with these conflicts.

■ writing about a friendship that's bothering you. Using Jesus' plan as a model, write your own plan for improving the friendship. What will you do and say?

F O R   M O R E ,   S E E . . .

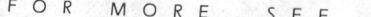

■ Genesis 4:1–15 (p. 7)
■ Luke 6:27–36 (p. 1013)

■ Galatians 2:11–14 (p. 1207)

threw the other servant into prison until he could pay everything he owed. ³¹When the other servants saw what had happened, they were very sorry. So they went and told their master all that had happened.

³²"Then the master called his servant in and said, 'You evil servant! Because you begged me to forget what you owed, I told you that you did not have to pay anything. ³³You should have showed mercy to that other servant, just as I showed mercy to you.' ³⁴The master was very angry and put the servant in prison to be punished until he could pay everything he owed.

³⁵"This king did what my heavenly Father will do to you if you do not forgive your brother or sister from your heart."

Jesus Teaches About Divorce

19 After Jesus said all these things, he left Galilee and went into the area of Judea on the other side of the Jordan River. ²Large crowds followed him, and he healed them there.

³Some Pharisees[d] came to Jesus and tried to trick him. They asked, "Is it right for a man to divorce his wife for any reason he chooses?"

⁴Jesus answered, "Surely you have read in the Scriptures:[d] When God made the world, 'he made them male and female.'[n] ⁵And God said, 'So a man will leave his father and mother and be united with his wife, and the two will become one body.'[n] ⁶So there are not two, but one. God has joined the two together, so no one should separate them."

⁷The Pharisees asked, "Why then did Moses give a command for a man to divorce his wife by giving her divorce papers?"

⁸Jesus answered, "Moses allowed you to divorce your wives because you refused to accept God's teaching, but divorce was not allowed in the beginning. ⁹I tell you that anyone who di-

'he made . . . female.' Quotation from Genesis 1:27 or 5:2.
'So . . . body.' Quotation from Genesis 2:24.

FORGIVENESS

So Sorry

Kerrie Trent was in trouble, and she knew it. She hadn't even cracked the textbook, and the history exam would determine her grade in the class.

She sat behind Matt Kimmerly, who was a smart student. He would help, she thought. "Psst, Matt," she whispered, poking him with her pencil. "Question five. Gimme a clue."

Matt shrugged.

Kerrie poked him again with the pencil. Matt turned. "Cut it out," he hissed.

"Matt, come up here, and bring your exam," interrupted Ms. Miller, the history teacher. As Matt walked to Ms. Miller's desk, Kerrie pretended to work on her exam.

"I won't tolerate cheating," Ms. Miller said quietly to Matt. She tossed the exam into the wastebasket. Matt tried to explain what had happened, but she didn't believe him. "Take your seat, and be quiet for the rest of the period," she snapped.

Kerrie saw Matt's face as he walked back toward his seat. His eyes showed his deep anger and hurt. "Why?" he whispered. Kerrie looked away.

As school let out, Kerrie saw Matt in the hall and tried to tell him how sorry she was. But Matt ignored her. At midnight, she still couldn't get Matt's hurt out of her mind. She knew what to do. "Tomorrow," she thought, "I'll tell Ms. Miller what really happened, but will Matt ever forgive me?"

Both Kerrie and Matt could learn from the story Jesus told in **Matthew 18:21–35**.

■ How is Kerrie's and Matt's struggle similar to the one in Jesus' story?
■ Which character in Jesus' parable do you identify with most often? Why?

C O N S I D E R . . .

■ listing things you find difficult to forgive. Put them in order, from least to most difficult to forgive. What factors make forgiveness difficult?
■ thinking of two people: one who has hurt you most, and one you have hurt the most. Pray for strength, and then do one thing to help bring forgiveness to both people.

F O R   M O R E ,   S E E . . .

■ Jonah 3 (p. 858)
■ Micah 7:18–20 (p. 868)
■ Luke 17:1–4 (p. 1039)

vorces his wife and marries another woman is guilty of adultery.[d] The only reason for a man to divorce his wife is if his wife has sexual relations with another man."

[10]The followers said to him, "If that is the only reason a man can divorce his wife, it is better not to marry."

[11]Jesus answered, "Not everyone can accept this teaching, but God has made some able to accept it. [12]There are different reasons why some men cannot marry. Some men were born without the ability to become fathers. Others were made that way later in life by other people. And some men have given up marriage because of the kingdom of heaven. But the person who can marry should accept this teaching about marriage."[n]

> ### ☀ SIDELIGHT: Divorce has always been a controversial subject—even in Jesus' day. While some religious leaders said someone could only get a divorce because of unfaithfulness, others argued that a husband could divorce a wife for burning supper, wearing the wrong thing in public, or even talking to another man. Jesus entered the debate in Matthew 19:1–12.

Jesus Welcomes Children

[13]Then the people brought their little children to Jesus so he could put his hands on them[n] and pray for them. His followers told them to stop, [14]but Jesus said, "Let the little children come to me. Don't stop them, because the kingdom of heaven belongs to people who are like these children." [15]After Jesus put his hands on the children, he left there.

A Rich Young Man's Question

[16]A man came to Jesus and asked, "Teacher, what good thing must I do to have life forever?"

[17]Jesus answered, "Why do you ask me about what is good? Only God is good. But if you want to have life forever, obey the commands."

[18]The man asked, "Which commands?"

Jesus answered, " 'You must not murder anyone; you must not be guilty of adultery;[d] you must not steal; you must not tell lies about your neighbor; [19]honor your father and mother;[n] and love your neighbor as you love yourself.' "[n]

[20]The young man said, "I have obeyed all these things. What else do I need to do?"

[21]Jesus answered, "If you want to be perfect, then go and sell your possessions and give the money to the poor. If you do this, you will have treasure in heaven. Then come and follow me."

[22]But when the young man heard this, he left sorrowfully, because he was rich.

[23]Then Jesus said to his followers, "I tell you the truth, it will be hard for a rich person to enter the kingdom of heaven. [24]Yes, I tell you that it is easier for a camel to go through the eye of a needle than for a rich person to enter the kingdom of God."

[25]When Jesus' followers heard this, they were very surprised and asked, "Then who can be saved?"

[26]Jesus looked at them and said, "This is something people cannot do, but God can do all things."

[27]Peter said to Jesus, "Look, we have left everything and followed you. So what will we have?"

[28]Jesus said to them, "I tell you the truth, when the age to come has arrived, the Son of Man[d] will sit on his great throne. All of you who followed me will also sit on twelve thrones, judging the twelve tribes[d] of Israel. [29]And all those who have left houses, brothers, sisters, father, mother, children, or farms to follow me will get much more than they left, and they will have life forever. [30]Many who have the highest place now will have the lowest place in the future. And many who have the lowest place now will have the highest place in the future.

A Story About Workers

20 "The kingdom of heaven is like a person who owned some land. One morning, he went out very early to hire some people to work in his vineyard. [2]The man agreed to pay the workers one coin[n] for working that day. Then he sent them into the vineyard to work. [3]About nine o'clock the man went to the marketplace and saw some other people standing there, doing nothing. [4]So he said to them, 'If you go and work in my vineyard, I will pay you what your work is worth.' [5]So they went to work in the vineyard. The man went out again about twelve o'clock and three o'clock and did the same thing. [6]About five o'clock the man went to the marketplace again and saw others standing there. He asked them, 'Why did you stand here all day doing nothing?' [7]They answered, 'No one gave us a job.' The man said to them, 'Then you can go and work in my vineyard.'

[8]"At the end of the day, the owner of the vine-

But . . . marriage.   This may also mean, "The person who can accept this teaching about not marrying should accept it."
put his hands on them   Showing that Jesus gave special blessings to these children.
'You . . . mother.'   Quotation from Exodus 20:12-16; Deuteronomy 5:16-20.
'love . . . yourself.'   Quotation from Leviticus 19:18.
coin   A Roman denarius. One coin was the average pay for one day's work.

yard said to the boss of all the workers, 'Call the workers and pay them. Start with the last people I hired and end with those I hired first.'

⁹"When the workers who were hired at five o'clock came to get their pay, each received one coin. ¹⁰When the workers who were hired first came to get their pay, they thought they would be paid more than the others. But each one of them also received one coin. ¹¹When they got their coin, they complained to the man who owned the land. ¹²They said, 'Those people were hired last and worked only one hour. But you paid them the same as you paid us who worked hard all day in the hot sun.' ¹³But the man who owned the vine-

yard said to one of those workers, 'Friend, I am being fair to you. You agreed to work for one coin. ⁴So take your pay and go. I want to give the man who was hired last the same pay that I gave you. ⁵I can do what I want with my own money. Are you jealous because I am good to those people?'

¹⁶"So those who have the last place now will have the first place in the future, and those who have the first place now will have the last place in the future."

Jesus Talks About His Own Death

¹⁷While Jesus was going to Jerusalem, he took his twelve followers aside privately and said to

---

It's Not Fair!

For months, Laura Steiner, seventeen, prepared her chemistry project for the area science fair competition. In previous years Laura had won several ribbons, but she had never won a chance to go to state. As a senior, this was her last chance.

Laura's fourteen-year-old brother, Kenneth, a freshman, also entered the science fair. Scientific concepts came to him easier than they did to Laura. Kenneth put together his project on the solar system in just a few days.

On the opening day of the fair, Laura, Kenneth, and their parents arrived in the family car. Laura rushed to see her project that simulated a nuclear reaction, while her brother and parents went to see Kenneth's entry. Laura couldn't wait to see the prize she expected from the judges.

But there was no ribbon. "Have the judges been here?" she cried. Yes, they have, she was told. "Then there's been some mistake!"

Kenneth ran up to Laura. "I won first prize!" yelled Kenneth. "I'm going to state!"

"That's unfair!" wailed Laura, who started sobbing. "Your project isn't even unique."

When she had settled down a bit, her parents tried to comfort her, but weren't very successful. "It just isn't fair," Laura muttered time and again. "I worked so hard, but Kenneth just threw his together at the last minute."

Then Mom reminded her of a time when Laura and Kenneth were younger. "Remember when you beat Kenneth in the skiing competition, after he had taught you to ski?" Mom asked. "He didn't think that was fair, but you didn't mind winning."

Laura was still disappointed, but started feeling happy for her brother. "Congratulations, and good luck at state," she finally told him.

No doubt you have been told, "Life isn't fair." Laura obviously found this out. God's view of justice and fairness puzzled many of the people in Jesus' time. Many assumed God would be better to them than to others. Read Jesus' response to their assumption in **Matthew 20:1–16**.

■ How are Laura's complaints similar to those of the vineyard workers in Jesus' parable?

■ If you were one of the first workers hired, how would you have felt? What would your reaction have been if you were among the last hired?

C O N S I D E R . . .

■ looking for examples of "fairness" and "justice" in the news. Talk with your friends about whether these examples fit their views.

■ asking a lawyer or judge to define justice. Ask your pastor to define justice. Then come up with your own definition.

F O R   M O R E   S E E . . .

■ Job 8:3–6 (p. 457)
■ Luke 14:12–24 (p. 1032)

■ 2 Thessalonians 1:3–12 (p. 1252)

them, [18]"Look, we are going to Jerusalem. The Son of Man[d] will be turned over to the leading priests and the teachers of the law, and they will say that he must die. [19]They will give the Son of Man to the non-Jewish people to laugh at him and beat him with whips and crucify him. But on the third day, he will be raised to life again."

A Mother Asks Jesus a Favor

[20]Then the wife of Zebedee came to Jesus with her sons. She bowed before him and asked him to do something for her.

[21]Jesus asked, "What do you want?"

She said, "Promise that one of my sons will sit at your right side and the other will sit at your left side in your kingdom."

[22]But Jesus said, "You don't understand what you are asking. Can you drink the cup that I am about to drink?"[n]

The sons answered, "Yes, we can."

[23]Jesus said to them, "You will drink from my cup. But I cannot choose who will sit at my right or my left; those places belong to those for whom my Father has prepared them."

[24]When the other ten followers heard this, they were angry with the two brothers.

SIDELIGHT: James and John, the sons of Zebedee, were nicknamed "the sons of thunder" (Matthew 20:20–24; see Mark 3:17, p. 969). The nicknames may have come from their booming voices or their short tempers. Either way, the name would look great on a wrestling team roster.

---

[25]Jesus called all the followers together and said, "You know that the rulers of the non-Jewish people love to show their power over the people. And their important leaders love to use all their authority. [26]But it should not be that way among you. Whoever wants to become great among you must serve the rest of you like a servant. [27]Whoever wants to become first among you must serve the rest of you like a slave. [28]In the same way, the Son of Man[d] did not come to be served. He came to serve others and to give his life as a ransom for many people."

Jesus Heals Two Blind Men

[29]When Jesus and his followers were leaving Jericho, a great many people followed him. [30]Two blind men sitting by the road heard that Jesus was

going by, so they shouted, "Lord, Son of David,[d] have mercy on us!"

[31]The people warned the blind men to be quiet, but they shouted even more, "Lord, Son of David, have mercy on us!"

[32]Jesus stopped and said to the blind men, "What do you want me to do for you?"

[33]They answered, "Lord, we want to see."

[34]Jesus felt sorry for the blind men and touched their eyes, and at once they could see. Then they followed Jesus.

Jesus Enters Jerusalem as a King

21 As Jesus and his followers were coming closer to Jerusalem, they stopped at Bethphage at the hill called the Mount of Olives.[d] From there Jesus sent two of his followers [2]and said to them, "Go to the town you can see there. When you enter it, you will quickly find a donkey tied there with its colt. Untie them and bring them to me. [3]If anyone asks you why you are taking the donkeys, say that the Master needs them, and he will send them at once."

[4]This was to bring about what the prophet[d] had said:

[5]"Tell the people of Jerusalem,
  'Your king is coming to you.
He is gentle and riding on a donkey,
  on the colt of a donkey.' "

Isaiah 62:11; Zechariah 9:9

[6]The followers went and did what Jesus told them to do. [7]They brought the donkey and the colt to Jesus and laid their coats on them, and Jesus sat on them. [8]Many people spread their coats on the road. Others cut branches from the trees and spread them on the road. [9]The people were walking ahead of Jesus and behind him, shouting,

"Praise[n] to the Son of David![d]
God bless the One who comes in the name
  of the Lord!   *Psalm 118:26*
Praise to God in heaven!"

[10]When Jesus entered Jerusalem, all the city was filled with excitement. The people asked, "Who is this man?"

[11]The crowd said, "This man is Jesus, the prophet from the town of Nazareth in Galilee."

Jesus Goes to the Temple

[12]Jesus went into the Temple[d] and threw out all the people who were buying and selling there. *He turned over the tables of those who were exchanging different kinds of money, and he upset the benches of those who were selling doves.

---

drink ... drink Jesus used the idea of drinking from a cup to ask if they could accept the same terrible things that would happen to him.

Praise Literally, "Hosanna," a Hebrew word used at first in praying to God for help. At this time it was probably a shout of joy used in praising God or his Messiah.

[13]Jesus said to all the people there, "It is written in the Scriptures,[d] 'My Temple will be called a house for prayer.'[n] But you are changing it into a 'hideout for robbers.' "[n]

[14]The blind and crippled people came to Jesus in the Temple, and he healed them. [15]The leading priests and the teachers of the law saw that Jesus was doing wonderful things and that the children were praising him in the Temple, saying, "Praise[n] to the Son of David."[d] All these things made the priests and the teachers of the law very angry.

[16]They asked Jesus, "Do you hear the things these children are saying?"

Jesus answered, "Yes. Haven't you read in the Scriptures, 'You have taught children and babies to sing praises'?"[n]

[17]Then Jesus left and went out of the city to Bethany, where he spent the night.

The Power of Faith

[18]Early the next morning, as Jesus was going back to the city, he became hungry. [19]Seeing a fig tree beside the road, Jesus went to it, but there were no figs on the tree, only leaves. So Jesus said to the tree, "You will never again have fruit." The tree immediately dried up.

[20]When his followers saw this, they were amazed. They asked, "How did the fig tree dry up so quickly?"

[21]Jesus answered, "I tell you the truth, if you have faith and do not doubt, you will be able to do what I did to this tree and even more. You will be able to say to this mountain, 'Go, fall into the sea.' And if you have faith, it will happen. [22]If you believe, you will get anything you ask for in prayer."

Leaders Doubt Jesus' Authority

[23]Jesus went to the Temple,[d] and while he was teaching there, the leading priests and the older leaders of the people came to him. They said, "What authority do you have to do these things? Who gave you this authority?"

[24]Jesus answered, "I also will ask you a question. If you answer me, then I will tell you what authority I have to do these things. [25]Tell me: When John baptized people, did that come from God or just from other people?"

They argued about Jesus' question, saying, "If we answer, 'John's baptism was from God,' Jesus will say, 'Then why didn't you believe him?' [26]But if we say, 'It was from people,' we are afraid of what the crowd will do because they all believe that John was a prophet."[d]

[27]So they answered Jesus, "We don't know."

Jesus said to them, "Then I won't tell you what authority I have to do these things.

A Story About Two Sons

[28]"Tell me what you think about this: A man had two sons. He went to the first son and said, 'Son, go and work today in my vineyard.' [29]The son answered, 'I will not go.' But later the son changed his mind and went. [30]Then the father went to the other son and said, 'Son, go and work today in my vineyard.' The son answered, 'Yes, sir, I will go and work,' but he did not go. [31]Which of the two sons obeyed his father?"

The priests and leaders answered, "The first son."

Jesus said to them, "I tell you the truth, the tax collectors and the prostitutes[d] will enter the kingdom of God before you do. [32]John came to show you the right way to live. You did not believe him, but the tax collectors and prostitutes believed him. Even after seeing this, you still refused to change your ways and believe him.

A Story About God's Son

[33]"Listen to this story: There was a man who owned a vineyard. He put a wall around it and dug a hole for a winepress[d] and built a tower. Then he leased the land to some farmers and left for a trip. [34]When it was time for the grapes to be picked, he sent his servants to the farmers to get his share of the grapes. [35]But the farmers grabbed the servants, beat one, killed another, and then killed a third servant with stones. [36]So the man sent some other servants to the farmers, even more than he sent the first time. But the farmers did the same thing to the servants that they had done before. [37]So the man decided to send his son to the farmers. He said, 'They will respect my son.' [38]But when the farmers saw the son, they said to each other, 'This son will inherit the vineyard. If we kill him, it will be ours!' [39]Then the farmers grabbed the son, threw him out of the vineyard, and killed him. [40]So what will the owner of the vineyard do to these farmers when he comes?"

[41]The priests and leaders said, "He will surely kill those evil men. Then he will lease the vineyard to some other farmers who will give him his share of the crop at harvest time."

'**My Temple ... prayer.**' Quotation from Isaiah 56:7.
'**hideout for robbers.**' Quotation from Jeremiah 7:11.
Praise Literally, "Hosanna," a Hebrew word used at first in praying to God for help. At this time it was probably a shout of joy used in praising God or his Messiah.
'**You ... praises**' Quotation from the Septuagint (Greek) version. cf Psalm 8:2.

42Jesus said to them, "Surely you have read this in the Scriptures:*d*

'The stone that the builders rejected
became the cornerstone.*d*
The Lord did this,
    and it is wonderful to us.'   *Psalm 118:22-23*

43"So I tell you that the kingdom of God will be taken away from you and given to people who do the things God wants in his kingdom. 44The person who falls on this stone will be broken, and on whomever that stone falls, that person will be crushed." *n*

45When the leading priests and the Pharisees*d* heard these stories, they knew Jesus was talking about them. 46They wanted to arrest him, but they were afraid of the people, because the people believed that Jesus was a prophet.*d*

Verse 44   Some copies do not have verse 44.

A Story About a Wedding Feast

22 Jesus again used stories to teach the people. He said, 2"The kingdom of heaven is like a king who prepared a wedding feast for his son. 3The king invited some people to the feast. When the feast was ready, the king sent his servants to tell the people, but they refused to come.

4"Then the king sent other servants, saying, 'Tell those who have been invited that my feast is ready. I have killed my best bulls and calves for the dinner, and everything is ready. Come to the wedding feast.'

5"But the people refused to listen to the servants and left to do other things. One went to work in his field, and another went to his business. 6Some of the other people grabbed the servants, beat them, and killed them. 7The king was

---

Sunday Christians

It was Saturday night and Jay Nelson was ready to party. On Saturday nights all streets led to the warehouse. After a tough week at school, it was party time!

The warehouse was in a secluded spot at the edge of town. The party was in full swing when Jay arrived. Beer flowed freely. People danced wildly to the full-volume music.

"Hey, Jay," a familiar voice cried.

Jay turned to see Chris Freedman, a new kid at school.

"I didn't know you'd be here," Chris said.

"Oh, yeah," Jay said easily as he hoisted a can of beer. "This is the place for all the cool people."

The next morning Jay's head was pounding. He dragged himself off to Sunday school. The teacher met him at the door. "Jay," she said. "There's someone new I'd like you to meet, Chris Freedman."

Chris's eyes widened. "This is great!" he said. "My folks made me come. But you're here, so this must be the cool place to be, huh?"

"Class," the teacher said. "Today's lesson will focus on telling others about God's love. Jay, would you please lead us in prayer?"

As he prayed, Jay had to come face-to-face with his own hypocrisy. Jesus told stories about living with integrity. Read one in **Matthew 21:28–32**.

■ Which son in Jesus' story is most like Jay? Why?
■ How are you like the son who said he wouldn't work but went anyway?
■ How are you like the son who said he would work but didn't?

CONSIDER . . .

■ looking up "hypocrite" in a dictionary. Jot down the definitions. Read what Jesus says about hypocrisy in Matthew 7:1–5, p. 918, and Matthew 23:1–12, p. 948. Write Jesus' advice under the definitions. Keep the paper as a reminder to guard against hypocrisy in your life.
■ noticing the sets on TV shows you watch this week—how the sets make the show seem "real" when it isn't at all. Then think of one "set" in your life and do one thing today to be more authentic.

FOR MORE, SEE . . .

■ Psalm 51 (p. 511)
■ Matthew 7:1–5 (p. 918)
■ Luke 11:37–44 (p. 1026)

furious and sent his army to kill the murderers and burn their city.

8"After that, the king said to his servants, 'The wedding feast is ready. I invited those people, but they were not worthy to come. 9So go to the street corners and invite everyone you find to come to my feast.' 10So the servants went into the streets and gathered all the people they could find, both good and bad. And the wedding hall was filled with guests.

11"When the king came in to see the guests, he saw a man who was not dressed for a wedding.

12The king said, 'Friend, how were you allowed to come in here? You are not dressed for a wedding.' But the man said nothing. 13So the king told some servants, 'Tie this man's hands and feet. Throw him out into the darkness, where people will cry and grind their teeth with pain.'

14"Yes, many people are invited, but only a few are chosen."

Is It Right to Pay Taxes or Not?

15Then the Pharisees[d] left that place and made plans to trap Jesus in saying something wrong.

What Are You Worth?

"I'm worth $353.21 today," Craig Madison remarked as he modeled the clothes he had purchased during his shopping binge. "These," he said as he removed new sunglasses. "$40."

"This leather jacket—$100. Check out these running shoes—$80." Craig continued to tick off his value in new goods, including sales tax.

A few months later, Craig joined his church's drama group, which traveled all summer across the country. When the group arrived in a town, members would set up a huge circus tent and perform several times. It was hard work, but lots of fun.

The least favorite part for Craig was the afternoon matinee, a play especially for young children. Craig didn't like little kids. They "bugged" him, he said. Until the group performed at an orphanage.

Almost immediately, six-year-old Billy liked Craig. Wherever Craig sat, Billy climbed in his lap. During the performance, Billy watched the play with awe. At one point, Billy yelled, "Hi, Craig!"

After the performance, Billy was back in Craig's lap. "Do you believe in this Jesus guy?" Billy asked.

"Yeah, I think so," Craig said.

"You think he'd love me?" Billy pressed.

"He loves everyone," Craig said.

"No one ever loved me before," Billy said.

Craig didn't know what to say. Suddenly all his possessions didn't seem so important. He handed his sunglasses to Billy. "Are these worth a lot?" Billy asked.

"Just $40," said Craig. "But Billy, you're worth much, much more. That's what Jesus is about."

Sometimes it's easy to forget what's really important. To help keep us on track, Jesus told a parable in **Matthew 22:1–14** about life's priorities. He wanted the people to know that his top priority is to live for God and do his will.

■ How is Craig's initial love of stuff like the attitude of the wedding guests? Why did his priorities change?

■ How are your priorities sometimes like those of the wedding guests?

CONSIDER . . .

■ reviewing your activities of the past week. Which of them reflect your desires for the best use of time? Which ones don't?

■ inviting your parent to list his or her priorities for you while you list your own. Compare the lists and discuss differences and similarities.

FOR MORE, SEE . . .

■ Ecclesiastes 2:1–11 (p. 599)
■ Luke 12:13–21 (p. 1027)

■ 1 Timothy 6:17–19 (p. 1261)

16They sent some of their own followers and some people from the group called Herodians. *n* They said, "Teacher, we know that you are an honest man and that you teach the truth about God's way. You are not afraid of what other people think about you, because you pay no attention to who they are. 17So tell us what you think. Is it right to pay taxes to Caesar*d* or not?"

18But knowing that these leaders were trying to trick him, Jesus said, "You hypocrites!*d* Why are you trying to trap me? 19Show me a coin used for paying the tax." So the men showed him a coin. *n* 20Then Jesus asked, "Whose image and name are on the coin?"

21The men answered, "Caesar's."

Then Jesus said to them, "Give to Caesar the things that are Caesar's, and give to God the things that are God's."

22When the men heard what Jesus said, they were amazed and left him and went away.

Some Sadducees Try to Trick Jesus

23That same day some Sadducees*d* came to Jesus and asked him a question. (Sadducees believed that people would not rise from the dead.) 24They said, "Teacher, Moses said if a married man dies without having children, his brother must marry the widow and have children for him. 25Once there were seven brothers among us. The first one married and died. Since he had no children, his brother married the widow. 26Then the second brother also died. The same thing happened to the third brother and all the other brothers. 27Finally, the woman died. 28Since all seven men had married her, when people rise from the dead, whose wife will she be?"

29Jesus answered, "You don't understand, because you don't know what the Scriptures*d* say, and you don't know about the power of God. 30When people rise from the dead, they will not marry, nor will they be given to someone to marry. They will be like the angels in heaven. 31Surely you have read what God said to you about rising from the dead. 32God said, 'I am the God of Abraham, the God of Isaac, and the God of Jacob.' *n* God is the God of the living, not the dead."

33When the people heard this, they were amazed at Jesus' teaching.

The Most Important Command

34When the Pharisees*d* learned that the Sadducees*d* could not argue with Jesus' answers to them, the Pharisees met together. 35One Pharisee, who was an expert on the law of Moses, asked Jesus this question to test him: 36"Teacher, which command in the law is the most important?"

37Jesus answered, " 'Love the Lord your God with all your heart, all your soul, and all your mind.' *n* 38This is the first and most important command. 39And the second command is like the first: 'Love your neighbor as you love yourself.' *n* 40All the law and the writings of the prophets*d* depend on these two commands."

Jesus Questions the Pharisees

41While the Pharisees*d* were together, Jesus asked them, 42"What do you think about the Christ?*d* Whose son is he?"

They answered, "The Christ is the Son of David."*d*

43Then Jesus said to them, "Then why did David call him 'Lord'? David, speaking by the power of the Holy Spirit,*d* said,

44'The Lord said to my Lord:

Sit by me at my right side,

until I put your enemies under your
    control.'   *Psalm 110:1*

45David calls the Christ 'Lord,' so how can the Christ be his son?"

46None of the Pharisees could answer Jesus' question, and after that day no one was brave enough to ask him any more questions.

Jesus Accuses Some Leaders

23 Then Jesus said to the crowds and to his followers, 2"The teachers of the law and the Pharisees*d* have the authority to tell you what the law of Moses says. 3So you should obey and follow whatever they tell you, but their lives are not good examples for you to follow. They tell you to do things, but they themselves don't do them. 4They make strict rules and try to force people to obey them, but they are unwilling to help those who struggle under the weight of their rules.

5"They do good things so that other people will see them. They make the boxes *n* of Scriptures*d* that they wear bigger, and they make their special prayer clothes very long. 6Those Pharisees and teachers of the law love to have the most important seats at feasts and in the synagogues.*d* 7They love people to greet them with respect in the marketplaces, and they love to have people call them 'Teacher.'

Herodians A political group that followed Herod and his family.
coin A Roman denarius. One coin was the average pay for one day's work.
'I am ... Jacob.' Quotation from Exodus 3:6.
'Love ... mind.' Quotation from Deuteronomy 6:5.
'Love ... yourself.' Quotation from Leviticus 19:18.
boxes Small leather boxes containing four important Scriptures. Some Jews tied these to the forehead and left arm, probably to show they were very religious.

8"But you must not be called 'Teacher,' because you have only one Teacher, and you are all brothers and sisters together. 9And don't call any person on earth 'Father,' because you have one Father, who is in heaven. 10And you should not be called 'Master,' because you have only one Master, the Christ.*d* 11Whoever is your servant is the greatest among you. 12Whoever makes himself great will be made humble. Whoever makes himself humble will be made great.

13"How terrible for you, teachers of the law and Pharisees! You are hypocrites!*d* You close the door for people to enter the kingdom of heaven. You yourselves don't enter, and you stop others who are trying to enter. 14 *n*

15"How terrible for you, teachers of the law and Pharisees! You are hypocrites! You travel across land and sea to find one person who will change to your ways. When you find that person, you make him more fit for hell than you are.

16"How terrible for you! You guide the people,

but you are blind. You say, 'If people swear by the Temple*d* when they make a promise, that means nothing. But if they swear by the gold that is in the Temple, they must keep that promise.' 17You are blind fools! Which is greater: the gold or the Temple that makes that gold holy? 18And you say, 'If people swear by the altar when they make a promise, that means nothing. But if they swear by the gift on the altar, they must keep that promise.' 19You are blind! Which is greater: the gift or the altar that makes the gift holy? 20The person who swears by the altar is really using the altar and also everything on the altar. 21And the person who swears by the Temple is really using the Temple and also everything in the Temple. 22The person who swears by heaven is also using God's throne and the One who sits on that throne.

23"How terrible for you, teachers of the law and Pharisees! You are hypocrites! You give to God one-tenth of everything you earn—even your

Verse 14   Some Greek copies add verse 14: "How terrible for you, teachers of the law and Pharisees. You are hypocrites. You take away widows' houses, and you say long prayers so that people will notice you. So you will have a worse punishment."

HYPOCRISY

Being an Example

Stuart Jacobs attended the same high school as David Springer. Stuart was a "brain." He got A's in all his courses except gym. He wore thick glasses, stuttered, and looked like an unmade bed. He had few friends. Stuart didn't fit in.

David heard about a game some guys had started to play at lunch at one of the school's doorways. A long, sloping ramp led to the door. David arrived and found Stuart chasing quarters down the ramp. The guys took turns rolling quarters. Stuart, who longed for acceptance from the guys, always chased the quarters. If he caught them before a certain crack in the ramp, he got to keep them. He didn't realize he was being laughed at.

"C'mon, David!" his friends called. "It's your turn to roll a quarter for Stuart." David didn't know what to do. He didn't want to disappoint the guys, but he didn't want to hurt Stuart's feelings, either.

His pastor's words during a recent sermon came back to him, "You may be the only one through whom others see Christ."

"What am I going to do?" David wondered.

Jesus told his followers that their words needed to reflect their actions. Read how Jesus taught about the differences between real faith and fake faith in **Matthew 23:1–12**.

■ If David followed his pastor's advice and Jesus' teachings, what did he do?

■ Have you ever sensed your faith was just an act? How can you change?

C O N S I D E R . . .

■ writing a variety of conclusions to David's story based on Jesus' teachings in the passage.

■ identifying one way you can "make yourself humble" this week, and do it.

F O R   M O R E ,   S E E . . .

■ Leviticus 19:15–18 (p. 116)   ■ Luke 6:37–42 (p. 1013)
■ Mark 12:28–44 (p. 988)

mint, dill, and cumin.[n] But you don't obey the really important teachings of the law—justice, mercy, and being loyal. These are the things you should do, as well as those other things. [24]You guide the people, but you are blind! You are like a person who picks a fly out of a drink and then swallows a camel![n]

> **SIDELIGHT:** When Jesus criticized the Pharisees for picking flies out of their drinks (Matthew 23:24), he mentioned one of the five smallest items in the Bible. Others are fleas (1 Samuel 24:14, p. 267), ants (Proverbs 6:6, p. 572), tiny pen marks (Matthew 5:18, p. 912), and mustard seeds (Mark 4:31, p. 972).

[25]"How terrible for you, teachers of the law and Pharisees! You are hypocrites! You wash the outside of your cups and dishes, but inside they are full of things you got by cheating others and by pleasing only yourselves. [26]Pharisees, you are blind! First make the inside of the cup clean, and then the outside of the cup can be truly clean.

[27]"How terrible for you, teachers of the law and Pharisees! You are hypocrites! You are like tombs that are painted white. Outside, those tombs look fine, but inside, they are full of the bones of dead people and all kinds of unclean things. [28]It is the same with you. People look at you and think you are good, but on the inside you are full of hypocrisy and evil.

[29]"How terrible for you, teachers of the law and Pharisees! You are hypocrites! You build tombs for the prophets,[d] and you show honor to the graves of those who lived good lives. [30]You say, 'If we had lived during the time of our ancestors, we would not have helped them kill the prophets.' [31]But you give proof that you are children of those who murdered the prophets. [32]And you will complete the sin that your ancestors started.

[33]"You are snakes! A family of poisonous snakes! How are you going to escape God's judgment? [34]So I tell you this: I am sending to you prophets and wise men and teachers. Some of them you will kill and crucify. Some of them you will beat in your synagogues and chase from town to town. [35]So you will be guilty for the death of all the good people who have been killed on earth—from the murder of that good man Abel to the murder of Zechariah[n] son of Berakiah, whom you murdered between the Temple and the altar. [36]I tell you the truth, all of these things will happen to you people who are living now.

Jesus Feels Sorry for Jerusalem

[37]"Jerusalem, Jerusalem! You kill the prophets[d] and stone to death those who are sent to you. Many times I wanted to gather your people as a hen gathers her chicks under her wings, but you did not let me. [38]Now your house will be left completely empty. [39]I tell you, you will not see me again until that time when you will say, 'God bless the One who comes in the name of the Lord.' "[n]

The Temple Will Be Destroyed

24 As Jesus left the Temple[d] and was walking away, his followers came up to show him the Temple's buildings. [2]Jesus asked, "Do you see all these buildings? I tell you the truth, not one stone will be left on another. Every stone will be thrown down to the ground."

[3]Later, as Jesus was sitting on the Mount of Olives,[d] his followers came to be alone with him. They said, "Tell us, when will these things happen? And what will be the sign that it is time for you to come again and for this age to end?"

[4]Jesus answered, "Be careful that no one fools you. [5]Many will come in my name, saying, 'I am the Christ,'[d] and they will fool many people. [6]You will hear about wars and stories of wars that are coming, but don't be afraid. These things must happen before the end comes. [7]Nations will fight against other nations; kingdoms will fight against other kingdoms. There will be times when there is no food for people to eat, and there will be earthquakes in different places. [8]These things are like the first pains when something new is about to be born.

[9]"Then people will arrest you, hand you over to be hurt, and kill you. They will hate you because you believe in me. [10]At that time, many will lose their faith, and they will turn against each other and hate each other. [11]Many false prophets[d] will come and cause many people to believe lies. [12]There will be more and more evil in the world, so most people will stop showing their love for each other. [13]But those people who keep their faith until the end will be saved. [14]The Good News[d] about God's kingdom will be preached in all the world, to every nation. Then the end will come.

---

mint, dill, and cumin Small plants grown in gardens and used for spices. Only very religious people would be careful enough to give a tenth of these plants.
You . . . camel! Meaning, "You worry about the smallest mistakes but commit the biggest sin."
Abel . . . Zechariah In the order of the books of the Hebrew Old Testament, the first and last men to be murdered.
'God . . . Lord.' Quotation from Psalm 118:26.

15"Daniel the prophet spoke about 'the destroying terror.'ⁿ You will see this standing in the holy place." (You who read this should understand what it means.) 16"At that time, the people in Judea should run away to the mountains. 17If people are on the roofsⁿ of their houses, they must not go down to get anything out of their houses. 18If people are in the fields, they must not go back to get their coats. 19At that time, how terrible it will be for women who are pregnant or have nursing babies! 20Pray that it will not be winter or a Sabbathᵈ day when these things happen and you have to run away, 21because at that time there will be much trouble. There will be more trouble than there has ever been since the beginning of the world until now, and nothing as bad will ever happen again. 22God has decided to make that terrible time short. Otherwise, no one would go on living. But God will make that time short to help the people he has chosen. 23At that time, someone might say to you, 'Look, there is the Christ!' Or another person might say, 'There he is!' But don't believe them. 24False Christs and false prophets will come and perform great wonders and miracles.ᵈ They will try to fool even the people God has chosen, if that is possible. 25Now I have warned you about this before it happens.

26"If people tell you, 'The Christ is in the desert,' don't go there. If they say, 'The Christ is in the inner room,' don't believe it. 27When the

'the destroying terror' Mentioned in Daniel 9:27; 12:11 (see also Daniel 11:31).
roof In Bible times houses were built with flat roofs. The roof was used for drying things such as flax and fruit. And it was used as an extra room, as a place for worship, and as a place to sleep in the summer.

Leading a Just Cause

On November 1, 1872, Susan B. Anthony walked into a polling place, demanding to be registered to vote. She voted in the national election. Two weeks later a U.S. marshal arrested her for "voting without lawful right." The judge wouldn't allow a jury trial. Her sentence was to pay a $100 fine and the cost of the trial. "Your Honor," declared Anthony. "I shall never pay one dollar of your unjust penalty."

She never did.

Anthony was long-familiar with the controversy and conflict of reform movements. Years earlier, she had worked for the American Anti-Slavery Society. She regarded slavery as evil and un-Christian. She published the first women's newspaper and organized the first women's union. Now Anthony was at the front of the National Women's Suffrage Movement, working tirelessly for women's voting rights.

The work was often discouraging. The press mocked her. She was denied entry into meetings. She was attacked by angry mobs. But these persecutions didn't stop her. She lectured, lobbied Congress and organized petitions.

In 1920, Anthony's efforts helped to pass the Nineteenth Amendment to the U.S. Constitution, assuring everyone the right to vote regardless of gender. But Anthony never got the chance to vote under the new amendment. She had died fourteen years earlier.

Those who lead movements for justice usually suffer ridicule, persecution, and sometimes death. Read in **Matthew 23:34–39**, what Jesus thinks about those who persecute the prophets of God.

■ Why do you think people fear and persecute leaders such as Susan B. Anthony and the ones Jesus describes?
■ When has your unpopular stance caused you persecution?

CONSIDER...
■ reading through one of the prophets of the Old Testament such as Amos (p. 842), trying to understand why his messages were ridiculed and rejected.
■ listening to leaders who have differing opinions, keeping your mind open for truth—even if it's uncomfortable.

FOR MORE, SEE...
■ Jeremiah 3:11–13 (p. 694)   ■ 2 Timothy 3:1–9 (p. 1265)
■ Ezekiel 20:13–20 (p. 776)

Son of Man*d* comes, he will be seen by everyone, like lightning flashing from the east to the west. 28Wherever the dead body is, there the vultures will gather.

29"Soon after the trouble of those days,

'the sun will grow dark,
    and the moon will not give its light.
The stars will fall from the sky.
And the powers of the heavens will be
    shaken.'   *Isaiah 13:10; 34:4*

30"At that time, the sign of the Son of Man will appear in the sky. Then all the peoples of the world will cry. They will see the Son of Man coming on clouds in the sky with great power and glory. 31He will use a loud trumpet to send his angels all around the earth, and they will gather his chosen people from every part of the world.

32"Learn a lesson from the fig tree: When its branches become green and soft and new leaves appear, you know summer is near. 33In the same

way, when you see all these things happening, you will know that the time is near, ready to come. 34I tell you the truth, all these things will happen while the people of this time are still living. 35Earth and sky will be destroyed, but the words I have said will never be destroyed.

When Will Jesus Come Again?

36"No one knows when that day or time will be, not the angels in heaven, not even the Son. Only the Father knows. 37When the Son of Man*d* comes, it will be like what happened during Noah's time. 38In those days before the flood, people were eating and drinking, marrying and giving their children to be married, until the day Noah entered the boat. 39They knew nothing about what was happening until the flood came and destroyed them. It will be the same when the Son of Man comes. 40Two men will be in the field. One will be taken, and the other will be left. 41Two women will be grinding grain with a mill. *n* One will be taken, and the other will be left.

[42]"So always be ready, because you don't know the day your Lord will come. [43]Remember this: If the owner of the house knew what time of night a thief was coming, the owner would watch and not let the thief break in. [44]So you also must be ready, because the Son of Man will come at a time you don't expect him.

[45]"Who is the wise and loyal servant that the master trusts to give the other servants their food at the right time? [46]When the master comes and finds the servant doing his work, the servant will be blessed. [47]I tell you the truth, the master will choose that servant to take care of everything he owns. [48]But suppose that evil servant thinks to himself, 'My master will not come back soon,' [49]and he begins to beat the other servants and eat and get drunk with others like him? [50]The master will come when that servant is not ready and is not expecting him. [51]Then the master will cut him in pieces and send him away to be with the hypocrites, *d* where people will cry and grind their teeth with pain.

A Story About Ten Bridesmaids

25 "At that time the kingdom of heaven will be like ten bridesmaids who took their lamps and went to wait for the bridegroom. [2]Five of them were foolish and five were wise. [3]The five foolish bridesmaids took their lamps, but they did not take more oil for the lamps to burn. [4]The wise

mill   Two large, round, flat rocks used for grinding grain to make flour.

DECISION MAKING

Always Be Ready

Kent Andrews was discouraged as he drove to work. He could hear Mom's words from a few months ago echo in his mind. "Kent, you must get your act together," she'd said. "It's your senior year and time is running out. You need to decide about college. Don't you want to go?"

What a worry wart, he had thought at the time. Of course he wanted to go to college. His grades were okay. He just needed to decide where to go. Weren't they all the same? Kent was sick of school anyway, and wanted to have fun with his friends in his senior year.

Kent hadn't counted on the state standardized test. The state allowed students to graduate only if they passed the basic skills test. Fairly easy stuff—if you were ready. But it had seemed a better idea to Kent to party than to study.

Kent had failed the test. He had missed the admissions deadlines for most colleges anyway, and most of the financial aid had already been doled out.

So, instead of receiving his diploma with his friends, Kent had watched graduation from the bleachers in the school gym. Instead of packing for college in the fall like his friends, he was sacking groceries at a local supermarket.

As Kent tied his apron for work, he thought about his friends in college. He realized it was his own fault he wasn't there with them. Next year, Kent vowed, I'll be ready.

Jesus told a story about poor preparation and poor decisions. Read it in **Matthew 25:1–13**.

- How are the stories of Kent and the ten girls similar? How did poor decision making play a role in both stories?
- When have you had to live with the consequences of a poor decision similar to that of the ten girls in Jesus' story? How would better decisions have helped you?

C O N S I D E R . . .

- dividing a piece of paper in half. On the left side list things about which you have made poor decisions in the past. On the right side write one thing you could do in each instance to make a better choice next time.
- asking a parent to tell about a tough decision he or she has made and what happened as a result of the choice.

F O R   M O R E ,   S E E . . .

- Proverbs 8:10 (p. 573)
- Luke 12:35–48 (p. 1028)
- John 7:16–18 (p. 1069)

bridesmaids took their lamps and more oil in jars. ⁵Because the bridegroom was late, they became sleepy and went to sleep.

⁶"At midnight someone cried out, 'The bridegroom is coming! Come and meet him!' ⁷Then all the bridesmaids woke up and got their lamps ready. ⁸But the foolish ones said to the wise, 'Give us some of your oil, because our lamps are going out.' ⁹The wise bridesmaids answered, 'No, the oil we have might not be enough for all of us. Go to the people who sell oil and buy some for yourselves.'

¹⁰"So while the five foolish bridesmaids went to buy oil, the bridegroom came. The bridesmaids who were ready went in with the bridegroom to the wedding feast. Then the door was closed and locked.

¹¹"Later the others came back and said, 'Sir, sir, open the door to let us in.' ¹²But the bridegroom answered, 'I tell you the truth, I don't want to know you.'

¹³"So always be ready, because you don't know the day or the hour the Son of Man[d] will come.

A Story About Three Servants

¹⁴"The kingdom of heaven is like a man who was going to another place for a visit. Before he left, he called for his servants and told them to take care of his things while he was gone. ¹⁵He gave one servant five bags of gold, another servant two bags of gold, and a third servant one bag of gold, to each one as much as he could handle. Then he left. ¹⁶The servant who got five bags went quickly to invest the money and earned five more bags. ¹⁷In the same way, the servant who had two bags invested them and earned two more. ¹⁸But the servant who got one bag went out and dug a hole in the ground and hid the master's money.

¹⁹"After a long time the master came home and asked the servants what they did with his money. ²⁰The servant who was given five bags of gold brought five more bags to the master and said, 'Master, you trusted me to care for five bags of gold, so I used your five bags to earn five more.' ²¹The master answered, 'You did well. You are a good and loyal servant. Because you were loyal with small things, I will let you care for much greater things. Come and share my joy with me.'

²²"Then the servant who had been given two bags of gold came to the master and said, 'Master, you gave me two bags of gold to care for, so I used your two bags to earn two more.' ²³The master answered, 'You did well. You are a good and loyal servant. Because you were loyal with small things, I will let you care for much greater things. Come and share my joy with me.'

²⁴"Then the servant who had been given one bag of gold came to the master and said, 'Master,

I knew that you were a hard man. You harvest things you did not plant. You gather crops where you did not sow any seed. ²⁵So I was afraid and went and hid your money in the ground. Here is your bag of gold.' ²⁶The master answered, 'You are a wicked and lazy servant! You say you knew that I harvest things I did not plant and that I gather crops where I did not sow any seed. ²⁷So you should have put my gold in the bank. Then, when I came home, I would have received my gold back with interest.'

²⁸"So the master told his other servants, 'Take the bag of gold from that servant and give it to the servant who has ten bags of gold. ²⁹Those who have much will get more, and they will have much more than they need. But those who do not have much will have everything taken away from them.' ³⁰Then the master said, 'Throw that useless servant outside, into the darkness where people will cry and grind their teeth with pain.'

The King Will Judge All People

³¹"The Son of Man[d] will come again in his great glory, with all his angels. He will be King and sit on his great throne. ³²All the nations of the world will be gathered before him, and he will separate them into two groups as a shepherd separates the sheep from the goats. ³³The Son of Man will put the sheep on his right and the goats on his left.

³⁴"Then the King will say to the people on his right, 'Come, my Father has given you his blessing. Receive the kingdom God has prepared for you since the world was made. ³⁵I was hungry, and you gave me food. I was thirsty, and you gave me something to drink. I was alone and away from home, and you invited me into your house. ³⁶I was without clothes, and you gave me something to wear. I was sick, and you cared for me. I was in prison, and you visited me.'

³⁷"Then the good people will answer, 'Lord, when did we see you hungry and give you food, or thirsty and give you something to drink? ³⁸When did we see you alone and away from home and invite you into our house? When did we see you without clothes and give you something to wear? ³⁹When did we see you sick or in prison and care for you?'

⁴⁰"Then the King will answer, 'I tell you the truth, anything you did for even the least of my people here, you also did for me.'

⁴¹"Then the King will say to those on his left, 'Go away from me. You will be punished. Go into the fire that burns forever that was prepared for the devil and his angels. ⁴²I was hungry, and you gave me nothing to eat. I was thirsty, and you gave me nothing to drink. ⁴³I was alone and away from home, and you did not invite me into your house. I was without clothes, and

you gave me nothing to wear. I was sick and in prison, and you did not care for me.'

44"Then those people will answer, 'Lord, when did we see you hungry or thirsty or alone and away from home or without clothes or sick or in prison? When did we see these things and not help you?'

45"Then the King will answer, 'I tell you the truth, anything you refused to do for even the least of my people here, you refused to do for me.'

46"These people will go off to be punished forever, but the good people will go to live forever."

The Plan to Kill Jesus

26 After Jesus finished saying all these things, he told his followers, 2"You know that the day after tomorrow is the day of the Passover*d* Feast. On that day the Son of Man*d* will be given to his enemies to be crucified."

3Then the leading priests and the older Jewish leaders had a meeting at the palace of the high priest, named Caiaphas. 4At the meeting, they planned to set a trap to arrest Jesus and kill him. 5But they said, "We must not do it during the feast, because the people might cause a riot."

Perfume for Jesus' Burial

6Jesus was in Bethany at the house of Simon, who had a skin disease. 7While Jesus was there, a woman approached him with an alabaster*d* jar filled with expensive perfume. She poured this perfume on Jesus' head while he was eating.

SERVICE

Are You Jesus?

Eric Schwartz dressed in army surplus fatigues and roared through the city on his motorcycle. He wore his hair long and his beard full, which made him look older than his eighteen years. Eric was proud of his tough image—it was his "style."

Because of his tough image, it was no surprise when he was arrested for shoplifting. Since Eric was a first-time offender, the judge sentenced him to several hours of community service instead of jail.

Eric chose to "do his time" at The Shepherd's Table, a soup kitchen for the homeless. He peeled potatoes, served food, and mopped floors. The sights, sounds, and smells depressed him. It was a place for the poor, broken, lonely, and afraid—people who reminded him a lot of himself.

Eric began to talk with the people. He had expected to find just a bunch of drunken bums, but, instead, he met a surprising variety of people caught in the poverty trap. There was a Vietnam War veteran who worked, but never had money at month's end. An older woman had lost her home after her husband had died. A young mother with three small children lived in one room. A family who had lost a farm struggled to find work in the city. The stories broke his heart.

He didn't feel so "tough" after a while. In fact, he began to enjoy how he felt when he served others. One evening after supper, he was wiping tables when he felt a tug at his camouflage pants. A young girl looked up to him.

"Mister," whispered the child. "Are you Jesus?"

The question startled him. "Huh?" he asked, confused.

"You must be Jesus," she insisted. "Momma told me Jesus loves poor people like us."

When Eric shared the story with the soup kitchen manager, she showed him **Matthew 25:31—46**. "That's why we're here," she said.

- What did serving teach Eric about being Jesus' follower?
- When have you seen someone as Jesus describes: hungry, thirsty, sick, without warm clothes, alone, or imprisoned? What was your reaction?

CONSIDER . . .

- listing all the people with whom you come in contact in a typical day. Decide something you can do to serve those people.
- thinking of Jesus each time you see someone in need. How do your thoughts affect your attitude toward that person?

FOR MORE, SEE . . .

- Lamentations 3:26–27 (p. 757)
- Luke 10:25–37 (p. 1022)
- John 13:1–17 (p. 1080)

⁸His followers were upset when they saw the woman do this. They asked, "Why waste that perfume? ⁹It could have been sold for a great deal of money and the money given to the poor."

¹⁰Knowing what had happened, Jesus said, "Why are you troubling this woman? She did an excellent thing for me. ¹¹You will always have the poor with you, but you will not always have me. ¹²This woman poured perfume on my body to prepare me for burial. ¹³I tell you the truth, wherever the Good News^d is preached in all the world, what this woman has done will be told, and people will remember her."

Judas Becomes an Enemy of Jesus

¹⁴Then one of the twelve apostles, Judas Iscariot, went to talk to the leading priests. ¹⁵He said, "What will you pay me for giving Jesus to you?" And they gave him thirty silver coins. ¹⁶After that, Judas watched for the best time to turn Jesus in.

Jesus Eats the Passover Meal

¹⁷On the first day of the Feast^d of Unleavened Bread, the followers came to Jesus. They said, "Where do you want us to prepare for you to eat the Passover^d meal?"

¹⁸Jesus answered, "Go into the city to a certain man and tell him, 'The Teacher says: The chosen

---

FRIENDS

Diary of a Backstabber

November 1: I knew something was wrong when I came out from work and saw Drew. He should have been at basketball practice. "I need to talk to you," he said, and my stomach tightened. "Lisa, I hate to do this, but there's no good way to break up. . . ."

He droned on, but I didn't hear anything past the "break up" part. "And I want to still be friends," he said. FRIENDS! He dumps me and still wants to be friends!

November 30: I can't stand seeing Drew at school. And now he's hanging around the mall with his skateboarding friends.

December 6: Tonight I saw some workers dismantling a Winter Wonderland display at the mall lobby. When I got to the store, I asked my manager what happened.

"It was skateboarders," she said. "A bunch of 'em sneaked in after hours and trashed the whole thing. They rode their skateboards all over, using the fake snowdrifts as ramps."

December 11: During prayer requests at youth group, I spoke up. "I think we should pray for Drew, since the incident at the mall with the skateboarders and all."

December 13: The rumors about Drew spread to school. Then in fifth hour, he was called out of class. After school let out, I ran into him. He didn't look good.

"Are you okay?" I asked, surprised that I felt so concerned.

"Yeah, I guess so," Drew answered. "Have you heard what everyone's saying about me, Lisa?"

"Uh, yeah," I stammered, not looking him in the eye.

"It wasn't us!" he says. "Sure, we hang around the mall some, but we'd never do something like that. I can't imagine who'd think we had. You don't know who turned in our names, do you?"

"No, Drew I don't," I said. Because she felt hurt, Lisa betrayed Drew and got him into a lot of trouble. We don't know Judas's motives for betraying Jesus, but we do know what happened. Read about it in **Matthew 26:14–25**.

■ What feelings might Lisa and Judas have experienced as each betrayed a friend?

■ If you had been in the room with Jesus and the disciples, what would you have said or done?

C O N S I D E R

■ making a commitment not to betray your friends by spreading rumors or gossip about them.

■ forgiving a friend who has betrayed you. Try to settle your differences.

F O R   M O R E ,   S E E . . .

■ Isaiah 53:4–6 (p. 672)
■ Mark 14:10–21 (p. 991)

■ Acts 1:12–26 (p. 1098)

time is near. I will have the Passover with my followers at your house.' " ¹⁹The followers did what Jesus told them to do, and they prepared the Passover meal.

²⁰In the evening Jesus was sitting at the table with his twelve followers. ²¹As they were eating, Jesus said, "I tell you the truth, one of you will turn against me."

²²This made the followers very sad. Each one began to say to Jesus, "Surely, Lord, I am not the one who will turn against you, am I?"

²³Jesus answered, "The man who has dipped his hand with me into the bowl is the one who will turn against me. ²⁴The Son of Man*d* will die, just as the Scriptures*d* say. But how terrible it will be for the person who hands the Son of Man over to be killed. It would be better for him if he had never been born."

²⁵Then Judas, who would give Jesus to his enemies, said to Jesus, "Teacher, surely I am not the one, am I?"

Jesus answered, "Yes, it is you."

The Lord's Supper

²⁶While they were eating, Jesus took some bread and thanked God for it and broke it. Then he gave it to his followers and said, "Take this bread and eat it; this is my body."

²⁷Then Jesus took a cup and thanked God for it and gave it to the followers. He said, "Every one of you drink this. ²⁸This is my blood which is the new agreement that God makes with his people. This blood is poured out for many to forgive their sins. ²⁹I tell you this: I will not drink of this fruit of the vine*n* again until that day when I drink it new with you in my Father's kingdom."

³⁰After singing a hymn, they went out to the Mount of Olives.*d*

Jesus' Followers Will Leave Him

³¹Jesus told his followers, "Tonight you will all stumble in your faith on account of me, because it is written in the Scriptures:*d*

'I will kill the shepherd,
    and the sheep will scatter.'   *Zechariah 13:7*

³²But after I rise from the dead, I will go ahead of you into Galilee."

³³Peter said, "Everyone else may stumble in their faith because of you, but I will not."

³⁴Jesus said, "I tell you the truth, tonight before the rooster crows you will say three times that you don't know me."

³⁵But Peter said, "I will never say that I don't know you! I will even die with you!" And all the other followers said the same thing.

Jesus Prays Alone

³⁶Then Jesus went with his followers to a place called Gethsemane. He said to them, "Sit here while I go over there and pray." ³⁷He took Peter and the two sons of Zebedee with him, and he began to be very sad and troubled. ³⁸He said to them, "My heart is full of sorrow, to the point of death. Stay here and watch with me."

³⁹After walking a little farther away from them, Jesus fell to the ground and prayed, "My Father, if it is possible, do not give me this cup*n* of suffering. But do what you want, not what I want." ⁴⁰Then Jesus went back to his followers and found them asleep. He said to Peter, "You men could not stay awake with me for one hour? ⁴¹Stay awake and pray for strength against temptation. The spirit wants to do what is right, but the body is weak."

⁴²Then Jesus went away a second time and prayed, "My Father, if it is not possible for this painful thing to be taken from me, and if I must do it, I pray that what you want will be done."

⁴³Then he went back to his followers, and again he found them asleep, because their eyes were heavy. ⁴⁴So Jesus left them and went away and prayed a third time, saying the same thing.

⁴⁵Then Jesus went back to his followers and said, "Are you still sleeping and resting? The time has come for the Son of Man*d* to be handed over to sinful people. ⁴⁶Get up, we must go. Look, here comes the man who has turned against me."

Jesus Is Arrested

⁴⁷While Jesus was still speaking, Judas, one of the twelve apostles,*d* came up. With him were many people carrying swords and clubs who had been sent from the leading priests and the older Jewish leaders of the people. ⁴⁸Judas had planned to give them a signal, saying, "The man I kiss is Jesus. Arrest him." ⁴⁹At once Judas went to Jesus and said, "Greetings, Teacher!" and kissed him.

⁵⁰Jesus answered, "Friend, do what you came to do."

Then the people came and grabbed Jesus and arrested him. ⁵¹When that happened, one of Jesus' followers reached for his sword and pulled it out. He struck the servant of the high priest and cut off his ear.

⁵²Jesus said to the man, "Put your sword back in its place. All who use swords will be killed with swords. ⁵³Surely you know I could ask my Father, and he would give me more than twelve armies of angels. ⁵⁴But it must happen this way to bring about what the Scriptures*d* say."

---

fruit of the vine Product of the grapevine; this may also be translated "wine."
cup Jesus is talking about the terrible things that will happen to him. Accepting these things will be very hard, like drinking a cup of something bitter.

⁵⁵Then Jesus said to the crowd, "You came to get me with swords and clubs as if I were a criminal. Every day I sat in the Temple*d* teaching, and you did not arrest me there. ⁵⁶But all these things have happened so that it will come about as the prophets*d* wrote." Then all of Jesus' followers left him and ran away.

Jesus Before the Leaders

⁵⁷Those people who arrested Jesus led him to the house of Caiaphas, the high priest, where the teachers of the law and the older Jewish leaders were gathered. ⁵⁸Peter followed far behind to the courtyard of the high priest's house, and he sat down with the guards to see what would happen to Jesus.

⁵⁹The leading priests and the whole Jewish council tried to find something false against Jesus so they could kill him. ⁶⁰Many people came and told lies about him, but the council could find no real reason to kill him. Then two people came and said, ⁶¹"This man said, 'I can destroy the Temple*d* of God and build it again in three days.' "

⁶²Then the high priest stood up and said to Jesus, "Aren't you going to answer? Don't you have something to say about their charges against you?" ⁶³But Jesus said nothing.

✳ SIDELIGHT: Practically every legal rule was broken to convict Jesus (Matthew 26:57–67). Jewish law prohibited trials at night, during Passover, and without legitimate witnesses—all of which happened in Jesus' trial. Any good judge would declare a mistrial today.

Again the high priest said to Jesus, "I command you by the power of the living God: Tell us if you are the Christ,*d* the Son of God."

⁶⁴Jesus answered, "Those are your words. But I tell you, in the future you will see the Son of Man*d* sitting at the right hand of God, the Powerful One, and coming on clouds in the sky."

⁶⁵When the high priest heard this, he tore his clothes and said, "This man has said things that are against God! We don't need any more witnesses; you all heard him say these things against God. ⁶⁶What do you think?"

The people answered, "He should die."

⁶⁷Then the people there spat in Jesus' face and beat him with their fists. Others slapped him. ⁶⁸They said, "Prove to us that you are a prophet,*d* you Christ! Tell us who hit you!"

Peter Says He Doesn't Know Jesus

⁶⁹At that time, as Peter was sitting in the courtyard, a servant girl came to him and said, "You also were with Jesus of Galilee."

⁷⁰But Peter said to all the people there that he was never with Jesus. He said, "I don't know what you are talking about."

⁷¹When he left the courtyard and was at the gate, another girl saw him. She said to the people there, "This man was with Jesus of Nazareth."

⁷²Again, Peter said he was never with him, saying, "I swear I don't know this man Jesus!"

⁷³A short time later, some people standing there went to Peter and said, "Surely you are one of those who followed Jesus. The way you talk shows it."

⁷⁴Then Peter began to place a curse on himself and swear, "I don't know the man." At once, a rooster crowed. ⁷⁵And Peter remembered what Jesus had told him: "Before the rooster crows, you will say three times that you don't know me." Then Peter went outside and cried painfully.

Jesus Is Taken to Pilate

27 Early the next morning, all the leading priests and older leaders of the people decided that Jesus should die. ²They tied him, led him away, and turned him over to Pilate, the governor.

Judas Kills Himself

³Judas, the one who had given Jesus to his enemies, saw that they had decided to kill Jesus. Then he was very sorry for what he had done. So he took the thirty silver coins back to the priests and the leaders, ⁴saying, "I sinned; I handed over to you an innocent man."

The leaders answered, "What is that to us? That's your problem, not ours."

⁵So Judas threw the money into the Temple.*d* Then he went off and hanged himself.

⁶The leading priests picked up the silver coins in the Temple and said, "Our law does not allow us to keep this money with the Temple money, because it has paid for a man's death." ⁷So they decided to use the coins to buy Potter's Field as a place to bury strangers who died in Jerusalem. ⁸That is why that field is still called the Field of Blood. ⁹So what Jeremiah the prophet*d* had said came true: "They took thirty silver coins. That is how little the Israelites thought he was worth. ¹⁰They used those thirty silver coins to buy the potter's field, as the Lord commanded me."*n*

Pilate Questions Jesus

¹¹Jesus stood before Pilate the governor, and

"They . . . commanded me."   See Zechariah 11:12-13 and Jeremiah 32:6-9.

Pilate asked him, "Are you the king of the Jews?"

Jesus answered, "Those are your words."

[12]When the leading priests and the older leaders accused Jesus, he said nothing.

[13]So Pilate said to Jesus, "Don't you hear them accusing you of all these things?"

[14]But Jesus said nothing in answer to Pilate, and Pilate was very surprised at this.

Pilate Tries to Free Jesus

[15]Every year at the time of Passover[d] the governor would free one prisoner whom the people chose. [16]At that time there was a man in prison, named Barabbas, who was known to be very bad. [17]When the people gathered at Pilate's house, Pilate said, "Whom do you want me to set free: Barabbas or Jesus who is called the Christ?"[d] [18]Pilate knew that the people turned Jesus in to him because they were jealous.

[19]While Pilate was sitting there on the judge's seat, his wife sent this message to him: "Don't do anything to that man, because he is innocent. Today I had a dream about him, and it troubled me very much."

[20]But the leading priests and older leaders convinced the crowd to ask for Barabbas to be freed and for Jesus to be killed.

[21]Pilate said, "I have Barabbas and Jesus. Which do you want me to set free for you?"

The people answered, "Barabbas."

[22]Pilate asked, "So what should I do with Jesus, the one called the Christ?"

They all answered, "Crucify him!"

[23]Pilate asked, "Why? What wrong has he done?"

But they shouted louder, "Crucify him!"

[24]When Pilate saw that he could do nothing about this and that a riot was starting, he took some water and washed his hands[n] in front of the crowd. Then he said, "I am not guilty of this man's death. You are the ones who are causing it!"

[25]All the people answered, "We and our children will be responsible for his death."

[26]Then he set Barabbas free. But Jesus was beaten with whips and handed over to the soldiers to be crucified.

[27]The governor's soldiers took Jesus into the governor's palace, and they all gathered around him. [28]They took off his clothes and put a red robe on him. [29]Using thorny branches, they made a crown, put it on his head, and put a stick in his right hand. Then the soldiers bowed before Jesus and made fun of him, saying, "Hail, King of the Jews!" [30]They spat on Jesus. Then they took his stick and began to beat him on the head. [31]After they finished, the soldiers took off the robe and put his own clothes on him again. Then they led him away to be crucified.

Jesus Is Crucified

[32]As the soldiers were going out of the city with Jesus, they forced a man from Cyrene, named Simon, to carry the cross for Jesus. [33]They all came to the place called Golgotha, which means the Place of the Skull. [34]The soldiers gave Jesus wine mixed with gall[n] to drink. He tasted the wine but refused to drink it. [35]When the soldiers had crucified him, they threw lots[d] to decide who would get his clothes. [36]The soldiers sat there and continued watching him. [37]They put a sign above Jesus' head with a charge against him. It said: THIS IS JESUS, THE KING OF THE JEWS. [38]Two robbers were crucified beside Jesus, one on the right and the other on the left. [39]People walked by and insulted Jesus and shook their heads, [40]saying, "You said you could destroy the Temple[d] and build it again in three days. So save yourself! Come down from that cross if you are really the Son of God!"

[41]The leading priests, the teachers of the law, and the older Jewish leaders were also making fun of Jesus. [42]They said, "He saved others, but he can't save himself! He says he is the king of Israel! If he is the king, let him come down now from the cross. Then we will believe in him. [43]He trusts in God, so let God save him now, if God really wants him. He himself said, 'I am the Son of God.'"

[44]And in the same way, the robbers who were being crucified beside Jesus also insulted him.

Jesus Dies

[45]At noon the whole country became dark, and the darkness lasted for three hours. [46]About three o'clock Jesus cried out in a loud voice, "Eli, Eli, lama sabachthani?" This means, "My God, my God, why have you rejected me?"

[47]Some of the people standing there who heard this said, "He is calling Elijah."

[48]Quickly one of them ran and got a sponge and filled it with vinegar and tied it to a stick and gave it to Jesus to drink. [49]But the others said, "Don't bother him. We want to see if Elijah will come to save him."

[50]But Jesus cried out again in a loud voice and died.

[51]Then the curtain in the Temple[n] was torn into two pieces, from the top to the bottom. Also, the earth shook and rocks broke apart. [52]The

washed his hands He did this as a sign to show that he wanted no part in what the people did.
gall Probably a drink of wine mixed with drugs to help a person feel less pain.
curtain in the Temple A curtain divided the Most Holy Place from the other part of the Temple. That was the special building in Jerusalem where God commanded the Jewish people to worship him.

graves opened, and many of God's people who had died were raised from the dead. ⁵³They came out of the graves after Jesus was raised from the dead and went into the holy city, where they appeared to many people.

⁵⁴When the army officer and the soldiers guarding Jesus saw this earthquake and everything else that happened, they were very frightened and said, "He really was the Son of God!"

⁵⁵Many women who had followed Jesus from Galilee to help him were standing at a distance from the cross, watching. ⁵⁶Mary Magdalene, and Mary the mother of James and Joseph, and the mother of James and John were there.

Jesus Is Buried

⁵⁷That evening a rich man named Joseph, a follower of Jesus from the town of Arimathea, came to Jerusalem. ⁵⁸Joseph went to Pilate and asked to have Jesus' body. So Pilate gave orders for the soldiers to give it to Joseph. ⁵⁹Then Joseph took the body and wrapped it in a clean linen cloth. ⁶⁰He put Jesus' body in a new tomb that he had cut out of a wall of rock, and he rolled a very large stone to block the entrance of the tomb. Then Joseph went away. ⁶¹Mary Magdalene and the other woman named Mary were sitting near the tomb.

The Tomb of Jesus Is Guarded

⁶²The next day, the day after Preparation*d* Day, the leading priests and the Pharisees*d* went to Pilate. ⁶³They said, "Sir, we remember that while that liar was still alive he said, 'After three days I will rise from the dead.' ⁶⁴So give the order for the tomb to be guarded closely till the third day. Otherwise, his followers might come and steal the body and tell people that he has risen from the dead. That lie would be even worse than the first one."

⁶⁵Pilate said, "Take some soldiers and go guard the tomb the best way you know." ⁶⁶So they all went to the tomb and made it safe from thieves

---

SADNESS

Does Anybody Care?

"Louise!" Mom yelled. "Joyce is on the phone!" Joyce Berg was Louise Stone's best friend. They were inseparable.

Joyce's voice was soft when Louise picked up the phone. It didn't sound like her. "Louise, my dad died," Joyce said.

Silence.

Louise's mind raced. She knew he had been sick. But Joyce and Louise were only sixteen. Parents don't die now!

"What can I do?" Louise asked.

"Can you come over?" Joyce replied.

Louise went. The sadness was overwhelming. Joyce was quiet. Her mom cried a lot. Her brother stayed in his room. Louise babysat, answered phones, collected casseroles from visitors. She went to the funeral and hugged Joyce a lot.

Back home Mom and Louise talked. "I couldn't do anything," Louise said as she wept. "It was awful. I couldn't take away her sadness. I didn't know how to tell her I cared."

For several weeks both Joyce and Louise remained sad. Although they knew this was temporary, they didn't realize that the death of Joyce's dad would leave them vulnerable to sad feelings for months, even years. There was no way to avoid their grief; it was just something to go through.

Sadness and grief are normal feelings when someone close to you dies. After Jesus was crucified, his friends were terribly sad. Read what they did in **Matthew 27:57–61**.

■ What feelings seem common to Jesus' friends and Louise?
■ What ways might this passage suggest for helping hurting friends?

CONSIDER . . .

■ making a list of your hurting friends. Carry it with you. It will remind you to reach out to those friends, especially after the immediate crisis has passed.
■ memorizing Romans 8:38–39, p. 1153. Use it to strengthen you in sad times.

FOR MORE. SEE . . .

■ Ecclesiastes 7:2–4 (p. 603)
■ Luke 23:44–56 (p. 1053)
■ John 11:28–44 (p. 1077)

by sealing the stone in the entrance and putting soldiers there to guard it.

Jesus Rises from the Dead

28 The day after the Sabbath*d* day was the first day of the week. At dawn on the first day, Mary Magdalene and another woman named Mary went to look at the tomb.

²At that time there was a strong earthquake. An angel of the Lord came down from heaven, went to the tomb, and rolled the stone away from the entrance. Then he sat on the stone. ³He was shining as bright as lightning, and his clothes were white as snow. ⁴The soldiers guarding the tomb shook with fear because of the angel, and they became like dead men.

⁵The angel said to the women, "Don't be afraid. I know that you are looking for Jesus, who has been crucified. ⁶He is not here. He has risen from the dead as he said he would. Come and see

the place where his body was. ⁷And go quickly and tell his followers, 'Jesus has risen from the dead. He is going into Galilee ahead of you, and you will see him there.' " Then the angel said, "Now I have told you."

> **SIDELIGHT:** The stones in front of tombs in Jesus' day were large, disk-shaped boulders (Matthew 28:2). They were placed in grooves so that they would roll down and block the entrance to the cave-like tombs, making them difficult to move.

⁸The women left the tomb quickly. They were afraid, but they were also very happy. They ran to tell Jesus' followers what had happened. ⁹Suddenly, Jesus met them and said, "Greetings." The

---

FOLLOWING GOD

Not Me, Lord!

"How do I know what God wants me to do?" Beth Berger asked her pastor. Beth was a college junior struggling with her future. She was home on Christmas break, looking for a summer job.

"Obviously, you want to follow God," Pastor Jones said. "Try listening. You'll be surprised at what you hear."

"I don't want to be a pastor!" Beth shot back. "I'm not sure I feel called to do that."

"You don't have to be in full-time ministry to follow God," he said quietly. "Following God takes different paths. Why not explore other possibilities?"

Beth stayed open to God's calling. She was offered a position for the summer at a church camp. She accepted. She worked with children, led Bible studies, planned and led worship and music, cared for animals and camped outdoors. She listened for God and learned what it meant to be a follower.

She returned to college energized for her senior year. "I discovered I'm good at things like teaching. I even like Bible studies," she wrote to Pastor Jones. "I still don't know what I'll do. But I'll keep finding ways to follow God."

Beth learned that following God may at first seem scary. But after the initial "Yes, send me," serving God brings adventure, growth and true joy. Read **Matthew 28:16–20** to find Jesus' commission and promise for those who agree to follow him.

■ What did Beth learn about following God? How is this similar to Jesus' command?

■ How do you follow God? How do you seek to make others followers of God?

C O N S I D E R . . .

■ writing a scenario in which you befriend people who have never heard about Jesus. How will you teach them about faith?

■ listing the ways the careers you're interested in could minister and spread God's kingdom.

F O R   M O R E ,   S E E . . .

■ Exodus 3 (p. 60)   ■ Acts 1:7–11 (p. 1098)
■ John 21 (p. 1094)

women came up to him, took hold of his feet, and worshiped him. [10]Then Jesus said to them, "Don't be afraid. Go and tell my followers to go on to Galilee, and they will see me there."

The Soldiers Report to the Leaders

[11]While the women went to tell Jesus' followers, some of the soldiers who had been guarding the tomb went into the city to tell the leading priests everything that had happened. [12]Then the priests met with the older Jewish leaders and made a plan. They paid the soldiers a large amount of money [13]and said to them, "Tell the people that Jesus' followers came during the night and stole the body while you were asleep. [14]If the governor hears about this, we will satisfy him and save you from trouble." [15]So the soldiers kept the

money and did as they were told. And that story is still spread among the Jewish people even today.

Jesus Talks to His Followers

[16]The eleven followers went to Galilee to the mountain where Jesus had told them to go. [17]On the mountain they saw Jesus and worshiped him, but some of them did not believe it was really Jesus. [18]Then Jesus came to them and said, "All power in heaven and on earth is given to me. [19]So go and make followers of all people in the world. Baptize them in the name of the Father and the Son and the Holy Spirit.[d] [20]Teach them to obey everything that I have taught you, and I will be with you always, even until the end of this age."

MARK

Why Read This Book:

- Learn about the healings and miracles Jesus performed (Mark 2—8).
- Listen to Jesus' teachings about following him (Mark 9—12).
- See how Jesus was victorious even though people killed him (Mark 14—16).

Behind the Scenes:

The Gospel of Mark is a lot like an evening newscast. It's filled with short, quick "news bites" about Jesus' life. It moves quickly from scene to scene, and is filled with action and drama.

Unlike a newsmagazine, it doesn't linger on any scene. Instead, it cuts quickly from one scene to the next. So Mark is packed with simple, vivid stories. The Greek word translated "immediately" or "then" appears more than forty times in just sixteen chapters!

The book begins with a short segment on John the Baptist, who announced Jesus' coming. Then it tells about Jesus' miracles and activities in the region of Lake Galilee. Finally, the action moves to Jerusalem, where Jesus was arrested and killed. Then he rose from the grave.

Unlike the other three Gospels, this book appears to be addressed to people

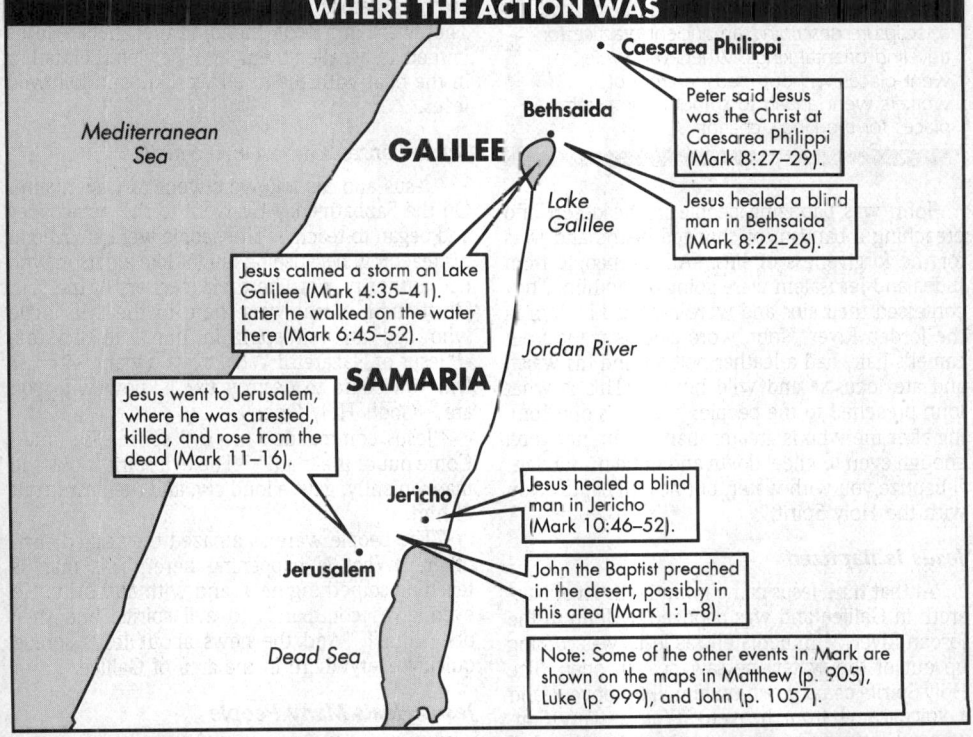

WHERE THE ACTION WAS

- **Caesarea Philippi**
  - Peter said Jesus was the Christ at Caesarea Philippi (Mark 8:27–29).
- **Bethsaida**
  - Jesus healed a blind man in Bethsaida (Mark 8:22–26).
- *Mediterranean Sea*
- **GALILEE**
- *Lake Galilee*
- Jesus calmed a storm on Lake Galilee (Mark 4:35–41). Later he walked on the water here (Mark 6:45–52).
- *Jordan River*
- **SAMARIA**
- Jesus went to Jerusalem, where he was arrested, killed, and rose from the dead (Mark 11–16).
- **Jericho**
  - Jesus healed a blind man in Jericho (Mark 10:46–52).
- **Jerusalem**
  - John the Baptist preached in the desert, possibly in this area (Mark 1:1–8).
- *Dead Sea*
- Note: Some of the other events in Mark are shown on the maps in Matthew (p. 905), Luke (p. 999), and John (p. 1057).

WHEN THE ACTION WAS

Jesus was born	Jesus was crucified, rose from the dead, and went to heaven	Paul began his missionary work	Fire destroyed Rome	
BC/AD	**25AD**	**50AD**	**75AD**	**100AD**
	Jesus began his ministry		Romans destroyed the Temple in Jerusalem	

Behind the Scenes (cont.):

who weren't from the area where Jesus lived. Since this audience wasn't as familiar with stories about Jesus, this book is a simple introduction to who Jesus was, what he did and why he came into the world.
So it's a great place to begin learning the basics!

John Prepares for Jesus

1 This is the beginning of the Good News*d* about Jesus Christ, the Son of God,*n* 2as the prophet*d* Isaiah wrote:
"I will send my messenger ahead of you,
    who will prepare your way."   *Malachi 3:1*
3"This is a voice of one
    who calls out in the desert:
'Prepare the way for the Lord.
    Make the road straight for him.'"   *Isaiah 40:3*

> ✸ **SIDELIGHT:** John the Baptist quoted from Isaiah about preparing the way for the Lord (Mark 1:2–3), a passage of scripture describing an ancient practice for traveling oriental kings. Whenever a ruler went places without roads, a crew of workers went ahead to smooth out rough places for the king's chariot.

4John was baptizing people in the desert and preaching a baptism of changed hearts and lives for the forgiveness of sins. 5All the people from Judea and Jerusalem were going out to him. They confessed their sins and were baptized by him in the Jordan River. 6John wore clothes made from camel's hair, had a leather belt around his waist, and ate locusts*d* and wild honey. 7This is what John preached to the people: "There is one coming after me who is greater than I; I am not good enough even to kneel down and untie his sandals. 8I baptize you with water, but he will baptize you with the Holy Spirit."*d*

Jesus Is Baptized

9At that time Jesus came from the town of Nazareth in Galilee and was baptized by John in the Jordan River. 10Immediately, as Jesus was coming up out of the water, he saw heaven open. The Holy Spirit*d* came down on him like a dove, 11and a voice came from heaven: "You are my Son, whom I love, and I am very pleased with you."
12Then the Spirit sent Jesus into the desert. 13He was in the desert forty days and was tempted by Satan. He was with the wild animals, and the angels came and took care of him.

Jesus Chooses Some Followers

14After John was put in prison, Jesus went into Galilee, preaching the Good News*d* from God. 15He said, "The right time has come. The kingdom of God is near. Change your hearts and lives and believe the Good News!"
16When Jesus was walking by Lake Galilee, he saw Simon*n* and his brother Andrew throwing a net into the lake because they were fishermen. 17Jesus said to them, "Come follow me, and I will make you fish for people." 18So Simon and Andrew immediately left their nets and followed him.
19Going a little farther, Jesus saw two more brothers, James and John, the sons of Zebedee. They were in a boat, mending their nets. 20Jesus immediately called them, and they left their father in the boat with the hired workers and followed Jesus.

Jesus Forces Out an Evil Spirit

21Jesus and his followers went to Capernaum. On the Sabbath*d* day He went to the synagogue*d* and began to teach. 22The people were amazed at his teaching, because he taught like a person who had authority, not like their teachers of the law. 23Just then, a man was there in the synagogue who had an evil spirit in him. He shouted, 24"Jesus of Nazareth! What do you want with us? Did you come to destroy us? I know who you are—God's Holy One!"
25Jesus commanded the evil spirit, "Be quiet! Come out of the man!" 26The evil spirit shook the man violently, gave a loud cry, and then came out of him.
27The people were so amazed they asked each other, "What is happening here? This man is teaching something new, and with authority. He even gives commands to evil spirits, and they obey him." 28And the news about Jesus spread quickly everywhere in the area of Galilee.

Jesus Heals Many People

29As soon as Jesus and his followers left the synagogue,*d* they went with James and John to the home of Simon*n* and Andrew. 30Simon's mother-in-law was sick in bed with a fever, and the people told Jesus about her. 31So Jesus went to her

the Son of God Some Greek copies omit these words.
Simon Simon's other name was Peter.

bed, took her hand, and helped her up. The fever left her, and she began serving them.

³²That evening, after the sun went down, the people brought to Jesus all who were sick and had demons*d* in them. ³³The whole town gathered at the door. ³⁴Jesus healed many who had different kinds of sicknesses, and he forced many demons to leave people. But he would not allow the demons to speak, because they knew who he was.

³⁵Early the next morning, while it was still dark, Jesus woke and left the house. He went to a lonely place, where he prayed. ³⁶Simon and his friends went to look for Jesus. ³⁷When they found him, they said, "Everyone is looking for you!"

³⁸Jesus answered, "We should go to other towns around here so I can preach there too. That is the reason I came." ³⁹So he went everywhere in Galilee, preaching in the synagogues and forcing out demons.

Moses . . . well   Read about this in Leviticus 14:1-32.

Jesus Heals a Sick Man

⁴⁰A man with a skin disease came to Jesus. He fell to his knees and begged Jesus, "You can heal me if you will."

⁴¹Jesus felt sorry for the man, so he reached out his hand and touched him and said, "I will. Be healed!" ⁴²Immediately the disease left the man, and he was healed.

⁴³Jesus told the man to go away at once, but he warned him strongly, ⁴⁴"Don't tell anyone about this. But go and show yourself to the priest. And offer the gift Moses commanded for people who are made well.*n* This will show the people what I have done." ⁴⁵The man left there, but he began to tell everyone that Jesus had healed him, and so he spread the news about Jesus. As a result, Jesus could not enter a town if people saw him. He stayed in places where nobody lived, but people came to him from everywhere.

Leaving Everything

Li Tang grew up in the Chinese capital of Beijing. All her life, Li's family and friends had taught her that God was not real. Li believed what others told her, but she hoped that someday she would find that there really is a God.

When Li was seventeen years old, she found a Bible in an old library. She opened it and began reading about God loving people and sending his Son to the world.

Li was amazed. Why had she never heard about this before? She wanted to know more about this God and follow him. How could she? She decided she would leave everything—her family, her friends and even her country—to follow Jesus.

Her parents weren't thrilled with Li's decision to study Christianity, but they wanted her to be happy. Many of her friends couldn't understand why she wanted to leave. Wasn't ancestor worship good enough for her?

Li moved to England to study and learn more about Jesus so she could someday return to tell others about him. While there, she met Christians who helped her learn and grow.

"You really experience the change in your life," Li reflected after she decided to follow Jesus. "It's really a difference."

Jesus asked people to follow him. Often, following meant leaving many things behind. Yet following also meant gaining a friend like Jesus. Read about Jesus' first followers in **Mark 1:14–20.**

■ How did what Li had to give up compare with what the disciples had to give up to follow Jesus?

■ What have you had to give up to follow Jesus? What do you need to give up now to follow Jesus more fully?

CONSIDER . . . .

■ making a small, wooden cross to carry in your pocket or purse as a reminder of what it means to follow Jesus.

■ interviewing two Christian friends about what it means to them to follow Jesus.

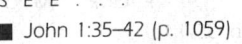

FOR MORE, SEE . . .

■ Ruth 1:11–18 (p. 240)   ■ John 1:35–42 (p. 1059)
■ Matthew 4:12–22 (p. 912)

Jesus Heals a Paralyzed Man

2 A few days later, when Jesus came back to Capernaum, the news spread that he was at home. ²Many people gathered together so that there was no room in the house, not even outside the door. And Jesus was teaching them God's message. ³Four people came, carrying a paralyzed man. ⁴Since they could not get to Jesus because of the crowd, they dug a hole in the roof right above where he was speaking. When they got through, they lowered the mat with the paralyzed man on it. ⁵When Jesus saw the faith of these people, he said to the paralyzed man, "Young man, your sins are forgiven."

⁶Some of the teachers of the law were sitting there, thinking to themselves, ⁷"Why does this man say things like that? He is speaking as if he were God. Only God can forgive sins."

⁸Jesus knew immediately what these teachers of the law were thinking. So he said to them, "Why are you thinking these things? ⁹Which is easier: to tell this paralyzed man, 'Your sins are forgiven,' or to tell him, 'Stand up. Take your mat and walk'? ¹⁰But I will prove to you that the Son of Man*d* has authority on earth to forgive sins." So Jesus said to the paralyzed man, ¹¹"I tell you, stand up, take your mat, and go home." ¹²Immediately the paralyzed man stood up, took his mat, and walked out while everyone was watching him.

The people were amazed and praised God. They said, "We have never seen anything like this!"

¹³Jesus went to the lake again. The whole crowd followed him there, and he taught them. ¹⁴While he was walking along, he saw a man named Levi son of Alphaeus, sitting in the tax collector's booth. Jesus said to him, "Follow me," and he stood up and followed Jesus.

¹⁵Later, as Jesus was having dinner at Levi's

FORGIVENESS

The Christmas Gift

"I can't stand him! He's the one who left us. Why should I have to ruin my Christmas by spending it with him?" Juanita shouted at her mother through sobs.

"Honey, that was three years ago," Ellen Gonzales said. She put her hand on her daughter's shoulder. "A lot has happened since then. We're different people now—and happier too."

"That doesn't make it right. He still left us," Juanita countered.

Ellen sat down beside Juanita. "Your father needed work, and there was nothing here for him. He had to go someplace where he could feel useful and needed. I never believed he really wanted to leave us."

"But he did leave us," Juanita said. "And he never came back."

"You're right. But that doesn't mean he doesn't love you. Now he wants you to understand, to forgive him, and to get to know him again. Could you please forgive your father and go to his house for a few days for Christmas?" Ellen asked sympathetically.

"I guess I never really understood why he left, Mom." Juanita thought for a moment, then said, "I don't really want to, but I guess I could spend part of my Christmas vacation with Dad."

As Juanita reached for the phone, Ellen smiled and said quietly, "Maybe forgiveness can be your Christmas gift to your dad."

Forgiveness can bring healing to people and relationships. Read **Mark 2:1–12** to see how Jesus' miracle resulted in forgiveness and healing.
■ How did Jesus' and Juanita's forgiveness bring about healing?
■ Who needs a healing word of forgiveness from you?

CONSIDER . . .
■ calling someone you've not talked with for a long time because of a misunderstanding.
■ listing people you need to forgive, forgiving each person and then performing an act of service for each one to bring about healing.

FOR MORE, SEE . . .
■ Psalm 130 (p. 557)
■ Luke 5:17–26 (p. 1011)
■ Hebrews 12:14–15 (p. 1290)

house, many tax collectors and "sinners" were eating there with Jesus and his followers. Many

> **SIDELIGHT:** Most of Jesus' ministry took place around Lake Galilee (for example, see Mark 2:13–14). This lake is the world's lowest fresh-water lake, with a surface 680 feet below sea level. Despite the lake's prominence in Jesus' ministry, it's only mentioned three times in the Old Testament (Numbers 34:11, p. 157; Joshua 12:3, p. 205; and Joshua 13:27, p. 206).

people like this followed Jesus. [16]When the teachers of the law who were Pharisees[d] saw Jesus eating with the tax collectors and "sinners," they asked his followers, "Why does he eat with tax collectors and sinners?"

[17]Jesus heard this and said to them, "It is not the healthy people who need a doctor, but the sick. I did not come to invite good people but to invite sinners."

Jesus' Followers Are Criticized

[18]Now the followers of John[n] and the Pharisees[d] often gave up eating for a certain time.[n] Some people came to Jesus and said, "Why do John's followers and the followers of the Phari-

John John the Baptist, who preached to the Jewish people about Christ's coming (Mark 1:4-8).
gave ... time This is called "fasting." The people would give up eating for a special time of prayer and worship to God. It was also done to show sadness and disappointment.

CELEBRATING

Party Blues

Allison Vollaro's graduation party really drew a crowd. She had invited all her friends, which came to around thirty. Beyond that, her parents had invited several relatives and friends.

People filled every nook and corner in the house. A group of guys talked and joked on the sun deck. Several of the girls gathered in the kitchen and laughed at each other's stories. And a large assortment of other people crammed into the living room, talking about the graduation ceremony and chuckling at the antics of some of the kids.

Everyone was having a great time. Everyone, that is, except Allison. She stood quietly in a corner of the kitchen, only half-listening to the girls' conversation.

"What's wrong, Al?" asked Kriss Mitchell, walking quietly over to Allison. "You seem lost in your thoughts."

"Yeah, I guess I am," Allison said with a weak smile. "It's just that now that I'm out of school, I don't know what's going to happen to my friendships. I love you all so much; it makes me sad to think of you not being in my life anymore."

Kriss touched Allison on the arm. "Hey, listen, none of us knows what's going to happen from one day to the next. We may all get to stay together forever, or we may not. We just can't know for sure. But," Kriss added with a smile, "we're here today. So let's go join the others and have some fun, okay? After all, it is your party."

"Okay, okay," Allison said jokingly. Then she reached out and grabbed Kriss's hand. "Thanks, Kriss. I needed to hear that."

Kriss helped Allison realize the importance of celebrating good things that come along, even though they may not last. Jesus helped his disciples understand the same truth. Read the story Jesus used in **Mark 2:18–22**.

■ How was Allison like the Pharisees' disciples in this passage?
■ How can you celebrate Jesus' presence in your life, as this passage directs?

C O N S I D E R . . .

■ writing all the ways Jesus reveals his presence in your life, then thanking God for being so real to you.
■ throwing a party to celebrate friendship and God's love.

F O R   M O R E ,   S E E . . .

■ Isaiah 62:1–9 (p. 682)   ■ John 3:25–30 (p. 1062)
■ Matthew 9:14–17 (p. 923)

sees often give up eating, but your followers don't?"

¹⁹Jesus answered, "The friends of the bridegroom do not give up eating while the bridegroom is still with them. As long as the bridegroom is with them, they cannot give up eating. ²⁰But the time will come when the bridegroom will be taken from them, and then they will give up eating.

²¹"No one sews a patch of unshrunk cloth over a hole in an old coat. Otherwise, the patch will shrink and pull away—the new patch will pull away from the old coat. Then the hole will be worse. ²²Also, no one ever pours new wine into old leather bags. Otherwise, the new wine will break the bags, and the wine will be ruined along with the bags. But new wine should be put into new leather bags."

Jesus Is Lord of the Sabbath

²³One Sabbath*ᵈ* day, as Jesus was walking through some fields of grain, his followers began to pick some grain to eat. ²⁴The Pharisees*ᵈ* said to Jesus, "Why are your followers doing what is not lawful on the Sabbath day?"

²⁵Jesus answered, "Have you never read what David did when he and those with him were hungry and needed food? ²⁶During the time of Abiathar the high priest, David went into God's house and ate the holy bread, which is lawful only for priests to eat. And David also gave some of the bread to those who were with him."

²⁷Then Jesus said to the Pharisees, "The Sabbath day was made to help people; they were not made to be ruled by the Sabbath day. ²⁸So then, the Son of Man*ᵈ* is Lord even of the Sabbath day."

FREEDOM

Free to Choose

Angela Ferrara stared out the window of her second-story bedroom. Her father had just told the family he was taking a job in California. They would move at the end of February.

Angela cried as she thought about the friends she would have to leave and the basketball team she would have to quit. It wasn't fair. She wanted to be angry at her dad for moving during her last year in junior high school. If only they could wait until June.

She had pleaded with her parents not to move, but they wouldn't change their minds. Angela had no choice. The family would have to stay together, and she knew her parents expected her to cooperate.

"Can I come in?"

Surprised, Angela turned and saw her dad standing in the doorway of her room. Angela hesitated. "Yeah, I guess," she said finally.

"Your mother and I have been thinking. And we think you're old enough to make good decisions about your life, Angela," her dad began. "You may stay with your Aunt Sarah until school is out if you'd like to."

Angela's expression changed from disgust to a smile. "You mean I have a choice?" Angela asked incredulously. "I can decide for myself?"

"We don't want the family to be separated," her dad said. "But, on the other hand, we don't want to force you to make a move in the middle of the school year. It's up to you."

Angela's parents trusted her to make a responsible decision. In a similar way, God gives us guidelines for our lives, but trusts us to use those guidelines responsibly. Read **Mark 2:23—3:6** to see how Jesus encouraged people to follow those guidelines.

■ What similarities are there between Jesus' use of guidelines and Angela's parents' decision to let Angela decide for herself?

■ What kind of judging attitudes have you had toward people that are similar to the Pharisees' attitudes?

CONSIDER . . .

■ talking to your parents about the purpose of family rules you don't understand.

■ *asking kids from other Christian churches about their beliefs.* Celebrate the freedom you each have to be different!

FOR MORE, SEE . . .

■ Amos 5:21–24 (p. 845)

■ Matthew 12:1–14 (p. 928)

■ Luke 6:1–11 (p. 1012)

Jesus Heals a Man's Hand

3 Another time when Jesus went into a synagogue,[d] a man with a crippled hand was there. [2]Some people watched Jesus closely to see if he would heal the man on the Sabbath[d] day so they could accuse him.

[3]Jesus said to the man with the crippled hand, "Stand up here in the middle of everyone."

[4]Then Jesus asked the people, "Which is lawful on the Sabbath day: to do good or to do evil, to save a life or to kill?" But they said nothing to answer him.

[5]Jesus was angry as he looked at the people, and he felt very sad because they were stubborn. Then he said to the man, "Hold out your hand." The man held out his hand and it was healed. [6]Then the Pharisees[d] left and began making plans with the Herodians[n] about a way to kill Jesus.

Many People Follow Jesus

[7]Jesus left with his followers for the lake, and a large crowd from Galilee followed him. [8]Also many people came from Judea, from Jerusalem, from Idumea, from the lands across the Jordan River, and from the area of Tyre and Sidon. When they heard what Jesus was doing, many people came to him. [9]When Jesus saw the crowds, he told his followers to get a boat ready for him to keep people from crowding against him. [10]He had healed many people, so all the sick were pushing toward him to touch him. [11]When evil spirits saw Jesus, they fell down before him and shouted, "You are the Son of God!" [12]But Jesus strongly warned them not to tell who he was.

Jesus Chooses His Twelve Apostles

[13]Then Jesus went up on a mountain and called to him the men he wanted, and they came to him. [14]Jesus chose twelve men and called them apostles.[d] He wanted them to be with him, and he wanted to send them out to preach [15]and to have the authority to force demons[d] out of people. [16]These are the twelve men he chose: Simon (Jesus named him Peter), [17]James and John, the sons of Zebedee (Jesus named them Boanerges, which means "Sons of Thunder"), [18]Andrew, Philip, Bartholomew, Matthew, Thomas, James the son of Alphaeus, Thaddaeus, Simon the Zealot,[d] [19]and Judas Iscariot, who later turned against Jesus.

Some People Say Jesus Has a Devil

[20]Then Jesus went home, but again a crowd gathered. There were so many people that Jesus and his followers could not eat. [21]When his family heard this, they went to get him because they thought he was out of his mind. [22]But the teachers of the law from Jerusalem were saying, "Beelzebul[d] is living inside him! He uses power from the ruler of demons[d] to force demons out of people."

[23]So Jesus called the people together and taught them with stories. He said, "Satan will not force himself out of people. [24]A kingdom that is divided cannot continue, [25]and a family that is divided cannot continue. [26]And if Satan is against himself and fights against his own people, he cannot continue; that is the end of Satan. [27]No one can enter a strong person's house and steal his things unless he first ties up the strong person. Then he can steal things from the house. [28]I tell you the truth, all sins that people do and all the things people say against God can be forgiven. [29]But anyone who speaks against the Holy Spirit[d] will never be forgiven; he is guilty of a sin that continues forever."

[30]Jesus said this because the teachers of the law said that he had an evil spirit inside him.

Jesus' True Family

[31]Then Jesus' mother and brothers arrived. Standing outside, they sent someone in to tell him to come out. [32]Many people were sitting around Jesus, and they said to him, "Your mother and brothers are waiting for you outside."

[33]Jesus asked, "Who are my mother and my brothers?" [34]Then he looked at those sitting around him and said, "Here are my mother and my brothers! [35]My true brother and sister and mother are those who do what God wants."

A Story About Planting Seed

4 Again Jesus began teaching by the lake. A great crowd gathered around him, so he sat down in a boat near the shore. All the people stayed on the shore close to the water. [2]Jesus taught them many things, using stories. He said, [3]"Listen! A farmer went out to plant his seed. [4]While he was planting, some seed fell by the road, and the birds came and ate it up. [5]Some seed fell on rocky ground where there wasn't much dirt. That seed grew very fast, because the ground was not deep. [6]But when the sun rose, the plants dried up because they did not have deep roots. [7]Some other seed fell among thorny weeds, which grew and choked the good plants. So those plants did not produce a crop. [8]Some other seed fell on good ground and began to grow. It got taller and produced a crop. Some plants made thirty times more, some made sixty times more, and some made a hundred times more."

[9]Then Jesus said, "You people who can hear me, listen!"

Herodians A political group that followed Herod and his family.

Jesus Tells Why He Used Stories

[10]Later, when Jesus was alone, the twelve apostles[d] and others around him asked him about the stories.

> **SIDELIGHT:** Jesus' story about planting seeds (Mark 4:1–9) not only has spiritual truth, but tells a lot about farming in those days. After plowing a field, farmers would walk through the field scattering seeds around the field. Then they would go back over the field dragging branches across to cover the seeds and protect them from birds and strong winds.

[11]Jesus said, "You can know the secret about the kingdom of God. But to other people I tell everything by using stories [12]so that:
'They will look and look, but they will not
    learn.
They will listen and listen, but they will not
    understand.
If they did learn and understand,
    they would come back to me and be
       forgiven.' "   *Isaiah 6:9-10*

Jesus Explains the Seed Story

[13]Then Jesus said to his followers, "Don't you understand this story? If you don't, how will you understand any story? [14]The farmer is like a person who plants God's message in people. [15]Sometimes the teaching falls on the road. This is like the people who hear the teaching of God, but Satan quickly comes and takes away the teaching that was planted in them. [16]Others are like the seed planted on rocky ground. They hear the teaching and quickly accept it with joy. [17]But since they don't allow the teaching to go deep into their lives, they keep it only a short time. When trouble or persecution comes because of the teaching they accepted, they quickly give up. [18]Others are like the seed planted among the thorny weeds. They hear

---

EVIL

Fearful Escape

Susan Platt was small, tired, and afraid. Her troubled eyes continually darted around the crowded bus stop. Everyone looked suspicious to Susan and made her want to run somewhere—anywhere—to get away from those who might find her and take her back.

Susan had a good reason to be afraid. Although she looked like any other teenager in Los Angeles, Susan was different from most. For the past six years, Susan had been involved in a coven that pledged itself to worship Satan. It had seemed fun when she started. Now, at eighteen, she wanted out.

Susan pulled at the sleeves of her sweater. Her arms must not be seen. They would expose her. Carved into her flesh were Satanic symbols to identify her as a devout Satanist. These marks were only an outward sign of the evil she had witnessed.

Susan had met some Christians a few years earlier. They had tried to tell her the truth about God's love and had offered to help her escape to a new way of life. She had refused then, but now she was going to find them.

Susan scanned the bus stop one last time. Seeing that no one was following her, she breathed a sigh of relief. As she climbed up the bus steps, Susan thought about how each step she took brought her closer to the freedom Jesus offered.

Since the beginning of time, Satan has lied to people, telling them his way is right and God's way is evil. **Mark 3:20–35** shows one instance when Satan convinced people that Jesus himself had an evil spirit.

■ Why did Susan and the people in Jesus' day fear Satan?
■ What promise do you see in this passage that helps you in the face of evil?

C O N S I D E R . . .
■ praying for your church and family to be united so they can stand against evil.
■ identifying an evil influence in your life and working to get rid of it.

F O R   M O R E ,   S E E . . . .
■ Genesis 3 (p. 4)
■ Matthew 9:32–34 (p. 923)
■ John 10:19–21 (p. 1075)

the teaching, [19]but the worries of this life, the temptation of wealth, and many other evil desires keep the teaching from growing and producing fruit[n] in their lives. [20]Others are like the seed planted in the good ground. They hear the teaching and accept it. Then they grow and produce fruit—sometimes thirty times more, sometimes sixty times more, and sometimes a hundred times more."

Use What You Have

[21]Then Jesus said to them, "Do you hide a lamp under a bowl or under a bed? No! You put the lamp on a lampstand. [22]Everything that is hidden will be made clear and every secret thing will be made known. [23]You people who can hear me, listen!

[24]"Think carefully about what you hear. The way you give to others is the way God will give to you, but God will give you even more. [25]Those who have understanding will be given more. But those who do not have understanding, even what they have will be taken away from them."

Jesus Uses a Story About Seed

[26]Then Jesus said, "The kingdom of God is like someone who plants seed in the ground. [27]Night and day, whether the person is asleep or awake, the seed still grows, but the person does not know how it grows. [28]By itself the earth produces grain. First the plant grows, then the head, and then all the grain in the head. [29]When the grain is ready, the farmer cuts it, because this is the harvest time."

A Story About Mustard Seed

[30]Then Jesus said, "How can I show you what the kingdom of God is like? What story can I use to explain it? [31]The kingdom of God is like a mustard seed, the smallest seed you plant in the ground. [32]But when planted, this seed grows and becomes the largest of all garden plants. It produces large branches, and the wild birds can make nests in its shade."

[33]Jesus used many stories like these to teach the crowd God's message—as much as they could understand. [34]He always used stories to

producing fruit   To produce fruit means to have in your life the good things God wants.

FAITH

It's Alive!

Witness, if you will, one of the most efficient, self-contained structures in nature. It possesses—on its own—almost everything it needs to survive and grow. It has its own coat, its own embryo and its own food supply.

It can even impregnate itself. That's right; each one has the male and female components it needs to create a fertilized egg.

The reproductive system is incredible, but it does need extra help to grow. After fertilization, it remains dormant until warm, moist conditions promote germination.

Then its coat softens and the metabolism rate in the cells increases. It drinks water and even starts "breathing," while a simple digestion begins. The digested food travels to new areas of growth that emerge when cell division begins.

And congratulations, Mr. and Mrs. Seed, it's a plant!

The incredible seed is a lot like the kingdom of God. Read **Mark 4:26–34** to see how.

■ How is a seed's reproductive system like faith's growth process in you?
■ According to this passage, what benefits can come from faith's growth in you? What benefits can come from many people growing in faith?

C O N S I D E R . . .

■ working in a garden and drawing other parallels between the plant world and faith. Write your own parable to illustrate those parallels.
■ choosing one quality from 2 Peter 1:5–9 (p. 1311) to add to your faith. Create one project to help develop that quality.

F O R   M O R E ,   S E E . . .

■ Ecclesiastes 11:1–6 (p. 606)
■ Matthew 13:24–32 (p. 931)
■ Luke 13:18–20 (p. 1031)

teach them. But when he and his followers were alone, Jesus explained everything to them.

Jesus Calms a Storm

[35]That evening, Jesus said to his followers, "Let's go across the lake." [36]Leaving the crowd behind, they took him in the boat just as he was. There were also other boats with them. [37]A very strong wind came up on the lake. The waves came over the sides and into the boat so that it was already full of water. [38]Jesus was at the back of the boat, sleeping with his head on a cushion. His followers woke him and said, "Teacher, don't you care that we are drowning!"

[39]Jesus stood up and commanded the wind and said to the waves, "Quiet! Be still!" Then the wind stopped, and it became completely calm.

[40]Jesus said to his followers, "Why are you afraid? Do you still have no faith?"

[41]The followers were very afraid and asked each other, "Who is this? Even the wind and the waves obey him!"

A Man with Demons Inside Him

5 Jesus and his followers went to the other side of the lake to the area of the Gerasene people. [2]When Jesus got out of the boat, instantly a man with an evil spirit came to him from the burial caves. [3]This man lived in the caves, and no one could tie him up, not even with a chain. [4]Many times people had used chains to tie the man's hands and feet, but he always broke them off. No one was strong enough to control him. [5]Day and night he would wander around the burial caves and on the hills, screaming and cutting himself with stones. [6]While Jesus was still far away, the man saw him, ran to him, and fell down before him.

[7]The man shouted in a loud voice, "What do you want with me, Jesus, Son of the Most High God? I command you in God's name not to torture me!" [8]He said this because Jesus was saying to him, "You evil spirit, come out of the man."

[9]Then Jesus asked him, "What is your name?"

He answered, "My name is Legion,[n] because we are many spirits." [10]He begged Jesus again and again not to send them out of that area.

[11]A large herd of pigs was feeding on a hill near there. [12]The demons[d] begged Jesus, "Send us into the pigs; let us go into them." [13]So Jesus allowed them to do this. The evil spirits left the man and went into the pigs. Then the herd of pigs — about two thousand of them — rushed down the hill into the lake and were drowned.

[14]The herdsmen ran away and went to the town and to the countryside, telling everyone about this. So people went out to see what had happened. [15]They came to Jesus and saw the man who used to have the many evil spirits, sitting, clothed, and in his right mind. And they were frightened. [16]The people who saw this told the others what had happened to the man who had the demons living in him, and they told about the pigs. [17]Then the people began to beg Jesus to leave their area.

[18]As Jesus was getting back into the boat, the man who was freed from the demons begged to go with him.

[19]But Jesus would not let him. He said, "Go home to your family and tell them how much the Lord has done for you and how he has had mercy on you." [20]So the man left and began to tell the people in the Ten Towns[n] about what Jesus had done for him. And everyone was amazed.

Jesus Gives Life to a Dead Girl and Heals a Sick Woman

[21]When Jesus went in the boat back to the other side of the lake, a large crowd gathered around him there. [22]A leader of the synagogue,[d] named Jairus, came there, saw Jesus, and fell at his feet. [23]He begged Jesus, saying again and again, "My daughter is dying. Please come and put your hands on her so she will be healed and will live." [24]So Jesus went with him.

A large crowd followed Jesus and pushed very close around him. [25]Among them was a woman who had been bleeding for twelve years. [26]She had suffered very much from many doctors and had spent all the money she had, but instead of improving, she was getting worse. [27]When the woman heard about Jesus, she came up behind him in the crowd and touched his coat. [28]She thought, "If I can just touch his clothes, I will be healed." [29]Instantly her bleeding stopped, and she felt in her body that she was healed from her disease.

[30]At once Jesus felt power go out from him. So he turned around in the crowd and asked, "Who touched my clothes?"

[31]His followers said, "Look at how many people are pushing against you! And you ask, 'Who touched me?' "

[32]But Jesus continued looking around to see who had touched him. [33]The woman, knowing that she was healed, came and fell at Jesus' feet. Shaking with fear, she told him the whole truth. [34]Jesus said to her, "Dear woman, you are made well because you believed. Go in peace; be healed of your disease."

Legion Means very many. A legion was about five thousand men in the Roman army.
Ten Towns In Greek, called "Decapolis." It was an area east of Lake Galilee that once had ten main towns.

³⁵While Jesus was still speaking, some people came from the house of the synagogue leader. They said, "Your daughter is dead. There is no need to bother the teacher anymore."

³⁶But Jesus paid no attention to what they said. He told the synagogue leader, "Don't be afraid; just believe."

³⁷Jesus let only Peter, James, and John the brother of James go with him. ³⁸When they came to the house of the synagogue leader, Jesus found many people there making lots of noise and crying loudly. ³⁹Jesus entered the house and said to them, "Why are you crying and making so much noise? The child is not dead, only asleep." ⁴⁰But they laughed at him. So, after throwing them out of the house, Jesus took the child's father and mother and his three followers into the room where the child was. ⁴¹Taking hold of the girl's hand, he said to her, "Talitha, koum!" (This means, "Young girl, I tell you to stand up!") ⁴²At once the girl stood right up and began walking. (She was twelve years old.) Everyone was completely amazed. ⁴³Jesus gave them strict orders not to tell people about this. Then he told them to give the girl something to eat.

Jesus Goes to His Hometown

6 Jesus left there and went to his hometown, and his followers went with him. ²On the Sabbath*d* day he taught in the synagogue.*d* Many people heard him and were amazed, saying, "Where did this man get these teachings? What is this wisdom that has been given to him? And where did he get the power to do miracles?*d* ³He is just the carpenter, the son of Mary and the brother of James, Joseph, Judas, and Simon. And his sisters are here with us." So the people were upset with Jesus.

⁴Jesus said to them, "A prophet*d* is honored everywhere except in his hometown and with his own people and in his own home." ⁵So Jesus was not able to work any miracles there except to heal a few sick people by putting his hands on them. ⁶He was amazed at how many people had no faith.

Then Jesus went to other villages in that area and taught. ⁷He called his twelve followers together and got ready to send them out two by two and gave them authority over evil spirits. ⁸This is what Jesus commanded them: "Take nothing for your trip except a walking stick. Take no bread,

---

no bag, and no money in your pockets. ⁹Wear sandals, but take only the clothes you are wearing. ¹⁰When you enter a house, stay there until you leave that town. ¹¹If the people in a certain place refuse to welcome you or listen to you, leave that place. Shake its dust off your feet[n] as a warning to them."

¹²So the followers went out and preached that people should change their hearts and lives. ¹³They forced many demons[d] out and put olive oil on many sick people and healed them.

How John the Baptist Was Killed

¹⁴King Herod heard about Jesus, because he was now well known. Some people said, "He is John the Baptist,[d] who has risen from the dead. That is why he can work these miracles."[d]

¹⁵Others said, "He is Elijah."[n]

Other people said, "Jesus is a prophet,[d] like the prophets who lived long ago."

¹⁶When Herod heard this, he said, "I killed John by cutting off his head. Now he has risen from the dead!"

¹⁷Herod himself had ordered his soldiers to arrest John and put him in prison in order to please his wife, Herodias. She had been the wife of Philip, Herod's brother, but then Herod had married her. ¹⁸John had been telling Herod, "It is not lawful for you to be married to your brother's wife." ¹⁹So Herodias hated John and wanted to kill him. But she couldn't, ²⁰because Herod was afraid of John and protected him. He knew John was a good and holy man. Also, though John's preaching always bothered him, he enjoyed listening to John.

²¹Then the perfect time came for Herodias to cause John's death. On Herod's birthday, he gave a dinner party for the most important government leaders, the commanders of his army, and the most important people in Galilee. ²²When the daughter of Herodias came in and danced, she pleased Herod and the people eating with him.

So King Herod said to the girl, "Ask me for anything you want, and I will give it to you." ²³He promised her, "Anything you ask for I will give to you — up to half of my kingdom."

²⁴The girl went to her mother and asked, "What should I ask for?"

Her mother answered, "Ask for the head of John the Baptist."[d]

²⁵At once the girl went back to the king and said to him, "I want the head of John the Baptist *right now on a platter.*"

²⁶Although the king was very sad, he had made a promise, and his dinner guests had heard it. So he did not want to refuse what she asked. ²⁷Immediately the king sent a soldier to bring John's head. The soldier went and cut off John's head in the prison ²⁸and brought it back on a platter. He gave it to the girl, and the girl gave it to her mother. ²⁹When John's followers heard this, they came and got John's body and put it in a tomb.

More than Five Thousand Fed

³⁰The apostles[d] gathered around Jesus and told him about all the things they had done and taught. ³¹Crowds of people were coming and going so that Jesus and his followers did not even have time to eat. He said to them, "Come away by yourselves, and we will go to a lonely place to get some rest."

³²So they went in a boat by themselves to a lonely place. ³³But many people saw them leave and recognized them. So from all the towns they ran to the place where Jesus was going, and they got there before him. ³⁴When he arrived, he saw a great crowd waiting. He felt sorry for them, because they were like sheep without a shepherd. So he began to teach them many things.

³⁵When it was late in the day, his followers came to him and said, "No one lives in this place, and it is already very late. ³⁶Send the people away so they can go to the countryside and towns around here to buy themselves something to eat."

³⁷But Jesus answered, "You give them something to eat."

They said to him, "We would all have to work a month to earn enough money to buy that much bread!"

³⁸Jesus asked them, "How many loaves of bread do you have? Go and see."

When they found out, they said, "Five loaves and two fish."

³⁹Then Jesus told his followers to have the people sit in groups on the green grass. ⁴⁰So they sat in groups of fifty or a hundred. ⁴¹Jesus took the five loaves and two fish and, looking up to heaven, he thanked God for the food. He divided the bread and gave it to his followers for them to give to the people. Then he divided the two fish among them all. ⁴²All the people ate and were satisfied. ⁴³The followers filled twelve baskets

---

Shake . . . feet A warning. It showed that they were rejecting these people.
Elijah A man who spoke for God and who lived hundreds of years before Christ. See 1 Kings 17.

with the leftover pieces of bread and fish. ⁴⁴There were five thousand men who ate.

Jesus Walks on the Water

⁴⁵Immediately Jesus told his followers to get into the boat and go ahead of him to Bethsaida across the lake. He stayed there to send the people home. ⁴⁶After sending them away, he went into the hills to pray.

⁴⁷That night, the boat was in the middle of the lake, and Jesus was alone on the land. ⁴⁸He saw his followers struggling hard to row the boat, because the wind was blowing against them. Between three and six o'clock in the morning, Jesus came to them, walking on the water, and he wanted to walk past the boat. ⁴⁹But when they saw him walking on the water, they thought he was a ghost and cried out. ⁵⁰They all saw him and were afraid. But quickly Jesus spoke to them and said, "Have courage! It is I. Do not be afraid." ⁵¹Then he got into the boat with them, and the wind became calm. The followers were greatly amazed. ⁵²They did not understand about the miracle of the five loaves, because their minds were closed.

⁵³When they had crossed the lake, they came to shore at Gennesaret and tied the boat there. ⁵⁴When they got out of the boat, people immedi-

---

HUNGER AND POVERTY

The Multiplication Principle

"We have only three thousand cans. I wanted to collect ten thousand," Kristen Green complained to Mr. Rossetti, the principal of St. Francis De Sales High School in Columbus, Ohio. Mr. Rossetti was the one who had asked Kristen to chair her school's canned food drive for the soup kitchen.

Mr. Rossetti listened but didn't say much. Later that day during the school pep rally, he surprised Kristen by asking her to speak to the students about the food drive.

Kristen spoke about a man she had met at the local soup kitchen who each night asked for an extra plate of food for his dying wife. Kristen also told about a hungry woman who shared her orange with the person sitting beside her. She continued, "We think of starving people being in Ethiopia, but these people live three blocks from this school." Kristen challenged the students to meet the goal of ten thousand cans of food in the next week.

After the pep rally, students asked Kristen how they could help. Suddenly everyone was mobilized: The football team went door to door in the Columbus neighborhoods, asking for donations of canned goods. The Fellowship of Christian Athletes collected $1,500 worth of food in one night. Kristen and a friend asked area grocers for food donations.

By Wednesday, the goal of ten thousand cans was met—a goal people had thought was unrealistic. (Only four thousand cans had been collected the year before.) Kristen decided not to tell anyone the goal was reached before the deadline. On Friday, people cheered when she announced the total: 17,299 cans!

Kristen and others filled three school buses with the food. As they delivered the food to the soup kitchen, people standing in line thanked them and patted them on the back.

"We knew we were making a difference," Kristen says. "People were going to be able to eat."

Jesus and his disciples were also confronted with the challenge of feeding hungry people. Read **Mark 6:30–44** to see how Jesus fed a hungry mob.

■ How is the multiplication of canned food at De Sales High similar to Jesus multiplying food for the multitude? How is it different?

■ How have you seen Jesus increase your gifts or resources to help others?

C O N S I D E R . . . .

■ giving up eating a meal and spending time in prayer for those who have less to eat than you do. Donate the money you would have spent on the meal to World Vision, Special Programs, Pasadena, CA 91131, or to another relief agency.

■ organizing a canned food drive at your church or school.

F O R   M O R E   S E E . . .

■ 2 Kings 4:42–44 (p. 337)   ■ John 6:1–15 (p. 1066)

■ Matthew 14:13–21 (p. 934)

ately recognized Jesus. [55]They ran everywhere in that area and began to bring sick people on mats wherever they heard he was. [56]And everywhere he went — into towns, cities, or countryside — the people brought the sick to the marketplaces. They begged him to let them touch just the edge of his coat, and all who touched it were healed.

Obey God's Law

7 When some Pharisees[d] and some teachers of the law came from Jerusalem, they gathered around Jesus. [2]They saw that some of Jesus' followers ate food with hands that were not clean,[d] that is, they hadn't washed them. [3](The Pharisees and all the Jews never eat before washing their hands in a special way according to their unwritten laws. [4]And when they buy something in the market, they never eat it until they wash themselves in a special way. They also follow many other unwritten laws, such as the washing of cups, pitchers, and pots.)

[5]The Pharisees and the teachers of the law said to Jesus, "Why don't your followers obey the unwritten laws which have been handed down to us? Why do your followers eat their food with hands that are not clean?"

[6]Jesus answered, "Isaiah was right when he spoke about you hypocrites.[d] He wrote,

'These people show honor to me with words, but their hearts are far from me.
[7]Their worship of me is worthless.
The things they teach are nothing but human rules.'   *Isaiah 29:13*

[8]You have stopped following the commands of God, and you follow only human teachings."

[9]Then Jesus said to them, "You cleverly ignore the commands of God so you can follow your own teachings. [10]Moses said, 'Honor your father and your mother,'[n] and 'Anyone who says cruel things to his father or mother must be put to death.'[n] [11]But you say a person can tell his father or mother, 'I have something I could use to help you, but it is Corban — a gift to God.' [12]You no longer let that person use that money for his fa-

---

'Honor ... mother'   Quotation from Exodus 20:12; Deuteronomy 5:16.
'Anyone ... death.'   Quotation from Exodus 21:17.

HYPOCRISY

An Open Letter to God

Craig Mackey was tired of seeing what he called "the Dr. Jekyll and Mr. Hyde" sides of his father. In his frustration, he wrote this letter to God.

Dear God,

There are a few things I just don't understand about people and the way they act. Let me tell you what I mean.

Take my dad, for example. Don't get me wrong. He's a nice guy; he goes to church with us and everything. But when it comes to his business, he really changes. Dad's always talking about how he really "got the best of that guy" in a business deal or how he "beat her out of a contract." It just doesn't seem very Christian.

Oh, and another place is on the highway. My dad gets really angry at other drivers and sometimes even yells at them.

And, oh well, I guess I just don't understand. It just doesn't seem very Christian.

Can you help me understand, God?

Craig

Hypocrisy is common. Even in Jesus' day, Jesus' followers were troubled by hypocrites. Read **Mark 7:1–23** to learn more about the situation.

■ What was hypocritical about Craig's dad's actions and the Pharisees' actions?

■ According to this passage, what's the cure for hypocrisy?

CONSIDER...

■ evaluating your own life for any hypocrisies and applying the "cure" to get rid of them.
■ writing a letter to Craig that responds to his frustrations.

FOR MORE, SEE...

■ Isaiah 29:13–14 (p. 645)
■ Matthew 15:1–20 (p. 934)

■ Romans 14:13–18 (p. 1160)

ther or his mother. [13]By your own rules, which you teach people, you are rejecting what God said. And you do many things like that."

[14]After Jesus called the crowd to him again, he said, "Every person should listen to me and understand what I am saying. [15]There is nothing people put into their bodies that makes them unclean. People are made unclean by the things that come out of them." [16] n

[17]When Jesus left the people and went into the house, his followers asked him about this story. [18]Jesus said, "Do you still not understand? Surely you know that nothing that enters someone from the outside can make that person unclean. [19]It does not go into the mind, but into the stomach. Then it goes out of the body." (When Jesus said this, he meant that no longer was any food unclean for people to eat.)

[20]And Jesus said, "The things that come out of people are the things that make them unclean. [21]All these evil things begin inside people, in the mind: evil thoughts, sexual sins, stealing, murder, adultery,[d] [22]greed, evil actions, lying, doing sinful things, jealousy, speaking evil of others, pride, and foolish living. [23]All these evil things come from inside and make people unclean."

Jesus Helps a Non-Jewish Woman

[24]Jesus left that place and went to the area around Tyre. When he went into a house, he did not want anyone to know he was there, but he could not stay hidden. [25]A woman whose daughter had an evil spirit in her heard that he was there. So she quickly came to Jesus and fell at his feet. [26]She was Greek, born in Phoenicia, in Syria. She begged Jesus to force the demon[d] out of her daughter.

[27]Jesus told the woman, "It is not right to take the children's bread and give it to the dogs. First let the children eat all they want."

[28]But she answered, "Yes, Lord, but even the dogs under the table can eat the children's crumbs."

[29]Then Jesus said, "Because of your answer, you may go. The demon has left your daughter."

[30]The woman went home and found her daughter lying in bed; the demon was gone.

Jesus Heals a Deaf Man

[31]Then Jesus left the area around Tyre and went through Sidon to Lake Galilee, to the area of the Ten Towns. n [32]While he was there, some people brought a man to him who was deaf and could not talk plainly. The people begged Jesus to put his hand on the man to heal him.

[33]Jesus led the man away from the crowd, by himself. He put his fingers in the man's ears and then spit and touched the man's tongue. [34]Looking up to heaven, he sighed and said to the man, "Ephphatha!" (This means, "Be opened.") [35]Instantly the man was able to hear and to use his tongue so that he spoke clearly.

[36]Jesus commanded the people not to tell anyone about what happened. But the more he commanded them, the more they told about it. [37]They were completely amazed and said, "Jesus does everything well. He makes the deaf hear! And those who can't talk he makes able to speak."

More than Four Thousand People Fed

8 Another time there was a great crowd with Jesus that had nothing to eat. So Jesus called his followers and said, [2]"I feel sorry for these people, because they have already been with me for three days, and they have nothing to eat. [3]If I send them home hungry, they will faint on the way. Some of them live a long way from here."

[4]Jesus' followers answered, "How can we get enough bread to feed all these people? We are far away from any town."

[5]Jesus asked, "How many loaves of bread do you have?"

They answered, "Seven."

[6]Jesus told the people to sit on the ground. Then he took the seven loaves, gave thanks to God, and divided the bread. He gave the pieces to his followers to give to the people, and they did so. [7]The followers also had a few small fish. After Jesus gave thanks for the fish, he told his followers to give them to the people also. [8]All the people ate and were satisfied. Then his followers filled seven baskets with the leftover pieces of food. [9]There were about four thousand people who ate. After they had eaten, Jesus sent them home. [10]Then right away he got into a boat with his followers and went to the area of Dalmanutha.

The Leaders Ask for a Miracle

[11]The Pharisees[d] came to Jesus and began to ask him questions. Hoping to trap him, they asked Jesus for a miracle[d] from God. [12]Jesus sighed

---

Verse 16 Some Greek copies add verse 16: "You people who can hear me, listen!"
Ten Towns In Greek, called "Decapolis." It was an area east of Lake Galilee that once had ten main towns.

deeply and said, "Why do you people ask for a miracle as a sign? I tell you the truth, no sign will be given to you." [13]Then Jesus left the Pharisees and went in the boat to the other side of the lake.

Guard Against Wrong Teachings

[14]His followers had only one loaf of bread with them in the boat; they had forgotten to bring more. [15]Jesus warned them, "Be careful! Beware of the yeast of the Pharisees[d] and the yeast of Herod."

[16]His followers discussed the meaning of this, saying, "He said this because we have no bread."

[17]Knowing what they were talking about, Jesus asked them, "Why are you talking about not having bread? Do you still not see or understand? Are your minds closed? [18]You have eyes, but you don't really see. You have ears, but you don't really listen. Remember when [19]I divided five loaves of bread for the five thousand? How many

baskets did you fill with leftover pieces of food?"

They answered, "Twelve."

[20]"And when I divided seven loaves of bread for the four thousand, how many baskets did you fill with leftover pieces of food?"

They answered, "Seven."

[21]Then Jesus said to them, "Don't you understand yet?"

Jesus Heals a Blind Man

[22]Jesus and his followers came to Bethsaida. There some people brought a blind man to Jesus and begged him to touch the man. [23]So Jesus took the blind man's hand and led him out of the village. Then he spit on the man's eyes and put his hands on the man and asked, "Can you see now?"

[24]The man looked up and said, "Yes, I see people, but they look like trees walking around."

[25]Again Jesus put his hands on the man's eyes.

SICKNESS

She Made a Difference

In the 1940s, more than 500,000 people in the city of Calcutta (5 percent of the city's population) literally lived and died in the streets. With summer temperatures normally above 115 degrees and winter temperatures hovering in the high 90s, the city could seem like hell on earth. It was there that the "poorest of the poor" lived, plagued by leprosy, tuberculosis, pneumonia and, most of all, poverty.

What hope was there in such a place? Surely no one could make a difference there. But Agnes thought differently. She believed that God was calling her to bring hope to these poor and downtrodden people.

In her journal, Agnes, now known as Mother Teresa, described her first day in the slums as a day of meeting Christ. She met Christ face to face there—the hungry Christ, the naked Christ, the sick Christ, the homeless Christ. She said the touch of him in this distressing disguise gave her great joy, peace, and strength.

So, clad in a white sari edged with blue, Mother Teresa began her work. She and a group of nuns taught the children of the poor. They provided care for lepers who could get help nowhere else. They built shelters and hospitals so the poor would have a place out of the streets. They fed the hungry and loved the unlovable. They literally changed the face of Calcutta.

Jesus' love flowed through Mother Teresa to touch people. Jesus' love always makes a difference. When Jesus touches sick people, their lives are never the same. Read **Mark 7:31–37** and imagine how the sick people who met Jesus must have felt.

■ How is Mother Teresa's hands-on approach to ministry like Jesus' approach?

■ Which of Jesus' actions in this passage are most important to people who are sick?

C O N S I D E R . . .

■ doing a task that you don't like to do (such as cleaning a bathroom) for a homebound member of your church.

■ talking to your pastor about how your church can minister to people with AIDS.

F O R   M O R E ,   S E E . . .

■ Leviticus 13 (p. 108)
■ Matthew 8:1–4 (p. 920)
■ Luke 17:11–19 (p. 1040)

Then the man opened his eyes wide and they were healed, and he was able to see everything clearly. [26]Jesus told him to go home, saying, "Don't go into the town."

Peter Says Jesus Is the Christ

[27]Jesus and his followers went to the towns around Caesarea Philippi. While they were traveling, Jesus asked them, "Who do people say I am?"

[28]They answered, "Some say you are John the Baptist.[d] Others say you are Elijah,[n] and others say you are one of the prophets."[d]

[29]Then Jesus asked, "But who do you say I am?"

Peter answered, "You are the Christ."[d]

[30]Jesus warned his followers not to tell anyone who he was.

[31]Then Jesus began to teach them that the Son of Man[d] must suffer many things and that he would be rejected by the older Jewish leaders, the leading priests, and the teachers of the law. He told them that the Son of Man must be killed and then rise from the dead after three days. [32]Jesus told them plainly what would happen. Then Peter took Jesus aside and began to tell him not to talk like that. [33]But Jesus turned and looked at his followers. Then he told Peter not to talk that way. He said, "Go away from me, Satan![n] You don't care about the things of God, but only about things people think are important."

[34]Then Jesus called the crowd to him, along with his followers. He said, "If people want to follow me, they must give up the things they want. They must be willing even to give up their lives to follow me. [35]Those who want to save their lives will give up true life. But those who give up their lives for me and for the Good News[d] will have true life. [36]It is worth nothing for them to have the whole world if they lose their souls. [37]They could never pay enough to buy back their souls. [38]The people who live now are living in a sinful and evil time. If people are ashamed of me and my teaching, the Son of Man[d] will be ashamed of them when he comes with his Father's glory and with the holy angels."

9 Then Jesus said to the people, "I tell you the truth, some people standing here will see the kingdom of God come with power before they die."

Jesus Talks with Moses and Elijah

[2]Six days later, Jesus took Peter, James, and John up on a high mountain by themselves. While they watched, Jesus' appearance was changed. [3]His clothes became shining white, whiter than any person could make them. [4]Then Elijah and Moses[n] appeared to them, talking with Jesus.

[5]Peter said to Jesus, "Teacher, it is good that we are here. Let us make three tents—one for you, one for Moses, and one for Elijah." [6]Peter did not know what to say, because he and the others were so frightened.

[7]Then a cloud came and covered them, and a voice came from the cloud, saying, "This is my Son, whom I love. Listen to him!"

[8]Suddenly Peter, James, and John looked around, but they saw only Jesus there alone with them.

[9]As they were coming down the mountain, Jesus commanded them not to tell anyone about what they had seen until the Son of Man[d] had risen from the dead.

[10]So the followers obeyed Jesus, but they discussed what he meant about rising from the dead.

[11]Then they asked Jesus, "Why do the teachers of the law say that Elijah must come first?"

[12]Jesus answered, "They are right to say that Elijah must come first and make everything the way it should be. But why does the Scripture[d] say that the Son of Man will suffer much and that people will treat him as if he were nothing? [13]I tell you that Elijah has already come. And people did to him whatever they wanted to do, just as the Scriptures said it would happen."

Jesus Heals a Sick Boy

[14]When Jesus, Peter, James, and John came back to the other followers, they saw a great crowd around them and the teachers of the law arguing with them. [15]But as soon as the crowd saw Jesus, the people were surprised and ran to welcome him.

[16]Jesus asked, "What are you arguing about?"

[17]A man answered, "Teacher, I brought my son to you. He has an evil spirit in him that stops him from talking. [18]When the spirit attacks him, it throws him on the ground. Then my son foams at the mouth, grinds his teeth, and becomes very stiff. I asked your followers to force the evil spirit out, but they couldn't."

[19]Jesus answered, "You people have no faith. How long must I stay with you? How long must I put up with you? Bring the boy to me."

[20]So the followers brought him to Jesus. As soon as the evil spirit saw Jesus, it made the boy lose control of himself, and he fell down and rolled on the ground, foaming at the mouth.

Elijah   A man who spoke for God and who lived hundreds of years before Christ. See 1 Kings 17.
Satan   Name for the devil meaning "the enemy." Jesus means that Peter was talking like Satan.
Elijah and Moses   Two of the most important Jewish leaders in the past. Moses had given them the law, and Elijah was an important prophet.

²¹Jesus asked the boy's father, "How long has this been happening?"

The father answered, "Since he was very young. ²²The spirit often throws him into a fire or into water to kill him. If you can do anything for him, please have pity on us and help us."

²³Jesus said to the father, "You said, 'If you can!' All things are possible for the one who believes."

²⁴Immediately the father cried out, "I do believe! Help me to believe more!"

²⁵When Jesus saw that a crowd was quickly gathering, he ordered the evil spirit, saying, "You spirit that makes people unable to hear or speak, I command you to come out of this boy and never enter him again!"

²⁶The evil spirit screamed and caused the boy to fall on the ground again. Then the spirit came out. The boy looked as if he were dead, and many people said, "He is dead!" ²⁷But Jesus took hold of the boy's hand and helped him to stand up.

²⁸When Jesus went into the house, his followers began asking him privately, "Why couldn't we force that evil spirit out?"

²⁹Jesus answered, "That kind of spirit can only be forced out by prayer."

Jesus Talks About His Death

³⁰Then Jesus and his followers left that place and went through Galilee. He didn't want anyone to know where he was, ³¹because he was teaching his followers. He said to them, "The Son of Manᵈ will be handed over to people, and they will kill him. After three days, he will rise from the dead." ³²But the followers did not understand what Jesus meant, and they were afraid to ask him.

Who Is the Greatest?

³³Jesus and his followers went to Capernaum. When they went into a house there, he asked them, "What were you arguing about on the road?" ³⁴But the followers did not answer, because their argument on the road was about which one of them was the greatest.

³⁵Jesus sat down and called the twelve apostlesᵈ to him. He said, "Whoever wants to be the most important must be last of all and servant of all."

FAITH

Over a Cliff

Ethan Magness peered anxiously over his shoulder down the steep cliff. The bottom of the deep ravine appeared to be miles away. Standing on the edge of the rocks, he heard the rappelling instructor yell, "Just lean straight back into the air; the ropes will hold you."

"I can't lean back," Ethan thought. "How do I know the ropes will hold me?"

"Come on, Ethan, are you afraid?" Ellie asked.

Sweat poured down his face as he thought about the cliff. He was afraid, but he didn't want anyone to know it—especially not Ellie.

"Come on, Ethan," the instructor encouraged. "It's all right; just have faith in the ropes. They'll hold you."

Ethan held his breath and leaned back. He was swinging in the air, but the ropes did hold! Cautiously, he let out the tension on the rope and slid down. Finally he reached the bottom. Whew!

Just as it took faith for Ethan to rappel, it also took faith for the disciples to believe in Jesus. Read **Mark 9:1—9** to see an experience the disciples had with Jesus.

■ How is Ethan's faith in his ropes similar to the faith the disciples needed to believe in Jesus?

■ How can you overcome hard-to-believe things that stand in the way of your faith in Jesus?

CONSIDER . . .

■ listing obstacles to your faith on separate sheets of paper and tearing up each sheet.

■ doing one risky thing to demonstrate your faith. For example, tell a non-Christian friend about Jesus or take a stand for or against a social issue.

FOR MORE . SEE . . .

■ Psalm 130 (p. 557)
■ Matthew 17:1–9 (p. 937)
■ Luke 9:28–36 (p. 1019)

³⁶Then Jesus took a small child and had him stand among them. Taking the child in his arms, he said, ³⁷"Whoever accepts a child like this in my name accepts me. And whoever accepts me accepts the One who sent me."

Anyone Not Against Us Is for Us

³⁸Then John said, "Teacher, we saw someone using your name to force demons*d* out of a person. We told him to stop, because he does not belong to our group."

³⁹But Jesus said, "Don't stop him, because anyone who uses my name to do powerful things will not easily say evil things about me. ⁴⁰Whoever is not against us is with us. ⁴¹I tell you the truth, whoever gives you a drink of water because you belong to the Christ*d* will truly get his reward.

⁴²"If one of these little children believes in me, and someone causes that child to sin, it would be better for that person to have a large stone tied around his neck and be drowned in the sea. ⁴³If your hand causes you to sin, cut it off. It is better for you to lose part of your body and live forever than to have two hands and go to hell, where the fire never goes out. ⁴⁴ *n* ⁴⁵If your foot causes you to sin, cut it off. It is better for you to lose part of your body and to live forever than to have two feet and be thrown into hell. ⁴⁶ *n* ⁴⁷If your eye causes you to sin, take it out. It is better for you to enter the kingdom of God with only one eye than to have two eyes and be thrown into hell. ⁴⁸In hell the worm does not die; the fire is never put out. ⁴⁹Every person will be salted with fire.

⁵⁰"Salt is good, but if the salt loses its salty taste, you cannot make it salty again. So, be full of salt, and have peace with each other."

Verse 44   Some Greek copies of Mark add verse 44, which is the same as verse 43.
Verse 46   Some Greek copies of Mark add verse 46, which is the same as verse 43.

POPULARITY

Everyone Is Going

Sam Collins slammed his locker shut. It was Friday afternoon: the final bell had rung. He needed to catch Roy and Justin before they got on their bus to be sure all of them were meeting at the football game that night.

As Sam turned from his locker, his foot caught on a wheel. It was Alex O'Brien's wheelchair. Alex had broken his neck the previous spring in a diving accident and was paralyzed from the shoulders down.

"Hey, Sam, what are you guys doin' tonight?" Alex asked.

"Well, uh. . . ." Sam hesitated as his eyes searched the hall for the other guys, but Alex didn't wait for an answer.

"Would you like to come over to my place? My mom said she'd pick up some videos. Could you open my locker and put away the books in my backpack, please?"

Sam impatiently unloaded the backpack, opened the locker, and deposited the books. As Sam closed the locker, Alex asked again, "Well? What about tonight?"

Sam glanced down the empty hallway. The buses were pulling away. It was too late to make plans with Justin and Roy. Alex needed a friend. But everyone would be going to the game.

Sam thought for a moment and then smiled at Alex. "What time do you want me to come over?"

The disciples also had to make a decision about what it meant to be popular. They were arguing about who was the greatest or most popular. **Read Mark 9:30—37** to see how Jesus turned the tables on them.

■ How would Sam's actions make him important in the kingdom of God?
■ When have you had to decide between doing what's popular and what's right? How was that experience like the incident in this passage?

CONSIDER . . .

■ having lunch with an unpopular classmate.
■ doing a household chore that everyone in your family dislikes doing.

FOR MORE, SEE . . .

■ Proverbs 11:24—26 (p. 577)   ■ Philippians 2:5—7 (p. 1230)
■ Matthew 18:1—5 (p. 939)

Jesus Teaches About Divorce

10 Then Jesus left that place and went into the area of Judea and across the Jordan

River. Again, crowds came to him, and he taught them as he usually did.

[2]Some Pharisees[d] came to Jesus and tried to trick him. They asked, "Is it right for a man to divorce his wife?"

[3]Jesus answered, "What did Moses command you to do?"

[4]They said, "Moses allowed a man to write out divorce papers and send her away."[n]

[5]Jesus said, "Moses wrote that command for you because you were stubborn. [6]But when God made the world, 'he made them male and female.'[n] [7]'So a man will leave his father and mother and be united with his wife, [8]and the two will become one body.'[n] So there are not two, but one. [9]God has joined the two together, so no one should separate them."

[10]Later, in the house, his followers asked Jesus again about the question of divorce. [11]He answered, "Anyone who divorces his wife and marries another woman is guilty of adultery[d] against her. [12]And the woman who divorces her husband and marries another man is also guilty of adultery."

Jesus Accepts Children

[13]Some people brought their little children to Jesus so he could touch them, but his followers told them to stop. [14]When Jesus saw this, he was upset and said to them, "Let the little children come to me. Don't stop them, because the kingdom of God belongs to people who are like these children. [15]I tell you the truth, you must accept the kingdom of God as if you were a little child, or you will never enter it." [16]Then Jesus took the

children in his arms, put his hands on them, and blessed them.

A Rich Young Man's Question

[17]As Jesus started to leave, a man ran to him and fell on his knees before Jesus. The man asked, "Good teacher, what must I do to have life forever?"

[18]Jesus answered, "Why do you call me good? Only God is good. [19]You know the commands: 'You must not murder anyone. You must not be guilty of adultery.[d] You must not steal. You must not tell lies about your neighbor. You must not cheat. Honor your father and mother.' "[n]

[20]The man said, "Teacher, I have obeyed all these things since I was a boy."

[21]Jesus, looking at the man, loved him and said, "There is one more thing you need to do. Go and sell everything you have, and give the money to the poor, and you will have treasure in heaven. Then come and follow me."

[22]He was very sad to hear Jesus say this, and he left sorrowfully, because he was rich.

[23]Then Jesus looked at his followers and said, "How hard it will be for the rich to enter the kingdom of God!"

[24]The followers were amazed at what Jesus said. But he said again, "My children, it is very hard to enter the kingdom of God! [25]It is easier for a camel to go through the eye of a needle than for a rich person to enter the kingdom of God."

[26]The followers were even more surprised and said to each other, "Then who can be saved?"

[27]Jesus looked at them and said, "This is something people cannot do, but God can. God can do all things."

[28]Peter said to Jesus, "Look, we have left everything and followed you."

[29]Jesus said, "I tell you the truth, all those who have left houses, brothers, sisters, mother, father, children, or farms for me and for the Good News[d] [30]will get more than they left. Here in this world they will have a hundred times more homes, brothers, sisters, mothers, children, and fields. And with those things, they will also suffer for their belief. But in the age that is coming they will have life forever. [31]Many who have the highest place now will have the lowest place in the future. And many who have the lowest place now will have the highest place in the future."

Jesus Talks About His Death

[32]As Jesus and the people with him were on the

"Moses . . . away." Quotation from Deuteronomy 24:1.
'he made . . . female.' Quotation from Genesis 1:27.
'So . . . body.' Quotation from Genesis 2:24.
'You . . . mother.' Quotation from Exodus 20:12-16; Deuteronomy 5:16-20.

road to Jerusalem, he was leading the way. His followers were amazed, but others in the crowd who followed were afraid. Again Jesus took the twelve apostles[d] aside and began to tell them what was about to happen in Jerusalem. ³³He said, "Look, we are going to Jerusalem. The Son of Man[d] will be turned over to the leading priests and the teachers of the law. They will say that he must die, and they will turn him over to the non-Jewish people, ³⁴who will laugh at him and spit on him. They will beat him with whips and crucify him. But on the third day, he will rise to life again."

Two Followers Ask Jesus a Favor

³⁵Then James and John, sons of Zebedee, came to Jesus and said, "Teacher, we want to ask you to do something for us."

³⁶Jesus asked, "What do you want me to do for you?"

³⁷They answered, "Let one of us sit at your right side and one of us sit at your left side in your glory in your kingdom."

³⁸Jesus said, "You don't understand what you are asking. Can you drink the cup that I must drink? And can you be baptized with the same kind of baptism that I must go through?"[n]

³⁹They answered, "Yes, we can."

Jesus said to them, "You will drink the same cup that I will drink, and you will be baptized with the same baptism that I must go through. ⁴⁰But I cannot choose who will sit at my right or my left; those places belong to those for whom they have been prepared."

⁴¹When the other ten followers heard this, they began to be angry with James and John.

⁴²Jesus called them together and said, "The non-Jewish people have rulers. You know that those rulers love to show their power over the people, and their important leaders love to use all their authority. ⁴³But it should not be that way among you. Whoever wants to become great among you must serve the rest of you like a servant. ⁴⁴Whoever wants to become the first among you must serve all of you like a slave. ⁴⁵In the same way, the Son of Man[d] did not come to be served. He came to serve others and to give his life as a ransom for many people."

Can you ... through?   Jesus was asking if they could suffer the same terrible things that would happen to him.

Christmas In June, July . . .

Corky Adams is unique. He's a real trendsetter. For example, he always wears one red sock and one green sock to remind himself that every day is Christmas. His socks are a perfect reflection of the way he lives his Christian faith with others.

Corky often plays with children and talks with elderly folks in his neighborhood. Once he drove a thousand miles to comfort someone whose friend had died suddenly. He is also a gifted photographer who captures the best of each person he photographs.

Corky is a joy to be around. His beaming smile lights up his cheeks as though he were Santa Claus himself. When friends see him, their natural reaction is to smile and give him a hug. His faith is alive with wonder and joy—much like the excitement of a child who has just discovered that dirt and water make mud.

What's most amazing about Corky, though, is that he's thirty-five years old!

Jesus, himself, challenges us, no matter how old or young we are, to live the childlike faith and joy that Corky lives each day. Read **Mark 10:13–16** to see how Jesus requires childlike faith.

■ How does Corky reflect the kingdom of God in a childlike way?
■ In what ways do you feel challenged to be more childlike in your own faith?

C O N S I D E R . . .
■ listing the questions you had about God as a child, then writing the answers you have discovered as you've grown.
■ playing with a little child. Build with blocks; paint with your fingers. Read stories. Notice the childlike qualities, such as curiosity, innocence, and trust. Then work at applying those qualities to your faith.

F O R   M O R E ,   S E E . . .
■ Isaiah 11:1–6 (p. 629)   ■ Romans 8:14–17 (p. 1150)
■ Mark 9:33–37 (p. 980)

Jesus Heals a Blind Man

⁴⁶Then they came to the town of Jericho. As Jesus was leaving there with his followers and a great many people, a blind beggar named Bartimaeus son of Timaeus was sitting by the road. ⁴⁷When he heard that Jesus from Nazareth was walking by, he began to shout, "Jesus, Son of David,*d* have mercy on me!"

⁴⁸Many people warned the blind man to be quiet, but he shouted even more, "Son of David, have mercy on me!"

⁴⁹Jesus stopped and said, "Tell the man to come here."

So they called the blind man, saying, "Cheer up! Get to your feet. Jesus is calling you." ⁵⁰The blind man jumped up, left his coat there, and went to Jesus.

⁵¹Jesus asked him, "What do you want me to do for you?"

The blind man answered, "Teacher, I want to see."

⁵²Jesus said, "Go, you are healed because you believed." At once the man could see, and he followed Jesus on the road.

Jesus Enters Jerusalem as a King

11 As Jesus and his followers were coming closer to Jerusalem, they came to the towns of Bethphage and Bethany near the Mount of Olives.*d* From there Jesus sent two of his followers ²and said to them, "Go to the town you can see there. When you enter it, you will quickly find a colt tied, which no one has ever ridden. Untie it and bring it here to me. ³If anyone asks you why you are doing this, tell him its Master needs the colt, and he will send it at once. "

⁴The followers went into the town, found a colt tied in the street near the door of a house, and untied it. ⁵Some people were standing there and asked, "What are you doing? Why are you untying that colt?" ⁶The followers answered the way Jesus told them to answer, and the people let them take the colt.

⁷They brought the colt to Jesus and put their coats on it, and Jesus sat on it. ⁸Many people spread their coats on the road. Others cut branches in the fields and spread them on the road. ⁹The people were walking ahead of Jesus and behind him, shouting,

---

MONEY

What's Important?

"I have made many millions, but they have brought me no happiness. I would barter them all for the days I sat on an office stool in Cleveland and counted myself rich on $3 a week." —John Rockefeller, a multi-millionaire

"The care of $200 million is too great a load for any brain or back to bear. It is enough to kill anyone. There is no pleasure in it." —W.H. Vanderbilt, who inherited a fortune

"I am the most miserable man on earth." —John Jacob Astor, who died leaving $5 million

"Millionaires seldom smile." —Andrew Carnegie, a millionaire

Each of these people, who had lots of money, knew other things were more important than money. Jesus tried to teach the same lesson to the young man in **Mark 10:17–30**. Read how he responded.
■ How is what Jesus said similar to the quotes from these millionaires?
■ How does your "wealth" help or hinder your faith?

CONSIDER . . .
■ drawing a treasure chest and "filling" it with all the things that are most valuable to you. Evaluate what Jesus would think of your treasure.
➤ giving someone $10 with no strings attached and for no particular reason—just for the fun of it. How does it make you feel?

FOR MORE, SEE . . .
■ Deuteronomy 14:22–29 (p. 174)
■ Luke 21:1–4 (p. 1047)
■ Acts 3:1–10 (p. 1100)

"Praise[n] God!

God bless the One who comes in the name
of the Lord!   *Psalm 118:26*

[10]God bless the kingdom of our father David!

That kingdom is coming!

Praise to God in heaven!"

[11]Jesus entered Jerusalem and went into the Temple.[d] After he had looked at everything, since it was already late, he went out to Bethany with the twelve apostles.[d]

[12]The next day as Jesus was leaving Bethany, he became hungry. [13]Seeing a fig tree in leaf from far away, he went to see if it had any figs on it. But he found no figs, only leaves, because it was not the right season for figs. [14]So Jesus said to the tree, "May no one ever eat fruit from you again." And Jesus' followers heard him say this.

Jesus Goes to the Temple

[15]When Jesus returned to Jerusalem, he went into the Temple[d] and began to throw out those who were buying and selling there. He turned over the tables of those who were exchanging different kinds of money, and he upset the benches of those who were selling doves. [16]Jesus refused to allow anyone to carry goods through the Temple courts. [17]Then he taught the people, saying, "It is written in the Scriptures,[d] 'My Temple will be called a house for prayer for people from all nations.'[n] But you are changing God's house into a 'hideout for robbers.' "[n]

[18]The leading priests and the teachers of the law heard all this and began trying to find a way to kill Jesus. They were afraid of him, because all the people were amazed at his teaching. [19]That evening, Jesus and his followers left the city.

Praise   Literally, "Hosanna," a Hebrew word used at first in praying to God for help, but at this time it was probably a shout of joy used in praising God or his Messiah.

'My Temple . . . nations.'   Quotation from Isaiah 56:7.

'hideout for robbers.'   Quotation from Jeremiah 7:11.

SERVICE

Volunteer of the Year

Wanted: Class clown. Poor study habits a must.

If you asked her teachers, this job advertisement fit Denise Delgado perfectly. She never did her homework, and she was constantly cutting up in class. Denise had a definite gift of getting people to notice her.

Yet, Denise also had a gift her teachers failed to recognize. During her senior year, Denise volunteered at a special school for autistic children. Autistic children are difficult to work with because they seldom respond to those around them. However, Denise loved working with the kids. She soaked in any affirmation they would give her—a nod of the head, the glance of an eye, or a rare smile. Teachers and parents alike marveled at Denise's success in helping their children.

When she graduated, the special school awarded Denise a scholarship to study special education. The "class clown" even became a celebrity when the local United Way recognized her as the Youth Volunteer of the Year.

Like Denise early in high school, Jesus' followers sometimes searched for recognition among their peers. They didn't understand that Jesus required them to be servants first of all. John and James were two such people. Read about their encounter with Jesus in **Mark 10:35—45**.

■ How was Denise's response similar to the challenge Jesus gave his followers?

■ Which servant characteristics that Jesus talks about in this passage do you have?

C O N S I D E R . . .

■ encouraging someone you usually compete with, and being excited when he or she does something better than you.

■ going to a sports event and writing down the encouraging things people say to their favorite team. Use those things to encourage the people around you.

F O R   M O R E ,   S E E . . .

■ 1 Samuel 3:1–10 (p. 247)   ■ John 13:1–17 (p. 1080)

■ Luke 22:24–27 (p. 1049)

The Power of Faith

20The next morning as Jesus was passing by with his followers, they saw the fig tree dry and dead, even to the roots. 21Peter remembered the tree and said to Jesus, "Teacher, look! The fig tree you cursed is dry and dead!"

⚜ **SIDELIGHT:** The people whom Jesus threw out of the Temple were merchants who took advantage of those in Jerusalem on religious pilgrimages (Mark 11:15–17). They exchanged foreign currency for money to use in the Temple—with an extra charge, of course. Others sold doves to be used in Temple sacrifices.

22Jesus answered, "Have faith in God. 23I tell you the truth, you can say to this mountain, 'Go, fall into the sea.' And if you have no doubts in your mind and believe that what you say will hap-pen, God will do it for you. 24So I tell you to be-lieve that you have received the things you ask for in prayer, and God will give them to you. 25When you are praying, if you are angry with someone, forgive him so that your Father in heaven will also forgive your sins." 26 *n*

Leaders Doubt Jesus' Authority

27Jesus and his followers went again to Jerusa-lem. As Jesus was walking in the Temple,*d* the leading priests, the teachers of the law, and the older leaders came to him. 28They said to him, "What authority do you have to do these things? Who gave you this authority?"

29Jesus answered, "I will ask you one question. If you answer me, I will tell you what authority I have to do these things. 30Tell me: When John baptized people, was that authority from God or just from other people?"

31They argued about Jesus' question, saying, "If we answer, 'John's baptism was from God,' Jesus will say, 'Then why didn't you believe him?' 32But

---

Verse 26 Some early Greek copies add verse 26: "But if you don't forgive other people, then your Father in heaven will not forgive your sins."

PERSISTENCE

The Long Run

"We don't know if your baby will live through the night," the doctors told two-pound Patti Maslowski's new parents. She was born in 1966, when few babies born three months premature survived.

But Patti was a fighter from the start.

By the time she reached high school, she was an excellent student and an all-district volleyball star. She was also the regional track champion in the 3,200-meter run. When she finished eighth in her first state track meet, everyone was confident she had a great running future.

But then a back injury before her junior year changed her plans. No longer could she run like she used to. So she found a new way to give of herself—by becoming the track team manager.

Patti explains why she perseveres: "My persistence comes from making the most of each opportunity I'm given. I wasn't expected to live in the first place, so now I just want to use the gifts I've been blessed with to the best of my ability."

At one point in Jesus' ministry, he met a blind man who also exhibited Patti's perseverance. Read about the blind man in **Mark 10:46–52**.

■ Why did Patti and the blind man persevere?

■ How does your faith in Jesus help you persevere in pursuing your goals?

C O N S I D E R . . .

■ making a plan of action to improve performance in one area of your life.
Then spend the time needed to make progress. Evaluate your progress every month.

◀ *setting short- and long-term goals. Write them in a pocket calendar, and keep the* calendar in your purse or wallet.

F O R   M O R E ,   S E E . . .

■ Isaiah 35:1–10 (p. 650)
■ Luke 5:17–25 (p. 1011)   ■ Hebrews 10:32–39 (p. 1287)

if we say, 'It was from other people,' the crowd will be against us." (These leaders were afraid of the people, because all the people believed that John was a prophet.*d*)

[33]So they answered Jesus, "We don't know."

Jesus said to them, "Then I won't tell you what authority I have to do these things."

A Story About God's Son

12 Jesus began to use stories to teach the people. He said, "A man planted a vineyard. He put a wall around it and dug a hole for a winepress*d* and built a tower. Then he leased the land to some farmers and left for a trip. [2]When it was time for the grapes to be picked, he sent a servant to the farmers to get his share of the grapes. [3]But the farmers grabbed the servant and beat him and sent him away empty-handed. [4]Then the man sent another servant. They hit him on the head and showed no respect for him. [5]So the man sent another servant, whom they killed. The man sent many other servants; the farmers beat some of them and killed others.

[5]"The man had one person left to send, his son whom he loved. He sent him last of all, saying, 'They will respect my son.'

[7]"But the farmers said to each other, 'This son will inherit the vineyard. If we kill him, it will be ours.' [8]So they took the son, killed him, and threw him out of the vineyard.

[9]"So what will the owner of the vineyard do? He will come and kill those farmers and will give the vineyard to other farmers. [10]Surely you have read this Scripture:*d*

'The stone that the builders rejected
   became the cornerstone.*d*
[11]The Lord did this,
   and it is wonderful to us.' "   *Psalm 118:22-23*

[12]The Jewish leaders knew that the story was about them. So they wanted to find a way to arrest Jesus, but they were afraid of the people. So the leaders left him and went away.

Is It Right to Pay Taxes or Not?

[13]Later, the Jewish leaders sent some Phari-

---

sees[d] and Herodians[n] to Jesus to trap him in saying something wrong. [14]They came to him and said, "Teacher, we know that you are an honest man. You are not afraid of what other people think about you, because you pay no attention to who they are. And you teach the truth about God's way. Tell us: Is it right to pay taxes to Caesar[d] or not? [15]Should we pay them, or not?"

But knowing what these men were really trying to do, Jesus said to them, "Why are you trying to trap me? Bring me a coin to look at." [16]They gave Jesus a coin, and he asked, "Whose image and name are on the coin?" •

They answered, "Caesar's."

[17]Then Jesus said to them, "Give to Caesar the things that are Caesar's, and give to God the things that are God's." The men were amazed at what Jesus said.

Some Sadducees Try to Trick Jesus

[18]Then some Sadducees[d] came to Jesus and asked him a question. (Sadducees believed that people would not rise from the dead.) [19]They said, "Teacher, Moses wrote that if a man's brother dies, leaving a wife but no children, then that man must marry the widow and have children for his brother. [20]Once there were seven brothers. The first brother married and died, leaving no children. [21]So the second brother married the widow, but he also died and had no children. The same thing happened with the third brother. [22]All seven brothers married her and died, and none of the brothers had any children. Finally the woman died too. [23]Since all seven brothers had married her, when people rise from the dead, whose wife will she be?"

[24]Jesus answered, "Why don't you understand? Don't you know what the Scriptures[d] say, and don't you know about the power of God? [25]When people rise from the dead, they will not marry, nor will they be given to someone to marry. They will be like the angels in heaven. [26]Surely you have read what God said about people rising from the dead. In the book in which Moses wrote about the burning bush,[n] it says that God told Moses, 'I am the God of Abraham, the God of Isaac, and the God of Jacob.'[n] [27]God is the God of the living, not the dead. You Sadducees are wrong!"

The Most Important Command

[28]One of the teachers of the law came and heard Jesus arguing with the Sadducees.[d] Seeing that Jesus gave good answers to their questions,

he asked Jesus, "Which of the commands is most important?"

[29]Jesus answered, "The most important command is this: 'Listen, people of Israel! The Lord our God is the only Lord. [30]Love the Lord your God with all your heart, all your soul, all your mind, and all your strength.'[n] [31]The second command is this: 'Love your neighbor as you love yourself.'[n] There are no commands more important than these."

[32]The man answered, "That was a good answer, Teacher. You were right when you said God is the only Lord and there is no other God besides him. [33]One must love God with all his heart, all his mind, and all his strength. And one must love his neighbor as he loves himself. These commands are more important than all the animals and sacrifices we offer to God."

[34]When Jesus saw that the man answered him wisely, Jesus said to him, "You are close to the kingdom of God." And after that, no one was brave enough to ask Jesus any more questions.

[35]As Jesus was teaching in the Temple,[d] he asked, "Why do the teachers of the law say that the Christ[d] is the son of David? [36]David himself, speaking by the Holy Spirit,[d] said:

'The Lord said to my Lord:
  Sit by me at my right side,
  until I put your enemies under your
    control.'   *Psalm 110:1*

[37]David himself calls the Christ 'Lord,' so how can the Christ be his son?" The large crowd listened to Jesus with pleasure.

[38]Jesus continued teaching and said, "Beware of the teachers of the law. They like to walk around wearing fancy clothes, and they love for people to greet them with respect in the marketplaces. [39]They love to have the most important seats in the synagogues[d] and at feasts. [40]But they cheat widows and steal their houses and then try to make themselves look good by saying long prayers. They will receive a greater punishment."

True Giving

[41]Jesus sat near the Temple[d] money box and watched the people put in their money. Many rich people gave large sums of money. [42]Then a poor widow came and put in two small copper coins, which were only worth a few cents.

[43]Calling his followers to him, Jesus said, "I tell you the truth, this poor widow gave more than all those rich people. [44]They gave only what they did not need. This woman is very poor, but she gave all she had; she gave all she had to live on."

Herodians   A political group that followed Herod and his family.
burning bush   Read Exodus 3:1-12 in the Old Testament.
'I am . . . Jacob.'   Quotation from Exodus 3:6.
'Listen . . . strength.'   Quotation from Deuteronomy 6:4-5.
'Love . . . yourself.'   Quotation from Leviticus 19:18.

The Temple Will Be Destroyed

13 As Jesus was leaving the Temple,*d* one of his followers said to him, "Look, Teacher! How beautiful the buildings are! How big the stones are!"

²Jesus said, "Do you see all these great buildings? Not one stone will be left on another. Every stone will be thrown down to the ground."

❋ **SIDELIGHT:** Jesus' prediction that the Temple would be destroyed (Mark 13:1–2) came true within about forty years. In A.D. 70, the Romans surrounded and sacked Jerusalem, burning the Temple to the ground. Today, the Muslim shrine called the "Dome of the Rock" stands on the Temple site.

---

³Later, as Jesus was sitting on the Mount of Olives,*d* opposite the Temple, he was alone with Peter, James, John, and Andrew. They asked Jesus,

⁴"Tell us, when will these things happen? And what will be the sign that they are going to happen?"

⁵Jesus began to answer them, "Be careful that no one fools you. ⁶Many people will come in my name, saying, 'I am the One,' and they will fool many people. ⁷When you hear about wars and stories of wars that are coming, don't be afraid. These things must happen before the end comes. ⁸Nations will fight against other nations, and kingdoms against other kingdoms. There will be earthquakes in different places, and there will be times when there is no food for people to eat. These things are like the first pains when something new is about to be born.

⁹"You must be careful. People will arrest you and take you to court and beat you in their synagogues.*d* You will be forced to stand before kings and governors, to tell them about me. This will happen to you because you follow me. ¹⁰But before these things happen, the Good News*d* must be told to all people. ¹¹When you are arrested and judged, don't worry ahead of time about what you should say. Say whatever is given you to say

---

GIVING

Under Construction

Stephen Chang was shy and short. He was one of those teenagers who seemed to slip into the background at big events. He was so quiet that most of the time no one noticed he was even there.

One thing, however, that did stand out about Stephen was how hard he worked. When the youth group picked up leaves for a fund-raiser, Stephen had the most bags of leaves. And when litter filled the youth group room during a meeting, Stephen stayed after to clean up.

It was Stephen's hard work that Joe Heaton recalled when he asked him to design a planter box for a youth group prayer service. Stephen responded enthusiastically, immediately drawing up blueprints for the planter. He created a large cross-shaped planter box. It was beautiful.

The youth group members then planted mustard seeds in the box. As the seeds grew, tended by Stephen's loving care, they reminded the class members of their own growth as Christians.

Aside from Joe, few people knew it was Stephen who had created the planter. No one even knew Stephen had cared for the plants.

In some ways, Stephen is like the widow Jesus talked about in **Mark 12:38–44**. Read this passage to discover Jesus' message.

■ How were Stephen's gifts like the kind of giving Jesus described?
■ According to this passage, what are things we should not do to be "religious"?

C O N S I D E R . . .

■ doing something anonymously to help someone. For example, you could send money to someone, or you could rake someone's leaves without his knowing about it.
■ committing to contribute a percentage of your income to your church.

F O R   M O R E ,   S E E . . .

■ Malachi 3:8–12 (p. 901)
■ Matthew 6:19–24 (p. 918)
■ 1 Timothy 6:6–10 (p. 1260)

at that time, because it will not really be you speaking; it will be the Holy Spirit.[d]

[12]"Brothers will give their own brothers to be killed, and fathers will give their own children to be killed. Children will fight against their own parents and cause them to be put to death. [13]All people will hate you because you follow me, but those people who keep their faith until the end will be saved.

[14]"You will see 'the destroying terror'[n] standing where it should not be." (You who read this should understand what it means.) "At that time, the people in Judea should run away to the mountains. [15]If people are on the roofs[n] of their houses, they must not go down or go inside to get anything out of their houses. [16]If people are in the fields, they must not go back to get their coats. [17]At that time, how terrible it will be for women who are pregnant or have nursing babies! [18]Pray that these things will not happen in winter, [19]be-cause those days will be full of trouble. There will be more trouble than there has ever been since the beginning, when God made the world, until now, and nothing as bad will ever happen again. [20]God has decided to make that terrible time short. Otherwise, no one would go on living. But God will make that time short to help the people he has chosen. [21]At that time, someone might say to you, 'Look, there is the Christ!'[d] Or another person might say, 'There he is!' But don't believe them. [22]False Christs and false prophets[d] will come and perform great wonders and miracles.[d] They will try to fool even the people God has chosen, if that is possible. [23]So be careful. I have warned you about all this before it happens.

[24]"During the days after this trouble comes,
'the sun will grow dark,
and the moon will not give its light.
[25]The stars will fall from the sky.

'the destroying terror' Mentioned in Daniel 9:27; 12:11 (cf. Daniel 11:31).
roofs In Bible times houses were built with flat roofs. The roof was used for drying things such as flax and fruit. And it was used as an extra room, as a place for worship, and as a place to sleep in the summer.

FUTURE

Be Prepared

NEW MADRID, MO.—In November 1990, grocery store shelves were cleared and ice chests packed with emergency items such as food, water, first-aid kits, flashlights and radios. People were frightened. Some people wouldn't even sleep in their own homes; they slept in their cars and pick-up trucks instead. Many residents even left the area.

"I'm terrified of this," resident Anna Harper said. "I feel like it's some terminal illness. I don't want to believe it, but there is so much talk about it."

Residents of this small town were preparing for the earthquake that Iben Browning, a business consultant from New Mexico, had predicted. He said tidal forces were unusually high and could trigger an earthquake of 6.5 to 7.5 on the Richter scale forty-eight hours before or after December 3, along the New Madrid Fault.

While many residents of the small town scurried about to prepare for the catastrophe, others were calm about it. After all, these residents said, it's not as though they didn't already know they were living on a fault line.

December 3 came and went, and there was no earthquake.

In **Mark 13:24–33**, Jesus warns his followers of a certain day they need to be prepared for in the future.

■ According to this passage, no one knows when Jesus will return. To prepare for that day, which people should we be like—the people who prepared at the last minute or those who were ready at all times?

■ If Jesus were to return today, would you be ready?

C O N S I D E R . . .

■ deciding what things you would put in an "emergency kit" to prepare for the end of the world; for example, faith or courage. Think about what you need to do to have those things ready.

■ asking your pastor or youth leader to teach a course on the "end times."

F O R   M O R E ,   S E E . . .

■ Genesis 9:1–17 (p. 10)
■ Luke 21:25–36 (p. 1048)
■ 1 Thessalonians 4:13–5:11 (p. 1248)

And the powers of the heavens will be
shaken.'   *Isaiah 13:10; 34:4*
²⁶"Then people will see the Son of Man*ᵈ* coming in clouds with great power and glory. ²⁷Then
he will send his angels all around the earth to
gather his chosen people from every part of the
earth and from every part of heaven.

²⁸"Learn a lesson from the fig tree: When its
branches become green and soft and new leaves
appear, you know summer is near. ²⁹In the same
way, when you see these things happening, you
will know that the time is near, ready to come. ³⁰I
tell you the truth, all these things will happen
while the people of this time are still living.
³¹Earth and sky will be destroyed, but the words
I have said will never be destroyed.

³²"No one knows when that day or time will
be, not the angels in heaven, not even the Son.
Only the Father knows. ³³Be careful! Always be
ready, because you don't know when that time
will be. ³⁴It is like a man who goes on a trip. He
leaves his house and lets his servants take care of
it, giving each one a special job to do. The man
tells the servant guarding the door always to be
watchful. ³⁵So always be ready, because you don't
know when the owner of the house will come
back. It might be in the evening, or at midnight,
or in the morning while it is still dark, or when
the sun rises. ³⁶Always be ready. Otherwise he
might come back suddenly and find you sleeping.
³⁷I tell you this, and I say this to everyone: 'Be
ready!' "

The Plan to Kill Jesus

14 It was now only two days before the
Passover*ᵈ* and the Feast*ᵈ* of Unleavened
Bread. The leading priests and teachers of the law
were trying to find a trick to arrest Jesus and kill
him. ²But they said, "We must not do it during
the feast, because the people might cause a riot."

A Woman with Perfume for Jesus

³Jesus was in Bethany at the house of Simon,
who had a skin disease. While Jesus was eating
there, a woman approached him with an alabaster*ᵈ* jar filled with very expensive perfume, made
of pure nard.*ᵈ* She opened the jar and poured the
perfume on Jesus' head.

⁴Some who were there became upset and said
to each other, "Why waste that perfume? ⁵It was
worth a full year's work. It could have been sold
and the money given to the poor." And they got
very angry with the woman.

⁶Jesus said, "Leave her alone. Why are you
troubling her? She did an excellent thing for me.
⁷You will always have the poor with you, and you
can help them anytime you want. But you will not
always have me. ⁸This woman did the only thing
she could do for me; she poured perfume on my

body to prepare me for burial. ⁹I tell you the truth,
wherever the Good News*ᵈ* is preached in all the
world, what this woman has done will be told,
and people will remember her."

☀ **SIDELIGHT:** The perfume the
woman poured on Jesus' feet at
Bethany (Mark 14:3–9) might have made
many modern perfumes seem cheap. Called
spikenard, it was taken from pink-blossomed
plants in the Himalayan Mountains of
northern India.

Judas Becomes an Enemy of Jesus

¹⁰One of the twelve apostles, Judas Iscariot,
went to talk to the leading priests to offer to hand
Jesus over to them. ¹¹These priests were pleased
about this and promised to pay Judas money. So
he watched for the best time to turn Jesus in.

Jesus Eats the Passover Meal

¹²It was now the first day of the Feast*ᵈ* of Unleavened Bread when the Passover*ᵈ* lamb was sacrificed. Jesus' followers said to him, "Where do
you want us to go and prepare for you to eat the
Passover meal?"

¹³Jesus sent two of his followers and said to
them, "Go into the city and a man carrying a jar
of water will meet you. Follow him. ¹⁴When he
goes into a house, tell the owner of the house,
'The Teacher says: Where is my guest room in
which I can eat the Passover meal with my followers?' ¹⁵The owner will show you a large room upstairs that is furnished and ready. Prepare the food
for us there."

¹⁶So the followers left and went into the city.
Everything happened as Jesus had said, so they
prepared the Passover meal.

¹⁷In the evening, Jesus went to that house with
the twelve. ¹⁸While they were all eating, Jesus
said, "I tell you the truth, one of you will turn
against me—one of you eating with me now."

¹⁹The followers were very sad to hear this.
Each one began to say to Jesus, "I am not the one,
am I?"

²⁰Jesus answered, "It is one of the twelve—the
one who dips his bread into the bowl with me.
²¹The Son of Man*ᵈ* will die, just as the Scriptures*ᵈ*
say. But how terrible it will be for the person who
hands the Son of Man over to be killed. It would
be better for him if he had never been born."

The Lord's Supper

²²While they were eating, Jesus took some
bread and thanked God for it and broke it. Then
he gave it to his followers and said, "Take it; this
is my body."

23Then Jesus took a cup and thanked God for it and gave it to the followers, and they all drank from the cup. 24Then Jesus said, "This is my blood which is the new agreement that God makes with his people. This blood is poured out for many. 25I tell you the truth, I will not drink of this fruit of the vine[n] again until that day when I drink it new in the kingdom of God." 26After singing a hymn, they went out to the Mount of Olives.[d]

Jesus' Followers Will Leave Him

27Then Jesus told the followers, "You will all stumble in your faith, because it is written in the Scriptures:[d]
'I will kill the shepherd,
    and the sheep will scatter.'   Zechariah 13:7
28But after I rise from the dead, I will go ahead of you into Galilee." 29Peter said, "Everyone else may stumble in their faith, but I will not."

30Jesus answered, "I tell you the truth, tonight before the rooster crows twice you will say three times you don't know me." 31But Peter insisted, "I will never say that I don't know you! I will even die with you!" And all the other followers said the same thing.

Jesus Prays Alone

32Jesus and his followers went to a place called Gethsemane. He said to them, "Sit here while I pray." 33Jesus took Peter, James, and John with him, and he began to be very sad and troubled. 34He said to them, "My heart is full of sorrow, to the point of death. Stay here and watch." 35After walking a little farther away from them, Jesus fell to the ground and prayed that, if possible, he would not have this time of suffering. 36He prayed, "Abba,[n] Father! You can do all things. Take away this cup[n] of suffering. But do what you want, not what I want." 37Then Jesus went back to his followers and found them asleep. He said to Peter, "Simon, are

fruit of the vine   Product of the grapevine; this may also be translated "wine."
Abba   Name that a child called his father.
cup   Jesus is talking about the terrible things that will happen to him. Accepting these things will be very hard, like drinking a cup of something bitter.

DEATH

Loving Memories

"Peace I leave with you." That's the message Rudy Beranek lived and died.

Peace and hope. Those were Rudy's constant themes in life. And as he prepared for his death, he continued to share those gifts.

He invited two funeral homes to work together on his funeral services, because the funeral director of each was his close friend. He then asked two flower shops to design floral arrangements, again, because he valued each shop owner's friendship.

For Rudy, the most important thing in life was people working together for the good of all, sharing their gifts and appreciating others' gifts. It was as if by inviting businesses to collaborate in preparing with him for his death that he was inviting them to recognize what was most important in life.

Rudy also asked people at each church he had served to donate college scholarships for children to have a Christian education. And he invited each church's choir to share its gift of song at his funeral.

He wanted no one to be left out. In short, Rudy said "I love you" to the people whom his life had touched.

Jesus, like Rudy, shared his life as he gathered his friends together for his last meal. Read about this special gathering in **Mark 14:12–26**.

■ How did Jesus, like Rudy, prepare people for his death?
■ How can you remember Jesus' death for you every day?

CONSIDER . . .

■ visiting the grave or a favorite spot of a friend or relative who has died. Recall the ways that person taught you through his or her life.
■ creating a symbol of Jesus' death and carrying it in your pocket or purse every day.

FOR MORE, SEE . . .

■ Exodus 12:1–17 (p. 67)
■ Luke 22:7–20 (p. 1049)
■ John 13:21–30 (p. 1081)

you sleeping? Couldn't you stay awake with me for one hour? 38Stay awake and pray for strength against temptation. The spirit wants to do what is right, but the body is weak."

39Again Jesus went away and prayed the same thing. 40Then he went back to his followers, and again he found them asleep, because their eyes were very heavy. And they did not know what to say to him.

41After Jesus prayed a third time, he went back to his followers and said to them, "Are you still sleeping and resting? That's enough. The time has come for the Son of Man*d* to be handed over to sinful people. 42Get up, we must go. Look, here comes the man who has turned against me."

Jesus Is Arrested

43At once, while Jesus was still speaking, Judas, one of the twelve apostles,*d* came up. With him were many people carrying swords and clubs who had been sent from the leading priests, the teachers of the law, and the older Jewish leaders.

44Judas had planned a signal for them, saying, "The man I kiss is Jesus. Arrest him and guard him while you lead him away." 45So Judas went straight to Jesus and said, "Teacher!" and kissed him. 46Then the people grabbed Jesus and arrested him. 47One of his followers standing nearby pulled out his sword and struck the servant of the high priest and cut off his ear.

48Then Jesus said, "You came to get me with swords and clubs as if I were a criminal. 49Every day I was with you teaching in the Temple,*d* and you did not arrest me there. But all these things have happened to make the Scriptures*d* come true." 50Then all of Jesus' followers left him and ran away.

51A young man, wearing only a linen cloth, was following Jesus, and the people also grabbed him. 52But the cloth he was wearing came off, and he ran away naked.

Jesus Before the Leaders

53The people who arrested Jesus led him to the house of the high priest, where all the leading priests, the older Jewish leaders, and the teachers of the law were gathered. 54Peter followed far behind and entered the courtyard of the high priest's house. There he sat with the guards, warming himself by the fire.

55The leading priests and the whole Jewish council tried to find something that Jesus had done wrong so they could kill him. But the council could find no proof of anything. 56Many people came and told false things about him, but all said different things — none of them agreed.

57Then some people stood up and lied about Jesus, saying, 58"We heard this man say, 'I will destroy this Temple*d* that people made. And three days later, I will build another Temple not made by people.' " 59But even the things these people said did not agree.

60Then the high priest stood before them and asked Jesus, "Aren't you going to answer? Don't you have something to say about their charges against you?" 61But Jesus said nothing; he did not answer.

The high priest asked Jesus another question: "Are you the Christ,*d* the Son of the blessed God?"

62Jesus answered, "I am. And in the future you will see the Son of Man*d* sitting at the right hand of God, the Powerful One, and coming on clouds in the sky."

63When the high priest heard this, he tore his clothes and said, "We don't need any more witnesses! 64You all heard him say these things against God. What do you think?"

They all said that Jesus was guilty and should die. 65Some of the people there began to spit at Jesus. They blindfolded him and beat him with their fists and said, "Prove you are a prophet!"*d* Then the guards led Jesus away and beat him.

Peter Says He Doesn't Know Jesus

66While Peter was in the courtyard, a servant girl of the high priest came there. 67She saw Peter warming himself at the fire and looked closely at him.

Then she said, "You also were with Jesus, that man from Nazareth."

68But Peter said that he was never with Jesus. He said, "I don't know or understand what you are talking about." Then Peter left and went toward the entrance of the courtyard. And the rooster crowed.*n*

69The servant girl saw Peter there, and again she said to the people who were standing nearby, "This man is one of those who followed Jesus."

70Again Peter said that it was not true.

A short time later, some people were standing near Peter saying, "Surely you are one of those who followed Jesus, because you are from Galilee, too."

71Then Peter began to place a curse on himself and swear, "I don't know this man you're talking about!"

72At once, the rooster crowed the second time. Then Peter remembered what Jesus had told him: "Before the rooster crows twice, you will say three times that you don't know me." Then Peter lost control of himself and began to cry.

And ... crowed.   A few, early Greek copies leave out this phrase.

Pilate Questions Jesus

15 Very early in the morning, the leading priests, the older leaders, the teachers of the law, and all the Jewish council decided what to do with Jesus. They tied him, led him away, and turned him over to Pilate, the governor.

²Pilate asked Jesus, "Are you the king of the Jews?"

Jesus answered, "Those are your words."

³The leading priests accused Jesus of many things. ⁴So Pilate asked Jesus another question, "You can see that they are accusing you of many things. Aren't you going to answer?"

⁵But Jesus still said nothing, so Pilate was very surprised.

Pilate Tries to Free Jesus

⁶Every year at the time of the Passover[d] the governor would free one prisoner whom the people chose. ⁷At that time, there was a man named Barabbas in prison who was a rebel and had committed murder during a riot. ⁸The crowd came to

---

PEER PRESSURE

Curfew Capers

"It's our last night at camp. Can't we please stay up late to talk?" Missy Goette and Michael Davenport begged.

The two spokespeople had been designated by their peers to negotiate an extended curfew with Wayne Broderick, the camp director. Wayne listened patiently. Then he reminded them that "we all agreed on Sunday evening that the camp curfew would be midnight. We still have one day's activities to rest up for, so we will not change the curfew."

Missy and Michael reluctantly agreed and relayed the news to their friends. Most accepted the verdict.

Nonetheless, Mary McCain and Justin Weimer convinced Missy to secretly rendezvous at 4 A.M. to celebrate their last night together.

Just after leaving their dorms, the three friends came face-to-face with Wayne.

"What are you doing out here?" he growled.

Missy tried to explain: "We were just talking. We wanted to have more time together before we have to leave."

"What about curfew?" asked Wayne.

"We agreed to a midnight curfew," Justin admitted.

Wayne continued by asking, "What are the consequences for breaking a guideline?"

Mary spoke quietly as tears filled her eyes. "We have to call our parents to pick us up from camp early."

After daybreak, Wayne had the three call their parents. Soon they were heading homeward with their families.

Peer pressure, like that Mary, Justin, and Missy experienced, can be destructive. Read **Mark 15:1–20** to see how a type of peer pressure led to Jesus' death.

■ Why did Pilate, the crowd who shouted for Barabbas to be released, and the kids who came together at 4 A.M. give in to pressure?

■ If you had been in the shouting crowd, how would you have withstood the pressure to kill Jesus? How can you use those same actions to withstand peer pressure today?

CONSIDER . . .

■ listing situations in which you experience strong peer pressure to do wrong. Beside each situation, write what you can do or say to withstand the pressure.

■ forming a "Pressure Valve Team" with friends. Whenever a teammate is pressured to do something wrong, relieve that negative pressure by providing positive pressure to do what's right.

FOR MORE, SEE . . .

■ Proverbs 1:10–19 (p. 568)
■ Luke 23:1–25 (p. 1052)   ■ John 18:28—19:16 (p. 1091)

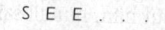

Pilate and began to ask him to free a prisoner as he always did.

⁹So Pilate asked them, "Do you want me to free the king of the Jews?" ¹⁰Pilate knew that the leading priests had turned Jesus in to him because they were jealous. ¹¹But the leading priests had persuaded the people to ask Pilate to free Barabbas, not Jesus.

¹²Then Pilate asked the crowd again, "So what should I do with this man you call the king of the Jews?"

¹³They shouted, "Crucify him!"

¹⁴Pilate asked, "Why? What wrong has he done?"

But they shouted even louder, "Crucify him!"

¹⁵Pilate wanted to please the crowd, so he freed Barabbas for them. After having Jesus beaten with whips, he handed Jesus over to the soldiers to be crucified.

SIDELIGHT: The kind of beating Jesus experienced (Mark 15:15) was a gruesome practice among the Romans. The whip was made of leather, lead, and bone, and could tear out eyes, sever veins, and rip open stomachs. It was a customary part of the death sentence.

---

¹⁶The soldiers took Jesus into the governor's palace (called the Praetorium) and called all the other soldiers together. ¹⁷They put a purple robe on Jesus and used thorny branches to make a crown for his head. ¹⁸They began to call out to him, "Hail, King of the Jews!" ¹⁹The soldiers beat Jesus on the head many times with a stick. They spit on him and made fun of him by bowing on their knees and worshiping him. ²⁰After they finished, the soldiers took off the purple robe and put his own clothes on him again. Then they led him out of the palace to be crucified.

Jesus Is Crucified

²¹A man named Simon from Cyrene, the father of Alexander and Rufus, was coming from the fields to the city. The soldiers forced Simon to carry the cross for Jesus. ²²They led Jesus to the place called Golgotha, which means the Place of the Skull. ²³The soldiers tried to give Jesus wine mixed with myrrh*d* to drink, but he refused. ²⁴The soldiers crucified Jesus and divided his clothes among themselves, throwing lots*d* to decide what each soldier would get.

²⁵It was nine o'clock in the morning when they

crucified Jesus. ²⁶There was a sign with this charge against Jesus written on it: THE KING OF THE JEWS. ²⁷They also put two robbers on crosses beside Jesus, one on the right, and the other on the left. ²⁸ ⁿ ²⁹People walked by and insulted Jesus and shook their heads, saying, "You said you could destroy the Temple*d* and build it again in three days. ³⁰So save yourself! Come down from that cross!"

³¹The leading priests and the teachers of the law were also making fun of Jesus. They said to each other, "He saved other people, but he can't save himself. ³²If he is really the Christ,*d* the king of Israel, let him come down now from the cross. When we see this, we will believe in him." The robbers who were being crucified beside Jesus also insulted him.

Jesus Dies

³³At noon the whole country became dark, and the darkness lasted for three hours. ³⁴At three o'clock Jesus cried in a loud voice, "Eloi, Eloi, lama sabachthani." This means, "My God, my God, why have you rejected me?"

³⁵When some of the people standing there heard this, they said, "Listen! He is calling Elijah."

³⁶Someone there ran and got a sponge, filled it with vinegar, tied it to a stick, and gave it to Jesus to drink. He said, "We want to see if Elijah will come to take him down from the cross."

³⁷Then Jesus cried in a loud voice and died.

³⁸The curtain in the Temple*n* was torn into two pieces, from the top to the bottom. ³⁹When the army officer who was standing in front of the cross saw what happened when Jesus died, he said, "This man really was the Son of God!"

⁴⁰Some women were standing at a distance from the cross, watching; among them were Mary Magdalene, Salome, and Mary the mother of James and Joseph. (James was her youngest son.) ⁴¹These women had followed Jesus in Galilee and helped him. Many other women were also there who had come with Jesus to Jerusalem.

Jesus Is Buried

⁴²This was Preparation*d* Day. (That means the day before the Sabbath*d* day.) That evening, ⁴³Joseph from Arimathea was brave enough to go to Pilate and ask for Jesus' body. Joseph, an important member of the Jewish council, was one of the people who was waiting for the kingdom of God to come. ⁴⁴Pilate was amazed that Jesus would have already died, so he called the army officer who had guarded Jesus and asked him if Jesus had already died. ⁴⁵The officer told Pilate that he was

---

Verse 28 Some Greek copies add verse 28: "And the Scripture came true that says, 'They put him with criminals.' "
curtain in the Temple A curtain divided the Most Holy Place from the other part of the Temple. That was the special building in Jerusalem where God commanded the Jewish people to worship him.

dead, so Pilate told Joseph he could have the body. [46]Joseph bought some linen cloth, took the body down from the cross, and wrapped it in the linen. He put the body in a tomb that was cut out of a wall of rock. Then he rolled a very large stone to block the entrance of the tomb. [47]And Mary Magdalene and Mary the mother of Joseph saw the place where Jesus was laid.

SIDELIGHT: Most people who were crucified in Jesus' day were left on the cross or were simply discarded in a mass grave. By requesting Jesus' body for burial, Joseph saved Jesus from that final indignity (Mark 15:42–47).

Jesus Rises from the Dead

16 The day after the Sabbath[d] day, Mary Magdalene, Mary the mother of James, and Salome bought some sweet-smelling spices to put on Jesus' body. [2]Very early on that day, the first day of the week, soon after sunrise, the women were on their way to the tomb. [3]They said to each other, "Who will roll away for us the stone that covers the entrance of the tomb?" [4]Then the women looked and saw that the stone had already been rolled away, even though it was very large. [5]The women entered the tomb and saw a young man wearing a white robe and sitting on the right side, and they were afraid.

[6]But the man said, "Don't be afraid. You are looking for Jesus from Nazareth, who has been crucified. He has risen from the dead; he is not here. Look, here is the place they laid him. [7]Now go and tell his followers and Peter, 'Jesus is going into Galilee ahead of you, and you will see him there as he told you before.' "

[8]The women were confused and shaking with fear, so they left the tomb and ran away. They did not tell anyone about what happened, because they were afraid.

Verses 9-20 are not included in two of the best and oldest Greek manuscripts of Mark.

Some Followers See Jesus

[[9]After Jesus rose from the dead early on the first day of the week, he showed himself first to Mary Magdalene. One time in the past, he had forced seven demons[d] out of her. [10]After Mary saw Jesus, she went and told his followers, who were very sad and were crying. [11]But Mary told

---

Unexpected Savior

Jesus painted no pictures. Yet some of the greatest artists were inspired by him to paint their greatest works.

Jesus wrote no poetry. Yet hundreds of the world's greatest poems pay tribute to him.

Jesus composed no music. Yet Haydn, Handel, Beethoven, Bach, and other great musicians wrote some of their greatest music to praise him.

Jesus preached and taught for only three years. The philosopher Socrates taught for forty years, Plato for fifty years, and Aristotle for forty years. Yet more people follow what Jesus taught than follow the three philosophers combined.

Jesus died on a cross as a criminal. Yet even a guard who helped put him to death recognized that he was God's Son. Read **Mark 15:33–39** to see how Jesus showed he was God's Son even in his death.

■ What unexpected things do you see in Jesus' life as described by the passage and by the comparisons above?

■ How does this passage strengthen your faith in Jesus as God's Son?

CONSIDER . . . .

■ listing everything you would expect a king to do. Then compare it to what you read in the Bible about Jesus. Identify similarities and differences.

■ rereading the passage, putting yourself in the place of the officer. How would you have responded to this situation? What would you have said?

FOR MORE, SEE . . .

■ Isaiah 53 (p. 672)
■ Matthew 16:21–28 (p. 937)
■ John 19:28–37 (p. 1092)

them that Jesus was alive. She said that she had seen him, but the followers did not believe her.

12Later, Jesus showed himself to two of his followers while they were walking in the country, but he did not look the same as before. 13These followers went back to the others and told them what had happened. but again, the followers did not believe them.

Jesus Talks to the Apostles

14Later Jesus showed himself to the eleven apostles while they were eating, and he criticized them because they had no faith. They were stubborn and refused to believe those who had seen him after he had risen from the dead.

15Jesus said to his followers, "Go everywhere in the world, and tell the Good News*d* to everyone. 16Anyone who believes and is baptized will be saved, but anyone who does not believe will be punished. 17And those who believe will be able to do these things as proof: They will use my name to force out demons.*d* They will speak in new languages.*n* 18They will pick up snakes and drink poison without being hurt. They will touch the sick, and the sick will be healed."

19After the Lord Jesus said these things to his followers, he was carried up into heaven, and he sat at the right side of God. 20The followers went everywhere in the world and told the Good News to people, and the Lord helped them. The Lord proved that the Good News they told was true by giving them power to work miracles.*d*]

languages This can also be translated "tongues."

A Light in the Darkness

Devon Sparks was heavily into drugs by the time he was fourteen. After being arrested for helping his friends steal a radio, he was placed in an alternative school. But he kept slipping further and further downhill.

He became more distant from his family and friends. And he started using drugs daily to try to escape the pain he felt inside.

One day Devon couldn't stand the pain any longer. He hated himself, and he didn't want to go on living. He felt trapped. The darkness was overwhelming, and he just couldn't see a way out.

Finally, he cried out to God. "Please," he pleaded. "please help me."

Almost immediately he sensed a peace and calm inside, as if the darkness was replaced with a new hope. In the next weeks, he began attending Narcotics Anonymous support meetings and joined a Christian fellowship. Devon had a new beginning.

"Turning my life over to God's direction is the toughest decision I've ever made," Devon later explained. "But my faith is beginning to pay off. I'm making new friends. I found a job. I'm taking art classes. I feel alive. It's a day-to-day struggle to stay free of drugs, but I'm headed in the right direction for once in my life."

Devon was beginning to experience the life and power of Jesus' resurrection. Read about the resurrection in **Mark 16:1–8**.
■ How was Devon's new life similar to Jesus' resurrection? How was it different?
■ How is your response to Jesus' resurrection like or unlike the women's reactions in this passage?

C O N S I D E R . . .
■ asking God to "roll away" an obstacle in your life with his resurrection power.
■ listing the ways you can "stop the pain" you may be experiencing like Devon stopped his pain. Ask others for help if you need to.

F O R   M O R E ,   S E E . . .
■ Exodus 14 (p. 70)   ■ John 20:1–18 (p. 1093)
■ Matthew 28:1–10 (p. 961)

SHARING FAITH

Pass It On!

Geri Rainbolt was frightened when she stepped up to the microphone. She wasn't sure God could use her story to help other people. But she began speaking anyway.

"Two years ago I went out drinking with several friends. I drank so much I passed out. My friends panicked. Was I dying? Would I be okay? They didn't know what to do.

"So they drove me to Kristi Coll's house. Her parents would know what to do. They were always around when we needed them.

"Kristi's parents called my dad. He came and picked me up, drove me home and carried me to my room. I don't remember anything—just waking up the next morning.

"My dad came in to talk with me. Tears filled his eyes. He was so afraid of losing me.

"Right then, I realized I never knew how much I could hurt my father. I really love him, but I had hurt him.

"And that's the message I want to share with you today. The things that keep me—that keep us—from loving our parents or friends are the same things that can keep us from growing in our relationship with God."

The room was silent as the teenagers soaked in the truth of Geri's message. Geri could sense God's power as she stepped away from the microphone. She had indeed passed on a truth about faith they all needed to hear.

In **Mark 16:19–20**, Jesus' first followers experienced the same power in telling others about Jesus.

■ How is Geri's talk similar to the disciples telling the Good News? How is it different?

■ How can you tell others the Good News?

C O N S I D E R . . .

■ telling a non-Christian friend about Jesus.
■ asking your pastor or youth leader to lead a training course on telling others about Christ.

F O R   M O R E ,   S E E . . .

■ 1 Kings 18 (p. 323)
■ Luke 24:44–53 (p. 1056)

■ Acts 1:1–14 (p. 1098)

LUKE

Why Read This Book:

- Discover the Bible's only stories about Jesus' childhood (Luke 2).
- See how Jesus ministered to all people, especially the poor and the outcast (Luke 4—8).
- Enjoy some of Jesus' most famous stories (Luke 10, 15—16).
- Learn how Jesus gave his life for our sins (Luke 22—24).

Behind the Scenes:

Imagine never hearing that Jesus was laid in a manger when he was born (Luke 2:7—11). Imagine not knowing the parable of the Good Samaritan (Luke 10:25—37). Or the parable of the son who left home, which is also known as the Prodigal Son (Luke 15:11—32). Imagine not knowing about Jesus' encounter with Zacchaeus (Luke 19:1—10).

We wouldn't have any of these stories without the Gospel of Luke.

Though the books of Matthew, Mark, and John tell many stories about Jesus, they don't include about one-third of the material in Luke. Luke is the most complete account of Jesus' life. Written by a doctor, it's a detailed, organized picture of Jesus' life and ministry.

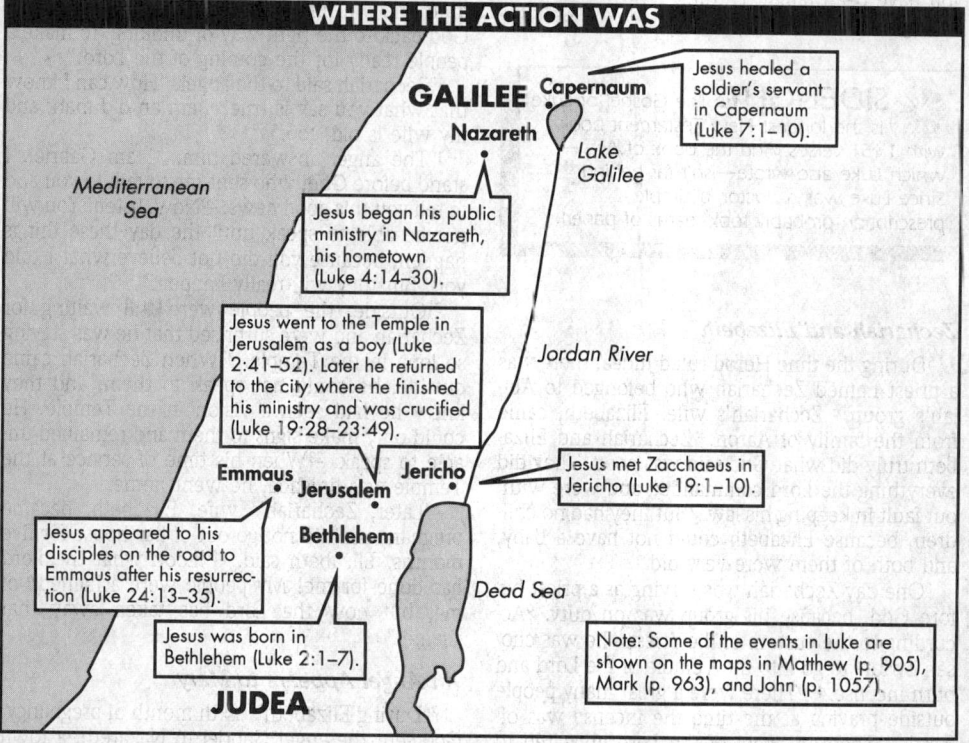

WHERE THE ACTION WAS

GALILEE

Capernaum

Jesus healed a soldier's servant in Capernaum (Luke 7:1—10).

Nazareth

Lake Galilee

Mediterranean Sea

Jesus began his public ministry in Nazareth, his hometown (Luke 4:14—30).

Jesus went to the Temple in Jerusalem as a boy (Luke 2:41—52). Later he returned to the city where he finished his ministry and was crucified (Luke 19:28—23:49).

Jordan River

Emmaus

Jerusalem

Jericho

Jesus met Zacchaeus in Jericho (Luke 19:1—10).

Jesus appeared to his disciples on the road to Emmaus after his resurrection (Luke 24:13—35).

Bethlehem

Dead Sea

Jesus was born in Bethlehem (Luke 2:1—7).

JUDEA

Note: Some of the events in Luke are shown on the maps in Matthew (p. 905), Mark (p. 963), and John (p. 1057).

WHEN THE ACTION WAS

Jesus was born	Jesus was crucified, rose from the dead, and went to heaven	Paul began his missionary work	Fire destroyed Rome		
BC/AD	25AD	50AD		75AD	100AD
	Jesus began his ministry			Romans destroyed the Temple in Jerusalem	

Behind the Scenes (cont.): As you read the Gospel of Luke, you'll discover some important emphases. First, this book emphasizes that Jesus came for all people, not just the Jews. You'll also see Jesus' particular concern for women, the poor and the outcasts of the world. Then the book shows Jesus as God's Spirit-led Son who came to offer eternal life to all people who follow him.

Luke 19:10 says that "the Son of Man came to find lost people and save them." This book tells, in detail, the story of his coming. If you like the Gospel of Luke, check out the sequel: the book of Acts (p. 1097). It's written by the same author, and continues the story where Luke leaves off.

Luke Writes About Jesus' Life

1 Many have tried to report on the things that happened among us. [2]They have written the same things that we learned from others — the people who saw those things from the beginning and served God by telling people his message. [3]Since I myself have studied everything carefully from the beginning, most excellent[n] Theophilus, it seemed good for me to write it out for you. I arranged it in order [4]to help you know that what you have been taught is true.

> **SIDELIGHT:** The Gospel of Luke is the longest New Testament book, with 1,151 verses. And the book of Acts— which Luke also wrote—isn't far behind. Since Luke was a doctor, a simple prescription probably took reams of paper!

Zechariah and Elizabeth

[5]During the time Herod ruled Judea, there was a priest named Zechariah who belonged to Abijah's group.[n] Zechariah's wife, Elizabeth, came from the family of Aaron. [6]Zechariah and Elizabeth truly did what God said was good. They did everything the Lord commanded and were without fault in keeping his law. [7]But they had no children, because Elizabeth could not have a baby, and both of them were very old.

[8]One day Zechariah was serving as a priest before God, because his group was on duty. [9]According to the custom of the priests, he was chosen by lot[d] to go into the Temple of the Lord and burn incense.[d] [10]There were a great many people outside praying at the time the incense was offered. [11]Then an angel of the Lord appeared to Zechariah, standing on the right side of the incense table. [12]When he saw the angel, Zechariah was startled and frightened. [13]But the angel said

to him, "Zechariah, don't be afraid. God has heard your prayer. Your wife, Elizabeth, will give birth to a son, and you will name him John. [14]He will bring you joy and gladness, and many people will be happy because of his birth. [15]John will be a great man for the Lord. He will never drink wine or beer, and even from birth, he will be filled with the Holy Spirit.[d] [16]He will help many people of Israel return to the Lord their God. [17]He will go before the Lord in spirit and power like Elijah. He will make peace between parents and their children and will bring those who are not obeying God back to the right way of thinking, to make a people ready for the coming of the Lord."

[18]Zechariah said to the angel, "How can I know that what you say is true? I am an old man, and my wife is old, too."

[19]The angel answered him, "I am Gabriel. I stand before God, who sent me to talk to you and to tell you this good news. [20]Now, listen! You will not be able to speak until the day these things happen, because you did not believe what I told you. But they will really happen."

[21]Outside, the people were still waiting for Zechariah and were surprised that he was staying so long in the Temple. [22]When Zechariah came outside, he could not speak to them, and they knew he had seen a vision in the Temple. He could only make signs to them and remained unable to speak. [23]When his time of service at the Temple was finished, he went home.

[24]Later, Zechariah's wife, Elizabeth, became pregnant and did not go out of her house for five months. Elizabeth said, [25]"Look what the Lord has done for me! My people were ashamed[n] of me, but now the Lord has taken away that shame."

An Angel Appears to Mary

[26]During Elizabeth's sixth month of pregnancy, God sent the angel Gabriel to Nazareth, a town in Galilee, [27]to a virgin.[d] She was engaged to marry a man named Joseph from the family of David. Her name was Mary. [28]The angel came to

---

excellent This word was used to show respect to an important person like a king or ruler.
Abijah's group The Jewish priests were divided into twenty-four groups. See 1 Chronicles 24.
ashamed The Jewish people thought it was a disgrace for women not to have children.

her and said, "Greetings! The Lord has blessed you and is with you."

²⁹But Mary was very startled by what the angel said and wondered what this greeting might mean.

³⁰The angel said to her, "Don't be afraid, Mary; God has shown you his grace. ³¹Listen! You will become pregnant and give birth to a son, and you will name him Jesus. ³²He will be great and will be called the Son of the Most High. The Lord God will give him the throne of King David, his ancestor. ³³He will rule over the people of Jacob forever, and his kingdom will never end."

³⁴Mary said to the angel, "How will this happen since I am a virgin?"

³⁵The angel said to Mary, "The Holy Spirit*d* will come upon you, and the power of the Most High will cover you. For this reason the baby will be holy and will be called the Son of God. ³⁶Now Elizabeth, your relative, is also pregnant with a son though she is very old. Everyone thought she could not have a baby, but she has been pregnant for six months. ³⁷God can do anything!"

³⁸Mary said, "I am the servant of the Lord. Let this happen to me as you say!" Then the angel went away.

Mary Visits Elizabeth

³⁹Mary got up and went quickly to a town in the hills of Judea. ⁴⁰She came to Zechariah's house and greeted Elizabeth. ⁴¹When Elizabeth heard Mary's greeting, the unborn baby inside her jumped, and Elizabeth was filled with the Holy Spirit.*d* ⁴²She cried out in a loud voice, "God has blessed you more than any other woman, and he has blessed the baby to which you will give birth. ⁴³Why has this good thing happened to me, that the mother of my Lord comes to me? ⁴⁴When I heard your voice, the baby inside me jumped with joy. ⁴⁵You are blessed because you believed that what the Lord said to you would really happen."

Mary Praises God

⁴⁶Then Mary said,
"My soul praises the Lord;
⁴⁷ my heart rejoices in God my Savior,
⁴⁸because he has shown his concern for his
       humble servant girl.

Power in Letting Go

Joni Eareckson loved to swim when she was young. She was an excellent diver too, and had even thought about trying out for the Olympics.

When she was seventeen, Joni and her friends went swimming in Chesapeake Bay. Joni dove into the unfamiliar waters, expecting to feel that cool, free-floating feeling she had come to love. Instead, she felt nothing. As her head struck the bottom, her spinal cord snapped—leaving her paralyzed from the neck down for the rest of her life.

Joni felt depressed and angry at the prospect of spending the rest of her life in a wheelchair. Most of her anger was aimed at God. "Oh God, how can you do this to me?" she prayed. "What have you done to me?"

Though God has never healed her physically, he did heal Joni's soul. And over the years she has grown into a beautiful free spirit. She sums it up this way: "When I had no choice but acceptance, trust, and surrender . . . it was as if I had finally gained emotional independence—through complete dependence on God."

Read **Luke 1:26–38** to see how God brought forth life in another teenage girl because she was ready to accept, trust, and surrender.

■ How was Mary's response to God's actions different from or similar to Joni's?

■ In what specific ways would you like to see God's power change your life?

C O N S I D E R . . .

■ underlining the verses in this passage that speak most to you, and memorizing them.

■ asking God to help you understand his unlimited power and the ways he chooses to use (or not to use) it.

F O R   M O R E ,   S E E . . .

■ Psalm 31:14–24 (p. 500)   ■ James 1:1–5 (p. 1294)
■ 2 Corinthians 12:7–10 (p. 1203)

From now on, all people will say that I am
  blessed,
49 because the Powerful One has done great
  things for me.
  His name is holy.
50God will show his mercy forever and ever
  to those who worship and serve him.
51He has done mighty deeds by his power.
  He has scattered the people who are
  proud
  and think great things about themselves.
52He has brought down rulers from their
  thrones
  and raised up the humble.
53He has filled the hungry with good things
  and sent the rich away with nothing.
54He has helped his servant, the people of
  Israel,
  remembering to show them mercy
55as he promised to our ancestors,
  to Abraham and to his children forever."
56Mary stayed with Elizabeth for about three
months and then returned home.

The Birth of John

57When it was time for Elizabeth to give birth,
she had a boy. 58Her neighbors and relatives heard
how good the Lord was to her, and they rejoiced
with her.

59When the baby was eight days old, they came
to circumcise[d] him. They wanted to name him
Zechariah because this was his father's name,
60but his mother said, "No! He will be named
John."

61The people said to Elizabeth, "But no one in
your family has this name." 62Then they made
signs to his father to find out what he would like
to name him.

63Zechariah asked for a writing tablet and
wrote, "His name is John," and everyone was surprised. 64Immediately Zechariah could talk again,
and he began praising God. 65All their neighbors
became alarmed, and in all the mountains of Judea people continued talking about all these
things. 66The people who heard about them wondered, saying, "What will this child be?" because
the Lord was with him.

Zechariah Praises God

67Then Zechariah, John's father, was filled with
the Holy Spirit and prophesied:[d]
68"Let us praise the Lord, the God of Israel,
  because he has come to help his people and
  has given them freedom.

---

⁶⁹He has given us a powerful Savior
    from the family of God's servant David.
⁷⁰He said that he would do this
    through his holy prophets*d* who lived long
        ago:
⁷¹He promised he would save us from our
        enemies
    and from the power of all those who hate
        us.
⁷²He said he would give mercy to our fathers
    and that he would remember his holy
        promise.
⁷³God promised Abraham, our father,
⁷⁴ that he would save us from the power of
        our enemies
    so we could serve him without fear,
⁷⁵being holy and good before God as long as
        we live.

⁷⁶"Now you, child, will be called a prophet of
        the Most High God.
    You will go before the Lord to prepare his
        way.
⁷⁷You will make his people know that they will
        be saved
    by having their sins forgiven.
⁷⁸With the loving mercy of our God,
    a new day from heaven will dawn upon
        us.
⁷⁹It will shine on those who live in darkness,
        in the shadow of death.
    It will guide us into the path of peace."

⁸⁰And so the child grew up and became strong
in spirit. John lived in the desert until the time
when he came out to preach to Israel.

The Birth of Jesus

2 At that time, Augustus Caesar*d* sent an order
    that all people in the countries under Roman
rule must list their names in a register. ²This was
the first registration;*n* it was taken while Quirinius was governor of Syria. ³And all went to their
own towns to be registered.

⁴So Joseph left Nazareth, a town in Galilee, and
went to the town of Bethlehem in Judea, known
as the town of David. Joseph went there because
he was from the family of David. ⁵Joseph registered with Mary, to whom he was engaged*n* and
who was now pregnant. ⁶While they were in
Bethlehem, the time came for Mary to have the
baby, ⁷and she gave birth to her first son. Because
there were no rooms left in the inn, she wrapped
the baby with pieces of cloth and laid him in a box
where animals are fed

Shepherds Hear About Jesus

⁸That night, some shepherds were in the fields
nearby watching their sheep. ⁹Then an angel of

> **SIDELIGHT:** When Mary
> wrapped Jesus with cloths (Luke 2:7),
> he probably couldn't move his arms because
> he was wrapped so tightly. In biblical times,
> people believed a good six-month
> "wrapping" prevented arms and legs from
> becoming crooked.

the Lord stood before them. The glory of the Lord
was shining around them, and they became very
frightened. ¹⁰The angel said to them, "Do not be
afraid. I am bringing you good news that will be
a great joy to all the people. ¹¹Today your Savior
was born in the town of David. He is Christ,*d* the
Lord. ¹²This is how you will know him: You will
find a baby wrapped in pieces of cloth and lying
in a feeding box."

¹³Then a very large group of angels from
heaven joined the first angel, praising God and
saying:
¹⁴"Give glory to God in heaven,
    and on earth let there be peace among the
        people who please God."

¹⁵When the angels left them and went back to
heaven, the shepherds said to each other, "Let's
go to Bethlehem. Let's see this thing that has happened which the Lord has told us about."
¹⁶So the shepherds went quickly and found
Mary and Joseph and the baby, who was lying in
a feeding box. ¹⁷When they had seen him, they
told what the angels had said about this child.
¹⁸Everyone was amazed at what the shepherds
said to them. ¹⁹But Mary treasured these things
and continued to think about them. ²⁰Then the
shepherds went back to their sheep, praising God
and thanking him for everything they had seen
and heard. It had been just as the angel had told
them.
²¹When the baby was eight days old, he was
circumcised*d* and was named Jesus, the name
given by the angel before the baby began to grow
inside Mary.

Jesus Is Presented in the Temple

²²When the time came for Mary and Joseph to
do what the law of Moses taught about being
made pure,*n* they took Jesus to Jerusalem to
present him to the Lord. ²³(It is written in the law

---

registration Census. A counting of all the people and the things they own.
engaged For the Jewish people, an engagement was a lasting agreement. It could only be broken by divorce.
pure The law of Moses said that forty days after a Jewish woman gave birth to a son, she must be cleansed by a ceremony at
    the Temple. Read Leviticus 12:2-8.

of the Lord: "Every firstborn*d* male shall be given to the Lord.") *n* 24Mary and Joseph also went to offer a sacrifice, as the law of the Lord says: "You must sacrifice two doves or two young pigeons." *n*

Simeon Sees Jesus

25In Jerusalem lived a man named Simeon who was a good man and godly. He was waiting for the time when God would take away Israel's sorrow, and the Holy Spirit*d* was in him. 26Simeon had been told by the Holy Spirit that he would not die before he saw the Christ*d* promised by the Lord. 27The Spirit led Simeon to the Temple.*d* When Mary and Joseph brought the baby Jesus to the Temple to do what the law said they must do, 28Simeon took the baby in his arms and thanked God:

29"Now, Lord, you can let me, your servant,
    die in peace as you said.
30With my own eyes I have seen your
    salvation,
31 which you prepared before all people.
32It is a light for the non-Jewish people to see
    and an honor for your people, the
    Israelites."

33Jesus' father and mother were amazed at what Simeon had said about him. 34Then Simeon blessed them and said to Mary, "God has chosen this child to cause the fall and rise of many in Israel. He will be a sign from God that many people will not accept 35so that the thoughts of many will be made known. And the things that will happen will make your heart sad, too."

Anna Sees Jesus

36There was a prophetess,*d* Anna, from the family of Phanuel in the tribe*d* of Asher. Anna was very old. She had once been married for seven years. 37Then her husband died, and she was a widow for eighty-four years. Anna never left the Temple but worshiped God, going without food and praying day and night. 38Standing there at that time, she thanked God and spoke about Jesus to all who were waiting for God to free Jerusalem.

Joseph and Mary Return Home

39When Joseph and Mary had done everything the law of the Lord commanded, they went home to Nazareth, their own town in Galilee. 40The little child grew and became strong. He was filled with wisdom, and God's goodness was upon him.

"**Every ... Lord.**"   Quotation from Exodus 13:2.
"**You ... pigeons.**"   Quotation from Leviticus 12:8.

WORSHIP

Awesome Stuff

When you look up at the sky on a clear night, did you know:
- the nearest star to earth is four light-years away?
- the light your eyeball sees from a star may have begun its journey toward you—at 186,000 miles per second—before the birth of Christ?
- some of the stars you see in a night sky may not be stars but whole galaxies? They may be millions of stars that are so incredibly far away they appear to be just one pinpoint of light.
- our little corner of the universe is one of only a few places with light and activity? Most of space is vast emptiness with no stars or planets.
- the earth's place in the universe may be comparable to the place occupied by a grain of sand in our world? Awe-inspiring, isn't it? In **Luke 2:8–21** the shepherds also learned how worship can grow out of seeing beyond ourselves into God's awesome realm.
- How do the facts of Jesus' birth and the vastness of our universe compare or contrast?
- What does it tell you to know that the same God who made and watches over us became a human just so we could know him?

CONSIDER . . .
◗ *listing five ways you can worship God more, then doing them.*
- sitting under a starry sky and pondering God's vast power.

FOR MORE, SEE . . .
- Psalm 8:3–9 (p. 486)
- Habbakuk 3:17–19 (p. 878)
- Acts 4:24–31 (p. 1104)

Jesus As a Boy

⁴¹Every year Jesus' parents went to Jerusalem for the Passover*d* Feast. ⁴²When he was twelve years old, they went to the feast as they always did. ⁴³After the feast days were over, they started home. The boy Jesus stayed behind in Jerusalem, but his parents did not know it. ⁴⁴Thinking that Jesus was with them in the group, they traveled for a whole day. Then they began to look for him among their family and friends. ⁴⁵When they did not find him, they went back to Jerusalem to look for him there. ⁴⁶After three days they found Jesus sitting in the Temple*d* with the teachers, listening to them and asking them questions. ⁴⁷All who heard him were amazed at his understanding and answers. ⁴⁸When Jesus' parents saw him, they were astonished. His mother said to him, "Son, why did you do this to us? Your father and I were very worried about you and have been looking for you."

⁴⁹Jesus said to them, "Why were you looking for me? Didn't you know that I must be in my Father's house?" ⁵⁰But they did not understand the meaning of what he said.

⁵¹Jesus went with them to Nazareth and was obedient to them. But his mother kept in her mind all that had happened. ⁵²Jesus became wiser and grew physically. People liked him, and he pleased God.

The Preaching of John

3 It was the fifteenth year of the rule of Tiberius Caesar.*d* These men were under Caesar: Pontius Pilate, the ruler of Judea; Herod, the ruler of Galilee; Philip, Herod's brother, the ruler of Iturea and Trachonitis; and Lysanias, the ruler of Abilene. ²Annas and Caiaphas were the high priests. At this time, the word of God came to John son of Zechariah in the desert. ³He went all over the area around the Jordan River preaching a baptism of changed hearts and lives for the forgiveness of sins. ⁴As it is written in the book of Isaiah the prophet:*d*

"This is a voice of one
who calls out in the desert:

Laboratory of Faith

"Jen, I don't want to leave." Jen Peters knew Kay Stone was serious. "Christianity is so much easier here. Everyone follows God, gets along, and it feels so good to get away from the pressure."

Kay's youth group had spent a weekend together in a mountain cabin. They had had a lot of fun and spent time learning about God. But now it was time to go home.

"Maybe I should take time off from school and stay here—or maybe even go to school in another town," Kay wondered aloud.

A few caring questions from Jen helped Kay talk about the real issue in her life. She was under stress at home, and the weekend away had provided a sense of escape. She didn't want to go back to the way it was.

"Kay, God has taught you much this weekend. And for every lesson he teaches, he provides a laboratory to test your new understanding and put it to work. Your family just might be your laboratory."

Kay thought for a moment, then nodded in agreement.

"Yeah," Kay sighed. "I guess there's no better place for God to help me grow."

Good or bad, families can challenge you to grow as a person and a Christian. **Luke 2:22–40** speaks of how God used Jesus' family to help him.

■ Why does Kay need her family, even though things are hard? Why did Jesus need his family?

■ Who are the "Simeons" and "Annas" in your life who help you see God's work in your life and your family? Why are these people important to you?

CONSIDER . . .

■ telling your parent one good lesson you have learned because of your family.
■ talking to a trusted adult if your family struggles feel overwhelming.

FOR MORE, SEE . . .

■ Proverbs 22:6 (p. 586)　　　　■ Ephesians 6:1–3 (p. 1225)
■ Matthew 12:46–50 (p. 930)

'Prepare the way for the Lord.
Make the road straight for him.
⁵Every valley should be filled in,
and every mountain and hill should be
made flat.
Roads with turns should be made straight,
and rough roads should be made smooth.
⁶And all people will know about the salvation
of God!' "   *Isaiah 40:3-5*

⁷To the crowds of people who came to be baptized by John, he said, "You are all snakes! Who warned you to run away from God's coming punishment? ⁸Do the things that show you really have changed your hearts and lives. Don't begin to say to yourselves, 'Abraham is our father.' I tell you that God could make children for Abraham from these rocks. ⁹The ax is now ready to cut down the trees, and every tree that does not produce good fruit will be cut down and thrown into the fire." *n*

¹⁰The people asked John, "Then what should we do?"

¹¹John answered, "If you have two shirts, share with the person who does not have one. If you have food, share that also."

¹²Even tax collectors came to John to be baptized. They said to him, "Teacher, what should we do?"

¹³John said to them, "Don't take more taxes from people than you have been ordered to take."

¹⁴The soldiers asked John, "What about us? What should we do?"

John said to them, "Don't force people to give you money, and don't lie about them. Be satisfied with the pay you get."

¹⁵Since the people were hoping for the Christ*d* to come, they wondered if John might be the one.

¹⁶John answered everyone, "I baptize you with water, but there is one coming who is greater

The ax . . . fire.   This means that God is ready to punish his people who do not obey him.

SPIRITUAL GROWTH

Who Am I?

When Brian Ziegler was a boy, he used to love to make mud pies by the outdoor faucet on the side of his house. His mom would give him old pie pans, and he'd fill them with just the right mix of dirt and water.

"You had to be careful to mix it right," Brian recalls. "Too much dirt, and your pie would crumble. Too much water, and it would ooze."

As Brian got older, he didn't make mud pies as often. But he still enjoyed working with his hands to create. In junior high, Brian got into an art class and learned the basics of sculpture design.

"I was hooked from then on," Brian says with a smile. "I loved the idea of taking an image in my hands, and making it a reality in the clay. It's been fun ever since!"

Brian now works as a sculptor part-time after school. He has won several awards for his work through the school system, and plans to attend an art school in New York after he graduates.

"I want to design sculptures like you see around big corporate skyscrapers," says Brian, "and still have my own business."

Brian grins. "Wow, I never realized you could turn making mud pies into a career."

Brian's interest and skill in sculpting grew as he got older. In the same way, our ability to understand and appreciate God grows as we get older and expose ourselves to more of God's ways. Jesus also experienced this spiritual growth process. Read about it in **Luke 2:41–52**, especially verse 52.

■ What do Jesus and Brian have in common based on the passage?
■ How have you "continued to learn more and more" in the past year?

C O N S I D E R . . .

■ thinking about all the ways you have changed in the past year, and thanking *God for helping you grow spiritually;*
■ keeping a prayer journal to help log spiritual growth in your life.

F O R   M O R E ,   S E E . . .
■ 1 Samuel 2:26 (p. 247)
■ Ephesians 4:4–16 (p. 1222)
■ 1 Corinthians 13:11–13 (p. 1184)

than I am. I am not good enough to untie his sandals. He will baptize you with the Holy Spirit[d] and fire. [17]He will come ready to clean the grain, separating the good grain from the chaff.[d] He will put the good part of the grain into his barn, but he will burn the chaff with a fire that cannot be put out."[n] [18]And John continued to preach the Good News,[d] saying many other things to encourage the people.

[19]But John spoke against Herod, the governor, because of his sin with Herodias, the wife of Herod's brother, and because of the many other evil things Herod did. [20]So Herod did something even worse: He put John in prison.

Jesus Is Baptized by John

[21]When all the people were being baptized by John, Jesus also was baptized. While Jesus was praying, heaven opened [22]and the Holy Spirit[d] came down on him in the form of a dove. Then a voice came from heaven, saying, "You are my Son, whom I love, and I am very pleased with you."

The Family History of Jesus

[23]When Jesus began his ministry, he was about thirty years old. People thought that Jesus was Joseph's son.

Joseph was the son[n] of Heli.
[24]Heli was the son of Matthat.
Matthat was the son of Levi.
Levi was the son of Melki.
Melki was the son of Jannai.
Jannai was the son of Joseph.
[25]Joseph was the son of Mattathias.
Mattathias was the son of Amos.
Amos was the son of Nahum.
Nahum was the son of Esli.
Esli was the son of Naggai.
[26]Naggai was the son of Maath.
Maath was the son of Mattathias.
Mattathias was the son of Semein.
Semein was the son of Josech.
Josech was the son of Joda.
[27]Joda was the son of Joanan.
Joanan was the son of Rhesa.
Rhesa was the son of Zerubbabel.

He will . . . out. This means that Jesus will come to separate good people from bad people, saving the good and punishing the bad.
son "Son" in Jewish lists of ancestors can sometimes mean grandson or more distant relative.

Quiet Disasters

If forty thousand people were to die from an earthquake or hurricane, would it make the news? Of course.

But forty thousand people die every day—from hunger. And when was the last time you saw that on the news?

If you saw a rich person feasting while a poor child starved at the doorstep, would you be angry? Of course.

But did you know that the United States has less than 6 percent of the world's population, yet consumes more than 33 percent of the world's resources?

It may be hard to see yourself as superwealthy, especially when you compare your income with those of kids around you. But when compared to the average world citizen, you have great wealth. And you have a lot to offer a hurting world.

Luke 3:1–18 records John's advice to the people of his day who practiced "religion," but weren't supporting "justice." Read the passage to hear the warning he gives them—and us.

■ What group of people might John relay his message to today?
■ According to this passage, how should we define justice?

CONSIDER . . .

■ writing a short speech that John the Baptist might deliver to your church.
■ doing something to promote justice in the world. For example, spearhead a canned food drive, or volunteer at a local relief agency.

FOR MORE, SEE . . .

■ Jeremiah 2:34–35 (p. 694)
■ Matthew 3:1–12 (p. 910)
■ John 1:19–34 (p. 1059)

Zerubbabel was the grandson of Shealtiel.
Shealtiel was the son of Neri.
28Neri was the son of Melchi.
Melchi was the son of Addi.
Addi was the son of Cosam.
Cosam was the son of Elmadam.
Elmadam was the son of Er.
29Er was the son of Joshua.
Joshua was the son of Eliezer.
Eliezer was the son of Jorim.
Jorim was the son of Matthat.
Matthat was the son of Levi.
30Levi was the son of Simeon.
Simeon was the son of Judah.
Judah was the son of Joseph.
Joseph was the son of Jonam.
Jonam was the son of Eliakim.
31Eliakim was the son of Melea.
Melea was the son of Menna.
Menna was the son of Mattatha.
Mattatha was the son of Nathan.
Nathan was the son of David.
32David was the son of Jesse.
Jesse was the son of Obed.
Obed was the son of Boaz.
Boaz was the son of Salmon.
Salmon was the son of Nahshon.
33Nahshon was the son of Amminadab.
Amminadab was the son of Admin.
Admin was the son of Arni.
Arni was the son of Hezron.
Hezron was the son of Perez.
Perez was the son of Judah.
34Judah was the son of Jacob.
Jacob was the son of Isaac.
Isaac was the son of Abraham.
Abraham was the son of Terah.
Terah was the son of Nahor.
35Nahor was the son of Serug.
Serug was the son of Reu.
Reu was the son of Peleg.
Peleg was the son of Eber.
Eber was the son of Shelah.
36Shelah was the son of Cainan.
Cainan was the son of Arphaxad.
Arphaxad was the son of Shem.
Shem was the son of Noah.
Noah was the son of Lamech.
37Lamech was the son of Methuselah.
Methuselah was the son of Enoch.
Enoch was the son of Jared.
Jared was the son of Mahalalel.
Mahalalel was the son of Kenan.
38Kenan was the son of Enosh.
Enosh was the son of Seth.

Seth was the son of Adam.
Adam was the son of God.

Jesus Is Tempted by the Devil

4 Jesus, filled with the Holy Spirit,*d* returned from the Jordan River. The Spirit led Jesus into the desert 2where the devil tempted Jesus for forty days. Jesus ate nothing during that time, and when those days were ended, he was very hungry.

3The devil said to Jesus, "If you are the Son of God, tell this rock to become bread."

4Jesus answered, "It is written in the Scriptures:*d* 'A person does not live by eating only bread.' "*n*

5Then the devil took Jesus and showed him all the kingdoms of the world in an instant. 6The devil said to Jesus, "I will give you all these kingdoms and all their power and glory. It has all been given to me, and I can give it to anyone I wish. 7If you worship me, then it will all be yours."

8Jesus answered, "It is written in the Scriptures: 'You must worship the Lord your God and serve only him.' "*n*

9Then the devil led Jesus to Jerusalem and put him on a high place of the Temple.*d* He said to Jesus, "If you are the Son of God, jump down. 10It is written in the Scriptures:

'He has put his angels in charge of you
    to watch over you.'   *Psalm 91:11*

11It is also written:

'They will catch you in their hands
    so that you will not hit your foot on a
        rock.' "   *Psalm 91:12*

12Jesus answered, "But it also says in the Scriptures: 'Do not test the Lord your God.' "*n*

13After the devil had tempted Jesus in every way, he left him to wait until a better time.

Jesus Teaches the People

14Jesus returned to Galilee in the power of the Holy Spirit,*d* and stories about him spread all through the area. 15He began to teach in their synagogues,*d* and everyone praised him.

> **SIDELIGHT:** If you don't like being noticed when you visit different churches, you wouldn't have visited many synagogues in Jesus' day. It was customary for the synagogue leader to invite visitors to address the congregation. Jesus took advantage of the opportunity to preach in Luke 4:14–19.

'A person . . . bread.' Quotation from Deuteronomy 8:3.
'You . . . him.' Quotation from Deuteronomy 6:13.
'Do . . . God.' Quotation from Deuteronomy 6:16.

16Jesus traveled to Nazareth, where he had grown up. On the Sabbath*d* day he went to the synagogue, as he always did, and stood up to read. 17The book of Isaiah the prophet*d* was given to him. He opened the book and found the place where this is written:

18"The Lord has put his Spirit in me,
   because he appointed me to tell the Good
      News*d* to the poor.
He has sent me to tell the captives they are
      free
and to tell the blind that they can see
      again.   *Isaiah 61:1*
God sent me to free those who have been
      treated unfairly   *Isaiah 58:6*

19 and to announce the time when the Lord
      will show his kindness."   *Isaiah 61:2*

20Jesus closed the book, gave it back to the assistant, and sat down. Everyone in the synagogue was watching Jesus closely. 21He began to say to them, "While you heard these words just now, they were coming true!"

22All the people spoke well of Jesus and were amazed at the words of grace he spoke. They asked, "Isn't this Joseph's son?"

23Jesus said to them, "I know that you will tell me the old saying: 'Doctor, heal yourself.' You want to say, 'We heard about the things you did in Capernaum. Do those things here in your own

SIN

Proving Self

In his small high school in upstate New York, Josh Hartley was a star. He played everything from baseball to football, and enjoyed knowing he had helped win most of the trophies in the school display case. Some people thought he was stuck-up, but that didn't bother him much. The important thing was that everyone knew who Josh Hartley was.

Then things changed. Josh's mother got a new job in another part of the state. So Josh had to move from his small-town school to a supersize suburban school near New York City.

No problem, thought Josh. I may not be able to play every sport here, but I can still make my mark somewhere.

But time after time, Josh met with disappointment. He would try out, but when teams were posted, his name never appeared. And even if he had made the teams, the trophy case filled an entire hallway of the school. No chance of recognition there.

For the first time in his life Josh began to get in trouble. It was little things at first—skipping school and picking fights between classes. But then the problems began to get worse. Josh seemed out of control. He didn't care about school anymore, or much of anything else.

One year later Josh was put in the county correctional center for arson. He had torched the high school field house.

Josh was released from prison on the condition that he receive counseling. After much therapy and prayer, Josh's attitude and outlook on life improved.

After Josh got out of prison, he told his parents, "I just didn't know who I was anymore. I wasn't an athlete. I didn't belong anywhere. So I found other ways to prove myself and get noticed."

Josh tried to prove himself in unhealthy ways. In **Luke 4:1–13** Satan also tempted Jesus to prove his identity by sinning against God. Read the passage to see how Jesus defeated the temptation to sin.
■ What temptations did both Josh and Jesus face?
■ Based on Jesus' example, what can you do to keep from sinning the next time you're tempted?

                    C O N S I D E R . . .
■ identifying ways you want to "prove yourself and get noticed." Talk about one of the ways with a parent or trusted friend.
■ telling a trusted friend about a sin you struggle with and asking him or her to pray for you.

              F O R   M O R E ,   S E E . . .
■ Genesis 3:1–6 (p. 4)   ■ Mark 12:28–34 (p. 988)
■ Matthew 4:1–11 (p. 910)

town!' " 24Then Jesus said, "I tell you the truth, a prophet is not accepted in his hometown. 25But I tell you the truth, there were many widows in Israel during the time of Elijah. It did not rain in Israel for three and one-half years, and there was no food anywhere in the whole country. 26But Elijah was sent to none of those widows, only to a widow in Zarephath, a town in Sidon. 27And there were many with skin diseases living in Israel during the time of the prophet Elisha. But none of them were healed, only Naaman, who was from the country of Syria."

28When all the people in the synagogue heard these things, they became very angry. 29They got up, forced Jesus out of town, and took him to the edge of the cliff on which the town was built. They planned to throw him off the edge, 30but Jesus walked through the crowd and went on his way.

Jesus Forces Out an Evil Spirit

31Jesus went to Capernaum, a city in Galilee, and on the Sabbath*d* day, he taught the people. 32They were amazed at his teaching, because he spoke with authority. 33In the synagogue*d* a man who had within him an evil spirit shouted in a loud voice, 34"Jesus of Nazareth! What do you want with us? Did you come to destroy us? I know who you are—God's Holy One!"

35Jesus commanded the evil spirit, "Be quiet! Come out of the man!" The evil spirit threw the man down to the ground before all the people and then left the man without hurting him.

36The people were amazed and said to each other, "What does this mean? With authority and power he commands evil spirits, and they come out." 37And so the news about Jesus spread to every place in the whole area.

Jesus Heals Many People

38Jesus left the synagogue*d* and went to the home of Simon. *n* Simon's mother-in-law was sick with a high fever, and they asked Jesus to help her. 39He came to her side and commanded the

Simon   Simon's other name was Peter.

GOD'S WILL

Against the Grain

In the spring of 1981, a worker at a nuclear weapons plant near Amarillo, Texas, made an appointment to see Bishop Leroy Matthiesen of the diocese of Amarillo.

"I'm pushing sixty," said Bill Hobbles. "I've worked for Pantex for seventeen years, and I'm worried that, as a Christian, what I'm doing with my life may be morally wrong."

Bishop Matthiesen listened to Bill's dilemma, and decided to take action. Knowing that the plant was a cornerstone of the local economy, the bishop issued a public statement calling for workers in the nuclear-weapons industry to search their consciences and consider quitting and finding other jobs.

He was accused of treason in the papers and was publicly invited to accept a one-way ticket to the totalitarian country of his choice. Moreover, a local agency cut off all funds for one of his social-service programs.

An important part of living out our faith means following God's will as we understand it—even when our view is unpopular. And as Jesus found in **Luke 4:16—30**, sometimes it's hardest to follow God's will when we are with those who know us best.

■ How is the bishop's experience like Jesus' experience in the passage? How are their experiences different?

■ Drawing from the passage, how should you respond when you feel you must take a stand that others—even Christians—disagree with?

C O N S I D E R . . .

■ choosing one way you will stand up for your beliefs at school, even though it may be unpopular with some people. For example, stick up for someone who is being picked on or take a stand on a controversial issue.

✒ writing out all the questions you have about God's will for your life and then talking to your youth pastor about them.

F O R   M O R E ,   S E E . . .

■ Jeremiah 1:4—10 (p. 691)
■ Mark 6:1—6 (p. 973)
                                            ■ Romans 12:1—2 (p. 1157)

fever to leave. It left her, and immediately she got up and began serving them.

⁴⁰When the sun went down, the people brought those who were sick to Jesus. Putting his hands on each sick person, he healed every one of them. ⁴¹Demonsᵈ came out of many people, shouting, "You are the Son of God." But Jesus commanded the demons and would not allow them to speak, because they knew Jesus was the Christ.ᵈ

⁴²At daybreak, Jesus went to a lonely place, but the people looked for him. When they found him, they tried to keep him from leaving. ⁴³But Jesus said to them, "I must preach about God's kingdom to other towns, too. This is why I was sent." ⁴⁴Then he kept on preaching in the synagoguesᵈ of Judea.

Jesus' First Followers

5 One day while Jesus was standing beside Lake Galilee, many people were pressing all around him to hear the word of God. ²Jesus saw two boats at the shore of the lake. The fishermen had left them and were washing their nets. ³Jesus got into one of the boats, the one that belonged to Simon,ⁿ and asked him to push off a little from the land. Then Jesus sat down and continued to teach the people from the boat.

⁴When Jesus had finished speaking, he said to Simon, "Take the boat into deep water, and put your nets in the water to catch some fish."

⁵Simon answered, "Master, we worked hard all night trying to catch fish, and we caught nothing. But you say to put the nets in the water, so I will." ⁶When the fishermen did as Jesus told them, they caught so many fish that the nets began to break. ⁷They called to their partners in the other boat to come and help them. They came and filled both boats so full that they were almost sinking.

⁸When Simon Peter saw what had happened, he bowed down before Jesus and said, "Go away from me, Lord. I am a sinful man!" ⁹He and the other fishermen were amazed at the many fish they caught, as were ¹⁰James and John, the sons of Zebedee, Simon's partners.

Jesus said to Simon, "Don't be afraid. From now on you will fish for people." ¹¹When the men brought their boats to the shore, they left everything and followed Jesus.

Jesus Heals a Sick Man

¹²When Jesus was in one of the towns, there was a man covered with a skin disease. When he saw Jesus, he bowed before him and begged him, "Lord, you can heal me if you will."

¹³Jesus reached out his hand and touched the man and said, "I will. Be healed!" Immediately the disease disappeared. ¹⁴Then Jesus said, "Don't tell anyone about this, but go and show yourself to the priestⁿ and offer a gift for your healing, as Moses commanded.ⁿ This will show the people what I have done."

¹⁵But the news about Jesus spread even more. Many people came to hear Jesus and to be healed of their sicknesses, ¹⁶but Jesus often slipped away to be alone so he could pray.

Jesus Heals a Paralyzed Man

¹⁷One day as Jesus was teaching the people, the Phariseesᵈ and teachers of the law from every town in Galilee and Judea and from Jerusalem were there. The Lord was giving Jesus the power to heal people. ¹⁸Just then, some men were carrying on a mat a man who was paralyzed. They tried to bring him in and put him down before Jesus. ¹⁹But because there were so many people there, they could not find a way in. So they went up on the roof and lowered the man on his mat through the ceiling into the middle of the crowd right before Jesus. ²⁰Seeing their faith, Jesus said, "Friend, your sins are forgiven."

> ❋ **SIDELIGHT:** If you think access to buildings is a new problem for disabled people, read Luke 5:18–20. The friends probably had to dig through layers of clay, reeds, grass, and branches to make a hole in the roof, since that's how most roofs were made in Jesus' time. The roofs were supported by wooden beams, which stretched from wall to wall.

²¹The Jewish teachers of the law and the Pharisees thought to themselves, "Who is this man who is speaking as if he were God? Only God can forgive sins."

²²But Jesus knew what they were thinking and said, "Why are you thinking these things? ²³Which is easier: to say, 'Your sins are forgiven,' or to say, 'Stand up and walk'? ²⁴But I will prove to you that the Son of Manᵈ has authority on earth to forgive sins." So Jesus said to the paralyzed man, "I tell you, stand up, take your mat, and go home."

²⁵At once the man stood up before them, picked up his mat, and went home, praising God. ²⁶All the people were fully amazed and began to praise God. They were filled with much re-

---

Simon　Simon's other name was Peter.
show . . . priest　The law of Moses said a priest must say when a Jewish person with a skin disease was well.
Moses commanded　Read about this in Leviticus 14:1-32.

spect and said, "Today we have seen amazing things!"

Levi Follows Jesus

27After this, Jesus went out and saw a tax collector named Levi sitting in the tax collector's booth. Jesus said to him, "Follow me!" 28So Levi got up, left everything, and followed him.

29Then Levi gave a big dinner for Jesus at his house. Many tax collectors and other people were eating there, too. 30But the Pharisees*d* and the men who taught the law for the Pharisees began to complain to Jesus' followers, "Why do you eat and drink with tax collectors and sinners?"

31Jesus answered them, "It is not the healthy people who need a doctor, but the sick. 32I have not come to invite good people but sinners to change their hearts and lives."

Jesus Answers a Question

33They said to Jesus, "John's followers often give up eating*n* for a certain time and pray, just as the Pharisees*d* do. But your followers eat and drink all the time."

34Jesus said to them, "You cannot make the friends of the bridegroom give up eating while he is still with them. 35But the time will come when the bridegroom will be taken away from them, and then they will give up eating."

36Jesus told them this story: "No one takes cloth off a new coat to cover a hole in an old coat. Otherwise, he ruins the new coat, and the cloth from the new coat will not be the same as the old cloth. 37Also, no one ever pours new wine into old leather bags. Otherwise, the new wine will break the bags, the wine will spill out, and the leather bags will be ruined. 38New wine must be put into new leather bags. 39No one after drinking old wine wants new wine, because he says, 'The old wine is better.' "

Jesus Is Lord over the Sabbath

6 One Sabbath*d* day Jesus was walking through some fields of grain. His followers picked the heads of grain, rubbed them in their hands, and ate them. 2Some Pharisees*d* said, "Why do you do what is not lawful on the Sabbath day?"

3Jesus answered, "Have you not read what David did when he and those with him were hungry? 4He went into God's house and took and ate the holy bread, which is lawful only for priests to eat. And he gave some to the people who were with him." 5Then Jesus said to the Pharisees, "The Son of Man*d* is Lord of the Sabbath day."

Jesus Heals a Man's Hand

6On another Sabbath*d* day Jesus went into the synagogue*d* and was teaching, and a man with a crippled right hand was there. 7The teachers of the law and the Pharisees*d* were watching closely to see if Jesus would heal on the Sabbath day so they could accuse him. 8But he knew what they were thinking, and he said to the man with the crippled hand, "Stand up here in the middle of everyone." The man got up and stood there. 9Then Jesus said to them, "I ask you, which is lawful on the Sabbath day: to do good or to do evil, to save a life or to destroy it?" 10Jesus looked around at all of them and said to the man, "Hold out your hand." The man held out his hand, and it was healed.

11But the Pharisees and the teachers of the law were very angry and discussed with each other what they could do to Jesus.

Jesus Chooses His Apostles

12At that time Jesus went off to a mountain to pray, and he spent the night praying to God. 13The next morning, Jesus called his followers to him and chose twelve of them, whom he named apostles:*d* 14Simon (Jesus named him Peter), his brother Andrew, James, John, Philip, Bartholomew, 15Matthew, Thomas, James son of Alphaeus, Simon (called the Zealot*d*), 16Judas son of James, and Judas Iscariot, who later turned Jesus over to his enemies.

Jesus Teaches and Heals

17Jesus and the apostles*d* came down from the mountain, and he stood on level ground. A large group of his followers was there, as well as many people from all around Judea, Jerusalem, and the seacoast cities of Tyre and Sidon. 18They all came to hear Jesus teach and to be healed of their sicknesses, and he healed those who were troubled by evil spirits. 19All the people were trying to touch Jesus, because power was coming from him and healing them all.

20Jesus looked at his followers and said,

"You people who are poor are happy,
    because the kingdom of God belongs to
      you.
21You people who are now hungry are happy,
    because you will be satisfied.
You people who are now crying are happy,
    because you will laugh with joy.
22"People will hate you, shut you out, insult you, and say you are evil because you follow the Son of Man.*d* But when they do, you will be happy. 23Be full of joy at that time, because you have a great reward waiting for you in heaven.

---

give up eating This is called "fasting." The people would give up eating for a special time of prayer and worship to God. It was also done to show sadness and disappointment.

Their ancestors did the same things to the prophets.*d*

24"But how terrible it will be for you who are rich,

because you have had your easy life.

25How terrible it will be for you who are full now,

because you will be hungry.

How terrible it will be for you who are laughing now,

because you will be sad and cry.

26"How terrible when everyone says only good things about you, because their ancestors said the same things about the false prophets.

Love Your Enemies

27"But I say to you who are listening, love your enemies. Do good to those who hate you, 28bless those who curse you, pray for those who are cruel to you. 29If anyone slaps you on one cheek, offer him the other cheek, too. If someone takes your coat, do not stop him from taking your shirt. 30Give to everyone who asks you, and when someone takes something that is yours, don't ask for it back. 31Do to others what you would want them to do to you. 32If you love only the people who love you, what praise should you get? Even sinners love the people who love them. 33If you do good only to those who do good to you, what praise should you get? Even sinners do that! 34If you lend things to people, always hoping to get something back, what praise should you get? Even sinners lend to other sinners so that they can get back the same amount! 35But love your enemies, do good to them, and lend to them without hoping to get anything back. Then you will have a great reward, and you will be children of the Most High God, because he is kind even to people who are ungrateful and full of sin. 36Show mercy, just as your Father shows mercy.

Look at Yourselves

37"Don't judge other people, and you will not be judged. Don't accuse others of being guilty, and you will not be accused of being guilty. Forgive, and you will be forgiven. 38Give, and you will receive. You will be given much. Pressed down, shaken together, and running over, it will spill into your lap. The way you give to others is the way God will give to you."

39Jesus told them this story: "Can a blind person lead another blind person? No! Both of them will fall into a ditch. 40A student is not better than the teacher, but the student who has been fully trained will be like the teacher.

41"Why do you notice the little piece of dust in your friend's eye, but you don't notice the big piece of wood in your own eye? 42How can you say to your friend, 'Friend, let me take that little piece of dust out of your eye' when you cannot see that big piece of wood in your own eye! You hypocrite!*d* First, take the wood out of your own eye. Then you will see clearly to take the dust out of your friend's eye.

Two Kinds of Fruit

43"A good tree does not produce bad fruit, nor does a bad tree produce good fruit. 44Each tree is known by its own fruit. People don't gather figs from thornbushes, and they don't get grapes from bushes. 45Good people bring good things out of the good they stored in their hearts. But evil people bring evil things out of the evil they stored in their hearts. People speak the things that are in their hearts.

Two Kinds of People

46"Why do you call me, 'Lord, Lord,' but do not do what I say? 47I will show you what everyone is like who comes to me and hears my words and obeys. 48That person is like a man building a house who dug deep and laid the foundation on rock. When the floods came, the water tried to wash the house away, but it could not shake it, because the house was built well. 49But the one who hears my words and does not obey is like a man who built his house on the ground without a foundation. When the floods came, the house quickly fell and was completely destroyed."

Jesus Heals a Soldier's Servant

7 When Jesus finished saying all these things to the people, he went to Capernaum. 2There was an army officer who had a servant who was very important to him. The servant was so sick he was nearly dead. 3When the officer heard about Jesus, he sent some older Jewish leaders to him to ask Jesus to come and heal his servant. 4The men went to Jesus and begged him, saying, "This officer is worthy of your help. 5He loves our people, and he built us a synagogue."*d*

6So Jesus went with the men. He was getting near the officer's house when the officer sent friends to say, "Lord, don't trouble yourself, because I am not worthy to have you come into my house. 7That is why I did not come to you myself. But you only need to command it, and my servant will be healed. 8I, too, am a man under the authority of others, and I have soldiers under my command. I tell one soldier, 'Go,' and he goes. I tell another soldier, 'Come,' and he comes. I say to my servant, 'Do this,' and my servant does it."

9When Jesus heard this, he was amazed. Turning to the crowd that was following him, he said, "I tell you, this is the greatest faith I have found anywhere, even in Israel."

10Those who had been sent to Jesus went back to the house where they found the servant in good health.

Jesus Brings a Man Back to Life

11Soon afterwards Jesus went to a town called Nain, and his followers and a large crowd traveled with him. 12When he came near the town gate, he saw a funeral. A mother, who was a widow, had lost her only son. A large crowd from the town was with the mother while her son was being carried out. 13When the Lord saw her, he felt very sorry for her and said, "Don't cry." 14He went up and touched the coffin, and the people who were carrying it stopped. Jesus said, "Young man, I tell you, get up!" 15And the son sat up and began to talk. Then Jesus gave him back to his mother.

16All the people were amazed and began praising God, saying, "A great prophet*d* has come to us! God has come to help his people."

17This news about Jesus spread through all Judea and into all the places around there.

John Asks a Question

18John's followers told him about all these things. He called for two of his followers 19and sent them to the Lord to ask, "Are you the One who is to come, or should we wait for someone else?"

> **SIDELIGHT:** The coffin where the boy lay when Jesus brought him back to life (Luke 7:11–15) wasn't like coffins today. In fact, it was probably just a board on which they laid the body. Just like today, wealthier people sometimes had more elaborate "funeral biers," as they were called.

20When the men came to Jesus, they said, "John the Baptist*d* sent us to you with this question: 'Are you the One who is to come, or should we wait for someone else?'"

21At that time, Jesus healed many people of

LEADERSHIP

Fish Out of Water

"Whales Commit Mass Suicide"

The 1986 newspaper headline alerted the community in Cape Cod about the baffling incident that had happened the night before. A herd, or "pod," of ninety-four whales beached themselves on the shores of Cape Cod. They just swam up onto the sand . . . and died.

That wasn't the first or last time whales have committed this strange act around the world. Newspapers periodically report stories of whales beaching themselves.

Several theories try to explain why whales do this. One of them is that the whales are following a basic herd instinct. Every pod has a leader. And if the leader becomes ill or disoriented, it might react by beaching itself. But since it's the leader, the other whales simply follow, even though it means death.

Sound crazy? Maybe, but it's not so unlike the way many people act. It's easy to follow leaders who say they have got the right answers, or know the truth.

People who pretend to have life's answers but live destructively are called hypocrites. In **Luke 6:39–49**, Jesus was saddened and angered to find hypocrisy in the religious leaders around him.

■ How is the lead whale like the blind leaders Jesus talks about in this passage?

■ What leaders do kids follow, even though the leaders' lifestyles seem destructive?

CONSIDER . . .

■ listing "good fruits" and "bad fruits" you see in your own life, then asking God to take away the bad fruit.

■ telling people whom you look to as leaders about the "good fruits" you see in their lives.

FOR MORE, SEE . . .

■ Isaiah 29:13 (p. 645)
■ Amos 8:4–8 (p. 848)
■ James 1:19–27 (p. 1294)

their sicknesses, diseases, and evil spirits, and he gave sight to many blind people. ²²Then Jesus answered John's followers, "Go tell John what you saw and heard here. The blind can see, the crippled can walk, and people with skin diseases are healed. The deaf can hear, the dead are raised to life, and the Good News*d* is preached to the poor. ²³Those who do not stumble in their faith because of me are blessed!"

²⁴When John's followers left, Jesus began talking to the people about John: "What did you go out into the desert to see? A reed*n* blown by the wind? ²⁵What did you go out to see? A man dressed in fine clothes? No, people who have fine clothes and much wealth live in kings' palaces. ²⁶But what did you go out to see? A prophet?*d* Yes, and I tell you, John is more than a prophet. ²⁷This was written about him:

'I will send my messenger ahead of you,
   who will prepare the way for you.' *Malachi 3:1*
²⁸I tell you, John is greater than any other person ever born, but even the least important person in the kingdom of God is greater than John."

²⁹(When the people, including the tax collectors, heard this, they all agreed that God's teaching was good, because they had been baptized by John. ³⁰But the Pharisees*d* and experts on the law refused to accept God's plan for themselves; they did not let John baptize them.)

³¹Then Jesus said, "What shall I say about the people of this time? What are they like? ³²They are like children sitting in the marketplace, calling to one another and saying,

'We played music for you, but you did not
   dance;
we sang a sad song, but you did not cry.'
³³John the Baptist came and did not eat bread or drink wine, and you say, 'He has a demon*d* in him.' ³⁴The Son of Man*d* came eating and drinking, and you say, 'Look at him! He eats too much and drinks too much wine, and he is a friend of tax collectors and sinners!' ³⁵But wisdom is proved to be right by what it does."

A Woman Washes Jesus' Feet

³⁶One of the Pharisees*d* asked Jesus to eat with

---

reed   It means that John was not ordinary or weak like grass blown by the wind.

FAITH

Surrender

In Officer's Training School, Roger Curtis learned to speak to an officer in a specific way. First you say, "Sir." Then you say your name, "Candidate Curtis." Then you answer the question or respond to the officer. Then finish with, "Sir." Officers try their hardest to confuse you. For example:

Officer: "Candidate Curtis!"
Candidate: "Sir, Candidate Curtis, yes, Sir!"
Officer: "You've got a thread on your uniform, Curtis!"
Candidate: "Sir, Candidate Curtis, yes, Sir!"
Officer: "Tell you what I'm gonna do; I'm gonna pull it, and I want you to make a noise like a cannon."
Candidate: "Sir, Candidate Curtis, yes, Sir!"
Officer: "I pulled it!"
Candidate: "Sir, Candidate Curtis, boom, Sir!"

Maybe this approach sounds foolish to you. But in battle, the most important thing soldiers can do is to place themselves completely under the authority of their superior—even if they don't understand the reasoning behind the orders. That's real faith. **Luke 7:1–10** describes another soldier who understood that kind of faith, and reaped the benefits of it.

■ How is the soldier in this passage like Candidate Curtis?
■ Is your faith as strong as the officer's in this passage? Why or why not?

C O N S I D E R . . .
■ trusting God with a part of your life you have never had the faith to let go of before.
■ memorizing Hebrews 11:1 (p. 1287), to learn God's definition of faith.

F O R   M O R E ,   S E E . . .
■ Genesis 22:1–18 (p. 25)   ■ Hebrews 11 (p. 1287)
■ Matthew 14:22–35 (p. 934)

him, so Jesus went into the Pharisee's house and sat at the table. [37]A sinful woman in the town learned that Jesus was eating at the Pharisee's house. So she brought an alabaster[d] jar of perfume [38]and stood behind Jesus at his feet, crying. She began to wash his feet with her tears, and she dried them with her hair, kissing them many times and rubbing them with the perfume. [39]When the Pharisee who asked Jesus to come to his house saw this, he thought to himself, "If Jesus were a prophet,[d] he would know that the woman touching him is a sinner!"

[40]Jesus said to the Pharisee, "Simon, I have something to say to you."

Simon said, "Teacher, tell me."

[41]Jesus said, "Two people owed money to the same banker. One owed five hundred coins[n] and the other owed fifty. [42]They had no money to pay what they owed, but the banker told both of them they did not have to pay him. Which person will love the banker more?"

[43]Simon, the Pharisee, answered, "I think it would be the one who owed him the most money."

Jesus said to Simon, "You are right." [44]Then Jesus turned toward the woman and said to Simon, "Do you see this woman? When I came into your house, you gave me no water for my feet, but she washed my feet with her tears and dried them with her hair. [45]You gave me no kiss of greeting, but she has been kissing my feet since I came in. [46]You did not put oil on my head, but she

coins Roman denarii. One coin was the average pay for one day's work.

Beyond the Great Divide

Janice Jenson was a riot. There was just no denying that. Tasha Smith hated her world history course, but Janice, who sat next to her, had a way of summing up every lecture that made it all seem like a funny movie. Her silly faces and off-the-wall comments sent Tasha rolling every time.

Tasha had to admit she liked Janice. But that made Tasha uneasy. She wasn't sure she was supposed to like Janice.

Janice had a reputation for wildness around school. She was a heavy drinker and usually had a whole string of boyfriends begging for her attention—which she freely gave. She was bad news, and everybody knew it.

"Tasha, why are hanging around with that girl?" her church friends would sometimes ask. "She could hurt your Christian witness."

Before long, Tasha began to get angry about her friends' attitude—and the internal struggle over Janice she still fought.

"How will people who don't know you ever get the chance if I'm unwilling to get to know them first?" Tasha asked God one day.

"They won't," a voice seemed to respond. Tasha smiled. She knew what she had to do now. She gladly spends time with her non-Christian friends—and shares Christ's love with them.

Tasha struggled with accepting non-Christians when others thought it was wrong. Jesus had to deal with the same problem within the religious community of his time. Read about his encounter with a "sinful woman" in **Luke 7:36—50**.

■ What feelings do Tasha's church friends and the Pharisee in the passage share?

■ If Jesus were a student in your school, whom might he spend the most time with?

C O N S I D E R . . .

■ scanning your yearbook and asking God to lead you to people he wants you to spend time with.

■ talking with your youth pastor about doing a youth group study on friendship evangelism.

F O R   M O R E ,   S E E . . .

■ Isaiah 61:1–2 (p. 680)
■ John 4:1–41 (p. 1063)

■ 2 Corinthians 6:14–18 (p. 1199)

poured perfume on my feet. 47I tell you that her many sins are forgiven, so she showed great love. But the person who is forgiven only a little will love only a little."

48Then Jesus said to her, "Your sins are forgiven."

49The people sitting at the table began to say among themselves, "Who is this who even forgives sins?"

50Jesus said to the woman, "Because you believed, you are saved from your sins. Go in peace."

The Group with Jesus

8 After this, while Jesus was traveling through some cities and small towns, he preached and told the Good News*d* about God's kingdom. The twelve apostles*d* were with him, 2and also some women who had been healed of sicknesses and evil spirits: Mary, called Magdalene, from whom seven demons*d* had gone out; 3Joanna, the wife of Chuza (the manager of Herod's house); Susanna; and many others. These women used their own money to help Jesus and his apostles.

A Story About Planting Seed

4When a great crowd was gathered, and people were coming to Jesus from every town, he told them this story:

5"A farmer went out to plant his seed. While he was planting, some seed fell by the road. People walked on the seed, and the birds ate it up. 6Some seed fell on rock, and when it began to grow, it died because it had no water. 7Some seed fell among thorny weeds, but the weeds grew up with it and choked the good plants. 8And some seed fell on good ground and grew and made a hundred times more."

As Jesus finished the story, he called out, "You people who can hear me, listen!"

9Jesus' followers asked him what this story meant.

10Jesus said, "You have been chosen to know the secrets about the kingdom of God. But I use stories to speak to other people so that:

'They will look, but they may not see.
They will listen, but they may not
    understand.'   *Isaiah 6:9*

11"This is what the story means: The seed is God's message. 12The seed that fell beside the road is like the people who hear God's teaching, but the devil comes and takes it away from them so they cannot believe it and be saved. 13The seed that fell on rock is like those who hear God's teaching and accept it gladly, but they don't allow the teaching to go deep into their lives. They believe for a while, but when trouble comes, they give up. 14The seed that fell among the thorny weeds is like those who hear God's teaching, but

they let the worries, riches, and pleasures of this life keep them from growing and producing good fruit. 15And the seed that fell on the good ground is like those who hear God's teaching with good, honest hearts and obey it and patiently produce good fruit.

Use What You Have

16"No one after lighting a lamp covers it with a bowl or hides it under a bed. Instead, the person puts it on a lampstand so those who come in will see the light. 17Everything that is hidden will become clear, and every secret thing will be made known. 18So be careful how you listen. Those who have understanding will be given more. But those who do not have understanding, even what they think they have will be taken away from them."

Jesus' True Family

19Jesus' mother and brothers came to see him, but there was such a crowd they could not get to him. 20Someone said to Jesus, "Your mother and your brothers are standing outside, wanting to see you."

21Jesus answered them, "My mother and my brothers are those who listen to God's teaching and obey it!"

Jesus Calms a Storm

22One day Jesus and his followers got into a boat, and he said to them, "Let's go across the lake." And so they started across. 23While they were sailing, Jesus fell asleep. A very strong wind blew up on the lake, causing the boat to fill with water, and they were in danger.

24The followers went to Jesus and woke him, saying, "Master! Master! We will drown!"

Jesus got up and gave a command to the wind and the waves. They stopped, and it became calm. 25Jesus said to his followers, "Where is your faith?"

The followers were afraid and amazed and said to each other, "Who is this that commands even the wind and the water, and they obey him?"

A Man with Demons Inside Him

26Jesus and his followers sailed across the lake from Galilee to the area of the Gerasene people. 27When Jesus got out on the land, a man from the town who had demons*d* inside him came to Jesus. For a long time he had worn no clothes and had lived in the burial caves, not in a house. 28When he saw Jesus, he cried out and fell down before him. He said with a loud voice, "What do you want with me, Jesus, Son of the Most High God? I beg you, don't torture me!" 29He said this because Jesus was commanding the evil spirit to come out of the man. Many times it had taken hold of him. Though he had been kept under guard and chained hand and foot, he had broken his chains and had been forced by the demon out into a lonely place.

[30]Jesus asked him, "What is your name?"

He answered, "Legion,"[n] because many demons were in him. [31]The demons begged Jesus not to send them into eternal darkness.[n] [32]A large herd of pigs was feeding on a hill, and the demons begged Jesus to allow them to go into the pigs. So Jesus allowed them to do this. [33]When the demons came out of the man, they went into the pigs, and the herd ran down the hill into the lake and was drowned.

[34]When the herdsmen saw what had happened, they ran away and told about this in the town and the countryside. [35]And people went to see what had happened. When they came to Jesus, they found the man sitting at Jesus' feet, clothed and in his right mind, because the demons were gone. But the people were frightened. [36]The people who saw this happen told the others how Jesus had made the man well. [37]All the people of the Gerasene country asked Jesus to leave, because they were all very afraid. So Jesus got into the boat and went back to Galilee.

[38]The man whom Jesus had healed begged to go with him, but Jesus sent him away, saying, [39]"Go back home and tell people how much God has done for you." So the man went all over town telling how much Jesus had done for him.

Jesus Gives Life to a Dead Girl and Heals a Sick Woman

[40]When Jesus got back to Galilee, a crowd welcomed him, because everyone was waiting for him. [41]A man named Jairus, a leader of the synagogue,[d] came to Jesus and fell at his feet, begging him to come to his house. [42]Jairus' only daughter, about twelve years old, was dying.

While Jesus was on his way to Jairus' house, the people were crowding all around him. [43]A woman was in the crowd who had been bleeding for twelve years, but no one was able to heal her. [44]She came up behind Jesus and touched the edge of his coat, and instantly her bleeding stopped. [45]Then Jesus said, "Who touched me?"

When all the people said they had not touched him, Peter said, "Master, the people are all around you and are pushing against you."

[46]But Jesus said, "Someone did touch me, because I felt power go out from me." [47]When the woman saw she could not hide, she came forward, shaking, and fell down before Jesus. While all the people listened, she told why she had

touched him and how she had been instantly healed. [48]Jesus said to her, "Dear woman, you are made well because you believed. Go in peace."

[49]While Jesus was still speaking, someone came from the house of the synagogue leader and said to him, "Your daughter is dead. Don't bother the teacher anymore."

[50]When Jesus heard this, he said to Jairus, "Don't be afraid. Just believe, and your daughter will be well."

[51]When Jesus went to the house, he let only Peter, John, James, and the girl's father and mother go inside with him. [52]All the people were crying and feeling sad because the girl was dead, but Jesus said, "Stop crying. She is not dead, only asleep."

[53]The people laughed at Jesus because they knew the girl was dead. [54]But Jesus took hold of her hand and called to her, "My child, stand up!" [55]Her spirit came back into her, and she stood up at once. Then Jesus ordered that she be given something to eat. [56]The girl's parents were amazed, but Jesus told them not to tell anyone what had happened.

Jesus Sends Out the Apostles

9 Jesus called the twelve apostles[d] together and gave them power and authority over all demons[d] and the ability to heal sicknesses. [2]He sent the apostles out to tell about God's kingdom and to heal the sick. [3]He said to them, "Take nothing for your trip, neither a walking stick, bag, bread, money, or extra clothes. [4]When you enter a house, stay there until it is time to leave. [5]If people do not welcome you, shake the dust off of your feet[n] as you leave the town, as a warning to them."

[6]So the apostles went out and traveled through all the towns, preaching the Good News[d] and healing people everywhere.

Herod Is Confused About Jesus

[7]Herod, the governor, heard about all the things that were happening and was confused, because some people said, "John the Baptist[d] has risen from the dead." [8]Others said, "Elijah has come to us." And still others said, "One of the prophets[d] who lived long ago has risen from the dead." [9]Herod said, "I cut off John's head, so who is this man I hear such things about?" And Herod kept trying to see Jesus.

More than Five Thousand Fed

[10]When the apostles[d] returned, they told Jesus

"Legion" Means very many. A legion was about five thousand men in the Roman army.
eternal darkness Literally, "the abyss," something like a pit or a hole that has no end.
shake . . . feet A warning. It showed that they had rejected these people.

everything they had done. Then Jesus took them with him to a town called Bethsaida where they could be alone together. [11]But the people learned where Jesus went and followed him. He welcomed them and talked with them about God's kingdom and healed those who needed to be healed.

[12]Late in the afternoon, the twelve apostles came to Jesus and said, "Send the people away. They need to go to the towns and countryside around here and find places to sleep and something to eat, because no one lives in this place."

[13]But Jesus said to them, "You give them something to eat."

They said, "We have only five loaves of bread and two fish, unless we go buy food for all these people." [14](There were about five thousand men there.)

Jesus said to his followers, "Tell the people to sit in groups of about fifty people."

[15]So the followers did this, and all the people sat down. [16]Then Jesus took the five loaves of bread and two fish, and looking up to heaven, he thanked God for the food. Then he divided the food and gave it to the followers to give to the people. [17]They all ate and were satisfied, and what was left over was gathered up, filling twelve baskets.

Jesus Is the Christ

[18]One time when Jesus was praying alone, his followers were with him, and he asked them, "Who do the people say I am?"

[19]They answered, "Some say you are John the Baptist.[d] Others say you are Elijah.[n] And others say you are one of the prophets[d] from long ago who has come back to life."

[20]Then Jesus asked, "But who do you say I am?"

Peter answered, "You are the Christ[d] from God."

[21]Jesus warned them not to tell anyone, saying, [22]"The Son of Man[d] must suffer many things. He will be rejected by the older Jewish leaders, the leading priests, and the teachers of the law. He will be killed and after three days will be raised from the dead."

[23]Jesus said to all of them, "If people want to follow me, they must give up the things they want. They must be willing to give up their lives daily to follow me. [24]Those who want to save their lives will give up true life. But those who give up their lives for me will have true life. [25]It

is worth nothing for them to have the whole world if they themselves are destroyed or lost. [26]If people are ashamed of me and my teaching, then the Son of Man[d] will be ashamed of them when he comes in his glory and with the glory of the Father and the holy angels. [27]I tell you the truth, some people standing here will see the kingdom of God before they die."

Jesus Talks with Moses and Elijah

[28]About eight days after Jesus said these things, he took Peter, John, and James and went up on a mountain to pray. [29]While Jesus was praying, the appearance of his face changed, and his clothes became shining white. [30]Then two men, Moses and Elijah,[n] were talking with Jesus. [31]They appeared in heavenly glory, talking about his departure which he would soon bring about in Jerusalem. [32]Peter and the others were very sleepy, but when they awoke fully, they saw the glory of Jesus and the two men standing with him. [33]When Moses and Elijah were about to leave, Peter said to Jesus, "Master, it is good that we are here. Let us make three tents — one for you, one for Moses, and one for Elijah." (Peter did not know what he was talking about.)

[34]While he was saying these things, a cloud came and covered them, and they became afraid as the cloud covered them. [35]A voice came from the cloud, saying, "This is my Son, whom I have chosen. Listen to him!"

[36]When the voice finished speaking, only Jesus was there. Peter, John, and James said nothing and told no one at that time what they had seen.

Jesus Heals a Sick Boy

[37]The next day, when they came down from the mountain, a large crowd met Jesus. [38]A man in the crowd shouted to him, "Teacher, please come and look at my son, because he is my only child. [39]An evil spirit seizes my son, and suddenly he screams. It causes him to lose control of himself and foam at the mouth. The evil spirit keeps on hurting him and almost never leaves him. [40]I begged your followers to force the evil spirit out, but they could not do it."

[41]Jesus answered, "You people have no faith, and your lives are all wrong. How long must I stay with you and put up with you? Bring your son here."

[42]While the boy was coming, the demon[d] threw him on the ground and made him lose control of himself. But Jesus gave a strong command to the evil spirit and healed the boy and gave him

---

Elijah   A man who spoke for God and who lived hundreds of years before Christ. See 1 Kings 17.
Moses and Elijah   Two of the most important Jewish leaders in the past. Moses had given them the law, and Elijah was an important prophet.

back to his father. [43]All the people were amazed at the great power of God.

Jesus Talks About His Death

While everyone was wondering about all that Jesus did, he said to his followers, [44]"Don't forget what I tell you now: The Son of Man[d] will be handed over to people." [45]But the followers did not understand what this meant; the meaning was hidden from them so they could not understand. But they were afraid to ask Jesus about it.

Who Is the Greatest?

[46]Jesus' followers began to have an argument about which one of them was the greatest. [47]Jesus knew what they were thinking, so he took a little child and stood the child beside him. [48]Then Jesus said, "Whoever accepts this little child in my name accepts me. And whoever accepts me accepts the One who sent me, because whoever is least among you all is really the greatest."

Anyone Not Against Us Is for Us

[49]John answered, "Master, we saw someone using your name to force demons[d] out of people. We told him to stop, because he does not belong to our group."

[50]But Jesus said to him, "Don't stop him, because whoever is not against you is for you."

A Town Rejects Jesus

[51]When the time was coming near for Jesus to depart, he was determined to go to Jerusalem. [52]He sent some men ahead of him, who went into a town in Samaria to make everything ready for him. [53]But the people there would not welcome him, because he was set on going to Jerusalem. [54]When James and John, followers of Jesus, saw this, they said, "Lord, do you want us to call fire down from heaven and destroy those people?" [n]

Verse 54 Here, some Greek copies add: ". . . as Elijah did."

DECISION MAKING

A Soldier Decides

On June 5, 1944, Dwight Eisenhower sat at a table surrounded by all his advisers. The decision, however, was his alone.

It appeared there just might be a brief break in the horrible weather they were having. The question was whether to send the largest amphibious invasion force ever assembled across the stormy English Channel to attack Hitler's "Fortress Europe." Their efforts had been fruitless before, but the success of this mission was essential if the war was to be won.

Conditions of tide and moon wouldn't be right again for weeks, and by then the element of surprise could be lost. On the other hand, the predicted gale force winds in the channel could swamp the landing crafts and drown the entire army before it reached shore. All the eyes looked to General Eisenhower. He knew if he made the wrong choice, the results could be disastrous. After long minutes of silence, he spoke.

"We go!" he said.

The D-Day invasion was on, and the outcome of the war was decided—in favor of Britain and the Allies.

Making big decisions is hard, especially since we usually don't know all the consequences of our choices. In **Luke 9:51–62**, Jesus pointed out that important decisions can involve letting go of the past and taking a stand.

■ How was General Eisenhower unlike the would-be followers in this passage?

■ Are you willing to say to Jesus, "I'll follow you any place you go"? If not, what's holding you back?

CONSIDER . . .

■ writing out all the important decisions you need to make soon and asking advice from several people you trust.

◢ asking your parent or youth leader to give his or her insight on how you can make better decisions.

FOR MORE, SEE . . .

■ Joshua 24:14–15 (p. 214)
■ Proverbs 8 (p. 573)

■ Acts 5:1–11 (p. 1104)

[55]But Jesus turned and scolded them. [56]Then[n] they went to another town.

> **SIDELIGHT:** The disciples' reaction to Jesus' not being welcomed in a Samaritan town (Luke 9:51–56) would have been common in Jesus' day, given the hatred between Jews and Samaritans at that time. A hundred years earlier, Jews had destroyed a Samaritan temple. Then, during the night, Samaritans had strewn human bones on the steps of the Jewish Temple in Jerusalem. To see Jesus' attitude toward the Samaritans, read John 4:5–10 (p. 1063).

Following Jesus

[57]As they were going along the road, someone said to Jesus, "I will follow you any place you go."

[58]Jesus said to them, "The foxes have holes to live in, and the birds have nests, but the Son of Man[d] has no place to rest his head."

[59]Jesus said to another man, "Follow me!"

But he said, "Lord, first let me go and bury my father."

[60]But Jesus said to him, "Let the people who are dead bury their own dead. You must go and tell about the kingdom of God."

[61]Another man said, "I will follow you, Lord, but first let me go and say good-bye to my family."

[62]Jesus said, "Anyone who begins to plow a field but keeps looking back is of no use in the kingdom of God."

Jesus Sends Out the Seventy-Two

10 After this, the Lord chose seventy-two[n] others and sent them out in pairs ahead of him into every town and place where he planned to go. [2]He said to them, "There are a great many people to harvest, but there are only a few workers. So pray to God, who owns the harvest, that he will send more workers to help gather his harvest. [3]Go now, but listen! I am sending you out like sheep among wolves. [4]Don't carry a purse, a bag, or sandals, and don't waste time talking with people on the road. [5]Before you go into a house, say, 'Peace be with this house.' [6]If peaceful people live there, your blessing of peace will stay with them, but if not, then your blessing will come back to you. [7]Stay in the peace-ful house, eating and drinking what the people there give you. A worker should be given his pay. Don't move from house to house. [8]If you go into a town and the people welcome you, eat what they give you. [9]Heal the sick who live there, and tell them, 'The kingdom of God is near you.' [10]But if you go into a town, and the people don't welcome you, then go into the streets and say, [11]'Even the dirt from your town that sticks to our feet we wipe off against you.[n] But remember that the kingdom of God is near.' [12]I tell you, on the Judgment Day it will be better for the people of Sodom[n] than for the people of that town.

Jesus Warns Unbelievers

[13]"How terrible for you, Korazin! How terrible for you, Bethsaida! If the miracles[d] I did in you had happened in Tyre and Sidon,[n] those people would have changed their lives long ago. They would have worn rough cloth and put ashes on themselves to show they had changed. [14]But on the Judgment Day it will be better for Tyre and Sidon than for you. [15]And you, Capernaum,[n] will you be lifted up to heaven? No! You will be thrown down to the depths!

[16]"Whoever listens to you listens to me, and whoever refuses to accept you refuses to accept me. And whoever refuses to accept me refuses to accept the One who sent me."

Satan Falls

[17]When the seventy-two[n] came back, they were very happy and said, "Lord, even the demons[d] obeyed us when we used your name!"

[18]Jesus said, "I saw Satan fall like lightning from heaven. [19]Listen, I have given you power to walk on snakes and scorpions, power that is greater than the enemy has. So nothing will hurt you. [20]But you should not be happy because the spirits obey you but because your names are written in heaven."

Jesus Prays to the Father

[21]Then Jesus rejoiced in the Holy Spirit[d] and said, "I praise you, Father, Lord of heaven and earth, because you have hidden these things from the people who are wise and smart. But you have shown them to those who are like little children. Yes, Father, this is what you really wanted.

[22]"My Father has given me all things. No one knows who the Son is, except the Father. And no

---

Verse 55-56 Some copies read: "But Jesus turned and scolded them. And Jesus said, 'You don't know what kind of spirit you belong to. [56]The Son of Man did not come to destroy the souls of people but to save them.' Then"

seventy-two Many Greek copies read seventy.

dirt . . . you A warning. It showed that they had rejected these people.

Sodom City that God destroyed because the people were so evil.

Tyre and Sidon Towns where wicked people lived.

Korazin, Bethsaida, Capernaum Towns by Lake Galilee where Jesus preached to the people.

one knows who the Father is, except the Son and those whom the Son chooses to tell."

23Then Jesus turned to his followers and said privately, "You are blessed to see what you now see. 24I tell you, many prophets[d] and kings wanted to see what you now see, but they did not, and they wanted to hear what you now hear, but they did not."

The Good Samaritan

25Then an expert on the law stood up to test Jesus, saying, "Teacher, what must I do to get life forever?"

26Jesus said, "What is written in the law? What do you read there?"

27The man answered, "Love the Lord your God with all your heart, all your soul, all your strength, and all your mind."[n] Also, "Love your neighbor as you love yourself."[n]

28Jesus said to him, "Your answer is right. Do this and you will live."

29But the man, wanting to show the importance of his question, said to Jesus, "And who is my neighbor?"

30Jesus answered, "As a man was going down from Jerusalem to Jericho, some robbers attacked him. They tore off his clothes, beat him, and left him lying there, almost dead. 31It happened that a Jewish priest was going down that road. When he saw the man, he walked by on the other side. 32Next, a Levite[n] came there, and after he went over and looked at the man, he walked by on the

"Love . . . mind." Quotation from Deuteronomy 6:5.
"Love . . . yourself." Quotation from Leviticus 19:18.
Levite Levites were members of the tribe of Levi who helped the Jewish priests with their work in the Temple. Read 1 Chronicles 23:24-32.

SHARING FAITH

Unknown Soldiers

Spitballs and paper airplanes were flying everywhere. One student was demonstrating his amazing mastery of crude sounds. Poor Edward Kimball. He was only nineteen, but he was responsible for this Sunday school class of half-crazed junior high boys. He did his best, but they were more concerned about spitballs, practical jokes, and nasty sounds than about God.

Ed was warm, gentle, and shy. But to the boys, he came across as dull. Many adults had serious doubts about Ed's future as a Sunday school teacher.

But Ed was persistent. He really cared about those boys. Realizing his weaknesses as a teacher, he decided he might be more successful meeting the boys one-to-one. One sunny day in April he paced up and down a Boston street, trying to get up nerve to walk into a shoe store where Dwight, one of his students, worked. Finally he did. In frightened, faltering words he told Dwight how God had made a difference in his life. When he looked up the boy was crying.

Not many people today remember what Ed did. Thousands of lives, however, were touched by Dwight L. Moody, the famous evangelist, who on that day in 1855 was led to faith in Christ by Edward Kimball.

It wasn't easy for Ed to share his faith. In **Luke 10:1–12**, Jesus explains that the way won't be easy, but his heart will guide and strengthen us as we obey him.

■ Do you think some of the seventy-two people in this passage felt as "ungifted" as Ed did? Why did Jesus choose them? (See especially verse 2.)

■ According to this passage, which quality was most important to Jesus: talent or obedience? Why is that?

C O N S I D E R . . .

■ asking God to show you how you can be more obedient to him in *sharing your faith.*

■ reading a book about Dwight L. Moody's life and ministry.

F O R   M O R E ,   S E E . . .

■ Isaiah 6:1–8 (p. 622)
■ Matthew 28:16–20 (p. 962)
■ Mark 6:7–13 (p. 973)

other side of the road. ³³Then a Samaritanⁿ traveling down the road came to where the hurt man was. When he saw the man, he felt very sorry for him. ³⁴The Samaritan went to him, poured olive oil and wine^z on his wounds, and bandaged them. Then he put the hurt man on his own donkey and took him to an inn where he cared for him. ³⁵The next day, the Samaritan brought out two coins,ⁿ gave them to the innkeeper, and said, 'Take care of this man. If you spend more money on him, I will pay it back to you when I come again.' "

³⁶Then Jesus said, "Which one of these three men do you think was a neighbor to the man who was attacked by the robbers?"

³⁷The expert on the law answered, "The one who showed him mercy."

> **SIDELIGHT:** The Jerusalem-to-Jericho road where the man was robbed in Jesus' story (Luke 10:30) was notoriously dangerous. With a 3,600 foot drop in only seventeen miles, this narrow, steep, twisting path—nicknamed "The Bloody Way"—was the notorious hangout of robbers.

Samaritan   Samaritans were people from Samaria. These people were part Jewish, but the Jews did not accept them as true Jews. Samaritans and Jews disliked each other.
olive oil and wine   Oil and wine were used like medicine to soften and clean wounds.
coins   Roman denarii. One coin was the average pay for one day's work.

SERVICE

Sweating on a Shingle

Minnie Burgeon wasn't looking forward to the rainy season.

"Oh, it's worse now than it was before they worked on it," says Minnie, who last year paid $2,000 to replace the roof on her home.

The roofing company Minnie used had done several jobs in her area— mostly for the elderly—and then had disappeared.

Minnie had no money to get the roof replaced again, so she contacted the Samaritan Connection, a service organization that matches people in need with volunteer labor.

The timing was bad. It was June, and hot. Everyone wanted to be swimming and boating, not baking on a rooftop. One youth group volunteered its time and energy for Minnie, but once the group members had spent a few hours tearing shingles off the sweltering roof, their resolve to help others waned.

"Hey, I'm sorry, but I don't think I can stay very long. I've got stuff around the house I'm supposed to do."

"Yeah, I've got a date tonight, and I've gotta do my hair."

"I told a friend I'd meet her at the mall in a little while, so I can't stay long."

The leader knew he had to do something or lose the whole work crew. He brought them downstairs to meet Minnie. She pointed to the water stains above her bed and talked about how she would lie in bed and worry as water dripped on her. Then she said, "Jesus has been good to me to send me you Samaritans."

Nobody left. Nobody complained again. They all finished the job and felt great. Minnie was no longer just a "service project." She was a neighbor.

Read **Luke 10:25–37** to find out who God says your neighbor is.

■ How is your youth group like the one in the story? How is it like the men who encountered the hurt man in the passage?

■ What can you do to become more like the Samaritan in the passage?

CONSIDER . . .

■ helping a friend or neighbor with a job around the house.
■ listing four ways you could serve others better and then doing one each week for the next four weeks.

FOR   MORE,   SEE . . .

■ Matthew 22:34–46 (p. 948)   ■ Philippians 2:1–4 (p. 1230)
■ Mark 12:28–34 (p. 983)

Jesus said to him, "Then go and do what he did."

Mary and Martha

38While Jesus and his followers were traveling, Jesus went into a town. A woman named Martha let Jesus stay at her house. 39Martha had a sister named Mary, who was sitting at Jesus' feet and listening to him teach. 40But Martha was busy with all the work to be done. She went in and said, "Lord, don't you care that my sister has left me alone to do all the work? Tell her to help me."

41But the Lord answered her, "Martha, Martha, you are worried and upset about many things. 42Only one thing is important. Mary has chosen the better thing, and it will never be taken away from her."

Jesus Teaches About Prayer

11 One time Jesus was praying in a certain place. When he finished, one of his fol-

lowers said to him, "Lord, teach us to pray as John taught his followers."

2Jesus said to them, "When you pray, say:
'Father, may your name always be kept holy.
 May your kingdom come.
3Give us the food we need for each day.
4Forgive us for our sins,
 because we forgive everyone who has done
 wrong to us.
And do not cause us to be tempted.' "

Continue to Ask

5Then Jesus said to them, "Suppose one of you went to your friend's house at midnight and said to him, 'Friend, loan me three loaves of bread. 6A friend of mine has come into town to visit me, but I have nothing for him to eat.' 7Your friend inside the house answers, 'Don't bother me! The door is already locked, and my children and I are in bed. I cannot get up and give you anything.' 8I tell you, if friendship is not enough to make him get up to give you the bread, your boldness will make

---

WORRYING

First Letter Home

Dear Mom and Dad,
 I hate college! I wish I were back home in Toledo in high school. I worry about tests. I worry about dates. I worry if anyone likes me. My studying never feels like it does me any good. I don't feel comfortable with friends like I did in high school. I even wake up and worry about the weather.
 I never used to worry! What's happening to me?
 Love, Moira

Dear Moira,
 Sorry to hear you're so worried. We could tell you "don't worry," but even we know better.
 One suggestion: Don't rely on others, or your accomplishments, or your busyness for your self-concept. If you do, there'll be lots of worry in your future. Take some time and sit still with God. He has less worrisome ways of helping us know who we are—apart from those other things. Rely on him to show you what he thinks of you.
 Love, Mom & Dad
 P.S. Don't worry!

Moira Jackson needed to see that she was loved and accepted just as she was, without doing anything. Read how Jesus helped another busy, fretful, worrying woman see that truth in **Luke 10:38–42**.
 ■ Can you think of a time you acted like Martha in this passage?
 ■ How would your "worry level" change if you had a better sense of God's love for you?

CONSIDER...
 ◢ *sitting for five minutes in God's presence and just listening.*
 ■ writing out all your concerns and then talking to God about each one.

FOR MORE, SEE...
 ■ Psalm 131 (p. 558)
 ■ Matthew 6:25–34 (p. 918)
 ■ 1 Peter 5:6–7 (p. 1308)

him get up and give you whatever you need. ⁹So I tell you, ask, and God will give to you. Search, and you will find. Knock, and the door will open for you. ¹⁰Yes, everyone who asks will receive. The one who searches will find. And everyone who knocks will have the door opened. ¹¹If your children ask for a fish, which of you would give them a snake instead? ¹²Or, if your children ask for an egg, would you give them a scorpion? ¹³Even though you are bad, you know how to give good things to your children. How much more your heavenly Father will give the Holy Spirit*d* to those who ask him!"

Jesus' Power Is from God

¹⁴One time Jesus was sending out a demon*d* that could not talk. When the demon came out, the man who had been unable to speak, then spoke. The people were amazed. ¹⁵But some of them said, "Jesus uses the power of Beelzebul,*d* the ruler of demons, to force demons out of people."

¹⁶Other people, wanting to test Jesus, asked him to give them a sign from heaven. ¹⁷But knowing their thoughts, he said to them, "Every kingdom that is divided against itself will be destroyed. And a family that is divided against itself will not continue. ¹⁸So if Satan is divided against himself, his kingdom will not continue. You say that I use the power of Beelzebul to force out demons. ¹⁹But if I use the power of Beelzebul to force out demons, what power do your people use to force demons out? So they will be your judges. ²⁰But if I use the power of God to force out demons, then the kingdom of God has come to you.

²¹"When a strong person with many weapons guards his own house, his possessions are safe. ²²But when someone stronger comes and defeats him, the stronger one will take away the weapons the first man trusted and will give away the possessions.

²³"Anyone who is not with me is against me, and anyone who does not work with me is working against me.

The Empty Person

²⁴"When an evil spirit comes out of a person, it travels through dry places, looking for a place to rest. But when it finds no place, it says, 'I will go back to the house I left.' ²⁵And when it comes

back, it finds that house swept clean and made neat. ²⁶Then the evil spirit goes out and brings seven other spirits more evil than it is, and they go in and live there. So the person has even more trouble than before."

People Who Are Truly Happy

²⁷As Jesus was saying these things, a woman in the crowd called out to Jesus, "Happy is the mother who gave birth to you and nursed you."

²⁸But Jesus said, "No, happy are those who hear the teaching of God and obey it."

The People Want a Miracle

²⁹As the crowd grew larger, Jesus said, "The people who live today are evil. They want to see a miracle*d* for a sign, but no sign will be given them, except the sign of Jonah.*n* ³⁰As Jonah was a sign for those people who lived in Nineveh, the Son of Man*d* will be a sign for the people of this time. ³¹On the Judgment Day the Queen of the South*n* will stand up with the people who live now. She will show they are guilty, because she came from far away to listen to Solomon's wise teaching. And I tell you that someone greater than Solomon is here. ³²On the Judgment Day the people of Nineveh will stand up with the people who live now, and they will show that you are guilty. When Jonah preached to them, they were sorry and changed their lives. And I tell you that someone greater than Jonah is here.

Be a Light for the World

³³"No one lights a lamp and puts it in a secret place or under a bowl, but on a lampstand so the people who come in can see. ³⁴Your eye is a light for the body. When your eyes are good, your whole body will be full of light. But when your eyes are evil, your whole body will be full of darkness. ³⁵So be careful not to let the light in you become darkness. ³⁶If your whole body is full of light, and none of it is dark, then you will shine bright, as when a lamp shines on you."

Jesus Accuses the Pharisees

³⁷After Jesus had finished speaking, a Pharisee*d* asked Jesus to eat with him. So Jesus went in and sat at the table. ³⁸But the Pharisee was surprised when he saw that Jesus did not wash his hands*n* before the meal. ³⁹The Lord said to him, "You Pharisees clean the outside of the cup and the dish, but inside you are full of greed and evil. *40You foolish people! The same one who made* what is outside also made what is inside. ⁴¹So give

what is in your dishes to the poor, and then you will be fully clean. ⁴²How terrible for you Pharisees! You give God one-tenth of even your mint, your rue, and every other plant in your garden. But you fail to be fair to others and to love God. These are the things you should do while continuing to do those other things. ⁴³How terrible for you Pharisees, because you love to have the most important seats in the synagogues,*d* and you love to be greeted with respect in the marketplaces. ⁴⁴How terrible for you, because you are like hidden graves, which people walk on without knowing."

Jesus Talks to Experts on the Law

⁴⁵One of the experts on the law said to Jesus, "Teacher, when you say these things, you are insulting us, too."

⁴⁶Jesus answered, "How terrible for you, you experts on the law! You make strict rules that are very hard for people to obey, but you yourselves don't even try to follow those rules. ⁴⁷How terrible for you, because you build tombs for the prophets*d* whom your ancestors killed! ⁴⁸And now you show that you approve of what your ancestors did. They killed the prophets, and you build tombs for them! ⁴⁹This is why in his wisdom God said, 'I will send prophets and apostles*d* to them. They will kill some, and they will treat others cruelly.' ⁵⁰So you who live now will be punished for the deaths of all the prophets who were killed since the beginning of the world — ⁵¹from the killing of Abel to the killing of Zechariah,*n* who died between the altar and the Temple.*d* Yes, I tell you that you who are alive now will be punished for them all.

⁵²"How terrible for you, you experts on the law. You have taken away the key to learning about God. You yourselves would not learn, and you stopped others from learning, too."

⁵³When Jesus left, the teachers of the law and the Pharisees*d* began to give him trouble, asking him questions about many things, ⁵⁴trying to catch him saying something wrong.

Don't Be Like the Pharisees

12 So many thousands of people had gathered that they were stepping on each other. Jesus spoke first to his followers, saying, "Beware of the yeast of the Pharisees,*d* because they are hypocrites.*d* ²Everything that is hidden will be shown, and everything that is secret will *be made known. 3What you have said in the dark* will be heard in the light, and what you have

---

sign of Jonah Jonah's three days in the fish are like Jesus' three days in the tomb. See Matthew 12:40.
Queen of the South The Queen of Sheba. She traveled a thousand miles to learn God's wisdom from Solomon. Read 1 Kings 10:1-3.
wash his hands This was a Jewish religious custom that the Pharisees thought was very important.
Abel . . . Zechariah In the Hebrew Old Testament, the first and last men to be murdered.

whispered in an inner room will be shouted from the housetops.

⁴"I tell you, my friends, don't be afraid of people who can kill the body but after that can do nothing more to hurt you. ⁵I will show you the one to fear. Fear the one who has the power to kill you and also to throw you into hell. Yes, this is the one you should fear.

⁶"Five sparrows are sold for only two pennies, and God does not forget any of them. ⁷But God even knows how many hairs you have on your head. Don't be afraid. You are worth much more than many sparrows.

Don't Be Ashamed of Jesus

⁸"I tell you, all those who stand before others and say they believe in me, I, the Son of Man,*ᵈ* will say before the angels of God that they be-long to me. ⁹But all who stand before others and say they do not believe in me, I will say be-fore the angels of God that they do not belong to me.

¹⁰"Anyone who speaks against the Son of Man*ᵈ* can be forgiven, but anyone who speaks against the Holy Spirit*ᵈ* will not be forgiven.

¹¹"When you are brought into the synagogues*ᵈ* before the leaders and other powerful people, don't worry about how to defend yourself or what to say. ¹²At that time the Holy Spirit will teach you what you must say."

Jesus Warns Against Selfishness

¹³Someone in the crowd said to Jesus, "Teacher, tell my brother to divide with me the property our father left us."

¹⁴But Jesus said to him, "Who said I should

BRAGGING

Cliffhangers

Pugslie Selman was by far the biggest kid around, and he didn't mind letting everyone know it. In a neighborhood full of tough guys, this loner was the undisputed champion. His real name was John, but nobody used it. The few guys he hung around with called him "Pugs," and most everyone else simply tried to stay out of his way.

Today was different, though. Instead of pushing people around, Pugs was on a ledge forty feet high, crying like a baby. He had come rock climbing with his buddies, and now he was stuck. He was afraid to try to go back down the way he had come up, but he couldn't trust the rope around his waist (or the boy who was holding it) enough to lean out and grab the rock above his head. So he clung to the cliff and cried.

Predictably, everyone on the ground laughed at Pugslie. They were yelling and joking about the "giant wimp." But then things changed. Paul Woods, a little guy that Pugslie liked to push around, climbed up the cliff face. "Everything will be all right, Pugs, " said Paul. "You'll be fine. Just follow me."

Then Paul climbed ahead of Pugslie, showing him each place to put his feet and hands. Before long, the guys on the ground were cheering Pugslie as he climbed over the top of the cliff and raised his fist into the air.

Pugslie is still big, and he's still tough. But because of Paul, Pugslie doesn't brag about his size so much. Paul showed Pugs that everyone has special gifts.

Jesus told a story about another man who thought he was big and tough. Like Pugslie, he had an "I'm the best" attitude. Read about his "fall" in **Luke 12:13–21**.

■ What similarities can you see between Pugslie and the rich man in the passage?

■ In what ways do you "store things up" for yourself? What does this passage say to you about that?

C O N S I D E R . . .

■ listing the positive qualities of three of your friends and thanking God for giving them those gifts.

■ looking up the word humility in the dictionary, and asking God to help you be humble.

F O R   M O R E ,   S E E . . .

■ Daniel 4:19–37 (p. 811)   ■ Ephesians 2:8–9 (p. 1219)
■ 1 Corinthians 1:26–31 (p. 1168)

judge or decide between you?" 15Then Jesus said to them, "Be careful and guard against all kinds of greed. Life is not measured by how much one owns."

16Then Jesus told this story: "There was a rich man who had some land, which grew a good crop. 17He thought to himself, 'What will I do? I have no place to keep all my crops.' 18Then he said, 'This is what I will do: I will tear down my barns and build bigger ones, and there I will store all my grain and other goods. 19Then I can say to myself, "I have enough good things stored to last for many years. Rest, eat, drink, and enjoy life!"'

20"But God said to him, 'Foolish man! Tonight your life will be taken from you. So who will get those things you have prepared for yourself?'

21"This is how it will be for those who store up things for themselves and are not rich toward God."

SIDELIGHT: The rich man in Jesus' story (Luke 12:16–21) would probably have been a millionaire today. Most farmers stored their food supply in clay jars of various sizes. To have a barn or grain silo would indicate extreme wealth. Archaeologists have discovered some underground grain silos that are twenty-five feet wide and more than twenty feet deep.

Don't Worry

22Jesus said to his followers, "So I tell you, don't worry about the food you need to live, or about the clothes you need for your body. 23Life is more than food, and the body is more than clothes. 24Look at the birds. They don't plant or harvest, they don't have storerooms or barns, but God feeds them. And you are worth much more than birds. 25You cannot add any time to your life by worrying about it. 26If you cannot do even the little things, then why worry about the big things? 27Consider how the lilies grow; they don't work or make clothes for themselves. But I tell you that even Solomon with his riches was not dressed as beautifully as one of these flowers. 28God clothes the grass in the field, which is alive today but tomorrow is thrown into the fire. So how much more will God clothe you? Don't have so little faith! 29Don't always think about what you will eat or what you will drink, and don't keep worrying. 30All the people in the world are trying to get these things, and your Father knows you need them. 31But seek God's kingdom, and all the other things you need will be given to you.

Don't Trust in Money

32"Don't fear, little flock, because your Father wants to give you the kingdom. 33Sell your possessions and give to the poor. Get for yourselves purses that will not wear out, the treasure in heaven that never runs out, where thieves can't steal and moths can't destroy. 34Your heart will be where your treasure is.

Always Be Ready

35"Be dressed, ready for service, and have your lamps shining. 36Be like servants who are waiting for their master to come home from a wedding party. When he comes and knocks, the servants immediately open the door for him. 37They will be blessed when their master comes home, because he sees that they were watching for him. I tell you the truth, the master will dress himself to serve and tell the servants to sit at the table, and he will serve them. 38Those servants will be happy when he comes in and finds them still waiting, even if it is midnight or later.

39"Remember this: If the owner of the house knew what time a thief was coming, he would not allow the thief to enter his house. 40So you also must be ready, because the Son of Man[d] will come at a time when you don't expect him!"

Who Is the Trusted Servant?

41Peter said, "Lord, did you tell this story to us or to all people?"

42The Lord said, "Who is the wise and trusted servant that the master trusts to give the other servants their food at the right time? 43When the master comes and finds the servant doing his work, the servant will be blessed. 44I tell you the truth, the master will choose that servant to take care of everything he owns. 45But suppose the servant thinks to himself, 'My master will not come back soon,' and he begins to beat the other servants, men and women, and to eat and drink and get drunk. 46The master will come when that servant is not ready and is not expecting him. Then the master will cut him in pieces and send him away to be with the others who don't obey.

47"The servant who knows what his master wants but is not ready, or who does not do what the master wants, will be beaten with many blows! 48But the servant who does not know what his master wants and does things that should be punished will be beaten with few blows. From everyone who has been given much, much will be demanded. And from the one trusted with much, much more will be expected.

Jesus Causes Division

49"I came to set fire to the world, and I wish it were already burning! 50I have a baptism[n] to suffer through, and I feel very troubled until it is over. [51]Do you think I came to give peace to the earth? No, I tell you, I came to divide it. [52]From now on, a family with five people will be divided, three against two, and two against three. [53]They will be divided: father against son and son against father, mother against daughter and daughter against mother, mother-in-law against daughter-in-law and daughter-in-law against mother-in-law."

I . . . baptism   Jesus was talking about the suffering he would soon go through.

Understanding the Times

[54]Then Jesus said to the people, "When you see clouds coming up in the west, you say, 'It's going to rain,' and it happens. [55]When you feel the wind begin to blow from the south, you say, 'It will be a hot day,' and it happens. [56]Hypocrites![d] You know how to understand the appearance of the earth and sky. Why don't you understand what is happening now?

MONEY

It's Only Money!

By the time he was thirty, Millard Fuller had achieved the American Dream. He was worth more than $1 million and lived a lifestyle that showed it. He drove a fancy car, lived in a huge house, owned lots of land, and generally enjoyed the things his money could buy. He and his wife, Linda, had just about anything that a young couple could want, except . . .

Except what? Well, they weren't sure. All Millard and Linda did know was that they weren't happy.

"We just thought there must be something more to life," Millard explains.

On the advice of a friend, Millard and Linda turned to God. They spent time reading the Bible and praying with other Christians at Koinonia Farms. What could they do? What should they do?

"By seeing other Christians' lifestyles," explains Linda, "we quickly saw there was much more to life than the success money can bring. We realized God had a purpose for us. And we were determined to find out what it was."

Finally, they received the answer to their prayers. They believed God wanted them to start something new. Something big. They believed God wanted them to start over.

So they did. They sold off their businesses and their big house, and gave the money away. They sold their land, their boats, their horses, their cattle. In fact, they got rid of just about everything.

After this, they didn't go on tour to brag about how kind they were, or how many points they had earned with God. Instead, they continued to pray about what God was calling them toward. For more than five years, they worked at various mission stations, continuing to pray. Finally, at God's prompting, they formed Habitat for Humanity, a world-wide group that seeks to eliminate all substandard housing. Because the Fullers were able to give everything away and listen to God, thousands of families go to bed each night in safe, secure homes.

One of the passages that helped the Fullers make their decision was **Luke 12:32–40**. Read it and see if you can understand their actions.

■ How did these verses influence the Fullers?

■ What can you do to apply Jesus' words in this passage?

C O N S I D E R . . .

■ deciding to give a specific portion of your money to your church or other charity.

■ keeping a list of all the money you spend in a week. Sit down with your list and see who really determines how you spend it. Then pray for the freedom to give everything to God.

F O R   M O R E ,   S E E . . .

■ Isaiah 58:6–11 (p. 677)   ■ 2 Corinthians 9:6–9 (p. 1201)

■ Matthew 6:19–21 (p. 918)

Settle Your Problems

[57]"Why can't you decide for yourselves what is right? [58]If your enemy is taking you to court, try hard to settle it on the way. If you don't, your enemy might take you to the judge, and the judge might turn you over to the officer, and the officer might throw you into jail. [59]I tell you, you will not get out of there until you have paid everything you owe."

Change Your Hearts

13 At that time some people were there who told Jesus that Pilate[n] had killed some people from Galilee while they were worshiping. He mixed their blood with the blood of the animals they were sacrificing to God. [2]Jesus answered, "Do you think this happened to them because they were more sinful than all others from Galilee? [3]No, I tell you. But unless you change your hearts and lives, you will be destroyed as they were! [4]What about those eighteen people who died when the tower of Siloam fell on them? Do you think they were more sinful than all the others who live in Jerusalem? [5]No, I tell you. But unless you change your hearts and lives, you will all be destroyed too!"

The Useless Tree

[6]Jesus told this story: "A man had a fig tree planted in his vineyard. He came looking for some fruit on the tree, but he found none. [7]So the man said to his gardener, 'I have been looking for fruit on this tree for three years, but I never find any. Cut it down. Why should it waste the ground?' [8]But the servant answered, 'Master, let the tree have one more year to produce fruit. Let me dig

Pilate   Pontius Pilate was the Roman governor of Judea from A.D. 26 to A.D. 36.

SPIRITUAL GROWTH

Every Day Counts

Tim Richard was a friend of mine, in an unusual way. We met by accident and had very little in common. We liked different foods, different sports, different girls, and we each had our own definition of a "good time." We did share two things, though: we had the same birthday and we loved the same God. Sometimes this was all we could agree on, but we usually enjoyed our time together.

When we were eighteen, Tim died suddenly of a heart attack. He said he wasn't feeling well, and he passed out by the time the paramedics got to him. He was dead hours later. Through my tears, I realized that I didn't have anyone to share my birthday with. And I wasn't so sure about the God that I loved. Why did this happen? Everybody knows that teenagers aren't supposed to die, right?

A few days later, Tim's family and friends got together to mourn his death. As we sat around talking, somebody told a story about Tim that brought a smile to our faces. Before long, all of Tim's old jokes were flying, along with stories of how his short life had touched each of us. In that conversation, we saw that Tim had tried to live each day as though it were an important chance to serve God and others.

I think of my friend Tim often, because his life and death challenged me. I realized I don't know what will happen. So I must work to make each day count.

When people asked Jesus about their friends who had died, he gave them a challenge to use their days well. Read about it in **Luke 13:1–9**.

■ How is Tim's story like the stories in the passage?
■ What can you do to prepare yourself to "bear fruit" and so avoid being like the useless tree in the passage?

CONSIDER . . .

■ imagining that you have only two weeks to live. Decide what your priorities would be, then do them.
■ buying two small potted plants and taking one to a person who is sick, elderly or shut-in. Keep the other in your room as a reminder to pray for your special friend—and as a reminder to always try to bear fruit for God's kingdom.

FOR MORE, SEE . . .

■ Psalm 90 (p. 535)
■ Matthew 7:15–23 (p. 920)

■ Galatians 6:7–10 (p. 1214)

up the dirt around it and put on some fertilizer. 9If the tree produces fruit next year, good. But if not, you can cut it down.' "

Jesus Heals on the Sabbath

10Jesus was teaching in one of the synagogues*d* on the Sabbath*d* day. 11A woman was there who, for eighteen years, had an evil spirit in her that made her crippled. Her back was always bent; she could not stand up straight. 12When Jesus saw her, he called her over and said, "Woman, you are free from your sickness." 13Jesus put his hands on her, and immediately she was able to stand up straight and began praising God.

14The synagogue leader was angry because Jesus healed on the Sabbath day. He said to the people, "There are six days when one has to work. So come to be healed on one of those days, and not on the Sabbath day."

15The Lord answered, "You hypocrites!*d* Doesn't each of you untie your work animals and lead them to drink water every day — even on the Sabbath day? 16This woman that I healed, a daughter of Abraham, has been held by Satan for eighteen years. Surely it is not wrong for her to be freed from her sickness on a Sabbath day!" 17When Jesus said this, all of those who were criticizing him were ashamed, but the entire crowd rejoiced at all the wonderful things Jesus was doing.

Stories of Mustard Seed and Yeast

18Then Jesus said, "What is God's kingdom like? What can I compare it with? 19It is like a mustard seed that a man plants in his garden. The seed grows and becomes a tree, and the wild birds build nests in its branches."

20Jesus said again. "What can I compare God's kingdom with? 21It is like yeast that a woman took and hid in a large tub of flour until it made all the dough rise."

The Narrow Door

22Jesus was teaching in every town and village as he traveled toward Jerusalem. 23Someone said to Jesus, "Lord, will only a few people be saved?"

Jesus said, 24"Try hard to enter through the narrow door, because many people will try to enter there, but they will not be able. 25When the owner of the house gets up and closes the door, you can stand outside and knock on the door and say, 'Sir, open the door for us.' But he will answer, 'I don't know you or where you come from.' 26Then you will say, 'We ate and drank with you, and you taught in the streets of our town.' 27But he will say to you, 'I don't know you

or where you come from. Go away from me, all you who do evil!' 28You will cry and grind your teeth with pain when you see Abraham, Isaac, Jacob, and all the prophets*d* in God's kingdom, but you yourselves thrown outside. 29People will come from the east, west, north, and south and will sit down at the table in the kingdom of God. 30There are those who have the lowest place in life now who will have the highest place in the future. And there are those who have the highest place now who will have the lowest place in the future."

Jesus Will Die in Jerusalem

31At that time some Pharisees*d* came to Jesus and said, "Go away from here! Herod wants to kill you!"

32Jesus said to them, "Go tell that fox Herod, 'Today and tomorrow I am forcing demons*d* out and healing people. Then, on the third day, I will reach my goal.' 33Yet I must be on my way today and tomorrow and the next day. Surely it cannot be right for a prophet*d* to be killed anywhere except in Jerusalem.

34"Jerusalem, Jerusalem! You kill the prophets and stone to death those who are sent to you. Many times I wanted to gather your people as a hen gathers her chicks under her wings, but you would not let me. 35Now your house is left completely empty. I tell you, you will not see me until that time when you will say, 'God bless the One who comes in the name of the Lord.' "*n*

Healing on the Sabbath

14 On a Sabbath*d* day, when Jesus went to eat at the home of a leading Pharisee,*d* the people were watching Jesus very closely. 2And in front of him was a man with dropsy.*n* 3Jesus said to the Pharisees and experts on the law, "Is it right or wrong to heal on the Sabbath day?" 4But they would not answer his question. So Jesus took the man, healed him, and sent him away. 5Jesus said to the Pharisees and teachers of the law, "If your child or ox falls into a well on the Sabbath day, will you not pull him out quickly?" 6And they could not answer him.

Don't Make Yourself Important

7When Jesus noticed that some of the guests were choosing the best places to sit, he told this story: 8"When someone invites you to a wedding feast, don't take the most important seat, because someone more important than you may have been invited. 9The host, who invited both of you, will come to you and say, 'Give this person your seat.' Then you will be embarrassed and will have

---

'**God . . . Lord.**' Quotation from Psalm 118:26.
dropsy A sickness that causes the body to swell larger and larger.

to move to the last place. [10]So when you are invited, go sit in a seat that is not important. When the host comes to you, he may say, 'Friend, move up here to a more important place.' Then all the other guests will respect you. [11]All who make themselves great will be made humble, but those who make themselves humble will be made great."

You Will Be Rewarded

[12]Then Jesus said to the man who had invited him, "When you give a lunch or a dinner, don't invite only your friends, your family, your other relatives, and your rich neighbors. At another time they will invite you to eat with them, and you will be repaid. [13]Instead, when you give a feast, invite the poor, the crippled, the lame, and the blind. [14]Then you will be blessed, because they have nothing and cannot pay you back. But you will be repaid when the good people rise from the dead."

A Story About a Big Banquet

[15]One of those at the table with Jesus heard these things and said to him, "Happy are the people who will share in the meal in God's kingdom."

[16]Jesus said to him, "A man gave a big banquet

Good Enough

Terry Wilson's favorite saying seemed to be "good enough."

"Hey, Terry!" his friend, Josh Simms, yelled. "How'd baseball tryouts go?"

"Good enough," he said.

"Did you clean your room?" Terry's mom would ask.

"Good enough," was the inevitable response.

"What about that song you were working on for Sunday, Terry?" his youth minister asked. "Will it be ready for Sunday service?"

The amazing thing about Terry is that whatever he did, it almost always was good enough. He usually did make the team or pass the test or win the award. If he wanted to, Terry could make anything he tried come out "good enough." It was even more surprising that he usually accomplished these feats without trying too hard. If a particular task was too demanding or required too much commitment, Terry simply shifted his energy into something else that promised an easier victory.

One summer Terry asked his friend Josh to be his prayer partner. They arranged to meet each week, and it started out well.

But then Terry started coming late, or not at all. Josh was always there, but Terry eventually quit. The commitment was too much, it seemed. That fall, after leaving home for the first time, Terry called Josh, in tears. He was so lonely and felt so "dead" inside. Josh sympathized with his friend and prayed for him, but there was little else he could do. If Terry's faith wasn't "good enough," it was his own fault.

Terry discovered that living the Christian life wasn't as easy as other things he had tried. And he had trouble paying the price to follow God. When Jesus talked about living with God forever, he said that it starts with giving your all to live for God here on earth. Listen to his words in **Luke 13:22–30**.

- What did Jesus say to the people who, like Terry, thought their lives were "good enough" to be worthy of eternal life?
- What are obstacles that keep you from the "narrow road" that leads to living with God forever?

CONSIDER . . .

- writing a short story or poem that describes what you think life in heaven will be like.
- selecting five goals that will help you walk the "narrow road" of eternal life with God. *Put a copy of them in an envelope and give it to a trusted friend. Ask him or her to* mail it to you in six months. Do your best to achieve the goals!

FOR MORE, SEE . . .

- Hosea 6:1–6 (p. 827)
- Matthew 7:13–23 (p. 919)
- Hebrews 6:7–12 (p. 1281)

and invited many people. [17]When it was time to eat, the man sent his servant to tell the guests, 'Come. Everything is ready.'

[18]"But all the guests made excuses. The first one said, 'I have just bought a field, and I must go look at it. Please excuse me.' [19]Another said, 'I have just bought five pairs of oxen; I must go and try them. Please excuse me.' [20]A third person said, 'I just got married; I can't come.' [21]So the servant returned and told his master what had happened. Then the master became angry and said, 'Go at once into the streets and alleys of the town, and bring in the poor, the crippled, the blind, and the lame.' [22]Later the servant said to him, 'Master, I did what you commanded, but we still have room.' [23]The master said to the servant, 'Go out to the roads and country lanes, and urge the people there to come so my house will be full. [24]I tell you, none of those whom I invited first will eat with me.' "

SIDELIGHT: A party invitation in Jesus' day (Luke 14:15–24) included the day but never the hour. When the party was ready, slaves would go get the guests. To reject an invitation you had earlier accepted was the ultimate insult—as this story illustrates!

FRIENDS

A New Kind of Friend

Seventeen-year-old Amanda Hughes doesn't worry much about friends. Her attractive smile, engaging personality and sincere personal warmth make people simply want to be with her.

When she went on the service project, Amanda wasn't concerned about being in a new group. Questions like "will they like me?" never entered her mind. She was just excited about this new experience.

Amanda was surprised the first day she worked. She had expected to work on new home construction, interacting only with her crew. But her crew was renovating an existing home—a home full of people, one of whom, Charles, was close to her own age. For perhaps the first time in her life, she was nervous about making a friend. Her skin was a different color, and her life experience was vastly different. She and Charles seemed to have little in common.

Amanda cried as she told her prayer group of her desire to befriend Charles and his family. How could she do it? They were just so different.

One day, instead of taking her break with the work crew, she challenged Charles to a game of basketball. It was no contest, but they had a great time. The next day, he offered to help her paint, and again they had a lot of fun.

On their last work day, Amanda asked Charles if she could have his address and write to him.

"That'd be great," he exclaimed.

After exchanging addresses and phone numbers, they exchanged hugs. Amanda laughed inside as she thought about her confusion, and thanked God for helping bring two of his children just a little bit closer.

Sometimes we're friends only with those who are just like us. See how Jesus felt about that subject by reading **Luke 14:7–14**.

■ How did Amanda demonstrate her understanding of Jesus' words in this passage?

■ What do these verses say about you and your circle of friends?

C O N S I D E R . . .

■ sending an anonymous letter to one of your friends. Fill it with encouragement from scripture, as well as other affirmations.

■ arranging for your youth group to visit another church, preferably one of a different tradition and location (for instance, if you're in the suburbs, visit a city church). See what you can learn from each other.

F O R   M O R E ,   S E E . . .

■ Ruth 1 (p. 239)   ■ 1 John 4:13–21 (p. 1319)

■ Philemon 4–7 (p. 1274)

The Cost of Being Jesus' Follower

²⁵Large crowds were traveling with Jesus, and he turned and said to them, ²⁶"If anyone comes to me but loves his father, mother, wife, children, brothers, or sisters — or even life — more than me, he cannot be my follower. ²⁷Whoever is not willing to carry the cross and follow me cannot be my follower. ²⁸If you want to build a tower, you first sit down and decide how much it will cost, to see if you have enough money to finish the job. ²⁹If you don't, you might lay the foundation, but you would not be able to finish. Then all who would see it would make fun of you, ³⁰saying, 'This person began to build but was not able to finish.' ³¹"If a king is going to fight another king, first he will sit down and plan. He will decide if he and his ten thousand soldiers can defeat the other king who has twenty thousand soldiers. ³²If he can't, then while the other king is still far away, he will send some people to speak to him and ask for peace. ³³In the same way, you must give up everything you have to be my follower.

Don't Lose Your Influence

³⁴"Salt is good, but if it loses its salty taste, you cannot make it salty again. ³⁵It is no good for the soil or for manure; it is thrown away.

"You people who can hear me, listen."

A Lost Sheep, a Lost Coin

15 The tax collectors and sinners all came to listen to Jesus. ²But the Pharisees*d* and the teachers of the law began to complain: "Look, this man welcomes sinners and even eats with them."

³Then Jesus told them this story: ⁴"Suppose one of you has a hundred sheep but loses one of them. Then he will leave the other ninety-nine sheep in the open field and go out and look for the

---

The Choice to Follow

André Bolte is a likable guy. He's athletic, funny, good-looking, and charming. In fact, when André joined the youth group at First Church, attendance went up. He was eager to learn more about following God and making friends.

André was also eager to please others. So it wasn't long before he agreed to participate in Bible study, Sunday school and other activities. After a few years, you couldn't go to any youth group event without seeing André or hearing how wonderful he was. And he was a great follower of God.

As time passed, André stayed active in the group. But new things came up, too. He started playing sports at school. He joined a couple of academic clubs. He got a new girlfriend. He got a job and a car.

André didn't want his friends to think he had forgotten them, so he kept volunteering for jobs in the group. He got so busy, though, that he began to do them poorly, or just *forgot* about them.

He still comes around the youth group occasionally. Not long ago, he came to encourage the younger kids to keep active—"Just like I am," he said. They didn't say much, though. Afterward, Michelle Jones commented: "André is a lot of talk and no action. He never does what he says he will. It seems pretty useless to me."

André wanted to follow God, but his overloaded lifestyle got in the way. When people asked Jesus what it takes to truly follow God, he had them make some hard choices. Read Jesus' requirements in **Luke 14:25–33**.

■ How is André's situation like that of the king mentioned in the passage?
■ What does this passage say about your priorities and following God?

CONSIDER . . .

■ listing your top five priorities in life and taping the list to your mirror. Each day, pray for the chance to follow God in those areas of your life.
■ keeping a daily log for the coming week, writing down everything you do and how *long it takes. At the end of the week,* compare your daily log to your priorities. What does it say about your schedule?

FOR MORE, SEE . . .

■ Psalm 119:105–115 (p. 553)
■ Luke 9:23–26 (p. 1019)

■ Philippians 3:8–11 (p. 1232)

lost sheep until he finds it. [5]And when he finds it, he happily puts it on his shoulders [6]and goes home. He calls to his friends and neighbors and says, 'Be happy with me because I found my lost sheep.' [7]In the same way, I tell you there is more joy in heaven over one sinner who changes his heart and life, than over ninety-nine good people who don't need to change.

[8]"Suppose a woman has ten silver coins, [n] but loses one. She will light a lamp, sweep the house, and look carefully for the coin until she finds it. [9]And when she finds it, she will call her friends and neighbors and say, 'Be happy with me because I have found the coin that I lost.' [10]In the same way, there is joy in the presence of the angels of God when one sinner changes his heart and life."

The Son Who Left Home

[11]Then Jesus said, "A man had two sons. [12]The younger son said to his father, 'Give me my share of the property.' So the father divided the property between his two sons. [13]Then the younger son gathered up all that was his and traveled far away to another country. There he wasted his money in foolish living. [14]After he had spent everything, a time came when there was no food anywhere in the country, and the son was poor

---

silver coins Roman denarii. One coin was the average pay for one day's work.

Stubborn Love

Stan Geary sat dumbfounded at the dining room table in Arlo Lane's house. For years Arlo had told stories about how he hated his mom because she didn't really care about him. Arlo had accused her of trying to control him, choose his friends for him, even determine the music he listened to.

He didn't really believe his mother loved him.

Arlo's mom had wanted him to stop smoking marijuana. She told him how hurtful the drug is, how addictive it can be. But Arlo claimed it was all a front—his mom just wanted to control him. She got her pleasure out of ruling his life, he thought.

But now, Stan didn't know what to believe. He knew at least some of Arlo's stories must have been true, but a quick glance around the table told him that they weren't true anymore. As Arlo and his mom laughed and joked, it was obvious that something—no, everything—had changed.

Stan didn't understand it, but he liked it. Later, when the guys were outside working on Arlo's ten-speed bike, Stan asked what had changed.

"It was awesome," Arlo said. "After one of our battles, Mom and I were both really upset. She started crying, you know? I yelled something like, 'What do you have to cry about?' She said she was crying because she loved me, and the drugs were hurting me."

"At that moment I looked at her and realized she was telling the truth. I don't know how—something just clicked inside. I realized she really does love me. So we decided to start all over again. It hasn't been easy, but I've quit smoking marijuana. Things have gotten a lot better!"

Arlo discovered how God's love can change things for the better. Jesus told stories that show how God's love can change people's lives. Check them out in **Luke 15:1–10.**

■ How do you think the love Jesus talked about in this passage helped Arlo's relationship with his mom to change?

■ What can you do to help you feel God's love for you?

C O N S I D E R . . . .

■ writing what you think God's love is like, then comparing your ideas with 1 Corinthians 13:4–7.

■ reading the words to "Amazing Grace" from a hymnal. Rewrite them to fit your own life. Then sing your own song of thanks to God for his love!

F O R   M O R E ,   S E E . . .

■ Zephaniah 3:14–17 (p. 884)   ■ 1 John 3:1–3 (p. 1318)

■ John 3:16 (p. 1062)

and hungry. ¹⁵So he got a job with one of the citizens there who sent the son into the fields to feed pigs. ¹⁶The son was so hungry that he wanted to eat the pods the pigs were eating, but no one gave him anything. ¹⁷When he realized what he was doing, he thought, 'All of my father's servants have plenty of food. But I am here, almost dying with hunger. ¹⁸I will leave and return to my father and say to him, "Father, I have sinned against God and have done wrong to you. ¹⁹I am no longer worthy to be called your son, but let me be like one of your servants." ' ²⁰So the son left and went to his father.

"While the son was still a long way off, his father saw him and felt sorry for his son. So the father ran to him and hugged and kissed him. ²¹The son said, 'Father, I have sinned against God and have done wrong to you. I am no longer worthy to be called your son.' ²²But the father said to his servants, 'Hurry! Bring the best clothes and put them on him. Also, put a ring on his finger

and sandals on his feet. ²³And get our fat calf and kill it so we can have a feast and celebrate. ²⁴My son was dead, but now he is alive again! He was lost, but now he is found!' So they began to celebrate.

²⁵"The older son was in the field, and as he came closer to the house, he heard the sound of music and dancing. ²⁶So he called to one of the servants and asked what all this meant. ²⁷The servant said, 'Your brother has come back, and your father killed the fat calf, because your brother came home safely.' ²⁸The older son was angry and would not go in to the feast. So his father went out and begged him to come in. ²⁹But the older son said to his father, 'I have served you like a slave for many years and have always obeyed your commands. But you never gave me even a young goat to have at a feast with my friends. ³⁰But your other son, who wasted all your money on prostitutes,ᵈ comes home, and you kill the fat calf for him!' ³¹The father said to him, 'Son, you are al-

---

REBELLION

I'm Outta Here

"Have you seen Liz?" the nervous voice asked. "It's past midnight and she's not home yet. We had another argument. . . . Her mother and I are . . . worried."

How could this be happening? Liz Cole was great—very popular and liked by everyone in her group. Her parents were model church members. They seemed like the "perfect" family. But this night revealed that they weren't so "perfect" after all.

Three hours later, Liz came up the front steps. She looked angry. "I'm outta here. I just came home for some clothes."

"Your dad and I were worried, " her mother said.

She sneered. "I've got nothing to say to you."

But then she sat down, crying. She cried for a long time. In fact, all three of them did. And it turned out that they had plenty to say to each other. Before long, they were talking about how this "perfect" family had been spending a lot of energy concentrating on the rules and regulations involved with being so perfect, and not enough time telling how much they loved each other. The word love was used a lot more that night than it had been in a long time.

The Coles now know they don't have the perfect family. But they do love each other and have created a family where rebellion has been replaced by gentleness, respect, and forgiveness.

Liz's family was almost torn apart by rebellion. Jesus told a story about another family that dealt with rebellion. Read about it in **Luke 15:11–32**.
- What similarities and differences do you see between Liz's story and the one Jesus told?
- What things make you feel like rebelling? What might this passage say to you?

CONSIDER . . .
- walking around your block three times. Each time, pray about a different problem in your family life that makes you feel like rebelling.
- rewriting the story in Luke 15:11–32 to fit your family situation.

FOR MORE, SEE . . .
- Daniel 9:3–19 (p. 816)
- John 3:16–21 (p. 1062)
- Hebrews 3:12—4:13 (p. 1279)

ways with me, and all that I have is yours. ³²We had to celebrate and be happy because your brother was dead, but now he is alive. He was lost, but now he is found.' "

True Wealth

16 Jesus also said to his followers, "Once there was a rich man who had a manager to take care of his business. This manager was accused of cheating him. ²So he called the manager in and said to him, 'What is this I hear about you? Give me a report of what you have done with my money, because you can't be my manager any longer.' ³The manager thought to himself, 'What will I do since my master is taking my job away from me? I am not strong enough to dig ditches, and I am ashamed to beg. ⁴I know what I'll do so that when I lose my job people will welcome me into their homes.'

⁵"So the manager called in everyone who owed the master any money. He asked the first one, 'How much do you owe?' ⁶He answered, 'Eight hundred gallons of olive oil.' The manager said to him, 'Take your bill, sit down quickly, and write four hundred gallons.' ⁷Then the manager asked another one, 'How much do you owe?' He answered, 'One thousand bushels of wheat.' Then the manager said to him, 'Take your bill and write eight hundred bushels.' ⁸So, the master praised the dishonest manager for being smart. Yes, worldly people are smarter with their own kind than spiritual people are.

⁹"I tell you, make friends for yourselves using worldly riches so that when those riches are gone, you will be welcomed in those homes that continue forever. ¹⁰Whoever can be trusted with a little can also be trusted with a lot, and whoever is dishonest with a little is dishonest with a lot. ¹¹If you cannot be trusted with worldly riches, then who will trust you with true riches? ¹²And if you cannot be trusted with things that belong to someone else, who will give you things of your own?

¹³"No servant can serve two masters. The servant will hate one master and love the other, or

---

MONEY

Tool or Master?

Money was tight for John Wesley. When he began his ministry in the 1700s, he had to budget to survive. After making careful calculations, he determined that he would need about sixty-five dollars a year to live on. Remember, this was a long time ago! Because there was little inflation during that time, John stayed on that yearly budget for the rest of his life. When he first made that decision, his annual income was about seventy dollars. John was able to give away five dollars that first year.

Later in his life, after he had written several books and become a famous minister, his income often exceeded three thousand dollars per year. But John still held to his budget and lived on sixty-five dollars. He gave the rest of the money to people who needed it or to charities that would help tell others about God's love for them.

How could John do this? Was it hard? We don't know the answers to those questions. All we do know is that at an early age John Wesley decided to make sure that money would be his servant, not his master.

John Wesley, who started the Christian movement we know as Methodism, understood the truth Jesus talks about in **Luke 16:1–13**. Read the passage to learn Jesus' view on money.

■ How did John Wesley apply Jesus' teaching in this passage to his own life?
■ How would heeding these verses change your spending habits?

C O N S I D E R . . .

■ looking through the advertisements of two or three current magazines to see what they reveal about our society's view of money and material goods. How does society's view of money compare with Jesus'?
■ making a commitment to give money to a worthwhile organization, such as your denomination's hunger-relief program, or an interdenominational hunger-relief organization.

F O R   M O R E ,   S E E . . .

■ Proverbs 30:7–9 (p. 594)   ■ James 1:9–11 (p. 1294)
■ Luke 16:19–31 (p. 1038)

will follow one master and refuse to follow the other. You cannot serve both God and worldly riches."

God's Law Cannot Be Changed

14The Pharisees,[d] who loved money, were listening to all these things and made fun of Jesus. 15He said to them, "You make yourselves look good in front of people, but God knows what is really in your hearts. What is important to people is hateful in God's sight.

16"The law of Moses and the writings of the prophets[d] were preached until John[n] came. Since then the Good News[d] about the kingdom of God is being told, and everyone tries to enter it by force. 17It would be easier for heaven and earth to pass away than for the smallest part of a letter in the law to be changed.

Divorce and Remarriage

18"If a man divorces his wife and marries another woman, he is guilty of adultery,[d] and the man who marries a divorced woman is also guilty of adultery."

The Rich Man and Lazarus

19Jesus said, "There was a rich man who always dressed in the finest clothes and lived in luxury every day. 20And a very poor man named Lazarus, whose body was covered with sores, was laid at the rich man's gate. 21He wanted to eat only the small pieces of food that fell from the rich man's table. And the dogs would come and lick his sores. 22Later, Lazarus died, and the angels carried him to the arms of Abraham.[d] The rich man died, too, and was buried. 23In the place of the dead, he was in much pain. The rich man saw

John John the Baptist, who preached to people about Christ's coming (Matthew 3, Luke 3).

DECISION MAKING

But I Didn't Think . . .

Sixteen-year-old Alan McPherson was in a daze as he walked out of Mr. Lloyd's English class. His friends and classmates swirled by him in a rush to get to sixth period for their final exam of the day.

"How was I supposed to know all that stuff?" he asked out loud.

"Oh, come on, Alan," said his friend, Casey Adams. "You've known for weeks that our whole exam would come from Moby Dick. Don't act surprised now."

"Yeah, but it all seemed so complicated. There were so many details!"

"Tell the truth, Alan. Did you even read the book?" he asked.

He moaned. "Of course not! You know I watched the movie. It's a stupid book anyway. What do I care about Ahab and the Pequod or whatever? I didn't have time. I thought all I'd need was the basic plot, not every little detail."

"You know whose fault that is," Casey sighed as he left Alan by the lockers. "See ya later."

Alan did know whose fault it was. If only he could turn back the clock, he thought. If only he had made the right decision. Then he could have passed the test.

Alan made the wrong decision, and suffered for it. Fortunately, Alan's test was not a life-or-death matter. **Luke 16:19–31** records a story about another man's exam. But this man's test had eternal consequences.

■ What similarities do you think exist between Alan and the rich man in the passage?

■ How was the decision the rich man faced like decisions you face in life?

CONSIDER . . .

■ using a concordance to find times Jesus talked about the importance of making wise choices. Look up "wisdom," "choice," "decide," or "decision."

■ listing all the decisions you face right now, and asking your youth leader for advice on what choices would be best.

FOR MORE, SEE . . .

■ Proverbs 8:10–11 (p. 573)
■ Isaiah 58:3–9 (p. 676)

■ Romans 7:15–25 (p. 1148)

Abraham far away with Lazarus at his side. ²⁴He called, 'Father Abraham, have mercy on me! Send Lazarus to dip his finger in water and cool my tongue, because I am suffering in this fire!' ²⁵But Abraham said, 'Child, remember when you were alive you had the good things in life, but bad things happened to Lazarus. Now he is comforted here, and you are suffering. ²⁶Besides, there is a big pit between you and us, so no one can cross over to you, and no one can leave there and come here.' ²⁷The rich man said, 'Father, then please send Lazarus to my father's house. ²⁸I have five brothers, and Lazarus could warn them so that they will not come to this place of pain.' ²⁹But Abraham said, 'They have the law of Moses and the writings of the prophets;^d let them learn from them.' ³⁰The rich man said, 'No, father Abraham! If someone goes to them from the dead, they would believe and change their hearts and lives.' ³¹But Abraham said to him, 'If they will not listen to Moses and the prophets, they will not listen to someone who comes back from the dead.' "

SIDELIGHT: To say that the rich man in Luke 16:19–31 wore "the finest clothes" would indicate the man spent a lot of money on his wardrobe. The outer clothes were purple, a sign of true wealth and royalty. Some of his clothes might have been made out of an Egyptian yellowed flax that was so luxurious it was called "woven air."

Sin and Forgiveness

17 Jesus said to his followers, "Things that cause people to sin will happen, but how terrible for the person who causes them to happen! ²It would be better for you to be thrown into the sea with a large stone around your neck than to cause one of these little ones to sin. ³So be careful!

"If another follower sins, warn him, and if he is sorry and stops sinning, forgive him. ⁴If he sins against you seven times in one day and says that he is sorry each time, forgive him."

FRIENDS

Helping Each Other

Everyone wants friends, and those friends have a great influence on our lives. That influence can be harmful, as it is when people push us to vandalize property, get sexually involved, or use drugs. But—as students in an Atlanta, Georgia, high school discovered—friends can also be positive influences.

Older teenagers decided they could use their influence on younger teenagers to make a positive difference. So they started a program to convince junior high kids that they could avoid sex before marriage and still be popular.

Did it make a difference?

■ By the end of the eighth grade, students who didn't participate in the program were five times more likely to be sexually active than those who participated.

■ A year later, the rate of sexual activity among those who had gone through this "peer-to-peer" program was 33 percent less than the rate of those not in the program.

Jesus talked about how friends can affect each other's behavior. He told people to use "positive peer pressure," rather than give in to others' sin. Read all about it in **Luke 17:1–10**.

■ How does the Atlanta high school story relate to this passage?

■ How does this passage help you evaluate your friendships? How does it challenge you to help your friends?

C O N S I D E R . . .

■ listing activities you could do with your friends that would be both fun and positive.

■ spending more time with the strong Christians in your youth group.

F O R   M O R E ,   S E E . . .

■ Exodus 32:1–29 (p. 89)   ■ James 5:19–20 (p. 1300)
■ Romans 1:11–12 (p. 1141)

How Big Is Your Faith?

⁵The apostles*d* said to the Lord, "Give us more faith!"

⁶The Lord said, "If your faith were the size of a mustard seed, you could say to this mulberry tree, 'Dig yourself up and plant yourself in the sea,' and it would obey you.

Be Good Servants

⁷"Suppose one of you has a servant who has been plowing the ground or caring for the sheep. When the servant comes in from working in the field, would you say, 'Come in and sit down to eat'? ⁸No, you would say to him, 'Prepare something for me to eat. Then get yourself ready and serve me. After I finish eating and drinking, you can eat.' ⁹The servant does not get any special thanks for doing what his master commanded.

¹⁰It is the same with you. When you have done everything you are told to do, you should say, 'We are unworthy servants; we have only done the work we should do.' "

Be Thankful

¹¹While Jesus was on his way to Jerusalem, he was going through the area between Samaria and Galilee. ¹²As he came into a small town, ten men who had a skin disease met him there. They did not come close to Jesus ¹³but called to him, "Jesus! Master! Have mercy on us!"

¹⁴When Jesus saw the men, he said, "Go and show yourselves to the priests." *n*

As the ten men were going, they were healed. ¹⁵When one of them saw that he was healed, he went back to Jesus, praising God in a loud voice. ¹⁶Then he bowed down at Jesus' feet and thanked

show ... priests   The law of Moses said a priest must say when a Jewish person with a skin disease became well.

THANKFULNESS

Attitude of Gratitude

Bruce Hallman's father shook his head doubtfully. "I don't see how we can do it, son," he said.

Bruce knew his father was right, but it still hurt to think about missing the big trip. All of the guys in the jazz band were looking forward to that summer trip, but Bruce's dad had been unemployed for a while. So money was tight—too tight to allow an eleventh grader to go to Europe for a month.

As Bruce left the room, he asked God to somehow show him a way. He continued to pray about it, and not long afterward a family in his church asked him to do some yardwork. Not much, but it was something. Soon more jobs came in, mostly from families who knew that Bruce was saving his money for the trip.

All spring, Bruce was busier than he had ever been. And that summer, he went to Europe with the band. The families he had worked for had provided the means to get there.

That was a long time ago, but Bruce hasn't forgotten those families. He's a youth minister now, committed to helping kids find their way out of rough spots. "I know I can't go back and thank all those families who helped me," Bruce says. "I don't even remember some of their names. But I figure I can express my thanks to God for all the good things in my life by helping others."

Sometimes we only think of thankfulness when something really special happens to us. People like Bruce, though, understand what Jesus said about always being thankful. Read Jesus' words in **Luke 17:11–19**.

■ How is Bruce like the leper who returned to Jesus?

■ What things in your life make you feel like running after Jesus just to say "thanks!"?

CONSIDER...

■ writing a letter to God, thanking him for all the good things in your life.

■ *keeping stamps and blank postcards handy all the time. When people do something nice for you, send them a note of thanks.*

FOR MORE, SEE...

■ Psalm 100 (p. 539)
■ Acts 3:1–10 (p. 1100)

■ 1 Thessalonians 5:15–18 (p. 1249)

him. (And this man was a Samaritan.*d*) [17]Jesus said, "Weren't ten men healed? Where are the other nine? [18]Is this Samaritan the only one who came back to thank God?" [19]Then Jesus said to him, "Stand up and go on your way. You were healed because you believed."

SIDELIGHT: The "skin disease" described in Luke 17:11–19 is often called leprosy. It was a dreaded disease, and people who had it were isolated from other people because they were unclean (see Leviticus 13:42–46, p. 109). Most scholars agree leprosy in the Bible isn't the same disease we call leprosy today, but it's not clear exactly what the disease was.

God's Kingdom Is Within You

[20]Some of the Pharisees*d* asked Jesus, "When will the kingdom of God come?"

Jesus answered, "God's kingdom is coming, but not in a way that you will be able to see with your eyes. [21]People will not say, 'Look, here it is!' or, 'There it is!' because God's kingdom is within*n* you."

[22]Then Jesus said to his followers, "The time will come when you will want very much to see one of the days of the Son of Man.*d* But you will not see it. [23]People will say to you, 'Look, there he is!' or, 'Look, here he is!' Stay where you are; don't go away and search.

When Jesus Comes Again

[24]"When the Son of Man*d* comes again, he will shine like lightning, which flashes across the sky and lights it up from one side to the other. [25]But first he must suffer many things and be rejected by the people of this time. [26]When the Son of Man comes again, it will be as it was when Noah lived. [27]People were eating, drinking, marrying, and giving their children to be married until the day Noah entered the boat. Then the flood came and killed them all. [28]It will be the same as during the time of Lot. People were eating, drinking, buying, selling, planting, and building. [29]But the day Lot left Sodom,*n* fire and sulfur rained down from the sky and killed them all. [30]This is how it will be when the Son of Man comes again.

[31]"On that day, a person who is on the roof and whose belongings are in the house should not go inside to get them. A person who is in the field should not go back home. [32]Remember Lot's wife.*n* [33]Those who try to keep their lives will lose them. But those who give up their lives will save them. [34]I tell you, on that night two people will be sleeping in one bed; one will be taken and the other will be left. [35]There will be two women grinding grain together; one will be taken, and the other will be left." [36] *n*

[37]The followers asked Jesus, "Where will this be, Lord?"

Jesus answered, "Where there is a dead body, there the vultures will gather."

God Will Answer His People

18 Then Jesus used this story to teach his followers that they should always pray and never lose hope. [2]"In a certain town there was a judge who did not respect God or care about people. [3]In that same town there was a widow who kept coming to this judge, saying, 'Give me my rights against my enemy.' [4]For a while the judge refused to help her. But afterwards, he thought to himself, 'Even though I don't respect God or care about people, [5]I will see that she gets her rights. Otherwise she will continue to bother me until I am worn out.'"

[6]The Lord said, "Listen to what the unfair judge said. [7]God will always give what is right to his people who cry to him night and day, and he will not be slow to answer them. [8]I tell you, God will help his people quickly. But when the Son of Man*d* comes again, will he find those on earth who believe in him?"

Being Right with God

[9]Jesus told this story to some people who thought they were very good and looked down on everyone else: [10]"A Pharisee*d* and a tax collector both went to the Temple*d* to pray. [11]The Pharisee stood alone and prayed, 'God, I thank you that I am not like other people who steal, cheat, or take part in adultery,*d* or even like this tax collector. [12]I give up eating*n* twice a week, and I give one-tenth of everything I get!'

[13]"The tax collector, standing at a distance, would not even look up to heaven. But he beat on his chest because he was so sad. He said, 'God, have mercy on me, a sinner.' [14]I tell you, when this man went home, he was right with God, but the Pharisee was not. All who make themselves great will be made humble, but all who make themselves humble will be made great."

---

within Or "among."
Sodom City that God destroyed because the people were so evil.
Lot's wife A story about what happened to Lot's wife is found in Genesis 19:15-17, 26.
Verse 36 A few Greek copies add verse 36: "Two people will be in the field. One will be taken, and the other will be left."
give up eating This is called "fasting." The people would give up eating for a special time of prayer and worship to God. It was also done to show sadness and disappointment.

Who Will Enter God's Kingdom?

[15]Some people brought even their babies to Jesus so he could touch them. When the followers saw this, they told them to stop. [16]But Jesus called for the children, saying, "Let the little children come to me. Don't stop them, because the kingdom of God belongs to people who are like these children. [17]I tell you the truth, you must accept the kingdom of God as if you were a child, or you will never enter it."

A Rich Man's Question

[18]A certain leader asked Jesus, "Good Teacher, what must I do to have life forever?"

[19]Jesus said to him, "Why do you call me good? Only God is good. [20]You know the commands: 'You must not be guilty of adultery.[d] You must not murder anyone. You must not steal. You must not tell lies about your neighbor. Honor your father and mother.' "[n]

[21]But the leader said, "I have obeyed all these commands since I was a boy."

[22]When Jesus heard this, he said to him, "There is still one more thing you need to do. Sell everything you have and give it to the poor, and you will have treasure in heaven. Then come and follow me." [23]But when the man heard this, he became very sad, because he was very rich.

[24]Jesus looked at him and said, "It is very hard for rich people to enter the kingdom of God. [25]It is easier for a camel to go through the eye of a needle than for a rich person to enter the kingdom of God."

Who Can Be Saved?

[26]When the people heard this, they asked, "Then who can be saved?"

[27]Jesus answered, "God can do things that are not possible for people to do."

'You ... mother.'   Quotation from Exodus 20:12-16; Deuteronomy 5:16-20.

BRAGGING

Maximum Ruler

In October 1989, pictures of General Manuel Noriega shaking his fist at the world made headlines everywhere. As dictator of the country of Panama, he'd just thwarted an attempt to remove him from power. Some reports indicated he tortured and murdered as many as seventy-five rebel soldiers after the attempted coup.

Noriega controlled the Panamanian government pridefully, as if he owned it. He held mock elections where his people frightened away voters. He reportedly financed his lifestyle through illegal drug trade and commonly mocked and belittled his enemies, including the United States.

In December, his arrogance reached its peak. He boasted that he was Panama's "maximum leader," daring anyone to disagree.

Someone did.

That month the United States invaded Panama and removed Noriega from power. Within days, he was on his way to face drug charges in a Florida courtroom.

On New Year's Day, the world again saw Manuel Noriega's picture in the headlines. This time, though, the pictures showed a handcuffed man dressed in prison clothes being taken away to jail.

Jesus talked about how God views bragging and prideful people. Read what he said in **Luke 18:9–14**.

■ What attitude did both General Noriega and the Pharisee in this passage display?

■ How can pride interfere in your relationship with Christ?

C O N S I D E R . . .

■ looking up the word pride in a dictionary and thinking about what part pride plays in bragging.

■ writing the second half of Luke 18:14 on a 4" X 6" card and placing it on your mirror as an encouragement to avoid arrogance.

F O R   M O R E ,   S E E . . .

■ Jeremiah 9:23–24 (p. 703)
■ 1 Corinthians 4:6–7 (p. 1172)

■ James 4:13–17 (p. 1298)

²⁸Peter said, "Look, we have left everything and followed you."

²⁹Jesus said, "I tell you the truth, all those who have left houses, wives, brothers, parents, or children for the kingdom of God ³⁰will get much more in this life. And in the age that is coming, they will have life forever."

Jesus Will Rise from the Dead

³¹Then Jesus took the twelve apostles* aside and said to them, "We are going to Jerusalem. Everything the prophets* wrote about the Son of Man* will happen. ³²He will be turned over to those who are not Jews. They will laugh at him, insult him, spit on him, ³³beat him with whips, and kill him. But on the third day, he will rise to life again." ³⁴The apostles did not understand this; the meaning was hidden from them, and they did not realize what was said.

Jesus Heals a Blind Man

³⁵As Jesus came near the city of Jericho, a blind man was sitting beside the road, begging. ³⁶When he heard the people coming down the road, he asked, "What is happening?"

³⁷They told him, "Jesus, from Nazareth, is going by."

³⁸The blind man cried out, "Jesus, Son of David,* have mercy on me!"

³⁹The people leading the group warned the blind man to be quiet. But the blind man shouted even more, "Son of David, have mercy on me!"

⁴⁰Jesus stopped and ordered the blind man to be brought to him. When he came near, Jesus asked him, ⁴¹"What do you want me to do for you?"

He said, "Lord, I want to see."

⁴²Jesus said to him, "Then see. You are healed because you believed."

⁴³At once the man was able to see, and he followed Jesus, thanking God. All the people who saw this praised God.

Zacchaeus Meets Jesus

19 Jesus was going through the city of Jericho. ²A man was there named

---

Zacchaeus, who was a very important tax collector, and he was wealthy. [3]He wanted to see who Jesus was, but he was not able because he was too short to see above the crowd. [4]He ran ahead to a place where Jesus would come, and he climbed a sycamore tree so he could see him. [5]When Jesus came to that place, he looked up and said to him, "Zacchaeus, hurry and come down! I must stay at your house today."

[6]Zacchaeus came down quickly and welcomed him gladly. [7]All the people saw this and began to complain, "Jesus is staying with a sinner!"

[8]But Zacchaeus stood and said to the Lord, "I will give half of my possessions to the poor. And if I have cheated anyone, I will pay back four times more."

[9]Jesus said to him, "Salvation has come to this house today, because this man also belongs to the family of Abraham. [10]The Son of Man[d] came to find lost people and save them."

SIDELIGHT: Asking to stay at Zacchaeus's house, as Jesus did in Luke 19:1–10, would have been seen as scandalous. As a tax collector, Zacchaeus was thought of as a thief or a swindler. Many tax collectors would charge more than the fair amount and keep the "profits" for themselves—a practice approved by the Roman government.

A Story About Three Servants

[11]As the people were listening to this, Jesus told them a story because he was near Jerusalem and they thought God's kingdom would appear immediately. [12]He said: "A very important man went to a country far away to be made a king and then to return home. [13]So he called ten of his servants and gave a coin[n] to each servant. He said, 'Do business with this money until I get back.' [14]But the people in the kingdom hated the man. So they

---

coin   A Greek "mina." One mina was enough money to pay a person for working three months.

MONEY

Earning Potential

Norm Wakefield has a lot to be proud of.

His son Joel earns a good salary during the school year as a physical education teacher. During summers Joel works as a trainer for baseball's Oakland Athletics. Through his work in Oakland, he has earned a World Series championship ring, valued at seven thousand dollars.

Norm's daughter Annette may never make as much money as Joel. Hampered by a learning disability, she'll take a little longer than usual to finish high school. During the summer she earns the minimum wage working with kids at the community center. She also gets income from babysitting. When she took part in the Special Olympics, she did well enough to win a second-place ribbon.

When Norm was asked to speak at a junior high graduation, he took with him to show both Joel's championship ring and Annette's track ribbon. Their abilities brought them different rewards monetarily. But in their father's eyes, they are both champions.

Annette and Joel both did their best. Jesus talks about God's view of making the most of what you have. Read his words in **Luke 19:11–27**.

■ Which character in the passage is most like Joel? like Annette? like you?
■ According to this passage, what does God expect you to do with the gifts he has given you?

CONSIDER . . .

■ evaluating how thoughtfully you spend your money.
■ looking for ways you can invest what God has given you—whether it's money or talents—to make the most of what God has given to you.

FOR MORE, SEE . . .

■ Ecclesiastes 5:10–17 (p. 603)
■ Matthew 6:31–33 (p. 918)
■ Matthew 25:14–30 (p. 954)

sent a group to follow him and say, 'We don't want this man to be our king.'

[15]"But the man became king. When he returned home, he said, 'Call those servants who have my money so I can know how much they earned with it.'

[16]"The first servant came and said, 'Sir, I earned ten coins with the one you gave me.' [17]The king said to the servant, 'Excellent! You are a good servant. Since I can trust you with small things, I will let you rule over ten of my cities.'

[18]"The second servant said, 'Sir, I earned five coins with your one.' [19]The king said to this servant, 'You can rule over five cities.'

[20]"Then another servant came in and said to the king, 'Sir, here is your coin which I wrapped in a piece of cloth and hid. [21]I was afraid of you, because you are a hard man. You even take money that you didn't earn and gather food that you didn't plant.' [22]Then the king said to the servant, 'I will condemn you by your own words, you evil servant. You knew that I am a hard man, taking money that I didn't earn and gathering food that I didn't plant. [23]Why then didn't you put my money in the bank? Then when I came back, my money would have earned some interest.'

[24]"The king said to the men who were standing by, 'Take the coin away from this servant and give it to the servant who earned ten coins.' [25]They said, 'But sir, that servant already has ten coins.' [26]The king said, 'Those who have will be given more, but those who do not have anything will have everything taken away from them. [27]Now where are my enemies who didn't want me to be king? Bring them here and kill them before me.' "

Jesus Enters Jerusalem as a King

[28]After Jesus said this, he went on toward Jerusalem. [29]As Jesus came near Bethphage and Bethany, towns near the hill called the Mount of Olives,[d] he sent out two of his followers. [30]He said, "Go to the town you can see there. When you enter it, you will find a colt tied there, which no one has ever ridden. Untie it and bring it here to me. [31]If anyone asks you why you are untying it, say that the Master needs it."

[32]The two followers went into town and found the colt just as Jesus had told them. [33]As they were untying it, its owners came out and asked the followers, "Why are you untying our colt?"

[34]The followers answered, "The Master needs it." [35]So they brought it to Jesus, threw their coats on the colt's back, and put Jesus on it. [36]As Jesus rode toward Jerusalem, others spread their coats on the road before him.

[37]As he was coming close to Jerusalem, on the way down the Mount of Olives, the whole crowd of followers began joyfully shouting praise to God for all the miracles[d] they had seen. [38]They said,

"God bless the king who comes in the name of the Lord!   *Psalm 118:26*
There is peace in heaven and glory to God!"

[39]Some of the Pharisees[d] in the crowd said to Jesus, "Teacher, tell your followers not to say these things."

[40]But Jesus answered, "I tell you, if my followers didn't say these things, then the stones would cry out."

Jesus Cries for Jerusalem

[41]As Jesus came near Jerusalem, he saw the city and cried for it, [42]saying, "I wish you knew today what would bring you peace. But now it is hidden from you. [43]The time is coming when your enemies will build a wall around you and will hold you in on all sides. [44]They will destroy you and all your people, and not one stone will be left on another. All this will happen because you did not recognize the time when God came to save you."

Jesus Goes to the Temple

[45]Jesus went into the Temple[d] and began to throw out the people who were selling things there. [46]He said, "It is written in the Scriptures,[d] 'My Temple will be a house for prayer.'[n] But you have changed it into a 'hideout for robbers'!"[n]

[47]Jesus taught in the Temple every day. The leading priests, the experts on the law, and some of the leaders of the people wanted to kill Jesus. [48]But they did not know how they could do it, because all the people were listening closely to him.

Jewish Leaders Question Jesus

20 One day Jesus was in the Temple,[d] teaching the people and telling them the Good News.[d] The leading priests, teachers of the law, and older Jewish leaders came up to talk with him, [2]saying, "Tell us what authority you have to do these things? Who gave you this authority?"

[3]Jesus answered, "I will also ask you a question. Tell me: [4]When John baptized people, was that authority from God or just from other people?"

[5]They argued about this, saying, "If we answer, 'John's baptism was from God,' Jesus will say, 'Then why did you not believe him?' [6]But if we say, 'It was from other people,' all the people will stone us to death, because they believe John was a prophet."[d] [7]So they answered that they didn't know where it came from.

'**My Temple . . . prayer.**' Quotation from Isaiah 56:7.
'**hideout for robbers**' Quotation from Jeremiah 7:11.

8Jesus said to them, "Then I won't tell you what authority I have to do these things."

A Story About God's Son

9Then Jesus told the people this story: "A man planted a vineyard and leased it to some farmers. Then he went away for a long time. 10When it was time for the grapes to be picked, he sent a servant to the farmers to get some of the grapes. But they beat the servant and sent him away empty-handed. 11Then he sent another servant. They beat this servant also, and showed no respect for him, and sent him away empty-handed. 12So the man sent a third servant. The farmers wounded him and threw him out. 13The owner of the vineyard said, 'What will I do now? I will send my son whom I love. Maybe they will respect him.' 14But when the farmers saw the son, they said to each other, 'This son will inherit the vineyard. If we kill him, it will be ours.' 15So the farmers threw the son out of the vineyard and killed him.

"What will the owner of this vineyard do to them? 16He will come and kill those farmers and will give the vineyard to other farmers."

When the people heard this story, they said, "Let this never happen!"

17But Jesus looked at them and said, "Then what does this verse mean:

'The stone that the builders rejected
became the cornerstone'?d   Psalm 118:22

18Everyone who falls on that stone will be broken, and the person on whom it falls, that person will be crushed!"

19The teachers of the law and the leading priests wanted to arrest Jesus at once, because they knew the story was about them. But they were afraid of what the people would do.

Is It Right to Pay Taxes or Not?

20So they watched Jesus and sent some spies who acted as if they were sincere. They wanted to trap Jesus in saying something wrong so they could hand him over to the authority and power of the governor. 21So the spies asked Jesus, "Teacher, we know that what you say and teach

---

is true. You pay no attention to who people are, and you always teach the truth about God's way. 22Tell us, is it right for us to pay taxes to Caesar*d* or not?"

23But Jesus, knowing they were trying to trick him, said, 24"Show me a coin. Whose image and name are on it?"

They said, "Caesar's."

25Jesus said to them, "Then give to Caesar the things that are Caesar's, and give to God the things that are God's."

26So they were not able to trap Jesus in anything he said in the presence of the people. And being amazed at his answer, they became silent.

Some Sadducees Try to Trick Jesus

27Some Sadducees,*d* who believed people would not rise from the dead, came to Jesus. 28They asked, "Teacher, Moses wrote that if a man's brother dies and leaves a wife but no children, then that man must marry the widow and have children for his brother. 29Once there were seven brothers. The first brother married and died, but had no children. 30Then the second brother married the widow, and he died. 31And the third brother married the widow, and he died. The same thing happened with all seven brothers; they died and had no children. 32Finally, the woman died also. 33Since all seven brothers had married her, whose wife will she be when people rise from the dead?"

34Jesus said to them, "On earth, people marry and are given to someone to marry. 35But those who will be worthy to be raised from the dead and live again will not marry, nor will they be given to someone to marry. 36In that life they are like angels and cannot die. They are children of God, because they have been raised from the dead. 37Even Moses clearly showed that the dead are raised to life. When he wrote about the burning bush,*n* he said that the Lord is 'the God of Abraham, the God of Isaac, and the God of Jacob.'*n* 38God is the God of the living, not the dead, because all people are alive to him."

39Some of the teachers of the law said,

"Teacher, your answer was good." 40No one was brave enough to ask him another question.

Is the Christ the Son of David?

41Then Jesus said, "Why do people say that the Christ*d* is the Son of David?*d* 42In the book of Psalms, David himself says:

'The Lord said to my Lord:
  Sit by me at my right side,
43 until I put your enemies under your
    control.'*n*   *Psalm 110:1*

44David calls the Christ 'Lord,' so how can the Christ be his son?"

Jesus Accuses Some Leaders

45While all the people were listening, Jesus said to his followers, 46"Beware of the teachers of the law. They like to walk around wearing fancy clothes, and they love for people to greet them with respect in the marketplaces. They love to have the most important seats in the synagogues*d* and at feasts. 47But they cheat widows and steal their houses and then try to make themselves look good by saying long prayers. They will receive a greater punishment."

True Giving

21 As Jesus looked up, he saw some rich people putting their gifts into the Temple*d* money box.*n* 2Then he saw a poor widow putting two small copper coins into the box. 3He said, "I tell you the truth, this poor widow gave more than all those rich people. 4They gave only what they did not need. This woman is very poor, but she gave all she had to live on."

The Temple Will Be Destroyed

5Some people were talking about the Temple*d* and how it was decorated with beautiful stones and gifts offered to God.

But Jesus said, 6"As for these things you are looking at, the time will come when not one stone will be left on another. Every stone will be thrown down."

7They asked Jesus, "Teacher, when will these things happen? What will be the sign that they are about to take place?"

8Jesus said, "Be careful so you are not fooled. Many people will come in my name, saying, 'I am the One' and, 'The time has come!' But don't follow them. 9When you hear about wars and riots, don't be afraid, because these things must happen first, but the end will come later."

10Then he said to them, "Nations will fight

---

burning bush   Read Exodus 3:1-12 in the Old Testament.
'the God of . . . Jacob'   These words are taken from Exodus 3:6.
until . . . control   Literally, "until I make your enemies a footstool for your feet."
money box   A special box in the Jewish place of worship where people put their gifts to God.

against other nations, and kingdoms against other kingdoms. ¹¹In various places there will be great earthquakes, sicknesses, and a lack of food. Fearful events and great signs will come from heaven.

¹²"But before all these things happen, people will arrest you and treat you cruelly. They will judge you in their synagogues*d* and put you in jail and force you to stand before kings and governors, because you follow me. ¹³But this will give you an opportunity to tell about me. ¹⁴Make up your minds not to worry ahead of time about what you will say. ¹⁵I will give you the wisdom to say things that none of your enemies will be able to stand against or prove wrong. ¹⁶Even your parents, brothers, relatives, and friends will turn against you, and they will kill some of you. ¹⁷All people will hate you because you follow me. ¹⁸But none of these things can really harm you. ¹⁹By continuing to have faith you will save your lives.

Jerusalem Will Be Destroyed

²⁰"When you see armies all around Jerusalem, you will know it will soon be destroyed. ²¹At that time, the people in Judea should run away to the mountains. The people in Jerusalem must get out, and those who are near the city should not go in. ²²These are the days of punishment to bring about all that is written in the Scriptures.*d* ²³How terrible it will be for women who are pregnant or have nursing babies! Great trouble will come upon this land, and God will be angry with these people. ²⁴They will be killed by the sword and taken as prisoners to all nations. Jerusalem will be crushed by non-Jewish people until their time is over.

Don't Fear

²⁵"There will be signs in the sun, moon, and stars. On earth, nations will be afraid and confused because of the roar and fury of the sea. ²⁶People will be so afraid they will faint, wondering what is happening to the world, because the powers of the heavens will be shaken. ²⁷Then people will see the Son of Man*d* coming in a cloud with power and great glory. ²⁸When these things begin to happen, look up and hold your heads

---

PEER PRESSURE

Friends in Deed

Lance O'Pry was a student at Lamar High School in Rosenberg, Texas, when he learned he had cancer. He was told he would have to undergo painful chemotherapy if he hoped to live.

For Lance the pain was even harder to take knowing the treatment would make his hair fall out. Would he fit in at school? What would his friends say? Would they avoid him because they were embarrassed by his baldness? Would he be laughed at and mocked? He knew his classmates' reactions could make having the awful disease even more unbearable.

What he didn't know—but soon discovered—was that his friends really cared. To make sure Lance would fit in, Jason, Korl, Mac, Tim, Johnny, Donnie, Jeff, and Doug all shaved their heads.

A stranger to Rosenberg might wonder why nine students at Lamar High study, laugh, joke and go on dates wearing shiny, bald heads. But one of those bald heads knows the power of positive peer pressure. That makes all the difference.

Peer pressure can be good or bad. The Bible talks about a negative kind of peer pressure that many Christians will face. Read **Luke 21:5–19**, especially verse 16, to find out more about it.

■ Lance faced rejection at school. How will Christians face rejection by the world, according to this passage?

■ What encouragement does this passage give you to stand up to pressure from people who try to get you to compromise what you believe?

C O N S I D E R . . .

■ making a list of pressures that challenge your relationships with God and your friends, then asking your youth leader for advice on how to overcome those pressures.

■ making a pact with your friends to always encourage each other to follow God.

F O R   M O R E ,   S E E . . .

■ 1 Samuel 20:28–42 (p. 264)
■ Matthew 10:16–23 (p. 924)

■ 1 Corinthians 15:33 (p. 1188)

high, because the time when God will free you is near!"

Jesus' Words Will Live Forever

²⁹Then Jesus told this story: "Look at the fig tree and all the other trees. ³⁰When their leaves appear, you know that summer is near. ³¹In the same way, when you see these things happening, you will know that God's kingdom is near.

³²"I tell you the truth, all these things will happen while the people of this time are still living. ³³Earth and sky will be destroyed, but the words I have spoken will never be destroyed.

Be Ready All the Time

³⁴"Be careful not to spend your time feasting, drinking, or worrying about worldly things. If you do, that day might come on you suddenly, ³⁵like a trap on all people on earth. ³⁶So be ready all the time. Pray that you will be strong enough to escape all these things that will happen and that you will be able to stand before the Son of Man."*d*

³⁷During the day, Jesus taught the people in the Temple,*d* and at night he went out of the city and stayed on the Mount of Olives.*d* ³⁸Every morning all the people got up early to go to the Temple to listen to him.

Judas Becomes an Enemy of Jesus

22 It was almost time for the Feast*d* of Unleavened Bread, called the Passover*d* Feast. ²The leading priests and teachers of the law were trying to find a way to kill Jesus, because they were afraid of the people.

³Satan entered Judas Iscariot, one of Jesus' twelve apostles.*d* ⁴Judas went to the leading priests and some of the soldiers who guarded the Temple*d* and talked to them about a way to hand Jesus over to them. ⁵They were pleased and agreed to give Judas money. ⁶He agreed and watched for the best time to hand Jesus over to them when he was away from the crowd.

Jesus Eats the Passover Meal

⁷The Day of Unleavened*d* Bread came when the Passover*d* lambs had to be sacrificed. ⁸Jesus said to Peter and John, "Go and prepare the Passover meal for us to eat."

⁹They asked, "Where do you want us to prepare it?" ¹⁰Jesus said to them, "After you go into the city, a man carrying a jar of water will meet you. Follow him into the house that he enters, ¹¹and tell the owner of the house, 'The Teacher says: Where is the guest room in which I may eat the Passover meal with my followers?' ¹²Then he will show you a large, furnished room upstairs. Prepare the Passover meal there."

¹³So Peter and John left and found everything as Jesus had said. And they prepared the Passover meal.

The Lord's Supper

¹⁴When the time came, Jesus and the apostles*d* were sitting at the table. ¹⁵He said to them, "I wanted very much to eat this Passover*d* meal with you before I suffer. ¹⁶I will not eat another Passover meal until it is given its true meaning in the kingdom of God."

¹⁷Then Jesus took a cup, gave thanks, and said, "Take this cup and share it among yourselves. ¹⁸I will not drink again from the fruit of the vine*n* until God's kingdom comes."

¹⁹Then Jesus took some bread, gave thanks, broke it, and gave it to the apostles, saying, "This is my body, which I am giving for you. Do this to remember me." ²⁰In the same way, after supper, Jesus took the cup and said, "This cup is the new agreement that God makes with his people. This new agreement begins with my blood which is poured out for you.

Who Will Turn Against Jesus?

²¹"But one of you will turn against me, and his hand is with mine on the table. ²²What God has planned for the Son of Man*d* will happen, but how terrible it will be for that one who turns against the Son of Man."

²³Then the apostles*d* asked each other which one of them would do that.

Be Like a Servant

²⁴The apostles*d* also began to argue about which one of them was the most important. ²⁵But Jesus said to them, "The kings of the non-Jewish people rule over them, and those who have authority over others like to be called 'friends of the people.' ²⁶But you must not be like that. Instead, the greatest among you should be like the youngest, and the leader should be like the servant. ²⁷Who is more important: the one sitting at the table or the one serving? You think the one at the table is more important, but I am like a servant among you.

²⁸"You have stayed with me through my struggles. ²⁹Just as my Father has given me a kingdom, I also give you a kingdom ³⁰so you may eat and drink at my table in my kingdom. And you will sit on thrones, judging the twelve tribes*d* of Israel.

Don't Lose Your Faith!

³¹"Simon, Simon, Satan has asked to test all of you as a farmer sifts his wheat. ³²I have prayed that you will not lose your faith! Help your brothers be stronger when you come back to me."

---

fruit of the vine   Product of the grapevine; this may also be translated "wine."

33But Peter said to Jesus, "Lord, I am ready to go with you to prison and even to die with you!"

34But Jesus said, "Peter, before the rooster crows this day, you will say three times that you don't know me."

Be Ready for Trouble

35Then Jesus said to the apostles,*d* "When I sent you out without a purse, a bag, or sandals, did you need anything?"

They said, "No."

36He said to them, "But now if you have a purse or a bag, carry that with you. If you don't have a sword, sell your coat and buy one. 37The Scripture*d* says, 'He was treated like a criminal,'*n* and I tell you this scripture must have its full meaning. It was written about me, and it is happening now."

38His followers said, "Look, Lord, here are two swords."

He said to them, "That is enough."

Jesus Prays Alone

39Jesus left the city and went to the Mount of Olives,*d* as he often did, and his followers went with him. 40When he reached the place, he said to them, "Pray for strength against temptation."

41Then Jesus went about a stone's throw away from them. He kneeled down and prayed, 42"Father, if you are willing, take away this cup*n* of suffering. But do what you want, not what I want." 43Then an angel from heaven appeared to him to strengthen him. 44Being full of pain, Jesus prayed even harder. His sweat was like drops of blood falling to the ground. 45When he finished praying, he went to his followers and found them asleep because of their sadness. 46Jesus said to them, "Why are you sleeping? Get up and pray for strength against temptation."

Jesus Is Arrested

47While Jesus was speaking, a crowd came up, and Judas, one of the twelve apostles,*d* was leading them. He came close to Jesus so he could kiss him.

48But Jesus said to him, "Judas, are you using the kiss to give the Son of Man*d* to his enemies?"

49When those who were standing around him

'He ... criminal'   Quotation from Isaiah 53:12.
cup   Jesus is talking about the painful things that will happen to him. Accepting these things will be hard, like drinking a cup of something bitter.

JEALOUSY

When Others Succeed

"Few men have the strength to honor a friend's success without envy." —Aeschylus

"Lots of people know a good thing the minute the other fellow sees it first." —Job E. Hedges

"The man who keeps busy helping the man below him won't have time to envy the man above him—and there may not be anybody above him anyway." —Henrietta C. Mears

"The greatest among you should be like the youngest, and the leader should be like the servant." —Jesus Christ

For more about what Jesus said to his jealous disciples—who were arguing about prestige—read **Luke 22:24–30**.
■ What similarities and differences are there between what Jesus said and what these famous people said about jealousy?
■ How are you like and unlike the disciples in the passage? What would Jesus say to you?

CONSIDER . . .
■ stopping yourself next time you feel jealous toward someone. Instead, do an act of service for that person.
■ setting three goals for the coming week that will help you overcome jealous feelings you have toward someone you know.

FOR MORE, SEE . . .
■ Genesis 37:2–28 (p. 42)
■ 1 Samuel 18:6–11 (p. 262)
■ 1 Peter 2:1 (p. 1303)

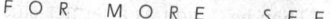

saw what was happening, they said, "Lord, should we strike them with our swords?" ⁵⁰And one of them struck the servant of the high priest and cut off his right ear.

⁵¹Jesus said, "Stop! No more of this." Then he touched the servant's ear and healed him.

⁵²Those who came to arrest Jesus were the leading priests, the soldiers who guarded the Temple,ᵈ and the older Jewish leaders. Jesus said to them, "You came out here with swords and clubs as though I were a criminal. ⁵³I was with you every day in the Temple, and you didn't arrest me there. But this is your time — the time when darkness rules."

Peter Says He Doesn't Know Jesus

⁵⁴They arrested Jesus, and led him away, and brought him into the house of the high priest. Peter followed far behind them. ⁵⁵After the soldiers started a fire in the middle of the courtyard and sat together, Peter sat with them. ⁵⁶A servant girl saw Peter sitting there in the firelight, and looking closely at him, she said, "This man was also with him."

⁵⁷But Peter said this was not true; he said, "Woman, I don't know him."

⁵⁸A short time later, another person saw Peter and said, "You are also one of them."

But Peter said, "Man, I am not!"

⁵⁹About an hour later, another man insisted, "Certainly this man was with him, because he is from Galilee, too."

⁶⁰But Peter said, "Man, I don't know what you are talking about!"

At once, while Peter was still speaking, a rooster crowed. ⁶¹Then the Lord turned and looked straight at Peter. And Peter remembered what the Lord had said: "Before the rooster crows this day, you will say three times that you don't know me." ⁶²Then Peter went outside and cried painfully.

The People Make Fun of Jesus

⁶³The men who were guarding Jesus began making fun of him and beating him.

⁶⁴They blindfolded him and said, "Prove that you are a prophet,ᵈ and tell us who hit you." ⁶⁵They said many cruel things to Jesus.

GOD'S WILL

Daring to Follow

Bruce Olson believed strongly that God wanted him to live with the savage Motilone Indians in the jungles of South America. So, this skinny, shy, Minnesota boy set out to find them.

The Motilones were an isolated and fierce group. They hated white people and had killed or wounded all who tried to contact them. Bruce's first encounter with them came when they shot an arrow through his thigh. Then they captured him and forced him to walk hours to their village.

The months that followed were filled with pain, hunger and loneliness. But Bruce wouldn't give up. God had sent him. Eventually Bruce learned the Motilones' language and began communicating with his captors. They called him "Bruchko."

The Motilones have now come to love and respect Bruchko. Through him many people have met Jesus and have benefited from Bruchko's medical and agricultural expertise.

All because he dared to follow God.

Bruce knew what God wanted him to do, and he wouldn't stop until he had accomplished it. Jesus also refused to give up on God's will. Read about his experience in **Luke 22:39–46**, when he prayed the night before he was to suffer beatings and a cruel death.

■ Knowing it would be hard, why do you think both Jesus and Bruchko insisted on following God's leadership?

■ Jesus followed God's will all his life. What makes following God's will possible even when it's tough for you?

C O N S I D E R . . .

■ placing an object in your room that will remind you to seek God's desires.

■ reading Bruce Olson's autobiography, titled Bruchko, published by Creation House.

F O R   M O R E ,   S E E . . .

■ Psalm 143:8–11 (p. 562)　　　　■ Mark 14:32–42 (p. 992)
■ Matthew 26:36–46 (p. 957)

Jesus Before the Leaders

66When day came, the council of the older leaders of the people, both the leading priests and the teachers of the law, came together and led Jesus to their highest court. 67They said, "If you are the Christ,*d* tell us."

Jesus said to them, "If I tell you, you will not believe me. 68And if I ask you, you will not answer. 69But from now on, the Son of Man*d* will sit at the right hand of the powerful God."

70They all said, "Then are you the Son of God?" Jesus said to them, "You say that I am."

71They said, "Why do we need witnesses now? We ourselves heard him say this."

Pilate Questions Jesus

23 Then the whole group stood up and led Jesus to Pilate.*n* 2They began to accuse Jesus, saying, "We caught this man telling things that mislead our people. He says that we should not pay taxes to Caesar,*d* and he calls himself the Christ,*d* a king."

3Pilate asked Jesus, "Are you the king of the Jews?"

Jesus answered, "Those are your words."

4Pilate said to the leading priests and the people, "I find nothing against this man."

5They were insisting, saying, "But Jesus makes trouble with the people, teaching all around Judea. He began in Galilee, and now he is here."

Pilate Sends Jesus to Herod

6Pilate heard this and asked if Jesus was from Galilee. 7Since Jesus was under Herod's authority, Pilate sent Jesus to Herod, who was in Jerusalem at that time. 8When Herod saw Jesus, he was very glad, because he had heard about Jesus and had wanted to meet him for a long time. He was hoping to see Jesus work a miracle.*d* 9Herod asked Jesus many questions, but Jesus said nothing.

Pilate Pontius Pilate was the Roman governor of Judea from A.D. 26 to A.D. 36.

The Price of Goals

In West Perrine, Florida, Lee Lawrence had a dream.

"Can you imagine," he said, "all the churches in the neighborhood . . . marching up Homestead Avenue to let the drug pushers know we won't take it anymore?"

The drug dealers didn't like Lee or his vision. Twice he was shot at while getting out of his car. The grocery store he owned was vandalized; then someone tried to burn it down. Refusing to give up, Lee got several pushers arrested. His store became a drug-free haven for the neighborhood kids.

The dealers vowed to strike back.

In March 1989, Lee walked outside his store and was met by a man shooting a semiautomatic rifle. The first shot knocked Lee to the ground. A second man shot Lee again as he lay on the pavement. Minutes later he was dead. But his vision was not.

On Lee Lawrence's funeral day, more than three thousand people from area churches linked arms and marched up Homestead Avenue singing, "We shall overcome: drugs and crime must go!"

It was a dream come true. And the start of a turnaround in West Perrine.

Lee was willing to face hardship—even death—to see his goal become a reality. Jesus also endured hardship because of his mission to reclaim humanity from sin. Read about it in **Luke 22:63–71**.

■ What price were both Lee and Jesus willing to pay to see their goals become reality?

■ How was Jesus' response in this passage like the way you respond when others attack your faith? How is your response different from Jesus'?

CONSIDER . . .

■ writing down three goals you would be willing to suffer for.

▟ looking through a newspaper to find three people who are suffering for doing right, and praying for them each day this week.

FOR MORE, SEE . . .

■ Exodus 3:6–10 (p. 60)
■ Mark 14:62–65 (p. 993)

■ 1 Peter 2:18–25 (p. 1305)

[10]The leading priests and teachers of the law were standing there, strongly accusing Jesus. [11]After Herod and his soldiers had made fun of Jesus, they dressed him in a kingly robe and sent him back to Pilate. [12]In the past, Pilate and Herod had always been enemies, but on that day they became friends.

Jesus Must Die

[13]Pilate called the people together with the leading priests and the Jewish leaders. [14]He said to them, "You brought this man to me, saying he makes trouble among the people. But I have questioned him before you all, and I have not found him guilty of what you say. [15]Also, Herod found nothing wrong with him; he sent him back to us. Look, he has done nothing for which he should die. [16]So, after I punish him, I will let him go free." [17] [n]

[18]But the people shouted together, "Take this man away! Let Barabbas go free!" [19](Barabbas was a man who was in prison for his part in a riot in the city and for murder.)

[20]Pilate wanted to let Jesus go free and told this to the crowd. [21]But they shouted again, "Crucify him! Crucify him!"

[22]A third time Pilate said to them, "Why? What wrong has he done? I can find no reason to kill him. So I will have him punished and set him free."

[23]But they continued to shout, demanding that Jesus be crucified. Their yelling became so loud that [24]Pilate decided to give them what they wanted. [25]He set free the man who was in jail for rioting and murder, and he handed Jesus over to them to do with him as they wished.

Jesus Is Crucified

[26]As they led Jesus away, Simon, a man from Cyrene, was coming in from the fields. They forced him to carry Jesus' cross and to walk behind him.

[27]A large crowd of people was following Jesus, including some women who were sad and crying for him. [28]But Jesus turned and said to them, "Women of Jerusalem, don't cry for me. Cry for yourselves and for your children. [29]The time is coming when people will say, 'Happy are the women who cannot have children and who have no babies to nurse.' [30]Then people will say to the mountains, 'Fall on us!' And they will say to the hills, 'Cover us!' [31]If they act like this now when

life is good, what will happen when bad times come?" [n]

[32]There were also two criminals led out with Jesus to be put to death. [33]When they came to a place called the Skull, the soldiers crucified Jesus and the criminals — one on his right and the other

> **SIDELIGHT:** If Jesus had been crucified like most Roman prisoners were executed, he was probably nailed to a capital T-shaped (Roman) cross rather than the Italian cross that most churches now display (Luke 23:32–33).

on his left. [34]Jesus said, "Father, forgive them, because they don't know what they are doing." [n] The soldiers threw lots[d] to decide who would get his clothes. [35]The people stood there watching. And the leaders made fun of Jesus, saying, "He saved others. Let him save himself if he is God's Chosen One, the Christ."[d]

[36]The soldiers also made fun of him, coming to Jesus and offering him some vinegar. [37]They said, "If you are the king of the Jews, save yourself!" [38]At the top of the cross these words were written: THIS IS THE KING OF THE JEWS.

[39]One of the criminals on a cross began to shout insults at Jesus: "Aren't you the Christ? Then save yourself and us."

[40]But the other criminal stopped him and said, "You should fear God! You are getting the same punishment he is. [41]We are punished justly, getting what we deserve for what we did. But this man has done nothing wrong." [42]Then he said, "Jesus, remember me when you come into your kingdom."

[43]Jesus said to him, "I tell you the truth, today you will be with me in paradise." [n]

Jesus Dies

[44]It was about noon, and the whole land became dark until three o'clock in the afternoon, [45]because the sun did not shine. The curtain in the Temple[n] was torn in two. [46]Jesus cried out in a loud voice, "Father, I give you my life." After Jesus said this, he died.

[47]When the army officer there saw what happened, he praised God, saying, "Surely this was a good man!"

[48]When all the people who had gathered there

Verse 17 A few Greek copies add verse 17: "Every year at the Passover Feast, Pilate had to release one prisoner to the people."
If . . . come? Literally, "If they do these things in the green tree, what will happen in the dry?"
Verse 34 Some early Greek copies do not have this part of the verse.
paradise A place where people who are obedient to God go when they die.
curtain in the Temple A curtain divided the Most Holy Place from the other part of the Temple, the special building in Jerusalem where God commanded the Jewish people to worship him.

to watch saw what happened, they returned home, beating their chests because they were so sad. [49]But those who were close friends of Jesus, including the women who had followed him from Galilee, stood at a distance and watched.

Joseph Takes Jesus' Body

[50]There was a good and religious man named Joseph who was a member of the Jewish council. [51]But he had not agreed to the other leaders' plans and actions against Jesus. He was from the Jewish town of Arimathea and was waiting for the kingdom of God to come. [52]Joseph went to Pilate to ask for the body of Jesus. [53]He took the body down from the cross, wrapped it in cloth, and put it in a tomb that was cut out of a wall of rock. This tomb had never been used before. [54]This was late on Preparation[d] Day, and when the sun went down, the Sabbath[d] day would begin.

[55]The women who had come from Galilee with Jesus followed Joseph and saw the tomb and how Jesus' body was laid. [56]Then the women left to prepare spices and perfumes.

On the Sabbath day they rested, as the law of Moses commanded.

Jesus Rises from the Dead

24 Very early on the first day of the week, at dawn, the women came to the tomb, bringing the spices they had prepared. [2]They found the stone rolled away from the entrance of the tomb, [3]but when they went in, they did not find the body of the Lord Jesus. [4]While they were wondering about this, two men in shining clothes suddenly stood beside them. [5]The women were very afraid and bowed their heads to the ground. The men said to them, "Why are you looking for a living person in this place for the dead? [6]He is not here; he has risen from the dead. Do you remember what he told you in Galilee? [7]He said the Son of Man[d] must be handed over to sinful people, be crucified, and rise from the dead on the

---

Lasting Impact

Dr. Boris Kornfeld was a prisoner in Siberia. Because of his medical skills, he regularly performed surgery for both prisoners and staff.

One day while repairing a guard's artery, which had been cut by a knife wound, he seriously considered stitching the wound in a way that would cause the guard to bleed to death. Shocked by his own hatred and bitterness, he quietly said the words from the Lord's Prayer:

"Forgive us for our sins, just as we have forgiven those who sinned against us."

Weeks later, Dr. Kornfeld was examining a patient who had just had surgery for cancer. Sensing a spiritual depth in the man, Kornfeld retold the story of the earlier incident. He shared his secret faith with the patient.

That night, someone who was angry at the doctor sneaked into his sleeping quarters and smashed his head. Kornfeld died a few hours later.

But his confession did not die. The patient who heard it became a Christian. When he left the prison camp, he went on to tell the world of his experiences there.

The patient was the Christian writer Aleksandr Solzhenitsyn.

Dr. Kornfeld's forgiveness of guards in the terrible prison camps had a great impact on Solzhenitsyn's life—and, as a result, on the world. The Bible tells of an even greater sacrifice and act of forgiveness—Jesus dying on the cross for all people's sins. Read about the forgiveness in **Luke 23:26–43**.

■ How was Dr. Kornfeld's forgiveness of the guard like and unlike Jesus' forgiveness of the thief in the passage?

■ If you were watching Jesus on the cross, and knew he was God's son, what would you ask forgiveness for?

C O N S I D E R . . .

■ writing a short song to thank God for forgiving you.

▶ creating a symbol of forgiveness and putting it in your locker or on your notebooks at school to remind you that God's forgiveness is always available.

F O R   M O R E .   S E E . . .

■ Isaiah 53:1–12 (p. 672)

■ Mark 15:21–21 (p. 995)

■ John 19:17–27 (p. 1092)

third day." [8]Then the women remembered what Jesus had said.

[9]The women left the tomb and told all these things to the eleven apostles[d] and the other followers. [10]It was Mary Magdalene, Joanna, Mary the mother of James, and some other women who told the apostles everything that had happened at the tomb. [11]But they did not believe the women, because it sounded like nonsense. [12]But Peter got up and ran to the tomb. Bending down and looking in, he saw only the cloth that Jesus' body had been wrapped in. Peter went away to his home, wondering about what had happened.

Jesus on the Road to Emmaus

[13]That same day two of Jesus' followers were going to a town named Emmaus, about seven miles from Jerusalem. [14]They were talking about everything that had happened. [15]While they were talking and discussing, Jesus himself came near and began walking with them, [16]but they were kept from recognizing him. [17]Then he said, "What are these things you are talking about while you walk?"

The two followers stopped, looking very sad. [18]The one named Cleopas answered, "Are you the only visitor in Jerusalem who does not know what just happened there?"

[19]Jesus said to them, "What are you talking about?"

They said, "About Jesus of Nazareth. He was a prophet[d] who said and did many powerful things before God and all the people. [20]Our leaders and the leading priests handed him over to be sentenced to death, and they crucified him. [21]But we were hoping that he would free Israel. Besides this, it is now the third day since this happened. [22]And today some women among us amazed us. Early this morning they went to the tomb, [23]but they did not find his body there. They came and told us that they had seen a vision of angels who said that Jesus was alive! [24]So some of our group went to the tomb, too. They found it just as the women said, but they did not see Jesus."

[25]Then Jesus said to them, "You are foolish and slow to believe everything the prophets said. [26]They said that the Christ[d] must suffer these things before he enters his glory." [27]Then starting with what Moses and all the prophets had said about him, Jesus began to explain everything that had been written about himself in the Scriptures.[d]

[28]They came near the town of Emmaus, and Jesus acted as if he were going farther. [29]But they begged him, "Stay with us, because it is late; it is almost night." So he went in to stay with them.

[30]When Jesus was at the table with them, he took some bread, gave thanks, divided it, and

---

LIFE

Good News

Bob Delker's family members mourned the day he died, but they also knew others would live now because of him. Bob had decided to give his body to medicine. That meant that people who desperately needed organ donations would receive them. For these people, Bob's death brought new life.

A few received badly needed bone transplants. Some critically injured burn victims received skin grafts. Corneas from Bob's eyes allowed two blind people to see.

In all, Bob's final gift helped thirty-four people. Countless others have been inspired to become organ donors because of Bob's example.

Bob's death brought new life to many people. Similarly, the sad news of Jesus' death meant the possibility of new life for all people everywhere, for Jesus rose from the dead. But unlike Bob Delker, Jesus didn't stay dead. Read **Luke 24:1–11** to discover what happened.

■ How is an organ transplant a little like Jesus' coming back from the dead?
■ How does Jesus' rising from the dead make a difference in your life?

C O N S I D E R . . .
■ listing the ways that Christ's death has given you life.
■ growing a plant in your room as a reminder of the spiritual life Jesus gives you.

F O R   M O R E ,   S E E . . .
■ Psalm 36:7–9 (p. 502)   ■ John 20:1–13 (p. 1093)
■ Mark 16:1–8 (p. 996)

gave it to them. ³¹And then, they were allowed to recognize Jesus. But when they saw who he was, he disappeared. ³²They said to each other, "It felt like a fire burning in us when Jesus talked to us on the road and explained the Scriptures to us."

³³So the two followers got up at once and went back to Jerusalem. There they found the eleven apostles*d* and others gathered. ³⁴They were saying, "The Lord really has risen from the dead! He showed himself to Simon."

³⁵Then the two followers told what had happened on the road and how they recognized Jesus when he divided the bread.

Jesus Appears to His Followers

³⁶While the two followers were telling this, Jesus himself stood right in the middle of them and said, "Peace be with you."

³⁷They were fearful and terrified and thought they were seeing a ghost. ³⁸But Jesus said, "Why are you troubled? Why do you doubt what you see? ³⁹Look at my hands and my feet. It is I myself! Touch me and see, because a ghost does not have a living body as you see I have."

⁴⁰After Jesus said this, he showed them his hands and feet. ⁴¹While they still could not believe it because they were amazed and happy, Jesus said to them, "Do you have any food here?" ⁴²They gave him a piece of broiled fish. ⁴³While the followers watched, Jesus took the fish and ate it.

⁴⁴He said to them, "Remember when I was with you before? I said that everything written about me must happen — everything in the law of Moses, the books of the prophets,*d* and the Psalms."

⁴⁵Then Jesus opened their minds so they could understand the Scriptures.*d* ⁴⁶He said to them, "It is written that the Christ*d* would suffer and rise from the dead on the third day ⁴⁷and that a change of hearts and lives and forgiveness of sins would be preached in his name to all nations, starting at Jerusalem. ⁴⁸You are witnesses of these things. ⁴⁹I will send you what my Father has promised, but you must stay in Jerusalem until you have received that power from heaven."

Jesus Goes Back to Heaven

⁵⁰Jesus led his followers as far as Bethany, and he raised his hands and blessed them. ⁵¹While he was blessing them, he was separated from them and carried into heaven. ⁵²They worshiped him and returned to Jerusalem very happy. ⁵³They stayed in the Temple*d* all the time, praising God.

JOHN

Why Read This Book:

■ Be reminded that Jesus Christ is fully human and fully divine (John 1).
■ Find stories that reveal Jesus' glory as giver of eternal life (John 2—11).
■ Learn the importance of Jesus' death and resurrection (John 13—21).

Behind the Scenes:

Imagine meeting someone for the first time. The conversation begins with "Hi, I'm Barb. I go to Central High. I live in Rogers Park." If the conversation continues, you might talk about hobbies, interests, background, and other information.

But you still wouldn't really know that person. If you saw each other regularly, you would begin to understand each other's personality, values, and uniquenesses.

In some ways, the first three Gospels (Matthew, p. 906; Mark, p. 964; and Luke, p. 1000) are like the first part of a relationship with Jesus Christ. Through these books, we get to know stories about Jesus and what he did. But the Gospel of John digs deeper into who Jesus was, why he lived and the meaning of his life.

WHERE THE ACTION WAS

The Gospel of John focuses primarily on events that took place in Jerusalem, which is shown here.

Jesus healed the sick man near the pool of Bethzatha (John 5:1–13).

Jesus entered Jerusalem riding on a donkey (John 12:12–16).

Jesus was tried and sentenced to death at the Roman governor's palace (John 18:28–40).

In John's account, Jesus began his ministry by kicking the merchants out of the Temple (John 2:13–16).

Jesus was crucified at The Place of the Skull (John 19:17–24).

Temple

Jesus was arrested on the Mount of Olives (John 18:1–11).

Jerusalem

Jesus and his followers ate their last meal together (John 13:1–20).

City wall

Jesus told the blind man to wash his eyes in the Pool of Siloam and be healed (John 9:1–11).

WHEN THE ACTION WAS

Jesus was born	Jesus was crucified, rose from the dead, and went to heaven	Fire destroyed Rome	
BC/AD	**25AD**	**50AD**	**75AD** **100AD**
	Jesus began his ministry		Romans destroyed the Temple in Jerusalem

This fourth Gospel is quite different from the other three. Like the others, it tells about what Jesus said and did. But it goes a step further by interpreting Jesus' significance as God's Son.

Many new believers turn first to this Gospel to discover what it means to be a Christian. That's not surprising, given the book's purpose as stated in John 20:31: "These [things] are written so that you may believe that Jesus is the Christ, the Son of God. Then, by believing, you may have life through his name."

Christ Comes to the World

1 In the beginning there was the Word. [n] The Word was with God, and the Word was God. [2]He was with God in the beginning. [3]All things were made by him, and nothing was made without him. [4]In him there was life, and that life was the light of all people. [5]The Light shines in the darkness, and the darkness has not overpowered it.

[6]There was a man named John [n] who was sent by God. [7]He came to tell people the truth about the Light so that through him all people could

Word   The Greek word is "logos," meaning any kind of communication; it could be translated "message." Here, it means Christ, because Christ was the way God told people about himself.

John   John the Baptist, who preached to people about Christ's coming (Matthew 3, Luke 3).

JESUS CHRIST

Point to the Light

All the kids called him "Grandpa." He was a plumber with an eighth-grade education. But no one was more articulate about Jesus Christ than Grandpa Craig.

Kids from all over spent a lot of time with Grandpa—eating popcorn in his living room, having Bible studies, praying, just "shooting the breeze." No matter where the conversation wandered, though, Grandpa would always bring it around to Jesus.

Whenever we were talking about school or dating or the future, Grandpa would say, "That reminds me of something Jesus said . . ." or, "That's just like when Jesus . . ." and he would reveal new insights to us about Jesus.

Grandpa's life was filled with the reality of Jesus' presence. On Saturday afternoons, we would sometimes take long walks with Grandpa. He would point to the countryside and say, "Now, that's Jesus' way of showing us how much he loves us. He made all these things for us to enjoy."

Grandpa saw Jesus in everything around him. "See how the sun goes down so faithfully every evening?" he would ask. "That shows how faithful Jesus is to us. Just like the sun, he never lets us down."

When anyone wondered how to act toward a new kid in school, Grandpa would ask, "How would Jesus act if he were in school?" Problems with parents? "What would Jesus do in your shoes?" His advice was always simple: "Focus on Jesus. Figure it out from there."

In the same way that Grandpa experienced Jesus in everything, **John 1:1—18** reminds us that Jesus is central to everything.

■ How did Grandpa reflect Jesus' light to others?

■ How can your life be a light pointing others to Jesus?

C O N S I D E R . . .

■ pointing people to Jesus by noticing God's work in the world and by asking yourself what Jesus would do in different situations. If you're not sure, talk with a Christian friend or church member about the issue.

◢ taking a nature walk and sitting down to list all the ways Jesus is revealed through creation and then sharing your list with a friend.

F O R   M O R E ,   S E E . . .

■ Isaiah 53:1—12 (p. 672)
■ Philippians 2:5—11 (p. 1230)
■ Colossians 1:15—20 (p. 1239)

hear about the Light and believe. [8]John was not the Light, but he came to tell people the truth about the Light. [9]The true Light that gives light to all was coming into the world!

[10]The Word was in the world, and the world was made by him, but the world did not know him. [11]He came to the world that was his own, but his own people did not accept him. [12]But to all who did accept him and believe in him he gave the right to become children of God. [13]They did not become his children in any human way — by any human parents or human desire. They were born of God.

[14]The Word became a human and lived among us. We saw his glory — the glory that belongs to the only Son of the Father — and he was full of

---

SIDELIGHT: Did you know Jesus was a great camper? When John 1:14 says "The Word became a human and lived among us," the literal Greek words say he "pitched his tent" among us. No fancy houses here!

---

grace and truth. [15]John tells the truth about him and cries out, saying, "This is the One I told you about: 'The One who comes after me is greater than I am, because he was living before me.' "

[16]Because he was full of grace and truth, from him we all received one gift after another. [17]The law was given through Moses, but grace and truth came through Jesus Christ. [18]No one has ever seen God. But God the only Son is very close to the Father, [n] and he has shown us what God is like.

John Tells People About Jesus

[19]Here is the truth John[n] told when the Jews in Jerusalem sent priests and Levites to ask him, "Who are you?"

[20]John spoke freely and did not refuse to answer. He said, "I am not the Christ."[d]

[21]So they asked him, "Then who are you? Are you Elijah?"[n]

He answered, "No, I am not."

"Are you the Prophet?"[n] they asked.

He answered, "No."

[22]Then they said, "Who are you? Give us an answer to tell those who sent us. What do you say about yourself?"

[23]John told them in the words of the prophet Isaiah:

"I am the voice of one
    calling out in the desert:
'Make the road straight for the Lord.' "

Isaiah 40:3

[24]Some Pharisees[d] who had been sent asked John: [25]"If you are not the Christ or Elijah or the Prophet, why do you baptize people?"

[26]John answered, "I baptize with water, but there is one here with you that you don't know about. [27]He is the One who comes after me. I am not good enough to untie the strings of his sandals."

[28]This all happened at Bethany on the other side of the Jordan River, where John was baptizing people.

[29]The next day John saw Jesus coming toward him. John said, "Look, the Lamb of God,[n] who takes away the sin of the world! [30]This is the One I was talking about when I said, 'A man will come after me, but he is greater than I am, because he was living before me.' [31]Even I did not know who he was, although I came baptizing with water so that the people of Israel would know who he is."

[32-33]Then John said, "I saw the Spirit come down from heaven in the form of a dove and rest on him. Until then I did not know who the Christ was. But the God who sent me to baptize with water told me, 'You will see the Spirit[d] come down and rest on a man; he is the One who will baptize with the Holy Spirit.' [34]I have seen this happen, and I tell you the truth: This man is the Son of God."

The First Followers of Jesus

[35]The next day John[n] was there again with two of his followers. [36]When he saw Jesus walking by, he said, "Look, the Lamb of God!"[n]

[37]The two followers heard John say this, so they followed Jesus. [38]When Jesus turned and saw them following him, he asked, "What are you looking for?"

They said, "Rabbi, where are you staying?" ("Rabbi" means "Teacher.")

[39]He answered, "Come and see." So the two men went with Jesus and saw where he was staying and stayed there with him that day. It was about four o'clock in the afternoon.

[40]One of the two men who followed Jesus after they heard John speak about him was Andrew, Simon Peter's brother. [41]The first thing Andrew

---

But ... Father This could be translated, "But the only God is very close to the Father." Also, some Greek copies say, "But the only Son is very close to the Father."

John John the Baptist, who preached to people about Christ's coming (Matthew 3, Luke 3).

Elijah A man who spoke for God. He lived hundreds of years before Christ and was expected to return before Christ (Malachi 4:5-6).

Prophet They probably meant the prophet that God told Moses he would send (Deuteronomy 18:15-19).

Lamb of God Name for Jesus. Jesus is like the lambs that were offered for a sacrifice to God.

did was to find his brother Simon and say to him, "We have found the Messiah." ("Messiah" means "Christ."[d])

[42]Then Andrew took Simon to Jesus. Jesus looked at him and said, "You are Simon son of John. You will be called Cephas." ("Cephas" means "Peter."[n])

[43]The next day Jesus decided to go to Galilee. He found Philip and said to him, "Follow me."

[44]Philip was from the town of Bethsaida, where Andrew and Peter lived. [45]Philip found Nathanael and told him, "We have found the man that Moses wrote about in the law, and the prophets[d] also wrote about him. He is Jesus, the son of Joseph, from Nazareth."

[46]But Nathanael said to Philip, "Can anything good come from Nazareth?"

Philip answered, "Come and see."

[47]As Jesus saw Nathanael coming toward him, he said, "Here is truly an Israelite. There is nothing false in him."

[48]Nathanael asked, "How do you know me?"

Jesus answered, "I saw you when you were under the fig tree, before Philip told you about me."

[49]Then Nathanael said to Jesus, "Teacher, you are the Son of God; you are the King of Israel."

[50]Jesus said to Nathanael, "Do you believe simply because I told you I saw you under the fig tree? You will see greater things than that." [51]And Jesus said to them, "I tell you the truth, you will all see heaven open and 'angels of God going up and coming down'[n] on the Son of Man."[d]

The Wedding at Cana

2 Two days later there was a wedding in the town of Cana in Galilee. Jesus' mother was there, [2]and Jesus and his followers were also invited to the wedding. [3]When all the wine was gone, Jesus' mother said to him, "They have no more wine."

[4]Jesus answered, "Dear woman, why come to me? My time has not yet come."

[5]His mother said to the servants, "Do whatever he tells you to do."

[6]In that place there were six stone water jars that the Jews used in their washing ceremony.[n] Each jar held about twenty or thirty gallons.

[7]Jesus said to the servants, "Fill the jars with water." So they filled the jars to the top.

[8]Then he said to them, "Now take some out and give it to the master of the feast."

So they took the water to the master. [9]When *he tasted it, the water had become wine. He did* not know where the wine came from, but the

servants who had brought the water knew. The master of the wedding called the bridegroom [10]and said to him, "People always serve the best wine first. Later, after the guests have been drinking awhile, they serve the cheaper wine. But you have saved the best wine till now."

[11]So in Cana of Galilee Jesus did his first miracle.[d] There he showed his glory, and his followers believed in him.

SIDELIGHT: The wedding at Cana (John 2:1–11) wouldn't have involved a short ceremony followed by a cake-and-punch reception. In Jesus' day, weddings usually lasted about a week. On the first day, the couple exchanged vows under a canopy. Then, for the next six days or more, the couple and all the guests celebrated with dancing, games, music, food, and wine.

Jesus in the Temple

[12]After this, Jesus went to the town of Capernaum with his mother, brothers, and followers. They stayed there for just a few days. [13]When it was almost time for the Jewish Passover[d] Feast, Jesus went to Jerusalem. [14]In the Temple[d] he found people selling cattle, sheep, and doves. He saw others sitting at tables, exchanging different kinds of money. [15]Jesus made a whip out of cords and forced all of them, both the sheep and cattle, to leave the Temple. He turned over the tables and scattered the money of those who were exchanging it. [16]Then he said to those who were selling pigeons, "Take these things out of here! Don't make my Father's house a place for buying and selling!"

[17]When this happened, the followers remembered what was written in the Scriptures:[d] "My strong love for your Temple completely controls me."[n]

[18]The Jews said to Jesus, "Show us a miracle[d] to prove you have the right to do these things."

[19]Jesus answered them, "Destroy this temple, and I will build it again in three days."

[20]The Jews answered, "It took forty-six years to build this Temple! Do you really believe you can build it again in three days?"

[21](But the temple Jesus meant was his own *body. [22]After Jesus was raised from the dead, his* followers remembered that Jesus had said this.

Peter   The Greek name "Peter," like the Aramaic name "Cephas," means "rock."
'angels . . . down'   These words are from Genesis 28:12.
washing ceremony   The Jewish people washed themselves in special ways before eating, before worshiping in the Temple, and at other special times.
"My . . . me."   Quotation from Psalm 69:9.

Then they believed the Scripture*d* and the words Jesus had said.)

²³When Jesus was in Jerusalem for the Passover Feast, many people believed in him because they saw the miracles he did. ²⁴But Jesus did not trust himself to them because he knew them all. ²⁵He did not need anyone to tell him about people, because he knew what was in people's minds.

Nicodemus Comes to Jesus

3 There was a man named Nicodemus who was one of the Pharisees*d* and an important Jewish leader. ²One night Nicodemus came to Jesus and said, "Teacher, we know you are a teacher sent from God, because no one can do the miracles*d* you do unless God is with him."

³Jesus answered, "I tell you the truth, unless one is born again, he cannot be in God's kingdom."

⁴Nicodemus said, "But if a person is already old, how can he be born again? He cannot enter his mother's body again. So how can a person be born a second time?"

⁵But Jesus answered, "I tell you the truth, unless one is born from water and the Spirit,*d* he cannot enter God's kingdom. ⁶Human life comes from human parents, but spiritual life comes from the Spirit. ⁷Don't be surprised when I tell you, 'You must all be born again.' ⁸The wind blows where it wants to and you hear the sound of it, but you don't know where the wind comes from or where it is going. It is the same with every person who is born from the Spirit."

⁹Nicodemus asked, "How can this happen?"

¹⁰Jesus said, "You are an important teacher in Israel, and you don't understand these things? ¹¹I tell you the truth, we talk about what we know, and we tell about what we have seen, but you don't accept what we tell you. ¹²I have told you about things here on earth, and you do not be-

---

Constructive Anger

They wander the streets late at night in the toughest parts of town. Jackets with their emblem let anyone who can see know exactly who they are.

They are not the Crips or Bloods. They are not even a gang. They are "Mad Dads"—men who have dedicated themselves to fight the influences of gangs and substance abuse in Omaha, Nebraska.

Neighborhoods feel the difference when the Mad Dads come around. These men educate adults about the needs of young people. They clean up gang graffiti, work with local businesses to find jobs for kids who need them, and encourage kids to stay in school and out of trouble.

Often, volunteer patrols of Mad Dads watch for gang or drug-related activities, and then report them to the police.

Mad Dads formed out of the founders' shared anger against gang violence and drug pushing in their neighborhoods. They finally got angry enough to take positive action.

Eddie Staton, one of the founders, said, "For too long, we, as black men, were silent. And people took our silence to mean we didn't care about drugs, alcohol, or gangs. So we took action. As parents, as black fathers in particular . . . we are actively involved in preventative measures against the influences of gangs, drugs, and alcohol."

Jesus became angry at bad influences too. Read **John 2:12–22** to see what Jesus did with his anger.

■ How are the Mad Dads' actions like Jesus' actions in this passage? How are they different?

■ When have you been so angry at wrongdoing that you took action against it like Jesus or the Mad Dads did?

CONSIDER . . .

■ stopping the next time you get angry, and praying that your anger will produce something positive.

■ memorizing Ephesians 4:26, p. 1224. What does the verse mean to you? Meditate on it so it can help you the next time you are angry.

FOR MORE, SEE . . .

■ Psalm 103:7–13 (p. 540)　　　　　　　■ James 1:19–20 (p. 1294)
■ Ephesians 4:26–27 (p. 1224)

lieve me. So you will not believe me if I tell you about things of heaven. [13]The only one who has ever gone up to heaven is the One who came down from heaven—the Son of Man.[d]

[14]"Just as Moses lifted up the snake in the desert,[n] the Son of Man must also be lifted up. [15]So that everyone who believes can have eternal life in him.

[16]"God loved the world so much that he gave his one and only Son so that whoever believes in him may not be lost, but have eternal life. [17]God did not send his Son into the world to judge the world guilty, but to save the world through him. [18]People who believe in God's Son are not judged guilty. Those who do not believe have already been judged guilty, because they have not believed in God's one and only Son. [19]They are judged by this fact: The Light has come into the world, but they did not want light. They wanted darkness, because they were doing evil things. [20]All who do evil hate the light and will not come to the light, because it will show all the evil things they do. [21]But those who follow the true way come to the light, and it shows that the things they do were done through God."

Jesus and John the Baptist

[22]After this, Jesus and his followers went into the area of Judea, where he stayed with his followers and baptized people. [23]John was also baptizing in Aenon, near Salim, because there was plenty of water there. People were going there to be baptized. [24](This was before John was put into prison.)

[25]Some of John's followers had an argument with a Jew about religious washing.[n] [26]So they came to John and said, "Teacher, remember the man who was with you on the other side of the Jordan River, the one you spoke about so much? He is baptizing, and everyone is going to him."

[27]John answered, "A man can get only what God gives him. [28]You yourselves heard me say, 'I

Moses ... desert When the Israelites were dying from snake bites, God told Moses to put a brass snake on a pole. The people who looked at the snake were healed (Numbers 21:4-9).

religious washing The Jewish people washed themselves in special ways before eating, before worshiping in the Temple, and at other special times.

ETERNAL LIFE

The Ultimate Price

Brian Watkins had been in New York City before. Brian loved the annual trip his family made from Provo, Utah, to watch the U.S. Open together in New York.

One Sunday during the 1990 tournament, Brian was waiting with his parents in a Manhattan subway station when a gang approached them. Surrounding the Watkinses, they robbed Brian's father, then began beating Brian's mother.

Brian fought back to defend his mother. The attackers turned from Brian's mother to Brian. In the struggle, one of the robbers pulled a knife and stabbed Brian to death.

Brian Watkins paid the ultimate price because he couldn't stand watching the ones he loved be hurt. Jesus, God's Son, willingly paid the ultimate price for us because he doesn't want us to be hurt forever.

In **John 3:1–21**, Jesus talks about the gift of eternal life that his death would provide.

■ How were Brian's feelings for his parents like God's desires for us? How were they different?

■ According to this passage (especially verses 16–18), what must we do to receive all God desires for us?

C O N S I D E R . . .

■ writing John 3:16 on paper, placing it in a box, and gift wrapping the box. Give the box to a friend to keep in his or her room as a reminder of God's gift of eternal life.

◢ asking your pastor or youth leader what eternal life is, then comparing the answer to what Jesus said in this passage.

F O R   M O R E .   S E E . . .

■ Isaiah 12 (p. 631)
■ 1 Timothy 1:12–17 (p. 1256)

■ 1 John 5:1–12 (p. 1319)

am not the Christ,[d] but I am the one sent to prepare the way for him.' [29]The bride belongs only to the bridegroom. But the friend who helps the bridegroom stands by and listens to him. He is thrilled that he gets to hear the bridegroom's voice. In the same way, I am really happy. [30]He must become greater, and I must become less important.

The One Who Comes from Heaven

[31]"The One who comes from above is greater than all. The one who is from the earth belongs to the earth and talks about things on the earth. But the One who comes from heaven is greater than all. [32]He tells what he has seen and heard, but no one accepts what he says. [33]Whoever accepts what he says has proven that God is true. [34]The One whom God sent speaks the words of God, because God gives him the Spirit[d] fully. [35]The Father loves the Son and has given him power over everything. [36]Those who believe in the Son have eternal life, but those who do not obey the Son will never have life. God's anger stays on them."

Jesus and a Samaritan Woman

4 The Pharisees[d] heard that Jesus was making and baptizing more followers than John, [2]although Jesus himself did not baptize people, but his followers did. [3]Jesus knew that the Pharisees had heard about him, so he left Judea and went back to Galilee. [4]But on the way he had to go through the country of Samaria.

[5]In Samaria Jesus came to the town called Sychar, which is near the field Jacob gave to his son Joseph. [6]Jacob's well was there. Jesus was tired from his long trip, so he sat down beside the well. It was about twelve o'clock noon. [7]When a Samaritan[d] woman came to the well to get some water, Jesus said to her, "Please give me a drink." [8](This happened while Jesus' followers were in town buying some food.)

[9]The woman said, "I am surprised that you ask me for a drink, since you are a Jewish man and I am a Samaritan woman." (Jewish people are not friends with Samaritans.[n])

[10]Jesus said, "If you only knew the free gift of God and who it is that is asking you for water, you would have asked him, and he would have given you living water."

[11]The woman said, "Sir, where will you get this living water? The well is very deep, and you have nothing to get water with. [12]Are you greater than Jacob, our father, who gave us this well and drank from it himself along with his sons and flocks?"

[13]Jesus answered, "Everyone who drinks this water will be thirsty again, [14]but whoever drinks the water I give will never be thirsty. The water I give will become a spring of water gushing up inside that person, giving eternal life."

[15]The woman said to him, "Sir, give me this water so I will never be thirsty again and will not have to come back here to get more water."

[16]Jesus told her, "Go get your husband and come back here."

[17]The woman answered, "I have no husband."

Jesus said to her, "You are right to say you have no husband. [18]Really you have had five husbands, and the man you live with now is not your husband. You told the truth."

[19]The woman said, "Sir, I can see that you are a prophet.[d] [20]Our ancestors worshiped on this mountain, but you Jews say that Jerusalem is the place where people must worship."

[21]Jesus said, "Believe me, woman. The time is coming when neither in Jerusalem nor on this mountain will you actually worship the Father. [22]You Samaritans worship something you don't understand. We understand what we worship, because salvation comes from the Jews. [23]The time is coming when the true worshipers will worship the Father in spirit and truth, and that time is here already. You see, the Father too is actively seeking such people to worship him. [24]God is spirit, and those who worship him must worship in spirit and truth."

[25]The woman said, "I know that the Messiah is coming." (Messiah is the One called Christ.[d]) "When the Messiah comes, he will explain everything to us."

[25]Then Jesus said, "I am he — I, the one talking to you."

[27]Just then his followers came back from town and were surprised to see him talking with a woman. But none of them asked, "What do you want?" or "Why are you talking with her?"

[28]Then the woman left her water jar and went back to town. She said to the people, [29]"Come and see a man who told me everything I ever did. Do you think he might be the Christ?" [30]So the people left the town and went to see Jesus.

※ **SIDELIGHT:** Jesus risked getting into lots of trouble when he talked with the Samaritan woman (see John 4:1–30). Jewish law forbade teachers to speak to women, Jews to talk to Samaritans, and the "righteous" to mingle with "sinners." Kinda made it hard to have any friends, don't you think?

Jewish people . . . Samaritans. This can also be translated "Jewish people don't use things that Samaritans have used."

³¹Meanwhile, his followers were begging him, "Teacher, eat something."

³²But Jesus answered, "I have food to eat that you know nothing about."

³³So the followers asked themselves, "Did somebody already bring him food?"

³⁴Jesus said, "My food is to do what the One who sent me wants me to do and to finish his work. ³⁵You have a saying, 'Four more months till harvest.' But I tell you, open your eyes and look at the fields ready for harvest now. ³⁶Already, the one who harvests is being paid and is gathering crops for eternal life. So the one who plants and the one who harvests celebrate at the same time.

³⁷Here the saying is true, 'One person plants, and another harvests.' ³⁸I sent you to harvest a crop that you did not work on. Others did the work, and you get to finish up their work." [n]

³⁹Many of the Samaritans in that town believed in Jesus because of what the woman said: "He told me everything I ever did." ⁴⁰When the Samaritans came to Jesus, they begged him to stay with them, so he stayed there two more days. ⁴¹And many more believed because of the things he said.

⁴²They said to the woman, "First we believed in Jesus because of your speech, but now we believe because we heard him ourselves. We know

But I . . . their work. As a farmer sends workers to harvest grain, Jesus sends his followers out to bring people to God.

JUDGING OTHERS

Prejudice

The bell rang. Creative writing was over for another day. Burt Moore stared at his short story.

His classmates walked by, some commenting as they passed. "What an imagination you have in there!" Burt wasn't sure if it was a compliment or not. "I'd love to hear you try reading it yourself, freak." He was sure that wasn't a compliment.

Burt waited for the classroom traffic to clear, then made his way to his next class: trigonometry.

Mr. Springer, his teacher, greeted him at the doorway. "Hi, Burt!" he yelled. "How are you today?"

Burt just nodded and wondered, once again, why people treated him like he was deaf.

When Burt began attending public school in junior high, one of the toughest adjustments was learning how to interact with others. Some people were great. They shared Burt's interest in chess and science fiction, and made special efforts to make him their friend. Others, though, openly insulted him for being different.

Burt learned a lot about prejudice in junior high and high school. Because of his severe cerebral palsy, some people expected Burt to be stupid. He always took special pleasure in blowing away stereotypes by writing a creative short story or taking the toughest math class offered.

Burt was different from others in some ways. His speech was often difficult to understand. He communicated by typing with touchsticks strapped to his hands. And he traveled by moving a joystick attached to his wheelchair.

But Burt had a lot more in common with those around him than many people thought. A lot of them refused to see beyond his wheelchair or his inability to speak as they did. And their prejudice was tough on Burt.

Jesus also had to overcome people's prejudice. Read **John 4:5—42** about how Jesus dealt with prejudice toward himself and others.

■ How did Burt break down prejudice in the same way Jesus did?
■ What prejudices do you have? How would Jesus respond to those prejudices?

C O N S I D E R . . .

■ writing a letter to the editor of your school or local newspaper concerning a prejudice *you see. Describe ways to combat that prejudice.*
■ regularly eating lunch at school with someone who has been hurt by prejudice.

F O R   M O R E ,   S E E . . .

■ Psalm 9:7–10 (p. 487)
■ Acts 10:1–33 (p. 1114)
■ Galatians 3:26–29 (p. 1210)

that this man really is the Savior of the world."

Jesus Heals an Officer's Son

[43]Two days later, Jesus left and went to Galilee. [44](Jesus had said before that a prophet[d] is not respected in his own country.) [45]When Jesus arrived in Galilee, the people there welcomed him. They had seen all the things he did at the Passover[d] Feast in Jerusalem, because they had been there, too.

[46]Jesus went again to visit Cana in Galilee where he had changed the water into wine. One of the king's important officers lived in the city of Capernaum, and his son was sick. [47]When he heard that Jesus had come from Judea to Galilee, he went to Jesus and begged him to come to Capernaum and heal his son, because his son was almost dead. [48]Jesus said to him, "You people must see signs and miracles[d] before you will believe in me."

[49]The officer said, "Sir, come before my child dies."

[50]Jesus answered, "Go. Your son will live."

The man believed what Jesus told him and went home. [51]On the way the man's servants came and met him and told him, "Your son is alive."

[52]The man asked, "What time did my son begin to get well?"

They answered, "Yesterday at one o'clock the fever left him."

[53]The father knew that one o'clock was the exact time that Jesus had said, "Your son will live." So the man and all the people who lived in his house believed in Jesus.

[54]That was the second miracle Jesus did after coming from Judea to Galilee.

Jesus Heals a Man at a Pool

5 Later Jesus went to Jerusalem for a special Jewish feast. [2]In Jerusalem there is a pool with five covered porches, which is called Bethzatha[n] in the Jewish language.[n] This pool is near the Sheep Gate. [3]Many sick people were lying on the porches beside the pool. Some were blind, some were crippled, and some were paralyzed.[n] [5]A man was lying there who had been sick for thirty-eight years. [6]When Jesus saw the man and knew that he had been sick for such a long time, Jesus asked him, "Do you want to be well?"

[7]The sick man answered, "Sir, there is no one to help me get into the pool when the water starts moving. While I am coming to the water, someone else always gets in before me."

[8]Then Jesus said, "Stand up. Pick up your mat and walk." [9]And immediately the man was well; he picked up his mat and began to walk.

The day this happened was a Sabbath[d] day. [10]So the Jews said to the man who had been healed, "Today is the Sabbath. It is against our law for you to carry your mat on the Sabbath day."

[11]But he answered, "The man who made me well told me, 'Pick up your mat and walk.' "

[12]Then they asked him, "Who is the man who told you to pick up your mat and walk?"

[13]But the man who had been healed did not know who it was, because there were many people in that place, and Jesus had left.

[14]Later, Jesus found the man at the Temple[d] and said to him, "See, you are well now. Stop sinning so that something worse does not happen to you."

[15]Then the man left and told the Jews that Jesus was the one who had made him well.

[16]Because Jesus was doing this on the Sabbath day, the Jews began to persecute him. [17]But Jesus said to them, "My Father never stops working, and so I keep working, too."

[18]This made the Jews try still harder to kill him. They said, "First Jesus was breaking the law about the Sabbath day. Now he says that God is his own Father, making himself equal with God!"

Jesus Has God's Authority

[19]But Jesus said, "I tell you the truth, the Son can do nothing alone. The Son does only what he sees the Father doing, because the Son does whatever the Father does. [20]The Father loves the Son and shows the Son all the things he himself does. But the Father will show the Son even greater things than this so that you can all be amazed. [21]Just as the Father raises the dead and gives them life, so also the Son gives life to those he wants to. [22]In fact, the Father judges no one, but he has given the Son power to do all the judging [23]so that all people will honor the Son as much as they honor the Father. Anyone who does not honor the Son does not honor the Father who sent him.

[24]"I tell you the truth, whoever hears what I say and believes in the One who sent me has eternal life. That person will not be judged guilty but has already left death and entered life. [25]I tell you the truth, the time is coming and is already here when the dead will hear the voice of the Son of God, and those who hear will have life. [26]Life comes from the Father himself, and he has allowed the Son to have life in himself as well.

Bethzatha Also called Bethsaida or Bethesda, a pool of water north of the Temple in Jerusalem.
Jewish language Hebrew or Aramaic, the languages of the Jewish people in the first century.
Verse 3 Some Greek copies add "and they waited for the water to move." A few later copies add verse 4: "Sometimes an angel of the Lord came down to the pool and stirred up the water. After the angel did this, the first person to go into the pool was healed from any sickness he had."

27And the Father has given the Son the power to judge, because he is the Son of Man.*d* 28Don't be surprised at this: A time is coming when all who are dead and in their graves will hear his voice. 29Then they will come out of their graves. Those who did good will rise and have life forever, but those who did evil will rise to be judged guilty.

Jesus Is God's Son

30"I can do nothing alone. I judge only the way I am told, so my judgment is fair. I don't try to please myself, but I try to please the One who sent me.

31"If only I tell people about myself, what I say is not true. 32But there is another who tells about me, and I know that the things he says about me are true.

33"You have sent people to John, and he has told you the truth. 34It is not that I accept such human telling; I tell you this so you can be saved. 35John was like a burning and shining lamp, and you were happy to enjoy his light for a while.

36"But I have a proof about myself that is greater than that of John. The things I do, which are the things my Father gave me to do, prove that the Father sent me. 37And the Father himself who sent me has given proof about me. You have never heard his voice or seen what he looks like. 38His teaching does not live in you, because you don't believe in the One the Father sent. 39You carefully study the Scriptures*d* because you think they give you eternal life. They do in fact tell about me, 40but you refuse to come to me to have that life.

41"I don't need praise from people. 42But I know you—I know that you don't have God's love in you. 43I have come from my Father and speak for him, but you don't accept me. But when another person comes, speaking only for himself, you will accept him. 44You try to get praise from each other, but you do not try to get the praise that comes from the only God. So how can you believe? 45Don't think that I will stand before the Father and say you are wrong. The one who says you are wrong is Moses, the one you hoped would save you. 46If you really believed Moses, you would believe me, because Moses wrote about me. 47But if you don't believe what Moses wrote, how can you believe what I say?"

More than Five Thousand Fed

6 After this, Jesus went across Lake Galilee (or, Lake Tiberias). 2Many people followed him because they saw the miracles*d* he did to heal the sick. 3Jesus went up on a hill and sat down there with his followers. 4It was almost the time for the Jewish Passover*d* Feast.

5When Jesus looked up and saw a large crowd coming toward him, he said to Philip, "Where can we buy enough bread for all these people to eat?" 6(Jesus asked Philip this question to test him, because Jesus already knew what he planned to do.)

7Philip answered, "We would all have to work a month to buy enough bread for each person to have only a little piece."

8Another one of his followers, Andrew, Simon Peter's brother, said, 9"Here is a boy with five loaves of barley bread and two little fish, but that is not enough for so many people."

> ✳ **SIDELIGHT:** There were three types of bread in Jesus' day: small loaves (that would look like our biscuits), round loaves (about the size of basketballs), and flat loaves (large, bread-like pancakes). The boy who gave loaves to Jesus gave the first type (John 6:9). His were made from barley, indicating he was probably poor.

10Jesus said, "Tell the people to sit down." This was a very grassy place, and about five thousand men sat down there. 11Then Jesus took the loaves of bread, thanked God for them, and gave them to the people who were sitting there. He did the same with the fish, giving as much as the people wanted.

12When they had all had enough to eat, Jesus said to his followers, "Gather the leftover pieces of fish and bread so that nothing is wasted." 13So they gathered up the pieces and filled twelve baskets with the pieces left from the five barley loaves.

14When the people saw this miracle*d* that Jesus did, they said, "He must truly be the Prophet*n* who is coming into the world."

15Jesus knew that the people planned to come and take him by force and make him their king, so he left and went into the hills alone.

Jesus Walks on the Water

16That evening Jesus' followers went down to Lake Galilee. 17It was dark now, and Jesus had not yet come to them. The followers got into a boat and started across the lake to Capernaum. 18By now a strong wind was blowing, and the waves on the lake were getting bigger. 19When they had *rowed the boat about three or four miles, they* saw Jesus walking on the water, coming toward the boat. The followers were afraid, 20but Jesus said to them, "It is I. Do not be afraid." 21Then they were glad to take him into the boat. At once

Prophet   They probably meant the prophet that God told Moses he would send (Deuteronomy 18:15-19).

the boat came to land at the place where they wanted to go.

The People Seek Jesus

22The next day the people who had stayed on the other side of the lake knew that Jesus had not gone in the boat with his followers but that they had left without him. And they knew that only one boat had been there. 23But then some boats came from Tiberias and landed near the place where the people had eaten the bread after the Lord had given thanks. 24When the people saw that Jesus and his followers were not there now, they got into boats and went to Capernaum to find Jesus.

Jesus, the Bread of Life

25When the people found Jesus on the other side of the lake, they asked him, "Teacher, when did you come here?"

26Jesus answered, "I tell you the truth, you aren't looking for me because you saw me do miracles.d You are looking for me because you ate the bread and were satisfied. 27Don't work for the food that spoils. Work for the food that stays good always and gives eternal life. The Son of Mand will give you this food, because on him God the Father has put his power."

28The people asked Jesus, "What are the things God wants us to do?"

29Jesus answered, "The work God wants you to do is this: Believe the One he sent."

30So the people asked, "What miracle will you do? If we see a miracle, we will believe you. What will you do? 31Our fathers ate the mannad in the

Proms and Personalities

"So who are you going to the prom with this year?" Heather Keith asked.

"I'm waiting for Brett to ask me. He's got the greatest car, and his parents have loads of money. So I know we'd have a blast," Laurie Hull answered.

"I didn't know you liked Brett Howard. How long has this been going on?"

Laurie tossed her hair back. "Oh, I don't like him."

Heather didn't have to say anything. Her shocked look said it all.

"I don't have to like him to go to the prom with him," Laurie explained. "I just think we'd look good together. And he can afford the kind of evening I want."

Over the next few weeks, Laurie asked her friends to drop hints to Brett. She even teased him at lunch one day, asking if he had anyone with whom to share his Trans Am for the prom.

A week before the prom, though, Brett hadn't asked Laurie to the prom. Three other guys had asked the bubbly cheerleader, but Laurie thought they were too weird. They didn't have very much money, and she wasn't about to be seen with any of them.

Prom night came, and Laurie stayed home watching television. While her friends had a great time, Laurie ate popcorn and wondered why Brett had never asked her.

Laurie had focused on what she could get from people, rather than on the people themselves. But when she did, she came up empty-handed.

Jesus frequently challenged people to make people rather than things a priority. Read **John 6:24—51** to see how people tended to give Jesus' miracles higher priority than they gave Jesus himself

■ What was most important to Laurie and the people in this passage?

■ How can you make people a priority in your life?

C O N S I D E R . . .

■ looking at your class members' photographs in a recent yearbook. Ask God to help you focus on your classmates as people and not on what you can get from them.

■ telling five friends or family members the things you appreciate about them. Focus only on inner qualities and not on what you can get from them.

F O R   M O R E ,   S E E . . .

■ 1 Samuel 16:6–13 (p. 258)   ■ James 2:1–9 (p. 1294)

■ Matthew 6:25–34 (p. 918)

desert. This is written in the Scriptures: *d* 'He gave them bread from heaven to eat.' " *n*

³²Jesus said, "I tell you the truth, it was not Moses who gave you bread from heaven; it is my Father who is giving you the true bread from heaven. ³³God's bread is the One who comes down from heaven and gives life to the world."

³⁴The people said, "Sir, give us this bread always."

³⁵Then Jesus said, "I am the bread that gives life. Whoever comes to me will never be hungry, and whoever believes in me will never be thirsty. ³⁶But as I told you before, you have seen me and still don't believe. ³⁷The Father gives me my people. Every one of them will come to me, and I will always accept them. ³⁸I came down from heaven to do what God wants me to do, not what I want to do. ³⁹Here is what the One who sent me wants me to do: I must not lose even one whom God gave me, but I must raise them all on the last day. ⁴⁰Those who see the Son and believe in him have eternal life, and I will raise them on the last day. This is what my Father wants."

⁴¹The Jews began to complain about Jesus because he said, "I am the bread that comes down from heaven." ⁴²They said, "This is Jesus, the son of Joseph. We know his father and mother. How can he say, 'I came down from heaven'?"

⁴³But Jesus answered, "Stop complaining to each other. ⁴⁴The Father is the One who sent me. No one can come to me unless the Father draws him to me, and I will raise that person up on the last day. ⁴⁵It is written in the prophets, *d* 'They will all be taught by God.' *n* Everyone who listens to the Father and learns from him comes to me. ⁴⁶No one has seen the Father except the One who is from God; only he has seen the Father. ⁴⁷I tell you the truth, whoever believes has eternal life. ⁴⁸I am the bread that gives life. ⁴⁹Your ancestors ate the manna in the desert, but still they died. ⁵⁰Here is the bread that comes down from heaven. Anyone who eats this bread will never die. ⁵¹I am the living bread that came down from heaven. Anyone who eats this bread will live forever. This bread is my flesh, which I will give up so that the world may have life."

⁵²Then the Jews began to argue among themselves, saying, "How can this man give us his flesh to eat?"

⁵³Jesus said, "I tell you the truth, you must eat the flesh of the Son of Man and drink his blood. Otherwise, you won't have real life in you. ⁵⁴Those who eat my flesh and drink my blood have eternal life, and I will raise them up on the last day. ⁵⁵My flesh is true food, and my blood is true drink. ⁵⁶Those who eat my flesh and drink

my blood live in me, and I live in them. ⁵⁷The living Father sent me, and I live because of the Father. So whoever eats me will live because of me. ⁵⁸I am not like the bread your ancestors ate. They ate that bread and still died. I am the bread that came down from heaven, and whoever eats this bread will live forever." ⁵⁹Jesus said all these things while he was teaching in the synagogue *d* in Capernaum.

The Words of Eternal Life

⁶⁰When the followers of Jesus heard this, many of them said, "This teaching is hard. Who can accept it?"

⁶¹Knowing that his followers were complaining about this, Jesus said, "Does this teaching bother you? ⁶²Then will it also bother you to see the Son of Man *d* going back to the place where he came from? ⁶³It is the Spirit that gives life. The flesh doesn't give life. The words I told you are spirit, and they give life. ⁶⁴But some of you don't believe." (Jesus knew from the beginning who did not believe and who would turn against him.) ⁶⁵Jesus said, "That is the reason I said, 'If the Father does not bring a person to me, that one cannot come.' "

⁶⁶After Jesus said this, many of his followers left him and stopped following him.

⁶⁷Jesus asked the twelve followers, "Do you want to leave, too?"

⁶⁸Simon Peter answered him, "Lord, where would we go? You have the words that give eternal life. ⁶⁹We believe and know that you are the Holy One from God."

⁷⁰Then Jesus answered, "I chose all twelve of you, but one of you is a devil." ⁷¹Jesus was talking about Judas, the son of Simon Iscariot. Judas was one of the twelve, but later he was going to turn against Jesus.

Jesus' Brothers Don't Believe

7 After this, Jesus traveled around Galilee. He did not want to travel in Judea, because the Jews there wanted to kill him. ²It was time for the Jewish Feast *d* of Shelters. ³So Jesus' brothers said to him, "You should leave here and go to Judea so your followers there can see the miracles *d* you do. ⁴Anyone who wants to be well known does not hide what he does. If you are doing these things, show yourself to the world." ⁵(Even Jesus' brothers did not believe in him.)

⁶Jesus said to his brothers, "The right time for me has not yet come, but any time is right for you. ⁷The world cannot hate you, but it hates me, because I tell it the evil things it does. ⁸So you go to the feast. I will not go yet to this feast, because the

'He gave ... eat.' Quotation from Psalm 78:24.
'They ... God.' Quotation from Isaiah 54:13.

right time for me has not yet come." ⁹After saying this, Jesus stayed in Galilee.

¹⁰But after Jesus' brothers had gone to the feast, Jesus went also. But he did not let people see him. ¹¹At the feast the Jews were looking for him and saying, "Where is that man?"

¹²Within the large crowd there, many people were whispering to each other about Jesus. Some said, "He is a good man."

Others said, "No, he fools the people." ¹³But no one was brave enough to talk about Jesus openly, because they were afraid of the Jews.

Jesus Teaches at the Feast

¹⁴When the feast was about half over, Jesus went to the Temple[d] and began to teach. ¹⁵The Jews were amazed and said, "This man has never studied in school. How did he learn so much?"

¹⁶Jesus answered, "The things I teach are not my own, but they come from him who sent me. ¹⁷If people choose to do what God wants, they will know that my teaching comes from God and not from me. ¹⁸Those who teach their own ideas are trying to get honor for themselves. But those who try to bring honor to the one who sent him speak the truth, and there is nothing false in them. ¹⁹Moses gave you the law,[n] but none of you obeys that law. Why are you trying to kill me?"

²⁰The people answered, "A demon[d] has come into you. We are not trying to kill you."

²¹Jesus said to them, "I did one miracle,[d] and you are all amazed. ²²Moses gave you the law about circumcision.[d] (But really Moses did not give you circumcision; it came from our ancestors.) And yet you circumcise a baby on a Sabbath[d] day. ²³If a baby can be circumcised on a Sabbath day to obey the law of Moses, why are you angry at me for healing a person's whole body on the Sabbath day? ²⁴Stop judging by the way things look, but judge by what is really right."

Is Jesus the Christ?

²⁵Then some of the people who lived in Jerusa-

---

law Moses gave God's people the law that God gave him on Mount Sinai (Exodus 34:29-32).

---

lem said, "This is the man they are trying to kill. [26]But he is teaching where everyone can see and hear him, and no one is trying to stop him. Maybe the leaders have decided he really is the Christ.[d] [27]But we know where this man is from. And when the real Christ comes, no one will know where he comes from."

[28]Jesus, teaching in the Temple,[d] cried out, "Yes, you know me, and you know where I am from. But I have not come by my own authority. I was sent by the One who is true, whom you don't know. [29]But I know him, because I am from him, and he sent me."

[30]When Jesus said this, the people tried to take him. But no one was able to touch him, because it was not yet the right time. [31]But many of the people believed in Jesus. They said, "When the Christ comes, will he do more miracles[d] than this man has done?"

The Leaders Try to Arrest Jesus

[32]The Pharisees[d] heard the crowd whispering these things about Jesus. So the leading priests and the Pharisees sent some Temple[d] guards to arrest him. [33]Jesus said, "I will be with you a little while longer. Then I will go back to the One who sent me. [34]You will look for me, but you will not find me. And you cannot come where I am."

[35]The Jews said to each other, "Where will this man go so we cannot find him? Will he go to the Greek cities where our people live and teach the Greek people there? [36]What did he mean when he said, 'You will look for me, but you will not find me,' and 'You cannot come where I am'?"

Jesus Talks About the Spirit

[37]On the last and most important day of the feast Jesus stood up and said in a loud voice, "Let anyone who is thirsty come to me and drink. [38]If anyone believes in me, rivers of living water will flow out from that person's heart, as the Scripture[d] says." [39]Jesus was talking about the Holy Spirit.[d] The Spirit had not yet been given, because Jesus had not yet been raised to glory. But later, those who believed in Jesus would receive the Spirit.

The People Argue About Jesus

[40]When the people heard Jesus' words, some of them said, "This man really is the Prophet."[n] [41]Others said, "He is the Christ."[d]

Still others said, "The Christ will not come from Galilee. [42]The Scripture[d] says that the Christ will come from David's family and from Bethlehem, the town where David lived." [43]So the peo-

ple did not agree with each other about Jesus. [44]Some of them wanted to arrest him, but no one was able to touch him.

Some Leaders Won't Believe

[45]The Temple[d] guards went back to the leading priests and the Pharisees,[d] who asked, "Why didn't you bring Jesus?"

[46]The guards answered, "The words he says are greater than the words of any other person who has ever spoken!"

[47]The Pharisees answered, "So Jesus has fooled you also! [48]Have any of the leaders or the Pharisees believed in him? No! [49]But these people, who know nothing about the law, are under God's curse."

[50]Nicodemus, who had gone to see Jesus before, was in that group.[n] He said, [51]"Our law does not judge a man without hearing him and knowing what he has done."

[52]They answered, "Are you from Galilee, too? Study the Scriptures,[d] and you will learn that no prophet[d] comes from Galilee."

Some early Greek manuscripts do not contain 7:53 — 8:11.

[[53]And everyone left and went home.

The Woman Caught in Adultery

8 Jesus went to the Mount of Olives.[d] [2]But early in the morning he went back to the Temple,[d] and all the people came to him, and he sat and taught them. [3]The teachers of the law and the Pharisees[d] brought a woman who had been caught in adultery.[d] They forced her to stand before the people. [4]They said to Jesus, "Teacher, this woman was caught having sexual relations with a man who is not her husband. [5]The law of Moses commands that we stone to death every woman who does this. What do you say we should do?" [6]They were asking this to trick Jesus so that they could have some charge against him.

But Jesus bent over and started writing on the ground with his finger. [7]When they continued to ask Jesus their question, he raised up and said, "Anyone here who has never sinned can throw the first stone at her." [8]Then Jesus bent over again and wrote on the ground.

[9]Those who heard Jesus began to leave one by one, first the older men and then the others. Jesus was left there alone with the woman standing before him. [10]Jesus raised up again and asked her,

---

Prophet They probably meant the prophet God told Moses he would send (Deuteronomy 18:15-19).
Nicodemus ... group. The story about Nicodemus going and talking to Jesus is in John 3:1-21.

"Woman, where are they? Has no one judged you guilty?"

¹¹She answered, "No one, sir."

Then Jesus said, "I also don't judge you guilty. You may go now, but don't sin anymore."]

Jesus Is the Light of the World

¹²Later, Jesus talked to the people again, saying, "I am the light of the world. The person who follows me will never live in darkness but will have the light that gives life."

¹³The Pharisees* said to Jesus, "When you talk about yourself, you are the only one to say these things are true. We cannot accept what you say."

¹⁴Jesus answered. "Yes, I am saying these things about myself, but they are true. I know where I came from and where I am going. But you don't know where I came from or where I am

going. ¹⁵You judge by human standards. I am not judging anyone. ¹⁶But when I do judge, my judging is true, because I am not alone. The Father

> ✳ **SIDELIGHT:** When the teachers of the law and the Pharisees brought the woman caught in adultery to Jesus, they were more interested in tricking Jesus than in doing what was right (John 8:1–11). Though the woman was "caught in adultery," they didn't accuse the man involved—even though the law demanded that both be executed if guilty (Leviticus 20:10, p. 117).

who sent me is with me. ¹⁷Your own law says that when two witnesses say the same thing, you must accept what they say. ¹⁸I am one of the witnesses who speaks about myself, and the Father who sent me is the other witness."

SEXUALITY

Once Forgiven, What Then?

Stephanie Broussard silently wept as Ross Walker sat next to her in the front seat of his dad's Buick, buttoning his shirt. The silence seemed to swallow them.

"Ross, we said we'd never do this again," she finally said through her tears.

"Well, we didn't mean to. . . . It just happened," Ross responded

"That's what you always say." The two sat silently for a long time, and then Stephanie finally spoke, "I don't think we should see each other anymore."

Ross didn't say anything. He just stared out the window. But Stephanie knew by his sniffling that he was crying.

Stephanie reached across and touched his arm. "I'm sorry, Ross, but I just can't keep doing this to us—or to God. We just keep doing it over and over, and then asking God to forgive us."

Ross jerked his head around and looked at Stephanie. "But God does forgive us, Steph," Ross argued. "We won't do it again."

Stephanie started crying even harder. "No, Ross, we say that every time. I'm serious this time. We can't keep sinning and expect God to forgive us. I love you, but this hurts too much. Please take me home."

In **John 8:1–11**, Jesus faced a woman caught in sexual sin. Read what he said to her.

■ How are Ross and Stephanie similar to the woman caught in adultery? How are they different?

■ What does this passage tell us about Jesus' perspective on sexual sin and the person who commits it? What is there in your life that needs to hear his "don't sin anymore"?

CONSIDER . . .

■ evaluating the movies you watch or music you listen to and deciding what view of sexuality they promote.

■ acting on one area of your life where Jesus is telling you to "go and not sin anymore." Tell a friend or parent about the area, and ask that person to support you in your decision.

FOR MORE, SEE . . .

■ Psalm 51:1–19 p. 511)

■ I Corinthians 6:12–20 (p. 1174)

■ Ephesians 6:10–18 (p. 1226)

¹⁹They asked, "Where is your father?"

Jesus answered, "You don't know me or my Father. If you knew me, you would know my Father, too." ²⁰Jesus said these things while he was teaching in the Temple,*d* near where the money is kept. But no one arrested him, because the right time for him had not yet come.

The People Misunderstand Jesus

²¹Again, Jesus said to the people, "I will leave you, and you will look for me, but you will die in your sins. You cannot come where I am going."

²²So the Jews asked, "Will Jesus kill himself? Is that why he said, 'You cannot come where I am going'?"

²³Jesus said, "You people are from here below, but I am from above. You belong to this world, but I don't belong to this world. ²⁴So I told you that you would die in your sins. Yes, you will die in your sins if you don't believe that I am he."

²⁵They asked, "Then who are you?"

Jesus answered, "I am what I have told you from the beginning. ²⁶I have many things to say and decide about you. But I tell people only the things I have heard from the One who sent me, and he speaks the truth."

²⁷The people did not understand that he was talking to them about the Father. ²⁸So Jesus said to them, "When you lift up the Son of Man,*d* you will know that I am he. You will know that these things I do are not by my own authority but that I say only what the Father has taught me. ²⁹The One who sent me is with me. I always do what is pleasing to him, so he has not left me alone." ³⁰While Jesus was saying these things, many people believed in him.

Freedom from Sin

³¹So Jesus said to the Jews who believed in him, "If you continue to obey my teaching, you are truly my followers. ³²Then you will know the truth, and the truth will make you free."

³³They answered, "We are Abraham's children, and we have never been anyone's slaves. So why do you say we will be free?"

³⁴Jesus answered, "I tell you the truth, everyone who lives in sin is a slave to sin. ³⁵A slave does not stay with a family forever, but a son belongs to the family forever. ³⁶So if the Son makes you free, you will be truly free. ³⁷I know you are Abraham's children, but you want to kill me because you don't accept my teaching. ³⁸I am telling you what my Father has shown me, but you do what your father has told you."

³⁹They answered, "Our father is Abraham."

Jesus said, "If you were really Abraham's children, you would do the things Abraham did. ⁴⁰I am a man who has told you the truth which I heard from God, but you are trying to kill me. Abraham did nothing like that. ⁴¹So you are doing the things your own father did."

But they said, "We are not like children who never knew who their father was. God is our Father; he is the only Father we have."

⁴²Jesus said to them, "If God were really your Father, you would love me, because I came from God and now I am here. I did not come by my own authority; God sent me. ⁴³You don't understand what I say, because you cannot accept my teaching. ⁴⁴You belong to your father the devil, and you want to do what he wants. He was a murderer from the beginning and was against the truth, because there is no truth in him. When he tells a lie, he shows what he is really like, because he is a liar and the father of lies. ⁴⁵But because I speak the truth, you don't believe me. ⁴⁶Can any of you prove that I am guilty of sin? If I am telling the truth, why don't you believe me? ⁴⁷The person who belongs to God accepts what God says. But you don't accept what God says, because you don't belong to God."

Jesus Is Greater than Abraham

⁴⁸The Jews answered, "We say you are a Samaritan*d* and have a demon*d* in you. Are we not right?"

⁴⁹Jesus answered, "I have no demon in me. I give honor to my Father, but you dishonor me. ⁵⁰I am not trying to get honor for myself. There is One who wants this honor for me, and he is the judge. ⁵¹I tell you the truth, whoever obeys my teaching will never die."

⁵²The Jews said to Jesus, "Now we know that you have a demon in you! Even Abraham and the prophets*d* died. But you say, 'Whoever obeys my teaching will never die.' ⁵³Do you think you are greater than our father Abraham, who died? And the prophets died, too. Who do you think you are?"

⁵⁴Jesus answered, "If I give honor to myself, that honor is worth nothing. The One who gives me honor is my Father, and you say he is your God. ⁵⁵You don't really know him, but I know him. If I said I did not know him, I would be a liar like you. But I do know him, and I obey what he says. ⁵⁶Your father Abraham was very happy that he would see my day. He saw that day and was glad."

⁵⁷The Jews said to him, "You have never seen Abraham! You are not even fifty years old."

⁵⁸Jesus answered, "I tell you the truth, before Abraham was even born, I am!" ⁵⁹When Jesus said this, the people picked up stones to throw at him. But Jesus hid himself, and then he left the Temple.*d*

Jesus Heals a Man Born Blind

9 As Jesus was walking along, he saw a man who had been born blind. ²His followers asked him, "Teacher, whose sin caused this man to be born blind—his own sin or his parents' sin?"

³Jesus answered, "It is not this man's sin or his parents' sin that made him be blind. This man was born blind so that God's power could be shown in him. ⁴While it is daytime, we must continue doing the work of the One who sent me. Night is coming, when no one can work. ⁵While I am in the world, I am the light of the world."

⁶After Jesus said this, he spit on the ground and made some mud with it and put the mud on the man's eyes. ⁷Then he told the man, "Go and wash in the Pool of Siloam." (Siloam means Sent.) So the man went, washed, and came back seeing.

⁸The neighbors and some people who had earlier seen this man begging said, "Isn't this the same man who used to sit and beg?"

⁹Some said, "He is the one," but others said, "No, he only looks like him."

The man himself said, "I am the man."

¹⁰They asked, "How did you get your sight?"

¹¹He answered, "The man named Jesus made some mud and put it on my eyes. Then he told me to go to Siloam and wash. So I went and washed, and then I could see."

¹²They asked him, "Where is this man?"

"I don't know," he answered.

SIDELIGHT: Sending the blind man to wash in the Pool of Siloam would clearly have been symbolic for the people in Jesus' day (John 9:7). This pool was the source for water used for religious ceremonies. It was also Jerusalem's primary water source.

Pharisees Question the Healing

¹³Then the people took to the Pharisees[d] the

SIN

Blind Side

"I actually thought no one could tell I was drinking." Josh Perez studied his hands for a moment before he looked up at the group. "I got caught the first time I got drunk. I thought about quitting then. But my friends were into it, so I kept drinking with them."

Josh paused and took a deep breath. Then he continued, "Before long, I didn't need them as an excuse to drink. I enjoyed it so much I drank every chance I could." A few other teenagers in the group nodded knowingly. Josh relaxed a bit.

"I figured I was maintaining pretty well. I kept my position on the baseball team and my grades hadn't slipped too far. I tried to be careful with curfews and covering the alcohol on my breath.

"One day, my dad made some comment to me about how I was gonna end up just like him. That shocked me! Dad's an alcoholic. And it scared me.

"So I talked to my youth leader, and he suggested I get into this support group," Josh said as his eyes swept over the teenagers seated in a circle. "I really thought I had everyone fooled. I guess the only one blind to my drinking problem was me."

Jesus encountered blind people of all kinds. Read **John 9:1–41** to see the key to true sight.

■ What are the similarities and differences between Josh's blindness and the Pharisees' blindness? Between Josh's blindness and that of the man blind from birth?

■ What does this Bible passage tell us about being blind to sin?

CONSIDER . . .

■ asking God to open your eyes to areas where you are blind to sin.
■ asking a good friend to tell you about a blind spot in your life, then working to change it.

FOR MORE, SEE . . .

■ Isaiah 6:9–10 (p. 623)   ■ Ephesians 5:6–15 (p. 1224)
■ Matthew 15:1–20 (p. 934)

man who had been blind. ¹⁴The day Jesus had made mud and healed his eyes was a Sabbath*d* day. ¹⁵So now the Pharisees asked the man, "How did you get your sight?"

He answered, "He put mud on my eyes, I washed, and now I see."

¹⁶So some of the Pharisees were saying, "This man does not keep the Sabbath day, so he is not from God."

But others said, "A man who is a sinner can't do miracles*d* like these." So they could not agree with each other.

¹⁷They asked the man again, "What do you say about him since it was your eyes he opened?"

The man answered, "He is a prophet."*d*

¹⁸The Jews did not believe that he had been blind and could now see again. So they sent for the man's parents ¹⁹and asked them, "Is this your son who you say was born blind? Then how does he now see?"

²⁰His parents answered, "We know that this is our son and that he was born blind. ²¹But we don't know how he can now see. We don't know who opened his eyes. Ask him. He is old enough to speak for himself." ²²His parents said this because they were afraid of the Jews, who had already decided that anyone who said Jesus was the Christ*d* would be put out of the synagogue.*d* ²³That is why his parents said, "He is old enough. Ask him."

²⁴So for the second time, they called the man who had been blind. They said, "You should give God the glory by telling the truth. We know that this man is a sinner."

²⁵He answered, "I don't know if he is a sinner. One thing I do know: I was blind, and now I see."

²⁶They asked, "What did he do to you? How did he make you see again?"

²⁷He answered, "I already told you, and you didn't listen. Why do you want to hear it again? Do you want to become his followers, too?"

²⁸Then they insulted him and said, "You are his follower, but we are followers of Moses. ²⁹We know that God spoke to Moses, but we don't even know where this man comes from."

³⁰The man answered, "This is a very strange thing. You don't know where he comes from, and yet he opened my eyes. ³¹We all know that God does not listen to sinners, but he listens to anyone who worships and obeys him. ³²Nobody has ever heard of anyone giving sight to a man born blind. *³³If this man were not from God, he could do nothing.*"

³⁴They answered, "You were born full of sin! Are you trying to teach us?" And they threw him out.

Spiritual Blindness

³⁵When Jesus heard that they had thrown him out, Jesus found him and said, "Do you believe in the Son of Man?"*d*

³⁶He asked, "Who is the Son of Man, sir, so that I can believe in him?"

³⁷Jesus said to him, "You have seen him. The Son of Man is the one talking with you."

³⁸He said, "Lord, I believe!" Then the man worshiped Jesus.

³⁹Jesus said, "I came into this world so that the world could be judged. I came so that the blind*n* would see and so that those who see will become blind."

⁴⁰Some of the Pharisees*d* who were nearby heard Jesus say this and asked, "Are you saying we are blind, too?"

⁴¹Jesus said, "If you were blind, you would not be guilty of sin. But since you keep saying you see, your guilt remains."

The Shepherd and His Sheep

10 Jesus said, "I tell you the truth, the person who does not enter the sheepfold by the door, but climbs in some other way, is a thief and a robber. ²The one who enters by the door is the shepherd of the sheep. ³The one who guards the door opens it for him. And the sheep listen to the voice of the shepherd. He calls his own sheep by name and leads them out. ⁴When he brings all his sheep out, he goes ahead of them, and they follow him because they know his voice. ⁵But they will never follow a stranger. They will run away from him because they don't know his voice." ⁶Jesus told the people this story, but they did not understand what it meant.

> ✳ **SIDELIGHT:** When Jesus described a sheepfold in John 10:1–6, his listeners would have understood immediately, since sheep were the most common animal of that region. Sheepfolds consisted of low buildings to protect the flock during bad weather, and an outdoor pen that had a wall around it. The wall was covered with sharp thorny brush to keep out thieves and predators.

Jesus Is the Good Shepherd

⁷So Jesus said again, "I tell you the truth, I am the door for the sheep. ⁸All the people who came before me were thieves and robbers. The sheep did not listen to them. ⁹I am the door, and the person who enters through me will be saved and

---

blind   Jesus is talking about people who are spiritually blind, not physically blind.

will be able to come in and go out and find pasture. ¹⁰A thief comes to steal and kill and destroy, but I came to give life—life in all its fullness.

¹¹"I am the good shepherd. The good shepherd gives his life for the sheep. ¹²The worker who is paid to keep the sheep is different from the shepherd who owns them. When the worker sees a wolf coming, he runs away and leaves the sheep alone. Then the wolf attacks the sheep and scatters them. ¹³The man runs away because he is only a paid worker and does not really care about the sheep.

¹⁴⁻¹⁵"I am the good shepherd. I know my sheep, as the Father knows me. And my sheep know me, as I know the Father. I give my life for the sheep. ¹⁶I have other sheep that are not in this flock, and I must bring them also. They will listen to my voice, and there will be one flock and one shepherd. ¹⁷The Father loves me because I give my life so that I can take it back again. ¹⁸No one takes it away from me; I give my own life freely. I have the right to give my life, and I have the right to take it back. This is what my Father commanded me to do."

¹⁹Again the Jews did not agree with each other because of these words of Jesus. ²⁰Many of them said, "A demon ᵈ has come into him and made him crazy. Why listen to him?"

²¹But others said, "A man who is crazy with a demon does not say things like this. Can a demon open the eyes of the blind?"

Jesus Is Rejected

²²The time came for the Feastᵈ of Dedication at Jerusalem. It was winter, ²³and Jesus was walking in the Templeᵈ in Solomon's Porch.ᵈ ²⁴The Jews gathered around him and said, "How long will you make us wonder about you? If you are the Christ,ᵈ tell us plainly."

²⁵Jesus answered, "I told you already, but you did not believe. The miraclesᵈ I do in my Father's name show who I am. ²⁶But you don't believe, because you are not my sheep. ²⁷My sheep listen to my voice; I know them, and they follow me. ²⁸I give them eternal life, and they will never die, and no one can steal them out of my hand. ²⁹My Father gave my sheep to me. He is greater than all, and no person can steal my sheep out of my Father's hand. ³⁰The Father and I are one."

GOD'S LOVE

Shepherds and Sheep

Sheep can be incredibly smart. For instance, most sheep can distinguish their shepherd's voice from any other voice. A few exceptional sheep can even be taught how to come when called and how to sit like a dog (well, almost) on command.

On the other hand, sheep can seem completely brainless. It's not unusual to see sheep trying to walk through a barbed wire fence or casually strolling straight off the edge of a cliff. To make matters worse, where one goes, others tend to follow.

The hardest thing about being a shepherd is keeping the sheep where they should be. Certain sheep seem determined to go where they could be harmed. Modern shepherds use a device called a "hobbler" on sheep's hind legs to keep them from moving freely. Before hobblers were invented, shepherds often broke a sheep's leg to keep it from the great danger of wandering away from the flock. It was all part of caring for the sheep.

Jesus seemed to understand sheep well. Read **John 10:1–30** to discover how Jesus saw his followers as sheep and himself as their shepherd.

- How is Jesus' care of his people similar to the care of a shepherd for sheep?
- How are people today—including yourself—like sheep?

CONSIDER . . .

- underlining the things in this passage that the shepherd does and circling the things sheep do. Then turn to Psalm 23, p. 495, and do the same thing.
- reading A Shepherd Looks at Psalm 23 by W. Phillip Keller (Zondervan) to learn more about sheep and their shepherd.

FOR MORE, SEE . . .

- Psalm 23 (p. 495)
- Ezekiel 34:11–31 (p. 790)
- Luke 15:1–7 (p. 1034)

31Again the Jews picked up stones to kill Jesus. 32But he said to them, "I have done many good works from the Father. Which of these good works are you killing me for?"

33The Jews answered, "We are not killing you because of any good work you did, but because you speak against God. You are only a human, but you say you are the same as God!"

34Jesus answered, "It is written in your law that God said, 'I said, you are gods.'n 35This Scripture*d* called those people gods who received God's message, and Scripture is always true. 36So why do you say that I speak against God because I said, 'I am God's Son'? I am the one God chose and sent into the world. 37If I don't do what my Father does, then don't believe me. 38But if I do what my Father does, even though you don't believe in me, believe what I do. Then you will know and understand that the Father is in me and I am in the Father."

39They tried to take Jesus again, but he escaped from them.

40Then he went back across the Jordan River to the place where John had first baptized. Jesus stayed there, 41and many people came to him and said, "John never did a miracle, but everything John said about this man is true." 42And in that place many believed in Jesus.

The Death of Lazarus

11 A man named Lazarus was sick. He lived in the town of Bethany, where Mary and her sister Martha lived. 2Mary was the woman who later put perfume on the Lord and wiped his feet with her hair. Mary's brother was Lazarus, the man who was now sick. 3So Mary and Martha sent someone to tell Jesus, "Lord, the one you love is sick."

4When Jesus heard this, he said, "This sickness will not end in death. It is for the glory of God, to bring glory to the Son of God." 5Jesus loved Martha and her sister and Lazarus. 6But when he heard that Lazarus was sick, he stayed where he was for two more days. 7Then Jesus said to his followers, "Let's go back to Judea."

8The followers said, "But Teacher, the Jews

'I . . . gods.' Quotation from Psalm 82:6.

Sharing Sadness

They went through the church doors, signed the guest registry and made their way to a back pew. Neither of them knew Polly's father, but they had decided to go to his funeral because Polly Brinkman was their classmate.

It wasn't a comfortable situation for Steve Parks or Don Shackelford, but they couldn't begin to imagine how tough it must have been for Polly. As they filed past the open coffin after the service, Polly looked up at them and kind of smiled and cried at the same time.

The next Thursday Polly came back to school and made it a point to talk with Don and Steve before class. "I really want to thank you guys for being at my dad's funeral Saturday. It means a lot to me," Polly said.

"We didn't know what else we could do to help," Don offered.

"That was enough," Polly said. "Just knowing I had friends there made a difference. I didn't feel so alone. Your being around made the service easier to take. It was like you shared some of the hurt."

Jesus understood what it was like to grieve with friends. Read **John 11:1—45** to see how Jesus shared his friends' grief and how Jesus' presence at a funeral made a difference.

■ How did Steve's and Don's actions compare with Jesus' actions?

■ What does Jesus' reactions to Lazarus's death teach us about dealing with sadness?

C O N S I D E R . . .

■ telling a trusted friend about the death of someone who was important to you. Openly express your emotions.

◀ asking your pastor or youth leader to help you and a group of friends devise things you can do when a friend's family member dies.

F O R   M O R E ,   S E E . . .

■ Isaiah 61:1–3 (p. 680)
■ Romans 12:9–15 (p. 1157)

■ Revelation 21:1–4 (p. 1347)

there tried to stone you to death only a short time ago. Now you want to go back there?"

9Jesus answered, "Are there not twelve hours in the day? If anyone walks in the daylight, he will not stumble, because he can see by this world's light. 10But if anyone walks at night, he stumbles because there is no light to help him see."

11After Jesus said this, he added, "Our friend Lazarus has fallen asleep, but I am going there to wake him."

12The followers said, "But Lord, if he is only asleep, he will be all right."

13Jesus meant that Lazarus was dead, but his followers thought he meant Lazarus was really sleeping. 14So then Jesus said plainly, "Lazarus is dead. 15And I am glad for your sakes I was not there so that you may believe. But let's go to him now."

16Then Thomas (the one called Didymus) said to the other followers, "Let us also go so that we can die with him."

Jesus in Bethany

17When Jesus arrived, he learned that Lazarus had already been dead and in the tomb for four days. 18Bethany was about two miles from Jerusalem. 19Many of the Jews had come there to comfort Martha and Mary about their brother.

20When Martha heard that Jesus was coming, she went out to meet him, but Mary stayed home. 21Martha said to Jesus, "Lord, if you had been here, my brother would not have died. 22But I know that even now God will give you anything you ask."

23Jesus said, "Your brother will rise and live again."

24Martha answered, "I know that he will rise and live again in the resurrection[n] on the last day."

25Jesus said to her, "I am the resurrection and the life. Those who believe in me will have life even if they die. 26And everyone who lives and believes in me will never die. Martha, do you believe this?"

27Martha answered, "Yes, Lord. I believe that you are the Christ,[d] the Son of God, the One coming to the world."

Jesus Cries

28After Martha said this, she went back and talked to her sister Mary alone. Martha said, "The Teacher is here and he is asking for you." 29When Mary heard this, she got up quickly and went to Jesus. 30Jesus had not yet come into the town but was still at the place where Martha had met him. 31The Jews were with Mary in the house, comforting her. When they saw her stand and leave quickly, they followed her, thinking she was going to the tomb to cry there.

32But Mary went to the place where Jesus was. When she saw him, she fell at his feet and said, "Lord, if you had been here, my brother would not have died."

33When Jesus saw Mary crying and the Jews who came with her also crying, he was upset and was deeply troubled. 34He asked, "Where did you bury him?"

"Come and see, Lord," they said.

35Jesus cried.

36So the Jews said, "See how much he loved him."

37But some of them said, "If Jesus opened the eyes of the blind man, why couldn't he keep Lazarus from dying?"

Jesus Raises Lazarus

38Again feeling very upset, Jesus came to the tomb. It was a cave with a large stone covering the entrance. 39Jesus said, "Move the stone away."

Martha, the sister of the dead man, said, "But, Lord, it has been four days since he died. There will be a bad smell."

> **SIDELIGHT:** Lazarus had been dead four days before Jesus arrived (John 11:39). That would have made bringing him back to life particularly miraculous to people in Jesus' day. They believed that a soul stayed with a body for three days and then left.

40Then Jesus said to her, "Didn't I tell you that if you believed you would see the glory of God?"

41So they moved the stone away from the entrance. Then Jesus looked up and said, "Father, I thank you that you heard me. 42I know that you always hear me, but I said these things because of the people here around me. I want them to believe that you sent me." 43After Jesus said this, he cried out in a loud voice, "Lazarus, come out!" 44The dead man came out, his hands and feet wrapped with pieces of cloth, and a cloth around his face.

Jesus said to them, "Take the cloth off of him and let him go."

The Plan to Kill Jesus

45Many of the Jews, who had come to visit Mary and saw what Jesus did, believed in him. 46But some of them went to the Pharisees[d] and told them what Jesus had done. 47Then the lead-

---

resurrection   Being raised from the dead to live again.

ing priests and Pharisees called a meeting of the Jewish council. They asked, "What should we do? This man is doing many miracles.*d* 48If we let him continue doing these things, everyone will believe in him. Then the Romans will come and take away our Temple*d* and our nation."

49One of the men there was Caiaphas, the high priest that year. He said, "You people know nothing! 50You don't realize that it is better for one man to die for the people than for the whole nation to be destroyed."

51Caiaphas did not think of this himself. As high priest that year, he was really prophesying*d* that Jesus would die for the Jewish nation 52and for God's scattered children to bring them all together and make them one.

53That day they started planning to kill Jesus. 54So Jesus no longer traveled openly among the Jews. He left there and went to a place near the desert, to a town called Ephraim and stayed there with his followers.

55It was almost time for the Jewish Passover*d* Feast. Many from the country went up to Jerusalem before the Passover to do the special things to make themselves pure. 56The people looked for Jesus and stood in the Temple asking each other,

"Is he coming to the Feast? What do you think?" 57But the leading priests and the Pharisees had given orders that if anyone knew where Jesus was, he must tell them. Then they could arrest him.

Jesus with Friends in Bethany

12 Six days before the Passover*d* Feast, Jesus went to Bethany, where Lazarus lived. (Lazarus is the man Jesus raised from the dead.) 2There they had a dinner for Jesus. Martha served the food, and Lazarus was one of the people eating with Jesus. 3Mary brought in a pint of very expensive perfume made from pure nard.*d* She poured the perfume on Jesus' feet, and then she wiped his feet with her hair. And the sweet smell from the perfume filled the whole house.

4Judas Iscariot, one of Jesus' followers who would later turn against him, was there. Judas said, 5"This perfume was worth three hundred coins.*n* Why wasn't it sold and the money given to the poor?" 6But Judas did not really care about the poor; he said this because he was a thief. He was the one who kept the money box, and he often stole from it.

7Jesus answered, "Leave her alone. It was right

coins One coin, a denarius, was the average pay for one day's work.

SERVICE

Life on the Altar

Chuckie Johnston could be making a lot of money selling drugs. Or he could have a steady job as a bodyguard in his old neighborhood. Instead, he lives and works with former addicts at Boston Outreach, a Christian rehabilitation program.

Chuckie could have been part of a network that destroyed thousands of lives. Instead, he is helping hundreds of people break the bondage of drug abuse.

Gertrude Falk could have been a school administrator in a good school in the United States. She could have lived in a beautiful home and retired with a great pension. Rather, she has spent all of her adult life living in a modest home on a little island in Haiti. Thousands of kids over the years have received an education, medical care, adequate nutrition, and a chance to hear about Jesus Christ because of Gertrude's gifts.

Chuckie and Gertrude have given their lives to serve others. They have no regrets, because they know the secret of service—gratitude. In **John 12:1–11**, we read that Mary also knew the secret of service.

■ In what ways is Mary's service similar to or different from Chuckie's and Gertrude's service to the Lord?

■ If Jesus were in your house today, how might you serve him?

CONSIDER . . . .

■ listing all the things God has done for you and thanking him for those things.

◀ becoming involved in an ongoing act of service to others by joining a volunteer service organization.

FOR MORE, SEE . . . . .

■ Isaiah 1:11–17 (p. 617)

■ Romans 12:1–2 (p. 1157)

■ James 1:26–27 (p. 1294)

for her to save this perfume for today, the day for me to be prepared for burial. ⁸You will always have the poor with you, but you will not always have me."

The Plot Against Lazarus

⁹A large crowd of Jews heard that Jesus was in Bethany. So they went there to see not only Jesus but Lazarus, whom Jesus raised from the dead. ¹⁰So the leading priests made plans to kill Lazarus, too. ¹¹Because of Lazarus many of the Jews were leaving them and believing in Jesus.

Jesus Enters Jerusalem

¹²The next day a great crowd who had come to Jerusalem for the Passover*d* Feast heard that Jesus was coming there. ¹³So they took branches of palm trees and went out to meet Jesus, shouting,
"Praise*n* God!
God bless the One who comes in the name
    of the Lord!
God bless the King of Israel!"   *Psalm 118:25-26*
¹⁴Jesus found a colt and sat on it. This was as the Scripture*d* says,
¹⁵"Don't be afraid, people of Jerusalem!
    Your king is coming,
    sitting on the colt of a donkey."   *Zechariah 9:9*
¹⁶The followers of Jesus did not understand this at first. But after Jesus was raised to glory, they remembered that this had been written about him and that they had done these things to him.

People Tell About Jesus

¹⁷There had been many people with Jesus when he raised Lazarus from the dead and told him to come out of the tomb. Now they were telling others about what Jesus did. ¹⁸Many people went out to meet Jesus, because they had heard about this miracle.*d* ¹⁹So the Pharisees*d* said to each other, "You can see that nothing is going right for us. Look! The whole world is following him."

Jesus Talks About His Death

²⁰There were some Greek people, too, who came to Jerusalem to worship at the Passover*d* Feast. ²¹They went to Philip, who was from Bethsaida in Galilee, and said, "Sir, we would like to see Jesus." ²²Philip told Andrew, and then Andrew and Philip told Jesus.
²³Jesus said to them, "The time has come for the Son of Man*d* to receive his glory. ²⁴I tell you the truth, a grain of wheat must fall to the ground and die to make many seeds. But if it never dies, it remains only a single seed. ²⁵Those who love their lives will lose them, but those who hate their

lives in this world will keep true life forever. ²⁶Whoever serves me must follow me. Then my servant will be with me everywhere I am. My Father will honor anyone who serves me.
²⁷"Now I am very troubled. Should I say, 'Father, save me from this time'? No, I came to this time so I could suffer. ²⁸Father, bring glory to your name!"
Then a voice came from heaven, "I have brought glory to it, and I will do it again."
²⁹The crowd standing there, who heard the voice, said it was thunder.
But others said, "An angel has spoken to him."
³⁰Jesus said, "That voice was for your sake, not mine. ³¹Now is the time for the world to be judged; now the ruler of this world will be thrown down. ³²If I am lifted up from the earth, I will draw all people toward me." ³³Jesus said this to show how he would die.
³⁴The crowd said, "We have heard from the law that the Christ*d* will live forever. So why do you say, 'The Son of Man must be lifted up'? Who is this 'Son of Man'?"
³⁵Then Jesus said, "The light will be with you for a little longer, so walk while you have the light. Then the darkness will not catch you. If you walk in the darkness, you will not know where you are going. ³⁶Believe in the light while you still have it so that you will become children of light." When Jesus had said this, he left and hid himself from them.

Some People Won't Believe in Jesus

³⁷Though Jesus had done many miracles*d* in front of the people, they still did not believe in him. ³⁸This was to bring about what Isaiah the prophet*d* had said:
"Lord, who believed what we told them?
    Who saw the Lord's power in this?"
                                        Isaiah 53:1
³⁹This is why the people could not believe: Isaiah also had said,
⁴⁰"He has blinded their eyes,
    and he has closed their minds.
Otherwise they would see with their eyes
    and understand in their minds
    and come back to me and be healed."
                                        Isaiah 6:10
⁴¹Isaiah said this because he saw Jesus' glory and spoke about him.
⁴²But many believed in Jesus, even many of the leaders. But because of the Pharisees,*d* they did not say they believed in him for fear they would be put out of the synagogue.*d* ⁴³They loved praise from people more than praise from God.
⁴⁴Then Jesus cried out, "Whoever believes in

Praise Literally, "Hosanna," a Hebrew word used at first in praying to God for help, but at this time it was probably a shout of joy used in praising God or his Messiah.

me is really believing in the One who sent me. 45Whoever sees me sees the One who sent me. 46I have come as light into the world so that whoever believes in me would not stay in darkness.

47"Anyone who hears my words and does not obey them, I do not judge, because I did not come to judge the world, but to save the world. 48There is a judge for those who refuse to believe in me and do not accept my words. The word I have taught will be their judge on the last day. 49The things I taught were not from myself. The Father who sent me told me what to say and what to teach. 50And I know that eternal life comes from what the Father commands. So whatever I say is what the Father told me to say."

Jesus Washes His Followers' Feet

13 It was almost time for the Jewish Passover*d* Feast. Jesus knew that it was time for him to leave this world and go back to the Father. He had always loved those who were his own in the world, and he loved them all the way to the end.

2Jesus and his followers were at the evening meal. The devil had already persuaded Judas Is-

cariot, the son of Simon, to turn against Jesus. 3Jesus knew that the Father had given him power over everything and that he had come from God and was going back to God. 4So during the meal Jesus stood up and took off his outer clothing. Taking a towel, he wrapped it around his waist. 5Then he poured water into a bowl and began to wash the followers' feet, drying them with the towel that was wrapped around him.

6Jesus came to Simon Peter, who said to him, "Lord, are you going to wash my feet?"

7Jesus answered, "You don't understand now what I am doing, but you will understand later."

8Peter said, "No, you will never wash my feet."

Jesus answered, "If I don't wash your feet, you are not one of my people."

9Simon Peter answered, "Lord, then wash not only my feet, but wash my hands and my head, too!"

10Jesus said, "After a person has had a bath, his whole body is clean. He needs only to wash his feet. And you men are clean,*d* but not all of you."

11Jesus knew who would turn against him, and that is why he said, "Not all of you are clean."

12When he had finished washing their feet, he

DEATH

Life From the Ashes

Forest fires swept through nearly half of Yellowstone National Park's 2.2 million acres in the summer of 1988. At first, it seemed life in the park could never be the same. The fire seemed like a total disaster.

But it wasn't. Foresters pointed out that lodgepole pine trees had cones on them that would only open under intense heat—almost as though they were designed to respond to a forest fire. Yellowstone's dry climate kept dead wood from decaying quickly, so the ashes from the fire provided nutrients to the ground that could actually mean better growth for years to come. Bluebirds and woodpeckers would benefit from open areas the fire had created. Other animals would flourish with the nearly tenfold increase in plant species that the newly fortified and uncovered earth could offer.

No one at Yellowstone looks forward to forest fires. But it is known that fires, however devastating they seem, don't mean the end of things.

The devastation of death can be sudden and tragic—like the devastation of a forest. But new life can result. Read **John 12:20–36** to discover what Jesus said about death and new growth.

■ How might an ecologist's attitude toward forest fires be like Jesus' attitude toward death?

■ What does the Bible passage say to you about death?

                    C O N S I D E R . . .

■ writing on a sheet of paper about an area of your life in which you need to give something up and then burying the paper in your backyard. A week later, dig it up and evaluate your progress in letting go.

■ walking through a park or forest to notice examples in nature of how death gives way to new growth.

                F O R   M O R E ,   S E E . . .

■ Ecclesiastes 3:1–8 (p. 600)

■ 2 Corinthians 4:16—5:10 (p. 1196)

■ 1 John 1:5–7 (p. 1316)

put on his clothes and sat down again. He asked, "Do you understand what I have just done for you? [13]You call me 'Teacher' and 'Lord,' and you are right, because that is what I am. [14]If I, your Lord and Teacher, have washed your feet, you also should wash each other's feet. [15]I did this as an example so that you should do as I have done for you. [16]I tell you the truth, a servant is not greater than his master. A messenger is not greater than the one who sent him. [17]If you know these things, you will be happy if you do them.

[18]"I am not talking about all of you. I know those I have chosen. But this is to bring about what the Scripture[d] said: 'The man who ate at my table has turned against me.'[n] [19]I am telling you this now before it happens so that when it happens, you will believe that I am he. [20]I tell you the truth, whoever accepts anyone I send also accepts me. And whoever accepts me also accepts the One who sent me."

Jesus Talks About His Death

[21]After Jesus said this, he was very troubled. He said openly, "I tell you the truth, one of you will turn against me."

[22]The followers all looked at each other, because they did not know whom Jesus was talking about. [23]One of the followers sitting[n] next to

'The man ... me.' Quotation from Psalm 41:9.
sitting Literally, "lying." The people of that time ate lying down and leaning on one arm.

SERVICE

The Lowly Star

Jerry Richardson was an all-state running back and linebacker for a high school football team that was considered one of the best in the nation. He was fast. He was remarkably strong. And opposing players hated to see him walk onto the field

Jerry's teammate, Scott Cunningham, on the other hand, was nothing special on the football field. He played Jerry's same position on offense—running back. He made the team only because the head coach found a place for every player who lasted through the rigorous two-a-day practices. Scott boasted few athletic skills, but he did have the courage to pick himself up after each ferocious hit and do it all again.

Since he rarely played in games, Scott never knew the thrill of the crowd chanting his name after a big play. What he heard, most often, was "Jer-ry! Jer-ry! Jer-ry!"

That's why what happened at the yearbook-signing party after Scott and Jerry's senior year was so remarkable. Scott saw Jerry walking toward him with a smile on his face.

Softly Jerry said, "I'd like to sign your yearbook, Scott. Would you sign mine?"

Scott nervously handed over his yearbook. A couple of minutes later, Jerry handed it back, smiled and squeezed Scott's shoulder. Scott never saw Jerry again. But he will always remember what Jerry wrote in his yearbook: "You have to be the greatest influence on me because of the size of your heart. You are the best player I know, from the standpoint of desire and heart. Glad to have you on my side. Luck always, Jerry."

Just as Jerry humbled himself in front of his classmates, Jesus humbled himself and washed his disciples' feet—a task normally reserved for servants, not kings. Read about it in **John 13:1−17**.

■ How was Jerry's note to Scott similar to Jesus' washing the disciple's feet?
■ At first, some of Jesus' disciples were uncomfortable with Jesus washing their feet. How would you feel if someone like Jerry washed your feet or did something equal to that?

C O N S I D E R . . .
■ thinking about someone in your life who could use some encouragement. Write a note to that person, listing the qualities you appreciate about him or her. Sign the note and then secretly slip it into his or her locker or notebook.
■ planning a get-together for your friends and inviting someone who is normally not invited to parties or events.

F O R   M O R E ,   S E E . . .
■ Nehemiah 5:1–13 (p. 431)   ■ Galatians 5:13–15 (p. 1212)
■ Matthew 20:20–28 (p. 944)

Jesus was the follower Jesus loved. [24]Simon Peter motioned to him to ask Jesus whom he was talking about.

[25]That follower leaned closer to Jesus and asked, "Lord, who is it?"

> ### SIDELIGHT: Parents may tell
> kids to wash their hands before dinner, but they probably don't insist on clean feet. In Jesus' day, washing feet was important, since people wore sandals and their feet got sore from walking everywhere. But, more importantly, washing a guest's feet was a sign of hospitality (John 13:1–20). Try it next time you have a party!

[26]Jesus answered, "I will dip this bread into the dish. The man I give it to is the man who will turn against me." So Jesus took a piece of bread, dipped it, and gave it to Judas Iscariot, the son of Simon. [27]As soon as Judas took the bread, Satan entered him. Jesus said to him, "The thing that you will do — do it quickly." [28]No one at the table understood why Jesus said this to Judas. [29]Since he was the one who kept the money box, some of the followers thought Jesus was telling him to buy what was needed for the feast or to give something to the poor.

[30]Judas took the bread Jesus gave him and immediately went out. It was night.

[31]When Judas was gone, Jesus said, "Now the Son of Man[d] receives his glory, and God receives glory through him. [32]If God receives glory through him, then God will give glory to the Son

FRIENDS

The Tough Choice

Melissa Spencer had a secret problem. Two months earlier, she and her boyfriend Matt had had sexual intercourse. It was her first time. Now she was pregnant. And Matt, immature and desperate, was pressuring her to "get rid" of the baby. When Melissa refused, he beat her. Life seemed dark and hopeless to her. She was afraid to tell anyone about her problems, especially her single mom.

But Melissa's best friend, Jessica Bullard, knew, and that secret tormented Jessica. Melissa had made Jessica promise to keep quiet about her secret.

"If you tell anyone," warned Melissa, "I'll hate you forever." But Jessica could barely contain her rage when she saw how Matt was abusing Melissa.

Though she knew she was risking a strong friendship, Jessica decided to get help for Melissa before it was too late. She asked to meet with Melissa's aunt and uncle and, sobbing, told them Melissa's story.

They thanked Jessica for her honesty and courage, then they found Melissa and gently confronted her with the truth. After Melissa's initial shock, she broke down crying, asking them for help.

Melissa was angry with Jessica for violating her trust. But in less than a week, she forgave Jessica and told her how relieved she was that Jessica had told.

Melissa got the help she needed. And she gave birth to a healthy little girl who was adopted by a couple who could never have children.

Just as Jessica risked something important to her for the good of her friend, Jesus encourages those who follow him to love each other with a self-sacrificing love. Read about this kind of love in **John 13:31–35**.

■ How is Jessica's decision to tell Melissa's secret similar to Jesus' decision to go to the cross?

■ What's one way you can love your best friend the way Jesus loved his disciples?

CONSIDER...

■ talking to a friend who has been doing something that concerns you.
◤ making a pact with a friend, promising each other to be open to criticism and direction regarding the choices you each make in life.

FOR MORE, SEE...

■ 1 Samuel 20 (p. 263)
■ Proverbs 17:17 (p. 582)

■ 1 John 4:7–8 (p. 1319)

through himself. And God will give him glory quickly."

33Jesus said, "My children, I will be with you only a little longer. You will look for me, and what I told the Jews, I tell you now: Where I am going you cannot come.

34"I give you a new command: Love each other. You must love each other as I have loved you. 35All people will know that you are my followers if you love each other."

Peter Will Say He Doesn't Know Jesus

36Simon Peter asked Jesus, "Lord, where are you going?"

Jesus answered, "Where I am going you cannot follow now, but you will follow later."

37Peter asked, "Lord, why can't I follow you now? I am ready to die for you!"

38Jesus answered, "Are you ready to die for me? I tell you the truth, before the rooster crows, you will say three times that you don't know me."

Jesus Comforts His Followers

14 Jesus said, "Don't let your hearts be troubled. Trust in God, and trust in me. 2There are many rooms in my Father's house; I would not tell you this if it were not true. I am going there to prepare a place for you. 3After I go and prepare a place for you, I will come back and take you to be with me so that you may be where I am. 4You know the way to the place where I am going."

5Thomas said to Jesus, "Lord, we don't know where you are going. So how can we know the way?"

6Jesus answered, "I am the way, and the truth, and the life. The only way to the Father is through me. 7If you really knew me, you would know my Father, too. But now you do know him, and you have seen him."

8Philip said to him, "Lord, show us the Father. That is all we need."

DOUBT

Riding Out the Storm

Robin Graham is the youngest person in history to sail around the world alone. But success didn't come easily for him. He left on his three-year odyssey as a sixteen-year-old boy thrill-seeker. Adventure was like a drug to him.

His trip changed something deep inside him. A violent storm almost capsized his little sloop, the Dove. In the midst of the torrent, the Dove's mast snapped in two, and Robin barely survived a waterspout—a water-filled tornado.

But that wasn't the worst of it. When his boat entered the doldrums, a windless, currentless part of the ocean near the equator, Robin almost went crazy with despair and doubt. At one point, he completely gave up hope that he would ever make it out of the doldrums, so he splashed kerosene all over his boat and set it on fire. Fortunately, Robin snapped to his senses and doused the fire before it did serious damage.

Three years after his departure, Robin sailed into the Los Angeles harbor to cheering crowds, honking cars, and blasting steam whistles. He had made it. And, more importantly, he had wrestled two great enemies—doubt and despair—and found himself stronger as a result.

Robin Graham is a courageous hero. But he had crippling doubts about himself, just like the "heroes of the faith" who first followed Jesus. Read about them in **John 14:1–14**.

- How were Robin's doubts like the doubts the disciples experienced after Jesus told them he was leaving them?
- What doubts have you had about your life that seem impossible for God to solve?

C O N S I D E R . . .

- writing on paper, "The one thing I doubt the most is. . ." and finishing the sentence. Then ask a friend to pray with you about your doubt.
- writing out one nagging doubt you have about God. Then tape your "doubt" to a specific date on a calendar at least a week from today. Ask God to give you insight into your doubt by that date.

F O R   M O R E ,   S E E . . .

- Jonah (p. 857)
- Matthew 14:22–33 (p. 934)

- James 1:2–8 (p. 1294)

[9]Jesus answered, "I have been with you a long time now. Do you still not know me, Philip? Whoever has seen me has seen the Father. So why do you say, 'Show us the Father'? [10]Don't you believe that I am in the Father and the Father is in me? The words I say to you don't come from me, but the Father lives in me and does his own work. [11]Believe me when I say that I am in the Father and the Father is in me. Or believe because of the miracles[d] I have done. [12]I tell you the truth, whoever believes in me will do the same things that I do. Those who believe will do even greater things than these, because I am going to the Father. [13]And if you ask for anything in my name, I will do it for you so that the Father's glory will be shown through the Son. [14]If you ask me for anything in my name, I will do it.

The Promise of the Holy Spirit

[15]"If you love me, you will obey my commands. [16]I will ask the Father, and he will give you another Helper[n] to be with you forever— [17]the Spirit[d] of truth. The world cannot accept him, because it does not see him or know him. But you know him, because he lives with you and he will be in you.

[18]"I will not leave you all alone like orphans; I will come back to you. [19]In a little while the world will not see me anymore, but you will see me. Because I live, you will live, too. [20]On that day

Helper "Counselor" or "Comforter." Jesus is talking about the Holy Spirit.

PEACE

The True Champion

Four decades after his death, an obscure Scottish sprinter named Eric Liddell became a household name after the Oscar-winning movie Chariots of Fire profiled his heroics in the 1924 Olympic Games. The movie told of Liddell's strong Christian convictions, his competitive spirit that was harnessed by his love for God, and his decision to drop out of the Olympic 100-meter dash because the race was scheduled for Sunday, a day he believed was to be a day of rest for Christians.

Later, Liddell shocked the sports world by competing in and winning the Olympic 400-meter race—an event he had not intended to enter. The actor who played Liddell in the film, Ian Charleson, said, "What I admired about him was his serenity. My whole personality changed during the time I was doing the part. I became very slow and laconic."

After his Olympic victory, Liddell returned to China where he continued his work as a Christian missionary. When war broke out, he and other Westerners were rounded up by Japanese troops and held as "civil internees." During Liddell's two years in the camp, he was cut off from his wife and children. Liddell worked long hours—with little complaint—to organize a sports and recreation program for teenagers. He also helped people in any way he could and tutored students at night.

Toward the end of the war, Liddell died fighting the onslaught of a brain tumor. He died the same way he always ran—fighting for every inch on the outside, but at peace inside.

Annie Buchan, a close friend, was with him when he died. Before slipping into a coma from which he would never recover, Eric told his friend, "Annie, it's complete surrender."

Eric Liddell knew by experience the kind of peace Jesus promises those who follow him. Read about that peace in **John 14:15–29**.
- Have you experienced the kind of peace Eric Liddell knew and Jesus talked about?
- What does the passage tell you about how to know God's peace? What's one thing in your life you feel you need peace about?

CONSIDER . . .
- watching for times you don't feel at peace, then stopping to pray for fifteen seconds.
- planning to take a few hours or even a day or two for a "personal retreat" with God. Spend the time reading the Bible, praying and worshiping.

FOR MORE, SEE . . .
- Psalm 119:162–165 (p. 554)
- Philippians 4:6–9 (p. 1234)
- James 3:13–18 (p. 1297)

you will know that I am in my Father, and that you are in me and I am in you. [21]Those who know my commands and obey them are the ones who love me, and my Father will love those who love me. I will love them and will show myself to them."

[22]Then Judas (not Judas Iscariot) said, "But, Lord, why do you plan to show yourself to us and not to the rest of the world?"

[23]Jesus answered, "If people love me, they will obey my teaching. My Father will love them, and we will come to them and make our home with them. [24]Those who do not love me do not obey my teaching. This teaching that you hear is not really mine; it is from my Father, who sent me.

[25]"I have told you all these things while I am with you. [26]But the Helper will teach you everything and will cause you to remember all that I told you. This Helper is the Holy Spirit whom the Father will send in my name.

[27]"I leave you peace; my peace I give you. I do not give it to you as the world does. So don't let your hearts be troubled or afraid. [28]You heard me say to you, 'I am going, but I am coming back to you.' If you loved me, you should be happy that I am going back to the Father, because he is greater than I am. [29]I have told you this now, before it happens, so that when it happens, you will believe. [30]I will not talk with you much longer, because the ruler of this world is coming. He has no power over me, [31]but the world must know that I love the Father. so I do exactly what the Father told me to do.

"Come now, let us go.

Jesus Is Like a Vine

15 "I am the true vine; my Father is the gardener. [2]He cuts off every branch of mine that does not produce fruit. And he trims and cleans every branch that produces fruit so that it will produce even more fruit. [3]You are already clean[d] because of the words I have spoken to you. [4]Remain in me, and I will remain in you. A branch cannot produce fruit alone but must remain in the vine. In the same way, you cannot produce fruit alone but must remain in me.

[5]"I am the vine, and you are the branches. If any remain in me and I remain in them, they produce much fruit. But without me they can do nothing. [6]If any do not remain in me, they are like a branch that is thrown away and then dies. People pick up dead branches, throw them into the fire, and burn them. [7]If you remain in me and follow my teachings, you can ask anything you want, and it will be given to you. [8]You should produce much fruit and show that you are my followers, which brings glory to my Father. [9]I

loved you as the Father loved me. Now remain in my love. [10]I have obeyed my Father's commands, and I remain in his love. In the same way, if you obey my commands, you will remain in my love. [11]I have told you these things so that you can have the same joy I have and so that your joy will be the fullest possible joy.

---

[12]"This is my command: Love each other as I have loved you. [13]The greatest love a person can show is to die for his friends. [14]You are my friends if you do what I command you. [15]I no longer call you servants, because a servant does not know what his master is doing. But I call you friends, because I have made known to you everything I heard from my Father. [16]You did not choose me; I chose you. And I gave you this work: to go and produce fruit, fruit that will last. Then the Father will give you anything you ask for in my name. [17]This is my command: Love each other.

Jesus Warns His Followers

[18]"If the world hates you, remember that it hated me first. [19]If you belonged to the world, it would love you as it loves its own. But I have chosen you out of the world, so you don't belong to it. That is why the world hates you. [20]Remember what I told you: A servant is not greater than his master. If people did wrong to me, they will do wrong to you, too. And if they obeyed my teaching, they will obey yours, too. [21]They will do all this to you on account of me, because they do not know the One who sent me. [22]If I had not come and spoken to them, they would not be guilty of sin, but now they have no excuse for their sin. [23]Whoever hates me also hates my Father. [24]I did works among them that no one else has ever done. If I had not done these works, they would not be guilty of sin. But now they have seen what I have done, and yet they have hated both me and my Father. [25]But this happened so that what is written in their law would be true: 'They hated me for no reason.'[n]

'**They . . . reason.'** These words could be from Psalm 35:19 or Psalm 69:4.

26"I will send you the Helper[n] from the Father; he is the Spirit of truth who comes from the Father. When he comes, he will tell about me, 27and you also must tell people about me, because you have been with me from the beginning.

16 "I have told you these things to keep you from giving up. 2People will put you out of their synagogues.[d] Yes, the time is coming when those who kill you will think they are offering service to God. 3They will do this because they have not known the Father and they have not known me. 4I have told you these things now

so that when the time comes you will remember that I warned you.

The Work of the Holy Spirit

"I did not tell you these things at the beginning, because I was with you then. 5Now I am going back to the One who sent me. But none of you asks me, 'Where are you going?' 6Your hearts are filled with sadness because I have told you these things. 7But I tell you the truth, it is better for you that I go away. When I go away, I will send the Helper[n] to you. If I do not go away, the Helper

Helper   "Counselor" or "Comforter." Jesus is talking about the Holy Spirit.

SPIRITUAL GROWTH

Cheri's Gift

Michele remembers exactly why she tried to meet Cheri Bruce the first time. They sang together in the Girls Performance Choir their senior year, and Cheri's talent dazzled Michele. Cheri wrote her own songs and could play piano with the kind of intensity and skill Michele envied.

But there was something about Cheri that defied description. She had an honesty about her—a fearless security that made Michele feel safe and challenged at the same time.

One day Michele decided to stay after choir and talk to Cheri. That became the first of many long, intense conversations. The inner strength Michele had always sensed in Cheri was rooted, she found, in a deep faith in Christ.

She seemed to know more about God than anyone Michele had ever met. Michele herself had grown up going to church, and had opinions about God. But Cheri told Michele about a God she had come to know personally.

One day as they rode together in her car, Cheri said, "The Bible says God hates sin, and that's why it's so important for us to recognize our sin and ask God's forgiveness."

"So what?" Michele said. "I don't drink, swear, smoke, or do drugs. I don't have anything to confess."

But Cheri didn't miss a beat. "Michele, all of us sin. I know you've lied to your parents about going out with that older actor guy you met. Don't you realize that lying to your parents is sin in God's eyes?"

Cheri was getting a little too bold, and suddenly Michele felt very uncomfortable. "If I'm a Christian and you're a Christian, why are we so different?" Michele asked.

"The big question is, 'How much do you need God in your life?' " Cheri responded. "Everyone needs God, but not everyone knows they need him."

That conversation in the car has been locked in Michele's memory since that day, because that day she really put her faith in Christ and began spending time in prayer, Bible reading, and church so as to grow closer to Jesus—as Jesus told all Christians to do in **John 15:1–17**.

■ Did Cheri love Michele the way Jesus commanded his followers to love? Why or why not?

■ What kind of "spiritual fruit" do you see ripening in your life?

       C O N S I D E R . . . .

■ inviting someone you respect spiritually to have lunch with you.

■ asking someone who gardens to explain how a plant produces fruit. Then ask God to make you produce more "spiritual fruit" in your life.

     F O R   M O R E ,   S E E . . . .

■ Psalm 1 (p. 482)

■ Matthew 7:24–27 (p. 920)

■ Matthew 13:3–23 (p. 930)

will not come. ⁸When the Helper comes, he will prove to the people of the world the truth about sin, about being right with God, and about judgment. ⁹He will prove to them that sin is not believing in me. ¹⁰He will prove to them that being right with God comes from my going to the Father and not being seen anymore. ¹¹And the Helper will prove to them that judgment happened when the ruler of this world was judged.

¹²"I have many more things to say to you, but they are too much for you now. ¹³But when the Spirit*d* of truth comes, he will lead you into all truth. He will not speak his own words, but he will speak only what he hears, and he will tell you what is to come. ¹⁴The Spirit of truth will bring glory to me, because he will take what I have to say and tell it to you. ¹⁵All that the Father has is mine. That is why I said that the Spirit will take what I have to say and tell it to you.

Sadness Will Become Happiness

¹⁶"After a little while you will not see me, and then after a little while you will see me again."

¹⁷Some of the followers said to each other, "What does Jesus mean when he says, 'After a little while you will not see me, and then after a little while you will see me again'? And what does he mean when he says, 'Because I am going to the Father'?" ¹⁸They also asked, "What does he mean by 'a little while'? We don't understand what he is saying."

¹⁹Jesus saw that the followers wanted to ask

HOLY SPIRIT

The Improbable Disciple

Nicky Cruz was a murderous, uncontrollable gang leader who had killed before and would likely kill again. Without overstating the truth, Cruz was the most unlikely prospect for Christian conversion. He was also one of the first gang members whom David Wilkerson, a rural minister, met on the rough streets of New York City.

Wilkerson left his comfortable surroundings and started a missionary outreach to gang members in New York during the late 1960s. He was idealistic, and sometimes his efforts to gain a foothold for Christ among the vicious gang culture failed miserably.

Time after time, Nicky rejected David's pleas to seek God's forgiveness—once threatening the thin, quaking minister with a knife to his throat. But David replied, "You can cut me to pieces, Nicky, but every piece will still cry out, 'I love you.' "

David invited Nicky to attend a city-wide revival meeting he was organizing for gang members. Impressed by the man's courage, Nicky told David he and his gang would be there.

Nicky did show up at the revival, and David invited him to collect the offering. Nicky and his gang did and then headed for the backstage exit, snickering at the gullible preacher.

But on the way out, Nicky felt a heavy, almost overpowering weight on his shoulders. He stopped. He couldn't escape the fearful truth: The Jesus about whom David had spoken required something of him. Nicky and his gang returned to meet David on stage. At the end of the meeting, Nicky told David, "I've given my heart to God.'

Today Nicky works with tough, inner-city teenagers, helping them turn from drugs and violence and follow Christ. Jesus said one of the Holy Spirit's main responsibilities is to prove the truth to people who are like Nicky Cruz used to be. Read about the Holy Spirit in **John 16:4–15**.

■ According to verse 8, how did the Holy Spirit influence Nicky Cruz's change of heart?

■ When have you felt the Holy Spirit working with you? Explain.

CONSIDER . . .

■ listing ten words that could replace the word "Holy" and ten words that could replace the word "Spirit." Mix and match the words to come up with combinations such as "Perfect Presence" or "Pure Companion."

■ spending five minutes at the end of each day, thinking of ways the Holy Spirit was with you throughout the day.

FOR MORE, SEE . . .

■ Psalm 51:10–13 (p. 511)   ■ Acts 2:1–36 (p. 1098)
■ Luke 11:5–13 (p. 1024)

him about this, so he said to them, "Are you asking each other what I meant when I said, 'After a little while you will not see me, and then after a little while you will see me again'? ²⁰I tell you the truth, you will cry and be sad, but the world will be happy. You will be sad, but your sadness will become joy. ²¹When a woman gives birth to a baby, she has pain, because her time has come. But when her baby is born, she forgets the pain, because she is so happy that a child has been born into the world. ²²It is the same with you. Now you are sad, but I will see you again and you will be happy, and no one will take away your joy. ²³In that day you will not ask me for anything. I tell you the truth, my Father will give you anything you ask for in my name. ²⁴Until now you have not asked for anything in my name. Ask and you will receive, so that your joy will be the fullest possible joy.

Victory over the World

²⁵"I have told you these things, using stories that hide the meaning. But the time will come when I will not use stories like that to tell you things; I will speak to you in plain words about the Father. ²⁶In that day you will ask the Father for things in my name. I mean, I will not need to ask the Father for you. ²⁷The Father himself loves you. He loves you because you loved me and believed that I came from God. ²⁸I came from the Father into the world. Now I am leaving the world and going back to the Father."

²⁹Then the followers of Jesus said, "You are speaking clearly to us now and are not using stories that are hard to understand. ³⁰We can see now that you know all things. You can answer a person's question even before it is asked. This makes us believe you came from God."

³¹Jesus answered, "So now you believe? ³²Listen to me; a time is coming when you will be scattered, each to his own home. That time is now here. You will leave me alone, but I am never really alone, because the Father is with me. ³³"I told you these things so that you can have peace in me. In this world you will have trouble, but be brave! I have defeated the world."

SIDELIGHT: Jesus' prayer in John 17 is the longest prayer in the New Testament. But Nehemiah holds the record for the longest Bible prayer with his prayer of praise, confession, and covenant in Nehemiah 9:5–37 (p. 434).

Jesus Prays for His Followers

17 After Jesus said these things, he looked toward heaven and prayed, "Father, the time has come. Give glory to your Son so that the

---

PRAYER

Do You Have a Prayer?

Does prayer have a place in your life? Read about other teenagers' prayer attitudes and practices as discovered in a Search Institute survey:

■ Eighty-three percent say they often pray for God's help when they have problems.
■ Eighty-three percent say they often pray that God will help other people.
■ Sixty-five percent say they pray at least once a week outside church and other than before meals.
■ Yet only 15 percent say personal prayer is an important influence in their life.
■ No wonder 90 percent of teenagers are interested in learning how to pray. Read **John 17:1–26** to see how Jesus prayed.
■ What might the teenagers in the survey ask Jesus if they talked to him about his prayer?
■ What does Jesus' prayer in this passage reveal about what is most important to him? How are your own priorities reflected in your prayers?

CONSIDER . . .
■ making a prayer list of the people and things you consider most important to pray for. Use it daily, and keep track of answers.
■ forming a prayer group to study prayer and pray together each week.

FOR MORE, SEE . . .
■ 2 Samuel 7:18–29 (p. 280)
■ Ephesians 6:18–19 (p. 1226)   ■ Hebrews 4:14–16 (p. 1279)

Son can give glory to you. ²You gave the Son power over all people so that the Son could give eternal life to all those you gave him. ³And this is eternal life: that people know you, the only true God, and that they know Jesus Christ, the One you sent. ⁴Having finished the work you gave me to do, I brought you glory on earth. ⁵And now, Father, give me glory with you; give me the glory I had with you before the world was made.

⁶"I showed what you are like to those you gave me from the world. They belonged to you, and you gave them to me, and they have obeyed your teaching. ⁷Now they know that everything you gave me comes from you. ⁸I gave them the teachings you gave me, and they accepted them. They knew that I truly came from you, and they believed that you sent me. ⁹I am praying for them. I am not praying for people in the world but for those you gave me, because they are yours. ¹⁰All I have is yours, and all you have is mine. And my glory is shown through them. ¹¹I am coming to you; I will not stay in the world any longer. But they are still in the world. Holy Father, keep them safe by the power of your name, the name you gave me, so that they will be one, just as you and I are one. ¹²While I was with them, I kept them safe by the power of your name, the name you gave me. I protected them, and only one of them, the one worthy of destruction, was lost so that the Scripture^d would come true.

¹³"I am coming to you now. But I pray these things while I am still in the world so that these followers can have all of my joy in them. ¹⁴I have given them your teaching. And the world has hated them, because they don't belong to the world, just as I don't belong to the world. ¹⁵I am not asking you to take them out of the world but to keep them safe from the Evil One. ¹⁶They don't belong to the world, just as I don't belong to the world. ¹⁷Make them ready for your service through your truth; your teaching is truth. ¹⁸I have sent them into the world, just as you sent me into the world. ¹⁹For their sake, I am making myself ready to serve so that they can be ready for their service of the truth.

²⁰"I pray for these followers, but I am also praying for all those who will believe in me because of their teaching. ²¹Father, I pray that they can be one. As you are in me and I am in you, I pray that they can also be one in us. Then the world will believe that you sent me. ²²I have given these people the glory that you gave me so that they can be one, just as you and I are one. ²³I will be in them and you will be in me so that they will be com-

pletely one. Then the world will know that you sent me and that you loved them just as much as you loved me.

²⁴"Father, I want these people that you gave me to be with me where I am. I want them to see my glory, which you gave me because you loved me before the world was made. ²⁵Father, you are the One who is good. The world does not know you, but I know you, and these people know you sent me. ²⁶I showed them what you are like, and I will show them again. Then they will have the same love that you have for me, and I will live in them."

Jesus Is Arrested

18 When Jesus finished praying, he went with his followers across the Kidron Valley. On the other side there was a garden, and Jesus and his followers went into it.

²Judas knew where this place was, because Jesus met there often with his followers. Judas was the one who turned against Jesus. ³So Judas came there with a group of soldiers and some guards from the leading priests and the Pharisees.^{d} They were carrying torches, lanterns, and weapons.

⁴Knowing everything that would happen to him, Jesus went out and asked, "Who is it you are looking for?"

⁵They answered, "Jesus from Nazareth."

"I am he," Jesus said. (Judas, the one who turned against Jesus, was standing there with them.) ⁶When Jesus said, "I am he," they moved back and fell to the ground.

⁷Jesus asked them again, "Who is it you are looking for?"

They said, "Jesus of Nazareth."

⁸"I told you that I am he," Jesus said. "So if you are looking for me, let the others go." ⁹This happened so that the words Jesus said before would come true: "I have not lost any of the ones you gave me."

¹⁰Simon Peter, who had a sword, pulled it out and struck the servant of the high priest, cutting off his right ear. (The servant's name was Malchus.) ¹¹Jesus said to Peter, "Put your sword back. Shouldn't I drink the cup^n the Father gave me?"

Jesus Is Brought Before Annas

¹²Then the soldiers with their commander and the Jewish guards arrested Jesus. They tied him ¹³and led him first to Annas, the father-in-law of Caiaphas, the high priest that year. ¹⁴Caiaphas was the one who told the Jews that it would be better if one man died for all the people.

---

cup Jesus is talking about the painful things that will happen to him. Accepting these things will be very hard, like drinking a cup of something bitter.

Peter Says He Doesn't Know Jesus

[15]Simon Peter and another one of Jesus' followers went along after Jesus. This follower knew the high priest, so he went with Jesus into the high priest's courtyard. [16]But Peter waited outside near the door. The follower who knew the high priest came back outside, spoke to the girl at the door, and brought Peter inside. [17]The girl at the door said to Peter, "Aren't you also one of that man's followers?"

Peter answered, "No, I am not!"

[18]It was cold, so the servants and guards had built a fire and were standing around it, warming themselves. Peter also was standing with them, warming himself.

The High Priest Questions Jesus

[19]The high priest asked Jesus questions about his followers and his teaching. [20]Jesus answered, "I have spoken openly to everyone. I have always

---

FEAR

Letting Go

Brad Parks, Dean Brown, and Eric Unrau grew up together. In the summer they played football, rode trail bikes, and shot BB guns. In the fall they signed up for the same classes and held all-night Monopoly tournaments. In the winter they skied; in the spring they went camping. The years they had spent together made them feel like brothers.

But during their senior year in high school, something changed. Dean and Eric started drinking. They insisted on seeing the raunchiest movies in town. They each talked about how far they had gotten with their girlfriends.

All the while, Brad went along with them. But he felt worse and worse about himself. The changes he saw in Dean and Eric disgusted him. But Brad didn't have many friends in school. He couldn't risk alienating the ones he did have. He was afraid they would reject him. For months, this fear overpowered the sick feeling he had whenever he was with his friends.

One night, Dean called Brad and told him to be ready to leave for the movies in a half-hour.

"What are we going to see?" asked Brad.

"Eric found out how to sneak into a steamy show downtown. It starts in an hour."

Something broke in Brad. He was angry about his wasted weekends, about the terrible things he had said and done with his friends, and about letting God down.

"I'm sorry. I just can't go with you guys tonight," Brad said. "I can't stand the kind of movies we've seen lately. I'm not going to do that kind of stuff with you anymore."

Shocked, Dean tried to convince Brad to come anyway. But Brad wouldn't budge. Furious, Dean hung up the phone.

Dean and Eric abruptly broke off all contact with Brad. They spread terrible rumors about him at school and threatened to beat him up. A five-minute conversation had cost Brad his two closest friends. But it won him something far more valuable: the ability to face his fears and overcome them.

Just as Brad struggled to stand up to his friends, the apostle Peter was too afraid to admit he followed Jesus when he thought his life might be threatened. Read about Peter's struggle in **John 18:1–27**.

■ How were Brad's fears similar to the apostle Peter's fears? How were they different?

■ If you had been in Peter's shoes, what would you have said to the people who asked if you knew Jesus?

C O N S I D E R . . .

■ writing one thing you have been afraid to tell a friend this last month, then thinking of a creative way to face your fear.

■ listing the activities and topics of conversation you have participated in with your friends this last week. Circle things Jesus would never do or say, and mark a star beside things he would do or say.

F O R   M O R E ,   S E E . . .

■ Psalm 118:5–9 (p. 549)

■ Matthew 10:26–32 (p. 925)

■ Acts 2:14–42 (p. 1099)

taught in synagogues*d* and in the Temple,*d* where all the Jews come together. I never said anything in secret. 21So why do you question me? Ask the people who heard my teaching. They know what I said."

22When Jesus said this, one of the guards standing there hit him. The guard said, "Is that the way you answer the high priest?"

> ### SIDELIGHT: The sword Simon
> Peter used in John 18:10–11 was probably similar to a modern machete. Roman soldiers of this time used lightweight, well-balanced swords that were about two feet long for close-range combat. The sword is the most common weapon mentioned in the Bible, appearing more than four hundred times from Genesis to Revelation.

23Jesus answered him, "If I said something wrong, then show what it was. But if what I said is true, why do you hit me?"

24Then Annas sent Jesus, who was still tied, to Caiaphas the high priest.

Peter Says Again He Doesn't Know Jesus

25As Simon Peter was standing and warming himself, they said to him, "Aren't you one of that man's followers?"

Peter said it was not true; he said, "No, I am not."

26One of the servants of the high priest was there. This servant was a relative of the man whose ear Peter had cut off. The servant said, "Didn't I see you with him in the garden?"

27Again Peter said it wasn't true. At once a rooster crowed.

Jesus Is Brought Before Pilate

28Early in the morning they led Jesus from Caiaphas's house to the Roman governor's palace. They would not go inside the palace, because they did not want to make themselves unclean;*n* they wanted to eat the Passover*d* meal. 29So Pilate went outside to them and asked, "What charges do you bring against this man?"

30They answered, "If he were not a criminal, we wouldn't have brought him to you."

31Pilate said to them, "Take him yourselves and judge him by your own law."

"But we are not allowed to put anyone to death," the Jews answered. 32(This happened so that what Jesus said about how he would die would come true.)

33Then Pilate went back inside the palace and called Jesus to him and asked, "Are you the king of the Jews?"

34Jesus said, "Is that your own question, or did others tell you about me?"

35Pilate answered, "I am not Jewish. It was your own people and their leading priests who handed you over to me. What have you done wrong?"

36Jesus answered, "My kingdom does not belong to this world. If it belonged to this world, my servants would fight so that I would not be given over to the Jews. But my kingdom is from another place."

37Pilate said, "So you are a king!"

Jesus answered, "You are the one saying I am a king. This is why I was born and came into the world: to tell people the truth. And everyone who belongs to the truth listens to me."

38Pilate said, "What is truth?" After he said this, he went out to the Jews again and said to them, "I find nothing against this man. 39But it is your custom that I free one prisoner to you at Passover time. Do you want me to free the 'king of the Jews'?"

40They shouted back, "No, not him! Let Barabbas go free!" (Barabbas was a robber.)

19 Then Pilate ordered that Jesus be taken away and whipped. 2The soldiers made a crown from some thorny branches and put it on Jesus' head and put a purple robe around him. 3Then they came to him many times and said, "Hail, King of the Jews!" and hit him in the face.

4Again Pilate came out and said to them, "Look, I am bringing Jesus out to you. I want you to know that I find nothing against him." 5So Jesus came out, wearing the crown of thorns and the purple robe. Pilate said to them, "Here is the man!"

6When the leading priests and the guards saw Jesus, they shouted, "Crucify him! Crucify him!"

But Pilate answered, "Crucify him yourselves, because I find nothing against him."

7The Jews answered, "We have a law that says he should die, because he said he is the Son of God."

8When Pilate heard this, he was even more afraid. 9He went back inside the palace and asked Jesus, "Where do you come from?" But Jesus did not answer him. 10Pilate said, "You refuse to speak to me? Don't you know I have power to set you free and power to have you crucified?"

11Jesus answered, "The only power you have over me is the power given to you by God. The

---

unclean Going into a non-Jewish place would make them unfit to eat the Passover Feast, according to Jewish law.

man who turned me in to you is guilty of a greater sin."

¹²After this, Pilate tried to let Jesus go. But the Jews cried out, "Anyone who makes himself king is against Caesar. If you let this man go, you are no friend of Caesar."

¹³When Pilate heard what they were saying, he brought Jesus out and sat down on the judge's seat at the place called The Stone Pavement. (In the Jewish language[n] the name is Gabbatha.) ¹⁴It was about noon on Preparation[d] Day of Passover[d] week. Pilate said to the Jews, "Here is your king!"

¹⁵They shouted, "Take him away! Take him away! Crucify him!"

Pilate asked them, "Do you want me to crucify your king?"

The leading priests answered, "The only king we have is Caesar."

¹⁶So Pilate handed Jesus over to them to be crucified.

Jesus Is Crucified

The soldiers took charge of Jesus. ¹⁷Carrying his own cross, Jesus went out to a place called The Place of the Skull, which in the Jewish language[n] is called Golgotha. ¹⁸There they crucified Jesus. They also crucified two other men, one on each side, with Jesus in the middle. ¹⁹Pilate wrote a sign and put it on the cross. It read: JESUS OF NAZARETH, THE KING OF THE JEWS. ²⁰The sign was written in the Jewish language, in Latin, and in Greek. Many of the Jews read the sign, because the place where Jesus was crucified was near the city. ²¹The leading Jewish priests said to Pilate, "Don't write, 'The King of the Jews.' But write, 'This man said, "I am the King of the Jews." ' "

²²Pilate answered, "What I have written, I have written."

²³After the soldiers crucified Jesus, they took his clothes and divided them into four parts, with each soldier getting one part. They also took his long shirt, which was all one piece of cloth, woven from top to bottom. ²⁴So the soldiers said to each other, "We should not tear this into parts. Let's throw lots[d] to see who will get it." This happened so that this Scripture would come true:[d]

"They divided my clothes among them,
  and they threw lots[d] for my clothing."

Psalm 22:18

So the soldiers did this.

²⁵Standing near his cross were Jesus' mother, his mother's sister, Mary the wife of Clopas, and Mary Magdalene. ²⁶When Jesus saw his mother and the follower he loved standing nearby, he said to his mother, "Dear woman, here is your son." ²⁷Then he said to the follower, "Here is your mother." From that time on, the follower took her to live in his home.

Jesus Dies

²⁸After this, Jesus knew that everything had been done. So that the Scripture[d] would come true, he said, "I am thirsty."[n] ²⁹There was a jar full of vinegar there, so the soldiers soaked a sponge in it, put the sponge on a branch of a hyssop plant, and lifted it to Jesus' mouth. ³⁰When Jesus tasted the vinegar, he said, "It is finished." Then he bowed his head and died.

³¹This day was Preparation[d] Day, and the next day was a special Sabbath[d] day. Since the Jews did not want the bodies to stay on the cross on the Sabbath day, they asked Pilate to order that the legs of the men be broken[n] and the bodies be taken away. ³²So the soldiers came and broke the legs of the first man on the cross beside Jesus. Then they broke the legs of the man on the other cross beside Jesus. ³³But when the soldiers came to Jesus and saw that he was already dead, they did not break his legs. ³⁴But one of the soldiers stuck his spear into Jesus' side, and at once blood and water came out. ³⁵(The one who saw this happen is the one who told us this, and whatever he says is true. And he knows that he tells the truth, and he tells it so that you might believe.) ³⁶These things happened to make the Scripture come true: "Not one of his bones will be broken."[n] ³⁷And another Scripture says, "They will look at the one they stabbed."[n]

Jesus Is Buried

³⁸Later, Joseph from Arimathea asked Pilate if he could take the body of Jesus. (Joseph was a secret follower of Jesus, because he was afraid of the Jews.) Pilate gave his permission, so Joseph

---

Jewish language   Hebrew or Aramaic, the languages of the Jewish people in the first century.
"I am thirsty."   Read Psalms 22:15; 69:21.
broken   The breaking of their bones would make them die sooner.
"Not one . . . broken."   Quotation from Psalm 34:20. The idea is from Exodus 12:46; Numbers 9:12.
"They . . . stabbed."   Quotation from Zechariah 12:10.

came and took Jesus' body away. ³⁹Nicodemus, who earlier had come to Jesus at night, went with Joseph. He brought about seventy-five pounds of myrrh*ᵈ* and aloes.*ᵃ* ⁴⁰These two men took Jesus' body and wrapped it with the spices in pieces of linen cloth, which is how the Jewish people bury the dead. ⁴¹In the place where Jesus was crucified, there was a garden. In the garden was a new tomb that had never been used before. ⁴²The men laid Jesus in that tomb because it was nearby, and the Jews were preparing to start their Sabbath*ᵈ* day.

Jesus' Tomb Is Empty

20 Early on the first day of the week, Mary Magdalene went to the tomb while it was still dark. When she saw that the large stone had been moved away from the tomb, ²she ran to Simon Peter and the follower whom Jesus loved. Mary said, "They have taken the Lord out of the tomb, and we don't know where they have put him."

³So Peter and the other follower started for the tomb. ⁴They were both running, but the other follower ran faster than Peter and reached the tomb first. ⁵He bent down and looked in and saw the strips of linen cloth lying there, but he did not go in. ⁶Then following him, Simon Peter arrived and went into the tomb and saw the strips of linen lying there. ⁷He also saw the cloth that had been around Jesus' head, which was folded up and laid in a different place from the strips of linen. ⁸Then the other follower, who had reached the tomb first, also went in. He saw and believed. ⁹(They did not yet understand from the Scriptures*ᵈ* that Jesus must rise from the dead.)

DEATH

Good-bye to a Pigtail-Puller

Danny Finnegan was Irish through and through. His red hair clashed with his light blue eyes—eyes that always seemed to laugh with mischief. Danny and his wife were Christine's parents' best friends. And he was the only adult she can remember who made a special effort to make her feel important.

In church on Sundays he would always sit behind Christine, where he could tug on her pigtails without ever taking his eyes off the minister. He would ride with Christine's family in the station wagon after church because he had never learned how to drive. And always, he would lean back and shout over the dull roar created by her brothers and sisters, "Christine, please sing 'Danny Boy' for me. You have such a beautiful voice. Please, Christine, sing for me."

Beaming with pride, she would always oblige. And when she had sung the last note, she always heard Danny's hearty laugh amid her brothers' and sisters' groans.

Danny loved Christine. He was one of those people you're sure will live forever just because a world without Danny wouldn't seem a whole world at all.

But one day Danny's doctor told him he was dying of cancer. Though years had passed since Danny had pulled on Christine's pigtails in church, she was stunned. She wrote Danny a long, loving letter when she heard he wouldn't last much longer.

A month later Danny died. But before he slipped away, he made one last phone call to Christine's parents to tell them about "the most beautiful letter."

It was hard to see someone die who had been so full of life. Joseph and Nicodemus knew what it was like to lose somebody who made life worth living. Read about what they did for Jesus in **John 19:38–42**.

■ How was the letter to Danny Finnegan like Joseph's and Nicodemus's burying Jesus?

■ If you had been there, what would have been your first reaction to Jesus' death? What would you have done for Jesus?

CONSIDER . . . .

■ writing a letter to a friend or relative, telling him or her how your life has been enriched by his or her presence in it.

■ asking someone who has lost a loved one to talk about that loved one.

FOR MORE, SEE . . .

■ Psalm 116 (p. 548)
■ Luke 24:1–8 (p. 1054)

■ Hebrews 9:23–28 (p. 1285)

Jesus Appears to Mary Magdalene

10Then the followers went back home. 11But Mary stood outside the tomb, crying. As she was crying, she bent down and looked inside the tomb. 12She saw two angels dressed in white, sitting where Jesus' body had been, one at the head and one at the feet.

13They asked her, "Woman, why are you crying?"

She answered, "They have taken away my Lord, and I don't know where they have put him." 14When Mary said this, she turned around and saw Jesus standing there, but she did not know it was Jesus.

15Jesus asked her, "Woman, why are you crying? Whom are you looking for?"

Thinking he was the gardener, she said to him, "Did you take him away, sir? Tell me where you put him, and I will get him."

16Jesus said to her, "Mary."

Mary turned toward Jesus and said in the Jewish language, *n* "Rabboni." (This means Teacher.)

17Jesus said to her, "Don't hold on to me, because I have not yet gone up to the Father. But go to my brothers and tell them, 'I am going back to my Father and your Father, to my God and your God.' "

18Mary Magdalene went and said to the followers, "I saw the Lord!" And she told them what Jesus had said to her.

Jesus Appears to His Followers

19When it was evening on the first day of the week, the followers were together. The doors were locked, because they were afraid of the Jews. Then Jesus came and stood right in the middle of them and said, "Peace be with you." 20After he said this, he showed them his hands and his side. The followers were thrilled when they saw the Lord.

21Then Jesus said again, "Peace be with you. As the Father sent me, I now send you." 22After he said this, he breathed on them and said, "Receive the Holy Spirit.*d* 23If you forgive anyone his sins, they are forgiven. If you don't forgive them, they are not forgiven."

Jesus Appears to Thomas

24Thomas (called Didymus), who was one of the twelve, was not with them when Jesus came. 25The other followers kept telling Thomas, "We saw the Lord."

But Thomas said, "I will not believe it until I see the nail marks in his hands and put my finger where the nails were and put my hand into his side."

26A week later the followers were in the house again, and Thomas was with them. The doors were locked, but Jesus came in and stood right in the middle of them. He said, "Peace be with you." 27Then he said to Thomas, "Put your finger here, and look at my hands. Put your hand here in my side. Stop being an unbeliever and believe."

28Thomas said to him, "My Lord and my God!"

29Then Jesus told him, "You believe because you see me. Those who believe without seeing me will be truly happy."

Why John Wrote This Book

30Jesus did many other miracles*d* in the presence of his followers that are not written in this book. 31But these are written so that you may believe that Jesus is the Christ,*d* the Son of God. Then, by believing, you may have life through his name.

Jesus Appears to Seven Followers

21 Later, Jesus showed himself to his followers again—this time at Lake Galilee.*n* This is how he showed himself: 2Some of the followers were together: Simon Peter, Thomas (called Didymus), Nathanael from Cana in Galilee, the two sons of Zebedee, and two other followers. 3Simon Peter said, "I am going out to fish."

The others said, "We will go with you." So they went out and got into the boat. They fished that night but caught nothing.

4Early the next morning Jesus stood on the shore, but the followers did not know it was Jesus. 5Then he said to them, "Friends, did you catch any fish?"

They answered, "No."

6He said, "Throw your net on the right side of the boat, and you will find some." So they did, and they caught so many fish they could not pull the net back into the boat.

7The follower whom Jesus loved said to Peter, "It is the Lord!" When Peter heard him say this, he wrapped his coat around himself. (Peter had taken his clothes off.) Then he jumped into the water. 8The other followers went to shore in the boat, dragging the net full of fish. They were not very far from shore, only about a hundred yards. 9When the followers stepped out of the boat and onto the shore, they saw a fire of hot coals. There were fish on the fire, and there was bread.

10Then Jesus said, "Bring some of the fish you just caught."

11Simon Peter went into the boat and pulled the net to the shore. It was full of big fish, one

Jewish language   Hebrew or Aramaic, the languages of the Jewish people in the first century.
Lake Galilee   Literally, "Sea of Tiberias."

hundred fifty-three in all, but even though there were so many, the net did not tear. [12]Jesus said to them, "Come and eat." None of the followers dared ask him, "Who are you?" because they knew it was the Lord. [13]Jesus came and took the bread and gave it to them, along with the fish.

[14]This was now the third time Jesus showed himself to his followers after he was raised from the dead.

Jesus Talks to Peter

[15]When they finished eating, Jesus said to Simon Peter, "Simon son of John do you love me more than these?"

He answered, "Yes, Lord, you know that I love you."

Jesus said, "Feed my lambs."

[16]Again Jesus said, "Simon son of John do you love me?"

He answered, "Yes, Lord, you know that I love you."

Jesus said, "Take care of my sheep."

[17]A third time he said, "Simon son of John do you love me?"

❋ **SIDELIGHT:** Barbecued fish for breakfast, anyone? That's what Jesus served when he appeared to his disciples (see John 21:4–13). Cooking fish on an open, charcoal fire was common in Jesus' day. He may have served them musht fish (now known as St. Peter's fish), which is one of the most common fish in Lake Galilee.

DOUBT

The Death of Doubt

Tim Simpson and his brothers had fought with their dad through the years. He was a salesman, a community leader, a church leader and a strong disciplinarian. He expected a lot from his four sons; his standards were high and generally inflexible. Going to church wasn't an option; it was expected.

Tim loved his dad, but it had always been a fearful, distant love. He had never really known, deep inside, whether his dad loved him. He saw God the same way—as a fearful, distant ruler he was forced to obey. So he wasn't sure if God loved him either. Until one cold November day.

Tim's dad had asked Tim to go out to breakfast with him—just the two of them. Tim didn't know what to think. What have I done? he wondered.

So Tim and his dad climbed into the family's beat-up station wagon and went to breakfast together. They didn't say much in the car, and Tim could see that his dad had something important to tell him.

After a tense, awkward breakfast, his dad laid down his fork, looked at Tim and said: "I know we haven't always seen eye to eye. And I know I've made life tough on you. But I don't ever want you to forget what I'm about to say to you. I love you as much as a father can love his son. And nothing will ever change that."

The words came with a power and a peace that enveloped Tim. Something changed between him and his dad in that moment. And something changed between Tim and God in that moment. Tim felt, for the first time, the assurance of God's love for him.

Like Tim, the disciples sometimes had a hard time believing God. They doubted many of the promises Jesus had told them. And the chief doubter among them was Thomas. Read about Thomas's doubt in **John 20:19–31**.

■ How did Tim's doubts about his father's love for him compare to Thomas's doubts about Jesus rising from the dead?

■ When have you doubted the love of someone close to you?

C O N S I D E R . . .

■ taking a twenty-minute walk and asking God to demonstrate his love for you in something you see.

■ reaffirming your love to a friend or family member who may be doubting your love.

F O R   M O R E ,   S E E . . .

■ Job 40–41 (p. 477)
■ Luke 24:13–53 (p. 1055)

■ Romans 14:14–23 (p. 1160)

Peter was hurt because Jesus asked him the third time, "Do you love me?" Peter said, "Lord, you know everything; you know that I love you!"

He said to him, "Feed my sheep. [18]I tell you the truth, when you were younger, you tied your own belt and went where you wanted. But when you are old, you will put out your hands and someone else will tie you and take you where you don't want to go." [19](Jesus said this to show how Peter would die to give glory to God.) Then Jesus said to Peter, "Follow me!"

[20]Peter turned and saw that the follower Jesus loved was walking behind them. (This was the follower who had leaned against Jesus at the supper and had said, "Lord, who will turn against you?") [21]When Peter saw him behind them, he asked Jesus, "Lord, what about him?"

[22]Jesus answered, "If I want him to live until I come back, that is not your business. You follow me."

[23]So a story spread among the followers that this one would not die. But Jesus did not say he would not die. He only said, "If I want him to live until I come back, that is not your business."

[24]That follower is the one who is telling these things and who has now written them down. We know that what he says is true.

[25]There are many other things Jesus did. If every one of them were written down, I suppose the whole world would not be big enough for all the books that would be written.

CELEBRATING

A Dark Victory

All year long, Tracy Howell's volleyball coach assured the team they were the best in the state. For most of the year, the state rankings agreed with her. Hilltop High's varsity volleyball team ranked Number One going into the district playoffs. Winning the district championship was the first step on the way to the state championship.

But Hilltop lost its first three playoff matches. One more, and they were out. With each loss, the girls became more depressed. Before their fourth match, the coach couldn't even get them "up" for it. The fans stayed away when they began losing.

Privately, Tracy told her best friend, "I know we're good, but I don't think we can win."

Hilltop's ranking slipped to sixth in state, and the experts labeled them the "dark horse" in the state playoffs. Seeded next to last in the tournament, Hilltop was paired against the best teams in state. They won their first match and surprised even themselves. In the second match, they lost their first game, but won the last two. They went into the state finals with renewed fan support.

In the third match, the games were tight. Hilltop won the first game, 18–16, but lost the second, 17–15. When the last point was scored in the final game, Hilltop had won 19–17.

The fans rushed onto the court and mobbed the Hilltop players. In the middle of the screaming crowd, Tracy felt out of place. She expected to feel all the ecstatic emotions she had dreamed of. But she felt more relief than anything.

That same joyful relief is what Jesus' disciples must have felt when Jesus rose from the dead and showed himself to them. Read about the disciples' experience in **John 21:1–14**.

■ How do Tracy's up-and-down emotions compare with the disciples' emotions after Jesus was crucified and then appeared to them?

■ When have you felt the kind of joy the disciples experienced on the shores of Lake Galilee? Explain.

C O N S I D E R . . .

■ sending a "Celebrate Life" box to a faraway friend. Include confetti, party hats, party favors, snacks, and notes of encouragement to celebrate life.

■ celebrating Christmas—the birth of Jesus—one day during the next two weeks. Plan a party, invite your friends, decorate in Christmas colors and ornaments, watch Christmas movies on video, and close by thanking God for his goodness in sending Christ.

F O R   M O R E ,   S E E . . .

■ Psalm 126 (p. 555)
■ Luke 15:1–7 (p. 1034)
■ James 1:2–4 (p. 1294)

ACTS

Why Read This Book:

- Discover how the Christian church was born (Acts 1—9).
- Recognize that God wants all people to have faith in him (Acts 10—12).
- Be encouraged to tell others about your faith, as the early Christians did (Acts 13—28).

Behind the Scenes:

It looked like everything was over. Jesus was dead—executed by the Romans. After three years with Jesus, the disciples weren't sure what to do next. Maybe go back to fishing and tax-collecting and the other things they did before Jesus came along.

But three days later, Jesus rose from the dead, and the world has never been the same. The book of Acts tells how that event began changing the world.

Written by Luke, Acts picks up where the Gospel of Luke (p. 1000) leaves off. It tells how Jesus went up into heaven, then sent his Holy Spirit fifty days later (Acts 2). The rest of the book tells how the Good News of Jesus Christ spread rapidly throughout the world. Most of the book focuses on two people: Peter and Paul. Peter had been Jesus' disciple, and he quickly became a prominent leader in the early church. Through the book of Acts, we see him struggling to learn—and teach others—what it means to follow Jesus. Peter became a courageous leader who risked his life many times to share his faith.

Unlike Peter, Paul began as an enemy of Christians. But through a miraculous conversion (Acts 9), he became a devout Christian and great church leader. Acts tells about his travels to spread the Good News. And Acts provides the context for many of the topics Paul writes about in his letters (such as 1 Corinthians, p. 1167 and Philippians, p. 1229).

Acts tells about a time Christians were endangered by religious and political authorities. Many churches had to meet in hiding, and Christian leaders were

WHERE THE ACTION WAS

- **Rome** • **ITALY**
  - Paul was taken by sea to Rome as a prisoner (Acts 27–28).
- **MACEDONIA**
  - Thessalonica • **Philippi**
  - • Troas
  - Athens •
  - Corinth
  - **MALTA**
- **ASIA**
  - People caused a riot when Paul preached at Ephesus (Acts 19:23–41).
  - • Lystra
  - Derbe • • Tarsus
  - • Ephesus
  - **CYPRUS**
  - **CRETE**
  - *Mediterranean Sea*
  - Paul and Barnabas were sent on their first missionary journey by the church at Antioch (Acts 13:1–3).
  - Antioch
  - Damascus
  - Sidon •
  - Tyre •
  - Caesarea •
  - Jerusalem •
  - Saul (whose name became Paul) was converted on the road from Jerusalem to Damascus (Acts 9:1–19).
- Paul traveled to Macedonia on his second and third missionary journeys (Acts 16–20).
- The church began in Jerusalem and then spread throughout the Mediterranean region (Acts 1:6–5:42).

WHEN THE ACTION WAS

Jesus was born	The church began soon after Jesus went to heaven	Paul began his missionary work	Fire destroyed Rome	
BC/AD	**25AD**	**50AD**	**75AD**	**100AD**
	Jesus began his ministry	Paul became a Christian	Romans destroyed the Temple in Jerusalem	

regularly thrown in jail—or killed—for what they believed and taught. Yet the early
Christians didn't back down. Their determination can encourage us to live our faith
and tell others about it—even when we are tempted to hide it.

Luke Writes Another Book

1 To Theophilus.
The first book I wrote was about everything
Jesus began to do and teach ²until the day he was
taken up into heaven. Before this, with the help
of the Holy Spirit,ᵈ Jesus told the apostles he had
chosen what they should do. ³After his death, he
showed himself to them and proved in many
ways that he was alive. The apostles saw Jesus
during the forty days after he was raised from the
dead, and he spoke to them about the kingdom of
God. ⁴Once when he was eating with them, he
told them not to leave Jerusalem. He said, "Wait
here to receive the promise from the Father
which I told you about. ⁵John baptized people
with water, but in a few days you will be baptized
with the Holy Spirit."

Jesus Is Taken Up Into Heaven

⁶When the apostlesᵈ were all together, they
asked Jesus, "Lord, are you now going to give the
kingdom back to Israel?"
⁷Jesus said to them, "The Father is the only
One who has the authority to decide dates and
times. These things are not for you to know. ⁸But
when the Holy Spiritᵈ comes to you, you will receive power. You will be my witnesses—in Jerusalem, in all of Judea, in Samaria, and in every
part of the world."
⁹After he said this, as they were watching, he
was lifted up, and a cloud hid him from their
sight. ¹⁰As he was going, they were looking into
the sky. Suddenly, two men wearing white
clothes stood beside them. ¹¹They said, "Men of
Galilee, why are you standing here looking into
the sky? Jesus, whom you saw taken up from you
into heaven, will come back in the same way you
saw him go."

A New Apostle Is Chosen

¹²Then they went back to Jerusalem from the
Mount of Olives.ᵈ (This mountain is about half a
mile from Jerusalem.) ¹³When they entered the
city, they went to the upstairs room where they
were staying. Peter, John, James, Andrew, Philip,
Thomas, Bartholomew, Matthew, James son of
Alphaeus, Simon (known as the Zealotᵈ), and Judas son of James were there. ¹⁴They all continued

praying together with some women, including
Mary the mother of Jesus, and Jesus' brothers.
¹⁵During this time there was a meeting of the
believers (about one hundred twenty of them).
Peter stood up and said, ¹⁶⁻¹⁷"Brothers and sisters,ⁿ in the Scripturesᵈ the Holy Spiritᵈ said
through David something that must happen involving Judas. He was one of our own group and
served together with us. He led those who arrested Jesus." ¹⁸(Judas bought a field with the
money he got for his evil act. But he fell to his
death, his body burst open, and all his intestines
poured out. ¹⁹Everyone in Jerusalem learned
about this so they named this place Akeldama. In
their language Akeldama means "Field of Blood.")
²⁰"In the Book of Psalms," Peter said, "this is written:

'May his place be empty;
leave no one to live in it.'   *Psalm 69:25*

And it is also written:

'Let another man replace him as leader.'

Psalm 109:8

²¹⁻²²"So now a man must become a witness
with us of Jesus' being raised from the dead. He
must be one of the men who were part of our
group during all the time the Lord Jesus was
among us—from the time John was baptizing
people until the day Jesus was taken up from us
to heaven."
²³They put the names of two men before the
group. One was Joseph Barsabbas, who was also
called Justus. The other was Matthias. ²⁴⁻²⁵The
apostles prayed, "Lord, you know the thoughts of
everyone. Show us which one of these two you
have chosen to do this work. Show us who should
be an apostleᵈ in place of Judas, who turned away
and went where he belongs." ²⁶Then they used
lotsᵈ to choose between them, and the lots
showed that Matthias was the one. So he became
an apostle with the other eleven.

The Coming of the Holy Spirit

2 When the day of Pentecostᵈ came, they were
all together in one place. ²Suddenly a noise
like a strong, blowing wind came from heaven
and filled the whole house where they were sitting. ³They saw something like flames of fire that
were separated and stood over each person there.

Brothers and sisters Although the Greek text says "Brothers" here and throughout this book, the words of the speakers were
meant for the entire church, including men and women.

[4]They were all filled with the Holy Spirit,[d] and they began to speak different languages[n] by the power the Holy Spirit was giving them.

> **SIDELIGHT:** Before the birth of the church, Pentecost (Acts 2:1–4) was a major time of celebration among Jews. This festival celebrated the wheat harvest with religious ceremonies, eating, drinking, and music. The festivities surrounding the event may be why skeptics thought the disciples were drunk (Acts 2:13).

---

[5]There were some religious Jews staying in Jerusalem who were from every country in the world. [6]When they heard this noise, a crowd came together. They were all surprised, because each one heard them speaking in his own language. [7]They were completely amazed at this. They said, "Look! Aren't all these people that we hear speaking from Galilee? [8]Then how is it possible that we each hear them in our own languages? We are from different places: [9]Parthia,

languages This can also be translated "tongues."

Media, Elam, Mesopotamia, Judea, Cappadocia, Pontus, Asia, [10]Phrygia, Pamphylia, Egypt, the areas of Libya near Cyrene, Rome [11](both Jews and those who had become Jews), Crete, and Arabia. But we hear them telling in our own languages about the great things God has done!" [12]They were all amazed and confused, asking each other, "What does this mean?"

[13]But others were making fun of them, saying, "They have had too much wine."

Peter Speaks to the People

[14]But Peter stood up with the eleven apostles,[d] and in a loud voice he spoke to the crowd: "My fellow Jews, and all of you who are in Jerusalem, listen to me. Pay attention to what I have to say. [15]These people are not drunk, as you think; it is only nine o'clock in the morning! [16]But Joel the prophet[d] wrote about what is happening here today:

[17]"God says: In the last days
I will pour out my Spirit[d] on all kinds of people.
Your sons and daughters will prophesy.[d]
Your young men will see visions,
and your old men will dream dreams.

HOLY SPIRIT

The Third Rail

The largest subway in the world is in New York City. It is an electric-powered, underground railway system. Every day, the system's 6,200 cars carry 3.5 million people to their destinations. Each year, more than a billion people use the subway.

The subway trains get their power through a "third rail," which runs alongside the 723 miles of subway tracks and supplies 600 volts of electricity to each train.

Without the third rail's power, the whole system would fail, and millions of people would be stranded. At all times, the successful operation of the subway system depends on the power of the third rail. Like the third rail is the subway's source of power, the Holy Spirit is the source of power for Christians. As we connect with the Spirit, we have the power we need to live the Christian life. Read **Acts 2:1–21** to discover how the Holy Spirit first empowered Christians.

■ As the third rail empowers the subway, how does the Holy Spirit empower Christians?

■ According to this passage, what are some evidences of the Holy Spirit's power?

CONSIDER . . .

■ telling people from another culture about Jesus. Depend on the Holy Spirit to help you communicate clearly.

■ finding out about the beginning of your congregation. What similarities do you see between that beginning and the beginning of the church in Acts 2?

FOR MORE, SEE . . .

■ Joel 2:28–29 (p. 838)   ■ 1 Corinthians 12:1–11 (p. 1181)
■ John 14:15–26 (p. 1084)

18At that time I will pour out my Spirit
 also on my male slaves and female slaves,
 and they will prophesy.
19I will show miracles*d*
 in the sky and on the earth:
 blood, fire, and thick smoke.
20The sun will become dark,
 the moon red as blood,
 before the overwhelming and glorious day
  of the Lord will come.
21Then anyone who calls on the Lord
 will be saved.'   *Joel 2:28-32*

22"People of Israel, listen to these words: Jesus from Nazareth was a very special man. God clearly showed this to you by the miracles,*d* wonders, and signs he did through Jesus. You all know this, because it happened right here among you. 23Jesus was given to you, and with the help of those who don't know the law, you put him to death by nailing him to a cross. But this was God's plan which he had made long ago; he knew all this would happen. 24God raised Jesus from the dead and set him free from the pain of death, because death could not hold him. 25For David said this about him:

'I keep the Lord before me always.
 Because he is close by my side,
 I will not be hurt.
26So I am glad, and I rejoice.
 Even my body has hope,
27because you will not leave me in the grave.
 You will not let your Holy One rot.
28You will teach me how to live a holy life.
 Being with you will fill me with joy.'
                                   Psalm 16:8-11

29"Brothers and sisters, I can tell you truly that David, our ancestor, died and was buried. His grave is still here with us today. 30He was a prophet*d* and knew God had promised him that he would make a person from David's family a king just as he was.*n* 31Knowing this before it happened, David talked about the Christ*d* rising from the dead. He said:

'He was not left in the grave.
 His body did not rot.'
32So Jesus is the One whom God raised from the dead. And we are all witnesses to this. 33Jesus was lifted up to heaven and is now at God's right side. The Father has given the Holy Spirit*d* to Jesus as he promised. So Jesus has poured out that Spirit, and this is what you now see and hear. 34David was not the one who was lifted up to heaven, but he said:

'The Lord said to my Lord,
 "Sit by me at my right side,
35 until I put your enemies under your
  control." '*n*   *Psalm 110:1*

36"So, all the people of Israel should know this truly: God has made Jesus — the man you nailed to the cross — both Lord and Christ."

37When the people heard this, they felt guilty and asked Peter and the other apostles, "What shall we do?" 38Peter said to them, "Change your hearts and lives and be baptized, each one of you, in the name of Jesus Christ for the forgiveness of your sins. And you will receive the gift of the Holy Spirit. 39This promise is for you, for your children, and for all who are far away. It is for everyone the Lord our God calls to himself."

40Peter warned them with many other words. He begged them, "Save yourselves from the evil of today's people!" 41Then those people who accepted what Peter said were baptized. About three thousand people were added to the number of believers that day. 42They spent their time learning the apostles' teaching, sharing, breaking bread,*n* and praying together.

The Believers Share

43The apostles*d* were doing many miracles*d* and signs, and everyone felt great respect for God. 44All the believers were together and shared everything. 45They would sell their land and the things they owned and then divide the money and give it to anyone who needed it. 46The believers met together in the Temple*d* every day. They ate together in their homes, happy to share their food with joyful hearts. 47They praised God and were liked by all the people. Every day the Lord added those who were being saved to the group of believers.

Peter Heals a Crippled Man

3 One day Peter and John went to the Temple*d* at three o'clock, the time set each day for the afternoon prayer service. 2There, at the Temple gate called Beautiful Gate, was a man who had been crippled all his life. Every day he was carried to this gate to beg for money from the people going into the Temple. 3The man saw Peter and John going into the Temple and asked them for money. 4Peter and John looked straight at him and said, "Look at us!" 5The man looked at them, *thinking they were going to give him some*

God . . . was   See 2 Samuel 7:13; Psalm 132:11.
until . . . control   Literally, "until I make your enemies a footstool for your feet."
breaking bread   This may mean a meal as in verse 46, or the Lord's Supper, the special meal Jesus told his followers to eat to remember him (Luke 22:14-20).

money. ⁶But Peter said, "I don't have any silver or gold, but I do have something else I can give you. By the power of Jesus Christ from Nazareth, stand up and walk." ⁷Then Peter took the man's right hand and lifted him up. Immediately the man's feet and ankles became strong. ⁸He jumped up, stood on his feet, and began to walk. He went into the Temple with them, walking and jumping and praising God. ⁹⁻¹⁰All the people recognized him as the crippled man who always sat by the Beautiful Gate begging for money. Now they saw this same man walking and praising God, and they were amazed. They wondered how this could happen.

Peter Speaks to the People

¹¹While the man was holding on to Peter and John, all the people were amazed and ran to them at Solomon's Porch.*d* ¹²When Peter saw this, he said to them, "People of Israel, why are you surprised? You are looking at us as if it were our own power or goodness that made this man walk. ¹³The God of Abraham, Isaac, and Jacob, the God of our ancestors, gave glory to Jesus, his servant. But you handed him over to be killed. Pilate decided to let him go free, but you told Pilate you did not want Jesus. ¹⁴You did not want the One who is holy and good but asked Pilate to give you

---

CHURCH

The Place to Belong

Rebecca Fisher yearned to fit in. She wanted people to like her and be her friend. That's why she joined every organization she could at school. She still didn't feel like she fit in, but at least she was busy.

During French club meeting one day, Lee Brungardt invited Rebecca to church. She grimaced at the thought, remembering the church she had attended with her mother years before. Each service had been one long, boring sermon with her mom telling her to be quiet. That was not Rebecca's idea of fun. She "had a commitment already," she lied to Lee.

But Lee persisted. Finally Rebecca agreed to endure one service—just to get him to leave her alone.

She didn't say much to him. When Lee and Rebecca arrived for Sunday school the next Sunday morning, the kids were standing around talking and laughing. Several of them recognized Rebecca and welcomed her. During the Bible study, the teacher called Rebecca by name and asked her opinion. Several kids invited Rebecca and Lee to sit with them during the worship service. And during the sermon, the pastor told interesting stories. Rebecca never felt bored.

After the worship service, all the kids went to Jason Hawley's house for lunch and to complete plans for their mission project. Rebecca helped make posters.

All the way home, Rebecca couldn't stop talking about how much she had liked Lee's church. "It just seems like I fit there, you know?" she commented.

"Yeah, I know." Lee smiled. "So, I guess you'll need a ride next week?"

Rebecca laughed and asked, "What do you think?"

People are attracted to places where people really care and teach God's Word. Read **Acts 2:36–47** to see how the first church attracted people by the way its people lived and worshiped together.

■ How does the church in Acts compare with Lee's church?
■ Which qualities does the Acts church have in common with your church? Which qualities of this church are different from your church's?

CONSIDER . . .
■ befriending visitors who come to your church. Ask them to sit with you or invite them to other church activities.
■ doing a specific job in your church, such as greeting visitors or writing for the newsletter. Become one of the people who makes church more of what God wants it to be.

FOR MORE, SEE . . .

■ Isaiah 2:2–5 (p. 618)   ■ Romans 12 (p. 1157)
■ Acts 4:32–35 (p. 1104)

a murderer[n] instead. ¹⁵And so you killed the One
who gives life, but God raised him from the dead.
We are witnesses to this. ¹⁶It was faith in Jesus
that made this crippled man well. You can see this
man, and you know him. He was made completely well because of trust in Jesus, and you all
saw it happen!

¹⁷"Brothers and sisters, I know you did those
things to Jesus because neither you nor your leaders understood what you were doing. ¹⁸God said
through the prophets[d] that his Christ[d] would suffer and die. And now God has made these things
come true in this way. ¹⁹So you must change your
hearts and lives! Come back to God, and he will
forgive your sins. Then the Lord will send the
time of rest. ²⁰And he will send Jesus, the One he

chose to be the Christ. ²¹But Jesus must stay in
heaven until the time comes when all things will
be made right again. God told about this time long
ago when he spoke through his holy prophets.
²²Moses said, 'The Lord your God will give you a
prophet like me, who is one of your own people.
You must listen to everything he tells you. ²³Any-
one who does not listen to that prophet will die,
cut off from God's people.'[n] ²⁴Samuel, and all the
other prophets who spoke for God after Samuel,
told about this time now. ²⁵You are descendants[d]
of the prophets. You have received the agreement
God made with your ancestors. He said to your
father Abraham, 'Through your descendants[d] all
the nations on the earth will be blessed.'[n] ²⁶God
has raised up his servant Jesus and sent him to

murderer   Barabbas, the man the crowd asked Pilate to set free instead of Jesus (Luke 23:18).
'The Lord . . . people.'   Quotation from Deuteronomy 18:15, 19.
'Through . . . blessed.'   Quotation from Genesis 22:18; 26:4.

GOD'S LOVE

Power to Heal

"Hey, freak! Why don't you join the circus?"

"Aaagh! It's Frankenstein's brother."

Rocky Dennis had heard cruel jeers like this all his life. Rocky had been born with a
disease known as lionitis. This disease multiplied calcium deposits at an abnormal rate
throughout Rocky's skull and progressively disfigured Rocky's face.

But Rocky displayed remarkable friendship, joy, and confidence—even with the people
who were most cruel. He wouldn't accept rejection. When people made fun of his face, he
responded with better jokes. Rocky loved people in a way that made them forget what he
looked like. His comfort with himself put other people at ease.

Mask, the movie about Rocky's life, portrays how Rocky loved a blind and beautiful
teenage girl. Because the girl couldn't see his physical deformity, his inner beauty captured
her heart. Rocky opened up the world to her. He showed her color by placing things in her
hands: Blue was an ice cube; red was a hot rock; the hot rock cooled to pink; white was a
mass of cotton balls.

But not everyone could see Rocky's beauty. After meeting Rocky, the blind
girl's parents blocked further contact with him. The only girl who had ever
really seen Rocky was taken away from him.

Rocky had reason to be frustrated, angry and sad. But he overcame bad
with good. He continued to care for people and was patient with those who
were blinded by his deformity.

Jesus also knew the pain of rejection, but he kept loving people anyway,
as we see in **Acts 3:11—19**.

■ How were Rocky's attitude and actions similar to Jesus' attitude and
actions?

■ According to this passage, what is the Christlike way to respond to
rejection?

C O N S I D E R . . . .

■ listing things you could say to people who reject you.

■ developing a friendship with someone other people reject.

F O R   M O R E ,   S E E . . . .

■ Isaiah 53:1–6 (p. 672)

■ Matthew 5:43–48 (p. 916)

■ 1 Peter 4:12–19 (p. 1307)

you first to bless you by turning each of you away from doing evil."

Peter and John at the Council

4 While Peter and John were speaking to the people, Jewish priests, the captain of the soldiers that guarded the Temple,*d* and Sadducees*d* came up to them. ²They were upset because the two apostles*d* were teaching the people and were preaching that people will rise from the dead through the power of Jesus. ³The Jewish leaders grabbed Peter and John and put them in jail. Since it was already night, they kept them in jail until the next day. ⁴But many of those who had heard Peter and John preach believed the things they said. There were now about five thousand in the group of believers.

⁵The next day the Jewish rulers, the older Jewish leaders, and the teachers of the law met in Jerusalem. ⁶Annas the high priest, Caiaphas, John, and Alexander were there, as well as everyone from the high priest's family. ⁷They made Peter and John stand before them and then asked them,

"By what power or authority did you do this?"

⁸Then Peter, filled with the Holy Spirit,*d* said to them, "Rulers of the people and you older leaders, ⁹are you questioning us about a good thing that was done to a crippled man? Are you asking us who made him well? ¹⁰We want all of you and all the Jewish people to know that this man was made well by the power of Jesus Christ from Nazareth. You crucified him, but God raised him from the dead. This man was crippled, but he is now well and able to stand here before you because of the power of Jesus. ¹¹Jesus is

'the stone *n* that you builders rejected,
which has become the cornerstone.'*d*

Psalm 118:22

¹²Jesus is the only One who can save people. His name is the only power in the world that has been given to save people. We must be saved through him."

¹³The Jewish leaders saw that Peter and John were not afraid to speak, and they understood that these men had no special training or education. So they were amazed. Then they realized

stone   A symbol meaning Jesus.

SHARING FAITH

Responding to Opportunities

"C'mon, Manuel. Don't let me down! Mrs. Reece trusts you," Rick Jantzen pleaded. "She would let you into the classroom to use the lab at night, and you could copy the test key while you're there. She'd never know."

"I just can't. I can't use Mrs. Reece's trust that way," Manuel Salazar said. "And besides, it's wrong to cheat."

"Why can't you do it just this once? No one will know!" Rick persisted.

"I will know and so will Jesus," Manuel answered.

"But Jesus wants you to make good grades, doesn't he?" Rick challenged.

"Yeah, he does. This just isn't the way to make those good grades."

Rick finally quit pressuring Manuel to compromise his faith. In fact, over time Rick even started asking Manuel questions about "this Jesus who runs your life."

Caught in a tough situation, Manuel shared his faith by showing how it influenced his actions. Read how Peter and John took advantage of an opportunity to talk about Jesus in **Acts 4:1–13**.

■ What obstacles did Manuel and Peter have to overcome to talk about their faith?

■ What basic facts about Jesus did Peter consider essential in discussing his faith?

CONSIDER . . . .

■ writing down ways you could share your faith with a non-Christian. Use one of these ways with someone this week.

■ enlisting a friend to role-play faith-sharing situations. Role-play talking to people who are skeptical, open, rebellious or interested.

FOR MORE, SEE . . .

■ Daniel 1:3–16 (p. 807)   ■ Colossians 4:5–6 (p. 1243)
■ Matthew 10:16–20 (p. 924)

that Peter and John had been with Jesus. ¹⁴Because they saw the healed man standing there beside the two apostles, they could say nothing against them. ¹⁵After the Jewish leaders ordered them to leave the meeting, they began to talk to each other. ¹⁶They said, "What shall we do with these men? Everyone in Jerusalem knows they have done a great miracle,ᵈ and we cannot say it is not true. ¹⁷But to keep it from spreading among the people, we must warn them not to talk to people anymore using that name."

¹⁸So they called Peter and John in again and told them not to speak or to teach at all in the name of Jesus. ¹⁹But Peter and John answered them, "You decide what God would want. Should we obey you or God? ²⁰We cannot keep quiet. We must speak about what we have seen and heard." ²¹The Jewish leaders warned the apostles again and let them go free. They could not find a way to punish them, because all the people were praising God for what had been done. ²²The man who received the miracle of healing was more than forty years old.

SIDELIGHT: The council before which Peter appeared in Acts 4:1–22 was the Sanhedrin, the Jewish equivalent of the Supreme Court. It was likely composed of Jerusalem's religious and political leaders. Its main job was to protect Jewish life, custom, and law.

The Believers Pray

²³After Peter and John left the meeting of Jewish leaders, they went to their own group and told them everything the leading priests and the older Jewish leaders had said to them. ²⁴When the believers heard this, they prayed to God together, "Lord, you are the One who made the sky, the earth, the sea, and everything in them. ²⁵By the Holy Spirit,ᵈ through our father David your servant, you said:

'Why are the nations so angry?
    Why are the people making useless plans?
²⁶The kings of the earth prepare to fight,
    and their leaders make plans together
    against the Lord
        and his Christ.'ᵈ   *Psalm 2:1-2*

²⁷These things really happened when Herod, Pontius Pilate, those who are not Jews, and the Jewish people all came together against Jesus here in Jerusalem. Jesus is your holy servant, the One you made to be the Christ. ²⁸These people made your plan happen because of your power and your will. ²⁹And now, Lord, listen to their threats. Lord, help us, your servants, to speak your word with-

out fear. ³⁰Help us to be brave by showing us your power to heal. Give proofs and make miraclesᵈ happen by the power of Jesus, your holy servant."

³¹After they had prayed, the place where they were meeting was shaken. They were all filled with the Holy Spirit,ᵈ and they spoke God's word without fear.

The Believers Share

³²The group of believers were united in their hearts and spirit. All those in the group acted as though their private property belonged to everyone in the group. In fact, they shared everything. ³³With great power the apostlesᵈ were telling people that the Lord Jesus was truly raised from the dead. And God blessed all the believers very much. ³⁴No one in the group needed anything. From time to time those who owned fields or houses sold them, brought the money, ³⁵and gave it to the apostles. Then the money was given to anyone who needed it.

³⁶One of the believers was named Joseph, a Levite born in Cyprus. The apostles called him Barnabas (which means "one who encourages"). ³⁷Joseph owned a field, sold it, brought the money, and gave it to the apostles.

Ananias and Sapphira Die

5 But a man named Ananias and his wife Sapphira sold some land. ²He kept back part of the money for himself; his wife knew about this and agreed to it. But he brought the rest of the money and gave it to the apostles.ᵈ ³Peter said, "Ananias, why did you let Satan rule your thoughts to lie to the Holy Spiritᵈ and to keep for yourself part of the money you received for the land? ⁴Before you sold the land, it belonged to you. And even after you sold it, you could have used the money any way you wanted. Why did you think of doing this? You lied to God, not to us!" ⁵⁻⁶When Ananias heard this, he fell down and died. Some young men came in, wrapped up his body, carried it out, and buried it. And everyone who heard about this was filled with fear.

⁷About three hours later his wife came in, but she did not know what had happened. ⁸Peter said to her, "Tell me, was the money you got for your field this much?"

Sapphira answered, "Yes, that was the price."

⁹Peter said to her, "Why did you and your husband agree to test the Spirit of the Lord? Look! The men who buried your husband are at the door, and they will carry you out." ¹⁰At that moment Sapphira fell down by his feet and died. When the young men came in and saw that she was dead, they carried her out and buried her beside her husband. ¹¹The whole church and all the others who heard about these things were filled with fear.

The Apostles Heal Many

[12]The apostles[d] did many signs and miracles[d] among the people. And they would all meet together on Solomon's Porch.[d] [13]None of the others dared to join them but all the people respected them. [14]More and more men and women believed in the Lord and were added to the group of believers. [15]The people placed their sick on beds and mats in the streets, hoping that when Peter passed by at least his shadow might fall on them. [16]Crowds came from all the towns around Jerusalem, bringing their sick and those who were bothered by evil spirits, and all of them were healed.

Leaders Try to Stop the Apostles

[17]The high priest and all his friends (a group called the Sadducees[d]) became very jealous. [18]They took the apostles[d] and put them in jail. [19]But during the night, an angel of the Lord opened the doors of the jail and led the apostles outside. The angel said, [20]"Go stand in the Tem-

---

PRIORITIES

Who's the Boss?

Richard Wurmbrand fidgeted in his chair as he listened to Gheorghe Gheorghiu-Dej, the Communist Party boss, deliver his speech. Gheorghe promised the post-World War II clergy of Romania that his government would pay the clergy from tax revenues if communism and Christianity would work together.

Most of the audience cheered, and a leader promised that the clergy would cooperate with the state.

But Richard didn't cheer. He had already been imprisoned and beaten several times for his faith. He knew speaking out could again cost him his freedom.

Richard's wife, Sabrina, sat beside him. "Go and wash this shame from the face of Christ!" she demanded.

Richard pleaded that he would probably be taken away if he spoke out against the communists.

"I don't need a coward," Sabrina replied.

Gathering his courage, Richard asked permission to speak and was welcomed forward by the organizers, who apparently anticipated a unity speech. Instead, Richard began by saying it was the duty of pastors to glorify God, not earthly powers. He encouraged the clergy to support the eternal kingdom of God, not the fleeting powers of Romania.

As he continued, someone suddenly began to clap. And another person also clapped. Soon, the clapping erupted into waves of applause.

"Stop! Your right to speak has been withdrawn," ordered the Minister of Cults ("cults" included religious bodies of all kinds in Romania).

"My right to speak comes from God," Richard declared. He kept speaking until his microphone was disconnected.

Soon after, Richard was imprisoned. The Romanian communists instituted their state religion and the Ministry of Cults ran the church.

Like Richard, the apostles recognized the priority of obeying God and speaking out for him. Read **Acts 5:17–32** to see how they spoke out for Jesus even when threatened by imprisonment.

■ Based on the story and the Bible passage, what were the top priorities for Richard Wurmbrand and the apostles?

■ When have you faced opposition for your faith? How was that experience like and unlike the scripture passage?

C O N S I D E R . . .

■ making a poster of Acts 5:29 and writing around the border five priorities you believe God wants you to follow. Then make a weekly schedule that reflects those priorities.

■ talking with a friend about times you have had to do something unpopular to make your faith your top priority.

F O R   M O R E ,   S E E . . .

■ Psalm 119:17–24 (p. 550)

■ 2 Corinthians 11:23–29 (p. 1202)

■ Matthew 10:32–35 (p. 925)

pled and tell the people everything about this new life." 21When the apostles heard this, they obeyed and went into the Temple early in the morning and continued teaching.

When the high priest and his friends arrived, they called a meeting of the Jewish leaders and all the important older Jewish men. They sent some men to the jail to bring the apostles to them. 22But, upon arriving, the officers could not find the apostles. So they went back and reported to the Jewish leaders. 23They said, "The jail was closed and locked, and the guards were standing at the doors. But when we opened the doors, the jail was empty!" 24Hearing this, the captain of the Temple guards and the leading priests were confused and wondered what was happening.

25Then someone came and told them, "Listen! The men you put in jail are standing in the Temple teaching the people." 26Then the captain and his men went out and brought the apostles back. But the soldiers did not use force, because they were afraid the people would stone them to death.

27The soldiers brought the apostles to the meeting and made them stand before the Jewish leaders. The high priest questioned them, 28saying, "We gave you strict orders not to continue teaching in that name. But look, you have filled Jerusalem with your teaching and are trying to make us responsible for this man's death."

29Peter and the other apostles answered, "We must obey God, not human authority! 30You killed Jesus by hanging him on a cross. But God, the God of our ancestors, raised Jesus up from the dead! 31Jesus is the One whom God raised to be on his right side, as Leader and Savior. Through him, all Jewish people could change their hearts and lives and have their sins forgiven. 32We saw all these things happen. The Holy Spirit,d whom God has given to all who obey him, also proves these things are true."

33When the Jewish leaders heard this, they became angry and wanted to kill them. 34But a Phariseed named Gamaliel stood up in the meeting. He was a teacher of the law, and all the people respected him. He ordered the apostles to leave the meeting for a little while. 35Then he said, "People of Israel, be careful what you are planning to do to these men. 36Remember when Theudas appeared? He said he was a great man, and about four hundred men joined him. But he was killed, and all his followers were scattered; they were able to do nothing. 37Later, a man named Judas came from Galilee at the time of the registration.n He also led a group of followers and was

killed, and all his followers were scattered. 38And so now I tell you: Stay away from these men, and leave them alone. If their plan comes from human authority, it will fail. 39But if it is from God, you will not be able to stop them. You might even be fighting against God himself!"

The Jewish leaders agreed with what Gamaliel said. 40They called the apostles in, beat them, and told them not to speak in the name of Jesus again. Then they let them go free. 41The apostles left the meeting full of joy because they were given the honor of suffering disgrace for Jesus. 42Every day in the Temple and in people's homes they continued teaching the people and telling the Good News — that Jesus is the Christ.d

---

SIDELIGHT: Relationships between Jews and non-Jewish people were strained in Bible times. This prejudice shows up in Acts 6:1 where Greek (non-Jewish) Christians complained that their widows weren't receiving a fair share of the church's distributions. The book of Acts is filled with other stories that highlight the tensions between Jewish and non-Jewish Christians.

Seven Leaders Are Chosen

6 The number of followers was growing. But during this same time, the Greek-speaking followers had an argument with the other Jewish followers. The Greek-speaking widows were not getting their share of the food that was given out every day. 2The twelve apostlesd called the whole group of followers together and said, "It is not right for us to stop our work of teaching God's word in order to serve tables. 3So, brothers and sisters, choose seven of your own men who are good, full of the Spiritd and full of wisdom. We will put them in charge of this work. 4Then we can continue to pray and to teach the word of God."

5The whole group liked the idea, so they chose these seven men: Stephen (a man with great faith and full of the Holy Spirit), Philip,n Procorus, Nicanor, Timon, Parmenas, and Nicolas (a man from Antioch who had become a Jew). 6Then they put these men before the apostles, who prayed and laid their handsn on them.

7The word of God was continuing to spread. The group of followers in Jerusalem increased, and a great number of the Jewish priests believed and obeyed.

---

registration Census. A counting of all the people and the things they own.
Philip Not the apostle named Philip.
laid their hands The laying on of hands had many purposes, including the giving of a blessing, power, or authority.

Stephen Is Accused

[8]Stephen was richly blessed by God who gave him the power to do great miracles[d] and signs among the people. [9]But some Jewish people were against him. They belonged to the synagogue[d] of Free Men[n] (as it was called), which included Jewish people from Cyrene, Alexandria, Cilicia, and Asia. They all came and argued with Stephen.

[10]But the Spirit[d] was helping him to speak with wisdom, and his words were so strong that they could not argue with him. [11]So they secretly urged some men to say, "We heard Stephen speak against Moses and against God."

[12]This upset the people, the older Jewish leaders, and the teachers of the law. They came and grabbed Stephen and brought him to a meeting of the Jewish leaders. [13]They brought in some people to tell lies about Stephen, saying, "This man is always speaking against this holy place and the law of Moses. [14]We heard him say that Jesus from Nazareth will destroy this place and that Jesus will change the customs Moses gave us." [15]All the people in the meeting were watching Stephen closely and saw that his face looked like the face of an angel.

Stephen's Speech

7 The high priest said to Stephen, "Are these things true?"

[2]Stephen answered, "Brothers and fathers, lis-

Free Men Jewish people who had been slaves or whose fathers had been slaves, but were now free.

Rumors

"Shhhhh! There she is."

The girls in the back of the room stopped giggling and whispering when Zoe Ketner arrived at her first-period world history class on Monday morning.

"What's going on?" Zoe asked uncomfortably as she sat next to her best friend, Marlene Riddle.

Marlene shot a dirty look at the girls in the back of the room: "Someone is saying you're 'easy,' " she said. "There's a note in the guys' bathroom that says 'Zoe's fine, so get in line.' "

Zoe couldn't believe it. She felt like someone had just kicked her in the chest.

Just then, Mark Warren leaned across the aisle and asked, "Hey, Zoe, can I be next in line?"

Zoe burst into tears and ran from the room. Her mind raced as she stumbled through the empty hallway. Where could such a false rumor have come from? Who could say such ugly things?

Then she remembered what Ben Pullman, her ex-boyfriend, had said. After begging her not to break up, he warned that she would be sorry if she did.

"This must be what he meant," Zoe thought as she leaned against a locker and slid down to sit on the floor.

Zoe knew it would take a long time to clear her reputation. But she was determined that, no matter what, it would be cleared.

"Lord," she prayed, "help me be strong." Zoe maintained her high standards in dating, and in time the rumors died down.

Stephen was also a victim of lies and rumors, but he remained faithful to God, as we read in **Acts 6:8–15**.

■ How could Zoe and Stephen be strong in the face of lies and rumors?
■ When has someone told lies about you the way these people did about Stephen? How did you respond?

C O N S I D E R . . .

■ thinking of a tactful way to respond to people who spread rumors. Always talk to the person who is being talked about rather than spread rumors.
■ deciding what you will do to clear your reputation if someone spreads dishonest rumors about you.

F O R   M O R E ,   S E E . . .

■ Leviticus 19:16–17 (p. 116)
■ Matthew 26:57–68 (p. 958)
■ James 3:1–12 (p. 1296)

ten to me. Our glorious God appeared to Abraham, our ancestor, in Mesopotamia before he lived in Haran. [3]God said to Abraham, 'Leave your country and your relatives, and go to the land I will show you.'[n] [4]So Abraham left the country of Chaldea and went to live in Haran. After Abraham's father died, God sent him to this place where you now live. [5]God did not give Abraham any of this land, not even a foot of it. But God promised that he would give this land to him and his descendants,[d] even before Abraham had a child. [6]This is what God said to him: 'Your descendants will be strangers in a land they don't own. The people there will make them slaves and will mistreat them for four hundred years. [7]But I will punish the nation where they are slaves. Then your descendants will leave that land and will worship me in this place.'[n] [8]God made an agreement with Abraham, the sign of which was circumcision.[d] And so when Abraham had his son Isaac, Abraham circumcised him when he was eight days old. Isaac also circumcised his son Jacob, and Jacob did the same for his sons, the twelve ancestors[n] of our people.

[9]"Jacob's sons became jealous of Joseph and sold him to be a slave in Egypt. But God was with him [10]and saved him from all his troubles. The king of Egypt liked Joseph and respected him because of the wisdom God gave him. The king made him governor of Egypt and put him in charge of all the people in his palace.

[11]"Then all the land of Egypt and Canaan became so dry that nothing would grow, and the people suffered very much. Jacob's sons, our ancestors, could not find anything to eat. [12]But when Jacob heard there was grain in Egypt, he sent his sons there. This was their first trip to Egypt. [13]When they went there a second time, Joseph told his brothers who he was, and the king learned about Joseph's family. [14]Then Joseph sent messengers to invite Jacob, his father, to come to Egypt along with all his relatives (seventy-five persons altogether). [15]So Jacob went down to Egypt, where he and his sons died. [16]Later their bodies were moved to Shechem and put in a grave there. (It was the same grave Abraham had bought for a sum of money from the sons of Hamor in Shechem.)

[17]"The promise God made to Abraham was soon to come true, and the number of people in Egypt grew large. [18]Then a new king, who did not know who Joseph was, began to rule Egypt.

[19]This king tricked our people and was cruel to our ancestors, forcing them to leave their babies outside to die. [20]At this time Moses was born, and he was very beautiful. For three months Moses was cared for in his father's house. [21]When they put Moses outside, the king's daughter adopted him and raised him as if he were her own son. [22]The Egyptians taught Moses everything they knew, and he was a powerful man in what he said and did.

[23]"When Moses was about forty years old, he thought it would be good to visit his own people, the people of Israel. [24]Moses saw an Egyptian mistreating an Israelite, so he defended the Israelite and punished the Egyptian by killing him. [25]Moses thought his own people would understand that God was using him to save them, but they did not. [26]The next day when Moses saw two men of Israel fighting, he tried to make peace between them. He said, 'Men, you are brothers. Why are you hurting each other?' [27]The man who was hurting the other pushed Moses away and said, 'Who made you our ruler and judge? [28]Are you going to kill me as you killed the Egyptian yesterday?'[n] [29]When Moses heard him say this, he left Egypt and went to live in the land of Midian where he was a stranger. While Moses lived in Midian, he had two sons.

[30]"Forty years later an angel appeared to Moses in the flames of a burning bush as he was in the desert near Mount Sinai. [31]When Moses saw this, he was amazed and went near to look closer. Moses heard the Lord's voice say, [32]'I am the God of your ancestors, the God of Abraham, Isaac, and Jacob.'[n] Moses began to shake with fear and was afraid to look. [33]The Lord said to him, 'Take off your sandals, because you are standing on holy ground. [34]I have seen the troubles my people have suffered in Egypt. I have heard their cries and have come down to save them. And now, Moses, I am sending you back to Egypt.'[n]

[35]"This Moses was the same man the two men of Israel rejected, saying, 'Who made you a ruler and judge?'[n] Moses is the same man God sent to be a ruler and savior, with the help of the angel that Moses saw in the burning bush. [36]So Moses led the people out of Egypt. He worked miracles[d] and signs in Egypt, at the Red Sea,[d] and then in the desert for forty years. [37]This is the same Moses that said to the people of Israel, 'God will give you a prophet[d] like me, who is one of your own

---

'Leave . . . you.' Quotation from Genesis 12:1.
'Your descendants . . . place.' Quotation from Genesis 15:13-14 and Exodus 3:12.
twelve ancestors Important ancestors of the Jewish people; the leaders of the twelve Jewish tribes.
'Who . . . yesterday?' Quotation from Exodus 2:14.
'I am . . . Jacob.' Quotation from Exodus 3:6.
'Take . . . Egypt.' Quotation from Exodus 3:5-10.
'Who . . . judge?' Quotation from Exodus 2:14.

people.'[n] [33]This is the Moses who was with the gathering of the Israelites in the desert. He was with the angel that spoke to him at Mount Sinai, and he was with our ancestors. He received commands from God that give life, and he gave those commands to us.

[39]"But our ancestors did not want to obey Moses. They rejected him and wanted to go back to Egypt. [40]They said to Aaron, 'Make us gods who will lead us. Moses led us out of Egypt, but we don't know what has happened to him.'[n] [41]So the people made an idol that looked like a calf. Then they brought sacrifices to it and were proud of what they had made with their own hands. [42]But God turned against them and did not try to stop them from worshiping the sun, moon, and stars. This is what is written in the book of the prophets: God says,

'People of Israel, you did not bring me
　　sacrifices and offerings
while you traveled in the desert for forty
　　years.
[43]You have carried with you
　　the tent to worship Molech[d]
and the idols of the star god Rephan that
　　you made to worship.
So I will send you away beyond Babylon.'

Amos 5:25-27

[44]"The Holy Tent[d] where God spoke to our ancestors was with them in the desert. God told Moses how to make this Tent, and he made it like the plan God showed him. [45]Later, Joshua led our ancestors to capture the lands of the other nations. Our people went in, and God forced the other people out. When our people went into this new land, they took with them this same Tent they had received from their ancestors. They kept it until the time of David, [46]who pleased God and asked God to let him build a house for him, the God of Jacob. [47]But Solomon was the one who built the Temple.[d]

[48]"But the Most High does not live in houses that people build with their hands. As the prophet says:
[49]'Heaven is my throne,
　　and the earth is my footstool.
So do you think you can build a house for
　　me? says the Lord.
Do I need a place to rest?
[50]Remember, my hand made all these things!' "

Isaiah 66:1-2

[51]Stephen continued speaking: "You stubborn people! You have not given your hearts to God, nor will you listen to him! You are always against what the Holy Spirit[d] is trying to tell you, just as

your ancestors were. [52]Your ancestors tried to hurt every prophet who ever lived. Those prophets said long ago that the One who is good would come, but your ancestors killed them. And now you have turned against and killed the One who is good. [53]You received the law of Moses, which God gave you through his angels, but you haven't obeyed it."

Stephen Is Killed

[54]When the leaders heard this, they became furious. They were so mad they were grinding their teeth at Stephen. [55]But Stephen was full of the Holy Spirit.[d] He looked up to heaven and saw the glory of God and Jesus standing at God's right side. [56]He said, "Look! I see heaven open and the Son of Man[d] standing at God's right side."

[57]Then they shouted loudly and covered their ears and all ran at Stephen. [58]They took him out of the city and began to throw stones at him to kill him. And those who told lies against Stephen left their coats with a young man named Saul. [59]While they were throwing stones, Stephen prayed, "Lord Jesus, receive my spirit." [60]He fell on his knees and cried in a loud voice, "Lord, do not hold this sin against them." After Stephen said this, he died.

8 Saul agreed that the killing of Stephen was good.

Troubles for the Believers

On that day the church of Jerusalem began to be persecuted,[d] and all the believers, except the apostles,[d] were scattered throughout Judea and Samaria.

[2]And some religious people buried Stephen and cried loudly for him. [3]Saul was also trying to destroy the church, going from house to house, dragging out men and women and putting them in jail. [4]And wherever they were scattered, they told people the Good News.[d]

Philip Preaches in Samaria

[5]Philip[n] went to the city of Samaria and preached about the Christ.[d] [6]When the people there heard Philip and saw the miracles[d] he was doing, they all listened carefully to what he said. [7]Many of these people had evil spirits in them, but Philip made the evil spirits leave. The spirits made a loud noise when they came out. Philip also healed many weak and crippled people there. [8]So the people in that city were very happy.

[9]But there was a man named Simon in that city. Before Philip came there, Simon had practiced magic and amazed all the people of Samaria.

'God . . . people.'　Quotation from Deuteronomy 18:15.
'Make . . . him.'　Quotation from Exodus 32:1.
Philip　Not the apostle named Philip.

He bragged and called himself a great man. ¹⁰All the people — the least important and the most important — paid attention to Simon, saying, "This man has the power of God, called 'the Great Power'!" ¹¹Simon had amazed them with his magic so long that the people became his followers. ¹²But when Philip told them the Good News*d* about the kingdom of God and the power of Jesus Christ, men and women believed Philip and were baptized. ¹³Simon himself believed, and after he was baptized, he stayed very close to Philip. When he saw the miracles and the powerful things Philip did, Simon was amazed.

¹⁴When the apostles*d* who were still in Jerusalem heard that the people of Samaria had accepted the word of God, they sent Peter and John to them. ¹⁵When Peter and John arrived, they prayed that the Samaritan believers might receive the Holy Spirit.*d* ¹⁶These people had been baptized in the name of the Lord Jesus, but the Holy Spirit had not yet come upon any of them. ¹⁷Then, when the two apostles began laying their hands on the people, they received the Holy Spirit.

¹⁸Simon saw that the Spirit was given to people when the apostles laid their hands on them. So he offered the apostles money, ¹⁹saying, "Give me also this power so that anyone on whom I lay my hands will receive the Holy Spirit."

²⁰Peter said to him, "You and your money should both be destroyed, because you thought you could buy God's gift with money. ²¹You cannot share with us in this work since your heart is not right before God. ²²Change your heart! Turn away from this evil thing you have done, and pray to the Lord. Maybe he will forgive you for thinking this. ²³I see that you are full of bitter jealousy and ruled by sin."

²⁴Simon answered, "Both of you pray for me to the Lord so the things you have said will not happen to me."

²⁵After Peter and John told the people what they had seen Jesus do and after they had spoken the message of the Lord, they went back to Jerusalem. On the way, they went through many Samaritan towns and preached the Good News to the people.

ANGER

Rage

Ann, thirteen, appeared to be a model student and a devoted daughter. But one night, Ann brought two guys into her bedroom and called her father to come upstairs. Using a knife and a length of pipe, the three teenagers slashed and bludgeoned him to death. Ann had been psychologically abused by her father.

Alan, fourteen, was the school scapegoat. Gangly and clumsy, with few friends, he was the target of daily harassment and beatings. One morning in late January, Alan headed to school carrying one of his father's high-power rifles and ammunition. When he got there, he opened fire in the hallway, killing the school's principal and wounding two teachers and one student. He thought his actions might win his harsh father's approval.

A group of Jewish leaders, religious and proper, faithfully practiced the regulations of their faith. When Stephen, a Christian disciple, started preaching about Jesus, the Jewish leaders went berserk. They carried Stephen out of the city and hurled stones at him until he was dead.

Read **Acts 7:51–60** to get the full story of how these Jewish leaders let their anger lead to destruction.

■ What caused Ann's, Alan's, and the Jewish leaders' rage?

■ Why was Stephen able to respond to his killers the way he did?

CONSIDER . . .

■ counting to ten before expressing your anger so you won't do something you'll later regret.

✒ *seeking professional help if your anger turns to rage. Protect yourself and others by learning how to handle anger.*

FOR MORE, SEE . . .

■ Deuteronomy 13:6–11 (p. 173)

■ Ephesians 4:26–32 (p. 1224)

■ James 1:19–20 (p. 1294)

Philip Teaches an Ethiopian

26An angel of the Lord said to Philip,ⁿ "Get ready and go south to the road that leads down to Gaza from Jerusalem — the desert road." 27So Philip got ready and went. On the road he saw a man from Ethiopia, a eunuch.ᵈ He was an important officer in the service of Candace, the queen of the Ethiopians; he was responsible for taking care of all her money. He had gone to Jerusalem to worship. 28Now, as he was on his way home, he was sitting in his chariot reading from the Book of Isaiah, the prophet.ᵈ 29The Spiritᵈ said to Philip, "Go to that chariot and stay near it."

30So when Philip ran toward the chariot, he heard the man reading from Isaiah the prophet. Philip asked, "Do you understand what you are reading?"

31He answered, "How can I understand unless someone explains it to me?" Then he invited Philip to climb in and sit with him. 32The portion of Scriptureᵈ he was reading was this:

"He was like a sheep being led to be killed.
He was quiet, as a lamb is quiet while its
wool is being cut;
he never opened his mouth.
33 He was shamed and was treated unfairly.
He died without children to continue his
family.
His life on earth has ended."   *Isaiah 53:7-8*

34The officer said to Philip, "Please tell me, who is the prophet talking about — himself or someone else?" 35Philip began to speak, and starting with this same Scripture, he told the man the Good Newsᵈ about Jesus.

36While they were traveling down the road, they came to some water. The officer said, "Look, here is water. What is stopping me from being

Philip Not the apostle named Philip.

Creative Questions

"Lately I've been wondering if there really is a God," Kevin Morgan said and looked down at his shoes. "I mean, how do I know Christianity isn't just wishful thinking?"

Kevin looked around the room for someone to answer his questions. Everyone was silent.

Finally, Jeremy Coffey spoke up. "I like to hit it from the opposite point of view. I try to prove there isn't a God."

Then everyone started talking at once.

"That leads to even harder questions," said someone in the corner. "How can you explain everything in this world if there isn't a Creator?"

"And why do people get mad at things like murder and child abuse if there isn't a God who shows the difference between right and wrong?"

"Yeah! And what about people's need for religion? Why would they want to worship God if there is no God?"

The questions went on and on. Finally, the kids were silent. Jeremy looked around and smiled. "Believing there is no God takes more faith than realizing there is one," he said. "Thanks for stretching my faith."

There's nothing wrong with sincere questions because they lead to real answers. An Ethiopian asked questions that led to faith in Jesus in **Acts 8:26—40**.

■ How do you think his questions led Kevin to deeper faith? How did the Ethiopian's questions lead him to God's salvation?

■ What questions would you ask about the passage the Ethiopian had read?

C O N S I D E R . . .

■ listing the questions you have about God and searching for answers to those questions.

■ writing down questions as you read the Bible. Ask these questions during Sunday school or youth group.

F O R M O R E , S E E . . .

■ Isaiah 53:7–8 (p. 672)   ■ Hebrews 6: –3 (p. 1280)
■ John 20:24–29 (p. 1094)

baptized?" [37] [n] [38]Then the officer commanded the chariot to stop. Both Philip and the officer went down into the water, and Philip baptized him. [39]When they came up out of the water, the Spirit of the Lord took Philip away; the officer never saw him again. And the officer continued on his way home, full of joy. [40]But Philip appeared in a city called Azotus and preached the Good News in all the towns on the way from Azotus to Caesarea.

> ✺ **SIDELIGHT:** Acts 8:26–40 tells of what is likely the conversion of the first African. He came from an area south of Egypt called Nubia. Philip had traveled about fifty miles from Jerusalem to witness to this man.

Saul Is Converted

9 In Jerusalem Saul was still threatening the followers of the Lord by saying he would kill them. So he went to the high priest [2]and asked him to write letters to the synagogues[d] in the city of Damascus. Then if Saul found any followers of Christ's Way, men or women, he would arrest them and bring them back to Jerusalem.

[3]So Saul headed toward Damascus. As he came near the city, a bright light from heaven suddenly flashed around him. [4]Saul fell to the ground and heard a voice saying to him, "Saul, Saul! Why are you persecuting me?"

[5]Saul said, "Who are you, Lord?"

The voice answered, "I am Jesus, whom you are persecuting. [6]Get up now and go into the city. Someone there will tell you what you must do."

[7]The people traveling with Saul stood there but said nothing. They heard the voice, but they saw

Verse 37   Some late copies of Acts add verse 37: "Philip answered, 'If you believe with all your heart, you can.' The officer said, 'I believe that Jesus Christ is the Son of God.'"

FOLLOWING GOD

Show and Tell

Charles Blondin stretched an eleven-hundred-foot tightrope across Niagara Falls on June 30, 1859. About twenty-five thousand spectators gathered to watch the incredible stunt. Charles stood in front of the crowd and asked, "How many believe I can walk across Niagara Falls?"

"We believe!" the crowd roared. And so Charles walked safely across Niagara Falls, one hundred sixty feet in the air.

Five days later, he asked, "How many believe I can walk across Niagara Falls blindfolded and pushing a wheelbarrow?"

The crowd cheered. And Charles did it again.

Two weeks later, the crowd gathered again. "How many believe I can walk across with a person on my back?" he asked.

The crowd screamed: "Of course! We believe!"

Charles looked straight at a person in the front. "You, sir. Climb on!" The man refused.

There's a big difference between talking about faith and acting on that faith. In **Acts 9:1–20**, Saul and Ananias both learned what it meant to act on their faith.

■ Which was most difficult to act on: Charles's challenge or Jesus' instructions to Saul and Ananias? Why?

■ What did Ananias's actions communicate to Saul?

C O N S I D E R . . .

■ becoming an "Ananias" to a friend who is struggling with his or her faith. Provide encouragement and support as that person searches for what it means to follow God.

▰ writing the story of a time when you have experienced God's love. Then tell a friend your story.

F O R   M O R E ,   S E E . . .

■ Exodus 4:1–17 (p. 62)
■ Acts 22:1–16 (p. 1132)
■ James 2:14–18 (p. 1295)

no one. [8]Saul got up from the ground and opened his eyes, but he could not see. So those with Saul took his hand and led him into Damascus. [9]For three days Saul could not see and did not eat or drink.

[10]There was a follower of Jesus in Damascus named Ananias. The Lord spoke to Ananias in a vision, "Ananias!"

Ananias answered, "Here I am, Lord."

[11]The Lord said to him, "Get up and go to Straight Street. Find the house of Judas,[n] and ask for a man named Saul from the city of Tarsus. He is there now, praying. [12]Saul has seen a vision in which a man named Ananias comes to him and lays his hands on him. Then he is able to see again."

[13]But Ananias answered, "Lord, many people have told me about this man and the terrible things he did to your holy people in Jerusalem. [14]Now he has come here to Damascus, and the leading priests have given him the power to arrest everyone who worships you."

[15]But the Lord said to Ananias, "Go! I have chosen Saul for an important work. He must tell about me to those who are not Jews, to kings, and to the people of Israel. [16]I will show him how much he must suffer for my name."

[17]So Ananias went to the house of Judas. He laid his hands on Saul and said, "Brother Saul, the Lord Jesus sent me. He is the one you saw on the road on your way here. He sent me so that you can see again and be filled with the Holy Spirit."[d] [18]Immediately, something that looked like fish scales fell from Saul's eyes, and he was able to see again! Then Saul got up and was baptized. [19]After he ate some food, his strength returned.

Saul Preaches in Damascus

Saul stayed with the followers of Jesus in Damascus for a few days. [20]Soon he began to preach about Jesus in the synagogues,[d] saying, "Jesus is the Son of God."

[21]All the people who heard him were amazed. They said, "This is the man who was in Jerusalem trying to destroy those who trust in this name! He came here to arrest the followers of Jesus and take them back to the leading priests."

[22]But Saul grew more powerful. His proofs that Jesus is the Christ[d] were so strong that the Jewish people in Damascus could not argue with him.

[23]After many days, some Jewish people made plans to kill Saul. [24]They were watching the city gates day and night, but Saul learned about their plan. [25]One night some followers of Saul helped him leave the city by lowering him in a basket through an opening in the city wall.

Saul Preaches in Jerusalem

[26]When Saul went to Jerusalem, he tried to join the group of followers, but they were all afraid of him. They did not believe he was really a follower. [27]But Barnabas accepted Saul and took him to the apostles.[c] Barnabas explained to them that Saul had seen the Lord on the road and the Lord had spoken to Saul. Then he told them how boldly Saul had preached in the name of Jesus in Damascus.

[28]And so Saul stayed with the followers, going everywhere in Jerusalem, preaching boldly in the name of the Lord. [29]He would often talk and argue with the Jewish people who spoke Greek, but they were trying to kill him. [30]When the followers learned about this, they took Saul to Caesarea and from there sent him to Tarsus.

[31]The church everywhere in Judea, Galilee, and Samaria had a time of peace and became stronger. Respecting the Lord by the way they lived, and being encouraged by the Holy Spirit,[c] the group of believers continued to grow.

Peter Heals Aeneas

[32]As Peter was traveling through all the area, he visited God's people who lived in Lydda. [33]There he met a man named Aeneas, who was paralyzed and had not been able to leave his bed for the past eight years. [34]Peter said to him, "Aeneas, Jesus Christ heals you. Stand up and make your bed." Aeneas stood up immediately. [35]All the people living in Lydda and on the Plain of Sharon saw him and turned to the Lord.

Peter Heals Tabitha

[36]In the city of Joppa there was a follower named Tabitha (whose Greek name was Dorcas). She was always doing good deeds and kind acts. [37]While Peter was in Lydda, Tabitha became sick and died. Her body was washed and put in a room upstairs. [38]Since Lydda is near Joppa and the followers in Joppa heard that Peter was in Lydda, they sent two messengers to Peter. They begged him, "Hurry, please come to us!" [39]So Peter got ready and went with them. When he arrived, they took him to the upstairs room where all the widows stood around Peter, crying. They showed him the shirts and coats Tabitha had made when she was still alive. [40]Peter sent everyone out of the room and kneeled and prayed. Then he turned to the body and said, "Tabitha, stand up." She opened her eyes, and when she saw Peter, she sat up. [41]He gave her his hand and helped her up. Then he called the saints[d] and the widows into the room and showed them that Tabitha was alive. [42]People everywhere in Joppa learned about

Judas   This is not either of the apostles named Judas.

this, and many believed in the Lord. ⁴³Peter stayed in Joppa for many days with a man named Simon who was a tanner.

Peter Teaches Cornelius

10 At Caesarea there was a man named Cornelius, an officer in the Italian group of the Roman army. ²Cornelius was a religious man. He and all the other people who lived in his house worshiped the true God. He gave much of his money to the poor and prayed to God often. ³One afternoon about three o'clock, Cornelius clearly saw a vision. An angel of God came to him and said, "Cornelius!"

⁴Cornelius stared at the angel. He became afraid and said, "What do you want, Lord?"

The angel said, "God has heard your prayers. He has seen that you give to the poor, and he remembers you. ⁵Send some men now to Joppa to bring back a man named Simon who is also called Peter. ⁶He is staying with a man, also named Simon, who is a tanner and has a house beside the sea." ⁷When the angel who spoke to Cornelius left, Cornelius called two of his servants and a soldier, a religious man who worked for him. ⁸Cornelius explained everything to them and sent them to Joppa.

⁹About noon the next day as they came near Joppa, Peter was going up to the roof*ⁿ* to pray. ¹⁰He was hungry and wanted to eat, but while the food was being prepared, he had a vision. ¹¹He saw heaven opened and something coming down that looked like a big sheet being lowered to earth by its four corners. ¹²In it were all kinds of animals, reptiles, and birds. ¹³Then a voice said to Peter, "Get up, Peter; kill and eat."

¹⁴But Peter said, "No, Lord! I have never eaten food that is unholy or unclean."*ᵈ*

¹⁵But the voice said to him again, "God has made these things clean so don't call them 'unholy'!" ¹⁶This happened three times, and at once the sheet was taken back to heaven.

¹⁷While Peter was wondering what this vision meant, the men Cornelius sent had found Simon's house and were standing at the gate. ¹⁸They asked, "Is Simon Peter staying here?"

¹⁹While Peter was still thinking about the vision, the Spirit*ᵈ* said to him, "Listen, three men are looking for you. ²⁰Get up and go downstairs. Go with them without doubting, because I have sent them to you."

²¹So Peter went down to the men and said, "I am the one you are looking for. Why did you come here?"

²²They said, "A holy angel spoke to Cornelius, an army officer and a good man; he worships God. All the Jewish people respect him. The angel told Cornelius to ask you to come to his house so that he can hear what you have to say." ²³So Peter asked the men to come in and spend the night.

The next day Peter got ready and went with them, and some of the followers from Joppa joined him. ²⁴On the following day they came to Caesarea. Cornelius was waiting for them and had called together his relatives and close friends. ²⁵When Peter entered, Cornelius met him, fell at his feet, and worshiped him. ²⁶But Peter helped him up, saying, "Stand up. I too am only a human." ²⁷As he talked with Cornelius, Peter went inside where he saw many people gathered. ²⁸He said, "You people understand that it is against our Jewish law for Jewish people to associate with or visit anyone who is not Jewish. But God has shown me that I should not call any person 'unholy' or 'unclean.' ²⁹That is why I did not argue when I was asked to come here. Now, please tell me why you sent for me."

³⁰Cornelius said, "Four days ago, I was praying in my house at this same time — three o'clock in the afternoon. Suddenly, there was a man standing before me wearing shining clothes. ³¹He said, 'Cornelius, God has heard your prayer and has seen that you give to the poor and remembers you. ³²So send some men to Joppa and ask Simon Peter to come. Peter is staying in the house of a man, also named Simon, who is a tanner and has a house beside the sea.' ³³So I sent for you immediately, and it was very good of you to come. Now we are all here before God to hear everything the Lord has commanded you to tell us."

³⁴Peter began to speak: "I really understand now that to God every person is the same. ³⁵In every country God accepts anyone who worships him and does what is right. ³⁶You know the message that God has sent to the people of Israel is the Good News*ᵈ* that peace has come through Jesus Christ. Jesus is the Lord of all people! ³⁷You know what has happened all over Judea, beginning in Galilee after John*ⁿ* preached to the people about baptism. ³⁸You know about Jesus from Nazareth, that God gave him the Holy Spirit*ᵈ* and power. You know how Jesus went everywhere doing good and healing those who were ruled by the devil, because God was with him. ³⁹We saw what Jesus did in Judea and in Jerusalem, but the Jews in Jerusalem killed him by hanging him on a cross. ⁴⁰Yet, on the third day, God raised Jesus to life and caused him to be seen, ⁴¹not by all the people, but only by the witnesses God had already cho-

---

roof In Bible times houses were built with flat roofs. The roof was used for drying things such as flax and fruit. And it was used as an extra room, as a place for worship, and as a place to sleep in the summer.
John John the Baptist, who preached to people about Christ's coming (Luke 3).

sen. And we are those witnesses who ate and drank with him after he was raised from the dead. ⁴²He told us to preach to the people and to tell them that he is the one whom God chose to be the judge of the living and the dead. ⁴³All the prophets say it is true that all who believe in Jesus will be forgiven of their sins through Jesus' name."

⁴⁴While Peter was still saying this, the Holy Spirit*d* came down on all those who were listening. ⁴⁵The Jewish believers who came with Peter were amazed that the gift of the Holy Spirit had been given even to those who were not Jews. ⁴⁶These Jewish believers heard them speaking in different languages*n* and praising God. Then Peter said, ⁴⁷"Can anyone keep these people from being baptized with water? They have received the Holy Spirit just as we did!" ⁴⁸So Peter ordered that they be baptized in the name of Jesus Christ. Then they asked Peter to stay with them for a few days.

languages This can also be translated "tongues."

Peter Returns to Jerusalem

11 The apostles*d* and the believers in Judea heard that some who were not Jewish had accepted God's teaching too. ²But when Peter came to Jerusalem, some Jewish believers argued with him. ³They said, "You went into the homes of people who are not circumcised*d* and ate with them!"

⁴So Peter explained the whole story to them. ⁵He said, "I was in the city of Joppa, and while I was praying, I had a vision. I saw something that looked like a big sheet being lowered from heaven by its four corners. It came very close to me. ⁶I looked inside it and saw animals, wild beasts, reptiles, and birds. ⁷I heard a voice say to me, 'Get up, Peter. Kill and eat.' ⁸But I said, 'No, Lord! I have never eaten anything that is unholy or unclean.'*d* ⁹But the voice from heaven spoke again, 'God has made these things clean, so don't call them unholy.' ¹⁰This happened three times. Then the whole thing was taken back to heaven.

JUDGING OTHERS

The Color of Hatred

"It's not that blacks are bad," John Metzger says. "There are quite a few, well, not quite a few, but a sizable number of nonwhites who are intelligent."

John is a racist. He believes whites are the "chosen people"—that all nonwhite races should live in their own territories, away from whites. He is also the leader of the Aryan Youth Movement, otherwise known as "skinheads."

John doesn't look like a skinhead. His blond hair is cut conservatively. He has a respectable job and dresses like most guys his age.

But John's racist beliefs are deeply ingrained. His father leads a group of adult racists called the White Aryan Resistance. When other kids were growing up with stories about Goldilocks and the three bears, John listened to stories of hatred and prejudice at his father's knee.

Skinheads in John's Aryan Youth Movement have been linked to such brutalities as beating people to death, terrorizing people of nonwhite origin, and even nailing a former skinhead to a cross. And they have done these things all in the name of preserving their race.

Prejudice has blinded John and other racists to the fact that God loves all people the same. In **Acts 10:34–48**, Peter challenges the people of his day to see others from God's perspective and lay aside their prejudices.

■ How was prejudice in Peter's day different from John Metzger's prejudice? How are they similar?

■ According to this passage, what is the cure for prejudice?

C O N S I D E R . . . .

■ observing people in a mall. Evaluate which people you do or don't have prejudices toward. Then ask God to remove any prejudices you may have.

■ getting to know someone you have prejudged. Think about the ways the person is different from what you had expected.

F O R   M O R E ,   S E E . . .

■ Genesis 3:20 (p. 6)   ■ Acts 11:1–18 (p. 1115)
■ John 4:1–27 (p. 1063)

[11]Right then three men who were sent to me from Caesarea came to the house where I was staying. [12]The Spirit[d] told me to go with them without doubting. These six believers here also went with me, and we entered the house of Cornelius. [13]He told us about the angel he saw standing in his house. The angel said to him, 'Send some men to Joppa and invite Simon Peter to come. [14]By the words he will say to you, you and all your family will be saved.' [15]When I began my speech, the Holy Spirit came on them just as he came on us at the beginning. [16]Then I remembered the words of the Lord. He said, 'John baptized with water, but you will be baptized with the Holy Spirit.' [17]Since God gave them the same gift he gave us who believed in the Lord Jesus Christ, how could I stop the work of God?"

[18]When the Jewish believers heard this, they stopped arguing. They praised God and said, "So God is allowing even those who are not Jewish to turn to him and live."

The Good News Comes to Antioch

[19]Many of the believers were scattered when they were persecuted after Stephen was killed. Some of them went as far as Phoenicia, Cyprus, and Antioch telling the message to others, but only to Jews. [20]Some of these believers were people from Cyprus and Cyrene. When they came to Antioch, they spoke also to Greeks, telling them the Good News[d] about the Lord Jesus. [21]The Lord was helping the believers, and a large group of people believed and turned to the Lord.

[22]The church in Jerusalem heard about all of this, so they sent Barnabas to Antioch. [23-24]Barnabas was a good man, full of the Holy Spirit[d] and full of faith. When he reached Antioch and saw how God had blessed the people, he was glad. He encouraged all the believers in Antioch always to obey the Lord with all their hearts, and many people became followers of the Lord.

[25]Then Barnabas went to the city of Tarsus to look for Saul, [26]and when he found Saul, he

---

---

brought him to Antioch. For a whole year Saul and Barnabas met with the church and taught many people there. In Antioch the followers were called Christians for the first time.

[27]About that time some prophets[d] came from Jerusalem to Antioch. [28]One of them, named Agabus, stood up and spoke with the help of the Holy Spirit. He said, "A very hard time is coming to the whole world. There will be no food to eat." (This happened when Claudius ruled.) [29]The believers all decided to help the followers who lived in Judea, as much as each one could. [30]They gathered the money and gave it to Barnabas and Saul, who brought it to the elders[d] in Judea.

Herod Agrippa Hurts the Church

12 During that same time King Herod began to mistreat some who belonged to the church. [2]He ordered James, the brother of John, to be killed by the sword. [3]Herod saw that the Jewish people liked this, so he decided to arrest Peter, too. (This happened during the time of the Feast[d] of Unleavened Bread.)

[4]After Herod arrested Peter, he put him in jail and handed him over to be guarded by sixteen soldiers. Herod planned to bring Peter before the people for trial after the Passover[d] Feast. [5]So Peter was kept in jail, but the church prayed earnestly to God for him.

Peter Leaves the Jail

[6]The night before Herod was to bring him to trial, Peter was sleeping between two soldiers, bound with two chains. Other soldiers were guarding the door of the jail. [7]Suddenly, an angel of the Lord stood there, and a light shined in the cell. The angel struck Peter on the side and woke him up. "Hurry! Get up!" the angel said. And the chains fell off Peter's hands. [8]Then the angel told him, "Get dressed and put on your sandals." And Peter did. Then the angel said, "Put on your coat and follow me." [9]So Peter followed him out, but he did not know if what the angel was doing was real; he thought he might be seeing a vision. [10]They went past the first and second guards and came to the iron gate that separated them from the city. The gate opened by itself for them, and they went through it. When they had walked down one street, the angel suddenly left him.

[11]Then Peter realized what had happened. He thought, "Now I know that the Lord really sent his angel to me. He rescued me from Herod and from all the things the Jewish people thought would happen."

[12]When he considered this, he went to the home of Mary, the mother of John Mark. Many people were gathered there, praying. [13]Peter knocked on the outside door, and a servant girl named Rhoda came to answer it. [14]When she recognized Peter's voice, she was so happy she forgot to open the door. Instead, she ran inside and told the group, "Peter is at the door!"

[15]They said to her, "You are crazy!" But she

kept on saying it was true, so they said, "It must be Peter's angel."

[16]Peter continued to knock, and when they opened the door, they saw him and were amazed. [17]Peter made a sign with his hand to tell them to be quiet. He explained how the Lord led him out of the jail, and he said, "Tell James and the other believers what happened." Then he left to go to another place.

[18]The next day the soldiers were very upset and wondered what had happened to Peter. [19]Herod looked everywhere for him but could not find him. So he questioned the guards and ordered that they be killed.

The Death of Herod Agrippa

Later Herod moved from Judea and went to the city of Caesarea, where he stayed. [20]Herod was very angry with the people of Tyre and Sidon, but the people of those cities all came in a group to him. After convincing Blastus, the king's personal servant, to be on their side, they asked Herod for peace, because their country got its food from his country.

[21]On a chosen day Herod put on his royal robes, sat on his throne, and made a speech to the people. [22]They shouted, "This is the voice of a god, not a human!" [23]Because Herod did not give the glory to God, an angel of the Lord immediately caused him to become sick, and he was eaten by worms and died.

[24]God's message continued to spread and reach people.

[25]After Barnabas and Saul finished their task in Jerusalem, they returned to Antioch, taking John Mark with them.

Barnabas and Saul Are Chosen

13 In the church at Antioch there were these prophets[d] and teachers: Barnabas, Simeon (also called Niger), Lucius (from the city of Cyrene), Manaen (who had grown up with Herod, the ruler), and Saul. [2]They were all worshiping the Lord and giving up eating for a certain time.[n] During this time the Holy Spirit[d] said to them, "Set apart for me Barnabas and Saul to do a special work for which I have chosen them."

[3]So after they gave up eating and prayed, they laid their hands on[n] Barnabas and Saul and sent them out.

Barnabas and Saul in Cyprus

[4]Barnabas and Saul, sent out by the Holy Spirit,[d] went to the city of Seleucia. From there they sailed to the island of Cyprus. [5]When they came to Salamis, they preached the Good News[d] of God in the Jewish synagogues.[d] John Mark was with them to help.

[6]They went across the whole island to Paphos where they met a Jewish magician named Bar-Jesus. He was a false prophet[d] [7]who always stayed close to Sergius Paulus, the governor and a smart man. He asked Barnabas and Saul to come to him, because he wanted to hear the message of God. [8]But Elymas, the magician, was against them. (Elymas is the name for Bar-Jesus in the Greek language.) He tried to stop the governor from believing in Jesus. [9]But Saul, who was also called Paul, was filled with the Holy Spirit. He looked straight at Elymas [10]and said, "You son of the devil! You are an enemy of everything that is right! You are full of evil tricks and lies, always trying to change the Lord's truths into lies. [11]Now the Lord will touch you, and you will be blind. For a time you will not be able to see anything—not even the light from the sun."

Then everything became dark for Elymas, and he walked around trying to find someone to lead him by the hand. [2]When the governor saw this, he believed because he was amazed at the teaching about the Lord.

Paul and Barnabas Leave Cyprus

[13]Paul and those with him sailed from Paphos and came to Perga, in Pamphylia. There John Mark left them to return to Jerusalem. [14]They continued their trip from Perga and went to Antioch, a city in Pisidia. On the Sabbath[d] day they went into the synagogue[d] and sat down. [15]After the law of Moses and the writings of the prophets[d] were read, the leaders of the synagogue sent a message to Paul and Barnabas: "Brothers, if you have any message that will encourage the people, please speak."

[16]Paul stood up, raised his hand, and said, "You Israelites and you who worship God, please listen! [17]The God of the Israelites chose our ancestors. He made the people great during the time they lived in Egypt, and he brought them out of that country with great power. [18]And he was patient with them for forty years in the desert. [19]God destroyed seven nations in the land of Canaan and gave the land to his people. [20]All this happened in about four hundred fifty years.

"After this, God gave them judges until the time of Samuel the prophet. [21]Then the people asked for a king, so God gave them Saul son of Kish. Saul was from the tribe[d] of Benjamin and was king for forty years. [22]After God took him away, God made David their king. God said about

---

giving up . . . time This is called "fasting." The people would give up eating for a special time of prayer and worship to God. It was also done to show sadness and disappointment.

laid their hands on The laying on of hands had many purposes, including the giving of a blessing, power, or authority.

him: 'I have found in David son of Jesse the kind of man I want. He will do all I want him to do.' ²³So God has brought Jesus, one of David's descendants,ᵈ to Israel to be its Savior,ᵈ as he promised. ²⁴Before Jesus came, Johnⁿ preached to all the people of Israel about a baptism of changed hearts and lives. ²⁵When he was finishing his work, he said, 'Who do you think I am? I am not the Christ.ᵈ He is coming later, and I am not worthy to untie his sandals.'

²⁶"Brothers, sons of the family of Abraham, and those of you who are not Jews who worship God, listen! The news about this salvation has been sent to us. ²⁷Those who live in Jerusalem and their leaders did not realize that Jesus was the Savior. They did not understand the words that the prophets wrote, which are read every Sabbathᵈ day. But they made them come true when they said Jesus was guilty. ²⁸They could not find any real reason for Jesus to be put to death, but they asked Pilate to have him killed. ²⁹When they had done to him all that the Scripturesᵈ had said, they took him down from the cross and laid him in a tomb. ³⁰But God raised him up from the dead! ³¹After this, for many days, those who had gone with Jesus from Galilee to Jerusalem saw him.

They are now his witnesses to the people. ³²We tell you the Good Newsᵈ about the promise God made to our ancestors. ³³God has made this promise come true for us, his children, by raising Jesus from the dead. We read about this also in Psalm 2:

'You are my Son.
Today I have become your Father.'   *Psalm 2:7*
³⁴God raised Jesus from the dead, and he will never go back to the grave and become dust. So God said:
'I will give you the holy and sure blessings
that I promised to David.'   *Isaiah 55:3*
³⁵But in another place God says:
'You will not let your Holy One rot.'
   Psalm 16:10
³⁶David did God's will during his lifetime. Then he died and was buried beside his ancestors, and his body did rot in the grave. ³⁷But the One God raised from the dead did not rot in the grave. ³⁸˒³⁹Brothers, understand what we are telling you: You can have forgiveness of your sins through Jesus. The law of Moses could not free you from your sins. But through Jesus everyone who believes is free from all sins. ⁴⁰Be careful! Don't let what the prophets said happen to you:

John   John the Baptist, who preached to people about Christ's coming (Luke 3).

BIBLE STUDY

Putting the Pieces Together

Jigsaw puzzles can drive you crazy. When first you dump hundreds of jigsaw puzzle pieces from the box, you fear you will never get the puzzle together. But because you know the pieces have to fit together eventually, you separate border pieces from inside pieces. The border goes together reasonably well, so you move on to notice pieces that are related and may form a figure in the puzzle.

Each time you fit a piece, you feel more hopeful. Completing certain sections may bring cries of victory and, "Come see what we finished!" Sometimes along the way, it gets discouraging, but you keep at it. Bit by bit, the picture begins to take shape. The pieces are no longer meaningless but related and relevant. When only a few pieces remain, you can see exactly where they belong. The triumph of the final assembly makes the hours of work worth it.

Sometimes Bible study can be like a jigsaw puzzle. Understanding the Bible and the God described in it also happens piece by piece. In **Acts 13:22–33**, Paul put together some pieces about Jesus for his listeners.
■ How is this passage like the picture on the front of a puzzle box?
■ What are the three most important pieces to you in this passage?

CONSIDER...
■ listing at least ten things you already understand about Jesus.
■ keeping a journal of discoveries you make during group and individual Bible studies. Reread this journal to remind yourself of the pieces of truth you've learned.

FOR MORE, SEE...
■ Deuteronomy 6:4–9 (p. 167)
■ Romans 15:4 (p. 1161)
■ 2 Timothy 3:14–17 (p. 1266)

41'Listen, you people who doubt!
    You can wonder, and then die.
I will do something in your lifetime
    that you won't believe even when you are
        told about it!' "   *Habakkuk 1:5*

42While Paul and Barnabas were leaving the synagogue, the people asked them to tell them more about these things on the next Sabbath. 43When the meeting was over, many Jews and those who had changed to the Jewish religion and who worshiped God followed Paul and Barnabas from that place. Paul and Barnabas were persuading them to continue trusting in God's grace.

44On the next Sabbath day, almost everyone in the city came to hear the word of the Lord. 45Seeing the crowd, the Jewish people became very jealous and said insulting things and argued against what Paul said. 46But Paul and Barnabas spoke very boldly, saying, "We must speak the message of God to you first. But you refuse to listen. You are judging yourselves not worthy of having eternal life! So we will now go to the people of other nations. 47This is what the Lord told us to do, saying:

'I have made you a light for the nations;
    you will show people all over the world the
        way to be saved.' "   *Isaiah 49:6*

48When those who were not Jewish heard Paul say this, they were happy and gave honor to the message of the Lord. And the people who were chosen to have life forever believed the message.

49So the message of the Lord was spreading through the whole country. 50But the Jewish people stirred up some of the important religious women and the leaders of the city. They started trouble against Paul and Barnabas and forced them out of their area. 51So Paul and Barnabas shook the dust off their feet*n* and went to Ico-

---

shook . . . feet A warning. It showed that they had rejected these people.

---

nium. [52]But the followers were filled with joy and the Holy Spirit.[d]

Paul and Barnabas in Iconium

14 In Iconium, Paul and Barnabas went as usual to the Jewish synagogue.[d] They spoke so well that a great many Jews and Greeks believed. [2]But some of the Jews who did not believe excited the non-Jewish people and turned them against the believers. [3]Paul and Barnabas stayed in Iconium a long time and spoke bravely for the Lord. He showed that their message about his grace was true by giving them the power to work miracles[d] and signs. [4]But the city was divided. Some of the people agreed with the Jews, and others believed the apostles.[d]

[5]Some who were not Jews, some Jews, and some of their rulers wanted to mistreat Paul and Barnabas and to stone them to death. [6]When Paul and Barnabas learned about this, they ran away to Lystra and Derbe, cities in Lycaonia, and to the areas around those cities. [7]They announced the Good News[d] there, too.

Paul in Lystra and Derbe

[8]In Lystra there sat a man who had been born crippled; he had never walked. [9]As this man was listening to Paul speak, Paul looked straight at him and saw that he believed God could heal him. [10]So he cried out, "Stand up on your feet!" The man jumped up and began walking around. [11]When the crowds saw what Paul did, they shouted in the Lycaonian language, "The gods have become like humans and have come down to us!" [12]Then the people began to call Barnabas "Zeus"[n] and Paul "Hermes,"[n] because he was

"Zeus"   The Greeks believed in many gods, of whom Zeus was most important.
"Hermes"   The Greeks believed he was a messenger for the other gods.

HEROES

Admire, Don't Worship

Mandy Rios admired everything about her pastor. When he first came to her church, she was immediately drawn to his dynamic personality, warm smile and genuine concern for people.

The pastor always had time to listen. He always talked about how great the young people of the church were, praising their character and service. Mandy believed that God must be just like her pastor.

Whenever the youth group had a controversial discussion, Mandy would go to her pastor later and ask what he thought. Mandy would explain what he said in the next youth group meeting. To Mandy, he knew everything.

Eleven months after coming to Mandy's church, her pastor left suddenly to go to another church. He answered none of Mandy's letters, nor did he return her phone calls. He never even said good-bye.

Mandy was crushed and heartbroken. How could he treat her church like this? How could he treat her like this when she had respected him so much? Mandy felt betrayed. Could she ever trust a pastor again?

Worshiping a person always leads to disappointment. Her pastor turned out to be human—with human faults and inconsistencies. In **Acts 14:8–18**, God used Paul and Barnabas to work miracles, but even they weren't worthy of worship.

■ What led Mandy to worship her pastor, and the people to worship Paul and Barnabas?
■ Based on Paul's and Barnabas's words, what are appropriate ways to treat spiritual leaders?

C O N S I D E R . . .
■ thanking God for the good qualities of people you admire. Ask God to help you keep your admiration in proper perspective.
✎ getting to know someone you admire and learning about his or her human and less-admirable qualities as well.

F O R   M O R E ,   S E E . . .
■ Exodus 20:2–6 (p. 78)
■ Daniel 3 (p. 809)   ■ 1 Corinthians 4:1–7 (p. 1172)

the main speaker. [13]The priest in the temple of Zeus, which was near the city, brought some bulls and flowers to the city gates. He and the people wanted to offer a sacrifice to Paul and Barnabas. [14]But when the apostles,[d] Barnabas and Paul, heard about it, they tore their clothes. They ran in among the people, shouting, [15]"Friends, why are you doing these things? We are only human beings like you. We are bringing you the Good News[d] and are telling you to turn away from these worthless things and turn to the living God. He is the One who made the sky, the earth, the sea, and everything in them. [16]In the past, God let all the nations do what they wanted. [17]Yet he proved he is real by showing kindness, by giving you rain from heaven and crops at the right times, by giving you food and filling your hearts with joy." [18]Even with these words, they were barely able to keep the crowd from offering sacrifices to them.

SIDELIGHT: Paul and Barnabas faced a real case of mistaken identity when they visited Lystra, a town in the center of modern-day Turkey (Acts 14:8–18). The people in the region believed a myth that the Greek gods Zeus and Hermes had previously visited the area. When Paul and Barnabas healed a cripple, the people thought the gods had returned, putting the Christian missionaries in an awkward situation.

---

[19]Then some Jewish people came from Antioch and Iconium and persuaded the people to turn against Paul. So they threw stones at him and dragged him out of town, thinking they had killed him. [20]But the followers gathered around him, and he got up and went back into the town. The next day he and Barnabas left and went to the city of Derbe.

The Return to Antioch in Syria

[21]Paul and Barnabas told the Good News[d] in Derbe, and many became followers. Paul and Barnabas returned to Lystra, Iconium, and Antioch, [22]making the followers of Jesus stronger and helping them stay in the faith. They said, "We must suffer many things to enter God's kingdom." [23]They chose elders[d] for each church, by praying and giving up eating for a certain time.[n] These elders had trusted the Lord, so Paul and Barnabas put them in the Lord's care.

[24]Then they went through Pisidia and came to Pamphylia. [25]When they had preached the mes-

sage in Perga, they went down to Attalia. [26]And from there they sailed away to Antioch where the believers had put them into God's care and had sent them out to do this work. Now they had finished.

[27]When they arrived in Antioch, Paul and Barnabas gathered the church together. They told the church all about what God had done with them and how God had made it possible for those who were not Jewish to believe. [28]And they stayed there a long time with the followers.

The Meeting at Jerusalem

15 Then some people came to Antioch from Judea and began teaching the non-Jewish believers: "You cannot be saved if you are not circumcised[d] as Moses taught us." [2]Paul and Barnabas were against this teaching and argued with them about it. So the church decided to send Paul, Barnabas, and some others to Jerusalem where they could talk more about this with the apostles[d] and elders.[d]

[3]The church helped them leave on the trip, and they went through the countries of Phoenicia and Samaria, telling all about how those who were not Jewish had turned to God. This made all the believers very happy. [4]When they arrived in Jerusalem, they were welcomed by the apostles, the elders, and the church. Paul, Barnabas, and the others told about everything God had done with them. [5]But some of the believers who belonged to the Pharisee[d] group came forward and said, "The non-Jewish believers must be circumcised. They must be told to obey the law of Moses."

[6]The apostles and the elders gathered to consider this problem. [7]After a long debate, Peter stood up and said to them, "Brothers, you know that in the early days God chose me from among you to preach the Good News[d] to those who are not Jewish. They heard the Good News from me, and they believed. [8]God, who knows the thoughts of everyone, accepted them. He showed this to us by giving them the Holy Spirit,[d] just as he did to us. [9]To God those people are not different from us. When they believed, he made their hearts pure. [10]So now why are you testing God by putting a heavy load around the necks of the non-Jewish believers? It is a load that neither we nor our ancestors were able to carry. [11]But we believe that we and they too will be saved by the grace of the Lord Jesus."

[12]Then the whole group became quiet. They listened to Paul and Barnabas tell about all the miracles[d] and signs that God did through them among the non-Jewish people. [13]After they finished speaking, James said, "Brothers, listen to

---

giving ... time This is called "fasting." The people would give up eating for a special time of prayer and worship to God. It was also done to show sadness and disappointment.

me. [14]Simon has told us how God showed his love for the non-Jewish people. For the first time he is accepting from among them a people to be his own. [15]The words of the prophets[d] agree with this too:

[16]'After these things I will return.
The kingdom of David is like a fallen tent.
But I will rebuild its ruins,
and I will set it up.
[17]Then those people who are left alive may ask the Lord for help,
and the other nations that belong to me, says the Lord,
who will make it happen.
[18] And these things have been known for a long time.'   *Amos 9:11-12*

[19]"So I think we should not bother the non-Jewish people who are turning to God. [20]Instead, we should write a letter to them telling them these things: Stay away from food that has been offered to idols (which makes it unclean[d]), any kind of sexual sin, eating animals that have been strangled, and blood. [21]They should do these things, because for a long time in every city the law of Moses has been taught. And it is still read in the synagogue[d] every Sabbath[d] day."

Letter to Non-Jewish Believers

[22]The apostles,[d] the elders,[d] and the whole church decided to send some of their men with Paul and Barnabas to Antioch. They chose Judas Barsabbas and Silas, who were respected by the believers. [23]They sent the following letter with them:

From the apostles and elders, your brothers.

To all the non-Jewish believers in Antioch, Syria, and Cilicia:

Greetings!
[24]We have heard that some of our group have come to you and said things that trouble and upset you. But we did not tell them to do this. [25]We have all agreed to choose some messengers and send them to you with our dear friends Barnabas and Paul — [26]people who have given their lives to serve our Lord Jesus Christ. [27]So we are sending Judas and Silas, who will tell you the same things. [28]It has pleased the Holy Spirit[d] that you should not have a heavy load to carry, and we agree. You need to do only these things: [29]Stay away from any food that has been offered to idols; eating any animals that have been strangled, and blood, and any kind of sexual sin. If you stay away from these things, you will do well.

Good-bye.

[30]So they left Jerusalem and went to Antioch where they gathered the church and gave them the letter. [31]When they read it, they were very happy because of the encouraging message. [32]Judas and Silas, who were also prophets,[d] said many things to encourage the believers and make them stronger. [33]After some time Judas and Silas were sent off in peace by the believers, and they went back to those who had sent them. [34] *n*

[35]But Paul and Barnabas stayed in Antioch and, along with many others, preached the Good News[d] and taught the people the message of the Lord.

Paul and Barnabas Separate

[36]After some time, Paul said to Barnabas, "We should go back to all those towns where we preached the message of the Lord. Let's visit the believers and see how they are doing."

[37]Barnabas wanted to take John Mark with them, [38]but he had left them at Pamphylia; he did not continue with them in the work. So Paul did not think it was a good idea to take him. [39]Paul and Barnabas had such a serious argument about this that they separated and went different ways. Barnabas took Mark and sailed to Cyprus, [40]but Paul chose Silas and left. The believers in Antioch put Paul into the Lord's care, [41]and he went through Syria and Cilicia, giving strength to the churches.

Timothy Goes with Paul

16 Paul came to Derbe and Lystra, where a follower named Timothy lived. Timothy's mother was Jewish and a believer, but his father was a Greek. [2]The believers in Lystra and Iconium respected Timothy and said good things about him. [3]Paul wanted Timothy to travel with him, but all the Jews living in that area knew that Timothy's father was Greek. So Paul circumcised[d] Timothy to please the Jews. [4]Paul and those with him traveled from town to town and gave the decisions made by the apostles[d] and elders[d] in Jerusalem for the people to obey. [5]So the churches became stronger in the faith and grew larger every day.

Paul Is Called Out of Asia

[6]Paul and those with him went through the areas of Phrygia and Galatia since the Holy Spirit[d] did not let them preach the Good News[d] in the country of Asia. [7]When they came near the country of Mysia, they tried to go into Bithynia, but the Spirit of Jesus did not let them. [8]So they passed by Mysia and went to Troas. [9]That night Paul saw in

Verse 34 Some Greek copies add verse 34: ". . . but Silas decided to remain there."

a vision a man from Macedonia. The man stood and begged, "Come over to Macedonia and help us." [10]After Paul had seen the vision, we immediately prepared to leave for Macedonia, understanding that God had called us to tell the Good News to those people.

Lydia Becomes a Christian

[11]We left Troas and sailed straight to the island of Samothrace. The next day we sailed to Neapolis.[n] [12]Then we went by land to Philippi, a Roman colony[n] and the leading city in that part of Macedonia. We stayed there for several days.

[13]On the Sabbath[d] day we went outside the city gate to the river where we thought we would find a special place for prayer. Some women had gathered there, so we sat down and talked with them. [14]One of the listeners was a woman named Lydia from the city of Thyatira whose job was selling purple cloth. She worshiped God, and he opened her mind to pay attention to what Paul was saying. [15]She and all the people in her house were baptized. Then she invited us to her home, saying, "If you think I am truly a believer in the Lord, then come stay in my house." And she persuaded us to stay with her.

Neapolis City in Macedonia. It was the first city Paul visited on the continent of Europe.
Roman colony A town begun by Romans with Roman laws, customs and privileges.

GOD'S WILL

Close to Your Heart

Sandra Graham was one semester away from high school graduation, and she had no idea what she would do with her life. She had been praying for God to show her his will, but still there were no answers.

One Sunday after church, Ted Holt, a Sunday school teacher, asked Sandra to come home with his family of eight for dinner.

All through the meal, they talked about Sandra's plans after graduation. "What do you think God wants you to do, Sandra?" Ted asked as they finished dessert.

"I don't know. I've been praying about it, but God just doesn't seem to answer," Sandra lamented.

Ted's voice softened. "What do you want to do?" he asked.

"God's will," she answered.

Again, Ted asked, "But what do you want to do?"

Sandra was confused. "That's it. I want to do God's will."

Ted smiled. "Sandra, I have six kids, and I want nothing more than for each of my kids to be happy. I'll do almost anything to make that happen."

Sandra nodded, not sure what this had to do with her decision.

Ted laughed heartily when he saw her confusion. "Sandra, God is your father, and he wants you to be happy. He's probably been showing you all the time what his will is."

"He has?" Sandra asked incredulously.

"Yes, he has. Look into your heart. I'll bet your desires will point you toward God's will."

Sandra did find God's will. After she graduated from college, she used her love for drama to teach others how to communicate their faith. In **Acts 16:6–10**, Paul also found God's will.

■ What was Ted trying to help Sandra learn about finding God's will? In the passage, how did God show his will to Paul and the others?
■ Do you think God still reveals his will to people as he did in the passage? In what other ways do people learn God's will?

CONSIDER...

■ keeping track of what happens to you in the coming week. See if any patterns emerge that show God leading you in a particular direction.
■ interviewing an older person in your church about what he or she has learned about discovering and doing God's will.

FOR MORE, SEE...

■ Psalm 32:6–11 (p. 500)   ■ Luke 22:41–43 (p. 1050)
■ Matthew 6:9–13 (p. 918)

Paul and Silas in Jail

16Once, while we were going to the place for prayer, a servant girl met us. She had a special spirit*n* in her, and she earned a lot of money for her owners by telling fortunes. 17This girl followed Paul and us, shouting, "These men are servants of the Most High God. They are telling you how you can be saved."

18She kept this up for many days. This bothered Paul, so he turned and said to the spirit, "By the power of Jesus Christ, I command you to come out of her!" Immediately, the spirit came out.

19When the owners of the servant girl saw this, they knew that now they could not use her to make money. So they grabbed Paul and Silas and dragged them before the city rulers in the marketplace. 20They brought Paul and Silas to the Roman rulers and said, "These men are Jews and are making trouble in our city. 21They are teaching things that are not right for us as Romans to do."

22The crowd joined the attack against them. The Roman officers tore the clothes of Paul and Silas and had them beaten with rods. 23Then Paul and Silas were thrown into jail, and the jailer was ordered to guard them carefully. 24When he heard this order, he put them far inside the jail and pinned their feet down between large blocks of wood.

25About midnight Paul and Silas were praying and singing songs to God as the other prisoners listened. 26Suddenly, there was a strong earthquake that shook the foundation of the jail. Then all the doors of the jail broke open, and all the prisoners were freed from their chains. 27The jailer woke up and saw that the jail doors were open. Thinking that the prisoners had already escaped, he got his sword and was about to kill himself.*n* 28But Paul shouted, "Don't hurt yourself! We are all here."

29The jailer told someone to bring a light. Then he ran inside and, shaking with fear, fell down before Paul and Silas. 30He brought them outside and said, "Men, what must I do to be saved?"

31They said to him, "Believe in the Lord Jesus and you will be saved — you and all the people in your house." 32So Paul and Silas told the message of the Lord to the jailer and all the people in his house. 33At that hour of the night the jailer took Paul and Silas and washed their wounds. Then he and all his people were baptized immediately. 34After this the jailer took Paul and Silas home and gave them food. He and his family were very happy because they now believed in God.

35The next morning, the Roman officers sent the police to tell the jailer, "Let these men go free."

36The jailer said to Paul, "The officers have sent an order to let you go free. You can leave now. Go in peace."

37But Paul said to the police, "They beat us in public without a trial, even though we are Roman citizens.*n* And they threw us in jail. Now they want to make us go away quietly. No! Let them come themselves and bring us out."

38The police told the Roman officers what Paul said. When the officers heard that Paul and Silas were Roman citizens, they were afraid. 39So they came and told Paul and Silas they were sorry and took them out of jail and asked them to leave the city. 40So when they came out of the jail, they went to Lydia's house where they saw some of the believers and encouraged them. Then they left.

Paul and Silas in Thessalonica

17 Paul and Silas traveled through Amphipolis and Apollonia and came to Thessalonica where there was a Jewish synagogue.*d* 2Paul went into the synagogue as he always did, and on each Sabbath*d* day for three weeks, he talked with the Jews about the Scriptures.*d* 3He explained and proved that the Christ*d* must die and then rise from the dead. He said, "This Jesus I am telling you about is the Christ." 4Some of the Jews were convinced and joined Paul and Silas, along with many of the Greeks who worshiped God and many of the important women.

5But the Jews became jealous. So they got some evil men from the marketplace, formed a mob, and started a riot. They ran to Jason's house, looking for Paul and Silas, wanting to bring them out to the people. 6But when they did not find them, they dragged Jason and some other believers to the leaders of the city. The people were yelling, "These people have made trouble everywhere in the world, and now they have come here too! 7Jason is keeping them in his house. All of them do things against the laws of Caesar,*d* saying there is another king, called Jesus."

8When the people and the leaders of the city heard these things, they became very upset. 9They made Jason and the others put up a sum of money. Then they let the believers go free.

Paul and Silas Go to Berea

10That same night the believers sent Paul and Silas to Berea where they went to the Jewish syna-

---

spirit   This was a spirit from the devil, which caused her to say she had special knowledge.
kill himself   He thought the leaders would kill him for letting the prisoners escape.
Roman citizens   Roman law said that Roman citizens must not be beaten before they had a trial.

gogue.*d* *11*These Jews were more willing to listen than the Jews in Thessalonica. The Bereans were eager to hear what Paul and Silas said and studied the Scriptures*d* every day to find out if these things were true. *12*So, many of them believed, as well as many important Greek women and men. *13*But the Jews in Thessalonica learned that Paul was preaching the word of God in Berea, too. So they came there, upsetting the people and making trouble. *14*The believers quickly sent Paul away to the coast, but Silas and Timothy stayed in Berea. *15*The people leading Paul went with him to Athens. Then they carried a message from Paul back to Silas and Timothy for them to come to him as soon as they could.

Paul Preaches in Athens

*16*While Paul was waiting for Silas and Timothy in Athens, he was troubled because he saw that the city was full of idols. *17*In the synagogue,*d* he talked with the Jews and the Greeks who worshiped God. He also talked every day with people in the marketplace.

*18*Some of the Epicurean and Stoic philosophers*n* argued with him, saying, "This man

---

Epicurean and Stoic philosophers   Philosophers were those who searched for truth. Epicureans believed that pleasures, especially pleasures of the mind, were the goal of life. Stoics believed that life should be without feelings of joy or grief.

A Way Out

Keivan McClure was delighted to land a job at the steak house. He needed every penny he could earn for college. Few of his co-workers were Christians, but Keivan didn't let that bother him. He tried to make friends with them, and he talked about faith and church when he had a chance.

One night after closing, the entire crew decided to go to a drive-in movie and out for pizza. The chosen movie was one with lots of violence and nudity, so Keivan decided not to go.

"I'll meet you after the movie for pizza," Keivan said.

"What's the matter? Our movie choice not good enough for Mr. Holier-Than-Thou?" one of the crew chided.

Keivan knew he didn't deserve that, so he just repeated his request: "That's not what I said or meant. I'll see you for pizza."

"Yeah, right, church-boy," another crew member taunted. "You can't handle the scary stuff, so you're running away."

Most of the other crew members laughed. Keivan didn't know what to say.

Finally, Conrad Largley, the crew leader, spoke up. "Hey, get off his back," he said. "Keivan's a Christian and doesn't watch that junk. I'm a Christian too, and I'm not going either."

The crew was silent. Keivan was surprised. He knew Conrad was a nice guy, but Conrad had never said anything about being a Christian before.

After that night, things got better at work. Keivan and Conrad became close friends, and the crew members showed more respect for their beliefs.

Committed Christian friends. They're a great help when the going gets rough. In **Acts 17:1–15**, Paul and Silas were rescued from discouraging circumstances by friends who cared.

■ How was the way Conrad helped Keivan similar to the way the believers helped Paul?

■ When has someone helped you in the same way the believers helped Paul? When have you supported another Christian?

C O N S I D E R . . .

■ keeping a journal where you write about times you are discouraged. Later, re-read entries and reflect on how God pulled you through.

■ encouraging a Christian friend who is in a difficult situation to be strong and hang in there.

F O R   M O R E ,   S E E . . .

■ Ecclesiastes 4:9–12 (p. 602)
■ Matthew 10:21–23 (p. 924)
■ 1 Timothy 1:1–3 (p. 1256)

doesn't know what he is talking about. What is he trying to say?" Others said, "He seems to be telling us about some other gods," because Paul was telling them about Jesus and his rising from the dead. [19]They got Paul and took him to a meeting of the Areopagus, [n] where they said, "Please explain to us this new idea you have been teaching. [20]The things you are saying are new to us, and we want to know what this teaching means." [21](All the people of Athens and those from other countries who lived there always used their time to talk about the newest ideas.)

[22]Then Paul stood before the meeting of the Areopagus and said, "People of Athens, I can see you are very religious in all things. [23]As I was going through your city, I saw the objects you worship. I found an altar that had these words written on it: TO A GOD WHO IS NOT KNOWN. You worship a god that you don't know, and this is the God I am telling you about! [24]The God who made the whole world and everything in it is the Lord of the land and the sky. He does not live in temples built by human hands. [25]This God is the One who gives life, breath, and everything else to people. He does not need any help from them; he has every-

thing he needs. [26]God began by making one person, and from him came all the different people who live everywhere in the world. God decided exactly when and where they must live. [27]God wanted them to look for him and perhaps search all around for him and find him, though he is not far from any of us: [28]'We live in him. We walk in him. We are in him.' Some of your own poets have said: 'For we are his children.' [29]Since we are God's children, you must not think that God is like something that people imagine or make from gold, silver, or rock. [30]In the past, people did not understand God, and he ignored this. But now, God tells all people in the world to change their hearts and lives. [31]God has set a day that he will judge all the world with fairness, by the man he chose long ago. And God has proved this to everyone by raising that man from the dead!"

[32]When the people heard about Jesus being raised from the dead, some of them laughed. But others said, "We will hear more about this from you later." [33]So Paul went away from them. [34]But some of the people believed Paul and joined him. Among those who believed was Dionysius, a member of the Areopagus, a woman named Damaris, and some others.

Areopagus   A council or group of important leaders in Athens. They were like judges.

NON-CHRISTIANS

A Starting Place

Jay Dugan is a talented musician. His friend explained God as a director who "conducts" every element of life to move in harmony.

Amanda Roady has moved nine times in eleven years. Her friend explained God as the friend who goes with us no matter where we move or what new situation we face.

Jason Gaddy is a soccer star. His friend explained God as a coach who insists on practice, works to tone our life muscles, teaches strategy for difficult experiences, and cheers every play from the sidelines.

Some Greek leaders thought there must be a god they did not know. In **Acts 17:22–31**, Paul focused on their understanding of that god to guide them to a full knowledge of the true God.

■ Why is it effective to explain God by using things people already understand?

■ What images did Paul use to describe God in this passage?

CONSIDER...

■ underlining phrases about God in Acts 17:22–31 that someone who has never been in church could understand. Use these phrases to explain God to your non-Christian friends.

◢ thinking of a way to explain Jesus to a non-Christian friend. Begin with an image your friend will relate to.

FOR MORE, SEE...

■ Exodus 3:12–15 (p. 60)
■ John 4:5–25 (p. 1063)

■ 1 Corinthians 9:19–23 (p. 1178)

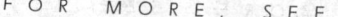

Paul in Corinth

18 Later Paul left Athens and went to Corinth. [2]Here he met a Jew named Aquila who had been born in the country of Pontus. But Aquila and his wife, Priscilla, had recently moved to Corinth from Italy, because Claudius[n] commanded that all Jews must leave Rome. Paul went

> **SIDELIGHT:** Claudius (Acts 18:2) ruled Rome thirteen years and was partially paralyzed. He kicked Christians out of Rome for allegedly starting riots that threatened the Roman peace—a common charge against early Christians.

to visit Aquila and Priscilla. [3]Because they were tentmakers, just as he was, he stayed with them and worked with them. [4]Every Sabbath[d] day he talked with the Jews and Greeks in the synagogue,[d] trying to persuade them to believe in Jesus.

[5]Silas and Timothy came from Macedonia and joined Paul in Corinth. After this, Paul spent all his time telling people the Good News,[d] showing the Jews that Jesus is the Christ.[d] [6]But they would not accept Paul's teaching and said some evil things. So he shook off the dust from his clothes[n] and said to them, "If you are not saved, it will be your own fault! I have done all I can do! After this, I will go only to those who are not Jewish." [7]Paul left the synagogue and moved into the home of Titius Justus, next to the synagogue. This man worshiped God. [8]Crispus was the leader of that synagogue, and he and all the people living in his house believed in the Lord. Many others in Corinth also listened to Paul and believed and were baptized.

[9]During the night, the Lord told Paul in a vision: "Don't be afraid. Continue talking to people and don't be quiet. [10]I am with you, and no one will hurt you because many of my people are in this city." [11]Paul stayed there for a year and a half, teaching God's word to the people.

Paul Is Brought Before Gallio

[12]When Gallio was the governor of the country of Southern Greece, some of the Jews came together against Paul and took him to the court. [13]They said, "This man is teaching people to worship God in a way that is against our law."

[14]Paul was about to say something, but Gallio spoke to the Jews, saying, "I would listen to you Jews if you were complaining about a crime or some wrong. [15]But the things you are saying are only questions about words and names—arguments about your own law. So you must solve this problem yourselves. I don't want to be a judge of these things." [16]And Gallio made them leave the court.

[17]Then they all grabbed Sosthenes, the leader of the synagogue,[d] and beat him there before the court. But this did not bother Gallio.

Paul Returns to Antioch

[18]Paul stayed with the believers for many more days. Then he left and sailed for Syria, with Priscilla and Aquila. At Cenchrea Paul cut off his hair,[n] because he had made a promise to God. [19]Then they went to Ephesus, where Paul left Priscilla and Aquila. While Paul was there, he went into the synagogue[d] and talked with the Jews. [20]When they asked him to stay with them longer, he refused. [21]But as he left, he said, "I will come back to you again if God wants me to." And so he sailed away from Ephesus.

[22]When Paul landed at Caesarea, he went and gave greetings to the church in Jerusalem. After that, Paul went to Antioch. [23]He stayed there for a while and then left and went through the regions of Galatia and Phrygia. He traveled from town to town in these regions, giving strength to all the followers.

Apollos in Ephesus and Corinth

[24]A Jew named Apollos came to Ephesus. He was born in the city of Alexandria and was a good speaker who knew the Scriptures[d] well. [25]He had been taught about the way of the Lord and was always very excited when he spoke and taught the truth about Jesus. But the only baptism Apollos knew about was the baptism that John[n] taught. [26]Apollos began to speak very boldly in the synagogue,[d] and when Priscilla and Aquila heard him, they took him to their home and helped him better understand the way of God. [27]Now Apollos wanted to go to the country of Southern Greece. So the believers helped him and wrote a letter to the followers there, asking them to accept him. These followers had believed in Jesus because of God's grace, and when Apollos arrived, he helped them very much. [28]He argued very strongly with the Jews before all the people, clearly proving with the Scriptures that Jesus is the Christ.[d]

Claudius The emperor (ruler) of Rome, A.D. 41-54.
shook ... clothes This was a warning to show that Paul was finished talking to the Jews in that city.
cut ... hair Jews did this to show that the time of a special promise to God was finished.
John John the Baptist, who preached to people about Christ's coming (Luke 3).

Paul in Ephesus

19 While Apollos was in Corinth, Paul was visiting some places on the way to Ephesus. There he found some followers [2]and asked them, "Did you receive the Holy Spirit[d] when you believed?"

They said, "We have never even heard of a Holy Spirit."

[3]So he asked, "What kind of baptism did you have?"

They said, "It was the baptism that John[n] taught."

[4]Paul said, "John's baptism was a baptism of changed hearts and lives. He told people to believe in the one who would come after him, and that one is Jesus."

[5]When they heard this, they were baptized in the name of the Lord Jesus. [6]Then Paul laid his hands on them, [n] and the Holy Spirit came upon them. They began speaking different languages [n] and prophesying.[d] [7]There were about twelve people in this group.

[8]Paul went into the synagogue[d] and spoke out boldly for three months. He talked with the Jews and persuaded them to accept the things he said about the kingdom of God. [9]But some of the Jews became stubborn. They refused to believe and said evil things about the Way of Jesus before all the people. So Paul left them, and taking the followers with him, he went to the school of a man named Tyrannus. There Paul talked with people every day [10]for two years. Because of his work, every Jew and Greek in the country of Asia heard the word of the Lord.

John John the Baptist, who preached to people about Christ's coming (Luke 3).
laid his hands on them The laying on of hands had many purposes, including the giving of a blessing, power, or authority.
languages This can also be translated "tongues."

FAITH

Growing Up

Checkmark the items that are true of your relationship with God. I understand God better now than when I first started learning about him. I genuinely enjoy being involved in activities related to my faith. God helps me love and care for people. My relationships are better as a result of my faith in God. I understand scripture better than I used to. I ask God to help me solve problems. My friends and family know I'm a Christian. I take time each day to pray. I know God loves me. I ask God to forgive me when I do something wrong. I am honest with God about my feelings. I tell people about Jesus. My relationship with God deeply influences my actions.

Now rate yourself:
- 6 to 13 checkmarks—Your faith is definitely growing. You are experiencing the type of growth described in Acts 19:1–7.
- 3 to 5 checkmarks—Be careful that your faith is not stagnating. Read the items you didn't checkmark, and begin building those things into your life. Be encouraged by Acts 19:1–7.
- 0 to 2 checkmarks—Your faith is wilting. Water it with the Word of God and get involved with other Christians soon—before your faith withers. Be challenged by Acts 19:1–7.

In **Acts 19:1–7**, Paul explained truth that the followers did not know. When they heard all that God had done for them, they were changed—and their faith could grow.
- How did Paul help people's faith grow? What items in the checklist would be true for the people in the passage?
- How did the people in this passage express their faith?

C O N S I D E R . . .
- pretending it's yearbook signing time. Write an entry to Jesus telling ways your relationship has grown, what you appreciate about him and how you hope your relationship will grow in the next year.
- choosing one item from the checklist to begin building into your life.

F O R   M O R E ,   S E E . . .
- Psalm 15 (p. 488)
- 1 Corinthians 3:1–9 (p. 1169)
- Colossians 1:9–14 (p. 1238)

The Sons of Sceva

[11]God used Paul to do some very special miracles.[d] [12]Some people took handkerchiefs and clothes that Paul had used and put them on the sick. When they did this, the sick were healed and evil spirits left them.

[13]But some Jews also were traveling around and making evil spirits go out of people. They tried to use the name of the Lord Jesus to force the evil spirits out. They would say, "By the same Jesus that Paul talks about, I order you to come out!" [14]Seven sons of Sceva, a leading Jewish priest, were doing this.

[15]But one time an evil spirit said to them, "I know Jesus, and I know about Paul, but who are you?"

[16]Then the man who had the evil spirit jumped on them. Because he was so much stronger than all of them, they ran away from the house naked and hurt. [17]All the people in Ephesus — Jews and Greeks — learned about this and were filled with fear and gave great honor to the Lord Jesus. [18]Many of the believers began to confess openly and tell all the evil things they had done. [19]Some of them who had used magic brought their magic books and burned them before everyone. Those books were worth about fifty thousand silver coins.[n]

[20]So in a powerful way the word of the Lord kept spreading and growing.

[21]After these things, Paul decided to go to Jerusalem, planning to go through the countries of Macedonia and Southern Greece and then on to Jerusalem. He said, "After I have been to Jerusalem, I must also visit Rome." [22]Paul sent Timothy and Erastus, two of his helpers, ahead to Macedonia, but he himself stayed in Asia for a while.

Trouble in Ephesus

[23]And during that time, there was some serious trouble in Ephesus about the Way of Jesus. [24]A man named Demetrius, who worked with silver, made little silver models that looked like the temple of the goddess Artemis.[n] Those who did this work made much money. [25]Demetrius had a meeting with them and some others who did the same kind of work. He told them, "Men, you know that we make a lot of money from our business. [26]But look at what this man Paul is doing. He has convinced and turned away many people in Ephesus and in almost all of Asia! He says the gods made by human hands are not real. [27]There is a danger that our business will lose its good name, but there is also another danger: People will begin to think that the temple of the great

goddess Artemis is not important. Her greatness will be destroyed, and Artemis is the goddess that everyone in Asia and the whole world worships."

[28]When the others heard this, they became very angry and shouted, "Artemis, the goddess of Ephesus, is great." [29]The whole city became confused. The people grabbed Gaius and Aristarchus, who were from Macedonia and were traveling with Paul, and ran to the theater. [30]Paul wanted to go in and talk to the crowd, but the followers did not let him. [31]Also, some leaders of Asia who were friends of Paul sent him a message, begging him not to go into the theater. [32]Some people were shouting one thing, and some were shouting another. The meeting was completely confused; most of them did not know why they had come together. [33]The Jews put a man named Alexander in front of the people, and some of them told him what to do. Alexander waved his hand so he could explain things to the people. [34]But when they saw that Alexander was a Jew, they all shouted the same thing for two hours: "Great is Artemis of Ephesus!"

[35]Then the city clerk made the crowd be quiet. He said, "People of Ephesus, everyone knows that Ephesus is the city that keeps the temple of the great goddess Artemis and her holy stone[n] that fell from heaven. [36]Since no one can say this is not true, you should be quiet. Stop and think before you do anything. [37]You brought these men here, but they have not said anything evil against our goddess or stolen anything from her temple. [38]If Demetrius and those who work with him have a charge against anyone they should go to the courts and judges where they can argue with each other. [39]If there is something else you want to talk about, it can be decided at the regular town meeting of the people. [40]I say this because some people might see this trouble today and say that we are rioting. We could not explain this, because there is no real reason for this meeting." [41]After the city clerk said these things, he told the people to go home.

Paul In Macedonia and Greece

20 When the trouble stopped, Paul sent for the followers to come to him. After he encouraged them and then told them good-bye, he left and went to the country of Macedonia. [2]He said many things to strengthen the followers in the different places on his way through Macedonia. Then he went to Greece, [3]where he stayed for three months. He was ready to sail for Syria, but some Jews were planning something against him. So Paul decided to go back through Macedo-

---

fifty thousand silver coins   Probably drachmas. One coin was enough to pay a worker for one day's labor.
Artemis   A Greek goddess that the people of Asia Minor worshiped.
holy stone   Probably a meteorite or stone that the people thought looked like Artemis.

nia to Syria. [4]The men who went with him were Sopater son of Pyrrhus, from the city of Berea; Aristarchus and Secundus, from the city of Thessalonica; Gaius, from Derbe; Timothy; and Tychicus and Trophimus, two men from the country of Asia. [5]These men went on ahead and waited for us at Troas. [6]We sailed from Philippi after the Feast[d] of Unleavened Bread. Five days later we met them in Troas, where we stayed for seven days.

Paul's Last Visit to Troas

[7]On the first day of the week,[n] we all met together to break bread,[n] and Paul spoke to the group. Because he was planning to leave the next day, he kept on talking until midnight. [8]We were all together in a room upstairs, and there were many lamps in the room. [9]A young man named Eutychus was sitting in the window. As Paul continued talking, Eutychus was falling into a deep sleep. Finally, he went sound asleep and fell to the ground from the third floor. When they picked him up, he was dead. [10]Paul went down to Eutychus, knelt down, and put his arms around him. He said, "Don't worry. He is alive now." [11]Then Paul went upstairs again, broke bread, and ate. He spoke to them a long time, until it was early morning, and then he left. [12]They took the young man home alive and were greatly comforted.

The Trip from Troas to Miletus

[13]We went on ahead of Paul and sailed for the city of Assos, where he wanted to join us on the ship. Paul planned it this way because he wanted to go to Assos by land. [14]When he met us there, we took him aboard and went to Mitylene. [15]We sailed from Mitylene and the next day came to a place near Chios. The following day we sailed to Samos, and the next day we reached Miletus. [16]Paul had already decided not to stop at Ephesus, because he did not want to stay too long in the country of Asia. He was hurrying to be in Jerusalem on the day of Pentecost,[d] if that were possible.

The Elders from Ephesus

[17]Now from Miletus Paul sent to Ephesus and called for the elders[d] of the church. [18]When they came to him, he said, "You know about my life from the first day I came to Asia. You know the way I lived all the time I was with you. [19]The Jews made plans against me, which troubled me very much. But you know I always served the Lord unselfishly, and I often cried. [20]You know I

preached to you and did not hold back anything that would help you. You know that I taught you in public and in your homes. [21]I warned both Jews and Greeks to change their lives and turn to God and believe in our Lord Jesus. [22]But now I must obey the Holy Spirit[d] and go to Jerusalem. I don't know what will happen to me there. [23]I know only that in every city the Holy Spirit tells me that troubles and even jail wait for me. [24]I don't care about my own life. The most important thing is that I complete my mission, the work that the Lord Jesus gave me — to tell people the Good News[d] about God's grace.

[25]"And now, I know that none of you among whom I was preaching the kingdom of God will ever see me again. [26]So today I tell you that if any of you should be lost, I am not responsible, [27]because I have told you everything God wants you to know. [28]Be careful for yourselves and for all the people the Holy Spirit has given to you to care for. You must be like shepherds to the church of God,[n] which he bought with the death of his own son. [29]I know that after I leave, some people will come like wild wolves and try to destroy the flock. [30]Also, some from your own group will rise up and twist the truth and will lead away followers after them. [31]So be careful! Always remember that for three years, day and night, I never stopped warning each of you, and I often cried over you.

[32]"Now I am putting you in the care of God and the message about his grace. It is able to give you strength, and it will give you the blessings God has for all his holy people. [33]When I was with you, I never wanted anyone's money or fine clothes. [34]You know I always worked to take care of my own needs and the needs of those who were with me. [35]I showed you in all things that you should work as I did and help the weak. I taught you to remember the words Jesus said: 'It is more blessed to give than to receive.' "

[36]When Paul had said this, he knelt down with all of them and prayed. [37-38]And they all cried because Paul had said they would never see him again. They put their arms around him and kissed him. Then they went with him to the ship.

Paul Goes to Jerusalem

21 After we all said good-bye to them, we sailed straight to the island of Cos. The next day we reached Rhodes, and from there we went to Patara. [2]There we found a ship going to Phoenicia, so we went aboard and sailed away. [3]We sailed near the island of Cyprus, seeing it to

first day of the week Sunday, which for the Jews began at sunset on our Saturday. But if in this part of Asia a different system of time was used, then the meeting was on our Sunday night.
break bread Probably the Lord's Supper, the special meal that Jesus told his followers to eat to remember him (Luke 22:14-20).
of God Some Greek copies say, "of the Lord."

the north, but we sailed on to Syria. We stopped at Tyre because the ship needed to unload its cargo there. [4]We found some followers in Tyre and stayed with them for seven days. Through the Holy Spirit[d] they warned Paul not to go to Jerusalem. [5]When we finished our visit, we left and continued our trip. All the followers, even the women and children came outside the city with us. After we all knelt on the beach and prayed, [6]we said good-bye and got on the ship, and the followers went back home.

[7]We continued our trip from Tyre and arrived at Ptolemais, where we greeted the believers and stayed with them for a day. [8]The next day we left Ptolemais and went to the city of Caesarea. There we went into the home of Philip the preacher,[d] one of the seven helpers,[n] and stayed with him. [9]He had four unmarried daughters who had the gift of prophesying.[d] [10]After we had been there for some time, a prophet named Agabus arrived from Judea. [11]He came to us and borrowed Paul's belt and used it to tie his own hands and feet. He said, "The Holy Spirit says, 'This is how the Jews in Jerusalem will tie up the man who wears this belt. Then they will give him to those who are not Jews.'"

[12]When we all heard this, we and the people there begged Paul not to go to Jerusalem. [13]But he said, "Why are you crying and making me so sad? I am not only ready to be tied up in Jerusalem, I am ready to die for the Lord Jesus!" [14]We could not persuade him to stay away from Jerusalem. So we stopped begging him and said, "We pray that what the Lord wants will be done."

[15]After this, we got ready and started on our way to Jerusalem. [16]Some of the followers from Caesarea went with us and took us to the home of Mnason, where we would stay. He was from Cyprus and was one of the first followers.

Paul Visits James

[17]In Jerusalem the believers were glad to see us. [18]The next day Paul went with us to visit James, and all the elders[d] were there. [19]Paul greeted them and told them everything God had done among the non-Jewish people through him. [20]When they heard this, they praised God. Then they said to Paul, "Brother, you can see that many thousands of Jews have become believers. And they think it is very important to obey the law of Moses. [21]They have heard about your teaching, that you tell the Jews who live among those who are not Jews to leave the law of Moses. They have heard that you tell them not to circumcise[d] their children and not to obey Jewish customs. [22]What

should we do? They will learn that you have come. [23]So we will tell you what to do: Four of our men have made a promise to God. [24]Take these men with you and share in their cleansing ceremony.[n] Pay their expenses so they can shave their heads.[n] Then it will prove to everyone that what they have heard about you is not true and that you follow the law of Moses in your own life. [25]We have already sent a letter to the non-Jewish believers. The letter said: 'Do not eat food that has been offered to idols, or blood, or animals that have been strangled. Do not take part in sexual sin.'"

[26]The next day Paul took the four men and shared in the cleansing ceremony with them. Then he went to the Temple[d] and announced the time when the days of the cleansing ceremony would be finished. On the last day an offering would be given for each of the men.

[27]When the seven days were almost over, some Jews from Asia saw Paul at the Temple. They caused all the people to be upset and grabbed Paul. [28]They shouted, "People of Israel, help us! This is the man who goes everywhere teaching against the law of Moses, against our people, and against this Temple. Now he has brought some Greeks into the Temple and has made this holy

---

> ✳ **SIDELIGHT:** When Paul was accused of making the Temple unclean, he was being accused of a crime punishable by death (Acts 21:28). Archaeologists have found a temple inscription that says: "No foreigner is to enter. . . . Whoever is caught will render himself liable to the consequent penalty of death."

---

place unclean!"[d] [29](The Jews said this because they had seen Trophimus, a man from Ephesus, with Paul in Jerusalem. The Jews thought that Paul had brought him into the Temple.)

[30]All the people in Jerusalem became upset. Together they ran, took Paul, and dragged him out of the Temple. The Temple doors were closed immediately. [31]While they were trying to kill Paul, the commander of the Roman army in Jerusalem learned that there was trouble in the whole city. [32]Immediately he took some officers and soldiers and ran to the place where the crowd was gathered. When the people saw them, they stopped beating Paul. [33]The commander went to Paul and arrested him. He told his soldiers to tie Paul with

---

helpers   The seven men chosen for a special work described in Acts 6:1-6.
cleansing ceremony   The special things Jews did to end the Nazirite promise.
shave their heads   The Jews did this to show that their promise was finished.

two chains. Then he asked who he was and what he had done wrong. [34]Some in the crowd were yelling one thing, and some were yelling another. Because of all this confusion and shouting, the commander could not learn what had happened. So he ordered the soldiers to take Paul to the army building. [35]When Paul came to the steps, the soldiers had to carry him because the people were ready to hurt him. [36]The whole mob was following them, shouting, "Kill him!"

[37]As the soldiers were about to take Paul into the army building, he spoke to the commander, "May I say something to you?"

The commander said, "Do you speak Greek? [38]I thought you were the Egyptian who started some trouble against the government not long ago and led four thousand killers out to the desert."

[39]Paul said, "No, I am a Jew from Tarsus in the country of Cilicia. I am a citizen of that important city. Please, let me speak to the people."

[40]The commander gave permission, so Paul stood on the steps and waved his hand to quiet the people. When there was silence, he spoke to them in the Jewish language. [n]

Paul Speaks to the People

22 Paul said, "Friends, fellow Jews, listen to my defense to you." [2]When the Jews heard him speaking the Jewish language, [n] they became very quiet. Paul said, [3]"I am a Jew, born in Tarsus in the country of Cilicia, but I grew up in this city. I was a student of Gamaliel, [n] who carefully taught me everything about the law of our ancestors. I was very serious about serving God, just as are all of you here today. [4]I persecuted the people who followed the Way of Jesus, and some of them were even killed. I arrested men and women and put them in jail. [5]The high priest and the whole council of older Jewish leaders can tell you this is true. They gave me letters to the Jewish brothers in Damascus. So I was going there to arrest these people and bring them back to Jerusalem to be punished.

[6]"About noon when I came near Damascus, a bright light from heaven suddenly flashed all around me. [7]I fell to the ground and heard a voice saying, 'Saul, Saul, why are you persecuting me?' [8]I asked, 'Who are you, Lord?' The voice said, 'I am Jesus from Nazareth whom you are persecuting.' [9]Those who were with me did not hear the voice, but they saw the light. [10]I said, 'What shall I do, Lord?' The Lord answered, 'Get up and go to Damascus. There you will be told about all the things I have planned for you to do.' [11]I could not see, because the bright light had made me blind. So my companions led me into Damascus.

[12]"There a man named Ananias came to me. He was a religious man; he obeyed the law of Moses, and all the Jews who lived there respected him. [13]He stood by me and said, 'Brother Saul, see again!' Immediately I was able to see him. [14]He said, 'The God of our ancestors chose you long ago to know his plan, to see the Righteous One, and to hear words from him. [15]You will be his witness to all people, telling them about what you have seen and heard. [16]Now, why wait any longer? Get up, be baptized, and wash your sins away, trusting in him to save you.'

[17]"Later, when I returned to Jerusalem, I was praying in the Temple, [d] and I saw a vision. [18]I saw the Lord saying to me, 'Hurry! Leave Jerusalem now! The people here will not accept the truth about me.' [19]But I said, 'Lord, they know that in every synagogue [d] I put the believers in jail and beat them. [20]They also know I was there when Stephen, your witness, was killed. I stood there agreeing and holding the coats of those who were killing him!' [21]But the Lord said to me, 'Leave now. I will send you far away to the non-Jewish people.' "

[22]The crowd listened to Paul until he said this. Then they began shouting, "Kill him! Get him out of the world! He should not be allowed to live!" [23]They shouted, threw off their coats, [n] and threw dust into the air. [n]

[24]Then the commander ordered the soldiers to take Paul into the army building and beat him. He wanted to make Paul tell why the people were shouting against him like this. [25]But as the soldiers were tying him up, preparing to beat him, Paul said to an officer nearby, "Do you have the right to beat a Roman citizen [n] who has not been proven guilty?"

[26]When the officer heard this, he went to the commander and reported it. The officer said, "Do you know what you are doing? This man is a Roman citizen."

[27]The commander came to Paul and said, "Tell me, are you really a Roman citizen?"

He answered, "Yes."

[28]The commander said, "I paid a lot of money to become a Roman citizen."

But Paul said, "I was born a citizen."

[29]The men who were preparing to question Paul moved away from him immediately. The commander was frightened because he had already tied Paul, and Paul was a Roman citizen.

Jewish language Hebrew or Aramaic, the languages of the Jews in the first century.
Gamaliel A very important teacher of the Pharisees, a Jewish religious group (Acts 5:34).
threw off their coats This showed that the Jews were very angry with Paul.
threw dust into the air This showed even greater anger.
Roman citizen Roman law said that Roman citizens must not be beaten before they had a trial.

Paul Speaks to Jewish Leaders

30The next day the commander decided to learn why the Jews were accusing Paul. So he ordered the leading priests and the Jewish council to meet. The commander took Paul's chains off. Then he brought Paul out and stood him before their meeting.

23 Paul looked at the Jewish council and said, "Brothers, I have lived my life without guilt feelings before God up to this day." 2Ananias,*n* the high priest, heard this and told the men who were standing near Paul to hit him on the mouth. 3Paul said to Ananias, "God will hit you, too! You are like a wall that has been painted white. You sit there and judge me, using the law of Moses, but you are telling them to hit me, and that is against the law."

4The men standing near Paul said to him, "You cannot insult God's high priest like that!"

5Paul said, "Brothers, I did not know this man was the high priest. It is written in the Scriptures,*d* 'You must not curse a leader of your people.' "*n*

6Some of the men in the meeting were Sadducees,*d* and others were Pharisees.*d* Knowing this, Paul shouted to them, "My brothers, I am a Pharisee, and my father was a Pharisee. I am on trial here because I believe that people will rise from the dead."

7When Paul said this, there was an argument between the Pharisees and the Sadducees, and the group was divided. 8(The Sadducees do not believe in angels or spirits or that people will rise from the dead. But the Pharisees believe in them all.) 9So there was a great uproar. Some of the teachers of the law, who were Pharisees, stood up and argued, "We find nothing wrong with this man. Maybe an angel or a spirit did speak to him."

10The argument was beginning to turn into such a fight that the commander was afraid the Jews would tear Paul to pieces. So he told the soldiers to go down and take Paul away and put him in the army building.

11The next night the Lord came and stood by Paul. He said, "Be brave! You have told people in Jerusalem about me. You must do the same in Rome."

12In the morning some of the Jews made a plan to kill Paul, and they took an oath not to eat or drink anything until they had killed him. 13There were more than forty Jews who made this plan. 14They went to the leading priests and the older Jewish leaders and said, "We have taken an oath not to eat or drink until we have killed Paul. 15So this is what we want you to do: Send a message to the commander to bring Paul out to you as though you want to ask him more questions. We

will be waiting to kill him while he is on the way here."

16But Paul's nephew heard about this plan and went to the army building and told Paul. 17Then Paul called one of the officers and said, "Take this young man to the commander. He has a message for him."

18So the officer brought Paul's nephew to the commander and said, "The prisoner, Paul, asked me to bring this young man to you. He wants to tell you something."

19The commander took the young man's hand and led him to a place where they could be alone. He asked, "What do you want to tell me?"

20The young man said, "The Jews have decided to ask you to bring Paul down to their council meeting tomorrow. They want you to think they are going to ask him more questions. 21But don't believe them! More than forty men are hiding and waiting to kill Paul. They have all taken an oath not to eat or drink until they have killed him. Now they are waiting for you to agree."

22The commander sent the young man away, ordering him, "Don't tell anyone that you have told me about their plan."

Paul Is Sent to Caesarea

23Then the commander called two officers and said, "I need some men to go to Caesarea. Get two hundred soldiers, seventy horsemen, and two hundred men with spears ready to leave at nine o'clock tonight. 24Get some horses for Paul to ride so he can be taken to Governor Felix safely." 25And he wrote a letter that said:

> 26From Claudius Lysias.
> To the Most Excellent Governor Felix: Greetings.
> 27The Jews had taken this man and planned to kill him. But I learned that he is a Roman citizen, so I went with my soldiers and saved him. 28I wanted to know why they were accusing him, so I brought him before their council meeting. 29I learned that the Jews said Paul did some things that were wrong by their own laws, but no charge was worthy of jail or death. 30When I was told that some of the Jews were planning to kill Paul, I sent him to you at once. I also told those Jews to tell you what they have against him.

31So the soldiers did what they were told and took Paul and brought him to the city of Antipatris that night. 32The next day the horsemen went with Paul to Caesarea, but the other soldiers went back to the army building in Jerusalem. 33When

---

Ananias   This is not the same man named Ananias in Acts 22:12.
'You ... people.'   Quotation from Exodus 22:28.

the horsemen came to Caesarea and gave the letter to the governor, they turned Paul over to him. 34The governor read the letter and asked Paul, "What area are you from?" When he learned that Paul was from Cilicia, 35he said, "I will hear your case when those who are against you come here, too." Then the governor gave orders for Paul to be kept under guard in Herod's palace.

Paul Is Accused

24 Five days later Ananias, the high priest, went to the city of Caesarea with some of the older Jewish leaders and a lawyer named Tertullus. They had come to make charges against Paul before the governor. 2Paul was called into the meeting, and Tertullus began to accuse him, saying, "Most Excellent Felix! Our people enjoy much peace because of you, and many wrong things in our country are being made right through your wise help. 3We accept these things always and in every place, and we are thankful for them. 4But not wanting to take any more of your time, I beg you to be kind and listen to our few words. 5We have found this man to be a troublemaker, stirring up the Jews everywhere in the world. He is a leader of the Nazarene*d* group. 6Also, he was trying to make the Temple*d* unclean,*d* but we stopped him.*n* 8By asking him questions yourself, you can decide if all these things are true." 9The other Jews agreed and said that all of this was true.

10When the governor made a sign for Paul to speak, Paul said, "Governor Felix, I know you have been a judge over this nation for a long time. So I am happy to defend myself before you. 11You can learn for yourself that I went to worship in Jerusalem only twelve days ago. 12Those who are accusing me did not find me arguing with anyone in the Temple or stirring up the people in the synagogues*d* or in the city. 13They cannot prove the things they are saying against me now. 14But I will tell you this: I worship the God of our ancestors as a follower of the Way of Jesus. The Jews say that the Way of Jesus is not the right way. But I believe everything that is taught in the law of Moses and that is written in the books of the Prophets.*d* 15I have the same hope in God that they have—the hope that all people, good and bad, will surely be raised from the dead. 16This is why I always try to do what I believe is right before God and people.

17"After being away from Jerusalem for several years, I went back to bring money to my people and to offer sacrifices. 18I was doing this when they found me in the Temple. I had finished the cleansing ceremony and had not made any trou-

ble; no people were gathering around me. 19But there were some Jews from the country of Asia who should be here, standing before you. If I have really done anything wrong, they are the ones who should accuse me. 20Or ask these Jews here if they found any wrong in me when I stood before the Jewish council in Jerusalem. 21But I did shout one thing when I stood before them: 'You are judging me today because I believe that people will rise from the dead!' "

22Felix already understood much about the Way of Jesus. He stopped the trial and said, "When commander Lysias comes here, I will decide your case." 23Felix told the officer to keep Paul guarded but to give him some freedom and to let his friends bring what he needed.

Paul Speaks to Felix and His Wife

24After some days Felix came with his wife, Drusilla, who was Jewish, and asked for Paul to be brought to him. He listened to Paul talk about believing in Christ Jesus. 25But Felix became afraid when Paul spoke about living right, self-control, and the time when God will judge the world. He said, "Go away now. When I have more time, I will call for you." 26At the same time Felix hoped that Paul would give him some money, so he often sent for Paul and talked with him.

SIDELIGHT: The Judean governor Felix was greedy, brutal, and incompetent. He once killed four hundred men suspected of terrorist activities—without a trial. When Paul wouldn't pay him a bribe, Felix left the apostle in jail for two years, until Felix was succeeded in office (Acts 24:1–27).

27But after two years, Felix was replaced by Porcius Festus as governor. But Felix had left Paul in prison to please the Jews.

Paul Asks to See Caesar

25 Three days after Festus became governor, he went from Caesarea to Jerusalem. 2There the leading priests and the important Jewish leaders made charges against Paul before Festus. 3They asked Festus to do them a favor. They wanted him to send Paul back to Jerusalem, because they had a plan to kill him on the way. 4But Festus answered that Paul would be kept in Caesarea and that he himself was returning there soon. 5He said, "Some of your leaders should go

Verse 6 Some Greek copies add 6b-8a: "And we wanted to judge him by our own law. 7But the officer Lysias came and used much force to take him from us. 8And Lysias commanded those who wanted to accuse Paul to come to you."

with me. They can accuse the man there in Caesarea, if he has really done something wrong."

⁶Festus stayed in Jerusalem another eight or ten days and then went back to Caesarea. The next day he told the soldiers to bring Paul before him. Festus was seated on the judge's seat ⁷when Paul came into the room. The Jewish people who had come from Jerusalem stood around him, making serious charges against him, which they could not prove. ⁸This is what Paul said to defend himself: "I have done nothing wrong against the Jewish law, against the Temple,ᵈ or against Caesar."ᵈ

⁹But Festus wanted to please the Jews. So he asked Paul, "Do you want to go to Jerusalem for me to judge you there on these charges?"

¹⁰Paul said, "I am standing at Caesar's judgment seat now, where I should be judged. I have done nothing wrong to the Jews; you know this is true. ¹¹If I have done something wrong and the law says I must die, I do not ask to be saved from death. But if these charges are not true, then no one can give me to them. I want Caesar to hear my case!"

¹²Festus talked about this with his advisors. Then he said, "You have asked to see Caesar, so you will go to Caesar!"

Paul Before King Agrippa

¹³A few days later King Agrippa and Bernice came to Caesarea to visit Festus. ¹⁴They stayed there for some time, and Festus told the king about Paul's case. Festus said, "There is a man that Felix left in prison. ¹⁵When I went to Jerusalem, the leading priests and the older Jewish leaders there made charges against him, asking me to sentence him to death. ¹⁶But I answered, 'When a man is accused of a crime, Romans do not hand him over until he has been allowed to face his accusers and defend himself against their charges.' ¹⁷So when these Jews came here to Caesarea for the trial, I did not waste time. The next day I sat on the judge's seat and commanded that the man be brought in. ¹⁸The Jews stood up and accused him, but not of any serious crime as I thought they would. ¹⁹The things they said were about their own religion and about a man named Jesus who died. But Paul said that he is still alive. ²⁰Not knowing how to find out about these questions, I asked Paul, 'Do you want to go to Jerusalem and be judged there?' ²¹But he asked to be kept in Caesarea. He wants a decision from the emperor.ⁿ So I ordered that he be held until I could send him to Caesar.ᵗ"

²²Agrippa said to Festus, "I would also like to hear this man myself."

Festus said, "Tomorrow you will hear him."

²³The next day Agrippa and Bernice appeared with great show, acting like very important people. They went into the judgment room with the army leaders and the important men of Caesarea. Then Festus ordered the soldiers to bring Paul in. ²⁴Festus said, "King Agrippa and all who are gathered here with us, you see this man. All the Jewish people, here and in Jerusalem, have complained to me about him, shouting that he should not live any longer. ²⁵When I judged him, I found no reason to order his death. But since he asked to be judged by Caesar, I decided to send him. ²⁶But I have nothing definite to write the emperor about him. So I have brought him before all of you—especially you, King Agrippa. I hope you can question him and give me something to write. ²⁷I think it is foolish to send a prisoner to Caesar without telling what charges are against him."

Paul Defends Himself

26 Agrippa said to Paul, "You may now speak to defend yourself."

Then Paul raised his hand and began to speak. ²He said, "King Agrippa, I am very happy to stand before you and will answer all the charges the Jewish people make against me. ³You know so much about all the Jewish customs and the things the Jews argue about, so please listen to me patiently.

⁴"All the Jewish people know about my whole life, how I lived from the beginning in my own country and later in Jerusalem. ⁵They have known me for a long time. If they want to, they can tell you that I was a good Pharisee.ᵈ And the Pharisees obey the laws of the Jewish religion more carefully than any other group. ⁶Now I am on trial because I hope for the promise that God made to our ancestors. ⁷This is the promise that the twelve tribesᵈ of our people hope to receive as they serve God day and night. My king, the Jews have accused me because I hope for this same promise! ⁸Why do any of you people think it is impossible for God to raise people from the dead?

⁹"I, too, thought I ought to do many things against Jesus from Nazareth. ¹⁰And that is what I did in Jerusalem. The leading priests gave me the power to put many of God's people in jail, and when they were being killed, I agreed it was a good thing. ¹¹In every synagogue,ᵈ I often punished them and tried to make them speak against Jesus. I was so angry against them I even went to other cities to find them and punish them.

¹²"One time the leading priests gave me permission and the power to go to Damascus. ¹³On the way there, at noon, I saw a light from heaven. It was brighter than the sun and flashed all around me and those who were traveling with me. ¹⁴We

---

emperor   The ruler of the Roman Empire, which was almost all the known world.

all fell to the ground. Then I heard a voice speaking to me in the Jewish language,[n] saying, 'Saul, Saul, why are you persecuting me? You are only hurting yourself by fighting me.' [15]I said, 'Who are you, Lord?' The Lord said, 'I am Jesus, the one you are persecuting. [16]Stand up! I have chosen you to be my servant and my witness—you will tell people the things that you have seen and the things that I will show you. This is why I have come to you today. [17]I will keep you safe from your own people and also from those who are not Jewish. I am sending you to them [18]to open their eyes so that they may turn away from darkness to the light, away from the power of Satan and to God. Then their sins can be forgiven, and they can have a place with those people who have been made holy by believing in me.'

[19]"King Agrippa, after I had this vision from heaven, I obeyed it. [20]I began telling people that they should change their hearts and lives and turn to God and do things to show they really had changed. I told this first to those in Damascus, then in Jerusalem, and in every part of Judea, and also to those who are not Jewish. [21]This is why the Jews took me and were trying to kill me in the Temple.[d] [22]But God has helped me, and so I stand here today, telling all people, small and great, what I have seen. But I am saying only what Moses and the prophets[d] said would happen— [23]that the Christ[d] would die, and as the first to rise from the dead, he would bring light to the Jewish and non-Jewish people."

Paul Tries to Persuade Agrippa

[24]While Paul was saying these things to defend himself, Festus said loudly, "Paul, you are out of your mind! Too much study has driven you crazy!"

[25]Paul said, "Most excellent Festus, I am not crazy. My words are true and sensible. [26]King Agrippa knows about these things, and I can speak freely to him. I know he has heard about all of these things, because they did not happen off in a corner. [27]King Agrippa, do you believe what the prophets[d] wrote? I know you believe."

[28]King Agrippa said to Paul, "Do you think you can persuade me to become a Christian in such a short time?"

[29]Paul said, "Whether it is a short or a long time, I pray to God that not only you but every person listening to me today would be saved and be like me—except for these chains I have."

[30]Then King Agrippa, Governor Festus, Bernice, and all the people sitting with them stood up [31]and left the room. Talking to each other, they said, "There is no reason why this man should die or be put in jail." [32]And Agrippa said to Festus, "We could let this man go free, but he has asked Caesar[d] to hear his case."

Paul Sails for Rome

27 It was decided that we would sail for Italy. An officer named Julius, who served in the emperor's[n] army, guarded Paul and some other prisoners. [2]We got on a ship that was from the city of Adramyttium and was about to sail to different ports in the country of Asia. Aristarchus, a man from the city of Thessalonica in Macedonia, went with us. [3]The next day we came to Sidon. Julius was very good to Paul and gave him freedom to go visit his friends, who took care of his needs. [4]We left Sidon and sailed close to the island of Cyprus, because the wind was blowing against us. [5]We went across the sea by Cilicia and Pamphylia and landed at the city of Myra, in Lycia. [6]There the officer found a ship from Alexandria that was going to Italy, so he put us on it.

[7]We sailed slowly for many days. We had a hard time reaching Cnidus because the wind was blowing against us, and we could not go any farther. So we sailed by the south side of the island of Crete near Salmone. [8]Sailing past it was hard. Then we came to a place called Fair Havens, near the city of Lasea.

[9]We had lost much time, and it was now dangerous to sail, because it was already after the Day of Cleansing.[n] So Paul warned them, [10]"Men, I can see there will be a lot of trouble on this trip. The ship, the cargo, and even our lives may be lost." [11]But the captain and the owner of the ship did not agree with Paul, and the officer believed what the captain and owner of the ship said. [12]Since that harbor was not a good place for the ship to stay for the winter, most of the men decided that the ship should leave. They hoped we could go to Phoenix and stay there for the winter. Phoenix, a city on the island of Crete, had a harbor which faced southwest and northwest.

The Storm

[13]When a good wind began to blow from the south, the men on the ship thought, "This is the wind we wanted, and now we have it." So they pulled up the anchor, and we sailed very close to the island of Crete. [14]But then a very strong wind named the "northeaster" came from the island. [15]The ship was caught in it and could not sail against it. So we stopped trying and let the wind

carry us. [16]When we went below a small island named Cauda, we were barely able to bring in the lifeboat. [17]After the men took the lifeboat in, they tied ropes around the ship to hold it together. The men were afraid that the ship would hit the sandbanks of Syrtis, [n] so they lowered the sail and let the wind carry the ship. [18]The next day the storm was blowing us so hard that the men threw out some of the cargo. [19]A day later with their own hands they threw out the ship's equipment. [20]When we could not see the sun or the stars for many days, and the storm was very bad, we lost all hope of being saved.

[21]After the men had gone without food for a long time, Paul stood up before them and said, "Men, you should have listened to me. You should not have sailed from Crete. Then you would not have all this trouble and loss. [22]But now I tell you to cheer up because none of you will die. Only the ship will be lost. [23]Last night an angel came to me from the God I belong to and worship. [24]The angel said, 'Paul, do not be afraid. You must stand before Caesar.[d] And God has promised you that he will save the lives of everyone sailing with you.' [25]So men, have courage. I trust in God that everything will happen as his angel told me. [26]But we will crash on an island."

[27]On the fourteenth night we were still being carried around in the Adriatic Sea.[n] About midnight the sailors thought we were close to land, [28]so they lowered a rope with a weight on the end of it into the water. They found that the water was one hundred twenty feet deep. They went a little farther and lowered the rope again. It was ninety feet deep. [29]The sailors were afraid that we would hit the rocks, so they threw four anchors into the water and prayed for daylight to come. [30]Some of the sailors wanted to leave the ship, and they lowered the lifeboat, pretending they were throwing more anchors from the front of the ship. [31]But Paul told the officer and the other soldiers, "If these men do not stay in the ship, your lives cannot be saved." [32]So the soldiers cut the ropes and let the lifeboat fall into the water.

[33]Just before dawn Paul began persuading all the people to eat something. He said, "For the past fourteen days you have been waiting and watching and not eating. [34]Now I beg you to eat something. You need it to stay alive. None of you will lose even one hair off your heads." [35]After he said this, Paul took some bread and thanked God for it before all of them. He broke off a piece and began eating. [36]They all felt better and started eating, too. [37]There were two hundred seventy-six people on the ship. [38]When they had eaten all

they wanted, they began making the ship lighter by throwing the grain into the sea.

The Ship Is Destroyed

[39]When daylight came, the sailors saw land. They did not know what land it was, but they saw a bay with a beach and wanted to sail the ship to the beach if they could. [40]So they cut the ropes to the anchors and left the anchors in the sea. At the same time, they untied the ropes that were holding the rudders. Then they raised the front sail into the wind and sailed toward the beach. [41]But the ship hit a sandbank. The front of the ship stuck there and could not move, but the back of the ship began to break up from the big waves.

[42]The soldiers decided to kill the prisoners so none of them could swim away and escape. [43]But Julius, the officer, wanted to let Paul live and did not allow the soldiers to kill the prisoners. Instead he ordered everyone who could swim to jump into the water first and swim to land. [44]The rest were to follow using wooden boards or pieces of the ship. And this is how all the people made it safely to land.

SIDELIGHT: Paul often experienced rough waters while sailing (Acts 27:13–44). Storms, a common occurrence in the Mediterranean Sea, made travel hazardous for wooden trading ships. Today, one Greek island, only nine miles long, has four hundred churches that were built by sailors who were fulfilling vows they made to God in the midst of perilous storms.

Paul on the Island of Malta

28 When we were safe on land, we learned that the island was called Malta. [2]The people who lived there were very good to us. Because it was raining and very cold, they made a fire and welcomed all of us. [3]Paul gathered a pile of sticks and was putting them on the fire when a poisonous snake came out because of the heat and bit him on the hand. [4]The people living on the island saw the snake hanging from Paul's hand and said to each other, "This man must be a murderer! He did not die in the sea, but Justice[n] does not want him to live." [5]But Paul shook the snake off into the fire and was not hurt. [5]The people thought that Paul would swell up or fall down dead. They waited and watched him for a long time, but nothing bad happened to him. So they changed their minds and said, "He is a god!"

Syrtis   Shallow area in the sea near the Libyan coast.
Adriatic Sea   The sea between Greece and Italy, including the central Mediterranean.
Justice   The people thought there was a god named Justice who would punish bad people.

⁷There were some fields around there owned by Publius, an important man on the island. He welcomed us into his home and was very good to us for three days. ⁸Publius' father was sick with a fever and dysentery.ⁿ Paul went to him, prayed, and put his hands on the man and healed him. ⁹After this, all the other sick people on the island came to Paul, and he healed them, too. ¹⁰⁻¹¹The people on the island gave us many honors. When we were ready to leave, three months later, they gave us the things we needed.

Paul Goes to Rome

We got on a ship from Alexandria that had stayed on the island during the winter. On the front of the ship was the sign of the twin gods.ⁿ ¹²We stopped at Syracuse for three days. ¹³From there we sailed to Rhegium. The next day a wind began to blow from the south, and a day later we came to Puteoli. ¹⁴We found some believers there who asked us to stay with them for a week. Finally, we came to Rome. ¹⁵The believers in Rome heard that we were there and came out as far as the Market of Appiusⁿ and the Three Innsⁿ to meet us. When Paul saw them, he was encouraged and thanked God.

Paul in Rome

¹⁶When we arrived at Rome, Paul was allowed to live alone, with the soldier who guarded him.

¹⁷Three days later Paul sent for the Jewish leaders there. When they came together, he said, "Brothers, I have done nothing against our people or the customs of our ancestors. But I was arrested in Jerusalem and given to the Romans. ¹⁸After they asked me many questions, they could find no reason why I should be killed. They wanted to let me go free, ¹⁹but the Jewish people there argued against that. So I had to ask to come to Rome to have my trial before Caesar.ᵈ But I have no charge to bring against my own people. ²⁰That is why I wanted to see you and talk with you. I am bound with this chain because I believe in the hope of Israel."

²¹They answered Paul, "We have received no letters from Judea about you. None of our Jewish brothers who have come from there brought news or told us anything bad about you. ²²But we want to hear your ideas, because we know that people everywhere are speaking against this religious group."

²³Paul and the Jewish people chose a day for a meeting and on that day many more of the Jews met with Paul at the place he was staying. He spoke to them all day long. Using the law of Moses and the prophets'ᵈ writings, he explained the kingdom of God, and he tried to persuade them to believe these things about Jesus. ²⁴Some believed what Paul said, but others did not. ²⁵So they argued and began leaving after Paul said one more thing to them: "The Holy Spiritᵈ spoke the truth to your ancestors through Isaiah the prophet, saying,

²⁶'Go to this people and say:
You will listen and listen, but you will not
    understand.
You will look and look, but you will not
    learn,
²⁷because these people have become stubborn.
They don't hear with their ears,
    and they have closed their eyes.
Otherwise, they might really understand
    what they see with their eyes
    and hear with their ears.
They might really understand in their minds
    and come back to me and be healed.'
Isaiah 6:9-10

²⁸"I want you to know that God has also sent his salvation to those who are not Jewish, and they will listen!" ²⁹ ⁿ

³⁰Paul stayed two full years in his own rented house and welcomed all people who came to visit him. ³¹He boldly preached about the kingdom of God and taught about the Lord Jesus Christ, and no one tried to stop him.

---

dysentery   A sickness like diarrhea.
twin gods   Statues of Castor and Pollux, gods in old Greek tales.
Market of Appius   A town about twenty-seven miles from Rome.
Three Inns   A town about thirty miles from Rome.
Verse 29   Some late Greek copies add verse 29: "After Paul said this, the Jews left. They were arguing very much with each other."

ROMANS

Why Read This Book:

- Understand that all people have sinned (Romans 1—3).
- Learn how Jesus Christ pays for our sins (Romans 4—8).
- Be challenged to live the Christian life (Romans 12—15).

Behind the Scenes:

Suppose a school friend sat down with you in the cafeteria and asked, out of the blue, "What do you believe?" What would you say?

The Book of Romans is the apostle Paul's answer to that question: What do you believe? For more than twenty years, he had been a missionary, spreading the good news about Jesus Christ. He wanted to visit the Roman church, but before he went, he wanted the Roman Christians to understand what he believed.

So he wrote them this letter, which many people believe is the best, most powerful summary of Christian beliefs in the Bible. The letter explains how all people have sinned and how God sent Jesus to pay for those sins and make people right with God (Romans 3:22–28). Then it explains what it means to live as Christians.

The Book of Romans is packed with powerful statements about God and faith. From this book we can learn how God's love for us overcomes the power of sin in our lives and how we can live lives that please God.

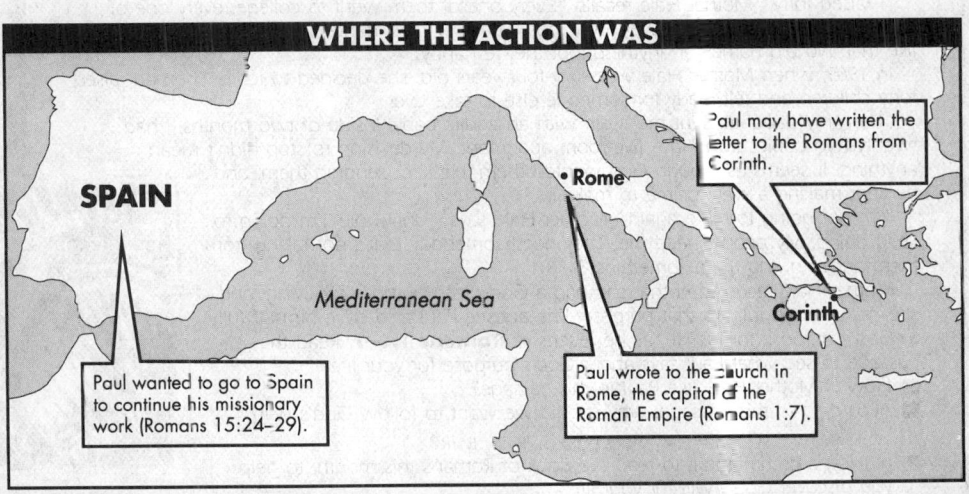

WHERE THE ACTION WAS

SPAIN

Rome

Mediterranean Sea

Corinth

Paul may have written the letter to the Romans from Corinth.

Paul wanted to go to Spain to continue his missionary work (Romans 15:24–29).

Paul wrote to the church in Rome, the capital of the Roman Empire (Romans 1:7).

WHEN THE ACTION WAS

Jesus was born	The church began soon after Jesus went to heaven	Paul began his missionary work	Fire destroyed Rome
BC/AD	25AD	50AD	75AD 100AD
	Jesus began his ministry Paul became a Christian		Paul wrote Romans Romans destroyed the Temple in Jerusalem

1 From Paul, a servant of Christ Jesus. God called me to be an apostle^d and chose me to tell the Good News.^d

²God promised this Good News long ago through his prophets,^d as it is written in the Holy Scriptures.^d ³⁴The Good News is about God's Son, Jesus Christ our Lord. As a man, he was born from the family of David. But through the Spirit^d of holiness he was appointed to be God's Son with great power by rising from the dead. ⁵Through Christ, God gave me the special work of an apostle, which was to lead people of all nations to believe and obey. I do this work for him. ⁶And you

who are in Rome are also called to belong to Jesus Christ.

⁷To all of you in Rome whom God loves and has called to be his holy people:

Grace and peace to you from God our Father and the Lord Jesus Christ.

A Prayer of Thanks

⁸First I want to say that I thank my God through Jesus Christ for all of you, because people everywhere in the world are talking about your faith. ⁹God, whom I serve with my whole heart by telling the Good News^d about his Son, knows

---

GOD'S WILL

Mother Hale

"My husband and I had dreams of what we were going to do with our children," recalls Clara McBride Hale of her life in the early part of the 1900s. "We dreamed that they'd grow up and be what they want to be and have a good life."

But Clara's husband died when their children, Lorraine and Nathan, were five and six. And during that time, untrained women could only work domestic jobs, such as housecleaning. Clara had to support her children, but she didn't want to leave them alone all day while she went to work.

"So I decided to take in other people's children," Clara continues. "They were coming for five days and going home Saturday and Sunday. But they got so they didn't want to go home. They wanted to stay with me altogether. So the parents would give me an extra dollar, and that meant I kept them all the time."

What started as a "survival" business bloomed into a lifetime ministry for Clara, who came to be known by the children and their parents as "Mother Hale."

"I raised forty," Mother Hale recalls. "Every one of them went to college, every one of them graduated, and they have lovely jobs. I have singers, dancers, preachers, and things like that. No big names or anything, but they're happy."

In 1969, when Mother Hale was sixty-four years old, she decided to retire. She had raised forty children and felt ready for someone else to take over.

"Then my daughter sent me a girl with an addict baby. Inside of two months, I had twenty-two babies living in a five-room apartment. My decision to stop didn't mean anything. It seems as though God wanted them. He kept sending them, and he kept making a way for me to make it.

"I'm not going to retire again," Mother Hale says. "Until I die, I'm going to keep doing. My people need me. They need somebody that's not taking from them and is giving them something."

Mother Hale recognized that she had a God-given purpose for living, and she gave herself fully to that purpose. The apostle Paul also gave himself fully to God's purpose for his life, as he asserts in **Romans 1:1–7**. Read the passage to see what Paul says about God's purpose for your life.

■ How is Mother Hale like Paul in this passage?
■ According to this passage, why should we want to follow God's will?

C O N S I D E R . . .
■ making a commitment to read the Book of Romans this month, to help you discover God's will for your life.
■ writing out God's purpose for your life according to the passage. Then pray for God to make his purpose become reality in your life.

F O R   M O R E ,   S E E . . .
■ Jeremiah 1:4–8 (p. 691)
■ Matthew 12:46–50 (p. 930)   ■ 1 Thessalonians 4:3–8 (p. 1247)

that I always mention you [10]every time I pray. I pray that I will be allowed to come to you, and

this will happen if God wants it. [11]I want very much to see you, to give you some spiritual gift to make you strong. [12]I mean that I want us to help each other with the faith we have. Your faith will help me, and my faith will help you. [13]Brothers and sisters,[n] I want you to know that I planned many times to come to you, but this has not been possible. I wanted to come so that I could help you grow spiritually as I have helped the other non-Jewish people.

[14]I have a duty to all people — Greeks and those who are not Greeks, the wise and the foolish. [15]That is why I want so much to preach the Good News to you in Rome.

[16]I am proud of the Good News, because it is the power God uses to save everyone who believes — to save the Jews first, and also to save those who are not Jews. [17]The Good News shows how God makes people right with himself — that it begins and ends with faith. As the Scripture[d] says, "But those who are right with God will live by trusting in him."[n]

All People Have Done Wrong

[18]God's anger is shown from heaven against all the evil and wrong things people do. By their own evil lives they hide the truth. [19]God shows his anger because some knowledge of him has been made clear to them. Yes, God has shown himself to them. [20]There are things about him that people cannot see — his eternal power and all the things that make him God. But since the beginning of the world those things have been easy to understand by what God has made. So people have no excuse for the bad things they do. [21]They knew God, but they did not give glory to God or thank him. Their thinking became useless. Their foolish minds were filled with darkness. [22]They said they were wise, but they became fools. [23]They traded the glory of God who lives forever for the worship of idols made to look like earthly people, birds, animals, and snakes.

[24]Because they did these things, God left them and let them go their sinful way, wanting only to do evil. As a result, they became full of sexual sin, using their bodies wrongly with each other. [25]They traded the truth of God for a lie. They worshiped and served what had been created instead of the God who created those things, who should be praised forever. Amen.

[26]Because people did those things, God left them and let them do the shameful things they wanted to do. Women stopped having natural sex and started having sex with other women. [27]In the same way, men stopped having natural sex and began wanting each other. Men did shameful things with other men, and in their bodies they received the punishment for those wrongs.

[28]People did not think it was important to have a true knowledge of God. So God left them and allowed them to have their own worthless thinking and to do things they should not do. [29]They are filled with every kind of sin, evil, selfishness, and hatred. They are full of jealousy, murder, fighting, lying, and thinking the worst about each other. They gossip [30]and say evil things about each other. They hate God. They are rude and conceited and brag about themselves. They invent ways of doing evil. They do not obey their parents. [31]They are foolish, they do not keep their promises, and they show no kindness or mercy to others. [32]They know God's law says that those who live like this should die. But they themselves not only continue to do these evil things, they applaud others who do them.

You People Also Are Sinful

2 If you think you can judge others, you are wrong. When you judge them, you are really judging yourself guilty, because you do the same things they do. [2]God judges those who do wrong things, and we know that his judging is right. [3]You judge those who do wrong, but you do wrong yourselves. Do you think you will be able to escape the judgment of God? [4]He has been very kind and patient, waiting for you to change, but you think nothing of his kindness. Perhaps you do not understand that God is kind to you so you will change your hearts and lives. [5]But you are stubborn and refuse to change, so you are making your own punishment even greater on the day he shows his anger. On that day everyone will see God's right judgments. [6]God will reward or punish every person for what that person has done. [7]Some people, by always continuing to do good, live for God's glory, for honor, and for life that has no end. God will give them life forever. [8]But other

---

Brothers and sisters Although the Greek text says "Brothers" here and throughout this book, Paul's words were meant for the entire church, including men and women.
"But those . . . him." Quotation from Habakkuk 2:4.

people are selfish. They refuse to follow truth and, instead, follow evil. God will give them his punishment and anger. ⁹He will give trouble and suffering to everyone who does evil — to the Jews first and also to those who are not Jews. ¹⁰But he will give glory, honor, and peace to everyone who does good — to the Jews first and also to those who are not Jews. ¹¹For God judges all people in the same way.

¹²People who do not have the law and who are sinners will be lost, although they do not have the law. And, in the same way, those who have the law and are sinners will be judged by the law. ¹³Hearing the law does not make people right with God. It is those who obey the law who will be right with him. ¹⁴(Those who are not Jews do not have the law, but when they freely do what the law commands, they are the law for themselves. This is true even though they do not have the law. ¹⁵They show that in their hearts they know what is right and wrong, just as the law commands. And they show this by their consciences. Sometimes their thoughts tell them they did wrong, and sometimes their thoughts tell them they did right.) ¹⁶All these things will happen on the day when God, through Christ Jesus, will judge people's secret thoughts. The Good News*d* that I preach says this.

The Jews and the Law

¹⁷What about you? You call yourself a Jew. You trust in the law of Moses and brag that you are close to God. ¹⁸You know what he wants you to do and what is important, because you have learned the law. ¹⁹You think you are a guide for the blind and a light for those who are in darkness. ²⁰You think you can show foolish people what is right and teach those who know nothing. You have the law; so you think you know everything and have all truth. ²¹You teach others, so why don't you teach yourself? You tell others not to steal, but you steal. ²²You say that others must not take part in adultery,*d* but you are guilty of that sin. You hate idols, but you steal from temples. ²³You brag about having God's law, but you bring shame to God by breaking his law, ²⁴just as the Scriptures*d* say: "Those who are not Jews speak against God's name because of you." *n*

²⁵If you follow the law, your circumcision*d* has meaning. But if you break the law, it is as if you were never circumcised. ²⁶People who are not Jews are not circumcised, but if they do what the law says, it is as if they were circumcised. ²⁷You Jews have the written law and circumcision, but you break the law. So those who are not circumcised in their bodies, but still obey the law, will show that you are guilty. ²⁸They can do this be-

"Those . . . you." Quotation from Isaiah 52:5; Ezekiel 36:20.

cause a person is not a true Jew if he is only a Jew in his physical body; true circumcision is not only on the outside of the body. ²⁹A person is a Jew only if he is a Jew inside; true circumcision is done in the heart by the Spirit,*d* not by the written law. Such a person gets praise from God rather than from people.

3 So, do Jews have anything that other people do not have? Is there anything special about being circumcised? ²Yes, of course, there is in every way. The most important thing is this: God trusted the Jews with his teachings. ³If some Jews were not faithful to him, will that stop God from doing what he promised? ⁴No! God will continue to be true even when every person is false. As the Scriptures*d* say:

"So you will be shown to be right when you
    speak,
and you will win your case."   *Psalm 51:4*

⁵When we do wrong, that shows more clearly that God is right. So can we say that God is wrong to punish us? (I am talking as people might talk.) ⁶No! If God could not punish us, he could not judge the world.

⁷A person might say, "When I lie, it really gives him glory, because my lie shows God's truth. So why am I judged a sinner?" ⁸It would be the same to say, "We should do evil so that good will come." Some people find fault with us and say we teach this, but they are wrong and deserve the punishment they will receive.

All People Are Guilty

⁹So are we Jews better than others? No! We have already said that Jews and those who are not Jews are all guilty of sin. ¹⁰As the Scriptures*d* say:

"There is no one who always does what is
    right,
    not even one.
¹¹ There is no one who understands.
    There is no one who looks to God for help.
¹²All have turned away.
    Together, everyone has become useless.
There is no one who does anything good;
    there is not even one."   *Psalm 14:1-3*
¹³"Their throats are like open graves;
    they use their tongues for telling lies."
                                    Psalm 5:9
"Their words are like snake poison." *Psalm 140:3*
¹⁴ "Their mouths are full of cursing and hate."
                                    Psalm 10:7
¹⁵"They are always ready to kill people.
¹⁶ Everywhere they go they cause ruin and
    misery.
¹⁷They don't know how to live in peace."
                                    Isaiah 59:7-8
¹⁸ "They have no fear of God."   *Psalm 36:1*

[19]We know that the law's commands are for those who have the law. This stops all excuses and brings the whole world under God's judgment, [20]because no one can be made right with God by following the law. The law only shows us our sin.

How God Makes People Right

[21]But God has a way to make people right with him without the law, and he has now shown us that way which the law and the prophets[d] told us about. [22]God makes people right with himself through their faith in Jesus Christ. This is true for all who believe in Christ, because all people are the same: [23]All have sinned and are not good enough for God's glory, [24]and all need to be made right with God by his grace, which is a free gift. They need to be made free from sin through Jesus Christ. [25]God gave him as a way to forgive sin through faith in the blood of Jesus' death. This showed that God always does what is right and fair, as in the past when he was patient and did not punish people for their sins. [26]And God gave Jesus to show today that he does what is right. God did this so he could judge rightly and so he could make right any person who has faith in Jesus.

[27]So do we have a reason to brag about ourselves? No! And why not? It is the way of faith that stops all bragging, not the way of trying to obey the law. [28]A person is made right with God through faith, not through obeying the law. [29]Is God only the God of the Jews? Is he not also the God of those who are not Jews? [30]Of course he is, because there is only one God. He will make Jews right with him by their faith, and he will also make those who are not Jews right with him through their faith. [31]So do we destroy the law by following the way of faith? No! Faith causes us to be what the law truly wants.

The Example of Abraham

4 So what can we say that Abraham,[n] the father of our people, learned about faith? [2]If

---

Abraham   Most respected ancestor of the Jews. Every Jew hoped to see Abraham.

Abraham was made right by the things he did, he had a reason to brag. But this is not God's view, [3]because the Scripture[d] says, "Abraham believed God, and God accepted Abraham's faith, and that faith made him right with God."[n]

[4]When people work, their pay is not given as a gift, but as something earned. [5]But people cannot do any work that will make them right with God. So they must trust in him, who makes even evil people right in his sight. Then God accepts their faith, and that makes them right with him.

"**Abraham ... God.**" Quotation from Genesis 15:6.

[6]David said the same thing. He said that people are truly blessed when God, without paying attention to good deeds, makes people right with himself.
[7]"Happy are they
whose sins are forgiven,
whose wrongs are pardoned.
[8]Happy is the person
whom the Lord does not consider guilty."

Psalm 32:1-2

[9]Is this blessing only for those who are circum-

FAITH

Free Approval

Ed Marx really liked Julie Hempstead. In fact, he was totally crazy about her.

Julie was funny, smart, beautiful—everything Ed wanted in a girl. For weeks, Ed watched Julie as she went from class to class. He watched her while she ate lunch. He watched her as she walked home from school.

Finally, after weeks of planning, he got up the nerve to ask her out.

"Hi, Ed. What's up?" Julie asked with that smile Ed loved so much.

"Um, I was wondering . . ." he said, clearing his throat. "I was wondering if you'd like to go do something Friday night." Ed couldn't believe his heart could pound so hard.

"Sure, I'd love to," Julie responded without missing a beat.

That was the first of many evenings together for the new couple. Julie really liked Ed. He was funny and sensitive. And, of course, Ed liked Julie, but he couldn't believe she could be interested in him.

As they continued to date, Ed kept doing things for Julie to keep her interested. He bought her gifts. He offered to run errands for her. One day, he even offered her his car so she wouldn't have to walk to school.

"Ed, I don't want your car," Julie said.

"It's okay, really," Ed assured her. "I want you to have it."

"No, Ed, you don't understand." Julie took a deep breath. "You don't need to try so hard. I already like you. You really don't need to do anything to win my love. So just relax, okay? You're starting to drive me crazy."

Ed felt embarrassed. "It's hard to believe, that's all," he said.

"Well, believe it," Julie said, grinning, and she kissed him.

Ed had a hard time believing Julie could love him unless he did things to earn her affection. **Romans 4:1–12** tells a similar story about Abraham, who discovered that God's favor is also based on believing. Read the passage to see why we can't earn God's approval through our actions.

■ How does Ed's response to Julie differ from Abraham's response to God in the passage?

■ According to the passage, what does God require for you to have a relationship with him?

CONSIDER . . .

■ thinking of ways you might try to earn God's love and then asking God to help you accept his love by faith.

■ writing out how you think God sees you, and having your youth leader do the same.

■ Compare the two descriptions, and ask God to increase your faith to believe the truth about how he sees you.

FOR MORE, SEE . . .

■ Genesis 15:1–6 (p. 16)
■ Galatians 3:6–27 (p. 1209)
■ Ephesians 2:8–9 (p. 1219)

cised[d] or also for those who are not circumcised? We have already said that God accepted Abraham's faith and that faith made him right with God. [10]So how did this happen? Did God accept Abraham before or after he was circumcised? It was before his circumcision. [11]Abraham was circumcised to show that he was right with God through faith before he was circumcised. So Abraham is the father of all those who believe but are not circumcised; he is the father of all believers who are accepted as being right with God. [12]And Abraham is also the father of those who have been circumcised and who live following the faith that our father Abraham had before he was circumcised.

God Keeps His Promise

[13]Abraham[n] and his descendants[d] received the promise that they would get the whole world. He did not receive that promise through the law, but through being right with God by his faith. [14]If people could receive what God promised by following the law, then faith is worthless. And God's promise to Abraham is worthless, [15]because the law can only bring God's anger. But if there is no law, there is nothing to disobey.

[16]So people receive God's promise by having faith. This happens so the promise can be a free gift. Then all of Abraham's children can have that promise. It is not only for those who live under the law of Moses but for anyone who lives with faith like that of Abraham, who is the father of us all. [17]As it is written in the Scriptures:[d] "I am making you a father of many nations."[n] This is true before God, the God Abraham believed, the God who gives life to the dead and who creates something out of nothing.

[18]There was no hope that Abraham would have children. But Abraham believed God and continued hoping, and so he became the father of many nations. As God told him, "Your descendants also will be too many to count."[n] [19]Abraham was almost a hundred years old, much past the age for having children, and Sarah could not have children. Abraham thought about all this, but his faith in God did not become weak. [20]He never doubted that God would keep his promise, and he never stopped believing. He grew stronger in his faith and gave praise to God. [21]Abraham felt sure that God was able to do what he had promised. [22]So, "God accepted Abraham's faith, and that faith made him right with God."[n] [23]Those words ("God accepted Abraham's faith") were written

not only for Abraham [24]but also for us. God will accept us also because we believe in the One who raised Jesus our Lord from the dead. [25]Jesus was given to die for our sins, and he was raised from the dead to make us right with God.

Right with God

5 Since we have been made right with God by our faith, we have peace with God. This happened through our Lord Jesus Christ, [2]who has brought us into that blessing of God's grace that we now enjoy. And we are happy because of the hope we have of sharing God's glory. [3]We also have joy with our troubles, because we know that these troubles produce patience. [4]And patience produces character, and character produces hope. [5]And this hope will never disappoint us, because God has poured out his love to fill our hearts. He gave us his love through the Holy Spirit,[d] whom God has given to us.

[6]When we were unable to help ourselves, at the moment of our need, Christ died for us, although we were living against God. [7]Very few people will die to save the life of someone else. Although perhaps for a good person someone might possibly die [8]But God shows his great love for us in this way: Christ died for us while we were still sinners.

[9]So through Christ we will surely be saved from God's anger, because we have been made right with God by the blood of Christ's death. [10]While we were God's enemies, he made friends with us through the death of his Son. Surely, now that we are his friends, he will save us through his Son's life. [11]And not only that, but now we are also very happy in God through our Lord Jesus Christ. Through him we are now God's friends again.

Adam and Christ Compared

[12]Sin came into the world because of what one man did, and with sin came death. This is why everyone must die — because everyone sinned. [13]Sin was in the world before the law of Moses, but sin is not counted against us as breaking a command when there is no law. [14]But from the time of Adam to the time of Moses, everyone had to die, even those who had not sinned by breaking a command, as Adam had.

Adam was like the One who was coming in the future. [15]But God's free gift is not like Adam's sin. Many people died because of the sin of that one man. But the grace from God was much greater;

Abraham   Most respected ancestor of the Jews. Every Jew hoped to see Abraham.
"I . . . nations."   Quotation from Genesis 17:5.
"Your . . . count."   Quotation from Genesis 15:5.
"God . . . God."   Quotation from Genesis 15:6.

many people received God's gift of life by the grace of the one man, Jesus Christ. ¹⁶After Adam sinned once, he was judged guilty. But the gift of God is different. God's free gift came after many sins, and it makes people right with God. ¹⁷One man sinned, and so death ruled all people because of that one man. But now those people who accept God's full grace and the great gift of being made right with him will surely have true life and rule through the one man, Jesus Christ.

¹⁸So as one sin of Adam brought the punishment of death to all people, one good act that Christ did makes all people right with God. And that brings true life for all. ¹⁹One man disobeyed God, and many became sinners. In the same way, one man obeyed God, and many will be made right. ²⁰The law came to make sin worse. But when sin grew worse, God's grace increased. ²¹Sin once used death to rule us, but God gave people more of his grace so that grace could rule by making people right with him. And this brings life forever through Jesus Christ our Lord.

Dead to Sin but Alive in Christ

6 So do you think we should continue sinning so that God will give us even more grace?

> **SIDELIGHT:** Adam—the man in the Garden of Eden (Genesis 1–4, p. 2)—seems to get blamed for more than his share of sin in Romans 5:12–21. But don't feel too sorry for him. Paul uses Adam to represent all people. That's not surprising when you know that "adam" means "human."

²No! We died to our old sinful lives, so how can we continue living with sin? ³Did you forget that all of us became part of Christ when we were baptized? We shared his death in our baptism. ⁴When we were baptized, we were buried with Christ and shared his death. So, just as Christ was

---

FRIENDS

What Are Friends For?

Sometimes Lisa Kretch got frustrated with her friends. It seemed like she was constantly bailing them out of something.

Take Coreen Mills for instance. She was flunking algebra. And Nancy Olton had just broken up with her boyfriend and was depressed all the time. Luann Winger was gaining weight like crazy, and all she did was complain about it and eat.

And as if that weren't enough, last week all three of these friends had gone to a party and had drunk several beers. Lisa had to drive them home so they wouldn't have a wreck.

Sometimes it seemed like Lisa's friends were trying to cause her problems. It was all getting to be too much. Too much concern, too much pain.

Maybe she should just find new friends, she thought. It would sure make her life easier. But . . .

"Hi, Lisa!" Coreen said, setting her tray down beside Lisa's at the cafeteria table. "Boy, this algebra is a bear. Can you help me with a couple of things?"

This was it. The true test. Was Lisa strong enough? She gathered her courage, took a deep breath, paused, and said, "Sure, Coreen. What are friends for?" And she meant it.

Lisa learned that friendship means commitment, even when friends disappoint you. **Romans 5:1–19** calls God our friend. Read the passage to discover how committed he is to us.

■ How is Lisa's friendship with her friends like God's friendship with us in Jesus Christ?

■ How can you model your friendship with God in human friendships?

CONSIDER . . .

■ writing down the names of three friends and praying for them each day this week.

■ writing a card, buying a flower, or doing a favor for a friend, just to say I'm committed to you.

FOR MORE, SEE . . .

■ Job 2:11–13 (p. 453)
■ Proverbs 17:17 (p. 582)
■ John 15:13–16 (p. 1085)

raised from the dead by the wonderful power of the Father, we also can live a new life.

[5]Christ died, and we have been joined with him by dying too. So we will also be joined with him by rising from the dead as he did. [6]We know that our old life died with Christ on the cross so that our sinful selves would have no power over us and we would not be slaves to sin. [7]Anyone who has died is made free from sin's control.

[8]If we died with Christ, we know we will also live with him. [9]Christ was raised from the dead, and we know that he cannot die again. Death has no power over him now. [10]Yes, when Christ died, he died to defeat the power of sin one time — enough for all time. He now has a new life, and his new life is with God. [11]In the same way, you should see yourselves as being dead to the power of sin and alive with God through Christ Jesus.

[12]So, do not let sin control your life here on earth so that you do what your sinful self wants to do. [13]Do not offer the parts of your body to serve sin, as things to be used in doing evil. Instead, offer yourselves to God as people who have died and now live. Offer the parts of your body to God to be used in doing good. [14]Sin will not be your master, because you are not under law but under God's grace.

Be Slaves of Righteousness

[15]So what should we do? Should we sin because we are under grace and not under law? No! [16]Surely you know that when you give yourselves

A Slave to Freedom

Tom Stipe wouldn't have been late for Biology 101 if he hadn't fallen. And he wouldn't have fallen if he hadn't been running. And he wouldn't have been running if he had gotten out of bed on time.

But he didn't get out of bed on time. He had forgotten to set his alarm. And his roommate—a guy he could hardly stand—hadn't bothered to wake him up, even though they were in the same class.

College wasn't everything Tom had hoped it would be.

It wasn't the classes. They were hard, sure, but Tom was no stranger to the books. And it wasn't the basketball practice. Practice was always rough, but you expected that and planned for it. It wasn't even Jack, the bothersome roommate. Tom had roomed with his brother at home, and they had rarely gotten along for more than a few minutes at a time.

It was the freedom, Tom realized with a start. Or, more to the point, it was the responsibility that came with the freedom. That was the part Tom disliked.

In high school, Tom had resented the way everyone controlled his time. His mother woke him in the morning. His teachers prodded him to work during the day and sent work home with him at night. Tom longed to be free.

But now that he was in college, Tom discovered that the freedom he had longed for came with one looming catch: responsibility. He was free to do what he wanted, but he also had to live with the consequences of his actions.

Tom learned that freedom and responsibility always come together.

Romans 6:1–12 talks about freedom too, and the responsibility that comes with it.

■ How is Tom's struggle with freedom similar to the struggle for freedom Paul writes about in the passage?

■ What does the passage say we need to do to gain freedom?

C O N S I D E R . . .

■ drawing a line down the center of a page. On the left side, list all the freedoms you want to gain. On the right, list all the responsibilities that will come with those freedoms. With a parent, design a plan for helping you gain those freedoms responsibly.

■ evaluating how you use your free time to see if you use it responsibly. If not, start using some of your time to do something on a regular basis to serve others.

F O R   M O R E ,   S E E . . .

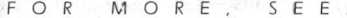

■ Psalm 119:41–48 (p. 551)
■ John 8:31–32, 34–36 (p. 1072)

■ 1 Peter 2:16 (p. 1304)

like slaves to obey someone, then you are really slaves of that person. The person you obey is your master. You can follow sin, which brings spiritual death, or you can obey God, which makes you right with him. [17]In the past you were slaves to sin — sin controlled you. But thank God, you fully obeyed the things that you were taught. [18]You were made free from sin, and now you are slaves to goodness. [19]I use this example because this is hard for you to understand. In the past you offered the parts of your body to be slaves to sin and evil; you lived only for evil. In the same way now you must give yourselves to be slaves of goodness. Then you will live only for God.

[20]In the past you were slaves to sin, and goodness did not control you. [21]You did evil things, and now you are ashamed of them. Those things only bring death. [22]But now you are free from sin and have become slaves of God. This brings you a life that is only for God, and this gives you life forever. [23]When people sin, they earn what sin pays — death. But God gives us a free gift — life forever in Christ Jesus our Lord.

An Example from Marriage

7 Brothers and sisters, all of you understand the law of Moses. So surely you know that the law rules over people only while they are alive. [2]For example, a woman must stay married to her husband as long as he is alive. But if her husband dies, she is free from the law of marriage. [3]But if she marries another man while her husband is still alive, the law says she is guilty of adultery.[d] But if her husband dies, she is free from the law of marriage. Then if she marries another man, she is not guilty of adultery.

[4]In the same way, my brothers and sisters, your old selves died, and you became free from the law through the body of Christ. This happened so that you might belong to someone else — the One who was raised from the dead — and so that we might be used in service to God. [5]In the past, we were ruled by our sinful selves. The law made us want to do sinful things that controlled our bodies, so the things we did were bringing us death. [6]In the past, the law held us like prisoners, but our old selves died, and we were made free from the law. So now we serve God in a new way with the Spirit,[d] and not in the old way with written rules.

Our Fight Against Sin

[7]You might think I am saying that sin and the law are the same thing. That is not true. But the law was the only way I could learn what sin meant. I would never have known what it means to want to take something belonging to someone else if the law had not said, "You must not want

to take your neighbor's things." [n] [8]And sin found a way to use that command and cause me to want all kinds of things I should not want. But without the law, sin has no power. [9]I was alive before I knew the law. But when the law's command came to me, then sin began to live, [10]and I died. The command was meant to bring life, but for me it brought death. [11]Sin found a way to fool me by using the command to make me die.

[12]So the law is holy, and the command is holy and right and good. [13]Does this mean that something that is good brought death to me? No! Sin used something that is good to bring death to me. This happened so that I could see what sin is really like; the command was used to show that sin is very evil.

The War Within Us

[14]We know that the law is spiritual, but I am not spiritual since sin rules me as if I were its slave. [15]I do not understand the things I do. I do not do what I want to do, and I do the things I hate. [16]And if I do not want to do the hated things I do, that means I agree that the law is good. [17]But I am not really the one who is doing these hated things; it is sin living in me that does them. [18]Yes, I know that nothing good lives in me — I mean nothing good lives in the part of me that is earthly and sinful. I want to do the things that are good, but I do not do them. [19]I do not do the good things I want to do, but I do the bad things I do not want to do. [20]So if I do things I do not want to do, then I am not the one doing them. It is sin living in me that does those things.

[21]So I have learned this rule: When I want to do good, evil is there with me. [22]In my mind, I am happy with God's law. [23]But I see another law working in my body, which makes war against the law that my mind accepts. That other law working in my body is the law of sin, and it makes me its prisoner. [24]What a miserable man I am! Who will save me from this body that brings me death? [25]I thank God for saving me through Jesus Christ our Lord!

So in my mind I am a slave to God's law, but in my sinful self I am a slave to the law of sin.

Be Ruled by the Spirit

8 So now, those who are in Christ Jesus are not judged guilty. [2]Through Christ Jesus the law of the Spirit[d] that brings life made me free from the law that brings sin and death. [3]The law was without power, because the law was made weak by our sinful selves. But God did what the law could not do. He sent his own Son to earth with the same human life that others use for sin. By sending his Son to be an offering to pay for sin,

---

"You . . . things." Quotation from Exodus 20:17.

God used a human life to destroy sin. [4]He did this so that we could be the kind of people the law correctly wants us to be. Now we do not live following our sinful selves, but we live following the Spirit.

[5]Those who live following their sinful selves think only about things that their sinful selves want. But those who live following the Spirit are thinking about the things the Spirit wants them to do. [6]If people's thinking is controlled by the sinful self, there is death. But if their thinking is controlled by the Spirit, there is life and peace. [7]When people's thinking is controlled by the sinful self, they are against God, because they refuse to obey God's law and really are not even able to obey God's law. [8]Those people who are ruled by their sinful selves cannot please God.

[9]But you are not ruled by your sinful selves. You are ruled by the Spirit, if that Spirit of God really lives in you. But the person who does not have the Spirit of Christ does not belong to Christ. [10]Your body will always be dead because of sin.

Not Alone . . .

Seven years, five months, three days. That's how long Shelly Everett had been sober. Counting today. And she didn't mind talking about it to her fellow Alcoholics Anonymous (AA) members. It helped her stick with recovery.

"I started drinking in high school," she explained. "But I didn't start abusing it until I was in college. By the time I was out of school and in a career position, I was an alcoholic."

Shelly went on to tell how a marriage and the addition of two children didn't change her drinking habits much. "I managed to keep up with my responsibilities, both at home and at work," she said. "As long as I did that, I convinced myself that I had it under control."

But then things changed. A messy divorce. Trouble at work. And a daughter who almost died from rheumatic fever.

"I began to drink more often—for comfort, and sometimes, to forget. Eventually, events in my life began to blur together. I was never sober.

"And the worse I felt about myself the more I drank. Finally, I just wanted to die. So I tried to drink myself to death. Five days later I woke up in a hospital room attached to a bunch of machines. The doctors say I didn't even know who I was. I lay there and cried. I couldn't eat. I couldn't sleep. I was a failure. I couldn't even kill myself right." Shelly pulled a tissue from the box beside her. The AA leader motioned her to continue.

"Then," she went on, "the hospital chaplain walked in, and there's this little dumpy woman with him. They both just sit down by my bed. And this little dumpy woman asked, 'You wanna quit drinking?' "

Now Shelly's tears came in full flood. "I just bawled like a baby. I wanted to quit, but I didn't know how! Then she says, 'You don't have to do it alone. You've got me and Reverend Benjamin here and a whole flock of folks willing to help. And you've got God, too, honey. Don't forget about God.' "

Shelly blew her nose on the tissue and looked around at the faces of her friends. "For the first time I realized I wasn't alone. And I haven't had a drink since that day—all because you, and God, are keeping me sober."

Shelly learned she wasn't alone in her struggle. And God made a difference in her life. The apostle Paul made a similar discovery. Read about it in **Romans 7:14–25**.

■ How is Shelly's addiction like the "battle" Paul describes in this passage?
■ What are ways God shows that he is with you when you're pressured to use alcohol or drugs?

C O N S I D E R . . .
■ encouraging a friend who is dealing with issues like Shelly's to seek professional help.
■ finding an appropriate support group in your community if you struggle with a drinking or drug problem. Your pastor or a counselor can help you.

F O R   M O R E ,   S E E . . .

■ Proverbs 23:29–32 (p. 588)   ■ Luke 21:34–36 (p. 1049)
■ Isaiah 5:11–12 (p. 621)

But if Christ is in you, then the Spirit gives you life, because Christ made you right with God. [11]God raised Jesus from the dead, and if God's Spirit is living in you, he will also give life to your bodies that die. God is the One who raised Christ from the dead, and he will give life through his Spirit that lives in you.

[12]So, my brothers and sisters, we must not be ruled by our sinful selves or live the way our sinful selves want. [13]If you use your lives to do the wrong things your sinful selves want, you will die spiritually. But if you use the Spirit's help to stop doing the wrong things you do with your body, you will have true life.

[14]The true children of God are those who let God's Spirit lead them. [15]The Spirit we received does not make us slaves again to fear; it makes us children of God. With that Spirit we cry out, "Father." [n] [16]And the Spirit himself joins with our spirits to say we are God's children. [17]If we are God's children, we will receive blessings from God together with Christ. But we must suffer as Christ suffered so that we will have glory as Christ has glory.

"Father"   Literally, "Abba, Father." Jewish children called their fathers "Abba."

SPIRITUAL GROWTH

Living for God

To buy or not to buy. That was the question.

Carrie Munson was the only one in her class who didn't have a school jacket. Well, nearly the only one. Most of the kids had them—navy blue and white, with a hood that rolled up into the zippered collar when you didn't want it over your head.

And Cline's Sporting Goods had a special offer this weekend. They would put the school name on the back of the coat and your initials on the front—no charge. But only if you bought it this weekend.

"Let's see," Carrie thought aloud. "That's a savings of . . . $8 for the school name and $3 for my initials . . . that's $11 savings!"

True, it wasn't a fortune, but with Carrie's meager allowance, every penny counted.

There was just one problem. Carrie had pledged to give $13 each month to the church to help fund the new homeless shelter. And if she bought the jacket, she would have only $11 left.

That's $2 short, Carrie thought. And the pledge is due this Sunday.

"Ugh!" Carrie grunted in frustration. Why had she made such a big pledge? Thirteen dollars! That was almost a fourth of her income! And besides, the jacket was on sale now. If Carrie didn't buy it this weekend, it would cost her $11 dollars more next week, and she wouldn't have enough money then—especially if she paid her pledge.

"What should I do?" Carrie asked, looking at the ceiling of the sporting goods store. Slowly, her eyebrows unfurled, her tense shoulders relaxed, and she walked out of the store—away from the jacket she wanted.

When Carrie got home, she went to her bedroom, pulled $13 out of her purse, and put it in the Bible next to her bed.

"If you want me to have the jacket, you'll provide a way," she prayed. "But I don't want to break my promise to you just to get what I want."

Carrie discovered it's not always easy to do what's right, especially when our own desires get in the way. **Romans 8:6–17** talks about why spiritual growth is sometimes hard.

■ How is the conflict described in this passage like what happened to Carrie?

■ According to this passage, what should you do the next time your own desires conflict with God's?

CONSIDER . . .

■ asking God's forgiveness for times you have chosen your desires over his.

➤ listing all the ways your desires might conflict with God's and asking God to help you grow through following his desires for your life.

FOR MORE, SEE . . .

■ Psalm 1:1–3 (p. 482)
■ Colossians 3:1–10 (p. 1241)

■ Hebrews 12:1–13 (p. 1289)

Our Future Glory

¹⁸The sufferings we have now are nothing compared to the great glory that will be shown to us. ¹⁹Everything God made is waiting with excitement for God to show his children's glory completely. ²⁰Everything God made was changed to become useless, not by its own wish but because God wanted it and because all along there was this hope: ²¹that everything God made would be set free from ruin to have the freedom and glory that belong to God's children.

²²We know that everything God made has been waiting until now in pain, like a woman ready to give birth. ²³Not only the world, but we also have been waiting with pain inside us. We have the Spirit*ᵈ* as the first part of God's promise. So we are waiting for God to finish making us his own children, which means our bodies will be made free. ²⁴We were saved, and we have this hope. If we see what we are waiting for, that is not really hope. People do not hope for something they already have. ²⁵But we are hoping for something we do not have yet, and we are waiting for it patiently.

²⁶Also, the Spirit helps us with our weakness. We do not know how to pray as we should. But the Spirit himself speaks to God for us, even begs God for us with deep feelings that words cannot explain. ²⁷God can see what is in people's hearts. And he knows what is in the mind of the Spirit, because the Spirit speaks to God for his people in the way God wants.

²⁸We know that in everything God works for the good of those who love him. They are the

---

Looking Back

Pierce Richman had been a Christian about six months before the problems started. What problems? "Well, I lost my job," Pierce recalls. "Then the transmission on my car went out, and I had no money to repair it. But that wasn't the real problem. My girlfriend broke up with me. I really wanted to marry this girl, but she said I wasn't what she wanted in a husband. That really hurt."

About that time Pierce's old desires began to well up. Before he had become a Christian at age eighteen, he had lived a loose lifestyle, filled with drinking and taking drugs and sleeping with girlfriends.

"I came to Christ to get away from all that," he recalls. "But when all these problems started, I began to feel really insecure. It was all I could do not to go out and get drunk or call up one of my old girlfriends. I felt gross inside. I began to wonder whether I was really a Christian."

But Pierce didn't go back to his old lifestyle. Even though he didn't understand why all these things were happening to him, he knew God was in control. So he waited.

"Things didn't get better right away," Pierce says, "but I knew I had made the right decision. And that helped me believe even more that, if I was patient, God would come through for me. And he did!"

Pierce and his girlfriend got back together, and he got a new job—better than the other one. Now Pierce knows the value of obeying God even when you don't know what God is doing.

Pierce learned that becoming like Christ takes patience. Paul talked about how all creation is waiting patiently for us to become like Christ. Read why in **Romans 8:22–30.**

■ How does Pierce demonstrate the patience the passage describes?
■ According to the passage, what is God's ultimate purpose for you? Why do we need patience to wait for his purpose to be fulfilled?

C O N S I D E R . . .

■ dreaming about the kind of person you want to be ten years from now. Then ask God to give you patience to let him make you into the person he wants you to be.
■ working on a project that takes a long time to finish, such as a quilt or a model ship. Use the experience to learn more about patience.

F O R   M O R E ,   S E E . . .

■ Lamentations 3:25–26 (p. 757)　　　■ James 5:7–11 (p. 1299)
■ Hebrews 11:8–16 (p. 1288)

people he called, because that was his plan. [29]God knew them before he made the world, and he decided that they would be like his Son so that Jesus would be the firstborn[n] of many brothers. [30]God planned for them to be like his Son; and those he planned to be like his Son, he also called; and those he called, he also made right with him; and those he made right, he also glorified.

God's Love in Christ Jesus

[31]So what should we say about this? If God is with us, no one can defeat us. [32]He did not spare his own Son but gave him for us all. So with Jesus,

God will surely give us all things. [33]Who can accuse the people God has chosen? No one, because God is the One who makes them right. [34]Who can say God's people are guilty? No one, because Christ Jesus died, but he was also raised from the dead, and now he is on God's right side, begging God for us. [35]Can anything separate us from the love Christ has for us? Can troubles or problems or sufferings or hunger or nakedness or danger or violent death? [36]As it is written in the Scriptures:[d]

"For you we are in danger of death all the time.

---

firstborn   Here this probably means that Christ was the first in God's family to share God's glory.

WORRYING

Let It Rain!

When Ray Jordon was a teenager, his friend Scott Wright and he would help bale hay each summer for seventy-year-old Bailey Tag, a rancher who lived near their town. Mr. Tag baled the hay onto the ground. Then he would drive the tractor, and Ray would walk behind it, picking up bales and throwing them up to Scott on the wagon, where he would stack them.

It was hot, miserable, sticky, dirty work. But the pay was good.

One day as the three ate their lunches under a big oak tree, the sky began to darken in the west and the sound of thunder rolled toward them.

Mr. Tag sat, eating his apple and looking at the clouds. "Beautiful, aren't they?" he remarked. "Rain'll cool things off a might, I 'spect."

"What about the hay?" Scott asked.

Mr. Tag looked at his apple. "Let me finish this, and we'll get the hay to the barn. We've got time."

Scott looked at Ray, and they both looked out over the field where the other bales waited to be picked up.

"Mr. Tag," said Ray, "those clouds look like they're moving this way."

He looked at them, paused, then nodded. "Maybe."

Ray swept the field with his arm. "But, what about the other bales? I mean, what if the rain is moving this way? What'll we do?"

Mr. Tag looked at Ray, smiled around a bite of his apple and winked. "Why, we'll let it rain," he said. "What else can we do?"

So that's what they did. They let it rain. The bales got wet, and they had to dry in the sun for a few days before they could be picked up. But they got picked up. What else could have been done?

After all, worrying wouldn't stop the rain. **Romans 8:31–39** says there are some things we never have to worry about. Read the passage to find out what we can be sure of.

■ How does worrying about the hay differ from worrying about God's love?
■ What assurance do these verses offer you when you worry about losing your special relationship with God?

CONSIDER . . .
■ writing down all the things you worry about, then crossing out the ones you can't do anything about. Create a plan for doing something about the others.
■ reading a fun novel, going camping, or doing something similar—to help you let go of your worries and trust God.

FOR MORE, SEE . . .
■ Psalm 91 (p. 535)
■ Psalm 131 (p. 558)   ■ Matthew 6:25–34 (p. 918)

People think we are worth no more than
 sheep to be killed."   *Psalm 44:22*

[37]But in all these things we have full victory through God who showed his love for us. [38]Yes, I am sure that neither death, nor life, nor angels, nor ruling spirits, nothing now, nothing in the future, no powers, [39]nothing above us, nothing below us, nor anything else in the whole world will ever be able to separate us from the love of God that is in Christ Jesus our Lord.

God and the Jewish People

9 I am in Christ, and I am telling you the truth; I do not lie. My conscience is ruled by the Holy Spirit,[d] and it tells me I am not lying. [2]I have great sorrow and always feel much sadness. [3]I wish I could help my Jewish brothers and sisters, my people. I would even wish that I were cursed and cut off from Christ if that would help them. [4]They are the people of Israel, God's chosen children. They have seen the glory of God, and they have the agreements that God made between himself and his people. God gave them the law of Moses and the right way of worship and his promises. [5]They are the descendants[d] of our great ancestors, and they are the earthly family into which Christ was born, who is God over all. Praise him forever![n] Amen.

[6]It is not that God failed to keep his promise to them. But only some of the people of Israel are truly God's people,[n] [7]and only some of Abraham's[n] descendants are true children of Abraham. But God said to Abraham: "The descendants I promised you will be from Isaac."[n] [8]This means that not all of Abraham's descendants are God's true children. Abraham's true children are those who become God's children because of the promise God made to Abraham. [9]God's promise to Abraham was this: "At the right time I will return, and Sarah will have a son."[n] [10]And that is not all. Rebekah's sons had the same father, our father Isaac. [11-12]But before the two boys were born, God told Rebekah, "The older will serve the younger."[n] This was before the boys had done anything good or bad. God said this so that the one chosen would be chosen because of God's own plan. He was chosen because he was the one God wanted to call, not because of anything he did. [13]As the Scripture[d] says, "I loved Jacob, but I hated Esau."[n]

[14]So what should we say about this? Is God unfair? In no way. [15]God said to Moses, "I will show kindness to anyone to whom I want to show kindness, and I will show mercy to anyone to whom I want to show mercy."[n] [16]So God will choose the one to whom he decides to show mercy; his choice does not depend on what people want or try to do. [17]The Scripture says to the king of Egypt: "I made you king for this reason: to show my power in you so that my name will be talked about in all the earth."[n] [18]So God shows mercy where he wants to show mercy, and he makes stubborn the people he wants to make stubborn.

[19]So one of you will ask me: "Then why does God blame us for our sins? Who can fight his will?" [20]You are only human, and human beings have no right to question God. An object should not ask the person who made it, "Why did you make me like this?" [21]The potter can make anything he wants to make. He can use the same clay to make one thing for special use and another thing for daily use.

[22]It is the same way with God. He wanted to show his anger and to let people see his power. But he patiently stayed with those people he was angry with — people who were made ready to be destroyed. [23]He waited with patience so that he could make known his rich glory to the people who receive his mercy. He has prepared these people to have his glory, [24]and we are those people whom God called. He called us not from the Jews only but also from those who are not Jews. [25]As the Scripture says in Hosea:

"I will say, 'You are my people'
 to those I had called 'not my people.'
And I will show my love
 to those people I did not love."   *Hosea 2:1, 23*
[26]"They were called,
 'You are not my people,'
but later they will be called
 'children of the living God.' "   *Hosea 1:10*
[27]And Isaiah cries out about Israel:
"The people of Israel are many,
 like the grains of sand by the sea.
But only a few of them will be saved,
[28] because the Lord will quickly and
        completely punish the people on the
        earth."   *Isaiah 10:22-23*
[29]It is as Isaiah said:

---

born ... forever! This can also mean, "born. May God, who rules over all things, be praised forever!"
God's people Literally, "Israel," the people God chose to bring his blessings to the world.
Abraham Most respected ancestor of the Jews. Every Jew hoped to see Abraham
"The descendants ... Isaac." Quotation from Genesis 21:12.
"At ... son." Quotation from Genesis 18:10, 14.
"The older ... younger." Quotation from Genesis 25:23.
"I ... Esau." Quotation from Malachi 1:2-3.
"I ... mercy." Quotation from Exodus 33:19.
"I ... earth." Quotation from Exodus 9:16.

"The Lord All-Powerful
    allowed a few of our descendants to live.
Otherwise we would have been completely
    destroyed
like the cities of Sodom and Gomorrah." *n*

Isaiah 1:9

30So what does all this mean? Those who are not Jews were not trying to make themselves right with God, but they were made right with God because of their faith. 31The people of Israel tried to follow a law to make themselves right with God. But they did not succeed, 32because they tried to make themselves right by the things they did instead of trusting in God to make them right. They stumbled over the stone that causes people to stumble. 33As it is written in the Scripture:

"I will put in Jerusalem a stone that causes
            people to stumble,
    a rock that makes them fall.
Anyone who trusts in him will never be
    disappointed."   *Isaiah 8:14; 28:16*

SIDELIGHT: Early Christians often argued about what was required to be a Christian (Romans 9:1–33). Some Jewish Christians wanted the non-Jewish ones to obey all the Jewish laws. If their beliefs had won the day, we would all have to eat kosher pickles!

---

10 Brothers and sisters, the thing I want most is for all the Jews to be saved. That is my prayer to God. 2I can say this about them: They really try to follow God, but they do not know the right way. 3Because they did not know the way that God makes people right with him, they tried to make themselves right in their own way. So they did not accept God's way of making people right. 4Christ ended the law so that everyone who believes in him may be right with God.

5Moses writes about being made right by following the law. He says, "A person who obeys these things will live because of them." *n* 6But this is what the Scripture says about being made right through faith: "Don't say to yourself, 'Who will go up into heaven?' " (That means, "Who will go up to heaven and bring Christ down to earth?") 7"And do not say, 'Who will go down into the world below?' " (That means, "Who will

go down and bring Christ up from the dead?") 8This is what the Scripture says: "The word is near you; it is in your mouth and in your heart." *n* That is the teaching of faith that we are telling. 9If you use your mouth to say, "Jesus is Lord," and if you believe in your heart that God raised Jesus from the dead, you will be saved. 10We believe with our hearts, and so we are made right with God. And we use our mouths to say that we believe, and so we are saved. 11As the Scripture says, "Anyone who trusts in him will never be disappointed." *n* 12That Scripture says "anyone" because there is no difference between those who are Jews and those who are not. The same Lord is the Lord of all and gives many blessings to all who trust in him, 13as the Scripture says, "Anyone who calls on the Lord will be saved." *n*

14But before people can ask the Lord for help, they must believe in him; and before they can believe in him, they must hear about him; and for them to hear about the Lord, someone must tell them; 15and before someone can go and tell them, that person must be sent. It is written, "How beautiful is the person who comes to bring good news." *n*

16But not all the Jews accepted the good news. Isaiah said, "Lord, who believed what we told them?" *n* 17So faith comes from hearing the Good News, *d* and people hear the Good News when someone tells them about Christ.

18But I ask: Didn't people hear the Good News? Yes, they heard — as the Scripture says:
"Their message went out through all the
            world;
    their words go everywhere on earth."

Psalm 19:4

19Again I ask: Didn't the people of Israel understand? Yes, they did understand. First, Moses says:
"I will use those who are not a nation to
            make you jealous.
    I will use a nation that does not understand
            to make you angry."   *Deuteronomy 32:21*
20Then Isaiah is bold enough to say:
"I was found by those who were not asking
            me for help.
    I made myself known to people who were
            not looking for me."   *Isaiah 65:1*
21But about Israel God says,
"All day long I stood ready to accept
    people who disobey and are stubborn."

Isaiah 05:2

Sodom and Gomorrah Two cities that God destroyed because the people were so evil.
"A person . . . them." Quotation from Leviticus 18:5.
Verses 6-8 Quotations from Deuteronomy 9:4; 30:12-14; Psalm 107:26.
"Anyone . . . disappointed." Quotation from Isaiah 28:16.
"Anyone . . . saved." Quotation from Joel 2:32.
"How . . . news." Quotation from Isaiah 52:7.
"Lord, . . . them?" Quotation from Isaiah 53:1.

God Shows Mercy to All People

11 So I ask: Did God throw out his people? No! I myself am an Israelite from the family of Abraham, from the tribe[d] of Benjamin. [2]God chose the Israelites to be his people before they were born, and he has not thrown his people out. Surely you know what the Scripture[d] says about Elijah, how he prayed to God against the people of Israel. [3]"Lord," he said, "they have killed your prophets,[d] and they have destroyed your altars. I am the only prophet left, and now they are trying to kill me, too."[n] [4]But what answer did God give Elijah? He said, "But I have left seven thousand people in Israel who have never bowed down before Baal."[n] [5]It is the same now. There are a few people that God has chosen by his grace. [6]And if he chose them by grace, it is not for the things they have done. If they could be made God's people by what they did, God's gift of grace would not really be a gift.

"They . . . too."   Quotation from 1 Kings 19:10, 14.
"But . . . Baal."   Quotation from 1 Kings 19:18.

SHARING FAITH

Why Didn't You Say Something?

Mark Shipp went to church on Sundays. He didn't make a big thing of it, but he sang in the choir and went to Bible study. He was even on the youth council. Mark was trying to do what was right without being . . . pushy.

Just about every Friday, his school buddy, Jack, would invite him to play touch football: "So, what'cha got planned this weekend, Mark?"

Mark would shrug, "Oh, you know . . ."

"Tell me about it! Clean this, straighten that, mow the grass, wash the car! I work harder on Saturdays than I do on school days."

Mark would smile knowingly and shrug, "That's the truth."

"That's why I take Sunday off. Me, Tim, Larry, and some other guys get together in the morning to play football. Do ya wanna come?"

Mark would evade the question, "Oh, I'd like to, Jack. I really would, but I can't. I've already made plans."

"Sure. Well, if you ever change your mind, the invitation stands," Jack would say and then off he would go with a smile.

Then one Friday late in the year, the ritual took a different turn.

Mark had just evaded the question, explaining that he really wanted to play touch football but couldn't, and Jack just nodded as usual. But this time, Jack didn't walk away. He just stood there, looking at Mark.

Finally, he spoke. "Mark, for the past year I've invited you to play touch football, but you can't because you go to church."

Mark was caught off guard. "Oh, well, yeah, I go to church, but that . . ."

"For a year I've been inviting you to play football, and never once have you invited me to church," Jack continued, scratching his head. "Why?"

Mark needed to read Paul's admonition in **Romans 10:8–18** to learn how important it is to tell others about your faith in Christ and not just assume they don't want to know.

■ What does this passage say about Mark's attitude toward telling others about his faith in Christ?
■ According to the passage, why is it important that you tell others about your faith in Christ?

C O N S I D E R . . .
■ putting your faith story into words. How, in a hundred words, has your faith affected your life?
■ inviting a non-Christian friend to go to church with you this Sunday.

F O R   M O R E ,   S E E . . .

■ Jeremiah 1:4–8 (p. 691)   ■ Acts 2 (p. 1098)
■ Matthew 10:32–33 (p. 925)

[7] So this is what has happened: Although the Israelites tried to be right with God, they did not succeed, but the ones God chose did become right with him. The others were made stubborn and refused to listen to God. [8] As it is written in the Scriptures:[d]

"God gave the people a dull mind so they
    could not understand."   *Isaiah 29:10*
"He closed their eyes so they could not see
    and their ears so they could not hear.
This continues until today."   *Deuteronomy 29:4*

[9] And David says:

"Let their own feasts trap them and cause
    their ruin; ·
    let their feasts cause them to stumble and
    be paid back.
[10] Let their eyes be closed so they cannot see
    and their backs be forever weak from
    troubles."   *Psalm 69:22-23*

[11] So I ask: When the Jews fell, did that fall destroy them? No! But their mistake brought salvation to those who are not Jews, in order to make the Jews jealous. [12] The Jews' mistake brought rich blessings for the world, and the Jews' loss brought rich blessings for the non-Jewish people. So surely the world will receive much richer blessings when enough Jews become the kind of people God wants.

[13] Now I am speaking to you who are not Jews. I am an apostle[d] to those who are not Jews, and since I have that work, I will make the most of it. [14] I hope I can make my own people jealous and, in that way, help some of them to be saved. [15] When God turned away from the Jews, he became friends with other people in the world. So when God accepts the Jews, surely that will bring them life after death.

[16] If the first piece of bread is offered to God, then the whole loaf is made holy. If the roots of a tree are holy, then the tree's branches are holy too.

[17] It is as if some of the branches from an olive tree have been broken off. You non-Jewish people are like the branch of a wild olive tree that has been joined to that first tree. You now share the strength and life of the first tree, the Jews. [18] So do not brag about those branches that were broken off. If you brag, remember that you do not support the root, but the root supports you. [19] You will say, "Branches were broken off so that I could be joined to their tree." [20] That is true. But those branches were broken off because they did not *believe, and you continue to be part of the tree* only because you believe. Do not be proud, but be afraid. [21] If God did not let the natural branches of that tree stay, then he will not let you stay if you don't believe.

[22] So you see that God is kind and also very strict. He punishes those who stop following him. But God is kind to you, if you continue following in his kindness. If you do not, you will be cut off from the tree. [23] And if the Jews will believe in God again, he will accept them back. God is able to put them back where they were. [24] It is not natural for a wild branch to be part of a good tree. And you who are not Jews are like a branch cut from a wild olive tree and joined to a good olive tree. But since those Jews are like a branch that grew from the good tree, surely they can be joined to their own tree again.

[25] I want you to understand this secret, brothers and sisters, so you will understand that you do not know everything: Part of Israel has been made stubborn, but that will change when many who are not Jews have come to God. [26] And that is how all Israel will be saved. It is written in the Scriptures:

"The Savior will come from Jerusalem;
    he will take away all evil from the family of
    Jacob.[n]
[27] And I will make this agreement with those
    people
    when I take away their sins."
         Isaiah 59:20-21; 27:9

[28] The Jews refuse to accept the Good News,[d] so they are God's enemies. This has happened to help you who are not Jews. But the Jews are still God's chosen people, and he loves them very much because of the promises he made to their ancestors. [29] God never changes his mind about the people he calls and the things he gives them. [30] At one time you refused to obey God. But now you have received mercy, because those people refused to obey. [31] And now the Jews refuse to obey, because God showed mercy to you. But this happened so that they also can receive mercy from him. [32] God has given all people over to their stubborn ways so that he can show mercy to all.

Praise to God

[33] Yes, God's riches are very great, and his wisdom and knowledge have no end! No one can explain the things God decides or understand his ways. [34] As the Scripture[d] says,

"Who has known the mind of the Lord,
    or who has been able to give him advice?"
         Isaiah 40:13

35 "No one has ever given God anything
    that he must pay back."   *Job 41:11*
[36] Yes, God made all things, and everything continues through him and for him. To him be the glory forever! Amen.

Jacob Father of the twelve family groups of Israel, the people God chose to be his people.

Give Your Lives to God

12 So brothers and sisters, since God has shown us great mercy, I beg you to offer your lives as a living sacrifice to him. Your offering must be only for God and pleasing to him, which is the spiritual way for you to worship. ²Do not change yourselves to be like the people of this world, but be changed within by a new way of thinking. Then you will be able to decide what God wants for you; you will know what is good and pleasing to him and what is perfect. ³Because God has given me a special gift, I have something to say to everyone among you. Do not think you are better than you are. You must decide what you really are by the amount of faith God has given you. ⁴Each one of us has a body with many parts, and these parts all have different uses. ⁵In the same way, we are many, but in Christ we are all one body. Each one is a part of that body, and each part belongs to all the other parts. ⁶We all have different gifts, each of which came because of the grace God gave us. The person who has the gift of prophecy*ᵈ* should use that gift in agreement with the faith. ⁷Anyone who has the gift of serving should serve. Anyone who has the gift of teaching should teach. ⁸Whoever has the gift of encouraging others should encourage. Whoever has the gift of giving to others should give freely. Anyone who has the gift of being a leader should try hard when he leads. Whoever has the gift of showing mercy to others should do so with joy.

⁹Your love must be real. Hate what is evil, and hold on to what is good. ¹⁰Love each other like brothers and sisters. Give each other more honor than you want for yourselves. ¹¹Do not be lazy but work hard, serving the Lord with all your heart. ¹²Be joyful because you have hope. Be patient when trouble comes, and pray at all times.

GOD'S LOVE

Free Gifts

Aaron Spell volunteered in an inner-city free store, where he sorted used clothing and helped people pick out things they needed.

One Friday while Aaron was walking to the bus stop near the store, he passed a house that was having a yard sale. He recognized one of the kids as the child of a woman who often came to the free store. After a few moments of talking to the child, he began to recognize more than just the little boy.

There, piled on the old card tables, were stacks of blue jeans, sweatshirts, socks, shoes, and mittens that Aaron had seen earlier that week at the free store. He was outraged! These people didn't take the clothing from the store because they needed it. They took it so they could sell it! What a rip-off!

"It just doesn't seem right," Aaron complained to Jim Knudson, the store manager, later that week. "We gave them those clothes so they'd have something to wear, not so they could sell them."

"Well, it seems they needed the clothes either way," responded Jim. "They needed the clothes to sell for cash so they could buy other things. Besides, we help these people because we care about them, not because they always respond the way we want them to."

"It sounds risky," Aaron said.

"Love always is," answered Jim.

Jim helped Aaron see that their love wasn't something people should have to earn. God's love is like that too. Read **Romans 11:29–36** to find a description of God's merciful gift of love for us.

■ How is the free store like God's love for us?

■ What would happen to your relationship with God if his love depended on your doing what he wanted?

C O N S I D E R . . .

■ writing out five reasons God's love can never be taken away from you. Read Romans 8:31–39 for a few hints.

■ giving a dollar to someone you meet who is in need—without knowing how that person will use the money.

F O R   M O R E ,   S E E . . .

■ Psalm 103:6–14 (p. 540)   ■ 1 John 4:7–12 (p. 1319)
■ Ephesians 2:4–7 (p. 1219)

13Share with God's people who need help. Bring strangers in need into your homes.

14Wish good for those who harm you; wish them well and do not curse them. 15Be happy with those who are happy, and be sad with those who are sad. 16Live in peace with each other. Do not be proud, but make friends with those who seem unimportant. Do not think how smart you are.

17If someone does wrong to you, do not pay him back by doing wrong to him. Try to do what

everyone thinks is right. 18Do your best to live in peace with everyone. 19My friends, do not try to punish others when they wrong you, but wait for God to punish them with his anger. It is written: "I will punish those who do wrong; I will repay them,"n says the Lord. 20But you should do this:

"If your enemy is hungry, feed him;
 if he is thirsty, give him a drink.
Doing this will be like pouring burning coals
 on his head."   *Proverbs 25:21-22*

"I . . . them" Quotation from Deuteronomy 32:35.

FOLLOWING GOD

Bouncing Betties

The Bouncing Betty was the worst kind of land mine in the Vietnam War. It was loaded with a spring so when you stepped on it, it flew into the air, about waist high, then exploded. It was designed to blow people apart and to strike terror in the hearts of young soldiers.

The plan worked on Craig Morrison.

He was on patrol one day with five other guys and this little Vietnamese guy who was supposed to be their guide. They had been out about three hours, walking quietly through the bush, just looking and listening and trying not to get shot.

Then they came to a clearing, maybe a hundred feet across. The situation had "Bouncing Betty" written all over it. And Craig just knew snipers were hiding in the jungle on the other side, waiting for him and his buddies to step into that clearing. But the bush was too thick to go around the clearing, so they had no choice but to go through.

The Vietnamese guide signaled for quiet and pointed to his feet then spread his fingers on both hands. "Stay quiet," he whispered. "Follow me. Place your feet where I place mine. Stay ten yards behind the guy in front of you."

Craig had never been so scared in his life. The guide went ten yards out into the clearing and then motioned for Craig to follow.

Slowly now. Despite his fears, he managed to keep putting his feet in the impressions left by the guide. He kept his head down, waiting for a sniper's bullet to send him to the ground.

And then it was over. He took a deep breath and realized he had made it across. Shaking violently, he looked up and saw the little Vietnamese guy smiling at him. It was nice to have someone in whose steps you could walk.

Craig learned that to get through rough times he had to deny his own desires and follow someone he could trust, someone who knew the way. **Romans 12:1–16** talks about God as the one who knows the way for our lives. Read the passage to see how we can walk in his steps.

■ How is the way Craig followed the guide similar to the way you follow God?

■ According to the passage, why should you follow God? (See verses 1–2.)

C O N S I D E R . . .

■ asking your youth leader to read Romans 12:6–8. Have the leader tell you which gifts he thinks you have. Then ask God to give you more opportunities to use your gift.

■ *writing how your life would change if you walked each day in Christ's steps by* following his instructions in this passage.

F O R M O R E , S E E . . .

■ Psalm 119:9–16 (p. 550)
■ Luke 9:23–26 (p. 1019)

■ Luke 14:25–33 (p. 1034)

²¹Do not let evil defeat you, but defeat evil by doing good.

Christians Should Obey the Law

13 All of you must yield to the government rulers. No one rules unless God has given him the power to rule, and no one rules now without that power from God. ²So those who are against the government are really against what God has commanded. And they will bring punishment on themselves. ³Those who do right do not have to fear the rulers; only those who do wrong fear them. Do you want to be unafraid of the rulers? Then do what is right, and they will praise you. ⁴The ruler is God's servant to help you. But if you do wrong, then be afraid. He has the power to punish; he is God's servant to punish those who do wrong. ⁵So you must yield to the government, not only because you might be punished, but because you know it is right.

⁶This is also why you pay taxes. Rulers are working for God and give their time to their

---

GOVERNMENT

An Inch Is as Good as a Mile

Darren Smithers wrote a column for his high school newspaper. It wasn't a big column, but it was fun. He wrote humorously about cafeteria food, class workload, or the latest bungle of the notoriously bad basketball team. He had gotten the job because his best friend, Mitch Salinas, was the editor. And much to their surprise, the column had become one of the paper's most popular features, even among kids who attended other schools.

One Monday on the way to class, Darren saw a student in a wheelchair and an older woman trying—unsuccessfully—to push the wheelchair over the curb.

When Darren stopped to help, he noticed a wheelchair ramp cut into the curb just a few yards away. But the yellow paint that marked it off had faded, and someone had parked in front of it.

"Unbelievable," Darren said, shaking his head.

"Believe it," said the student in the wheelchair, whose name was Bruce McCoy. "It happens all the time. That's why my mom has to come with me. More than half the ramps haven't been painted in five years. People just ignore them."

Darren smelled a story. He agreed to meet Bruce and his mom the next day. They would bring their extra wheelchair, and Darren would spend the day trying to get around school in it.

That's how Darren discovered that the main elevator stopped two inches below the floor level (as good as two miles when you're in a wheelchair). He had trouble negotiating the super-narrow doors in the band room. And he discovered high water fountains everywhere and over a hundred obstacles all over the campus. And that was in just six hours!

The next day, Darren wrote about his experiences, but somehow that just didn't seem like enough. He also attended student council meetings and talked to the principal about the problem.

A few months later, Darren talked to Bruce again. But this time his mom wasn't with him. "She doesn't need to come with me anymore," he said. "For some reason, the principal just seemed to wake up."

"Maybe somebody tapped him on the shoulder," Darren said.

Romans 13:1–10 encourages us to do what's right in serving our government. In Paul's day, that meant carefully following the laws laid out by Rome. But in today's democracy, it can mean helping to shape policy—just as Darren did. Read the passage to see what else Paul said about your relationship with the government.

■ Would Paul have approved of Darren's actions? Why or why not?
■ What's one thing you can do to apply this passage to your situation?

CONSIDER . . .

■ running for a place in your school's student council.
■ writing a letter to your congressional representative, relating your concerns about the disabled, education, or some other issue you care about.

FOR MORE, SEE . . .

■ 1 Samuel 8:1–22 (p. 251)   ■ 1 Peter 2:13–17 (p. 1304)
■ Matthew 22:17–21 (p. 948)

work. [7]Pay everyone, then, what you owe. If you owe any kind of tax, pay it. Show respect and honor to them all.

> **SIDELIGHT:** Relations with the government were important to Roman Christians, since they lived in the capital city. When Paul wrote Romans 13:1–7, about obeying the government, Christians were tolerated—sometimes even protected—by the state. Within a few years, though, Christians would face the constant threat of torture and execution.

Loving Others

[8]Do not owe people anything, except always owe love to each other, because the person who loves others has obeyed all the law. [9]The law says, "You must not be guilty of adultery.[d] You must not murder anyone. You must not steal. You must not want to take your neighbor's things."[n] All these commands and all others are really only one rule: "Love your neighbor as you love yourself."[n] [10]Love never hurts a neighbor, so loving is obeying all the law.

[11]Do this because we live in an important time. It is now time for you to wake up from your sleep, because our salvation is nearer now than when we first believed. [12]The "night"[n] is almost finished, and the "day"[n] is almost here. So we should stop doing things that belong to darkness and take up the weapons used for fighting in the light. [13]Let us live in a right way, like people who belong to the day. We should not have wild parties or get drunk. There should be no sexual sins of any kind, no fighting or jealousy. [14]But clothe yourselves with the Lord Jesus Christ and forget about satisfying your sinful self.

Do Not Criticize Other People

14 Accept into your group someone who is weak in faith, and do not argue about opinions. [2]One person believes it is right to eat all kinds of food.[n] But another, who is weak, believes it is right to eat only vegetables. [3]The one who knows that it is right to eat any kind of food must not reject the one who eats only vegetables. And the person who eats only vegetables must not think that the one who eats all foods is wrong,

because God has accepted that person. [4]You cannot judge another person's servant. The master decides if the servant is doing well or not. And the Lord's servant will do well because the Lord helps him do well.

[5]Some think that one day is more important than another, and others think that every day is the same. Let all be sure in their own mind. [6]Those who think one day is more important than other days are doing that for the Lord. And those who eat all kinds of food are doing that for the Lord, and they give thanks to God. Others who refuse to eat some foods do that for the Lord, and they give thanks to God. [7]We do not live or die for ourselves. [8]If we live, we are living for the Lord, and if we die, we are dying for the Lord. So living or dying, we belong to the Lord.

[9]The reason Christ died and rose from the dead to live again was so he would be Lord over both the dead and the living. [10]So why do you judge your brothers or sisters in Christ? And why do you think you are better than they are? We will all stand before God to be judged, [11]because it is written in the Scriptures:[d]

" 'As surely as I live,' says the Lord,
 'Everyone will bow before me;
 everyone will say that I am God.' "

Isaiah 45:23

[12]So each of us will have to answer to God.

Do Not Cause Others to Sin

[13]For that reason we should stop judging each other. We must make up our minds not to do anything that will make another Christian sin. [14]I am in the Lord Jesus, and I know that there is no food that is wrong to eat. But if a person believes something is wrong, that thing is wrong for him. [15]If you hurt your brother's or sister's faith because of something you eat, you are not really following the way of love. Do not destroy someone's faith by eating food he thinks is wrong, because Christ died for him. [16]Do not allow what you think is good to become what others say is evil. [17]In the kingdom of God, eating and drinking are not important. The important things are living right with God, peace, and joy in the Holy Spirit.[d] [18]Anyone who serves Christ by living this way is pleasing God and will be accepted by other people.

[19]So let us try to do what makes peace and helps one another. [20]Do not let the eating of food destroy the work of God. All foods are all right to

---

"You . . . things." Quotation from Exodus 20:13-15, 17.
"Love . . . yourself." Quotation from Leviticus 19:18.
"night" This is used as a symbol of the sinful world we live in. This world will soon end.
"day" This is used as a symbol of the good time that is coming, when we will be with God.
all . . . food The Jewish law said there were some foods Jews should not eat. When Jews became Christians, some of them did not understand they could now eat all foods.

eat, but it is wrong to eat food that causes someone else to sin. [21]It is better not to eat meat or drink wine or do anything that will cause your brother or sister to sin.

[22]Your beliefs about these things should be kept secret between you and God. People are happy if they can do what they think is right without feeling guilty. [23]But those who eat something without being sure it is right are wrong because they did not believe it was right. Anything that is done without believing it is right is a sin.

15 We who are strong in faith should help the weak with their weaknesses, and not please only ourselves. [2]Let each of us please our neighbors for their good, to help them be stronger

in faith. [3]Even Christ did not live to please himself. It was as the Scriptures[d] said: "When people insult you, it hurts me."[n] [4]Everything that was written in the past was written to teach us. The Scriptures give us patience and encouragement so that we can have hope. [5]Patience and encouragement come from God. And I pray that God will help you all agree with each other the way Christ Jesus wants. [6]Then you will all be joined together, and you will give glory to God the Father of our Lord Jesus Christ. [7]Christ accepted you, so you should accept each other, which will bring glory to God. [8]I tell you that Christ became a servant of the Jews to show that God's promises to the Jewish ancestors are true. [9]And he also did this so

"When . . . me." Quotation from Psalm 69:9.

DRUGS AND ALCOHOL

The Lost Weekend

"It was just beer. It wasn't like they were alcoholics or drug addicts or anything, right?"

The teenagers in the small Sunday school class nodded their heads, but they didn't speak. What was there to say? So JoAnn Pearson kept talking.

"Well, so we'd do it every weekend. We'd usually go to a ball game or a dance or a party or something on Friday night. Then we'd go get some beer and chips and stuff and go back to Lonnie Brock's house. Her parents were never home.

"Then we'd just drink beer all weekend. Just, you know, get a buzz on Friday and keep it until Sunday night. Then, after a while it was more than a buzz. We started getting really drunk. And we'd just stay drunk all weekend.

"To tell you the truth, it was getting kinda scary, but I didn't know what to do. Then, one day I woke up with a terrible hangover. I was so wasted. And it was Sunday and I didn't know where I was. I mean, I couldn't remember anything that had happened since Friday night. That really scared me.

"I remember kneeling next to the commode in the bathroom and thinking, whoa, this has gone too far. I lost a whole weekend.

"And that's why I'm here," JoAnn concluded. "I decided to go to church more and see if God could help me straighten out my life. He can, can't he?"

"Yes, he can," said Chip Shoenig. "And we'll be there to help too. Right, guys?"

And everyone nodded.

JoAnn learned the hard way that to be free she had to turn away from alcohol. **Romans 13:11–14** also talks about the need to turn away from drunkenness to follow God. Read the passage to see what it says about drinking and drugs.

■ According to this passage, how did JoAnn's decision move her from darkness to light?

■ What reasons does the passage give for avoiding drunkenness?

CONSIDER . . .

■ examining your own drug or alcohol use in light of this passage. What would God want you to do (or stop doing)?

■ helping a drug-abusing friend find help through a local substance abuse program or your church.

FOR MORE SEE . . .

■ Proverbs 23:19–21 (p. 587)   ■ Galatians 5:16–25 (p. 1212)

■ Luke 21:34–36 (p. 1049)

that those who are not Jews could give glory to God for the mercy he gives to them. It is written in the Scriptures:

"So I will praise you among the non-Jewish
  people.
  I will sing praises to your name."   *Psalm 18:49*

10The Scripture also says,

"Be happy, you who are not Jews, together
  with his people."   *Deuteronomy 32:43*

11Again the Scripture says,

"All you who are not Jews, praise the Lord.
  All you people, sing praises to him."
                    Psalm 117:1

12And Isaiah says,

"A new king will come from the family of
  Jesse. *n*

He will come to rule over the non-Jewish
  people,
and they will have hope because of him."
                    Isaiah 11:10

13I pray that the God who gives hope will fill you with much joy and peace while you trust in him. Then your hope will overflow by the power of the Holy Spirit. *d*

Paul Talks About His Work

14My brothers and sisters, I am sure that you are full of goodness. I know that you have all the knowledge you need and that you are able to teach each other. 15But I have written to you very openly about some things I wanted

Jesse   Jesse was the father of David, king of Israel. Jesus was from their family.

DECISION MAKING

Different Strokes for Different Folks

"I'd be mortified!" Rachael Whalen said.

"Everyone would laugh at us!" Dora Parolini shouted.

"We can't let her do it. We'll just have to talk to her, that's all," Janeen Holt reasoned.

Laura Booker shook her head and tried to calm them. "It won't do any good. Her church says you can't wear skirts or dresses above the knee."

"But that's stupid," said Dora. "How can you be a cheerleader and not wear a short skirt? Everyone does it!"

"Yeah," Janeen added. "And besides, Linda knew when she tried out that we wore short skirts."

"Why can't we just let her wear her skirt longer than ours?" Laura asked. "Is it really such a big deal? I mean, I don't think there's anything wrong with our outfits. But if she does, why can't we let her do it her way?"

Rachael sighed loudly. "They're called uniforms! We're supposed to look the same."

"I still don't think it's that big a deal," Laura said. "We're talking about two inches of fabric. No one's asking us to lengthen our skirts. She just wants to be allowed to wear hers longer."

There was a long pause as Laura looked at the other girls. Finally Rachael said, "Okay! Okay, I guess it's all right. Different strokes for different folks, huh?"

Laura smiled. It was nice to know that sometimes everyone could "win."

Linda had made a decision based on her beliefs, even though she knew others would disagree. **Romans 14:5–12** challenges us all to make decisions based on our faith.

■ How is Linda like the people mentioned in the passage?
■ How might this passage affect the way you make decisions about your faith?

C O N S I D E R . . .

■ talking to your youth leader about your church's beliefs. Ask how your church decided to believe the things it does.
■ *making decisions about your lifestyle based on what the Bible teaches. Work toward changing activities that go against your beliefs.*

F O R   M O R E ,   S E E . . .

■ 1 Kings 12:1–20 (p. 316)
■ Matthew 7:13–14 (p. 919)

■ Acts 5:12–32 (p. 1105)

you to remember. I did this because God gave me this special gift [16]to be a minister of Christ Jesus to those who are not Jews. I served God by teaching his Good News,[d] so that the non-Jewish people could be an offering that God would accept — an offering made holy by the Holy Spirit.[d]

[17]So I am proud of what I have done for God in Christ Jesus. [18]I will not talk about anything except what Christ has done through me in leading those who are not Jews to obey God. They have obeyed God because of what I have said and done, [19]because of the power of miracles[d] and the great things they saw, and because of the power of the Holy Spirit. I preached the Good News from Jerusalem all the way around to Illyricum, and so I have finished that part of my work. [20]I always want to preach the Good News in places where people have never heard of Christ, because I do not want to build on the work someone else has already started. [21]But it is written in the Scriptures:[d]

"Those who were not told about him will
    see,

FRIENDS

Accepted

Karen Flock carried her tray into the cafeteria, looking for her friends. As usual, they were sitting by the windows, in the traditional "senior corner." Karen carried her tray to the table and sat down, but she had trouble staying with their conversation. Her mind was on something else.

A girl named Amy.

Amy Powell was a freshman whom Karen had seen at church. Amy was new to the school and, Karen could see, desperately lonely. Amy ate her lunch alone every day. Not because she wanted to—you could see that in her eyes. She ate alone because sophomores, juniors, and seniors didn't eat with underclassmen, and other freshmen were afraid to eat with her.

They weren't afraid of Amy. It was Kara Holland they were afraid of. Kara was queen of the freshman class. She and her "court" of five pretty girls ruled freshman society. They decided who was "in" and who was "out," and, for undisclosed reasons, Amy was definitely "out."

The more Karen thought about Amy's situation, the more angry she became. It's time to stop this dumb game, she thought. So Karen picked up her tray and walked across the cafeteria to where Amy was sitting. Amy wouldn't look up at her, so she said, "Hi, Amy."

"Hi."

"Is this seat saved?" she asked, pulling out a chair and sitting down.

"No." She looked up briefly, then back to her plate.

"So, how do you like the school?"

Amy shrugged.

"Hi, Amy!" two voices said as they walked by. Girls. Freshmen. Then they giggled.

Now Amy looked up at Karen. She smiled, shyly.

It would be okay, now, she knew. No freshman ever questioned the acceptance of a senior.

Karen accepted Amy even though others had rejected her. Paul talks about the foolishness of rejecting others, since we have all been accepted equally by Christ. Read what else Paul said about accepting others in **Romans 15:4–13**.

- Based on this passage, what might Paul have said to Karen and her friends?
- How does knowing that Christ has accepted other people help you accept them too?

CONSIDER . . .

- sitting by people you don't know this week and getting to know them.
- thinking of people at school or church whom you don't like and asking God to help you accept them as he does.

FOR MORE, SEE . . .

- Job 2:11–13 (p. 453)
- 1 Samuel 18:1–4 (p. 262)
- John 13:20 (p. 1081)

and those who have not heard about him will understand." *Isaiah 52:15*

Paul's Plan to Visit Rome

22This is the reason I was stopped many times from coming to you. 23Now I have finished my work here. Since for many years I have wanted to come to you, 24I hope to visit you on my way to Spain. After I enjoy being with you for a while, I hope you can help me on my trip. 25Now I am going to Jerusalem to help God's people. 26The believers in Macedonia and Southern Greece were happy to give their money to help the poor among God's people at Jerusalem. 27They were happy to do this, and really they owe it to them. These who are not Jews have shared in the Jews' spiritual blessings, so they should use their material possessions to help the Jews. 28After I am sure the poor in Jerusalem get the money that has been given for them, I will leave for Spain and stop and visit you. 29I know that when I come to you I will bring Christ's full blessing.

30Brothers and sisters, I beg you to help me in my work by praying to God for me. Do this because of our Lord Jesus and the love that the Holy Spirit*d* gives us. 31Pray that I will be saved from the non-believers in Judea and that this help I bring to Jerusalem will please God's people there. 32Then, if God wants me to, I will come to you with joy, and together you and I will have a time of rest. 33The God who gives peace be with you all. Amen.

Greetings to the Christians

16 I recommend to you our sister Phoebe, who is a helper*n* in the church in Cenchrea. 2I ask you to accept her in the Lord in the way God's people should. Help her with anything she needs, because she has helped me and many other people also.

3Give my greetings to Priscilla and Aquila, who work together with me in Christ Jesus 4and who risked their own lives to save my life. I am thank-

ful to them, and all the non-Jewish churches are thankful as well. 5Also, greet for me the church that meets at their house.

Greetings to my dear friend Epenetus, who was the first person in the country of Asia to follow Christ. 6Greetings to Mary, who worked very hard for you. 7Greetings to Andronicus and Junia, my relatives, who were in prison with me. They are very important apostles. They were believers in Christ before I was. 8Greetings to Ampliatus, my dear friend in the Lord. 9Greetings to Urbanus, a worker together with me for Christ. And greetings to my dear friend Stachys. 10Greetings to Apelles, who was tested and proved that he truly loves Christ. Greetings to all those who are in the family of Aristobulus. 11Greetings to Herodion, my fellow citizen. Greetings to all those in the family of Narcissus who belong to the Lord. 12Greetings to Tryphena and Tryphosa, women who work very hard for the Lord. Greetings to my dear friend Persis, who also has worked very hard for the Lord. 13Greetings to Rufus, who is a special person in the Lord, and to his mother, who has been like a mother to me also. 14Greetings to Asyncritus, Phlegon, Hermes, Patrobas, Hermas, and all the brothers who are with them. 15Greetings to Philologus and Julia, Nereus and his sister, and Olympas, and to all God's people with them. 16Greet each other with a holy kiss. All of Christ's churches send greetings to you.

17Brothers and sisters, I ask you to look out for those who cause people to be against each other and who upset other people's faith. They are against the true teaching you learned, so stay away from them. 18Such people are not serving our Lord Christ but are only doing what pleases themselves. They use fancy talk and fine words to fool the minds of those who do not know about evil. 19All the believers have heard that you obey, so I am very happy because of you. But I want you to be wise in what is good and innocent in what is evil.

20The God who brings peace will soon defeat Satan and give you power over him.

The grace of our Lord Jesus be with you.

21Timothy, a worker together with me, sends greetings, as well as Lucius, Jason, and Sosipater, my relatives.

22I am Tertius, and I am writing this letter from Paul. I send greetings to you in the Lord.

23Gaius is letting me and the whole church here use his home. He also sends greetings to you, as do Erastus, the city treasurer, and our brother Quartus. 24 *n*

25Glory to God who can make you strong in

SIDELIGHT: Since the early Christians didn't have churches to go to, they usually met in homes (Romans 16:3–5). Priscilla and Aquila might have been wealthy and had a large house where Christians could gather for worship. You would probably have to clean your room more often if this were still standard practice.

---

helper Literally, "deaconess." This might mean the same as one of the special women helpers in 1 Timothy 3:11.
Verse 24 Some Greek copies add verse 24: "The grace of our Lord Jesus Christ be with all of you. Amen."

faith by the Good News[d] that I tell people and by the message about Jesus Christ. The message about Christ is the secret that was hidden for long ages past but is now made known. [26]It has been made clear through the writings of the prophets.[d]

And by the command of the eternal God it is made known to all nations that they might believe and obey.

[27]To the only wise God be glory forever through Jesus Christ! Amen.

Recipe

Ray Marx had baked bread before. Hundreds of times.

Well, two times anyway.

"It's a simple loaf of white bread. How hard could that be?" Ray wondered aloud. "A little yeast, a little oil, a little flour—nothing to it."

Ray put all the ingredients into the big bowl his mother always used, added more flour until the mixture was a big ball, and dumped it onto the counter.

As Ray kneaded the dough he imagined how surprised and happy his parents would be when he presented his homemade bread for breakfast the next morning. It was their twenty-fifth anniversary.

Ray covered the big ball of dough with a light coating of butter, flipped it into the bowl, covered it with plastic wrap, and set it aside in a warm corner of the room to rise.

"See, nothing to it," he said smugly. "Didn't even have to look at the recipe."

Now all he had to do was wait for it to rise. Thirty minutes. Nothing. An hour. Nothing.

"It just sat there in the bowl like a . . . like a big lump of dough. Why wasn't it rising?" Ray asked himself.

He checked the expiration date on the yeast package. No problem; it wouldn't expire for another three months. So what could it be?

Reluctantly, he went to the cookbook.

"Let's see," he mused. "Flour, oil, yeast, sugar . . .

"Sugar! Of course!"

Without sugar, the yeast couldn't do its job. No wonder the bread wasn't rising! He had left out a small but vital ingredient.

Ray's bread couldn't rise without sugar. In the same way, Paul says that a Christian can't reach a mature faith without having the right ingredients in his or her life. Read **Romans 16:22–27** to see what those ingredients are.

■ What, according to Paul, is the effect of God's message on people's lives?

■ According to this passage, what ingredients might you be lacking to bring you to Christian maturity?

C O N S I D E R . . .

■ asking your parent or Sunday school teacher to give you a recipe for Bible study. Ask what steps you should follow in studying the Bible.

■ regularly attending your youth group's weekly Bible study. If you don't have one, ask your youth leader to start one.

F O R   M O R E ,   S E E . . .

■ Joshua 1:8 (p. 195)
■ Psalm 19:7–11 (p. 492)
■ Revelation 1:1–3 (p. 1332)

1 CORINTHIANS

Why Read This Book:

- Hear down-to-earth advice about dealing with church problems (1 Corinthians 1—10).
- Learn the importance of working together as Christians (1 Corinthians 11—13).
- Discover the promise of Christ's victory over death (1 Corinthians 14—16).

Behind the Scenes:

If you have ever gone on a road trip with a band, youth group, or sports team, you know what it's like. At first, everything goes well. Everyone has fun being together. But as the miles and days pass, things get tense. Roommates have fights. Bossy people get on other people's nerves. Clowns become irritating. By the time you're home, you're glad you only see those people a few hours a day!

The Christians at Corinth may have had similar feelings. Located in one of the largest and most important cities in Greece, church members came from all over the world. Their backgrounds were different. Their incomes were different. Their beliefs were different. And those differences were dividing the church. To complicate things, many were immature Christians.

In this letter to the Corinthians, the apostle Paul addresses the issues that were dividing the church. These included competition, pride, differences in theology, sexual immorality, lawsuits, marriage and singleness, food offered to idols, and worship. He expresses his beliefs on the issues, challenging the church to follow Christ in all things.

At the heart of the letter, Paul focuses on what it means to be Christians together (1 Corinthians 12—13), respecting each other's uniqueness and gifts, and, above all, loving each other with God's love.

This letter is a problem-solving letter. As you read, you can almost picture Paul referring to a list of questions he has heard from the people, then answering each one. His advice is specific and practical.

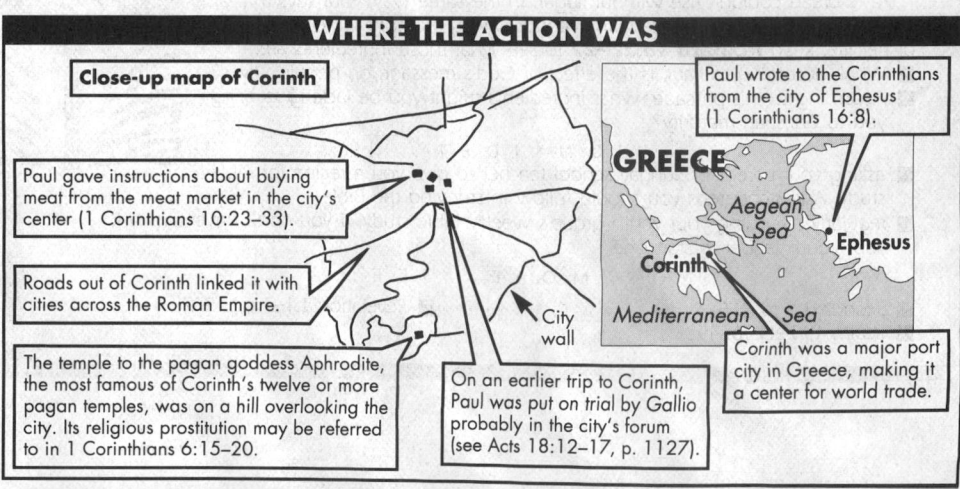

WHERE THE ACTION WAS

Close-up map of Corinth

Paul wrote to the Corinthians from the city of Ephesus (1 Corinthians 16:8).

Paul gave instructions about buying meat from the meat market in the city's center (1 Corinthians 10:23–33).

Roads out of Corinth linked it with cities across the Roman Empire.

The temple to the pagan goddess Aphrodite, the most famous of Corinth's twelve or more pagan temples, was on a hill overlooking the city. Its religious prostitution may be referred to in 1 Corinthians 6:15–20.

On an earlier trip to Corinth, Paul was put on trial by Gallio probably in the city's forum (see Acts 18:12–17, p. 1127).

City wall

Corinth was a major port city in Greece, making it a center for world trade.

GREECE

Aegean Sea

Ephesus

Corinth

Mediterranean Sea

WHEN THE ACTION WAS

Jesus was born	The church began soon after Jesus went to heaven	Paul began his missionary work	Fire destroyed Rome	
BC/AD	25AD	50AD	75AD	100AD
	Jesus began his ministry	Paul founded the church in Corinth	Paul wrote 1 Corinthians	Romans destroyed the Temple in Jerusalem

Behind the Scenes (cont.): In many ways, the Corinthian Christians lived in a culture a lot like ours. They faced many of the same temptations and problems we face today. This book gives a unique glimpse into their world. And it gives us practical insights into how to live in our complex world today.

---

1 From Paul. God called me to be an apostle[d] of Christ Jesus because that is what God wanted. Also from Sosthenes, our brother in Christ.

²To the church of God in Corinth, to you who have been made holy in Christ Jesus. You were called to be God's holy people with all people everywhere who pray in the name of the Lord Jesus Christ—their Lord and ours: ³Grace and peace to you from God our Father and the Lord Jesus Christ.

Paul Gives Thanks to God

⁴I always thank my God for you because of the grace God has given you in Christ Jesus. ⁵I thank God because in Christ you have been made rich

---

HEROES

How Hard They Fall

Phil Edwards's youth group was selected to sing at a Christian music conference. The young people were so excited; they would be singing on the same stage as many contemporary Christian artists.

Phil hoped to meet some of the musicians—especially those in one particular band. Phil had their albums, and he had gone to a few of their concerts. He had T-shirts with their group logo on them, and his room was plastered with their posters. Phil was even a trivia expert on the group. He could tell you the band members' birthdays, birthplaces, favorite foods and even their pet peeves. Phil practically worshiped this band!

On the day of the performance, when Phil and his youth group went backstage to prepare for the performance, Phil was distracted. He searched the area to get a glimpse of the band.

He didn't have to look far. He heard arguing from a back corner and looked to see the lead guitarist yelling at a stagehand. Two other band members were smoking under a No Smoking sign by the door, and the lead singer was walking right toward Phil.

As the singer walked past, Phil touched the singer's shoulder to get his attention.

"Hey, punk! What do you think this is? Public property?" the singer growled and jerked away.

Phil couldn't even speak. He just melted back into his group in shock.

When Phil went home that night, he tore down all his posters and shoved them into his trash can. He couldn't believe he had been so stupid. Phil had thought these guys were perfect just because they could sing. Phil vowed he would never again forget that even famous people are just human, and can disappoint others.

Knowing whom to trust and admire isn't a new problem. People back in Bible times also had a hard time figuring out just who should be their hero. Read about one such struggle in **1 Corinthians 1:1–17**.

■ In what ways is Phil's "hero worship" similar to that of the Corinthians in this passage? In what ways is it different?

■ According to this passage (especially verses 10–13), what happens if we worship human heroes?

C O N S I D E R . . .

■ evaluating whether people whom you admire deserve your respect. Then look for heroes that point you toward Christ.

■ going out with your best friend for "hero" sandwiches at your local sub shop. With every bite, give one reason that only Jesus can be a real hero.

F O R   M O R E ,   S E E . . .

■ Proverbs 4:20–27 (p. 571)　　■ 1 Timothy 4:12–16 (p. 1259)
■ Romans 15:1–6 (p. 1161)

in every way, in all your speaking and in all your knowledge. ⁶Just as our witness about Christ has been guaranteed to you, ⁷so you have every gift from God while you wait for our Lord Jesus Christ to come again. ⁸Jesus will keep you strong until the end so that there will be no wrong in you on the day our Lord Jesus Christ comes again. ⁹God, who has called you to share everything with his Son, Jesus Christ our Lord, is faithful.

☀ SIDELIGHT: You have heard of the Suez Canal in Egypt and the Panama Canal in Panama. But have you heard of the Corinth Track? Because Corinth was located on a small strip of land (see map, p. 1166), the city built a five-mile rock track across the land to roll cargo and small ships. By using this track, sailors not only had a shorter trip, but they avoided a dangerous sea journey.

Problems in the Church

¹⁰I beg you, brothers and sisters,ⁿ by the name of our Lord Jesus Christ that all of you agree with each other and not be split into groups. I beg that you be completely joined together by having the same kind of thinking and the same purpose. ¹¹My brothers and sisters, some people from Chloe's family have told me quite plainly that there are quarrels among you. ¹²This is what I mean: One of you says, "I follow Paul"; another says, "I follow Apollos"; another says, "I follow Peter"; and another says, "I follow Christ." ¹³Christ has been divided up into different groups! Did Paul die on the cross for you? No! Were you baptized in the name of Paul? No! ¹⁴I thank God I did not baptize any of you except Crispus and Gaius ¹⁵so that now no one can say you were baptized in my name. ¹⁶(I also baptized the family of Stephanas, but I do not remember that I baptized anyone else.) ¹⁷Christ did not send me to baptize people but to preach the Good News.ᵈ And he sent me to preach the Good News without using words of human wisdom so that the crossⁿ of Christ would not lose its power.

Christ Is God's Power and Wisdom

¹⁸The teaching about the cross is foolishness to *those who are being lost, but to us who are being*

saved it is the power of God. ¹⁹It is written in the Scriptures:ᵈ

"I will cause the wise men to lose their
  wisdom;
I will make the wise men unable to
  understand."   *Isaiah 29:14*

²⁰Where is the wise person? Where is the educated person? Where is the skilled talker of this world? God has made the wisdom of the world foolish. ²¹In the wisdom of God the world did not know God through its own wisdom. So God chose to use the message that sounds foolish to save those who believe. ²²The Jews ask for miracles,ᵈ and the Greeks want wisdom. ²³But we preach a crucified Christ. This is a big problem to the Jews, and it is foolishness to those who are not Jews. ²⁴But Christ is the power of God and the wisdom of God to those people God has called — Jews and Greeks. ²⁵Even the foolishness of God is wiser than human wisdom, and the weakness of God is stronger than human strength.

²⁶Brothers and sisters, look at what you were when God called you. Not many of you were wise in the way the world judges wisdom. Not many of you had great influence. Not many of you came from important families. ²⁷But God chose the foolish things of the world to shame the wise, and he chose the weak things of the world to shame the strong. ²⁸He chose what the world thinks is unimportant and what the world looks down on and thinks is nothing in order to destroy what the world thinks is important. ²⁹God did this so that no one can brag in his presence. ³⁰Because of God you are in Christ Jesus, who has become for us wisdom from God. In Christ we are put right with God, and have been made holy, and have been set free from sin. ³¹So, as the Scriptureᵈ says, "If someone wants to brag, he should brag only about the Lord."ⁿ

The Message of Christ's Death

2 Dear brothers and sisters, when I came to you, I did not come preaching God's secret with fancy words or a show of human wisdom. ²I decided that while I was with you I would forget about everything except Jesus Christ and his death on the cross. ³So when I came to you, I was weak and fearful and trembling. ⁴My teaching and preaching were not with words of human wisdom that persuade people but with proof of the power that the Spiritᵈ gives. ⁵This was so that your faith would be in *God's power and not in human wisdom.*

---

brothers and sisters   Although the Greek text says "brothers" here and throughout this book, Paul's words were meant for the entire church, including men and women.
cross   Paul uses the cross as a picture of the gospel, the story of Christ's death and rising from the dead to pay for people's sins. The cross, or Christ's death, was God's way to save people.
"If . . . Lord."   Quotation from Jeremiah 9:24.

God's Wisdom

[6]However, I speak a wisdom to those who are mature. But this wisdom is not from this world or from the rulers of this world, who are losing their power. [7]I speak God's secret wisdom, which he has kept hidden. Before the world began, God planned this wisdom for our glory. [8]None of the rulers of this world understood it. If they had, they would not have crucified the Lord of glory. [9]But as it is written in the Scriptures:[d]

"No one has ever seen this,
    and no one has ever heard about it.
No one has ever imagined
    what God has prepared for those
    who love him."   *Isaiah 64:4*

[10]But God has shown us these things through the Spirit.[d]

The Spirit searches out all things, even the deep secrets of God. [11]Who knows the thoughts that another person has? Only a person's spirit that lives within him knows his thoughts. It is the same with God. No one knows the thoughts of God except the Spirit of God. [12]Now we did not receive the spirit of the world, but we received the Spirit that is from God so that we can know all that God has given us. [13]And we speak about these things, not with words taught us by human wisdom but with words taught us by the Spirit. And so we explain spiritual truths to spiritual people. [14]A person who does not have the Spirit does not accept the truths that come from the Spirit of God. That person thinks they are foolish and cannot understand them, because they can only be judged to be true by the Spirit. [15]The spiritual person is able to judge all things, but no one can judge him. The Scripture says:

[16]"Who has known the mind of the Lord?
    Who has been able to teach him?"   *Isaiah 40:13*

But we have the mind of Christ.

Following People Is Wrong

3 Brothers and sisters, in the past I could not talk to you as I talk to spiritual people. I had to talk to you as I would to people without the Spirit — babies in Christ. [2]The teaching I gave you was like milk, not solid food, because you were

PRIORITIES

Is This All There Is?

When Howard Hughes was forty-five, he was one of the most glamorous men in America. He owned an airline and hotels around the world. He dated actresses, flew exotic test aircraft, and worked on top-secret CIA contracts.

Twenty years later, Howard Hughes was the world's richest man—with $2.3 billion. But he was also one of the world's most pathetic. He lived in small, dark rooms in his hotels. He preferred to keep his life without sun and without joy. He had a scraggly beard down to his waist, long hair, and two-inch-long fingernails. His body had wasted away to a mere one hundred pounds.

He spent most of his time watching movies over and over—sometimes watching the same movie 150 times. He lay naked in bed, deathly afraid of germs. Life had lost its meaning for him.

Finally, emaciated and hooked on drugs, Howard Hughes died at age sixty-seven, because he didn't have a medical device his company had helped to develop.

Howard Hughes had it all—worldly wisdom, wealth, power, fame. He had all the things the world considers important. But they weren't enough. Read **1 Corinthians 1:18–31** to see what Paul says is really important in life.

■ How was Howard Hughes's life an illustration of this passage?
■ According to this passage, what does God say is most important for Christians?

C O N S I D E R . . .

■ doing something "foolish"—such as helping someone who doesn't deserve it—as a sign of your faith.
■ tearing out words and pictures from a magazine that show what the world says is important and what God says is important. Make a separate pile for each category.

F O R   M O R E ,   S E E . . .

■ Psalm 139:1–18 (p. 561)   ■ 1 John 3:1–3 (p. 1318)
■ 2 Corinthians 11:16–31 (p. 1202)

not able to take solid food. And even now you are not ready. ³You are still not spiritual, because there is jealousy and quarreling among you, and this shows that you are not spiritual. You are acting like people of the world. ⁴One of you says, "I belong to Paul," and another says, "I belong to Apollos." When you say things like this, you are acting like people of the world.

⁵Is Apollos important? No! Is Paul important? No! We are only servants of God who helped you believe. Each one of us did the work God gave us to do. ⁶I planted the seed, and Apollos watered it. But God is the One who made it grow. ⁷So the one who plants is not important, and the one who waters is not important. Only God, who makes things grow, is important. ⁸The one who plants and the one who waters have the same purpose, and each will be rewarded for his own work. ⁹We

are God's workers, working together; you are like God's farm, God's house.

> **SIDELIGHT:** Even though Apollos isn't mentioned much in the Bible, he appears to have been an influential church leader. For a while he was a leader in Corinth, and may have been a better preacher than Paul (1 Corinthians 3:1–9).

¹⁰Using the gift God gave me, I laid the foundation of that house like an expert builder. Others are building on that foundation, but all people should be careful how they build on it. ¹¹The foundation that has already been laid is Jesus Christ, and no one can lay down any other foun-

---

SCHOOL

The Powerful Way

It was disgusting! While Scott Douglas was at the evening play practice, someone had smeared animal guts all over his car. Scott just stood in the parking lot, looking shocked.

Things had not been the same since he had seriously committed his life to Christ. Many of his friends didn't understand. They thought Scott was snubbing them when he wouldn't party with them. The verbal abuse came first. Then a few flattened tires. Then vicious rumors.

But this? This was sick!

Scott's best friend, Jeff Stevens, walked up behind him. When he noticed the car, Jeff blew up. "Man! . . . I can't believe . . . the nerve of those. . . ." Jeff was so angry he couldn't even finish his sentences. "We know who's behind this," he fumed. "Enough is enough! Let's go bash some heads!"

Scott shook his head and began to smile. "No way. Two bucks and some elbow grease, and we'll never know it happened. Besides, aren't we supposed to act more like Jesus? Do you think Jesus would bash heads now?"

Jeff looked at his friend and began to smile. "You're something, buddy. You're also right. Okay. To the car wash we go!"

Scott Douglas had plenty of reasons to take revenge. But, instead, Scott prayed for those people and treated them as he would anyone else. People noticed. During his final months at high school, people who knew what Scott had been through asked what his secret was.

It was tough for Scott to live the Christian life at school. But because he didn't fight back, Scott's actions demonstrated God's power. To find out more about demonstrating God's power at school, read **1 Corinthians 2:1–11**.

■ How do Scott's actions show the difference between God's wisdom and the world's wisdom?

■ According to this passage, what should be our attitude as we talk about and demonstrate our faith?

CONSIDER . . .

■ imagining you were with Paul when he was experiencing some of the feelings he talks about in this passage. Write what you would say to encourage him.

■ demonstrating God's power at school by not getting angry if people ridicule your faith.

FOR MORE, SEE . . .

■ Joshua 6 (p. 198)
■ Ephesians 3:14–21 (p. 1222)
■ 2 Timothy 1:6–8 (p. 1263)

dation. [12]But if people build on that foundation, using gold, silver, jewels, wood, grass, or straw, [13]their work will be clearly seen, because the Day of Judgment[n] will make it visible. That Day will appear with fire, and the fire will test everyone's work to show what sort of work it was. [14]If the building that has been put on the foundation still stands, the builder will get a reward. [15]But if the building is burned up, the builder will suffer loss. The builder will be saved, but it will be as one who escaped from a fire.

[16]Don't you know that you are God's temple and that God's Spirit[d] lives in you? [17]If anyone destroys God's temple, God will destroy that person, because God's temple is holy and you are that temple.

[18]Do not fool yourselves. If you think you are wise in this world, you should become a fool so that you can become truly wise, [19]because the wisdom of this world is foolishness with God. It is written in the Scriptures,[d] "He catches those who are wise in their own clever traps."[n] [20]It is also written in the Scriptures, "The Lord knows what wise people think. He knows their thoughts are just a puff of wind."[n] [21]So you should not brag about human leaders. All things belong to you: [22]Paul, Apollos, and Peter; the world, life, death, the present, and the future—all these be-

---

Day of Judgment　The day Christ will come to judge all people and take his people home to live with him.
"He . . . traps."　Quotation from Job 5:13.
"The Lord . . . wind."　Quotation from Psalm 94:11.

It's Not Who You Know . . .

Even in grade school, Steven Curtis Chapman faced a dilemma: to be popular by the "in" crowd's terms or to be popular on his own terms. Steven's faith was important to him, and he didn't want to compromise it.

At the same time, he just wanted to be everyone's friend. "I wanted to get along with everybody," Steven, the 1990 Gospel Music Association's Artist of the Year, explains now. So he decided to live what he believed and hope people would like him anyway.

It wasn't easy. He used to get together to play guitars with one guy. "Then [this guy] went the direction of the jock crowd," Steven recalls. "I went into music. He was the cool sports guy that everybody wanted to be friends with, and I saw this split happening and it really bothered me."

It didn't seem right that they couldn't be friends, just because they had different interests.

So Steven challenged the system. He continued to be himself and pursue interests even if they were "unpopular." He tried to be the best Christian he could be, and he treated people the same—no matter what clique they were in.

By the end of his high school years, people recognized what Steven had done. Steven's classmates voted to give him the highest honors possible at Heath High School, naming him "Mr. Heath" and "Mr. Senior."

Steven thinks he got the awards, "not so much for myself, but as a representative of a group of people who said, 'We are going to stand for what's good and right.' "

Steven had proven that it's not whom you know but who you are that matters most of all. Read **1 Corinthians 3:1–23** to see how Paul helped the Corinthian church understand this principle.

■ Why do people such as Steven's classmates and the Corinthians value having the right connections? How does this attitude divide people?

■ What does this passage tell us we should focus on, instead of focusing on popularity?

CONSIDER . . .

■ evaluating whether your efforts to be popular please God.
■ working with friends to create a "Popularity/Clique Survey" to distribute at school. Determine how cliques affect relationships.

FOR MORE, SEE . . .

■ Daniel 1:1–21 (p. 807)
■ Mark 10:42–45 (p. 983)

■ 3 John 2–8 (p. 1326)

long to you. ²³And you belong to Christ, and Christ belongs to God.

Apostles Are Servants of Christ

4 People should think of us as servants of Christ, the ones God has trusted with his secrets. ²Now in this way those who are trusted with something valuable must show they are worthy of that trust. ³As for myself, I do not care if I am judged by you or by any human court. I do not even judge myself. ⁴I know of no wrong I have done, but this does not make me right before the Lord. The Lord is the One who judges me. ⁵So do not judge before the right time; wait until the Lord comes. He will bring to light things that are now hidden in darkness, and will make known the secret purposes of people's hearts. Then God will praise each one of them.

⁶Brothers and sisters, I have used Apollos and myself as examples so you could learn through us the meaning of the saying, "Follow only what is written in the Scriptures."ᵈ Then you will not be more proud of one person than another. ⁷Who says you are better than others? What do you have that was not given to you? And if it was given to you, why do you brag as if you did not receive it as a gift?

⁸You think you already have everything you need. You think you are rich. You think you have become kings without us. I wish you really were kings so we could be kings together with you. ⁹But it seems to me that God has put us apostlesᵈ in last place, like those sentenced to die. We are

---

Worthy of the Trust

"Son, please don't go."

Bill Dukes's eyes met his father's. "Dad, I believe God wants me in Brazil this year. We've been waiting on the missionary board for a long time. Now the appointment is here. I've got to go."

Bill nearly broke down as he watched his dad's eyes fill with tears. The doctors didn't think Bill's dad had long to live. If Bill left for Brazil, his father might die before Bill could come home.

"Look, Dad, I know you want me to stay. I want to be around you too. But I have to ask what God wants. And as far as I can tell now, he wants me in Brazil."

As Bill drove away from his parents' house, his mind replayed doubts others had expressed about his decision:

"A wife, one boy, and a baby on the way. You're crazy!"

"Do you really think God would call you away from your father now?"

"We need pastors in this country. Why don't you stay?"

Bill weighed his options. Jesus had given him so much that Bill felt he had a responsibility to fulfill.

For eight years, Bill and his family worked in South America. And, against all predictions by doctors and the expectations of Bill's family, Bill's father was alive to welcome him home.

"I'm convinced that God is faithful," Bill says, "especially in those times when someone has to make a hard choice to be faithful in serving God."

The Corinthian Christians needed to be reminded of the same thing, and so do we. Read how Paul makes the point clear in **1 Corinthians 4:1–5**.

■ How would Bill's feelings about his life compare with Paul's feelings in this passage?

■ How do you feel about God's knowing and judging the secrets of your heart?

CONSIDER . . .

■ thanking God for a servant whose faithfulness has helped you in some way. Ask God to help you do the same for someone else.

■ evaluating any commitments to serve you have made and haven't kept. Begin fulfilling those commitments this week.

FOR MORE, SEE . . .

■ Joshua 24:14–15 (p. 214)
■ Luke 16:10–12 (p. 1037)

■ Ephesians 4:11–16 (p. 1223)

like a show for the whole world to see — angels and people. [10]We are fools for Christ's sake, but you are very wise in Christ. We are weak, but you are strong. You receive honor, but we are shamed. [11]Even to this very hour we do not have enough to eat or drink or to wear. We are often beaten, and we have no homes in which to live. [12]We work hard with our own hands for our food. When people curse us, we bless them. When they hurt us, we put up with it. [13]When they tell evil lies about us, we speak nice words about them. Even today, we are treated as though we were the garbage of the world — the filth of the earth.

[14]I am not trying to make you feel ashamed. I am writing this to give you a warning as my own dear children. [15]For though you may have ten thousand teachers in Christ, you do not have many fathers. Through the Good News[d] I became your father in Christ Jesus, [16]so I beg you, please follow my example. [17]That is why I am sending to you Timothy, my son in the Lord. I love Timothy, and he is faithful. He will help you remember my way of life in Christ Jesus, just as I teach it in all the churches everywhere.

[18]Some of you have become proud, thinking that I will not come to you again. [19]But I will come to you very soon if the Lord wishes. Then I will know what the proud ones do, not what they say, [20]because the kingdom of God is present not in talk but in power. [21]Which do you want: that I come to you with punishment or with love and gentleness?

Wickedness in the Church

5 It is actually being said that there is sexual sin among you. And it is a kind that does not happen even among people who do not know God. A man there has his father's wife. [2]And you are proud! You should have been filled with sadness so that the man who did this should be put out of your group. [3]I am not there with you in person, but I am with you in spirit. And I have already judged the man who did that sin as if I were really there. [4]When you meet together in the name of our Lord Jesus, and I meet with you in spirit with the power of our Lord Jesus, [5]then hand this man over to Satan. So his sinful self[n] will be destroyed, and his spirit will be saved on the day of the Lord.

[6]Your bragging is not good. You know the saying, "Just a little yeast makes the whole batch of dough rise." [7]Take out all the old yeast so that you will be a new batch of dough without yeast, which you really are. For Christ, our Passover[d] lamb, has been sacrificed. [8]So let us celebrate this feast, but not with the bread that has the old

yeast — the yeast of sin and wickedness. Let us celebrate this feast with the bread that has no yeast — the bread of goodness and truth.

[9]I wrote you in my earlier letter not to associate with those who sin sexually. [10]But I did not mean you should not associate with those of this world who sin sexually, or with the greedy, or robbers, or those who worship idols. To get away from them you would have to leave this world. [11]I am writing to tell you that you must not associate with those who call themselves believers in Christ but who sin sexually, or are greedy, or worship idols, or abuse others with words, or get drunk, or cheat people. Do not even eat with people like that.

[12-13]It is not my business to judge those who are not part of the church. God will judge them. But you must judge the people who are part of the church. The Scripture[d] says, "You must get rid of the evil person among you."[n]

SIDELIGHT: Corinth was known for lawsuits (1 Corinthians 6:1). Trials were social events, and sitting on the jury was a privilege. One record tells of a jury with six thousand people on it.

Judging Problems Among Christians

6 When you have something against another Christian, how can you bring yourself to go before judges who are not right with God? Why do you not let God's people decide who is right? [2]Surely you know that God's people will judge the world. So if you are to judge the world, are you not able to judge small cases as well? [3]You know that in the future we will judge angels, so surely we can judge the ordinary things of this life. [4]If you have ordinary cases that must be judged, are you going to appoint people as judges who mean nothing to the church? [5]I say this to shame you. Surely there is someone among you wise enough to judge a complaint between believers. [6]But now one believer goes to court against another believer — and you do this in front of unbelievers!

[7]The fact that you have lawsuits against each other shows that you are already defeated. Why not let yourselves be wronged? Why not let yourselves be cheated? [8]But you yourselves do wrong and cheat, and you do this to other believers!

[9-10]Surely you know that the people who do wrong will not inherit God's kingdom. Do not be fooled. Those who sin sexually, worship idols, take part in adultery,[d] those who are male prosti-

---

sinful self Literally, "flesh." This could also mean his body.
"You . . . you." Quotation from Deuteronomy 17:7; 19:19; 22:21, 24; 24:7.

tutes,[d] or men who have sexual relations with other men, those who steal, are greedy, get drunk, lie about others, or rob — these people will not inherit God's kingdom. [11]In the past, some of you were like that, but you were washed clean. You were made holy, and you were made right with God in the name of the Lord Jesus Christ and in the Spirit of our God.

Use Your Bodies for God's Glory

[12]"I am allowed to do all things," but all things are not good for me to do. "I am allowed to do all things," but I will not let anything make me its slave. [13]"Food is for the stomach, and the stomach for food," but God will destroy them both. The body is not for sexual sin but for the Lord, and the Lord is for the body. [14]By his power God has raised the Lord from the dead and will also raise us from the dead. [15]Surely you know that your bodies are parts of Christ himself. So I must never take the parts of Christ and join them to a prostitute![d] [16]It is written in the Scriptures,[d] "The two

will become one body."[n] So you should know that anyone who joins with a prostitute becomes one body with the prostitute. [17]But the one who joins with the Lord is one spirit with the Lord.

[18]So run away from sexual sin. Every other sin people do is outside their bodies, but those who sin sexually sin against their own bodies. [19]You should know that your body is a temple for the Holy Spirit[d] who is in you. You have received the Holy Spirit from God. So you do not belong to yourselves, [20]because you were bought by God for a price. So honor God with your bodies.

About Marriage

7 Now I will discuss the things you wrote me about. It is good for a man not to have sexual relations with a woman. [2]But because sexual sin is a danger, each man should have his own wife, and each woman should have her own husband. [3]The husband should give his wife all that he owes her as his wife. And the wife should give her husband all that she owes him as her husband.

"The two ... body."   Quotation from Genesis 2:24.

4The wife does not have full rights over her own body; her husband shares them. And the husband does not have full rights over his own body; his wife shares them. 5Do not refuse to give your bodies to each other, unless you both agree to stay away from sexual relations for a time so you can give your time to prayer. Then come together again so Satan cannot tempt you because of a lack of self-control. 6I say this to give you permission to stay away from sexual relations for a time. It is not a command to do so. 7I wish that everyone were like me, but each person has his own gift from God. One has one gift, another has another gift.

8Now for those who are not married and for the widows I say this: It is good for them to stay unmarried as I am. 9But if they cannot control themselves, they should marry. It is better to marry than to burn with sexual desire.

10Now I give this command for the married people. (The command is not from me; it is from the Lord.) A wife should not leave her husband. 11But if she does leave, she must not marry again, or she should make up with her husband. Also the husband should not divorce his wife.

12For all the others I say this (I am saying this, not the Lord): If a Christian man has a wife who is not a believer, and she is happy to live with him, he must not divorce her. 13And if a Christian woman has a husband who is not a believer, and he is happy to live with her, she must not divorce him. 14The husband who is not a believer is made holy through his believing wife. And the wife who is not a believer is made holy through her believing husband. If this were not true, your children would not be clean,d but now your children are holy.

15But if those who are not believers decide to leave, let them leave. When this happens, the Christian man or woman is free. But God called us to live in peace. 16Wife, you don't know; maybe you will save your husband. And husband, you don't know; maybe you will save your wife.

Live as God Called You

17But in any case each one of you should continue to live the way God has given you to live — the way you were when God called you. This is a rule I make in all the churches. 18If a man was already circumcisedd when he was called, he should not undo his circumcision. If a man was without circumcision when he was called, he should not be circumcised. 19It is not important if a man is circumcised or not. The important thing is obeying God's commands. 20Each one of you should stay the way you were when God called you. ²¹If you were a slave when God called you, do not let that bother you. But if you can be free, then make good use of your freedom. ²²Those who were slaves when the Lord called them are free persons who belong to the Lord. In the same way, those who were free when they were called are now Christ's slaves. ²³You all were bought at a great price, so do not become slaves of people. ²⁴Brothers and sisters, each of you should stay as you were when you were called, and stay there with God.

Questions About Getting Married

²⁵Now I write about people who are not married. I have no command from the Lord about this; I give my opinion. But I can be trusted, because the Lord has shown me mercy. ²⁶The present time is a time of trouble, so I think it is good for you to stay the way you are. ²⁷If you have a wife, do not try to become free from her. If you are not married, do not try to find a wife. ²⁸But if you decide to marry, you have not sinned. And if a girl who has never married decides to marry, she has not sinned. But those who marry will have trouble in this life, and I want you to be free from trouble.

²⁹Brothers and sisters, this is what I mean: We do not have much time left. So starting now, those who have wives should live as if they had no wives. ³⁰Those who are crying should live as if they were not crying. Those who are happy should live as if they were not happy. Those who buy things should live as if they own nothing. ³¹Those who use the things of the world should live as if they were not using them, because this world in its present form will soon be gone.

³²I want you to be free from worry. A man who is not married is busy with the Lord's work, trying to please the Lord. ³³But a man who is married is busy with things of the world, trying to please his wife. ³⁴He must think about two things — pleasing his wife and pleasing the Lord. A woman who is not married or a girl who has never married is busy with the Lord's work. She wants to be holy in body and spirit. But a married woman is busy with things of the world, as to how she can please her husband. ³⁵I am saying this to help you, not to limit you. But I want you to live in the right way, to give yourselves fully to the Lord without concern for other things.

³⁶If a man thinks he is not doing the right thing with the girl he is engaged to, if she is almost past the best age to marry and he feels he should marry her, he should do what he wants. They should get married. It is no sin. ³⁷But if a man is sure in his mind that there is no need for marriage, and has

---

LOVE

Keeping in Focus

- The best way to draw a straight line is to focus on its ending point.
- The best way to take a test is to shut out all distractions and focus only on the questions.
- The best way to drive a car safely is to focus on the road and the traffic around you.
- The best way to become an accomplished musician or athlete is to focus your time and talent on training and practice.
- The best way to build lifelong friendships is to focus on being friendly and communicating honestly.
- The best way to accomplish things is to focus on goals.
- The best way to love God is to focus on knowing Christ and doing his will. For more about the importance of keeping love's focus, read

1 Corinthians 7:29–35.

- How does focusing on loving God affect the way you use your time?
- What things listed in this passage distract you from focusing your love on God?

CONSIDER . . .

- asking God to reveal any distractions in your life that keep you from focusing your love on him.
- transforming the relationships in your life to help you focus on loving God. For example, you and a friend could have a Bible study together, or you and your mom or dad could pray together once a week.

FOR MORE, SEE . . .

- Genesis 5:21–24 (p. 8)
- Matthew 10:34–38 (p. 925)
- Philippians 3:12–14 (p. 1232)

his own desires under control, and has decided not to marry the one to whom he is engaged, he is doing the right thing. ³⁸So the man who marries his girl does right, but the man who does not marry will do better.

³⁹A woman must stay with her husband as long as she lives. But if her husband dies, she is free to marry any man she wants, but she must marry in the Lord. ⁴⁰The woman is happier if she does not marry again. This is my opinion, but I believe I also have God's Spirit.

About Food Offered to Idols

8 Now I will write about meat that is sacrificed to idols. We know that "we all have knowledge." Knowledge puffs you up with pride, but love builds up. ²If you think you know something, you do not yet know anything as you should. ³But if any person loves God, that person is known by God.

⁴So this is what I say about eating meat sacrificed to idols: We know that an idol is really nothing in the world, and we know there is only one God. ⁵Even though there are things called gods, in heaven or on earth (and there are many "gods" and "lords"), ⁶for us there is only one God—our Father. All things came from him, and we live for him. And there is only one Lord—Jesus Christ. All things were made through him, and we also were made through him.

⁷But not all people know this. Some people are still so used to idols that when they eat meat, they still think of it as being sacrificed to an idol. Because their conscience is weak, when they eat it, they feel guilty. ⁸But food will not bring us closer to God. Refusing to eat does not make us less pleasing to God and eating does not make us better in God's sight.

⁹But be careful that your freedom does not cause those who are weak in faith to fall into sin. ¹⁰You have "knowledge," so you eat in an idol's temple.ⁿ But someone who is weak in faith might see you eating there and be encouraged to eat meat sacrificed to idols while thinking it is

idol's temple   Building where a god is worshiped.

Free to Do Good

Holly Boyd was overweight. All the kids made fun of her when she tried to play games with them. And when refreshments were served, they would say things such as "Hurry! Hide the food. Here comes Holly."

One night after youth group, youth leader Max Barrett found Holly crying in an empty room.

She told Max about how much it hurt when kids made fun of her and how she wanted to lose weight but couldn't. Max couldn't relate to Holly's weight problem; he was a runner and never seemed to gain weight. But he could empathize with the pain she felt.

"I'll tell you what, Holly," he offered, "you give up sweets and so will I. And why don't you start running with me?"

Holly agreed. The two ran together three times a week. And at youth group meetings while the kids were eating junk food, Max and Holly munched on veggies.

In four months, Holly had lost thirty pounds. She felt better about herself. Holly told Max she couldn't have done it without him.

Max could have eaten whatever he wanted, but he gave up his freedom to help Holly. Read **1 Corinthians 8:1–13** to see how Paul encourages Christians to use their freedom to help others.

■ How do Max's actions demonstrate the principles of this passage?
■ How would your friends describe your use of the freedom you have in Jesus Christ?

C O N S I D E R . . .
■ changing an area of your life if your freedom is hurting others.
■ talking to a new Christian and asking what he or she thinks about how Christians use their freedom.

F O R   M O R E ,   S E E . . .

■ Deuteronomy 30:11–20 (p. 187)   ■ 1 Timothy 4:10–12 (p. 1259)
■ 1 Corinthians 10:23–24 (p. 1180)

wrong to do so. [11]This weak believer for whom Christ died is ruined because of your "knowledge." [12]When you sin against your brothers and sisters in Christ like this and cause them to do what they feel is wrong, you are also sinning against Christ. [13]So if the food I eat causes them to fall into sin, I will never eat meat again so that I will not cause any of them to sin.

Paul Is like the Other Apostles

9 I am a free man. I am an apostle.[d] I have seen Jesus our Lord. You people are all an example of my work in the Lord. [2]If others do not accept me as an apostle, surely you do, because you are proof that I am an apostle in the Lord.

[3]This is the answer I give people who want to judge me: [4]Do we not have the right to eat and drink? [5]Do we not have the right to bring a believing wife with us when we travel as do the other apostles and the Lord's brothers and Peter? [6]Are Barnabas and I the only ones who must work to earn our living? [7]No soldier ever serves in the army and pays his own salary. No one ever plants a vineyard without eating some of the grapes. No person takes care of a flock without drinking some of the milk.

[8]I do not say this by human authority; God's law also says the same thing. [9]It is written in the law of Moses: "When an ox is working in the grain, do not cover its mouth to keep it from eating." [n] When God said this, was he thinking only about oxen? No. [10]He was really talking about us. Yes, that Scripture[d] was written for us, because it goes on to say: "The one who plows and the one who works in the grain should hope to get some of the grain for their work." [11]Since we planted spiritual seed among you, is it too much if we should harvest from you some things for this life? [12]If others have the right to get something from you, surely we have this right, too. But we do not use it. No, we put up with everything ourselves so that we will not keep anyone from believing the Good News[d] of Christ. [13]Surely you know that those who work at the Temple[d] get their food from the Temple, and those who serve at the altar get part of what is offered at the altar. [14]In the same way, the Lord has commanded that those who tell the Good News should get their living from this work.

[15]But I have not used any of these rights. And I am not writing this now to get anything from you. I would rather die than to have my reason for bragging taken away. [16]Telling the Good News does not give me any reason for bragging. Telling the Good News is my duty—something I must do. And how terrible it will be for me if I do not tell the Good News. [17]If I preach because it is my own choice, I have a reward. But if I preach and it is not my choice to do so, I am only doing the duty that was given to me. [18]So what reward do I get? This is my reward: that when I tell the Good News I can offer it freely. I do not use my full rights in my work of preaching the Good News.

[19]I am free and belong to no one. But I make myself a slave to all people to win as many as I can. [20]To the Jews I became like a Jew to win the Jews. I myself am not ruled by the law. But to those who are ruled by the law I became like a person who is ruled by the law. I did this to win those who are ruled by the law. [21]To those who are without the law I became like a person who is without the law. I did this to win those people who are without the law. (But really, I am not without God's law—I am ruled by Christ's law.) [22]To those who are weak, I became weak so I could win the weak. I have become all things to all people so I could save some of them in any way possible. [23]I do all this because of the Good News and so I can share in its blessings.

[24]You know that in a race all the runners run, but only one gets the prize. So run to win! [25]All those who compete in the games use self-control so they can win a crown. That crown is an earthly thing that lasts only a short time, but our crown will never be destroyed. [26]So I do not run without a goal. I fight like a boxer who is hitting something—not just the air. [27]I treat my body hard and make it my slave so that I myself will not be disqualified after I have preached to others.

> ※ **SIDELIGHT:** Paul's reference to "running the race" in 1 Corinthians 9:24–27 would have reminded the Corinthians of the Isthmian Games, held every two years in Corinth's coliseum. These games were the most famous athletic competition of their time except for the ancient Olympics. The games might have included wrestling, boxing, chariot races, and foot races.

Warnings from Israel's Past

10 Brothers and sisters, I want you to know what happened to our ancestors who followed Moses. They were all under the cloud and all went through the sea. [2]They were all baptized as followers of Moses in the cloud and in the sea. [3]They all ate the same spiritual food, [4]and all drank the same spiritual drink. They drank from that spiritual rock that followed them, and that

---

"When an ox . . . eating." Quotation from Deuteronomy 25:4.

rock was Christ. [5]But God was not pleased with most of them, so they died in the desert.

[6]And these things happened as examples for us, to stop us from wanting evil things as those people did. [7]Do not worship idols, as some of them did. Just as it is written in the Scriptures:[d] "They sat down to eat and drink, and then they got up and sinned sexually."[n] [8]We must not take part in sexual sins, as some of them did. In one day twenty-three thousand of them died because of their sins. [9]We must not test Christ as some of them did; they were killed by snakes. [10]Do not complain as some of them did; they were killed by the angel that destroys.

[11]The things that happened to those people are examples. They were written down to teach us, because we live in a time when all these things of the past have reached their goal. [12]If you think you are strong, you should be careful not to fall. [13]The only temptation that has come to you is that which everyone has. But you can trust God, who

will not permit you to be tempted more than you can stand. But when you are tempted, he will also give you a way to escape so that you will be able to stand it.

[14]So, my dear friends, run away from the worship of idols. [15]I am speaking to you as to intelligent people; judge for yourselves what I say. [16]We give thanks for the cup of blessing,[n] which is a sharing in the blood of Christ. And the bread that we break is a sharing in the body of Christ. [17]Because there is one loaf of bread, we who are many are one body, because we all share that one loaf.

[18]Think about the Israelites: Do not those who eat the sacrifices share in the altar? [19]I do not mean that the food sacrificed to an idol is important. I do not mean that an idol is anything at all. [20]But I say that what is sacrificed to idols is offered to demons,[d] not to God. And I do not want you to share anything with demons. [21]You cannot drink the cup of the Lord and the cup of demons also. You cannot share in the Lord's table and the

"They . . . sexually."   Quotation from Exodus 32:6.
cup of blessing   The cup of the fruit of the vine that Christians thank God for and drink at the Lord's Supper.

Giving It All

In 1873, Lottie Moon went to China as a missionary. She reached out to the Chinese people in the face of tremendous persecution, and she challenged Christians back in the United States to give more money to help people hear the gospel.

In 1911, war and famine hit China. Lottie was evacuated to Japan, but she regularly gave a large part of her small salary to her starving Chinese friends.

She wrote to her mission board asking for help time and again. But the board was heavily in debt and could hardly pay its missionary salaries. Nothing was budgeted for famine relief.

The famine worsened. Lottie drew out the last of her savings from a bank to send to relief workers. "I pray that no missionary will ever be as lonely as I have been," she wrote in her bank book.

Lottie vowed not to eat as long as her Chinese friends were starving. On Christmas Eve night, 1912, she lapsed into unconsciousness. The nurse who was with her watched her clasping and unclasping her hands in the Chinese fashion of greeting. The nurse bent over her and heard her saying the name of a Chinese friend. Even in her last minutes, Lottie's heart and mind were focused on the people she loved.

Lottie Moon died, having given everything she had to the Chinese people. Paul writes about this kind of love in **1 Corinthians 9:16—27**.

■ How did Lottie Moon demonstrate this passage with her life?
■ How can the methods in this passage help you effectively reach a non-Christian friend?

CONSIDER . . .

■ getting to know a non-Christian friend so you can share your faith.
■ giving to a missionary organization to help spread the gospel.

FOR MORE, SEE . . .

■ Isaiah 61 (p. 680)
■ Matthew 10:1–15 (p. 923)

■ Matthew 28:16–20 (p. 962)

table of demons. [22]Are we trying to make the Lord jealous? We are not stronger than he is, are we?

How to Use Christian Freedom

[23]"We are allowed to do all things," but all things are not good for us to do. "We are allowed to do all things," but not all things help others grow stronger. [24]Do not look out only for yourselves. Look out for the good of others also.

[25]Eat any meat that is sold in the meat market. Do not ask questions to see if it is meat you think is wrong to eat. [26]You may eat it, "because the earth belongs to the Lord, and everything in it."[n]

[27]Those who are not believers may invite you to eat with them. If you want to go, eat anything that is put before you. Do not ask questions to see if you think it might be wrong to eat. [28]But if anyone says to you, "That food was offered to idols," do not eat it. Do not eat it because of that person who told you and because eating it might be thought to be wrong. [29]I don't mean you think it

is wrong, but the other person might. But why, you ask, should my freedom be judged by someone else's conscience? [30]If I eat the meal with thankfulness, why am I criticized because of something for which I thank God?

[31]The answer is, if you eat or drink, or if you do anything, do it all for the glory of God. [32]Never do anything that might hurt others—Jews, Greeks, or God's church— [33]just as I, also, try to please everybody in every way. I am not trying to do what is good for me but what is good for most people so they can be saved.

11 Follow my example, as I follow the example of Christ.

Being Under Authority

[2]I praise you because you remember me in everything, and you follow closely the teachings just as I gave them to you. [3]But I want you to understand this: The head of every man is Christ, the head of a woman is the man,[n] and the head of

"because ... it"   Quotation from Psalms 24:1; 50:12; 89:11.
the man   This could also mean "her husband."

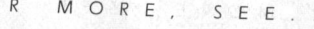

Christ is God. [4]Every man who prays or prophesies[d] with his head covered brings shame to his head. [5]But every woman who prays or prophesies with her head uncovered brings shame to her head. She is the same as a woman who has her head shaved. [6]If a woman does not cover her head, she should have her hair cut off. But since it is shameful for a woman to cut off her hair or to shave her head, she should cover her head. [7]But a man should not cover his head, because he is the likeness and glory of God. But woman is man's glory. [8]Man did not come from woman, but woman came from man. [9]And man was not made for woman, but woman was made for man. [10]So that is why a woman should have a symbol of authority on her head, because of the angels.

[11]But in the Lord women are not independent of men, and men are not independent of women. [12]This is true because woman came from man, but also man is born from woman. But everything comes from God. [13]Decide this for yourselves: Is it right for a woman to pray to God with her head uncovered? [14]Even nature itself teaches you that wearing long hair is shameful for a man. [15]But long hair is a woman's glory. Long hair is given to her as a covering. [16]Some people may still want to argue about this, but I would add that neither we nor the churches of God have any other practice.

The Lord's Supper

[17]In the things I tell you now I do not praise you, because when you come together you do more harm than good. [18]First, I hear that when you meet together as a church you are divided, and I believe some of this. [19](It is necessary to have differences among you so that it may be clear which of you really have God's approval.) [20]When you come together, you are not really eating the Lord's Supper.[n] [21]This is because when you eat, each person eats without waiting for the others. Some people do not get enough to eat, while others have too much to drink. [22]You can eat and drink in your own homes! You seem to think God's church is not important, and you embarrass those who are poor. What should I tell you? Should I praise you? I do not praise you for doing this.

[23]The teaching I gave you is the same teaching I received from the Lord: On the night when the Lord Jesus was handed over to be killed, he took bread [24]and gave thanks for it. Then he broke the bread and said, "This is my body; it is for you. Do this to remember me." [25]In the same way, after they ate, Jesus took the cup. He said, "This cup is the new agreement that is sealed with the blood

of my death. When you drink this, do it to remember me." [26]Every time you eat this bread and drink this cup you are telling others about the Lord's death until he comes.

[27]So a person who eats the bread or drinks the cup of the Lord in a way that is not worthy of it will be guilty of sinning against the body and the blood of the Lord. [28]Look into your own hearts before you eat the bread and drink the cup, [29]because all who eat the bread and drink the cup without recognizing the body eat and drink judgment against themselves. [30]That is why many in your group are sick and weak, and many have died. [31]But if we judged ourselves in the right way, God would not judge us. [32]But when the Lord judges us, he punishes us so that we will not be destroyed along with the world.

[33]So my brothers and sisters, when you come together to eat, wait for each other. [34]Anyone who is too hungry should eat at home so that in meeting together you will not bring God's judgment on yourselves. I will tell you what to do about the other things when I come.

Gifts from the Holy Spirit

12 Now, brothers and sisters, I want you to understand about spiritual gifts. [2]You know the way you lived before you were believers. You let yourselves be influenced and led away to worship idols — things that could not speak. [3]So I want you to understand that no one who is speaking with the help of God's Spirit says, "Jesus be cursed." And no one can say, "Jesus is Lord," without the help of the Holy Spirit.[d]

[4]There are different kinds of gifts, but they are all from the same Spirit. [5]There are different ways to serve but the same Lord to serve. [6]And there are different ways that God works through people but the same God. God works in all of us in everything we do. [7]Something from the Spirit can be seen in each person for the common good. [8]The Spirit gives one person the ability to speak with wisdom, and the same Spirit gives another the ability to speak with knowledge. [9]The same Spirit gives faith to one person. And, to another, that one Spirit gives gifts of healing. [10]The Spirit gives to another person the power to do miracles,[d] to another the ability to prophesy.[d] And he gives to another the ability to know the difference between good and evil spirits. The Spirit gives one person the ability to speak in different kinds of languages[n] and to another the ability to interpret those languages. [11]One Spirit, the same Spirit, does all these things, and the Spirit decides what to give each person.

Lord's Supper   The meal Jesus told his followers to eat to remember him (Luke 22:14-20).
languages   This can also be translated "tongues."

The Body of Christ Works Together

¹²A person's body is only one thing, but it has many parts. Though there are many parts to a body, all those parts make only one body. Christ is like that also. ¹³Some of us are Jews, and some are Greeks. Some of us are slaves, and some are free. But we were all baptized into one body through one Spirit.ᵈ And we were all made to share in the one Spirit.

¹⁴The human body has many parts. ¹⁵The foot might say, "Because I am not a hand, I am not part of the body." But saying this would not stop the foot from being a part of the body. ¹⁶The ear might say, "Because I am not an eye, I am not part of the body." But saying this would not stop the ear from being a part of the body. ¹⁷If the whole body were an eye, it would not be able to hear. If the whole body were an ear, it would not be able to smell. ¹⁸⁻¹⁹If each part of the body were the same part, there would be no body. But truly God put all the parts, each one of them, in the body

as he wanted them. ²⁰So then there are many parts, but only one body.

²¹The eye cannot say to the hand, "I don't need you!" And the head cannot say to the foot, "I don't need you!" ²²No! Those parts of the body that seem to be the weaker are really necessary. ²³And the parts of the body we think are less deserving are the parts to which we give the most honor. We give special respect to the parts we want to hide. ²⁴The more respectable parts of our body need no special care. But God put the body together and gave more honor to the parts that need it ²⁵so our body would not be divided. God wanted the different parts to care the same for each other. ²⁶If one part of the body suffers, all the other parts suffer with it. Or if one part of our body is honored, all the other parts share its honor.

²⁷Together you are the body of Christ, and each one of you is a part of that body. ²⁸In the church God has given a place first to apostles,ᵈ second to prophets,ᵈ and third to teachers. Then God has

WORSHIP

Remember Me?

The second Sunday in March is a special day for Sharon Ebell's family. Each year on this date, her family gathers for a meal. When the table is cleared, the family photo albums are brought out and passed around.

Everyone smiles and giggles to see how each family member has changed from picture to picture over the years. The giggles sometimes erupt into laughter when the pictures prompt funny stories about family members. Sharon's favorite is the one about her dad being chased by a skunk when he was a teenager.

And there are always tears when the family sees the photos of its absent members. No eye is dry when photos of Jonathan, Sharon's younger brother, are passed around. He died of cystic fibrosis when he was five.

Some of Sharon's friends think her family's habit is a little weird. A few have even wondered if it isn't like worshiping the dead.

But Sharon shrugs off their comments. "It's just how we remember the people who've been important to our family. I never met my grandparents, but I feel like I know them. I've seen their pictures and heard stories about them at least once a year for as long as I can remember," she explains. "I don't think we worship our dead relatives; we just celebrate their lives."

As Christians, we don't worship the dead. But we do worship one who died and rose from the dead. Read **1 Corinthians 11:23–26** to see how Paul explains one way in which Christians can celebrate Jesus' life and work.

■ How is the celebration Paul describes similar to the celebration in Sharon's family? How is it different?

■ What do you do in your church and life to remember Jesus?

CONSIDER . . .

■ creating other celebrations to remember Jesus. For example, a candlelight dinner could remind you that Jesus is the light of the world.

■ talking with your pastor about the ways your church follows this scripture.

FOR MORE, SEE . . .

■ Exodus 12:14–20 (p. 68)
■ Exodus 16:31–36 (p. 74)

■ Luke 22:14–20 (p. 1049)

given a place to those who do miracles,*d* those who have gifts of healing, those who can help others, those who are able to govern, and those who can speak in different languages.*n* 29Not all are apostles. Not all are prophets. Not all are teachers. Not all do miracles. 30Not all have gifts of healing. Not all speak in different languages. Not all interpret those languages. 31But you should truly want to have the greater gifts.

Love Is the Greatest Gift

And now I will show you the best way of all.

13 I may speak in different languages*n* of people or even angels. But if I do not

have love, I am only a noisy bell or a crashing cymbal. 2I may have the gift of prophecy.*d* I may understand all the secret things of God and have

languages This can also be translated "tongues."

SELF-ESTEEM

Be Yourself

Susan Klopp wanted to be like Melody Malen. Melody was smart. She was in the National Honor Society. And teachers said Melody was the best student in their classes.

Susan wanted that recognition too. So she started doing what Melody did. When Melody got a wedge haircut, Susan did the same. When Melody joined the yearbook staff, so did Susan.

But as Susan got involved with the yearbook staff, she began to doubt herself. She felt out of place. Susan hated matching all the mug shots with the names of the students. She liked talking, not working by herself writing about the rifle team's accomplishments.

Susan's best friend, Gina Andrews, confronted Susan one day.

"What are you trying to do? You looked better in long hair," Gina said.

"What's wrong with my hair?" Susan asked.

"It's just not you," Gina replied. "Just like you should be on the debate team, not the yearbook staff. You're a better debater than a writer. In fact, if you didn't have that nose, I'd swear you were just another Melody."

"That's not true!" Susan sputtered.

"Oh, no?" Gina asked. "Just look in the mirror sometime. And ask yourself who you are."

At first Susan dismissed Gina's comments. But the more she worked on the yearbook, the emptier she felt. Susan missed her friend Gina. She missed being on the debate team. She missed her old self.

So Susan quit the yearbook staff, realizing that she had to choose her own life—not copy Melody's. Susan started hanging around with Gina and joined the debate team again. It felt good to be back.

Susan finally recognized the importance of being herself and using her own talents. Read **1 Corinthians 12:1–11** to see what Paul says about gifts.

■ What does this passage say about whether it was wise for Susan to copy Melody?

■ How does this passage make you feel about your own gifts, or about the gifts of others?

CONSIDER . . .

■ meeting with your Christian friends to identify each other's gifts.

■ rereading this passage with your family, substituting your name and other family members' names who best fit the gifts described.

FOR MORE, SEE . . .

■ Genesis 49:2–28 (p. 54)   ■ Ephesians 4:1 –12 (p. 1223)

■ Romans 12:4–8 (p. 1157)

all knowledge, and I may have faith so great I can move mountains. But even with all these things, if I do not have love, then I am nothing. ³I may give away everything I have, and I may even give my body as an offering to be burned. *ⁿ* But I gain nothing if I do not have love.

⁴Love is patient and kind. Love is not jealous, it does not brag, and it is not proud. ⁵Love is not rude, is not selfish, and does not get upset with others. Love does not count up wrongs that have been done. ⁶Love is not happy with evil but is happy with the truth. ⁷Love patiently accepts all things. It always trusts, always hopes, and always remains strong.

⁸Love never ends. There are gifts of prophecy, *ᵈ* but they will be ended. There are gifts of speaking in different languages, but those gifts will stop. There is the gift of knowledge, but it will come to an end. ⁹The reason is that our knowledge and our ability to prophesy are not perfect. ¹⁰But when perfection comes, the things that are not perfect will end. ¹¹When I was a child, I talked like a child, I thought like a child, I reasoned like a child. When I became a man, I stopped those childish ways. ¹²It is the same with us. Now we see a dim reflection, as if we were looking into a mirror, but then we shall see clearly. Now I know only a part, but then I will know fully, as God has known me. ¹³So these three things continue forever: faith, hope, and love. And the greatest of these is love.

Desire Spiritual Gifts

14 You should seek after love, and you should truly want to have the spiritual gifts, especially the gift of prophecy. *ᵈ* ²I will explain why. Those who have the gift of speaking in different languages *ⁿ* are not speaking to people; they are speaking to God. No one understands

Verse 3 Other Greek copies read: "hand over my body in order that I may brag."
languages This can also be translated "tongues."

Watching Every Detail

Michelangelo spent four years painting the 132-foot-long by 44-foot-wide ceiling of the Sistine Chapel. Every day for hours, Michelangelo would lie on his back on the scaffolding, perfecting the details of the continuous, unbroken compositions that contained hundreds of figures from the book of Genesis.

The color. The curves of the lines. The facial expressions. The shadows. The hair. The noses. The fingers. Every detail was important.

But the ceiling was sixty feet from the floor. Those admiring Michelangelo's work could see the mastery of his work, but they couldn't see the details from so far away.

One day one of Michelangelo's friends asked Michelangelo why he spent so many hours painstakingly perfecting each detail—details no one would ever be able to see. "After all, who will know whether it is perfect or not?" Michelangelo's friend asked.

"I will," Michelangelo replied.

Michelangelo saw the many possibilities of details for the ceiling of the Sistine Chapel. And he knew when all those details came together, they would make a masterpiece.

That's what **1 Corinthians 12:12–27** is all about. Read what Paul says about the importance of many parts making one body—the church.

■ According to the passage, why are details so important?
■ How can this passage help you see the important gifts each person brings to your church?

CONSIDER . . .

■ asking a teenager, a middle-aged adult, and a senior citizen ways they contribute to church and why those contributions are important. Then evaluate your own contributions.
■ getting involved in the church and using your talents. If you sing, join the choir. If you're good at art, make posters to publicize events.

FOR MORE, SEE . . .

■ 1 Kings 5:5–18 (p. 308)
■ Colossians 3:11–17 (p. 1241)
■ 1 Peter 4:7–11 (p. 1306)

them; they are speaking secret things through the Spirit.*d* ³But those who prophesy are speaking to people to give them strength, encouragement, and comfort. ⁴The ones who speak in different languages are helping only themselves, but those who prophesy are helping the whole church. ⁵I wish all of you had the gift of speaking in different kinds of languages, but more, I wish you would prophesy. Those who prophesy are greater than those who can only speak in different languages—unless someone is there who can explain what is said so that the whole church can be helped.

⁶Brothers and sisters, will it help you if I come to you speaking in different languages? No! It will help you only if I bring you a new truth or some new knowledge, or prophecy, or teaching. ⁷It is the same as with lifeless things that make sounds—like a flute or a harp. If they do not make clear musical notes, you will not know what is being played. ⁸And in a war, if the trumpet does not give a clear sound, who will prepare for battle? ⁹It is the same with you. Unless you speak clearly with your tongue, no one can understand what you are saying. You will be talking into the air! ¹⁰It may be true that there are all kinds of sounds in the world, and none is without meaning. ¹¹But unless I understand the meaning of what someone says to me, I will be a foreigner to him, and he will be a foreigner to me. ¹²It is the

---

LOVE

Love Never Ends

Everyone knew Lisa Wilson and Gregg Hillburn as Lisa and Gregg—almost as though their names were one word. They had been dating for four years. They cheered for the football team together. They ate lunch together. They did everything together. Nothing could separate them.

Until Gregg started to party.

At first he and Lisa went to parties to be with their friends. Sure there was alcohol, but Lisa and Gregg didn't drink.

After a while, though, Gregg began accepting a glass of beer. Then he started getting drunk. Lisa hated it.

Sometimes Lisa tried talking to Gregg about the problem. But he always got mad. One time he even broke up with her on the spot and called her nasty names. Lisa wanted to scream back at him, but instead she went to his parents.

Tears streaked Lisa's face as she told Gregg's mom and dad what was happening. After she finished, Gregg's dad told Lisa about his own former drinking problem. He knew Gregg needed professional help.

Over the next few months, Lisa wanted to give up on Gregg. Although he was seeing a professional counselor, he was furious at Lisa for "turning him in." He accused her of ruining his life. And he said he never wanted to see her again.

But Lisa patiently waited for Gregg to recover. Although Gregg's words hurt her, Lisa hung on to her memories of the Gregg she first knew. When Gregg eventually admitted his problem, he thanked Lisa for loving him during the times when he was so unlovable.

Lisa loved Gregg with the kind of love described in **1 Corinthians 13:1–13**. Through the tough times, Lisa stuck with Gregg, and a few years later they were married. Gregg has remained sober to this day.

■ How do Lisa's actions reflect the message of this scripture?
■ How can this passage help you know what true love is all about?

CONSIDER...

■ copying this scripture passage onto the inside cover of a notebook. The next time someone stretches your patience, read this scripture for advice on how to respond.
■ hanging in there with a friend or relative you are about to give up on. Keep loving this person through a difficult time.

FOR MORE, SEE...

■ Song of Solomon 8:6–7 (p. 614)   ■ Romans 13:9–10 (p. 1160)
■ Matthew 5:43–48 (p. 916)

same with you. Since you want spiritual gifts very much, seek most of all to have the gifts that help the church grow stronger.

[13]The one who has the gift of speaking in a different language should pray for the gift to interpret what is spoken. [14]If I pray in a different language, my spirit is praying, but my mind does nothing. [15]So what should I do? I will pray with my spirit, but I will also pray with my mind. I will sing with my spirit, but I will also sing with my mind. [16]If you praise God with your spirit, those persons there without understanding cannot say amen[n] to your prayer of thanks, because they do not know what you are saying. [17]You may be thanking God in a good way, but the other person is not helped.

[18]I thank God that I speak in different kinds of languages more than all of you. [19]But in the church meetings I would rather speak five words

I understand in order to teach others than thousands of words in a different language.

[20]Brothers and sisters, do not think like children. In evil things be like babies, but in your thinking you should be like adults. [21]It is written in the Scriptures:[d]

"With people who use strange words and
    foreign languages
I will speak to these people.
But even then they will not listen to me,"
                                    Isaiah 28:11-12

says the Lord.

[22]So the gift of speaking in different kinds of languages is a proof for those who do not believe, not for those who do believe. And prophecy is for people who believe, not for those who do not believe. [23]Suppose the whole church meets together and everyone speaks in different languages. If some people come in who do not understand or

amen   To say amen means to agree with the things that were said.

Inside Lingo

What do the following acronyms mean?

- MS-DOS
- SIMM
- SCSI
- MB
- ROM
- RAM

- DPI
- RGB
- PC
- CD-ROM
- CPU

If you know computers, you probably know what most of these acronyms stand for. And when you talk with other computer people, you might rattle off these abbreviations and have a great conversation.

But if you don't work with computers, few of these abbreviations make any sense. And you may feel left out when others use them around you.

Cliques work in a similar way. People on the "inside" may talk the same way, act the same way, and like the same kinds of things. They easily exclude others and make them feel unwanted.

In **1 Corinthians 14:13–20**, Paul talks about including other people in worship, and his advice has a lot to say about cliques.

- According to this passage, why is it better to speak five understandable words than thousands of words that no one understands? What does this say about cliques?
- How did you feel not knowing what the words at the beginning of this devotion were all about? What does the Scripture say to you about "insiders" and "outsiders"?

C O N S I D E R . . .

- getting together with your friends and discussing ways you exclude others. Choose one way to improve.
- *thumbing through your yearbook, looking for someone who used to be—but is no longer—in your group of friends. Call that person and ask how he or she is doing.*

F O R   M O R E ,   S E E . . .

- Ruth 2 (p. 240)
- Jonah 4 (p. 859)

- Philemon (p. 1274)

do not believe, they will say you are crazy. 24But suppose everyone is prophesying and some people come in who do not believe or do not understand. If everyone is prophesying, their sin will be shown to them, and they will be judged by all that they hear. 25The secret things in their hearts will be made known. So they will bow down and worship God saying, "Truly, God is with you."

Meetings Should Help the Church

26So, brothers and sisters, what should you do? When you meet together, one person has a song, and another has a teaching. Another has a new truth from God. Another speaks in a different language,*n* and another person interprets that language. The purpose of all these things should be to help the church grow strong. 27When you meet together, if anyone speaks in a different language, it should be only two, or not more than three, who speak. They should speak one after the other, and someone else should interpret. 28But if there is no interpreter, then those who speak in a different language should be quiet in the church meeting. They should speak only to themselves and to God.

29Only two or three prophets*d* should speak, and the others should judge what they say. 30If a message from God comes to another person who is sitting, the first speaker should stop. 31You can all prophesy one after the other. In this way all the people can be taught and encouraged. 32The spirits of prophets are under the control of the prophets themselves. 33God is not a God of confusion but a God of peace.

As is true in all the churches of God's people, 34women should keep quiet in the church meetings. They are not allowed to speak, but they must yield to this rule as the law says. 35If they want to learn something, they should ask their own husbands at home. It is shameful for a woman to speak in the church meeting. 36Did God's teaching come from you? Or are you the only ones to whom it has come?

37Those who think they are prophets or spiritual persons should understand that what I am writing to you is the Lord's command. 38Those who ignore this will be ignored by God.

39So my brothers and sisters, you should truly want to prophesy. But do not stop people from using the gift of speaking in different kinds of languages. 40But let everything be done in a right and orderly way.

The Good News About Christ

15

Now, brothers and sisters, I want you to remember the Good News*d* I brought to you. You received this Good News and continue

strong in it. 2And you are being saved by it if you continue believing what I told you. If you do not, then you believed for nothing.

3I passed on to you what I received, of which this was most important: that Christ died for our sins, as the Scriptures*d* say; 4that he was buried and was raised to life on the third day as the Scriptures say; 5and that he was seen by Peter and then by the twelve apostles.*d* 6After that, Jesus was seen by more than five hundred of the believers at the same time. Most of them are still living today, but some have died. 7Then he was seen by James and later by all the apostles. 8Last of all he was seen by me — as by a person not born at the normal time. 9All the other apostles are greater than I am. I am not even good enough to be called an apostle, because I persecuted the church of God. 10But God's grace has made me what I am, and his grace to me was not wasted. I worked harder than all the other apostles. (But it was not I really; it was God's grace that was with me.) 11So if I preached to you or the other apostles preached to you, we all preach the same thing, and this is what you believed.

We Will Be Raised from the Dead

12Now since we preached that Christ was raised from the dead, why do some of you say that people will not be raised from the dead? 13If no one is ever raised from the dead, then Christ has not been raised. 14And if Christ has not been raised, then our preaching is worth nothing, and your faith is worth nothing. 15And also, we are guilty of lying about God, because we testified of him that he raised Christ from the dead. But if people are not raised from the dead, then God never raised Christ. 16If the dead are not raised, Christ has not been raised either. 17And if Christ has not been raised, then your faith has nothing to it; you are still guilty of your sins. 18And those in Christ who have already died are lost. 19If our hope in Christ is for this life only, we should be pitied more than anyone else in the world.

20But Christ has truly been raised from the dead — the first one and proof that those who sleep in death will also be raised. 21Death has come because of what one man did, but the rising from death also comes because of one man. 22In Adam all of us die. In the same way, in Christ all of us will be made alive again. 23But everyone will be raised to life in the right order. Christ was first to be raised. When Christ comes again, those who belong to him will be raised to life, 24and then the end will come. At that time Christ will destroy all rulers, authorities, and powers, and he will hand over the kingdom to God the Father. 25Christ must rule until he puts all enemies under his con-

---

language   This can also be translated "tongue."

trol. 26The last enemy to be destroyed will be death. 27The Scripture*d* says that God put all things under his control.*n* When it says "all things" are under him, it is clear this does not include God himself. God is the One who put everything under his control. 28After everything has been put under the Son, then he will put himself under God, who had put all things under him. Then God will be the complete ruler over everything.

29If the dead are never raised, what will people do who are being baptized for the dead? If the dead are not raised at all, why are people being baptized for them?

30And what about us? Why do we put ourselves in danger every hour? 31I die every day. That is true, brothers and sisters, just as it is true that I brag about you in Christ Jesus our Lord. 32If I fought wild animals in Ephesus only with human hopes, I have gained nothing. If the dead are not raised, "Let us eat and drink, because tomorrow we will die."*n*

33Do not be fooled: "Bad friends will ruin good habits." 34Come back to your right way of thinking and stop sinning. Some of you do not know God—I say this to shame you.

> ⚜ **SIDELIGHT:** Though Paul probably didn't fight wild animals himself (1 Corinthians 15:32), it's likely he is referring to the Roman "sport" of putting prisoners in an arena, then releasing wild animals to maul the prisoners while huge crowds watched. Animals used in this activity included lions, bears, leopards, rhinoceroses, crocodiles, tigers, and elephants. A decade after Paul wrote this letter, Christians faced this kind of persecution.

What Kind of Body Will We Have?

35But someone may ask, "How are the dead raised? What kind of body will they have?" 36Foolish person! When you sow a seed, it must die in

God put . . . control. From Psalm 8:6.
"Let us . . . die." Quotation from Isaiah 22:13; 56:12.

FAITH

Stick With It

It's not easy to become an emperor butterfly. To emerge into the world, the butterfly must force its way through the neck of a flask-shaped cocoon. Getting through this opening takes hours of intense struggle. The insect must squirm and wiggle to push its way through the confining threads.

If you watched an emperor butterfly's struggle, you might feel sorry for the struggling insect and snip the confining threads to make an easier exit. But if you did, the butterfly would never develop its wings. Instead, it would spend most of its life crawling, never able to spread its wings and fly.

Entomologists who study this butterfly believe the pressure on the insect's body forces the essential juices into the wings, thus preparing the wings for flight. Without the pressure, the wings would never become strong.

Sometimes having faith is difficult. Like the emperor butterfly, we struggle. We feel overwhelmed—tested. And we wish someone could step in and take away the struggle.

But our faith grows through those struggles, as Paul reminds us in
1 Corinthians 15:1–11.

■ According to this passage, what are we to continue to believe in?
■ How can the example of the people's faith in this passage encourage you when you struggle with your faith?

C O N S I D E R . . .
■ calling one of your grandparents or an older person in your congregation. Ask that *person about his or her faith journey—including the ups and downs.*
■ talking to a friend about the ways you have grown after a difficult time.

F O R   M O R E ,   S E E . . .
■ Genesis 22 (p. 25)
■ Daniel 3 (p. 809)
■ Hebrews 11 (p. 1287)

the ground before it can live and grow. [37]And when you sow it, it does not have the same "body" it will have later. What you sow is only a bare seed, maybe wheat or something else. [38]But God gives it a body that he has planned for it, and God gives each kind of seed its own body. [39]All things made of flesh are not the same: People have one kind of flesh, animals have another, birds have another, and fish have another. [40]Also there are heavenly bodies and earthly bodies. But the beauty of the heavenly bodies is one kind, and the beauty of the earthly bodies is another. [41]The sun has one kind of beauty, the moon has another beauty, and the stars have another. And each star is different in its beauty.

[42]It is the same with the dead who are raised to life. The body that is "planted" will ruin and decay, but it is raised to a life that cannot be destroyed. [43]When the body is "planted," it is without honor, but it is raised in glory. When the body is "planted," it is weak, but when it is raised, it is powerful. [44]The body that is "planted" is a physical body. When it is raised, it is a spiritual body.

There is a physical body, and there is also a spiritual body. [45]It is written in the Scriptures:[d] "The first man, Adam, became a living person."[n] But the last Adam became a spirit that gives life. [46]The spiritual did not come first, but the physical

and then the spiritual. [47]The first man came from the dust of the earth. The second man came from heaven. [48]People who belong to the earth are like the first man of earth. But those people who belong to heaven are like the man of heaven. [49]Just as we were made like the man of earth, so we will also be made like the man of heaven.

[50]I tell you this, brothers and sisters: Flesh and blood cannot have a part in the kingdom of God. Something that will ruin cannot have a part in something that never ruins. [51]But look! I tell you this secret: We will not all sleep in death, but we will all be changed. [52]It will take only a second — as quickly as an eye blinks — when the last trumpet sounds. The trumpet will sound, and those who have died will be raised to live forever, and we will all be changed. [53]This body that can be destroyed must clothe itself with something that can never be destroyed. And this body that dies must clothe itself with something that can never die. [54]So this body that can be destroyed will clothe itself with that which can never be destroyed, and this body that dies will clothe itself with that which can never die. When this happens, this Scripture will be made true:

"Death is destroyed forever in victory."

Isaiah 25:8

[55]"Death, where is your victory?
    Death, where is your pain?"   *Hosea 13:14*

"The first . . . person."   Quotation from Genesis 2:7.

---

⁵⁶Death's power to hurt is sin, and the power of sin is the law. ⁵⁷But we thank God! He gives us the victory through our Lord Jesus Christ.

⁵⁸So my dear brothers and sisters, stand strong. Do not let anything change you. Always give yourselves fully to the work of the Lord, because you know that your work in the Lord is never wasted.

The Gift for Other Believers

16 Now I will write about the collection of money for God's people. Do the same thing I told the Galatian churches to do: ²On the first day of every week, each one of you should put aside money as you have been blessed. Save it up so you will not have to collect money after I come. ³When I arrive, I will send whomever you approve to take your gift to Jerusalem. I will send them with letters of introduction, ⁴and if it seems good for me to go also, they will go along with me.

Paul's Plans

⁵I plan to go through Macedonia, so I will come to you after I go through there. ⁶Perhaps I will stay with you for a time or even all winter. Then you can help me on my trip, wherever I go. ⁷I do not want to see you now just in passing. I hope to stay a longer time with you if the Lord allows it. ⁸But I will stay at Ephesus until Pentecost,ᵈ ⁹because a good opportunity for a great and growing work has been given to me now. And there are many people working against me.

¹⁰If Timothy comes to you, see to it that he has nothing to fear with you, because he is working for the Lord just as I am. ¹¹So none of you should treat Timothy as unimportant, but help him on his trip in peace so that he can come back to me. I am expecting him to come with the brothers.

¹²Now about our brother Apollos: I strongly encouraged him to visit you with the other brothers. He did not at all want to come now; he will come when he has the opportunity.

Paul Ends His Letter

¹³Be alert. Continue strong in the faith. Have courage, and be strong. ¹⁴Do everything in love.

¹⁵You know that the family of Stephanas were the first believers in Southern Greece and that they have given themselves to the service of God's people. I ask you, brothers and sisters, ¹⁶to follow the leading of people like these and anyone else who works and serves with them.

ETERNAL LIFE

We Will All Be Changed

Coal, buried deep within the earth, sometimes encounters intense pressure and heat. When it does, over time, a diamond results.

Under the right conditions, the mineral beryl transforms into an emerald, another precious stone. But if beryl contains impurities and undergoes the same conditions, the result is aquamarine—which is only a semiprecious stone.

When rocks with specks of gold are melted, the weighty gold deposits sink to the bottom, and the impurities are scraped from the top. After the process is repeated several times, only pure gold remains.

As minerals change under the right conditions, our bodies will change at death. In **1 Corinthians 15:35–58**, Paul talks about the transformation and refining that will occur in our bodies.

■ How will the change in our bodies be similar to what happens to coal, beryl, and gold-specked rocks? How will it be different?

■ How does the value of eternal life compare to the value of precious stones?

CONSIDER . . .

■ drawing a picture of what you think heaven will be like.

■ *hanging a "We Will All Be Changed" sign in your closet to remind you how our* earthly bodies will change.

FOR MORE, SEE . . .

■ Psalm 73:23–28 (p. 525)
■ Job 19:25–27 (p. 463)

■ Revelation 22:1–5 (p. 1348)

17I am happy that Stephanas, Fortunatus, and Achaicus have come. You are not here, but they have filled your place. 18They have refreshed my spirit and yours. You should recognize the value of people like these.

19The churches in the country of Asia send greetings to you. Aquila and Priscilla greet you in the Lord, as does the church that meets in their house. 20All the brothers and sisters here send greetings. Give each other a holy kiss when you meet.

21I, Paul, am writing this greeting with my own hand.

22If anyone does not love the Lord, let him be separated from God — lost forever!

Come, O Lord!

23The grace of the Lord Jesus be with you.

24My love be with all of you in Christ Jesus.

2 CORINTHIANS

Why Read This Book:

- Explore what it means to be a minister for Christ (2 Corinthians 1—7).
- Be challenged to give generously to God's work (2 Corinthians 8—9).
- See what Christians have to brag about (2 Corinthians 10—13).

Behind the Scenes:

"One of the striking differences between a cat and a lie is that the cat has only nine lives." —Mark Twain, American humorist

The apostle Paul wouldn't have laughed at that quote while he was writing 2 Corinthians. Any mention of lying would not have been a laughing matter.

Just three or four years earlier, Paul had started the church in Corinth, a major city in modern-day Greece. He had carefully guided and helped the people grow in their faith, as can be seen in 1 Corinthians (p. 1166). The church was special to him.

But then someone started spreading lies and rumors about Paul, trying to discredit him. He was inconsistent, they said. He was deceptive, arrogant, and boastful. He didn't have the right credentials. He was emotionally unstable. And the list continued. Even worse, the people believed the lies, and were turning to other, false leaders for guidance.

The slanderous lies angered and upset Paul personally. But he worried most that the church was being led away from Jesus Christ. Though he didn't like doing it, Paul's enemies had forced him to defend his ministry. He sent a harsh, stinging letter, which we don't have (see 2 Corinthians 2:3-4). He demanded that the church turn away from the false teachers and discipline the person who insulted him. Much to the apostle's relief, the church followed his advice and reaffirmed its loyalty to him (see 2 Corinthians 7:6-16). The crisis was over.

In 2 Corinthians, a thankful Paul rebuilds the relationship that had been strained by the sharp words. He also clears up any remaining misunderstanding that might

WHERE THE ACTION WAS

MACEDONIA

Paul was probably in Macedonia when he wrote 2 Corinthians (2 Corinthians 7:5).

ITALY

Rome

ASIA

The boundary of the Roman Empire in Paul's day.

Mediterranean Sea

Corinth

Paul wrote to the church in the Greek city of Corinth (2 Corinthians 1:1).

Jerusalem

Paul urged the Corinthians to give generously to the church in Jerusalem (2 Corinthians 8-9).

AFRICA

WHEN THE ACTION WAS

Jesus was born	The church began soon after Jesus went to heaven	Paul began his missionary work	Fire destroyed Rome	
BC/AD	25AD	50AD	75AD	100AD
	Jesus began his ministry	Paul founded the church in Corinth	Paul wrote 2 Corinthians	Romans destroyed the Temple in Jerusalem

Behind the
Scenes (cont.): be present in the church. Finally, he urges the Corinthians to give generously to the offering he was collecting for the struggling church in Jerusalem.

Because of the conflict that prompted the letter, 2 Corinthians gives us an intimate picture of the struggles and dangers Paul faced because of his ministry. In the process, the book gives us a detailed picture of what it means to follow Christ and to be a minister of the Good News.

Though the book focuses on being a minister, its insights and guidance apply to all Christians. It gives courage to overcome discouragement. It encourages us to share freely with others. And it reminds us to find our strength in Christ. That's good advice for all people!

---

1 From Paul, an apostle[d] of Christ Jesus. I am an apostle because that is what God wanted. Also from Timothy our brother in Christ.

To the church of God in Corinth, and to all of God's people everywhere in Southern Greece:

²Grace and peace to you from God our Father and the Lord Jesus Christ.

SIDELIGHT: The Corinthian church was made up of a diverse group of people who came to this major city from around the world. Paul hints at this when he addresses them in 2 Corinthians 1:2 with "grace," a Greek greeting, and "peace," a Hebrew greeting.

Paul Gives Thanks to God

³Praise be to the God and Father of our Lord Jesus Christ. God is the Father who is full of mercy and all comfort. ⁴He comforts us every time we have trouble, so when others have trouble, we can comfort them with the same comfort God gives us. ⁵We share in the many sufferings of Christ. In the same way, much comfort comes to us through Christ. ⁶If we have troubles, it is for your comfort and salvation, and if we have comfort, you also have comfort. This helps you to accept patiently the same sufferings we have. ⁷Our hope for you is strong, knowing that you share in our sufferings and also in the comfort we receive.

⁸Brothers and sisters,[n] we want you to know about the trouble we suffered in Asia. We had great burdens there that were beyond our own strength. We even gave up hope of living. ⁹Truly, in our own hearts we believed we would die. But this happened so we would not trust in ourselves but in God, who raises people from the dead. ¹⁰God saved us from these great dangers of death, and he will continue to save us. We have put our hope in him, and he will save us again. ¹¹And you can help us with your prayers. Then many people

will give thanks for us — that God blessed us because of their many prayers.

The Change in Paul's Plans

¹²This is what we are proud of, and I can say it with a clear conscience: In everything we have done in the world, and especially with you, we have had an honest and sincere heart from God. We did this by God's grace, not by the kind of wisdom the world has. ¹³ ¹⁴We write to you only what you can read and understand. And I hope that as you have understood some things about us, you may come to know everything about us. Then you can be proud of us, as we will be proud of you on the day our Lord Jesus Christ comes again.

¹⁵I was so sure of all this that I made plans to visit you first so you could be blessed twice. ¹⁶I planned to visit you on my way to Macedonia and again on my way back. I wanted to get help from you for my trip to Judea. ¹⁷Do you think that I made these plans without really meaning it? Or maybe you think I make plans as the world does, so that I say yes, yes and at the same time no, no.

¹⁸But if you can believe God, you can believe that what we tell you is never both yes and no. ¹⁹The Son of God, Jesus Christ, that Silas and Timothy and I preached to you, was not yes and no. In Christ it has always been yes. ²⁰The yes to all of God's promises is in Christ, and through Christ we say yes to the glory of God. ²¹Remember, God is the One who makes you and us strong in Christ. God made us his chosen people. ²²He put his mark on us to show that we are his, and he put his Spirit[d] in our hearts to be a guarantee for all he has promised.

²³I tell you this, and I ask God to be my witness that this is true: The reason I did not come back to Corinth was to keep you from being punished or hurt. ²⁴We are not trying to control your faith. You are strong in faith. But we are workers with you for your own joy.

2 So I decided that my next visit to you would not be another one to make you sad. ²If I

Brothers and sisters Although the Greek text says "Brothers" here and throughout this book, Paul's words were meant for the entire church, including men and women.

make you sad, who will make me glad? Only you can make me glad — particularly the person whom I made sad. [3]I wrote you a letter for this reason: that when I came to you I would not be made sad by the people who should make me happy. I felt sure of all of you, that you would share my joy. [4]When I wrote to you before, I was very troubled and unhappy in my heart, and I wrote with many tears. I did not write to make you sad, but to let you know how much I love you.

Forgive the Sinner

[5]Someone there among you has caused sadness, not to me, but to all of you. I mean he caused sadness to all in some way. (I do not want to make it sound worse than it really is.) [6]The punishment that most of you gave him is enough for him. [7]But now you should forgive him and comfort him to keep him from having too much sadness and giving up completely. [8]So I beg you to show that you love him. [9]I wrote you to test you and to see if you obey in everything. [10]If you forgive someone, I also forgive him. And what I have forgiven — if I had anything to forgive — I forgave it for you, as if Christ were with me. [11]I did this so that Satan would not win anything from us, because we know very well what Satan's plans are.

Paul's Concern in Troas

[12]When I came to Troas to preach the Good News[d] of Christ, the Lord gave me a good opportunity there. [13]But I had no peace, because I did not find my brother Titus. So I said good-bye to them at Troas and went to Macedonia.

Victory Through Christ

[14]But thanks be to God, who always leads us in victory through Christ. God uses us to spread his knowledge everywhere like a sweet-smelling perfume. [15]Our offering to God is this: We are the sweet smell of Christ among those who are being saved and among those who are being lost. [16]To those who are lost, we are the smell of death that brings death, but to those who are being saved, we are the smell of life that brings life. So who is able to do this work? [17]We do not sell the word of God for a profit as many other people do. But in Christ we speak the truth before God, as messengers of God.

Servants of the New Agreement

3 Are we starting to brag about ourselves again? Do we need letters of introduction to you or from you, like some other people? [2]You yourselves are our letter, written on our hearts,

known and read by everyone. [3]You show that you are a letter from Christ sent through us. This letter is not written with ink but with the Spirit[d] of the living God. It is not written on stone tablets[n] but on human hearts.

[4]We can say this, because through Christ we feel certain before God. [5]We are not saying that we can do this work ourselves. It is God who makes us able to do all that we do. [6]He made us able to be servants of a new agreement from himself to his people. This new agreement is not a written law, but it is of the Spirit. The written law brings death, but the Spirit gives life.

[7]The law that brought death was written in words on stone. It came with God's glory, which made Moses' face so bright that the Israelites could not continue to look at it. But that glory later disappeared. [8]So surely the new way that brings the Spirit has even more glory. [9]If the law that judged people guilty of sin had glory, surely the new way that makes people right with God has much greater glory. [10]That old law had glory, but it really loses its glory when it is compared to the much greater glory of this new way. [11]If that law which disappeared came with glory, then this new way which continues forever has much greater glory.

[12]We have this hope, so we are very bold. [13]We are not like Moses, who put a covering over his face so the Israelites would not see it. The glory was disappearing, and Moses did not want them to see it end. [14]But their minds were closed, and even today that same covering hides the meaning when they read the old agreement. That covering is taken away only through Christ. [15]Even today, when they read the law of Moses, there is a covering over their minds. [16]But when a person changes and follows the Lord, that covering is taken away. [17]The Lord is the Spirit, and where the Spirit of the Lord is, there is freedom. [18]Our faces, then, are not covered. We all show the Lord's glory, and we are being changed to be like him. This change in us brings ever greater glory, which comes from the Lord, who is the Spirit.

Preaching the Good News

4 God, with his mercy, gave us this work to do, so we don't give up. [2]But we have turned away from secret and shameful ways. We use no trickery, and we do not change the teaching of God. We teach the truth plainly, showing everyone who we are. Then they can know in their hearts what kind of people we are in God's sight. [3]If the Good News[d] that we preach is hidden, it is hidden only to those who are lost. [4]The devil who rules this world has blinded the minds of those who do not believe. They cannot see the

---

stone tablets   Meaning the law of Moses that was written on stone tablets (Exodus 24:12; 25:16).

light of the Good News—the Good News about the glory of Christ, who is exactly like God. ⁵We do not preach about ourselves, but we preach that Jesus Christ is Lord and that we are your servants for Jesus. ⁶God once said, "Let the light shine out of the darkness!" This is the same God who made his light shine in our hearts by letting us know the glory of God that is in the face of Christ.

Spiritual Treasure in Clay Jars

⁷We have this treasure from God, but we are like clay jars that hold the treasure. This shows that the great power is from God, not from us.

⁸We have troubles all around us, but we are not defeated. We do not know what to do, but we do not give up the hope of living. ⁹We are persecuted, but God does not leave us. We are hurt

> ✺ **SIDELIGHT:** Hiding treasures in clay jars was a common practice in biblical times, since people wouldn't suspect anything valuable was in the cheap jar (2 Corinthians 4:7). It's sort of like hiding your money in a sock.

NON-CHRISTIANS

Trying Too Hard

Dave Hildebrant tried to live a perfect Christian life. He went to church and was active in his youth group. He faithfully read the Bible and shared his faith with others.

Dave's problem was that he got carried away.

At school Dave constantly talked about his beliefs. In history class he challenged everything his teacher said. In science class he blasted theories and ideas as un-Christian. During lunch he commented on others' food, telling them that God wanted them to treat their bodies like a temple. Between classes he witnessed in the halls.

At first, teachers and students listened to him. But soon, people around him grew irritated. Teachers began to cut him off, and students just laughed. The more they laughed or ignored him the harder he tried. Finally, even other Christians began to sneer. They started calling him "the preacher" and "super Christian."

Holly Myers was also a Christian. Although she, too, was tired of Dave's style, she felt sorry when others put him down. One day Dave complained to Holly that no one ever listened.

"Maybe you're trying too hard," Holly suggested. "After all, we don't have to be preaching all the time. We just need to let God's love shine through."

Over the next few weeks, whenever Holly saw Dave she just smiled. For a long time Dave didn't seem to have heard her. He just kept on preaching and witnessing, and students kept on making fun of him.

Slowly, Dave began following Holly's advice. He still lived out his faith, but instead of being obnoxious, he expressed it with a smile, a kind word or an offer of help. And, for the first time, people began responding positively to Dave's efforts.

Sometimes we get so tied up in trying to convert others that we don't let God's love show through us to non-Christians. Read **2 Corinthians 4:3–12** to discover more about the treasure of God's love and how to share your faith with the world.

■ How does Dave's discovery relate to Paul's belief that we are clay jars holding the treasure of God's love?

■ How have you shared God's treasure with a non-Christian?

CONSIDER...

■ asking God to teach you how to respect others while you share your beliefs with them.

■ inviting a friend who doesn't go to church to come with you to worship. Introduce him or her to your Christian friends.

FOR MORE, SEE...

■ Genesis 18:16–33 (p. 20)
■ Matthew 28:16–20 (p. 962)

■ Colossians 3:12–17 (p. 1241)

sometimes, but we are not destroyed. [10]We carry the death of Jesus in our own bodies so that the life of Jesus can also be seen in our bodies. [11]We are alive, but for Jesus we are always in danger of death so that the life of Jesus can be seen in our bodies that die. [12]So death is working in us, but life is working in you.

[13]It is written in the Scriptures,[d] "I believed, so I spoke." [n] Our faith is like this, too. We believe, and so we speak. [14]God raised the Lord Jesus from the dead, and we know that God will also raise us with Jesus. God will bring us together with you, and we will stand before him. [15]All these things are for you. And so the grace of God that is being given to more and more people will bring increasing thanks to God for his glory.

"**I . . . spoke.**"   Quotation from Psalm 116:10.

Living by Faith

[16]So we do not give up. Our physical body is becoming older and weaker, but our spirit inside us is made new every day. [17]We have small troubles for a while now, but they are helping us gain an eternal glory that is much greater than the troubles. [18]We set our eyes not on what we see but on what we cannot see. What we see will last only a short time, but what we cannot see will last forever.

5 We know that our body—the tent we live in here on earth—will be destroyed. But when that happens, God will have a house for us. It will not be a house made by human hands; instead, it will be a home in heaven that will last forever. [2]But now we groan in this tent. We want God to

---

FAITH

Unseen Water

Frank Zeigler's ranch in Wyoming had been in his family for years, but had never been used. It was full of cactus and rocks. Surely the land could be used for something, Frank thought. He thought of raising sheep, but sheep couldn't live there without water. He thought of mining the minerals that had been discovered long ago, but there was no water to process the ore.

Frank felt he was missing something—something he couldn't see. He just needed water, but there was none for miles around.

"I know there is more," he told his wife. "I just know there is. God is always giving us gifts, but half the time we don't see them."

One day as he rode across the barren range, he suddenly stopped. He piled up five or six rocks and called a drilling company. Frank told them to drill a deep water well where he had piled the rocks.

At first the owners laughed. "There's no water on that land. You know that," they teased.

But he insisted. "I just have a feeling it's there," he said. Finally they agreed to drill. Months later, they hit water almost one mile underground.

Astonished, the drilling crew asked how he knew water was down there. Frank shrugged. "I just knew," he said. "I guess I had the faith that there was more there than my eyes could see."

As Frank did, it's important for us to have faith not just in things seen but in things unseen as well. To learn more, read **2 Corinthians 4:13–18**.

■ How does Frank's search for water parallel the faith described in the passage? How does it differ?

■ Which part of this passage gives you the greatest sense of hope in your faith?

C O N S I D E R . . .

■ thinking about things you know exist even though you can't see them, such as air and electricity. List ways you know God exists even though you can't see him.

◀ stepping out in faith in an area where you may not have all the "facts" but still believe what you're doing is God's will.

F O R   M O R E ,   S E E . . .

■ Psalm 116 (p. 548)
■ Romans 8:18–28 (p. 1151)

■ Colossians 3:1–4 (p. 1241)

give us our heavenly home, ³because it will clothe us so we will not be naked. ⁴While we live in this body, we have burdens, and we groan. We do not want to be naked, but we want to be clothed with our heavenly home. Then this body that dies will be fully covered with life. ⁵This is what God made us for, and he has given us the Spirit*d* to be a guarantee for this new life.

⁶So we always have courage. We know that while we live in this body, we are away from the Lord. ⁷We live by what we believe, not by what we can see. ⁸So I say that we have courage. We really want to be away from this body and be at home with the Lord. ⁹Our only goal is to please God whether we live here or there, ¹⁰because we must all stand before Christ to be judged. Each of us will receive what we should get — good or bad — for the things we did in the earthly body.

Becoming Friends with God

¹¹Since we know what it means to fear the Lord, we try to help people accept the truth about us. God knows what we really are, and I hope that in your hearts you know, too. ¹²We are not trying to prove ourselves to you again, but we are telling you about ourselves so you will be proud of us. Then you will have an answer for those who are proud about things that can be seen rather than what is in the heart. ¹³If we are out of our minds, it is for God. If we have our right minds, it is for you. ¹⁴The love of Christ controls us, because we know that One died for all, so all have died. ¹⁵Christ died for all so that those who live would not continue to live for themselves. He died for them and was raised from the dead so that they would live for him.

¹⁶From this time on we do not think of anyone as the world does. In the past we thought of Christ as the world thinks, but we no longer think of him in that way. ¹⁷If anyone belongs to Christ, there is a new creation. The old things have gone; everything is made new! ¹⁸All this is from God. Through Christ, God made peace between us and himself, and God gave us the work of telling ev-

---

FOLLOWING GOD

Daring to Believe

Christopher Wren, a young English architect in the early 1700s, had the chance of a lifetime. He had won the job of building a new cathedral in London. He prayed and worked to design a cathedral with a magnificently arched ceiling stretching toward heaven.

But when the church was almost finished, other architects in London claimed the building was flawed. They said six additional pillars were needed or else the roof would fall.

Wren genuinely believed God was guiding him in building the cathedral. Still, the other architects were older and more experienced. So, instead of reacting angrily, he listened and prayed. After much discussion he agreed to add the pillars.

At least that's what everyone thought.

After the cathedral was finished, Wren left London. Fifty years later, after his death, workers were repainting the ceiling when they discovered something strange. Each of the six additional pillars was a few inches short of the vaulted ceiling.

Wren had been right. And he had proven it.

Like Christopher Wren we are called to follow God as best we know how, which often requires courage and creativity. To learn more about following God read **2 Corinthians 5:6–17**.

■ How does Christopher Wren's decision to follow God's call in his heart relate to Paul's advice to live by believing in Christ?

■ How have you made choices that reflect the challenge of verse 7? What happened?

C O N S I D E R . . .

■ choosing a creative way to follow God this week, such as writing, drawing, painting, or singing.

■ interviewing your pastor, a teacher, or a friend about times he or she struggled with decisions to follow God, and what happened.

F O R   M O R E ,   S E E . . .

■ Isaiah 65:17–25 (p. 686)
■ John 14:1–7 (p. 1083)
■ Philippians :19–20 (p. 1230)

eryone about the peace we can have with him. [19]God was in Christ, making peace between the world and himself. In Christ, God did not hold the world guilty of its sins. And he gave us this message of peace. [20]So we have been sent to speak for Christ. It is as if God is calling to you through us. We speak for Christ when we beg you to be at peace with God. [21]Christ had no sin, but God made him become sin so that in Christ we could become right with God.

6 We are workers together with God, so we beg you: Do not let the grace that you received from God be for nothing. [2]God says,

"At the right time I heard your prayers.
 On the day of salvation I helped you."

Isaiah 49:8

I tell you that the "right time" is now, and the "day of salvation" is now.

[3]We do not want anyone to find fault with our work, so nothing we do will be a problem for anyone. [4]But in every way we show we are servants of God: in accepting many hard things, in troubles, in difficulties, and in great problems. [5]We are beaten and thrown into prison. We meet those who become upset with us and start riots. We work hard, and sometimes we get no sleep or food. [6]We show we are servants of God by our pure lives, our understanding, patience, and kind-

SERVICE

Doing What We Can

Joanni Glade wasn't like the other kids in the youth group. Born with the neuromuscular disease Charcot-marie-toothe, she couldn't walk without crutches.

This was her first year in the youth group, and though she had been very active, the other kids assumed she wouldn't go on the two-week summer service project. But Joanni shocked them when she made it clear she was going.

A few youth group members went to Joanni. "We know you want to go, but don't you think it would be better for everyone if you stayed at home?" they asked. "Aren't you afraid you'll get hurt?" Joanni firmly replied she was going.

When the group arrived at the service project, their assignment was to repair a home in the middle of a dry, treeless yard. Everyone had an assignment. Some kids repaired the roof, some replaced siding, and some painted.

Joanni began painting, but quickly discovered she didn't have the strength to lift the brush over and over. By the end of the first day she felt like a failure. "I guess everyone was right. I really am useless here," she thought.

The same people who had talked to her earlier approached her again. "Maybe it would be better if you went home," they urged. "It's not that we don't care; it's just that we're here to help these other people." After a while Joanni disappeared, and no one could find her. Later she reappeared with a tired but happy smile on her face.

The next day Joanni didn't go with the group to the work site. An hour later, a supply truck arrived at the work site with lumber, nails, shingles and water. Joanni sat in the cab with a list of supplies. For two weeks Joanni kept track of supplies and saw to it that work groups had what they needed. By the end of the project, the project directors talked about hiring her the next year as their supply coordinator.

Joanni took the message of **2 Corinthians 5:20—6:10** seriously. In spite of the doubts of others she served God in her own unique way.

■ How were Joanni's actions similar to the kind of service the passage talks about?

■ When have you served God and others in ways that are reflected in this passage? What was the result?

CONSIDER . . .

■ taking an inventory of your skills, gifts and abilities, and deciding how you can use them in God's service.

▮ including people with disabilities as full and equal servants in your youth group and church.

FOR MORE, SEE . . .

■ Jeremiah 1:4–10 (p. 691)
■ Matthew 4:16–19 (p. 912)

■ James 2:14–26 (p. 1295)

ness, by the Holy Spirit,[d] by true love, [7]by speaking the truth, and by God's power. We use our right living to defend ourselves against everything. [8]Some people honor us, but others blame

> ## ✸ SIDELIGHT: Paul was no
> stranger to the local bars—prison bars, that is (2 Corinthians 6:5). According to Clement of Rome, Paul was imprisoned at least seven times. Among the places he was locked up were Philippi, Jerusalem, and Rome. Paul's life ended in prison when he was executed by the Roman government.

us. Some people say evil things about us, but others say good things. Some people say we are liars, but we speak the truth. [9]We are not known, but we are well known. We seem to be dying, but we continue to live. We are punished, but we are not killed. [10]We have much sadness, but we are always rejoicing. We are poor, but we are making many people rich in faith. We have nothing, but really we have everything.

[11]We have spoken freely to you in Corinth and have opened our hearts to you. [12]Our feelings of love for you have not stopped, but you have stopped your feelings of love for us. [13]I speak to you as if you were my children. Do to us as we have done—open your hearts to us.

Warning About Non-Christians

[14]You are not the same as those who do not believe. So do not join yourselves to them. Good and bad do not belong together. Light and darkness cannot share together. [15]How can Christ and Belial, the devil, have any agreement? What can a believer have together with a nonbeliever? [16]The temple of God cannot have any agreement with idols, and we are the temple of the living God. As God said: "I will live with them and walk with them. And I will be their God, and they will be my people." [n]

[17]"Leave those people,
    and be separate, says the Lord.
Touch nothing that is unclean,[d]
    and I will accept you."

Isaiah 52:11; Ezekiel 20:34, 41

[18]"I will be your father,
    and you will be my sons and daughters,
    says the Lord Almighty."   *2 Samuel 7:14; 7:8*

7 Dear friends, we have these promises from God, so we should make ourselves pure—

free from anything that makes body or soul unclean. We should try to become holy in the way we live, because we respect God.

Paul's Joy

[2]Open your hearts to us. We have not done wrong to anyone, we have not ruined the faith of anyone, and we have not cheated anyone. [3]I do not say this to blame you. I told you before that we love you so much we would live or die with you. [4]I feel very sure of you and am very proud of you. You give me much comfort, and in all of our troubles I have great joy.

[5]When we came into Macedonia, we had no rest. We found trouble all around us. We had fighting on the outside and fear on the inside. [6]But God, who comforts those who are troubled, comforted us when Titus came. [7]We were comforted, not only by his coming but also by the comfort you gave him. Titus told us about your wish to see me and that you are very sorry for what you did. He also told me about your great care for me, and when I heard this, I was much happier.

[8]Even if my letter made you sad, I am not sorry I wrote it. At first I was sorry, because it made you sad, but you were sad only for a short time. [9]Now I am happy, not because you were made sad, but because your sorrow made you change your lives. You became sad in the way God wanted you to, so you were not hurt by us in any way. [10]The kind of sorrow God wants makes people change their hearts and lives. This leads to salvation, and you cannot be sorry for that. But the kind of sorrow the world has brings death. [11]See what this sorrow—the sorrow God wanted you to have—has done to you: It has made you very serious. It made you want to prove you were not wrong. It made you angry and afraid. It made you want to see me. It made you care. It made you want the right thing to be done. You proved you were innocent in the problem. [12]I wrote that letter, not because of the one who did the wrong or because of the person who was hurt. I wrote the letter so you could see, before God, the great care you have for us. [13]That is why we were comforted.

Not only were we very comforted, we were even happier to see that Titus was so happy. All of you made him feel much better. [14]I bragged to Titus about you, and you showed that I was right. Everything we said to you was true, and you have proved that what we bragged about to Titus is true. [15]And his love for you is stronger when he remembers that you were all ready to obey. You welcomed him with respect and fear. [16]I am very happy that I can trust you fully.

"I ... people." Quotation from Leviticus 26:11-12; Jeremiah 32:38; Ezekiel 37:27.

Christian Giving

8 And now, brothers and sisters, we want you to know about the grace God gave the churches in Macedonia. [2]They have been tested by great troubles, and they are very poor. But they gave much because of their great joy. [3]I can tell you that they gave as much as they were able and even more than they could afford. No one told them to do it. [4]But they begged and pleaded with us to let them share in this service for God's people. [5]And they gave in a way we did not expect: They first gave themselves to the Lord and to us. This is what God wants. [6]So we asked Titus to help you finish this special work of grace since he is the one who started it. [7]You are rich in everything—in faith, in speaking, in knowledge, in truly wanting to help, and in the love you learned

from us. In the same way, be strong also in the grace of giving.

[8]I am not commanding you to give. But I want to see if your love is true by comparing you with others that really want to help. [9]You know the grace of our Lord Jesus Christ. You know that Christ was rich, but for you he became poor so that by his becoming poor you might become rich.

[10]This is what I think you should do: Last year you were the first to want to give, and you were the first who gave. [11]So now finish the work you started. Then your "doing" will be equal to your "wanting to do." Give from what you have. [12]If you want to give, your gift will be accepted. It will be judged by what you have, not by what you do not have. [13]We do not want you to have troubles while other people are at ease, but we want ev-

---

GIVING

The Little Things

Linda Dale was Judy Grantham's friend, and she had come on the ski trip to be with Judy. The Bible studies and prayertimes were okay, but she had really come to ski. After a day of skiing, Linda was on the bus, feeling exhausted and cold. Her socks were soaked and the bus was freezing. Shivering and surrounded by people she barely knew, she hoped Judy would come soon.

Jennifer Davis was cold, too. She was a regular group member, and noticed Linda sitting alone, cold and miserable. Going over to Linda, she asked, "Are you okay? You look like a Popsicle."

"I'm just so cold," Linda said. "My feet are freezing. Maybe Judy will have an extra pair of dry socks she can loan me."

"I have an extra pair of socks I'd be glad to give you," Jennifer said.

Linda hesitated, but then she said, "Would you? That would be wonderful."

Jennifer found the socks and gave them to Linda, along with some dry gloves and a scarf. By the time Judy boarded the bus, Linda and Jennifer were laughing about their day of skiing.

Later that night Linda asked Judy, "Why did Jennifer give me all those clothes when she was just as cold as I was?"

"Because giving is a part of being a Christian," Judy said. Then they talked for hours about why Judy was a Christian, and what it meant to give.

After the ski trip, Linda began coming to youth group regularly. While she still enjoyed the fun stuff, she also began asking more questions during Bible studies and offered prayers during worship. It took a while, but slowly she developed a solid faith.

In a world that assumes life's purpose is to take and keep, Jennifer's giving showed Linda that Christianity is different. Jennifer took **2 Corinthians 8:5–15** to heart.

■ Looking at the passage, why did Jennifer share dry socks with Linda?
■ In what ways does the passage challenge you to give to others?

CONSIDER . . .

◢ doing one unexpected chore around the house as a way to give of yourself.
■ organizing a benefit fund-raiser to help a Christian mission or service project.

FOR MORE, SEE . . .

■ Exodus 22:25–27 (p. 81)
■ Acts 20:32–35 (p. 1130)

■ Philippians 2:5–7 (p. 1230)

erything to be equal. [14]At this time you have plenty. What you have can help others who are in need. Then later, when they have plenty, they can help you when you are in need, and all will be equal. [15]As it is written in the Scriptures,[d] "The person who gathered more did not have too much, nor did the person who gathered less have too little."[n]

Titus and His Companions Help

[16]I thank God because he gave Titus the same love for you that I have. [17]Titus accepted what we asked him to do. He wanted very much to go to you, and this was his own idea. [18]We are sending with him the brother who is praised by all the churches because of his service in preaching the Good News.[d] [19]Also, this brother was chosen by the churches to go with us when we deliver this gift of money. We are doing this service to bring glory to the Lord and to show that we really want to help.

[20]We are being careful so that no one will criticize us for the way we are handling this large gift. [21]We are trying hard to do what the Lord accepts as right and also what people think is right.

[22]Also, we are sending with them our brother, who is always ready to help. He has proved this to us in many ways, and he wants to help even more now, because he has much faith in you.

[23]Now about Titus — he is my partner who is working with me to help you. And about the other brothers — they are sent from the churches, and they bring glory to Christ. [24]So show these men the proof of your love and the reason we are proud of you. Then all the churches can see it.

Help for Fellow Christians

9 I really do not need to write you about this help for God's people. [2]I know you want to help. I have been bragging about this to the people in Macedonia, telling them that you in Southern Greece have been ready to give since last year. And your desire to give has made most of them ready to give also. [3]But I am sending the brothers to you so that our bragging about you in this will not be empty words. I want you to be ready, as I said you would be. [4]If any of the people from Macedonia come with me and find that you are not ready, we will be ashamed that we were so sure of you. (And you will be ashamed, too!) [5]So I thought I should ask these brothers to go to you before we do. They will finish getting in order the generous gift you promised so it will be ready when we come. And it will be a generous gift — not one that you did not want to give.

[6]Remember this: The person who plants a little will have a small harvest, but the person who plants a lot will have a big harvest. [7]Each one should give as you have decided in your heart to give. You should not be sad when you give, and you should not give because you feel forced to give. God loves the person who gives happily. [8]And God can give you more blessings than you need. Then you will always have plenty of everything — enough to give to every good work. [9]It is written in the Scriptures:[d]

"He gives freely to the poor.
    The things he does are right and will
        continue forever." *Psalm 112.9*

[10]God is the One who gives seed to the farmer and bread for food. He will give you all the seed you need and make it grow so there will be a great harvest from your goodness. [11]He will make you rich in every way so that you can always give freely. And your giving through us will cause many to give thanks to God. [12]This service you do not only helps the needs of God's people, it also brings many more thanks to God. [13]It is a proof of your faith. Many people will praise God because you obey the Good News[d] of Christ — the gospel you say you believe — and because you freely share with them and with all others. [14]And when they pray, they will wish they could be with you because of the great grace that God has given you. [15]Thanks be to God for his gift that is too wonderful for words.

Paul Defends His Ministry

10 I, Paul, am begging you with the gentleness and the kindness of Christ. Some people say that I am easy on you when I am with you and bold when I am away. [2]They think we live in a worldly way, and I plan to be very bold with them when I come. I beg you that when I come I will not need to use that same boldness with you. [3]We do live in the world, but we do not fight in the same way the world fights. [4]We fight with weapons that are different from those the world uses. Our weapons have power from God that can destroy the enemy's strong places. We destroy people's arguments [5]and every proud thing that raises itself against the knowledge of God. We capture every thought and make it give up and obey Christ [6]We are ready to punish anyone there who does not obey, but first we want you to obey fully.

[7]You must look at the facts before you. If you feel sure that you belong to Christ, you must remember that we belong to Christ just as you do. [8]It is true that we brag freely about the authority the Lord gave us. But this authority is to build you up, not to tear you down. So I will not be ashamed. [9]I do not want you to think I am trying to scare you with my letters. [10]Some people say,

---

"The person . . . little." Quotation from Exodus 16:18.

"Paul's letters are powerful and sound important, but when he is with us, he is weak. And his speaking is nothing." [11]They should know this: We are not there with you now, so we say these things in letters. But when we are there with you, we will show the same authority that we show in our letters.

SIDELIGHT: Paul may have been a great missionary, but he would have never made it on the front of a fashion magazine. A nonbiblical book called Acts of Paul and Thecla described him as "a man small of stature, with bald head and crooked legs . . . with eyebrows meeting and nose somewhat hooked." His critics said: "He is weak. And his speaking is nothing" (2 Corinthians 10:10).

---

[12]We do not dare to compare ourselves with those who think they are very important. They use themselves to measure themselves, and they judge themselves by what they themselves are. This shows that they know nothing. [13]But we will not brag about things outside the work that was given us to do. We will limit our bragging to the work that God gave us, and this includes our work with you. [14]We are not bragging too much, as we would be if we had not already come to you. But we have come to you with the Good News[d] of Christ. [15]We limit our bragging to the work that is ours, not what others have done. We hope that as your faith continues to grow, you will help our work to grow much larger. [16]We want to tell the Good News in the areas beyond your city. We do not want to brag about work that has already been done in another person's area. [17]But, "If someone wants to brag, he should brag only about the Lord." [n] [18]It is not those who say they are good who are accepted but those who the Lord thinks are good.

Paul and the False Apostles

11 I wish you would be patient with me even when I am a little foolish, but you are already doing that. [2]I am jealous over you with a jealousy that comes from God. I promised to give you to Christ, as your only husband. I want to give you as his pure bride. [3]But I am afraid that your minds will be led away from your true and pure following of Christ just as Eve was tricked by the snake with his evil ways. [4]You are very patient with anyone who comes to you and preaches a

different Jesus from the one we preached. You are very willing to accept a spirit or gospel that is different from the Spirit[d] and Good News[d] you received from us.

[5]I do not think that those "great apostles" are any better than I am. [6]I may not be a trained speaker, but I do have knowledge. We have shown this to you clearly in every way.

[7]I preached God's Good News to you without pay. I made myself unimportant to make you important. Do you think that was wrong? [8]I accepted pay from other churches, taking their money so I could serve you. [9]If I needed something when I was with you, I did not trouble any of you. The brothers who came from Macedonia gave me all that I needed. I did not allow myself to depend on you in any way, and I will never depend on you. [10]No one in Southern Greece will stop me from bragging about that. I say this with the truth of Christ in me. [11]And why do I not depend on you? Do you think it is because I do not love you? God knows that I love you.

[12]And I will continue doing what I am doing now, because I want to stop those people from having a reason to brag. They would like to say that the work they brag about is the same as ours. [13]Such men are not true apostles[d] but are workers who lie. They change themselves to look like apostles of Christ. [14]This does not surprise us. Even Satan changes himself to look like an angel of light. [n] [15]So it does not surprise us if Satan's servants also make themselves look like servants who work for what is right. But in the end they will be punished for what they do.

Paul Tells About His Sufferings

[16]I tell you again: No one should think I am a fool. But if you think so, accept me as you would accept a fool. Then I can brag a little, too. [17]When I brag because I feel sure of myself, I am not talking as the Lord would talk but as a fool. [18]Many people are bragging about their lives in the world. So I will brag too. [19]You are wise, so you will gladly be patient with fools! [20]You are even patient with those who order you around, or use you, or trick you, or think they are better than you, or hit you in the face. [21]It is shameful to me to say this, but we were too "weak" to do those things to you!

But if anyone else is brave enough to brag, then I also will be brave and brag. (I am talking as a fool.) [22]Are they Hebrews? [n] So am I. Are they Israelites? So am I. Are they from Abraham's family? So am I. [23]Are they serving Christ? I am serving him more. (I am crazy to talk like this.) I have

---

"If . . . Lord." Quotation from Jeremiah 9:24.
angel of light Messenger from God. The devil fools people so that they think he is from God.
Hebrews A name for the Jews that some Jews were very proud of.

worked much harder than they. I have been in prison more often. I have been hurt more in beatings. I have been near death many times. [24]Five times the Jews have given me their punishment of thirty-nine lashes with a whip. [25]Three different times I was beaten with rods. One time I was almost stoned to death. Three times I was in ships that wrecked, and one of those times I spent a night and a day in the sea. [26]I have gone on many travels and have been in danger from rivers, thieves, my own people, the Jews, and those who are not Jews. I have been in danger in cities, in places where no one lives, and on the sea. And I have been in danger with false Christians. [27]I have done hard and tiring work, and many times I did not sleep. I have been hungry and thirsty, and many times I have been without food. I have been cold and without clothes. [28]Besides all this, there is on me every day the load of my concern for all the churches. [29]I feel weak every time someone is weak, and I feel upset every time someone is led into sin.

[30]If I must brag, I will brag about the things that show I am weak. [31]God knows I am not lying. He is the God and Father of the Lord Jesus Christ, and he is to be praised forever. [32]When I was in Damascus, the governor under King Aretas wanted to arrest me, so he put guards around the city. [33]But my friends lowered me in a basket through a hole in the city wall. So I escaped from the governor.

A Special Blessing in Paul's Life

12 I must continue to brag. It will do no good, but I will talk now about visions and revelations[n] from the Lord. [2]I know a man in Christ who was taken up to the third heaven fourteen years ago. I do not know whether the man was in his body or out of his body, but God knows. [3-4]And I know that this man was taken up to paradise.[n] I don't know if he was in his body or away from his body, but God knows. He heard things he is not able to explain, things that no human is allowed to tell. [5]I will brag about a man like that, but I will not brag about myself, except about my weaknesses. [6]But if I wanted to brag about myself, I would not be a fool, because I would be telling the truth. But I will not brag about myself. I do not want people to think more of me than what they see me do or hear me say.

[7]So that I would not become too proud of the wonderful things that were shown to me, a painful physical problem[a] was given to me. This problem was a messenger from Satan, sent to beat me and keep me from being too proud. [8]I begged

the Lord three times to take this problem away from me. [9]But he said to me, "My grace is enough for you. When you are weak, my power is made perfect in you." So I am very happy to brag about my weaknesses. Then Christ's power can live in me. [10]For this reason I am happy when I have weaknesses, insults, hard times, sufferings, and all kinds of trouble for Christ. Because when I am weak, then I am truly strong.

Paul's Love for the Christians

[11]I have been talking like a fool, but you made me do it. You are the ones who should say good things about me. I am worth nothing, but those "great apostles" are not worth any more than I am! [12]When I was with you, I patiently did the things that prove I am an apostle[d]—signs, wonders, and miracles.[d] [13]So you received everything that the other churches have received. Only one thing was different: I was not a burden to you. Forgive me for this!

[14]I am now ready to visit you the third time, and I will not be a burden to you. I want nothing from you, except you. Children should not have to save up to give to their parents. Parents should save to give to their children. [15]So I am happy to give everything I have for you, even myself. If I love you more, will you love me less?

[16]It is clear I was not a burden to you, but you think I was tricky and lied to catch you. [17]Did I cheat you by using any of the messengers I sent to you? No, you know I did not. [18]I asked Titus to go to you, and I sent our brother with him. Titus did not cheat you, did he? No, you know that Titus and I did the same thing and with the same spirit.

[19]Do you think we have been defending ourselves to you all this time? We have been speaking in Christ and before God. You are our dear friends, and everything we do is to make you stronger. [20]I am afraid that when I come, you will not be what I want you to be, and I will not be what you want me to be. I am afraid that among you there may be arguing, jealousy, anger, selfish fighting, evil talk, gossip, pride, and confusion. [21]I am afraid that when I come to you again, my God will make me ashamed before you. I may be saddened by many of those who have sinned because they have not changed their hearts or turned from their sexual sins and the shameful things they have done.

Final Warnings and Greetings

13 I will come to you for the third time. "Every case must be proved by two or

---

revelations   Revelation is making known a truth that was hidden.
paradise   A place where good people go when they die.
painful physical problem   Literally, "thorn in the flesh."

three witnesses." [n] [2]When I was with you the second time, I gave a warning to those who had sinned. Now I am away from you, and I give a warning to all the others. When I come to you again, I will not be easy with them. [3]You want proof that Christ is speaking through me. My proof is that he is not weak among you, but he is powerful. [4]It is true that he was weak when he was killed on the cross, but he lives now by God's power. It is true that we are weak in Christ, but for you we will be alive in Christ by God's power.

[5]Look closely at yourselves. Test yourselves to see if you are living in the faith. You know that Jesus Christ is in you — unless you fail the test. [6]But I hope you will see that we ourselves have not failed the test. [7]We pray to God that you will not do anything wrong. It is not important to see that we have passed the test, but it is important that you do what is right, even if it seems we have failed. [8]We cannot do anything against the truth, but only for the truth. [9]We are happy to be weak, if you are strong, and we pray that you will become complete. [10]I am writing this while I am away from you so that when I come I will not

have to be harsh in my use of authority. The Lord gave me this authority to build you up, not to tear you down.

[11]Now, brothers and sisters, I say good-bye. Try to be complete. Do what I have asked you to do. Agree with each other, and live in peace. Then the God of love and peace will be with you.

> ## ☀ SIDELIGHT: Want to start
> rumors in your youth group? Then put 2 Corinthians 13:12 into practice. This custom of kissing other Christians arose spontaneously in the early church, and later became a regular part of worship. It's still a custom in some Near Eastern cultures.

[12]Greet each other with a holy kiss. [13]All of God's holy people send greetings to you.

[14]The grace of the Lord Jesus Christ, the love of God, and the fellowship of the Holy Spirit[d] be with you all.

"Every ... witnesses." Quotation from Deuteronomy 19:15.

GALATIANS

Why Read This Book:

■ See the dangers of listening to false teachers (Galatians 1—2).
■ Discover the freedom we have through faith in Christ (Galatians 3).
■ Find out how Christians should use their freedom (Galatians 5—6).

Behind the Scenes:

What do you have to do to be a Christian? Do you have to practice certain rituals? Do you have to follow certain rules?

Those were controversial questions in the early church, as we discover in Paul's letter to the Galatians. Not long before, Paul had started the churches in Galatia. But soon after he left, people began questioning his beliefs and authority. They said non-Jewish people who became Christians also had to follow Jewish laws and rituals to be true Christians—a perspective that was splitting the early church (see Acts 15, p. 1121).

When Paul heard what was happening, he wrote this letter to confront the problem. "You have already accepted the Good News. If anyone is preaching something different to you, he should be judged guilty!" he blasts in Galatians 1:9. Then Paul gets to the heart of the Christian faith. He explains that people can't do anything to earn God's promises. Those promises are free gifts for all people, to be received by faith in Christ. Instead of being the law's prisoners, Christians live in freedom.

Someone always seems to be telling us that serving God means following a long list of dos and don'ts. Paul's letter to the Galatians reminds us that being a Christian isn't a matter of what we do or don't do; it's a matter of accepting what Jesus Christ did for us. Now that's Good News!

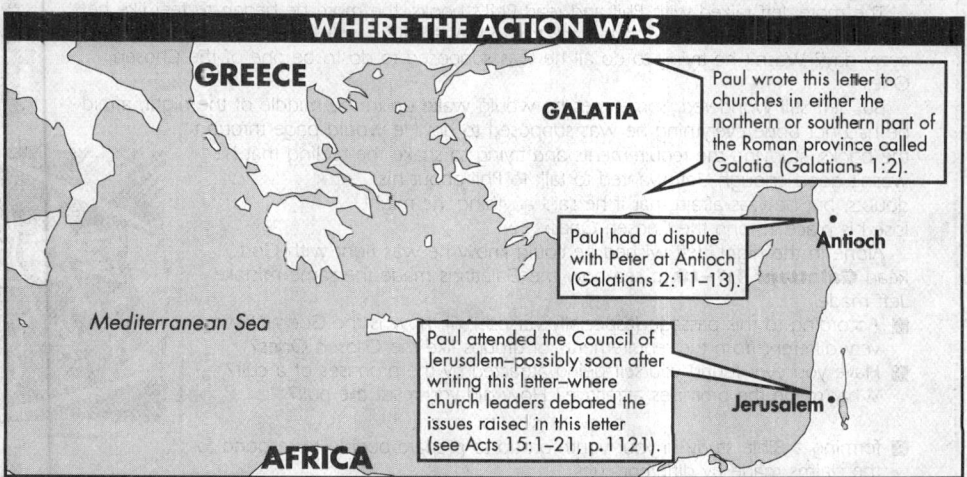

WHERE THE ACTION WAS

GREECE

GALATIA

Paul wrote this letter to churches in either the northern or southern part of the Roman province called Galatia (Galatians 1:2).

Paul had a dispute with Peter at Antioch (Galatians 2:11–13).

Antioch

Mediterranean Sea

Paul attended the Council of Jerusalem—possibly soon after writing this letter—where church leaders debated the issues raised in this letter (see Acts 15:1–21, p.1121).

Jerusalem

AFRICA

WHEN THE ACTION WAS

Jesus was born	The church began soon after Jesus went to heaven		Paul started churches in Galatia	Fire destroyed Rome
BC/AD	**20AD**	**30AD**	**40AD**	**50AD**	**60AD**	**70AD**
	Jesus began his ministry	Paul became a Christian		Paul wrote Galatians	Romans destroyed the Temple in Jerusalem

1 From Paul, an apostle.*d* I was not chosen to be an apostle by human beings, nor was I sent from human beings. I was made an apostle through Jesus Christ and God the Father who raised Jesus from the dead. ²This letter is also from all those of God's family*n* who are with me.

To the churches in Galatia:*n*

³Grace and peace to you from God our Father and the Lord Jesus Christ. ⁴Jesus gave himself for our sins to free us from this evil world we live in, as God the Father planned. ⁵The glory belongs to God forever and ever. Amen.

The Only Good News

⁶God, by his grace through Christ, called you to become his people. So I am amazed that you are turning away so quickly and believing something different than the Good News.*d* ⁷Really, there is no other Good News. But some people are confusing you; they want to change the Good News

those ... family The Greek text says "brothers."
Galatia Probably the same country where Paul preached and began churches on his first missionary trip. Read the book of Acts, chapters 13 and 14.

CULTS

Good News, Bad News

Jeff Davis had gone to church off and on since he was little, but he had never felt he really needed God. That is, until last summer. Nearly everything Jeff did seemed to go wrong. He got fired from his summer job, then he totaled his car. Now his dad had moved out and wanted a divorce. Jeff began to wonder if maybe he could use help with his life.

He immediately thought of Phil Rogers. Nothing seemed to faze him. He seemed to have an inside track on the supernatural. He constantly read spiritual books and encouraged other kids to read them.

So Jeff started talking with Phil during lunch. Phil had an answer for every question Jeff asked. He made everything seem so simple and clear-cut. Phil talked about what it took to be one of the "Chosen Ones"—a new religious group Phil was involved with. "Wow," Jeff thought. "This guy really knows his stuff!"

Of course, Phil explained the Bible differently than Jeff had ever heard, but Phil seemed to know what he was talking about. It all seemed so simple. All you had to do is follow a list of rules and requirements, and you would be fine.

The more Jeff talked with Phil and read Phil's books, the more he began to feel like he, too, might finally be on the inside track to God. After all, wasn't he learning new things every day? Wasn't he trying to do all he was supposed to do to be one of the Chosen Ones?

But Jeff still wondered. Sometimes he would wake up in the middle of the night, afraid he had not done everything he was supposed to do. He would page through the books, studying the requirements and trying to shake the feeling that he wasn't good enough. Jeff wanted to talk to Phil about his doubts, but he was afraid that if he said anything, he might lose his place among the Chosen Ones.

Alone in the night, Jeff wished he could know he was right with God.

Read **Galatians 1:1–10** to see how the Galatians made the same mistake Jeff made.

- According to this passage (especially verses 4–6), how is the Good News very different from the requirements of groups like the Chosen Ones?
- Have you ever found yourself being attracted by the promises of a cult? What made the promises attractive? How did you resist the pull?

C O N S I D E R . . .

- forming a Bible study in your youth group to prepare people to respond to the claims made by different cults.
- sharing the Good News with someone in a cult. Take an older Christian with you who knows about the specific cult.

F O R   M O R E ,   S E E . . .

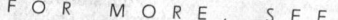

- Deuteronomy 13:1–4 (p. 173)
- Matthew 7:13–20 (p. 919)
- 1 John 4:1–6 (p. 1319)

of Christ. [8]We preached to you the Good News. So if we ourselves, or even an angel from heaven, should preach to you something different, we should be judged guilty! [9]I said this before, and now I say it again: You have already accepted the Good News. If anyone is preaching something different to you, he should be judged guilty!

> **SIDELIGHT:** If Paul wrote Galatians early in his missionary career—as some scholars believe—it may have been the first New Testament book written, dated less than twenty years after Jesus lived. Other scholars think either 1 Thessalonians (p. 1244) or James (p. 1293) was the first book written.

[10]Do you think I am trying to make people accept me? No, God is the One I am trying to please. Am I trying to please people? If I still wanted to please people, I would not be a servant of Christ.

Paul's Authority Is from God

[11]Brothers and sisters,[n] I want you to know that the Good News[d] I preached to you was not made up by human beings. [12]I did not get it from humans, nor did anyone teach it to me, but Jesus Christ showed it to me.

[13]You have heard about my past life in the Jewish religion. I attacked the church of God and tried to destroy it. [14]I was becoming a leader in the Jewish religion, doing better than most other Jews of my age. I tried harder than anyone else to follow the teachings handed down by our ancestors.

[15]But God had special plans for me and set me apart for his work even before I was born. He called me through his grace [16]and showed his son to me so that I might tell the Good News about him to those who are not Jewish. When God called me, I did not get advice or help from any person. [17]I did not go to Jerusalem to see those who were apostles[d] before I was. But, without waiting, I went away to Arabia and later went back to Damascus.

[18]After three years I went to Jerusalem to meet Peter and stayed with him for fifteen days. [19]I met no other apostles, except James, the brother of the Lord. [20]God knows that these things I write are not lies. [21]Later, I went to the areas of Syria and Cilicia.

[22]In Judea the churches in Christ had never met me. [23]They had only heard it said, "This man who was attacking us is now preaching the same faith that he once tried to destroy." [24]And these believers praised God because of me.

Other Apostles Accepted Paul

2 After fourteen years I went to Jerusalem again, this time with Barnabas. I also took Titus with me. [2]I went because God showed me I should go. I met with the believers there, and in private I told them leaders the Good News[d] that I preach to the non-Jewish people. I did not want my past work and the work I am now doing to be wasted. [3]Titus was with me, but he was not forced to be circumcised,[d] even though he was a Greek. [4]We talked about this problem because some false believers had come into our group secretly. They came in like spies to overturn the freedom we have in Christ Jesus. They wanted to make us slaves. [5]But we did not give in to those false believers for a minute. We wanted the truth of the Good News to continue for you.

[6]Those leaders who seemed to be important did not change the Good News that I preach. (It doesn't matter to me if they were "important" or not. To God everyone is the same.) [7]But these leaders saw that I had been given the work of telling the Good News to those who are not Jewish, just as Peter had the work of telling the Jews. [8]God gave Peter the power to work as an apostle[d] for the Jewish people. But he also gave me the power to work as an apostle for those who are not Jews. [9]James, Peter, and John, who seemed to be the leaders, understood that God had given me this special grace, so they accepted Barnabas and me. They agreed that they would go to the Jewish people and that we should go to those who are not Jewish. [10]The only thing they asked us was to remember to help the poor—something I really wanted to do.

Paul Shows that Peter Was Wrong

[11]When Peter came to Antioch, I challenged him to his face, because he was wrong. [12]Peter ate with the non-Jewish people until some Jewish people sent from James came to Antioch. When they arrived, Peter stopped eating with those who weren't Jewish, and he separated himself from them. He was afraid of the Jews. [13]So Peter was a hypocrite,[d] as were the other Jewish believers who joined with him. Even Barnabas was influenced by what these Jewish believers did. [14]When I saw they were not following the truth of the Good News,[d] I spoke to Peter in front of them all.

Brothers and sisters   Although the Greek text says "Brothers" here and throughout this book, Paul's words were meant for the entire church, including men and women.

I said, "Peter, you are a Jew, but you are not living like a Jew. You are living like those who are not Jewish. So why do you now try to force those who are not Jewish to live like Jews?"

15We were not born as non-Jewish "sinners," but as Jews. 16Yet we know that a person is made right with God not by following the law, but by trusting in Jesus Christ. So we, too, have put our faith in Christ Jesus, that we might be made right with God because we trusted in Christ. It is not because we followed the law, because no one can be made right with God by following the law.

17We Jews came to Christ, trying to be made right with God, and it became clear that we are sinners, too. Does this mean that Christ encourages sin? No! 18But I would really be wrong to begin teaching again those things that I gave up. 19It was the law that put me to death, and I died to the law so that I can now live for God. 20I was put to death on the cross with Christ, and I do not live anymore—it is Christ who lives in me. I still live in my body, but I live by faith in the Son of God who loved me and gave himself to save me. 21By saying these things I am not going against God's grace. Just the opposite, if the law could make us right with God, then Christ's death would be useless.

FAITH

You'd Better Believe It!

Pastor Crosby offered to take everyone out for pizza after Bible study. The kids cheered. Then the pastor disappeared upstairs to make a phone call.

"Did you hear that?" David asked James. "He's gonna buy us pizza!"

"There's no such thing as a free lunch, Dave. Look over there." James pointed toward a pile of brand new brooms, mops, buckets and sponges stacked against the wall. "When Crosby gets back, he's gonna tell us we've gotta clean the basement to pay for our lunch."

David had to admit James's theory made sense.

"Well, I'm starving," James continued. "If we gotta clean up, we might as well get going." He walked over and picked up one of the brooms.

"What are you guys doing?" Laura Moore asked.

"Well, what are you doing?" David asked sarcastically.

Laura was confused. "I'm waiting to go to lunch."

The boys laughed. "The sooner we get this basement cleaned, the sooner we can eat," David said, raising a storm of dust with his broom.

Laura started coughing. "You guys are making a big mess."

A few minutes later, Pastor Crosby walked into the dust storm. "What's going on down here? I thought I told you guys we were going out to lunch."

David stepped forward with a sheepish grin. "We figured you'd have us clean the basement before lunch, so we decided to get a head start."

"I just ordered pizzas at that new restaurant across town," Pastor Crosby said. "Let's go!"

James and David didn't believe their pastor's promise. Read **Galatians 2:11–21** to see how the apostle Peter didn't have faith in God's promises to him.

■ How is the boys' lack of faith in their pastor's promise similar to Peter's lack of faith in God's promises?

■ How have you acted like Peter in this passage and not believed God loves you and accepts you?

C O N S I D E R . . .

■ making a list of good deeds you have done to make God love and accept you. Then tear up the list to symbolize that faith—not good deeds—earns eternal life.

■ looking for "free" offers of things that really aren't free. Compare these things to God's free gift of eternal life through faith. Think about why it's hard for people to believe God's gift is really free.

F O R   M O R E ,   S E E . . .

■ Genesis 15:1–6 (p. 16)
■ Romans 3:21–31 (p. 1143)
■ Ephesians 2:4–10 (p. 1219)

Blessing Comes Through Faith

3 You people in Galatia were told very clearly about the death of Jesus Christ on the cross. But you were foolish; you let someone trick you. [2]Tell me this one thing: How did you receive the Holy Spirit?[d] Did you receive the Spirit by following the law? No, you received the Spirit because you heard the Good News[d] and believed it. [3]You began your life in Christ by the Spirit. Now are you trying to make it complete by your own power? That is foolish. [4]Were all your experiences wasted? I hope not! [5]Does God give you the Spirit and work miracles[d] among you because you follow the law? No, he does these things because you heard the Good News and believed it.

[6]The Scriptures[d] say the same thing about Abraham: "Abraham believed God, and God accepted Abraham's faith, and that faith made him right with God."[n] [7]So you should know that the true children of Abraham are those who have faith. [8]The Scriptures, telling what would happen in the future, said that God would make the non-Jewish people right through their faith. This Good News was told to Abraham beforehand, as the Scripture says: "All nations will be blessed through you."[n] [9]So all who believe as Abraham believed are blessed just as Abraham was. [10]But those who depend on following the law to make them right are under a curse, because the Scriptures say, "Anyone will be cursed who does not always obey what is written in the Book of the Law."[n] [11]Now it is clear that no one can be made right with God by the law, because the Scriptures say, "Those who are right with God will live by trusting in him."[n] [12]The law is not based on faith. It says, "A person who obeys these things will live because of them."[n] [13]Christ took away the curse the law put on us. He changed places with us and put himself under that curse. It is written in the Scriptures, "Anyone whose body is displayed on a tree[n] is cursed." [14]Christ did this so that God's blessing promised to Abraham might come through Jesus Christ to those who are not Jews. Jesus died so that by our believing we could receive the Spirit that God promised.

The Law and the Promise

[15]Brothers and sisters, let us think in human terms: Even an agreement made between two persons is firm. After that agreement is accepted by both people, no one can stop it or add anything to it. [16]God made promises both to Abraham and to his descendant.[d] God did not say, "and to your descendants." That would mean many people. But God said, "and to your descendant." That means only one person; that person is Christ. [17]This is what I mean: God had an agreement with Abraham and promised to keep it. The law, which came four hundred thirty years later, cannot change that agreement and so destroy God's promise to Abraham. [18]If the law could give us Abraham's blessing, then the promise would not be necessary. But that is not possible, because God freely gave his blessings to Abraham through the promise he had made.

[19]So what was the law for? It was given to show that the wrong things people do are against God's will. And it continued until the special descendant, who had been promised, came. The law was given through angels who used Moses for a mediator[n] to give the law to people. [20]But a mediator is not needed when there is only one side, and God is only one.

The Purpose of the Law of Moses

[21]Does this mean that the law is against God's promises? Never! That would be true only if the law could make us right. But God did not give a law that can bring life. [22]Instead, the Scriptures[d] showed that the whole world is bound by sin. This was so the promise would be given through faith to people who believe in Jesus Christ.

SIDELIGHT: The Greek word translated "guardian" in Galatians 3:24 could almost be translated "babysitter." It refers to the person—usually a slave—who was responsible for taking care of young children (see also Galatians 4:1–7, p. 1210). Possibly half of the population of the Roman Empire were slaves during New Testament times.

---

[23]Before this faith came, we were all held prisoners by the law. We had no freedom until God showed us the way of faith that was coming. [24]In other words, the law was our guardian leading us to Christ so that we could be made right with God through faith. [25]Now the way of faith has come, and we no longer live under a guardian.

"Abraham . . . God." Quotation from Genesis 15:6.
"All . . . you." Quotation from Genesis 12:3 and 18:18.
"Anyone . . . Law." Quotation from Deuteronomy 27:26.
"Those . . . him." Quotation from Habakkuk 2:4.
"A person . . . them." Quotation from Leviticus 18:5.
displayed on a tree Deuteronomy 21:22-23 says that when a person was killed for doing wrong, the body was hung on a tree to show shame. Paul means that the cross of Jesus was like that.
mediator A person who helps one person talk to or give something to another person.

26-27You were all baptized into Christ, and so you were all clothed with Christ. This means that you are all children of God through faith in Christ Jesus. 28In Christ, there is no difference between Jew and Greek, slave and free person, male and female. You are all the same in Christ Jesus. 29You belong to Christ, so you are Abraham's descendants.*d* You will inherit all of God's blessings because of the promise God made to Abraham.

4 I want to tell you this: While those who will inherit their fathers' property are still children, they are no different from slaves. It does not matter that the children own everything. 2While they are children, they must obey those who are chosen to care for them. But when the children reach the age set by their fathers, they are free. 3It is the same for us. We were once like children, slaves to the useless rules of this world. 4But when the right time came, God sent his Son who was born of a woman and lived under the law. 5God did this so he could buy freedom for those who were under the law and so we could become his children.

6Since you are God's children, God sent the Spirit of his Son into your hearts, and the Spirit*d* cries out, "Father." *n* 7So now you are not a slave; you are God's child, and God will give you the blessing he promised, because you are his child.

"Father"   Literally, "Abba, Father." Jewish children called their fathers "Abba."

JUDGING OTHERS

Inside Out

In this corner: Harold Milburn, Sunday school superintendent, board member, businessman. Gray suit and tie, starched shirt, thick glasses.

In that corner: Josh Kincaid, would-be radical, always off on some wild project to save the world, usually involving loud music. Orange-dyed mohawk, ripped jeans, T-shirt, earring.

Mohawk sizes up Starched Shirt. "He'll turn me down before I even ask. Old people are like that. Narrow-minded, afraid of anything new."

Starched Shirt sizes up Mohawk: "Oh, boy. Here we go. Another crazy idea. And if I say no, he'll call me old-fashioned."

"Hi, Josh. What's up?"

"We want to fix up the old fellowship hall for a place to have a weekly Bible study."

Starched Shirt frowns.

So does Mohawk. "I knew it," he thinks. "You think anybody who doesn't look like you can't be trusted."

"Hmmm," Starched Shirt muses. "These kids sure dress funny, but their hearts are in the right place."

"Sounds like a great idea to me," Starched Shirt finally says. "What's your first topic?"

Mohawk is down for the count. "Uh, the importance of prayer," he manages to get out.

"Now there's a subject I could always use some help with," Starched Shirt says.

"Well, Mr. Milburn," Mohawk grins, "why don't you join us sometime?"

Though people may be different on the outside, they are the same in Jesus Christ. Read this truth in **Galatians 3:23–29**.

■ How are Starched Shirt and Mohawk—or as it says in this passage, a Jew and a Greek—no different in Christ?

■ What criteria besides what is in this passage have you used to judge another Christian?

C O N S I D E R . . .

■ tearing out pictures of five people from a magazine. On each picture, write five preconceptions you have about people like that person. Check your perceptions by getting to know people in each category.

◄ visiting a church with a different culture. For example, if you are from a Spanish-speaking church, visit a Vietnamese church.

F O R   M O R E ,   S E E . . .

■ 1 Samuel 16:1–13 (p. 258)
■ Romans 2:28–29 (p. 1142)
■ 2 Corinthians 5:11–12 (p. 1197)

Paul's Love for the Christians

⁸In the past you did not know God. You were slaves to gods that were not real. ⁹But now you know the true God. Really, it is God who knows you. So why do you turn back to those weak and useless rules you followed before? Do you want to be slaves to those things again? ¹⁰You still follow teachings about special days, months, seasons, and years. ¹¹I am afraid for you, that my work for you has been wasted.

¹²Brothers and sisters, I became like you, so I beg you to become like me. You were very good to me before. ¹³You remember that it was because of an illness that I came to you the first time, preaching the Good News.ᵈ ¹⁴Though my sickness was a trouble for you, you did not hate me or make me leave. But you welcomed me as an angel from God, as if I were Jesus Christ himself! ¹⁵You were very happy then, but where is that joy now? I am ready to testify that you would have taken out your eyes and given them to me if that were possible. ¹⁶Now am I your enemy because I tell you the truth?

¹⁷Those peopleⁿ are working hard to persuade

Those people   They are the false teachers who were bothering the believers in Galatia (Galatians 1:7).

GOD'S LOVE

Too Good to Be True?

"Yours Free! Just Call and Claim Your Prize! No Obligation!" It was a once-in-a-lifetime offer that Jackie Sondheim couldn't refuse when it arrived in the mail.

Sure, Jackie had heard that some of these offers were scams. But this looked like a sure bet. It guaranteed she would get "a luxurious fur coat" or a "limited edition Mercedes sports car with all the extras."

"Everyone's a winner" the card boasted. "Call now to learn what you won!"

"What could it hurt," Jackie thought to herself, picking up the phone.

Sure enough, she had won! The fur coat was being packed for her. And, the contest's agent asked if she would also consider another special offer. For only $395 (charge it, if you like), she could receive beauty tips from "the nation's foremost beauty experts" in an exclusive newsletter for teenage girls called "Lookin' Good."

Plus, she would have access to a toll-free "Looks Line." She could call the number any time, day or night, and receive personal consultations on anything from shoes to eye shadow—for the rest of her life. It was just a one-time fee, Jackie told herself. And it was good for a lifetime. So she placed her order with her mom's credit card.

Jackie's excitement turned to displeasure when she received the genuine dyed rabbit fur coat. She knew she had been taken when the one-page "Lookin' Good" newsletter arrived, complete with revolutionary beauty tips such as "thoroughly wash your face each night before going to bed."

Something that had seemed like a dream just a few days earlier now seemed like a nightmare. It had sounded too good to be true. And it was.

All around us are too-good-to-be-true offers. Most are hoaxes. **Galatians 4:4–7** tells about an offer of God's love that seems too good to be true, but really is true!

■ What differences do you see between the once-in-a-lifetime offer Jackie fell for and the once-for-all-times offer of God's love that's described in the passage?

■ What parts of God's offer of love are most appealing to you? How have you responded to that offer?

C O N S I D E R . . .

■ using the form and style of a junk-mail offer to write a postcard about God's offer of love. Send it to a friend who needs some encouragement.

■ talking to a friend who was adopted about what it feels like to be specially chosen by parents. Discuss similarities and differences between that experience and the experience of being a child of God.

F O R   M O R E ,   S E E . . .

■ Isaiah 64:8–9 (p. 685)   ■ Romans 8:31–39 (p. 1152)

■ Matthew 7:7–11 (p. 919)

you, but this is not good for you. They want to persuade you to turn against us and follow only them. [18]It is good for people to show interest in you, but only if their purpose is good. This is always true, not just when I am with you. [19]My little children, again I feel the pain of childbirth for you until you truly become like Christ. [20]I wish I could be with you now and could change the way I am talking to you, because I do not know what to think about you.

The Example of Hagar and Sarah

[21]Some of you still want to be under the law. Tell me, do you know what the law says? [22]The Scriptures[d] say that Abraham had two sons. The mother of one son was a slave woman, and the mother of the other son was a free woman. [23]Abraham's son from the slave woman was born in the normal human way. But the son from the free woman was born because of the promise God made to Abraham.

[24]This story teaches something else: The two women are like the two agreements between God and his people. One agreement is the law that God made on Mount Sinai,[n] and the people who are under this agreement are like slaves. The mother named Hagar is like that agreement. [25]She is like Mount Sinai in Arabia and is a picture of the earthly Jewish city of Jerusalem. This city and its people, the Jews, are slaves to the law. [26]But the heavenly Jerusalem, which is above, is like the free woman. She is our mother. [27]It is written in the Scriptures:

"Be happy, Jerusalem.
　　You are like a woman who never gave
　　　　birth to children.
Start singing and shout for joy.
　　You never felt the pain of giving birth,
but you will have more children
　　than the woman who has a husband."

Isaiah 54:1

[28]My brothers and sisters, you are God's children because of his promise, as Isaac was then. [29]The son who was born in the normal way treated the other son badly. It is the same today. [30]But what does the Scripture say? "Throw out the slave woman and her son. The son of the slave woman should not inherit anything. The son of the free woman should receive it all."[n] [31]So, my brothers and sisters, we are not children of the slave woman, but of the free woman.

Keep Your Freedom

5 We have freedom now, because Christ made us free. So stand strong. Do not change and go back into the slavery of the law. [2]Listen, I Paul tell you that if you go back to the law by being circumcised,[d] Christ does you no good. [3]Again, I warn every man: If you allow yourselves to be circumcised, you must follow all the law. [4]If you try to be made right with God through the law, your life with Christ is over — you have left God's grace. [5]But we have the true hope that comes from being made right with God, and by the Spirit we wait eagerly for this hope. [6]When we are in Christ Jesus, it is not important if we are circumcised or not. The important thing is faith — the kind of faith that works through love.

> ⚘ **SIDELIGHT:** Circumcision (Galatians 5:2–6) was an important ritual for Jews, symbolizing bringing a baby boy into God's family. A festive occasion marked each circumcision, which was usually performed by the boy's father.

[7]You were running a good race. Who stopped you from following the true way? [8]This change did not come from the One who chose you. [9]Be careful! "Just a little yeast makes the whole batch of dough rise." [10]But I trust in the Lord that you will not believe those different ideas. Whoever is confusing you with such ideas will be punished.

[11]My brothers and sisters, I do not teach that a man must be circumcised. If I teach circumcision, why am I still being attacked? If I still taught circumcision, my preaching about the cross would not be a problem. [12]I wish the people who are bothering you would castrate[n] themselves!

[13]My brothers and sisters, God called you to be free, but do not use your freedom as an excuse to do what pleases your sinful self. Serve each other with love. [14]The whole law is made complete in this one command: "Love your neighbor as you love yourself."[n] [15]If you go on hurting each other and tearing each other apart, be careful, or you will completely destroy each other.

The Spirit and Human Nature

[16]So I tell you: Live by following the Spirit.[d] Then you will not do what your sinful selves want. [17]Our sinful selves want what is against the

---

Mount Sinai   Mountain in Arabia where God gave his laws to Moses (Exodus 19 and 20).
"Throw ... all."   Quotation from Genesis 21:10.
castrate   To cut off part of the male sex organ. Paul uses this word because it is similar to "circumcision." Paul wanted to show that he is very upset with the false teachers.
"Love ... yourself."   Quotation from Leviticus 19:18.

Spirit, and the Spirit wants what is against our sinful selves. The two are against each other, so you cannot do just what you please. ¹⁸But if the Spirit is leading you, you are not under the law.

¹⁹The wrong things the sinful self does are clear: being sexually unfaithful, not being pure, taking part in sexual sins, ²⁰worshiping gods, doing witchcraft,ᵈ hating, making trouble, being jealous, being angry, being selfish, making people angry with each other, causing divisions among people, ²¹feeling envy, being drunk, having wild and wasteful parties, and doing other things like these. I warn you now as I warned you before: Those who do these things will not inherit God's kingdom. ²²But the Spirit produces the fruit of love, joy, peace, patience, kindness, goodness, faithfulness, ²³gentleness, self-control. There is no law that says these things are wrong. ²⁴Those who belong to Christ Jesus have crucified their own

sinful selves. They have given up their old selfish feelings and the evil things they wanted to do. ²⁵We get our new life from the Spirit, so we should follow the Spirit. ²⁶We must not be proud or make trouble with each other or be jealous of each other.

Help Each Other

6 Brothers and sisters, if someone in your group does something wrong, you who are spiritual should go to that person and gently help make him right again. But be careful, because you might be tempted to sin, too. ²By helping each other with your troubles, you truly obey the law of Christ. ³If anyone thinks he is important when he really is not, he is only fooling himself. ⁴Each person should judge his own actions and not compare himself with others. Then he can be proud for what he himself has done. ⁵Each person must be responsible for himself.

SERVICE

Free to Serve

The 1970s. "Feathered" hair, disco, the Bee Gees.
And Watergate.

The scandal of Watergate led to the first resignation by an American president since the nation was founded. It was a turbulent time, full of suspicion, intrigue, distrust, and power-hungry leaders. In the middle of it was Charles W. Colson.

Chuck Colson was a presidential aide for Richard Nixon. He was one of several White House personnel who were sentenced to prison for their involvement in the Watergate scandal. Colson served seven months.

Before he was sent to prison, Colson became a Christian. And while in prison, he saw firsthand the tremendous obstacles facing prisoners, ex-prisoners, and their families. "Rather than rehabilitating, prisons have become breeding grounds for crime," he says.

After his release from prison, Colson could have done like many people. He could have forgotten about his prison experience and gone on with his life. But he chose not to forget. He founded Prison Fellowship, a Christian outreach to inmates. Today, Colson regularly visits prisons and works for prison reform in the United States and in countries around the world.

Because of Colson's organization, nearly forty thousand volunteers work in more than six hundred prisons in the United States alone. His dedicated concern has resulted in the changed lives of thousands of inmates and families.

Chuck Colson turned his freedom into an opportunity to help those in prison. **Galatians 5:13–26** talks about the relationship between freedom and service. Read the passage to discover why God sets people free.

■ How does Colson's choice to serve prisoners reflect this passage?
■ How have you used your freedom in Christ as an avenue to serve others?

C O N S I D E R . . .
■ using some of your "free time" to serve other people.
■ becoming a pen pal with a prison inmate, or contacting Prison Fellowship, Box 17500, Washington, DC 20041, to see how you can serve in your area.

F O R   M O R E ,   S E E . . .
■ Leviticus 19:17–18 (p. 116)
■ 1 Corinthians 10:23–24 (p. 1180)
■ Philippians 2:4–7 (p. 1230)

⁶Anyone who is learning the teaching of God should share all the good things he has with his teacher.

Life Is like Planting a Field

⁷Do not be fooled: You cannot cheat God. People harvest only what they plant. ⁸If they plant to satisfy their sinful selves, their sinful selves will bring them ruin. But if they plant to please the Spirit,ᵈ they will receive eternal life from the Spirit. ⁹We must not become tired of doing good. We will receive our harvest of eternal life at the right time if we do not give up. ¹⁰When we have the opportunity to help anyone, we should do it. But we should give special attention to those who are in the family of believers.

Paul Ends His Letter

¹¹See what large letters I use to write this myself. ¹²Some people are trying to force you to be circumcisedᵈ so the Jews will accept them. They are afraid they will be attacked if they follow only

> **SIDELIGHT:** Paul may have had a lot to say, but he probably didn't have good handwriting (Galatians 6:11). From Galatians 4:13–15 (p. 1211), some scholars think he might have had poor eyesight, because he thanks them for their generosity in being willing to take out their eyes and give them to him.

FRIENDS

When Friends Fail

Scott Perkins couldn't believe his eyes. There was Jason Haas, smoking a cigarette and laughing with the rest of the lunchtime crowd in the student parking lot.

"Didn't I tell you he was a phony?" Denise Rambo whispered. "I wish he'd stop coming to church altogether and hang out with his real friends."

"Hmmm," Scott thought. "I wonder what's going on here."

The next morning, he bumped into Jason between classes. "Wanna grab a burger for lunch?" Scott asked.

Jason looked down. "I don't think so."

Scott put his hand on Jason's shoulder. "Hey, you haven't been yourself lately. I wish we could talk about it."

Jason brushed him off. "I know what you want to talk about—you and Denise and everyone else. You're gonna be all nice and buy me a burger and then jump all over my case for being a big, bad sinner. Well, I don't want to hear it."

He turned to leave, but Scott grabbed his arm. "Wait a second. Number one, you're no bigger or worse a sinner than I am. Number two, I know if I suddenly had a total personality change I'd want my friends to investigate. And number three, you're buying your own burger."

Jason smiled. "Okay. You win. There are a couple of things I wouldn't mind talking about. And you're probably the only guy I know who'd care enough to listen."

Scott understood what it meant to be a real friend. Read **Galatians 6:1–10** to learn about the responsibilities of Christian friendship.

■ Who most closely lived out this scripture: Scott or Denise?

■ When have you acted out this scripture to help a fellow Christian who's done something wrong? When has another Christian gently corrected you? What were the results of either time?

CONSIDER . . .

■ developing a friendship with an older Christian. Discuss your own areas of weakness with your new friend and ask him or her to help you avoid stumbling into sin.

■ starting a prayer group with your friends. Discuss ways to draw closer and watch out for one another.

FOR MORE, SEE . . .

■ Proverbs 27:6, 9–10 (p. 591)
■ Luke 22:31–32 (p. 1049)
■ Hebrews 10:24–25 (p. 1286)

the cross of Christ.[n] [13]Those who are circumcised do not obey the law themselves, but they want you to be circumcised so they can brag about what they forced you to do. [14]I hope I will never brag about things like that. The cross of our Lord Jesus Christ is my only reason for bragging. Through the cross of Jesus my world was crucified, and I died to the world. [15]It is not important if a man is circumcised or uncircumcised. The important thing is being the new people God has made. [16]Peace and mercy to those who follow this rule—and to all of God's people.

[17]So do not give me any more trouble. I have scars on my body that show[n] I belong to Christ Jesus.

[18]My brothers and sisters, the grace of our Lord Jesus Christ be with your spirit. Amen.

---

cross of Christ   Paul uses the cross as a picture of the gospel, the story of Christ's death and rising from the dead to pay for our sins. The cross, or Christ's death, was God's way to save us.

that show   Many times Paul was beaten and whipped by people who were against him because he was teaching about Christ. The scars were from these beatings.

EPHESIANS

Why Read This Book:

■ Discover the blessings we have because we belong to Christ (Ephesians 1—3).
■ Learn how to be united in our relationships with others (Ephesians 4—6:4).
■ Gather the armor you need to follow God (Ephesians 6:10–20).

Behind the Scenes:

Has anything ever happened to you that was so great that you couldn't help but burst into song? When you read the book of Ephesians, you get the feeling the author felt that way about being a Christian.

The book is like a grand musical celebration of the Christian faith. It sings about God, Christ, human redemption, the church, God's power, and unity in Christ. Many people describe it as the climax of the New Testament.

Probably intended for several churches in Asia, including Ephesus, the book focuses on God's eternal purpose in establishing the universal church on earth. No matter what their background or nationality, all people are called to become part of Christ's body, which is both a privilege and a responsibility.

The first part of the book (Ephesians 1—3) uses prayers and praise to describe God's plan to unite all things in Christ. The second part (Ephesians 4—6) describes Christians' role in fulfilling God's plan.

As Christians, we come from various backgrounds, and attend different churches. Yet we share in the same blessings from God, and are called to live our lives according to Christ's example.

WHERE THE ACTION WAS

The temple of the goddess Artemis (see Acts 19:35–37, p. 1129) was one of the seven wonders of the ancient world.

The city of Ephesus was the fourth largest city in the Roman Empire. Paul spent more than two years there (see Acts 19:1–20:1, p. 1128).

An inland harbor (now filled in with silt) made Ephesus a major trading center.

Ephesus

GREECE

Mediterranean Sea

Silversmiths rioted in the theater because Paul challenged the power of the idols they made (see Acts 19:23-41, p. 1129). The theater would seat 24,000 people.

City wall

WHEN THE ACTION WAS

Jesus was born	The church began soon after Jesus went to heaven		Paul began his missionary work	Paul may have written Ephesians in prison	Fire destroyed Rome
BC/AD	20AD	30AD	40AD	50AD	60AD	70AD
	Jesus began his ministry	Paul became a Christian		Paul worked in Ephesus for more than two years	Romans destroyed the Temple in Jerusalem

1 From Paul, an apostle*d* of Christ Jesus. I am an apostle because that is what God wanted.

To God's holy people living in Ephesus, believers in Christ Jesus:

²Grace and peace to you from God our Father and the Lord Jesus Christ.

Spiritual Blessings in Christ

³Praise be to the God and Father of our Lord Jesus Christ. In Christ, God has given us every spiritual blessing in the heavenly world. ⁴That is, in Christ, he chose us before the world was made so that we would be his holy people — people without blame before him. ⁵Because of his love, God had already decided to make us his own children through Jesus Christ. That was what he wanted and what pleased him, ⁶and it brings praise to God because of his wonderful grace. God gave that grace to us freely, in Christ, the One he loves. ⁷In Christ we are set free by the blood of his death, and so we have forgiveness of sins. How rich is God's grace, ⁸which he has given to us so fully and freely. God, with full wisdom and understanding, ⁹let us know his secret purpose. This was what God wanted, and he planned to do it through Christ ¹⁰His goal was to carry out his plan, when the right time came, that all things in

---

FORGIVENESS

Putting Up Bail

"Now I've done it," Bob Logan thought as he slammed his fist into the dashboard. The nose of his car was buried in someone's hedge, and red and blue lights were flashing in his rear-view mirror.

To make matters worse, Bob had been drinking. He hoped the police officer would be kind. More than that, he hoped his dad would be. This was the third time this year Bob had wrecked his car, and he figured his dad would explode when he found out.

Bob was arrested and allowed one phone call home. His mother cried as he told her what had happened. No one bailed Bob out; he spent the night in jail. He thought he would never be able to face his parents again.

In the morning, an officer yelled at Bob to get up and follow him. Bob left the stench of the cell and stepped into the white light of the police station. The first person Bob saw was his dad, standing with his hat in his hands, looking at the floor.

"Thanks . . ." Bob started and then stopped, unsure of how his dad would react. His dad looked up, and Bob saw the compassion in his eyes.

"Come on, Son," he said, "let's get out of here."

As they walked out of the station, Bob tried to explain. "Dad, I'm so sorry. It'll never happen again. I promise."

"Bob, you've made some big mistakes—mistakes that could've killed you," his dad responded.

Bob tried to speak, but his dad stopped him. "Son, I love you, and we're going to get through this together."

Although Bob's father forgave him, Bob still suffered some heavy consequences: He lost his license for ninety days, and it took him six months to repay the bail money. But Bob's relationship with his dad remained strong.

Being forgiven by his dad set Bob free. **Ephesians 1:1–10** describes how our Heavenly Father has set us free.

■ How is Bob's experience of forgiveness like the forgiveness described in this passage? How is it different?

■ According to this passage, what are the benefits of God's forgiveness to those who are in Christ?

CONSIDER . . .

■ forgiving someone and setting that person free.

■ making a card that says "Christians Aren't Perfect, Just Forgiven." Put it by your bed and think about its meaning each time you see it this week.

FOR MORE, SEE . . .

■ Psalm 103 (p. 540)   ■ Colossians 1:13–14 (p. 1239)

■ Romans 3:21–26 (p. 1143)

heaven and on earth would be joined together in Christ as the head.

[11]In Christ we were chosen to be God's people, because from the very beginning God had decided this in keeping with his plan. And he is the One who makes everything agree with what he decides and wants. [12]We are the first people who hoped in Christ, and we were chosen so that we would bring praise to God's glory. [13]So it is with you. When you heard the true teaching—the Good News[d] about your salvation—you believed in Christ. And in Christ, God put his special mark of ownership on you by giving you the Holy Spirit[d] that he had promised. [14]That Holy Spirit is the guarantee that we will receive what God promised for his people until God gives full freedom to those who are his—to bring praise to God's glory.

Paul's Prayer

[15]That is why since I heard about your faith in the Lord Jesus and your love for all God's people, [16]I have not stopped giving thanks to God for you. I always remember you in my prayers, [17]asking the God of our Lord Jesus Christ, the glorious Father, to give you a spirit of wisdom and revelation[d] so that you will know him better. [18]I pray also that you will have greater understanding in your heart so you will know the hope to which he has called us and that you will know how rich and glorious are the blessings God has promised his holy people. [19]And you will know that God's

---

GOD'S POWER

Batteries Included

Tony DeFazio might never have turned around except for the ministry of Richard Parks. A street kid, Tony ran away from his home in Newport, Oregon, when he was only eleven years old. He lived on handouts for a while but soon found that selling drugs earned him a better living. He was in and out of various homes and schools for seven years.

Then when he was eighteen, he met Richard on a street corner in Portland. Richard, a reformed street kid himself, was dedicated to getting kids off the streets through his work in an inner-city church. Richard found Tony a place to live and helped him get a job in a nearby gas station. He helped turn Tony around.

Tony was just one of many kids whom Richard reached with his love. When the local police heard about Richard's ministry, they asked how they could get involved. They figured their additional resources would expand the program, add energy and make it more effective.

After learning about the program, one officer remarked: "That's great. We'd be glad to help. But can we leave out the stuff about Jesus?"

Overhearing the question, Tony replied: "Hey man, you might as well take out the batteries. Jesus is what makes it work!"

Tony knew God's power was what had changed his life. This same power is available to all Christians, as we read in **Ephesians 1:15–23**.

■ According to this passage, how is God's power different from earthly powers?

■ How does this passage say to tap into God's power supply?

C O N S I D E R . . .

■ writing a radio commercial announcing the benefits of God's power. Read the commercial to a friend or family member.

◗ applying God's power to your life in an area in which you have felt weak. Pray and work together with God to change that weakness.

F O R   M O R E ,   S E E . . .

■ 1 Chronicles 29:11–12 (p. 384)
■ Acts 1:7–8 (p. 1098)

■ Ephesians 3:20–21 (p. 1222)

power is very great for us who believe. That power is the same as the great strength ²⁰God used to raise Christ from the dead and put him at his right side in the heavenly world. ²¹God has put Christ over all rulers, authorities, powers, and kings, not only in this world but also in the next. ²²God put everything under his power and made him the head over everything for the church, ²³which is Christ's body. The church is filled with Christ, and Christ fills everything in every way.

We Now Have Life

2 In the past you were spiritually dead because of your sins and the things you did against God. ²Yes, in the past you lived the way the world lives, following the ruler of the evil powers that are above the earth. That same spirit is now work-ing in those who refuse to obey God. ³In the past all of us lived like them, trying to please our sinful selves and doing all the things our bodies and minds wanted. We should have suffered God's anger because of the way we were. We were the same as all other people.

⁴But God's mercy is great, and he loved us very much. ⁵Though we were spiritually dead because of the things we did against God, he gave us new life with Christ. You have been saved by God's grace. ⁶And he raised us up with Christ and gave us a seat with him in the heavens. He did this for those in Christ Jesus ⁷so that for all future time he could show the very great riches of his grace by being kind to us in Christ Jesus. ⁸I mean that you have been saved by grace through believing. You did not save yourselves; it was a gift from God. ⁹It was not the result of your own efforts, so you can-

PEACE

Enemy in My House

Ellie Gamble and her father were best friends. She had always run to him when she was hurt. But when Ellie was in junior high, everything changed. Her father began spending more time away from home. And when he was home, he and Ellie's mother fought all the time.

One day after school, Ellie found her mother lying across her bed, crying. The closet doors hung open, and her father's clothes were gone. Ellie's father had been having an affair and had moved out. Ellie couldn't believe it. She felt betrayed. How could her dad walk out on her like this?

Within three months, Ellie's parents were together, trying to restore their marriage. But Ellie couldn't see herself loving her father again. She avoided him. She even put a "No Men Allowed" sign on her bedroom door.

When Ellie went away to college, she was relieved to get away from the tense relationship with her dad. But during her freshman year, she heard the gospel and decided to follow Christ.

Her life began to change. She realized God wanted to rebuild her relationship with her dad. While home one weekend, Ellie cried as she told her dad she forgave him and asked him to forgive her.

From that point on, there was peace in Ellie's home—the kind of peace that made her homesick for time with her father.

God's love brought peace between Ellie and her dad. Read **Ephesians 2:4–22** to see how Christ also broke down the walls and established peace between the Jews and those who were not Jews.

■ How was Ellie's broken relationship with her dad like the broken relationship between Jewish and non-Jewish people? How was it different?
■ How can Christ break down walls of hatred between you and other people you know?

C O N S I D E R . . .
■ asking God to reveal any walls in your relationships that need to be broken down.
■ making peace with someone from whom you feel separated by giving that person a brick or rock and explaining that you want to break down the "wall" between you.

F O R   M O R E ,   S E E . . .
■ Psalm 120:6–7 (p. 554)   ■ Hebrews 12:14–15 (p. 1290)
■ Romans 9 (p. 1153)

not brag about it. [10]God has made us what we are. In Christ Jesus, God made us to do good works, which God planned in advance for us to live our lives doing.

One in Christ

[11]You were not born Jewish. You are the people the Jews call "uncircumcised."[n] Those who call you "uncircumcised" call themselves "circumcised."[d] (Their circumcision is only something they themselves do on their bodies.) [12]Remember that in the past you were without Christ. You were not citizens of Israel, and you had no part in the agreements[n] with the promise that God made to his people. You had no hope, and you did not know God. [13]But now in Christ Jesus, you who were far away from God are brought near through the blood of Christ's death. [14]Christ himself is our peace. He made both Jewish people and those who are not Jews one people. They were separated as if there were a wall between them, but Christ broke down that wall of hate by giving his own body. [15]The Jewish law had many com-

mands and rules, but Christ ended that law. His purpose was to make the two groups of people become one new people in him and in this way make peace. [16]It was also Christ's purpose to end the hatred between the two groups, to make them into one body, and to bring them back to God. Christ did all this with his death on the cross. [17]Christ came and preached peace to you who were far away from God, and to those who were near to God. [18]Yes, it is through Christ we all have the right to come to the Father in one Spirit.[d]

[19]Now you who are not Jewish are not foreigners or strangers any longer, but are citizens together with God's holy people. You belong to God's family. [20]You are like a building that was built on the foundation of the apostles[d] and prophets.[d] Christ Jesus himself is the most important stone[n] in that building, [21]and that whole building is joined together in Christ. He makes it grow and become a holy temple in the Lord. [22]And in Christ you, too, are being built together with the Jews into a place where God lives through the Spirit.

uncircumcised   People not having the mark of circumcision as the Jews had.
agreements   The agreements that God gave to his people in the Old Testament.
most important stone   Literally, "cornerstone." The first and most important stone in a building.

Paul's Work in Telling the Good News

3 So I, Paul, am a prisoner of Christ Jesus for you who are not Jews. [2]Surely you have heard that God gave me this work through his grace to help you. [3]He let me know his secret by showing it to me. I have already written a little

---

SIDELIGHT: To describe Jesus as the "most important stone" or cornerstone (Ephesians 2:20) makes him essential for the "building." When construction workers started building, they would first place one stone—the cornerstone—and then line up all the walls based on this stone.

---

about this. [4]If you read what I wrote then, you can see that I truly understand the secret about the Christ.[d] [5]People who lived in other times were not told that secret. But now, through the Spirit,[d] God has shown that secret to his holy apostles[d] and prophets.[d] [6]This is that secret: that

through the Good News[d] those who are not Jews will share with the Jews in God's blessing. They belong to the same body, and they share together in the promise that God made in Christ Jesus.

[7]By God's special gift of grace given to me through his power, I became a servant to tell that Good News. [8]I am the least important of all God's people, but God gave me this gift — to tell those who are not Jews the Good News about the riches of Christ, which are too great to understand fully. [9]And God gave me the work of telling all people about the plan for his secret, which has been hidden in him since the beginning of time. He is the One who created everything. [10]His purpose was that through the church all the rulers and powers in the heavenly world will now know God's wisdom, which has so many forms. [11]This agrees with the purpose God had since the beginning of time, and he carried out his plan through Christ Jesus our Lord. [12]In Christ we can come before God with freedom and without fear. We can do this through faith in Christ. [13]So I ask you not to become discouraged because of the sufferings I am having for you. My sufferings are for your glory.

CHURCH

Friends or Foes?

After several months of fighting among Westside Church members, the get-rid-of-the-pastor side won. Pastor Howard fought back tears as he announced his resignation on Sunday morning. He packed up his office and home. and moved away within a month.

Many church members on the keep-the-pastor side were angry and disillusioned; most of them left the Westside Church within six months. Some went to other churches. But some stayed away from the church for years.

Those who stayed at Westside Church hired a new pastor—one they were sure they would like much better than Pastor Howard. But in less than two years, the church members were fighting again. They ordered the new pastor to leave, and the cycle began again.

After watching the church destroy itself for the second time, one of the young people commented, "I don't think you can even call this place a church—anyway, I don't think it's what God meant for the church to be."

This teenager's perception fits the description of the church in **Ephesians 4:1–6**. Read this scripture to see what God wants the church to be like.
- If Westside Church members had applied these verses to their situation, how would the outcome have been different?
- How can you use this passage to promote unity within your church?

CONSIDER . . .
- encouraging your youth group to pray weekly for your church to be united.
- talking to your pastor about creating an annual "Unity Award" for church members who consistently promote unity in your church.

FOR MORE, SEE . . .
- Psalm 133 (p. 558)
- Titus 3:9–11 (p. 1271)
- 1 Peter 3:8–12 (p. 1306)

The Love of Christ

¹⁴So I bow in prayer before the Father ¹⁵from whom every family in heaven and on earth gets its true name. ¹⁶I ask the Father in his great glory to give you the power to be strong inwardly through his Spirit.ᵈ ¹⁷I pray that Christ will live in your hearts by faith and that your life will be strong in love and be built on love. ¹⁸And I pray that you and all God's holy people will have the power to understand the greatness of Christ's love — how wide and how long and how high and how deep that love is. ¹⁹Christ's love is greater than anyone can ever know, but I pray that you will be able to know that love. Then you can be filled with the fullness of God.

²⁰With God's power working in us, God can do much, much more than anything we can ask or imagine. ²¹To him be glory in the church and in Christ Jesus for all time, forever and ever. Amen.

The Unity of the Body

4 I am in prison because I belong to the Lord. God chose you to be his people, so I urge you now to live the life to which God called you. ²Always be humble, gentle, and patient, accepting each other in love. ³You are joined together with peace through the Spirit,ᵈ so make every effort to continue together in this way. ⁴There is one body and one Spirit, and God called you to have one hope. ⁵There is one Lord, one faith, and one baptism. ⁶There is one God and Father of everything. He rules everything and is everywhere and is in everything.

> **SIDELIGHT:** Christian unity is central to the book of Ephesians. The word "one" appears seven times in Ephesians 4:4–6 alone!

⁷Christ gave each one of us the special gift of grace, showing how generous he is. ⁸That is why it says in the Scriptures,ᵈ

"When he went up to the heights,
  he led a parade of captives,
  and he gave gifts to people."   *Psalm 68:18*

CULTS

Hazardous to Your Health

Jim Jones was an ordained minister who thought he was the messiah. Jones demanded total allegiance from his followers, telling them he was going to create the perfect society—free from hate, crime, and lack of anything.

People believed him. They sold everything they had and gave it to Jones. Nearly a thousand people followed Jones to Guyana in South America, where he established a settlement called Jonestown.

In 1978, Leo Ryan, a United States representative from California traveled to Jonestown to investigate rumors that Jones was holding some people against their will. In fear of being caught, Jones had Ryan and three journalists who accompanied Ryan killed. Then to destroy all evidence of his lies and deceit, Jones ordered his followers to take poison in a religious ceremony. More than nine hundred people—including Jones himself—died in what is now called the "Jonestown Massacre."

The people in Jonestown didn't recognize Jim Jones's lies. **Ephesians 4:11–16** warns us to be mature so we can recognize false teachings.
- How were the people in Jim Jones's church like the babies described in this passage?
- Has anyone ever tried to lead you down the wrong path like this passage talks about? How did the truth help you stay on God's path?

CONSIDER...
- talking to your pastor or other church leader about the elements of truth that your own church emphasizes.
- asking your pastor or youth leader to lead a study on a new "religious movement" to discover whether or not it is founded on the truth.

FOR MORE, SEE...
- Proverbs 4 (p. 570)
- Romans 1:18–32 (p. 1141)
- Philippians 4:8–9 (p. 1234)

[9]When it says, "He went up," what does it mean? It means that he first came down to the earth. [10]So Jesus came down, and he is the same One who went up above all the sky. Christ did that to fill everything with his presence. [11]And Christ gave gifts to people — he made some to be apostles,[d] some to be prophets,[d] some to go and tell the Good News,[d] and some to have the work of caring for and teaching God's people. [12]Christ gave those gifts to prepare God's holy people for the work of serving, to make the body of Christ stronger. [13]This work must continue until we are all joined together in the same faith and in the same knowledge of the Son of God. We must become like a mature person, growing un- until we become like Christ and have his perfec- tion.

[14]Then we will no longer be babies. We will not be tossed about like a ship that the waves carry one way and then another. We will not be influenced by every new teaching we hear from people who are trying to fool us. They make plans and try any kind of trick to fool people into follow- ing the wrong path. [15]No! Speaking the truth with love, we will grow up in every way into Christ, who is the head. [16]The whole body depends on Christ, and all the parts of the body are joined and held together. Each part does its own work to make the whole body grow and be strong with love.

The Way You Should Live

[17]In the Lord's name, I tell you this. Do not continue living like those who do not believe. Their thoughts are worth nothing. [18]They do not understand, and they know nothing, because they refuse to listen. So they cannot have the life that God gives. [19]They have lost all feeling of shame, and they use their lives for doing evil. They con- tinually want to do all kinds of evil. [20]But what you learned in Christ was not like this. [21]I know that you heard about him, and you are in him, so you were taught the truth that is in Jesus. [22]You were taught to leave your old self — to stop living the evil way you lived before. That old self be- comes worse, because people are fooled by the evil things they want to do. [23]But you were taught to be made new in your hearts, [24]to become a new person. That new person is made to be like God — made to be truly good and holy.

[25]So you must stop telling lies. Tell each other the truth, because we all belong to each other in

---

ANGER

Handle With Care

Clarisse Olson wasn't having a good day. Her boyfriend broke up with her before her first class. She got her math test back and knew her parents would not be pleased with the score. She missed lunch. And then she mouthed off at her P.E. teacher.

She shook her head as she recalled the incident.

"Come on, Clarisse," Mr. Eaton had yelled. "You can't do push-ups with your fanny in the air. Try fifty more, and do them right this time!"

Clarisse felt the anger well up inside her as she started over again. "One . . . two . . . three . . ." she counted.

"I'd like to see you do fifty push-ups, you fat slob," Clarisse mumbled — a little louder than she intended.

Now she was sitting in the detention room while everyone else in school was in a pep assembly for the homecoming game.

"If only I'd kept my mouth shut," Clarisse moaned.

Sometimes our anger can get us into trouble. Read the warning about anger in **Ephesians 4:25 — 5:2**.

■ According to this passage, did Clarisse's anger lead to sin or not?
■ How can you be angry, and yet not sin?

CONSIDER . . .

■ listing three things that make you angry. Beside each one, write a brief description of how you can handle the situation without sinning.
■ resolving to deal quickly with things that make you angry.

FOR MORE, SEE . . .

■ Psalm 4 (p. 483)
■ Proverbs 22:24–25 (p. 587)

■ James 1:19–20 (p. 1294)

the same body.*n* *26*When you are angry, do not sin, and be sure to stop being angry before the end of the day. *27*Do not give the devil a way to defeat you. *28*Those who are stealing must stop stealing and start working. They should earn an honest living for themselves. Then they will have something to share with those who are poor.

*29*When you talk, do not say harmful things, but say what people need — words that will help others become stronger. Then what you say will do good to those who listen to you. *30*And do not make the Holy Spirit*d* sad. The Spirit is God's proof that you belong to him. God gave you the Spirit to show that God will make you free when the final day comes. *31*Do not be bitter or angry or mad. Never shout angrily or say things to hurt others. Never do anything evil. *32*Be kind and loving to each other, and forgive each other just as God forgave you in Christ.

Living in the Light

5 You are God's children whom he loves, so try to be like him. *2*Live a life of love just as Christ loved us and gave himself for us as a sweet-smelling offering and sacrifice to God.

*3*But there must be no sexual sin among you, or any kind of evil or greed. Those things are not right for God's holy people. *4*Also, there must be no evil talk among you, and you must not speak foolishly or tell evil jokes. These things are not right for you. Instead, you should be giving thanks to God. *5*You can be sure of this: No one will have a place in the kingdom of Christ and of God who sins sexually, or does evil things, or is greedy. Anyone who is greedy is serving a false god.

*6*Do not let anyone fool you by telling you things that are not true, because these things will bring God's anger on those who do not obey him. *7*So have nothing to do with them. *8*In the past you were full of darkness, but now you are full of light in the Lord. So live like children who belong to the light. *9*Light brings every kind of goodness, right living, and truth. *10*Try to learn what pleases the Lord. *11*Have nothing to do with the things done in darkness, which are not worth anything. But show that they are wrong. *12*It is shameful even to talk about what those people do in secret. *13*But the light makes all things easy to see, *14*and everything that is made easy to see can become light. This is why it is said:

"Wake up, sleeper!
  Rise from death,
and Christ will shine on you."

*15*So be very careful how you live. Do not live

Tell . . . body. Quotation from Zechariah 8:16.

Who's Gonna Know?

Rob was having the time of his life on tour in Germany with his community orchestra — and no parents! There were chaperones, of course, but Rob was making his own decisions and loving every minute of it.

On Saturday night, Rob's friends went out to get their first taste of German beer. Most band members were excited to take advantage of Germany's lax alcohol laws.

Rob wasn't sure. He didn't feel quite right about going. It seemed to be an okay thing to do in Germany, but it wasn't something he would do at home.

But then he thought, "Who's gonna know?"

"I'd know," Rob finally told himself, after remembering the advice in **Ephesians 5:6–20**. See how this passage can help you make tough decisions.

■ What principles do you find in this passage that Rob may have used in making his decision?

■ How can you use the passage's advice in a decision you face now?

C O N S I D E R . . .

■ praying and writing about what God wants you to do with your life.

✒ writing a letter to a friend who's facing a tough decision. Include the passage's advice on decision making.

F O R   M O R E ,   S E E . . .

■ 1 Kings 18:1–40 (p. 323)
■ Romans 12:1–2 (p. 1157)
■ James 1:5–8 (p. 1294)

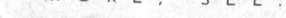

like those who are not wise, but live wisely. ¹⁶Use every chance you have for doing good, because these are evil times. ¹⁷So do not be foolish but learn what the Lord wants you to do. ¹⁸Do not be drunk with wine, which will ruin you, but be filled with the Spirit.ᵈ ¹⁹Speak to each other with psalms, hymns, and spiritual songs, singing and making music in your hearts to the Lord. ²⁰Always give thanks to God the Father for everything, in the name of our Lord Jesus Christ.

Wives and Husbands

²¹Yield to obey each other because you respect Christ.

²²Wives, yield to your husbands, as you do to the Lord, ²³because the husband is the head of the wife, as Christ is the head of the church. And he is the Savior of the body, which is the church. ²⁴As the church yields to Christ, so you wives should yield to your husbands in everything.

²⁵Husbands, love your wives as Christ loved the church and gave himself for it ²⁶to make it

belong to God. Christ used the word to make the church clean by washing it with water. ²⁷He died so that he could give the church to himself like a bride in all her beauty. He died so that the church could be pure and without fault, with no evil or sin or any other wrong thing in it. ²⁸In the same way, husbands should love their wives as they love their own bodies. The man who loves his wife loves himself. ²⁹No one ever hates his own body, but feeds and takes care of it. And that is what Christ does for the church, ³⁰because we are parts of his body. ³¹The Scripture says, "So a man will leave his father and mother and be united with his wife, and the two will become one body."ⁿ ³²That secret is very important—I am talking about Christ and the church. ³³But each one of you must love his wife as he loves himself, and a wife must respect her husband.

Children and Parents

6 Children, obey your parents as the Lord wants, because this is the right thing to do. ²The command says, "Honor your father and

"**So ... body.**" Quotation from Genesis 2:24.

Wolf Packs

When people think of wolves, they sometimes visualize a lonely silhouette on a hill, howling at the moon. Some picture the predator, sneaking up on an unsuspecting flock of sheep.

Much the opposite is true of wolves. While wolves do hunt, they most often prey on the sick or old animals in a herd, leaving the healthy animals to reproduce and protect the others. And wolves are seldom lonely. They live together with other wolves in families called packs.

Within the pack, adult wolves work together to hunt and to feed the younger members of the family. After a time of training, the young wolves take their place alongside the adults to hunt and to care for the next generation. Wolves rarely fight among themselves. But they will stand together, defending their home from attack by outsiders.

Experts believe wolves stay together as families because they have a kind of love for each other. Human family members also have certain responsibilities that help maintain order. Read about these responsibilities in **Ephesians 6:1–4**.

■ How is a wolf pack like the family described in this passage? How is it different?
■ From this passage, what is your role in your family?

C O N S I D E R . . .
■ writing out one thing you could do to improve your role in your family. Then do it.
■ obeying your parents this week, even when they ask you to do something you don't want to.

F O R   M O R E ,   S E E . . .

■ Proverbs 23:22–25 (p. 588)   ■ Colossians 3:13–21 (p. 1242)
■ Matthew 15:3–9 (p. 934)

mother." *n* This is the first command that has a promise with it— ³"Then everything will be well with you, and you will have a long life on the earth." *n*

⁴Fathers, do not make your children angry, but raise them with the training and teaching of the Lord.

Slaves and Masters

⁵Slaves, obey your masters here on earth with fear and respect and from a sincere heart, just as you obey Christ. ⁶You must do this not only while they are watching you, to please them. With all your heart you must do what God wants as people who are obeying Christ. ⁷Do your work with enthusiasm. Work as if you were serving the Lord, not as if you were serving only men and women. ⁸Remember that the Lord will give a reward to everyone, slave or free, for doing good.

⁹Masters, in the same way, be good to your slaves. Do not threaten them. Remember that the One who is your Master and their Master is in heaven, and he treats everyone alike.

Wear the Full Armor of God

¹⁰Finally, be strong in the Lord and in his great power. ¹¹Put on the full armor of God so that you can fight against the devil's evil tricks. ¹²Our fight is not against people on earth but against the rulers and authorities and the powers of this world's darkness, against the spiritual powers of evil in the heavenly world. ¹³That is why you need to put on God's full armor. Then on the day of evil you will be able to stand strong. And when you have finished the whole fight, you will still be standing. ¹⁴So stand strong, with the belt of truth tied around your waist and the protection of right living on your chest. ¹⁵On your feet wear the Good News *d* of peace to help you stand strong. ¹⁶And also use the shield of faith with which you can stop all the burning arrows of the Evil One. ¹⁷Accept God's salvation as your helmet, and take the sword of the Spirit, *d* which is the word of God. ¹⁸Pray in the Spirit at all times with all kinds of prayers, asking for everything you need. To do this you must always be ready and never give up. Always pray for all God's people.

"Honor ... mother."   Quotation from Exodus 20:12; Deuteronomy 5:16.
"Then ... earth."   Quotation from Exodus 20:12; Deuteronomy 5:16.

Spiritual Armor-All

Kremmling, Colorado, was a small mountain town of fifteen hundred where nothing out of the ordinary ever happened. Then police found a graffiti-emblazoned shack where someone had set up an altar with a satanic bible and plotted to vandalize churches and sacrifice animals.

"Major things like this never happen in Kremmling," Jody Cordova said. "It's kind of scary. I wrack my brain trying to figure out the people in town who would do this."

The townspeople were frightened. Some were even hysterical, threatening to carry handguns while taking children trick-or-treating on Halloween.

People were puzzled and concerned. They couldn't believe the dark side of the spiritual world could invade their little town the way it had.

Ephesians 6:10–20 warns not to be caught off guard in spiritual battles. Read the passage to see how Christians can protect themselves.

■ How might this passage help the people of Kremmling respond to their situation? Which piece of armor would help them most?
■ Which pieces of your armor are weakest? Which are strongest?

CONSIDER . . .

■ writing on a bookmark the words to represent each of the pieces of armor in the passage. Keep the bookmark in one of your school books to remind you to stay prepared.

◀ choosing the pieces of your armor that are weakest. Begin to strengthen those pieces this week.

FOR MORE, SEE . . .

■ 1 Samuel 17 (p. 260)
■ Matthew 8:28–34 (p. 921)
■ James 4:7–10 (p. 1298)

¹⁹Also pray for me that when I speak, God will give me words so that I can tell the secret of the Good News without fear. ²⁰I have been sent to preach this Good News, and I am doing that now,

here in prison. Pray that when I preach the Good News I will speak without fear, as I should.

Final Greetings

²¹I am sending to you Tychicus, our brother whom we love and a faithful servant of the Lord's work. He will tell you everything that is happening with me. Then you will know how I am and what I am doing. ²²I am sending him to you for this reason — so that you will know how we are, and he can encourage you.

²³Peace and love with faith to you from God the Father and the Lord Jesus Christ. ²⁴Grace to all of you who love our Lord Jesus Christ with love that never ends.

SIDELIGHT: The "shield of faith" in Ephesians 6:16 is a comparison to the large Roman shield used by heavily armed soldiers. This shield was designed to protect against burning darts, one of the most dangerous weapons of the time. When the dart hit the shield, it sunk into wood, and the flame was extinguished.

PHILIPPIANS

Why Read This Book?

■ Discover how serving other people serves Christ (Philippians 1—2).
■ Learn why growing in faith is so important (Philippians 3).
■ Learn Paul's secret of having joy amidst suffering (Philippians 4).

Behind the Scenes:

Paul spent his life telling the Good News of Jesus Christ and starting new churches. But what did he get for it? He was put on trial, run out of town, stoned, beaten with rods, and thrown in prison several times. In addition, other Christians misunderstood and opposed him.

In short, Paul had plenty of reason to be gloomy and depressed. But, as we learn in Philippians, Paul felt just the opposite. In fact, this short letter from Paul is probably the most upbeat, cheerful book in the Bible.

Part of the reason he was happy was that the Christians in Philippi had heard about his imprisonment and had taken up a collection for him. Their love and concern made Paul deeply grateful, and Paul thanks them in this letter.

But the most important reason for Paul's happiness is clear in the letter. "To me the only important thing about living is Christ," he writes, "and dying would be profit for me" (Philippians 1:21).

The Romans could chain Paul's body, but they couldn't chain Paul's heart. And in this letter to his friends at Philippi, the apostle shares his secret for facing difficult circumstances with a song on his lips and joy in his heart.

WHERE THE ACTION WAS

Rome
ITALY
GREECE
Philippi
Christians in Philippi received Paul's letter (Philippians 1:1).
Ephesus
AFRICA
Mediterranean Sea
Jerusalem
Paul wrote Philippians from his prison cell, probably in Rome or Ephesus (Philippians 1:13).

WHEN THE ACTION WAS

Jesus was born	The church began soon after Jesus went to heaven	Paul began his missionary work	Fire destroyed Rome	
BC/AD	**25AD**	**50AD**	**75AD**	**100AD**
	Jesus began his ministry	Paul started the church in Philippi	Paul wrote Philippians	Romans destroyed the Temple in Jerusalem

1 From Paul and Timothy, servants of Christ Jesus.

To all of God's holy people in Christ Jesus who live in Philippi, including your elders*d* and deacons:*d*

²Grace and peace to you from God our Father and the Lord Jesus Christ.

Paul's Prayer

³I thank my God every time I remember you, ⁴always praying with joy for all of you. ⁵I thank God for the help you gave me while I preached the Good News*d*—help you gave from the first day you believed until now. ⁶God began doing a good work in you, and I am sure he will continue it until it is finished when Jesus Christ comes again.

⁷And I know that I am right to think like this

about all of you, because I have you in my heart. All of you share in God's grace with me while I am in prison and while I am defending and proving the truth of the Good News. ⁸God knows that I want to see you very much, because I love all of you with the love of Christ Jesus.

⁹This is my prayer for you: that your love will grow more and more; that you will have knowl-

FRIENDS

First-String Help

Wyatt Jordan was a sure bet to make second-string quarterback, right behind his best friend Todd Andrews. That is, until Todd suddenly quit the team.

Steve Lowry congratulated Wyatt the morning after Todd quit. Steve was especially excited: now he would be second-string quarterback, right behind Wyatt.

"Yeah, thanks," Wyatt said with a lot less enthusiasm. He knew there was only one reason his friend would quit the team: Things must be getting worse at home. It had been a rough summer at the Andrews's family farm, with financial problems and Todd's dad being sick.

Of course, Todd's mom had insisted that her son play football. "Your brothers can bring in the harvest without you or your father," she had said. But at the first practice, Todd warned Wyatt that he might have to give up football to work on the farm.

During Wyatt's first practice as the starting quarterback, Coach Larson put the ball in Wyatt's hands.

"You're my man now," the coach said and blew his whistle.

"This is ridiculous," Wyatt thought. "The only reason I picked up a football in the first place was because of Todd. How can I do this when I know he's having a tough time right now?"

Wyatt walked off the field toward the coach, stopping first to give Steve the football. "Where are you going?" an astonished Steve asked.

"Farming," Wyatt answered.

Wyatt is the kind of friend we all want when we are having problems.

Read **Philippians 1:3–11** to discover how Paul felt about friends who helped him when life was difficult.

■ How do Wyatt's actions reflect the kind of friendship Paul is thankful for in this passage?

■ How does the kind of friendship displayed in this passage make a difference in relationships?

CONSIDER . . .

■ praying Philippians 1:9–11 for each of your friends.
■ making a scrapbook for a friend, with mementos of what his or her friendship has meant to you. Then present the scrapbook to your friend.

FOR MORE, SEE . . .

■ Exodus 17:8–13 (p. 75)
■ Mark 14:32–42 (p. 992)
■ Philemon 10–14 (p. 1274)

edge and understanding with your love; [10]that you will see the difference between good and bad and will choose the good; that you will be pure and without wrong for the coming of Christ; [11]that you will do many good things with the help of Christ to bring glory and praise to God.

Paul's Troubles Help the Work

[12]I want you brothers and sisters[n] to know that what has happened to me has helped to spread the Good News.[d] [13]All the palace guards and everyone else knows that I am in prison because I am a believer in Christ. [14]Because I am in prison, most of the believers have become more bold in Christ and are not afraid to speak the word of God.

[15]It is true that some preach about Christ because they are jealous and ambitious, but others preach about Christ because they want to help. [16]They preach because they have love, and they know that God gave me the work of defending the Good News. [17]But the others preach about Christ for selfish and wrong reasons, wanting to make trouble for me in prison.

[18]But it doesn't matter. The important thing is that in every way, whether for right or wrong reasons, they are preaching about Christ. So I am happy, and I will continue to be happy. [19]Because you are praying for me and the Spirit of Jesus Christ is helping me, I know this trouble will bring my freedom. [20]I expect and hope that I will not fail Christ in anything but that I will have the courage now, as always, to show the greatness of Christ in my life here on earth, whether I live or die. [21]To me the only important thing about living is Christ, and dying would be profit for me. [22]If I continue living in my body, I will be able to work for the Lord. I do not know what to choose — living or dying. [23]It is hard to choose between the two. I want to leave this life and be with Christ, which is much better, [24]but you need me here in my body. [25]Since I am sure of this, I know I will stay with you to help you grow and have joy in your faith. [26]You will be very happy in Christ Jesus when I am with you again.

[27]Only one thing concerns me: Be sure that you live in a way that brings honor to the Good News of Christ. Then whether I come and visit you or am away from you, I will hear that you are standing strong with one purpose, that you work together as one for the faith of the Good News, [28]and that you are not afraid of those who are against you. All of this is proof that your enemies will be destroyed but that you will be saved by God. [29]God gave you the honor not only of believing in Christ but also of suffering for him, both of

which bring glory to Christ. [30]When I was with you, you saw the struggles I had, and you hear about the struggles I am having now. You yourselves are having the same kind of struggles.

2 Does your life in Christ give you strength? Does his love comfort you? Do we share together in the spirit? Do you have mercy and kindness? [2]If so, make me very happy by having the same thoughts, sharing the same love, and having one mind and purpose. [3]When you do things, do not let selfishness or pride be your guide. Instead, be humble and give more honor to others than to yourselves. [4]Do not be interested only in your own life, but be interested in the lives of others.

Be Unselfish like Christ

[5]In your lives you must think and act like Christ Jesus.

[6]Christ himself was like God in everything.
　But he did not think that being equal with
　　God was something to be used for his
　　own benefit.
[7]But he gave up his place with God and made
　　himself nothing.
　He was born to be a man
　and became like a servant.
[8]And when he was living as a man,
　he humbled himself and was fully obedient
　　to God,
　even when that caused his death — death
　　on a cross.
[9]So God raised him to the highest place.
　God made his name greater than every
　　other name
[10]so that every knee will bow to the name of
　　Jesus —
　everyone in heaven, on earth, and under
　　the earth.
[11]And everyone will confess that Jesus Christ is
　　Lord
　and bring glory to God the Father.

Be the People God Wants You to Be

[12]My dear friends, you have always obeyed God when I was with you. It is even more important that you obey now while I am away from you. Keep on working to complete your salvation with fear and trembling, [13]because God is working in you to help you want to do and be able to do what pleases him.

[14]Do everything without complaining or arguing. [15]Then you will be innocent and without any wrong. You will be God's children without fault. But you are living with crooked and mean people all around you, among whom you shine like stars in the dark world. [16]You offer the teaching that

---

brothers and sisters Although the Greek text says "brothers" here and throughout this book, Paul's words were meant for the entire church, including men and women.

gives life. So when Christ comes again, I can be happy because my work was not wasted. I ran the race and won.

17Your faith makes you offer your lives as a sacrifice in serving God. If I have to offer my own blood with your sacrifice, I will be happy and full of joy with all of you. 18You also should be happy and full of joy with me.

Timothy and Epaphroditus

19I hope in the Lord Jesus to send Timothy to you soon. I will be happy to learn how you are. 20I have no one else like Timothy, who truly cares for you. 21Other people are interested only in their own lives, not in the work of Jesus Christ. 22You know the kind of person Timothy is. You know he has served with me in telling the Good News,*d* as

a son serves his father. 23I plan to send him to you quickly when I know what will happen to me. 24I am sure that the Lord will help me to come to you soon.

25Epaphroditus, my brother in Christ, works and serves with me in the army of Christ. When I needed help, you sent him to me. I think now that I must send him back to you, 26because he wants very much to see all of you. He is worried because you heard that he was sick. 27Yes, he was sick, and nearly died, but God had mercy on him and me too so that I would not have more sadness. 28I want very much to send him to you so that when you see him you can be happy, and I can stop worrying about you. 29Welcome him in the Lord with much joy. Give honor to people like him, 30because he almost died for the work of

---

DEATH

After AIDS

For Dale Pullen, a childhood filled with rejection became a life of rejection. His parents' failed marriage contributed to his own broken marriages. A need to escape problems led to drug and alcohol addictions. A desire for some kind of acceptance led to homosexuality. And homosexuality led to AIDS.

Abandoned by family and friends, Dale faced death alone. He was ready to end his life when Jeanne Cottrell, a Christian friend, invited Dale into her home. Through Jeanne's caring, Dale eventually decided to follow Christ.

What changes occurred in the heart of this beaten, lonely man! He experienced the release of forgiveness from his past. For the first time in his life, he felt genuine acceptance and unconditional love. And he had a place to belong with people who cared for him.

As his body weakened, Dale's spirit grew stronger and stronger. He was revitalized by his newfound hope in Christ. Dale directed his energy to reaching out with the love of Jesus to those who needed it most.

He visited AIDS patients at a local hospital and shared his story with many dying people who had also been rejected. He spoke at churches and support groups, and he explained how God's love reaches even those whom some find unlovable. He spent his time eagerly giving and receiving love.

"I don't know how long I'm going to live, but I want to live the rest of my days for the Lord," Dale told his friends.

After several months, Dale died. Those who were touched by Dale's life felt a tremendous loss. But at the same time, they rejoiced because they knew Dale was at peace and happy to be with Jesus.

Paul faced death peacefully under different circumstances. Read
Philippians 1:21–27 to see Paul's attitude toward living and dying.
- How were Dale's and Paul's attitudes about life affected by what they thought about death?
- According to this passage, what is the purpose of life and death?

CONSIDER...
- thinking of the number one reason you have to live, then putting more energy into that activity.
- discussing your feelings about death with a Christian friend. Think about how your priorities look from a heavenly perspective.

FOR MORE, SEE...
- Psalm 42 (p. 507)
- Romans 14:7–8 (p. 1160)
- Galatians 2:20–21 (p. 1208)

Christ. He risked his life to give me the help you could not give in your service to me.

The Importance of Christ

3 My brothers and sisters, be full of joy in the Lord. It is no trouble for me to write the same things to you again, and it will help you to be more ready. [2]Watch out for those who do evil, who are like dogs, who demand to cut[n] the body. [3]We are the ones who are truly circumcised.[d] We worship God through his Spirit,[d] and our pride is in Christ Jesus. We do not put trust in ourselves or anything we can do, [4]although I might be able to put trust in myself. If anyone thinks he has a reason to trust in himself, he should know that I have greater reason for trusting in myself. [5]I was circumcised eight days after my birth. I am from the people of Israel and the tribe[d] of Benjamin. I am a Hebrew, and my parents were Hebrews. I had a strict view of the law, which is why I became a Pharisee.[d] [6]I was so enthusiastic I tried to hurt the church. No one could find fault with the way I obeyed the law of Moses. [7]Those things were important to me, but now I think they are worth nothing because of Christ. [8]Not only those things, but I think that all things are worth nothing compared with the greatness of knowing Christ Jesus my Lord. Because of him, I have lost all those things, and now I know they are worthless trash. This allows me to have Christ [9]and to belong to him. Now I am right with God, not because I followed the law, but because I believed in Christ. God uses my faith to make me right with him. [10]I want to know Christ and the power that raised him from the dead. I want to share in his sufferings and become like him in his death. [11]Then I have hope that I myself will be raised from the dead.

Continuing Toward Our Goal

[12]I do not mean that I am already as God wants me to be. I have not yet reached that goal, but I continue trying to reach it and to make it mine.

cut   The word in Greek is like the word "circumcise," but it means "to cut completely off."

Sticking Together

When a flock of geese fly south for the winter, they fly in a V-shaped formation. If they didn't, they would never reach their destination.

Researchers have found that the V-shaped formation helps geese fly at least 71 percent farther than they could fly alone, because each bird creates an updraft for the one behind it, making flying easier.

If one goose falls out of formation, the wind resistance slows down the bird. If it doesn't act quickly, it will not be able to keep up with its flock. So, it quickly gets back into formation.

Like geese, Christians need to work together in the church. Read **Philippians 2:1–11** to learn how.

■ How is the geese's V-shaped formation like the passage's description of Christians working together?

■ How does being with other Christians encourage you in your faith?

C O N S I D E R . . .

■ writing your name and the names of other people in a V-shaped pattern to symbolize how you support each other. Thank God for people in the church who lead and support you.

■ talking to your youth leader or a Sunday school teacher about how you can create an "updraft" to support and encourage others in your church.

F O R   M O R E ,   S E E . . .

■ Psalm 133:1–3 (p. 558)

■ Mark 9:33–37 (p. 980)

■ Acts 2:44–47 (p. 1100)

Christ wants me to do that, which is the reason he made me his. [13]Brothers and sisters, I know that I have not yet reached that goal, but there is one thing I always do. Forgetting the past and straining toward what is ahead, [14]I keep trying to reach the goal and get the prize for which God called me through Christ to the life above.

[15]All of us who are spiritually mature should think this way, too. And if there are things you do not agree with, God will make them clear to you. [16]But we should continue following the truth we already have.

[17]Brothers and sisters, all of you should try to follow my example and to copy those who live the way we showed you. [18]Many people live like enemies of the cross of Christ. I have often told you about them, and it makes me cry to tell you about them now. [19]In the end, they will be destroyed. They do whatever their bodies want, they are proud of their shameful acts, and they think only about earthly things. [20]But our homeland is in heaven, and we are waiting for our Savior, the Lord Jesus Christ, to come from heaven. [21]By his power to rule all things, he will change our simple bodies and make them like his own glorious body.

POPULARITY

Impressive!

Mark Lester was assigned to work with class president Barry Clark on a biology class project. Who could have foreseen that working together a few nights a week for a month might actually lead to a friendship?

Barry and Mark had little in common. Barry was popular, owned a fancy car, and partied with the "in" crowd. Mark had a few friends from church, rode a bike, and spent his weekends with the youth group.

But one Friday night at the basketball game, Barry asked Mark to sit with him in the bleacher section informally reserved for football players, cheerleaders—anybody but Mark Lester. Not even in his wildest dreams could Mark have pictured himself sitting in the bleachers right in front of Tracy Watkins and spending more time talking to her than watching the game!

Mark was so enamored with his sudden change of fortune that he had to ask Tracy to repeat herself. The next time, she said it so loudly everyone heard her—including Barry. "If you can find a way to get us some beer, I'll go out with you after the game," she shouted above the crowd's roar.

Barry's expression said he was very impressed. Mark pretended to watch the basketball game for a second. It was the final quarter, and time was running out. But another clock was ticking in the bleachers. Mark knew the more important contest was taking place right where he sat.

"Well," he began, then hesitated.

Tracy frowned and glanced at Barry, who grinned, leaned forward, and teased, "If you won't take her out, Mark, I guess I'll have to."

Mark gripped the bleacher with both hands and, with all the enthusiasm he could muster, grinned back at Barry through gritted teeth. "Go for it, Barry," he stuttered. The clock ran out. The buzzer sounded. The game had been close, but Mark knew he had won.

Mark had chosen to be popular with God rather than people. Read **Philippians 3:8–11** to see how Paul had a similar attitude.

■ How does Mark's decision reflect Paul's philosophy in this passage?
■ How can "knowing Christ" be greater than what the world offers?

C O N S I D E R . . .

■ giving up something that might make you popular if it stands in the way of your knowing Christ.
■ asking a parent to recall the popular people in his or her high school, then finding out what has happened to them.

F O R   M O R E ,   S E E . .

■ Joshua 24:14–27 (p. 214)
■ John 5:41–44 (p. 1066)
■ Galatians 1:9–10 (p. 1207)

What the Christians Are to Do

4 My dear brothers and sisters, I love you and want to see you. You bring me joy and make me proud of you, so stand strong in the Lord as I have told you.

[2] I ask Euodia and Syntyche to agree in the Lord. [3] And I ask you, my faithful friend, to help these women. They served with me in telling the Good News,[d] together with Clement and others who worked with me, whose names are written in the book of life. [n]

[4] Be full of joy in the Lord always. I will say again, be full of joy.

[5] Let everyone see that you are gentle and kind. The Lord is coming soon. [6] Do not worry about anything, but pray and ask God for everything you need, always giving thanks. [7] And God's peace, which is so great we cannot understand it, will keep your hearts and minds in Christ Jesus.

[8] Brothers and sisters, think about the things

SIDELIGHT: When Paul said our "homeland is in heaven" (Philippians 3:20), he literally said Christians live in a colony of heaven. The Philippian Christians would have seen this as a great privilege, since Philippi was a colony of the Roman Empire (see Acts 16:12, p. 1123). Being a colony meant Philippi had special privileges, including self-government, exemption from control by regional governments, and exemption from many taxes.

---

book of life   God's book that has the names of all God's chosen people (Revelation 3:5; 21:27).

PERSISTENCE

Sticking With It

Wilma Rudolph dreamed of competing in the Olympics. But she had everything stacked against her.

She was born prematurely in a Tennessee shack, weighing only four and one-half pounds. Scarlet fever and polio struck, partially paralyzing her left leg, and forcing her to wear a steel brace.

Wilma remembers: "My father was the one who sort of babied me and was sympathetic. . . . My mother was the one who made me work, made me believe that one day it would be possible for me to walk without braces." Wilma's mother told her that, with persistence, she could follow her dreams in life.

So at age nine, Wilma did away with the braces. Four years later she developed a rhythmic stride and entered her first race. She came in last.

But she didn't give up.

"I worked very hard for the next four years," Wilma recalls. "I was self-motivated and motivated by my family. It took sheer determination to be able to run a hundred yards and remember all of the mechanics that go along with it. It takes steady nerves and being a fighter to stay out there."

In the 1960 Olympics, Wilma Rudolph set the world record in the 100-meter dash. She also won the 200-meter sprints and ran the anchor leg for the United States 400-meter relay team. She was the first American woman to win three gold medals in track and field at a single Olympiad.

Wilma Rudolph learned the lesson of **Philippians 3:12–21**. Read the passage to discover the key to persistence.

■ In light of the passage, why was Wilma persistent?
■ What was Paul's spiritual goal, according to this passage? How can this passage help you persist in reaching such a goal?

CONSIDER . . .

■ watching part of a sports event on television. Look for evidences of persistence, then apply what you learn to a challenge you face.
◀ setting a specific goal to help you grow in your faith and persisting to meet that goal this week.

FOR MORE, SEE . . .

■ Psalm 37:23–24 (p. 504)
■ Luke 9:57–62 (p. 1021)
■ 1 Timothy 6:11–16 (p. 1260)

that are good and worthy of praise. Think about the things that are true and honorable and right and pure and beautiful and respected. ⁹Do what you learned and received from me, what I told you, and what you saw me do. And the God who gives peace will be with you.

❋ SIDELIGHT: The words joy and rejoice occur in some form sixteen times in Philippians (for example, Philippians 4:4). Even in prison, Paul's thoughts were focused on joy!

Paul Thanks the Christians

¹⁰I am very happy in the Lord that you have shown your care for me again. You continued to care about me, but there was no way for you to show it. ¹¹I am not telling you this because I need anything. I have learned to be satisfied with the things I have and with everything that happens. ¹²I know how to live when I am poor, and I know how to live when I have plenty. I have learned the secret of being happy at any time in everything that happens, when I have enough to eat and when I go hungry, when I have more than I need and when I do not have enough. ¹³I can do all things through Christ, because he gives me strength.

¹⁴But it was good that you helped me when I needed it. ¹⁵You Philippians remember when I first preached the Good News*d* there. When I left Macedonia, you were the only church that gave me help. ¹⁶Several times you sent me things I needed when I was in Thessalonica. ¹⁷Really, it is

---

PEACE

Beyond Understanding

The ringing telephone pierced the night. "Hello, Mrs. Gibson. This is Officer Rogers with the highway patrol."

Norma's throat tightened, but she managed to gulp: "Yes, what is it?"

"It's your daughter, Cassandra. There's been an accident." Shocked, Norma sobbed uncontrollably and dropped the phone. Her husband, Neil, grabbed it and learned that Cassandra was still alive, but that she had extensive head injuries and was unconscious. The Flight for Life helicopter was flying her to an Oklahoma City hospital.

When Neil and Norma arrived at the hospital, Cassandra was in a coma. Her head was bruised and swollen. Her back was broken, and her body lay lifeless. Her heart had stopped once in the helicopter, but the paramedics had restarted it. Surgeons were inserting a catheter into Cassandra's skull to relieve the pressure on her brain.

During the surgery, Norma prayed in the hospital chapel. As she read her Bible, an overwhelming peace filled her. She couldn't explain what she felt, especially with her daughter so close to death. All she knew was that God seemed near and that he would take care of Cassandra.

For days, Neil and Norma rarely left Cassandra's side. Norma's prayers surprised even her, because they were filled with thanksgiving rather than questioning or pleading. Her heart was filled with God's peace.

It took a long time for Cassandra to recover, and much of what happened in the weeks after the accident is now a blur to her. But every hour is vivid to Neil and Norma. They were joyful that their daughter was alive.

In **Philippians 4:1–9**, Paul describes the secret to having a joy that is greater than life's difficulties. Read it to understand Norma's experience.

■ Which actions or attitudes from this passage did Norma have that resulted in peace?

■ Which ones can most help you experience God's peace?

CONSIDER . . .

■ listing the nine steps to peace—one step from each verse in this passage. Choose one step you can take to experience God's peace.

■ planning with a friend to pray together during difficult times.

FOR MORE, SEE . . .

■ Psalm 25 (p. 496)   ■ John 14:27–29 (p. 1085)

■ Luke 6:17–23 (p. 1012)

not that I want to receive gifts from you, but I want you to have the good that comes from giving. [18]And now I have everything, and more. I have all I need, because Epaphroditus brought your gift to me. It is like a sweet-smelling sacrifice offered to God, who accepts that sacrifice and is pleased with it. [19]My God will use his wonderful riches in Christ Jesus to give you everything you need. [20]Glory to our God and Father forever and ever! Amen.

[21]Greet each of God's people in Christ. Those who are with me send greetings to you. [22]All of God's people greet you, particularly those from the palace of Caesar.[d]

[23]The grace of the Lord Jesus Christ be with you all.

COLOSSIANS

Why Read This Book?

- Learn the importance of following only Jesus Christ (Colossians 1).
- Discover how to respond to false teachers (Colossians 2).
- Find guidelines for living a Christian life (Colossians 3—4).

Behind the Scenes:

ESP. Astrology. Witchcraft. Ghosts. UFOs. Tarot cards. Ouija boards. The Loch Ness monster. Mysterious things can intrigue and attract us.

We are not the only people who can be fascinated with these kinds of things. Early Christians in Colosse were attracted to the same kinds of mysterious or supernatural things. Someone apparently came into the church and began teaching people to worship angels and cosmic powers. Jesus is fine, they argued, but these other mysterious powers controlled human destiny and gave secret knowledge (Colossians 2:16–23).

This letter to the Colossians challenges these false teachers. But instead of picking apart their arguments, the letter goes on the offensive, telling the Colossians the truth about Jesus Christ. "He ranks higher than everything that has been made," the letter states. "Christ is all that is important" (Colossians 1:15, 3:11).

The letter's advice to the Colossians is good advice for all people in all times. When we feel tempted to look for power in other, mysterious things, this book reminds us of the source of true power. And when someone suggests we need to do something else for salvation, Colossians assures us that Jesus is all we need.

WHERE THE ACTION WAS

Rome • ITALY

GREECE

TURKEY

Laodicea
• Colosse

The Colossians were told to share the letter with the Christians in nearby Laodicea (Colossians 4:16).

Christians in Colosse, a small city in modern-day Turkey, received this letter (Colossians 1:2).

Mediterranean Sea

Jerusalem •

AFRICA

WHEN THE ACTION WAS

Jesus was born	The church began soon after Jesus went to heaven	Paul began his missionary work	Fire destroyed Rome	
BC/AD	**25AD**	**50AD**	**75AD**	**100AD**
	Jesus began his ministry	Paul became a Christian	Paul wrote this letter to the Colossians	Romans destroyed the Temple in Jerusalem

1 From Paul, an apostle*d* of Christ Jesus. I am an apostle because that is what God wanted. Also from Timothy, our brother.

²To the holy and faithful brothers and sisters *n* in Christ that live in Colosse:

Grace and peace to you from God our Father.

³In our prayers for you we always thank God, the Father of our Lord Jesus Christ, ⁴because we have heard about the faith you have in Christ Jesus and the love you have for all of God's people. ⁵You have this faith and love because of your hope, and what you hope for is kept safe for you in heaven. You learned about this hope when you heard the message about the truth, the Good News*d* ⁶that was told to you. Everywhere in the world that Good News is bringing blessings and is growing. This has happened with you, too, since you heard the Good News and understood the truth about the grace of God. ⁷You learned about God's grace from Epaphras, whom we love. He works together with us and is a faithful servant of Christ for us. ⁸He also told us about the love you have from the Holy Spirit.*d*

⁹Because of this, since the day we heard about you, we have continued praying for you, asking God that you will know fully what he wants. We pray that you will also have great wisdom and understanding in spiritual things ¹⁰so that you will live the kind of life that honors and pleases the Lord in every way. You will produce fruit in every good work and grow in the knowledge of God. ¹¹God will strengthen you with his own great

brothers and sisters   Although the Greek text says "brothers" here and throughout this book, Paul's words were meant for the entire church, including men and women.

A Life Pleasing God

From childhood, Robert Beck knew he wanted to be a missionary to Africa. Every day he kept his goal foremost in his mind. He read magazine articles and books and watched TV news reports and documentaries on Africa. In school he wrote stories and reports about the African people.

After graduating from high school, Robert earned a bachelor's degree, then completed seminary. After almost twenty years of education, Robert finally was ready to start on his goal. He began a church in Africa.

Robert preached regularly at the mission church. He taught children about God's love. He befriended the people when they were sick and lonely, and cheerfully devoted all his time to his vision of God's will.

But after only one year in Africa, Robert contracted malaria and died of complications.

Some of Robert's friends and relatives wondered if he had wasted his life. "How's it fair that this happened to such a promising young man?" they asked bitterly. "Can this really be God's will?"

Back at Robert's seminary, the news of his death shocked and saddened the whole community. The professors asked whether any graduating student would consider serving the church Robert had started.

Eight signed up to serve.

Although Robert died young, he lived "the kind of life that honors and pleases the Lord in every way" and produced "fruit in every good work" (Colossians 1:10). He followed God's will, just as Paul urged his readers to do in **Colossians 1:1–14**.

■ In light of this passage, how was God's will accomplished with Robert?

■ How can this passage help you discover God's will for your life?

CONSIDER . . .

■ praying that God will let you "know fully what he wants" for your future (Colossians 1:9).

■ keeping a journal about God's will for your life. Read Bible verses about God's will (see below) and write your thoughts as you apply those verses to decisions you are facing.

FOR MORE, SEE . . .

■ Psalm 40:8–10 (p. 505)
■ Matthew 6:9–13 (p. 918)
■ Mark 3:31–35 (p. 969)

power so that you will not give up when troubles come, but you will be patient. 12And you will joyfully give thanks to the Father who has made you able to have a share in all that he has prepared for his people in the kingdom of light. 13God has freed us from the power of darkness, and he brought us into the kingdom of his dear Son. 14The Son paid for our sins, and in him we have forgiveness.

The Importance of Christ

15No one can see God, but Jesus Christ is exactly like him. He ranks higher than everything that has been made. 16Through his power all things were made—things in heaven and on earth, things seen and unseen, all powers, authorities, lords, and rulers. All things were made through Christ and for Christ. 17He was there before anything was made, and all things continue because of him. 18He is the head of the body, which is the church. Everything comes from him. He is the first one who was raised from the dead. So in all things Jesus has first place. 19God was pleased for all of himself to live in Christ. 20And through Christ, God has brought all things back

to himself again—things on earth and things in heaven. God made peace through the blood of Christ's death on the cross.

SIDELIGHT: The city of Colosse (Colossians 1:2) was once a major mill town, known for its wool-working and cloth-dying industries. In fact, a widely used dark red wool cloth was known as colossinum. However, the city had declined by the time this letter was written, and may have been devastated by a major earthquake in A.D. 60 or 61.

21At one time you were separated from God. You were his enemies in your minds, and the evil things you did were against God. 22But now God has made you his friends again. He did this through Christ's death in the body so that he might bring you into God's presence as people who are holy, with no wrong, and with nothing of which God can judge you guilty. 23This will

---

FORGIVENESS

The Face of Hatred

Just before Leonardo da Vinci began painting the Last Supper, he argued bitterly with a fellow painter. Da Vinci was so enraged that he decided to paint the face of his enemy as the face of Judas Iscariot. That way the hated painter's face would be preserved for ages in the face of the disciple who betrayed Jesus.

Da Vinci painted the face of Judas quickly. At first he took delight as everyone who came by recognized the face of the other painter in Judas.

Work on the other disciples' portraits continued. Da Vinci tried several times to start Jesus' face, but couldn't make any progress. Something seemed to baffle him, frustrating his best efforts.

In time, da Vinci saw his hatred of the other painter as the problem holding him back from finishing his work. Only after repainting the face of Judas was he able to paint Jesus' face and complete his masterpiece.

In his work on the Last Supper, da Vinci learned something important about forgiveness. **Colossians 1:15–29** has a similar lesson as it explains how Christ came to forgive—to end the separation between God and people.

■ How was Leonardo da Vinci's separation from his fellow painter like humanity's separation from God as described in the passage?

■ How do you feel when you are forgiven? How do you feel when you forgive someone else?

C O N S I D E R . . .

■ confessing your sin to God, and, if you can, to an adult you trust. It may help you feel God's forgiveness.

■ closing your eyes and thinking about the face of someone you need to forgive. Then imagine the face of Jesus next to that person's, and ask God to help you forgive that person.

F O R   M O R E ,   S E E . . .

■ Psalm 79:8–9 (p. 529)   ■ Romans 5:1–11 (p. 1145)
■ Luke 6:37–38 (p. 1013)

happen if you continue strong and sure in your faith. You must not be moved away from the hope brought to you by the Good News that you heard. That same Good News has been told to everyone in the world, and I, Paul, help in preaching that Good News.

Paul's Work for the Church

24I am happy in my sufferings for you. There are things that Christ must still suffer through his body, the church. I am accepting, in my body, my part of these things that must be suffered. 25I became a servant of the church because God gave me a special work to do that helps you, and that work is to tell fully the message of God. 26This message is the secret that was hidden from everyone since the beginning of time, but now it is made known to God's holy people. 27God decided to let his people know this rich and glorious secret which he has for all people. This secret is Christ himself, who is in you. He is our only hope for glory. 28So we continue to preach Christ to each person, using all wisdom to warn and to teach everyone, in order to bring each one into God's presence as a mature person in Christ. 29To do this, I work and struggle, using Christ's great strength that works so powerfully in me.

2 I want you to know how hard I work for you, those in Laodicea, and others who have never seen me. 2I want them to be strengthened and joined together with love so that they may be rich in their understanding. This leads to their knowing fully God's secret, that is, Christ himself. 3In him all the treasures of wisdom and knowledge are safely kept.

4I say this so that no one can fool you by arguments that seem good, but are false. 5Though I am absent from you in my body, my heart is with you,

---

CULTS

Fatal Attraction

DeAnne Shackly was an average high school senior. Her grades were average: Bs and Cs in most subjects. Her interest in school was average: She thought school was okay, but she would much rather play tennis or watch television. Her social life was average: an occasional date or evening out with some friends.

DeAnne couldn't wait to graduate from high school and get on with life. She didn't know what she wanted, but she knew it had to be more interesting than what she was doing.

One day after school, DeAnne went to the beach. There, some members of a religious group approached her. DeAnne had never heard of the group. But because they offered her a chance to belong, to take part in something greater than herself, she joined them.

After two years DeAnne decided the cult had manipulated her for its own ends. The group had offered "answers" to tough questions, but then told her to stop asking questions—to "just believe." It used her to raise money by selling flowers, candy, and other things, but when she asked where all the money was going, she was told it wasn't her concern.

Finally, she dropped out. She felt sick about the two years she had wasted. "Why was I attracted to that group?" she later asked herself. "I was a typical kid with a comfortable lifestyle. Why did I change my life so drastically? I wasn't that unhappy."

The Colossian Christians experienced a similar attraction to false beliefs. **Colossians 2:1–15** warns the early Christians not to be fooled by empty teachings.

■ How might DeAnne's response to the cult have been different if she had listened to the warnings in this passage?

■ How can you recognize false teachers today, according to the passage?

C O N S I D E R . . .

■ making a list of Paul's warnings about false teachers. Refer to it when someone offers you quick, appealing answers to tough questions.

◢ asking your pastor or youth leader to get literature from cult groups and asking his help evaluating the groups' claims in light of scripture.

F O R   M O R E ,   S E E . . .

■ Deuteronomy 13:1–5 (p. 173)
■ Matthew 24:23–25 (p. 951)

■ 2 Peter 2:17–22 (p. 1312)

and I am happy to see your good lives and your strong faith in Christ

Continue to Live in Christ

[6]As you received Christ Jesus the Lord, so continue to live in him. [7]Keep your roots deep in him and have your lives built on him. Be strong in the faith, just as you were taught, and always be thankful.

[8]Be sure that no one leads you away with false and empty teaching that is only human, which comes from the ruling spirits of this world, and not from Christ. [9]All of God lives in Christ fully (even when Christ was on earth), [10]and you have a full and true life in Christ, who is ruler over all rulers and powers.

[11]Also in Christ you had a different kind of circumcision,[d] a circumcision not done by hands. It was through Christ's circumcision, that is, his death, that you were made free from the power of your sinful self. [12]When you were baptized, you were buried with Christ, and you were raised up with him through your faith in God's power that was shown when he raised Christ from the dead. [13]When you were spiritually dead because of your sins and because you were not free from the power of your sinful self, God made you alive with Christ, and he forgave all our sins. [14]He canceled the debt, which listed all the rules we failed to follow. He took away that record with its rules and nailed it to the cross. [15]God stripped the spiritual rulers and powers of their authority. With the cross, he won the victory and showed the world that they were powerless.

Don't Follow People's Rules

[16]So do not let anyone make rules for you about eating and drinking or about a religious feast, a New Moon[d] Festival, or a Sabbath[d] day. [17]These things were like a shadow of what was to come. But what is true and real has come and is found in Christ. [18]Do not let anyone disqualify you by making you humiliate yourself and worship angels. Such people enter into visions, which fill

them with foolish pride because of their human way of thinking. [19]They do not hold tightly to Christ, the head. It is from him that all the parts of the body are cared for and held together. So it grows in the way God wants it to grow.

[20]Since you died with Christ and were made free from the ruling spirits of the world, why do you act as if you still belong to this world by following rules like these: [21]"Don't eat this," "Don't taste that," "Don't even touch that thing"? [22]These rules refer to earthly things that are gone as soon as they are used. They are only man-made commands and teachings. [23]They seem to be wise, but they are only part of a man-made religion. They make people pretend not to be proud and make them punish their bodies, but they do not really control the evil desires of the sinful self.

Your New Life in Christ

3 Since you were raised from the dead with Christ, aim at what is in heaven, where Christ is sitting at the right hand of God. [2]Think only about the things in heaven, not the things on earth. [3]Your old sinful self has died, and your new life is kept with Christ in God. [4]Christ is our life, and when he comes again, you will share in his glory.

[5]So put all evil things out of your life: sexual sinning, doing evil, letting evil thoughts control you, wanting things that are evil, and greed. This is really serving a false god. [6]These things make God angry.[n] [7]In your past, evil life you also did these things.

[8]But now also put these things out of your life: anger, bad temper, doing or saying things to hurt others, and using evil words when you talk. [9]Do not lie to each other. You have left your old sinful life and the things you did before. [10]You have begun to live the new life, in which you are being made new and are becoming like the One who made you. This new life brings you the true knowledge of God. [11]In the new life there is no difference between Greeks and Jews, those who are circumcised[d] and those who are not circumcised, or people who are foreigners, or Scythians.[n] There is no difference between slaves and free people. But Christ is in all believers, and Christ is all that is important.

[12]God has chosen you and made you his holy people. He loves you. So always do these things: Show mercy to others, be kind, humble, gentle, and patient. [13]Get along with each other, and forgive each other. If someone does wrong to you, forgive that person because the Lord forgave you. [14]Do all these things; but most important, love each other. Love is what holds you all together in

---

These ... angry   Some Greek copies add: "against the people who do not obey God."
Scythians   The Scythians were known as very wild and cruel people.

perfect unity. ¹⁵Let the peace that Christ gives control your thinking, because you were all called together in one body*ⁿ* to have peace. Always be thankful. ¹⁶Let the teaching of Christ live in you richly. Use all wisdom to teach and instruct each other by singing psalms, hymns, and spiritual songs with thankfulness in your hearts to God. ¹⁷Everything you do or say should be done to obey Jesus your Lord. And in all you do, give thanks to God the Father through Jesus.

Your New Life with Other People

¹⁸Wives, yield to the authority of your husbands, because this is the right thing to do in the Lord.

¹⁹Husbands, love your wives and be gentle with them.

²⁰Children, obey your parents in all things, because this pleases the Lord.

²¹Fathers, do not nag your children. If you are too hard to please, they may want to stop trying.

> ☀ **SIDELIGHT:** If you feel like you have read some of Colossians somewhere else, you might be right. The book is filled with passages that closely parallel Ephesians (for example, compare Colossians 3:16–17 with Ephesians 5:19–20, p. 1225). In fact, about half of Ephesians' 155 verses also have similarities to verses in Colossians.

²²Slaves, obey your masters in all things. Do not obey just when they are watching you, to gain their favor, but serve them honestly, because you respect the Lord. ²³In all the work you are doing,

body The spiritual body of Christ, meaning the church or his people.

FOLLOWING GOD

Wake Up!

In high school, George shyly kept to himself. His few friends thought he was a nice guy, but nobody, including himself, thought he had much talent or potential. In fact, they seemed rarely to think anything of him. That was okay with George, since he rarely thought about anything anyway. He was content just to exist without any goals, dreams, or ideas.

About the only thing George enjoyed was driving around town in his car. It seemed a way to pass empty hours. But one day another car slammed into George's, sending his car off the road toward a tree. George was thrown from the car just before it smashed into the tree.

When George regained consciousness, he kept hearing the police say how lucky he was. George suffered minor injuries, but the car was totaled.

George's near tragedy awakened him to the reality of his empty life. Deciding he wanted to live for more than driving his car, he poured himself into many new interests, including filmmaking. A few years after his accident, George Lucas entertained millions with American Graffiti, the Star Wars trilogy, and the Indiana Jones movies.

George Lucas was lucky: He lost his car, but gained a new purpose in life. **Colossians 3:1–10** tells Christians to "wake up" to a whole, new life that is far more important than any new career.

■ How does George Lucas's awakening to life illustrate Paul's challenge to live a different way in Christ? How is it different?

■ In light of this passage, how is your "old life" different from your "new life in Christ"?

C O N S I D E R . . .

■ writing on one side of a sheet of paper things that are different because of your "new life in Christ." On the back, write out temptations you can avoid because of this new life. Thank God for giving you strength.

■ trying a new skill or interest that might help you follow God's will. Focus your attention on gifts you believe God has given you.

F O R   M O R E ,   S E E . . .

■ Habakkuk 3:2 (p. 878)
■ Luke 9:24 (p. 1019)

■ Revelation 21:1–5 (p. 1347)

work the best you can. Work as if you were doing it for the Lord, not for people. [24]Remember that you will receive your reward from the Lord, which he promised to his people. You are serving the Lord Christ. [25]But remember that anyone who does wrong will be punished for that wrong, and the Lord treats everyone the same.

4 Masters, give what is good and fair to your slaves. Remember that you have a Master in heaven.

What the Christians Are to Do

[2]Continue praying, keeping alert, and always thanking God. [3]Also pray for us that God will give us an opportunity to tell people his message. Pray that we can preach the secret that God has made known about Christ. This is why I am in prison. [4]Pray that I can speak in a way that will make it clear, as I should.

[5]Be wise in the way you act with people who are not believers, making the most of every opportunity. [6]When you talk, you should always be kind and pleasant so you will be able to answer everyone in the way you should.

News About the People with Paul

[7]Tychicus is my dear brother in Christ and a faithful minister and servant with me in the Lord. He will tell you all the things that are happening to me. [8]This is why I am sending him: so you may know how we are and he may encourage you. [9]I send him with Onesimus, a faithful and dear brother in Christ, and one of your group. They will tell you all that has happened here.

[10]Aristarchus, a prisoner with me, and Mark, the cousin of Barnabas, greet you. (I have already told you what to do about Mark. If he comes, welcome him.) [11] Jesus, who is called Justus, also greets you. These are the only Jewish believers who work with me for the kingdom of God, and they have been a comfort to me.

[12]Epaphras, a servant of Jesus Christ, from your group, also greets you. He always prays for you that you will grow to be spiritually mature and have everything God wants for you. [13]I know he has worked hard for you and the people in Laodicea and in Hierapolis. [14]Demas and our dear friend Luke, the doctor, greet you.

[15]Greet the brothers in Laodicea. And greet Nympha and the church that meets in her house. [16]After this letter is read to you, be sure it is also read to the church in Laodicea. And you read the letter that I wrote to Laodicea. [17]Tell Archippus, "Be sure to finish the work the Lord gave you."

[18]I, Paul, greet you and write this with my own hand. Remember me in prison. Grace be with you.

1 THESSALONIANS

Why Read This Book:

- Be encouraged to stand up for your faith even when those around you make fun of you (1 Thessalonians 2—3).
- See the importance of growing strong in faith (1 Thessalonians 4—5).

Behind the Scenes:

Summer camp was sensational. You had fun. You made friends. You grew in your faith. Around the campfire the final night, you were sure your life would never be the same because of your renewed faith. Then you went home. Your enthusiasm wore off as you faced the realities of everyday life. Would your new commitment last?

The Thessalonians might have felt the same way. Paul had come to their city, and they had become Christians. Then, suddenly, Paul was run out of town, and the new Christians were left in a hostile city without their leader. Could they stick to their faith? Would their faith keep growing?

Paul wrote this letter to encourage the new Christians and to explain why he left so quickly. He says how happy he is that they are "hanging in there" through all the troubles they face. He challenges them to keep growing in their faith. And he encourages them to look beyond persecution to the day when the Lord will come again.

Just as the letter encouraged the Thessalonians, it encourages new (and longtime) Christians today. It challenges us to hold firmly to our faith and to press on toward becoming mature Christians—even when we don't feel the spiritual "highs" we might have experienced at first.

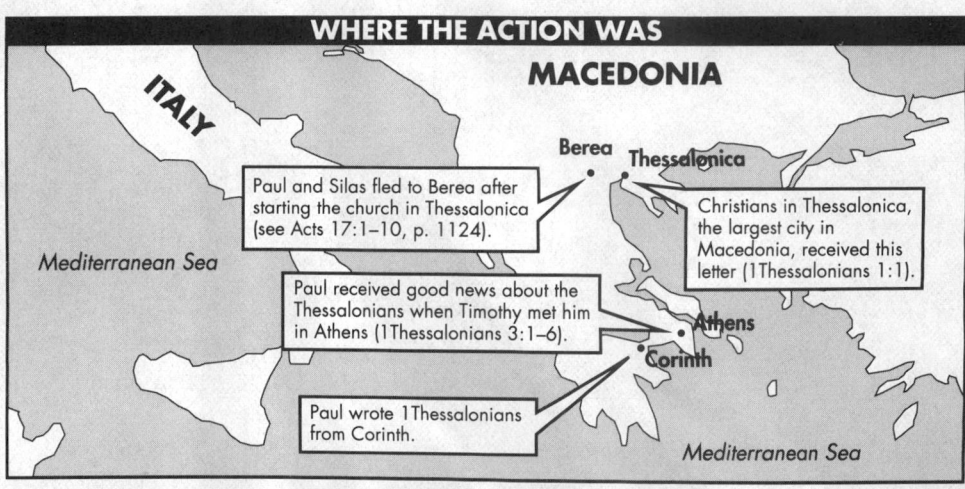

WHERE THE ACTION WAS

MACEDONIA

ITALY

Mediterranean Sea

Berea

Thessalonica

Paul and Silas fled to Berea after starting the church in Thessalonica (see Acts 17:1-10, p. 1124).

Christians in Thessalonica, the largest city in Macedonia, received this letter (1 Thessalonians 1:1).

Paul received good news about the Thessalonians when Timothy met him in Athens (1 Thessalonians 3:1-6).

Athens

Corinth

Paul wrote 1 Thessalonians from Corinth.

Mediterranean Sea

WHEN THE ACTION WAS

Jesus was born	The church began soon after Jesus went to heaven	Paul began his missionary work	Fire destroyed Rome	
BC/AD	**25AD**	**50AD**	**75AD**	**100AD**
	Jesus began his ministry	Paul became a Christian	Paul wrote 1 Thessalonians	Romans destroyed the Temple in Jerusalem

1 From Paul, Silas, and Timothy.
To the church in Thessalonica, the church in God the Father and the Lord Jesus Christ:
Grace and peace to you.

The Faith of the Thessalonians

[2]We always thank God for all of you and mention you when we pray. [3]We continually recall before God our Father the things you have done because of your faith and the work you have done because of your love. And we thank him that you continue to be strong because of your hope in our Lord Jesus Christ.

[4]Brothers and sisters,[n] God loves you, and we know he has chosen you, [5]because the Good News[d] we brought to you came not only with words, but with power, with the Holy Spirit,[d] and

with sure knowledge that it is true. Also you

>
> ### ☀ SIDELIGHT: If all the New
> Testament books appeared in the Bible in the order they were actually written, 1 Thessalonians might come first (with the possible exception of Galatians, p. 1206 or James, p. 1294. It is believed to have been written only twenty years after Jesus was crucified and rose from the dead.

know how we lived when we were with you in order to help you. [6]And you became like us and like the Lord. You suffered much, but still you accepted the teaching with the joy that comes

Brothers and sisters Although the Greek text says "Brothers" here and throughout this book, Paul's words were meant for the entire church, including men and women.

SPIRITUAL GROWTH

Spreading Love Around

Maria Mayo sat quietly in her pew through the whole organ postlude. She couldn't get the pastor's sermon on using God-given talents out of her head. She knew she had talents such as playing the guitar, but she had never thought of how she might use them for God.

Then Maria began remembering all her church friends. One friend played the piano, another played drums, and two could sing. Maybe they should form a Christian band.

Maria approached her friends, and they agreed. After practicing for several months, the band began volunteering to perform at retreats, youth gatherings, children's camps, and church services. Maria thoroughly enjoyed the band and hoped the music was helping people grow in faith.

But she really couldn't tell.

Several years later, Maria was asked to lead music for a denominational youth gathering. After an opening service, one teenager grabbed her and asked, "Did you lead music at Circle R seven summers ago?"

Maria vaguely remembered that the old band had played there. The young person continued, "That summer was the first time I heard about Jesus. I'm starting college now and want to go into the ministry. Thanks for the seed you planted."

Even though Maria didn't know how God was using her at the time, Maria spread the Good News—just as Paul spread the Good News. In **1 Thessalonians 1:1–10** we read about how the Thessalonians heard the Good News, grew in faith, and "became an example to all the believers."

■ How might Paul say Maria's faith is like the Thessalonians' faith?
■ The passage describes how the Thessalonians grew through several stages in their faith. What stage is your faith in?

C O N S I D E R . . .

■ deciding how God might use you to be an example of faith to those around you. Look in the passage for specific ideas.
■ taking a potted plant to someone who needs cheering up—as a symbol of your spiritual growth.

F O R   M O R E ,   S E E . . .

■ Jeremiah 17:7–8 (p. 711)   ■ Hebrews 5: 2–14 (p. 1280)
■ 1 Corinthians 12:1–11 (p. 1181)

from the Holy Spirit. ⁷So you became an example to all the believers in Macedonia and Southern Greece. ⁸And the Lord's teaching spread from you not only into Macedonia and Southern Greece, but now your faith in God has become known everywhere. So we do not need to say anything about it. ⁹People everywhere are telling about the way you accepted us when we were there with you. They tell how you stopped worshiping idols and began serving the living and true God. ¹⁰And you wait for God's Son, whom God raised from the dead, to come from heaven. He is Jesus, who saves us from God's angry judgment that is sure to come.

Paul's Work in Thessalonica

2 Brothers and sisters, you know our visit to you was not a failure. ²Before we came to you, we suffered in Philippi. People there insulted us, as you know, and many people were against us. But our God helped us to be brave and to tell you his Good News.ᵈ ³Our appeal does not come from lies or wrong reasons, nor were we trying to trick you. ⁴But we speak the Good News because God tested us and trusted us to do it. When we speak, we are not trying to please people, but

God, who tests our hearts. ⁵You know that we never tried to influence you by saying nice things about you. We were not trying to get your money; we had no selfishness to hide from you.

✺ SIDELIGHT: Most pastors and missionaries are not in it for the money. Paul certainly wasn't (1 Thessalonians 2:5, 9). In addition to his missionary work, Paul also worked as a tentmaker (see Acts 18:3, p. 1127) so he wouldn't have to take money from the churches he started.

God knows that this is true. ⁶We were not looking for human praise, from you or anyone else, ⁷even though as apostlesᵈ of Christ we could have used our authority over you.

But we were very gentle with you, like a mother caring for her little children. ⁸Because we loved you, we were happy to share not only God's Good News with you, but even our own lives. You had become so dear to us! ⁹Brothers and sisters, I know you remember our hard work and difficulties. We worked night and day so we

---

LEADERSHIP

Gentle Leadership

She didn't look like a dynamic leader. She didn't look like a dynamic anything. In fact, you probably wouldn't notice her in a crowd—smoky gray hair, out-of-fashion glasses, thin figure, pencil behind her ear. Yet in the twenty years she taught high school English, Elsie Cannery powerfully influenced her students' lives. She gently prodded and encouraged them to use their creativity and sharpen their thinking skills.

Elsie was available to her students night and day. She told them to call her at home any time they needed to talk to someone about school or any part of their lives.

Ninety percent of her students went on to graduate from college.

As Elsie Cannery made a difference in her students' lives, the apostles made a difference in the new Christians' lives. See the similarities in
1 Thessalonians 2:1–13.

■ How are Elsie Cannery's leadership qualities like those of the apostles?
■ How is your leadership style similar to the one Paul describes in the passage? How is it different?

CONSIDER...

■ listing all the words you can to describe Christian leadership. Read the passage to give you ideas. Check the "leadership" words that also describe you. How strong is your leadership ability?
■ thinking about one leader you admire a lot (a family member, friend, pastor, teacher). Talk to that person. Ask how he or she chose a profession. Ask about the qualities to strive for as a leader.

FOR MORE, SEE...

■ Proverbs 12:14 (p. 577)
■ Ephesians 2:9–10 (p. 1219)
■ James 2:14–17 (p. 1295)

would not burden any of you while we preached God's Good News to you.

[10]When we were with you, we lived in a holy and honest way, without fault. You know this is true, and so does God. [11]You know that we treated each of you as a father treats his own children. [12]We encouraged you, we urged you, and we insisted that you live good lives for God, who calls you to his glorious kingdom.

[13]Also, we always thank God because when you heard his message from us, you accepted it as the word of God, not the words of humans. And it really is God's message which works in you who believe. [14]Brothers and sisters, your experiences have been like those of God's churches in Christ that are in Judea.[n] You suffered from the people of your own country, as they suffered from the Jews, [15]who killed both the Lord Jesus and the prophets[d] and forced us to leave that country. They do not please God and are against all people. [16]They try to stop us from teaching those who are not Jews so they may be saved. By doing this, they are increasing their sins to the limit. The anger of God has come to them at last.

Paul Wants to Visit Them Again

[17]Brothers and sisters, though we were separated from you for a short time, our thoughts were still with you. We wanted very much to see you and tried hard to do so. [18]We wanted to come to you. I, Paul, tried to come more than once, but Satan stopped us. [19]You are our hope, our joy, and the crown we will take pride in when our Lord Jesus Christ comes. [20]Truly you are our glory and our joy.

3 When we could not wait any longer, we decided it was best to stay in Athens alone [2]and send Timothy to you. Timothy, our brother, works with us for God and helps us tell people the Good News[d] about Christ. We sent him to strengthen and encourage you in your faith [3]so none of you would be upset by these troubles. You yourselves know that we must face these troubles. [4]Even when we were with you, we told you we all would have to suffer, and you know it has happened. [5]Because of this, when I could wait no longer, I sent Timothy to you so I could learn about your faith. I was afraid the devil had tempted you, and then our hard work would have been wasted.

[6]But Timothy now has come back to us from you and has brought us good news about your faith and love. He told us that you always remember us in a good way and that you want to see us just as much as we want to see you. [7]So, brothers

and sisters, while we have much trouble and suffering, we are encouraged about you because of your faith. [8]Our life is really full if you stand strong in the Lord. [9]We have so much joy before our God because of you. We cannot thank him enough for all the joy we feel. [10]Night and day we continue praying with all our heart that we can see you again and give you all the things you need to make your faith strong.

[11]Now may our God and Father himself and our Lord Jesus prepare the way for us to come to you. [12]May the Lord make your love grow more and multiply for each other and for all people so that you will love others as we love you. [13]May your hearts be made strong so that you will be holy and without fault before our God and Father when our Lord Jesus comes with all his holy ones.

A Life that Pleases God

4 Brothers and sisters, we taught you how to live in a way that will please God, and you are living that way. Now we ask and encourage you in the Lord Jesus to live that way even more. [2]You know what we told you to do by the authority of the Lord Jesus. [3]God wants you to be holy and to stay away from sexual sins. [4]He wants each of you to learn to control your own body[n] in a way that is holy and honorable. [5]Don't use your body for sexual sin like the people who do not know God. [6]Also, do not wrong or cheat another Christian in this way. The Lord will punish people who do those things as we have already told you and warned you. [7]God called us to be holy and does not want us to live in sin. [8]So the person who refuses to obey this teaching is disobeying God, not simply a human teaching. And God is the One who gives us his Holy Spirit.[d]

SIDELIGHT: The church in Thessalonica would have been in an excellent position to love all the "Christians in all of Macedonia" (1 Thessalonians 4:10). The city was the capital of its province, so its residents had contact with people from all over the province.

---

[9]We do not need to write you about having love for your Christian family, because God has already taught you to love each other. [10]And truly you do love the Christians in all of Macedonia. Brothers and sisters, now we encourage you to love them even more.

[11]Do all you can to live a peaceful life. Take

Judea The Jewish land where Jesus lived and taught and where the church first began.
learn ... body This might also mean "learn to live with your own wife."

care of your own business, and do your own work as we have already told you. [12]If you do, then people who are not believers will respect you, and you will not have to depend on others for what you need.

The Lord's Coming

[13]Brothers and sisters, we want you to know about those Christians who have died so you will not be sad, as others who have no hope. [14]We believe that Jesus died and that he rose again. So, because of him, God will raise with Jesus those who have died. [15]What we tell you now is the Lord's own message. We who are living when the Lord comes again will not go before those who have already died. [16]The Lord himself will come down from heaven with a loud command, with the voice of the archangel, [n] and with the trumpet call of God. And those who have died believing in Christ will rise first. [17]After that, we who are still alive will be gathered up with them in the clouds to meet the Lord in the air. And we will be with the Lord forever. [18]So encourage each other with these words.

Be Ready for the Lord's Coming

5 Now, brothers and sisters, we do not need to write you about times and dates. [2]You know

---

archangel The leader among God's angels or messengers.

HAPPINESS

Creating Happiness

Jorge and Juanita Hernandez were having a horrible spring as they watched their parents' unhappy marriage disintegrate. Dinners were filled with tension, evenings filled with fighting, mornings filled with angry silence.

In time, their parents decided to divorce.

On one hand, Jorge and Juanita were relieved because the constant tension would end. But they were sad because their family, as they knew it, would also end. They would have to live with one parent and visit the other.

Jorge spent the next several weeks stewing about the divorce, watching television, being alone, and skipping church and school activities. "I don't care what my parents do, and I don't care what I do," Jorge told Juanita.

Juanita thought just the opposite. "I'm hurting, but I know others are hurting worse than I am," she replied. "I want to help some of those people."

So Juanita signed up for a youth group trip to Mexico. On the trip, Juanita and other group members sang songs in prisons, presented puppet plays, read stories, and played with the village kids. Although she was sad about her parents, she dealt with that sadness by reaching out to others.

Her Mexico experience gave Juanita a new perspective on happiness. "I saw how others with a lot less than I have are happy," she said. "In some ways we need to make our own happiness."

In the midst of her sadness, Juanita created happiness for herself by reaching out to others. Read about similar feelings of happiness and joy in **1 Thessalonians 3:9–13**.

■ What encouragement would Juanita find by reading this passage? What parts of this passage show the meaning of true happiness, even when things aren't going well?

C O N S I D E R . . .

■ writing on your calendar what makes you happiest each day of the upcoming week. See if there's a pattern. Are you happiest when you are reaching out to others?

■ choosing one thing that makes you happy and doing that for someone else. For example, if you're happy when a friend calls you on the phone and says, "I was just thinking about you," think of another person, and call him or her.

F O R   M O R E   S E E . . .

■ Psalm 43:4–5 (p. 507)
■ Proverbs 8:3–36 (p. 573)
■ James 5:7–11 (p. 1299)

very well that the day the Lord comes again will be a surprise, like a thief that comes in the night. ³While people are saying, "We have peace and we are safe," they will be destroyed quickly. It is like pains that come quickly to a woman having a baby. Those people will not escape. ⁴But you, brothers and sisters, are not living in darkness, and so that day will not surprise you like a thief. ⁵You are all people who belong to the light and to the day. We do not belong to the night or to darkness. ⁶So we should not be like other people who are sleeping, but we should be alert and have self-control. ⁷Those who sleep, sleep at night. Those who get drunk, get drunk at night. ⁸But we belong to the day, so we should control ourselves. We should wear faith and love to protect us, and the hope of salvation should be our helmet. ⁹God did not choose us to suffer his anger but to have salvation through our Lord Jesus Christ. ¹⁰Jesus died for us so that we can live together with him, whether we are alive or dead when he comes. ¹¹So encourage each other and give each other strength, just as you are doing now.

Final Instructions and Greetings

¹²Now, brothers and sisters, we ask you to appreciate those who work hard among you, who lead you in the Lord and teach you. ¹³Respect them with a very special love because of the work they do.

Live in peace with each other. ¹⁴We ask you, brothers and sisters, to warn those who do not work. Encourage the people who are afraid. Help those who are weak. Be patient with everyone. ¹⁵Be sure that no one pays back wrong for wrong, but always try to do what is good for each other and for all people.

¹⁶Always be joyful. ¹⁷Pray continually, ¹⁸and give thanks whatever happens. That is what God wants for you in Christ Jesus.

¹⁹Do not hold back the work of the Holy Spirit.ᵈ ²⁰Do not treat prophecyᵈ as if it were unimportant. ²¹But test everything. Keep what is good, ²²and stay away from everything that is evil.

²³Now may God himself, the God of peace, make you pure, belonging only to him. May your

---

DEATH

We Have Hope

Dennis Harwell was in high school when his parents had a baby girl. The birth was a major celebration because Dennis's parents had wanted another child since he was four years old. Years of trying, years of crying, years of suffering through three miscarriages finally produced Dennis's baby sister, whom they named Sarah.

Dennis and his parents were overjoyed with the new addition to their family. They fixed up a nursery and designed a playroom. They planned a special outing each weekend. They thoroughly enjoyed their new family member.

Their joy lasted six short months. One morning they woke up to discover Sarah had died in her sleep. Dennis and his parents were numb with grief. The doctors determined the cause of death was Sudden Infant Death Syndrome (SIDS). They told the family not to blame themselves, that it is virtually impossible to prevent a SIDS death.

Although Dennis and his parents felt a bit comforted by the doctors, they were still devastated by Sarah's death. As Dennis tried to work through his grief, he read **1 Thessalonians 4:13–14**. Dennis shared the passage with his parents, and they were all comforted by its words of hope.

■ How were Dennis and his family comforted by this passage?
■ How does it feel to know that someday you will see Christian loved ones who have died?

C O N S I D E R . . .

■ writing a memorial letter to someone you loved who has died. Keep the letter as a reminder of this special person.
■ thinking of someone who has recently lost a loved one. Call, write, visit, or take that person out to eat. Offer a little comfort.

F O R   M O R E ,   S E E . . .

■ Isaiah 25:7–8 (p. 640)　　　　　　■ 2 Timothy 1:9–10 (p. 1263)
■ Romans 8:37–39 (p. 1153)

whole self — spirit, soul, and body — be kept safe and without fault when our Lord Jesus Christ comes. 24You can trust the One who calls you to do that for you.

25Brothers and sisters, pray for us.

26Give each other a holy kiss when you meet. 27I tell you by the authority of the Lord to read this letter to all the believers.

28The grace of our Lord Jesus Christ be with you.

Get Ready!

A beginning-of-the-year notice was issued to all seniors at Franklin High: "A surprise senior fitness test will be given near the end of the school year," the notice read. "You won't know the exact day or time. You will be tested on strength, flexibility, and endurance. The highest scorer will receive a $1,000 scholarship to the college of his or her choice. This is your only notice. Be prepared!"

Steven Killain read the notice and decided to prepare right away for the test. He wanted to win the scholarship money, so it meant getting in shape, staying in shape, and staying alert for the test.

He regularly jogged, stretched, and lifted weights. He ate nutritious foods. Some of his friends thought he was crazy. "Why don't you relax a while?" they asked. "You'll have plenty of time to get ready later."

But Steve wanted to be ready whenever or wherever the test was announced. He wanted to win.

When the test was announced, all seniors competed. Most were not physically fit. Most could not even finish the long-distance run, jumping jacks, or push-ups. Not only did Steve complete all test areas, he took first place in all of them. Steve won the $1,000.

In **1 Thessalonians 5:1–11** we read about being alert and ready for the Lord's coming. Like Steve, we don't want to be caught unprepared.

■ What "be prepared" qualities did Steve possess that you also see recommended for believers in this passage?

■ How can you grow more awake and alert in following God so that you are not caught unprepared when the Lord comes?

C O N S I D E R . . .

■ consciously going through one day's activities as if it were the day Jesus were coming. How did you act differently? The same?

■ hanging a "Be Prepared" sign in your closet to remind you to live each day to the fullest and be ready for Christ's return.

F O R   M O R E ,   S E E . . .

■ Daniel 12:1–13 (p. 820)

■ Matthew 22:1–14 (p. 946)

■ 2 Peter 3:8–13 (p. 1313)

2 THESSALONIANS

Why Read This Book:

■ Learn how God is with us now and in the future (2 Thessalonians 1).
■ Find hope and comfort in God's love in the midst of life's tough times (2 Thessalonians 2—3).

Behind the Scenes:

You are about to graduate. You have passed all your classes, but you still have one English test left to go. You don't think the test will make any difference on your grade or transcript. How hard will you study?

The Thessalonian Christians were in a similar situation. They had been told that "the day of the Lord" (Christ's Second Coming) had already come, and some believed it. As a result, they didn't think they had anything to worry about, since they would all go to heaven soon. So they quit work, sat around lazily, meddled in other people's business, and depended on the church for charity. Worst of all, people decided they didn't really have to worry about growing spiritually.

Second Thessalonians challenged these actions, saying the day of the Lord had not come and would not come for some time. Instead of sitting lazily, waiting for the end, Christians should be working hard and seeking to grow in their faith.

Sometimes it can be tempting to be so excited about God's gift of eternal life that we stop working. Second Thessalonians reminds us that God has a purpose for us on earth, and we are called to do God's work in this world. We are called to keep growing in our faith even in the face of persecution.

WHEN THE ACTION WAS			
Jesus was born	The church began soon after Jesus went to heaven	Paul began his missionary work	Fire destroyed Rome
BC/AD	**25AD**	**50AD**	**75AD** ... **100AD**
	Jesus began his ministry	2 Thessalonians may have been written	Romans destroyed the Temple in Jerusalem

1 From Paul, Silas, and Timothy. To the church in Thessalonica in God our Father and the Lord Jesus Christ:

²Grace and peace to you from God the Father and the Lord Jesus Christ.

Paul Talks About God's Judgment

³We must always thank God for you, brothers and sisters. *n* This is only right, because your faith is growing more and more, and the love that every one of you has for each other is increasing. ⁴So we brag about you to the other churches of God. We tell them about the way you continue to be strong and have faith even though you are being treated badly and are suffering many troubles.

⁵This is proof that God is right in his judgment. He wants you to be counted worthy of his kingdom for which you are suffering. ⁶God will do what is right. He will give trouble to those who trouble you. ⁷And he will give rest to you who are troubled and to us also when the Lord Jesus appears with burning fire from heaven with his powerful angels. ⁸Then he will punish those who do not know God and who do not obey the Good News*d* about our Lord Jesus Christ. ⁹Those people will be punished with a destruction that continues forever. They will be kept away from the Lord

brothers and sisters   Although the Greek text says "brothers" here and throughout this book, Paul's words were meant for the entire church, including men and women.

SUFFERING

When a Dream Dies

It was unbelievable! Doug Hutchcraft would be able to play junior varsity football. And he was just a sophomore. His summer of intense training and his "killer instinct" were paying off. Maybe he would reach his lifelong dream of playing professional football.

During preseason workouts, Doug was ruthless. Once he noticed another guy's blood on his jersey after a workout, and he wouldn't let his mom wash the jersey.

Then one day during the cool-down drills after a scrimmage, Doug caught a cleat in the turf, spun around, and fell—with another guy on top of him. He heard a snap. "I tried to stand," Doug said. "It was impossible. My right knee felt like water."

Doug spent his whole sophomore year waiting for the badly torn ligament in his knee to heal. But at the beginning of the next season, Doug's coaches said he would need a doctor's release to play. So he went to see the team doctor of the New York Giants. "I can't sign a release allowing you to play," the doctor told him. "If you play football with this injury, you won't get through the season without ruining your knee for the rest of your life."

Doug's dream of playing football died. "I felt bitter," he later said. "I didn't think I deserved it. I had led a clean life, unlike most of the other players I knew. So why did God seem to be coming down so hard on me?"

The answer to Doug's question came later when he realized how football had replaced God in his life. "It hit me: I hadn't been living for the only thing that endures," he said. "Even if I'd been successful in the sport, the glory might have lasted six or eight years more, only if I got to the pros. But what was that compared to eternity?"

When the Thessalonians received this letter, they also were wondering why they had to suffer for their faith. **Second Thessalonians 1:1–12** encourages them to hang on because God will be victorious in the end.

■ What perspective on their suffering might Doug and the Thessalonians have gotten from this letter?

■ How might knowing you will experience peace with God in the future help you through troubles right now?

CONSIDER . . .

■ praying for God's comfort and strength to help you through troubles you are facing at home, school, church, or work.

■ writing all of the troubles you're now experiencing. Pray that God will strengthen you and help you grow in your faith through these troubles.

FOR MORE, SEE . . .

■ Isaiah 9:2–7 (p. 626)
■ Matthew 7:7–11 (p. 919)

■ 1 Peter 3:8–22 (p. 1306)

and from his great power. [10]This will happen on the day when the Lord Jesus comes to receive glory because of his holy people. And all the people who have believed will be amazed at Jesus. You will be in that group, because you believed what we told you.

> **SIDELIGHT:** In the first century, being a Christian could be hazardous to your health (2 Thessalonians 1:4). The Roman historian Tacitus describes how Emperor Nero tortured Christians in Rome by dipping them in tar and setting them on fire to illuminate his race track at night.

---

[11]That is why we always pray for you, asking our God to help you live the kind of life he called you to live. We pray that with his power God will help you do the good things you want and perform the works that come from your faith. [12]We pray all this so that the name of our Lord Jesus Christ will have glory in you, and you will have glory in him. That glory comes from the grace of our God and the Lord Jesus Christ.

Evil Things Will Happen

2 Brothers and sisters, we have something to say about the coming of our Lord Jesus Christ and the time when we will meet together with him. [2]Do not become easily upset in your thinking or afraid if you hear that the day of the Lord has already come. Someone may say this in a prophecy[d] or in a message or in a letter as if it came from us. [3]Do not let anyone fool you in any way. That day of the Lord will not come until the turning away[n] from God happens and the Man of Evil, who is on his way to hell, appears. [4]He will be against and put himself above anything called God or anything that people worship. And that Man of Evil will even go into God's Temple[d] and sit there and say that he is God.

[5]I told you when I was with you that all this would happen. Do you not remember? [6]And now you know what is stopping that Man of Evil so he will appear at the right time. [7]The secret power of evil is already working in the world, but there is one who is stopping that power. And he will continue to stop it until he is taken out of the way. [8]Then that Man of Evil will appear, and the Lord Jesus will kill him with the breath that comes from his mouth and will destroy him with the glory of his coming. [9]The Man of Evil will come by the power of Satan. He will have great power, and he will do many different false miracles,[d]

signs, and wonders. [10]He will use every kind of evil to trick those who are lost. They will die, because they refused to love the truth. (If they loved the truth, they would be saved.) [11]For this reason God sends them something powerful that leads them away from the truth so they will believe a lie. [12]So all those will be judged guilty who did not believe the truth, but enjoyed doing evil.

You Are Chosen for Salvation

[13]Brothers and sisters, whom the Lord loves, God chose you from the beginning to be saved. So we must always thank God for you. You are saved by the Spirit[d] that makes you holy and by your faith in the truth. [14]God used the Good News[d] that we preached to call you to be saved so you can share in the glory of our Lord Jesus Christ. [15]So, brothers and sisters, stand strong and continue to believe the teachings we gave you in our speaking and in our letter.

[16-17]May our Lord Jesus Christ himself and God our Father encourage you and strengthen you in every good thing you do and say. God loved us, and through his grace he gave us a good hope and encouragement that continues forever.

Pray for Us

3 And now, brothers and sisters, pray for us that the Lord's teaching will continue to spread quickly and that people will give honor to that teaching, just as happened with you. [2]And pray that we will be protected from stubborn and evil people, because not all people believe. [3]But the Lord is faithful and will give you strength and will protect you from the Evil One. [4]The Lord makes us feel sure that you are doing and will continue to do the things we told you. [5]May the Lord lead your hearts into God's love and Christ's patience.

The Duty to Work

[6]Brothers and sisters, by the authority of our Lord Jesus Christ we command you to stay away from any believer who refuses to work and does not follow the teaching we gave you. [7]You yourselves know that you should live as we live. We were not lazy when we were with you. [8]And when we ate another person's food, we always paid for it. We worked very hard night and day so we would not be an expense to any of you. [9]We had the right to ask you to help us, but we worked to take care of ourselves so we would be an example for you to follow. [10]When we were with you, we gave you this rule: "Anyone who refuses to work should not eat."

[11]We hear that some people in your group refuse to work. They do nothing but busy them-

---

turning away Or "the rebellion."

selves in other people's lives. ¹²We command those people and beg them in the Lord Jesus Christ to work quietly and earn their own food. ¹³But you, brothers and sisters, never become tired of doing good.

SIDELIGHT: Slouches, beware! If you don't work, you don't eat. That's what 2 Thessalonians 3:11–13 says to people who sat around waiting for Christ's Second Coming. The original Greek language is a pun. It could be translated, "No loaf for loafers!"

---

¹⁴If some people do not obey what we tell you in this letter, then take note of them. Have nothing to do with them so they will feel ashamed. ¹⁵But do not treat them as enemies. Warn them as fellow believers.

Final Words

¹⁶Now may the Lord of peace give you peace at all times and in every way. The Lord be with all of you.

¹⁷I, Paul, end this letter now in my own handwriting. All my letters have this to show they are from me. This is the way I write.

¹⁸The grace of our Lord Jesus Christ be with you all.

GOD'S LOVE

Tough Times

The Jefferson family experienced the pits of despair. Mr. Jefferson, a fantastic, energetic, loving husband and father, was killed in a car accident. He left a wife, an eighteen-year-old daughter, and a sixteen-year-old son. How would the family survive this horribly lonely and tough time?

Their church rallied around them. People volunteered to mow their yard and repair their house. Church members cooked and served meals every day right after the death and once a week throughout the following year. The church collected a special offering for their immediate expenses and found a job for Mrs. Jefferson. Church friends supported the family throughout that tough first year with phone calls, visits, cards, and gifts.

The Jeffersons wrote this thank-you to their congregation: "Through your prayers, dear friends, we have been comforted. Through your kind acts we have been soothed. We experienced God's love through you and your love. You made an unbearable experience bearable."

As the church comforted the Jeffersons, **2 Thessalonians 2:13—3:5** promises that God's love will comfort Christians who suffer.

■ How is the love shown to the Jeffersons by their congregation like the love that comforted the early Christians?
■ How does God's love comfort you through tough times?

C O N S I D E R . . .

■ circling the word love each time you read your Bible over the next several days. Count the number of "loves." Notice how God's love for you is stressed throughout the Bible. Consider starting your reading with the passages listed below.
■ letting God's love shine through you. Think of someone who is sad or lonely (for example, a new person at school or an elderly church member who has lost a spouse). Surprise that person with a present or a card.

F O R   M O R E ,   S E E . . .

■ Psalm 89:1–2 (p. 534)
■ Matthew 11:28–30 (p. 928)
■ Romans 5:6–8 (p. 1145)

1 TIMOTHY

Why Read This Book:

- Learn how to guard against false teaching (1 Timothy 1).
- Find out what to look for in a good church leader (1 Timothy 2—5).
- See what is really important in life (1 Timothy 6).

Behind the Scenes:

When you begin using a computer, you could just turn it on and start punching keys, hoping you will hit the right ones to make something happen. But, more likely, you will begin by reading the machine's operations manual. There you will find step-by-step things to do to use the machine correctly.

The first Christians didn't have experience running a church. Many times they tried different things, hoping they were right. But they also needed an "operations manual."

First Timothy was just what they needed. It gives church leaders specific guidance on running a church: choosing leaders, dealing with false teachings, and order in worship, for example. It's called a "pastoral letter" because it focuses on the work of pastors. The two other pastoral letters in the Bible are 2 Timothy (p. 1263) and Titus (p. 1270).

Just because 1 Timothy was originally written about church leaders doesn't mean pastors are the only ones who can benefit from reading it. The book helps all Christians learn the differences between true and false teachings. And it gives practical guidance on how to live as Christians.

WHERE THE ACTION WAS

Rome • ITALY
GREECE
ASIA MINOR
Ephesus
Lystra
Mediterranean Sea
AFRICA

Timothy was teaching the Christians in Ephesus (1 Timothy 1:3).

Timothy was a native of Lystra, (Acts 16:1, p. 1122).

WHEN THE ACTION WAS

Jesus was born	The church began soon after Jesus went to heaven	Timothy traveled with Paul on numerous trips	Fire destroyed Rome
BC/AD	**25AD**	**50AD**	**75AD**	**100AD**
	Jesus began his ministry	Paul became a Christian	I Timothy may have been written	Romans destroyed the Temple in Jerusalem

1 From Paul, an apostle[d] of Christ Jesus, by the command of God our Savior and Christ Jesus our hope.

[2]To Timothy, a true child to me because you believe:

Grace, mercy, and peace from God the Father and Christ Jesus our Lord.

> ✺ **SIDELIGHT:** Genealogies were hot fads in Bible times (1 Timothy 1:4). Alexander the Great even made up his own family tree, linking him with such Greek gods as Hercules and Achilles.

Warning Against False Teaching

[3]I asked you to stay longer in Ephesus when I went into Macedonia so you could command some people there to stop teaching false things. [4]Tell them not to spend their time on stories that are not true and on long lists of names in family histories. These things only bring arguments; they do not help God's work, which is done in faith. [5]The purpose of this command is for people to have love, a love that comes from a pure heart and a good conscience and a true faith. [6]Some people have missed these things and turned to useless talk. [7]They want to be teachers of the law, but they do not understand either what they are talking about or what they are sure about.

[8]But we know that the law is good if someone uses it lawfully. [9]We also know that the law is not made for good people but for those who are against the law and for those who refuse to follow it. It is for people who are against God and are sinful, who are not holy and have no religion, who kill their fathers and mothers, who murder, [10]who take part in sexual sins, who have sexual relations with people of the same sex, who sell slaves, who tell lies, who speak falsely, and who do anything against the true teaching of God. [11]That teaching is part of the Good News[d] of the blessed God that he gave me to tell.

Thanks for God's Mercy

[12]I thank Christ Jesus our Lord, who gave me strength, because he trusted me and gave me this work of serving him. [13]In the past I spoke against Christ and persecuted him and did all kinds of things to hurt him. But God showed me mercy, *because I did not know what I was doing. I did* not believe. [14]But the grace of our Lord was fully given to me, and with that grace came the faith and love that are in Christ Jesus.

[15]What I say is true, and you should fully accept it: Christ Jesus came into the world to save sinners, of whom I am the worst. [16]But I was given

mercy so that in me, the worst of all sinners, Christ Jesus could show that he has patience without limit. His patience with me made me an example for those who would believe in him and have life forever. [17]To the King that rules forever, who will never die, who cannot be seen, the only God, be honor and glory forever and ever. Amen.

[18]Timothy, my child, I am giving you a command that agrees with the prophecies[d] that were given about you in the past. I tell you this so you can follow them and fight the good fight. [19]Continue to have faith and do what you know is right. Some people have rejected this, and their faith has been shipwrecked. [20]Hymenaeus and Alexander have done that, and I have given them to Satan so they will learn not to speak against God.

Some Rules for Men and Women

2 First, I tell you to pray for all people, asking God for what they need and being thankful to him. [2]Pray for rulers and for all who have authority so that we can have quiet and peaceful lives full of worship and respect for God. [3]This is good, and it pleases God our Savior, [4]who wants all people to be saved and to know the truth. [5]There is one God and one way human beings can reach God. That way is through Christ Jesus, who is himself human. [6]He gave himself as a payment to free all people. He is proof that came at the right time. [7]That is why I was chosen to tell the Good News[d] and to be an apostle.[d] (I am telling the truth; I am not lying.) I was chosen to teach those who are not Jews to believe and to know the truth.

[8]So, I want the men everywhere to pray, lifting up their hands in a holy manner, without anger and arguments.

> ✺ **SIDELIGHT:** Though many Christians kneel and fold their hands to pray, the early Christians often stood with their hands raised when they prayed (1 Timothy 2:8). In the art of the Christian catacombs—underground burial places—praying figures are always depicted standing.

[9]Also, women should wear proper clothes that show respect and self-control, not using braided hair or gold or pearls or expensive clothes. [10]Instead, *they should do good deeds, which is right* for women who say they worship God.

[11]Let a woman learn by listening quietly and being ready to cooperate in everything. [12]But I do not allow a woman to teach or to have authority over a man, but to listen quietly, [13]because Adam was formed first and then Eve. [14]And Adam was

not tricked, but the woman was tricked and became a sinner. [15]But she will be saved through having children if they continue in faith, love, and holiness, with self-control.

Elders in the Church

3 What I say is true: Anyone wanting to become an elder[d] desires a good work. [2]An elder must not give people a reason to criticize him, and he must have only one wife. He must be self-controlled, wise, respected by others, ready to welcome guests, and able to teach. [3]He must not drink too much wine or like to fight, but rather be gentle and peaceable, not loving money. [4]He must be a good family leader, having children who cooperate with full respect. [5](If someone does not know how to lead the family, how can that person take care of God's church?) [6]But an elder must not be a new believer, or he might be too proud of himself and be judged guilty just as the devil was. [7]An elder must also have the respect of people who are not in the church so he will not be criticized by others and caught in the devil's trap.

Deacons in the Church

[8]In the same way, deacons[d] must be respected by others, not saying things they do not mean. They must not drink too much wine or try to get rich by cheating others. [9]With a clear conscience

---

Accidents Happen

Tyler Hanson and Troy Carr crouched low when they heard a twig snap. Peering through the brush, they saw the buck.

"I'll circle to his left. You circle to his right," Troy whispered.

Tyler nodded and started crawling to the right.

As the buck wandered closer, Tyler slowly rose and pointed his rifle.

But Troy's shot pierced the silence first, and Tyler fell to the ground before he could shoot.

When Tyler awoke eight hours later at the hospital, he couldn't see. He had been shot in the eye, his doctors explained. A glass eye would replace his destroyed eye.

Tyler seethed. "How could his best friend do this to him?" he asked himself.

When Troy visited Tyler for the first time, Tyler refused to speak to him. He folded his arms and wouldn't face Troy. When Troy hung around too long, Tyler exploded. "Get out of here! Leave me alone!"

After Tyler settled down, he and Troy talked. The buck had jumped right before Troy pulled the trigger. "It was an accident. I jerked the gun to hit him," Troy explained. "But instead, I hit you. Please, don't hate me."

It took weeks for Tyler to talk to Troy—let alone forgive him. But finally Tyler realized forgiveness was the only way to heal the bitterness inside him. And when he forgave Troy, the two became close again.

"Yes, I lost my eye," Tyler told Troy two months after the accident, "but I didn't need to lose a friend, too."

Tyler and Troy understood the importance of mercy and forgiveness, which is what **1 Timothy 1:12–17** is all about. Read what the writer says about mercy.

- How is Troy like the writer in this passage? How are they different? Why were Troy and the writer of 1 Timothy thankful for the forgiveness they received?
- How might God's forgiveness help you deal with the sins you've committed?

C O N S I D E R . . .

- praying about the wrongs you have done and asking God for forgiveness. Write "You are forgiven" on a note, and post it on your mirror.
- inviting someone you need to forgive to an ice cream shop. Buy the person a treat, talk about the problem, and forgive the person. Ask your forgiven friend to forgive you.

F O R   M O R E ,   S E E . . .

- Genesis 50:15–21 (p. 56)
- Matthew 6:14–15 (p. 918)
- 2 Corinthians 2:5–10 (p. 1194)

they must follow the secret of the faith that God made known to us. [10]Test them first. Then let them serve as deacons if you find nothing wrong in them. [11]In the same way, women[n] must be respected by others. They must not speak evil of others. They must be self-controlled and trustworthy in everything. [12]Deacons must have only one wife and be good leaders of their children and their own families. [13]Those who serve well as deacons are making an honorable place for themselves, and they will be very bold in their faith in Christ Jesus.

The Secret of Our Life

[14]Although I hope I can come to you soon, I am writing these things to you now. [15]Then, even if I am delayed, you will know how to live in the family of God. That family is the church of the living God, the support and foundation of the truth. [16]Without doubt, the secret of our life of worship is great:

He was shown to us in a human body,
proved right in spirit,[d]

and seen by angels.
He was preached to those who are not Jews,
believed in by the world,
and taken up in glory.

A Warning About False Teachers

4 Now the Holy Spirit[d] clearly says that in the later times some people will stop believing the faith. They will follow spirits that lie and teachings of demons.[d] [2]Such teachings come from the false words of liars whose consciences are destroyed as if by a hot iron. [3]They forbid people to marry and tell them not to eat certain foods which God created to be eaten with thanks by people who believe and know the truth. [4]Everything God made is good, and nothing should be refused if it is accepted with thanks, [5]because it is made holy by what God has said and by prayer.

Be a Good Servant of Christ

[6]By telling these things to the brothers and sis-

---

women This might mean the wives of the deacons, or it might mean women who serve in the same way as deacons.

PRAYER

Pray for All People

"I'm shipping out tonight to Saudi Arabia. I'll see you when I get back."

Darlene Wachs hung up the phone. Saudi Arabia? Her boyfriend Greg Richter was going to Saudi Arabia with the U.S. armed forces. She didn't even know where Saudi Arabia was! She said a quick prayer, asking God to keep Greg safe.

Darlene swallowed the lump in her throat and searched for a world atlas. She was terrified something could happen to Greg, but she wanted at least to know where he was going.

During the worship service on Sunday, her pastor said, "Let's pray for all people," and then listed different parts of the world, including Saudi Arabia. Darlene's mind usually wandered during those prayers, since the places seemed so far away and irrelevant to her life. But this time she paid attention. What happened in Saudi Arabia really did affect her life.

When Darlene's boyfriend suddenly went overseas, she understood the importance of praying for all people. **1 Timothy 2:1–4** expands our prayer concerns beyond ourselves and reminds us God cares for the whole world.

■ How does praying for a country such as Saudi Arabia fit the message of this scripture?
■ Which countries and rulers should you pray for today?

CONSIDER . . .

■ reading the international section of your newspaper. Ask members of your church to pray for the people mentioned there.
■ looking at a world atlas, and praying for people in different parts of the world. Pray for them each evening.

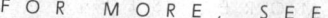

FOR MORE, SEE . . .

■ Psalm 46 (p. 508)
■ Ephesians 6:18–20 (p. 1226)

■ James 5:13–18 (p. 1299)

ters,[n] you will be a good servant of Christ Jesus. You will be made strong by the words of the faith and the good teaching which you have been following. [7]But do not follow foolish stories that disagree with God's truth, but train yourself to serve God. [8]Training your body helps you in some ways, but serving God helps you in every way by bringing you blessings in this life and in the future

SIDELIGHT: When 1 Timothy 4:8 talks about training your body, the original Greek word for training is the same as gymnastics in English. And the word gymnastics comes from the word for nude, since athletes worked out in the nude. Today we just have to put up with gang showers!

life, too. [9]What I say is true, and you should fully accept it. [10]This is why we work and struggle: We hope in the living God who is the Savior of all people, especially of those who believe.

[11]Command and teach these things. [12]Do not let anyone treat you as if you are unimportant because you are young. Instead, be an example to the believers with your words, your actions, your love, your faith, and your pure life. [13]Until I come, continue to read the Scriptures[d] to the people, strengthen them, and teach them. [14]Use the gift you have, which was given to you through prophecy[d] when the group of elders[d] laid their hands on[n] you. [15]Continue to do those things; give your life to doing them so your progress may be seen by everyone. [16]Be careful in your life and in your teaching. If you continue to live and teach rightly, you will save both yourself and those who listen to you.

Rules for Living with Others

5 Do not speak angrily to an older man, but plead with him as if he were your father. Treat younger men like brothers, [2]older women like mothers, and younger women like sisters. Always treat them in a pure way.

[3]Take care of widows who are truly widows. [4]But if a widow has children or grandchildren, let them first learn to do their duty to their own family and to repay their parents or grandparents. That pleases God. [5]The true widow, who is all alone, puts her hope in God and continues to pray night and day for God's help. [6]But the widow

who uses her life to please herself is really dead while she is alive. [7]Tell the believers to do these things so that no one can criticize them. [8]Whoever does not care for his own relatives, especially his own family members, has turned against the faith and is worse than someone who does not believe in God.

[9]To be on the list of widows, a woman must be at least sixty years old. She must have been faithful to her husband. [10]She must be known for her good works — works such as raising her children, welcoming strangers, washing the feet of God's people, helping those in trouble, and giving her life to do all kinds of good deeds.

[11]But do not put younger widows on that list. After they give themselves to Christ, they are pulled away from him by their physical needs, and then they want to marry again. [12]They will be judged for not doing what they first promised to do. [13]Besides that, they learn to waste their time, going from house to house. And they not only waste their time but also begin to gossip and busy themselves with other people's lives, saying things they should not say. [14]So I want the younger widows to marry, have children, and manage their homes. Then no enemy will have any reason to criticize them. [15]But some have already turned away to follow Satan.

[16]If any woman who is a believer has widows in her family, she should care for them herself. The church should not have to care for them. Then it will be able to take care of those who are truly widows.

[17]The elders[d] who lead the church well should receive double honor, especially those who work hard by speaking and teaching, [18]because the Scripture[d] says: "When an ox is working in the grain, do not cover its mouth to keep it from eating,"[n] and "A worker should be given his pay."[a]

[19]Do not listen to someone who accuses an elder, without two or three witnesses. [20]Tell those who continue sinning that they are wrong. Do this in front of the whole church so that the others will have a warning.

[21]Before God and Christ Jesus and the chosen angels, I command you to do these things without showing favor of any kind to anyone.

[22]Think carefully before you lay your hands on[a] anyone, and don't share in the sins of others. Keep yourself pure.

[23]Stop drinking only water, but drink a little wine to help your stomach and your frequent sicknesses.

---

brothers and sisters Although the Greek text says "brothers" here and throughout this book, Paul's words refer to the entire church, including men and women.
laid their hands on The laying on of hands had many purposes, including the giving of a blessing, power, or authority.
"When . . . eating," Quotation from Deuteronomy 25:4.
"A worker . . . pay." Quotation from Luke 10:7.
lay your hands on The laying on of hands had many purposes, including the giving of a blessing, power, or authority.

²⁴The sins of some people are easy to see even before they are judged, but the sins of others are seen only later. ²⁵So also good deeds are easy to see, but even those that are not easily seen cannot stay hidden.

6 All who are slaves under a yoke*d* should show full respect to their masters so no one will speak against God's name and our teaching. ²The slaves whose masters are believers should not show their masters any less respect because they are believers. They should serve their masters even better, because they are helping believers they love.

You must teach and preach these things.

False Teaching and True Riches

³Anyone who has a different teaching does not agree with the true teaching of our Lord Jesus Christ and the teaching that shows the true way to serve God. ⁴This person is full of pride and understands nothing, but is sick with a love for arguing and fighting about words. This brings jealousy, fighting, speaking against others, evil mistrust, ⁵and constant quarrels from those who have evil

minds and have lost the truth. They think that serving God is a way to get rich.

⁶Serving God does make us very rich, if we are satisfied with what we have. ⁷We brought nothing into the world, so we can take nothing out. ⁸But, if we have food and clothes, we will be satisfied with that. ⁹Those who want to become rich bring temptation to themselves and are caught in a trap. They want many foolish and harmful things that ruin and destroy people. ¹⁰The love of money causes all kinds of evil. Some people have left the faith, because they wanted to get more money, but they have caused themselves much sorrow.

Some Things to Remember

¹¹But you, man of God, run away from all those things. Instead, live in the right way, serve God, have faith, love, patience, and gentleness. ¹²Fight the good fight of faith, grabbing hold of the life that continues forever. You were called to have that life when you confessed the good confession before many witnesses. ¹³In the sight of God, who gives life to everything, and of Christ Jesus, I give

MONEY

More and More

Disappointed by her mom's refusal to buy the expensive dress she wanted for her junior prom, Janice Nielsen vowed her senior prom would be different.

So, at the start of her senior year, Janice landed a job as a cashier in a video store. All year she worked hard. From each paycheck, she diligently put away money for the prom dress and other prom expenses.

During March and April, Janice tried on dress after dress. She wanted to buy just the right one—the one that would make her happy.

The morning after the prom, Janice sat in her room and cried. The night had been wonderful. Her dress was beautiful. The limousine ride was fun. But now it was all over. The hundreds of dollars she had spent had not brought the happiness she expected.

She felt betrayed, especially when she compared her senior prom to her junior prom. After all, she had had just as much fun at the junior prom, even though her dress had cost much less.

Janice thought money would buy her happiness. As you read **1 Timothy 6:6–16**, consider what truly makes Christians rich.

■ What advice in this passage could help Janice understand the ultimate result of the love of money?

■ When do you get caught up in wanting more? How could the advice in the passage help you avoid that trap?

C O N S I D E R . . .

■ analyzing your use of money in three categories: spending, saving and giving. Based on what you read in the passage, what do you need to do with your money?

■ beginning a tithe (giving 10 percent of your income) to your church.

F O R   M O R E ,   S E E . . .

■ Joshua 7:19–26 (p. 200)   ■ Hebrews 13:5–6 (p. 1291)
■ Proverbs 15:27 (p. 581)

you a command. Christ Jesus made the good confession when he stood before Pontius Pilate. [14]Do what you were commanded to do without wrong or blame until our Lord Jesus Christ comes again. [15]God will make that happen at the right time. He is the blessed and only Ruler, the King of all kings and the Lord of all lords. [16]He is the only One who never dies. He lives in light so bright no one can go near it. No one has ever seen God, or can see him. May honor and power belong to God forever. Amen.

[17]Command those who are rich with things of this world not to be proud. Tell them to hope in God, not in their uncertain riches. God richly gives us everything to enjoy. [18]Tell the rich people to do good, to be rich in doing good deeds, to be generous and ready to share. [19]By doing that, they will be saving a treasure for themselves as a strong foundation for the future. Then they will be able to have the life that is true life.

[20]Timothy, guard what God has trusted to you. Stay away from foolish, useless talk and from the arguments of what is falsely called "knowledge." [21]By saying they have that "knowledge," some have missed the true faith.

Grace be with you.

SIDELIGHT: Saying that Jesus Christ is "King of all kings and the Lord of all lords" (1 Timothy 6:15) was a bold statement in the midst of the persecution the early Christians faced. Near the end of the first century, the Roman emperor Domitian demanded that his subjects address him as "Lord and God." Christians who refused were threatened, exiled, and put to death.

2 TIMOTHY

Why Read This Book:

- Be encouraged to keep following God, even when you face danger for doing it (2 Timothy 1—2).
- Find out how to make it through tough times (2 Timothy 3—4).

Behind the Scenes:

People who know they are soon to die often divide up their belongings and ask those around them to finish the projects they have started. Paul knew he was facing death (2 Timothy 4:6–8), so he wrote this letter to hand off the baton of ministry for Timothy to carry on.

Second Timothy captures what a retiring leader would say to a new leader. It gives lots of encouragement. It gives advice on how to become a leader. And it says that the road will be rocky and rough at times, but we should remain strong anyway.

While 1 Timothy gives instructions on how to run a church, 2 Timothy is a personal letter—like one you would write to a close friend. It encourages Christians facing tough times, since the Roman leader was persecuting Christians. And it can encourage us to stick to our faith today, even when people try to pull us away.

WHERE THE ACTION WAS

Nero was one of the emperors who ruled the Roman Empire, which controlled this territory.

SPAIN

Rome

AFRICA

Mediterranean Sea

Ephesus

Timothy was teaching the Christians in Ephesus (1 Timothy 1:3, p. 1256).

Paul died as a prisoner in Rome (2 Timothy 4:6–8).

WHEN THE ACTION WAS

Jesus was born	The church began soon after Jesus went to heaven	Timothy traveled with Paul on numerous trips	Fire destroyed Rome	
BC/AD	**25AD**	**50AD**	**75AD**	**100AD**
	Jesus began his ministry	Paul became a Christian	2 Timothy may have been written	Romans destroyed the Temple in Jerusalem

1 From Paul, an apostle*d* of Christ Jesus by the will of God. God sent me to tell about the promise of life that is in Christ Jesus. ²To Timothy, a dear child to me:

Grace, mercy, and peace to you from God the Father and Christ Jesus our Lord.

Encouragement for Timothy

³I thank God as I always mention you in my prayers, day and night. I serve him, doing what I know is right as my ancestors did. ⁴Remembering that you cried for me, I want very much to see you so I can be filled with joy. ⁵I remember your true faith. That faith first lived in your grandmother Lois and in your mother Eunice, and I know you now have that same faith. ⁶This is why I remind you to keep using the gift God gave you when I laid my hands on*ⁿ* you. Now let it grow, as a small flame grows into a fire. ⁷God did not give us a spirit that makes us afraid but a spirit of power and love and self-control.

⁸So do not be ashamed to tell people about our Lord Jesus, and do not be ashamed of me, in prison for the Lord. But suffer with me for the Good News.*d* God, who gives us the strength to do that, ⁹saved us and made us his holy people. That was not because of anything we did ourselves but because of God's purpose and grace. That grace was given to us through Christ Jesus before time began, ¹⁰but it is now shown to us by the coming of our Savior Christ Jesus. He de-

---

laid my hands on   The laying on of hands had many purposes, including the giving of a blessing, power, or authority.

SHARING FAITH

What to Say?

Megan Taylor abruptly dropped out of church. She had been going regularly for several months, so the group noticed her absence immediately. Her friend Jeanne Murray went over to Megan's house to ask what was wrong.

"I'm just not good enough to be a Christian," Megan replied. "I sometimes swear when I get mad. I think bad things sometimes. And I just don't feel like I set a good example for other people."

"But you don't need to be perfect or know all the answers," Jeanne said.

Megan just shook her head, and Jeanne struggled to find the right words to help her friend. "You're always so giving, and Christians are giving," Jeanne said.

"I'm not more giving than anybody else," Megan replied.

Jeanne didn't know how to respond. The more she thought, the more frustrated she became. She finally blurted out, "You are a Christian, Megan. But if I were really a good friend, I'd know how to help you."

Megan paused. "You're right. You're absolutely right."

"Huh?" a puzzled Jeanne asked.

"You just told me why I can still be a Christian," Megan said. "We've been friends a long time, right? But sometimes we don't feel like we're good friends. It's the same with being a Christian. At times, I may feel like a failure. But as long as I'm trying, I'm doing okay. You really helped me, Jeanne. Thanks."

As Jeanne walked home, she still wondered how she had helped Megan. So, she simply thanked God for giving her the words to say. Jeanne's willingness to witness was a lot like **2 Timothy 1:3–14**.

■ How did Jeanne share her faith with Megan? How was her experience like and unlike the passage?

■ What does this passage say about sharing your faith with others?

C O N S I D E R . . .

■ telling your family why you are a Christian. Ask how family members see you sharing your faith.

■ dropping a postcard to someone struggling with his or her faith, encouraging that person like 2 Timothy offers encouragement.

F O R   M O R E ,   S E E . . .

■ Exodus 4:1–12 (p. 62)   ■ 1 Corinthians 1:18–31 (p. 1168)
■ Luke 9:1–6 (p. 1018)

stroyed death, and through the Good News he showed us the way to have life that cannot be destroyed. [11]I was chosen to tell that Good News and to be an apostle[d] and a teacher. [12]I am suffering now because I tell the Good News, but I am not ashamed, because I know Jesus, the One in whom I have believed. And I am sure he is able to protect what he has trusted me with until that day.[n] [13]Follow the pattern of true teachings that you heard from me in faith and love, which are in Christ Jesus. [14]Protect the truth that you were given; protect it with the help of the Holy Spirit[d] who lives in us.

SIDELIGHT: Like his mentor Paul (2 Timothy 1:8), Timothy also experienced persecution for his faith, according to Hebrews 13:23 (p. 1292). He was imprisoned but released. Paul was apparently executed while a prisoner in Rome.

---

[15]You know that everyone in the country of Asia has left me, even Phygelus and Hermogenes. [16]May the Lord show mercy to the family of Onesiphorus, who has often helped me and was not ashamed that I was in prison. [17]When he came to Rome, he looked eagerly for me until he found me. [18]May the Lord allow him to find mercy from the Lord on that day. You know how many ways he helped me in Ephesus.

A Loyal Soldier of Christ Jesus

2 You then, Timothy, my child, be strong in the grace we have in Christ Jesus. [2]You should teach people whom you can trust the things you and many others have heard me say. Then they will be able to teach others. [3]Share in the troubles we have like a good soldier of Christ Jesus. [4]A soldier wants to please the enlisting officer, so no one serving in the army wastes time with everyday matters. [5]Also an athlete who takes part in a contest must obey all the rules in order to win. [6]The farmer who works hard should be the first person to get some of the food that was grown. [7]Think about what I am saying, because the Lord will give you the ability to understand everything.

[8]Remember Jesus Christ, who was raised from the dead, who is from the family of David. This *is the Good News[d] I preach,* [9]*and I am suffering* because of it to the point of being bound with chains like a criminal. But God's teaching is not

in chains. [10]So I patiently accept all these troubles so that those whom God has chosen can have the salvation that is in Christ Jesus. With that salvation comes glory that never ends.
[11]This teaching is true:
  If we died with him, we will also live with
    him.
[12] If we accept suffering, we will also rule
    with him.
  If we refuse to accept him, he will refuse to
    accept us.
[13] If we are not faithful, he will still be
    faithful,
  because he cannot be false to himself.

A Worker Pleasing to God

[14]Continue teaching these things, warning people in God's presence not to argue about words. It does not help anyone, and it ruins those who listen. [15]Make every effort to give yourself to God as the kind of person he will accept. Be a worker who is not ashamed and who uses the true teaching in the right way. [16]Stay away from foolish, useless talk, because that will lead people further away from God. [17]Their evil teaching will spread like a sickness inside the body. Hymenaeus and Philetus are like that. [18]They have left the true teaching, saying that the rising from the dead has already taken place, and so they are destroying the faith of some people. [19]But God's strong foundation continues to stand. These words are written on the seal: "The Lord knows those who belong to him,"[n] and "Everyone who wants to belong to the Lord must stop doing wrong."

[20]In a large house there are not only things made of gold and silver, but also things made of wood and clay. Some things are used for special purposes, and others are made for ordinary jobs. [21]All who make themselves clean[d] from evil will be used for special purposes. They will be made holy, useful to the Master, ready to do any good work.

[22]But run away from the evil young people like to do. Try hard to live right and to have faith, love, and peace, together with those who trust in the Lord from pure hearts. [23]Stay away from foolish and stupid arguments, because you know they grow into quarrels. [24]And a servant of the Lord must not quarrel but must be kind to everyone, a good teacher, and patient. [25]The Lord's servant must gently teach those who disagree. Then maybe God will let them change their minds so they can accept the truth. [26]And they may wake up and escape from the trap of the devil, who catches them to do what he wants.

---

day The day Christ will come to judge all people and take his people to live with him.
"The Lord ... him" Quotation from Numbers 16:5.

The Last Days

3 Remember this! In the last days there will be many troubles, [2]because people will love themselves, love money, brag, and be proud. They will say evil things against others and will not obey their parents or be thankful or be the kind of people God wants. [3]They will not love others, will refuse to forgive, will gossip, and will not control themselves. They will be cruel, will hate what is good, [4]will turn against their friends, and will do foolish things without thinking. They will be conceited, will love pleasure instead of God, [5]and will act as if they serve God but will not have his power. Stay away from those people. [6]Some of them go into homes and get control of silly women who are full of sin and are led by many evil desires. [7]These women are always learning new teachings, but they are never able to understand the truth fully. [8]Just as Jannes and Jambres were against Moses, these people are against the truth. Their thinking has been ruined, and they have failed in trying to follow the faith. [9]But they will not be successful in what they do,

PATIENCE

Worth the Wait

For thirty years, Rosa Parks bristled at the inequalities all around her. Because she was black, she had to ride in the back of the bus. Her skin color made everything more difficult for her in the segregated South.

On her way home from work in 1955, in Montgomery, Alabama, Rosa boarded a bus and filled a vacant seat. She was exhausted. Her neck, shoulders and back ached from sewing alterations all day. A few white people boarded the bus after Rosa, and they all found seats, except for one white man.

The bus driver asked someone to give up a seat, meaning that a black person was to give up a seat for the white person. Since Rosa sat in a seat closest to the front and closest to the aisle, everyone looked at her. But Rosa would not budge. Finally two police officers arrested her.

Rosa's arrest stirred an uproar in the black community. People were furious at the unfairness of forcing a black woman to give up her seat on a bus to a white man just because of her skin color.

People gathered at Dexter Avenue Baptist Church to organize a bus boycott that made history and brought Martin Luther King, Jr., to national attention. The 381-day boycott required intense patience and endurance as the organizers set up car pools to transport workers who relied on bus transportation. The boycott succeeded when Montgomery buses were ordered desegregated in 1956. No longer would blacks be forced to give up their seats for whites.

Because of Rosa Parks's patience and the patience of the boycott leaders, the civil rights movement of the 1950s and 1960s was born. By refusing to budge and by being patient to see segregation crumble, Rosa showed the patience reflected in **2 Timothy 2:8–13**.

■ How are the patience and suffering mentioned in this passage like the patience and suffering of blacks in the boycott?

■ How could this passage help you to be more patient during tough times?

C O N S I D E R . . .

■ asking God for patience to deal with a problem you are facing, and then being patient.

■ talking with your family about creating a rule for silently counting to fifteen when someone tries a family member's patience.

F O R   M O R E ,   S E E . . .

■ Numbers 11:4–20 (p. 136)
■ Romans 8:16–18 (p. 1150)

■ 1 Peter 4:12–19 (p. 1307)

because as with Jannes and Jambres, everyone will see that they are foolish.

Obey the Teachings

¹⁰But you have followed what I teach, the way I live, my goal, faith, patience, and love. You know I never give up. ¹¹You know how I have been hurt and have suffered, as in Antioch, Iconium, and Lystra. I have suffered, but the Lord saved me from all those troubles. ¹²Everyone who wants to live as God desires, in Christ Jesus, will be hurt. ¹³But people who are evil and cheat others will go from bad to worse. They will fool others, but they will also be fooling themselves.

¹⁴But you should continue following the teachings you learned. You know they are true, because you trust those who taught you. ¹⁵Since you were a child you have known the Holy Scriptures*d* which are able to make you wise. And that wisdom leads to salvation through faith in Christ Jesus. ¹⁶All Scripture is given by God and is useful for teaching, for showing people what is wrong in their lives, for correcting faults, and for teaching how to live right. ¹⁷Using the Scriptures, the person who serves God will be capable, having all that is needed to do every good work.

4 I give you a command in the presence of God and Christ Jesus, the One who will judge the living and the dead, and by his coming and his kingdom: ²Preach the Good News.*d* Be ready at all times, and tell people what they need to do. Tell them when they are wrong. Encourage them with great patience and careful teaching, ³because the time will come when people will not listen to the true teaching but will find many more teachers who please them by saying the things they want to hear. ⁴They will stop listening to the truth and will begin to follow false stories. ⁵But you should control yourself at all times, accept troubles, do the work of telling the Good News, and complete all the duties of a servant of God.

BIBLE STUDY

Take Time to Learn

Reading the Bible is important, right? But do you do it? Many Christian teenagers don't, indicates Teenage Magazine:

■ Thirteen percent of Christian teenagers say they never read their Bible.
■ Only eight percent say they read the Bible every day.
■ Forty-four percent say they read the Bible only when they feel like it.
■ And the rest, thirty-five percent, read the Bible a few times a week, or less.

Why don't Christian teenagers read the Bible? Teenagers say the top five reasons are:
1. They get busy.
2. They would rather do something else.
3. They think the Bible is boring.
4. They don't know how to study the Bible.
5. They forget to read it.

The Bible has been called the most printed and the least read of all books. Adults and teenagers alike cannot grow as Christians without the life-changing guidance of the Bible. Teenagers might get a lot from the Bible if they read it knowing the value of scripture as described in **2 Timothy 3:14—4:5**.

■ According to this passage, of what value is Bible study to the Christian's life?
■ What can you do to make Bible study an important part of your everyday life?

C O N S I D E R . . .

■ asking your youth minister or pastor for tips on how to make Bible study easier and more effective.
■ spending one week reading through one of the Gospels (Matthew, Mark, Luke, or John) with a friend, meeting every day at lunch to discuss what you have learned in your reading.

F O R   M O R E ,   S E E . . .

■ Psalm 119:97–104 (p. 552)
■ John 5:39 (p. 1066)
■ 2 Timothy 1:13–14 (p. 1264)

⁶My life is being given as an offering to God, and the time has come for me to leave this life. ⁷I have fought the good fight, I have finished the race, I have kept the faith. ⁸Now, a crown is being held for me — a crown for being right with God. The Lord, the judge who judges rightly, will give the crown to me on that day *n* — not only to me but to all those who have waited with love for him to come again.

Personal Words

⁹Do your best to come to me as soon as you can, ¹⁰because Demas, who loved this world, left me and went to Thessalonica. Crescens went to Galatia, and Titus went to Dalmatia. ¹¹Luke is the only one still with me. Get Mark and bring him with you when you come, because he can help me in my work here. ¹²I sent Tychicus to Ephesus. ¹³When I was in Troas, I left my coat there with Carpus. So when you come, bring it to me, along with my books, particularly the ones written on parchment. *n*

 SIDELIGHT: Have trouble misplacing things? Take heart. So did the apostle Paul. He left his coat in Troas (2 Timothy 4:13), which was more than a hundred miles from Ephesus, and close to a thousand miles from Rome — the two places he might have been when he asked the people to send the coat to him. This coat was probably a heavy cloak that would have kept Paul warmer in a damp prison cell.

¹⁴Alexander the metalworker did many harmful things against me. The Lord will punish him for what he did. ⁵You also should be careful that

day The day Christ will come to judge all people and take his people to live with him.
parchment A writing paper made from the skins of sheep.

PERSISTENCE

Dream Big

He always dreamed of playing football, but many obstacles blocked his dream.

His church discouraged playing the game. His parents weren't keen on the idea, but eventually they let him try out for the sport. In seventh grade, he went out for the team — even though he was too small to fit in a uniform.

Once on the field playing defense, the odds of his making the team seemed even worse. "The coach put me up against the biggest fullback on the team," he recalls. "I didn't know what to do. I yelled and grabbed him around the legs. He carried me for a few yards, and I finally tackled him."

After that first courageous tackle, the coach let the boy play. Although he lacked size, the coach saw a "won't-give-up" persistence in the kid. And he showed an intensity the coach rarely saw.

Many years later, after high school and college football, this persistent player was drafted by the Chicago Bears. And in 1985 and 1988 Mike Singletary, the 6-foot, 230-pound linebacker, was named the NFL Defensive Player of the Year.

His seventh-grade persistence paid off for Mike Singletary. He lives the message of persistence in **2 Timothy 4:6–18**.

- How is Mike Singletary like the writer of 2 Timothy, especially in verse 16 of this passage?
- What hobby, sport, or talent have you considered giving up on? How should you decide whether to stick with it or not?

CONSIDER . . .

- identifying someone who has stuck with something after almost quitting. Write or call that person, encouraging him or her to hang in there.
- looking at the people around you — friends, family, teachers. Choose one person you can talk to when you feel like quitting.

FOR MORE, SEE . . .

- 1 Samuel 17:1–54 (p. 260)
- Acts 20:24 (p. 1130)
- 1 Corinthians 9:24–27 (p. 1178)

he does not hurt you, because he fought strongly against our teaching.

[16]The first time I defended myself, no one helped me; everyone left me. May they be forgiven. [17]But the Lord stayed with me and gave me strength so I could fully tell the Good News[d] to all those who are not Jews. So I was saved from the lion's mouth. [18]The Lord will save me when anyone tries to hurt me, and he will bring me safely to his heavenly kingdom. Glory forever and ever be the Lord's. Amen.

Final Greetings

[19]Greet Priscilla and Aquila and the family of Onesiphorus. [20]Erastus stayed in Corinth, and I left Trophimus sick in Miletus. [21]Try as hard as you can to come to me before winter.

Eubulus sends greetings to you. Also Pudens, Linus, Claudia, and all the brothers and sisters in Christ greet you.

[22]The Lord be with your spirit. Grace be with you.

TITUS

Why Read
This Book:

■ Find out what it takes to be a Christian leader (Titus 1).
■ Discover how to live as a Christian (Titus 2—3).

**Behind the
Scenes:**

Suppose you knew a group of people who lied, bickered, and were greedy? Most likely you would write them off as evil people and wouldn't hang around with them. And what if these people said they were Christians? You would probably call them hypocrites—then switch churches.

Yet that is the kind of people Titus encountered when he went to Crete, an island infamous for its tough people. Years earlier, a poet from the island had written: "Cretans are always liars, evil animals, and lazy people who do nothing but eat" (Titus 1:12).

But instead of writing off these people, Titus had gone to work with them, helping them grow in their faith. It was a tough missionary assignment. The letter to Titus encourages the leader and gives the people practical advice on how to overcome their past, sinful practices and to begin living a new life in Christ.

This short letter is full of help for effective Christian living. It summarizes the basics of the Christian faith, and encourages all people to live lives that are pleasing to God.

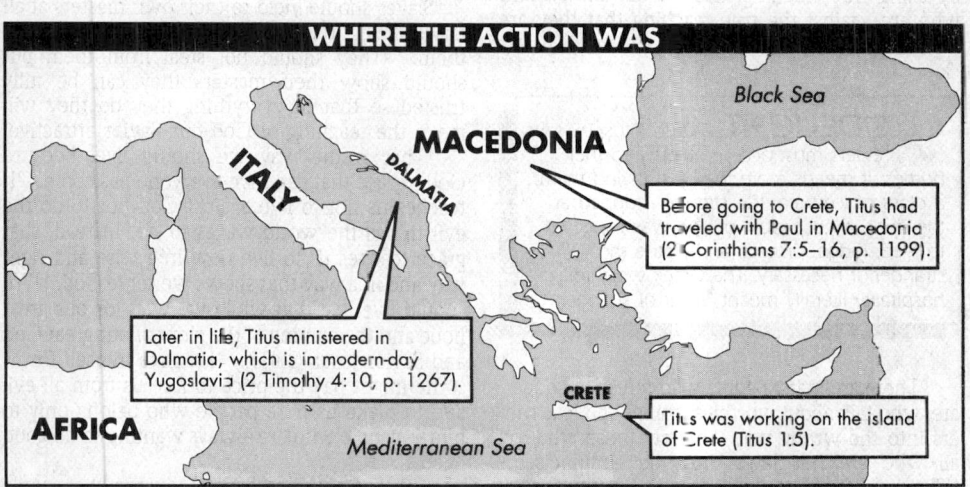

WHERE THE ACTION WAS

Black Sea

MACEDONIA

ITALY

DALMATIA

Before going to Crete, Titus had traveled with Paul in Macedonia (2 Corinthians 7:5–16, p. 1199).

Later in life, Titus ministered in Dalmatia, which is in modern-day Yugoslavia (2 Timothy 4:10, p. 1267).

AFRICA

CRETE

Titus was working on the island of Crete (Titus 1:5).

Mediterranean Sea

WHEN THE ACTION WAS

Jesus was born	The church began soon after Jesus went to heaven	Paul began his missionary work	Fire destroyed Rome	
BC/AD	**25AD**	**50AD**	**75AD**	**100AD**
	Jesus began his ministry	Paul became a Christian	Titus may have been written	Romans destroyed the Temple in Jerusalem

1 From Paul, a servant of God and an apostle[d] of Jesus Christ. I was sent to help the faith of God's chosen people and to help them know the truth that shows people how to serve God. [2]That faith and that knowledge come from the hope for life forever, which God promised to us before time began. And God cannot lie. [3]At the right time God let the world know about that life through preaching. He trusted me with that work, and I preached by the command of God our Savior.

[4]To Titus, my true child in the faith we share:

Grace and peace from God the Father and Christ Jesus our Savior.

Titus' Work in Crete

[5]I left you in Crete so you could finish doing the things that still needed to be done and so you could appoint elders[d] in every town, as I directed you. [6]An elder must not be guilty of doing wrong, must have only one wife, and must have believing children. They must not be known as children who are wild and do not cooperate. [7]As God's manager, an elder must not be guilty of doing wrong, being selfish, or becoming angry quickly. He must not drink too much wine, like to fight, or try to get rich by cheating others. [8]An elder must be ready to welcome guests, love what is good, be wise, live right, and be holy and self-controlled. [9]By holding on to the trustworthy word just as we teach it, an elder can help people by using true teaching, and he can show those who are against the true teaching that they are wrong.

> ✳ **SIDELIGHT:** When Titus 1:8 says elders must accept others into their homes, it means more than just giving them a glass of iced tea. If a stranger stopped at the door, a hospitable person was expected to feed, lodge, protect, and clothe the stranger, if necessary. The Greek word for hospitality literally meant "lover of strangers."

[10]There are many people who refuse to cooperate, who talk about worthless things and lead others into the wrong way—mainly those who say all who are not Jews must be circumcised.[d] [11]These people must be stopped, because they are upsetting whole families by teaching things they should not teach, which they do to get rich by cheating people. [12]Even one of their own prophets said, "Cretans are always liars, evil animals, and lazy people who do nothing but eat." [13]The words that prophet said are true. So firmly tell those people they are wrong so they may become

strong in the faith, [14]not accepting Jewish false stories and the commands of people who reject the truth. [15]To those who are pure, all things are pure, but to those who are full of sin and do not believe, nothing is pure. Both their minds and their consciences have been ruined. [16]They say they know God, but their actions show they do not accept him. They are hateful people, they refuse to obey, and they are useless for doing anything good.

Following the True Teaching

2 But you must tell everyone what to do to follow the true teaching. [2]Teach older men to be self-controlled, serious, wise, strong in faith, in love, and in patience.

[3]In the same way, teach older women to be holy in their behavior, not speaking against others or enslaved to too much wine, but teaching what is good. [4]Then they can teach the young women to love their husbands, to love their children, [5]to be wise and pure, to be good workers at home, to be kind, and to yield to their husbands. Then no one will be able to criticize the teaching God gave us.

[6]In the same way, encourage young men to be wise. [7]In every way be an example of doing good deeds. When you teach, do it with honesty and seriousness. [8]Speak the truth so that you cannot be criticized. Then those who are against you will be ashamed because there is nothing bad to say about us.

[9]Slaves should yield to their own masters at all times, trying to please them and not arguing with them. [10]They should not steal from them but should show their masters they can be fully trusted so that in everything they do they will make the teaching of God our Savior attractive. [11]That is the way we should live, because God's grace that can save everyone has come. [12]It teaches us not to live against God nor to do the evil things the world wants to do. Instead, that grace teaches us to live now in a wise and right way and in a way that shows we serve God. [13]We should live like that while we wait for our great hope and the coming of the glory of our great God and Savior Jesus Christ. [14]He gave himself for us so he might pay the price to free us from all evil and to make us pure people who belong only to him—people who are always wanting to do good deeds.

[15]Say these things and encourage the people and tell them what is wrong in their lives, with all authority. Do not let anyone treat you as if you were unimportant.

The Right Way to Live

3 Remind the believers to yield to the authority of rulers and government leaders, to obey them, to be ready to do good, [2]to speak no evil about anyone, to live in peace, and to be gentle and polite to all people.

[3]In the past we also were foolish. We did not obey, we were wrong, and we were slaves to many things our bodies wanted and enjoyed. We spent our lives doing evil and being jealous. People hated us, and we hated each other. [4]But when the kindness and love of God our Savior was shown, [5]he saved us because of his mercy. It was not because of good deeds we did to be right with him. He saved us through the washing that made us new people through the Holy Spirit.[d] [6]God poured out richly upon us that Holy Spirit through Jesus Christ our Savior. [7]Being made right with God by his grace, we could have the hope of receiving the life that never ends.

[8]This teaching is true, and I want you to be sure the people understand these things. Then those who believe in God will be careful to use their lives for doing good. These things are good and will help everyone.

[9]But stay away from those who have foolish arguments and talk about useless family histories and argue and quarrel about the law. Those things are worth nothing and will not help anyone. [10]After a first and second warning, avoid someone who causes arguments. [11]You can know that such people are evil and sinful; their own sins prove them wrong.

Some Things to Remember

[12]When I send Artemas or Tychicus to you, make every effort to come to me at Nicopolis, because I have decided to stay there this winter. [13]Do all you can to help Zenas the lawyer and

---

The Fun Factor

Tom Harrington didn't think Christianity was much fun. There were so many rules and commandments. No getting drunk. No swearing. No messing around with girls. No making fun of other people. To be a Christian, he thought, meant wearing a stern face, singing slow hymns and eating tuna casseroles at potluck dinners.

His view of Christianity brightened when he saw in his youth minister's office a painting of a laughing Jesus.

Tom never imagined Jesus laughing before. He had always thought of Jesus as quiet and somber—someone who never smiled and spoke only in wise-sounding tones. Could Jesus really be fun?

This image of Jesus laughing made Tom look again at the stories of Jesus in the Gospels. He saw hints of Jesus' humor and began to see in the stories the Jesus of the painting. He started going to youth group, where he met Christians who had fun. They had joy, too, even when life wasn't great.

As Tom grew in faith, his own view of fun changed. Instead of calling friends to go get drunk, he called a Christian friend. Sometimes they just talked and laughed. Other times they watched comedies. Whatever they did, they enjoyed it, without hurting themselves.

Like Tom, the early Christians also had trouble knowing how Christians should live. **Titus 2:11—3:7** describes the joy of living a Christian life that is freeing and hopeful, not dull and rigid.

■ How does the picture of a laughing Jesus match the good news of God's gift that is described in this passage?
■ How could you implement these guidelines in your life and enjoy following them at the same time? What in the passage gives reason to celebrate following God?

C O N S I D E R . . .
■ looking around your church for positive, fun, or joyful images of faith in paintings, pictures, banners, and books. Think about how these images of joy compare to the world's view of fun.
■ meeting with your Christian friends and thinking of ideas for joyful ways to follow Christ.

F O R   M O R E ,   S E E . . .
■ Isaiah 6:1–8 (p. 622)   ■ Philippians 4:4–9 (p. 1234)
■ Ephesians 4:31–32 (p. 1224)

Apollos on their journey so that they have everything they need. [14]Our people must learn to use their lives for doing good deeds to provide what is necessary so that their lives will not be useless.

[15]All who are with me greet you. Greet those who love us in the faith.

Grace be with you all.

SIDELIGHT: The reason Paul says he plans to spend the winter in Nicopolis (Titus 3:12) was that ships stopped sailing during the stormy winter months. The practice would have made it hard to get to Grandma's for Christmas!

PHILEMON

**Behind the
Scenes:**

Onesimus, a slave, deserved to die. He had stolen from his master, then run away. Under Roman law, a runaway slave had no rights. Disobedience meant possible beatings, tortuous brandings on the face and even crucifixion.

But something had happened since Onesimus had left his master. He had become a Christian through Paul's influence. And making the matter even more complicated, his master Philemon was also a Christian. Onesimus knew he should return to his master, but he also knew he could die if he went back.

So Paul wrote this letter to persuade Philemon to forgive Onesimus and welcome him back as a Christian friend. Instead of telling Philemon to punish Onesimus, Paul asked that the wrongdoing be charged to Paul.

Though we no longer live with slavery, we, like Philemon, may be tempted to look down on people because of the color of their skin, the amount of money they have, or what they wear. And we may treat them as second-class citizens and think we are first class. Philemon challenges all of us to rethink those prejudices.

WHERE THE ACTION WAS

Black Sea

MACEDONIA

ITALY

Rome

Ephesus
Colosse

AFRICA

Mediterranean Sea

Paul was in prison in Rome or Ephesus when he wrote Philemon (Philemon 23).

Philemon lived in Colosse when Paul wrote him this letter (Philemon 15; Colossians 4:9, p. 1243).

WHEN THE ACTION WAS

Jesus was born	The church began soon after Jesus went to heaven	Paul began his missionary work	Fire destroyed Rome	
BC/AD	**25AD**	**50AD**	**75AD**	**100AD**
	Jesus began his ministry	Paul became a Christian	Paul wrote Philemon	Romans destroyed the Temple in Jerusalem

¹From Paul, a prisoner of Christ Jesus, and from Timothy, our brother.

To Philemon, our dear friend and worker with us; ²to Apphia, our sister; to Archippus, a worker with us; and to the church that meets in your home:

³Grace and peace to you from God our Father and the Lord Jesus Christ.

Philemon's Love and Faith

⁴I always thank my God when I mention you in my prayers, ⁵because I hear about the love you have for all God's holy people and the faith you have in the Lord Jesus. ⁶I pray that the faith you share may make you understand every blessing we have in Christ. ⁷I have great joy and comfort, my brother, because the love you have shown to God's people has refreshed them.

Accept Onesimus as a Brother

⁸So, in Christ, I could be bold and order you to do what is right. ⁹But because I love you, I am pleading with you instead. I, Paul, an old man now and also a prisoner for Christ Jesus, ¹⁰am pleading with you for my child Onesimus, who became my child while I was in prison. ¹¹In the past he was useless to you, but now he has become useful for both you and me.

¹²I am sending him back to you, and with him I am sending my own heart. ¹³I wanted to keep him with me so that in your place he might help me while I am in prison for the Good News.ᵈ ¹⁴But I did not want to do anything without asking you first so that any good you do for me will be because you want to do it, not because I forced you. ¹⁵Maybe Onesimus was separated from you

> ✳ **SIDELIGHT:** Slavery was common in the Roman Empire in Paul's day. According to some estimates, there were about sixty million slaves in the Empire—up to half the total population.

for a short time so you could have him back forever— ¹⁶no longer as a slave, but better than a slave, as a loved brother. I love him very much, but you will love him even more, both as a person and as a believer in the Lord.

¹⁷So if you consider me your partner, welcome

FRIENDS

A Friend in Everyone

Everyone liked Connie Klein. But nobody liked Sam Bush—except Connie.

After school, Connie would visit Sam. They would go biking, go for long walks in the park, or listen to music.

No one understood what Connie saw in Sam. People made fun of Sam because his socks didn't match. His shirt was usually buttoned wrong, and his hair wasn't always combed. And when Sam sang duets with Connie, people would rather plug their ears than listen to Sam sing.

Sam was mentally disabled. And when he tried to sing, he moaned. And the more fun he had, the louder he moaned.

But Connie didn't mind. In fact, she loved it. She loved to see him smile and laugh. She loved to see his eyes light up every time she showed up. And every time, she would give Sam a big hug before going home.

Connie didn't dismiss Sam because he was different from herself. Instead she saw him as an important friend. Consider her reasons as you read Paul's view on Christian relationships in **Philemon 4–21**.

■ How are Onesimus and Sam alike? Why did Paul stand up for Onesimus?
■ How can this passage help you befriend someone who is friendless?

CONSIDER . . .

■ investing your time in getting to know kids in special education programs. For example, you might volunteer to tutor elementary-age kids with learning disabilities.

■ asking someone you don't like very well to join you for popcorn. Get to know the person by asking a lot of questions.

FOR MORE, SEE . . .
■ 1 Samuel 20:1–42 (p. 263)
■ Matthew 25:34–46 (p. 954)
■ 1 Timothy 6:11–16 (p. 1260)

Onesimus as you would welcome me. [18]If he has done anything wrong to you or if he owes you anything, charge that to me. [19]I, Paul, am writing this with my own hand. I will pay it back, and I will say nothing about what you owe me for your own life. [20]So, my brother, I ask that you do this for me in the Lord: Refresh my heart in Christ. [21]I write this letter, knowing that you will do what I ask you and even more.

[22]One more thing—prepare a room for me in which to stay, because I hope God will answer your prayers and I will be able to come to you.

Final Greetings

[23]Epaphras, a prisoner with me for Christ Jesus, sends greetings to you. [24]And also Mark, Aristarchus, Demas, and Luke, workers together with me, send greetings.

[25]The grace of our Lord Jesus Christ be with your spirit.

HEBREWS

Why Read This Book:

Behind the Scenes:

Imagine a courtroom scene. The jury has heard persuasive testimony from many different people. Now the jury is about to go behind closed doors to come to a verdict about whether Christianity does hold the truth. But first the lawyers will present their closing arguments.

The book of Hebrews is like a closing argument in defense of Christianity. Using careful logic and referring often to testimony, the writer shows that Jesus Christ is the Son of God and worthy of our faith. The book compares and contrasts Jesus with all of Old Testament history and argues that Jesus is the climax of everything in the past.

So, the author concludes, "Let us look only to Jesus, the One who began our faith and who makes it perfect. . . . Think about Jesus' example. . . . So do not get tired and stop trying" (Hebrews 12:2–3).

We don't know how the original readers responded to the eloquent argument in Hebrews. But we do know that the book has become a treasured source of encouragement and hope for Christians through the centuries. Just as this letter encouraged its first readers to hold strong to their faith, it can do the same for us today.

WHEN THE ACTION WAS

Jesus was born	The church began soon after Jesus went to heaven	Paul began his missionary work	Fire destroyed Rome
BC/AD	**25AD**	**50AD**	**75AD** **100AD**
	Jesus began his ministry	Paul became a Christian	Hebrews was written	Romans destroyed the Temple in Jerusalem

God Spoke Through His Son

1 In the past God spoke to our ancestors through the prophets[d] many times and in many different ways. [2]But now in these last days God has spoken to us through his Son. God has chosen his Son to own all things, and through him he made the world. [3]The Son reflects the glory of God and shows exactly what God is like. He holds everything together with his powerful word. When the Son made people clean from their sins, he sat down at the right side of God, the Great One in heaven. [4]The Son became much greater than the angels, and God gave him a name that is much greater than theirs.

SIDELIGHT: No one really knows who wrote Hebrews. Suggestions have included Paul, Apollos, Luke, Barnabas, Clement of Rome, Silas, Philip, and Priscilla. In the third century, Origen probably had the right idea when he wrote, "Who wrote the epistle God alone knows certainly."

---

[5]This is because God never said to any of the angels,
"You are my Son.
Today I have become your Father."   *Psalm 2:7*
Nor did God say of any angel,
"I will be his Father,
and he will be my Son."   *2 Samuel 7:14*
[6]And when God brings his firstborn Son into the world, he says,
"Let all God's angels worship him." [n]   *Psalm 97:7*
[7]This is what God said about the angels:
"God makes his angels become like winds.
He makes his servants become like flames
of fire."   *Psalm 104:4*
[8]But God said this about his Son:
"God, your throne will last forever and ever.
You will rule your kingdom with fairness.
[9]You love right and hate evil,
so God has chosen you from among your
friends;
he has set you apart with much joy."
  Psalm 45:6-7
[10]God also says,
"Lord, in the beginning you made the earth,
and your hands made the skies.
[11]They will be destroyed, but you will remain.
They will all wear out like clothes.

[12]You will fold them like a coat.
And, like clothes, you will change them.
But you never change,
and your life will never end."   *Psalm 102:25-27*
[13]And God never said this to an angel:
"Sit by me at my right side
until I put your enemies under your
control." [n]   *Psalm 110:1*
[14]All the angels are spirits who serve God and are sent to help those who will receive salvation.

Our Salvation Is Great

2 So we must be more careful to follow what we were taught. Then we will not stray away from the truth. [2]The teaching God spoke through angels was shown to be true, and anyone who did not follow it or obey it received the punishment that was earned. [3]So surely we also will be punished if we ignore this great salvation. The Lord himself first told about this salvation, and it was proven true to us by those who heard him. [4]God also proved it by using wonders, great signs, many kinds of miracles,[d] and by giving people gifts through the Holy Spirit,[d] just as he wanted.

Christ Became like Humans

[5]God did not choose angels to be the rulers of the new world that was coming, which is what we have been talking about. [6]It is written in the Scriptures,[d]
"Why are people important to you?
Why do you take care of human beings?
[7]You made them a little lower than the angels
and crowned them with glory and honor.
[8] You put all things under their control."
  Psalm 8:4-6
When God put everything under their control, there was nothing left that they did not rule. Still, we do not yet see them ruling over everything. [9]But we see Jesus, who for a short time was made lower than the angels. And now he is wearing a crown of glory and honor because he suffered and died. And by God's grace, he died for everyone.

[10]God is the One who made all things, and all things are for his glory. He wanted to have many children share his glory, so he made the One who leads people to salvation perfect through suffering.

[11]Jesus, who makes people holy, and those who are made holy are from the same family. So he is not ashamed to call them his brothers and sisters. [n] [12]He says,
"Then, I will tell my fellow Israelites about
you;

"Let . . . him."   These words are found in Deuteronomy 32:43 in the Septuagint, the Greek version of the Old Testament, and in a Hebrew copy among the Dead Sea Scrolls.
until . . . control   Literally, "until I make your enemies a footstool for your feet."
brothers and sisters   Although the Greek text says "brothers" here and throughout this book, the writer's words were meant for the entire church, including men and women.

I will praise you in the public meeting."

Psalm 22:22

[13]He also says,

"I will trust in God."   Isaiah 8:17

And he also says,

"I am here, and with me are the children
    God has given me."   Isaiah 8:18

[14]Since these children are people with physical bodies, Jesus himself became like them. He did this so that, by dying, he could destroy the one who has the power of death—the devil— [15]and free those who were like slaves all their lives because of their fear of death. [16]Clearly, it is not angels that Jesus helps, but the people who are from Abraham.[n] [17]For this reason Jesus had to be made like his brothers in every way so he could be their merciful and faithful high priest in service to God. Then Jesus could bring forgiveness for their sins. [18]And now he can help those who are tempted, because he himself suffered and was tempted.

Jesus Is Greater than Moses

3 So all of you holy brothers and sisters, who were called by God, think about Jesus, who

was sent to us and is the high priest of our faith. [2]Jesus was faithful to God as Moses was in God's family. [3]Jesus has more honor than Moses, just as the builder of a house has more honor than the house itself. [4]Every house is built by someone, but the builder of everything is God himself. [5]Moses was faithful in God's family as a servant, and he told what God would say in the future. [6]But Christ is faithful as a Son over God's house. And we are God's house if we keep on being very sure about our great hope.

We Must Continue to Follow God

[7]So it is as the Holy Spirit[d] says:
"Today listen to what he says.
[8]Do not be stubborn as in the past
    when you turned against God,
when you tested God in the desert.
[9]There your ancestors tried me and tested me
    and saw the things I did for forty years.
[10]I was angry with them.
    I said, 'They are not loyal to me
    and have not understood my ways.'
[11]I was angry and made a promise,

Abraham   Most respected ancestor of the Jews. Every Jew hoped to see Abraham.

SHARING FAITH

Can You Tell the Difference?

When she graduated from college, Bev Johnson became a short-term missionary at a school in Japan. Each day she led a Bible study and taught English to the Japanese.

Each day an elderly woman came to the Bible study. She sat quietly in the back of the room and rushed out when it ended. And each day Bev grew more curious about the silent woman.

One day after the Bible study, Bev walked quickly to the woman and began a conversation. The woman spoke excellent English. She told Bev she had heard of Jesus since she was a young girl. The woman owned a Bible and knew much of it by heart.

"Are you a Christian?" Bev asked.

"No, no I'm not," the woman said, "but I've seen Christians, and I'm watching to see if Jesus makes any difference in their lives."

From that incident, Bev learned how people need to see Jesus in Christians. Read how Jesus can shine through us in **Hebrews 2:9–18**.

■ How does the older woman's statement to Bev relate to this passage?

■ Why do you think God, in Jesus, became a person for us to know?

CONSIDER . . .

■ listing all the ways Jesus showed what God is like, such as loving all people, and so on. Choose one of those ways to show how you follow Christ.

✔ letting at least one other person know this week how Christ has made a difference in your life.

FOR MORE, SEE . . .

■ Isaiah 57:14–21 (p. 676)

■ Matthew 20:29–34 (p. 944)

■ John 11:28–43 (p. 1077)

'They will never enter my rest.' " *n*

Psalm 95:7-11

[12]So brothers and sisters, be careful that none of you has an evil, unbelieving heart that will turn you away from the living God. [13]But encourage each other every day while it is "today." *n* Help each other so none of you will become hardened because sin has tricked you. [14]We all share in Christ if we keep till the end the sure faith we had in the beginning. [15]This is what the Scripture[d] says:

"Today listen to what he says.
　Do not be stubborn as in the past
　when you turned against God."　*Psalm 95:7-8*

[16]Who heard God's voice and was against him? It was all those people Moses led out of Egypt. [17]And with whom was God angry for forty years? He was angry with those who sinned, who died in the desert. [18]And to whom was God talking when he promised that they would never enter his rest? He was talking to those who did not obey him. [19]So we see they were not allowed to enter and have God's rest, because they did not believe.

SIDELIGHT: If Hebrews had been submitted as a term paper, it probably would have gotten a good grade for research and documentation. The book quotes from the Old Testament more than eighty times, including Psalm 95:7-11 (p. 537) in Hebrews 3:7-11.

---

4 Now, since God has left us the promise that we may enter his rest, let us be very careful so none of you will fail to enter. [2]The Good News[d] was preached to us just as it was to them. But the teaching they heard did not help them, because they heard it but did not accept it with faith. [3]We who have believed are able to enter and have God's rest. As God has said,

"I was angry and made a promise,
　'They will never enter my rest.' "　*Psalm 95:11*

But God's work was finished from the time he made the world. [4]In the Scriptures[d] he talked about the seventh day of the week: "And on the seventh day God rested from all his works." *n*
[5]And again in the Scripture God said, "They will never enter my rest."

[6]It is still true that some people will enter God's rest, but those who first heard the way to be saved did not enter, because they did not obey. [7]So God planned another day, called "today." He spoke about that day through David a long time later in the same Scripture used before:

"Today listen to what he says.
　Do not be stubborn."　*Psalm 95:7-8*

[8]We know that Joshua *n* did not lead the people into that rest, because God spoke later about another day. [9]This shows that the rest *n* for God's people is still coming. [10]Anyone who enters God's rest will rest from his work as God did. [11]Let us try as hard as we can to enter God's rest so that no one will fail by following the example of those who refused to obey.

[12]God's word is alive and working and is sharper than a double-edged sword. It cuts all the way into us, where the soul and the spirit are joined, to the center of our joints and bones. And it judges the thoughts and feelings in our hearts. [13]Nothing in all the world can be hidden from God. Everything is clear and lies open before him, and to him we must explain the way we have lived.

Jesus Is Our High Priest

[14]Since we have a great high priest, Jesus the Son of God, who has gone into heaven, let us hold on to the faith we have. [15]For our high priest is able to understand our weaknesses. When he lived on earth, he was tempted in every way that we are, but he did not sin. [16]Let us, then, feel very sure that we can come before God's throne where there is grace. There we can receive mercy and grace to help us when we need it.

5 Every high priest is chosen from among other people. He is given the work of going before God for them to offer gifts and sacrifices for sins. [2]Since he himself is weak, he is able to be gentle with those who do not understand and who are doing wrong things. [3]Because he is weak, the high priest must offer sacrifices for his own sins and also for the sins of the people.

[4]To be a high priest is an honor, but no one chooses himself for this work. He must be called by God as Aaron *n* was. [5]So also Christ did not choose himself to have the honor of being a high priest, but God chose him. God said to him,

"You are my Son.
　Today I have become your Father."　*Psalm 2:7*

[6]And in another Scripture[d] God says,

"You are a priest forever,

---

rest　A place of rest God promised to give his people.
"today"　This word is taken from verse 7. It means that it is important to do these things now.
"And . . . works."　Quotation from Genesis 2:2.
Joshua　After Moses died, Joshua became leader of the Jewish people and led them into the land that God promised to give them.
rest　Literally, "sabbath rest," meaning a sharing in the rest that God began after he created the world.
Aaron　Aaron was Moses' brother and the first Jewish high priest.

a priest like Melchizedek." *n*   *Psalm 110:4*

[7]While Jesus lived on earth, he prayed to God and asked God for help. He prayed with loud cries and tears to the One who could save him from death, and his prayer was heard because he trusted God. [8]Even though Jesus was the Son of God, he learned obedience by what he suffered. [9]And because his obedience was perfect, he was able to give eternal salvation to all who obey him. [10]In this way God made Jesus a high priest, a priest like Melchizedek.

Warning Against Falling Away

[11]We have much to say about this, but it is hard to explain because you are so slow to understand.

[12]By now you should be teachers, but you need someone to teach you again the first lessons of God's message. You still need the teaching that is like milk. You are not ready for solid food. [13]Anyone who lives on milk is still a baby and knows nothing about right teaching. [14]But solid food is for those who are grown up. They have practiced in order to know the difference between good and evil.

6 So let us go on to grown-up teaching. Let us not go back over the beginning lessons we learned about Christ. We should not again start teaching about faith in God and about turning away from those acts that lead to death. [2]We should not return to the teaching about bap-

Melchizedek   A priest and king who lived in the time of Abraham. (Read Genesis 14:17-24.)

FOLLOWING GOD

When the Going Gets Tough . . .

Isabella Baumfree was an African-American slave born to a Dutch owner in Ulster County, New York, about 1797. She was separated from her family and sold twice before she was twelve. Slave life was never easy. Even after she was set free in 1827, she barely survived as a domestic helper in New York City.

After the Civil War began, Isabella left New York to "travel up an' down the land showin' the people their sins an' bein' a sign unto them." She even changed her name to Sojourner Truth.

Sojourner Truth became famous for her unique style of preaching. Although she couldn't read or write, she preached a message of freedom for slaves, women, and the poor. She spoke in a heavy Dutch accent, knew the Bible well, and drew stares by wrapping a turban around her head.

Because blacks—especially black women—were routinely oppressed, Sojourner Truth found the going difficult. But she kept at it, hardened by her life of slavery and struggle. Her fame spread; she even met with President Lincoln in 1864.

Fame doesn't always equal popularity, as Sojourner Truth found out. She often preached and lectured before hostile audiences. Many times she was told her mission was hopeless. "I don't care any more for your talk than I do for the bite of a flea," someone told her.

"Perhaps not," she replied, "but the Lord willing, I'll keep you scratchin'."

Sojourner Truth knew following God requires commitment and endurance. So did the writer of Hebrews. And, in **Hebrews 4:1–13**, the writer promises that endurance and commitment will not go unrewarded.

■ How was Sojourner Truth's persistence in her mission like the challenge of the passage to stay obedient to God? How did she embody the theme of verses 12–13?

■ What does the passage say about those who truly follow God versus those who just say they do?

CONSIDER . . .
■ taking an unpopular stand on an issue because you believe it's what God wants you to do.
■ listing things you would honestly die for. Decide how to follow those priorities better this week.

FOR MORE, SEE . . .
■ Deuteronomy 33:26–29 (p. 193)
■ Luke 10:25–37 (p. 1022)
■ Acts 7:51–60 (p. 1109)

tisms, [n] about laying on of hands, [n] about the raising of the dead and eternal judgment. ³And we will go on to grown-up teaching if God allows.

⁴Some people cannot be brought back again to a changed life. They were once in God's light, and enjoyed heaven's gift, and shared in the Holy Spirit. [d] ⁵They found out how good God's word is, and they received the powers of his new world. ⁶But they fell away from Christ. It is impossible to bring them back to a changed life again, because they are nailing the Son of God to a cross again and are shaming him in front of others.

⁷Some people are like land that gets plenty of rain. The land produces a good crop for those who work it, and it receives God's blessings. ⁸Other people are like land that grows thorns and weeds and is worthless. It is in danger of being cursed by God and will be destroyed by fire.

⁹Dear friends, we are saying this to you, but we really expect better things from you that will lead to your salvation ¹⁰God is fair; he will not forget the work you did and the love you showed for him by helping his people. And he will remember that you are still helping them. ¹¹We want each

---

baptisms The word here may refer to Christian baptism, or it may refer to the Jewish ceremonial washings.
laying on of hands The laying on of hands had many purposes, including the giving of a blessing, power, or authority.

GOD'S LOVE

Storm Trackers

When people on the Atlantic coast hear hurricane warnings, most board up their windows and evacuate the coastline. They know hurricanes can whip across the ocean with winds of more than 150 miles per hour and raise the ocean level by twenty feet.

But while most people are getting away from a hurricane, storm trackers aboard their WC-130 aircraft are headed straight into the storm. It takes ten to forty-five seconds to fly through the swirling clouds around the eye of the storm. Once in the storm's eye, the crew flies from one end of the eye to the other, tracking the hurricane's path and measuring its conditions.

These missions are extremely dangerous. The plane can be struck by lightning, or its jet engines sometimes stall because of the sheets of water kicked up by the storm. At times the winds are so strong that one pilot cannot steer the plane alone.

"Everything is whipping around," says storm tracker Scott Maddox describing a typical mission. "You have one pilot with both hands on the throttle and the other one on the automatic pilot, using it to bring the plane straight and level in air that is battering it in all directions."

Why do they go on these dangerous missions? Because without their efforts, more people would lose their lives in hurricanes. While satellite pictures warn when a hurricane is approaching land, they cannot measure wind speeds, barometric pressure, temperatures, or sea swells in the middle of the storm. That information is vital for forecasting when, where, and with how much force a hurricane will hit land.

Because they risk their lives on dangerous missions, storm trackers gain information that saves people's lives. Because of his love, God sent his Son Jesus on an even more deadly mission: to come to earth to save us and pay for our sins. Read about this unbelievable love in **Hebrews 4:14—5:10**.
■ How do the storm trackers illustrate the kind of self-sacrificing love that is described in this passage? What makes God's love even more amazing?
■ How does knowing about God's love and Christ's sacrifice for you affect the way you live?

CONSIDER...
■ looking in the newspaper this week for stories of people who take great risks to save the lives of others. Thank God for these human examples of the kind of love God has for people.
■ writing "Thanks for Your Love, God" at the top of a sheet of paper. Then fill the paper with words that show how you have experienced God's love. Keep the sheet in your Bible as a reminder, and add to it when you think of something new.

FOR MORE, SEE...
■ Daniel 9:1–9 (p. 816)
■ Matthew 7:7–11 (p. 919)
■ Romans 3:21–26 (p. 1143)

of you to go on with the same hard work all your lives so you will surely get what you hope for. [12]We do not want you to become lazy. Be like those who through faith and patience will receive what God has promised.

SIDELIGHT: Many scholars believe Hebrews may have originally been a sermon, partly because the author mentions speaking in several places (for example, Hebrews 6:9). If it was originally a sermon, it would have taken about fifty minutes to read aloud—not too long for an early Christian worship service. Their services often included "breaking bread" (communion), teaching, preaching, singing, praying, prophesying, and reading letters. Hope they had padded pews!

---

[13]God made a promise to Abraham. And as there is no one greater than God, he used himself when he swore to Abraham, [14]saying, "I will surely bless you and give you many descendants."[n] [15]Abraham waited patiently for this to happen, and he received what God promised.

[16]People always use the name of someone greater than themselves when they swear. The oath proves that what they say is true, and this ends all arguing. [17]God wanted to prove that his promise was true to those who would get what he promised. And he wanted them to understand clearly that his purposes never change, so he made an oath. [18]These two things cannot change: God cannot lie when he makes a promise, and he cannot lie when he makes an oath. These things encourage us who came to God for safety. They give us strength to hold on to the hope we have been given. [19]We have this hope as an anchor for the soul, sure and strong. It enters behind the curtain in the Most Holy Place in heaven, [20]where Jesus has gone ahead of us and for us. He has become the high priest forever, a priest like Melchizedek.[n]

The Priest Melchizedek

7 Melchizedek[n] was the king of Salem and a priest for God Most High. He met Abraham when Abraham was coming back after defeating the kings. When they met, Melchizedek blessed Abraham, [2]and Abraham gave him a tenth of everything he had brought back from the battle. First, Melchizedek's name means "king of good-

ness," and he is king of Salem, which means "king of peace." [3]No one knows who Melchizedek's father or mother was,[n] where he came from, when he was born, or when he died. Melchizedek is like the Son of God; he continues being a priest forever.

[4]You can see how great Melchizedek was. Abraham, the great father, gave him a tenth of everything that he won in battle. [5]Now the law says that those in the tribe[d] of Levi who become priests must collect a tenth from the people — their own people — even though the priests and the people are from the family of Abraham. [6]Melchizedek was not from the tribe of Levi, but he collected a tenth from Abraham. And he blessed Abraham, the man who had God's promises. [7]Now everyone knows that the more important person blesses the less important person. [8]Priests receive a tenth, even though they are only men who live and then die. But Melchizedek, who received a tenth from Abraham, continues living, as the Scripture[d] says. [9]We might even say that Levi, who receives a tenth, also paid it when Abraham paid Melchizedek a tenth. [10]Levi was not yet born, but he was in the body of his ancestor when Melchizedek met Abraham.

SIDELIGHT: If you think Melchizedek (Hebrews 7:1) is a hard name to say, try the Bible's longest name: Maher-Shalal-Hash-Baz, the name of Isaiah's son (Isaiah 8:1, p. 625).

---

[11]The people were given the law[n] based on a system of priests from the tribe of Levi, but they could not be made perfect through that system. So there was a need for another priest to come, a priest like Melchizedek, not Aaron. [12]And when a different kind of priest comes, the law must be changed, too. [13]We are saying these things about Christ, who belonged to a different tribe. No one from that tribe ever served as a priest at the altar. [14]It is clear that our Lord came from the tribe of Judah, and Moses said nothing about priests belonging to that tribe.

Jesus Is like Melchizedek

[15]And this becomes even more clear when we see that another priest comes who is like Melchizedek.[n] [16]He was not made a priest by human rules and laws but through the power of his life, which continues forever. [17]It is said about him,

---

"I ... descendants." Quotation from Genesis 22:17.
Melchizedek A priest and king who lived in the time of Abraham. (Read Genesis 14:17-24.)
No ... was Literally, "Melchizedek was without father, without mother, without genealogy."
The ... law This refers to the people of Israel who were given the law of Moses.

"You are a priest forever,
  a priest like Melchizedek."   *Psalm 110:4*

[18]The old rule is now set aside, because it was weak and useless. [19]The law of Moses could not make anything perfect. But now a better hope has been given to us, and with this hope we can come near to God. [20]It is important that God did this with an oath. Others became priests without an oath, [21]but Christ became a priest with God's oath. God said:

"The Lord has made a promise
  and will not change his mind.
'You are a priest forever.' "   *Psalm 110:4*

[22]This means that Jesus is the guarantee of a better agreement[n] from God to his people.

[23]When one of the other priests died, he could not continue being a priest. So there were many priests. [24]But because Jesus lives forever, he will never stop serving as priest. [25]So he is able always to save those who come to God through him because he always lives, asking God to help them.

[26]Jesus is the kind of high priest we need. He is holy, sinless, pure, not influenced by sinners, and he is raised above the heavens. [27]He is not like the other priests who had to offer sacrifices every day, first for their own sins, and then for the sins of the people. Christ offered his sacrifice only once and for all time when he offered himself. [28]The law chooses high priests who are people with weaknesses, but the word of God's oath came later than the law. It made God's Son to be the high priest, and that Son has been made perfect forever.

Jesus Is Our High Priest

8 Here is the point of what we are saying: We have a high priest who sits on the right side of God's throne in heaven. [2]Our high priest serves in the Most Holy Place, the true place of worship that was made by God, not by humans.

[3]Every high priest has the work of offering gifts and sacrifices to God. So our high priest must also offer something to God. [4]If our high priest were now living on earth, he would not be a priest, because there are already priests here who follow the law by offering gifts to God. [5]The work they do as priests is only a copy and a shadow of what is in heaven. This is why God warned Moses when he was ready to build the Holy Tent:[d] "Be very careful to make everything by the plan I showed you on the mountain."[n] [6]But the priestly work that has been given to Jesus is much greater than the work that was given to the other priests. In the same way, the new agreement that Jesus

brought from God to his people is much greater than the old one. And the new agreement is based on promises of better things.

[7]If there had been nothing wrong with the first agreement,[n] there would have been no need for a second agreement. [8]But God found something wrong with his people. He says:

"Look, the time is coming, says the Lord,
  when I will make a new agreement
with the people of Israel
  and the people of Judah.
[9]It will not be like the agreement
  I made with their ancestors
when I took them by the hand
  to bring them out of Egypt.
But they broke that agreement,
  and I turned away from them, says the
    Lord.
[10]This is the agreement I will make
  with the people of Israel at that time, says
    the Lord.
I will put my teachings in their minds
  and write them on their hearts.
I will be their God,
  and they will be my people.
[11]People will no longer have to teach their
    neighbors and relatives
  to know the Lord,
because all people will know me,
  from the least to the most important.
[12]I will forgive them for the wicked things they
    did,
  and I will not remember their sins
    anymore."   *Jeremiah 31:31-34*

[13]God called this a new agreement, so he has made the first agreement old. And anything that is old and worn out is ready to disappear.

The Old Agreement

9 The first agreement[n] had rules for worship and a man-made place for worship. [2]The Holy Tent[d] was set up for this. The first area in the Tent was called the Holy Place. In it were the lamp and the table with the bread that was made holy for God. [3]Behind the second curtain was a room called the Most Holy Place. [4]In it was a golden altar for burning incense[d] and the Ark[d] covered with gold that held the old agreement. Inside this Ark was a golden jar of manna,[d] Aaron's rod that once grew leaves, and the stone tablets of the old agreement. [5]Above the Ark were the creatures that showed God's glory, whose wings reached over the lid. But we cannot tell everything about these things now.

---

agreement   God gives a contract or agreement to his people. For the Jews, this agreement was the law of Moses. But now God has given a better agreement to his people through Christ.
"Be ... mountain."   Quotation from Exodus 25:40.
first agreement   The contract God gave the Jewish people when he gave them the law of Moses.

⁶When everything in the Tent was made ready in this way, the priests went into the first room every day to worship. ⁷But only the high priest could go into the second room, and he did that only once a year. He could never enter the inner room without taking blood with him, which he offered to God for himself and for sins the people did without knowing they did them. ⁸The Holy Spirit[d] uses this to show that the way into the Most Holy Place was not open while the system of the old Holy Tent was still being used. ⁹This is an example for the present time. It shows that the gifts and sacrifices offered cannot make the conscience of the worshiper perfect. ¹⁰These gifts and sacrifices were only about food and drink and special washings. They were rules for the body, to be followed until the time of God's new way.

The New Agreement

¹¹But when Christ came as the high priest of the good things we now have, he entered the greater and more perfect tent. It is not made by humans and does not belong to this world. ¹²Christ entered the Most Holy Place only once — and for all time. He did not take with him the blood of goats and calves. His sacrifice was his own blood, and by it he set us free from sin forever. ¹³The blood of goats and bulls and the ashes of a cow are sprinkled on the people who are unclean,[d] and this makes their bodies clean again. ¹⁴How much more is done by the blood of Christ. He offered himself through the eternal Spirit[n] as a perfect sacrifice to God. His blood will make our consciences pure from useless acts so we may serve the living God.

¹⁵For this reason Christ brings a new agreement from God to his people. Those who are called by God can now receive the blessings he has promised, blessings that will last forever. They can have those things because Christ died so that

Spirit   This refers to the Holy Spirit, to Christ's own spirit, or to the spiritual and eternal nature of his sacrifice.

Unexpected Forgiveness

Dawn Hammond and Craig Meadows had been dating for about a year. Both were sixteen. When Dawn stopped coming to youth group meetings, Donna Richards, her youth leader, dropped by after school to see if she was okay.

She obviously wasn't.

Dawn confessed her relationship with Craig had gotten very physical. "I think I'm pregnant," she said.

She and Craig had had sex on a date four weeks earlier. "It just happened. We didn't plan it," she kept saying.

"Have you told your parents?" Donna asked.

"No!" she screamed. "They would absolutely die if they knew!"

"That's not the main issue," Donna said. "They need to know, and you need their help."

Donna promised to stay with Dawn until her parents came home from work. When Dawn told them the news, they were upset at first, but they assured Dawn they loved her. What she had done was wrong, but it didn't change the way they felt about her. She was their daughter.

Dawn learned a hard lesson about sex before marriage. She also learned a lot about the kind of forgiveness and acceptance written about in **Hebrews 9:11—28**.

■ How was forgiveness by Dawn's parents like and unlike the forgiveness described in this passage? How did the price Dawn's parents paid in the story differ from the price Christ paid in the passage?

■ How are our sins forgiven, according to the passage?

CONSIDER . . .

■ talking with a trusted adult about a sin you're struggling with.

■ defining the word "sin," using this passage and the ones listed in "For More, See . . ." for guidance. Find out whether your friends agree with your definition. Check it out with your youth leader too.

FOR MORE, SEE . . .

■ Genesis 4:1–12 (p. 7)

■ Romans 3:21–26 (p. 1143)

■ Romans 6:12–14 (p. 1147)

the people who lived under the first agreement could be set free from sin.

[16]When there is a will,[n] it must be proven that the one who wrote that will is dead. [17]A will means nothing while the person is alive; it can be used only after the person dies. [18]This is why even the first agreement could not begin without blood to show death. [19]First, Moses told all the people every command in the law. Next he took the blood of calves and mixed it with water. Then he used red wool and a branch of the hyssop plant to sprinkle it on the book of the law and on all the people. [20]He said, "This is the blood that begins the Agreement that God commanded you to obey."[n] [21]In the same way, Moses sprinkled the blood on the Holy Tent[d] and over all the things used in worship. [22]The law says that almost everything must be made clean by blood, and sins cannot be forgiven without blood to show death.

Christ's Death Takes Away Sins

[23]So the copies of the real things in heaven had to be made clean[d] by animal sacrifices. But the real things in heaven need much better sacrifices. [24]Christ did not go into the Most Holy Place made by humans, which is only a copy of the real one. He went into heaven itself and is there now before God to help us. [25]The high priest enters the Most Holy Place once every year with blood that is not his own. But Christ did not offer himself many times. [26]Then he would have had to suffer many times since the world was made. But Christ came only once and for all time at just the right time to take away all sin by sacrificing himself. [27]Just as everyone must die once and be judged, [28]so Christ was offered as a sacrifice one time to take away the sins of many people. And he will come a second time, not to offer himself for sin, but to bring salvation to those who are waiting for him.

10 The law is only an unclear picture of the good things coming in the future; it is not the real thing. The people under the law offer the same sacrifices every year, but these sacrifices can never make perfect those who come near to worship God. [2]If the law could make them perfect, the sacrifices would have already stopped. The worshipers would be made clean, and they would no longer have a sense of sin. [3]But these sacrifices remind them of their sins every year, [4]because it is impossible for the blood of bulls and goats to take away sins.

[5]So when Christ came into the world, he said:
"You do not want sacrifices and offerings,

but you have prepared a body for me.
[6]You do not ask for burnt offerings
and offerings to take away sins.
[7]Then I said, 'Look, I have come.
It is written about me in the book.
God, I have come to do what you want.' "

Psalm 40:6-8

[8]In this Scripture[d] he first said, "You do not want sacrifices and offerings. You do not ask for burnt offerings and offerings to take away sins." (These are all sacrifices that the law commands.) [9]Then he said, "Look, I have come to do what you want." God ends the first system of sacrifices so he can set up the new system. [10]And because of this, we are made holy through the sacrifice Christ made in his body once and for all time.

[11]Every day the priests stand and do their religious service, often offering the same sacrifices. Those sacrifices can never take away sins. [12]But after Christ offered one sacrifice for sins, forever, he sat down at the right side of God. [13]And now Christ waits there for his enemies to be put under his power. [14]With one sacrifice he made perfect forever those who are being made holy.

> **SIDELIGHT:** When Hebrews 10:1 talks about making "the same sacrifices every year," it refers to the annual Jewish holiday of Yom Kippur. On this day, the high priest would symbolically transfer the sins of Israel to a goat (known as a scapegoat). Then the goat would be carried away to the desert where it—along with the sins—would be lost and forgotten (see Leviticus 16:7-10, 20-22, p. 113).

[15]The Holy Spirit[c] also tells us about this. First he says:
[16]"This is the agreement[n] I will make
with them at that time, says the Lord.
I will put my teachings in their hearts
and write them on their minds." *Jeremiah 31:33*
[17]Then he says:
"Their sins and the evil things they do—
I will not remember anymore." *Jeremiah 31:34*
[18]Now when these have been forgiven, there is no more need for a sacrifice for sins.

Continue to Trust God

[19]So, brothers and sisters, we are completely free to enter the Most Holy Place without fear

---

will A legal document that shows how a person's money and property are to be distributed at the time of death. This is the same word in Greek as "agreement" in verse 15.
"This ... obey." Quotation from Exodus 24:8.
agreement God gives a contract or agreement to his people. For the Jews, this agreement was the law of Moses. But now God has given a better agreement to his people through Christ.

because of the blood of Jesus' death. [20]We can enter through a new and living way that Jesus opened for us. It leads through the curtain—Christ's body. [21]And since we have a great priest over God's house, [22]let us come near to God with a sincere heart and a sure faith, because we have been made free from a guilty conscience, and our bodies have been washed with pure water. [23]Let us hold firmly to the hope that we have confessed, because we can trust God to do what he promised.

[24]Let us think about each other and help each other to show love and do good deeds. [25]You should not stay away from the church meetings, as some are doing, but you should meet together and encourage each other. Do this even more as you see the day[n] coming.

[26]If we decide to go on sinning after we have learned the truth, there is no longer any sacrifice for sins. [27]There is nothing but fear in waiting for the judgment and the terrible fire that will destroy all those who live against God. [28]Anyone who refused to obey the law of Moses was found guilty from the proof given by two or three witnesses. He was put to death without mercy. [29]So what do you think should be done to those who do not

day   The day Christ will come to judge all people and take his people to live with him.

CHURCH

Family of Friends

Jeremy Carr had had a rough life. His parents were divorced, and he had bounced between one parent and the other. When he signed up for summer youth camp, everyone was surprised, since he had shown little interest in church before.

After they arrived at the camp, the campers were split into groups of ten, each including an adult counselor. The group would stay together for a week.

Jeremy started acting up immediately. His counselor and the other kids tried to include him, but he ignored their kind gestures. He acted rude, obnoxious and selfish.

Finally the camp director, Cheryl Bolte, met with him after supper. When she asked Jeremy what he didn't like about his group, he said, "All they do is sit around and talk about their problems. I'm bored."

Cheryl explained to Jeremy that they were trying to build relationships, and that he was choosing not to be a part. "You don't have to participate, but you must respect other people's feelings," she said.

Jeremy spent the next day listening. He watched the group care for each other. Before he knew it, he told the group about his family and how much he hated moving back and forth between parents.

The group listened. Then one of the guys spoke. "We will be family for you, if you'll let us," he offered Jeremy, and the others agreed.

Jeremy couldn't believe it at first. But through the week, the campers' concern and their openness to him convinced him.

On the last day of camp, Jeremy thanked the group. "I've never known what it meant to have a real family, until this week," he said. "I know things still won't be easy at home, but I know at least ten people who care."

Fortunately for Jeremy, he experienced the love of a group of committed Christians who wouldn't give up on him. In **Hebrews 10:19–39**, the writer talks about this kind of commitment to the family of God.

■ While at camp, how well did Jeremy's group live up to this passage's message?

■ According to this passage, why do we need the church?

C O N S I D E R . . .

■ praying for someone at church whom you think is incredibly rude or obnoxious. Then pray for help in understanding that person.

 accepting the care and concern of others if they invite you to church youth group meetings or outings. You may find new friends there.

F O R   M O R E ,   S E E . . .

■ Isaiah 65:1–2 (p. 685)
■ Matthew 16:13–20 (p. 937)

■ Acts 2:43–47 (p. 1100)

respect the Son of God, who look at the blood of the agreement that made them holy as no different from others' blood, who insult the Spirit*d* of God's grace? Surely they should have a much worse punishment. [30]We know that God said, "I will punish those who do wrong; I will repay them." *n* And he also said, "The Lord will judge his people." *n* [31]It is a terrible thing to fall into the hands of the living God.

[32]Remember those days in the past when you first learned the truth. You had a hard struggle with many sufferings, but you continued strong. [33]Sometimes you were hurt and attacked before crowds of people, and sometimes you shared with those who were being treated that way. [34]You helped the prisoners. You even had joy when all that you owned was taken from you, because you knew you had something better and more lasting.

[35]So do not lose the courage you had in the past, which has a great reward. [36]You must hold on, so you can do what God wants and receive what he has promised. [37]For in a very short time,

"The One who is coming will come
    and will not be delayed.
[38]The person who is right with me
    will live by trusting in me.
But if he turns back with fear,
    I will not be pleased with him." *Habakkuk 2:3-4*

[39]But we are not those who turn back and are lost. We are people who have faith and are saved.

What Is Faith?

11 Faith means being sure of the things we hope for and knowing that something is real even if we do not see it. [2]Faith is the reason we remember great people who lived in the past.

[3]It is by faith we understand that the whole world was made by God's command so what we

"I ... them."   Quotation from Deuteronomy 32:35.
"The Lord ... people."   Quotation from Deuteronomy 32:36; Psalm 135:14.

FAITH

A Voice in the Dark

A youth group was enjoying a week of climbing and cave exploration at Flat Rock, near Fredericksburg, Texas. David Yankton, an experienced wilderness guide, led the group. He'd brought along his six-year-old daughter, Kelly Jo, to hike with them.

On the second day, David led the group as it explored a nearby cave. He allowed just one flashlight. At the entrance there was plenty of light and the group moved along rapidly. As they sank deeper into the cave, however, the darkness thickened. Finally, the cave was so dark the hikers couldn't walk a step without clear directions from the person in front of them.

At one point in the darkness, Kelly Jo panicked and screamed out what the rest of the group felt: "Daddy, don't leave me!"

From the darkness came David's calming voice. "Kelly Jo, I'm right in front of you, leading the way." That was all she needed to hear. In fact, the whole group felt better after hearing David's voice.

The writer of Hebrews wanted Christians to understand how faith sometimes requires believing in things that can't be seen or heard. The writer gives examples in **Hebrews 11:1–16** of others who acted in faith even though they didn't know exactly where or how God was leading them.

■ How were Kelly Jo and the group like some of the examples the writer mentions in this passage?
■ When have you trusted in God even though you didn't know what was going to happen? How does that experience help you trust God now?

C O N S I D E R . . .

■ trying something new in your faith, such as singing in the choir, or helping with mission or service projects.
■ listing the ways you trust others, such as letting someone drive you somewhere or relying on others for food. Compare the list with the ways you trust God will take care of you.

F O R   M O R E ,   S E E . . .

■ Genesis 12:1–5 (p. 14)
■ Mark 4:35–41 (p. 972)
■ Romans 4:13–25 (p. 1145)

see was made by something that cannot be seen.

⁴It was by faith that Abel offered God a better sacrifice than Cain did. God said he was pleased with the gifts Abel offered and called Abel a good man because of his faith. Abel died, but through his faith he is still speaking.

⁵It was by faith that Enoch was taken to heaven so he would not die. He could not be found, because God had taken him away. Before he was taken, the Scripture*d* says that he was a man who truly pleased God. ⁶Without faith no one can please God. Anyone who comes to God must believe that he is real and that he rewards those who truly want to find him.

⁷It was by faith that Noah heard God's warnings about things he could not yet see. He obeyed God and built a large boat to save his family. By his faith, Noah showed that the world was wrong, and he became one of those who are made right with God through faith.

⁸It was by faith Abraham obeyed God's call to go to another place God promised to give him. He left his own country, not knowing where he was to go. ⁹It was by faith that he lived like a foreigner in the country God promised to give him. He lived in tents with Isaac and Jacob, who had received that same promise from God. ¹⁰Abraham was waiting for the city*n* that has real foundations — the city planned and built by God.

¹¹He was too old to have children, and Sarah could not have children. It was by faith that Abraham was made able to become a father, because he trusted God to do what he had promised. ¹²This man was so old he was almost dead, but from him came as many descendants as there are stars in the sky. Like the sand on the seashore, they could not be counted.

¹³All these great people died in faith. They did not get the things that God promised his people, but they saw them coming far in the future and were glad. They said they were like visitors and strangers on earth. ¹⁴When people say such things, they show they are looking for a country that will be their own. ¹⁵If they had been thinking about the country they had left, they could have gone back. ¹⁶But they were waiting for a better country — a heavenly country. So God is not ashamed to be called their God, because he has prepared a city for them.

¹⁷It was by faith that Abraham, when God tested him, offered his son Isaac as a sacrifice. God made the promises to Abraham, but Abraham was ready to offer his own son as a sacrifice. ¹⁸God had said, "The descendants I promised you will be from Isaac."*n* ¹⁹Abraham believed that

God could raise the dead, and really, it was as if Abraham got Isaac back from death.

²⁰It was by faith that Isaac blessed the future of Jacob and Esau. ²¹It was by faith that Jacob, as he was dying, blessed each one of Joseph's sons. Then he worshiped as he leaned on the top of his walking stick.

²²It was by faith that Joseph, while he was dying, spoke about the Israelites leaving Egypt and gave instructions about what to do with his body.

²³It was by faith that Moses' parents hid him for three months after he was born. They saw that Moses was a beautiful baby, and they were not afraid to disobey the king's order.

²⁴It was by faith that Moses, when he grew up, refused to be called the son of the king of Egypt's daughter. ²⁵He chose to suffer with God's people instead of enjoying sin for a short time. ²⁶He thought it was better to suffer for the Christ*d* than to have all the treasures of Egypt, because he was looking for God's reward. ²⁷It was by faith that Moses left Egypt and was not afraid of the king's anger. Moses continued strong as if he could see the God that no one can see. ²⁸It was by faith that Moses prepared the Passover*d* and spread the blood on the doors so the one who brings death would not kill the firstborn*d* sons of Israel.

²⁹It was by faith that the people crossed the Red Sea as if it were dry land. But when the Egyptians tried it, they were drowned.

³⁰It was by faith that the walls of Jericho fell after the people had marched around them for seven days.

³¹It was by faith that Rahab, the prostitute,*d* welcomed the spies and was not killed with those who refused to obey God.

✳ **SIDELIGHT:** If you think you have had a hard life, read Hebrews 11:32–38. When verse 37 talks about being "cut in half," it may refer to the prophet Isaiah (p. 617), who, according to tradition, met this fate.

---

³²Do I need to give more examples? I do not have time to tell you about Gideon, Barak, Samson, Jephthah, David, Samuel, and the prophets.*d* ³³Through their faith they defeated kingdoms. They did what was right, received God's promises, and shut the mouths of lions. ³⁴They stopped great fires and were saved from being killed with swords. They were weak, and yet were made

---

city The spiritual "city" where God's people live with him. Also called "the heavenly Jerusalem." (See Hebrews 12:22.)
"The descendants ... Isaac." Quotation from Genesis 21:12.

strong. They were powerful in battle and defeated other armies. ³⁵Women received their dead relatives raised back to life. Others were tortured and refused to accept their freedom so they could be raised from the dead to a better life. ³⁶Some were laughed at and beaten. Others were put in chains and thrown into prison. ³⁷They were stoned to death, they were cut in half, and they were killed with swords. Some wore the skins of sheep and goats. They were poor, abused, and treated badly. ³⁸The world was not good enough for them! They wandered in deserts and mountains, living in caves and holes in the earth.

³⁹All these people are known for their faith, but none of them received what God had promised.

⁴⁰God planned to give us something better so that they would be made perfect, but only together with us.

Follow Jesus' Example

12 We have around us many people whose lives tell us what faith means. So let us run the race that is before us and never give up. We should remove from our lives anything that would get in the way and the sin that so easily holds us back. ²Let us look only to Jesus, the One who began our faith and who makes it perfect. He suffered death on the cross. But he accepted the shame as if it were nothing because of the joy that

---

PERSISTENCE

Learning to Win

It seemed to Sylvia Snyder that Coach Riker had no trust in the girls' basketball team. "The woman's impossible to please," Sylvia complained to her parents.

Sylvia remembered the end of the previous season when Coach Riker said they had the talent to be one of the state's best teams. "The question is, do you want to be the best?" she had asked.

"Yes!" they had all shouted. So, Sylvia and her teammates dedicated themselves to that goal.

When practice began again, Coach Riker worked the girls hard. Each daily practice turned into three grueling hours of pain and sweat. The coach never let up on them. She made them run extra laps, enforced a curfew, and monitored their grades. Sylvia was so frustrated she was ready to quit.

"I don't think I can take it anymore," Sylvia told her youth minister. "Coach Riker won't let up on us. She thinks practice is the most important thing in the world."

Sylvia's youth minister heard her frustration. "I know it's tough for you," he said. "But you and the rest of the team made a commitment at the end of last season. You knew it wouldn't be easy, so hang in there at least until the end of this season."

The season did end. The girls played hard and won the district. They went on to win third place at the state tournament. At the end of their final game, they carried out Coach Riker on their shoulders.

The next Sunday, the youth minister asked Sylvia whether she was glad she didn't quit. "I just didn't realize at the time that Coach Riker knew what she was doing," Sylvia said. "All of it—the practices, drills, monitoring our homework—helped us achieve our goal."

The writer of Hebrews knew life is often difficult. Things don't always go the way we plan. **Hebrews 12:1–13** explains the importance of being persistent in our lives as Christians.

■ How could Sylvia's attitude have been different if she had read this passage?

■ How does this passage apply to being persistent in your own life?

C O N S I D E R . . .

■ taking on the next step of the hardest task, school project, or job you are facing.

■ making a goal for your spiritual life for the next week (such as reading from your Bible three times). Tell your goal to two friends so they can pray for you and encourage you to stick with your goal. Talk about what you are learning from your reading.

F O R   M O R E ,   S E E . . .

■ Isaiah 42:1–4 (p. 657)

■ Luke 18:1–5 (p. 1041)

■ Ephesians 6:10–18 (p. 1226)

God put before him. And now he is sitting at the right side of God's throne. [3]Think about Jesus' example. He held on while wicked people were doing evil things to him. So do not get tired and stop trying.

God Is like a Father

[4]You are struggling against sin, but your struggles have not yet caused you to be killed. [5]You have forgotten the encouraging words that call you his children:

"My child, don't think the Lord's discipline is
     worth nothing,
and don't stop trying when he corrects you.
[6]The Lord disciplines those he loves,
     and he punishes everyone he accepts as his
     child."   *Proverbs 3:11-12*

[7]So hold on through your sufferings, because they are like a father's discipline. God is treating you as children. All children are disciplined by their fathers. [8]If you are never disciplined (and every child must be disciplined), you are not true children. [9]We have all had fathers here on earth who disciplined us, and we respected them. So it is even more important that we accept discipline from the Father of our spirits so we will have life. [10]Our fathers on earth disciplined us for a short time in the way they thought was best. But God disciplines us to help us, so we can become holy as he is. [11]We do not enjoy being disciplined. It is painful, but later, after we have learned from it, we have peace, because we start living in the right way.

Be Careful How You Live

[12]You have become weak, so make yourselves strong again. [13]Live in the right way so that you will be saved and your weakness will not cause you to be lost.

[14]Try to live in peace with all people, and try to live free from sin. Anyone whose life is not holy will never see the Lord. [15]Be careful that no one fails to receive God's grace and begins to cause trouble among you. A person like that can ruin many of you. [16]Be careful that no one takes part in sexual sin or is like Esau and never thinks about God. As the oldest son, Esau would have received everything from his father, but he sold all that for a single meal. [17]You remember that after Esau did this, he wanted to get his father's blessing, but his father refused. Esau could find no way to change

what he had done, even though he wanted the blessing so much that he cried.

[18]You have not come to a mountain that can be touched and that is burning with fire. You have not come to darkness, sadness, and storms. [19]You have not come to the noise of a trumpet or to the sound of a voice like the one the people of Israel heard and begged not to hear another word. [20]They did not want to hear the command: "If anything, even an animal, touches the mountain, it must be put to death with stones." [n] [21]What they saw was so terrible that Moses said, "I am shaking with fear." [n]

[22]But you have come to Mount Zion, [n] to the city of the living God, the heavenly Jerusalem. You have come to thousands of angels gathered together with joy. [23]You have come to the meeting of God's firstborn [n] children whose names are written in heaven. You have come to God, the judge of all people, and to the spirits of good people who have been made perfect. [24]You have come to Jesus, the One who brought the new agreement from God to his people, and you have come to the sprinkled blood [n] that has a better message than the blood of Abel. [n]

[25]So be careful and do not refuse to listen when God speaks. Others refused to listen to him when he warned them on earth, and they did not escape. So it will be worse for us if we refuse to listen to God who warns us from heaven. [26]When he spoke before, his voice shook the earth, but now he has promised, "Once again I will shake not only the earth but also the heavens." [n] [27]The words "once again" clearly show us that everything that was made—things that can be shaken—will be destroyed. Only the things that cannot be shaken will remain.

[28]So let us be thankful, because we have a kingdom that cannot be shaken. We should worship God in a way that pleases him with respect and fear, [29]because our God is like a fire that burns things up.

13 Keep on loving each other as brothers and sisters. [2]Remember to welcome strangers, because some who have done this have welcomed angels without knowing it. [3]Remember those who are in prison as if you were in prison with them. Remember those who are suffering as if you were suffering with them.

[4]Marriage should be honored by everyone, and husband and wife should keep their marriage

---

"If ... stones."   Quotation from Exodus *19:12-13*.
"I ... fear."   Quotation from Deuteronomy 9:19.
Mount Zion   Another name for Jerusalem, here meaning the spiritual city of God's people.
firstborn   The first son born in a Jewish family was given the most important place in the family and received special blessings. All of God's children are like that.
sprinkled blood   The blood of Jesus' death.
Abel   The son of Adam and Eve, who was killed by his brother Cain (Genesis 4:8).
"Once ... heavens."   Quotation from Haggai 2:6, 21.

pure. God will judge as guilty those who take part in sexual sins. [5]Keep your lives free from the love of money, and be satisfied with what you have. God has said,

"I will never leave you;
  I will never forget you." *Deuteronomy 31:6*
[6]So we can be sure when we say,
"I will not be afraid, because the Lord is my helper.
  People can't do anything to me." *Psalm 118:6*
[7]Remember your leaders who taught God's message to you. Remember how they lived and died, and copy their faith. [8]Jesus Christ is the same yesterday, today, and forever.

[9]Do not let all kinds of strange teachings lead you into the wrong way. Your hearts should be strengthened by God's grace, not by obeying rules about foods, which do not help those who obey them.

[10]We have a sacrifice, but the priests who serve in the Holy Tent[d] cannot eat from it. [11]The high priest carries the blood of animals into the Most Holy Place where he offers this blood for sins. But the bodies of the animals are burned outside the camp. [12]So Jesus also suffered outside the city to make his people holy with his own blood. [13]So let us go to Jesus outside the camp, holding on as he did when we are abused.

[14]Here on earth we do not have a city that lasts forever, but we are looking for the city that we will have in the future. [15]So through Jesus let us always offer to God our sacrifice of praise, coming from lips that speak his name. [16]Do not forget to do good to others, and share with them, because such sacrifices please God.

[17]Obey your leaders and act under their authority. They are watching over you, because they are responsible for your souls. Obey them so that they will do this work with joy, not sadness. It will not help you to make their work hard.

[18]Pray for us. We are sure that we have a clear conscience, because we always want to do the right thing. [19]I especially beg you to pray so that God will send me back to you soon.

[20-21]I pray that the God of peace will give you every good thing you need so you can do what he

---

WORSHIP

Why Doesn't God Talk?

On the Thursday before Easter at the children's home, the children enjoyed a candlelight service in the chapel. The kids entered in their usual loud way. But, as soon as they saw the candles they became very quiet. Their eyes showed anticipation, as if something were about to happen.

After a moving service, Jason, Jenny, and Tina—three older children who lived at the home—came to talk to the chaplain. They wanted to know why God doesn't always seem as close as he was that evening.

"If God would talk to me, you know, out loud, it would be a lot easier to be a Christian," Jenny said.

The others agreed. "Why doesn't God just speak to us in church?" Jason asked.

Seven-year-old Kimberly, who had been listening, suddenly spoke up. "God does talk to you," she said to the other three. "Maybe you just don't always listen."

The writer of Hebrews describes how God speaks to us in worship. The writer of Hebrews knew that his readers, like the kids at the children's home, needed guidance for hearing God's message in worship. In **Hebrews 12:18–25** you will find more on hearing God in worship.

■ Would the writer of Hebrews agree or disagree with Kimberly? Why or why not?
■ How might you be more open to God's talking with you, according to the passage?

CONSIDER . . .

■ spending a few minutes in prayer just before you go to a worship service this week, asking God to help you hear him better.
■ volunteering to take a more active role one week in your church's worship service. See your pastor or minister of worship to see how you can participate.

FOR MORE, SEE . . .

■ Exodus 3:1–6 (p. 60)   ■ Matthew 21:12–16 (p. 944)
■ Psalm 95 (p. 537)

wants. God raised from the dead our Lord Jesus, the Great Shepherd of the sheep, because of the blood of his death. His blood began the eternal agreement that God made with his people. I pray that God will do in us what pleases him, through Jesus Christ, and to him be glory forever and ever. Amen.

22My brothers and sisters, I beg you to listen patiently to this message I have written to encourage you, because it is not very long. 23I want you to know that our brother Timothy has been let out of prison. If he arrives soon, we will both come to see you.

24Greet all your leaders and all of God's people. Those from Italy send greetings to you.

25Grace be with you all.

SERVICE

When You See It

The Seventh Street Church youth group regularly went on outings. One night when the kids were returning in a church van from a pizza party, they saw an elderly woman waving for help in a bad section of town. Her car was broken down and she was alone. The kids immediately wanted to stop and help.

The car's battery was dead, and no one had jumper cables. The woman was afraid to leave her car there, and the kids didn't want to leave her there. So they decided to push her car to the nearest service station.

Eleven kids and one youth minister began pushing the woman's old Ford LTD through two miles of the worst section of town. More than once, people offered to take the car off their hands. The group pushed for what seemed forever. When a service station came into view, everyone cheered.

The woman was so grateful that she cried. "Not even my neighbors are so kind to me," she said. She took each member of the group by the hand and gave each one a hug and a smile.

As the group boarded the van for home, the woman thanked them again. "It takes special people to see a need and meet it where it is," she said.

The writer of Hebrews reminds Christians that serving each other is important. **Hebrews 13:1–8** offers several examples of how to love and care for others.

■ How does the youth group's willingness to help compare with the message of the passage?
■ What specific teachings from the passage apply to your life today?

C O N S I D E R . . .

■ calling someone who has done something for you recently and letting that person know you appreciate the caring.
■ doing something for someone in need. Look for needs you can meet, such as cutting grass or running an errand.

F O R M O R E , S E E . . .

■ Psalm 146 (p. 563)   ■ Luke 7:1–10 (p. 1013)
■ Matthew 15:21–28 (p. 935)

JAMES

Why Read This Book:

- Learn how to handle temptation, testing and trouble (James 1).
- Understand the connection between what you believe and what you do (James 2—3).
- See what can happen when you let God be in charge of your life (James 4—5).

Behind the Scenes:

If someone says, "Would you mind taking out the garbage?" it's easy to forget or find some excuse for not doing it. But suppose someone says, "Take out the garbage!" It's hard to ignore the demand or find an excuse not to do it.

The book of James is like the second example. Its guidance is so clear that it is hard to ignore. "Do not become angry easily" (James 1:19). "Never think some people are more important than others" (James 2:1). "Do not tell evil lies about each other" (James 4:11). In fact, James has more than fifty direct commands in just five chapters!

While much of the New Testament focuses on what Christians believe, James focuses on how Christians behave. Some early Christians apparently thought they could do whatever they wanted because God would forgive them anyway. But James warns them that "if people say they have faith, but do nothing, their faith is worth nothing" (James 2:14).

This short book is loaded with advice on putting our faith into action. It covers many areas of life we continue to struggle with: handling money, relations between the rich and poor, bragging, judging others, being patient. The book is as practical today as when it was written almost two thousand years ago.

WHERE THE ACTION WAS

Black Sea

SPAIN

Rome

Philippi

Athens

Corinth

Ephesus

AFRICA

Mediterranean Sea

Jerusalem

James was written to all Christians everywhere. The dotted line on this map shows how far Christianity had spread by the end of the first century A.D.
• These cities had a Christian community in them.

WHEN THE ACTION WAS

Jesus was born	The church began soon after Jesus went to heaven		Paul began his missionary work		Fire destroyed Rome	
BC/AD	20AD	30AD	40AD	50AD	60AD	70AD
	Jesus began his ministry	Paul became a Christian		James may have been written		Romans destroyed the Temple in Jerusalem

1 From James, a servant of God and of the Lord Jesus Christ.

To all of God's people who are scattered everywhere in the world:

Greetings.

Faith and Wisdom

2My brothers and sisters, [n] when you have many kinds of troubles, you should be full of joy, 3because you know that these troubles test your

---

> **☀ SIDELIGHT:** James was a common name in the first century, so we are not positive who wrote this letter. One theory is that the author was a brother of Jesus. This James became the leader of the Jerusalem church and later was put to death because of his faith.

---

faith, and this will give you patience. 4Let your patience show itself perfectly in what you do. Then you will be perfect and complete and will have everything you need. 5But if any of you needs wisdom, you should ask God for it. He is generous and enjoys giving to all people, so he will give you wisdom. 6But when you ask God, you must believe and not doubt. Anyone who doubts is like a wave in the sea, blown up and down by the wind. 7-8Such doubters are thinking two different things at the same time, and they cannot decide about anything they do. They should not think they will receive anything from the Lord.

True Riches

9Believers who are poor should be proud, because God has made them spiritually rich. 10Those who are rich should be proud, because God has shown them that they are spiritually poor. The rich will die like a wild flower in the grass. 11The sun rises with burning heat and dries up the plants. The flower falls off, and its beauty is gone. In the same way the rich will die while they are still taking care of business.

Temptation Is Not from God

12When people are tempted and still continue strong, they should be happy. After they have proved their faith, God will reward them with life forever. God promised this to all those who love him. 13When people are tempted, they should not say, "God is tempting me." Evil cannot tempt God, and God himself does not tempt anyone.

14But people are tempted when their own evil desire leads them away and traps them. 15This desire leads to sin, and then the sin grows and brings death.

16My dear brothers and sisters, do not be fooled about this. 17Every good action and every perfect gift is from God. These good gifts come down from the Creator of the sun, moon, and stars, who does not change like their shifting shadows. 18God decided to give us life through the word of truth so we might be the most important of all the things he made.

Listening and Obeying

19My dear brothers and sisters, always be willing to listen and slow to speak. Do not become angry easily, 20because anger will not help you live the right kind of life God wants. 21So put out of your life every evil thing and every kind of wrong. Then in gentleness accept God's teaching that is planted in your hearts, which can save you. 22Do what God's teaching says; when you only listen and do nothing, you are fooling yourselves. 23Those who hear God's teaching and do nothing are like people who look at themselves in a mirror. 24They see their faces and then go away and quickly forget what they looked like. 25But the truly happy people are those who carefully study God's perfect law that makes people free, and they continue to study it. They do not forget what they heard, but they obey what God's teaching says. Those who do this will be made happy.

The True Way to Worship God

26People who think they are religious but say things they should not say are just fooling themselves. Their "religion" is worth nothing. 27Religion that God accepts as pure and without fault is this: caring for orphans or widows who need help, and keeping yourself free from the world's evil influence.

Love All People

2 My dear brothers and sisters, as believers in our glorious Lord Jesus Christ, never think some people are more important than others. 2Suppose someone comes into your church meeting wearing nice clothes and a gold ring. At the same time a poor person comes in wearing old, dirty clothes. 3You show special attention to the one wearing nice clothes and say, "Please, sit here in this good seat." But you say to the poor person, "Stand over there," or, "Sit on the floor by my feet." 4What are you doing? You are making some people more important than others, and with evil

---

brothers and sisters Although the Greek text says "brothers" here and throughout this book, James' words were meant for the entire church, including men and women.

thoughts you are deciding that one person is better.

⁵Listen, my dear brothers and sisters! God chose the poor in the world to be rich with faith and to receive the kingdom God promised to those who love him. ⁶But you show no respect to the poor. The rich are always trying to control your lives. They are the ones who take you to court. ⁷And they are the ones who speak against Jesus, who owns you.

⁸This royal law is found in the Scriptures:*d* "Love your neighbor as you love yourself."*n* If you obey this law, you are doing right. ⁹But if you treat one person as being more important than another, you are sinning. You are guilty of breaking God's law. ¹⁰A person who follows all of God's law but fails to obey even one command is guilty of breaking all the commands in that law. ¹¹The same God who said, "You must not be guilty of adultery,"*d, n* also said, "You must not murder anyone."*n* So if you do not take part in adultery but you murder someone, you are guilty of breaking all of God's law. ¹²In everything you say and do, remember that you will be judged by the law that makes people free. ¹³So you must show mercy to others, or God will not show mercy to you when he judges you. But the person who shows mercy can stand without fear at the judgment.

Faith and Good Works

¹⁴My brothers and sisters, if people say they have faith, but do nothing, their faith is worth nothing. Can faith like that save them? ¹⁵A brother or sister in Christ might need clothes or food. ¹⁶If you say to that person, "God be with you! I hope you stay warm and get plenty to eat," but you do not give what that person needs, your

---

"Love ... yourself."   Quotation from Leviticus 19:18.
"You ... adultery."   Quotation from Exodus 20:14 and Deuteronomy 5:18.
"You ... anyone."   Quotation from Exodus 20:13 and Deuteronomy 5:17.

BIBLE STUDY

A Word From Your Sponsor

If you're a typical teenager, by the time you graduate from high school, you'll have watched eighteen to twenty thousand hours of television. An hour of television may carry fifteen to twenty-five advertisements. Thus, a typical eighteen year old has seen about three to four hundred thousand advertisements.

How many of those ads do you think eighteen year olds can remember?

Probably no one could recall more than a few hundred. Even lower would be the number of acts to which the typical teenager responded by purchasing the product.

We simply tune out much of what we hear.

But **James 1:17–27** says we can't afford to "tune out" when we hear God's teaching. Tune in the passage.

- What does James say about those "who hear God's teaching and do nothing"—the way most of us treat commercials?
- According to James, who is "the truly happy person?" How might your life change if you were to remember and act on more of God's teaching?

CONSIDER . . .

- telling a Christian friend what you read in the Bible today. Doing so can help you remember it and apply it to your own life.
- taking notes the next time you hear a sermon in church.

FOR MORE, SEE . . .

- Joshua 1:6–9 (p. 195)
- Luke 11:27–28 (p. 1026)
- Psalm 119:1–16 (p. 550)

words are worth nothing. [17]In the same way, faith that is alone—that does nothing—is dead.

[18]Someone might say, "You have faith, but I have deeds." Show me your faith without doing anything, and I will show you my faith by what I do. [19]You believe there is one God. Good! But the demons[d] believe that, too, and they tremble with fear.

[20]You foolish person! Must you be shown that faith that does nothing is worth nothing? [21]Abraham, our ancestor, was made right with God by what he did when he offered his son Isaac on the altar. [22]So you see that Abraham's faith and the things he did worked together. His faith was made perfect by what he did. [23]This shows the full meaning of the Scripture[d] that says: "Abraham believed God, and God accepted Abraham's faith, and that faith made him right with God."[n] And Abraham was called God's friend.[n] [24]So you see that people are made right with God by what they do, not by faith only.

[25]Another example is Rahab, a prostitute,[d] who was made right with God by something she did. She welcomed the spies into her home and helped them escape by a different road.

[26]Just as a person's body that does not have a spirit is dead, so faith that does nothing is dead!

Controlling the Things We Say

3 My brothers and sisters, not many of you should become teachers, because you know that we who teach will be judged more strictly. [2]We all make many mistakes. If people never said anything wrong, they would be perfect and able to control their entire selves, too. [3]When we put bits into the mouths of horses to make them obey

"**Abraham . . . God.**"　Quotation from Genesis 15:6.
God's friend　These words about Abraham are found in 2 Chronicles 20:7 and Isaiah 41:8.

JUDGING OTHERS

A Perfect Ten?

Peggy Reynolds and her friends moved down the food line in the music camp dining hall. Two guys serving food watched Peggy and the other girls, and grinned. When she got near them, they reached under the counter, pulled out two cardboard signs with numbers, and put them on a high ledge behind them. "Nine" and "five," Peggy thought, reading the cards. "I wonder what they mean?"

When Peggy's friend Marie got to the same place in line, the guys changed the numbers to an "eight" and a "six." By now everybody had stopped eating to watch. When the next girl in line received a "nine" and a "seven," people cheered. "They're rating us," Peggy suddenly realized. Her face turned red.

Peggy and her friends laughed uncomfortably as the two guys continued to rate girls as they passed in line. Then Terri Smith got in line. She wasn't "perfect" looking and was a bit overweight. Peggy dreaded how the guys might rate Terri. But as she passed through the line, the guys just ignored her. They didn't rate her at all. Then, when other "better looking" girls came up in the line, the guys resumed their rating game.

But the game wasn't funny to Peggy. She felt judged, and imagined how hurt Terri probably felt.

Sometimes it may seem like fun to judge other people, but being judged is rarely funny. Read in **James 2:1–17** what James wrote about treating people as though they are more important than others.

■ What does James say is wrong with judging people like the guys were rating the girls at the camp?
■ When have you unfairly judged someone because of clothes or grades or skill at sports? What makes us fall into doing things like that?

C O N S I D E R . . .
■ thinking about one person you have judged. The next time you see this person, say, "Hi."
■ watching this week how often you put people down. Whenever you realize you have put someone down, quickly say something that builds the person up too.

F O R　M O R E ,　S E E . . .
■ 1 Samuel 16:7 (p. 258)
■ Matthew 7:1–5 (p. 918)
■ Romans 12:14–16 (p. 1158)

us, we can control their whole bodies. ⁴Also a ship is very big, and it is pushed by strong winds. But a very small rudder controls that big ship, making it go wherever the pilot wants. ⁵It is the same with the tongue. It is a small part of the body, but it brags about great things.

A big forest fire can be started with only a little flame. ⁶And the tongue is like a fire. It is a whole world of evil among the parts of our bodies. The tongue spreads its evil through the whole body. The tongue is set on fire by hell, and it starts a fire that influences all of life. ⁷People can tame every kind of wild animal, bird, reptile, and fish, and they have tamed them, ⁸but no one can tame the tongue. It is wild and evil and full of deadly poison. ⁹We use our tongues to praise our Lord and Father, but then we curse people, whom God made like himself. ¹⁰Praises and curses come from the same mouth! My brothers and sisters, this should not happen. ¹¹Do good and bad water flow from the same spring? ¹²My brothers and sisters, can a fig tree make olives, or can a grapevine make figs? No! And a well full of salty water cannot give good water.

True Wisdom

¹³Are there those among you who are truly wise and understanding? Then they should show it by living right and doing good things with a gentleness that comes from wisdom. ¹⁴But if you are selfish and have bitter jealousy in your hearts, do not brag. Your bragging is a lie that hides the truth. ¹⁵That kind of "wisdom" does not come from God but from the world. It is not spiritual; it is from the devil. ¹⁶Where jealousy and selfishness are, there will be confusion and every kind of evil. ¹⁷But the wisdom that comes from God is first of all pure, then peaceful, gentle, and easy to please. This wisdom is always ready to help those who are troubled and to do good for others. It is always fair and honest. ¹⁸People who work for peace in a peaceful way plant a good crop of right-living.

Give Yourselves to God

4 Do you know where your fights and arguments come from? They come from the selfish desires that war within you. ²You want things, but you do not have them. So you are ready to kill and are jealous of other people, but you still cannot get what you want. So you argue and fight. You do not get what you want, because you do not ask God. ³Or when you ask, you do not receive because the reason you ask is wrong.

You want things so you can use them for your own pleasures.

⁴So, you are not loyal to God! You should know that loving the world is the same as hating God. Anyone who wants to be a friend of the world becomes God's enemy. ⁵Do you think the Scripture[d] means nothing that says, "The Spirit[d] that God made to live in us wants us for himself alone."[n] ⁶But God gives us even more grace, as the Scripture says,

"God is against the proud,
  but he gives grace to the humble."

Proverbs 3:34

⁷So give yourselves completely to God. Stand against the devil, and the devil will run from you. ⁸Come near to God, and God will come near to you. You sinners, clean sin out of your lives. You who are trying to follow God and the world at the same time, make your thinking pure. ⁹Be sad, cry, and weep! Change your laughter into crying and your joy into sadness. ¹⁰Don't be too proud in the Lord's presence, and he will make you great.

You Are Not the Judge

¹¹Brothers and sisters, do not tell evil lies about each other. If you speak against your fellow believers or judge them, you are judging and speaking against the law they follow. And when you are judging the law, you are no longer a follower of the law. You have become a judge. ¹²God is the only Lawmaker and Judge. He is the only One who can save and destroy. So it is not right for you to judge your neighbor.

Let God Plan Your Life

¹³Some of you say, "Today or tomorrow we will go to some city. We will stay there a year, do business, and make money." ¹⁴But you do not know what will happen tomorrow! Your life is like a mist. You can see it for a short time, but then it goes away. ¹⁵So you should say, "If the Lord wants, we will live and do this or that." ¹⁶But now you are proud and you brag. All of this bragging is wrong. ¹⁷Anyone who knows the right thing to do, but does not do it, is sinning.

"The Spirit . . . alone." These words may be from Exodus 20:5.

GOD'S WILL

Lump on an All-Star's Arm

"Cancer came into my life as a small thing," remembers all-star baseball pitcher Dave Dravecky, talking about the small lump that had appeared on his throwing arm.

"The San Francisco Giants had clinched the division," Dave says. "We were making ready for what every baseball player works for, and most never experience: postseason play. So I had things on my mind other than a little, painless lump."

But the lump on his arm didn't go away. It grew. The next year the tumor had to be removed, along with 50 percent of Dave's deltoid muscle. "Short of a miracle," the cancer specialist said, "Dave will never pitch again."

Through therapy and exercise, Dave did come back. But in his second game the next season, he broke his arm, and his career came to an abrupt and painful halt.

"There's a bittersweet quality to my retirement from baseball," he says. "I've learned to put my life in God's hands. I had to learn to do what was within my grasp, one day at a time, and leave control of the rest to God."

James 4:13–17 reminds us that the future is in God's hands.

■ What would both Dave Dravecky and James say we should expect from the future?

■ What are you hoping and planning to do in the next several months? When you think about these plans, does God come into your mind?

C O N S I D E R . . .

■ evaluating your dreams for the future in light of this passage on God's will.

■ writing on an envelope, "It's in God's hands." Whenever you are worried about something in the future you cannot control, write out your worry on a slip of paper and place it in the envelope.

F O R   M O R E ,   S E E . . .

■ Psalm 139 (p. 561)
■ Proverbs 16:1, 9 (p. 581)
■ Luke 12:22–31 (p. 1028)

A Warning to the Rich

5 You rich people, listen! Cry and be very sad because of the troubles that are coming to you. ²Your riches have rotted, and your clothes have been eaten by moths. ³Your gold and silver have rusted, and that rust will be a proof that you were wrong. It will eat your bodies like fire. You saved your treasure for the last days. ⁴The pay you did not give the workers who mowed your fields cries out against you, and the cries of the workers have been heard by the Lord All-Powerful. ⁵Your life on earth was full of rich living and pleasing yourselves with everything you wanted. You made yourselves fat, like an animal ready to be killed. ⁶You have judged guilty and then murdered innocent people, who were not against you.

Be Patient

⁷Brothers and sisters, be patient until the Lord comes again. A farmer patiently waits for his valuable crop to grow from the earth and for it to receive the autumn and spring rains. ⁸You, too, must be patient. Do not give up hope, because the Lord is coming soon. ⁹Brothers and sisters, do not complain against each other or you will be judged guilty. And the judge is ready to come! ¹⁰Brothers and sisters, follow the example of the prophets*ᵈ* who spoke for the Lord. They suffered many hard things, but they were patient. ¹¹We say they are happy because they did not give up. You have heard about Job's patience, and you know the Lord's purpose for him in the end. You know the Lord is full of mercy and is kind.

Be Careful What You Say

¹²My brothers and sisters, above all, do not use an oath when you make a promise. Don't use the name of heaven, earth, or anything else to prove what you say. When you mean yes, say only yes, and when you mean no, say only no so you will not be judged guilty.

The Power of Prayer

¹³Anyone who s having troubles should pray.

Endless Paddling

"Come on, guys! Hurry up!" Sherri Rohrer's youth leader called from a silver canoe a hundred yards ahead. Sherri felt she would never catch up, let alone finish the ten-day trip.

They had broken camp at 9:00 A.M. It was now 3:00 P.M., and they still had miles to paddle. The wind blew against them, and the hard paddling took its toll on many out-of-shape bodies. "I can't wait to get there," Sherri complained to her canoeing partner. "Where's a motor for this thing? My arms feel dead."

As Sherri lifted her paddle out of the water, she watched the drops fall back into the dark Maine river. She thought about how she had waited all year for this trip. She and the other group members had worked hard—spaghetti dinners, car washes, bake sales. Her excitement had grown as the trip date approached. It had been hard to wait.

Now that the trip was here, she sometimes wondered whether it had been worth all the excitement. She grew tired of still waiting—for rest, for dinner, and for free time to relax.

As Sherri had trouble being patient on the canoe trip, Christians sometimes tire of waiting for things to get better. **James 5:7–11** encourages believers to keep a patient faith, because things will get better.

- How might James's advice help Sherri?
- What does James say we can look forward to if we are patient? How can knowing that Jesus is coming help you be patient today?

CONSIDER . . .

- listing things you are waiting for. Ask God to give you hope while you wait.
- getting a calendar and marking the date of an upcoming "big event" in your life. Sprinkle short notes on dates along the way to encourage you while you wait.

FOR MORE, SEE . . .

- Job 2:11–13 (p. 453) and 42:10–17 (p. 479)
- Isaiah 40:27–31 (p. 656)
- Matthew 7:7–11 (p. 919)

Anyone who is happy should sing praises. [14]Anyone who is sick should call the church's elders.[d] They should pray for and pour oil on the person[n]

---

in the name of the Lord. [15]And the prayer that is said with faith will make the sick person well; the Lord will heal that person. And if the person has sinned, the sins will be forgiven. [16]Confess your sins to each other and pray for each other so God can heal you. When a believing person prays, great things happen. [17]Elijah was a human being just like us. He prayed that it would not rain, and it did not rain on the land for three and a half years! [18]Then Elijah prayed again, and the rain came down from the sky, and the land produced crops again.

Saving a Soul

[19]My brothers and sisters, if one of you wanders away from the truth, and someone helps that person come back, [20]remember this: Anyone who brings a sinner back from the wrong way will save that sinner's soul from death and will cause many sins to be forgiven.

---

pour oil on the person Oil was used in the name of the Lord as a sign that the person was now set apart for God's special attention and care.

1 PETER

Behind the Scenes:

You may have experienced the old prank: Someone writes "KICK ME" on a sheet of paper, then puts it on your back without your knowing it. Suddenly everyone starts laughing at you. Some kick you. You feel angry and embarrassed.

The Christians who received 1 Peter had similar feelings, though the reasons were much different and much more serious. They had become Christians in a pagan culture. And the Christian label brought ridicule, persecution, and suffering.

Some of these Christians might have felt embarrassed about their faith. They may have been tempted to get rid of the Christian "label." Maybe being a Christian wasn't worth all this pain.

This letter encourages the early Christians to stick with their faith, even in the midst of their suffering. It gives them practical advice on how to live with the pain. It reminds them that their circumstances don't have to control their joy and hope in life. God is in control, and he cares about their suffering.

Sometimes it is hard being a Christian. People may make fun of our choices. They may call us names. But this letter encourages us to stay strong in our faith, for in the end God will give victory to his faithful.

WHERE THE ACTION WAS

Black Sea

ITALY

Rome

The churches in Asia Minor (modern-day Turkey) received this letter (1 Peter 1:1).

BITHYNIA   PONTUS

GALATIA   CAPPADOCIA

ASIA MINOR

Many people believe Peter wrote this letter from Rome, where he died for his faith.

AFRICA

Mediterranean Sea

WHEN THE ACTION WAS

Jesus was born	The church began soon after Jesus went to heaven	Fire destroyed Rome, and Roman persecution of Christians began	
BC/AD	**25AD**	**50AD**	**75AD** **100AD**
	Jesus began his ministry	Paul began his missionary work	1 Peter may have been written	The Roman emperor increased persecution of Christians

1 From Peter, an apostle[d] of Jesus Christ. To God's chosen people who are away from their homes and are scattered all around the countries of Pontus, Galatia, Cappadocia, Asia, and Bithynia. [2]God planned long ago to choose you by making you his holy people, which is the Spirit's[d] work. God wanted you to obey him and to be made clean by the blood of the death of Jesus Christ.

Grace and peace be yours more and more.

We Have a Living Hope

[3]Praise be to the God and Father of our Lord Jesus Christ. In God's great mercy he has caused us to be born again into a living hope, because Jesus Christ rose from the dead. [4]Now we hope for the blessings God has for his children. These blessings, which cannot be destroyed or be spoiled or lose their beauty, are kept in heaven for you. [5]God's power protects you through your faith until salvation is shown to you at the end of

---

The Hope Giver

Tony Melendez amazed 100 million TV viewers in 1987 as he played the guitar with his feet and sang for Pope John Paul II. "Tony," the Pope said, after embracing the performer, "you are giving hope to all of us. My wish to you is to continue giving this hope to all the people."

Born without arms, Tony is normal in every other way. But he had struggled for years to be accepted.

Without persistence, Tony might never have graduated from high school. When he transferred from special education into a "normal" English class, all eyes watched him when he walked into the classroom. He shrugged off his backpack, pulled out a notebook with his toes and put it on the floor. Then he grabbed a pencil between his two biggest toes and began taking notes. Even the teacher had stopped the discussion of Moby Dick to watch. Everyone stared in silence.

"Somebody had to break the silence," Tony recalled. "Hope the floor is clean," he said with a grin. "If it isn't, I'll have to turn in a dirty paper." The students and teacher roared with laughter, then class continued. It was one of the many awkward times he had to show his strength.

Still, Tony was afraid to go to school dances—afraid he would be rejected by girls. But he finally faced his fears and went alone. He stood along the side watching, wondering if everyone was watching him. Then all of a sudden a girl from his English class walked up, looked him in the eye, and said "Go!" Seconds later the couple was tearing up the floor. "I've been dancing almost nonstop ever since," Tony says.

"I don't think that girl will ever know how important she was to me that night. At various times in my life people like her have come along to say or do just the right thing when I needed it. These sensitive ones are the hope givers."

By the time he played for the Pope, Tony had learned how to face obstacles with persistence and a sense of humor. Tony's enduring happiness is like the message of **1 Peter 1:3–9**.

■ How did the girl give Tony hope? According to the passage, who gives every Christian "living hope"?

■ How does being a Christian give you hope? How does your being a Christian give hope to others?

CONSIDER . . .

■ writing down five good and five bad things that could happen to you and thinking how faith in Christ could give you happiness in any situation.

◀ interviewing someone who has suffered great tragedy, but whose life still is characterized by joy.

FOR MORE, SEE . . .

■ Job 5:17 (p. 454)
■ John 15:11 (p. 1085)
     ■ James 1:2–4 (p. 1294)

time. ⁶This makes you very happy, even though now for a short time different kinds of troubles may make you sad. ⁷These troubles come to prove that your faith is pure. This purity of faith is worth more than gold, which can be proved to be pure by fire but will ruin. But the purity of your faith will bring you praise and glory and honor when Jesus Christ is shown to you. ⁸You have not seen Christ, but still you love him. You cannot see him now, but you believe in him. So you are filled with a joy that cannot be explained, a joy full of glory. ⁹And you are receiving the goal of your faith — the salvation of your souls.

¹⁰The prophets*d* searched carefully and tried to learn about this salvation. They prophesied about the grace that was coming to you. ¹¹The Spirit*d* of Christ was in the prophets, telling in advance about the sufferings of Christ and about the glory that would follow those sufferings. The prophets tried to learn about what the Spirit was showing them, when those things would happen, and what the world would be like at that time. ¹²It was shown them that their service was not for themselves but for you when they told about the truths you have now heard. Those who preached the Good News*d* to you told you those things with the help of the Holy Spirit who was sent from heaven — things into which angels desire to look.

A Call to Holy Living

¹³So prepare your minds for service and have self-control. All your hope should be for the gift of grace that will be yours when Jesus Christ is shown to you. ¹⁴Now that you are obedient children of God do not live as you did in the past. You did not understand, so you did the evil things you wanted. ¹⁵But be holy in all you do, just as God, the One who called you, is holy. ¹⁶It is written in the Scriptures:*d* "You must be holy, because I am holy." *n*

¹⁷You pray to God and call him Father, and he judges each person's work equally. So while you are here on earth, you should live with respect for God. ¹⁸You know that in the past you were living in a worthless way, a way passed down from the people who lived before you. But you were saved from that useless life. You were bought, not with something that ruins like gold or silver, ¹⁹but with the precious blood of Christ, who was like a pure and perfect lamb. ²⁰Christ was chosen before the world was made, but he was shown to the world in these last times for your sake. ²¹Through Christ you believe in God, who raised Christ from the dead and gave him glory. So your faith and your hope are in God.

²²Now that you have made your souls pure by obeying the truth, you can have true love for your Christian brothers and sisters. *n* So love each other deeply with all your heart. ²³You have been born again, and this new life did not come from something that dies, but from something that cannot die. You were born again through God's living message that continues forever. ²⁴The Scripture says,

"All people are like the grass,
    and all their glory is like the flowers of the
        field.
The grass dies and the flowers fall,
²⁵ but the word of the Lord will live forever."
                                                    Isaiah 40:6-8

And this is the word that was preached to you.

Jesus Is the Living Stone

2 So then, rid yourselves of all evil, all lying, hypocrisy,*d* jealousy, and evil speech. ²As newborn babies want milk, you should want the pure and simple teaching. By it you can grow up and be saved, ³because you have already examined and seen how good the Lord is.

⁴Come to the Lord Jesus, the "stone" *n* that lives. The people of the world did not want this stone, but he was the stone God chose, and he was precious. ⁵You also are like living stones, so let yourselves be used to build a spiritual temple — to be holy priests who offer spiritual sacrifices to God. He will accept those sacrifices through Jesus Christ. ⁶The Scripture*d* says:

"I will put a stone in the ground in
        Jerusalem.
    Everything will be built on this important
        and precious rock.
Anyone who trusts in him
    will never be disappointed." *Isaiah 28:16*

⁷This stone is worth much to you who believe. But to the people who do not believe,

"the stone that the builders rejected
    has become the cornerstone."*d* *Psalm 118:22*

⁸Also, he is

"a stone that causes people to stumble,
    a rock that makes them fall." *Isaiah 8:14*

They stumble because they do not obey what God says, which is what God planned to happen to them.

⁹But you are a chosen people, royal priests, a holy nation, a people for God's own possession. You were chosen to tell about the wonderful acts of God, who called you out of darkness into his wonderful light. ¹⁰At one time you were not a people, but now you are God's people. In the past

---

"You must be . . . holy." Quotation from Leviticus 11:45; 19:2; 20:7.
brothers and sisters Although the Greek text says "brothers" here and throughout this book, Peter's words were meant for the entire church, including men and women.
"stone" The most important stone in God's spiritual temple or house (his people).

you had never received mercy, but now you have received God's mercy.

Live for God

¹¹Dear friends, you are like foreigners and strangers in this world. I beg you to avoid the evil things your bodies want to do that fight against your soul. ¹²People who do not believe are living all around you and might say that you are doing wrong. Live such good lives that they will see the good things you do and will give glory to God on the day when Christ comes again.

Yield to Every Human Authority

¹³For the Lord's sake, yield to the people who have authority in this world: the king, who is the highest authority, ¹⁴and the leaders who are sent by him to punish those who do wrong and to praise those who do right. ¹⁵It is God's desire that by doing good you should stop foolish people from saying stupid things about you. ¹⁶Live as free people, but do not use your freedom as an excuse to do evil. Live as servants of God. ¹⁷Show respect for all people: Love the brothers and sisters of God's family, respect God, honor the king.

LOVE

Given, Not Earned

The argument was brutal. Rochelle Mattison's parents didn't want her to go to the party. They didn't know the guy throwing it, didn't know his parents, didn't know who was going to be there, and didn't know what the teenagers would be doing.

"You're eighteen years old, Rochelle," her father said. "We won't forbid you to go. But if you ignore our wishes on this, don't expect us to honor your wishes on other things . . . including the use of the car."

They thought withholding the car would stop her.

But it didn't. "I'm tired of you using the car to force me to do what you want," she shot back. "Just keep the car! I don't need it! I've got friends who'll take me to parties!"

With that, she stormed out, called her friends from a pay phone, and headed for the party. Rochelle savored her apparent victory.

But then she arrived at the party. It was wild. Heavy drinking. Too many people. No adults around. She wanted to leave. But her "friends" had left without her, and everyone else at the party had been drinking. She was left to walk seven miles home. She stood alone outside, wondering what to do.

"Hey, Beautiful! Want a lift?" a voice said from a car pulling up behind her. Rochelle felt a surge of fear, and looked for somewhere to run. But when she glanced over her shoulder at the car, she saw her dad's smiling face.

She got in. Dad spoke first. "Dina called," he explained. "She said they tried to find you before they left but it was too crowded. They wanted to get out of there before their car got blocked in."

"I didn't think you'd be willing to come and get me," Rochelle said. "Not after the things I said and did."

Dad pulled the car over and turned to look at her. "Hey," he said. "You're my daughter. I love you. Nothing you say or do can ever change that."

Rochelle learned something about true love that night. **First Peter 1:17–23** talks about the kind of love Rochelle felt from her dad.

■ According to the passage, how is Rochelle's dad's love for her like God's love for us?

■ How might your life change if you trusted and accepted God's love as described in 1 Peter?

CONSIDER . . .

■ comparing your parents' love with God's love. Share your observations with your mom or dad.

➦ talking with a grandparent, aunt, or uncle about times when someone had to discipline your mom or dad. How was that person's love like God's love for you?

FOR MORE SEE . . .

■ Deuteronomy 7:7–9 (p. 168)
■ Romans 4:1–8 (p. 1143)

■ 1 John 4:7–10 (p. 1319)

Follow Christ's Example

[18]Slaves, yield to the authority of your masters with all respect, not only those who are good and kind, but also those who are dishonest. [19]A person might have to suffer even when it is unfair, but if he thinks of God and stands the pain, God is pleased. [20]If you are beaten for doing wrong, there is no reason to praise you for being patient in your punishment. But if you suffer for doing good, and you are patient then God is pleased. [21]This is what you were called to do, because Christ suffered for you and gave you an example to follow. So you should do as he did.

[22]"He had never sinned,
　　and he had never lied." *Isaiah 53:9*

[23]People insulted Christ, but he did not insult them in return. Christ suffered, but he did not threaten. He let God, the One who judges rightly, take care of him. [24]Christ carried our sins in his body on the cross so we would stop living for sin and start living for what is right. And you are healed because of his wounds. [25]You were like sheep that wandered away, but now you have come back to the Shepherd and Protector of your souls.

> **SIDELIGHT:** Because the early Christians were viewed suspiciously, 1 Peter 2:12 urges them to "live good lives" so people would not accuse them of wrongdoing. Among other things, early Christians were falsely accused of eating children because they followed Jesus' command to eat his body and drink his blood in the Communion (also called the Lord's Supper) (see 1 Corinthians 11:23–26, p. 1181).

SELF-ESTEEM

Paying the Price

More than anything, Frank Simms wanted to join the Lords. What a great feeling it would be, he thought, to wear the gang jacket, to be accepted by the guys, to be tough.

But membership in the Lords came with a price. One of the initiation rites was to beat up another guy, steal his expensive shoes, then wear those shoes the next day.

Jimmy Pantelli was chosen as Frank's target. Frank worked out a plan for the attack and left home late one afternoon with a baseball bat. He cornered Jimmy and told him to hand over his shoes.

But Jimmy refused, and a fight broke out. By the time it was over, Frank had been arrested, and Jimmy had been taken to the hospital.

Three months later, Frank still sat in jail, awaiting trial for attempted murder. Jimmy still lay in a coma. Frank wondered why it had all backfired. Why hadn't Jimmy just given him the shoes?

"I wanted to be somebody, that's all," Frank explained. "I just wanted to belong." But nothing could help him feel less guilty for wrecking Jimmy's life, nor reduce the serious consequences of his crime.

Frank was paying the price for his violent attempts to be accepted. **First Peter 2:2–10** shows how Jesus offers a different foundation for building self-esteem.

■ If Frank were to read and follow this passage, what would it tell him about feeling chosen, accepted, and important?
■ Whenever you feel shaky in your self-esteem, how might this passage help you improve your view?

C O N S I D E R . . .

■ listing the groups you would like to belong to, along with the need they could fill for you. What price would you pay to belong, and how would your self-esteem benefit from belonging?
■ choosing one person whom you think would truly help you change for the better, and befriend that person.

F O R　M O R E ,　S E E . . .

■ Isaiah 8:12–14 (p. 626)
■ Hosea 2:23 (p. 825)
■ 2 Corinthians 6:3–10 (p. 1198)

Wives and Husbands

3 In the same way, you wives should yield to your husbands. Then, if some husbands do not obey God's teaching, they will be persuaded to believe without anyone's saying a word to them. They will be persuaded by the way their wives live. [2]Your husbands will see the pure lives you live with your respect for God. [3]It is not fancy hair, gold jewelry, or fine clothes that should make you beautiful. [4]No, your beauty should come from within you — the beauty of a gentle and quiet spirit that will never be destroyed and

---

SIDELIGHT: When 1 Peter 3:3–4 says true beauty comes from the inside, it would not have made the jewelry merchants happy. In those times, women would decorate their hair with elaborate combs and hairpins, some of which were made of gold.

---

is very precious to God. [5]In this same way the holy women who lived long ago and followed God made themselves beautiful, yielding to their own husbands. [6]Sarah obeyed Abraham, her husband, and called him her master. And you women are true children of Sarah if you always do what is right and are not afraid.

[7]In the same way, you husbands should live with your wives in an understanding way, since they are weaker than you. But show them respect, because God gives them the same blessing he gives you — the grace that gives true life. Do this so that nothing will stop your prayers.

Suffering for Doing Right

[8]Finally, all of you should be in agreement, understanding each other, loving each other as family, being kind and humble. [9]Do not do wrong to repay a wrong, and do not insult to repay an insult. But repay with a blessing, because you yourselves were called to do this so that you might receive a blessing. [10]The Scripture[d] says,

"A person must do these things
to enjoy life and have many happy days.
He must not say evil things,
and he must not tell lies.
[11]He must stop doing evil and do good.
He must look for peace and work for it.
[12]The Lord sees the good people
and listens to their prayers.
But the Lord is against
those who do evil."
      Psalm 34:12-16

[13]If you are trying hard to do good, no one can really hurt you. [14]But even if you suffer for doing right, you are blessed.

"Don't be afraid of what they fear;
do not dread those things."   *Isaiah 8:12-13*
[15]But respect Christ as the holy Lord in your hearts. Always be ready to answer everyone who asks you to explain about the hope you have, [16]but answer in a gentle way and with respect. Keep a clear conscience so that those who speak evil of your good life in Christ will be made ashamed. [17]It is better to suffer for doing good than for doing wrong if that is what God wants. [18]Christ himself suffered for sins once. He was not guilty, but he suffered for those who are guilty to bring you to God. His body was killed, but he was made alive in the spirit. [19]And in the spirit he went and preached to the spirits in prison [20]who refused to obey God long ago in the time of Noah. God was waiting patiently for them while Noah was building the boat. Only a few people — eight in all — were saved by water. [21]And that water is like baptism that now saves you — not the washing of dirt from the body, but the promise made to God from a good conscience. And this is because Jesus Christ was raised from the dead. [22]Now Jesus has gone into heaven and is at God's right side ruling over angels, authorities, and powers.

Change Your Lives

4 Since Christ suffered while he was in his body, strengthen yourselves with the same way of thinking Christ had. The person who has suffered in the body is finished with sin. [2]Strengthen yourselves so that you will live here on earth doing what God wants, not the evil things people want. [3]In the past you wasted too much time doing what nonbelievers enjoy. You were guilty of sexual sins, evil desires, drunkenness, wild and drunken parties, and hateful idol worship. [4]Nonbelievers think it is strange that you do not do the many wild and wasteful things they do, so they insult you. [5]But they will have to explain this to God, who is ready to judge the living and the dead. [6]For this reason the Good News[d] was preached to those who are now dead. Even though they were judged like all people, the Good News was preached to them so they could live in the spirit as God lives.

Use God's Gifts Wisely

[7]The time is near when all things will end. So think clearly and control yourselves so you will be able to pray. [8]Most importantly, love each other *deeply, because love will cause many sins to be* forgiven. [9]Open your homes *to each other, with*out complaining. [10]Each of you has received a gift to use to serve others. Be good servants of God's various gifts of grace. [11]Anyone who speaks should speak words from God. Anyone who

serves should serve with the strength God gives so that in everything God will be praised through Jesus Christ. Power and glory belong to him forever and ever. Amen.

Suffering as a Christian

¹²My friends, do not be surprised at the terrible trouble which now comes to test you. Do not think that something strange is happening to you. ¹³But be happy that you are sharing in Christ's sufferings so that you will be happy and full of joy when Christ comes again in glory. ¹⁴When people insult you because you follow Christ, you are blessed, because the glorious Spirit,*d* the Spirit of God, is with you. ¹⁵Do not suffer for murder, theft, or any other crime, nor because you trouble other people. ¹⁶But if you suffer because you are a Christian, do not be ashamed. Praise God because you wear that name. ¹⁷It is time for judgment to begin with God's family. And if that judging begins with us, what will happen to those people who do not obey the Good News*d* of God? ¹⁸"If it is very hard for a good person to be saved,

the wicked person and the sinner will surely be lost!" *n*

¹⁹So those who suffer as God wants should trust their souls to the faithful Creator as they continue to do what is right.

The Flock of God

5 Now I have something to say to the elders*d* in your group. I also am an elder. I have seen Christ's sufferings, and I will share in the glory that will be shown to us. I beg you to ²shepherd God's flock, for whom you are responsible. Watch over them because you want to, not because you are forced. That is how God wants it. Do it because you are happy to serve, not because you want money. ³Do not be like a ruler over people you are responsible for, but be good examples to them. ⁴Then when Christ, the Chief Shepherd,

---

"If . . . lost!"   Quotation from Proverbs 11:31 in the Septuagint, the Greek version of the Old Testament.

SUFFERING

The Cost of Faith

"Hey, man," said Bill Miller to his friend Jose Castano. "I don't want to hear about your Jesus! Leave me alone!"

The words broke Jose's heart. Bill had been his best friend since eighth grade. But now, three years later, their friendship was in jeopardy because Jose had become a Christian and had let his friends know.

Bill had confronted Jose at a friend's party, accusing him of "thinking you're better than everyone else" because Jose had chosen not to drink anymore.

"Let me know when you get over this religion stuff," Bill had said. "Maybe then we can be friends again." At that, Bill left Jose standing alone. Jose feared he had just lost his best friend.

"No one ever told me that being a Christian could hurt this bad or cost so much," Jose muttered to himself as he went home after the party. "Maybe it's just not worth it. I thought being a Christian meant life got better, not more painful."

As we grow in faith, we change. Sometimes friends change with us. Sometimes they don't. This change may cause some pain. **First Peter 4:12–19** reminds us that being a Christian does not insulate us from pain and suffering. In fact, Peter lets us know that we can expect it as we grow in Christ. He also reminds us that some things are worth suffering for.

■ What comfort or understanding might this passage give to Jose in the loss of his friendship with Bill?

■ When have you paid a cost for your faith? How did you grow from that experience?

CONSIDER . . .
■ praying for a friend whom you know is suffering right now.
■ reading about the life of a Christian martyr. Your pastor can help you find such a story.

FOR MORE, SEE . . .

■ Psalm 56:1–4 (p. 514)
■ John 15:18–21 (p. 1085)

■ 1 Peter 2:19–25 (p. 1305)

comes, you will get a glorious crown that will never lose its beauty.

⁵In the same way, younger people should be willing to be under older people. And all of you should be very humble with each other.

"God is against the proud,
but he gives grace to the humble."

Proverbs 3:34

⁶Be humble under God's powerful hand so he will lift you up when the right time comes. ⁷Give all your worries to him, because he cares about you.

⁸Control yourselves and be careful! The devil, your enemy, goes around like a roaring lion looking for someone to eat. ⁹Refuse to give in to him, by standing strong in your faith. You know that your Christian family all over the world is having the same kinds of suffering.

¹⁰And after you suffer for a short time, God, who gives all grace, will make everything right. He will make you strong and support you and keep you from falling. He called you to share in his glory in Christ, a glory that will continue forever. ¹¹All power is his forever and ever. Amen.

Final Greetings

¹²I wrote this short letter with the help of Silas, who I know is a faithful brother in Christ. I

WORRYING

Weighty Worries

Dwight Evans has played baseball with the Boston Red Sox for almost two decades. He has hit more than 350 home runs, batted in 1,200 runs and had 2,000 hits. His salary matches his accomplishments. He shouldn't have much to worry about, right?

But he does. His two teenage sons suffer from neurofibromatosis, a genetic disorder that causes tumors on the skin. Both sons have had numerous surgeries and radiation treatments. Since the disease is incurable, their future remains uncertain.

"It's very easy to feel sorry for ourselves," Evans says. What keeps Evans and his wife from being overwhelmed with worries? Their faith. "I can't tell you the number of times we've just gotten down on our knees and prayed," he explains. "We have faith in God to carry us through."

Like the Evans family, the early Christians needed assurance that God would deliver them from worries. Bible texts such as **1 Peter 5:6–11** helped them put life in perspective.

■ How might this passage give hope and comfort to the Evans family?
■ How does the passage, especially verse 7, speak to whatever worries you right now?

CONSIDER . . .
■ memorizing verse 7 to encourage you when worries get you down.
▶ keeping a list of troubles and prayers. Over time, review the list, remembering how God helped you endure various problems.

FOR MORE, SEE . . .
■ Proverbs 3:3–5 (p. 570)
■ Matthew 11:28–30 (p. 928)
■ Revelation 2:8–11 (p. 1333)

wrote to encourage you and to tell you that this is the true grace of God. Stand strong in that grace.

¹³The church in Babylon, who was chosen like you, sends you greetings. Mark, my son in Christ, also greets you. ¹⁴Give each other a kiss of Christian love when you meet.

Peace to all of you who are in Christ.

2 PETER

Why Read This Book:

■ Be assured that the Christian faith is true (2 Peter 1).
■ Learn how to respond to false teaching (2 Peter 2).
■ Anticipate Christ's return (2 Peter 3).

Behind the Scenes:

Walking on rocks is fairly easy if you have a good pair of shoes. But what happens when even a small pebble inches its way inside your shoe? The pain and annoyance are almost unbearable. Something has to be done!

Think of 2 Peter as dealing with a pebble in the church's shoe. The early church expected false teachings outside the church, and these Christians had learned to protect themselves from those false teachings. But then, like an annoying pebble, false teachings entered the church. Some people were accepting the teachings as truth. But 2 Peter challenged them to get rid of the "pebble" before it caused more problems.

This hard-hitting letter urges believers to counteract false "knowledge" with true knowledge. It exposes the false beliefs of those who said Jesus would not come again. And it attacks those who lived sinful lives by abusing their freedom in Christ. Christ is coming again, the letter proclaims. And Christians should live moral lives as they wait for that return.

This short letter challenges us today, just as it challenged its original readers. Watch out for false teachers. Live lives that follow God's commands. And wait with anticipation for Christ to come again.

WHEN THE ACTION WAS			
Jesus was born	The church began soon after Jesus went to heaven	Paul began his missionary work	Fire destroyed Rome
BC/AD	25AD	50AD	75AD 100AD
	Jesus began his ministry	2 Peter may have been written	The Roman emperor increased persecution of Christians

1

From Simon Peter, a servant and apostle[d] of Jesus Christ.

To you who have received a faith as valuable as ours, because our God and Savior Jesus Christ does what is right.

[2]Grace and peace be given to you more and more, because you truly know God and Jesus our Lord.

SIDELIGHT: If you want to read a short version of 2 Peter, check out Jude (p. 1329). About nineteen of the twenty-five verses in Jude are similar to verses in 2 Peter.

God Has Given Us Blessings

[3]Jesus has the power of God, by which he has given us everything we need to live and to serve God. We have these things because we know him. Jesus called us by his glory and goodness. [4]Through these he gave us the very great and precious promises. With these gifts you can share in being like God, and the world will not ruin you with its evil desires.

[5]Because you have these blessings, do your best to add these things to your lives: to your faith, add goodness; and to your goodness, add knowledge; [6]and to your knowledge, add self-control; and to your self-control, add patience; and to your patience, add service for God; [7]and to your service for God, add kindness for your brothers and sisters in Christ and to this kindness, add love. [8]If all these things are in you and are growing, they will help you to be useful and productive in your knowledge of our Lord Jesus Christ. [9]But anyone who does not have these things cannot see clearly. He is blind and has forgotten that he was made clean from his past sins.

[10]My brothers and sisters,[n] try hard to be certain that you really are called and chosen by God. If you do all these things, you will never fall. [11]And you will be given a very great welcome into the eternal kingdom of our Lord and Savior Jesus Christ.

[12]You know these things, and you are very strong in the truth, but I will always help you remember them. [13]I think it is right for me to help you remember as long as I am in this body. [14]I know I must soon leave this body, as our Lord Jesus Christ has shown me. [15]I will try my best so that you may be able to remember these things even after I am gone.

We Saw Christ's Glory

[16]When we told you about the powerful coming of our Lord Jesus Christ, we were not telling just smart stories that someone invented. But we saw the greatness of Jesus with our own eyes. [17]Jesus heard the voice of God, the Greatest Glory, when he received honor and glory from God the Father. The voice said, "This is my Son, whom I love, and I am very pleased with him." [18]We heard that voice from heaven while we were with Jesus on the holy mountain.

[19]This makes us more sure about the message the prophets[d] gave. It is good for you to follow closely what they said as you would follow a light shining in a dark place, until the day begins and the morning star rises in your hearts. [20]Most of all, you must understand this: No prophecy in the Scriptures[d] ever comes from the prophet's own interpretation. [21]No prophecy ever came from what a person wanted to say, but people led by the Holy Spirit[d] spoke words from God.

False Teachers

2

There used to be false prophets[d] among God's people, just as you will have some false teachers in your group. They will secretly teach things that are wrong—teachings that will cause people to be lost. They will even refuse to accept the Master, Jesus, who bought their freedom. So they will bring quick ruin on themselves. [2]Many will follow their evil ways and say evil things about the way of truth. [3]Those false teachers only want your money, so they will use you by telling you lies. Their judgment spoken against them long ago is still coming, and their ruin is certain.

[4]When angels sinned, God did not let them go free without punishment. He sent them to hell and put them in caves of darkness where they are being held for judgment. [5]And God punished the world long ago when he brought a flood to the world that was full of people who were against him. But God saved Noah, who preached about being right with God, and seven other people with him. [6]And God also destroyed the evil cities of Sodom and Gomorrah[n] by burning them until they were ashes. He made those cities an example of what will happen to those who are against God. [7]But he saved Lot from those cities. Lot, a good man, was troubled because of the filthy lives of evil people. [8](Lot was a good man, but because he lived with evil people every day, his good heart was hurt by the evil things he saw and heard.) [9]So the Lord knows how to save those who serve him when troubles come. He will hold evil people and

brothers and sisters Although the Greek text reads "brothers" here and throughout this book, Peter's words were meant for the entire church, including men and women.
Sodom and Gomorrah Two cities God destroyed because the people were so evil.

punish them, while waiting for the Judgment Day. [10]That punishment is especially for those who live by doing the evil things their sinful selves want and who hate authority.

These false teachers are bold and do anything they want. They are not afraid to speak against the angels. [11]But even the angels, who are much stronger and more powerful than false teachers, do not accuse them with insults before the Lord. [12]But these people speak against things they do not understand. They are like animals that act without thinking, animals born to be caught and killed. And, like animals, these false teachers will be destroyed. [13]They have caused many people to suffer, so they themselves will suffer. That is their pay for what they have done. They take pleasure in openly doing evil, so they are like dirty spots and stains among you. They delight in trickery while eating meals with you. [14]Every time they look at a woman they want her, and their desire for sin is never satisfied. They lead weak people into the trap of sin, and they have taught their hearts to be greedy. God will punish them! [15]These false teachers left the right road and lost

their way, following the way Balaam went. Balaam was the son of Beor, who loved being paid for doing wrong. [16]But a donkey, which cannot talk, told Balaam he was sinning. It spoke with a man's voice and stopped the prophet's crazy thinking.

[17]Those false teachers are like springs without water and clouds blown by a storm. A place in the blackest darkness has been kept for them. [18]They brag with words that mean nothing. By their evil desires they lead people into the trap of sin — people who are just beginning to escape from others who live in error. [19]They promise them freedom, but they themselves are not free. They are slaves of things that will be destroyed. For people are slaves of anything that controls them. [20]They were made free from the evil in the world by knowing our Lord and Savior Jesus Christ. But if they return to evil things and those things control them, then it is worse for them than it was before. [21]Yes, it would be better for them to have never known the right way than to know it and to turn away from the holy teaching that was given to them. [22]What they did is like this true saying: "A

God's Love Letter

Have you ever received love letters? No doubt you read them differently than you would read junk mail or a form letter inviting you to join Latin club. Indeed, author Mortimer Adler says that when we read a love letter, we:

■ read every word three ways,
■ read between the lines,
■ weigh each sentence,
■ perceive the color of each word, and,
■ look for deep meaning, even in the punctuation.

When you are in love, you read a love letter over and over, carefully, and in depth.

If the Bible were a letter, what kind of letter would it be for you? Would it be "junk mail"? Would it be boring "required reading" such as a literature assignment? Or, would it be a "love letter" from God to you?

The writer of **2 Peter 1:16–21** guarantees that the life and message of Jesus Christ is not "junk mail." It's a love letter from God.

■ Why might someone who loves God learn more from the Bible than someone who doesn't love God?
■ How might reading more of God's "love letters" in the Bible help you face life's problems and decisions?

CONSIDER . . .

■ listing reasons why people study the Bible, and then choosing which one is your top reason.
 reading the Gospel of Matthew over the next month (one chapter per day) as if it were addressed particularly to you.

FOR MORE, SEE . . .

■ Jeremiah 23:25–29 (p. 717)
■ Acts 17:11 (p. 1125)
■ Hebrews 4:12–16 (p. 1279)

dog goes back to what it has thrown up,"[n] and, "After a pig is washed, it goes back and rolls in the mud."

Jesus Will Come Again

3 My friends, this is the second letter I have written you to help your honest minds remember. [2] I want you to think about the words the holy prophets[d] spoke in the past, and remember the command our Lord and Savior gave us through your apostles.[d] [3] It is most important for you to understand what will happen in the last days. People will laugh at you. They will live doing the evil things they want to do. [4] They will say, "Jesus promised to come again. Where is he? Our fathers have died, but the world continues the way it has been since it was made." [5] But they do not want to remember what happened long ago. By the word of God heaven was made, and the earth was made from water and with water. [6] Then the world was flooded and destroyed with water. [7] And that same word of God is keeping heaven and earth that we now have in order to be destroyed by fire. They are being kept for the Judgment Day and the destruction of all who are against God.

[8] But do not forget this one thing, dear friends: To the Lord one day is as a thousand years, and a thousand years is as one day. [9] The Lord is not slow in doing what he promised — the way some people understand slowness. But God is being patient with you. He does not want anyone to be lost, but he wants all people to change their hearts and lives.

[10] But the day of the Lord will come like a thief. The skies will disappear with a loud noise. Everything in them will be destroyed by fire, and the earth and everything in it will be burned up.[n]

"A dog ... up" Quotation from Proverbs 26:11.
will be burned up Many Greek copies say, "will be found." One copy says, "will disappear."

FUTURE

Party Now?

"Why shouldn't I party?" protested sixteen-year-old Joe Williams at a youth group meeting. "The world might not even be around when I'm twenty."

Joe didn't see much hope for the future. He read newspapers and newsmagazines to keep up with world events. The more Joe read, the more he became a sarcastic pessimist.

"We're either gonna die in a nuclear war or from poisoning our environment," he would say. His cynical attitude began to affect his views on life issues. He still received good grades, but he no longer enjoyed learning

At one time in junior high, Joe had held to high values about issues such as sex, alcohol use, and the environment. In his dark gloom about the future, however, those values seemed irrelevant to him.

"I just hang out, watch some TV, and look out for a good time," he said. "I want to live it up now while I still can."

Joe said his dark view of the future might have something to do with his uncertainty about God. "I don't even know if God can get us out of this mess, or even if he cares," he said. "I'm living for now and for me. I wish there were hope somewhere, but I don't see any right now."

Joe's views of the future negatively affected how he lived every day. In contrast, **2 Peter 3:8–13** offers a hopeful message that can positively affect how we live now.

■ If Joe were to read this passage, what hope or encouragement about the future might he find?
■ How does knowing that the future rests in God's hands influence the way you live your life?

C O N S I D E R . . .

■ living like God is in complete control of your day.
■ setting three important goals to reach in the next five years, based on your reading of the passage.

F O R   M O R E ,   S E E . . .

■ Isaiah 65:17–25 (p. 686)   ■ Revelation 21:1–5 (p. 1347)
■ Mark 13:32–37 (p. 991)

11In that way everything will be destroyed. So what kind of people should you be? You should live holy lives and serve God, 12as you wait for and look forward to the coming of the day of God. When that day comes, the skies will be destroyed with fire, and everything in them will melt with heat. 13But God made a promise to us, and we are waiting for a new heaven and a new earth where goodness lives.

> ✳ **SIDELIGHT:** According to 2 Peter 3:15–16, you are in good company if you sometimes have trouble understanding Romans (p. 1140) or other books that Paul wrote. Peter did too. This passage is a rare example of a New Testament author giving another New Testament book the authority of scripture.

14Dear friends, since you are waiting for this to happen, do your best to be without sin and without fault. Try to be at peace with God. 15Remember that we are saved because our Lord is patient. Our dear brother Paul told you the same thing when he wrote to you with the wisdom that God gave him. 16He writes about this in all his letters. Some things in Paul's letters are hard to understand, and people who are ignorant and weak in faith explain these things falsely. They also falsely explain the other Scriptures,*d* but they are destroying themselves by doing this.

17Dear friends, since you already know about this, be careful. Do not let those evil people lead you away by the wrong they do. Be careful so you will not fall from your strong faith. 18But grow in the grace and knowledge of our Lord and Savior Jesus Christ. Glory be to him now and forever! Amen.

1 JOHN

Why Read This Book:

- Find out how to grow closer to God (1 John 1—2).
- See what it's like to be part of God's family (1 John 3—4).
- Be assured of life with God after death (1 John 5).

Behind the Scenes:

When you read the book of 1 John, you almost have the feeling that a grandfather has gathered his grandchildren around a fire to talk. You can see his love for them sparkling in his eyes, and you know from the way they look at him that they respect him a great deal.

As he talks to his "children," as he calls them, you can feel the warmth. He reassures them of God's love for them. He gently coaxes them to believe in and follow God.

But he also has another purpose. He is worried that the younger Christians are hearing mixed messages about Jesus Christ. People—known as gnostics—are saying that Jesus wasn't really human; he was only divine. Furthermore, they were arguing that they could do whatever they wanted to do with their bodies, because the physical body was separate from the spiritual nature.

The grandfather knows these ideas are wrong. Jesus was both fully human and fully divine. And what the body does certainly affects the spirit—for better or worse. So the grandfather challenges the false teaching and urges his children to stick to the truth.

Of course, 1 John isn't really a fireside chat between a grandfather and his grandchildren. It's a letter or sermon written to Christians to help them grow in their faith and to counteract the false teaching that was gaining influence among the early Christians.

Yet the true spirit of the letter comes through when we imagine the love and warmth that comes when we sit around a fireplace, listening to the advice of a wise grandfather. Not only did the words encourage and challenge the original hearers to keep following God, but they challenge and encourage us today.

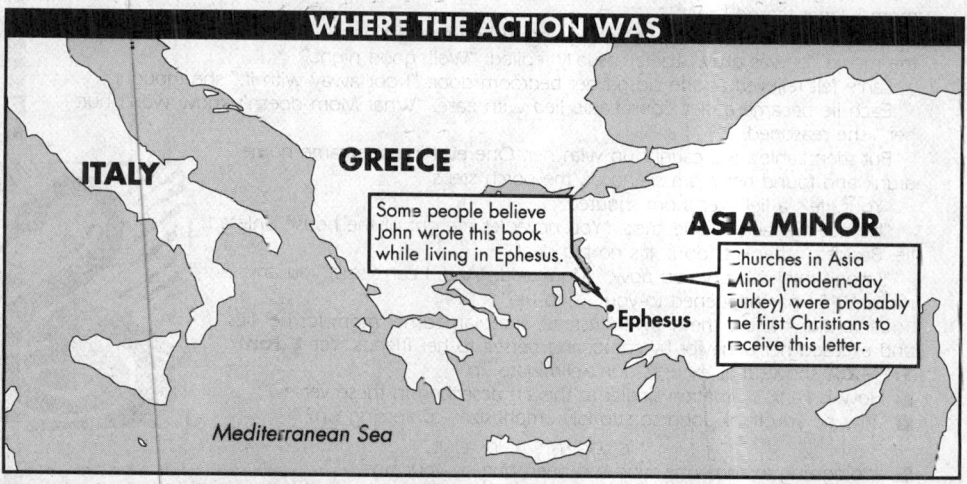

WHERE THE ACTION WAS

ITALY

GREECE

Some people believe John wrote this book while living in Ephesus.

ASIA MINOR

Churches in Asia Minor (modern-day Turkey) were probably the first Christians to receive this letter.

Ephesus

Mediterranean Sea

WHEN THE ACTION WAS

Jesus was born	The church began soon after Jesus went to heaven	Paul began his missionary work	Fire destroyed Rome	1 John was written
BC/AD	25AD	50AD	75AD	100AD
	Jesus began his ministry	Paul became a Christian	Romans destroyed the Temple in Jerusalem	

1 We write you now about what has always existed, which we have heard, we have seen with our own eyes, we have looked at, and we have touched with our hands. We write to you about the Word[n] that gives life. [2]He who gives life was shown to us. We saw him and can give proof about it. And now we announce to you that he has life that continues forever. He was with God the Father and was shown to us. [3]We announce to you what we have seen and heard, because we want you also to have fellowship with us. Our fellowship is with God the Father and with his Son, Jesus Christ. [4]We write this to you so you can be full of joy with us.

God Forgives Our Sins

[5]Here is the message we have heard from Christ and now announce to you: God is light,[n] and in him there is no darkness at all. [6]So if we say we have fellowship with God, but we continue living in darkness, we are liars and do not follow the truth. [7]But if we live in the light, as God is in the light, we can share fellowship with each other. Then the blood of Jesus, God's Son, cleanses us from every sin.

[8]If we say we have no sin, we are fooling ourselves, and the truth is not in us. [9]But if we confess our sins, he will forgive our sins, because we can trust God to do what is right. He will cleanse us from all the wrongs we have done. [10]If we say we have not sinned, we make God a liar, and we do not accept God's teaching.

Jesus Is Our Helper

2 My dear children, I write this letter to you so you will not sin. But if anyone does sin, we have a helper in the presence of the Father—Jesus Christ, the One who does what is right. [2]He

---

Word The Greek word is "logos," meaning any kind of communication. Here, it means Christ, who was the way God told people about himself.
light Here, this word is used as a symbol of God's goodness or truth.

SIN

No Excuses

Lanie Pritchard remembers the first time she lied to her mom about where she was going. "Janet, Kate, and I are going to a movie," she lied without looking straight into her mom's eyes.

Could her mom tell she was lying? Lanie couldn't tell, so she quickly left the house.

The party blared away when the three girls arrived. "See, it wasn't so hard to fool your mom," Janet teased Lanie.

Still, Lanie was tense the whole evening. When she got home, her mom asked about the movie. "It was okay," Lanie casually replied. "Well, good night."

Lanie felt relieved as she closed her bedroom door. "I got away with it," she thought.

Each lie became easier. Soon Lanie lied with ease. "What Mom doesn't know won't hurt her," she reasoned.

But then Lanie's lies caught up with her. One evening she came home drunk and found her mom sitting on the porch steps.

"Your life's a lie!" her mom shouted.

"It's not my fault," Lanie cried. "You never let me out of the house unless I lie. Besides, other kids do it. It's no big deal."

"I don't think I know you now," Mom said. "And, I can't trust you anymore. What has happened to you . . . to us?"

Lanie didn't know the answer. Instead, she blamed her mom for her lies and excused her behavior by comparing herself to her friends. Yet **1 John 1:1—2:2** shows that excuses don't eliminate sin.

■ How is Lanie's situation similar to the sin described in these verses?
■ Why do you think John so strongly emphasizes confessing sin?

CONSIDER . . .
■ apologizing to someone who has been hurt by your sins.
■ selecting a verse from the passage that conveys the "no excuses" idea. Write the verse on a small card and memorize it.

FOR MORE, SEE . . .
■ Genesis 3:1–13 (p. 4)
■ Psalm 51:1–13 (p. 511)
■ Luke 15:11–24 (p. 1035)

is the way our sins are taken away, and not only our sins but the sins of all people.

> **SIDELIGHT:** Perhaps the biggest heresy (wrong doctrine) that the early church faced involved the gnostic understanding of evil. Gnostics—whose name came from the word for "knowledge"—believed evil was simply an error that grew out of ignorance; the person who did wrong was not really responsible. First John responded that people are responsible for their sins and must be forgiven to be right with God (1 John 1:9; 2:2).

[3]We can be sure that we know God if we obey his commands. [4]Anyone who says, "I know God," but does not obey God's commands is a liar, and the truth is not in that person. [5]But if someone obeys God's teaching, then in that person God's love has truly reached its goal. This is how we can be sure we are living in God: [6]Whoever says that he lives in God must live as Jesus lived.

The Command to Love Others

[7]My dear friends, I am not writing a new command to you but an old command you have had from the beginning. It is the teaching you have already heard. [8]But also I am writing a new command to you, and you can see its truth in Jesus and in you, because the darkness is passing away, and the true light is already shining.

[9]Anyone who says, "I am in the light," *n* but hates a brother or sister, *n* is still in the darkness. [10]Whoever loves a brother or sister lives in the light and will not cause anyone to stumble in his faith. [11]But whoever hates a brother or sister is in darkness, lives in darkness, and does not know where to go, because the darkness has made that person blind.

[12]I write to you, dear children,
  because your sins are forgiven through Christ.
[13]I write to you, parents,
  because you know the One who existed
    from the beginning.
I write to you, young people,
  because you have defeated the Evil One.
[14]I write to you, children,
  because you know the Father.

I write to you, parents,
  because you know the One who existed
    from the beginning.
I write to you, young people,
  because you are strong;
  the teaching of God lives in you,
  and you have defeated the Evil One.

[15]Do not love the world or the things in the world. If you love the world, the love of the Father is not in you. [16]These are the ways of the world: wanting to please our sinful selves, wanting the sinful things we see, and being too proud of what we have. None of these come from the Father, but all of them come from the world. [17]The world and everything that people want in it are passing away, but the person who does what God wants lives forever.

Reject the Enemies of Christ

[18]My dear children, these are the last days. You have heard that the enemy of Christ[d] is coming, and now many enemies of Christ are already here. This is how we know that these are the last days. [19]These enemies of Christ were in our fellowship, but they left us. They never really belonged to us; if they had been a part of us, they would have stayed with us. But they left, and this shows that none of them really belonged to us. [20]You have the gift[n] that the Holy One gave you, so you all know the truth. [21]I do not write to you because you do not know the truth but because you do know the truth. And you know that no lie comes from the truth.

[22]Who is the liar? It is the person who does not accept Jesus as the Christ. This is the enemy of Christ: the person who does not accept the Father and his Son. [23]Whoever does not accept the Son does not have the Father. But whoever confesses the Son has the Father, too.

[24]Be sure you continue to follow the teaching you heard from the beginning. If you continue to follow what you heard from the beginning, you will stay in the Son and in the Father. [25]And this is what the Son promised to us—life forever.

[26]I am writing this letter about those people who are trying to lead you the wrong way. [27]Christ gave you a special gift that is still in you, so you do not need any other teacher. His gift teaches you about everything, and it is true, not false. So continue to live in Christ, as his gift taught you.

[28]Yes, my dear children, live in him so that when Christ comes back, we can be without fear and not be ashamed in his presence. [29]If you

---

light   Here, this word is used as a symbol of God's goodness or truth.
brother or sister   Although the Greek text says "brother" here and throughout this book, the writer's words were meant for the entire church, including men and women.
gift   This might mean the Holy Spirit, or it might mean teaching or truth as in verse 24.

know that Christ is all that is right, you know that all who do right are God's children.

We Are God's Children

3 The Father has loved us so much that we are called children of God. And we really are his children. The reason the people in the world do not know us is that they have not known him. ²Dear friends, now we are children of God, and we have not yet been shown what we will be in the future. But we know that when Christ comes again, we will be like him, because we will see him as he really is. ³Christ is pure, and all who have this hope in Christ keep themselves pure like Christ.

⁴The person who sins breaks God's law. Yes, sin is living against God's law. ⁵You know that Christ came to take away sins and that there is no sin in Christ. ⁶So anyone who lives in Christ does not go on sinning. Anyone who goes on sinning has never really understood Christ and has never known him.

⁷Dear children, do not let anyone lead you the wrong way. Christ is all that is right. So to be like Christ a person must do what is right. ⁸The devil has been sinning since the beginning, so anyone who continues to sin belongs to the devil. The Son of God came for this purpose: to destroy the devil's work.

⁹Those who are God's children do not continue sinning, because the new life from God remains in them. They are not able to go on sinning, because they have become children of God. ¹⁰So we can see who God's children are and who the devil's children are: Those who do not do what is right are not God's children, and those who do not love their brothers and sisters are not God's children.

We Must Love Each Other

¹¹This is the teaching you have heard from the beginning: We must love each other. ¹²Do not be like Cain who belonged to the Evil One and killed his brother. And why did he kill him? Because the things Cain did were evil, and the things his brother did were good.

FOLLOWING GOD

Life at the Top

Lynn Hill has always been at the top of everything. When she was a kid, she was at the top of trees, telephone poles, even street lights. Now she is on top of cliffs and mountains as one of the world's leading rock climbers. She is one of the few people who has defied gravity and scaled cliffs that are "steeper" than vertical.

Lynn has gotten to be so good because she dedicates her life to her climbing. A picture taken the day after her wedding shows how important climbing is to her. It shows her and her new husband—also a climber, of course—in full wedding attire hanging from a rope off cliffs near their home.

Lynn knows how important it is to not become lax in her climbing techniques. Once she fell seventy-five feet down a cliff because she forgot to tie a simple knot on her safety rope. A tree branch slowed her fall and saved her life, though she was injured.

"The rock is a tool for learning and understanding," she says. "When you get to the top, you've conquered something inside as well."

Lynn's dedication to climbing illustrates the kind of dedication Christians should have in following God. **First John 3:1–24** encourages Christians not to be distracted from following God.

■ What parallels do you see between Lynn's dedication to rock climbing and the passage's guidance about being a Christian?
■ How have other Christians encouraged you and kept you dedicated to following God?

C O N S I D E R . . .

■ thinking about everything you did in the past twenty-four hours. Decide which things helped you follow God and which ones did not.
■ asking a Christian friend to help you overcome a sin that keeps you from following God, with the kind of dedication Lynn has for rock climbing.

F O R   M O R E ,   S E E . . .

■ Psalm 95:1–11 (p. 537)
■ Romans 7:14–25 (p. 1148)

■ Ephesians 5:1–11 (p. 1224)

[13]Brothers and sisters, do not be surprised when the people of the world hate you. [14]We know we have left death and have come into life because we love each other. Whoever does not love is still dead. [15]Everyone who hates a brother or sister is a murderer,[n] and you know that no murderers have eternal life in them. [16]This is how we know what real love is: Jesus gave his life for us. So we should give our lives for our brothers and sisters. [17]Suppose someone has enough to live and sees a brother or sister in need, but does not help. Then God's love is not living in that person. [18]My children, we should love people not only with words and talk, but by our actions and true caring.

> ✲ **SIDELIGHT:** When 1 John 3:13 told believers not to be surprised that the world hates them, it was speaking to an everyday reality for Christians at that time in Asia Minor. Even the Roman historian Tacitus, who lived during that time, wrote that Romans hated the Christians.

[19-20]This is the way we know that we belong to the way of truth. When our hearts make us feel guilty, we can still have peace before God. God is greater than our hearts, and he knows everything. [21]My dear friends, if our hearts do not make us feel guilty, we can come without fear into God's presence. [22]And God gives us what we ask for because we obey God's commands and do what pleases him. [23]This is what God commands: that we believe in his Son, Jesus Christ, and that we love each other, just as he commanded. [24]The people who obey God's commands live in God, and God lives in them. We know that God lives in us because of the Spirit[d] God gave us.

Warning Against False Teachers

4 My dear friends, many false prophets[d] have gone out into the world. So do not believe every spirit, but test the spirits to see if they are from God. [2]This is how you can know God's Spirit:[d] Every spirit who confesses that Jesus Christ came to earth as a human is from God. [3]And every spirit who refuses to say this about Jesus is not from God. It is the spirit of the enemy of Christ,[d] which you have heard is coming, and now he is already in the world.

[4]My dear children, you belong to God and have defeated them; because God's Spirit, who is in you, is greater than the devil, who is in the world. [5]And they belong to the world, so what they say

is from the world, and the world listens to them. [6]But we belong to God, and those who know God listen to us. But those who are not from God do not listen to us. That is how we know the Spirit that is true and the spirit that is false.

Love Comes from God

[7]Dear friends, we should love each other, because love comes from God. Everyone who loves has become God's child and knows God. [8]Whoever does not love does not know God, because God is love. [9]This is how God showed his love to us: He sent his one and only Son into the world so that we could have life through him. [10]This is what real love is: It is not our love for God; it is God's love for us in sending his Son to be the way to take away our sins.

[11]Dear friends, if God loved us that much we also should love each other. [12]No one has ever seen God, but if we love each other, God lives in us, and his love is made perfect in us.

[13]We know that we live in God and he lives in us, because he gave us his Spirit.[d] [14]We have seen and can testify that the Father sent his Son to be the Savior of the world. [15]Whoever confesses that Jesus is the Son of God has God living inside, and that person lives in God. [16]And so we know the love that God has for us, and we trust that love.

God is love. Those who live in love live in God, and God lives in them. [17]This is how love is made perfect in us: that we can be without fear on the day God judges us, because in this world we are like him. [18]Where God's love is, there is no fear, because God's perfect love drives out fear. It is punishment that makes a person fear, so love is not made perfect in the person who fears.

[19]We love because God first loved us. [20]If people say, "I love God," but hate their brothers or sisters, they are liars. Those who do not love their brothers and sisters, whom they have seen, cannot love God, whom they have never seen. [21]And God gave us this command: Those who love God must also love their brothers and sisters.

Faith in the Son of God

5 Everyone who believes that Jesus is the Christ[d] is God's child, and whoever loves the Father also loves the Father's children. [2]This is how we know we love God's children: when we love God and obey his commands. [3]Loving God means obeying his commands. And God's commands are not too hard for us, [4]because everyone who is a child of God conquers the world. And this is the victory that conquers the world — our faith. [5]So the one who wins against the world is

---

Everyone . . . murderer If one person hates a brother or sister, then in the heart that person has killed that brother or sister. Jesus taught about this sin to his followers (Matthew 5:21-26).

the person who believes that Jesus is the Son of God.

[6]Jesus Christ is the One who came by water[n] and blood.[n] He did not come by water only, but by water and blood. And the Spirit[d] says that this is true, because the Spirit is the truth. [7]So there are three witnesses that tell us about Jesus: [8]the Spirit, the water, and the blood; and these three witnesses agree. [9]We believe people when they say something is true. But what God says is more important, and he has told us the truth about his own Son. [10]Anyone who believes in the Son of God has the truth that God told us. Anyone who does not believe makes God a liar, because that person does not believe what God told us about his Son. [11]This is what God told us: God has given us eternal life, and this life is in his Son. [12]Who-

ever has the Son has life, but whoever does not have the Son of God does not have life.

We Have Eternal Life Now

[13]I write this letter to you who believe in the Son of God so you will know you have eternal life. [14]And this is the boldness we have in God's presence: that if we ask God for anything that agrees with what he wants, he hears us. [15]If we know he hears us every time we ask him, we know we have what we ask from him.

[16]If anyone sees a brother or sister sinning (sin that does not lead to eternal death), that person should pray, and God will give the sinner life. I am talking about people whose sin does not lead to eternal death. There is sin that leads to death. I do not mean that a person should pray about

water This probably means the water of Jesus' baptism.
blood This probably means the blood of Jesus' death.

LOVE

The First Step

"But I don't even like her," Michelle Benson complained to Angie Stone after the camp Bible study. "So how am I going to love her?"

No one could remember what started the feud between Cindy and Michelle. They had known each other since childhood, and seemed always in conflict. They accused each other of telling lies; they fought over boyfriends; they over-competed in classes.

Angie suggested that Christian love goes beyond liking what others do. "It's a conscious decision to care," Angie explained.

Michelle frowned. "No matter what she does, I have to love her?"

"Loving people who love us is easy," said Angie. "Loving difficult people makes Christian love unique."

Michelle walked away, frustrated by Angie's words. During the week at camp, however, Michelle watched others build new relationships and mend damaged ones. People who had not gotten along at first seemed to make peace with each other.

At the last campfire, the camp director urged the kids to settle differences with those whom they had hurt during the year. Michelle wanted to go to Cindy, but held back, fearing rejection.

Suddenly she saw Cindy coming straight toward her with tears in her eyes. "I'm sorry," Michelle heard Cindy say. The girls hugged and cried. Healing began.

Loving others even when you don't like them is tough, but it is possible. In **1 John 4:7–12**, look for unique qualities of Christian love in action.

■ How did Michelle's initial attitude toward Cindy influence her relationship with God, according to this passage?

■ Why is loving others easier when you understand how God loves you?

CONSIDER . . .

■ making the first move to mend a damaged relationship with a family member or friend.

■ asking several friends to go out for hamburgers, including someone who is difficult for you to love. Try to get to know that person better.

FOR MORE, SEE . . .

■ Deuteronomy 6:5 (p. 167)
■ Matthew 5:43–48 (p. 916)

■ 1 Peter 4:8–9 (p. 1306)

that sin. ¹⁷Doing wrong is always sin, but there is sin that does not lead to eternal death.

¹⁸We know that those who are God's children do not continue to sin. The Son of God keeps them safe, and the Evil One cannot touch them. ¹⁹We know that we belong to God, but the Evil One controls the whole world. ²⁰We also know

that the Son of God has come and has given us understanding so that we can know the True One. And our lives are in the True One and in his Son, Jesus Christ. He is the true God and the eternal life.

²¹So, dear children, keep yourselves away from gods.

DISCOURAGEMENT

Hope Breakers and Makers

Did you ever experience a day when everything went wrong? Sometimes the day seems like one disappointing event after another. These disappointments can be called "hope breakers." Hope breakers can lead to outright discouragement if they persist. Which of these hope breakers seem familiar to you?

- threats of war in the world
- fights with your parents
- an accident in the family car
- breaking up with a girlfriend/boyfriend
- making a poor grade on a test
- doubting your Christian beliefs
- too much homework
- criticism from others
- feeling alone

Hope can overcome discouragement. Hope reminds you of a brighter future. Which of the events below are hope makers for you?

- feeling good about your life
- scoring high on a hard test
- giving and receiving Christian love from others
- making the team
- enjoying a beautiful day
- knowing God loves you
- getting a fantastic job
- having a great time with friends
- renewing a broken friendship

John offered reassurance and hope to Christians who had experienced too many hope breakers. Read John's hope-making ideas in **1 John 5:1–15**.

- How do the hope breakers and hope makers described above compare to the ones in this passage?
- What phrases in this passage offer you the most hope?

C O N S I D E R . . .

- writing out the promises and assurances in this passage. Post the list on your locker door.
- acting as a hope maker to a discouraged friend by offering encouragement, time or help.

F O R   M O R E ,   S E E . . .

- Psalm 42 (p. 507)
- John 15:18–27 (p. 1085)
- Romans 8:35–39 (p. 1152)

2 JOHN

Why Read This Book:

- Learn ways to show Christian love (2 John 1–6).
- Examine the danger of listening to false teachers (2 John 7–11).

Behind the Scenes:

The musical-movie The Music Man tells about a swindling, traveling salesman who goes into gullible towns offering to start bands for the kids. Then when people get excited and give him money for uniforms and instruments, he slips out of town, laughing about the trick.

The early Christians faced a similar situation. Because they were always open and loving to strangers, false teachers would take advantage of their openness. These teachers would get into the church and begin spreading false teachings. (For a description of the teachings, see the introduction to 1 John, p. 1315.)

Second John was written to warn churches not to welcome people who bring false teaching into the church. The short letter encourages them to keep loving each other. But, at the same time, it urges them to stay far away from false teachers.

As Christians, we too need to be open and loving to each other. But we also need to be on guard against people who present teachings that contradict the Bible. Second John challenges us to carefully evaluate others' statements before accepting them as true.

While 2 John warns against welcoming false teachers, 3 John (p. 1325) gives the other side of the issue. It focuses on the importance of being hospitable toward fellow believers. Read the two letters together for a balanced picture.

WHEN THE ACTION WAS				
Jesus was born	The church began soon after Jesus went to heaven	Paul began his missionary work	Fire destroyed Rome	2 John was written
BC/AD	25AD	50AD	75AD	100AD
	Jesus began his ministry	Paul became a Christian	Romans destroyed the Temple in Jerusalem	

¹From the Elder.ⁿ

To the chosen lady*ⁿ* and her children:

I love all of you in the truth,*ⁿ* and all those who know the truth love you. ²We love you because of the truth that lives in us and will be with us forever.

³Grace, mercy, and peace from God the Father and his Son, Jesus Christ, will be with us in truth and love.

⁴I was very happy to learn that some of your children are following the way of truth, as the Father commanded us. ⁵And now, dear lady, this is not a new command but is the same command we have had from the beginning. I ask you that we all love each other. ⁶And love means living the way God commanded us to live. As you have heard from the beginning, his command is this: Live a life of love.

⁷Many false teachers are in the world now who do not confess that Jesus Christ came to earth as a human. Anyone who does not confess this is a

> ☀ **SIDELIGHT:** If other books in the New Testament are letters (such as 1 Corinthians, p. 1167), then 2 John is more like a postcard. With only thirteen verses, it is the shortest book in the Bible. One reason it may have been short is so it could fit on a single sheet of papyrus, the paper of the day (2 John 12).

false teacher and an enemy of Christ.*ᵈ* ⁸Be careful yourselves that you do not lose everything you have worked for, but that you receive your full reward.

Elder "Elder" means an older person. It can also mean a special leader in the church (as in Titus 1:5).
lady This might mean a woman, or in this letter it might mean a church. If it is a church, then "her children" would be the people of the church.
truth The truth or "Good News" about Jesus Christ that joins all believers together.

CULTS

Christian Frauds

Amy Vanderhoof had just turned sixteen when she was approached by a friendly guy at the mall who engaged her in a conversation about God. The guy's enthusiasm about his beliefs impressed Amy. He invited her to a Bible study the next Tuesday evening. Already active in her church, Amy thought it sounded fun, so she went.

The Bible study began with upbeat songs. Then the teacher began his talk. He started calmly, but grew more energized as he taught. He held the Bible while he spoke, and he even referred to a Bible story Amy recognized. It all sounded real, acceptable, and safe.

Amy grew more involved. After attending several more Bible studies, she agreed to go with the group on a weekend retreat.

She never returned home.

Frantically, her parents tried to contact her, but the leaders kept them away. Soon her parents learned that she had "voluntarily" moved to a cult center in another state. Despite constant effort, Amy's parents never heard from her again.

Although the cult leaders used scripture, prayer, and other Christian-sounding ideas, Jesus Christ wasn't their focus. Since the beginning, false teachers have plagued the church. False teachers greatly concerned the writer of 2 John. Check out John's criteria for a false teacher in **2 John 7–11**.

- How could John's warning have helped Amy?
- What current false teachers or groups do you recognize from John's description?

C O N S I D E R . . .

- becoming aware of cults operating in your area. What do they believe? How do they recruit?
- seeking to understand more of Christ's teachings so that you will know when a false teacher "goes beyond" them (verse 9).

F O R   M O R E ,   S E E . . .

- Daniel 6:7–23 (p. 813)
- John 14:5–7 (p. 1083)
- 2 Timothy 4:3–5 (p. 1266)

[9]Anyone who goes beyond Christ's teaching and does not continue to follow only his teaching does not have God. But whoever continues to follow the teaching of Christ has both the Father and the Son. [10]If someone comes to you and does not bring this teaching, do not welcome or accept that person into your house. [11]If you welcome such a person, you share in the evil work.

[12]I have many things to write to you, but I do not want to use paper and ink. Instead, I hope to come to you and talk face to face so we can be full of joy. [13]The children of your chosen sister [n] greet you.

3 JOHN

Why Read This Book:

■ Consider how Christians can support one another (3 John 1–8).
■ See how much damage one negative leader can do (3 John 9–11)

Behind the Scenes:

Suppose a visitor walked in to your Sunday school class. Would you welcome him or her? Would you invite the visitor home for dinner? And suppose the visitor expressed different views from yours during the discussion. Would you be open to those views? Or would you cut the person off?

The two central characters in 3 John would answer those questions quite differently. Gaius (3 John 1) would probably welcome the visitor and listen closely to his or her views. Diotrephes (3 John 9) would probably shun the visitor and squelch his or her opinions.

The situation in 3 John was different from a Sunday school class, of course. Gaius was welcoming missionaries sent by "the Elder" (3 John 1), and the writer thanks him for it. Diotrephes refused to welcome these missionaries. In fact, he tried to kick out of the church anyone who did welcome them.

Like 2 John (p. 1323), 3 John focuses on welcoming and showing love to fellow Christians. Taken together, these two letters tell a lot about the church. On the one hand, Christians are called to love, accept and serve one another in Christ. At the same time, Christians are to be on guard against false teachers. These two themes are as relevant to Christians today as they were back then.

WHEN THE ACTION WAS				
Jesus was born	The church began soon after Jesus went to heaven	Paul began his missionary work	Fire destroyed Rome	3 John was written
BC/AD	25AD	50AD	75AD	100AD
	Jesus began his ministry	Paul became a Christian		Romans destroyed the Temple in Jerusalem

¹From the Elder.ⁿ

To my dear friend Gaius, whom I love in the truth:ⁿ

²My dear friend, I know your soul is doing fine, and I pray that you are doing well in every way and that your health is good. ³I was very happy when some brothers and sistersⁿ came and told me about the truth in your life and how you are following the way of truth. ⁴Nothing gives me greater joy than to hear that my children are following the way of truth.

⁵My dear friend, it is good that you help the brothers and sisters, even those you do not know. ⁶They told the church about your love. Please help them to continue their trip in a way worthy of God. ⁷They started out in service to Christ, and they have been accepting nothing from nonbeliev-

ers. ⁸So we should help such people; when we do, we share in their work for the truth.

> ✳ SIDELIGHT: Since motels in ancient times were notoriously dirty, flea-infested, and expensive, travelers often stayed in people's homes—without any advance notice (3 John 5–8). "Oh, Mom! Guess who's coming to dinner."

⁹I wrote something to the church, but Diotrephes, who loves to be their leader, will not listen to us. ¹⁰So if I come, I will talk about what Diotrephes is doing, about how he lies and says evil things about us. But more than that, he refuses to

Elder   "Elder" means an older person. It can also mean a special leader in the church (as Titus 1:5).
truth   The truth or "Good News" about Jesus Christ that joins all believers together.
brothers and sisters   Although the Greek text says "brothers" here and throughout this book, the writer's words were meant for the entire church, including men and women.

SERVICE

Thanks for Coming

"Dear Mack,

"Thank you for coming so far away to teach me 'bout Jesus. I have fun. I miss you, but I'll read the Bible you gave me. I love you!— Wesley."

Mack Kemper smiled when he read the scrawled words on notebook paper. The unexpected thanks made Mack's week.

For five busy days, five hundred miles from home, twenty-two teenagers had used songs, crafts, and recreation to show Jesus' love to children in a small church. Eight-year-old Wesley Wilke was among the children who heard the exciting news about Jesus.

The summer trip had been Mack's first mission project. He didn't know what to expect, or whether the kids would like him. But Wesley had taken a special liking to Mack. Toward week's end, Wesley had asked Mack how he could make Jesus his friend.

Mack had handed his own Bible to Wesley and had prayed with him. On the last day, Wesley had given Mack the short letter.

At the teenagers' final meeting before returning home, Mack read Wesley's letter. "I think I understand a little more about the song 'Jesus Loves Me, This I Know,' " Mack explained. "Now, I've seen it in action." From the back of the room the simple song began and grew as others joined in.

Mack found out how Christian service often helps the giver as much as the receiver. Read how John stressed the value of Christian service in **3 John 5–8**.

■ How did Wesley benefit from Mack's serving? How did Mack benefit from the serving?

■ How can John's idea of Christian service help both those receiving and those giving the service?

CONSIDER . . .

■ serving someone who needs help this week.

■ asking to serve on your youth group's or church's missions or outreach committee.

FOR MORE, SEE . . .

■ Proverbs 11:24–25 (p. 577)

■ John 13:4–17 (p. 1080)

■ 1 Peter 5:2–7 (p. 1307)

accept the other brothers and sisters; he even stops those who do want to accept them and puts them out of the church.

11My dear friend, do not follow what is bad; follow what is good. The one who does good belongs to God. But the one who does evil has never known God.

12Everyone says good things about Demetrius, and the truth agrees with what they say. We also speak well of him, and you know what we say is true.

13I have many things I want to write you, but I do not want to use pen and ink. 14I hope to see you soon and talk face to face. 15Peace to you. The friends here greet you. Please greet each friend there by name.

JUDE

Why Read
This Book:

- Test others' beliefs against the truth of Jesus Christ (Jude 1–4).
- Focus on the dangers of listening to false teachers (Jude 5–16).
- Be challenged to stay strong in your faith (Jude 17–24).

**Behind the
Scenes:**

Termites can destroy a building before you even know they are there. The wood might look fine from the outside, but inside the termites have hollowed the beams. If you don't discover the damage soon enough and get rid of the insects, the building can become so weak that it can't be salvaged.

The early church had to deal with false teachers who were like termites in the church. They had sneaked into the church with lies about Jesus and salvation. Unless the church got rid of the false teachers, they could weaken or even destroy the church.

Jude urges the church to get rid of the termites!—"to fight hard for the faith that was given the holy people of God" (Jude 3). These false teachers evidently believed that their freedom encouraged them to follow the modern philosophy: "If it feels good, do it." These people will be punished by God in the end, the author says, but in the meantime their loose morals, hypocrisy, rejection of authority, and divisiveness were infecting the church.

How should the Christians deal with the false teachers? By being strong in their own faith, Jude says. By praying. By focusing on God's love. By waiting patiently for Jesus Christ. And even though Christians hate and avoid what these sinful people do, Christians should reach out to them with God's love (Jude 20–23).

As Christians, we regularly encounter people who believe and act differently from us. How do we respond to them? The book of Jude offers positive guidance.

WHEN THE ACTION WAS				
Jesus was born	The church began soon after Jesus went to heaven	Paul began his missionary work	Fire destroyed Rome	
BC/AD	25AD	50AD	75AD	100AD
	Jesus began his ministry / Paul became a Christian		Jude may have been written / Romans destroyed the Temple in Jerusalem	

¹From Jude, a servant of Jesus Christ and a brother of James.

To all who have been called by God. God the Father loves you, and you have been kept safe in Jesus Christ:

²Mercy, peace, and love be yours richly.

God Will Punish Sinners

³Dear friends, I wanted very much to write you about the salvation we all share. But I felt the need to write you about something else: I want to encourage you to fight hard for the faith that was given the holy people of God once and for all time. ⁴Some people have secretly entered your group. Long ago the prophets*d* wrote about these people who will be judged guilty. They are against God and have changed the grace of our God into a reason for sexual sin. They also refuse to accept Jesus Christ, our only Master and Lord.

⁵I want to remind you of some things you already know: Remember that the Lord saved his people by bringing them out of the land of Egypt. But later he destroyed all those who did not believe. ⁶And remember the angels who did not keep their place of power but left their proper home. The Lord has kept these angels in darkness, bound with everlasting chains, to be judged on the great day. ⁷Also remember the cities of

---

FOLLOWING GOD
Standing Alone

At a large youth convention, thirty-two teams competed for a -500 prize in a Bible quiz game called the "Holy Word Squares." Most teams had five members. But one team had only one person, a shy thirteen-year-old named Chris Bailey.

Chris was short, skinny and wore heavy glasses. He had been so excited about the Bible quiz that he had tried to find four other youth-group kids to team up with him. But they were not interested; they had other things to do besides practice for a Bible game.

Their rejection didn't stop Chris. He entered the competition alone—a one-person "team." For weeks before the contest, Chris studied the Bible and "scrimmaged" with his youth minister. He got better and better.

When Chris's youth group got to the convention, the other kids went swimming while Chris began to compete. No one took him seriously, until he won a preliminary round. Then he won the next round. Then the semifinals. By the final game, everyone was curious about this one-person team.

More than seven hundred people eagerly awaited the final round with Chris against a five-member team. First, the other team won. Then Chris won. The tournament all came down to one, tie-breaking game.

Each side answered question after question. When the round was almost over, Chris took the lead. Then he correctly answered the final question. He had won!

As Chris raised his arms in victory, his youth group swarmed around him in celebration. The crowd gave him a screaming, standing ovation.

His group cheered again when he announced that he was giving the prize money to the group. Pizza was on him!

Despite the way he was treated at first, Chris stuck with what he believed. His story illustrates the kind of determination and faith **Jude 17–25** urges all Christians to have as they seek to follow God.

■ How was Chris's solitary stand like the ways Jude tells believers to keep following God?

■ What situations do you encounter in which this passage can encourage you to keep following God?

C O N S I D E R . . .

■ rating from one to ten your willingness to act on your faith, with ten as the highest. Why did you rate yourself as you did?

■ practicing sharing your faith with a Christian friend. Then share it with a non-Christian friend.

F O R   M O R E ,   S E E . .

■ Psalm 113 (p. 547)   ■ 1 Peter 2:—10 (p. 1303)
■ 1 Thessalonians 5:12–22 (p. 1249)

Sodom and Gomorrah[n] and the other towns around them. In the same way they were full of sexual sin and people who desired sexual relations that God does not allow. They suffer the punishment of eternal fire, as an example for all to see.

[8]It is the same with these people who have entered your group. They are guided by dreams and make themselves filthy with sin. They reject God's authority and speak against the angels. [9]Not even the archangel[n] Michael, when he argued with the devil about who would have the body of Moses, dared to judge the devil guilty. Instead, he said, "The Lord punish you." [10]But these people speak against things they do not understand. And what they do know, by feeling, as dumb animals know things, are the very things that destroy them. [11]It will be terrible for them. They have followed the way of Cain, and for money they have given themselves to doing the wrong that Balaam did. They have fought against God as Korah did, and like Korah, they surely will be destroyed. [12]They are like dirty spots in your special Christian meals you share. They eat with you and have no fear, caring only for themselves. They are clouds without rain, which the wind blows around. They are autumn trees without fruit that are pulled out of the ground. So they are

They are like stars that wander in the sky. A place in the blackest darkness has been kept for them forever.

[14]Enoch, the seventh descendant[d] from Adam, said about these people: "Look, the Lord is coming with many thousands of his holy angels to [15]judge every person. He is coming to punish all who are against God for all the evil they have done against him. And he will punish the sinners who are against God for all the evil they have said against him."

[16]These people complain and blame others, doing the evil things they want to do. They brag about themselves, and they flatter others to get what they want.

A Warning and Things to Do

[17]Dear friends, remember what the apostles[d] of our Lord Jesus Christ said before. [18]They said to you, "In the last times there will be people who laugh about God, following their own evil desires which are against God." [19]These are the people who divide you, people whose thoughts are only of this world, who do not have the Spirit.[d]

[20]But dear friends, use your most holy faith to build yourselves up, praying in the Holy Spirit. [21]Keep yourselves in God's love as you wait for the Lord Jesus Christ with his mercy to give you life forever.

[22]Show mercy to some people who have doubts. [23]Take others out of the fire, and save them. Show mercy mixed with fear to others, hating even their clothes which are dirty from sin.

Praise God

[24]God is strong and can help you not to fall. He can bring you before his glory without any wrong in you and can give you great joy. [25]He is the only God, the One who saves us. To him be glory, greatness, power, and authority through Jesus Christ our Lord for all time past, now, and forever. Amen.

> ☀ **SIDELIGHT:** Don't look for the quotation by Enoch in the Old Testament (Jude 14–15). This is a direct quote from a book known as 1 Enoch, which is part of the sixty-five documents known as the Pseudepigrapha. Christians don't consider these books part of scripture, but the books were widely read and quoted in New Testament times.

twice dead. [13]They are like wild waves of the sea, tossing up their own shameful actions like foam.

Sodom and Gomorrah Two cities God destroyed because they were so evil.
archangel The leader among God's angels or messengers.

REVELATION

Why Read This Book:

■ Hear warnings about problems in churches (Revelation 1—3).
■ See God's power against the forces of evil (Revelation 4—11).
■ Be comforted by God's promise of hope for all his people (Revelation 12—22).

Behind the Scenes:

A blood-red moon. A lamb with seven horns and seven eyes. Locusts with golden crowns. White, red, black, and pale horses. A giant, red dragon. A sea of glass mixed with fire.

These images sound like they are straight out of a science-fiction movie. But they are not; they are from the book of Revelation, the last book of the Bible. They make the book exciting and mysterious . . . and confusing.

This book can be so difficult to understand because it is "apocalyptic" literature. This literature uses mysterious visions and symbolic language to describe God's victory over the troubles of this world. Most often, this kind of literature was written during tough times, when the church was being persecuted. One reason for using the images and symbols was to use symbols that Christians would understand, but others would not.

That's certainly true of the book of Revelation. At the time, Christians were under attack by the Roman authorities. The Romans demanded that all people worship the emperor. Many Christians refused, and many were executed.

The book of Revelation was written to give hope and courage to these persecuted Christians. Scholars view the symbols, events and visions in Revelation in different ways. Some of the major perspectives include:

■ The book describes the first-century situation, and all the events described in it have taken place.
■ The book contains predictions for a long chain of events that will conclude with Christ's Second Coming.

WHERE THE ACTION WAS

ITALY
•Rome

Revelation was originally sent to seven churches in Asia Minor (Revelation 1:4).

GREECE

ASIA MINOR

The emperor in Rome persecuted the Christians.

Pergamum
• Thyatira
Smyrna • Sardis
•Ephesus • Philadelphia
• Laodicea

Patmos

John wrote Revelation on the island of Patmos Revelation 1:9.

Mediterranean Sea

WHEN THE ACTION WAS

Jesus was born	The church began soon after Jesus went to heaven	Paul began his missionary work	Fire destroyed Rome	The book of Revelation was written
BC/AD	25AD	50AD	75AD	100AD
	Jesus began his ministry · Paul became a Christian		Romans destroyed the Temple in Jerusalem	

Behind the Scenes (cont.):

- The visions describe the final days before the end of the world, and do not relate directly to biblical times.
- The book does not predict the future; rather, it uses symbolic language to teach religious truth about God's victory over evil.

Regardless of the specific perspective, central themes are clear. God is powerful. Jesus Christ reigns forever. Those who suffer for Christ will ultimately share his victory. Revelation gives a message of hope and encouragement for all people in all times.

John Tells About This Book

1 This is the revelation*n* of Jesus Christ, which God gave to him, to show his servants what must soon happen. And Jesus sent his angel to show it to his servant John, [2]who has told everything he has seen. It is the word of God; it is the message from Jesus Christ. [3]Happy is the one who reads the words of God's message, and happy are the people who hear this message and do what is written in it. The time is near when all of this will happen.

Jesus' Message to the Churches

[4]From John.
To the seven churches in the country of Asia:

revelation   A making known of truth that has been hidden.

Grace and peace to you from the One who is and was and is coming, and from the seven spirits before his throne, [5]and from Jesus Christ. Jesus is the faithful witness, the first among those raised from the dead. He is the ruler of the kings of the earth.

He is the One who loves us, who made us free from our sins with the blood of his death. [6]He made us to be a kingdom of priests who serve God his Father. To Jesus Christ be glory and power forever and ever! Amen.

[7]Look, Jesus is coming with the clouds, and everyone will see him, even those who stabbed him. And all peoples of the earth will cry loudly because of him. Yes, this will happen! Amen.

[8]The Lord God says, "I am the Alpha and the

GOD'S POWER

The World's Strongest Man

As a teenager, Paul Anderson concentrated on one big goal: to become the world's strongest man. He turned down a full college football scholarship to work on his weight-lifting goal. By age twenty-one, Anderson had packed 300 rock-hard pounds on his 5-foot, 10-inch body.

In 1956 Anderson won the Olympic gold medal in heavyweight weight-lifting. One year later in Toccoa, Georgia, he back-lifted a table holding 6,270 pounds of auto parts and a safe full of lead. This weight-lifting feat remains unbroken in the Guinness Book of World Records.

Anderson turned professional and moved from weight-lifting to power-lifting. As a professional he could squat-lift 1,200 pounds and dead-lift 820 pounds. Anderson's popularity soared, and in 1974 he was inducted into the Georgia Sports Hall of Fame.

Paul Anderson's amazing power earned him the title of the world's strongest man. His strength, however, is small compared to God's power. See what God's all-powerful nature involves as you read **Revelation 1:4–18**.

- What power does God have that no human can claim?
- How does this passage's expression of God's power affect your life?

CONSIDER . . .

- *watching for evidence of God's power around you while you go through this day.*
- designing a symbol or logo representing God's power described in these verses.

FOR MORE, SEE . . .

- Psalm 46 (p. 508)
- Isaiah 40:12–31 (p. 655)
- Luke 18: 27–39 (p. 1042)

Omega.[n] I am the One who is and was and is coming. I am the Almighty."

[9]I, John, am your brother. All of us share with Christ in suffering, in the kingdom, and in patience to continue. I was on the island of Patmos,[n] because I had preached the word of God

and the message about Jesus. [10]On the Lord's day I was in the Spirit,[d] and I heard a loud voice behind me that sounded like a trumpet. [11]The voice said, "Write what you see in a book and send it to the seven churches: to Ephesus, Smyrna, Pergamum, Thyatira, Sardis, Philadelphia, and Laodicea."

[12]I turned to see who was talking to me. When I turned, I saw seven golden lampstands [13]and someone among the lampstands who was "like a Son of Man."[n] He was dressed in a long robe and had a gold band around his chest. [14]His head and hair were white like wool, as white as snow, and his eyes were like flames of fire. [15]His feet were like bronze that glows hot in a furnace, and his voice was like the noise of flooding water. [16]He held seven stars in his right hand, and a sharp double-edged sword came out of his mouth. He looked like the sun shining at its brightest time.

[17]When I saw him, I fell down at his feet like a dead man. He put his right hand on me and said, "Do not be afraid. I am the First and the Last. [18]I am the One who lives; I was dead, but look, I am alive forever and ever! And I hold the keys to death and to the place of the dead. [19]So write the things you see, what is now and what will happen later. [20]Here is the secret of the seven stars that you saw in my right hand and the seven golden lampstands: The seven lampstands are the seven churches, and the seven stars are the angels of the seven churches.

To the Church in Ephesus

2 "Write this to the angel of the church in Ephesus:

"The One who holds the seven stars in his right hand and walks among the seven golden lampstands says this: [2]I know what you do, how you

work hard and never give up. I know you do not put up with the false teachings of evil people. You have tested those who say they are apostles[d] but really are not, and you found they are liars. [3]You have patience and have suffered troubles for my name and have not given up.

[4]"But I have this against you: You have left the love you had in the beginning. [5]So remember where you were before you fell. Change your hearts and do what you did at first. If you do not change, I will come to you and will take away your lampstand from its place. [6]But there is something you do that is right: You hate what the Nicolaitans[n] do, as much as I.

[7]"Every person who has ears should listen to what the Spirit[e] says to the churches. To those who win the victory I will give the right to eat the fruit from the tree of life, which is in the garden of God.

To the Church in Smyrna

[8]"Write this to the angel of the church in Smyrna:

"The One who is the First and the Last, who died and came to life again, says this: [9]I know your troubles and that you are poor, but really you are rich! I know the bad things some people say about you. They say they are Jews, but they are not true Jews. They are a synagogue[d] that belongs to Satan. [10]Do not be afraid of what you are about to suffer. I tell you, the devil will put some of you in prison to test you, and you will suffer for ten days. But be faithful, even if you have to die, and I will give you the crown of life.

[11]"Everyone who has ears should listen to what the Spirit[d] says to the churches. Those who win the victory will not be hurt by the second death.

To the Church in Pergamum

[12]"Write this to the angel of the church in Pergamum:

"The One who has the sharp, double-edged sword says this: [13]I know where you live. It is where Satan has his throne. But you are true to me. You did not refuse to tell about your faith in me even during the time of Antipas, my faithful witness who was killed in your city, where Satan lives.

[14]"But I have a few things against you: You have some there who follow the teaching of Balaam. He taught Balak how to cause the people of Israel to sin by eating food offered to idols and by taking part in sexual sins. [15]You also have some who follow the teaching of the Nicolaitans.[n] [16]So

---

Alpha and the Omega The first and last letters of the Greek alphabet. This means "the beginning and the end."
Patmos A small island in the Aegean Sea, near the coast of Asia Minor (modern Turkey).
"like . . . Man" "Son of Man" is a name Jesus called himself. See dictionary.
Nicolaitans This is the name of a religious group that followed false beliefs and ideas.

change your hearts and lives. If you do not, I will come to you quickly and fight against them with the sword that comes out of my mouth.

[17]"Everyone who has ears should listen to what the Spirit[d] says to the churches.

"I will give some of the hidden manna[d] to everyone who wins the victory. I will also give to each one who wins the victory a white stone with a new name written on it. No one knows this new name except the one who receives it.

To the Church in Thyatira

[18]"Write this to the angel of the church in Thyatira:

"The Son of God, who has eyes that blaze like fire and feet like shining bronze, says this: [19]I know what you do. I know about your love, your faith, your service, and your patience. I know that you are doing more now than you did at first.

[20]"But I have this against you: You let that woman Jezebel spread false teachings. She says she is a prophetess,[d] but by her teaching she leads my people to take part in sexual sins and to eat food that is offered to idols. [21]I have given her time to change her heart and turn away from her sin, but she does not want to change. [22]So I will throw her on a bed of suffering. And all those who take part in adultery[d] with her will suffer greatly if they do not turn away from the wrongs she does. [23]I will also kill her followers. Then all the churches will know I am the One who searches hearts and minds, and I will repay each of you for what you have done.

[24]"But others of you in Thyatira have not followed her teaching and have not learned what some call Satan's deep secrets. I say to you that I will not put any other load on you. [25]Only continue in your loyalty until I come.

[26]"I will give power over the nations to everyone who wins the victory and continues to be obedient to me until the end.

[27]'You will rule over them with an iron rod,
   as when pottery is broken into pieces.'

Psalm 2:9

[28]This is the same power I received from my Father. I will also give him the morning star. [29]Everyone who has ears should listen to what the Spirit[d] says to the churches.

To the Church in Sardis

3 "Write this to the angel of the church in Sardis:

"The One who has the seven spirits and the seven stars says this: I know what you do. People say that you are alive, but really you are dead. [2]Wake up! Make yourselves stronger before what you have left dies completely. I have found that

what you are doing is less than what my God wants. [3]So do not forget what you have received and heard. Obey it, and change your hearts and

lives. So you must wake up, or I will come like a thief, and you will not know when I will come to you. [4]But you have a few there in Sardis who have kept their clothes unstained, so they will walk with me and will wear white clothes, because they are worthy. [5]Those who win the victory will be dressed in white clothes like them. And I will not erase their names from the book of life, but I will say they belong to me before my Father and before his angels. [6]Everyone who has ears should listen to what the Spirit[d] says to the churches.

To the Church in Philadelphia

[7]"Write this to the angel of the church in Philadelphia:

"This is what the One who is holy and true, who holds the key of David, says. When he opens a door, no one can close it. And when he closes it, no one can open it. [8]I know what you do. I have put an open door before you, which no one can close. I know you have a little strength, but you have obeyed my teaching and were not afraid to speak my name. [9]Those in the synagogue[a] that belongs to Satan say they are Jews, but they are not true Jews; they are liars. I will make them come before you and bow at your feet, and they will know that I have loved you. [10]You have obeyed my teaching about not giving up your faith. So I will keep you from the time of trouble that will come to the whole world to test those who live on earth.

[11]"I am coming soon. Continue strong in your faith so no one will take away your crown. [12]I will make those who win the victory pillars in the temple of my God, and they will never have to leave it. I will write on them the name of my God and the name of the city of my God, the new Jerusalem,[n] that comes down out of heaven from my God. I will also write on them my new name. [13]Everyone who has ears should listen to what the Spirit[d] says to the churches.

Jerusalem This name is used to mean the spiritual city God built for his people. See Revelation 21-22.

To the Church in Laodicea

14"Write this to the angel of the church in Laodicea:

"The Amen,[n] the faithful and true witness, the beginning of all God has made, says this: 15I know what you do, that you are not hot or cold. I wish that you were hot or cold! 16But because you are lukewarm — neither hot, nor cold — I am ready to spit you out of my mouth. 17You say, 'I am rich, and I have become wealthy and do not need anything.' But you do not know that you are really miserable, pitiful, poor, blind, and naked. 18I advise you to buy from me gold made pure in fire so you can be truly rich. Buy from me white clothes so you can be clothed and so you can cover your shameful nakedness. Buy from me medicine to put on your eyes so you can truly see.

19"I correct and punish those whom I love. So be eager to do right, and change your hearts and lives. 20Here I am! I stand at the door and knock. If you hear my voice and open the door, I will come in and eat with you, and you will eat with me.

21"Those who win the victory will sit with me on my throne in the same way that I won the victory and sat down with my Father on his throne. 22Everyone who has ears should listen to what the Spirit[d] says to the churches."

John Sees Heaven

4 After the vision of these things I looked, and there before me was an open door in heaven. And the same voice that spoke to me before, that sounded like a trumpet, said, "Come up here, and I will show you what must happen after this." 2Immediately I was in the Spirit,[d] and before me was a throne in heaven, and someone was sitting on it. 3The One who sat on the throne looked like precious stones, like jasper and carnelian. All around the throne was a rainbow the color of an emerald. 4Around the throne there were twenty-four other thrones with twenty-four elders sitting on them. They were dressed in white and had golden crowns on their heads. 5Lightning flashes and noises and thundering came from the throne. Before the throne seven lamps were burning, which are the seven spirits of God. 6Also before the throne there was something that looked like a sea of glass, clear like crystal.

In the center and around the throne were four living creatures with eyes all over them, in front and in back. 7The first living creature was like a lion. The second was like a calf. The third had a face like a man. The fourth was like a flying eagle. 8Each of these four living creatures had six wings

and was covered all over with eyes, inside and out. Day and night they never stop saying:

"Holy, holy, holy is the Lord God Almighty.
He was, he is, and he is coming."

9These living creatures give glory, honor, and thanks to the One who sits on the throne, who lives forever and ever. 10Then the twenty-four elders bow down before the One who sits on the throne, and they worship him who lives forever and ever. They put their crowns down before the throne and say:

11"You are worthy, our Lord and God,
to receive glory and honor and power,
because you made all things.
Everything existed and was made,
because you wanted it."

5 Then I saw a scroll in the right hand of the One sitting on the throne. The scroll had writing on both sides and was kept closed with

---

❋ **SIDELIGHT:** Ancient scrolls (Revelation 5:1) were created by beating papyrus (a reed found in the Nile River) into sheets (often about 8" × 10") and sewing them together. A scroll of Revelation—written on both sides to save money—would have been about fifteen feet long.

---

seven seals. 2And I saw a powerful angel calling in a loud voice, "Who is worthy to break the seals and open the scroll?" 3But there was no one in heaven or on earth or under the earth who could open the scroll or look inside it. 4I cried hard because there was no one who was worthy to open the scroll or look inside. 5But one of the elders said to me, "Do not cry! The Lion[n] from the tribe[d] of Judah, David's descendant,[d] has won the victory so that he is able to open the scroll and its seven seals."

6Then I saw a Lamb standing in the center of the throne and in the middle of the four living creatures and the elders. The Lamb looked as if he had been killed. He had seven horns and seven eyes, which are the seven spirits of God that were sent into all the world. 7The Lamb came and took the scroll from the right hand of the One sitting on the throne. 8When he took the scroll, the four living creatures and the twenty-four elders bowed down before the Lamb. Each one of them had a harp and golden bowls full of incense,[d] which are the prayers of God's holy people. 9And they all sang a new song to the Lamb:

Amen Used here as a name for Jesus; it means to agree fully that something is true.
Lion Here refers to Christ.

"You are worthy to take the scroll
and to open its seals,
because you were killed,
and with the blood of your death you
bought people for God
from every tribe, language, people, and
nation.
¹⁰You made them to be a kingdom of priests
for our God,
and they will rule on the earth."
¹¹Then I looked, and I heard the voices of many
angels around the throne, and the four living creatures, and the elders. There were thousands and
thousands of angels, ¹²saying in a loud voice:
"The Lamb who was killed is worthy
to receive power, wealth, wisdom, and
strength,
honor, glory, and praise!"
¹³Then I heard all creatures in heaven and on
earth and under the earth and in the sea saying:
"To the One who sits on the throne
and to the Lamb
be praise and honor and glory and power
forever and ever."

¹⁴The four living creatures said, "Amen," and
the elders bowed down and worshiped.

6 Then I watched while the Lamb opened the
first of the seven seals. I heard one of the
four living creatures say with a voice like thunder,
"Come!" ²I looked, and there before me was a
white horse. The rider on the horse held a bow,
and he was given a crown, and he rode out, determined to win the victory.

³When the Lamb opened the second seal, I
heard the second living creature say, "Come!"
⁴Then another horse came out, a red one. Its rider
was given power to take away peace from the
earth and to make people kill each other, and he
was given a big sword.

⁵When the Lamb opened the third seal, I heard
the third living creature say, "Come!" I looked,
and there before me was a black horse, and its
rider held a pair of scales in his hand. ⁶Then I
heard something that sounded like a voice coming from the middle of the four living creatures.
The voice said, "A quart of wheat for a day's pay,
and three quarts of barley for a day's pay, and do
not damage the olive oil and wine!"

WORSHIP

Worship's Many Faces

Christians are free to worship in varied and unique ways. There is no one right way to worship, as evidenced by the thousands of denominations and churches through the ages. Many churches today worship in ways shaped by traditions hundreds of years old. For example:

■ Some Christians lift their voices in song, but use no musical instruments in their worship services.
■ Many Christians sing hymns accompanied by pipe organs. They may use familiar prayers and liturgies through the service.
■ Other Christians have informal worship styles that include contemporary music and spontaneous applause.
■ Some Christians raise their hands above their heads when they pray and worship.
■ And some Christians hold meetings without a formal program or a minister. Instead of a set order of worship, they gather in silence. They speak when they feel moved to pray, read a Bible passage or share a thought.

As these examples show, Christians worship God in many different ways. But they all have the central purpose of worship in mind that is found in **Revelation 5:11–14**.

■ How do different expressions of worship capture the worship described in this vision?
■ What feelings about worship does the passage bring out in you?

CONSIDER . . .
■ finding ways your church has incorporated this passage in its worship services.
■ planning a worship service with other young people. Ask your pastor to let you share in leading worship for the whole church.

FOR MORE, SEE . . .
■ Psalm 100 (p. 539)
■ Isaiah 6:1–8 (p. 622)
■ John 4:19–24 (p. 1063)

[7]When the Lamb opened the fourth seal, I heard the voice of the fourth living creature say, "Come!" [8]I looked and there before me was a pale horse. Its rider was named death, and Hades[n] was following close behind him. They were given power over a fourth of the earth to kill people by war, by starvation, by disease, and by the wild animals of the earth.

[9]When the Lamb opened the fifth seal, I saw under the altar the souls of those who had been killed because they were faithful to the word of God and to the message they had received. [10]These souls shouted in a loud voice, "Holy and true Lord, how long until you judge the people of the earth and punish them for killing us?" [11]Then each one of them was given a white robe and was told to wait a short time longer. There were still some of their fellow servants and brothers and sisters[n] in the service of Christ who must be killed as they were. They had to wait until all of this was finished.

[12]Then I watched while the Lamb opened the sixth seal, and there was a great earthquake. The sun became black like rough black cloth, and the whole moon became red like blood. [13]And the stars in the sky fell to the earth like figs falling from a fig tree when the wind blows. [14]The sky disappeared as a scroll when it is rolled up, and every mountain and island was moved from its place.

[15]Then the kings of the earth, the rulers, the generals, the rich people, the powerful people, the slaves, and the free people hid themselves in caves and in the rocks on the mountains. [16]They called to the mountains and the rocks, "Fall on us. Hide us from the face of the One who sits on the throne and from the anger of the Lamb! [17]The great day for their anger has come, and who can stand against it?"

The 144,000 People of Israel

7 After the vision of these things I saw four angels standing at the four corners of the earth. The angels were holding the four winds of the earth to keep them from blowing on the land or on the sea or on any tree. [2]Then I saw another angel coming up from the east who had the seal of the living God. And he called out in a loud voice to the four angels to whom God had given power to harm the earth and the sea. [3]He said to them, "Do not harm the land or the sea or the trees until we mark with a sign the foreheads of the people who serve our God." [4]Then I heard

how many people were marked with the sign. There were one hundred forty-four thousand from every tribe[d] of the people of Israel.

[5]From the tribe of Judah twelve thousand
were marked with the sign,
from the tribe of Reuben twelve thousand,
from the tribe of Gad twelve thousand,
[6]from the tribe of Asher twelve thousand,
from the tribe of Naphtali twelve thousand,
from the tribe of Manasseh twelve thousand,
[7]from the tribe of Simeon twelve thousand,
from the tribe of Levi twelve thousand,
from the tribe of Issachar twelve thousand,
[8]from the tribe of Zebulun twelve thousand,
from the tribe of Joseph twelve thousand,
and from the tribe of Benjamin twelve thousand were marked with the sign.

The Great Crowd Worships God

[9]After the vision of these things I looked, and there was a great number of people, so many that no one could count them. They were from every nation, tribe,[d] people, and language of the earth. They were all standing before the throne and before the Lamb, wearing white robes and holding palm branches in their hands. [10]They were shouting in a loud voice, "Salvation belongs to our God, who sits on the throne, and to the Lamb." [11]All the angels were standing around the throne and the elders and the four living creatures. They all bowed down on their faces before the throne and worshiped God, [12]saying, "Amen! Praise, glory, wisdom, thanks, honor, power, and strength belong to our God forever and ever. Amen!"

[13]Then one of the elders asked me, "Who are these people dressed in white robes? Where did they come from?"

[14]I answered, "You know, sir."

And the elder said to me, "These are the people who have come out of the great distress. They have washed their robes[n] and made them white in the blood of the Lamb. [15]Because of this, they are before the throne of God. They worship him day and night in his temple. And the One who sits on the throne will be present with them. [16]Those people will never be hungry again, and they will never be thirsty again. The sun will not hurt them, and no heat will burn them, [17]because the Lamb at the center of the throne will be their shepherd. He will lead them to springs of water that give life. And God will wipe away every tear from their eyes."

Hades The unseen world of the dead.
brothers and sisters Although the Greek text says "brothers" here and throughout this book, both men and women would have been included.
washed their robes This means they believed in Jesus so that their sins could be forgiven by Christ's blood.

The Seventh Seal

8 When the Lamb opened the seventh seal, there was silence in heaven for about half an hour. ²And I saw the seven angels who stand before God and to whom were given seven trumpets.

³Another angel came and stood at the altar, holding a golden pan for incense.*d* He was given much incense to offer with the prayers of all God's holy people. The angel put this offering on the golden altar before the throne. ⁴The smoke from the incense went up from the angel's hand to God with the prayers of God's people. ⁵Then the angel filled the incense pan with fire from the altar and threw it on the earth, and there were

SIDELIGHT: Since no one had invented lick-and-seal envelopes in Bible times, people would fold or roll up documents, tie string around them, and press a lump of clay over the knot (Revelation 8:1). Then the sender would stamp the hardening clay with a special ring or seal, which was intended to be broken only by the appropriate person.

SADNESS

The Worst Year of Her Life

Lexie Byers had looked forward to her junior year. She did not know it would be her life's worst.

Early in the fall her mother was diagnosed with leukemia. Her dad quit his job to help care for her mom. Money, time, and energy were scarce. And, Lexie carried a difficult class load.

"I had to take care of the house, feed everyone, and plow through my schoolwork," she recalls. "It was tough, but I got along somehow."

One day, however, her mother entered the hospital for one final, risky operation to fight the leukemia. "When the surgeons came out of the operating room, I could tell by the way they looked at me that she was gone," she says.

After the funeral, Lexie's life changed dramatically. Her father, in deep grief, wandered about the house. One day Lexie found a For Sale sign in their front yard. "It's too painful for me to live here," her father said.

Lexie watched her dad fall apart. Unable to find work and desperately lonely, her father returned to his hometown. Lexie faced the difficult choice: either live with her older sister and finish at her present school, or go with her father. Even though she missed her dad, Lexie stayed with her sister.

What sustained her through this sad time? "Christian friends and a caring church got me through the experience," she says. "I couldn't pray, because I was mad at God. All I'd do was cry. These friends just kept loving me, even when I was unlovely."

Lexie went on to college, where she's majoring in engineering. Her father, in time, overcame his grief and went on with his life. "My world fell apart in eleventh grade," Lexie reflects. "Our family suffered a lot. But with God's help, we made it through, and that's what matters."

Everyone experiences pain, disappointment, and uncontrollable events. When those sad times seem overwhelming, Christians can turn to passages such as **Revelation 7:9–17** for a message of hope.

■ What hope could Lexie gain from these verses?
■ How could these verses help you deal with sadness in your life?

CONSIDER . . .

■ doing something positive to help you get out of the blues. Try visiting a friend, watching a comedy film, or exercising.
■ visiting someone who is having a sad time. Take fresh flowers, cookies, or a small gift to show you care.

FOR MORE, SEE . . .

■ Psalm 40:1–3 (p. 505)
■ Ecclesiastes 3:1–8 (p. 600)

■ Hebrews 10:23–25 (p. 1286)

flashes of lightning, thunder and loud noises, and an earthquake.

The Seven Angels and Trumpets

6Then the seven angels who had the seven trumpets prepared to blow them.

7The first angel blew his trumpet, and hail and fire mixed with blood were poured down on the earth. And a third of the earth, and all the green grass, and a third of the trees were burned up.

8Then the second angel blew his trumpet, and something that looked like a big mountain, burning with fire, was thrown into the sea. And a third of the sea became blood, 9a third of the living things in the sea died, and a third of the ships were destroyed.

10Then the third angel blew his trumpet, and a large star, burning like a torch, fell from the sky. It fell on a third of the rivers and on the springs of water. 11The name of the star is Wormwood.n And a third of all the water became bitter, and many people died from drinking the water that was bitter.

12Then the fourth angel blew his trumpet, and a third of the sun and a third of the moon, and a third of the stars were struck. So a third of them became dark, and a third of the day was without light, and also the night.

13While I watched, I heard an eagle that was flying high in the air cry out in a loud voice, "Trouble! Trouble! Trouble for those who live on the earth because of the remaining sounds of the trumpets that the other three angels are about to blow!"

9 Then the fifth angel blew his trumpet, and I saw a star fall from the sky to the earth. The star was given the key to the deep hole that leads to the bottomless pit. 2Then it opened up the hole that leads to the bottomless pit, and smoke came up from the hole like smoke from a big furnace. Then the sun and sky became dark because of the smoke from the hole. 3Then locustsd came down to the earth out of the smoke, and they were given the power to sting like scorpions.n 4They were told not to harm the grass on the earth or any plant or tree. They could harm only the people who did not have the sign of God on their foreheads. 5These locusts were not given the power to kill anyone, but to cause pain to the people for five months. And the pain they felt was like the pain a scorpion gives when it stings someone. 6During those days people will look for a way to die, but they will not find it. They will want to die, but death will run away from them.

7The locusts looked like horses prepared for battle. On their heads they wore what looked like crowns of gold, and their faces looked like human faces. 8Their hair was like women's hair, and their teeth were like lions' teeth. 9Their chests looked like iron breastplates, and the sound of their wings was like the noise of many horses and chariots hurrying into battle. 10The locusts had tails with stingers like scorpions, and in their tails was their power to hurt people for five months. 11The locusts had a king who was the angel of the bottomless pit. His name in the Hebrew language is Abaddon and in the Greek language is Apollyon.n

12The first trouble is past; there are still two other troubles that will come.

13Then the sixth angel blew his trumpet, and I heard a voice coming from the horns on the golden altar that is before God. 14The voice said to the sixth angel who had the trumpet, "Free the four angels who are tied at the great river Euphrates." 15And they let loose the four angels who had been kept ready for this hour and day and month and year so they could kill a third of all people on the earth. 16I heard how many troops on horses were in their army — two hundred million.

17The horses and their riders I saw in the vision looked like this: They had breastplates that were fiery red, dark blue, and yellow like sulfur. The heads of the horses looked like heads of lions, with fire, smoke, and sulfur coming out of their mouths. 18A third of all the people on earth were killed by these three terrible disasters coming out of the horses' mouths: the fire, the smoke, and the sulfur. 19The horses' power was in their mouths and in their tails; their tails were like snakes with heads, and with them they hurt people.

20The other people who were not killed by these terrible disasters still did not change their hearts and turn away from what they had made with their own hands. They did not stop worshiping demonsd and idols made of gold, silver, bronze, stone, and wood — things that cannot see or hear or walk. 21These people did not change their hearts and turn away from murder or evil magic, from their sexual sins or stealing.

The Angel and the Small Scroll

10 Then I saw another powerful angel coming down from heaven dressed in a cloud with a rainbow over his head. His face was like the sun, and his legs were like pillars of fire. 2The angel was holding a small scroll open in his

---

Wormwood Name of a very bitter plant; used here to give the idea of bitter sorrow.
scorpions A scorpion is an insect that stings with a bad poison.
Abaddon, Apollyon Both names mean "Destroyer."

hand. He put his right foot on the sea and his left foot on the land. ³Then he shouted loudly like the roaring of a lion. And when he shouted, the voices of seven thunders spoke. ⁴When the seven thunders spoke, I started to write. But I heard a voice from heaven say, "Keep hidden what the seven thunders said, and do not write them down."

⁵Then the angel I saw standing on the sea and on the land raised his right hand to heaven, ⁶and he made a promise by the power of the One who lives forever and ever. He is the One who made the skies and all that is in them, the earth and all that is in it, and the sea and all that is in it. The angel promised, "There will be no more waiting! ⁷In the days when the seventh angel is ready to blow his trumpet, God's secret will be finished. This secret is the Good News*ᵈ* God told to his servants, the prophets."*ᵈ*

⁸Then I heard the same voice from heaven again, saying to me: "Go and take the open scroll that is in the hand of the angel that is standing on the sea and on the land."

⁹So I went to the angel and told him to give me the small scroll. And he said to me, "Take the scroll and eat it. It will be sour in your stomach, but in your mouth it will be sweet as honey." ¹⁰So I took the small scroll from the angel's hand and ate it. In my mouth it tasted sweet as honey, but after I ate it, it was sour in my stomach. ¹¹Then I was told, "You must prophesy*ᵈ* again about many peoples, nations, languages, and kings."

The Two Witnesses

11 I was given a measuring stick like a rod, and I was told, "Go and measure the temple*ᵈ* of God and the altar, and count the people worshiping there. ²But do not measure the yard outside the temple. Leave it alone, because it has been given to those who are not God's people. And they will trample on the holy city for forty-two months. ³And I will give power to my two witnesses to prophesy*ᵈ* for one thousand two hundred sixty days, and they will be dressed in rough cloth to show their sadness."

⁴These two witnesses are the two olive trees and the two lampstands that stand before the Lord of the earth. ⁵And if anyone tries to hurt them, fire comes from their mouths and kills their enemies. And if anyone tries to hurt them in whatever way, in that same way that person will die. ⁶These witnesses have the power to stop the sky from raining during the time they are prophesying. And they have power to make the waters become blood, and they have power to send every kind of trouble to the earth as many times as they want.

⁷When the two witnesses have finished telling their message, the beast that comes up from the bottomless pit will fight a war against them. He will defeat them and kill them. ⁸The bodies of the two witnesses will lie in the street of the great city where the Lord was killed. This city is named Sodom*ⁿ* and Egypt, which has a spiritual meaning. ⁹Those from every race of people, tribe,*ᵈ* language, and nation will look at the bodies of the two witnesses for three and one-half days, and they will refuse to bury them. ¹⁰People who live on the earth will rejoice and be happy because these two are dead. They will send each other gifts, because these two prophets brought much suffering to those who live on the earth.

¹¹But after three and one-half days, God put the breath of life into the two prophets again. They stood on their feet, and everyone who saw them became very afraid. ¹²Then the two prophets heard a loud voice from heaven saying, "Come up here!" And they went up into heaven in a cloud as their enemies watched.

¹³In the same hour there was a great earthquake, and a tenth of the city was destroyed. Seven thousand people were killed in the earthquake, and those who did not die were very afraid and gave glory to the God of heaven.

¹⁴The second trouble is finished. Pay attention: The third trouble is coming soon.

The Seventh Trumpet

¹⁵Then the seventh angel blew his trumpet. And there were loud voices in heaven, saying:
"The power to rule the world
    now belongs to our Lord and his Christ,*ᵈ*
and he will rule forever and ever."
¹⁶Then the twenty-four elders, who sit on their thrones before God, bowed down on their faces and worshiped God. ¹⁷They said:
"We give thanks to you, Lord God Almighty,
    who is and who was,
because you have used your great power
    and have begun to rule!
¹⁸The people of the world were angry,
    but your anger has come.
The time has come to judge the dead
and to reward your servants the prophets*ᵈ*
    and your holy people,
all who respect you, great and small.
The time has come to destroy those who
    destroy the earth!"
¹⁹Then God's temple*ᵈ* in heaven was opened. The Ark*ᵈ* that holds the agreement God gave to his people could be seen in his temple. Then there were flashes of lightning, noises, thunder, an earthquake, and a great hailstorm.

Sodom City that God destroyed because the people were so evil.

The Woman and the Dragon

12 And then a great wonder appeared in heaven: A woman was clothed with the sun, and the moon was under her feet, and a crown of twelve stars was on her head. [2]She was pregnant and cried out with pain, because she was about to give birth. [3]Then another wonder appeared in heaven: There was a giant red dragon with seven heads and seven crowns on each head. He also had ten horns. [4]His tail swept a third of the stars out of the sky and threw them down to the earth. He stood in front of the woman who was ready to give birth so he could eat her baby as soon as it was born. [5]Then the woman gave birth to a son who will rule all the nations with an iron rod. And her child was taken up to God and to his throne. [6]The woman ran away into the desert to a place God prepared for her where she would be taken care of for one thousand two hundred sixty days.

[7]Then there was a war in heaven. Michael[n] and his angels fought against the dragon, and the dragon and his angels fought back. [8]But the dragon was not strong enough, and he and his angels lost their place in heaven. [9]The giant dragon was thrown down out of heaven. (He is that old snake called the devil or Satan, who tricks the whole world.) The dragon with his angels was thrown down to the earth.

[10]Then I heard a loud voice in heaven saying:
"The salvation and the power and the
   kingdom of our God
  and the authority of his Christ[d] have now
   come.
The accuser of our brothers and sisters,
  who accused them day and night before
   our God,
  has been thrown down.
[11]And our brothers and sisters defeated him
  by the blood of the Lamb's death
  and by the message they preached.
They did not love their lives so much
  that they were afraid of death.
[12]So rejoice, you heavens
  and all who live there!
But it will be terrible for the earth and the
   sea,
  because the devil has come down to you!
He is filled with anger,
  because he knows he does not have much
   time."

[13]When the dragon saw he had been thrown down to the earth, he hunted for the woman who had given birth to the son. [14]But the woman was given the two wings of a great eagle so she could fly to the place prepared for her in the desert.

There she would be taken care of for three and one-half years, away from the snake. [15]Then the snake poured water out of its mouth like a river toward the woman so the flood would carry her away. [16]But the earth helped the woman by opening its mouth and swallowing the river that came from the mouth of the dragon. [17]Then the dragon was very angry at the woman, and he went off to make war against all her other children — those who obey God's commands and who have the message Jesus taught.

[18]And the dragon stood on the seashore.

SIDELIGHT: The reign of the Roman Emperor Nero (often paralleled with the first beast in Revelation 13) was marked by terrible crimes, destruction, and persecution of Christians. When he sent someone to murder his own mother, she bared her body and cried, "Strike my womb because it bore a Nero!"

The Two Beasts

13 Then I saw a beast coming up out of the sea. It had ten horns and seven heads, and there was a crown on each horn. A name against God was written on each head. [2]This beast looked like a leopard, with feet like a bear's feet and a mouth like a lion's mouth. And the dragon gave the beast all of his power and his throne and great authority. [3]One of the heads of the beast looked as if it had been killed by a wound, but this death wound was healed. Then the whole world was amazed and followed the beast. [4]People worshiped the dragon because he had given his power to the beast. And they also worshiped the beast, asking, "Who is like the beast? Who can make war against it?"

[5]The beast was allowed to say proud words and words against God and it was allowed to use its power for forty-two months. [6]It used its mouth to speak against God, against God's name, against the place where God lives, and against all those who live in heaven. [7]It was given power to make war against God's holy people and to defeat them. It was given power over every tribe,[d] people, language, and nation. [8]And all who live on earth will worship the beast — all the people since the beginning of the world whose names are not written in the Lamb's book of life. The Lamb is the One who was killed.

[9]Anyone who has ears should listen:
[10]If you are to be a prisoner,
  then you will be a prisoner.

Michael The archangel—leader among God's angels or messengers (Jude 9).

If you are to be killed with the sword,
    then you will be killed with the sword.
This means that God's holy people must have patience and faith.

[11] Then I saw another beast coming up out of the earth. It had two horns like a lamb, but it spoke like a dragon. [12] This beast stands before the first beast and uses the same power the first beast has. By this power it makes everyone living on earth worship the first beast, who had the death wound that was healed. [13] And the second beast does great miracles[d] so that it even makes fire come down from heaven to earth while people are watching. [14] It fools those who live on earth by the miracles it has been given the power to do. It does these miracles to serve the first beast. The second beast orders people to make an idol to honor the first beast, the one that was wounded by the deadly sword but sprang to life again. [15] The second beast was given power to give life to the idol of the first one so that the idol could speak. And the second beast was given power to command all who will not worship the image of the beast to be killed. [16] The second beast also forced all people, small and great, rich and poor, free and slave, to have a mark on their right hand or on their forehead. [17] No one could buy or sell without this mark, which is the name of the beast or the number of its name. [18] This takes wisdom. Let the one who has understanding find the meaning of the number, which is the number of a person. Its number is six hundred sixty-six.

The Song of the Saved

14 Then I looked, and there before me was the Lamb standing on Mount Zion.[n] With him were one hundred forty-four thousand people who had his name and his Father's name written on their foreheads. [2] And I heard a sound from heaven like the noise of flooding water and like the sound of loud thunder. The sound I heard was like people playing harps. [3] And they sang a new song before the throne and before the four living creatures and the elders. No one could learn the new song except the one hundred forty-four thousand who had been bought from the earth. [4] These are the ones who did not do sinful things with women, because they kept themselves pure. They follow the Lamb every place he goes. These one hundred forty-four thousand were bought from among the people of the earth *as people to be offered to God and the Lamb.* [5] They were not guilty of telling lies; they are without fault.

The Three Angels

[6] Then I saw another angel flying high in the air. He had the eternal Good News[d] to preach to those who live on earth — to every nation, tribe,[d] language, and people. [7] He preached in a loud voice, "Fear God and give him praise, because the time has come for God to judge all people. So worship God who made the heavens, and the earth, and the sea, and the springs of water."

[8] Then the second angel followed the first angel and said, "Ruined, ruined is the great city of Babylon! She made all the nations drink the wine of the anger of her adultery."[d]

[9] Then a third angel followed the first two angels, saying in a loud voice: "If anyone worships the beast and his idol and gets the beast's mark on the forehead or on the hand, [10] that one also will drink the wine of God's anger, which is prepared with all its strength in the cup of his anger. And that person will be put in pain with burning sulfur before the holy angels and the Lamb. [11] And the smoke from their burning pain will rise forever and ever. There will be no rest, day or night, for those who worship the beast and his idol or who get the mark of his name." [12] This means God's holy people must be patient. They must obey God's commands and keep their faith in Jesus.

[13] Then I heard a voice from heaven saying, "Write this: Happy are the dead who die from now on in the Lord."

The Spirit[d] says, "Yes, they will rest from their hard work, and the reward of all they have done stays with them."

The Earth Is Harvested

[14] Then I looked, and there before me was a white cloud, and sitting on the white cloud was One who looked like a Son of Man.[n] He had a gold crown on his head and a sharp sickle[n] in his hand. [15] Then another angel came out of the temple and called out in a loud voice to the One who was sitting on the cloud, "Take your sickle and harvest from the earth, because the time to harvest has come, and the fruit of the earth is ripe." [16] So the One who was sitting on the cloud swung his sickle over the earth, and the earth was harvested.

[17] Then another angel came out of the temple in heaven, and he also had a sharp sickle. [18] And then another angel, who has power over the fire, came from the altar. This angel called to the angel with *the sharp sickle, saying,* "Take your sharp sickle and gather the bunches of grapes from the earth's vine, because its grapes are ripe." [19] Then the an-

Mount Zion   Another name for Jerusalem; here meaning the spiritual city of God's people.
Son of Man   "Son of Man" is a name Jesus called himself. See dictionary.
sickle   A farming tool with a curved blade. It was used to harvest grain.

gel swung his sickle over the earth. He gathered the earth's grapes and threw them into the great winepress[d] of God's anger. 20They were trampled in the winepress outside the city, and blood flowed out of the winepress as high as horses' bridles for a distance of about one hundred eighty miles.

The Last Troubles

15 Then I saw another wonder in heaven that was great and amazing. There were seven angels bringing seven disasters. These are the last disasters, because after them, God's anger is finished.

2I saw what looked like a sea of glass mixed with fire. All of those who had won the victory over the beast and his idol and over the number of his name were standing by the sea of glass. They had harps that God had given them. 3They sang the song of Moses, the servant of God, and the song of the Lamb:

"You do great and wonderful things, *Psalm 111:2*
Lord God Almighty. *Amos 3:13*
Everything the Lord does is right and true,
Psalm 145:17
King of the nations.
4Everyone will respect you, Lord, *Jeremiah 10:7*
and will honor you.
Only you are holy.
All the nations will come
and worship you, *Psalm 86:9-10*
because the right things you have done
are now made known." *Deuteronomy 32:4*

5After this I saw that the temple (the Tent[d] of the Agreement) in heaven was opened. 6And the seven angels bringing the seven disasters came out of the temple. They were dressed in clean, shining linen and wore golden bands tied around their chests. 7Then one of the four living creatures gave to the seven angels seven golden bowls filled with the anger of God, who lives forever and ever. 8The temple was filled with smoke from the glory and the power of God, and no one could enter the temple until the seven disasters of the seven angels were finished.

The Bowls of God's Anger

16 Then I heard a loud voice from the temple saying to the seven angels, "Go and pour out the seven bowls of God's anger on the earth."

2The first angel left and poured out his bowl on the land. Then ugly and painful sores came upon all those who had the mark of the beast and who worshiped his idol.

3The second angel poured out his bowl on the sea, and it became blood like that of a dead man, and every living thing in the sea died.

4The third angel poured out his bowl on the rivers and the springs of water, and they became blood. 5Then I heard the angel of the waters saying:

"Holy One, you are the One who is and who was.
You are right to decide to punish these evil people.
6They have poured out the blood of your holy people and your prophets.[d]
So now you have given them blood to drink as they deserve."

7And I heard a voice coming from the altar saying:
"Yes, Lord God Almighty,
the way you punish evil people is right and fair."

8The fourth angel poured out his bowl on the sun, and he was given power to burn the people with fire. 9They were burned by the great heat, and they cursed the name of God, who had control over these disasters. But the people refused to change their hearts and lives and give glory to God.

10The fifth angel poured out his bowl on the throne of the beast, and darkness covered its kingdom. People gnawed their tongues because of the pain. 11They also cursed the God of heaven because of their pain and the sores they had, but they refused to change their hearts and turn away from the evil things they did.

12The sixth angel poured out his bowl on the great river Euphrates so that the water in the river was dried up to prepare the way for the kings from the east to come. 13Then I saw three evil spirits that looked like frogs coming out of the mouth of the dragon, out of the mouth of the beast, and out of the mouth of the false prophet.[d] 14These evil spirits are the spirits of demons,[d] which have power to do miracles.[d] They go out to the kings of the whole world to gather them together for the battle on the great day of God Almighty.

15"Listen! I will come as a thief comes! Happy are those who stay awake and keep their clothes on so that they will not walk around naked and have people see their shame."

15Then the evil spirits gathered the kings to-

☀ SIDELIGHT: Revelation 16:15 isn't a warning to wear pajamas in bed. According to Jewish laws of the time, the captain of the Temple would check up on the Temple police at night. If someone was asleep on duty, his clothes were taken off and burned, and he was sent away naked and disgraced. Anyone want an extra cup of coffee?

gether to the place that is called Armageddon in the Hebrew language.

17The seventh angel poured out his bowl into the air. Then a loud voice came out of the temple from the throne, saying, "It is finished!" 18Then there were flashes of lightning, noises, thunder, and a big earthquake — the worst earthquake that has ever happened since people have been on earth. 19The great city split into three parts, and the cities of the nations were destroyed. And God remembered the sins of Babylon the Great, so he gave that city the cup filled with the wine of his terrible anger. 20Then every island ran away, and mountains disappeared. 21Giant hailstones, each weighing about a hundred pounds, fell from the sky upon people. People cursed God for the disaster of the hail, because this disaster was so terrible.

The Woman on the Animal

17 Then one of the seven angels who had the seven bowls came and spoke to me. He said, "Come, and I will show you the punishment that will be given to the great prostitute,*d* the one sitting over many waters. 2The kings of the earth sinned sexually with her, and the people of the earth became drunk from the wine of her sexual sin."

3Then the angel carried me away by the Spirit*d* to the desert. There I saw a woman sitting on a red beast. It was covered with names against God written on it, and it had seven heads and ten horns. 4The woman was dressed in purple and red and was shining with the gold, precious jewels, and pearls she was wearing. She had a golden cup in her hand, a cup filled with evil things and the uncleanness of her sexual sin. 5On her forehead a title was written that was secret. This is what was written:

THE GREAT BABYLON
MOTHER OF PROSTITUTES
AND OF THE EVIL THINGS OF THE EARTH

6Then I saw that the woman was drunk with the blood of God's holy people and with the blood of those who were killed because of their faith in Jesus.

When I saw the woman, I was very amazed. 7Then the angel said to me, "Why are you amazed? I will tell you the secret of this woman and the beast she rides — the one with seven heads and ten horns. 8The beast you saw was once alive but is not alive now. But soon it will come up out of the bottomless pit and go away to be destroyed. There are people who live on earth whose names have not been written in the book of life since the beginning of the world. They will be amazed when they see the beast, because he was once alive, is not alive now, but will come again.

9"You need a wise mind to understand this. The seven heads on the beast are seven mountains where the woman sits. 10And they are seven kings. Five of the kings have already been destroyed, one of the kings lives now, and another has not yet come. When he comes, he must stay a short time. 11The beast that was once alive, but is not alive now, is also an eighth king. He belongs to the first seven kings, and he will go away to be destroyed.

12"The ten horns you saw are ten kings who have not yet begun to rule, but they will receive power to rule with the beast for one hour. 13All ten of these kings have the same purpose, and they will give their power and authority to the beast. 14They will make war against the Lamb, but the Lamb will defeat them, because he is Lord of lords and King of kings. He will defeat them with his called, chosen, and faithful followers."

15Then the angel said to me, "The waters that you saw, where the prostitute sits, are peoples, races, nations, and languages. 16The ten horns and the beast you saw will hate the prostitute. They will take everything she has and leave her naked. They will eat her body and burn her with fire. 17God made the ten horns want to carry out his purpose by agreeing to give the beast their power to rule, until what God has said comes about. 18The woman you saw is the great city that rules over the kings of the earth."

Babylon Is Destroyed

18 After the vision of these things, I saw another angel coming down from heaven. This angel had great power, and his glory made the earth bright. 2He shouted in a powerful voice:
"Ruined, ruined is the great city of Babylon!
   She has become a home for demons*d*
and a prison for every evil spirit,
   and a prison for every unclean*d* bird and
      unclean beast.
3She has been ruined, because all the peoples
      of the earth
   have drunk the wine of the desire of her
      sexual sin.
She has been ruined also because the kings of
      the earth
   have sinned sexually with her,
and the merchants of the earth
   have grown rich from the great wealth of
      her luxury."

4Then I heard another voice from heaven saying:
"Come out of that city, my people,
   so that you will not share in her sins,
   so that you will not receive the disasters
      that will come to her.
5Her sins have piled up as high as the sky,

and God has not forgotten the wrongs she
has done.
⁶Give that city the same as she gave to others.
Pay her back twice as much as she did.
Prepare wine for her that is twice as strong
as the wine she prepared for others.
⁷She gave herself much glory and rich living.
Give her that much suffering and sadness.
She says to herself, 'I am a queen sitting on
my throne.
I am not a widow; I will never be sad.'
⁸So these disasters will come to her in one
day:
death, and crying, and great hunger,
and she will be destroyed by fire,
because the Lord God who judges her is
powerful."
⁹The kings of the earth who sinned sexually
with her and shared her wealth will see the
smoke from her burning. Then they will cry and
be sad because of her death. ¹⁰They will be afraid
of her suffering and stand far away and say:
"Terrible! How terrible for you, great city,
powerful city of Babylon,
because your punishment has come in one
hour!"
¹¹And the merchants of the earth will cry and
be sad about her, because now there is no one to
buy their cargoes — ¹²cargoes of gold, silver, jewels, pearls, fine linen, purple cloth, silk, red cloth;
all kinds of citron wood and all kinds of things
made from ivory, expensive wood, bronze, iron,
and marble; ¹³cinnamon, spice, incense,ᵈ myrrh,ᵈ
frankincense,ᵈ wine, olive oil, fine flour, wheat,
cattle, sheep, horses, carriages, slaves, and human
lives.
¹⁴The merchants will say,
"Babylon, the good things you wanted are
gone from you.
All your rich and fancy things have
disappeared.
You will never have them again."
¹⁵The merchants who became rich from selling to
her will be afraid of her suffering and will stand
far away. They will cry and be sad ¹⁶and say:
"Terrible! How terrible for the great city!
She was dressed in fine linen, purple and
red cloth,
and she was shining with gold, precious
jewels, and pearls!
¹⁷All these riches have been destroyed in one
hour!"
Every sea captain, every passenger, the sailors,
and all those who earn their living from the sea
stood far away from Babylon. ¹⁸As they saw the
smoke from her burning, they cried out loudly,
"There was never a city like this great city!" ¹⁹And

they threw dust on their heads and cried out,
weeping and being sad. They said:
"Terrible! How terrible for the great city!
All the people who had ships on the sea
became rich because of her wealth!
But she has been destroyed in one hour!
²⁰Be happy because of this, heaven!
Be happy, God's holy people and apostlesᵈ
and prophets!ᵈ
God has punished her because of what she
did to you."
²¹Then a powerful angel picked up a large
stone, like one used for grinding grain, and threw
it into the sea. He said:
"In the same way, the great city of Babylon
will be thrown down,
and it will never be found again.
²²The music of people playing harps and other
instruments, flutes, and trumpets,
will never be heard in you again.
No workman doing any job
will ever be found in you again.
The sound of grinding grain
will never be heard in you again.
²³The light of a lamp
will never shine in you again,
and the voices of a bridegroom and bride
will never be heard in you again.
Your merchants were the world's great
people,
and all the nations were tricked by your
magic.
²⁴You are guilty of the death of the prophets
and God's holy people
and all who have been killed on earth."

People in Heaven Praise God

19 After this vision and announcement I
heard what sounded like a great many
people in heaven saying:
"Hallelujah!ⁿ
Salvation, glory, and power belong to our
God,
² because his judgments are true and right.
He has punished the prostituteᵈ
who made the earth evil with her sexual
sin.
He has paid her back for the death of his
servants."
³Again they said
"Hallelujah!
She is burning, and her smoke will rise
forever and ever."
⁴Then the twenty-four elders and the four living creatures bowed down and worshiped God,
who sits on the throne. They said:
"Amen, Hallelujah!"

Hallelujah | This means "praise God!"

5Then a voice came from the throne, saying: "Praise our God, all you who serve him

and all you who honor him, both small and great!"

6Then I heard what sounded like a great many people, like the noise of flooding water, and like the noise of loud thunder. The people were saying:

"Hallelujah!

Our Lord God, the Almighty, rules.

7Let us rejoice and be happy

and give God glory,

because the wedding of the Lamb has come,

and the Lamb's bride has made herself ready.

8Fine linen, bright and clean, was given to her to wear."

(The fine linen means the good things done by God's holy people.)

9And the angel said to me, "Write this: Happy are those who have been invited to the wedding meal of the Lamb!" And the angel said, "These are the true words of God."

10Then I bowed down at the angel's feet to worship him, but he said to me, "Do not worship me! I am a servant like you and your brothers and sisters who have the message of Jesus. Worship God, because the message about Jesus is the spirit that gives all prophecy."d

The Rider on the White Horse

11Then I saw heaven opened, and there before me was a white horse. The rider on the horse is called Faithful and True, and he is right when he judges and makes war. 12His eyes are like burning fire, and on his head are many crowns. He has a name written on him, which no one but himself knows. 13He is dressed in a robe dipped in blood, and his name is the Word of God. 14The armies of heaven, dressed in fine linen, white and clean, were following him on white horses. 15Out of the rider's mouth comes a sharp sword that he will use to defeat the nations, and he will rule them with a rod of iron. He will crush out the wine in the winepressd of the terrible anger of God the Almighty. 16On his robe and on his upper leg was

written this name: KING OF KINGS AND LORD OF LORDS.

17Then I saw an angel standing in the sun, and he called with a loud voice to all the birds flying in the sky: "Come and gather together for the great feast of God 18so that you can eat the bodies of kings, generals, mighty people, horses and their riders, and the bodies of all people—free, slave, small, and great."

19Then I saw the beast and the kings of the earth. Their armies were gathered together to make war against the rider on the horse and his army. 20But the beast was captured and with him the false prophetd who did the miraclesd for the beast. The false prophet had used these miracles to trick those who had the mark of the beast and worshiped his idol. The false prophet and the beast were thrown alive into the lake of fire that burns with sulfur. 21And their armies were killed with the sword that came out of the mouth of the rider on the horse, and all the birds ate the bodies until they were full.

The Thousand Years

20 I saw an angel coming down from heaven. He had the key to the bottomless pit and a large chain in his hand. 2The angel grabbed the dragon, that old snake who is the devil and Satan, and tied him up for a thousand years. 3Then he threw him into the bottomless pit, closed it, and locked it over him. The angel did this so he could not trick the people of the earth anymore until the thousand years were ended. After a thousand years he must be set free for a short time.

4Then I saw some thrones and people sitting on them who had been given the power to judge. And I saw the souls of those who had been killed because they were faithful to the message of Jesus and the message from God. They had not worshiped the beast or his idol, and they had not received the mark of the beast on their foreheads or on their hands. They came back to life and ruled with Christ for a thousand years. 5(The others that were dead did not live again until the thousand years were ended.) This is the first raising of the dead. 6Happy and holy are those who share in this first raising of the dead. The second death has no power over them. They will be priests for God and for Christ and will rule with him for a thousand years.

7When the thousand years are over, Satan will be set free from his prison. 8Then he will go out to trick the nations in all the earth—Gog and Magog—to gather them for battle. There are so many people they will be like sand on the seashore. 9And Satan's army marched across the earth and gathered around the camp of God's people and the city God loves. But fire came down from heaven and burned them up. [10]And Satan, who tricked them, was thrown into the lake of burning sulfur with the beast and the false prophet.[d] There they will be punished day and night forever and ever.

People of the World Are Judged

[11]Then I saw a great white throne and the One who was sitting on it. Earth and sky ran away from him and disappeared. [12]And I saw the dead, great and small, standing before the throne. Then books were opened, and the book of life was opened. The dead were judged by what they had done, which was written in the books. [13]The sea gave up the dead who were in it, and Death and Hades[n] gave up the dead who were in them. Each person was judged by what he had done. [14]And Death and Hades were thrown into the lake of fire. The lake of fire is the second death. [15]And anyone whose name was not found written in the book of life was thrown into the lake of fire.

The New Jerusalem

21 Then I saw a new heaven and a new earth. The first heaven and the first earth had disappeared, and there was no sea anymore.

Hades The place of the dead.
new Jerusalem The spiritual city where God's people live with him.

[2]And I saw the holy city, the new Jerusalem,[n] coming down out of heaven from God. It was prepared like a bride dressed for her husband. [3]And I heard a loud voice from the throne, saying, "Now God's presence is with people, and he will live with them, and they will be his people. God himself will be with them and will be their God. [4]He will wipe away every tear from their eyes, and there will be no more death, sadness, crying, or pain, because all the old ways are gone."

> ☀ **SIDELIGHT:** To dress the bride (Revelation 21:2) in Bible times was about as expensive as it can be today. The bride's face was made up to look glossy and shiny. Her hair was braided with gold and pearls. She was dressed in inherited family treasures. People borrowed what they couldn't buy.

[5]The One who was sitting on the throne said, "Look! I am making everything new!" Then he said, "Write this because these words are true and can be trusted."

---

⁶The One on the throne said to me, "It is finished. I am the Alpha and the Omega,ⁿ the Beginning and the End. I will give free water from the spring of the water of life to anyone who is thirsty. ⁷Those who win the victory will receive this, and I will be their God, and they will be my children. ⁸But cowards, those who refuse to believe, who do evil things, who kill, who sin sexually, who do evil magic, who worship idols, and who tell lies—all these will have a place in the lake of burning sulfur. This is the second death."

⁹Then one of the seven angels who had the seven bowls full of the seven last troubles came to me, saying, "Come with me, and I will show you the bride, the wife of the Lamb." ¹⁰And the angel carried me away by the Spiritᵈ to a very large and high mountain. He showed me the holy city, Jerusalem, coming down out of heaven from God. ¹¹It was shining with the glory of God and was bright like a very expensive jewel, like a jasper, clear as crystal. ¹²The city had a great high wall with twelve gates with twelve angels at the gates, and on each gate was written the name of one of the twelve tribesᵈ of Israel. ¹³There were three gates on the east, three on the north, three on the south, and three on the west. ¹⁴The walls of the city were built on twelve foundation stones, and on the stones were written the names of the twelve apostlesᵈ of the Lamb.

¹⁵The angel who talked with me had a measuring rod made of gold to measure the city, its gates, and its wall. ¹⁶The city was built in a square, and its length was equal to its width. The angel measured the city with the rod. The city was twelve thousand stadiaⁿ long, twelve thousand stadia wide, and twelve thousand stadia high. ¹⁷The angel also measured the wall. It was one hundred forty-four cubitsⁿ high, by human measurements, which the angel was using. ¹⁸The wall was made of jasper, and the city was made of pure gold, as pure as glass. ¹⁹The foundation stones of the city walls were decorated with every kind of jewel. The first foundation was jasper, the second was sapphire, the third was chalcedony, the fourth was emerald, ²⁰the fifth was onyx, the sixth was carnelian, the seventh was chrysolite, the eighth was beryl, the ninth was topaz, the tenth was chrysoprase, the eleventh was jacinth, and the twelfth was amethyst. ²¹The twelve gates were twelve pearls, each gate having been made from a single pearl. And the street of the city was made of pure gold as clear as glass.

²²I did not see a temple in the city, because the Lord God Almighty and the Lamb are the city's temple. ²³The city does not need the sun or the moon to shine on it, because the glory of God is its light, and the Lamb is the city's lamp. ²⁴By its light the people of the world will walk, and the kings of the earth will bring their glory into it. ²⁵The city's gates will never be shut on any day, because there is no night there. ²⁶The glory and the honor of the nations will be brought into it. ²⁷Nothing uncleanᵈ and no one who does shameful things or tells lies will ever go into it. Only those whose names are written in the Lamb's book of life will enter the city.

22 Then the angel showed me the river of the water of life. It was shining like crystal and was flowing from the throne of God and of the Lamb ²down the middle of the street of the city. The tree of life was on each side of the river. It produces fruit twelve times a year, once each month. The leaves of the tree are for the healing of all the nations. ³Nothing that God judges guilty will be in that city. The throne of God and of the Lamb will be there, and God's servants will worship him. ⁴They will see his face, and his name will be written on their foreheads. ⁵There will never be night again. They will not need the light of a lamp or the light of the sun, because the Lord God will give them light. And they will rule as kings forever and ever.

⁶The angel said to me, "These words can be trusted and are true." The Lord, the God of the spirits of the prophets,ᵈ sent his angel to show his servants the things that must happen soon.

⁷"Listen! I am coming soon! Happy is the one who obeys the words of prophecy in this book."

⁸I, John, am the one who heard and saw these things. When I heard and saw them, I bowed down to worship at the feet of the angel who showed these things to me. ⁹But the angel said to me, "Do not worship me! I am a servant like you, your brothers the prophets, and all those who obey the words in this book. Worship God!"

¹⁰Then the angel told me, "Do not keep secret the words of prophecy in this book, because the time is near for all this to happen. ¹¹Let whoever is doing evil continue to do evil. Let whoever is unclean continue to be unclean. Let whoever is doing right continue to do right. Let whoever is holy continue to be holy."

¹²"Listen! I am coming soon! I will bring my reward with me, and I will repay each one of you for what you have done. ¹³I am the Alpha and the Omega,ⁿ the First and the Last, the Beginning and the End.

¹⁴"Happy are those who wash their robesⁿ so

Alpha and the Omega The first and last letters of the Greek alphabet. This means "the beginning and the end."
stadia One stadion was a distance of about two hundred yards; about one-eighth of a Roman mile.
cubits A cubit is about half a yard, the length from the elbow to the tip of the little finger.
wash their robes This means they believed in Jesus so that their sins could be forgiven by Christ's blood.

that they will receive the right to eat the fruit from the tree of life and may go through the gates into the city. [15]Outside the city are the evil people, those who do evil magic, who sin sexually, who murder, who worship idols, and who love lies and tell lies.

[16]"I, Jesus, have sent my angel to tell you these things for the churches. I am the descendant[d] from the family of David, and I am the bright morning star."

[17]The Spirit[d] and the bride say, "Come!" Let the one who hears this say, "Come!" Let whoever is thirsty come; whoever wishes may have the water of life as a free gift.

[18]I warn everyone who hears the words of the prophecy of this book: If anyone adds anything to these words, God will add to that person the disasters written about in this book. [19]And if anyone takes away from the words of this book of prophecy, God will take away that one's share of the tree of life and of the holy city, which are written about in this book.

[20]Jesus, the One who says these things are true, says, "Yes, I am coming soon."

Amen. Come, Lord Jesus!

[21]The grace of the Lord Jesus be with all. Amen.

ETERNAL LIFE

A Bit of Heaven

Three hundred teenage tourists gathered in the Swiss Alps, 7,100 feet above sea level. Rising even higher on one side were craggy, snow-capped peaks. A huge glacier stretched out on the other side, seemingly unaffected by the warm July day.

The group gathered for outdoor worship, which began with a trio of alpine horns echoing hymns across the valley. The minister shared the Good News of Christ. Then voices joined together to close the service with familiar choruses of praise to God.

The day passed quickly, filled with hugs, songs, shouts of pleasure, helping hands, huge smiles, and incredible sights. As the teenagers waited to return to Grindelwald on Europe's longest chair lift, several girls talked about the experience.

"I hope heaven's like this," said one of the girls.

"Heaven's going to be even better!" said another.

God's promise of eternal life in heaven is even better! Read the promise in **Revelation 22:12–21**.

■ What do you think made the girls think of heaven during their outing in Switzerland? How do you think the mountain experience compares to heaven itself?

■ What difference does God's promise of eternal life make in your everyday living?

CONSIDER...

■ remembering a time when you felt overwhelmed by nature's majesty as a reminder of God's greatness.

■ asking yourself what you need to do to respond to the invitation in verse 17: "Let whoever is thirsty come; whoever wishes may have the water of life as a free gift."

FOR MORE, SEE...

■ Psalm 16:9–11 (p. 489)   ■ John 4:5–42 (p. 1063)
■ Matthew 19:15–30 (p. 942)

DICTIONARY

A

Aaron (AIR-ohn) *older brother of Moses.*
- before the king of Egypt, Exodus 4:14-16; 5:1-5; 7:1-2
- death of, Numbers 20:22-29

Abba (AB-uh) *word for "father" in Aramaic.*
- Jesus called God "Abba," Mark 14:36
- we can call God "Abba," Romans 8:15; Galatians 4:6

Abednego (a-BED-nee-go) *one of the three friends of Daniel whom God protected from the fiery furnace.*
- refused the king of Babylon's food, Daniel 1:3-17
- thrown into the fiery furnace, Daniel 3

Abel (AY-bul) *the second son of Adam and Eve.*
- born to Adam and Eve, Genesis 4:2
- approved by God, Genesis 4:3-4; Hebrews 11:4
- murdered by Cain, Genesis 4:8; 1 John 3:12

Abib (ah-BEEB) *first month of the Jewish calendar, about the time of year as our March or April; also called "Nisan"; means "young ears of grain."*
- the time the Israelites left Egypt, Exodus 13:3-4
- the time for the Feast of Unleavened Bread, Exodus 23:15; 34:18

Abigail, sister of David (AB-eh-gale) 1 Chronicles 2:13-17

Abigail, wife of Nabal
- brought food to David, 1 Samuel 25:14-35
- became David's wife, 1 Samuel 25:36-42

Abijah, king of Judah (a-BY-jah) 1 Kings 15:1-8; 2 Chronicles 13:1–14:1

Abijah, son of Jeroboam
- death of, 1 Kings 14:1-18

Abijah, son of Samuel, 1 Samuel 8:1-3

ability
- given by God, 2 Corinthians 3:5-6
- through Christ, Philippians 4:13
- differing abilities, 1 Corinthians 12:7-11

Abimelech, king of Gerar (a-BIM-eh-lek)
- tried to take Sarah as his wife, Genesis 20

Abimelech, king of the Philistines
- tried to take Rebekah as his wife, Genesis 26:6-11

Abimelech, son of Gideon
- birth of, Judges 8:29-31
- murdered his brothers, Judges 9:1-6
- defeated the people of Shechem, Judges 9:22-45
- burned the Tower of Shechem, Judges 9:46-49
- death of, Judges 9:50-55

Abishai (a-BISH-eye) *nephew of King David.*
- served in David's army, 2 Samuel 23:18-19; 1 Chronicles 18:12-13
- saved David's life, 2 Samuel 21:15-17

Abner (AB-nur) *commander of Saul's army.*
- at Goliath's defeat, 1 Samuel 17:55-57
- made Ish-Bosheth king of Israel, 2 Samuel 2:8-10
- later loyal to David, 2 Samuel 3:6-21
- killed by Joab, 2 Samuel 3:22-27

Abraham (AY-bra-ham) *father of the Jewish nation.*
- called from Ur by God, Genesis 12:1-4
- lied about Sarai, Genesis 12:10-20
- separated from Lot, Genesis 13
- God's agreement with, Genesis 15; 17
- name changed, Genesis 17:3-6
- father of Isaac, Genesis 21:1-7
- offered Isaac as a sacrifice, Genesis 22:1-19
- father of the faithful, Romans 4
- God's friend, James 2:23

Absalom (AB-sah-lum) *one of David's sons.*
- turned against David, 2 Samuel 15–18:8
- killed by Joab, 2 Samuel 18:9-15

abstain (ab-STAIN) *to keep from doing something.*
- from food offered to idols, Acts 15:20
- from evil, 1 Thessalonians 5:22
- from lust, 1 Peter 2:11

abyss (uh-BISS) See "bottomless pit."

accept
- a prophet not accepted, Luke 4:24
- accepted by God, Acts 10:35; 15:7-8; Romans 14:3
- each other, Romans 14:1; 15:7
- Jesus, John 12:48

accuse
- Jesus accused by the Jews, Matthew 27:12-13; Mark 15:3; Luke 6:7
- Paul accused by the Jews, Acts 23:27-29; 26:7
- the Devil, as the accuser, Revelation 12:10

Achaia (a-KA-yuh) See "Greece."

Achan (AY-can) *an Israelite who disobeyed God during the battle of Jericho, Joshua 7*

Achish (AY-kish) *king of the Philistine city of Gath.*
- David pretends to be insane, 1 Samuel 21:10-15
- David in his army, 1 Samuel 27; 29

actions
- judged by, Proverbs 20:11; Matthew 11:19; Galatians 6:4
- of love, 1 John 3:18
- of goodness, Matthew 5:16

Adam (AD-um) *the first man.*
- created by God, Genesis 1:26–2:25
- disobeyed God, Genesis 3
- compared to Christ, 1 Corinthians 15:21-22,45-49

adder, *a poisonous snake.* See "snake."

Adonijah (ad-oh-NY-jah) *David's fourth son.*
- son of Haggith, 2 Samuel 3:4
- tried to become king, 1 Kings 1
- killed by Solomon, 1 Kings 2:12-25

Adoni-Zedek (a-DOH-ny-ZEE-dek) *an Amorite king of Jerusalem.*
- defeated by Joshua, Joshua 10:1-28

Adullam (a-DOO-lum) *a city about thirteen miles from Bethlehem.*
- David hid in a cave there, 2 Samuel 23:13

adultery (ah-DUL-ter-ee) *breaking a marriage promise by having sexual relations with someone other than your husband or wife.*
- "You must not be guilty of adultery," Exodus 20:14
- Christ teaches about, Matthew 5:27-32; Luke 16:18
- woman caught in adultery, John 8:1-11

advice
- given by Ahithophel, 2 Samuel 15:30–17:23
- given to Rehoboam, 1 Kings 12:1-15
- teachings about, Proverbs 11:14; 12:5,15; 19:20

Agabus (AG-uh-bus) *a Christian prophet.*
- warned the people, Acts 11:27-30
- warned Paul about going to Jerusalem, Acts 21:10-11

Agag (AY-gag) *king of the Amalekites.*
- captured by Saul, 1 Samuel 15

agreement *a contract, promise, or covenant.*
- with Noah, Genesis 9:1-7
- with Abraham, Genesis 15; 17:1-14
- Ark of the Agreement, Exodus 25:10-22; 1 Samuel 4–5; 2 Samuel 6:1-15
- with the Israelites, Exodus 19:3-8,24; Deuteronomy 29
- new agreement, 2 Corinthians 2:12–3:18
- difference between the old and new agreements, Hebrews 8–10

Agrippa (uh-GRIP-pah) See "Herod Agrippa."

Ahab (AY-hab) *evil king of Israel who was married to Jezebel.*
- worshiped Baal, 1 Kings 16:29-33
- had Naboth killed, 1 Kings 21
- death of, 1 Kings 22:1-40

Ahasuerus (ah-HAZ-oo-EE-rus) *Hebrew word for the Greek name Xerxes.* See "Xerxes."

Ahaz, *twelfth king of Judah,* 2 Kings 16; 2 Chronicles 28

Ahaziah, king of Judah (ay-ha-ZY-uh) 2 Chronicles 22:1-9

Ahaziah, son of Ahab
- king of Israel, 1 Kings 22:40-53

Ahijah, great-grandson of Eli (a-HY-jah) 1 Samuel 14:1-23

Ahijah, the prophet
- told Jeroboam the kingdom would be divided, 1 Kings 11:29-39
- told that Jeroboam's son would die, 1 Kings 14:1-18

Ahimelech, the high priest (a-HIM-eh-lex)
- helped David, 1 Samuel 21:1-9

Ahimelech, the Hittite warrior, 1 Samuel 26:6

Ahithophel (a-HITH-oh fel) *gave advice to King David.*
- helped Absalom rebel against David, 1 Samuel 15:31; 16:15–17:23

Ai (AY-eye) *a city completely destroyed by the Israelites,* Joshua 7–8:28

Akeldama (a-KEL-dah-mah) *field bought with the money Judas received for betraying Jesus,* Matthew 27:3-10; Acts 1:18-19

alabaster (AL-a-bass-ter) *light-colored stone with streaks or stripes through it,* Matthew 26:7; Mark 14:3; Luke 7:37

alamoth (AL-a-moth) *a musical word, which may mean "like a flute" or "high-pitched,"* Psalm 46

All-Powerful, *a name for God,* 1 Chronicles 11:9; Psalm 24:10; Isaiah 6:3-5; Malachi 3:1-17

Almighty, *a name for God.*
- "I am God Almighty,' Genesis 17:1
- "I appeared to Abraham . . . by the name, God Almighty," Exodus 6:3
- "Holy, holy, holy is the Lord God Almighty," Revelation 4:8

almond
- design of the lampstands in Holy Tent, Exodus 25:31-36
- Aaron's stick produced, Numbers 17:8

aloes (AL-ohs) *oils from sweet-smelling sap of certain trees; used to make perfume and medicine and to prepare bodies for burial,* Psalm 45:8; Proverbs 7:17
- used to prepare Jesus' body for burial, John 19:39

Alpha and Omega (AL-fah and oh-MAY-guh) *the first and last letters of the Greek alphabet, like our A and Z.*
- used to describe Jesus, Revelation 1:8; 21:6; 22:13

altar (ALL-ter) *a place where sacrifices, gifts, or prayers were offered to a god.*
- built by Noah, Genesis 8:20
- built by Abraham, Genesis 22:9
- for burnt offerings, Exodus 27:1-8
- for incense, Exodus 30:1-10
- corners of, Exodus 27:2; 30:10; 1 Kings 1:50
- for the Temple, 2 Chronicles 4:1

Amalekites (AM-a-lah-kites) *fierce, fighting people who descended from Esau; they were enemies of Israel and were finally wiped out during the time of Hezekiah.*
- enemies of Israel, Exodus 17:8-16; 1 Samuel 15
- destroyed by King Hezekiah, 1 Chronicles 4:43

Amasa (AM-a-sa) *leader of Absalom's army when he rebelled against David,* 2 Samuel 17:25
- made leader of David's army, 2 Samuel 19:13
- killed by Joab, 2 Samuel 20:1-10

Amaziah (am-ah-ZY-uh) *the ninth king of Judah,* 2 Kings 14; 2 Chronicles 25

amen (AY-MEN or AH-MEN) *Hebrew word for "that is right,"* 1 Chronicles 16:36; Psalm 106:48; 1 Corinthians 14:15
- "Amen. Come, Lord Jesus!" Revelation 22:20

Ammonites (AM-on-ites) *descendants of Lot's son, Ben-Ammi,* Genesis 19:36-38
- enemies of Israel, Judges 10:6–11:33; 1 Samuel 11; 2 Samuel 10:1-14
- worshiped Molech, 1 Kings 11:5

Amon (AM-on) *the fifteenth king of Judah,* 2 Kings 21:18-26; 2 Chronicles 33:20-25
- an ancestor of Jesus, Matthew 1:10

Amorites (AM-or-ites) *a group of wicked people who worshiped false gods and lived in Canaan when the Israelites arrived.*
- defeated by Israel, Numbers 21:21-32; Joshua 10:1–11:14

Amos (AY-mos) *a prophet who warned Israel of God's punishment for disobedience.*
- a shepherd from Tekoa, Amos 1:1
- his visions, Amos 7–9:10

Anak/Anakites (A-nak/AN-uh-kites) *a group of large, fighting people who lived in Canaan when the Israelites arrived.*
- feared by the twelve spies, Numbers 13:22,28,33; Deuteronomy 1:26-28
- defeated by Joshua, Joshua 11:21-23

Ananias, husband of Sapphira (an-uh-NY-us)
- killed for lying to the Holy Spirit, Acts 5:1-6

Ananias, a Christian in Damascus
- helped Saul of Tarsus, Acts 9:10-19; 22:12-16

Ananias, the high priest
- at Paul's trial, Acts 23:1-5

Andrew, *a fisherman and brother of the apostle Peter.*
- chosen by Jesus to be an apostle, Mark 1:16-18; 3:13-19
- brought Peter to Jesus, John 1:40-42
- waited with the apostles in Jerusalem, Acts 1:13

angel (AIN-jel) *a heavenly being.*
- rescued Lot from Sodom, Genesis 19:1-22
- led Israel to Canaan, Exodus 23:20-23; 32:34
- announced Jesus' birth, Matthew 1:20-21; Luke 1:26-37; 2:8-15
- helped Jesus, Matthew 4:11; Luke 22:43
- helped the apostles, Acts 5:19-20; 12:6-10
- will bring judgment, Matthew 13:24-50; 24:31
- archangel, 1 Thessalonians 4:16; Jude 9
- less than Christ, Hebrews 1:4-14; 1 Peter 3:22
- rebellious angels, 2 Peter 2:4; Jude 6
- serving in heaven, Revelation 7–10

anger, *wrath.*
- of God toward people, John 3:36; Romans 1:18; 2:5-6; Colossians 3:5-6
- saved from God's anger by Christ, Romans 5:9; 1 Thessalonians 1:10; 5:9
- warnings against, Matthew 5:21-22; Ephesians 4:26,31; James 1:19-20

animal
- created by God, Genesis 1:20-25
- to be ruled by people, Genesis 1:26
- named by Adam, Genesis 2:19-20
- saved by Noah, Genesis 6:19-20
- clean, Leviticus 11:1-3,9; Deuteronomy 14:3-6
- unclean, Leviticus 11:4-8,10-12,26-44; Deuteronomy 14:7-8

Annas (AN-us) *a high priest of the Jews during Jesus' lifetime,* Luke 3:2; John 18:13
- questioned Peter and John, Acts 4:5-22

anoint (uh-NOINT) *to pour oil on.*
- to appoint a priest, Exodus 28:41; 40:13
- to appoint a king, 1 Samuel 10:1; 16:12-13; 2 Kings 9:6
- the Holy Tent, Numbers 7:1
- to heal sickness, Mark 6:13; James 5:14

Anti-Christ (AN-tee KRYST) See "enemy of Christ."

Antioch in Pisidia (AN-tee-ahk) *a small city in the country of Pisidia.*
- Paul preached there, Acts 13:14-15

Antioch in Syria, *third largest city in the Roman Empire.*
- Saul and Barnabas preached there, Acts 11:19-26
- followers first called "Christians" there, Acts 11:26
- Peter in Antioch, Galatians 2:11-12

- Paul preached there, Acts 13:14-15

Apollos (uh-POL-us) *an educated Jew from Alexandria.*
- taught by Aquila and Priscilla, Acts 18:24-28
- preached to the Corinthians, 1 Corinthians 1:12; 3:4-6
- friend of Paul, Titus 3:13

apostle (uh-POS-'l) *someone who is sent off. Jesus chose these twelve special followers and sent them to tell the Good News about him to the whole world.*
- twelve chosen by Jesus, Mark 3:14-19
- Matthias chosen, Acts 1:12-26
- Paul chosen, 1 Corinthians 15:3-11; 2 Corinthians 12:11-12
- duties and powers of, Luke 9:1-6; Acts 5:12-16; 8:18
- leaders of the church, Acts 15; 16:4; 1 Corinthians 12:28
- false apostles, 2 Corinthians 11:13; Revelation 2:2

appearance
- not to judge by, 1 Samuel 16:7; John 7:24
- deceiving, Matthew 23:27-28
- of Jesus, Isaiah 53:2; Philippians 2:7

Aquila (AK-wi-lah) *a Jewish Christian from Rome.*
- friend of Paul, Acts 18:2-3; Romans 16:3-5
- taught Apollos, Acts 18:24-28

Arabah (AIR-uh-bah) *the Hebrew word for the Jordan Valley.* See "Jordan Valley."

Arabah, Sea of, See "Dead Sea."

Aram (AIR-um) *a country northeast of Israel,* 1 Kings 11:25; 15:18; 2 Kings 5:1; Isaiah 7:1
- known as "Syria" in the New Testament, Matthew 4:24; Acts 15:23

Aramaic (AIR-uh-MAY-ik) *the language of the people in the nation of Aram.*
- common language of the Jews, 2 Kings 18:26; John 19:13,17,20; Acts 21:40

Ararat (AIR-uh-rat) *a group of mountains located in what is now Turkey and the Soviet Union.*
- Noah's boat landed there, Genesis 8:14

Araunah (a-RAW-nah) *a Jebusite who was also called Ornan.*
- sold his threshing floor to King David, 2 Samuel 24:15-25; 1 Chronicles 21:18-28

archangel (ark-AIN-jel) *the leader of God's angels,* 1 Thessalonians 4:16; Jude 9

Areopagus (AI R-ee-OP-uh-gus) *a council or group of important leaders in Athens.*
- Paul spoke there, Acts 17:16-34

argue
- the apostles argued, Mark 9:33-37; Luke 9:46-48
- avoid arguments, Philippians 2:14; 2 Timothy 2:23-26; Titus 3:9
- Michael argued with the devil, Jude 9

Aristarchus (air-i-STAR-kus) *a man from Thessalonica who often traveled with Paul,* Acts 27:2; Colossians 4:10; Philemon 24

ark, Noah's, *the huge boat that Noah built to save his family from the flood God sent to cover the earth.* See "boat."

Ark of the Agreement, *a special box made of acacia wood and gold. Inside were the stone tablets on which the Ten Commandments were written. Later, a pot of manna and Aaron's walking stick were also put into the Ark. It was to remind the people of Israel of God's promise to be with them.*
- building of, Exodus 25:10-22; 37:1-9
- crossing the Jordan River, Joshua 3:1-17
- captured by the Philistines, 1 Samuel 4–7:1
- *touched by Uzzah, 2 Samuel 6:1-8; 1 Chronicles 13*
- placed in the Temple, 2 Chronicles 5:2-10
- contents of, Hebrews 9:4-5

Ark of the Covenant, See "Ark of the Agreement."

armor
- of Saul, 1 Samuel 17:38-39; 31:9-10

- of God, Ephesians 6:10-17

arrest
- John the Baptist arrested, Matthew 14:3; Mark 6:17
- Jesus arrested, Matthew 26:50-57; Mark 14:44-50; John 18:1-14
- Peter arrested, Acts 12:1-4
- Paul arrested, Acts 28:17-20

Artaxerxes (ar-tah-ZERK-sees) *the title or name of Persian kings,* Ezra 4:7; Nehemiah 2:1
- his letter to Ezra, Ezra 7:11-26

Artemis (AR-tuh-mis) *a goddess that many Greeks worshiped,* Acts 19:23-41

Asa (AY-sah) *the third king of Judah,* 1 Kings 15:9-24; 2 Chronicles 14–16

Asaph (AY-saf) *a leader of singers when David was king,* 1 Chronicles 16:5,7; 25:1-2; 2 Chronicles 5:12
- songs of, Psalms 73–83

ascension (uh-SIN-shun) *lifted up; used to describe Jesus' return to heaven,* Acts 1:2-11; 2:32-33

ashamed
- of Jesus, Mark 8:38; Luke 9:26; 2 Timothy 1:8
- for suffering as a Christian, 1 Peter 4:16

Ashdod (ASH-dahd) *one of the five strong, walled cities of the Philistines; called Azotus in the New Testament.*
- Ark of the Agreement there, 1 Samuel 5:1-8
- later called "Azotus," Acts 8:40

Asherah (ah-SHIR-ah) *a Canaanite goddess thought to be the wife of the god Baal.*
- worshiped by Israelites, 1 Kings 14:14-15,22-23; 15:13
- worship forbidden, Exodus 34:13-14; Deuteronomy 16:21-22

Ashkelon (ASH-keh-lon) *one of the five important cities of the Philistines,* Judges 1:18; Zephaniah 2:4,7
- thirty of its men killed by Samson, Judges 14:19

Ashtoreth (ASH-toh-reth) *a goddess of the people of Assyria and Canaan. At times the Israelites forgot God and built idols to worship her.* Judges 2:13; 1 Samuel 7:3-4; 12:10
- worshiped by Solomon, 1 Kings 11:5,33

Asia (AY-zhuh) *the western part of the country now called "Turkey."*
- Paul preached there, Acts 19:10,26
- seven churches of, Revelation 1:4

assembly (a-SEM-blee) *a meeting; a group of people gathered for a purpose.*
- of the church, Hebrews 10:24-25
- conduct in, James 2:1-4

assurance (uh-SHURE-ans) *with confidence; without doubts.*
- about the gospel, 1 Thessalonians 1:5
- before God, Hebrews 10:22-23; 1 John 5:14-15
- faith as, Hebrews 11:1

Assyria (uh-SEER-ee-uh) *a powerful nation north and east of Israel.*
- enemy of Israel, 2 Kings 15:19-20; 17:3-6
- enemy of Judah, 2 Kings 18:13–19:36; Isaiah 36–37:37

Astarte (ah-STAR-tay) *another name for the goddess Ashtoreth.* See "Ashtoreth."

Athaliah (ath-uh-LY-uh) *the only woman who ruled over Judah,* 2 Kings 11; 2 Chronicles 22:10–23:21

Athens (ATH-enz) *the leading city of the country of Greece.*
- Paul preached there, Acts 17:16-34

atonement (uh-TONE-ment) *to remove or forgive sins.*
- through animal sacrifices, Exodus 30:10; Leviticus 17:11; Numbers 25:13
- *through faith in the blood of Jesus' death, Romans 3:25; Hebrews 2:17; 9:22; 10:11-12*

Atonement, Day of, See "Cleansing, Day of."

Augustus Caesar (aw-GUS-tus SEE-zer) *or Caesar Augustus, the first Roman emperor,* Luke 2:1

authority (uh-THAR-uh-tee) *power or right to control.*

- proper use of, Matthew 20:25-26; Luke 22:24-30; Titus 2:15
- respect for, Luke 20:20-26; Romans 13:1-7; 1 Timothy 2:2; 1 Peter 2:13-17; Hebrews 13:17
- Jesus' authority, Matthew 7:29; 9:6; Mark 11:27-33; Luke 5:24; John 5:19-29

B

Baal (BAY-el) *a god of the Canaanites; "Baal" was the common word for "master, lord." He was known as the son of Dagon, or the son of El, who was known as the father of the false gods.*
- worshiped by Israelites, Judges 2:10-11; Jeremiah 11:13
- Elijah defeated prophets of Baal, 1 Kings 18:1-40
- Baal worship destroyed by Jehu, 2 Kings 10:18-28

Baal-Zebub, See "Beelzebul."

Baasha (BAY-ah-shah) *the third king of Israel,* 1 Kings 15:27–16:7; 2 Chronicles 16:1-6; Jeremiah 41:9

Babel (BAY-bel) *a tower built to reach the sky,* Genesis 11:1-9

baby
- Moses as, Exodus 2:1-10
- Solomon determined mother of, 1 Kings 3:16-28
- Elizabeth's, Luke 1:39-44
- Jesus as, Luke 2:6-21
- as a symbol of new Christians, 1 Peter 2:2

Babylon (BAB-uh-lun) *city on the Euphrates River; capital of Babylonia.*
- captives in Babylon, Psalm 137:1; Jeremiah 29:10
- destruction predicted, Jeremiah 51:36-37
- as a symbol of evil, Revelation 14:8; 17:5

Babylonians (bab-e-LONE-e-unz) *people of the country Babylonia. Also called "Chaldeans."*
- capture warned by Jeremiah, Jeremiah 21; 25
- captured the people of Judah, 2 Kings 20:12-18; 24–25; Jeremiah 39:1-10
- Daniel in Babylon, Daniel 1–4
- released Israelite captives, Ezra 2

Balaam (BAY-lum) *a prophet from Midian.*
- asked by Balak to prophesy, Numbers 22–24; 2 Peter 2:15-16; Revelation 2:14
- death of, Numbers 31:8

balm, *oil from a plant used as medicine,* Genesis 37:25; Jeremiah 8:22; 51:8; Ezekiel 27:17

Baptist, John the (BAP-tist) *someone who baptizes. John, a relative of Jesus, was called this because he baptized many people.* Matthew 3:1-6
- condemned Pharisees and Sadducees, Matthew 3:7-10
- preached about Jesus, Matthew 3:11-12
- baptized Jesus, Matthew 3:13-17
- in prison, Matthew 11:1-6; Luke 7:18-23
- described by Jesus, Matthew 11:7-12; 17:10-13; Luke 7:24-28
- death of, Matthew 14:1-12; Mark 6:14-29
- baptism of, Matthew 21:25-26; Acts 10:37; 18:25; 19:3-4
- Jesus mistaken for, Matthew 16:13-14; Mark 8:27-28; Luke 9:18-19

baptism (BAP-tiz-em) *dipping or immersing.*
- by John, Matthew 3:6; Mark 1:4; Luke 3; Acts 19:3
- of Jesus, Matthew 3:13-17
- examples of, Acts 2:38-41; 8:36-38; 16:15,33
- with fire, Matthew 3:11; Luke 3:16
- with the Holy Spirit, Mark 1:5; 11:16

Barabbas (bah-RAB-us) *a robber who had murdered someone in Jerusalem. He was freed instead of Jesus.* Matthew 27:15-26; Mark 15:6-11

Barak (BAY-rak) *a leader of Israel's army when Deborah was judge,* Judges 4–5

Bar-Jesus, See "Elymas."

barley (BAR-lee) *a type of grain.*
- harvest of, Ruth 1:22; 2:17,23; 2 Samuel 21:9

- loaves of, John 6:9-13

barn
- storing in, Matthew 6:26
- rich man's, Luke 12:16-20

Barnabas (BAR-nah-bus) *an encourager who helped the apostles,* Acts 4:36; 11:23
- worked with Paul, Acts 11:26; 13–15
- influenced by hypocrites, Galatians 2:13

Bartholomew (bar-THOL-oh-mew) *one of the twelve apostles of Jesus,* Matthew 10:3; Mark 3:18; Luke 6:14; Acts 1:13

Bartimaeus (bar-teh-MAY-us) *a blind man who was healed by Jesus,* Mark 10:46-52

Baruch (BAH-rook) *a friend of the prophet Jeremiah,* Jeremiah 36

Bathsheba (bath-SHE-buh) *the mother of Solomon and wife of David,* 2 Samuel 11–12:25; 1 Kings 1–2; 22

beatitude (bee-A-ti-yood) *blessed or happy; often used for Jesus' teaching in Matthew 5:3-12; Luke 6:20-22.*

Beelzebul (bee-EL-ze-bull) *false god of the Philistines; in the New Testament it often refers to the devil.*
- name for Satan, Matthew 12:24; Mark 3:22; Luke 11:15

Beersheba (beer-SHE-buh) *the town farthest south in the land of Judah,* 2 Samuel 3:10; 2 Chronicles 30:5
- Abraham made an agreement there, Genesis 21:14-34

beg
- Jesus begged by demons, Matthew 8:28-34; Mark 5:1-13; Luke 8:26-33
- Jesus begged by people, Matthew 14:36; Mark 7:24-26,32; 8:22

beggar
- Bartimaeus, Mark 10:46-52
- Lazarus, Luke 16:19-31
- at Beautiful Gate, Acts 3:1-10
- man born blind, John 9:1-12

Bel, a false god of the Babylonians, Jeremiah 50:2; 51:44

believe
- in God, Acts 16:34; Romans 4:24
- in Jesus, Matthew 18:6; John 12:44; 14:11-12; 1 John 5:10
- in the Good News, Mark 1:15; 11:24; Acts 15:7
- rewards of believing, Matthew 21:22; John 20:31; 1 Thessalonians 2:13
- a lie, 2 Thessalonians 2:11

believers (be-LEE-vers) *the followers of Jesus,* John 3:16; Acts 4:32; 5:14; Galatians 6:10

Belshazzar (bell-SHAZ-er) *a ruler of Babylon,* Daniel 5

Belteshazzar (BELL-teh-SHAZ-er) *the Babylonian name that Nebuchadnezzar gave to Daniel,* Daniel 4:8; 5:12

Benaiah (bee-NAY-uh) *the captain of David's bodyguard,* 2 Samuel 23:20-23
- commander of Solomon's army, 1 Kings 2:34-35

Ben-Hadad (ben-HAY-dad) *two or three Syrian kings who often fought against Israel,* 1 Kings 20:1-34; 2 Kings 6:24–8:15

Benjamin (BEN-jah-min) *the youngest son of Jacob and Rachel.*
- birth of, Genesis 35:16-20
- reunited with Joseph, Genesis 42–45

Bernice (bur-NY-see) *the oldest daughter of Herod Agrippa I,* Acts 25:13–26:32

Bethany (BETH-uh-nee) *a small town about two miles from Jerusalem.*
- home of Mary, Martha, and Lazarus, John 11:1; 12:1
- home of Simon, Mark 14:3

Bethel (BETH-el) *a town about twelve miles north of Jerusalem.*
- named by Jacob, Genesis 28:10-19
- Jeroboam built idols there, 1 Kings 12:26-33

Bethesda (be-THES-da) See "Bethzatha, pool of."
Bethlehem (BETH-le-hem) *a small town five miles from Jerusalem.*
• hometown of King David, 1 Samuel 16:1,13
• birthplace of Jesus, Matthew 2:1; Luke 2:15-17
Bethsaida (beth-SAY-ih-duh) *a city in Galilee and home of Peter, Andrew, and Philip,* John 1:44; 12:21
• rejected Jesus, Matthew 11:20-21; Luke 10:13
Bethzatha, pool of (beth-ZAY-tha) *a pool in Jerusalem near the Sheep Gate.*
• Jesus healed a man there, John 5:1-18
betray (be-TRAY) *to turn against.*
• families against each other, Mark 13:12-13
• Jesus betrayed, Matthew 26:20-25; Mark 14:18-46; John 13:2-30
birds
• created by God, Genesis 1:20-21
• saved by Noah, Genesis 6:19-20; 7:1-3
• unclean, Leviticus 11:13-19
• cared for by God, Matthew 6:25-27; Luke 12:24
birth
• spiritual birth, John 1:13; 3:3-8; 1 Peter 1:23
bishop, See "elder."
bitter
• water, Exodus 15:22-25; Numbers 5:18-27; Revelation 8:11
• herbs, Exodus 12:8
bitterness (BIT-er-nes) *sorrow or pain; anger or hatred.*
• warning against, Acts 8:23; Ephesians 4:31; James 3:14
blasphemy (BLAS-feh-mee) *saying things against God or not showing respect for God.*
• examples of, 1 Timothy 1:13; Revelation 13:6
• warnings against, Matthew 12:31-32; Mark 3:28-29
• Jesus accused of, Matthew 9:3; 26:65; Mark 2:6-7; John 10:36
blessing (BLES-ing) *a gift from God; asking God's favor on.*
• promised to Abraham, Genesis 12:1-3
• Isaac blessed Jacob, Genesis 27:1-41
• from God, Acts 3:25; Romans 10:12; 15:27; Hebrews 6:7
• by Jesus, Mark 10:16; Luke 24:50; John 1:16
• by each other, Luke 6:28; 1 Corinthians 4:12; 1 Peter 3:9
blind
• the blind healed, Matthew 9:27-31; 15:30; Mark 8:22-26; John 9
• Saul struck blind, Acts 9:8-9
• spiritually blind, Matthew 23:16-26; John 9:35-41; 2 Peter 1:5-9
blood, *sometimes used to mean "death."*
• water turned into, Exodus 7:14-24
• used in the Passover, Exodus 12:13-23
• not to be eaten, Leviticus 3:17; Deuteronomy 12:16; 1 Samuel 14:31-34
• of animal sacrifices, Leviticus 1; 3; 4; Hebrews 9:12-13; 10:4
• of Christ, Matthew 26:28; Romans 5:9; Hebrews 9:14; 1 John 1:7
boasting, See "bragging."
boat, *ark.*
• built by Noah, Genesis 6:11-21
• of the apostles, Matthew 4:21-22; John 21:3-11
• used by Jesus, Matthew 8:23; 13:2; 14:13-34
body
• made of dust, Genesis 2:7; 3:19
• health of, Proverbs 3:7-8; 4:20-22; 14:30
• *attitudes toward, Matthew 6:25; Romans 6:13;* Ephesians 5:29
• warnings against misuse, Romans 8:13; 1 Corinthians 6:18-20; 1 Thessalonians 4:5
body of Christ, *sometimes means Jesus' human body; also a way of describing Christians.*

• Christ's physical body, John 2:19-21; 19:38; Acts 2:31; 1 Corinthians 11:24; 1 Timothy 3:16; 1 Peter 3:18
• the Church as Christ's spiritual body, Romans 12:5; 1 Corinthians 12:12-31; Ephesians 1:23; 4:4; 5:23
bone
• "whose bones came from my bones," Genesis 2:23
• Ezekiel's vision of, Ezekiel 37:1-14
• none of Jesus' bones to be broken, John 19:36
book, *parchments, scroll.*
• Book of the Teachings, Deuteronomy 30:10; Joshua 1:8; 2 Chronicles 34:14-32; Ezra 8
• book of life, Philippians 4:3; Revelation 3:5; 13:8; 20:12; 21:27
• "Jesus did many other miracles. . .not written in this book." John 20:30
• "the whole world would not be big enough for all the books," John 21:25
bottomless pit, *the place where the devil and his demons live,* Luke 8:31; Revelation 9:1-11; 11:7; 17:8; 20:1-3
box of Scriptures, *small leather boxes that some Jews tied to their foreheads and left arms; also called "phylacteries" or "frontlets."*
• held the Law of Moses, Deuteronomy 6:6-8
• Jesus criticized misuse of, Matthew 23:5
bragging, *boasting.*
• warnings against, Proverbs 27:1; 2 Corinthians 10:12-18; James 4:16; Jude 16
• about the Lord, 1 Corinthians 1:31; 2 Corinthians 10:17; Galatians 6:14
bread, *the most important food in New Testament times; usually made of barley or wheat.*
• to feed 5,000 people, Matthew 14:13-21; Mark 6:30-44; Luke 9:10-17; John 6:1-13
• to feed 4,000 people, Matthew 15:32-39; Mark 8:1-10
• Jesus, the bread of life, John 6:25-59
• "A person does not live by eating only bread." Matthew 4:4; Luke 4:4
• "Give us the food we need for each day." Luke 11:3
• in the Lord's Supper, Luke 22:19; Acts 20:7; 1 Corinthians 10:16; 11:17-34
bread that shows we are in God's presence, *twelve loaves of bread that were kept on the table in the Holy Tent and later in the Temple; also called "Bread of the Presence" or "showbread,"* Leviticus 24:5-9
• eaten by David, Matthew 12:3-4; Mark 2:25-26; Luke 6:4
bride, Song of Solomon 4:8-12
• belongs to the bridegroom, John 3:29
• of Christ, Revelation 21:2,9
bridegroom
• sun compared to, Psalm 19:5
• Jesus compared to, Matthew 9:15; Mark 2:19-20; Luke 5:34
• Jesus' story of, Matthew 25:1-13
• at Jesus' first miracle, John 2:9
brother, *a family member; people from the same country; or Christians.*
• physical brothers, Proverbs 18:24; Matthew 19:29; Mark 12:18-23
• Jesus' brothers, Matthew 13:55; Mark 3:31; John 2:12; 7:3; Acts 1:14; 1 Corinthians 9:5
• spiritual brothers, Romans 8:29; 12:10; 1 Timothy 6:2; Hebrews 2:11; 1 Peter 2:17
burn
• *sacrifices, Exodus 29:10-42; Leviticus 1-4*
• incense, Exodus 30:7-8; Numbers 16:40; Jeremiah 48:35; Luke 1:9
• Jericho burned by Israelites, Joshua 6:24
• idols burned by Josiah, 2 Kings 23:4-20
• jealousy like a fire, Psalm 79:5

- chaff, Matthew 3:12; Luke 3:17
- lake of burning sulfur, Revelation 21:8

burnt offerings, *a whole animal sacrificed as a gift to God.*
- rules about, Leviticus 1; 6:8-13; Numbers 28–29
- less important than obedience, 1 Samuel 15:22; Psalm 51:16-19
- less important than love, Hosea 6:6; Mark 12:32-33

bury, Matthew 8:21-22; Luke 9:59-60
- Abraham buried Sarah, Genesis 23
- Jacob not to be buried in Egypt, Genesis 47:29-30; 50:1-14
- strangers, Matthew 27:7
- in baptism, Romans 6 4

C

Caesar (SEE-zer) *a famous Roman family; used as the title of the Roman emperors.*
- Augustus, Luke 2:1
- Tiberius, Luke 3:1; 20:22; John 19:12
- Claudius, Acts 11:28; 17:7; 18:2
- Nero, Acts 25:8; 27:24; Philippians 4:22

Caesarea (SES-uh-REE-uh) *a city on the Mediterranean Sea,* Acts 10:1; 21:8; 23:32

Caesarea Philippi (SES-uh-REE-uh fih-LIP-eye) *a city at the base of Mount Hermon,* Matthew 16:13; Mark 8:27

Caiaphas (KAY-uh-fus) *the Jewish high priest from A.D. 18 to 36.*
- plotted to kill Jesus, Matthew 26:3-5; John 11:45-54
- father-in-law to Annas, John 18:13
- at Jesus' trial, Matthew 26:57-67
- questioned Peter and John, Acts 4:5-22

Cain, *the first son of Adam and Eve.*
- killed his brother Abel, Genesis 4:1-24; 1 John 3:12

Caleb (KAY-leb) *one of the twelve men Moses sent to spy out Canaan.*
- explored Canaan, Numbers 13–14
- given the city of Hebron, Joshua 14:6-15

calf
- gold idol, Exodus 32 1-20; 1 Kings 12:26-30; 2 Kings 10:28-29
- fatted, Luke 15:23,27,30

camel, Genesis 37:25; 1 Samuel 30:17; 1 Kings 10:2
- Rebekah watered Abraham's camels, Genesis 24:10-20
- "easier for a camel to go through the eye of a needle," Matthew 19:24; Mark 10:25; Luke 18:25
- "swallows a camel," Matthew 23:24

Cana (KAY-nah) *a small town near the city of Nazareth in Galilee.*
- place of Jesus' first miracle, John 2:1-11

Canaan (KAY-nun) *land God promised to the Israelites,* Leviticus 25:38; Numbers 13:2; 33:51; Psalm 105:11

Capernaum (kay-PUR-nay-um) *a city on the western shore of Lake Galilee.*
- Jesus lived there, Matthew 4:12-13
- Jesus healed there, Matthew 8:5-13; Luke 4:31-41
- rejected Jesus, Matthew 11:23-24

capital, *the top of a pillar, usually decorated with beautiful carvings.*
- in the Temple, 1 Kings 7:16-20; 2 Kings 25:17

captive
- Israelites as captives, Deuteronomy 28:41; 2 Kings 25:21; Jeremiah 30:3

cassia (CASH-ah) *a pleasant-smelling powder. Its odor is like the bark of the cinnamon plant.* Exodus 30:23-24; Psalm 45:8

census (SIN-sus) *a count of the number of people who live in an area.*
- the Israelites counted, Numbers 1:2; 26:2
- ordered by David, 1 Chronicles 21:1-2
- ordered by Augustus Caesar, Luke 2:1-3

centurion (sin-TUR-ee-un) *a Roman army officer who commanded a hundred soldiers.*
- centurion's servant healed by Jesus, Matthew 8:5-13; Luke 7:1-10
- at Jesus' death, Matthew 27:54; Mark 15:39; Luke 23:47
- Cornelius, Acts 10

Cephas (SEE-fuss) *the Aramaic word for "rock"; in Greek, "Peter." Jesus gave this name to the apostle Simon.* John 1:42

chaff (CHAF) *the husk of a head of grain. Farmers would toss the grain and chaff into the air. Since the chaff is lighter, the wind would blow it away, and the good grain would fall back to the threshing floor.*
- sinners to be destroyed like chaff, Psalms 1:4; 35:5; Matthew 3:12; Luke 3:17

Chaldeans, See "Babylonians."

change of heart and life, *repentance.*
- commanded, Matthew 3:2; Mark 1:15; Luke 13:3; Acts 3:19; 17:30
- causes of, Romans 2:4; 2 Corinthians 7:9-10
- examples of, Matthew 12:41; Luke 11:32

chariot
- Egyptians' chariots destroyed, Exodus 14:5-23
- of fire, 2 Kings 2:11; 6:17
- Ethiopian taught in a chariot, Acts 8:27-31

Chemosh (KEE-mosh) *a god of the Moabites,* Jeremiah 48:13
- worshiped by Solomon, 1 Kings 11:7

cherubim (CHAIR-uh-bim) *heavenly beings with wings and the faces of men and animals.*
- guarded the garden of Eden, Genesis 3:24
- on the Ark of the Agreement, Exodus 25:18-22; 1 Kings 6:23-28
- seen by Ezekiel, Ezekiel 10:1-20

children
- of God, John 1: 2; Romans 8:14; 1 Peter 1:14; 1 John 3:1-10
- training of, Ephesians 6:4; Colossians 3:21
- obedience of, Ephesians 6:1; Colossians 3:20; 1 Timothy 3:4
- become like, Matthew 18:3-4
- "Let the little children come to me," Matthew 19:14; Mark 10:14; Luke 18:16

chosen
- Israelites chosen by God, Deuteronomy 7:7-8; 9:4-5; Isaiah 44:1
- people chosen by God, Romans 8:33; Ephesians 1:4-5; 2 Timothy 2:10; 1 Peter 1:2; 2:9
- Jesus chosen by God, Hebrews 1:2; 1 Peter 2:4

Christ (KRYST) *anointed (or chosen) one. Jesus is the Christ, chosen by God to save people from their sins.*
- active in creation, John 1:1-3; Colossians 1:15-17; Hebrews 1:2 10
- equal with God, John 5:23; 10:30; Philippians 2:6; Colossians 2:9; Hebrews 1:3
- purpose of his death, Romans 5:6; 14:9; Hebrews 9:28; 1 Peter 3:18
- gives life, John 5:21; 6:35; 10:28; 11:25; 14:6
- as Savior, Matthew 1:21; John 12:47
- as judge, Matthew 10:32-33; 25:31-46; John 5:22; Acts 17:31
- living in Christians, John 17:23; Romans 8:10; 2 Corinthians 1:21; Ephesians 3:17
- his return, John 1:11; 1 Thessalonians 5:1-11; Hebrews 9:28; 2 Peter 3:10
- enemy of, 1 John 2:18,22; 4:3; 2 John 7

Christians (KRIS-chuns) *Christ's followers,* Acts 11:26; 26:28; 1 Peter 4:16

church
- established by Christ, Matthew 16:18
- Christ as its head, Ephesians 1:22; 5:23; Colossians 1:18

- Christ died for, Ephesians 5:25
- activities of, Acts 12:5; 1 Corinthians 14:26-40; 1 Timothy 5:16; Hebrews 10:24-25

circumcision (SIR-kum-SIH-zhun) *the cutting off of the foreskin of the male sex organ; each Jewish boy was circumcised on the eighth day after he was born; this was done as a sign of the agreement God had made with his people, the Jews.*
- commanded by God, Genesis 17; Leviticus 12:1-3
- spiritual circumcision, Philippians 3:3; Colossians 2:11

city of refuge, See "safety, city of."

Claudius (CLAW-dee-us) *the fourth Roman emperor. He ruled from A.D. 41 to 54.* Acts 11:28; 17:7; 18:2

clean, *the state of a person, animal, or action that is pleasing to God. Under the Teachings of Moses, unclean animals could not be eaten. People who were considered clean could live and serve God normally.*
- clean and unclean animals, Deuteronomy 14:1-21; Mark 7:19; Acts 10
- clean and unclean people, Leviticus 13
- spiritually clean, Ephesians 5:26; Hebrews 9:14; 2 Peter 1:9

Cleansing, Day of, *the Day of Atonement; the most special day of the year for the Israelites when the high priest could go into the Most Holy Place. Animals were sacrificed for the sins of the people as a sign that people were cleansed of their sins for a year.*
- rules about, Leviticus 23:26-32; 25:9

cloud
- Israel led by pillar of cloud, Exodus 13:21
- cloud as small as a fist, 1 Kings 18:44
- Jesus leaves and will return in clouds, Luke 21:27; Acts 1:9; 1 Thessalonians 4:17; Revelation 1:7

Colossae (koh-LAH-see) *a city in the country of Turkey,* Colossians 1:1-2

comfort, *to help ease someone's pain, grief, or trouble.*
- bad comforters, Job 16:2
- by shepherd's rod, Psalm 23:4
- from God, Isaiah 49:13; Matthew 5:4; 2 Corinthians 1:3-4
- from the Holy Spirit, John 14:16-18

commands
- to be taught, Deuteronomy 6:1-7; Matthew 5:19
- to be obeyed, Deuteronomy 8:6; Proverbs 19:16; John 15:10
- a new command, John 13:34
- to love, Galatians 5:14; 1 Timothy 1:5; 2 John 6

communion (KUH-myu-nyun) See "Lord's Supper."

complain
- Pharisees complained, Luke 5:30
- disciples complained, John 6:61
- warnings against, Philippians 2:14

concubine (KON-kyu-bine) See "slave woman."

condemn (kun-DIM) *to judge someone guilty of doing wrong,* John 3:16-18; Romans 2:1; 8:1

coney, See "rock badger."

confess
- admitting sin, Psalm 32:5; Proverbs 28:13; James 5:16; 1 John 1:9
- admitting Christ is Lord, Romans 10:9-10; Philippians 2:11; 1 Timothy 6:12; 1 John 4:2-3

confidence (KON-fuh-dens) *a feeling of assurance; trust.*
- from the Lord, 2 Thessalonians 3:4; 2 Timothy 1:7
- in Christ, Philippians 4:13
- *before God, 1 John 3:21*

conscience (KON-shunts) *a person's belief about what is right and wrong.*
- Paul's good conscience, Acts 23:1
- commanded to have a good conscience, 1 Timothy 3:9; Hebrews 9:14

- a troubled conscience, Hebrews 10:22; 1 John 3:20
- a corrupt conscience, 1 Timothy 4:2; Titus 1:15

contentment, *satisfaction.*
- Paul learned, Philippians 4:11
- with possessions, Luke 3:14; 1 Timothy 6:6; Hebrews 13:5

conversion (kon-VER-zhun) *a person's turning toward God and becoming a Christian.*
- examples of, Acts 9:1-22; 11:19-21; 1 Thessalonians 1:9

coral (KOR-al) *a type of limestone that forms in the ocean,* Job 28:18; Ezekiel 27:16

Corinth (KOR-inth) *a large seaport in the country of Greece.*
- Paul preached there, Acts 18:1-11
- Paul's letters to the church there, 1 and 2 Corinthians

Cornelius (kor-NEEL-yus) *a Roman army officer in charge of a hundred soldiers,* Acts 10

cornerstone, *the most important stone at the corner of the base of a building; Jesus is called the cornerstone of the new law.*
- Christ as the cornerstone, Ephesians 2:20; 1 Peter 2:4-8

council (KOWN-s'l) *or meeting; the highest Jewish court in the days of Jesus.*
- Jesus before the council, Matthew 26:57-68; Mark 14:53-65
- apostles before the council, Acts 4:1-22; 22:30–23:10
- Stephen before the council, Acts 6:18–7

courage
- need for, Joshua 1:6-9; Psalm 27:14; 1 Corinthians 16:13; Philippians 1:20
- examples of, Acts 4:13; 5:17-32; 20:22-24

court, courtyard, *part of a building that has walls, but no roof. The Temple had four courts:*
- the Court of the Non-Jews (Gentiles), a large open area just inside the walls of Herod's Temple, Mark 11:15-17; John 10:23; Acts 3:11
- the Court of Women, the next area, where both men and women were allowed, Mark 12:41-44
- the Court of Israel, the inner area of the Temple, where only Jewish men were allowed
- the Court of the Priests, the innermost court in the Temple, where only priests were allowed, Matthew 23:35

covenant (KUV-eh-nant) See "agreement."

covet (KUV-et) *to want strongly something that belongs to someone else.*
- forbidden by God, Exodus 20:17; Romans 13:9; Hebrews 13:5

creation
- of the world, Genesis 1–2; Job 38–41; Psalm 8; Isaiah 40:21-26; John 1:1-3; Hebrews 11:3

creator, *one who makes something out of nothing.*
- God as our Maker, Deuteronomy 32:6
- "Remember your Creator," Ecclesiastes 12:1

Crete (KREET) *an island in the Mediterranean Sea.*
- Paul visited there, Acts 27:7; Titus 1:5

cross, *two rough beams of wood nailed together; criminals were killed on crosses.*
- Jesus died on a cross, Matthew 27:31-50; Mark 15:20-37; Luke 23:26-46; John 19:16-30
- importance of, 1 Corinthians 1:18; 2:2; Galatians 6:14; Ephesians 2:16; Colossians 2:13-14
- as a symbol of death to oneself, Matthew 10:38; Luke 9:23; Romans 6:6; Galatians 5:24

crown, *a special band worn around the head.*
- a king's crown, Psalm 21:2-3; Song of Solomon 3:11; Revelation 12:3
- of thorns, Matthew 27:29; Mark 15:17; John 19:2
- of victory, 1 Corinthians 9:25; 2 Timothy 4:8; 1 Peter 5:4

crucifixion (kroo-suh-FIK-shun) *to be killed on a cross. See "cross."*

cubit (KU-bit) *a measurement in Bible times; about eighteen inches,* Revelation 21:17
cud, *an animal's food that is chewed slightly, swallowed, brought up, then chewed more completely a second time,* Leviticus 11; Deuteronomy 14
cup
 • of the king of Egypt, Genesis 40:11
 • of Joseph, Genesis 44: -17
 • of Lord's Supper, Matthew 26:27-29; Mark 14:22-25; Luke 22:17-20; 1 Corinthians 11:25-29
 • of anger, Isaiah 51:17-23
 • of water, Matthew 10:42; Mark 9:41
cupbearer, *the officer who tasted and served the king his wine.*
 • to the king of Egypt, Genesis 40
 • Nehemiah, cupbearer to Artaxerxes, Nehemiah 1:11
curse
 • from God, Deuteronomy 11:26-29; John 7:49; Galatians 3:10-13
 • forbidden to people, Matthew 15:4; Romans 12:14; James 3:9-10
 • response to, Luke 6:28 1 Corinthians 4:12
curtain
 • of the Holy Tent, Exodus 26:1-2; 36:9
 • of the Temple, Matthew 27:51; Mark 15:38; Luke 23:45
Cush, *a country in Africa,* Genesis 2:13; Psalm 68:31; Isaiah 18; 20
Cush, grandson of Noah, Genesis 10
Cyprus (SY-prus) *an island in the Mediterranean Sea,* Acts 11:19-20; 13:4; 15:39
Cyrene (sy-REE-nee) *a city in North Africa,* Acts 2:10; 6:9
 • Simon of, Matthew 27:32; Mark 15:21; Luke 23:26
Cyrus (SY-rus) *a king of Persia,* Daniel 1:21
 • sent captives home, Ezra 1; 6
 • chosen by God, Isaiah 44:28–45:13

D

Dagon (DAY-gon) *a false god of the Philistines,* Judges 16:23; 1 Samuel 5:2-7; 1 Chronicles 10:10
Damascus (duh-MAS-kus) *a city forty miles east of Lake Galilee.*
 • a chief city of Syria, 1 Kings 15:18; 2 Chronicles 24:23
 • condemned by Amos, Amos 1:3,5
 • Paul converted there, Acts 9:1-22
Dan, a city
 • Israel's most northern city, Judges 20:1; 2 Samuel 16:11
Dan, son of Jacob, Genesis 30:6; 49:16-17; Joshua 19:40-48
Daniel (DAN-yel) *a Hebrew captive taken to Babylon as a young man.*
 • taken to Babylon, Daniel 1:1-6
 • became king's servant, Daniel 1:7-21
 • explained Nebuchadnezzar's dreams, Daniel 2; 4
 • read the writing on the wall, Daniel 5
 • thrown into lions' den, Daniel 6
 • his visions, Daniel 7; 8; 10
 • a prophet, Matthew 24:15
Darius Hystaspes (dah-RYE-us his-TAHS-peez) *a ruler of Persia who allowed the Jews to finish rebuilding the Temple,* Ezra 5–6
Darius the Mede, *the king of Persia who made Daniel an important ruler under him,* Daniel 5:31–6:28; Haggai 1:1; Zechariah 1:1
darkness, *having no light; a symbol of evil.*
 • before creation, Genesis 1:2
 • as a plague, Exodus 10:21-23
 • at Jesus' death, Matthew 27:45; Mark 15:33; Luke 23:44-45
 • spiritual, John 1:5; Romans 13:12; Colossians 1:13
 • as punishment, Matthew 8:12; 2 Peter 2:17; Jude 6; 13
David (DAY-vid) *Israel's greatest king.*
 • son of Jesse, 1 Samuel 16:13-23

 • played harp for Saul, 1 Samuel 16:14-23
 • killed Goliath, 1 Samuel 17
 • friend of Jonathan, 1 Samuel 18:1-4; 19:1-7; 20
 • chased by Saul, 1 Samuel 18–19; 23:7-29
 • protected Saul, 1 Samuel 24; 26
 • became king, 2 Samuel 2:1-7; 5:1-14
 • married Bathsheba, 2 Samuel 11–12:25
 • reign of, 2 Samuel 5–1 Kings 1
 • not allowed to build the Temple, 2 Samuel 7:1-17
 • death of, 1 Kings 2:1-11
 • Jesus as son of David, Matthew 22:42-45; Luke 1:27; 20:41-44
deacon (DEE-kun) *a person chosen to serve the church in special ways,* Philippians 1:1; 1 Timothy 3:8-13
Dead Sea, *large lake at the south end of the Jordan River. Several small streams flow into it, but it has no outlet. It is so salty that nothing lives in it. It is also called the "Sea of Arabah," the "Salt Sea," and the "Eastern Sea."* Genesis 14:3; Numbers 34:3,12; Joshua 3:16
deaf, *unable or unwilling to hear.*
 • healed, Matthew 11:5; Luke 7:22
 • and dumb spirit, Mark 9:25
death
 • a result of sin, Genesis 2:16-17; Romans 5:12; 6:23; 1 Corinthians 15:21
 • Christ's victory over, 1 Corinthians 15:24-26,54-57; 2 Timothy 1:10; Hebrews 2:14; Revelation 1:18
 • spiritual death, Ephesians 2:1; Colossians 2:13
Deborah (DEB-oh-rah) *the only woman judge over Israel,* Judges 4–5
Decapolis (dee-KAP-oh-lis) *ten towns in an area southeast of Lake Galilee,* Matthew 4:25; Mark 5:20; 7:31
Delilah (dee-LYE-luh) *an evil Philistine woman whom Samson loved,* Judges 16:4-20
Demas (DEE-mus) *a Christian who helped the apostle Paul when Paul was in prison.*
 • worked with Paul, Colossians 4:14; Philemon 24
 • left Paul, 2 Timothy 4:10
Demetrius (deh-MEE-tree-us) *a silver worker in Ephesus,* Acts 19:23-27,38
demon, *an evil spirit from the devil. Sometimes demons lived in people, but Jesus could force them out.*
 • people possessed by, Matthew 8:28-32; 9:32-33; Mark 7:24-30; 9:17-29
 • Jesus accused of demon possession, Mark 3:22; John 7:20; 8:48; 10:20-21
 • demons recognized Jesus, Mark 1:23-26; 3:11-12; 5:7-8; Acts 19:15; James 2:19
deny (di-NY) *refusing to believe the truth.*
 • denying Christ, Matthew 10:32-33; 2 Timothy 2:12; 1 John 2:22-23
 • Peter denied Christ, Matthew 26:34-35,69-75
descendants (de-SEN-dants) *family members who are born to a person or his children; grandchildren, great-grandchildren, great-great-grandchildren and so on,* Genesis 13:14-16; 15:12-16
devil (DEV-'l) *Satan; a spirit and the enemy of God and humans.*
 • Jesus tempted by, Matthew 4:1-11; Luke 4:1-13
 • children of, John 8:41-44; Acts 13:10; 1 John 3:7-10
 • people to oppose, Ephesians 4:27; 6:11; James 4:7
Didymus (DID-ee-mus) *another name for Thomas, one of Jesus' apostles,* John 11:16; 20:24; 21:2
disciple (dih-SYE-p'l) See "follower."
disease
 • a result of sin, Exodus 15:26; Deuteronomy 7:15; 28:60-61
 • healed by Jesus, Matthew 4:23-24; 15:30-31; 21:14; Luke 7:21
 • healed by apostles, Acts 5:12-16; 9:32-35; 14:8-10; 19:11-12; 28:8-9

disobedience
- brought sin, Romans 5:19
- to be punished, 2 Corinthians 10:6; Hebrews 4:11

divide
- heavens and earth, Genesis 1:6-8
- Red Sea, Exodus 14:16,21
- family against itself, Matthew 12:25; Mark 3:25; Luke 11:17

divorce
- teachings about, Deuteronomy 22:13-19,28-29; 24:1-4; Matthew 5:31-32; 19:1-12; 1 Corinthians 7:10-16

dog
- drinking water like a dog, Judges 7:5-6
- returns to its vomit, Proverbs 26:11; 2 Peter 2:22
- licked Ahab's blood, 1 Kings 22:38
- licked Lazarus's sores, Luke 16:20-21

door
- Jesus as the door, John 10:1
- "Knock, and the door will open," Luke 11:9-10
- "I stand at the door and knock." Revelation 3:20

donkey
- Balaam's, Numbers 22:21-30
- jawbone of, Judges 15:15-17
- ridden by Jesus, Matthew 21:1-7

Dorcas (DOR-kus) *Tabitha; a Christian woman known for helping the poor.*
- raised from the dead, Acts 9:36-43

dove, *a small bird similar to a pigeon; often a symbol for love, peace, and the Holy Spirit.*
- sent out by Noah, Genesis 8:8-12
- form taken by the Spirit of God, Matthew 3:16; Mark 1:10
- sellers of, John 2:14-16

dreams
- Joseph's, Genesis 37:1-11
- the king of Egypt's, Genesis 41:1-36
- Nebuchadnezzar's, Daniel 2; 4
- angel appeared to Joseph, Matthew 1:20-21; 2:13,19
- "your old men will dream dreams," Acts 2:17

drunkenness
- Noah became drunk, Genesis 9:20-23
- warnings against, Romans 13:13; 1 Corinthians 6:10; Ephesians 5:18; 1 Peter 4:3

E

eagle
- "to rise up as an eagle," Isaiah 40:31

earth
- creation of, Genesis 1:9-10; Jeremiah 51:15
- belongs to God, Exodus 19:5; Psalm 24:1

earthquake
- experienced by Elijah, 1 Kings 19:11-12
- at the death of Jesus, Matthew 27:51-54
- at Jesus' resurrection, Matthew 28:2
- experienced by Paul and Silas, Acts 16:25-26

Ebal (EE-buhl) *a mountain in Samaria next to Mount Gerizim.*
- place to announce curses, Deuteronomy 11:29; 27:12-13; Joshua 8:30-35

Eden, garden of (EE-den) *the home God created for Adam and Eve,* Genesis 2:8–3:24; Ezekiel 36:35; Joel 2:3

Edom (EE-dum) *Esau; the land where Esau's descendants lived.*
- the land of Esau, Genesis 36:8-9
- refused to let Israelites pass through, Numbers 20:14-21; Judges 11:17-18
- broke away from Judah, 2 Kings 8:20-22
- to be punished, Jeremiah 49:7-22; Ezekiel 25:12-14; Obadiah

education
- of Moses, Acts 7:22
- of children, Deuteronomy 6:1-7

- brings wisdom, Proverbs 8:33; 22:6

Eglon (EGG-lon) *a king of Moab,* Judges 3:12-25

Egypt (EE-jipt) *a country in the northeast part of Africa.*
- Joseph there, Genesis 39–50
- Israelites there, Genesis 46:5-34; Exodus 1; Acts 7:9-38
- Israelites left, Exodus 12:31-51
- Jesus there, Matthew 2:13-15

Ehud (EE-hud) *the second judge of Israel,* Judges 3:12-30

elder (EL-der) *older men who led God's people; appointed leaders in the church.*
- leaders of the Jews, Numbers 11:16-25; Deuteronomy 19:11-12; Matthew 21:23; Acts 4:5-7
- leaders of the church, Acts 11:30; 14:23; 15:2; 16:4
- duties and qualities, Acts 20:28; 1 Timothy 3:1-7; Titus 1:6-9; 1 Peter 5:1-3

Eleazar (el-ee-A-zar) *son of Aaron.*
- birth of, Exodus 6:23-25
- Moses became angry with, Leviticus 10:16-20
- a high priest, Numbers 3:32
- divided the promised land, Numbers 34:17

election, *process of selecting.* See "chosen."

Eli (EE-lye) *a priest and the next-to-last judge of Israel.*
- trained Samuel, 1 Samuel 1:9-28; 2:11; 3
- didn't discipline his sons, 1 Samuel 2:12-36
- death of, 1 Samuel 4:1-18

Elihu (ee-LYE-hew) *the fourth of Job's friends to try to explain Job's troubles,* Job 32–37

Elijah (ee-LIE-juh) *a prophet who spoke for God.*
- fed by ravens, 1 Kings 17:1-6
- brought boy to life, 1 Kings 17:7-24
- against prophets of Baal, 1 Kings 18:1-40
- condemned Ahab, 1 Kings 21:17-29
- taken to heaven, 2 Kings 2:1-12
- appeared with Jesus, Matthew 17:1-13; Mark 9:2-13; Luke 9:28-36

Elisha (ee-LYE-shuh) *the prophet who took Elijah's place as God's messenger.*
- received Elijah's spirit, 2 Kings 2:9-14
- helped a Shunammite woman, 2 Kings 4:1-36
- miracles of, 2 Kings 2:19-22; 4:38-44; 6:1-7
- healed Naaman, 2 Kings 5
- death of, 2 Kings 13:14-20

Elizabeth (ee-LIZ-uh-beth) *the wife of Zechariah, a priest.*
- mother of John the Baptist, Luke 1:5-25,57-66
- visited by Mary, Luke 1:39-45

Elkanah (el-KAY-nuh) *the father of Samuel,* 1 Samuel 1–2:11

Elymas (EL-ih-mus) *Bar-Jesus; magician in the city of Paphos in Cyprus,* Acts 13:4-12

Emmaus (ee-MAY-us) *a town seven miles from Jerusalem.*
- Jesus appeared to disciples near there, Luke 24:13-39

encourage
- encouragement from God, Romans 15:4-5
- Christians to encourage each other, 1 Thessalonians 5:14; 2 Timothy 4:2; Hebrews 3:13; 10:24-25
- examples of encouragement, Acts 11:23; 13:15; 15:31-32

endurance, See "patience."

enemy
- attitude toward, Exodus 23:4-5; Matthew 5:43-48; Luke 6:27-36; Romans 12:20
- God's enemies, Romans 5:10; Philippians 3:18-19; James 4:4

enemy of Christ, *the anti-Christ,* 1 John 2:18,22; 4:3; 2 John 7

Enoch (E-nuk) *a man who walked with God,* Genesis 5:21-24; Hebrews 11:5

enrollment, See "census."

envy, See "jealousy."

Epaphras (EP-ah-fruhs) *a Christian who started the church at Colossae,* Colossians 1:7-8; 4:12-13; Philemon 23

Epaphroditus (ee-PAF-ro-DYE-tus) *a Christian in the church at Philippi,* Philippians 2:25-30; 4:18

ephah (EE-fah) *a common measurement for dry materials, about twenty quarts,* Exodus 16:36

Ephesus [EF-eh-sus] *the capital city in the Roman state of Asia.*
• Paul's work there, Acts 18:18-20; 1 Corinthians 16:8-9
• church there, Ephesians 1:1; Revelation 2:1-7

ephod (EE-ahd) See "vest, holy."

Ephraim (EE-frah-im) *Joseph's younger son,* Genesis 41:50-52; 48:8-20
• descendants of, Numbers 26:35; Joshua 16:5-10

equality (ee-KWAHL-eh-tee) *being identical in value.*
• in death, Ecclesiastes 3:19-20
• of Jewish and non-Jewish people, Romans 10:12
• in Christ, Galatians 3:26-28

Esau (EE-saw) See "Edom."

Esther (ES-ter) *a Jewish girl who became the wife of Ahasuerus, King of Persia,* Esther 1–10
• became queen, Esther 1–2:18
• learned of the plan to kill the Jews, Esther 3–4
• saved the Jews, Esther 5–8

eternal, See "forever."

eternal life, *the new kind of life promised to those who follow Jesus.*
• conditions for, Mark 10:17-31; John 3:14-15; 12:25; 17:3; Galatians 6:7-8
• source of, John 6:27-29; 10:28; Titus 1:2; 1 John 5:11-12

Ethiopia, *earlier called "Cush."* See "Cush."

eunuch (YOU-nuk) *a man who cannot have sexual relations. In Bible times, eunuchs were often high officers in royal palaces or armies.* 2 Kings 9:32; Esther 2:3; Isaiah 56:3-5; Acts 8:26-40

Euphrates (you-FRAY-teez) *a long, important river in Bible lands.*
• in the garden of Eden, Genesis 2:10-14
• a boundary, Genesis 15:18; 1 Kings 4:21; 2 Kings 24:7

Eutychus (YOU-ti-cus) *a young man in the city of Troas who was brought back to life,* Acts 20:7-12

evangelist (ee-VAN-juh-list) *someone who tells the Good News.*
• Philip, the evangelist, Acts 21:8
• as a gift from Christ, Ephesians 4:11

Eve (EEV) *the first woman.*
• created by God, Genesis 2:18-25
• tricked by Satan, Genesis 3; 2 Corinthians 11:3; 1 Timothy 2:13-14

everlasting, *living forever; eternal.*
• God, Genesis 21:33; Nehemiah 9:5; Isaiah 40:28
• Christ, Isaiah 9:6
• kingdom, Daniel 4:3; 2 Peter 1:11
• fire, Matthew 18:8,25,41
• gospel, Revelation 14:6

evil
• warnings against, Amos 5:15; Romans 12:9; 1 Thessalonians 5:22
• to be punished, Proverbs 24:20; Isaiah 13:11

evil spirit, See "demon."

eye
• "eye for eye," Exodus 21:23-24; Matthew 5:38
• wood in, Matthew 7:3-5; Luke 6:41-42

eyewitness, *one who sees an occurrence and reports on it.*
• of Jesus' life, Luke 1:2; 2 Peter 1:16; 1 John 1:1

Ezekiel (ee-ZEEK-yel) *a prophet during the time the Jews were captured by the Babylonians,* Ezekiel 1:3
• his vision of dry bones, Ezekiel 37:1-14

Ezra (EZ-ra) *the leader of a group of Israelites who were allowed to return to Jerusalem from Babylon,* Ezra 7–10; Nehemiah 8

F

faith (FAYTH) *belief and trust.*
• definition of, Hebrews 11:1

• sources of, Romans 1:20; 10:17
• examples of, Matthew 8:5-10; 15:21-28; Hebrews 11
• power of, Matthew 17:20-21; Ephesians 6:16
• made right with God by, Romans 4:3; 5:1; Philippians 3:9
• salvation by, Mark 16:15-16; John 5:24; 20:31; Romans 10:9; Galatians 2:16
• blessings by, Galatians 3:1-14; Ephesians 3:12; 1 Peter 1:5
• continue in, 2 Corinthians 13:5; Colossians 1:23; 1 Timothy 1:19; 2 Timothy 2:22
• lack of, Matthew 8:26; 14:31; 16:8

faithful (FAYTH-ful) *honest, loyal, true.*
• God is faithful, Deuteronomy 32:3-4; Isaiah 49:7; 2 Timothy 2:13; Hebrews 3:6; Revelation 19:11
• God's people must be faithful, Matthew 25:21; Revelation 2:10; 14:12; 17:14

fall, *sometimes used to describe the first sin.*
• Adam and Eve sinned, Genesis 3

false
• gods, Exodus 20:3; Deuteronomy 4:28; 1 Chronicles 16:26
• prophets, Deuteronomy 13:1-11; 18:22; Jeremiah 14:13-16; Matthew 7:15
• Christs, Matthew 24:24; Mark 13:22
• apostles, 2 Corinthians 11:13
• brothers, Galatians 2:4
• teachers, 2 Peter 2:1

family
• of believers, Galatians 6:10; Hebrews 2:11; 1 Peter 4:17

famine (FAM-un) *a time of hunger when there is very little food.*
• in Egypt, Genesis 41:30-31,53-57
• in Moab, Ruth 1:1
• in Israel, 1 Kings 17:1
• in Jerusalem during Claudius's rule, Acts 11:27-28

fasting (FAST-ing) *giving up food for a while.*
• to show sorrow, 1 Samuel 1:11-12; 2 Samuel 12:15-22
• of Jesus, Matthew 4:1-2
• how to fast, Matthew 6:16-18
• combined with prayer, Ezra 8:23; Luke 5:33; Acts 13:1-3

father
• to be honored, Exodus 20:12; Ephesians 6:2
• commands to, Colossians 3:21
• God as Father, Matthew 6:9; 23:9; 2 Corinthians 6:18; Galatians 4:6; Hebrews 12:4-11

fear, *a feeling of being afraid, or one of deep respect.*
• of God, Matthew 10:26-31; Luke 23:40
• overcoming, 2 Timothy 1:7; Hebrews 13:6; 1 John 4:18
• "your salvation. . .with fear and trembling," Philippians 2:12

feast (FEEST) *a special meal and celebration for a certain purpose.*
• Feast of Dedication, an eight-day celebration for the Jews that showed they were thankful that the Temple had been cleansed again, John 10:22
• Feast of Harvest, see "Feast of Weeks."
• Feast of Purim (PURE-rim) reminded the Israelites of how they were saved from death during the time of Queen Esther, Esther 9:18-32
• Feast of Shelters, "Feast of Booths" or "Feast of Tents"; reminded the Israelites of how God had taken care of them when they left Egypt and lived in tents in the wilderness, Exodus 23:16; Deuteronomy 16:13-17
• Feast of Unleavened Bread, or "Passover"; reminded the Israelites how God brought them out of Egyptian slavery, Exodus 12:1-30; Numbers 28:16-25; Deuteronomy 16:1-8
• Feast of Weeks, or "Pentecost," the "Feast of Harvest," or the "Day of Firstfruits"; a feast of thanksgiving for the summer harvest, Exodus 34:22; Leviticus 23:15-22; Numbers 28:26-31

Felix (FEE-lix) *the Roman governor of Judea from A.D. 52 to 54.*
• put Paul on trial, Acts 23:23-24; 24
fellowship (FEL-o-ship) *sharing friendship and love with others.*
• with Christ, Matthew 18:20; 1 Corinthians 1:9; 1 John 1:3
• with the Holy Spirit, 2 Corinthians 13:14; Philippians 2:1
• with believers, Acts 2:42; 1 John 1:7
Festus (FES-tus) *governor of Judea after Felix.*
• put Paul on trial, Acts 25–26
fighting
• against evil, 2 Corinthians 10:3-6; Ephesians 6:12
• "fight the good fight," 1 Timothy 1:18
• "I have fought the good fight." 2 Timothy 4:7
fire, *used by God as a sign of his presence and power.*
• the burning bush, Exodus 3:1-6
• pillar of, Exodus 13:21-22
• chariot of, 2 Kings 2:11
• wrong kind of, Numbers 26:61
• fiery furnace, Daniel 3:25
• baptism of, Matthew 3:11
• of punishment, Matthew 5:22; 13:41-42; Mark 9:43; 2 Thessalonians 1:8; Hebrews 10:27
• everything destroyed by fire, 2 Peter 3:10
• evidence of the Holy Spirit, Acts 2:3
firstborn (FIRST-born) *the oldest child in a family; the firstborn son in a Jewish family received a double share of his father's wealth and became the leader of the family when his father died.*
• Esau sold his rights, Genesis 25:27-34
• Israelites as God's firstborn, Exodus 4:22; Jeremiah 31:9
• death of, Exodus 11:1-8
• given to God, Exodus 13:1-16
firstfruits (FIRST-fruits) *the first and best crops and animals the Israelites raised and gave to God at harvest time,* Exodus 34:26; Numbers 28:26; Deuteronomy 18:3-4
fish
• clean and unclean, Deuteronomy 14:9-10
• used in miracles, Matthew 14:17; Luke 5:1-7; John 21:1-13
flax (FLAKS) *a plant used to make clothing and ropes,* Exodus 9:31; Isaiah 19:9
• used by Rahab, Joshua 2:6
flood, Genesis 6:9–8; Matthew 24:37-39; 2 Peter 3:5-6
follower (FAHL-o-wer) *a person who is learning from someone else; a "disciple."*
• of John, Matthew 9:14; 11:2; Mark 2:18
• of Christ, Matthew 11:1; 28:18-20; John 19:38; Acts 6:1-7; 11:26
fool, *someone who is not wise,* Proverbs 10:8-23; 17:7-28; 26:1-12
• examples of, Matthew 7:24-27; 25:1-13
• rejects God, Psalms 14:1; 53:1; Romans 1:20-23
footwashing, *done as an act of hospitality in Bible times because people wore sandals.*
• examples of, 1 Samuel 25:41; Luke 7:44; John 13:1-17
forever
• God's love continues forever, 1 Chronicles 16:34; Psalm 136
• praise God forever, Psalm 44:8; Romans 9:5
• be with God forever, 1 Thessalonians 4:17; 1 John 2:17
• Jesus lives forever, Hebrews 7:24
• "word of the Lord will live forever," 1 Peter 1:25
forgiveness
• *of others, Matthew 6:14-15; 18:21-35; Mark 11:25;* Luke 17:3-4
• by God, Luke 24:47-48; Acts 10:43; Ephesians 1:7; 1 John 1:9
• not given, Matthew 12:31-32; Mark 3:28-29; Luke 12:10; John 20:19-23

• "Father, forgive them," Luke 23:34
fornication (for-ni-KAY-shun) *having sexual relations with someone to whom you are not married.* See "adultery."
fountain, Proverbs 10:11; 13:14; 14:27; 16:22
frankincense (FRANK-in-senz) *a very expensive, sweet smelling perfume,* Exodus 30:34; Revelation 18:13
• given to Jesus, Matthew 2:11
freedom, *having liberty; not being a slave.*
• given to Jesus, Matthew 2:11
• in Christ, 2 Corinthians 3:17; Galatians 5:1; Hebrews 2:15
• from sin, Romans 6; 8:2; Hebrews 9:15
• to be used wisely, 1 Corinthians 8:9; Galatians 5:13; 1 Peter 2:16
• "truth will make you free," John 8:32
friend
• characteristics of, Proverbs 17:17; 18:24
• of Jesus, John 15:13-15
• Abraham, as a friend of God, James 2:23
frontlet, See "box of Scriptures."
fruit, *often used to mean "result."*
• spiritual, Matthew 7:15-20; John 15:1-17; Colossians 1:10
• of the Spirit, Galatians 5:22
fulfill (full-FILL) *to give the full meaning or to cause something to come true.*
• prophecy fulfilled, Matthew 2:14-15,17-18; Luke 4:16-21; 24:44-46; John 19:24
furnace
• Shadrach, Meshach, and Abednego thrown into, Daniel 3
• hell compared to, Matthew 13:42

G

Gabriel (GAY-bree-el) *an angel of God.*
• seen in a vision, Daniel 8:16; 9:21-27
• announced Jesus' birth, Luke 1:8-20,26-38
Gad, *a prophet*
• David's seer, 1 Samuel 22:5; 2 Samuel 24:11-19
Gad, son of Jacob
• birth of, Genesis 30:9-11
• land of, Deuteronomy 33:20-21; Joshua 22:1-4
• tribe of, Numbers 26:15
Gadarenes (gad-uh-REENZ) *people who lived in Gadara, southeast of Lake Galilee,* Matthew 8:28-34
Galatia (guh-LAY-shuh) *a district of Asia,* Acts 16:6; 18:23; Galatians 1:2; 1 Corinthians 16:1
Galilee (GAL-i-lee) *the country between the Jordan River and the Mediterranean Sea,* 2 Kings 15:29; Matthew 4:23; 21:11; John 7:1
Galilee, Lake (GAL-i-lee) *or "Sea of Galilee," "Sea of Kinnereth," "Lake of Gennesaret," "Sea of Tiberias"; a lake thirteen miles long and eight miles wide.*
• Jesus preached there, Matthew 4:12-22; 8:23-27; John 6:1-2,16-21
Gallio (GAL-ee-oh) *a Roman governor in the country of Achaia.*
• refused to punish Paul, Acts 18:12-17
Gamaliel (guh-MAY-lee-el) *a Pharisee and Jewish teacher of the Law of Moses.*
• prevented deaths of Peter and John, Acts 5:17-40
• Paul's teacher, Acts 22:1-3
gate
• Samson removed, Judges 16:3
• narrow, Matthew 7:13-14
• *of heaven, Revelation 21:21*
Gath, *one of the Philistines' five strong cities,* Joshua 13:3; 1 Samuel 21:10-12
• captured Ark taken there, 1 Samuel 5:1-10
• home of Goliath, 1 Samuel 17:4
Gaza (GAY-zuh) *one of the Philistines' five strong cities,*

Joshua 13:3; Judges 1:18; 1 Samuel 6:17; Amos 1:6; Acts 8:26
- Samson in prison there, Judges 16

gazelle (gah-ZEL) *an animal of the antelope family; known for its beauty and speed,* Deuteronomy 12:15; 1 Chronicles 12:8

Gedaliah (ged-uh-LYE-uh) *made governor of Judah by Nebuchadnezzar after capturing Jerusalem,* 2 Kings 25:22-26; Jeremiah 39:14–41:18

Gehazi (geh-HAY-zye) *a servant of the prophet Elisha.*
- and the Shunammite woman, 2 Kings 4:8-37
- and Naaman, 2 Kings 5:1-27

Gehenna, See "Hinnom."

genealogy (jee-nee-AHL-o-jee) *a list of the descendants in a family.*
- of Jesus, Matthew 1:1-17; Luke 3:23-38

generosity (jen-uh-RAHS-et-ee) *unselfishness.*
- shown to Ruth, Ruth 2:14-16
- to the needy, Nehemiah 8:10
- rewarded, Proverbs 11:25; Matthew 7:11

Gennesaret, Lake of, See "Galilee, Lake."

Gentiles (JEN-tiles) *anyone not Jewish.*
- received the Good News, Acts 10:44-45; 11:18; Romans 11:11-15; Ephesians 3:6-8
- conflict with the Jews, Acts 15:5-11; Galatians 2:11-14

Gerasenes (GER-un-seenz) or *"Gadarenes."* See "Gadarenes."

Gerizim (GER-i-zim) *a mountain next to Mount Ebal about thirty miles north of Jerusalem.*
- blessings announced from there, Deuteronomy 11:29; 27:12; Joshua 8:33

Gethsemane (geth-SEM-uh-nee) *a garden of olive trees just outside Jerusalem.*
- Jesus arrested there, Matthew 26:36-56; Mark 14:32-50

Gibeah (GIB-ee-uh) *a city about three miles north of Jerusalem.* Judges 19:12–20:43; 1 Samuel 10:26

Gibeon (GIB-ee-uhn) *a town about six miles northwest of Jerusalem.*
- Joshua defeated Amorites there, Joshua 9–10

Gideon (GID-ee-uhn) *the judge who led Israel to defeat the Midianites,* Judges 6:1–8:35
- angel appeared to, Judges 6:11-24
- destroyed Baal idol, Judges 6:25-32
- defeated Midianites, Judges 6:33–8:21
- the sign of the fleece, Judges 6:36-40
- built an idol, Judges 8:22-27
- death of, Judges 8:28-32
- hero of faith, Hebrews 11:32-34

gifts, *talents or abilities.*
- spiritual, Romans 12:6-8; 1 Corinthians 7:7; 12; 14:1-25; Ephesians 4:7

Gihon (GYE-hohn) *a spring outside the walls of Jerusalem,* 1 Kings 1:38-39; 2 Chronicles 32:30; 33:14

Gilead (GIL-ee-ad) *the area that Israel owned east of the Jordan River,* Numbers 32; Deuteronomy 3:10-16

Gilgal (GIL-gal) *the first place the Israelites camped after entering the promised land,* Joshua 4:19–5:12

gittith (GIT-tith) *probably a musical word and a musical instrument,* Psalms 3; 81; 84

giving
- examples of generous giving, Mark 12:43; Acts 10:2; 11:29-30; 2 Corinthians 8:3-5
- proper attitude toward, Matthew 6:3-4; Romans 12:8; 1 Corinthians 13:3; 2 Corinthians 9:7

gleaning (GLEEN-ing) *to gather grain left in the field after harvest,* Ruth 2

glory, *visible sign of God's greatness.*
- appeared in a cloud, Exodus 16:10; 24:16-17
- seen by Moses, Exodus 33:18-23
- "The heavens tell the glory of God," Psalm 19:1
- seen by Ezekiel, Ezekiel 1:26-28; 3:23; 8:4
- at Jesus' birth, Luke 2:8-14

- of Jesus, Luke 9:28-32
- seen by Stephen, Acts 7:55
- in the temple in heaven, Revelation 15:8

gluttony (GLUH-tun-ee) *eating too much.*
- warnings against, Deuteronomy 21:20; Proverbs 23:20-21
- Jesus accused of, Matthew 11:19; Luke 7:34

goat
- for a sin offering, Leviticus 9:3
- divided from sheep, Matthew 25:32-33
- blood of, Hebrews 9:12-13; 10:4

God, *the One who made the world and everything in it.* See also "glory."
- the creator, Genesis 1; Acts 17:24; Romans 1:25
- nearness of, Acts 17:27-28; James 4:8
- goodness of, Matthew 19:17; Acts 14:17; Romans 2:4; 1 John 4:7-11
- eternal nature of, Psalm 102:24-28; 1 Timothy 1:17; 6:16
- names of, Exodus 3:13-14; 1 Timothy 6:15; Hebrews 12:9; James 1:17; 5:4
- power of, Job 9:4-9; Isaiah 40:12-31; Matthew 19:26
- mercy of, Exodus 20:6; Numbers 14:18; Ephesians 2:4
- justice of, Psalm 67:4; Acts 17:31; Romans 2:2

golden calf, *an idol made to worship false gods.*
- made by Aaron, Exodus 32:1-24
- made by Jeroboam, 1 Kings 12:26-33

golden rule, *a name often used for Jesus' command: "Do to others what you want them to do to you,"* Matthew 7:12; Luke 6:31

Golgotha (GOL-guh-thuh) *Calvary; the hill where Jesus was crucified,* Matthew 27:33; Mark 15:22; John 19:17

Goliath (go-LYE-eth) *the giant from Gath whom David killed,* 1 Samuel 17

Gomorrah (goh-MOR-ruh) *an evil city near Sodom.*
- destroyed by God, Genesis 18:17–19:29; Matthew 10:11-15; 2 Peter 2:6

Good News, *also called the "gospel." Jesus died on the cross, was buried, and came back to life so people can be saved.* Mark 1:1; Acts 5:42; 13:26-39
- power of, Romans 1:16-17; Colossians 1:5-6; 1 Corinthians 15:2
- preached by the apostles, Luke 9:6; Acts 8:25; Philippians 1:5,12-14

Goshen (GO-shen) *an area in the Nile delta of Egypt.*
- home for Joseph's family, Genesis 45:9-10; 47:1-6,27

gospel (GOS-p'l) *"good news." The first four books of the New Testament are called the gospels because they tell the good news of what Jesus has done for us.* See "Good News."

gossip
- to be avoided, Romans 1:28-32; 2 Corinthians 12:20; 1 Timothy 5:13

government (GUV-er-ment) *group of people in charge of managing and making laws for people in a country, state, or city.*
- to be obeyed, Matthew 22:15-21; Romans 13:1-7; Titus 3:1; 1 Peter 2:13-17

governor
- Joseph, governor of Egypt, Genesis 42:6
- Nehemiah, governor of Judah, Nehemiah 5:14
- Pilate, governor of Judea, Matthew 27:2
- Felix, governor of Judea, Acts 23:26

grace, *God's kindness and love shown to us, even though we do not deserve them.*
- source of, Ephesians 3:7; Hebrews 4:14-16
- saved by, Acts 15:11; Romans 3:24; Ephesians 2:5-8; 2 Timothy 1:9
- misuse of, Romans 6; Galatians 5:4; Jude 4

grandchildren
- a blessing, Ruth 4:15; Proverbs 17:6
- inherit grandparents' wealth, Proverbs 13:22

grave, See "tomb."

Great Sea, See "Mediterranean Sea."

Greece, *once the most powerful nation in southeast Europe. Northern Greece was called "Macedonia." Southern Greece was called "Achaia."*
• Paul preached there, Acts 16:11-12; 20:1-6
greed, *selfish desire for more than one's share of something.*
• never satisfied, Proverbs 27:20
• beware of, Luke 12:15
• love of money, 1 Timothy 6:10
Greek
• the language of Greece, John 19:20; Acts 21:37; Revelation 9:11
• the people from Greece, Acts 14:1; 16:1; Colossians 3:11
grief
• of David for Absalom, 2 Samuel 18:33
• of the disciples, Matthew 17:23; John 16:6
guidance (GYD-ns) *direction.*
• by God, Exodus 13:21
• of the humble, Psalm 25:9
• of the Holy Spirit, John 16:15
guilt, *fact of having done wrong; regret, shame.*
• for improper worship, 1 Corinthians 11:27
• for breaking the Law, James 2:10
• cleansed of, Job 33:9; Isaiah 6:7; Hebrews 10:22

H

Habakkuk (ha-BAK-uk) *a prophet who wrote about the same time as Jeremiah,* Habakkuk 1–3
Hades (HAY-deez) *the world of the dead,* Revelation 6:8; 20:13-14
Hagar (HAY-gar) *Sarah's slave girl.*
• gave birth to Ishmael, Genesis 16
• sent away by Sarah, Genesis 21:8-21
Haggai (HAG-ay-eye) *a prophet in Jerusalem when the Israelites came back from Babylon,* Ezra 5:1; 6:14; Haggai 1–2
half-tribe, *one of the two parts of the tribe of Manasseh. One half-tribe settled east of the Jordan and the other settled west of the Jordan.* Joshua 1:12-15; 13:8-9; 22
Ham, *the son of Noah,* Genesis 6:10; 9:18-19; 10:6
Haman (HAY-man) *the chief officer under Ahasuerus, King of Persia.*
• planned to kill the Jews, Esther 3–6
• hanged, Esther 7
hands, laying on, *a ceremony where a person places his hands upon another.*
• for healing, Mark 5:23; 6:5; Luke 4:40
• to receive the Holy Spirit, Acts 8:17-19; 19:6
• for blessing, Mark 10:16; Acts 13:3
Hannah (HAN-uh) *the mother of Samuel,* 1 Samuel 1–2:21
happiness
• of the people of God, Psalms 144:15; 146:5; Proverbs 16:20; Matthew 5:3-12
• comes from wisdom, Proverbs 3:13
Haran (HAY-ran)
• Abraham's brother, Genesis 11:26-31
• home of Abraham, Genesis 11:31–12:5
harlot, See "prostitute."
harp, *the favorite musical instrument of the Jews.*
• first played, Genesis 4:21
• played by David, 1 Samuel 16:23; 18:10-11
• to praise God, Psalms 33:2; 71:22; 150:3
harvest
• of the poor, Ruth 2
• *as a symbol, Matthew 9:37-38; 13:24-30,39; Revelation 14:14-16*
hate
• seven things God hates, Proverbs 6:16-19
• a time to, Ecclesiastes 3:8
• of the world toward Jesus, John 15:18

• equal to murder, 1 John 3:15
• commands against, Galatians 5:19-21; 1 John 4:19-21
head
• a part of the body, Genesis 3:15; Psalm 23:5; Matthew 8:20; 1 Corinthians 12:21; Revelation 14:14
• a leader, Ephesians 1:22; 5:23; Colossians 1:18
heal
• a time to, Ecclesiastes 3:3
• by faith, Matthew 9:21-22; James 5:15
• "Doctor, heal yourself." Luke 4:23
heart, *the mind or feelings; not the physical heart that pumps blood,* Deuteronomy 6:5; Matthew 22:37
heaven
• *the home of God,* Matthew 5:34; Mark 16:19; John 3:13; Revelation 4
• angel spoke from, Genesis 21:17; 22:11
• opened, Matthew 3:16; Acts 7:56; 10:11
• fire from, 2 Kings 1:10-14; 1 Chronicles 21:26
• third heaven, 2 Corinthians 12:2
• the new heaven, Revelation 21:1-4
• kingdom of, Matthew 3:2; 5:3,19-20
Hebrews (HEE-brooz) *another name for the Jewish people,* Exodus 7:16; 2 Corinthians 11:22; Philippians 3:5
Hebron (HEE-bron) *a city about twenty miles southwest of Jerusalem,* Genesis 13:18; Numbers 13:22; 2 Samuel 2:1-11
heir (AIR) *the person who inherits what belongs to a relative. Because through Christ we can be adopted children of God, Christians are heirs to God's riches.*
• Abraham's heir, Genesis 15:3-4
• heir of God, Romans 8:17; Galatians 4:7
hell
• home of the devil and his angels, 2 Peter 2:4
• future home of sinners, Matthew 10:28; 23:33; Revelation 21:8
• descriptions of, Matthew 13:42; Mark 9:47-48; James 3:6; Revelation 14:11
helmet
• worn in battle, 1 Samuel 17:5; Ezekiel 23:24
• a symbol of salvation, Isaiah 59:17; Ephesians 6:17; 1 Thessalonians 5:8
help
• the stone of help, 1 Samuel 7:12
• the Holy Spirit as helper, Romans 8:26; Philippians 1:19
• from God, Psalms 46:1; 121:1-2; Isaiah 41:10
• commanded, 1 Thessalonians 5:14; Hebrews 6:10
Herod I (HEH-rud) *"Herod the Great"; king of Palestine from 40 to 4 B.C.,* Matthew 2:1; Luke 1:5
Herod Agrippa I (uh-GRIP-a) *King of Palestine from A.D. 41 to 44,* Acts 12:1
Herod Agrippa II, *King of Palestine from A.D. 52 to 70,* Acts 25:13–26:32
Herod Antipas (AN-ti-pus) *King of Palestine from 4 B.C. to about A.D. 39,* Matthew 14:1; Mark 6:14; Luke 23:7
Herodias (heh-ROW-dee-us) *the granddaughter of Herod I.*
• asked for John's head, Matthew 14:3-12; Mark 6:17-28; Luke 3:19
Hezekiah (hez-eh-KY-uh) *one of the good kings of Judah.*
• destroyed idols, 2 Kings 18:1-8; 2 Chronicles 29–31
• attacked by Assyria, 2 Kings 18:9–19:37; 2 Chronicles 32:1-23; Isaiah 36–37
• life extended by God, 2 Kings 20:1-11; Isaiah 38
• death of, 2 Kings 20:12-21; 2 Chronicles 32:24-33
higgaion (hig-GI-on) *probably a time to think quietly during a song,* Psalm 9:16
high place, *a place to worship gods,* 1 Kings 14:23; *2 Chronicles 31:1; 33:3*
high priest, *the most important religious leader of the Jewish people.*
• rules for, Leviticus 21:10-15
• of the Jews, Exodus 29:30; Numbers 35:25; Matthew 26:3; Acts 23:2

• Jesus as, Hebrews 2:17; 3:1; 4:14–5:10; 8:1-6

Hilkiah (hil-KY-ah) *high priest when Josiah was King,* 2 Kings 22–23; 2 Chronicles 34

Hinnom, Valley of (HIN-num) *an area where trash was burned just outside of Jerusalem; also called "Gehenna,"* Joshua 15:8; 18:16; Nehemiah 11:30

Hiram (HY-rum) *King of Tyre when David and Solomon were kings over Israel.*
• supplied trees for Solomon's Temple, 2 Samuel 5:11; 1 Kings 5:1-18; 9:11-27; 10:22

Hittites (HIT-tites) *people who lived in what is now Turkey,* Genesis 23:1-16; Exodus 3:8; Joshua 1:4; 1 Samuel 11:3

holy (HO-lee) *pure, belonging to and willing to serve God.*
• holiness of God, Leviticus 11:45; Isaiah 6:3; Hebrews 12:10; Revelation 4:8
• holy kiss, Romans 16:16
• people to be holy, Ephesians 1:4; Colossians 1:22-23; 3:2; 1 Peter 1:15-16

Holy of Holies, See "Most Holy Place."

Holy Place, *a room in the Holy Tent and the Temple,* Exodus 25:31-35; 28:29; Leviticus 6:30; 1 Kings 8:10-11

Holy Spirit (HO-lee SPIH-rit) *one of the three persons of God. The Holy Spirit helped the apostles do miracles and led men to write God's word; he lives in Christians today.*
• in creation, Genesis 1:2
• living in Christians, John 14:15-17; 1 Corinthians 6:19; Galatians 4:6
• as a helper, John 14:25-26; 16:7-15; Romans 8:1-27; Galatians 5:22-25
• filled with, Luke 1:15; Acts 2:4; 7:55; 11:23-24
• sin against, Matthew 12:31; Acts 5:3; 1 Thessalonians 5:19; Hebrews 10:29

Holy Tent, See "Meeting Tent."

honest
• heart, Luke 8:15
• people, 2 Kings 12:15
• answer, Proverbs 24:26
• commanded, Mark 10:19; Philippians 4:8

honor
• for the old, Leviticus 19:32
• from God, 1 Samuel 2:30
• comes from humility, Proverbs 15:33
• to the deserving, Romans 13:7
• shown to parents, Exodus 20:12; Matthew 15:4
• shown to God, Proverbs 3:9; John 5:23; Revelation 4:9
• not shown to a prophet in his own town, Matthew 13:57

hope, *looking forward to something you really expect to happen.*
• reason for, Romans 5:3-5; 15:4; 2 Thessalonians 2:16; 1 Peter 1:13
• nature of, Romans 8:24-25
• results of, Colossians 1:5; Hebrews 6:18

Hophni (HOF-nee) *an evil son of Eli the priest,* 1 Samuel 2:12-34; 3:11–4:18

Horeb, Mount, See "Sinai."

horses, Exodus 14:9; 1 Kings 10:26-29; Psalm 33:16-17; James 3:3

Hosanna (ho-ZAN-ah) *a shout of joy in praising God,* Matthew 21:9,15; Mark 11:9; John 12:13

Hosea (ho-SEE-uh) *a prophet who lived about seven hundred years before Christ.*
• his unfaithful wife, Hosea 1
• his warnings to Israel, Hosea 2; 4–14

hospitality
• of Abraham, Genesis 18:1-16
• teachings about, Romans 12:13; 1 Timothy 3:2; 5:9-10; 1 Peter 4:9

hosts, *armies; God is called the "Lord of hosts."* See "Lord of hosts."

Huldah (HUL-duh) *a woman prophet,* 2 Kings 22:14-20; 2 Chronicles 34:22-28

humble (HUM-bul) *not bragging or calling attention to yourself.*
• Moses as example of, Numbers 12:3
• humility commanded, Luke 14:7-11; 22:24-27; Ephesians 4:2; Philippians 2:3
• Jesus' humility, Philippians 2:5-8

hunger
• feeding the hungry, Matthew 25:34-35; Romans 12:20
• spiritual, John 6:35; 1 Peter 2:2

husband
• responsibilities of, 1 Corinthians 7:3-5; Ephesians 5:25-33; Colossians 3:19; 1 Peter 3:7

hymn (HIM) *a song that teaches us about God or praises him,* Matthew 26:30; Ephesians 5:19; Colossians 3:16
• Jesus and apostles sang, Matthew 26:30; Mark 14:26
• teachings about, Ephesians 5:19; Colossians 3:16

hypocrisy (hi-POK-r-see) *acting as if one is good when that is not true,* Matthew 23:28; 1 Peter 2:1

hypocrite (HIP-oh-krit) *a person who acts as if he is good but isn't.*
• warnings about, Matthew 6:2,5,16; 7:3-5; Luke 13:15-17
• Pharisees as hypocrites, Matthew 15:1-9; 23:13-32

hyssop (HIS-op) *a small bushy plant; marjoram,* Exodus 12:22; Leviticus 14:4,6; John 19:29

I

Iconium (eye-KOH-ree-um) *a city in Galatia where Paul preached,* Acts 14:1-7,19-23

idol (EYE-d'l) *a statue of a false god.* See also "Baal," "Chemosh," "Molech."
• worship of, 2 Kings 17:12-17; Acts 17:16-23; 19:24; Romans 1:25
• warnings against worship of, Leviticus 19:4; Deuteronomy 6:14-15; 1 Corinthians 5:10-11; 6:9-10
• Baal, 1 Kings 18:17-40
• Chemosh, Numbers 21:29
• Molech, Jeremiah 32:35

ignorance (IG-nur-rance) *a lack of knowledge.*
• not an excuse, Leviticus 5:17

image, *likeness.*
• God's, Genesis 1:26-27
• Caesar's, Luke 20:24
• the Lord's, 2 Corinthians 3:18
• Jesus in God's image, Hebrews 1:3

immorality (IM-mor-RAL-i-tee) *evil; sinfulness.* See also "sin."
• warnings against, 1 Corinthians 5:9-11; 6:9-10; Galatians 5:19-21; Ephesians 5:5

immortality (IM-mor-TAL-i-tee) *life after death,* Job 14:1-14; Daniel 12:1-2; 1 Corinthians 15:12-58; 2 Timothy 1:10. See also "eternal life."

impossible
• people cannot do, Matthew 19:26
• for God to lie, Hebrews 6:18
• without faith to please God, Hebrews 11:6

incense (IN-sents) *a spice burned to make a sweet smell.*
• altar of, Exodus 30:1-10,34-38; Revelation 8:3-5
• used in worship, Psalm 141:2
• as a gift, Matthew 2:11

inheritance (in-HEH-ri-tence) *something valuable that is handed down within a family.*
• of land, Numbers 36:8; Deuteronomy 3:28; Psalm 25:13

iniquity, See "sin."

inn, *a place for travelers to spend the night,* Luke 2:7; 10:34

innocence (IN-uh-sens) *not guilty of sin.*
• of Adam and Eve, Genesis 2:25
• declared by Job, Job 34:5

- declared by Pilate, Matthew 27:24

inspiration (IN-spi-RAY-shun) *"God-breathed." It is used to mean that the Bible writers wrote what God wanted them to write.* 2 Timothy 3:16; 2 Peter 1:20-21

Isaac (EYE-zak) *the son of Abraham and Sarah.*
- birth of, Genesis 21:1-4
- offered as a sacrifice, Genesis 22:1-19
- married Rebekah, Genesis 24
- tricked by Jacob, Genesis 27
- hero of faith, Hebrews 11:20

Isaiah (eye-ZAY-uh) *prophet who lived about seven hundred years before Christ.*
- became a prophet, Isaiah 6:1-8
- prophesied to Hezekiah, 2 Kings 19–20
- prophecies fulfilled, Matthew 3:3; 4:14; 13:14-15

Ish-Bosheth (ish-BOW-sheth) *son of Saul,* 2 Samuel 2:8–4

Ishmael (ISH-may-el) *son of Abraham and Hagar.*
- birth of, Genesis 16:2-16
- sent away from Abraham's camp, Genesis 21:8-21

Israel, kingdom of (IZ-rah-el) *the northern kingdom which had ten tribes.*
- beginning of, 1 Kings 11:27–12
- fall of, 2 Kings 17:1-18
- rulers of, 1 Kings 15:25–16; 22:51-53; 2 Kings 13; 14:23–17:6

Israel, son of Isaac, *Hebrew for "he who wrestles with God." Jacob's name was changed to Israel when he struggled with an angel at Bethel.* Genesis 32:22-28; 35:9-10. See also "Jacob."
- name given to Jacob's descendants, Genesis 49:28; Exodus 4:22; Psalm 22:23; Romans 9:3-5

Issachar (IS-uh-car) *a son of Jacob and Leah,* Genesis 30:18
- his descendants, Numbers 1:28-29; 26:23

ivory (EYE-voh-ree) *a creamy white bone that comes from elephant tusks,* 1 Kings 10:18; 22:39; Psalm 45:8

J

Jabbok River (JAB-ok) *a stream about fifty miles long that runs into the Jordan River,* Numbers 21:24; Joshua 12:2; Judges 11:13

Jabesh Gilead (JAY-besh GIL-ee-ad) *a small town on the east side of the Jordan River,* Judges 21:6-14; 2 Samuel 2:4-7

Jabin, king of Hazor (JAY-bin) *led a group of kings against the Israelites,* Joshua 11:1-11

Jabin, king of Canaan, *defeated by Israel when Deborah was judge,* Judges 4

Jacob (JAY-cub) *one of the sons of Isaac.*
- cheated Esau, Genesis 25:29-34
- tricked Isaac, Genesis 27:1-29
- his dream of a ladder to heaven, Genesis 28:10-22
- tricked by his sons, Genesis 37:10-22
- moved to Egypt, Genesis 45:25–47:12
- hero of faith, Hebrews 11:20-21

Jacob's Portion (JAY-cubs POR-shun) *a name for God, meaning he cares for Jacob's people,* Jeremiah 10:16; 51:19

jailer, *a keeper of a jail.*
- of Paul and Silas, Acts 16:23

Jairus (jay-EYE-rus) *a ruler of the synagogue.*
- Jesus brought his daughter back to life, Matthew 9:18-26; Mark 5:21-43; Luke 8:40-56

James, brother of Jesus, Matthew 13:55; Acts 12:17; 21:18
- *later an apostle,* Galatians 1:19

James, son of Alphaeus, *an apostle,* Matthew 10:3; Mark 3:18; Luke 6:15; Acts 1:13

James, son of Zebedee, *an apostle of Jesus and a brother of the apostle John,* Matthew 10:2; Mark 10:35; Acts 12:2

Japheth (JAY-fith) *one of Noah's three sons,* Genesis 5:32; 7:13; 9:18-27; 10:1-5

Jashar, Book of, *a book mentioned in the Bible, but not part of it,* Joshua 10:12-13; 2 Samuel 1:17-27

Jason (JAY-son) *a Christian in Thessalonica,* Acts 17:5-9

jealousy
- to describe God, Exodus 20:5; 34:14; Deuteronomy 5:9
- examples of, Genesis 37:11; 1 Samuel 18:19; Matthew 27:18; Acts 5:17
- warnings against, Romans 13:13; 1 Corinthians 13:4; 1 Timothy 6:4; 1 Peter 2:1

Jebusites (JEB-you-sites) *people who lived around Jerusalem before the time of David,* Joshua 15:63; Judges 19:10-11; 2 Samuel 4:6-8

Jehoahaz, son of Jehu (jeh-HO-uh-haz) *King of Israel who lived about eight hundred years before Christ,* 2 Kings 13:1-9

Jehoahaz, son of Josiah, *King of Judah for only three months,* 2 Kings 23:31-34; 2 Chronicles 36:1-4

Jehoash (jeh-HO-ash) *a king of Israel,* 2 Kings 13:10–14:16

Jehoiachin (jeh-HO-uh-kin) *the next-to-last king of Judah.*
- surrendered to Babylon, 2 Kings 24:8-17
- in Babylon, 2 Kings 25:27-30

Jehoiada (jeh-HO-yah-duh) *the chief priest in Jerusalem during Joash's rule,* 2 Kings 11–12; 2 Chronicles 22:11–24

Jehoiakim (jeh-HO-uh-kim) *king of Judah about 600 B.C.,* 2 Kings 23:34–24:6
- tried to kill Jeremiah, Jeremiah 26:1-23
- burned Jeremiah's scroll, Jeremiah 36:1-23

Jehoram (jeh-HOR-am) *or "Joram"; the fifth king of Judah,* 2 Kings 8:16-29; 2 Chronicles 21:4-20

Jehoshaphat (jeh-HOSH-uh-fat) *one of the good kings of Judah.*
- faithful to God, 2 Chronicles 17:1-9
- appointed judges, 2 Chronicles 19:4-11
- defeated Moab and Ammon, 2 Chronicles 20

Jehovah (jeh-HOVE-uh) *a name for God; also translated "LORD,"* Exodus 3:15; 6:3; Deuteronomy 28:58; Psalm 83:18

Jehu (JEE-hew) *an army captain who became king of Israel.*
- appointed as king, 2 Kings 9:1-13
- killed Joram and Ahaziah, 2 Kings 9:14-29
- stopped Baal worship, 2 Kings 10:18-35

Jephthah (JEF-thuh) *one of the judges of Israel.*
- fought the Ammonites, Judges 11:1-29,32-33
- his vow, Judges 11:30-31,34-39
- fought the people of Ephraim, Judges 12:2-7

Jeremiah (jer-eh-MY-ah) *a prophet who warned the people of Judah,* Jeremiah 1–52
- became a prophet, Jeremiah 1:1-10
- songs of, 2 Chronicles 35:25
- his prophecies fulfilled, 2 Chronicles 36:21-22; Matthew 2:17; 27:9
- wrote a scroll, Jeremiah 36

Jericho (JEHR-ih-ko) *probably the oldest city in the world,* Mark 10:46; Luke 10:30; 19:1
- fall of, Joshua 2–6
- rebuilt, 1 Kings 16:34

Jeroboam, son of Jehoash (jeh-ro-BO-am) *a king of Israel,* 2 Kings 14:23-29; Amos 7:7-17

Jeroboam, son of Nebat, *first ruler of the northern kingdom of Israel.*
- given ten tribes by God, 1 Kings 11:26-40
- built idols, 1 Kings 12:26-33
- warned by God, 1 Kings 13:1-34
- death of his son, 1 Kings 14:1-20

Jerusalem (jeh-ROO-suh-lem) *"Zion" or "City of David"; the greatest city of Palestine.*
- the City of David, 2 Samuel 5:6-7
- captured by Babylonians, 2 Chronicles 36:15-23

- Jews returned to, Ezra 1–2
- the new Jerusalem, Galatians 4:26; Hebrews 12:22; Revelation 3:12; 21–22

Jesse (JEH-see) *father of King David,* 1 Samuel 16–17; 1 Chronicles 2:13-15; Luke 3:32; Romans 15:12

Jesus (JEE-zus) *"Savior"; the son of God.* See also "Christ," "Son of David," "Son of Man."
- birth and childhood of Matthew 1–2; Luke 1–2
- temptation of, Matthew 4:1-11; Mark 1:12-13; Luke 4:1-13
- miracles of, Matthew 8–9; Mark 6:30-56; Luke 17:11; 22:50-51; John 2:1; 11
- appeared with Moses and Elijah, Matthew 17:1-13; Mark 9:2-13; Luke 9:28-36
- forced men from the Temple, Matthew 21:12-13; John 2:13-17
- the Last Supper, Matthew 26:17-30; Luke 22:1-20; John 13
- trial and death of, Matthew 26:57–27:66; Mark 15; Luke 22:66–23:56; John 18–19
- appearances after resurrection, Matthew 28; Mark 16; Luke 24; John 20–21; 1 Corinthians 15:5-8
- Son of God, Matthew 3:16-17; 26:63-64; John 1:14

Jethro (JETH-row) *father of Moses' wife,* Exodus 2:16-21
- advised Moses, Exodus 18

Jews (JOOZ) *first, the tribe of Judah; later, any of the twelve tribes,* Ezra 4:12; Esther 3–10; Acts 2:5
- against Jesus, John 5:15-18; 7:1,32-36; 1C:25-42
- Jesus, king of, Matthew 2:2; 27:11-14,29; John 19:17-22
- and non-Jewish people, 1 Corinthians 12:13; Galatians 3:28; Colossians 3:11

Jezebel (JEZ-eh-bell) *the evil wife of King Ahab.*
- married Ahab, 1 Kings 16:31
- killed the Lord's prophets, 1 Kings 18:4-14
- killed Naboth, 1 Kings 21:1-23
- death of, 2 Kings 9:30-37

Jezreel (JEZ-reel) *the name of a town and a valley near the Jordan River,* Judges 6:33; 1 Kings 21:1; 2 Kings 8:29

Joab (JO-ab) *the commander of King David's army,* 2 Samuel 2:12–3; 10–11: 14; 18– 20; 24; 1 Kings 1–2

Joanna (jo-ANN-uh) *a woman Jesus healed,* Luke 8:2-3; 23:55–24:11

Joash, Gideon's father (JO-ash)
- protected Gideon, Judges 6:28-32

Joash, son of Ahaziah, *became king of Judah when he was seven,* 2 Kings 11–12; 2 Chronicles 22:10–24

Job (JOBE) *a wealthy man who honored God.*
- ruined by Satan, Job 1–2:10
- wealth restored, Job 42:7
- example of patience, James 5:11

Joel (JO-el) *a prophet who wrote the book of Joel,* Joel 1–3; Acts 2:16

Johanan (jo-HAY-nan) *a Jewish army captain,* Jeremiah 40:8–43

John, the apostle, *one of the sons of Zebedee.*
- called by Jesus, Mark 1:19-20
- at Jesus' transfiguration, Mark 9:2
- with Jesus in Gethsemane, Mark 14:33-42
- in the early church, Acts 3–4
- writer of Revelation, Revelation 1:1-4,9

John the Baptist, *Jesus' relative and the son of Elizabeth and Zechariah the priest.*
- birth of, Luke 1:5-25,57-80
- preached at the Jordan River, Matthew 3:1-12
- baptized Jesus, Matthew 3:13-17
- killed by Herod, Matthew 14:1-12

John Mark, See "Mark."

Jonah (JO-nah) *a prophet whom God told to preach to the city of Nineveh.*
- ran from God, Jonah 1:1-3
- swallowed by a fish, Jonah 1:4–2:10
- went to Nineveh, Jonah 3

- complained to God, Jonah 4
- the sign of, Matthew 12:38-41; 16:4; Luke 11:29-32

Jonathan (JAH-nah-thun) *the oldest son of King Saul.*
- David's friend, 1 Samuel 18:1-4
- saved David's life, 1 Samuel 19:1-7; 20
- death of, 1 Samuel 31:2

Joppa (JOP-uh) *a city on the coast of Palestine,* Jonah 1:3
- Peter preached there, Acts 9:36-42; 10:9-36

Joram (JO-ram) *son of Ahab; also a king of Israel,* 2 Kings 3:1-3; 8:29; 9: 4-29

Jordan (JOR-d'n) *the only large river in Palestine.*
- Israelites crossed, Joshua 3
- Jesus baptized in, Matthew 3:13-17; Mark 1:9-11

Jordan Valley, *the valley along the Jordan River,* Deuteronomy :1; 3:17; Joshua 11:2

Joseph of Arimathea (JOZ-uf) *took the body of Jesus down from the cross and buried it in a tomb Joseph had dug for himself,* Matthew 27:57-60; Mark 15:42-46; Luke 23:50-54

Joseph of Nazareth, *husband of Mary, Jesus' mother.*
- angel appeared to, Matthew 1:18-24
- went to register in Bethlehem, Luke 2:4-7
- took Jesus to the Temple, Luke 2:21-52

Joseph, son of Jacob, *one of the twelve sons of Israel.*
- sold into slavery, Genesis 37
- put into prison, Genesis 39
- interpreted dreams, Genesis 40–41
- reunited with family, Genesis 42–50

Joshua (JAH-shoo-ah) *leader of the Israelites into the promised land.*
- spied out Canaan, Numbers 13
- chosen to replace Moses, Numbers 27:12-23; Deuteronomy 34:9-10
- conquered Canaan, Joshua 1: 3–12
- death of, Joshua 23–24

Josiah (jo-SY-uh) *king of Judah about 640 to 609 B.C.*
- became king, 2 Kings 22:1-2
- found the lost laws of God, 2 Kings 22:3-20
- gave the law to the people, 2 Kings 23:1-30

Jotham, youngest son of Gideon (JO-tham) Judges 9:1-21,57

Jotham, son of Uzziah, *a king of Judah,* 2 Kings 15:32-38; 2 Chronicles 27

joy, Psalm 43:4; John 15:11; 17:13; 1 Thessalonians 1:6
- a fruit of the Holy Spirit, Galatians 5:22
- God as the source, Psalms 43:4; 45:7; Romans 15:13
- joy from the Holy Spirit, Luke 10:21; Romans 14:17; Galatians 5:22; 1 Thessalonians 1:6

Jubilee (JOO-bih-lee) *a Jewish celebration that took place once every fifty years. Israelites were to let the soil rest, to free their slaves, and to return land and houses to their first owners or their descendants,* Leviticus 25; 27:17-24; Numbers 36:4

Judah, son of Jacob (JOO-duh) Genesis 29:35
- saved Joseph, Genesis 37:26-27
- deceived by Tamar, Genesis 38
- reunited with Joseph, Genesis 43–44
- tribe of, Numbers 1:26-27; 26:20-22; Joshua 15
- Jesus, a descendant of, Matthew 1:2-3; Luke 3:33-34; Revelation 5:5

Judah, kingdom of, *the southern kingdom when Israel split in two.*
- beginning of, 1 Kings 11:27–12:20
- rulers of, 1 Kings 14:21–15:24; 22:41-50; 2 Kings 8:16-29; 11–12; 14–16; 18–24
- fall of, 2 Kings 24:18–25:22

Judas Iscariot (JOO-dus is-CARE-ee-ut) *apostle who handed Jesus over to be killed.*
- chosen by Jesus, Matthew 10:4; Mark 3:19
- apostles' treasurer, John 12:4-6; 13:27-29
- betrayed Jesus, Matthew 26:14-16,47-50; Luke 22:1-6; John 6:70-71, 13:2,21-30

• death of, Matthew 27:3-5
Judas, brother of Jesus, Matthew 13:55; Mark 6:3
Judas, son of James
• an apostle, Luke 6:16; Acts 1:13
Jude (JOOD) *brother of James,* Jude 1
Judea (joo-DEE-uh) *the land of the Jews,* Matthew 2:1;
   3:1; Luke 1:5; 3:1; Acts 1:8
judges (JUHG-es) *leaders of Israel prior to the kings,*
   Judges 2:16-19; 3:7–4; 10–12; 1 Samuel 8:1-5
judging
• warnings against, Matthew 7:1-5; 1 Corinthians 4:5;
   James 4:11-12
• good kinds of judging, 1 Corinthians 5:12; 6:2; 10:15
• God's judging of people, Matthew 11:22; Acts 17:31;
   2 Peter 2:9; 3:7
Judgment Day (JUJ-ment) *the day Christ will judge all
   people,* Matthew 11:20-24; 12:33-37; 2 Peter 2:9-
   10; 3:7-13
Julius (JOOL-yus) *a Roman soldier in charge of Paul while
   Paul was taken to Rome,* Acts 27:1-3
justify (JUS-teh-fy) *to make someone right with God,*
   Romans 3:24; 5:1; Galatians 2:16; Titus 3:7

K

Kadesh/Kadesh Barnea (KAY-desh BAR-nee-uh) *a town
   in the Desert of Zin,* Numbers 20:1-21; Joshua
   10:41
Kenites (KEE-nites) *a tribe of early metal workers,* Genesis
   15:19; Judges 1:16; 4:11; 1 Samuel 27:10
Kerethites (KAIR-uh-thites) *King David's bodyguards,*
   2 Samuel 8:18; 1 Kings 1:38
Keturah (keh-TOO-ruh) *Abraham's second wife,* Genesis
   25:1-4; 1 Chronicles 1:32-33
key, *something that solves or explains.*
• to God's kingdom, Matthew 16:19
• to death, Revelation 1:18
Kidron Valley (KEH-dron) *a valley between Jerusalem and
   the Mount of Olives,* 2 Samuel 15:23; John 18:1
• idols burned there, 1 Kings 15:13; 2 Kings 23:4
kill
• Cain killed, Genesis 4:10-11
• laws against, Exodus 20:13
• of baby boys, Exodus 1:16; Matthew 2:16
• Jesus killed, Matthew 27:31-50; Mark 15:20-37; Luke
   23:25-46; John 19:16-30
kindness
• of God, Exodus 34:6-7; Jeremiah 9:24; Romans 2:4;
   Ephesians 2:4-7
• commanded, 2 Corinthians 6:6; Ephesians 4:32;
   Colossians 3:12; 2 Peter 1:5-7
king
• King of kings, 1 Timothy 6:15; Revelation 17:14
kingdom (KING-d'm) *the kingdom of heaven is God
   ruling in the lives of his people.*
• the nature of, Matthew 5:19-20; 19:14; Luke 17:20-21;
   Romans 14:17
• parables of, Matthew 13:24-52; 18:23-35; 20:1-16;
   25:1-30; Mark 4:30-33; Luke 13:18-21
• belongs to, Matthew 5:3,10; 19:14
Kiriath Jearim (KEER-yath JEE-ah-rim) *a town in the hills
   about twelve miles west of Jerusalem,* 1 Samuel
   6:20–7:20; 1 Chronicles 13:5-6; 2 Chronicles 1:4
Kish, *father of Saul,* 1 Samuel 9:1-2
Kishon (KY-shon) *the name of a valley and a stream,*
   Judges 4:13; 5:21; 1 Kings 18:40
kiss, *a greeting of friendship, love, or respect.*
• *of Judas, Matthew 26:48-49; Mark 14:44-45; Luke
   22:47-48*
• holy kiss, Romans 16:16; 1 Corinthians 16:20; 1 Peter
   5:14
Kittim (KEH-tim) *the island of Cyprus,* Genesis 10:4;
   Numbers 24:24; 1 Chronicles 1:7; Isaiah 23:1,12

kneel
• Solomon kneeled before God, 1 Kings 8:54
• Daniel kneeled before God, Daniel 6:10
• everyone to kneel before Jesus, Philippians 2:10
knock
• "knock, and the door will open," Matthew 7:7
• at the door, Luke 13:25
• Peter knocked, Acts 12:13,16
• Jesus knocks, Revelation 3:20
knowledge
• tree of, Genesis 2:9,17
• value of, Proverbs 1:7; 8:10; 18:15; 24:5; 2 Peter 1:5-6
• lack of, Hosea 4:6; Romans 1:28
• limitations of, 1 Corinthians 8:1-2; 13:2,8-10
Kohath (KO-hath) *a son of Levi,* Exodus 6:16-20; Numbers
   3:17-19
Kohathites (KO-hath-ites) *descendants of Kohath.*
• worked in the Holy Tent and Temple, Numbers 3:27-
   31; 4:1-20; 1 Chronicles 9:17-32
Korah (KO-ruh) *the musician,* Psalms 42; 44–49; 84
Korah, son of Izhar, *rebelled against Moses,* Numbers
   16:1-40

L

Laban (LAY-ban) *father of Leah and Rachel.*
• Jacob worked for, Genesis 29:13-30
• divided his flocks with Jacob, Genesis 30:29-43
• chased Jacob, Genesis 31:19-55
Lachish (LAY-kish) *a city about thirty miles southwest of
   Jerusalem.*
• Joshua defeated, Joshua 10
lake
• of Galilee, Luke 5:1-2; 8:22-23,33
• of fire, Revelation 19:20
• of sulfur, Revelation 20:10; 21:8
lamb (LAM) *an animal that the Jews often offered as a gift
   to God.*
• as sacrifice, Genesis 4:4; Exodus 12:3-10; Leviticus 3:6-
   11; 4:32-35; 5:6; 14:24-25
• Jesus, the lamb of God, John 1:29,36; 1 Corinthians
   5:7; 1 Peter 1:19; Revelation 5–7
Lamech, a descendant of Cain (LAY-mek) Genesis 4:18-
   24
Lamech, son of Methuselah, *the father of Noah,* Genesis
   5:28-31
lamp, *a small bowl that held a wick and burned olive oil,
   thus giving light,* Matthew 25:1-13; Luke 8:16-18
• "Your word is like a lamp for my feet," Psalm 119:105
lampstand, *a holder for a lamp.*
• in the Holy Tent, Exodus 25:31-40; Numbers 8:1-4
• in the Temple, 1 Kings 7:49
• symbol of the church, Revelation 1:12-13,20
language
• world spoke only one, Genesis 11:1,6
• confused at Babel, Genesis 11:7,9
• Aramaic, 2 Kings 18:26; Ezra 4:7; John 19:20
• Latin, John 19:20
• Greek, John 19:20; Acts 21:37
Laodicea (lay-ah-deh-SEE-uh) *a town in what is now
   Turkey,* Colossians 4:13-16; Revelation 3:14-22
Last Supper, *the meal Jesus ate with his followers the
   night before his death,* Matthew 26:17-30; Mark
   14:12-26; Luke 22:7-20; 1 Corinthians 11:23-26
Latin (LAT-in) *the language spoken by the Romans during
   New Testament times,* John 19:20
laughter
• *Sarah laughed, Genesis 18:12*
• mouths filled with, Psalm 126:2
• sorrow better than, Ecclesiastes 7:3
• changed into crying, James 4:9
law
• as rules, Romans 4:15; 6:14-15; Galatians 5:18

- as God's rules or teachings, Psalm 119; Romans 7:22; 8:7; James 1:25; 1 John 3:4

Law of Moses, See "Teachings of Moses."

laying on of hands, See "hands, laving on."

Lazarus of Bethany (LAZ-uh-rus) *a brother to Mary and Martha and a friend of Jesus,* John 11:1-45; 12:1-11

Lazarus, the beggar, Luke 16:19-31

laziness
- brings poverty, Proverbs 10:4
- not to be fed, 2 Thessalonians 3:10

leadership
- blind, Matthew 15:14
- of own family, 1 Timothy 3:5
- elders worthy of honor, 1 Timothy 5:17

Leah (LEE-uh) *a wife of Jacob,* Genesis 29:15-35; 30:9-21; 49:31

leather, Leviticus 13:47-59; Matthew 3:4

leaven, See "yeast."

Lebanon (LEH-beh-nun) *a country north of Israel.*
- cedars of, 1 Kings 5:1-11; Ezra 3:7
- prophecy of Lebanon's fall, Isaiah 10:34

Legion (LEE-jun) *a man who had many evil spirits in him,* Mark 5:9; Luke 8:30

lend
- money, Exodus 22:25
- borrower, a servant to lender, Proverbs 22:7
- sinners to sinners, Luke 6:34
- to enemies, Luke 6:35

leprosy (LEH-prah-see) *bad skin disease. A person with leprosy was called a leper and had to live outside the city.* Leviticus 13:45-46
- disease of Naaman, 2 Kings 5:1-27
- healed by Jesus, Matthew 8:2-3; Luke 7:11-19

Leviathan (lee-VI-ah-than) *a sea monster; possibly a crocodile,* Job 3:8; 41:1; Psalm 74:14; Isaiah 27:1

Levites (LEE-vites) *descendants of Levi, one of Jacob's sons.*
- served as priests, Numbers 1:47-53; 8:5-26; Deuteronomy 10:8-9; 18:1-8
- towns assigned to, Joshua 21

liar
- better to be poor, Proverbs 19:22
- Satan as a, John 8:44
- Cretans as, Titus 1:12
- to be punished, Revelation 21:8

lid on the Ark of the Agreement, *the mercy seat; the gold lid on the Ark of the Agreement,* Exodus 25:17-22; Hebrews 9:5

life
- breath of, Genesis 2:7
- book of, Philippians 4:3; Revelation 3:5; 21:27
- in the blood, Leviticus 17:14
- length of, Psalm 90:10
- true life, John 12:25
- "I am the. . .life." John 14:6
- eternal, John 5:24-29; 6:35-51

light
- creation of, Genesis 1:3-4
- of the world, Matthew 5:14
- God is, 1 Timothy 6:16; 1 John 1:5
- Jesus is, John 1:4-9; 3:19-20; 8:12; 12:46
- God's word is light, Psalm 119:105
- symbol of God's presence, 2 Corinthians 4:6; Ephesians 5:8-9; 1 Peter 2:9

linen (LEH-nin) *a type of cloth made from the flax plant.*
- used for priests' clothes, Exodus 28:39-42; Leviticus 6:10
- used for royal clothes, Esther 8:15
- Jesus' body wrapped in, Matthew 27:59

lion
- killed by Samson, Judges 14:5-18
- killed by David, 1 Samuel 17:34-37

- devil like a lion, 1 Peter 5:8

lips
- touched by hot coal, Isaiah 6:5-7

loaves
- used to feed five thousand, Matthew 14:17-19
- used to feed four thousand, Matthew 15:34-38

locust (LO-cust) *an insect that looks like a grasshopper. They travel in large groups and can destroy crops.*
- as a plague, Exodus 10:3-19; Deuteronomy 28:38-42; Joel 1:1-4; Nahum 3:15-17
- food for John the Baptist, Matthew 3:4; Mark 1:6

Lord, *master or one who is in control; ruler of all the world and universe.*
- God as Lord, Exodus 3:15; 7:16; Psalms 31:5; 106:48
- Jesus as Lord, Acts 2:36; 1 Corinthians 8:6; Philippians 2:11; 1 Peter 3:15
- Holy Spirit as Lord, 2 Corinthians 3:18

Lord of hosts, *one of the names used for God; also called "Lord All-Powerful" and "Lord Sabaoth,"* 1 Chronicles 11:9; Psalm 24:10; Isaiah 6:3-5; Malachi 3:1-17

Lord's day
- the first day of the week, Acts 20:7; Revelation 1:10
- as the Judgment Day, 1 Corinthians 5:5; 2 Corinthians 1:14; 1 Thessalonians 5:2; 2 Peter 3:10

Lord's Prayer, *the name often given to the model prayer Jesus taught his followers,* Matthew 6:9-13; Luke 11:1-4

Lord's Supper, *the meal Jesus' followers eat to remember how he died for them; also called "communion."*
- beginning of, Matthew 26:26-29; Mark 14:22-25; Luke 22:14-20
- examples of, Acts 20:7; 1 Corinthians 10:16; 11:17-34

Lot, *Abraham's nephew,* Genesis 11:27-30
- divided land with Abram, Genesis 13
- captured, Genesis 14:1-16
- escaped destruction of Sodom, Genesis 19:1-29
- death of wife, Genesis 19:15-26

lots, *sticks, stones, or pieces of bone thrown like dice to decide something. Often God controlled the result of the lots to let people know what he wanted them to do.*
- Canaan divided by, Numbers 26:55-56
- Jonah found guilty by, Jonah 1:7
- Jesus' clothes divided by, Luke 23:34
- Matthias chosen by, Acts 1:26

love. *a strong feeling of affection, loyalty and concern for someone.*
- love of God commanded, Deuteronomy 6:5; 11:1; Matthew 22:36-38
- of God for people, Psalm 36; John 3:16; Romans 5:8; 8:39; Ephesians 1:4; 1 John 4:10-11
- of people for God, 1 Corinthians 8:3; 1 John 5:3
- of Christ for people, John 13:1; 15:9; Romans 8:35; Galatians 2:20; 1 John 3:16
- of people for Christ, Matthew 10:37; 1 Corinthians 16:22; 1 Peter 1:8
- of people for each other, Leviticus 19:18; Luke 6:27-35; John 13:34-35; 1 Corinthians 13; 1 John 4:7

Luke, *a non-Jewish doctor who often traveled with the apostle Paul,* Colossians 4:14; 2 Timothy 4:11

lust, *wanting something evil.*
- to be avoided, Proverbs 6:25; Matthew 5:28; Colossians 3:5; 1 Thessalonians 4:5
- typical of the ungodly, Romans 1:26; 1 Peter 4:3

Lydia (LID-ee-uh) *a woman from the city of Thyatira who sold purple cloth,* Acts 16:13-15,40

lying
- warnings against, Ephesians 4:25; Colossians 3:9; Revelation 21:8
- devil as a liar, John 8:44
- to the Holy Spirit, Acts 5:1-6

lyre (LIRE) *a musical instrument with strings, similar to a harp,* 1 Chronicles 15:16; Psalms 33:2; 81:2

Lystra (LIS-tra) *a city of Lycaonia.*
- Paul preached there, Acts 14:6-20; 16:1; 2 Timothy 3:11

M

Macedonia (mas-eh-DOH-nee-uh) *the northern part of Greece.*
- Paul preached there, Acts 16:6-10; 20:1-6; 1 Corinthians 16:5-9; Philippians 4:15

Machpelah (mack-PEE-luh) *the land Abraham bought from Ephron, the Hittite.*
- Sarah buried there, Genesis 23:7-19
- Abraham buried there, Genesis 25:7-10
- Jacob buried there, Genesis 49:29-33; 50:12-13

magic (MAJ-ik) *trying to use the power of evil spirits to make unnatural things happen.*
- magicians of Egypt, Genesis 41:8; Exodus 7:11-12
- condemned, Leviticus 19:26; 20:27; Deuteronomy 18:10-12
- Simon the magician, Acts 8:9-24
- Elymas the magician, Acts 13:6-11
- Ephesian magicians burn their books, Acts 19:17-19

mahalath (mah-HAY-lath) *probably a musical word; may be the name of a tune or may mean to dance and shout,* Psalms 53; 88

Malachi (MAL-uh-ky) *a prophet who lived about the time of Nehemiah. He wrote the last book of the Old Testament.* Malachi 1:1

man, *humankind; a male.*
- created by God, Genesis 1:26-27; 2:7-23
- born of woman, Job 14:1
- important to God, Psalm 8:4-8
- woman created for, 1 Corinthians 11:9

Manasseh, son of Hezekiah (mah-NASS-uh) *a king of Judah for fifty-five years,* 2 Kings 21:1-17; 2 Chronicles 33:1-20

Manasseh, son of Joseph, *older brother of Ephraim. His descendants were the tribe of Manasseh.* Genesis 41:51; 46:20; 48:1-20
- descendants of, Numbers 1:34; 26:29-34; Joshua 13:8-13; 17
- eastern half-tribe, Joshua 1:12-17; 22
- western half-tribe, Joshua 21:5,25; 22:7

manger (MAIN-jur) *a box where animals are fed,* Luke 2:6-17

manna (MAN-ah) *the white, sweet-tasting food God gave the people of Israel in the wilderness. It appeared on the ground during the night so they could gather it in the morning.*
- God sent to Israel, Exodus 16:11-36; Joshua 5:10-12
- kept in the Ark, Exodus 16:31-34; Hebrews 9:1-4

Manoah (mah-NO-uh) *the father of Samson,* Judges 13

Marduk (MAR-dook) *a god of the Babylonians. The Babylonians believed that people were evil because Marduk had created them from the blood of an evil god.* Jeremiah 50:2

Mark, *John Mark; a cousin to Barnabas; traveled with Paul and Barnabas and wrote the Gospel of Mark,* Acts 12:12,25; 13:5; Colossians 4:10; 2 Timothy 4:11
- left Paul, Acts 13:13
- traveled with Barnabas, Acts 15:36-41

marketplace, *usually a large open area inside a city where people came to buy and sell goods,* Matthew 20:3; Mark 7:4; 12:38; Luke 7:32; Acts 16:19

marriage
- teachings about, Mark 10:6-9; 1 Corinthians 7:1-16; Hebrews 13:4; 1 Timothy 5:14
- authority in, Ephesians 5:21; Colossians 3:18

Mars Hill, See "Areopagus."

Martha (MAR-thuh) *the sister of Mary and Lazarus who lived in Bethany.*
- criticized Mary, Luke 10:38-42
- at death of Lazarus, John 11:17-44

martyr (MAR-ter) *"witness"; one who knows about something. Later, martyr came to mean a person who was killed for being a witness.*
- Stephen, first Christian martyr, Acts 7:54-60
- James killed, Acts 12:2
- heroes of faith killed, Hebrews 11:32-37

Mary Magdalene (MAG-duh-lun) *a follower of Jesus from the town of Magdala; the first person to see Jesus after he came back to life.*
- at Jesus' death, Matthew 27:55-56,61
- saw Jesus after his resurrection, Matthew 28:1-10; Mark 16:1-11; John 20:10-18

Mary, mother of Jesus
- engaged to marry Joseph, Matthew 1:18-25; Luke 2:4-5
- angel appeared to, Luke 1:26-45
- birth of Jesus, Luke 2:6-21
- with Jesus in Jerusalem, Luke 2:41-52
- at wedding in Cana, John 2:1-10
- at Jesus' death, John 19:25-27
- with the apostles, Acts 1:14

Mary of Bethany, *sister of Martha and Lazarus, and a friend of Jesus.*
- sat at Jesus' feet, Luke 10:38-42
- at death of Lazarus, John 11:1-45
- poured oil on Jesus' feet, John 12:1-8

maskil (MAS-kil) *probably a description of the kind of song that some of the Psalms were,* Psalms 32, 42, 44, 45

master, *lord; ruler.*
- "No one can serve two masters." Matthew 6:24
- not to be called, Matthew 23:10
- to be obeyed, Ephesians 6:5
- how to treat slaves, Ephesians 6:9
- in heaven, Ephesians 6:9; Colossians 4:1
- Jesus as, Luke 5:5; 8:24; 17:13

Matthew (MATH-you) *also called Levi; a tax collector; wrote the Gospel of Matthew,* Matthew 9:9-10; 10:3; Acts 1:13

Matthias (muh-THY-us) *chosen to be an apostle after Judas Iscariot killed himself,* Acts 1:15-26

meat
- given by God in the wilderness, Exodus 16:1-15; Numbers 11:4-34; Psalm 78:27
- eating meat sacrificed to idols, Acts 15:20; 1 Corinthians 8; 10:25-32

Medes (MEEDS) *the people who lived in Media, which is called "Iran" today,* 2 Kings 17:6; Ezra 6:2; Esther 1:3-19; Daniel 5:28; 6:8-15

mediator (MEE-dee-a-ter) *a go-between.*
- Jesus as, 1 Timothy 2:5

medicine
- happy heart as, Proverbs 17:22

Mediterranean Sea (med-ih-teh-RANE-ih-an) *a large sea west of Canaan; also called the "Great Sea" or the "Western Sea,"* Numbers 34:6-7; Joshua 1:4

medium (MEED-ee-um) *a person who tries to help living people talk to the spirits of the dead.*
- condemned, Leviticus 19:31; Deuteronomy 18:11-13; Isaiah 8:19-20
- of Endor, 1 Samuel 28
- Josiah destroyed mediums, 2 Kings 23:24

Meeting Tent, *"Tabernacle" or "Holy Tent"; a special tent where the Israelites worshiped God. It was used from the time they left Egypt until Solomon built the Temple in Jerusalem.*
- description of, Exodus 25–27
- set up, Exodus 39:32–40:36

Megiddo (meh-GID-oh) *important town in northern Israel where many battles were fought. The book of Revelation tells about a great battle between good and evil at "Armageddon," which means "the hill of*

Megiddo." Joshua 12:8-21; 2 Kings 23:29-30; Revelation 16:16

Melchizedek (mel-KIZ-ih-dek) *priest and king who worshiped God in the time of Abraham,* Genesis 14:17-24
• Christ compared to, Hebrews 5:4-10; 7

Mene, mene, tekel, parsin (MEE-nee, TEE-kul, PAR-sun) *the words written on the wall by a mysterious hand at Belshazzar's feast,* Daniel 5

Mephibosheth (me-FIB-o-sheth) *crippled son of Jonathan,* 2 Samuel 4:4
• David's agreement with, 2 Samuel 9
• tricked by Ziba, 2 Samuel 16:1-4; 19:24-30

Merab (MEE-rab) *daughter of King Saul,* 1 Samuel 14:49; 18:17-19

Merarites (mee-RAY-rites) *descendants of Merari, a son of Levi; they were responsible for caring for the frame of the Holy Tent,* Numbers 3:17,33-37; 4:29-33

mercy (MUR-see) *kindness and forgiveness.*
• God's mercy to people, Exodus 34:6; Deuteronomy 4:31; Luke 1:50; Ephesians 2:4
• people's mercy to each other, Matthew 5:7; James 2:13

mercy seat, See "lid on the Ark of the Agreement."

Mesha (MEE-shuh) *an evil king of Moab,* 2 Kings 3:4-27

Meshach (MEE-shack) *friend of Daniel who was put in the fiery furnace,* Daniel 1-3

messenger, 1 Samuel 23:27; 1 Kings 19:2
• John the Baptist as, Matthew 11:10; Mark 1:2; Luke 7:27
• of Satan, 2 Corinthians 12:7

Messiah (muh-SYE-uh) *"anointed one"; the Greek word for Messiah is "Christ." Christians believe that Jesus is the Messiah or the Christ.* John 1:40-41; 4:25-26

Methuselah (meh-THOO-zeh-lah) *lived 969 years, longer than anyone else in the Bible; the son of Enoch and the grandfather of Noah,* Genesis 5:21-27

Micah (MY-cuh) *a prophet who told the people of Israel and Judah about their sins,* Micah 1-7

Micaiah (mi-KAY-uh) *a prophet of God,* 1 Kings 22:8-28; 2 Chronicles 18

Michael (MY-kul) *the archangel of God,* Jude 9; Revelation 12:7

Michal (MY-kul) *a daughter of Saul and wife of David,* 1 Samuel 18:20-29; 19:11-17; 2 Samuel 3:13-16
• criticized David, 2 Samuel 6:16-23

Michmash (MIK-mash) *a hilly area about seven miles northeast of Jerusalem,* 1 Samuel 13:23-14:23; Isaiah 10:28

Midian (MID-ee-un) *a son of Abraham; his descendants were called "Midianites,"* Genesis 25:1-6
• Joseph sold to, Genesis 37:18-36
• Jethro, a descendant of, Exodus 2:15-21
• enemy of Israel, Judges 6-7

midnight
• when the firstborn of Egypt died, Exodus 12:29
• Paul and Silas freed from jail, Acts 16:25-26
• Paul preached until, Acts 20:7

miktam (MIK-tam) *a kind of song that may describe some of the Psalms. It may mean that it is a sad song or a song about danger.* Psalms 16; 56-60

mildew (MIL-doo) *a growth that appears on things that have been damp for a long time,* Leviticus 13:47-59; 14:33-54

milk, 1 Peter 2:2

millstones, *huge stones used for grinding grain into flour or meal,* Deuteronomy 24:6; Matthew 18:6; Luke 17:1-2
• used to kill Abimelech, Judges 9:53; 2 Samuel 11:21

minister (MIN-ister) *servant; one who lives serving God and others,* Romans 15:15-16; Colossians 4:7

miracle (MEER-ih-k'l) *"wonderful thing"; a great event which can be done only by God's help. Miracles are special signs to show God's power.*

• purpose of, Exodus 10:1-2; Mark 2:8-12; John 2:11; Acts 3:1-10
• over nature, Exodus 14:21-22; Joshua 10:12-13; Matthew 8:23-27; 14:22-32; 21:18-22
• of healing, Matthew 8:14-17; 9:27-31; Mark 7:31-37; Acts 14:3
• of bringing people back to life, Mark 5:21-43; John 11:1-44; Acts 9:36-43

Miriam (MEER-ee-um) *the sister of Moses and Aaron.*
• watched over Moses, Exodus 2:1-8
• song of, Exodus 15:19-21
• punished, Numbers 12:1-15
• death of, Numbers 20:1

mistress (MISS-tres) *a female head of the household,* Proverbs 30:21-23
• Hagar as, Genesis 16:4-9

Mizpah (MIZ-pah) *the place where Jacob and Laban made a pile of stones to remind them of their agreement not to be angry with each other,* Genesis 31:44-49

Mizpah, *the city, a few miles north of Jerusalem,* Judges 11:29-34; 1 Samuel 7:5-16; 2 Kings 25:23

Moab (MO-ab) *the country on the east side of the Dead Sea.*
• fought with Israel, Numbers 22:1-25:9; Judges 3:12-30
• home of Ruth, Ruth 1:2,4
• rebelled against Israel, 2 Kings 3:4-27

mob
• against Paul, Acts 17:5; 21:30-36

Molech (MO-lek) *a god of the Canaanite people. Those who worshiped Molech often sacrificed their own children to him by burning them on altars.* Leviticus 18:21; 20:1-5; 2 Kings 23:10; Jeremiah 32:35

money, *Many kinds of money were used in Bible days—gold, silver, and copper.*
• proper attitudes toward, Luke 16:13; Hebrews 13:5; 1 Timothy 3:3; 6:10

moneychangers, *people who traded money from other countries for Jewish money.*
• of the Temple, Matthew 21:12-13; Mark 11:15-17; Luke 19:45-45; John 2:13-16

Mordecai (MOR-deh-kye) *a man who helped Esther to save the Jews from death.*
• discovered a plot, Esther 2:19-23
• asked Esther to help, Esther 4
• honored by the king, Esther 6

Moriah (moh-RYE-uh) *the land where Abraham went to sacrifice Isaac,* Genesis 22:2
• site of the Temple, 2 Chronicles 3:1

mortar (MORE-tar) *a stone bowl where grain is ground into flour by pounding; also, the sticky material that holds bricks together,* Genesis 11:3; Exodus 1:14

Moses (MO-zez) *the man who led God's people out of the land of Egypt; the author of the first five books of the Old Testament.*
• birth of, Exodus 2:1-10
• in Midian, Exodus 2:11-4:17
• led Israel out of Egypt, Exodus 4:18-12:51; 13:17-31
• received the law, Exodus 20-31
• struck the rock, Numbers 20:1-13
• death of, Deuteronomy 31:14-34:12

Most Holy Place, *the inner and most special room in the Holy Tent and the Temple.*
• rules about, Leviticus 16:2-20
• in the Temple, 1 Kings 6:16-35
• entered by Christ, Hebrews 9:3-25

mother-in-law
• law about, Deuteronomy 27:23
• of Ruth, Ruth 1:3-4
• Peter's, Matthew 8:14-15; Luke 4:38-39
• family against, Matthew 10:35; Luke 12:53

mothers
• treatment of, Exodus 20:12; 21:15,17; Leviticus 19:3;

Proverbs 1:8; 13:1; 23:22, 25; Matthew 15:4;
1 Timothy 5:2,4

Mount of Olives, *a hill covered with olive trees near Jerusalem; site of the garden of Gethsemane,* Matthew 21:1; 24:3; John 8:1
- David cried there, 2 Samuel 15:30
- Jesus prayed there, Luke 22:39-53
- Jesus ascended from there, Acts 1:6-12

Mount Sinai (SYE-nye) *a mountain in the Sinai Peninsula.*
- Lord spoke with Moses there, Exodus 24:16; Acts 7:30,38
- law given on, Exodus 31:18

Mount Zion (ZI-on) *one of the hills on which Jerusalem was built; later, it became another name for the whole city of Jerusalem; also a name for heaven.*
- hill of Jerusalem, 2 Kings 19:31; Psalm 48:2,11; Isaiah 24:23
- as heaven, Hebrews 12:22; Revelation 14:1

mourning (MORN-ing) *showing sadness, especially when someone has died.*
- examples of, Genesis 50:3; Deuteronomy 34:8; 1 Samuel 31:11-13

murder
- laws against, Exodus 20:13; Deuteronomy 5:17; Matthew 5:21
- committed by Barabbas, Mark 15:7
- devil as a murderer, John 8:44
- full of, Romans 1:29

music
- to the Lord, Judges 5:3; Ephesians 5:19
- in the Temple, 1 Chronicles 25:6-7

myrrh (MUR) *sweet-smelling liquid taken from certain trees and shrubs; used as a perfume and a painkiller,* Genesis 37:25; 43:11; Proverbs 7:17
- given to Jesus, Matthew 2:11; Mark 15:23
- used in Jesus' burial, John 19:39-40

mystery (MIH-ster-ee) *a secret.*
- revealed by God, Daniel 2:28
- of the message of Christ, Romans 16:25-26; Colossians 2:2; 4:3
- of Gentiles also being saved, Ephesians 3:1-6; Colossians 1:25-27
- of life after death, 1 Corinthians 15:51

N

Naaman (NAY-uh-mun) *a commander of the Aramean army; healed by Elisha of a skin disease,* 2 Kings 5; Luke 4:27

Nabal (NAY-bal) *husband of Abigail.*
- refused to help David, 1 Samuel 25:2-13
- saved by Abigail, 1 Samuel 25:14-35
- death of, 1 Samuel 25:36-38

Naboth (NAY-both) *killed by Jezebel so she could steal his vineyard,* 1 Kings 21

Nadab (NAY-dab) *son of Aaron.*
- saw God, Exodus 24:1-11
- death of, Leviticus 10:1; Numbers 3:4; 26:61

Nahum (NAY-hum) *a prophet of God; wrote the book of Nahum,* Nahum 1–3

naked
- Adam and Eve, Genesis 2:25
- realization of nakedness, Genesis 3:7-10
- born, Job 1:21

Naomi (nay-OH-me) *mother-in-law of Ruth,* Ruth 1:1-5
- returned to Bethlehem, Ruth 1:6-22
- encouraged Ruth, Ruth 2:19–3:4
- became a grandmother, Ruth 4:13-17

Naphtali (NAF-tuh-lye) the sixth son of Jacob; his descendants were the tribe of Naphtali, Genesis 30:7-8; Numbers 26:48-50; Joshua 19:32-39

nard, *an expensive perfume which was imported from India,* Song of Solomon 4:13; Mark 14:3; John 12:3

Nathan (NAY-thun) *a prophet during the time of David and Solomon,* 1 Kings 1
- told David not to build the Temple, 2 Samuel 7:1-17
- told David the parable of the lamb, 2 Samuel 12:1-25

Nathanael (nuh-THAN-yul) *one of Jesus' twelve apostles; probably called "Bartholomew."* John 1:43-51

nation
- formed and spread, Genesis 10:32
- against nation, Mark 13:8
- Good News preached to every one, Revelation 14:6

Nazarene (NAZ-uh-reen) *a person from the town of Nazareth. Jesus was called a Nazarene, so his followers sometimes were also called Nazarenes.* Matthew 2:21-23; Acts 24:5

Nazareth (NAZ-uh-reth) *the city in Galilee where Jesus grew up,* Matthew 2:21-23; Luke 4:16-30; John 1:45-46

Nazirite (NAZ-e-rite) *a special promise made to God, which had rules about eating certain foods and cutting the hair.*
- rules for, Numbers 6:1-21
- made by Samson, Judges 13:2-7; 16:17

Nebo, god of the Babylonians (NEE-boh) Isaiah 46:1

Nebo, the mountain
- Moses died there, Deuteronomy 34:1-5

Nebuchadnezzar (neb-you-kud-NEZ-zur) *a Babylonian king.*
- conquered Jerusalem, 2 Kings 24–25; 2 Chronicles 36
- his dreams, Daniel 2; 4
- and fiery furnace, Daniel 3

Nebuzaradan (NEB-you-ZAR-ah-dan) *the commander of Nebuchadnezzar's army.*
- captured Jerusalem, 2 Kings 25:8-12; Jeremiah 39:8-14; 40:1-6

Neco (NECK-o) *king of Egypt from 609 to 594 B.C.*
- killed King Josiah, 2 Kings 23:29-37; 2 Chronicles 35:20-27
- captured Jehoahaz, 2 Chronicles 36:1-4
- defeated by Nebuchadnezzar, Jeremiah 46:2

Nehemiah (NEE-uh-MY-uh) *led the first group of Israelites back to Jerusalem from Babylon.*
- sent to Jerusalem, Nehemiah 2
- rebuilt walls of Jerusalem, Nehemiah 3–4; 6
- as governor, Nehemiah 8:9; 10:1

neighbor
- teachings about, Exodus 20:16-17; Leviticus 19:13-18; Proverbs 3:27-29; Matthew 19:19; Luke 10:25-37

Nephilim (NEF-eh-lim) *people who were famous for being large and strong. The ten spies who were afraid to enter Canaan had seen the Nephilim who lived there.* Genesis 6:4; Numbers 13:30-33

Ner (NUR) *father of Kish,* 1 Chronicles 8:33; 9:36,39

net
- fishing with, Matthew 4:18; Luke 5:5,6; John 21:6-11
- kingdom of heaven like, Matthew 13:47

new
- a new song, Psalms 40:3; 98:1
- a new name, Isaiah 62:2; Revelation 2:17
- new mercies every morning, Lamentations 3:22-23
- a new heart, Ezekiel 18:31; 36:26
- a new life, Romans 6:4; Ephesians 4:23-24; Colossians 3:10; 1 Peter 1:3
- a new agreement, Jeremiah 31:31; 1 Corinthians 11:25; Hebrews 8:8; 9:15; 12:24
- a new heaven and earth, 2 Peter 3:13; Revelation 21:1

New Moon, *a Jewish feast held on the first day of the month. It was celebrated with animal sacrifices and the blowing of trumpets. It was to dedicate the month to the Lord.* Numbers 10:10; 2 Chronicles 2:4; 8:13; Psalm 81:3; Isaiah 1:11-17

Nicodemus (nick-uh-DEE-mus) *an important Jewish ruler*

and teacher. Jesus taught him about spiritual life.
John 3:1-21; 7:45-53; 19:38-42

night, *can refer to ordinary darkness or be a symbol of distress, judgment, or evil.*
- created by God, Genesis 1:5; Psalm 19:1-2
- time of distress, Psalms 30:5; 42:8; 77:6
- time of judgment, John 9:4
- symbol of evil, 1 Thessalonians 5:5
- no night in heaven, Revelation 21:25

Nile River, *a river in Africa more than twenty-five hundred miles long.*
- baby Moses placed there, Exodus 2:1-10
- turned to blood, Exodus 7:14-25
- produced plague of frogs, Exodus 8:1-15

Nineveh (NIN-eh-vuh) *one of the oldest and most important cities in the world. For many years it was the capital of Assyria.* Genesis 10:8-11
- Jonah preached there, Jonah 1:1-2; 3–4; Matthew 12:41
- Nahum prophesied against, Nahum 1–3

Noah (NO-uh) *saved his family and the animals from the flood.*
- built the boat, Genesis 6:8-22
- saved from the flood, Genesis 7–8
- agreement with God, Genesis 9:1-17

Nob, *a town where priests lived during the days of King Saul,* 1 Samuel 21:1

noise
- joyful, Psalm 66:1
- of many people, Isaiah 17:12
- skies will disappear with, 2 Peter 3:10

noon
- sun to go down at, Amos 8:9
- bright light at, Acts 22:6

O

oath, *a promise or vow.*
- rules about, Matthew 5:33-37; 23:16-22; James 5:12
- God's oath, Hebrews 6:16-18
- examples of, 1 Samuel 14:24-28; 1 Kings 1:29-30; Psalm 132:1-12

Obadiah (oh-buh-DYE-uh) *a prophet of God who warned the Edomites they would be punished.* Obadiah 1-21

obedience
- to God, Leviticus 25:18; Deuteronomy 27:10; Acts 5:29
- to parents, Ephesians 6:1; Colossians 3:20
- to government, Romans 13:1-7; Titus 3:1-2; Matthew 22:17-21
- punishment for disobedience, Ephesians 5:6; 2 Thessalonians 1:8; 1 Timothy 1:9

offering (AW-fer-ing) *a gift or sacrifice. See "sacrifice."*
- brought by Cain, Genesis 4:3-5
- of non-Jewish people, Romans 15:16
- of Christ, Hebrews 10:5-18

Og (AHG) *the king of Bashan who was defeated by the Israelites,* Numbers 21:33-35; Deuteronomy 3:1-11

oil, *in Bible times usually means olive oil; used for cooking, medicine, burning in lamps, and anointing. See "anoint."*
- for lamps, Exodus 25:5-6; Matthew 25:1-10
- as medicine, Luke 10:34
- in offerings, Leviticus 2; 14:12-31
- in cooking, 1 Kings 17:10-16

ointment, See "perfume."

olive (OL-iv) *a small fruit; its oil was used in anointing ceremonies and as medicine. See "oil."*
- leaf, Genesis 8:11
- trees, Deuteronomy 6:11; 1 Samuel 8:14; Habakkuk 3:17; John 18:1

Omega, See "Alpha and Omega."

Omri (AHM-rih) *an evil king of Israel,* 1 Kings 16:15-28

Onesimus (oh-NES-ih-mus) *the slave of a Christian named Philemon,* Colossians 4:9; Philemon

Onesiphorus (OH-nih-SIF-uh-russ) *a Christian friend of Paul who lived in Ephesus,* 2 Timothy 1:16-18; 4:19

onyx (AHN-ix) *a precious stone with layers of black and white running through it,* Genesis 2:12; Job 28:16
- used in the holy vest, Exodus 25:7; 28:9-14; 39:6-7,13

Orpah (OR-pah) *the sister-in-law of Ruth,* Ruth 1:3-14

Ophir (OH-fur) *a land known for its gold and beautiful trees. Its location is uncertain.* Psalm 45:9; Isaiah 13:12
- Solomon traded with Ophir, 1 Kings 9:28; 10:11; 1 Chronicles 29:4

oven, *fire was built in the bottom of a clay barrel to bake bread,* Exodus 8:3; Leviticus 2:4; Hosea 7:4

oxen
- not to be coveted, Exodus 20:17
- as offering, Numbers 7:12-83
- not to be denied food, Deuteronomy 25:4; 1 Corinthians 9:9
- Elisha plowed with, 1 Kings 19:19-21
- pulled the cart containing the Ark, 1 Chronicles 13:9

P

pain
- of a woman in childbirth, Genesis 3:16; Isaiah 13:8; Romans 8:22; Galatians 4:19,27
- not found in the new Jerusalem, Revelation 21:4

palace
- of David, 2 Samuel 5:11-12
- of Solomon, 1 Kings 7:1-12

palm tree, *a tall tree with long, fan-shaped branches growing out of the top; gives dates for food and wood for building,* Exodus 15:27; Nehemiah 8:15
- Jericho, city of, Deuteronomy 34:3; Judges 1:16; 3:13
- branches spread before Jesus, John 12:12-13

papyrus (puh-PY-rus) *a tall reed that grows in swampy places; used to make paper,* Job 8:11; 9:26

parable (PARE-uh-b'l) *a story that teaches a lesson by comparing two things.*
- of the kingdom of God, Matthew 13; 20:1-16
- of the lost sheep, coin, and son, Luke 15:1-31
- of the Judgment Day, Matthew 25

Paradise (PARE-uh-dice) *"garden"; a place where God's people go when they die,* Luke 23:43; 2 Corinthians 12:3-4

Paran (PAY-ran) *a desert area between Egypt and Canaan,* Genesis 21:20; Numbers 10:12; 12:16; 13:1-26

parchment (PARCH-ment) *a writing material made from the skin of sheep or goats,* 2 Timothy 4:13

parents
- responsibilities of, Ephesians 6:4; Colossians 3:21

Passover Feast (PASS-o-ver FEEST) *an important holy day for the Jews in the spring of each year. They ate a special meal on this day to remind them that God had freed them from being slaves in Egypt.*
- first Passover, Exodus 12:1-30
- commanded, Numbers 9:1-14
- celebrated by Jesus, Matthew 26:2,17-19

patience (PAY-shentz) *to handle pain or difficult times calmly and without complaining.*
- of God, Romans 2:4; 2 Peter 3:9
- teachings about, 1 Corinthians 13:4,7; Hebrews 6:12
- comes from the Holy Spirit, Galatians 5:22
- commanded, Romans 12:12; Ephesians 4:2; 1 Thessalonians 5:14; James 5:7-8

Patmos (PAT-mus) *a small, rocky island in the Aegean Sea between Greece and Turkey,* Revelation 1:9

Paul, *the Roman name for "Saul." Saul was a Jew, born in the city of Tarsus. He became an apostle and a great servant of God.*
- conversion of, Acts 9:1-22

peace
- name changed from "Saul," Acts 13:9
- healings by, Acts 14:8-10; 19:11-12; 20:7-12; 28:1-11
- imprisoned, Acts 23:35–28:31
- death of, 2 Timothy 4:6-8

peace
- from God, Psalm 29:11; John 14:27; Romans 5:1
- commanded, Romans 12:18; 14:17-19; Colossians 3:15
- Prince of Peace, Isaiah 9:6
- from the Holy Spirit, Galatians 5:22

pearl (PURL), Matthew 7:6; 1 Timothy 2:9; Revelation 21:21
- parable of, Matthew 13:45-46

Pekah (PEE-kuh) *an evil king of Israel,* 2 Kings 15:25–16:9; Isaiah 7:1-10

Pekahiah (peck-uh-HI-uh) *an evil king of Israel,* 2 Kings 15:22-26

Pelethites (PELL-eh-thites) *King David's bodyguards,* 2 Samuel 15:18; 20:6-7,23

Peninnah (pe-NIN-uh) *a wife of Elkanah,* 1 Samuel 1:2-6

Pentecost (PEN-tee-cost) *a Jewish feast day celebrating the summer harvest. The apostles began telling the Good News on Pentecost after Jesus died.* Acts 2:1-41; 20:16; 1 Corinthians 16:8

perfect
- describing Jesus, Hebrews 2:10; 5:9; 7:28
- describing God, Psalm 18:30; Matthew 5:48
- God's perfect law, James 1:25
- will of God, Romans 12:2
- love, 1 John 4:18
- people made perfect, 2 Corinthians 13:11; Hebrews 10:1-14; 11:40; 12:23

perfume
- used in idol worship, Isaiah 57:9
- poured on Jesus' feet, Mark 14:3-9; Luke 7:36-39; John 12:3

Pergamum (PER-guh-mum) *a town in the Roman province of Asia in what is now Turkey,* Revelation 2:12-17

persecution (PUR-seh-CUE-shun) *trying to hurt people. Christians in the New Testament times were often persecuted by being put in jail or killed.*
- blessings with, Matthew 5:11-12; 1 Peter 3:8-17
- examples of, Acts 8:1-4; 1 Peter 3:13-15
- response to, Matthew 5:44; Romans 12:14; 1 Corinthians 4:12; 2 Corinthians 12:2
- of Christians, Matthew 13:21; 2 Timothy 3:12

Persia (PUR-zhuh) *a powerful country during the last years of the Old Testament; now called "Iran."*
- defeated Babylon, 2 Chronicles 36:20-23
- let captives return to Jerusalem, Ezra 1:1-11

Peter, *a fisherman; he and his brother, Andrew, were the first two apostles Jesus chose. First called " Simon" or "Peter," Jesus changed his name to "Cephas," which means "rock."*
- called to follow Jesus, Matthew 4:18-20
- walked on water, Matthew 14:22-33
- at the Last Supper, John 13:1-11
- defended Jesus, John 18:10-11
- denied Jesus, Mark 14:66-72; Luke 22:54-62
- preached the Good News, Acts 2:14-40
- an elder in the church, 1 Peter 5:1

pharaoh (FAY-row) *the title given to the kings of Egypt.*
- made Joseph ruler of Egypt, Genesis 40–47
- made Israelites slaves, Exodus 1–14

Pharisees (FARE-ih-seez) *"the separate people"; they followed the Jewish religious laws and customs very strictly. Jesus often spoke against them for their religious teachings and traditions.*
- practices of, Matthew 9:14; 15:1-9; Mark 7:1-13; Luke 7:30
- against Jesus, Matthew 12:14; 22:15; John 8:1-6
- criticized by Jesus, Matthew 5:20; Matthew 23

Philadelphia (fill-uh-DEL-fee-uh) *a city in the country now called "Turkey,"* Revelation 3:7-13

Philemon (fih-LEE-mun) *a Christian in the city of Colossae,* Philemon 1-25

Philip, the apostle (FIL-ip) *friend of Peter and Andrew.*
- called by Jesus, John 1:43
- brought Nathanael to Jesus, John 1:44-50
- brought Greeks to Jesus, John 12:21-22

Philip, the evangelist, *a Greek-speaking Jew chosen to serve in the church in Jerusalem.*
- preached in Samaria, Acts 8:5-13
- preached to the Ethiopian, Acts 8:26-39
- his daughters prophesied, Acts 21:8-9

Philip, the tetrarch, *son of Herod I and Cleopatra.*
- ruler of Iturea and Trachonitis, Luke 3:1

Philippi (fih-LIP-eye) *a city in northeastern Greece,* Philippians 1:1; 4:15
- Paul in jail there, Acts 16:11-40

Philistines (FIL-ih-steens) *people who were Israel's enemy for many years; worshiped false gods.*
- Samson defeated, Judges 15–16
- captured the Ark of the Agreement, 1 Samuel 4–6
- David defeated, 1 Samuel 17–18; 2 Samuel 5:17-25; 21:15-22

Phinehas, son of Eleazar (FIN-ee-us) *a priest and grandson of Aaron,* Numbers 25:1-13

Phinehas, son of Eli, *an evil priest,* 1 Samuel 1:3; 2:34; 4:4-11

Phoebe (FEE-beh) *a woman in the church in Cenchrea,* Romans 16:1

Phoenicia (foh-NEE-shuh) *an early name for the land on the east coast of the Mediterranean Sea; called "Lebanon" today,* Mark 7:26; Acts 11:19; 15:3

phylactery (fil-LAK-tur-ee) See "box of Scriptures."

pigs
- considered unclean, Leviticus 11:7
- snout of, Proverbs 11:22
- "don't throw your pearls before pigs." Matthew 7:6
- demons sent into, Matthew 8:30-33; Mark 5:11-13; Luke 8:32-33
- fed by prodigal son, Luke 15:15-16

Pilate, Pontius (PIE-lut, PON-shus) *the Roman governor of Judea from A.D. 26 to 36,* Luke 3:1; 13:1
- handed Jesus over to be killed, Matthew 27; Mark 15; Luke 23; John 18:28–19:38

pillar (PILL-ur) *a large stone that is set upright; also a tall column of stone that supports the roof of a building.*
- of Jacob, Genesis 28:18-22
- to worship false gods, 2 Kings 17:9-12
- in the Temple, 1 Kings 7:6,15-22
- of cloud and fire, Exodus 13:21-22; 14:19-24; 33:8-10

Pisgah, Mount (PIS-guh) *one of the high spots on Mount Nebo where Moses stood to see into the promised land,* Numbers 23:14; Deuteronomy 3:27; 34:1

plague (PLAYG) *a disaster. God sent ten plagues on the land of Egypt so the Egyptians would set the Israelites free.*
- on the Egyptians, Exodus 7–11
- on the Israelites, Exodus 32:35; Numbers 11:31-33; 16:41-50; 25:1-9

plumb line (PLUM LINE) *a string with a rock or other weight on one end. People used it to see if a wall was straight.*
- symbol for God's judging, 2 Kings 21:10-13; Amos 7:7-8

pomegranate (PAHM-gran-it) *a reddish fruit about the size of an apple,* Numbers 13:23; Joel 1:12
- design on priests' clothing, Exodus 28:33-34
- design of Temple decorations, 1 Kings 7:18-20

poor
- God's care for, Psalm 140:12; Proverbs 22:22-23; Matthew 11:5; James 2:5

• treatment of, Leviticus 19:9-10; Matthew 25:34-36;
   Luke 14:12-14
possessions
   • promised land given to Israelites, Genesis 17:8;
      Numbers 32:22; Joshua 1:11
   • proper attitudes toward, Ecclesiastes 5:10– 6:6; Luke
      12:13-21; Acts 2:45; 1 John 3:17
   • danger of, Matthew 19:22
   • sold by Christians, Acts 2:45
Potiphar (POT-ih-fur) *an officer for the king of Egypt. He
   put Joseph in charge of his household.* Genesis 39
pottage (POT-edge) *a thick vegetable soup or stew,*
   Genesis 25:29-34; 2 Kings 4:38-41
potter (POT-ur) *a person who makes pots and dishes out
   of clay.*
   • as a symbol of God, Jeremiah 18:1-6
power
   • of Jesus, Matthew 24:30; 28:18; Luke 6:19
   • of the Spirit, Luke 4:14; Acts 1:8; Romans 15:19
   • of Satan, Acts 26:18
   • of the apostles, Luke 9 1; Acts 4:33
praetorium (pray-TORE-ee-um) *the governor's palace in
   New Testament times,* Matthew 27:27; Acts 23:35
praise (PRAYZ) *to say good things about someone or
   something. God's people can praise him by singing,
   praying, and by living the way he tells us to live.*
   1 Chronicles 16:4-7; Psalms 103; 104; 145–150
prayer
   • teachings about, Matthew 5:44-45; 21:18-22;
      Philippians 4:6; James 5:15-16
   • Jesus' model prayer, Matthew 6:5-15
preach, *to give a talk on a religious subject; to tell the
   Good News.*
   • Jonah preached to Nineveh, Jonah 3:2-4
   • John preached, Matthew 3:1; Mark 1:4; Luke 3:3
   • Jesus preached, Matthew 4:17; Mark 2:2; Luke 4:43-44
   • Good News preached, Acts 8:25,40; Galatians 2:7;
      1 Thessalonians 2:9
   • preaching commanded, 2 Timothy 4:2
Preparation Day (prep-a-RAY-shun DAY) *the day before
   the Sabbath day. On that day the Jews prepared for
   the Sabbath.* Luke 23:54; John 19:14,31
pride
   • warnings against, Romans 12:3; 1 Corinthians 13:4;
      Philippians 2:3; James 4:6
priest (PREEST) *in the Old Testament, a servant of God
   who worked in the Holy Tent or Temple. See also
   "high priest."*
   • clothes for, Exodus 28
   • appointing of, Exodus 29:1-37
   • rules for, Leviticus 21–22:16
Priscilla (prih-SIL-uh) *a friend of Paul,* Acts 18:1-4,18-19;
   Romans 16:3-4
   • taught Apollos, Acts 18:24-26
prison
   • Joseph in prison, Genesis 39:20–41:40
   • Peter in prison, Acts 5:17-20
   • Paul in prison, Acts 16:23-34
prodigal (PRAH-dih-gul) *careless and wasteful.*
   • the prodigal son, Luke 15:11-32
promise
   • from God, Joshua 1:3; 1 Kings 8:20; Galatians 3:14;
      Ephesians 3:6
   • first commandment with, Ephesians 6:2
   • Lord is not slow in keeping, 2 Peter 2:9
prophecy (PRAH-feh-see) *a message; God speaking
   through chosen people called "prophets,"* Ezekiel
   14:9; 1 Thessalonians 5:20; 2 Peter 1:20-21
prophesy (PRAH-fes-sy) *to speak a prophecy,* Acts 2:17-
   18. See "prophecy."
   • a spiritual gift, 1 Corinthians 14:1-5
prophet (PRAH-fet) *a messenger; one who is able, with*

God's help, to tell God's message correctly.
   Sometimes prophets told what would happen in the
   future. Matthew 11:13-14
   • how to judge, Deuteronomy 13:1-5; 18:21-22
   • examples of, Ezra 5:1; Jeremiah 1:1-9; Matthew 3:3
   • false prophets, Deuteronomy 13:1-5
prophetess (PRAH-feh-tess) *a female prophet,* Exodus
   15:20; Judges 4:4; 2 Kings 22:14; Luke 2:36. See
   "prophet."
prostitute (PRAH-sti-toot) *a person who sells his or her
   body for sex.*
   • warnings against, 1 Corinthians 6:15
   • examples of, Genesis 38:15-16; Jeremiah 3:1-3; Hosea
      3:2-3; Matthew 21:32
proverbs (PRAH-verbs) *wise sayings. The book of Proverbs
   contains many wise sayings that tell how to live a
   good and happy life.* 1 Kings 4:32; Proverbs
psalm (SAHM) *a song. The book of Psalms is like a
   songbook.* Ephesians 5:19; Colossians 3:16
publican (PUB-leh-kun) See "tax collector."
Publius (POOB-lih-us) *an important man of the island of
   Malta,* Acts 28:7-8
Pul, See "Tiglath-Pileser."
punishment
   • of Cain, Genesis 4:13
   • everlasting, Matthew 25:46; 2 Thessalonians 1:8-9
   • for rejecting Jesus, Hebrews 10:29
   • by government, Romans 13:4; 1 Peter 2:14
pure
   • gold, Exodus 25:11-39; 37; 1 Kings 6:20-21
   • heart, Psalm 51:10; Matthew 5:8
   • describing Jesus, Hebrews 7:26
   • describing people, Job 4:17; 15:14; Philippians 1:10;
      Titus 1:15
   • water, Hebrews 10:22
Purim, See "Feast of Purim."
purple, *a color that, in Bible times, was worn by kings,
   queens, and other rich people. Purple cloth was
   expensive because the purple dye came from special
   shellfish.* Exodus 25:1-4; Judges 8:26; Mark 15:17;
   Acts 16:14

Q

quail (KWALE) *a brownish-white bird.*
   • given by God to Israel, Exodus 16:11-13; Numbers
      11:31-34; Psalm 105:40
quarrel
   • Israelites quarreled with Moses, Exodus 17:1-7
Queen Goddess, *Ishtar; a goddess of the Babylonians,*
   Jeremiah 7:18; 44:15-29
Queen of Heaven, See "Queen Goddess."
queen of Sheba, See "Sheba, queen of."
question
   • Solomon questioned by queen of Sheba, 1 Kings 10:1-3
   • Jesus questioned, Mark 8:11; Luke 23:9; John 8:6
   • asked by Jesus, Matthew 21:24
   • apostles questioned by Jews, Acts 4:7; 5:27
quiet
   • words, Ecclesiastes 9:17
   • riot quieted, Acts 19:35-36
   • life, 1 Thessalonians 4:11; 1 Timothy 2:2
Quirinius (kwy-RIN-ee-us) *the Roman governor of Syria
   when Jesus was born,* Luke 2:1-3
quiver (KWIH-vur) *a bag to hold arrows,* Psalm 127:5;
   Isaiah 49:2

R

Rabbah (RAB-uh) *the capital city of the Ammonites,*
   2 Samuel 11:1; 12:26-29; Ezekiel 25:5
rabbi/rabboni (RAB-eye/rah-BONE-eye) *teacher. Jesus'
   followers often called him "rabbi" as a sign of
   respect.* John 1:38; 20:16

Rachel (RAY-chel) *a wife of Jacob and the mother of Benjamin and Joseph.*
• married Jacob, Genesis 29:1-30
• gave birth to Joseph, Genesis 30:22-24
• stole Laban's idols, Genesis 31:19-35
• death of, Genesis 35:16-20
Rahab, the dragon (RAY-hab) *In a well-known story, Rahab was defeated. Egypt was sometimes called Rahab to show that it would be defeated.* Job 9:13; Isaiah 30:7
Rahab, the prostitute, *a woman in Jericho. She hid the Israelite spies and helped them escape.*
• hid the spies, Joshua 2:1-21
• rescued from Jericho, Joshua 6:16-25
• an example of faith, Hebrews 11:31; James 2:25
rainbow
• a sign of God's agreement with people, Genesis 9:8-17
raisin, 1 Samuel 25:18; 30:12; 1 Chronicles 12:40
ram, *a male sheep.*
• offered instead of Isaac, Genesis 22:13
• used for burnt offerings, Exodus 29; Leviticus 8:18-29; Numbers 28:11–29:37
• with two horns, Daniel 8:3-22
Ramah (RAY-muh) *a town about five miles north of Jerusalem,* Jeremiah 31:15; Matthew 2:18
Rameses (RAM-eh-seez) *one of the cities built by the Israelites when they were slaves in Egypt,* Exodus 1:11; 12:37; Numbers 33:3
Ramoth Gilead (RAY-moth GIL-ee-ad) *one of the cities of safety on the east side of the Jordan River,* Joshua 20:8; 1 Kings 4:13; 2 Kings 8:28–9:14
ransom, *a payment that frees a captive.*
• Jesus as a ransom for sins, Matthew 20:28; 1 Timothy 2:6; Hebrews 9:15
Rapha (RAY-fa) *a leader of a group of people in Canaan who may have been giants. The descendants of Rapha are called "Rephaites."* 2 Samuel 21:15-22; Joshua 13:12
raven, *a large black bird similar to a crow which eats dead things.*
• sent out by Noah, Genesis 8:7
• fed Elijah, 1 Kings 17:4-6
read
• the Book of the Teachings, Joshua 8:34-35; Nehemiah 8:2-9
• reading the teachings commanded, Deuteronomy 17:18-19; 31:9-13
• brings happiness, Revelation 1:3
Rebekah (ree-BEK-uh) *the wife of Isaac and the mother of Jacob and Esau.*
• married Isaac, Genesis 24
• gave birth to Jacob and Esau, Genesis 25:19-26
• helped deceive Isaac, Genesis 27
• buried at Machpelah, Genesis 49:31
redeem (ree-DEEM) *to buy something back or to buy a slave's freedom.*
• property, Leviticus 25:23-34; Ruth 4:3-6
• slave, Leviticus 25:47-49
• redeemed by God, 1 Corinthians 6:20; Galatians 4:5; Titus 2:14
Red Sea, *Sea of Reeds; a large body of water between Africa and Arabia.*
• Israelites crossed, Exodus 13:17–14:31
refuge, *a place of safety or protection.*
• God as our refuge, Deuteronomy 33:27; 2 Samuel 22:3; Psalms 18:2; 31:2; 71:3; 91:2
• *city of, Numbers 35:6-34; Joshua 20*
Rehoboam (ree-ho-BO-um) *son of Solomon who took his place as king.*
• became king, 1 Kings 11:41-43
• Israel rebelled against, 1 Kings 12:1-24
• strengthened Judah, 2 Chronicles 11:5-17

• disobeyed God, 2 Chronicles 12
rejoice
• commanded to, Matthew 5:11-12; Romans 12:15; Philippians 4:4; 1 Peter 4:13
• examples of, 1 Samuel 6:13; Nehemiah 12:43
remission (rih-MISH-un) See "forgiveness."
remnant (REM-nant) *a small part that is left; a name used for the Jews who were left alive after their captivity in Babylon.*
• of Israelites who returned to Jerusalem, Ezra 9:15; Nehemiah 1:2; Isaiah 10:20-22
repent (ree-PENT) *being sorry for doing something wrong and not continuing to do that wrong. See "change of heart and life."*
Rephaites, See "Rapha."
respect
• to parents, Leviticus 19:3; 1 Timothy 3:4
• between husbands and wives, Ephesians 5:33; 1 Peter 3:7
• to all people, 1 Peter 2:17; 3:16
rest
• on the seventh day, Genesis 2:2; Exodus 31:15; Hebrews 4:4
• given by the Lord, Psalm 95:11; Jeremiah 6:16; Matthew 11:28
• heaven as a place of rest, Revelation 14:13
resurrection (REZ-uh-REK-shun) *a dead person's coming back to life.*
• of Jesus, Matthew 28:1-10; Mark 16; Luke 24; John 20–21; Acts 2:24-32; Romans 1:4
• of God's people, John 6:39; Acts 24:15; 1 Corinthians 15; Philippians 3:10-11; Hebrews 11:35
Reuben (ROO-ben) *oldest of Jacob's twelve sons.*
• birth of, Genesis 29:32
• tried to save Joseph, Genesis 37:18-29
• descendants of, Exodus 6:14; Numbers 1:20; Joshua 13:15-23
revelation (rev-uh-LAY-shun) *showing plainly something that has been hidden,* 2 Corinthians 12:1; Revelation 1:1-3
revenge
• warnings against, Leviticus 19:18; Romans 12:19; 1 Thessalonians 5:15; 1 Peter 3:9
reward
• in heaven, Matthew 5:12
• for obedience, Psalm 19:11
• for what a person does, Matthew 6:1-18; 10:42; 16:27; Colossians 3:24
• children as a reward, Psalm 127:3
Rhoda (ROAD-uh) *a servant girl in the home of John Mark's mother,* Acts 12:6-17
righteousness (RY-chuss-ness) *being right with God and doing what is right.*
• explained, Romans 3:19-26; 2 Corinthians 5:21; 6:4-7; Philippians 3:8-9
• Abraham as an example of, Romans 4:3
• right living, 2 Corinthians 6:7; Ephesians 5:9; 1 Timothy 6:11; 1 Peter 2:24
robber
• Temple as a hideout for, Jeremiah 7:11; Matthew 21:13
• attacked man on road to Jericho, Luke 10:30
• killed with Jesus, Matthew 27:38-44; John 18:40
roof
• spies hid there, Joshua 2:6
• David saw Bathsheba from there, 2 Samuel 11:2
• built room for Elisha there, 2 Kings 4:8-10
• *man lowered through, Mark 2:3-4*
• Peter prayed there, Acts 10:9
Rock, *often used as a name for God. As a large rock is strong and provides a hiding place, so God is strong and protects us from our enemies.* Genesis 49:24; 2 Samuel 22:32-49; Psalm 19:14

rock badger (ROK BAD-jur) *a coney; a small, tailless animal like a rabbit that hides among the mountain gorges and rocky areas of Arabia,* Psalm 104:18; Proverbs 30:26

Rome, *the capital city of the Roman Empire at the time of Christ,* Acts 2:10; 18:2; Romans 1:7
• Paul sent there, Acts 23:11; 28:14-15

Ruth (ROOTH) *a widow from Moab.*
• moved to Judah, Ruth 1
• worked in Boaz's field Ruth 2
• married Boaz, Ruth 3–4
• birth of Obed, Ruth 4:13-22

S

Sabbath (SAB-uth) *means "rest"; the seventh day of the Jewish week; the Jews' day to worship God. They were not allowed to work on this day.*
• commands about, Exodus 20:8-11; 31:12-17
• Jesus is Lord of, Matthew 12:1-13; Mark 2:23-28; Luke 6:1-11

sackcloth (SAK-cloth) *a type of clothing made from rough cloth; worn by people to show their sadness,* Genesis 37:33-35; Esther 4:1; Matthew 11:21

sacrifice (SAK-rih-fice) *to give something valuable to God.*
• burnt sacrifices, Leviticus 6:8-13
• drink sacrifices, Leviticus 23:13; Numbers 15:5; 28:7
• penalty sacrifices, Leviticus 7:1-10
• fellowship sacrifices, Leviticus 3; 7:11-27
• sin sacrifices, Leviticus 4
• limits of, Hebrews 9; 10
• living sacrifice, Romans 12:1

Sadducees (SAD-you-seez) *a Jewish religious group that didn't believe in angels or resurrection; they believed only the first five books of the Old Testament were true.*
• challenged Jesus, Matthew 22:23-33
• arrested Peter and John, Acts 4:1-3
• arrested the apostles, Acts 5:17-42
• Paul spoke to the council, Acts 23:1-9

safety, city of, *city of refuge. In Bible times, someone who had accidentally killed another person could go to a city of safety for protection. As long as he was there, the dead person's relative could not punish him.*
• rules about, Numbers 35:6-34; Joshua 20

saffron (SAF-ron) *a purple flower; parts of it are used as a spice,* Song of Solomon 4:14

saint, *holy person; another word for "Christian,"* Acts 9:41; Romans 1:7; 1 Corinthians 14:33

Salem (SAY-lem) *means "peace"; an old name for Jerusalem.*
• home of Melchizedek, Genesis 14:18; Hebrews 7:1-2

Salome, daughter of Herodias (sah-LO-mee)
• had John the Baptist killed, Matthew 14:3-12; Mark 6:17-29

Salome, wife of Zebedee, *the mother of the apostles James and John,* Mark 15:40; 16:1

salt
• used to preserve foods, Job 6:6; Mark 9:50
• Lot's wife turned into salt, Genesis 19:15-26
• "You are the salt of the earth," Matthew 5:13

Salt Sea, See "Dead Sea."

salvation (sal-VAY-shun) *being rescued from danger; being saved from sin and its punishment.*
• as God's gift, John 3:16; Ephesians 2:8; Titus 2:11
• through Christ, Acts 4:12; 1 Thessalonians 5:9; 1 Timothy 1:15; Hebrews 5:7-9
• as a helmet, Ephesians 6:17; 1 Thessalonians 5:8
• urgency of, 2 Corinthians 6:2; Hebrews 2:3
• rejoice in, Psalms 9:14; 13:5; 51:12; Isaiah 25:9

Samaritan (sah-MEHR-ih-ton) *a person from the area of Samaria in Palestine. These people were only partly*

Jewish, so the Jews hated them. John 4:9
• Jesus taught a Samaritan woman, John 4:1-42
• story of the good Samaritan, Luke 10:25-37

Samson (SAM-son) *one of Israel's judges; he was famous for his great strength.*
• birth of, Judges 13
• married a Philistine, Judges 14–15
• tricked by Delilah, Judges 16:4-22
• death of, Judges 16:23-31
• hero of faith, Hebrews 11:32

Samuel (SAM-u-el) *the last judge in Israel.*
• birth of, 1 Samuel 1:1-20
• worked in the Temple, 1 Samuel 1:21–2:26
• became a prophet, 1 Samuel 3
• appointed Saul as king, 1 Samuel 10
• appointed David as king, 1 Samuel 16:1-13
• death of, 1 Samuel 25:1

Sanballat (san-BAL-lat) *governor of Samaria who tried to stop Nehemiah from rebuilding the walls of Jerusalem,* Nehemiah 4–6

sanctify (SANK-teh-fy) *to make holy or ready for service to God,* John 17: 7-19; 1 Corinthians 6:11; 1 Peter 1:2

sanctuary (SANK-choo-air-ee) See "Holy Place."

sand
• Abraham's descendants as numerous as, Genesis 22:17; 32:12
• Job's days as numerous as, Job 29:18
• house built on, Matthew 7:26-27

Sanhedrin (san-HEE-drin) See "council."

Sapphira (sah-FY-ruh) *wife of Ananias.*
• lied to the Holy Spirit, Acts 5:1-11

Sarah (SAIR-uh) *wife of Abraham,* Genesis 11:29-30
• gave Hagar to Abraham, Genesis 16:1-6
• name changed from "Sarai," Genesis 17:15-16
• gave birth to Isaac, Genesis 21:1-7
• death of, Genesis 23

Satan (SAY-ton) *means "enemy"; the devil; the enemy of God and man.*
• encouraged David to sin, 1 Chronicles 21:1
• tested Job, Job 1:5-12; 2:1-7
• tempted Jesus, Luke 4:1-13
• a fallen angel, Luke 10:18-19
• to be thrown into lake of fire, Revelation 20:10

Saul, king of Israel
• appointed king, 1 Samuel 9–10
• disobeyed God, 1 Samuel 15
• tried to kill David, 1 Samuel 19; 23:7-29
• death of, 1 Samuel 31

Saul of Tarsus, Acts 13:9. See "Paul."

savior
• God as Savior, Psalm 25:5; Isaiah 45:21; Luke 1:47; 1 Timothy 1:1
• Christ as Savior, Luke 2:11; John 4:42; Ephesians 5:23; Titus 2:13

scarlet (SCAR-let) *a bright red color,* Exodus 26:1; Joshua 2:18; Isaiah 1:18; Matthew 27:28

scepter (SEP-tur) *a wand or a rod that the king holds; a sign of his power,* Esther 4:11; Psalm 60:7

scourge (SKURJ) *to beat someone with a whip or stick,* 1 Kings 12:11
• Jesus scourged, Matthew 27:26; Mark 15:15
• Paul scourged, Acts 21:32; 2 Corinthians 11:24

scribe, *to write, to count, and to put in order. In New Testament times scribes were men who wrote copies of the Scriptures.*
• Ezra as scribe, Nehemiah 8:1
• against Jesus, Matthew 15:1-9
• condemned by Jesus, Matthew 23:13-36

Scriptures (SCRIP-churs) *special writings of God's word for people. When the word Scriptures is used in the New Testament, it usually means the Old Testament. Later, it came to mean the whole Bible.*

- fulfilled, Matthew 26:52-54; John 19:24,28,36
- given by God, 2 Timothy 3:16

scroll, *a long roll of paper used for writing,* Deuteronomy 17:18; Jeremiah 36; Revelation 5:1-5

Scythians (SITH-ee-unz) *a group of wandering people who lived near the Black Sea,* Colossians 3:11

Sea of Galilee, See "Galilee, Lake."

Sea of Reeds, See "Red Sea."

seal, *a tool with a design or picture carved on it. Kings pressed this seal into wax and used it like a signature. Sometimes these seals were worn as rings.*
- examples of, 1 Kings 21:8; Esther 8:8

seed
- created by God, Genesis 1:11,12,29
- parables of, Matthew 13:1-43

seer, *another name for prophet.* See "prophet."

Selah (SEE-lah) *probably a musical direction; used in the Psalms. It may mean to pause. The word was not intended to be spoken when reading the psalm.* Psalms 3:2,4,8; 89:4,37,45,48

Sennacherib (sen-AK-ur-ib) *king of Assyria from 705 to 681 B.C.*
- attacked Jerusalem, 2 Kings 18:13–19; 2 Chronicles 32:1-23; Isaiah 36–37

Sermon on the Mount, *a sermon Jesus preached as he was sitting on the side of a mountain near Lake Galilee,* Matthew 5–7

serpent, See "snake."

servant
- of the Lord, Deuteronomy 34:5; Joshua 2:8; 1 Kings 11:32; Luke 1:38
- Jesus as a, Philippians 2:7
- parable of, Matthew 25:14-30
- Jesus' followers to be, Matthew 20:25-27

Seth, *the third son of Adam and Eve,* Genesis 4:25-26; 5:6-8; Luke 3:38

Shadrach (SHAYD-rak) *a friend of Daniel.*
- taken into captivity, Daniel 1
- became a leader, Daniel 2:49
- saved from the furnace, Daniel 3

Shallum, king of Israel (SHAL-um) *ruled for only one month in 752 B.C.,* 2 Kings 15:10-15

Shalmaneser (shal-mah-NEE-zer) *a king of Assyria,* 2 Kings 17:1-6; 18:9

Shaphan (SHAY-fan) *an assistant to King Josiah,* 2 Kings 22:3-14; 2 Chronicles 34:8-21

sharing
- commanded, Luke 3:11; Romans 12:13; 1 Timothy 6:18
- examples of, Acts 2:42-47; 4:32; 2 Corinthians 8:1-4

Sharon (SHAIR-un) *the plain in Palestine along the coast of the Mediterranean Sea,* 1 Chronicles 5:16; 27:29; Song of Solomon 2:1; Isaiah 33:9

sheaf (SHEEF) *a bundle of grain stalks that have been cut and tied together,* Genesis 37:7; Leviticus 23:10; Job 24:10

Sheba, queen of (SHE-buh) *a queen who came to visit Solomon and see his wealth,* 1 Kings 10:1-13

Shebna (SHEB-nuh) *the manager of the palace for King Hezekiah,* 2 Kings 18:17–19:4; Isaiah 36:1–37:4

sheep
- God's people compared to, Ezekiel 34; John 10:1-18; 1 Peter 2:25
- parable of, Luke 15:1-7

Shem, *Noah's oldest son,* Genesis 6:10; 7:13; 10:21-31

sheminith (SHEM-ih-nith) *a musical term in the Psalms that means an octave (eight notes); may mean to use an instrument with eight strings,* Psalms 6; 12

shepherd
- David as, 1 Samuel 17:15,34-36
- Lord as, Psalm 23

- Jesus, the good shepherd, John 10:1-18
- elders as, 1 Peter 5:1-4

Sheshbazzar (shesh-BAZ-ur) *governor of the Jews in 538 B.C.,* Ezra 1:7-11; 5:13-16

shiggaion (shi-GY-on) *probably a musical term; used in the Psalms; may mean that the psalm is a sad song,* Psalm 7

shigionoth (shi-GY-o-noth) *probably a musical term,* Habakkuk 3:1

Shiloh (SHY-lo) *a town north of Jerusalem.*
- location of the Holy Tent, Joshua 18:1,8; Judges 18:31; Jeremiah 7:12

Shimei (SHIM-ee-i) *a relative of King Saul.*
- cursed David, 2 Samuel 16:5-14
- asked forgiveness, 2 Samuel 19:16-23
- death of, 1 Kings 2:36-46

ship, 1 Kings 9:26-28; 22:48; Acts 27

Shishak (SHY-shak) *king of Egypt during the time of Solomon and Rehoboam.*
- attacked Jerusalem, 1 Kings 14:25-28; 2 Chronicles 12:1-9

showbread, See "bread that shows we are in God's presence."

Shunammite (SHOO-nah-mite) *a person from Shunem, a town in northern Israel.*
- Shunammite woman took care of Elisha, 2 Kings 4:8-17
- her son raised from the dead, 2 Kings 4:18-37
- given back her land, 2 Kings 8:1-6

sickle (SICK-ul) *a tool for cutting grain,* Revelation 14:14-19

Sidon (SY-don) *a Phoenician city on the coast of the Mediterranean Sea,* Genesis 10:19; Matthew 11:21-22; Mark 7:31; Acts 27:3-4

siege mound (SEEJ) *dirt piled against a city wall to make it easier for attackers to climb up and attack the city,* 2 Samuel 20:15; Isaiah 37:33; Jeremiah 6:6

signet ring (SIG-net RING) *a ring worn by a king or other important person. It had his seal on it.* Genesis 41:42; Esther 3:10; 8:2-10; Daniel 6:17. See "seal."

Sihon (SY-hon) *a king of the Amorites when the Israelites came out of Egypt.*
- refused to let Israelites pass, Numbers 21:21-31; Deuteronomy 2:24-37

Silas (SY-lus) *also "Silvanus"; a teacher in the church in Jerusalem who often traveled with Paul.*
- sent to the Gentiles, Acts 15:22-23; 17:16
- joined Paul in Corinth, Acts 18:5
- helped with Peter's letter, 1 Peter 5:12

Siloam, pool of (sy-LO-um) *a pool of water in Jerusalem,* John 9:1-12

Silvanus (sil-VAY-nus) See "Silas."

Simeon of Jerusalem (SIM-ee-un) *a godly man who saw baby Jesus in the Temple,* Luke 2:25-35

Simeon, son of Israel, *one of the twelve sons of Israel,* Genesis 29:33; 42:23-36
- descendants of, Numbers 1:22-23; 26:12-14

Simon, brother of Jesus (SY-mun) Matthew 13:55

Simon of Cyrene (sy-REE-ni) *carried the cross of Jesus,* Matthew 27:32; Mark 15:21; Luke 23:26

Simon Peter, See "Peter."

Simon, the magician, *tried to buy the power of the Holy Spirit,* Acts 8:9-24

Simon, the Zealot, *an apostle of Jesus,* Matthew 10:4; Mark 3:18; Luke 6:15; Acts 1:13

sin, *a word, thought, or act against the law of God.*
- offering for, Leviticus 4; 6:24-30; Hebrews 7:27; 10:4-12
- committed by everyone, Romans 3:23; 1 John 1:8-10
- Christ died for, Romans 4:25; 1 Corinthians 15:3; 1 Peter 2:24; 1 John 2:2; 3:5
- results of, Isaiah 59:2; Romans 6:23; Ephesians 2:1; Hebrews 12:1

Sinai (SY-ny) *a mountain in the desert between Egypt and Canaan.*
- Moses received the Ten Commandments there, Exodus 19–20

singing, *a way of praising God and teaching each other,* Judges 5:3; Psalm 30:4; Ephesians 5:19; Colossians 3:16

Sisera (SIS-er-uh) *captain of a Canaanite army,* Judges 4

slave
- rules about, Exodus 21:1-11,16,26-32; Ephesians 6:5-9; 1 Timothy 6:1-2

slave woman, *concubine; she bore children for her master but was not considered equal to a wife.*
- Hagar as, Genesis 16:1-3
- of Solomon, 1 Kings 11:2-3

sleep
- God never sleeps, Psalm 121:4
- danger of, Proverbs 6 10-11
- Eutychus fell asleep, Acts 20:9
- to awake from, Romans 13:11
- a gift from the Lord, Psalm 127:2

sling, *a weapon for throwing rocks,* Judges 20:16; 1 Samuel 17:39-50; 2 Kings 3:24-25

slothful (SLAWTH-ful) *lazy and undependable,* Proverbs 6:6-11; 13:4; Matthew 25:26; Hebrews 6:12

sluggard, See "slothful."

snake
- sticks became snakes, Exodus 7:8-13
- bronze snake made by Moses, Numbers 21:4-9; John 3:14
- Paul bitten by, Acts 28:1-6

Sodom (SOD-um) *a town known for its evil people.*
- destroyed, Genesis 13:17–19:29
- symbol of evil, Matthew 10:11-15; 11:20-24; Revelation 11:8

soldier
- arrested Jesus, John 18:12-13
- made fun of Jesus, Matthew 27:27-31; Luke 23:11
- at Jesus' death, Matthew 27:32-37; Luke 23:26-38,47; John 19:1-3,16-24,28-35
- lied about Jesus' resurrection, Matthew 28:11-15
- Cornelius, Acts 10:1
- guarded Peter, Acts 12:6
- Christian compared to, 2 Timothy 2:3-4

Solomon (SOL-o-mon) *a son of David; famous for his wisdom.*
- became king, 1 Kings 1:28-53
- wisdom of, 1 Kings 3:1-15; 4:29-34
- made a wise decision, 1 Kings 3:16-28
- built the Temple, 1 Kings 6; 7:13-51
- visited by the queen of Sheba, 1 Kings 10:1-13; Matthew 12:42
- married many women, 1 Kings 11:1-8
- death of, 1 Kings 11:40-41

Solomon's Porch (SOL-o-mon's PORCH) *a covered courtyard on the east side of the Temple,* 1 Kings 7:6; John 10:23; Acts 3:11; 5:12

Son of David, *a name the Jews used for the Christ because the Savior was to come from the family of King David,* Matthew 1:1; 9:27; 15:22; 21:9

Son of Man, *a name Jesus called himself. It showed that he was God's Son, but he was also a human being.* Matthew 24:30; Mark 13:26; Luke 21:27; 22:69-70

sorcery (SOR-sir-ee) *trying to put magical spells on people or harming them by magic,* Acts 8:9-25; 19:18-19
- warnings against, Leviticus 19:26; Deuteronomy 18:14-15; 2 Kings 17:17

soul (SOLE) *what makes a person alive. Sometimes the Bible writers used words like "heart" and "soul" to mean a person's whole being or the person himself.*
- "destroy the soul and the body," Matthew 10:28
- losing, Matthew 15:26

- "all your heart and all your soul," Matthew 22:37
- joined with the spirit, Hebrews 4:12

sower, *someone who plants seeds to grow into crops,* Matthew 13:1-43; 2 Corinthians 9:6

Spirit (SPIH-rit) See "Holy Spirit."

spirit, *the part of humans that was made to be like God because God is spirit. The New Testament also talks about evil spirits.* Isaiah 26:9; 1 Thessalonians 5:23; James 2:26
- evil spirit, Matthew 12:43; Mark 1:23; 5:2; Luke 4:33

spiritual gifts, *special talents or abilities that God gives his people,* Romans 12:6-8; 1 Corinthians 12:1-11; 14; Ephesians 4:7-13

spring, *a natural fountain,* Genesis 7:11; Exodus 15:27

staff, *a shepherd's walking stick,* Exodus 4:1-5; 7:8-12; Numbers 20:6-11; Psalm 23:4

steal, See also "robber."
- commands against, Exodus 20:15; Matthew 19:18; Romans 13:9; Ephesians 4:28

Stephen (STEE-ven) *one of the seven men chosen to serve the church in Jerusalem; the first martyr for Christ.*
- chosen to serve the church, Acts 6:5-6
- killed by the Jews, Acts 6:8–7:60

stoning, *a way of killing someone by throwing rocks at him.*
- commanded, Deuteronomy 17:2-7
- Naboth stoned, 1 Kings 21:13
- Stephen stoned, Acts 7:54-60
- Paul stoned, Acts 14:19

strength
- love God with all your strength, Deuteronomy 6:5; Mark 12:30
- God as the source, Psalms 18:1; 73:26; Philippians 4:13; 1 Peter 4:11

stronghold, *a fortress, a well protected place,* 1 Samuel 22:4; 2 Samuel 5:17

suffering
- proper attitude toward, 2 Corinthians 1:3-7; James 5:10
- value of, Romans 8:17-18; 1 Peter 3:8-17
- of Jesus, Isaiah 53:3-10; Luke 24:26,46; Philippians 3:10; Hebrews 2:18

swaddling clothes, *pieces of cloth that were wrapped around a newborn baby in Jesus' time,* Luke 2:7-12

sword
- of fire, Genesis 3:24
- a weapon, Joshua 5:13; 1 Samuel 17:45; Matthew 26:51-52
- the word of God, Ephesians 6:17; Hebrews 4:12

Sychar (SY-kar) *a small town in Samaria near Jacob's well,* John 4:5-6

synagogue (SIN-uh-gog) *"a meeting." By the first century, the Jews met in synagogues to read and study the Scriptures. The building was also used as the Jewish court and as a school.*
- Jesus taught in, Matthew 4:23; Mark 1:21; Luke 4:16-17
- Paul spoke there, Acts 17:1,10

Syria (SEER-ee-uh) *an area north of Galilee and east of the Mediterranean Sea; called "Aram" in Old Testament times.* See "Aram."
- enemy of Israel, 1 Kings 11:25; 20:1-34; 2 Kings 13:22-25
- learned about Jesus, Matthew 4:24

T

tabernacle (TAB-er-NAK-'l) See "Meeting Tent."

tablets of the agreement, *two flat stones on which God wrote the Ten Commandments.*
- given to Moses, Exodus 19–20; 24:12-18
- broken by Moses, Exodus 32:15-19
- the second tablets, Exodus 34:1-4

• in the Most Holy Place, Hebrews 9:4

Tabitha (TAB-eh-thuh) See "Dorcas."

Tabor, Mount (TAY-bur) *in the Valley of Jezreel about twelve miles from Lake Galilee,* Judges 4:6-16; Psalm 89:12

tambourine (tam-bah-REEN) *a musical instrument that is beaten to keep rhythm,* Exodus 15:20; 1 Samuel 18:6; Psalm 81:2

Tarshish (TAR-shish) *a city somewhere on the western side of the Mediterranean Sea,* Jonah 1:3; 4:2

Tarsus (TAR-sus) *the most important city in Cilicia, which is now the country of Turkey,* Acts 9:30; 11:25-26
• home of Paul, Acts 9:11; 21:39; 22:3

tax collector, *a Jew hired by the Romans to collect taxes,* Matthew 9:10-11
• Matthew, Matthew 10:3; Luke 5:27
• Zacchaeus, Luke 19:1-10

teacher
• Jesus called a, Matthew 8:19; Mark 10:17; John 1:38; 3:2
• in the church, Romans 12:7; Ephesians 4:11; 1 Timothy 4:13
• false, 1 Timothy 4:1-5; 2 Peter 2:1
• to be judged more strictly, James 3:1

teaching
• commanded, Deuteronomy 6:1-7; Matthew 28:20; 2 Timothy 2:2,14-15; Titus 2

Teachings of Moses, *or the "Law of Moses,"* Deuteronomy 31:24-26; Joshua 23:6; Nehemiah 8
• purpose of, Romans 3:20; 5:20; Galatians 3:21-25
• limitations of, Romans 8:3; Galatians 2:19; Hebrews 10:1

temple (TEM-p'l) *a building where people worship. God told the Jewish people to worship him at the Temple in Jerusalem.*
• Solomon's Temple, 1 Kings 6–8; 2 Chronicles 2–7
• the Temple rebuilt, Ezra 3
• the body as a temple, John 2:19-22; 1 Corinthians 3:16-17; 6:19-20; 2 Corinthians 6:16

temptation (temp-TAY-shun) *the devil's attempt to get us to do something wrong.*
• Jesus tempted, Matthew 4:1-11; Luke 4:1-13; Hebrews 4:15-16
• a way of escape from, 1 Corinthians 10:13
• source of, James 1:13-15

Ten Commandments, *the rules God gave Moses on Mount Sinai,* Exodus 20:1-20; 31:18; 34:1-28; Deuteronomy 5:1-22

tent
• Abram's tents, Genesis 13:18
• peg, Judges 4:21-22
• makers of, Acts 18:3

Tent, See "Meeting Tent."

Thaddaeus (THAD-ee-us) *one of the twelve apostles,* Matthew 10:3; Mark 3:18

thankfulness, Psalm 107:1; 1 Thessalonians 5:8; Hebrews 12:28

Theophilus (thee-AHF-ih-lus) *the person to whom the books of Luke and Acts were written,* Luke 1:1-4; Acts 1:1

Thessalonica (THES-ah-lah-NY-kah) *the capital of the country of Macedonia, which is now northern Greece,* 1 Thessalonians 1:1; 2 Thessalonians 1:1
• Paul preached there, Acts 17:1-9

Thomas (TOM-us) *Didymus; one of the twelve apostles,* Matthew 10:2-3
• questioned Jesus, John 14:5-7
• saw Jesus after resurrection, John 20:24-29; 21:2

thorn, *sharp points on a branch or stem of a plant.*
• as a curse on Adam, Genesis 3:17-18
• crown of, Matthew 27:29; Mark 15:17; John 19:2-5

threshing floor, *a place where farmers separated grain*

from chaff. This was done by beating the stalks on the hard ground, throwing them in the air, and letting the wind blow the chaff away.
• angel visited Gideon there, Judges 6:11
• David bought, 2 Samuel 24:16-25

throne
• king's throne, 1 Kings 10:18-19
• God's throne, Matthew 5:34; Hebrews 4:16; Revelation 3:21; 4

Thummim (THUM-im) *the Urim and Thummim may have been gems. They were attached to the holy vest of the high priest and were used to learn God's will.* Exodus 28:29-30; Leviticus 8:8; Deuteronomy 33:8

Thyatira (THY-ah-TY-rah) *an important city in Asia famous for its purple cloth,* Acts 16:13-14; Revelation 1:11; 2:18-29

Tiberius Caesar (tie-BEER-ee-us SEE-zur) *Roman emperor during the last half of Jesus' life,* Luke 3:1

Tiglath-Pileser (TIG-lath-peh-LEE-zur) *king of Assyria who helped Ahaz; also called "Pul."*
• attacked Israel, 2 Kings 15:19-20
• rescued Ahaz, 2 Kings 16:7-10

Tigris (TY-gris) *a great river in the eastern part of the Bible lands,* Genesis 2:14; Daniel 10:4

Timothy (TIM-oh-thee) *close friend and helper of the apostle Paul.*
• helped Paul, Acts 16:1-3; 17:13-16; 1 Corinthians 4:17; 2 Corinthians 1:19
• instructed by Paul, 1 and 2 Timothy

tithe (TIETH) *"tenth." The Jews were told to give one-tenth of what they earned to God.* Leviticus 27:30-32; Deuteronomy 12:1-6; Luke 11:42; 18:12

Titus (TIE-tus) *trusted friend and helper of the apostle Paul.*
• helped Corinthians, 2 Corinthians 7:6-7,13-15; 8:6,16,23
• appointed elders, Titus 1:4-5
• Paul's instructions to, Titus 1–3

Tobiah (toe-BY-uh) *tried to keep Nehemiah from rebuilding the walls of Jerusalem,* Nehemiah 2:10-20; 6:10-19; 13:4-9

tomb
• of Lazarus, John 11:38-44
• of Jesus, Matthew 27:57–28:15; Mark 15:42–16:30; Luke 23:50–24:12; John 19:38–20:9

tongue
• lying tongue hated by God, Proverbs 6:16-17
• cannot be tamed, James 3:2-12

tower of Babel, See "Babel."

transfiguration (tranz-fig-you-RAY-shun) *"to change." Jesus was transfigured in front of Peter, James, and John when his face and clothes began to shine brightly.* Matthew 17:1-9; Mark 9:2-9; Luke 9:28-36

tree
• of knowledge of good and evil, Genesis 2:9; 3:3
• of life, Genesis 2:9; Revelation 2:7; 22:2,14
• people compared to, Psalms 1:3; 92:12; Jeremiah 17:8; Matthew 3:10; 12:33
• cross described as a tree, Galatians 3:13

trespass, See "sin."

tribe, *all descendants of a certain person. The twelve tribes of Israel were descendants of the twelve sons of Jacob, who was later named "Israel."* Numbers 1–2
• Canaan divided among, Joshua 13:7-33; 15–19

triumphal entry (tri-UMF-ul) *the time Jesus entered Jerusalem just before his death,* Matthew 21;)-11; Mark 11:1-10; Luke 19:28-44; John 12:12-15

Troas (TRO-az) *one of the most important cities in northwest Asia,* Acts 16:8-10; 20:5-12; 2 Corinthians 2:12

Trophimus (TROF-eh-mus) *non-Jewish Christian who*

traveled with Paul, Acts 20:3-4; 21:27-29; 2 Timothy 4:20

trumpet (TRUM-pet) *in Bible times it was made from animal horns; used to call an army together or announce something important,* Numbers 10:2-10; Joshua 6:4-20; 1 Corinthians 15:52

trust
* a duty, Luke 16:11; 1 Corinthians 4:2; Titus 2:10
* in God, Psalm 20:7; Proverbs 3:5; 16:20; Romans 4:5; 10:11; 1 Peter 2:6
* in lesser things, Psalms 49:13-14; 118:9; Proverbs 11:28; Isaiah 2:22

truth
* speaking honestly, Psalm 15:2; Proverbs 16:13
* God's message, John 17:17; Romans 1:25; Ephesians 1:13; 1 John 1:6

tunic (TOO-nik) *a kind of coat,* Exodus 28:39-40; John 19:23

Tychicus (TIK-ih-kus) *Christian from Asia who did important jobs for Paul,* Acts 20:4; Ephesians 6:21-22; Colossians 4:7-9

Tyre (TIRE) *large, important city in Phoenicia, which is now part of the country of Lebanon,* Mark 7:24-31; Acts 12:20
* Hiram, king of, 2 Samuel 5:11; 1 Kings 9:10-14; 2 Chronicles 2
* a wicked city, Matthew 11:21-22; Luke 10:13-14

U

uncircumcised, See "circumcision."

unclean, *the state of a person, animal or action that was not pleasing to God. In the Old Testament God said certain animals were unclean and were not to be eaten. If a person disobeyed the rules about being clean, he was called unclean and could not serve God until he was made clean again.* See "clean."
* unclean animals, Leviticus 11; Acts 10:9-15
* unclean people, Leviticus 12-15
* God declared everyone to be clean, Acts 10

unleavened bread (un-LEV-'nd BREAD) *bread made without yeast.*
* used in the Passover Feast, Exodus 12:20; Deuteronomy 16:1-4

Unleavened Bread, Day of, *the first day of the Feast of Unleavened Bread or Passover,* Matthew 26:17; Luke 22:7

upper room, *upstairs room in a house.*
* Jesus and his followers met there, Mark 14:14-15; Luke 22:9-12

Ur, *a great city thousands of years ago; today in the country of Iraq.*
* home of Abram, Genesis 11:28-31

Uriah (you-RY-uh) *a soldier in King David's army.*
* killed by David, 2 Samuel 11

Urim (YOUR-im) See "Thummim."

Uzzah (UZ-uh) *touched the Ark of the Agreement and died,* 2 Samuel 6:1-8; 1 Chronicles 13:1-14

Uzziah (uh-ZY-uh) *a king of Judah,* 2 Kings 15:13-15; 2 Chronicles 26; Isaiah 6:1

V

Vashti (VASH-ty) *the wife of Ahasuerus, king of Persia,* Esther 1:1-20

veil (VALE) *a head covering usually worn by women; also, a curtain in the Temple.*
* worn by women, Genesis 24:65; Song of Solomon 4:1; Isaiah 3:19
* the Temple veil, Matthew 27:51; Mark 15:38; Luke 23:45

vest, holy, "ephod"; *a special type of clothing for the priests in the Old Testament. The holy vest for the high priest had gold and gems on it.*

---

* description of, Exodus 25:7; 28:6-14; 39:2-7
* one made by Micah, Judges 17:1-5; 18:14-20
* worn by David, 2 Samuel 6:14

vine
* fruit of the, Matthew 26:29; Mark 14:25; Luke 22:18
* Jesus as the, John 15:1-11

vineyard
* Naboth's, 1 Kings 21
* parables of, Matthew 20:1-16; 21:28-46; Mark 12:1-12; Luke 20:9-19

virgin (VUR-jin) *person who has not had sexual relations,* Deuteronomy 22:13-29; Isaiah 7:14; Matthew 1:23; Luke 1:34

vision (VIZ-zhun) *like a dream. God often spoke to his people in visions.*
* of Abram, Genesis 15:1
* of Daniel, Daniel 2:19
* of Peter and Cornelius, Acts 10:1-16
* of Paul, Acts 16:9

vow, *a special and serious promise often made to God.*
* rules about, Numbers 30; Deuteronomy 23:21-23
* the Nazirite, Numbers 6:1-21
* of Jephthah, Judges 11:29-40
* of Paul, Acts 18:18

W

war
* rumors of, Matthew 24:6-7; Mark 13:7-8; Luke 21:9-10
* spiritual, 2 Corinthians 10:3-4
* will end, Micah 4:1-3

watchman
* examples of, 2 Samuel 18:24-27; Psalm 130:6
* prophets as watchmen, Ezekiel 3:17; Micah 7:4

water
* in creation, Genesis 1:1-2,6-10
* bitter, Exodus 5:22-27
* from a rock, Exodus 17:1-7
* for David, 2 Samuel 23:15-17
* drink of, Matthew 10:42; Mark 9:41
* Jesus walked on, Matthew 14:22-36
* turned to wine, John 2:1-11
* living water, John 4:1-15

"Way, the," *one of the earliest names given to Christians. Jesus said he was "the way" to reach God.* Acts 9:1-2; 19:9,23; 22:4; 24:14,22

wedding, Matthew 22:1-14; Luke 14:8; John 2:1-11

Western Sea, See "Mediterranean Sea."

widow
* examples of, Ruth 4:10; 1 Kings 17:8-24; Luke 21:2-4
* care for, Deuteronomy 24:17-22; 1 Timothy 5:3-16; James 1:27

wife
* man united with, Genesis 2:24
* the good wife, Proverbs 31:10-31
* teachings about, 1 Corinthians 7:1-16
* responsibility of, Ephesians 5:21-24,33; Colossians 3:18; 1 Peter 3:1

wine
* danger of, Proverbs 20:1; Ephesians 5:18
* at wedding in Cana, John 2:1-11
* for the stomach, 1 Timothy 5:23

winepress, *a pit where grapes were mashed to get the juice out. The winepress is sometimes used to describe how enemy armies will defeat people as if they were grapes crushed in a winepress.*
* examples of, Judges 6:11; Matthew 21:33
* as a symbol of punishment, Lamentations 1:15; Revelation 14:19-20; 19:15

wisdom (WIZ-d'm) *understanding what is really important in life. This wisdom comes from God.* Proverbs 1:1-2,7; 2; 4
* Solomon asked for, 1 Kings 4:29-34

- source of, James 1:5
- a parable about, Matthew 25:1-13

wise men, "magi"; *men who studied the stars,* Genesis 41:8; Exodus 7:11; Matthew 2:1-12

witchcraft, *using the power of the devil to do magic.*
- warnings against, Deuteronomy 18:10-12; Galatians 5:19-21
- examples of, 2 Kings 9:22; 2 Chronicles 33:6

witness, Acts 1:8,22; 2:32; 22:14-15

woman
- created by God, Genesis 2:22-23
- how to treat a, 1 Timothy 5:2,14

word, *in the Bible often means God's message to us in the Scriptures. Jesus is called the "Word" because he shows us what God is like.*
- like a lamp, Psalm 119:105
- like a sword, Hebrews 4:12
- living in God's people, John 15:7; Colossians 3:16; 1 John 2:14
- lasts forever, Matthew 24:35; 1 Peter 1:25
- people's words, Proverbs 12:25; 25:11; Matthew 12:36-37
- as a message, 1 Peter 1:24-25; 1 John 2:14
- Jesus as the "Word," John 1:1-5,14; 1 John 1:1-2

world, *the planet Earth; also the people on this earth who follow Satan.*
- as the Earth, 2 Samuel 22:16; Psalm 18:15
- as a symbol of wickedness, Romans 12:2; Ephesians 2:2

worship, *to praise and serve God.*
- commanded, Exodus 34:14; Luke 4:8; John 4:20-24

X-Y

Xerxes (ZERK-sees) *a king of Persia; also called "Ahasuerus,"* Esther 1-10

yeast (YEEST) *an ingredient used to make breads and cakes rise; used in the New Testament to stand for a person's influence over others.* See also "unleavened bread."
- as a symbol for influence, Mark 8:15; Luke 13:21

yoke, *a wooden frame that fits on the necks of animals to hold them together while working.*
- examples of, Deuteronomy 21:3; 1 Kings 19:19-21

youth
- "Remember your Creator," Ecclesiastes 12:1
- teachings about, 1 Timothy 4:12

Z

Zacchaeus (za-KEE-us) *Jewish tax collector in the city of Jericho,* Luke 19:1-8

Zadok (ZAY-dok) *priest who helped King David,* 2 Samuel 15:24-36; 17:15-21; 1 Kings 1:18-45

Zarephath (ZAIR-eh-fath) *a Canaanite town where the prophet Elijah helped a widow,* 1 Kings 17:8-24; Luke 4:25-26

Zealots (ZEL-ots) *a group of Jewish men also called "Enthusiasts." They hated the Romans for controlling their home country, and they planned to force the Romans out.*
- Simon, the Zealot, Matthew 10:4; Mark 3:18; Luke 6:15; Acts 1:13

Zebedee (ZEB-uh-dee) *a fisherman on Lake Galilee,* Matthew 4:21-22; 20:20; Mark 1:19-20; Luke 5:10; John 21:2

Zechariah, father of John the Baptist, (ZEK-uh-RY-uh) *a Jewish priest,* Luke 1:5-25,57-80

Zechariah, king of Israel, *ruled for only six months; killed by Shallum,* 2 Kings 14:29; 15:8-11

Zechariah, son of Berekiah, *a prophet who wrote the next-to-the-last book in the Old Testament,* Ezra 5:1; Zechariah 1-14

Zechariah, son of Jehoiada, *a priest who taught the people to serve God,* 2 Chronicles 24:20-25

Zedekiah, son of Josiah, (zed-ee-KY-uh) *the last king of Judah,* 2 Kings 24:16-25:7

Zedekiah, son of Kenaanah, *a false prophet during the time of King Ahab,* 1 Kings 22:1-24

Zedekiah, son of Maaseiah, *a false prophet in Babylon during the time of Jeremiah,* Jeremiah 29:21-23

Zephaniah (zef-uh-NY-uh) *a prophet who lived when Josiah was king of Judah; wrote the short book of Zephaniah,* Zephaniah 1:1

Zerubbabel (zeh-RUB-uh-bull) *governor of Jerusalem after the Jews had been in captivity in Babylon for seventy years.*
- returned from exile, Ezra 2:2
- built the altar of God, Ezra 3:1-6
- rebuilt the Temple, Ezra 3:7-10; 5:2

Ziba (ZY-buh) *a servant of Saul,* 2 Samuel 9:1-11; 16:1-4; 19:24-30

Zimri (ZIM-rye) *a king of Israel,* 1 Kings 16:11-20

Zion (ZY-on) *a hill inside the city of Jerusalem.* See "Mount Zion."

Ziph (ZIF) *a city about twenty-five miles south of Jerusalem,* 1 Samuel 23:14-28; 26:1-25

Zipporah (zih-PO-ruh) *the wife of Moses,* Exodus 2:15-22; 4:24-26; 18:1-3

zither (ZITH-ur) *a type of musical instrument that had about forty strings on it,* Ezekiel 3:5,7,10,15

Abraham's Journey

▲ ▲ ▲ Possible route
that Abraham followed

Caspian Sea

▲ Mount Ararat?

Persian Gulf

• Susa

• Nineveh

Tigris River

• Nuzi

• Babylon

• Erech

• Ur

• Kanish

• Asshur

Euphrates River

• Mari

MESOPOTAMIA

• Haran

PADAN ARAM

HITTITES

• Carchemish

• Ebla

• Ugarit

• Kadesh

CYPRUS

Sidon •

Tyre •

• Damascus

• Hazor

• Dothan

Shechem •

CANAAN

Bethel •

• Jerusalem

Dead Sea

Mediterranean Sea

Beersheba •

▲ Mount Sinai

Red Sea

EGYPT

• On

• Memphis

The Desert Wanderings

Jordan River

· Joppa

· Ai
Jericho ·

· Ashdod   Heshbon

· Ashkelon

Mediterranean Sea

· Gaza   *Dead Sea*

Hebron ·

· Beersheba

· Rameses

Baal · · Zilu
Zephon

DESERT OF SHUR   **DESERT OF ZIN**   **EDOM**

· Succoth

GOSHEN   Kadesh Barnea ·

Bitter Lakes

EGYPT

· Marah   · Ezion Geber

· Elim

DESERT OF SIN

Red Sea   · Dophkah   Hazeroth ·

· Rephidim

MIDIAN

Mount Sinai

Possible route of the desert wanderings.

The Twelve Tribes During the Judges

The Kingdoms of Judah and Israel

- Damascus
- Sidon
- Dan
- Tyre
SIDON
- Hazor
ARAM
Lake Galilee

Mediterranean Sea

- Dor
Megiddo
- Jezreel
- Ramoth Gilead

Jordan River

- Samaria
- Shechem
- Succoth

KINGDOM OF ISRAEL

- Joppa

AMMON

Gibeah
- Gezer
- Jericho

- Ashdod
- Jerusalem
Ashkelon
Beth Shemesh
Adullam

- Lachish
- Hebron
- Gaza
- Ziklag
- Beersheba
Dead Sea

PHILISTIA

MOAB

Brook of Egypt

KINGDOM OF JUDAH

EDOM

- Kadesh Barnea

Palestine in Jesus' Life

Mediterranean Sea

• Tyre

• Caesarea Philippi

SYRIA

GALILEE

• Korazin

Capernaum •

• Bethsaida

Magdala •

Lake Galilee

• Cana

Nazareth •

▲ *Mt. Tabor*

• Nain

• Gadara

DECAPOLIS

• Caesarea

Jordan River

• Samaria

• Sychar

SAMARIA

• Antipatris

• Arimathea?

Philadelphia •

PEREA

• Emmaus

• Jericho

JUDEA

• Jerusalem

• Bethany

• Bethlehem

IDUMEA

Dead Sea

Jesus' Last Week in Jerusalem

- Pool of Bethzatha
- Mount of Olives ▸
- Gethsemane ▸

Fortress Antonia

Gordon's Calvary & Garden Tomb

Sheep Gate

Temple

Water Gate

Court of the Gentiles

Herod Family Palace

Herod's Palace

UPPER CITY

Gihon Spring

Home of Caiaphas

Kidron Valley

Mt. Zion

Upper Room

LOWER CITY

HILL OPHEL

Pool of Siloam

Hinnom Valley

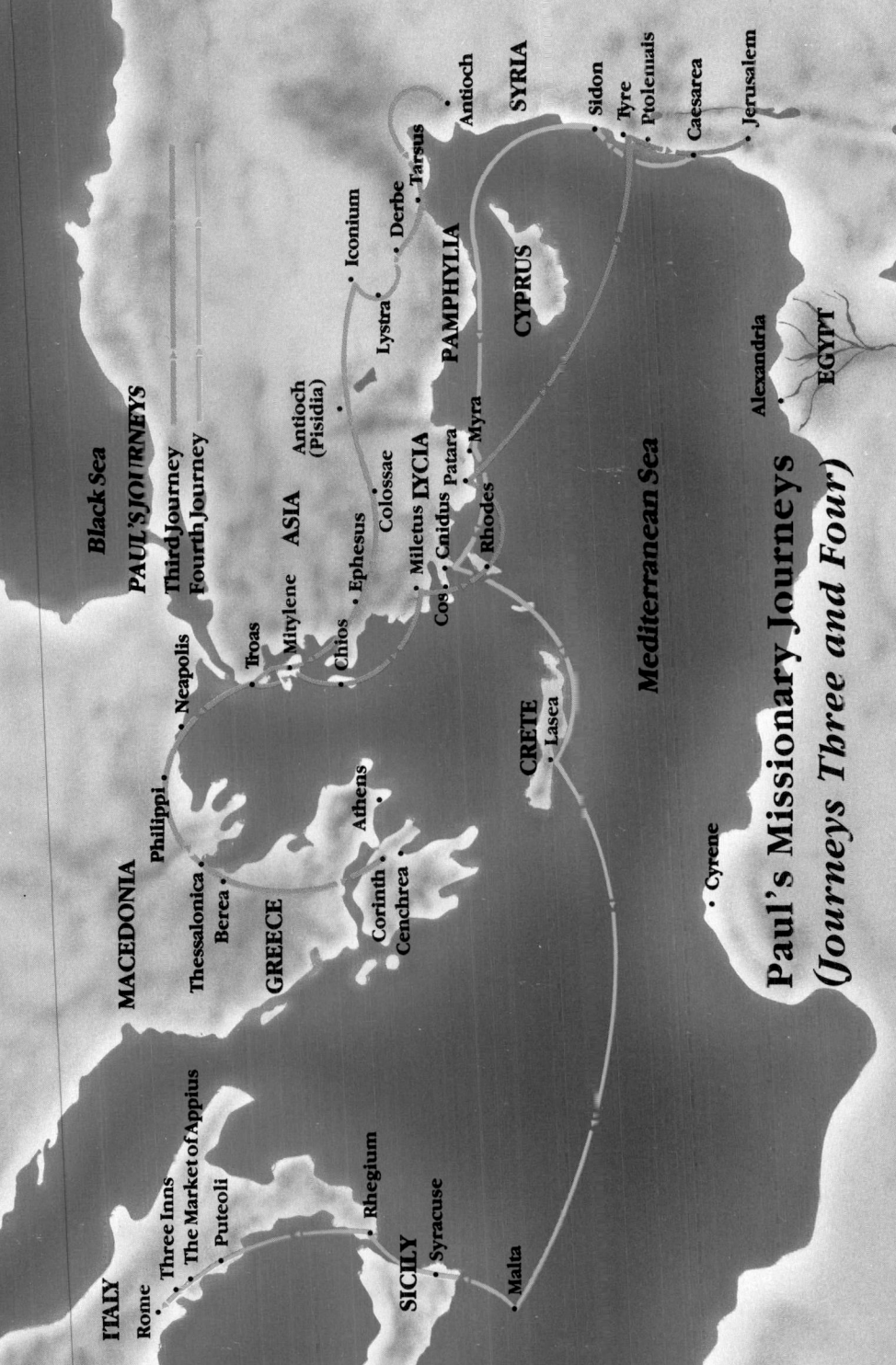

Paul's Missionary Journeys
(Journeys Three and Four)

Paul's Missionary Journeys
(Journeys One and Two)

PAUL'S JOURNEYS
First Journey
Second Journey

Black Sea

ITALY

SICILY

MACEDONIA
Philippi • Neapolis
Amphipolis • Samothrace
Thessalonica • Berea • Apollonia

GREECE
Athens
Corinth • Cenchrea

Troas

ASIA

Ephesus

Antioch
(Pisidia)

LYCIA
Cnidus

Iconium
Lystra • Derbe • Tarsus

Perga
Attalia

PAMPHYLIA

CYPRUS
Salamis
Paphos

Antioch
Seleucia

SYRIA
Sidon
Tyre
Caesarea
Jerusalem

CRETE

Mediterranean Sea

Cyrene

Alexandria

EGYPT